S0-AXY-570

Herman Summers

THIRTEENTH EDITION

Criminal Justice Today

AN INTRODUCTORY TEXT FOR THE TWENTY-FIRST CENTURY

Frank Schmalleger, Ph.D.
Distinguished Professor Emeritus, The University of North Carolina at Pembroke

PEARSON

Boston Columbus Indianapolis New York San Francisco Upper Saddle River
Amsterdam Cape Town Dubai London Madrid Milan Munich Paris Montreal Toronto
Delhi Mexico City São Paulo Sydney Hong Kong Seoul Singapore Taipei Tokyo

THE CRIMINAL

POLICE

COURTS

ENTRY INTO THE SYSTEM

PROSECUTION & PRETRIAL SERVICES

ADJUDICATION

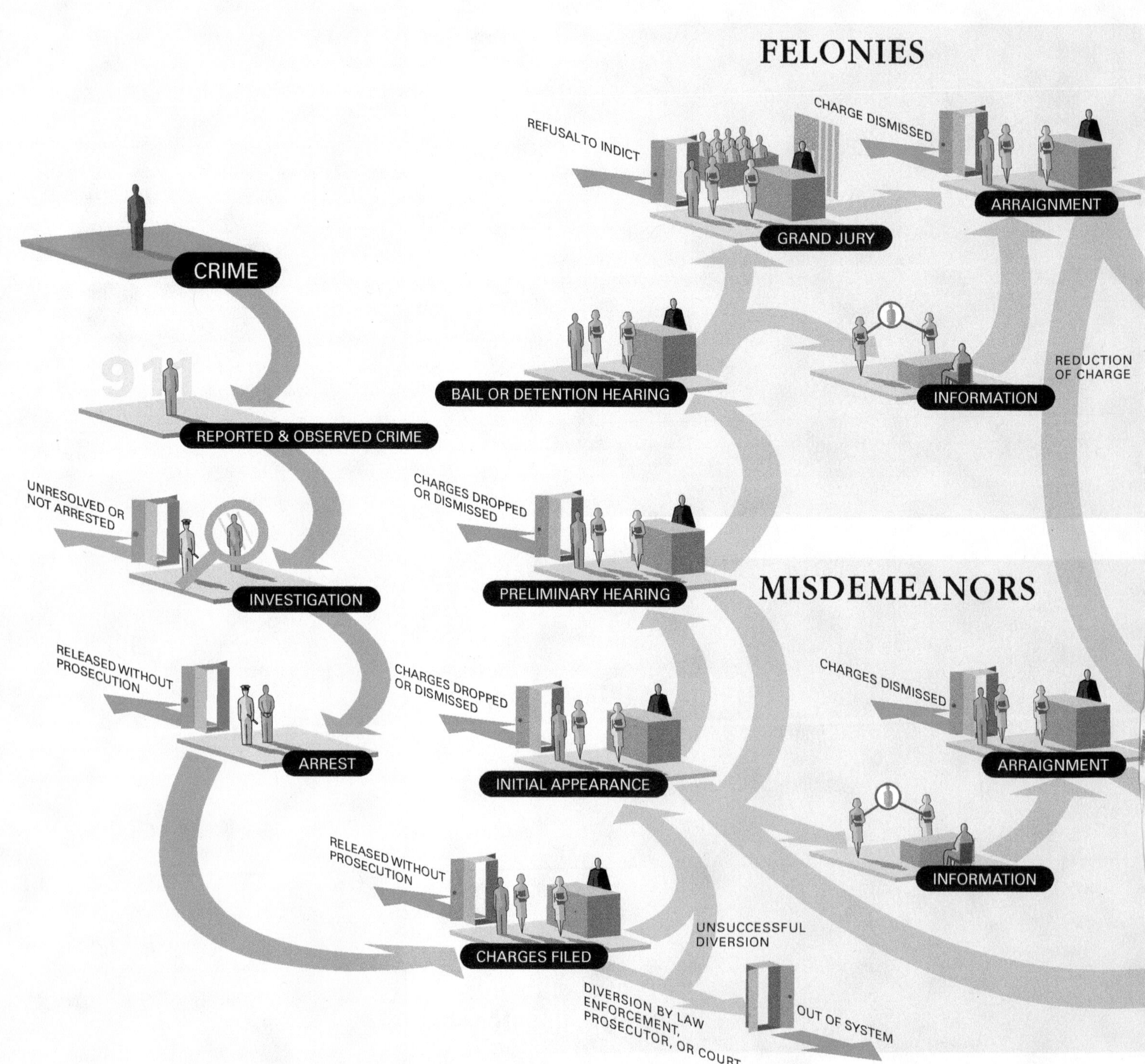

JUSTICE SYSTEM

CORRECTIONS

SENTENCING & SANCTIONS | **PROBATION** | **PRISON** | **PAROLE**

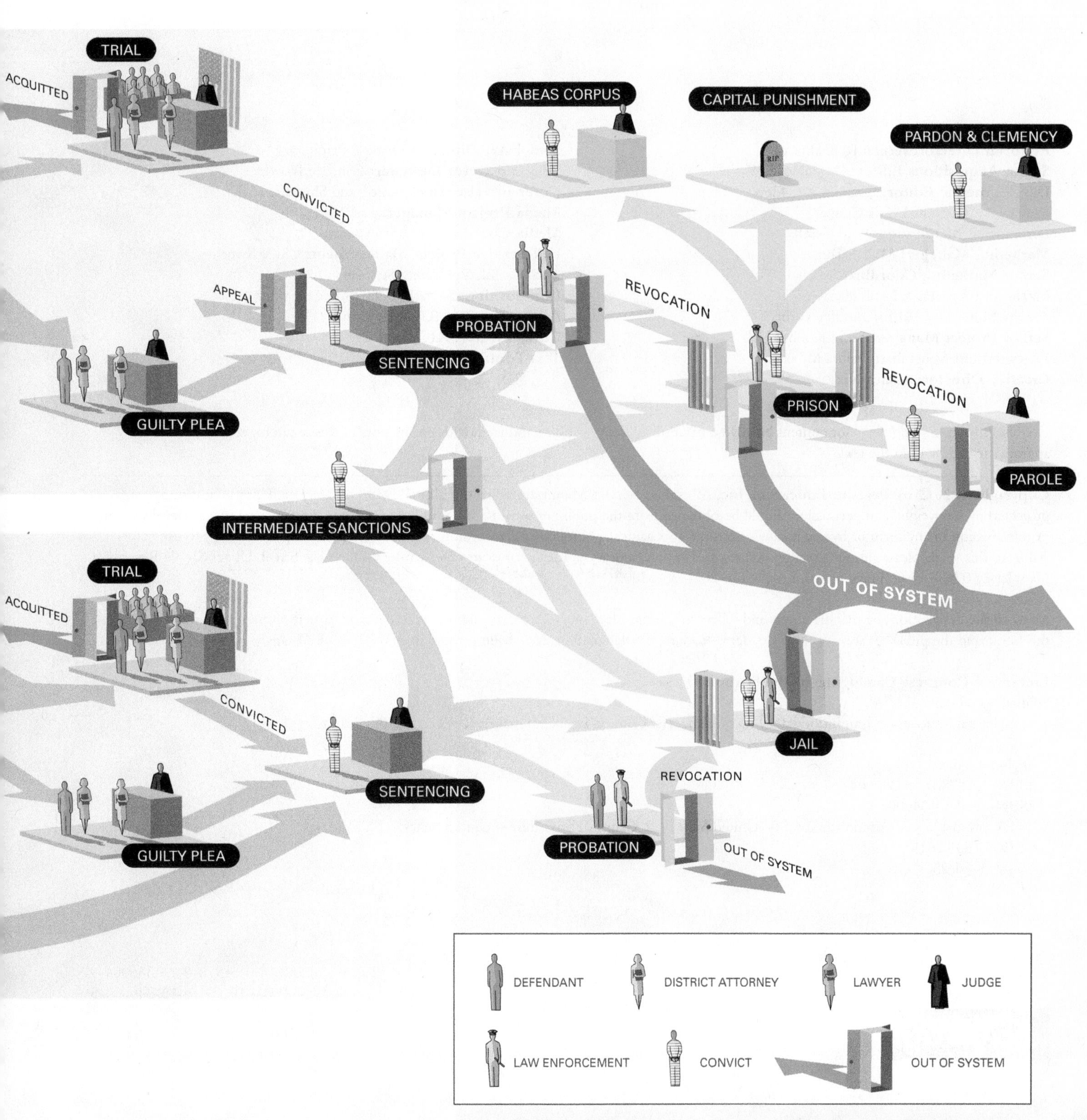

Editorial Director: Vernon R. Anthony
Senior Acquisitions Editor: Gary Bauer
Developmental Editor: Elisa Rogers, 4development
Editorial Assistant: Lynda Cramer
Director of Marketing: David Gesell
Marketing Manager: Mary Salzman
Senior Marketing Coordinator: Alicia Wozniak
Marketing Assistant: Les Roberts
Senior Managing Editor: JoEllen Gohr
Senior Project Manager: Steve Robb
Procurement Specialist: Deidra M. Skahill
Creative Director: Andrea Nix
Senior Art Director: Diane Y. Ernsberger
Text and Cover Designer: Candace Rowley
Cover Images: iStockphoto® and Shutterstock®
Media Project Manager: Leslie Brado
Media Coordinator: April Cleland
Full-Service Project Management: Cindy Sweeney, S4Carlisle Publishing Services
Composition: S4Carlisle Publishing Services
Printer/Binder: RR Donnelley
Cover Printer: RR Donnelley
Text Font: Bembo Std

Credits and acknowledgments for content borrowed from other sources and reproduced, with permission, in this textbook appear on the appropriate page within the text.

Library of Congress Cataloging-in-Publication Data
Schmalleger, Frank.
Criminal justice today : an introductory text for the 21st century/Frank Schmalleger.—Thirteenth edition.
pages cm
Includes index.
ISBN-13: 978-0-13-346004-9
ISBN-10: 0-13-346004-5
1. Criminal justice, Administration of—United States. 2. Criminal procedure—United States. I. Title.
HV9950.S35 2015
364.973—dc23

2013030693

2 16

Paper bound ISBN 13: 978-0-13-346004-9
ISBN 10: 0-13-346004-5

Loose leaf ISBN 13: 978-0-13-346011-7
ISBN 10: 0-13-346011-8

This book is dedicated to my beautiful wife
Ellen Willow Szirandi Schmalleger, my true companion,
whose wonderful, happy, and free spirit
is a gift to all who know her.

Brief Contents

Contents

Chapter 4 | Criminal Law 106

PART TWO ■ Policing 135

PART THREE ■ Adjudication 272

Chapter 9 | The Courts: Structure and Participants 273

Chapter 18 | The Future of Criminal Justice 594

New to This Edition

General Changes

- "Paying for It" feature boxes are now included in the text, emphasizing the financial realities of today's world—including the need of justice system components to deal with budget shortfalls and limits on available resources.
- Evidence-based practices are introduced in early chapters and are stressed throughout the text, including in the book's sections on policing, the courts, and corrections.
- This new edition makes use of enhanced graphics, and many photos have been updated.
- "CJ News" boxes are now based on author-created content, and integrate information from a number of new sources.
- New chapter-opening stories have been added in most chapters, along with new photographs related to those stories.

Chapter-Specific Changes

Chapter 1: What Is Criminal Justice?

- The changing nature of crime is recognized, and students are asked to consider what crime rates would look like if all types of crime today could be captured by traditional crime reporting systems.
- The chapter opens with a new story about Adam Lanza, the Sandy Hook Elementary School shooter.
- Issues of gun control, mental illness, and random mass shootings are now discussed.
- The case of Texas billionaire R. Allen Stanford, 61, convicted by a federal jury in a $7 billion Ponzi scheme, is now included.
- California's Chelsea's Law, a bill intended to increase prison sentences and extend parole terms for offenders who commit sex crimes against minors, is now discussed.
- A new "CJ News" box on surveillance technology has been added.
- The concept of budgetary constraints facing criminal justice agencies is introduced and a new "Paying for It" box is included in the chapter to illustrate the significance of cost-effective justice administration.
- The new U.S. Department of Justice website, **www.crimesolutions.gov,** is introduced and its importance is explained.

Chapter 2: The Crime Picture

- All crime statistics from the Uniform Crime Reporting Program and the National Criminal Victimization Survey have been updated, and updated information from the Southern Poverty Law Center on hate groups in America is included.
- The updated identity theft section now includes Mark Zuckerberg's ID-theft victimization.
- A revised story opens the chapter.
- The changing nature of criminal offenses is recognized, and questions are raised about crime-data-gathering programs and their ability to keep pace with changes now occurring.
- Random mass shootings now receive more complete coverage.
- The "Freedom or Safety" box has been updated and revised.
- Changes in the Federal Bureau of Investigation's definition of the terms "rape" and "forcible rape" for statistical reporting purposes are described, and their impact on crime statistics is discussed.
- A new "CJ News" box on "flash robs" is included.
- The discussion of race and crime has been revised to include the concept of "modern racism," which refers to assumptions that issues of race have been resolved when, in fact, they have not.
- The new NCVS Victimization Analysis Tool (NVAT) is discussed and a Web link is provided.
- The discussion of the VAWA has been revised to recognize its 2013 reauthorization.
- The case of Tyler Clementi is described in the hate crimes section of the chapter.
- The discussion of gun control issues has been updated and expanded, and links to President Obama's executive orders relating to gun control are included.

Chapter 3: The Search for Causes

- The chapter-opening story and statistics on male/female arrests have been updated.
- Routine activities theory is explained in greater detail.
- A new section on biosocial theories of crime is included, and these theories are elucidated.
- A discussion of Terri Moffit's social development theory has been added to the chapter.
- A discussion of trait theory has been added to the section on psychological theories of crime, to include the Big Five personality traits.
- A new "CJ News" box on the "warrior gene" has been added in order to emphasize the importance to new and emerging biosocial theories.

Chapter 4: Criminal Law

- A new chapter-opening story is included.
- The "CJ News" box has been rewritten using multiple sources.
- The case of *Holder* v. *Humanitarian Law Project*, in which the U.S. Supreme Court decided what constitutes criminal support of terrorist organizations, is now discussed.
- The section on espionage has been updated using the example of Stewart Nozette, 54, who was recently sentenced to 13 years in prison after pleading guilty to federal espionage charges.
- The practice of "flaking," or the planting of drugs on innocent people, is now discussed.

Chapter 5: Policing: History and Structure

- The London Metropolitan Police Service (MPS) is now described by its new name.
- The number of women FBI agents has been updated.
- Information on CODIS has been updated.
- The "CJ News" box has been replaced with one describing falling crime rates in Los Angeles.
- Statistics on the number of local police departments have been updated.
- A new "Paying for It" box on cost-efficient policing has been added.
- Information on the cost of securing the 2012 London Olympics is now included.
- A new "CJ Careers" box on working as a security professional has been added.

Chapter 6: Policing: Purpose and Organization

- The chapter-opening story now features the Occupy Wall Street movement.
- The chapter now includes a "Paying for It" box focused on policing in an economic downturn.
- Additional information on intelligence-led policing and fusion centers is now included.
- The "Ethics and Professionalism" box describing the Law Enforcement Oath of Honor has been moved to this chapter (from Chapter 8).
- A link to Discover Policing (**www.discoverpolicing.org**) has been added for those interested in employment in the law enforcement field.

Chapter 7: Policing: Legal Aspects

- The new chapter-opening story describes a recent lawsuit brought against the LAPD in the shooting death of a 19-year-old.
- Discussion of the 2013 U.S. Supreme Court case of *Baily* v. *U.S.*, which limited the power of police to detain people who are away from their homes when police conduct a search of their residence, is now discussed.
- Plain-view searches in the area of electronic evidence are now discussed.
- The 2012 U.S. Supreme Court case of *Howes* v. *Fields*, in which the Court explained that "custody is a term of art that specifies circumstances that are thought generally to present a serious danger of coercion," is now discussed.
- The 2012 U.S. Supreme Court case of *Perry* v. *New Hampshire*, in which the Court recognized problems with eyewitness identification, especially when such identification is obtained by skilled law enforcement interrogators, is now discussed.
- The discussion of public-safety exceptions to the *Miranda* rule has been expanded with the addition of the case of 19-year-old Dzhokhar Tsarnaev, the surviving Boston Marathon bomber.
- The "CJ News" box on GPS tracking has been replaced with one written by the author.
- A new "Freedom or Safety" box on the USA PATRIOT Act has been added.
- The National Institute of Justice's Electronic Crime Technology Center of Excellence (ECTCoE), which serves to assist in building the capacity for electronic crime prevention and digital evidence collection and examination of state and local law enforcement agencies, is now discussed.

Chapter 8: Policing: Issues and Challenges

- A new story now opens the chapter, and describes the recent act of kindness by NYPD officer Larry DePrimo, who gave a homeless person clean socks and shoes on a cold winter's night.
- The section on police corruption and integrity has been revised.
- A discussion of *Garrity* rights—which are protections that police officers have against self-incrimination in the face of questioning by their superiors—has been added to the chapter.

- The "Freedom or Safety" box in this chapter has been updated.
- Discussion of the Badge of Life, an organization that promotes mental health services for police officers, has been added.
- Discussion of the federal consent decree involving the New Orleans Police Department has been updated.
- A new "CJ News" box on the video recording of police activity in a public place has been added.
- Racial profiling is now distinguished from *behavioral profiling*.
- A "Freedom or Safety" box on the NYPD's monitoring of Muslim groups has been added to the chapter.
- A 2013 story on police civil liability involving a civil settlement by the city of Chicago has been added.
- A brief discussion of the use of unmanned aerial vehicles by police agencies is now included.

Chapter 9: The Courts: Structure and Participants

- The discussion on community courts has been expanded, and the phrases *community courts* and *specialized courts* are now key terms.
- A new "CJ News" box on how budget cuts are affecting America's courts has been added to the chapter.
- A new "Paying for It" box describes cost-efficient courts.
- The discussion of the Casey Anthony trial has been updated and revised.
- A new "CJ Careers" box features an assistant district attorney.
- New line art showing indigent defense expenditures in the United States from 1986 to 2008 is now included.
- The discussion of the U.S. Supreme Court case of *Daubert* v. *Merrell Dow Pharmaceuticals*, which eased the criteria for the introduction of scientific evidence at both civil and criminal trials, has been moved here from Chapter 18.
- The 2010 U.S. Supreme Court case of *Melendez-Diaz* v. *Massachusetts*, defining the role of forensic analysts, has been moved here from Chapter 18.

Chapter 10: Pretrial Activities and the Criminal Trial

- A new chapter-opening story, describing the Jodi Arias trial, now begins the chapter.
- Additional information on plea bargaining has been added in the chapter.
- Two U.S. Supreme Court cases expanding the authority of judges in the plea-bargaining process are now included.
- A new "Paying for It" box describes cost-efficient courts.
- A new "CJ News" box on the use of social media by the courts is included.

Chapter 11: Sentencing

- Offender risk and needs assessment is now discussed in greater detail.
- A new "Paying for It" box describing cost-efficient corrections and sentencing is now included in the chapter.
- The discussion of the death penalty has been revised to include recent changes in state law in Connecticut, Illinois, and Maryland.
- Discussion on the use of the death penalty internationally has been expanded.
- DNA collection laws are now discussed, including recently enacted statutes at the state and federal levels.
- A new NIJ study of factors that can lead to wrongful convictions is now discussed.
- The status of innocence projects across the nation is described.
- A new meta-analysis focused on the deterrent effect of the death penalty by the National Academies of Sciences is reviewed.
- A new "CJ News" box on the high cost of the death penalty is included.
- The 2008 U.S. Supreme Court case of *Kennedy* v. *Louisiana*, is now included. The decision bars states from imposing the death penalty for the rape of a child where the crime did not result, and was not intended to result, in the victim's death.
- A new "CJ News" box on the use of DNA to expose flaws in the legal system is now included.

Chapter 12: Probation, Parole, and Intermediate Sanctions

- The title of the chapter has been changed to recognize its expanded coverage of intermediate sanctions.
- A new chapter-opening story examines the shooting death of Tom Clements, chief of Colorado's corrections department.
- New statistics on probation and parole are integrated into the chapter.

- The federal Probation and Pretrial Services Automated Case Tracking System (PACTS) is discussed. This system collects records from the electronic files of thousands of probation officers in all 94 federal districts and stores those records in a single data warehouse called the National PACTS Reporting (NPR) System.
- California's 2011 Criminal Justice Realignment Act is described. The Act shifted the supervision of most parolees, under what the state calls the Post-Release Community Supervision program, from state parole officers to county probation officers.
- A 2006 comprehensive review of state parole practices in California is now included.
- The discontinuation of the use of prison boot camps in many jurisdictions is discussed.
- A new "CJ News" box on GPS tracking of sex offenders has been added to the chapter.
- New statistics on the use of electronic monitoring of convicted offenders has been added.
- The results of new NIJ studies of the GPS monitoring of offenders has been included.
- Discussion of the impact of budgetary cutbacks on reintegration efforts is now included.
- SVORI program results are included now that funding for the program has effectively ended.
- Reentry courts are now discussed and defined.
- The discussion on the evidence-based movement in probation and parole has been expanded.
- A new "CJ Issues" box on remote reporting problems in probation services is now part of the chapter.
- Discussion of Hawaii's HOPE program is now included.

Chapter 13: Prisons and Jails

- The "CJ Careers" box has been removed.
- The evidence-based era in corrections is described and explored.
- A new "CJ News" box describing federal oversight of California prisons is included.
- A "CJ Issues" box now discusses California's Public Safety Realignment Program.
- New material is presented on who is in prison and why—including new line art.
- A new "Paying for It" box describes how budget shortfalls have led to cost-saving measures, resulting in declining prison populations.
- Statistics on overcrowding in federal correctional facilities have been updated.
- A new "CJ News" box on the state of California's efforts to end federal oversight of its prisons is included.
- Revised statistics on jails and jail populations are included.
- The 2011 U.S. Supreme court case of *Minneci* v. *Pollard* is discussed. In that ruling, the Court held that a *Bivens* action against employees of a privately run federal prison in California could not proceed because state tort law already "authorizes adequate alternative damages actions."

Chapter 14: Prison Life

- The chapter now begins with a new story about Miss America 2012, Laura Kaeppeler, and her support for mentoring the children of incarcerated parents.
- The section on the children of parents who are incarcerated has been updated.
- Statistics on sexual victimization and the Prison Rape Elimination Act have been updated.
- The term *gender responsiveness* has been more fully defined.
- The section on prison riots has been updated.
- Prison gangs (security threat groups) are discussed in more detail, and the death of Tom Clements, the Colorado prison chief, is described as it relates to gang activity.
- A "Paying for It" box discussing the online Cost-Benefit Knowledge Bank in Criminal Justice has been added.
- Discussion of the 2012 U.S. Supreme Court case of *Howes* v. *Fields*, which dealt with inmates facing questioning by law enforcement officers while incarcerated, has been added.
- Discussion of the 2012 U.S. Supreme Court case of *Florence* v. *Burlington County*, which dealt with the strip searching of those arrested before admitting them to jail, has been added to the chapter.
- A new "CJ Careers" box has been added to the chapter.
- Statistics on the rate of HIV/AIDS infection in prisons and jails have been updated.
- Other data throughout the chapter have also been updated.
- The section on video visitation for prison inmates has been enhanced.

Chapter 15: Juvenile Justice

- Arrest statistics and data on case processing and institutionalization have been updated throughout the chapter.
- A new chapter-opening story is included.

- The overview of juvenile arrests and juvenile court caseloads has been revised and updated.
- The "CJ News" box on bullying has been completely revised.
- The 2012 U.S. Supreme Court case of *Miller* v. *Alabama* is discussed. The Court held that *mandatory* life-without-parole sentences for individuals 17 or younger convicted of homicide violate the Eighth Amendment.
- The 2012 Georgetown Center on Poverty, Inequality and Public Policy report on improving the juvenile justice system for girls is now discussed.
- A new "CJ Careers" box has been added to the chapter.
- The ages of juvenile court jurisdiction across the country have been updated.
- The state of California's policy of juvenile justice realignment is discussed, and its implications for the justice system in that state are explored.
- A new "CJ Issues" box on evidence-based juvenile justice has been added to the chapter.

Chapter 16: Drugs and Crime

- The chapter now begins with a new story about drug lord Joaquin "El Chapo" Guzman.
- Statistics on drug use and abuse have been updated throughout the chapter.
- All data relating to the National Survey on Drug Use and Health have been updated.
- The table describing major controlled substances has been updated.
- A new "CJ News" box on "bath salts" has been added.
- The National Office of Control Policy's (ONDCP) 2013 publication, the *National Drug Control Strategy*, is now discussed.
- A recent National Institute of Justice study, the Multisite Adult Drug Court Evaluation, is now discussed.
- Recent action by Washington state and Colorado to legalize the possession of small amounts of marijuana for personal use is now discussed.

Chapter 17: Terrorism and Multinational Criminal Justice

- The chapter begins with a new opening story.
- A discussion of the Twelfth United Nations Crime Congress is now included.
- Interpol's Eighty-First General Assembly (in 2012) is now discussed.
- Data throughout the chapter have been updated.
- A new "CJ News" box on violent jihadism is now included in the chapter.
- The Obama administration's strategy to combat terrorism is presented and discussed.
- The list of designated foreign terrorist organizations has been updated.

Chapter 18: The Future of Criminal Justice

- The chapter begins with a new story.
- The list of the most significant computer viruses and malware has been updated.
- The discussion of the law related to stem cells and embryonic stem cell research has been updated.
- The 2013 Social Media Internet Law Enforcement (SMILE) national conference is now discussed.
- The new National Commission on Forensic Science is discussed as it relates to the National Institute of Standards and Technology's activities.
- A new "CJ News" box discusses Kim Dotcom of the infamous file-sharing site Megaupload.
- General Electric's new advanced behavior recognition system for use in crowded environments is discussed. This system employs computer software to analyze the images sent from surveillance cameras to interpret and predict the behavior of individuals and groups in social settings.
- The 2012 report by the Washington, D.C.–based Sentencing Project, entitled *To Build a Better Criminal Justice System,* is discussed in some detail.

Preface

The attacks of September 11, 2001, changed our nation's course and tested the moral fiber of Americans everywhere. Nowhere outside the armed forces has the terrorist threat been felt more keenly than in the criminal justice profession. The 2001 attacks led many to look to our system of justice, and to the people who serve it, for protection and reassurance—protection from threats both internal and external and reassurance that a justice system rooted in the ideals of democracy will continue to offer fairness and equality to all who come before the law.

In the years since 9/11, strict new laws have been enacted, security efforts have been greatly enhanced, and practitioners of American criminal justice (especially those in law enforcement agencies) have recognized their important role as the first line of defense against threats to the American way of life. As a consequence, the study of criminal justice is more relevant today than ever before.

For many, personal involvement in the criminal justice field has become a way of serving our nation and helping protect our communities. I understand that motivation and applaud it—partially because of the heroism and personal sacrifice it involves, but also because it adds to the important "moral sense" of what we, as Americans, are all about. The profession's service role has expanded to include college and university students who, in large numbers, are declaring majors in criminal justice. Participation in the criminal justice system and in the study of criminal justice offers students a way of personally and meaningfully contributing to our society. It allows those who meet the challenging criteria for successful studies and employment to give something back to the nation and to the communities that nurtured them, and it reaffirms the American way of life by reinforcing the social values on which it is based.

Many students are also attracted to criminal justice because it provides a focus for the tension that exists within our society between individual rights and freedoms, on the one hand, and the need for public safety, security, and order, on the other. That tension—between individual rights and public order—is the theme around which all editions of this textbook have been built. That same theme is all the more relevant today because of the important question we have all been asking in recent years: How much personal freedom are we willing to sacrifice to achieve a solid sense of security?

Although there are no easy answers to this question, this textbook guides criminal justice students in the struggle to find a satisfying balance between freedom and security. True to its origins, the 13th edition focuses on the crime picture in America and on the three traditional elements of the criminal justice system: police, courts, and corrections. This edition has been enhanced with additional "Freedom or Safety" boxes, which time and again question the viability of our freedoms in a world that has grown increasingly more dangerous. This edition also asks students to evaluate the strengths and weaknesses of the American justice system as it struggles to adapt to an increasingly multicultural society and to a society in which the rights of a few can threaten the safety of many.

It is my hope that this book will ground students in the important issues that continue to evolve from the tension between the struggle for justice and the need for safety. For it is on that bedrock that the American system of criminal justice stands, and it is on that foundation that the future of the justice system—and of this country—will be built.

FRANK SCHMALLEGER, Ph.D.
Distinguished Professor Emeritus,
The University of North Carolina at Pembroke

Key Features Include

Freedom or Safety? You Decide boxes in each chapter highlight the book's ever-evolving theme of individual rights versus public order, a hallmark feature of this text since the first edition. In each chapter of the text, Freedom or Safety boxes build on this theme by illustrating some of the personal rights issues that challenge policymakers today. Each box includes critical-thinking questions that ask readers to ponder whether and how the criminal justice system balances individual rights and public safety.

freedom OR **safety?** YOU **decide**

Clarence Thomas Says: "Freedom Means Responsibility"

In 2009, U.S. Supreme Court Justice Clarence Thomas spoke to a group of high school essay contest winners in a Washington, D.C., hotel ballroom. Thomas used the occasion, which was dedicated to our nation's Bill of Rights, to point out the importance of obligations as well as rights. "Today there is much focus on our rights," said Thomas. "Indeed, I think there is a proliferation of rights." But then he went on to say, "I am often surprised by the virtual nobility that seems to be accorded those with grievances. Shouldn't there at least be equal time for our Bill of Obligations and our Bill of Responsibilities?"

Today, the challenge for the criminal justice system, it seems, is to balance individual rights and personal freedoms with social control and respect for legitimate authority. Years ago, during the height of what was then a powerful movement to win back control of our nation's cities and to rein in skyrocketing crime rates, the *New York Post* sponsored a conference on crime and civil rights. The keynote speaker at that conference was New York City's mayor, Rudolph W. Giuliani. In his speech, Giuliani identified the tension between personal freedoms and individual responsibilities as the crux of the crime problem then facing his city and the nation. We mistakenly look to government and elected officials, Giuliani said, to assume responsibility for solving the problem of crime when, instead, each individual citizen must become accountable for fixing what is wrong with our society. "We only see the oppressive side of authority. . . . What we don't see is that freedom is not a concept in which people can do anything they want, be anything they can be. Freedom is about authority. Freedom is about the willingness of every single human being to cede to lawful authority a great deal of discretion about what you do."

You Decide

How can we, as Justice Thomas suggests, achieve a balance of rights and obligations in American society? What did Giuliani mean when he said, "What we don't see is that freedom is not a concept in which people can do anything they want, be anything they can be"? Is it possible to balance individual rights and personal freedoms with social control and respect for legitimate authority?

References: Adam Liptak, "Reticent Justice Opens Up to a Group of Students," *New York Times*, April 13, 2009, http://www.nytimes.com/2009/04/14/us/14bar.html (accessed September 2, 2009); and Philip Taylor, "Civil Libertarians: Giuliani's Efforts Threaten First Amendment," *Freedom Forum Online*, http://www.freedomforum.org (accessed September 5, 2007).

CJ Careers boxes outline the characteristics of a variety of criminal justice careers in a Q&A format, to introduce today's pragmatic students to an assortment of potential career options and assist them in making appropriate career choices.

CJ | CAREERS
Police Officer

Christian Tomas

Name. Narcotics Agent Christian Tomas

Position. QRT Agent (Quick Response Team/Narcotics) City of West Palm Beach, Florida

Colleges attended. Palm Beach State College

Majors. Psychology

Year hired. 2007

Please give a brief description of your job. As a narcotics agent, my co-workers and I target street-level drug dealers and other quality of life issues, to include prostitution as well as other illegal business practices. We use our own initiative to begin investigations throughout the city. We buy narcotics in an undercover capacity and work with the S.W.A.T. team by writing search warrants for them to execute.

What is a typical day like? Typical day involves doing research and identifying a target. Once an investigation is complete, we move on to another. Some days are spent primarily on surveillance; while on others we are directly involved with drug dealers.

What qualities/characteristics are most helpful for this job? Common sense, honesty, integrity, confidence, self-discipline, dedication, humility, composure, physical and mental toughness, Tactical awareness and the ability to work with minimal, to no, supervision.

What is a typical starting salary? The West Palm Beach Police Department starting salary is $45,324 annually, with excellent benefits

What is the salary potential as you move up into higher-level jobs? An officer reaching PFC (Patrolman first Class) and MPO (Master Patrol Officer) will receive a 2 and 1/2% raise for each level attained. Promotion in rank produces significant raises over time.

What advice would you give someone in college beginning studies in criminal justice? This isn't a job for someone expecting to win all of the battles. You try as hard as you can, but you have to be prepared for some disappointments when a case doesn't go the way you wanted it to. Get your degree, as it will help you get promoted. When choosing a department, make sure that it's the kind of department that you are looking for. I came to West Palm Beach for the experience and to be busy; I wanted to be challenged and to do as much as I possibly could. Policing is a very rewarding career if you have the motivation and determination to succeed.

CJ News boxes in each chapter present case stories from the media to bring a true-to-life dimension to the study of criminal justice and allow insight into the everyday workings of the justice system.

CJ | NEWS
LAPD Adds Officers and Crime Falls—But Is There a Connection?

AURELIA VENTURA/LA OPINION/Newscom

New officers graduate from the LAPD academy. Why does the IACP say that the optimum ratio of police officers to citizens in a city depends on local conditions? What conditions would those be?

Ever since he successfully ran for office in 2005, Los Angeles Mayor Antonio Villaraigosa has been intent on adding more sworn officers to the Los Angeles Police Department (LAPD) and reaching a record level of 10,000.

Battling huge budget shortfalls, he succeeded in adding a few hundred new officers through 2012, putting the LAPD just shy of the 10,000 mark. Facing the end of his tenure due to term limits, the mayor finally reached his goal on January 1, 2013, through a maneuver that didn't put any new officers on the streets. The LAPD simply annexed the city's General Services Department, which oversees parks, libraries, and other municipal buildings, and its 60 officers were sworn into the LAPD.

"I know some people think that 10,000 cops is a magical illusion, a meaningless number, that more officers don't necessarily lead to a reduction in crime," the mayor said. "Those critics talk a lot, but they're just plain wrong."

City officials noted that from 2011–2012, gang crime, one of the city's greatest scourges, fell by 10.5%. By 2012, Los Angeles had the lowest overall crime rate of any major city. Using extra officers early in Villaraigosa's tenure, the LAPD could put more of them on the streets and open new stations, and response times fell from eight to nine minutes to six to seven minutes for calls for assistance.

But were extra officers the key factor in reducing crime? Skeptics point to other factors, such as a nationwide decline in crime rates and reshuffling existing officers into a new LAPD office targeting gang violence. Also, the city's budget shortages led to cutbacks in overtime, reducing the possible positive impact of having more officers on the payroll.

And if more officers reduce crime, then why do Chicago and New York, which have much higher ratios of officers to residents, have higher crime rates than LA? In 2005, the LAPD's ratio of officers to residents was about half the rate of the NYPD, even though Los Angeles has a much larger geographic area that should make it harder to patrol. Chicago, with markedly fewer people and a smaller area to patrol, actually has more officers than LA.

The varying circumstances among big-city police departments show there is no single ratio of officers to population that can be applied to all cities. The optimum ratio depends on local conditions, according to the International Association of Chiefs of Police (IACP). "Defining patrol staffing allocation and deployment requirements is a complex endeavor which requires consideration of an extensive series of factors and a sizable body of reliable, current data," the group says.

Therefore, a low crime rate might allow a city to have fewer officers. But without a universal standard for officer-to-population ratios, there will always be debate on what the right level for a city should be. For example, Charlie Beck, the current LAPD chief, insisted in a 2010 interview that LA should have 12,000 officers. With a lower number, "You're not able to spend any time working on solutions," he said. "You're just constantly chasing the symptoms."

But by January 2013, Beck was concerned about just maintaining the 10,000-officer level. If voters do not approve a sales tax increase in an upcoming ballot initiative, Beck warned that the number of officers might have to be cut.

Resources: David Zahniser, "LAPD Force Exceeds 10,000 for the First Time, Officials Say," *Los Angeles Times*, January 8, 2013, http://articles.latimes.com/2013/jan/08/local/la-me-lapd-size-20130108; Philip Rosenbaum, "LAPD Chief: The Thin Blue Line Keeps Getting Thinner," *CNN*, February 16, 2010, http://articles.cnn.com/2010-02-16/justice/california.lapd.beck_1_beck-transparency-cnn?_s=PM:CRIME; and Jerry Berrios, "LAPD Sees Force Grow to Record High," *Los Angeles Daily News*, March 2, 2009, http://www.dailynews.com/ci_11822848.

NEW! Paying for It boxes in the first four parts of the text explore how the criminal justice system is affected by today's financial realities. Financial necessity in the form of budget shortfalls and limits on available resources is leading police, courts, and corrections to become more cost-efficient.

paying for it
Cost-Efficient Criminal Justice

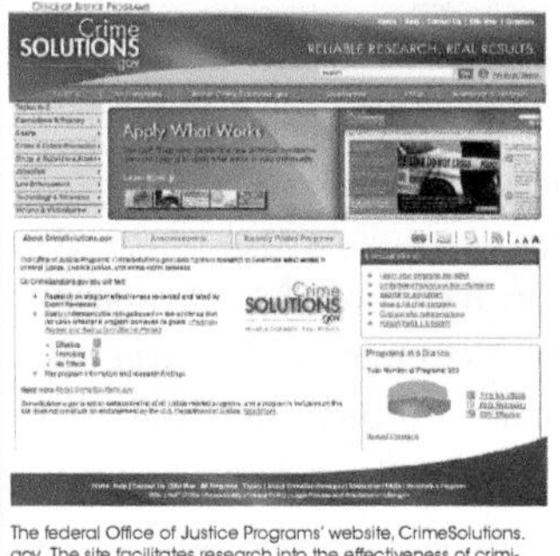

The federal Office of Justice Programs' website, CrimeSolutions.gov. The site facilitates research into the effectiveness of criminal justice-related programs. How can the site be of help to policymakers?

The Great Recession of the past few years has forced state and local governments to make some hard choices about budgets. As government revenues declined due to a drop in taxable income, consumer spending, lower property values, and fewer licensing fees, officials in many locales have been forced to reduce expenditures and to curb services. Criminal justice agencies have not been immune to the impact of budget cuts, and many are looking for ways to offer quality services at a lower cost. Noteworthy is the fact that today's emphasis on the efficient use of resources has combined with calls for greater accountability and transparency in government spending.

To discuss today's concern with cost efficiency throughout the justice system, a number of boxes like this one appear throughout the text and describe what police departments, courts, and corrections agencies are doing as they move toward increasingly responsible stewardship of taxpayer dollars. Noteworthy is the fact that today's emphasis on the efficient use of resources has combined with calls for greater accountability and transparency in government spending.

In an effort to help justice agencies utilize resources wisely, the U.S. Department of Justice announced a new website in 2012. Located at **http://crimesolutions.gov,** the site is designed to provide policymakers, justice system administrators, and taxpayers with the ability to assess the effectiveness of state and local anticrime programs. The site, run by the Washington, D.C.-based National Institute of Justice (NIJ), has been described by federal officials as a "single, credible, online resource to inform practitioners and policymakers about what works in criminal justice, juvenile justice, and crime victim services."

Once criminal justice programs have been selected for review, experts working with the NIJ analyze available research documenting the program's effectiveness and cost efficiency. Programs are then scored on CrimeSolutions.gov according to established criteria and identified as either: (1) effective, (2) promising, or (3) no effect. Where evidence on a program is insufficient or inconsistent, it receives no ranking. As of this writing, 33% of programs reviewed have been scored as "effective," whereas another 57% were identified as "promising."

Finally, the concept of **sustainable justice** was advanced by Melissa Hickman Barlow, in her 2012 presidential address to the Academy of Criminal Justice Sciences. Sustainable justice, said Barlow, can be defined as "criminal laws and criminal justice institutions, policies, and practices that achieve justice in the present without compromising the ability of future generations to have the benefits of a just society." Sustainable justice, in other words, refers to criminal justice practices and institutions that are affordable now, and into the future. Visit the topics page of CrimeSolutions.gov at **http://www.crimesolutions.gov/topics.aspx** to learn more about the categories of programs being evaluated.

References: CrimeSolutions.gov; Melissa Hickman Barlow, "Sustainable Justice: 2012 Presidential Address to the Academy of Criminal Justice Sciences," *Justice Quarterly*, Vol. 30, No. 1 (2013), pp. 1–17.

Issues boxes throughout the text showcase selected issues in the field of criminal justice, including topics related to multiculturalism, diversity, and technology.

CJ | ISSUES
Investigating Crime in a Multicultural Setting

In the mid-1990s, the Washington, D.C.–based National Crime Prevention Council (NCPC) published an important guide for American law enforcement officers who work with multicultural groups. The principles it contains can be applied equally to most foreign-born individuals living in the United States and are especially important to patrol officers and criminal investigators.

The NCPC guide points out that it is important for well-intentioned newcomers to this country to learn that the law enforcement system in the United States is not a national police force but a series of local, state, and federal agencies that take seriously their obligation to "serve and protect" law-abiding residents. Newcomers need to know that police officers can teach them how to protect themselves and their families from crime. Many immigrants, especially political refugees, come from countries in which the criminal justice system is based on tyranny, repression, and fear.

The NCPC suggests that law enforcement officers and other members of the criminal justice system can help ease this transition by working not only to communicate with immigrants but also to understand them and the complexities of their native cultures. The mere absence of conflict in a neighborhood does not mean that residents of different cultures have found harmony and a cooperative working relationship, says the NCPC. True multicultural integration occurs when various cultures reach a comfortable day-to-day interaction marked by respect, interest, and caring.

Communities in which immigrants and law enforcement have established close positive ties benefit considerably, according to the NCPC. Immigrants gain greater access to police and other services, such as youth programs, victims' assistance, parenting classes, medical assistance programs, business networking, and neighborhood groups. Crime decreases in communities where law enforcement officers help immigrants learn to protect themselves against crime.

For police officers working in communities in which "language is a serious barrier between cultures," the NCPC suggests the following pointers for communicating more effectively:

- Be patient when speaking with someone who does not clearly understand your language. Speak slowly and distinctly. Be willing to repeat words or phrases if necessary. Remember that shouting never helps a nonnative speaker understand better.
- Be careful with your choice of words, selecting those that are clear, straightforward, and simple to understand. Avoid colloquialisms and slang.
- Allow extra time for investigation when the people involved have not mastered English.
- Be sure that anyone who serves as an interpreter is fully qualified and has had experience. Interpreting under pressure is a difficult task; lack of training can lead to mistakes.
- Be candid about your ability to speak or understand a language. Trying to "fake it" just leads to confusion, misunderstanding, and misspent time.
- Never assume that someone is less intelligent just because he or she doesn't speak English well.

Visit the National Crime Prevention Council via http://www.ncpc.org.

Reference: Adapted from National Crime Prevention Council, *Building and Crossing Bridges: Refugees and Law Enforcement Working Together* (Washington, DC: NCPC, 1994).

Supplements

The 13th edition of *Criminal Justice Today* is supported by a complete package of instructor and student resources:

- ***eBooks.*** *Criminal Justice Today* is available in three eBook formats, *CourseSmart*, ePub, and Adobe Reader. *CourseSmart* is an exciting new choice for students looking to save money. As an alternative to purchasing the printed textbook, students can purchase an electronic version of the same content. With a *CourseSmart* eTextbook, students can search the text, make notes online, print out reading assignments that incorporate lecture notes, and bookmark important passages for later review. For more information, or to purchase access to the *CourseSmart* eTextbook, visit **www.coursesmart.com.**
- ***TestBank*** and ***MyTest.*** These supplements represent a new standard in testing material. Whether you use the basic *TestBank* in the Instructor's Manual or generate questions electronically through *MyTest*, every question is linked to the a chapter learning objective and includes the text page number and level of difficulty. This allows for quick reference in the text and an easy way to check the difficulty level and variety of your questions. *MyTest* can be accessed at **www.PearsonMyTest.com.**
- ***The Pearson Criminal Justice Online Community.*** Available at **www.mycriminaljusticecommunity.com**, this site is a place for educators to connect and to exchange ideas and advice on courses, content, *Criminal Justice Interactive* and *Criminology Interactive,* and so much more.

Other Supplements

- Standard PowerPoint Presentation and Classroom Response System PowerPoint Presentation
- Annotated Instructor's Edition
- Instructor's Manual with Test Bank

To access supplementary materials online, instructors need to request an instructor access code. Go to **www.pearsonhighered.com**, click the Instructor Resource Center link, and then click Request IRC access for an instructor access code. Within 48 hours of registering you will receive a confirming e-mail including an instructor access code. Once you have received your code, go to the site and log on for full instructions on downloading the materials you wish to use.

Pearson Online Course Solutions

Criminal Justice Today is supported by online course solutions that include interactive learning modules, a variety of assessment tools, videos, simulations, and current event features. Go to **www.pearsonhighered.com** or contact your local representative for the latest information.

Acknowledgments

My thanks to all who assisted in so many different ways in the development of this textbook. Thanks also to Leslie Brado, April Cleland, Lynda Cramer, Alicia Wozniak, David Gesell, JoEllen Gohr, Megan Moffo, Steve Robb, Elisa Rogers, Kevin Cecil, Deidra Skahill, and all the past and present Pearson staff with whom I have worked. They are true professionals and have made the task of manuscript development enjoyable.

A very special thank-you goes to Leah Jewel, David Gesell, and Vern Anthony for their stewardship and support; and to my editor, Gary Bauer; marketing manager Mary Salzman; senior marketing coordinator Alicia Wozniak, and marketing assistant Les Robert; and to the Course Connect team for their invaluable insights, perseverance, and dedication to this project.

I am grateful to my supplements authors for their support of this new edition: Bill Shaw for the Instructor's Manual; Derek Licata, Interactive PowerPoints; David Pasick, CRS PowerPoints; and William Hanna, MyTest and Test Bank. I am grateful, as well, to the manuscript reviewers involved in this and previous editions for holding me to the fire when I might have opted for a less rigorous coverage of some topics—especially Darl Champion of Methodist College, Jim Smith at West Valley College, Cassandra L. Renzi of Keiser University, and Bryan J. Vila formerly of the National Institute of Justice for their insightful suggestions as this book got under way.

I thank the reviewers of the manuscript for this 13th edition. They include:

Stephanie Abramoske-James, Collin County Community College
Jonathan Appel, Tiffin University
Earl Ballou, Palo Alto College
Kevin Beaver, Florida State University
Robert Bing, University of Texas - Arlington
Michael Bisciglia, Southeastern Louisiana University
Gary Boyer, Dabney S. Lancaster CC
Chip Burns, Texas Christian University
Dr. Joseph Ciccone, WWCC
Lisa Clayton, Community College of Southern Nevada
Tomasina Cook, Erie Community College
William Corbet, New Mexico State University
Catherine Cowling, Campbell University
Fredrick Crawford, Missouri Baptist University
Robert Franzese, University of Oklahoma
Barry Langford, Columbia College
Tony LaRose, University of Tampa
Francis Marrocco, Triton College
Theresa McGuire, DeVry University
Melanie Norwood, Southeastern Louisiana University
Christopher Rosbough, Florida State University
Tim Schuetzle, University of Mary
Bart Scroggins, Columbia College
Francis Williams, Plymouth State University

I also thank the following reviewers of previous editions, including:

Howard Abadinsky, St. Johns University
Reed Adams, Elizabeth City State University
Earl Ballou, Jr., Palo Alto College
Kevin Barrett, Palomar College
Larry Bassi, State University of New York (SUNY)–Brockport
Richard Becker, North Harris College
Todd Beitzel, University of Findlay
Gad Bensinger, Loyola University–Chicago
Gary Boyer, Sr., Dabney S. Lancaster Community College
Mindy Bradley, University of Arkansas
Alton Braddock, University of Louisiana–Monroe
Pauline Brennan, University of Nebraska
Ronald Burns, Texas Christian University
Theodore P. Byrne, California State University–Dominguez Hills
W. Garret Capune, California State University–Fullerton
Mike Carlie, Southwest Missouri State University
Geary Chlebus, James Sprunt Community College
Steven Christiansen, Joliet Junior College
Joseph Ciccone, WWCC & CCI/Everest College
Jon E. Clark, Temple University
Lora C. Clark, Pitt Community College
Warren Clark, California State University–Bakersfield
Lisa Clayton, College of Southern Nevada
Ellen G. Cohn, Florida International University
Gary Colboth, California State University–Long Beach
Kimberly Collica, Monroe College
Tomasina Cook, Erie Community College
Susan C. Craig, University of Central Florida
Jannette O. Domingo, John Jay College of Criminal Justice
Vicky Doworth, Montgomery College
Daniel P. Doyle, University of Montana
Martha Earwood, University of Alabama–Birmingham
Steven Egger, University of Houston–Clearlake
Ron Fagan, Pepperdine University
Alan S. Frazier, Glendale Community College
Harold A. Frossard, Moraine Valley Community College

Barry J. Garigen, Genesee Community College
S. Marlon Gayadeen, Buffalo State College
Michael Gray, Wor-Wic Community College
Alex Greenberg, Niagara County Community College
Tim Griffin, St. Xavier University
Julia Hall, Drexel University
Ed Heischmidt, Rend Lake College
Gary Herwald, Central Texas College and University of Phoenix
Dennis Hoffman, University of Nebraska at Omaha
Michael Hooper, California Department of Justice
William D. Hyatt, Western Carolina University
Nicholas H. Irons, County College of Morris
Galan M. Janeksela, University of Tennessee at Chattanooga
Jeffrie Jinian, Florida Gulf Coast University
Steve Johnson, Eastern Arizona College
Terry L. Johnson, Owens Community College
David M. Jones, University of Wisconsin–Oshkosh
Victor Kappeler, Eastern Kentucky State University
P. Ray Kedia, Grambling State University
David Keys, New Mexico State University
Lloyd Klein, Louisiana State University–Shreveport
Sylvia Kuennen, Briar Cliff College
Karel Kurst-Swanger, Oswego State University of New York
Hamid R. Kusha, Texas A&M International University
David Legere, New England College
David S. Long, St. Francis College
Joan Luxenburg, University of Central Oklahoma
Michael Lyman, Columbia College
Adam Martin, South Florida Community College
Dena Martin, Ivy Tech Community College of Indiana
Richard H. Martin, Elgin Community College
David C. May, Eastern Kentucky University
G. Larry Mays, New Mexico State University
Thomas P. McAninch, Scott Community College
William McGovern, Sussex County Community College
Susan S. McGuire, San Jacinto College North
Robert J. Meadows, California Lutheran University
Jim Mezhir, Niagara County Community College
Rick Michelson, Grossmont College
Jeffrey D. Monroe, Xavier University
Harvey Morley, California State University–Long Beach
Jacqueline Mullany, Indiana University Northwest
Charles Myles, California State University–Los Angeles
Bonnie Neher, Harrisburg Area Community College
David Neubauer, University of New Orleans–Lakefront
Melanie Norwood, Southeastern Louisiana University
Ken O'Keefe, Prairie State College
David F. Owens, Onondaga Community College
Michael J. Palmiotto, Wichita State University
Lance Parr, Grossmont College
William H. Parsonage, Penn State University
Allison Payne, Villanova University
Ken Peak, University of Nevada–Reno
Joseph M. Pellicciotti, Indiana University Northwest
Roger L. Pennel, Central Missouri State University
Joseph L. Peterson, University of Illinois at Chicago
Morgan Peterson, Palomar College
Caryl Poteete, Illinois Central College
Gary Prawel, Keuka College
Philip J. Reichel, University of Northern Colorado
Albert Roberts, Rutgers University
Carl E. Russell, Scottsdale Community College
Paul Sarantakos, Parkland College
Wayne J. Scamuffa, ITT Technical Institute
Benson Schaffer, IVAMS Arbitration and Mediation Services
Stephen J. Schoenthaler, California State University–Stanislaus
Jeff Schrink, Indiana State University
Scott Senjo, Weber State University
Judith M. Sgarzi, Mount Ida College
Louis F. Shepard, West Georgia Technical College
John Siler, Georgia Perimeter College
Ira Silverman, University of South Florida
Loretta J. Stalans, Loyola University–Chicago
Domenick Stampone, Raritan Valley Community College
Z. G. Standing Bear, University of Colorado
Mark A. Stetler, Montgomery College
B. Grant Stitt, University of Nevada–Reno
Norma Sullivan, College of DuPage; Troy University
Robert W. Taylor, University of North Texas
Lawrence F. Travis III, University of Cincinnati
Ron Vogel, California State University–Long Beach
David Whelan, Western Carolina University
Dianne A. Williams, North Carolina A&T State University
Kristin Williams, Ball State University
Lois Wims, Salve Regina University
L. Thomas Winfree, Jr., New Mexico State University
John M. Wyant, Illinois Central College
Jeffrey Zack, Fayetteville Technical Community College

My thanks to everyone! I would also like to extend a special thanks to the following individuals for their invaluable comments and suggestions along the way: Gordon Armstrong, Avon Burns, Kathy Cameron-Hahn, Alex Obi Ekwuaju, Gene Evans, Joe Graziano, Donald J. Melisi, Greg Osowski, Phil Purpura, Victor Quiros, John Robich, Barry Schreiber, Dave Seip, Ted Skotnicki, Stewart Stanfield, Bill Tafoya, Tom Thackery, Joe Trevalino, Howard Tritt, Bill Tyrrell, Tim Veiders, and Bob Winslow.

Thanks are also due to everyone who assisted in artistic arrangements, including Sergeant Michael Flores of the New York City Police Department's Photo Unit, Michael L. Hammond of the Everett (Washington) Police Department, Mikael Karlsson of Arresting Images, Assistant Chief James M. Lewis of the Bakersfield (California) Police Department, Tonya Matz of the University of Illinois at Chicago, and Monique Smith of the National Institute of Justice—all of whom were especially helpful in providing a wealth of photo resources. I am especially indebted to University of Illinois Professor Joseph L. Peterson for his assistance with sections on scientific evidence and to George W. Knox of the National Gang Crime Research Center for providing valuable information on gangs and gang activity.

I'd also like to acknowledge Chief J. Harper Wilson and Nancy Carnes of the FBI's Uniform Crime Reporting Program; Mark Reading of the Drug Enforcement Administration's Office of Intelligence; Kristina Rose at the National Institute of Justice; Marilyn Marbrook and Michael Rand at the Office of Justice Programs; Wilma M. Grant of the U.S. Supreme Court's Project Hermes; Ken Kerle at the American Jail Association; Lisa Bastian, survey statistician with the National Crime Victimization Survey Program; Steve Shackelton with the U.S. Parks Service; Ronald T. Allen, Steve Chaney, Bernie Homme, and Kenneth L. Whitman, all with the California Peace Officer Standards and Training Commission; Dianne Martin at the Drug Enforcement Administration; and George J. Davino of the New York City Police Department for their help in making this book both timely and accurate.

Last, but by no means least, Taylor Davis, H. R. Delaney, Jannette O. Domingo, Al Garcia, Rodney Hennigsen, Norman G. Kittel, Robert O. Lampert, and Joseph M. Pellicciotti should know that their writings, contributions, and valuable suggestions at the earliest stages of manuscript development continue to be very much appreciated. Thank you, everyone!

FRANK SCHMALLEGER, Ph.D.

About the Author

Frank Schmalleger, Ph.D., is Distinguished Professor Emeritus at the University of North Carolina at Pembroke. He holds degrees from the University of Notre Dame and The Ohio State University, having earned both a master's (1970) and a doctorate in sociology (1974) from The Ohio State University with a special emphasis in criminology. From 1976 to 1994, he taught criminology and criminal justice courses at the University of North Carolina at Pembroke. For the last 16 of those years, he chaired the university's Department of Sociology, Social Work, and Criminal Justice. The university named him Distinguished Professor in 1991.

Schmalleger has taught in the online graduate program of the New School for Social Research, helping build the world's first electronic classrooms in support of distance learning through computer telecommunications. As an adjunct professor with Webster University in St. Louis, Missouri, Schmalleger helped develop the university's graduate program in security administration and loss prevention. He taught courses in that curriculum for more than a decade. An avid Web user and website builder, Schmalleger is also the creator of a number of award-winning websites, including some that support this textbook.

Frank Schmalleger is the author of numerous articles and more than 40 books, including the widely used *Criminal Justice: A Brief Introduction* (Pearson, 2014), *Criminology Today* (Pearson, 2015), and *Criminal Law Today* (Pearson, 2014).

Schmalleger is also founding editor of the journal *Criminal Justice Studies.* He has served as editor for the Pearson series *Criminal Justice in the Twenty-First Century* and as imprint adviser for Greenwood Publishing Group's criminal justice reference series.

Schmalleger's philosophy of both teaching and writing can be summed up in these words: "In order to communicate knowledge we must first catch, then hold, a person's interest—be it student, colleague, or policymaker. Our writing, our speaking, and our teaching must be relevant to the problems facing people today, and they must in some way help solve those problems." Visit the author's website at **http://www.schmalleger.com**.

Justice is truth in action!

—Benjamin Disraeli (1804–1881)

Injustice anywhere is a threat to justice everywhere.

—Martin Luther King, Jr. (1929–1968)

PART

1

CRIME IN AMERICA

INDIVIDUAL RIGHTS VERSUS PUBLIC ORDER

The accused has these common law, constitutional, statutory, and humanitarian rights:

- Justice for the individual
- Personal liberty
- Dignity as a human being
- The right to due process

Those individual rights must be effectively balanced against these community concerns:

- Social justice
- Equality before the law
- The protection of society
- Freedom from fear

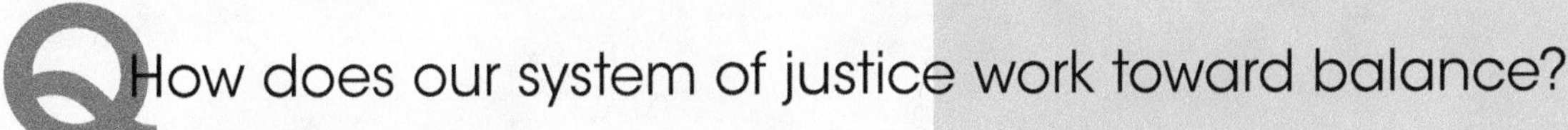

Q How does our system of justice work toward balance?

The Will of the People Is the Best Law

The great American statesman and orator Daniel Webster (1782–1852) once wrote, "Justice is the great interest of man on earth. It is the ligament which holds civilized beings and civilized nations together." Although Webster lived in a relatively simple time with few problems and many shared rules, justice has never been easily won. Unlike Webster's era, society today is highly complex. It is populated by groups with a wide diversity of interests, and it faces threats and challenges unimaginable in Webster's day. It is within this challenging context that the daily practice of American criminal justice occurs.

The criminal justice system has three central components: police, courts, and corrections. The history, the activities, and the legal environment surrounding the police are discussed in Part 2 of this book. Part 3 describes the courts, and Part 4 deals with prisons, probation, and parole. Part 5 provides a guide to the future of the justice system and describes the impact of the threat of terrorism on enforcement agencies. We begin here in Part 1, however, with an overview of that grand ideal that we call *justice*, and we consider how the justice ideal relates to the everyday practice of criminal justice in the United States today. To that end, in the four chapters that make up this section, we will examine how and why laws are made. We will look at the wide array of interests that impinge upon the justice system, and we will examine closely the dichotomy that distinguishes citizens who are primarily concerned with individual rights from those who emphasize the need for individual responsibility and social accountability—a dichotomy that has existed since the start of our country, but has become especially significant in the wake of the September 11, 2001, terrorist attacks. In the pages that follow, we will see how justice can mean personal freedom and protection from the power of government to some people and greater safety and security to others. In this section, we will also lay the groundwork for the rest of the text by painting a picture of crime in America today, suggesting possible causes for it, and showing how policies for dealing with crime have evolved.

As you read about the complex tapestry that is the practice of criminal justice in America today, you will learn of a system in flux, perhaps less sure of its purpose than at any time in its history. You may also catch the sense, however, that very soon a new and reborn institution of justice may emerge from the ferment that now exists. Whatever the final outcome, it can only be hoped that *justice*, as proffered by the American system of criminal justice, will be sufficient to hold our civilization together—and to allow it to prosper in the twenty-first century and beyond.

Tony Avelar-Pool/Getty Images

1 WHAT IS CRIMINAL JUSTICE?

OUTLINE

- Introduction
- A Brief History of Crime in America
- The Theme of this Book
- Criminal Justice and Basic Fairness
- American Criminal Justice: System and Functions
- American Criminal Justice: The Process
- Due Process and Individual Rights
- Evidence-Based Practice in Criminal Justice
- Multiculturalism and Diversity in Criminal Justice

LEARNING OBJECTIVES

After reading this chapter, you should be able to

- Summarize the history of crime in America and corresponding changes in the American criminal justice system.
- Describe the public-order (crime-control) and individual-rights (due process) perspectives of criminal justice, concluding with how the criminal justice system balances the two perspectives.
- Explain the relationship of criminal justice to general concepts of equity and fairness.
- Describe the American criminal justice system in terms of its three major components and their respective functions.
- Describe the process of American criminal justice, including the stages of criminal case processing.
- Define *due process of law,* including where the American legal system guarantees due process.
- Describe the role of evidence-based practice in contemporary criminal justice.
- Explain how multiculturalism and diversity present challenges to and opportunities for the American system of criminal justice.

People expect both safety and justice and do not want to sacrifice one for the other.

CHRISTOPHER STONE, President, Open Society Foundations[1]

Introduction

On December 14, 2012, 20-year-old Adam Lanza, a socially awkward young man, went on a shooting rampage at Sandy Hook Elementary School in Newtown, Connecticut. In a matter of minutes, Lanza had shot to death 20 kindergarten students, four teachers, a principal, and the school's psychologist. The shooting spree ended when Lanza turned one of his three guns on himself. Before the massacre, Lanza shot his mother to death at the house they shared only minutes from the school. The horrific shooting was covered by media services for days, and reignited an intense national debate about gun control.

Although the Newton shooting stood out as especially horrific because it ended so many innocent young lives, it is but one of a number of random mass shootings in the United States in recent years. In 2012 alone, there were 12 other random mass killings—including a July attack by a lone gunman in an Aurora, Colorado, movie theater where 12 people were killed and another 58 injured during a midnight showing of the movie *The Dark Knight Rises.*[2] In that crime, the admitted shooter, 24-year-old James Eagan Holmes, who dressed as the Joker (a nefarious character from the film) during the shooting spree, was arrested outside of the theater. He remains jailed as this book goes to press.

Experts tell us that the number of random mass shootings is on the increase. According to the *Wall Street Journal*, there "were 18 random mass shootings in the 1980s, 54 in the 1990s, and 87 in the 2000s."[3] The *Journal's* emphasis was on *random shootings*, but a 2013 *USA Today* report on *mass killings* found that the number of all mass killings since 2006—including those in which at least some of the victims were known to the killers—totaled 146, and that 900 lives were lost in such incidents.[4] The FBI defines a mass killing as an incident in which at least four people lost their lives.[5]

A fair question would be to ask why the number of incidents, especially those identified as random, is increasing. Some answers might be found in the personal characteristics of the shooters. Lanza and Holmes shared a number of things in common. Both were middle-class white males in their early 20s who were regarded by their peers as unnervingly intelligent. Holmes had been a former neuroscience graduate student at the University of Colorado's Anschutz Campus, whose academic career unraveled shortly before the movie theater shooting. Lanza, once a prominent member of his high school's technology club and an honor student, was said to have been extraordinarily bright by former teachers. Neither shooter had a previous criminal record.[6]

REUTERS/Bill Robles

James Eagan Holmes, who killed 12 people and wounded 58 others at an Aurora, Colorado, movie theater in 2012. Would stricter gun control laws or better mental health treatment be effective at reducing incidents of random violence in America?

Kateleen Foy/Getty Images

Adam Lanza, the Sandy Hook Elementary School shooter who killed 20 kindergarten students and six others in Newtown, Connecticut in 2012—shown when he was a boy. Lanza also shot and killed his mother and himself. What can be done to prevent mass shootings?

After the Newtown shooting, investigators learned that Lanza had created a huge spreadsheet listing the identities of previous mass killers—including details about each crime, the number of people killed, the weapons used, the locations of the shootings, and so on. A senior investigator involved in gathering evidence at Lanza's home told a police audience that Lanza appeared to be trying to "win" the record for the most people killed, and that he may have been planning the attack for years.[7]

What may have contributed to both incidents, however, were two additional features the two men shared—social alienation and a disordered personality.[8] According to the American Psychiatric Association, most mentally ill people do not turn to violence, although some forms of mental illness have been associated with aggression and criminal activity, especially when combined with illegal drug use.[9]

Questions about Lanza's mental health were quickly raised following the Sandy Hook shootings by former friends and family members who knew him to be a painfully shy, reclusive, and socially isolated individual. Described by personal acquaintances as "very bright" but emotionally troubled, Lanza may have suffered from a form of Asperger's syndrome and was said to be impervious to physical pain. He had been on numerous medications intended to lower the anxiety that he experienced in everyday social situations, and prior to the Newtown shootings, his mother had repeatedly sought help in controlling her increasingly unresponsive and emotionally withdrawn son.

■ **crime** Conduct in violation of the criminal laws of a state, the federal government, or a local jurisdiction for which there is no legally acceptable justification or excuse.[i]

■ **Follow the author's tweets about the latest crime and justice news @schmalleger.**

Holmes, the Colorado shooter, met with at least three mental health professionals prior to the movie theater shooting, and CBS news reports that the fact "adds to the picture of Holmes being clearly on [psychiatrists'] radar in the time period leading up the shooting."[10]

Once we understand that guns, social disengagement, and certain forms of mental illness can prove to be a dangerous combination, it is important to ask whether something can be done to predict and prevent episodes of random mass violence. Two days after the Newtown shooting President Obama, for example, told those gathered at a memorial service at the town's high school, "We can't tolerate this anymore,"[11] and promised to examine federal gun control options.[12]

Yet the answer may not be as simple as gun control. Some say that the focus should be on violence rather than guns, and that Americans must ask themselves why ours is such a violent society, and what can be done to curb the many murderous attacks on innocents that have been filling the media in recent years.

Mental health issues also need to be explored. Lanza and Holmes were known to have serious mental health problems, yet they were able to live freely in society, to arm themselves without alarming authorities, and to attack unprotected and innocent people in what should have been safe public places. As this chapter will later explain in some detail, American society is built upon a delicate balance between the demand for *personal freedoms* and the need for *public safety*. It is in the cracks that appear within the social and legal fabric woven from the attempt to achieve balance between these two contrasting goals that crimes like random mass shootings emerge.

A dozen years before the mass shootings described here, a very different kind of criminal event thrust itself on American society and our justice system with the September 11, 2001, terrorist attacks that targeted New York City's World Trade Center and the Pentagon. Those attacks, including one on an airliner that crashed in the Pennsylvania countryside, left nearly 3,000 people dead and caused billions of dollars in property damage. They have since been classified as the most destructive criminal activity ever to have been perpetrated on U.S. soil. The resulting "war on terrorism" changed the face of world politics and ushered in a new era in American society. Before the attacks, most Americans lived relatively secure lives, largely unfettered by fear of random personal attack. The attacks of 9-11, however, share something in common with the mass shootings of recent years. Following 9-11, a heated debate took place between those wanting to enforce powerful crime-prevention and security measures and others seeking to preserve the individual rights and freedoms that have long been characteristic of American life. This issue, which is also central to recent efforts to reduce the number of random mass killings, continues to feed TV talk shows, newspaper editorials, and Web blogs nationwide. It asks Americans to determine which rights, freedoms, and conveniences (if any) they are willing to sacrifice to increase personal and public safety.

American society is built upon a delicate balance between the demand for *personal freedoms* and the need for *public safety*.

Regardless of your personal position in the ongoing debate between freedom and safety, it is important to recognize that terrorism, like mass shootings, is a potentially horrendous **crime**. Many states and the federal government have statutes outlawing terrorism, although terrorism itself can involve many other kinds of crimes. In the case of the World Trade Center and Pentagon attacks, for example, the crimes committed included murder, kidnapping, hijacking, grand theft, felonious assault, battery, conspiracy, and arson.

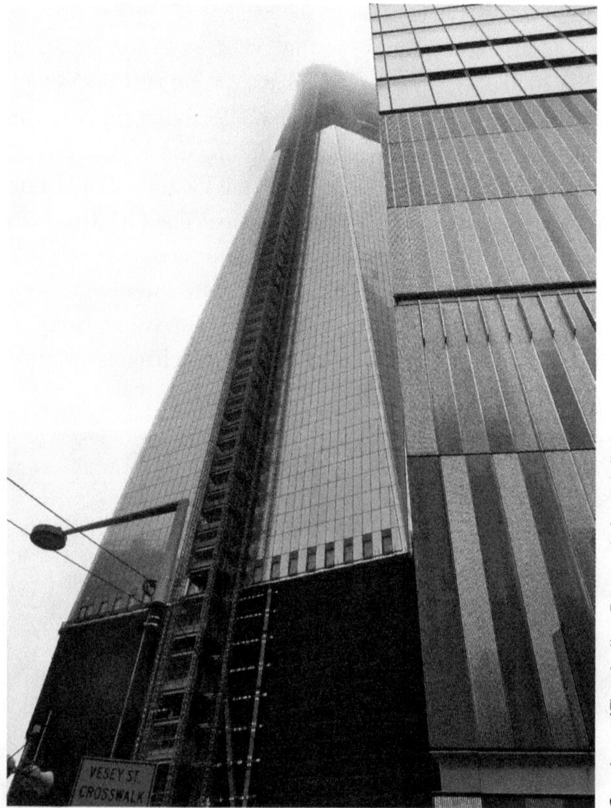

Courtesy of The Justice Research Association

Freedom Tower under construction at the World Trade Center site in New York City. When completed, the tower will stand 1,776 feet tall and be surrounded by several other buildings, and a memorial to the nearly 3,000 people who were killed in the terrorist attacks that demolished the Twin Towers in 2001. How did those attacks change the American justice system?

A Brief History of Crime in America

What we call *criminal activity* has undoubtedly been with us since the dawn of history, and crime control has long been a primary concern of politicians and government leaders worldwide. Still, the American experience with crime during the last half century has been especially influential in shaping the criminal justice system of today (Figure 1-1). In this country, crime waves have come and gone, including an 1850–1880 crime epidemic, which was apparently related to social upheaval caused by large-scale immigration and the Civil War.[13] A spurt of widespread organized criminal activity was associated with the Prohibition years of the early twentieth century. Following World War II, however, American crime rates remained relatively stable until the 1960s.

The 1960s and 1970s saw a burgeoning concern for the rights of ethnic and racial minorities, women, people with physical and mental challenges, and many other groups. The civil rights movement of the period emphasized equality of opportunity and respect for individuals, regardless of race, color, creed, gender, or personal attributes. As new laws were passed and suits filed, court involvement in the movement grew. Soon a plethora of hard-won individual rights and prerogatives, based on the U.S. Constitution, the Bill of Rights, and new federal and state legislation, were recognized and guaranteed. By the 1980s, the civil rights movement had profoundly affected all areas of social life—from education and employment to the activities of the criminal justice system.

1850–1880 A crime epidemic spurred by social upheaval brought on by large-scale immigration and the Civil War.

1920–1933 Prohibition spurs the growth of organized crime.

Following World War II, American crime rates remained relatively stable until the 1960s.

1960–1970 The civil rights movement of the period emphasized equality of opportunity and respect for individuals regardless of race, color, creed, gender, or personal attributes. This period also saw a dramatic increase in reported criminal activity.

1970s Reports of crimes such as murder, rape, and assault increased considerably.

1980s By the mid-1980s the dramatic increase in sale and use of illicit drugs led to increased crime. Large cities became havens for drug gangs and cities experienced dramatic declines in property values and quality of life. President Reagan declared a "war on drugs."

1992 The videotaped beating of Rodney King, an African American, by Los Angeles–area police officers was seen as an example of the abuse of police power.

By the late **1990s** the public perception was that crime rates were growing and that many offenders went unpunished. This led to a growing emphasis on responsibility and punishment and the development of a "get tough on crime" era.

The incidence of personal crime declined throughout the 1990s.

2001 A series of terrorist attacks on New York City, Washington, D.C., and elsewhere changed the focus of law enforcement to a proactive and more global approach.

2001 **USA PATRIOT Act** dramatically increases the investigatory authority of federal, state, and local police agencies.

2009 Bernard Madoff plead guilty to the largest Ponzi scheme in history. The crimes of Madoff, and widespread suspicions about the activities of Wall Street financiers, led to a number of white-collar crime investigations. White-collar crime came into focus as a serious threat to the American way of life.

2011 FBI most-wanted terrorist Osama Bin Laden was killed by U.S. special operations forces in Pakistan, leading to fears of a renewed terrorist onslaught on American targets throughout the world.

2012–2014 Epidemic of mass shootings and random violence sweeps public venues across the U.S.

Photo sources (from top): Courtesy of the Library of Congress; Darryl Jacobson / Everett Collection / Superstock; Darryl Jacobson / Superstock; Steven Hirsch/ Newscom; NetPics / Alamy

FIGURE 1-1 | Milestones in Crime History

■ **individual rights** The rights guaranteed to all members of American society by the U.S. Constitution (especially those found in the first ten amendments to the Constitution, known as the *Bill of Rights*). These rights are particularly important to criminal defendants facing formal processing by the criminal justice system.

■ **social disorganization** A condition said to exist when a group is faced with social change, uneven development of culture, maladaptiveness, disharmony, conflict, and lack of consensus.

This emphasis on **individual rights** was accompanied by a dramatic increase in reported criminal activity. Although some researchers doubted the accuracy of official accounts, reports by the Federal Bureau of Investigation (FBI) of "traditional" crimes like murder, rape, and assault increased considerably during the 1970s and into the 1980s. Many theories were advanced to explain this leap in observed criminality. Some analysts of American culture, for example, suggested that the combination of newfound freedoms and long-pent-up hostilities of the socially and economically deprived worked to produce **social disorganization**, which in turn increased criminality.

By the mid-1980s, the dramatic increase in the sale and use of illicit drugs threatened the foundation of American society. Cocaine, and later laboratory-processed "crack," spread to every corner of America. Large cities became havens for drug gangs, and many inner-city areas were all but abandoned to highly armed and well-financed drug racketeers. Cities experienced dramatic declines in property values, and residents wrestled with an eroding quality of life.

The American experience with crime during the last half century has been especially influential in shaping the criminal justice system of today.

By the close of the 1980s, neighborhoods and towns were fighting for their communal lives. Huge rents had been torn in the national social fabric, and the American way of life, long taken for granted, was under the gun. Traditional values appeared in danger of going up in smoke along with the "crack" being consumed openly in some parks and resorts. Looking for a way to stem the tide of increased criminality, many took up the call for "law and order." In response, President Ronald Reagan created a cabinet-level "drug czar" position to coordinate the "war on drugs." Careful thought was given at the highest levels to using the military to patrol the sea-lanes and air corridors through which many of the illegal drugs entered the country. President George H. W. Bush, who followed Reagan into office, quickly embraced and expanded the government's antidrug efforts.

A decade later, a few spectacular crimes that received widespread coverage in the news media fostered a sense among the American public that crime in the United States was out of hand and that strict new measures were needed to combat it. One such crime was the 1995 bombing of the Alfred P. Murrah Federal Building in Oklahoma City by antigovernment extremists. Another was the 1999 Columbine High School massacre in Colorado that left 12 students and one teacher dead.[14]

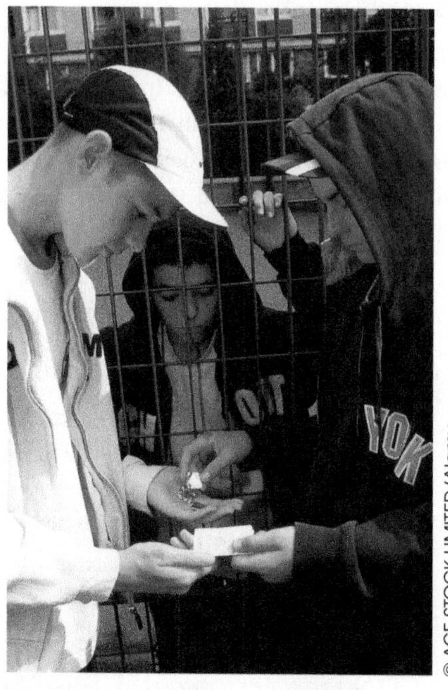

© ACE STOCK LIMITED/Alamy

A street-corner drug deal. By the mid-1980s, the American criminal justice system had become embroiled in a war against illicit drugs, filling the nation's prisons and jails with drug dealers, traffickers, and users. Has the war been won?

The public's perception that crime rates were growing, coupled with a belief that offenders frequently went unpunished or received only a judicial slap on the wrist, led to a burgeoning emphasis on responsibility and punishment. By the late 1990s, a newfound emphasis on individual accountability began to blossom among an American public fed up with crime and fearful of its own victimization. Growing calls for enhanced responsibility quickly began to replace the previous emphasis on individual rights. As a juggernaut of conservative opinion made itself felt on the political scene, Senator Phil Gramm of Texas observed that the public wants to "grab violent criminals by the throat, put them in prison [and] stop building prisons like Holiday Inns."[15]

By the late 1990s, a newfound emphasis on individual accountability began to blossom among an American public fed up with crime and fearful of its own victimization.

Then, in an event that changed the course of our society, public tragedy became forever joined with private victimization in our collective consciousness after a series of highly destructive and well-coordinated terrorist attacks on New York City and Washington, D.C., on September 11, 2001. Those attacks resulted in the collapse and total destruction of the twin 110-story towers of the World Trade Center and a devastating explosion at the Pentagon. Thousands of people perished, and many were injured. Although law enforcement and security agencies were unable to prevent the September 11 attacks, many have since moved from a reactive to a proactive posture in the fight against terrorism—a change that is discussed in more detail in Chapter 6, "Policing: Purpose and Organization."

The September 11 attacks also made clear that adequate law enforcement involves a global effort at controlling crime and reducing the risk of injury and loss to law-abiding people both at home and abroad. The attacks showed that criminal incidents that take place on the other side of the globe can affect those of us living in the United States, and they illustrated how the acquisition of skills needed to understand diverse cultures can help in the fight against crime and terrorism.

As Chapter 17, "Terrorism and Multinational Criminal Justice," points out, terrorism is a criminal act, and preventing terrorism and investigating terrorist incidents after they occur are highly important roles for local, state, and federal law enforcement agencies.

A different kind of offending, corporate, and white-collar crime took center stage in 2002 and 2003 as Congress stiffened penalties for unscrupulous business executives who knowingly falsify their company's financial reports.[16] The changes came amidst declining stock market values, shaken investor confidence, and threats to the viability of employee pension plans in the wake of a corporate crime wave involving criminal activities that had been planned and undertaken by executives at a number of leading corporations. In an effort to restore order to American financial markets, President George W. Bush signed the Sarbanes-Oxley Act on July 30, 2002.[17] The law, which has been called "the single most important piece of legislation affecting corporate governance, financial disclosure and the practice of public accounting since the US securities laws of the early 1930s,"[18] is intended to deter corporate fraud and to hold business executives accountable for their actions.

Today, white-collar crime continues to be a focus of federal prosecutors. In 2012, for example, Texas billionaire R. Allen Stanford, 61, was convicted by a federal jury in a $7 billion Ponzi scheme that he ran for almost 20 years.[19] Prosecutors convinced the jury that Stanford illegally funneled money from investors in his financial services firm to his personal accounts, allowing him to pay for an extravagant lifestyle including private jets, yachts, and a number of mansions for himself and his family. Following conviction, Stanford received a sentence of 110 years in prison.

Similarly, in a 2009 story that most readers will remember, investment fund manager Bernard Madoff pleaded guilty to operating a Ponzi scheme that defrauded investors out of as much as $50 billion.[20] Madoff pleaded guilty to 11 felony counts, including securities fraud, mail fraud, wire fraud, money laundering, and perjury. Madoff was sentenced to serve 150 years in federal prison—three times as long as federal probation officers had recommended.[21] White-collar crime is discussed in more detail in Chapter 2, "The Crime Picture."

Lucas Jackson/Reuters/Landov Media

Ponzi schemer Bernard Madoff is escorted by police and photographed by the media as he departs U.S. federal court after a hearing in New York, January 5, 2009. Madoff, whose financial crimes may have cost investors as much as $50 billion, was sentenced to 150 years in prison in 2009. What happened to the money he stole?

The current era is characterized by low and declining rates of "traditional" crimes such as rape, robbery, and burglary (see Chapter 2 for more details), but the specter of random mass shootings, a high number of inner-city murders, and novel forms of criminal activity complicates today's crime picture. In 2012, for example, the year of the mass shootings in Aurora, Colorado, and Newtown, Connecticut, both Camden, New Jersey, and Detroit, Michigan, reported more murders than at any time in their history, and other cities, including Chicago, Illinois, were seeing record homicide rates.[22] Similarly, as Chapter 2 explains in greater detail, many other types of crimes today are Internet-based or involve other forms of high-technology. Criminal perpetrators who illegally gain access to digital information (and money) through social media or Internet-based transactions are responsible for a significant level of criminal activity in the virtual world. Such crimes can

If we were to examine all forms of criminal activity, and if we were to become fully aware of all of today's hidden offenses, we would probably find that crimes today have undergone a significant shift away from historical forms of offending to more innovative schemes involving computers and other digital devices.

have very significant impacts on people's lives. Moreover, crimes committed through the medium of cyberspace frequently remain undiscovered, or are found out only with the passage of time. Computer-related crimes are discussed in Chapter 18, "The Future of Criminal Justice." For a detailed look at crimes, both historical and contemporary, visit **http://www.trutv.com/library/crime**.

The Theme of this Book

This book examines the American system of criminal justice and the agencies and processes that constitute it. It builds on a theme that is especially valuable for studying criminal justice today: *individual rights versus public order.* This theme draws on historical developments that have shaped our legal system and our understandings of crime and justice. It is one of the primary determinants of the nature of contemporary criminal justice—including criminal law, police practice, sentencing, and corrections.

A strong emphasis on individual rights rose to the forefront of American social thought during the 1960s and 1970s, a period known as the *civil rights era*. The civil rights era led to the recognition of fundamental personal rights that had previously been denied illegally to many people on the basis of race, ethnicity, gender, sexual preference, or disability. The civil rights movement soon expanded to include the rights of many other groups, including criminal suspects, parolees and probationers, trial participants, prison and jail inmates, and victims. As the emphasis on civil rights grew, new laws and court decisions broadened the rights available to many.

The treatment of criminal suspects was afforded special attention by those who argued that the purpose of any civilized society should be to secure rights and freedoms for each of its citizens—including those suspected and convicted of crimes. Rights advocates feared unnecessarily restrictive government action and viewed it as an assault on basic human dignity and individual liberty. They believed that at times it was necessary to sacrifice some degree of public safety and predictability to guarantee basic freedoms. Hence criminal rights activists demanded a justice system that limits police powers and that holds justice agencies accountable to the highest procedural standards.

During the 1960s and 1970s, the dominant philosophy in American criminal justice focused on guaranteeing the rights of criminal defendants while seeking to understand the root causes of crime and violence. The past 30 years, however, have witnessed increased interest in an ordered society, in public safety, and in the rights of crime victims. This change in attitudes was likely brought about by national frustration with the perceived inability of our society and its justice system to prevent crimes and to consistently hold offenders to heartfelt standards of right and wrong. Increased conservatism in the public-policy arena was given new life by the September 11, 2001, terrorist attacks and by widely publicized instances of sexual offenses targeting children. It continues to be sustained by the many stories of violent victimization, like random mass shootings, that seem to be the current mainstay of the American media.

Public perspectives in the late 20th century largely shifted away from seeing the criminal as an unfortunate victim of poor social and personal circumstances who is inherently protected by fundamental human and constitutional rights to seeing him or her as a dangerous social predator who usurps the rights and privileges of law-abiding citizens. Reflecting the "get tough on crime" attitudes of recent times, many Americans demanded to know how offenders can better be held accountable for violations of the criminal law. In late 2010, for example, California state senators unanimously passed Chelsea's Law, a bill intended to increase prison sentences and extend parole terms for offenders who commit sex crimes against minors. The bill, named after 17-year-old Chelsea King, who was raped and murdered by a convicted sex offender earlier in 2010, was signed into law by the state's governor soon after it passed the legislature.[23] Even in an era of difficult budgetary challenges, some states are continuing to extend prison sentences for sex offenders, restrict where released sex offenders can live, and improve public notification of the whereabouts of sex offenders.[24]

Public perspectives in the late 20th century largely shifted away from seeing the criminal as an unfortunate victim of poor social and personal circumstances who is inherently protected by fundamental human and constitutional rights to seeing him or her as a dangerous social predator who usurps the rights and privileges of law-abiding citizens.

Although financial constraints have tempered the zeal of legislators to expand criminal punishments, the tension between individual rights and social responsibility still forms the basis for much policymaking activity in the criminal justice arena. Those

■ **individual-rights advocate** One who seeks to protect personal freedoms within the process of criminal justice.

■ **social order** The condition of a society characterized by social integration, consensus, smooth functioning, and lack of interpersonal and institutional conflict. Also, a lack of social disorganization.

freedom OR safety? YOU decide

Clarence Thomas Says: "Freedom Means Responsibility"

In 2009, U.S. Supreme Court Justice Clarence Thomas spoke to a group of high school essay contest winners in a Washington, D.C., hotel ballroom. Thomas used the occasion, which was dedicated to our nation's Bill of Rights, to point out the importance of obligations as well as rights. "Today there is much focus on our rights," said Thomas. "Indeed, I think there is a proliferation of rights." But then he went on to say, "I am often surprised by the virtual nobility that seems to be accorded those with grievances. Shouldn't there at least be equal time for our Bill of Obligations and our Bill of Responsibilities?"

Today, the challenge for the criminal justice system, it seems, is to balance individual rights and personal freedoms with social control and respect for legitimate authority. Years ago, during the height of what was then a powerful movement to win back control of our nation's cities and to rein in skyrocketing crime rates, the *New York Post* sponsored a conference on crime and civil rights. The keynote speaker at that conference was New York City's mayor, Rudolph W. Giuliani. In his speech, Giuliani identified the tension between personal freedoms and individual responsibilities as the crux of the crime problem then facing his city and the nation. We mistakenly look to government and elected officials, Giuliani said, to assume responsibility for solving the problem of crime when, instead, each individual citizen must become accountable for fixing what is wrong with our society. "We only see the oppressive side of authority. . . . What we don't see is that freedom is not a concept in which people can do anything they want, be anything they can be. Freedom is about authority. Freedom is about the willingness of every single human being to cede to lawful authority a great deal of discretion about what you do."

You Decide

How can we, as Justice Thomas suggests, achieve a balance of rights and obligations in American society? What did Giuliani mean when he said, "What we don't see is that freedom is not a concept in which people can do anything they want, be anything they can be"? Is it possible to balance individual rights and personal freedoms with social control and respect for legitimate authority?

References: Adam Liptak, "Reticent Justice Opens Up to a Group of Students," *New York Times*, April 13, 2009, http://www.nytimes.com/2009/04/14/us/14bar.html (accessed September 2, 2009); and Philip Taylor, "Civil Libertarians: Giuliani's Efforts Threaten First Amendment," *Freedom Forum Online*, http://www.freedomforum.org (accessed September 5, 2007).

who fight for individual rights continue to carry the banner of civil and criminal rights for the accused and the convicted, while public-order activists loudly proclaim the rights of the victimized and call for an increased emphasis on social responsibility and criminal punishment for convicted criminals. In keeping with these realizations, the theme of this book can be stated as follows:

> There is widespread recognition in contemporary society of the need to balance (1) the freedoms and privileges of our nation's citizens and the respect accorded the rights of individuals faced with criminal prosecution against (2) the valid interests that society has in preventing future crimes, in public safety, and in reducing the harm caused by criminal activity. While the personal freedoms guaranteed to law-abiding citizens as well as to criminal suspects by the Constitution, as interpreted by the U.S. Supreme Court, must be closely guarded, the urgent social needs of communities to control unacceptable behavior and to protect law-abiding citizens from harm must be recognized. Still to be adequately addressed are the needs and interests of victims and the fear of crime and personal victimization that is often prevalent in the minds of many law-abiding citizens. It is important to recognize, however, that the drama between individual rights and public safety advocates now plays out in a tenuous economic environment characterized by financial constraints and a concern with effective public policy.

Figure 1-2 represents our theme and shows that most people today who intelligently consider the criminal justice system assume one of two viewpoints. We will refer to those who seek to protect personal freedoms and civil rights within society, and especially within the criminal justice process, as **individual-rights advocates**. Those who suggest that under certain circumstances involving criminal threats to public safety, the interests of society, especially crime control and **social order**, should take precedence

In this book, we seek to look at ways in which the individual-rights and public-order perspectives can be balanced to serve both sets of needs.

■ **public-order advocate** One who believes that under certain circumstances involving a criminal threat to public safety, the interests of society should take precedence over individual rights.
■ **justice** The principle of fairness; the ideal of moral equity.
■ **social justice** An ideal that embraces all aspects of civilized life and that is linked to fundamental notions of fairness and to cultural beliefs about right and wrong.

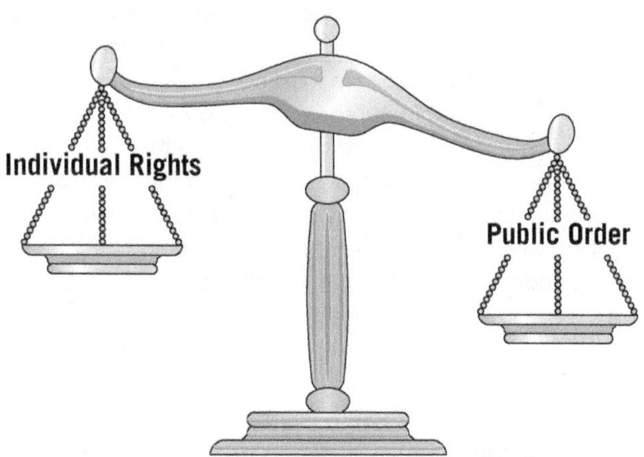

FIGURE 1-2 | The Theme of This Book
Balancing the concern for individual rights with the need for public order through the administration of criminal justice is the theme of this book.

over individual rights will be called **public-order advocates**. Recently, retired U.S. Supreme Court Justice Sandra Day O'Connor summed up the differences between these two perspectives by asking, "At what point does the cost to civil liberties from legislation designed to prevent terrorism [and crime] outweigh the added security that that legislation provides?"[25] In this book, we seek to look at ways in which the individual-rights and public-order perspectives can be balanced to serve both sets of needs. Hence you will find our theme discussed throughout this text, and within "Freedom or Safety?" boxes.

Criminal Justice and Basic Fairness

On the eve of the national election in November 2008, as final votes were being counted, President-elect Barack H. Obama gave an inspiring victory speech addressed to the nation and the world. In it he said, "A new dawn of American leadership is at hand. To those who would tear this world down—we will defeat you. To those who seek peace and security—we support you. And to all those who have wondered if America's beacon still burns as bright—tonight we proved once more that the true strength of our nation comes not from the might of our arms or the scale of our wealth, but from the enduring power of our ideals: democracy, liberty, opportunity, and unyielding hope." The president concluded that night's remarks with an enduring phrase, telling listeners that "the arc of the moral universe is long, but it bends toward justice." The phrase, a favorite of the president's, had been adapted from remarks that Martin Luther King, Jr., made before the Southern Christian Leadership Conference in 1967.[26]

There is no denying that the word *justice* is powerful, and—at the time—the president's choice of words spoke to all Americans. The reality, however, is that *justice* is an elusive term. Although most listeners came away inspired that night, few who heard the president's speech knew exactly what *justice* might mean and what form it might eventually take. Even to those living within the same society, *justice* means different things. And just as *justice* can be an ambiguous term for politicians, it is not always clear how justice can be achieved in the criminal justice system. For example, is "justice for all" a reasonable expectation of today's—or tomorrow's—system of criminal justice? The answer is unclear because individual interests and social needs often diverge. From the perspective of a society or an entire nation, justice can look very different than it does from the perspective of an individual or a small group of people. Because of this dilemma, we now turn our attention to the nature of justice.

British philosopher and statesman Benjamin Disraeli (1804–1881) defined **justice** as "truth in action." A popular dictionary defines it as "the principle of moral rightness, or conformity to truth."[27] **Social justice** is a concept that embraces all aspects of civilized life. It is linked to notions of fairness and to cultural beliefs about right and wrong. Questions of social justice can arise about relationships between individuals, between parties (such as corporations and agencies of government), between the rich and the poor, between the sexes, between ethnic groups and minorities—between social connections of all sorts. In the abstract, the concept of social justice embodies the highest personal and cultural ideals.

■ **civil justice** The civil law, the law of civil procedure, and the array of procedures and activities having to do with private rights and remedies sought by civil action. Civil justice cannot be separated from social justice because the justice enacted in our nation's civil courts reflects basic American understandings of right and wrong.

■ **criminal justice** In the strictest sense, the criminal (penal) law, the law of criminal procedure, and the array of procedures and activities having to do with the enforcement of this body of law. Criminal justice cannot be separated from social justice because the justice enacted in our nation's criminal courts reflects basic American understandings of right and wrong.

■ **administration of justice** The performance of any of the following activities: detection, apprehension, detention, pretrial release, post-trial release, prosecution, adjudication, correctional supervision, or rehabilitation of accused persons or criminal offenders.[ii]

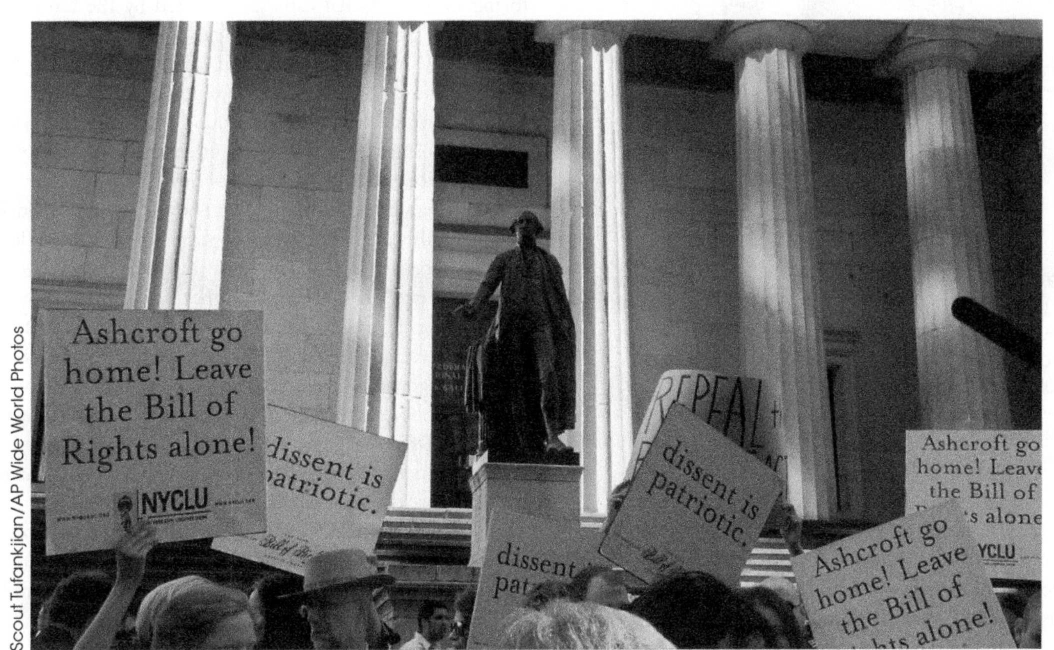

Demonstrators gathering on the steps of New York City's Federal Hall to protest provisions of the USA PATRIOT Act. Federal Hall served as the venue for President George Washington's inauguration in 1789 and was the meeting place of the First Congress, which wrote our nation's Bill of Rights. The PATRIOT Act was passed by Congress with little debate just 45 days after the terrorist attacks of September 11, 2001. Rights advocates claim that the act unfairly restricts individual liberties. What do you think?

Civil justice, one component of social justice, concerns itself with fairness in relationships between citizens, government agencies, and businesses in private matters, such as those involving contractual obligations, business dealings, hiring, and equality of treatment. **Criminal justice**, on the other hand, refers to the aspects of social justice that concern violations of the criminal law. As mentioned earlier, community interests in the criminal justice sphere demand the apprehension and punishment of law violators. At the same time, criminal justice ideals extend to the protection of the innocent, the fair treatment of offenders, and fair play by the agencies of law enforcement, including courts and correctional institutions.

Criminal justice, ideally speaking, is "truth in action" within the process that we call the **administration of justice**. It is therefore vital to remember that justice, in the truest and most satisfying sense of the word, is the ultimate goal of criminal justice—and of the day-to-day practices and challenges that characterize the American criminal justice system. Reality, unfortunately, typically falls short of the ideal and is severely complicated by the fact that justice seems to wear different guises when viewed from diverse vantage points. To some people, the criminal justice system and criminal justice agencies often seem biased in favor of the powerful. The laws they enforce seem to emanate more from well-financed, organized, and vocal interest groups than they do from any idealized sense of social justice. As a consequence, disenfranchised groups, those who do not feel as though they share in the political and economic power of society, are often wary of the agencies of justice, seeing them more as enemies than as benefactors.

On the other hand, justice practitioners, including police officers, prosecutors, judges, and corrections officials,

CJ | NEWS

Surveillance Technology Has Been Blanketing the Nation Since 9-11

Charles Rex Arbogast/AP Wide World Photos

A Chicago Police Department surveillance camera system and microphone unit positioned high above the street. This surveillance system includes a camera, high-bandwidth wireless communication, a strobe light, and a gunshot-recognition system, all in a bulletproof enclosure. The city is installing the surveillance system to spot crimes or terrorist activity. Do such units infringe on the personal freedoms of Chicago residents?

In *1984*, a book written more than 60 years ago, George Orwell envisioned a totalitarian regime that created an extensive surveillance network to monitor people's every move. Today, in the wake of the terrorist attacks of September 11, 2001, America has built a surveillance network that rivals that of *1984*, but without a totalitarian regime involved.

A decade after 9-11, there were an estimated 30 million surveillance cameras in the United States, says IMS Research. U.S. law enforcement is also implementing facial recognition technology, license plate readers, and gunfire alert systems. These developments prompted Jay Stanley of the American Civil Liberties Union to warn that the nation is heading toward "a total surveillance society in which your every move, your every transaction, is duly registered and recorded by some computer."

Most Americans, however, are not alarmed and actually welcome the trend. A 2007 ABC News/Washington Post poll showed that 71% of respondents favored increased video surveillance. In addition, courts have indicated that surveillance cameras, placed in plain view in public spaces, do not violate the Fourth Amendment, which bars governments from conducting unreasonable searches or seizures.

Technology has come a long way since surveillance cameras took small, grainy photos of two 9-11 hijackers boarding their plane at Boston's Logan Airport. Today's cameras collect and store images with many more pixels of information, making it possible to enlarge the photographs and capture previously undetected details.

In 2003, the city of Chicago began building what has become one of the most extensive surveillance systems in the United States, with 2,000 cameras operated by the police department and central monitoring over additional cameras operated by the transit system, school system, and private entities.

A 2011 study by the Urban Institute examining the use of surveillance cameras in three Chicago neighborhoods found they reduced crime in two of the neighborhoods. In the Humboldt Park neighborhood, for example, drug-related offenses and robberies fell by nearly 33% and violent crime declined by 20%.

Chicago has spent more than $60 million on its video surveillance network. Although that cost was supplemented by federal Homeland Security grants, such systems have high maintenance costs and compete for scarce tax dollars with other law enforcement activities, such as patrolling. The Urban Institute, however, found that Chicago saved $4.30 for every dollar spent on cameras in Humboldt Park.

Chicago uses wireless cameras mounted on poles with a "pan-tilt-zoom" technology that allows operators to follow subjects and focus in on them. Officers can do this manually, but as images proliferate, law enforcement has been increasingly turning to video analytic software that can sort through thousands of pictures to look for a specific image. This involves use of sophisticated software that recognizes faces or specific shapes and colors. The same technology is also used for scanners that read license plates and automatically check the number through a direct feed with state car license databases.

Police departments across the country are also implementing new sound-wave technology to monitor gunshots. This type of system, the best known of which is Shotspotter™, requires installing sensors throughout the city that can triangulate sound waves and identify the location of the gunshot within 5 yards. The Boston Police Department spent about $1.5 million to install gunshot detection systems and spends $150,000 to $175,000 in annual maintenance fees.

The effectiveness of gunfire alert systems has not been independently studied. According to the manufacturer, about one-third of reports are false alarms involving backfiring cars, construction, and other urban noises. But one definite advantage is that gunshot reports arrive in one to two minutes faster than 911 calls, bringing officers to the scene more quickly. And sometimes the systems pick up gunshots that were never called in.

Resources: "Surveillance Society: New High-Tech Cameras Are Watching You," *Popular Mechanics*, October 2, 2009, http://www.popularmechanics.com/technology/military/4236865; "Surveillance Cameras Cost-Effective Tools for Cutting Crime, 3-Year Study Concludes," *Urban Institute*, September 19, 2011, http://www.urban.org/publications/901450.html; and "Surveillance Technology Helps Boston Police Find Location of Gunfire," *WBUR*, December 23, 2011, http://www.wbur.org/2011/12/23/shotspotter.

frequently complain that their efforts to uphold the law garner unfair public criticism. The realities of law enforcement and of "doing justice," they say, are often overlooked by critics of the system who have little experience in dealing with offenders and victims. We must recognize, practitioners often tell us, that those accused of violating the criminal law face an elaborate process built around numerous legislative, administrative, and organizational concerns. Viewed realistically, although the criminal justice process can be fine-tuned to take into consideration the interests of ever-larger numbers of people, it rarely pleases everyone. The outcome of the criminal justice process in any particular case is a social product, and like any product that is the result of group effort, it must inevitably be a patchwork quilt of human emotions, reasoning, and concerns.

■ **criminal justice system** The aggregate of all operating and administrative or technical support agencies that perform criminal justice functions. The basic divisions of the operational aspects of criminal justice are law enforcement, courts, and corrections.

■ **consensus model** A criminal justice perspective that assumes that the system's components work together harmoniously to achieve the social product we call *justice*.

■ **conflict model** A criminal justice perspective that assumes that the system's components function primarily to serve their own interests. According to this theoretical framework, justice is more a product of conflicts among agencies within the system than it is the result of cooperation among component agencies.

Whichever side we choose in the ongoing debate over the nature and quality of criminal justice in America, it is vital that we recognize the plethora of pragmatic issues involved in the administration of justice while also keeping a clear focus on the justice ideal.[28] Was justice done, for example, in the 2013 first-degree murder trial of Jodi Arias on charges that she killed her boyfriend, Travis Alexander (the case is discussed in more detail in Chapter 10, "Pretrial Activities and the Criminal Trial"). What about in the 2005 criminal trial of pop-music superstar Michael Jackson on charges of child molestation? After Jackson's death, was the 2011 trial of his personal physician, Conrad Murray, just? Has justice been served in the case of Casey Anthony, whom authorities say killed her young daughter? Similarly, we might ask, was justice done in the arrest and lengthy detention of hundreds of Muslims after September 11, 2001—even though most were later released when no evidence could be found linking them to any crime?[29] Although answers to such questions may reveal a great deal about the American criminal justice system, they also have much to say about the perspectives of those who provide them.

American Criminal Justice: System and Functions

The Consensus Model

So far, we have described a **criminal justice system**[30] consisting of the component agencies of police, courts, and corrections. Each of these components can, in turn, be described in terms of its functions and purpose (Figure 1-3).

The systems perspective on criminal justice is characterized primarily by its assumption that the various parts of the justice system work together by design to achieve the wider purpose we have been calling *justice*. Hence the systems perspective on criminal justice generally encompasses a point of view called the **consensus model**. The consensus model assumes that each of the component parts of the criminal justice system strives toward a common goal and that the movement of cases and people through the system is smooth due to cooperation between the various components of the system.

The systems model of criminal justice is more an analytic tool than a reality, however. An analytic model, whether in the hard sciences or in the social sciences, is simply a convention chosen for its explanatory power. By explaining the actions of criminal justice officials—such as arrest, prosecution, and sentencing—as though they were systematically related, we are able to envision a fairly smooth and predictable process (which is described in more detail later in this chapter).

The systems model has been criticized for implying a greater level of organization and cooperation among the various agencies of justice than actually exists. The word *system* calls to mind a near-perfect form of social organization. The modern mind associates the idea of a system with machine-like precision in which the problems of wasted effort, redundancy, and conflicting actions are quickly corrected. In practice, the justice system has nowhere near this level of perfection, and the systems model is admittedly an oversimplification. Conflicts among and within agencies are rife, individual actors within the system often do not share immediate goals, and the system may move in different directions depending on political currents, informal arrangements, and personal discretion.

The Conflict Model

The **conflict model** provides another approach to the study of American criminal justice. The conflict model says that the interests of criminal justice agencies tend to make actors within the system self-serving. According to this model, the goals of individual agencies often conflict, and pressures for success, promotion, pay increases, and general accountability fragment the efforts of the system as a whole, leading to a criminal justice *non*system.[31]

A classic study of clearance rates by criminologist Jerome H. Skolnick provides support for the idea of a criminal justice nonsystem.[32] Clearance rates are a measure of crimes solved by the police. The more crimes the police can show they have solved,

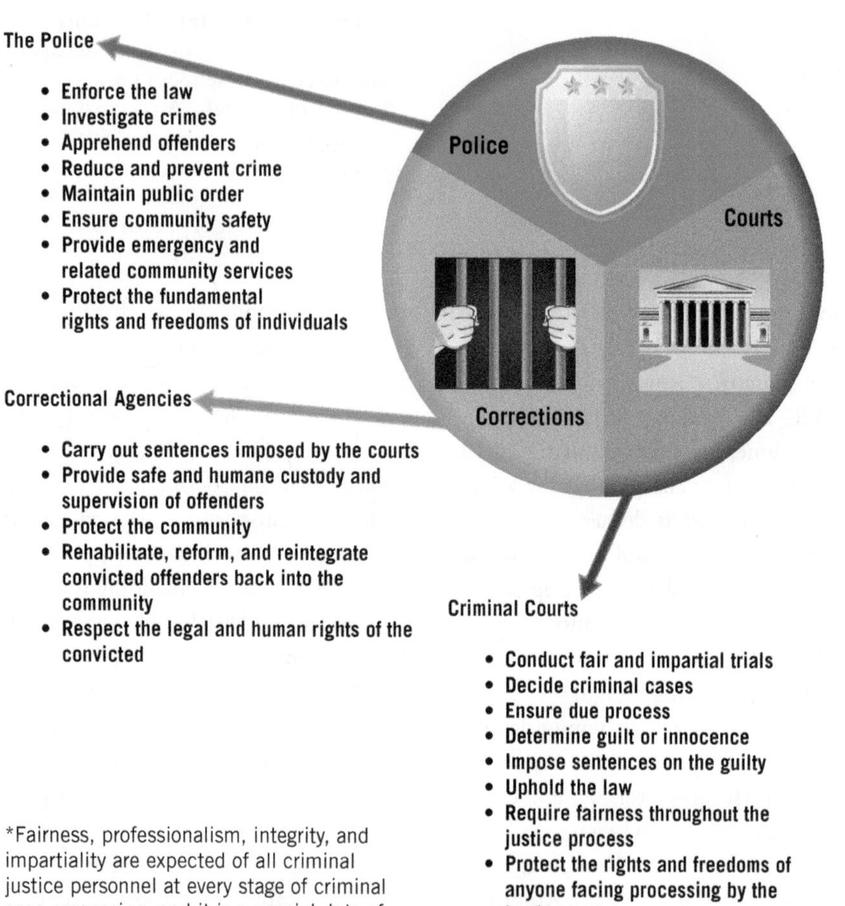

The Police
• Enforce the law
• Investigate crimes
• Apprehend offenders
• Reduce and prevent crime
• Maintain public order
• Ensure community safety
• Provide emergency and related community services
• Protect the fundamental rights and freedoms of individuals
Police
Courts
Corrections
Correctional Agencies
• Carry out sentences imposed by the courts
• Provide safe and humane custody and supervision of offenders
• Protect the community
• Rehabilitate, reform, and reintegrate convicted offenders back into the community
• Respect the legal and human rights of the convicted
Criminal Courts
• Conduct fair and impartial trials
• Decide criminal cases
• Ensure due process
• Determine guilt or innocence
• Impose sentences on the guilty
• Uphold the law
• Require fairness throughout the justice process
• Protect the rights and freedoms of anyone facing processing by the justice system
• Provide a check on the exercise of power by other justice system agencies*
*Fairness, professionalism, integrity, and impartiality are expected of all criminal justice personnel at every stage of criminal case processing, and it is a special duty of the courts to ensure that these expectations are met.

FIGURE 1-3 | The Core Components of the American Criminal Justice System and Their Functions

the better they look to the public they serve. Skolnick discovered an instance in which a burglar was caught red-handed during the commission of a burglary. After his arrest, the police suggested that he confess to many unsolved burglaries that they knew he had not committed. In effect they said, "Help us out, and we will try to help you out!" The burglar did confess—to more than 400 other burglaries. Following the confession, the police were satisfied because they could say they had "solved" many burglaries, and the suspect was pleased as well because the police and the prosecutor agreed to speak on his behalf before the judge.

Both models have something to tell us. Agencies of justice with a diversity of functions (police, courts, and corrections) and at all levels (federal, state, and local) are linked closely enough for the term *system* to be meaningfully applied to them. On the other hand, the very size of the criminal justice undertaking makes effective cooperation between component agencies difficult. The police, for example, have an interest in seeing offenders put behind bars. Prison officials, on the other hand, are often working with extremely overcrowded facilities. They may favor early-release programs for certain categories of offenders, such as those judged to be nonviolent. Who wins out in the long run might just be a matter of internal politics and quasi-official wrangling. Everyone should be concerned, however, when the goal of justice is affected, and sometimes even sacrificed, because of conflicts within the system.

Everyone should be concerned when the goal of justice is affected, and sometimes even sacrificed, because of conflicts within the system.

■ **sustainable justice** Criminal laws and criminal justice institutions, policies, and practices that achieve justice in the present without compromising the ability of future generations to have the benefits of a just society.[iii]

paying for it

Cost-Efficient Criminal Justice

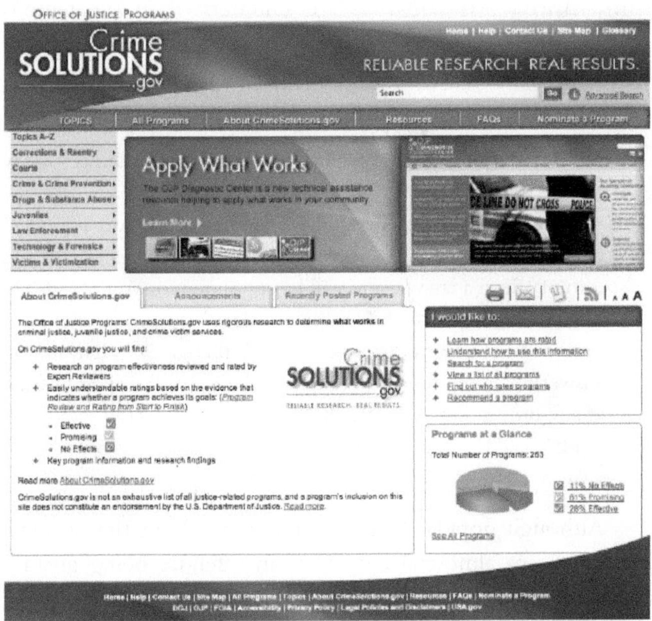

The federal Office of Justice Programs' website, CrimeSolutions.gov. The site facilitates research into the effectiveness of criminal justice–related programs. How can the site be of help to policymakers?

The Great Recession of the past few years has forced state and local governments to make some hard choices about budgets. As government revenues declined due to a drop in taxable income, consumer spending, lower property values, and fewer licensing fees, officials in many locales have been forced to reduce expenditures and to curb services. Criminal justice agencies have not been immune to the impact of budget cuts, and many are looking for ways to offer quality services at a lower cost. Noteworthy is the fact that today's emphasis on the efficient use of resources has combined with calls for greater accountability and transparency in government spending.

To discuss today's concern with cost efficiency throughout the justice system, a number of boxes like this one appear throughout the text and describe what police departments, courts, and corrections agencies are doing as they move toward increasingly responsible stewardship of taxpayer dollars. Noteworthy is the fact that today's emphasis on the efficient use of resources has combined with calls for greater accountability and transparency in government spending.

In an effort to help justice agencies utilize resources wisely, the U.S. Department of Justice announced a new website in 2012. Located at **http://crimesolutions.gov,** the site is designed to provide policymakers, justice system administrators, and taxpayers with the ability to assess the effectiveness of state and local anticrime programs. The site, run by the Washington, D.C.–based National Institute of Justice (NIJ), has been described by federal officials as a "single, credible, online resource to inform practitioners and policymakers about what works in criminal justice, juvenile justice, and crime victim services."

Once criminal justice programs have been selected for review, experts working with the NIJ analyze available research documenting the program's effectiveness and cost efficiency. Programs are then scored on CrimeSolutions.gov according to established criteria and identified as either: (1) effective, (2) promising, or (3) no effect. Where evidence on a program is insufficient or inconsistent, it receives no ranking. As of this writing, 33% of programs reviewed have been scored as "effective," whereas another 57% were identified as "promising."

Finally, the concept of **sustainable justice** was advanced by Melissa Hickman Barlow, in her 2012 presidential address to the Academy of Criminal Justice Sciences. Sustainable justice, said Barlow, can be defined as "criminal laws and criminal justice institutions, policies, and practices that achieve justice in the present without compromising the ability of future generations to have the benefits of a just society." Sustainable justice, in other words, refers to criminal justice practices and institutions that are affordable now, and into the future. Visit the topics page of CrimeSolutions.gov at **http://www.crimesolutions.gov/topics.aspx** to learn more about the categories of programs being evaluated.

References: CrimeSolutions.gov; Melissa Hickman Barlow, "Sustainable Justice: 2012 Presidential Address to the Academy of Criminal Justice Sciences," *Justice Quarterly*, Vol. 30, No. 1 (2013), pp. 1–17.

■ **warrant** In criminal proceedings, a writ issued by a judicial officer directing a law enforcement officer to perform a specified act and affording the officer protection from damages if he or she performs it.

American Criminal Justice: The Process

Whether part of a system or a nonsystem, the agencies of criminal justice must process the cases that come before them. An analysis of criminal justice case processing provides both a useful guide to this book and a "road map" to the criminal justice system itself. The figure in the front matter of this book illustrates the processing of a criminal case through the federal justice system in some detail, beginning with the investigation of reported crimes; while Figure 1-4 provides a summary of the process. The process in most state systems is similar.

Investigation and Arrest

The modern justice process begins with investigation. After a crime has been discovered, evidence is gathered at the scene when possible, and a follow-up investigation attempts to reconstruct the sequence of activities. Although a few offenders are arrested at the scene of the crime, most are apprehended later. In such cases, an arrest **warrant** issued by a judge provides the legal basis for an apprehension by police.

An arrest, in which a person is taken into custody, limits the arrestee's freedom. Arrest is a serious step in the process of justice and involves a discretionary decision made by the police seeking to bring criminal sanctions to bear. Most arrests are made peacefully, but if a suspect tries to resist, a police officer may need to use force. Only about half of all people arrested are eventually convicted, and of those, only about a quarter are sentenced to a year or more in prison.

The *Miranda* decision requires only that police advise a person of his or her rights prior to questioning. An arrest without questioning does not require a warning.

During arrest and before questioning, defendants are usually advised of their constitutional rights, as enumerated in the famous U.S. Supreme Court decision of *Miranda* v. *Arizona*.[33] Defendants are told:

> (1) "You have the right to remain silent." (2) "Anything you say can and will be used against you in court." (3) "You have the right to talk to a lawyer for advice before we ask you any questions, and to have him with you during questioning." (4) "If you cannot afford a lawyer, one will be appointed for you before any questioning if you wish." (5) "If you decide to answer questions now without a lawyer present, you will still have the right to stop answering at any time. You also have the right to stop answering at any time and may talk with a lawyer before deciding to speak again." (6) "Do you wish to talk or not?" and (7) "Do you want a lawyer?"[34]

Although popular television programs about the criminal justice system almost always show an offender being given a rights advisement at the time of arrest, the *Miranda* decision requires only that police advise a person of his or her rights prior to questioning. An arrest without questioning does not require a warning. When an officer interrupts a crime in progress, public-safety considerations may make it reasonable for the officer to ask a few questions prior to a rights advisement. Many officers, however, feel they are on sound legal ground only by advising suspects of their rights immediately after arrest. Investigation and arrest are discussed in detail in Chapter 7, "Policing: Legal Aspects."

Investigation ▶
After a crime has been discovered, evidence is gathered and follow-up investigations attempt to reconstruct the sequence of activities leading up to and including the criminal event. Efforts to identify suspects are initiated.

Warrant ▶
An arrest warrant issued by a judge provides the legal basis for an apprehension of suspects by police.

Arrest ▶
In an arrest, a person is taken into custody, limiting the arrestee's freedom. Arrest is a serious step in the process of justice. During arrest and before questioning, defendants are usually advised of their constitutional rights, or Miranda rights.

Booking ▶
Following arrest, suspects are booked. Booking is an administrative procedure where pictures, fingerprints, and personal information are obtained. A record of the events leading up to and including the arrest is created. In some jurisdictions, DNA evidence may be collected from arrestees.

FIGURE 1-4 | The American Criminal Justice Process

■ **booking** A law enforcement or correctional administrative process officially recording an entry into detention after arrest and identifying the person, the place, the time, the reason for the arrest, and the arresting authority.

■ **bail** The money or property pledged to the court or actually deposited with the court to effect the release of a person from legal custody.

■ **preliminary hearing** A proceeding before a judicial officer in which three matters must be decided: (1) whether a crime was committed, (2) whether the crime occurred within the territorial jurisdiction of the court, and (3) whether there are reasonable grounds to believe that the defendant committed the crime.

■ **probable cause** A set of facts and circumstances that would induce a reasonably intelligent and prudent person to believe that a specified person has committed a specified crime. Also, reasonable grounds to make or believe an accusation. Probable cause refers to the necessary level of belief that would allow for police seizures (arrests) of individuals and full searches of dwellings, vehicles, and possessions.

Booking

Following arrest, suspects are booked. During **booking**, which is an administrative procedure, pictures are taken, fingerprint records are made, and personal information such as address, date of birth, weight, and height is gathered. Details of the charges are recorded, and an administrative record of the arrest is created. At this time suspects are often advised of their rights again and are asked to sign a form on which each right is written. The written form generally contains a statement acknowledging the advisement of rights and attesting to the fact that the suspect understands them.

Pretrial Activities

First Appearance

Within hours of arrest, suspects must be brought before a magistrate (a judicial officer) for an initial appearance. The judge will tell them of the charges against them, will again advise them of their rights, and may sometimes provide the opportunity for **bail**.

Most defendants are released on recognizance into their own care or the care of another or are given the chance to post a bond during their first appearance. A bond may take the form of a cash deposit or a property bond in which a house or other property serves as collateral against flight. Those who flee may be ordered to forfeit the posted cash or property. Suspects who are not afforded the opportunity for bail because their crimes are very serious or who do not have the needed financial resources are taken to jail to await the next stage in the justice process.

If a defendant doesn't have a lawyer, one will be appointed at the first appearance. To retain a court-appointed lawyer, the defendant may have to demonstrate financial hardship. The names of assigned lawyers are usually drawn off the roster of practicing defense attorneys in the county. Some jurisdictions use public defenders to represent indigent defendants.

All aspects of the first appearance, including bail bonds and possible pretrial release, are discussed in detail in Chapter 10, "Pretrial Activities and the Criminal Trial."

Preliminary Hearing

The primary purpose of a **preliminary hearing**, also sometimes called a *preliminary examination*, is to establish whether sufficient evidence exists against a person to continue the justice process. At the preliminary hearing, the hearing judge will seek to determine whether there is **probable cause** to believe that (1) a crime has been committed and (2) the defendant committed it. The decision is a judicial one, but the process provides the prosecutor with an opportunity to test the strength of the evidence at his or her disposal.

First Appearance ▶
Within hours of arrest suspects must be brought before a magistrate (a judicial officer) for an initial appearance. The judge will tell them of the charges against them, advise them of their rights, and may provide the opportunity for bail.

Preliminary Hearing ▶
The purpose of a preliminary hearing is to establish whether sufficient evidence exists against a person to continue the justice process. At the preliminary hearing, the hearing judge will seek to determine whether there is probable cause. The process provides the prosecutor with an opportunity to test the strength of the evidence.

Information or Indictment ▶
In some states the prosecutor may seek to continue the case against a defendant by filing an information with the court. Other states require an indictment be returned by a grand jury. The grand jury hears evidence presented by the prosecutor and decides whether the case should go to trial.

Arraignment ▶
At arraignment the accused stands before a judge and hears the information or indictment against him. Defendants are again notified of their rights and asked to enter a plea. Pleas include not guilty, guilty, and no contest. No contest may result in a conviction but cannot be used in trial as an admission of guilt.

■ **information** A formal, written accusation submitted to a court by a prosecutor, alleging that a specified person has committed a specified offense.

■ **indictment** A formal, written accusation submitted to the court by a grand jury, alleging that a specified person has committed a specified offense, usually a felony.

■ **grand jury** A group of jurors who have been selected according to law and have been sworn to hear the evidence and to determine whether there is sufficient evidence to bring the accused person to trial, to investigate criminal activity generally, or to investigate the conduct of a public agency or official.

■ **arraignment** Strictly, the hearing before a court having jurisdiction in a criminal case in which the identity of the defendant is established, the defendant is informed of the charge and of his or her rights, and the defendant is required to enter a plea. Also, in some usages, any appearance in criminal court before trial.

The preliminary hearing also allows defense counsel the chance to assess the strength of the prosecution's case. As the prosecution presents evidence, the defense is said to "discover" what it is. Hence the preliminary hearing serves a discovery function for the defense. If the defense attorney thinks the evidence is strong, he or she may suggest that a plea bargain be arranged. All defendants, including those who are indigent, have a right to be represented by counsel at the preliminary hearing.

Information or Indictment

In some states, the prosecutor may seek to continue the case against a defendant by filing an **information** with the court. An information, which is a formal written accusation, is filed on the basis of the outcome of the preliminary hearing.

Other states require that an **indictment** be returned by a **grand jury** before prosecution can proceed. The grand jury hears evidence from the prosecutor and decides whether the case should go to trial. In effect, the grand jury is the formal indicting authority. It determines whether probable cause exists to charge the defendant formally with the crime. Grand juries can return an indictment on less than a unanimous vote.

The grand jury system has been criticized because it is one-sided. The defense has no opportunity to present evidence; the grand jury is led only by the prosecutor, often through an appeal to emotions or in ways that would not be permitted in a trial. At the same time, the grand jury is less bound by specific rules than a trial jury. For example, a grand jury member once told the author that a rape case had been dismissed because the man had taken the woman to dinner first. Personal ignorance and subcultural biases are far more likely to play a role in grand jury hearings than in criminal trials. In defense of the grand jury system, however, defendants who are clearly innocent will likely not be indicted. A grand jury's refusal to indict can save the system considerable time and money by preventing cases lacking in evidence from further processing by the criminal justice system.

Arraignment

The **arraignment** is "the first appearance of the defendant before the court that has the authority to conduct a trial."[35] At arraignment, the accused individuals stand before a judge and hear the information, or indictment, against them as it is read. Defendants are again notified of their rights and are asked to enter a plea. Acceptable pleas generally include (1) not guilty, (2) guilty, and (3) no contest (*nolo contendere*), which may result in conviction but can't be used later as an admission of guilt in civil proceedings. Civil proceedings, or private lawsuits, while not covered in detail in this book, provide an additional avenue of relief for victims or their survivors. Convicted offenders increasingly face suits brought against them by victims seeking to collect monetary damages.

The Federal Rules of Criminal Procedure specify that "arraignment shall be conducted in open court and shall consist of reading the indictment or information to the defendant or stating to him the substance of the charge and calling on him to plead thereto. He shall be given a copy of the indictment or information before he is called upon to plead."[36]

Adjudication ▶
A criminal trial may be held, or the defendant may decide to enter a guilty plea. A criminal trial involves an adversarial process that pits the prosecution against the defense. In most trials, a jury hears the evidence and decides issues of guilt or innocence, while the judge ensures the fairness of the proceedings.

Sentencing ▶
After the person has been convicted it is up to the judge to determine the punishment. Prior to sentencing, a sentencing hearing is sometimes held in which attorneys for both sides can present information to influence the judge's decision.

Corrections ▶
The corrections period begins following sentencing. Corrections involves a variety of sentences that can be imposed on a defendant.

Reentry
Not everyone who has been convicted of a crime goes to prison. Probation imposes requirements or restrictions upon offenders. Offenders are required to check in with a probation officer on a regular basis.

Similarly, after a defendant has served a portion of his prison term he may be freed on parole. Like probation, parole may come with obligations and requires the offender to check in with a parole officer.

Photo sources (from left): Dave King © Dorling Kindersley; Gibson/Shutterstock; and Marc Dietrich/Shutterstock

FIGURE 1-4 | (continued)

■ **trial** In criminal proceedings, the examination in court of the issues of fact and relevant law in a case for the purpose of convicting or acquitting the defendant.

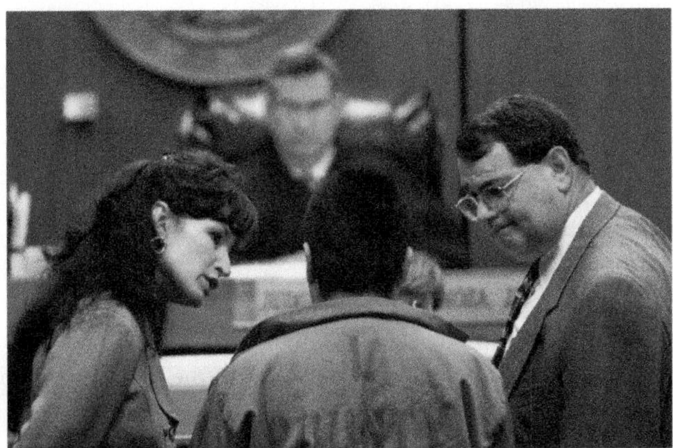

Newscom

A criminal defendant in a Tampa, Florida, courtroom conferring with his attorney and a Spanish-language interpreter. Everyone facing criminal prosecution in the United States is guaranteed a constitutional right to due process, meaning that defendants must be afforded a fair opportunity to participate in every stage of criminal proceedings. Should due process rights extend to all offenders—even accused terrorists?

Guilty pleas are not always accepted by the judge. If the judge believes a guilty plea is made under duress or is due to a lack of knowledge on the part of the defendant, the plea will be rejected and a plea of "not guilty" will be substituted for it. Sometimes defendants "stand mute"—that is, they refuse to speak or to enter a plea of any kind. In that case, the judge will enter a plea of "not guilty" on their behalf.

The arraignment process is discussed in detail in Chapter 10, "Pretrial Activities and the Criminal Trial."

Adjudication

Under the Sixth Amendment to the U.S. Constitution, every criminal defendant has a right to a **trial** by jury. The U.S. Supreme Court, however, has held that petty offenses are not covered by the Sixth Amendment guarantee and that the seriousness of a case is determined by the way in which "society regards the offense." For the most part, "offenses for which the maximum period of incarceration is six months or less are presumptively petty."[37] In *Blanton* v. *City of North Las Vegas* (1989), the Court held that "a defendant can overcome this presumption and become entitled to a jury trial, only by showing that . . . additional penalties [such as fines and community service] viewed together with the maximum prison term, are so severe that the legislature clearly determined that the offense is a serious one."[38] The *Blanton* decision was further reinforced in the case of *U.S.* v. *Nachtigal* (1993).[39]

In most jurisdictions, many criminal cases never come to trial. Most are "pleaded out"; that is, they are dispensed of as the result of a bargained plea, or they are dismissed for one of a variety of reasons. Studies have found that as many as 82% of all sentences are imposed in criminal cases because of guilty pleas rather than trials.[40]

In cases that do come to trial, the procedures governing the submission of evidence are tightly controlled by procedural law and precedent. *Procedural law* specifies the type of evidence that may be submitted, the credentials of those allowed to represent the state or the defendant, and what a jury is allowed to hear.

Precedent refers to understandings built up through common usage and also to decisions rendered by courts in previous cases. Precedent in the courtroom, for example, requires that lawyers request permission from the judge before approaching a witness. It also can mean that excessively gruesome items of evidence may not be used or must be altered in some way so that their factual value is not lost in the strong emotional reactions they may create.

Some states allow trials for less serious offenses to occur before a judge if defendants waive their right to a trial by jury. This is called a *bench trial*. Other states require a jury trial for all serious criminal offenses.

Trials are expensive and time consuming. They pit defense attorneys against prosecutors. Regulated conflict is the rule, and jurors are required to decide the facts and apply the law as the judge explains it to them. In some cases, however, a jury may be unable to decide. Such a jury is said to be *deadlocked*, and the judge declares a mistrial. The defendant may be tried again when a new jury is impaneled.

Precedent refers to understandings built up through common usage and also to decisions rendered by courts in previous cases.

The criminal trial and its participants are described fully in Chapter 9, "The Courts: Structure and Participants," and Chapter 10, "Pretrial Activities and the Criminal Trial."

Sentencing

Once a person has been convicted, it becomes the responsibility of the judge to impose some form of punishment. The sentence may take the form of supervised probation in the community, a fine, a prison term, or some combination of these. Defendants will often be ordered to pay the costs of the court or of their own defense if they are able.

consecutive sentence One of two or more sentences imposed at the same time, after conviction for more than one offense, and served in sequence with the other sentence. Also, a new sentence for a new conviction, imposed upon a person already under sentence for a previous offense, which is added to the previous sentence, thus increasing the maximum time the offender may be confined or under supervision.

concurrent sentence One of two or more sentences imposed at the same time, after conviction for more than one offense, and served at the same time. Also, a new sentence for a new conviction, imposed upon a person already under sentence for a previous offense, served at the same time as the previous sentence.

due process A right guaranteed by the Fourth, Fifth, Sixth, and Fourteenth Amendments of the U.S. Constitution and generally understood, in legal contexts, to mean the due course of legal proceedings according to the rules and forms established for the protection of individual rights. In criminal proceedings, due process of law is generally understood to include the following basic elements: a law creating and defining the offense, an impartial tribunal having jurisdictional authority over the case, accusation in proper form, notice and opportunity to defend, trial according to established procedure, and discharge from all restraints or obligations unless convicted.

Prior to sentencing, a sentencing hearing may be held in which lawyers on both sides present information concerning the defendant. The judge may also ask a probation or parole officer to compile a presentence report, which contains information on the defendant's family and business situation, emotional state, social background, and criminal history. This report helps the judge make an appropriate sentencing decision.

Judges traditionally have had considerable discretion in sentencing, although new state and federal laws now place limits on judicial discretion in some cases, requiring that a sentence "presumed" by law be imposed. Judges still retain enormous discretion, however, in specifying whether sentences on multiple charges are to run consecutively or concurrently. Offenders found guilty of more than one charge may be ordered to serve one sentence after another is completed, called a **consecutive sentence**, or may be told that their sentences will run at the same time, which is called a **concurrent sentence**.

Many convictions are appealed. The appeals process can be complex and can involve both state and federal judiciaries. An appeal is based on the defendant's claim that rules of procedure were not followed properly at some earlier stage in the justice process or that the defendant was denied the rights guaranteed by the U.S. Constitution.

Chapter 11, "Sentencing," outlines modern sentencing practices and describes the many modern alternatives to imprisonment.

Corrections

Once an offender has been sentenced, the corrections stage begins. Some offenders are sentenced to prison, where they "do time" for their crimes. Once in the correctional system, they are classified according to local procedures and are assigned to confinement facilities and treatment programs. Newer prisons today bear little resemblance to the massive bastions of the past, which isolated offenders from society behind huge stone walls. Many modern prisons, however, still suffer from a "lock psychosis" (a preoccupation with security) among top- and mid-level administrators as well as a lack of significant rehabilitation programs.

Chapter 13, "Prisons and Jails," discusses the philosophy behind prisons and sketches their historical development. Chapter 14, "Prison Life," portrays life on the inside and delineates the social structures that develop in response to the pains of imprisonment.

Reentry

Not everyone who is convicted of a crime and sentenced ends up in prison. Some offenders are ordered to prison only to have their sentences suspended and a probationary term imposed. They may also be ordered to perform community-service activities as a condition of their probation. During the term of probation, these offenders are required to submit to supervision by a probation officer and to meet other conditions set by the court. Failure to do so results in revocation of probation and imposition of the original prison sentence.

Offenders who have served a portion of their prison sentences may be freed on parole. They are supervised by a parole officer and assisted in their readjustment to society. As in the case of probation, failure to meet the conditions of parole may result in revocation of parole and a return to prison.

Chapter 11, "Sentencing," and Chapter 12, "Probation, Parole, and Intermediate Sanctions," deal with the practice of probation and parole and with the issues surrounding reentry. Learn more about the criminal justice process at **http://www.justicestudies.com/pubs/perspectives.pdf**. For a critical look at the justice system, visit **http://www.360degrees.org**.

Due Process and Individual Rights

The U.S. Constitution requires that criminal justice case processing be conducted with fairness and equity; this requirement is referred to as **due process**. Simply put, *due process* means procedural fairness.[41] It recognizes the individual rights of criminal defendants facing prosecution by a state or the federal government. Under the due process standard, rights violations may

TABLE 1-1 | **Individual Rights Guaranteed by the Bill of Rights[a]**

A right to be assumed innocent until proven guilty
A right against unreasonable searches of person and place of residence
A right against arrest without probable cause
A right against unreasonable seizure of personal property
A right against self-incrimination
A right to fair questioning by the police
A right to protection from physical harm throughout the justice process
A right to an attorney
A right to trial by jury
A right to know the charges
A right to cross-examine prosecution witnesses
A right to speak and present witnesses
A right not to be tried twice for the same crime
A right against cruel or unusual punishment
A right to due process
A right to a speedy trial
A right to assistance of counsel in criminal proceedings
A right against excessive bail
A right against excessive fines
A right to be treated the same as others, regardless of race, sex, religious preference, and other personal attributes

[a]As interpreted by the U.S. Supreme Court.

become the basis for the dismissal of evidence or of criminal charges, especially at the appellate level. Table 1-1 outlines the basic rights to which defendants in criminal proceedings are generally entitled.

Due process underlies the first ten amendments to the Constitution, which are collectively known as the *Bill of Rights.* Due process is specifically guaranteed by the Fourth, Fifth, Sixth, and Fourteenth Amendments and is succinctly stated in the Fifth, which reads, "No person shall be . . . deprived of life, liberty, or property, without due process of law." The Fourteenth Amendment makes due process binding on the states—that is, it requires individual states to respect the due process rights of U.S. citizens who come under their jurisdiction.

The courts, and specifically the U.S. Supreme Court, have interpreted and clarified the guarantees of the Bill of Rights. The due process standard was set in the 1960s by the Warren Court (1953–1969), following a number of far-reaching Supreme Court decisions that affected criminal procedure. Led by Chief Justice Earl Warren, the Warren Court is remembered for its concern with protecting the innocent against the massive power of the state in criminal proceedings.[42] As a result of its tireless efforts to institutionalize the Bill of Rights, the daily practice of modern American criminal justice is now set squarely upon the due process standard.

The Role of the Courts in Defining Rights

Although the Constitution deals with many issues, what we have been calling *rights* are open to interpretation. Many modern rights, although written into the Constitution, would not exist in practice were it not for the fact that the U.S. Supreme Court decided, at some point in history, to recognize them in cases brought before it. In the well-known case of *Gideon* v. *Wainwright* (1963),[43] for example, the Supreme Court embraced the Sixth Amendment guarantee of a right to a lawyer for all criminal defendants and mandated that states provide lawyers for defendants who are unable to pay for them. Before *Gideon* (which is discussed in detail in Chapter 9, "The Courts: Structure and Participants"), court-appointed attorneys for defendants unable to afford their own counsel were practically unknown, except in capital cases and in some federal courts. After the *Gideon* decision, court-appointed counsel became commonplace, and measures were instituted in jurisdictions across the nation to select attorneys fairly for indigent defendants. It is important to note, however, that although the Sixth Amendment specifically says, among other things, that "in all criminal prosecutions, the accused shall enjoy the right . . . to have the Assistance of Counsel for his defense," it does not say, in so many words, that the state is *required* to provide counsel. It is the U.S. Supreme Court, interpreting the Constitution, that has said that.

The U.S. Supreme Court is very powerful, and its decisions often have far-reaching consequences.

The U.S. Supreme Court is very powerful, and its decisions often have far-reaching consequences. The decisions rendered by the justices in cases like *Gideon* become, in effect, the law of the land. For all practical purposes, such decisions often carry as much weight as legislative action. For this reason, we speak of "judge-made law" (rather than legislated law) in describing judicial precedents that affect the process of justice.

■ **crime-control model** A criminal justice perspective that emphasizes the efficient arrest and conviction of criminal offenders.

■ **due process model** A criminal justice perspective that emphasizes individual rights at all stages of justice system processing.

■ **social control** The use of sanctions and rewards within a group to influence and shape the behavior of individual members of that group. Social control is a primary concern of social groups and communities, and it is their interest in the exercise of social control that leads to the creation of both criminal and civil statutes.

■ **evidence-based practice** Crime-fighting strategies that have been scientifically tested and are based on social science research.

Rights that have been recognized by court decisions are subject to continual refinement, and although the process of change is usually very slow, new interpretations may broaden or narrow the scope of applicability accorded to constitutional guarantees.

The Ultimate Goal: Crime Control through Due Process

Two primary goals were identified in our discussion of this book's theme: (1) the need to enforce the law and to maintain public order and (2) the need to protect individuals from injustice, especially at the hands of the criminal justice system. The first of these principles values the efficient arrest and conviction of criminal offenders. It is often referred to as the **crime-control model** of justice. The crime-control model was first brought to the attention of the academic community in Stanford University law professor Herbert Packer's cogent analysis of the state of criminal justice in the late 1960s.[44] For that reason, it is sometimes referred to as *Packer's crime-control model*.

The second principle is called the **due process model** because of its emphasis on individual rights. Due process is intended to ensure that innocent people are not convicted of crimes; it is a fundamental part of American criminal justice. It requires a careful and informed consideration of the facts of each individual case. Under the due process model, police are required to recognize the rights of suspects during arrest, questioning, and handling. Similarly, prosecutors and judges must recognize constitutional and other guarantees during trial and the presentation of evidence.

The dual goals of crime control and due process are often assumed to be opposing goals. Indeed, some critics of American criminal justice argue that the practice of justice is too often concerned with crime control at the expense of due process. Other analysts of the American scene maintain that our type of justice coddles offenders and does too little to protect the innocent. Although it is impossible to avoid ideological conflicts like these, it is also realistic to think of the American system of justice as representative of *crime control through due process*—that is, as a system of **social control** that is fair to those whom it processes. This model of *law enforcement infused with the recognition of individual rights* provides a workable conceptual framework for understanding the American system of criminal justice.

Evidence-Based Practice in Criminal Justice

In 2011, John H. Laub, then-director of the National Institute of Justice (NIJ), called for the creation of a "culture of science and research within the institute." What that means, said Laub, "is embracing empirical data, embracing transparency and also embracing a critical perspective." Science, Laub continued, challenges conventional wisdom and has the ability to evaluate programs and strategies to show what works in the area of criminal justice. The NIJ, said Laub, should be thought of "as a science agency." You can view Laub's comments online at **http://nij.ncjrs.gov/multimedia/video-laub1.htm**.

Only a year earlier, in June 2010, Assistant Attorney General Laurie O. Robinson announced a new initiative at the Office of Justice Programs (OJP), an arm of the U.S. Department of Justice that funds implementation of state-of-the-art practices in criminal justice agencies across the country.[45] The initiative, which Robinson said was intended to help "criminal and juvenile justice professionals expand their base of scientific knowledge and transform research into practice," is known as the Evidence Integration Initiative (E2I). E2I is an ongoing, OJP-wide effort to integrate science and research throughout the agency and the work it sponsors. "Most importantly," Robinson said, "we are working to move evidence into practice by funding evidence-based programs."

As the word is used here, *evidence* does not refer to evidence of a crime but means, instead, findings that are supported by studies. Hence, **evidence-based practice** refers to crime-fighting strategies that have been scientifically tested and are based on social science research. Scientific research has become a major element in the increasing

Evidence-based practices can be expected to play an expanded role in policymaking and in the administration of criminal justice in the years to come.

CJ | CAREERS

Careers in Criminal Justice

Throughout this book, you will find a number of "CJ Career" boxes showcasing individuals currently working in the justice field. Those boxes highlight job opportunities within various kinds of criminal justice agencies, and provide brief interviews with people employed in the field. A list of some of the many kinds of criminal justice career opportunities available today is provided in this table.

Arson/fire investigator
Bailiff
Bounty hunter
Computer forensic technician
Correctional officer
Correctional treatment specialist
Court clerk
Court reporter
Crime laboratory analyst
Crime prevention specialist
Crime scene investigator
Crime scene technician
Criminal investigator
Criminalist
Criminologist
Criminology researcher/research associate
Deputy sheriff
Electronic crime scene investigator
Federal Bureau of Investigation (FBI) forensic accountant
Federal Bureau of Investigation (FBI) special agent
Federal Protective Service (FPS) officer
Fish and game warden
Forensic nurse
Forensic psychologist
Forensic science technician
Fraud investigator
Gaming surveillance officer
Highway patrol officer
Information security manager
Judge
Juvenile probation officer
K-9 officer
Lawyer/attorney
Legal clerk
Loss prevention specialist (retail)
Magistrate
Motorcycle officer
National Security Agency (NSA) police officer
Native American tribal police officer
Nuclear security officer
Paralegal
Park ranger
Parole officer
Penologist
Police detective
Police dispatcher
Police officer
Police sniper
Private detective
Private investigator
Private security manager
Probation officer
Railroad police officer
Sheriff
Social worker
State trooper
Substance abuse counselor
Surveillance officer
SWAT team member
Transit Authority police officer
University/College Campus Police Officer
U.S. Air Force Office of Special Investigations (OSI) special agent
U.S. Air Marshal
U.S. Army criminal investigator (CID)
U.S. Army military police officer
U.S. Bureau of Alcohol, Tobacco, Firearms and Explosives (ATF) special agent
U.S. Bureau of Indian Affairs (BIA) correctional officer
U.S. Bureau of Indian Affairs (BIA) drug enforcement special agent
U.S. Bureau of Indian Affairs (BIA) investigator
U.S. Bureau of Indian Affairs (BIA) police officer
U.S. Bureau of Reclamation Security, Safety, and Law Enforcement officer
U.S. Coast Guard (USCG) compliance officer
U.S. Coast Guard (USCG) sea marshal
U.S. Customs and Border Protection (CBP) special agent
U.S. Department of Agriculture (USDA) compliance officer
U.S. Department of Agriculture (USDA) criminal investigator
U.S. Department of Agriculture (USDA) investigative attorney
U.S. Department of State Civilian Response Corps team member
U.S. Department of State diplomatic security officer
U.S. Department of Veterans Affairs (VA) police officer
U.S. Drug Enforcement Administration (DEA) special agent
U.S. Fish and Wildlife Service, Division of Refuge Law Enforcement officer
U.S. Immigration and Customs Enforcement (ICE) special agent
U.S. Internal Revenue Service (IRS) special agent
U.S. Marine Corps criminal investigator
U.S. Marine Corps military police officer
U.S. marshal
U.S. Navy criminal investigator (NCIS)
U.S. Navy law enforcement officer
U.S. Navy security officer
U.S. Park Police
U.S. Secret Service special agent
U.S. Secret Service uniformed division officer
U.S. Transportation Security Administration (TSA) screener

■ **criminology** The scientific study of the causes and prevention of crime and the rehabilitation and punishment of offenders.

professionalization of criminal justice, both as a career field and as a field of study. As Robinson recognized, there is a strong call today within criminal justice policymaking circles for the application of evidence-based practices throughout the justice field.

As noted in the "Paying for It" feature, in 2012, in support of the evidence-based movement in criminal justice, the U.S. Department of Justice announced a new website, **http://crimesolutions.gov**, featuring an innovative online program evaluation tool created by the federal Office of Justice Programs (OJP). The website, which is meant to help citizens and policymakers assess the effectiveness of state and local crime-fighting programs, has been described as a "single, credible, online resource to inform practitioners and policymakers about what works in criminal justice, juvenile justice, and crime victim services."[46]

As Chapter 5, "Policing: History and Structure," of this text points out, evidence-based practices can be expected to play an expanded role in policymaking and in the administration of criminal justice in the years to come. For additional insight into some of the issues facing criminal justice policymakers today, visit the Smart on Crime Coalition at **http://www.besmartoncrime.org** and read the Coalition's 2011 recommendations to Congress and the president.

The Start of Academic Criminal Justice

The study of criminal justice as an academic discipline began in this country in the late 1920s, when August Vollmer (1876–1955), the former police chief of the Los Angeles Police Department (LAPD), persuaded the University of California to offer courses on the subject.[47] Vollmer was joined by his former student Orlando W. Wilson (1900–1972) and by William H. Parker (who later served as chief of the LAPD from 1950 to 1966) in calling for increased professionalism in police work through better training.[48] Largely as a result of Vollmer's influence, early criminal justice education was practice oriented; it was a kind of extension of on-the-job training for working practitioners. Hence, in the early days of the discipline, criminal justice students were primarily focused on the application of general management principles to the administration of police agencies. Criminal justice came to be seen as a practical field of study concerned largely with issues of organizational effectiveness.

By the 1960s, however, police training came to be augmented by criminal justice education[49] as students of criminal justice began to apply the techniques of social scientific research—many of them borrowed from sister disciplines like **criminology**, sociology, psychology, and political science—to the study of all aspects of the justice system. Scientific research into the operation of the criminal justice system was encouraged by the 1967 President's Commission on Law Enforcement and Administration of Justice, which influenced passage of the Safe Streets and Crime Control Act of 1968. The Safe Streets Act led to the creation of the National Institute of Law Enforcement and Criminal Justice, which later became the National Institute of Justice (NIJ). As a central part of its mission, the NIJ continues to support research in the criminal justice field through substantial funding for scientific explorations into all aspects of the discipline, and it funnels much of the $3 billion spent annually by the U.S. Department of Justice to local communities to help fight crime.

Now, almost 100 years after its beginnings as a field of study, criminal justice is being revitalized by an evidence-based approach to its subject matter (described earlier). Former Assistant Attorney General Robinson put it this way: "Justice professionals have been collecting, analyzing, and using evidence for centuries—in laboratories and courtrooms. As financial realities demand more innovative approaches, social science research is forming the basis for new programs in areas ranging from reentry to victim services. Evidence has found a new home: in the field."[50]

Multiculturalism and Diversity in Criminal Justice

In 2011, polygamist Warren Jeffs, a former leader of the Fundamentalist Church of Jesus Christ of Latter-day Saints (FLDS), an offshoot of the mainstream Mormon church, was sentenced to life in prison for sexually assaulting two underage female followers whom he took as wives. During his trial, prosecutors played an audio recording of what they said was Jeffs raping a 12-year-old girl. Jeffs, who had been on the FBI's Ten Most Wanted list, won't be eligible for parole for at least 45 years.[51]

The FLDS brought plural marriage to Utah in the early nineteenth century, but the state legislature banned the practice more than 100 years ago. Today, the church officially excommunicates polygamists, although members of the FLDS practice polygamy as a central tenet of their religion. Some estimate the number of polygamists living in Utah and Arizona today at over 30,000.[52] The existence of such alternative family lifestyles is just one indicator that the United States is a multicultural and diverse society.

■ **multiculturalism** The existence within one society of diverse groups that maintain unique cultural identities while frequently accepting and participating in the larger society's legal and political systems.[iv] *Multiculturalism* is often used in conjunction with the term *diversity* to identify many distinctions of social significance.

Multiculturalism describes a society that is home to a multitude of different cultures, each with its own set of norms, values, and routine behaviors. Although American society today is truly a multicultural society, composed of a wide variety of racial and ethnic heritages, diverse religions, incongruous values, disparate traditions, and distinct languages, multiculturalism in America is not new. For thousands of years before Europeans arrived in the Western Hemisphere, tribal nations of Native Americans each spoke their own language, were bound to customs that differed significantly from one another, and practiced a wide range of religions. European immigration, which began in earnest in the seventeenth century, led to greater diversity still. Successive waves of immigrants, along with the slave trade of the early and mid-nineteenth century,[53] brought a diversity of values, beliefs, and patterns of behavior to American shores that frequently conflicted with prevailing cultures. Differences in languages and traditions fed the American melting pot of the late nineteenth and early twentieth centuries and made effective communication between groups difficult.

The face of multiculturalism in America today is quite different than it was in the past, due largely to relatively high birthrates among some minority populations and the huge but relatively recent immigration of Spanish-speaking people from Mexico, Cuba, Central America, and South America. Part of that influx consists of substantial numbers of undocumented immigrants who have entered the country illegally and who, because of experiences in their home countries, may have a special fear of police authority and a general distrust for the law. Such fears make members of this group hesitant to report being victimized, and their undocumented status makes them easy prey for illegal scams involving extortion, blackmail, and documentation crimes. Learn more about immigration and crime via **http://www.justicestudies.com/pubs/immcrime.pdf**.

Diversity characterizes both immigrant and U.S.-born individuals. Census Bureau statistics show that people identifying themselves as white account for 71% of the U.S. population—a percentage that has been dropping steadily for at least the past 40 years. People of Hispanic origin constitute approximately 12%

Jim Lo Scalzo/Newscom

A group of immigrants who have just completed taking the pledge of allegiance during a naturalization ceremony in Washington, D.C. American society is multicultural, composed of a wide variety of racial and ethnic heritages, diverse religions, incongruous values, disparate traditions, and distinct languages. What impact does the multicultural nature of our society have on the justice system?

of the population and are the fastest-growing group in the country. Individuals identifying themselves as African American make up another 12% of the population, and people of Asian and Pacific Island origin make up almost 4% of the total. Native Americans, including American Indians, Eskimos, and Aleuts, account for slightly less than 1% of all Americans.[54] Statistics like these, however, are only estimates, and their interpretation is complicated by the fact that surveyed individuals may be of mixed race. Nonetheless, it is clear that American society today is ethnically and racially quite diverse.

Race and *ethnicity* are only buzzwords that people use when they talk about multiculturalism. After all, neither race nor ethnicity determines a person's values, attitudes, or behavior. Just as there is no uniquely identifiable "white culture" in American society, it is a mistake to think that all African Americans share the same values or that everyone of Hispanic descent honors the same traditions or even speaks Spanish.

Multiculturalism, as the term is used today, is but one form of *diversity*. Taken together, these two concepts—multiculturalism and diversity—encompass many distinctions of social significance. The broad brush of contemporary multiculturalism and social diversity draws attention to variety along racial, ethnic, subcultural, generational, faith, economic, and gender lines. Lifestyle diversity is also important. The fact that influential elements of the wider society are less accepting of some lifestyles than others doesn't mean that such lifestyles aren't recognized from the viewpoint of multiculturalism. It simply means that at least for now, some lifestyles are accorded less official acceptability than others. As a result, certain lifestyle choices, even within a multicultural society that generally respects and encourages diversity, may still be criminalized, as in the case of polygamy.

> The demands and expectations placed on justice agencies in multicultural societies involve the dilemma of how to protect the rights of individuals to self-expression while ensuring social control and the safety and security of the public.

Multiculturalism and diversity will be discussed in various chapters throughout this textbook. For now, it is sufficient to recognize that the diverse values, perspectives, and behaviors characteristic of various groups within society have a significant impact on the justice system. Whether it is the confusion that arises from a police officer's commands to a non-English-speaking suspect, the need for interpreters in the courtroom, a deep-seated distrust of the police in some minority communities, a lack of willingness among some immigrants to report crime, the underrepresentation of women in criminal justice agencies, or some people's irrational suspicions of Arab Americans following the September 11 terrorist attacks, diversity and multiculturalism present special challenges to the everyday practice of criminal justice in America. Finally, as we shall see, the demands and expectations placed on justice agencies in multicultural societies involve a dilemma that is closely associated with the theme of this text: how to protect the rights of individuals to self-expression while ensuring social control and the safety and security of the public.

For an overview of crime rates, corrections statistics, and additional resources about crime and justice in the United States, see the 181-page *Crime and Justice Atlas* created by the U.S. Department of Justice at **http://www.jrsa.org/programs/Crime_Atlas_2000.pdf**. An updated version of the atlas is available at **http://www.jrsa.org/programs/Crime_Atlas_2001-update.pdf**.

SUMMARY

- The American experience with crime during the last half century has been especially influential in shaping the criminal justice system of today. Although crime waves have come and gone, some events during the past century stand out as especially significant, including a spurt of widespread organized criminal activity associated with the Prohibition years of the early twentieth century, the substantial increase in "traditional" crimes during the 1960s and 1970s, the threat to the American way of life represented by illicit drugs around the same time, and the terrorist attacks of September 11, 2001.
- The theme of this book is one of individual rights versus public order. As this chapter points out, the personal freedoms guaranteed to law-abiding citizens as well as to criminal suspects by the Constitution must be closely guarded. At the same time, the urgent social needs of communities for controlling unacceptable behavior and protecting law-abiding citizens from harm must be recognized. This theme is represented by two opposing groups: individual-rights advocates and public-order advocates. The fundamental challenge facing the practice of American criminal justice is in achieving efficient and cost-effective enforcement of the laws while simultaneously recognizing and supporting the legal rights of suspects and the legitimate personal differences and prerogatives of individuals.
- Although justice may be an elusive concept, it is important to recognize that criminal justice is tied closely to other notions of justice, including personal and cultural beliefs about equity and fairness. As a goal to be achieved, criminal justice refers to those aspects of social justice that concern violations of the criminal law. Although community interests in the administration of criminal justice demand the apprehension and punishment of law violators, criminal justice ideals extend to the protection of the innocent, the fair treatment of offenders, and fair play by justice administration agencies.

- In this chapter, we described the process of American criminal justice as a system with three major components—police, courts, and corrections—all of which can be described as working together toward a common goal. We warned, however, that a systems viewpoint is useful primarily for the simplification that it provides. A more realistic approach to understanding criminal justice may be the nonsystem approach. As a nonsystem, the criminal justice process is depicted as a fragmented activity in which individuals and agencies within the process have interests and goals that at times coincide but often conflict.
- The stages of criminal case processing include investigation and arrest, booking, a first appearance in court, the defendant's preliminary hearing, the return of an indictment by the grand jury or the filing of an information by the prosecutor, arraignment of the defendant before the court, adjudication or trial, sentencing, and corrections. As a field of study, corrections includes jails, probation, imprisonment, and parole.
- The principle of due process, which underlies the first ten amendments to the U.S. Constitution, is central to American criminal justice. Due process (also called *due process of law*) means procedural fairness and requires that criminal case processing be conducted with fairness and equity. The ultimate goal of the criminal justice system in America is achieving crime control through due process.
- The study of criminal justice as an academic discipline began in this country in the late 1920s and is well established today. Scientific research has become a major element in the increasing professionalization of criminal justice, and there is an increasingly strong call for the application of evidence-based practices in the justice field. Evidence-based practices are crime-fighting strategies that have been scientifically tested and that are based on social science research.
- American society today is a multicultural society, composed of a wide variety of racial and ethnic heritages, diverse religions, incongruous values, disparate traditions, and distinct languages. Multiculturalism complicates the practice of American criminal justice because there is rarely universal agreement in our society about what is right or wrong or about what constitutes "justice." As such, multiculturalism represents both challenges and opportunities for today's justice practitioners.

KEY TERMS

administration of justice, 11
arraignment, 18
bail, 17
booking, 17
civil justice, 11
concurrent sentence, 20
conflict model, 13
consecutive sentence, 20
consensus model, 13
crime, 4
crime-control model, 22
criminal justice, 11
criminal justice system, 13
criminology, 24
due process, 20
due process model, 22
evidence-based practice, 22
grand jury, 18
indictment, 18
individual rights, 6
individual-rights advocate, 9
information, 18
justice, 10
multiculturalism, 25
preliminary hearing, 17
probable cause, 17
public-order advocate, 10
social control, 22
social disorganization, 6
social justice, 10
social order, 9
sustainable justice, 15
trial, 19
warrant, 16

QUESTIONS FOR REVIEW

1. Describe the American experience with crime during the last half century. What noteworthy criminal incidents or activities can you identify during that time, and what social and economic conditions might have produced them?
2. What is the theme of this book? According to that theme, what are the differences between the individual-rights perspective and the public-order perspective?
3. This chapter also says that the drama of individual rights versus public order plays out in an economic environment constrained by today's financial considerations. How can evidence-based strategies help to meet the goals of both individual-rights and public-order advocates?
4. What is justice? What aspects of justice does this chapter discuss? How does criminal justice relate to other, wider notions of equity and fairness?
5. What are the main components of the criminal justice system? How do they interrelate? How might they conflict?
6. List the stages of case processing that characterize the American system of criminal justice, and describe each stage.
7. What is meant by *due process of law*? Where in the American legal system are guarantees of due process found?
8. What is the role of research in criminal justice? What is evidence-based practice? How can research influence crime-control policy?
9. What is multiculturalism? What is social diversity? What impact do multiculturalism and diversity have on the practice of criminal justice in contemporary American society?

QUESTIONS FOR REFLECTION

1. Reiterate the theme of this textbook. How might this book's theme facilitate the study of criminal justice?
2. Why is public order necessary? Do we have enough public order or too little? How can we tell? What might a large, complex society like ours be like without laws and without a system of criminal justice? Would you want to live in such a society? Why or why not?
3. What must we, as individuals, sacrifice to facilitate public order? Do we ever give up too much in the interest of public order? If so, when?
4. This chapter describes two models of the criminal justice system. What are they, and how do they differ? Which model do you think is more useful? Which is more accurate? Why?

NOTES

i. All boldfaced terms are explained whenever possible using definitions provided by the Bureau of Justice Statistics under a mandate of the Justice System Improvement Act of 1979. That mandate found its most complete expression in the *Dictionary of Criminal Justice Data Terminology* (Washington, DC: Bureau of Justice Statistics, 1982), the second edition of which provides the wording for many definitions in this text.

ii. Adapted from U.S. Code, Title 28, Section 20.3 (2[d]). Title 28 of the U.S. Code defines the term administration of criminal justice.

iii. Melissa Hickman Barlow, "Sustainable Justice: 2012 Presidential Address to the Academy of Criminal Justice Sciences," *Justice Quarterly*, Vol. 30, No. 1 (2013), pp. 1–17.

iv. Adapted from Robert M. Shusta et al., *Multicultural Law Enforcement*, 2nd ed. (Upper Saddle River, NJ: Prentice Hall, 2002), p. 443.

1. As quoted in "Communities: Mobilizing Against Crime," *National Institute of Justice Journal*, August 1996.
2. "U.S. Mass Shootings in 2012," *Washington Post*, December 14, 2012, http://www.washingtonpost.com/wp-srv/special/nation/us-mass-shootings-2012 (accessed March, 20, 2013). The same article, however, notes that there has been no long-term increase in mass shootings, only in *random* mass shootings.
3. David Kopel, "Guns, Mental Illness and Newtown," *Wall Street Journal*, December 17, 2012 (accessed March 21, 2013).
4. "Mass Shooting Toll Exceeds 900 in Past Seven Years," *USA Today*, February 22, 2013, http://www.usatoday.com/story/news/nation/2013/02/21/mass-shootings-domestic-violence-nra/1937041 (accessed July 19, 2013).
5. Ibid.
6. Holly Yan, "Gunman's Family at a Loss to Explain Connecticut Shooting," December 17, 2012, http://www.cnn.com/2012/12/16/justice/connecticut-shooting-suspect-profile/index.html (accessed March 20, 2013).
7. "Lupica: Morbid Find Suggests Murder-Obsessed Gunman Adam Lanza Plotted Newtown, Conn.'s Sandy Hook Massacre for Years," *New York Daily News*, March 18, 2013, http://www.nydailynews.com/news/national/lupica-lanza-plotted-massacre-years-article-1.1291408 (accessed March 18, 2013).
8. The Autism Research Institute's Autistic Global Initiative Project notes that autism and Asperger's syndrome are neurodevelopmental issues, and does not consider them to be mental health disorders.
9. American Psychiatric Association, Council on Law and Psychiatry, *Access to Firearms by People with Mental Illness: Resource Document* (Arlington, VA: American Psychiatric Association, 2009).
10. Rick Sallinger, "James Holmes Saw Three Mental Health Professionals before Shooting," CBS News, August 21, 2012, http://www.cbsnews.com/8301-201_162-57497820/james-holmes-saw-three-mental-health-professionals-before-shooting/ (accessed March 21, 2013).
11. Transcript: "'We have Wept with You'; Obama Says in Newtown Speech," CNN, December 16, 2012, http://politicalticker.blogs.cnn.com/2012/12/16/breaking-we-have-wept-with-you-obama-says-in-newtown-speech (accessed March 20, 2013).
12. Jared A. Favole, "Obama Says All Gun Buyers Should Face Checks," *Wall Street Journal*, December 19, 2012, http://professional.wsj.com/article/SB10001424127887324461604578188680585236550.html?mod=WSJPRO_hps_MIDDLEThirdNews (accessed March 22, 2013).
13. For a thorough discussion of immigration as it relates to crime, see Ramiro Martinez, Jr., and Matthew T. Lee, "On Immigration and Crime," in National Institute of Justice, *Criminal Justice 2000, Vol. 1: The Nature of Crime—Continuity and Change* (Washington, DC: U.S. Dept. of Justice, Office of Justice Programs, 2000).
14. "Inside Columbine," *Rocky Mountain News*, http://www.rockymountainnews.com/drmn/columbine (accessed July 4, 2007).
15. "Cries of Relief," *Time*, April 26, 1993, p. 18; and "King II: What Made the Difference?" *Newsweek*, April 26, 1993, p. 26.
16. Laurence McQuillan, "Bush to Urge Jail for Execs Who Lie," *USA Today*, July 9, 2002, http://www.usatoday.com/news/washdc/2002/07/09/bush-business.htm (accessed July 9, 2006).
17. Sarbanes-Oxley Act of 2002 (officially known as the Public Company Accounting Reform and Investor Protection Act), Public Law 107–204, 116 Stat. 745 (July 30, 2002).
18. PricewaterhouseCoopers, "The Sarbanes-Oxley Act," http://www.pwcglobal.com/Extweb/NewCoAtWork.nsf/docid/D0D7F79003C6D64485256CF30074D66C (accessed July 8, 2007).
19. "Texas Tycoon R. Allen Stanford Convicted of $7 Billion Ponzi Fraud," CBS News Crimesider, http://www.cbsnews.com/8301-504083_162-57391629-504083/texas-tycoon-r-allen-stanford-convicted-of-$7-billion-ponzi-fraud. March 6, 2012 (accessed March 9, 2012).
20. Richard Esposito, Eloise Harper, and Maddy Sauer, "Bernie Madoff Pleads Guilty to Ponzi Scheme, Goes Straight to Jail, Says He's 'Deeply Sorry,'" ABCNews.com, March 12, 2009, http://abcnews.go.com/Blotter/WallStreet/Story?id=7066715&page=1 (accessed July 4, 2009).
21. Robert Lenzner, "Bernie Madoff's $50 Billion Ponzi Scheme," Forbes.com, December 12, 2008, http://www.forbes.com/2008/12/12/madoff-ponzi-hedge-pf-ii-in_rl_1212croesus_inl.html (accessed September 28, 2009).
22. Jeremy Gorner, "In Chicago, Killings and Questions on the Rise," *Chicago Tribune*, December 30, 2012, http://www.chicagotribune.com/news/local/ct-met-chicago-violence-2012-20121230,0,186137.story (accessed January 3, 2013); Darran Simon, "Cracking Camden's Killings," *Philadelphia Inquirer*, December 30, 2012, http://articles.philly.com/2012-12-30/news/36065156_1_homicide-unit-reluctant-witnesses-killings (accessed January 3, 2013); and George Hunter and Mike Wilkinson, "Detroit Homicides Climb 10%," *The Detroit News*, December 31, 2012 (accessed January 4, 2013).
23. Elliot Spagat, "Chelea's Law Signed by Schwarzenegger, Will Give Some Sex Offenders Life in Prison," *Huffington Post*, September 9, 2010, http://www.huffingtonpost.com/2010/09/09/chelseas-law-signed-by-sc_n_711115.html (accessed April 4, 2012).
24. Wendy Koch, "States Get Tougher with Sex Offenders," *USA Today*, May 24, 2006, p. 1A.
25. See "Justice Questions Should Terrorists Be Treated Differently Than Criminals," Free Library, http://www.thefreelibrary.com/Justice+questions+should+terrorists+be+treated+differently+than...-a079412926 (accessed September 12, 2009).
26. Martin Luther King, Jr., in an address to the Tenth Anniversary Convention of the Southern Christian Leadership Conference in Atlanta, Georgia, on August 16, 1967. It was abolitionist and Unitarian minister Theodore Parker who first used a similar phrase in the mid-1800s, saying "I do not pretend to understand the moral universe; the arc is a long one. . . . And from what I see I am sure it bends toward justice."
27. The American Heritage Dictionary on CD-ROM (Boston: Houghton Mifflin, 1991).

28. For a good overview of the issues involved, see Judge Harold J. Rothwax, *Guilty: The Collapse of Criminal Justice* (New York: Random House, 1996).
29. For one perspective on the detention of Muslims following September 11, 2001, see the plaintiff's motion to stay proceedings on defendant's summary judgment motion pending discovery, in *Center for National Security Studies* v. *U.S. Department of Justice*, U.S. District Court for the District of Columbia (Civil Action No. 01-2500; January 2002), http://www.aclu.org/court/cnssjan22.pdf (accessed September 24, 2007).
30. The systems model of criminal justice is often attributed to the frequent use of the term *system* by the 1967 Presidential Commission in its report *The Challenge of Crime in a Free Society* (Washington, DC: U.S. Government Printing Office, 1967).
31. One of the first published works to use the nonsystem approach to criminal justice was the American Bar Association's *New Perspective on Urban Crime* (Washington, DC: ABA Special Committee on Crime Prevention and Control, 1972).
32. Jerome H. Skolnick, *Justice without Trial* (New York: John Wiley, 1966), p. 179.
33. *Miranda* v. *Arizona*, 384 U.S. 436, 16 L.Ed.2d 694, 86 S.Ct. 1602 (1966).
34. North Carolina Justice Academy, *Miranda Warning Card* (Salemburg: North Carolina Justice Academy, n.d.).
35. John M. Scheb and John M. Scheb II, *American Criminal Law* (St. Paul, MN: West, 1996), p. 32.
36. Federal Rules of Criminal Procedure, 10.
37. *Blanton* v. *City of North Las Vegas*, 489 U.S. 538, 103 L.Ed.2d 550, 109 S.Ct. 1289 (1989).
38. Ibid.
39. *U.S.* v. *Nachtigal*, 122 L.Ed.2d 374, 113 S.Ct. 1072, 1073 (1993), per curiam.
40. Barbara Borland and Ronald Sones, *Prosecution of Felony Arrests* (Washington, DC: Bureau of Justice Statistics, 1991).
41. "The Defendants' Rights at a Criminal Trial," http://www.mycounsel.com/content/arrests/court/rights.html (accessed February 10, 2007).
42. For a complete and now-classic analysis of the impact of decisions made by the Warren Court, see Fred P. Graham, *The Due Process Revolution: The Warren Court's Impact on Criminal Law* (New York: Hayden Press, 1970).
43. *Gideon* v. *Wainwright*, 372 U.S. 353 (1963).
44. Herbert Packer, *The Limits of the Criminal Sanction* (Stanford, CA: Stanford University Press, 1968).
45. "Understanding and Using Evidence-Based Practices," Justice Resource Update, http://www.ojp.gov/justiceresourceupdate/june2010 (accessed June 3, 2010).
46. "Criminal Justice: What Works? What Doesn't?" *The Crime Report*, June 21, 2011, http://www.thecrimereport.org/archive/criminal-justice-reform-what-works-what-doesnt-what-dont-we-know (accessed August 13, 2011).
47. For an excellent history of policing in the United States, see Edward A. Farris, "Five Decades of American Policing, 1932–1982," *Police Chief* (November 1982), pp. 30–36.
48. Gene Edward Carte, "August Vollmer and the Origins of Police Professionalism," *Journal of Police Science and Administration*, Vol. 1, No. 1 (1973), pp. 274–281.
49. Chris Eskridge distinguishes between police training, which is "job specific" and is intended to teach trainees how to do something (like fire a weapon), and justice education, whose purpose is to "develop a general spirit of inquiry." See C. W. Eskridge, "Criminal Justice Education and Its Potential Impact on the Sociopolitical-Economic Climate of Central European Nations," *Journal of Criminal Justice Education*, Vol. 14, No. 1 (spring 2003), pp. 105–118; and James O. Finckenauer, "The Quest for Quality in Criminal Justice Education," *Justice Quarterly*, Vol. 22, No. 4 (December 2005), pp. 413–426.
50. "Understanding and Using Evidence-Based Practices."
51. "Polygamist Jeffs Gets Life for Underage Sex Assault," *USA Today*, August 10, 2011, p. 5A.
52. "Polygamist Wins Parole from Utah State Prison," Associated Press, August 27, 2007.
53. On March 22, 1794, the U.S. Congress barred American citizens from transporting slaves from the United States to another nation or between foreign nations. On January 1, 1808, the importation of slaves into the United States became illegal, and Congress charged the U.S. Revenue Cutter Service (now known as the U.S. Coast Guard) with enforcing the law on the high seas. Although some slave ships were seized, the importation of Africans for sale as slaves apparently continued in some southern states until the early 1860s. See U.S. Coast Guard, "U.S. Coast Guard in Illegal Immigration (1794–1971)," http://www.uscg.mil/hq/g-o/g-opl/mle/amiohist.htm (accessed October 13, 2007).
54. U.S. Census Bureau website, http://www.census.gov (accessed March 22, 2006). Population statistics are estimates because race is a difficult concept to define and because Census Bureau interviewers allow individuals to choose more than one race when completing census forms.

© David R. Frazier Photolibrary, Inc./Alamy

2 THE CRIME PICTURE

OUTLINE

- Introduction
- The UCR/NIBRS Program
- The National Crime Victimization Survey
- Comparisons of the UCR and NCVS
- Special Categories of Crime

LEARNING OBJECTIVES

After reading this chapter, you should be able to

- Describe the FBI's UCR/NIBRS Program, including its purpose, history, and what it tells us about crime in the United States today.
- Describe the National Crime Victimization Survey (NCVS) program, including its purpose, history, and what it tells us about crime in the United States today.
- Compare and contrast the UCR and NCVS data collection and reporting programs.
- Describe how the special categories of crime discussed in this chapter are significant today.

No one way of describing crime describes it well enough.

PRESIDENT'S COMMISSION ON LAW ENFORCEMENT AND ADMINISTRATION OF JUSTICE

Introduction

The CBS TV megahit *CSI: Miami* garnered 50 million regular viewers in more than 55 countries and ran for ten seasons before going off the air in 2012. But CSI programming extends well beyond the Miami-based series, and the CSI franchise, which now includes shows featuring New York City, Las Vegas, and other locales, is available in both real time and on demand to a global audience of nearly 2 billion viewers in 200 countries around the globe.[1] In 2012, the CSI series was named the most watched TV show in the world for the fifth time.[2] Another popular crime show, *Law and Order*, ran for 20 seasons before ending in 2010, and was succeeded by the spin-offs *Law and Order: Criminal Intent* and *Law and Order: Special Victims Unit*. Today's most popular crime shows, *NCIS* and *NCIS: Los Angeles* (CBS), average more than 21 million viewers per episode,[3] and dozens of other media programs focusing on crime are available to the nation's viewing audience.

Social commentators say that the plethora of crime shows produced today reveals a penchant among American TV viewers for crime-related entertainment and a fascination with police work and the criminal justice system. Many add that it's not the violence of crime dramas that attracts viewers, but rather the sense of justice and fair play as the perpetrator gets caught. Visit *CSI* online at CBS's web site, or become a fan of *NCIS* on Facebook via **http://www.facebook.com/NCIS.**

Statistical aggregates of reported crime, whatever their source, do not reveal the lost lives, human suffering, lessened productivity, and reduced quality of life that crime causes.

This chapter has a dual purpose. First, it provides a statistical overview of crime in contemporary America by examining information on reported and discovered crimes. Second, it identifies special categories of crime that are of particular interest today, including crime against women, crime against the elderly, hate crime, corporate and white-collar crime, organized crime, gun crime, drug crime, cybercrime, and terrorism.

Although we will look at many crime statistics in this chapter, it is important to remember that statistical aggregates of reported crime, whatever their source, do not reveal the lost lives, human suffering, lessened productivity, and reduced quality of life that crime causes. Unlike the fictional characters on TV crime shows, real-life crime victims as well as real-life offenders lead intricate lives—they have families, hold jobs, and dream dreams. As we examine the crime statistics, we must not lose sight of the people behind the numbers.

CBS/Cliff Lipson/Landov

A scene from the CBS-TV show *NCIS: Los Angeles*. The American public has long been enthralled with crime shows, and since the terrorist attacks of 2001, the public's concern with personal safety has surged. Why do so many people like to watch crime shows?

Crime Data and Social Policy

Crime statistics provide an overview of criminal activity. If used properly, a statistical picture of crime can serve as a powerful tool for creating social policy. Decision makers at all levels, including legislators, other elected officials, and administrators throughout the criminal justice system, rely on crime data to analyze and evaluate existing programs, to fashion and design new crime-control initiatives, to develop funding requests, and to plan new laws and crime-control legislation. Many "get tough" policies, such as the three-strikes movement that swept the country during the 1990s, have been based in large part on the measured ineffectiveness of existing programs to reduce the incidence of repeat offending.

However, some people question just how objective—and therefore how useful—crime statistics are. Social events, including crime, are complex and difficult to quantify. Even the decision of which crimes should be included and which excluded in statistical reports is itself a judgment reflecting the interests and biases of policymakers. As mentioned in Chapter 1, the number of Internet-based offenses and crimes making use of other forms of high technology are constantly increasing, and statistical reporting programs that were designed years ago may not fully count such crimes. As famed criminologist Herbert Packer once observed, "We can have as much or as little crime as we please; depending on what we choose to count as criminal."[4]

How much crime we have depends on what we count as criminal.

■ **Uniform Crime Reporting (UCR) Program**
A statistical reporting program run by the FBI's Criminal Justice Information Services (CJIS) division. The UCR Program publishes *Crime in the United States*, which provides an annual summation of the incidence and rate of reported crimes throughout the United States.

■ **National Crime Victimization Survey (NCVS)**
An annual survey of selected American households conducted by the Bureau of Justice Statistics to determine the extent of criminal victimization—especially unreported victimization—in the United States.

■ **Bureau of Justice Statistics (BJS)** A U.S. Department of Justice agency responsible for the collection of criminal justice data, including the annual National Crime Victimization Survey.

■ **self-reports** Crime measures based on surveys that ask respondents to reveal any illegal activity in which they have been involved.

Finally, we should note that public opinion about crime is not always realistic. As well-known criminologist Norval Morris points out, the news media do more to influence public perceptions of crime than any official data do.[5] During the four-year period (in the mid-1990s) covered by Morris's study, for example, the frequency of crime stories reported in the national media increased fourfold. During the same time period, crime was at the top of the list in subject matter covered in news stories at both the local and national levels. The irony, says Morris, is that "the grossly increasing preoccupation with crime stories came at a time of steadily declining crime and violence." However, as Morris adds, "aided and abetted by this flood of misinformation, the politicians, federal and state and local, fostered the view that the public demands . . . 'get tough' policies."

The Collection of Crime Data

Nationally, crime statistics come from two major sources: (1) the Federal Bureau of Investigation's (FBI's) **Uniform Crime Reporting (UCR) Program** (also known today as the UCR/NIBRS Program), which produces an annual overview of major crime titled *Crime in the United States;* and (2) the **National Crime Victimization Survey (NCVS)** of the **Bureau of Justice Statistics (BJS)**. The most widely quoted numbers purporting to describe crime in America today probably come from the UCR/NIBRS Program, although the statistics it produces are based largely on *reports* to the police by victims of crime.

Social events, including crime, are complex and difficult to quantify. Even the decision of which crimes should be included and which excluded in statistical reports is itself a judgment reflecting the interests and biases of policymakers.

A third source of crime data is offender **self-reports** based on surveys that ask respondents to reveal any illegal activity in which they have been involved. Offender self-reports are not discussed in detail in this chapter because surveys utilizing them are not national in scope and are not undertaken regularly. Moreover, offenders are often reluctant to accurately report ongoing or recent criminal involvement, making information derived from these surveys somewhat unreliable and less than current. However, the available information from offender self-reports reveals that serious criminal activity is considerably more widespread than most "official" surveys show (Figure 2-1).

Other data sources also contribute to our knowledge of crime patterns throughout the nation. One important source is the *Sourcebook of Criminal Justice Statistics*—an annual compilation of national information on crime and on the criminal justice system. *Sourcebook* data is produced by the BJS, and made available on the Web through the auspices of the State University of New York at Albany. The National Institute of Justice (NIJ), which is the primary research arm of the U.S. Department of Justice, the Office of Juvenile Justice and Delinquency Prevention (OJJDP), the Federal Justice Statistics Resource Center, and the National Victim's Resource Center provide still more information on crime patterns. The *Sourcebook* is available online at **http://www.albany.edu/sourcebook**.

The UCR/NIBRS Program

Development of the UCR Program

In 1930, Congress authorized the U.S. attorney general to survey crime in America, and the FBI was designated to implement the program. In short order, the bureau built on earlier efforts by the International Association of Chiefs of Police (IACP) to create a national system of uniform crime statistics. As a practical measure, the IACP had recommended the use of readily available information, and so it was that citizens' crime reports to the police became the basis of the FBI's plan.[6]

During its first year of operation, the FBI's Uniform Crime Reporting Program received reports from 400 cities in 43 states. Twenty million people were covered by that first comprehensive survey. Today, approximately 18,000 law enforcement agencies provide crime information for the program, with data coming from city, county, and state departments. To ensure uniformity

■ **Crime Index** A now defunct but once inclusive measure of the UCR Program's violent and property crime categories, or what are called *Part I offenses*. The Crime Index, long featured in the FBI's publication *Crime in the United States*, was discontinued in 2004. The index had been intended as a tool for geographic (state-to-state) and historical (year-to-year) comparisons via the use of crime rates (the number of crimes per unit of population). However, criticism that the index was misleading arose after researchers found that the largest of the index's crime categories, larceny-theft, carried undue weight and led to an underappreciation of changes in the rates of more violent and serious crimes.

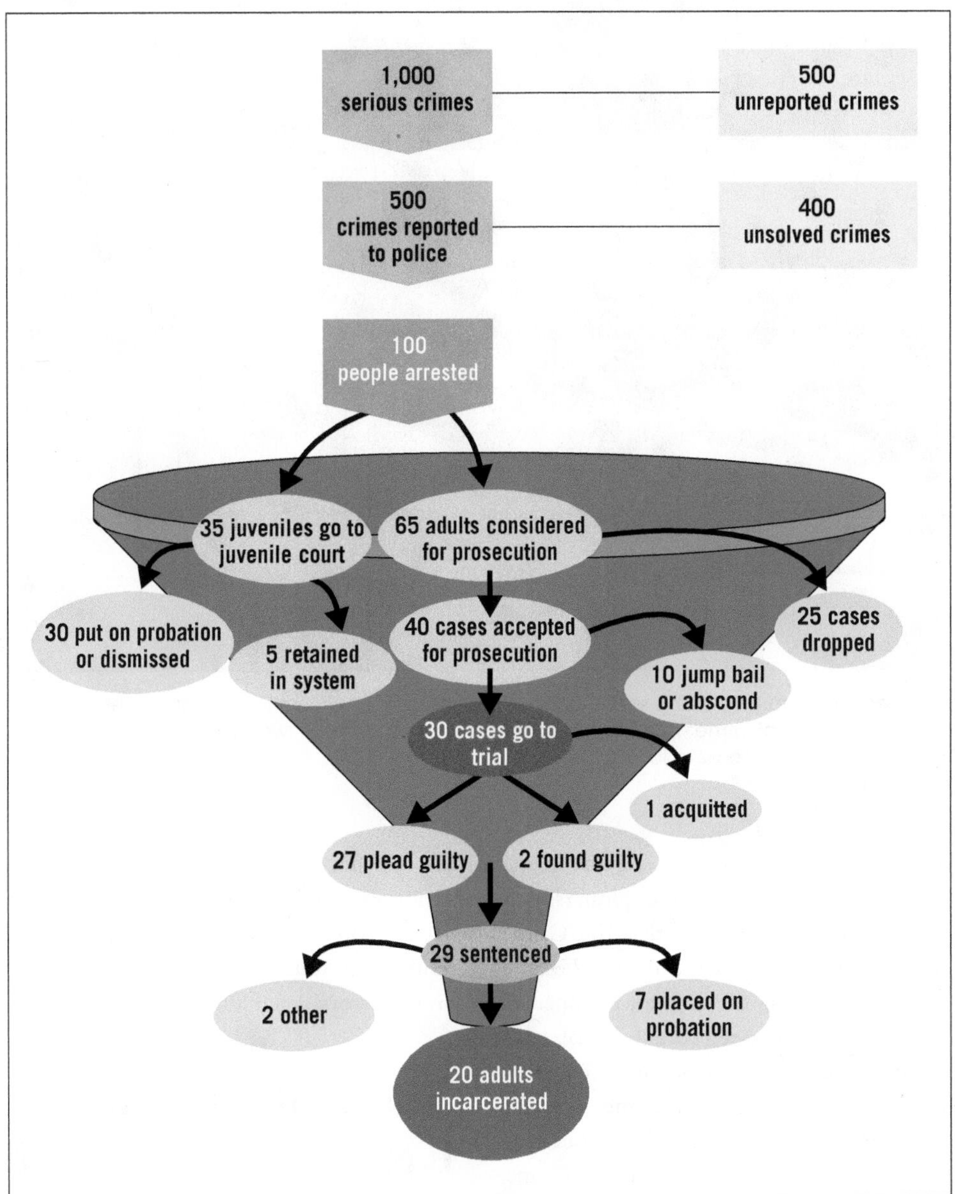

FIGURE 2-1 | The Criminal Justice Funnel

Source: Based on data from Tracey Kyckelhahn and Thomas H. Cohen, *Felony Defendants in Large Urban Counties, 2004* (Washington, DC: Bureau of Justice Statistics, 2008), and updated with more recent estimates by the author.

in reporting, the FBI has developed standardized definitions of offenses and terminologies used in the program. Numerous publications, including the *Uniform Crime Reporting Handbook* and the *Manual of Law Enforcement Records*, are supplied to participating agencies, and training for effective reporting is available through FBI-sponsored seminars and instructional literature.

Following IACP recommendations, the original UCR Program was designed to permit comparisons over time through construction of a **Crime Index**. The index summed the occurrences of seven major offenses—murder, forcible rape, robbery, aggravated assault, burglary, larceny-theft, and motor vehicle theft—and expressed the result as a crime rate based on population. In 1979, by congressional mandate, an eighth offense—arson—was added to the index. The Crime Index, first published in *Crime in the United States* in 1960, was the title used for a simple aggregation of the seven main offense

■ **Follow the author's tweets about the latest crime and justice news @schmalleger.**

■ **National Incident-Based Reporting System (NIBRS)** An incident-based reporting system that collects detailed data on every single crime occurrence. NIBRS data are replacing the kinds of summary data that have traditionally been provided by the FBI's Uniform Crime Reporting Program.

Andrew McKenzie/AP Images

Los Angeles emergency personnel working at the scene of an apparent gang-related shooting at Sunset Boulevard and Pacific Coast Highway. Some experts fear that violent crime may be starting to rise in big cities after two decades of decline. What would be the consequences for American cities if crime were to increase?

classifications (called Part I offenses). The Modified Crime Index refers to the original Crime Index offenses plus arson.

Over the years, however, concern grew that the Crime Index did not provide a clear picture of criminality because it was skewed by the offense with the highest number of reports—typically larceny-theft. The sheer volume of larceny-theft offenses overshadowed more serious but less frequently committed offenses, skewing perceptions of crime rates for jurisdictions with high numbers of larceny-thefts, but low numbers of serious crimes such as murder and forcible rape. In June 2004, the FBI's Criminal Justice Information Services (CJIS) Advisory Policy Board officially discontinued the use of the Crime Index in the UCR/NIBRS Program and in its publications and directed the FBI to instead publish simple violent crime totals and property crime totals until a more viable index could be developed.[7]

Although work to develop such an index is still ongoing, UCR/NIBRS Program crime categories continue to provide useful comparisons of specific reported crimes over time and between jurisdictions. It is important to recognize, as you read through the next few pages, that today's UCR/NIBRS Program categories tend to parallel statutory definitions of criminal behavior, but they are not legal classifications—only conveniences created for statistical-reporting purposes. Because many of the offense used in this textbook are derived from official UCR/NIBRS Program terminology, you should remember that these definitions may differ from statutory definitions of crimes.

The National Incident-Based Reporting System (NIBRS)

Beginning in 1988, the FBI's UCR Program initiated development of a new national crime-collection effort called the **National Incident-Based Reporting System (NIBRS)**. NIBRS represents a significant redesign of the original Uniform Crime Reporting Program. Whereas the original UCR system was "summary based," the enhanced National Incident-Based Reporting System is incident driven (Table 2-1). Under NIBRS, city, county, state, and federal law enforcement agencies throughout the country furnish detailed data on crime and arrest activities at the incident level either to the individual state incident-based reporting programs or directly to the federal NIBRS program.

TABLE 2-1 | Differences between the Traditional UCR and Enhanced UCR/NIBRS Reporting

TRADITIONAL UCR	ENHANCED UCR/NIBRS
Consists of monthly aggregate crime counts	Consists of individual incident records for the 8 major crimes and 38 other offenses, with details on offense, victim, offender, and property involved
Records one offense per incident, as determined by the hierarchy rule, which suppresses counts of lesser offenses in multiple-offense incidents	Records each offense occurring in an incident
Does not distinguish between attempted and completed crimes	Distinguishes between attempted and completed crimes
Collects assault information in five categories	Restructures definition of assault
Collects weapon information for murder, robbery, and aggravated assault	Collects weapon information for all violent offenses
Provides counts on arrests for the 8 major crimes and 21 other offenses	Provides details on arrests for the 8 major crimes and 49 other offenses

Source: Adapted from *Effects of NIBRS on Crime Statistics*, BJS Special Report (Washington, DC: Bureau of Justice Statistics, 2000), p. 1.

NIBRS is not a separate report; rather, it is the new methodology underlying the contemporary UCR system—hence our use of the term *UCR/NIBRS* in describing today's Uniform Crime Reporting Program. Whereas the old UCR system depended on statistical tabulations of crime data, which were often little more than frequency counts, the new UCR/NIBRS system gathers many details about each criminal incident. Included is information on place of occurrence, weapon used, type and value of property damaged or stolen, the personal characteristics of the offender and the victim, the nature of any relationship between the two, and the disposition of the complaint.

Under UCR/NIBRS, the traditional distinctions between Part I and Part II offenses are being replaced with 22 general offenses: arson, assault, bribery, burglary, counterfeiting, embezzlement, extortion, forcible sex offenses, fraud, gambling, homicide, kidnapping, larceny, motor vehicle theft, narcotics offenses, nonforcible sex offenses, pornography, prostitution, receiving stolen property, robbery, vandalism, and weapons violations. Other offenses on which UCR/NIBRS data are being gathered include bad checks, vagrancy, disorderly conduct, driving under the influence, drunkenness, nonviolent family offenses, liquor-law violations, "peeping Tom" activity, trespass, and a general category of all "other" criminal law violations. UCR/NIBRS also collects data on an expanded array of attributes involved in the commission of offenses, including whether the offender is suspected of using alcohol, drugs, or narcotics, or a computer, in the commission of the offense.

The FBI began accepting crime data in NIBRS format in January 1989. Although the bureau intended to have NIBRS fully in place by 1999, delays have been routine, and the NIBRS format has not yet been fully adopted. Because it is a flexible system, changes continue to be made in the data gathered under UCR/NIBRS. In 2003, for example, three new data elements were added to the survey to collect information on law enforcement officers killed and assaulted. Another new data element has been added to indicate the involvement of gang members in reported offenses.

The goals of the innovations introduced under NIBRS are to enhance the quantity, quality, and timeliness of crime-data collection by law enforcement agencies and to improve the methodology used for compiling, analyzing, auditing, and publishing the collected data. A major advantage of UCR/NIBRS, beyond the sheer increase in the volume of data collected, is the ability that NIBRS provides to break down and combine crime offense data into specific information.[8] The latest crime statistics from the FBI can be viewed at **http://www.fbi.gov/stats-services/crimestats**.

Other changes in crime reporting were brought about by the 1990 Crime Awareness and Campus Security Act, which requires colleges to publish annual security reports.[9] Most campuses share crime data with the FBI, increasing the reported national incidence of a variety of offenses. The U.S. Department of Education reported that 15 murders and 2,934 forcible sex offenses occurred on U.S. college campuses in 2010—the most recent year for which data are available. Also reported were 1,817 robberies, 2,531 aggravated assaults, 22,202 burglaries, and 3,623 motor vehicle thefts.[10] Although these numbers may seem high, it is important to realize that, except for the crimes of rape and sexual assault, college students experience violence at average annual rates that are lower than those for nonstudents in the same age group.[11] Rates of rape and sexual assault do not differ statistically between students and nonstudents. For the latest campus crime information, see **http://www.securityoncampus.org**.

Historical Trends

Most UCR/NIBRS information is reported as a rate of crime. Rates are computed as the number of crimes *per* some unit of population. National reports generally make use of large units of population, such as 100,000 people. Hence the rate of rape reported by the UCR/NIBRS Program for 2012 was 26.4 forcible rapes per every 100,000 inhabitants of the United States (or 52.9 per 100,000 females, although some rape victims are male).[12] Rates allow for a meaningful comparison over areas and across time. The rate of reported rape for 1960, for example, was only about 10 per 100,000 inhabitants. We expect the number of crimes to increase as population grows, but rate increases are cause for concern because they indicate that reports of crime are increasing faster than the population is growing. Rates, however, require interpretation. Although there is a tendency to judge an individual's risk of victimization based on rates, such judgments tend to be inaccurate because they are based purely on averages and do not take into consideration individual life circumstances, such as place of residence, wealth, and educational level. Although rates may tell us about aggregate conditions and trends, we must be very careful when applying them to individual cases.

A fourth shift in crime trends may be on the horizon and could lead to sustained increases in crime.

Since the FBI's Uniform Crime Reporting Program began, there have been three major shifts in crime rates—and we now seem to be witnessing the beginning of a fourth (Figure 2-2). The first occurred during the early 1940s, when crime decreased sharply due to the large number of young men who entered military service during World War II. Young males make up the most "crime-prone" segment of the population, and their deployment overseas did much to lower crime rates at home. From 1933 to 1941, the Crime Index declined from 770 to 508 offenses per every 100,000 members of the American population.[13]

The second noteworthy shift in offense statistics was a dramatic increase in most forms of crime between 1960 and the early 1990s. Several factors contributed to the increase in reported crime during this period. One was also linked to World War II. With the end of the war and the return of millions of young men to civilian life, birthrates skyrocketed between 1945 and 1955, creating a postwar baby boom. By 1960, the first baby boomers were teenagers—and had entered a crime-prone age. This disproportionate number of young people produced a dramatic increase in most major crimes.

Other factors contributed to the increase in reported crime during the same period. Modified reporting requirements made it less stressful for victims to file police reports, and the publicity associated with the rise in crime sensitized victims to the importance of reporting. Crimes that might have gone undetected in the past began to figure more prominently in official statistics. Similarly, the growing professionalization of some police

1933–1959
From 1933 to 1941, the crime rate declined from 770 to 508 offenses per every 100,000 Americans.
In 1941 crime decreased sharply based on the large numbers of young men entering the military during WWII.
Young men make up the most crime-prone segment of the population, and their removal to European and Pacific theaters of war reduced the incidence of offending throughout the country.
1960–1989
From 1960 to 1980, crime rates rose from 1,887 to 5,950 offenses per every 100,000 Americans.
Starting around 1960, crime rates began to increase based on several factors.
The end of the war brought many young men home to the U.S., and birthrates skyrocketed in the years between 1945 and 1955. By 1960 these baby boomers had become teenagers and had entered a crime-prone age.
Also, reporting procedures were simplified and publicity surrounding crime increased the number of reports. Police agencies were becoming more professional, resulting in increased data and more accurate data collection.
Moreover, the 1960s were tumultuous years. The Vietnam War, civil rights struggles, and an influx of drugs combined to create an imbalance in society that led to an increase in crime.
1933 1937 1941 1945 1949 1963 1967 1960 1963 1967 1975 1979 1983 1987

FIGURE 2-2 | American Crime Rates: Historical Trends

Sources: Photo sources (from left): Everett Collection/SuperStock, Inc.; SuperSTock; Michael Mathews-Police Images/Alamy; Jim West/Alamy.

departments resulted in greater and more accurate data collection, making some of the most progressive departments appear to be associated with the largest crime increases.[14]

The 1960s were tumultuous years. The Vietnam War, a vibrant civil rights struggle, the heady growth of secularism, a dramatic increase in the divorce rate, diverse forms of "liberation," and the influx of psychedelic and other drugs all combined to fragment existing institutions. Social norms were blurred, and group control over individual behavior declined substantially. The "normless" quality of American society in the 1960s contributed greatly to the rise in crime.

From 1960 to 1980, crime rates rose from 1,887 to 5,950 offenses per every 100,000 U.S. residents. In the early 1980s, when postwar boomers began to age out of the crime-prone years and American society emerged from the cultural drift that had characterized the previous 20 years, crime rates leveled out briefly. Soon, however, an increase in drug-related criminal activity led crime rates—especially violent crime rates—to soar once again. Crime rates peaked during the early 1990s.

A third major shift came with a significant decline in the rates of most major crimes being reported between 1991 and 2012. During these years, the rate of reported crime dropped from 5,897 to 3,246 offenses per every 100,000 residents—sending it down to levels not seen since 1975. The U.S. Department of Justice suggests various reasons for the decline, including[15]

- A coordinated, collaborative, and well-funded national effort to combat crime, beginning with the Safe Streets Act of 1968 and continuing through the USA PATRIOT Act of 2001
- Stronger, better-prepared criminal justice agencies, resulting from increased spending by federal and state governments on crime-control programs
- The growth in popularity of innovative police programs, such as community policing (see Chapter 6, "Policing: Purpose and Organization")
- A strong victims' movement and enactment of the 1984 federal Victims of Crime Act (see Chapter 11, "Sentencing") and the 1994 Violence against Women Act (discussed later in this chapter), which established the Office for Victims of Crime in the U.S. Department of Justice
- Sentencing reform, including various "get tough on crime" initiatives (see Chapter 11)
- A substantial growth in the use of incarceration (see Chapter 13, "Prisons and Jails") due to changes in sentencing law practice (see Chapter 11)
- The "war on drugs," begun in the 1970s,[16] which resulted in stiff penalties for drug dealers and repeat drug offenders
- Advances in forensic science and enforcement technology, including the increased use of real-time communications, the growth of the Internet, and the advent of DNA evidence (see Chapter 11)

More important than new strict laws, an expanded justice system, police funding, or changes in crime-fighting technologies, however, may have been influential economic and demographic factors that were largely beyond the control of policymakers but that combined to produce substantial decreases in rates of crime—including economic expansion and a significant shift in demographics caused by an aging of the population. During the

1990–2012 ▶

From 1991 to 2012, crime rates dropped from 5,897 to 3,246 offenses per every 100,000 Americans.

Strict laws, an expanded justice system, and increased police funding for personnel and for crime-fighting technologies are cited as reasons for the drop in crime. Other changes beyond the control of the police may have played a role as well and include economic expansion and an aging population. During the 1990s, unemployment decreased by 36% and likely contributed to the decline in crime rates.

2013–present

In recent years some cities have experienced increases in homicides and other violent crimes.

A fourth shift in crime trends may be about to begin. Economic uncertainty, increased jobless rates, a growing number of ex-convicts back on the streets as well as an increase in teen populations and gang activity may soon lead to sustained increases in crime.

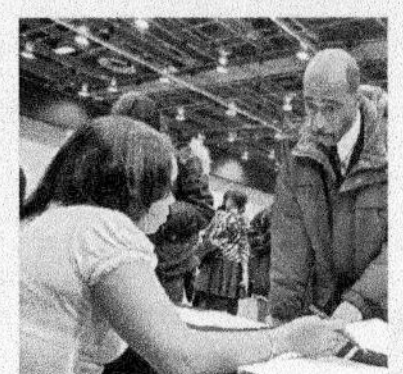

1990 1994 1997 2001 2005 2009 2010 2011 2012 2014

FIGURE 2-2 | (continued)

1990s, unemployment decreased by 36% in the United States, while the number of people ages 20 to 34 declined by 18%. Hence it may have been the ready availability of jobs combined with demographic shifts in the population—not the official efforts of policymakers—that produced a noteworthy decrease in crime during the 1990s.

Confounding matters even more, the digital age has brought with it a plethora of new criminal opportunities—many of which were inconceivable only a decade or two ago. Shifts in crime patterns away from more "traditional" crimes (like those measured by the UCR and NCVS), and toward innovative forms of law violation using high technology, may mask the true face of crime in America—leading to a mistaken sense that the total number of criminal offenses in our society is lower than it actually is. Bank robbery, for example, is a "traditional" crime and is scored by the FBI as one form of "robbery" in the crime statistics that it reports; but while bank robberies have fallen in number over the years, illicit computer attempts to access and misappropriate funds held by banks have risen significantly. In 2013, for example, an international ring of computer criminals stole $45 million from thousands of ATM machines around the globe in a matter of hours. In New York City alone, members of the ring struck 2,904 ATM machines over a ten-hour period, illegally withdrawing more than $2.4 million leading the *New York Times* to comment that "the criminals never wore ski masks, threatened a teller or set foot in a vault."[17] Still, some computer crimes are not reportable under historical crime categories.[18]

It is important to recognize that today's law enforcement administrators often feel judged by their success in lowering crime rates. Consequently, police departments may put pressure on officers to artificially reduce crime rates through techniques such as downgrading crimes to lesser offenses when completing official paperwork. In fact, a 2012 study of nearly 2,000 retired New York Police Department (NYPD) officers found that the manipulation of crime reports has become a part of police culture in the NYPD.[19] Indications are that the underreporting of crime statistics by the police may be a nationwide phenomenon. Another 2012 investigation, for example, this one into the crime reporting practices of Milwaukee police officers, found hundreds of violent assaults that were misreported as minor offenses, and that were not counted in the city's violent crime rate. Following the report, Milwaukee Police Chief Edward Flynn ordered 70 members of the department to complete a refresher training course offered by the FBI on crime reporting.[20]

A fourth shift in crime trends may be on the horizon. Some think that recent economic uncertainty, an increased jobless rate among unskilled workers, the growing number of ex-convicts who are back on the streets, the recent growth in the teenage population in this country, the increasing influence of gangs, copycat crimes, and the lingering social disorganization brought on by natural disasters like Hurricane Katrina in 2005 and Super Storm Sandy in 2012 may lead to sustained increases in crime.[21] "We're probably done seeing declines in crime rates for some time to come," says Jack Riley, director of the Public Safety and Justice Program at RAND Corporation in Santa Monica, California. "The question," says Riley, "is how strong and how fast will those rates [rise], and what tools do we have at our disposal to get ahead of the curve."[22]

The specter of frequent but random mass shootings, and a high number of inner-city murders, is also changing the face of crime in America. One recent study, for example, showed that while rates of traditional crimes have been falling, some cities are experiencing dramatically higher rates of murder. Cities and towns showing a more than 200% increase in year-over-year murders in 2012 included El Paso, Texas; Chula Vista, California; and Madison, Wisconsin. Increases of around 100% could be found in Anaheim, California; Lincoln, Nebraska; San Jose, California; and Reno, Nevada.[23] In 2012, the year of the mass shootings in Aurora, Colorado, and Newtown, Connecticut, both Camden, New Jersey, and Detroit, Michigan, reported more murders than at any time in their history, and other cities, including Chicago, Illinois, were seeing record homicide rates.[24]

Finally, it is important to realize that while official U.S. crime rates may be close to multi-year lows, a number of other countries are experiencing high levels of criminal activity. Mexico, for example, where an ongoing war between the government and drug cartels has led to the deaths of more than 70,000 people and the disappearance of 27,000 more in the past eight years, is caught up in a rapid rate of violent crime escalation.[25] Violent crime, much of it associated with tribal and political conflicts, now extends across borders in Africa, the Middle East, and parts of Europe, leading one English writer

Reuters/Jose Luis Gonzales

Morgue workers place a coffin holding an unidentified body into a grave on the outskirts of the Mexican border city of Ciudad Juarez. Mexico's drug war has claimed more than 70,000 lives in the past eight years. Should cross-national killings be a concern of American law enforcement officials?

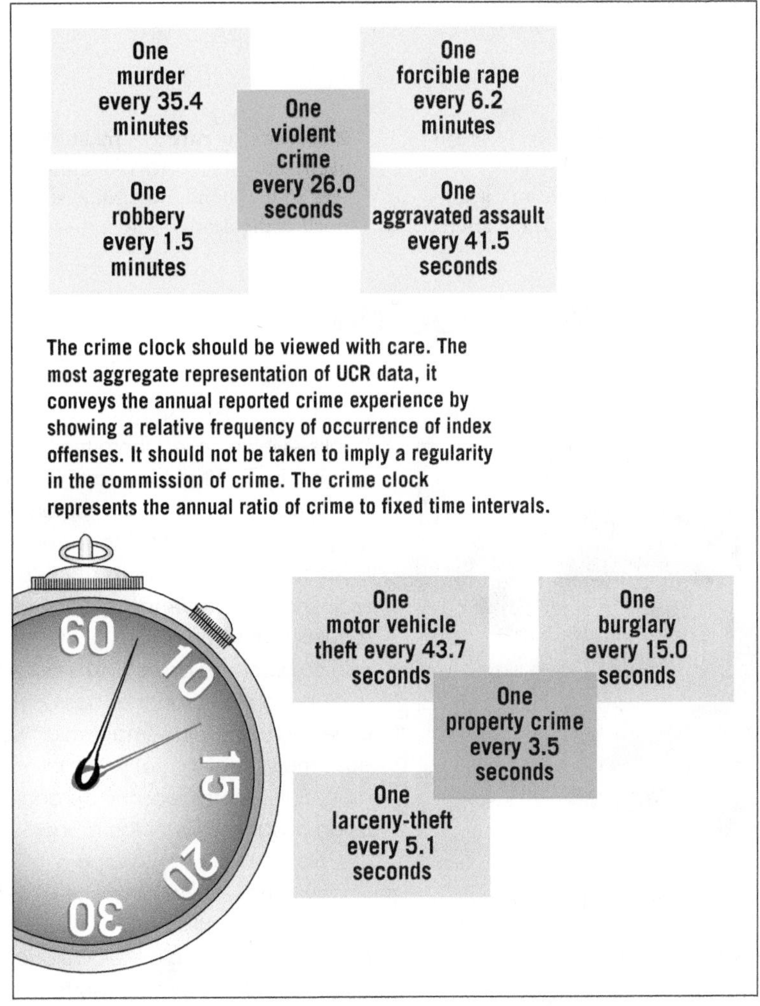

One murder every 35.4 minutes
One forcible rape every 6.2 minutes
One violent crime every 26.0 seconds
One robbery every 1.5 minutes
One aggravated assault every 41.5 seconds
The crime clock should be viewed with care. The most aggregate representation of UCR data, it conveys the annual reported crime experience by showing a relative frequency of occurrence of index offenses. It should not be taken to imply a regularity in the commission of crime. The crime clock represents the annual ratio of crime to fixed time intervals.
60
10
15
20
30
One motor vehicle theft every 43.7 seconds
One burglary every 15.0 seconds
One property crime every 3.5 seconds
One larceny-theft every 5.1 seconds

FIGURE 2-3 | The FBI Crime Clock, Which Shows the Frequency of the Commission of Major Crimes in 2012

Source: Adapted from Federal Bureau of Investigation, *Crime in the United States, 2012* (Washington, DC: U.S. Department of Justice, 2013).

to comment in 2012 that "crime has become a global anxiety, alongside climate change, banking crises, and outbreaks of disease."[26] Keep up with headlines in the Mexican drug war via the *Los Angeles Times* at **http://projects.latimes.com/mexico-drug-war/#/its-a-war.**

UCR/NIBRS in Transition

Reports of U.S. crime data available through the UCR/NIBRS Program are now going through a transitional phase, as the FBI integrates more NIBRS-based data into its official summaries. The transition to NIBRS reporting is complicated by the fact that not only does NIBRS gather more kinds of data than the older summary UCR Program did, but the definitions used for certain kinds of criminal activity under NIBRS differ from what they were under the traditional UCR Program. The standard reference publication that the FBI designates for use by police departments in scoring and reporting crimes that occur within their jurisdiction is the *Uniform Crime Reporting Handbook*, and it is the most recent edition of that *Handbook* that guides and informs the discussion of crime statistics in the pages that follow. You can access the entire 164-page *Uniform Crime Reporting Handbook* at **http://www.justicestudies.com/pubs/ucrhandbook.pdf**. A thorough review of that document shows that much of the traditional UCR summary data reporting terminology and structure remains in place.

Figure 2-3 shows the FBI crime clock, which has long been calculated annually as a shorthand way of diagramming crime frequency in the United States. Note that crime clock data imply a regularity to crime that, in reality, does not exist.[27] Also, although the crime clock is a useful diagrammatic tool, it is not a rate-based measure of criminal activity and does not allow easy comparisons over time. Seven major crimes are included in the figure: murder, forcible rape, robbery, aggravated assault, burglary, larceny-theft, and motor vehicle theft.

■ **violent crime** A UCR/NIBRS summary offense category that includes murder, rape, robbery, and aggravated assault.

■ **property crime** A UCR/NIBRS summary offense category that includes burglary, larceny-theft, motor vehicle theft, and arson.

■ **clearance rate** A traditional measure of investigative effectiveness that compares the number of crimes reported or discovered to the number of crimes solved through arrest or other means (such as the death of the suspect).

freedom OR safety? YOU decide

A Dress Code for Bank Customers?

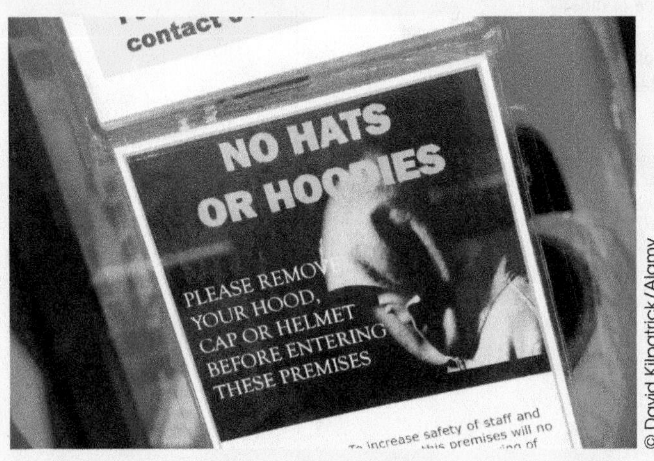

© David Kilpatrick/Alamy

Many banks and some retail establishments require customers to remove hats, hoodies, and sunglasses before entering their place of business. Do you see such requests as limitations on personal rights and freedoms, or as reasonable and necessary precautions?

Hoodies, or hooded sweatshirts, made the national news in 2012 following the fatal shooting of Trayvon Martin in Florida. Martin, a black 17-year-old, was wearing a hoodie when he was apparently confronted by George Zimmerman, a Hispanic community-watch volunteer working in a gated community. Following the shooting, hooded sweatshirts became a symbol of racial profiling, and inspired protests, including one by U.S. Representative Bobby Rush (D-Ill.), who wore sunglasses and a hoodie on the House floor.

Even before the Martin shooting, however, dark glasses, hooded sweatshirts, and hats had been banned by some banks—which called them the "uniform of choice" for bank robbers. In an effort to thwart an increase in robberies, many banks post requests for customers to remove hats, hoods, and sunglasses before entering financial establishments. In 2009, for example, Houston-area banks began putting up signs requiring that customers remove even their cowboy hats—a request that some saw as going too far. Since Sterling Bank, with 60 branches across Texas, asked customers to follow such rules, none of its branches has been robbed. Graham Painter, a Sterling Bank spokesman, said, "We don't want our regular customers thinking that we're telling them how they ought to dress. But it seems reasonable and not too much to ask to give us an advantage over the robber."

Not all banks, however, are following the trend. "I think what you have to weigh is convenience to customers versus the added benefits in terms of identifying suspects with a measure like this," said Melodie Jackson, spokeswoman for Citizens Bank of Massachusetts. "We're taking a very close look at things."

Nonetheless, dress code signs are now commonplace at banks throughout the country, and it is likely that this request will soon become the *de facto* standard at all financial venues.

You Decide

Are bank "dress codes" asking too much of customers? How would you feel about doing business with a bank that posts requests like those described here? Would *you* discriminate against certain members of the public if they dressed in ways that you considered suspicious? If so, what type of clothing would arouse your suspicions?

References: Cindy Horswell, "Some Banks Strike Hats, Sunglasses from Dress Code," *Houston Chronicle*, April 23, 2009; Michael S. Rosenwald and Emily Ramshaw, "Banks Post Dress Code to Deter Robbers," *Boston Globe*, July 13, 2002; and "Missouri Banks Attempt Unmasking Robbers," *Police Magazine* online, October 25, 2002, http://www.policemag.com/t_newspick.cfm?rank571952 (accessed August 8, 2013).

The crime clock distinguishes between two categories of offenses: violent crimes and property crimes. **Violent crimes** (also called *personal crimes*) include murder, forcible rape, robbery, and aggravated assault. It is worth noting that in California and in some other states, almost all violent crimes are referred to as "strikable," as two- and three-strikes laws in those states can result in long prison terms for anyone who commits two or more such crimes. **Property crimes** are motor vehicle theft, burglary, and larceny-theft. Other than the use of this simple dichotomy, UCR/NIBRS data do not provide a clear measure of the severity of the crimes they cover.

Like most UCR/NIBRS statistics, crime clock data are based on crimes reported to (or discovered by) the police. For a few offenses, the numbers reported are probably close to the numbers that actually occur. Murder, for example, is a crime that is difficult to conceal because of its seriousness. Even where the

■ **murder** The unlawful killing of a human being. *Murder* is a generic term that in common usage may include first- and second-degree murder, manslaughter, involuntary manslaughter, and other similar offenses.

■ **Part I offenses** A UCR/NIBRS offense group used to report murder, rape, robbery, aggravated assault, burglary, larceny-theft, motor vehicle theft, and arson, as defined under the FBI's UCR/NIBRS Program.

crime is not immediately discovered, the victim is often quickly missed by family members, friends, and associates, and someone files a "missing persons" report with the police. Auto theft is another crime that is reported in numbers similar to its actual rate of occurrence, probably because insurance companies require that the victim file a police report before they will pay the claim.

A commonly used term in today's UCR/NIBRS reports is **clearance rate**, which refers to the proportion of reported crimes that have been "solved." Clearances are judged primarily on the basis of arrests and do not involve judicial disposition. Once an arrest has been made, a crime is regarded as having been "cleared" for reporting purposes. Exceptional clearances (sometimes called *clearances by exceptional means*) can result when law enforcement authorities believe they know who committed a crime but cannot make an arrest. The perpetrator may, for example, have fled the country or died. Table 2-2 summarizes UCR/NIBRS Program statistics for 2012.

TABLE 2-2 | Major Crimes Known to the Police, 2012 (UCR/NIBRS Part I Offenses)

OFFENSE	NUMBER	RATE PER 100,000	CLEARANCE RATE
Personal/Violent Crimes			
Murder	14,827	4.7	62.5%
Forcible rape	84,376	26.9	40.1
Robbery	354,520	112.9	28.1
Aggravated assault	760,739	242.3	55.8
Property Crimes			
Burglary	2,103,787	670.2	12.7
Larceny-theft	6,150,598	1,959.3	22.0
Motor vehicle theft	721,053	229.7	11.9
Arson[a]	52,766	18.7	20.4
U.S. Total	**10,242,666**	**3,264.7**	

[a]Arson can be classified as either a property crime or a violent crime, depending on whether personal injury or loss of life results from its commission. It is generally classified as a property crime, however. Arson statistics are incomplete for 2012.

Source: Adapted from Federal Bureau of Investigation, *Crime in the United States, 2012* (Washington, DC: U.S. Dept. of Justice, 2013).

Part I Offenses

Murder

Murder is the unlawful killing of one human being by another.[28] UCR/NIBRS statistics on murder describe the yearly incidence of all willful and unlawful homicides within the United States. Included in the count are all cases of nonnegligent manslaughter that have been reported to or discovered by the police. Not included in the count are suicides, justifiable homicides (that is, those committed in self-defense), deaths caused by negligence or accident, and murder attempts. In 2012, some 14,827 murders came to the attention of police departments across the United States. First-degree murder is a criminal homicide that is planned. Second-degree murder is an intentional and unlawful killing but one that is generally unplanned and that happens "in the heat of the moment."

Murder is the smallest numerical category in the **Part I offenses**. The 2012 murder rate was 4.7 homicides for every 100,000 residents of the United States. Generally, murder rates peak in the warmest months; in 2012, the greatest number of murders occurred in August. Geographically, murder is most common in the southern states. However, because those states are also the most populous, a meaningful comparison across regions of the country is difficult.

Age is no barrier to murder. Statistics for 2012 reveal that 144 infants (children under the age of one) were victims of homicide, as were 271 people age 75 and over.[29] Young adults between 20 and 24 were the most likely to be murdered. Murder perpetrators were also most common in this age group.

Firearms are the weapon used most often to commit murder. In 2012, guns were used in 69.3% of all killings. Handguns outnumbered shotguns almost 15 to 1 in the murder statistics, with rifles used almost as often as shotguns. Knives were used in approximately 12.5% of all murders. Other weapons included explosives, poison, narcotics overdose, blunt objects like clubs, hands, feet and fists.

Only 12.2% of all murders in 2012 were perpetrated by offenders classified as "strangers." In 45.1% of all killings, the relationship between the parties had not yet been determined. The largest category of killers was officially listed as "acquaintances,"

Because murder is such a serious crime, it consumes substantial police resources. Consequently, over the years, the offense has shown the highest clearance rate of any index crime.

which probably includes a large number of former friends. Arguments cause most murders (41.8%), but murders also occur during the commission of other crimes, such as robbery, rape, and burglary. Homicides that follow from other crimes are more likely to be impulsive rather than planned.

Murders may occur in sprees, which "involve killings at two or more locations with almost no time break between murders."[30] One spree killer, a former police officer of the Los Angeles Police Department (LAPD), killed three people over the course of a few days in 2013, and fled into the mountains of Southern California before being killed in a cabin hideaway. Dorner was seeking revenge for his firing from the department after having falsely accused another officer of using excessive[31] force. Another spree killer, John Allen Muhammad, 41, part of the "sniper team" that terrorized the Washington, D.C., area in 2002, was arrested along with 17-year-old Jamaican immigrant Lee Boyd Malvo in the random shootings of 13 people in Maryland, Virginia, and Washington over a three-week period. Ten of the victims died.[32] In 2003, Muhammad and Malvo were convicted of capital murder; Muhammad was sentenced to die. Malvo was given a second sentence of life without the possibility of parole in 2006 after he struck a deal with prosecutors in an effort to avoid the death penalty.[33]

In contrast to spree killing, mass murder entails "the killing of four or more victims at one location, within one event."[34] Recent mass murderers have included Newtown, Connecticut, shooter Adam Lanza (who killed 20 first graders and six adults at Sandy Hook Elementary School); Aurora, Colorado, movie theater shooter James Eagan Holmes (who killed 12 people and injured 58 others); Seung-Hui Cho (who killed 33 people and wounded 20 on the campus of Virginia Polytechnic Institute and State University in Blacksburg, Virginia, in 2007); Timothy McVeigh (the antigovernment Oklahoma City bomber); and Mohammed Atta and the terrorists whom he led in the September 11, 2001, attacks against American targets.

Yet another kind of murder, serial murder, happens over time and officially "involves the killing of several victims in three or more separate events."[35] In cases of serial murder, days, months, or even years may elapse between killings.[36] Some of the more infamous serial killers of recent years are confessed Wichita BTK[37] murderer Dennis Rader; Jeffrey Dahmer, who received 936 years in prison for the murders of 15 young men (and who was himself later murdered in prison); Ted Bundy, who killed many college-aged women; Henry Lee Lucas, now in a Texas prison, who confessed to 600 murders but later recanted (yet was convicted of 11 murders and linked to at least 140 others);[38] Ottis Toole, Lucas's partner in crime; cult leader Charles Manson, still serving time for ordering followers to kill seven Californians, including famed actress Sharon Tate; Andrei Chikatilo, the Russian "Hannibal Lecter," who killed 52 people, mostly schoolchildren;[39] David Berkowitz, also known as the "Son of Sam," who killed six people on lovers' lanes around New York City; Theodore Kaczynski, the Unabomber, who perpetrated a series of bomb attacks on "establishment" figures; Seattle's Green River Strangler, Gary Leon Ridgway, a 54-year-old painter who in 2003 confessed to killing 48 women in the 1980s; and the infamous "railroad killer" Angel Maturino Resendiz. Although Resendiz was convicted of only one murder—that of Dr. Claudia Benton, which occurred in 1998—he is suspected of many more.[40]

Federal homicide laws changed in 2004, when President George Bush signed the Unborn Victims of Violence Act.[41] The act, which passed the Senate by only one vote, made it a separate federal crime to "kill or attempt to kill" a fetus "at any stage of development" during an assault on a pregnant woman. The fetal homicide statute, better known as Laci and Conner's Law, after homicide victims Laci Peterson and her unborn son (whom she had planned to name Conner), specifically prohibits the prosecution of "any person for conduct relating to an abortion for which the consent of the pregnant woman, or a person authorized by law to act on her behalf, has been obtained."

Because murder is such a serious crime, it consumes substantial police resources. Consequently, over the years, the offense has shown the highest clearance rate of any index crime. More than 62.5% of all homicides were cleared in 2012. Figure 2-4 shows expanded homicide data from the FBI.

Elaine Thompson/Reuters/Landov Media

Self-confessed serial killer Gary L. Ridgway. The 54-year-old man, known as the Green River Strangler, is said to be the nation's worst captured serial killer. In 2003, Ridgway admitted to killing 48 women over a 20-year period in the Pacific Northwest. He is now serving life in prison without possibility of parole. What's the difference between serial killers and mass murderers?

■ **rape** Unlawful sexual intercourse achieved through force and without consent. Broadly speaking, the term *rape* has been applied to a wide variety of sexual attacks and may include same-sex rape and the rape of a male by a female. Some jurisdictions refer to same-sex rape as *sexual battery*.

■ **forcible rape (UCR/NIBRS)** The carnal knowledge of a person, forcibly and against his or her will. More specifically, penetration, no matter how slight, of the vagina or anus with any body part or object, or oral penetration by a sex organ of another person, without the consent of the victim. Statutory rape differs from forcible rape in that it generally involves nonforcible sexual intercourse with a minor.

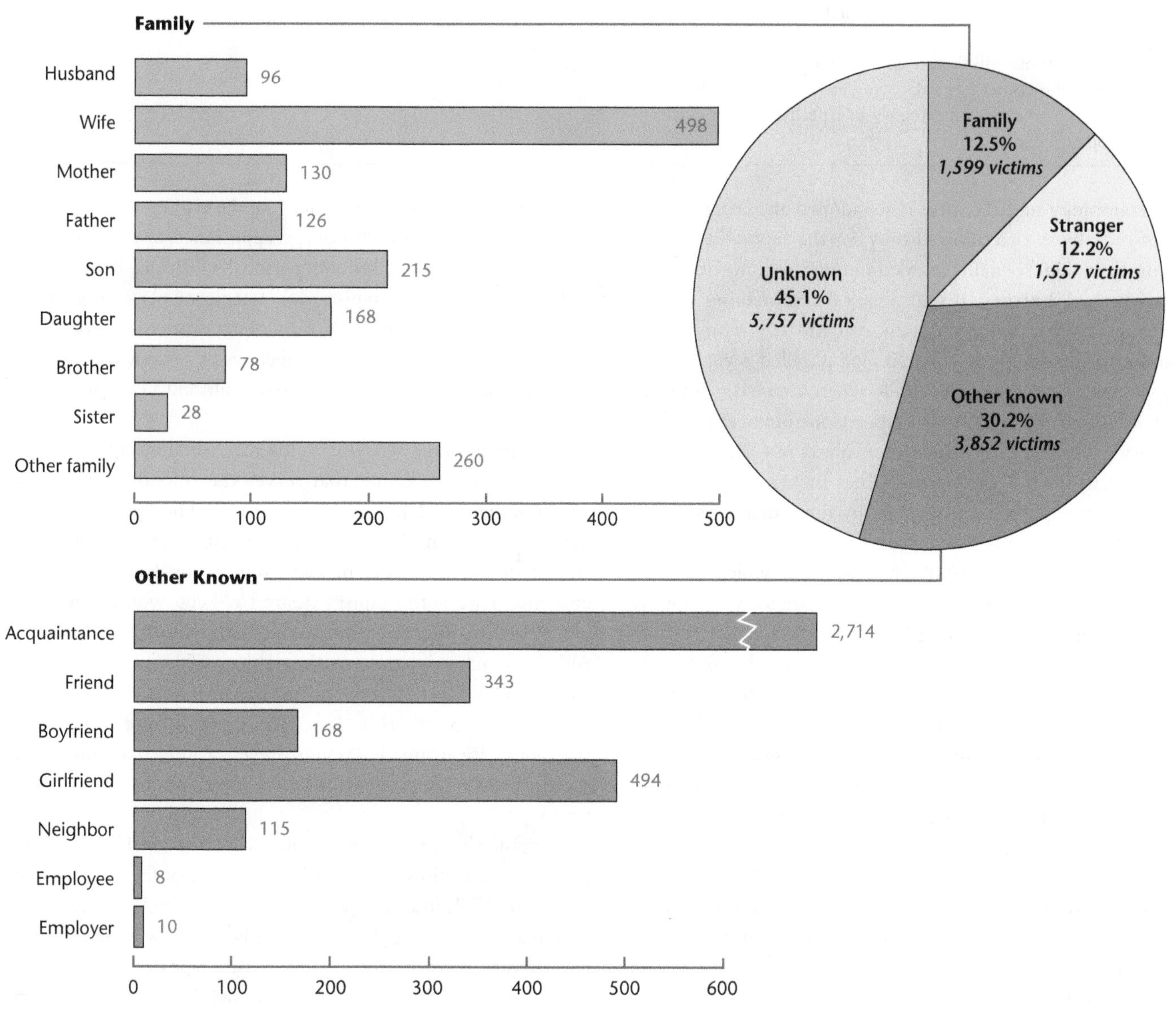

NOTE: Relationship is that of victim to offender. Percentages may not total 100 due to rounding.

FIGURE 2-4 | Murder by Relationship, 2012

Source: Federal Bureau of Investigation, *Crime in the United States, 2012* (Washington, DC: U.S. Dept. of Justice, 2013).

Forcible Rape

The terms **rape** and *forcible rape* are often applied to a wide variety of sexual attacks, including same-sex rape and the rape of a male by a female. Under the FBI's UCR program the term **forcible rape** generally means "the carnal knowledge of a person forcibly and against their will."[42] More specifically, forcible rape is defined by the UCR program as "penetration, no matter how slight, of the vagina or anus with any body part or object, or oral penetration by a sex organ of another person, without the consent of the victim."[43] The FBI began using

sexual battery Intentional and wrongful physical contact with a person, without his or her consent, that entails a sexual component or purpose.

date rape Unlawful forced sexual intercourse that occurs within the context of a dating relationship. Date rape, or acquaintance rape, is a subcategory of rape that is of special concern today.

that terminology in 2012, after it abandoned an earlier definition of the phrase that allowed only for the rape of a female. Previously, violent sexual crimes committed against men were termed **sexual battery**, sexual assault, or something similar under the FBI's reporting program. It is worth noting that, in a number of jurisdictions, forcible rape is called *sexual assault* or *aggravated sexual assault* (especially when the victim is under a certain age or if the victim suffers serious physical injuries). Statutory rape, where no force is involved but the victim is younger than the age of consent, is not included in rape statistics, but attempts to commit rape by force or the threat of force are.

Forcible rape is the least reported of all violent crimes. Estimates are that only one out of every four forcible rapes is reported to the police. An even lower figure was reported by a 1992 government-sponsored study, which found that only 16% of rapes were reported.[44] The victim's fear of embarrassment was the most commonly cited reason for nonreports. In the past, many states routinely permitted a person's past sexual history to be revealed in detail in the courtroom if a trial ensued. But the past few decades have seen many changes designed to facilitate accurate reporting of rape and other sex offenses. Trained female detectives often interview female victims, physicians have become better educated in handling the psychological needs of victims, and sexual histories are no longer regarded as relevant in most trials.

UCR/NIBRS statistics show 84,376 reported forcible rapes for 2012, a slight decrease over the number of offenses reported for the previous year. Rape reports, however, have sometimes increased, even in years when reports of other violent crimes have been on the decline. The offense of rape follows homicide in its seasonal variation. The greatest numbers of forcible rapes in 2012 were reported in the hot summer months, and the lowest numbers were recorded in January, February, November, and December.

Rape is frequently committed by a person known to the victim, as in the case of **date rape**. Victims may be held captive and subjected to repeated assaults.[45] In the crime of heterosexual rape, any female—regardless of age, appearance, or occupation—is a potential victim. Through personal violation, humiliation, and physical battering, rapists seek a sense of personal aggrandizement and dominance. Victims of rape often experience a lessened sense of personal worth; feelings of despair, helplessness, and vulnerability; a misplaced sense of guilt; and a lack of control over their personal lives.

Contemporary wisdom holds that forcible rape is often a planned violent crime that serves the offender's need for power rather than sexual gratification.[46] The "power thesis" has its origins in the writings of Susan Brownmiller, who argued in 1975 that the primary motivation leading to heterosexual rape is the rapist's desire to "keep women in their place" and to preserve gender inequality through violence.[47] Although many writers on the subject of heterosexual rape have generally accepted the power thesis, at least one study has caused some to rethink it. In a 1995 survey of imprisoned serial rapists, for example, Dennis Stevens found that "lust" was reported most often (41%) as "the primary motive for predatory rape."[48]

Statistically speaking, most rapes are committed by acquaintances of the victims and often betray a trust or friendship. Date rape, which falls into this category, appears to be far more common than previously believed. Recently, the growing number of rapes perpetrated with the use of the "date rape drug" Rohypnol have alarmed law enforcement personnel. Rohypnol, which is discussed in Chapter 16, "Drugs and Crime," is an illegal pharmaceutical substance that is virtually tasteless. Available on the black market, it dissolves easily in drinks and can leave anyone who consumes it unconscious for hours, making them vulnerable to sexual assault.

Rape within marriage, which has not always been recognized as a crime, is a growing area of concern in American criminal justice, and many laws have been enacted during the past few decades to deter it. Similarly, even though some state laws on rape continue to encompass only the rape or attempted rape of a

■ **robbery (UCR/NIBRS)** The unlawful taking or attempted taking of property that is in the immediate possession of another by force or violence and/or by putting the victim in fear. Armed robbery differs from unarmed, or strong-arm, robbery in that it involves a weapon. Contrary to popular conceptions, highway robbery does not necessarily occur on a street—and rarely in a vehicle. The term *highway robbery* applies to any form of robbery that occurs outdoors in a public place.

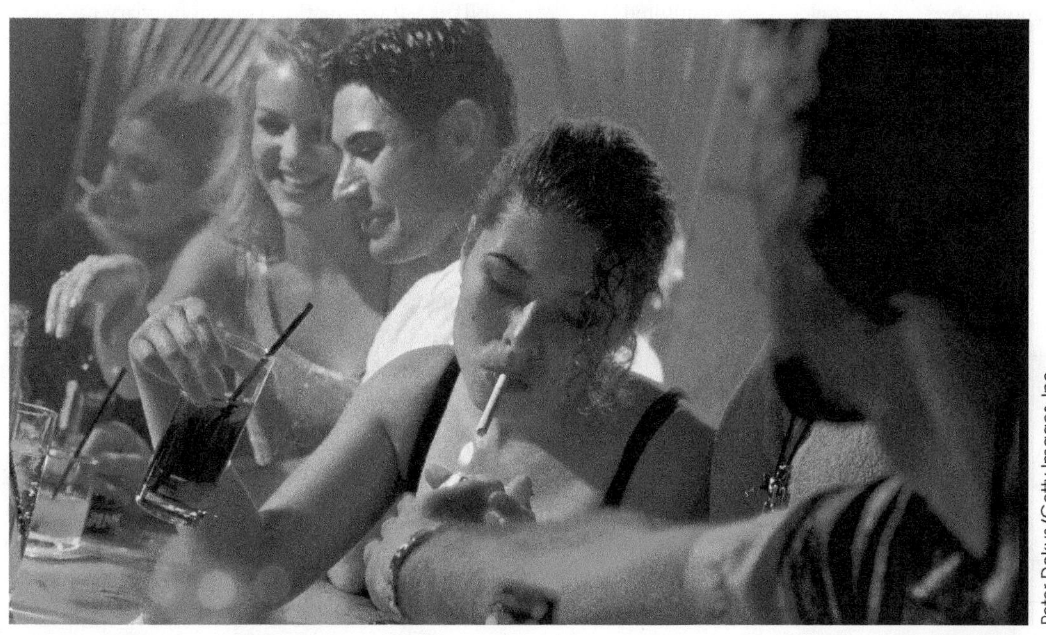

Peter Dokus/Getty Images, Inc.

A crime in progress? Date rape is unlawful sexual intercourse that occurs within the context of a dating relationship. "Date rape drugs" like Rohypnol are sometimes secretly placed in drinks, rendering victims unable to resist. How can people guard against being victimized?

female by a male, they also criminalize the sexual abuse of a male by a female. When it occurs, this offense is typically charged as statutory rape, or falls under some other state statute. In 2011, for example 28-year-old former English teacher Tina Marie Amato, of Fredericksburg, Virginia, pleaded guilty to four felony courts of having sexual relations with a 15-year-old male student under her care.[49] Amato, a teacher at Gar-Field High School, pleaded guilty in Prince William Circuit Court to three counts of taking indecent liberties with a minor by a custodian and one count of crimes against nature.

Robbery

Robbery is a personal crime involving a face-to-face confrontation between a victim and a perpetrator. It is often confused with burglary, which is primarily a property crime. (We'll examine burglary later.) Weapons may be used in robbery, or strong-arm robbery may occur through intimidation. Purse snatching and pocket picking are not classified as robbery by the UCR/NIBRS Program but are included under the category of larceny-theft.

In 2012, as Figure 2-5 shows, individuals were the most common target of robbers (shown under the category of "street/highway" robbery). Banks, gas stations, convenience stores, and other businesses were the second most common target, with residential robberies accounting for only 16.9% of the total. In 2012, 354,520 robberies were reported to the police. Of that number, 43.5% were highway robberies, meaning that the crime occurred outdoors, most commonly as the victim was walking in a public place. Strong-arm robberies, in which the victim was intimidated but no weapon was used, accounted for 42.5% of the total robberies reported. Guns were used in 41.0% of all robberies, and knives were used in 7.8%. Armed robbers are dangerous; guns are actually discharged in 20% of all robberies.[50]

When a robbery occurs, the UCR/NIBRS Program scores the event as one robbery, even when numerous victims were robbed during the event. With the move toward incident-driven reporting, however, the revised UCR/NIBRS Program will soon make data available on the number of individuals robbed in each incident. Because statistics on crime follow what's known

■ **assault (UCR/NIBRS)** An unlawful attack by one person upon another. Historically, *assault* meant only the attempt to inflict injury on another person; a completed act constituted the separate offense of battery. Under modern statistical usage, however, attempted and completed acts are grouped together under the generic term *assault*.

■ **aggravated assault** The unlawful, intentional inflicting, or attempted or threatened inflicting, of serious injury upon the person of another. Although *aggravated assault* and *simple assault* are standard terms for reporting purposes, most state penal codes use labels like *first-degree* and *second-degree* to make such distinctions.

■ **burglary (UCR/NIBRS)** The unlawful entry of a structure to commit a felony or a theft (excludes tents, trailers, and other mobile units used for recreational purposes). Under the UCR/NIBRS Program, the crime of burglary can be reported if (1) an unlawful entry of an unlocked structure has occurred, (2) a breaking and entering (of a secured structure) has taken place, or (3) a burglary has been attempted.

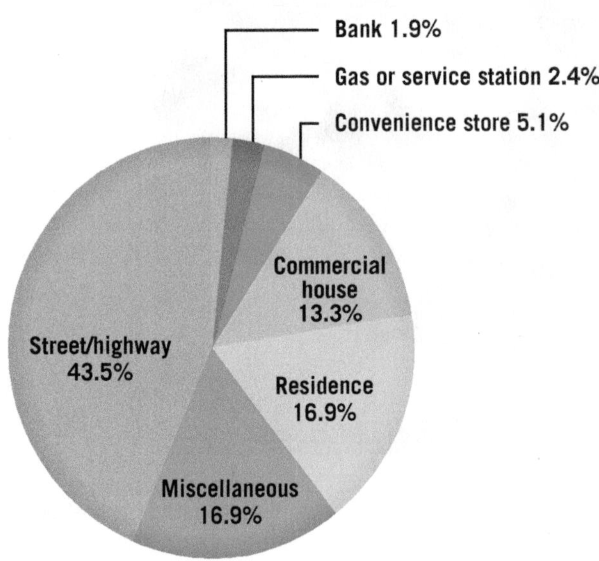

FIGURE 2-5 | Robbery Locations, 2012

Source: Based on data from Federal Bureau of Investigation, *Crime in the United States, 2012* (Washington, DC: U.S. Dept. of Justice, 2013).

as the *hierarchy rule*, they show only the most serious offense that occurred during a particular episode. Hence robberies are often hidden when they occur in conjunction with more serious crimes. For example, 3% of robbery victims are also raped, and a large number of homicide victims are robbed.[51]

Robbery is primarily an urban offense, and most arrestees are young male minorities. The robbery rate in large cities in 2012 was 293.6 per every 100,000 inhabitants, whereas it was much lower in rural areas. Of those arrested for robbery in 2012, 87% were male, 60% were under the age of 25, and 57% were minorities.[52]

Aggravated Assault

In April 2006, Arthur J. McClure, 22, of Fort Myers, Florida, was arrested when he allegedly took the head off an Easter Bunny costume that he was wearing and punched Erin Johansson of Cape Coral, Florida, after the young mother apparently became upset that a mall photo set was closing 10 minutes early.[53] The incident was witnessed by dozens of people, including many children who had gathered to have their pictures taken with the rabbit. McClure, who denied he struck Johansson, was fired after the incident.

Assaults are of two types: simple (misdemeanor) and aggravated (felonious). For statistical-reporting purposes, simple assaults typically involve pushing and shoving. Although simple assault may also at times include fistfights, the correct legal term to describe such incidents is *battery*. **Aggravated assaults** are distinguished from simple assaults in that either a weapon is used or the assault victim requires medical assistance. When a deadly weapon is employed, an aggravated assault may be charged as attempted murder even if no injury results.[54] In some cases, the UCR/NIBRS Program scores these attempted assaults as aggravated assault because of the potential for serious consequences.

In 2012, 760,739 cases of aggravated assault were reported to law enforcement agencies in the United States. Assault reports were most frequent in summer months and least frequent in February, November, December, and January. Most aggravated assaults were committed with blunt objects or objects near at hand, and hands, feet, and fists were also commonly used (27%). Less frequently used were knives (19%) and firearms (22%). Because those who commit assaults are often known to their victims, aggravated assaults are relatively easy to solve. About 56% of all aggravated assaults reported to the police in 2012 were cleared by arrest.

Burglary

Although it may involve personal and even violent confrontation, **burglary** is primarily a property crime. Burglars are interested in financial gain and usually fence (that is, illegally sell) stolen items, recovering a fraction of their cash value. About 2.1 million burglaries were reported to the police in 2012. Dollar losses to burglary victims totaled $4.7 billion, with an average loss per offense of $2,230.

The UCR/NIBRS Program employs three classifications of burglary: (1) forcible entry, (2) unlawful entry where no force is used, and (3) attempted forcible entry. In most jurisdictions,

CJ | NEWS

"Flash Robs"—The Next Social Media Phenomenon

Richard Sennott/Newscom

The immediate aftermath of a flash robbery showing young people streaming out of a store that they just attacked. How have social media changed the nature of criminal activity in this country?

"Flash mobs," where text messaging or Twitter brings together large groups of people for spontaneous events, have irked police because they lack permits and may be disruptive. Now, however, police are facing a more serious problem: "flash robs," where social media directs people—often teenagers—to go to retail stores and rob them.

Unlike conventional robberies, flash robs have the feel of a mob looting a store. When social media bring people together, the individuals often don't even know each other and very little planning has taken place. Videos on YouTube show scores of jubilant teenagers filing into a convenience store and helping themselves to snacks and sodas, as employees helplessly look on. It all lasts a matter of minutes.

This is "mob behavior but it has some pre-meditation, which is a new thing," said Read Hayes, a University of Florida research scientist, in an interview with the *Wall Street Journal.*

According to a July 2011 poll by the National Retail Federation, 10% of storeowners reported they were victims of flash robs in the past 12 months, and half of them said they experienced two to five incidents in that period. Social media or texting was involved in at least 42% of cases where suspects were apprehended, and 83% of incidents involved juveniles.

Because flash robs involve as many as 50 people, store employees can do little to stop them and may even suffer injury. Participants have been known to punch an employee on the way out. In addition to the loss of merchandise, retailers are concerned about losing customers. "A frenzied group of teens snatching merchandise and running through store aisles creates panic and potential safety issues for customers and store employees," according to a 2011 white paper by the National Retail Federation.

One flash robbery at a convenience store can involve hundreds of dollars worth of goods, and the toll can be far greater at high-end retailers. About 20 flash robbers stole $20,000 worth of merchandise from a Washington, D.C., clothing store in April 2011.

Swarms of young people assembled through social media may also commit acts of violence or vandalism, without stealing. In Philadelphia, for example, teens knocked down passers-by and assaulted shoppers in an upscale department store. Such incidents prompted Mayor Michael A. Nutter to intensify police patrols and move a curfew for teens to 9 p.m. in 2011.

In many cases, flash robbers are recorded by surveillance cameras, making it easier to arrest and convict them. They may also be identified on social media or be apprehended leaving the scene. Police simply have to look for large groups of young people who have items from the store but no receipts (although the legal issues involved in stopping and searching people can pose problems for law enforcers).

Even though the total value of stolen goods can be high, the value of what each person stole is often quite low, making it difficult to charge the participants with a serious crime. Typically, the charges are third-degree theft and riot. Guns are not used and criminal conspiracy charges don't apply when participants don't even know each other.

After several flash robs occurred in Maryland in 2011, a bill introduced in the state legislature would make each participant in a flash rob responsible for the total value stolen, thus allowing for harsher sentences. In a different tack, the city of Cleveland considered making it a criminal offense to summon any kind of flash mob through social media, but the proposal was withdrawn.

Resources: "Flash Mobs Aren't Just for Fun Anymore," NPR, May 26, 2011, http://www.npr.org/2011/05/26/136578945/flash-mobs-arent-just-for-fun-anymore; "Flash Robs" Vex Retailers, *Wall Street Journal*, October 21, 2011, http://online.wsj.com/article/SB10001424052970203752604576643422390552158.html; and "Multiple Offender Crimes," *National Retail Federation White Paper*, August 2011, http://www.nrf.com/modules.php?name=News&op=viewlive&sp_id=1167.

force need not be employed for a crime to be classified as burglary. Unlocked doors and open windows are invitations to burglars, and the legal essence of burglary consists not so much of a forcible entry as it does of the intent to trespass and steal. In 2012, 60.5% of all burglaries were forcible entries, 33.2% were unlawful entries, and 6.3% were attempted forcible entries.[55] The most dangerous burglaries were those in which a household member was home (about 10% of all burglaries).[56] Residents who were home during a burglary suffered a greater than 30% chance of becoming the victim of a violent crime.[57] However, although burglary may evoke images of dark-clothed strangers breaking into houses in which families lie sleeping, burglaries more often are of unoccupied homes and take place during daylight hours.

The clearance rate for burglary, as for other property crimes that we'll look at later, is generally low. In 2012, the clearance rate for burglary was only 12.4%. Burglars usually do not know their victims, and in cases where they do, burglars conceal their identity by committing their crime when the victim is not present.

larceny-theft (UCR/NIBRS) The unlawful taking or attempted taking, carrying, leading, or riding away of property, from the possession or constructive possession of another. Motor vehicles are excluded. Larceny is the most common of the eight major offenses, although probably only a small percentage of all larcenies are actually reported to the police because of the small dollar amounts involved.

Larceny-Theft

In 2013, Natalie Heil of West Palm Beach, Florida, was arrested and charged with grand theft for renting out a home that she didn't own.[58] According to police, the house that Heil rented was in foreclosure and had been vacant for over a year. Two women rented the home from Heil by answering an advertisement that Heil had placed on Craigslist. They signed a rental agreement with Heil and paid her more than $13,000 before the scheme was discovered by a woman who was checking on the property.

Because larceny has traditionally been considered a crime that requires physical possession of the item appropriated, some computer crimes, including thefts engineered through online access or thefts of software and information, have not been scored as larcenies unless computer equipment, electronic circuitry, or computer media were actually stolen.

Larceny is another name for theft and, as is true in this example, almost anything of value can be stolen. The UCR/NIBRS Program uses the term **larceny-theft** to describe theft offenses (Figure 2-6) of all kinds. Some states distinguish between simple larceny and grand larceny, categorizing the crime based on the dollar value of what is stolen. Larceny-theft, as defined by the UCR/NIBRS Program, includes the theft of valuables of any dollar amount. The reports specifically list the following offenses as types of larceny (listed here in order of declining frequency):

- Thefts from motor vehicles
- Shoplifting
- Thefts from buildings
- Thefts of motor vehicle parts and accessories
- Bicycle thefts
- Thefts from coin-operated machines
- Purse snatching
- Pocket picking

Thefts of farm animals (known as *rustling*) and thefts of most types of farm machinery also fall into the larceny category. In fact, larceny is such a broad category that it serves as a kind of catchall in the UCR/NIBRS Program. In 1995, for example, Yale University officials filed larceny charges against 25-year-old-student Lon Grammer, claiming that he had fraudulently obtained university funds.[59] The university maintained that Grammer had stolen his education by forging college and high school transcripts and concocting letters of recommendation prior to admission. Grammer's alleged misdeeds, which Yale University officials said misled them into thinking that Grammer, a poor student before attending Yale, had an exceptional scholastic record, permitted him to receive $61,475 in grants and loans during the time he attended the school. Grammer was expelled.

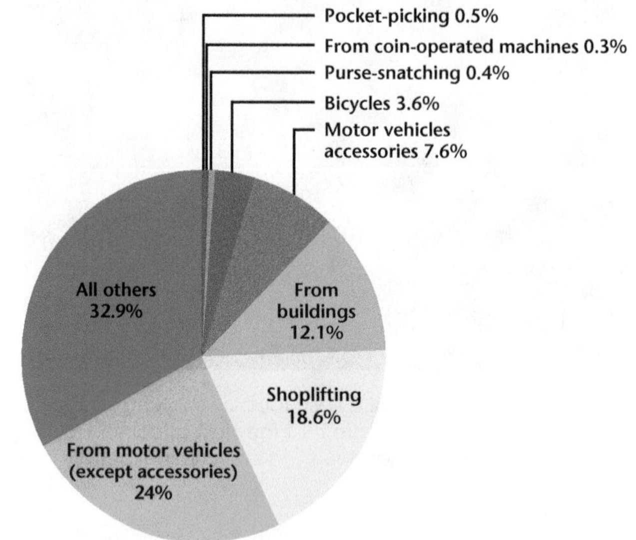

FIGURE 2-6 | Larceny-Theft Distribution, 2012

Note: Due to rounding, the percentages may not total 100.

Source: Based on data from Federal Bureau of Investigation, *Crime in the United States, 2012* (Washington, DC: U.S. Dept. of Justice, 2013).

Reported thefts vary widely, in terms of both the objects stolen and their value. Stolen items range from pocket change to a $100 million aircraft. For reporting purposes, crimes entailing embezzlement, con games, forgery, and worthless checks are specifically excluded from the count of larceny. Because larceny has traditionally been considered a crime that requires physical possession of the item appropriated, some computer crimes, including thefts engineered through online access or thefts of software and information, have not been scored as larcenies unless computer equipment, electronic circuitry, or computer media were actually stolen. In 2004, however, the FBI confirmed that it was working with Cisco Systems, Inc., to investigate the possible theft of some of the company's intellectual property.[60]

CJ | ISSUES

Race and the Criminal Justice System

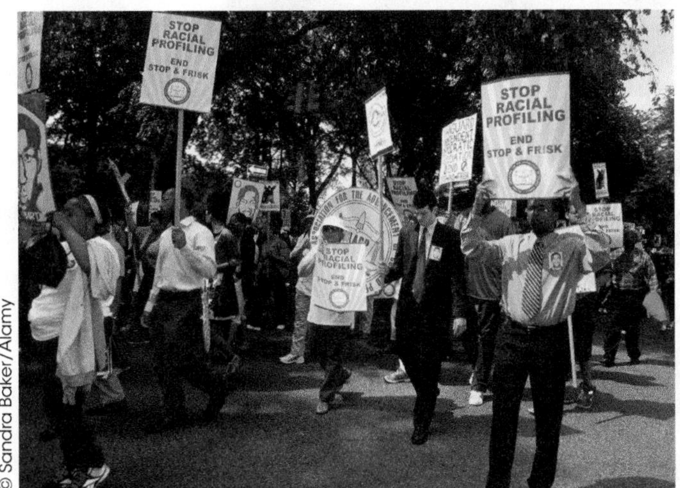

© Sandra Baker/Alamy

A protest in New York City over the "stop and frisk" policies of the NYPD, which some claim puts members of underrepresented groups at risk for unfair treatment. Others that such police activity deploys enforcement resources to areas that need it the most and protects members of minority communities. Is the American criminal justice system equitable?

Several years ago, Professor Lani Guinier of the University of Pennsylvania School of Law was interviewed on *Think Tank*, a public television show. Guinier was asked by Ben Wattenberg, the program's moderator, "When we talk about crime, crime, crime, are we really using a code for black, black, black?" Guinier responded this way: "To a great extent, yes, and I think that's a problem, not because we shouldn't deal with the disproportionate number of crimes that young black men may be committing, but because if we can't talk about race, then when we talk about crime, we're really talking about other things, and it means that we're not being honest in terms of acknowledging what the problem is and then trying to deal with it."[1]

Crimes, of course, are committed by individuals of all races. The link between crime—especially violent, street, and predatory crimes—and race, however, shows a striking pattern. In most crime categories, arrests of black offenders equal or exceed arrests of whites. In any given year, arrests of blacks account for approximately 38% of all arrests for violent crimes, and 50% of arrests for murder. Blacks, however, comprise only 12% of the U.S. population. When *rates* (which are based upon the relative proportion of racial groups) are examined, the statistics are even more striking. The murder rate among blacks, for example, is ten times that of whites. Similar rate comparisons, when calculated for other violent crimes, show that far more blacks than whites are involved in other street crimes, such as assault, burglary, and robbery. Related studies show that 30% of all young black men in America are under correctional supervision on any given *day*—a far greater percentage than for members of any other race in the country.[2] Not only do statistics on arrest indicate an overabundance of black and minority offenders, but, according to a report by the American Sociological Association, "black men and women are victims of serious violent crimes at far higher rates than whites."[3]

The real question for anyone interested in justice system fairness is how to explain such huge race-based disparities. Contemporary research appears to disprove claims that today's American justice system is intentionally racist. Recently, for example, Pauline K. Brennan, a criminologist at the University of Nebraska at Omaha, examined the effects of race and ethnicity on the sentencing of female misdemeanants and found that "race/ethnicity did not directly affect sentencing."[4] Brennan discovered, however, that black and Hispanic females "were more likely to receive jail sentences than their White counterparts due to differences in" things like prior record and charge severity.

Some authors continue to maintain, however, that racial differences in arrests and in rates of imprisonment are due to the differential treatment of African Americans at the hands of a discriminatory criminal justice system. Marvin D. Free, Jr., for example, says that the fact that African Americans are underrepresented as criminal justice professionals results in their being overrepresented in arrest and confinement statistics. Some police officers, says Free, are more prone to arrest blacks than whites, frequently arrest blacks without sufficient evidence to support criminal charges, and overcharge in criminal cases involving black defendants.

Other writers disagree. In *The Myth of a Racist Criminal Justice System*, for example, William Wilbanks claims that although the practice of American criminal justice may have been significantly racist in the past, the system today is by and large objective in its processing of criminal defendants.[5] Using statistical data, Wilbanks shows that "at every point from arrest to parole there is little or no evidence of an overall racial effect, in that the percentage outcomes for blacks and whites are not very different." Wilbanks is careful to counter claims advanced by those who continue to suggest that the system is racist. He says that "the best evidence on this question comes from the National Crime Survey which interviews 130,000 Americans each year about crime victimization. . . . The percent of offenders described by victims as being black is generally consistent with the percent of offenders who are black according to arrest figures."

The question of *actual* fairness of the justice system can be quite different from one of *perceived* fairness. As University of Maryland Professor Katheryn K. Russell points out, "Study after study has shown that blacks and whites hold contrary views on the fairness of the criminal justice system's operation; blacks tend to be more cautious in their praise and frequently view the system as unfair and racially biased; by contrast whites have a favorable impression of the justice system. . . . The point is not that whites are completely satisfied with the justice system, but rather that, relative to blacks, they have faith in the system."[6]

In short, the justice system of today must be race-neutral if it is to win acceptance by the wider community—and the old saying that "justice is blind" would likely serve well to guide the actions of justice system participants in all racially charged areas.

[1]Quoted in "For the Record," *Washington Post* wire service, March 3, 1994.

[2]Marvin D. Free, Jr., *African-Americans and the Criminal Justice System* (New York: Garland, 1996).

[3]Katherine J. Rosich, *Race, Ethnicity, and the Criminal Justice System* (Washington, DC: American Sociological Association, 2007), p. 4.

[4]Pauline K. Brennan, "Sentencing Female Misdemeanants: An Examination of the Direct and Indirect Effects of Race/Ethnicity," *Justice Quarterly*, Vol. 23, No. 1 (March 2006), pp. 60–95.

[5]William Wilbanks, *The Myth of a Racist Criminal Justice System* (Monterey, CA: Brooks/Cole, 1987).

[6]Katheryn K. Russell, "The Racial Hoax as Crime: The Law as Affirmation," *Indiana Law Journal*, Vol. 71 (1996), pp. 593–621.

© Aygul Bulté/Fotolia

High speed commuter trains. The FBI defines motor vehicles as self-propelled vehicles that run on the ground and not on rails. How might the theft of a train be classified under the UCR?

The theft involved approximately 800 megabytes of proprietary software code used to control the company's Internet routers. Because hardware manufactured by Cisco Systems accounts for more than 60% of all routers used on the Internet,[61] officials feared that the lost software could represent a major security threat for the entire Internet.

Larceny-theft is the most frequently reported major crime, according to the UCR/NIBRS Program. It may also be the program's most underreported crime category because small thefts rarely come to the attention of the police.

From a statistical standpoint, the most common form of larceny in recent years has been theft of motor vehicle parts, accessories, and contents. Tires, wheels, hubcaps, radar detectors, stereos, satellite radios, CD players, compact discs, and cellular phones account for many of the items reported stolen.

Reports to the police in 2012 showed 6,150,598 larcenies nationwide, with the total value of property stolen placed at $6 billion. Larceny-theft is the most frequently reported major crime, according to the UCR/NIBRS Program. It may also be the program's most underreported crime category because small thefts rarely come to the attention of the police. The average value of items reported stolen in 2012 was about $987.

© Mandoga Media/Alamy

Facebook founder Mark Zuckerberg. Companies like Facebook are always working to upgrade personal security to prevent crimes such as identity theft. Why is identity theft so prevalent today? How can it be stopped?

Identity Theft: A New Kind of Larceny In May 2010, 26-year-old Facebook founder and billionaire Mark Zuckerberg announced that his company would provide users with the ability to significantly upgrade personal security settings.[62] Facebook, said Zuckerberg, would enhance privacy choices in order to reduce the amount of personal information that is publicly available by default. Online settings, which Zuckerberg pledged would become easier to find and to change, would also allow users to opt out of third-party applications associated

identity theft A crime in which an impostor obtains key pieces of information, such as Social Security and driver's license numbers, to obtain credit, merchandise, and services in the name of the victim. The victim is often left with a ruined credit history and the time-consuming and complicated task of repairing the financial damage.[i]

motor vehicle theft (UCR/NIBRS) The theft or attempted theft of a motor vehicle. A *motor vehicle* is defined as a self-propelled road vehicle that runs on land surface and not on rails. The stealing of trains, planes, boats, construction equipment, and most farm machinery is classified as larceny under the UCR/NIBRS Program, not as motor vehicle theft.

with Facebook.[63] The announcement came after users, privacy advocates, and lawmakers voiced their concerns over lax security features on the highly popular site. Many were concerned that criminals could use Facebook to acquire information about its users and steal their identities.[64]

Identity theft, which involves obtaining credit, merchandise, or services by fraudulent personal representation, is a special kind of larceny. According to a recent federal survey, 11.7 million Americans were victims of identity theft in 2008, although most did not report the crime.[65] Information from the Bureau of Justice Statistics (BJS) shows that 7.0% of all households in the United States had at least one member who had been a victim of one or more types of identity theft in 2010.[66] The BJS also says that identity theft is the fastest-growing type of crime in America.[67]

Identity theft became a federal crime in 1998 with the passage of the Identity Theft and Assumption Deterrence Act.[68] The law makes it a crime whenever anyone "knowingly transfers or uses, without lawful authority, a means of identification of another person with the intent to commit, or to aid or abet, any unlawful activity that constitutes a violation of federal law, or that constitutes a felony under any applicable state or local law."

The 2004 Identity Theft Penalty Enhancement Act[69] added two years to federal prison sentences for criminals convicted of using stolen credit card numbers and other personal data to commit crimes. It also prescribed prison sentences for those who use identity theft to commit other crimes, including terrorism, and it increased penalties for defendants who exceed or abuse the authority of their positions in unlawfully obtaining or misusing means of personal identification.

According to the National White Collar Crime Center, identity thieves use several common techniques. Some engage in "dumpster diving," going through trash bags, cans, or dumpsters to get copies of checks, credit card and bank statements, credit card applications, or other records that typically bear identifying information. Others use a technique called "shoulder surfing," which involves looking over the victim's shoulder as he or she enters personal information into a computer or on a written form. Eavesdropping is another simple, yet effective, technique that identity thieves often use. Eavesdropping can occur when the victim is using an ATM machine, giving credit card or other personal information over the phone, or dialing the number for a telephone calling card. Criminals can also obtain personal identifying information from potential victims through the Internet. Some Internet users, for example, reply to "spam" (unsolicited e-mail) that promises them all sorts of attractive benefits while requesting identifying data, such as checking account or credit card numbers and expiration dates, along with their name and address.[70] Identity theft perpetrated through the use of high technology depends on the fact that a person's legal and economic identity in contemporary society is largely "virtual" and supported by technology. Read the National Strategy to Combat Identity Theft at **http://www.justicestudies.com/pubs/natlstrategy.pdf**.

Motor Vehicle Theft

For record-keeping purposes, the UCR/NIBRS Program defines *motor vehicles* as self-propelled vehicles that run on the ground and not on rails. Included in the definition are automobiles, motorcycles, motor scooters, trucks, buses, and snowmobiles. Excluded are trains, airplanes, bulldozers, most farm and construction machinery, ships, boats, and spacecraft; the theft of these would be scored as larceny-theft.[71] Vehicles that are temporarily taken by individuals who have lawful access to them are not thefts. Hence spouses who jointly own all property may drive the family car, even though one spouse may think of the vehicle as his or her exclusive personal property.

As we said earlier, because most insurance companies require police reports before they will reimburse car owners for their losses, most occurrences of **motor vehicle theft** are reported to law enforcement agencies. Some reports of motor vehicle thefts, however, may be false. People who have damaged their own vehicles in single-vehicle crashes or who have been unable to sell them may try to force insurance companies to "buy" them through reports of theft.

In 2012, 721,053 motor vehicles were reported stolen. The average value per stolen vehicle was $6,019, making motor vehicle theft a $4.3 billion crime. The clearance rate for motor vehicle theft was only 11.9% in 2012. Large city agencies reported the lowest rates of clearance, and rural counties had the highest rate. Many stolen vehicles are quickly disassembled and the parts resold, as auto parts are much more difficult to identify

■ **arson (UCR/NIBRS)** Any willful or malicious burning or attempt to burn, with or without intent to defraud, a dwelling house, public building, motor vehicle or aircraft, personal property of another, and so on. Some instances of arson result from malicious mischief, some involve attempts to claim insurance money, and some are committed in an effort to disguise other crimes, such as murder, burglary, or larceny.

■ **Part II offenses** A UCR/NIBRS offense group used to report arrests for less serious offenses. Agencies are limited to reporting only arrest information for Part II offenses, with the exception of simple assault.

■ **dark figure of crime** Crime that is not reported to the police and that remains unknown to officials.

and trace than are intact vehicles. In some parts of the country, chop shops—which take stolen vehicles apart and sell their components—operate like big businesses, and one shop may strip a dozen or more cars per day.

Motor vehicle theft can turn violent, as in cases of carjacking—a crime in which offenders usually force the car's occupants onto the street before stealing the vehicle. The BJS estimates that around 34,000 carjackings occur annually and account for slightly more than 1% of all motor vehicle thefts.[72] Arrest reports for motor vehicle theft show that the typical offender is a young male. Nearly 42% of all arrestees in 2012 were under the age of 25, and 81.1% were male.

Arson

The UCR/NIBRS Program received crime reports from more than 15,000 law enforcement agencies in 2012.[73] Of these, only 14,782 submitted expanded **arson** data. Even fewer agencies provided complete data as to the type of arson (the nature of the property burned), the estimated monetary value of the property, the ownership, and so on. Arson data include only the fires that are determined through investigation to have been willfully or maliciously set. Fires of unknown or suspicious origin are excluded from arson statistics.[74]

The intentional and unlawful burning of structures (houses, storage buildings, manufacturing facilities, and so on) was the type of arson reported most often in 2012 (21,494 instances). The arson of vehicles was the second most common category, with 10,609 such burnings reported. The average dollar loss per instance of arson in 2012 was $12,796, and total nationwide property damage was placed at close to $1 billion.[75] As with most property crimes, the clearance rate for arson was low—only 20% nationally. The crime of arson exists in a kind of statistical limbo. In 1979, Congress ordered that it be added as an eighth Part I offense. Today, however, many law enforcement agencies still have not begun making regular reports to the FBI on arson offenses in their jurisdictions.

Some of these difficulties have been resolved through the Special Arson Program, authorized by Congress in 1982. In conjunction with the National Fire Data Center, the FBI now operates a Special Arson Reporting System, which focuses on fire departments across the nation. The reporting system is designed to provide data to supplement yearly UCR arson tabulations.[76]

Part II Offenses

The Uniform Crime Reporting Program also includes information on what the FBI calls **Part II offenses**. Part II offenses, which are generally less serious than those that make up the Part I offense category, include a number of social-order, or so-called victimless, crimes. The statistics on Part II offenses are for *recorded arrests*, not for crimes reported to the police. The logic inherent in this form of scoring is that most Part II offenses would never come to the attention of the police were it not for arrests. Part II offenses are shown in Table 2-3, with the number of estimated arrests made in each category for 2012. You can access the BJS data analysis tool at **http://www.bjs.gov/index.cfm?ty=datool&surl=/arrests/index.cfm** to view customized national and local arrest data by age, sex, and race for many different offenses.

A Part II arrest is counted each time a person is taken into custody. As a result, the statistics in Table 2-3 do not report the number of suspects arrested but rather the number of arrests made. Some suspects were arrested more than once.

The National Crime Victimization Survey

A second major source of statistical data about crime in the United States is the National Crime Victimization Survey (NCVS), which is based on victim self-reports rather than on police reports. The NCVS is designed to estimate the occurrence of all crimes, whether reported or not.[77] The NCVS was first conducted in 1972. It built on efforts in the late 1960s by both the National Opinion Research Center and the President's Commission on Law Enforcement and the Administration of Justice to uncover what some had been calling the **dark figure of crime**. This term refers to those crimes that are not reported to the police and that remain

TABLE 2-3 | **UCR/NIBRS Part II Offenses, 2012**

OFFENSE CATEGORY	NUMBER OF ARRESTS
Simple assault	1,199,476
Forgery and counterfeiting	67,046
Fraud	153,535
Embezzlement	16,023
Stolen property (e.g., receiving)	97,670
Vandalism	228,463
Weapons (e.g., carrying)	149,286
Prostitution and related offenses	56,575
Sex offenses (e.g., statutory rape)	68,355
Drug-law violations	1,552,432
Gambling	7,868
Offenses against the family (e.g., nonsupport)	107,018
Driving under the influence	1,282,957
Liquor-law violations	441,532
Public drunkenness	511,271
Disorderly conduct	543,995
Vagrancy	27,003
Curfew violation/loitering	70,190

Source: Adapted from Federal Bureau of Investigation, *Crime in the United States, 2012* (Washington, DC: U.S. Dept. of Justice, 2013).

unknown to officials. Before the development of the NCVS, little was known about such unreported and undiscovered offenses.

Early data from the NCVS changed the way criminologists thought about crime in the United States. The use of victim self-reports led to the discovery that crimes of all types were more prevalent than UCR statistics indicated. Many cities were shown to have victimization rates that were more than twice the rate of reported offenses. Others, like Saint Louis, Missouri, and Newark, New Jersey, were found to have rates of victimization that very nearly approximated reported crime. New York, often thought of as a high-crime city, was discovered to have one of the lowest rates of self-reported victimization. The NCVS for 2012 data showed that 56% of all violent victimizations, and 88% of thefts, were not reported to the police.[78]

NCVS data are gathered by the BJS through a cooperative arrangement with the U.S. Census Bureau.[79] Twice each year, Census Bureau personnel interview household members in a nationally representative sample of approximately 90,000 households (about 160,000 people). Only individuals age 12 or older are interviewed. Households stay in the sample for three years, and new households rotate into the sample regularly.

The NCVS collects information on crimes suffered by individuals and households, whether or not those crimes were reported to law enforcement. It estimates the proportion of each crime type reported to law enforcement, and it summarizes the reasons that victims give for reporting or not reporting. BJS statistics are published in annual reports made available on the Internet titled *Criminal Victimization* and *Crime and the Nation's Households*.

Using definitions similar to those employed by the UCR/NIBRS Program, the NCVS includes data on the national incidence of rape, sexual assault, robbery, assault, burglary, personal and household larceny, and motor vehicle theft. Not included are murder, kidnapping, and victimless crimes (crimes that, by their nature, tend to involve willing participants). Commercial robbery and the burglary of businesses were dropped from NCVS reports in 1977. The NCVS employs a hierarchical counting system similar to that of the pre-NIBRS system: It counts only the most "serious" incident in any series of criminal events perpetrated against the same individual. Both completed and attempted offenses are counted, although only people 12 years of age and older are included in household surveys.

NCVS statistics for recent years reveal the following:

- Approximately 15% of American households are touched by crime every year.
- About 22 million victimizations occur each year.
- City residents are almost twice as likely as rural residents to be victims of crime.
- About half of all violent crimes, and slightly more than one-third of all property crimes, are reported to police.[80]
- Victims of crime are more often men than women.
- Younger people are more likely than the elderly to be victims of crime.
- Blacks are more likely than whites or members of other racial groups to be victims of violent crimes.
- Violent victimization rates are highest among people in lower-income families.

A report by the BJS found that in 2010, NCVS crime rates had reached their lowest level since the survey began.[81] Declines began in the mid-1990s, with violent crime rates dropping over 60% between 1993 and 2010.[82] NCVS rates have begun to rise during the past two years, and UCR statistics, which go back almost another 40 years, show that today's crime rate is still many

TABLE 2-4 | Comparison of UCR/NIBRS and NCVS Data, 2012

OFFENSE	UCR/NIBRS	NCVS[a]
Personal/Violent Crimes		
Homicide	14,827	—
Forcible rape[b]	84,376	346,830
Robbery	354,520	741,760
Aggravated assault	760,739	996,110
Property Crimes		
Burglary[c]	2,103,787	3,764,540
Larceny	6,150,598	15,224,700
Motor vehicle theft	721,053	633,740
Arson[d]	52,766	—
Total of All Crimes Recorded	10,242,666	26,465,570[e]

[a]NCVS data cover "households touched by crime," not absolute numbers of crime occurrences. More than one victimization may occur per household, but only the number of households in which victimizations occur enters the tabulations.
[b]NCVS statistics include both rape and sexual assault.
[c]NCVS statistics include only household burglary and attempts.
[d]Arson data are incomplete in the UCR/NIBRS and are not reported by the NCVS.
[e]Includes NCVS crimes not shown in the table, including 4.8 million simple assaults.

Source: Based on data from Compiled from U.S. Department of Justice, *Criminal Victimization, 2012* (Washington, DC: Bureau of Justice Statistics, 2013); and Federal Bureau of Investigation, *Crime in the United States, 2012* (Washington, DC: U.S. Dept. of Justice, 2013).

times what it was in the early and middle years of the twentieth century.[83] Like the UCR, however, NCVS major data categories do not fully encompass the shifting nature of criminal activity in the United States. Nonetheless, some researchers trust NCVS data more than UCR/NIBRS data because they believe that victim self-reports provide a more accurate gauge of criminal incidents than do police reports in which victims had to initiate the reporting process. A comparison of UCR/NIBRS and NCVS data for 2012 can be found in Table 2-4.

You can also explore the NCVS Victimization Analysis Tool (NVAT) at **http://www.bjs.gov/index.cfm?ty=nvat**. The tool, which became available in 2012, analyzes data on victims, households, and incidents, and instantly generates tables with national estimates of the numbers, rates, and percentages of both violent and property victimization from 1993 to the most recent year for which NCVS data are available.

Comparisons of the UCR and NCVS

As mentioned earlier in this chapter, crime statistics from the UCR/NIBRS and the NCVS reveal crime patterns that are often the bases for social policies that intend to deter or reduce crime. These policies also build on explanations for criminal behavior found in more elaborate interpretations of the statistical information. Unfortunately, however, researchers too often forget that statistics, which are merely descriptive, can be weak in explanatory power. For example, NCVS data show that "household crime rates" are highest for households (1) headed by blacks, (2) headed by younger people, (3) with six or more members, (4) headed by renters, and (5) located in central cities.[84] Such findings, combined with statistics that show that most crime occurs among members of the same race, have led some researchers to conclude that values among certain black subcultural group members both propel them into crime and make them targets of criminal victimization. The truth may be, however, that crime is more a function of inner-city location than of culture. From simple descriptive statistics, it is difficult to know which is the case.

Like most statistical data-gathering programs in the social sciences, the UCR/NIBRS and the NCVS programs are not without problems.

Like most statistical data-gathering programs in the social sciences, the UCR/NIBRS and the NCVS programs are not without problems. Because UCR/NIBRS data are based primarily on citizens' crime reports to the police, there are several inherent difficulties. First, not all people report when they are victimized. Some victims are afraid to contact the police, whereas others may not believe that the police can do anything about the offense. Second, certain kinds of crimes are reported rarely, if at all. These include victimless crimes, also known as *social-order offenses*, such as drug use, prostitution, and gambling. Similarly, white-collar offenses, such as embezzlement—because they often go undiscovered, or because they are difficult to score in terms of traditional UCR categories—probably enter the official statistics only rarely. The FBI acknowledges such shortcomings by saying that "it is well documented that the major limitation of the traditional Summary Reporting System is its failure to keep up with the changing face of crime and criminal activity. The inability to grasp the extent of white-collar crime is a specific example of that larger limitation."[85] Third, high-technology and computer crime, like white-collar crime, don't always "fit" well with traditional reporting categories, leading to their possible underrepresentation in today's crime statistics.[86] Finally, victims' reports may not be entirely accurate. A victim's memory may be faulty, victims may feel the need to impress or please the police, or they may be under pressure from others to misrepresent the facts. Finally, all reports are filtered through a number of bureaucratic levels, which increases the likelihood that inaccuracies will enter the data. As noted methodologist Frank Hagan points out, "The government is very keen on amassing statistics. They collect them, add to them, raise them to the nth power, take the cube root, and prepare wonderful diagrams. But what you must never forget is that every one of these figures comes in the first instance from the *chowty dar* [village watchman], who puts down what he damn pleases."[87]

■ **crime typology** A classification of crimes along a particular dimension, such as legal categories, offender motivation, victim behavior, or the characteristics of individual offenders.

In contrast to the UCR/NIBRS dependence on crimes reported by victims who seek out the police, the National Crime Victimization Survey relies on door-to-door surveys and personal interviews for its data. Survey results, however, may be skewed for several reasons. First, no matter how objective survey questions may appear to be, survey respondents inevitably provide their personal interpretations and descriptions of what may or may not have been a criminal event. Second, by its very nature, the survey includes information from those people who are most willing to talk to surveyors; more reclusive people are less likely to respond regardless of the level of victimization they may have suffered. Also, some victims are afraid to report crimes even to nonpolice interviewers, and others may invent victimizations for the interviewer's sake. As the first page of the NCVS report admits, "Details about the crimes come directly from the victims, and no attempt is made to validate the information against police records or any other source."[88]

Finally, because both the UCR/NIBRS and the NCVS are human artifacts, they contain only data that their creators think appropriate. UCR/NIBRS statistics for 2001, for example, do not include a tally of those who perished in the September 11, 2001, terrorist attacks because FBI officials concluded that the events were too "unusual" to count. Although the FBI's 2001 *Crime in the United States* acknowledges "the 2,830 homicides reported as a result of the events of September 11, 2001," it goes on to say that "these figures have been removed" from the reported data.[89] Crimes that result from an anomalous event, but are excluded from reported data, highlight the arbitrary nature of the data collection process itself.

Special Categories of Crime

A **crime typology** is a classification scheme used in the study and description of criminal behavior. There are many typologies, all of which have an underlying logic. The system of classification that derives from any particular typology may be based on legal criteria, offender motivation, victim behavior, the characteristics of individual offenders, or the like. Criminologists Terance D. Miethe and Richard C. McCorkle note that crime typologies "are designed primarily to simplify social reality by identifying homogeneous groups of crime behaviors that are different from other clusters of crime behaviors."[90] Hence one common but simple typology contains only two categories of crime: violent and property. In fact, many crime typologies contain overlapping or nonexclusive categories—just as violent crimes may involve property offenses, and property offenses may lead to violent crimes. Thus no one typology is likely to capture all of the nuances of criminal offending.

Social relevance is a central distinguishing feature of any meaningful typology, and it is with that in mind that the remaining sections of this chapter briefly highlight crimes of special importance today. They are crime against women, crime against the elderly, hate crime, corporate and white-collar crime, organized crime, gun crime, drug crime, cybercrime, and terrorism.

Crime against Women

The victimization of women is a special area of concern, and both the NCVS and the UCR/NIBRS contain data on gender as it relates to victimization. Statistics show that women are victimized less frequently than men in every major personal crime category other than rape.[91] The overall U.S. rate of violent victimization is about 15.7 per 1,000 males age 12 or older, and 14.2 per 1,000 females.[92] When women become victims of violent crime, however, they are more likely than men to be injured (29% vs. 22%, respectively).[93] Moreover, a larger proportion of women than men make modifications in the way they live because of the threat of crime.[94] Women, especially those living in cities, have become increasingly careful about where they travel and the time of day they leave their homes—particularly if they are unaccompanied—and in many settings are often wary of unfamiliar males.

Many crime typologies contain overlapping or nonexclusive categories—just as violent crimes may involve property offenses, and property offenses may lead to violent crimes. Thus no one typology is likely to capture all of the nuances of criminal offending.

■ **stalking** Repeated harassing and threatening behavior by one individual against another, aspects of which may be planned or carried out in secret. Stalking might involve following a person, appearing at a person's home or place of business, making harassing phone calls, leaving written messages or objects, or vandalizing a person's property. Most stalking laws require that the perpetrator make a credible threat of violence against the victim or members of the victim's immediate family.

■ **cyberstalking** The use of the Internet, e-mail, and other electronic communication technologies to stalk another person.[ii]

Date rape, familial incest, spousal abuse, **stalking**, and the exploitation of women through social-order offenses like prostitution and pornography are major issues facing American society today. Testimony before Congress tagged domestic violence as the largest cause of injury to American women.[95] Former Surgeon General C. Everett Koop once identified violence against women by their partners as the number one health problem facing women in America.[96] Findings from the National Violence against Women Survey (NVAWS) reveal the following:[97]

- Physical assault is widespread among American women. Fifty-two percent of surveyed women said that they had been physically assaulted as a child or as an adult.
- Approximately 1.9 million women are physically assaulted in the United States each year.
- Eighteen percent of women experienced a completed or attempted rape at some time in their lives.
- Of those reporting rape, 22% were under 12 years old, and 32% were between 12 and 17 years old when they were first raped.
- Native American and Alaska Native women were most likely to report rape and physical assault, and Asian/Pacific Islander women were least likely to report such victimization. Hispanic women were less likely to report rape than non-Hispanic women.
- Women report significantly more partner violence than men. Twenty-five percent of surveyed women, and only 8% of surveyed men, said they had been raped or physically assaulted by a current or former spouse, cohabiting partner, or date.
- Violence against women is primarily partner violence. Seventy-six percent of the women who had been raped or physically assaulted since age 18 were assaulted by a current or former husband, cohabiting partner, or date, compared with 18% of the men.
- Women are significantly more likely than men to be injured during an assault. Thirty-two percent of the women and 16% of the men who had been raped since age 18 were injured during their most recent rape; 39% of the women and 25% of the men who were physically assaulted since age 18 were injured during their most recent physical assault.
- Eight percent of surveyed women and 2% of surveyed men said they had been stalked at some time in their lives. According to survey estimates, approximately 1 million women and 371,000 men are stalked annually in the United States.

Survey findings like these show that more must be done to alleviate the social conditions that result in the victimization of women. Suggestions already under consideration call for expansion in the number of federal and state laws designed to control domestic violence, a broadening of the federal Family Violence Prevention and Services Act, federal help in setting up state advocacy offices for battered women, increased funding for battered women's shelters, and additional funds for prosecutors and courts to develop spousal abuse units. The federal Violent Crime Control and Law Enforcement Act of 1994 was designed to meet many of these needs through a subsection titled the Violence against Women Act (VAWA). That act signified a major shift in our national response to domestic violence, stalking (which is often part of the domestic violence continuum), and sexual assault crimes. For the first time in our nation's history, violent crimes against women were addressed in relation to the more general problem of gender inequality.[98] VAWA is discussed in greater detail in a "CJ Issues" box in this chapter.

Finally, the passage of antistalking legislation by all 50 states and the District of Columbia provides some measure of additional protection to women (as women comprise 80% of all stalking victims[99]). On the federal level, the seriousness of stalking was addressed when Congress passed the interstate stalking law in 1996.[100] The law[101] also addresses **cyberstalking**, or the use of the Internet by perpetrators seeking to exercise power and control over their victims by threatening them directly or by posting misleading and harassing information about them Cyberstalking can be especially insidious because it does not require that the perpetrator and the victim be in the same geographic area. Similarly, electronic communication technologies lower the barriers to harassment and threats; a cyberstalker does not need to confront the victim physically.[102]

Crime against the Elderly

Relative to other age groups, older victims rarely appear in the crime statistics. Criminal victimization seems to decline with age, suggesting that older people are only infrequently targeted by violent and property criminals. Moreover, older people are more likely than younger individuals to live in secure areas and to have the financial means to provide for their own personal security.

■ **hate crime (UCR/NIBRS)** A criminal offense committed against a person, property, or society that is motivated, in whole or in part, by the offender's bias against a race, religion, disability, sexual orientation, or ethnicity/national origin.

Victimization data pertaining to older people come mostly from the NCVS, which, for such purposes, looks at people age 65 and older. The elderly generally experience the lowest rate of victimization of any age group in both violent and property crime categories.[103] Some aspects of crime against older people are worth noting. In general, elderly crime victims are more likely than younger victims to

- Be victims of property crime—nine out of ten crimes committed against the elderly are property crimes, compared to fewer than four in ten crimes against people between age 12 and 24.
- Face offenders who are armed with guns
- Be victimized by strangers
- Be victimized in or near their homes during daylight hours
- Report their victimization to the police, especially when they fall victim to violent crime
- Be physically injured

In addition, elderly people are less likely to attempt to protect themselves when they are victims of violent crime.

The elderly face special kinds of victimizations that only rarely affect younger adults, such as physical abuse at the hands of caregivers. Criminal physical abuse of the elderly falls into two categories: domestic and institutional. Domestic abuse often occurs at the hands of caregivers who are related to their victims; institutional abuse occurs in residential settings such as retirement centers, nursing homes, and hospitals. Both forms of elder abuse may also involve criminal sexual victimization.

The elderly are also more often targeted by con artists. Confidence schemes center on commercial and financial fraud (including telemarketing fraud), charitable donation fraud, funeral and cemetery fraud, real estate fraud, caretaker fraud, automobile and home repair fraud, living trust fraud, health-care fraud (e.g., promises of "miracle cures"), and health-provider fraud (overbilling and unjustified repeat billing by otherwise legitimate health-care providers). "False friends" may intentionally isolate elderly targets from others in the hopes of misappropriating money through short-term secret loans or outright theft. Similarly, a younger person may feign romantic involvement with an elderly victim or pretend to be devoted to the senior in order to solicit money or receive an inappropriate gift or inheritance.

Finally, crime against the elderly will likely undergo a significant increase as baby boomers enter their retirement years. Not only will the elderly comprise an increasingly larger segment of the population as boomers age, but it is anticipated that they will be wealthier than any preceding generation of retirees, making them attractive targets for scam artists and property criminals.[104] The National Center for Elder Abuse, which provides additional information for researchers and justice system participants, can be reached at **http://www.ncea.aoa.gov/ncearoot/Main_Site/index.aspx.**

Hate Crime

A significant change in crime reporting practices resulted from the Hate Crime Statistics Act,[105] signed into law by President George H. W. Bush in 1990. The act mandates a statistical tally of **hate crimes**; data collection under the law began in 1991. Congress defined *hate crime* as an offense "in which the defendant's conduct was motivated by hatred, bias, or prejudice, based on the actual or perceived race, color, religion, national origin, ethnicity, gender, or sexual orientation of another individual or group of individuals."[106] In 2011, police agencies reported a total of 6,222 hate-crime incidents, including eight murders, across the country. As Figure 2-7 shows, approximately 20.0% of the incidents were motivated by religious bias, 47% were caused by racial hatred, and 12% were driven by prejudice against ethnicity or national origin. Another 21% of all hate crimes were based on sexual orientation, most committed against males believed by their victimizers to be homosexuals.[107] A relatively small number of hate crimes targeted people with physical or mental disabilities.

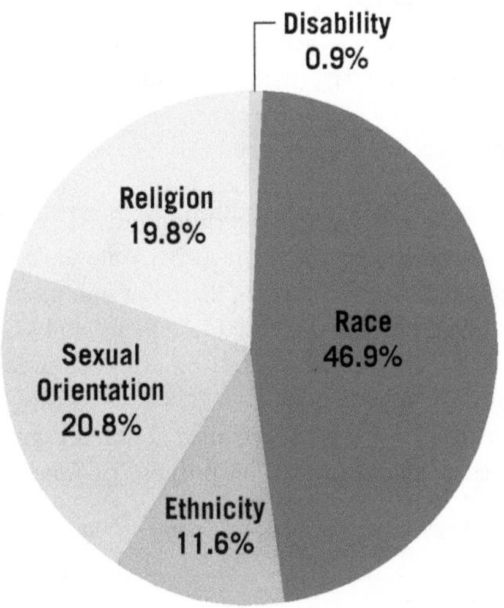

FIGURE 2-7 | Motivation of Hate-Crime Offenders, 2011

Note: Total may be more than 100% due to rounding.

Source: Based on data from Federal Bureau of Investigation, "Hate Crime Statistics: Incidents and Offenses, 2012," http://www.fbi.gov/about-us/cjis/ucr/hate-crime/2012/narratives/hate-crime-2012-incidents-and-offenses (accessed October 7, 2013).

CJ | ISSUES
Gender Issues in Criminal Justice

© HHS Photos/Alamy

President Obama signing the Violence against Women Act (VAWA) reauthorization legislation in 2013. Intimate partner violence is a problem of special concern to the criminal justice system, and violence against women is an area that is receiving legislative attention, as evidenced by the federal VAWA. How might laws designed to protect women be improved?

The Violent Crime Control and Law Enforcement Act of 1994 included significant provisions intended to enhance gender equality throughout the criminal justice system. Title IV of the Violent Crime Control and Law Enforcement Act, known as the Violence against Women Act (VAWA) of 1994, contains the Safe Streets for Women Act. This act increased federal penalties for repeat sex offenders and requires mandatory restitution for sex crimes, including costs related to medical services (including physical, psychiatric, and psychological care); physical and occupational therapy or rehabilitation; necessary transportation, temporary housing, and child-care expenses; lost income; attorneys' fees, including any costs incurred in obtaining a civil protection order; and any other losses suffered by the victim as a result of the offense. The act requires that compliance with a restitution order be made a condition of probation or supervised release (if such a sentence is imposed by the court) and provides that violation of the order will result in the offender's imprisonment. The law also extends "rape shield law" protections to civil cases and to all criminal cases in order to bar irrelevant inquiries into a victim's sexual history.

Chapter 2 of the VAWA provided funds for grants to combat violent crimes against women. The purpose of funding was to assist states and local governments to "develop and strengthen effective law enforcement and prosecution strategies to combat violent crimes against women, and to develop and strengthen victim services in cases involving violent crimes against women." The law also provided funds for the "training of law enforcement officers and prosecutors to more effectively identify and respond to violent crimes against women, including the crimes of sexual assault and domestic violence"; for "developing, installing, or expanding data collection and communication systems, including computerized systems, linking police, prosecutors, and courts or for the purpose of identifying and tracking arrests, protection orders, violations of protection orders, prosecutions, and convictions for violent crimes against women, including the crimes of sexual assault and domestic violence"; and for developing and strengthening "victim services programs, including sexual assault and domestic violence programs."

The act also created the crime of crossing state lines in violation of a protection order and the crime of crossing state lines to commit assault on a domestic partner. It established federal penalties for the latter offense of up to life in prison in cases where death results.

Chapter 3 of the act provided funds to increase the "safety for women in public transit and public parks." It authorized up to $10 million in grants through the Department of Transportation to enhance lighting, camera surveillance, and security telephones in public transportation systems used by women.

Chapter 5 of VAWA funded the creation of hotlines, educational seminars, informational materials, and training programs for professionals who provide assistance to victims of sexual assault. Another portion of the law, titled the Safe Homes for Women Act, increased grants for battered women's shelters, encouraged arrest in cases of domestic violence, and provided for the creation of a national domestic violence hotline to provide counseling, information, and assistance to victims of domestic violence. The act also mandates that any protection order issued by a state court must be recognized by the other states and by the federal government and must be enforced "as if it were the order of the enforcing state."

The VAWA was reauthorized by Congress in 2000, 2005, and again in 2013.[1] The 2005 VAWA reauthorization included a new statute known as the International Marriage Broker Regulation Act (IMBRA), which provides potential life-saving protections to prospective foreign brides who may immigrate to the United States. Finally, the 2013 reauthorization made $659 million available each year for five years for programs that strengthen the justice system's response to crimes against women and some men, including protections for gays, lesbians, bisexual, and transgender Americans.

[1]VAWA 2013 was signed into law by President Obama on March 7, 2013. It is officially known as the Violence against Women Reauthorization Act of 2013.

Following the terrorist attacks of September 11, 2001, authorities in some jurisdictions reported a dramatic shift in the nature of hate crime, with race-motivated crimes declining and crimes motivated by religion or ethnicity increasing sharply.[108] Islamic individuals, in particular, became the target of many such crimes.

Most hate crimes consist of intimidation, although vandalism, simple assault, and aggravated assault also account for a

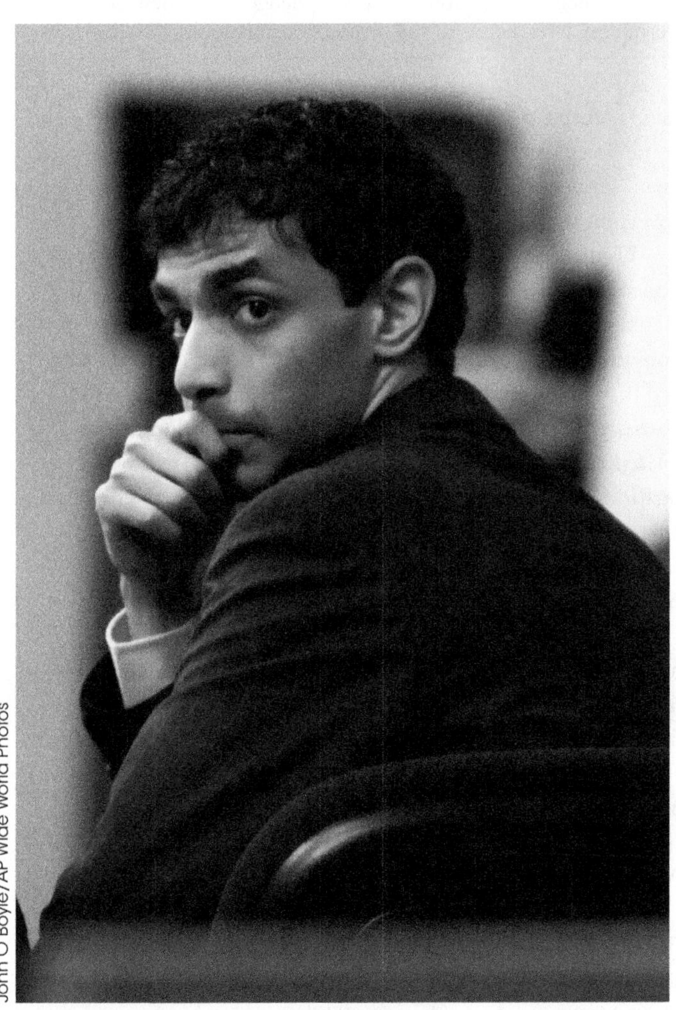
John O'Boyle/AP Wide World Photos

Former Rutgers University student Dharun Ravi, 20, at Superior Court in Middlesex County, New Jersey, as he listens to the verdict in his 2012 trial. Ravi, 20, was convicted of 15 criminal charges, including bias intimidation and invasion of privacy, by a New Jersey jury following the 2010 suicide death of his gay roommate, Tyler Clementi. Why are hate crimes given special attention under the law?

number of hate-crime offenses. A few robberies and rapes were also classified as hate crimes in 2012.

Although hate crimes are popularly conceived of as crimes motivated by racial enmity, the Violent Crime Control and Law Enforcement Act of 1994 created a new category of "crimes of violence motivated by gender." Congress defined this crime as "a crime of violence committed because of gender or on the basis of gender, and due, at least in part, to an animus based on the victim's gender." The 1994 act did not establish separate penalties for gender-motivated crimes, anticipating that they would be prosecuted as felonies under existing laws. The 1994 act also mandated that crimes motivated by biases against people with disabilities be considered hate crimes.

In 2010 President Obama signed the Matthew Shepard and James Byrd, Jr. Hate Crimes Prevention Act into law. The act expanded the definition of federal hate crimes to include crimes based on sexual orientation, gender identity, or disability. The law also amended the Hate Crimes Statistics Act to include crimes motivated by gender and gender identity, as well as hate crimes committed by and against juveniles.

Some states have imitated federal law in crafting their own bias-crime statutes. In 2012, in a case involving just such a law, former Rutgers University student Dharun Ravi, 20, was convicted of 15 criminal charges, including bias intimidation and invasion of privacy, by a New Jersey jury following the 2010 suicide death of his roommate, Tyler Clementi.[109] A fearful and embarrassed Clementi took his life after Ravi, who was his roommate, used a webcam to secretly transmit live videos onto the Internet of Clementi being intimate with another man. Prosecutors in the case said that Ravi's crime fell into the category of a hate crime because it maliciously targeted gays.

Hate crimes are sometimes called *bias crimes*. One form of bias crime that bears special mention is homophobic homicide—the murder of homosexuals by those opposed to their lifestyles. The Southern Poverty Law Center, which tracks hate groups, recently identified 1,002 such groups operating in the United States.[110] The center, which is based in Montgomery, Alabama, says that the number of hate groups has jumped 66% since 2000, mostly because of the formation of new anti-immigrant and antigovernment "patriot" organizations. So-called patriot groups are "sovereign citizen" extremists who don't recognize government authority, including its power to tax and to enforce laws. According to the center, California has the most hate groups (68). Nationwide, the center identified 170 neo-Nazi, 136 white nationalist, 136 racist skinhead, 26 Christian identity, 149 black separatist, 42 neoconfederate, and 221 Ku Klux Klan groups in 2010. Another 122 general hate groups—or those that "espouse a variety of hateful doctrines"—were also identified. Learn more about hate crime and what can be done to address it at **http://www.justicestudies.com/pubs/hcv0311.pdf** and **http://www.justicestudies.com/pubs/hatecrimes.pdf**.

Corporate and White-Collar Crime

In 2012 Texas financier R. Allen Stanford was convicted by a federal trial jury of 13 out of 14 counts of financial fraud for his involvement in an illegal investment scheme that cost nearly 30,000 investors in 113 countries $7 billion.[111] Stanford's fraud occurred over more than 20 years, and included staged hoaxes designed to convince clients that their investments were safe.

■ **corporate crime** A violation of a criminal statute by a corporate entity or by its executives, employees, or agents acting on behalf of and for the benefit of the corporation, partnership, or other form of business entity.[iii]

■ **white-collar crime** Violations of the criminal law committed by a person of respectability and high social status in the course of his or her occupation. Also, nonviolent crime for financial gain utilizing deception and committed by anyone who has special technical or professional knowledge of business or government, irrespective of the person's occupation.

The most infamous financial crime of recent years involved investment fund manager Bernard ("Bernie") Madoff, who pled guilty in 2009 to operating a Ponzi scheme that defrauded investors out of as much as $50 billion.[112] Called "Wall Street's biggest fraud" by some, Madoff's shenanigans purportedly cost investors $50 billion in money that seemed to simply disappear.[113] Madoff, a former chairman of the NASDAQ stock market, pleaded guilty to 11 felony counts, including securities fraud, mail fraud, wire fraud, money laundering, and perjury. He was sentenced to 150 years in prison.[114]

The recent economic downturn, combined with the collapse of the housing market and a loss of jobs in many sectors of the economy, sparked a rapid growth in mortgage fraud scams. Mortgage fraud, which is a federal crime, can involve making false or misleading statements about one's identity, personal income, assets, or debts during the mortgage application process. It also includes efforts to knowingly overvalue land or property to defraud purchasers and lenders.

Essentially, there are three types of mortgage fraud. The first, "fraud for profit," involves a scheme by "ghost buyers" to collect cash, with no interest in owning the property against which money is being borrowed. The second is "fraud for housing," or application fraud, in which otherwise legitimate homebuyers fake documents in order to appear eligible for a loan that they would not otherwise get. According to one report, 61% of all reported mortgage frauds in 2008 involved misrepresentations made on applications for a mortgage. The third type of mortgage fraud involves overestimating a property's value or submitting a false appraisal.

The recent economic downturn, combined with the collapse of the housing market and a loss of jobs in many sectors of the economy, sparked a rapid growth in mortgage fraud scams.

A recent study by the Mortgage Asset Research Institute concluded that mortgage fraud was more prevalent at the time of the study than it had been at the height of the nation's building boom just a few years earlier.[115] Federal agencies, already inundated with mortgage fraud cases, are starting to look into a new breed of scams perpetrated by those who offer to refinance homes or save them from foreclosure. In one of the new scams, criminals offer to help people who are about to lose their homes, collect several thousand dollars up front, and then disappear.[116] In early 2009, the Federal Trade Commission announced a wave of law enforcement actions against operations using deceptive tactics to market mortgage modification and home foreclosure relief services, including firms that marketed their "services" by falsely implying an affiliation with the federal government.[117]

Under the American system of criminal justice, corporations can be treated as separate legal entities and can be convicted of violations of the criminal law under a legal principle known as the *identification doctrine*. In 2002, for example, a federal jury convicted global accounting firm Arthur Andersen of obstruction of justice after its employees shredded documents related to Enron's bankruptcy in an effort to impede an investigation by securities regulators. The conviction, which was overturned by a unanimous U.S. Supreme Court in 2005,[118] capped the firm's demise, and it ended U.S. operations in August 2002.[119]

Although corporations may be convicted of a crime, the human perpetrators of **corporate crime** are business executives known as *white-collar criminals*. **White-collar crime** was first defined in 1939 by Edwin H. Sutherland in his presidential address to the American Sociological Society.[120] Sutherland proposed that "crime in the suites" (a reference to corporate offices) rivaled the importance of street crime in its potential impact on American society.

In July 2002, President George W. Bush created a Corporate Fraud Task Force within the federal government and proposed a new law providing criminal penalties for corporate fraud. He told corporate leaders on Wall Street, "At this moment, America's greatest economic need is higher ethical standards—standards enforced by strict laws and upheld by responsible business leaders."[121] A few months later, the president signed into law the Sarbanes-Oxley Act.[122] The new law created tough provisions designed to deter and punish corporate and accounting fraud and corruption and to protect the interests of workers and shareholders. Under the Sarbanes-Oxley Act, corporate officials (chief executive officers and chief financial officers) must personally vouch for the truth and accuracy of their companies' financial statements. The act also substantially increased federal penalties for obstructing justice and, specifically, for shredding or destroying documents that might aid in a criminal investigation of business practices. Learn more about corporate and white-collar crime at the National White Collar Crime Center (NW3C) via **http://www.nw3c.org**. Established in 1992, the NW3C provides a national support system for the prevention, investigation, and prosecution of multijurisdictional economic crimes.

■ **organized crime** The unlawful activities of the members of a highly organized, disciplined association engaged in supplying illegal goods or services, including gambling, prostitution, loan-sharking, narcotics, and labor racketeering, and in other unlawful activities.[iv]

■ **transnational organized crime** Unlawful activity undertaken and supported by organized criminal groups operating across national boundaries.

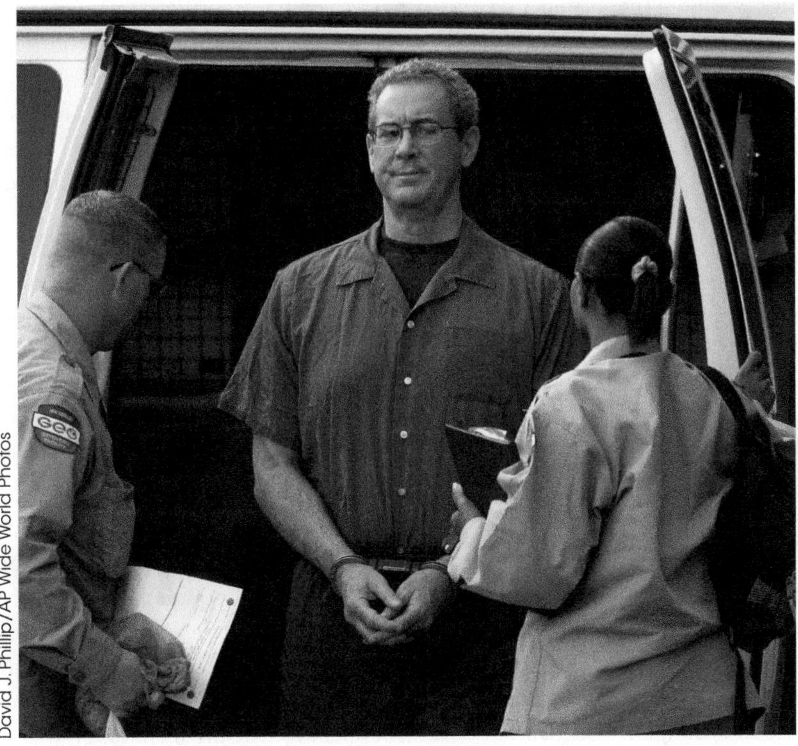

David J. Phillip/AP Wide World Photos

Texas financier R. Allen Stanford, who was convicted by a federal trial jury in 2012 of 13 out of 14 counts of financial fraud for his involvement in an illegal investment scheme that cost nearly 30,000 investors in 113 countries $7 billion. Stanford received a sentence of 110 years in prison. Are you worried that you might become a victim of financial crime like the ones Stanford committed?

Organized Crime

For many people, the term **organized crime** conjures up images of the Mafia (also called the *Cosa Nostra*) or the hit HBO TV series *The Sopranos* and *Boardwalk Empire*. Although organized criminal activity is decidedly a group phenomenon, the groups involved in such activity in the United States today display a great deal of variation. During the past few decades in the United States, the preeminence of traditional Sicilian American criminal organizations has fallen to such diverse criminal associations as the Black Mafia, the Cuban Mafia, the Haitian Mafia, the Colombian cartels, and Asian criminal groups like the Chinese Tongs and street gangs, Japanese yakuza, and Vietnamese gangs. Included here as well might be inner-city gangs, the best known of which are probably the Los Angeles Crips and Bloods and the Chicago Vice Lords; international drug rings; outlaw motorcycle gangs like the Hell's Angels and the Pagans; and other looser associations of small-time thugs, prison gangs, and drug dealers. Noteworthy among these groups—especially for their involvement in the lucrative drug trade—are the Latino organized bands, including the Dominican, Colombian, Mexican, and Cuban importers of cocaine, heroin, marijuana, and other controlled substances.

The unlawful activities of organized groups that operate across national boundaries are especially significant. Such activity is referred to as **transnational organized crime**. Transnational criminal associations worthy of special mention are the Hong Kong–based Triads, the South American cocaine cartels, the Italian Mafia, the Japanese yakuza, the Russian *Mafiya*, and the West African crime groups—each of which extends its reach well beyond its home country. In some parts of the world, close links between organized crime and terrorist groups involve money laundering, which provides cash to finance the activities of terrorist cells and to finance paramilitary efforts to overthrow established governments.

Former Central Intelligence Agency (CIA) Director R. James Woolsey points out that "while organized crime is not a new phenomenon today, some governments find their authority besieged at home and their foreign policy interests imperiled abroad. Drug trafficking, links between drug traffickers and terrorists, smuggling of illegal aliens, massive financial and bank fraud, arms smuggling, potential involvement in the theft and sale of nuclear material, political intimidation, and corruption all constitute a poisonous brew—a mixture potentially as deadly as what we faced during the cold war."[123] The challenge for today's criminal justice student is to recognize that crime does not respect national boundaries. Crime is global, and what happens in one part of the world could affect us all.[124]

Gun Crime

Guns and gun crime seem to pervade American culture. The story that opened Chapter 1 described the 2012 Newtown, Connecticut, school shootings in which 28 people died, including the shooter and 20 first graders. A month earlier, on July 20, 2012, a gunman who apparently identified with the Joker, a character in Batman movies, attacked a crowded theater in Aurora, Colorado, during a midnight showing of the movie *The Dark Knight Rises*, killing 12 people and injuring 58 others. The shooter, James Egan Holmes, used a shotgun, a semiautomatic rife with a 100-round magazine, and a handgun. Eighteen months earlier, in January 2011, another random mass shooting claimed the lives of six people and wounded 13 people, including U.S. Representative Gabrielle Giffords, who was shot through the head. These three events, happening in rapid succession, led to strident calls for gun control at both the state and national level.

Guns and gun crime seem to pervade American culture.

Constitutional guarantees of the right to bear arms have combined with historical circumstances to make ours a well-armed society. Guns are used in many types of crimes. Each year, approximately 1 million serious crimes—including homicide, rape, robbery, and assault—involve the use of a handgun. In a typical year, approximately 8,800 murders are committed in the United States with firearms. A recent report by the BJS found that 18% of state prison inmates and 15% of federal inmates were armed at the time they committed the crime for which they were imprisoned.[125] Nine percent of those in state prisons said they fired a gun while committing the offense for which they were serving time.[126]

Both federal and state governments have responded to the public concern over the ready availability of handguns. In 1994, Congress passed the Brady Handgun Violence Prevention Act, which President Bill Clinton signed into law. The law was named for former Press Secretary James Brady, who was shot and severely wounded in an attempt on President Ronald Reagan's life on March 30, 1981. The law mandated a five-day waiting period before the purchase of a handgun, and it established a national instant criminal background check system that firearms dealers must use before selling a handgun. The five-day waiting period was discontinued in 1998 when the instant computerized background checking system became operational.

Although the Brady law may limit retail purchases of handguns by felons, a BJS study found that most offenders obtain weapons from friends or family members or "on the street" rather than attempt to purchase them at retail establishments.[127] In 2001, undercover congressional investigators were able to show that applicants using fake forms of identification, such as counterfeit driver's licenses with fictitious names, could easily circumvent Brady law provisions.[128] Moreover, according to these studies, ever-growing numbers of violent criminals are now carrying handguns.

In Congress, debate continues about whether to require gun manufacturers to create and retain "ballistic fingerprints" (the marks left on a bullet by the barrel of the gun from which it was fired) of each weapon they produce. Although a national ballistics fingerprinting requirement may still be years away, three states—California, Maryland, and New York—and the District of Columbia already require that a record be kept of the "fingerprint" characteristics of each new handgun sold.[129]

Microstamping uses laser engraving to encode a weapon's serial number on each cartridge that it fires, and California authorities believe that the technology will allow handguns to be traced to their manufacturer and then to the first purchaser, using only spent cartridges left at crime scenes.

For the latest information on gun violence and gun laws, visit the Brady Center to Prevent Gun Violence via **http://www.bradycenter.org**. The National Rifle Association site at **http://home.nra.org** provides support for responsible access to firearms.

Drug Crime

Unlike many crimes tracked by the FBI, drug-related crime continues to rise even in many years when other crimes decrease. The seemingly relentless increase in drug violations largely accounts for the continued growth in America's prison populations, even when official crime rates (which count the eight major crimes discussed earlier) have been declining. Chapter 16, "Drugs and Crime," discusses illicit drugs and drug-law violations in detail. As that chapter shows, the rate of drug-related crime commission has more than doubled in the United States since 1975.

Alone, drug-law violations are themselves criminal, but more and more studies are linking drug abuse to other serious crimes. An early study by the RAND Corporation found that most of the "violent predators" among prisoners had extensive histories of heroin abuse, often in combination with alcohol

■ **cybercrime** Any crime perpetrated through the use of computer technology. Also, any violation of a federal or state cybercrime statute.

and other drugs.[130] Some cities reported that a large percentage of their homicides were drug related.[131] More recent studies also link drug abuse to other serious crimes. Community leaders perceive, and data analyses confirm, that crack cocaine has a profound impact on violent crime, with homicide rates closely tracking cocaine-use levels among adult male arrestees.[132] Prisoner survey data show that 19% of state inmates and 16% of federal prisoners reported committing their current offense to obtain money for drugs.[133] A 2000 study found that 13.3% of convicted jail inmates said that they had committed their offense to get money for drugs.[134]

Criminal justice system costs associated with the handling of drug offenders have increased substantially in recent years. Between 1984 and 2002, for example, the annual number of defendants charged with a drug offense in federal courts increased from 11,854 to more than 30,000.[135] Similarly, between 1984 and 2002, drug offenses accounted for an increased proportion of the federal criminal caseload, even when charges weren't brought. During 1984, 18% of referrals to U.S. attorneys were drug related, compared with 31% during 2002.[136] Some of the increase stems from changes in federal drug laws. Whatever the cause, the drug–crime link is costly to society and shows few signs of abating.

Cybercrime, sometimes called *computer crime* or *information-technology crime*, uses computers and computer technology as tools in crime commission.

Cybercrime

Cybercrime, sometimes called *computer crime* or *information-technology crime*, uses computers and computer technology as tools in crime commission. Computer criminals manipulate the information stored in computer systems in ways that violate the law. (Thefts of computer equipment, although sometimes spectacular, are not computer crimes but are instead classified as larcenies.) The incidence of cybercrime is shown graphically in Figure 2-8, which displays the number of complaints filed with the Internet Crime Complaint Center (IC3) from 2000 to 2012.

Many crimes committed via the Internet, such as prostitution, drug sales, theft, and fraud, are not new forms of offending. Rather, they are traditional offenses that use technology in their commission or that build on the possibilities for criminal activity that new technologies make possible. In 2013, for example, an international operation led by U.S. Immigration and Customs Enforcement agents led to arrest of 245 suspected child pornographers who communicated through the Internet.[137] Of those arrested, 213 were from the United States, and 23 from other countries. The enforcement effort, known as Operation Sunflower, led to the identification of 123 victims of child exploitation and the removal of 44 children from the control of alleged abusers. Five of the rescued children were three years old, and nine were between the ages of four and six.

U.S. Customs and Border Protection Senior Special Agent Donald Daufenbach, an international expert in child pornography and the Internet, points out that "the Internet is like anything else: It can be bent or perverted for nefarious purposes. . . . The Internet has absolutely changed the way people communicate with each other, changed the way people conduct commerce, changed the way people do research, changed the way people entertain themselves and changed the way people break the law. . . . People are catching on pretty quick, but law enforcement is lagging behind miserably in this whole endeavor."[138] Chapter 18, "The Future of Criminal Justice," provides additional information about cybercrime, including computer

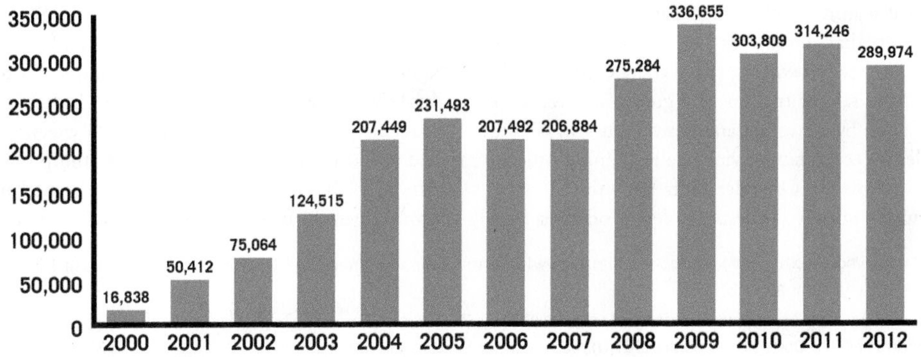

FIGURE 2-8 | Computer Crime Complaints, 2000–2012

Source: Based on data from Internet Crime Complaint Center.

CJ | ISSUES

Gun Control

The issue of gun control took center stage on January 30, 2013, when Senator Dianne Feinstein, astronaut Mark Kelly (husband of former Representative Gabrielle Giffords, who was seriously injured at a mass shooting in Arizona), National Rifle Association (NRA) vice president Wayne LaPierre, and others testified before the U.S. Senate Judiciary in a hearing on gun violence. During the hearing, LaPierre emphasized the constitutional right of people to bear arms, while Feinstein and others told committee members that the American people have a fundamental right to be safe. As with so many other issues in criminal justice, the debate that the committee heard that day centered on the tension between individual rights and public safety.

By the time the hearing had ended, the committee heard pleas to stiffen federal gun control legislation by outlawing the possession of assault weapons, to place limits on the capacity of ammunition magazines, and to increase the range of background checks to which potential gun owners would be subjected.

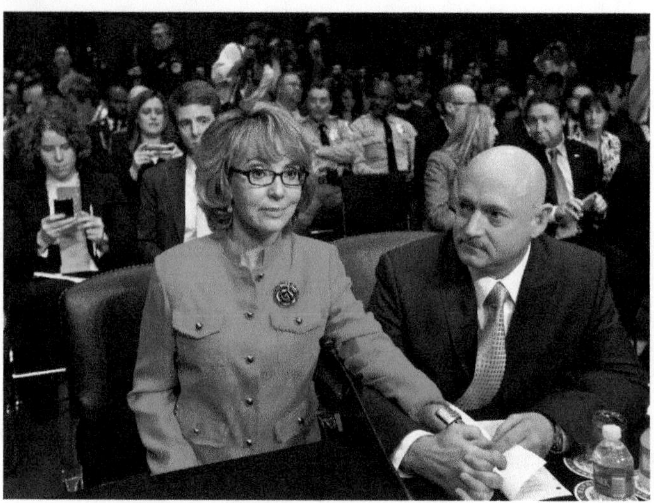

AP Photo/J. Scott Applewhite

Former Arizona Representative Gabrielle Giffords, who was seriously injured in a Tucson, Arizona, mass shooting in 2011, testifies with her husband before a U.S. Senate Judiciary Committee in 2013. The committee was examining issues of gun violence. What's your position on gun ownership and gun control?

Only a few years earlier, however, the U.S. Supreme Court came down heavily in support of the individual's right to bear arms. The Second Amendment to the U.S. Constitution reads, "A well regulated Militia, being necessary to the security of a free State, the right of the people to keep and bear Arms, shall not be infringed." In the 2008 case of *District of Columbia* v. *Heller*, the U.S. Supreme Court struck down a District of Columbia gun control regulation and ruled that "the Second Amendment protects an individual's right to possess firearms and that the city's total ban on handguns, as well as its requirement that firearms in the home be kept nonfunctional even when necessary for self-defense, violated that right."[1] The Court's holding in *Heller* was sweeping and unambiguous. The decision clearly declared the Second Amendment protection of "an individual right to possess a firearm unconnected with service in a militia, and to use that arm for traditionally lawful purposes, such as self-defense within the home."

Following Heller, some questioned whether the Court's ruling might be limited to federal enclaves, like the District of Columbia, or whether it was applicable to other jurisdictions. In 2010, in the case of *McDonald* v. *City of Chicago*,[2] the U.S. Supreme Court answered that question when it struck down gun-banning ordinances in Chicago and the city of Oak Park, Illinois. The Justices found that "the right to keep and bear arms must be regarded as a substantive guarantee" inherent in the U.S. Constitution.

One of the most significant laws enacted prior to *Heller* was the Violent Crime Control and Law Enforcement Act of 1994,[3] which regulated the sale of firearms within the United States and originally banned the manufacture of 19 military-style assault weapons, including those with specific combat features, such as high-capacity ammunition clips capable of holding more than ten rounds. The ban on assault weapons ended in 2004, however, when it was not renewed by Congress. The 1994 law also prohibited the sale or transfer of a gun to a juvenile, as well as the possession of a gun by a juvenile, and it prohibits gun sales to, and possession by, people subject to family violence restraining orders.

The 1996 Domestic Violence Offender Gun Ban[4] prohibits individuals convicted of misdemeanor domestic violence offenses from owning or using firearms. Following the 1999 Columbine High School shooting, a number of states moved to tighten controls over handguns and assault weapons. The California legislature, for example, restricted gun purchases to one per month and tightened a ten-year-old ban on assault weapons. Similarly, Illinois passed a law requiring that gun owners lock their weapons away from anyone under age 14.

In 2004, at the urging of major police organizations, the U.S. Senate scuttled plans for a gun-industry protection bill. However, the bill was revived in 2005 and passed both houses of Congress before being signed into law by President George W. Bush on October 31. Known as the Protection of Lawful Commerce in Firearms Act, the law grants gunmakers and most gun dealers immunity from lawsuits brought by victims of gun crimes and their survivors. The law removes negligence as viable grounds for a civil suit against a gun dealer who carelessly sells a gun to someone who is at risk for using it in a crime; the law states that the dealer can be sued only if he or she knew of the gun buyer's criminal intent before the purchase. Gunmakers were made similarly immune from suits alleging product liability for having manufactured potentially lethal items.

By 2013, however, as signaled by the Senate hearings with which this box opened, the need for greater gun control measures was highlighted by a series of random mass shootings that shocked the nation (and that are described earlier in this chapter and in Chapter 1). Consequently, President Obama signed 23 executive orders on gun safety and called upon Congress to address the problem of gun violence in America.[5] Read the executive orders signed by President Obama at http://justicestudies.com/pubs/wh_orders.pdf.

[1] *District of Columbia, et al.* v. *Dick Anthony Heller* (2008). Available at http://www.law.cornell.edu/supct/html/07-290.ZO.html (accessed August 4, 2009).

[2] *McDonald* v. *Chicago*, 561 U.S. 3025, 130 S.Ct. 3020 (2010).

[3] Public Law 103-322, 108 Stat. 1796 (codified as amended in scattered sections of 18, 21, 28, 42, etc., U.S.).

[4] Public Law 104-208, an amendment to U.S. Code, Title 18, Section 921(a). Also known as the Lautenberg Amendment.

[5] Rick Ungar, "Here Are the 23 Executive Orders on Gun Safety Signed Today by the President," *Forbes*, January 16, 2013, http://www.forbes.com/sites/rickungar/2013/01/16/here-are-the-23-executive-orders-on-gun-safety-signed-today-by-the-president/ (accessed January 16, 2013).

malware, software piracy, and phishing, and the law enforcement technologies used to fight it.

Terrorism

Following the September 11, 2001, attacks on the World Trade Center and the Pentagon, terrorism and its prevention became primary concerns of American justice system officials. Long before September 11, however, terrorism was far from unknown. In 2001, for example, terrorist attacks totaled 864 worldwide—down from the 1,106 reported a year earlier.[139]

To assist in developing protection for the nation's critical infrastructure, the Homeland Security Act of 2002 created the Department of Homeland Security and made its director a cabinet member. Visit the Department of Homeland Security via **http://www.dhs.gov**. Terrorism and efforts to combat it are discussed in detail in Chapter 17, "Terrorism and Multinational Criminal Justice."

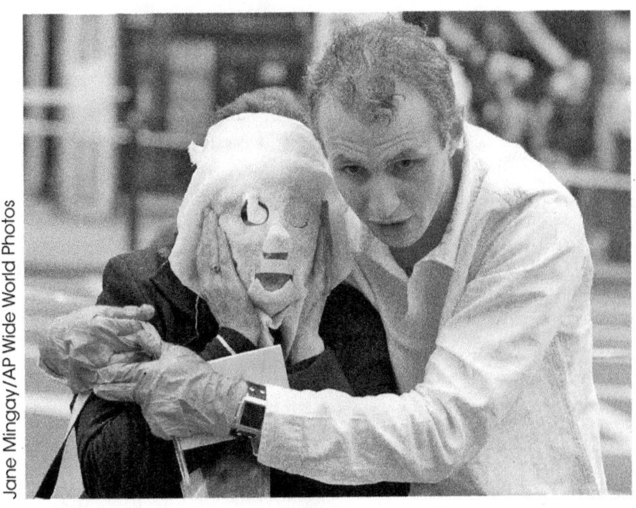

Jane Mingay/AP Wide World Photos

A commuter being helped away from the Edgware Road Underground Station following terrorist bombings in London's subway system in 2005. How might future acts of terrorism be prevented?

SUMMARY

- The FBI's Uniform Crime Reporting Program began in the 1930s when Congress authorized the U.S. attorney general to survey crime in America. Today's UCR/NIBRS Program provides annual data on the number of reported Part I offenses, or major crimes, as well as information about arrests that have been made for less serious Part II offenses. The Part I offenses are murder, forcible rape, robbery, aggravated assault, burglary, larceny-theft, motor vehicle theft, and arson. The Part II offense category covers many more crimes, including drug offenses, driving under the influence, and simple assault. Modifications to the UCR Program, which has traditionally provided only summary crime data, are occurring with the implementation of the new National Incident-Based Reporting System (NIBRS). NIBRS, which represents a significant redesign of the original UCR Program, gathers many details about each criminal incident, such as place of occurrence, weapon used, type and value of property damaged or stolen, the personal characteristics of the offender and the victim, the nature of any relationship between the two, and the disposition of the complaint.
- The National Crime Victimization Survey (NCVS) is the second major source of statistical data about crime in the United States. The NCVS, which was first conducted in 1972, is based on victim self-reports rather than on police reports. The NCVS originally built on efforts by both the National Opinion Research Center and the 1967 President's Commission on Law Enforcement and the Administration of Justice to uncover what some had been calling the *dark figure of crime*—that is, those crimes that are not reported to the police and that are relatively hidden from justice system officials. An analysis of victim self-report data led to the realization that crimes of all types were more prevalent than UCR statistics had previously indicated.
- Significant differences exist between the UCR/NIBRS and the NCVS. For example, UCR/NIBRS data are primarily based on citizens' crime reports to the police, whereas NCVS data are gathered by field researchers who interview randomly selected households throughout the country. These and other differences lead to significant variation in the crime rates reported under both programs.
- It is important to recognize that UCR/NIBRS and NCVS data do not necessarily provide a complete picture of crime in America not only because they fail to capture what we have called the dark figure of crime, but also because the traditional reporting categories that they employ do not always encompass more innovative forms of crime such as those committed through the use of high technology or certain forms of white-collar crime.
- This chapter discusses a number of special categories of crime, including crime against women, crime against the elderly, hate crime, corporate and white-collar crime, organized crime, gun crime, drug crime, cybercrime, and terrorism. Each of these categories is of special concern in contemporary society.

KEY TERMS

aggravated assault, 46
arson, 52
assault, 46
Bureau of Justice Statistics (BJS), 32
burglary, 46
clearance rate, 41
corporate crime, 60
Crime Index, 33
crime typology, 55
cybercrime, 63
cyberstalking, 56
dark figure of crime, 52
date rape, 44
forcible rape, 43
hate crime, 57
identity theft, 51
larceny-theft, 48
motor vehicle theft, 51
murder, 41
National Crime Victimization Survey (NCVS), 32
National Incident-Based Reporting System (NIBRS), 34
organized crime, 61
Part I offenses, 41
Part II offenses, 52
property crime, 40
rape, 43
robbery, 45
self-reports, 32
sexual battery, 44
stalking, 56
transnational organized crime, 61
Uniform Crime Reporting (UCR) Program, 32
violent crime, 40
white-collar crime, 60

QUESTIONS FOR REVIEW

1. Describe the historical development of the FBI's Uniform Crime Reporting Program, and list the crimes on which it reports. How is the ongoing implementation of the National Incident-Based Reporting System (NIBRS) changing the UCR Program? How will data reported under the new UCR/NIBRS differ from the crime statistics reported under the traditional UCR Program?
2. Describe the history of the National Crime Victimization Survey (NCVS). What do data from the NCVS tell us about crime in the United States today?
3. What significant differences between the UCR/NIBRS and NCVS programs can be identified?
4. What are the special categories of crime discussed in this chapter? Why are they important?

QUESTIONS FOR REFLECTION

1. What can crime statistics tell us about the crime picture in America? How has that picture changed over time?
2. What are the potential sources of error in the nation's major crime reports? Can you think of some popular use of crime statistics today that might be especially misleading?
3. Why are many crime statistics expressed as rates? How does the use of crime rates instead of simple numerical tabulations improve the usefulness of crime data?
4. Do "traditional" UCR/NIBRS and NCVS categories accurately reflect the changing nature of crime in America? Why or why not?
5. This chapter recognizes the changing nature of crime. What might crime rates look like if all types of crime today could be captured by traditional crime reporting systems?
6. Do some property crimes have a violent aspect? Are there any personal crimes that could be nonviolent? If so, what might they be?
7. What is a clearance rate? What does it mean to say that a crime has been "cleared"? What are the different ways in which a crime can be cleared?

NOTES

i. Identity Theft Resource Center website, http://www.idtheftcenter.org (accessed April 24, 2011).
ii. Ibid.
iii. Andrew Backover, "Two Former WorldCom Execs Charged," *USA Today* online, August 1, 2002, http://www.usatoday.com/money/industries/telecom/2003-08-01-worldcom-execs-surrender_x.htm (accessed August 2, 2006).
iv. The Organized Crime Control Act of 1970.

1. Gerard Gilbert "CSI: The Cop Show That Conquered the World," *The (London) Independent*, December 19, 2006, http://www.findarticles.com/p/articles/mi_qn4158/is_20061219/ai_n17081057 (accessed March 10, 2007).
2. Sara Bibel, "'CSI: Crime Scene Investigation' Is the Most-Watched Show in the World," TV by the Numbers, June 14, 2012, http://tvbythenumbers.zap2it.com/2012/06/14/csi-crime-scene-investigation-is-the-most-watched-show-in-the-world-2/138212/ (accessed July 26, 2012).
3. "'NCIS' and 'NCIS: Los Angeles' Top Tuesday as CBS Sweeps Night," TV by the Numbers, February 6, 2013, http://tvbythenumbers.zap2it.com/2013/02/06/ncis-and-ncis-los-angeles-top-tuesday-as-cbs-sweeps-night/168370 (accessed February 12, 2013).
4. Herbert Packer, *The Limits of Criminal Sanction* (Stanford: Stanford University Press, 1968), p. 364.
5. Norval Morris, "Crime, the Media, and Our Public Discourse," National Institute of Justice, Perspectives on Crime and Justice video series, recorded May 13, 1997.
6. Federal Bureau of Investigation, *Crime in the United States, 1987* (Washington, DC: U.S. Dept. of Justice, 1988), p. 1.
7. Federal Bureau of Investigation, "Uniform Crime Reports," http://www2.fbi.gov/ucr/ucr.htm (accessed October 7, 2011).
8. See the FBI's UCR/NIBRS website at http://www.fbi.gov/hq/cjisd/ucr.htm (accessed August 27, 2013).
9. The 1990 Crime Awareness and Campus Security Act (Public Law 101-542) required college campuses to commence publishing annual security reports beginning in September 1992.
10. The National Center for Victims of Crime, "Campus Crime," http://www.ncvc.org/ncvc/main.aspx?dbName=DocumentViewer&DocumentID=47695 (accessed October 7, 2011).
11. Katrina Baum and Patsy Klaus, *Violent Victimization of College Students, 1995–2002* (Washington, DC: Bureau of Justice Statistics, 2005).
12. Federal Bureau of Investigation, *Crime in the United States, 2012* (Washington, DC: U.S. Dept. of Justice, 2013).
13. The President's Commission on Law Enforcement and Administration of Justice, *The Challenge of Crime in a Free Society* (Washington, DC: U.S. Government Printing Office, 1967). The

commission relied on Uniform Crime Reports data. The other crime statistics reported in this section come from Uniform Crime Reports for various years.

14. Frank Hagan, *Research Methods in Criminal Justice and Criminology* (New York: Macmillan, 1982).
15. U.S. Department of Justice, *Fiscal Years 2000–2005 Strategic Plan* (Washington, DC: U.S. Government Printing Office, 2000).
16. The "war on drugs," and the use of that term, can be traced back to the Nixon administration. See Dan Baum, *Smoke and Mirrors: The War on Drugs and the Politics of Failure*, reprint ed. (Boston: Little, Brown, 1997).
17. Marc Santora, "In Hours, Thieves Took $45 Million in A.T.M. Scheme," *The New York Times*, May 9, 2013.
18. Some such crimes are reportable as crimes of theft. See, Jack Nicas, "Crime That No Longer Pays," *Wall Street Journal*, February 4, 2013, professional.wsj.com/article/SB1000142412 788732392610457827454116l239474.html (accessed March 3, 2013).
19. Wendy Ruderman, "Crime Report Manipulation Is Common among New York Police, Study Finds," *New York Times*, June 28, 2012, http://www.nytimes.com/2012/06/29/nyregion/new-york-police-department-manipulates-crime-reports-study-finds .html (accessed July 10, 2012).
20. Ben Poston and John Diedrich, "Flynn Orders Training on FBI Crime Reporting Standards," *Milwaukee Journal Sentinel*, http://www.jsonline.com/watchdog/watchdogreports/flynn-orders-training-on-fbi-crime-reporting-standards-db628gg-162006545.html (accessed June 11, 2012).
21. John J. DiIulio, Jr., "The Question of Black Crime," *Public Interest* (fall 1994), pp. 3–12.
22. Quoted in Dan Eggen, "Major Crimes in U.S. Increase: 2001 Rise Follows Nine Years of Decline," *Washington Post*, June 23, 2002.
23. Scott Thurm, Justin Scheck, and Bobby White, "Cities See Murder Slide End," *Wall Street Journal*, March 30, 2012, http://professional.wsj.com/article/SB10001424052702303812904577297801570813854.html (accessed April 2, 2012).
24. Jeremy Gorner, "In Chicago, Killings and Questions on the Rise," *Chicago Tribune*, December 30, 2012, http://www .chicagotribune.com/news/local/ct-met-chicago-violence-2012-20121230,0,186137.story (accessed January 3, 2013); Darran Simon, "Cracking Camden's Killings," *Philadelphia Inquirer*, December 30, 2012, http://articles.philly.com/2012-12-30/news/36065156_1_homicide-unit-reluctant-witnesses-killings (accessed January 3, 2013); and George Hunter and Mike Wilkinson, "Detroit Homicides Climb 10%," *The Detroit News*, December 31, 2012 (accessed January 4, 2013).
25. See Tim Johnson, "Mexico's War on Crime Now Ranks among Latin America's Bloodiest Conflicts," *McClatchy Newspapers*, February 21, 2013, www.mcclatchydc .com/2013/02/21/183820/mexicos-war-on-crime-now-ranks .html (accessed May 2, 2013); and Alan Taylor, "Mexico's Drug War: 50,000 Dead in Six Years," *The Atlantic*, May 17, 2012, http://www.theatlantic.com/infocus/2012/05/mexicos-drug-war-50-000-dead-in-6-years/100299/ (accessed May 2, 2013).
26. Paul Knepper, "Measuring the Threat of Global Crime: Insights from Research by the League of Nations into the Traffic in Women," *Criminology*, April 2012, doi: 10.1111/j.1745-9125.2012.00277.x.
27. That is, whereas crime clock data may imply that one murder occurs every half hour or so, most murders actually occur during the evening, and only a very few take place around sunrise.
28. Most offense definitions in this chapter are derived from those used by the UCR/NIBRS Program and are taken from the FBI's *Crime in the United States, 2012* or from the Bureau of Justice Statistics, *Criminal Justice Data Terminology*, 2nd ed. (Washington, DC: BJS, 1981).
29. These and other statistics in this chapter are derived primarily from the FBI's *Crime in the United States, 2012*.
30. Bureau of Justice Statistics, *Report to the Nation on Crime and Justice*, 2nd ed. (Washington, DC: U.S. Government Printing Office, 1988), p. 4.
31. Hannah Karp and Erica E. Phillips, "Officers Are Shot as Fugitive Is Cornered," *Wall Street Journal*, February 12, 2013, http://professional.wsj.com/article/SB10001424127887324196204578300442616103464.html?mod=WSJPRO_hpp_LEFTTopStories (accessed March 13, 2013).
32. "Feds Deny Thwarting Sniper Suspect's Confession," CNN.com, October 31, 2002, http://www.cnn.com/2002/US/10/30/snipers.interrogation/index.html (accessed October 31, 2002).
33. "Sniper Malvo Given Second Life Sentence," *USA Today*, October 27, 2004.
34. BJS, *Report to the Nation on Crime and Justice*, p. 4.
35. Ibid.
36. For excellent coverage of serial killers, see Steven Egger, *The Killers among Us: An Examination of Serial Murder and Its Investigation* (Upper Saddle River, NJ: Prentice Hall, 1998); Steven A. Egger, *Serial Murder: An Elusive Phenomenon* (Westport, CT: Praeger, 1990); and Stephen J. Giannangelo, *The Psychopathology of Serial Murder: A Theory of Violence* (New York: Praeger, 1996).
37. "BTK" stands for "Bind, Torture, and Kill," an acronym that Rader applied to himself in letters he sent to the media during the 1970s.
38. Several years ago, Lucas recanted all of his confessions, saying that he had never killed anyone—except possibly his mother, a killing he said he didn't remember. See "Condemned Killer Admits Lying, Denies Slayings," *Washington Post*, October 1, 1995.
39. Chikatilo was executed in 1994.
40. See Mark Babineck, "Railroad Killer Gets Death Penalty," Associated Press, May 22, 2000, http://cnews.tribune.com/news/tribune/story/0,1235,tribune-nation-37649,00.html (accessed March 3, 2002).
41. Public Law 108-212.
42. Email communication with the Criminal Justice Information Services Division of the FBI, January 6, 2012.
43. FBI, "UCR Offense Definitions," http://ucrdatatool.gov/offenses.cfm (accessed May 5, 2013).
44. "Study: Rape Vastly Underreported," Associated Press, April 26, 1992.
45. Ronald Barri Flowers, *Women and Criminality: The Woman as Victim, Offender, and Practitioner* (Westport, CT: Greenwood Press, 1987), p. 36.
46. A. Nichols Groth, *Men Who Rape: The Psychology of the Offender* (New York: Plenum Press, 1979).
47. Susan Brownmiller, *Against Our Will: Men, Women, and Rape* (New York: Simon and Schuster, 1975).
48. Dennis J. Stevens, "Motives of Social Rapists," *Free Inquiry in Creative Sociology*, Vol. 23, No. 2 (November 1995), pp. 117–126.
49. Amanda Stewart, "Former Gar-Field Teacher Pleads Guilty to Sex with Student," Insidenova.com, March 21, 2012, http://www2.insidenova.com/news/2011dec/15/4/former-gar-field-teacher-pleads-guilty-having-sex--ar-1546539 (accessed March 21, 2012).

50. BJS, *Report to the Nation on Crime and Justice*, p. 5.
51. Ibid.
52. FBI, *Crime in the United States, 2012*. For UCR reporting purposes, minorities are defined as African Americans, Native Americans, Asians, Pacific Islanders, and Alaska Natives.
53. "Easter Bunny Charged with Battery for Mall Attack," Associated Press, April 18, 2006.
54. This offense is sometimes called assault with a deadly weapon with intent to kill (AWDWWITK).
55. FBI, *Crime in the United States, 2012*.
56. BJS, *Report to the Nation on Crime and Justice*, p. 6.
57. Ibid.
58. "Natalie Heil Accused of Renting a Home She Didn't Own and Pocketing More Than $13,000, Police Say," WPTV, http://www.wptv.com/dpp/news/region_c_palm_beach_county/west_palm_beach/natalie-heil-accused-of-renting-a-home-she-didnt-own-and-pocketing-more-than-13000, February 5, 2013 (accessed May 12, 2013).
59. "Yale Says Student Stole His Education," *USA Today*, April 12, 1995.
60. Steven J. Vaughan-Nichols, "Cisco Source Code Reportedly Stolen," eWeek, May 18, 2004, http://www.eweek.com/article2/0,1759,1593862,00.asp (accessed May 17, 2007).
61. Ibid.
62. Jon Swartz, "Facebook Simplifies Its Privacy Controls," *USA Today*, May 27, 2010, p. 1B.
63. David Gelles and Richard Waters, "Facebook Backtracks on Privacy Controls," *Financial Times*, May 27, 2010, 1A.
64. "Facebook Warns of Gift Card Scam," MSN Money, April 13, 2010, http://articles.moneycentral.msn.com/Banking/FinancialPrivacy/facebook-warns-of-gift-card-scam.aspx (accessed May 27, 2010).
65. Lynn Langton and Michael Planty, *Victims of Identity Theft, 2008* (Washington, DC: Bureau of Justice Statistics, 2010).
66. Lynn Langton, *Identity Theft Reported by Households*, 2005–2010 (Washington, DC: Bureau of Justice Statistics, 2011).
67. Katrina Baum, *Identity Theft, 2005* (Washington, DC: Bureau of Justice Statistics, 2007).
68. U.S. Code, Title 18, Section 1028.
69. Public Law 108–275.
70. Much of the information in this paragraph is adapted from National White Collar Crime Center, "Identity Theft," http://www.nw3c.org/research/site_files.cfm?fileid=935cdacc-b138-483a-8d05-83e6fd3d9004&mode=w (accessed May 18, 2012).
71. FBI, *Uniform Crime Reporting Handbook, 2004*, p. 28.
72. Patsy Klaus, *Carjacking, 1993–2002* (Washington, DC: Bureau of Justice Statistics, July 2004).
73. FBI, *Crime in the United States, 2012*.
74. As indicated in the UCR definition of arson. See Federal Bureau of Investigation, *Crime in the United States, 1998* (Washington, DC: U.S. Dept. of Justice, 1999).
75. FBI, *Crime in the United States, 2012*.
76. Ibid.
77. "Trends in Crime and Victimization," *Criminal Justice Research Reports*, Vol. 2, No. 6 (July/August 2001), p. 83.
78. Jennifer Truman, Lynn Langton, and Michael Planty, *Criminal Victimization, 2012* (Washington, DC: Bureau of Justice Statistics, October 2013).
79. For additional information, see Jennifer L. Truman, et al., *Criminal Victimization, 2012* (Washington, DC: Bureau of Justice Statistics, 2013); and Patsy A. Klaus, *Crime and the Nation's Households, 2006* (Washington, DC: Bureau of Justice Statistics, 2007).
80. Klaus, *Crime and the Nation's Households, 2006*.
81. Truman, *Criminal Victimization, 2013*.
82. Ibid., p. 1.
83. See, for example, President's Commission on Law Enforcement and Administration of Justice, *The Challenge of Crime in a Free Society*, pp. 22–23.
84. BJS, *Report to the Nation on Crime and Justice*, p. 27.
85. FBI, Criminal Justice Information Services Division, *The Measurement of White-Collar Crime Using Uniform Crime Reporting (UCR) Data* (Washington, DC: FBI, no date), http://www.fbi.gov/about-us/cjis/ucr/nibrs/nibrs_wcc.pdf (accessed May 2, 2013).
86. It is the national UCR Program's official position that "Computer crime actually involves the historical common-law offenses of larceny, embezzlement, trespass, etc., which are being perpetrated through the use of a new tool, the computer." Therefore, according to the FBI, "if larcenies, embezzlements, and trespasses relating to computers were to be reported under a new classification called Computer Crime, the national UCR Program's traditional time series relating to such crimes would be distorted." To avoid such a result, NIBRS provides the capability to indicate whether a computer was the object of the crime and/or to indicate whether the offenders used computer equipment to perpetrate a crime. The FBI says that "this ensures the continuance of the traditional crime statistics and at the same time flags incidents that involve Computer Crime." FBI, Criminal Justice Information Services Division, *National Incident-Based Reporting System, Volume 1: Data Collection Guidelines* (Washington, DC: USDOJ, 2000), pp. 19–20.
87. Hagan, *Research Methods in Criminal Justice and Criminology*, p. 89.
88. Bureau of Justice Statistics, *Criminal Victimization in the United States, 1985* (Washington, DC: U.S. Government Printing Office, 1987), p. 1.
89. FBI, *Crime in the United States, 2001*, preliminary data, http://www.fbi.gov./ucr/01prelim.pdf (accessed August 27, 2002).
90. Terance D. Miethe and Richard C. McCorkle, *Crime Profiles: The Anatomy of Dangerous Persons, Places, and Situations* (Los Angeles: Roxbury, 1998), p. 19.
91. The definition of rape employed by the UCR/NIBRS Program, however, automatically excludes crimes of homosexual rape such as might occur in prisons and jails. As a consequence, the rape of males is excluded from the official count for crimes of rape.
92. Truman, *Criminal Victimization, 2012*, p. 6.
93. Thomas Simon et al., *Injuries from Violent Crime, 1992–98* (Washington, DC: Bureau of Justice Statistics, 2001), p. 5.
94. See, for example, Elizabeth Stanko, "When Precaution Is Normal: A Feminist Critique of Crime Prevention," in Loraine Gelsthorpe and Allison Morris, eds., *Feminist Perspectives in Criminology* (Philadelphia: Open University Press, 1990).
95. For more information, see Eve S. Buzawa and Carl G. Buzawa, *Domestic Violence: The Criminal Justice Response* (Thousand Oaks, CA: Sage, 1996).
96. "Battered Women Tell Their Stories to the Senate," *Charlotte (NC) Observer*, July 10, 1991, p. 3A.
97. Patricia Tjaden and Nancy Thoennes, *Full Report of the Prevalence, Incidence, and Consequences of Violence against Women: Findings from the National Violence against Women Survey* (Washington, DC: National Institute of Justice, 2000).
98. VAWA 2005 was signed into law by President George W. Bush on January 5, 2006. It is officially known as the Violence against Women and Department of Justice Reauthorization Act of 2005 (Public Law 109–162).
99. Violence against Women Office, *Stalking and Domestic Violence: Report to Congress* (Washington, DC: U.S. Dept. of Justice, 2001).
100. U.S. Code, Title 18, Section 2261A.
101. As modified through VAWA 2000.

102. Violence against Women Office, *Stalking and Domestic Violence.*
103. Many of the data in this section come from Bureau of Justice Statistics, *Crimes against Persons Age 65 or Older, 1993–2002* (Rockville, MD: BJS, 2005).
104. Lamar Jordan, "Law Enforcement and the Elderly: A Concern for the Twenty-First Century," *FBI Law Enforcement Bulletin*, May 2002, pp. 20–23.
105. Public Law 101–275.
106. H.R. 4797, 102d Cong. 2d Sess. (1992).
107. FBI, "Hate Crime Statistics: Incidents and Offenses, 2011," http://www.fbi.gov/about-us/cjis/ucr/hate-crime/2011/narratives/incidents-and-offenses (accessed September 23, 2013).
108. "Sept. 11 Attacks Cited in Nearly 25 Percent Increase in Florida Hate Crimes," Associated Press, August 30, 2002.
109. "To Understand Dharun Ravi Verdict, Define Bias," NJ.com, March 23, 2012, http://blog.nj.com/ledgerletters/2012/03/to_understand_dharun_ravi_verd.html (accessed March 23, 2012).
110. Mark Potok, "The Year in Hate and Extremism," Intelligence Report (spring 2011), pp. 41–49.
111. Clifford Krauss, "Jury Convicts Stanford in $7 Billion Ponzi Fraud," *New York Times*, March 6, 2012, http://www.nytimes.com/2012/03/07/business/jury-convicts-stanford-in-7-billion-ponzi-fraud.html (accessed May 15, 2012).
112. Richard Esposito, Eloise Harper, and Maddy Sauer, "Bernie Madoff Pleads Guilty to Ponzi Scheme, Goes Straight to Jail, Says He's 'Deeply Sorry,'" ABC News, March 12, 2009, http://abcnews.go.com/Blotter/WallStreet/Story?id=7066715&page=1 (accessed July 4, 2009).
113. Joanna Chung and Henny Sender, "Investors Fear $50bn Loss in Madoff's 'Big Lie,'" *Financial Times*, December 14, 2008.
114. Diana B. Henriques, "Madoff Is Sentenced to 150 Years for Ponzi Scheme," *New York Times*, June 29, 2009, http://www.nytimes.com/2009/06/30/business/30madoff.html (accessed September 28, 2010).
115. Dina ElBoghdady, "Mortgage Fraud Up as Credit Tightens," *Washington Post*, March 17, 2009, http://www.washingtonpost.com/wp-dyn/content/article/2009/03/16/AR2009031601612.html (accessed May 13, 2009).
116. Jennifer Liberto, "More Muscle Sought in Fraud Fight," CNNMoney.com, May 8, 2009, http://money.cnn.com/2009/05/08/news/economy/mortgage_fraud/index.htm (accessed May 13, 2009).
117. Federal Trade Commission, "Federal and State Agencies Crack Down on Mortgage Modification and Foreclosure Rescue Scams," http://www.ftc.gov/opa/2009/04/hud.shtm (accessed May 13, 2009).
118. *Andersen* v. *U.S.*, 544 U.S. 696 (2005).
119. Public Broadcasting System, "Enron: After the Collapse," http://www.pbs.org/newshour/bb/business/enron/player6.html (accessed August 27, 2005).
120. Edwin H. Sutherland, "White-Collar Criminality," *American Sociological Review* (February 1940), p. 12.
121. Scott Lindlaw, "Bush to Propose Crackdown on Corporate Abuses: President's Own Business Dealings Come under Scrutiny," Associated Press, July 9, 2002, http://www.washingtonpost.com/wp-dyn/articles/A43384-2002Jul9.html (accessed May 17, 2005).
122. Public Law 107-204.
123. R. James Woolsey, as quoted on the Transnational Threats Initiative home page of the Center for Strategic and International Studies (CSIS), http://www.csis.org/tnt/index.htm (accessed August 22, 2007).
124. These ideas were originally expressed by Assistant U.S. Attorney General Laurie Robinson in an address given at the Twelfth International Congress on Criminology, Seoul, Korea, August 28, 1998.
125. Caroline Wolf Harlow, *Firearm Use by Offenders* (Washington, DC: Bureau of Justice Statistics, 2001).
126. Ibid, p. 1.
127. Ibid.
128. *Firearms Purchased from Federal Firearm Licensees Using Bogus Identification* (Washington, DC: General Accounting Office, 2001).
129. Sarah Brady, "Statement on the Sniper Shootings," October 8, 2002, http://www.bradycampaign.org/press/release.asp?Record 5429 (accessed October 16, 2005).
130. J. M. Chaiken and M. R. Chaiken, *Varieties of Criminal Behavior* (Santa Monica, CA: RAND Corporation, 1982).
131. D. McBride, "Trends in Drugs and Death," paper presented at the annual meeting of the American Society of Criminology, Denver, 1983.
132. National Criminal Justice Reference Service, "The Micro Domain: Behavior and Homicide," p. 140, http://www.ncjrs.org/pdffiles/167262-3.pdf (accessed February 23, 2007).
133. Bureau of Justice Statistics, *Substance Abuse and Treatment: State and Federal Prisoners* (Washington, DC: U.S. Dept. of Justice, January 1999).
134. Bureau of Justice Statistics, *Drug Use, Testing, and Treatment in Jails* (Washington, DC: U.S. Dept. of Justice, May 2000).
135. Administrative Office of the United States Courts, "Criminal Defendants Commenced, by Offense," (Table D-2), http://www.uscourts.gov/uscourts/Statistics/JudicialBusiness/2012/appendices/D02DSep12.pdf (accessed October 14, 2013).
136. Federal Criminal Case Processing, 2002.
137. Details for this story come from Carol Cratty, "245 Arrested in U.S.-Led Child Sex Abuse Operation," CNN, January 4, 2013, http://www.cnn.com/2013/01/03/us/ice-child-abuse-arrests (accessed March 14, 2013).
138. Ibid.
139. Emergency Response and Research Institute, "Summary of Emergency Response and Research Institute Terrorism Statistics: 2000 and 2001," http://www.emergency.com/2002/terroris00-01.pdf (accessed August 22, 2007).

© Ice Tea Media/Alamy

3 THE SEARCH FOR CAUSES

OUTLINE

- Introduction
- Criminological Theory
- Classical and Neoclassical Theory
- Early Biological Theories
- Biosocial Theories
- Psychological Theories
- Sociological Theories
- Social Process Theories
- Conflict Theories
- Emergent Perspectives

LEARNING OBJECTIVES

After reading this chapter, you should be able to

- Summarize the development of criminological theory, including the role of social research in that development.
- Describe the Classical School of criminology, including how it continues to influence criminological theorizing through neoclassical thought.
- Describe the basic features of biological theories of crime causation and their shortcomings.
- Explain biosocial criminology and show how biosocial understanding of criminal behavior focus on the interaction between biology and the social and physical environments.
- Describe the fundamental assumptions of psychological explanations for crime and their shortcomings.
- Describe the basic features of sociological theories of crime causation.
- Describe social process theories of criminology, including the kinds of crime-control policies that might be based on them.
- Describe conflict theories of criminality, including the kinds of crime-control policies that might be based on them.
- Summarize two emerging theories of criminology.

Society prepares the crime; the criminal commits it.

HENRY THOMAS BUCKLE

■ **Follow the author's tweets about the latest crime and justice news @schmalleger.**

■ **deviance** A violation of social norms defining appropriate or proper behavior under a particular set of circumstances. Deviance often includes criminal acts.

Introduction

In 2013, someone fired a number of shots at well-known hip-hop artist Rick Ross (born William Roberts) and his girlfriend, fashion designer Shateria Morange-el, as Ross was driving his Rolls-Royce on Las Olas Boulevard, in Fort Lauderdale, Florida.[1] Ross—whose albums include *God Forgives, I Don't*; *Teflon Don*; *Deeper Than Rap*; *Port of Miami*; and *Trilla*—had recently performed with Clipse co-lyricist Pusha T (Terrence Thornton). He's also known for his work with Nipsey Hussle (born Ermias Asghedom) and with Kanye West's G.O.O.D. Music team. Prior to the shooting, Ross (sometimes called Rozay or The Bawse) had celebrated his 37th birthday at a nearby restaurant, which was hit by some of the bullets that were fired at his car. Spectators reported hearing around 15 shots at about 5 a.m., and seeing Ross's vehicle careen into the side of an apartment complex. Although neither Ross nor his girlfriend was hurt, the incident illustrates the link to violence that is inherent in the music genre sometimes referred to as gangsta rap.

Violent crime is no stranger to the world of hard-core rap music. In 2013, aspiring Oakland (California) rapper Kenny Clutch (Kenneth Cherry, Jr.) died after the Maserati he was driving was peppered with bullets from a passing Range Rover and crashed into a Yellow cab at a Las Vegas intersection, causing a fiery explosion.[2] The shooting, which happened at 4:20 a.m. on Las Vegas Boulevard, apparently stemmed from a dispute at a nearby hotel. The incident happened just two blocks from the location of a 1996 shooting in which rapper Tupac Shakur was killed.

© Randy Miramontez/Alamy

Rapper Rick Ross (William Roberts) performs in Sacramento, California, in 2012. Ross was targeted by a shooter in 2013 in Ft. Lauderdale, Florida, but survived without serious injury after wrecking his car to flee his attacker. Some claim that rap and some forms of hip-hop music lead to crime. What do you think?

Similarly, in an event that is still discussed today, hip-hop artist Curtis "50 Cent" Jackson, a rising star in the world of hard-core rap music, was shot nine times in front of his grandmother's home in New York City in 2000.[3] One of the bullets hit him in the face. "50," as the singer is known to his fans, survived the shooting but spent months recovering. Murdered rap stars include Tupac Shakur, Notorious B.I.G., Big L., and the Lost Boyz's hip-hop hype man Raymond "Freaky Tah" Rogers.

Whether rap music merely reflects the social conditions under which its artists come of age or whether it is a direct cause of the violence that surrounds them is a question to which we will return shortly. One clue is provided by Pusha T (aka Push), who has performed with Ross, as he explains: "It's tough out here as an artist and being in rap it's like this is the only profession where you don't really leave your core. You don't really leave your upbringing. You don't really leave that behind; you stay in it lyrically and so on and so forth. So it's like you can't really get out of it, you can't really get away from it. I don't care how much money you have."[4]

No discussion of crime and of the criminal justice system would be complete without considering the *causes* of crime and **deviance**, and the idea that certain types of music lead to law violation provides one theory of crime causation. Criminologists search for answers to the fundamental questions about what causes crime: Why do people commit crime? What are the root causes of violence and aggression? Are people basically good, or are they motivated only by self-interest? More precisely, we might ask why a particular person commits a particular crime on a given occasion and under specific circumstances.

In this chapter, we will look at the causes of crime. Before we begin, however, some brief definitions are in order. *Crime*, as noted in Chapter 1, is a violation of the criminal law without acceptable legal justification,[5] whereas *deviant behavior* is a violation of social norms that specify appropriate or proper behavior under a particular set of circumstances. Deviant behavior is a broad category that often includes crime.

Many theories have been advanced to explain all sorts of rule-violating behavior. As is the case with the story that opened this chapter, some observers of the contemporary scene blame much of today's crime on commonplace episodes of violence in the American media—especially on television, in music, and on film. Experts who study the media estimate that the average American child watches 8,000 murders and 100,000 acts of violence while growing up.[6] At an international conference, Suzanne Stutman, president of the Institute for Mental Health Initiatives, a nonprofit organization

Deviant behavior is a broad category that often includes crime, but not all deviance is criminal.

■ **theory** A set of interrelated propositions that attempt to describe, explain, predict, and ultimately control some class of events. A theory is strengthened by its logical consistency and is "tested" by how well it describes and predicts reality.

in Washington, D.C., reported that studies consistently show that the extent of exposure to television violence in childhood is a good predictor of future criminal behavior.[7] One particular study found that watching just one hour of television a day can make a person more violent toward others.[8] The study, which was conducted over a 25-year period at New York's Columbia University and published in 2002, used police records to confirm that 45% of young men who had watched three or more hours of television a day went on to commit at least one aggressive act against another person, compared to 9% of young men who had watched TV for less than one hour per day.

Robert Brown, executive director of the Washington, D.C., Children's Trust Neighborhood Initiative, lays much of the blame for contemporary violence on rap music, especially "gangsta rap" and some forms of hip-hop. "So many of our young men," says Brown, "have accepted false icons of manhood for themselves . . . because the popular culture of videos and rap . . . reinforces that this is the correct way to be. Guys . . . try to exude an aura that says, 'I am so bad that I am not afraid to take your life or to offer mine up in the process.'"[9]

An African American critic of gangsta rap puts it this way: "The key element is aggression—in rappers' body language, tone, and witty rhymes—that often leaves listeners hyped, on edge, angry about . . . something. Perhaps the most important element in gangsta rap is its messages, which center largely around these ideas: that women are no more than 'bitches and ho's,' disposable playthings who exist merely for men's abusive delight; that it's cool to use any means necessary to get the material things you want; and most importantly, it's admirable to be cold-blooded and hard."[10] The Reverend Arthur L. Cribbs, Jr., an African American social commentator, agrees. Cribbs calls gangsta rap "nothing but modern-day violence and vulgarity wrapped and packaged in blackface."[11]

Most people agree that media violence harms society. According to one survey, "57% of the public thinks violence in the media is a major factor in real-life violence" of all kinds.[12] But it is less than clear whether violence in the media and aggressive themes in popular music are indeed a cause of crime, as many believe, or merely a reflection of the social conditions that exist in many American communities today. Findings from studies on the effect of television viewing, for example, may be inadvertently spotlighting existing criminal tendencies among lower-class undereducated teenagers with enough time on their hands for extensive TV viewing. Hence getting legislators to address the issue of violence in the media is sometimes difficult. Moreover, in 2011, the U.S. Supreme Court weighed in with an important decision in the case of *Brown* v. *Entertainment Merchants Association*, in which it ruled that a state law in California restricting the sale or rental of violent computer games to minors was a violation of the First Amendment's guarantee of free speech.[13] The majority of justices held that computer games, "like protected books, plays, and movies, communicate ideas through familiar literary devices and features distinctive to the medium."[14]

Criminological Theory

It is easy to understand why the entertainment industry and the media are often targeted as the cause of crime and criminal violence. However, many other types of explanations for crime are also viable, such as individual psychological differences, including personality disorders; variations in patterns of early socialization that may predispose some people to crime and violence; and biosocial perspectives that say crime arises out of a causal brew formed by the interaction of biological predispositions and the social environment. Similarly, it is prudent to examine social institutions such as the family, schools, churches, and even the police for their role in reducing or enhancing the likelihood of criminality among people.

There is no single cause of crime; it is rooted in a diversity of causes and takes a variety of forms, depending on the situation in which it occurs.

One thing is certain: There is no single cause of crime; it is rooted in a diversity of causes and takes a variety of forms, depending on the situation in which it occurs. Nonetheless, some theories of human behavior help us understand why certain people engage in acts that society defines as criminal or deviant, while others do not. A **theory** is a kind of model. Theories posit relationships, often of a causal sort, between events and things under study. A theory's explanatory power derives primarily from its inherent logical consistency, and theories are tested by how well they describe and predict reality. In other words, a good theory fits the facts, and it stands up to continued scrutiny. Figure 3-1 uses the association between poverty and crime as an example to diagram the important aspects of theory creation in the social sciences.

History is rife with theories purporting to explain rule-violating behavior. For example, an old Roman theory, based

■ **hypothesis** An explanation that accounts for a set of facts and that can be tested by further investigation. Also, something that is taken to be true for the purpose of argument or investigation.[i]

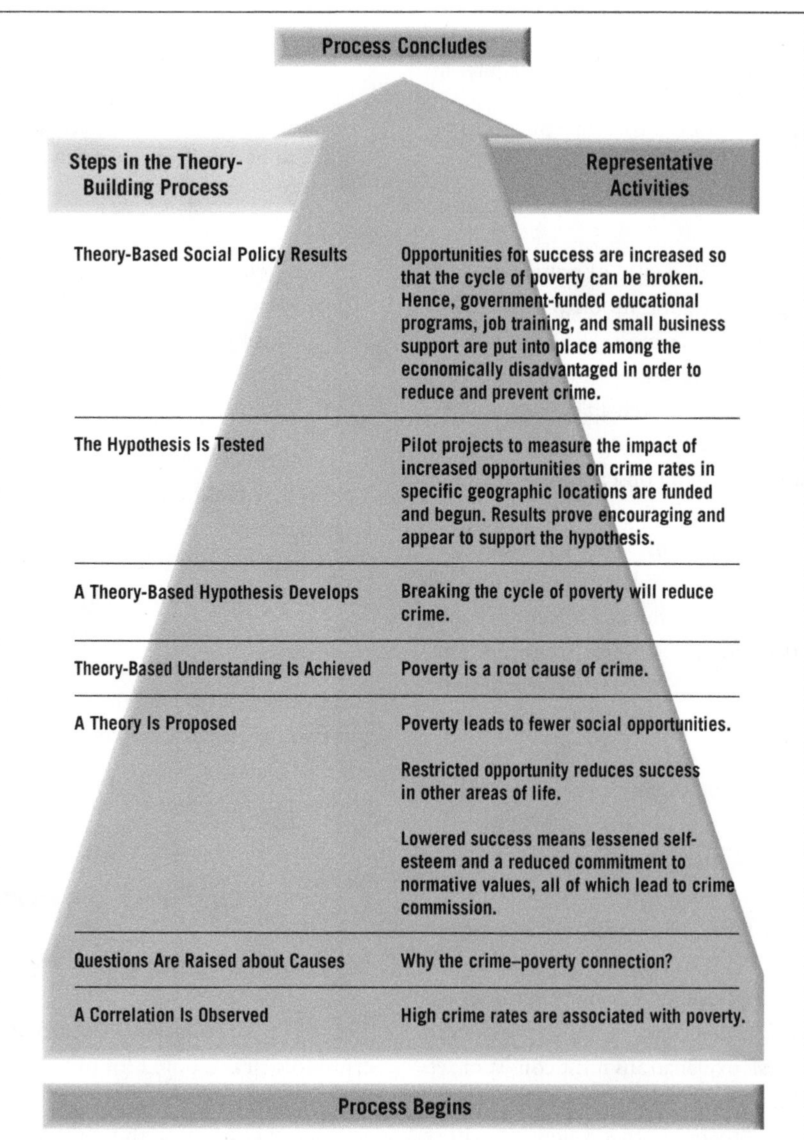

FIGURE 3-1 | Steps in Criminological Theory Building and Social Policy Creation

on ancient observations that more crime and deviance occur on nights with a full moon, proposed that the moon causes a kind of temporary insanity, or *lunacy*. According to this theory, deviant behavior isn't random; it waxes and wanes in cadence with the lunar cycle. Although modern statisticians have noted an association between phases of the moon and crime rates, the precise mechanism by which the moon influences behavior—if it does—has never been adequately explained.

As mentioned, a complete theory attempts to flesh out all of the causal links between phenomena that are associated, or *correlated*. For example, some comprehensive theories of lunacy suggest that light from the full moon stimulates the reticular-activating system (RAS) in the limbic portion of the human brain, which makes people more excitable and hyperactive—and thus more likely to behave in deviant ways and to commit crime. Others have suggested, quite simply, that people commit more crimes when the moon is full because it is easier to see.

Theories, once created, must be tested to determine whether they are valid, and modern criminology has become increasingly scientific.[15] Theory testing usually involves the development of **hypotheses** based on what the theory under scrutiny would predict. A theory of lunacy, for example, might be tested in a

■ **research** The use of standardized, systematic procedures in the search for knowledge.
■ **interdisciplinary theory** An approach that integrates a variety of theoretical viewpoints in an attempt to explain something, such as crime and violence.

■ **Classical School** An eighteenth-century approach to crime causation and criminal responsibility that grew out of the Enlightenment and that emphasized the role of free will and reasonable punishment. Classical thinkers believed that punishment, if it is to be an effective deterrent, has to outweigh the potential pleasure derived from criminal behavior.

variety of ways, including (1) observing rates of crime and deviance on nights when the light of the full moon is obscured by clouds (we would expect no rise in crime rates if the RAS or visibility explanations are correct) and (2) examining city crime rates on full-moon nights—especially in well-lit city areas where the light of the moon hardly increases visibility. If the predictions made by a theory are validated by careful observation, the theory gains greater acceptability.

Generally accepted research designs—coupled with careful data-gathering strategies and statistical techniques for data analysis—have yielded considerable confidence in certain explanations for crime, while at the same time disproving others. Theories of crime causation that have met rigorous scientific tests for acceptability give policymakers the intellectual basis they need to create informed crime-control strategies. The ultimate goal of **research** and theory building in criminology is to provide models that permit a better understanding of criminal behavior and that enhance the development of strategies, or policies, intended to address the problem of crime.

Although we will use the word *theory* in describing various explanations for crime throughout this chapter, it should be recognized that the word is only loosely applicable to some of the perspectives we will discuss. As noted, many social scientists insist that to be considered "theories," explanations must consist of sets of clearly stated, logically interrelated, and measurable propositions. The fact that few of the "theories" that follow rise above the level of organized conjecture, and that many others are not readily amenable to objective scrutiny through scientific testing, is one of the greatest failures of social science today.

Also, many contemporary theories of deviant and criminal behavior are far from complete, offering only limited ideas rather than comprehensive explanations for the behavior in question. Moreover, when we consider the wide range of behaviors regarded as criminal—from murder to drug use to terrorism to white-collar crime—it is difficult to imagine a theory that can explain them all.

For our purposes, explanations of criminal behavior fall into eight general categories:

- Classical and neoclassical
- Early biological
- Biosocial
- Psychological
- Sociological
- Social process
- Conflict
- Emergent

The differences among these approaches are summarized in Table 3-1. A ninth category could be **interdisciplinary theories**. Interdisciplinary approaches integrate a variety of theoretical viewpoints in an attempt to explain crime and violence. The Project on Human Development in Chicago Neighborhoods (PHDCN) is one example of an ongoing interdisciplinary study of the causes of crime. Described in more detail later in this chapter, the PHDCN project involves an examination of the roles of personality, school, and community as they contribute to juvenile delinquency and criminal behavior. See **http://www.justicestudies.com/pubs/phdcn.pdf** for more information on the project.

Classical and Neoclassical Theory

Theories of the **Classical School** of crime causation dominated criminological thought for much of the late eighteenth and early nineteenth centuries. These theories represented a noteworthy advance over previous thinking about crime because they moved beyond superstition and mysticism as explanations for deviance. As noted criminologist Stephen Schafer puts it, "In the eighteenth-century individualistic orientation of criminal law, the act was judged and the man made responsible."[16] A product of the Enlightenment then sweeping through Europe, the Classical School demanded recognition of rationality and the ability to exercise informed choice in human social life.

Most classical theories of crime causation, both old and new, make certain basic assumptions. Among them are these:

- Crime is caused by the individual exercise of free will. Human beings are fundamentally rational, and most human behavior is the result of free will coupled with rational choice.
- Pain and pleasure are the two central determinants of human behavior.

TABLE 3-1 | Types of Criminological Theory

TYPE & CONCEPTS	THEORISTS	CHARACTERISTICS
Classical and Neoclassical		
Free will theories	Beccaria	Crime is caused by the individual exercise of free will.
Hedonistic calculus Rational choice theory	Bentham Cohen & Felson	Prevention is possible through swift and certain punishment that offsets any gains to be had through criminal behavior.
Routine activities theory	Cohen & Felson	Lifestyles significantly affect both the amount and type of crime found in any society, and the risk of criminal victimization varies according to the circumstances and locations in which people place themselves and their property.
Early Biological		
Phrenology Atavism Criminal families Somatotypes Body types	Gall Lombroso Dugdale Goddard Sheldon	"Criminal genes" cause deviant behavior. Criminals are identifiable through physical characteristics or genetic makeup. Treatment is generally ineffective, but aggression may be usefully redirected.
Biosocial		
Gender ratio problem Genetics/chromosomes Hormones Nutrition Body chemistry Heredity/heritability Brain dysfunction	Wilson & Herrnstein Beaver Ellis Walsh Jacobs Raine	The interactions between human biology and the physical and social environments are key to understanding human behavior, including criminality.
Psychological		
Behavioral conditioning Psychoanalysis Psychopathology	Pavlov Freud Cleckley	Crime is the result of inappropriate behavioral conditioning or a diseased mind. Treatment necessitates extensive behavioral therapy.
Sociological		
Social disorganization Anomie	Park & Burgess Shaw & McKay Durkheim Merton	The structure of society and its relative degree of organization or disorganization are important actors contributing to the prevalence of criminal behavior.
Subcultures Focal concerns Subculture of violence	Cohen Miller Wolfgang & Ferracuti	Group dynamics, group organization, and subgroup relationships form the causal nexus out of which crime develops. Effective social policy may require basic changes in patterns of socialization and an increase in accepted opportunities for success.
Social Process		
Differential association Social learning Containment Social control Neutralization	Sutherland Burgess & Akers Reckless Hirschi Sykes & Matza	Crime results from the failure of self-direction, inadequate social roles, or association with defective others. Social policy places responsibility for change on the offender.
Labeling	Becker	The source of criminal behavior is unknown, but an understanding of crime requires recognition that the definition of crime is imposed on behavior by the wider society. Individuals defined as "criminal" may be excluded by society from "normal" opportunities. Therapy requires a total reorientation of the offender.
Social development Life course perspective	Terrie Moffitt Sampson & Laub	Human development occurs simultaneously on many levels, including psychological, biological, familial, interpersonal, cultural, societal, and ecological. The life course perspective notes that criminal behavior tends to follow an identifiable pattern throughout a person's life cycle.
Conflict		
Radical criminology	Turk Vold Chambliss	Conflict is fundamental to social life. Crime is a natural consequence of social, political, and economic inequities.
Peacemaking criminology	Pepinsky Quinney	Fundamental changes to the structure of society are needed to eliminate crime.
Emergent		
Feminist criminology	Adler Simon Daly & Chesney-Lind	Feminist criminology emphasizes the need for gender awareness in the criminological enterprise.
Postmodern criminology	Henry & Milovanovic	Deconstructionist approaches challenge existing theories in order to replace them with perspectives more relevant to the modern era.

■ **neoclassical criminology** A contemporary version of classical criminology that emphasizes deterrence and retribution and that holds that human beings are essentially free to make choices in favor of crime and deviance or conformity to the law.

■ **rational choice theory** A perspective on crime causation that holds that criminality is the result of conscious choice. Rational choice theory predicts that individuals will choose to commit crime when the benefits of doing so outweigh the costs of disobeying the law.

■ **routine activities theory (RAT)** A neoclassical perspective that suggests that lifestyles contribute significantly to both the amount and the type of crime found in any society.

- Crime erodes the bond that exists between individuals and society and is therefore an immoral form of behavior.
- Punishment, a necessary evil, is sometimes required to deter law violators from repeating their crimes and to serve as an example to others who would also violate the law.
- Crime prevention is possible through swift and certain punishment that offsets any gains to be had through criminal behavior.

Cesare Beccaria: Crime and Punishment

In 1764, Cesare Beccaria (1738–1794) published his *Essays on Crimes and Punishment*. The book was an immediate success and stirred a hornet's nest of controversy over the treatment of criminal offenders. Beccaria proposed basic changes in the criminal laws of his day to make them more "humanitarian." He called for the abolition of physical punishment and an end to the death penalty. Beccaria is best remembered for his suggestion that punishment should be just sufficient to deter criminal behavior but should never be excessive. Because Beccaria's writings stimulated many other thinkers throughout the eighteenth and early nineteenth centuries, he is referred to today as the founder of the Classical School of criminology.

Jeremy Bentham: Hedonistic Calculus

Among those influenced by Beccaria was the Englishman Jeremy Bentham (1748–1832). Bentham devised a "hedonistic calculus," which essentially said that the exercise of free will would cause an individual to avoid committing a crime as long as the punishment for committing that crime outweighed the benefits to be derived from committing it. Bentham termed this philosophy of social control *utilitarianism*. Both Bentham and Beccaria agreed that punishment had to be "swift and certain"—as well as just—to be effective. Learn more about Jeremy Bentham at **http://www.ucl.ac.uk/Bentham-Project**.

The Neoclassical Perspective

A contemporary theory with roots in the Classical School, **neoclassical criminology** is a perspective that owes much to the early classical thinkers. Although classical criminology focuses primarily on pleasure and pain as motivators of human behavior, neoclassical criminology places greater emphasis on rationality and cognition. Central to such perspectives is **rational choice theory**, which holds that criminality is largely the result of conscious choices that people make. According to the theory, offenders choose to violate the law when they believe that the benefits of doing so outweigh the costs.

Rational choice theory is represented by a somewhat narrower perspective called **routine activities theory**, and referred to by the somewhat humorous acronym, **RAT**. Routine activities theory was first proposed by Lawrence Cohen and Marcus Felson in 1979.[17] Cohen and Felson argued that lifestyles significantly affect both the amount and type of crime found in any society, and they noted that "the risk of criminal victimization varies dramatically among the circumstances and locations in which people place themselves and their property."[18] Lifestyles that contribute to criminal opportunities are likely to result in crime because they increase the risk of potential victimization.[19] For example, a person who routinely uses an ATM late at night in an isolated location is far more likely to be preyed on by robbers than is someone who stays home after dark. Rational choice theorists concentrate on "the decision-making process of offenders confronted with specific contexts" and have shifted "the focus of the effort to prevent crime . . . from broad social programs to target hardening, environmental design or any impediment that would [dissuade] a motivated offender from offending."[20]

Although classical criminology focuses primarily on pleasure and pain as determinants of human behavior, neoclassical criminology places greater emphasis on rationality and cognition.

Central to the routine activities approach is the claim that crime is likely to occur when a motivated offender and a suitable target come together in the absence of a *capable guardian*. Capable guardians are those who effectively discourage crime and prevent it from occurring. Members of neighborhood watch groups, for example, might be capable guardians. Capable guardians do not necessarily have to confront would-be offenders directly but might be people who have completed classes in crime prevention and who have taken steps to reduce their chances of victimization.

■ **Biological School** A perspective on criminological thought that holds that criminal behavior has a physiological basis.
■ **phrenology** The study of the shape of the head to determine anatomical correlates of human behavior.

Social Policy and Classical Theories

Much of the practice of criminal justice in America today is built on concepts provided by Classical School theorists. Many contemporary programs designed to prevent crime, for example, have their philosophical roots in the classical axioms of deterrence and punishment. Modern heirs of the Classical School see punishment as central to criminal justice policy, use evidence of high crime rates to argue that punishment is a necessary crime preventive, and believe punishment is a natural and deserved consequence of criminal activity. Such thinkers call for greater prison capacity and new prison construction. In Chapter 1, we used the term *public-order advocate*, which can be applied to modern-day proponents of classical theory who frequently seek stiffer criminal laws and greater penalties for criminal activity. The emphasis on punishment as an appropriate response to crime, however, whether founded on principles of deterrence or revenge, and the resulting packed courtrooms and overcrowded prisons, has left many contemporary criminal justice policy initiatives floundering.

Much of the practice of criminal justice in America today is built on concepts provided by Classical School theorists.

Early Biological Theories

Biological theories of crime causation, which had fallen into disrepute during the past few decades, are beginning to experience something of a contemporary resurgence. It is important to distinguish, however, between early biological perspectives, which have been largely discounted by contemporary criminologists, and the rather sophisticated biosocial perspectives offered by some cutting-edge criminologists today. Biosocial theories will be discussed later in this chapter, but most early theories of the **Biological School** of crime causation built on inherited or bodily characteristics and features and made certain fundamental assumptions. Among them are these:

- Basic determinants of human behavior, including criminal tendencies, are constitutionally or genetically based.
- The basic determinants of human behavior, including criminality, may be passed on from generation to generation. In other words, a penchant for crime may be inherited.
- At least some human behavior is the result of biological propensities inherited from more primitive developmental stages in the evolutionary process. Some human beings may be further along the evolutionary ladder than others, and their behavior may reflect it.

Franz Joseph Gall: Phrenology

The idea that the quality of a person can be judged by a study of the person's face is as old as antiquity. Even today, we often judge people on their looks, saying, "He has an honest face" or "She has tender eyes." Horror movies play on unspoken cultural themes to shape the way a "maniac" might look. Jack Nicholson's portrayal of a crazed killer in *The Shining* and Anthony Hopkins's role as a serial killer in *The Silence of the Lambs* turned that look into fortunes at the box office. More recently, TV series such as NBC's *Hannibal* have capitalized on scary looks and frightening scenes.

Franz Joseph Gall (1758–1828) was one of the first thinkers to theorize about the idea that bodily constitution might reflect personality. Gall was writing at a time when it was thought that organs throughout the body determined one's mental state and behavior. People were said to be "hard-hearted" or to have a "bad spleen" that filled them with bile. Gall focused on the head and the brain and called his approach *cranioscopy*. It can be summarized in four propositions:

- The brain is the organ of the mind.
- The brain consists of localized faculties or functions.
- The shape of the skull reveals the underlying development (or lack of development) of areas within the brain.
- The personality can be revealed by a study of the skull.

Gall never systematically tested his theory in a way that would meet contemporary scientific standards. Even so, his approach to predicting behavior, which came to be known as **phrenology**, quickly spread throughout Europe. Gall's student, Johann Gaspar Spurzheim (1776–1853), brought phrenology to America in a series of lectures and publications on the subject. By 1825, 29 phrenological journals were being produced in the United States and Britain.[21] Until the turn of the twentieth century, phrenology remained popular in some American circles, where it was used in diagnostic schemes to classify new prisoners.

■ **atavism** A condition characterized by the existence of features thought to be common in earlier stages of human evolution.

■ **Positivist School** An approach that stresses the application of scientific techniques to the study of crime and criminals.

Cesare Lombroso: Atavism

Gall's theory was "deterministic" in the sense that it left little room for choice. What a person did depended more on the shape of the skull than on the exercise of free will. Other biological theories would soon build on that premise. One of the best known is that created by the Italian psychologist Cesare Lombroso (1835–1909).

Lombroso began his criminal anthropology with a postmortem evaluation of famous criminals, including one by the name of Vilella. Before Vilella died, Lombroso had the opportunity to interview him on a number of occasions. After Vilella's death, Lombroso correlated earlier observations of personality traits with measurable physical abnormalities. As a result of this and other studies, Lombroso concluded that criminals were atavistic human beings—throwbacks to earlier stages of evolution who were not sufficiently mentally advanced for successful life in the modern world. **Atavism** was identifiable in suspicious individuals, Lombroso suggested, through measures designed to reveal "primitive" physical characteristics.

In the late nineteenth century, Charles Darwin's theory of evolution was rapidly being applied to a wide range of fields. It was not surprising, therefore, that Lombroso linked evolution and criminality. What separated Lombroso from his predecessors, however, was that he continually refined his theory through ongoing observation. Based on studies of known offenders, whom he compared to conformists, Lombroso identified a large number of atavistic traits, which he claimed characterized criminals. Among them were long arms, large lips, crooked noses, an abnormally large amount of body hair, prominent cheekbones, two eyes of different colors, and ears that lacked clearly defined lobes.

Atavism implies that certain people are born criminals. Throughout his life, Lombroso grappled with the task of determining what proportion of the total population of offenders were born criminals. His estimates ranged at different times between 70% and 90%. Career criminals and those who committed crimes of opportunity without atavistic features he termed *criminaloids*, and he recognized the potential causative roles of greed, passion, and circumstance in their behavior.

Today, Lombroso is known as the founder of the **Positivist School** of criminology because of the role observation played in the formulation of his theories. Stephen Schafer calls Lombroso "the father of modern criminology"[22] because most contemporary criminologists follow in the tradition that Lombroso began—scientific observation and a comparison of theory with fact.

© Mary Evans Picture Library/Alamy

Cesare Lombroso, who has been dubbed "the father of modern criminology," in a rare photograph from 1909. What concepts developed by Lombroso might still be applicable today?

The Evidence for and against Atavism

After Lombroso died, two English physicians, Charles Goring and Karl Pearson, conducted a test of atavism, studying more than 3,000 prisoners and comparing them along physiological criteria to an army detachment known as the Royal Engineers. No significant differences were found between the two groups, and Lombroso's ideas rapidly began to fall into disrepute.

A further study of atavism was published in 1939 by Earnest A. Hooton, a distinguished Harvard University anthropologist. Hooton spent 12 years constructing anthropometric profiles—profiles based on human body measurements—of 13,873 male convicts in ten different American states. He measured each inmate in 107 different ways and compared them to 3,203 volunteers from National Guard units, firehouses, beaches, and hospitals. Surprisingly, Hooton did find some basis for Lombroso's beliefs,

■ **somatotyping** The classification of human beings into types according to body build and other physical characteristics.

and he concluded that the inmate population in his study demonstrated a decided physical "inferiority."

However, Hooton never recognized that the prisoners he studied were only a subgroup of the population of all offenders throughout the country. They were, in fact, the least successful offenders—the ones who had been caught and imprisoned. Hooton may have unknowingly measured other criminals—the ones who had avoided capture—among his "conformist" population. Hence the "inferiority" Hooton observed may have been an artificial product of a process of selection (arrest) by the justice system.

Criminal Families

The concept of biological inheritance has been applied to "criminal families" as well as to individuals. The idea of mental degeneration as an inherited contributor to crime was first explored by Richard Dugdale.[23] Dugdale used the family tree method to study a family he called the Jukes, publishing his findings in 1877. The Juke lineage had its beginning in America with "Max" (whose last name is unknown), a descendant of Dutch immigrants to New Amsterdam in the early eighteenth century. Two of Max's sons married into the notorious "Juke family of girls," six sisters, all of whom were illegitimate. Male Jukes were reputed to have been "vicious," while Ada, one of the sisters, had an especially bad reputation and eventually came to be known as "the mother of criminals."

Dugdale found that, during the next 75 years, Ada's heirs included 1,200 people, most of whom were "social degenerates." Only a handful of socially productive progeny could be identified. In 1915, Dugdale's study of the Jukes was continued by Arthur A. Estabrook, who extended the line to include 2,094 descendants and found just as few conformists.

A similar study was published by Henry Goddard in 1912.[24] Goddard examined the Kallikak family, which contained two clear lines of descent. One emanated from an affair that Revolutionary War soldier Martin Kallikak had with a "feebleminded" barmaid. She bore a son, and the line eventually produced 480 identifiable descendants. After the war, Kallikak returned home and married a "virtuous" Quaker woman in Philadelphia. This legitimate line produced 496 offspring by 1912, of whom only 3 were abnormal; not one was criminal. The illegitimate group, however, contained over half "feebleminded" or deviant progeny.

The underlying suppositions of these studies are that degenerate and feebleminded people are produced and propagated through bad genetic material and that crime is an outlet for degenerate urges. However, these studies fail to recognize any effect that socialization and life circumstances have on the development of criminal behavior.

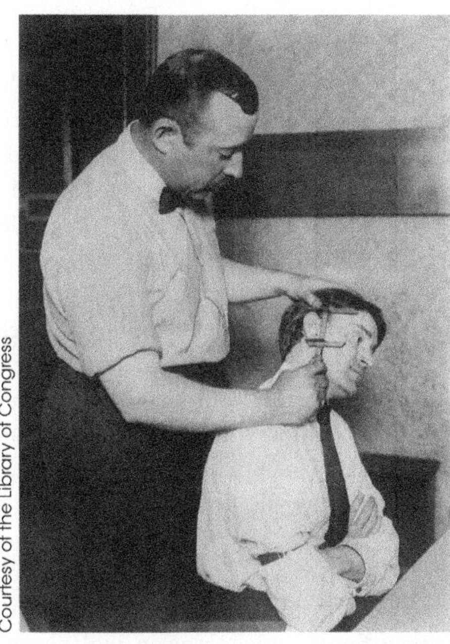

Courtesy of the Library of Congress

The Bertillion system of identification being applied to a subject in the years before the development of fingerprinting. The theory of atavism, based on the ideas of Charles Darwin, supported the use of physical anthropology in the identification of offenders. Why have sociological theories largely replaced simple biological approaches to explaining crime?

William Sheldon: Somatotypes

"Constitutional" theories of crime causation refer to the *physical constitution*, or bodily characteristics, of offenders. The last of the famous constitutional theorists was William Sheldon (1893–1977), who developed the idea of **somatotyping**.

Sheldon studied 200 juvenile delinquents between the ages of 15 and 21 at the Hayden Goodwill Institute in Boston and decided that the young men possessed one of three somatotypes (or body types). The types of bodies described by Sheldon were (in his words):

- *Mesomorphs* with a relative predominance of muscle, bone, and connective tissue
- *Endomorphs* with a soft roundness throughout the various regions of the body; short tapering limbs; small bones; and soft, smooth, velvety skin
- *Ectomorphs* characterized by thinness, fragility, and delicacy of body

■ **biosocial criminology** A theoretical perspective that sees the interaction between biology and the physical and social environments as key to understanding human behavior, including criminality.

■ **gender ratio problem** The need for an explanation of the fact that the number of crimes committed by men routinely far exceeds the number of crimes committed by women in almost all categories.

Sheldon developed a system of measurements by which an individual's physique could be expressed as a combination of numbers, and believed that predominantly mesomorphic individuals were most prone to aggression, violence, and delinquency.[25]

Social Policy and Early Biological Theories

Because traditional biological theories of crime causation attribute the cause of crime to fundamental physical characteristics that are not easily modified, they suggest the need for extreme social policies. During the 1920s and early 1930s, for example, biological theories of crime causation, especially those focusing on inherited mental degeneration, led to the eugenics movement, under which mentally handicapped people were sometimes sterilized to prevent them from bearing offspring. The eugenics movement was institutionalized by the 1927 U.S. Supreme Court case of *Buck* v. *Bell*, in which Justice Oliver Wendell Holmes, Jr., writing in support of a Virginia statute permitting sterilization, said, "It is better for all the world, if instead of waiting to execute degenerate offspring for crime, or to let them starve for their imbecility, society can prevent those persons who are manifestly unfit from continuing their kind."[26] Visit **http://www.crimetimes.org** to learn more about early biological theories of crime and violence.

Biosocial Theories

During the past few years, numerous researchers have taken a sophisticated approach to biological theorizing. Consequently, most contemporary biological theories of crime causation fall under the heading of **biosocial criminology**. The biosocial perspective sees the interaction between biology and the physical and social environments as key to understanding human behavior, including criminality. While recognizing the role of human DNA, heritability, environmental contaminants, nutrition, hormones, physical trauma (especially to the brain), and body chemistry in human cognition, feeling, and behavior, biosocial theorists emphasize that it is the *interaction* between biology and the cultural and social environments that produces behavior, and that both conformity and criminality are a consequence of such interaction. Some biosocial theories, including those offered by University of Pennsylvania criminologist Adrian Raine, stress the importance of the interaction between a cluster of biological markers—including brain dysfunction, glucose metabolism, poor nutrition, and physiological reactivity (such as skin resistance and heart rate)—with the social environment in producing deviance and criminality.[27] Raine argues that measurements of biological indicators and observations of the social environment can be used to accurately predict which people will turn to crime in later life.[28]

The biosocial perspective sees the interaction between biology and the physical and social environments as key to understanding human behavior, including criminality.

The Gender Ratio Problem

One of the most telling issues in contemporary criminology is what biosocial criminologists Kevin Beaver and Anthony Walsh call the **gender ratio problem**. The gender ratio problem refers to the fact that in all societies, regardless of the historical period, men are always far more involved in criminal activity than are women. That is not to say that some forms of crime, like prostitution, do not disproportionately involve women (although there are likely far more male "Johns" than there are female prostitutes), or that women commit a few specific types of crimes more often than men (but such crimes, like teller theft, are usually associated with a significant gender imbalance, as in the case of bank tellers, who are predominately women).

Anthony Walsh explains the gender ratio problem this way: "In virtually every study ever conducted, males are much more likely than females to engage in violence, aggression, and serious crimes. As the seriousness of the offense/behavior increases, the gender gap also tends to increase, such that the most violent criminal acts are almost exclusively a male phenomenon." Figure 3-2 shows, for example, gender differences in the rate of arrests for homicides in the United States from 1960 to 2010.

■ **chromosomes** Bundles of genes.
■ **genes** Distinct portions of a cell's DNA that carry coded instructions for making everything the body needs.

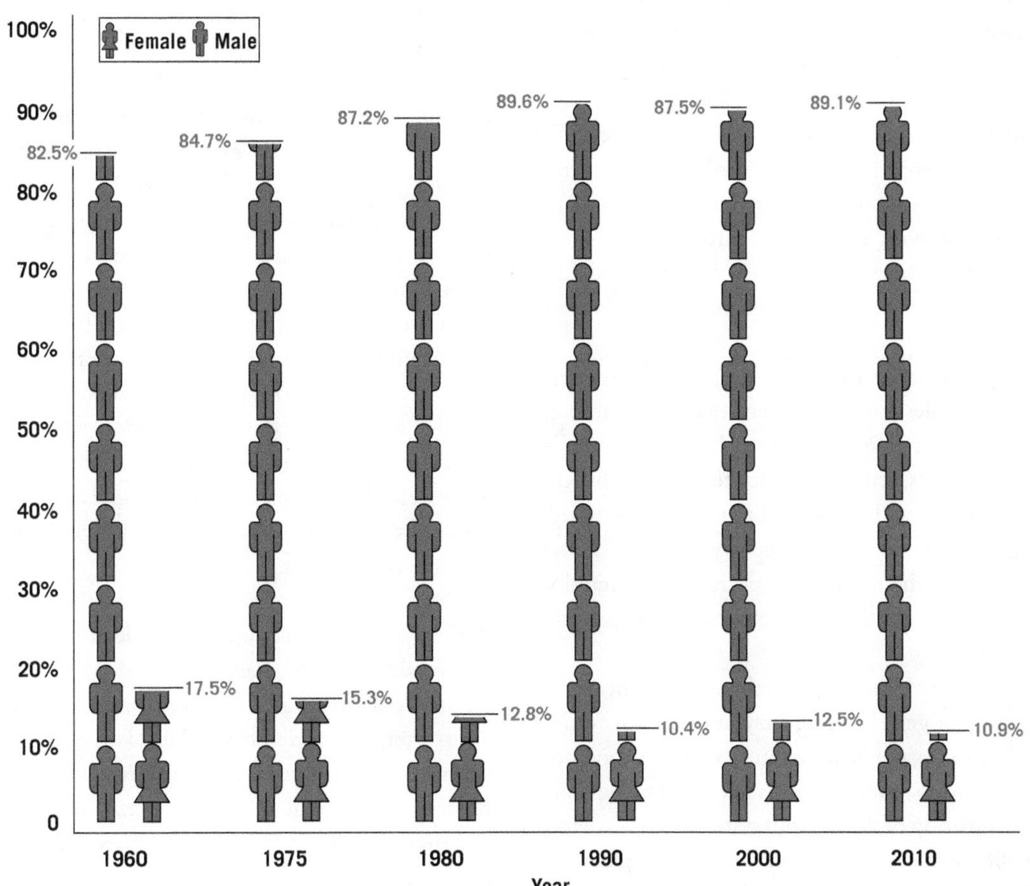

FIGURE 3-2 | Male and Female Murder Perpetrators as a Percentage of All Arrests for Homicide, 1960–2010

Source: Frank Schmalleger, *Criminology*, 2d ed. (Upper Saddle River, NJ: Pearson, 2014), Figure 3-6, p. 53.

As Walsh explains, the gender ratio problem is only a problem if biological explanations for criminality are ignored. Sociological theories, psychological perspectives, and approaches such as the Classical School tend to deny the important role that inherent physiological differences between the sexes can play in crime causation. Primary among such differences is the role that the male sex hormone testosterone plays in increasing the propensity toward violence and aggression among men. A few authors have suggested that testosterone is the agent primarily responsible for male criminality and that its relative lack in women leads them to commit fewer crimes. A growing body of evidence supports just such a hypothesis. Studies have shown, for example, that female fetuses exposed to elevated testosterone levels during gestation develop masculine characteristics, including a muscular build and a demonstrably greater tendency toward aggression later in life. Other studies show that testosterone strongly influences behavior, and that it creates what some have called "sexually dismorphic brains"—including physical and functional differences between the brains of men and women.

Chromosome Theory

In 2013, Connecticut Chief Medical Examiner H. Wayne Carver, ordered the testing of Newton, Connecticut, school shooter Adam Lanza's DNA in an effort to determine "if he possessed any genetic abnormalities that could have led to his violent behavior." The detailed mapping of human DNA and other recent advances in the field of recombinant DNA have rekindled interest in genetic correlates of deviant behavior. More sophisticated than their historical counterparts, the biosocial theories of today often draw on the latest medical advances or build on popular health concerns.

Chromosomes are bundles of genes, and **genes** are distinct portions of a cell's DNA that carry coded instructions for making everything the body needs.[29] The links between chromosome patterns and crime were first explored in the 1960s. A normal female has a chromosome structure often diagrammed as "XX" because of how the sex-determining gene pair looks

■ **supermale** A male individual displaying the XYY chromosome structure.

in an electron microscope. A male has a Y chromosome in place of the second X, for a typical male XY pattern. Although it had been known for some time that a few people have abnormal patterns that include "extra" chromosomes (such as XXX females, XXY males with Klinefelter's syndrome, and XXYY "double males"), it wasn't until 1965 that the respected English journal *Nature* reported on the work of Patricia Jacobs, who identified **supermales**—men with an extra Y chromosome whose chromosome structure is diagrammed XYY. Jacobs found that supermales were more common in prisons than in the general population.[30]

Other early studies claimed that the XYY male was more aggressive than other males and that he possessed a number of specific physical and psychological traits, such as height (taller than 6 feet, 1 inch), thinness, acne, a tendency toward homosexuality, a somewhat low IQ, and "a marked tendency to commit a succession of apparently motiveless property crimes."[31] Later studies disputed many of these findings, and today's criminologists largely disregard the relationship between XYY patterns and criminal behavior.

Instead, contemporary biosocial researchers have turned their attention to the study of gene deficits, enzymes, and hormones. Some recent studies, for example, have found that an overabundance of the enzyme monoamine oxidase A (MAOA) in the brain may lead to overstimulation of the nervous system, and to a defect in the DRD2 A1 allele gene, which some have called the pleasure-seeking gene. This combination can result in uncontrollable urges and, ultimately, criminal behavior (see the "CJ News" box in this chapter).[32] Defects in the DRD2 A1 allele gene can drive a person to seek stimulation and to engage in dangerous or threatening behavior.[33] Similarly, in 2007, researchers at the University of Texas Southwestern Medical Center discovered that mice carrying certain mutations in what is called the clock gene exhibited manic behaviors, such as recklessness and hyperactivity, and also displayed a preference for addictive substances, such as cocaine.

Unfortunately, things are not as simple as they might seem when considering the link between genes and crime. New understandings about how genes operate seem to call into question previous notions that genes are strong determinants of human behavior. Researchers in the field of neurobiology, for example, have found 17 genes, known as CREB genes, that are switched on and off in response to environmental influences. The CREB genes lay down neural pathways in the brain and form the basis of memory; the act of learning turns the CREB genes on and is made possible by them.[34] Hence, the CREB genes respond to human experience rather than determine it. One writer explains it this way: "These genes are at the mercy of our behavior, not the other way around."[35]

Biochemical Factors and Imbalances

Research in the area of nutrition has produced some limited evidence that the old maxim "You are what you eat" may contain more than a grain of truth. Some biocriminologists have linked violent or disruptive behavior to eating habits, vitamin deficiencies, genetics, and other conditions that affect body tissues.

One of the first studies to focus on chemical imbalances in the body as a cause of crime was reported in the British medical journal *Lancet* in 1943.[36] Authors of the study linked murder to hypoglycemia (low blood sugar), which is caused by too much insulin in the blood or by near-starvation diets. Some researchers believe that hypoglycemia reduces the mind's capacity to reason effectively or to judge the long-term consequences of behavior.

Allergic reactions to common foods have been reported as the cause of violence and homicide in a number of studies.[37] Foods said to produce allergic reactions in sensitive individuals, leading to a swelling of the brain and brain stem, include milk, citrus fruit, chocolate, corn, wheat, and eggs. Involvement of the central nervous system in such allergies, it has been suggested, reduces the amount of learning that occurs during childhood and may contribute to delinquency as well as to adult criminal behavior. Some studies have implicated food additives, such as monosodium glutamate, dyes, and artificial flavorings, in producing criminal behavior.[38]

Other research has found that the amount of coffee and sugar consumed by inmates is considerably greater than in the outside population.[39] Theorists have suggested that high blood levels of caffeine and sugar produce antisocial behavior.[40] It is unclear whether inmates consume more coffee due to boredom or whether those with "excitable" personalities need the kind of stimulation coffee drinking produces. On the other hand, habitual coffee drinkers in nonprison populations have not been linked to crime, and other studies, such as that conducted by Mortimer Gross of the University of Illinois, show no link between the amount of sugar consumed and hyperactivity.[41] Similarly, studies "have not yielded evidence that a change in diet will result in [a] significant reduction in aggressive or antisocial behavior" among inmate populations.[42] Nonetheless, some prison programs have limited the intake of dietary stimulants through nutritional management and the substitution of artificial sweeteners for refined sugar.

Vitamins have also been examined for their impact on delinquency. Abram Hoffer found that disruptive children consumed far less than the optimum levels of vitamins B_3 and B_6 than did

■ **heritability** A statistical construct that estimates the amount of variation in the traits of a population that is attributable to genetic factors.

nonproblem youths.[43] He claimed that the addition of these vitamins to the diets of children who were deficient in them could control unruly behavior and improve school performance.

Recently, Ap Zaalberg, an official at the Dutch Ministry of Justice, implemented a program of nutritional supplementation in 14 prisons in the Netherlands. Under the program, inmates were provided with healthy diets, devoid of added sugar, and supplemented with vitamins and important micronutrients, including fish oils.[44] Zaalberg's study, which showed a reduction in rule-breaking among prisoners,[45] followed on the heels of a nutritional experiment conducted a few years earlier in British prisons by Oxford University professor C. Bernard Gesch.[46] Gesch added dietary supplements to prisoners' diets, and reported finding a significant decrease in violent incidents and other offenses among study participants.

Hormones have also come under scrutiny as potential behavioral determinants. The male sex hormone, testosterone, has been linked to aggressiveness in males. Some studies of blood-serum levels of testosterone have shown a direct relationship[47] between the amount of hormone present and the degree of violence used by sex offenders,[48] and steroid abuse among bodybuilders has been linked to destructive urges and psychosis.[49] One 1998 study found that high levels of testosterone, especially when combined with low socioeconomic status, produced antisocial personalities, resulting in deviance and criminality.[50] In 2007, researchers at the University of Michigan at Ann Arbor found that the higher the blood levels of testosterone in young men, the more they enjoyed provoking anger in others.[51]

Research in the area of nutrition has produced some limited evidence that the old maxim "You are what you eat" may contain more than a grain of truth.

Some studies of brain chemistry have led researchers to conclude that low levels of certain neurotransmitters, especially serotonin, are directly related to a person's inability to control aggressive impulses.[52] The presence of adequate serotonin levels in the human brain buffers irritating experiences that might otherwise result in anger and aggression. Low serotonin levels may result from the ingestion of toxic pollutants, such as the metals lead and manganese, according to one study.[53] Reduced serotonin levels, say other researchers, are sometimes found in men with an extra Y chromosome.[54]

Researchers have also implicated a malfunctioning endocrine system as a cause of physical abuse, antisocial behavior, and psychopathology. One Swedish study that focused on variations in blood-serum levels of two thyroid hormones, triiodothyronine (T_3) and thyroxine (FT_4), found that elevated T_3 levels were related to alcoholism and criminality.[55] Serum levels of FT_4 were found to be negatively correlated to such behavior.

Heredity and Heritability

Studies have shown that the behavior of biological children of criminals who are adopted at birth tends to reflect the criminality of biological parents, independent of the environment in which the children were raised.[56] Also, identical twins exhibit a greater similarity in behavior than do nonidentical (or "fraternal") twins, and studies have shown that identical twins are more alike in patterns and degree of criminal involvement than are fraternal twins.[57]

One of the earliest modern-day biological perspectives on crime was proposed by James Q. Wilson and Richard Herrnstein in their book *Crime and Human Nature*, published in 1985.[58] Wilson and Herrnstein argue that inherited traits, such as maleness, aggressiveness, mesomorphic body type, and low intelligence, combine with environmental influences, including poor schools and strained family life, to produce crime. Although the authors reject a firm determinism, asserting that it is the interaction between genetics and environment that determines behavior, they do claim that children who will eventually grow up to be criminals can sometimes be identified early in their lives.

In 2011, making a genetic argument for at least some forms of callous-unemotional behavior, Nathalie Fontaine of Indiana University and colleagues reported that **heritability** (which is a statistical construct that estimates the amount of variation in the traits of a population that is attributable to genetic factors) leads to persistently high levels of such behavior among twin boys. The data on which Fontaine reported were derived from the United Kingdom's ongoing Twin Early Development Study (TEDS), which uses information gathered from over 15,000 families to explore how people change through childhood and adolescence.

Social Policy and Biological Theories

Early criminologists concerned with crime and its causes had hoped to find biological techniques that could be applied to the prevention and control of crime. If a crime-causing gene or chemical imbalance could somehow be identified, such researchers hoped that a drug or gene alteration might turn off criminal behavior.

Psychological School A perspective on criminological thought that views offensive and deviant behavior as the product of dysfunctional personality. Psychological thinkers identify the conscious, and especially the subconscious, contents of the human psyche as major determinants of behavior.

behavioral conditioning A psychological principle that holds that the frequency of any behavior can be increased or decreased through reward, punishment, and association with other stimuli.

personality The relatively stable characteristic patterns of thoughts, feelings, and behaviors that make a person unique, and that influence that person's behavior.

psychoanalysis A theory of human behavior, based on the writings of Sigmund Freud, that sees personality as a complex composite of interacting mental entities.

However, at least in the case of gene alterations, today's criminologists do not see such an easy solution. Lee Ellis and Anthony Walsh, two contemporary biosocial researchers, note that "in the case of behavior, nearly all of the effects of genes are quite indirect because they are mediated through complex chains of events occurring in the brain. This means that there are almost certainly no genes for something as complex as criminal behavior. Nevertheless," Ellis and Walsh concluded, "many genes may affect brain functioning in ways that either increase or reduce the chances of individuals learning various complex behavior patterns, including behavior patterns that happen to be so offensive to others that criminal sanctions have been instituted to minimize their recurrence."[59] In sum, it is important to recognize that genes are both the cause and the consequence of our actions—and that they do not so much *determine* human action as *enable* it.

Psychological Theories

Sociological theories are the most common approach to explaining crime today. Some, however, have pointed out that it is individuals who actually commit crimes. They argue that "ecological and societal factors must be included in any full explanation of crime," but that "individual factors always intervene between them and a criminal act."[60] For this reason, they say, "individual factors need to be at the center of any description of the causes of crime." Theories of the **Psychological School** of crime causation make certain fundamental assumptions. Among them are these:

- The individual is the primary unit of analysis.
- Personality is the major motivational element within individuals, as it is the source of drives and motives.
- Crimes result from inappropriately conditioned behavior or from abnormal, dysfunctional, or inappropriate mental processes within the personality.
- Defective or abnormal mental processes may have a variety of causes, including a diseased mind and inappropriate learning or improper conditioning—often occurring in early childhood.

Behavioral Conditioning

Two threads were woven through early psychological theories. One emphasized **behavioral conditioning**, while the other focused on **personality**—including personality disturbances and diseases of the mind. Taken together, these two foci constituted the early field of psychological criminology.

Conditioning is a psychological principle that holds that the frequency of any behavior, including criminal or deviant behavior, can be increased or decreased through reward, punishment, and association with other stimuli. The concept of conditioned behavior was popularized through the work of the Russian physiologist Ivan Pavlov (1849–1936), whose research with dogs won him the Nobel Prize in physiology and medicine in 1904. Similarly, behavioral psychologists suggest that criminal behavior, which may be inherently rewarding under many circumstances, tends to be more common in those who are able to avoid punishment when involved in rule-breaking behavior.

Freudian Psychoanalysis

The name most widely associated with the field of psychology is that of Sigmund Freud (1856–1939). Freudian theory posits the existence of an id, an ego, and a superego within the personality.[61] The id is the source of drives, which are seen as primarily sexual. The ego is a rational mental entity, which outlines paths through which the desires of the id can be fulfilled. The ego is often called the *reality principle* because of the belief that it relates desires to practical behavioral alternatives. The superego is a guiding principle, often compared to conscience, that judges the quality of the alternatives presented by the ego according to the standards of right and wrong acquired by the personality of which it is a part. Freud wrote very little about crime, but his followers, who developed the school of Freudian **psychoanalysis**, believe that crime can result from at least three conditions.

The first possible source of criminal behavior is a weak superego, which cannot responsibly control the drives that emanate from the id. Sex crimes, crimes of passion, murder, and other violent crimes are thought to follow inadequate superego development. People who lack fully developed superegos are often called *psychopaths* or *sociopaths* to indicate that they cannot see beyond their own interests. Canadian criminologist Gwynn Nettler observes that "civilization is paid for through development of a sense of guilt."[62]

Freud also created the concept of sublimation to explain the process by which one thing is symbolically substituted for another. He believed that sublimation was necessary when the direct pursuit of one's desires was not possible. Freud

■ **psychopathology** The study of pathological mental conditions—that is, mental illness.

■ **psychopath** A person with a personality disorder, especially one manifested in aggressively antisocial behavior, which is often said to be the result of a poorly developed superego.

suggested, for example, that many children learned to sublimate negative feelings about their mothers. In the society in which Freud developed his theories, mothers closely controlled the lives of their children, and Freud saw the developing child as continually frustrated in seeking freedom to act on his or her own. The strain produced by this conflict could not be directly expressed by the child because the mother also controlled rewards and punishments. Hence dislike for one's mother (which Freud thought was especially strong in boys) might show itself symbolically later in life. Crimes against women could then be explained as being committed by men expressing a symbolic hatred.

A final Freudian explanation for criminality is based on the death instinct, or Thanatos, which Freud believed each of us carries. Thanatos is the often-unrecognized desire of animate matter to return to the inanimate. Potentially self-destructive activities, including smoking, speeding, skydiving, bad diets, "picking fights," and so on, can be explained by Thanatos. The self-destructive wish may also motivate offenders to commit crimes that are themselves dangerous or self-destructive—such as burglary, assault, murder, prostitution, and drug use—or it may result in unconscious efforts to be caught. Criminals who leave evidence behind may be responding to some basic need for apprehension and punishment.

Psychopathology and Crime

From a psychiatric point of view, crime might also occur because of a diseased mind or a disordered personality—conditions that may collectively be referred to as *psychopathy*. The study of psychopathic mental conditions is called **psychopathology**. The role of a disordered personality in crime causation was central to early psychiatric theorizing. In 1944, for example, the well-known psychiatrist David Abrahamsen wrote, "When we seek to explain the riddle of human conduct in general and of antisocial behavior in particular, the solution must be sought in the personality."[63] Later, some psychiatrists went so far as to claim that criminal behavior itself is only a symptom of a more fundamental psychiatric disorder.[64]

Cleckley described the psychopath as a "moral idiot" whose central defining characteristic is the inability to empathize with others.

By the 1930s, psychiatrists had begun to develop the concept of a psychopathic personality. This personality type, which by its very definition is asocial, was fully developed by Hervey Cleckley in his 1941 book *The Mask of Sanity*.[65] Cleckley described the **psychopath**, also called a *sociopath*, as a "moral idiot" whose central defining characteristic is the inability to empathize with others. Hence it becomes possible for a psychopath to inflict pain and engage in cruelty without appreciation for the victim's suffering. Charles Manson, for example, whom some have called a psychopath, once told a television reporter, "I could take this book and beat you to death with it, and I wouldn't feel a thing. It'd be just like walking to the drugstore." According to Cleckley, psychopathic indicators appear early in life, often in the teenage years. They include lying, fighting, stealing, and vandalism. Even earlier signs may be found, according to some authors, in bed-wetting, cruelty to animals, sleepwalking, and fire setting.[66]

Although the terms *psychopath* and *criminal* are not synonymous, individuals manifesting characteristics of a psychopathic personality are likely, sooner or later, to run afoul of the law.

Although the terms *psychopath* and *criminal* are not synonymous, individuals manifesting characteristics of a psychopathic personality are likely, sooner or later, to run afoul of the law. As one writer says, "The impulsivity and aggression, the selfishness in achieving one's own immediate needs, and the disregard for society's rules and laws bring these people to the attention of the criminal justice system."[67]

Although much studied, the causes of psychopathy are unclear. Somatogenic causes, or those that are based on physiological aspects of the human organism, include (1) a malfunctioning central nervous system characterized by a low state of arousal, which drives the sufferer to seek excitement, and

AP Wide World Photos

Charles Manson, one of the most photographed criminal offenders of all time, is shown at a parole hearing years after he and his "family" shocked the world with their gruesome crimes. What can we learn from offenders like Manson?

■ **psychosis** A form of mental illness in which sufferers are said to be out of touch with reality.
■ **schizophrenic** A mentally ill individual who suffers from disjointed thinking and possibly from delusions and hallucinations.

■ **traits** Stable personality patterns that tend to endure throughout the life course and across social and cultural contexts.

(2) brain abnormalities, which may be present in most psychopaths from birth. Psychogenic causes, or those rooted in early interpersonal experiences, include the inability to form attachments to parents or other caregivers early in life, sudden separation from the mother during the first six months of life, and other forms of insecurity during the first few years of life. In short, a lack of love or the sensed inability to unconditionally depend on one central loving figure (typically the mother in most psychological literature) immediately following birth is often posited as a major psychogenic factor contributing to psychopathic development.

The Psychotic Offender

Another form of mental disorder is called **psychosis**. Psychotic people, according to psychiatric definitions, are out of touch with reality in some fundamental way. They may suffer from hallucinations, delusions, or other breaks with reality. For example, a psychotic may believe that he or she is a famous historical figure or may see spiders crawling on a bare wall. Psychoses may be either organic (that is, caused by physical damage to, or abnormalities in, the brain) or functional (that is, with no known physical cause). Psychotic people have also been classified as schizophrenic or paranoid schizophrenic. **Schizophrenics** are characterized by disordered or disjointed thinking, in which the types of logical associations they make are atypical of those of other people. Paranoid schizophrenics suffer from delusions and hallucinations.

Psychoses may lead to crime in a number of ways. Following the Vietnam War, for example, a number of former American soldiers suffering from a kind of battlefield psychosis killed friends and family members, thinking they were enemy soldiers. These men, who had been traumatized by battlefield experiences in Southeast Asia, relived their past on American streets.

Trait Theory

In 1964, Hans J. Eysenck, a British psychologist, published *Crime and Personality*, a book in which he explained crime as the result of fundamental personality characteristics, or **traits**, which he believed are largely inherited.[68] Psychological traits are stable personality patterns that tend to endure throughout the life course and across social and cultural contexts. According to trait theory, as an individual grows older or moves from one place to another, his or her personality remains largely intact—defined by the traits that comprise it. Trait theory links personality (and associated traits) to behavior, and holds that it is an individual's personality, combined with his or her intelligence and natural abilities,[69] that determines his or her behavior in a given situation.[70]

Trait theories of personality build on five basic traits known as the Big Five.

Generally speaking, trait theories of personality build on five basic traits: (1) openness to experience, (2) extraversion, (3) conscientiousness, (4) neuroticism, and (5) agreeableness. People are said to possess more or less of any one trait, and the combination of traits and the degree to which they are characteristic of an individual define that person's personality. Psychologists call these traits the Big Five, and they are referenced in most contemporary literature on personality. According to many psychologists, "the Big Five are strongly genetically influenced, and the genetic factor structure of the Big Five appears to be invariant across European, North American, and East Asian samples,"[71] which suggests that personality traits, to a greater or lesser degree, are universally shared by all peoples.

Eysenck, in contrast, believed that the degree to which just three universal supertraits are present in an individual accounts for his or her unique personality. He termed these supertraits (1) introversion/extraversion, (2) neuroticism/emotional stability, and (3) psychoticism. Eysenck, like many other psychologists, accepted the fact that personality holds steady throughout much of life, but stressed that it is largely determined by genetics. In support of his idea of the genetic basis of personality, Eysenck pointed to twin studies, which showed that identical twins display strikingly similar behavioral tendencies, whereas fraternal twins demonstrate far less likelihood of similar behaviors. Eysenck also argued that psychological conditioning occurs more rapidly in some people than in others because of biological differences, and that antisocial individuals are difficult to condition (or to socialize) because of underlying genetic characteristics. He believed that up to two-thirds of all "behavioral variance" could be strongly attributed to genetics.[72]

Of Eysenck's three personality dimensions, one in particular—psychoticism—was thought to be closely correlated with criminality at all stages.[73] According to Eysenck, psychoticism is defined by such characteristics as lack of empathy, creativeness, tough-mindedness, and antisociability. Psychoticism, added Eysenck, is also frequently characterized by hallucinations and delusions, leading to the personality type described as psychotic. Extroverts, Eysenck's second personality group that was associated with criminality, are described as carefree, dominant, and venturesome, operating with high levels of energy. "The typical extrovert," Eysenck wrote, "is sociable, likes parties, has many friends, needs to have people to talk to, and does not like reading or studying by himself."[74] Neuroticism, the third of the

■ **psychological profiling** The attempt to categorize, understand, and predict the behavior of certain types of offenders based on behavioral clues they provide.

■ **dangerousness** The likelihood that a given individual will later harm society or others. Dangerousness is often measured in terms of recidivism, or the likelihood that an individual will commit another crime within five years following arrest or release from confinement.

■ **Chicago School** A sociological approach that emphasizes demographics (the characteristics of population groups) and geographics (the mapped location of such groups relative to one another) and that sees the social disorganization that characterizes delinquency areas as a major cause of criminality and victimization.

personality characteristics Eysenck described, is said to be typical of people who are irrational, shy, moody, and emotional.

According to Eysenck, psychotics are the most likely to be criminal because they combine high degrees of emotionalism with similarly high levels of extroversion; individuals with such characteristics are especially difficult to socialize and to train and do not respond well to the external environment. Eysenck cited many studies in which children and others who harbored characteristics of psychoticism performed poorly on conditioning tests designed to measure how quickly they would respond appropriately to external stimuli. Because conscience is fundamentally a conditioned reflex, Eysenck said, an individual who does not take well to conditioning will not fully develop a conscience and will continue to exhibit the asocial behavioral traits of a very young child. In essence, criminality can be seen as a personality type characterized by self-centeredness, indifference to the suffering and needs of others, impulsiveness, and low self-control—which, taken together, lead to law-violating behavior.

Psychological Profiling

Psychological profiling is the attempt to derive a composite picture of an offender's social and psychological characteristics from the crime he or she committed and from the manner in which it was committed. Psychological profiling began during World War II as an effort by William Langer (1896–1977), a government psychiatrist hired by the Office of Strategic Services, to predict Adolf Hitler's actions.[75] Profiling in criminal investigations is based on the belief that criminality, because it is a form of behavior, can be viewed as symptomatic of the offender's personality. Psychological evaluations of crime scenes, including the analysis of evidence, are used to re-create the offender's frame of mind during the commission of the crime. A profile of the offender is then constructed to help in the investigation of suspects.

During the 1980s, the Federal Bureau of Investigation (FBI) led the movement toward psychological profiling[76] through its focus on violent sex offenses[77] and arson.[78] FBI profilers described "lust murderers" and serial arsonists. Often depicted as loners with an aversion to casual social contact, lust murderers were shown to rarely arouse suspicions in neighbors or employers. Other personality types became the focus of police efforts to arrest such offenders through a prediction of what they might do next.

New areas for psychological profiling include hostage negotiation[79] and international terrorism.[80] Right-wing terrorist groups in the United States have also been the subject of profiling efforts.

Social Policy and Psychological Theories

Crime-control policies based on psychological perspectives are primarily individualistic. They are oriented toward individualized treatment, characteristically exposing the individual offender to various forms of therapy intended to overcome the person's propensity for criminality.

Most crime-control strategies based on psychological theories emphasize assessing personal **dangerousness**, through psychological testing and other efforts to identify personality-based characteristics that predict interpersonal aggression. Although the ability to accurately predict future dangerousness is of great concern to today's policymakers, definitions of *dangerousness* are fraught with difficulty. As some authors have pointed out, "Dangerousness is not an objective quality like obesity or brown eyes; rather it is an ascribed quality like trustworthiness."[81] Hence, dangerousness is not necessarily a personality trait that is stable or easily identifiable. Even if it were, some studies of criminal careers show that involvement in crime decreases with age.[82] As one author puts it, if "criminality declines more or less uniformly with age, then many offenders will be 'over the hill' by the time they are old enough to be plausible candidates for preventive incarceration."[83]

Before crime-control policies can be based on present understandings of dangerousness, research must answer several questions: Can past behavior predict future behavior? Do former instances of criminality foretell additional ones? Are there other identifiable characteristics that violent offenders might manifest that could serve as warning signs to criminal justice decision makers faced with the dilemma of whether to release convicted felons?

Sociological Theories

Sociological theories are largely an American contribution to the study of crime causation. In the 1920s and 1930s, the famous **Chicago School** of sociology explained criminality as a product

■ **social disorganization** A condition said to exist when a group is faced with social change, uneven development of culture, maladaptiveness, disharmony, conflict, and lack of consensus.

■ **anomie** A socially pervasive condition of normlessness. Also, a disjunction between approved goals and means.

of society's impact on the individual. The structure of prevailing social arrangements, the interaction between individuals and groups, and the social environment were all seen as major determinants of criminal behavior.

Sociological perspectives on crime causation are quite diverse. Most, however, build on certain fundamental assumptions. Among them are these:

- Social groups, social institutions, the arrangements of society, and social roles all provide the proper focus for criminological study.
- Group dynamics, group organization, and subgroup relationships form the causal nexus out of which crime develops.
- The structure of society and the relative degree of social organization or **social disorganization** are important factors contributing to the prevalence of criminal behavior.

All sociological perspectives on crime share the foregoing characteristics, but particular theories may give greater or lesser weight to the following aspects of social life:

- The clash of norms and values among variously socialized groups
- Socialization and the process of association between individuals
- The existence of subcultures and varying types of opportunities

Social Ecology Theory

In the 1920s, during the early days of sociological theorizing, the University of Chicago brought together such thinkers as Robert Park, Ernest Burgess,[84] Clifford Shaw, and Henry McKay.[85] Park and Burgess recognized that Chicago, like most cities, could be mapped according to its social characteristics. Their map resembled a target with a bull's-eye in the center. Shaw and McKay adapted these concentric zones to the study of crime when they realized that the zones nearest the center of the city had the highest crime rates. In particular, zone 2 (once removed from the center) consistently showed the highest crime rate over time, regardless of the groups or nationalities inhabiting it. This "zone of transition"—so called because new immigrant groups moved into it as earlier ones became integrated into American culture and moved out—demonstrated that crime was dependent to a considerable extent on aspects of the social structure of the city itself. Structural elements identified by Shaw and McKay included poverty, illiteracy, lack of schooling, unemployment, and illegitimacy. In combination, these elements were seen to lead to social disorganization, which in turn produced crime.

Anomie Theory

The French word **anomie** has been loosely translated as a condition of "normlessness." Anomie entered the literature as a sociological concept with the writings of Émile Durkheim (1858–1917) in the late nineteenth century.[86] Robert Merton (1910–2003) applied anomie to criminology in 1938 when he used the term to describe a disjunction between socially acceptable goals and means in American society.[87]

Opportunities are not equally distributed throughout society, and some people turn to illegitimate means to achieve the goals they feel pressured to reach.

Merton believed that although the same goals and means are held out by society as desirable for everyone, they are not equally available to all. Socially approved goals in American society, for example, include wealth, status, and political power. The acceptable means to achieve these goals are education, wise investment, and hard work. Unfortunately, however, opportunities are not equally distributed throughout society, and some people turn to illegitimate means to achieve the goals they feel pressured to reach. Still others reject both acceptable goals and legitimate means of reaching them.

Merton represented his theory with a chart, shown in Table 3-2. *Conformists* accept both the goals and means that society holds out as legitimate, whereas *innovators* accept the goals but reject the means, instead using illegal means to gain money, power, and success. It is the innovators whom Merton identified as criminal. The inherent logic of the model led Merton to posit other social types. *Ritualists* are those who reject success goals but still perform their daily tasks in conformity with social expectations. They might hold regular jobs but lack the desire to advance in their careers or in other aspects of their lives. *Retreatists* reject both the goals and the means and usually drop out of society by becoming derelicts, drug users, hermits, or the like. *Rebels* constitute a special category. Their desire to replace the existing system of socially approved goals and means with some other system more to their liking makes them the revolutionaries of the theory.

CJ | NEWS

Evidence of "Warrior Gene" May Help Explain Violence

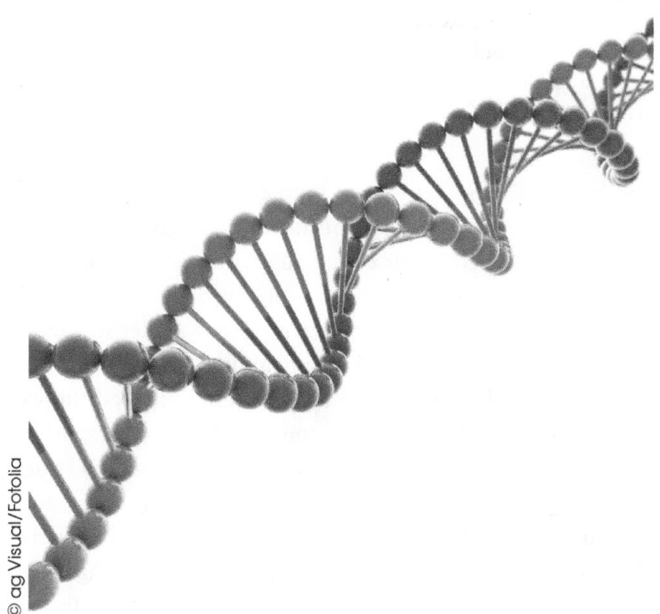

© ag Visual/Fotolia

An artist's representation of human DNA. Biosocial criminology tells us that genes may harbor certain behavioral predispositions, but that it is the interaction between genes and the environment that produces behavior. What forms might such interaction take?

As scientists study the DNA of the mass shooter at the elementary school in Newtown, Connecticut, some experts are hoping that it might lead to discovery of a gene that identifies violent criminals and helps prevent future killings. But be careful what you wish for. If a genetic link to violence were firmly identified, could it be used to falsely stigmatize people who haven't committed any crime at all? Or could such a link help convicted criminals get reduced sentences?

The argument that "my DNA made me do it" has, in fact, already been successfully used in the courts for a particular gene linked to violence. Monoamine oxidase A, known as MAOA, produces an enzyme that breaks down serotonin and other neurotransmitters in the brain that are identified with aggression. Studies have shown that a variant of the gene, known as MAOA-L, can lead to violent behavior when coupled with serious mistreatment in childhood. The link has only been identified in men, leaving women seemingly immune from the effects of this genetic anomaly.

The media nicknamed MAOA-L the "warrior gene" after it was identified as highly prevalent in a constantly warring Maori tribe. Another study found that boys with an MAOA variation were more likely to join gangs and become some of the most violent members. Researchers now know that MAOA-L may alter the very structure of the brain. Using structural magnetic resonance imaging (MRI) scanning, a 2006 study found that men with the gene variant were much more likely to have abnormalities in an area of the brain associated with behavior than were other men. Functional MRI scanning then showed that these men had difficulty inhibiting strong emotional impulses. Lawyers for violent defendants have latched on to the growing science. In the 2009 murder trial of Bradley Waldroup, who was convicted of chopping up his wife with a machete (she survived) and shooting her female friend to death, lawyers were able to demonstrate that Waldroup had the MAOA gene variant. Although the jury convicted him of murder and of attempted murder, its members concluded that his actions weren't premeditated due to the influence that his genes had on him—sparing him the death penalty. Also in 2009, an Italian appeals court cut the sentence of a convicted murderer by one year on the grounds that he, too, had the MAOA-L gene.

Judges are warming up to genetic defenses. In a 2012 study in *Science*, when trial judges were given the MAOA variant as evidence in mock trials, they tended to reduce sentences by one year in comparison to cases with no such evidence. Critics, however, argue that these defendants should be behind bars longer. Because their trait is baked into their DNA, such people say, they are likely to commit violence again. "Trying to absolve people of responsibility by attributing their behavior to their genes or environment is not new," wrote Ronald Bailey, author of the book *Liberation Biology*. He urged courts to take a tough stance against defendants with a genetic predilection to violence: "Knowing that you will be held responsible for criminal acts helps inhibit antisocial impulses that we all feel from time to time." Also, scientists want their findings to be taken with a grain of salt in the courts, arguing that science and the law have different aims. "Science is focused on understanding universal phenomena; we do this by averaging data across groups of individuals," wrote Joshua Buckholtz for the NOVA series on PBS. "Law, on the other hand, only cares about specific individual people—the individual on trial." Buckholtz observed that "Genetic differences rarely affect human behavior with the kind of selectivity or specificity desired and required by the law."

Resources: Mark Lallanilla, "Genetics May Provide Clues to Newtown Shooting," *Live Science*, December 28, 2012, http://www.livescience.com/25853-newtown-shooter-dna.html; Joshua W. Buckholtz, "Neuroprediction and Crime," *NOVA*, October 18, 2012, http://www.pbs.org/wgbh/nova/body/neuroprediction-crime.html; and Patricia Cohen, "Genetic Basis for Crime: A New Look," *New York Times*, June 19, 2011, http://www.nytimes.com/2011/06/20/arts/genetics-and-crime-at-institute-of-justice-conference.html?pagewanted=all&_r=0.

Merton believed that categories are not intentionally selected by the individuals who occupy them but rather are imposed on people by structural aspects of society. Where people live, how wealthy their families are, and what ethnic background they come from are all significant determinants of the "box" into which people are placed.

Modern writers on anomie recognize that normlessness is not likely to be expressed as criminality unless people who experience it also feel that they are capable of doing something to change their lives. As Catherine Ross and John Mirowsky put it, "A person who has high levels of normlessness and powerlessness is less likely to get in trouble with the law than a

■ **reaction formation** The process whereby a person openly rejects that which he or she wants or aspires to but cannot obtain or achieve.

■ **subculture of violence** A cultural setting in which violence is a traditional and often accepted method of dispute resolution.

■ **defensible space theory** The belief that an area's physical features may be modified and structured so as to reduce crime rates in that area and to lower the fear of victimization that residents experience.

■ **broken windows theory** A perspective on crime causation that holds that the physical deterioration of an area leads to higher crime rates and an increased concern for personal safety among residents.

TABLE 3-2 | Merton's Anomie Theory and Implied Types of Criminality

CATEGORY	GOALS	MEANS	EXAMPLES
Conformist	+	+	Law-abiding behavior
Innovator	+	–	Property offenses, white-collar crimes
Retreatist	–	–	Drug use/addiction, vagrancy, some "victimless" crimes
Ritualist	–	+	A repetitive and mundane lifestyle
Rebel	±	±	Political crime (for example, environmental activists who violate the law, violence-prone antiabortionists)

Source: Adapted from Robert K. Merton, "Social Structure and Anomie," *American Sociological Review*, Vol. 3, No. 5 (October 1938), pp. 672–682.

person who has a high level of normlessness and a high level of instrumentalism."[88]

Merton's anomie theory drew attention to the lack of equal opportunity that existed in society at the time he was writing. Although considerable efforts have been made to eradicate it, much of that inequality continues today.

Subcultural Theory

Another sociological contribution to criminological theory is the idea of a subculture. A subculture is a group of people who participate in a shared system of values and norms that are at variance with those of the larger culture. Subcultural explanations of crime posit the existence of group values that support criminal behavior. Subcultures were first recognized in the enclaves formed by immigrants who came to America during the early part of the twentieth century. Statistics have shown that certain immigrant groups had low crime rates.[89] Among them were the Scandinavians, Chinese, Dutch, Germans, and Japanese. Other immigrant groups, including the Italians, Mexicans, Puerto Ricans, and Africans, demonstrated a significantly greater propensity for involvement in crime.[90]

Albert Cohen (b. 1918) coined the term **reaction formation** to encompass the rejection of middle-class values by status-seeking lower-class youths who find they are not permitted access to approved opportunities for success.[91] In Cohen's eyes, reaction formation leads to the development of gangs and perpetuates the existence of subcultures. Walter Miller described the focal concerns of subcultural participants in terms of "trouble," "toughness," "excitement," "smartness," "fate," and "autonomy."[92] It is a focus on such concerns, Miller suggested, that leads members of criminal subcultures into violations of the law. Richard Cloward and Lloyd Ohlin proposed the existence of an illegitimate opportunity structure that permits delinquent youths to achieve in ways that are outside of legitimate avenues to success.[93]

During the 1950s, Marvin Wolfgang and Franco Ferracuti examined homicide rates in Philadelphia and found that murder was a way of life among certain groups.[94] They discovered a "wholesale" and a "retail" price for murder—which depended on who was killed and who did the killing. Killings that occurred within violent subgroups were more likely to be partially excused than those that happened elsewhere. The term **subculture of violence** has come to be associated with their work and has since been applied to other locations across the country.

Critiques of subcultural theory have been numerous. A major difficulty for these theories lies in the fact that studies involving self-reports of crime commission have shown that much violence and crime occur outside of "criminal" subcultures. Many middle- and upper-class lawbreakers are able to avoid the justice system and therefore do not enter the "official" crime statistics. Hence, criminal subcultures may be those in which crime is more visible rather than more prevalent.

Social Policy and Sociological Theories

Theoretical approaches that fault the social environment as the root cause of crime point to social action as a panacea. A contemporary example of intervention efforts based on sociological theories can be found in Targeted Outreach,[95] a program operated by the Boys and Girls Clubs of America. The program's philosophy is based on studies undertaken at the University of Colorado that showed that at-risk youths could be effectively diverted from the juvenile justice system through the provision of positive alternatives. The program recruits at-risk youngsters—many as young as seven years old—and diverts them into activities that

CJ | ISSUES

The Physical Environment and Crime

Social ecology theory—an outgrowth of the Chicago School of sociological thought, which flourished during the 1920s and 1930s—posited a link between physical location and crime. A modern perspective, called *crime prevention through environmental design* (CPTED), bears a strong resemblance to such earlier ecological theories. CPTED, which was first formulated in the 1960s and 1970s, focuses on the settings in which crimes occur and on techniques for reducing vulnerability within those settings. Because defensible space concepts are being increasingly applied to the design of physical facilities, including housing, parking garages, public buildings, and even entire neighborhoods, it is highly likely that applications of CPTED will accelerate throughout the twenty-first century.

Second-generation **defensible space theory**, upon which contemporary CPTED is built, developed around 1980 and considered more carefully how the impact of physical features on fear and victimization depends on other social and cultural features in the setting. Second-generation defensible space theory employed the **broken windows theory**, which holds that physical deterioration and an increase in unrepaired buildings lead to increased concerns for personal safety among area residents. Heightened concerns, in turn, lead to further decreases in maintenance and repair and to increased delinquency, vandalism, and crime among local residents, which spawn even further deterioration both in a sense of safety and in the physical environment. Offenders from other neighborhoods are then increasingly attracted by the area's perceived vulnerability.

Research on CPTED has shown environmental design to be effective in lowering crime and crime-related public-order problems. Effective use of CPTED to alter features of the physical environment can affect potential offenders' perceptions about a possible crime site, their evaluations of the opportunities associated with that site, and the availability and visibility of one or more natural guardians at or near the site. CPTED is based on the belief that offenders decide whether to commit a crime in a particular location after they evaluate the area's features, including (1) the ease of entry to the area, (2) the visibility of the target to others—that is, the chance of being seen, (3) the attractiveness or vulnerability of the target, (4) the likelihood that criminal behavior will be challenged or thwarted if discovered, and (5) the ease of egress—that is, the ability to quickly and easily leave the area once the crime has been committed.

According to the National Institute of Justice, CPTED suggests four approaches to making a location more resistant to crime and to crime-related public-order problems:

- *Housing design or block layout*—making it more difficult to commit crimes by (1) reducing the availability of crime targets, (2) removing barriers that prevent easy detection of potential offenders or of an offense in progress, and (3) increasing physical obstacles to committing a crime.
- *Land use and circulation patterns*—creating safer use of neighborhood space by reducing routine exposure of potential offenders to crime targets. This can be accomplished through careful attention to walkways, paths, streets, traffic patterns, and locations and hours of operation of public spaces and facilities. Street closings or revised traffic patterns that decrease vehicular volume may, under some conditions, encourage residents to better maintain the sidewalks and streets in front of their houses.
- *Territorial features*—encouraging the use of territorial markers or fostering conditions that will lead to more extensive marking to indicate that the block or site is occupied by vigilant residents. Sponsoring cleanup and beautification contests and creating controllable, semiprivate outdoor locations may encourage such activities. This strategy focuses on small-scale, private, and semipublic sites, usually within predominantly residential locales. It is most relevant at the street-block level and below. It enhances the chances that residents themselves will generate semifixed features that demonstrate their involvement in and watchfulness over a particular delimited location.
- *Physical maintenance*—controlling physical deterioration to reduce offenders' perceptions that areas are vulnerable to crime and that residents are so fearful they would do nothing to stop a crime. Physical improvements may reduce the signals of vulnerability and increase commitment to joint protective activities. Physical deterioration, in all probability, not only influences the cognition and behavior of potential offenders but also shapes how residents behave and what they think about other residents.

For additional information on CPTED via the Crime Mapping Research Center, see **http://www.justicestudies.com/pubs/cpted.pdf**.

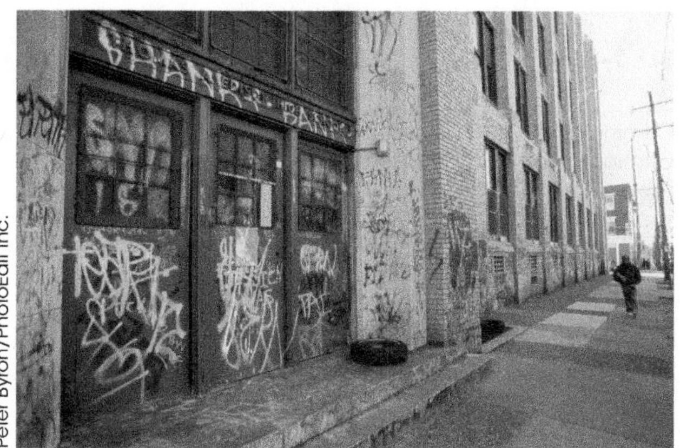

Peter Byron/PhotoEdit Inc.

A run-down city street. To explain crime, criminologists sometimes use the "broken windows" approach, which says that neighborhood deterioration leads to rising crime rates. Similarly, poverty, unemployment, a relative lack of formal education, and low skill levels, which often characterize inner-city populations, seem to be linked to criminality. Why?

References: Derek J. Paulsen and Matthew B. Robinson, *Spatial Aspects of Crime: Theory and Practice* (Boston: Allyn and Bacon, 2004); Oscar Newman, *Defensible Space* (New York: Macmillan, 1972); Oscar Newman, *Creating Defensible Space* (Washington, DC: HUD, 1996); James Q. Wilson and George Kelling, "Broken Windows," *Atlantic Monthly*, March 1982; Dan Fleissner and Fred Heinzelmann, *Crime Prevention through Environmental Design and Community Policing* (Washington, DC: NIJ, 1996); Ralph B. Taylor and Adele V. Harrell, *Physical Environment and Crime* (Washington, DC: NIJ, 1996); Mary S. Smith, *Crime Prevention through Environmental Design in Parking Facilities* (Washington, DC: NIJ, 1996); and Corey L. Gordon and William Brill, *The Expanding Role of Crime Prevention through Environmental Design in Premises Liability* (Washington, DC: NIJ, 1996).

■ **social process theory** A perspective on criminological thought that highlights the process of interaction between individuals and society. Most social process theories highlight the role of social learning.

are intended to promote a sense of belonging, competence, usefulness, and power. Social programs like Targeted Outreach are intended to change the cultural conditions and societal arrangements that are thought to lead people into crime.

Social Process Theories

Whereas psychological approaches to crime causation seek to uncover aspects of the personality hidden even from the mind in which they reside, and sociological theories look to institutional arrangements in the social world to explain crime, social process approaches focus on the interaction between individuals and society. Most **social process theories** highlight the role of social learning. They build on the premise that behavior—both "good" and "bad"—is learned, and they suggest that "bad" behavior can be unlearned. Social process theories are often the most attractive to contemporary policymakers because they demand that responsibility be placed on the offender for actively participating in rehabilitation efforts and because they are consistent with popular cultural and religious values centered on teaching right from wrong.

Differential Association Theory

In 1939, Edwin Sutherland (1883–1950) published the third edition of his *Principles of Criminology*. It contained, for the first time, a formalized statement of his theory of differential association, a perspective that Sutherland based on the "laws of imitation" described by Gabriel Tarde (1843–1904), a French sociologist.

The theory of differential association explains crime as a natural consequence of the interaction with criminal lifestyles. Sutherland suggested that children raised in crime-prone environments were often isolated and unable to experience the values that would otherwise lead to conformity. Differential association provides the basis for much research in modern criminology.[96] Even popular stories of young drug pushers, for instance, often refer to the fact that inner-city youths imitate what they see. Some residents of poverty-ridden ghettos learn quickly that fast money can be made in the illicit drug trade, and they tend to follow the examples of material "success" that they see around them.

Differential association views crime as the product of socialization and sees it as being acquired by criminals according to the same principles that guide the learning of law-abiding behavior in conformists. Differential association removes criminality from the framework of the abnormal and places it squarely within a general perspective applicable to all behavior. In the 1947 edition of his text, Sutherland wrote, "Criminal behavior is a part of human behavior, has much in common with non-criminal behavior, and must be explained within the same general framework as any other human behavior."[97] A study of the tenets of differential association (listed in Table 3-3) shows that Sutherland believed that even the sources of behavioral motivation are much the same for conformists and criminals—that is, both groups strive for money and success but choose different paths to the same goal.

However, differential association theory fails to explain why people have the associations they do and why some associations affect certain individuals more than others. Why, for example, are most prison guards unaffected by their constant association with offenders, while a few take advantage of their position to smuggle contraband? The theory has also been criticized for being so general and imprecise as to allow for little testing.[98] Complete testing of the theory would require that all of the associations a person has ever had be recorded and analyzed from the standpoint of the individual—a clearly impossible task.

Other theorists continue to build on Sutherland's early work. Robert Burgess and Ronald Akers, for example, have

TABLE 3-3 | Sutherland's Principles of Differential Association

1. Criminal behavior is learned.
2. Criminal behavior is learned in interaction with others in a process of communication.
3. The principal part of the learning of criminal behavior occurs within intimate personal groups.
4. When criminal behavior is learned, the learning includes (a) techniques of committing the crime, which are sometimes very complicated, sometimes very simple, and (b) the specific direction of motives, drives, rationalizations, and attitudes.
5. The specific direction of motives and drives is learned from definitions of the legal codes as favorable or unfavorable.
6. A person becomes delinquent because of an excess of definitions favorable to violations of law over definitions unfavorable to violations of law.
7. Differential associations may vary in frequency, duration, priority, and intensity.
8. The process of learning criminal behavior by association with criminal and anticriminal patterns involves all the mechanisms that are involved in any other learning.
9. Although criminal behavior is an expression of general needs and values, it is not explained by those general needs and values because noncriminal behavior is an expression of the same needs and values.

■ **social learning theory** A psychological perspective that says that people learn how to behave by modeling themselves after others whom they have the opportunity to observe.

■ **containment** The aspects of the social bond and of the personality that act to prevent individuals from committing crimes and engaging in deviance.

constructed a differential association–reinforcement theory that seeks to integrate Sutherland's original propositions with the work of American psychologist B. F. Skinner's work on conditioning.[99] Burgess and Akers suggest that although values and behavior patterns are learned in association with others, the primary mechanism through which such learning occurs is operant conditioning. Reinforcement is the key, they say, to understanding any social learning as it takes place. The name **social learning theory** has been widely applied to the work of Burgess and Akers. It is somewhat of a misnomer, however, because the term can easily encompass a wide range of approaches and should not be limited to one specific combination of the ideas found in differential association and reinforcement theory.

Restraint Theories

As we have seen throughout this chapter, most criminological theories posit a cause of crime.[100] Some theories, however, focus less on causes than on constraints—those forces that keep people from committing a crime. These theories are called *restraint theories*. However, because they focus primarily on why people do not break the law, restraint theories provide only half of the causal picture. They are especially weak in identifying the social-structural sources of motivations to commit crimes.[101] Also, the ways in which bonds with different institutions interact with one another and with personal attributes, as well as the variety of bonds that operate throughout the life cycle, have yet to be clarified.[102]

Containment Theory

Containment theory, a type of restraint theory offered by Walter Reckless (1899–1988), assumes that all of us are subject to inducements to crime.[103] Some of us resist these "pushes" toward criminal behavior, whereas others do not. The difference, according to Reckless, can be found in forces that contain, or control, behavior.

Reckless described two types of **containment**: outer and inner. Outer containment depends on social roles and the norms and expectations that apply to them. People who occupy significant roles in society find themselves insulated from deviant tendencies. A corporate executive, for example, is less apt to hold up a liquor store than is a drifter. The difference, according to Reckless, is not due solely to income, but also to the pressure the executive feels to conform.

Inner containment involves a number of factors, such as conscience, a positive self-image, a tolerance for frustration, and aspirations that are in line with reality. Reckless believed that inner containment is more powerful than outer containment; inner containment functions even in secret. For example, an inner-directed person who comes across a lost purse feels compelled to locate its rightful owner and return it. If theft or greed crosses the mind of an inner-directed person, he will say to himself, "I'm not that kind of person. That would be wrong."

Reckless studied small close-knit societies—including the Hutterites, Mennonites, and Amish—in developing his theory. He realized that the "containment of behavior . . . is . . . maximized under conditions of isolation and homogeneity of culture, class, and population."[104] Hence its applicability to modern American society, with its considerable heterogeneity of values and perspectives, is questionable.

Social Control Theory

Travis Hirschi emphasized the bond between individuals and society as the primary operative mechanism in his *social control theory*.[105] Hirschi identified four components of that bond: (1) emotional attachments to significant others, (2) a commitment to appropriate lifestyles, (3) involvement or immersion in conventional values, and (4) a belief in the "correctness" of social obligations and the rules of the larger society. These components act as social controls on deviant and criminal behavior; as they weaken, social control suffers, and the likelihood of crime and deviance increases. Using self-reports of delinquency from high school students in California, Hirschi concluded that youngsters who were less attached to teachers and parents and who had few positive attitudes about their own accomplishments were more likely to engage in crime and deviance than were others.[106]

Neutralization Techniques

Complementing restraint theory is the *neutralization approach* of Gresham Sykes and David Matza.[107] The neutralization approach centers on rationalizations that allow offenders to shed feelings of guilt and responsibility for their behavior. Sykes and Matza believed that most people drift into and out of criminal behavior but will not commit a crime unless they have available to them techniques of neutralization. Their study primarily concerned juveniles for whom, they suggested, neutralization techniques provided only a temporary respite from guilt. That respite, however, lasted long enough to avoid the twinges of conscience while a crime was being committed. Neutralization techniques include the following:

- Denial of responsibility ("I'm a product of my background.")
- Denial of injury ("No one was really hurt.")
- Denial of the victim ("They deserved it.")
- Condemnation of the condemners ("The cops are corrupt.")
- Appeal to higher loyalties ("I did it for my friends.")

■ **labeling theory** A social process perspective that sees continued crime as a consequence of the limited opportunities for acceptable behavior that follow from the negative responses of society to those defined as offenders.

■ **moral enterprise** The process undertaken by an advocacy group to have its values legitimated and embodied in law.

■ **social development theory** An integrated view of human development that points to the process of interaction among and between individuals and society as the root cause of criminal behavior.

■ **life course perspective** An approach to explaining crime and deviance that investigates developments and turning points in the course of a person's life.

Like containment theory, restraint theories tend to depend on a general agreement as to values, or they assume that offenders are simply conformists who suffer temporary lapses. Neutralization techniques, by definition, are needed only when the delinquent has been socialized into middle-class values or where conscience is well developed. Even so, neutralization techniques do not in themselves explain crime. Such techniques are available to us all, if we make only a slight effort to conjure them up. The real question is why some people readily allow proffered neutralizations to affect their behavior, while others effortlessly discount them.

Labeling Theory

As we saw earlier in this chapter, the worth of any theory of behavior is proved by how well it reflects the reality of the social world. In practice, however, theoretical perspectives find acceptance in the academic environment via a number of considerations. **Labeling theory**, for example, became fashionable in the 1960s. Its popularity may have been due more to the cultural environment into which it was introduced rather than to any inherent quality of the theory itself.

Labeling theory was first introduced by Frank Tannenbaum (1893–1969) in 1938 under the rubric of *tagging*.[108] He wrote, "The young delinquent becomes bad because he is defined as bad and because he is not believed if he is good." He went on to say, "The process of making the criminal, therefore, is a process of tagging. . . . It becomes a way of stimulating . . . and evolving the very traits that are complained of. . . . The person becomes the thing he is described as being."[109] Tannenbaum focused on society's power to *define* an act or an individual as bad and drew attention to the group need for a scapegoat in explaining crime. The search for causes inherent in individuals was not yet exhausted, however, and Tannenbaum's theory fell mostly on deaf ears.

By the 1960s, the social and academic environments in America had changed, and the issue of responsibility was seen more in terms of the group than the individual. In his book *Outsiders*, published in 1963, Howard Becker pointed out that criminality is not a quality inherent in an act or in a person. Crime, said Becker, results from a social definition, through law, of unacceptable behavior. That definition arises through **moral enterprise**, by which groups on both sides of an issue debate and eventually legislate their notion of what is moral and what is not. Becker wrote, "The central fact about deviance [is that] it is created by society. . . . Social groups create deviance by making the rules whose infraction constitutes deviance."[110]

The criminal label, however, produces consequences for labeled individuals that may necessitate continued criminality. In describing the criminal career, Becker wrote, "To be labeled a criminal one need only commit a single criminal offense. . . . Yet the word carries a number of connotations specifying auxiliary traits characteristic of anyone bearing the label."[111] The first time a person commits a crime, the behavior is called *primary deviance* and may be a merely transitory form of behavior.

However, in the popular mind, a "known" criminal is not to be trusted, should not be hired because of the potential for crimes on the job, and would not be a good candidate for the military, marriage, or any position requiring responsibility. Society's tendency toward such thinking, Becker suggested, closes legitimate opportunities, ensuring that the only new behavioral alternatives available to the labeled criminal are deviant ones. Succeeding episodes of criminal behavior are seen as a form of secondary deviance that eventually becomes stabilized in the behavioral repertoire and self-concept of the labeled person.[112]

Labeling theory can be critiqued along a number of dimensions. First, it is not really a "theory" in that labeling does not uncover the genesis of criminal behavior. It is more useful in describing how such behavior continues than in explaining how it originates. Second, labeling theory does not recognize the possibility that the labeled individual may make successful attempts at reform and may shed the negative label. Finally, the theory does not provide an effective way of dealing with offenders. Should people who commit crimes not be arrested and tried so as to avoid the consequences of negative labels? It would be exceedingly naïve to suggest that all repeat criminal behavior would cease, as labeling theory might predict, if people who commit crimes are not officially "handled" by the system.

Social Development and the Life Course

Some of the most recent perspectives on crime causation belong to a subcategory of social process thought called **social development theory**. According to the social development perspective, human development occurs simultaneously on many levels, including the psychological, biological, familial, interpersonal, cultural, societal, and ecological levels. Hence social development theories tend to be integrated theories—that is, theories that combine various points of view on the process of development. Theories that fall into this category, however, highlight the process of interaction between individuals and society as the root cause of criminal behavior. In particular, they emphasize that a critical period of transition occurs in a person's life as he or she moves from childhood to adulthood.

One social development approach is the dual taxonomy theory of offending offered by Terrie Moffitt in the 1990s.[113] Moffitt identifies two types of offenders: *adolescent limited offenders* and *life course persistent offenders*. The first type, adolescent limited offenders, are prone to antisocial behavior only during adolescence; the second type, life course persisters, continue to reoffend throughout life. Moffitt was interested in explaining the continuity and stability of antisocial behavior, and noted that life course persisters evidence significant antisocial attitudes and behavior early on in life. Moffitt's theory, while it is concerned with the development of antisocial behavior, combines biological factors (genetic influences, brain injury, and the like) with social ones (childhood abuse and neglect, bad parenting, and other factors) and proposes that initial biological predispositions can combine with a negative childhood environment to produce antisocial behavior that persists over time.

Another social development perspective of special significance is the **life course perspective**. According to Robert Sampson and John Laub, who named the life course perspective in 1993, criminal behavior typically follows an identifiable pattern throughout a person's life cycle.[114] In the lives of those who eventually become criminal, crime-like or deviant behavior is relatively rare during early childhood, tends to begin as sporadic instances during early adolescence, becomes more common during the late-teen and early-adult years, and then gradually diminishes as the person gets older.

Initial biological predispositions can combine with a negative childhood environment to produce antisocial behavior that persists over time.

Sampson and Laub also use the idea of *transitions* in the life course, or turning points that identify significant events in a person's life and represent the opportunity for people to turn either away from or toward deviance and crime. An employer who gives an employee a second chance, for example, may provide a unique opportunity that helps determine the future course of that person's life. Similarly, the principle of *linked lives*, also common to life course theories, highlights the fact that no one lives in isolation. Events in the life course are constantly being influenced by family members, friends, acquaintances, employers, teachers, and so on. Not only might such influences determine the life course of any given individual, but they are active throughout the life course. Figure 3-3 diagrams some of the life

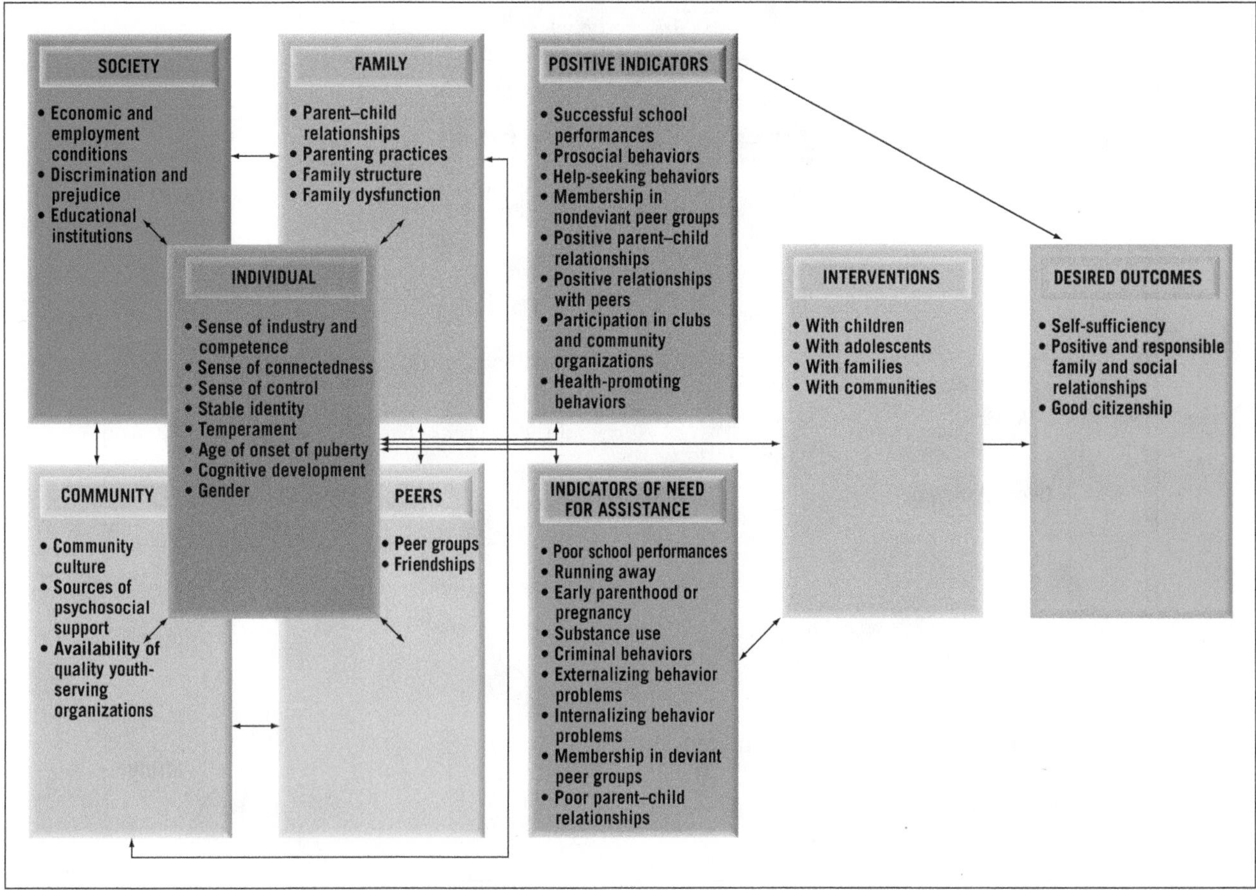

FIGURE 3-3 | A Conceptual Model of Adolescent Development

Source: Family and Youth Services Bureau, *Understanding Youth Development: Promoting Positive Pathways of Growth* (Washington, DC: U.S. Dept. of Health and Human Services, 2000).

course influences experienced by most adolescents. Also shown in the diagram are desired outcomes and positive and negative indicators of development.

In 1986, the federal Office of Juvenile Justice and Delinquency Prevention (OJJDP) began funding a study of life pathways as they lead to criminality. The Program of Research on the Causes and Correlates of Delinquency continues to produce results.[115] Researchers have been examining how delinquency, violence, and drug use develop within and are related to various social contexts, including the family, peer groups, schools, and the surrounding community. To date, the study has identified three distinct pathways to delinquency, which are shown in Figure 3-4. These pathways are not mutually exclusive and can sometimes converge:

- The *authority conflict pathway*, along which children begin to move during their early years (as early as three or four years old), involves stubborn behavior and resistance to parental authority. Defiance of authority begins around age 11, and authority avoidance (that is, truancy, running away) begins about the same time.
- The *covert pathway*, which starts around age ten with minor covert acts such as shoplifting and lying, quickly progresses to acts of vandalism involving property damage. Moderate to severe delinquency frequently begins a year or two later.
- The *overt pathway* is marked by minor aggression, such as bullying, that develops around age 11 or 12. The overt pathway leads to fighting and physical violence during the teenage years and tends to eventuate in serious violent criminality that may include rape, robbery, and assault.

A similar study is under way at the Project on Human Development in Chicago Neighborhoods (PHDCN), mentioned earlier in this chapter. PHDCN researchers are "tracing how

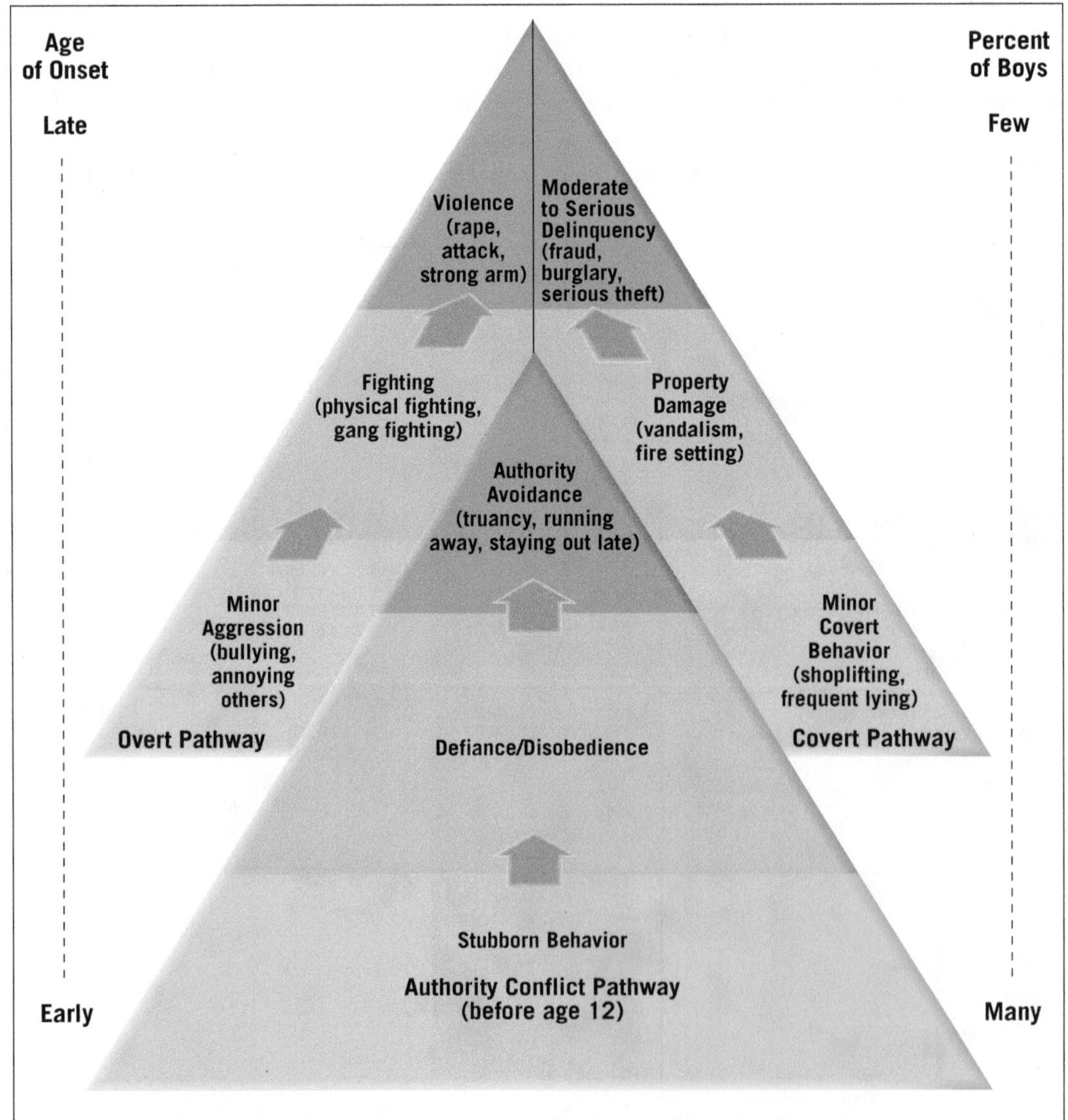

FIGURE 3-4 | Three Pathways to Disruptive Behavior and Delinquency

Source: Barbara Tatem Kelley et al., *Developmental Pathways in Boys' Disruptive and Delinquent Behavior* (Washington, DC: Office of Juvenile Justice and Delinquency Prevention, 1997).

■ **conflict perspective** A theoretical approach that holds that crime is the natural consequence of economic and other social inequities. Conflict theorists highlight the stresses that arise among and within social groups as they compete with one another for resources and for survival. The social forces that result are viewed as major determinants of group and individual behavior, including crime.

■ **radical criminology** A conflict perspective that sees crime as engendered by the unequal distribution of wealth, power, and other resources, which adherents believe is especially characteristic of capitalist societies.

criminal behavior develops from birth to age 32."[116] Participating researchers come from a variety of scientific backgrounds and include psychiatrists, developmental psychologists, sociologists, criminologists, physicians, educators, statisticians, and public health officials. The study focuses on the influence of communities, peers, families, and health-related, cognitive, and emotional factors to decipher the lines along which crime and delinquency are likely to develop. Learn more about the OJJDP's causes and correlates study at **http://www.justicestudies.com/pubs/ccdp.pdf**, and find out more about the PHDCN project at **http://ccf.tc.columbia.edu/neighborhood03.html**.

Conflict Theories

Basic to the **conflict perspective** is the belief that conflict is a fundamental aspect of social life and can never be fully resolved. From the conflict point of view, formal agencies of social control at best merely coerce the unempowered or the disenfranchised to comply with the rules established by those in power. Laws become tools of the powerful, tools that are useful in keeping others from wresting control over important social institutions. Social order, rather than being the result of any consensus or process of dispute resolution, rests on the exercise of power through law. The conflict perspective can be described in terms of four key elements:[117]

- Society is composed of diverse social groups, and diversity is based on distinctions that people hold to be significant, such as gender, sexual orientation, and social class.
- Conflict among groups is unavoidable because of differing interests and differing values. Hence conflict is inherent in social life.
- The fundamental nature of group conflict centers on the exercise of political power. Political power is the key to the accumulation of wealth and to other forms of power.
- Laws are the tools of power and further the interests of those powerful enough to make them. Laws allow those in control to gain what they define (through the law) as legitimate access to scarce resources and to deny (through the law) such access to the politically disenfranchised.

Radical Criminology

Criminological theory took a new direction during the 1960s and 1970s, brought about in part by the turmoil that characterized American society during that period. **Radical criminology** placed the blame for criminality and deviant behavior squarely on officially sanctioned cultural and economic arrangements. The distribution of wealth and power in society was held to be the primary cause of criminal behavior, especially among those who were disenfranchised. Poverty and discrimination were seen to lead to frustration and pent-up hostilities that were expressed through murder, rape, theft, and other crimes.

Radical criminology had its roots in early conflict theories and in the thought of Dutch criminologist Willem Bonger (1876–1940). Some authors have distinguished between conflict theory and radical criminology by naming them "conservative conflict theory" and "radical conflict theory," respectively.[118] The difference between the two theories, however, is mostly in the rhetoric of the times. Conservative conflict theories held that conflict was a natural part of any society and that struggles for power and control would always occur. "Losers" of conflicts were defined as "criminal," and constraints on their behavior would be

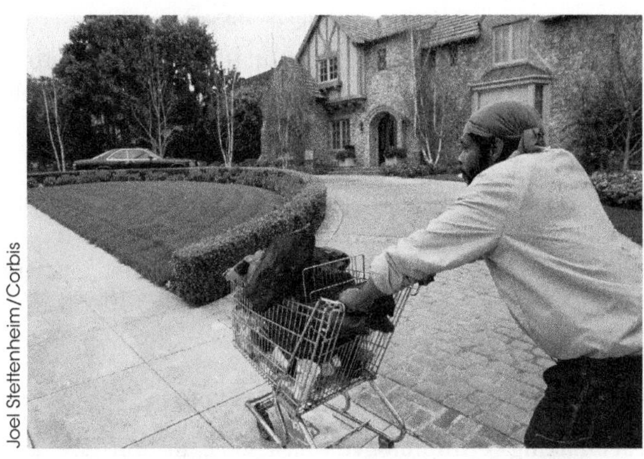
Joel Stettenheim/Corbis

A homeless man walking by an expensive home. Radical criminologists claim that the inequitable distribution of wealth in society produces frustrations and pent-up hostilities that lead to criminality. In this view, the powerful use the criminal law as a tool to maintain their privileged place in the social world. Do you agree? Why or why not?

■ **peacemaking criminology** A perspective that holds that crime-control agencies and the citizens they serve should work together to alleviate social problems and human suffering and thus reduce crime.

legislated. Characteristic of this perspective are the approaches of Austin Turk[119] (b. 1934) and George Vold (1896–1967). An even earlier conflict perspective can be found in the culture conflict notions of Thorsten Sellin (1896–1994), who was concerned with the clash of immigrant values and traditions with those of established American culture.[120]

Radical criminology went a step further. It recognized that the struggle to control resources is central to society, and it encompassed the notion that the law is a tool of the powerful. The focus of radical criminology, however, was capitalism and the evils that capitalism was believed to entail. The ideas of Karl Marx (1818–1883) entered the field of criminology through the writings of William Chambliss[121] (b. 1933) and Richard Quinney[122] (b. 1934). According to Marx, the labor of the lower classes provides the basis for the accumulated wealth of the upper classes, and the lower classes are always exploited by the "owners" in society. The poor were trained to believe that capitalism was in their best interests and the working classes suffered under the consequences of a "false class consciousness" perpetrated by the powerful. Marx believed that only when the exploited workers realized their exploitation would they rebel and change society for the better.

American radical criminology built on the ideals of the 1960s and charged that the "establishment," controlled by the upper classes, perverted justice through the unequal application of judicial sanctions. As David Greenberg observes, "Many researchers attributed the overrepresentation of blacks and persons from impoverished family backgrounds in arrest and conviction statistics to the discriminatory practices of the enforcement agencies. It was not that the poor stole more, but rather that when they did, the police were more likely to arrest them."[123] Conflict theories of criminality face the difficulty of realistic implementation. Radical criminology, in particular, is flawed by its narrow emphasis on capitalist societies. It fails to recognize adequately the role of human nature in the creation of social classes and in the perpetuation of the struggle for control of resources. Radical criminology implies that a utopian social arrangement—perhaps communism—would eliminate most crime. Such a belief is contrary to historical experience: A close look at any contemporary communist society will reveal both social conflict and crime.

Peacemaking Criminology

Peacemaking criminology, which some theorists see as a mature expression of earlier conflict theories, holds that crime-control agencies and the citizens they serve should work together to alleviate social problems and human suffering and thus reduce crime.[124] Criminology as peacemaking has its roots in ancient Christian and Eastern philosophies, as well as in traditional conflict theory. Peacemaking criminology, which includes the notion of service and has also been called *compassionate criminology*, suggests that "compassion, wisdom, and love are essential for understanding the suffering of which we are all a part, and for practicing a criminology of nonviolence."[125] Peacemaking criminology also holds that official agents of social control need to work with both the victimized and the victimizers to achieve a new world order that is more just and fair to all who live in it. In a fundamental sense, peacemaking criminologists exhort their colleagues to transcend personal dichotomies to end the political and ideological divisiveness that separates people. "If we ourselves cannot know peace . . . how will our acts disarm hatred and violence?" they ask.[126]

Criminology as peacemaking has its roots in ancient Christian and Eastern philosophies, as well as in traditional conflict theory.

Peacemaking criminology was popularized by the works of Harold Pepinsky[127] and Richard Quinney[128] beginning in 1986. Both Pepinsky and Quinney restate the problem of crime control from one of "how to stop crime" to one of "how to make peace" within society and among citizens and criminal justice agencies. Peacemaking criminology draws attention to many issues, among them the perpetuation of violence through the continuation of social policies based on dominant forms of criminological theory, the role of education in peacemaking, "common sense theories of crime," crime control as human rights enforcement, and conflict resolution within community settings.[129]

Social Policy and Conflict Theories

Because radical and conflict criminologists view social inequality as the cause of crime, many suggest that the only way to achieve real change in the rate of crime is through revolution. Revolution—because it holds the promise of greater equality for underrepresented groups and because it mandates a redistribution of wealth and power—is thought necessary for any lasting reduction in crime.

Some contemporary writers on radical criminology, however, have attempted to address the issue of what can be done under our current system, because they recognize that a sudden and total reversal of existing political arrangements within the United States is highly unlikely. Hence they have begun to focus on promoting "middle-range policy alternatives" to the present system, including "equal justice in the bail system, the abolition of mandatory sentences, prosecution of corporate crimes, increased employment opportunities,

■ **feminist criminology** A developing intellectual approach that emphasizes gender issues in criminology.

and promoting community alternatives to imprisonment."[130] Likewise, programs to reduce prison overcrowding, efforts to highlight injustices within the current system, the elimination of racism and other forms of inequality in the handling of both victims and offenders, growing equality in criminal justice system employment, and the like are all frequently mentioned as mid-range strategies for bringing about a justice system that is fairer and closer to the radical ideal.

Raymond Michalowski summarizes the policy directions envisioned by today's radical criminologists when he says, "We cannot be free from the crimes of the poor until there are no more poor; we cannot be free from domination of the powerful until we reduce the inequalities that make domination possible; and we cannot live in harmony with others until we begin to limit the competition for material advantage over others that alienates us from one another."[131]

Emergent Perspectives

A number of new and developing criminological perspectives deserve special mention. They include feminist, biosocial, and postmodern criminology. Biosocial criminology has already been discussed earlier in this chapter. Now, however, we will briefly discuss feminist and postmodern criminology.

Feminist Criminology

As some writers in the developing field of **feminist criminology** have observed, "Women have been virtually invisible in criminological analysis until recently and much theorizing has proceeded as though criminality is restricted to men."[132] Another puts it this way: "[Traditional] criminological theory assumes a woman is like a man."[133] Feminist criminologists are now working to change long-cherished notions of crime and of criminal justice so that the role of women in both crime causation and crime control might be better appreciated.[134]

One of the first writers to attempt a definitive explanation of the criminality of women was Otto Pollak. Pollak's book, *The Criminality of Women*,[135] written in 1950, suggested that women commit the same number of offenses as men but that most of their criminality is hidden. Pollak claimed that women's roles at the time, primarily those of homemaker and mother, served to disguise their criminal undertakings. He also proposed that chivalrous treatment by a male-dominated justice system acted to bias every stage of criminal justice processing in favor of women. Hence, according to Pollak, although women are just as criminal as men, they are rarely arrested, tried, or imprisoned. In fact, although the criminality of women may approach or exceed that of men in selected offense categories, today it is safe to say that Pollak was incorrect in his assessment of the degree of female criminality; overall, women commit far fewer crimes than men.

Early works in the field of feminist criminology include Freda Adler's *Sisters in Crime*[136] and Rita Simon's *Women and Crime*.[137] Both books were published in 1975, and in them the authors claimed that the existing divergences in crime rates between men and women were due primarily to socialization rather than biology. Women, claimed these authors, were taught to believe in personal limitations, faced reduced socioeconomic opportunities, and, as a result, suffered from lowered aspirations. As gender equality increased, they said, it could be expected that male and female criminality would take on similar characteristics. More recent researchers, however, have not found this to be true; substantial differences between the criminality of men and women remain, even as gender equality grows.[138]

Contemporary feminist thinking in criminology is represented by the works of writers like Kathleen Daly and Meda Chesney-Lind.[139] Daly and Chesney-Lind emphasize the need for a "gender-aware" criminology and stress the usefulness of applying feminist thinking to criminological analysis. Gender, say these writers, is a central organizing principle of contemporary life. Feminist criminology suggests that theories of crime causation and prevention must include women and that more research on gender-related issues in the field is badly needed. Additionally, some authors say, "Criminologists should begin to appreciate that their discipline and its questions are a product of white, economically privileged men's experiences."[140] They suggest that rates of female criminality, which are lower than those of males, may show that criminal behavior is not as "normal" as once thought. Because modern-day criminological perspectives were mostly developed by white middle-class males, the propositions and theories they advance fail to take into consideration women's "ways of knowing."[141] Hence the fundamental challenge posed by feminist criminology is this: Do existing theories of crime causation apply as well to women as they do to men? Or, as Daly and Chesney-Lind put it, given the current situation in theory development, "do theories of men's crime apply to women?"[142]

Recent perspectives on female criminality stress that "a key to understanding and responding to women as offenders is understanding their status as crime victims."[143] Psychologist Cathy Spatz Widom, for example, examined the life cycle of female offenders, looking for links between childhood abuse and neglect and later criminality. Widom suggests that the successful socialization of girls can be "derailed" by early victimization through mechanisms such as "running away, deficits in cognitive ability and achievement, growing up without traditional social controls, engaging in relationships with deviant or delinquent individuals, and failing to learn the social and psychological skills necessary for successful adult development."[144]

■ **postmodern criminology** A branch of criminology that developed after World War II and that builds on the tenets of postmodern social thought.
■ **deconstructionist theory** One of the emerging approaches that challenges existing criminological perspectives to debunk them and that works toward replacing them with concepts more applicable to the postmodern era.

Contemporary statistics tell us that although females make up 51% of the population of the United States, they are arrested for only 19.5% of all violent crimes and 37.6% of property crimes. The relatively limited involvement of women in the FBI's eight major crimes can be seen in Table 3-4. Data show that the number of female offenders is increasing faster than the number of male offenders, however. Between 1970 and 2000, for example, the number of crimes committed by men grew by 46%, while crimes committed by women increased 144%. Violent crimes by men increased 82% during the period; by women, 260%. Property crimes perpetrated by men grew by 3%; by women, 85%.[145]

Relative increases in the FBI's Part II offenses tell a similar story. Arrests of women for embezzlement, for example, increased by more than 228% between 1970 and 2000, versus only 8.5% for men—reflecting women's increased entry into positions of financial responsibility. Arrests of women for drug abuse grew by 289%, and liquor-law violations by women increased 285% (versus 96% for men).[146] In two officially reported categories—prostitution and runaways—women outnumber men in the volume of offenses committed.[147] Other crimes in which significant numbers of women (relative to men) are involved include larceny-theft (where 43.9% of reported crimes are committed by women), forgery and counterfeiting (37.6%), fraud (41.5%), and embezzlement (50.5%).[148] Nonetheless, as Table 3-4 shows, female offenders still account for only a small proportion of all serious crimes. Statistics on female criminality are difficult to interpret because reports of increasing female criminality may reflect the greater equality of treatment accorded women in contemporary society more than they do actual increases in criminal activity. In the past, when women committed crimes, they were dealt with less formally than is likely to be the case today.

TABLE 3-4 | **Male and Female Involvement in Crime: Offense Patterns, 2012**

	PERCENTAGE OF ALL ARRESTS	
UCR INDEX CRIME	**MALES**	**FEMALES**
Murder and nonnegligent manslaughter	88.7	11.3
Rape	99.1	0.9
Robbery	87.0	13.0
Aggravated assault	77.1	22.9
Burglary	83.6	16.4
Larceny-theft	56.9	43.1
Motor vehicle theft	81.1	18.9
Arson	82.0	18.0

Gender Differences

- Men are more likely than women to be arrested for serious crimes, such as murder, rape, robbery, and burglary.
- Arrest, jail, and prison data all suggest that more women than men who commit crimes are involved in property crimes, such as larceny, forgery, fraud, and embezzlement, and in drug offenses.

Source: Based on data from: Federal Bureau of Investigation, *Crime in the United States, 2012* (Washington, DC: U.S. Dept. of Justice, 2013).

When women do commit serious crimes, they are more often followers than leaders. A study of women in correctional settings, for example, found that women are far more likely to assume "secondary follower roles during criminal events" than "dominant leadership roles."[149] Only 14% of women surveyed played primary roles, but those who did "felt that men had little influence in initiating or leading them into crime." African American women were found to be more likely to play "primary and equal crime roles" with men or with female accomplices than were white or Hispanic women. Statistics such as these dispel the myth that the female criminal in America has taken her place alongside the male offender—in terms of either leadership roles or the absolute number of crimes committed.

Postmodern Criminology

Before concluding this chapter, it is important to note that **postmodern criminology** is a term applied to a wide variety of novel perspectives that have developed in recent decades. It encompasses evolving paradigms with such intriguing names as *chaos theory*, *discourse analysis*, *topology theory*, *critical theory*, *realist criminology*, *constitutive theory*, and *anarchic criminology*.[150] Postmodern criminology builds on the belief that past criminological approaches have failed to realistically assess the true causes of crime and have therefore failed to offer workable solutions for crime control—or if they have, that such theories and solutions may have been appropriate at one time but no longer apply to the postmodern era. Because postmodern criminology challenges and debunks existing perspectives, it is referred to as *deconstructionist*, and such theories are sometimes called **deconstructionist theories**.

SUMMARY

- A theory is a proposed model of causal relationships between events and things under study. This chapter defines *theory* as a series of interrelated propositions that attempt to describe, explain, predict, and ultimately control some class of events. A good theory fits the facts and stands up to continued scrutiny. The goal of social research in criminology is to assist in the development of theoretical models that permit a better understanding of criminal behavior and that enhance the development of strategies intended to address the problem of crime.
- The Classical School of criminology, which was in vogue throughout the late eighteenth and early nineteenth centuries, held that crime is caused by the individual exercise of free will and that it can be deterred through the promise of swift and certain punishment. Classical criminology continues to be influential through today's neoclassical thought, represented by rational choice and routine activities theories.
- Traditional biological theories of crime posit a genetic or a physiological basis for deviant and criminal behavior. The notion of a "weak" gene that might predispose some people toward criminal activity has been expanded to include the impact of environmental contaminants, poor nutrition, and food additives on behavior. Studies of fraternal twins and chromosome structure have helped bring biological theories into the modern day. Such theories, however, have their shortcomings, including attributing the cause of crime to fundamental physical characteristics that are not easily modified.
- Biosocial criminology, a contemporary biological perspective, sees the interaction between biology and the physical, cultural, and social environments as key to understanding human behavior, including criminality. Biosocial criminology recognizes the role that human DNA, environmental contaminants, nutrition, hormones, physical trauma, and body chemistry play in behavior that violates the law. The detailed mapping of human DNA and other recent advances in the field of recombinant DNA have rekindled interest in genetic correlates of criminal behavior.
- Psychological explanations of crime are individualistic. Some psychoanalytic theories see offenders as psychotic, psychopathic, or sociopathic. Other psychological theories claim that criminal behavior is a type of conditioned response. The stimulus-response model sees criminal behavior as the consequence of a conditioning process that extends over the entire life span of an individual. Trait theory links personality (and associated traits) to behavior, and holds that it is an individual's personality, combined with his or her intelligence and natural abilities that produces criminality. Psychological traits are stable personality patterns that tend to endure throughout the life course and across social and cultural contexts. As with most other theories, psychological perspectives remain plagued by shortcomings. Among them are questions about whether past behavior can accurately predict future behavior and whether there are identifiable characteristics that violent offenders might manifest that could serve as warning signs of impending criminal activity.
- Sociological theories hold that the individual is a product of his or her social environment. They emphasize the role that social structure, inequality, and socialization play in criminality. Although they are today's perspective of choice, the danger of most sociological approaches is that they tend to deny the significance of any influences beyond those that are mediated through social interaction.
- Social process theories of criminology claim that crime results from the failure of self-direction, from inadequate social roles, or from associating with others who are already criminal. Social policies based on such theories place responsibility for change largely on the offender.
- Conflict perspectives attempt to explain crime by noting that conflict is fundamental to social life and by claiming that crime is a natural consequence of social, political, and economic inequity. Conflict criminologists believe that fundamental changes in the structure of society are needed if crime is to be eliminated or curtailed.
- Included among emergent approaches to explaining crime are feminist criminology and postmodern criminology. Feminist criminology challenges some long-held notions of crime and criminal justice that have been based solely on understandings of male criminality. Postmodern criminology, the last of the approaches discussed in this chapter, is often more an effort to debunk previous perspectives than it is a theoretical perspective in its own right.

KEY TERMS

reaction formation, 90
research, 74
routine activities theory (RAT), 76
schizophrenic, 86
social development theory, 94
social disorganization, 88
social learning theory, 93
social process theory, 92
somatotyping, 79
subculture of violence, 90
supermale, 82
theory, 72
traits, 86

QUESTIONS FOR REVIEW

1. What is a theory? Describe the steps in criminological theory building, and explain the role that social research plays in the development of theories about crime.
2. List the basic assumptions of classical theories of crime causation, and describe the neoclassical perspective.
3. Describe the basic features of biological theories of crime causation. What shortcomings of the biological perspective can you identify?
4. What is biosocial criminology? How do biosocial theories of criminality differ from other biological theories?
5. Describe the basic features of psychological explanations for crime. What are the shortcomings of this perspective?
6. Describe the basic features of sociological explanations for crime. What are the shortcomings of this perspective?
7. Describe social process theories of crime causation, including labeling theory and the life course perspective. What types of crime-control policies might be based on such theories?
8. Describe conflict theories of crime causation, including radical criminology and peacemaking criminology. What sorts of crime-control policies might be predicated on the basis of such theories?
9. What is meant by "emergent perspectives"? List and describe two emergent perspectives on crime causation.

QUESTIONS FOR REFLECTION

1. Chapter 1 referred briefly to evidence-based practices. What evidence-based practices might be developed as a result of the studies discussed in this chapter?
2. What is the relationship between punishment and classical and neoclassical thought? With what types of offenders might punishment be the most effective in reducing recidivism?
3. Do you think that biological theories successfully explain the causes of crime? Why or why not?
4. How do biosocial theories of crime differ from early biological theories? What is the central feature of biosocial theories?
5. Do you think that psychological theories of crime causation are sound? Why or why not?
6. Do you think that sociological theories of crime causation are sound? Why or why not?

NOTES

i. The American Heritage Dictionary and Electronic Thesaurus on CD-ROM (Boston: Houghton Mifflin, 1987).

1. "Rick Ross Shooting: Rapper's Rolls Royce Crashes into Fort Lauderdale Building during Drive-By Attempt," *Huffington Post*, January 28, 2013, http://www.huffingtonpost.com/2013/01/28/rick-ross-shooting-rapper-rolls-royce-lauderdale_n_2566509.html (accessed January 29, 2013).
2. "Oakland Rapper 'Kenny Clutch' Killed in Las Vegas Strip Shooting," *Los Angeles Times*, February 22, 2013, http://latimesblogs.latimes.com/lanow/2013/02/oakland-rapper-kenny-clutch-killed-in-vegas-strip-shooting.html (accessed March 14, 2013).
3. "50 Cent Biography," Sing365.com, http://www.sing365.com/music/lyric.nsf/50-Cent-Biography/83CE63737F6CE6CB48256C79000EA96F (accessed June 1, 2013).
4. Rob Markman, "Rick Ross Is 'Layin' Back' after Shooting, Pusha T Says," MTV.com, January 29, 2013, http://www.mtv.com/news/articles/1700995/rick-ross-shooting-pusha-t-comments.jhtml (accessed January 29, 2013).
5. As we will see in Chapter 4, behavior that violates the criminal law may not be "crime" if accompanied by an acceptable legal justification or excuse. Justifications and excuses that are recognized by the law may serve as defenses to a criminal charge.
6. This and many of the statistics in these opening paragraphs come from Jonathan Wright, "Media Are Mixed Blessing, Criminologists Say," Reuters, May 2, 1995.
7. See "Comments of James T. Hamilton before the Federal Communications Commission, in the Matter of Industry Proposal for Rating Video Programming," May 23, 1997, citing Suzanne Stutman, Joanne Cantor, and Victoria Duran, *What Parents Want in a Television Rating System: Results of a National Survey* (Madison: University of Wisconsin, 1996); Wes Shipley and Gary Cavender, "Murder and Mayhem at the Movies," *Journal of Criminal Justice and Popular Culture*, Vol. 9, No. 1 (2001), pp. 1–14; and Suzanne Stutman, Joanne Cantor, and Victoria Duran, *What Parents Want in a Television Rating System: Results of a National Survey* (Washington, DC: National Parent Teacher Association, 2002), http://www.pta.org/ptacommunity/tvreport.asp (accessed August 21, 2007).
8. Jeffrey Johnson, "Television Viewing and Aggressive Behavior during Adolescence and Adulthood," *Science*, Vol. 295 (2002), pp. 2468–2471.
9. Wright, "Media Are Mixed Blessing, Criminologists Say."
10. Nathan McCall, "My Rap against Rap," Washington Post wire service, November 14, 1993.
11. Arthur L. Cribbs, Jr., "Gangsta Rappers Sing White Racists' Tune," *USA Today*, December 27, 1993.
12. U.S. News/UCLA Survey on the Media and Violence, reported in "Hollywood: Right Face," *U.S. News and World Report*, May 15, 1995.
13. *Brown* v. *Entertainment Merchants Association*, U.S. Supreme Court, No. 08–1448 (decided June 27, 2011).
14. Ibid.
15. The word *scientific* is used here to refer to the application of generally accepted research strategies designed to reject explanations that rival the one under study.
16. Stephen Schafer, *Theories in Criminology* (New York: Random House, 1969), p. 109.

17. L. E. Cohen and Marcus Felson, "Social Change and Crime Rate Trends: A Routine Activity Approach," *American Sociological Review*, Vol. 44, No. 4 (August 1979), pp. 588–608. Also see Marcus Felson and L. E. Cohen, "Human Ecology and Crime: A Routine Activity Approach," *Human Ecology*, Vol. 8, No. 4 (1980), pp. 389–406; Marcus Felson, "Linking Criminal Choices, Routine Activities, Informal Control, and Criminal Outcomes," in Derek B. Cornish and Ronald V. Clarke, eds., *The Reasoning Criminal: Rational Choice Perspectives on Offending* (New York: Springer-Verlag, 1986), pp. 119–128; and Ronald V. Clarke and Marcus Felson, eds., *Advances in Criminological Theory: Routine Activity and Rational Choice* (New Brunswick, NJ: Transaction, 1993).
18. Cohen and Felson, "Social Change and Crime Rate Trends," p. 595.
19. For a test of routine activities theory as an explanation for victimization in the workplace, see John D. Wooldredge, Francis T. Cullen, and Edward J. Latessa, "Victimization in the Workplace: A Test of Routine Activities Theory," *Justice Quarterly*, Vol. 9, No. 2 (June 1992), pp. 325–335.
20. Werner Einstadter and Stuart Henry, *Criminological Theory: An Analysis of Its Underlying Assumptions* (Fort Worth, TX: Harcourt Brace, 1995), p. 70.
21. For a modern reprint of a widely read nineteenth-century work on phrenology, see Orson Squire Fowler and Lorenzo Niles Fowler, *Phrenology: A Practical Guide to Your Head* (New York: Chelsea House, 1980).
22. Schafer, *Theories in Criminology*, p. 123.
23. Richard Louis Dugdale, *The Jukes: A Study in Crime, Pauperism, Disease, and Heredity*, 3rd ed. (New York: G. P. Putnam's Sons, 1985).
24. Henry Herbert Goddard, *The Kallikak Family: A Study in the Heredity of Feeblemindedness* (New York: Macmillan, 1912).
25. For more information, see Richard Herrnstein, "Crime File: Biology and Crime," a study guide (Washington, DC: National Institute of Justice, n.d.).
26. *Buck* v. *Bell*, 274 U.S. 200, 207 (1927).
27. Adrian Raine et al., "Prefrontal Glucose Deficits in Murderers Lacking Psychosocial Deprivation," *Neuropsychiatry, Neuropsychology, and Behavioral Neurology*, Vol. 11, No. 1 (1998), pp. 1–7.
28. Josh Fischman, "Criminal Minds," *Chronicle of Higher Education*, June 12, 2011, http://chronicle.com/article/Can-This-Man-Predict-Whether/127792 (accessed June 2, 2013).
29. Mary Kugler, "What Are Genes, DNA and Chromosomes?" About.com, http://rarediseases.about.com/od/geneticdisorders/a/genesbasics.htm (accessed December 6, 2012).
30. Patricia Jacobs et al., "Aggressive Behavior, Mental Subnormality, and the XYY Male," *Nature*, Vol. 208 (1965), pp. 1351–1352.
31. Schafer, *Theories in Criminology*, p. 193.
32. H. G. Brunner, M. Nelen, X. O. Breakefield, H. H. Ropers, and B. A. van Oost, "Abnormal Behavior Associated with a Point Mutation in the Structural Gene for Monoamine Oxidase A," *Science*, Vol. 262, No. 5133 (October 22, 1993), pp. 578–580.
33. A. E. Baum et al., "A Genome-Wide Association Study Implicates Diacylglycerol Kinase Eta (DGKH) and Several Other Genes in the Etiology of Bipolar Disorder," *Molecular Psychiatry*, advance online publication, http://doi:10.1038/sj.mp.4002012 (accessed May 8, 2007).
34. See "The Genome Changes Everything: A Talk with Matt Ridley," http://www.edge.org/3rd_culture/ridley03/ridley_print.html (accessed February 10, 2007).
35. Matt Ridley, "What Makes You Who You Are?" *Time*, June 2, 2003, pp. 55–63.
36. D. Hill and W. Sargent, "A Case of Matricide," *Lancet*, Vol. 244 (1943), pp. 526–527.
37. See, for example, A. R. Mawson and K. J. Jacobs, "Corn Consumption, Tryptophan, and Cross-National Homicide Rates," *Journal of Orthomolecular Psychiatry*, Vol. 7 (1978), pp. 227–230; and A. Hoffer, "The Relation of Crime to Nutrition," *Humanist in Canada*, Vol. 8 (1975), p. 8.
38. See, for example, C. Hawley and R. E. Buckley, "Food Dyes and Hyperkinetic Children," *Academy Therapy*, Vol. 10 (1974), pp. 27–32; and Alexander Schauss, *Diet, Crime, and Delinquency* (Berkeley, CA: Parker House, 1980).
39. "Special Report: Measuring Your Life with Coffee Spoons," *Tufts University Diet and Nutrition Letter*, Vol. 2, No. 2 (April 1984), pp. 3–6.
40. See, for example, "Special Report: Does What You Eat Affect Your Mood and Actions?" *Tufts University Diet and Nutrition Letter*, Vol. 2, No. 12 (February 1985), pp. 4–6.
41. See *Tufts University Diet and Nutrition Letter*, Vol. 2, No. 11 (January 1985), p. 2; and "Special Report: Why Sugar Continues to Concern Nutritionists," *Tufts University Diet and Nutrition Letter*, Vol. 3, No. 3 (May 1985), pp. 3–6.
42. Diana H. Fishbein and Susan E. Pease, "Diet, Nutrition, and Aggression," in Marc Hillbrand and Nathaniel J. Pallone, eds., *The Psychobiology of Aggression: Engines, Measurement, Control* (New York: Haworth Press, 1994), pp. 114–117.
43. A. Hoffer, "Children with Learning and Behavioral Disorders," *Journal of Orthomolecular Psychiatry*, Vol. 5 (1976), p. 229.
44. See, Megan Visscher, "How Food Can Cut Crime," *Ode Magazine*, February 9, 2010, http://www.care2.com/greenliving/how-food-can-cut-crime.html?page=4 (accessed March 11, 2012).
45. Ap Zaalberg, Henk Nijman, Erik Bulten, Luwe Stroosma, and Cees van der Staak, "Effects of Nutritional Supplements on Aggression, Rule-Breaking, and Psychopathology Among Young Adult Prisoners," *Aggressive Behavior*, Vol. 35 (2009), pp. 1–10.
46. C. B. Gesch, S. M. Hammond, S. E. Hampson, A. Eves, and M. J. Crowder, "Influence of Supplementary Vitamins, Minerals and Essential Fatty Acids on the Antisocial Behavior of Young Adult Prisoners: Randomized, Placebo-Controlled Trial," *British Journal of Psychiatry*, Vol. 181 (July 2002), pp. 22–28.
47. See, for example, R. T. Rada, D. R. Laws, and R. Kellner, "Plasma Testosterone Levels in the Rapist," *Psychomatic Medicine*, Vol. 38 (1976), pp. 257–268.
48. Later studies, however, have been less than clear. See, for example, J. M. Dabbs, Jr., "Testosterone Measurements in Social and Clinical Psychology," *Journal of Social and Clinical Psychology*, Vol. 11 (1992), pp. 302–321.
49. "The Insanity of Steroid Abuse," *Newsweek*, May 23, 1988, p. 75.
50. E. G. Stalenheim et al., "Testosterone as a Biological Marker in Psychopathy and Alcoholism," *Psychiatry Research*, Vol. 77, No. 2 (February 1998), pp. 79–88.
51. Michelle M. Wirth and Oliver C. Schultheiss, "Basal Testosterone Moderates Responses to Anger Faces in Humans," *Physiology and Behavior*, Vol. 90 (2007), pp. 496–505.
52. For a summary of such studies, see Serena-Lynn Brown, Alexander Botsis, and Herman M. Van Praag, "Serotonin and Aggression," in Hillbrand and Pallone, eds., *The Psychobiology of Aggression*, pp. 28–39.
53. Roger D. Masters, Brian Hone, and Anil Doshi, "Environmental Pollution, Neurotoxicity, and Criminal Violence," in J. Rose, ed., *Environmental Toxicology* (London and New York: Gordon and Breach, 1997).
54. B. Bioulac et al., "Serotonergic Functions in the XYY Syndrome," *Biological Psychiatry*, Vol. 15 (1980), pp. 917–923.
55. E. G. Stalenheim, L. von Knorring, and L. Wide, "Serum Levels of Thyroid Hormones as Biological Markers in a Swedish Forensic

Psychiatric Population," *Biological Psychiatry*, Vol. 43, No. 10 (May 15, 1998), pp. 755–761.
56. R. B. Cattell, *The Inheritance of Personality and Ability: Research Methods and Findings* (New York: Academic Press, 1982).
57. Karl Christiansen, "A Preliminary Study of Criminality among Twins," in Sarnoff Mednick and Karl O. Christiansen, eds., *Biosocial Bases of Criminal Behavior* (New York: Gardner Press, 1977).
58. James Q. Wilson and Richard J. Herrnstein, *Crime and Human Nature* (New York: Simon and Schuster, 1985).
59. Lee Ellis and Anthony Walsh, "Gene-Based Evolutionary Theories in Criminology," *Criminology*, Vol. 35, No. 2 (1997), pp. 229–230.
60. Peter J. Richerson, "Crime and Criminality," http://www.des.ucdavis.edu/faculty/Richerson/BooksOnline/He16-95.pdf (accessed March 1, 2013).
61. Sigmund Freud, *A General Introduction to Psychoanalysis* (New York: Boni and Liveright, 1920).
62. Nettler, *Killing One Another*, p. 79.
63. David Abrahamsen, *Crime and the Human Mind* (reprint, Montclair, NJ: Patterson Smith, 1969), p. 23.
64. See Adrian Raine, *The Psychopathology of Crime: Criminal Behavior as a Clinical Disorder* (Orlando, FL: Academic Press, 1993).
65. Hervey M. Cleckley, *The Mask of Sanity: An Attempt to Reinterpret the So-Called Psychopathic Personality* (St. Louis, MO: Mosby, 1941).
66. Nettler, *Killing One Another*, p. 179.
67. Albert I. Rabin, "The Antisocial Personality—Psychopathy and Sociopathy," in Hans Toch, ed., *Psychology of Crime and Criminal Justice* (Prospect Heights, IL: Waveland Press, 1979), p. 330.
68. Hans J. Eysenck, *Crime and Personality* (Boston: Houghton Mifflin, 1964).
69. Intelligence may also be seen as an ability. See, for example, Colin G. DeYoung, "Intelligence and Personality," in R. J. Sternberg and S. B. Kaufman, eds., *The Cambridge Handbook of Intelligence* (New York: Cambridge University Press, 2011), pp. 711–737.
70. Some early personality theorists considered intelligence to be part of personality. See, for example, R. B. Cattell, *Personality* (New York: McGraw-Hill, 1950); and J. P. Guilford, *Personality* (New York: McGraw-Hill, 1959).
71. Colin G. DeYoung, "Intelligence and Personality."
72. Eysenck, *Crime and Personality*, p. 92.
73. Hans J. Eysenck, "Personality and Criminality: A Dispositional Analysis," in William S. Laufer and Freda Adler, eds., *Advances in Criminology Theory*, Vol. 1 (New Brunswick, NJ: Transaction, 1989), p. 90.
74. Eysenck, *Crime and Personality*, pp. 35–36.
75. Richard L. Ault and James T. Reese, "A Psychological Assessment of Crime Profiling," *FBI Law Enforcement Bulletin* (March 1980), pp. 22–25.
76. John E. Douglas and Alan E. Burgess, "Criminal Profiling: A Viable Investigative Tool against Violent Crime," *FBI Law Enforcement Bulletin* (December 1986), pp. 9–13.
77. Robert R. Hazelwood and John E. Douglass, "The Lust Murderer," *FBI Law Enforcement Bulletin* (April 1980), pp. 18–22.
78. A. O. Rider, "The Firesetter—A Psychological Profile," *FBI Law Enforcement Bulletin* (June 1980), pp. 4–11.
79. M. Reiser, "Crime-Specific Psychological Consultation," *Police Chief* (March 1982), pp. 53–56.
80. Thomas Strentz, "A Terrorist Psychosocial Profile: Past and Present," *FBI Law Enforcement Bulletin* (April 1988), pp. 13–19.
81. Jill Peay, "Dangerousness—Ascription or Description," in M. P. Feldman, ed., *Violence*, Vol. 2 of *Developments in the Study of Criminal Behavior* (New York: John Wiley, 1982), p. 211, citing N. Walker, "Dangerous People," *International Journal of Law and Psychiatry*, Vol. 1 (1978), pp. 37–50.
82. See, for example, Michael Gottfredson and Travis Hirschi, *A General Theory of Crime* (Stanford, CA: Stanford University Press, 1990); and Travis Hirschi and Michael Gottfredson, "Age and the Explanation of Crime," *American Journal of Sociology*, Vol. 89 (1983), pp. 552–584.
83. David F. Greenberg, "Modeling Criminal Careers," *Criminology*, Vol. 29, No. 1 (1991), p. 39.
84. Robert E. Park and Ernest Burgess, *Introduction to the Science of Sociology*, 2nd ed. (Chicago: University of Chicago Press, 1924); and Robert E. Park, ed., *The City* (Chicago: University of Chicago Press, 1925).
85. Clifford R. Shaw and Henry D. McKay, "Social Factors in Juvenile Delinquency," in *Report on the Causes of Crime, National Commission on Law Observance and Enforcement*, report no. 13, Vol. 2 (Washington, DC: U.S. Government Printing Office, 1931); and Clifford R. Shaw, *Juvenile Delinquency in Urban Areas* (Chicago: University of Chicago Press, 1942).
86. Émile Durkheim, *Suicide* (reprint, New York: Free Press, 1951).
87. Robert K. Merton, "Social Structure and Anomie," *American Sociological Review*, Vol. 3 (1938), pp. 672–682.
88. Catherine E. Ross and John Mirowsky, "Normlessness, Powerlessness, and Trouble with the Law," *Criminology*, Vol. 25, No. 2 (May 1987), p. 257.
89. See Nettler, *Killing One Another*, p. 58.
90. This is not to say that all members of these groups engaged in criminal behavior, but rather that statistics indicated higher average crime rates for these groups than for certain others immediately after immigration to the United States.
91. Albert K. Cohen, *Delinquent Boys: The Culture of the Gang* (Glencoe, IL: Free Press, 1958).
92. Walter B. Miller, "Lower Class Culture as a Generating Milieu of Gang Delinquency," *Journal of Social Issues*, Vol. 14 (1958), pp. 5–19.
93. Richard Cloward and Lloyd Ohlin, *Delinquency and Opportunity: A Theory of Delinquent Gangs* (New York: Free Press, 1960).
94. Marvin Wolfgang, *Patterns in Criminal Homicide* (Philadelphia: University of Pennsylvania Press, 1958). See also Marvin Wolfgang and Franco Ferracuti, *The Subculture of Violence: Toward an Integrated Theory in Criminology* (London: Tavistock, 1967).
95. "Gang Prevention through Targeted Outreach—Boys and Girls Clubs of America," http://ojjdp.ncjrs.org/pubs/gun_violence/sect08-k.html (accessed April 10, 2007).
96. See, for example, James D. Orcutt, "Differential Association and Marijuana Use: A Closer Look at Sutherland (with a Little Help from Becker)," *Criminology*, Vol. 25, No. 2 (1987), pp. 341–358.
97. Edwin Sutherland, *Principles of Criminology*, 4th ed. (Chicago: J. B. Lippincott, 1947), p. 4.
98. John E. Conklin, *Criminology*, 3rd ed. (New York: Macmillan, 1989), p. 278.
99. Robert L. Burgess and Ronald L. Akers, "A Differential Association-Reinforcement Theory of Criminal Behavior," *Social Problems*, Vol. 14 (fall 1996), pp. 128–147.
100. Some theories are multicausal and provide explanations for criminal behavior that include a diversity of "causes."
101. For a more elaborate criticism of this sort, see Conklin, *Criminology*, p. 260.
102. Ibid.
103. Walter C. Reckless, *The Crime Problem*, 4th ed. (New York: Appleton-Century-Crofts, 1961).
104. Ibid., p. 472.

105. Travis Hirschi, *Causes of Delinquency* (Berkeley: University of California Press, 1969).
106. Ibid., p. 472.
107. Gresham Sykes and David Matza, "Techniques of Neutralization: A Theory of Delinquency," *American Sociological Review*, Vol. 22 (1957), pp. 664–670.
108. Many of the concepts used by Howard Becker in explicating his theory of labeling were, in fact, used previously not only by Frank Tannenbaum but also by Edwin M. Lemert. Lemert wrote of "societal reaction" and "primary and secondary deviance" and even used the word *labeling* in his book *Social Pathology* (New York: McGraw-Hill, 1951).
109. Frank Tannenbaum, *Crime and the Community* (Boston: Ginn, 1938), pp. 19–20.
110. Howard Becker, *Outsiders: Studies in the Sociology of Deviance* (New York: Free Press, 1963), pp. 8–9.
111. Ibid.
112. Ibid., p. 33.
113. Terrie E. Moffitt, "Adolescence-Limited and Life-Course Persistent Antisocial Behavior: A Developmental Taxonomy," *Psychological Review*, Vol. 100 (1993), pp. 674–701.
114. Robert J. Sampson and John H. Laub, *Crime in the Making: Pathways and Turning Points through the Life Course* (Cambridge, MA: Harvard University Press, 1993).
115. Katharine Browning et al., "Causes and Correlates of Delinquency Program," *OJJDP Fact Sheet* (Washington, DC: U.S. Dept. of Justice, April 1999).
116. MacArthur Foundation, "The Project on Human Development in Chicago Neighborhoods," http://www.macfound.org/research/hcd/hcd_5.htm (accessed January 5, 2007).
117. Adapted from Raymond Michalowski, "Perspectives and Paradigm: Structuring Criminological Thought," in Robert F. Meier, ed., *Theory in Criminology* (Beverly Hills, CA: Sage, 1977).
118. See George B. Vold, *Theoretical Criminology* (New York: Oxford University Press, 1986).
119. Austin T. Turk, *Criminality and the Legal Order* (Chicago: Rand McNally, 1969).
120. Thorsten Sellin, *Culture Conflict and Crime* (New York: Social Science Research Council, 1938).
121. William J. Chambliss and Robert B. Seidman, *Law, Order, and Power* (Reading, MA: Addison-Wesley, 1971).
122. Richard Quinney, *The Social Reality of Crime* (Boston: Little, Brown, 1970).
123. David F. Greenberg, *Crime and Capitalism* (Palo Alto, CA: Mayfield, 1981), p. 3.
124. For examples of how this might be accomplished, see F. H. Knopp, "Community Solutions to Sexual Violence: Feminist/Abolitionist Perspectives," in Harold E. Pepinsky and Richard Quinney, eds., *Criminology as Peacemaking* (Bloomington: Indiana University Press, 1991), pp. 181–193; and S. Caringella-MacDonald and D. Humphries, "Sexual Assault, Women, and the Community: Organizing to Prevent Sexual Violence," in Pepinsky and Quinney, eds., *Criminology as Peacemaking*, pp. 98–113.
125. Richard Quinney, "Life of Crime: Criminology and Public Policy as Peacemaking," *Journal of Crime and Justice*, Vol. 16, No. 2 (1993), pp. 3–9.
126. Ram Dass and P. Gorman, *How Can I Help? Stories and Reflections on Service* (New York: Alfred A. Knopf, 1985), p. 165, as cited in Richard Quinney and John Wildeman, *The Problem of Crime: A Peace and Social Justice Perspective*, 3rd ed. (Mayfield, CA: Mountain View Press, 1991), p. 116, originally published as *The Problem of Crime: A Critical Introduction to Criminology* (New York: Bantam, 1977).
127. See, for example, Harold E. Pepinsky, "This Can't Be Peace: A Pessimist Looks at Punishment," in W. B. Groves and G. Newman, eds., *Punishment and Privilege* (Albany, NY: Harrow and Heston, 1986); Harold E. Pepinsky, "Violence as Unresponsiveness: Toward a New Conception of Crime," *Justice Quarterly*, Vol. 5 (1988), pp. 539–563; and Pepinsky and Quinney, eds., *Criminology as Peacemaking*.
128. See, for example, Richard Quinney, "Crime, Suffering, Service: Toward a Criminology of Peacemaking," *Quest*, Vol. 1 (1988), pp. 66–75; Richard Quinney, "The Theory and Practice of Peacemaking in the Development of Radical Criminology," *Critical Criminologist*, Vol. 1, No. 5 (1989), p. 5; and Quinney and Wildeman, *The Problem of Crime*.
129. All of these themes are addressed, for example, in Pepinsky and Quinney, eds., *Criminology as Peacemaking*.
130. Michael J. Lynch and W. Byron Groves, *A Primer in Radical Criminology*, 2nd ed. (Albany, NY: Harrow and Heston, 1989), p. 128.
131. Raymond J. Michalowski, *Order, Law, and Crime: An Introduction to Criminology* (New York: Random House, 1985), p. 410.
132. Don C. Gibbons, Talking about Crime and Criminals: Problems and Issues in Theory Development in Criminology (Upper Saddle River, NJ: Prentice Hall, 1994), p. 165, citing Loraine Gelsthorpe and Alison Morris, eds., *Feminist Perspectives in Criminology* (Bristol, England: Open University Press, 1990).
133. Sally S. Simpson, "Feminist Theory, Crime, and Justice," *Criminology*, Vol. 27, No. 4 (1989), p. 605.
134. For an excellent overview of feminist theory in criminology and for a comprehensive review of research regarding female offenders, see Joanne Belknap, *The Invisible Woman: Gender Crime and Justice* (Belmont, CA: Wadsworth, 1996).
135. Otto Pollak, *The Criminality of Women* (Philadelphia: University of Pennsylvania Press, 1950).
136. Freda Adler, *Sisters in Crime: The Rise of the New Female Criminal* (New York: McGraw-Hill, 1975).
137. Rita J. Simon, *Women and Crime* (Lexington, MA: Lexington Books, 1975).
138. See, for example, Darrell J. Steffensmeir, "Sex Differences in Patterns of Adult Crime, 1965–1977: A Review and Assessment," *Social Forces*, Vol. 58 (1980), pp. 1098–1099.
139. See, for example, Kathleen Daly and Meda Chesney-Lind, "Feminism and Criminology," *Justice Quarterly*, Vol. 5, No. 5 (December 1988), pp. 497–535.
140. Ibid., p. 506.
141. Ibid.
142. Ibid., p. 514.
143. Cathy Spatz Widom, "Childhood Victimization and the Derailment of Girls and Women to the Criminal Justice System," in Beth E. Richie et al., eds., *Research on Women and Girls in the Justice System* (Washington, DC: National Institute of Justice, 2000), p. iii.
144. Ibid., pp. 27–36.
145. Federal Bureau of Investigation, *Crime in the United States, 1970* (Washington, DC: U.S. Dept. of Justice, 1971); and Federal Bureau of Investigation, *Crime in the United States, 2000* (Washington, DC: U.S. Dept. of Justice, 2001).
146. Ibid.
147. Federal Bureau of Investigation, *Crime in the United States, 2000*.
148. Federal Bureau of Investigation, *Crime in the United States, 2010* (Washington, DC: U.S. Dept. of Justice, 2011).
149. Leanne Fiftal Alarid et al., "Women's Roles in Serious Offenses: A Study of Adult Felons," *Justice Quarterly*, Vol. 13, No. 3 (September 1996), pp. 432–454.
150. For an excellent and detailed discussion of many of these approaches, see Milovanovic, *Postmodern Criminology*.

Alamy

4 CRIMINAL LAW

OUTLINE

LEARNING OBJECTIVES

After reading this chapter, you should be able to

- Summarize the purpose, primary sources, and development of law.
- Define the *rule of law,* including its importance in Western democratic societies.
- Summarize the various categories of law, including the purpose of each.
- Describe five categories of crimes and their characteristics.
- Describe the eight general features of crime.
- Explain what is meant by the elements of a specific criminal offense.
- Compare and contrast the four general categories of accepted criminal defense.

Law is the art of the good and the fair.

ULPIAN, ROMAN JUDGE (CIRCA A.D. 200)

Every law is an infraction of liberty.

JEREMY BENTHAM (1748–1832)

■ **law** A rule of conduct, generally found enacted in the form of a statute, that proscribes or mandates certain forms of behavior.

Introduction

In October, 2012, seven prominent Italian seismologists were convicted of manslaughter and sentenced to six years in prison for failing to warn residents of the historic town of L'Aquila of a coming earthquake.[1] The scientists, who denied responsibility by claiming that earthquake prediction is not an exact science, were also ordered to pay court costs and to reimburse the city for $10.2 million in damages. The trial and verdict came more than three years after a 6.3-magnitude earthquake destroyed L'Aquila's city center, in the Abruzzo region—a bucolic area east of Rome. The earthquake left 309 people dead, and thousands more homeless or injured. In rendering the verdict, the court agreed with prosecution arguments that "it is possible to predict risk and to adopt measures that mitigate that risk." The scientists' failure to do so resulted in the manslaughter convictions against them.[2]

A society needs laws to uphold fairness and to prevent the victimization of innocents.

Laws govern many aspects of our lives, and we are expected to know what the **law** *says* as it applies to our daily lives and to *follow* it. As this chapter will show, laws provide for predictability because people can study the law and know exactly what is required of them. In the case of the convicted scientists, however, no one had ever been found guilty of a crime for failing to make an accurate seismic prediction, and their murder convictions jolted the international scientific community into fearing an onslaught of criminal trials for failed or inaccurate scientific assessments.

REUTERS/Alessandro Bianchi

L'Aquila, Italy, damaged by an earthquake in October, 2012. Seven prominent Italian seismologists were convicted of manslaughter and sentenced to six years in prison for failing to warn residents of the historic town of the coming quake. Were their conviction and sentence just?

The Nature and Purpose of Law

Imagine a society without laws. Without civil law, people would not know what to expect from one another, nor would they be able to plan for the future with any degree of certainty. Without criminal law, people wouldn't feel safe because the more powerful could take what they wanted from the less powerful. Without constitutional law, people could not exercise the basic rights that are available to them as citizens of a free nation. A society needs laws to uphold fairness and to prevent the victimization of innocents.

Practically speaking, laws regulate relationships between people and also between parties, such as government agencies and individuals. They channel and simultaneously constrain human behavior, and they empower individuals while contributing to public order. Laws also serve other purposes. They ensure that the philosophical, moral, and economic perspectives of their creators are protected and made credible. They maintain values and uphold established patterns of social privilege. They sustain existing power relationships, and, finally, they support a system for the punishment and rehabilitation of offenders. (See Table 4-1.) Modifications of the law, when gradually introduced, promote orderly change in the rest of society.

Our laws are found in statutory provisions and constitutional enactments,[3] as well as in hundreds of years of rulings by courts at all levels. According to the authoritative *Black's Law Dictionary*, the word *law* "generally contemplates both statutory and case law."[4]

TABLE 4-1 | What Do Laws Do?

- Laws maintain order in society.
- Laws regulate human interaction.
- Laws enforce moral beliefs.
- Laws define the economic environment.
- Laws enhance predictability.
- Laws support the powerful.
- Laws promote orderly social change.
- Laws sustain individual rights.
- Laws redress wrongs.
- Laws identify wrongdoers.
- Laws mandate punishment and retribution.

■ **statutory law** Written or codified law; the "law on the books," as enacted by a government body or agency having the power to make laws.
■ **penal code** The written, organized, and compiled form of the criminal laws of a jurisdiction.
■ **case law** The body of judicial precedent, historically built on legal reasoning and past interpretations of statutory laws, that serves as a guide to decision making, especially in the courts.
■ **common law** Law originating from usage and custom rather than from written statutes. The term refers to an unwritten body of judicial opinion, originally developed by English courts, that is based on nonstatutory customs, traditions, and precedents that help guide judicial decision making.

■ **rule of law** The maxim that an orderly society must be governed by established principles and known codes that are applied uniformly and fairly to all of its members.
■ **jurisprudence** The philosophy of law. Also, the science and study of the law.

Statutory law is "the law on the books." It results from legislative action and is often thought of as "the law of the land." Written laws exist in both criminal and civil areas and are called *codes*. Once laws have been written down in an organized fashion, they are said to be *codified*. Federal statutes are compiled in the U.S. Code (U.S.C.), which is available online in its entirety at **http://uscode.house.gov**. State codes and municipal ordinances are also readily available in written, or statutory, form. The written form of the criminal law is called the **penal code**. **Case law**, which we will discuss in detail a bit later, is the law that results from judicial decisions.

But the laws of our country are not unambiguous. If all of "the law" could be found in written legal codes, it would be plain to nearly everyone, and we would need far fewer lawyers than are practicing today. But some laws—the precedents established by courts—do not exist "on the books," and even those that do are open to interpretation. This is where common law comes into play. **Common law** is the traditional body of unwritten historical precedents created from everyday social customs, rules, and practices, many of which were supported by judicial decisions during early times. Common law principles are still used to interpret many legal issues in quite a few states. Hence it is not uncommon to hear of jurisdictions within the United States referred to as "common law jurisdictions" or "common law states."

The Rule of Law

The social, economic, and political stability of any society depends largely on the development and institutionalization of a predictable system of laws. Western democratic societies adhere to the **rule of law**, which is sometimes also referred to as the *supremacy of law*. The rule of law centers on the belief that an orderly society must be governed by established principles and known codes that are applied uniformly and fairly to all of its members. Under this tenet, no one is above the law, and those who make or enforce the law must also abide by it. The principle was well illustrated when, in 2011, former House Majority Leader Tom DeLay was sentenced to three years in prison for taking part in a money-laundering scheme stemming from the 2002 elections. Delay was convicted of illegally funneling almost $200,000 in corporate donations through the Republican National Committee in an effort to elect Republicans to the Texas Legislature.[5]

The rule of law has been called the greatest political achievement of our culture.

The rule of law has been called the greatest political achievement of our culture. Without it, few other human achievements—especially those that require the coordinated efforts of a large number of people—would be possible. President John F. Kennedy eloquently explained the rule of law, saying, "Americans are free to disagree with the law, but not to disobey it; for [in] a government of laws and not of men, no man, however prominent and powerful, no mob, however unruly or boisterous, is entitled to defy a court of law."[6]

The rule of law has also been called "the foundation of liberties in the Western world,"[7] for it means that due process (which was discussed in Chapter 1) has to be followed in any criminal prosecution, and it is due process that serves as a check on arbitrary state power.

The American Bar Association notes that the rule of law includes these elements:[8]

- Freedom from private lawlessness provided by the legal system of a politically organized society
- A relatively high degree of objectivity in the formulation of legal norms and a like degree of evenhandedness in their application
- Legal ideas and juristic devices for the attainment of individual and group objectives within the bounds of ordered liberty
- Substantive and procedural limitations on governmental power in the interest of the individual for the enforcement of which there are appropriate legal institutions and machinery

Jurisprudence is the philosophy of law or the science and study of the law, including the rule of law. To learn more about the rule of law, including its historical development, visit **http://www.lexisnexis.com/about-us/rule-of-law**.

Types of Law

Criminal and civil law are the best-known types of modern law. However, scholars and philosophers have drawn numerous distinctions between categories of law that rest on the source, intent, and application of the law (Figure 4-1).

CJ | NEWS

Politicians Who Violate the "Rule of Law" Get Tough Prison Sentences

Former Detroit Mayor Kwame Kilpatrick (left), former Illinois Governor Rod Blagojevich (second from left), former U.S. House Majority Leader Tom DeLay (right), and former U.S. Representative William Jefferson (second from right). As their cases demonstrate, the rule of law means that no one is above the law—not even those who make it. Kilpatrick, charged with ten felony counts, pleaded guilty to reduced charges and served 99 days in jail before being released in February 2009; he reentered prison in 2010 for violating probation, and was again found guilty in 2013 of using his office as mayor to execute a wide-ranging racketeering conspiracy. Blagojevich was tried in 2011 on federal criminal charges and convicted on 17 counts of wire fraud, attempted extortion, soliciting bribes, and conspiracy. Jefferson served nine terms in the U.S. House of Representatives prior to being sentenced in 2009 to 13 years in prison for using his office to solicit bribes. DeLay was sentenced in 2011 to three years in prison for taking part in a money-laundering scheme. How would you explain the rule of law to someone who is unfamiliar with it?

Source: From left to right: Getty Images, Inc./Bill Pugliano; AP Wide World Photos/Seth Perlman; AP Wide World Photos/Kevin Wolf; and Chuck Kennedy/KRT/Newscom.

The United States has always embraced the principle that no one, not even a powerful politician, can violate the law with impunity. As President Theodore Roosevelt said, "No man is above the law and no man is below it."

Today, enforcement of "the rule of law" appears to be stricter than ever, producing some eye-popping prison terms for convicted politicians. Illinois Democratic Gov. Rod Blagojevich was sentenced to 14 years in prison in 2011, more than twice the 6½-year term given to his predecessor, former Republican Gov. George Ryan.

Blagojevich made headlines for his most notable crime: trying to sell President Obama's former senate seat—and he was unrepentant until almost the end. But was he twice as guilty as Ryan, who sold truck drivers' licenses to unqualified people, leading to highway deaths? And was Ryan twice as guilty as former Democratic Gov. Otto Kerner of Illinois, who got three years in prison in 1973 for accepting bribes from a racetrack owner?

Sentencing is a matter for individual judges to decide, but the overall trend for convicted politicians is increased prison time. In 2009, former Rep. William J. Jefferson (D-La.), who famously stored bribe money in his freezer, was given 13 years in prison. It was the longest sentence ever given to a former congressman, easily topping the eight years and four months in prison given in 2006 to former Rep. Randy Cunningham (R-Calif.), who accepted bribes for tens of millions of dollars in defense contracts.

Pleas for mercy now seem to fall on deaf ears. In the 1970s, Kerner was released early due to terminal cancer, but in 2011 a judge refused a request from former Governor Ryan to leave to visit his wife who was dying of cancer. The only way Ryan got to see her at all was through the mercy of his prison warden.

Some judges compare the destruction of citizens' trust in the political system to violent crimes. According to former U.S. Attorney Patrick Collins, who prosecuted Ryan, "judges are now looking at these corruption cases like guns and drug cases." As U.S. District Judge James Zagel put it in sentencing Blagojevich: "When it is the governor who goes bad, the fabric of Illinois is torn and disfigured and not easily or quickly repaired."

Some errant politicians still get relatively short sentences but are hammered if convicted again. In 2008, former Democratic Mayor Kwame Kilpatrick of Detroit was sentenced to four months in prison for covering up an affair with his chief of staff and assaulting a police officer. But when he violated parole, the judge lambasted him for his "lack of contriteness and lack of humility," and he received 18 months to 5 years in prison in 2010. In 2012, Kilpatrick was convicted by a federal jury of using his position as mayor and as a Michigan State House Representative to execute a wide-ranging racketeering conspiracy.

Politicians embrace high standards for their enemies, but not so much for themselves. When President Bill Clinton was impeached in 1978, Rep. Tom Delay (D-Texas), the House Majority Whip at the time, advocated "the higher road of the rule of law." He continued: "Sometimes hard, sometimes unpleasant, this path relies on truth, justice and the rigorous application of the principle that no man is above the law."

Then in 2011, Delay was convicted of money laundering and sentenced to three years in prison. He has never accepted blame for what he did, arguing that he was the victim of political enemies in Texas.

Resources: "Former Detroit Mayor Kwame Kilpatrick, His Father Bernard Kilpatrick, and City Contractor Bobby Ferguson Convicted on Racketeering, Extortion, Bribery, Fraud, and Tax Charges," *FBI press release*, March 11, 2013, http://www.fbi.gov/detroit/press-releases/2013/former-detroit-mayor-kwame-kilpatrick-his-father-bernard-kilpatrick-and-city-contractor-bobby-ferguson-convicted-on-racketeering-extortion-bribery-fraud-and-tax-charges; "'Sorry' Blagojevich Gets 14-Year Prison Sentence," *Chicago Sun-Times*, December 7, 2011, http://www.suntimes.com/news/metro/blagojevich/9300810-452/sorry-blagojevich-gets-14-year-prison-sentence.html; "Tom DeLay Gets 3 Years in Prison for Money Laundering," *Fox News*, January 10, 2011, http://www.foxnews.com/politics/2011/01/10/tom-delay-gets-years-prison-money-laundering/; and "Former Rep. William Jefferson Sentenced to 13 Years in Prison," *Christian Science Monitor*, November 13, 2009, http://www.csmonitor.com/USA/Politics/2009/1113/former-rep-william-jefferson-sentenced-to-13-years-in-prison.

criminal law The body of rules and regulations that define and specify the nature of and punishments for offenses of a public nature or for wrongs committed against the state or society. Also called *penal law*.

Follow the author's tweets about the latest crime and justice news @schmalleger.

substantive criminal law The part of the law that defines crimes and specifies punishments.

CRIMINAL LAW

Criminal law is defined as the body of rules and regulations that define and specify the nature of and punishments for offenses of a public nature or for wrongs committed against the state or society. Fundamental to the concept of criminal law is the assumption that criminal acts injure not just individuals but society as a whole. Criminal law is also called *penal law.*

These crimes not only offend their victims but also disrupt the peaceful order of society. It is for this reason that the state begins the official process of bringing the offender to justice. The state will be the plaintiff in the criminal proceeding. Those found guilty of violating a criminal law are punished.

EXAMPLES: Murder, rape, robbery, and assault are examples of criminal offenses against which there are laws.

ADMINISTRATIVE LAW

Administrative law is the body of regulations that governments create to control the activities of industries, businesses, and individuals. For the most part, a breach of administrative law is not a crime.

Administrative agencies will sometimes arrange settlements that fall short of court action but that are considered binding on individuals or groups that have not followed the rules of administrative law.

EXAMPLES: Tax laws, health codes, restrictions on pollution and waste disposal, vehicle regulation laws, and building codes are examples of administrative laws.

STATUTORY LAW

Refers to the law on the books; written, codified laws.

EXAMPLE: The acts of legislatures.

Substantive criminal law is a form of statutory law that describes what constitutes particular crimes and specifies the appropriate punishment for the offense.

Procedural law is a type of statutory law. It is a body of rules that determines the proceedings by which legal rights are enforced. These laws regulate the gathering of evidence and the processing of offenders by the criminal justice system.

CIVIL LAW

Civil law governs relationships between and among people, businesses and other organizations, and agencies of government. In contrast to the criminal law, whose violation is against the state or the nation, civil law governs relationships between parties.

Typically civil suits seek compensation (usually in the form of property or money). A violation of the civil law is not a crime. It may be a contract violation or a tort. A tort is a wrongful act, damage, or injury not involving a breach of contract. Because a tort is a personal wrong and not a crime, it is left to the aggrieved individual to bring the case to court. Civil law is more concerned with assessing liability than it is with intent. Civil suits can also be brought against a crime where the intent is clear. His or her victim may decide to seek monetary compensation.

EXAMPLES: Includes things such as rules for contracts, divorces, child support and custody, the creation of wills, property transfers, libel, and many other contractual and social obligations.

CASE LAW

Case law comes from judicial decisions and is also referred to as the law of precedent. It represents the accumulated wisdom of trial and appellate courts. Once a court decision is rendered, it is written down. At the appellate level, the reasoning behind the decision is recorded as well.

The Supreme Court is the highest-level appellate court. *Stare decisis* refers to the principle of recognizing previous decisions as precedents for guiding future deliberations.

A vertical rule requires that decisions made by a higher court be taken into consideration by lower courts.

The horizontal dimension refers to cases handled by the same court that should be decided in a similar way.

EXAMPLES: Under the law of precedent, the reasonings of previous courts should be taken into consideration by other courts in settling similar future cases.

COMMON LAW

Common law is that body of law originating from usage and custom rather than from written statutes.

EXAMPLE: English common law is the basis for much American criminal law, although most states have codified common law principles in their written statutes.

FIGURE 4-1 | Types of Law

Criminal Law

Criminal law, also called *penal law*, refers to the body of rules and regulations that define and specify the nature of and punishments for offenses of a public nature or for wrongs committed against the state or society. Public order is compromised whenever a criminal act occurs, and those found guilty of violating the criminal law are punished. Punishment for crime is philosophically justified by the fact that the offender *intended* the harm and is responsible for it. Criminal law, which is built on constitutional principles and operates within an established set of procedures applicable to the criminal justice system, is composed of both statutory (written law) and case law.

Statutory Law

Written law, or statutory law, is of two types: substantive and procedural. **Substantive criminal law** describes what constitutes particular crimes, such as murder, rape, robbery, and assault, and specifies the appropriate punishment for each particular offense.

■ **procedural law** The part of the law that specifies the methods to be used in enforcing substantive law.
■ **civil law** The branch of modern law that governs relationships between parties.
■ **tort** A wrongful act, damage, or injury not involving a breach of contract. Also, a private or civil wrong or injury.

■ **precedent** A legal principle that ensures that previous judicial decisions are authoritatively considered and incorporated into future cases.
■ ***stare decisis*** A legal principle requiring that, in subsequent cases on similar issues of law and fact, courts be bound by their own earlier decisions and by those of higher courts having jurisdiction over them. The term literally means "standing by decided matters."

Procedural law is a body of rules that determines the proceedings by which legal rights are enforced. The law of criminal procedure, for example, regulates the gathering of evidence and the processing of offenders by the criminal justice system. General rules of evidence, search and seizure, procedures to be followed in an arrest, trial procedures, and other specified processes by which the justice system operates are all contained in procedural law. Each state has its own set of criminal procedure laws, as does the federal government. Laws of criminal procedure balance a suspect's rights against the state's interests in the speedy and efficient processing of criminal defendants. View the Federal Rules of Criminal Procedure at **http://www.law.cornell.edu/rules/frcrmp** and the Federal Rules of Evidence at **http://www.uscourts.gov/uscourts/rules/rules-evidence.pdf.**

Civil Law

Civil law, much of which takes the form of statutory law, stands in contrast to criminal law. Civil law governs relationships between and among people, businesses and other organizations, and agencies of government. It contains rules for contracts, divorces, child support and custody, the creation of wills, property transfers, negligence, libel, unfair practices in hiring, the manufacture and sale of consumer goods with hidden hazards for the user, and many other contractual and social obligations. When the civil law is violated, a civil suit may follow. Typically, civil suits seek compensation (usually in the form of property or monetary damages), not punishment. A violation of the civil law is not a crime. It may be a contract violation or a **tort**—which is a wrongful act, damage, or injury not involving a breach of contract. Because a tort is a personal wrong and not a crime, it is left to the aggrieved individual to set the machinery of the court in motion—that is, to bring a suit. The parties to a civil suit are referred to as the *plaintiff*, who seeks relief, and the *defendant*, against whom relief is sought. Civil suits are also sometimes brought by crime victims against those whose criminal intent is clear. Once the perpetrator of a crime has been convicted, the victim may decide to seek monetary compensation from him or her through our system of civil laws.

Administrative Law

Still another kind of law, *administrative law,* is the body of regulations that governments create to control the activities of industries, businesses, and individuals. Tax laws, health codes, restrictions on pollution and waste disposal, vehicle registration laws, and building codes are examples of administrative laws. Other administrative laws cover practices in the areas of customs (imports and exports), immigration, agriculture, product safety, and most areas of manufacturing. For the most part, a breach of administrative law is not a crime. However, criminal law and administrative regulations may overlap. For instance, organized criminal activity is prevalent in the area of toxic waste disposal—an area covered by many administrative regulations—which has led to criminal prosecutions in several states.

Case Law

Legal experts also talk about case law, or the law of **precedent**. Case law comes from judicial decisions and represents the accumulated wisdom of trial and appellate courts (those that hear appeals) in criminal, civil, and administrative law cases over the years. Once a court decision is rendered, it is written down. At the appellate level, the reasoning behind the decision is recorded as well. Under the law of precedent, this reasoning is then taken into consideration by other courts in settling similar future cases. The principle of recognizing previous decisions as precedents to guide future deliberations, called ***stare decisis***, forms the basis for our modern law of precedent. *Stare decisis* makes for predictability in the law. The court with the greatest influence, of course, is the U.S. Supreme Court, and the precedents it establishes are used as guidelines in the process of legal reasoning by which lower courts reach conclusions.

Learn more about the evolution of American criminal law at **http://schmalleger.com/pubs/evolution.pdf**. Some online criminal law journals may be accessed at **http://www.law.berkeley.edu/228.htm** and **http://wings.buffalo.edu/law/bclc/bclr.htm**.

General Categories of Crime

Violations of the *criminal* law can be of many different types and can vary in severity. Six general categories of criminal law violations can be identified: (1) felonies, (2) misdemeanors, (3) offenses, (4) treason, (5) espionage, and (6) inchoate offenses (Figure 4-2).

■ **felony** A criminal offense punishable by death or by incarceration in a prison facility for at least one year.
■ **misdemeanor** An offense punishable by incarceration, usually in a local confinement facility, for a period whose upper limit is prescribed by statute in a given jurisdiction, typically one year or less.

■ **offense** A violation of the criminal law. Also, in some jurisdictions, a minor crime, such as jaywalking, that is sometimes described as *ticketable*.
■ **infraction** A minor violation of state statute or local ordinance punishable by a fine or other penalty or by a specified, usually limited, term of incarceration.
■ **treason** A U.S. citizen's actions to help a foreign government overthrow, make war against, or seriously injure the United States.[i] Also, the attempt to overthrow the government of the society of which one is a member.

FELONY
A criminal offense punishable by death or by incarceration in a prison facility for at least one year.

INCHOATE OFFENSE
An offense not yet completed. Also, an offense that consists of an action or conduct that is a step toward the intended commission of another offense.

OFFENSE
A violation of the criminal law. Also, in some jurisdictions, a minor crime, such as jaywalking, that is sometimes described as *ticketable.* Such minor offenses are also known as *infractions.*

MISDEMEANOR
An offense punishable by incarceration, usually in a local confinement facility, for a period whose upper limit is prescribed by statute in a given jurisdiction, typically one year or less.

TREASON
A U.S. citizen's actions to help a foreign government overthrow, make war against, or seriously injure the United States. Also, the attempt to overthrow the government of the society of which one is a member.

ESPIONAGE
The "gathering, transmitting, or losing" of information related to the national defense in such a manner that the information becomes available to enemies of the United States and may be used to their advantage.

FIGURE 4-2 | General Categories of Crime

Felonies

Felonies are serious crimes; they include murder, rape, aggravated assault, robbery, burglary, and arson. Today, many felons receive prison sentences, although the range of potential penalties includes everything from probation and a fine to capital punishment in many jurisdictions. Under common law, felons could be sentenced to death, could have their property confiscated, or both. Following common law tradition, people who are convicted of felonies today usually lose certain privileges. Some states, for example, make a felony conviction and incarceration grounds for uncontested divorce. Others prohibit offenders from voting, running for public office, or owning a firearm and exclude them from some professions, such as medicine, law, and police work.

Misdemeanors

Misdemeanors are relatively minor crimes, consisting of offenses such as petty theft, which is stealing items of little worth; simple assault, in which the victim suffers no serious injury and in which none was intended; breaking and entering; possessing burglary tools; being disorderly in public; disturbing the peace; filing a false crime report; and writing bad checks, although the amount for which the check is written may determine the classification of this offense. In general, misdemeanors are any crime punishable by a year or less in prison. In fact, most misdemeanants receive suspended sentences involving a fine and supervised probation.

Offenses

A third category of crime is the **offense**. Although, strictly speaking, all violations of the criminal law can be called *criminal offenses*, the term *offense* is sometimes used to refer specifically to minor violations of the law that are less serious than misdemeanors. When the term is used in that sense, it refers to such things as jaywalking, spitting on the sidewalk, littering, and committing certain traffic violations, including the failure to wear a seat belt. Another word used to describe such minor law violations is **infraction**. People committing infractions are typically ticketed and released, usually on a promise to appear later in court. Court appearances may often be waived through payment of a small fine that can be mailed to the court.

Treason and Espionage

Felonies, misdemeanors, offenses, and the people who commit them constitute the daily work of the justice system. However, special categories of crime do exist and should be recognized. They include treason and espionage, two crimes that are often regarded as the most serious of felonies. **Treason** can be defined

freedom OR **safety?** YOU **decide**

Should Violent Speech Be Free Speech?

In 2005, a state jury in Alexandria, Virginia, convicted 42-year-old Muslim scholar Ali al-Timimi of a number of offenses, including the crime of incitement, conspiring to carry firearms and explosives, and soliciting others to make war against the United States. The U.S.-born Islamic spiritual adviser had spoken frequently at the Center for Islamic Information and Education—also known as the Dar al Arqam Islamic Center—in Falls Church, Virginia. Prosecutors told jurors that al-Timimi had verbally encouraged his followers to train with terrorist organizations and to engage in violent Jihad, or holy war, against America and its allies. al-Timimi, who lived much of his life in the Washington, D.C., area, earned a doctorate in computational biology from George Mason University and is the author of at least 12 articles published in scientific journals, most dealing with how to use computers to analyze genes found in various kinds of cancer. As a teenager, al-Timimi had spent two years in Saudi Arabia with his family, where he became interested in Islam.

Following conviction, al-Timimi was sentenced to life in prison without the possibility of parole, plus 70 years—a sentence meant to guarantee that he would never leave prison. He is currently appealing, and there is some chance that his case will be sent back for retrial based on claims that the National Security Agency illegally gathered information about his activities.

The al-Timimi case raises a number of interesting issues—among them the issue of when violent speech crosses the line from free expression into criminal advocacy.

The First Amendment to the U.S. Constitution guarantees the right to free speech. It is a fundamental guarantee of our democratic way of life. So, for example, the speech of those who advocate a new form of government in the United States is protected, even though their ideas may appear anti-American and ill considered.

In the 1957 case of *Roth* v. *United States*, the U.S. Supreme Court held that "the protection given speech and press was fashioned to assure unfettered interchange of ideas for the bringing about of political and social changes desired by the people."

It is important to remember, however, that constitutional rights are not without limit—that is, they have varying applicability under differing conditions. Some forms of speech are too dangerous to be allowed, even under our liberal rules.

Freedom of speech does not mean, for example, that you have a protected right to stand up in a crowded theater and yell "Fire!" That's because the panic that would follow such an exclamation would likely cause injuries and would put members of the public at risk of harm.

Hence, the courts have held that although freedom of speech is guaranteed by the Constitution, there are limits to it. (Shouting "Fire!" in a public park would likely not be considered an actionable offense.)

Similarly, saying, "The president deserves to die," horrific as it may sound, may be merely a matter of personal opinion. Anyone who says, "I'm going to kill the president," however, can wind up in jail because threatening the life of the president is a crime—as is the act of communicating threats of imminent violence in most jurisdictions.

al-Timimi's mistake may have been the timing of his remarks, which were made to a public gathering in Virginia five days after the September 11, 2001, attacks. In his speech, al-Timimi called for a "holy war" and "violent Jihad" against the West. He was later quoted by converts with whom he met as referring to American forces in Afghanistan as "legitimate targets."

Critics of al-Timimi's conviction point to a seeming double standard under which people can be arrested for unpopular speech, but not for popular speech—regardless of the degree of violence it implies. They note, for example, that conservative columnist Ann Coulter has suggested in writing that "we should invade (Muslim) countries, kill their leaders and convert them to Christianity," but she was never arrested for what she said.

In 2010, in an effort to distinguish what would otherwise be protected free speech from speech that constitutes criminal support of terrorist organization, the U.S. Supreme Court decided the case of *Holder* v. *Humanitarian Law Project*. In that case, Chief Justice John G. Roberts, Jr., wrote that for speech to constitute criminal support of terrorist organizations, "it has to take the form of training, expert advice or assistance conveyed in coordination with or under the direction of a foreign terrorist organization."

You Decide

Should al-Timimi's advocacy of violence be unlawful? Why or why not? Do you think that al-Timimi's rhetoric rises to the level of criminal support of terrorist organizations according to the standard set in Holder v. Humanitarian Law Project? Might we have more to fear from the suppression of speech (even speech like al-Timimi's) than from its free expression? If so, how?

References: "Virginia Man Convicted of Urging War on U.S.," *USA Today*, April 27, 2005; Jonathan Turley, "When Is Violent Speech Still Free Speech?" *USA Today*, May 3, 2005; Eric Lichtblau, "Administration Continues Eavesdropping Defense," *The New York Times*, January 24, 2006; and *Holder* v. *Humanitarian Law Project*, 561 U.S. ___ (2010).

■ **espionage** The "gathering, transmitting, or losing"[ii] of information related to the national defense in such a manner that the information becomes available to enemies of the United States and may be used to their advantage.

■ **inchoate offense** An offense not yet completed. Also, an offense that consists of an action or conduct that is a step toward the intended commission of another offense.

■ ***actus reus*** An act in violation of the law. Also, a guilty act.

as "a U.S. citizen's actions to help a foreign government overthrow, make war against, or seriously injure the United States."[9]

Espionage, an offense akin to treason but that can be committed by noncitizens, is the "gathering, transmitting, or losing" of information related to the national defense in such a manner that the information becomes available to enemies of the United States and may be used to their advantage.[10] In 2012, for example, former U.S. government scientist Stewart Nozette, 54, was sentenced to 13 years in prison after pleading guilty to federal espionage charges. Nozette has been arrested during a Federal Bureau of Investigation (FBI) sting operation and later admitted that he had tried to provide classified information about U.S. early-warning systems and secret satellites to FBI agents posing as Israeli intelligence officers.[11] Nozette had once worked at the esteemed Lawrence Livermore National Laboratory.

Inchoate Offenses

Another special category of crime is called *inchoate*. The word *inchoate* means "incomplete or partial," and **inchoate offenses** are those that have not been fully carried out. Conspiracies are an example. When a person conspires to commit a crime, any action undertaken in furtherance of the conspiracy is generally regarded as a sufficient basis for arrest and prosecution. For instance, a woman who intends to kill her husband may make a phone call or conduct an Internet search to find a hit man to carry out her plan. The call or search are themselves evidence of her intent and can result in her imprisonment for conspiracy to commit murder.

Conventional legal wisdom holds that the essence of crime consists of three conjoined elements: (1) the criminal act, which in legal parlance is termed the *actus reus*; (2) a culpable mental state, or *mens rea*; and (3) a concurrence of the two.

Another type of inchoate offense is the attempt to commit a crime, which occurs when an offender is unable to complete the intended crime. For example, homeowners may arrive just as a burglar is beginning to enter their residence, causing the burglar to drop his tools and run. In most jurisdictions, this frustrated burglar can be arrested and charged with attempted burglary.

AP Wide World Photos

Former U.S. government scientist Stewart Nozette, 54, shown in undercover video from a Federal Bureau of Investigation (FBI) sting operation. Nozette was sentenced in 2012 to 13 years in prison after pleading guilty to federal espionage charges. He had once worked at the esteemed Lawrence Livermore National Laboratory, and admitted that he had tried to provide classified information about U.S. early-warning systems and secret satellites to FBI agents posing as Israeli intelligence officers. What's the difference between espionage and treason?

General Features of Crime

From the perspective of Western jurisprudence, all crimes can be said to share certain features (Figure 4-3), and the notion of crime itself can be said to rest on such general principles. Taken together, these features, which are described in this section, make up the legal essence of the concept of crime. Conventional legal wisdom holds that the essence of crime consists of three conjoined elements: (1) the criminal act, which in legal parlance is termed the *actus reus*; (2) a culpable mental state, or *mens rea*; and (3) a concurrence of the two. Hence, as we shall see in the following paragraphs, the essence of criminal conduct consists of a concurrence of a criminal act with a culpable mental state.

The Criminal Act (*Actus Reus*)

A necessary first feature of any crime is some act in violation of the law. Such an act is termed the ***actus reus*** of a crime. The term means "guilty act." Generally, a person must commit some voluntary act before he or she is subject to criminal sanctions. To *be something* is not a crime; to *do something* may be.

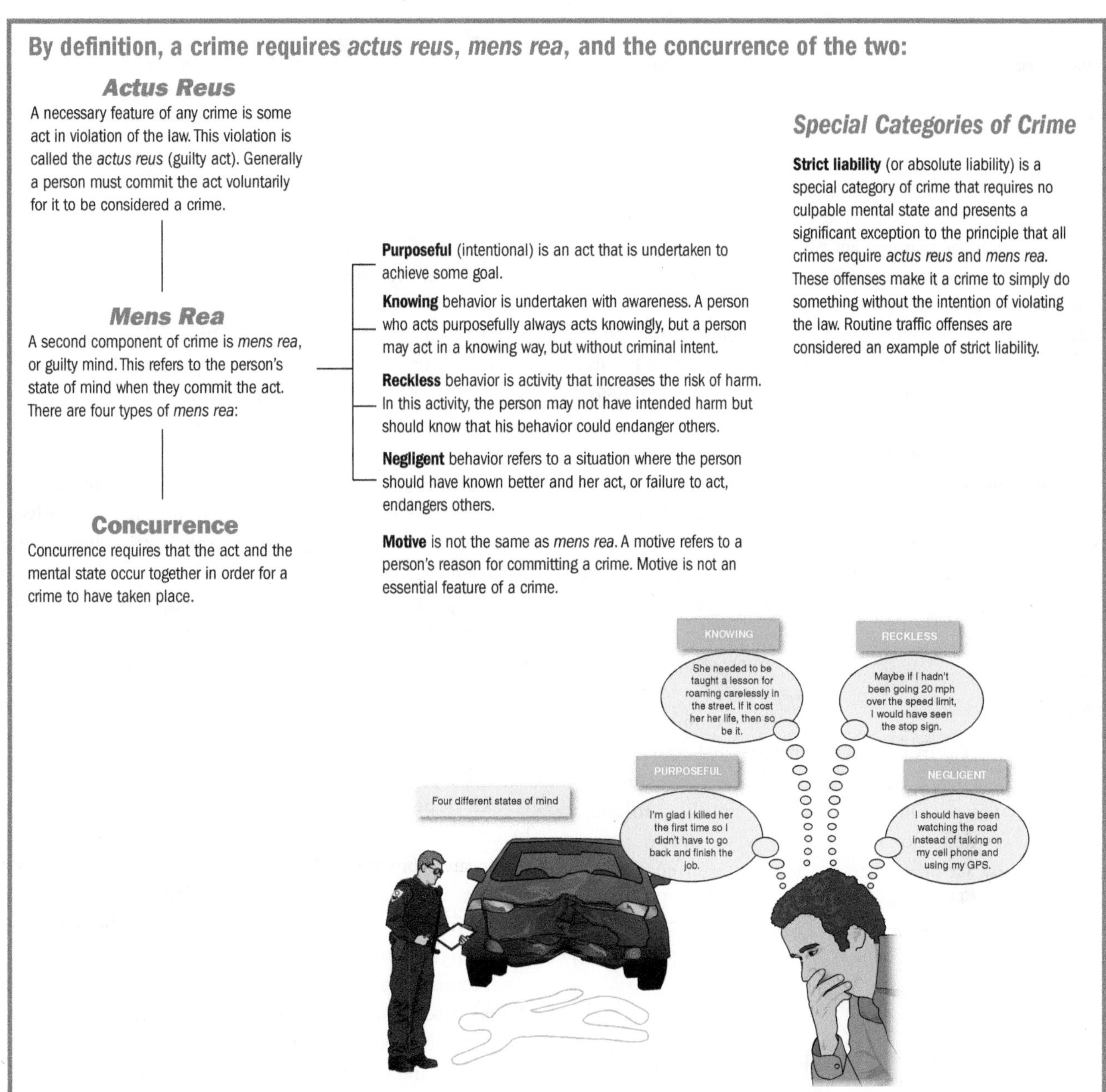

By definition, a crime requires actus reus, mens rea, and the concurrence of the two:
Actus Reus
A necessary feature of any crime is some act in violation of the law. This violation is called the actus reus (guilty act). Generally a person must commit the act voluntarily for it to be considered a crime.
Mens Rea
A second component of crime is mens rea, or guilty mind. This refers to the person's state of mind when they commit the act. There are four types of mens rea:
Purposeful (intentional) is an act that is undertaken to achieve some goal.
Knowing behavior is undertaken with awareness. A person who acts purposefully always acts knowingly, but a person may act in a knowing way, but without criminal intent.
Reckless behavior is activity that increases the risk of harm. In this activity, the person may not have intended harm but should know that his behavior could endanger others.
Negligent behavior refers to a situation where the person should have known better and her act, or failure to act, endangers others.
Motive is not the same as mens rea. A motive refers to a person's reason for committing a crime. Motive is not an essential feature of a crime.
Concurrence
Concurrence requires that the act and the mental state occur together in order for a crime to have taken place.
Special Categories of Crime
Strict liability (or absolute liability) is a special category of crime that requires no culpable mental state and presents a significant exception to the principle that all crimes require actus reus and mens rea. These offenses make it a crime to simply do something without the intention of violating the law. Routine traffic offenses are considered an example of strict liability.
KNOWING
She needed to be taught a lesson for roaming carelessly in the street. If it cost her her life, then so be it.
RECKLESS
Maybe if I hadn't been going 20 mph over the speed limit, I would have seen the stop sign.
PURPOSEFUL
I'm glad I killed her the first time so I didn't have to go back and finish the job.
NEGLIGENT
I should have been watching the road instead of talking on my cell phone and using my GPS.
Four different states of mind

FIGURE 4-3 | Features of a Crime

Source: Illustration from Frank A. Schmalleger, Daniel E. Hall, and John J. Dolatowski, *Criminal Law Today,* 4th ed. (Upper Saddle River, NJ: Pearson Education, 2010), p. 46. Reprinted by permission of Pearson Education, Inc., Upper Saddle River, NJ.

For example, someone who is caught using drugs can be arrested, whereas someone who simply admits that he or she is a drug user (perhaps on a TV talk show or in a tweet) cannot be arrested on that basis. Police who hear the drug user's admission might begin gathering evidence to prove some specific law violation in that person's past, or perhaps they might watch that individual for future behavior in violation of the law. A subsequent arrest would then be based on a specific action in violation of the law pertaining to controlled substances.

Vagrancy laws, popular in the early part of the twentieth century, have generally been invalidated by the courts because they did not specify what act violated the law. In fact, the less a person did, the more vagrant he or she was. An omission to act, however, may be criminal where the person in question is required by law to do something. Child-neglect laws, for example, focus on parents and child guardians who do not live up to their responsibility to care for their children.

Threatening to act can be a criminal offense. For example, threatening to kill someone can result in an arrest for the offense of communicating threats. Such threats against the president of the United States are taken seriously by the Secret Service, and individuals are arrested for boasting about planned violence

■ ***mens rea*** The state of mind that accompanies a criminal act. Also, a guilty mind.
■ **reckless behavior** Activity that increases the risk of harm.
■ **criminal negligence** Behavior in which a person fails to reasonably perceive the substantial and unjustifiable risks of dangerous consequences.
■ **motive** A person's reason for committing a crime.

directed at the president. Attempted criminal activity is also illegal. An attempt to murder or rape, for example, is a serious crime, even when the planned act is not accomplished.

Conspiracies, mentioned earlier in this chapter, are another criminal act. When a conspiracy unfolds, the ultimate act that it aims to bring about does not have to occur for the parties to the conspiracy to be arrested. When people plan to bomb a public building, for example, they can be legally stopped before the bombing. As soon as they take steps to "further" their plan, they have met the requirement for an act. Buying explosives, telephoning one another, and drawing plans of the building may all be actions in furtherance of the conspiracy. But not all conspiracy statutes require actions in furtherance of the "target crime" before an arrest can be made. Technically speaking, crimes of conspiracy can be seen as entirely distinct from the target crimes that the conspirators are contemplating. For example, in 1994 the U.S. Supreme Court upheld the drug-related conviction of Reshat Shabani when it ruled that, in the case of certain antidrug laws,[12] "it is presumed that Congress intended to adopt the common law definition of conspiracy, which does not make the doing of any act other than the act of conspiring a condition of liability."[13] Hence, according to the Court, "The criminal agreement itself," even in the absence of actions directed toward realizing the target crime, can be grounds for arrest and prosecution.

The importance of *mens rea* as a component of crime cannot be overemphasized.

A Guilty Mind (*Mens Rea*)

Mens rea is the second general component of crime. The term, which literally means "guilty mind," refers to the defendant's specific mental state at the time the behavior in question occurred. The importance of *mens rea* as a component of crime cannot be overemphasized. It can be seen in the fact that some courts have held that "[a]ll crime exists primarily in the mind."[14] The extent to which a person can be held criminally responsible for his or her actions generally depends on the nature of the mental state under which he or she was laboring at the time of the offense.

Four levels, or types, of *mens rea* can be distinguished: (1) purposeful (or intentional), (2) knowing, (3) reckless, and (4) negligent. Purposeful or intentional action is that which is undertaken to achieve some goal. Sometimes the harm that results from intentional action may be unintended; however, this does not reduce criminal liability. The doctrine of *transferred intent*, for example, which operates in all U.S. jurisdictions, holds a person guilty of murder if that individual took aim and shot at an intended victim but missed, killing another person instead. The philosophical notion behind the concept of transferred intent is that the killer's intent to kill, which existed at the time of the crime, transferred from the intended victim to the person who was struck by the bullet and died.

Knowing behavior is action undertaken with awareness. A person who acts purposefully always acts knowingly, but a person may act in a knowingly criminal way but for a purpose other than criminal intent. For example, an airline captain who allows a flight attendant to transport cocaine aboard an airplane may do so to gain sexual favors from the attendant, but without the purpose of drug smuggling. Knowing behavior involves near certainty. In this scenario, if the airline captain allows the flight attendant to carry cocaine aboard the plane, it *will* be transported, and the pilot knows it. In another example, if an HIV-infected individual knowingly has unprotected sexual intercourse with another person, the partner *will* be exposed to the virus.

Reckless Behavior and Criminal Negligence

Reckless behavior is activity that increases the risk of harm. In contrast to knowing behavior, knowledge may be part of recklessness, but it exists more in the form of probability than certainty. As a practical example, reckless driving is a frequent charge in many jurisdictions; it is generally brought when a driver engages in risky activity that endangers others.

Nevertheless, *mens rea* is said to be present when a person should have known better, even if the person did not directly intend the consequences of his or her action. A person who acts negligently and thereby endangers others may be found guilty of **criminal negligence** when harm occurs, even though no negative consequences were intended. For example, a parent who leaves a 12-month-old child alone in the tub can be prosecuted for negligent homicide if the child drowns.[15] It should be emphasized, however, that negligence in and of itself is not a crime. Negligent conduct can be evidence of crime only when it falls below some acceptable standard of care. That standard is applied today in criminal courts through the fictional creation of a *reasonable person*. The question to be asked in a given case is whether a reasonable person, in the same situation, would have known better and acted differently from the defendant. The reasonable person criterion provides a yardstick for juries faced with thorny issues of guilt or innocence.

It is important to note that *mens rea*, even in the sense of intent, is not the same thing as motive. A **motive** refers to a person's reason for committing a crime. Although evidence of motive may be admissible during a criminal trial to help prove

■ **strict liability** Liability without fault or intention. Strict liability offenses do not require *mens rea.*
■ **concurrence** The coexistence of (1) an act in violation of the law, and (2) a culpable mental state.

■ **legal cause** A legally recognizable cause. A legal cause must be demonstrated in court in order to hold an individual criminally liable for causing harm.

a crime, motive itself is not an essential element of a crime. As a result, we cannot say that a bad or immoral motive makes an act a crime.

Mens rea is a tricky concept. Not only is it philosophically and legally complex, but a person's state of mind during the commission of an offense can rarely be known directly unless the person confesses. Hence, *mens rea* must generally be inferred from a person's actions and from all the circumstances surrounding those actions. Pure accident, however, which involves no recklessness or negligence, cannot serve as the basis for either criminal or civil liability. "Even a dog," the famous Supreme Court Justice Oliver Wendell Holmes once wrote, "distinguishes between being stumbled over and being kicked."[16]

Strict Liability

A special category of crimes, called **strict liability** offenses, requires no culpable mental state and presents a significant exception to the principle that all crimes require a concurrence of *actus reus* and *mens rea*. Strict liability offenses, also called *absolute liability offenses*, make it a crime simply to *do* something, even if the offender has no intention of violating the law. Strict liability is philosophically based on the presumption that causing harm is in itself blameworthy, regardless of the actor's intent.

Routine traffic offenses are generally considered strict liability offenses. Driving 65 miles per hour in a 55-mph zone is a violation of the law, even though the driver may be listening to music, thinking, or simply going with the flow of traffic, entirely unaware that his or her vehicle is exceeding the posted speed limit. Statutory rape is another example of strict liability.[17] This crime generally occurs between two consenting individuals; it requires only that the offender have sexual intercourse with a person under the age of legal consent. Statutes describing the crime routinely avoid any mention of a culpable mental state. In many jurisdictions, it matters little whether the "perpetrator" knew the exact age of the "victim" or whether the "victim" lied about his or her age or had given consent, as statutory rape laws are "an attempt to prevent the sexual exploitation of persons deemed legally incapable of giving consent."[18]

Concurrence

The concurrence of an unlawful act and a culpable mental state provides the third basic component of crime. **Concurrence** requires that the act and the mental state occur together in order for a crime to take place. If one precedes the other, the requirements of the criminal law have not been met. A person may intend to kill a rival, for example. He drives to the intended victim's house, with his gun, fantasizing about how he will commit the murder. Just as he nears the victim's home, the victim crosses the street on the way to the grocery store. If the two accidentally collide and the intended victim dies, there has been no concurrence of act and intent.

Other Features of Crime

Some scholars contend that the three features of crime that we have just outlined—*actus reus*, *mens rea*, and concurrence—are sufficient to constitute the essence of the legal concept of crime. Other scholars, however, see modern Western law as more complex. They argue that recognition of five additional principles is necessary to fully appreciate contemporary understandings of crime. These five principles are (1) causation, (2) resulting harm, (3) the principle of legality, (4) the principle of punishment, and (5) necessary attendant circumstances. We will now discuss each of these additional features in turn.

Causation

Causation refers to the fact that the concurrence of a guilty mind and a criminal act may cause harm. Whereas some statutes criminalize only conduct, others require that the offender *cause* a particular result before criminal liability can be incurred. Sometimes, however, a causal link is unclear. For example, let's consider a case of assault with a deadly weapon with intent to kill. A person shoots another, and the victim is seriously injured but is not immediately killed. The victim, who remains in the hospital, survives for more than a year. The victim's death occurs due to a blood clot that forms from lack of activity. In such a case, it is likely that defense attorneys will argue that the defendant did not cause the death; rather, the death occurred because of disease. If a jury agrees with the defense's claim, the shooter may go free or be found guilty of a lesser charge, such as assault.

To clarify the issue of causation, the American Law Institute suggests use of the term **legal cause** to emphasize the notion of a legally recognizable cause and to preclude any assumption that such a cause must be close in time and space to the result it produces. Legal causes can be distinguished from those causes that may have produced the result in question but do not provide the basis for a criminal prosecution because they are too complex, too indistinguishable from other causes, not knowable, or not provable in a court of law.

■ ***ex post facto*** Latin for "after the fact." The Constitution prohibits the enactment of *ex post facto* laws, which make acts committed before the laws in question were passed punishable as crimes.

■ **attendant circumstances** The facts surrounding an event.

■ **element (of a crime)** In a specific crime, one of the essential features of that crime, as specified by law or statute.

Harm

A harm occurs in any crime, although not all harms are crimes. When a person is murdered or raped, harm can be clearly identified. Some crimes, however, can be said to be *victimless*. Perpetrators (and their attorneys) maintain that in committing such crimes they harm no one but themselves; rather, they say, the crime may actually be pleasurable for those involved. Prostitution, gambling, and drug use are commonly classified as "victimless." What these offenders fail to recognize, say legal theorists, is the social harm caused by their behavior. In areas afflicted with chronic prostitution, drug use, and illegal gambling, property values fall, family life disintegrates, and other, more traditional crimes increase as money is sought to support the "victimless" activities. Law-abiding citizens abandon the area.

In a criminal prosecution, however, it is rarely necessary to prove harm as a separate element of a crime because it is subsumed under the notion of a guilty act. In the crime of murder, for example, the "killing of a human being" brings about a harm but is, properly speaking, an act. When committed with the requisite *mens rea*, it becomes a crime. A similar type of reasoning applies to the criminalization of *attempts* that cause no harm. A scenario commonly raised to illustrate this dilemma is one in which attackers throw rocks at a blind person, but because of bad aim, the rocks hit no one, and the intended target remains unaware that anyone is trying to harm him. In such a case, should throwing rocks provide a basis for criminal liability? As one authority on the subject observes, "Criticism of the principle of harm has . . . been based on the view that the harm actually caused may be a matter of sheer accident and that the rational thing to do is to base the punishment on the *mens rea*, and the action, disregarding any actual harm or lack of harm or its degree."[19] This observation also shows why we have said that the essence of crime consists only of three things: (1) *actus reus*, (2) *mens rea*, and (3) the concurrence of an illegal act and a culpable mental state.

Legality

The principle of legality highlights the fact that a behavior cannot be criminal if no law exists that defines it as such. For example, as long as you are of drinking age, it is all right to drink beer because there is no statute on the books prohibiting it. During Prohibition, of course, the situation was quite different. (In fact, some parts of the United States are still "dry," and the purchase or public consumption of alcohol can be a law violation regardless of age.) The principle of legality also includes the notion that ***ex post facto*** laws are not binding, which means that a law cannot be created tomorrow that will hold a person legally responsible for something he or she does today. Rather, laws are binding only from the date of their creation or from some future date at which they are specified as taking effect.[20]

Punishment

The principle of punishment holds that no crime can be said to occur where punishment has not been specified in the law. Larceny, for example, would not be a crime if the law simply said, "It is illegal to steal." Punishment for the crime must be specified so that if a person is found guilty of violating the law, sanctions can be lawfully imposed.

Necessary Attendant Circumstances

Finally, statutes defining some crimes specify that certain additional elements, called **attendant circumstances**, must be present for a conviction to be obtained. Generally speaking, attendant circumstances are the "facts surrounding an event"[21] and include such things as time and place. Attendant circumstances that are specified by law as necessary elements of an offense are sometimes called *necessary attendant circumstances*, indicating that the existence of such circumstances is necessary, along with the other elements included in the relevant statute, for a crime to have been committed. Florida law, for example, makes it a crime to "[k]nowingly commit any lewd or lascivious act in the presence of any child under the age of 16 years."[22] In this case, the behavior in question might not be a crime if committed in the presence of someone who is older than 16. Sometimes attendant circumstances increase the degree, or level of seriousness, of an offense.

Circumstances surrounding a crime can also be classified as aggravating or mitigating and may, by law, increase or lessen the penalty that can be imposed on a convicted offender. Aggravating and mitigating circumstances are not elements of an offense, however, because they are primarily relevant at the sentencing stage of a criminal prosecution. They are discussed in Chapter 11.

Elements of a Specific Criminal Offense

Now that we have identified the principles that constitute the *general* notion of crime, we can examine individual statutes to see what particular statutory **elements** constitute a *specific* crime. Written laws specify exactly what conditions are necessary for a person to be charged in a given instance of criminal activity,

■ ***corpus delicti*** The facts that show that a crime has occurred. The term literally means "the body of the crime."

and they do so for every offense. Hence, elements of a crime are specific legal aspects of a criminal offense that the prosecution must prove to obtain a conviction. In almost every jurisdiction in the United States, for example, the crime of first-degree murder involves four quite distinct elements:

1. An unlawful killing
2. Of a human being
3. Intentionally
4. With planning (or "malice aforethought")

The elements of any specific crime are the statutory minimum without which that crime cannot be said to have occurred. Because statutes differ between jurisdictions, the specific elements of a particular crime may vary. To convict a defendant of a particular crime, prosecutors must prove to a judge or jury that all of the required statutory elements are present[23] and that the accused was responsible for producing them. If even one element of an offense cannot be established beyond a reasonable doubt, criminal liability will not have been demonstrated, and the defendant will be found not guilty.

The Example of Murder

Every statutory element of a crime serves a purpose. As mentioned, the crime of first-degree murder includes an *unlawful killing* as one of its required elements. Not all killings are unlawful. In war, for instance, human beings are killed. These killings are committed with planning and sometimes with "malice." They are certainly intentional. Yet killing in war is not unlawful as long as the belligerents wage war according to international conventions.

The second element of first-degree murder specifies that the killing must be *of a human being*. People kill all the time. They kill animals for meat, they hunt, and they practice euthanasia on aged and injured pets. Even if the killing of an animal is planned and involves malice (perhaps a vendetta against a neighborhood dog that overturns trash cans), it does not constitute first-degree murder. Such a killing, however, may violate statutes pertaining to cruelty to animals.

The third element of first-degree murder, *intentionality*, is the basis for the defense of accident. An unintentional or nonpurposeful killing is not first-degree murder, although it may violate some other statute.

Finally, murder has not been committed unless *malice* is involved. There are different kinds of malice. Second-degree murder involves malice in the sense of hatred or spite. A more extreme form of malice is necessary for a finding of first-degree murder. Sometimes the phrase used to describe this requirement is *malice aforethought*. This extreme kind of malice can be demonstrated by showing that planning was involved in the commission of the murder. Often, first-degree murder is described as "lying in wait," a practice that shows that thought and planning went into the illegal killing.

A charge of second-degree murder in most jurisdictions would necessitate proving that a voluntary (or intentional) killing of a human being had taken place—although without the degree of malice necessary for it to be classified as first-degree murder. A crime of passion is an example of second-degree murder. In a crime of passion, the malice felt by the perpetrator is hatred or spite, which is considered less severe than malice aforethought. Manslaughter, or third-degree murder, another type of homicide, can be defined simply as the unlawful killing of a human being. Not only is malice lacking in third-degree murder cases, but so is intention; in fact, the killer may not have intended that *any* harm come to the victim.

Manslaughter charges are often brought when a defendant acted in a negligent or reckless manner. The 2001 sentencing of 21-year-old Nathan Hall to 90 days in jail on charges of criminally negligent homicide following a fatal collision with another ski racer on Vail Mountain near Eagle, Colorado, provides such an example.[24] Hall had been tried on a more serious charge of reckless manslaughter, which carries a sentence of up to 16 years under Colorado law, but the jury convicted him of the lesser charge.

Manslaughter statutes, however, frequently necessitate some degree of negligence on the part of the killer. When a wanton disregard for human life is present—legally defined as "gross negligence"—some jurisdictions permit the offender to be charged with a more serious count of murder.

The *Corpus Delicti* of a Crime

The term ***corpus delicti*** literally means "the body of the crime." One way to understand the concept of *corpus delicti* is to realize that a person cannot be tried for a crime unless it can first be shown that the offense has, in fact, occurred. In other words, to establish the *corpus delicti* of a crime, the state has to demonstrate that a criminal law has been violated and that someone violated it (Figure 4-4). This term is often confused with the statutory elements of a crime, and sometimes it is mistakenly thought to refer to the body of a murder victim or some other physical result of criminal activity. It actually means something quite different.

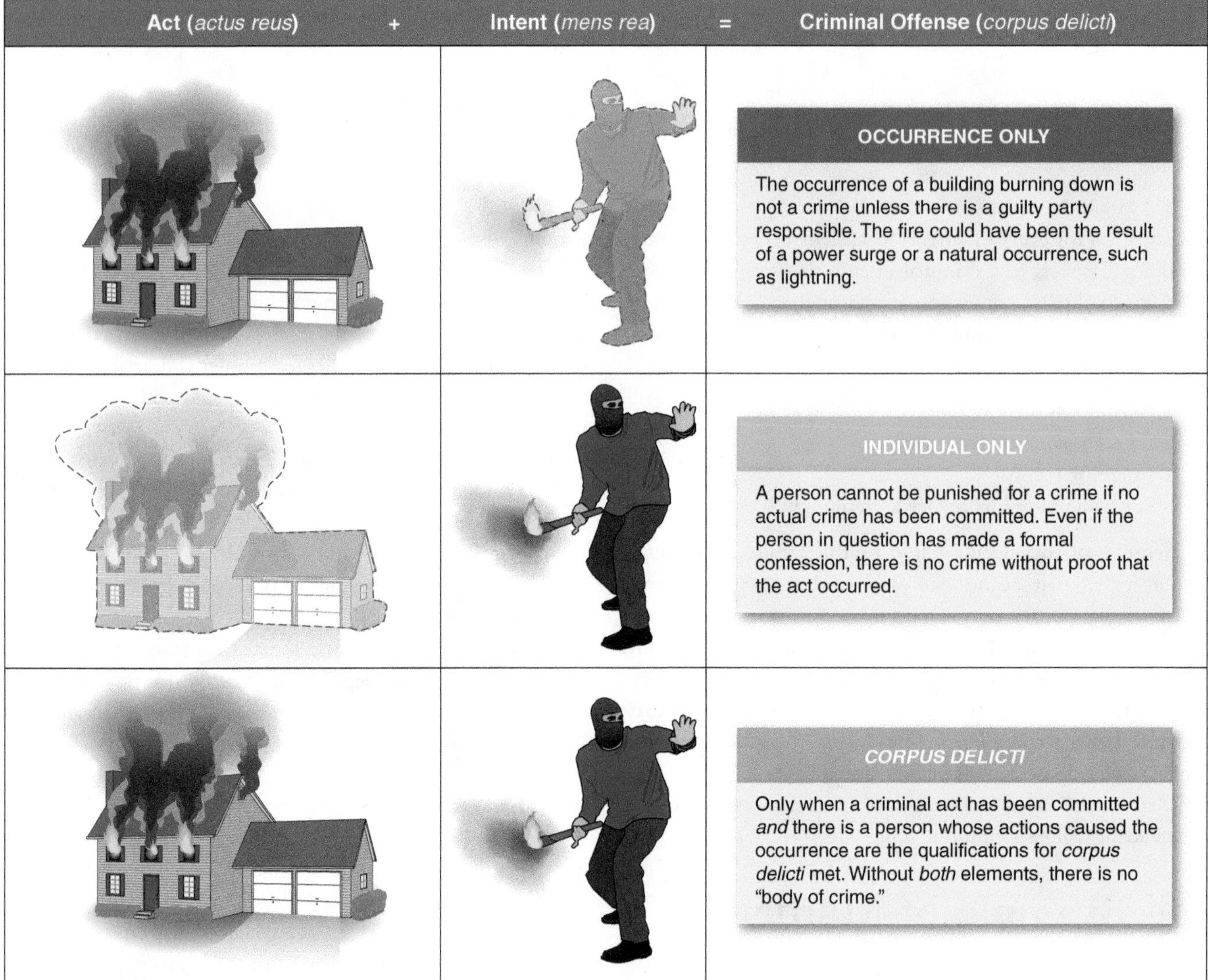

Act (actus reus) + Intent (mens rea) = Criminal Offense (corpus delicti)
OCCURRENCE ONLY
The occurrence of a building burning down is not a crime unless there is a guilty party responsible. The fire could have been the result of a power surge or a natural occurrence, such as lightning.
INDIVIDUAL ONLY
A person cannot be punished for a crime if no actual crime has been committed. Even if the person in question has made a formal confession, there is no crime without proof that the act occurred.
CORPUS DELICTI
Only when a criminal act has been committed and there is a person whose actions caused the occurrence are the qualifications for corpus delicti met. Without both elements, there is no "body of crime."

FIGURE 4-4 | Body of Crime

Source: Frank A. Schmalleger, Daniel E. Hall, and John J. Dolatowski, *Criminal Law Today,* 4th ed. (Upper Saddle River, NJ: Pearson Education, 2010), p. 61. Reprinted by permission of Pearson Education, Inc., Upper Saddle River, NJ.

There are two aspects to the *corpus delicti* of an offense: (1) that a certain result has been produced, and (2) that a person is criminally responsible for its production. For example, the crime of larceny requires proof that the property of another has been stolen—that is, unlawfully taken by someone whose intent it was to permanently deprive the owner of its possession.[25] Hence, evidence offered to prove the *corpus delicti* in a trial for larceny is insufficient if it fails to prove that any property was stolen or if property found in a defendant's possession cannot be identified as having been stolen. Similarly, "[i]n an arson case, the *corpus delicti* consists of (1) a burned building or other property, and (2) some criminal agency which caused the burning. . . . In other words, the *corpus delicti* includes not only the fact of burning, but it must also appear that the burning was by the willful act of some person, and not as a result of a natural or accidental cause."[26]

We should note that the identity of the perpetrator is not an element of the *corpus delicti* of an offense. Hence, the fact that a crime has occurred can be established without having any idea who committed it or even why it was committed. This principle was clearly enunciated in a Montana case when that state's supreme court held that "the identity of the perpetrator is not an element of the *corpus delicti*." In *State* v. *Kindle* (1924),[27] the court said, "We stated that '[i]n a prosecution for murder, proof of the *corpus delicti* does not necessarily carry with it the identity of the slain nor of the slayer.' . . . The essential elements of the *corpus delicti* are . . . establishing the death and the fact that the death was caused by a criminal agency, nothing more." *Black's Law Dictionary* puts it another way: "The *corpus delicti* [of a crime] is the fact of its having been actually committed."[28]

■ **defense (to a criminal charge)** Evidence and arguments offered by a defendant and his or her attorney to show why the defendant should not be held liable for a criminal charge.

■ **alibi** A statement or contention by an individual charged with a crime that he or she was so distant when the crime was committed, or so engaged in other provable activities, that his or her participation in the commission of that crime was impossible.

■ **justification** A legal defense in which the defendant admits to committing the act in question but claims it was necessary in order to avoid some greater evil.

■ **excuse** A legal defense in which the defendant claims that some personal condition or circumstance at the time of the act was such that he or she should not be held accountable under the criminal law.

■ **procedural defense** A defense that claims that the defendant was in some significant way discriminated against in the justice process or that some important aspect of official procedure was not properly followed in the investigation or prosecution of the crime charged.

Types of Defenses to a Criminal Charge

When a person is charged with a crime, he or she typically offers some defense (Figure 4-5). A **defense** consists of evidence and arguments offered by the defendant to show why he or she should not be held liable for a criminal charge. Our legal system generally recognizes four broad categories of defenses: (1) **alibi**, (2) **justifications**, (3) **excuses**, and (4) **procedural defenses**. An alibi, if shown to be valid, means that the defendant could not have committed the crime in question because he or she was somewhere else (and generally with someone else) at the time of the crime. When a defendant offers a justification as a defense, he or she admits committing the act in question but claims that it was necessary to avoid some greater evil. A defendant who offers an excuse as a defense, on the other hand, claims that some personal condition or circumstance at the time of the act was such that he or she should not be held accountable under the criminal law. Procedural defenses make the claim that the defendant was in some significant way discriminated against in the justice process or that some important aspect of official procedure was not properly followed in the investigation or prosecution of the crime charged.

Alibi

A reference book for criminal trial lawyers says, "Alibi is different from all of the other defenses . . . because . . . it is based upon the premise that the defendant is truly innocent."[29] The defense of alibi denies that the defendant committed the act in question. All of the other defenses we are about to discuss grant that the defendant committed the act, but they deny that he or she should be held criminally responsible. Whereas justifications and excuses may produce findings of "not guilty," the defense of alibi claims outright innocence.

Alibi is best supported by witnesses and documentation. A person charged with a crime can use the defense of alibi to show that he or she was not present at the scene when the crime was alleged to have occurred. Hotel receipts, eyewitness identification, and participation in social events have all been used to prove alibis.

ALIBI: The defendant could not have committed the offense because he or she was somewhere else at the time of the crime.

EXCUSE: Some personal condition or circumstance at the time of the act was such that the actor should not be held accountable under the criminal law.

EXAMPLES: Duress, age, mistake, involuntary intoxication, unconsciousness, provocation, insanity, diminished capacity, and mental incompetence are examples of excuse defenses.

JUSTIFICATION: The defendant admits committing the act in question but claims that it was necessary to avoid some greater evil.

EXAMPLES: Self-defense, necessity, defense of others, consent, defense of home and property, and resisting unlawful arrest are examples of justification defenses.

PROCEDURAL DEFENSE: The defendant was in some significant way discriminated against in the justice process, or some important aspect of official procedure was not properly followed in the investigation or prosecution of the crime charged.

EXAMPLES: Entrapment, denial of a speedy trial, double jeopardy, prosecutorial misconduct, *collateral estoppel*, police fraud, and selective prosecution are examples of procedural defenses.

FIGURE 4-5 | Types of Defenses to a Criminal Charge

■ **self-defense** The protection of oneself or of one's property from unlawful injury or from the immediate risk of unlawful injury. Also, the justification that the person who committed an act that would otherwise constitute an offense reasonably believed that the act was necessary to protect self or property from immediate danger.

■ **reasonable force** A degree of force that is appropriate in a given situation and is not excessive. Also, the minimum degree of force necessary to protect oneself, one's property, a third party, or the property of another in the face of a substantial threat.

Justifications

As defenses, justifications claim a kind of moral high ground. Justifications may be offered by people who find themselves forced to choose between "two evils." Generally speaking, conduct that a person believes is necessary to avoid harm to him- or herself or to another is justifiable if the harm he or she is trying to avoid is greater than the harm the law defining the offense seeks to avoid. For example, a firefighter might set a controlled fire to create a firebreak to head off a conflagration threatening a community. Although intentionally setting a fire might constitute arson, destroying property to save a town by creating a firebreak may be justifiable behavior in the eyes of the community and in the eyes of the law. Included under the broad category of justifications are (1) self-defense, (2) defense of others, (3) defense of home and property, (4) necessity, (5) consent, and (6) resisting unlawful arrest.

Self-Defense

In May 2009, when Oklahoma City pharmacist Jerome Ersland was confronted by two holdup men, he pulled a gun and shot one of them in the head.[30] The second man ran away. Then, in a scene recorded by the drugstore's security camera, Ersland went behind the counter, got another gun, and pumped five more bullets into the wounded robber as he lay on the floor, killing him. Following the incident, Ersland, whose store had been robbed before and is located in a crime-ridden part of the city, was charged with first-degree murder in a case that stirred a furious debate over vigilante justice and self-defense. Many people praised him for defending himself and for his actions in protecting two female employees at the store. Not everyone thought that Ersland was a hero, however. In 2011, more than two years after the shooting, the 59-year-old Ersland was found guilty of first-degree murder by an Oklahoma City jury, and was sentenced to life in prison without the possibility of parole.[31]

Self-defense is probably the best known of the justifications. This defense strategy makes the claim that it was necessary to inflict harm on another to ensure one's own safety in the face of near-certain injury or death. A person who harms an attacker can generally use this defense. However, the courts have generally held that where a "path of retreat" exists for a person being attacked, it should be taken. In other words, the safest use of self-defense, legally speaking, is only when cornered, with no path of escape. Some states, such as Florida, have enacted "stand-your-ground" laws, which remove the retreat requirement, and allow for the use of force without the need for a victim to evade his or her attacker or to give ground. By 2013, close to 30 states had passed stand your ground laws,[32] although the statutes came under close scrutiny after the acquittal on murder charges of Florida neighborhood watchman George Zimmerman, who shot and killed 17-year-old Trayvon Martin during a physical confrontation. Ironically, Zimmerman's defense did not invoke any stand-your-ground claims, but relied instead on a traditional self-defense strategy.

"Stand your ground" laws remove the retreat requirement, and allow for the use of force without the need for a victim to evade his or her attacker or to give ground.

The amount of defensive force used must be proportional to the amount of force or the perceived degree of threat that one is seeking to defend against. Hence, **reasonable force** is the degree of force that is appropriate in a given situation and that is not excessive. Reasonable force can also be thought of as the minimum degree of force necessary to protect oneself, one's property, a third party, or the property of another in the face of a substantial threat. Deadly force, the highest degree of force, is considered reasonable only when used to counter an immediate threat of death or great bodily harm. Deadly force cannot be used against nondeadly force.

Gary Green/UPI/Newscom

George Zimmerman is shown wearing restraints as he is escorted by a sheriff's deputy to his chair in the Seminole County courthouse in Orlando, Florida. Zimmerman was acquitted in 2013 on charges of second-degree murder and manslaughter in the Florida shooting death of 17-year-old Trayvon Martin. If you were on the jury, would you have found Zimmerman guilty?

■ **alter ego rule** In some jurisdictions, a rule of law that holds that a person can defend a third party only under circumstances and only to the degree that the third party could legally act on his or her own behalf.

Force, as the term is used within the context of self-defense, means physical force and does not extend to emotional, psychological, economic, psychic, or other forms of coercion. A person who turns the tables on a robber and assaults him during a robbery attempt, for example, may be able to claim self-defense, but a businessperson who physically assaults a financial rival to prevent a hostile takeover of her company will have no such recourse.

Self-defense has sometimes been claimed in killings of abusive spouses. A jury is likely to accept as justified a killing that occurs while the physical abuse is in progress, especially where a history of such abuse can be shown. On the other hand, wives who suffer repeated abuse but coldly plan the killing of their husbands have not fared well in court.

Defense of Others

The use of force to defend oneself has generally been extended to permit the use of reasonable force to defend others who are or who appear to be in imminent danger. The defense of others, sometimes called *defense of a third person*, is circumscribed in some jurisdictions by the **alter ego rule**. The alter ego rule holds that a person can defend a third party only under circumstances and only to the degree that the third party could act. In other words, a person who aids another whom he or she sees being attacked may become criminally liable if that person initiated the attack or if the assault is a lawful one—for example, the use of physical force by a law enforcement officer conducting a lawful arrest of a person who is resisting. A few jurisdictions, however, do not recognize the alter ego rule and allow a person to act in defense of another if the actor reasonably believes that his or her intervention is immediately necessary to protect the third person.

Defense of others cannot be claimed by an individual who joins an illegal fight merely to assist a friend or family member. Likewise, one who intentionally aids an offender in an assault, even though the tables have turned and the offender is losing the battle, cannot claim defense of others. Under the law, defense of a third person always requires that the defender be free from fault and that he or she act to aid an innocent person who is in the process of being victimized. The same restrictions that apply to self-defense also apply to the defense of a third party. Hence a defender may act only in the face of an immediate threat to another person, cannot use deadly force against nondeadly force, and must act only to the extent and use only the degree of force needed to repel the attack.

Defense of Home and Property

In most jurisdictions, the owner of property can justifiably use reasonable, *nondeadly* force to prevent others from unlawfully taking or damaging it. As a general rule, the preservation of human life outweighs the protection of property, and the use of deadly force to protect property is not justified unless the perpetrator of the illegal act may intend to commit, or is in the act of committing, a violent act against another human being. A person who shoots and kills an unarmed trespasser, for example, could not claim "defense of property" to avoid criminal liability.[33] However, a person who shoots and kills an armed robber while being robbed can make such a claim.

The use of mechanical devices to protect property is a special area of law. Because deadly force is usually not permitted in defense of property, the setting of booby traps, such as spring-loaded shotguns, electrified gates, and explosive devices, is generally not permitted to protect property that is unattended and unoccupied. If an individual is injured as a result of a mechanical device intended to cause death or injury in the protection of property, criminal charges may be brought against the person who set the device.

On the other hand, acts that would otherwise be criminal may carry no criminal liability if undertaken to protect one's home. For purposes of the law, one's "home" is one's dwelling, whether owned, rented, or merely borrowed. Hotel rooms, rooms aboard vessels, and rented rooms in houses belonging to others are all considered, for purposes of the law, one's home. The retreat rule referred to earlier, which requires a person under attack to retreat when possible before resorting to deadly force, is subject to what some call the *castle exception*. The castle exception can be traced to the writings of the sixteenth-century English jurist Sir Edward Coke, who said, "A man's house is his castle—for where shall a man be safe if it be not in his house?"[34] The castle exception generally recognizes that a person has a fundamental right to be in his or her home and that the home is a final and inviolable place of retreat (that is, the home offers a place of retreat from which a person can be expected to retreat no further). Hence, it is not necessary for one to retreat from one's home in the face of an immediate threat, even where such retreat is possible, before resorting to deadly force in protection of the home. Court decisions have extended the castle exception to include one's place of business, such as a store or an office.

Necessity

Necessity, or the claim that some illegal action was needed to prevent an even greater harm, is a useful defense in cases that do not involve serious bodily harm. A famous but unsuccessful use of this defense occurred in *The Crown* v. *Dudly & Stephens* in the late nineteenth century.[35] This British case involved a shipwreck in which three sailors and a cabin boy were set adrift in a lifeboat.

After a number of days at sea without food, two of the sailors decided to kill and eat the cabin boy. At their trial, they argued that it was necessary to do so, or none of them would have survived. The court, however, reasoned that the cabin boy was not a direct threat to the survival of the men and rejected this defense. Convicted of murder, they were sentenced to death, although they were spared the gallows by royal intervention. Although cannibalism is usually against the law, courts have sometimes recognized the necessity of consuming human flesh where survival was at issue. Those cases, however, involved only "victims" who had already died of natural causes.

Consent

The defense of consent claims that whatever harm was done occurred only after the injured person gave his or her permission for the behavior in question.

In the "Condom Rapist Case," for example, Joel Valdez was found guilty of rape in 1993 after a jury in Austin, Texas, rejected his claim that the act became consensual once he complied with his victim's request to use a condom. Valdez, who was drunk and armed with a knife at the time of the offense, claimed that his victim's request was a consent to sex. After that, he said, "we were making love."[36]

The castle exception generally recognizes that a person has a fundamental right to be in his or her home and that the home is a final and inviolable place of retreat.

Resisting Unlawful Arrest

All jurisdictions make resisting arrest a crime. Resistance, however, may be justifiable, especially if the arresting officer uses excessive force. Some states have statutory provisions detailing the limits imposed on such resistance and the conditions under which it can be used. Such laws generally say that a person may use a reasonable amount of force, other than deadly force, to resist arrest or an unlawful search by a law enforcement officer if the officer uses or attempts to use greater force than necessary to make the arrest or search. The rationale underlying such laws is that officers are no longer engaged in the performance of their duties under the law once they exceed the legal authority afforded to them under the law. Under California law, for example, an officer is not lawfully performing his or her duties when he or she "detains an individual without reasonable suspicion or arrests an individual without probable cause."[37] Resisting unlawful arrest as a defense is inapplicable in cases where the defendant is the first to resort to force. Deadly force to resist arrest is never justified unless the law enforcement officer resorts to deadly force when it is not called for.

Excuses

In contrast to a justification, an excuse does not claim that the conduct in question is justified by the situation or that it is moral. An excuse claims, rather, that the actor who engaged in the unlawful behavior was, at the time, not legally responsible for his or her actions and should not be held accountable under the law. For example, a person who assaults a police officer, thinking that the officer is really a disguised space alien who has come to abduct him, may be found "not guilty" of the charge of assault and battery by reason of insanity. Actions for which excuses are offered do not morally outweigh the wrong committed, but criminal liability may still be negated on the basis of some personal disability of the actor or because of some special circumstances that characterize the situation. Excuses recognized by the law include (1) duress, (2) age, (3) mistake, (4) involuntary intoxication, (5) unconsciousness, (6) provocation, (7) insanity, (8) diminished capacity, and (9) mental incompetence.

Duress

The defense of duress depends on an understanding of the situation. *Duress* has been defined as "any unlawful threat or coercion used by a person to induce another to act (or to refrain from acting) in a manner he or she otherwise would not (or would)."[38] A person may act under duress if, for example, he or she steals an employer's payroll to meet a ransom demand for kidnappers holding the person's children. Should the person later be arrested for larceny or embezzlement, the person can claim that he or she felt compelled to commit the crime to help ensure the safety of the children. Duress is generally not a useful defense when the crime committed involves serious physical harm, as the harm committed may outweigh the coercive influence in the minds of jurors and judges. Duress is sometimes also called *coercion*.

Age

Age offers another kind of excuse to a criminal charge, and the defense of "infancy"—as it is sometimes known in legal jargon—has its roots in the ancient belief that children cannot reason logically until around the age of seven. Early doctrine in the Christian church sanctioned that belief by declaring that rationality develops around that age. As a consequence, only older children could be held responsible for their crimes.

The defense of infancy today has been expanded to include young people well beyond the age of seven. Many states set the 16th birthday as the age at which a person becomes an adult for purposes of criminal prosecution. Others use the age of 17, and still others 18. When a person younger than the age required for adult prosecution commits a "crime," it is termed a *juvenile offense* (see Chapter 15). He or she is not guilty of a criminal violation of the law by virtue of youth.

In most jurisdictions, children below the age of 7 cannot be charged even with juvenile offenses, no matter how serious their actions may appear to others.

Mistake

Two types of mistakes can serve as a defense. One is mistake of law, and the other is mistake of fact. Rarely is mistake of

■ **insanity defense** A legal defense based on claims of mental illness or mental incapacity.

law held to be an acceptable defense. Most people realize that it is their responsibility to know the law as it applies to them. "Ignorance of the law is no excuse" is an old dictum still heard today. On occasion, however, cases do arise in which such a defense is accepted by authorities. For example, an elderly woman raised marijuana plants because they could be used to make a tea that relieved her arthritis pain. When her garden was discovered, she was not arrested but was advised as to how the law applied to her.[39]

Mistake of fact is a much more useful form of the mistake defense. In 2000, for example, the statutory rape conviction of 39-year-old Charles Ballinger of Bradley County, Tennessee, was reversed by Tennessee's Court of Criminal Appeals at Knoxville on a mistake-of-fact claim.[40] Ballinger admitted that he had had sex with his 15-year-old neighbor, who was under the age of legal consent at the time of the act in 1998. In his defense, however, Ballinger claimed that he had had good reason to mistake the girl's age.

Involuntary Intoxication

The claim of involuntary intoxication may form the basis for another excuse defense. Either drugs or alcohol may produce intoxication. Voluntary intoxication itself is rarely a defense to a criminal charge because it is a self-induced condition. It is widely recognized in our legal tradition that an altered mental condition that is the product of voluntary activity cannot be used to exonerate guilty actions that follow from it. Some state statutes formalize this general principle of law and specifically state that voluntary intoxication cannot be offered as a defense against a charge of criminal behavior.[41]

Involuntary intoxication, however, is another matter. A person might be tricked into consuming an intoxicating substance. Secretly "spiked" punch, popular aphrodisiacs, or drug-laced desserts might be ingested unknowingly. Because the effects and taste of alcohol are so widely known in our society, the defense of involuntary intoxication due to alcohol consumption can be difficult to demonstrate.

Unconsciousness

A very rarely used excuse is that of unconsciousness. An individual cannot be held responsible for anything he or she does while unconscious. Because unconscious people rarely do anything at all, this defense is almost never seen in the courts. However, people afflicted with sleepwalking, epileptic seizure, or neurological dysfunction may unintentionally cause injuries to others. Under such circumstances, a defense of unconsciousness might be argued with success.

Provocation

Provocation recognizes that a person can be emotionally enraged by another who intends to elicit just such a reaction. Should the person then strike out at the tormentor, some courts have held, he or she may not be guilty of criminality or may be guilty of a lesser degree of criminality than might otherwise be the case. The defense of provocation is commonly used in cases arising from barroom brawls in which a person's parentage was called into question, although most states don't look favorably on verbal provocation alone. This defense has also been used in some spectacular cases where wives have killed their husbands, or children their fathers, citing years of verbal and physical abuse. In these latter instances, perhaps because the degree of physical harm inflicted—the death of the husband or father—appears to be out of proportion to the abuse suffered by the wife or child, the courts have not readily accepted the defense of provocation. As a rule, the defense of provocation is generally more acceptable in minor offenses than in serious violations of the law.

Insanity

From the point of view of the criminal law, *insanity* has a legal definition and not a medical one. This legal definition often has very little to do with psychological or psychiatric understandings of mental illness; rather, it is a concept developed to enable the judicial system to assign guilt or innocence to particular defendants. As a consequence, medical conceptions of mental illness do not always fit well into the legal categories of mental illness created by courts and legislatures. The differences between psychiatric and legal conceptualizations of insanity often lead to disagreements among expert witnesses who, in criminal court, may provide conflicting testimony as to the sanity of a defendant.

The **insanity defense** is given a lot of play in the entertainment industry; movies and television shows regularly employ it because it makes for good drama. In practice, however, the defense of insanity is rarely raised. According to an eight-state study funded by the National Institute of Mental Health, the insanity defense was used in less than 1% of the cases that came before county-level courts.[42] The study showed that only 26% of all insanity pleas were argued successfully and that 90% of those who employed the defense had been previously diagnosed with a mental illness. As the American Bar Association says, "The best evidence suggests that the mental nonresponsibility defense is raised in less than one percent of all felony cases in the United States and is successful in about a fourth of these."[43] Even so, there are several rules that guide the legal definition of insanity.

■ **M'Naghten rule** A rule for determining insanity, which asks whether the defendant knew what he or she was doing or whether the defendant knew that what he or she was doing was wrong.

The M'Naghten Rule The insanity defense, as we know it today, was nonexistent prior to the nineteenth century. Until then, insane people who committed crimes were punished in the same way as other law violators. It was Daniel M'Naghten (sometimes spelled McNaughten or M'Naughten), a woodworker from Glasgow, Scotland, who, in 1844, became the first person to be found not guilty of a crime by reason of insanity. M'Naghten had tried to assassinate Sir Robert Peel, the British prime minister. He mistook Edward Drummond, Peel's secretary, for Peel himself and killed Drummond instead. At his trial, defense attorneys argued that M'Naghten suffered from vague delusions centered on the idea that the Tories, a British political party, were persecuting him. Medical testimony at the trial supported the defense's assertion that he didn't know what he was doing at the time of the shooting. The jury accepted M'Naghten's claim, and the insanity defense was born. Later, the House of Lords defined the criteria necessary for a finding of insanity. The **M'Naghten rule**, as it is called, holds that *a person is not guilty of a crime if, at the time of the crime, the person either didn't know what he or she was doing or didn't know that what he or she was doing was wrong.* The inability to distinguish right from wrong must be the result of some mental defect or disability.

Today, the M'Naghten rule is still followed in many U.S. jurisdictions (Figure 4-6). In those states, the burden of proving insanity falls on the defendant. Just as defendants are assumed to be innocent, they are also assumed to be sane at the outset of any criminal trial. Learn more about the M'Naghten rule at **http://tinyurl.com/6yfbybh**.

Irresistible Impulse The M'Naghten rule worked well for a time. Eventually, however, some cases arose in which defendants clearly knew what they were doing, and they knew it was wrong. Even so, they argued in their defense that they couldn't stop doing what they knew was wrong. Such people are said to suffer from an *irresistible impulse*, and in a number of states today, they may be found not guilty by reason of that particular brand of insanity. Some states that do not use the irresistible-impulse test in determining insanity may still allow the successful demonstration of such an impulse to be considered in sentencing decisions.

In a spectacular 1994 Virginia trial, Lorena Bobbitt successfully employed the irresistible-impulse defense against charges of malicious wounding stemming from an incident in which she cut off her husband's penis with a kitchen knife as he slept. In the case, which made headlines around the world, Bobbitt's defense attorney told the jury, "What we have is Lorena Bobbitt's life juxtaposed against John Wayne Bobbitt's penis. The evidence will show that in her mind it was his penis from which she could not escape, that caused her the most pain, the most fear, the most humiliation."[44] The impulse to sever the organ, said the lawyer, became irresistible.

AP Wide World Photos/Bill Robles

Jared Loughner, 22, makes an initial court appearance at the Sandra Day O'Connor U.S. Courthouse in Phoenix, Arizona, on January 10, 2011. In 2012 Loughner plead guilty to 19 felonies, including shooting Democratic congresswoman Gabrielle Giffords in the head during a street-corner political rally in Tucson, Arizona. Six people died and 14 were wounded during the incident. He was sentenced by a federal judge to life in prison with no eligibility of parole. Press accounts of Loughner's strange behavior preceding the shooting led many to think that Loughner lawyers would use an insanity defense if his case went to trial. What does *insanity* mean for purposes of the criminal law? What does *incompetence* mean?

The irresistible-impulse test has been criticized on a number of grounds. Primary among them is the belief that all of us suffer from compulsions. Most of us, however, learn to control them. If we give in to a compulsion, the critique goes, then why not just say it was unavoidable so as to escape any legal consequences?

The Durham Rule Another rule for gauging insanity is called the *Durham rule*. Originally created in 1871 by a New Hampshire court, it was later adopted by Judge David Bazelon in 1954 as he decided the case of *Durham* v. *U.S.* for the court of appeals in the District of Columbia.[45] The Durham rule states that *a person is not criminally responsible for his or her behavior if the person's illegal actions were the result of some mental disease or defect.*

> The Durham rule is especially vague, and provides fertile ground for conflicting claims.

Courts that follow the Durham rule typically hear from an array of psychiatric specialists as to the mental state of the defendant. Their testimony is inevitably clouded by the need to address the question of cause. A successful defense

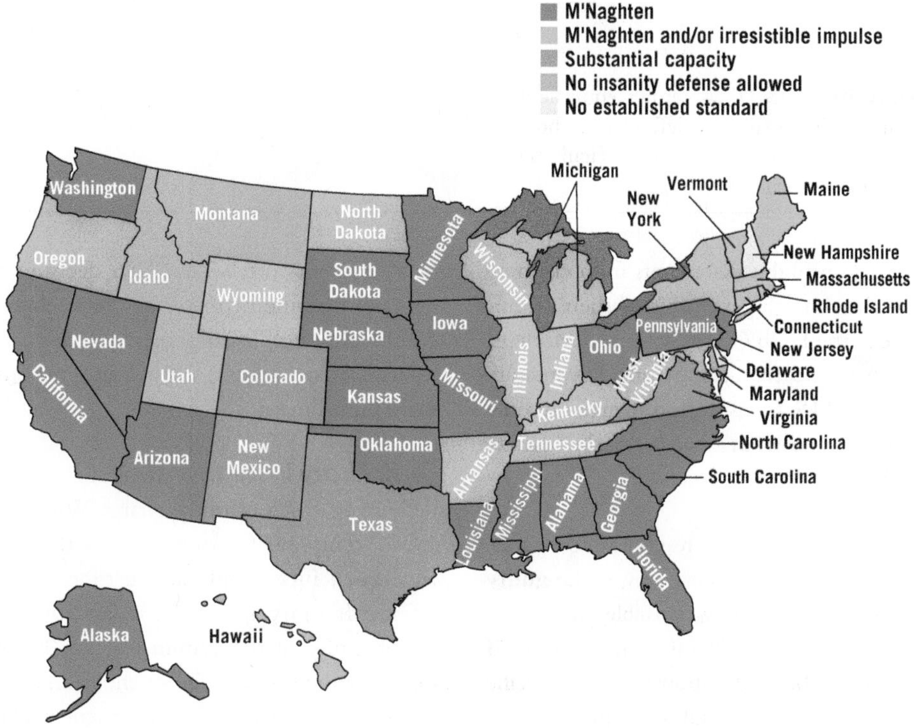

FIGURE 4-6 | Standards for Insanity Determinations by Jurisdiction

Source: Adapted from David B. Rottman and Shauna M. Strickland, *State Court Organization, 2004* (Washington, DC: Bureau of Justice Statistics, 2006), pp. 199–202.

under the Durham rule necessitates that jurors be able to see the criminal activity in question as the *product* of the defendant's mental deficiencies. And yet many people who suffer from mental diseases or defects never commit crimes. In fact, low IQ, mental retardation, and lack of general mental capacity are not allowable excuses for criminal behavior. Because the Durham rule is especially vague, it provides fertile ground for conflicting claims.

The Substantial-Capacity Test Nineteen states follow another guideline—the substantial-capacity test—as found in the Model Penal Code (MPC) of the American Law Institute (ALI).[46] Also called the *ALI rule* or the *MPC rule*, it suggests that insanity should be defined as the lack of a substantial capacity to control one's behavior. This test requires a judgment to the effect that the defendant either had or lacked "the mental capacity needed to understand the wrongfulness of his act or to conform his behavior to the requirements of the law."[47] The substantial-capacity test is a blending of the M'Naghten rule and the irresistible-impulse standard. "Substantial capacity" does not require total mental incompetence, nor does the rule require the behavior in question to live up to the criterion of total irresistibility. However, the problem of establishing just what constitutes "substantial mental capacity" has plagued this rule from its conception.

The Brawner Rule Judge Bazelon, apparently dissatisfied with the application of the Durham rule, created a new criterion for gauging insanity in the 1972 case of *U.S.* v. *Brawner*.[48] The Brawner rule, as it has come to be called, places responsibility for deciding insanity squarely with the jury. Bazelon suggested that the jury should be concerned with whether the defendant could justly be held responsible for the criminal act in the face of any claims of insanity. Under this proposal, juries are left with few rules to guide them other than their own sense of fairness.

The Insanity Defense and Social Reaction The insanity defense originated as a way to recognize the social reality of mental disease. However, the history of this defense has been rife with difficulty and contradiction. First, psychiatric testimony is expensive, and "expert" witnesses are often at odds with one another. Another difficulty with this defense is society's acceptance of it. When "not guilty due to insanity" findings have been made, the public has not always been satisfied that justice has been served. Dissatisfaction with the jumble of rules defining legal insanity peaked in 1982, when John Hinckley was acquitted of trying to assassinate then-President Ronald Reagan. At his trial, Hinckley's lawyers claimed that a series of delusions brought about by a history of schizophrenia left him unable to control his behavior. Government prosecutors were unable to counter defense contentions of insanity. The resulting acquittal shocked the nation and resulted in calls for a review of the insanity defense.

One response has been to ban the insanity defense from use at trial. A ruling by the U.S. Supreme Court in support of a

■ **guilty but mentally ill (GBMI)** A verdict, equivalent to a finding of "guilty," that establishes that the defendant, although mentally ill, was in sufficient possession of his or her faculties to be morally blameworthy for his or her acts.

Montana law allows states to prohibit defendants from claiming that they were insane at the time they committed their crimes. In 1994, without comment, the High Court let stand a Montana Supreme Court ruling that held that eliminating the insanity defense does not violate the U.S. Constitution. Currently, only three states—Montana, Idaho, and Utah—bar use of the insanity defense.[49]

Guilty But Mentally Ill Another response to public frustration with the insanity and responsibility issue is the **guilty but mentally ill (GBMI)** verdict, now possible in at least 11 states. (In a few states, the finding is "guilty but insane.") A GBMI verdict means that a person can be held responsible for a specific criminal act even though a degree of mental incompetence may be present in his or her personality. In most GBMI jurisdictions, a jury must return a finding of "guilty but mentally ill" if (1) every element necessary for a conviction has been proved beyond a reasonable doubt, (2) the defendant is found to have been *mentally ill* at the time the crime was committed, and (3) the defendant was *not* found to have been *legally insane* at the time the crime was committed. The difference between mental illness and legal insanity is a crucial one, as a defendant can be mentally ill by standards of the medical profession but sane for purposes of the law.

Upon return of a GBMI verdict, a judge may impose any sentence possible under the law for the crime in question. Mandated psychiatric treatment, however, is often part of the commitment order. Once cured, the offender is usually placed in the general prison population to serve any remaining sentence.

In 1997, Pennsylvania multimillionaire John E. du Pont was found guilty but mentally ill in the shooting death of former Olympic gold medalist David Schultz during a delusional episode. Although defense attorneys were able to show that du Pont sometimes saw Nazis in his trees, heard the walls talking, and had cut off pieces of his skin to remove bugs from outer space, he was held criminally liable for Schultz's death and was sentenced to 13 to 30 years in confinement.

As some authors have observed, the GBMI finding has three purposes: "first, to protect society; second, to hold some offenders who were mentally ill accountable for their criminal acts; [and] third, to make treatment available to convicted offenders suffering from some form of mental illness."[50] The U.S. Supreme Court case of *Ford* v. *Wainwright* recognized an issue of a different sort.[51] The 1986 decision specified that prisoners who become insane while incarcerated cannot be executed. Hence, although insanity may not always be a successful defense to criminal prosecution, it can later become a block to the ultimate punishment.

Temporary Insanity Temporary insanity is another possible defense against a criminal charge. Widely used in the 1940s and 1950s, temporary insanity means that the offender claims to have been insane only at the time of the commission of the offense. If a jury agrees, the defendant goes free. The defendant is not guilty of the criminal action by virtue of having been insane at the time, yet he or she cannot be ordered to undergo psychiatric counseling or treatment because the insanity is no longer present. This type of plea has become less popular as legislatures have regulated the circumstances under which it can be made.

The Insanity Defense under Federal Law Yet another response to the public's concern with the insanity defense and responsibility issues is the federal Insanity Defense Reform Act (IDRA). In 1984, Congress passed this act, which created major revisions in the federal insanity defense. Insanity under the law is now defined as a condition in which the defendant can be shown to have been suffering under a "severe mental disease or defect" and, as a result, "was unable to appreciate the nature and quality or the wrongfulness of his acts."[52] This definition of insanity comes close to that set forth in the old M'Naghten rule.

The act also places the burden of proving the insanity defense squarely on the defendant—a provision that has been challenged a number of times since the act was passed. The Supreme Court supported a similar requirement prior to the act's passage. In 1983, in the case of *Jones* v. *U.S.*,[53] the Court ruled that defendants can be required to prove their insanity when it becomes an issue in their defense. Shortly after the act became law, the Court held, in *Ake* v. *Oklahoma* (1985),[54] that the government must ensure access to a competent psychiatrist whenever a defendant indicates that insanity will be an issue at trial.

Consequences of an Insanity Ruling The insanity defense today is not an "easy way out" of criminal prosecution, as some people assume. Once a verdict of "not guilty by reason

■ **diminished capacity** A defense based on claims of a mental condition that may be insufficient to exonerate the defendant of guilt but that may be relevant to specific mental elements of certain crimes or degrees of crime.

■ **incompetent to stand trial** In criminal proceedings, a finding by a court that, as a result of mental illness, defect, or disability, a defendant is incapable of understanding the nature of the charges and proceedings against him or her, of consulting with an attorney, and of aiding in his or her own defense.

of insanity" is returned, the judge may order the defendant to undergo psychiatric treatment until cured. Because psychiatrists are reluctant to declare any potential criminal "cured," such a sentence may result in more time spent in a psychiatric institution than would have been spent in a prison. In *Foucha* v. *Louisiana* (1992),[55] however, the U.S. Supreme Court held that a defendant found not guilty by reason of insanity in a criminal trial could not thereafter be institutionalized indefinitely without a showing that he or she was either dangerous or mentally ill.

Diminished Capacity

Diminished capacity, or *diminished responsibility*, is a defense available in some jurisdictions. In 2003, the U.S. Sentencing Commission issued a policy statement saying that *diminished capacity* may mean that "the defendant, although convicted, *has a significantly impaired ability* to (A) understand the wrongfulness of the behavior comprising the offense or to exercise the power of reason; or (B) control behavior that the defendant knows is wrongful."[56] Still, "the terms 'diminished responsibility' and 'diminished capacity' do not have a clearly accepted meaning in [many] courts."[57] Some defendants who offer diminished-capacity defenses do so in recognition of the fact that such claims may be based on a mental condition that would not qualify as mental disease or mental defect nor be sufficient to support the defense of insanity but that might still lower criminal culpability. According to Peter Arenella, professor of law at UCLA, "the defense [of diminished capacity] was first recognized by Scottish common law courts to reduce the punishment of the 'partially insane' from murder to culpable homicide, a non-capital offense."[58]

The diminished-capacity defense is similar to the defense of insanity in that it depends on a showing that the defendant's mental state was impaired at the time of the crime.

The diminished-capacity defense is similar to the defense of insanity in that it depends on a showing that the defendant's mental state was impaired at the time of the crime. As a defense, diminished capacity is most useful when it can be shown that because of some defect of reason or mental shortcoming, the defendant's capacity to form the *mens rea* required by a specific crime was impaired. Unlike an insanity defense, however, which can result in a finding of "not guilty," a diminished-capacity defense is built on the recognition that "[m]ental condition, though insufficient to exonerate, may be relevant to specific mental elements of certain crimes or degrees of crime."[59] For example, a defendant might present evidence of mental abnormality in an effort to reduce first-degree murder to second-degree murder, or second-degree murder to manslaughter, when a killing occurs under extreme emotional disturbance. Similarly, in some jurisdictions, very low intelligence will, if proved, serve to reduce first-degree murder to manslaughter.[60]

As is the case with the insanity defense, some jurisdictions have entirely eliminated the diminished-capacity defense. The California Penal Code, for example, abolished the defense of diminished capacity,[61] stating that "[a]s a matter of public policy there shall be no defense of diminished capacity, diminished responsibility, or irresistible impulse in a criminal action or juvenile adjudication hearing."[62]

Mental Incompetence

In January 2007, King County (Washington) Superior Court Judge Helen Halpert dismissed murder charges against 39-year-old Marie Robinson, finding her mentally **incompetent to stand trial** in the deaths of her two baby sons.[63] The sons, 6-week-old Raiden and 16-month-old Justice, were found dead in Robinson's apartment by police who were called to check on the family. The boys were later determined to have died from starvation and dehydration, and Robinson was discovered passed out in a bedroom amid hundreds of empty beer cans. Her blood alcohol level at the time of discovery was five times Washington's legal limit for intoxication.

Although she was charged with two counts of second-degree murder, Halpert declared that "Ms. Robinson is clearly incompetent to stand trial. Every psychiatrist or psychologist who has examined her during the past two years has reached this conclusion." Interviews with Robinson showed that she believed her children were still alive and had been kidnapped by a secret police organization that wanted to prevent her from doing some kind of imagined scientific research.

Halpert found Robinson to be dangerously mentally ill and ordered her committed to a state mental hospital. Months later, however, doctors at Washington's Western State Hospital determined that she was not sick enough to be held for additional treatment and prosecutors refiled murder charges against her.[64] In late 2007, Robinson pleaded guilty to two reduced counts of manslaughter and one count of reckless endangerment and was sentenced to 34 years in prison.[65]

In Washington, as in most states, a person deemed competent to stand trial must be capable of understanding the nature of the proceedings and must be able to assist in his or her own legal defense. Hence, whereas insanity refers to an assessment of the offender's mental condition at the time the crime was

■ **entrapment** An improper or illegal inducement to crime by agents of law enforcement. Also, a defense that may be raised when such inducements have occurred.

■ **double jeopardy** A common law and constitutional prohibition against a second trial for the same offense.

committed, mental incompetence refers to his or her condition immediately before prosecution.

Mental illness that falls short of incompetence to stand trial can bar a defendant from self-representation. In 2008, in the case of *Indiana* v. *Edwards*, the U.S. Supreme Court held that even defendants found competent to stand trial can be prohibited from representing themselves before the court if they are too mentally disturbed to conduct trial proceedings by themselves.[66]

Procedural Defenses

Procedural defenses make the claim that the defendant was in some manner discriminated against in the justice process or that some important aspect of official procedure was not properly followed. As a result, those offering this defense say, the defendant should be released from any criminal liability. The procedural defenses we will discuss here are (1) entrapment, (2) double jeopardy, (3) *collateral estoppel*, (4) selective prosecution, (5) denial of a speedy trial, (6) prosecutorial misconduct, and (7) police fraud.

Entrapment

Entrapment is an improper or illegal inducement to crime by enforcement agents. Entrapment defenses argue that enforcement agents effectively created a crime where there would otherwise have been none. For entrapment to occur, the idea for the criminal activity must originate with official agents of the criminal justice system. Entrapment can also result when overzealous undercover police officers convince a defendant that the contemplated law-violating behavior is not a crime. To avoid claims of entrapment, officers must not engage in activity that would cause a person to commit a crime that he or she would not otherwise commit. Merely providing an opportunity for a willing offender to commit a crime, however, is not entrapment.

Double Jeopardy

The Fifth Amendment to the U.S. Constitution makes it clear that no person may be tried twice for the same offense. People who have been acquitted or found innocent may not again be "put in jeopardy of life or limb" for the same crime. The same is true of those who have been convicted: They cannot be tried again for the same offense. Cases that are dismissed for a lack of evidence also come under the double jeopardy rule and cannot result in a new trial. The U.S. Supreme Court has ruled that "the Double Jeopardy Clause protects against three distinct abuses: a second prosecution for the same offense after acquittal; a second prosecution for the same offense after conviction; and multiple punishments for the same offense."[67]

Double jeopardy does not apply in cases of trial error. Hence a defendant whose conviction was set aside because of some error in proceedings at a lower court level (for example, inappropriate instructions to the jury by the trial court judge) can be retried on the same charges. Similarly, when a defendant's motion for a mistrial is successful, or when members of the jury cannot agree on a verdict (resulting in a hung jury), a second trial may be held. Defendants, however, may be tried in both federal and state courts without necessarily violating the principle of double jeopardy.

Generally, because civil law and criminal law differ as to purpose, it is possible to try someone in civil court to collect damages for a possible violation of civil law, even if he or she was found "not guilty" in criminal court, without violating the principle of double jeopardy. For example, the 2005 civil trial of actor Robert Blake, following his acquittal at a criminal trial for murdering his wife, resulted in Blake's being ordered to pay $30 million to his wife's children.[68] In cases where civil penalties are "so punitive in form and effect as to render them criminal,"[69] however, a person sanctioned by a court in a civil case may not be tried in criminal court.

Collateral Estoppel

Collateral estoppel is similar to double jeopardy, but it applies to facts that have been determined by a "valid and final judgment."[70] Such facts cannot become the object of new litigation.

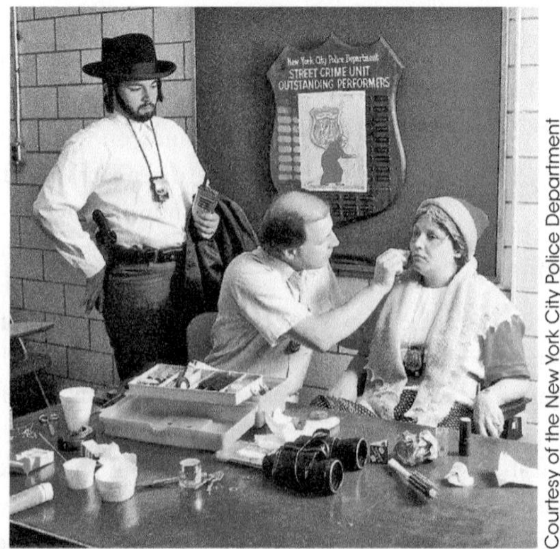

Courtesy of the New York City Police Department

Members of the New York City Police Department's Street Crimes Unit preparing for a day's work. Entrapment will likely not be an effective defense for muggers who attack these decoys. Why not?

For example, if a defendant has been acquitted of a murder charge by virtue of an alibi, it would not be permissible to try that person again for the murder of a second person killed along with the first.

Selective Prosecution

The procedural defense of selective prosecution is based on the Fourteenth Amendment's guarantee of "equal protection of the laws." This defense may be available where two or more individuals are suspected of criminal involvement, but not all are actively prosecuted. Selective prosecution based fairly on the strength of available evidence is not the object of this defense. But when prosecution proceeds unfairly on the basis of some arbitrary and discriminatory attribute, such as race, sex, friendship, age, or religious preference, this defense may offer protection. In 1996, however, in a case that reaffirmed reasonable limits on claims of selective prosecution, the U.S. Supreme Court ruled that for a defendant to successfully "claim that he was singled out for prosecution on the basis of his race, he must make a . . . showing that the Government declined to prosecute similarly situated suspects of other races."[71]

Denial of a Speedy Trial

The Sixth Amendment to the Constitution guarantees a right to a speedy trial. The purpose of the guarantee is to prevent unconvicted and potentially innocent people from languishing in jail. The federal government[72] and most states have laws (generally referred to as *speedy trial acts*) that define the time limit necessary for a trial to be "speedy." They generally set a reasonable period, such as 90 or 120 days following arrest. Excluded from the total number of days are delays that result from requests by the defense to prepare the defendant's case. If the limit set by law is exceeded, the defendant must be set free, and no trial can occur.

The Sixth Amendment to the Constitution guarantees a right to a speedy trial.

Speedy trial claims became an issue in New Orleans after it was ravaged by Hurricane Katrina in August 2005 because hundreds of inmates in parish jails who had been arrested before the hurricane hit never came to trial. Nine months after the storm battered the city, Chief District Judge Calvin Johnson told reporters that his staff was continuing to find people who shouldn't have been in jail and who were doing "Katrina time."[73] "We're still finding people—they bubble up weekly," Johnson said. Most pre-Katrina arrestees discovered by Johnson's staff had been taken into custody for misdemeanors before the storm hit, and the judge said that he released them when they were found. "We can't have people in jail indeterminately," he said. Speedy trial laws are discussed in more detail in Chapter 10.

Prosecutorial Misconduct

Another procedural defense is prosecutorial misconduct. Generally speaking, legal scholars use the term *prosecutorial misconduct* to describe actions undertaken by prosecutors that give the government an unfair advantage or that prejudice the rights of a defendant or a witness. Prosecutors are expected to uphold the highest ethical standards in the performance of their roles. When they knowingly permit false testimony, when they hide information that would clearly help the defense, or when they make unduly biased statements to the jury in closing arguments, the defense of prosecutorial misconduct may be available to the defendant.

Police Fraud

The defense of police fraud is available to defendants victimized by the police through planted evidence, the fabrication of "facts" uncovered during police investigations, and false arrests. In 2011, for example, Stephen Anderson, a former New York Police Department (NYPD) narcotics detective, testified in court that the practice of "flaking," or the planting of drugs on innocent people, was common practice in the NYPD's narcotics division. Flaking, said Anderson, was a quick and easy way to boost arrest numbers and to impress supervisors.[74]

Similarly, during the 1995 double-murder trial of O. J. Simpson, defense attorneys suggested that evidence against Simpson had been concocted and planted by police officers with a personal dislike of the defendant.

Not all claims of police fraud are supportable, however, and some defendants will claim fraud as a defense even when they know that they are guilty. As one observer put it, however, the defense of police fraud builds on extreme paranoia about the government and police agencies. This type of defense, said Francis Fukuyama, carries "to extremes a distrust of government and the belief that public authorities are in a vast conspiracy to violate the rights of individuals."[75] As a defense strategy, the claim of police fraud, when it is not warranted, can subject otherwise well-meaning public servants to intense public scrutiny, effectively shifting attention away from criminal defendants and onto the police officers—sometimes with disastrous personal results. Anthony Pellicano, a private investigator hired by Fuhrman's lawyers, put it this way: "[Fuhrman's] life right now is in the toilet. He has no job, no future. People think he's a racist. He can't do anything to help himself. He's been ordered not to talk. His family and friends, he's told them not to get involved. . . . Mark Fuhrman's life is ruined. For what? Because he found a key piece of evidence."[76] The 43-year-old Fuhrman retired from police work before the Simpson trial concluded and has since written two books.

SUMMARY

- Laws are rules of conduct, usually found enacted in the form of statutes, that regulate relationships between people and also between parties. One of the primary functions of the law is to maintain public order. Laws also serve to regulate human interaction, enforce moral beliefs, define the economic environment of a society, enhance predictability, promote orderly social change, sustain individual rights, identify wrongdoers and redress wrongs, and mandate punishment and retribution. Because laws are made by those in power and are influenced by those with access to power brokers, they tend to reflect and support the interest of society's most powerful members.
- The rule of law, which is sometimes referred to as the *supremacy of law*, encompasses the principle that an orderly society must be governed by established principles and known codes that are applied uniformly and fairly to all of its members. It means that no one is above the law, and it mandates that those who make or enforce the law must also abide by it. The rule of law is regarded as a vital underpinning in Western democracies, for without it disorder and chaos might prevail.
- This chapter identified various types of law, including criminal law, civil law, administrative law, case law, and procedural law. We were concerned primarily with criminal law, which is the form of the law that defines, and specifies punishments for, offenses of a public nature or for wrongs committed against the state or against society.
- Violations of the criminal law can be of many different types and can vary in severity. Five categories of violations were discussed in this chapter: (1) felonies, (2) misdemeanors, (3) offenses, (4) treason and espionage, and (5) inchoate offenses.
- From the perspective of Western jurisprudence, all crimes can be said to share certain features. Taken together, these features make up the legal essence of the concept of crime. The essence of crime consists of three conjoined elements: (1) the criminal act, which in legal parlance is termed the *actus reus*; (2) a culpable mental state, or *mens rea*; and (3) a concurrence of the two. Hence the essence of criminal conduct consists of a concurrence of a criminal act with a culpable mental state. Five additional principles, added to these three, allow us to fully appreciate contemporary understandings of crime. These five principles are (1) causation, (2) a resulting harm, (3) the principle of legality, (4) the principle of punishment, and (5) necessary attendant circumstances.
- Written laws specify exactly what conditions are required for a person to be charged in a given instance of criminal activity. Hence the elements of a crime are specific legal aspects of the criminal offense that the prosecution must prove to obtain a conviction. Guilt can be demonstrated, and criminal offenders convicted, only if all of the statutory elements of the particular crime can be proved in court.
- Our legal system recognizes four broad categories of defenses to a criminal charge: (1) alibi, (2) justifications, (3) excuses, and (4) procedural defenses. An alibi, if shown to be valid, means that the defendant could not have committed the crime in question because he or she was not present at the time of the crime. When a defendant offers a justification as a defense, he or she admits committing the act in question but claims that it was necessary to avoid some greater evil. A defendant who offers an excuse as a defense claims that some personal condition or circumstance at the time of the act was such that he or she should not be held accountable under the criminal law. Procedural defenses make the claim that the defendant was in some significant way discriminated against in the justice process or that some important aspect of official procedure was not properly followed in the investigation or prosecution of the crime charged.

KEY TERMS

actus reus, 114
alibi, 121
alter ego rule, 123
attendant circumstances, 118
case law, 108
civil law, 111
common law, 108
concurrence, 117
corpus delicti, 119
criminal law, 110
criminal negligence, 116
defense (to a criminal charge), 121
diminished capacity, 129
double jeopardy, 130
element (of a crime), 118
entrapment, 130
espionage, 114
excuse, 121
ex post facto, 118
felony, 112
guilty but mentally ill (GBMI), 128
inchoate offense, 114
incompetent to stand trial, 129
infraction, 112
insanity defense, 125
jurisprudence, 108
justification, 121
law, 107
legal cause, 117
mens rea, 116
misdemeanor, 112
M'Naghten rule, 126
motive, 116
offense, 112
penal code, 108
precedent, 111
procedural defense, 121
procedural law, 111
reasonable force, 122
reckless behavior, 116
rule of law, 108
self-defense, 122
stare decisis, 111
statutory law, 108
strict liability, 117
substantive criminal law, 110
tort, 111
treason, 112

KEY CASES

***Ake* v. *Oklahoma*, 128**
***The Crown* v. *Dudly & Stephens*, 123**
***Durham* v. *U.S.*, 126**
***Ford* v. *Wainwright*, 128**
***Foucha* v. *Louisiana*, 129**
***Holder* v. *Humanitarian Law Project*, 113**
***U.S.* v. *Brawner*, 127**

QUESTIONS FOR REVIEW

1. What is the purpose of law? What would a society without laws be like?
2. What is the rule of law? What is its importance in Western democracies? What does it mean to say that "nobody is above the law"?
3. What types of law does this chapter discuss? What purpose does each serve?
4. What are the five categories of criminal law violations? Describe each, and rank the categories in terms of seriousness.
5. List and describe the eight general features of crime. What are the "three conjoined elements" that comprise the legal essence of the concept of crime?
6. What is meant by the *corpus delicti* of a crime? How does the *corpus delicti* of a crime differ from the statutory elements that must be proved to convict a particular defendant of committing that crime?
7. What four broad categories of criminal defenses does our legal system recognize? Under what circumstances might each be employed?

QUESTIONS FOR REFLECTION

1. What is common law? What impact does common law have on contemporary American criminal justice?
2. How does the legal concept of insanity differ from psychiatric explanations of mental illness?
3. Does the insanity defense serve a useful function today? If you could create your own rule for determining insanity in criminal trials, what would it be? How would it differ from existing rules?

NOTES

i. Daniel Oran, *Oran's Dictionary of the Law* (St. Paul, MN: West, 1983), p. 306.
ii. Henry Campbell Black, Joseph R. Nolan, and Jacqueline M. Nolan-Haley, *Black's Law Dictionary*, 6th ed. (St. Paul, MN: West, 1990), p. 24.

1. Elisabetta Povoledo and Henry Fountain, "Italy Orders Jail Terms for 7 Who Didn't Warn of Deadly Earthquake," *New York Times*, October 22, 2012, http://www.nytimes.com/2012/10/23/world/europe/italy-convicts-7-for-failure-to-warn-of-quake.html?_r=0 (accessed May 2, 2013).
2. Ibid.
3. Henry Campbell Black, Joseph R. Nolan, and Jacqueline M. Nolan-Haley, *Black's Law Dictionary*, 6th ed. (St. Paul, MN: West, 1990), p. 884.
4. Ibid.
5. Catalina Camia, "DeLay Gets 3-Year Sentence for Corruption," *USA Today*, January 11, 2011, p. 2A.
6. John F. Kennedy, *Profiles in Courage* (New York: Harper and Row, 1956).
7. Fareed Zakaria, "The Enemy Within," *New York Times*, December 17, 2006.
8. American Bar Association Section of International and Comparative Law, *The Rule of Law in the United States* (Chicago: American Bar Association, 1958).
9. Daniel Oran, *Oran's Dictionary of the Law* (St. Paul, MN: West, 1983), p. 306.
10. Black, Nolan, and Nolan-Haley, *Black's Law Dictionary*, p. 24.
11. "Former Fed Scientist Sentenced to 13 Years in Espionage Case," *The Blog of Legal Times*, March 21, 2012, http://legaltimes.typepad.com/blt/2012/03/former-fed-scientist-sentenced-to-13-years-in-espionage-case.html (accessed March 3, 2013).
12. Specifically, U.S. Code, Title 21, Section 846.
13. *U.S.* v. *Shabani*, 510 U.S. 1108 (1994).
14. *Gordon* v. *State*, 52 Ala. 3008, 23 Am. Rep. 575 (1875).
15. But not for a more serious degree of homicide, as leaving a young child alone in a tub of water, even if intentional, does not necessarily mean that the person who so acts intends the child to drown.
16. O. W. Holmes, *The Common Law*, Vol. 3 (Boston: Little, Brown, 1881).
17. There is disagreement among some jurists as to whether the crime of statutory rape is a strict liability offense. Some jurisdictions treat it as such and will not accept a reasonable mistake about the victim's age. Others, however, do accept such a mistake as a defense.
18. *State* v. *Stiffler*, 763 P.2d 308 (Idaho App. 1988).
19. John S. Baker, Jr., et al., *Hall's Criminal Law*, 5th ed. (Charlottesville, VA: Michie, 1993), p. 138.
20. The same is not true for procedures within the criminal justice system, which can be modified even after a person has been sentenced, and hence become retroactive. See, for example, the U.S. Supreme Court case of *California Department of Corrections* v. *Morales*, 514 U.S. 499 (1995), in which the Court allowed changes in the length of time between parole hearings, even though those changes applied to offenders who had already been sentenced.
21. Black, Nolan, and Nolan-Haley, *Black's Law Dictionary*, p. 127.
22. The statute also says, "A mother's breastfeeding of her baby does not under any circumstance violate this section."
23. Common law crimes, of course, are not based on statutory elements.
24. "*People* v. *Hall*—Final Analysis," SkiSafety.com, http://www.skisafety.com/amicuscases-hall2.html (accessed August 28, 2013).
25. See *Maughs* v. *Commonwealth*, 181 Va. 117, 120, 23 S.E.2d 784, 786 (1943).
26. *State* v. *Stephenson*, Opinion No. 24403 (South Carolina, 1996). See also *State* v. *Blocker*, 205 S.C. 303, 31 S.E.2d 908 (1944).
27. *State* v. *Kindle*, 71 Mont. 58, 64, 227 (1924).
28. Black, Nolan, and Nolan-Haley, *Black's Law Dictionary*, p. 343.
29. Patrick L. McCloskey and Ronald L. Schoenberg, *Criminal Law Deskbook* (New York: Matthew Bender, 1988), Section 20.03[13].
30. Details for this story come from Tim Talley, "Folk Hero or Killer: Druggist Who Killed Robber," Associated Press, May 30, 2009, http://abcnews.go.com/US/wireStory?id=7713776 (accessed May 31, 2009).
31. "Pharmacist Gets Life for Killing Robber," *USA Today*, July 12, 2001, p. 3A.
32. Greg Allen, "Florida Governor Stands Firm on 'Stand Your Ground' Law," NPR, July 19, 2013, http://www.npr.org/2013/07/19/203594004/florida-governor-stands-firm-on-stand-your-ground-law (accessed July 19, 2013).
33. The exception, of course, is that of a trespasser who trespasses in order to commit a more serious crime.

34. Sir Edward Coke, *3 Institute*, 162.
35. *The Crown* v. *Dudly & Stephens*, 14 Q.B.D. 273, 286, 15 Cox C. C. 624, 636 (1884).
36. "Jury Convicts Condom Rapist," *USA Today*, May 14, 1993.
37. *Nuño* v. *County of San Bernardino* (C.D.Cal.1999) 58 F.Supp.2d 1127, 1134.
38. Black, Nolan, and Nolan-Haley, *Black's Law Dictionary*, p. 504.
39. Story originally appeared in the *Santa Cruz Sentinel* at http://forums.santacruzsentinel.com/cgi-bin/forums/ultimatebb.cgi?ubb=get_topic;f=7;t=000301. Link no longer available.
40. *State of Tennessee* v. *Charles Arnold Ballinger*, No. E2000-01339-CCA-R3-CD (Tenn.Crim.App. 01/09/2000).
41. See, for example, *Montana* v. *Egelhoff*, 116 S.Ct. 2013, 135 L.Ed.2d 361 (1996).
42. L. A. Callahan et al., "The Volume and Characteristics of Insanity Defense Pleas: An Eight-State Study," *Bulletin of the American Academy of Psychiatry and the Law*, Vol. 19, No. 4 (1991), pp. 331–338.
43. American Bar Association Standing Committee on Association Standards for Criminal Justice, *Proposed Criminal Justice Mental Health Standards* (Chicago: American Bar Association, 1984).
44. "Mrs. Bobbitt's Defense: 'Life Worth More Than Penis,'" Reuters, January 10, 1994.
45. *Durham* v. *U.S.*, 214 F.2d 867, 875 (D.C. Cir. 1954).
46. American Law Institute, *Model Penal Code: Official Draft and Explanatory Notes* (Philadelphia: American Law Institute, 1985).
47. Ibid.
48. *U.S.* v. *Brawner*, 471 F.2d 969, 973 (D.C. Cir. 1972).
49. See Joan Biskupic, "Insanity Defense: Not a Right; In Montana Case, Justices Give States Option to Prohibit Claim," *Washington Post* wire service, March 29, 1994.
50. Ibid.
51. *Ford* v. *Wainwright*, 477 U.S. 399, 106 S.Ct. 2595, 91 L.Ed.2d 335 (1986).
52. U.S. Code, Title 18, Section 401.
53. *Jones* v. *U.S.*, U.S. Sup. Ct., 33 CrL. 3233 (1983).
54. *Ake* v. *Oklahoma*, 470 U.S. 68, 105 S.Ct. 1087, 84 L.Ed.2d 53 (1985).
55. *Foucha* v. *Louisiana*, 504 U.S. 71 (1992).
56. U.S. Sentencing Commission, "Supplement to the 2002 Federal Sentencing Guidelines: Section 5K2.13. Diminished Capacity (Policy Statement)," April 30, 2003, http://www.ussc.gov/2002suppb/5K2_13.htm (accessed May 8, 2010). Italics added.
57. *U.S.* v. *Pohlot*, 827 F.2d 889 (1987).
58. Peter Arenella, "The Diminished Capacity and Diminished Responsibility Defenses: Two Children of a Doomed Marriage," *Columbia Law Review*, Vol. 77 (1977), p. 830.
59. *U.S.* v. *Brawner*, 471 F.2d 969 (1972).
60. Black, Nolan, and Nolan-Haley, *Black's Law Dictionary*, p. 458.
61. California Penal Code, Section 25(a).
62. Ibid., Section 28(b).
63. Tracy Johnson, "Charges Dropped against Mom Whose Kids Starved to Death," *Seattle Post-Intelligencer*, January 31, 2007, http://seattlepi.nwsource.com/local/301852_mom31ww.html (accessed June 15, 2010).
64. Natalie Singer, "Competence Issue Creates Dilemma in '04 Murder Case," *Seattle Times*, March 16, 2007.
65. Nancy Bartley, "Child Abuser Given 34 Years," *Seattle Times*, November 17, 2007, http://seattletimes.nwsource.com/html/localnews/2004019371_robinson17m.html (accessed August 8, 2009).
66. *Indiana* v. *Edwards*, U.S. Supreme Court, No. 07–208 (decided June 19, 2008).
67. *U.S.* v. *Halper*, 490 U.S. 435 (1989).
68. "Robert Blake Found Liable for Wife's Death," *Associated Press*, November 18, 2005.
69. See, for example, *Hudson* v. *U.S.*, 18 S.Ct. 488 (1997); and *U.S.* v. *Ursery*, 518 U.S. 267 (1996).
70. McCloskey and Schoenberg, *Criminal Law Deskbook*, Section 20.02[4].
71. *U.S.* v. *Armstrong*, 116 S.Ct. 1480, 134 L.Ed.2d 687 (1996).
72. Speedy Trial Act, U.S. Code, Title 18, Section 3161. Significant cases involving the U.S. Speedy Trial Act are those of *U.S.* v. *Carter*, 476 U.S. 1138, 106 S.Ct. 2241, 90 L.Ed.2d 688 (1986); and *Henderson* v. *U.S.*, 476 U.S. 321, 106 S.Ct. 1871, 90 L.Ed.2d 299 (1986).
73. Peter Whoriskey, "New Orleans Justice System Besieged," *Boston Globe*, April 17, 2006, http://www.boston.com/news/nation/articles/2006/04/17/new_orleans_justice_system_besieged/ (accessed May 10, 2007).
74. Stephen Anderson, "Ex-NYPD Cop: We Planted Evidence, Framed Innocent People to Reach Quotas," *Huffington Post*, October 13, 2011, http://www.huffingtonpost.com/2011/10/13/ex-nypd-cop-we-planted-ev_n_1009754.html?view=print&comm_ref=false (accessed March 23, 2012).
75. Francis Fukuyama, "Extreme Paranoia about Government Abounds," *USA Today*, August 24, 1995.
76. Lorraine Adams, "Simpson Trial Focus Shifts to Detective with Troubling Past," *Washington Post* wire service, August 22, 1995.

PART 2 POLICING

Chapter 5
Policing: History and Structure

Chapter 6
Policing: Purpose and Organization

Chapter 7
Policing: Legal Aspects

Chapter 8
Policing: Issues and Challenges

RIGHTS OF THE ACCUSED UNDER INVESTIGATION

The accused has these common law, constitutional, statutory, and humanitarian rights:

- A right against unreasonable searches
- A right against unreasonable arrest
- A right against unreasonable seizures of property
- A right to fair questioning by authorities
- A right to protection from personal harm

These individual rights must be effectively balanced against these community concerns:

- The efficient apprehension of offenders
- The prevention of crimes

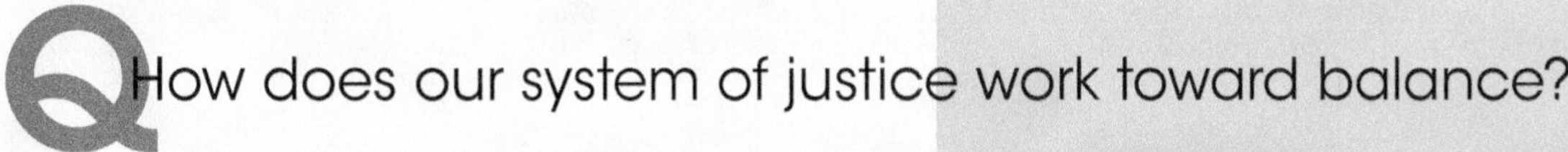

How does our system of justice work toward balance?

To Protect and to Serve

Famed police administrator and former New York City Police Commissioner Patrick V. Murphy once said, "It is a privilege to be a police officer in a democratic society." Although Murphy's words still ring true, many of today's law enforcement officers might hear in them only the echo of a long-dead ideal, unrealistic for today's times.

America's police officers form the front line in the unending battle against crime, drugs, and terrorism—a battle that seems to get more sinister and more demanding with each passing day. It is the police who are called when a crime is in progress or when one has been committed. They are the first responders to a terrorist event that strikes the homeland. The police are expected to objectively and impartially investigate law violations, gather evidence, solve crimes, and make arrests resulting in the successful prosecution of suspects—all the while adhering to the strict due process standards set forth in the U.S. Constitution and enforced by the courts. They are also expected to aid the injured, give succor to victims, and protect the innocent. The chapters in this section of *Criminal Justice Today* provide an overview of the historical development of policing; describe law enforcement agencies at the federal, state, and local levels; explore issues related to police administration; and discuss the due process and legal environments surrounding police activity.

As you will see, although the police are ultimately charged with protecting the public, they often believe that members of the public do not accord them the respect they deserve, and they feel that the distance between the police and the public is not easily bridged. Within the last few decades, however, an image of policing has emerged that may do much to heal that divide. This model, known as *community policing*, goes well beyond traditional conceptions of the police as mere law enforcers and encompasses the idea that police agencies should take counsel from the communities they serve. Under this model, the police are expected to prevent crime, as well as solve it, and to help members of the community deal with other pressing social issues.

5 POLICING: HISTORY AND STRUCTURE

OUTLINE

- Introduction
- Historical Development of the Police
- American Policing Today: From the Federal to the Local Level
- Federal Agencies
- State-Level Agencies
- Local Agencies
- Private Protective Services

LEARNING OBJECTIVES

After reading this chapter, you should be able to

- Summarize the historical development of policing in America.
- Describe the three major levels of public law enforcement in the United States today.
- Briefly describe three federal law enforcement agencies, including their responsibilities.
- Identify the two major models of state law enforcement organization.
- Describe the various kinds of local law enforcement agencies and their roles in enforcing the law.
- Describe private protective services in the United States and their possible future roles.

Fidelity, bravery, and integrity.

MOTTO OF THE FEDERAL BUREAU OF INVESTIGATION

■ ***comes stabuli*** A nonuniformed mounted law enforcement officer of medieval England. Early police forces were small and relatively unorganized but made effective use of local resources in the formation of posses, the pursuit of offenders, and the like.

■ **night watch** An early form of police patrol in English cities and towns.

■ **Statute of Winchester** A law, written in 1285, that created a watch and ward system in English cities and towns and that codified early police practices.

Introduction

Many of the techniques used by today's police differ quite a bit from those employed in days gone by. Listen to how a police officer, writing in the mid-1800s, describes the way pickpockets were caught in London 250 years ago: "I walked forth the day after my arrival, rigged out as the very model of a gentleman farmer, and with eyes, mouth, and pockets wide open, and a stout gold-headed cane in my hand, strolled leisurely through the fashionable thoroughfares, the pump-rooms, and the assembly-rooms, like a fat goose waiting to be plucked. I wore a pair of yellow gloves well wadded, to save me from falling, through a moment's inadvertency, into my own snare, which consisted of about fifty fish-hooks, large black hackles, firmly sewn barb downward, into each of the pockets of my brand new leather breeches. The most blundering 'prig' alive might have easily got his hand to the bottom of my pockets, but to get it out again, without tearing every particle of flesh from the bones, was a sheer impossibility. . . . I took care never to see any of my old customers until the convulsive tug at one or other of the pockets announced the capture of a thief. I then coolly linked my arm in that of the prisoner, and told him in a confidential whisper who I was."[1]

> The rise of the police as an organized force in the Western world coincided with the evolution of strong centralized governments.

Historical Development of the Police

Police tactics and strategy have changed substantially since historical times, and many different kinds of police agencies—some of them highly specialized—function within the modern criminal justice system. This chapter describes the development of organized policing in Western culture and discusses the function of contemporary American police forces at the federal, state, and local levels. Agency examples are given at each level. The promise held by private protective services, the recent rapid growth of private security organizations, and the quasi-private system of justice are also discussed.

English Roots

The rise of the police as an organized force in the Western world coincided with the evolution of strong centralized governments. Although police forces have developed throughout the world, often in isolation from one another, the historical growth of the English police is of special significance to students of criminal justice in America, for it was on the British model that much of early American policing was based.

Law enforcement in early Britain, except for military intervention in the pursuit of bandits and habitual thieves, was not well organized until around the year 1200.[2] When a person committed an offense and could be identified, he or she was usually pursued by an organized posse. All able-bodied men who could hear a victim's cry for help were obligated to join the posse in a common effort to apprehend the offender. The posse was led by the shire reeve (the leader of the county) or by a mounted officer (the ***comes stabuli***). Our modern words *sheriff* and *constable* are derived from these early terms. The *comites stabuli* (the plural form of the term) were not uniformed, nor were they numerous enough to perform all the tasks we associate today with law enforcement. This early system, employing a small number of mounted officers, depended for its effectiveness on the ability to organize and direct the efforts of citizens toward criminal apprehension.

The offender, cognizant of a near-certain end at the hands of the posse, often sought protection from trusted friends and family. As a consequence, feuds developed among organized groups of citizens, some seeking revenge and some siding with the offender. Suspects who lacked the shelter of a sympathetic group might flee into a church and invoke the time-honored custom of sanctuary. Sanctuary was rarely an ideal escape, however, as pursuers could surround the church and wait out the offender, preventing food and water from being carried inside. The offender, once caught, became the victim. Guilt was usually assumed, and trials were rare. Public executions, often involving torture, typified this early justice and served to provide a sense of communal solidarity as well as group retribution.

The development of law enforcement in English cities and towns grew out of an early reliance on bailiffs, or watchmen. Bailiffs were assigned the task of maintaining a **night watch**, primarily to detect fires and spot thieves. Although too few in number to handle most emergencies, bailiffs were able to rouse the sleeping population, which could then deal with whatever crisis was at hand. Larger cities expanded the idea of bailiffs by creating both a night watch and a day ward.

British police practices became codified in the **Statute of Winchester**, written in 1285. The statute (1) specified the creation of the watch and the ward in cities and towns; (2) mandated the draft of eligible males to serve those forces; (3) institutionalized the use of the *hue and cry*, making citizens

■ **Follow the author's tweets about the latest crime and justice news @schmalleger.**

■ **Bow Street Runners** An early English police unit formed under the leadership of Henry Fielding, magistrate of the Bow Street region of London.

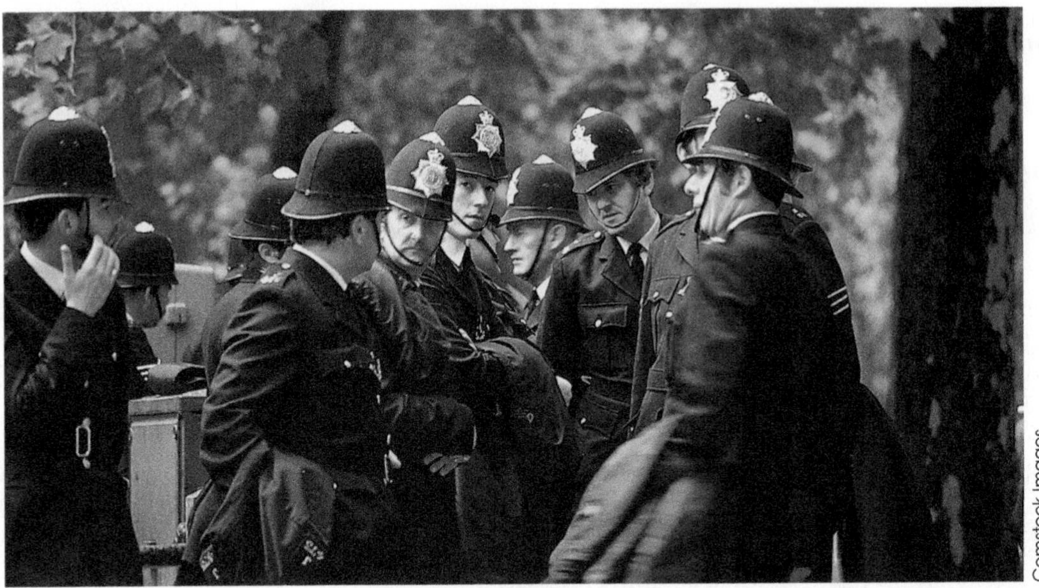

Comstock Images

British bobbies. Today's uniformed English police officers have a recognizable appearance rooted in the time of Sir Robert Peel. In what way were early American law enforcement efforts influenced by the British experience?

who disregarded a call for help subject to criminal penalties; and (4) required that citizens maintain weapons in their home for answering the call to arms.

Some authors have attributed the growth of modern police forces to the gin riots that plagued London and other European cities in the eighteenth and nineteenth centuries. The invention of gin around 1720 provided, for the first time, a potent and inexpensive alcoholic drink readily available to the massed populations gathered in the early industrial ghettos of eighteenth-century cities. Seeking to drown their troubles, huge numbers of people, far beyond the ability of the bailiffs to control, began binges of drinking and rioting. During the next hundred years, these gin riots created an immense social problem for British authorities. By this time, the bailiff system had broken down and was staffed by groups of woefully inadequate substitutes, hired by original draftees to perform duties in their stead. Incompetent and unable to depend on the citizenry for help in enforcing the laws, bailiffs became targets of mob violence and were often attacked and beaten for sport.

The development of law enforcement in English cities and towns grew out of an early reliance on bailiffs, or watchmen.

The Bow Street Runners

The early eighteenth century saw the emergence in London of a large criminal organization led by Jonathan Wild. Wild ran a type of fencing operation built around a group of loosely organized robbers, thieves, and burglars who would turn their plunder over to him. Wild would then negotiate with the legitimate owners for a ransom of their possessions.

The police response to Wild was limited by disinterest and corruption. However, change began when Henry Fielding, a well-known writer, became the magistrate of the Bow Street region of London. Fielding attracted a force of dedicated officers, dubbed the **Bow Street Runners**, who soon stood out as the best and most disciplined enforcement agents that London had to offer. Fielding's personal inspiration and his ability to communicate what he saw as the social needs of the period may have accounted for his success.

In February 1725, Wild was arrested and arraigned on the following charges: "(1) that for many years past he had been a confederate with great numbers of highwaymen, pickpockets, housebreakers, shop-lifters, and other thieves, (2) that he had formed a kind of corporation of thieves, of which he was the head or director . . . , (3) that he had divided the town and country into so many districts, and appointed distinct gangs for each, who regularly accounted with him for their robberies . . . , (4) that the persons employed by him were for the most part felon convicts . . . , (5) that he had, under his care and direction, several warehouses for receiving and concealing stolen goods, and also a ship for carrying off jewels, watches, and other valuable goods, to Holland, where he had a superannuated thief for his benefactor, and (6) that he kept in his pay several artists to make alterations, and transform watches, seals, snuff-boxes, rings,

■ **new police** A police force formed in 1829 under the command of Sir Robert Peel. It became the model for modern-day police forces throughout the Western world.

■ **bobbies** The popular British name given to members of Sir Robert (Bob) Peel's Metropolitan Police Service.

and other valuable things, that they might not be known."[3] Convicted of these and other crimes, Wild attempted suicide by drinking a large amount of laudanum, an opium compound. The drug merely rendered him senseless, and he was hanged the following morning, having only partially recovered from its effects.

In 1754, Henry Fielding died. His brother John took over his work and occupied the position of Bow Street magistrate for another 25 years. The Bow Street Runners remain famous to this day for quality police work.

The New Police

In 1829, Sir Robert Peel, who later became prime minister of England, formed what many have hailed as the world's first modern police force. The passage of the Metropolitan Police Act that year allocated the resources for Peel's force of 1,000 handpicked men. The London Metropolitan Police Service (MPS), also known as the **new police** or more simply the *Met*, soon became a model for police forces around the world.

Members of the Metropolitan Police were quickly dubbed **bobbies**, after their founder. London's bobbies were organized around two principles: the belief that it was possible to discourage crime, and the practice of preventive patrol. Peel's police patrolled the streets by walking beats. Their predecessors, the watchmen, had occupied fixed posts throughout the city, awaiting a public outcry. The new police were uniformed, resembling a military organization, and adopted a military administrative style.

London's first two police commissioners were Colonel Charles Rowan, a career military officer, and Richard Mayne, a lawyer. Rowan believed that mutual respect between the police and the citizenry would be crucial to the success of the new force. As a consequence, early bobbies were chosen for their ability to reflect and inspire the highest personal ideals among young men in early-nineteenth-century Britain.

The new police were not immediately well received. Some elements of the population saw them as an occupying army, and open battles between the police and the citizenry ensued. The tide of sentiment turned, however, when an officer was viciously killed in the Cold Bath Fields riot of 1833. A jury, considering a murder charge against the killer, returned a verdict of "not guilty," inspiring a groundswell of public support for the much-maligned force.

The Early American Experience

Early American law enforcement efforts were based to some degree on the British experience. Towns and cities in colonial America depended on modified versions of the night watch and

Sang Tan/AP Wide World Photos

An English policewoman directing subway riders in London following four terrorist explosions on the underground rail system and a bus in 2005. How has policing changed since the time of Sir Robert Peel?

the day ward, but the unique experience of the American colonies quickly differentiated the needs of colonists from those of the masses remaining in Europe. Huge expanses of uncharted territory, vast wealth, a widely dispersed population engaged mostly in agriculture, and a sometimes ferocious frontier all combined to mold American law enforcement in a distinctive way. Recent writers on the history of the American police have observed that policing in America was originally "decentralized," "geographically dispersed," "idiosyncratic," and "highly personalized."[4]

The Frontier

One of the major factors determining the development of American law enforcement was the frontier, which remained vast and wild until late in the nineteenth century. The backwoods areas provided a natural haven for outlaws and bandits. Henry Berry Lowery, a famous outlaw of the Carolinas, the James Gang, and many lesser-known desperadoes felt at home in the unclaimed swamps and forests.

Only the boldest of settlers tried to police the frontier. Among them was Charles Lynch, a Virginia farmer of the late eighteenth century. Lynch and his associates tracked and punished offenders, often according to the dictates of the still well-known lynch law, or vigilante justice, which they originated. Citizen posses and vigilante groups were often the only law available to settlers on the western frontier. Judge Roy Bean ("the Law West of the Pecos"), "Wild Bill" Hickok, Bat Masterson, Wyatt Earp, and Pat Garrett

■ **vigilantism** The act of taking the law into one's own hands.

were other popular figures of the nineteenth century who took it upon themselves, sometimes in a semiofficial capacity, to enforce the law on the books as well as the standards of common decency.

Although today **vigilantism** has a negative connotation, most of the original vigilantes of the American West were honest men and women trying to forge an organized and predictable lifestyle out of the challenging situations that they encountered. Often faced with unscrupulous, money-hungry desperadoes, they did what they could to bring the standards of civilization, as they understood them, to bear in their communities.

Policing America's Early Cities

Small-scale organized law enforcement came into being quite early in America's larger cities. In 1658, paid watchmen were hired by the city of New York to replace drafted citizens.[5] By 1693, the first uniformed officer was employed by the city, and in 1731, the first neighborhood station, or precinct, was constructed. Boston, Cincinnati, and New Orleans were among the American communities to follow the New York model and hire a force of watchmen in the early nineteenth century.

In 1829, American leaders watched closely as Sir Robert Peel created London's new police. One year later, Stephen Girard, a wealthy manufacturer, donated a considerable amount of money to the city of Philadelphia to create a capable police force. The city hired 120 men to staff a night watch and 24 to perform similar duties during the day.

In 1844, New York's separate day and night forces were combined into the New York City Police Department. Boston followed suit in 1855. Further advances in American policing were precluded by the Civil War. Southern cities captured in the war came under martial law and were subject to policing by the military.

The coming of the twentieth century, coinciding as it did with numerous technological advances and significant social changes, brought a flood of reform. The International Association of Chiefs of Police (IACP) was formed in 1902; it immediately moved to create a nationwide clearinghouse for criminal identification. In 1915, the Fraternal Order of Police (FOP) initiated operations. It was patterned after labor unions but prohibited strikes; it accepted personnel of all ranks, from patrol officer to chief. In 1910, Alice Stebbins Wells became the first policewoman in the world, serving with the Los Angeles Police Department.[6] Prior to Wells's appointment, women had served as jail matrons, and widows had sometimes been carried on police department payrolls if their officer-husbands had died in the line of duty, but they had not been fully "sworn" with carrying out the duties of

In 1910, Alice Stebbins Wells became the first policewoman in the world, serving with the Los Angeles Police Department.

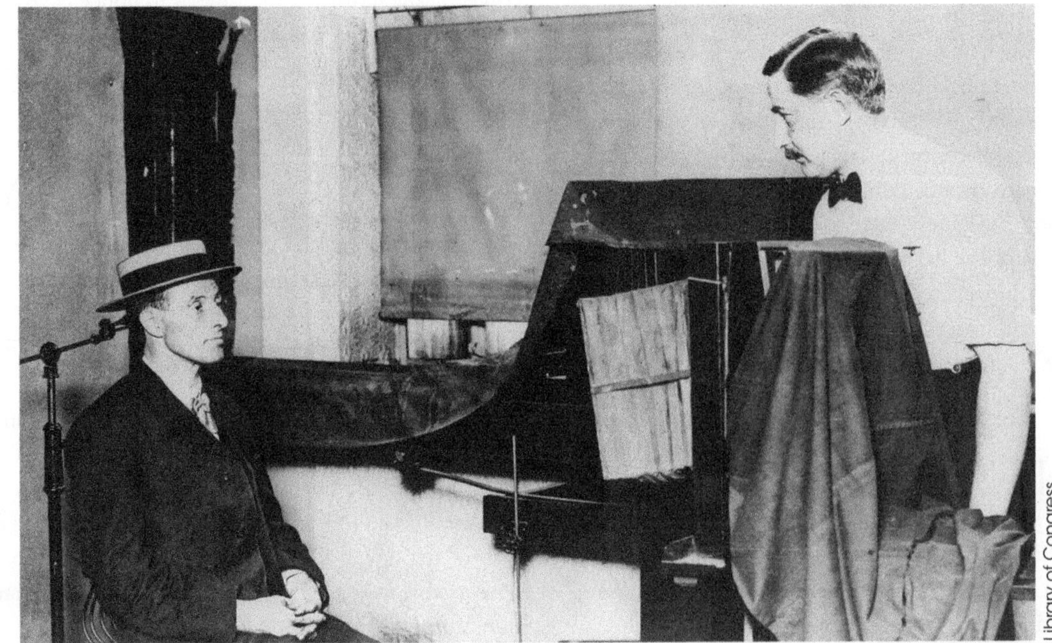
Library of Congress

A New York City police officer "mugging" a prisoner in the early days of police photography. How have advances in technology shaped policing?

■ **Wickersham Commission** The National Commission on Law Observance and Enforcement. In 1931, the commission issued a report stating that Prohibition was unenforceable and carried a great potential for police corruption.

■ **Law Enforcement Assistance Administration (LEAA)** A now-defunct federal agency established under Title I of the Omnibus Crime Control and Safe Streets Act of 1968 to funnel federal funding to state and local law enforcement agencies.

a police officer. Wells became an outspoken advocate for the hiring of more policewomen, and police departments across the country began to hire female officers, especially to provide police services to children and to women and to "protect male officers from delicate and troublesome situations"[7]—such as the need to physically restrain female offenders.

In 1915, the U.S. Census reported that 25 cities employed policewomen. In that year, coinciding with the creation of the FOP, the International Association of Policewomen (now the International Association of Women Police) was formed in the city of Baltimore. In 1918, Ellen O'Grady became the first woman to hold a high administrative post in a major police organization when she was promoted to the rank of deputy police commissioner for the city of New York. As Dorothy Moses Schulz, a contemporary commentator on women's entry into policing, has observed, "The Policewomen's movement was not an isolated phenomenon, but was part of women's movement into other newly created or newly professionalized fields."[8]

During the early twentieth century, telephones, automobiles, and radios all had their impact on the American police. Teddy Roosevelt, the 26th president of the United States, began his career by serving as a police commissioner in New York City from 1895 to 1897. While there, he promoted the use of a call-box system of telephones, which allowed citizens to report crimes rapidly and made it possible for officers to call quickly for assistance. As president, Roosevelt helped organize the Bureau of Investigation, which later became the Federal Bureau of Investigation (FBI). Federal law enforcement already existed in the form of U.S. marshals, created by an act of Congress in 1789, and in the form of postal inspectors, authorized by the U.S. Postal Act of 1829. The FBI became a national investigative service designed to quickly identify and apprehend offenders charged with a growing list of federal offenses. Automobiles created an era of affordable, rapid transportation and gave police forces far-reaching powers and high mobility. Telephones and radios provided the ability to maintain regular communication with central authorities. State police agencies arose to counter the threat of the mobile offender, with Massachusetts and Pennsylvania leading the way to statewide forces.

Prohibition and Police Corruption

A dark period for American law enforcement agencies began in 1920 with the passage of a constitutional prohibition against all forms of alcoholic beverages. Until Prohibition was repealed in 1933, most parts of the country were rife with criminal activity, much of it supporting the trade in bootlegged liquor. Bootleggers earned huge sums of money, and some of them became quite wealthy. Massive wealth in the hands of law violators greatly increased the potential for corruption among police officials, some of whom were "paid off" to support bootlegging operations.

In 1931, the **Wickersham Commission**, officially called the National Commission on Law Observance and Enforcement and led by former U.S. Attorney General George W. Wickersham, recognized that Prohibition was unenforceable and reported that it carried a great potential for police corruption.[9] The commission, which released a number of reports, also established guidelines for enforcement agencies that directed many aspects of American law enforcement until the 1970s. The most influential of the Wickersham Commission reports was titled *Report on the Enforcement of the Prohibition Laws of the United States*. That report, the release of which became one of the most important events in the history of American policing, can be read in its entirety at **http://www.druglibrary.org/schaffer/library/studies/wick**.

The Last Half of the Twentieth Century

The rapid cultural change that took place throughout America in the 1960s and 1970s forever altered the legal and social environment in which the police must work. During that period, in conjunction with a burgeoning civil rights movement, the U.S. Supreme Court frequently enumerated constitutionally based personal rights for those facing arrest, investigation, and criminal prosecution. Although a "chipping away" at those rights, which some say is continuing today, may have begun in the 1980s, the earlier emphasis placed on the rights of defendants undergoing criminal investigation and prosecution will have a substantial impact on law enforcement activities for many years to come.

The 1960s and 1970s were also a period of intense examination of police operations, from day-to-day enforcement decisions to administrative organization and police–community relations. In 1967, the President's Commission on Law Enforcement and Administration of Justice issued its report, *The Challenge of Crime in a Free Society*, which found that the police were often isolated from the communities they served.[10] In 1969, the **Law Enforcement Assistance Administration (LEAA)** was formed to assist police forces across the nation in acquiring

■ **scientific police management** The application of social science techniques to the study of police administration for the purpose of increasing effectiveness, reducing the frequency of citizen complaints, and enhancing the efficient use of available resources.

©The Protected Art Archive/Alamy

Prohibition agents pouring liquor down a drain in 1921. How did the constitutional prohibition against alcoholic beverages during the 1920s and early 1930s affect American policing?

the latest in technology and in adopting new enforcement methods. In 1973, the National Advisory Commission on Criminal Justice Standards and Goals issued a comprehensive report detailing strategies for combating and preventing crime and for improving the quality of law enforcement efforts at all levels.[11] Included in the report was a call for greater participation in police work by women and ethnic minorities and the recommendation that a college degree be made a basic prerequisite for police employment by the 1980s. The creation of a third major commission, the National Commission on Crime Prevention and Control, was authorized by the federal Violent Crime Control and Law Enforcement Act of 1994, but the commission never saw the light of day.[12]

Evidence-Based Policing

In 1968, with the passage of the Omnibus Crime Control and Safe Streets Act, the U.S. Congress created the Law Enforcement Assistance Administration. The LEAA was charged with combating crime through the expenditure of huge amounts of money in support of crime-prevention and crime-reduction programs. Some have compared the philosophy establishing the LEAA to that which supported the American space program's goal of landing people on the moon: Put enough money into any problem, and it will be solved! Unfortunately, the crime problem was more difficult to address than the challenge of a moon landing; even after the expenditure of nearly $8 billion, the LEAA had not come close to its goal. In 1982, the LEAA expired when Congress refused it further funding.

The legacy of the LEAA is an important one for police managers, however. The research-rich years of 1969 to 1982, supported largely through LEAA funding, have left a plethora of scientific findings relevant to police administration and, more important, have established a tradition of program evaluation within police management circles. This tradition, which is known as **scientific police management**, is a natural outgrowth of LEAA's insistence that every funded program contain a plan for its evaluation. *Scientific police management* refers to the application of social science techniques to the study of police administration for the purpose of increasing effectiveness, reducing the frequency of citizen complaints, and enhancing the efficient use of available resources. The heyday of scientific police management occurred in the 1970s, when federal monies were far more readily available to support such studies than they are today.

The LEAA was not alone in funding police research during the 1970s. On July 1, 1970, the Ford Foundation announced the establishment of a Police Development Fund totaling $30 million, to be spent during the following five years to support major crime-fighting strategies of police departments. This funding led to the establishment of the Police Foundation, which continues today with the mission of "fostering improvement and innovation in American policing."[13] Police Foundation–sponsored studies during the past 30 years have added to the growing body of scientific knowledge about policing.

Today, federal support for criminal justice research and evaluation continues under the National Institute of Justice (NIJ) and the Bureau of Justice Statistics (BJS), both part of the Office of Justice Programs (OJP). The OJP, created by Congress in 1984, provides federal leadership in developing the nation's capacity to prevent and control crime. The National Criminal Justice Reference Service (NCJRS), a part of the NIJ, assists researchers nationwide in locating information applicable to their research projects. "Custom searches" of the NCJRS computer database can be done online and yield abundant information in most criminal justice subject areas. The NIJ also publishes a series of informative periodic reports, such as the *NIJ Journal* and *NIJ*

■ **Kansas City experiment** The first large-scale scientific study of law enforcement practices. Sponsored by the Police Foundation, it focused on the practice of preventive patrol.

Research in Review, which serve to keep criminal justice practitioners and researchers informed about recent findings. View the NIJ recent online publication list at **http://nij.ncjrs.org/App/publications/pubs_db.aspx**.

The Kansas City Experiment

By far the most famous application of social research principles to police management was the Kansas City preventive patrol experiment.[14] The results of the year-long **Kansas City experiment** were published in 1974. The study, sponsored by the Police Foundation, divided the southern part of Kansas City into 15 areas. Five of these "beats" were patrolled in the usual fashion. In another group of five beats, patrol activities were doubled. The final third of the beats received a novel treatment indeed: No patrols were assigned to them, and no uniformed officers entered that part of the city unless they were called. The program was kept secret, and citizens were unaware of the difference between the patrolled and unpatrolled parts of the city.

The results of the Kansas City experiment were surprising. Records of "preventable crimes," those toward which the activities of patrol were oriented—such as burglary, robbery, auto theft, larceny, and vandalism—showed no significant differences in rate of occurrence among the three experimental beats. Similarly, citizens didn't seem to notice the change in patrol patterns in the two areas where patrol frequency was changed. Surveys conducted at the conclusion of the experiment showed no difference in citizens' fear of crime before and after the study. The 1974 study can be summed up in the words of the author of the final report: "The whole idea of riding around in cars to create a feeling of omnipresence just hasn't worked. . . . Good people with good intentions tried something that logically should have worked, but didn't."[15] This study has been credited with beginning the now-established tradition of scientific studies of policing.

A second Kansas City study focused on "response time."[16] It found that even consistently fast police response to citizen reports of crime had little effect on citizen satisfaction with the police or on the arrest of suspects. The study uncovered the fact that most reports made to the police came only after a considerable amount of time had passed. Hence, the police were initially

Shane Keyser/The Kansas City Star/Newscom

Kansas City, Missouri, police crime scene technicians unload equipment as officers and agents prepare to search the woods in an effort to find 11-month-old Lisa Irwin in 2011. The girl was not found. Scientific police management was first supported by studies of preventive patrol undertaken in Kansas City in 1974. How does today's evidence-based policing build on that tradition?

■ **directed patrol** A police-management strategy designed to increase the productivity of patrol officers through the scientific analysis and evaluation of patrol techniques.

■ **evidence-based policing (EBP)** The use of the best available research on the outcomes of police work to implement guidelines and evaluate agencies, units, and officers.[i]

handicapped by the timing of the report, and even the fastest police response was not especially effective.

Effects The Kansas City studies greatly affected managerial assumptions about the role of preventive patrol and traditional strategies for responding to citizen calls for assistance. As Joseph Lewis, then director of evaluation at the Police Foundation, said, "I think that now almost everyone would agree that almost anything you do is better than random patrol."[17]

Although the Kansas City studies called into question some basic assumptions about patrol, patrol remains the backbone of police work. New patrol strategies for the effective utilization of human resources have led to various kinds of **directed patrol** activities. One form of directed patrol varies the number of officers involved in patrolling according to the time of day or the frequency of reported crimes within an area, so as to put the most officers on the street where and when crime is most prevalent. Wilmington, Delaware, was one of the first cities to make use of split-force patrol, in which only a part of the patrol force performs routine patrol.[18] The remaining officers respond to calls for service, take reports, and conduct investigations.

As a result of the Kansas City study on response time, some cities have prioritized calls for service,[19] ordering a quick police response only when crimes are in progress or when serious crimes have occurred. Less significant offenses, such as minor larcenies and certain citizen complaints, are handled using the mail or by having citizens come to the police station to make a report.

Early policing studies, such as the Kansas City patrol experiment, were designed to identify and probe some of the basic assumptions that guided police work. The initial response to many such studies was "Why should we study that? Everybody knows the answer already!" As in the case of the Kansas City experiment, however, it soon became obvious that conventional wisdom was not always correct.

Evidence-Based Policing Today

At the close of the twentieth century, noted police researcher Lawrence W. Sherman addressed an audience of criminal justice policymakers, scholars, and practitioners at the Police Foundation in Washington, D.C., and called for a new approach to American policing that would use research to guide and evaluate practice. "Police practices should be based on scientific evidence about what works best," Sherman told his audience. Sherman's lecture, titled "Evidence-Based Policing: Policing Based on Science, Not Anecdote,"[20] popularized the term **evidence-based policing (EBP)**. EBP, says Sherman, "is the use of best available research on the outcomes of police work to implement guidelines and evaluate agencies, units, and officers."[21] In other words, evidence-based policing uses research into everyday police procedures to evaluate current practices and to guide officers and police executives in future decision making. In any discussion of evidence-based policing, it is important to remember that the word *evidence* refers to scientific evidence, not criminal evidence.

Today's EBP model has been called the single "most powerful force for change" in policing today.

"The basic premise of evidence-based practice," says Sherman, "is that we are all entitled to our own opinions, but not to our own facts."[22] Our own facts, or our beliefs about the way things should be done, says Sherman, often turn out to be wrong. During the civil rights movement of the 1960s and 1970s, for example, police executives in many areas took a heavy-handed approach in their attempts to control demonstrators. Images of tear-gas-filled streets, high-pressure fire hoses aimed at marchers, and police dogs biting fleeing demonstrators symbolize that era for many people. This heavy-handed approach had unintended consequences and served to inflame protesters. Situations that might have otherwise been contained with simple crowd-control tactics and the use of physical barriers became largely uncontrollable. Sherman reminds us that "the mythic power of subjective and unstructured wisdom holds back every field and keeps it from systematically discovering and implementing what works best in repeated tasks."

Some suggest that EBP offers a long-term approach for creating cost-effectiveness in policing that, in the current economic environment, "is the only alternative to current ways of operating."[23] "In an age of austerity and budget cuts," argue British writers Neil Wain and Alex Murray, it is necessary for police departments to invest wisely in programs and initiatives that have a proven track record at reducing or preventing crime.

Today's EBP model has been called the single "most powerful force for change" in policing today.[24] Leading the movement toward EBP are organizations like the FBI's Futures Working Group, the Campbell Crime and Justice Group, and the Center for Evidence-Based Crime Policy at George Mason University. FBI Supervisory Special Agent Carl J. Jensen III, a member of the Futures Working Group, notes that in the future "successful law enforcement executives will have to be consumers and appliers of research." They won't need to be researchers themselves, Jensen notes, "but they must use research in their everyday work."[25] The Campbell Crime and Justice Group, which emphasizes the use of experimental studies in crime and

■ **federal law enforcement agency** A U.S. government agency or office whose primary functional responsibility is to enforce federal criminal laws.

justice policymaking, can be accessed via the Campbell Collaboration web site.

A program of the Center for Evidence-Based Crime Policy (CEBCP) at George Mason University, the Evidence-Based Policing Hall of Fame, recognizes innovative law enforcement practitioners who have been central to the implementation of a high-quality research program in their respective agencies. Membership in the Hall of Fame highlights excellence in using and conducting policing research.

The Institute of Criminology at Cambridge University has identified the following questions in the area of policing as goals to be answered by evidence-based studies:[26]

- How can policing produce greater public safety without eroding civil liberties?
- How can more value for the money be returned from investments in policing to cut the costs of crime?
- Can crime be better forecast for preventive policing by time and place?
- Can unsuccessful police methods be distinguished from cost-effective ones?
- Can better policing reduce the high costs of a growing prison population?
- Can evaluation tools used in evidence-based medicine be adopted by police?
- What are the possibilities for a police service based on cost-effectiveness?
- What are the prospects for developing the knowledge base for such evidence?

Finally, in 2010, innovative British police professionals and academics founded the British Society of Policing (BSEBP) to promote and facilitate the increased use of the best available research evidence to solve policing problems and the production of new research by police practitioners and researchers, and to communicate research evidence to police practitioners and the public.

Visit the Center for Evidence-Based Crime Policy at **http://cebcp.org**, and explore the Evidence-Based Policing Hall of Fame at **http://cebcp.org/hall-of-fame**. Read about the new paradigm in police science at Harvard's Kennedy School of Government at **http://tinyurl.com/5rs26l5**. Also, an evidence-based policing matrix is available at **http://gemini.gmu.edu/cebcp/Matrix.html**. The matrix, provided by the Center for Evidence-Based Crime Policy, is a research-to-practice translation tool that visually organizes strong EBP studies.

American Policing Today: From the Federal to the Local Level

The organization of American law enforcement has been called the most complex in the world. Three major legislative and judicial jurisdictions exist in the United States—federal, state, and local—and each has created a variety of police agencies to enforce its laws. Unfortunately, there has been little uniformity among jurisdictions as to the naming, function, or authority of enforcement agencies. The matter is complicated still more by the rapid growth of private security firms, which operate on a for-profit basis and provide services that have traditionally been regarded as law enforcement activities.

Federal Agencies

Dozens of **federal law enforcement agencies** are distributed among 14 U.S. government departments and 28 nondepartmental entities (Table 5-1). In addition to the enforcement agencies listed in the table, many other federal government offices are involved in enforcement through inspection, regulation, and control activities. The Government Accounting Office (GAO) reports that nonmilitary federal agencies employ a total of 137,929 law enforcement officers, which it defines as individuals authorized to perform any of four specific functions: (1) conduct criminal investigations, (2) execute search warrants, (3) make arrests, or (4) carry firearms.[27]

Visit the home pages of many federal law enforcement agencies via **http://www.justicestudies.com/federal.html**.

The Federal Bureau of Investigation

The Federal Bureau of Investigation may be the most famous law enforcement agency in the country and in the world. The FBI has traditionally been held in high regard by many Americans, who think of it as an example of what a law enforcement organization should be and who believe that FBI agents are exemplary police officers. William Webster, former director

TABLE 5-1 | American Policing: Federal Law Enforcement Agencies

Department	Agencies
Department of Agriculture	U.S. Forest Service
Department of Commerce	Bureau of Export Enforcement National Marine Fisheries Administration
Department of Defense	Air Force Office of Special Investigations Army Criminal Investigation Division Defense Criminal Investigative Service Naval Investigative Service
Department of Energy	National Nuclear Safety Administration Office of Mission Operations Office of Secure Transportation
Department of Health and Human Services	Food and Drug Administration, Office of Criminal Investigations
Department of Homeland Security	Federal Law Enforcement Training Center Federal Protective Service Transportation Security Administration U.S. Coast Guard U.S. Customs and Border Protection—includes U.S. Border Patrol U.S. Immigration and Customs Enforcement U.S. Secret Service
Department of the Interior	Bureau of Indian Affairs Bureau of Land Management Fish and Wildlife Service National Park Service U.S. Park Police
Department of Justice	Bureau of Alcohol, Tobacco, Firearms and Explosives Bureau of Prisons Drug Enforcement Administration Federal Bureau of Investigation U.S. Marshals Service
Department of Labor	Office of Labor Racketeering
Department of State	Diplomatic Security Service Department of Transportation Federal Air Marshals Program
Department of the Treasury	Internal Revenue Service, Criminal Investigation Division Treasury Inspector General for Tax Enforcement
Department of Veterans Affairs	Office of Security and Law Enforcement
U.S. Postal Service	Postal Inspection Service Other Offices with Enforcement Personnel Administrative Office of the U.S. Courts AMTRAK Police Bureau of Engraving and Printing Police Environmental Protection Agency, Criminal Investigations Division Federal Reserve Board Tennessee Valley Authority U.S. Capitol Police U.S. Mint U.S. Supreme Court Police Washington, DC, Metropolitan Police Department

Note: Virtually every cabinet-level federal agency has its own Office of the Inspector General, which has enforcement authority—not all of which are listed here.

of the FBI, reflected this sentiment when he said, "Over the years the American people have come to expect the most professional law enforcement from the FBI. Although we use the most modern forms of management and technology in the fight against crime, our strength is in our people—in the character of the men and women of the FBI. For that reason we seek only those who have demonstrated that they can perform as professional people who can, and will, carry on our tradition of fidelity, bravery, and integrity."[28]

The Federal Bureau of Investigation may be the most famous law enforcement agency in the country and in the world.

The history of the FBI spans about 100 years. It began as the Bureau of Investigation in 1908, when it was designed to serve as the investigative arm of the U.S. Department of Justice. The creation of the bureau was motivated, at least in part, by the inability of other agencies to stem the rising tide of American political and business corruption.[29] Learn about the history of the FBI at **http://www.fbi.gov/about-us/history/brief-history**.

The official purpose of today's FBI is succinctly stated in the agency's mission statement: "The Mission of the FBI is to protect and defend the United States against terrorist and foreign intelligence threats, to uphold and enforce the criminal laws of the United States, and to provide leadership and criminal justice services to federal, state, municipal, and international agencies and partners."[30]

Women account for more than 2,600 of the FBI's agents (nearly 20%), and 11 of the FBI's field offices have female special agents in charge.

FBI headquarters are located in the J. Edgar Hoover Building on Pennsylvania Avenue in Washington, D.C. Special agents and support personnel who work at the agency's headquarters organize and coordinate FBI activities throughout the country and around the world. Headquarters staffers determine investigative priorities, oversee major cases, and manage the organization's resources, technology, and personnel.

The daily work of the FBI is done by approximately 13,500 special agents and 20,100 civilian employees assigned to 56 field offices and 400 satellite offices (known as *resident agencies*). A special agent in charge oversees each field office, except for the three largest field offices in Washington, D.C., Los Angeles, and New York City, each of which is headed by an assistant director.

Women account for more than 2,600 of the FBI's agents (nearly 20%), and 11 of the FBI's field offices have female special agents in charge.[31]

The FBI also operates "legal attaché offices" (called *Legats*) in a number of major cities around the world, including London and Paris. Such offices permit the international coordination of enforcement activities and facilitate the flow of law enforcement–related information between the FBI and police agencies in host countries. In 1995, a few years after the end of the cold war, the FBI opened a legal attaché office in Moscow. The Moscow office assists Russian police agencies in the growing battle against organized crime in that country and helps American officials track suspected Russian criminals operating in the United States. Also in 1995, an Eastern European version of the FBI Academy, known as the International Law Enforcement Academy (ILEA), opened in Budapest, Hungary. Its purpose is to train police administrators from all of Eastern Europe in the latest crime-fighting techniques.[32] Ten years later, in 2005, FBI director Robert S. Mueller III, spoke at the Budapest ILEA, telling gathered government ministers and diplomats that in times past, "Good fences make good neighbors." But today, he said, "seen from the perspective of the 21st-century global law enforcement community, dividing walls mean less security, not more. . . . Today, good bridges make good neighbors."[33]

The FBI also operates the Combined DNA Index System (CODIS), a computerized forensic database of DNA "profiles" of offenders convicted of serious crimes (such as rape, other sexual assaults, murder, and certain crimes against children), as well as DNA profiles from unknown offenders.[34] CODIS, now a part of the National DNA Index System (NDIS), was formally authorized by the federal DNA Identification Act of 1994.[35] It is being enhanced daily through the work of federal, state, and local law enforcement agencies that take DNA samples from biological evidence gathered at crime scenes and from offenders themselves. The computerized CODIS system can rapidly identify a perpetrator when it finds a match between an evidence sample and a stored profile. By 1998, every state had enacted legislation establishing a CODIS database and requiring that DNA from offenders convicted of certain serious crimes be entered into the system. By mid-2011, the CODIS database contained more than 8.5 million DNA profiles.[36] Learn more about CODIS at **http://www.dna.gov/dna-databases/codis**.

The FBI Laboratory Division, located in Quantico, Virginia, operates one of the largest and most comprehensive crime laboratories in the world. It provides services related to the scientific solution and prosecution of crimes throughout the country. It is also the only full-service federal forensic laboratory in the United States. Laboratory activities include crime scene searches, special surveillance photography, latent-fingerprint examination, forensic examination of evidence (including DNA testing), court testimony by laboratory personnel, and other scientific and technical services. The FBI offers laboratory services, free of charge, to all law enforcement agencies in the United States. Visit the FBI on the Web at **http://www.fbi.gov**.

Mark Milstein/Newscom

The International Law Enforcement Academy classroom building in Budapest, Hungary. The ILEA is run by the FBI and the Hungarian government and serves as a global training ground for police executives and criminal justice leaders from across Eastern Europe and much of Asia. Why is it important to build bridges in international policing?

The FBI also runs a National Academy Program, which is part of its Training Division. The program offered its first class in 1935 and had 23 students. It was then known as the FBI National Police Training School. In 1940, the school moved from Washington, D.C., to the U.S. Marine Amphibious Base at Quantico, Virginia. In 1972, the facility expanded to 334 acres, and the FBI Academy, as we know it today, officially opened.[37] According to the most recent statistics available, the academy program has produced 43,229 graduates since it began operations. This includes international graduates from 176 foreign countries as well as graduates from U.S. territories and possessions. More than 200 sessions have been offered since inception of the training program. The FBI offers support personnel a variety of training opportunities throughout their careers, including classroom training, distance learning via satellite, and courses offered through the "Virtual Academy" on the FBI's intranet.

The FBI and Counterterrorism

Soon after the attacks of September 11, 2001, the FBI reshaped its priorities to focus on preventing future terrorist attacks. This effort is managed by the Counterterrorism Division at FBI headquarters and is emphasized at every field office, resident agency, and Legat. Headquarters administers a national threat warning system that allows the FBI to instantly distribute important terrorism-related bulletins to law enforcement agencies and public-safety departments throughout the country. "Flying Squads" provide specialized counterterrorism knowledge and experience, language capabilities, and analytic support as needed to FBI field offices and Legats.

CJ | NEWS

LAPD Adds Officers and Crime Falls—But Is There a Connection?

AURELIA VENTURA/LA OPINION/Newscom

New officers graduate from the LAPD academy. Why does the IACP say that the optimum ratio of police officers to citizens in a city depends on local conditions? What conditions would those be?

Ever since he successfully ran for office in 2005, Los Angeles Mayor Antonio Villaraigosa has been intent on adding more sworn officers to the Los Angeles Police Department (LAPD) and reaching a record level of 10,000.

Battling huge budget shortfalls, he succeeded in adding a few hundred new officers through 2012, putting the LAPD just shy of the 10,000 mark. Facing the end of his tenure due to term limits, the mayor finally reached his goal on January 1, 2013, through a maneuver that didn't put any new officers on the streets. The LAPD simply annexed the city's General Services Department, which oversees parks, libraries, and other municipal buildings, and its 60 officers were sworn into the LAPD.

"I know some people think that 10,000 cops is a magical illusion, a meaningless number, that more officers don't necessarily lead to a reduction in crime," the mayor said. "Those critics talk a lot, but they're just plain wrong."

City officials noted that from 2011–2012, gang crime, one of the city's greatest scourges, fell by 10.5%. By 2012, Los Angeles had the lowest overall crime rate of any major city. Using extra officers early in Villaraigosa's tenure, the LAPD could put more of them on the streets and open new stations, and response times fell from eight to nine minutes to six to seven minutes for calls for assistance.

But were extra officers the key factor in reducing crime? Skeptics point to other factors, such as a nationwide decline in crime rates and reshuffling existing officers into a new LAPD office targeting gang violence. Also, the city's budget shortages led to cutbacks in overtime, reducing the possible positive impact of having more officers on the payroll.

And if more officers reduce crime, then why do Chicago and New York, which have much higher ratios of officers to residents, have higher crime rates than LA? In 2005, the LAPD's ratio of officers to residents was about half the rate of the NYPD, even though Los Angeles has a much larger geographic area that should make it harder to patrol. Chicago, with markedly fewer people and a smaller area to patrol, actually has more officers than LA.

The varying circumstances among big-city police departments show there is no single ratio of officers to population that can be applied to all cities. The optimum ratio depends on local conditions, according to the International Association of Chiefs of Police (IACP). "Defining patrol staffing allocation and deployment requirements is a complex endeavor which requires consideration of an extensive series of factors and a sizable body of reliable, current data," the group says.

Therefore, a low crime rate might allow a city to have fewer officers. But without a universal standard for officer-to-population ratios, there will always be debate on what the right level for a city should be. For example, Charlie Beck, the current LAPD chief, insisted in a 2010 interview that LA should have 12,000 officers. With a lower number, "You're not able to spend any time working on solutions," he said. "You're just constantly chasing the symptoms."

But by January 2013, Beck was concerned about just maintaining the 10,000-officer level. If voters do not approve a sales tax increase in an upcoming ballot initiative, Beck warned that the number of officers might have to be cut.

Resources: David Zahniser, "LAPD Force Exceeds 10,000 for the First Time, Officials Say," *Los Angeles Times*, January 8, 2013, http://articles.latimes.com/2013/jan/08/local/la-me-lapd-size-20130108; Philip Rosenbaum, "LAPD Chief: The Thin Blue Line Keeps Getting Thinner," *CNN*, February 16, 2010, http://articles.cnn.com/2010-02-16/justice/california.lapd.beck_1_beck-transparency-cnn?_s=PM:CRIME; and Jerry Berrios, "LAPD Sees Force Grow to Record High," *Los Angeles Daily News*, March 2, 2009, http://www.dailynews.com/ci_11822848.

An essential weapon in the FBI's battle against terrorism is the Joint Terrorism Task Force (JTTF).

To combat terrorism, the FBI's Counterterrorism Division collects, analyzes, and shares information and critical intelligence with various federal agencies and departments— including the Central Intelligence Agency (CIA), the National Security Agency (NSA), and the Department of Homeland Security (DHS)—and with law enforcement agencies throughout the country. An essential weapon in the FBI's battle against terrorism is the Joint Terrorism Task Force (JTTF). A National JTTF, located at the FBI's Washington headquarters, includes representatives from the Department of Defense, the Department of Energy, the Federal Emergency Management Agency, the Central Intelligence Agency, the Customs Service, the Secret Service, and U.S. Immigration and Customs Enforcement. In addition, through 66 local JTTFs, representatives from federal agencies, state and local law enforcement personnel, and first responders coordinate efforts to track down terrorists and to prevent acts of terrorism in the United States.

Hans Gutknecht/Newscom

The new Los Angeles Police Department's $437 million headquarters building that opened in 2009. The 500,000-square-foot building is home to 2,300 LAPD officers and civilian employees. How do the roles of federal, state, and municipal law enforcement agencies differ?

State-Level Agencies

Most state police agencies were created in the late nineteenth or early twentieth century to meet specific needs. The Texas Rangers, created in 1835 before Texas attained statehood, functioned as a military organization responsible for patrolling the republic's borders. The apprehension of Mexican cattle rustlers was one of its main concerns.[38] Massachusetts, targeting vice control, was the second state to create a law enforcement agency. Today, a wide diversity of state policing agencies exists. Table 5-2 lists typical state-sponsored law enforcement agencies.

Most state police agencies were created in the late nineteenth or early twentieth century to meet specific needs.

State law enforcement agencies are usually organized after one of two models. In the first, a centralized model, the tasks of major criminal investigations are combined with the patrol of state highways. Centralized state police agencies generally do the following:

- Assist local law enforcement departments in criminal investigations when asked to do so.
- Operate centralized identification bureaus.
- Maintain a centralized criminal records repository.
- Patrol the state's highways.
- Provide select training for municipal and county officers.

TABLE 5-2 | American Policing: State Law Enforcement Agencies

Alcohol law enforcement agencies	Port authorities	State police
Fish and wildlife agencies	State bureaus of investigation	State university police
Highway patrols	State park services	Weigh station operations

The Pennsylvania Constabulary, known today as the Pennsylvania State Police, was the first modern force to combine these duties and has been called the "first modern state police agency."[39] Michigan, New Jersey, New York, Vermont, and Delaware are a few of the states that patterned their state-level enforcement activities after the Pennsylvania model.

The second state model, the decentralized model of police organization, characterizes operations in the southern United States but is found as well in the Midwest and in some western states. The model draws a clear distinction between traffic enforcement on state highways and other state-level law enforcement functions by creating at least two separate agencies. North Carolina, South Carolina, and Georgia are a few of the many states that employ both a highway patrol and a state bureau of investigation. The names of the respective agencies may vary, however, even though their functions are largely the same. In North Carolina, for example, the two major state-level law enforcement agencies are the North Carolina Highway Patrol and the State Bureau of Investigation. Georgia fields a highway patrol and the Georgia Bureau of Investigation, and South Carolina operates a highway patrol and the South Carolina Law Enforcement Division.

■ **sworn officer** A law enforcement officer who is trained and empowered to perform full police duties, such as making arrests, conducting investigations, and carrying firearms.[ii]

■ **municipal police department** A city- or town-based law enforcement agency.

■ **sheriff** The elected chief officer of a county law enforcement agency. The sheriff is usually responsible for law enforcement in unincorporated areas and for the operation of the county jail.

States that use the decentralized model usually have a number of other adjunct state-level law enforcement agencies. North Carolina, for example, has created a State Wildlife Commission with enforcement powers, a Board of Alcohol Beverage Control with additional agents, and a separate Enforcement and Theft Bureau for enforcing certain motor vehicle and theft laws. Like government agencies everywhere, state police agencies have seen their budgets impacted by the recent recession.

Local Agencies

Local law enforcement agencies, including city and county agencies, represent a third level of police activity in the United States. The term *local police* encompasses a wide variety of agencies. Municipal departments, rural sheriff's departments, and specialized groups like campus police and transit police can all be grouped under the "local" rubric. Large municipal departments are highly visible because of their vast size, huge budgets, and innovative programs. The nation's largest law enforcement agency, the New York City Police Department (NYPD), for example, has about 45,000 full-time employees, including about 34,500 full-time **sworn officers**.[40] Learn more about the NYPD via "Inside the Department" podcasts available at **http://www.nyc.gov/html/nypd/html/pr/podcasts.shtml**.

Far greater in number, however, are small-town and county sheriff's departments. There are approximately 12,500 **municipal police departments** and 3,012 sheriff's departments in the United States.[41] Local police and sheriff's offices employ more than 1 million people, of which approximately 636,000 are sworn law enforcement officers.[42]

Every incorporated municipality in the country has the authority to create its own police force. Some very small communities hire only one officer, who fills the roles of chief, investigator, and night watch—as well as everything in between. About half of all local agencies employ fewer than ten full-time officers, and about 3,220 employ fewer than five full-time officers. These smaller agencies include 2,125 (or 12%) with just one full-time officer and 1,100 (or 6%) with only part-time officers.[43] A few communities contract with private security firms for police services, and still others have no active police force at all, depending instead on local sheriff's departments to deal with law violators.

City police chiefs are typically appointed by the mayor or selected by the city council. Their departments' jurisdictions are

Harry Cabluck/AP Wide World Photos

Texas Governor Rick Perry speaking to a group of Texas Rangers in Austin, Texas, in 2009. The Texas Rangers have long been held in high regard among state police agencies. How many levels of policing are there in the U.S.?

■ **private protective service** An independent or proprietary commercial organization that provides protective services to employers on a contractual basis.

limited by convention to the geographic boundaries of their communities. **Sheriffs**, on the other hand, are elected public officials whose agencies are responsible for law enforcement throughout the counties in which they function. Sheriff's deputies mostly patrol the "unincorporated" areas of the county, or those that lie between municipalities. They do, however, have jurisdiction throughout the county, and in some areas they routinely work alongside municipal police to enforce laws within towns and cities.

Sheriff's departments are generally responsible for serving court papers, including civil summonses, and for maintaining security within state courtrooms. Sheriffs also run county jails and are responsible for more detainees awaiting trial than any other type of law enforcement department in the country.

For example, the Los Angeles County Jail System, operated by the Custody Operations Division of the LA County Sheriff's Department (LASD), is the largest in the world.[44] With eight separate facilities, the custody division of the LASD has an average daily population of 18,423 inmates—considerably more than the number of inmates held in many state prison systems. More than 2,200 uniformed officers and 1,265 civilian employees work in the custody division of the LASD, and that division alone operates with a yearly budget in excess of $200 million.[45] Overall, the LASD has more than 10,000 sworn and 8,000 civilian personnel, plus more than 830 reserve deputies and over 4,000 civilian volunteers.[46]

Sheriff's departments remain strong across most of the country, although in parts of New England, deputies mostly function as court agents with limited law enforcement duties. One report found that most sheriff's departments are small, with more than half of them employing fewer than 25 sworn officers.[47] Only 18 departments employ more than 1,000 officers. Even so, southern and western sheriffs are still considered the "chief law enforcement officers" in their counties. A list of conventional police agencies found at the local level is shown in Table 5-3.

TABLE 5-3 | **American Policing: Local Law Enforcement Agencies**

Campus police	Housing authority agencies	Sheriff's departments
City/county agencies	Marine patrol agencies	Transit police
Constables	Municipal police departments	Tribal police
Coroners or medical examiners		

Private Protective Services

Private protective services constitute a fourth level of enforcement activity in the United States today. Whereas public police are employed by the government and enforce public laws, private security personnel work for corporate employers and secure private interests.

Private security has been defined as "those self-employed individuals and privately funded business entities and organizations providing security-related services to specific clientele for a fee, for the individual or entity that retains or employs them, or for themselves, in order to protect their persons, private property, or interests from various hazards."[48] The growth in the size of private security in recent years has been phenomenal. In 2004, for example, official estimates put the total amount spent to secure the Olympic Games in Athens at $1.5 billion—or $283 per paid ticket.[49] Given Greece's geopolitical situation and its proximity to the Balkans and the Middle East, officials in Athens wanted to be sure they could prevent terrorist attacks. Eight years later, in 2012, England spent around $13.8 billion to host the Thirtieth Olympiad, of which $870 million was spent on security (more than twice what had been originally budgeted).[50] The London games involved 23,700 security personnel securing more than 100 venues—supplemented by British troops and police, adding another $65 million in expenses.[51]

ASIS International, with more than 33,000 members, is the preeminent international organization for private security professionals.[52] ASIS International members include corporate security managers and directors, as well as architects, attorneys, and federal, state, and local law enforcement personnel. Founded in 1955, ASIS International, formerly known as the American Society for Industrial Security, is dedicated to increasing the effectiveness and productivity of security professionals by developing educational and certification programs and training materials that address the needs of the security profession. ASIS also actively promotes the value of security management to business, the media, governmental entities, and the public. The organization publishes the industry magazine *Security Management*.

With 204 chapters worldwide, ASIS administers three certification programs: (1) the Certified Protection Professional (CPP) program, which provides for board certification in security management; (2) the Physical Security Professional (PSP) program, which provides a technical certification opportunity for specialists in physical plant security; and (3) the Professional Certified Investigator (PCI) program. Holders of PCI

paying for it

Cost-Efficient Policing

In January 2011, Newark, New Jersey, ranked 23rd on the list of the most dangerous cities in America, laid off almost half of its police force as budget constraints forced the city to reduce the services it offered to its citizens. The layoffs came after city revenues dipped by one-third amid declining income from taxes on hotel stays and local payrolls, and parking fees collected by the city fell sharply. Adding to the city's woes was an additional decline of 40% in aid from the state of New Jersey.

In the four-month period immediately following the layoffs, crime in Newark surged. The murder rate climbed 73% above what it was in the same period for the previous year; auto thefts were up 40%; and carjackings increased fourfold. The number of shooting victims taken to area hospitals doubled. Although some claim that not all of those crime increases can be directly attributed to declines in police staffing, others are not so sure. As police personnel were cut, so were crime-prevention programs that had served the city well. One of them was Operation Impact, which targeted high-crime areas and resulted in a 35% decrease in crime in those neighborhoods. The program was eliminated as uniformed personnel were moved to street patrol.

The city of Newark, which has since rehired some of its officers, is not alone in facing financial pressures. A year after the layoffs were announced in Newark, Camden city officials, also in New Jersey, announced that they were considering eliminating the entire Camden Police Department, and were working to create a countywide police force to be named the Camden County Police Department. Theoretically, the department, which would include other cities and towns in the area, would bring about cost savings from a combination of resources and personnel that were previously performing redundant tasks. Current plans, however, which are still developing as this book goes to press, do not ask for the department to combine operations with the Camden County Sheriff's Office, which serves unincorporated areas of the county.

Although today's combined departments represent one approach to cost savings, others include the following: prioritizing activities, reducing services, and modifying service delivery; reorganizing and rightsizing agencies; partnering with other agencies and organizations; using proactive policing methods instead of reactive ones; adopting preventative and problem-solving service models; increasing efficiency; outsourcing services; and implementing force multipliers.

Force multipliers, the last of the options listed here, refers to using technologies that permit a few personnel to do the work of many. Cameras placed in crime-prone areas, for example, and monitored by police employees can sometimes reduce the need for active police patrols, thereby saving huge expenditures on personnel, vehicles, communications, and administrative expenses. Cross-training, in which personnel are trained to perform a number of roles—such as police officer, EMT, and firefighter—can also save money by eliminating duplicate positions.

Finally, another initiative, smart policing, makes use of techniques shown to work at both reducing and solving crimes. Hot-spot policing, in which agencies focus their resources on known areas of criminal activity, is one such technique; whereas predictive policing, which provides the ability to anticipate or predict crime through the use of statistical techniques, helps guide enforcement operations, and is an increasingly important concept in policing today (see the "CJ News box" in Chapter 6 for more information on hot-spot policing).

Two programs that support effective policing are the Smart Policing Initiative (SPI), and the National Law Enforcement and Corrections Technology Center (NLECTC). The NLECTC works to identify emerging technologies, as well as to assess their efficiency; the SPI, a collaborative consortium composed of the Bureau of Justice Assistance, the non-profit CNA Corporation, and over 30 local law enforcement agencies, works to build evidence-based law enforcement strategies that are effective, efficient, and economical. The SPI is also discussed in a "Paying for It" box in Chapter 6. Visit SPI on the Web at http://www.smartpolicinginitiative.com. The NLECTC can be accessed at http://www.justnet.org.

References: William Alden, "Newark Police Layoffs Threaten Crime-Fighting as Budget Cuts Spark Fears," *Huffington Post*, February 25, 2011, http://www.huffingtonpost.com/2011/02/25/newark-police-layoffs-budget-cuts_n_827993.html (accessed May 28, 2012); Claudia Vargas, "Camden City Council Urges Officials to Advance Plan for County Police Force," *The Philadelphia Inquirer*, December 28, 2011, http://articles.philly.com/2011-12-28/news/30565451_1_county-force-police-force-police-officers (accessed May 21, 2012); Joe Cordero, *Reducing the Costs of Quality Policing: Making Community Safety Cost Effective and Sustainable* (The Cordero Group), http://www.njlmef.org/policy-papers/FoLG_v_3_1.pdf (accessed May 29, 2012); Charlie Beck, "Predictive Policing: What Can We Learn from Wal-Mart and Amazon about Fighting Crime in a Recession?" *The Police Chief*, April 2012, http://www.policechiefmagazine.org/magazine/index.cfm?fuseaction=display_arch&article_id=1942&issue_id=112009 (accessed May 25, 2012); and JustNet, "About NLECTC," https://www.justnet.org/About_NLECTC.html (accessed May 29, 2012).

certification have satisfactorily demonstrated significant education and/or experience in the fields of case management, evidence collection, and case presentation. The ASIS also promotes the importance of ethical standards in the private security sector. The ASIS International Code of Ethics can be found in the "Ethics and Professionalism" box in this chapter. Visit ASIS online via **http://www.asisonline.org**.

A report released by the National Institute of Justice in 2001, titled *The New Structure of Policing*, found that "policing is being transformed and restructured in the modern world" in ways that were unanticipated only a few decades ago.[53] Much of the change is due to the development of private protective services as an important adjunct to public law enforcement activities in the United States and throughout much of the rest of the world. The NIJ report says that "the key to understanding the transformation is that policing, meaning the activity of making societies safe, is no longer carried out exclusively by governments" and that the distinction between private and public police has begun to blur. According to the NIJ, "gradually, almost imperceptibly, policing has been 'multilateralized,'" meaning that "a host of nongovernmental agencies have undertaken to provide security services." As a result, the NIJ report says, "policing has entered a new era, an era characterized by a transformation in the governance of security." The report concludes the following:

- In most countries, certainly in the democratic world, private police outnumber public police.
- In these same countries, people spend more time in their daily lives in places where visible crime prevention and control are provided by nongovernmental groups rather than by governmental police agencies.
- The reconstruction of policing is occurring worldwide despite differences in wealth and economic systems.

According to the National Center for Policy Analysis, private security personnel outnumber public law enforcement officers in the United States by nearly three to one.[54] The widely cited *Hallcrest Report II*,[55] another important document describing the private security industry, says that employment in the field of private security is anticipated to continue to expand by around 4% per year, whereas public police agencies are expected to grow by only 2.8% per year for the foreseeable future. Still faster growth is predicted in private security industry revenues, which are expected to increase about 7% per year, a growth rate almost three times greater than that projected for the gross national product. Table 5-4 lists the ten largest private security agencies in business today and some of the services they offer.

Major reasons for the quick growth of the American proprietary security sector include "(1) an increase in crimes in the workplace, (2) an increase in fear (real or perceived) of crime and terrorism, (3) the fiscal crises of the states, which have limited public protection, and (4) an increased public and business awareness and use of . . . more cost-effective private security products and services."[56]

Private agencies provide tailored policing funded by the guarded organization rather than through the expenditure of public monies. Experts estimate that the money spent on private security in this country exceeds the combined budgets of all law enforcement agencies—local, state, and federal.[57] Contributing to this vast expenditure is the federal government, which is itself a major employer of private security personnel, contracting for services that range from guards to highly specialized electronic

TABLE 5-4 | American Policing: Private Security Agencies

THE LARGEST PRIVATE SECURITY AGENCIES IN THE UNITED STATES		
Advance Security, Inc. Allied Security, Inc. American Protective Services Burns International Security Services	Globe Security Guardsmark, Inc. Pinkerton's, Inc.	Security Bureau, Inc. Wackenhut Corp. Wells Fargo Guard Services
PRIVATE SECURITY SERVICES		
Airport security ATM services Bank guards Company guards	Computer/information security Executive protection Hospital security Loss-prevention specialists	Nuclear facility security Railroad detectives School security Store/mall security
Source: Adapted from William C. Cunningham, John J. Strauchs, and Clifford W. Van Meter, *The Hallcrest Report II: Private Security Trends, 1970–2000* (McLean, VA: Hallcrest Systems, 1990).		

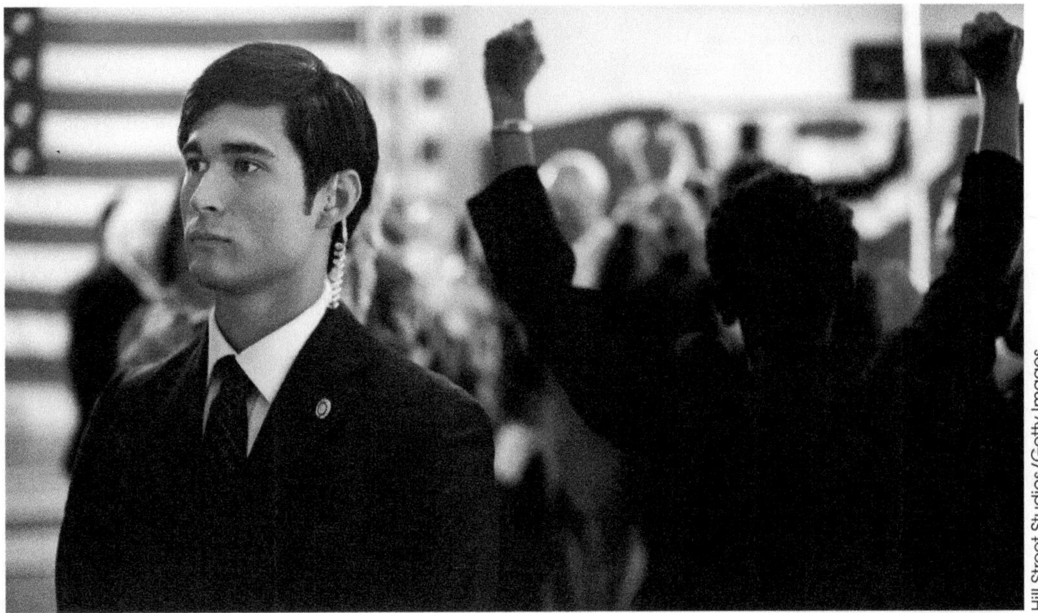

Hill Street Studios/Getty Images

A security guard at a political gathering. Why has the privatization of policing become a major issue facing governments and public justice agencies everywhere?

There are indications that private security activities are rapidly growing beyond traditional guard services to encompass dedicated efforts at security-related intelligence gathering.

snooping and computerized countermeasures at military installations and embassies throughout the world.

There are indications that private security activities are rapidly growing beyond traditional guard services to encompass dedicated efforts at security-related intelligence gathering. In August 2004, for example, the Department of Homeland Security warned that terrorists might be actively targeting Citigroup, Prudential, the New York Stock Exchange, and other large financial institutions on the East Coast of the United States. At the same time, however, Austin-based Stratfor, Inc., a low-profile private intelligence agency run by former CIA officers, was quietly assuring its clients that such an attack was very unlikely, saying that "Al Qaeda has never attacked into an alert."[58]

According to The Freedonia Group, a Cleveland-based industry research firm, U.S. demand for private contracted security services was around $66 billion in 2012.[59] The total includes spending on physical security, Internet safeguards, staff screening and training, and terrorist and related intelligence analysis. Not included are federal and state government expenditures on aviation security, homeland security, or border security.

Integrating Public and Private Security

As the private security field grows, its relationship to public law enforcement continues to evolve. Some argue that "today, a distinction between public and private policing is increasingly meaningless."[60] As a result, the focus has largely shifted from an analysis of competition between the sectors to the recognition that each form of policing can help the other.

As the private security field grows, its relationship to public law enforcement continues to evolve.

In 2012, Philip Cook, a professor of economics at Duke University, suggested that private security forces might have been largely responsible for the recent decade-long decline in reported crime. Although changes in crime rates are often attributed to effective policing, Cook reported that security contractors and anti-theft technology, such as LoJack devices and

Michael Newman/PhotoEdit Inc.

A private security officer conferring with a sworn public law enforcement officer. How can cooperation between private security agencies and public law enforcement offices help solve and prevent crimes?

CJ | CAREERS
Security Professional

The Justice Research Association

Ryan Strahan.

Name. Ryan James Strahan

Position. Security professional, Palm Beach Gardens, Florida

Colleges attended. Palm Beach State College Criminal Justice Institute/Vocational Certificate, Law Enforcement Officer Florida CMS Recruit Training Program

Majors. Basic Law Enforcement/Criminal Justice

Year hired. 2011

Please give a brief description of your job. As a security professional working in a private gated residential community, I deal with people on a day-to-day basis using the decision-making and problem-solving skills needed to maintain a harmonious and safe environment for the people living in, working in, and visiting the community.

What appealed to you most about the position when you applied for it? I have experience with event security for the Daytona Beach Bike Week and Biketoberfest for the last eight years. However, after my certification and training in law enforcement, I found that I need to be exposed to a more community-oriented style of enforcement. Working in a small community where people know each other and have a close intertwined living area is a great environment for a piece of the total experience of what anyone continuing to grow and learn should have.

How would you describe the interview process? I was directed to interview with the HOA operations supervisor. After a few emails and a face-to-face conversation, I was asked to fill out an application and provide an intake of certifications. I then had an interview with both the club manager and HOA operations supervisor. After a background check and drug test I was asked to start training in a watch-and-learn environment, until I was comfortable with the way the standard operating procedures (SOPs) worked.

What is a typical day like? Each day starts with a shift change where the guards read the activity log and discuss what is happening in the community since the last time they worked. We go over what needs to be done for the shift and communicate with our supervisor on any issues that need to be addressed. The shift is spent multitasking between taking information from people coming and going who are doing work or visiting the community, patrolling the community looking for anything out of the ordinary, and helping the residents with whatever we can do to give them the highest level of service.

Like most private communities, my employer has SOPs. This provides a structure that all employees are expected to use as performance guidelines. It is a format that we all follow in order to maintain high job performance standards. SOPs involve how we patrol, direct traffic, do perimeter checks, perform extra-duty house checks, and all other aspects of the job.

What qualities/characteristics are most helpful for this job? I have been a carpenter for over 12 years and still do a lot of side work as a woodworker; this puts me in a place to relate to the service workers who come into the community on a daily basis. With the training I have received in the police academy and experience I have from large-event security, I feel that I possess a well-rounded work history to provide a wide range of contributions.

What is a typical starting salary? $21,000–26,000, but much more can be earned through overtime work.

What is the salary potential as you move up into higher-level jobs? Up to $40,000 in my current position; but supervisory positions can pay well over $100,000 per year.

What career advice would you give someone in college beginning studies in criminal justice? Do not overlook getting experience in a field of work closely related to what you want to achieve. Any further experience can help you build a better résumé and become a desirable candidate for career employment.

---

video surveillance systems, limit criminal opportunity. "Private action," said Cook, is a way "of controlling opportunity to potential criminals."[61] He predicted that crime rates will continue to fall with improving security technology and wider involvement by the private sector in crime prevention.

One government-sponsored report recommends that the resources of proprietary and contract security should be brought to bear in cooperative, community-based crime-prevention and security-awareness programs. Doing so, says the report, would maximize the cooperative crime-fighting potential of existing private and public security resources.[62]

One especially important policy area involves building private security–public policing partnerships to prevent terrorism and to respond to threats of terrorism. A national policy summit report, jointly authored by the International Association of Chiefs of Police and the 30,000-member ASIS International, says that despite similar interests in protecting people and property in the United States, public police and private security agencies have rarely collaborated.[63] The report notes, however, that as much as 85% of the nation's critical infrastructure is protected by private security. It goes on to say that "the need for complex coordination, extra staffing, and special resources" in the light of possible terror attacks, "coupled with the significant demands of crime prevention and response, absolutely requires boosting the level of partnership between public policing and private security."[64] The full national policy summit report is available at **http://www.justicestudies.com/pubs/pubprivpart.pdf**.

ethics and professionalism

ASIS International Code of Ethics

Preamble

Aware that the quality of professional security activity ultimately depends upon the willingness of practitioners to observe special standards of conduct and to manifest good faith in professional relationships, the American Society for Industrial Security adopts the following Code of Ethics and mandates its conscientious observance as a binding condition of membership in or affiliation with the Society:

Code of Ethics

1. A member shall perform professional duties in accordance with the law and the highest moral principles.
2. A member shall observe the precepts of truthfulness, honesty, and integrity.
3. A member shall be faithful and diligent in discharging professional responsibilities.
4. A member shall be competent in discharging professional responsibilities.
5. A member shall safeguard confidential information and exercise due care to prevent its improper disclosure.
6. A member shall not maliciously injure the professional reputation or practice of colleagues, clients, or employers.

Article I

A member shall perform professional duties in accordance with the law and the highest moral principles.

Ethical Considerations

1. A member shall abide by the law of the land in which the services are rendered and perform all duties in an honorable manner.
2. A member shall not knowingly become associated in responsibility for work with colleagues who do not conform to the law and these ethical standards.
3. A member shall be just and respect the rights of others in performing professional responsibilities.

Article II

A member shall observe the precepts of truthfulness, honesty, and integrity.

Ethical Considerations

1. A member shall disclose all relevant information to those having the right to know.
2. A right to know is a legally enforceable claim or demand by a person for disclosure of information by a member. Such a right does not depend upon prior knowledge by the person of the existence of the information to be disclosed.
3. A member shall not knowingly release misleading information nor encourage or otherwise participate in the release of such information.

Article III

A member shall be faithful and diligent in discharging professional responsibilities.

Ethical Considerations

1. A member is faithful when fair and steadfast in adherence to promises and commitments.
2. A member is diligent when employing best efforts in an assignment.
3. A member shall not act in matters involving conflicts of interest without appropriate disclosure and approval.
4. A member shall represent services or products fairly and truthfully.

Article IV

A member shall be competent in discharging professional responsibilities.

Ethical Considerations

1. A member is competent who possesses and applies the skills and knowledge required for the task.
2. A member shall not accept a task beyond the member's competence nor shall competence be claimed when not possessed.

Article V

A member shall safeguard confidential information and exercise due care to prevent its improper disclosure.

Ethical Considerations

1. Confidential information is nonpublic information, the disclosure of which is restricted.
2. Due care requires that the professional must not knowingly reveal confidential information, or use a confidence to the disadvantage of the principal or to the advantage of the member or a third person, unless the principal

consents after full disclosure of all the facts. This confidentiality continues after the business relationship between the member and his principal has terminated.

3. A member who receives information and has not agreed to be bound by confidentiality is not bound from disclosing it. A member is not bound by confidential disclosures made of acts or omissions which constitute a violation of the law.
4. Confidential disclosures made by a principal to a member are not recognized by law as privileged in a legal proceeding. The member may be required to testify in a legal proceeding to the information received in confidence from his principal over the objection of his principal's counsel.
5. A member shall not disclose confidential information for personal gain without appropriate authorization.

Article VI

A member shall not maliciously injure the professional reputation or practice of colleagues, clients, or employers.

Ethical Considerations

1. A member shall not comment falsely and with malice concerning a colleague's competence, performance, or professional capabilities.
2. A member who knows, or has reasonable grounds to believe, that another member has failed to conform to the Society's Code of Ethics shall present such information to the Ethical Standards Committee in accordance with Article VIII of the Society's bylaws.

Thinking About Ethics

1. The ASIS code of ethics says, "A member shall observe the precepts of truthfulness, honesty, and integrity." Why are these qualities important in a security professional?
2. Why is it important for security personnel to "safeguard confidential information and exercise due care to prevent its improper disclosure"? What might happen if they didn't?

SUMMARY

- American police departments owe a historical legacy to Sir Robert Peel and the London Metropolitan Police Service (MPS). Although law enforcement efforts in the United States were based to some degree on the British experience, the unique character of the American frontier led to the growth of a decentralized form of policing throughout the United States.
- Police agencies in the United States function to enforce the statutes created by lawmaking bodies, and differing types and levels of legislative authority are reflected in the diversity of police forces in our country today. Consequently, American policing presents a complex picture that is structured along federal, state, and local lines.
- Dozens of federal law enforcement agencies are distributed among 14 U.S. government departments and 28 nondepartmental entities, and each federal agency empowered by Congress to enforce specific statutes has its own enforcement arm. The FBI may be the most famous law enforcement agency in the country and in the world. The mission of the FBI is to protect and defend the United States against terrorist and foreign intelligence threats, to uphold and enforce the criminal laws of the United States, and to provide leadership and criminal justice services to federal, state, municipal, and international agencies and partners.
- State law enforcement agencies have numerous functions, including assisting local law enforcement departments in criminal investigations when asked to do so, operating centralized identification bureaus, maintaining a centralized criminal records repository, patrolling the state's highways, and providing select training for municipal and county officers. State law enforcement agencies are usually organized after one of two models. In the first, a centralized model, the tasks of major criminal investigations are combined with the patrol of state highways. The second state model, the decentralized model, draws a clear distinction between traffic enforcement on state highways and other state-level law enforcement functions by creating at least two separate agencies.
- Local police agencies represent a third level of law enforcement activity in the United States. They encompass a wide variety of agencies, including municipal police departments, rural sheriff's departments, and specialized groups like campus police and transit police.
- Private protective services constitute another level of law enforcement. Whereas public police are employed by the government and enforce public laws, private security personnel work for corporate or private employers and secure private interests. Private security personnel outnumber public law enforcement officers in the United States by nearly three to one, and private agencies provide tailored protective services funded by the guarded organization rather than by taxpayers.

KEY TERMS

bobbies, 139
Bow Street Runners, 138
***comes stabuli*, 137**
directed patrol, 144
evidence-based policing (EBP), 144
federal law enforcement agency, 145
Kansas City experiment, 143
Law Enforcement Assistance Administration (LEAA), 141
municipal police department, 150
new police, 139
night watch, 137
private protective service, 151
scientific police management, 142
sheriff, 151
Statute of Winchester, 137
sworn officer, 150
vigilantism, 140
Wickersham Commission, 141

QUESTIONS FOR REVIEW

1. Describe the historical development of policing in America. What impact did the Prohibition era have on the development of American policing?
2. What are the three levels of public law enforcement described in this chapter?
3. Identify a number of significant federal law enforcement agencies, and describe the responsibilities of each.
4. Explain the role that state law enforcement agencies play in enforcing the law, and describe the two major models of state law enforcement organization.
5. What different kinds of local law enforcement agencies exist in the United States today? What role does each agency have in enforcing the law?
6. Describe the nature and extent of private protective services in the United States today. What role do you think they will play in the future?

QUESTIONS FOR REFLECTION

1. Why are there so many different types of law enforcement agencies in the United States? What problems, if any, do you think are created by having such a diversity of agencies?
2. What is evidence-based policing? What assumptions about police work have scientific studies of law enforcement called into question? What other assumptions made about police work today might be similarly questioned or studied?
3. Contrast the current deployment of private security personnel with the number of public law enforcement personnel.
4. How can the quality of private security services be ensured?
5. What is the relationship between private security and public policing in America today? How might the nature of that relationship be expected to change over time? Why?

NOTES

i. Lawrence W. Sherman, *Evidence-Based Policing* (Washington, DC: Police Foundation, 1998), p. 3.
ii. Adapted from Darl H. Champion and Michael K. Hooper, *Introduction to American Policing* (New York: McGraw-Hill, 2003), p. 166.

1. "A Reminiscence of a Bow-Street Officer," *Harper's New Monthly Magazine*, Vol. 5, No. 28 (September 1852), p. 484.
2. For a good discussion of the development of the modern police, see Sue Titus Reid, *Criminal Justice: Procedures and Issues* (St. Paul, MN: West, 1987), pp. 110–115; and Henry M. Wrobleski and Karen M. Hess, *Introduction to Law Enforcement and Criminal Justice*, 4th ed. (St. Paul, MN: West, 1993), pp. 3–51.
3. Camdem Pelham, *Chronicles of Crime*, Vol. 1 (London: T. Miles, 1887), p. 59.
4. Gary Sykes, "Street Justice: A Moral Defense of Order Maintenance Policing," *Justice Quarterly*, Vol. 3, No. 4 (December 1986), p. 504.
5. Law Enforcement Assistance Administration, *Two Hundred Years of American Criminal Justice: An LEAA Bicentennial Study* (Washington, DC: U.S. Government Printing Office, 1976), p. 15.
6. For an excellent discussion of the history of policewomen in the United States, see Dorothy Moses Schulz, *From Social Worker to Crimefighter: Women in United States Municipal Policing* (Westport, CT: Praeger, 1995); and Dorothy Moses Schulz, "Invisible No More: A Social History of Women in U.S. Policing," in Barbara R. Price and Natalie J. Sokoloff, eds., *The Criminal Justice System and Women: Offender, Victim, Worker*, 2nd ed. (New York: McGraw-Hill, 1995), pp. 372–382.
7. Schulz, *From Social Worker to Crimefighter*, p. 25.
8. Ibid., p. 27.
9. National Commission on Law Observance and Enforcement, *Wickersham Commission Reports*, 14 vols. (Washington, DC: U.S. Government Printing Office, 1931).
10. President's Commission on Law Enforcement and Administration of Justice, *The Challenge of Crime in a Free Society* (Washington, DC: U.S. Government Printing Office, 1967).
11. National Advisory Commission on Criminal Justice Standards and Goals, *A National Strategy to Reduce Crime* (Washington, DC: U.S. Government Printing Office, 1973).
12. Enacted as U.S. Code, Title 42, Chapter 136, Subchapter XII.
13. Thomas J. Deakin, "The Police Foundation: A Special Report," *FBI Law Enforcement Bulletin* (November 1986), p. 2.
14. George L. Kelling et al., *The Kansas City Patrol Experiment* (Washington, DC: Police Foundation, 1974).
15. Kevin Krajick, "Does Patrol Prevent Crime?" *Police Magazine* (September 1978), quoting Dr. George Kelling.
16. William Bieck and David Kessler, *Response Time Analysis* (Kansas City, MO: Board of Police Commissioners, 1977). See also J. Thomas McEwen et al., *Evaluation of the Differential*

Police Response Field Test: Executive Summary (Alexandria, VA: Research Management Associates, 1984); and Lawrence Sherman, "Policing Communities: What Works?" in Michael Tonry and Norval Morris, eds., *Crime and Justice: An Annual Review of Research*, Vol. 8 (Chicago: University of Chicago Press, 1986).

17. Krajick, "Does Patrol Prevent Crime?"
18. Ibid.
19. Ibid.
20. "Evidence-Based Policing," Police Foundation press release, March 17, 1998, http://www.policefoundation.org/docs/evidence.html (accessed January 5, 2009).
21. Lawrence W. Sherman, *Evidence-Based Policing* (Washington, DC: Police Foundation, 1998), p. 3.
22. Much of the information in this section comes from Sherman, *Evidence-Based Policing*.
23. Neil Wain and Alex Murray, "Gathering Evidence," Police-Professional.com, March 24, 2001, http://gemini.gmu.edu/cebcp/BritishSocietyEBPolicing.pdf (accessed May 18, 2011).
24. Carl J. Jensen III, "Consuming and Applying Research: Evidence-Based Policing," *Police Chief*, Vol. 73, No. 2 (February 2006), http://policechiefmagazine.org/magazine/index.cfm?fuseaction=display_arch&article_id=815&issue_id=22006 (accessed May 17, 2009).
25. Ibid.
26. University of Cambridge, "Evidence-Based Policing: Possibilities and Prospects," revised and final program announcement, June 30, 2008.
27. Government Accounting Office, *Federal Law Enforcement: Survey of Federal Civilian Law Enforcement Functions and Authorities* (Washington, DC: U.S. GAO, December 2006), p. 17.
28. U.S. Department of Justice, *A Proud History . . . a Bright Future: Careers with the FBI*, pamphlet (October 1986), p. 1.
29. Much of the information in this section comes from U.S. Department of Justice, *The FBI: The First Seventy-Five Years* (Washington, DC: U.S. Government Printing Office, 1986).
30. Some of the information in this section is adapted from Federal Bureau of Investigation, "Today's FBI: Facts and Figures, 2010–11," http://www.fbi.gov/stats-services/publications/facts-and-figures-2010-2011 (accessed May 18, 2011).
31. "Rising to the Occasion," FBI News Blog, October 22, 2012, http://www.fbi.gov/news/news_blog/in-new-interviews-women-agents-reflect-on-40-years (accessed February 15, 2013).
32. Telephone conversation with FBI officials, April 21, 1995.
33. Federal Bureau of Investigation, "The Budapest International Law Enforcement Academy Turns Ten," May 13, 2005, http://www.fbi.gov/news/stories/2005/may/ilea051305 (accessed July 10, 2013).
34. Information in this section comes from Christopher H. Asplen, "National Commission Explores Its Future," *NIJ Journal* (January 1999), pp. 17–24.
35. The DNA Identification Act is Section 210301 of the Violent Crime Control and Law Enforcement Act of 1994.
36. Federal Bureau of Investigation, "Combined DNA Index System (CODIS)," http://www.fbi.gov/about-us/lab/codis/ (accessed May 28, 2013).
37. Much of the information in this paragraph comes from the FBI Academy website at http://www.fbi.gov/hq/td/academy/academy.htm (accessed January 23, 2009).
38. Henry M. Wrobleski and Karen M. Hess, *Introduction to Law Enforcement and Criminal Justice*, 4th ed. (St. Paul, MN: West, 1993), p. 34.
39. Ibid., p. 35.
40. New York City Police Department website, http://www.nyc.gov/html/nypd/html/faq/faq_police.shtml (accessed June 21, 2011).
41. Brian A. Reaves, *Census of State and Local Law Enforcement Agencies, 2008* (Washington, DC: Bureau of Justice Statistics, 2011); and Andrea M. Burch, *Sheriffs' Offices, 2007*: Statistical Tables (Washington, D.C. Bureau of Justice Statistics, 2012), p. 1.
42. Andrea M. Burch, *Sheriffs' Offices, 2007: Statistical Tables* (Washington, D.C. Bureau of Justice Statistics, 2012), p. 6.
43. Reaves, *Census of State and Local Law Enforcement Agencies, 2008*.
44. Note, however, that New York City jails may have daily populations that, on a given day, exceed those of Los Angeles County.
45. The Police Assessment Resource Center, *The Los Angeles County Sheriff's Department—19th Semiannual Report* (Los Angeles: PARC, February 2005); and telephone communication with Deputy Ethan Marquez, Los Angeles County Sheriff's Department, Custodial Division, January 24, 2002.
46. Los Angeles County Sheriff's Department, "Employees," http://tinyurl.com/clq4eom (accessed February 15, 2013).
47. Burch, *Sheriffs' Offices, 2007: Statistical Tables*, p. 2.
48. *Private Security: Report of the Task Force on Private Security* (Washington, DC: U.S. Government Printing Office, 1976), p. 4.
49. "Securing the Olympic Games: $142,857 Security Cost per Athlete in Greece," *Wall Street Journal*, August 22, 2004, http://www.mindfully.org/Reform/2004/Olympic-Games-Security22aug04.htm (accessed May 17, 2007).
50. Christopher Elser, "London Olympics Doubles Spending on Security to $870 Million for Next Year," *Bloomberg*, December 5, 2011, http://www.bloomberg.com/news/2011-12-05/london-olympics-doubles-spending-on-security-to-870-million-for-next-year.html (accessed February 15, 2013).
51. John-Paul Ford Rojas, "£9 Billion Olympics 'Good Value,' Says Spending Watchdog," *The London Telegraph*, December 5, 2012 (accessed February 15, 2013).
52. The information and some of the wording in this paragraph come from the ASIS International website at http://www.asisonline.org (accessed August 5, 2009).
53. David H. Bayley and Clifford D. Shearing, *The New Structure of Policing: Description, Conceptualization, and Research Agenda* (Washington, DC: National Institute of Justice, 2001).
54. National Center for Policy Analysis, *Using the Private Sector to Deter Crime* (Washington, DC: NCPA, 2001).
55. William C. Cunningham, John J. Strauchs, and Clifford W. Van Meter, *The Hallcrest Report II: Private Security Trends, 1970–2000* (McLean, VA: Hallcrest Systems, 1990).
56. Ibid., p. 236.
57. See http://www.spyandsecuritystore.com.conex.html (accessed June 25, 2009).
58. Peter Lewis, "Companies Turn to Private Spies," *Fortune*, August 9, 2004, p. 24.

59. "U.S. Demand for Private Security Services to Approach $66 B in 2012," *Security Newswire*, July 29, 2008 (accessed February 15, 2013).
60. Bayley and Shearing, *The New Structure of Policing*, p. 15.
61. John Sodaro, "Move over, Police?" *The Crime Report*, http://www.thecrimereport.org/news/inside-criminal-justice/2012-02-move-over-police, February 10, 2012 (accessed February 15, 2013).
62. W. C. Cunningham, *Crime and Protection in America: A Study of Private Security and Law Enforcement Resources and Relationships* (Washington, DC: National Institute of Justice, 1985), pp. 59–72.
63. International Association of Chiefs of Police, *National Policy Summit: Building Private Security/Public Policing Partnerships to Prevent and Respond to Terrorism and Public Disorder: Vital Issues and Policy Recommendations, 2004* (Washington, DC: U.S. Dept. of Justice, 2004).
64. Ibid., p. 1.

UpperCut Images/Getty Images

6 POLICING: PURPOSE AND ORGANIZATION

OUTLINE

- Introduction
- The Police Mission
- Operational Strategies
- Managing Police Departments
- Policing Styles
- Terrorism's Impact on Policing
- Discretion and the Individual Officer
- Professionalism and Ethics
- Ethnic and Gender Diversity in Policing

LEARNING OBJECTIVES

After reading this chapter, you should be able to

- Explain the police mission in democratic societies.
- Discuss the five core operational strategies of today's police departments.
- Summarize the typical organizational structure of a police department.
- Compare and contrast the three most common policing styles.
- Compare the role of American police today in the post-9/11 environment with their pre-9/11 role.
- Explain how police discretion affects contemporary law enforcement.
- Summarize the importance of police professionalism and integrity as well as three methods for building them.
- Describe three ethnic and gender diversity issues in policing, including ways to resolve them.

The police in the United States are not separate from the people. They draw their authority from the will and consent of the people, and they recruit their officers from them.

NATIONAL ADVISORY COMMISSION ON CRIMINAL JUSTICE STANDARDS AND GOALS

■ **Follow the author's tweets about the latest crime and justice news @schmalleger.**

Introduction

In late March 2012, hundreds of demonstrators representing the Occupy Wall Street movement clashed with dozens of New York City Police Department (NYPD) officers, some of whom were equipped with riot gear. The protesters—concerned with what they called "the perceived injustices perpetuated by the economic and political elites"—were attempting to set up camp in New York City's Union Square Park, and called for the resignation of city Police Commissioner Ray Kelly.[1]

Although most demonstrators were peaceful, some appeared to want a confrontation with authorities. A few pulled down crowd-control barriers and scuffled with officers who were trying to dismantle the encampment. Before the melee ended, officers had to use batons, plastic shields, and pepper spray to gain control over unruly protesters. By the conclusion of the event, four people had been arrested and at least one protester was seriously injured. As the Union Square riot demonstrates, the maintenance of social order is an important part of police work today.

The Police Mission

The basic purposes of policing in democratic societies are to (1) enforce and support the laws of the society of which the police are a part, (2) investigate crimes and apprehend offenders, (3) prevent crime, (4) help ensure domestic peace and tranquility, and (5) provide the community with needed enforcement-related services. Simply put, as Sir Robert Peel, founder of the British system of policing, explained in 1822, "The basic mission for which the police exist is to reduce crime and disorder."[2]

Most police officers spend the majority of their time answering nonemergency public-service calls.

© Craig Ruttle / Alamy

An Occupy Wall Street protest in New York's financial district in 2012. What aspects of the police mission can you identify?

In the paragraphs that follow, we turn our attention to these five basic elements of the police mission.

Enforcing the Law

The police operate under an official public mandate that requires them to enforce the law. Collectively speaking, police agencies are the primary enforcers of federal, state, and local criminal laws. Not surprisingly, police officers see themselves as crime fighters, a view shared by the public and promoted by the popular media.

Although it is the job of the police to enforce the law, it is not their *only* job. Practically speaking, most officers spend the majority of their time answering nonemergency public-service calls,[3] controlling traffic, or writing tickets. Most are not involved in intensive, ongoing crime-fighting activities. Research shows that only about 10% to 20% of all calls to the police involve situations that actually require a law enforcement response—that is, situations that might lead to arrest and eventual prosecution.[4]

Even when the police are busy enforcing laws, they can't enforce them all. Police resources—including labor, vehicles, and investigative assets—are limited, causing officers to focus more on certain types of law violations than on others. Old laws prohibiting minor offenses like spitting on the sidewalk hold little social significance today and are typically relegated to the dustbin of statutory history. Even though they are still "on the books," few officers, if any, even think about enforcing such laws. Police tend to tailor their enforcement efforts to meet the contemporary concerns of the populace they serve.[5] For example, if a community is upset about a "massage parlor" operating in its neighborhood, the local police department may bring enforcement efforts to bear that lead to the relocation of the business. However, although community interests significantly influence the enforcement practices of police agencies, individual officers take their cue on enforcement priorities from their departments, their peers, and their supervisors.

The police are expected to not only enforce the law but also support it. The personal actions of law enforcement personnel should inspire others to respect and obey the law. Off-duty officers who speed down the highway or smoke marijuana at a party, for example, do a disservice to the police profession and engender disrespect for all agents of enforcement and for the law itself. Hence, in an important sense, we can say that respect for the law begins with the personal and public behavior of law enforcement officers.

■ **crime prevention** The anticipation, recognition, and appraisal of a crime risk and the initiation of action to eliminate or reduce it.

Apprehending Offenders

Some offenders are apprehended during the commission of a crime or immediately afterward. Fleeing Oklahoma City bomber Timothy McVeigh, for example, was stopped by an Oklahoma Highway Patrol officer on routine patrol only 90 minutes after the destruction of the Alfred P. Murrah federal building[6] for driving a car with no license plate. When the officer questioned McVeigh about a bulge in his jacket, McVeigh admitted that it was a gun. The officer then took McVeigh into custody for carrying a concealed weapon. Typically, McVeigh would then have made an immediate appearance before a judge and would have been released on bail. As fate would have it, however, the judge assigned to see McVeigh was involved in a protracted divorce case. The longer jail stay proved to be McVeigh's undoing. As the investigation into the bombing progressed, profiler Clinton R. Van Zandt of the Federal Bureau of Investigation's Behavioral Science Unit concluded that the bomber was likely a native-born white male in his 20s who had been in the military and was probably a member of a fringe militia group—all of which were true of McVeigh.[7] Working together, the Federal Bureau of Investigation (FBI) and the Oklahoma State Police realized that McVeigh was a likely suspect and questioned him. While McVeigh's capture was the result of a bit of good luck, many offenders are caught only as the result of extensive police work involving a painstaking investigation. (Investigation is described in more detail later in this chapter.)

Preventing Crime

Crime prevention is a proactive approach to the problem of crime; it is "the anticipation, recognition and appraisal of a crime risk and initiation of action to remove or reduce it."[8] In preventing crime, police agencies act before a crime happens, thus preventing victimization from occurring. Although the term *crime prevention* is relatively new, the idea is not. The techniques of securing valuables, limiting access to sensitive areas, and monitoring the activities of suspicious people were used long before Western police forces were established in the 1800s.

Modern crime-prevention efforts aim not only to reduce crime and criminal opportunities and to lower the potential rewards of criminal activity, but also to lessen the public's fear of crime.[9] Crime-prevention efforts led by law enforcement make use of both techniques and programs. Techniques include access control, including barriers to entryways and exits; video and other types of surveillance; the use of theft-deterrence devices like locks, alarms, and tethers; lighting; and visibility landscaping. In contrast to techniques, crime-prevention programs are organized efforts that focus resources on reducing a specific form of criminal threat. The Philadelphia Police Department's Operation Identification, for example, is designed to discourage theft and to help recover stolen property.[10] The program educates citizens on the importance of identifying, marking, and listing their valuables to deter theft (because marked items are more difficult to sell) and to aid in their recovery. Through Operation Identification, the police department provides engraving pens, suggests ways of photographing valuables, and provides window decals and car bumper stickers that identify citizens as participants in the program. Other crime-prevention programs typically target school-based crime, gang activity, drug abuse, violence, domestic abuse, identity theft, vehicle theft, and neighborhood crimes such as burglary.

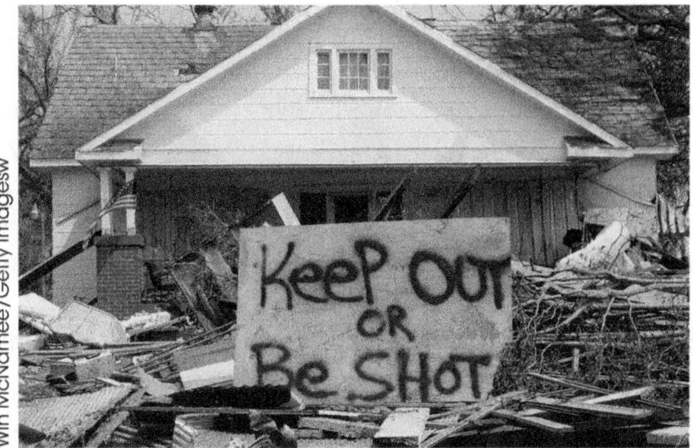

Win McNamee/Getty Imagesw

A warning sign telling looters to stay away from a flood-damaged home in Biloxi, Mississippi, following Hurricane Katrina in 2005. Effective law enforcement helps maintain social order and fills a critical need in the face of the widespread social disorganization that sometimes follows natural disasters or large-scale terrorist attacks. What other roles do the police fulfill?

Today's crime-prevention programs depend on community involvement and education and effective interaction between enforcement agencies and the communities they serve. For example, neighborhood watch programs build on active observation by homeowners and businesspeople on the lookout for anything unusual. Crime Stoppers International and Crime Stoppers USA are examples of privately sponsored programs that accept tips about criminal activity that they pass on to the appropriate law enforcement organization. Crime Stoppers International can be accessed via **http://www.c-s-i.org**, and the National Crime Prevention Council can be found at **http://www.ncpc.org**.

Predicting Crime

Law enforcement's ability to prevent crimes relies in part on the ability of police planners to predict when and where crimes will occur.

■ **CompStat** A crime-analysis and police management process, built on crime mapping, that was developed by the New York City Police Department in the mid-1990s.

■ **quality-of-life offense** A minor violation of the law (sometimes called a *petty crime*) that demoralizes community residents and businesspeople. Quality-of-life offenses involve acts that create physical disorder (for example, excessive noise or vandalism) or that reflect social decay (for example, panhandling and prostitution).

Effective prediction means that valuable police resources can be correctly assigned to the areas with the greatest need. One technique for predicting criminal activity is **CompStat**.[11] While CompStat may sound like a software program, it is actually a process of crime analysis and police management developed by the New York City Police Department in the mid-1990s[12] to help police managers better assess their performance and foresee the potential for crime. The CompStat process involves first collecting and analyzing the information received from 9-1-1 calls and officer reports.[13] Then, this detailed and timely information is mapped using special software developed for the purpose. The resulting map sequences, generated over time, reveal the time and place of crime patterns and identify "hot spots" of ongoing criminal activity. The maps also show the number of patrol officers active in an area, ongoing investigations, arrests made, and so on, thus helping commanders see which anticrime strategies are working.

CrimeStat, a Windows-based spatial statistics-analysis software program for analyzing crime-incident locations, is a second technique for predicting criminal activity. It produces results similar to CompStat's.[14] Developed by Ned Levine and Associates with grants from the National Institute of Justice (NIJ), CrimeStat provides statistical tools for crime mapping and analysis—including identification of crime hot spots, spatial distribution of incidents, and distance analysis—which help crime analysts target offenses that might be related to one another. A link to chicagocrime.org, which overlays crime statistics on maps of the city, is available at **http://chicago.everyblock.com/crime**.

Preserving the Peace

Enforcing the law, apprehending offenders, and preventing crime are all daunting tasks for police departments because there are many laws and numerous offenders. Still, crimes are clearly defined by statute and are therefore limited in number. Peacekeeping, however, is a virtually limitless police activity involving not only activities that violate the law (and hence the community's peace) but many others as well. Law enforcement officers who supervise parades, public demonstrations, and picketing strikers, for example, attempt to ensure that the behavior of everyone involved remains "civil" so that it does not disrupt community life.

Robert Langworthy, who has written extensively about the police, says that keeping the peace is often left up to individual officers.[15] Basically, he says, departments depend on patrol officers "to define the peace and decide how to support it," and an officer is doing a good job when his or her "beat is quiet, meaning there are no complaints about loiterers or traffic flow, and commerce is supported."

Many police departments focus on quality-of-life offenses as a crime-reduction and peacekeeping strategy. **Quality-of-life offenses** are minor law violations, sometimes called *petty crimes*, that demoralize residents and businesspeople by creating disorder. Examples of petty crimes include excessive noise, graffiti, abandoned cars, and vandalism. Other quality-of-life offenses reflect social decay and include panhandling and aggressive begging, public urination, prostitution, roaming youth gangs, public consumption of alcohol, and street-level substance abuse.[16] Homelessness, although not necessarily a violation of the law unless it involves some form of trespass,[17] is also typically addressed under quality-of-life programs. Through police interviews, many of the homeless are relocated to shelters or hospitals or are arrested for some other offense. Some researchers claim that reducing the number of quality-of-life offenses in a community can restore a sense of order, reduce the fear of crime, and lessen the number of serious crimes that occur. However, quality-of-life programs have been criticized by those who say that the police should not be taking a law enforcement approach to social and economic problems.[18]

A similar approach to keeping the peace can be found in the broken windows model of policing.[19] This thesis (which is

Watauga Democrat/Marie Freeman/AP Wide World Photos

Chief Deputy Paula Townsend of the Watauga County (North Carolina) Sheriff's Department carrying 11-month-old Breanna Chambers to safety in 2005 after the capture of the child's parents. The parents, who were already wanted on charges related to methamphetamine manufacture, were charged with additional counts of child abduction, felonious restraint, and assault with a gun after they abducted Breanna and her two-year-old brother, James Paul Chambers, from a foster home. Today's police officers are expected to enforce the law while meeting the needs of the community. Do those goals conflict? If so, how?

also discussed in the "CJ Issues" box in Chapter 3) is based on the notion that physical decay in a community, such as litter and abandoned buildings, can breed disorder and lead to crime by signaling that laws are not being enforced.[20] Such decay, the theory postulates, pushes law-abiding citizens to withdraw from the streets, which then sends a signal that lawbreakers can operate freely.[21] The broken windows theory suggests that by encouraging the repair of run-down buildings and controlling disorderly behavior in public spaces, police agencies can create an environment in which serious crime cannot easily flourish.[22]

Many police departments focus on quality-of-life offenses as a crime-reduction and peacekeeping strategy.

Although desirable, public order has its own costs. Noted police author Charles R. Swanson says, "The degree to which any society achieves some amount of public order through police action depends in part upon the price that society is willing to pay to obtain it."[23] Swanson goes on to describe the price to be paid in terms of (1) police resources paid for by tax dollars and (2) "a reduction in the number, kinds, and extent of liberties" that are available to members of the public.

Although desirable, public order has its own costs.

Providing Services

As writers for the National Institute of Justice observe, "any citizen from any city, suburb, or town across the United States can mobilize police resources by simply picking up the phone and placing a direct call to the police."[24] "Calling the cops" has been described as the cornerstone of policing in a democratic society. About 70% of the millions of daily calls to 9-1-1 systems across the country are directed to the police, although callers can also request emergency medical and fire services.

Calls received by 9-1-1 operators are prioritized and then relayed to patrol officers, specialized field units, or other emergency personnel. An online service, **http://crimereports.com**, provides a map overlaid with crime-related incidents and calls to 9-1-1 dispatchers. You can use it to view incidents in your neighborhood. Some cities have also adopted nonemergency "Citizen Service System" call numbers in addition to 9-1-1. More than a dozen metropolitan areas, including Baltimore, Dallas, Detroit, Las Vegas, New York, and San Jose, now staff 3-1-1 nonemergency systems around the clock. Plans are afoot in some places to adopt the 3-1-1 system statewide.

Operational Strategies

The police mission offers insight into general law enforcement goals, which help shape the various operational strategies that departments employ.[25] There are five core operational strategies—preventive patrol, routine incident response, emergency response, criminal investigation, and problem solving—and one ancillary operational strategy—support services.[26] The first four core strategies constitute the conventional way in which police have worked, at least since the 1930s; problem solving is relatively new. Each strategy has unique features, and each represents a particular way to approach situations that the police encounter.

Preventive Patrol

Preventive patrol, the dominant operational policing strategy,[27] has been the backbone of police work since the time of Sir Robert Peel. Routine patrol activities, which place uniformed police officers on the street in the midst of the public, consume most of the resources of local and state-level police agencies.

The purpose of patrol is fourfold: to deter crimes, to interrupt crimes in progress, to position officers for quick response to emergency situations, and to increase the public's feelings of safety and security. Patrol is the operational mode uniformed officers are expected to work in when not otherwise involved in answering calls for service. Most departments use a computer-aided dispatch (CAD) system to prioritize incoming service calls

A. Ramey/PhotoEdit Inc.

Mounted Los Angeles Police Department officers patrolling a beach within the city limits. Patrol, a typical police function, can take a variety of forms. What kinds of patrol activities does the public expect from the police?

■ **criminal investigation** "The process of discovering, collecting, preparing, identifying, and presenting evidence to determine *what happened and who is responsible*"[i] when a crime has occurred.

■ **crime scene** The physical area in which a crime is thought to have occurred and in which evidence of the crime is thought to reside.

■ **response time** A measure of the time that it takes for police officers to respond to calls for service.

into different categories and to record dispatches issued, time spent on each call, the identities of responding personnel, and so on.

The majority of police patrol activity is *interactive* because officers on patrol commonly interact with the public.

The majority of patrol activity is *interactive* because officers on patrol commonly interact with the public. Some forms of patrol, however, involve more interaction than others. The many types of patrol include foot, automobile, motorcycle, mounted, bicycle, boat, K-9, and aerial. Although some scientific studies of policing have questioned the effectiveness of preventive patrol in reducing crime (discussed in Chapter 5), most citizens expect police to patrol.

Routine Incident Response

Police officers on patrol frequently respond to routine incidents, such as minor traffic accidents. Routine incident responses comprise the second most common activity of patrol officers.[28] Officers responding to routine incidents must collect information and typically file a written report. As noted by the National Institute of Justice, "the specific police objective will . . . vary depending on the nature of the situation, but generally, the objective is to restore order, document information or otherwise provide some immediate service to the parties involved."[29]

One important measure of police success that is strongly linked to citizen satisfaction is **response time**—the time it takes for police officers to respond to calls for service. It is measured from the time a call for service is received by a dispatcher until an officer arrives on the scene. During the first four months of the 2007 fiscal year, for example, police response times in New York City to crimes in progress averaged 7 minutes and 6 seconds—24 seconds better than the same period in the previous year. The average time required for an NYPD officer to arrive on the scene when responding to an incident rated by dispatchers as "critical" was 4.3 minutes. Response times to both critical incidents and crimes in progress in New York City in 2007 were the quickest times recorded in the city in more than a decade.[30]

Emergency Response

In May 2003, Pomona, California, police officers on routine patrol responded to a dispatcher's instructions to assist in an emergency at a local coin-operated laundry.[31] On arrival, they found a two-year-old girl trapped inside an industrial-size washing machine. The officers used their batons to smash the locked glass-paned door. The girl, unconscious and nearly drowned when pulled from the machine, was taken to a local hospital where she was expected to recover. Her mother, 35-year-old Erma Osborne, was arrested at the scene and charged with child endangerment when the on-site video surveillance cameras showed her placing her daughter in the machine and shutting the door.

Although police respond to emergencies far less frequently than to routine incidents,[32] emergency response is a vital aspect of what police agencies do. Emergency responses, often referred to as *critical incidents*, are used for crimes in progress, traffic accidents with serious injuries, natural disasters, incidents of terrorism, officer requests for assistance, and other situations in which human life may be in jeopardy. Emergency responses take priority over all other police work, and until an emergency situation is secured and some order restored, the officers involved will not turn to other tasks. An important part of police training involves emergency response techniques, including first aid, hostage rescue, and the physical capture of suspects.

Criminal Investigation

Another operational strategy, criminal investigation, dominates media depictions of police work. Although central to the mission of the police, investigations actually constitute a relatively small proportion of police work. A **criminal investigation** is "the process of discovering, collecting, preparing, identifying, and presenting evidence to determine *what happened and who is responsible*"[33] when a crime occurs.

Criminal investigators are often referred to as *detectives*, and it is up to them to solve most crimes and to produce the evidence needed for the successful prosecution of suspects. But any police officer can be involved in the initial stages of the investigative process, especially those responding to critical incidents. First-on-the-scene officers, or first responders, can play a critical role in providing emergency assistance to the injured and in capturing suspects. First responders, however, also have an important responsibility to secure the crime scene, a duty that can later provide the basis for a successful criminal investigation. A **crime scene** is the physical area in which a crime is thought to have occurred and in which evidence of the crime is thought to reside (Figure 6-1). Securing the crime scene is

■ **preliminary investigation** All of the activities undertaken by a police officer who responds to the scene of a crime, including determining whether a crime has occurred, securing the crime scene, and preserving evidence.

Note: This diagram pertains to crime scene analysis, although a wider investigation will include identifying the victim, interviews with significant others in her life, and an examination of her background, recent activities and lifestyle. The area surrounding the swimming pool, to include the house and the electronic devices it contains, will also be searched for possible evidence, as will the victim's vehicle if she has one. The crime scene will be photographed and videos recordings will be made.

Computer forensic experts will examine the laptop found at the scene for possible digital evidence—including texts or email communications, especially those involving recent conversations. Ownership of the laptop will be established, and any GPS information will be collected showing where the computer might have been recently used. A record of Internet connections will be logged, and social media applications and other communications software will be evaluated for possible recent use.

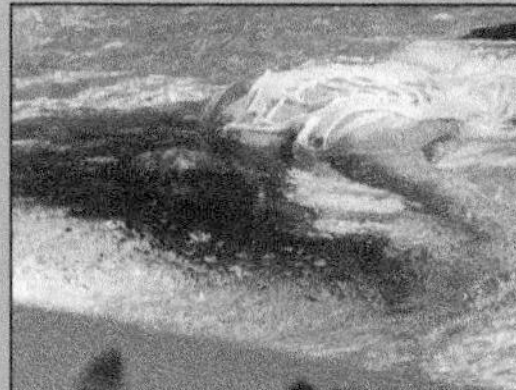

A medical examination by a pathologist will be ordered to determine the cause of death and to identify any injuries to (or marks on) the body. The pathologist will analyze the person's blood for the presence of prescription drugs, illegal substances, and alcohol. Evidence of any possible sexual activity will be recorded. Should the death be ruled a homicide, the evidence gathered in the other steps shown in this box will become relevant.

Persons living nearby or who were in the area at the time of the incident will be contacted and asked if they heard or saw anything of relevance to the investigation.

Pool water and pool equipment will be examined to see if they might have contributed to death (i.e., electrical shock, hair caught in drain, etc.).

The victim's clothing will be examined for possible trace evidence. Pocket contents, rents, and tears will be noted. Fingernails will be examined for any forensic DNA evidence resulting from a possible physical struggle.

The body of a young woman was found floating in a home swimming pool by neighbors who called 911; they also reported hearing screams and calls for help. First responders determined that the woman was dead, and crime scene investigators were called to examine and collect evidence to determine whether the death was an accident, a suicide, or a homicide. Although foul play was suspected, the investigators noted the absence of blood in the pool, and they considered that the woman could have been killed elsewhere and her body later dumped into the swimming pool.

The wine bottle and wine glass will be examined for fingerprints and for DNA traces—whether that of the victim or any possible perpetrators. Remnants of any toxic or other substances that might have been added to the wine will be identified.

The handgun found at the scene will be examined by ballistics experts to determine whether it has been fired recently, and the area will be searched for spent shell casings. Fingerprints might also be found on the weapon, and ownership of the pistol will be established.

FIGURE 6-1 | The Crime Scene Investigation Process

Source: Justice Research Association.

particularly crucial, for when a crime takes place, especially a violent one, confusion often results. People at the scene and curious onlookers may unwittingly (or sometimes intentionally) destroy physical evidence, obliterating important clues like tire tracks, fingerprints, or footprints.

The preliminary investigation is an important part of the investigatory process. An effective preliminary investigation is the foundation on which the entire criminal investigation process is built.[34] The Florida Highway Patrol's policy manual provides a broad definition of a **preliminary investigation**, saying

■ **crime scene investigator** An expert trained in the use of forensics techniques, such as gathering DNA evidence, collecting fingerprints, photographing the scene, sketching, and interviewing witnesses.

■ **solvability factor** Information about a crime that forms the basis for determining the perpetrator's identity.

that it refers to all of the activities undertaken by a police officer who responds to the scene of a crime.[35] Those activities include the following:

1. Responding to immediate needs and rendering aid to the injured
2. Noting such facts as the position of victims or injured subjects, recording spontaneous statements, noting unusual actions or activities, and notifying headquarters with an assessment of the scene
3. Determining that a crime has been committed
4. Initiating enforcement action, such as arresting or pursuing the offender or dispatching apprehension information
5. Securing the crime scene and protecting evidence, including limiting access, identifying and isolating witnesses, and protecting all evidence, especially short-lived evidence (such as impressions in sand or mud)
6. Determining the need for investigative specialists and arranging for their notification
7. Compiling a thorough and accurate report of activities

A preliminary investigation begins when the call to respond has been received. Even before they arrive at the crime scene, officers may observe important events related to the offense, such as fleeing vehicles or the presence of suspicious people nearby. After they arrive, first responders begin collecting information through observation and possibly through conversations with others who are already at the scene. Typically, it is at this point that officers determine whether there are sufficient grounds to believe that a crime has actually occurred. Even in suspected homicides, for example, it is important to rule out accidental death, suicide, and death by natural causes before the investigation can proceed beyond the preliminary stage.

Next, specially trained crime scene investigators arrive, and the detailed examination of a crime scene begins. **Crime scene investigators** are expert in the use of specific forensics techniques, such as gathering DNA evidence, collecting fingerprints, photographing the scene, making sketches to show the position of items at the scene, and interviewing witnesses.

Crime scene investigators are commonly promoted to their posts internally after at least a few years of patrol work. However, large local police departments and those at the state and federal levels may employ civilian crime scene investigators. Follow-up investigations, based on evidence collected at the scene, are conducted by police detectives. Important to any investigation are solvability factors. A **solvability factor** is information about a crime that can provide a basis for determining the perpetrator's identity. If few solvability factors exist, a continuing investigation is unlikely to lead to an arrest.

Problem Solving

Another operational strategy of police work is problem solving. Also called *problem-oriented policing*, problem solving seeks to reduce chronic offending in a community. NIJ authors note that "historically, [this operational strategy] is the least well-developed by the police profession. While the police have always used the mental processes of problem-solving, problem-solving as a formal operational strategy of police work has gained some structure and systematic attention only in the past 20 years."[36]

Problem-oriented policing seeks to reduce chronic offending in a community.

The methodology of police problem solving is known by acronyms such as SARA (scanning, analysis, response, and assessment) or CAPRA (clients, acquired/analyzed, partnerships, respond, assess). CAPRA was developed by the Royal Canadian Mounted Police, who built on the earlier SARA process. This is the CAPRA process:[37]

- The police begin by communicating with the *clients* most affected by community problems.
- Information is *acquired* and *analyzed* to determine the problem's causes.
- Solutions are developed through community *partnerships*.
- The police *respond* with a workable plan.
- After plan implementation, the police periodically *assess* the situation to ensure progress.

Support Services

Support services constitute the final operational strategy found in police organizations. They include such activities as dispatch, training, human resources management, property and evidence control, and record keeping. Support services keep police agencies running and help deliver the equipment, money, and resources necessary to support law enforcement officers in the field.

paying for it

Policing in an Economic Downturn

©Tom Grill/Corbis

First responders. In some cities, public-safety officers are cross-trained as police officers, firefighters, and in emergency medical services. What advantages accrue to communities who cross-train their first responders?

In 2013, the Police Executive Research Forum (PERF) released a report entitled *Policing and the Economic Downturn*. The subtitle of the publication was "Striving for Efficiency Is the New Normal." The 50-page document was based on a series of four surveys that PERF began sending to police administrators across the nation in 2008 asking about their department's economic situation. In the words of the report, "The first three surveys produced findings that could be summarized as 'grim', meaning that almost all agencies reported facing budget cutbacks and were making plans to reduce services or layoff officers."

PERF found that during the depths of the economic crisis around 2008, 32% of agencies had eliminated recruitment of new officers, while 72% reported a reduction in the amount of money being spent on training. Similarly, 67% of agencies had eliminated pay raises, and 58% of departments were implementing plans to decease services. Thirty-one percent of agencies that responded to the survey also said that response time to citizens' request for services had increased, or would likely increase due to budget cuts. Although not all agencies reported laying off officers, 45% reported hiring freezes. Finally, slightly more than half of all agencies responding to the early PERF surveys reported eliminating plans to acquire new technology.

Police departments have also been restructured in the face of budget cutbacks. Almost half of all departments reported discontinuing or significantly reducing specialty units such as bike patrols, and 22% said that they had consolidated some services with other departments. Many law enforcement agencies also said that they had shifted more officers into the field by staffing some internal positions, such as dispatch, crime analysis, and desk work, with civilian employees and volunteers. Finally, 34% of agencies said that patrol levels, meaning the number of officers assigned to an area at any given time, or the number of hours that an area was patrolled, had been lowered.

Since those initial surveys, however, trends in police funding have improved, with some departments reporting stable or increased monetary inflows. Today, only half as many agencies have cut back on recruiting efforts than those responding to earlier surveys, and agencies today are making fewer cuts to training. Almost half are instituting pay increases for their officers.

Many departments now report paying their officers overtime, rather than expanding the number of full-time officers on their payrolls. Funding overtime hours can be less expensive in the long run than hiring more full-time officers whose employment benefits, including health insurance and retirement expenses, can add substantially to an agency's costs.

One good thing that appears to have resulted from police budget cuts over the past six or more years has been increased efficiency in many areas of law enforcement. Some have used the term "smart policing" to describe the shift in attitude that came about as a result of the economic squeeze that law enforcement administrators have been facing.

According to the Smart Policing Initiative (SPI), the goal of smart policing is to "develop tactics and strategies that are effective, efficient and economical—as measured by reduced crime and high case closure rates." (SPI is also discussed in a "Paying for It" box in Chapter 5.)

SPI, which is a collaborative effort between the Bureau of Justice Assistance, the nonprofit CNA Corporation, and dozens of police departments, says that "effective policing requires a tightly focused, collaborative approach that is measurable; based on sound, detailed analysis; and includes policies and procedures that promote and support accountability."

One form of smart policing is being used in Sunnyvale, California, a city of around 140,000. There, police officers and firefighters are cross-trained so that, in a pinch, they can fill in for one another. In 2012, for example, the city was able to call upon firefighters who were finishing their shifts to switch into police uniforms and help canvas an area of the city looking for a man who had killed three people in a workplace shooting. Studies show that, because of cross-training, Sunnyvale is able to spend less on public safety than do surrounding communities—$519 per capita, versus $950 in Palo Alto and $683 in Mountain View (California).

Another form of smart policing was initiated two years ago in the Los Angeles Police Department (LAPD), where computer models alert officers to crimes that are likely to happen, and tell dispatchers to send officers to likely crime scenes. The program, called "predictive policing" by the LAPD, identifies potential "hot spots" of crime (sometimes as small as a 500-square-foot "zone") and makes predictions about the likelihood of future crime occurrences in those locations. Officers who are on patrol are then directed to "go in the box."

Unless municipalities can implement effective smart policing strategies, however, saving money on policing might not be such a good idea. In 2012, researchers at the University of California at Berkeley who studied crime in medium to large U.S. cities between 1960 and 2010 found that "each dollar spent on police is associated with approximately $1.60 in reduced victimization costs, suggesting that U.S. cities employ too few police."

Learn more about smart policing from the SPI website at http://www.smartpolicinginitiative.com.

Resources: Police Executive Research Forum, *Policing and the Economic Downturn: Striving for Efficiency Is the New Normal* (Washington, DC: PERF, February 2013); Aaron Chalfin and Justin McCrary, "The Effect of Police on Crime: New Evidence from U.S. Cities, 1960–2010," unpublished manuscript (University of California at Berkeley, November 8, 2012); Greg Risling, "Sci-Fi Policing: Predicting Crime before It Occurs," Associated Press, July 2, 2012, http://news.yahoo.com/sci-fi-policing-predicting-crime-occurs-150157831.html (accessed July 1, 2013); Lee Romney, "Cross-Training of Public Safety Workers Attracting More Interest," *The Los Angeles Times*, January 1, 2013, http://articles.latimes.com/2013/jan/01/local/la-me-sunnyvale-20130101 (accessed August 1, 2013); Paul Heaton, *Hidden in Plain Sight: What Cost-of-Crime Research Can Tell Us about Investing in Police* (RAND Center on Quality Policing, 2010), http://www.rand.org/content/dam/rand/pubs/occasional_papers/2010/RAND_OP279.pdf (accessed May 5, 2013); and Smart Policing Initiative, "Background," http://www.smartpolicinginitiative.com/background (accessed May 2, 2013).

■ **police management** The administrative activities of controlling, directing, and coordinating police personnel, resources, and activities in the service of preventing crime, apprehending criminals, recovering stolen property, and performing regulatory and helping services.[ii]

■ **line operations** In police organizations, the field activities or supervisory activities directly related to day-to-day police work.

■ **staff operations** In police organizations, activities (such as administration and training) that provide support for line operations.

■ **chain of command** The unbroken line of authority that extends through all levels of an organization, from the highest to the lowest.

■ **span of control** The number of police personnel or the number of units supervised by a particular commander.

Managing Police Departments

Police management entails administrative activities that control, direct, and coordinate police personnel, resources, and activities in an effort to prevent crime, apprehend criminals, recover stolen property, and perform a variety of regulatory and helping services.[38] Police managers include sworn law enforcement personnel with administrative authority, from the rank of sergeant to captain, chief, or sheriff, and civilians like police commissioners, attorneys general, state secretaries of crime control, and public-safety directors.

Police Organization and Structure

Almost all American law enforcement organizations are formally structured among divisions and along lines of authority. Roles within police agencies generally fall into one of two categories: line and staff. **Line operations** are field or supervisory activities directly related to daily police work. **Staff operations** include support roles, such as administration. In organizations that have line operations only, authority flows from the top down in a clear, unbroken line;[39] no supporting elements (media relations, training, fiscal management divisions, and so on) exist. All line operations are directly involved in providing field services. Because almost all police agencies need support, only the smallest departments have just line operations.

Most police organizations include both line and staff operations. In such organizations, line managers are largely unencumbered with staff operations like budgeting, training, the scientific analysis of evidence, legal advice, shift assignments, and personnel management. Support personnel handle these activities, freeing line personnel to focus on the day-to-day requirements of providing field services.

In a line and staff agency, divisions are likely to exist within both line operations and staff operations. For example, field services, a line operation, may be broken down into enforcement and investigation. Administrative services, a staff operation, may be divided into human resources management, training and education, materials supply, finance management, and facilities management. The line and staff structure easily accommodates functional areas of responsibility within line and staff divisions. An organizational chart showing the line and staff structure of the Los Angeles Sheriff's Department (LASD)—the largest sheriff's department in the world[40]—can be found in Figure 6-2.

Chain of Command

The organizational chart of any police agency shows a hierarchical **chain of command**, or the order of authority within the department. The chain of command clarifies who reports to whom. Usually, the chief of police or sheriff is at the top of the command chain—although his or her boss may be a police commissioner, city council, or mayor—followed by the subordinate leaders of each division.

Because law enforcement agencies employ a quasi-military chain-of-command structure, the titles assigned to personnel (captain, lieutenant, sergeant) are similar to those used by the military. It is important for individual personnel to know who is in charge; hence unity of command is an important principle that must be firmly established within the department. When unity of command exists, every individual has only one supervisor to answer to and, under normal circumstances, to take orders from. **Span of control** refers to the number of police personnel or the number of units supervised by a particular commander. For example, one sergeant may be in charge of five or six officers; they represent the sergeant's span of control.

Policing Styles

The history of American policing can be divided into four epochs,[41] each distinguishable by the relative dominance of a particular approach to police operations (Figure 6-3). The first period, the political era, was characterized by close ties between police and public officials. It began in the 1840s and ended around 1930. Throughout the period, American police agencies tended to serve the interests of powerful politicians and their cronies, providing public-order-maintenance services almost as an afterthought. The second period, the reform era, began in the 1930s and lasted until the 1970s. It was characterized by pride in professional crime fighting. Police departments during this period focused most of their resources on solving "traditional" crimes, such as murder, rape, and burglary, and on capturing offenders. The third period, which continues to characterize much of contemporary policing in America today, is the community policing era—an approach to policing that stresses

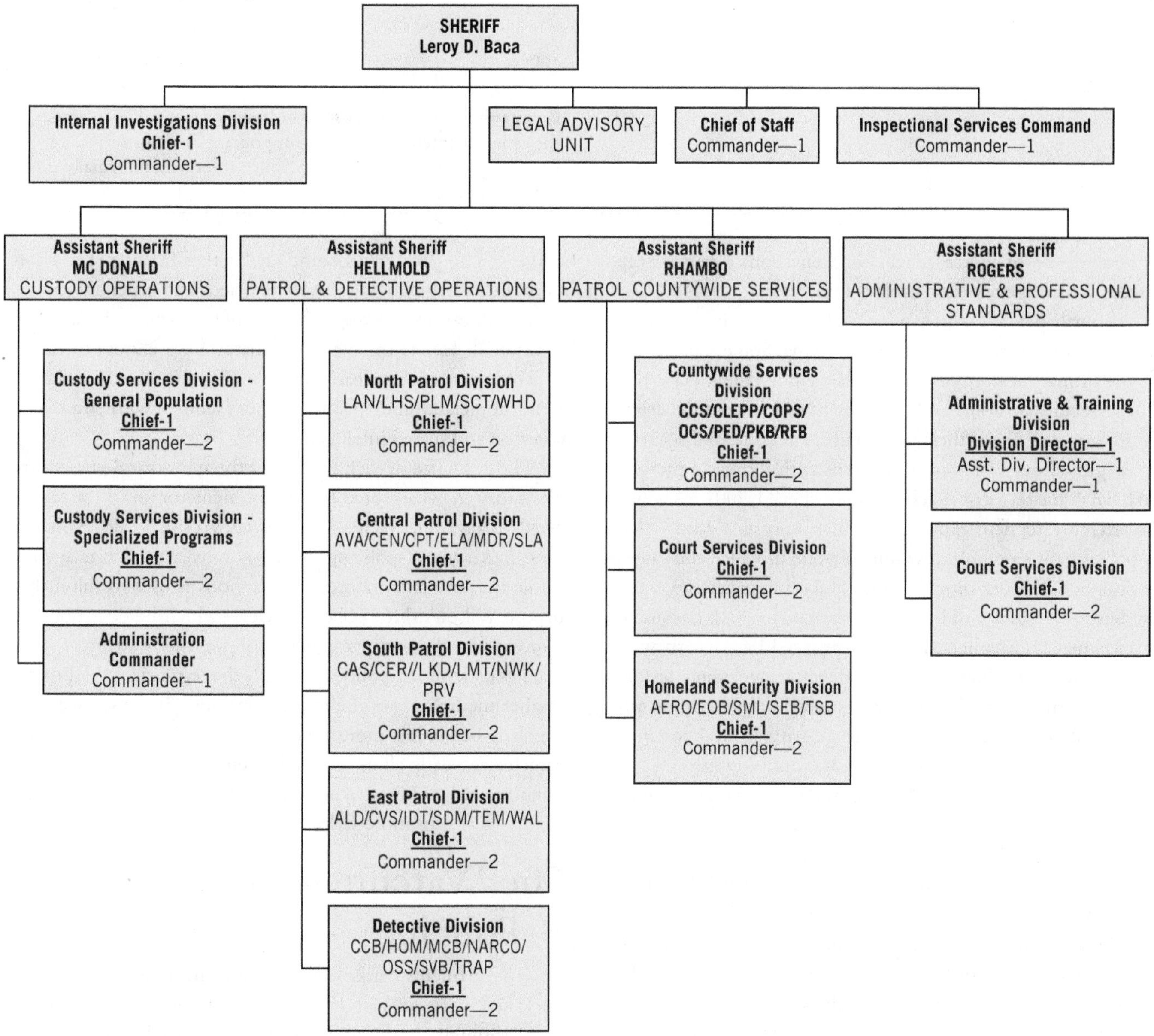

SHERIFF
Leroy D. Baca

- **Internal Investigations Division** — **Chief-1**, Commander—1
- LEGAL ADVISORY UNIT
- **Chief of Staff** — Commander—1
- **Inspectional Services Command** — Commander—1

Assistant Sheriff MC DONALD — CUSTODY OPERATIONS
- **Custody Services Division - General Population** — **Chief-1**, Commander—2
- **Custody Services Division - Specialized Programs** — **Chief-1**, Commander—2
- **Administration Commander** — Commander—1

Assistant Sheriff HELLMOLD — PATROL & DETECTIVE OPERATIONS
- **North Patrol Division** — LAN/LHS/PLM/SCT/WHD — **Chief-1**, Commander—2
- **Central Patrol Division** — AVA/CEN/CPT/ELA/MDR/SLA — **Chief-1**, Commander—2
- **South Patrol Division** — CAS/CER//LKD/LMT/NWK/PRV — **Chief-1**, Commander—2
- **East Patrol Division** — ALD/CVS/IDT/SDM/TEM/WAL — **Chief-1**, Commander—2
- **Detective Division** — CCB/HOM/MCB/NARCO/OSS/SVB/TRAP — **Chief-1**, Commander—2

Assistant Sheriff RHAMBO — PATROL COUNTYWIDE SERVICES
- **Countywide Services Division** — **CCS/CLEPP/COPS/OCS/PED/PKB/RFB** — **Chief-1**, Commander—2
- **Court Services Division** — **Chief-1**, Commander—2
- **Homeland Security Division** — AERO/EOB/SML/SEB/TSB — **Chief-1**, Commander—2

Assistant Sheriff ROGERS — ADMINISTRATIVE & PROFESSIONAL STANDARDS
- **Administrative & Training Division** — **Division Director—1**, Asst. Div. Director—1, Commander—1
- **Court Services Division** — **Chief-1**, Commander—2

FIGURE 6-2 | Organizational Chart of the Los Angeles County Sheriff's Department

Source: Los Angeles County Sheriff's Department. Reprinted with permission.

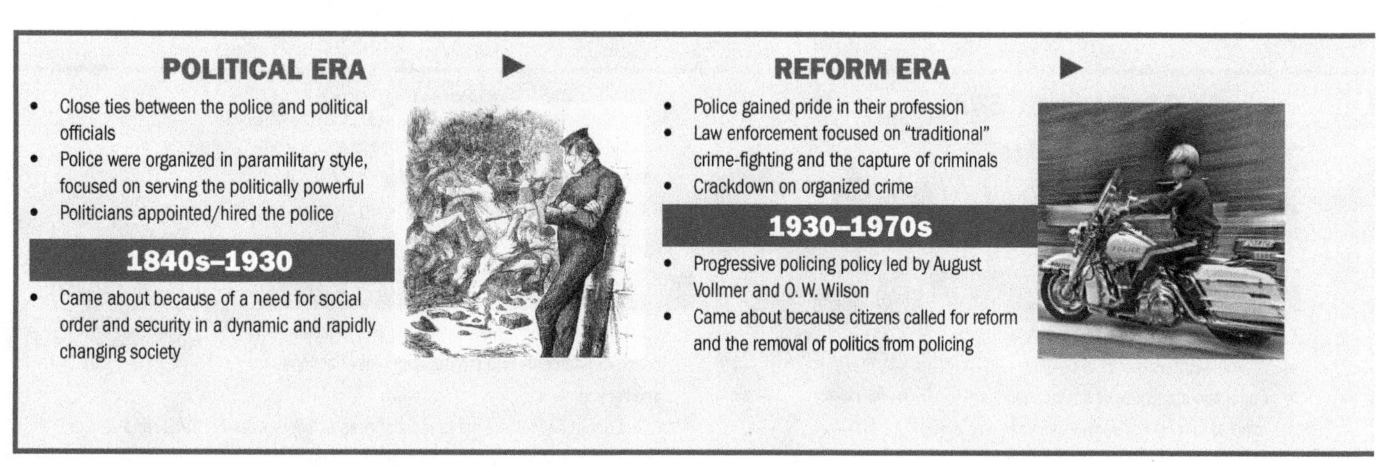

POLITICAL ERA
• Close ties between the police and political officials
• Police were organized in paramilitary style, focused on serving the politically powerful
• Politicians appointed/hired the police
1840s–1930
• Came about because of a need for social order and security in a dynamic and rapidly changing society
REFORM ERA
• Police gained pride in their profession
• Law enforcement focused on "traditional" crime-fighting and the capture of criminals
• Crackdown on organized crime
1930–1970s
• Progressive policing policy led by August Vollmer and O. W. Wilson
• Came about because citizens called for reform and the removal of politics from policing

FIGURE 6-3 | Historical Eras in American Policing

Source: (from left) Image Asset Management Ltd./SuperStock; Shutterstock; UpperCut Images/SuperStock; and AP Wide World Photos.

■ **watchman style** A style of policing marked by a concern for order maintenance. Watchman policing is characteristic of lower-class communities where police intervene informally into the lives of residents to keep the peace.

the service role of police officers and envisions a partnership between police agencies and their communities.

A fourth period, which we call the *new era*, has made its appearance only recently and is still evolving. Some scholars say that the primary feature of this new law enforcement era is policing to secure the homeland, and they have dubbed it the *homeland security era*.[42] From their perspective, the homeland security era has grown out of national concerns with terrorism prevention born of the terrorist attacks of September 11, 2001. As police scholar Gene Stephens explains it, "The twenty-first century has put policing into a whole new milieu—one in which the causes of crime and disorder often lie outside the immediate community, demanding new and innovative approaches."[43] A decline in street crime, says Stephens, has been replaced by concern with new and more insidious types of offending, including terrorism and Internet-assisted crimes. These new kinds of crimes, says Stephens, although they threaten the integrity of local communities, often involve offenders thousands of miles away.

Others, however, see the new era as underpinned by an emphasis on intelligence-led policing (ILP), and they refer to it as the *ILP era*. (ILP is discussed in detail later in this chapter.) Michael Downing, commanding officer of the LAPD's Counter-Terrorism and Special Operations Bureau (CTSOB), for example, says that ILP represents the next evolutionary stage in how law enforcement officers should approach their work. "The necessity to successfully shift into a fifth era, the intelligence-led policing era," says Downing, "with seamless precision has never been more important considering the great threat we face as a nation."[44] The good news, some say, "is that ILP is not only an important strategic tool to thwart al-Qaeda and other groups but also a practical one geared toward crime control and quality of life issues."[45] Hence the new era, whatever we choose to call it, is still emerging, but it clearly involves efforts to deal with threats to the homeland and to inform those efforts with situational awareness and shared intelligence.

The influence of each of the first three historical phases survives today in what noted social commentator and Presidential Medal of Freedom recipient James Q. Wilson[46] calls "policing styles."[47] A style of policing describes how a particular agency sees its purpose and chooses the methods it uses to fulfill that purpose. Wilson's three policing styles—which he does not link to any particular historical era—are (1) the watchman style (characteristic of the political era), (2) the legalistic style (professional crime fighting of the reform era), and (3) the service style (which is becoming more common today). These three styles characterize nearly all municipal law enforcement agencies now operating in the United States, although some departments are a mixture of two or more styles.

The Watchman Style of Policing

Police departments marked by the **watchman style** are chiefly concerned with achieving what Wilson calls "order maintenance" through control of illegal and disruptive behavior. Compared to the legalistic style, the watchman style uses discretion

COMMUNITY ERA ►

- Police departments work to identify and serve the needs of their communities
- Envisions a partnership between the police and the community

1970s–Today

- Police focus on quality-of-life offenses
- Broken windows model of policing
- Came about because of a realization that effective community partnerships can help prevent and solve crimes

THE NEW ERA

- Policing to secure the homeland; emphasis on terrorism prevention and intelligence-led policing
- Builds on partnership with the community to gather intelligence

2001–Today

- Creation of counterterrorism divisions and offices within police departments and the development of actionable intelligence
- Came about because of the terrorist attacks of September 11, 2001, and ongoing threats to the safety and security of Americans

FIGURE 6-3 | (Continued)

■ **legalistic style** A style of policing marked by a strict concern with enforcing the precise letter of the law. Legalistic departments may take a hands-off approach to disruptive or problematic behavior that does not violate the criminal law.

■ **service style** A style of policing marked by a concern with helping rather than strict enforcement. Service-oriented police agencies are more likely to use community resources, such as drug-treatment programs, to supplement traditional law enforcement activities than are other types of agencies.

■ **police–community relations (PCR)** An area of police activity that recognizes the need for the community and the police to work together effectively. PCR is based on the notion that the police derive their legitimacy from the communities they serve. Many police agencies began to explore PCR in the 1960s and 1970s.

liberally. Watchman-style departments keep order through informal police "intervention," which may include persuasion, threats, or even "roughing up" disruptive people. Some authors condemn this style of policing, suggesting that it is typically found in lower- or lower-middle-class communities, especially where interpersonal relations include a fair amount of violence or physical abuse.

The watchman style was typified by the Los Angeles police officers who took part in the infamous beating of Rodney King in 1992. After the ensuing riots, the Christopher Commission, the independent commission on the LAPD, found that the Los Angeles police "placed greater emphasis on crime control over crime prevention, a policy that distanced cops from the people they serve."[48]

The Legalistic Style of Policing

Departments operating under the **legalistic style** enforce the letter of the law. For example, an officer who tickets a person going 71 miles per hour in a 70-mph speed zone is likely a member of a department that adheres to the legalistic style of policing. Conversely, legalistic departments routinely avoid community disputes arising from violations of social norms that do not break the law. Police expert Gary Sykes calls this enforcement style "laissez-faire policing" in recognition of its hands-off approach to behaviors that are simply bothersome or inconsiderate of community principles.[49]

The Service Style of Policing

In service-oriented departments, which strive to meet the needs of the community and serve its members, the police see themselves more as helpers than as soldiers in a war on crime. This type of department works with social services and other agencies to provide counseling for minor offenders and to assist community groups in preventing crimes and solving problems. Prosecutors may support the **service style** by agreeing not to prosecute law violators who seek psychiatric help or who voluntarily participate in programs like Alcoholics Anonymous, family counseling, or drug treatment. The service style is supported in part by citizens who seek to avoid the embarrassment that might result from a public airing of personal problems, thereby reducing the number of criminal complaints filed, especially in minor disputes. Although the service style of policing may seem more appropriate to wealthy communities or small towns, it can also exist in cities with police departments that actively seek citizen involvement in identifying issues that the police can help address.

Police–Community Relations

The 1960s were fraught with riots, unrest, and student activism as the war in Vietnam, civil rights concerns, and other social issues produced large demonstrations and marches. The police, generally inexperienced in crowd control, were all too often embroiled in tumultuous encounters—even pitched battles—with citizen groups that viewed the police as agents of "the establishment." To manage these new challenges, the legalistic style of policing, so common in America until then, began to yield to the newer service-oriented policing.

As social disorganization increased, police departments across the nation, seeking to understand and better cope with the problems they faced, created **police–community relations (PCR)** programs. PCR programs represented a movement away from an exclusive emphasis on the apprehension of law violators toward an effort to increase the level of positive police–citizen interaction. At the height of the PCR movement, city police departments across the country opened storefront centers where citizens could air complaints and interact easily with police representatives. As police scholar Egon Bittner recognized in 1976, PCR programs need to reach to "the grassroots of discontent," where citizen dissatisfaction with the police exists,[50] if they are to be truly effective.

In many contemporary PCR programs, public-relations officers are appointed to provide an array of services, such as neighborhood watch programs, drug-awareness workshops, Project ID—using police equipment and expertise to mark valuables for identification in the event of theft—and victims' assistance programs. Modern PCR programs, however, often fail

■ **team policing** The reorganization of conventional patrol strategies into "an integrated and versatile police team assigned to a fixed district."[iii]

freedom OR safety? YOU decide

Watch Out: You're on Police TV

In 2011, 90 police officers with the city of Chesapeake, Virginia, were equipped with body cameras, small digital devices with extended recording capabilities that clipped to the officers' shirts. The body cameras, manufactured by Taser International, can record what an officer sees and hears during an eight-hour shift, and the recordings can be used as evidence in court.

Law enforcement officials say that body cameras are the next step in recording technology—supplementing the thousands of patrol car-mounted video cameras currently in use. Recently, for example, officials in Los Angeles installed video cameras in all 1,600 of the city's patrol cars. "It's a good accounting of what happened at the scene," said Bob Baker, president of the Los Angeles Police Protective League. "I think it's great for the officers, great for the community and great for the city."

Patrol cars equipped with video cameras have been on the nation's highways since the late 1980s, and the footage they've produced has been a staple of real-life police TV shows for years. In 2002, following the nationally televised airing of what appeared to be the physical abuse of a teenage suspect by an Inglewood, California, arresting officer, Inglewood Mayor Roosevelt Dorn called for cameras to be installed in all of his city's patrol cars. The alleged abuse had been videotaped by a bystander.

Many people believe that equipping both cars and personnel with continuous recording devices will lead to a reduction in police abuses, while serving to capture evidence of illegal behavior by suspects. Video footage can also be used for identification purposes and might be coupled with software that provides facial and license tag recognition, allowing officers to quickly identify stolen cars and wanted individuals.

Some, however, fear that the combination of video images and recognition software will lead to the creation of a suspect database that will inevitably include many otherwise innocent people and that might be improperly shared with other agencies or the popular media.

Since 2000, the Justice Department's Office of Community Oriented Policing Services has provided $15 million to state law enforcement agencies to equip 3,563 cruisers with cameras. A recent study by the International Association of Chiefs of Police surveyed 47 state law enforcement agencies that received federal grants to buy in-car cameras and concluded that such cameras substantially improved public trust in the police and protected officers against unfounded lawsuits.

You Decide

Do you think that equipping all of the nation's patrol cars with video cameras is a good idea? What about having patrol officers wear body cameras? What negative impact, if any, might such an initiative have on personal freedoms in our society? How might it affect policing?

References: Veronica Gonzales, "Chesapeake Police Expand Use of Body Cameras," *The Virginian-Pilot*, August 8, 2011, http://hamptonroads.com/2011/08/chesapeake-police-expand-use-body-cameras (accessed August 26, 2011); International Association of Chiefs of Police, *The Impact of Video Evidence on Modern Policing* (Alexandria, VA: IACP, 2005); Patrick McMahon, "Increased Clamor for Cameras in Cop Cars," *USA Today*, July 18, 2002; and "LAPD to Put Cameras in Patrol Cars," *USA Today*, March 19, 2007.

to achieve their goal of increased community satisfaction with police services because they focus on servicing groups already well satisfied with the police. PCR initiatives that do reach dis-affected community groups are difficult to manage and may even alienate participating officers from the communities they are assigned to serve. Thus, as Bittner noted, "while the first approach fails because it leaves out those groups to which the program is primarily directed, the second fails because it leaves out the police department."

Team Policing

During the 1960s and 1970s, some communities experimented with **team policing**, which rapidly became an extension of the PCR movement. With team policing, a team of police officers was assigned semipermanently to particular neighborhoods, where it was expected that the officers would become familiar with the inhabitants and with their problems and concerns. Patrol officers were given considerable authority in processing complaints, from receipt through resolution. Crimes were investigated and solved at the local level, with specialists called in only if the resources needed to continue an investigation were not available locally. Some authors called team policing a "technique to deliver total police services to a neighborhood."[51] Others, however, dismissed it as "little more than an attempt to return to the style of policing that was prevalent in the United States over a century ago."[52]

Community Policing

Over the past quarter-century, the role of the police in police–community relations has changed considerably. Originally, the

■ **strategic policing** A type of policing that retains the traditional police goal of professional crime fighting but enlarges the enforcement target to include nontraditional kinds of criminals, such as serial offenders, gangs and criminal associations, drug-distribution networks, and sophisticated white-collar and computer criminals. Strategic policing generally makes use of innovative enforcement techniques, including intelligence operations, undercover stings, electronic surveillance, and sophisticated forensic methods.

■ **problem-solving policing** A type of policing that assumes that crimes can be controlled by uncovering and effectively addressing the underlying social problems that cause crime. Problem-solving policing makes use of community resources, such as counseling centers, welfare programs, and job-training facilities. It also attempts to involve citizens in crime prevention through education, negotiation, and conflict management.

■ **community policing** "A collaborative effort between the police and the community that identifies problems of crime and disorder and involves all elements of the community in the search for solutions to these problems."[iv]

PCR model was based on the fact that many police administrators saw police officers as enforcers of the law who were isolated from, and often in opposition to, the communities they policed. As a result, PCR programs were often a shallowly disguised effort to overcome public suspicion and community hostility.

Today, increasing numbers of law enforcement administrators embrace the role of service provider. Modern departments frequently help citizens solve a vast array of personal problems, many of which involve no law-breaking activity. For example, officers regularly aid sick or distraught people, organize community crime-prevention efforts, investigate domestic disputes, regulate traffic, and educate children and teens about drug abuse. Service calls far exceed calls directly related to law violations, and officers make more referrals to agencies like Alcoholics Anonymous, domestic violence centers, and drug-rehabilitation programs than they make arrests.

In contemporary America, some say, police departments function a lot like corporations. According to Harvard University's Executive Session on Policing, three generic kinds of "corporate strategies" guide American policing: (1) strategic policing, (2) problem-solving policing, and (3) community policing.[53]

Jeff Greenberg/PhotoEdit Inc.

A police explorer volunteer hands out free sack lunches to participants in the Special Olympics Summer Games in North Miami, Florida. Activities like this help foster the community policing ideal through which law enforcement officers and members of the public become partners in controlling crime and keeping communities safe. How does such a partnership help the police? The community?

Strategic policing, something of a holdover from the reform era, "emphasizes an increased capacity to deal with crimes that are not well controlled by traditional methods."[54] Strategic policing retains the traditional police goal of professional crime fighting but enlarges the enforcement target to include nontraditional kinds of criminals, such as serial offenders, gangs and criminal associations, drug-distribution networks, and sophisticated white-collar and computer criminals. To meet its goals, strategic policing generally makes use of innovative enforcement techniques, including intelligence operations, undercover stings, electronic surveillance, and sophisticated forensic methods.

The other two strategies give greater recognition to Wilson's service style. **Problem-solving policing** (sometimes called *problem-oriented policing*) takes the view that many crimes are caused by existing social conditions in the communities. To control crime, problem-oriented police managers attempt to uncover and effectively address these underlying social problems. Problem-solving policing makes thorough use of community resources, such as counseling centers, welfare programs, and job-training facilities. It also attempts to involve citizens in crime prevention through education, negotiation, and conflict management. For example, police may ask residents of poorly maintained housing areas to clean up litter, install better lighting, and provide security devices for their houses and apartments in the belief that clean, well-lighted, secure areas are a deterrent to criminal activity.

The third and newest strategy, **community policing** (sometimes called *community-oriented policing*), goes a step beyond the other two. It has been described as "a philosophy based on forging a partnership between the police and the community, so that they can work together on solving problems of crime, [and] fear of crime and disorder, thereby enhancing the overall quality of life in their neighborhoods."[55] This approach addresses the causes of crime to reduce the fear of crime and social disorder through problem-solving strategies and police–community partnerships.

The community policing concept evolved from the early works of police researchers George Kelling and Robert Trojanowicz. Their studies of foot-patrol programs in Newark, New Jersey,[56] and Flint, Michigan,[57] showed that "police could develop more positive attitudes toward community members and could promote positive attitudes toward police if they spent time on foot in their neighborhoods."[58] Trojanowicz's *Community Policing*, published in 1990,[59] may be the definitive work on this topic.

Community policing seeks to actively involve citizens in the task of crime control by creating an effective working partnership between citizens and the police.[60] Under the community policing ideal, the public and the police share responsibility for establishing and maintaining peaceful neighborhoods.[61] As a result, community members participate more fully than ever before in defining the police role. Police expert Jerome Skolnick says that community policing is "grounded on the notion that, together, police and public are more effective and more humane coproducers of safety and public order than are the police alone."[62] According to Skolnick, community policing involves at least one of four elements: (1) community-based crime prevention, (2) the reorientation of patrol activities to emphasize the importance of nonemergency services, (3) increased police accountability to the public, and (4) a decentralization of command, including a greater use of civilians at all levels of police decision making.[63] As one writer explains, "Community policing seeks to integrate what was traditionally seen as the different law enforcement, order maintenance and social service roles of the police. Central to the integration of these roles is a working partnership with the community in determining what neighborhood problems are to be addressed, and how."[64] Table 6-1 highlights the differences between traditional and community policing.

Community policing is a two-way street. It requires not only police awareness of community needs but also both involvement and crime-fighting action on the part of citizens themselves. As Detective Tracie Harrison of the Denver Police Department explains, "When the neighborhood takes stock in their community and they're serious [that] they don't want crime, then you start to see crime go down. . . . They're basically fed up and know the police can't do it alone."[65]

Police departments throughout the country continue to join the community policing bandwagon. A 2001 report by the Bureau of Justice Statistics (BJS) showed that state and local law enforcement agencies across the United States had nearly 113,000 full-time sworn personnel regularly engaged in community policing activities.[66] The BJS noted that only about 21,000 officers would have been so categorized in 1997. At the

TABLE 6-1 | Traditional versus Community Policing

QUESTION	TRADITIONAL POLICING	COMMUNITY POLICING
Who are the police?	The police are a government agency principally responsible for law enforcement.	The police are the public, and the public are the police. Police officers are paid to give full-time attention to the duties of every citizen.
What is the relationship of the police force to other public-service departments?	Priorities often conflict.	The police are one department among many responsible for improving the quality of life.
What is the role of the police?	To solve crimes.	To solve problems.
How is police efficiency measured?	By detection and arrest rates	By the absence of crime and disorder.
What are the highest priorities?	Crimes that are high value (for example, bank robberies) and those involving violence.	Whatever problems disturb the community most.
What do police deal with?	Incidents.	Citizens' problems and concerns.
What determines the effectiveness of police?	Response times.	Public cooperation.
What view do police take of service calls?	They deal with them only if there is no "real" police work to do.	They view them as a vital function and a great opportunity.
What is police professionalism?	Providing a swift, effective response to serious crime.	Keeping close to the community.
What kind of intelligence is most important?	Crime intelligence (study of particular crimes or series of crimes).	Criminal intelligence (information about the activities of individuals or groups).
What is the essential nature of police accountability?	Highly centralized; governed by rules, regulations, and policy directives; accountable to the law.	Local accountability to community needs.
What is the role of headquarters?	To provide the necessary rules and policy directives.	To preach organizational values.
What is the role of the press liaison department?	To keep the "heat" off operational officers so they can get on with the job.	To coordinate an essential channel of communication with the community.
How do the police regard prosecutions?	As an important goal.	As one tool among many.

Source: Malcolm K. Sparrow, *Implementing Community Policing* (Washington, DC: National Institute of Justice, 1988), pp. 8–9.

time of the report, 64% of local police departments serving 86% of all residents had full-time officers engaged in some form of community policing activity, compared to 34% of departments serving 62% of all residents in 1997.

The Chicago Police Department launched its comprehensive community policing program, called Chicago's Alternative Policing Strategy (CAPS), in 1993. The development of a strategic plan for "reinventing the Chicago Police Department," from which CAPS evolved, included significant contributions by Mayor Richard M. Daley, who noted that community policing "means doing more than responding to calls for service and solving crimes. It means transforming the Department to support a new, proactive approach to preventing crimes before they occur. It means forging new partnerships among residents, business owners, community leaders, the police, and City services to solve long-range community problems."[67] Today, CAPS functions on a department-wide basis throughout the city. A review of Chicago's experience with community policing is available at **http://www.justicestudies.com/pubs/cpic.pdf**.

Although community policing efforts began in metropolitan areas, the community engagement and problem-solving spirit of these programs has spread to rural regions. Sheriff's departments operating community policing programs sometimes refer to them as "neighborhood-oriented policing" in recognition of the decentralized nature of rural communities. A Bureau of Justice Assistance (BJA) report on neighborhood-oriented policing notes that "the stereotypical view is that police officers in rural areas naturally work more closely with the public than do officers in metropolitan areas."[68] This view, warns the BJA, may not be entirely accurate, and rural departments would do well "to recognize that considerable diversity exists among rural communities and rural law enforcement agencies." Hence, as in metropolitan areas, effective community policing requires the involvement of all members of the community in identifying and solving problems.

Title I of the Violent Crime Control and Law Enforcement Act of 1994, known as the Public Safety Partnership and Community Policing Act of 1994, highlighted community policing's role in combating crime and funded (among other things) "increas[ing] the number of law enforcement officers involved in activities that are focused on interaction with members of the community on proactive crime control and prevention by redeploying officers to such activities." The avowed purposes of the Community Policing Act were to (1) substantially increase the number of law enforcement officers interacting directly with the public (through a program known as Cops on the Beat); (2) provide additional and more effective training to law enforcement officers to enhance their problem-solving, service, and other skills needed in interacting with community members; (3) encourage development and implementation of innovative programs to permit community members to assist local law enforcement agencies in the prevention of crime; and (4) encourage development of new technologies to assist local law enforcement agencies in reorienting their emphasis from reacting to crime to preventing crime.

In response to the 1994 law, the U.S. Department of Justice created the Office of Community Oriented Policing Services (COPS). The COPS Office administered the funds necessary to add 100,000 community policing officers to our nation's streets—the number originally targeted by law. In 1999, the Department of Justice and COPS reached an important milestone by funding the 100,000th officer ahead of schedule and under budget. Although the Community Policing Act originally provided COPS funding only through 2000, Congress has continued to fund COPS[69] In 2002, the COPS Office adopted the theme "Homeland Security through Community Policing," which emphasizes the local police officer's crucial role in gathering information on terrorist suspects—a topic that is discussed later in this chapter. For fiscal year 2012, the federal budget included $200 million in COPS Office funding. The majority of the money was used to make grants to local police departments to hire full-time sworn officers, or to rehire officers who had been laid off. The 2012 expenditures extended hiring preferences to military veterans returning from the Gulf.[70] Since its inception, the program has spent $12.4 billion and made grants to hire 117,000 police officers.[71] The federal COPS Office can be found at **http://www.cops.usdoj.gov**.

Critique of Community Policing

As some authors have noted, "Community policing has become the dominant theme of contemporary police reform in America,"[72] yet problems have plagued the movement since its inception.[73] For one thing, the range, complexity, and evolving nature of community policing programs make their effectiveness difficult to measure.[74] Moreover, "citizen satisfaction" with police performance can be difficult to conceptualize and quantify. Most early studies examined citizens' attitudes developed through face-to-face interaction with individual police officers. They generally found a far higher level of dissatisfaction with the police among African Americans than among most other groups. Recent findings continue to show that the attitudes

Recent findings continue to show that the attitudes of African Americans toward the police remain poor.

■ **police subculture** A particular set of values, beliefs, and acceptable forms of behavior characteristic of American police. Socialization into the police subculture begins with recruit training and continues thereafter.

RJ Sangosti/The Denver Post via Getty Images.

Los Angeles bike patrol officers conferring with a supervisor. The community policing concept requires that officers become an integral part of the communities they serve. How can community policing help to both prevent and solve crimes?

of African Americans toward the police remain poor. The wider reach of these studies, however, led evaluators to discover that this dissatisfaction may be rooted in overall quality of life and type of neighborhood.[75] Because, on average, African Americans continue to experience a lower quality of life than most other U.S. citizens, and because they often live in neighborhoods characterized by economic problems, drug trafficking, and street crime, recent studies conclude that it is these conditions of life, rather than race, that are most predictive of citizen dissatisfaction with the police.

Those who study community policing have often been stymied by ambiguity surrounding the concept of community.[76] Sociologists, who sometimes define a community as "any area in which members of a common culture share common interests,"[77] tend to deny that a community needs to be limited geographically. Police departments, on the other hand, tend to define communities "within jurisdictional, district or precinct lines, or within the confines of public or private housing developments."[78] Robert Trojanowicz and Mark Moore caution police planners that "the impact of mass transit, mass communications and mass media have widened the rift between a sense of community based on geography and one [based] on interest."[79]

Researchers who follow the police definition of *community* recognize that there may be little consensus within and between members of a local community about community problems and appropriate solutions. Robert Bohm and colleagues at the University of Central Florida have found, for example, that although there may be some "consensus about social problems and their solutions . . . the consensus may not be community-wide." It may, in fact, exist only among "a relatively small group of 'active' stakeholders who differ significantly about the seriousness of most of the problems and the utility of some solutions."[80]

Many citizens are not ready to accept a greater involvement of the police in their personal lives.

Finally, there is continuing evidence that not all police officers or managers are willing to accept nontraditional images of police work. One reason is that the goals of community policing often conflict with standard police performance criteria (such as arrests), leading to a perception among officers that community policing is inefficient at best and, at worst, a waste of time.[81] Similarly, many officers are loathe to take on new responsibilities as service providers whose role is more defined by community needs and less by strict interpretation of the law.

Some authors have warned that **police subculture** is so committed to a traditional view of police work, which is focused almost exclusively on crime fighting, that efforts to promote community policing can demoralize an entire department, rendering it ineffective at its basic tasks.[82] As the Christopher Commission found following the Rodney King riots, "Too many . . . patrol officers view citizens with resentment and hostility; too many treat the public with rudeness and disrespect."[83] Some analysts warn that only when the formal values espoused by today's innovative police administrators begin to match those of rank-and-file officers can any police agency begin to perform well in terms of the goals espoused by community policing reformers.[84]

Some public officials, too, are unwilling to accept community policing. Fifteen years ago, for example, New York City Mayor Rudolph W. Giuliani criticized the police department's Community Police Officer Program, saying that it "has resulted in officers doing too much social work and making too few arrests."[85] Similarly, many citizens are not ready to accept a greater involvement of the police in their personal lives. Although the turbulent, protest-prone years of the 1960s and early 1970s are long gone, some groups remain suspicious of the police. No matter how inclusive community policing programs become, it is doubtful that the gap between the police and the public will ever be entirely bridged. The police role of restraining behavior that violates the law will always produce friction between police departments and some segments of the community.

Reuters/Larry Downing/Landov Media

A Washington, D.C., Metro Transit police officer searching a train after subway bombings in London prompted increased security in 2005. How has the threat of terrorism altered the police role in America?

Terrorism's Impact on Policing

The terrorist attacks of September 11, 2001, have had a significant impact on policing in the United States. Although the core mission of American police departments has not changed, law enforcement agencies at all levels now devote an increased amount of time and resources to preparing for possible terrorist attacks and gathering the intelligence necessary to thwart them.

In today's post-9/11 world, local police departments play an especially important role in responding to the challenges of terrorism. They must help prevent attacks and respond when attacks occur, offering critical evacuation, emergency medical, and security functions to help stabilize communities following an incident. A survey of 250 police chiefs by the Police Executive Research Forum (PERF) found that the chiefs strongly believe that their departments can make valuable contributions to terrorism prevention by using community policing networks to exchange information with citizens and to gather intelligence.[86] Read the results of the PERF survey online at **http://tinyurl.com/69urerd**.

The Council on Foreign Relations, headquartered in New York City and Washington, D.C., agrees with PERF that American police departments can no longer assume that federal counterterrorism efforts alone will be sufficient to protect the communities they serve. Consequently, says the council, many police departments have responded to the terrorist threat by strengthening liaisons with federal, state, and local agencies (including fire departments and other police departments); by refining their training and emergency response plans; by creating antiterrorism divisions; and in a number of other ways.[87]

The extent of local departments' engagement in preventive activities depends substantially on budgetary considerations and is strongly influenced by the assessed likelihood of attack. The New York City Police Department (NYPD), for example, which has firsthand experience in responding to terrorist attacks (23 of its officers were killed when the World Trade Center towers collapsed), has created a special bureau headed by a deputy police commissioner responsible for counterterrorism training, prevention, and investigation.[88] One thousand officers have been reassigned to antiterrorism duties, and the department is training its entire 35,000-member force in how to respond to biological, radiological, and chemical attacks.[89] The NYPD has assigned detectives to work abroad with law enforcement agencies in Canada, Israel, Southeast Asia, and the Middle East to track terrorists who might target New York City,[90] and it now employs officers with a command of the Pashto, Farsi, and Urdu languages of the Middle East to monitor foreign television, radio, and Internet communications. The department has also invested heavily in new hazardous materials protective suits, gas masks, and portable radiation detectors.

■ **intelligence-led policing (ILP)** The collection and analysis of information to produce an intelligence end product designed to inform police decision making at both the tactical and strategic levels.[v]

■ **criminal intelligence** Information compiled, analyzed, or disseminated in an effort to anticipate, prevent, or monitor criminal activity.[vi]

In November 2004, in an effort to provide the law enforcement community and policymakers with guidance on critical issues related to antiterrorism planning and critical incident response, the International Association of Chiefs of Police (IACP) announced its Taking Command Initiative. The IACP described the initiative as "an aggressive project to assess the current state of homeland security efforts in the United States and to develop and implement the actions necessary to protect our communities from the specter of both crime and terrorism."[91] Initial deliberations under the initiative led the IACP to conclude that "the current homeland security strategy is handicapped by a fundamental flaw: It was developed without sufficiently seeking or incorporating the advice, expertise, or consent of public safety organizations at the state, tribal or local level."[92] Building on that premise, the IACP identified a number of key principles that it says must form the basis of any effective national homeland security strategy.[93]

Finally, in 2005, the IACP and its partners in the Post-9/11 Policing Project published *Assessing and Managing the Terrorism Threat*. The Post-9/11 Policing Project is a collaborative effort of the IACP, the National Sheriffs' Association (NSA), the National Organization of Black Law Enforcement Executives (NOBLE), the Major Cities Chiefs Association (MCCA), and the Police Foundation.[94] Download the publication *Assessing and Managing the Terrorism Threat* at **http://www.justicestudies.com/pubs/amterrth.pdf**.

Workable antiterrorism programs at the local level require effective sharing of critical information between agencies.

As the IACP recognizes, workable antiterrorism programs at the local level require effective sharing of critical information between agencies. FBI-sponsored Joint Terrorism Task Forces (JTTFs) facilitate this by bringing together federal and local law enforcement personnel to focus on specific threats. The FBI currently has established or authorized JTTFs in each of its 56 field offices. In addition to the JTTFs, the FBI has created Regional Terrorism Task Forces (RTTFs) to share information with local enforcement agencies. Through the RTTFs, FBI special agents assigned to terrorism prevention and investigation meet twice a year with their federal, state, and local counterparts for common training, discussion of investigations, and intelligence sharing. The FBI says that "the design of this non-traditional terrorism task force provides the necessary mechanism and structure to direct counterterrorism resources toward localized terrorism problems within the United States."[95] Six RTTFs are currently in operation: the Inland Northwest, South Central, Southeastern, Northeast Border, Deep South, and Southwest.

Another FBI counterterrorism component, Field Intelligence Groups (FIGs), were developed following recommendations of the 9/11 Commission. The commission said that the FBI should build a reciprocal relationship with state and local agencies, maximizing the sharing of information. FIGs, which now exist in all 56 FBI field offices, work closely with JTTFs to provide valuable services to law enforcement personnel at the state and local levels. According to the FBI, FIGs "generate intelligence products and disseminate them to the intelligence and law enforcement communities to help guide investigative, program, and policy decisions."[96]

Given the changes that have taken place in American law enforcement since the terrorist attacks of September 11, 2001, some say that traditional distinctions between crime, terrorism, and war are fading and that, at least in some instances, military action and civil law enforcement are becoming integrated. The critical question for law enforcement administrators in the near future may be one of discerning the role that law enforcement is to play in the emerging global context.

Intelligence-Led Policing and Antiterrorism

In 2005, the U.S. Department of Justice embraced the concept of **intelligence-led policing (ILP)** as an important technique to be employed by American law enforcement agencies in the battle against terrorism and organized and transnational crime.[97] Intelligence is information that has been analyzed and integrated into a useful perspective. The information used in the development of effective intelligence is typically gathered from many sources, such as surveillance, covert operations, financial records, electronic eavesdropping, interviews, newspapers, the Internet, and interrogations. Law enforcement intelligence, or **criminal intelligence**, is the result of a "process that evaluates information collected from diverse sources, integrates the relevant information into a cohesive package, and produces a conclusion or estimate about a criminal phenomenon by using the scientific approach to problem solving."[98] Although criminal investigation is typically part of the intelligence-gathering process, the intelligence function of a

Intelligence is information that has been analyzed and integrated into a useful perspective.

■ **NLETS** The International Justice and Public Safety Information Sharing Network.

police department is more exploratory and more broadly focused than a single criminal investigation.[99]

ILP (also known as *intelligence-driven policing*) is the use of criminal intelligence to guide policing. A 2012 Bureau of Justice Assistance study noted that "ILP relies on analytically understanding multijurisdictional crime threats, developing a pathway toward solving the crime problems, and relying on proactive information sharing, both within the agency and externally with other law enforcement agencies, to maximize the number of law enforcement personnel who may identify indicators of threats and intervene."[100]

A detailed description of ILP and its applicability to American law enforcement agencies is provided in the FBI publication *The Law Enforcement Intelligence Function* by David Carter of Michigan State University's School of Criminal Justice. The document is available at **http://tinyurl.com/6avb8fd**.

According to Carter, criminal intelligence "is a synergistic product intended to provide meaningful and trustworthy direction to law enforcement decision makers about complex criminality, criminal enterprises, criminal extremists, and terrorists." Carter goes on to point out that law enforcement intelligence consists of two types: tactical and strategic. Tactical intelligence "includes gaining or developing information related to threats of terrorism or crime and using this information to apprehend offenders, harden targets, and use strategies that will eliminate or mitigate the threat." Strategic intelligence, in contrast, provides information to decision makers about the changing nature of threats for the purpose of "developing response strategies and reallocating resources" to accomplish effective prevention.

Not every law enforcement agency has the staff or resources needed to create a dedicated intelligence unit. Even without an intelligence unit, however, a law enforcement organization should have the ability to effectively utilize the information and intelligence products that are developed and disseminated by organizations at all levels of government. In other words, even though a police agency may not have the resources necessary to analyze all the information it acquires, it should still be able to mount an effective response to credible threat information that it receives. Learn more about the law enforcement intelligence function and intelligence-led policing at **http://www.justicestudies.com/pubs/intelled.pdf**.

Information Sharing and Antiterrorism

The need to effectively share criminal intelligence across jurisdictions and between law enforcement agencies nationwide became apparent with the tragic events of September 11, 2001. Consequently, governments at all levels are today working toward the creation of a fully integrated criminal justice information system. According to a recent task force report, a fully integrated criminal justice information system is "a network of public safety, justice and homeland security computer systems which provides to each agency the information it needs, at the time it is needed, in the form that it is needed, regardless of the source and regardless of the physical location at which it is stored."[101] The information that is provided should be complete, accurate, and formatted in whatever way is most useful for the agency's tasks. In a fully integrated criminal justice information system, information would be made available at the practitioner's workstation, whether that workstation is a patrol car, desk, laptop, or judge's bench. Within such a system, each agency shares information not only with other agencies in its own jurisdiction but with multiple justice agencies on the federal, state, and local levels. In such an idealized justice information system, accurate information is also available to nonjustice agencies with statutory authority and a legal obligation to check criminal histories before licensing, employment, weapons purchase, and so on.

The need to effectively share criminal intelligence across jurisdictions and between law enforcement agencies nationwide became apparent with the tragic events of September 11, 2001.

One widely used information sharing system is Law Enforcement Online (LEO). LEO, an intranet intended exclusively for use by the law enforcement community, is a national interactive computer communications system and information service. This user-friendly system can be accessed by any approved employee of a duly constituted local, state, or federal law enforcement agency or by an approved member of an authorized law enforcement special-interest group. LEO provides a state-of-the-art communication mechanism to link all levels of law enforcement throughout the United States. Members use LEO to support investigative operations, send notifications and alerts, and remotely access a wide variety of law enforcement and intelligence systems and resources. LEO also allows federal agencies, including the FBI, to immediately disseminate sensitive but unclassified information across agency boundaries.[102] The system includes password-accessed e-mail, Internet chat, an electronic library, an online calendar, special-interest topical focus areas, and self-paced distance learning modules.[103]

Another important information-sharing resource is **NLETS**, the International Justice and Public Safety Information Sharing Network. NLETS members include all 50 states, most federal agencies and territories, and the Royal Canadian Mounted Police. NLETS, which has been in operation for nearly 40 years, was formerly called the National Law Enforcement Telecommunications System. It has recently been enhanced to facilitate a variety of encrypted digital communications, and it now links 30,000 agencies and over half a million access devices in the United States and Canada. The system facilitates nearly 41 million transmissions each month. Information available through NLETS includes state criminal histories, homeland alert messages, immigration databases, driver records and vehicle registrations, aircraft registrations, Amber Alerts, weather advisories, and hazardous materials notifications and regulations. You can reach NLETS on the Web via **http://www.nlets.org**.

Fusion Centers

In March 2011, more than 1,000 federal, state, and local law enforcement and Homeland Security officials attended the fifth National Fusion Center Conference in Denver, Colorado, to continue the process of standardizing fusion center operations.[104] The annual event supports the goal of establishing an integrated national network of state and major urban area fusion centers. Fusion centers, a new concept in policing, "fuse" intelligence from participating agencies to create a more comprehensive threat picture, locally and nationally. They don't just collect information. They integrate new data into existing information, evaluate it to determine its worth, analyze it for links and trends, and disseminate their findings to the agency in the best position to do something about it.

Slightly more than 70 fusion centers currently operate in all 50 states (there are another 20 regional centers) and have received $380 million in federal funding over the last five years. These centers are largely an outgrowth of one of the 9/11 Commission's criticisms that law enforcement agencies don't talk to each other as they should.

Guidelines for the development and operation of fusion centers have been created by a collaborative effort involving the U.S. Department of Justice (DOJ) and the U.S. Department of Homeland Security. According to those guidelines, a *fusion center* can be defined as a "collaborative effort of two or more agencies that provide resources, expertise, and information to the center with the goal of maximizing their ability to detect, prevent, investigate, and respond to criminal and terrorist activity."[105] Fusion centers vary greatly in size and in the equipment and personnel available to them. Some are small, consisting of little more than limited conference facilities and only a few participants. Others are large high-technology offices that make use of the latest information and computer technologies and that house representatives from many different organizations. Some fusion centers are physically located within the offices of other agencies. The Kentucky Fusion Center, for example, is housed within the state's Department of Transportation building in the state's capitol. Others operate out of stand-alone facilities and are physically separated from parent agencies.

Similarly, although information sharing is their central purpose, the activities of fusion centers are not uniform. Some centers perform investigations, some make arrests, and some exist only to share information. Certain fusion centers, such as the National Counterterrorism Center and the National Gang Intelligence Center, focus on clearly defined issues. Most of today's fusion centers do more than target terrorists, however; they work to collect information on a wide variety of offenders, gangs, immigrant smuggling operations, and other threats. Recognizing that actionable intelligence can come from seemingly unrelated areas, Michael Mines, the FBI's deputy assistant director of intelligence, says that the nation's network of fusion centers is intended to "maximize the ability to detect, prevent, investigate, and respond to criminal and terrorist activity."[106]

Many fusion centers are still developing, and a number of problems remain. Obtaining security clearances for employees of local law enforcement agencies, for example, has sometimes been difficult or time consuming. Even representatives of federal agencies such as the Department of Homeland Security and the FBI sometimes refuse to accept each other's clearances. Nonetheless, a recent hearing before the House Intelligence Subcommittee shows that federal lawmakers are hopeful about the success of fusion centers and are willing to find the federal dollars needed to continue to support them. As Jane Harman (D-Calif.), chairwoman of the House Intelligence Subcommittee, said recently, "Everyone recognizes that fusion centers hold tremendous promise."[107] Learn more about fusion centers at **http://justicestudies.com/pubs/intell_led.pdf**.

The National Criminal Intelligence Sharing Plan

Although information-sharing efforts continue to evolve, most experts agree that a fully integrated nationwide criminal justice information system does not yet exist.[108] Efforts to create one, however, began in 2003 with the National Criminal Intelligence Sharing Plan (NCISP). The NCISP was developed under the auspices of the U.S. Department of Justice's Global Justice Information Sharing Initiative and was authored by its Global Intelligence Working Group.[109] Federal, local, state, and tribal law enforcement representatives all had a voice in the development of the plan. The NCISP provides specific steps that law enforcement agencies can take to participate in the sharing of critical law enforcement and terrorism prevention information.

Plan authors note that not every agency has the staff or resources needed to create a formal intelligence unit. However, the plan says that even without a dedicated intelligence unit, every law enforcement organization needs the ability to effectively consume the intelligence available from a wide range of organizations at all levels of government.[110] The NCISP is available in its entirety at **http://www.justicestudies.com/pubs/ncisp.pdf**.

■ **police discretion** The opportunity for police officers to exercise choice in their enforcement activities.

CJ | NEWS

Fusion Centers: Unifying Intelligence to Protect Americans

AP Photo/Ed Andrieski

Inside the Miami-Dade Police Department's Fusion Center, which serves much of South Florida. The center's combined technologies enhance the power of instant collaboration and information sharing among analysts and investigators from various law enforcement agencies. Why did fusion centers develop?

In Arizona, an international terrorism case was referred to local law enforcement after it was determined that the subjects of the case were involved in local criminal activity. In New Mexico, several individuals linked to FBI investigations—including an MS-13 gang member—were identified. In Tennessee, the FBI developed—with its partners—a formal process for collecting, sharing, and analyzing suspicious activity reports, looking for trends and patterns.

These cooperative efforts—and many more like them—have been made possible through the work of intelligence fusion centers around the country. These centers, usually set up by states or major urban areas and run by state or local authorities, are often supported by federal law enforcement, including the FBI.

In March 2009, nearly 2,000 local, state, tribal, and federal representatives working in these centers gathered in Kansas City to continue the process of standardizing fusion center operations. The ultimate goal? To create a network of centers presenting a unified front against terrorism and other national security and criminal threats that put Americans at risk.

Speaking at the Kansas City conference, FBI Chief Intelligence Officer Don Van Duyn said that "while we still have work to do to make the information process more seamless," the FBI is committed to "expanding our interconnectedness" to help combat threats from terrorist and criminal networks. Van Duyn also said that during the past year the agency has rolled out—to all 56 field offices—standardized intelligence operations structures, roles, and procedures to enhance collaboration with its partners.

Although a few were already in existence before the terrorist attacks of September 11, 2001, fusion centers increased rapidly after the attacks when local and federal officials recognized the need to quickly coordinate information-sharing related to terrorism. Their number has been growing ever since. Today, there are some 70 centers around the country—50 state and 20 regional. Some have expanded their focus to include public-safety matters and major criminal threats.

Fusion center personnel "fuse" intelligence from participating agencies to create a more comprehensive threat picture, locally and nationally. They don't just collect information—they integrate new data into existing information, evaluate it to determine its worth, analyze it for links and trends, and disseminate their findings to the appropriate agency in the best position to do something about it.

The FBI currently has 114 employees working in 38 fusion centers—about 36% are agents, 61% are intelligence analysts, and the rest are language specialists, financial analysts, and the like. Fourteen of these centers also house an FBI *field intelligence group* or *joint terrorism task force*.

Elaine Cummins, the FBI's chief information-sharing officer, notes that "participating in a national network of fusion centers definitely helps us share timely, relevant, and actionable intelligence with our partners—an increasingly important component to our unique national-security and law enforcement mission."

The FBI says that "with fusion centers, everybody wins. State and local law enforcement agencies get access to certain federal databases and the benefit of big-picture terrorism and crime perspectives from their federal partners, along with grant funding, technical assistance, and training. Federal agencies like the FBI gain intelligence from the local level that may fuel terrorism or national security investigations elsewhere in the country or even overseas. And the public gets to sleep a little easier at night, knowing that their local, state, and federal officials are all working together to keep them safe."

Source: Adapted from Federal Bureau of Investigation, "Fusion Centers: Unifying Intelligence to Protect Americans," March 12, 2009, http://www.fbi.gov/page2/march09/fusion_031209.html (accessed May 6, 2013).

Discretion and the Individual Officer

Even as law enforcement agencies struggle to adapt to the threats posed by international terrorism, individual officers continue to retain considerable discretion in terms of their actions. **Police discretion** refers to the exercise of choice by law enforcement officers in the decision to investigate or apprehend, the disposition of suspects, the carrying out of official duties, and the application of sanctions. As one author has observed, "Police authority can be, at once, highly specific and exceedingly vague."[111] Decisions to stop and question someone, arrest a suspect, and perform many other police tasks are made solely by individual officers and must often be made quickly and in the absence of any close supervision. Kenneth Culp Davis, who pioneered the study of police discretion, says, "The police make policy about what law to enforce, how much to enforce it, against whom, and on what occasions."[112]

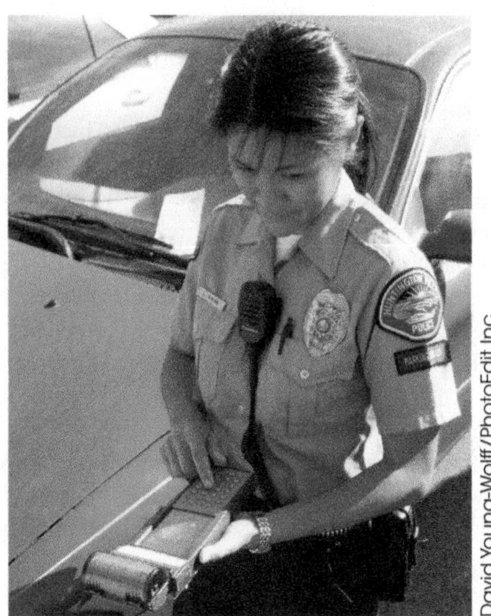

David Young-Wolff/PhotoEdit Inc.

An officer writing a traffic ticket. Police officers wield a great amount of discretion, and an individual officer's decision to enforce a particular law or to effect an arrest is based not just on the law's applicability to a particular set of circumstances but also on the officer's subjective judgment about the nature of appropriate enforcement activity. What other factors influence discretion?

To those who have contact with the police, the discretionary authority exercised by individual officers is of greater significance than all of the department manuals and official policy statements combined.

Patrolling officers often decide against a strict enforcement of the law, preferring instead to handle situations informally. Minor law violations, crimes committed out of the officer's presence where the victim refuses to file a complaint, and certain violations of the criminal law where the officer suspects that sufficient evidence to obtain a conviction is lacking may all lead to the discretionary action short of arrest. The widest exercise of discretion is in routine situations involving relatively less serious violations of the law, but serious criminal behavior may occasionally result in discretionary decisions not to make an arrest. Drunk driving, possession of controlled substances, and assault are examples of crimes in which on-the-scene officers may choose to issue a warning or offer a referral instead of making an arrest. Figure 6-4 illustrates a number of factors that studies of police discretion have found to influence the discretionary decisions of individual officers.

The widest exercise of police discretion is in routine situations involving relatively less serious violations of the law.

Professionalism and Ethics

A profession is an organized undertaking characterized by a body of specialized knowledge acquired through extensive education[113] and by a well-considered set of internal standards and ethical guidelines that hold members of the profession accountable to one another and to society. Contemporary policing has many of the attributes of a profession.

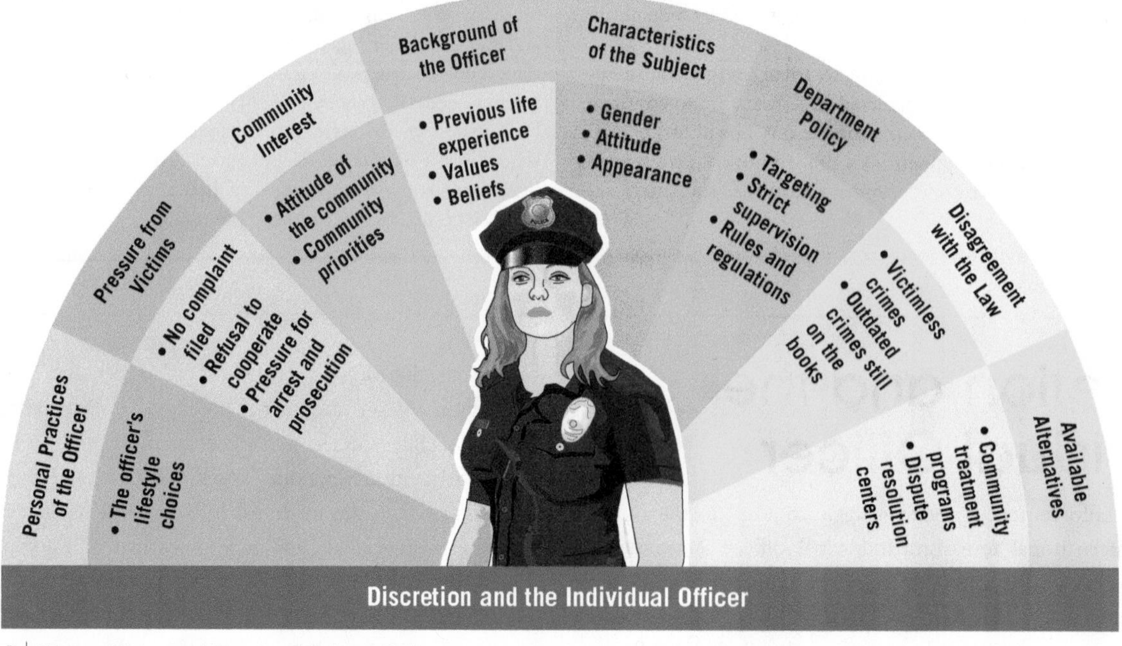

FIGURE 6-4 | Discretion and the Individual Officer

■ **police professionalism** The increasing formalization of police work and the accompanying rise in public acceptance of the police.

■ **police ethics** The special responsibility to adhere to moral duty and obligation that is inherent in police work.

ethics and professionalism

The Law Enforcement Code of Ethics

As a Law Enforcement Officer, my fundamental duty is to serve mankind; to safeguard lives and property; to protect the innocent against deception, the weak against oppression or intimidation, and the peaceful against violence or disorder; and to respect the Constitutional rights of all men to liberty, equality, and justice.

I will keep my private life unsullied as an example to all; maintain courageous calm in the face of danger, scorn, or ridicule; develop self-restraint; and be constantly mindful of the welfare of others. Honest in thought and deed in both my personal and official life, I will be exemplary in obeying the laws of the land and the regulations of my department. Whatever I see or hear of a confidential nature or that is confided to me in my official capacity will be kept secret unless revelation is necessary in the performance of my duty.

I will never act officiously or permit personal feelings, prejudices, animosities, or friendships to influence my decisions. With no compromise for crime and with relentless prosecution of criminals, I will enforce the law courteously and appropriately without fear or favor, malice or ill will, never employing unnecessary force or violence and never accepting gratuities.

I recognize the badge of my office as a symbol of public faith, and I accept it as a public trust to be held so long as I am true to the ethics of the police service. I will constantly strive to achieve these objectives and ideals, dedicating myself before God to my chosen profession . . . law enforcement.

Thinking About Ethics

1. Why does the Law Enforcement Code of Ethics ask law enforcement officers "to respect the Constitutional rights of all men to liberty, equality, and justice"? Does such respect further the goals of law enforcement? Why or why not?
2. Why is it important for law enforcement officers to "keep [their] private life unsullied as an example to all"? What are the potential consequences of *not* doing so?

Source: International Association of Chiefs of Police. Reprinted with permission.

Police professionalism requires that today's police officers have a great deal of specialized knowledge and that they adhere to the standards and ethics set out by the profession. Specialized knowledge in policing includes an understanding of criminal law, laws of procedure, constitutional guarantees, and relevant Supreme Court decisions; a working knowledge of weapons, hand-to-hand combat tactics, driving skills, vehicle maintenance, and radio communications; report-writing abilities; interviewing techniques; and media and human relations skills. Other specialized knowledge may include Breathalyzer operation, special weapons skills, polygraph operation, conflict resolution, and hostage negotiation. Supervisory personnel require an even wider range of skills, including administrative skills, management techniques, and strategies for optimum utilization of resources.

Police professionalism places important limits on the discretionary activities of individual enforcement personnel and helps officers and the departments they work for gain the respect and regard of the public they police. Police work is guided by an ethical code developed in 1956 by the Peace Officers Research Association of California (PORAC) in conjunction with Dr. Douglas M. Kelley of Berkeley's School of Criminology.[114] The Law Enforcement Code of Ethics is reproduced in the "Ethics and Professionalism" box in this chapter. You can learn more about police professionalism from Harvard University's Executive Session on Policing and Public Safety at **http://www.hks.harvard.edu/programs/criminaljustice/research-publications/executive-sessions/policing**.

Ethics training has been integrated into most basic law enforcement training programs, and calls for expanded training in **police ethics** are being heard from many corners. A comprehensive resource for enhancing awareness of law enforcement ethics, called the Ethics Toolkit, is available from the IACP and the federal Office of Community Oriented Policing Services at **http://tinyurl.com/3ucxnla**.

Many professional associations support police work. One such organization, the Arlington, Virginia–based International Association of Chiefs of Police, has done much to raise professional standards in policing and continually strives for improvements in law enforcement nationwide. In like manner, the Fraternal Order of Police (FOP) is one of the best-known

■ **peace officer standards and training (POST) program** The official program of a state or legislative jurisdiction that sets standards for the training of law enforcement officers. All states set such standards, although not all use the term *POST*.

ethics and professionalism

The FBI Oath

On their first day at the FBI Academy new-agent trainees raise their right hands and take this oath as they are sworn in:

> I [name] do solemnly swear (or affirm) that I will support and defend the Constitution of the United States against all enemies, foreign and domestic; that I will bear true faith and allegiance to the same; that I take this obligation freely, without any mental reservation or purpose of evasion; and that I will well and faithfully discharge the duties of the office on which I am about to enter. So help me God.

Similar ceremonies are conducted periodically in every state by every law enforcement agency for officers across the country, usually upon completion of their training. Although the wording of the oaths may vary, each officer promises to do one important thing—support and defend the Constitution of the United States.

Thinking About Ethics

1. How is the FBI oath similar to the Law Enforcement Code of Ethics presented earlier in this chapter? How does it differ?
2. What do the words "I will well and faithfully discharge the duties of the office" mean?

Source: "Our Oath of Office," *The FBI Law Enforcement Bulletin*, September, 2009.

organizations of public-service workers in the United States. The FOP is the world's largest organization of sworn law enforcement officers, with more than 318,000 members in more than 2,100 lodges.

Accreditation is another avenue toward police professionalism. The Commission on Accreditation for Law Enforcement Agencies (CALEA) was formed in 1979. Police departments seeking accreditation through the commission must meet hundreds of standards in areas as diverse as day-to-day operations, administration, review of incidents involving the use of a weapon by officers, and evaluation and promotion of personnel. As of January 1, 2010, more than 800 (almost 4%) of the nation's 17,784 law enforcement agencies were accredited,[115] and a number of others were undergoing the accreditation process. Many accredited agencies are among the nation's largest; as a result, 25% of full-time law enforcement officers in the United States at the state and local levels are members of CALEA-accredited agencies.[116] Although accreditation makes possible the identification of high-quality police departments, it is often not valued by agency leaders because it offers few incentives. Accreditation does not guarantee a department any rewards beyond that of peer recognition. Visit CALEA online via **http://www.calea.org**.

Education and Training

Basic law enforcement training requirements were established in the 1950s by the state of New York and through a voluntary **peace officer standards and training (POST) program** in California. (Information on California's POST program can be accessed via **http://www.post.ca.gov**.) Today, every jurisdiction mandates POST-like requirements, although these requirements vary considerably. Modern police education generally involves training in subjects as varied as self-defense, human relations, firearms and weapons, communications, legal aspects of policing, patrol, criminal investigations, administration, report writing, ethics, computers and information systems, and cultural diversity. According to a 2009 Bureau of Justice Statistics report, the median number of hours of training required of new officers is 881 in state police agencies, 965 in county departments, 883 in municipal departments, and 719 in sheriff's departments.[117] Standards continue to be modified.

Accreditation is another avenue toward police professionalism.

Federal law enforcement agents receive schooling at the Federal Law Enforcement Training Center (FLETC) in Glynco, Georgia. The center provides training for about 60 federal law enforcement agencies, excluding the FBI and the Drug Enforcement Administration (DEA), which have their own training academies in Quantico, Virginia. FLETC also offers advanced training to state and local police organizations through the National Center for State and Local Law Enforcement Training, located on the FLETC campus. Specialized schools, like Northwestern University's Traffic Institute, are also credited with raising the level of police practice from purely operational concerns to a more professional level.

In 1987, in a move to further professionalize police training, the American Society for Law Enforcement Trainers was formed at the Ohio Peace Officer Training Academy. Now known as the American Society for Law Enforcement Training (ASLET), the Frederick, Maryland–based agency works to ensure quality in peace officer training and confers the title Certified Law Enforcement Trainer (CLET) on police-training professionals who meet its high standards. ASLET also works with the Police Training Network to provide an ongoing and comprehensive nationwide calendar of law enforcement training activities.

A recent innovation in law enforcement training is the Police Training Officer (PTO) program, the development of which was funded by the COPS Office starting in 1999.[118] The PTO program was designed by the Reno (Nevada) Police Department, in conjunction with the Police Executive Research Forum (PERF), as an alternative model for police field training. In fact, it represents the first new postacademy field-training program for law enforcement agencies in more than 30 years. The PTO program uses contemporary methods of adult education and a version of problem-based learning that is specifically adapted to the police environment. It incorporates community policing and problem-solving principles and, according to the COPS Office, fosters "the foundation for life-long learning that prepares new officers for the complexities of policing today and in the future."

As the concern for quality policing builds, increasing emphasis is also being placed on the formal education of police officers. As early as 1931, the National Commission on Law Observance and Enforcement (the Wickersham Commission) highlighted the importance of a well-educated police force by calling for "educationally sound" officers.[119] In 1967, the President's Commission on Law Enforcement and Administration of Justice voiced the belief that "the ultimate aim of all police departments should be that all personnel with general enforcement powers have baccalaureate degrees."[120] At the time, the average educational level of police officers in the United States was 12.4 years—slightly beyond a high school degree. In 1973, the National Advisory Commission on Criminal Justice Standards and Goals made the following rather specific recommendation: "Every police agency should, no later than 1982, require as a condition of initial employment the completion of at least four years of education . . . at an accredited college or university."[121]

However, recommendations do not always translate into practice. One report found that 1 in 3 state agencies have a college requirement for new officers, with 12% requiring a two-year degree, and 2% requiring a four-year degree. About 1 in 4 municipal and county police departments have a college requirement, with about 1 in 10 requiring a degree.[122] One in seven sheriff's offices have a college requirement, including 6% that require a minimum of a two-year degree for new hires.[123] A 2002 report on police departments in large cities found that the percentage requiring new officers to have at least some college rose from 19% in 1990 to 37% in 2000, and the percentage requiring either a two-year or four-year degree grew from 6% to 14% over the same period.[124] A Dallas Police Department policy requiring a minimum of 45 semester hours of successful college-level study for new recruits[125] was upheld in 1985 by the Fifth U.S. Circuit Court of Appeals in the case of *Davis* v. *Dallas*.[126]

An early survey of police departments by the PERF found that police agencies that hire educated officers accrue these benefits:[127] (1) better written reports, (2) enhanced communications with the public, (3) more effective job performance, (4) fewer citizen complaints, (5) greater initiative, (6) wiser use of discretion, (7) heightened sensitivity to racial and ethnic issues, and (8) fewer disciplinary problems. However, there are drawbacks to having more educated police forces. Educated officers are more likely than noneducated officers to leave police work, question orders, and request reassignment.

Today, most federal agencies require a four-year college degree for entry-level positions, and those degrees must be obtained from a college or university accredited by one of the regional or national institutional associations recognized by the U.S. Department of Education. Among agencies with such a requirement are the FBI; the Drug Enforcement Agency (DEA); the Bureau of Alcohol, Tobacco, Firearms and Explosives (ATF); the Secret Service; the Bureau of Customs and Border Protection, and the Bureau of Immigration and Customs Enforcement (ICE).[128] Learn more about the close relationship between professionalism and training at **http://justicestudies.com/pubs/letraining.pdf**.

Recruitment and Selection

All professions need informed, dedicated, and competent personnel. In its 1973 report on the police, the National Advisory Commission on Criminal Justice Standards and Goals bemoaned the fact that "many college students are unaware of the varied, interesting, and challenging assignments and career opportunities that exist within the police service."[129] Today, police organizations consider education an important recruiting criterion, and they actively recruit new officers from two- and four-year colleges and universities, technical institutions, and professional organizations. The national commission report stressed the setting of high standards for police recruits and recommended a strong emphasis on minority recruitment, elimination of the requirement that new officers live in the area they were hired to serve,

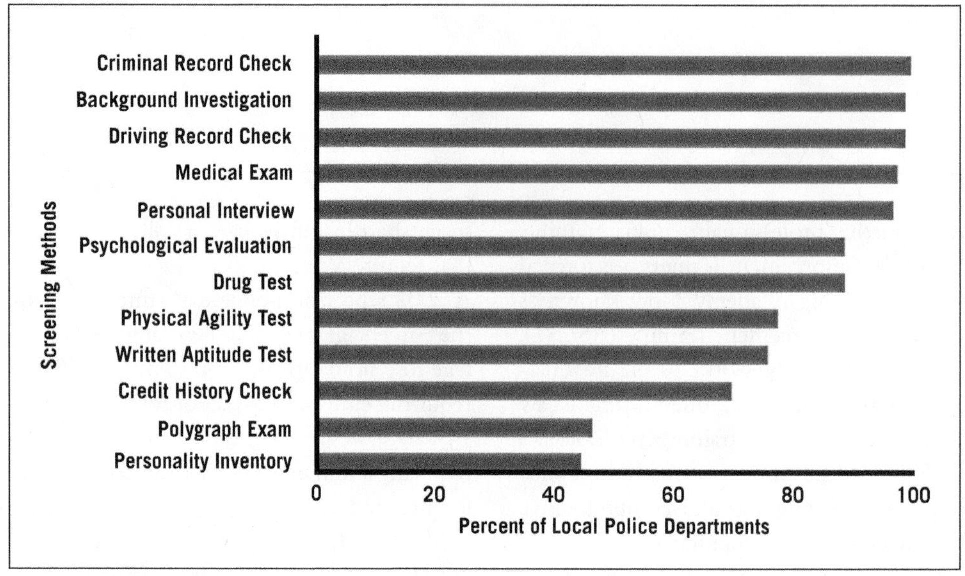

FIGURE 6-5 | Percentage of Local Police Departments Using Various Recruit-Screening Methods, 2003 and 2007

Source: Brian A. Reaves, *Local Police Departments, 2007* (Washington, DC: Bureau of Justice Statistics, 2010), p. 11.

decentralized application and testing procedures, and various recruiting incentives.

A recent Bureau of Justice Statistics study found that local police departments use a variety of applicant-screening methods.[130] Nearly all use personal interviews, and a large majority use basic skills tests, physical agility measurements, medical exams, drug tests, psychological evaluations, and background investigations into the personal character of applicants (see Figure 6-5). Among departments serving 25,000 or more residents, about eight in ten use physical agility tests and written aptitude tests, more than half check credit records, and about half use personality inventories and polygraph exams. After training, successful applicants are typically placed on probation for one year. The probationary period in police work has been called the "first true job-related test . . . in the selection procedure,"[131] providing the opportunity for supervisors to gauge the new officer's response to real-life situations.

Effective policing, however, may depend more on innate personal qualities than on educational attainment or credit history. One of the first people to attempt to describe the personal attributes necessary for a successful police officer, famed 1930s police administrator August Vollmer, said that the public expects police officers to have "the wisdom of Solomon, the courage of David, the strength of Samson, the patience of Job, the leadership of Moses, the kindness of the Good Samaritan, the strategic training of Alexander, the faith of Daniel, the diplomacy of Lincoln, the tolerance of the Carpenter of Nazareth, and finally, an intimate knowledge of every branch of the natural, biological, and social sciences."[132] More practically, Orlando (O. W.) Wilson, the well-known police administrator of the 1940s and 1950s, once enumerated some "desirable personal qualities of patrol officers": (1) initiative; (2) responsibility; (3) the ability to deal alone with emergencies; (4) the capacity to communicate effectively with people from diverse social, cultural, and ethnic backgrounds; (5) the ability to learn a variety of tasks quickly; (6) the attitude and ability necessary to adapt to technological changes; (7) the desire to help people in need; (8) an understanding of others; (9) emotional maturity; and (10) sufficient physical strength and endurance.[133]

High-quality police recruits, an emphasis on training with an eye toward ethical aspects of police performance, and higher levels of education are beginning to raise police pay, which has traditionally been low. The acceptance of police work as a true profession should contribute to significantly higher rates of pay in coming years. Learn more about a career in policing at **http://discoverpolicing.org**.

CBS/Cliff Lipson/Landov Media

La Toya Jackson showing off her wardrobe for the *Armed and Famous* TV show. The CBS series followed five stars through the Muncie, Indiana, police academy and on to patrol where they assisted in investigations and arrests. The show was canceled in 2007, but not before it gained the attention of many "wannabe" officers. What are the attractions of police work?

CJ | CAREERS
Police Officer

Christian Tomas

Name. Narcotics Agent Christian Tomas

Position. QRT Agent (Quick Response Team/Narcotics) City of West Palm Beach, Florida

Colleges attended. Palm Beach State College

Majors. Psychology

Year hired. 2007

Please give a brief description of your job. As a narcotics agent, my co-workers and I target street-level drug dealers and other quality of life issues, to include prostitution as well as other illegal business practices. We use our own initiative to begin investigations throughout the city. We buy narcotics in an undercover capacity and work with the S.W.A.T. team by writing search warrants for them to execute.

What is a typical day like? Typical day involves doing research and identifying a target. Once an investigation is complete, we move on to another. Some days are spent primarily on surveillance; while on others we are directly involved with drug dealers.

What qualities/characteristics are most helpful for this job? Common sense, honesty, integrity, confidence, self-discipline, dedication, humility, composure, physical and mental toughness, Tactical awareness and the ability to work with minimal, to no, supervision.

What is a typical starting salary? The West Palm Beach Police Department starting salary is $45,324 annually, with excellent benefits.

What is the salary potential as you move up into higher-level jobs? An officer reaching PFC (Patrolman first Class) and MPO (Master Patrol Officer) will receive a 2 and 1/2% raise for each level attained. Promotion in rank produces significant raises over time.

What advice would you give someone in college beginning studies in criminal justice? This isn't a job for someone expecting to win all of the battles. You try as hard as you can, but you have to be prepared for some disappointments when a case doesn't go the way you wanted it to. Get your degree, as it will help you get promoted. When choosing a department, make sure that it's the kind of department that you are looking for. I came to West Palm Beach for the experience and to be busy; I wanted to be challenged and to do as much as I possibly could. Policing is a very rewarding career if you have the motivation and determination to succeed.

Ethnic and Gender Diversity in Policing

In 2003, Annetta W. Nunn took the reins of the Birmingham (Alabama) Police Department. For many, Nunn, a 44-year-old African American mother and Baptist choir singer, symbolized the changes that had taken place in American policing during the past few decades. The new chief sat in a chair once occupied by Eugene "Bull" Connor, an arch segregationist and a national symbol of the South's fight against integration who jailed thousands of civil rights demonstrators during the 1960s. A 23-year veteran of the department, Nunn headed a force of 838 men and women. She left the department in 2008 to become an advocate for a domestic violence education program in municipal court.

More than 30 years before Nunn assumed the job of chief, a 1968 survey of police supervisors by the National Advisory Commission on Civil Disorders[134] (aka the Kerner Commission) found a marked disparity between the number of black and white officers in leadership positions. One of every 26 black police officers had been promoted to the rank of sergeant, whereas the ratio among whites was 1 in 12. Only 1 of every 114 black officers had become a lieutenant, whereas among whites the ratio was 1 in 26. At the level of captain, the disparity was even greater: One out of every 235 black officers had achieved the rank of captain, whereas 1 of every 53 whites had climbed to that rank.

David R. Frazier Photolibrary/Photo Researchers, Inc.

African American and Hispanic police officers in Los Angeles. Ethnic minorities, although still underrepresented in the criminal justice field, have many opportunities for employment throughout the system. Can the same be said for women?

Today, many departments, through dedicated recruitment efforts, have dramatically increased their complement of officers from underrepresented groups. The Metropolitan Detroit Police Department, for example, now has a force that is more than 30% black. Nationwide, racial and ethnic minorities comprised 22.7% of full-time sworn police personnel in 2000, up from 17.0% in 1990.[135] From 1990 to 2000, the number of African American local police officers increased by 13,300, or 35%, and the number of Hispanic officers increased by 17,600, or 93%. Moreover, a 2006 study of 123 African American police executives in the United States found that they were generally well accepted by their peers, well integrated into their leadership roles, and socially well adjusted.[136]

Although ethnic minorities are now employed in policing in numbers that approach their representation in the American population, women are still significantly underrepresented. The 2001 Status of Women in Policing Survey, conducted by the National Center for Women and Policing (NCWP), found that women fill only 12.7% of all sworn law enforcement positions nationwide.[137] On the other hand, the NCWP notes that women account for 46.5% of employed people over the age of 16 nationwide, meaning that they are "strikingly underrepresented within the field of sworn law enforcement."[138] Key findings from the survey show the following:[139]

- Women currently fill about 12.7% of all sworn law enforcement positions among municipal, county, and state agencies in the United States with 100 or more sworn officers. Women of color hold 4.8% of these positions.
- Between 1990 and 2001, the representation of women in sworn law enforcement ranks increased from 9% to 12.7%—a gain of less than 4%, or less than 0.5% each year.
- If the slow growth rate of women in policing holds, women will not achieve equal representation within the police profession for another 70 years, and many experts caution that time alone may not be sufficient to substantially increase the number of female officers.
- Women hold 7.3% of sworn top command law enforcement positions, 9.6% of supervisory positions, and 13.5% of line operation positions. Women of color hold 1.6% of sworn top command positions, 3.1% of supervisory positions, and 5.3% of line operation positions.
- Fifty-six percent of the agencies surveyed reported no women in top command positions, and 88% of the agencies reported no women of color in their highest ranks.
- State agencies trail municipal and county agencies by a wide margin in hiring and promoting women. Specifically, 5.9% of the sworn law enforcement officers in state agencies are women, which is significantly lower than the percentage reported by municipal agencies (14.2%) and county agencies (13.9%).
- Consent decrees mandating the hiring and promotion of women and minorities significantly affected the gains women have made in law enforcement. Of the 25 agencies with the highest percentage of sworn women, 10 are subject to such decrees. This contrasts sharply with just 4 of the 25 agencies with the lowest percentage of sworn women operating under consent decrees.
- On average, in agencies without a consent decree mandating the hiring and promotion of women and minorities, women comprise 9.7% of sworn personnel, whereas those agencies with a consent decree in force average 14.0% women in their ranks. The percentage of women of color is 6.3% in agencies without a consent decree and 11.7% in agencies operating under one.

It is unclear just how many women actually *want* to work in policing. Nonetheless, many departments aggressively recruit and retain women because they understand the benefits of having more women as sworn officers. Because female officers tend to use less physical force than male officers, for example, they are less likely to be accused of using excessive force. Female officers are also better at defusing and de-escalating potentially violent confrontations, often possess better communications skills than their male counterparts, and are better able to facilitate the cooperation and trust required to implement a community policing model. Moreover, the NCWP says that "female officers often respond more effectively to incidents of violence against women—crimes that represent one of the largest categories of calls to police departments. Increasing the representation of women on the force is also likely to address another costly problem for police administrators—the pervasive problem of sex discrimination and sexual harassment—by changing the climate of modern law enforcement agencies."[140] Finally, "because women frequently have different life experiences than men, they approach policing with a different perspective, and the very presence of women in the field will often bring about changes in policies and procedures that benefit both male and female officers."[141]

Women as Effective Police Officers

A recent report on female police officers in Massachusetts found that female officers (1) are "extremely devoted to their work," (2) "see themselves as women first, and then police officers," and (3) "are more satisfied when working in nonuniformed capacities."[142] The researcher identified two groups of female officers: (1) those who felt themselves to be well integrated into their departments and were confident in their jobs and (2) those who experienced strain and on-the-job isolation. The officers' children were cited as a significant influence on their perceptions of self and their jobs. The demands of child rearing in contemporary society were found to be a major factor contributing to the resignation of female officers. The study also found that the longer female officers stayed on the job, the greater the stress and frustration they tended to experience, primarily because of the uncooperative attitudes of male officers. Some of the female officers identified networking as a potential solution to the stresses encountered by female officers, but also said that when women get together to solve problems, they are seen as "crybabies" rather than professionals. Said one of the women in the study, "We've lost a lot of good women who never should have left the job. If we had helped each other, maybe they wouldn't have left."[143] For more information on working in policing, visit **http://discoverpolicing.org**.

Some studies found that female officers are often underutilized and that many departments hesitate to assign women to patrol and other potentially dangerous field activities.[144] Consequently, some policewomen experience frustration and a lack of job satisfaction. An analysis of the genderization of the criminal justice workplace by Susan Ehrlich Martin and Nancy Jurik, for example, points out that gender inequality is part of a historical pattern of entrenched forms of gender interaction relating to the division of labor, power, and culture.[145] Martin and Jurik contend that women working in the justice system are viewed in terms of such historically developed filters, causing them to be judged and treated according to normative standards developed for men. As a result, formal and informal social controls continue to disenfranchise women who wish to work in the system and make it difficult to recognize the specific contributions that they make as women.

ROGER L. WOLLENBERG/Newscom

Cathy Lanier, police chief of Washington, D.C. How do communities benefit from police agencies that are socially and culturally diverse?

SUMMARY

- The fundamental police mission in democratic societies includes five components: (1) enforcing the law (especially the criminal law), (2) investigating crimes and apprehending offenders, (3) preventing crime, (4) helping ensure domestic peace and tranquility, and (5) providing the community with needed enforcement-related services.
- This chapter presents five core law enforcement strategies: (1) preventive patrol, (2) routine incident response, (3) emergency response, (4) criminal investigation, and (5) problem solving. Support, an ancillary operational strategy, is also discussed.
- Police management involves the administrative activities of controlling, directing, and coordinating police personnel, resources, and activities in the service of preventing crime, apprehending criminals, recovering stolen property, and performing regulatory and helping services. Virtually all American law enforcement organizations are formally structured among divisions and along lines of authority. Roles within police agencies usually fall into one of two categories: line and staff. Line operations are field or supervisory activities directly related to daily police work. Staff operations include support roles, such as administration.
- Three policing styles are identified in this chapter: (1) the watchman style, (2) the legalistic style, and (3) the service style. The style of policing that characterizes a community tends to flow from the lifestyles of those who live there. Whereas the watchman style of policing, with its emphasis on order maintenance, was widespread during the mid-twentieth century, the service style, which is embodied in the community policing model, is commonplace today. Community policing is built on the principle that police departments and the communities they serve should work together as partners in the fight against crime.
- Policing in America was forever changed by the events of September 11, 2001. Local law enforcement agencies, many of which previously saw community protection and peacekeeping as their primary roles, are being called on to protect

against potential terrorist threats with international roots. The contemporary emphasis on terrorism prevention, along with the need for a rapid response to threats of terrorism, has led to what some see as a new era of policing to secure the homeland. Homeland security policing builds on the established framework of community policing for the purpose of gathering intelligence to prevent terrorism.

- Police discretion refers to the opportunity for police officers to exercise choice in their enforcement activities. Put another way, discretion refers to the exercise of choice by law enforcement officers in the decision to investigate or apprehend, the disposition of suspects, the carrying out of official duties, and the application of sanctions. The widest exercise of discretion can be found in routine situations involving relatively less serious violations of the law, but serious criminal behavior may also result in discretionary decisions not to make an arrest.
- Police professionalism requires that today's law enforcement officers adhere to ethical codes and standards established by the profession. Police professionalism places important limits on the discretionary activities of individual enforcement personnel and helps officers and the departments they work for gain the respect and regard of the public they police.
- This chapter points out that ethnic minorities are now employed in policing in numbers that approach their representation in the general population. Women, however, are still significantly underrepresented. Questions can be raised about the degree of minority participation in the command structure of law enforcement agencies, about the desire of significant numbers of women to work in policing, and about the respect accorded to women and members of other underrepresented groups who work in law enforcement by their fellow officers.

KEY TERMS

chain of command, 170
community policing, 175
CompStat, 164
crime prevention, 163
crime scene, 166
crime scene investigator, 168
criminal intelligence, 180
criminal investigation, 166
intelligence-led policing (ILP), 180
legalistic style, 173
line operations, 170
NLETS, 181
peace officer standards and training (POST) program, 186
police–community relations (PCR), 173
police discretion, 183
police ethics, 185
police management, 170
police professionalism, 185
police subculture, 178
preliminary investigation, 167
problem-solving policing, 175
quality-of-life offense, 164
response time, 166
service style, 173
solvability factor, 168
span of control, 170
staff operations, 170
strategic policing, 175
team policing, 174
watchman style, 172

QUESTIONS FOR REVIEW

1. What are the basic purposes of policing in democratic societies? How are they consistent with one another? In what ways might they be inconsistent?
2. What are the five core operational strategies that police departments use today? What is the ancillary operational strategy?
3. Define the term *police management*, and describe the different types of organizational structures typical of American police departments.
4. What are the three styles of policing described in this chapter? How do they differ? Which one characterizes the community in which you live?
5. What new responsibilities have American police agencies assumed since the September 11, 2001, terrorist attacks? What new challenges are they facing?
6. What is police discretion? How does the practice of discretion by today's officers reflect on their departments and on the policing profession as a whole?
7. What is police professionalism? How can you tell when police action is professional? Why are professionalism and ethics important in policing today?
8. What issues related to gender and ethnicity are important in American policing today? What problems still exist? How can those problems be addressed?

QUESTIONS FOR REFLECTION

1. Are there any aspects of the police mission that this chapter fails to recognize and that should be added to the basic purposes of policing identified here? If so, what are they?
2. How are police organizations managed? Might participatory or democratic management styles or the organizational styles of innovative high-technology firms be effective in policing? Why or why not?
3. What is community policing? How does it differ from what some might call traditional policing?
4. Does community policing offer an opportunity to improve policing services in the United States? Why or why not? Does it offer opportunities in the fight against terrorism? Why or why not?
5. Do you believe that policing is a true profession? How can the professionalism of today's law enforcement organizations be increased? Explain your answer.

NOTES

i. Wayne W. Bennett and Karen M. Hess, *Criminal Investigation*, 6th ed. (Belmont, CA: Wadsworth, 2001), p. 3 (italics in original).
ii. This definition draws on the classic work by O. W. Wilson, *Police Administration* (New York: McGraw-Hill, 1950), pp. 2–3.

iii. Sam S. Souryal, *Police Administration and Management* (St. Paul, MN: West, 1977), p. 261.

iv. Community Policing Consortium, *What Is Community Policing?* (Washington, DC: Community Policing Consortium, 1995).

v. Angus Smith, ed., *Intelligence-Led Policing* (Richmond, VA: International Association of Law Enforcement Intelligence Analysts, 1997), p. 1.

vi. Office of Justice Programs, *The National Criminal Intelligence Sharing Plan* (Washington, DC: U.S. Dept. of Justice, 2005), p. 27.

1. "Dozens of NYPD Cops Oust 300 Occupy Wall Street Protesters from Union Square Park," *The New York Daily News*, http://www.nydailynews.com/new-york/dozens-nypd-cops-oust-300-occupy-wall-street-protesters-union-square-park-article-1.1047996, March 21, 2012 (accessed June 3, 2012).
2. Andrew P. Sutor, *Police Operations: Tactical Approaches to Crimes in Progress* (St. Paul, MN: West, 1976), p. 68, citing Peel.
3. C. D. Hale, *Police Patrol: Operations and Management* (Upper Saddle River, NJ: Prentice Hall, 1994).
4. Victor Kappeler et al., *The Mythology of Crime and Criminal Justice* (Prospect Heights, IL: Waveland Press, 1996).
5. Darl H. Champion and Michael K. Hooper, *Introduction to American Policing* (New York: McGraw-Hill, 2003), p. 133.
6. Details for this story come from Ted Ottley, "Bad Day Dawning," Court TV's Crime Library, http://www.crimelibrary.com/serial_killers/notorious/mcveigh/dawning_1.html (accessed June 22, 2009).
7. Ibid.
8. This definition has been attributed to the National Crime Prevention Institute; see http://www.lvmpd.com/community/crmtip25.htm (accessed July 22, 2007).
9. See Steven P. Lab, *Crime Prevention at a Crossroads* (Cincinnati, OH: Anderson, 1997).
10. See the Philadelphia Police Department's Operation Identification website at http://www.ppdonline.org/ppd4_home_opid.htm (accessed July 25, 2008).
11. The term *CompStat* is sometimes thought to stand for computer statistics, comparative statistics, or computer comparative statistics, although it is not derived from any of those terms.
12. Learn more about CompStat from Vincent E. Henry, *The COMPSTAT Paradigm: Management Accountability in Policing, Business, and the Public Sector* (Flushing, NY: Looseleaf Law Publications, 2002).
13. Much of the information in this section comes from the Philadelphia Police Department, "The COMPSTAT Process," http://www.ppdonline.org/ppd_compstat.htm (accessed May 28, 2009).
14. See Ned Levine, *CrimeStat: A Spatial Statistics Program for the Analysis of Crime Incident Locations*, version 2.0 (Houston, TX: Ned Levine and Associates; Washington, DC: National Institute of Justice, May 2002).
15. Robert H. Langworthy and Lawrence P. Travis III, *Policing in America: A Balance of Forces*, 2nd ed. (Upper Saddle River, NJ: Prentice Hall, 1999), p. 194.
16. Adapted from Bronx County (New York) District Attorney's Office, "Quality of Life Offenses," December 24, 2002, http://www.bronxda.net/fighting_crime/quality_of_life_offenses.html (accessed June 20, 2006).
17. Other violations may be involved, as well. On December 29, 2000, for example, Judge John S. Martin, Jr., of the federal district court in Manhattan, ruled that homeless people in New York City could be arrested for sleeping in cardboard boxes in public. Judge Martin held that a city Sanitation Department regulation barring people from abandoning cars or boxes on city streets could be applied to the homeless who were sleeping in boxes.
18. Norman Siegel, executive director of the New York Civil Liberties Union, as reported in "Quality of Life Offenses Targeted," *Western Queens Gazette*, November 22, 2000, http://www.qgazette.com/News/2000/1122/Editorial_pages/e01.html (accessed June 12, 2007).
19. The broken windows thesis was first suggested by George L. Kelling and James Q. Wilson in "Broken Windows: The Police and Neighborhood Safety," *Atlantic Monthly*, March 1982. The article is available online at http://www.theatlantic.com/politics/crime/windows.htm (accessed June 22, 2005).
20. For a critique of the broken windows thesis, see Bernard E. Harcourt, *Illusion of Order: The False Promise of Broken Windows Policing* (Cambridge, MA: Harvard University Press, 2001).
21. Peter Schuler, "Law Professor Harcourt Challenges Popular Policing Method, Gun Violence Interventions," *Chicago Chronicle*, Vol. 22, No. 12 (March 20, 2003).
22. George L. Kelling, Catherine M. Coles, and James Q. Wilson, *Fixing Broken Windows: Restoring Order and Reducing Crime in Our Communities* (reprint, New York: Touchstone, 1998).
23. Charles R. Swanson, Leonard Territo, and Robert W. Taylor, *Police Administration: Structures, Processes, and Behavior*, 4th ed. (Upper Saddle River, NJ: Prentice Hall, 1998), p. 1.
24. Lorraine Mazerolle et al., *Managing Citizen Calls to the Police: An Assessment of Nonemergency Call Systems* (Washington, DC: National Institute of Justice, 2001), pp. 1–11.
25. The term *operational strategies* is taken from Michael S. Scott, *Problem-Oriented Policing: Reflections on the First 20 Years* (Washington, DC: U.S. Dept. of Justice, Office of Community Oriented Policing Services, 2000), p. 85, http://www.cops.usdoj.gov/Default.asp?Item5311 (accessed May 25, 2007).
26. Ibid., from which some of the wording and much of the material in this section is adapted.
27. Ibid., p. 86.
28. Ibid., from which much of this material is adapted.
29. Ibid., p. 86.
30. New York City Mayor's Office, *Fiscal 2007 Mayor's Management Report* (New York City: Office of the Mayor, 2007).
31. Details for this story come from Kurt Streeter, "Girl, 2, Rescued from Washer," *Los Angeles Times*, May 26, 2003, http://www.latimes.com/news/local/la-me-laundry 26may26,1,7334286.story (accessed May 27, 2003).
32. See Scott, *Problem-Oriented Policing*, from which much of this material is adapted.
33. Wayne W. Bennett and Karen M. Hess, *Criminal Investigation*, 6th ed. (Belmont, CA: Wadsworth, 2001), p. 3 (italics in original).
34. Chief Gordon F. Urlacher and Lieutenant Robert J. Duffy, Rochester (New York) Police Department, "The Preliminary Investigation Process," http://www.surviveall.net/preliminary_investigation_proces.htm (accessed May 27, 2009).
35. Florida Highway Patrol, "Policy Number 22.01," *Policy Manual*, February 1, 1996, http://www.fhp.state.fl.us/html/Manuals/fh22-01.pdf (accessed June 1, 2009).
36. Scott, *Problem-Oriented Policing*, p. 88.
37. Adapted from Michigan State Police, *Annual Report 2000*, p. 12.
38. This definition draws on the classic work by O. W. Wilson, *Police Administration* (New York: McGraw-Hill, 1950), pp. 2–3.
39. Charles R. Swanson, Leonard Territo, and Robert W. Taylor, *Police Administration: Structures, Processes, and Behavior* (Upper Saddle River, NJ: Prentice Hall, 1998), p. 167.

40. Los Angeles County Sheriff's Department, "About LASD," http://www.lasd.org/aboutlasd/about.html (accessed June 25, 2009).
41. For more information on the first three categories, see Francis X. Hartmann, "Debating the Evolution of American Policing," *Perspectives on Policing*, No. 5 (Washington, DC: National Institute of Justice, 1988).
42. Willard M. Oliver, "The Homeland Security Juggernaut: The End of the Community Policing Era," *Crime and Justice International*, Vol. 20, No. 79 (2004), pp. 4–10. See also Willard M. Oliver, "The Era of Homeland Security: September 11, 2001 to . . .," *Crime and Justice International*, Vol. 21, No. 85 (2005), pp. 9–17.
43. Gene Stephens, "Policing the Future: Law Enforcement's New Challenges," *The Futurist* (March/April 2005), pp. 51–57.
44. Cited in Bernie G. Thompson, *A Law Enforcement Assistance and Partnership Strategy* (Washington, DC: U.S. Congress, 2008), p. 5. Congressman Thompson is a ranking member of the Democratic staff of the Committee on Homeland Security.
45. Ibid., p. 5.
46. To learn more about Wilson, see "Presidential Medal of Freedom Recipient James Q. Wilson," http://www.medaloffreedom.com/JamesQWilson.htm (accessed January 5, 2006).
47. James Q. Wilson, *Varieties of Police Behavior: The Management of Law and Order in Eight Communities* (Cambridge, MA: Harvard University Press, 1968).
48. Independent Commission on the Los Angeles Police Department, *Report of the Independent Commission on the Los Angeles Police Department* (Los Angeles: The Commission, 1991).
49. Gary W. Sykes, "Street Justice: A Moral Defense of Order Maintenance Policing," *Justice Quarterly*, Vol. 3, No. 4 (December 1986), p. 505.
50. Egon Bittner, "Community Relations," in Alvin W. Cohn and Emilio C. Viano, eds., *Police Community Relations: Images, Roles, Realities* (Philadelphia: J. B. Lippincott, 1976), pp. 77–82.
51. Paul B. Weston, *Police Organization and Management* (Pacific Palisades, CA: Goodyear, 1976), p. 159.
52. Hale, *Police Patrol*.
53. Mark H. Moore and Robert C. Trojanowicz, "Corporate Strategies for Policing," *Perspectives on Policing*, No. 6 (Washington, DC: National Institute of Justice, 1988).
54. Ibid., p. 6.
55. Community Policing Consortium, *Community Policing Is Alive and Well* (Washington, DC: Community Policing Consortium, 1995), p. 1.
56. George L. Kelling, *The Newark Foot Patrol Experiment* (Washington, DC: Police Foundation, 1981).
57. Robert C. Trojanowicz, "An Evaluation of a Neighborhood Foot Patrol Program," *Journal of Police Science and Administration*, Vol. 11 (1983).
58. Bureau of Justice Assistance, *Understanding Community Policing: A Framework for Action* (Washington, DC: Bureau of Justice Statistics, 1994), p. 10.
59. Robert C. Trojanowicz and Bonnie Bucqueroux, *Community Policing* (Cincinnati, OH: Anderson, 1990).
60. Moore and Trojanowicz, "Corporate Strategies for Policing," p. 8.
61. S. M. Hartnett and W. G. Skogan, "Community Policing: Chicago's Experience," *National Institute of Justice Journal* (April 1999), pp. 2–11.
62. Jerome H. Skolnick and David H. Bayley, *Community Policing: Issues and Practices around the World* (Washington, DC: National Institute of Justice, 1988).
63. Ibid.
64. William L. Goodbody, "What Do We Expect New-Age Cops to Do?" *Law Enforcement News*, April 30, 1995, pp. 14, 18.
65. Sam Vincent Meddis and Desda Moss, "Many 'Fed-Up' Communities Cornering Crime," *USA Today*, May 22, 1995.
66. Matthew J. Hickman and Brian A. Reaves, *Community Policing in Local Police Departments, 1997 and 1999*, Bureau of Justice Statistics Special Report (Washington, DC: U.S. Dept. of Justice, 2001).
67. Richard M. Daley and Matt L. Rodriguez, *Together We Can: A Strategic Plan for Reinventing the Chicago Police Department* (Chicago: Chicago Police Department, 1993), http://www.ci.chi.il.us/CommunityPolicing/Statistics/Reports/TWC.pdf (accessed March 5, 2002).
68. Bureau of Justice Assistance, *Neighborhood-Oriented Policing in Rural Communities: A Program Planning Guide* (Washington, DC: Bureau of Justice Statistics, 1994), p. 4.
69. See the COPS Office website at http://www.cops.usdoj.gov (accessed September 6, 2012).
70. U.S. Department of Justice press release, "White House, Justice Department Announce Law Enforcement Grants for Hiring of Veterans," June 25, 2012.
71. "House Vote Expands Clinton-era Police Program," *USA Today*, April 23, 2009, http://www.usatoday.com/news/washington/2009-04-23-cops-program_N.htm (accessed May 19, 2011).
72. Jihong Zhao, Nicholas P. Lovrich, and Quint Thurman, "The Status of Community Policing in American Cities: Facilitators and Impediments Revisited," *Policing*, Vol. 22, No. 1 (1999), p. 74.
73. For a good critique and overview of community policing, see Geoffrey P. Alpert et al., *Community Policing: Contemporary Readings* (Prospect Heights, IL: Waveland Press, 1998).
74. Jack R. Greene, "Community Policing in America: Changing the Nature, Structure, and Function of the Police," in U.S. Department of Justice, *Criminal Justice 2000*, Vol. 3 (Washington, DC: U.S. Dept. of Justice, 2000).
75. Michael D. Reisig and Roger B. Parks, "Experience, Quality of Life, and Neighborhood Context: A Hierarchical Analysis of Satisfaction with Police," *Justice Quarterly*, Vol. 17, No. 3 (2000), p. 607.
76. Mark E. Correla, "The Conceptual Ambiguity of Community in Community Policing: Filtering the Muddy Waters," *Policing*, Vol. 23, No. 2 (2000), pp. 218–233.
77. Adapted from Donald R. Fessler, *Facilitating Community Change: A Basic Guide* (San Diego, CA: San Diego State University, 1976), p. 7.
78. Daniel W. Flynn, *Defining the "Community" in Community Policing* (Washington, DC: Police Executive Research Forum, 1998).
79. Robert C. Trojanowicz and Mark H. Moore, *The Meaning of Community in Community Policing* (East Lansing: Michigan State University's National Neighborhood Foot Patrol Center, 1988).
80. Robert M. Bohm, K. Michael Reynolds, and Stephen T. Holms, "Perceptions of Neighborhood Problems and Their Solutions: Implications for Community Policing," *Policing*, Vol. 23, No. 4 (2000), p. 439.
81. Ibid., p. 442.
82. Malcolm K. Sparrow, "Implementing Community Policing," *Perspectives in Policing*, No. 9 (Washington, DC: National Institute of Justice, 1988).
83. "L.A. Police Chief: Treat People Like Customers," *USA Today*, March 29, 1993.
84. Robert Wasserman and Mark H. Moore, "Values in Policing," *Perspectives in Policing*, No. 8 (Washington, DC: National Institute of Justice, 1988), p. 7.
85. "New York City Mayor Sparks Debate on Community Policing," *Criminal Justice Newsletter*, Vol. 25, No. 2 (January 18, 1994), p. 1.

86. Police Executive Research Forum, *Local Law Enforcement's Role in Preventing and Responding to Terrorism* (Washington, DC: PERF, October 2, 2001), http://www.policeforum.org/terrorismfinal.doc (accessed June 1, 2009).
87. Council on Foreign Relations, "Terrorism Questions and Answers: Police Departments," http://www.terrorismanswers.com/security/police.html (accessed April 19, 2005).
88. Ibid.
89. Michael Weissenstein, "NYPD Shifts Focus to Terrorism, Long Considered the Turf of Federal Agents," Associated Press, March 21, 2003, http://www.nj.com/newsflash/national/index.ssf?/cgi-free/getstory_ssf.cgi?a0801_BC_NYPD-Counterterror&&news&newsflash-national (accessed May 25, 2009).
90. Ibid.
91. International Association of Chiefs of Police, *From Hometown Security to Homeland Security: IACP's Principles for a Locally Designed and Nationally Coordinated Homeland Security Strategy* (Alexandria, VA: IACP, 2005).
92. Ibid.
93. Joseph G. Estey, *President's Message: Taking Command Initiative—An Update* (Washington, DC: International Association of Chiefs of Police, 2005), http://www.theiacp.org/documents/index.cfm?fuseaction5document&document_id5697 (accessed July 25, 2007).
94. Joel Leson, *Assessing and Managing the Terrorism Threat* (Washington, DC: Bureau of Justice Statistics, 2005).
95. Robert J. Jordan (FBI), Congressional Statement on Information Sharing before the U.S. Senate Committee on the Judiciary, Subcommittee on Administrative Oversight and the Courts, Washington, DC, April 17, 2002, http://www.fbi.gov/congress/congress02/jordan041702.htm (accessed April 19, 2003).
96. Suzel Spiller, "The FBI's Field Intelligence Groups and Police: Joining Forces," *FBI Law Enforcement Bulletin*, May 2006, pp. 2–6.
97. The concept of intelligence-led policing appears to have been first fully articulated in Angus Smith, ed., *Intelligence-Led Policing* (Richmond, VA: International Association of Law Enforcement Intelligence Analysts, 1997).
98. David L. Carter, *Law Enforcement Intelligence: A Guide for State, Local, and Tribal Law Enforcement Agencies* (Washington, DC: U.S. Dept. of Justice, 2004), p. 7.
99. Much of the information and some of the wording in this section is taken from Carter, *Law Enforcement Intelligence*.
100. *Reducing Crime through Intelligence-Led Policing* (Washington, DC: Bureau of Justice Assistance, 2012).
101. Governor's Commission on Criminal Justice Innovation, *Final Report* (Boston: The Commission, 2004), p. 57, from which much of the wording in the rest of this paragraph is taken.
102. Lesley G. Koestner, "LEO Roars into the Future," *FBI Law Enforcement Bulletin*, September 2006, p. 9.
103. Federal Bureau of Investigation, "Law Enforcement Online," http://www.fbi.gov/hq/cjisd/leo.htm (accessed September 1, 2006).
104. Information Sharing Environment, "Report from the 2011 National Fusion Center Conference," http://www.ise.gov/news/report-2011-national-fusion-center-conference (accessed May 19, 2011).
105. Bureau of Justice Assistance, *Fusion Center Guidelines: Developing and Sharing Information in a New Era* (Washington, DC: U.S. Dept. of Justice, 2006), p. 2.
106. Michael C. Mines, "Statement before the House Committee on Homeland Security, Subcommittee on Intelligence, Information Sharing, and Terrorism Risk Assessment," September 27, 2007.
107. "State and Local Fusion Centers Face Challenges as They Grow," *Criminal Justice Newsletter*, September 18, 2007, p. 1.
108. Bernard H. Levin, "Sharing Information: Some Open Secrets and a Glimpse at the Future," *Police Futurist*, Vol. 14, No. 1 (winter 2006), pp. 8–9.
109. The plan was an outgrowth of the IACP Criminal Intelligence Sharing Summit, held in Alexandria, VA, in March 2002. The results of the summit are documented in International Association of Chiefs of Police, *Recommendations from the IACP Intelligence Summit, Criminal Intelligence Sharing*.
110. Office of Justice Programs, *The National Criminal Intelligence Sharing Plan* (Washington, DC: U.S. Dept. of Justice, 2003).
111. Howard Cohen, "Overstepping Police Authority," *Criminal Justice Ethics* (summer/fall 1987), pp. 52–60.
112. Kenneth Culp Davis, *Police Discretion* (St. Paul, MN: West, 1975).
113. Michael Siegfried, "Notes on the Professionalization of Private Security," *Justice Professional* (spring 1989).
114. See Edward A. Farris, "Five Decades of American Policing, 1932–1982: The Path to Professionalism," *Police Chief* (November 1982), p. 34.
115. Commission on Accreditation for Law Enforcement Agencies, *Annual Report 2009* (Gainesville, VA: CALEA, 2010), p. 3.
116. *CALEA Update*, No. 81 (February 2003), http://www.calea.org/newweb/newsletter/No81/81index.htm (accessed May 21, 2003).
117. Brian A. Reaves, *State and Local Law Enforcement Training Academies, 2006* (Washington, DC: Bureau of Justice Statistics, 2009), p. 6.
118. Information in this paragraph comes from "PTO Program," COPS Office, U.S. Department of Justice, http://www.cops.usdoj.gov/print.asp?Item_461 (accessed June 3, 2007).
119. National Commission on Law Observance and Enforcement, *Report on Police* (Washington, DC: U.S. Government Printing Office, 1931).
120. President's Commission on Law Enforcement and Administration of Justice, *The Challenge of Crime in a Free Society* (Washington, DC: U.S. Government Printing Office, 1967).
121. National Advisory Commission on Criminal Justice Standards and Goals, *Report on the Police* (Washington, DC: U.S. Government Printing Office, 1973).
122. Brian A. Reaves and Matthew J. Hickman, *Law Enforcement Management and Administrative Statistics, 2000: Data for Individual State and Local Agencies with 100 or More Officers* (Washington, DC: Bureau of Justice Statistics, March 2004).
123. Ibid.
124. Brian A. Reaves and Matthew J. Hickman, *Police Departments in Large Cities, 1990–2000* (Washington, DC: Bureau of Justice Statistics, 2002), p. 1.
125. "Dallas PD College Rule Gets Final OK," *Law Enforcement News*, July 7, 1986, pp. 1, 13.
126. *Davis* v. *Dallas*, 777 F.2d 205 (5th Cir. 1985).
127. David L. Carter, Allen D. Sapp, and Darrel W. Stephens, *The State of Police Education: Policy Direction for the Twenty-First Century* (Washington, DC: Police Executive Research Forum, 1989), pp. xxii–xxiii.
128. The latter two were formerly part of the Immigration and Naturalization Service until its reorganization under the Homeland Security Act of 2002.
129. National Advisory Commission on Criminal Justice Standards and Goals, *Report on the Police*, p. 238.
130. Brian A. Reaves, *Local Police Departments, 2007* (Washington, DC: Bureau of Justice Statistics, 2010), p. 11.
131. Matthew J. Hickman and Brian A. Reaves, *Local Police Departments, 2003* (Washington, DC: Bureau of Justice Statistics, 2006), p. 270.

132. August Vollmer, *The Police and Modern Society* (Berkeley: University of California Press, 1936), p. 222.
133. O. W. Wilson and Roy Clinton McLaren, Police Administration, 4th ed. (New York: McGraw-Hill, 1977), p. 259.
134. *Report of the National Advisory Commission on Civil Disorders* (New York: E. P. Dutton, 1968), p. 332.
135. Hickman and Reaves, *Community Policing*.
136. R. Alan Thompson, "Black Skin–Brass Shields: Assessing the Presumed Marginalization of Black Law Enforcement Executives," *American Journal of Criminal Justice*, Vol. 30, No. 2 (2006), pp. 163–175.
137. National Center for Women and Policing, *Equality Denied: The Status of Women in Policing, 2001* (Los Angeles: NCWP, 2002), p. 2.
138. Ibid.
139. Ibid., pp. 4–5, from which some of the wording in the list is taken.
140. National Center for Women and Policing, *Recruiting and Retaining Women: A Self-Assessment Guide for Law Enforcement* (Los Angeles: NCWP, 2001), p. 22.
141. Ibid.
142. C. Lee Bennett, "Interviews with Female Police Officers in Western Massachusetts," paper presented at the annual meeting of the Academy of Criminal Justice Sciences, Nashville, TN, March 1991.
143. Ibid., p. 9.
144. Carole G. Garrison, Nancy K. Grant, and Kenneth L. J. McCormick, "Utilization of Police Women," *Police Chief*, Vol. 32, No. 7 (September 1998).
145. Susan Ehrlich Martin and Nancy C. Jurik, *Doing Justice, Doing Gender: Women in Law and Criminal Justice Occupations* (Thousand Oaks, CA: Sage, 1996).

AP Photo/Adam Lau

7 POLICING: LEGAL ASPECTS

OUTLINE

- Introduction
- The Abuse of Police Power
- Individual Rights
- Search and Seizure
- Arrest
- The Intelligence Function

LEARNING OBJECTIVES

After reading this chapter, you should be able to

- Explain how the Bill of Rights and democratically inspired legal restraints help protect our personal freedoms.
- Describe legal restraints on police action and instances of police abuse of power.
- Describe the circumstances under which police officers may conduct searches or seize property legally.
- Define *arrest*, and describe how popular depictions of the arrest process may not be consistent with legal understandings of the term.
- Describe the intelligence function, including the roles of police interrogation and the *Miranda* warning.

The touchstone of the Fourth Amendment is reasonableness. The Fourth Amendment does not proscribe all state-initiated searches and seizures. It merely proscribes those which are unreasonable.

FLORIDA V. JIMENO, 500 U.S. 248 (1991)

Introduction

In 2012, a $120 million civil suit alleging wrongful death was filed against the Los Angeles Police Department (LAPD) by the surviving parents of 19-year-old Abdul Arian, who was shot and killed by LAPD officers after he led them on a high-speed chase that ended when he swerved into the middle of the Hollywood Freeway in Woodland Hills, California. According to police reports supported by video taken from a helicopter at the scene, Arian fled his vehicle and repeatedly made threatening gestures toward pursuing officers, assuming the stance of a shooter and pointing what appeared to be a weapon at them.[1] Although he was later found to have been unarmed, he reportedly told 911 dispatchers, to whom he was speaking with during the chase, that he had a weapon and that he would "pull my gun out on them." Attorneys for the family explained that the amount of money asked for in the lawsuit was calculated using $1 million for each of the 120 bullets fired at Arian.

Law enforcement experts say that "contagious shooting"—gunfire that spreads "in the adrenaline-pumping, split-second heat of the moment"[2] among officers who believe that they, or their colleagues, are facing a deadly threat—likely explained the number of shots fired during the Arian shooting.[3] The incident was complicated by the fact that Arian had wanted to join the LAPD, but had been dismissed from its youth explorer program for disciplinary reasons.

Not all questionable cases of police use of force involve shootings. Two months after Hurricane Katrina devastated New Orleans, for example, members of the city's overworked police department became embroiled in a public-relations nightmare when an Associated Press Television News (APTN) crew working in the French Quarter filmed two white officers beating an apparently dazed and unresisting 64-year-old African American retired elementary school teacher named Robert Davis. A third officer could be seen grabbing and shoving an APTN producer working with the news team. As the incident ended, Davis, whose family had property in the city, was arrested and charged with public intoxication, resisting arrest, battery on a police officer, and public intimidation. He later told reporters that he hadn't had an alcoholic drink in 25 years and that the trouble began when he asked a mounted officer for directions.[4] New Orleans Police Superintendent Warren Riley was quick to condemn the officers' behavior. "The actions that were observed on this video are certainly unacceptable [to] this department," Riley said as he announced the firings of officers Lance Schilling and Robert Evangelist and the suspension without pay of another officer, S. M. Smith.

Not all questionable cases of police use of force involve shootings.

AP Photo/Reed Saxon

Mourners, many wearing T-shirts with images of Abdul Arian, a 19-year-old man shot and killed by members of the Los Angeles Police Department after a freeway chase, prepare to pray over his casket at his funeral at Valhalla Park in the North Hollywood district of Los Angeles, on April 17, 2012. Attorneys filed a $120 million claim against the city on behalf of the family. Might "contagious shooting" explain what happened on that fatal day?

Charges against Davis were dropped in April 2006, but he filed a federal lawsuit against the city claiming a denial of his civil rights resulting from the excessive use of police force. Lance Schilling was found dead on June 10, 2007, apparently from a self-inflicted gunshot wound. A month later, former officer Robert Evangelist was cleared of all criminal charges by Judge Frank Marullo, who said that the video evidence showed Davis struggling for several minutes with the police. "This event could have ended at any time if the man had put his hands behind his back," the judge wrote.[5] Finally, in late 2009, just as a civil trial was set to begin, a financial settlement was reached between the city and Davis. The terms of the settlement were not made public.[6]

The Abuse of Police Power

National publicity surrounding the Davis beating was considerably less intense than that which centered on the 1991 videotaped beating of motorist Rodney King by LAPD officers. King, an unemployed 25-year-old African American man, was stopped by LAPD officers for an alleged violation of motor vehicle laws. Police said King had been speeding and had refused to stop for a pursuing patrol car. Officers claimed to have clocked King's 1988 Hyundai at 115 miles per hour on suburban Los Angeles's Foothill Freeway—even though the car's manufacturer later said the vehicle was not capable of speeds over 100 mph.

No one is above the law—not even the police.

Eventually King did stop, but then officers of the LAPD appeared to attack him, shocking him twice with electronic stun guns and striking him with nightsticks and fists. Kicked in the stomach, face, and back, King was left with 11 skull fractures, missing teeth, a crushed cheekbone, and a broken ankle. A witness told reporters that she heard King begging officers to stop the beating but that they "were all laughing, like they just had a party."[7] King eventually underwent surgery for brain injuries. Officers involved in the beating claimed that King, at 6 feet, 3 inches and 225 pounds, appeared strung out on PCP and that he and his two companions made the officers feel threatened.[8]

The entire incident was captured on videotape by an amateur photographer on a nearby balcony who was trying out his new night-sensitive video camera. The two-minute videotape was repeatedly broadcast over national television and was picked up by hundreds of local TV stations. The furor that erupted over the tape led to the ouster of LAPD Chief Daryl Gates and initiated a Justice Department review of law enforcement practices across the country.[9]

In 1992, a California jury found four police defendants not guilty—a verdict that resulted in days of rioting across Los Angeles. A year later, however, in the spring of 1993, two of the officers, Sergeant Stacey Koon and Officer Laurence Powell, were found guilty in federal court of denying King his constitutional right "not to be deprived of liberty without due process of law, including the right to be . . . free from the intentional use of unreasonable force."[10] Later that year, both were sentenced to two and a half years in prison, far less than might have been expected under federal sentencing guidelines. They were released from prison in December 1995, and a three-year court battle over whether federal sentencing guidelines were violated was resolved in the officers' favor the next year. Officers Theodore Briseno and Timothy Wind were exonerated at the federal level.

In 1994, King settled a civil suit against the city of Los Angeles for a reported $3.8 million. Observers later concluded that King himself was not a model citizen. At the time of the beating, he was on parole after having served time in prison for robbery. Later, he was arrested on a variety of other charges, including battery, assault, drug use, and indecent exposure.[11] King was found dead at the bottom of a swimming pool in 2012. King's 1991 beating served for many years as a rallying point for individual-rights activists who wanted to ensure that citizens remain protected from the abuse of police power in what some see as an increasingly conservative society.

This chapter shows how no one is above the law—not even the police. It describes the legal environment surrounding police activities, from search and seizure through arrest and the interrogation of suspects. As we shall see throughout, democratically inspired legal restraints on the police help ensure individual freedoms in our society and prevent the development of a police state in America. Like anything else, however, the rules by which the police are expected to operate are in constant flux, and their continuing development forms the meat of this chapter. For a police perspective on these issues, visit **http://www.policedefense.org**.

■ **Follow the author's tweets about the latest crime and justice news @schmalleger.**

■ **Bill of Rights** The popular name given to the first ten amendments to the U.S. Constitution, which are considered especially important in the processing of criminal defendants.

TABLE 7-1 | **Constitutional Amendments of Special Significance to the American System of Justice**

THIS RIGHT IS GUARANTEED	BY THIS AMENDMENT
The right against unreasonable searches and seizures	Fourth
The right against arrest without probable cause	Fourth
The right against self-incrimination	Fifth
The right against "double jeopardy"	Fifth
The right to due process of law	Fifth, Sixth, Fourteenth
The right to a speedy trial	Sixth
The right to a jury trial	Sixth
The right to know the charges	Sixth
The right to cross-examine witnesses	Sixth
The right to a lawyer	Sixth
The right to compel witnesses on one's behalf	Sixth
The right to reasonable bail	Eighth
The right against excessive fines	Eighth
The right against cruel and unusual punishments	Eighth
The applicability of constitutional rights to all citizens, regardless of state law or procedure	Fourteenth

A Changing Legal Climate

The Constitution of the United States is designed—especially in its **Bill of Rights**—to protect citizens against abuses of police power (Table 7-1). However, the legal environment surrounding the police in modern America is much more complex than it was 50 years ago. Up until that time, the Bill of Rights was largely given only lip service in criminal justice proceedings around the country. In practice, law enforcement, especially on the state and local levels, revolved around tried-and-true methods of search, arrest, and interrogation that sometimes left little room for recognition of individual rights. Police operations during that period were often far more informal than they are today, and investigating officers frequently assumed that they could come and go as they pleased, even to the extent of invading someone's home without a search warrant. Interrogations could quickly turn violent, and the infamous "rubber hose," which was reputed to leave few marks on the body, was sometimes used during the questioning of suspects. Similarly, "doing things by the book" sometimes meant using thick telephone books to beat suspects, since the books spread out the force of blows and left few visible bruises. Although these abuses were not day-to-day practices in all police agencies and characterized just a small proportion of all officers, such conduct pointed to the need for greater control over police activities so that even the *potential* for abuse could be curtailed.

In the 1960s, the U.S. Supreme Court, under the direction of Chief Justice Earl Warren (1891–1974), accelerated the process of guaranteeing individual rights in the face of criminal prosecution. Warren Court rulings bound the police to strict procedural requirements in the areas of investigation, arrest, and interrogation. Later rulings scrutinized trial court procedure and enforced humanitarian standards in sentencing and punishment. The Warren Court also seized on the Fourteenth Amendment and made it the basis for judicial mandates requiring that both state and federal criminal justice agencies adhere to the Court's interpretation of the Constitution. The apex of the individual-rights emphasis in Supreme Court decisions was reached in the 1966 case of *Miranda* v. *Arizona*,[12] which established the famous requirement of a police "rights advisement" of suspects. In wielding its brand of idealism, the Warren Court (which held sway from 1953 until 1969) accepted that a few guilty people would go free in order to protect the rights of the majority of Americans.

In the decades since the Warren Court, a new conservative Court philosophy has resulted in Supreme Court decisions that have brought about what some call a "reversal" of Warren-era advances in the area of individual rights. By creating exceptions to some of the Warren Court's rules and restraints and by allowing for the emergency questioning of suspects before they are read their rights, a changed Supreme Court has recognized the realities attending day-to-day police work and the need to ensure public safety.

Individual Rights

The Constitution of the United States provides for a system of checks and balances among the legislative, judicial, and executive (presidential) branches of government. By this we mean that one branch of government is always held accountable to the other branches. The system is designed to ensure that no one individual or agency can become powerful enough to usurp the rights and freedoms guaranteed under the Constitution. Accountability rules out the possibility of a police state in which the power of law enforcement is absolute and is related more to political considerations and personal vendettas than to objective considerations of guilt or innocence.

Under our system of government, courts are the arena for dispute resolution, not just between individuals but between citizens and the agencies of government. People who feel they have

■ **landmark case** A precedent-setting court decision that produces substantial changes in both the understanding of the requirements of due process and the practical day-to-day operations of the justice system.

■ **illegally seized evidence** Evidence seized without regard to the principles of due process as described by the Bill of Rights. Most illegally seized evidence is the result of police searches conducted without a proper warrant or of improperly conducted interrogations.

not received the respect and dignity from the justice system that are due them under the law can appeal to the courts for redress. Such appeals are usually based on procedural issues and are independent of more narrow considerations of guilt or innocence in a particular case.

In this chapter, we focus on cases that are important for having clarified constitutional guarantees concerning individual liberties within the criminal justice arena. They involve issues that most of us have come to call *rights*. Rights are concerned with procedure, that is, with how police and other actors in the criminal justice system handle each part of the process of dealing with suspects. Rights violations have often become the basis for the dismissal of charges, the acquittal of defendants, or the release of convicted offenders after an appeal to a higher court.

Hill Street Studios/Glowimages

A female officer patting down a suspect. The legal environment surrounding the police helps ensure proper official conduct. In a stop like this, inappropriate behavior on the part of the officer can later become the basis for civil or criminal action against the officer and the police department. What might constitute inappropriate behavior?

Due Process Requirements

As you may recall from Chapter 1, the Fifth, Sixth, and Fourteenth Amendments to the U.S. Constitution require due process, which mandates that justice system officials respect the rights of accused individuals throughout the criminal justice process. Most due process requirements of relevance to the police pertain to three major areas: (1) evidence and investigation (often called *search and seizure*), (2) arrest, and (3) interrogation. Each of these areas has been addressed by a plethora of landmark U.S. Supreme Court decisions. **Landmark cases** produce substantial changes both in the understanding of the requirements of due process and in the practical day-to-day operations of the justice system. Landmark cases significantly clarify the "rules of the game"—the procedural guidelines by which the police and the rest of the justice system must abide.

The three areas we will discuss have been well defined by decades of court precedent. Keep in mind, however, that judicial interpretations of the constitutional requirement of due process are always evolving. As new decisions are rendered and as the composition of the Court itself changes, major changes and additional refinements may occur.

Search and Seizure

The Fourth Amendment to the U.S. Constitution declares that people must be secure in their homes and in their persons against unreasonable searches and seizures. This amendment reads, "The right of the people to be secure in their persons, houses, papers, and effects, against unreasonable searches and seizures, shall not be violated, and no Warrants shall issue, but upon probable cause, supported by Oath or affirmation, and particularly describing the place to be searched, and the persons or things to be seized." The Fourth Amendment, a part of the Bill of Rights, was adopted by Congress and became effective on December 15, 1791.

The language of the Fourth Amendment is familiar to all of us. "Warrants," "probable cause," and other phrases from the amendment are frequently cited in editorials, TV news shows, and daily conversation about **illegally seized evidence**. It is the interpretation of these phrases over time by the U.S. Supreme Court, however, that has given them the impact they have on the justice system today.

■ **exclusionary rule** The understanding, based on U.S. Supreme Court precedent, that incriminating information must be seized according to constitutional specifications of due process or it will not be allowed as evidence in a criminal trial.

■ **writ of *certiorari*** A writ issued from an appellate court for the purpose of obtaining from a lower court the record of its proceedings in a particular case. In some states, this writ is the mechanism for discretionary review. A request for review is made by petitioning for a writ of *certiorari*, and the granting of review is indicated by the issuance of the writ.

The Exclusionary Rule

The first landmark case concerning search and seizure was *Weeks* v. *U.S.* (1914).[13] Freemont Weeks was suspected of using the U.S. mail to sell lottery tickets, a federal crime. Weeks was arrested, and federal agents went to his home to conduct a search. Since at the time investigators did not routinely use warrants, the agents had no search warrant. Still, they confiscated many incriminating items of evidence, as well as some of the suspect's personal possessions, including clothes, papers, books, and even candy.

Prior to trial, Weeks's attorney asked that the personal items be returned, claiming that they had been illegally seized under Fourth Amendment guarantees. A judge agreed and ordered the materials returned. On the basis of the evidence that was retained, however, Weeks was convicted in federal court and was sentenced to prison. He appealed his conviction through other courts, and his case eventually reached the U.S. Supreme Court, where his lawyer reasoned that if some of his client's belongings had been illegally seized, then all were taken improperly. The Court agreed and overturned Weeks's earlier conviction.

The *Weeks* case forms the basis of what is now called the **exclusionary rule**, which holds that evidence illegally seized by the police cannot be used in a trial. The rule acts as a control over police behavior and specifically focuses on the failure of officers to obtain warrants authorizing them either to conduct searches or to make arrests, especially where arrest may lead to the acquisition of incriminating statements or to the seizure of physical evidence.

The decision of the Supreme Court in the *Weeks* case was binding, at the time, only on federal officers because it was federal agents who were involved in the illegal seizure. Learn more about *Weeks* v. *U.S.* at **http://tinyurl.com/59rsve**. See Figure 7-1 for more about the exclusionary rule and its development since *Weeks*.

Problems with Precedent

The *Weeks* case demonstrates the Supreme Court's power to enforce the "rules of the game," as well as the much more significant role that it plays in rule creation. Until the *Weeks* case was decided, federal law enforcement officers had little reason to think they were violating due process because they were not required to obtain a warrant before conducting searches. The rule that resulted from *Weeks* was new, and it would forever alter the enforcement activities of federal officers.

The *Weeks* case reveals that the present appeals system, focusing as it does on the "rules of the game," presents a ready-made channel for the guilty to go free. There is little doubt that Freemont Weeks had violated federal law. A jury had convicted him. Yet he escaped punishment because of the illegal behavior of the police—behavior that, until the Court ruled, had been widely regarded as legitimate. Even if the police knowingly violate the principles of due process, which they sometimes do, our sense of justice is compromised when the guilty go free. Famed Supreme Court Justice Benjamin Cardozo (1870–1938) once complained, "The criminal is to go free because the constable has blundered." One solution to the problem would be to allow the Supreme Court to address theoretical questions involving issues of due process. Concerned supervisors and officials could ask how the Court would rule "if . . ." As things now work, however, the Court can address only real cases and does so on a **writ of *certiorari***, in which the Court orders the record of a lower court case to be prepared for review.

The Fruit of the Poisonous Tree Doctrine

The Court continued to build on the rules concerning evidence with its decision in *Silverthorne Lumber Co.* v. *U.S.* (1920).[14]

The case against the Silverthornes, owners of a lumberyard, was built on evidence that was illegally seized. Although the tainted evidence was itself not used in court, its "fruits" (later evidence that derived from the illegal seizure) were and the Silverthornes were convicted. The Supreme Court overturned the decision, holding that any evidence that derives from a seizure that was in itself illegal cannot be used at trial.

■ **fruit of the poisonous tree doctrine** A legal principle that excludes from introduction at trial any evidence later developed as a result of an illegal search or seizure.

The *Silverthorne* case articulated a new principle of due process that today we call the **fruit of the poisonous tree doctrine**. This doctrine is potentially far-reaching. Complex cases developed after years of police investigative effort may be ruined if defense attorneys are able to demonstrate that the prosecution's case was originally based on a search or seizure that violated due process. In such cases, it is likely that all evidence will be declared "tainted" and will become useless.

THE FOURTH AMENDMENT TO THE U.S. CONSTITUTION

The right of the people to be secure in their persons, houses, papers, and effects, against unreasonable searches and seizures, shall not be violated, and no Warrants shall issue, but upon probable cause, supported by Oath or affirmation, and particularly describing the place to be searched, and the persons or things to be seized.

Based upon the Fourth Amendment, **the Exclusionary Rule** holds that evidence of an offense that is collected or obtained by law enforcement officers in violation of a defendant's constitutional rights is inadmissible for use in a criminal prosecution in a court of law.

SIGNIFICANT CASES

***Weeks* v. *U.S.* (1914)**

Established the exclusionary rule at the federal level, holding that evidence that is illegally obtained cannot be used in a criminal trial; and that federal officers must have a valid warrant before conducting searches or seizing evidence. Prior to *Weeks*, common practice generally allowed all relevant evidence, no matter how it was obtained, to be used in court.

***Silverthorne Lumber Co.* v. *U.S.* (1920)**

Set forth the **Fruit of the Poisonous Tree Doctrine**, which says that just as illegally seized evidence cannot be used in a trial, neither can evidence that *derives* from an illegal search or seizure. Under this doctrine, complex cases developed after years of police investigative effort may be ruined if defense attorneys are able to demonstrate that the prosecution's case was originally based on a search or seizure that, at the time it occurred, violated due process.

***Mapp* v. *Ohio* (1961)**

Applied the exclusionary rule to criminal prosecutions at the state level. The Court held that the due process clause of the Fourteenth Amendment to the U.S. Constitution makes Fourth Amendment provisions applicable to state proceedings.

SUBSTANTIAL SOCIAL COSTS

***U.S.* v. *Leon* (1984)** and ***Hudson* v. *Michigan* (2006)**

Recognized that the exclusionary rule generates "substantial social costs," which may include letting the guilty go free and setting the dangerous at large.

EXCEPTIONS TO THE EXCLUSIONARY RULE

THE GOOD-FAITH EXCEPTION

***U.S.* v. *Leon* (1984)**

Allowed evidence that officers had seized in "reasonable good faith" to be used in court, even though the search was later ruled illegal.

***Illinois* v. *Krull* (1987)**

The good-faith exception applied to a warrantless search supported by state law even though the state statute was later found to violate the Fourth Amendment.

***Maryland* v. *Garrison* (1987)**

The use of evidence obtained by officers with a search warrant that was inaccurate in its specifics was allowed.

THE PLAIN-VIEW DOCTRINE

***Harris* v. *U.S.* (1968)**

Police officers have the opportunity to begin investigations or to confiscate evidence, without a warrant, based on what they find in plain view and open to public inspection.

CLERICAL ERRORS EXCEPTION

***Arizona* v. *Evans* (1995)**

A traffic stop that led to the seizure of marijuana was legal even though officers conducted the stop based on an arrest warrant that should have been deleted from the computer database to which they had access.

***Herring* v. *U.S.* (2009)**

When police mistakes leading to an unlawful search are the result of isolated negligence rather than systemic error or reckless disregard of constitutional requirements, the exclusionary rule does not apply.

EMERGENCY SEARCHES OF PROPERTY/EMERGENCY ENTRY

***Brigham City* v. *Stuart* (2006)**

Certain emergencies may justify a police officer's decision to search or enter premises without a warrant.

FIGURE 7-1 | The Exclusionary Rule

freedom OR safety? YOU decide

Liberty Is a Double-Edged Sword

This chapter builds on the following theme: For police action to be "just," it must recognize the rights of individuals while holding them accountable to the social obligations defined by law. It is important to realize that many democratically inspired legal restraints on the police stem from the Bill of Rights, which comprises the first ten amendments to the U.S. Constitution. Such restraints help ensure individual freedoms in our society and prevent the development of a police state in America.

In police work and elsewhere, the principles of individual liberty and social justice are cornerstones on which the American way of life rests. Ideally, the work of police agencies, as well as the American system of criminal justice, is to ensure justice while guarding liberty. The liberty–justice issue is the dual thread that holds the tapestry of the justice system together—from the simplest daily activities of police officers on the beat to the often complex and lengthy renderings of the U.S. Supreme Court.

For the criminal justice system as a whole, the question becomes, How can individual liberties be maintained in the face of the need for official action, including arrest, interrogation, incarceration, and the like? The answer is far from simple, but it begins with the recognition that liberty is a double-edged sword, entailing obligations as well as rights.

You Decide

What does it mean to say that "for police action to be 'just,' it must recognize the rights of individuals while holding them accountable to the social obligations defined by law"? How can police agencies accomplish this? What can individual officers do to help their agencies in this regard?

The Warren Court (1953–1969)

Before the 1960s, the U.S. Supreme Court intruded only occasionally on the overall operation of the criminal justice system at the state and local levels. As one author observed, however, the 1960s were a time of idealism, and "without the distraction of a depression or world war, individual liberties were examined at all levels of society."[15] Hence, although the exclusionary rule became an overriding consideration in federal law enforcement from the time of its creation in 1914, it was not until 1961 that the Court, under Chief Justice Earl Warren, decided a case that changed the face of American law enforcement forever. Beginning with the now-famous *Mapp* v. *Ohio* (1961) case,[16] the Warren Court charted a course that would guarantee nationwide recognition of individual rights, as it understood them, by agencies at all levels of the criminal justice system. Learn more about the case of *Mapp* v. *Ohio* at **http://tinyurl.com/66yotaz**.

Searches Incident to Arrest

Another important Warren-era case, *Chimel* v. *California* (1969),[17] involved both arrest and search activities by local law enforcement officers. Ted Chimel was convicted of the burglary of a coin shop based on evidence gathered at his home, where he was arrested. Officers, armed with an arrest warrant but not a search warrant, took Chimel into custody when they arrived at his residence and proceeded with a search of his entire three-bedroom house, including the attic, a small workshop, and the garage. Although officers realized that the search might be challenged in court, they justified it by claiming that it was conducted not so much to uncover evidence but as part of the arrest process. Searches that are conducted incident to arrest, they argued, are necessary for the officers' protection and should not require a search warrant. Coins taken from the burglarized coin shop were found in various places in Chimel's residence, including the garage, and were presented as evidence against him at trial.

The Warren Court charted a course that would guarantee nationwide recognition of individual rights.

Chimel's appeal eventually reached the U.S. Supreme Court, which ruled that the search of Chimel's residence, although incident to arrest, became invalid when it went beyond the person arrested and the area subject to that person's "immediate control." The thrust of the Court's decision was that searches during arrest can be made to protect arresting officers but that without a search warrant, their scope must be strongly circumscribed. The legal implications of *Chimel* v. *California* are summarized in Table 7-2.

Since the early days of the exclusionary rule, other court decisions have highlighted the fact that "the Fourth Amendment protects people, not places."[18] In other words, people can reasonably expect privacy in their *homes*—even if those homes are not houses. "Homes" of all sorts—including apartments, duplex dwellings, motel rooms, and even the cardboard boxes or makeshift tents of the homeless—are protected places under

TABLE 7-2 | Implications of *Chimel* v. *California* (1969)

What Arresting Officers May Search
The defendant
The physical area within easy reach of the defendant
Valid Reasons for Conducting a Search
To protect the arresting officers
To prevent evidence from being destroyed
To keep the defendant from escaping
When a Search Becomes Illegal
When it goes beyond the defendant and the area within the defendant's immediate control
When it is conducted for other than a valid reason

the Fourth Amendment. In *Minnesota* v. *Olson* (1990),[19] for example, the U.S. Supreme Court extended the protection against warrantless searches to overnight guests residing in the home of another. The capacity to claim the protection of the Fourth Amendment, said the Court, depends on whether the *person* who makes that claim has a legitimate expectation of privacy in the place searched.

In 1998, in the case of *Minnesota* v. *Carter*,[20] the Court held that for a defendant to be entitled to Fourth Amendment protection, "he must demonstrate that he personally has an expectation of privacy in the place searched, and that his expectation is reasonable." The Court noted that "the extent to which the Amendment protects people may depend upon where those people are. While an overnight guest may have a legitimate expectation of privacy in someone else's home . . . one who is merely present with the consent of the householder may not." Hence an appliance repair person visiting a residence is unlikely to be accorded privacy protections while on the job.

In 2006, in the case of *Georgia* v. *Randolph*,[21] the Court ruled that police officers may not enter a home to conduct a warrantless search if one resident gives permission but the other refuses it. The *Randolph* ruling was a narrow one and centered on the stated refusal by a physically present co-occupant to permit warrantless entry in the absence of evidence of abuse or other circumstances that might otherwise justify an immediate police entry.[22]

Finally, in 2013, in the case of *Baily* v. *U.S.*, the Court limited the power of police to detain people who are away from their homes when police conduct a search of their residence, unless they have probable cause for an arrest. One expert commenting on *Bailey* noted that "if you allow this, then whenever you do a search, people associated with that home could be arrested, no matter where they are, and that just goes too far."[23]

The Burger Court (1969–1986) and the Rehnquist Court (1986–2005)

During the 1980s and 1990s, the United States experienced a swing toward conservatism, giving rise to a renewed concern with protecting the interests—financial and otherwise—of those who live within the law. The Reagan–Bush years, and the popularity of the two presidents who many thought embodied

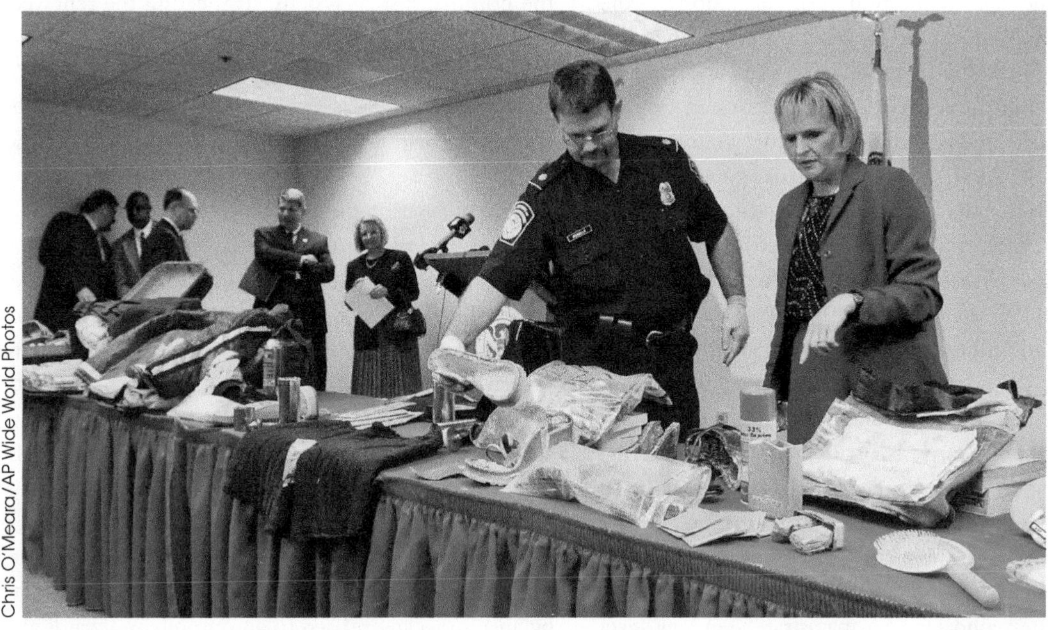

Chris O'Meara/AP Wide World Photos

Police officers examining suspected controlled substances after a drug raid. The exclusionary rule means that illegally gathered evidence cannot be used later in court, requiring that police officers pay close attention to how they gather and handle evidence. How did the exclusionary rule come into being?

■ **good-faith exception** An exception to the exclusionary rule. Law enforcement officers who conduct a search or who seize evidence on the basis of good faith (that is, when they believe they are operating according to the dictates of the law) and who later discover that a mistake was made (perhaps in the format of the application for a search warrant) may still provide evidence that can be used in court.

■ **probable cause** A set of facts and circumstances that would induce a reasonably intelligent and prudent person to believe that a particular other person has committed a specific crime. Also, reasonable grounds to make or believe an accusation. Probable cause refers to the necessary level of belief that would allow for police seizures (arrests) of individuals and full searches of dwellings, vehicles, and possessions.

"old-fashioned" values, reflected the tenor of a nation seeking a return to "simpler," less volatile times.

Throughout the late 1980s, the U.S. Supreme Court mirrored the nation's conservative tenor by distancing itself from some earlier decisions of the Warren Court. Whereas the Warren Court embodied the individual rights heyday in Court jurisprudence, Court decisions beginning in the 1970s were generally supportive of a "greater good" era—one in which the justices increasingly acknowledged the importance of social order and communal safety. Under Chief Justice Warren E. Burger, the new Court adhered to the principle that criminal defendants who claimed violations of their due process rights needed to bear most of the responsibility of showing that police went beyond the law in the performance of their duties. This tenet is still held by the Court today.

Good-Faith Exceptions to the Exclusionary Rule

The Burger Court, which held sway from 1969 until 1986, "chipped away" at the strict application of the exclusionary rule originally set forth in the *Weeks* and *Silverthorne* cases. In the 1984 case of *U.S.* v. *Leon*,[24] the Court recognized what has come to be called the **good-faith exception** to the exclusionary rule. In this case, the Court modified the exclusionary rule to allow evidence that officers had seized in "reasonable good faith" to be used in court, even though the search was later ruled illegal. The suspect, Alberto Leon, was placed under surveillance for drug trafficking following a tip from a confidential informant. Burbank (California) Police Department investigators applied for a search warrant based on information gleaned from the surveillance, believing that they were in compliance with the Fourth Amendment requirement that "no Warrants shall issue, but upon probable cause." **Probable cause** is a tricky but important concept. Its legal criteria are based on facts and circumstances that would cause a reasonable person to believe that a particular other person has committed a specific crime. Before a warrant can be issued, police officers must satisfactorily demonstrate probable cause in a written affidavit to a magistrate[25]—a low-level judge who ensures that the police establish the probable cause needed for warrants to be obtained. Upon a demonstration of probable cause, the magistrate will issue a warrant authorizing law enforcement officers to effect an arrest or conduct a search.

In *U.S.* v. *Leon*, a warrant was issued, and a search of Leon's three residences yielded a large amount of drugs and other evidence. Although Leon was convicted of drug trafficking, a later ruling in a federal district court resulted in the suppression of evidence against him on the basis that the original affidavit prepared by the police had not, in the opinion of the reviewing court, been sufficient to establish probable cause.

Before a warrant can be issued, police officers must satisfactorily demonstrate probable cause.

The federal government petitioned the U.S. Supreme Court to consider whether evidence gathered by officers acting in good faith as to the validity of a warrant should be fairly excluded at trial. The good-faith exception was presaged in the first paragraph of the Court's written decision: "When law enforcement officers have acted in objective good faith or their transgressions have been minor, the magnitude of the benefit conferred on such guilty defendants offends basic concepts of the criminal justice system." Reflecting the renewed conservatism of the Burger Court, the justices found for the government and reinstated Leon's conviction.

In that same year, the Supreme Court case of *Massachusetts* v. *Sheppard* (1984)[26] further reinforced the concept of good faith. In the *Sheppard* case, officers executed a search warrant that failed to accurately describe the property to be seized. Although they were aware of the error, a magistrate had assured them that the warrant was valid. After the seizure was complete and a conviction had been obtained, the Massachusetts Supreme Judicial Court reversed the finding of the trial court. Upon appeal, the U.S. Supreme Court reiterated the good-faith exception and reinstated the original conviction.

The cases of *Leon* and *Sheppard* represented a clear reversal of the Warren Court's philosophy, and the trend continued with the 1987 case of *Illinois* v. *Krull*.[27] In *Krull*, the Court, now under the leadership of Chief Justice William Rehnquist, held that the good-faith exception applied to a warrantless search permitted by an Illinois law related to automobile junkyards and vehicular parts sellers even though the state statute was later found to violate the Fourth Amendment. A 1987 Supreme Court case similar

■ **plain view** A legal term describing the ready visibility of objects that might be seized as evidence during a search by police in the absence of a search warrant specifying the seizure of those objects. To lawfully seize evidence in plain view, officers must have a legal right to be in the viewing area and must have cause to believe that the evidence is somehow associated with criminal activity.

to *Sheppard*, *Maryland* v. *Garrison*,[28] supported the use of evidence obtained with a search warrant that was inaccurate in its specifics. In *Garrison*, officers had procured a warrant to search an apartment, believing it was the only dwelling on the building's third floor. After searching the entire floor, they discovered that it housed more than one apartment. Even so, evidence acquired in the search was held to be admissible based on the reasonable mistake of the officers.

The 1990 case of *Illinois* v. *Rodriguez*[29] further diminished the scope of the exclusionary rule. In *Rodriguez*, a badly beaten woman named Gail Fischer complained to police that she had been assaulted in a Chicago apartment. Fischer led police to the apartment (which she indicated she shared with the defendant), produced a key, and opened the door to the dwelling. Inside, investigators found the defendant, Edward Rodriguez, asleep on a bed, with drug paraphernalia and cocaine spread around him. Rodriguez was arrested and charged with assault and possession of a controlled substance.

Upon appeal, Rodriguez demonstrated that Fischer had not lived with him for at least a month and argued that she could no longer be said to have legal control over the apartment. Hence, the defense claimed, Fischer had no authority to provide investigators with access to the dwelling. According to arguments made by the defense, the evidence, which had been obtained without a warrant, had not been properly seized. The Supreme Court disagreed, ruling that "even if Fischer did not possess common authority over the premises, there was no Fourth Amendment violation if the police *reasonably believed* at the time of their entry that Fischer possessed the authority to consent."

In 1995, in the case of *Arizona* v. *Evans*,[30] the U.S. Supreme Court created a "computer errors exception" to the exclusionary rule. In *Evans*, the Court held that a traffic stop that led to the seizure of marijuana was legal even though officers conducted the stop based on an arrest warrant that should have been deleted from their computer database. The arrest warrant reported to the officers by their computer had actually been quashed a few weeks earlier, but due to an oversight, a court employee had never removed it from the database.

In reaching its decision, the high court reasoned that police officers could not be held responsible for a clerical error made by a court worker and concluded that the arresting officers had acted in good faith. In addition, the majority opinion said that "the rule excluding evidence obtained without a warrant was intended to deter police misconduct, not mistakes by court employees." In 2009, in the case of *Herring* v. *U.S.*, the Court reinforced its ruling in *Evans*, holding that "when police mistakes leading to an unlawful search are the result of isolated negligence . . . rather than systemic error or reckless disregard of constitutional requirements, the exclusionary rule does not apply."[31]

A general listing of established exceptions to the exclusionary rule, along with other investigative powers created by court precedent, is provided in Table 7-3.

During Rehnquist's tenure as chief justice, the Court invoked a characteristically conservative approach to many important criminal justice issues—from limiting the exclusionary rule[32] and generally broadening police powers to sharply limiting the opportunities for state prisoners to bring appeals in federal courts.[33] Preventive detention, "no knock" police searches,[34] the death penalty,[35] and habitual offender statutes[36] (often known as *three-strikes laws*) all were decisively supported under Chief Justice Rehnquist.[37] The particular cases in which the Court addressed these issues are discussed elsewhere in this text.

Following Rehnquist's death in 2005, John G. Roberts, Jr., became the nation's seventeenth chief justice. Roberts had previously served as a judge on the U.S. Court of Appeals for the District of Columbia Circuit.

The Plain-View Doctrine

Police officers have the opportunity to begin investigations or to confiscate evidence, without a warrant, based on what they find in **plain view** and open to public inspection. The plain-view doctrine was succinctly stated in the U.S. Supreme Court case of *Harris* v. *U.S.* (1968),[38] in which a police officer inventorying an impounded vehicle discovered evidence of a robbery.[39] In the *Harris* case, the Court ruled that "objects falling in the plain view of an officer who has a right to be in the position to have that view are subject to seizure and may be introduced in evidence."[40]

The plain-view doctrine is applicable in common situations like crimes in progress, fires, accidents, and other emergencies. For example, police officers who enter a residence responding to a call for assistance and find drugs or other contraband in plain view are within their legitimate authority to confiscate the materials and to effect an arrest if the owner of the contraband can be identified. However, the plain-view doctrine applies only to sightings by the police under legal circumstances—that is, in places where the police have a legitimate right to be and, typically, only if the sighting was coincidental. Similarly, the incriminating nature of the evidence seized must have been "immediately apparent" to the officers making the seizure.[41] If officers conspired to avoid the necessity for a search warrant by helping create a

TABLE 7-3 | Selected Investigatory Activities Supported by Court Precedent

THIS POLICE ACTION	IS SUPPORTED BY
Search authorized by precedent, but subsequently ruled unconstitutional	*Davis* v. *U.S.* (2011)
Arrest based on isolated clerical error	*Herring* v. *U.S.* (2009) *Arizona* v. *Evans* (1995)
Authority to enter and/or search an "open field" without a warrant	*U.S.* v. *Dunn* (1987) *Oliver* v. *U.S.* (1984) *Hester* v. *U.S.* (1924)
Authority to search incident to arrest and/or to conduct a protective sweep in conjunction with an in-home arrest	*Maryland* v. *Buie* (1990) *U.S.* v. *Edwards* (1974) *Chimel* v. *California* (1969)
Gathering of incriminating evidence during interrogation in noncustodial circumstances	*Yarborough* v. *Alvarado* (2004) *Thompson* v. *Keohane* (1996) *Stansbury* v. *California* (1994) *U.S.* v. *Mendenhall* (1980) *Beckwith* v. *U.S.* (1976)
Gathering of incriminating evidence during *Miranda*-less custodial interrogation	*Montejo* v. *Louisiana* (2009) *U.S.* v. *Patane* (2004)
Inevitable discovery of evidence	*Nix* v. *Williams* (1984)
"No knock" searches or quick entry	*Brigham City* v. *Stuart* (2006) *Hudson* v. *Michigan* (2006) *U.S.* v. *Barnes* (2003) *Richards* v. *Wisconsin* (1997) *Wilson* v. *Arkansas* (1995)
Prompt action in the face of threat to public or personal safety or destruction of evidence	*U.S.* v. *Banks* (2003) *Borchardt* v. *U.S.* (1987) *New York* v. *Quarles* (1984) *Warden* v. *Hayden* (1967)
Seizure of evidence in good faith, even in the face of some exclusionary rule violations	*Illinois* v. *Krull* (1987) *U.S.* v. *Leon* (1984)
Seizure of evidence in plain view	*Horton* v. *California* (1990) *Coolidge* v. *New Hampshire* (1971) *Harris* v. *U.S.* (1968)
Stop and frisk/request personal identification	*Arizona* v. *Johnson* (2009) *Hiibel* v. *Sixth Judicial District Court of Nevada* (2004) *Terry* v. *Ohio* (1968)
Use of police informants in jail cells	*Arizona* v. *Fulminante* (1991) *Illinois* v. *Perkins* (1990) *Kuhlmann* v. *Wilson* (1986)
Warrantless naked-eye aerial observation of open areas and/or greenhouses	*Florida* v. *Riley* (1989) *California* v. *Ciraolo* (1986)
Warrantless search incident to a lawful arrest	*U.S.* v. *Rabinowitz* (1950)
Warrantless seizure of abandoned materials and refuse	*California* v. *Greenwood* (1988)
Warrantless vehicle search where probable cause exists to believe that the vehicle contains contraband and/or that the occupants have been lawfully arrested	*Thornton* v. *U.S.* (2004) *Ornelas* v. *U.S.* (1996) *California* v. *Acevedo* (1991) *California* v. *Carney* (1985) *U.S.* v. *Ross* (1982) *New York* v. *Belton* (1981) *Carroll* v. *U.S.* (1925)

plain-view situation through surveillance, duplicity, or other means, the doctrine likely would not apply.

The plain-view doctrine was restricted by later federal court decisions. In the 1982 case of *U.S.* v. *Irizarry*,[42] the First Circuit Court of Appeals held that officers could not move objects to gain a view of evidence otherwise hidden from view. In the U.S. Supreme Court case of *Arizona* v. *Hicks* (1987),[43] the requirement that evidence be in plain view, without requiring officers (who did not have a warrant, but who had been invited into a residence) to move or dislodge objects, was reiterated.

Most evidence seized under the plain-view doctrine is discovered "inadvertently"—that is, by accident.[44] However, in 1990, the U.S. Supreme Court ruled in the case of *Horton* v. *California*[45] that "even though inadvertence *is* a characteristic of most legitimate 'plain view' seizures, it is not a necessary condition."[46] In the *Horton* case, a warrant was issued authorizing the search of Terry

CJ | ISSUES
Plain-View Requirements

Following the opinion of the U.S. Supreme Court in the case of *Horton* v. *California* (1990), items seized under the plain-view doctrine may be admissible as evidence in a court of law if both of the following conditions are met:

1. The officer who seized the evidence was in the viewing area lawfully.
2. The officer had probable cause to believe that the evidence was somehow associated with criminal activity.

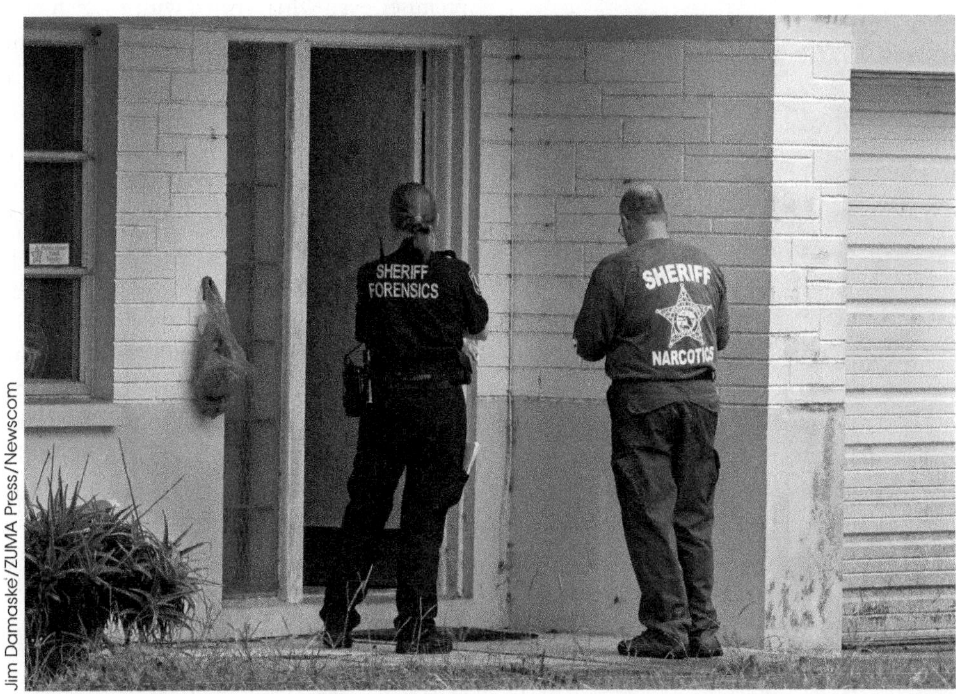

Jim Damaske/ZUMA Press/Newscom

Tarpon Springs, Florida, sheriff's deputies talk to a person inside of a home. How might the plain view doctrine apply to this situation? How would you explain the concept of plain view?

Brice Horton's home for stolen jewelry. The affidavit, completed by the officer who requested the warrant, alluded to an Uzi submachine gun and a stun gun—weapons purportedly used in the jewelry robbery. It did not request that those weapons be listed on the search warrant. Officers searched the defendant's home but did not find the stolen jewelry. They did, however, seize a number of weapons, among them an Uzi, two stun guns, and a .38-caliber revolver. Horton was convicted of robbery in a trial in which the seized weapons were introduced into evidence. He appealed his conviction, claiming that officers had reason to believe that the weapons were in his home at the time of the search and were therefore not seized inadvertently. His appeal was rejected by the Court. As a result of the *Horton* case, inadvertence is no longer considered a condition necessary to ensure the legitimacy of a seizure that results when evidence other than that listed in a search warrant is discovered.

Plain-view searches present a special problem in the area of electronic evidence (which is discussed in more detail later in this chapter). If, let's say, a police officer obtains a warrant to seize and search a computer that he suspects was used to commit a particular crime, he then has easy access to other documents and information stored on that computer. An officer conducting a fraud investigation, for example, might obtain a warrant to seize a personal computer, but then will need to examine individual files on it in order to determine which ones (if any) are related to the investigation. If, however, he discovers pirated videos stored on the machine, he can then generally charge the owner of the computer with illegally copying the digital media

emergency search A search conducted by the police without a warrant, which is justified on the basis of some immediate and overriding need, such as public safety, the likely escape of a dangerous suspect, or the removal or destruction of evidence.

because it is protected by copyright law. Consequently, some legal experts have called for limiting the range of potential types of prosecution available in such cases—and confining them to the offense specified in the original warrant.[47] That no such limitations are currently in place has prompted some commentators to propose "statutory solutions eliminating plain view for computer searches."[48] Read about some proposals at **http://www.harvardlawreview.org/media/pdf/kerr.pdf.**

Emergency Searches of Property and Emergency Entry

Certain emergencies may justify a police officer's decision to search or enter premises without a warrant. In 2006, for example, in the case of *Brigham City* v. *Stuart*,[49] the Court recognized the need for emergency warrantless entries under certain circumstances when it ruled that police officers "may enter a home without a warrant when they have an objectively reasonable basis for believing that an occupant is seriously injured or imminently threatened with such injury." The case involved police entry into a private home to break up a fight.

According to the Legal Counsel Division of the Federal Bureau of Investigation (FBI), there are three threats that "provide justification for emergency warrantless action":[50] clear dangers (1) to life, (2) of escape, and (3) of the removal or destruction of evidence. Any one of these situations may create an exception to the Fourth Amendment's requirement of a search warrant.

Emergency searches, or those conducted without a warrant when special needs arise, are legally termed *exigent circumstances searches*. When emergencies necessitate a quick search of premises, however, law enforcement officers are responsible for demonstrating that a dire situation existed that justified their actions. Failure to do so successfully in court will, of course, taint any seized evidence and make it unusable.

The U.S. Supreme Court first recognized the need for emergency searches in 1967 in the case of *Warden* v. *Hayden*.[51] In that case, the Court approved the warrantless search of a residence following reports that an armed robber had fled into the building. In *Hayden*,[52] the Supreme Court held that "the Fourth Amendment does not require police officers to delay in the course of an investigation if to do so would gravely endanger their lives or the lives of others."[53]

Certain emergencies may justify a police officer's decision to search or enter premises without a warrant.

A 1990 decision, rendered in the case of *Maryland* v. *Buie*,[54] extended the authority of police to search locations in a house where a potentially dangerous person could hide while an arrest warrant is being served. The *Buie* decision was meant primarily to protect investigators from potential danger and can apply even when officers lack a warrant, probable cause, or even reasonable suspicion.

In 1995, in the case of *Wilson* v. *Arkansas*,[55] the U.S. Supreme Court ruled that police officers generally must knock and announce their identity before entering a dwelling or other premises, even when armed with a search warrant. Under certain emergency circumstances, however, exceptions may be made, and officers may not need to knock or to identify themselves before entering.[56] In *Wilson*, the Court added that the Fourth Amendment requirement that searches be reasonable "should not be read to mandate a rigid rule of announcement that ignores countervailing law enforcement interests." Hence, officers need not announce themselves, the Court said, when suspects may be in the process of destroying evidence, officers are pursuing a recently escaped arrestee, or officers' lives may be endangered by such an announcement. Because the *Wilson* case involved an appeal from a drug dealer who was apprehended by police officers who entered her unlocked house while she was flushing marijuana down a toilet, some said that it establishes a "drug-law exception" to the knock-and-announce requirement.

In 1997, in *Richards* v. *Wisconsin*,[57] the Supreme Court clarified its position on "no knock" exceptions, saying that individual courts have the duty in each case to "determine whether the facts and circumstances of the particular entry justified dispensing with the requirement." The Court went on to say that "[a] 'no knock' entry is justified when the police have a reasonable suspicion that knocking and announcing their presence, under the particular circumstances, would be dangerous or futile, or that it would inhibit the effective investigation of the crime. This standard strikes the appropriate balance," said the Court, "between the legitimate law enforcement concerns at issue in the execution of search warrants and the individual privacy interests affected by no knock entries."

In 2001, in the case of *Illinois* v. *McArthur*,[58] the U.S. Supreme Court ruled that police officers with probable cause to believe that a home contains contraband or evidence of criminal activity may reasonably prevent a suspect found outside the home from reentering it while they apply for a search warrant; and in 2003, in a case involving drug possession, the Court held that a 15- to 20-second wait after officers knocked, announced themselves, and requested entry before breaking open a door was sufficient to satisfy Fourth Amendment requirements.[59]

■ **anticipatory warrant** A search warrant issued on the basis of probable cause to believe that evidence of a crime, while not presently at the place described, will likely be there when the warrant is executed.

■ **arrest** The act of taking an adult or juvenile into physical custody by authority of law for the purpose of charging the person with a criminal offense, a delinquent act, or a status offense, terminating with the recording of a specific offense. Technically, an arrest occurs whenever a law enforcement officer curtails a person's freedom to leave.

In the 2006 case of *Hudson* v. *Michigan*,[60] the Court surprised many when it ruled that evidence found by police officers who enter a home to execute a warrant without first following the knock-and-announce requirement can be used at trial despite that constitutional violation. In the words of the Court, "The interests protected by the knock-and-announce rule include human life and limb (because an unannounced entry may provoke violence from a surprised resident), property (because citizens presumably would open the door upon an announcement, whereas a forcible entry may destroy it), and privacy and dignity of the sort that can be offended by a sudden entrance." But, said the Court, "the rule has never protected one's interest in preventing the government from seeing or taking evidence described in a warrant." The justices reasoned that the social costs of strictly adhering to the knock-and-announce rule are considerable and may include "the grave adverse consequence that excluding relevant incriminating evidence always entails—the risk of releasing dangerous criminals." In a ruling that some said signaled a new era of lessened restraints on the police, the Court's majority opinion said that since the interests violated by ignoring the knock-and-announce rule "have nothing to do with the seizure of the evidence, the exclusionary rule is inapplicable."

In 2011, in the case of *Kentucky* v. *King*, the U.S. Supreme Court overruled a Kentucky Supreme Court decision and found that Lexington, Kentucky, police officers had legally entered a suspected drug dealer's apartment without a warrant when they smelled marijuana outside the residence.[61] After knocking loudly and announcing their presence, the officers heard noises coming from inside the apartment that they believed indicated the destruction of evidence. They then kicked in the door and saw evidence of drug use in plain view. Writing for the majority, Justice Samuel Alito said, "Occupants who choose not to stand on their constitutional rights but instead elect to attempt to destroy evidence have only themselves to blame for the warrantless exigent-circumstances search that may ensue." Learn more about another type of exception to the exclusionary rule via **http://www.justicestudies.com/pubs/emergency.pdf**.

Anticipatory Warrants

Anticipatory warrants are search warrants issued on the basis of probable cause to believe that evidence of a crime, although not presently at the place described, will likely be there when the warrant is executed. Such warrants anticipate the presence of contraband or other evidence of criminal culpability but do not claim that the evidence is present at the time that the warrant is requested or issued.

Anticipatory warrants are no different in principle from ordinary search warrants. They require an issuing magistrate to determine (1) that it is probable that (2) contraband, evidence of a crime, or a fugitive will be on the described premises (3) when the warrant is executed.

The constitutionality of anticipatory warrants was affirmed in 2006 in the U.S. Supreme Court case of *U.S.* v. *Grubbs*.[62] In *Grubbs*, an anticipatory search warrant had been issued for Grubbs's house based on a federal officer's affidavit stating that the warrant would not be executed until a parcel containing a videotape of child pornography—which Grubbs had ordered from an undercover postal inspector—was received at and physically taken into his residence. After the package was delivered, law enforcement officers executed the anticipatory search warrant, seized the videotape, and arrested Grubbs.

Arrest

Officers seize not only property but people as well—a process referred to as *arrest*. Although many people think of arrest in terms of what they see on popular TV crime shows—the suspect is chased, subdued, and "cuffed" after committing a loathsome act in view of the camera—most arrests are far more mundane.

In technical terms, an **arrest** occurs whenever a law enforcement officer restricts a person's freedom to leave. There may be no yelling "You're under arrest!" No *Miranda* warnings may be offered, and in fact, the suspect may not even consider himself or herself to be in custody. Some arrests evolve as a conversation between the officer and the suspect develops. Only when the suspect tries to leave and tests the limits of the police response may the suspect discover that he or she is really in custody. In the 1980 case of *U.S.* v. *Mendenhall*,[63] Justice Potter Stewart set forth the "free to leave" test for determining whether a person has been arrested. Stewart wrote, "A person has been 'seized' within the meaning of the Fourth Amendment only if in view of all the circumstances surrounding the incident, a reasonable person would have believed that he was not free to leave." The "free to leave" test "has been repeatedly adopted by the Court as the test for a seizure."[64] In 1994, in the case of *Stansbury* v. *California*,[65] the Court once again used such a test in determining the point at which an arrest had been made. In *Stansbury*, where the focus was on the interrogation of a suspected child molester and murderer, the Court ruled, "In determining whether an individual was in custody, a court must examine all of the circumstances surrounding the interrogation, but the ultimate inquiry is simply whether there [was] a formal arrest or restraint on freedom of movement of the degree associated with a formal arrest." More recently, in 2012, Justice Samuel A. Alito, Jr., in the case of *Howes* v. *Fields*, explained that "custody is a term of art that specifies

■ **search incident to an arrest** A warrantless search of an arrested individual conducted to ensure the safety of the arresting officer. Because individuals placed under arrest may be in possession of weapons, courts have recognized the need for arresting officers to protect themselves by conducting an immediate search of arrestees without obtaining a warrant.

circumstances that are thought generally to present a serious danger of coercion."[66]

Youth and inexperience do not automatically undermine a reasonable person's ability to assess when they are free to leave. Hence, in the 2004 case of *Yarborough* v. *Alvarado*,[67] the U.S. Supreme Court found that a 17-year-old boy's two-hour interrogation in a police station without a *Miranda* advisement was not custodial, even though the boy confessed to his involvement in a murder and was later arrested. The boy, said the Court, had not actually been in police custody, even though he was in a building used by the police for questioning, because actions taken by the interviewing officer indicated that the juvenile had been free to leave. Whether a person is actually free to leave, said the Court, can be determined only by examining the totality of the circumstances surrounding the interrogation.[68]

Probable cause is the basic minimum necessary for an arrest under any circumstances.

Arrests that follow the questioning of a suspect are probably the most common type of arrest. When the decision to arrest is reached, the officer has come to the conclusion that a crime has been committed and that the suspect is probably the one who committed it. The presence of these elements constitutes the probable cause needed for an arrest. Probable cause is the basic minimum necessary for an arrest under any circumstances.

Arrests may also occur when the officer comes upon a crime in progress. Although such situations sometimes require apprehension of the offender to ensure the safety of the public, most arrests made during crimes in progress are for misdemeanors rather than felonies. In fact, many states do not allow arrest for a misdemeanor unless it is committed in the presence of an officer, since visible crimes in progress clearly provide the probable cause necessary for an arrest. In 2001, in a case that made headlines nationwide,[69] the U.S. Supreme Court upheld a warrantless arrest made by a Lago Vista, Texas, police officer for a seat belt violation. In what many saw as an unfair exercise of discretion, Patrolman Bart Turek stopped, then arrested, Gail Atwater, a young local woman whom he observed driving a pickup truck in which she and her two small children (ages three and five) were unbelted. Facts in the case showed that Turek verbally berated the woman after stopping her vehicle and that he handcuffed her, placed her in his squad car, and drove her to the local police station, where she was made to remove her shoes, jewelry, and eyeglasses and empty her pockets. Officers took her "mug shot" and placed her alone in a jail cell for about an hour, after which she was taken before a magistrate and released on $310 bond. Atwater was charged with a misdemeanor violation of Texas seat belt law. She later pleaded no contest and paid a $50 fine. Soon afterward, she and her husband filed a Section 1983 lawsuit against the officer, his department, and the police chief, alleging that the actions of the officer violated Atwater's Fourth Amendment right to be free from unreasonable seizures. The Court, however, concluded that "the Fourth Amendment does not forbid a warrantless arrest for a minor criminal offense, such as a misdemeanor seat belt violation punishable only by a fine."

Most jurisdictions allow arrest for a felony without a warrant when a crime is not in progress, as long as probable cause can be established.[70] In jurisdictions that do require a warrant, arrest warrants are issued by magistrates when police officers can demonstrate probable cause. Magistrates will usually require that the officers seeking an arrest warrant submit a written affidavit outlining their reason for the arrest. In the case of *Payton* v. *New York* (1980),[71] the U.S. Supreme Court ruled that unless the suspect gives consent or an emergency exists, an arrest warrant is necessary if an arrest requires entry into a suspect's private residence.[72] In *Payton*, the justices held that "[a]bsent exigent circumstances," the "firm line at the entrance to the house . . . may not reasonably be crossed without a warrant." The Court reiterated its *Payton* holding in the 2002 case of *Kirk* v. *Louisiana*.[73] In *Kirk*, which involved an anonymous complaint about drug sales said to be taking place in the apartment of Kennedy Kirk, the justices reaffirmed their belief that "[t]he Fourth Amendment to the United States Constitution has drawn a firm line at the entrance to the home, and thus, the police need both probable cause to either arrest or search, and exigent circumstances to justify a nonconsensual warrantless intrusion into private premises."

Searches Incident to Arrest

The U.S. Supreme Court has established that police officers, to protect themselves from attack, have the right to conduct a search of a person being arrested, regardless of gender, and to search the area under the arrestee's immediate control. This rule regarding **search incident to an arrest** was created in the *Rabinowitz* and *Chimel* cases mentioned earlier. It became firmly established in other cases involving personal searches, such as the 1973 case of *U.S.* v. *Robinson*.[74] In Robinson, the Court upheld an officer's right to conduct a search without a warrant for purposes of personal protection and to use the fruits of the search when it turns up contraband. In the words of the Court, "A custodial arrest of a suspect based upon probable cause is a

■ **reasonable suspicion** The level of suspicion that would justify an officer in making further inquiry or in conducting further investigation. Reasonable suspicion may permit stopping a person for questioning or for a simple pat-down search. Also, a belief, based on a consideration of the facts at hand and on reasonable inferences drawn from those facts, that would induce an ordinarily prudent and cautious person under the same circumstances to conclude that criminal activity is taking place or that criminal activity has recently occurred. Reasonable suspicion is a *general* and reasonable belief that a crime is in progress or has occurred, whereas probable cause is a reasonable belief that a *particular* person has committed a *specific* crime.

© Michael Matthews/Alamy

Plain-clothes police detectives searching drug suspects in Harlem, New York City. The courts have generally held that to protect themselves and the public, officers have the authority to search suspects being arrested. What are the limits of such searches?

reasonable intrusion under the Fourth Amendment; that intrusion being lawful, a search incident to the arrest requires no additional jurisdiction."[75]

The Court's decision in *Robinson* reinforced an earlier ruling in *Terry* v. *Ohio* (1968),[76] involving a seasoned officer who conducted a pat-down search of two men whom he suspected were casing a store, about to commit a robbery. The arresting officer was a 39-year veteran of police work who testified that the men "did not look right." When he approached them, he suspected they were armed. Fearing for his life, he quickly spun the men around, put them up against a wall, patted down their clothing, and found a gun on one of the men. The man, Terry, was later convicted in Ohio courts of carrying a concealed weapon.

Terry's appeal was based on the argument that the suspicious officer had no probable cause to arrest him and therefore no cause to search him. The search, he argued, was illegal, and the evidence obtained should not have been used against him. The Supreme Court disagreed, saying, "In view of these facts, we cannot blind ourselves to the need for law enforcement officers to protect themselves and other prospective victims of violence in situations where they may lack probable cause for an arrest."

The *Terry* case set the standard for a brief stop and frisk based on reasonable suspicion. Attorneys refer to such brief encounters as *Terry-type stops*. **Reasonable suspicion** can be defined as a belief, based on a consideration of the facts at hand and on reasonable inferences drawn from those facts, that would induce an ordinarily prudent and cautious person under the same circumstances to conclude that criminal activity is taking place or that criminal activity has recently occurred. It is the level of suspicion needed to justify an officer in making further inquiry or in conducting further investigation. Reasonable suspicion, which is a *general* and reasonable belief that a crime is in progress or has occurred, should be differentiated from probable cause. Probable cause, as noted earlier, is a reasonable belief that a *particular* person has committed a *specific* crime. It is important to note that the *Terry* case, for all the authority it conferred on officers, also made it clear that officers must have reasonable grounds for any stop and frisk that they conduct. Read more about the case of *Terry* v. *Ohio* at **http://tinyurl.com/yf2jhc2**.

In 1989, in the case of *U.S.* v. *Sokolow*,[77] the Supreme Court clarified the basis on which law enforcement officers, lacking probable cause to believe that a crime has occurred, may stop and briefly detain a person for investigative purposes. In *Sokolow*, the Court ruled that the legitimacy of such a stop must be evaluated according to a "totality of circumstances" criterion—in which all aspects of the defendant's behavior, taken in concert, may provide the basis for a legitimate stop based on reasonable suspicion. In this case, the defendant, Andrew Sokolow, appeared suspicious to police because, while traveling under an alias from Honolulu, he had paid $2,100 in $20 bills (from a large roll of money) for two airplane tickets after spending a surprisingly small amount of time in Miami. In addition, the defendant was obviously nervous and checked no luggage. A warrantless airport investigation by Drug Enforcement Administration (DEA) agents uncovered more than 1,000 grams of cocaine in the defendant's belongings. In upholding Sokolow's conviction, the Court ruled that although no single behavior was proof of illegal activity, taken together his behaviors created circumstances under which suspicion of illegal activity was justified.

In 2002, the Court reinforced the *Sokolow* decision in *U.S.* v. *Arvizu* when it ruled that the "balance between the public interest and the individual's right to personal security"[78] "tilts in favor of a standard less than probable cause in brief investigatory stops of persons or vehicles . . . if the officer's action is supported by reasonable suspicion to believe that criminal activity may be afoot."[79] In the words of the Court, "This process allows officers to draw on their own experiences and specialized training to make inferences from and deductions about the cumulative information available."[80]

In 1993, in the case of *Minnesota* v. *Dickerson*,[81] the U.S. Supreme Court placed new limits on an officer's ability to seize evidence discovered during a pat-down search conducted for protective reasons when the search itself was based merely on suspicion and failed to immediately reveal the presence of a weapon. In this case, the high court ruled that "if an officer lawfully pats down a suspect's outer clothing and feels an object whose contour or mass makes its identity immediately apparent, there has been no invasion of the suspect's privacy beyond that already authorized by the officer's search for weapons." However, in *Dickerson*, the justices ruled, "the officer never thought that the lump was a weapon, but did not immediately recognize it as cocaine." The lump was determined to be cocaine only after the officer "squeezed, slid, and otherwise manipulated the pocket's contents." Hence, the Court held, the officer's actions in this case did not qualify under what might be called a "plain-feel" exception. In any case, said the Court, the search in *Dickerson* went far beyond what is permissible under *Terry*, where officer safety was the crucial issue. The Court summed up its ruling in *Dickerson* this way: "While *Terry* entitled [the officer] to place his hands on respondent's jacket and to feel the lump in the pocket, his continued exploration of the pocket after he concluded that it contained no weapon was unrelated to the sole justification for the search under *Terry*" and was therefore illegal.

Just as arrest must be based on probable cause, officers may not stop and question an unwilling citizen whom they have no reason to suspect of a crime. In the case of *Brown* v. *Texas* (1979),[82] two Texas law enforcement officers stopped the defendant and asked for identification. Ed Brown, they later testified, had not been acting suspiciously, nor did they think he might have a weapon. The stop was made simply because officers wanted to know who he was. Brown was arrested under a Texas statute that required a person to identify himself properly and accurately when asked to do so by peace officers. Eventually, his appeal reached the U.S. Supreme Court, which ruled that under the circumstances of the *Brown* case, a person "may not be punished for refusing to identify himself."

In the 2004 case of *Hiibel* v. *Sixth Judicial District Court of Nevada*,[83] however, the Court upheld Nevada's "stop-and-identify" law that requires a person to identify himself to police if they encounter him under circumstances that reasonably indicate that he "has committed, is committing or is about to commit a crime." The *Hiibel* case was an extension of the reasonable suspicion doctrine set forth earlier in *Terry*.

In *Smith* v. *Ohio* (1990),[84] the Court held that an individual has the right to protect his or her belongings from unwarranted police inspection. In *Smith*, the defendant was approached by two officers in plain clothes who observed that he was carrying a brown paper bag. The officers asked him to "come here a minute" and, when he kept walking, identified themselves as police officers. The defendant threw the bag onto the hood of his car and attempted to protect it from the officers' intrusion. Marijuana was found inside the bag, and the defendant was arrested. Because there was little reason to stop the suspect in this case and because control over the bag was not thought necessary for the officers' protection, the Court found that the Fourth Amendment protects both "the traveler who carries a toothbrush and a few articles of clothing in a paper bag" and "the sophisticated executive with the locked attaché case."[85]

The following year, however, in what some Court observers saw as a turnabout, the Court ruled in *California* v. *Hodari D.* (1991)[86] that suspects who flee from the police and throw away items as they retreat may later be arrested based on the incriminating nature of the abandoned items. The significance of *Hodari* for future police action was highlighted by California prosecutors who pointed out that cases like *Hodari* occur "almost every day in this nation's urban areas."[87]

Suspects who flee from the police and throw away items as they retreat may later be arrested based on the incriminating nature of the abandoned items.

In 2000, the Court decided the case of William Wardlow.[88] Wardlow had fled upon seeing a caravan of police vehicles converge on an area of Chicago known for narcotics trafficking. Officers caught him and, searching for weapons, conducted a pat-down search of his clothing. After discovering a handgun, the officers arrested Wardlow on weapons charges, but his lawyer argued that police had acted illegally in stopping him because they did not have reasonable suspicion that he had committed an offense. The Illinois Supreme Court agreed with Wardlow's attorney, holding that "sudden flight in a high crime area does not create a reasonable suspicion justifying a *Terry* stop because flight may simply be an exercise of the right to 'go on one's way.'"[89] The case eventually reached the U.S. Supreme Court, which overturned the Illinois court, finding, instead, that the officers' actions did not violate the Fourth Amendment. In the words of the Court, "This case, involving a brief encounter between a citizen and a police officer on a public street, is governed by *Terry*, under which an officer who has a reasonable, articulable suspicion that criminal activity is afoot may conduct a brief, investigatory stop. While 'reasonable suspicion' is a less demanding standard than probable cause, there must be at least a minimal level of objective justification for the stop. An individual's presence in a 'high crime area,' standing alone, is not enough to support a reasonable, particularized suspicion of criminal activity, but a location's characteristics are relevant in determining whether the circumstances are sufficiently suspicious to warrant further investigation. . . . In this case, moreover, it was also Wardlow's unprovoked flight that aroused the officers' suspicions. Nervous, evasive behavior is another pertinent factor in determining reasonable suspicion . . . and headlong flight is the consummate act of evasion."[90]

Emergency Searches of Persons

Situations in which officers have to search people based on quick decisions do arise. An emergency search of a person may be warranted when, for example, he matches the description of an armed robber, he is found unconscious, or he has what appears to be blood on his clothes. Such searches can save lives by disarming fleeing felons or by uncovering a medical reason for an emergency situation. They may also prevent criminals from escaping or destroying evidence.

Emergency searches of persons, like those of premises, fall under the exigent circumstances exception to the warrant requirement of the Fourth Amendment. In the 1979 case of *Arkansas* v. *Sanders*,[91] the Supreme Court recognized the need for such searches "where the societal costs of obtaining a warrant, such as danger to law officers or the risk of loss or destruction of evidence, outweigh the reasons for prior recourse to a neutral magistrate."[92]

The 1987 case of *U.S.* v. *Borchardt*,[93] decided by the Fifth Circuit Court of Appeals, held that Ira Eugene Borchardt could be prosecuted for heroin uncovered during medical treatment, even though the defendant had objected to the treatment.

The Legal Counsel Division of the FBI provides the following guidelines for conducting emergency warrantless searches of individuals, where the possible destruction of evidence is at issue.[94] (Keep in mind that there may be no probable cause to *arrest* the individual being searched.) All four conditions must apply:

1. At the time of the search there was probable cause to believe that evidence was concealed on the person searched.
2. At the time of the search there was probable cause to believe an emergency threat of destruction of evidence existed.
3. The officer had no prior opportunity to obtain a warrant authorizing the search.
4. The action was no greater than necessary to eliminate the threat of destruction of evidence.

Vehicle Searches

Vehicles present a special law enforcement problem. They are highly mobile, and when a driver or an occupant is arrested, the need to search the vehicle may be immediate.

The first significant Supreme Court case involving an automobile was *Carroll* v. *U.S.*[95] in 1925, in which a divided Court ruled that a warrantless search of an automobile or other vehicle is valid if it is based on a reasonable belief that contraband is present. In 1964, however, in the case of *Preston* v. *U.S.*,[96] the limits of warrantless vehicle searches were defined. Preston was arrested for vagrancy and taken to jail. His vehicle was impounded, towed to the police garage, and later searched. Two revolvers were uncovered in the glove compartment, and more incriminating evidence was found in the trunk. Preston, convicted on weapons possession and other charges, eventually appealed to the U.S. Supreme Court. The Court held that the warrantless search of Preston's vehicle had occurred while the automobile was in secure custody and had therefore been illegal. Time and circumstances would have permitted acquisition of a warrant to conduct the search, the Court reasoned. Similarly, in 2009, the Court, in the case of *Arizona* v. *Gant*, found that vehicle searches "incident to a recent occupant's arrest" cannot be authorized without a warrant if there is "no possibility the arrestee could gain access to the vehicle at the time of the search."[97]

When the search of a vehicle occurs after it has been impounded, however, that search may be legitimate if it is undertaken for routine and reasonable purposes. In the case of *South Dakota* v. *Opperman* (1976),[98] for example, the Court held that a warrantless search undertaken for purposes of inventorying and safekeeping the personal possessions of the car's owner was not illegal. The intent of the search, which turned up marijuana, had not been to discover contraband but to secure the owner's belongings from possible theft. Again, in *Colorado* v. *Bertine* (1987),[99] the Court supported the right of officers to open closed containers found in a vehicle while conducting

■ **fleeting-targets exception** An exception to the exclusionary rule that permits law enforcement officers to search a motor vehicle based on probable cause and without a warrant. The fleeting-targets exception is predicated on the fact that vehicles can quickly leave the jurisdiction of a law enforcement agency.

a routine search for inventorying purposes. In the words of the Court, such searches are "now a well-defined exception in the warrant requirement." In 1990, however, in the precedent-setting case of *Florida* v. *Wells*,[100] the Supreme Court agreed with a lower court's suppression of marijuana evidence discovered in a locked suitcase in the trunk of a defendant's impounded vehicle. In *Wells*, the Court held that standardized criteria authorizing the search of a vehicle for inventorying purposes were necessary before such a discovery could be legitimate. Standardized criteria, said the Court, could take the form of department policies, written general orders, or established routines.

Generally speaking, where vehicles are concerned, an investigatory stop is permissible under the Fourth Amendment if supported by reasonable suspicion,[101] and a warrantless search of a stopped car is valid if it is based on probable cause.[102] Reasonable suspicion can expand into probable cause when the facts in a given situation so warrant. In the 1996 case of *Ornelas* v. *U.S.*,[103] for example, two experienced Milwaukee police officers stopped a car with California license plates that had been spotted in a motel parking lot known for drug trafficking after the Narcotics and Dangerous Drugs Information System (NADDIS) identified the car's owner as a known or suspected drug trafficker. One of the officers noticed a loose panel above an armrest in the vehicle's backseat and then searched the car. A package of cocaine was found beneath the panel, and the driver and a passenger were arrested. Following conviction, the defendants appealed to the U.S. Supreme Court, claiming that no probable cause to search the car existed at the time of the stop. The majority opinion, however, noted that in the view of the court that originally heard the case, "the model, age, and source-State origin of the car, and the fact that two men traveling together checked into a motel at 4 o'clock in the morning without reservations, formed a drug-courier profile and . . . this profile together with the [computer] reports gave rise to a reasonable suspicion of drug-trafficking activity. . . . [I]n the court's view, reasonable suspicion became probable cause when [the deputy] found the loose panel."[104] Probable cause permits a warrantless search of a vehicle because it can quickly be driven out of a jurisdiction. This exception to the exclusionary rule is called the **fleeting-targets exception**.[105]

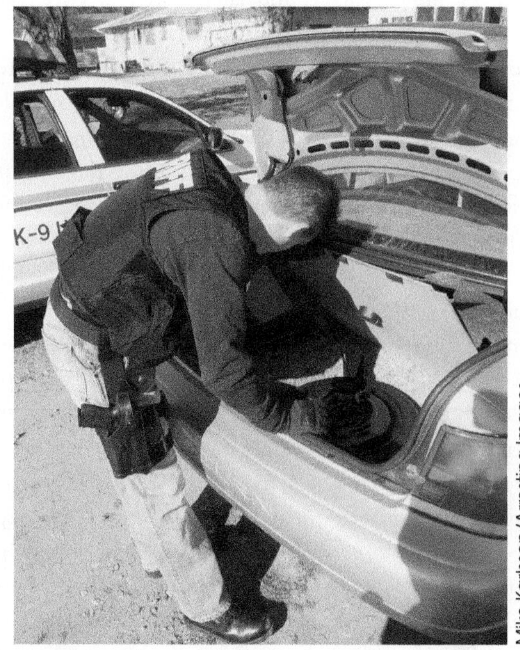

Mike Karlsson/Arresting Images

A police officer searching a vehicle in San Diego, California. Warrantless vehicle searches, where the driver is suspected of a crime, have generally been justified by the fact that vehicles are highly mobile and can quickly leave police jurisdiction. Can passengers in the vehicle also be searched?

Warrantless vehicle searches can extend to any area of the vehicle if officers have probable cause to conduct a purposeful search or if officers have been given permission to search the vehicle. In the 1991 case of *Florida* v. *Jimeno*,[106] arresting officers stopped a motorist who gave them permission to search his car. A bag on the floor of the car was found to contain cocaine, and the defendant was later convicted on a drug charge. On appeal to the U.S. Supreme Court, however, he argued that the permission given to search his car did not extend to bags and other items within the car. In a decision that may have implications beyond vehicle searches, the Court held that "[a] criminal suspect's Fourth Amendment right to be free from unreasonable searches is not violated when, after he gives police permission to search his car, they open a closed container found within the car that might reasonably hold the object of the search. The amendment is satisfied when, under the circumstances, it is objectively reasonable for the police to believe that the scope of the suspect's consent permitted them to open the particular container."[107]

In *U.S.* v. *Ross* (1982),[108] the Court found that officers had not exceeded their authority in opening a bag in the defendant's trunk that was found to contain heroin. The search was held to be justifiable on the basis of information developed from a search of the passenger compartment. The Court said, "If probable cause justifies the search of a lawfully stopped vehicle, it justifies the search of every part of the vehicle and its contents that may conceal the object of the search."[109] Moreover, according to the 1996 U.S. Supreme Court decision in *Whren* v. *U.S.*,[110] officers may stop a vehicle being driven suspiciously and then search it once probable cause has developed, even if their primary assignment centers on duties other than traffic enforcement or "if a reasonable officer would not have stopped the motorist absent some additional law enforcement objective" (which in the *Whren* case was drug enforcement).

Motorists and their passengers may be ordered out of stopped vehicles in the interest of officer safety, and any evidence developed as a result of such a procedure may be used in court.[111] In 1997, for example, in the case of *Maryland* v. *Wilson*,[112] the U.S. Supreme Court overturned a decision by a Maryland court that held that crack cocaine found during a traffic stop was seized illegally when it fell from the lap of a passenger ordered out of a stopped vehicle by a Maryland state trooper. The Supreme Court cited concerns for officer safety and held that the activities of passengers are subject to police control. Similarly, in 2007, in the case of *People* v. *Brendlin*, the Court ruled that passengers in stopped vehicles are necessarily detained as a result of the stop, and that they should expect that, for safety reasons, officers will exercise "unquestioned police command" over them for the duration of the stop.

In 1998, however, the U.S. Supreme Court placed clear limits on warrantless vehicle searches. In the case of *Knowles* v. *Iowa*,[113] an Iowa police officer stopped Patrick Knowles for speeding, issued him a citation, but did not make a custodial arrest. The officer then conducted a full search of his car without Knowles's consent and without probable cause. Marijuana was found, and Knowles was arrested. At the time, Iowa state law gave officers authority to conduct full-blown automobile searches when issuing only a citation. The Supreme Court found, however, that while concern for officer safety during a routine traffic stop may justify the minimal intrusion of ordering a driver and passengers out of a car, it does not by itself justify what it called "the considerably greater intrusion attending a full field-type search." Hence, whereas a search incident to arrest may be justifiable in the eyes of the Court, a search incident to citation clearly is not.

In the 1999 case of *Wyoming* v. *Houghton*,[114] the Court ruled that police officers with probable cause to search a car may inspect any passengers' belongings found in the car that are capable of concealing the object of the search. *Thornton* v. *U.S.* (2004) established the authority of arresting officers to search a car without a warrant even if the driver had previously exited the vehicle.[115]

In 2005, in the case of *Illinois* v. *Caballes*,[116] the Court held that the use of a drug-sniffing dog during a routine and lawful traffic stop is permissible and may not even be a search within the meaning of the Fourth Amendment. In writing for the majority, Justice John Paul Stevens said that "the use of a well-trained narcotics-detection dog—one that does not expose noncontraband items that otherwise would remain hidden from public view—during a lawful traffic stop generally does not implicate legitimate privacy interests."

Finally, in 2011, the Court created a good-faith exception to the exclusionary rule applicable to a search that was authorized by precedent at the time of the search but which was a type of search that was subsequently ruled unconstitutional. In that case, *Davis* v. *U.S.*, Willie Gene Davis was a passenger in a car stopped for a traffic violation in 2007.[117] He subsequently gave officers a false name, and was arrested for giving false information to a police officer. The vehicle in which he was riding was searched, and officers discovered a handgun in Davis's jacket, which he had left on the seat. Davis was charged and convicted for possession of an illegal weapon. Later, however, the U.S. Court of Appeals for the Eleventh Circuit found that the search was illegal, based on a previous Supreme Court ruling in the 2009 case of *Arizona* v. *Gant*.[118] Nonetheless, the lower court upheld Davis's conviction because the *Gant* ruling came after Davis's arrest. The Supreme Court agreed, saying "Searches conducted in objectively reasonable reliance on binding appellate precedent are not subject to the exclusionary rule."

Roadblocks and Motor Vehicle Checkpoints

The Fourth and Fourteenth Amendments to the U.S. Constitution guarantee liberty and personal security to all people residing within the United States. Courts have generally held that, in the absence of probable cause to believe that a crime has been committed, police officers have no legitimate authority to detain or arrest people who are going about their business in a peaceful manner. In a number of instances, however, the U.S. Supreme Court has decided that community interests may necessitate a temporary suspension of personal liberty, even when probable cause is lacking. One such case is *Michigan Dept. of State Police* v. *Sitz* (1990),[119] which involved the legality of highway sobriety checkpoints, including those at which nonsuspicious drivers are subjected to scrutiny. In *Sitz*, the Court ruled that such stops are reasonable insofar as they are essential to the welfare of the community as a whole.

> The Fourth and Fourteenth Amendments to the U.S. Constitution guarantee liberty and personal security to all people residing within the United States.

In a second case, *U.S.* v. *Martinez-Fuerte* (1976),[120] the Court upheld brief suspicionless seizures at a fixed international checkpoint designed to intercept illegal aliens. The Court noted that "to require that such stops always be based on reasonable suspicion would be impractical because the flow of traffic tends to be too heavy to allow the particularized study of a given car necessary to identify it as a possible carrier of illegal aliens. Such a requirement also would largely eliminate any deterrent to the conduct of well-disguised smuggling operations, even though smugglers are known to use these highways regularly."[121]

CJ | CAREERS
Patrol Officer

Name. Timothy D. Radtke

Position. Patrol officer, San Diego, California

Colleges attended. Winona State University (BS), University of Nevada–Las Vegas (MA)

Major. Criminal justice

Year hired. 2008

Please give a brief description of your job. Within a specified area of the city, I respond to radio calls for police service and perform self-initiated activities such as traffic stops and citizen contacts.

What appealed to you most about the position when you applied for it? While pursuing my degrees I worked closely with two police departments. The officers there inspired me to commit my life to a cause greater than myself—protecting communities. I was eager to put the knowledge I obtained through my education to practical use, to work closely with the community and apply the community-oriented policing and problem-oriented policing strategies I learned during my academic studies.

How would you describe the interview process? The testing process was strenuous. There were eight different tests: written test, preinvestigation questionnaire, physical ability test, comprehensive background investigation, polygraph, appointing authority interview, psychological screening, and medical exam.

The most challenging was the appointing authority interview, which was conducted by a lieutenant and a sergeant. They asked questions about my background and what I had done to prepare to serve as a police officer. I was asked to respond to a series of scenarios that police officers often encounter in the field. This process helped them determine whether I could quickly find a logical and appropriate response when presented with an unexpected or stressful situation.

What is a typical day like? Patrol officers begin with "lineup," in which they are briefed about recent crimes and events and assigned to the specific patrol beat they will work throughout their shift. Patrol officers must be prepared to handle the unexpected. One day they may respond to a domestic disturbance, the next help establish a driving under the influence (DUI) checkpoint to deter drunk drivers, and the next be asked to locate warrant suspects.

What qualities/characteristics are most helpful for this job? A successful officer must know how to speak with people. The people [the officer interacts] with daily often need immediate help or have difficulty controlling their emotions. An officer may be faced with an individual who is attempting suicide or an individual who is angry and showing signs of assaultive behavior, or [the officer may be] called upon to interview a child who has suffered abuse. The ability to speak tactfully and quickly build rapport with others is crucial.

What is a typical starting salary? Between \$40,000 and \$50,000.

What is the salary potential as you move up into higher-level jobs? An officer's salary will increase after graduating from the academy and when promoted within the department. Those with an BA or MA will also receive percentage increases in pay.

What career advice would you give someone in college beginning studies in criminal justice? Classroom instruction in college will help students understand the basics of police work and give them the skills to interpret and appropriately apply laws. It will also increase students' problem-solving and critical thinking skills, which are necessary for finding solutions to the complex problems officers encounter daily.

In fact, in 2004, in the case of *Illinois* v. *Lidster*,[122] the Court held that information-seeking highway roadblocks are permissible. The stop in *Lidster*, said the Court, was permissible because its intent was merely to solicit motorists' help in solving a crime. "The law," said the Court, "ordinarily permits police to seek the public's voluntary cooperation in a criminal investigation."

Watercraft and Motor Homes

The 1983 case of *U.S.* v. *Villamonte-Marquez*[123] widened the *Carroll* decision (the first U.S. Supreme Court case involving a vehicle, which was discussed earlier) to include watercraft. In this case, the Court reasoned that a vehicle on the water can easily leave the jurisdiction of enforcement officials, just as a car or truck can.

In *California* v. *Carney* (1985),[124] the Court extended police authority to conduct warrantless searches of vehicles to include motor homes. Earlier arguments had been advanced that a motor home, because it is more like a permanent residence than a vehicle, should not be considered a vehicle for purposes of search and seizure. In a 6–3 decision, the Court rejected those arguments, reasoning that a vehicle's appointments and size do not alter its basic function of providing transportation.

Houseboats were brought under the automobile exception to the Fourth Amendment warrant requirement in the 1988 Tenth Circuit Court case of *U.S.* v. *Hill*.[125] Learn about vehicle pursuits and the Fourth Amendment at **http://www.justicestudies.com/pubs/veh_pursuits.pdf**

■ **compelling interest** A legal concept that provides a basis for suspicionless searches when public safety is at stake. (Urinalysis tests of train engineers are an example.) It is the concept on which the U.S. Supreme Court cases of *Skinner* v. *Railway Labor Executives' Association* (1989) and *National Treasury Employees Union* v. *Von Raab* (1989) turned. In those cases, the Court held that public safety may sometimes provide a sufficiently compelling interest to justify limiting an individual's right to privacy.

■ **suspicionless search** A search conducted by law enforcement personnel without a warrant and without suspicion. Suspicionless searches are permissible only if based on an overriding concern for public safety.

Suspicionless Searches

In two 1989 decisions, the U.S. Supreme Court ruled for the first time that there may be instances when the need to ensure public safety provides a **compelling interest** that negates the rights of any individual to privacy, permitting **suspicionless searches**—those that occur when a person is not suspected of a crime. In the case of *National Treasury Employees Union* v. *Von Raab* (1989),[126] the Court, by a 5–4 vote, upheld a program of the U.S. Customs Service that required mandatory drug testing for all workers seeking promotions or job transfers involving drug interdiction and the carrying of firearms. The Court's majority opinion read, "We think the government's need to conduct the suspicionless searches required by the Customs program outweighs the privacy interest of employees engaged directly in drug interdiction, and of those who otherwise are required to carry firearms."

The second case, *Skinner* v. *Railway Labor Executives' Association* (1989),[127] was decided on the same day. In *Skinner*, the justices voted 7 to 2 to permit the mandatory testing of railway crews for the presence of drugs or alcohol following serious train accidents. The *Skinner* case involved evidence of drugs in a 1987 train wreck outside of Baltimore, Maryland, in which 16 people were killed and hundreds were injured.

The 1991 Supreme Court case of *Florida* v. *Bostick*,[128] which permitted warrantless "sweeps" of intercity buses, moved the Court deeply into conservative territory. The *Bostick* case came to the attention of the Court as a result of the Broward County (Florida) Sheriff's Department's routine practice of boarding buses at scheduled stops and asking passengers for permission to search their bags. Terrance Bostick, a passenger on one of the buses, gave police permission to search his luggage, which was found to contain cocaine. Bostick was arrested and eventually pleaded guilty to charges of drug trafficking. The Florida Supreme Court, however, found merit in Bostick's appeal, which was based on a Fourth Amendment claim that the search of his luggage had been unreasonable. The Florida court held that "a reasonable passenger in [Bostick's] situation would not have felt free to leave the bus to avoid questioning by the police," and it overturned the conviction.

The state appealed to the U.S. Supreme Court, which held that the Florida Supreme Court had erred in interpreting Bostick's *feelings* that he was not free to leave the bus. In the words of the Court, "Bostick was a passenger on a bus that was scheduled to depart. He would not have felt free to leave the bus even if the police had not been present. Bostick's movements were 'confined' in a sense, but this was the natural result of his decision to take the bus." In other words, Bostick was constrained not so much by police action as by his own feelings that he might miss the bus were he to get off. Following this line of reasoning, the Court concluded that warrantless, suspicionless "sweeps" of buses, "trains, planes, and city streets" are permissible as long as officers (1) ask individual passengers for permission before searching their possessions, (2) do not coerce passengers to consent to a search, and (3) do not convey the message that citizen compliance with the search request is mandatory. Passenger compliance with police searches must be voluntary for the searches to be legal.

In contrast to the tone of Court decisions more than two decades earlier, the justices did not require officers to inform passengers that they were free to leave nor that they had the right to deny officers the opportunity to search (although Bostick himself was so advised by Florida officers). Any reasonable person, the Court ruled, should feel free to deny the police request. In the words of the Court, "The appropriate test is whether, taking into account all of the circumstances surrounding the encounter, a reasonable passenger would feel free to decline the officers' requests or otherwise terminate the encounter." The Court continued, "Rejected, however, is Bostick's argument that he must have been seized because no reasonable person would freely consent to a search of luggage containing drugs, since the 'reasonable person' test presumes an innocent person."

Critics of the decision saw it as creating new "gestapo-like" police powers in the face of which citizens on public transportation will feel compelled to comply with police requests for search authority. Dissenting Justices Harry Blackmun, John Paul Stevens, and Thurgood Marshall held that "the bus sweep at issue in this case violates the core values of the Fourth Amendment." The Court's majority, however, defended its ruling by writing, "[T]he Fourth Amendment proscribes unreasonable searches and seizures; it does not proscribe voluntary cooperation." In mid-2000, however, in the case of *Bond* v. *U.S.*[129] the Court ruled that physical manipulation of a carry-on bag in the possession of a bus passenger without the owner's consent violates the Fourth Amendment's proscription against unreasonable searches.

In the case of *U.S.* v. *Drayton* (2002),[130] the U.S. Supreme Court reiterated its position that police officers are not required to advise bus passengers of their right to refuse to cooperate with officers conducting searches or of their right to refuse to be searched.

In 2004, the Court made it clear that suspicionless searches of vehicles at our nation's borders are permitted, even when the searches are extensive. In the case of *U.S.* v. *Flores-Montano*,[131] customs officials disassembled the gas tank of a car belonging to a man entering the country from Mexico and found that it contained 37 kilograms of marijuana. Although the officers admitted that their actions were not motivated by any particular belief that the search would reveal contraband, the Court held that Congress has always granted "plenary authority to conduct routine searches and seizures at the border without probable cause or a warrant." In the words of the Court, "the Government's authority to conduct suspicionless inspections at the border includes the authority to remove, disassemble and reassemble a vehicle's fuel tank." Learn more about public-safety exceptions to *Miranda* at **http://www.justicestudies.com/pubs/psafety.pdf**.

High-Technology Searches

The burgeoning use of high technology to investigate crime and to uncover violations of the criminal law is forcing courts throughout the nation to evaluate the applicability of constitutional guarantees in light of high-tech searches and seizures. In 1996, the California appellate court decision in *People* v. *Deutsch*[132] presaged the kinds of issues that are being encountered as American law enforcement expands its use of cutting-edge technology. In *Deutsch*, judges faced the question of whether a warrantless scan of a private dwelling with a thermal-imaging device constitutes an unreasonable search within the meaning of the Fourth Amendment. Such devices (also called *forward-looking infrared [FLIR] systems*) measure radiant energy in the radiant heat portion of the electromagnetic spectrum[133] and display their readings as thermographs. The "heat picture" that a thermal imager produces can be used, as it was in the case of Dorian Deutsch, to reveal unusually warm areas or rooms that might be associated with the cultivation of drug-bearing plants, such as marijuana. Two hundred cannabis plants, which were being grown hydroponically under high-wattage lights in two walled-off portions of Deutsch's home, were seized following an exterior thermal scan of her home by a police officer who drove by at 1:30 in the morning. Because no entry of the house was anticipated during the search, the officer had acted without a search warrant. The California court ruled that the scan was an illegal search because "society accepts a reasonable expectation of privacy" surrounding "nondisclosed activities within the home."[134]

In a similar case, *Kyllo* v. *U.S.* (2001),[135] the U.S. Supreme Court reached much the same conclusion. Based on the results of a warrantless search conducted by officers using a thermal-imaging device, investigators applied for a search warrant of Kyllo's home. The subsequent search uncovered more than 100 marijuana plants that were being grown under bright lights. In overturning Kyllo's conviction on drug-manufacturing charges, the Court held, "Where, as here, the Government uses a device that is not in general public use, to explore details of a private home that would previously have been unknowable without physical intrusion, the surveillance is a Fourth Amendment 'search,' and is presumptively unreasonable without a warrant."[136]

Learn more about the issues surrounding search and seizure at **http://caselaw.lp.findlaw.com/data/constitution/amendment04**.

The Intelligence Function

In law enforcement parlance, useful information is known as *intelligence*, and the need for intelligence leads police investigators to question both suspects and informants—and even more often, potentially knowledgeable citizens who may have been witnesses or victims. Data gathering is a crucial form of intelligence; without it, enforcement agencies would be virtually powerless to plan and effect arrests.

The importance of gathering intelligence in police work cannot be overstressed.

The importance of gathering intelligence in police work cannot be overstressed. Studies have found that the one factor most likely to lead to arrest in serious crimes is the presence of a witness who can provide information to the police. Undercover operations, neighborhood watch programs, "crime stopper" groups, and organized detective work all contribute this vital information.

Informants

Information gathering is a complex process, and many ethical questions have been raised about the techniques police use to gather information. The use of paid informants, for example, is an area of concern to ethicists who believe that informants are often paid while getting away with minor crimes that investigators are willing to overlook. Another concern is the police practice (endorsed by some prosecutors) of agreeing not to charge one offender out of a group if he or she will "talk" and testify against the others.

As we have seen, probable cause is an important aspect of both police searches and legal arrests. The successful use of informants in supporting requests for a warrant depends on the demonstrable reliability of their information. The case of *Aguilar* v. *Texas* (1964)[137] clarified the use of informants and established a two-pronged test. The U.S. Supreme Court ruled that informant information can establish probable cause if both of the following criteria are met:

1. The source of the informant's information is made clear.
2. The police officer has a reasonable belief that the informant is reliable.

interrogation The information-gathering activity of police officers that involves the direct questioning of suspects.

The two-pronged test of *Aguilar* v. *Texas* was intended to prevent the issuance of warrants on the basis of false or fabricated information. The case of *U.S.* v. *Harris* (1971)[138] provided an exception to the two-pronged *Aguilar* test. The *Harris* case recognized the fact that when an informant provides information that is damaging to him or her, it is probably true. In *Harris*, an informant told police that he had purchased non-tax-paid whiskey from another person. Because the information also implicated the informant in a crime, it was held to be accurate, even though it could not meet the second prong of the *Aguilar* test. "Admissions of crime," said the Court, "carry their own indicia of credibility—sufficient at least to support a finding of probable cause to search."[139]

In 1983, in the case of *Illinois* v. *Gates*,[140] the Court adopted a totality-of-circumstances approach and held that sufficient probable cause for issuing a warrant exists where an informant can be reasonably believed on the basis of everything that the police know. The *Gates* case involved an anonymous informant who provided incriminating information about another person through a letter to the police. Although the source of the information was not stated and the police were unable to say whether the informant was reliable, the overall sense of things, given what was already known to police, was that the information supplied was probably valid. In *Gates*, the Court held that probable cause exists when "there is a fair probability that contraband or evidence of a crime will be found in a particular place."

In the 1990 case of *Alabama* v. *White*,[141] the Supreme Court ruled that an anonymous tip, even in the absence of other corroborating information about a suspect, could form the basis for an investigatory stop if the informant accurately predicted the *future* behavior of the suspect. The Court reasoned that the ability to predict a suspect's behavior demonstrates a significant degree of familiarity with the suspect's affairs. In the words of the Court, "Because only a small number of people are generally privy to an individual's itinerary, it is reasonable for the police to believe that a person with access to such information is likely to also have access to reliable information about that individual's illegal activities."[142]

In 2000, in the case of *Florida* v. *J. L.*,[143] the Court held that an anonymous tip that a person is carrying a gun does not, without more evidence, justify a police officer's stop and frisk of that person. Ruling that such a search is invalid under the Fourth Amendment, the Court rejected the suggestion of a firearm exception to the general stop-and-frisk rule.[144] The identity of informants may be kept secret only if sources have been explicitly assured of confidentiality by investigating officers or if a reasonably implied assurance of confidentiality has been made. In *U.S. Dept. of Justice* v. *Landano* (1993),[145] the U.S. Supreme Court required that an informant's identity be revealed through a request made under the federal Freedom of Information Act. In that case, the FBI had not specifically assured the informant of confidentiality, and the Court ruled that "the government is not entitled to a presumption that all sources supplying information to the FBI in the course of a criminal investigation are confidential sources."

Police Interrogation

In 2003, Illinois became the first state in the nation to require the electronic recording of police interrogations and confessions in homicide cases.[146] State lawmakers hoped that the use of recordings would reduce the incidence of false confessions as well as the likelihood of convictions based on such confessions. Under the law, police interrogators must create videotape or audiotape recordings of any questioning of suspects. The law prohibits the courtroom introduction of statements and confessions that have not been taped. Proponents of the law say that it will prevent the police intimidation of murder suspects and will put an end to coerced confessions.

Some argue that the mandatory recording of police interrogations offers overwhelming benefits at minimal cost. "By creating an objective and reviewable record," says Richard A. Leo of the University of San Francisco Law School, "electronic recording promotes truth-finding in the criminal process, relegates 'swearing contests' to the past, and saves scarce resources at multiple levels of the criminal justice system."[147] According to Leo, requiring that all interrogations be recorded will benefit police and prosecutors by increasing the accuracy of confessions and convictions and "will also reduce the number of police-induced false confessions and the wrongful convictions they cause."

The U.S. Supreme Court has defined **interrogation** as any behaviors by the police "that the police should know are reasonably likely to elicit an incriminating response from the suspect."[148] Hence interrogation may involve activities that go well beyond mere verbal questioning, and the Court has held that interrogation may include "staged lineups, reverse lineups, positing guilt, minimizing the moral seriousness of crime, and casting blame on the victim or society" (Figure 7-2). The Court has also held that "police words or actions normally attendant to arrest and custody do not constitute interrogation" unless they involve pointed or directed questions. Hence, an arresting officer may instruct a suspect on what to do and may chitchat with him or her without engaging in interrogation within the meaning of the law. Once police officers make inquiries intended to elicit information about the crime in question, however, interrogation has begun. The interrogation of

■ **inherent coercion** The tactics used by police interviewers that fall short of physical abuse but that nonetheless pressure suspects to divulge information.

INTERROGATION

The U.S. Supreme Court has defined interrogation as any behaviors by the police "that the police should know are reasonably likely to elicit an incriminating response from the suspect." The Court also noted that "police words or actions normally attendant to arrest and custody do not constitute interrogation" unless they involve pointed or directed questions. The interrogation of suspects, like other areas of police activity, is subject to constitutional limits as interpreted by the courts, and a series of landmark decisions by the U.S. Supreme Court has focused on police interrogations.

Physical Abuse:
The first in a series of significant cases was ***Brown* v. *Mississippi***. In 1936 the court determined that physical abuse cannot be used to obtain a confession or elicit information from a suspect.

Inherent Coercion:
In the case of ***Ashcraft* v. *Tennessee*** (1944), the U.S. Supreme Court found that interrogation involving inherent coercion was not acceptable. Inherent coercion refers to any form of nonphysical coercion, hostility, or pressure to try to force a confession from a suspect.

Psychological Manipulation:
Interrogation should not involve sophisticated trickery or manipulation. In the case of ***Arizona* v. *Fulminante*** (1991) the U.S. Supreme Court determined that it was not legal to allow an FBI informant posing as a fellow inmate to trick the suspect into a confession. Interrogators do not have to be scrupulously honest in confronting suspects, but there must be limits to the lengths that can be pursued in questioning a suspect.

Right to Lawyer at Interrogation:
Escobedo* v. *Illinois (1964) and ***Minnick* v. *Mississippi*** (1990).

FIGURE 7-2 | Police Interrogation

suspects, like other areas of police activity, is subject to constitutional limits as interpreted by the courts, and a series of landmark decisions by the U.S. Supreme Court has focused on police interrogation.

Physical Abuse

The first in a series of significant cases regarding police interrogation was *Brown* v. *Mississippi*,[149] decided in 1936. The *Brown* case began with the murder of a white store owner in Mississippi in 1934 during a robbery. A posse formed and went to the home of a local African American man rumored to have been one of the perpetrators. They dragged the suspect from his home, put a rope around his neck, and hoisted and lowered him from a tree a number of times, hoping to get a confession from the man, but failing. The posse was headed by a deputy sheriff who then arrested other suspects in the case and laid them over chairs in the local jail and whipped them with belts and buckles until they "confessed." These confessions were used in the trial that followed, and all three defendants were convicted of murder. Their convictions were upheld by the Mississippi Supreme Court. In 1936, however, the case was reviewed by the U.S. Supreme Court, which overturned all of the convictions, saying that it was difficult to imagine techniques of interrogation more "revolting" to the sense of justice than those used in this case.

Inherent Coercion

Interrogation need not involve physical abuse for it to be contrary to constitutional principles. In the case of *Ashcraft* v. *Tennessee* (1944),[150] the U.S. Supreme Court found that interrogation involving **inherent coercion** was not acceptable. Ashcraft had been charged with the murder of his wife, Zelma. He was arrested on a Saturday night and interrogated by relays of skilled interrogators until Monday morning, when he purportedly made a statement implicating himself in the murder. During questioning, he had faced a blinding light but was not physically mistreated. Investigators later testified that when the suspect requested cigarettes, food, or water, they "kindly"

■ **psychological manipulation** Manipulative actions by police interviewers that are designed to pressure suspects to divulge information and that are based on subtle forms of intimidation and control.

provided them. The Court's ruling, which reversed Ashcraft's conviction, made it plain that the Fifth Amendment guarantee against self-incrimination excludes any form of official coercion or pressure during interrogation.

A similar case, *Chambers* v. *Florida*, was decided in 1940.[151] In that case, four black men were arrested without warrants as suspects in the robbery and murder of an aged white man. After several days of questioning in a hostile atmosphere, the men confessed to the murder. The confessions were used as the primary evidence against them at their trial, and all four were sentenced to die. On appeal, the U.S. Supreme Court held that "the very circumstances surrounding their confinement and their questioning without any formal charges having been brought, were such as to fill petitioners with terror and frightful misgivings."[152] Learn more about the case of *Chambers* v. *Florida* at **http://tinyurl.com/4uy3c2w**.

Psychological Manipulation

Not only must interrogation be free of coercion and hostility, but it also cannot involve sophisticated trickery designed to ferret out a confession. Interrogators do not necessarily have to be scrupulously honest in confronting suspects, and the expert opinions of medical and psychiatric practitioners may be sought in investigations. However, the use of professionals skilled in **psychological manipulation** to gain confessions was banned by the Court in the case of *Leyra* v. *Denno*[153] in 1954, during the heyday of psychiatric perspectives on criminal behavior.

In 1991, in the case of *Arizona* v. *Fulminante*,[154] the U.S. Supreme Court further curtailed the use of sophisticated techniques to gain a confession. Oreste Fulminante was an inmate in a federal prison when he was approached by a fellow inmate who was an FBI informant. The informant told Fulminante that other inmates were plotting to kill him because of a rumor that he had killed a child. The informant offered to protect Fulminante if he divulged the details of his crime. Fulminante then described his role in the murder of his 11-year-old stepdaughter. He was charged with that murder, tried, and convicted.

Not only must interrogation be free of coercion and hostility, but it also cannot involve sophisticated trickery designed to ferret out a confession.

On appeal to the U.S. Supreme Court, Fulminante's lawyers argued that their client's confession had been coerced because of the threat of violence communicated by the informant. The Court agreed that the confession had been coerced and ordered a new trial at which the confession could not be admitted into evidence. Simultaneously, however, the Court found that the admission of a coerced confession should be considered a harmless "trial error" that need not necessarily result in reversal of a conviction if other evidence still proves guilt. The decision was especially significant because it partially reversed the Court's earlier ruling, in *Chapman* v. *California* (1967),[155] where it was held that forced confessions were such a basic form of constitutional error that they automatically invalidated any conviction to which they related. Fulminante was convicted again at his second trial, where his confession was not entered into evidence, and he was sentenced to die. The Arizona Supreme Court, however, overturned his conviction, ruling that testimony describing statements the victim had made about fearing for her life prior to her murder, and which had been entered into evidence, were hearsay and had prejudiced the jury.[156]

Finally, the area of eyewitness identification bears discussion. In 2011, in the case of *State* v. *Henderson*,[157] the New Jersey Supreme Court held that the current legal standard for assessing eyewitness identifications must be revised because it did not offer adequate measures for reliability; did not sufficiently deter inappropriate police conduct; and overstated the jury's ability to evaluate identification evidence.

In 2012, in the case of *Perry* v. New *Hampshire*,[158] the U.S. Supreme Court recognized problems with eyewitness identification, especially when such identification is obtained by skilled law enforcement interrogators. Still, the court denied that the due process clause of the U.S. Constitution requires a preliminary judicial inquiry into the reliability of an eyewitness identification when the identification was not procured under unnecessarily suggestive circumstances arranged by law enforcement.

Learn more about detecting deception from the FBI at **http://www.justicestudies.com/pdf/truth_deception.pdf**.

The Right to a Lawyer at Interrogation

In 1964, in the case of *Escobedo* v. *Illinois*,[159] the right to have legal counsel present during police interrogation was formally recognized.

In 1981, the case of *Edwards* v. *Arizona*[160] established a "bright-line rule" (that is, specified a criterion that cannot be violated) for investigators to use in interpreting a suspect's right

■ ***Miranda* warnings** The advisement of rights due criminal suspects by the police before questioning begins. *Miranda* warnings were first set forth by the U.S. Supreme Court in the 1966 case of *Miranda* v. *Arizona*.

to counsel. In *Edwards*, the Supreme Court reiterated its *Miranda* concern that once a suspect who is in custody and is being questioned requests the assistance of counsel, all questioning must cease until an attorney is present. In 1990, the Court refined the rule in *Minnick* v. *Mississippi*,[161] when it held that after the suspect has had an opportunity to consult his or her lawyer, interrogation may not resume unless the lawyer is present.

The 1986 case of *Michigan* v. *Jackson*[162] provided further support for *Edwards*. In *Jackson*, the Court forbade police from initiating the interrogation of criminal defendants who have invoked their right to counsel at an arraignment or similar proceeding.

Similarly, according to *Arizona* v. *Roberson* (1988),[163] the police may not avoid the suspect's request for a lawyer by beginning a new line of questioning, even if it is about an unrelated offense.

In 1994, however, in the case of *Davis* v. *U.S.*,[164] the Court "put the burden on custodial suspects to make unequivocal invocations of the right to counsel." In the *Davis* case, a man being interrogated in the death of a sailor waived his *Miranda* rights but later said, "Maybe I should talk to a lawyer." Investigators asked the suspect clarifying questions, and he responded, "No, I don't want a lawyer." He appealed his conviction, claiming that interrogation should have ceased when he mentioned a lawyer. The Court, in affirming the conviction, stated that "it will often be good police practice for the interviewing officers to clarify whether or not [the suspect] actually wants an attorney."

In the 2009 case of *Montejo* v. *Louisiana*,[165] however, in something of an about-face, the U.S. Supreme Court held that "*Michigan* v. *Jackson* should be and now is overruled." The justices found that strict interpretations of *Jackson* could lead to practical problems. Montejo had been charged with first-degree murder, and appointment of counsel was ordered at his arraignment. He did not, however, ask to see his attorney. Later that same day, the police read Montejo his *Miranda* rights, and he agreed to accompany them on a trip to locate the murder weapon. During the trip, he wrote an incriminating letter of apology to the victim's widow. Upon returning, he met with his court-appointed attorney for the first time. At trial, his letter was admitted over defense objection, and he was convicted and sentenced to death. In the words of the Court, "Both *Edwards* and *Jackson* are meant to prevent police from badgering defendants into changing their minds about the right to counsel once they have invoked it, but a defendant who never asked for counsel has not yet made up his mind." In effect, although an attorney had been appointed to represent Montejo, he had never actually invoked his right to counsel.

Finally, in 2010, in the case of *Maryland* v. *Shatzer*,[166] the Court held that police could reopen the interrogation of a suspect who has invoked his right to counsel following a 14-day or longer break in questioning. Even though the defendant (Shatzer) had been in state prison during the break, the justices said, he had been free "from the coercive power of an interrogator" during that time.

Suspect Rights: The *Miranda* Decision

In the area of suspect rights, no case is as famous as *Miranda* v. *Arizona* (1966),[167] which established the well-known ***Miranda* warnings**. Many people regard *Miranda* as the centerpiece of the Warren Court due process rulings.

AP Wide World Photos

Ernesto Miranda, shown here after a jury convicted him for a second time. Miranda's conviction on rape and kidnapping charges after arresting officers failed to advise him of his rights led to the now-famous *Miranda* warnings. What do the *Miranda* warnings say?

The case involved Ernesto Miranda, who was arrested in Phoenix, Arizona, and was accused of having kidnapped and raped a young woman. At police headquarters, he was identified by the victim. After being interrogated for two hours, Miranda signed a confession that formed the basis of his later conviction on the charges.

On appeal, the U.S. Supreme Court rendered what some regard as the most far-reaching opinion to have affected criminal justice in the last half century. The Court ruled that Miranda's conviction was unconstitutional because "[t]he entire aura and atmosphere of police interrogation without notification of rights and an offer of assistance of counsel tends to subjugate the individual to the will of his examiner."

The Court continued, saying that the suspect "must be warned prior to any questioning that he has the right to remain silent, that anything he says can be used against him in a court of law, that he has the right to the presence of an attorney, and that if he cannot afford an attorney one will be appointed for him prior to any questioning if he so desires. Opportunity to exercise these rights must be afforded to him throughout the interrogation. After such warnings have been given, and such opportunity afforded him, the individual may knowingly and intelligently waive these rights and agree to answer the questions or make a statement. But unless and until such warnings and waiver are demonstrated by the prosecution at the trial, no evidence obtained as a result of interrogation can be used against him."

To ensure that proper advice is given to suspects at the time of their arrest, the now-famous *Miranda* rights are read before any questioning begins. These rights, as found on a *Miranda* warning card commonly used by police agencies, appear in the "CJ Issues" box.

Once suspects have been advised of their *Miranda* rights, they are commonly asked to sign a paper that lists each right, in order to confirm that they were advised of their rights and that they understand each right. Questioning may then begin, but only if suspects waive their rights not to talk and to have a lawyer present during interrogation.

In 1992, *Miranda* rights were effectively extended to illegal immigrants living in the United States. In a settlement of a class-action lawsuit against the Immigration and Naturalization Service, U.S. District Court Judge William Byrne, Jr., approved the printing of millions of notices in several languages to be given to arrestees. The approximately 1.5 million illegal aliens arrested each year must be told they may (1) talk with a lawyer, (2) make a phone call, (3) request a list of available legal services, (4) seek a hearing before an immigration judge, (5) possibly obtain release on bond, and (6) contact a diplomatic officer representing their country.[168] This was "long overdue," said Roberto Martinez of the American Friends Service Committee's Mexico–U.S. border program. "Up to now, we've had total mistreatment of civil rights of undocumented people."

When the *Miranda* decision was originally handed down, some hailed it as ensuring the protection of individual rights guaranteed under the Constitution. To guarantee those rights, they suggested, no better agency is available than the police themselves, since the police are present at the initial stages of the criminal justice process. Critics of *Miranda*, however, argued that the decision put police agencies in the uncomfortable and contradictory position not only of enforcing the law but also of having to offer defendants advice on how they might circumvent conviction and punishment. Under *Miranda*, the police partially assume the role of legal adviser to the accused.

In 1999, however, in the case of *U.S.* v. *Dickerson*,[169] the Fourth Circuit U.S. Court of Appeals upheld an almost-forgotten law that Congress had passed in 1968 with the intention of overturning *Miranda*. That law, Section 3501 of Chapter 223, Part II of Title 18 of the U.S. Code, says that "a confession . . . shall be admissible in evidence if it is voluntarily given." On appeal in 2000, the U.S. Supreme Court upheld its original *Miranda* ruling by a 7–2 vote and found that *Miranda* is a constitutional rule (that is, a fundamental right inherent in the U.S. Constitution) that cannot be dismissed by an act of Congress. "*Miranda* and its progeny," the majority wrote in *Dickerson* v. *U.S.* (2000), will continue to "govern the admissibility of statements made during custodial interrogation in both state and federal courts."[170]

On June 28, 2004, the U.S. Supreme Court handed down two important decisions—*U.S.* v. *Patane*[171] and *Missouri* v. *Seibert*[172]—in a continuing refinement of its original 1966 ruling in *Miranda* v. *Arizona*.[173]

As described in this chapter, *Miranda* created a presumption of coercion in all custodial interrogations. Generally speaking, only a demonstration that *Miranda* warnings have been provided to a suspect has been sufficient to counter that presumption and to allow legal proceedings based on the fruits of an interrogation to move forward. Consequently, some scholars were surprised by *Patane*, in which the Court found that "a mere failure to give *Miranda* warnings does not, by itself, violate a suspect's constitutional rights or even the *Miranda* rule."

The *Patane* case began with the arrest of a convicted felon after a federal agent told officers that the man owned a handgun illegally. At the time of arrest, the officers tried to advise the defendant of his rights, but he interrupted them, saying that he already knew his rights. The officers then asked him about the pistol, and he told them where it was. After the weapon was

CJ | ISSUES
The *Miranda* Warnings

Adult Rights Warning

Suspects 18 years old or older who are in custody must be advised of the following rights before any questioning begins:

1. You have the right to remain silent.
2. Anything you say can be used against you in a court of law.
3. You have the right to talk to a lawyer and to have a lawyer present while you are being questioned.
4. If you want a lawyer before or during questioning but cannot afford to hire a lawyer, one will be appointed to represent you at no cost before any questioning.
5. If you answer questions now without a lawyer here, you still have the right to stop answering questions at any time.

Waiver of Rights

After reading and explaining the rights of a person in custody, an officer must also ask for a waiver of those rights before any questioning. The following waiver questions must be answered affirmatively, either by express answer or by clear implication. Silence alone is not a waiver.

1. Do you understand each of these rights I have explained to you? (Answer must be YES.)
2. Having these rights in mind, do you now wish to answer questions? (Answer must be YES.)
3. Do you now wish to answer questions without a lawyer present? (Answer must be YES.)

   The following question must be asked of juveniles ages 14, 15, 16, and 17.

4. Do you now wish to answer questions without your parents, guardians, or custodians present? (Answer must be YES.)

---

recovered, the defendant was charged with illegal possession of a firearm by a convicted felon.

At first glance, *Patane* appears to contradict the fruit of the poisoned tree doctrine that the Court established in the 1920 case of *Silverthorne Lumber Co.* v. *U.S.*[174] and that *Wong Sun* v. *U.S.* (1963)[175] made applicable to verbal evidence derived immediately from an illegal search and seizure. An understanding of *Patane*, however, requires recognition of the fact that the *Miranda* rule is based on the self-incrimination clause of the Fifth Amendment to the U.S. Constitution. According to the Court in *Patane*, "that Clause's core protection is a prohibition on compelling a criminal defendant to testify against himself at trial." It cannot be violated, the Court said, "by the introduction of nontestimonial evidence obtained as a result of voluntary statements." In other words, according to the Court, only (1) coerced statements and (2) those voluntary statements made by a defendant that might directly incriminate him or her at a later trial are precluded by a failure to read a suspect his or her *Miranda* rights. Such voluntary statements would, of course, include such things as an outright confession.

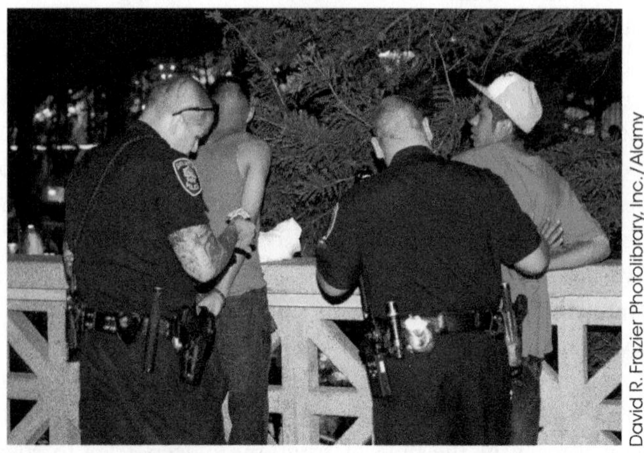
David R. Frazier Photolibrary, Inc./Alamy

A suspect being read his *Miranda* rights immediately after arrest. Officers often read *Miranda* rights from a card to preclude the possibility of a mistake. What might be the consequences of a mistake?

Significantly, however, oral statements must be distinguished, the Court said, from the "physical fruits of the suspect's unwarned but voluntary statements." In other words, if an unwarned suspect is questioned by police officers and tells the officers where they can find an illegal weapon or a weapon that has been used in a crime, the weapon can be recovered and later introduced as evidence at the suspect's trial. If the same unwarned suspect, however, tells police that he committed a murder, then his confession will not be allowed into evidence at trial. The line drawn by the court is against the admissibility of *oral statements* made by an unwarned defendant, not the *nontestimonial physical evidence* resulting from continued police investigation of such statements. Under *Patane*, the oral statements themselves cannot be admitted, but the physical evidence derived from them can be. "Thus," wrote the justices in *Patane*, "admission of nontestimonial physical fruits (the pistol here) does not run the risk of admitting into trial an accused's coerced incriminating statements against himself."

The *Seibert* case addressed a far different issue: that of the legality of a two-step police interrogation technique in which suspects were questioned and—if they made incriminating statements—were then advised of their *Miranda* rights and questioned again. The justices found that such a technique could not meet constitutional muster, writing, "When the [*Miranda*] warnings are inserted in the midst of coordinated and continuing interrogation, they are likely to mislead and deprive a defendant of knowledge essential to his ability to understand the nature of his rights and the consequences of abandoning them. . . . And it would be unrealistic to treat two spates of integrated and proximately conducted questioning as independent interrogations . . . simply because *Miranda* warnings formally punctuate them in the middle."

Waiver of *Miranda* Rights by Suspects

Suspects in police custody may legally waive their *Miranda* rights through a *voluntary* "knowing and intelligent" waiver. A *knowing waiver* can be made only if a suspect is advised of his or her rights and is in a condition to understand the advisement. A rights advisement made in English to a Spanish-speaking suspect, for example, cannot produce a knowing waiver. Likewise, an *intelligent waiver* of rights requires that the defendant be able to understand the consequences of not invoking the *Miranda* rights. In the case of *Moran* v. *Burbine* (1986),[176] the U.S. Supreme Court defined an intelligent and knowing waiver as one "made with a full awareness both of the nature of the right being abandoned and the consequences of the decision to abandon it." Similarly, in *Colorado* v. *Spring* (1987),[177] the Court held that an intelligent and knowing waiver can be made even though a suspect has not been informed of all the alleged offenses about which he or she is about to be questioned.

Inevitable-Discovery Exception to *Miranda*

The case of Robert Anthony Williams provides a good example of the change in the U.S. Supreme Court philosophy, alluded to earlier in this chapter, from an individual-rights perspective toward a public-order perspective. The case epitomizes what many consider a slow erosion of the advances in defendant rights, which reached their apex in *Miranda*. This case began in 1969, at the close of the Warren Court era. Williams was apprehended as a suspect in the murder of ten-year-old Pamela Powers around Christmas time and was advised of his rights. Later, as Williams rode in a car with detectives who were searching for the girl's body, one of the detectives made what has since become known as the "Christian burial speech." The detective told Williams that since Christmas was almost upon them, it would be "the Christian thing to do" to see to it that Pamela had a decent burial rather than having to lie in a field somewhere. Williams confessed and led detectives to the body. However, because Williams had not been reminded of his right to have a lawyer present during his conversation with the detective, the Supreme Court in *Brewer* v. *Williams* (1977)[178] overturned Williams's conviction, saying that the detective's remarks were "a deliberate eliciting of incriminating evidence from an accused in the absence of his lawyer."

In 1977, Williams was retried for the murder, but his remarks in leading detectives to the body were not entered into evidence. The discovery of the body was used, however, and Williams was convicted, prompting another appeal to the Supreme Court based on the argument that the body should not have been used as evidence because it was discovered due to the illegally gathered statements. This time, in the 1984 case of *Nix* v. *Williams*,[179] the Supreme Court affirmed Williams's second conviction, holding that the body would have been found anyway, since detectives were searching in the direction where it lay when Williams revealed its location. This ruling came during the heyday of the Burger Court and clearly demonstrates a tilt by the Court away from suspects' rights and an acknowledgment of the imperfect world of police procedure. The *Williams* case, as it was finally resolved, is said to have created the inevitable-discovery exception to the *Miranda* requirements. The inevitable-discovery exception means that evidence, even if it was otherwise gathered inappropriately, can be used in a court of law if it would have invariably turned up in the normal course of events.

Public-Safety Exception to *Miranda*

In 2013, U.S. officials announced that they would question 19-year-old Dzhokhar Tsarnaev, the surviving Boston Marathon bomber, before reading him his *Miranda* rights.[180] The Boston attack killed three people and wounded more than 170. Tsarnaev had been wounded and was captured after his brother had been killed in a police shootout. Law enforcement officials said that they would question the hospitalized Tsarnaev under the well-established *public-safety exception* to the *Miranda* rule which is intended to allow authorities to conduct an initial public-safety interview in order to quickly determine whether any danger to the public still exists. The *Tsarnaev* case raised questions, however, because it wasn't clear that taking the time for a rights advisement endangered public safety.

The public-safety exception was created in 1984, when the U.S. Supreme Court decided the case of *New York* v. *Quarles*.[181] That case centered on a rape in which the victim told police her assailant had a gun and had fled into a nearby supermarket. Two police officers entered the store and apprehended the suspect. One officer immediately noticed that the man was wearing an empty shoulder holster and, fearing that a child might find the discarded weapon, quickly asked, "Where's the gun?" Quarles was convicted of rape but appealed his conviction, requesting that the weapon be suppressed as evidence because officers had not advised him of his *Miranda* rights before asking him about it. The Supreme Court disagreed, stating that considerations of public safety were overriding and negated the need for rights advisement prior to limited questioning that focused on the need to prevent further harm. Following such reasoning, interrogators decided not to *Mirandize* Tsarnaev before questioning him, in the belief that he might be able to provide information about bombs or other plots that could pose an immediate danger to the public.

The U.S. Supreme Court has also held that in cases when the police issue *Miranda* warnings, a later demonstration that a person may have been suffering from mental problems does not necessarily negate a confession. *Colorado* v. *Connelly* (1986)[182] involved a man who approached a Denver police officer and said

■ ***Miranda* triggers** The dual principles of custody and interrogation, both of which are necessary before an advisement of rights is required.

© ZUMA Press, Inc./Alamy

The immediate aftermath of a terrorist explosion at the finish line of the 2013 Boston Marathon. Dzhokhar Tsarnaev, one of two brothers who planted the explosive devices among the crowd, survived a citywide manhunt, but authorities invoked the public-safety exception to the *Miranda* requirement in not advising him of his rights for a couple of days following his arrest. Why did they do that, and what information were they hoping to uncover by questioning Tsarnaev?

he wanted to confess to the murder of a young girl. The officer immediately informed him of his *Miranda* rights, but the man waived them and continued to talk. When a detective arrived, the man was again advised of his rights and again waived them. After being taken to the local jail, the man began to hear "voices" and later claimed that it was these voices that had made him confess. At the trial, the defense moved to have the earlier confession negated on the basis that it was not voluntarily or freely given because of the defendant's mental condition. On appeal, the U.S. Supreme Court disagreed, saying that "no coercive government conduct occurred in this case." Hence "self-coercion," due to either a guilty conscience or faulty thought processes, does not bar prosecution based on information revealed willingly by a suspect.

The 1986 case of *Kuhlmann* v. *Wilson*[183] represents another refinement of *Miranda*. In this case, the Court upheld a police informant's lawful ability to gather information for use at a trial from a defendant while the two were placed together in a jail cell. The passive gathering of information was judged to be acceptable, provided that the informant did not make attempts to elicit information.

In the case of *Illinois* v. *Perkins* (1990),[184] the Court expanded its position to say that under appropriate circumstances, even the active questioning of a suspect by an undercover officer posing as a fellow inmate does not require *Miranda* warnings. In *Perkins*, the Court found that, lacking other forms of coercion, the fact that the suspect was not aware of the questioner's identity as a law enforcement officer ensured that his statements were freely given. In the words of the Court, "The essential ingredients of a 'police-dominated atmosphere' and compulsion are not present when an incarcerated person speaks freely to someone that he believes to be a fellow inmate." Learn more about the public safety exception directly from the FBI at **http://www.justicestudies.com/pubs/public_safety.pdf**.

Miranda and the Meaning of Interrogation

Modern interpretations of the applicability of *Miranda* warnings turn on an understanding of interrogation. The *Miranda* decision, as originally rendered, specifically recognized the need for police investigators to make inquiries at crime scenes to determine facts or to establish identities. As long as the individual questioned is not yet in custody and as long as probable cause is lacking in the investigator's mind, such questioning can proceed without *Miranda* warnings. In such cases, interrogation, within the meaning of *Miranda*, has not yet begun.

The case of *Rock* v. *Zimmerman* (1982)[185] provides a different sort of example—one in which a suspect willingly made statements to the police before interrogation began. The suspect had set fire to his own house and shot and killed a neighbor. When the fire department arrived, he began shooting again and killed the fire chief. Cornered later in a field, the defendant, gun in hand, spontaneously shouted at police, "How many people did I kill? How many people are dead?"[186] This spontaneous statement was held to be admissible evidence at the suspect's trial.

It is also important to recognize that in the *Miranda* decision, the Supreme Court required that officers provide warnings only in those situations involving *both* arrest and custodial interrogation—what some call the ***Miranda* triggers**. In other words, it is generally permissible for officers to take a suspect into custody and listen, without asking questions, while he or she talks. Similarly, they may ask questions without providing a *Miranda* warning, even within the confines of a police station house, as long as the person questioned is not a suspect and is not under arrest.[187] Warnings are required only when officers begin to actively and deliberately elicit responses from a suspect whom they know has been indicted or who is in custody.

Officers were found to have acted properly in the case of *South Dakota* v. *Neville* (1983)[188] when they informed a man suspected of driving while intoxicated (DWI), without reading him his rights, that he would stand to lose his driver's license if he did not submit to a Breathalyzer test. When the driver responded, "I'm too drunk. I won't pass the test," his answer became evidence of his condition and was permitted at trial.

A third-party conversation recorded by the police after a suspect has invoked the *Miranda* right to remain silent may be used as evidence, according to a 1987 ruling in *Arizona* v. *Mauro*.[189] In *Mauro*, a man who willingly conversed with his wife in the presence of a police tape recorder, even after invoking his right to keep silent, was held to have effectively abandoned that right.

When a waiver is not made, however, in-court references to a defendant's silence following the issuing of *Miranda* warnings are unconstitutional. In the 1976 case of *Doyle* v. *Ohio*,[190] the U.S. Supreme Court definitively ruled that "a suspect's [post-*Miranda*] silence will not be used against him." Even so, according to the Court in *Brecht* v. *Abrahamson* (1993),[191] prosecution efforts to use such silence against a defendant may not invalidate a finding of guilt by a jury unless the "error had substantial and injurious effect or influence in determining the jury's verdict."[192]

Of course, when a person is *not* a suspect and is *not* charged with a crime, *Miranda* warnings need not be given. Such logic led to what some have called a "fractured opinion"[193] in the 2003 case of *Chavez* v. *Martinez*.[194] The case involved Oliverio Martinez, who was blinded and paralyzed in a police shooting after he grabbed an officer's weapon during an altercation. An Oxnard, California, police officer named Chavez persisted in questioning Martinez while he was awaiting treatment despite his pleas to stop and the fact that he was obviously in great pain. The Court held that "police questioning in [the] absence of *Miranda* warnings, even questioning that is overbearing to [the] point of coercion, does not violate constitutional protections against self-incrimination, as long as no incriminating statements are introduced at trial."[195] Nonetheless, the Court found that Martinez could bring a civil suit against Chavez and the Oxnard Police Department for violation of his constitutional right to due process.

In the 2010 case of *Florida* v. *Powell*, the U.S. Supreme Court held that although *Miranda* warnings are generally required prior to police interrogation, the wording of those warnings is not set in stone. The Court ruled that "in determining whether police warnings were satisfactory, reviewing courts are not required to examine them as if construing a will or defining the terms of an easement. The inquiry is simply whether the warnings reasonably convey to a suspect his rights as required by *Miranda*."

Also in 2010, in the case of *Berghuis* v. *Thompkins*, the Court held that a Michigan suspect did not invoke his Fifth Amendment right to remain silent by simply not answering questions that interrogators put to him.[196] Instead, the justices ruled, a suspect must unambiguously assert his right to remain silent before the police are required to end their questioning. In this case, the defendant, Van Chester Thompkins, was properly advised of his rights prior to questioning, and, although he was largely silent during a three-hour interrogation, he never said that he wanted to remain silent, that he did not want to talk with the police, or that he wanted an attorney. Near the end of the interrogation, however, he answered "yes" when asked whether he prayed to God to forgive him for the shooting death of a murder victim.

Finally, in 2013, in the case of *Salinas* v. *Texas*, the Supreme Court found that an offender must *expressly* invoke his Miranda privileges, and that failure to do so can later result in use at trial of the offender's silence as evidence of his guilt.[197] According to the Court, "A defendant normally does not invoke the privilege (against self-incrimination) by remaining silent."

Gathering Special Kinds of Nontestimonial Evidence

The role of law enforcement is complicated by the fact that suspects are often privy to special evidence of a nontestimonial sort. Nontestimonial evidence is generally physical evidence, and most physical evidence is subject to normal procedures of search and seizure. A special category of nontestimonial evidence, however, includes very personal items that may be within or part of a person's body, such as ingested drugs, blood cells, foreign objects, medical implants, and human DNA. Also included in this category are fingerprints and other kinds of biological residue. The gathering of such special kinds of nontestimonial evidence is a complex area rich in precedent. The Fourth Amendment guarantee that people be secure in their homes and in their persons has generally been interpreted by the courts to mean that the improper seizure of physical evidence of any kind is illegal and will result in exclusion of that evidence at trial. When very personal kinds of nontestimonial evidence are considered, however, the issue becomes more complicated.

The Right to Privacy

Two 1985 cases, *Hayes* v. *Florida*[198] and *Winston* v. *Lee*,[199] provide examples of limits the courts have placed on the seizure of very personal forms of nontestimonial evidence. The *Hayes* case established the right of suspects to refuse to be fingerprinted when probable cause necessary to effect an arrest does not exist. *Winston* demonstrated the inviolability of the body against surgical and other substantially invasive techniques that might be ordered by authorities against a suspect's will.

In the *Winston* case, Rudolph Lee, Jr., was found a few blocks from the scene of a robbery with a gunshot wound in his chest. The robbery had involved an exchange of gunshots by the store owner and the robber, with the owner noting that the robber had apparently been hit by a bullet. At the hospital, the store owner identified Lee as the robber. The prosecution sought to have Lee submit to surgery to remove the bullet in his chest, arguing that the bullet would provide physical evidence linking him to the crime. Lee refused the surgery, and in *Winston* v. *Lee*, the U.S. Supreme Court ruled that Lee could not be ordered to undergo surgery because intrusion into his body of that magnitude was unacceptable under the right to privacy guaranteed by the Fourth Amendment. The *Winston* case was based on precedent established in *Schmerber* v. *California* (1966).[200] The *Schmerber* case turned on the extraction against the defendant's will of a blood sample to be measured for alcohol content. In *Schmerber*, the Court ruled that warrants must be obtained for bodily intrusions unless fast action is necessary to prevent the destruction of evidence by natural physiological processes.

Body-Cavity Searches

In early 2005, officers of the Suffolk County (New York) Police Department arrested 36-year-old Terrance Haynes and charged him with marijuana possession.[201] After placing him in the back of a patrol car, Haynes appeared to choke and had difficulty breathing. Soon his breathing stopped, prompting officers to use the Heimlich maneuver, which dislodged a plastic bag from Haynes's windpipe. The bag contained 11 packets of cocaine. Although Haynes survived the ordeal, he now faces up to 25 years in prison.

Although some suspects might literally "cough up" evidence, some are more successful at hiding it *in* their bodies. Body-cavity searches are among the most problematic types of searches for police today. "Strip" searches of convicts in prison, including the search of body cavities, have generally been held to be permissible.

Body-cavity searches are among the most problematic types of searches for police today.

The 1985 Supreme Court case of *U.S.* v. *Montoya de Hernandez*[202] focused on the issue of "alimentary canal smuggling," in which the offender typically swallows condoms filled with cocaine or heroin and waits for nature to take its course to recover the substance. In the *Montoya* case, a woman known to be a "balloon swallower" arrived in the United States on a flight from Colombia. She was detained by customs officials and given a pat-down search by a female agent. The agent reported that the woman's abdomen was firm and suggested that X-rays be taken. The suspect refused and was given the choice of submitting to further tests or taking the next flight back to Colombia. No flight was immediately available, however, and the suspect was placed in a room for 16 hours, where she refused all food and drink. Finally, a court order for an X-ray was obtained. The procedure revealed "balloons," and the woman was detained another four days, during which time she passed numerous cocaine-filled plastic condoms. The Court ruled that the woman's confinement was not unreasonable, based as it was on the supportable suspicion that she was "body-packing" cocaine. Any discomfort she experienced, the Court ruled, "resulted solely from the method that she chose to smuggle illicit drugs."[203]

Electronic Eavesdropping

Modern technology makes possible increasingly complex forms of communication. One of the first Supreme Court decisions involving electronic communications was the 1928 case of *Olmstead* v. *U.S.*[204] In *Olmstead*, bootleggers used their home telephones to discuss and transact business. Agents tapped the lines and based their investigation and ensuing arrests on conversations they overheard. The defendants were convicted and eventually appealed to the high court, arguing that the agents had in effect seized information illegally without a search warrant in violation of the defendants' Fourth Amendment right to be secure in their homes. The Court ruled, however, that telephone lines were not an extension of the defendants' homes and therefore were not protected by the constitutional guarantee of security. However, subsequent federal statutes have substantially modified the significance of *Olmstead*.

Recording devices carried on the body of an undercover agent or an informant were ruled to produce admissible evidence in *On Lee* v. *U.S.* (1952)[205] and *Lopez* v. *U.S.* (1963).[206] The 1967 case of *Berger* v. *New York*[207] permitted wiretaps and "bugs" in instances where state law provided for the use of such devices and where officers obtained a warrant based on probable cause.

The Court appeared to undertake a significant change of direction in the area of electronic eavesdropping when it decided the case of *Katz* v. *U.S.* in 1967.[208] Federal agents had monitored a number of Katz's telephone calls from a public phone using a device separate from the phone lines and attached to the glass of the phone booth. The Court, in this case, stated that a warrant is required to unveil what a person makes an effort to keep private, even in a public place. In the words of the Court, "The government's activities in electronically listening to and recording the petitioner's words violated the privacy upon which he justifiably relied while using the telephone booth and thus constituted a 'search and seizure' within the meaning of the Fourth Amendment."

A warrant is required to unveil what a person makes an effort to keep private, even in a public place.

In 1968, with the case of *Lee* v. *Florida*,[209] the Court applied the Federal Communications Act[210] to telephone conversations that might be the object of police investigation and held that evidence obtained without a warrant could not be used in state proceedings if it resulted from a wiretap. The only person who

CJ | NEWS

Supreme Court Says Police Need Warrant for GPS Tracking

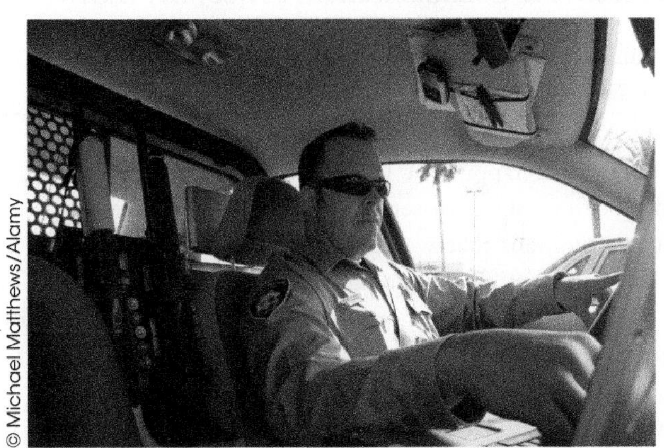
© Michael Matthews/Alamy

A Las Vegas police officer tracks a suspect vehicle using GPS tracking technology. What role did such devices play in the 2012 U.S. Supreme Court case of *U.S. v. Jones*? Following the justices' reasoning in that case, under what circumstances can the police use GPS devices to track suspects' vehicles?

Police have always needed a warrant from a judge to search a person's home, but until recently, they did not need one to attach a geographic positioning system (GPS) tracking device to a car and see where it went.

After all, some said, police don't need a warrant to get into their cars and follow suspects through the streets, and GPS systems are basically doing the same thing, only digitally.

In 2012, however, the Supreme Court decided that GPS devices are far more intrusive than tailing a car. In the case of *U.S. v. Jones* the justices voted 9–0 that the FBI needed a warrant when placing a GPS device on the vehicle of a suspected drug dealer.

"GPS monitoring generates a precise, comprehensive record of a person's public movement that reflects a wealth of detail about her familial, political, religious and sexual associations," wrote Justice Sonia Sotomayor.

The *Jones* case was the first time that the court dealt with GPSs, which have become a common police tool only in recent years. The court also signaled that it won't be the last time it deals with the booming field of high-tech surveillance, which also includes using signals emitted from cellphones to track someone down.

Although all the justices agreed that the FBI had violated the Fourth Amendment, which protects against unreasonable search and seizure, they were spilt on how the violation took place.

A five-member majority held that when the FBI agents attached the GPS device, they were in effect trespassing. This opinion, which will be the basis for all future court renderings, holds that a private vehicle cannot be touched, in the same way that a house cannot be entered, even when that car is out on public streets.

But Justice Samuel Alito, speaking for the four-member minority, contended that the real violation was not touching the car, but rather that it lay in violating the driver's expectation of privacy. This is part of a legal theory the court has been applying for 45 years, which holds that the Fourth Amendment "protects people, not places," he wrote.

Alito explained there would be future cases when the majority's concept of trespassing would no longer apply to high-tech tracking. For instance, when a car comes with a GPS device already in it, the police do not even have to touch the car to link into the device. He added that more than 322 million cell phones in the nation have chips in them allowing phone companies to track customers' locations. Again, without touching the cell phone, police can simply obtain tracking data from the phone companies involved.

Justice Sotomayor wrote that it could take a while for the courts to sort out all the implications of tracking technology. "In the course of carrying out mundane tasks," she wrote, Americans disclose which phone numbers they dial, which URLs they visit, and "the books, groceries and medications they purchase."

Following *U.S. v. Jones*, the FBI was forced to turn off about 3,000 GPS tracking devices. In some cases, the agency had to get court orders to briefly turn the devices back on so they could be located and retrieved.

The bureau, like other law enforcement agencies, can still use GPS trackers if it gets a search warrant, but Andrew Weissmann, the FBI's chief legal counsel, said this could be tricky. The FBI would first need to justify its suspicions to a judge, showing "probable cause," but often the ability to show probable cause depends on the information agents obtain from tracking techniques like GPS, he said.

Resources: "Justices Rein in Police on GPS Trackers," *Wall Street Journal*, January 24, 2012, http://online.wsj.com/article/SB10001424052970203806504577178811800873358.html; "Supreme Court: GPS Devices Equivalent of a Search, Police Must Get Warrant," *Fox News*, January 23, 2012, http://www.foxnews.com/politics/2012/01/23/supreme-court-gps-devices-equivalent-search-police-must-get-warrant-469182072/; and "FBI Still Struggling with Supreme Court's GPS Ruling," *NPR*, March 21, 2012, http://www.npr.org/2012/03/21/149011887/fbi-still-struggling-with-supreme-courts-gps-ruling.

---

has the authority to permit eavesdropping, according to that act, is the sender of the message.

The Federal Communications Act, originally passed in 1934, does not specifically mention the potential interest of law enforcement agencies in monitoring communications. Title III of the Omnibus Crime Control and Safe Streets Act of 1968, however, mostly prohibits wiretaps but does allow officers to listen to electronic communications when (1) an officer is one of the parties involved in the communication, (2) one of the parties is not the officer but willingly decides to share the communication with the officer, or (3) officers obtain a warrant based on probable cause. In the 1971 case of *U.S. v. White*,[211] the Court held that law enforcement officers may intercept electronic information when one of the parties involved in the communication gives consent, even without a warrant.

In 1984, the Supreme Court decided the case of *U.S. v. Karo*,[212] in which DEA agents had arrested James Karo for cocaine importation. Officers placed a radio transmitter inside a 50-gallon drum of ether purchased by Karo for use in processing the cocaine. The device was placed inside the drum with the consent of the seller of the ether but without a search warrant. The shipment of ether was followed to the Karo house, and

Electronic Communications Privacy Act (ECPA) A law passed by Congress in 1986 establishing the due process requirements that law enforcement officers must meet in order to legally intercept wire communications.

Karo was arrested and convicted of cocaine-trafficking charges. Karo appealed to the U.S. Supreme Court, claiming that the radio beeper had violated his reasonable expectation of privacy inside his premises and that, without a warrant, the evidence it produced was tainted. The Court agreed and overturned his conviction.

Minimization Requirement for Electronic Surveillance

The Supreme Court established a minimization requirement pertinent to electronic surveillance in the 1978 case of *U.S. v. Scott.*[213] Minimization means that officers must make every reasonable effort to monitor only those conversations, through the use of phone taps, body bugs, and the like, that are specifically related to the criminal activity under investigation. As soon as it becomes obvious that a conversation is innocent, then the monitoring personnel are required to cease their invasion of privacy. Problems arise if the conversation occurs in a foreign language, if it is "coded," or if it is ambiguous. It has been suggested that investigators involved in electronic surveillance maintain logbooks of their activities that specifically show monitored conversations, as well as efforts made at minimization.[214]

The Electronic Communications Privacy Act of 1986

Passed by Congress in 1986, the **Electronic Communications Privacy Act (ECPA)**[215] brought major changes in the requirements law enforcement officers must meet to intercept wire communications (those involving the human voice). The ECPA deals specifically with three areas of communication: (1) wiretaps and bugs; (2) pen registers, which record the numbers dialed from a telephone; and (3) tracing devices, which determine the number from which a call emanates. The act also addresses the procedures to be followed by officers in obtaining records relating to communications services, and it establishes requirements for gaining access to stored electronic communications and records of those communications. The ECPA basically requires that investigating officers must obtain wiretap-type court orders to eavesdrop on *ongoing communications*. The use of pen registers and recording devices, however, is specifically excluded by the law from court order requirements.[216]

A related measure, the Communications Assistance for Law Enforcement Act (CALEA) of 1994,[217] appropriated $500 million to modify the U.S. phone system to allow for continued wiretapping by law enforcement agencies. The law also specifies a standard-setting process for the redesign of existing equipment that would permit effective wiretapping in the face of coming technological advances. In the words of the FBI's Telecommunications Industry Liaison Unit, "This law requires telecommunications carriers, as defined in the Act, to ensure law enforcement's ability, pursuant to court order or other lawful authorization, to intercept communications notwithstanding advanced telecommunications technologies."[218] In 2010, 3,194 wiretap requests were approved by federal and state judges, and approximately 5 million conversations were intercepted by law enforcement agencies throughout the country.[219]

The Telecommunications Act of 1996

Title V of the Telecommunications Act of 1996[220] made it a federal offense for anyone engaged in interstate or international communications to knowingly use a telecommunications device "to create, solicit, or initiate the transmission of any comment, request, suggestion, proposal, image, or other communication which is obscene, lewd, lascivious, filthy, or indecent, with intent to annoy, abuse, threaten, or harass another person." The law also provided special penalties for anyone who "makes a telephone call . . . without disclosing his identity and with intent to annoy, abuse, threaten, or harass any person at the called number or who receives the communication" or who "makes or causes the telephone of another repeatedly or continuously to ring, with intent to harass any person at the called number; or makes repeated telephone calls" for the purpose of harassing a person at the called number.

A section of the law, known as the Communications Decency Act (CDA),[221] criminalized the transmission to minors of "patently offensive" obscene materials over the Internet or other computer telecommunications service. Portions of the CDA were invalidated by the U.S. Supreme Court in the case of *Reno* v. *ACLU* (1997).[222]

The USA Patriot Act of 2001

The USA PATRIOT Act of 2001, which is also discussed in a "CJ Issues" box in this chapter, made it easier for police investigators to intercept many forms of electronic communications. Under previous federal law, for example, investigators could not obtain a wiretap order to intercept *wire* communications for violations of the Computer Fraud and Abuse Act.[223] In several well-publicized cases, hackers had stolen teleconferencing services

■ **sneak-and-peek search** A search that occurs in the suspect's absence and without his or her prior knowledge.

CJ | ISSUES

The USA PATRIOT Act of 2001 and the USA PATRIOT Improvement and Reauthorization Act of 2005

On October 26, 2001, President George W. Bush signed into law the USA PATRIOT Act, also known as the Uniting and Strengthening America by Providing Appropriate Tools Required to Intercept and Obstruct Terrorism Act. The law, which was drafted in response to the September 11, 2001, terrorist attacks on the World Trade Center and the Pentagon, substantially increased the investigatory authority of federal, state, and local police agencies.

The act permits longer jail terms for certain suspects arrested without a warrant, broadens authority for **"sneak-and-peek" searches** (searches conducted without prior notice and in the absence of the suspect), and enhances the power of prosecutors. The law also increases the ability of federal authorities to tap phones (including wireless devices), share intelligence information, track Internet usage, crack down on money laundering, and protect U.S. borders. Many of the crime-fighting powers created under the legislation are not limited to acts of terrorism but apply to many different kinds of criminal offenses.

The 2001 law led individual-rights advocates to question whether the government unfairly expanded police powers at the expense of civil liberties. Although many aspects of the USA PATRIOT Act have been criticized as potentially unconstitutional, Section 213, which authorizes delayed notice of the execution of a warrant, may be the most vulnerable to court challenge. The American Civil Liberties Union (ACLU) maintains that under this section, law enforcement agents could enter a house, apartment, or office with a search warrant while the occupant is away, search through his or her property, and take photographs without having to tell the suspect about the search until later.[1] The ACLU also believes that this provision is illegal because the Fourth Amendment to the Constitution protects against unreasonable searches and seizures and requires the government to obtain a warrant and to give notice to the person whose property will be searched before conducting the search. The notice requirement enables the suspect to assert his or her Fourth Amendment rights.

In 2005, the U.S. Congress reauthorized most provisions of the USA PATRIOT Act, and in May 2011, President Barack Obama signed legislation providing for an extension of several terrorist surveillance provisions included in the USA PATRIOT Act and in the Intelligence Reform and Terrorism Prevention Act of 2004.

Read the original USA PATRIOT Act of 2001 in its entirety at **http://www.justicestudies.com/pubs/patriot.pdf**. Title 18 of the U.S. Code is available at **http://uscode.house.gov/download/title_18.shtml.**

[1] Much of the material in this paragraph is taken from American Civil Liberties Union, "How the Anti-Terrorism Bill Expands Law Enforcement 'Sneak and Peek' Warrants," http://www.aclu.org/congress/1102301b.html (accessed August 28, 2007).

References: "Congressional Committee Votes to Reauthorize PATRIOT Act Provisions," Examiner.com, May 20, 2011, http://www.examiner.com/public-safety-in-national/congressional-committee-votes-to-reauthorize-patriot-act-provisions#ixzz1N65VSX33 (accessed May 22, 2011); USA PATRIOT Improvement and Reauthorization Act of 2005 (Public Law 109-177); U.S. Department of Justice, *Field Guidance on Authorities (Redacted) Enacted in the 2001 Anti-Terrorism Legislation* (Washington, DC: U.S. Dept. of Justice, no date), http://www.epic.org/terrorism/DOJguidance.pdf (accessed August 28, 2010); and USA PATRIOT Act, 2001 (Public Law 107-56).

---

from telephone companies and then used those services to plan and execute hacking attacks.

The act[224] added felony violations of the Computer Fraud and Abuse Act to Section 2516(1) of Title 18 of the U.S. Code—the portion of federal law that lists specific types of crimes for which investigators may obtain a wiretap order for wire communications.

The USA PATRIOT Act also modified that portion of the ECPA that governs law enforcement access to stored electronic communications, such as e-mail, to include stored wire communications, such as voice mail. Before the modification, law enforcement officers needed to obtain a wiretap order rather than a search warrant to obtain unopened voice communications. Because today's e-mail messages may contain digitized voice "attachments," investigators were sometimes required to obtain both a search warrant and a wiretap order to learn the contents of a specific message. Under the act, the same rules now apply to both stored wire communications and stored electronic communications. Wiretap orders, which are often much more difficult to obtain than search warrants, are now required only to intercept real-time telephone conversations.

Before passage of the USA PATRIOT Act, federal law allowed investigators to use an administrative subpoena (that is, a subpoena authorized by a federal or state statute or by a federal or state grand jury or trial court) to compel Internet service providers to provide a limited class of information, such as a customer's name, address, length of service, and means of payment. Also under previous law, investigators could not subpoena certain records, including credit card numbers or details about other forms of payment for Internet service. Such information can be very useful in determining a suspect's true identity because, in some cases, users give false names to Internet service providers.

Before passage of the USA PATRIOT Act, federal law allowed investigators to use an administrative subpoena (that is, a subpoena authorized by a federal or state statute or by a federal or state grand jury or trial court) to compel Internet service providers to provide a limited class of information, such as a customer's name, address, length of service, and means of payment. Also under previous law, investigators could not subpoena certain records, including credit card numbers or details about other forms of payment for Internet service. Such information, however, can be highly relevant in determining a suspect's true identity because, in many cases, users register with Internet service providers using false names.

Previous federal law[225] was also technology specific, relating primarily to telephone communications. Local and long-distance telephone billing records, for example, could be subpoenaed, but not billing information for Internet communications or records of Internet session times and durations. Similarly, previous law allowed the government to use a subpoena to obtain the customer's "telephone number or other subscriber number or identity" but did not define what that phrase meant in the context of Internet communications.

The USA PATRIOT Act amended portions of this federal law[226] to update and expand the types of records that law enforcement authorities may obtain with a subpoena. "Records of session times and durations," as well as "any temporarily assigned network address" may now be gathered. Such changes should make the process of identifying computer criminals and tracing their Internet communications faster and easier.

Finally, the USA PATRIOT Act facilitates the use of roving, or multipoint, wiretaps. Roving wiretaps, issued with court approval, target a specific individual and not a particular telephone number or communications device. Hence, law enforcement agents armed with an order for a multipoint wiretap can follow the flow of communications engaged in by a person as he switches from one cellular phone to another or to a wired telephone.

In 2006, President George W. Bush signed the USA PATRIOT Improvement and Reauthorization Act of 2005[227] into law. Also referred to as PATRIOT II, the act made permanent 14 provisions of the original 2001 legislation that had been slated to expire and extended others for another four years (including the roving wiretap provision and a provision that allows authorities to seize business records). It also addressed some of the concerns of civil libertarians who had criticized the earlier law as too restrictive. Finally, the new law provided additional protections for mass transportation systems and seaports, closed some legal loopholes in laws aimed at preventing terrorist financing, and includes a subsection called the Combat Methamphetamine Epidemic Act (CMEA). The CMEA contains significant provisions intended to strengthen federal, state, and local efforts designed at curtailing the spread of methamphetamine use.

In May 2011, President Barack Obama signed into law legislation extending a number of provisions of the PATRIOT Act that would have otherwise expired. The president's signature gave new life to the roving wiretap and business records provisions of the act, as well as some others.[228]

Gathering Electronic Evidence

The Internet, computer networks, and automated data systems present many new opportunities for committing criminal

freedom OR safety? YOU decide

Presidential Candidates Debate the USA PATRIOT Act

The freedom-versus-safety issue was well summarized in a televised debate that took place on November 23, 2011 between then-Republican presidential candidates Newt Gingrich and Ron Paul. Here's the exchange that took place between the two candidates:

GINGRICH: I think it's desperately important that we preserve your right to be innocent until proven guilty, if it's a matter of criminal law. But if you're trying to find someone who may have a nuclear weapon that they are trying to bring into an American city, I think you want to use every tool that you can possibly use to gather the intelligence; and the PATRIOT Act has clearly been a key part of that.

PAUL: I think the PATRIOT Act is unpatriotic because it undermines our liberties. I'm as concerned as everybody else is about the terrorist attacks. Timothy McVeigh was a vicious terrorist. He was arrested. Terrorism is still on the books. Internationally and nationally it is a crime and we should deal with it. We dealt with it rather well with Timothy McVeigh.

GINGRICH: Timothy McVeigh succeeded. That's the whole point. Timothy McVeigh killed a lot of Americans. I don't want a law that says after you eliminate a major American city we are sure going to come and find you. I want a law that says "When you try to take out an American city, we're going to stop you."

You Decide

How does the USA PATRIOT Act limit the freedom of American citizens? Do the demands of public safety justify the kind of restriction on personal freedoms that the act allows?

Reference: Fred Lucas, "Gingrich vs. Paul on Patriot Act: 'That's the Whole Point. Timothy McVeigh Killed a Lot of Americans," November 23, 2011, http://cnsnews.com/news/article/gingrich-vs-paul-patriot-act-s-whole-point-timothy-mcveigh-killed-lot-americans (accessed March 23, 2012).

■ **electronic evidence** Information and data of investigative value that are stored in or transmitted by an electronic device.[i]

■ **latent evidence** Evidence of relevance to a criminal investigation that is not readily seen by the unaided eye.

■ **digital criminal forensics** The lawful seizure, acquisition, analysis, reporting, and safeguarding of data from digital devices that may contain information of evidentiary value to the trier of fact in criminal events.[ii]

activity.[229] Computers and other electronic devices are increasingly being used to commit, enable, or support crimes perpetrated against people, organizations, and property. Whether the crime involves attacks against computer systems or the information they contain or more traditional offenses like murder, money laundering, trafficking, or fraud, **electronic evidence** is increasingly important.

Electronic evidence is "information and data of investigative value that is stored in or transmitted by an electronic device."[230] Such evidence is often acquired when physical items like computers, removable disks, cameras, CDs, DVDs, magnetic tape, flash memory chips, cellular telephones, and other electronic devices are collected from a crime scene or are obtained from a suspect.

Electronic evidence has special characteristics: (1) It is latent; (2) it can transcend national and state borders quickly and easily; (3) it is fragile and can easily be altered, damaged, compromised, or destroyed by improper handling or improper examination; and (4) it may be time sensitive. Like DNA or fingerprints, electronic evidence is **latent evidence** because it is not readily visible to the human eye under normal conditions. Special equipment and software are required to "see" and evaluate electronic evidence. In the courtroom, expert testimony may be needed to explain the acquisition of electronic evidence and the examination process used to interpret it.

In 2002, in recognition of the special challenges posed by electronic evidence, the Computer Crime and Intellectual Property Section (CCIPS) of the Criminal Division of the U.S. Department of Justice released a how-to manual for law enforcement officers called *Searching and Seizing Computers and Obtaining Electronic Evidence in Criminal Investigations*.[231] The manual, which explains procedures for **digital criminal forensics**, can be accessed at **http://www.justicestudies.com/pubs/electronic.pdf**.

About the same time, the Technical Working Group for Electronic Crime Scene Investigation (TWGECSI) released a detailed guide for law enforcement officers to use in gathering electronic evidence. The manual, *Electronic Crime Scene Investigation: A Guide for First Responders*,[232] grew out of a partnership formed in 1998 between the National Cybercrime Training Partnership, the Office of Law Enforcement Standards, and the National Institute of Justice. The working group was asked to identify, define, and establish basic criteria to assist federal and state agencies in handling electronic investigations and related prosecutions.

TWGECSI guidelines say that law enforcement must take special precautions when documenting, collecting, and preserving electronic evidence to maintain its integrity. The guidelines also note that the first law enforcement officer on the scene should take steps to ensure the safety of everyone at the scene and to protect the integrity of all evidence, both traditional and electronic. The entire TWGECSI guide, which includes many practical instructions for investigators working with electronic evidence, is available at **http://www.justicestudies.com/pubs/ecsi.pdf**.

Once digital evidence has been gathered, it must be analyzed. Consequently, in 2004, the government-sponsored Technical Working Group for the Examination of Digital Evidence (TWGEDE) published *Forensic Examination of Digital Evidence: A Guide for Law Enforcement*. Among the guide's recommendations are that digital evidence should be acquired in a manner that protects and preserves the integrity of the original evidence and that examination should be conducted only on a *copy* of the original evidence. The entire guide, which is nearly 100 pages long, can be accessed at **http://www.justicestudies.com/pubs/forensicexam.pdf**. An even more detailed guide, titled *Investigations Involving the Internet and Computer Networks*, was published by the National Institute of Justice in 2007 and is available at **http://www.justicestudies.com/pubs/internet-invest.pdf**.

Recently, the National Institute of Justice established the Electronic Crime Technology Center of Excellence (ECT-CoE) to assist in building the capacity for electronic crime prevention and investigation and digital evidence collection and examination of state and local law enforcement. The ECTCoE works to identify electronic crime and digital evidence tools, technologies, and training gaps. In 2013, it developed a manual that outlines policies and procedures for gathering and analyzing digital evidence, which is available in Microsoft Word format through the National Law Enforcement and Corrections Technology Center (NLECTC) website at **http://www.justnet.org.**

Warrantless searches bear special mention in any discussion of electronic evidence. In the 1999 case of *U.S.* v. *Carey*,[233] a federal appellate court held that the consent a defendant had given to police for his apartment to be searched did not extend to the search of his computer once it was taken to a police station. Similarly, in *U.S.* v. *Turner* (1999),[234] the First Circuit Court of Appeals held that the warrantless police search of a defendant's personal computer while in his apartment exceeded the scope of the defendant's consent. Learn more about gathering digital evidence from the FBI at **http://www.justicestudies.com/digital_evidence.pdf**.

SUMMARY

- Legal restraints on police action stem primarily from the U.S. Constitution's Bill of Rights—especially the Fourth, Fifth, and Sixth Amendments, which, along with the Fourteenth Amendment, require due process of law. Most due process requirements of relevance to police work concern three major areas: (1) evidence and investigation (often called *search and seizure*), (2) arrest, and (3) interrogation. Each of these areas has been addressed by a number of important U.S. Supreme Court decisions, and it is the discussion of those decisions and their significance for police work that makes up the bulk of this chapter's content.
- The Bill of Rights was designed to protect citizens against abuses of police power. It does so by guaranteeing due process of law for everyone suspected of having committed a crime and by ensuring the availability of constitutional rights to all citizens, regardless of state or local law or procedure. Within the context of criminal case processing, due process requirements mandate that all justice system officials, not only the police, respect the rights of accused individuals throughout the criminal justice process.
- The Fourth Amendment to the Constitution declares that people must be secure in their homes and in their persons against unreasonable searches and seizures. Consequently, law enforcement officers are generally required to demonstrate probable cause in order to obtain a search warrant if they are to legally conduct searches and seize the property of criminal suspects. The Supreme Court has established that police officers, in order to protect themselves from attack, have the right to search a person being arrested and to search the area under the arrestee's immediate control.
- An arrest takes place whenever a law enforcement officer restricts a person's freedom to leave. Arrests may occur when an officer comes upon a crime in progress, but most jurisdictions also allow warrantless arrests for felonies when a crime is not in progress, as long as probable cause can later be demonstrated.
- Information that is useful for law enforcement purposes is called *intelligence*, and as this chapter has shown, intelligence gathering is vital to police work. The need for useful information often leads police investigators to question suspects, informants, and potentially knowledgeable citizens. When suspects who are in custody become subject to interrogation, they must be advised of their *Miranda* rights before questioning begins. The *Miranda* warnings, which were mandated by the Supreme Court in the 1966 case of *Miranda* v. *Arizona*, are listed in this chapter. They ensure that suspects know their rights—including the right to remain silent—in the face of police interrogation.

KEY TERMS

anticipatory warrant, 211
arrest, 211
Bill of Rights, 200
compelling interest, 219
digital criminal forensics, 235
Electronic Communications Privacy Act (ECPA), 232
electronic evidence, 235
emergency search, 210
exclusionary rule, 202
fleeting-targets exception, 216
fruit of the poisonous tree doctrine, 203
good-faith exception, 206
illegally seized evidence, 201
inherent coercion, 222
interrogation, 221
landmark case, 201
latent evidence, 235
***Miranda* triggers, 228**
***Miranda* warnings, 224**
plain view, 207
probable cause, 206
psychological manipulation, 223
reasonable suspicion, 213
search incident to an arrest, 212
sneak-and-peek search, 233
suspicionless search, 219
writ of *certiorari*, 202

KEY CASES

Alabama v. *White*, 221
Arizona v. *Fulminante*, 223
Brecht v. *Abrahamson*, 229
Brown v. *Mississippi*, 222
California v. *Hodari D.*, 214
Carroll v. *U.S.*, 215
Chimel v. *California*, 204
Dickerson v. *U.S.*, 225
Escobedo v. *Illinois*, 223
Florida v. *Bostick*, 219
Horton v. *California*, 208
Illinois v. *Perkins*, 228
Kyllo v. *U.S.*, 220
Mapp v. *Ohio*, 204
Minnick v. *Mississippi*, 224
Miranda v. *Arizona*, 224
Nix v. *Williams*, 227
Richards v. *Wisconsin*, 210
Silverthorne Lumber Co. v. *U.S.*, 202
Smith v. *Ohio*, 214
Terry v. *Ohio*, 213
U.S. v. *Drayton*, 219
U.S. v. *Patane*, 208
U.S. v. *Robinson*, 212
Weeks v. *U.S.*, 202
Wilson v. *Arkansas*, 210

QUESTIONS FOR REVIEW

1. Name some of the legal restraints on police action, and list some types of behavior that might be considered abuse of police authority.
2. How do the Bill of Rights and democratically inspired legal restraints on the police help ensure personal freedoms in our society?
3. Describe the legal standards for assessing searches and seizures conducted by law enforcement agents.
4. What is an arrest, and when does it occur? How do legal understandings of the term differ from popular depictions of the arrest process?
5. What is the role of interrogation in intelligence gathering? List each of the *Miranda* warnings. Which recent U.S. Supreme Court cases have affected *Miranda* warning requirements?

QUESTIONS FOR REFLECTION

1. What is the Bill of Rights, and how does it affect our understandings of due process?
2. On what constitutional amendments are due process guarantees based? Can we ensure due process in our legal system without substantially increasing the risk of criminal activity?
3. What is the exclusionary rule? What is the fruit of the poisonous tree doctrine? What is their importance in American criminal justice?
4. Under what circumstances may police officers search vehicles? What limits, if any, are there on such searches? What determines such limits?
5. What are suspicionless searches? How does the need to ensure public safety justify certain suspicionless searches?
6. What is electronic evidence? How should first-on-the-scene law enforcement personnel handle it?

NOTES

i. Adapted from Technical Working Group for Electronic Crime Scene Investigation, *Electronic Crime Scene Investigation*, p. 2.
ii. Adapted from Larry R. Leibrock, "Overview and Impact on 21st Century Legal Practice: Digital Forensics and Electronic Discovery," http://www.courtroom21.net/FDIC.pps (accessed July 5, 2005).

1. Video: "LAPD Pursuit Ends in Gunfire," April 12, 2012, http://www.policemag.com/Videos/Channel/Patrol/2012/04/LAPD-Pursuit-Ends-In-Gunfire.aspx (accessed May 20, 2012).
2. Marcus Baram, "How Common Is Contagious Shooting?" ABC News, November 17, 2006, http://abcnews.go.com/Politics/story?id=2681947&page=1 (accessed May 21, 2007).
3. Michael Wilson, "50 Shots Fired, and the Experts Offer a Theory," *New York Times*, November 27, 2006, http://www.nytimes.com/2006/11/27/nyregion/27fire.html (accessed August 28, 2008).
4. "Victim of Police Beating Says He Was Sober," Associated Press, October 10, 2005, http://www.msnbc.msn.com/id/9645260 (accessed July 10, 2008).
5. "Police Officer Acquitted of Beating Man in Hurricane Katrina's Aftermath," Associated Press, July 25, 2007, http://www.foxnews.com/story/0,2933,290662,00.html (accessed August 30, 2009).
6. Michael Kunzelman, "New Orleans to Settle Lawsuit over Taped Beating," Associated Press, August 7, 2009, http://www.wtopnews.com/?nid=104&sid=1735442 (accessed August 30, 2009).
7. "Police Brutality!" *Time*, March 25, 1991, p. 18.
8. "Police Charged in Beating Case Say They Feared for Their Lives," *Boston Globe*, May 22, 1991, p. 22.
9. Ibid., pp. 16–19.
10. "Cries of Relief," *Time*, April 26, 1993, p. 18.
11. "Rodney King Slams SUV into House, Breaks Pelvis," CNN.com, April 16, 2003, http://www.cnn.com/2003/US/West/04/15/rodney.king.ap/index.html (accessed August 5, 2007).
12. *Miranda* v. *Arizona*, 384 U.S. 436 (1966).
13. *Weeks* v. *U.S.*, 232 U.S. 383 (1914).
14. *Silverthorne Lumber Co.* v. *U.S.*, 251 U.S. 385 (1920).
15. Clemmens Bartollas, *American Criminal Justice* (New York: Macmillan, 1988), p. 186.
16. *Mapp* v. *Ohio*, 367 U.S. 643 (1961).
17. *Chimel* v. *California*, 395 U.S. 752 (1969).
18. *Katz* v. *U.S.*, 389 U.S. 347, 88 S.Ct. 507 (1967).
19. *Minnesota* v. *Olson*, 110 S.Ct. 1684 (1990).
20. *Minnesota* v. *Carter*, 525 U.S. 83 (1998).
21. *Georgia* v. *Randolph*, 547 U.S. 103 (2006).
22. The ruling left open the possibility that any evidence relating to criminal activity undertaken by the consenting party might be admissible in court. In the words of the Court, refusal by a co-occupant "renders entry and search unreasonable and invalid as to him."
23. Nina Totenberg, "High Court Rules on Detaining Suspects, Sniffer Dogs," NPR, February 19, 2013, http://www.npr.org/2013/02/19/172431555/latest-supreme-court-decisions-give-police-one-victory-one-loss, citing Cornell law professor Sherry Colb (accessed May 3, 2013).
24. *U.S.* v. *Leon*, 468 U.S. 897, 104 S.Ct. 3405, 82 L.Ed.2d 677, 52 U.S.L.W. 5155 (1984).
25. Judicial titles vary among jurisdictions. Many lower-level state judicial officers are called *magistrates*. Federal magistrates, however, generally have a significantly higher level of judicial authority.
26. *Massachusetts* v. *Sheppard*, 104 S.Ct. 3424 (1984).
27. *Illinois* v. *Krull*, 107 S.Ct. 1160 (1987).
28. *Maryland* v. *Garrison*, 107 S.Ct. 1013 (1987).
29. *Illinois* v. *Rodriguez*, 110 S.Ct. 2793 (1990).
30. *Arizona* v. *Evans*, 514 U.S. 1 (1995).
31. *Herring* v. *U.S.*, 555 U.S. 135 (2009).
32. See *California* v. *Acevedo*, 500 U.S. 565 (1991); *Ornelas* v. *U.S.*, 517 U.S. 690 (1996); and others.
33. See *Edwards* v. *Balisok*, 520 U.S. 641 (1997); *Booth* v. *Churner*, 532 U.S. 731 (2001); and *Porter* v. *Nussle*, 534 U.S. 516 (2002).
34. See *Wilson* v. *Arkansas*, 115 S.Ct. 1914 (1995); and *Richards* v. *Wisconsin*, 117 S.Ct. 1416 (1997).
35. See *McCleskey* v. *Kemp*, 481 U.S. 279, 107 S.Ct. 1756, 95 L.Ed.2d 262 (1987); *McCleskey* v. *Zant*, 499 U.S. 467, 493–494 (1991); *Coleman* v. *Thompson*, 501 U.S. 722 (1991); *Schlup* v. *Delo*, 115 S.Ct. 851, 130 L.Ed.2d 808 (1995); *Felker* v. *Turpin, Warden*, 117 S.Ct. 30, 135 L.Ed.2d 1123 (1996); *Boyde* v. *California*, 494 U.S. 370 (1990); and others.
36. See *Ewing* v. *California*, 538 U.S. 11 (2003); and *Lockyer* v. *Andrade*, 538 U.S. 63 (2003).
37. Richard Lacayo and Viveca Novak, "How Rehnquist Changed America," *Time*, June 30, 2003, pp. 20–25.
38. *Harris* v. *U.S.*, 390 U.S. 234 (1968).
39. The legality of plain-view seizures was also confirmed in earlier cases, including *Ker* v. *California*, 374 U.S. 23, 42–43 (1963); *U.S.* v. *Lee*, 274 U.S. 559 (1927); *U.S.* v. *Lefkowitz*, 285 U.S. 452, 465 (1932); and *Hester* v. *U.S.*, 265 U.S. 57 (1924).
40. As cited in Kimberly A. Kingston, "Look But Don't Touch: The Plain View Doctrine," *FBI Law Enforcement Bulletin*, December 1987, p. 18.
41. *Horton* v. *California*, 496 U.S. 128 (1990).
42. *U.S.* v. *Irizarry*, 673 F.2d 554, 556–567 (1st Cir. 1982).
43. *Arizona* v. *Hicks*, 107 S.Ct. 1149 (1987).
44. Inadvertence, as a requirement of legitimate plain-view seizures, was first cited in the U.S. Supreme Court case of *Coolidge* v. *New Hampshire*, 403 U.S. 443, 91 S.Ct. 2022 (1971).
45. *Horton* v. *California*, 496 U.S. 128 (1990).
46. Ibid.

47. Orin S. Kerr, "Searches and Seizures in a Digital World," *Harvard Law Review*, Vol. 119 (2005), p. 521, http://www.harvardlawreview.org/media/pdf/kerr.pdf (accessed May 1, 2013).
48. Caleb Mason, "Plain View Searches: Gen. Petraeus' Waterloo," *The Crime Report*, January 8, 2013, http://www.thecrimereport.org/viewpoints/2013-01-plain-view-searches-gen-petraeus-waterloo (accessed May 2, 2013).
49. *Brigham City* v. *Stuart*, 547 U.S. 398 (2006).
50. John Gales Sauls, "Emergency Searches of Premises, Part 1," *FBI Law Enforcement Bulletin*, March 1987, p. 23.
51. *Warden* v. *Hayden*, 387 U.S. 294 (1967).
52. Ibid.
53. Sauls, "Emergency Searches of Premises," p. 25.
54. *Maryland* v. *Buie*, 110 S.Ct. 1093 (1990).
55. *Wilson* v. *Arkansas*, 514 U.S. 927 (1995).
56. For additional information, see Michael J. Bulzomi, "Knock and Announce: A Fourth Amendment Standard," *FBI Law Enforcement Bulletin*, May 1997, pp. 27-31.
57. *Richards* v. *Wisconsin*, 117 S.Ct. 1416 (1997), syllabus.
58. *Illinois* v. *McArthur*, 531 U.S. 326, 330 (2001).
59. *U.S.* v. *Banks*, 540 U.S. 31 (2003).
60. *Hudson* v. *Michigan*, 547 U.S. 586 (2006).
61. *Kentucky* v. *King*, 563 U.S. ___ (2011).
62. *U.S.* v. *Grubbs*, 547 U.S. 90 (2006).
63. *U.S.* v. *Mendenhall*, 446 U.S. 544 (1980).
64. A. Louis DiPietro, "Voluntary Encounters or Fourth Amendment Seizures," *FBI Law Enforcement Bulletin*, January 1992, pp. 28–32.
65. *Stansbury* v. *California*, 114 S.Ct. 1526, 1529, 128 L.Ed.2d 293 (1994).
66. *Howes* v. *Fields*, U.S. Supreme Court, No. 10-680 (decided February 21, 2012).
67. *Yarborough* v. *Alvarado*, 541 U.S. 652 (2004).
68. *Thompson* v. *Keohane*, 516 U.S. 99, 112 (1996).
69. *Atwater* v. *Lago Vista*, 532 U.S. 318 (2001).
70. In 1976, in the case of *Watson* v. *U.S.* (432 U.S. 411), the U.S. Supreme Court refused to impose a warrant requirement for felony arrests that occur in public places.
71. *Payton* v. *New York*, 445 U.S. 573, 590 (1980).
72. In 1981, in the case of *U.S.* v. *Steagald* (451 U.S. 204), the Court ruled that a search warrant is also necessary when the planned arrest involves entry into a third party's premises.
73. *Kirk* v. *Louisiana*, 122 S.Ct. 2458, 153 L.Ed.2d 599 (2002).
74. *U.S.* v. *Robinson*, 414 U.S. 218 (1973).
75. Ibid.
76. *Terry* v. *Ohio*, 392 U.S. 1 (1968).
77. *U.S.* v. *Sokolow*, 109 S.Ct. 1581 (1989).
78. The Court was quoting from *U.S.* v. *Brignoni-Ponce*, 422 U.S. 873, 878 (1975).
79. 76 *U.S.* v. *Arvizu*, 534 U.S. 266 (2002).
80. Ibid.
81. *Minnesota* v. *Dickerson*, 113 S.Ct. 2130, 124 L.Ed.2d 334 (1993).
82. *Brown* v. *Texas*, 443 U.S. 47 (1979).
83. *Hiibel* v. *Sixth Judicial District Court of Nevada*, 542 U.S. 177 (2004).
84. *Smith* v. *Ohio*, 110 S.Ct. 1288 (1990).
85. Ibid., at 1289.
86. *California* v. *Hodari D.*, 111 S.Ct. 1547 (1991).
87. *Criminal Justice Newsletter*, May 1, 1991, p. 2.
88. *Illinois* v. *Wardlow*, 528 U.S. 119 (2000).
89. Ibid., syllabus, http://supct.law.cornell.edu/supct/html/98-1036.ZS.html (accessed April 1, 2009).
90. Ibid.
91. *Arkansas* v. *Sanders*, 442 U.S. 753 (1979).
92. Ibid.
93. *U.S.* v. *Borchardt*, 809 F.2d 1115 (5th Cir. 1987).
94. *FBI Law Enforcement Bulletin*, January 1988, p. 28.
95. *Carroll* v. *U.S.*, 267 U.S. 132 (1925).
96. *Preston* v. *U.S.*, 376 U.S. 364 (1964).
97. *Arizona* v. *Gant*, 556 U.S. 332 (2009).
98. *South Dakota* v. *Opperman*, 428 U.S. 364 (1976).
99. *Colorado* v. *Bertine*, 479 U.S. 367, 107 S.Ct. 741 (1987).
100. *Florida* v. *Wells*, 110 S.Ct. 1632 (1990).
101. *Terry* v. *Ohio*, 392 U.S. 1 (1968).
102. *California* v. *Acevedo*, 500 U.S. 565 (1991).
103. *Ornelas* v. *U.S.*, 517 U.S. 690, 696 (1996).
104. Ibid.
105. The phrase is usually attributed to the 1991 U.S. Supreme Court case of *California* v. *Acevedo* (500 U.S. 565 [1991]). See Devallis Rutledge, "Taking an Inventory," *Police*, November 1995, pp. 8–9. See also *Pennsylvania* v. *Labron*, 518 U.S. 938 (1996), in which the Court held that if a vehicle is readily mobile and probable cause exists to believe it contains contraband, the Fourth Amendment permits police to search the vehicle, and contraband seized from such a search should not be suppressed.
106. *Florida* v. *Jimeno*, 111 S.Ct. 1801 (1991).
107. Ibid., syllabus, http://laws.findlaw.com/us/500/248.html (accessed March 2, 2009).
108. *U.S.* v. *Ross*, 456 U.S. 798 (1982).
109. Ibid.
110. *Whren* v. *U.S.*, 517 U.S. 806 (1996).
111. See *Pennsylvania* v. *Mimms*, 434 U.S. 106 (1977).
112. *Maryland* v. *Wilson*, 117 S.Ct. 882 (1997).
113. *Knowles* v. *Iowa*, 525 U.S. 113 (1998).
114. *Wyoming* v. *Houghton*, 526 U.S. 295 (1999).
115. *Thornton* v. *U.S.*, 41 U.S. 615 (2004).
116. *Illinois* v. *Caballes*, 543 U.S. 405 (2005).
117. *Davis* v. *U.S.*, U.S. Supreme Court, No. 09-11328 (decided June 16, 2011).
118. *Arizona* v. *Gant*, 556 U.S. 332 (2009).
119. *Michigan Dept. of State Police* v. *Sitz*, 110 S.Ct. 2481 (1990).
120. *U.S.* v. *Martinez-Fuerte*, 428 U.S. 543 (1976).
121. Ibid., syllabus.
122. *Illinois* v. *Lidster*, 540 U.S. 419 (2004).
123. *U.S.* v. *Villamonte-Marquez*, 462 U.S. 579 (1983).
124. *California* v. *Carney*, 471 U.S. 386, 105 S.Ct. 2066, 85 L.Ed.2d 406, 53 U.S.L.W. 4521 (1985).
125. *U.S.* v. *Hill*, 855 F.2d 664 (10th Cir. 1988).
126. *National Treasury Employees Union* v. *Von Raab*, 489 U.S. 656 (1989).
127. *Skinner* v. *Railway Labor Executives' Association*, 489 U.S. 602 (1989).
128. *Florida* v. *Bostick*, 111 S.Ct. 2382 (1991).
129. *Bond* v. *U.S.*, 529 U.S. 334 (2000), http://supct.law.cornell.edu/supct/html/98-9349.ZS.html (accessed January 10, 2009).
130. *U.S.* v. *Drayton*, 122 S.Ct. 2105 (2002).
131. *U.S.* v. *Flores-Montano*, 541 U.S. 149 (2004).
132. *People* v. *Deutsch*, 96 C.D.O.S. 2827 (1996).
133. The thermal imager differs from infrared devices (such as night-vision goggles) in that infrared devices amplify the infrared spectrum of light, whereas thermal imagers register solely the portion of the infrared spectrum that we call heat.
134. *People* v. *Deutsch*, 96 C.D.O.S. 2827 (1996).
135. *Kyllo* v. *U.S.*, 533 U.S. 27 (2001).
136. Ibid.

137. *Aguilar* v. *Texas*, 378 U.S. 108 (1964).
138. *U.S.* v. *Harris*, 403 U.S. 573 (1971).
139. Ibid. at 584.
140. *Illinois* v. *Gates*, 426 U.S. 213 (1983).
141. *Alabama* v. *White*, 110 S.Ct. 2412 (1990).
142. Ibid., at 2417.
143. *Florida* v. *J. L.*, 529 U.S. 266 (2000).
144. Some of the wording in this paragraph is adapted from the *LII Bulletin*, "End of Term Wrap-Up," June 29, 2000 (e-mail bulletin of the Legal Information Institute, Cornell University School of Law).
145. *U.S. Dept. of Justice* v. *Landano*, 113 S.Ct. 2014, 124 L.Ed.2d 84 (1993).
146. Richard Willing, "Illinois Law First to Order Taping Murder Confessions," *USA Today*, July 18, 2003.
147. Richard A. Leo and Kimberly D. Richman, "Mandate the Electronic Recording of Police Interrogations," *Crime and Public Policy*, Vol. 6 (June 2008), http://ssrn.com/abstract=1141335 (accessed September 1, 2009).
148. *South Dakota* v. *Neville*, 103 S.Ct. 916 (1983).
149. *Brown* v. *Mississippi*, 297 U.S. 278 (1936).
150. *Ashcraft* v. *Tennessee*, 322 U.S. 143 (1944).
151. *Chambers* v. *Florida*, 309 U.S. 227 (1940).
152. Ibid.
153. *Leyra* v. *Denno*, 347 U.S. 556 (1954).
154. *Arizona* v. *Fulminante*, 111 S.Ct. 1246 (1991).
155. *Chapman* v. *California*, 386 U.S. 18 (1967).
156. *State* v. *Fulminante*, No. CR-95-0160.
157. State v. Henderson, August 24, 2011.
158. *Perry* v. *New Hampshire*, U.S. Supreme Court, No. 10-8974 (decided January 11, 2012).
159. *Escobedo* v. *Illinois*, 378 U.S. 478 (1964).
160. *Edwards* v. *Arizona*, 451 U.S. 477, 101 S.Ct. 1880, 68 L.Ed.2d 378 (1981).
161. *Minnick* v. *Mississippi*, 498 U.S. 146 (1990).
162. *Michigan* v. *Jackson*, 475 U.S. 625 (1986).
163. *Arizona* v. *Roberson*, 486 U.S. 675, 108 S.Ct. 2093 (1988).
164. *Davis* v. *U.S.*, 114 S.Ct. 2350 (1994).
165. *Montejo* v. *Louisiana*, 556 U.S. 778 (2009).
166. *Maryland* v. *Shatzer*, U.S. Supreme Court, No. 08-680 (2010).
167. *Miranda* v. *Arizona*, 384 U.S. 436 (1966).
168. "Immigrants Get Civil Rights," *USA Today*, June 11, 1992.
169. *U.S.* v. *Dickerson*, 166 F.3d 667 (1999).
170. *Dickerson* v. *U.S.*, 530 U.S. 428 (2000).
171. *U.S.* v. *Patane*, 542 U.S. 630 (2004).
172. *Missouri* v. *Seibert*, 542 U.S. 600 (2004).
173. *Miranda* v. *Arizona*, 384 U.S. 436 (1966).
174. *Silverthorne Lumber Co.* v. *U.S.*, 251 U.S. 385 (1920).
175. *Wong Sun* v. *U.S.*, 371 U.S. 471 (1963).
176. *Moran* v. *Burbine*, 475 U.S. 412, 421 (1986).
177. *Colorado* v. *Spring*, 479 U.S. 564, 107 S.Ct. 851 (1987).
178. *Brewer* v. *Williams*, 430 U.S. 387 (1977).
179. *Nix* v. *Williams*, 104 S.Ct. 2501 (1984).
180. "ACLU Eyes Boston Bombing Suspect's Miranda Rights," Associate Press, April 20, 2013, http://abcnews.go.com/US/wireStory/aclu-eyes-boston-bombing-suspects-miranda-rights-19007093#.UXPjlat4bYg (accessed April 21, 2013).
181. *New York* v. *Quarles*, 104 S.Ct. 2626, 81 L.Ed.2d 550 (1984).
182. *Colorado* v. *Connelly*, 107 S.Ct. 515, 93 L.Ed.2d 473 (1986).
183. *Kuhlmann* v. *Wilson*, 477 U.S. 436 (1986).
184. *Illinois* v. *Perkins*, 495 U.S. 292 (1990).
185. *Rock* v. *Zimmerman*, 543 F. Supp. 179 (M.D. Pa. 1982).
186. Ibid.
187. See *Oregon* v. *Mathiason*, 429 U.S. 492, 97 S.Ct. 711 (1977).
188. *South Dakota* v. *Neville*, 103 S.Ct. 916 (1983).
189. *Arizona* v. *Mauro*, 107 S.Ct. 1931, 95 L.Ed.2d 458 (1987).
190. *Doyle* v. *Ohio*, 426 U.S. 610 (1976).
191. *Brecht* v. *Abrahamson*, 113 S.Ct. 1710, 123 L.Ed.2d 353 (1993).
192. Citing *Kotteakos* v. *U.S.*, 328 U.S. 750 (1946).
193. See Linda Greenhouse, "The Supreme Court: Supreme Court Roundup—Police Questioning Allowed to the Point of Coercion," *New York Times*, May 28, 2003.
194. *Chavez* v. *Martinez*, 538 U.S. 760 (2003).
195. Ibid.
196. *Berghuis* v. *Thompson*, 560 U.S. ___ (2010).
197. *Salinas* v. *Texas*, U.S. Supreme Court, No. 12-246 (decided June 17, 2013).
198. *Hayes* v. *Florida*, 470 U.S. 811, 105 S.Ct. 1643 (1985).
199. *Winston* v. *Lee*, 470 U.S. 753, 105 S.Ct. 1611 (1985).
200. *Schmerber* v. *California*, 384 U.S. 757 (1966).
201. "Man Coughs Up Cocaine while in Custody," *Police Magazine* online, March 4, 2005, http://www.policemag.com/t_newspick.cfm?rank574703 (accessed January 4, 2006).
202. *U.S.* v. *Montoya de Hernandez*, 473 U.S. 531, 105 S.Ct. 3304 (1985).
203. Ibid.
204. *Olmstead* v. *U.S.*, 277 U.S. 438 (1928).
205. *On Lee* v. *U.S.*, 343 U.S. 747 (1952).
206. *Lopez* v. *U.S.*, 373 U.S. 427 (1963).
207. *Berger* v. *New York*, 388 U.S. 41 (1967).
208. *Katz* v. *U.S.*, 389 U.S. 347 (1967).
209. *Lee* v. *Florida*, 392 U.S. 378 (1968).
210. Federal Communications Act of 1934, U.S. Code, Title 47, Section 151.
211. *U.S.* v. *White*, 401 U.S. 745 (1971).
212. *U.S.* v. *Karo*, 468 U.S. 705 (1984).
213. *U.S.* v. *Scott*, 436 U.S. 128 (1978).
214. For more information, see *FBI Law Enforcement Bulletin*, June 1987, p. 25.
215. Electronic Communications Privacy Act of 1986, Public Law 99-508.
216. For more information on the ECPA, see Robert A. Fiatal, "The Electronic Communications Privacy Act: Addressing Today's Technology," *FBI Law Enforcement Bulletin*, April 1988, pp. 24–30.
217. Communications Assistance for Law Enforcement Act of 1994, Public Law 103-414.
218. U.S. Department of Justice, Office of the Inspector General, *Implementation of the Communications Assistance for Law Enforcement Act by the Federal Bureau of Investigation* (Washington, DC: U.S. Dept. of Justice, 2004).
219. Administrative Office of the United States Courts, "2010 Wiretap Report," http://www.uscourts.gov/Statistics/WiretapReports/WiretapReport2010.aspx (accessed June 1, 2013).
220. Telecommunications Act of 1996, Public Law 104-104, 110 Statute 56.
221. Title 47, U.S.C.A., Section 223(a)(1)(B)(ii) (Supp. 1997).
222. *Reno* v. *ACLU*, 117 S.Ct. 2329 (1997).
223. U.S. Code, Title 18, Section 1030.
224. Ibid., Section 202.
225. U.S. Code, Title 18, Section 2703(c).
226. Ibid.
227. Public Law 109-177.
228. "Obama Signs Last-Minute Patriot Act Extension," Fox News, http://www.foxnews.com/politics/2011/05/27/senate-clearing-way-extend-patriot-act, May 27, 2011 (accessed September 1, 2011).

229. Technical Working Group for Electronic Crime Scene Investigation, *Electronic Crime Scene Investigation: A Guide for First Responders* (Washington, DC: National Institute of Justice, 2001), from which much of the information in this section is taken.
230. Ibid., p. 2.
231. Computer Crime and Intellectual Property Section, U.S. Department of Justice, *Searching and Seizing Computers and Obtaining Electronic Evidence in Criminal Investigations* (Washington, DC: U.S. Dept. of Justice, 2002), http://www.usdoj.gov/criminal/cybercrime/s&smanual2002.htm (accessed August 4, 2007).
232. Technical Working Group, *Electronic Crime Scene Investigation*, p. 2.
233. *U.S. v. Carey*, 172 F. 3d 1268 (10th Cir. 1999).
234. *U.S. v. Turner*, 169 F. 3d 84 (1st Cir. 1999).

8 POLICING: ISSUES AND CHALLENGES

OUTLINE

- Introduction
- Police Personality and Culture
- Corruption and Integrity
- The Dangers of Police Work
- Police Use of Force
- Racial Profiling and Biased Policing
- Police Civil Liability

LEARNING OBJECTIVES

After reading this chapter, you should be able to

- Summarize the law enforcement code of ethics and police subculture.
- Describe different types of police corruption and possible methods for building police integrity.
- Describe the dangers, conflicts, challenges, and sources of stress that police officers face in their work.
- Summarize the guidelines for using force and for determining when excessive force has been used.
- Describe racial profiling and biased policing, including why they have become significant issues in policing.
- Summarize the civil, criminal, and nonjudicial remedies available to individuals who believe their rights have been violated.
- Describe civil liability issues associated with policing, including common sources of civil suits against the police.

The police at all times should maintain a relationship with the public that gives reality to the historic tradition that the police are the public and that the public are the police.

SIR ROBERT PEEL, 1829[1]

police working personality All aspects of the traditional values and patterns of behavior evidenced by police officers who have been effectively socialized into the police subculture. Characteristics of the police personality often extend to the personal lives of law enforcement personnel.

Introduction

On a cold evening in late November, 2012, a young New York City Police Department (NYPD) officer was caught on a tourist's cell phone camera giving clean socks and shoes to a homeless man sitting on a sidewalk in Times Square. The photo was posted to Facebook and soon went viral, causing an outpouring of well wishes for the officer, Larry DePrimo. What DePrimo did that night was not part of his job, but a personal act of kindness that demonstrated the human side of police work. Interviewed later by *People Magazine*, DePrimo said, "Honestly, I feel undeserving of so much thanks. I just love to help people. That's why I became a cop."[2]

Today's police officers and administrators face many complex issues, and not all of the stories involving police work end well. Some concerns, such as corruption, on-the-job dangers, and the use of deadly force, derive from the very nature of policing. Others, like racial profiling and exposure to civil liability, have arisen due to common practices, characteristic police values, public expectations, legislative action, and ongoing societal change. Certainly, one of the most significant challenges facing American law enforcement today is policing a multicultural society. All of these issues are discussed in the pages that follow. We begin, however, with the police recruit socialization process. It is vital to understand this process because the values and expectations learned through it not only contribute to the nature of many important police issues but also determine how the police view and respond to those issues.

Peter Kramer/NBC/NBC NewsWire via Getty Images

NYPD officer Larry DePrimo. DePrimo made headlines in 2012 when he was photographed by a tourist giving shoes and socks to a homeless man on a cold winter night, and the photo went viral on Facebook. Is DePrimo a typical police officer?

Police Personality and Culture

New police officers learn what is considered appropriate police behavior by working with seasoned veterans. Through conversations with other officers in the locker room, in a squad car, or over a cup of coffee, a new recruit is introduced to the value-laden subculture of police work. A definition of *police subculture* was given in Chapter 6. It can also be understood as "the set of informal values which characterize the police force as a distinct community with a common identity."[3] This process of informal socialization plays a much bigger role than formal police academy training in determining how rookies come to see police work. Through it, new officers gain a shared view of the world that can best be described as "streetwise." Streetwise cops know what official department policy is, but they also know the most efficient way to get a job done. By the time rookie officers become streetwise, they know which of the various informal means of accomplishing the job are acceptable to other officers. The police subculture creates few real mavericks, but it also produces few officers who view their jobs exclusively in terms of public mandates and official dictums.

In the 1960s, renowned criminologist Jerome Skolnick described what he called the **police working personality**.[4] Skolnick's description of the police personality was consistent with William Westley's classic study of the Gary (Indiana) Police Department, in which he found a police culture with its own "customs, laws, and morality,"[5] and with Arthur Niederhoffer's observation that cynicism was pervasive among officers in New York City.[6] More recent authors have claimed that the "big curtain of secrecy" surrounding much of police work shields knowledge of the nature of the police personality from outsiders.[7] Taken in concert, these writers offer a picture of the police working personality shown in Table 8-1.

TABLE 8-1 | The Police Personality

Authoritarian	Honorable	Loyal
Conservative	Hostile	Prejudiced
Cynical	Individualistic	Secret
Dogmatic	Insecure	Suspicious
Efficient		

Follow the author's tweets about the latest crime and justice news @schmalleger.

Some characteristics of the police working personality are essential for survival and effectiveness. For example, because officers are often exposed to highly emotional and potentially threatening confrontations with belligerent people, they must develop *efficient, authoritarian* strategies for gaining control over others. Similarly, a suspicious nature makes for a good police officer, especially during interrogations and investigations.

However, other characteristics of the police working personality are not so advantageous. For example, many officers are cynical, and some can be hostile toward members of the public who do not share their conservative values. These traits result from regular interaction with suspects, most of whom, even when they are clearly guilty in the eyes of the police, deny any wrongdoing. Eventually, personal traits that result from typical police work become firmly ingrained, setting the cornerstone of the police working personality.

There are at least two sources of the police personality. On the one hand, it may be that components of the police personality already exist in some individuals and draw them toward police work.[8] Supporting this view are studies that indicate that police officers who come from conservative backgrounds view themselves as defenders of middle-class morality.[9] On the other hand, some aspects of the police personality can be attributed to the socialization into the police subculture that rookie officers experience when they are inducted into police ranks.

Researchers have reported similar elements in police subculture throughout the United States. They have concluded that, like all cultures, police subculture is a relatively stable collection of beliefs and values that is unlikely to change from within. Police subculture may, however, be changed through external pressures, such as new hiring practices, investigations into police corruption or misuse of authority, and commission reports that create pressures for police reform. Learn more about police subculture and police behavior at **http://clontz.mc-companies.com/additional_readings/subculture.htm**.

Corruption and Integrity

In 2012, East Haven, Connecticut, police Sargent John Miller and three fellow officers, David Cari, Dennis Spaulding, and Jason Zullo, were arrested by agents of the Federal Bureau of Investigation (FBI) and charged with conspiracy, false arrest, excessive force, and obstruction of justice.[10] The men, authorities

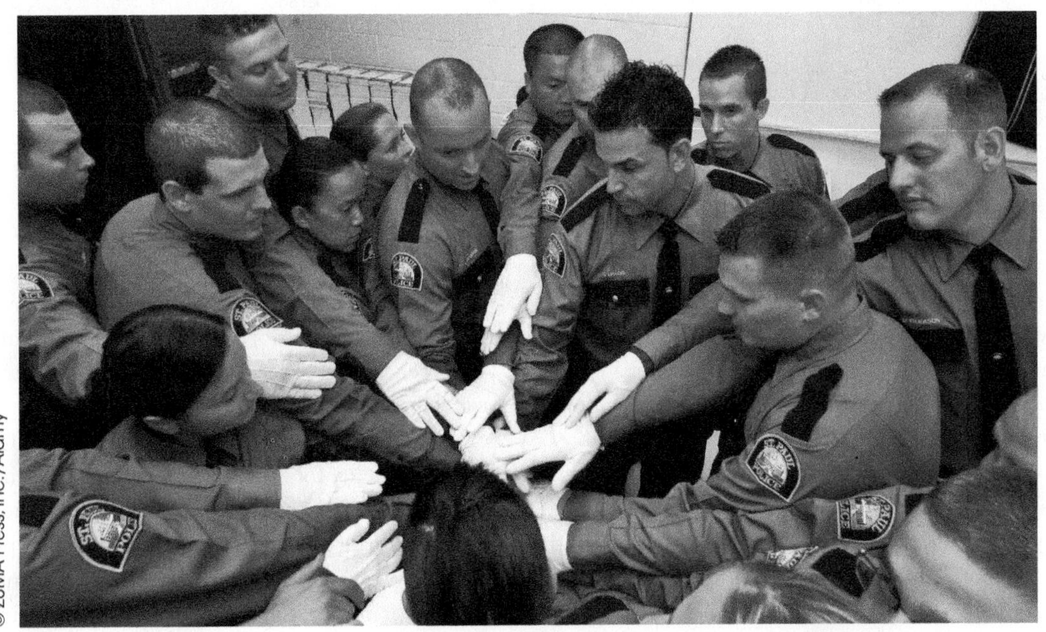

© ZUMA Press, Inc./Alamy

Police cadets in St. Paul, Minnesota, celebrate their graduation from the police academy. The police working personality has been characterized as authoritarian, suspicious, and conservative. How does the police working personality develop?

■ **police corruption** The abuse of police authority for personal or organizational gain.[i]

CJ | ISSUES
Policing a Multicultural Society

Members of some social groups have backgrounds, values, and perspectives that, although they do not directly support lawbreaking, contrast sharply with those of many police officials. Robert M. Shusta, a well-known writer on multicultural law enforcement, says that police officers "need to recognize the fact of poor police–minority relations historically, including *unequal* treatment under the law."[1] Moreover, says Shusta, "many officers and citizens are defensive with each other because their contact is tinged with negative historical 'baggage.'"

In other words, even though discrimination in the enforcement of the criminal law may not be commonplace today, it was in the past—and perceptions built on past experience are often difficult to change. Moreover, if the function of law enforcement is to "protect and serve" law-abiding citizens from all backgrounds, then it becomes vital for officers to understand and respect differences in habits, customs, beliefs, patterns of thought, and traditions.[2] Hence, as Shusta says, "the acts of approaching, communicating, questioning, assisting, and establishing trust with members of different groups require special knowledge and skills that have nothing to do with the fact that 'the law is the law' and must be enforced equally. Acquiring sensitivity, knowledge, and skills leads to [an increased appreciation for the position of others] that will contribute to improved communications with members of all groups."[3]

How can police officers acquire greater sensitivity to the issues involved in policing a diverse multicultural society? Some researchers suggest that law enforcement officers of *all* backgrounds begin by exploring their own prejudices. Prejudices, which are judgments or opinions formed before facts are known and which usually involve negative or unfavorable thoughts about groups of people, can lead to discrimination. Most people, including police officers, are able to reduce their tendency to discriminate against those who are different by exploring and uprooting their own personal prejudices.

One technique for identifying prejudices is cultural awareness training. As practiced in some police departments today, cultural awareness training explores the impact of culture on human behavior—and especially on lawbreaking behavior. Cultural awareness training generally involves four stages:[4]

- *Clarifying the relationship between cultural awareness and police professionalism.* As Shusta explains it, "The more professional a police officer is, the more sophisticated he or she is in responding to people of all backgrounds and the more successful he or she is in cross-cultural contact."[5]
- *Recognizing personal prejudices.* In the second stage of cultural awareness training, participating officers are asked to recognize and identify their own personal prejudices and biases. Once prejudices have been identified, trainers strive to show how they can affect daily behavior.
- *Acquiring sensitivity to police–community relations.* In this stage of training, participating officers learn about historical and existing community perceptions of the police. Training can often be enhanced through the use of carefully chosen and well-qualified guest speakers or participants from minority communities.
- *Developing interpersonal relations skills.* The goal of this last stage of training is to help officers develop the positive verbal and nonverbal communications skills necessary for successful interaction with community members. Many trainers believe that basic skills training will result in the continuing development of such skills because officers will quickly begin to see the benefits (in terms of lessened interpersonal conflict) of effective interpersonal skills.

[1]Robert M. Shusta et al., *Multicultural Law Enforcement: Strategies for Peacekeeping in a Diverse Society*, 2nd ed. (Upper Saddle River, NJ: Prentice Hall, 2002), p. 4.
[2]Ibid., p. 16.
[3]Ibid., p. 4.
[4]Ibid., pp. 104–106.
[5]Ibid., p. 4.

said, had spent years harassing and mistreating citizens, especially those of Hispanic origin, in the neighborhoods they patrolled. Known as Miller's Boys, the officers worked the shift from 4 p.m. to midnight, and allegedly used their authority to intimidate suspects into confessing to crimes they likely hadn't committed, and to harass immigrants living in the local Latino community. Only months before the officers' arrest, the U.S. Department of Justice issued a scathing indictment of the East Haven Police Department, saying that its members had engaged in widespread "biased policing, unconstitutional searches and seizures, and the use of excessive force."

Police corruption has been a problem in American society since the early days of policing. It is probably an ancient and natural tendency of human beings to attempt to placate or win over those in positions of authority over them, while some people in authority will always be tempted to abuse. These tendencies become even more complicated in today's materialistic society by greed and by the personal and financial benefits to be derived from evading the law. The temptations toward illegality offered to police range from a free cup of coffee from a restaurant owner to huge monetary bribes arranged by drug dealers to guarantee that the police will look the other way as an important shipment of contraband arrives. As noted criminologist Carl Klockars says, policing, by its very nature, "is an occupation that is rife with opportunities for misconduct. Policing is a highly discretionary, coercive activity

Ned Gerard/AP Wide World Photos

"No person is above the law," said David B. Fein, left, the U.S. attorney for Connecticut, at a 2012 news conference in Bridgeport, Connecticut, where he announced the arrest of "Miller's Boys"—an allegedly corrupt group of East Haven police officers. Are police officers subject to the rule of law?

that routinely takes place in private settings, out of the sight of supervisors, and in the presence of witnesses who are often regarded as unreliable."[11]

The effects of police corruption are far-reaching. As Michael Palmiotto of Wichita State University notes, "Not only does misconduct committed by an officer personally affect that officer, it also affects the community, the police department that employs the officer and every police department and police officer in America. Frequently, negative police actions caused by inappropriate police behavior reach every corner of the nation, and at times, the world."[12]

Exactly what constitutes corruption is not always clear. Ethicists say that police corruption ranges from minor offenses to serious violations of the law. In recognition of what some have called corruption's "slippery slope,"[13] most police departments now explicitly prohibit officers from accepting even minor gratuities. The slippery slope perspective holds that accepting even small thank-yous from members of the public can lead to a more ready acceptance of larger bribes. An officer who begins to accept, and then expect, gratuities may soon find that his or her practice of policing becomes influenced by such gifts and that larger ones soon follow. At that point, the officer may easily slide to the bottom of the moral slope, which was made slippery by previous small concessions.

Thomas Barker and David Carter, who have studied police corruption in depth, make the distinction between "occupational deviance," which is motivated by the desire for personal benefit, and "abuse of authority, which occurs most often to further the organizational goals of law enforcement, including arrest, ticketing, and the successful conviction of suspects."[14]

Police corruption ranges from minor offenses to serious violations of the law.

FBI Special Agent Frank Perry, former chief of the bureau's ethics unit, distinguishes between police deviance and police corruption. Police deviance, according to Perry, consists of "unprofessional on- and off-duty misconduct, isolated instances of misuse of position, improper relationships with informants or criminals, sexual harassment, disparaging racial or sexual comments, embellished/falsified reporting, time and attendance abuse, insubordination, nepotism, cronyism, and noncriminal unauthorized disclosure of information."[15] Deviance, says Perry, is a precursor to individual and organizational corruption. It may eventually lead to outright corruption unless police supervisors and internal affairs units are alert to the warning signs and actively intervene to prevent corruption from developing.

Figure 8-1 sorts examples of police corruption in terms of seriousness, though not everyone would agree with this ranking. In fact, a survey of 6,982 New York City police officers found that 65% did not classify excessive force, which we define later in this chapter, as a corrupt behavior.[16] Likewise, 71% of responding officers said that accepting a free meal is not a corrupt practice. Another 15% said that personal use of illegal drugs by law enforcement officers should not be considered corruption.

■ **knapp commission** A committee that investigated police corruption in New York City in the early 1970s.

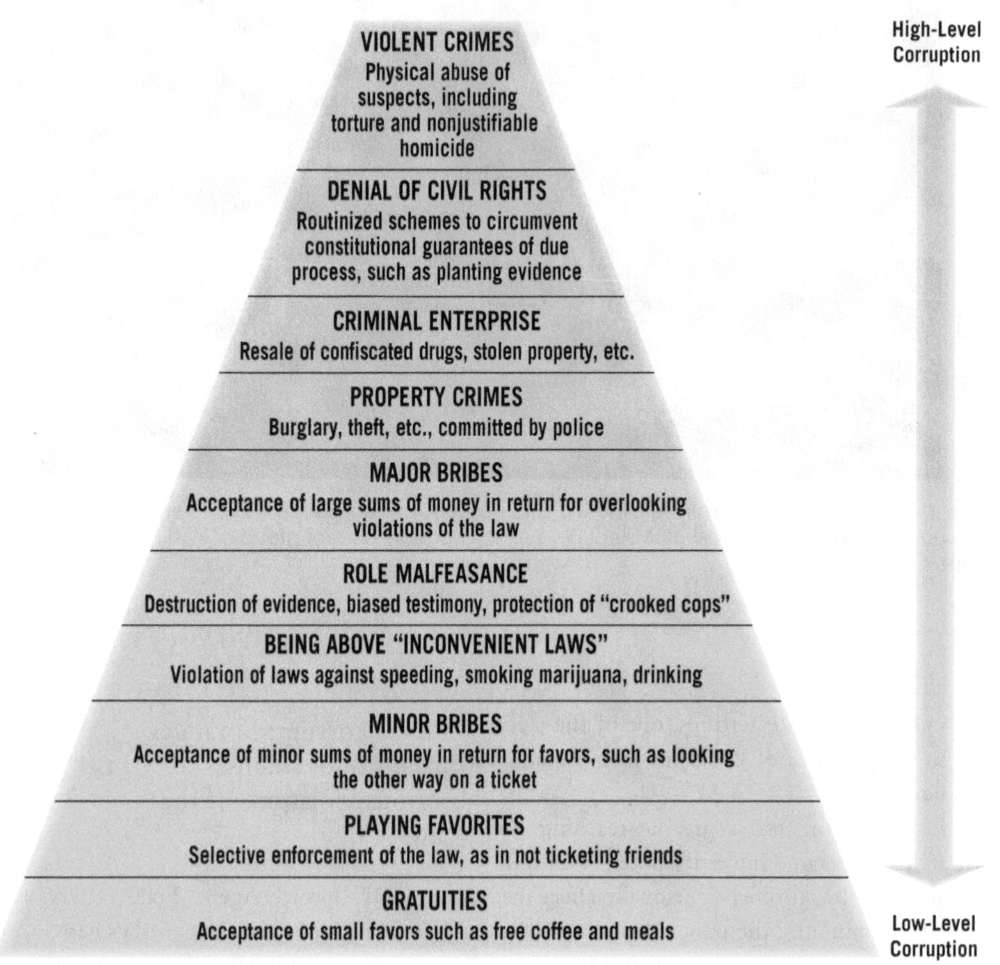

FIGURE 8-1 | Types and Examples of Police Corruption

In the early 1970s, Frank Serpico made headlines when he testified before the **Knapp Commission** on police corruption in New York City.[17] Serpico, an undercover operative within the police department, revealed a complex web of corruption in which money and services routinely changed hands in "protection rackets" created by unethical officers. The authors of the Knapp Commission report distinguished between two types of corrupt officers, which they termed "grass eaters" and "meat eaters."[18] "Grass eating," the more common form of police corruption, was described as illegitimate activity that occurs from time to time in the normal course of police work. It involves mostly small bribes or relatively minor services offered by citizens seeking to avoid arrest and prosecution. "Meat eating" is a much more serious form of corruption, involving an officer's actively seeking illicit moneymaking opportunities. Meat eaters solicit bribes through threat or intimidation, whereas grass eaters commit the less serious offense of failing to refuse bribes that are offered.

In 1993, during 11 days of corruption hearings reminiscent of the Knapp Commission era, a parade of crooked New York police officers testified before a commission headed by former judge and Deputy Mayor Milton Mollen. Among the many revelations, officers spoke of dealing drugs, stealing confiscated drug funds, stifling investigations, and beating innocent people. Officer Michael Dowd, for example, told the commission that he had run a cocaine ring out of his station house in Brooklyn and had bought three homes on Long Island and a Corvette with the money he made. Most shocking of all, however, were allegations that high-level police officials attempted to cover up embarrassing incidents and that many officials may have condoned unprofessional and even criminal practices by the officers under their command. Honest officers,

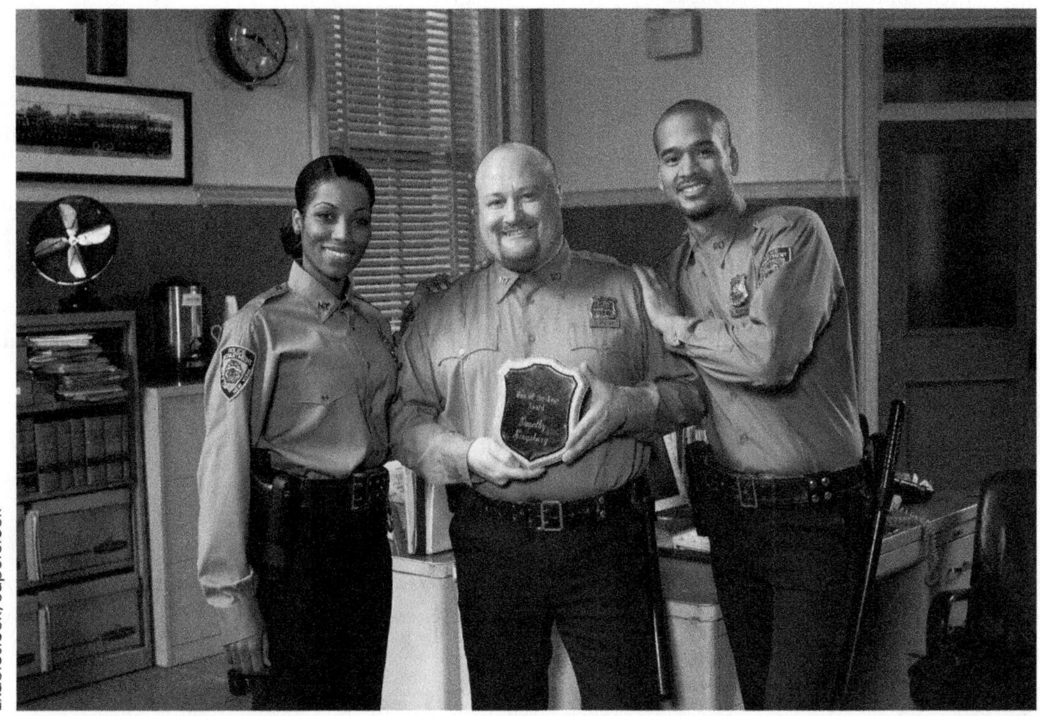

Exactostock/SuperStock

An award ceremony held in recognition of an outstanding law enforcement officer. The appropriate and timely recognition of outstanding and professional police activity can go a long way toward building police integrity and offsetting possible temptations for individual officers to engage in inappropriate behavior. What kinds of activities should be rewarded?

including internal affairs investigators, described how higher authorities had resisted their efforts to end corruption among their colleagues.

Repercussions from the Mollen Commission hearings continue to be felt. In 2004, for example, a New York State judge ruled that the city of New York had to pay special disability benefits to former police officer Jeffrey W. Baird, who served as an informant for the commission. Baird helped uncover corruption while working as an internal affairs officer but suffered from post-traumatic stress disorder after fellow officers threatened him, vandalized his work area, and sent obscene materials to his home.[19]

Money—The Root of Police Evil?

Years ago, Edwin Sutherland applied the concept of *differential association* (discussed in Chapter 3) to the study of deviant behavior.[20] Sutherland suggested that frequent, continued association of one person with another makes the associates similar. Of course, Sutherland was talking about criminals, not police officers. Consider, however, the dilemma of average officers: Their job entails issuing traffic citations to citizens who try to talk their way out of a ticket, dealing with prostitutes who feel hassled by police, and arresting drug users who think it should be their right to do what they want as long as "it doesn't hurt anyone." Officers regularly encounter personal hostility and experience consistent and often quite vocal rejection of society's formalized norms. They receive relatively low pay, which indicates to them that their work is not really valued. By looking at the combination of these factors, it is easy to understand how officers often develop a jaded attitude toward the society they are sworn to protect.

Police officers' low pay may be a critical ingredient of the corruption mix. Salaries paid to police officers in this country have been notoriously low compared to those of other professions that require personal dedication,

Police officers' low pay may be a critical ingredient of the corruption mix.

extensive training, high stress, and the risk of bodily harm. As police work becomes more professional, many police administrators hope that salaries will rise. However, no matter how much police pay increases, it will never be able to compete with the staggering amounts of money to be made through dealing in contraband. Working hand in hand with monetary pressures toward corruption are the moral dilemmas produced by unenforceable laws that provide the basis for criminal profit. During Prohibition, the Wickersham Commission warned of the potential for official corruption inherent in the legislative taboos on alcohol. The immense demand for drink called into question the wisdom of the law while simultaneously providing vast resources designed to circumvent it. Today's drug scene bears similarities to the Prohibition era. As long as there is a market for illegal drugs, the financial as well as societal pressures on the police to profit from the drug trade will remain substantial.

As long as there is a market for illegal drugs, the financial as well as societal pressures on the police to profit from the drug trade will remain substantial.

Building Police Integrity

The difficulties of controlling corruption can be traced to several factors, including the reluctance of police officers to report corrupt activities by their fellow officers, the reluctance of police administrators to acknowledge the existence of corruption in their agencies, the benefits of corrupt transactions to the parties involved, and the lack of immediate victims willing to report corruption. However, high moral standards embedded in the principles of the police profession and effectively communicated to individual officers through formal training and peer-group socialization can raise the level of integrity in any department. Some law enforcement training programs are increasingly determined to reinforce the high ideals many recruits bring to police work and to encourage veteran officers to retain their commitment to the highest professional standards. As one FBI publication explains it, "Ethics training must become an integral part of academy and in-service training for new and experienced officers alike."[21]

High moral standards embedded in the principles of the police profession and effectively communicated to individual officers through formal training and peer-group socialization can raise the level of integrity in any department.

Ethics training, which was discussed in Chapter 6, is part of a "reframing" strategy that emphasizes integrity to target police corruption. In 1997, for example, the National Institute of Justice (NIJ) released a report titled *Police Integrity: Public Service with Honor.*[22] The report, based on recommendations made by participants in a national symposium on police integrity, suggested (1) integrating ethics training into the programs offered by newly funded Regional Community Policing Institutes throughout the country, (2) broadening research activities in the area of ethics through NIJ-awarded grants for research on police integrity, and (3) conducting case studies of departments that have an excellent track record in the area of police integrity.

The NIJ report was followed in 2001 by a U.S. Department of Justice document titled *Principles for Promoting Police Integrity.*[23] The foreword to that document states, "For . . . policing to be successful, and crime reduction efforts to be effective, citizens must have trust in the police. All of us must work together to address the problems of excessive use of force and racial profiling, and—equally important—the perceptions of many minority residents that law enforcement treats them unfairly, if we are to build the confidence in law enforcement necessary for continued progress. Our goal must be professional law enforcement that gives all citizens of our country the feeling that they are being treated fairly, equally and with respect." The report covered such topics as the use of force; complaints and misconduct investigations; accountability and effective management; training; nondiscriminatory policing; and recruitment, hiring, and retention. Read the full report, which provides examples of promising police practices and policies that promote integrity, at **http://www.justicestudies.com/pubs/integrity.pdf**.

In 2000, the International Association of Chiefs of Police (IACP), in an effort to reinforce the importance of ethical standards in policing, adopted the Law Enforcement Oath of Honor, shown in the "Ethics and Professionalism" box in Chapter 6. The IACP suggests that the Law Enforcement Oath of Honor should be seen by individual officers as a statement of commitment to ethical behavior. It is meant to reinforce the principles embodied in the IACP's Law Enforcement Code of Ethics, which is printed in the "Ethics and Professionalism" box in Chapter 6.

In December 2005, the U.S. Department of Justice weighed in on the issue of police integrity with a Research for Practice report titled *Enhancing Police Integrity*.[24] The report said that "an agency's culture of integrity, as defined by clearly understood and implemented policies and rules, may be more important in shaping the ethics of police officers than hiring the 'right' people."[25] The report's authors also noted that officers tend to evaluate the seriousness of various types of misconduct by observing and assessing their department's response in detecting and disciplining it. If unwritten policies conflict with written policies, the authors observed, then the resulting confusion undermines an agency's overall integrity-enhancing efforts. *Enhancing Police Integrity* is available online at **http://www.justicestudies.com/pubs/epi.pdf**. An FBI-sponsored article on police corruption and ethics can be accessed at **http://www.justicestudies.com/pubs/policecorrup.pdf**.

■ **internal affairs** The branch of a police organization tasked with investigating charges of wrongdoing involving members of the department.

Most large-city law enforcement agencies have their own **internal affairs** divisions, which are empowered to investigate charges of wrongdoing made against officers. Where necessary, state police agencies may be called on to examine reported incidents. Federal agencies, including the FBI and the Drug Enforcement Administration, get involved when corruption violates federal statutes. The U.S. Department of Justice (DOJ), through various investigative offices, has the authority to examine possible violations of civil rights resulting from the misuse of police authority. The DOJ is often supported in these endeavors by the American Civil Liberties Union (ACLU), the National Association for the Advancement of Colored People (NAACP), and other watchdog groups.

Internal affairs divisions are empowered to investigate charges of wrongdoing made against officers.

Officers suspected of law violations may invoke their *Garrity rights*—which are protections that officers have against self-incrimination in the face of questioning. Like the *Miranda* rights guaranteed to civilian criminal suspects who face questioning by police officers, Garrity rights protect officers themselves when being questioned by representatives of their department's internal affairs division or by their superior officers.

Drug Testing of Police Employees

On November 17, 2000, the U.S. Court of Appeals for the Fourth Circuit found that the chief of police in Westminster, Maryland, had acted properly in asking a doctor to test an officer's urine for the presence of heroin without the officer's knowledge.[26] Westminster Police Officer Eric Carroll had gone to the local hospital complaining of tightness in his chest and fatigue. The doctor who examined Carroll diagnosed him as suffering from high blood pressure. Carroll was placed on disability leave for three days. While Carroll was gone, the police chief received a call from someone who said that the officer was using heroin. The chief verified the caller's identity and then called the department doctor and asked him to test Carroll for drugs—but without informing the officer of the test. When Carroll returned to the physician for a follow-up visit, the doctor took a urine sample, saying that it was to test for the presence of blood. Although no blood was found in Carroll's urine, it did test positive for heroin. As a consequence, Officer Carroll's employment with the department was terminated. He then sued in federal court, alleging conspiracy, defamation, and violations of his constitutional rights. The Fourth Circuit Court of Appeals, however, determined that the chief's actions were reasonable because, among other things, Carroll had signed a preemployment waiver that permitted the department to conduct drug tests at any time, with or without cause.[27]

The widespread potential for police corruption created by illicit drugs has led to focused efforts to combat drug use by officers. Drug-testing programs in local police departments are an example of such efforts. The IACP has developed a model drug-testing policy for police managers. The policy, designed to meet the needs of local departments, suggests the following:[28]

- Testing all applicants and recruits for drug or narcotics use
- Testing current employees when performance difficulties or documentation indicates a potential drug problem
- Testing current employees when they are involved in the use of excessive force or when they suffer or cause an on-duty injury
- Routine testing of all employees assigned to special "high-risk" areas, such as narcotics and vice

The courts have supported drug testing based on a reasonable suspicion that drug abuse has been or is occurring,[29] although random testing of officers was banned by the New York State Supreme Court in the case of *Philip Caruso, President of P.B.A.* v. *Benjamin Ward, Police Commissioner* (1986).[30] Citing overriding public interests, a 1989 decision by the U.S. Supreme Court upheld the testing of U.S. Customs personnel applying for transfer into drug-law enforcement positions or into positions requiring a firearm.[31] Many legal issues surrounding employee drug testing remain to be resolved in court, however.

Complicating this issue is the fact that drug and alcohol addictions are "handicaps" protected by the Federal Rehabilitation Act of 1973. As such, federal law enforcement employees, as well as those working for agencies with federal contracts, are entitled to counseling and treatment before action can be taken toward termination.

Employee drug testing in police departments, as in many other agencies, is a sensitive subject. Some claim that existing tests for drug use are inaccurate, yielding a significant number of "false positives." Repeated testing and high threshold levels for narcotic substances in the blood may eliminate many of these concerns. Less easy to address, however, is the belief that drug testing intrudes on the personal rights and professional dignity of individual employees.

The Dangers of Police Work

On October 15, 1991, the National Law Enforcement Officers' Memorial was unveiled in Washington, DC. The memorial contained the names of 12,561 law enforcement officers killed in the line of duty, including U.S. Marshals Service Officer Robert Forsyth, who in 1794 was the nation's first law enforcement officer to be killed on the job. More than 6,000 names have been added since opening day.[32] At the memorial, an interactive video system provides visitors with brief biographies and photographs of officers who have died. Tour the memorial by visiting **http://www.nleomf.com**.

As the memorial proves, police work is, by its very nature, dangerous. Although many officers never once fire their weapons in the line of duty, some die while performing their jobs. On-the-job police deaths occur from stress, training accidents, and auto crashes. However, it is violent death at the hands of criminal offenders that police officers and their families fear most.

Violence in the Line of Duty

Most officers who are shot are killed by lone suspects armed with a single weapon. In 2012, 119 American law enforcement officers were killed in the line of duty.[33] Figure 8-2 shows the number of officers killed in different types of incidents in 2012. In 2001, the attacks on the World Trade Center resulted in the greatest ever annual loss of life of on-duty law enforcement officers when 72 police officers perished.[34]

A study by the FBI found that, generally, slain officers were good natured and conservative in the use of physical force, "as compared to other law enforcement officers in similar situations. They were also perceived as being well-liked by the community and the department, friendly to everyone, laid back, and easy going."[35] Finally, the study, which was published before the September 11, 2001, terrorist attacks, also found that most officers who were killed failed to wear protective vests.

For statistics on police killings to have meaning beyond the personal tragedy they entail, it is necessary to place them within a larger framework. There are approximately 732,000 state and local (full- and part-time) sworn police employees in this country,[36] along with another 105,000 federal agents.[37] Such numbers demonstrate that the rate of violent death among law enforcement officers in the line of duty is small indeed.

Roger L. Wollenberg UPI Photo Service/Newscom

NYPD officer James Smith makes a rubbing of his wife Moira Smith's freshly engraved name at the National Law Enforcement Officers Memorial in Washington, D.C. Inscribed on the walls of the memorial are the names of the more than 18,000 police officers who gave their lives in the line of duty. In what other ways are fallen officers honored?

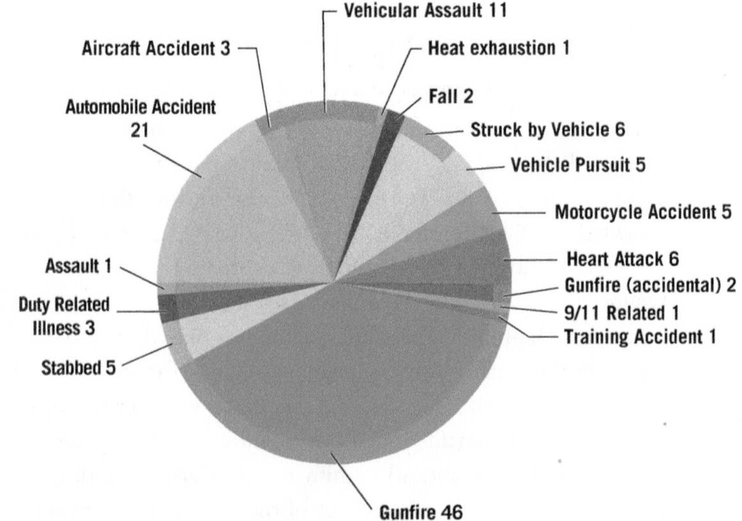

FIGURE 8-2 | U.S. Law Enforcement Officers Killed in the Line of Duty, 2012

Source: Based on data from the Officer Down Memorial Page website, http://www.odmp.org (accessed June 1, 2013).

■ **biological weapon** A biological agent used to threaten human life (for example, anthrax, smallpox, or any infectious disease).[ii]

Risk of Disease and Infected Evidence

Dangers other than violence also threaten law enforcement officers. The increase in serious diseases that can be transmitted by blood and other body fluids, the possible planned release of active **biological weapons** like anthrax or smallpox, and the fact that crime and accident scenes are inherently dangerous combine to make *caution* a necessary watchword among investigators and first responders. Routine criminal and accident investigations hold the potential for infection through minor cuts and abrasions resulting from contact with the broken glass and torn metal of a wrecked vehicle, the sharp edges of knives found at the scene of an assault or murder, and drug implements like razor blades and hypodermic needles secreted in vehicles, homes, and pockets. Such minor injuries, previously shrugged off by many police personnel, have become a focal point for warnings about the dangers of AIDS, hepatitis B, tuberculosis, and other diseases spread through contact with infected blood.

Infection can also occur from the use of breath alcohol instruments on infected persons, the handling of evidence of all types, seemingly innocuous implements like staples, the emergency delivery of babies in squad cars, and the attack (especially bites) by infected individuals who are being questioned or who are in custody. Understandably, officers are concerned about how to handle the threat of AIDS and other bloodborne diseases. However, as a publication of the NYPD reminds its officers, "Police officers have a professional responsibility to render assistance to those who are in need of our services. We cannot refuse to help. Persons with infectious diseases must be treated with the care and dignity we show all citizens."[38]

Of equal concern is the threat of biological agents. Although crime scenes and sites known to harbor (or that are suspected of harboring) dangerous active biological agents require a response by teams equipped with special protective equipment, all law enforcement officers should take reasonable precautions against exposure to the wide variety of infectious agents known to exist at even routine crime scenes. Emergency management agencies generally recommend a number of precautions, shown in Table 8-2, to defend against exposure to infectious substances.

All law enforcement officers should take reasonable precautions against exposure to the wide variety of infectious agents known to exist at even routine crime scenes.

To better combat the threat of infectious diseases among public-safety employees and health care professionals, the federal Bloodborne Pathogens Act of 1991[39] requires that police officers receive proper training in how to prevent contamination by bloodborne infectious agents. The act also requires that police officers undergo an annual refresher course on the topic.

Police departments will face an increasing number of legal challenges in the years to come in cases of infectious diseases like AIDS and in cases involving the release of biological agents. Predictable areas of concern include (1) the need to educate officers and other police employees about AIDS, anthrax, and other serious infectious diseases; (2) the responsibility of police departments to prevent the spread of AIDS and other infectious diseases in police lockups; and (3) the necessity of effective and nondiscriminatory enforcement activities and lifesaving measures by police officers in environments contaminated with active biological agents. With regard to nondiscriminatory activities, the National Institute of Justice has suggested that legal claims in support of an officer's refusal to render assistance to people with AIDS would probably not be effective in court.[40] The reason is twofold: The officer has a basic duty to render assistance to individuals in need of it, and the possibility of AIDS transmission by casual contact has been scientifically established as extremely remote. A final issue of growing concern involves activities by police officers infected with the AIDS virus. Few statistics are currently available on the number of officers with AIDS, but public reaction to those officers may be a developing problem that police managers will soon need to address.

Police departments will face an increasing number of legal challenges in the years to come in cases of infectious diseases like AIDS and in cases involving the release of biological agents.

Stress and Fatigue among Police Officers

Traumatic events, like hurricanes, terrorist attacks, and violent confrontations, are instantly stressful. But long-term stress, whose debilitating effects accumulate over years, may be the most

TABLE 8-2 | **Biological Incident Law Enforcement Concerns**

Suspicious material	Responding officers should not handle or come into close physical contact with suspicious material. If it is necessary to handle the material to evaluate it, officers should wear surgical gloves and masks and wash their hands thoroughly with soap and water after handling.
Human bites	The biter usually receives the victim's blood. Viral transmission through saliva is highly unlikely. If bitten by anyone, milk the wound to make it bleed, wash the area thoroughly, and seek medical attention.
Spitting	Viral transmission through saliva is highly unlikely.
Urine/feces	The virus has been isolated in only very low concentrations in urine and not at all in feces. No cases of AIDS or AIDS virus infection have been associated with either urine or feces.
Cuts/puncture wounds	Use caution in handling sharp objects and searching areas hidden from view. Needlestick studies show risk of infection is very low.
CPR/first aid	To eliminate the already minimal risk associated with CPR, use masks/airways. Avoid blood-to-blood contact by keeping open wounds covered and wearing gloves when in contact with bleeding wounds.
Body removal	Observe crime scene rules; do not touch anything. Those who must come in contact with blood or other body fluids should wear gloves.
Casual contact	No cases of AIDS or AIDS virus infection have been attributed to casual contact.
Any contact with blood or body fluids	Wear gloves if contact with blood or body fluids is considered likely. If contact occurs, wash thoroughly with soap and water; clean up spills with one part water to nine parts household bleach.
Contact with dried blood	No cases of infection have been traced to exposure to dried blood. The drying process itself appears to inactivate the virus. Despite low risk, however, caution dictates wearing gloves, a mask, and protective shoe coverings if exposure to dried blood particles is likely (for example, during a crime scene investigation).

References: Michigan Department of Community Health, "Anthrax (*Bacillus anthracis*) Information for Health Care Providers," http://www.michigan.gov/documents/Healthcare_provider_FAQ-anthrax_08-2004_104327_7.pdf (accessed June 11, 2010); Massachusetts Administrative Office of the Trial Court, "Personnel Policies and Procedures Manual, Section 24.000 (Statement of Policy and Procedures on AIDS)," http://www.state.ma.us/courts/admin/hr/section24.html (accessed June 5, 2013); and "Collecting and Handling Evidence Infected with Human Disease-Causing Organisms," *FBI Law Enforcement Bulletin*, July 1987.

insidious and least visible of all threats facing law enforcement personnel today. Although some degree of stress can be a positive motivator, serious stress, over long periods of time, is generally regarded as destructive, even life threatening.

Stress is a natural component of police work (Figure 8-3).[41] The American Institute of Stress, based in Yonkers, New York, ranks policing among the top ten stress-producing jobs in the country.[42] The Bureau of Justice Statistics points out that "exposure to violence, suffering, and death is inherent to the profession of the law enforcement officer. There are other sources of stress as well. Officers who deal with offenders on a daily basis may perceive the public's opinion of police performance to be unfavorable; they often are required to work mandatory, rotating shifts; and they may not have enough time to spend with their families. Police officers also face unusual, often highly disturbing, situations, such as dealing with a child homicide victim or the survivors of vehicle crashes."[43]

Some stressors in police work are particularly destructive. One is frustration brought on by the inability to be effective, regardless of the amount of personal effort expended. Arrests may not lead to convictions. Evidence available to the officer may not be allowed in court. Imposed sentences may seem inadequate to the arresting officer. The feelings of powerlessness that come from seeing repeat offenders back on the streets and from witnessing numerous injustices to innocent victims may greatly stress police officers and cause them to question the purpose of their professional lives. These feelings of frustration and powerlessness may also lead to desperate attempts to find relief. As one researcher observes, "The suicide rate of police officers is more than twice that of the general population."[44]

Stress is not unique to the police profession, but because of the "macho" attitude that is traditionally associated with police work, police officers deny their stress more often than those in other occupations do. Some individuals are more susceptible to the negative effects of stress than others. The Type A personality, first identified almost 40 years ago, is most likely to perceive life in terms of pressure and performance. Type B people are more laid back and less likely to suffer from the negative effects of stress. Police ranks, drawn as they are from the general population, are filled with both stress-sensitive and stress-resistant personalities.

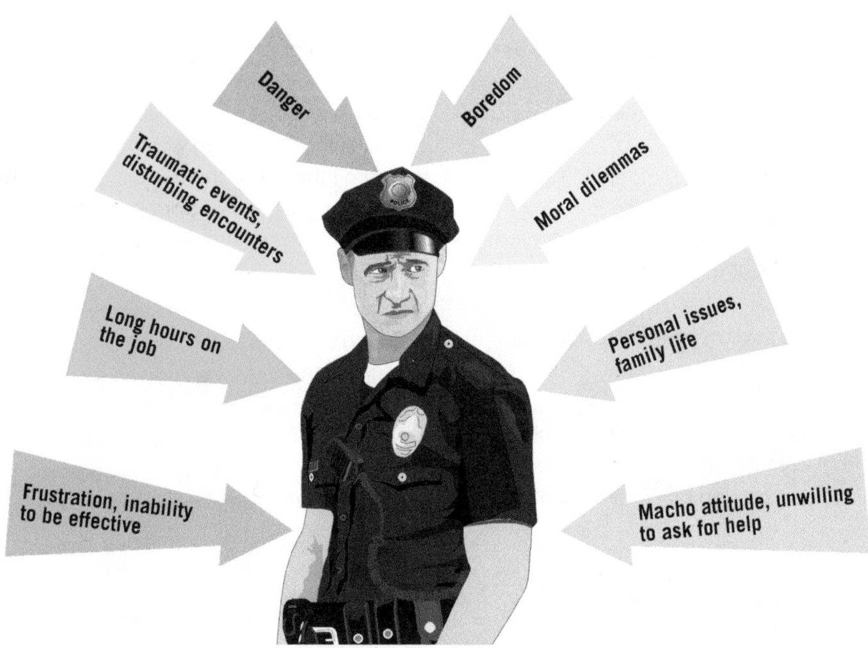

FIGURE 8-3 | Stress and Fatigue among Police Officers

Stress Reduction

It is natural to want to reduce stress.[45] Humor helps, even if it's somewhat cynical. Health-care professionals, for example, are noted for their ability to joke while caring for patients who are seriously ill or even dying. At times, police officers use humor similarly to defuse their reactions to dark or threatening situations. Keeping an emotional distance from stressful events is another way of coping with them, although such distance is not always easy to maintain. Police officers who have had to deal with serious cases of child abuse often report that they experience emotional turmoil as a consequence.

Exercise, meditation, abdominal breathing, biofeedback, self-hypnosis, guided imaging, induced relaxation, subliminal conditioning, music, prayer, and diet have all been cited as useful techniques for stress reduction. Devices to measure stress levels are available in the form of handheld heart rate monitors, blood pressure devices, "biodots" (which change color according to the amount of blood flow in the extremities), and psychological inventories.

A new approach to managing stress among police officers holds that the amount of stress that officers experience is directly related to their reactions to potentially stressful situations.[46]

Officers who can filter out extraneous stimuli and who can distinguish between truly threatening situations and those that

Robert Brenner/PhotoEdit Inc.

A New York City Police Department officer showing obvious signs of fatigue while working at a traffic barrier. Stress and fatigue are common problems in police work and can result from long work hours, grueling investigations, traumatic experiences, and even boredom. How can boredom be combated?

freedom OR safety? YOU decide

Religion and Public Safety

In April 2011, the French government initiated a ban on the wearing of veils, or Islamic burkas, following a number of terrorist incidents in that country. The new law gave French police the power to imposes fines on women who wear veils in public, although recent reports reveal that few women have actually been ticketed.

The French ban was preceded by an incident in Florida in 2003, when state judge Janet Thorpe ruled that a Muslim woman could not wear a veil while being photographed for a state driver's license. The woman, Sultaana Freeman, claimed that her religious rights were violated when the state department of motor vehicles required that she reveal her face for the photograph. She offered to show her eyes, but not the rest of her face, to the camera.

Judge Thorpe said, however, that a "compelling interest in protecting the public from criminal activities and security threats" did not place an undue burden on Freeman's ability to practice her religion.

After the hearing, Freeman's husband, Abdul-Maalik Freeman, told reporters, "This is a religious principle; this is a principle that's imbedded in us as believers. So, she's not going to do that." Howard Marks, the Freemans' attorney, supported by the American Civil Liberties Union (ACLU), filed an appeal claiming that the ruling was counter to guarantees of religious freedom inherent in the U.S. Constitution. Two years later, however, a Florida court of appeals denied further hearings in the case.

You Decide

Do the demands of public safety justify restrictions on religious practice? If so, would you go so far as the French practice of banning the wearing of veils in public? As an alternative, should photo IDs, such as driver's licenses, be replaced with other forms of identification (such as an individual's stored DNA profile) to accommodate the beliefs of individuals like the Freemans?

References: "Judge: No Veil in Driver's License Photo," Associated Press, June 6, 2003; Associated Press, "FL Appeals Court Upholds Ban of Veil in Driver's License Photo," September 7, 2005, http://www.newsday.com/news/nationworld/nation/orl-bk-freeman090705,0,2758466.story?coll=ny-leadnationalnews-headlines (accessed April 17, 2012); and Andrew Chung, "French Ban on Islamic Veil Turns Out to Be Toothless," *Toronto Star*, March 31, 2012, http://www.thestar.com/news/world/article/1154781–french-ban-on-islamic-veil-turns-out-to-be-toothless (accessed May 20, 2013).

are benign are much less likely to report job-related stressors than those lacking these abilities. Because stress-filtering abilities are often closely linked to innate personality characteristics, some researchers suggest careful psychological screening of police applicants to better identify those who have a natural ability to cope with situations that others might perceive as stressful.[47]

Police officers' family members often report feelings of stress that are directly related to the officers' work. As a result, some departments have developed innovative programs to allay family stress. The Collier County (Florida) Spousal Academy, for example, is a family support program that offers training to spouses and other domestic partners of deputies and recruits who are enrolled in the department's training academy. The ten-hour program deals directly with issues that are likely to produce stress and informs participants of department and community resources that are available to help them. Peer-support programs for spouses and life partners and for the adolescent children of officers are also beginning to operate nationwide. One organization, Badge of Life, promotes mental health services for police officers. The organization has created an Emotional Self-care Training (ESC) initiative that asks officers to perform a periodic mental health check by visiting a licensed therapist at least once a year. Badge of Life can be reached on the Web at **http://www.badgeoflife.com.**

Officer Fatigue

Like stress, fatigue can affect a police officer's performance. As criminologist Bryan Vila points out, "Tired, urban street cops are a national icon. Weary from overtime assignments, shift work, night school, endless hours spent waiting to testify, and the emotional and physical demands of the job, not to mention trying to patch together a family and social life during irregular islands of off-duty time, they fend off fatigue with coffee and hard-bitten humor."[48] Vila found levels of police officer fatigue to be six times as high as those of shift workers in industrial and mining jobs.[49] As Vila notes, few departments set work-hour standards, and fatigue associated with the pattern and length of work hours may be expected to contribute to police accidents, injuries, and misconduct.

To address the problem, Vila recommends that police departments "review the policies, procedures, and practices that affect shift scheduling and rotation, overtime moonlighting, the number of consecutive work hours allowed, and the way in which the department deals with overly tired employees."[50] Vila also suggests controlling the working hours of police officers, "just as we control the working hours of many other occupational groups."[51] Learn more about police fatigue from the FBI at **http://justicestudies.com/pubs/police_fatigue.pdf**.

■ **police use of force** The use of physical restraint by a police officer when dealing with a member of the public.[iii]

■ **excessive force** The application of an amount and/or frequency of force greater than that required to compel compliance from a willing or unwilling subject.[iv]

Police Use of Force

In early 2013, U.S. District Court Judge Susie Morgan officially entered a consent decree into judgment mandating a plan to instill sweeping reforms in the New Orleans Police Department (NOPD).[52] Two years earlier, the Civil Rights Division (CRD) of the U.S. Department of Justice issued a stinging indictment of the NOPD[53] in a 158-page report detailing inadequacies within the department that had led to what the report's authors called "a pattern or practice of conduct that deprives individuals of rights, privileges, or immunities secured or protected by the Constitution or laws of the United States." The CRD investigation, which had been requested by the municipal administration of the City of New Orleans, was part of efforts by elected officials and concerned citizens to bring about the "complete transformation" of the NOPD. One of the most significant findings of the investigation was that the "NOPD, for at least the past several years, has been all too frequently indifferent to its officers' improper use of force." The report's authors explained it this way: "Police-civilian interactions only rarely require the use of force. In the small portion of interactions where it is necessary for officers to use force, the Constitution requires that officers use only the amount of force that is reasonable under the circumstances. We found that officers in NOPD routinely use unnecessary and unreasonable force in violation of the Constitution and NOPD policy." You can access the complete report at **http://justicestudies.com/pdf/nolpd.pdf**. The 2013 consent decree can be found at **http://justicestudies.com/pdf/noldconsentdecree.pdf.**

Police use of force can be defined as the use of physical restraint by a police officer when dealing with a member of the public.[54] As the Justice Department report on the NOPD noted, law enforcement officers are authorized to use only the amount of force that is reasonable and necessary given the circumstances facing them. Most officers are trained in the use of force and typically encounter numerous situations during their careers when the use of force is appropriate—for example, when making some arrests, restraining unruly combatants, or controlling a disruptive demonstration. Force may involve hitting; holding or restraining; pushing; choking; threatening with a flashlight, baton, or chemical or pepper spray; restraining with a police dog; or threatening with a gun. Some definitions of police use of force include handcuffing. It important to note that some police departments no longer use the phrase "use of force," preferring instead to talk about "response to resistance."

The National Institute of Justice estimates that more than 43.5 million people nationwide have face-to-face contact with the police over a typical 12-month period (nearly 18 million as a result of traffic stops) and that approximately 1.6%, or about 700,000, of these people become subject to the use of force or the threat of force.[55] When handcuffing is included in the definition of force, the number of people subjected to force increases to 1.2 million, or slightly more than 2.5% of those having contact with the police. Other studies show that police use weaponless tactics in approximately 80% of use-of-force incidents and that about 88% of all use-of-force incidents involve merely grabbing or holding the suspect.[56]

Studies show that police use force in fewer than 20% of adult custodial arrests. Even in instances where force is used, the police primarily use weaponless tactics. Female officers have been found to be less likely to use physical force and firearms, and more likely to use chemical weapons (mostly pepper spray), than their male counterparts.[57] Figure 8-4 shows the types of encounters in which the use of force is most likely to be employed.

A more complex issue is the use of excessive force. The IACP defines **excessive force** as "the application of an amount and/or frequency of force greater than that required to compel compliance from a willing or unwilling subject."[58] When excessive force is employed, the activities of the police often come under public scrutiny and receive attention from the media and from legislators. Police officers' use of

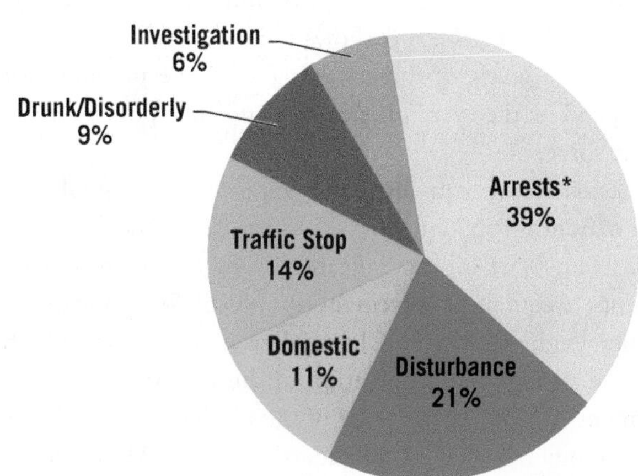

*Includes serving arrest warrants, making field arrests, and effecting other arrests.

FIGURE 8-4 | Police Use of Force by Type of Encounter

Source: International Association of Chiefs of Police, *Police Use of Force in America, 2001* (Alexandria, VA: IACP, 2001), p. iii. Reprinted with permission.

■ **problem police officer** A law enforcement officer who exhibits problem behavior, as indicated by high rates of citizen complaints and use-of-force incidents and by other evidence.[v]

■ **deadly force** Force likely to cause death or great bodily harm. Also, "the intentional use of a firearm or other instrument resulting in a high probability of death."[vi]

excessive force can also result in lawsuits by members of the public who feel that they have been treated unfairly. Whether the use of excessive force is aberrant behavior on the part of an individual officer or is a practice of an entire law enforcement agency, both the law and public opinion generally condemn it. Many police departments are now posting their use of force policy manuals online. See, for example, the UCLA Police Department's posting at **http://www.ucpd.ucla.edu/policy/300Use_of_force.pdf.**

Kenneth Adams, an associate dean at the University of Central Florida and an expert in the use of force by police, notes that there is an important difference between the terms *excessive force,* such as shoving or pushing when simply grabbing a suspect would be adequate, and *excessive use of force,* which refers to the phenomenon of force being used unacceptably, often on a department-wide basis. The term, says Adams, "deals with relative comparisons among police agencies, and there are no established criteria for judgment." *Use of excessive force* and the *excessive use of force* may be distinguished from the *illegal use of force,* which refers to situations in which the use of force by police violates a law or statute.[59]

In one study, Geoffrey Alpert and Roger Dunham found that the "force factor"—the level of force used by the police relative to the suspect's level of resistance—is a key element to consider in attempting to reduce injuries to both the police and suspects.[60] The force factor is calculated by measuring both the suspect's level of resistance and the officer's level of force on an equivalent scale and by then subtracting the level of resistance from the level of police force used. Results from the study indicate that, on average, the level of force that officers use is closely related to the type of training that their departments emphasize. Figure 8-5 shows a use of force continuum containing five levels of force starting with the potential for force implied by the mere physical presence of a police officer, to deadly force.

Excessive force can also be symptomatic of **problem police officers**. Problem police officers are those who exhibit problem behavior, as indicated by high rates of citizen complaints, frequent involvement in use-of-force incidents, and other evidence.[61] The Christopher Commission, which studied the structure and operation of the Los Angeles Police Department (LAPD) in the wake of the Rodney King beating, found a number of "repeat offenders" on the LAPD force.[62] According to the commission, approximately 1,800 LAPD officers were alleged to have used excessive force or improper tactics between 1986 and 1990. Of these officers, more than 1,400 had only one or two allegations against them. Another 183 officers had four or more allegations, 44 had six or more,

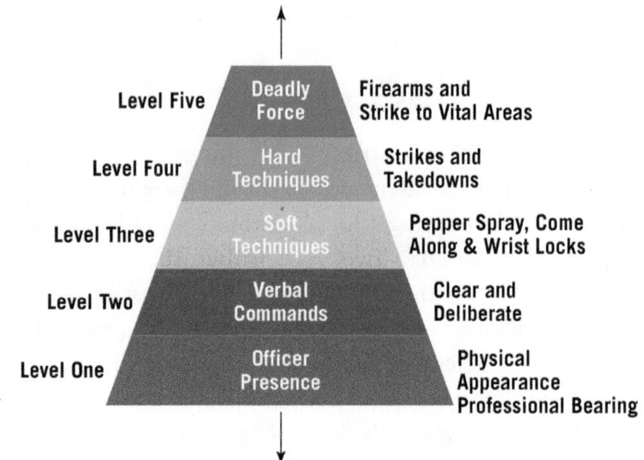

FIGURE 8-5 | Police Use of Force Continuum

16 had eight or more, and one had 16 such allegations. The commission also found that, generally speaking, the 44 officers with six complaints or more had received positive performance evaluations that failed to record "sustained" complaints or to discuss their significance.

Recent studies have found that problem police officers do not differ significantly in race or ethnicity from nonproblem officers, although they tend to be male and have disciplinary records that are more serious than those of other officers. Some departments are developing early-warning systems to allow police managers to identify potentially problematic officers and to reduce problem behavior. Learn more about police use of force, as well as force used against the police, from **http://www.justicestudies.com/pubs/force.pdf** and **http://www.justicestudies.com/pubs/measureforce.pdf**. Two FBI articles on excessive force are available at **http://www.justicestudies.com/pubs/excessiveforce.pdf** and **http://www.justicestudies.com/pubs/excessiveforce02.pdf**.

Deadly Force

Generally speaking, **deadly force** is likely to cause death or significant bodily harm. The FBI defines *deadly force* as "the intentional use of a firearm or other instrument resulting in a high probability of death."[63]

The use of deadly force by law enforcement officers, especially when it is *not* considered justifiable, is one area of potential civil liability that has received considerable attention in recent years. Historically, the fleeing-felon rule applied to most U.S. jurisdictions. It held that officers could use deadly force to prevent the escape of a suspected felon, even when that person represented no immediate threat to the officer or to the public.

The 1985 U.S. Supreme Court case of *Tennessee* v. *Garner*[64] specified the conditions under which deadly force could be used in the apprehension of suspected felons. Edward Garner, a 15-year-old suspected burglar, was shot to death by Memphis police after he refused their order to halt and attempted to climb over a chain-link fence. In an action initiated by Garner's father, who claimed that his son's constitutional rights had been violated, the Court held that the use of deadly force by the police to prevent the escape of a fleeing felon could be justified only where the suspect could reasonably be thought to represent a significant threat of serious injury or death to the public or to the officer and where deadly force is necessary to effect the arrest. In reaching its decision, the Court declared that "[t]he use of deadly force to prevent the escape of *all* felony suspects, whatever the circumstances, is constitutionally unreasonable."

In the 1989 case of *Graham* v. *Connor*,[65] the Supreme Court established the standard of "objective reasonableness." The Court said that whether deadly force has been used appropriately should be judged from the perspective of a reasonable officer on the scene and not with the benefit of "20/20 hindsight." The justices wrote, "The calculus of reasonableness must embody allowance for the fact that police officers are often forced to make split-second judgments—in circumstances that are tense, uncertain, and rapidly evolving—about the amount of force that is necessary in a particular situation."

In 1995, following investigations into the actions of federal agents at the deadly siege of the Branch Davidian compound at Waco, Texas, and the tragic deaths associated with a 1992 FBI assault on antigovernment separatists in Ruby Ridge, Idaho (a case that is discussed later in the chapter), the federal government announced that it was adopting an "imminent danger" standard for the use of deadly force by federal agents. The imminent danger standard restricts the use of deadly force to those situations in which the lives of agents or others are in danger. When the new standard was announced, federal agencies were criticized for taking so long to adopt it. The federal deadly force policy, as adopted by the FBI, contains the following elements:[66]

The imminent danger standard restricts the use of deadly force to those situations in which the lives of agents or others are in danger.

- *Defense of life.* Agents may use deadly force only when necessary—that is, only when they have probable cause to believe that the subject poses an imminent danger of death or serious physical injury to the agent or to others.
- *Fleeing subject.* Deadly force may be used to prevent the escape of a fleeing subject if there is probable cause to believe that the subject has committed a felony involving the infliction or threatened infliction of serious physical injury or death and that the subject's escape would pose an imminent danger of death or serious physical injury to the agent or to others.
- *Verbal warnings.* If feasible, and if doing so would not increase the danger to the agent or to others, a verbal warning to submit to the authority of the agent should be given prior to the use of deadly force.
- *Warning shots.* Agents may not fire warning shots.
- *Vehicles.* Agents may not fire weapons solely to disable moving vehicles. Weapons may be fired at the driver or other occupant of a moving motor vehicle only when the agent has probable cause to believe that the subject poses an imminent danger of death or serious physical injury to the agent or to others and when the use of deadly force does not create a danger to the public that outweighs the likely benefits of its use.

Studies of killings by the police have often focused on claims of discrimination—that is, that minority suspects are more likely to be shot than whites. But research has not provided solid support for such claims. While individuals shot by police are more likely to be minorities, an early study by James Fyfe found that police officers will generally respond with deadly force when mortally threatened and that minorities are considerably more likely to use weapons in assaults on officers than are whites.[67] Complicating the picture further, Fyfe's study showed that minority officers are involved in the shootings of suspects more often than other officers, a finding that may be due to the assignment of minority officers to inner-city and ghetto areas. However, a later study by Fyfe, which analyzed police shootings in Memphis, Tennessee, found that black property offenders were twice as likely as whites to be shot by police.[68]

Although relatively few police officers ever fire their weapons at suspects during the course of their careers, those who do may become embroiled in social, legal, and personal complications. It is estimated that in an average year, 600 suspects are killed by public police in America, while another 1,200 are shot and wounded, and 1,800 are shot at and missed.[69] The personal side of police shootings is well summarized in the title of an article that appeared in *Police Magazine.* The article "I've Killed That Man Ten Thousand Times" demonstrates how police officers who have to use their weapons may be haunted by years of depression and despair.[70] Not long ago, according to author Anne Cohen, all departments did to help an officer who had shot someone was to "give him enough bullets to reload his gun." The stress and trauma that police officers suffer from having shot someone are only now being realized, and many

The stress and trauma that police officers suffer from having shot someone are only now being realized, and many departments have yet to develop mechanisms for adequately dealing with them.

■ **less-lethal weapon** A weapon that is designed to disable, capture, or immobilize—but not kill—a suspect. Occasional deaths do result from the use of such weapons, however.

departments have yet to develop mechanisms for adequately dealing with them.[71]

Police officers have particular difficulty dealing with instances of "suicide by cop," in which individuals bent on dying engage in behavior that causes responding officers to resort to deadly force. On March 10, 2005, for example, John T. Garczynski, Jr., a father of two preteen boys, died in a hail of 26 bullets fired by police officers who had surrounded his vehicle in a Boca Raton, Florida, condominium parking lot.[72] Garczynski, a Florida Power and Light Company employee, had been separated from his wife months earlier and appeared to have been despondent over financial problems and the breakup of his marriage. The night before his death, Garczynski met his wife at a bowling alley and handed her a packet containing a suicide note, a typed obituary, and a eulogy to be read at his funeral. After he left, Garczynski's wife called police, and officers used the help of a cell phone company to locate Garczynski. As deputies surrounded his 2003 Ford Explorer, he attempted to start the vehicle. One of the officers yelled "Freeze" and then "Let me see your hands." It was at that point, deputies said, that Garczynski pointed a gun at them and they fired.

Rebecca Stincelli, author of the book *Suicide by Cop: Victims from Both Sides of the Badge,*[73] says an incident like that involving Garczynski can be devastating for police officers. "In the past, people have used rope, a gun, gas, jumped off a building. A police officer is just another method," said Stincelli. "They say it's nothing personal. [But] they are wrong. It's very personal" for the officers involved.[74] The FBI says that "suicide-by-cop incidents are painful and damaging experiences for the surviving families, the communities, and all law enforcement professionals."[75]

A study of fatal shootings by Los Angeles police officers found that an astonishingly large number—more than 10%—could be classified as "suicide by cop."[76] Recently, researchers have identified three main "suicide by cop" categories: direct confrontations, in which suicidal subjects instigate attacks on police officers for the purpose of dying; disturbed interventions, in which potentially suicidal subjects take advantage of police intervention in their suicide attempt in order to die; and criminal interventions, in which criminal suspects prefer death to capture and arrest.[77]

Less-Lethal Weapons

Less-lethal weapons offer what may be a problem-specific solution to potential incidents of "suicide by cop," as well as a generic solution to at least some charges of use of excessive force. Less-lethal weapons are designed to disable, capture, or immobilize a suspect rather than kill him or her. Efforts to provide law enforcement officers with less-lethal weapons like

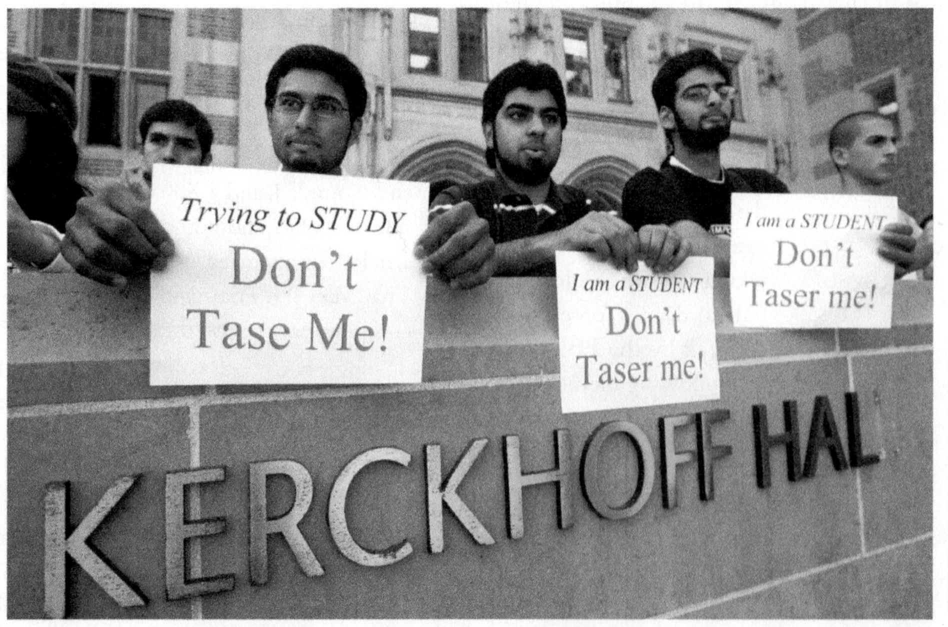

UCLA students protesting the police use of Tasers. This less-lethal weapon, manufactured by Taser International, incapacitates potential attackers by delivering an electrical shock to the person's nervous system. The technology is intended to reduce injury rates to both suspects and officers. Why do some people oppose its use?

CJ | NEWS

Is the Video Recording of Police Activity in a Public Place Legal?

STAN HONDA/Getty Images

New York City police officers arrest a demonstrator while a bevy of news photographers record the scene. Courts have held that the photographic recording of police activities that occur in public is permissible unless the recording interferes with or hinders those activities.

Simon Glik was walking in the Boston Common in 2007, when he saw police officers putting a suspected drug offender into a chokehold and heard someone yell, "You are hurting him, stop."

Glik pulled out his cell phone camera and began recording the scene, but the officers arrested him for filming them and confiscated the device. Taking him to jail, they charged him under a state law that bars secret recordings, even though the officers could plainly see the cell phone.

The charges against Glik were quickly dismissed in municipal court, but Boston Police continued over the next four years to seek qualified immunity for similar arrests. In August 2011, however, a federal appeals court once and for all denied any qualified immunity claims and confirmed that the video recording of an on-duty police officer is protected by the First Amendment, which also guarantees freedom of speech. An internal investigation by the Boston Police Department in January 2012 concluded that officers had shown poor judgment in arresting Glik, and the city agreed two months later to pay $170,000 to settle his civil rights lawsuit against the city.

Today, six years after the original incident, just about every cell phone in America has a camera built into it, and recordings like the one Glik's made are occurring regularly. Yet arrests continue. In May 2011, for example, a police officer in Rochester, New York, arrested a woman standing in her own yard, taking pictures of him searching a man's car.

Before arresting her, the officer said, "I don't feel safe with you standing behind me." Clearly, some officers are not comfortable being filmed, even when doing nothing wrong. Perhaps they recall that when camera phones didn't exist some 20 years ago, a bystander's filming of the Los Angeles police beating of Rodney King literally caused a riot in South Central LA, resulting in $1 billion in property damage. Two of the officers caught on videotape in the King incident were sentenced to 30 months in prison.

In the *Glik* decision, the appeals court welcomed the filming the police by citizens. "Ensuring the public's right to gather information about their officials," the court declared, "not only aids in the uncovering of abuses but also may have a salutary effect on the functioning of government more generally." In any case, officers who make such arrests today often end up suffering public scorn and undergoing investigation by their department's internal affairs division. The Rochester woman who was mentioned earlier was acquitted and, after her video went viral on the Internet, Rochester Police made an apology and initiated training programs about the right of people to record police activity that takes place in public.

Training programs may not be enough, however. Philadelphia police were trained on the use of cameras by members of the public, but in March 2012, they arrested a college student for taking photos of officers conducting a traffic stop in front of his house. He was charged with obstruction of justice, resisting arrest, and disorderly conduct.

Although the use of video cameras when recording police activity has generally been supported by the courts, the law on making recordings is not that easy to follow. For example, unlike photography and video, there is no general right to make audio recordings—especially those made without police knowledge. As Michael Allison found out in the tiny town of Bridgeport, Illinois, secret audio recordings are definitely out-of-bounds in many jurisdictions.

Told that there would be no court reporter provided for his legal hearing in late 2011, Allison taped it on a small digital recorder in his pocket, without telling the judge. When he was found out, Allison was arrested and charged with felony eavesdropping. Four more counts were added when other secret recordings were detected on his device, meaning he faced a possible 75-year prison sentence. The charges were thrown out, but the Illinois Attorney General later appealed the ruling to get them reinstated.

Resources: "Police Reverse Stance on Taping of Officers' Actions," *The Boston Globe*, January 10, 2012, http://www.bostonglobe.com/metro/2012/01/10/police-reverse-stance-taping-officers-actions/va6glfwq9L1mUElv6a33HK/story.html; "Chief Sheppard, the RPD, and Emily Good," *Rochester City Newspaper*, September 2, 2011, http://www.rochestercitynewspaper.com/news/blog/2011/09/Chief-Sheppard-the-RPD-and-Emily-Good/; and "Eavesdropping Case in Tiny Illinois Town Makes Big Waves," *Chicago Tribune*, January 2, 2012, http://articles.chicagotribune.com/2012-01-02/news/ct-met-eavesdropping-law-sidebar-20120102_1_eavesdropping-case-tiny-illinois-town-big-waves.

---

stun guns Tasers (aka conducted energy devices), rubber bullets, beanbag projectiles, and pepper spray began in 1987.[78] More exotic types of less-lethal weapons, however, are on the horizon. They include snare nets fired from shotguns, disabling sticky foam that can be sprayed from a distance, microwave beams that heat the tissue of people exposed to them until they desist in their illegal or threatening behavior or lose consciousness, and high-tech guns that fire bolts of electromagnetic energy at a target, causing painful sensory overload and violent muscle spasms. The National Institute of Justice says, "The goal is to give line officers effective and safe alternatives to lethal force."[79]

As their name implies, however, less-lethal weapons are not always safe. On October 21, 2004, for example, 21-year-old Emerson College student Victoria Snelgrove died hours after being hit in the eye with a plastic pepper-spray-filled projectile that police officers fired at a rowdy crowd celebrating the Red Sox victory over the New York Yankees in the final game of the American League Championship Series in 2004. Witnesses said that officers fired the projectile into the crowd after a reveler

racial profiling "Any police-initiated action that relies on the race, ethnicity, or national origin, rather than [1] the behavior of an individual, or [2] . . . information that leads the police to a particular individual who has been identified as being, or having been, engaged in criminal activity."[vii]

near Fenway Park threw a bottle at a mounted Boston police officer.[80] Learn more about less-lethal weapons from the FBI at **http://www.justicestudies.com/pubs/lesslethal.pdf**.

Racial Profiling and Biased Policing

As mentioned earlier in this chapter, the U.S. Department of Justice's Civil Rights Division released a 2011 report critical of the New Orleans Police Department's (NOPD) use of force. That same report identified discriminatory enforcement practices among many NOPD officers. The report's authors concluded, "We find reasonable cause to believe that NOPD engages in a pattern or practice of discriminatory policing in violation of constitutional and statutory law."[81] Discriminatory policing, said the writers, "occurs when police officers and departments unfairly enforce the law—or fail to enforce the law—based on characteristics such as race, ethnicity, national origin, sex, religion, or [sexual preference]."[82] Subjecting individuals to differential treatment, concluded the authors, "based on a belief that characteristics such as race, ethnicity, national origin, sex, or religion signal a higher risk of criminality or unlawful activity—constitutes unlawful discrimination, often called "profiling" or "biased policing."

Racial profiling first received national attention in the late 1990s. Racial profiling can be defined as any police action initiated on the basis of the race, ethnicity, or national origin of a suspect, rather than on the behavior of that individual or on information that leads the police to a particular individual who has been identified as being, or having been, engaged in criminal activity.[83]

It should be noted that racial profiling is significantly different from the practice of *behavioral profiling*, which makes use of a person's demeanor, actions, bearing, and manner to identify an offender before he can act.[84] As such, behavioral profiling can be both a useful predictive and proactive tool. Behavioral profiling has been successfully used, for example, by Israeli security forces to prevent acts of terrorism. In that country, potential offenders have been identified by their simple actions like wearing loose clothing (to conceal bombs or weapons), smoking on the Sabbath (something that Orthodox Jews would not do), or simply fidgeting and avoiding eye contact while standing in line.

Racial profiling is different because it uses a person's race as the sole or predominate factor in determining criminal intent or culpability.[85] The alleged use by police of racial profiling may take a number of forms. Minority accounts of disparate treatment at the hands of police officers include being stopped for being "in the wrong car" (for example, a police stop of an African American youth driving an expensive late-model BMW); being stopped and questioned for being in the wrong neighborhood (that is, police stops of members of minority groups driving through traditionally white residential neighborhoods); and perceived harassment at the hands of police officers for petty traffic violations like underinflated tires, failure to signal properly before switching lanes, vehicle equipment failures, driving less than 10 miles per hour above the speed limit, or having an illegible license plate.[86]

Racial profiling uses a person's race as the sole or predominate factor in determining criminal intent or culpability.

Profiling was originally intended to help catch drug couriers attempting to enter the country. The U.S. Customs Service and the Drug Enforcement Administration developed a number of "personal indicators" that seemed, from the agency's day-to-day enforcement experiences, to be associated with increased likelihood of law violation. Among the indicators were these: speaking Spanish; entering the United States on flights originating in particular Central and South American countries; being an 18- to 32-year-old male; having purchased tickets with cash; and having a short planned stay (often of only a day or two) in the United States. Federal agents frequently used these criteria in deciding which airline passengers to search and which bags to inspect.

Profiling was originally intended to help catch drug couriers attempting to enter the country.

Racial profiling has been derisively referred to as "driving while black" or "driving while brown," although it may also apply to situations other than those involving traffic violations. Racial profiling came to the attention of the public when police in New Jersey and Maryland were accused of unfair treatment of black motorists and admitted that race was a factor in traffic stops. Additional information about racial profiling studies focused on practices in New Jersey can be found in the expanded book.

In 2003, in response to widespread public outcry over racial profiling, the U.S. Department of Justice banned its practice in all federal law enforcement agencies, except in cases that involve the possible identification of terrorist suspects.[87] According to the DOJ, "the guidance provides that in making routine law enforcement decisions—such as deciding which motorists to stop for traffic infractions—consideration of the driver's race or ethnicity is absolutely forbidden."[88]

Those who defend the use of racial profiling by the police argue that it is not a bigoted practice when based on facts (such as when a police department decides to increase patrols in a housing area occupied primarily by minorities because of exceptionally high crime rates there) or when significant criminal potential exists among even a few members of a group. An example of the latter is the widespread public suspicions that focused on Arabs and Arab Americans following the terrorist attacks of September 11, 2001. As soon as it was publicly announced that the hijackers had been of Middle Eastern origin, some flight crews demanded that Arab-looking passengers be removed from their airplanes before takeoff, and passengers refused to fly with people who looked like Arabs.[89]

None of this is to say, of course, that race or ethnicity somehow inherently causes crime (or that it somehow causes poverty or increases the risk of victimization). If anything, race and ethnicity may simply display a significant correlation with certain types of crime, as they do with certain kinds of victimization. Hence, although the *real* causes of criminality may be socialization into criminal subcultures, economically deprived neighborhoods, a lack of salable job skills, and intergenerational poverty, and not race per se, to some law enforcement officers race provides one more indicator of the likelihood of criminality. David Cole, a professor at Georgetown University's Law Center, for example, notes that in the minds of many police officials, "racial and ethnic disparities reflect not discrimination [or bigotry] but higher rates of offenses among minorities."[90] "Nationwide," says Cole, "blacks are 13 times more likely to be sent to state prisons for drug convictions than are whites, so it would seem rational for police to assume that all other things being equal, a black driver is more likely than a white driver to be carrying drugs." Statistics like this, of course, may further enhance police focus on minorities and may result in even more arrests, thereby reinforcing the beliefs on which racial profiling by enforcement agents is based. Such observations led esteemed sociologist Amitai Etzioni following the turn of the century to declare that racial profiling, even though repugnant to most, is not necessarily racist.[91] Moreover, warned Etzioni, an end to racial profiling "would penalize those African-American communities with high incidences of violent crime" because they would lose the levels of policing that they need to remain relatively secure.

Regardless of arguments offered in support of racial profiling as an enforcement tool, the practice has been widely condemned as being contrary to basic ethical principles, and national public opinion polls conducted by the Gallup Organization show that more than 80% of respondents are morally opposed to the practice of racial profiling by the police,[92] although beliefs about the use of racial profiling vary widely by race (Figure 8-6). Figure 8-7 provides a map showing states that have officially banned the practice of racial profiling.[93] From a more pragmatic viewpoint, however, racial profiling is unacceptable because it weakens the public's confidence in the police, thereby decreasing police–citizen trust and cooperation.[94]

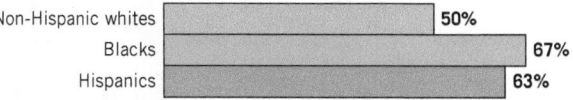

For each of the following situations, please say if you think the practice known as "racial profiling" is widespread, or not? How about.

Percentage saying "yes, widespread"

When motorists are stopped on roads and highways

When passengers are stopped at security checkpoints in airports

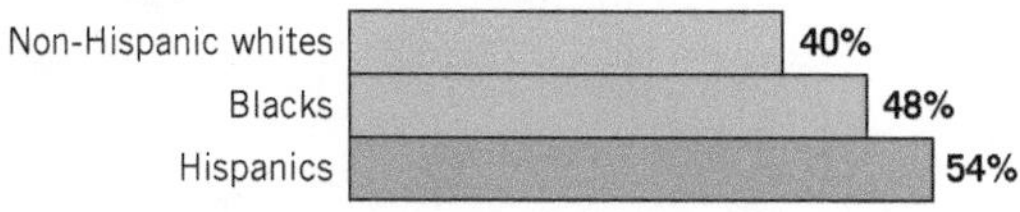

When shoppers in malls or stores are questioned about possible theft

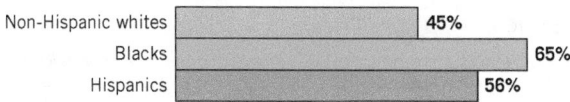

FIGURE 8-6 | Racial Profiling and Biased Policing, Perceptions by Race

Source: From The Gallup Poll, http://www.gallup.com. Reprinted with permission of The Gallup Organization.

Racially Biased Policing

A decade ago, the Police Executive Research Forum (PERF) released a detailed report titled *Racially Biased Policing: A Principled Response.*[95] PERF researchers surveyed more than 1,000 police executives, analyzed material from more than 250 law enforcement agencies, and sought input from law enforcement agency personnel, community activists, and civil rights leaders about racial bias in policing. Researchers concluded that "the vast majority of law enforcement officers—of all ranks, nationwide—are dedicated men and women committed to serving all citizens with fairness and dignity."[96] Most police officers, said the report, share an intolerance for racially biased policing. The report's authors noted that some police behaviors may be misinterpreted as biased when, in fact, the officer is just doing his or her job. "The good officer continually scans the environment for anomalies to normalcy—for conditions, people and behavior that are unusual for that environment," they said. "In learning and practicing their craft, officers quickly develop a sense for what is normal and expected, and conversely, for what is not."[97] Hence for officers of any race to take special notice of unknown young white males who unexpectedly appear in a traditionally African American neighborhood, for example, might be nothing other than routine police procedure. Such an observation, however, is not in itself sufficient for an investigatory stop but might be used in conjunction with other trustworthy and relevant information already in the officer's possession—such as the officer's prior knowledge that young white men have been visiting a particular apartment complex in the neighborhood to purchase drugs—to justify such a stop.

The PERF report makes many specific recommendations to help police departments be free of bias. One recommendation,

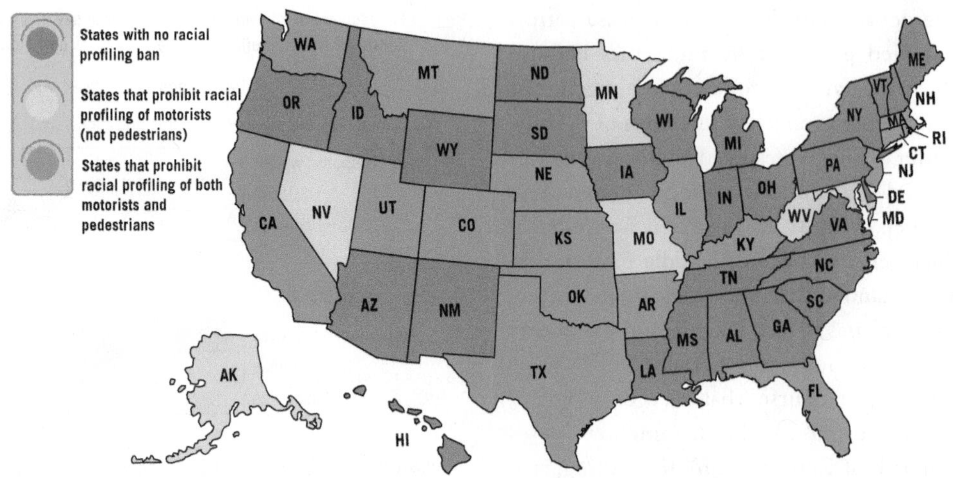

FIGURE 8-7 | States That Have Banned Racial Profiling

Source: Amnesty International USA, *Threat and Humiliation: Racial Profiling, Domestic Security, and Human Rights in the United States* (New York: Amnesty International USA Publications, 2004), p. 6. http://www.amnestyusa.org. © Amnesty International USA. Reprinted with permission.

for example, says that "supervisors should monitor activity reports for evidence of improper practices and patterns. They should conduct spot-checks and regular sampling of in-car videotapes, radio transmissions, and in-car computer and central communications records to determine if both formal and informal communications are professional and free from racial bias and other disrespect."[98] Read the entire PERF report at **http://www.justicestudies.com/pubs/rbiasp.pdf**.

freedom OR safety? YOU decide

Was the NYPD's Monitoring of Muslim Groups a Form of Religious Profiling?

In 2013, civil rights lawyers filed suit in federal court asking for the appointment of an independent commission to review the New York Police Department's monitoring of Muslim groups. Officials with the NYPD admitted to having conducted surveillance of Islamic mosques and Muslim groups in and around New York City over the past few years. At times, the surveillance involved planting undercover officers in Islamic groups and the monitoring of Muslim student groups at 16 colleges in the city and surrounding areas. The department was seeking to identify radical Islamists and al-Qaida sympathizers who might represent a danger to the city's inhabitants.

Once news of the program became public, it drew quick criticism from many corners. Islamic leaders felt that it was a thinly disguised form of racial and religious profiling and that it was aimed unfairly at them and at members of their communities. New York City Comptroller John Liu also questioned the monitoring program, saying, "We should not as a matter of policy profile people based on religion or race—it goes against everything this city stands for." Robert Jackson, the sole Muslim on the New York City council, added, "When you step on one religious group, Muslims, then you're stepping on every religious group."

Even some law enforcement officials questioned the program. Michael Ward, director of the FBI's Newark office, told reporters that his agency had spent years building up trust in Muslim neighborhoods. "What we have now," he said, "is (Muslim communities) . . . that they're not sure they trust law enforcement in general, they're fearing being watched, they're starting to withdraw their activities." "The impact of that sinking tide of cooperation," said Ward, "means that we don't have our finger on the pulse of what's going on in the community, as well—we're less knowledgeable, we have blind spots, and there's more risk."

New York Police Commissioner Raymond Kelly made no apologies for the intelligence program and said that he and Mayor Michael Bloomberg are committed to doing whatever is needed to lawfully protect the city. "It is not as if would-be terrorists aren't trying," Kelly told city council members. "To the contrary, they've attempted to kill New Yorkers in 14 different plots."

You Decide

Is the NYPD's monitoring program really a form of religious and ethnic profiling? If so, should such profiling be permitted in order to safeguard the city? Why or why not?

References: Joseph Goldstein, "Lawyers Say Surveillance of Muslims Flouts Accord," *New York Times*, http://www.nytimes.com/2013/02/04/nyregion/police-department-flouts-surveillance-guidelines-lawyers-say.html (accessed February 4, 2013); Adam Peck, "FBI Officials: News of NYPD Muslim Surveillance Program Is 'Starting to Have a Negative Impact,'" *Think Progress*, March 8, 2012, http://thinkprogress.org/security/2012/03/08/440780/fbi-official-nypd-muslim-surveillance/?mobile=nc (accessed May 1, 2012); Michael Howard Saul, "Speaker Quinn Voices Support for NYPD Monitoring of Muslims," *Wall Street Journal*, February 27, 2012, http://blogs.wsj.com/metropolis/2012/02/27/speaker-quinn-voices-support-for-nypd-monitoring-of-muslims (accessed May 1, 2012); "NYPD Police Commissioner Ray Kelly Not Sorry about NJ Muslim Surveillance," *Huffington Post*, February 27, 2012, http://www.huffingtonpost.com/2012/02/27/nypd-police-commissioner-_n_1304710.html (accessed May 1, 2012); and "Heated Exchanges Mark Ray Kelly's Testimony Before City Council," *CBS New York*, http://newyork.cbslocal.com/2012/03/15/nypds-ray-kelly-testifies-before-city-council-on-muslim-surveillance, March 15, 2012 (accessed May 1, 2012).

■ **civil liability** Potential responsibility for payment of damages or other court-ordered enforcement as a result of a ruling in a lawsuit. Civil liability is not the same as criminal liability, which means "open to punishment for a crime."[viii]

Henny Ray Abrams/AP Wide World Photos

An elderly woman shows her displeasure with Transportation Security Administration (TSA) security requirements. Some people fear that the use of profiling techniques could unfairly discriminate against members of certain racial and ethnic groups. Others suggest that the careful use of profiling can provide an important advantage in an age of scarce resources. With which perspective do you agree?

Police Civil Liability

In 2013, officials with the city of Chicago, Illinois, agreed to pay $22.5 million to settle a lawsuit brought against the city's police department.[99] The award, paid to Chistina Eilman, members of her family, and her attorneys, was thought to be the largest amount of money ever offered to a single victim of police misconduct. The civil suit against the city stemmed from the arrest and relatively quick release of Eilman after she had spent less than 24 hours in police custody. Eilman, who was a 21-year-old small diminutive white woman at the time of her arrest, had been taken into custody at Chicago's Midway airport in May 2006 after airport officials alerted police officers to her erratic and aggressive behavior. She was taken to a police station where officers learned that she was suffering from bipolar disorder. Released the next day around sundown, she was offered no assistance as stepped onto the streets of a gang-infested African American neighborhood. Soon after, she wandered away from the police station, and was lured into a high-crime housing project, where a number of young men threatened to attack her sexually. In what appears to have been an effort to escape, Eilman flung herself out of a seven-story window and suffered serious injury—including a shattered pelvis, many broken bones, and serious brain injury. Although she survived, she lives today in a permanent childlike mental state. Faulting the police department, Chief Judge Frank Easterbrook of the Seventh U.S. Circuit Court of Appeals wrote that officers "might as well have released her into the lion's den at the Brookfield Zoo."

Civil liability suits brought against law enforcement personnel are of two types: state and federal. Suits brought in state courts have generally been the more common form of civil litigation involving police officers. In recent years, however, an increasing number of suits have been brought in federal courts on the claim that the civil rights of the plaintiff, as guaranteed by federal law, were denied.

Common Sources of Civil Suits

Police officers may become involved in a variety of situations that could result in civil suits against the officers, their superiors, and their departments. Major sources of police civil liability are listed in Table 8-3. Charles Swanson, an expert in police procedure, says that the most common sources of lawsuits against the police are "assault, battery, false imprisonment, and malicious prosecution."[100]

Of all complaints brought against the police, assault charges are the best known, being, as they are, subject to high media visibility. Less visible, but not uncommon, are civil suits charging the police with false arrest or false imprisonment. In the 1986 case of *Malley* v. *Briggs*,[101] the U.S. Supreme Court held that a police officer who effects an arrest or conducts a search on the basis of an improperly issued warrant may be liable for monetary damages when a reasonably well-trained officer, under the same circumstances, "would have known that his affidavit failed to establish probable cause and that he should not have applied for the warrant." Significantly, the Court ruled that an officer "cannot excuse his own default by pointing to the greater incompetence of the magistrate."[102] That is, the officer, rather than the judge who issued the warrant, is ultimately responsible for establishing the basis for pursuing the arrest or search.

TABLE 8-3 | Major Sources of Police Civil Liability

Failure to protect property in police custody	Negligence in the care of suspects in police custody
Failure to render proper emergency medical assistance	Failure to prevent a foreseeable crime
Lack of due regard for the safety of others	False imprisonment
Failure to aid private citizens	Unnecessary assault or battery
False arrest	Violations of constitutional rights
Inappropriate use of deadly force	Racial profiling
Malicious prosecution	Patterns of unfair and inequitable treatment

CJ | ISSUES
Investigating Crime in a Multicultural Setting

In the mid-1990s, the Washington, D.C.–based National Crime Prevention Council (NCPC) published an important guide for American law enforcement officers who work with multicultural groups. The principles it contains can be applied equally to most foreign-born individuals living in the United States and are especially important to patrol officers and criminal investigators.

The NCPC guide points out that it is important for well-intentioned newcomers to this country to learn that the law enforcement system in the United States is not a national police force but a series of local, state, and federal agencies that take seriously their obligation to "serve and protect" law-abiding residents. Newcomers need to know that police officers can teach them how to protect themselves and their families from crime. Many immigrants, especially political refugees, come from countries in which the criminal justice system is based on tyranny, repression, and fear.

The NCPC suggests that law enforcement officers and other members of the criminal justice system can help ease this transition by working not only to communicate with immigrants but also to understand them and the complexities of their native cultures. The mere absence of conflict in a neighborhood does not mean that residents of different cultures have found harmony and a cooperative working relationship, says the NCPC. True multicultural integration occurs when various cultures reach a comfortable day-to-day interaction marked by respect, interest, and caring.

Communities in which immigrants and law enforcement have established close positive ties benefit considerably, according to the NCPC. Immigrants gain greater access to police and other services, such as youth programs, victims' assistance, parenting classes, medical assistance programs, business networking, and neighborhood groups. Crime decreases in communities where law enforcement officers help immigrants learn to protect themselves against crime.

For police officers working in communities in which "language is a serious barrier between cultures," the NCPC suggests the following pointers for communicating more effectively:

- Be patient when speaking with someone who does not clearly understand your language. Speak slowly and distinctly. Be willing to repeat words or phrases if necessary. Remember that shouting never helps a nonnative speaker understand better.
- Be careful with your choice of words, selecting those that are clear, straightforward, and simple to understand. Avoid colloquialisms and slang.
- Allow extra time for investigation when the people involved have not mastered English.
- Be sure that anyone who serves as an interpreter is fully qualified and has had experience. Interpreting under pressure is a difficult task; lack of training can lead to mistakes.
- Be candid about your ability to speak or understand a language. Trying to "fake it" just leads to confusion, misunderstanding, and misspent time.
- Never assume that someone is less intelligent just because he or she doesn't speak English well.

Visit the National Crime Prevention Council via http://www.ncpc.org.

Reference: Adapted from National Crime Prevention Council, *Building and Crossing Bridges: Refugees and Law Enforcement Working Together* (Washington, DC: NCPC, 1994).

When an officer makes an arrest without just cause or simply impedes an individual's right to leave the scene without good reason, he or she may also be liable for the charge of false arrest. Officers who "throw their weight around" are especially subject to this type of suit, grounded as it is on the abuse of police authority. Because generally employers may be sued for the negligent or malicious actions of their employees, many police departments are being named as codefendants in lawsuits today.

Civil suits are also brought against officers whose actions are deemed negligent. High-speed vehicle pursuits are especially dangerous because of the potential for injury to innocent bystanders. In the case of *Biscoe* v. *Arlington County* (1984),[103] for example, Alvin Biscoe was awarded \$5 million after he lost both legs as a consequence of a high-speed chase while he was waiting to cross the street. Biscoe, an innocent bystander, was struck by a police car that went out of control. The officer driving the car had violated department policies prohibiting high-speed chases, and the court found that he had not been properly trained.

High-speed vehicle pursuits are especially dangerous because of the potential for injury to innocent bystanders.

The FBI states that "a traffic accident constitutes the most common terminating event in an urban pursuit."[104] Some cities are actively replacing high-speed vehicle pursuits with surveillance technologies employing unmanned aerial vehicles (UAVs). Although helicopters have long been used in this capacity, the advent of UAV technology promises to make the tracking of fleeing suspects much quicker and far safer for all involved.

Departments may protect themselves from lawsuits to a significant degree by providing proper and adequate training to their personnel, and by creating regulations limiting the authority of employees. The Justice Department's investigation into the New Orleans Police Department, for example, which was mentioned earlier in this chapter, found that "the Department's failure to provide sufficient guidance, training, and support to its

■ **1983 lawsuit** A civil suit brought under Title 42, Section 1983, of the U.S. Code against anyone who denies others their constitutional right to life, liberty, or property without due process of law.

Tom Carter/Index Stock/AGE Fotostock

A police car destroyed during a high-speed chase. Research shows that most of the suspects chased by police are not violent criminals, and high-speed chases are especially dangerous because of their potential to injure innocent bystanders. When injuries do occur, a chase might provide a lawful basis for a civil suit against officers and their departments. How might a department protect itself from these kinds of suits?

officers," along with "its failure to implement systems to ensure officers are wielding their authority effectively and safely," could be addressed by implementing policies and practices to "properly recruit, train, and supervise officers."[105] "This understanding," the report's authors pointed out, "serves as the foundation upon which to build sustainable reform that will reduce . . . and prevent crime more effectively, police all parts of the New Orleans' community fairly, respect the rights of all New Orleans' residents and visitors, and prepare and protect officers."

Law enforcement supervisors may be the object of lawsuits by virtue of the fact that they are responsible for the actions of their officers. If it can be shown that supervisors were negligent in hiring (as when someone with a history of alcoholism, mental problems, sexual deviance, or drug abuse is employed) or if supervisors failed in their responsibility to properly train officers before arming and deploying them, they may be found liable for damages.

Law enforcement supervisors may be the object of lawsuits by virtue of the fact that they are responsible for the actions of their officers.

In the 1989 case of the *City of Canton, Ohio* v. *Harris*,[106] the U.S. Supreme Court ruled that a "failure to train" can become the basis for legal liability on the part of a municipality where the "failure to train amounts to deliberate indifference to the rights of persons with whom the police come in contact."[107] In that case, Geraldine Harris was arrested and taken to the Canton, Ohio, police station. While at the station, she slumped to the floor several times. Officers left her on the floor and did not call for medical assistance. Upon release, Harris's family took her to a local hospital, where she was found to be suffering from several emotional ailments. Harris was hospitalized for a week and received follow-up outpatient treatment for the next year.

In the 1997 case of *Board of the County Commissioners of Bryan County, Oklahoma* v. *Brown*, however, the Supreme Court ruled that to establish liability, plaintiffs must show that "the municipal action in question was not simply negligent, but was taken with 'deliberate indifference' as to its known or obvious consequences."[108] Learn more about vehicle pursuits and the Fourth Amendment at **http://www.justicestudies.com/ubs/pursuits.pdf**. Law enforcement training is the topic of the FBI article at **http://justicestudies.com/pubs/letraining.pdf**.

Federal Lawsuits

In April, 2012, five former officers of the New Orleans Police Department were sentenced to terms of imprisonment ranging from 6 to 65 years for violating the civil rights of unarmed residents on the city's Danziger Bridge during the breakdown of social order that followed Hurricane Katrina.[109] The officers, who claimed they thought that the residents were armed looters, shot six people, killing two of them.

Civil suits alleging police misconduct that are filed in federal courts are often called **1983 lawsuits** because they are

■ ***Bivens* action** A civil suit, based on the case of *Bivens* v. *Six Unknown Federal Agents*, brought against federal government officials for denying the constitutional rights of others.

based on Section 1983 of Title 42 of the U.S. Code—an act passed by Congress in 1871 to ensure the civil rights of men and women of all races. That act requires due process of law before any person can be deprived of life, liberty, or property and specifically provides redress for the denial of these constitutional rights by officials acting under color of state law. It reads as follows:

> Every person who, under color of any statute, ordinance, regulation, custom, or usage, of any State or Territory, subjects, or causes to be subjected, any citizen of the United States or other person within the jurisdiction thereof to the deprivation of any rights, privileges, or immunities secured by the Constitution and laws, shall be liable to the party injured in an action at law, suit in equity, or other proper proceeding for redress.[110]

A 1983 suit may be brought, for example, against officers who shoot suspects under questionable circumstances, thereby denying them their right to life without due process. Similarly, an officer who makes an arrest based on accusations that he or she knows to be untrue may be subject to a 1983 lawsuit.

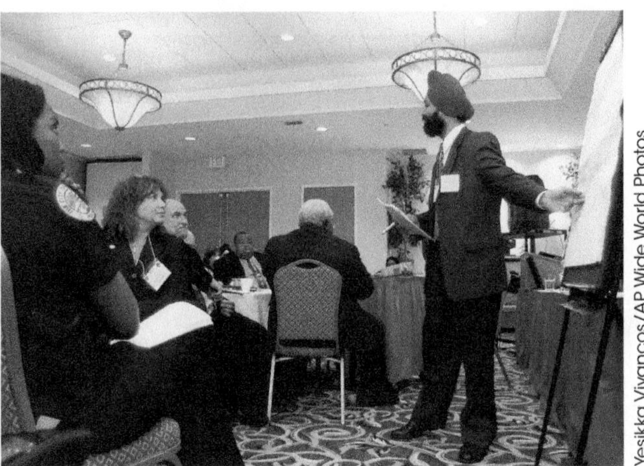

Yesikka Vivancos/AP Wide World Photos

Major Juanita Walker-Kirkland of the Miami Police Department, left, listening to Manjit Singh, right, chair of Sikh Mediawatch and Task Force, during a Building Cultural Competency training program in June 2003. The training program was sponsored by the U.S. Department of Justice in hopes of improving community relations between law enforcement officials and diverse cultural and religious groups. Why are such programs important?

Another type of liability action, this one directed specifically at federal officials or enforcement agents, is called a ***Bivens* action**. The case of *Bivens* v. *Six Unknown Federal Agents* (1971)[111] established a path for legal action against agents enforcing federal laws, which is similar to that found in a 1983 suit. *Bivens* actions may be addressed against individuals but not against the United States or its agencies.[112] Federal officers have generally been granted a court-created qualified immunity and have been protected from suits where they were found to have acted in the belief that their action was consistent with federal law.[113]

In the past, the doctrine of sovereign immunity barred legal actions against state and local governments. Sovereign immunity was a legal theory that held that a governing body could not be sued because it made the law and therefore could not be bound by it. Immunity is a much more complex issue today. Some states have officially abandoned any pretext of immunity through legislative action. New York State, for example, has declared that public agencies are equally as liable as private agencies for violations of constitutional rights. Other states, like California, have enacted statutory provisions that define and limit governmental liability.[114] A number of state immunity statutes have been struck down by court decision. In general, states are moving in the direction of setting dollar limits on liability and adopting federal immunity principles to protect individual officers, including "good-faith" and "reasonable-belief" rules.

At the federal level, the concept of sovereign immunity is embodied in the Federal Tort Claims Act (FTCA),[115] which grants broad immunity to federal government agencies engaged in discretionary activities. When a federal employee is sued for a wrongful or negligent act, the Federal Employees Liability Reform and Tort Compensation Act of 1988, commonly known as the Westfall Act, empowers the attorney general to certify that the employee was acting within the scope of his or her office or employment at the time of the incident. Upon certification, the employee is dismissed from the action, and the United States is substituted as defendant. The case then falls under the governance of the FTCA. (See Chapter 14 for more information on the FTCA.)

The U.S. Supreme Court has supported a type of qualified immunity for individual officers (as opposed to the agencies for which they work). This immunity "shields law enforcement officers from constitutional lawsuits if reasonable officers believe their actions to be lawful in light of clearly established law and the information the officers possess." The Supreme Court has also described qualified immunity as a defense "which shields public officials from actions for damages unless their conduct was unreasonable in light of clearly established law."[116] According to the Court, "[T]he qualified immunity doctrine's central objective is to protect public officials from undue interference with their duties and from potentially disabling threats of liability."[117] In the context of a warrantless arrest, the Court said in *Hunter* v. *Bryant* (1991),[118] "even law enforcement officials who reasonably but mistakenly conclude that probable cause is present are entitled to immunity."[119]

The doctrine of qualified immunity, as it exists today, rests largely on the 2001 U.S. Supreme Court decision of *Saucier* v. *Katz*,[120] in which the Court established a two-pronged test for assessing constitutional violations by government agents.[121] First, the court hearing the case must decide whether the facts, taken in the light most favorable to the party asserting the injury, show that the defendant's conduct violated a constitutional right. Second, the court must then decide whether that right was clearly established. For a right to be clearly established, the Court ruled, "it would be clear to a reasonable [defendant] that his conduct was unlawful in the situation he confronted." In summary, qualified immunity protects law enforcement agents from being sued for damages unless they violate clearly established law which a reasonable official in the agent's position would have known. The *Saucier* decision has recently faced substantial legal challenges, leading the Court to rule in *Pearson et al.* v. *Callahan*[122] (2009) that "the rigid *Saucier* procedure" has serious shortcomings. The Court noted that "*stare decisis* does not prevent this Court from determining whether the *Saucier* procedure should be modified or abandoned."

Criminal charges can also be brought against officers who appear to overstep legal boundaries or who act in violation of set standards. In 2001, for example, in the case of *Idaho* v. *Horiuchi*,[123] the Ninth U.S. Circuit Court of Appeals ruled that federal law enforcement officers are not immune from state prosecution where their actions violate state law "either through malice or excessive zeal." The case involved FBI sharpshooter Lon Horiuchi, who was charged with negligent manslaughter by prosecutors in Boundary County, Idaho, following the 1992 incident at Ruby Ridge.

Today, most police departments at both state and federal levels carry liability insurance to protect themselves against the severe financial damage that can result from the loss of a large civil suit. Some officers also acquire private policies that provide coverage in the event they are named as individuals in a civil suit. Both types of insurance policies generally cover legal fees up to a certain amount, regardless of the outcome of the case. Police departments that face civil prosecution because of the actions of an officer may find that legal and financial liability extends to supervisors, city managers, and the community itself. Where insurance coverage does not exist or is inadequate, city coffers may be nearly drained to meet the damages awarded.[124]

One study of a large sample of police chiefs throughout Texas found that most believed that lawsuits or the threat of civil litigation against the police makes it harder for individual officers to do their jobs. Most of the chiefs espoused the idea that adequate training, better screening of applicants, close supervision of officers, and "treating people fairly" all reduced the likelihood of lawsuits.[125]

SUMMARY

- The police personality is created through informal pressures on officers by a powerful police subculture that communicates values that support law enforcement interests. This chapter described the police personality as, among other things, authoritarian, conservative, honorable, loyal, cynical, dogmatic, hostile, prejudiced, secret, and suspicious.
- Various types of police corruption were described in this chapter, including "grass eating" and "meat eating." The latter includes the most serious forms of corruption, such as an officer's actively seeking illegal moneymaking opportunities through the exercise of his or her law enforcement duties. Ethics training was mentioned as part of a "reframing" strategy that emphasizes integrity in an effort to target police corruption. Also discussed was a recent U.S. Department of Justice report that focused on enhancing policing integrity and that cited a police department's culture of integrity as more important in shaping the ethics of police officers than hiring the "right" people.
- The dangers of police work are many and varied. They consist of violent victimization, disease, exposure to biological or chemical toxins, stressful encounters with suspects and victims, and on-the-job fatigue. Stress-management programs, combined with department policies designed to reduce exposure to dangerous situations and agency practices that support officers' needs, can all help combat the dangers and difficulties that police officers face in their day-to-day work.
- Law enforcement officers are authorized to use the amount of force that is reasonable and necessary in a particular situation. Many officers have encounters where the use of force is appropriate. Nonetheless, studies show that the police use force in fewer than 20% of adult custodial arrests. Even in instances where force is used, police officers primarily use weaponless tactics. Excessive force is the application of an amount and/or frequency of force greater than that required to compel compliance from a willing or unwilling subject.
- Racial profiling, or racially biased policing, is any police action initiated on the basis of the race, ethnicity, or national

origin of a suspect rather than on the behavior of that individual or on information that leads the police to a particular individual who has been identified as being, or having been, engaged in criminal activity. Racial profiling is a bigoted practice unworthy of the law enforcement professional. It has been widely condemned as contrary to basic ethical principles. Further, it weakens the public's confidence in the police, thereby decreasing police–citizen trust and cooperation. This chapter pointed out, however, that racial or ethnic indicators associated with particular suspects or suspect groups may have a place in legitimate law enforcement strategies if they accurately relate to suspects who are being sought for criminal law violations.

- Civil liability issues are very important in policing. They arise because officers and their agencies sometimes inappropriately use power to curtail the civil and due process rights of criminal suspects. Both police departments and individual police officers can be targeted by civil lawsuits. Federal suits based on claims that officers acted with disregard for an individual's right to due process are called *1983 lawsuits* because they are based on Section 1983 of Title 42 of the U.S. Code. Another type of civil suit that can be brought specifically against federal agents is a *Bivens* action. Although the doctrine of sovereign immunity barred legal action against state and local governments in the past, recent court cases and legislative activity have restricted the opportunity for law enforcement agencies and their officers to exercise claims of immunity.

KEY TERMS

1983 lawsuit, 265
biological weapon, 251
***Bivens* action, 266**
civil liability, 263
deadly force, 256
excessive force, 255
internal affairs, 249
Knapp Commission, 246
less-lethal weapon, 258
police corruption, 244
police use of force, 255
police working personality, 242
problem police officer, 256
racial profiling, 260

KEY CASES

***Biscoe* v. *Arlington County*, 264**
***Bivens* v. *Six Unknown Federal Agents*, 266**
***City of Canton, Ohio* v. *Harris*, 265**
***Graham* v. *Connor*, 257**
***Hunter* v. *Bryant*, 266**
***Idaho* v. *Horiuchi*, 267**
***Malley* v. *Briggs*, 263**
***Tennessee* v. *Garner*, 257**

QUESTIONS FOR REVIEW

1. What is the police working personality? What are its central features? How does it develop? How does it relate to police subculture?
2. What are the different types of police corruption? What themes run through the findings of the Knapp Commission and the Wickersham Commission? What innovative steps might police departments take to reduce or eliminate corruption among their officers?
3. What are the dangers of police work? What can be done to reduce those dangers?
4. In what kinds of situations are police officers most likely to use force? When has too much force been used?
5. What is racial profiling? What is racially biased policing? Why have they become significant issues in policing today?
6. What are some of the civil liability issues associated with policing? What are some of the common sources of civil suits against the police? How can civil liability be reduced?

QUESTIONS FOR REFLECTION

1. Do you think that this chapter has accurately described the police personality? Why or why not? Can you identify any additional characteristics of the police personality? Are there any listed here that you do not think are accurate?
2. What strategies can you think of for helping build police integrity? How might those strategies differ from one agency to another or from the local to the state or federal level?
3. What is it about racial profiling that most people find unacceptable? Are there any situations in which law enforcement's use of racial features or ethnic characteristics may be appropriate in targeting suspected criminals? If so, what would those situations be?

NOTES

i. Carl B. Klockars et al., "The Measurement of Police Integrity," *National Institute of Justice Research in Brief* (Washington, DC: National Institute of Justice, 2000), p. 1.
ii. Technical Working Group on Crime Scene Investigation, *Crime Scene Investigation: A Guide for Law Enforcement* (Washington, DC: National Institute of Justice, 2000), p. 12.
iii. National Institute of Justice, *Use of Force by Police: Overview of National and Local Data* (Washington, DC: National Institute of Justice, 1999).
iv. International Association of Chiefs of Police, *Police Use of Force in America, 2001* (Alexandria, VA: IACP, 2001), p. 1.
v. Samuel Walker, Geoffrey P. Albert, and Dennis J. Kenney, *Responding to the Problem Police Officer: A National Study of Early Warning Systems* (Washington, DC: National Institute of Justice, 2000).
vi. Sam W. Lathrop, "Reviewing Use of Force: A Systematic Approach," *FBI Law Enforcement Bulletin*, October 2000, p. 18.
vii. Deborah Ramierz, Jack McDevitt, and Amy Farrell, *A Resource Guide on Racial Profiling Data Collection Systems: Promising Practices and Lessons Learned* (Washington, DC: U.S. Dept. of Justice, 2000), p. 3.
viii. Adapted from Gerald Hill and Kathleen Hill, *The Real Life Dictionary of the Law*, http://www.law.com (accessed June 11, 2007).

1. Quoted in Jim Helihy, "Issues Affecting Irish Policing, 1922–1932," http://www.esatclear.ie/~garda/issues.html (accessed June 15, 2008).
2. "Caring and Courage: 2012 Heroes Among Us Awards," *People*, December 17, 2012, p. 95.
3. Janine Rauch and Etienne Marasis, "Contextualizing the Waddington Report," http://www.wits.ac.za/csvr/papers/papwadd.html (accessed January 5, 2009).
4. Jerome H. Skolnick, *Justice without Trial: Law Enforcement in a Democratic Society* (New York: John Wiley, 1966).
5. William A. Westley, *Violence and the Police: A Sociological Study of Law, Custom, and Morality* (Cambridge, MA: MIT Press, 1970); and William A. Westley, "Violence and the Police," *American Journal of Sociology*, Vol. 49 (1953), pp. 34–41.
6. Arthur Niederhoffer, *Behind the Shield: The Police in Urban Society* (Garden City, NY: Anchor, 1967).
7. Thomas Barker and David L. Carter, *Police Deviance* (Cincinnati, OH: Anderson, 1986). See also Christopher P. Wilson, *Cop Knowledge: Police Power and Cultural Narrative in Twentieth-Century America* (Chicago: University of Chicago Press, 2000).
8. Richard Bennett and Theodore Greenstein, "The Police Personality: A Test of the Predispositional Model," *Journal of Police Science and Administration*, Vol. 3 (1975), pp. 439–445.
9. James Teevan and Bernard Dolnick, "The Values of the Police: A Reconsideration and Interpretation," *Journal of Police Science and Administration* (1973), pp. 366–369.
10. Peter Applebome, "Police Gang Tyrannized Latinos, Indictment Says," *New York Times*, January 24, 2012, http://www.nytimes.com/2012/01/25/nyregion/connecticut-police-officers-accused-of-mistreating-latinos.html (accessed April 5, 2012).
11. Carl B. Klockars et al., "The Measurement of Police Integrity," *National Institute of Justice Research in Brief* (Washington, DC: NIJ, 2000), p. 1.
12. Michael J. Palmiotto, ed., *Police Misconduct: A Reader for the Twenty-First Century* (Upper Saddle River, NJ: Prentice Hall, 2001), preface.
13. Tim Prenzler and Peta Mackay, "Police Gratuities: What the Public Thinks," *Criminal Justice Ethics* (winter/spring 1995), pp. 15–25.
14. Thomas Barker and David L. Carter, *Police Deviance* (Cincinnati, OH: Anderson, 1986). For a detailed overview of the issues involved in police corruption, see Victor E. Kappeler, Richard D. Sluder, and Geoffrey P. Alpert, *Forces of Deviance: Understanding the Dark Side of Policing*, 2nd ed. (Prospect Heights, IL: Waveland Press, 1998); Dean J. Champion, *Police Misconduct in America: A Reference Handbook* (Santa Barbara, CA: Abo-Clio, 2002); and Kim Michelle Lersch, ed., *Policing and Misconduct* (Upper Saddle River, NJ: Prentice Hall, 2002).
15. L. Perry, "Repairing Broken Windows: Preventing Corruption within Our Ranks," *FBI Law Enforcement Bulletin*, February 2001, pp. 23–26.
16. "Nationline: NYC Cops—Excess Force Not Corruption," *USA Today*, June 16, 1995.
17. *Knapp Commission Report on Police Corruption* (New York: George Braziller, 1973).
18. Ibid.
19. Sabrina Tavernise, "Victory for Officer Who Aided Corruption Inquiry," *New York Times*, April 3, 2004.
20. Edwin H. Sutherland and Donald Cressey, *Principles of Criminology*, 8th ed. (Philadelphia: J. B. Lippincott, 1970).
21. Tim R. Jones, Compton Owens, and Melissa A. Smith, "Police Ethics Training: A Three-Tiered Approach," *FBI Law Enforcement Bulletin* (June 1995), pp. 22–26.
22. Stephen J. Gaffigan and Phyllis P. McDonald, *Police Integrity: Public Service with Honor* (Washington, DC: National Institute of Justice, 1997).
23. U.S. Department of Justice, *Principles for Promoting Police Integrity: Examples of Promising Police Practices* (Washington, DC: U.S. Dept. of Justice, 2001).
24. National Institute of Justice, *Enhancing Police Integrity* (Washington, DC: U.S. Dept. of Justice, 2005).
25. Ibid., p. ii.
26. *Carroll* v. *City of Westminster*, 4th Cir. No. 99-1556, November 17, 2000.
27. The material in this paragraph is adapted from Sharon Burrell, "Random Drug Testing of Police Officers Upheld," *Legal Views* (Office of the County Attorney, Montgomery County, Maryland), Vol. 6, No. 2 (February 2001), p. 4.
28. International Association of Chiefs of Police, *Employee Drug Testing* (St. Paul, MN: IACP, 1999).
29. *Maurice Turner* v. *Fraternal Order of Police*, 500 A.2d 1005 (D.C. 1985).
30. *Philip Caruso, President of P.B.A.* v. *Benjamin Ward, Police Commissioner*, New York State Supreme Court, Pat. 37, Index No. 12632-86, 1986.
31. *National Treasury Employees Union* v. *Von Raab*, 489 U.S. 656, 659 (1989).
32. National Law Enforcement Officers' Memorial Fund website, http://www.nleomf.com (accessed April 29, 2012).
33. From the Officer Down Memorial Page, http://www.odmp.org/year.php?year2012 (accessed July 15, 2013).
34. Ibid., http://www.odmp.org/year.php?year2001 (accessed January 16, 2011).
35. Anthony J. Pinizzotto and Edward F. Davis, "Cop Killers and Their Victims," *FBI Law Enforcement Bulletin*, December 1992, p. 10.
36. Brian A. Reaves, *Census of State and Local Law Enforcement Agencies, 2004* (Washington, DC: Bureau of Justice Statistics, 2007); and Matthew J. Hickman and Brian A. Reaves, *Local Police Departments, 2003* (Washington, DC: Bureau of Justice Statistics, 2006).
37. Brian A. Reaves, *Federal Law Enforcement Officers, 2004* (Washington, DC: Bureau of Justice Statistics, 2006).
38. *AIDS and Our Workplace*, New York City Police Department pamphlet, November 1987.
39. See Occupational Safety and Health Administration, OSHA Bloodborne Pathogens Act of 1991 (29 CFR 1910.1030).
40. *National Institute of Justice Reports*, No. 206 (November/December 1987).
41. See "On-the-Job Stress in Policing: Reducing It, Preventing It," *National Institute of Justice Journal* (January 2000), pp. 18–24.
42. "Stress on the Job," *Newsweek*, April 25, 1988, p. 43.
43. "On-the-Job Stress in Policing," p. 19.
44. Kevin Barrett, "Police Suicide: Is Anyone Listening?" *Journal of Safe Management of Disruptive and Assaultive Behavior* (spring 1997), pp. 6–9.
45. For an excellent review of coping strategies among police officers, see Robin N. Haarr and Merry Morash, "Gender, Race, and Strategies of Coping with Occupational Stress in Policing," *Justice Quarterly*, Vol. 16, No. 2 (June 1999), pp. 303–336.
46. Mark H. Anshel, "A Conceptual Model and Implications for Coping with Stressful Events in Police Work," *Criminal Justice and Behavior*, Vol. 27, No. 3 (2000), p. 375.
47. Ibid.
48. Bryan Vila, "Tired Cops: Probable Connections between Fatigue and the Performance, Health, and Safety of Patrol Officers," *American Journal of Police*, Vol. 15, No. 2 (1996), pp. 51–92.

49. Bryan Vila et al., *Evaluating the Effects of Fatigue on Police Patrol Officers: Final Report* (Washington, DC: National Institute of Justice, 2000).
50. Bryan Vila and Dennis Jay Kenney, "Tired Cops: The Prevalence and Potential Consequences of Police Fatigue," *NIJ Journal*, No. 248 (2002), p. 19.
51. Bryan Vila and Erik Y. Taiji, "Fatigue and Police Officer Performance," paper presented at the annual meeting of the American Society of Criminology, Chicago, 1996.
52. John Simerman, "Mayor Landrieu Fails in Bid to Halt Pending NOPD Reform Deal," *The Times-Picayune*, January 11, 2013, http://www.nola.com/crime/index.ssf/2013/01/mayor_landrieu_calls_halt_to_p.html#incart_m-rpt-2 (accessed March 11, 2013).
53. Civil Rights Division, U.S. Department of Justice, *Investigation of the New Orleans Police Department* (Washington, DC: USDOJ, 2011).
54. Some of the material in this section is adapted or derived from National Institute of Justice, *Use of Force by Police: Overview of National and Local Data* (Washington, DC: NIJ, 1999).
55. Matthew R. Durose, Erica L. Smith, and Patrick A. Langan, *Contacts between Police and the Public, 2005* (Washington, DC: Bureau of Justice Statistics, 2007).
56. Ibid, p. 10.
57. Not all studies agree on this point, and in 2005, researchers who examined the use of force by male and female officers in the Montgomery County Police Department in Maryland found that male and female officers were relatively comparable in their use of force. See Peter B. Hoffman and Edward R. Hickey, "Use of Force by Female Police Officers," *Journal of Criminal Justice*, Vol. 33, No. 2 (2005), p. 142.
58. International Association of Chiefs of Police, *Police Use of Force in America, 2001* (Alexandria, VA: IACP, 2001), p. 1.
59. Kenneth Adams, "What We Know about Police Use of Force," in National Institute of Justice, *Use of Force by Police: Overview of National and Local Data* (Washington, DC: NIJ, 1999), p. 4.
60. Geoffrey P. Alpert and Roger G. Dunham, *The Force Factor: Measuring Police Use of Force Relative to Suspect Resistance—A Final Report* (Washington, DC: National Institute of Justice, 2001).
61. Samuel Walker, Geoffrey P. Alpert, and Dennis J. Kenney, *Responding to the Problem Police Officer: A National Study of Early Warning Systems* (Washington, DC: National Institute of Justice, 2000).
62. See Human Rights Watch, "The Christopher Commission Report," from which some of the wording in this paragraph is adapted, http://www.hrw.org/reports98/police/uspo73.htm (accessed March 30, 2007).
63. Sam W. Lathrop, "Reviewing Use of Force: A Systematic Approach," *FBI Law Enforcement Bulletin*, October 2000, p. 18.
64. *Tennessee* v. *Garner*, 471 U.S. 1 (1985).
65. *Graham* v. *Connor*, 490 U.S. 386, 396–397 (1989).
66. John C. Hall, "FBI Training on the New Federal Deadly Force Policy," *FBI Law Enforcement Bulletin*, April 1996, pp. 25–32.
67. James Fyfe, *Shots Fired: An Examination of New York City Police Firearms Discharges* (Ann Arbor, MI: University Microfilms, 1978).
68. James Fyfe, "Blind Justice? Police Shootings in Memphis," paper presented at the annual meeting of the Academy of Criminal Justice Sciences, Philadelphia, March 1981.
69. It is estimated that American police shoot *at* approximately 3,600 people every year. See William Geller, "Crime File: Deadly Force," a study guide (Washington, DC: National Institute of Justice, n.d.).
70. Anne Cohen, "I've Killed That Man Ten Thousand Times," *Police Magazine*, July 1980.
71. For more information, see Joe Auten, "When Police Shoot," *North Carolina Criminal Justice Today*, Vol. 4, No. 4 (summer 1986), pp. 9–14.
72. Details for this story come from Stephanie Slater, "Suicidal Man Killed by Police Fusillade," *Palm Beach Post*, March 11, 2005.
73. Rebecca Stincelli, *Suicide by Cop: Victims from Both Sides of the Badge* (Folsom, CA: Interviews and Interrogations Institute, 2004).
74. Quoted in Slater, "Suicidal Man Killed by Police Fusillade."
75. Anthony J. Pinizzotto, Edward F. Davis, and Charles E. Miller III, "Suicide by Cop: Defining a Devastating Dilemma," *FBI Law Enforcement Bulletin*, Vol. 74, No. 2 (February 2005), p. 15.
76. "Ten Percent of Police Shootings Found to Be 'Suicide by Cop,'" *Criminal Justice Newsletter*, September 1, 1998, pp. 1–2.
77. Robert J. Homant and Daniel B. Kennedy, "Suicide by Police: A Proposed Typology of Law Enforcement Officer-Assisted Suicide," *Policing: An International Journal of Police Strategies and Management*, Vol. 23, No. 3 (2000), pp. 339–355.
78. David W. Hayeslip and Alan Preszler, "NIJ Initiative on Less-Than-Lethal Weapons," National Institute of Justice Research in Brief (Washington, DC: NIJ, 1993).
79. Ibid.
80. Thomas Farragher and David Abel, "Postgame Police Projectile Kills an Emerson Student," *Boston Globe*, October 22, 2004, http://www.boston.com/sports/baseball/redsox/articles/2004/10/22/postgame_police_projectile_kills_an_emerson_student (accessed July 25, 2005).
81. Civil Rights Division, U.S. Dept. of Justice, *Investigation of the New Orleans Police Department*, p. viii.
82. Ibid., p. ix.
83. Adapted from Deborah Ramirez, Jack McDevitt, and Amy Farrell, *A Resource Guide on Racial Profiling Data Collection Systems: Promising Practices and Lessons Learned* (Washington, DC: U.S. Dept. of Justice, 2000), p. 3.
84. Sid Heal, "The ABC3s," *The Tactical Edge*, Fall 2004, pp. 36–39.
85. Ibid.
86. David Harris, *Driving While Black: Racial Profiling on Our Nation's Highways* (Washington, DC: American Civil Liberties Union, 1999).
87. "Justice Department Bars Race Profiling, with Exception for Terrorism," *Criminal Justice Newsletter*, July 15, 2003, pp. 6–7.
88. "Justice Department Issues Policy Guidance to Ban Racial Profiling," U.S. Department of Justice press release (No. 355), June 17, 2003.
89. Blaine Harden and Somini Sengupta, "Some Passengers Singled Out for Exclusion by Flight Crew," *New York Times*, September 22, 2001.
90. David Cole and John Lambreth, "The Fallacy of Racial Profiling," *New York Times*, May 13, 2001, http://college1.nytimes.com/buests/articles/2001/05/13/846196.xml (accessed August 28, 2009).
91. Amitai Etzioni, "Another Side of Racial Profiling," *USA Today*, May 21, 2001, p. 15A.
92. Gallup Poll Organization, *Racial Profiling Is Seen as Widespread, Particularly among Young Black Men* (Princeton, NJ: Gallup Poll Organization, December 9, 1999), p. 1.
93. Gallup Poll Organization, "Racial Profiling Seen as Pervasive, Unjust," July 20, 2004, http://www.gallup.com/poll/12406/Racial-Profiling-Seen-Pervasive-Unjust.aspx (accessed August 1, 2010).

94. Ramirez, McDevitt, and Farrell, *A Resource Guide on Racial Profiling Data Collection Systems*, p. 3.
95. Police Executive Research Forum, *Racially Biased Policing: A Principled Response* (Washington, DC: PERF, 2001).
96. Ibid., foreword.
97. Ibid., p. 39.
98. Ibid., p. 47.
99. Details for this story come from David Heinzmann, "Committee to Consider Settling Cop Misconduct Cases for Nearly $33 Million," *Chicago Tribune*, http://www.chicagotribune.com/news/local/breaking/chi-emanuel-seeks-to-settle-2-cop-misconduct-cases-for-nearly-33-million-20130114,0,4742395,full.story, January 15, 2013.
100. Charles R. Swanson, Leonard Territo, and Robert W. Taylor, *Police Administration: Structures, Processes, and Behavior*, 2nd ed. (New York: Macmillan, 1988).
101. *Malley* v. *Briggs*, 475 U.S. 335, 106 S.Ct. 1092 (1986).
102. Ibid., at 4246.
103. *Biscoe* v. *Arlington County*, 238 U.S.App. D.C. 206, 738 F.2d 1352, 1362 (1984). See also 738 F.2d 1352 (D.C. Cir. 1984), cert. denied; 469 U.S. 1159; and 105 S.Ct. 909, 83 L.E.2d 923 (1985).
104. John Hill, "High-Speed Police Pursuits: Dangers, Dynamics, and Risk Reduction," *FBI Law Enforcement Bulletin* (July 2002), pp. 14–18.
105. Civil Rights Division, U.S. Dept. of Justice, *Investigation of the New Orleans Police Department*, p. xii.
106. *City of Canton, Ohio* v. *Harris*, 489 U.S. 378 (1989).
107. Ibid., at 1204.
108. *Board of the County Commissioners of Bryan County, Oklahoma* v. *Brown*, 520 U.S. 397 (1997).
109. Jeffrey Bloomer, "Ex-cops Handed Tough Sentences for Katrina Shootings," *The Slatest*, April 4, 2012, http://slatest.slate.com/posts/2012/04/04/katrina_police_shootings_convicted_new_orleans_police_officers_handed_stiff_sentences_in_shootings.html (accessed May 20, 2012).
110. U.S. Code, Title 42, Section 1983.
111. *Bivens* v. *Six Unknown Federal Agents*, 403 U.S. 388 (1971).
112. See *F.D.I.C.* v. *Meyer*, 510 U.S. 471 (1994), in which the U.S. Supreme Court reiterated its ruling under *Bivens*, stating that only government employees and not government agencies can be sued.
113. *Wyler* v. *U.S.*, 725 F.2d 157 (2d Cir. 1983).
114. California Government Code, Section 818.
115. Federal Tort Claims Act, U.S. Code, Title 28, Section 1346(b), 2671–2680.
116. *Elder* v. *Holloway*, 114 S.Ct. 1019, 127 L.Ed.2d 344 (1994).
117. Ibid.
118. *Hunter* v. *Bryant*, 112 S.Ct. 534 (1991).
119. William U. McCormack, "Supreme Court Cases: 1991–1992 Term," *FBI Law Enforcement Bulletin*, November 1992, p. 30.
120. *Saucier* v. *Katz*, 533 U.S. 194 (2001).
121. See also *Brosseau* v. *Haugen*, 543 U.S. 194 (2004).
122. *Pearson* v. *Callahan*, 555 U.S. 223 (2009).
123. *Idaho* v. *Horiuchi*, 266 F.3d 979 (9th Cir. 2001).
124. For more information on police liability, see Daniel L. Schofield, "Legal Issues of Pursuit Driving," *FBI Law Enforcement Bulletin*, May 1988, pp. 23–29.
125. Michael S. Vaughn, Tab W. Cooper, and Rolando V. del Carmen, "Assessing Legal Liabilities in Law Enforcement: Police Chiefs' Views," *Crime and Delinquency*, Vol. 47, No. 1 (2001), p. 3.

PART 3 ADJUDICATION

RIGHTS OF THE ACCUSED BEFORE THE COURT

The accused has these common law, constitutional, statutory, and humanitarian rights:

- The right to a speedy trial
- The right to legal counsel
- The right against self-incrimination
- The right not to be tried twice for the same offense
- The right to know the charges
- The right to cross-examine witnesses
- The right against excessive bail

These individual rights must be effectively balanced against these community concerns:

- Conviction of the guilty
- Exoneration of the innocent
- The imposition of appropriate punishment
- The protection of society
- Efficient and cost-effective procedures
- Seeing justice done

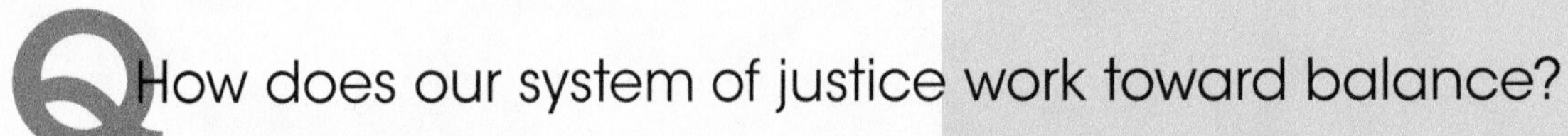

Q How does our system of justice work toward balance?

Equal Justice Under the Law

The well-known British philosopher and statesman Benjamin Disraeli (1804–1881) once defined justice as "truth in action." The study of criminal case processing by courts at all levels provides perhaps the best opportunity available to us from within the criminal justice system to observe what should ideally be "truth in action." The courtroom search for truth, which is characteristic of criminal trials, pits the resources of the accused against those of the state. The ultimate outcome of such procedures, say advocates of our adversarial-based system of trial practice, should be both truth and justice.

Others are not so sure. British novelist William McIlvanney (1936–) once wrote, "Who thinks the law has anything to do with justice? It's what we have because we can't have justice." Indeed, many critics of the present system claim that courts at all levels have become so concerned with procedure and with sets of formalized rules that they have lost sight of the truth. The chapters that make up this section of *Criminal Justice Today* provide an overview of American courts, including their history and present structure, and examine the multifaceted roles played by both professional and lay courtroom participants. Sentencing—the practice whereby juries recommend and judges impose sanctions on convicted offenders—is covered in the concluding chapter of this section. Whether American courts routinely uncover truth and therefore dispense justice, or whether they are merely locked into a pattern of hollow procedure that does little other than mock the justice ideal, will be for you to decide.

9 THE COURTS: STRUCTURE AND PARTICIPANTS

OUTLINE

- Introduction
- History and Structure of the American Court System
- The State Court System
- The Federal Court System
- The Courtroom Work Group
- Professional Courtroom Participants
- Outsiders: Nonprofessional Courtroom Participants

LEARNING OBJECTIVES

After reading this chapter, you should be able to

- Summarize the development of American courts, including the concept of the dual-court system.
- Describe a typical state court system, including some of the differences between the state and federal court systems.
- Describe the structure of the federal court system, including the various types of federal courts.
- Identify all typical job titles of the courtroom work group members.
- Describe the roles of professional members of the courtroom work group.
- Describe the roles of outsiders, or nonprofessional courtroom participants.

The criminal court is the central, crucial institution in the criminal justice system. . . . It is the institution around which the rest of the system has developed.

PRESIDENT'S COMMISSION ON LAW ENFORCEMENT AND ADMINISTRATION OF JUSTICE

federal court system The three-tiered structure of federal courts, comprising U.S. district courts, U.S. courts of appeal, and the U.S. Supreme Court.

Follow the author's tweets about the latest crime and justice news @schmalleger.

state court system A state judicial structure. Most states have at least three court levels: trial courts, appellate courts, and a state supreme court.

Introduction

On June 6, 2011, Donny Love was found guilty by a federal jury of ten criminal charges, including the use of a weapon of mass destruction, for his role in bombing the Edward J. Schwartz federal courthouse in San Diego, California, two years earlier.[1] Love was the mastermind behind a scheme to build and detonate three nail-filled pipe bombs at the entrance to the courthouse on May 4, 2008. The explosion shattered the building's glass door, damaged the lobby, and punched a hole in a window across the street. Although no one was injured, the FBI's San Diego Joint Terrorism Task Force conducted a vigorous investigation that resulted in the arrest of Love and two female accomplices. Love had filed more than 100 lawsuits in the courthouse that was attacked, and had also been sanctioned by a judge for frivolous filings, with the judge noting that "the lawsuits had been a lucrative cottage industry."[2] This time, according to prosecutors, Love planned and directed the bombing so that he could later provide investigators with bogus information about the incident in an effort to both obtain reward money and get a reduction in state charges that were pending against him.

Incidents like the San Diego bombing highlight the critical role that our nation's courts and the personnel who staff them play in the American system of justice. Without courts to decide guilt or innocence and to impose sentences on those convicted of crimes, the activities of law enforcement officials would become meaningless.

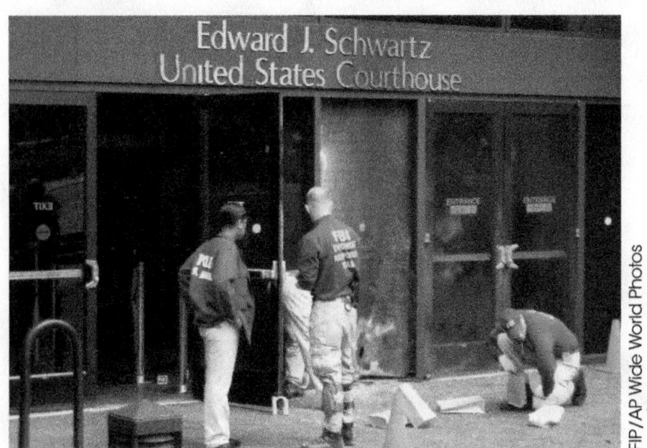

FIP/AP Wide World Photos

Federal Bureau of Investigation (FBI) and Alcohol, Tobacco, and Firearms (ATF) agents investigating damage to the Edward J. Schwartz federal courthouse in San Diego, California, following a bombing that targeted the facility in 2008. The bomber was later caught and convicted. What role do the courts play in the American criminal justice system?

There are many different levels of courts in the United States, but they all dispense justice and help ensure that officials in the justice system work within the law when carrying out their duties. At many points in this textbook and in three specific chapters (Chapters 7, 12, and 13), we take a close look at court precedents that have defined the legality of enforcement efforts and correctional action. In Chapter 4, we explored the law-making function of courts. This chapter provides a picture of how courts work by describing the American court system at both the state and federal levels. We will look at the roles of courtroom actors—from attorneys to victims and from jurors to judges. Then in Chapter 10, we will discuss pretrial activities and examine each of the steps in a criminal trial.

History and Structure of the American Court System

Two types of courts function within the American criminal justice system: (1) state courts and (2) federal courts. Figure 9-1 outlines the structure of today's **federal court system**, and Figure 9-2 diagrams a typical **state court system**. This dual-court system is the result of general agreement among the nation's founders about the need for individual states to retain significant legislative authority and judicial autonomy separate from federal control. Under this concept, the United States developed as a relatively loose federation of semi-independent provinces. New states joining the union were assured of limited federal intervention in local affairs. State legislatures were free to create laws, and state court systems were needed to hear cases in which violations of those laws occurred.

In the last 200 years, states' rights have gradually waned relative to the power of the federal government, but the dual-court system still exists. Even today, state courts do not hear cases involving alleged violations of federal law, nor do federal courts get involved in deciding issues of state law unless there is a conflict between local or state statutes and federal constitutional guarantees. When such conflicts arise, claimed violations of federal

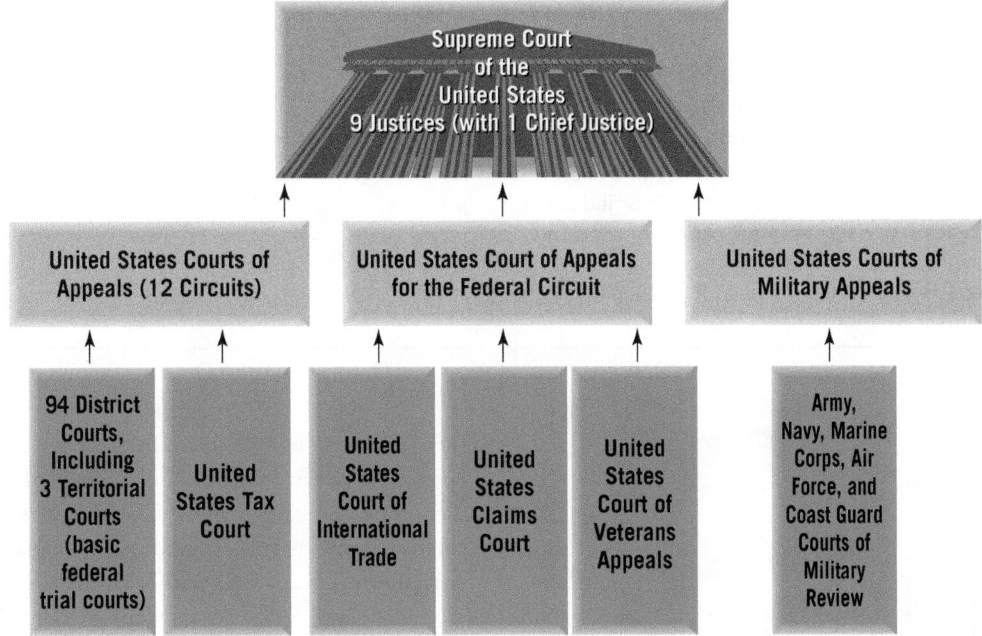

FIGURE 9-1 | The Structure of the Federal Courts

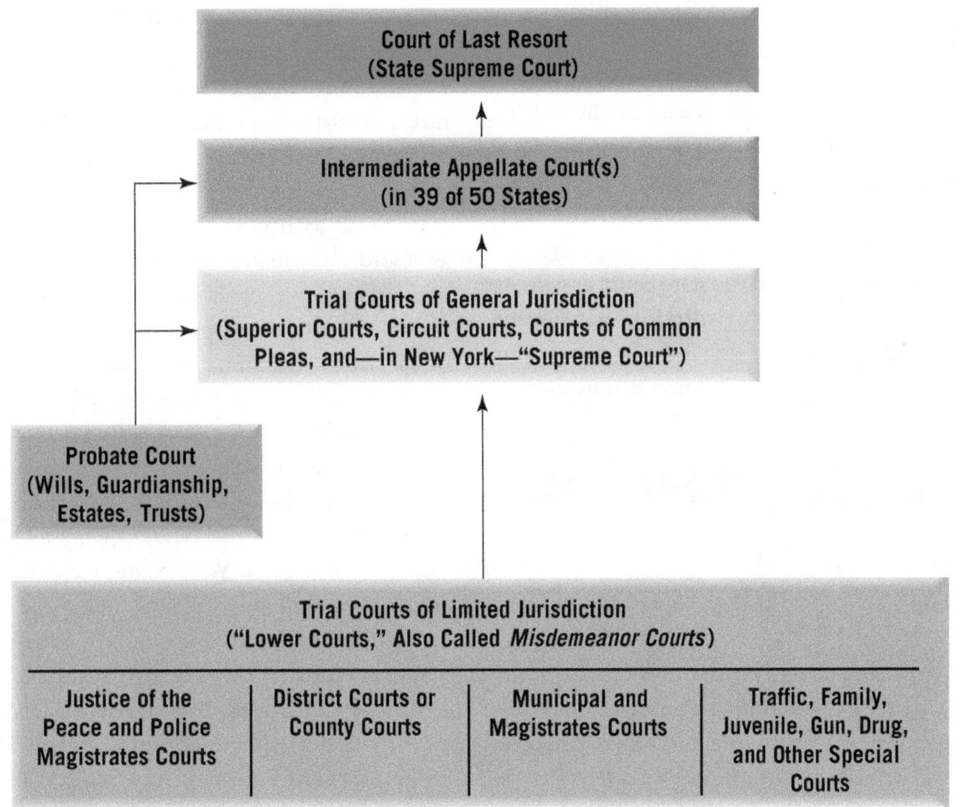

FIGURE 9-2 | A Typical State Court System

■ **jurisdiction** The territory, subject matter, or people over which a court or other justice agency may exercise lawful authority, as determined by statute or constitution.

■ **original jurisdiction** The lawful authority of a court to hear or to act on a case from its beginning and to pass judgment on the law and the facts. The authority may be over a specific geographic area or over particular types of cases.

■ **appellate jurisdiction** The lawful authority of a court to review a decision made by a lower court.

Jeff Greenberg/PhotoEdit Inc.

Junior high school children posing in the pillory in Williamsburg, Virginia. Just as criminal punishments have changed throughout the centuries, so too have criminal courts, which today provide civilized forums for exploring conflicting claims about guilt and innocence. How might our courts continue to evolve?

due process guarantees—especially those found in the Bill of Rights—can provide the basis for appeals made to federal courts by offenders convicted in state court systems. Learn more about the dual-court system in America at **http://public.findlaw.com/abaflg/flg-2-2a-1.html**.

This chapter describes both federal and state court systems in terms of their historical development, **jurisdiction**, and current structure. Because it is within state courts that the large majority of criminal cases originate, we turn our attention first to them.

The State Court System

The Development of State Courts

Each of the original American colonies had its own court system for resolving disputes, both civil and criminal. As early as 1629, the Massachusetts Bay Colony created a General Court, composed of the governor, his deputy, 18 assistants, and 118 elected officials. The General Court was a combined legislature and court that made laws, held trials, and imposed sentences.[3] By 1776, all of the American colonies had established fully functioning court systems.

Following the American Revolution, state court systems, were anything but uniform. Initially, most states made no distinction between **original jurisdiction**, the lawful authority of a court to hear cases that arise within a specified geographic area or that involve particular kinds of law violations, and **appellate jurisdiction**, the lawful authority of a court to review a decision made by a lower court. Many, in fact, had no provisions for appeal. Delaware, for example, did not allow appeals in criminal cases until 1897. States that did permit appeals often lacked any established appellate courts and sometimes used state legislatures for that purpose.

By the late nineteenth century, a dramatic increase in population, growing urbanization, the settlement of the West, and other far-reaching changes in the American way of life led to a tremendous increase in civil litigation and criminal arrests. Legislatures tried to keep pace with the rising tide of cases. States created a number of courts at the trial, appellate, and supreme court levels, calling them by a variety of names and assigning them functions that sometimes were completely different from those of similarly named courts in neighboring states. City courts, which were limited in their jurisdiction by community boundaries, arose to handle the special problems of urban life, such as disorderly conduct, property disputes, and the enforcement of restrictive and regulatory ordinances. Other tribunals, such as juvenile courts, developed to handle special kinds of problems or special clients. Some, like magistrate's courts or small-claims courts, handled only minor law violations and petty disputes. Still others, like traffic courts, were very narrow in focus. The result was a patchwork quilt of hearing bodies, some only vaguely resembling modern notions of a trial court.

State court systems developed by following several models. One was the New York State Field Code of 1848, which clarified jurisdictional claims and specified matters of court procedure. While many states copied the plan of the Field Code, it was later amended so extensively that its usefulness as a model dissolved. The federal Judiciary Act of 1789 and later the federal Reorganization Act of 1801 provided other models for state court systems. States that followed the federal model developed a three-tiered structure of (1) trial courts of limited jurisdiction, (2) trial courts of general jurisdiction, and (3) appellate courts.

■ **trial *de novo*** Literally, "new trial." The term is applied to cases that are retried on appeal, as opposed to those that are simply reviewed on the record.

State Court Systems Today

The three-tiered federal model was far from perfect, however. Within the structure it provided, many local and specialized courts proliferated. Traffic courts, magistrate's courts, municipal courts, recorder's courts, probate courts, and courts held by justices of the peace were but a few that functioned at the lower levels. In the early twentieth century, the American Bar Association (ABA) and the American Judicature Society led the movement toward simplification of state court structures. Proponents of state court reform sought to unify redundant courts that held overlapping jurisdictions. Most reformers suggested a uniform model for all states that would build on (1) a centralized court structure composed of a clear hierarchy of trial and appellate courts, (2) the consolidation of numerous lower-level courts with overlapping jurisdictions, and (3) a centralized state court authority that would be responsible for budgeting, financing, and managing all courts within a state.

The court reform movement continues today. Although reformers have made substantial progress in many states, there are still many differences between and among state court systems. Reform states, which early on embraced the reform movement, are now characterized by streamlined judicial systems consisting of precisely conceived trial courts of limited and general jurisdiction, supplemented by one or two appellate court levels. Nonreform, or traditional, states retain judicial systems that are a conglomeration of multilevel and sometimes redundant courts with poorly defined jurisdictions. Even in nonreform states, however, most criminal courts can be classified within the three-tiered structure of two trial court echelons and an appellate tier.

State Trial Courts

Trial courts are where criminal cases begin. The trial court conducts arraignments, sets bail, takes pleas, and conducts trials. (We will discuss each of these functions in more depth in the next chapter.) If the defendant pleads guilty or is found guilty, the trial court imposes sentence. Trial courts of limited, or special, jurisdiction are also called *lower courts*. Lower courts are authorized to hear only less serious criminal cases, usually involving misdemeanors, or to hear special types of cases, such as traffic violations, family disputes, and small claims. Courts of limited jurisdiction, which are depicted on TV shows like *Judge Judy* and *Judge Joe Brown*, rarely hold jury trials, depending instead on the hearing judge to make determinations of both fact and law. At the lower-court level, a detailed record of the proceedings is not maintained. Case files will include only information on the charge, the plea, the finding of the court, and the sentence. All but six of the states make use of trial courts of limited jurisdiction.[4] These lower courts are much less formal than courts of general jurisdiction.

Trial courts of general jurisdiction—variously called *high courts*, *circuit courts*, or *superior courts*—are authorized to hear any criminal case. In many states, they also provide the first appellate level for courts of limited jurisdiction. In most cases, superior courts offer

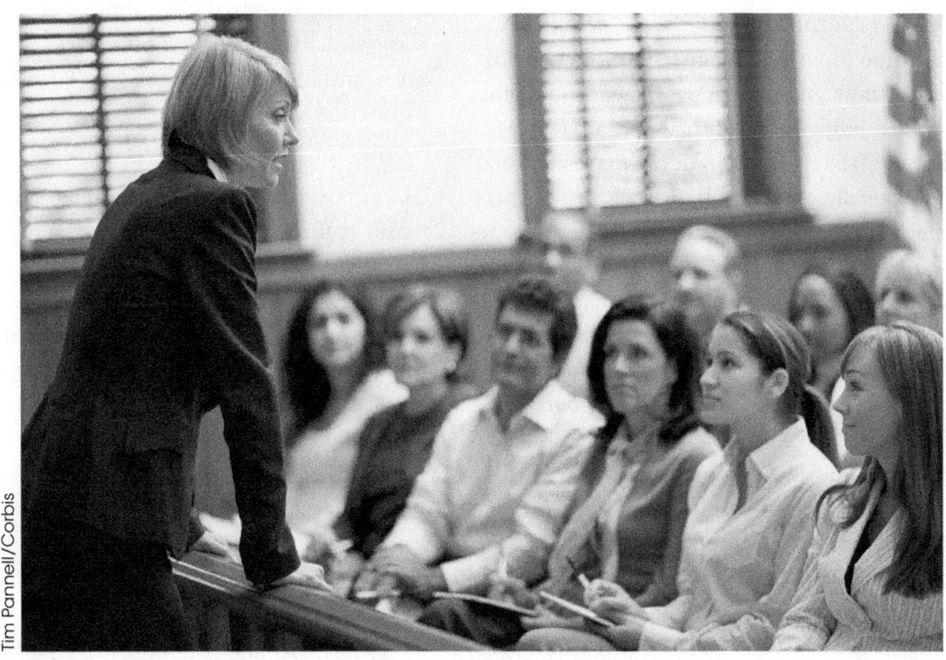
Tim Pannell/Corbis

An attorney making a closing argument to a jury. Why are courts sometimes called "the fulcrum of the criminal justice system"?

■ **court of last resort** The court authorized by law to hear the final appeal on a matter.

■ **appeal** Generally, the request that a court with appellate jurisdiction review the judgment, decision, or order of a lower court and set it aside (reverse it) or modify it.

■ **state court administrator** A coordinator who assists with case-flow management, operating funds budgeting, and court docket administration.

defendants whose cases originated in lower courts the chance for a new trial instead of a review of the record of the earlier hearing. When a new trial is held, it is referred to as **trial *de novo***.

Trial courts of general jurisdiction operate within a fact-finding framework called the *adversarial process*. That process pits the interests of the state, represented by prosecutors, against the professional skills and abilities of defense attorneys. The adversarial process is not a free-for-all; rather, it is constrained by procedural rules specified in law and sustained through tradition.

State Appellate Courts

Most states today have an appellate division where people can appeal a decision against them. The appellate division generally consists of an intermediate appellate court (often called the *court of appeals*) and a high-level appellate court (generally termed the *state supreme court*). High-level appellate courts are referred to as **courts of last resort**, indicating that a defendant can go no further with an appeal within the state court system once the high court rules on a case. All states have supreme courts, although only 39 have intermediate appellate courts.[5]

An **appeal** by a convicted defendant asks that a higher court review the actions of a lower court. Once they agree to review a decision, or accept an appeal, courts within the appellate division do not conduct a new trial. Instead, they review the case on the record, examining the written transcript of lower-court hearings to ensure that those proceedings were carried out fairly and in accordance with proper procedure and state law. These courts may also allow attorneys for both sides to make brief oral arguments and will generally consider other briefs or information filed by the appellant (the party initiating the appeal) or the appellee (the side opposed to the appeal). State statutes generally require that sentences of death or life imprisonment be automatically reviewed by the state supreme court.

Most convictions are affirmed on appeal. Occasionally, however, an appellate court will determine that the trial court erred in allowing certain kinds of evidence to be heard, that it failed to properly interpret the significance of a relevant statute, or that some other impropriety occurred. When that happens, the verdict of the trial court will be reversed, and the case may be sent back for a new trial, or *remanded*. When a conviction is overturned by an appellate court because of constitutional issues or when a statute is determined to be invalid, the state usually has recourse to the state supreme court or, when an issue of federal law is involved, as when a state court has ruled a federal law unconstitutional, to the U.S. Supreme Court.

Defendants who are not satisfied with the resolution of their case within the state court system may attempt an appeal to the U.S. Supreme Court. For such an appeal to have any chance of being heard, it must be based on claimed violations of the defendant's rights, as guaranteed under federal law or the U.S. Constitution. Under certain circumstances, federal district courts, which we will look at later in the chapter, may also provide a path of relief for state defendants who can show that their federal constitutional rights were violated. However, in the 1992 case of *Keeney* v. *Tamayo-Reyes*, the U.S. Supreme Court ruled that a "respondent is entitled to a federal evidentiary hearing [only] if he can show cause for his failure to develop the facts in the state-court proceedings and actual prejudice resulting from that failure, or if he can show that a fundamental miscarriage of justice would result from failure to hold such a hearing."[6] Justice Byron White, writing for the Court, said, "It is hardly a good use of scarce judicial resources to duplicate fact-finding in federal court merely because a petitioner has negligently failed to take advantage of opportunities in state-court proceedings."

Likewise, in *Herrera* v. *Collins* (1993),[7] the Court ruled that new evidence of innocence is no reason for a federal court to order a new state trial if constitutional grounds are lacking. The *Keeney* and *Herrera* decisions have severely limited access by state defendants to federal courts.

State Court Administration

To function efficiently, courts require uninterrupted funding, adequate staffing, trained support personnel, a well-managed case flow, and coordination between levels and among jurisdictions. To oversee these and other aspects of judicial management, every state has its own mechanism for court administration. Most have **state court administrators** who manage these operational functions.

State court administrators can receive assistance from the National Center for State Courts (NCSC) in Williamsburg, Virginia. The NCSC is an independent nonprofit organization dedicated to the improvement of the American court system. It was founded in 1971 at the behest of Chief Justice Warren E. Burger. You can visit the National Center for State Courts at **http://www.ncsc.org**.

At the federal level, the court system is administered by the Administrative Office of the United States Courts (AOUSC), in

■ **community court** A low-level court that focuses on quality-of-life crimes that erode a neighborhood's morale. Community courts emphasize problem solving rather than punishment and build on restorative principles such as community service and restitution.

■ **specialized court** A low-level court that focuses on relatively minor offenses and handles special populations or addresses special issues such as reentry. Specialized courts are often a form of community courts.

■ **dispute-resolution center** An informal hearing place designed to mediate interpersonal disputes without resorting to the more formal arrangements of a criminal trial court.

Washington, D.C. The AOUSC, created by Congress in 1939, prepares the budget and legislative agenda for federal courts. It also performs audits of court accounts, manages funds for the operation of federal courts, compiles and publishes statistics on the volume and type of business conducted by the courts, and recommends plans and strategies to efficiently manage court business. You can visit the Administrative Office of the United States Courts via **http://www.uscourts.gov/Home.aspx**.

Dispute-Resolution Centers and Specialized Courts

It is often possible to resolve minor disputes (in which minor criminal offenses might otherwise be charged) without a formal court hearing. Some communities have **dispute-resolution centers**, which hear victims' claims of minor wrongs such as passing bad checks, trespassing, shoplifting, and petty theft. Today, more than 200 centers throughout the country,[8] frequently staffed by volunteer mediators, work to resolve disagreements without assigning blame. Dispute-resolution programs began in the early 1970s, with the earliest being the Community Assistance Project in Chester, Pennsylvania; the Night Prosecutor Program in Columbus, Ohio; and the Arbitration as an Alternative Program in Rochester, New York. Following the lead of these programs, the U.S. Department of Justice helped promote the development of three experimental Neighborhood Justice Centers in Los Angeles; Kansas City, Missouri; and Atlanta. Each center accepted both minor civil and criminal cases.

Mediation centers are often closely integrated with the formal criminal justice process and may substantially reduce the caseload of lower-level courts. Some centers are, in fact, run by the courts and work only with court-ordered referrals. Others are semiautonomous but may be dependent on courts for endorsement of their decisions; others function with complete autonomy. Rarely, however, do dispute-resolution programs entirely supplant the formal criminal justice mechanism, and defendants who appear before a community mediator may later be charged with a crime. Community mediation programs have become a central feature of today's restorative justice movement (discussed in more detail in Chapter 11).

Courtesy of Gordon M. Armstrong

As a trainer observes, a counselor/trainee in a community dispute-resolution training program conducts a mock mediation session between an "offender" and his "victim." Staffed largely by volunteers, dispute-resolution centers facilitate cooperative solutions to relatively low-level disputes in which minor criminal offenses might otherwise be charged. How do dispute-resolution centers help relieve some of the pressures facing our criminal courts?

Unlike dispute-resolution centers, **community courts** are always *official* components of the formal justice system and can hand down sentences, including fines and jail time, without the need for further judicial review. Community courts began as grassroots movements undertaken by community residents and local organizations seeking to build confidence in the way offenders are handled for less serious offenses. A distinguishing feature of community courts is their focus on quality-of-life crimes that erode a neighborhood's morale. Like dispute-resolution centers they emphasize problem solving rather than punishment, and build on restorative principles such as community service and restitution.

Community courts generally sentence convicted offenders to work within the community, "where neighbors can see what they are doing."[9] A 2006 Center for Court Innovation study of the Red Hook Community Justice Center in Red Hook, New York, found that defendants considered the community court to be more fair than traditional courts.[10] According to the study, perceptions of fairness were primarily related to the more personal role played by community court judges, who dispense with much of the formality of traditional courts and who often offer support and praise to defendants who work within the parameters set by the court.

Recently, the community justice movement has led to the creation of innovative low-level courts in some parts of the country. These **specialized courts** focus on relatively minor offenses, and handle special populations or address special issues. Some hear only cases involving veterans, others focus on the needs of the mentally ill or the homeless. Still others handle only sex offenders charged with lessor offenses. The Brooklyn Mental Health Court provides an example of a specialized court that, in its own words, "seeks to craft a meaningful response to the problems posed by defendants with mental illness in the criminal justice system."[11] The Brooklyn court attempts to address both the needs of defendants with mental illness and public safety concerns. It uses the authority of the court to provide counseling and treatment for defendants with identified serious and persistent mental illnesses in lieu of jail or prison time. The court employs on-site clinical teams to assess the degree of mental illness from which a defendant suffers, and to gauge the risk that the defendant represents to the community were he or she to be released into a community-based supervision program.

Specialized courts that deal with specific offenses include gun courts, domestic violence courts, driving while intoxicated (DWI) or driving under the influence (DUI) courts, and drug courts. Other specialized courts, called reentry courts, utilizes the drug court model to facilitate the reintegration of drug-involved offenders paroled into the community after being released from prison. Using the authority of the court to apply graduated sanctions and positive reinforcement, reentry courts marshal resources to support positive reintegration by the returning offender. Reentry courts are discussed in more detail in Chapter 12.

Most specialized court programs are motivated by two sets of goals: (1) case management, in which the court works to expedite case processing and reduce caseloads, as well as to reduce time to disposition (thus increasing trial capacity for more serious crimes); and (2) therapeutic jurisprudence, in which the court works to reduce criminal offending through therapeutic and interdisciplinary approaches that address addiction and other underlying issues without jeopardizing public safety and due process.[12]

Specialized courts can be distinguished from other criminal courts by the fact that they operate according to a problem-solving model, rather than a retributive one—meaning that they seek to address the root causes of law violation, whether they lie within the individual, the community, or the larger culture.[13] Their purpose is not only to make justice more efficient, but more effective, as well.

The Federal Court System

Whereas state courts evolved from early colonial arrangements, federal courts were created by the U.S. Constitution. Article III, Section 1, of the Constitution provides for the establishment of "one supreme Court, and . . . such inferior Courts as the Congress may from time to time ordain and establish." Article III, Section 2, specifies that such courts are to have jurisdiction over cases arising under the Constitution, federal laws, and treaties. Federal courts are also to settle disputes between states and to have jurisdiction in cases where one of the parties is a state.

Today's federal court system represents the culmination of a series of congressional mandates that have expanded the federal judicial infrastructure so that it can continue to carry out the duties envisioned by the Constitution. Notable federal statutes that have contributed to the present structure of the federal court system include the Judiciary Act of 1789, the Judiciary Act of 1925, and the Magistrate's Act of 1968.

As a result of constitutional mandates, congressional actions, and other historical developments, today's federal judiciary consists of three levels: (1) U.S. district courts, (2) U.S. courts of appeals, and (3) the U.S. Supreme Court. Each is described in turn in the following sections.

CJ | NEWS

America's Judiciary: Courting Disaster

Newscom

The Schenectady (New York) County Courthouse. How might state budget shortfalls impact the important role of courts?

As states slash budgets to get through a still-sluggish economy, the courts under their jurisdiction are feeling the pain in the form of fewer personnel, shorter hours of operation and backed-up caseloads.

After years of cuts for courts, "we are now at the point where funding failures are not merely causing inconvenience, annoyances and burdens," said David Boies, co-chairman of an American Bar Association (ABA) commission looking into the problem. Altogether, 42 states cut judicial funding in 2011, according to the National Center for State Courts.

Covering 95% of all litigation, state-financed court systems are essential for prosecuting criminals, resolving personal conflicts, straightening out household finances, and getting business done. This work includes county-based trial courts that try criminal and civil cases, as well as special courts to address traffic accidents, small claims, family matters, and other issues.

Services are being cut at a time when case volumes are often on the rise due to the same economic forces driving the cuts. In tough economic times, courts tend to deal with increased foreclosures, bankruptcies, contract claims and embezzlement cases, the ABA reports. Between 2005 and 2010, the state of Maine, for example, experienced a 50% increase in civil cases.

Generally, when courts cut their budgets, criminal cases are least affected. Many jurisdictions have to meet mandated time limits on the period between arrest and arraignment, and the case may be thrown out if the limits are violated. Citing the time limit, Georgia courts recently dismissed indictments against several suspects accused of violent crimes.

The focus on meeting criminal time limits means the brunt of the cuts goes to civil cases, including foreclosures, divorces, traffic violations and civil disputes. According to the New York Bar Association, for example, it often takes a year to begin a civil trial in Ulster County, New York.

Even as the economy improves, many states are still struggling with their budgets and continue to cut back court services:

- In California, the Los Angeles County Superior Court system plans to lay off about 350 employees in June due to cuts in spending for courts across the state. California justices have warned that it may take up to five years to resolve civil cases.
- In Florida, the 2013 state budget included a 7% cut for court clerks, who are essential to efficient court operation. Clerks say the cuts could lead to 40-day delays in the processing of documents.
- In New York, judges have begun to cut hours, usually stopping court at 4:30 p.m., even when testimony is ongoing or a jury is deliberating, the state bar association reports.

At least 15 states reported reduced hours of court operations in 2011, the National Center for State Courts reported.

Budget-cutting tactics such as sending staff home in "furlough closures," however, just make the problem worse, said New Mexico Chief Justice Charles W. Daniels. "It's not like a furlough closure of a museum or a park or a tourist train, where you can actually save money by cutting services to the public on a given day," he said. "The work of busy courts just gets even more backed up and still takes the same resources, the same employee time, the same expense to process."

The ABA reports that state cuts for the judiciary started well before the recession and can be proportionately larger than cuts for other state-funded agencies. Back when state legislators were predominantly lawyers, Boies said they understood the courts' needs and routinely approved judicial funding, but fewer legislators are lawyers now.

Resources: "Task Force Finds Court Underfunding Still a Crisis, Business Partnership an Opportunity," *ABA Now*, February 6, 2012, http://www.abanow.org/2012/02/task-force-finds-court-underfunding-still-a-crisis-business-partnership-an-opportunity/; "Budget Cuts Clog Criminal Justice System," *Daily Herald*, October 27, 2011, http://www.heraldextra.com/news/national/article_9f1459ac-fb78-5a41-bd5e-8d930a28281b.html; and "Cuts Could Stall Sluggish Courts at Every Turn," *New York Times*, May 15, 2011, http://www.nytimes.com/2011/05/16/nyregion/budget-cuts-for-new-york-courts-likely-to-mean-delays.html?pagewanted=all.

U.S. District Courts

The U.S. district courts are the trial courts of the federal court system.[14] Within limits set by Congress and the Constitution, the district courts have jurisdiction to hear nearly all categories of federal cases, including both civil and criminal matters. There are 94 federal judicial districts, including at least one district in each state (some states, such as New York and California, have as many as four), the District of Columbia, and Puerto Rico. Each district includes a U.S. bankruptcy court as a unit of the district court. Three territories of the United States—the Virgin Islands, Guam, and the Northern Mariana Islands—have district courts that hear federal cases, including bankruptcy cases. There are two special trial courts that have nationwide jurisdiction over certain types of cases. The Court of International Trade addresses cases involving international trade and customs issues. The U.S. Court of Federal Claims has jurisdiction over most claims for monetary damages against the United States, disputes over federal contracts, unlawful "takings" of private property by the federal government, and a variety of other claims against the United States.

Federal district courts have original jurisdiction over all cases involving alleged violations of federal statutes. A district may be divided into divisions and may have several places where the court hears cases. District courts were first authorized by Congress through the Judiciary Act of 1789, which allocated one federal court to each state. Because of population increases over the years, new courts have been added in many states.

Nearly 650 district court judges staff federal district courts. Because some courts are much busier than others, the number of district court judges varies from a low of two in some jurisdictions to a high of 27 in others. District court judges are appointed by the president and confirmed by the Senate, and they serve for life. An additional 369 full-time and 110 part-time magistrate judges (referred to as *U.S. magistrates* before 1990) serve the district court system and assist the federal judges. Magistrate judges have the power to conduct arraignments and may set bail, issue warrants, and try minor offenders.

U.S. district courts handle tens of thousands of cases per year. During 2012, for example, 75,290 criminal cases[15] and 285,260 civil cases[16] were filed in U.S. district courts. Drug prosecution and the prosecution of illegal immigrants, especially in federal courts located close to the U.S.–Mexican border, has led to considerable growth in the number of cases filed. Federal drug prosecutions in the border states of California, Arizona, New Mexico, and Texas more than doubled between 1994 and 2000, from 2,864 to 6,116, and immigration prosecutions increased more than sevenfold, from 1,056 to 7,613.[17] During the past 20 years, the number of cases handled by the entire federal district court system has grown exponentially. The hiring of new judges and the creation of new courtroom facilities have not kept pace with the increase in caseload, and questions persist as to the quality of justice that overworked judges can deliver.

In 2011, in response to rapidly growing caseloads, Roslyn O. Silver, a federal judge in the Ninth Circuit's Tucson division, declared a federal court emergency in Arizona. The emergency declaration came in response to the rising number of illegal immigration and drug smuggling cases handled by federal courts in the state. In fact, federal criminal caseloads in Arizona rose 65% from 2008 to 2011 after the Department of Homeland Security established a policy of criminal prosecution for anyone caught crossing the border illegally.[18] Under the emergency declaration, federal courts can avoid certain Speedy Trial Act requirements and push the time limit for a trial to begin to 180 days (up from the 70 days normally required by the legislation).

Another pressing issue facing district court judges is the fact that their pay, which at around $174,000 in mid-2010[19] placed them in the top 1% of income-earning Americans, is low compared to what most could earn in private practice. Since 1992, the salaries of federal judges have remained relatively stagnant, leading many judges to leave the bench,[20] and in 2006, Chief Justice John Roberts called Congress's failure to raise judges' pay "a direct threat to judicial independence."[21] Because of low pay, said Roberts, "judges effectively serve for a term dictated by their financial position rather than for life." Learn more about the federal courts at **http://www.justicestudies.com/pubs/fedcourts.pdf**.

U.S. Courts of Appeals

The 94 judicial districts are organized into 12 regional circuits, each of which has a U.S. court of appeals.[22] A court of appeals hears appeals from the district courts located within its circuit, as well as appeals from decisions of federal administrative agencies. The Court of Appeals for the Federal Circuit has nationwide jurisdiction to hear appeals in special cases, such as those involving patent laws and cases decided by the Court of International Trade and the U.S. Court of Federal Claims.

The U.S. Court of Appeals for the Federal Circuit and the 12 regional courts of appeals are often referred to as *circuit courts*. Early in the nation's history, the judges of the first courts of appeals visited each of the courts in one region in a particular sequence, traveling by horseback and riding the "circuit." Today, the regional courts of appeals review matters from the district courts of their geographic regions, from the U.S. Tax Court, and from certain federal administrative agencies. A disappointed party in a district court usually has the right to have the case reviewed in the court of appeals for the circuit. The First through Eleventh Circuits all include three or more states, as illustrated in Figure 9-3.

Each court of appeals consists of six or more judges, depending on the caseload of the court. Circuit court judges are appointed for life by the president with the advice and consent of the Senate. The judge who has served on the court the longest and who is under-

Circuit court judges are appointed for life by the president with the advice and consent of the Senate.

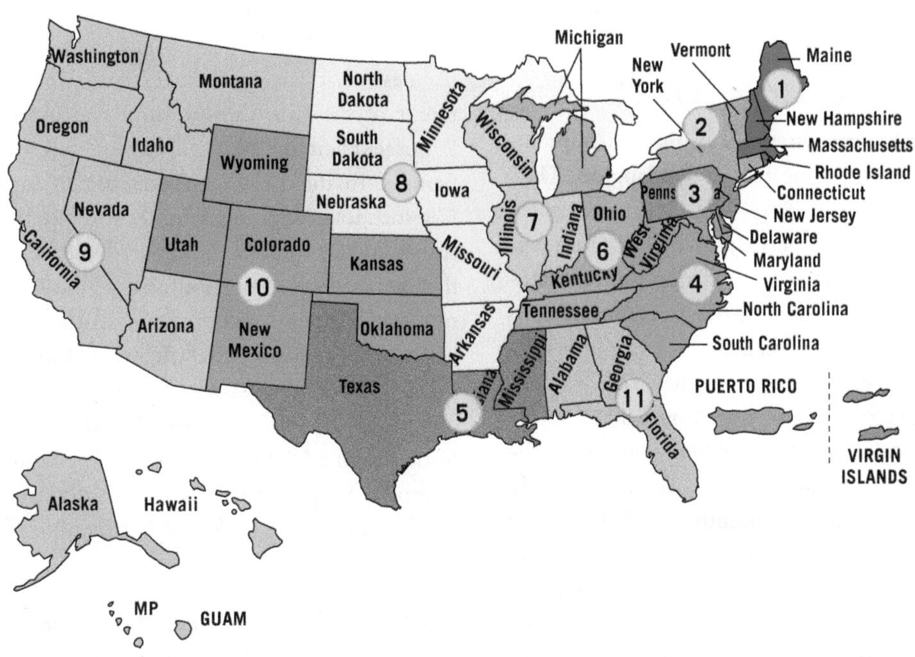

FIGURE 9-3 | Geographic Boundaries of the U.S. Courts of Appeals

65 years of age is designated as the chief judge and performs administrative duties in addition to hearing cases. The chief judge serves for a maximum term of seven years. There are 167 judges on the 12 regional courts of appeals.

The U.S. Court of Appeals for the District of Columbia, which is often called the Twelfth Circuit, hears cases arising in the District of Columbia and has appellate jurisdiction assigned by Congress in legislation concerning many departments of the federal government. The U.S. Court of Appeals for the Federal Circuit (in effect, the Thirteenth Circuit) was created in 1982 by the merging of the U.S. Court of Claims and the U.S. Court of Customs and Patent Appeals. The court hears appeals in cases from the U.S. Court of Federal Claims, the U.S. Court of International Trade, the U.S. Court of Veterans Appeals, the International Trade Commission, the Board of Contract Appeals, the Patent and Trademark Office, and the Merit Systems Protection Board. The Federal Circuit Court also hears appeals from certain decisions of the secretaries of the Department of Agriculture and the Department of Commerce and cases from district courts involving patents and minor claims against the federal government.

Almost all appeals from federal district courts go to the court of appeals serving the circuit in which the case was first heard. Federal appellate courts have mandatory jurisdiction over the decisions of district courts within their circuits. *Mandatory jurisdiction* means that U.S. courts of appeals are required to hear the cases brought to them. Criminal appeals from federal district courts are usually heard by panels of three judges sitting on a court of appeals rather than by all the judges of each circuit. A defendant's right to appeal, however, has been interpreted to mean the right to one appeal. Hence the U.S. Supreme Court need not necessarily hear the appeals of defendants who are dissatisfied with the decision of a federal appellate court.

Federal appellate courts operate under the Federal Rules of Appellate Procedure, although each has also created its own separate Local Rules. Local Rules may mean that one circuit, such as the Second, will depend heavily on oral arguments, while others may substitute written summary depositions in their place. Appeals generally fall into one of three categories: (1) frivolous appeals, which have little substance, raise no significant new issues, and are generally disposed of quickly; (2) ritualistic appeals, which are brought primarily because of the demands of litigants, even though the probability of reversal is negligible; and (3) nonconsensual appeals, which entail major questions of law and policy and on which there is considerable professional disagreement among the courts and within the legal profession.[23] The probability of reversal is highest in the case of nonconsensual appeals.

In 2011, the Judicial Conference of the United States, the primary policymaking arm of the federal courts, urged Congress to create 61 permanent new federal judgeships in appellate and district courts.[24] The conference cited a need for 8 new appeals court judges and 53 new federal judges at the district court level.

■ **judicial review** The power of a court to review actions and decisions made by other agencies of government.

The U.S. Supreme Court

At the apex of the federal court system stands the U.S. Supreme Court. The Supreme Court is located in Washington, D.C., across the street from the U.S. Capitol. The Court consists of nine justices, eight of whom are associate justices. The ninth presides over the Court as the chief justice of the United States. Supreme Court justices are nominated by the president, are confirmed by the Senate, and serve for life. Lengthy terms of service are a tradition among justices. One of the earliest chief justices, John Marshall, served the Court for 34 years, from 1801 to 1835. The same was true of Justice Stephen J. Field, who sat on the bench between 1863 and 1897. Justice Hugo Black passed the 34-year record, serving an additional month, before he retired in 1971. Justice William O. Douglas set a record for longevity on the bench, retiring in 1975 after 36 years and six months of service. You can view the biographies of today's Supreme Court justices via **http://www.supremecourt.gov/about/biographies.aspx**.

The Supreme Court of the United States wields immense power. The Court's greatest authority lies in its capacity for **judicial review** of lower-court decisions and state and federal statutes. By exercising its power of judicial review, the Court decides what laws and lower-court decisions keep with the intent of the U.S. Constitution. The power of judicial review is not explicit in the Constitution but was anticipated by its framers. In the *Federalist-Papers*, which urged adoption of the Constitution, Alexander Hamilton wrote that through the practice of judicial review, the Court would ensure that "the will of the whole people," as grounded in the Constitution, would be supreme over the "will of the legislature," which might be subject to temporary whims.[25] It was not until 1803, however, that the Court forcefully asserted its power of judicial review. In an opinion written for the case of *Marbury* v. *Madison* (1803),[26] Chief Justice John Marshall established the Court's authority as final interpreter of the U.S. Constitution, declaring, "It is emphatically the province of the judicial department to say what the law is."

The Supreme Court Today

The Supreme Court reviews the decisions of lower courts and may accept cases both from U.S. courts of appeals and from state supreme courts. It has limited original jurisdiction and does not conduct trials except in disputes between states and in some cases of attorney disbarment. For a case to be heard, at least four justices must vote in favor of a hearing. When the Court agrees to hear a case, it will issue a writ of *certiorari* to a lower court,

Demonstrators in support of a 2012 ruling by the Ninth Circuit Court of Appeals affirming a decision by U.S. District Court Judge Vaughn R. Walker that overturned California's ban on gay marriages. The Ninth Circuit also held that the fact that Walker is gay was immaterial. Do judges' personal perspectives influence their decisions? Should they?

SAUL LOEB/Getty Images

U.S. Supreme Court Justice Sonia Sotomayor (center) being applauded by President Barack Obama and Vice President Joe Biden at her 2009 nomination to the Court. Do you think that a justice's personal values and beliefs might influence his or her decisions on important matters that come before the court—or are such decisions always a matter of impersonal application of relevant law?

ordering it to send the records of the case forward for review. Once having granted *certiorari*, the justices can revoke the decision. In such cases, a writ is dismissed by ruling that it was improvidently granted.

The U.S. Supreme Court may review any decision appealed to it that it decides is worthy of review. In fact, however, the Court elects to review only cases that involve a substantial federal question. Of approximately 5,000 requests for review received by the Court yearly, only about 200 are heard.

The U.S. Supreme Court may review any decision appealed to it that it decides is worthy of review.

A term of the Supreme Court begins, by statute, on the first Monday in October and lasts until early July. The term is divided among sittings, when cases will be heard, and time for the writing and delivering of opinions. Between 22 and 24 cases are heard at each sitting (which may last days), with each side allotted 30 minutes for arguments before the justices. Intervening recesses allow justices time to study arguments and supporting documentation and to work on their opinions.

Decisions rendered by the Supreme Court are rarely unanimous. Instead, the opinion that a majority of the Court's justices agree on becomes the judgment of the Court. Justices who agree with the Court's judgment write concurring opinions if they agree for a different reason or if they feel that they have some new light to shed on a legal issue in the case. Justices who do not agree with the decision of the Court write dissenting opinions, which may offer new possibilities for successful appeals of future cases. Visit the U.S. Supreme Court via **http://www.supremecourt.gov**.

The Courtroom Work Group

On May 24, 2011, following an extended period of jury selection, the first-degree murder trial of 23-year-old Casey Anthony began at the Orange County courthouse in Orlando, Florida. On that day, prosecutors told a packed courtroom that they would prove that Casey was responsible for the death of

paying for it

Cost-Efficient Courts

It might seem strange to spend money in order to save it. Yet, that's just what the Washington, D.C.-based Justice Policy Institute recommended in 2011 with publication of its report *System Overload*. The Institute pointed out that nearly four out of five people charged with a crime in the United States are eligible for assistance from court-appointed counsel; yet the funding allocated to public defender's offices has historically been so poor in many areas that they have been in a state of "chronic crisis" for decades. It's only by upping the quality of America's public defense system, the Institute says, that innocent people can be prevented from being convicted and going to prison—which would ultimately cost taxpayers far more than funding quality public defender programs.

Special-purpose courts, which divert nonviolent offenders from prison, can also serve taxpayers effectively. In Champaign County, Illinois, for example, felony drug offenders are routinely adjudicated in the area's special drug court. If found guilty, most offenders are placed on probation and ordered to undergo treatment at county expense, especially when judged not to be a danger to themselves or to the community. Some of the money spent on treatment can be recouped when offenders are also ordered to participate in mandatory community service programs and to pay restitution. Experts estimate that imprisonment in Illinois costs the state $21,500 per year for every offender kept behind bars. In contrast, probation, combined with drug treatment, costs approximately $4,000.

Drug courts, like many other special-purpose courts, effectively divert nonviolent defendants not only from prison, but from the more elaborate, and far more expensive, formal processing of trial courts.

Treatment courts, which serve mentally ill populations, are another recent innovation, designed to divert offenders with mental issues from prison and place them into treatment programs. In 2012, the state of Michigan ran eight mental health courts, serving nearly 700 people per year. Typical defendants seen by Michigan's treatment court have gotten into trouble with the law for relatively minor offenses, but because of their frequently lengthy arrest records, they might have ended up in jail or prison when handled by traditional criminal courts. Instead, Michigan's treatment courts work with community-based nonprofit organizations, such as the Detroit Central City Community Mental Health agency, and order psychotherapy, medication, and even residential treatment for the most serious cases. The cost savings are obvious: In Detroit, community treatment costs about $10,000 per year, versus around $35,000 for incarceration.

Moreover, special-purpose courts hold the promise of breaking the revolving door of imprisonment. Many drug-involved and mentally ill offenders are bound to a vicious cycle of crime commission and, without the treatment options offered by these special courts, would keep the revolving door of prison spinning.

Special-purpose courts are not the only way that money can be saved in the court system. In 2012, the National Center for State Courts (NCSC) performed an analysis on the use of e-filings versus paper documents in selected courthouses. The NCSC found that effective e-filing systems could cut the costs of document intake and storage to as little as 11 cents per page compared with 69 cents per page for costs of paper intake and storage. Moreover, said the Center, "courthouses are incredibly expensive storage spaces."[27] A small file room measuring 20 by 60 feet, said the Center, "would cost $360,000 to construct and at 5% per year, cost $18,000 per year to heat/cool and maintain." A typical computer hard drive, which could contain all of that digitized data in that room, might be purchased for as little as $300, although backup and associated computer costs would raise the costs somewhat. Learn more about using technology to achieve greater efficiency in courtroom operation from the NCSC at **http://www.ncsc.org.**

References: Champaign County Drug Court, "General Information," http://www.co.champaign.il.us/circt/DrugCourt/Info.htm (accessed August 1, 2012); Jeff Gerritt, "Salvaging Lives, Saving Money: Eight Pilot Courts That Divert Mentally Ill Offenders from Prison," *Detroit Free Press*, March 4, 2012, http://www.freep.com/article/20120304 (accessed August 1, 2012); and James E. McMillan, Carole D. Pettijohn, and Jennifer K. Berg, "Calculating an E-Court Return on Investment (ROI)," *Court Technology Bulletin*, February 16, 2012, http://courttech bulletin.blogspot.com/2012/02/calculating-e-court-return-on.html (accessed August 2, 2013).

her two-year-old daughter, Caylee Marie Anthony. Caylee had been reported missing on June 15, 2008, by her grandmother—a month after her mother said she had disappeared.[28] According to prosecutors and law enforcement officials, Casey told a string of lies about her daughter's disappearance, and in October 2008, with Caylee still missing, she was charged with first-degree murder. Prosecutors also charged Casey with aggravated child abuse, aggravated manslaughter, and providing false information to law enforcement officers. Two months after the charges were brought, a utility worker found Caylee's remains among cloth laundry and plastic trash bags near her home. Glittery pink letters that spelled out the phrase "Big Trouble Comes Small" were found with the remains and appear to have been on the shirt that Caylee was wearing at the time of her death.

After a trial that lasted 36 days, Casey was acquitted of all of the serious charges that had been brought against her. The jury did, however, find her guilty of the relatively minor crime of lying to a law enforcement officer. See a complete timeline of events in the Casey Anthony case from the Huffington Post at **http://tinyurl.com/3epa8sr**.

Professional Courtroom Participants

To the public eye, criminal trials frequently appear to be well-managed events even though they may entail quite a bit of drama. Like plays on a stage, trials involve many participants, each

■ **courtroom work group** The professional courtroom actors, including judges, prosecuting attorneys, defense attorneys, public defenders, and others who earn a living serving the court.
■ **judge** An elected or appointed public official who presides over a court of law and who is authorized to hear and sometimes to decide cases and to conduct trials.

Joe Burbank/AP Wide World Photos

Casey Anthony in a Florida courtroom in 2011. After a six-week trial, Anthony was found guilty on charges that she had lied to police, but was found not guilty of first-degree murder and other serious charges. Why did some people feel that the verdict was unfair?

of whom has a different role to fill. Unlike such plays, however, they are real-life events, and the impact that a trial's outcome has on people's lives can be far-reaching.

Participants in a criminal trial can be divided into two categories (Figure 9-4): professionals and outsiders. The professionals are the official courtroom actors; they are well versed in criminal trial practice and set the stage for and conduct the business of the court. Judges, prosecuting attorneys, defense attorneys, public defenders, and others who earn a living serving the court fall into this category. Professional courtroom actors are also called the **courtroom work group**. Some writers have pointed out that aside from statutory requirements and ethical considerations, courtroom interaction among professionals involves an implicit recognition of informal rules of civility, cooperation, and shared goals.[29] Hence even within the adversarial framework of a criminal trial, the courtroom work group is dedicated to bringing the procedure to a successful close.[30]

In contrast, outsiders—those trial participants who are only temporarily involved with the court—are generally unfamiliar with courtroom organization and trial procedure. Outsiders, or nonjudicial personnel, include jurors and witnesses as well as defendants and victims. Although in this chapter we refer to these people as nonprofessional courtroom actors, they may have a greater personal investment in the outcome of the trial than anyone else.

The Judge

The trial **judge** has the primary duty of ensuring justice. The American Bar Association's *Standards for Criminal Justice* describes the duties of the trial judge as follows: "The trial judge has the responsibility for safeguarding both the rights of the accused and the interests of the public in the administration of criminal justice. . . . The purpose of a criminal trial is to determine whether the prosecution has established the guilt of the accused as required by law, and the trial judge should not allow the proceedings to be used for any other purpose."[31]

The trial judge has the primary duty of ensuring justice.

In the courtroom, the judge holds ultimate authority, ruling on matters of law, weighing objections from both sides, deciding on the admissibility of evidence, and disciplining anyone who challenges the order of the court. In most jurisdictions, judges also sentence offenders after a verdict has been returned; in some states, judges serve to decide guilt or innocence for defendants who waive a jury trial.

Most state jurisdictions have a chief judge who, besides serving as a trial judge, must also manage the court system. Management includes hiring staff, scheduling sessions of court, ensuring the adequate training of subordinate judges, and coordinating activities with other courtroom actors. Chief judges usually assume their position by virtue of seniority and rarely have any formal training in management. Hence the managerial effectiveness of a chief judge is often a matter of personality and dedication more than anything else.

Judicial Selection

As mentioned earlier, judges at the federal level are nominated by the president of the United States and take their place on the bench only after confirmation by the Senate. At the state level, things work somewhat differently. Depending on the jurisdiction, state judgeships are won either through popular election or by political (usually gubernatorial) appointment. The process of judicial selection at the state level is set by law.

Both judicial election and appointment have been criticized for allowing politics to enter the judicial arena.

Both judicial election and appointment have been criticized for allowing politics to enter the judicial arena, although in somewhat different ways.

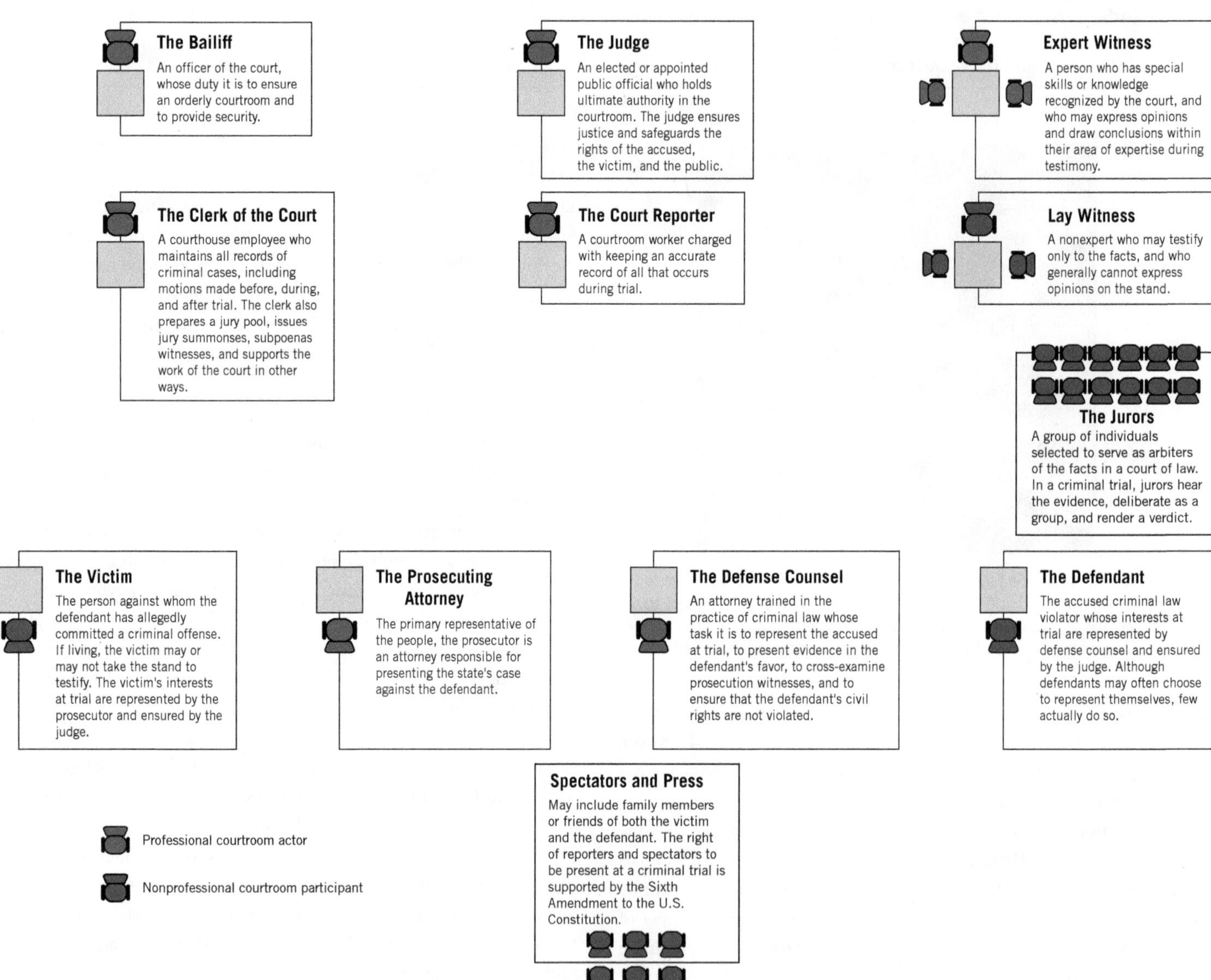

FIGURE 9-4 | Participants in a Criminal Trial

Source: Frank A. Schmalleger, *Criminal Justice: A Brief Introduction*, 9th Edition, © 2012. Reprinted by permission of Pearson Education, Inc., Upper Saddle River, NJ.

Under the election system, judicial candidates must receive the endorsement of their parties, generate contributions, and manage an effective campaign. Under the appointment system, judicial hopefuls must be in favor with incumbent politicians to receive appointments. Because partisan politics plays a role in both systems, critics have claimed that sitting judges can rarely be as neutral as they should be. They carry to the bench with them campaign promises, personal indebtedness, and possible political agendas.

To counter some of these problems, a number of states have adopted the Missouri Plan (or the Missouri Bar Plan) for judicial selection,[32] which combines elements of both election and appointment. It requires candidates for judicial vacancies to undergo screening by a nonpartisan state judicial nominating committee. Candidates selected by the committee are reviewed by an arm of the governor's office, which selects a final list of names for appointment. Incumbent judges must face the electorate after a specified term in office. They then run unopposed in nonpartisan elections in which only their records may be considered. Voters have the choice of allowing a judge to continue in office or asking that another be appointed to take his or her place. Because the Missouri Plan provides for periodic public review of judicial performance, it is also called the *merit plan of judicial selection*.

Judicial Qualifications

A few decades ago, many states did not require any special training, education, or other qualifications for judges. Anyone (even someone without a law degree) who won election or was appointed could assume a judgeship. Today, however, almost all states require that judges in general jurisdiction and appellate courts hold a law degree, be a licensed attorney, and be a member of their state bar association. Many states also require newly elected judges to attend state-sponsored training sessions on subjects like courtroom procedure, evidence, dispute resolution, judicial writing, administrative record keeping, and ethics.

While most states provide instruction to meet the needs of trial judges, some organizations also provide specialized training. The National Judicial College (NJC), located on the campus of the University of Nevada at Reno, is one such institution. It was established in 1963 by the Joint Committee for the Effective Administration of Justice, chaired by Justice Tom C. Clark of the U.S. Supreme Court.[33] More than 3,000 judges enroll annually in courses offered by NJC, and many courses are offered online. The NJC, in collaboration with the National Council of Juvenile and Family Court Judges and the University of Nevada at Reno, offers the nation's only advanced judicial degree programs, leading to a master's degree and PhD in judicial studies.[34] Visit the National Judicial College via **http://www.judges.org**.

In some parts of the United States, lower-court judges, such as justices of the peace, local magistrates, and "district" court judges, may still be elected without educational and other professional requirements. Today, in 43 states, some 1,300 nonlawyer judges are serving in mostly rural courts of limited jurisdiction.[35] In New York, for example, of the 3,511 judges in the state's unified court system, approximately 2,250 are part-time town or village justices, and about 80% of town and village justices are not lawyers.[36] The majority of cases that come before New York lay judges involve alleged traffic violations, although they may also include misdemeanors, small-claims actions, and civil cases of up to $3,000.

Even though some have defended lay judges as being closer to the citizenry in their understanding of justice,[37] in most jurisdictions, the number of lay judges is declining. States that continue to use lay judges in lower courts do require that candidates for judgeships not have criminal records, and most states require that they attend special training sessions if elected.

Judicial Misconduct

Most judges are highly professional in and out of the courtroom. Occasionally, however, a judge oversteps the limits of his or her authority; some unprofessional judicial behavior may even violate the law. In April 2011, for example, 67-year-old senior U.S. District Court Judge Jack Tarpley Camp was sentenced to 30 days in federal prison for committing a series of crimes with an exotic dancer.[38] The sentencing judge, U.S. District Judge Thomas Hogan, read the oath of office that Camp had taken 22 years earlier when he was sworn in, and said that Camp had disgraced his office. "He has denigrated the federal judiciary," said Hogan. "He has encouraged disrespect for the law." Camp's downfall came when he was arrested in 2010 for unlawful possession of controlled substances after paying an undercover law enforcement officer money for cocaine and a nonprescribed narcotic pain reliever. Authorities said that the judge intended to use the illegal drugs while partying with a stripper that he had befriended at the Goldrush Showbar in Atlanta, Georgia.[39] Evidence against Camp showed that he had had an ongoing affair with the woman, and had also given her his government-issued laptop computer—resulting in his conviction on a charge of unlawful conversion of government property.[40]

At the federal level, the Judicial Councils Reform and Judicial Conduct and Disability Act, passed by Congress in 1980, specifies the procedures necessary to register complaints against federal judges and, in serious cases, to begin the process of impeachment, or forced removal from the bench. Similarly, most states have their own commissions on judicial misconduct, while the Brenan Center for Justice at the New York University School of Law works to hold judges accountable for their conduct on the bench.

prosecutor An attorney whose official duty is to conduct criminal proceedings on behalf of the state or the people against those accused of having committed criminal offenses.

prosecutorial discretion The decision-making power of prosecutors, based on the wide range of choices available to them, in the handling of criminal defendants, the scheduling of cases for trial, the acceptance of negotiated pleas, and so on. The most important form of prosecutorial discretion lies in the power to charge, or not to charge, a person with an offense.

The Prosecuting Attorney

The **prosecutor**—called variously the *district attorney*, *state's attorney*, *county attorney*, *commonwealth attorney*, or *solicitor*—is responsible for presenting the state's case against the defendant. The prosecuting attorney is the primary representative of the people by virtue of the belief that violations of the criminal law are an affront to the public. Except for federal prosecutors (called *U.S. attorneys*) and solicitors in five states, prosecutors are elected and generally serve four-year terms with the possibility of continuing reelection.[41] Widespread criminal conspiracies, whether they involve government officials or private citizens, may require the services of a special prosecutor whose office can spend the time and resources needed for efficient prosecution.[42]

The prosecutor is responsible for presenting the state's case against the defendant.

In many jurisdictions, because the job of prosecutor entails too many duties for one person to handle, prosecutors supervise a staff of assistant district attorneys who do most in-court work. Assistants are trained attorneys, usually hired directly by the chief prosecutor and licensed to practice law in the state in which they work. Approximately 2,300 chief prosecutors, assisted by 24,000 deputy attorneys, serve the nation's counties and independent cities.[43]

Another prosecutorial role has traditionally been that of quasi-legal adviser to local police departments. Because prosecutors are sensitive to the kinds of information needed for conviction, they may help guide police investigations and will exhort detectives to identify credible witnesses, uncover additional evidence, and the like. This role is limited, however. Police departments are independent of the administrative authority of the prosecutor, and cooperation between them, although based on the common goal of conviction, is purely voluntary. Moreover, close cooperation between prosecutors and police may not always be legal. A 1998 federal law known as the McDade-Murtha Law,[44] for example, requires that federal prosecutors abide by all state bar ethics rules. In late 2000, in a reflection of the federal sentiment, the Oregon Supreme Court temporarily ended police–prosecutor collaboration in that state in instances involving potential deception by law enforcement officers.[45] The court, ruling in the Oregon State Bar disciplinary case of *In re Gatti*,[46] held that all lawyers within the state, including government prosecutors overseeing organized crime, child pornography, and narcotics cases, must abide by the Oregon State Bar's strictures against dishonesty, fraud, deceit, and misrepresentation.[47] Under the court's ruling, a prosecutor in Oregon who encourages an undercover officer or an informant to misrepresent himself or herself could be disbarred and prohibited from practicing law. As a result of the highly controversial ruling, the FBI and the Drug Enforcement Administration ended all big undercover operations in Oregon, and local police departments cancelled many ongoing investigations. In 2002, the Oregon Supreme Court accepted an amendment to the state bar association's disciplinary rules to allow a lawyer to advise and to supervise otherwise lawful undercover investigations of violations of civil law, criminal law, or constitutional rights as long as the lawyer "in good faith believes there is a reasonable possibility that unlawful activity has taken place, is taking place or will take place in the foreseeable future."[48]

Once a trial begins, the job of the prosecutor is to vigorously present the state's case against the defendant. Prosecutors introduce evidence against the accused, steer the testimony of witnesses "for the people," and argue in favor of conviction. Because defendants are presumed innocent until proven guilty, the burden of demonstrating guilt beyond a reasonable doubt rests with the prosecutor.

Prosecutorial Discretion

American prosecutors occupy a unique position in the nation's criminal justice system by virtue of the considerable **prosecutorial discretion** they exercise. As U.S. Supreme Court Justice Robert H. Jackson noted in 1940, "The prosecutor has more control over life, liberty, and reputation than any other person in America."[49] Before a case comes to trial, the prosecutor may decide to accept a plea bargain, divert the suspect to a public or private social service agency, ask the suspect to seek counseling, or dismiss the case entirely for lack of evidence or for a variety of other reasons. Studies have found that the prosecution dismisses from one-third to one-half of all felony cases before trial or before a plea bargain is made.[50] Prosecutors also play a significant role before grand juries. States that use the grand jury system depend on prosecutors to bring evidence before the grand jury and to be effective in seeing indictments returned against suspects.

In preparation for trial, the prosecutor decides what charges are to be brought against the defendant, examines the strength of the incriminating evidence, and decides which witnesses to call. Two important U.S. Supreme Court decisions have held that it is the duty of prosecutors to make available any evidence in their possession to, in effect, help the defense build its case. In the first case, *Brady* v. *Maryland* (1963),[51] the Court held that the prosecution is required to disclose to the defense evidence that

■ **exculpatory evidence** Any information having a tendency to clear a person of guilt or blame.

CJ | CAREERS
Assistant District Attorney

Heidi Jaegers

Name. Robert S. Jaegers

Position. Assistant State Attorney, Palm Beach County, Florida

Colleges attended. Ohio Northern University Pettit College of Law, Ada, Ohio; Pennsylvania State University

Majors. English and law

Year hired. Joined the State Attorney's Office in Palm Beach County, Florida, in 1988

Please give a brief description of your job. Currently Felony Division Trial Prosecutor with over 200 cases pending trial. Caseload includes aggravated batteries, drug trafficking, burglaries, robberies, and economic crimes.

What appealed to you most about the position when you applied for it? Immediately following law school, I was commissioned as Captain, Judge Advocate General's Department, U.S. Air Force, in 1977. In 1982, I left active duty and moved to Florida to become an associate at a law firm that had a general law practice, including criminal defense and appeals. After working for three years as a criminal appellate attorney for the Florida Attorney General's Office (1984–1988), I again wanted to argue cases before juries.

How would you describe the interview process? The current state attorney interview process involves an interview with three experienced prosecutors, then an interview with two of the three chief assistants, then an interview with the elected state attorney. The process has varied over the years, depending upon the wishes of the elected state attorney, from a single interview with the state attorney to the current process but without an interview with the state attorney. Law school internship experience is a plus, as is any prior experience as an attorney or legal support person.

What is a typical day like? A "typical" day begins at 8:30 a.m. with a morning-long session of short hearings (around 120 cases with sometimes as many different defendants), with four regularly assigned division prosecutors and as many as six specialty division prosecutors, and four public defender attorneys regularly assigned to the division, plus varying numbers of privately retained attorneys. All discuss arraignments, plea offers, demands for discovery from both sides, scheduling of trials, scheduling of motion hearings, scheduling of plea conferences, conducting plea conferences, demands by defendants to represent themselves, restitution hearings, requests to enter appearances by private attorneys, requests to withdraw from representation by private attorneys, requests to continue, demands for speedy trial, and so on. In short, we conduct all the proceedings necessary to move cases to conclusion, either by plea or by trial. If this is all concluded by 10 or 11 a.m., the judge may call for a jury pool and commence a trial. Following a lunch break, there are trials, or motions to suppress or dismiss with evidentiary hearings, or more lengthy hearings specially set by the parties and the judge.

What qualities/characteristics are most helpful for this job? The ability to be flexible in preparation, articulate in English, able to read opposing motions, and conduct research on legal opinions is paramount. Next is an ability to speak to groups of people from all backgrounds and abilities, and select a group of fair and impartial jurors to be your factfinders. You must be able to communicate your arguments, and help your witnesses convey the evidence they have to present to the factfinders in a readily understandable manner. Preparation is key. You must be able to work with and cooperate with your support staff of secretaries, investigators, information managers, judges' secretaries, clerks, and opposing counsel's secretaries, and do this even with opposing counsel. You must also be willing to devote the time to prepare for each trial and each hearing, even while knowing that the opposing side may decide at the last moment to concede and enter a plea. If you aren't prepared, the defense will sense that, and use it against you.

What is a typical starting salary? Starting salary as of 2012 is $40,000 per year. This is accompanied by medical benefits, retirement benefits, travel reimbursements, and continuing legal education opportunities.

What is the salary potential as you move up into higher-level jobs? The statutory maximum salary of the state attorney is $150,000 per year. Assistants are not usually compensated above this level.

What career advice would you give someone in college beginning studies in criminal justice? If you are contemplating a career as a prosecuting attorney, take every opportunity to study creative writing, English literature, psychology, public speaking and debate, and dramatics, and make sure to keep yourself physically fit. You may find yourself in many stressful situations, some physical and some mental, and a sound mind in a sound body gives you an advantage.

Source: Reprinted with permission of Robert S. Jaegers. Photo courtesy of Robert S. Jaegers. Logo courtesy of the Palm Beach County, Florida, State Attorney's Office.

directly relates to claims of either guilt or innocence. The second and more recent case is that of *U.S.* v. *Bagley*,[52] decided in 1985. In *Bagley*, the Court ruled that the prosecution must disclose any evidence that the defense requests. The Court reasoned that to withhold evidence, even when it does not relate directly to issues of guilt or innocence, may mislead the defense into thinking that such evidence does not exist.

In 2004, in a decision predicated upon *Brady*, the U.S. Supreme Court intervened to stop the execution of 45-year-old Texan Delma Banks ten minutes before it was scheduled to begin.

In finding that prosecutors had withheld vital **exculpatory evidence**, or information that might have cleared Banks of blame, during his trial for the 1980 shooting death of a 16-year-old boy, the Court said that "a rule declaring 'prosecutor may hide, defendant must seek,' is not tenable in a system constitutionally bound to accord defendants due process."[53] Banks had spent 24 years on death row.

One special decision that the prosecutor makes concerns the filing of separate or multiple charges. The decision to try a defendant simultaneously on multiple charges allows for the presentation of a considerable amount of evidence and permits an in-court demonstration of a complete sequence of criminal events. This strategy has additional practical advantages: It saves time and money by substituting one trial for what might otherwise be a number of trials if each charge were to be brought separately before the court. From the prosecutor's point of view, however, trying the charges one at a time carries the advantage of allowing for another trial on a new charge if a "not guilty" verdict is returned.

The activities of the prosecutor do not end with a finding of guilt or innocence. Following conviction, prosecutors are usually allowed to make sentencing recommendations to the judge. For example, they can argue that aggravating factors (discussed in Chapter 11), prior criminal record, or the especially heinous nature of the offense calls for strict punishment. When a convicted defendant appeals, prosecutors may need to defend their own actions and, in briefs filed with appellate courts, to argue that the conviction was properly obtained. Most jurisdictions also allow prosecutors to make recommendations when defendants they have convicted are being considered for parole or for early release from prison.

Until relatively recently, prosecutors generally enjoyed much of the same kind of immunity against liability in the exercise of their official duties that judges do. The 1976 Supreme Court case *Imbler* v. *Pachtman*[54] provided the basis for immunity with its ruling that "state prosecutors are absolutely immune from liability . . . for their conduct in initiating a prosecution and in presenting the State's case." However, in the 1991 case of *Burns* v. *Reed*,[55] the Court held that "[a] state prosecuting attorney is absolutely immune from liability for damages . . . for participating in a probable cause hearing, but not for giving legal advice to the police." The *Burns* case involved Cathy Burns of Muncie, Indiana, who shot her sleeping sons while laboring under a multiple personality disorder. To explore the possibility of multiple personality further, the police asked the prosecuting attorney if it would be appropriate for them to hypnotize the defendant. The prosecutor agreed that hypnosis would be a permissible avenue for investigation, and the suspect confessed to the murders while hypnotized. She later alleged in her complaint to the Supreme Court "that [the prosecuting attorney] knew or should have known that hypnotically induced testimony was inadmissible" at trial.[56]

Until relatively recently, prosecutors generally enjoyed much of the same kind of immunity against liability in the exercise of their official duties that judges do.

Finally, in 2009, in the case of *Van de Kamp* v. *Goldstein*,[57] the U.S. Supreme Court reaffirmed its holding in *Imbler* and found that a prosecutor's absolute immunity from Section 1983 claims (discussed in the last chapter) extends to (1) a failure to properly train prosecutors, (2) a failure to properly supervise prosecutors, and (3) a failure to establish an information system containing potential impeachment material about informants. In the words of the justices, a prosecutor is absolutely immune from liability in civil suits when his or her actions are "intimately associated with the judicial phase of the criminal process" and the prosecutor is serving as "an officer of the court."

The Abuse of Discretion

Because prosecutors have so much discretion in their decision making, there is considerable potential for abuse. Many types of discretionary decisions are always inappropriate. Examples include accepting guilty pleas to drastically reduced charges for personal considerations, deciding not to prosecute friends or political cronies, and being overzealous in prosecuting to support political ambitions.

Administrative decisions such as case scheduling, which can wreak havoc with the personal lives of defendants and the professional lives of defense attorneys, can also be used by prosecutors to harass defendants into pleading guilty. Some forms of abuse may be unconscious. At least one study suggests that some prosecutors tend toward leniency where female defendants are concerned and tend to discriminate against minorities when deciding whether to prosecute.[58]

Although the electorate is the final authority to which prosecutors must answer, gross misconduct by prosecutors may be addressed by the state supreme court or by the state attorney general's office. Short of addressing *criminal* misconduct, however, the options available to the court and to the attorney general are limited.

In 2011, in an effort to deter prosecutorial misconduct at the federal level, the U.S. Department of Justice created a new internal watchdog office to oversee the actions of federal prosecutors. Called the Professional Misconduct Review Unit, the office is responsible for disciplining federal prosecutors who engage in intentional or reckless misconduct.[59]

The Prosecutor's Professional Responsibility

As members of the legal profession, prosecutors are expected to abide by various standards of professional responsibility, such as those found in the Model Rules of Professional Conduct of the American Bar Association (ABA). Most state bar associations have adopted their own versions of the ABA rules and expect their members to respect those standards. Consequently,

■ **defense counsel** A licensed trial lawyer hired or appointed to conduct the legal defense of a person accused of a crime and to represent him or her before a court of law.

serious violations of the rules may result in a prosecutor's being disbarred from the practice of law. Official ABA commentary on Rule 3.8, *Special Responsibilities of the Prosecutor*, says that "a prosecutor has the responsibility of a minister of justice and not simply that of an advocate; the prosecutor's duty is to seek justice, not merely to convict. This responsibility carries with it specific obligations to see that the defendant is accorded procedural justice and that guilt is decided upon the basis of sufficient evidence."[60] Hence prosecutors are barred by the standards of the legal profession from advocating any fact or position that they know is untrue. Prosecutors have a voice in influencing public policy affecting the safety of America's communities through the National District Attorneys Association (NDAA). Visit the NDAA via **http://www.ndaa.org**.

The Defense Counsel

The **defense counsel** is a trained lawyer who may specialize in the practice of criminal law. The task of the defense counsel is to represent the accused as soon as possible after arrest and to ensure that the defendant's civil rights are not violated during processing by the criminal justice system. Other duties of the defense counsel include testing the strength of the prosecution's case, taking part in plea negotiations, and preparing an adequate defense to be used at trial. In the preparation of a defense, criminal lawyers may enlist private detectives, experts, witnesses to the crime, and character witnesses. Some lawyers perform aspects of the role of private detective or investigator themselves. Defense attorneys also review relevant court precedents to identify the best defense strategy.

Defense preparation often entails conversations between lawyer and defendant. Such discussions are recognized as privileged communications protected under the umbrella of attorney–client confidentiality. In other words, lawyers cannot be compelled to reveal information that their clients have confided to them.[61]

Lawyers cannot be compelled to reveal information that their clients have confided to them.

If the defendant is found guilty, the defense attorney will be involved in arguments at sentencing, may be asked to file an appeal, and may counsel the defendant and the defendant's family about any civil matters (payment of debts, release from contractual obligations, and so on) that must be arranged after sentence is imposed. Hence the work of the defense attorney encompasses many roles, including attorney, negotiator, investigator, confidant, family and personal counselor, social worker, and, as we shall see, bill collector.

The Criminal Lawyer

Three major categories of defense attorneys assist criminal defendants in the United States: (1) private attorneys, usually referred to as *retained counsel*; (2) *court-appointed counsel*; and (3) *public defenders*.

Private attorneys either have their own legal practices or work for law firms in which they are partners or employees. Private attorneys' fees can be high; most privately retained criminal lawyers charge from $100 to $250 per hour. Included in their bill is the time it takes to prepare for a case, as well as time spent in the courtroom. High-powered criminal defense attorneys who have a reputation for successfully defending their clients can be far more expensive. Fees charged by famous criminal defense attorneys can run into the hundreds of thousands of dollars—and sometimes exceed $1 million—for handling just one case!

Few law students choose to specialize in criminal law, even though the job of a criminal lawyer may appear glamorous. One reason may be that the collection of fees can be a significant source of difficulty for many defense attorneys. Most defendants are poor. Those who aren't are often reluctant to pay what they believe is an exorbitant fee, and woe be it to the defense attorney whose client is convicted before the fee has been paid! Visit the National Association of Criminal Defense Lawyers (NACDL) via **http://www.nacdl.org** and the Association of Federal Defense Attorneys (AFDA) web site to learn more about the practice of criminal law.

Court-Appointed Counsel

The Sixth Amendment to the U.S. Constitution guarantees criminal defendants the effective assistance of counsel. A series of U.S. Supreme Court decisions has established that defendants who are unable to pay for private criminal defense attorneys will receive adequate representation at all stages of criminal justice processing. In *Powell* v. *Alabama* (1932),[62] the Court held that the Fourteenth Amendment requires state courts to appoint counsel for defendants in capital cases who are unable to afford their own. In 1938, in *Johnson* v. *Zerbst*,[63] the Court overturned the conviction of an indigent federal inmate, holding that his Sixth Amendment due process right to counsel had been violated. The Court declared, "If the accused . . . is not represented by counsel and has not competently and intelligently waived his constitutional right, the Sixth Amendment stands as a jurisdictional bar to a valid conviction

The Sixth Amendment to the U.S. Constitution guarantees criminal defendants the effective assistance of counsel.

■ **public defender** An attorney employed by a government agency or subagency, or by a private organization under contract to a government body, for the purpose of providing defense services to indigents, or an attorney who has volunteered such service.

and sentence depriving him of his life or his liberty." The decision established the right of indigent defendants to receive the assistance of appointed counsel in all criminal proceedings in federal courts. The 1963 case of *Gideon* v. *Wainwright*[64] extended the right to appointed counsel to all indigent defendants charged with a felony in state courts. In *Argersinger* v. *Hamlin* (1972),[65] the Court required adequate legal representation for anyone facing a potential sentence of imprisonment. Juveniles charged with delinquent acts were granted the right to appointed counsel in the case of *In re Gault* (1967).[66]

In 2002, a closely divided U.S. Supreme Court expanded the Sixth Amendment right to counsel, ruling that defendants in state courts who are facing relatively minor charges must be provided with an attorney at government expense even when they face only the slightest chance of incarceration. The case, *Alabama* v. *Shelton*,[67] involved defendant LeReed Shelton, who was convicted of third-degree assault after taking part in a fistfight with another motorist following a minor traffic accident. Shelton had been advised of his right to have an attorney represent him at trial, and the judge who heard his case repeatedly suggested that he should hire an attorney and warned him of the dangers of serving as his own attorney, but at no time did the judge offer Shelton assistance of counsel. Unable to afford an attorney, Shelton proceeded to represent himself and was convicted and sentenced to 30 days in the county jail. The sentence was suspended, and he was placed on two years of unsupervised probation, fined $500, and ordered to make restitution and to pay the costs of court. Shelton soon appealed on Sixth Amendment grounds, however, and the Alabama Supreme Court ruled in his favor, reasoning that a suspended sentence constitutes a "term of imprisonment" no matter how unlikely it is that the term will ever be served. On appeal by the state of Alabama, the case made its way to the U.S. Supreme Court, which agreed that "[a] suspended sentence is a prison term" and requires appointed counsel when an indigent defendant desires legal representation.

States have responded to the federal mandate for indigent defense in a number of ways. Most now use one of three systems to deliver legal services to criminal defendants who are unable to afford their own: (1) court-appointed counsel, (2) public defenders, and (3) contractual arrangements. Most systems are administered at the county level, although funding arrangements may involve state, county, and municipal monies—as well as federal grants and court fees.

Assigned Counsel Assigned counsel, also known as *court-appointed defense attorneys*, are usually drawn from a roster of all practicing criminal attorneys within the jurisdiction of the trial court. Their fees are paid at a rate set by the state or local government. These fees are typically low, however, and may affect the amount of effort an assigned attorney puts into a case. In 2001, for example, New York's court-appointed attorneys were paid only $25 per hour for out-of-court preparation time and $40 an hour for time spent in the courtroom—a rate of pay that is 10 to 20 times less than what they normally earn for a private case.[68] So, although most attorneys assigned by the court to indigent defense take their jobs seriously, some feel only a loose commitment to their clients. Paying clients, in their eyes, deserve better representation.

Public Defenders A **public defender** is a state-employed lawyer defending indigent defendants. A public defender program relies on full-time salaried staff. Staff members include defense attorneys, defense investigators, and office personnel. Defense investigators gather information in support of the defense effort. They may interview friends, family members, and employers of the accused, with an eye toward effective defense. Public defender programs have become popular in recent years, and a 2010 report by the Bureau of Justice Statistics (BJS) found that 49 states and the District of Columbia use public defenders to provide legal representation for some or all indigent defendants.[69] The BJS noted that in 27 states and the District of Columbia, counties or local jurisdictions funded and administered public defender offices. In the remaining 22 states, one office oversaw indigent defense operations throughout the state. County-based public defender offices employed 71% of the nation's 15,026 public defenders in 2007. The 10,705 attorneys in county-based offices served a total population of approximately 167 million residents. County-based public defender offices received 4,081,030 cases in 2007, with a median of about 2,500 cases per office. These attorneys handled more than 4 million cases in 2007, which was 73% of the total number of public defender cases nationwide.

An earlier report by the BJS found that a public defender system is the primary method used to provide indigent counsel for criminal defendants and that 28% of state jurisdictions nationwide use public defender programs exclusively to provide indigent defense.[70] Critics charge that public defenders, because they are government employees, are not sufficiently independent from prosecutors and judges. For the same reason, clients may be suspicious of public defenders, viewing them as state functionaries. Finally, because of the huge

Critics charge that public defenders, because they are government employees, are not sufficiently independent from prosecutors and judges.

caseloads typical of public defender's offices, there is pressure to use plea bargaining excessively. Learn more about system overload in public defenders offices via **http://tinyurl.com/4yywlrt**.

Contractual Arrangements Through a third type of indigent defense, contract attorney programs, county and state officials arrange with local criminal lawyers to provide for indigent defense on a contractual basis. Individual attorneys, local bar associations, and multipartner law firms may all be tapped to provide services. Contract defense programs are the least widely used form of indigent defense at present, although their popularity is growing.

Critics of the current system of indigent defense point out that the system is woefully underfunded. As a consequence of limited funding, many public defender's offices employ what critics call a "plead 'em and speed 'em through" strategy, which can often mean that attorneys meet their clients for the first time in courtrooms as trials are about to begin and use plea bargaining to move cases along. Mary Broderick of the National Legal Aid and Defender Association says, "We aren't being given the same weapons. . . . It's like trying to deal with smart bombs when all you've got is a couple of cap pistols."[71]

Proposed enhancements to indigent defense systems are offered by the National Legal Aid and Defender Association (NLADA). You can visit the NLADA via **http://www.nlada.org**. A 200-page report by the National Symposium on Indigent Defense, showing what individual states spend on indigent defense, is available at **http://www.justicestudies.com/pubs/cjindig.pdf**. Total moneys spent on indigent defense in this country between 1986 and 2008 are shown in Figure 9-5.

Although state indigent defense services are sometimes significantly underfunded, the same is not true of the federal system. The defense of indigent Oklahoma City bomber Timothy McVeigh, for example, cost taxpayers an estimated \$13.8 million—which doesn't include the cost of his appeal or execution. McVeigh's expenses included \$6.7 million for attorneys, \$2 million for investigators, \$3 million for expert witnesses, and approximately \$1.4 million for office rent and secretarial assistance.[72]

Of course, defendants need not be represented by any counsel at all. Defendants may waive their right to an attorney and undertake their own defense—a right held by the U.S. Supreme Court to be inherent in the Sixth Amendment in the 1975 case of *Faretta* v. *California*.[73] Self-representation is uncommon, however, and only 1% of federal inmates and 3% of state inmates report having represented themselves.[74] Some famous instances of self-representation include the 1995 trial of Long Island Rail Road commuter train shooter Colin Ferguson, the 1999 assisted suicide trial of Dr. Jack Kevorkian, and the 2002 federal competency hearings of Zacarias Moussaoui.

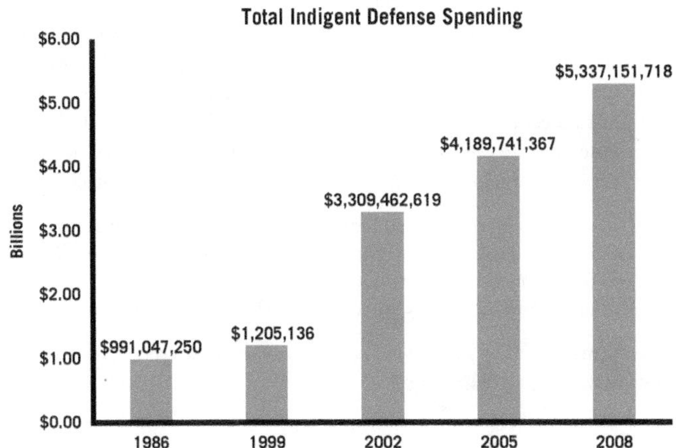

FIGURE 9-5 | Indigent Defense Spending in the United States, 1986–2008

References: Lynn Langton and Donald J. Farole, Jr., *Public Defender Offices, 2007—Statistical Tables* (Washington, DC: Bureau of Justice Statistics, 2009); Carol J. DeFrances and Marika F.X. Litras, *Indigent Defense Services in Large Counties, 1999*; and The Spangenberg Project at the Center for Justice, Law and Society at George Mason University, *State, County and Local Expenditures for Indigent Defense Services, Fiscal Year 2008* (Chicago, IL: American Bar Association, 2010), p. 72.

Defendants who are not pleased with the lawyer appointed to defend them are in a somewhat different situation. They may request, through the court, that a new lawyer be assigned to represent them, as Timothy McVeigh did following his conviction and death sentence in the Oklahoma City bombing case. However, unless there is clear reason for reassignment, such as an obvious personality conflict between defendant and attorney, few judges are likely to honor a request of this sort. Short of obvious difficulties, most judges will trust in the professionalism of appointed counsel.

State-supported indigent defense systems may also be called on to provide representation for clients upon appeal. An attorney who is appointed to represent an indigent defendant on appeal, however, may conclude that an appeal would be frivolous. If so, he or she may request that the appellate court allow him or her to withdraw from the case or that the court dispose of the case without requiring the attorney to file a brief arguing the merits of the appeal. In 1967, in the case of *Anders* v. *California*,[75] the U.S. Supreme Court found that to protect a defendant's constitutional right to appellate counsel, appellate courts must safeguard against the risk of accepting an attorney's negative assessment of a case where an appeal is not actually frivolous. The Court also found California's existing procedure for evaluating such requests to be inadequate, and the justices set forth an acceptable

CJ | ISSUES

Gideon v. *Wainwright* and Indigent Defense

Today, about three-fourths of state-level criminal defendants and one-half of federal defendants are represented in court by publicly funded counsel.[1] As recently as 40 years ago, however, the practice of publicly funded indigent defense was uncommon. That changed in 1963 when, in the case of *Gideon* v. *Wainwright*,[2] the U.S. Supreme Court extended the right to legal counsel to indigent defendants charged with a criminal offense. The reasoning of the Court is well summarized in this excerpt from the majority opinion written by Justice Hugo Black:

> Governments, both state and federal, quite properly spend vast sums of money to establish machinery to try defendants accused of crime. Lawyers to prosecute are everywhere deemed essential to protect the public's interest in an orderly society. Similarly, there are few defendants charged with crime, few indeed, who fail to hire the best lawyers they can get to prepare and present their defenses. That government hires lawyers to prosecute and defendants who have the money hire lawyers to defend are the strongest indications of the widespread belief that lawyers in criminal courts are necessities, not luxuries. The right of one charged with crime to counsel may not be deemed fundamental and essential to fair trials in some countries, but it is in ours. From the very beginning, our state and national constitutions and laws have laid great emphasis on procedural and substantive safeguards designed to assure fair trials before impartial tribunals in which every defendant stands equal before the law. This noble ideal cannot be realized if the poor man charged with crime has to face his accusers without a lawyer to assist him.

[1]Steven K. Smith and Carol J. DeFrances, *Indigent Defense* (Washington, DC: Bureau of Justice Statistics, 1996).
[2]*Gideon* v. *Wainwright*, 372 U.S. 335 (1963).

---

procedure. In 1979, in the case of *People* v. *Wende*,[76] the state of California adopted a new standardized procedure that, although not the same as the one put forth in *Anders*, was designed to protect the right of a criminal defendant to appeal.

The *Wende* standard was put to the test in the 2000 case of *Smith* v. *Robbins*.[77] The case began when convicted California murderer Lee Robbins told his court-appointed counsel that he wanted to file an appeal. His attorney concluded that the appeal would be frivolous and filed a brief with the state court of appeals to that effect. The court agreed with the attorney's assessment, and the appeal was not heard. The California Supreme Court denied further review of the case. After exhausting his state postconviction remedies, Robbins appealed to the federal courts, arguing that he had been denied effective assistance of appellate counsel because his counsel's brief did not comply with one of the requirements in *Anders*—specifically, the requirement that the brief must mention "anything in the record that might arguably support the appeal." A federal district court agreed, concluding that there were at least two issues that might have supported Robbins's appeal. The court found that the failure to include them in the brief deviated from the *Anders* procedure and thus amounted to deficient performance by counsel. The Ninth Circuit Court agreed, concluding that *Anders* established a mandatory procedure as a standard against which the performance of appointed counsel could be assessed. When the case finally reached the U.S. Supreme Court, the justices held that the *Anders* procedure is only one method of satisfying the Constitution's requirements for indigent criminal appeals and that the states are free to adopt different procedures as long as those procedures adequately safeguard a defendant's right to appellate counsel.

Finally, in 2001, in the case of *Texas* v. *Cobb*,[78] the Supreme Court ruled that the Sixth Amendment right to counsel is "offense specific" and applies only to the offense with which a defendant is charged—and not to other offenses, even if they are factually related to the charged offense.

The Ethics of Defense

The job of defense counsel, as we have already mentioned, is to prepare and offer a vigorous defense on behalf of the accused at trial and to appeal cases that have merit. A proper defense at trial often involves the presentation of evidence and the examination of witnesses, both of which require careful thought and planning. Good attorneys may become emotionally committed to the outcomes of trials in which they are involved. Some lawyers, however, cross the line when they lose their professional objectivity and embrace the wider cause of their clients. That's what happened to Lynne Stewart, 65, who was convicted in 2005 of smuggling messages from her jailed client, the radical Egyptian sheik Omar Abdel-Rahman (also known as the "blind sheik"), to his terrorist followers outside of prison.[79] Abdel-Rahman is serving life behind bars for his role in an unsuccessful 1993 plot to bomb New York City landmarks. Stewart, a 1960s-era radical, has often chosen to represent the most contemptible clients, believing that justice requires that everyone receive a vigorous defense. She was arrested after she issued a public statement on behalf of the sheik expressing her client's withdrawal of support for a cease-fire involving his supporters in Egypt. Stewart had known in advance that making the statement violated an order to restrict the sheik's communications, but she later testified that she believed that violence is sometimes necessary to achieve justice. Other evidence showed that she had facilitated forbidden communications between Abdel-Rahman and a translator by using prearranged cues such as tapping on a table, shaking a water bottle, and uttering key terms like "chocolate" and "heart attack" during prison visits. In 2006, she was sentenced to serve 28 months in prison;

Stephen Chernin/AP Wide World Photos

Defense attorney Lynne Stewart, who was sentenced to prison in 2006 for smuggling messages from her jailed client, the radical Egyptian sheik Omar Abdel-Rahman (aka the "blind sheik"), to his terrorist followers outside of prison. Our adversarial system requires that attorneys sometimes defend unpopular clients, but the defense role is carefully prescribed by ethical and procedural standards. How did Stewart's actions violate those standards?

but in 2010 a federal court ordered that she be resentenced due to new revelations about perjury and increased her sentence to ten years and a month.[80] Her appeal to the federal Court of Appeals for the Second Circuit was turned down in 2012.[81]

The nature of the adversarial process, fed by the emotions of the participants combined with the often privileged and extensive knowledge that defense attorneys have about their cases, is enough to tempt the professional ethics of some counselors. Because the defense counsel may often know more about the guilt or innocence of the defendant than anyone else prior to trial, the defense role is carefully prescribed by ethical and procedural considerations. Attorneys violate both law and the standards of their profession if they knowingly misrepresent themselves or their clients. As Michael Ratner, president of the Center for Constitutional Rights, put it when commenting on the *Stewart* case, "lawyers need to be advocates, but they don't need to be accomplices."[82]

To help attorneys understand what is expected of them, and what the appropriate limits of a vigorous defense might be, the American Bar Association provides significant guidance in the areas of legal ethics and professional responsibility. (See the "Ethics and Professionalism" box in this chapter.) Even so, some attorney–client interactions remain especially tricky. Defense attorneys, for example, are under no obligation to reveal information obtained from a client without the client's permission. However, all states permit defense lawyers to violate a client's confidentiality without fear of reprisal if they reasonably believe that doing so could prevent serious injury or death to another person. In 2004, with passage of a new evidence law broadening the state's evidence code, California joined the other 49 states in freeing attorneys to violate client confidentiality in such cases. California law makes disclosure discretionary, not mandatory. Kevin Mohr, a professor at Western State University College of Law in Fullerton, California, noted that the new law provides the first exception to the attorney–client privilege in California in more than 130 years. "A lawyer can now take action and intervene and prevent [a] criminal act from occurring," said Mohr.[83]

The California changes had been presaged by an action of the American Bar Association, which eased its secrecy rules surrounding attorney–client relationships in 2001.[84] Prior to that time, ABA rules permitted criminal defense attorneys to disclose incriminating information about a client only to prevent imminent death or substantial bodily harm. The 2001 rule change dispensed with the word *imminent*, allowing attorneys to reveal clients' secrets in order to stop future deaths or to prevent substantial bodily harm.

Somewhat earlier, the 1986 U.S. Supreme Court case of *Nix* v. *Whiteside*[85] clarified the duty of lawyers to reveal known instances of client perjury. The *Nix* case came to the Court upon the complaint of the defendant, Whiteside, who claimed that he was deprived of the assistance of effective counsel during his murder trial because his lawyer would not allow him to testify untruthfully. Whiteside wanted to testify that he had seen a gun or something metallic in his victim's hand before killing him. Before trial, however, Whiteside admitted to his lawyer that he had actually seen no weapon, but he believed that to testify to the truth would result in his conviction. The lawyer told Whiteside that, as a professional counselor, he would be forced to challenge Whiteside's false testimony if it occurred and to explain to the court the facts as he knew them. On the stand, Whiteside said only that he thought the victim was reaching for a gun but did not claim to have seen one. He was found guilty of second-degree murder and appealed to the Supreme Court on the claim of inadequate representation. The Court, recounting the development of ethical codes in the legal profession, held that a lawyer's duty to a client "is limited to legitimate, lawful conduct compatible with the very nature of a trial as a search for truth. . . . Counsel is precluded from taking steps or in any way assisting the client in presenting false evidence or otherwise violating the law."[86]

■ **bailiff** The court officer whose duties are to keep order in the courtroom and to maintain physical custody of the jury.

ethics and professionalism

American Bar Association's Model Rules of Professional Conduct

To help attorneys understand what is expected of them, the American Bar Association (ABA) has provided significant guidance in the areas of legal ethics and professional responsibility. Specifically, the ABA has developed professional standards intended to serve as models for state bar associations and to guide legislative bodies focused on ensuring ethical behavior among attorneys.

The ABA's first major foray into the area of ethical guidelines resulted in the adoption of its original Canons of Professional Ethics on August 27, 1908. In 1913, in an effort to keep the association informed about state and local bar activities concerning professional ethics, the ABA established its Standing Committee on Professional Ethics. The name of the group was changed to the Committee on Ethics and Professional Responsibility in 1971, and the committee continues to function under that name today.

In 1969, the committee's Model Code of Professional Responsibility was formally adopted by the ABA. Eventually, the majority of state and federal jurisdictions adopted their own versions of the Model Code.

In 1977, the ABA Commission on Evaluation of Professional Standards was created and charged with rethinking the ethical problems of the legal profession. Over the next six years, the Commission drafted the Model Rules of Professional Conduct, which the ABA adopted on August 2, 1983. The Model Rules effectively supplanted the Model Code of Professional Responsibility, and today most state and federal jurisdictions have adapted the Model Rules to their own particular circumstances.

The Model Rules have been periodically amended—most significantly in 2002—but continue to provide the touchstone ethical standards of the American legal profession today. Visit the American Bar Association on the Internet at **http://www.americanbar.org**, and learn about its Center for Professional Responsibility at **http://www.americanbar.org/groups/professional_responsibility.html**.

Thinking About Ethics

1. Should a defense attorney represent a client whom he or she knows to be guilty? Explain.
2. Would it be unethical for an attorney to refuse to represent such a client? Why or why not?

Reference: American Bar Association, *Model Rules of Professional Conduct—Preface*, http://www.abanet.org/cpr/mrpc/preface.html (accessed May 17, 2011).

The Bailiff

The **bailiff**, another member of the professional courtroom work group, is usually an armed law enforcement officer. The job of the bailiff, also called a *court officer*, is to ensure order in the courtroom, to announce the judge's entry into the courtroom, to call witnesses, and to prevent the escape of the accused (if the accused has not been released on bond). The bailiff also supervises the jury when it is sequestered and controls public and media access to jury members. Bailiffs in federal courtrooms are deputy U.S. marshals.

Courtrooms can be dangerous places, and bailiffs play a critical role in courtroom security. In an event that led to tightened courtroom security nationwide, George Lott opened fire in a courtroom in Tarrant County, Texas, in 1992, killing two lawyers and injuring three other people.[87] Lott, an attorney, was frustrated by the court's handling of his divorce and by child molestation charges that had been filed against him by his ex-wife. Lott was sentenced to die in 1993. Following the Lott incident and others like it, most courts began using metal detectors, and many now require visitors to leave packages, cellular phones, and objects that might conceal weapons in lockers or to check them with personnel before entering the courtroom.

A comprehensive courthouse security plan must, of course, extend beyond individual courtrooms. In 2005, the National Center for State Courts released a comprehensive plan for improving security in state courthouses.[88] The plan contained a list of ten essential elements for court safety that included the need to (1) assess existing and potential threats, (2) identify physical strengths and weaknesses of existing courts, (3) develop a comprehensive emergency response plan, (4) be aware of the latest technologies in court security, and (5) build strong and effective partnerships among state courts, law enforcement agencies, and county commissioners.

Trial Court Administrators

Many states now employ local court administrators whose job is to facilitate the smooth functioning of courts in a judicial district or area. A major impetus for the hiring of local court administrators came from the 1967 President's Commission on Law Enforcement and Administration of Justice. Examining state courts, the commission found "a system that treats defendants who are

■ **expert witness** A person who has special knowledge and skills recognized by the court as relevant to the determination of guilt or innocence. Unlike lay witnesses, expert witnesses may express opinions or draw conclusions in their testimony.

charged with minor offenses with less dignity and consideration than it treats those who are charged with serious crimes."[89] A few years later, the National Advisory Commission on Criminal Justice Standards and Goals recommended that all courts with five or more judges create the position of trial court administrator.[90]

Court administrators provide uniform court management, assuming many of the duties previously performed by chief judges, prosecutors, and court clerks. Where court administrators operate, the ultimate authority for running the court still rests with the chief judge. Administrators, however, are able to relieve the judge of many routine and repetitive tasks, such as record keeping, scheduling, caseflow analysis, personnel administration, space utilization, facilities planning, and budget management. They may also take the minutes at meetings of judges and their committees.

Where court administrators operate, the ultimate authority for running the court still rests with the chief judge.

Juror management is another area in which trial court administrators are becoming increasingly involved. Juror utilization studies can identify problems such as the overselection of citizens for the jury pool and the reasons for excessive requests to be excused from jury service. They can also suggest ways to reduce the time jurors waste waiting to be called or impaneled.

Effective court administrators are able to track lengthy cases and identify bottlenecks in court processing. They then suggest strategies to make the administration of justice more efficient for courtroom professionals and more humane for lay participants.

The Court Reporter

The role of the court reporter (also called the *court stenographer* or *court recorder*) is to create a record of all that occurs during a trial. Accurate records are very important in criminal trial courts because appeals may be based entirely on what went on in the courtroom. Especially significant are all verbal comments made in the courtroom, including testimony, objections, the judge's rulings, the judge's instructions to the jury, arguments made by lawyers, and the results of conferences between the lawyers and the judge. The official trial record, often taken on a stenotype machine or an audio recorder, may later be transcribed in manuscript form and will become the basis for any appellate review of the trial.

Today's court stenographers often employ computer-aided transcription (CAT) software, which translates typed stenographic shorthand into complete and readable transcripts. Court reporters may be members of the National Court Reporters Association, the United States Court Reporters Association, or the Association of Legal Administrators—all of which support the activities of these professionals. You can visit the National Court Reporters Association via **http://www.ncraonline.org**.

The Clerk of Court

The duties of the clerk of court (also known as the *county clerk*) extend beyond the courtroom. The clerk maintains all records of criminal cases, including all pleas and motions made both before and after the actual trial. The clerk also prepares a jury pool, issues jury summonses, and subpoenas witnesses for both the prosecution and the defense. During the trial, the clerk (or an assistant) marks physical evidence for identification as instructed by the judge and maintains custody of that evidence. The clerk also swears in witnesses and performs other functions as the judge directs. Some states allow the clerk limited judicial duties, such as the power to issue warrants, to handle certain matters relating to individuals declared mentally incompetent,[91] and to serve as judge of probate—overseeing wills and the administration of estates.

Expert Witnesses

Most of the "insiders" we've talked about so far either are employees of the state or have ongoing professional relationships with the court (as in the case of defense counsel). **Expert witnesses**, however, may not have that kind of status, although some do. Expert witnesses are recognized as having specialized skills and knowledge in an established profession or technical area. They must demonstrate their expertise through education, work experience, publications, and awards. Their testimony at trial provides an effective way of introducing scientific evidence in such areas as medicine, psychology, ballistics, crime scene analysis, photography, and many other disciplines. Expert witnesses, like the other courtroom actors described in this chapter, are generally paid professionals. And like all other witnesses, they are subject to cross-examination. Unlike lay witnesses, they are allowed to express opinions and to draw conclusions, but only within their particular area of expertise.

In the 1993 civil case of *Daubert* v. *Merrell Dow Pharmaceuticals*,[92] the U.S. Supreme Court established that the test for the admissibility of scientific expert testimony is for the trial judge to decide "at the outset ... whether the expert is proposing to testify to (1) scientific knowledge that (2) will assist the trier of

■ ***Daubert* standard** A test of scientific acceptability applicable to the gathering of evidence in criminal cases.

fact to understand or determine a fact in issue." The Court concluded that the task of the trial judge is one of "ensuring that an expert's testimony both rests on a reliable foundation and is relevant to the task at hand. Pertinent evidence based on scientifically valid principles," said the Court, "will satisfy those demands." The ***Daubert* standard** eased the criteria for the introduction of scientific evidence at both civil and criminal trials, effectively clearing the way for the use of DNA evidence in the courtroom.[93]

In 2010, in the case of *Melendez-Diaz* v. *Massachusetts*,[94] the Court further defined the role of forensic analysts, deciding that they are "witnesses" and their reports are "testimonial"—meaning that, under the Constitution's Confrontation Clause, they must personally testify at trial unless the defendant waives his or her right to cross-examine them. Similarly, in the 2011 U.S. Supreme Court case of *Bullcoming* v. *New Mexico*,[95] the Court found that the Confrontation Clause does not permit the introduction into evidence during trial of a forensic laboratory report through the in-court testimony of an analyst who did not sign the document or personally observe the test it describes. In effect, the Court held that a forensic analyst who testifies at a criminal trial must be the one who performed or witnessed the lab tests being described.

One difficulty with expert testimony is that it can be confusing to the jury. Sometimes the trouble is due to the nature of the subject matter and sometimes to disagreements between the experts themselves. Often, however, it arises from the strict interpretation given to expert testimony by procedural requirements. The difference between medical and legal definitions of insanity, for example, points to a divergence in both history and purpose between the law and science. Courts that attempt to apply criteria like the M'Naghten rule (discussed in Chapter 4) in deciding claims of "insanity" are often faced with the testimony of psychiatric experts who refuse to even recognize the word. Such experts may prefer, instead, to speak in terms of *psychosis* and *neurosis*—words that have no place in legal jargon. Because of the uncertainties they create, legal requirements may pit experts against one another and may confound the jury.

One difficulty with expert testimony is that it can be confusing to the jury.

Even so, most authorities agree that expert testimony is usually viewed by jurors as more trustworthy than other forms of evidence. In a study of scientific evidence, one prosecutor commented that if he had to choose between presenting a fingerprint or an eyewitness at trial, he would always go with the fingerprint.[96] As a consequence of the effectiveness of scientific evidence, the National Institute of Justice recommends that "prosecutors consider the potential utility of such information in all cases where such evidence is available."[97]

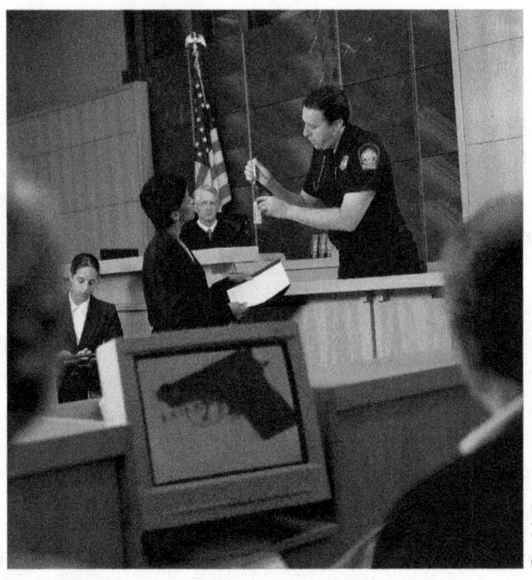
Corbis Images

A ballistics expert testifying on the witness stand in a criminal trial as jurors view evidence on nearby computer displays. Expert witnesses may express opinions and draw conclusions in their area of expertise; they need not limit their testimony to facts alone. Why are expert witnesses permitted such leeway?

Some expert witnesses traverse the country and earn very high fees by testifying at trials. DNA specialist John Gerdes, for example, was paid $100 per hour for his work in support of the defense in the 1995 O. J. Simpson criminal trial, and New York forensic pathologist Michael Baden charged $1,500 per day for time spent working for Simpson in Los Angeles. Baden billed Simpson more than $100,000, and the laboratory for which Gerdes worked received more than $30,000 from Simpson's defense attorneys.[98] In 2008, Simpson was convicted by a Las Vegas jury on 12 felony counts stemming from a confrontation in a hotel room in 2007. The convictions came 13 years to the day after his 1995 acquittal.

Outsiders: Nonprofessional Courtroom Participants

Defendants, victims, jurors, and most witnesses are usually unwilling or inadvertent participants in criminal trials. Although they are outsiders who lack the status of paid professional participants, these are precisely the people who provide the grist for the judicial mill. The press, a willing player in many criminal trials, makes up another group of outsiders. Let's look now at each of these courtroom actors.

■ **lay witness** An eyewitness, character witness, or other person called on to testify who is not considered an expert. Lay witnesses must testify to facts only and may not draw conclusions or express opinions.

■ **subpoena** A written order issued by a judicial officer or grand jury requiring an individual to appear in court and to give testimony or to bring material to be used as evidence. Some subpoenas mandate that books, papers, and other items be surrendered to the court.

■ **victims' assistance program** An organized program that offers services to victims of crime in the areas of crisis intervention and follow-up counseling and that helps victims secure their rights under the law.

Lay Witnesses

Nonexpert witnesses, also known as **lay witnesses**, may be called to testify by either the prosecution or the defense. Lay witnesses may be eyewitnesses who saw the crime being committed or who came upon the crime scene shortly after the crime occurred. Another type of lay witness is the character witness, who frequently provides information about the personality, family life, business acumen, and so on of the defendant in an effort to show that this is not the kind of person who would commit the crime with which he or she is charged. Of course, the victim may also be a witness, providing detailed and sometimes lengthy testimony about the defendant and the crime.

A written document called a **subpoena** officially notifies witnesses that they are to appear in court to testify. Subpoenas are generally served by an officer of the court or by a police officer, though they are sometimes mailed. Both sides in a criminal case may subpoena witnesses and might ask that individuals called to testify bring with them books, papers, photographs, videotapes, or other forms of physical evidence. Witnesses who fail to appear when summoned may face contempt-of-court charges.

The job of a witness is to provide accurate testimony concerning only those things of which he or she has direct knowledge. Normally, witnesses are not allowed to repeat things that others have told them unless they must do so to account for certain actions of their own. Because few witnesses are familiar with courtroom procedure, the task of testifying is fraught with uncertainty and can be traumatizing.

Everyone who testifies in a criminal trial must do so under oath, in which some reference to God is made, or after affirmation,[99] which is a pledge to tell the truth used by those who find either swearing or a reference to God objectionable.

Lay witnesses may be surprised to find that cross-examination can force them to defend their personal and moral integrity.

All witnesses are subject to cross-examination, a process that will be discussed in the next chapter. Lay witnesses may be surprised to find that cross-examination can force them to defend their personal and moral integrity. A cross-examiner may question a witness about past vicious, criminal, or immoral acts, even when such matters have never been the subject of a criminal proceeding.[100] As long as the intent of such questions is to demonstrate to the jury that the witness is not credible, the judge will normally permit them.

Witnesses have traditionally been shortchanged by the judicial process. Subpoenaed to attend court, they have often suffered from frequent and unannounced changes in trial dates. A witness who promptly responds to a summons to appear may find that legal maneuvering has resulted in unanticipated delays. Strategic changes by either side may make the testimony of some witnesses entirely unnecessary, and people who have prepared themselves for the psychological rigors of testifying often experience an emotional letdown.

To compensate witnesses for their time and to make up for lost income, many states pay witnesses for each day that they spend in court. Payments range from $5 to $40 per day,[101] although some states pay nothing at all. Juror pay is also quite low. In a 2004 Chicago murder case in which Oprah Winfrey served as a juror, for example, all jurors, including Winfrey—a billionaire—were paid $17.20 a day for their services.[102] The 1991 U.S. Supreme Court case of *Demarest* v. *Manspeaker et al.*[103] held that federal prisoners subpoenaed to testify are entitled to witness fees just as nonincarcerated witnesses would be.

In an effort to make the job of witnesses less onerous, 39 states and the federal government have laws or guidelines requiring that witnesses be notified of scheduling changes and cancellations in criminal proceedings.[104] In 1982, Congress passed the Victim and Witness Protection Act, which required the U.S. attorney general to develop guidelines to assist victims and witnesses in meeting the demands placed on them by the justice system. A number of **victims' assistance programs** (also called *victim/witness-assistance programs*) have also taken up a call for the rights of witnesses and are working to make the courtroom experience more manageable.

Jurors

The Cook County, Illinois, jury on which television host Oprah Winfrey served convicted a man of first-degree murder in 2004.

■ **juror** A member of a trial or grand jury who has been selected for jury duty and is required to serve as an arbiter of the facts in a court of law. Jurors are expected to render verdicts of "guilty" or "not guilty" as to the charges brought against the accused, although they sometimes fail to do so (as in the case of a hung jury).

"It was an eye-opener for all of us," Winfrey said after the three-day trial ended. "It was not an easy decision to make."[105]

Article III of the U.S. Constitution requires that "[t]he trial of all crimes . . . shall be by jury." States have the authority to determine the size of criminal trial juries. Most states use juries composed of 12 people and one or two alternates designated to fill in for **jurors** who are unable to continue due to accident, illness, or personal emergency. Some states allow for juries of fewer than 12, and juries with as few as six members have survived Supreme Court scrutiny.[106]

Jury duty is regarded as a responsibility of citizenship. Other than juveniles and people in certain occupations, such as police personnel, physicians, members of the armed services on active duty, and emergency services workers, those who are called for jury duty must serve unless they can convince a judge that they should be excused for overriding reasons. Aliens, convicted felons, and citizens who have served on a jury within the past two years are excluded from jury service in most jurisdictions.

The names of prospective jurors are often gathered from the tax register, motor vehicle records, or voter registration rolls of a county or municipality. Minimum qualifications for jury service include adulthood, a basic command of spoken English, citizenship, "ordinary intelligence," and local residency. Jurors are also expected to possess their "natural faculties," meaning that they should be able to hear, speak, see, move, and so forth. Some jurisdictions have recently allowed people with physical disabilities to serve as jurors, although the nature of the evidence to be presented in a case may preclude people with certain kinds of disabilities from serving.

Ideally, the jury should be a microcosm of society, reflecting the values, rationality, and common sense of the average person.

Ideally, the jury should be a microcosm of society, reflecting the values, rationality, and common sense of the average person. The U.S. Supreme Court has held that criminal defendants have a right to have their cases heard before a jury of their peers.[107] Peer juries are those composed of a representative cross section of the community in which the alleged crime occurred and where the trial is to be held. The idea of a peer jury stems from the Magna Carta's original guarantee of jury trials for "freemen." Freemen in England during the thirteenth century, however, were more likely to be of similar mind than is a cross section of Americans today. Hence, although the duty of the jury is to deliberate on the evidence and, ultimately, to determine guilt or innocence, social dynamics may play just as great a role in jury verdicts as do the facts of a case.

In a 1945 case, *Thiel* v. *Southern Pacific Co.*,[108] the Supreme Court clarified the concept of a "jury of one's peers" by noting that although it is not necessary for every jury to contain representatives of every conceivable racial, ethnic, religious, gender, and economic group in the community, court officials may not systematically and intentionally exclude any juror solely because of his or her social characteristics.

In 2005, the American Bar Association released a set of 19 principles intended to guide jury reform.[109] ABA President Robert J. Grey, Jr., said that the principles were aimed at improving the courts' treatment of jurors and to "move jury service into the 21st Century." Some of the principles sounded like a juror's bill of rights and included provisions to protect jurors' privacy and personal information, to inform jurors of trial schedules, and to "vigorously promote juror understanding of the facts and the law." Courts should instruct jurors "in plain and understandable language," the ABA report said. When trials conclude, the report continued, jurors should be advised by judges that they have the right to talk to anyone, including members of the press, and that they also have the right to refuse to talk to anyone about their jury service. Practical recommendations included allowing jurors to take notes, educating jurors regarding the essential aspects of a jury trial, and providing them with identical notebooks containing the court's preliminary instructions and selected exhibits that have been ruled admissible. Read the ABA's entire report, *Principles for Juries and Jury Trials*, at **http://tinyurl.com/43hzc8x**.

The Victim

Not all crimes have clearly identifiable victims, and in a murder case, the victim does not survive. Where there is an identifiable surviving victim, however, he or she is often one of the most forgotten people in the courtroom. Although the victim may have been profoundly affected by the crime itself and is often emotionally committed to the proceedings and trial outcome, he or she may not even be permitted to participate directly in the trial process. Although a powerful movement to recognize the interests of victims is in full swing in this country, it is still not unusual for crime victims to be totally unaware of the final outcome of a case that intimately concerns them.[110]

Not all crimes have clearly identifiable victims.

Hundreds of years ago, the situation surrounding victims was far different. During the early Middle Ages in much of Europe, victims or their survivors routinely played a central role in trial proceedings and in sentencing decisions. They testified, examined witnesses, challenged defense contentions, and pleaded with the judge or jury for justice, honor, and often revenge. Sometimes they were even expected to carry out the sentence of the court by flogging the offender or by releasing the trapdoor used for hangings. This "golden age" of the victim ended with the consolidation of power into the hands of monarchs, who declared that vengeance was theirs alone.

Today, victims, like witnesses, experience many hardships as they participate in the criminal court process. These are a few of the rigors they endure:

- Uncertainty as to their role in the criminal justice process
- A general lack of knowledge about the criminal justice system, courtroom procedure, and legal issues
- Trial delays that result in frequent travel, missed work, and wasted time
- Fear of the defendant or of retaliation from the defendant's associates
- The trauma of testifying and of cross-examination

The trial process itself can make for a bitter experience. If victims take the stand, defense attorneys may test their memory, challenge their veracity, or even suggest that they were somehow responsible for their own victimization. After enduring cross-examination, some victims report feeling as though they, and not the offender, were portrayed as the criminal to the jury. The difficulties encountered by victims have been compared to a second victimization at the hands of the criminal justice system.

After enduring cross-examination, some victims report feeling as though they, and not the offender, were portrayed as the criminal to the jury.

The Defendant

Generally, defendants must be present at their trials. The Federal Rules of Criminal Procedure, like state rules, require that a defendant must be present at every stage of a trial, except that a defendant who is initially present may be voluntarily absent after the trial has commenced.[111] In *Crosby* v. *U.S.* (1993),[112] the U.S. Supreme Court held that a defendant may not be tried in absentia, even if he or she was present at the beginning of a trial, if his or her absence is due to escape or failure to appear. In *Zafiro* v. *U.S.* (1993),[113] the justices held that, at least in federal courts, defendants charged with similar or related offenses may be tried together, even when their defenses differ substantially.

The majority of criminal defendants are poor, uneducated, and often alienated from the philosophy that undergirds the American justice system.

The majority of criminal defendants are poor, uneducated, and often alienated from the philosophy that undergirds the American justice system. Many are relatively powerless and are at the mercy of judicial mechanisms. However, experienced defendants, notably those who are career offenders, may be well versed in courtroom demeanor. As we discussed earlier, defendants in criminal trials may even choose to represent themselves, though such a choice may not be in their best interests.

Even without self-representation, every defendant who chooses to do so can substantially influence events in the courtroom. Defendants exercise choice in (1) selecting and retaining counsel, (2) planning a defense strategy in coordination with their attorney, (3) deciding what information to provide to (or withhold from) the defense team, (4) deciding what plea to enter, (5) deciding whether to testify personally, and (6) determining whether to file an appeal if convicted.

Nevertheless, even the most active defendants suffer from a number of disadvantages. One is the tendency of others to assume that anyone on trial must be guilty. Although a criminal defendant is "innocent until proven guilty," the very fact that the defendant is accused of an offense casts a shadow of suspicion that may foster biases in the minds of jurors and other courtroom actors. Another disadvantage lies in the often-substantial social and cultural differences that separate the offender from the professional courtroom staff. Whereas lawyers and judges tend to identify with upper-middle-class values and lifestyles, few offenders do. The consequences of such a gap between defendant and courtroom staff may be insidious and far-reaching.

Spectators and the Press

Spectators and the press are often overlooked because they do not have an official role in courtroom proceedings. Both spectators and media representatives may be present in large numbers at any trial. Spectators include members of the families of both victim and defendant, friends of either side, and curious onlookers—some of whom are avocational court watchers. Journalists, TV reporters, and other members of the press are apt to be present at "spectacular" trials (those involving an especially gruesome crime or a famous personality) and at those in which there is a great deal of community interest. The right of reporters and spectators to be present at a

■ **change of venue** The movement of a trial or lawsuit from one jurisdiction to another or from one location to another within the same jurisdiction. A change of venue may be made in a criminal case to ensure that the defendant receives a fair trial.

criminal trial is supported by the Sixth Amendment's requirement of a public trial.

Press reports at all stages of a criminal investigation and trial often create problems for the justice system. Significant pretrial publicity about a case may make it difficult to find jurors who have not already formed an opinion as to the guilt or innocence of the defendant. News reports from the courtroom may influence or confuse nonsequestered jurors who hear them, especially when they contain information brought to the bench but not heard by the jury.

In the 1976 case of *Nebraska Press Association* v. *Stuart*,[114] the U.S. Supreme Court ruled that trial court judges could not legitimately issue gag orders preventing the pretrial publication of information about a criminal case, as long as the defendant's right to a fair trial and an impartial jury could be ensured by traditional means.[115] These means include (1) a **change of venue**, whereby the trial is moved to another jurisdiction less likely to have been exposed to the publicity; (2) trial postponement, which would allow for memories to fade and emotions to cool; and (3) jury selection and screening to eliminate biased people from the jury pool. In 1986, the Court extended press access to preliminary hearings, which it said are "sufficiently like a trial to require public access."[116] In 1993, in the case of *Caribbean International News Corporation* v. *Puerto Rico*,[117] the Court effectively applied that requirement to territories under U.S. control.

Today, members of the press and their video, television, and still cameras are allowed into most state courtrooms. New York is one significant exception, and in 2004, a state court upheld the constitutionality of a 51-year-old law[118] prohibiting the use of cameras in that state's courts.[119] Forty-two states specifically allow cameras at most criminal trials,[120] although most require that permission be obtained from the judge before filming begins. Most states also impose restrictions on certain kinds of recording—of jurors or of juveniles, for example, or of conferences between an attorney and the defendant or between an attorney and the judge—although most states allow the filming of such proceedings without audio pickup. Only a few states ban television or video cameras outright. Indiana, Maryland, Mississippi, Nebraska, and Utah all prohibit audiovisual coverage of criminal trials. The District of Columbia prohibits cameras at trials and at appellate hearings.[121]

Forty-two states specifically allow cameras at most criminal trials.

The U.S. Supreme Court has been far less favorably disposed to television coverage than have most state courts. In 1981, a Florida defendant appealed his burglary conviction to the Supreme Court,[122] arguing that the presence of television cameras at his trial had turned the court into a circus for attorneys and made the proceedings more a sideshow than a trial. The Supreme Court, recognizing that television cameras have an untoward effect on many people, found in favor of the defendant. In the words of the Court, "Trial courts must be especially vigilant to guard against any impairment of the defendant's right to a verdict based solely upon the evidence and the relevant law."

Cameras of all kinds have been prohibited in all federal district criminal proceedings since 1946 by Rule 53 of the Federal Rules of Criminal Procedure.[123] In 1972, the Judicial Conference of the United States adopted a policy opposing broadcast of civil proceedings in district courts, and that policy was incorporated into the Code of Conduct for United States Judges. Nonetheless, some district courts have local rules that allow photographs and filming during selected proceedings.

A three-year pilot project that allowed television cameras into six U.S. district courts and two appeals courts closed on December 31, 1994, when the Judicial Conference voted to end the project. Conference members expressed concerns that cameras were a distracting influence and were having a "negative impact on jurors [and] witnesses"[124] by exposing them to possible harm by revealing their identities. Still, some federal appellate courts have created their own policy on the use of cameras and broadcast equipment in the courtroom. The official policy of the U.S. Court of Appeals for the Ninth Circuit, for example, permits cameras and media broadcasts that meet certain rules. The policy stipulates, "Three business days advance notice is required from the media of a request to be present to broadcast, televise, record electronically, or take photographs at a particular session. Such requests must be submitted to the Clerk of Court." The policy adds, "The presiding judge of the panel may limit or terminate media coverage, or direct the removal of camera coverage personnel when necessary to protect the rights of the parties or to assure the orderly conduct of the proceedings."[125]

Today's new personal technologies, however, which include cellular telephones with digital camera capabilities, streaming Web-based video, and miniaturized recording devices, all threaten courtroom privacy.

SUMMARY

- In the United States, there are two judicial systems. One is a state system made up of state and local courts established under the authority of state governments. The other is the federal court system, created by Congress under the authority of the U.S. Constitution. This dual-court system is the result of a general agreement among the nation's founders about the need for individual states to retain significant legislative authority and judicial autonomy separate from federal control.
- A typical state court system consists of trial courts of limited jurisdiction, trial courts of general jurisdiction, and appellate courts—usually including a state supreme court. State courts have virtually unlimited power to decide nearly every type of case, subject only to the limitations of the U.S. Constitution, their own state constitutions, and state law. It is within state courts that the large majority of criminal cases originate.
- The federal court system consists of three levels: U.S. district courts, U.S. courts of appeals, and the U.S. Supreme Court. U.S. district courts are the trial courts of the federal system and are located principally in larger cities. They decide only those cases over which the Constitution gives them authority. The highest federal court, the U.S. Supreme Court, is located in Washington, D.C., and hears cases only on appeal from lower courts.
- The courtroom work group comprises professional courtroom personnel, including the judge, the prosecuting attorney, the defense counsel, the bailiff, the local court administrator, the court reporter, the clerk of court, and expert witnesses. Also present in the courtroom for a trial are "outsiders"—nonprofessional courtroom participants like witnesses and jurors.
- The courtroom work group is guided by statutory requirements and ethical considerations, and its members are generally dedicated to bringing the criminal trial and other courtroom procedures to a successful close. This chapter describes the role that each professional participant plays in the courtroom. The judge, for example, has the primary duty of ensuring a fair trial—in short, seeing that justice prevails.
- Nonprofessional courtroom participants include lay witnesses, jurors, the victim, the defendant, and spectators and members of the press. Nonjudicial courtroom personnel, or outsiders, may be unwilling or inadvertent participants in a criminal trial.

KEY TERMS

appeal, 278
appellate jurisdiction, 276
bailiff, 298
change of venue, 304
community court, 279
court of last resort, 278
courtroom work group, 287
***Daubert* standard, 300**
defense counsel, 293
dispute-resolution center, 279
exculpatory evidence, 291
expert witness, 299
federal court system, 274
judge, 287
judicial review, 284
jurisdiction, 274
juror, 302
lay witness, 301
original jurisdiction, 276
prosecutor, 290
prosecutorial discretion, 290
public defender, 294
specialized courts, 279
state court administrator, 278
state court system, 274
subpoena, 301
trial *de novo*, 277
victims' assistance program, 301

KEY CASES

***Argersinger* v. *Hamlin*, 294**
***Burns* v. *Reed*, 292**
***Crosby* v. *U.S.*, 303**
***Daubert* v. *Merrell Dow Pharmaceuticals*, 299**
***Demarest* v. *Manspeaker et al.*, 301**
***Gideon* v. *Wainwright*, 294**
***Herrera* v. *Collins*, 278**
***Imbler* v. *Pachtman*, 292**
***Keeney* v. *Tamayo-Reyes*, 278**
***Marbury* v. *Madison*, 284**
***Melendez-Diaz* v. *Massachusetts*, 300**
***Van de Kamp* v. *Goldstein*, 292**
***Zafiro* v. *U.S.*, 303**

QUESTIONS FOR REVIEW

1. How did the American court system develop? What is the dual-court system? Why do we have a dual-court system in America?
2. What is a typical state court system like? What are some of the differences between the state and federal court systems?
3. How is the federal court system structured? What are the various types of federal courts?
4. What is meant by the *courtroom work group*? What two major subcategories comprise the courtroom work group?
5. Who are the professional members of the courtroom work group, and what are their roles?
6. Who are the nonprofessional courtroom participants, and what are their roles?

QUESTIONS FOR REFLECTION

1. What are the three forms of indigent defense used in the United States? Why might defendants prefer private attorneys over public counsel?
2. What is an expert witness? What is a lay witness? How might their testimony differ? What are some of the issues involved in deciding whether a person is an expert for purposes of testimony?
3. How do the professional and nonprofessional courtroom participants work together to bring most criminal trials to a successful close? What do you think a "successful close" might mean to the judge? To the defense attorney? To the prosecutor? To the jury? To the defendant? To the victim?

NOTES

1. "Federal Jury Convicts California Man in 2008 Courthouse Bombing," CNN, June 6, 2011, http://www.cnn.com/2011/CRIME/06/06/california.courthouse.blast/index.html?hptju_c2 (accessed June 7, 2011).
2. John Mattes, "Motives for Bombing Downtown Federal Courthouse?" August 8, 2008, http://www.sandiego6.com/content/unit6/story/Motives-for-Bombing-Downtown-Federal-Courthouse/ZGo7RgwzaUagS6XDW7cypQ.cspx (accessed July 1, 2009).
3. Law Enforcement Assistance Administration, *Two Hundred Years of American Criminal Justice* (Washington, DC: U.S. Government Printing Office, 1976), p. 31.
4. David B. Rottman and Shauna M. Strickland, *State Court Organization, 2004* (Washington, DC: Bureau of Justice Statistics, 2006), p. 7.
5. In 1957, only 13 states had permanent intermediate appellate courts. Now, all but 10 states have these courts. See Rottman and Strickland, *State Court Organization, 2004*, pp. 9–10.
6. *Keeney, Superintendent, Oregon State Penitentiary* v. *Tamayo-Reyes*, 113 S.Ct. 853, 122 L.Ed.2d 203 (1992).
7. *Herrera* v. *Collins*, 113 S.Ct. 853, 122 L.Ed.2d 203 (1993).
8. Martin Wright, *Justice for Victims and Offenders* (Bristol, PA: Open University Press, 1991), p. 56.
9. "Bridging the Gap between Communities and Courts," http://www.communityjustice.org (accessed November 22, 2009).
10. M. Somjen Frazer, *The Impact of the Community Court Model on Defendant Perceptions of Fairness: A Case Study at the Red Hook Community Justice Center* (New York: Center for Court Innovation, 2006).
11. Center for Court Innovation, "Brooklyn Mental Health Court," http://www.courtinnovation.org/project/brooklyn-mental-health-court (accessed March 5, 2013).
12. Adapted from National Institute of Justice, "Specialized Courts," http://www.nij.gov/topics/courts/specialized-courts.htm (accessed March 3, 2013).
13. Rekha Mirchandani, "What's So Special about Specialized Courts? The State and Social Change in Salt Lake City's Domestic Violence Court," *Law and Society Review*, Vol. 39, No. 2 (2005), p. 379.
14. Most of the information and some of the wording in this section come from Administrative Office of the U.S. Courts, "Understanding the Federal Courts," http://www.uscourts.gov/UFC99.pdf (accessed April 2, 2009).
15. Administrative Office of the U.S. Courts, "U.S. District Courts—Criminal Cases Commenced, Terminated, and Pending during the 12-Month Periods Ending March 31, 2011 and 2012," http://www.uscourts.gov/Viewer.aspx?doc=/uscourts/Statistics/FederalJudicialCaseloadStatistics/2012/tables/D00CMar12.pdf (accessed September 18, 2013).
16. Ibid.
17. Administrative Office of the U.S. Courts, "U.S. District Courts—Judicial Caseload Profile."
18. John R. Emshwiller and Alexandra Beerzon, "Decree in Arizona Eases Trial Limit," *Wall Street Journal*, January 28, 2011, http://online.wsj.com/article/SB10001424052748704013604576104510607653374.html (accessed June 2, 2011).
19. Administrative Office of the U.S. Courts, "Federal Judicial Pay Increase Fact Sheet," http://www.uscourts.gov/JudgesAndJudgeships/JudicialCompensation/JudicialPayIncreaseFact.aspx (accessed November 7, 2011).
20. Although the Ethics Reform Act of 1989 was supposed to allow for a cost-of-living increase in federal judicial salaries, Congress blocked the automatic increases from 1995 to 1999 because they also applied to the salaries of members of Congress and were seen as politically unpalatable.
21. Chief Justice John Roberts, "2005 Year-End Report on the Federal Judiciary," *Third Branch*, Vol. 38, No. 1 (January 2006), http://www.uscourts.gov/ttb/jan06ttb/yearend/index.html (accessed March 30, 2007).
22. Much of the information and some of the wording in this section come from Administrative Office of the U.S. Courts, "About the Federal Courts," http://www.uscourts.gov/about.html (accessed October 4, 2007).
23. Stephen L. Wasby, *The Supreme Court in the Federal Judicial System*, 3rd ed. (Chicago: Nelson-Hall, 1988), p. 58.
24. Judicial Conference of the United States, "Judgeship Recommendations, March 2011," http://www.uscourts.gov/Federal-Courts/JudicialConference/JudgeshipRecommendations.aspx (accessed March 3, 2013).
25. *The Supreme Court of the United States* (Washington, DC: U.S. Government Printing Office, no date), p. 4.
26. *Marbury* v. *Madison*, 1 Cranch 137 (1803).
27. National Center for State Courts, "Court Technology Bulletin," February 16, 2012, http://courttechbulletin.blogspot.com/2012/02/calculating-e-court-return-on.html (accessed July 26, 2012).
28. Many of the details for this story come from CBS News. See, for example, Mike Ballou, "Caylee Anthony Autopsy Reveals Grim Details But Sheds Little Light on Mystery," June 22, 2009, http://www.cbsnews.com/8301-504083_162-5103384-504083.html (accessed May 20, 2010).
29. See, for example, Jeffrey T. Ulmer, *Social Worlds of Sentencing: Court Communities under Sentencing Guidelines* (Ithaca: State University of New York Press, 1997); and Roy B. Flemming, Peter F. Nardulli, and James Eisenstein, *The Craft of Justice: Politics and Work in Criminal Court Communities* (Philadelphia: University of Pennsylvania Press, 1993).
30. See, for example, Edward J. Clynch and David W. Neubauer, "Trial Courts as Organizations," *Law and Policy Quarterly*, Vol. 3 (1981), pp. 69–94.
31. American Bar Association, *ABA Standards for Criminal Justice*, 2nd ed. (Chicago: ABA, 1980).
32. In 1940, Missouri became the first state to adopt a plan for the "merit selection" of judges based on periodic public review.
33. National Judicial College, "About the NJC," http://www.judges.org/about (accessed February 2, 2009).
34. See National Judicial College, "National Impact," 2006, http://www.judges.org/downloads/general_information/national_impact06 (accessed May 22, 2008).
35. Doris Marie Provine, *Judging Credentials: Nonlawyer Judges and the Politics of Professionalism* (Chicago: University of Chicago Press, 1986).
36. Town and village justices in New York State serve part-time and may or may not be lawyers; judges of all other courts must be lawyers, whether or not they serve full-time. From New York State Commission on Judicial Conduct, "2011 Annual Report," http://http://www.cjc.ny.gov/Publications/AnnualReports/nyscjc.2011annualreport.pdf (accessed March 10, 2013).
37. Ibid.
38. Bill Rankin, "Ex-judge Camp Sentenced to 30 Days in Prison," *Atlanta Journal-Constitution*, March 11, 2011, http://www.ajc.com/news/atlanta/ex-judge-camp-sentenced-867817.html (accessed June 2, 2011).
39. West Virginia Justice Watch, "Former Circuit Court Judge Joseph Troisi Made State and National Headlines for Biting the Nose of a Defendant (1997)," http://www.wvjusticewatch.org/ethics/bite_nose.htm (accessed July 5, 2005).

40. U.S. Department of Justice, Office of Public Affairs, Press Release, "Former Senior U.S. District Judge Sentenced to One Month in Prison for Misuse of Government Property and Drug Offenses," March 11, 2011, http://www.justice.gov/opa/pr/2011/March/11-crm-315.html (accessed June 1, 2011).
41. Bureau of Justice Statistics, *Report to the Nation on Crime and Justice: The Data* (Washington, DC: U.S. Dept. of Justice, 1983).
42. For a discussion of the resource limitations that district attorneys face in combating corporate crime, see Michael L. Benson et al., "District Attorneys and Corporate Crime: Surveying the Prosecutorial Gatekeepers," *Criminology*, Vol. 26, No. 3 (August 1988), pp. 505–517.
43. Carol J. DeFrances and Greg W. Steadman, *Prosecutors in State Courts, 1996* (Washington, DC: Bureau of Justice Statistics, 1998).
44. U.S. Code, Title 28, Section 530A.
45. Some of the wording in this paragraph is adapted from Kim Murphy, "Prosecutors in Oregon Find 'Truth' Ruling a Real Hindrance," *Los Angeles Times*, August 5, 2001.
46. *In re Gatti*, S45801, Oregon Supreme Court, August 17, 2000.
47. The ruling was based on Disciplinary Rule 1-102 of the Oregon State Bar, which says, in part, that it is professional misconduct for a lawyer to "engage in conduct involving dishonesty, fraud, deceit or misrepresentation." The rule also prohibits a lawyer from violating this dishonesty provision through the acts of another. Also at issue was Disciplinary Rule 7-102, which prohibits a lawyer from "knowingly making a false statement of law or fact."
48. Most of the information and some of the wording in this section come from Administrative Office of the U.S. Courts, "Understanding the Federal Courts," http://www.uscourts.gov/UFC99.pdf (accessed April 2, 2004).
49. Kenneth Culp Davis, *Discretionary Justice* (Baton Rouge: Louisiana State University Press, 1969), p. 190.
50. Barbara Borland, *The Prosecution of Felony Arrests* (Washington, DC: Bureau of Justice Statistics, 1983).
51. *Brady* v. *Maryland*, 373 U.S. 83 (1963).
52. *U.S.* v. *Bagley*, 473 U.S. 667 (1985).
53. *Banks* v. *Dretke*, 124 S.Ct. 1256, 1280 (2004).
54. *Imbler* v. *Pachtman*, 424 U.S. 409 (1976).
55. *Burns* v. *Reed*, 500 U.S. 478 (1991).
56. Ibid., complaint, p. 29.
57. *Van de Kamp* v. *Goldstein*, U.S. Supreme Court, No. 07-854 (decided January 26, 2009).
58. Cassia Spohn, John Gruhl, and Susan Welch, "The Impact of the Ethnicity and Gender of Defendants on the Decision to Reject or Dismiss Felony Charges," *Criminology*, Vol. 25, No. 1 (1987), pp. 175–191.
59. Brad Heath and Kevin McCoy, "Justice Dept. Office to Punish Prosecutors' Misconduct," *USA Today*, January 19, 2011, p. 1A.
60. American Bar Association Center for Professional Responsibility, *Model Rules of Professional Conduct* (Chicago: ABA, 2003), p. 87.
61. The same is true under federal law, and in almost all of the states, of communications between defendants and members of the clergy, psychiatrists and psychologists, medical doctors, and licensed social workers in the course of psychotherapy. See, for example, *Jaffee* v. *Redmond*, 116 S.Ct. 1923 (1996).
62. *Powell* v. *Alabama*, 287 U.S. 45 (1932).
63. *Johnson* v. *Zerbst*, 304 U.S. 458 (1938).
64. *Gideon* v. *Wainwright*, 372 U.S. 335 (1963).
65. *Argersinger* v. *Hamlin*, 407 U.S. 25 (1972).
66. *In re Gault*, 387 U.S. 1 (1967).
67. *Alabama* v. *Shelton*, 535 U.S. 654 (2002).
68. Jane Fritsch, "Pataki Rethinks Promise of a Pay Raise for Lawyers to the Indigent," *New York Times*, December 24, 2001.
69. Donald J. Farole, Jr., and Lynn Langton, *County-Based and Local Public Defender Offices, 2007* (Washington, DC: BJS, 2010).
70. Ibid.
71. Carol J. DeFrances, *State-Funded Indigent Defense Services, 1999* (Washington, DC: National Institute of Justice, 2001).
72. "Nationline: McVeigh's Defense Cost Taxpayers $13.8 Million," *USA Today*, July 3, 2001.
73. *Faretta* v. *California*, 422 U.S. 806 (1975).
74. Smith and DeFrances, *Indigent Defense*, pp. 2–3.
75. *Anders* v. *California*, 386 U.S. 738 (1967).
76. *People* v. *Wende*, 25 Cal.3d 436, 600 P.2d 1071 (1979).
77. *Smith* v. *Robbins*, 528 U.S. 259 (2000).
78. *Texas* v. *Cobb*, 532 U.S. 162 (2001).
79. Details for this story come from Chisun Lee, "Punishing Mmes. Stewart: The Parallel Universes of Martha and Lynne," *Village Voice*, February 15, 2005, http://www.refuseandresist.org/article-print.php?aid51757 (accessed January 5, 2006).
80. Scott Shifrel and James Fanelli, "Lynn Stewart, 70-year-old Radical Lawyer, Sentenced to 10 years in Prison for Aiding Bomb Plotter," *Daily News*, July 16, 2010, http://www.nydailynews.com/new-york/lynn-stewart-70-year-old-radical-lawyer-sentenced-10-years-prison-aiding-bomb-plotter-article-1.466192 (accessed July 31, 2013).
81. "Justice for Lynne Stewart," http://lynnestewart.org (accessed May 12, 2013).
82. "Lawyer Convicted of Terrorist Support," *USA Today*, February 11, 2005, p. 3A.
83. Mike McKee, "California State Bar to Allow Lawyers to Break Confidentiality," *Recorder*, May 17, 2004, http://www.law.com/jsp/article.jsp?id51084316038367 (accessed August 25, 2007).
84. "ABA Eases Secrecy Rules in Lawyer-Client Relationship," *USA Today*, August 7, 2001.
85. *Nix* v. *Whiteside*, 475 U.S. 157 (1986).
86. Ibid.
87. "Courtroom Killings Verdict," *USA Today*, February 15, 1993.
88. National Center for State Courts, "Improving Security in State Courthouses: Ten Essential Elements for Court Safety," http://www.ncsconline.org/whatsNew/TenPointPlan.htm (accessed October 20, 2007).
89. President's Commission on Law Enforcement and Administration of Justice, *The Challenge of Crime in a Free Society* (Washington, DC: U.S. Government Printing Office, 1967), p. 129.
90. National Advisory Commission on Criminal Justice Standards and Goals, *Courts* (Washington, DC: U.S. Government Printing Office, 1973), Standard 9.3.
91. See, for example, Joan G. Brannon, *The Judicial System in North Carolina* (Raleigh, NC: Administrative Office of the United States Courts, 1984), p. 14.
92. *Daubert* v. *Merrell Dow Pharmaceuticals, Inc.*, 509 U.S. 579, 113 S.Ct. 2786 (1993).
93. For the application of *Daubert* to DNA technology, see Barry Sheck, "DNA and *Daubert*," *Cardozo Law Review*, Vol. 15 (1994), p. 1959.
94. *Melendez-Diaz* v. *Massachusetts*, 557 U.S. 305 (2009).
95. *Bullcoming* v. *New Mexico*, U.S. Supreme Court, No. 09-10876 (decided June 23, 2011).
96. Joseph L. Peterson, "Use of Forensic Evidence by the Police and Courts," *National Institute of Justice Research in Brief* (Washington, DC: NIJ, 1987), p. 3.
97. Ibid., p. 6.
98. Jennifer Bowles, "Simpson-Paid Experts," Associated Press, August 12, 1995.

99. *California* v. *Green*, 399 U.S. 149 (1970).
100. Patrick L. McCloskey and Ronald L. Schoenberg, *Criminal Law Deskbook* (New York: Matthew Bender, 1988), Section 17, p. 123.
101. United States District Court, District of Massachusetts, "Additional Federal Jury Duty Information," http://www.mad.uscourts.gov/jurors/federal-information-more.htm (accessed May 22, 2012).
102. Anna Johnson, "Jury with Oprah Winfrey Convicts Man of Murder," Associated Press, August 19, 2004.
103. *Demarest* v. *Manspeaker et al.*, 498 U.S. 184, 111 S.Ct. 599, 112 L.Ed.2d 608 (1991).
104. Bureau of Justice Statistics, *Report to the Nation on Crime and Justice*, p. 82.
105. Johnson, "Jury with Oprah Winfrey Convicts Man of Murder."
106. *Williams* v. *Florida*, 399 U.S. 78, 90 S.Ct. 1893, 26 L.Ed.2d 446 (1970).
107. *Smith* v. *Texas*, 311 U.S. 128 (1940). That right does not apply when the defendants are facing the possibility of a prison sentence of less than six months in length or even when the potential aggregate sentence for multiple petty offenses exceeds six months (see *Lewis* v. *U.S.*, 518 U.S. 322 [1996]).
108. *Thiel* v. *Southern Pacific Co.*, 328 U.S. 217 (1945).
109. American Bar Association, *Principles for Juries and Jury Trials* (Chicago: ABA, 2005).
110. The author was himself the victim of a felony some years ago. His car was stolen in Columbus, Ohio, and recovered a year later in Cleveland. He was informed that the person who had taken it was in custody, but he never heard what happened to him, nor could he learn where or whether a trial was to be held.
111. Federal Rules of Criminal Procedure, Rule 43.
112. *Crosby* v. *U.S.*, 113 S.Ct. 748, 122 L.Ed.2d 25 (1993).
113. *Zafiro* v. *U.S.*, 113 S.Ct. 933, 122 L.Ed.2d 317 (1993).
114. *Nebraska Press Association* v. *Stuart*, 427 U.S. 539 (1976).
115. However, it is generally accepted that trial judges may issue limited gag orders aimed at trial participants.
116. *Press Enterprise Company* v. *Superior Court of California, Riverside County*, 478 U.S. 1 (1986).
117. *Caribbean International News Corporation* v. *Puerto Rico*, 508 U.S. 147 (1993).
118. N.Y. Civil Rights Law, Section 52.
119. Tom Perrotta, "New York Law Banning Cameras in State Courts Found Constitutional," *New York Law Journal*, May 23, 2004.
120. Charles L. Babcock et al., "Fifty-State Survey of the Law Governing Audio-Visual Coverage of Court Proceedings," http://www.jw.com/articles/details.cfm?articlenum5120 (accessed October 10, 2005).
121. See Radio-Television News Directors Association, "Summary of State Camera Coverage Rules," http://www.rtnda.org/issues/camerassummary.htm (accessed February 9, 2000).
122. *Chandler* v. *Florida*, 499 U.S. 560 (1981).
123. Rule 53 of the Federal Rules of Criminal Procedure reads, "The taking of photographs in the court room during the progress of judicial proceedings or radio broadcasting of judicial proceedings from the court room shall not be permitted by the court."
124. Harry F. Rosenthal, "Courts-TV," Associated Press, September 21, 1991. See also "Judicial Conference Rejects Cameras in Federal Courts," *Criminal Justice Newsletter*, September 15, 1994, p. 6.
125. Policy, U.S. Court of Appeals for the Ninth Circuit, http://www.ce9.uscourts.gov/web/OCELibra.nsf/504ca249c786e20f85256284006da7ab/ba060a3e537d2866882569760067ac8e?OpnDocument (accessed September 16, 2007).

moodboard/Getty Images

10 PRETRIAL ACTIVITIES AND THE CRIMINAL TRIAL

OUTLINE

- Introduction
- Pretrial Activities
- The Criminal Trial
- Stages in a Criminal Trial
- Improving the Adjudication Process

LEARNING OBJECTIVES

After reading this chapter, you should be able to

- Describe the pretrial steps and activities.
- State the purpose of the criminal trial.
- Describe the criminal trial process.
- Describe three approaches to improving the adjudication process.

Society asks much of the criminal court. The court is expected to meet society's demand that serious offenders be convicted and punished, and at the same time it is expected to insure that the innocent and unfortunate are not oppressed.

THE PRESIDENT'S COMMISSION ON LAW ENFORCEMENT AND ADMINISTRATION OF JUSTICE

■ **first appearance** An appearance before a magistrate during which the legality of the defendant's arrest is initially assessed and the defendant is informed of the charges on which he or she is being held. At this stage in the criminal justice process, bail may be set or pretrial release arranged.

Introduction

On May 8, 2013, Arizona jurors found 32-year-old Jodi Arias guilty of first-degree murder in the brutal killing of her former boyfriend, Travis Alexander. Arias, who admitted shooting and stabbing her then-30-year-old lover at his home in 2008, claimed that she had been trying to defend herself from emotional, physical, and sexual abuse. Arias appeared as a petite and demure woman during her widely-televised trial, and dressed like a schoolgirl while on the stand. Although her appearance might have been unremarkable, Arias's trial captured the attention of the nation and the world as it wound through five months of testimony, cross-examination, and jury debate. *USA Today* described it this way, "the Jodi Arias trial, which would ordinarily be a run-of-the-mill domestic murder case," drew a media circus that fed a large following of TV viewers who watched the trial unfold.[1] They were captivated by its intimate details of "love, lies, sex, and dirty secrets." At one point, an audio recording was played during the trail in which Alexander said that he wanted to tie Arias to a tree and commit deviant sex acts on her.

Alexander's body was found in the shower of his Mesa, Arizona, home. He had been shot in the face, stabbed 30 times, and his throat had been cut from ear to ear. Court testimony revealed that Arias was a jilted lover who turned into a stalker, even though Alexander continued to invite her to his house and have sex with her while he saw other women.

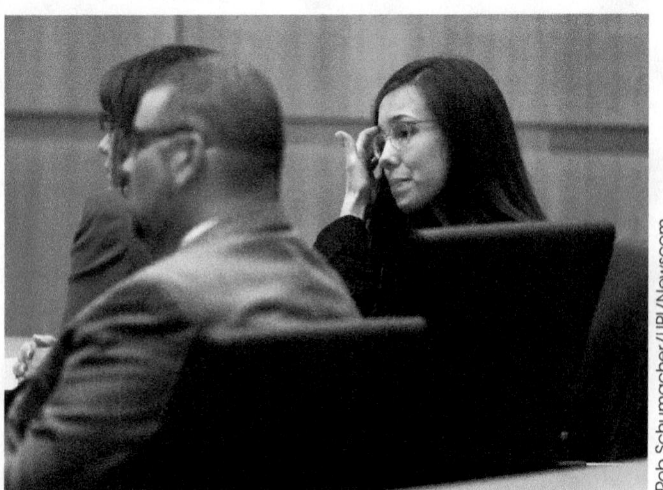

Rob Schumacher/UPI/Newscom

Jodi Arias, convicted in 2013 of the brutal murder of her boyfriend, Travis Alexander. Why did the televised trial draw such a large audience?

Pretrial Activities

In this chapter, we will describe the criminal trial process, highlighting each important stage in the procedure. First, however, we look at the court-related activities that routinely take place *before* trial can begin. These activities (as well as the names given to them) vary among jurisdictions. They are described generally in the pages that follow (see Figure 10-1).

The First Appearance

Following arrest, most defendants do not come into contact with an officer of the court until their **first appearance** before a magistrate or a lower-court judge.[2] A first appearance, sometimes called an *initial appearance* or *magistrate's review*, occurs when defendants are brought before a judge (1) to be given formal notice of the charges against them, (2) to be advised of their rights, (3) to be given the opportunity to retain a lawyer or to have one appointed to represent them, and (4) perhaps to be afforded the opportunity for bail.

According to the procedural rules of all jurisdictions, defendants who have been taken into custody must be offered an in-court appearance before a magistrate "without unnecessary delay." The 1943 U.S. Supreme Court case of *McNabb* v. *U.S.*[3] established that any unreasonable delay in an initial court appearance would make confessions inadmissible if interrogating officers obtained them during the delay. Based on the *McNabb* decision, 48 hours following arrest became the standard maximum time by which a first appearance should be held.

> Defendants who have been taken into custody must be offered an in-court appearance before a magistrate "without unnecessary delay."

The first appearance may also involve a probable cause hearing, although such hearings may be held separately because they do not require the defendant's presence. (In some jurisdictions, a probable cause hearing may be combined with the preliminary hearing, which we will look at later in this chapter.) Probable cause hearings are necessary when arrests are made without a warrant.[4] During a probable cause hearing, also called a *probable cause determination*, a judicial officer will review police documents and reports to ensure that probable cause supported the arrest. The review of the arrest proceeds in a relatively informal fashion, with the judge seeking to decide whether, at the time of apprehension, the arresting officer had reason to believe both (1) that a crime had been or was being committed and (2) that the defendant was the person who committed it. Most of the evidence presented to the judge comes either

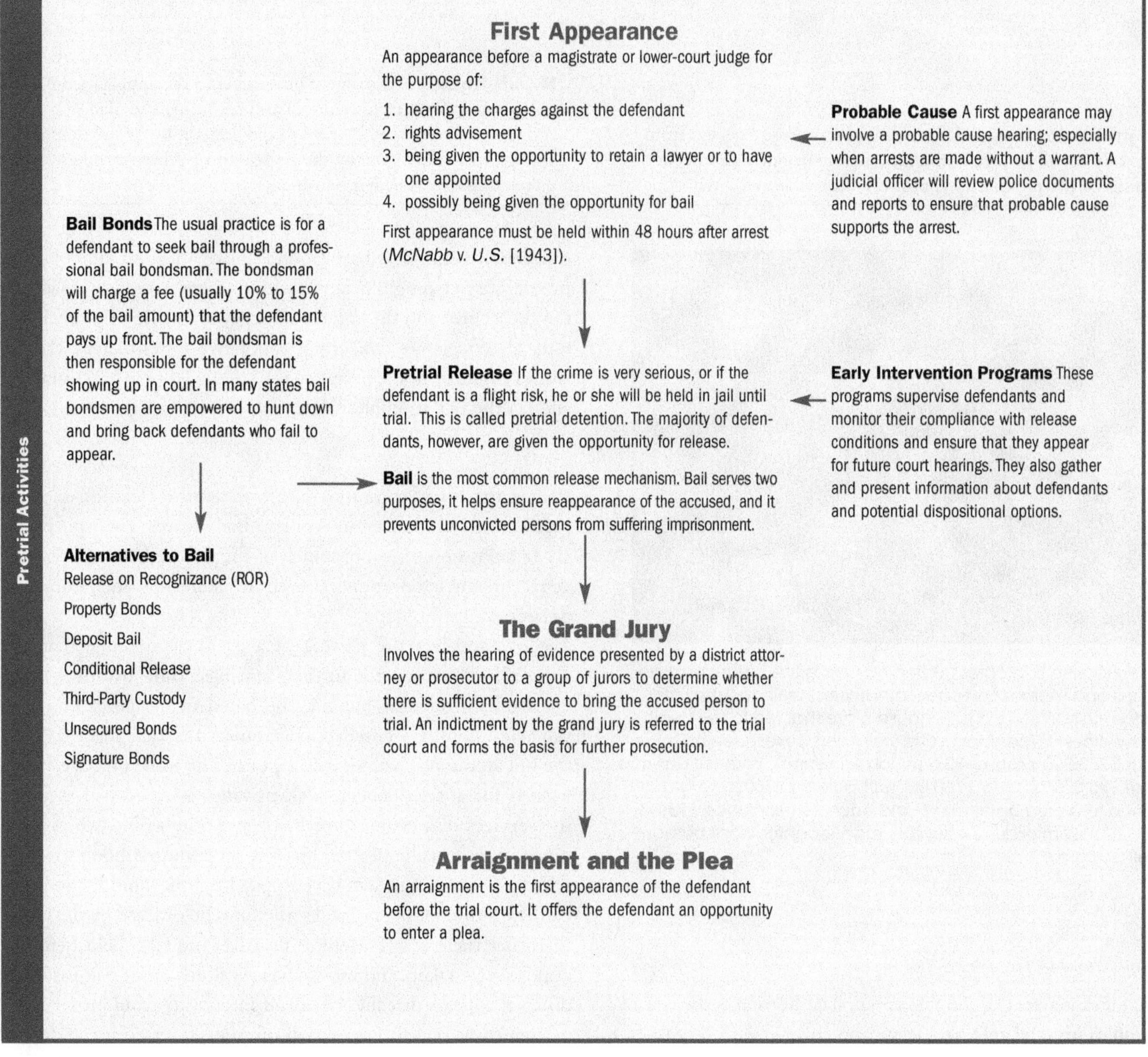

FIGURE 10-1 | Pretrial Activities

from the arresting officer or from the victim. If probable cause is not found, the suspect is released. As with a first appearance, a probable cause hearing should take place within 48 hours.

In 1991, in a class-action suit titled *County of Riverside* v. *McLaughlin,*[5] the U.S. Supreme Court imposed a promptness requirement on probable cause determinations for in-custody arrestees. The Court held that "a jurisdiction that provides judicial determinations of probable cause within 48 hours of arrest will, as a general matter, comply with the promptness requirement." The Court specified, however, that weekends and holidays could not be excluded from the 48-hour requirement (as they had been in Riverside County, California) and that, depending on the specifics of the case, delays of fewer than two days may still be unreasonable.

During a first appearance, the suspect is not given an opportunity to present evidence, although the U.S. Supreme Court has held that defendants are entitled to representation by counsel at their first appearance[6] and that an indigent person is entitled to have an attorney appointed for him or her at the initial appearance.[7] Following a reading of the charges and an advisement of rights, counsel may be appointed to represent indigent defendants and proceedings may be adjourned until counsel can be obtained. In cases where a suspect is unruly, intoxicated, or uncooperative, a judicial review may take place without the suspect's presence.

Some states waive a first appearance and proceed directly to arraignment (discussed later), especially when the defendant has been arrested on a warrant. In states that move directly to arraignment, the procedures undertaken to obtain a warrant are regarded as sufficient to demonstrate a basis for detention before arraignment.

■ **pretrial release** The release of an accused person from custody, for all or part of the time before or during prosecution, on his or her promise to appear in court when required.

■ **bail bond** A document guaranteeing the appearance of a defendant in court as required and recording the pledge of money or property to be paid to the court if he or she does not appear, which is signed by the person to be released and anyone else acting on his or her behalf.

AP Wide World Photos

A bail hearing in progress. Standing before the judge are Julie Barnes and Thomas Levesque, a homeless pair accused of accidentally starting a warehouse blaze that led to the deaths of six Worcester, Massachusetts, firefighters. Levesque's bail was set at $250,000 cash, or $2.5 million with surety; Barnes's bail was set at $75,000 cash, or $750,000 with surety. In 2002, the two agreed to a plea agreement, and each was sentenced to five years of probation for involuntary manslaughter. What purpose does bail serve?

Pretrial Release

A significant aspect of the first appearance hearing is the consideration of **pretrial release**. Defendants charged with very serious crimes, or those who are thought likely to escape or to injure others, are usually held in jail until trial. Such a practice is called *pretrial detention*. Most defendants, however, are afforded the opportunity for release. Many jurisdictions make use of pretrial service programs, which may also be called *early-intervention programs*.[8] Such programs, which are typically funded by the states or by individual counties, perform two critical functions: (1) They gather and present information about newly arrested defendants and about available release options for use by judicial officers in deciding what (if any) conditions are to be set for the defendants' release prior to trial, and (2) they supervise defendants who are released from custody during the pretrial period by monitoring their compliance with release conditions and by helping ensure that they appear for scheduled court events. Learn more about pretrial services at **http://www.justicestudies.com/pubs/pretrial.pdf**.

The initial pretrial release–detention decision is usually made by a judicial officer or by a specially appointed hearing officer who considers background information provided by the pretrial service program, along with the representations made by the prosecutor and the defense attorney. In making this decision, judicial officers are concerned about two types of risk: (1) the risk of flight or nonappearance for scheduled court appearances and (2) the risk to public safety.

Bail

Bail is the most common release–detention decision-making mechanism in American courts. Bail serves two purposes: (1) It helps ensure reappearance of the accused, and (2) it prevents unconvicted individuals from suffering imprisonment unnecessarily.

Bail involves the posting of a bond as a pledge that the accused will return for further hearings. **Bail bonds** usually involve cash deposits but may be based on property or other valuables. A fully secured bond requires the defendant to post the full amount of bail set by the court. The usual practice, however, is for a defendant to seek privately secured bail through the services of a professional bail agent. The agent will assess a percentage (usually 10% to 15%) of the required bond as a fee, which the defendant will have to pay up front. Those who "skip bail" by hiding or fleeing will sometimes be ordered by the court to forfeit their bail. Forfeiture hearings must be held before a bond can be taken, and most courts will not order bail forfeited unless it appears that the defendant intends to avoid prosecution permanently. Bail forfeiture will often be reversed if the defendant later appears willingly to stand trial.

In many states, bail bond agents are empowered to hunt down and bring back defendants who have fled. In some jurisdictions, bail bond agents hold virtually unlimited powers and have been permitted by courts to pursue, arrest, and forcibly extradite their charges from foreign jurisdictions without concern for the due process considerations or statutory limitations that apply to law enforcement officers.[9] Recently, however, some states have enacted laws that eliminate for-profit bail bond businesses, replacing them instead with state-operated pretrial service agencies. Visit the Professional Bail Agents of the United States via **http://www.pbus.com** to learn more about the job of bail bond agents and to view the group's code of ethics.

In many states, bail bond agents are empowered to hunt down and bring back defendants who have fled.

■ **release on recognizance (ROR)** The pretrial release of a criminal defendant on his or her written promise to appear in court as required. No cash or property bond is required.

■ **property bond** The setting of bail in the form of land, houses, stocks, or other tangible property. In the event that the defendant absconds prior to trial, the bond becomes the property of the court.

A typical bail bond office. Bail bond offices like this one are usually found near courthouses where criminal trials are held. Should all criminal suspects be afforded bail? Why or why not?

Alternatives to Bail

The Eighth Amendment to the U.S. Constitution does not guarantee the opportunity for bail but does state that "[e]xcessive bail shall not be required." Some studies, however, have found that many defendants who are offered the opportunity for bail are unable to raise the money. Thirty years ago, a report by the National Advisory Commission on Criminal Justice Standards and Goals found that as many as 93% of felony defendants in some jurisdictions were unable to make bail.[10]

To extend the opportunity for pretrial release to a greater number of nondangerous arrestees, many states and the federal government now offer various alternatives to the cash bond system, such as (1) release on recognizance, (2) property bond, (3) deposit bail, (4) conditional release, (5) third-party custody, (6) unsecured bond, and (7) signature bond.

Release on Recognizance (ROR) **Release on recognizance (ROR)** involves no cash bond, requiring as a guarantee only that the defendant agree in writing to return for further hearings as specified by the court. Release on recognizance was tested during the 1960s in a social experiment called the Manhattan Bail Project.[11] In the experiment, those arrested for serious crimes, including murder, rape, and robbery, and those with extensive prior criminal records were excluded from participating in the project. The rest of the defendants were scored and categorized according to a number of "ideal" criteria used as indicators of both dangerousness and the likelihood of pretrial flight. Criteria included (1) no previous convictions, (2) residential stability, and (3) a good employment record. Those likely to flee were not released.

Studies of the bail project revealed that it released four times as many defendants before trial as had been freed under the traditional cash bond system,[12] and that only 1% of those released fled from prosecution—the same percentage as for those set free on cash bond.[13] Later studies, however, were unclear as to the effectiveness of release on recognizance, with some finding a no-show rate as high as 12%.[14]

Property Bond **Property bonds** substitute other items of value in place of cash. Land, houses, automobiles, stocks, and so on may be consigned to the court as collateral against pretrial flight.

Deposit Bail Deposit bail is an alternative form of cash bond available in some jurisdictions. Deposit bail places the court in the role of the bail bond agent, allowing the defendant to post a percentage of the full bail with the court. Unlike private bail bond agents, court-run deposit bail programs usually return the amount of the deposit except for a small administrative fee (perhaps 1%). If the defendant fails to appear for court, the entire amount of court-ordered bail is forfeited.

■ **conditional release** The release by executive decision of a prisoner from a federal or state correctional facility who has not served his or her full sentence and whose freedom is contingent on obeying specified rules of behavior.

■ **danger law** A law intended to prevent the pretrial release of criminal defendants judged to represent a danger to others in the community.

Conditional Release **Conditional release** imposes requirements on the defendant, such as participating in a drug-treatment program; staying away from specified others, such as potential witnesses; and working at a regular job. *Release under supervision* is similar to conditional release but adds the stipulation that defendants report to an officer of the court or to a police officer at designated times.

Third-Party Custody Third-party custody is a bail bond alternative that assigns custody of the defendant to an individual or agency promising to ensure his or her later appearance in court.[15] Some pretrial release programs allow attorneys to assume responsibility for their clients in this fashion. If a defendant fails to appear, the attorney's privilege to participate in the program may be ended.

Unsecured Bonds An unsecured bond is based on a court-determined dollar amount of bail. Like a credit contract, it requires no monetary deposit with the court. The defendant agrees in writing that failure to appear will result in forfeiture of the entire amount of the bond, which might then be taken in the seizure of land, personal property, bank accounts, and so on.

Signature Bonds Signature bonds allow release based on the defendant's written promise to appear. Signature bonds involve no particular assessment of the defendant's dangerousness or likelihood of later appearance in court. They are used only in cases of minor offenses like traffic-law violations and some petty drug-law violations. Signature bonds may be issued by the arresting officer acting on behalf of the court.

Jim Ruymen/CORBIS-NY

Bounty hunter Duane "Dog" Chapman, owner of Bounty Hunter International, calls himself the "greatest bounty hunter in the world." Bounty hunters collect fees from bail bond agents, who otherwise stand to forfeit money they have posted for clients who do not appear in court. Chapman, an ex-con born-again Christian, makes a living pursuing felons who fail to appear for their court dates after posting bail through a bail bond agent. He has more than 6,000 captures to his credit. Read more about him at http://www.dogthebountyhunter.com. Would you want to be a bounty hunter?

Pretrial Release and Public Safety

Pretrial release is common practice. Approximately 57% of all state-level felony criminal defendants[16] and 66% of all federal felony defendants[17] are released before trial. At the state level, 43% percent of all defendants are detained until the court disposes of their case. Murder defendants (88%) are the most likely to be detained. A majority of defendants charged with motor vehicle theft (61%), robbery (58%), or burglary (54%) are also detained until case disposition. Defendants on parole (83%) are more likely to be detained.

A growing movement, arguing that defendants released before trial may be dangerous to themselves or to others, seeks to reduce the number of defendants released under any conditions. Advocates of this conservative policy cite a number of studies documenting crimes committed by defendants released on bond. One study found that 16% of defendants released before trial were rearrested; of those, 30% were arrested more than once.[18] Another study determined that as many as 41% of those released before trial for serious crimes, such as rape and robbery, were rearrested before their trial date.[19] Not surprisingly, such studies generally find that the longer the time spent free on bail prior to trial, the greater the likelihood of misconduct.

In response to findings like these, some states have enacted **danger laws**, which limit the right to bail to certain kinds of offenders.[20] Other states, including Arizona, California, Colorado, Florida, and Illinois, have approved constitutional amendments restricting the use of bail.[21] Most such provisions exclude defendants charged with certain crimes from being eligible for bail and demand that other defendants being considered for bail meet stringent conditions. Some states combine these strictures with tough release conditions designed to keep close control over defendants before trial.

The 1984 federal Bail Reform Act allows federal judges to assess the danger of an accused to the community and to deny bail to defendants who are thought to be dangerous. In the words of the act, a suspect held in pretrial custody on federal criminal charges must be detained if "after a hearing . . . he is found to pose a risk of flight and a danger to others or the community and if no condition of release can give reasonable assurances against these contingencies."[22] Defendants seeking bail must demonstrate a high likelihood of later court appearance. The act also requires that a defendant have a speedy first appearance and, if he or she is to be detained, that a *detention hearing* be held together with the initial appearance.

In the 1990 case of *U.S.* v. *Montalvo-Murillo,*[23] however, a defendant who was not provided with a detention hearing at the time of his first appearance and was subsequently released by an appeals court was found to have no "right" to freedom because of this "minor" statutory violation. The Supreme Court held that "unless it has a substantial influence on the outcome of the proceedings . . . failure to comply with the Act's prompt hearing provision does not require release of a person who should otherwise be detained" because "[a]utomatic release contravenes the statutory purpose of providing fair bail procedures while protecting the public's safety and assuring a defendant's appearance at trial."[24]

Court challenges to the constitutionality of pretrial detention legislation have not met with much success. The U.S. Supreme Court case of *U.S.* v. *Hazzard* (1984),[25] decided only a few months after enactment of federal bail reform, held that Congress was justified in providing for denial of bail to offenders who represent a danger to the community. Later cases have supported the presumption of flight, which federal law presupposes for certain types of defendants.[26]

The Grand Jury

The federal government and about half of the states use grand juries as part of the pretrial process. Grand juries comprise private citizens (often 23 in number) who hear evidence presented by the prosecution. Grand juries serve primarily as filters to eliminate cases for which there is not sufficient evidence for further processing.

In early times, grand juries served a far different purpose. The grand jury system began in England in 1166 as a way of identifying law violators. Lacking a law enforcement agency with investigative authority, the government looked to the grand jury as a source of information on criminal activity in the community. Even today, grand juries in most jurisdictions may initiate prosecution independently of the prosecutor, although they rarely do.

Grand jury hearings are held in secret, and the defendant is generally not afforded the opportunity to appear.[27] Similarly, the defense has no opportunity to cross-examine prosecution witnesses. Grand juries have the power to subpoena witnesses and to mandate a review of books, records, and other documents crucial to their investigation.

After hearing the evidence, the grand jury votes on the indictment presented to it by the prosecution. The indictment is a formal listing of proposed charges. If the majority of grand jury

Archives du 7eme Art/Alamy

A grand jury in action. Grand jury proceedings are generally very informal, as this picture shows. What is the grand jury's job?

■ **competent to stand trial** A finding by a court that the defendant has sufficient present ability to consult with his or her attorney with a reasonable degree of rational understanding and that the defendant has a rational as well as factual understanding of the proceedings against him or her.

■ **plea** In criminal proceedings, the defendant's formal answer in court to the charge contained in a complaint, information, or indictment that he or she is guilty of the offense charged, is not guilty of the offense charged, or does not contest the charge.

■ ***nolo contendere*** A plea of "no contest." A no-contest plea is used when the defendant does not wish to contest conviction. Because the plea does not admit guilt, however, it cannot provide the basis for later civil suits that might follow a criminal conviction.

members agree to forward the indictment to the trial court, it becomes a "true bill" on which further prosecution will turn.

The Preliminary Hearing

States that do not use grand juries rely instead on a preliminary hearing "for charging defendants in a fashion that is less cumbersome and arguably more protective of the innocent."[28] In these jurisdictions, the prosecutor files an accusatory document called an *information*, or complaint, against the accused. A preliminary hearing is then held to determine whether there is probable cause to hold the defendant for trial. A few states, notably Tennessee and Georgia, use both the grand jury mechanism and a preliminary hearing as a "double check against the possibility of unwarranted prosecution."[29]

Although the preliminary hearing is not nearly as elaborate as a criminal trial, it has many of the same characteristics. The defendant is taken before a lower-court judge who summarizes the charges and reviews the rights to which all criminal defendants are entitled. The prosecution may present witnesses and will offer evidence in support of the complaint. The defendant is afforded the right to testify and may also call witnesses.

The primary purpose of the preliminary hearing is to give the defendant an opportunity to challenge the legal basis for his or her detention. At this point, defendants who appear to be or claim to be mentally incompetent may be ordered to undergo further evaluation to determine whether they are **competent to stand trial**. Competence to stand trial, which was briefly discussed in Chapter 4, may become an issue when a defendant appears to be incapable of understanding the proceedings or is unable to assist in his or her own defense due to mental disease or defect.

In 2003, the U.S. Supreme Court placed strict limits on the government's power to forcibly medicate some mentally ill defendants to make them competent to stand trial.[30] In the case of *Sell* v. *U.S.*,[31] the Court ruled that the use of antipsychotic drugs on a nonviolent pretrial defendant who does not represent a danger while institutionalized must be in the defendant's best medical interest and must be "substantially unlikely" to cause side effects that might compromise the fairness of the trial.

Barring a finding of mental incompetence, all that is required for the wheels of justice to move forward is a demonstration "sufficient to justify a prudent man's belief that the suspect has committed or was committing an offense" within the jurisdiction of the court.[32] If the magistrate finds enough evidence to justify a trial, the defendant is bound over to the grand jury. In states that do not require grand jury review, the defendant is sent directly to the trial court. If the complaint against the defendant cannot be substantiated, he or she is released. A release is not a bar to further prosecution, however, and the defendant may be rearrested if further evidence comes to light.

Arraignment and the Plea

Once an indictment has been returned or an information has been filed, the accused will be formally arraigned. Arraignment is "the first appearance of the defendant before the court that has the authority to conduct a trial."[33] Arraignment is generally a brief process with two purposes: (1) to once again inform the defendant of the specific charges against him or her and (2) to allow the defendant to enter a **plea**. The Federal Rules of Criminal Procedure allow for one of three types of pleas to be entered: guilty, not guilty, and *nolo contendere*. A ***nolo contendere*** (no-contest) plea is much the same as a guilty plea. A defendant who pleads "no contest" is immediately convicted and may be sentenced just as though he or she had pleaded guilty. A no-contest plea, however, is not an admission of guilt and provides one major advantage to defendants: It may not be used later as a basis for civil proceedings that seek monetary or other damages against the defendant.

Some defendants refuse to enter any plea and are said to "stand mute." Standing mute is a defense strategy that is rarely employed. Defendants who choose this alternative simply do not answer the request for a plea. However, for procedural purposes, a defendant who stands mute is considered to have entered a plea of not guilty.

Plea Bargaining

In 2012, 53-yerar-old Kenneth Kassab, of Marquette, Michigan, was on the verge of pleading guilty to federal charges of illegally transporting thousands of pounds of explosives, but changed his mind at the last minute and decided to go to trial.[34] Kassab, who always maintained his innocence, was arrested after his employer had ordered him to use a truck to move a large number of 50-pound bags of fertilizer similar to those that had been used in the 1995 bombing of the Alfred P. Murrah federal building in Oklahoma City, Oklahoma. Kassab had thought of accepting

■ **plea bargaining** The process of negotiating an agreement among the defendant, the prosecutor, and the court as to an appropriate plea and associated sentence in a given case. Plea bargaining circumvents the trial process and dramatically reduces the time required for the resolution of a criminal case.

CJ | ISSUES

Nonjudicial Pretrial Release Decisions

In most American jurisdictions, judicial officers decide whether an arrested person will be detained or released. Some jurisdictions, however, allow others to make that decision. Some observers argue that the critical issue is not whether the decision maker is a judge, but whether there are clear and appropriate criteria for making the decision, whether the decision maker has adequate information, and whether he or she has been well trained in pretrial release–detention decision making.

Nonjudicial decision makers and release–detention mechanisms include the following:

- *Police officers and desk appearance tickets.* Desk appearance tickets, or citations, are summonses given to defendants at the police station, usually for petty offenses or misdemeanor charges. The tickets can greatly reduce the use of pretrial detention and can save the court system a great deal of time by avoiding initial pretrial release or bail hearings in minor cases. However, because they are typically based only on the current charge (and sometimes on a computer search to check for outstanding warrants), high-risk defendants could be released without supervision or monitoring. As computerized access to criminal history information becomes more readily available, enabling rapid identification of individuals with prior records who pose a risk to the community, desk appearance tickets may be more widely used.
- *Jail administrators.* In many jurisdictions, jail officials have the authority to release (or to refuse to book into jail) arrestees who meet certain criteria. In some localities, jail officials exercise this authority pursuant to a court order that specifies priorities with respect to the categories of defendants who can be admitted to the jail and those who are to be released when the jail population exceeds a court-imposed ceiling. The "automatic release" approach helps minimize jail crowding, but it does so at the risk of releasing some defendants who pose a high risk of becoming fugitives or committing criminal acts. To help minimize these risks, some sheriffs and jail administrators have developed their own pretrial services or "release on recognizance" units with staff who conduct risk assessments based on interviews with arrestees, information from references, and criminal history checks.
- *Bail schedules.* These predetermined schedules set levels of bail (from release on recognizance to amounts of surety bond) based solely on the offense charged. Depending on local practices, release pursuant to a bail schedule may take place at a police station, at the local jail, or at court. This practice saves time for judicial officers and allows rapid release of defendants who can afford to post the bail amount. However, release determinations based solely on the current charge are of dubious value because there is no proven relationship between a particular charge and risk of flight or subsequent crime. Release pursuant to a bail schedule depends simply on the defendant's ability to post the amount of the bond. Moreover, when a defendant is released by posting bond, there is generally no procedure for supervision to minimize the risks of nonappearance and subsequent crime.
- *Bail bond agents.* When a judicial officer sets the amount of bond that a defendant must produce to be released, or when bond is set mechanically on the basis of a bail schedule, the real decision makers are often the surety bail bond agents. If no bail bond agent will offer bond, the defendant without other sources of money will remain in jail. The defendant's ability to pay a bail bond agent the 10% fee (and sometimes to post collateral) bears no relationship to his or her risk of flight or danger to the community.
- *Pretrial service agencies.* In some jurisdictions, pretrial service agencies have the authority to release certain categories of defendants. The authority is usually limited to relatively minor cases, although agencies in a few jurisdictions can release some categories of felony defendants. Because the pretrial service agency can obtain information about the defendant's prior record, community ties, and other pending charges, its decision to release or detain is based on more extensive information and criteria than when the decision is based on a bail schedule. However, because these programs lack the independence that judicial officers are allowed, they are susceptible to political and public pressure.

Reference: Adapted from Barry Mahoney et al., *Pretrial Services Programs: Responsibilities and Potential* (Washington, DC: National Institute of Justice, 2001).

a plea deal offered by prosecutors in order to avoid what might have been a lengthy prison sentence—which a judge could have imposed had he been convicted at trial. Instead, a week after deciding to reject the plea arrangement, a federal jury found him not guilty and he was set free. Kassab's case is unusual because 97% of all federal criminal defendants agree to plead guilty rather than going to trial—a significant increase from the 84% who made that choice in 1990.[35]

Guilty pleas are often not straightforward and are typically arrived at only after complex negotiations known as *plea bargaining*. **Plea bargaining** is a process of negotiation that usually involves the defendant, the prosecutor, and the defense counsel. It is founded on the mutual interests of all involved. Defense attorneys and their clients will agree to a plea of guilty when they are unsure of their ability to win acquittal at trial. Prosecutors may be willing to bargain because the evidence they have against the defendant is weaker than they would like it to be. Plea bargaining offers prosecutors the additional advantage of a quick conviction without the need to commit the time and resources necessary for trial. Benefits to the accused include the possibility of reduced or combined charges, lower defense costs, and a shorter sentence than might otherwise be anticipated.

The U.S. Supreme Court has held that a guilty plea constitutes conviction.[36] To validate the conviction, negotiated pleas require judicial consent. Judges often accept pleas that are the result of a bargaining process because such pleas reduce the court's workload. Although few judges are willing to guarantee a sentence before a plea is entered, most prosecutors and criminal trial lawyers know what sentences to expect from typical pleas.

Bargained pleas are commonplace in both federal and state courts. Surveys have found that 94% of state criminal cases are eventually resolved through a negotiated plea.[37] In a study of 37 big-city prosecutors, the Bureau of Justice Statistics found that for every 100 adults arrested on a felony charge, half were eventually convicted of either a felony or a misdemeanor.[38] Of all convictions, fully 94% were the result of a plea. Only 6% of convictions were the result of a criminal trial. After a guilty plea has been entered, it may be withdrawn with the consent of the court.

Some Supreme Court decisions, however, have enhanced the prosecutor's authority in the bargaining process by declaring that defendants cannot capriciously withdraw negotiated pleas.[39] Other rulings have supported discretionary actions by prosecutors in which sentencing recommendations were retracted even after bargains had been struck.[40] Some lower-court cases have upheld the government's authority to withdraw from a negotiated plea when the defendant fails to live up to certain conditions.[41] Conditions may include requiring the defendant to provide information on other criminals, criminal cartels, and smuggling activities.

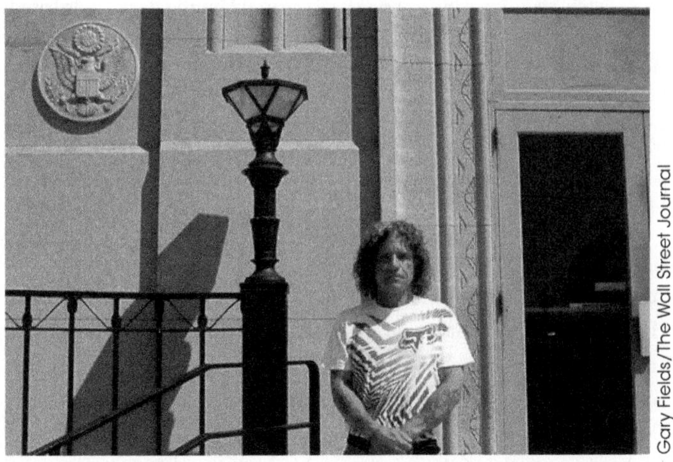

Gary Fields/The Wall Street Journal

Kenneth Kassab, the Michigan man who refused to accept a plea bargain offered by federal prosecutors in 2012 after he had been arrested and charged with illegally transporting explosives. Kassab was later acquitted at trial. Why was he initially tempted to plead guilty?

In 2012, in two decisions that expanded the authority of judges in the plea bargaining process, the U.S. Supreme Court held that the Sixth Amendment right to effective assistance of counsel applies to all critical states of criminal proceedings, including that of plea bargaining.[42] The Court also held that, "as a general rule, defense counsel has the duty to communicate formal prosecution offers to accept a plea on terms and conditions that may be favorable to the accused." Failure to communicate such offers to the defendant may be the basis for later appeal, but only where the defendant can demonstrate a reasonable probability that those offers would have been accepted and that the plea would have been entered without the prosecution's canceling it, or the trial court's refusing to accept it.

Although it is generally agreed that bargained pleas should relate in some way to the original charge, they are not always related. Entered pleas may be chosen for the punishments likely to be associated with them rather than for their accuracy in describing the criminal offense in which the defendant was involved.[43] This is especially true when the defendant wants to minimize the socially stigmatizing impact of the offense. A charge of indecent liberties, for example, in which the defendant is accused of sexual misconduct, may be pleaded out as assault. Such a plea, which takes advantage of the fact that indecent liberties can be considered a form of sexual assault, would effectively disguise the true nature of the offense.

Even though the Supreme Court has endorsed plea bargaining and protected suspects' rights during the process, the public sometimes views it suspiciously. Law-and-order advocates, who generally favor harsh punishments and long jail terms, claim that plea bargaining results in unjustifiably light sentences. As a consequence, prosecutors, almost all of whom regularly engage in the practice, rarely advertise it. Plea bargaining can be a powerful prosecutorial tool, but this power carries with it the potential for misuse. Because they circumvent the trial process, plea bargains can be abused by prosecutors and defense attorneys who are more interested in the speedy resolution of cases than they are in seeing justice done. Carried to the extreme, plea bargaining may result in defendants being convicted of crimes they did not commit. Although it is rare, innocent defendants (especially those with prior criminal records) who think a jury will convict them—for whatever reason—may plead guilty to reduced charges to avoid a trial. In an effort to protect defendants against hastily arranged pleas, the Federal Rules of

Even though the Supreme Court has endorsed plea bargaining and protected suspects' rights during the process, the public sometimes views it suspiciously.

paying for it

Cost-Efficient Courts

In 2013, California Supreme Court Chief Justice Tani Cantil-Sakauye reportedly remarked, "I hear people on television all the time saying, 'We'll have our day in court;' and I nudge my husband and say, 'Don't they know there aren't any courts anymore?'" Cantil-Sakauye's tongue-in-cheek remarks were a reaction to severe state budget cuts that have drastically reduced the number of courtrooms and court resources throughout the cash-strapped state. By the end of 2012, California's Judicial Council, the policymaking body of the California court system, had already shuttered 60 courtrooms in Los Angeles County alone, and was planning to close ten more courthouses, lay off additional courtroom staff, and halt construction on all new courts in ten of the state's counties. In 2013, the Council withdrew its proposal to create 50 new judgeships due to the state's failure to fund positions that had previously been recommended. The Council estimates that 264 additional judges are needed to effectively handle growing caseloads throughout the state.

One significant casualty of budget cuts was the California Case Management System (CCMS), a paperless computerized network that was once touted to potentially increase the efficiency of courts throughout the state by linking them electronically. The CCMS, which would have made court records easily available to judicial personnel throughout the state's court system, was opposed by court workers and unions due to their belief that jobs would be lost through automation. Estimates are that around half a billion dollars had been spent developing the system, and that it's full implementation would have cost the state an additional $120 million over the next two years.

Even Judge Lance Ito, the famous jurist who presided over O. J. Simpson's California murder trial in the 1990s, now finds himself shuttling between judicial chambers where much of the furniture has been stripped away and the heat is off to save money. Ito, who faces retirement in a few years, and whose former courtroom was closed because of cutbacks, observes: "This has been a slow-motion train wreck since 2008. . . . I have no staff, no bailiff, no court reporter and I have to persuade friendly clerks to enter minute orders."

Fortunately, not all states have had to cut back on court funding to the same degree as California. And even in that state, progress is being made to restore fiscal liquidity. In the late fall of 2012, for example, California's voters approved Proposition 30, increasing the state's sales tax and hiking income taxes on those earning over $250,000. That money has not yet made its way into state coffers, however, and in an effort to cover shortfalls in the state's judicial budget, Governor Jerry Brown announced an austerity plan for state courts that was scheduled to take effect in 2014. Many of the governor's proposals called for a doubling of court fees, including charging one dollar per page for every copy of a court record distributed to the public or to attorneys (the current rate is 50 cents per page). Other planned savings would accrue from not destroying dated public records or records relating to marijuana possession, and providing transcripts of preliminary hearings only in homicide cases.

Another effort to raise money for the state is a one-time amnesty program for persons who have failed to pay motor vehicle fines. The program permits violators to voluntarily pay 50% of unpaid fines that were imposed prior to January 1, 2009, in lieu of the full amount, without risking contempt-of-court citations or other criminal penalties. Other suggestions to raise money have included allowing a percentage of all criminal fines imposed to be used for court administration, and allowing a greater percentage of delinquent fines for criminal infractions to go to the courts. Estimates show that about $7.5 billion in delinquent court-ordered debt remains unpaid. One member of California's Administrative Office of the Courts notes that "if courts were receiving the money directly, they may have more of an incentive to collect." Critics fear, however, that such a move would only encourage judges to impose stiff fines more frequently than they have in the past.

References: California Vehicle Code, Section 42008.7, Infractions: One-Time Amnesty Program, http://www.dmv.ca.gov/pubs/vctop/d18/vc42008_7.htm (accessed March 3, 2013); Kendall Taggart, "Billions in Court-Ordered Debt Goes Uncollected," California Watch, June 5, http://californiawatch.org/dailyreport/billions-court-ordered-debt-goes-uncollected-16459 (accessed March 3, 2013); "California Judicial Council Halts Court Case Management System," *The Sacramento Bee*, http://blogs.sacbee.com/capitolalertlatest/2012/03/california-judicial-council-halts-controversial-court-case-management-system.html (accessed March 6, 2013); "Brown Looks to Fee Hikes to Fund Courts," *The Los Angeles Times*, January 15, 2013, http://latimesblogs.latimes.com/california-politics/2013/01/brown-looks-to-fee-hikes-to-fund-courts.html (accessed March 16, 2013); "State's Judicial Council Puts New Courthouses on Ice," *The Los Angeles Times*, http://latimesblogs.latimes.com/california-politics/2013/01/council-puts-new-courthouses-on-ice.html (accessed March 5, 2013); and "Judges Say Courts under Siege from Budget Cuts," Associated Press, January 20, 2013, http://www.appeal-democrat.com/news/judges-122737-say-angeles.html (accessed March 5, 2013).

Criminal Procedure require judges to (1) inform the defendant of the various rights he or she is surrendering by pleading guilty, (2) determine that the plea is voluntary, (3) require disclosure of any plea agreements, and (4) make sufficient inquiry to ensure there is a factual basis for the plea.[44]

The Criminal Trial

From arrest through sentencing, the criminal justice process is carefully choreographed. Arresting officers must follow proper procedure when gathering evidence and arresting and

■ **rules of evidence** Court rules that govern the admissibility of evidence at criminal hearings and trials.

■ **adversarial system** The two-sided structure under which American criminal trial courts operate. The adversarial system pits the prosecution against the defense. In theory, justice is done when the most effective adversary is able to convince the judge or jury that his or her perspective on the case is the correct one.

questioning suspects. Magistrates, prosecutors, jailers, and prison officials are all subject to their own strictures. Nowhere, however, is the criminal justice process more closely circumscribed than it is at the criminal trial.

Procedures in a modern courtroom are highly formalized. **Rules of evidence**, which govern the admissibility of evidence, and other procedural guidelines determine the course of a criminal hearing and trial. Although rules of evidence are partially based on tradition, all U.S. jurisdictions have formalized, written rules of evidence. Criminal trials at the federal level generally adhere to the requirements of the Federal Rules of Evidence.

Trials are also circumscribed by informal rules and professional expectations. An important component of law school education is the teaching of rules that structure and define appropriate courtroom demeanor. In addition to statutory rules, law students are thoroughly exposed to the ethical standards of their profession, as found in the American Bar Association standards and other writings.

Nature and Purpose of the Criminal Trial

In the remainder of this chapter, we will describe the chronology of a criminal trial and will explore some of the widely accepted rules of criminal procedure. Before we begin, however, it is good to keep two points in mind. One is that the primary purpose of any criminal trial is the determination of the defendant's guilt or innocence. In this regard, it is important to recognize the crucial distinction that scholars make between factual guilt and legal guilt. Factual guilt deals with the issue of whether the defendant is actually responsible for the crime of which he or she stands accused. If the defendant did it, then he or she is, in fact, guilty. Legal guilt is not as clear. Legal guilt is established only when the prosecutor presents sufficient evidence to convince the judge (where the judge determines the verdict) or the jury that the defendant is guilty as charged. The distinction between factual guilt and legal guilt is crucial because it points to the fact that the burden of proof rests with the prosecution, and it indicates the possibility that guilty defendants may nonetheless be found "not guilty."

The second point to remember is that criminal trials under our system of justice are built around an **adversarial system** and that central to this system is the advocacy model. Participating in the adversarial system are advocates for the state (the prosecutor or the district attorney) and for the defendant (the defense counsel, the public defender, and so on). The philosophy behind the adversarial system is that the greatest number of just resolutions in criminal trials will occur when both sides are allowed to argue their cases effectively and vociferously before a fair and impartial jury. The system requires that advocates for both sides do their utmost, within the boundaries set by law and professional ethics, to protect and advance the interests of their clients (that is, the defendant and the state). The advocacy model makes clear that it is not the job of the defense attorney or the prosecution to decide the guilt of any defendant. Hence, even defense attorneys who are convinced that their clients are guilty are still exhorted to offer the best possible defense and to counsel their clients as effectively as possible.

The adversarial system has been criticized by some thinkers who point to fundamental differences between law and science in the way the search for truth is conducted.[45] Whereas proponents of traditional legal procedure accept the belief that truth can best be uncovered through an adversarial process, scientists adhere to a painstaking process of research and replication to acquire knowledge. Most of us would agree that scientific advances in recent years may have made factual issues less difficult to ascertain. For example, some of the new scientific techniques in evidence analysis, such as DNA fingerprinting, can now unequivocally link a suspect to criminal activity or even show that someone who was once thought guilty is actually innocent. At least 328 convictions have been overturned using DNA evidence since 1989, when Gary Dotson of Illinois became the first person convicted of a crime to be exonerated through the use of such evidence.[46] According to Samuel Gross and colleagues at the University of Michigan Law School, who published a comprehensive study of exonerations in 2004, those 328 people "had spent more than 3400 years in prison for crimes for which they never should have been convicted."[47] Exonerations occur most frequently in cases where DNA evidence is relatively easy to acquire, such as rape and murder cases. False conviction rates for other crimes, such as robbery, are much more difficult to assess using DNA. Hence, says Gross, "the clearest and most important lesson from the recent spike in rape exonerations is that false convictions that come to light are the tip of the iceberg."[48]

At least 328 convictions have been overturned using DNA evidence since 1989.

Whether scientific findings should continue to serve a subservient role to the adversarial process is a question widely discussed. The answer will be determined by the results the

■ **Follow the author's tweets about the latest crime and justice news at @schmalleger.**

two processes are able to produce. If the adversarial model results in the acquittal of too many demonstrably guilty people because of legal "technicalities," or if the scientific approach identifies too many suspects inaccurately, either could be restricted.

Stages in a Criminal Trial

We turn now to a discussion of the steps in a criminal trial. As Figure 10-2 shows, trial chronology consists of eight stages:

1. Trial initiation
2. Jury selection
3. Opening statements
4. Presentation of evidence
5. Closing arguments
6. Judge's charge to the jury
7. Jury deliberations
8. Verdict

Jury deliberations and the verdict are discussed jointly. If the defendant is found guilty, a sentence is imposed by the judge at the conclusion of the trial. Sentencing is discussed in the next chapter.

Trial Initiation: The Speedy Trial Act

In 2005, a Louisiana state appeals court threw out murder charges against James Thomas and ordered him released. Thomas, an impoverished day laborer, had been arrested in 1996 and had spent eight and a half years in jail waiting for a trial that never came. The ruling by the appeals court was widely seen as an indictment of Louisiana's understaffed and underfunded public defender system; the public defenders had simply been too busy to work on Thomas's case. A private attorney managed to get Thomas set free after his mother scraped together $500 to pay his fee.

The U.S. Constitution contains a speedy trial provision in its Sixth Amendment.

The U.S. Constitution contains a speedy trial provision in its Sixth Amendment, which guarantees that "[i]n all criminal prosecutions, the accused shall enjoy the right to a speedy and public trial." Clogged court calendars, limited judicial resources, and general inefficiency, however, often combine to produce what appears to many to be unreasonable delays in trial initiation. The attention of the U.S. Supreme Court was brought to bear on trial delays in three precedent-setting cases: *Klopfer* v. *North Carolina* (1967),[49] *Barker* v. *Wingo* (1972),[50] and *Strunk* v. *U.S.* (1973).[51] The *Klopfer* case involved a Duke University professor who had engaged in civil disobedience to protest segregated facilities. In ruling on Klopfer's

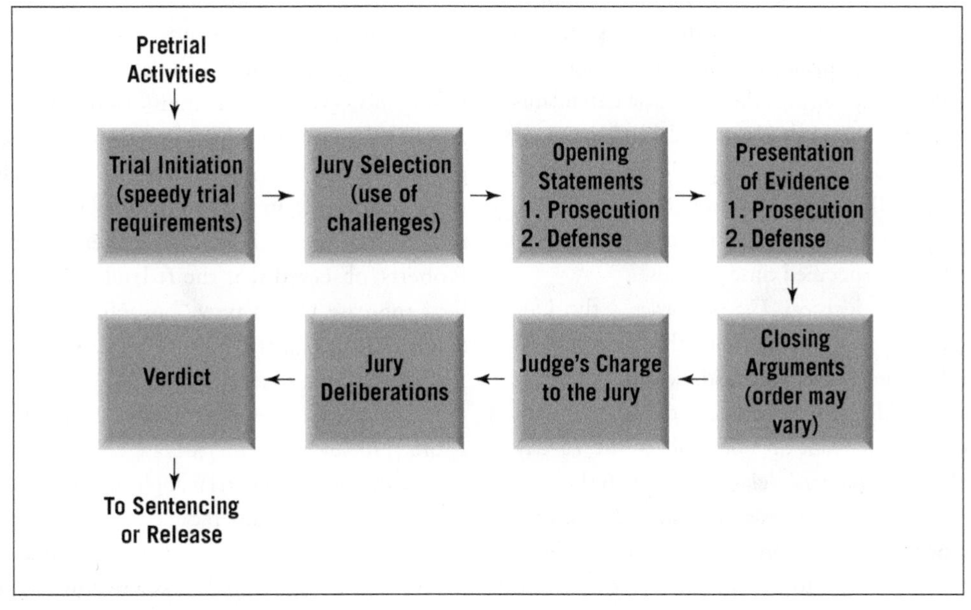

FIGURE 10-2 | Stages in a Criminal Trial

■ **Speedy Trial Act** A 1974 federal law requiring that proceedings against a defendant in a federal criminal case begin within a specified period of time, such as 70 working days after indictment. Some states also have speedy trial requirements.

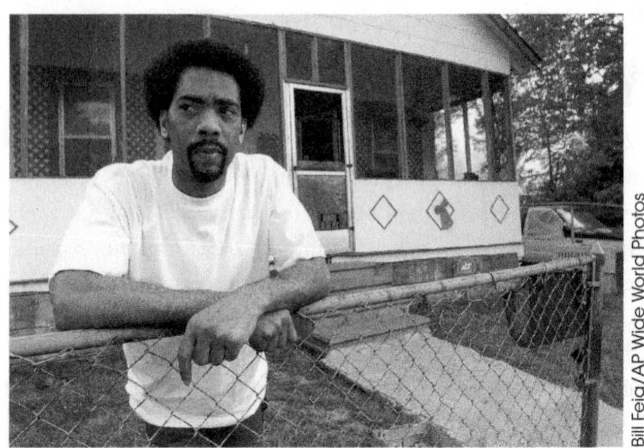
Bill Feig/AP Wide World Photos

James Thomas, who was charged with murder in 1996 and was freed in April 2005 after spending eight and a half years in a Louisiana jail waiting for his case to go to trial. A Louisiana state appeals court ruled that the state had taken too long to try him. Why does our system of justice require speedy trials?

long-delayed trial, the Court asserted that the right to a speedy trial is a fundamental guarantee of the Constitution. In the *Barker* case, the Court held that Sixth Amendment guarantees to a quick trial could be illegally violated even in cases where the accused did not explicitly object to delays. In *Strunk*, it found that the denial of a speedy trial should result in the dismissal of all charges.

In 1974, against the advice of the Justice Department, the U.S. Congress passed the federal **Speedy Trial Act**.[52] The act, which was phased in gradually and became fully effective in 1980, allows for the dismissal of federal criminal charges in cases in which the prosecution does not seek an indictment or information within 30 days of arrest (a 30-day extension is granted when the grand jury is not in session) or where a trial does not begin within 70 working days after indictment for defendants who plead "not guilty." If a defendant is not available for trial, or if witnesses cannot be called within the 70-day limit, the period may be extended up to 180 days. Delays brought about by the defendant, through requests for a continuance or because of escape, are not counted in the specified time periods.

In an important 1988 decision, *U.S.* v. *Taylor*,[53] the U.S. Supreme Court applied the requirements of the Speedy Trial Act to the case of a drug defendant who had escaped following arrest. The Court made it clear that trial delays that derive from the willful actions of the defendant do not apply to the 70-day period. The Court also held that trial delays, even when they result from government action, do not necessarily provide grounds for dismissal if they occur "without prejudice." Delays without prejudice are those that are due to circumstances beyond the control of criminal justice agencies.

In 1993, an Indiana prisoner, William Fex, appealed a Michigan conviction on armed robbery and attempted murder charges, claiming that he had to wait 196 days after submitting a request to Indiana prison authorities for his Michigan trial to commence. In *Fex* v. *Michigan* (1993),[54] the U.S. Supreme Court ruled that "common sense compel[s] the conclusion that the 180-day period does not commence until the prisoner's disposition request has actually been delivered to the court and prosecutor of the jurisdiction that lodged the detainer against him." In Fex's case, Indiana authorities had taken 22 days to forward his request to Michigan.

However, in a 1992 case, *Doggett* v. *U.S.*,[55] the Court held that a delay of eight and a half years violated speedy trial provisions because it resulted from government negligence. In *Doggett*, the defendant was indicted on a drug charge in 1980 but left the country for Panama, where he lived until 1982, when he reentered the United States. He lived openly in the United States until 1988, when a credit check revealed him to authorities. He was arrested, tried, and convicted of federal drug charges stemming from his 1980 indictment. In overturning his conviction, the U.S. Supreme Court ruled, "[E]ven delay occasioned by the Government's negligence creates prejudice that compounds over time, and at some point, as here, becomes intolerable."[56]

In 2006, the Court refused to hear an appeal by dirty bomb conspiracy suspect Jose Padilla, letting stand a lower court's decision that said the president could order a U.S. citizen who was arrested in this country for suspected ties to terrorism to be held indefinitely without charges and without going to trial.[57] Padilla, who was arrested in 2002, had been held for four years in a Navy brig without being charged with a crime. Shortly before Padilla's case was to come before the Court, however, he was transferred from military custody to a civilian jail, indicted on terrorism charges, and scheduled to go to trial—rendering his appeal moot. Although there was no official ruling in the case, Justice Anthony Kennedy, writing for himself, Justice John Paul Stevens, and Chief Justice John Roberts, observed that the federal district court scheduled to hear the case would now "be obliged to afford him the protection, including the right to a speedy trial, guaranteed to all federal criminal defendants."[58]

The federal Speedy Trial Act is applicable only to federal courts. However, the *Klopfer* case effectively made constitutional guarantees of a speedy trial applicable to state courts. In keeping with the trend toward reduced delays, many states have since enacted their own speedy trial legislation. Most state legislation sets a limit of 90 or 120 days as a reasonable period of time for a trial to commence.

■ **peremptory challenge** The right to challenge a potential juror without disclosing the reason for the challenge. Prosecutors and defense attorneys routinely use peremptory challenges to eliminate from juries individuals who, although they express no obvious bias, are thought to be capable of swaying the jury in an undesirable direction.

■ **jury selection** The process whereby, according to law and precedent, members of a trial jury are chosen.

■ **scientific jury selection** The use of correlational techniques from the social sciences to gauge the likelihood that potential jurors will vote for conviction or for acquittal.

Jury Selection

The Sixth Amendment guarantees the right to an impartial jury. An impartial jury is not necessarily an ignorant one. In other words, potential jurors will not always be excused from service on a jury if they have some knowledge of the case before them.[59] However, candidates who have already formed an opinion as to the guilt or innocence of the defendant are likely to be excused.

Some prospective jurors *try* to get excused, whereas others who would like to serve are excused because they are not judged to be suitable. Prosecution and defense attorneys use challenges to ensure the impartiality of the jury being impaneled. Three types of challenges are recognized in criminal courts: (1) challenges to the array, (2) challenges for cause, and (3) **peremptory challenges**.

Challenges to the array signify the belief, generally by the defense attorney, that the pool from which potential jurors are to be selected is not representative of the community or is biased in some significant way. A challenge to the array is argued before the hearing judge before **jury selection** begins.

During jury selection, both prosecution and defense attorneys question potential jurors in a process known as *voir dire* examination. Jurors are expected to be unbiased and free of preconceived notions of guilt or innocence. Challenges for cause, which may arise during *voir dire* examination, make the claim that an individual juror cannot be fair or impartial. A special issue of juror objectivity that has concerned the U.S. Supreme Court is whether jurors with philosophical opposition to the death penalty should be excluded from juries whose decisions might result in the imposition of capital punishment. In the case of *Witherspoon* v. *Illinois* (1968),[60] the Court ruled that a juror opposed to the death penalty could be excluded from such juries if it were shown that (1) the juror would automatically vote against conviction without regard to the evidence or (2) the juror's philosophical orientation would prevent an objective consideration of the evidence. The *Witherspoon* case left a number of issues unresolved, among them the concern that it is difficult to demonstrate how a juror would automatically vote, a fact that might not even be known to the juror before trial begins.

Another area of concern that the Supreme Court has addressed involves the potential that jurors could be influenced by pretrial news stories. In 1991, for example, the Court decided the case of *Mu'Min* v. *Virginia*.[61] Dawud Majud Mu'Min was a Virginia inmate who was serving time for first-degree murder. While accompanying a work detail outside the prison, he committed another murder. At the ensuing trial, 8 of the 12 jurors who were seated admitted that they had heard or read something about the case, although none indicated that he or she had formed an opinion in advance as to Mu'Min's guilt or innocence. Following his conviction, Mu'Min appealed to the Supreme Court, claiming that his right to a fair trial had been denied due to pretrial publicity. The Court disagreed and upheld his conviction, citing the jurors' claim not to be biased.

The third kind of challenge, the peremptory challenge, allows attorneys to remove potential jurors without having to give a reason. Peremptory challenges, used by both the prosecution and the defense, are limited in number. Federal courts allow each side up to 20 peremptory challenges in capital cases and as few as 3 in minor criminal cases.[62] States vary as to the number of peremptory challenges they permit.

A developing field that seeks to take advantage of peremptory challenges is **scientific jury selection**. Scientific jury selection uses correlational techniques from the social sciences to gauge the likelihood that a potential juror will vote for conviction or acquittal. It makes predictions based on the economic, ethnic, and other personal and social characteristics of each member of the juror pool. Such techniques generally remove potential jurors who have any knowledge or opinions about the case to be tried. Also removed are people who have been trained in the law or in criminal justice. Anyone working for a criminal justice agency or anyone who has a family member working for such an agency or for a defense attorney will likely be dismissed through peremptory challenges on the chance that they may be biased in favor of one side or the other. Additionally, scientific jury selection techniques may result in the dismissal of highly educated or professionally successful individuals to eliminate the possibility of such individuals exercising undue control over jury deliberations.

Critics of the jury-selection process charge that the end result is a jury composed of people who are uneducated, uninformed, and generally inexperienced at making any type of well-considered decision. Some jurors may not understand the charges against the defendant or may not comprehend what is required for a finding of guilt or innocence. Likewise, some may not even possess the attention span needed to hear all the testimony that will be offered in a case. As a consequence, critics say, decisions rendered by such a jury may be based more on emotion than on findings of fact.

■ **sequestered jury** A jury that is isolated from the public during the course of a trial and throughout the deliberation process.

Another emerging technique is the use of "shadow juries" to assess the impact of a defense attorney's arguments. Shadow jurors are hired court observers who sit in the courtroom and listen to what both sides in a criminal trial have to say. They hear evidence as it is presented and listen as witnesses are examined and cross-examined. Unlike professional legal experts, shadow jurors are laypeople who are expected to give defense attorneys a feel for what the "real" jurors are thinking and feeling as a case progresses, allowing for ongoing modifications in defense strategy. After wrangling over jury selection has run its course, the jury is sworn in, and alternate jurors are selected. Alternates may be called to replace jurors taken ill or dismissed from the jury because they don't conform to the requirements of jury service once trial has begun. At this point, the judge will decide whether the jury is to be sequestered during the trial. Members of **sequestered juries** are not permitted to have contact with the public and are often housed in a motel or hotel until the trial ends. Anyone who attempts to contact a sequestered jury or to influence members of a nonsequestered jury may be held accountable for jury tampering. Following jury selection, the stage is set for opening arguments[63] to begin.[64]

Jury Selection and Race

Race alone cannot provide the basis for jury selection, and juries may not be intentionally selected for racial balance. As long ago as 1880, the U.S. Supreme Court held that "a statute barring blacks from service on grand or petit juries denied equal protection of the laws to a black man convicted of murder by an all-white jury."[65] Even so, peremptory challenges continued to be used to strike racial imbalance on juries. In 1965, for example, a black defendant in Alabama was convicted of rape by an all-white jury. The local prosecutor had used his peremptory challenges to exclude blacks from the jury. The case eventually reached the Supreme Court, where the conviction was upheld.[66] At that time, the Court refused to limit the practice of peremptory challenges, reasoning that to do so would place these challenges under the same judicial scrutiny as challenges for cause.

However, in the 1986 case of *Batson* v. *Kentucky*,[67] following what many claimed was widespread abuse of peremptory challenges by prosecution and defense alike, the Supreme Court was forced to overrule its earlier decision. Batson, an African American man, had been convicted of second-degree burglary and other offenses by an all-white jury. The prosecutor had used his peremptory challenges to remove all blacks from jury service at the trial. The Court agreed that the use of peremptory challenges for purposeful discrimination constitutes a violation of the defendant's right to an impartial jury.

The *Batson* decision laid out the requirements that defendants must prove when seeking to establish the discriminatory use of peremptory challenges. They include the need to prove that the defendant is a member of a recognized racial group that was intentionally excluded from the jury and the need to raise a reasonable suspicion that the prosecutor used peremptory challenges in a discriminatory manner. Justice Thurgood Marshall, writing a concurring opinion in *Batson*, presaged what was to come: "The inherent potential of peremptory challenges to destroy the jury process by permitting the exclusion of jurors on racial grounds should ideally lead the Court to ban them entirely from the criminal justice system."

A few years later, in *Ford* v. *Georgia* (1991),[68] the Court moved much closer to Justice Marshall's position when it remanded a case for a new trial because the prosecutor had misused peremptory challenges. The prosecutor had used nine of the ten peremptory challenges available under Georgia law to eliminate black prospective jurors. Following his conviction on charges of kidnapping, raping, and murdering a white woman, the African American defendant, James Ford, argued that the prosecutor had demonstrated a systematic racial bias in other cases as well as his own. Specifically, Ford argued that his Sixth Amendment right to an impartial jury had been violated by the prosecutor's racially based method of jury selection. His appeal to the Supreme Court claimed that "the exclusion of members of the black race in the jury when a black accused is being tried is done in order that the accused will receive excessive punishment if found guilty, or to inject racial prejudice into the fact finding process of the jury." Although the Court did not find a basis for such a Sixth Amendment claim, it did determine that the civil rights of the jurors themselves had been violated under the Fourteenth Amendment due to a pattern of discrimination based on race.

In another 1991 case, *Powers* v. *Ohio*,[69] the Court found in favor of a white defendant who claimed that his constitutional rights had been violated by the intentional exclusion of blacks from his jury through the use of peremptory challenges. In *Powers*, the Court held that "[a]lthough an individual juror does not have the right to sit on any particular petit jury, he or she does possess the right not to be excluded from one on account of race."

In *Edmonson* v. *Leesville Concrete Co., Inc.* (1991),[70] a civil case with significance for the criminal justice system, the Court held that peremptory challenges in *civil* suits were not acceptable if based on race. Justice Anthony Kennedy, writing for the majority, said that race-based juror exclusions are forbidden in civil lawsuits because jury selection is a "unique governmental function delegated to private litigants" in a public courtroom.

■ **opening statement** The initial statement of the prosecutor or the defense attorney, made in a court of law to a judge or jury, describing the facts that he or she intends to present during trial to prove the case.

In the 1992 case of *Georgia* v. *McCollum*,[71] the Court barred *criminal* defendants and their attorneys from using peremptory challenges to exclude potential jurors on the basis of race. In *McCollum*, Justice Harry Blackmun, writing for the majority, said, "Be it at the hands of the state or defense, if a court allows jurors to be excluded because of group bias, it is a willing participant in a scheme that could only undermine the very foundation of our system of justice—our citizens' confidence in it."

Soon thereafter, peremptory challenges based on gender were similarly restricted (*J.E.B.* v. *Alabama*, 1994),[72] although the Court has refused to ban peremptory challenges that exclude jurors because of religious or sexual orientation.[73] Also, in 1996, the Court refused to review "whether potential jurors can be stricken from a trial panel because they are too fat."[74] The case involved Luis Santiago-Martinez, a drug defendant whose lawyer objected to the prosecution's use of peremptory challenges "because the government," he said, "had used such strikes to discriminate against the handicapped, specifically the obese." The attorney, who was himself obese, claimed that thin jurors might have been unfairly biased against his arguments.

In the 1998 case of *Campbell* v. *Louisiana*,[75] the Court held that a white criminal defendant can raise equal protection and due process objections to discrimination against blacks in the selection of grand jurors. Attorneys for Terry Campbell, who was white, objected to an apparent pattern of discrimination in the selection of grand jury foremen. The foreman of the Evangeline Parish, Louisiana, grand jury that heard second-degree murder charges against him (in the killing of another white man) was white, as had been all such foremen for the last 16 years. The Supreme Court reasoned that "regardless of skin color, an accused suffers a significant 'injury in fact' when the grand jury's composition is tainted by racial discrimination." The Court also said, "The integrity of the body's decisions depends on the integrity of the process used to select the grand jurors."

In the 2003 case of *Miller-El* v. *Cockrell*,[76] the Court found that a convicted capital defendant's constitutional rights had been violated by Dallas County, Texas, prosecutors who engaged in intentional efforts to remove eligible blacks from the pool of potential jurors. Ten out of 11 eligible blacks were excluded through the use of peremptory strikes. The Court said, "In this case, debate as to whether the prosecution acted with a race-based reason when striking prospective jurors was raised by the statistical evidence demonstrating that 91% of the eligible African Americans were excluded . . . ; and by the fact that three of the State's proffered race-neutral rationales for striking African Americans—ambivalence about the death penalty, hesitancy to vote to execute defendants capable of being rehabilitated, and the jurors' own family history of criminality—pertained just as well to some white jurors who were not challenged and who did serve on the jury."[77] The decision was reaffirmed in the 2005 U.S. Supreme Court case of *Miller-El* v. *Dretke*,[78] and again in the 2008 case of *Snyder* v. *Louisiana*.[79] The Court's decision in *Snyder* v. *Louisiana*, which provides a good summary of its position on the use of peremptory strikes to eliminate black prospective jurors, is available at **http://tinyurl.com/3zgqtjf**.

Opening Statements

The presentation of information to the jury begins with **opening statements** made by the prosecution and the defense. The purpose of opening statements is to advise the jury of what the attorneys intend to prove and to describe how such proof will be offered. Evidence is not offered during opening statements. Eventually, however, the jury will have to weigh the evidence presented during the trial and decide which side made the more effective arguments. When a defendant has little evidence to present, the main job of the defense attorney will be to dispute the veracity of the prosecution's version of the facts. Under such circumstances, defense attorneys may choose not to present any evidence or testimony at all, focusing instead on the burden-of-proof requirement facing the prosecution. Such plans will generally be made clear during opening statements. At this time, the defense attorney is also likely to stress the human qualities of the defendant and to remind jurors of the awesome significance of their task.

Lawyers for both sides are bound by a "good-faith" ethical requirement in their opening statements. Attorneys may mention only the evidence that they believe actually can and will be presented as the trial progresses. Allusions to evidence that an attorney has no intention of offering are regarded as unprofessional and have been defined by the U.S. Supreme Court as "professional misconduct."[80] When material alluded to in an opening statement cannot, for whatever reason, later be presented in court, opposing counsel gains an opportunity to discredit the other side.

The Presentation of Evidence

The crux of the criminal trial is the presentation of evidence. First, the state is given the opportunity to present evidence intended to prove the defendant's guilt. After prosecutors have rested their case, the defense is afforded the opportunity to provide evidence favorable to the defendant.

■ **evidence** Anything useful to a judge or jury in deciding the facts of a case. Evidence may take the form of witness testimony, written documents, videotapes, magnetic media, photographs, physical objects, and so on.

■ **direct evidence** Evidence that, if believed, directly proves a fact. Eyewitness testimony and videotaped documentation account for the majority of all direct evidence heard in the criminal courtroom.

■ **circumstantial evidence** Evidence that requires interpretation or that requires a judge or jury to reach a conclusion based on what the evidence indicates. From the proximity of the defendant to a smoking gun, for example, the jury might conclude that he or she pulled the trigger.

■ **real evidence** Evidence that consists of physical material or traces of physical activity.

■ **probative value** The degree to which a particular item of evidence is useful in, and relevant to, proving something important in a trial.

Types of Evidence

Evidence can be either direct or circumstantial. **Direct evidence**, if believed, proves a fact without requiring the judge or jury to draw inferences. For example, direct evidence may consist of the information contained in a photograph or a videotape. It might also consist of testimonial evidence provided by a witness on the stand. A straightforward statement by a witness ("I saw him do it!") is a form of direct evidence.

Circumstantial evidence is indirect. It requires the judge or jury to make inferences and to draw conclusions. At a murder trial, for example, a person who heard gunshots and moments later saw someone run by with a smoking gun in hand might testify to those facts. Even without an eyewitness to the actual homicide, the jury might conclude that the person seen with the gun was the one who pulled the trigger and committed the crime. Circumstantial evidence is sufficient to produce a conviction in a criminal trial. In fact, some prosecuting attorneys prefer to work entirely with circumstantial evidence, weaving a tapestry of the criminal act into their arguments to the jury.

Real evidence, which may be either direct or circumstantial, consists of physical material or traces of physical activity. Weapons, tire tracks, ransom notes, and fingerprints all fall into the category of real evidence. Real evidence, sometimes called *physical evidence*, is introduced in the trial by means of exhibits. *Exhibits* are objects or displays that, after having been formally accepted as evidence by the judge, may be shown to members of the jury. *Documentary evidence*, one type of real evidence, includes written evidence like business records, journals, written confessions, and letters. Documentary evidence can extend beyond paper and ink to include stored computer data and video and audio recordings.

The Evaluation of Evidence

One of the most significant decisions a trial court judge makes is which evidence can be presented to the jury. To make this determination, judges examine the relevance of the evidence to the case at hand. Relevant evidence has a bearing on the facts at issue. For example, decades ago, it was not unusual for a woman's sexual history to be brought out in rape trials. Under "rape shield statutes," most states today will not allow this practice, recognizing that these details have no bearing on the case. Rape shield statutes have been strengthened by recent U.S. Supreme Court decisions, including the 1991 case of *Michigan* v. *Lucas*.[81]

Colorado's rape shield law played a prominent role in the 2004 case of Kobe Bryant, a basketball superstar who was accused of sexually assaulting a 19-year-old Vail-area resort employee. Bryant admitted to having a sexual encounter with the woman but claimed it was consensual. Defense attorneys sought to have the Colorado law declared unconstitutional in an effort to show that injuries to the woman were the result of her having had sexual intercourse with multiple partners before and after her encounter with Bryant. The woman later dropped the criminal case against Bryant and settled a civil suit against him in 2005.[82] The terms of the suit were not disclosed.

In evaluating evidence, judges must also weigh the **probative value** of an item of evidence against its potential inflammatory or prejudicial qualities. Evidence has probative value when it is useful and relevant, but even useful evidence may unduly bias a jury if it is exceptionally gruesome or is presented in such a way as to imply guilt. For example, gory color photographs may be withheld from the jury's eyes. In one recent case, a new trial was ordered when photos of the crime scene were projected on a wall over the head of the defendant as he sat in the courtroom. An appellate court found the presentation to have prejudiced the jury.

Sometimes evidence is found to have only limited admissibility. This means that the evidence can be used for a specific purpose but that it might not be accurate in other details. Photographs, for example, may be admitted as evidence for the narrow purpose of showing spatial relationships between objects under discussion, even if the photographs were taken under conditions that did not exist when the offense was committed (such as daylight).

When judges allow the use of evidence that may have been illegally or unconstitutionally gathered, there may be grounds for a later appeal if the trial concludes with a "guilty" verdict. Even when evidence is improperly introduced at trial, however, certain Supreme Court decisions[83] have held that there may be no grounds for an effective appeal unless such introduction "had substantial and injurious effect or influence in determining the jury's verdict."[84] Called the *harmless error rule*,

■ **testimony** Oral evidence offered by a sworn witness on the witness stand during a criminal trial.

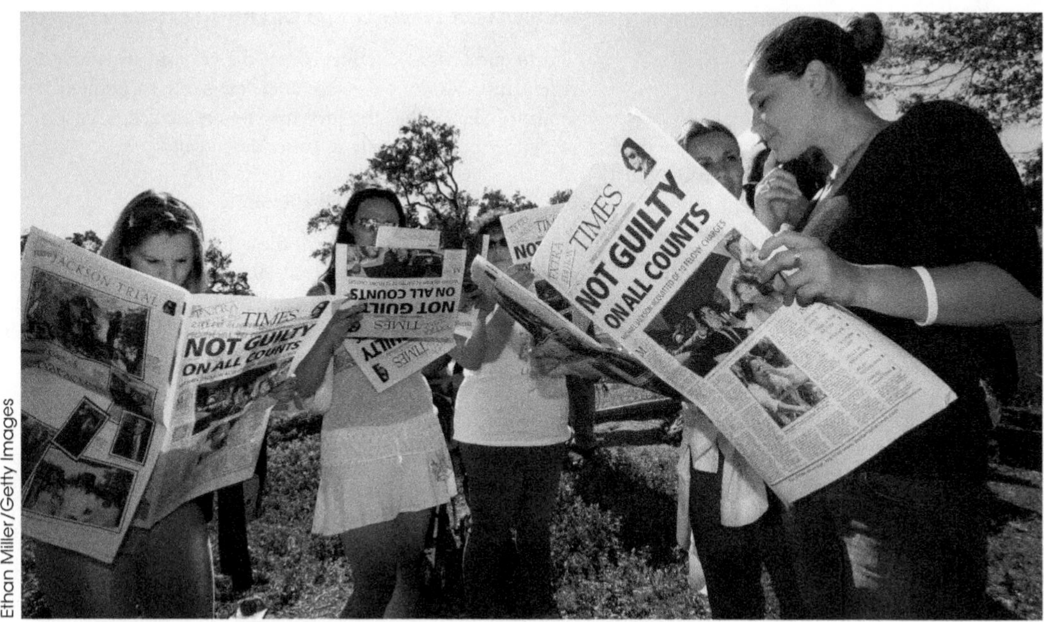

Ethan Miller/Getty Images

Michael Jackson fans reading copies of a special edition of the *Santa Maria Times* outside Jackson's Neverland Ranch in Los Olivos, California. The famous entertainer, who died in 2009, was found not guilty of child molestation and other charges in a 2005 trial that lasted almost four months and involved testimony from 140 witnesses. What is the primary purpose of a criminal trial?

this standard places the burden on the prosecution to show that the jury's decision would most likely have been the same even in the absence of the inappropriate evidence. The rule is not applicable when a defendant's constitutional guarantees are violated by "structural defects in the constitution of the trial mechanism" itself[85]—as when a judge gives constitutionally improper instructions to a jury. (We'll discuss those instructions later in this chapter.)

The Testimony of Witnesses

Witness **testimony** is generally the chief means by which evidence is introduced at trial. Witnesses may include victims, police officers, the defendant, specialists in recognized fields, and others with useful information to provide. Some of these witnesses may have been present during the commission of the offense, whereas most will have had only a later opportunity to investigate the situation or to analyze evidence.

Before a witness is allowed to testify to any fact, the questioning attorney must establish the person's competence. Competence to testify requires that witnesses have personal knowledge of the information they will discuss and that they understand their duty to tell the truth.

One of the defense attorney's most critical decisions is whether to put the defendant on the stand. Defendants have a Fifth Amendment right to remain silent and to refuse to testify. In the precedent-setting case of *Griffin* v. *California* (1965),[86] the U.S. Supreme Court declared that if a defendant refuses to testify, prosecutors and judges are enjoined from even commenting on this fact, although the judge should instruct the jury that such a failure cannot be held to indicate guilt. In the 2001 case of *Ohio* v. *Reiner*,[87] the U.S. Supreme Court extended Fifth Amendment protections to witnesses who deny any and all guilt in association with a crime for which another person is being prosecuted.

Direct examination of a witness takes place when a witness is first called to the stand. If the prosecutor calls the witness, the witness is referred to as a *witness for the prosecution*. If the direct examiner is a defense attorney, the witness is a *witness for the defense*.

The direct examiner may ask questions that require a "yes" or "no" answer or may ask narrative questions that allow the witness to tell a story in his or her own words. During direct examination, courts generally prohibit the use of leading questions or those that suggest answers to the witness.[88]

Cross-examination is the questioning of a witness by someone other than the direct examiner. Anyone who offers testimony in a criminal court has the duty to submit to cross-examination.[89] The purpose of cross-examination is to test the credibility and the memory of the witness.

Most states and the federal government restrict the scope of cross-examination to material covered during direct

CJ | ISSUES

Pretrial and Post-Trial Motions

A *motion* is "an oral or written request made to a court at any time before, during, or after court proceedings, asking the court to make a specified finding, decision, or order." Written motions are called *petitions*. The following are the most common motions made by both sides in a criminal case before and after trial.

Motion for Discovery

A motion for discovery, filed by the defense, asks the court to allow the defendant's lawyers to view the evidence that the prosecution intends to present at trial. Physical evidence, lists of witnesses, documents, photographs, and so on that the prosecution plans to introduce in court are usually made available to the defense as a result of a motion for discovery.

Motion to Suppress Evidence

The defense may file a motion to suppress evidence if it learns, in the preliminary hearing or through pretrial discovery, of evidence that it believes to have been unlawfully acquired.

Motion to Dismiss Charges

A variety of circumstances may result in the filing of a motion to dismiss charges. They include (1) an opinion, by defense counsel, that the indictment or information is not sound; (2) violations of speedy trial legislation; (3) a plea bargain with the defendant, which may require testimony against codefendants; (4) the death of an important witness or the destruction or disappearance of necessary evidence; (5) the confession, by a supposed victim, that the facts in the case were fabricated; and (6) the success of a motion to suppress evidence that effectively eliminates the prosecution's case.

Motion for Continuance

This motion seeks a delay in the start of the trial. Defense motions for continuance are often based on an inability to locate important witnesses, the illness of the defendant, or a change in defense counsel immediately prior to trial.

Motion for Change of Venue

In well-known cases, pretrial publicity may lessen the opportunity for a case to be tried before an unbiased jury. A motion for a change in venue asks that the trial be moved to some other area where prejudice against the defendant is less likely to exist.

Motion for Severance of Offenses

Defendants charged with a number of crimes may ask to be tried separately on all or some of the charges. Although consolidating charges for trial saves time and money, some defendants believe that it is more likely to make them appear guilty.

Motion for Severance of Defendants

This request asks the court to try the accused separately from any codefendants. Motions for severance are likely to be filed when the defendant believes that the jury may be prejudiced against him or her by evidence applicable only to other defendants.

Motion to Determine Present Sanity

A lack of "present sanity," even though it may be no defense against the criminal charge, can delay trial. A person cannot be tried, sentenced, or punished while insane. If a defendant is insane at the time a trial is to begin, this motion may halt the proceedings until treatment can be arranged.

Motion for a Bill of Particulars

This motion asks the court to order the prosecutor to provide detailed information about the charges that the defendant will be facing in court. Defendants charged with a number of offenses, or with a number of counts of the same offense, may make such a motion. They may, for example, seek to learn which alleged instances of an offense will become the basis for prosecution or which specific items of contraband allegedly found in their possession are held to violate the law.

Motion for a Mistrial

A mistrial may be declared at any time, and a motion for a mistrial may be made by either side. Mistrials are likely to be declared in cases in which highly prejudicial comments are made by either attorney. Defense motions for a mistrial do not provide grounds for a later claim of double jeopardy.

Motion for Arrest of Judgment

After the verdict of the jury has been announced, but before sentencing, the defense may make a motion for arrest of judgment. With this motion, the defense asserts that some legally acceptable reason exists as to why sentencing should not occur. Defendants who are seriously ill, who are hospitalized, or who have gone insane prior to judgment being imposed may file such a motion.

Motion for a New Trial

After a jury has returned a guilty verdict, the court may entertain a defense motion for a new trial. Acceptance of such a motion is usually based on the discovery of new evidence that is of significant benefit to the defense and that will set aside the conviction.

Reference: U.S. Department of Justice, *Dictionary of Criminal Justice Data Terminology*, 2nd ed. (Washington, DC: U.S. Government Printing Office, 1982).

---

examination. Questions about other matters, even though they may relate to the case before the court, are not allowed in most states, although a few states allow the cross-examiner to raise any issue as long as the court deems it relevant. Leading questions, generally disallowed in direct examination, are regarded as the mainstay of cross-examination. Such questions allow for a concise restatement of testimony that has already been offered and serve to focus efficiently on potential problems that the cross-examiner seeks to address.

Some witnesses commit **perjury**—that is, they make statements that they know are untrue. Reasons for perjured testimony vary, but most witnesses who lie on the stand do so in an

■ **perjury** The intentional making of a false statement as part of the testimony by a sworn witness in a judicial proceeding on a matter relevant to the case at hand.

■ **hearsay** Something that is not based on the personal knowledge of a witness. Witnesses who testify about something they have heard, for example, are offering hearsay by repeating information about a matter of which they have no direct knowledge.

■ **hearsay rule** The long-standing precedent that hearsay cannot be used in American courtrooms. Rather than accepting testimony based on hearsay, the court will ask that the person who was the original source of the hearsay information be brought in to be questioned and cross-examined. Exceptions to the hearsay rule may occur when the person with direct knowledge is dead or is otherwise unable to testify.

effort to help friends accused of crimes. Witnesses who perjure themselves are subject to impeachment, in which either the defense or the prosecution demonstrates that a witness has intentionally offered false testimony. For example, previous statements made by the witness may be shown to be at odds with more recent declarations. When it can be demonstrated that a witness has offered inaccurate or false testimony, the witness has been effectively impeached. Perjury is a serious offense in its own right, and dishonest witnesses may face fines or jail time.

At the conclusion of the cross-examination, the direct examiner may again question the witness. This procedure is called *redirect examination* and may be followed by a recross-examination and so on, until both sides are satisfied that they have exhausted fruitful lines of questioning.

Children as Witnesses

An area of special concern is the use of children as witnesses in a criminal trial, especially when the children are also victims. Currently, in an effort to avoid what may be traumatizing direct confrontations between child witnesses and the accused, 37 states allow the use of videotaped testimony in criminal courtrooms, and 32 permit the use of closed-circuit television, which allows the child to testify out of the presence of the defendant. In 1988, however, in the case of *Coy* v. *Iowa,*[90] the U.S. Supreme Court ruled that a courtroom screen, used to shield child witnesses from visual confrontation with a defendant in a child sex-abuse case, had violated the confrontation clause of the Constitution (found in the Sixth Amendment).

On the other hand, in the 1990 case of *Maryland* v. *Craig,*[91] the Court upheld the use of closed-circuit television to shield children who testify in criminal courts. The Court's decision was partially based on the realization that "a significant majority of States have enacted statutes to protect child witnesses from the trauma of giving testimony in child-abuse cases . . . [which] attests to the widespread belief in the importance of such a policy."

Although a face-to-face confrontation with a child victim may not be necessary in the courtroom, until 1992 the Supreme Court had been reluctant to allow into evidence descriptions of abuse and other statements made by children, even to child-care professionals, when those statements were made outside the courtroom. In *Idaho* v. *Wright* (1990),[92] the Court reasoned that such "statements [are] fraught with the dangers of unreliability which the Confrontation Clause is designed to highlight and obviate."

However, in *White* v. *Illinois* (1992),[93] the Court reversed its stance, ruling that in-court testimony provided by a medical provider and the child's babysitter, which repeated what the child had said to them concerning White's sexually abusive behavior, was permissible. The Court rejected White's claim that out-of-court statements should be admissible only when the witness is unavailable to testify at trial, saying instead, "A finding of unavailability of an out-of-court declarant is necessary only if the out-of-court statement was made at a prior judicial proceeding." Placing *White* within the context of generally established exceptions, the Court declared, "A statement that has been offered in a moment of excitement—without the opportunity to reflect on the consequences of one's exclamation—may justifiably carry more weight with a trier of fact than a similar statement offered in the relative calm of the courtroom. Similarly, a statement made in the course of procuring medical services, where the declarant knows that a false statement may cause misdiagnosis or mistreatment, carries special guarantees of credibility that a trier of fact may not think replicated by courtroom testimony."

The Hearsay Rule

Hearsay is anything not based on the personal knowledge of a witness. A witness may say, for example, "John told me that Fred did it!" Such a witness becomes a hearsay declarant, and following a likely objection by counsel, the trial judge will have to decide whether the witness's statement will be allowed to stand as evidence. In most cases, the judge will instruct the jury to disregard the witness's comment, thereby enforcing the **hearsay rule**, which prohibits the use of "secondhand evidence."

Exceptions to the hearsay rule have been established by both precedent and tradition. One exception is the dying declaration. A dying declaration is a statement made by a person who is about to die. When heard by a second party, it may usually be repeated in court, provided that certain conditions have been met. A dying declaration is generally a valid exception to the hearsay rule when it is made by someone who knows that he or she is about to die and when the statement made relates to the cause and circumstances of the impending death.

■ **closing argument** An oral summation of a case presented to a judge, or to a judge and jury, by the prosecution or by the defense in a criminal trial.

■ **reasonable doubt** In legal proceedings, an actual and substantial doubt arising from the evidence, from the facts or circumstances shown by the evidence, or from the lack of evidence.[108] Also, the state of a case such that, after the comparison and consideration of all the evidence, jurors cannot say they feel an abiding conviction of the truth of the charge.[109,110]

■ **reasonable doubt standard** The standard of proof necessary for conviction in criminal trials.

Spontaneous statements provide another exception to the hearsay rule. A statement is considered spontaneous when it is made in the heat of excitement before the person has had time to make it up. For example, a defendant who was injured and is just regaining consciousness following a crime may say something that could later be repeated in court by those who heard it.

Out-of-court statements, especially if they were recorded during a time of great excitement or while a person was under considerable stress, may also become exceptions to the hearsay rule. Many states, for example, permit juries to hear 9-1-1 tape recordings or to read police transcripts of victim interviews without requiring that the people who made them appear in court. In two recent cases, however, the U.S. Supreme Court barred admission of tape-recorded 9-1-1 calls when the people making them were alive and in good health but not available for cross-examination. In *Crawford* v. *Washington*,[94] a 2004 case, the Court disallowed a woman's tape-recorded eyewitness account of a fight in which her husband stabbed another man, holding that the Constitution bars admission of testimonial statements of a witness who did not appear at trial unless he or she was unable to testify and the defendant had a prior opportunity for cross-examination. In *Davis* v. *Washington*,[95] decided in 2006, the Court held that a 9-1-1 call made by a woman who said that her former boyfriend was beating her had been improperly introduced as testimonial evidence. The woman had been subpoenaed but failed to appear in court. The keyword in both cases is *testimonial*, and the Court indicated that "statements are nontestimonial when made in the course of police interrogation under circumstances objectively indicating that the primary purpose of interrogation is to enable police assistance to meet an ongoing emergency."[96]

The use of other out-of-court statements, such as writings or routine video or audio recordings, usually requires the witness to testify that the statements or depictions were accurate at the time they were made. Witnesses who so testify may be subject to cross-examination by the defendant's attorney. Nonetheless, this "past recollection recorded" exception to the hearsay rule is especially useful in drawn-out court proceedings that occur long after the crime. Under such circumstances, witnesses may no longer remember the details of an event. Their earlier statements to authorities, however, can be introduced into evidence as past recollection recorded.

Closing Arguments

At the conclusion of a criminal trial, both sides have the opportunity for a final narrative presentation to the jury in the form of a **closing argument**. This summation provides a review and analysis of the evidence. Its purpose is to persuade the jury to draw a conclusion favorable to the presenter. Testimony can be quoted, exhibits referred to, and attention drawn to inconsistencies in the evidence presented by the other side.

States vary as to the order of closing arguments. Nearly all allow the defense attorney to speak to the jury before the prosecution makes its final points. A few permit the prosecutor the first opportunity for summation. Some jurisdictions and the Federal Rules of Criminal Procedure[97] authorize a defense rebuttal. A rebuttal is a response to the closing argument of the other side.

Some specific issues may need to be addressed during summation. If, for example, the defendant has not taken the stand during the trial, the defense attorney's closing argument will inevitably stress that this failure to testify cannot be regarded as indicating guilt. Where the prosecution's case rests entirely on circumstantial evidence, the defense can be expected to stress the lack of any direct proof, and the prosecutor is likely to argue that circumstantial evidence can be stronger than direct evidence, as it is not as easily affected by human error or false testimony.

The Judge's Charge to the Jury

After closing arguments, the judge charges the jury to "retire," select one of its number as a foreman, and deliberate on the evidence that has been presented until it has reached a verdict. The words of the judge's "charge" vary somewhat between jurisdictions and among judges, but all judges will remind members of the jury of their duty to consider objectively only the evidence that has been presented and of the need for impartiality. Most judges also remind jury members of the statutory elements of the alleged offense, of the burden of proof that rests on the prosecution, and of the need for the prosecution to have proved the defendant's guilt beyond a **reasonable doubt** before the jury can return a guilty verdict. The **reasonable doubt standard** is the single most important criterion for determining the level of proof necessary for conviction in criminal trials. If the prosecutor fails to prove a defendant's guilt beyond a reasonable doubt, then the jury must return a not-guilty verdict.

In their charge, many judges also provide a summary of the evidence presented, usually from notes they took during

CJ | NEWS

Social Media Pose New Threats to Keeping Jurors Isolated during Trials

© dandaman/Fotolia

A young man uses an iPad. Digital devices are commonplace today. How might jurors' unauthorized use of modern technology influence their deliberations?

Growing use of the Internet and social media has made it much easier for jurors to violate age-old prohibitions against conversing with outsiders about a case, conducting outside research, and contacting plaintiffs or defendants.

The rise of Facebook, Twitter, and Wikipedia, combined with widespread use of smartphones, seems to have blurred the traditional line between jurors and the outside world. "This is a generational change, and I don't know if the legal system is ready for it," said Thaddeus Hoffmeister, a professor at the University of Dayton Law School who specializes in jury issues.

Violations that once took some effort, such as going to a library to look up a term or just making a phone call to a friend, now can be done with a few keystrokes. Research suggests very few violators are caught. But when they are, the courts take the matter very seriously. They may throw out the verdict, cite jurors for contempt, and even jail them.

A 2011 study by Reuters Legal found that Internet-related juror misconduct had led to 21 overturned verdicts or new trials since January 2009. Because violations can occur away from the courthouse and jurors' online use is rarely monitored, courts have identified very few violators. A national survey of federal judges by the Federal Judicial Center, released in November 2011, found that just 6% were aware of social media used during deliberations, but 79% admitted they would have no way of knowing about violations.

Jurors' use of Facebook can be easy to spot. In a few high-profile cases, jurors have improperly "friended" plaintiffs, defendants, and even each other in the period before jurors can get together to deliberate. One juror who friended the plaintiff in an auto accident case was sentenced to three days in jail.

In a Twitter violation in Arkansas, a murder conviction was thrown out on appeal in December 2011 because the juror tweeted after being asked to stop, and one of his tweets revealed the verdict before it was announced. The court ordered a new trial, but it did not punish the juror.

Although jurors have never been allowed to conduct outside research, Internet-based research is so second-nature that it may not occur to jurors they are violating the rules. When a juror in a 2009 Maryland rape trial looked up the term "oppositional defiant disorder" on the Internet and passed the information on to fellow jurors, the courts said he had "improperly and irreparably influenced the jury's deliberative process" and ordered a new trial.

To prevent violations, experts say jury instructions should specify each kind of prohibited Internet use, explain the reasoning behind the ban, and show how the legal process could be damaged. For example, even when nothing is revealed on a juror's blog or a posting on Facebook, just reading the comments to the posts might improperly influence jury members.

Experts also recommend that candidates in the jury-selection process be asked about their own online activities and whether they'd be comfortable stopping them for the duration of the trial. Some potential jurors who said they could not stop have withdrawn voluntarily. It has also been proposed that the courts ask jurors to name frequently used sites and to provide the passwords for them, so that they can be monitored during the trial.

In 2012, the federal Judicial Conference's Committee on Court Administration and Case Management (CACM) admonished federal judges to repeatedly warn jurors not to discuss cases that they are deliberating on social media or the Internet. The Committee's proposed model jury instructions can be accessed at **http://www.justicestudies.com/modelinst.pdf**.

Resources: "Jurors' Use of Social Media during Trials Leading to Mistrials," Martindale-Hubble, March 22 2012, http://blog.martindale.com/jurors-use-of-social-media-during-trials-leading-to-mistrials; "Jurors' Use of Social Media during Trials and Deliberations," Federal Judicial Center, November 22, 2011, http://www.fjc.gov/public/pdf.nsf/lookup/dunnjuror.pdf/$file/dunnjuror.pdf; and "Friend or Foe? Social Media, the Jury and You," The Jury Expert, September 26, 2011, http://www.thejuryexpert.com/2011/09/friend-or-foe-social-media-the-jury-and-you/.

---

the trial, as a means of refreshing the jurors' memories of events. About half of all the states allow judges the freedom to express their own views as to the credibility of witnesses and the significance of evidence. Other states only permit judges to summarize the evidence in an objective and impartial manner.

Recently, as the "CJ News" box in this section shows, the plethora of digital communications devices now available has made it difficult for courts to control jurors' access to out-of-court information. Read a set of jury instructions designed for federal courts to use in alleviating this problem at **http://www.justicestudies.com/pubs/electronic_instructions.pdf**.

Following the charge, the jury is removed from the courtroom and is permitted to begin its deliberations. In the absence of the jury, defense attorneys may choose to challenge portions of the judge's charge. If they feel that some oversight has occurred in the original charge, they may ask the judge to provide the jury with additional instructions or information. Such objections, if denied by the judge, often become the basis for an appeal when a conviction is returned.

verdict The decision of the jury in a jury trial or of a judicial officer in a nonjury trial.

Jury Deliberations and the Verdict

In cases in which the evidence is either very clear or very weak, jury deliberations may be brief, lasting only a matter of hours or even minutes. Some juries, however, deliberate days or sometimes weeks, carefully weighing all the nuances of the evidence they have seen and heard. Many jurisdictions require that juries reach a unanimous **verdict**, although the U.S. Supreme Court has ruled that unanimous verdicts are not required in noncapital cases.[98] Even so, some juries are unable to agree on any verdict. When a jury is deadlocked, it is said to be a *hung jury*. When a unanimous decision is required, juries may be deadlocked by the strong opposition of several members or of only one member to a verdict agreed on by all the others.

In some states, judges are allowed to add a boost to nearly hung juries by recharging them under a set of instructions that the Supreme Court put forth in the 1896 case of *Allen* v. *U.S.*[99] The *Allen* charge, as it is known, urges the jury to vigorous deliberations and suggests to obstinate jurors that their objections may be ill founded if they make no impression on the other jurors.

Problems with the Jury System

Judge Harold J. Rothwax, a well-known critic of today's jury system, tells the tale of a rather startling 1991 case over which he presided. The case involved a murder defendant, a handsome young man who had been fired by a New York company that serviced ATMs. After being fired, the defendant intentionally caused a machine in a remote area to malfunction. When two former colleagues arrived to fix it, he robbed them, stole the money inside the ATM, and shot both men repeatedly. One of the men survived long enough to identify his former coworker as the shooter. The man was arrested, and a trial ensued, but after three weeks of hearing the case, the jury deadlocked. Judge Rothwax later learned that the jury had voted 11 to 1 to convict the defendant, but the one holdout just couldn't believe that "someone so good-looking could . . . commit such a crime."[100]

Many routine cases as well as some highly publicized cases, like the murder trial of O. J. Simpson, have called into question the ability of the American jury system to do its job—that is, to sort through the evidence and to accurately determine the defendant's guilt or innocence. In a televised 1995 trial, Simpson was acquitted of the charge that he murdered his ex-wife Nicole Brown and her friend Ronald Goldman outside Brown's home in 1994. Many people believed that strong evidence tied Simpson to the crimes, and the criminal trial left many people feeling unsatisfied with the criminal justice system and with the criminal trial process. Later, a civil jury ordered Simpson to pay $33.5 million to the Goldman family and to Nicole Brown's estate.

Because jurors are drawn from all walks of life, many cannot be expected to understand modern legal complexities and to appreciate all the nuances of trial court practice. It is likely that even the best-intentioned jurors cannot understand and rarely observe some jury instructions.[101] In highly charged cases, emotions are often difficult to separate from fact, and during deliberations, some juries are dominated by one or two members with forceful personalities.

Jurors may be less than effective in cases where they fear personal retaliation. In the state-level trial of the police officers accused in the infamous 1991 Rodney King beating, for example, jurors reported being afraid for their lives due to the riots in Los Angeles that broke out after their not-guilty verdict was announced. Some slept with weapons by their side, and others sent their children away to safe locations.[102] Because of the potential for harm that jurors faced in the 1993 federal trial of the same officers, U.S. District Judge John G. Davies ruled that the names of the jurors be forever kept secret. Members of the press called the secrecy order "an unprecedented infringement of the public's right of access to the justice system."[103] Similarly, in the 1993 trial of three black men charged with the beating of white truck driver Reginald Denny during the Los Angeles riots that followed the Rodney King verdict, Los Angeles Superior Court Judge John Ouderkirk ordered that the identities of the jurors not be released.

Opponents of the jury system have argued that it should be replaced by a panel of judges who would both render a verdict and impose sentence.

Opponents of the jury system have argued that it should be replaced by a panel of judges who would both render a verdict and impose sentence. Regardless of how well considered such a suggestion may be, such a change could not occur without modification of the Constitution's Sixth Amendment right to trial by jury.

An alternative suggestion for improving the process of trial by jury has been the call for professional jurors. Professional jurors would be paid by the government, as are judges, prosecutors, and public defenders. They would be expected to have the expertise to sit on any jury. Professional jurors would be trained to listen objectively and would be taught the kinds of decision-making skills they would need to function effectively within an adversarial context. They would hear one case after another, perhaps moving between jurisdictions in cases of highly publicized crimes.

A professional jury system offers these advantages:

1. *Dependability.* Professional jurors could be expected to report to the courtroom in a timely fashion and to be good listeners, as both would be required by the nature of the job.
2. *Knowledge.* Professional jurors would be trained in the law, would understand what a finding of guilt requires, and would know what to expect from the other professionals in the courtroom.
3. *Equity.* Professional jurors would understand the requirements of due process and would be less likely to be swayed by the emotional content of a case, having been schooled in the need to separate matters of fact from personal feelings.

A professional jury system would not be without difficulties. Jurors under such a system might become jaded, deciding cases out of hand as routines lead to boredom. They might categorize defendants according to whether they "fit the type" for guilt or innocence based on the jurors' previous experiences. Job requirements for professional jurors would be difficult to establish without infringing on the jurors' freedom to decide cases as they understand them. For the same reason, any evaluation of the job performance of professional jurors would be a difficult call. Finally, professional jurors might not truly be peer jurors, as their social characteristics might be skewed by education, residence, and politics.

Improving the Adjudication Process

Courts today are coming under increasing scrutiny, and well-publicized trials, like those of Casey Anthony, Drew Peterson, Jodi Arias, Michael Jackson, O. J. Simpson, and John Allen Muhammad, have heightened awareness of problems with the American court system. One of today's most important issues is reducing the number of jurisdictions by unifying courts. The current multiplicity of jurisdictions frequently leads to what many critics believe are avoidable conflicts and overlaps in the handling of criminal defendants. In some states, problems are exacerbated by the lack of any centralized judicial authority that might resolve jurisdictional and procedural disputes.[104] Proponents of unification suggest eliminating overlapping jurisdictions, creating special-purpose courts, and establishing administrative offices to achieve economies of scale.[105]

The number of court-watch citizens' groups is also rapidly growing. Such organizations focus on the trial court level, but they are part of a general movement seeking greater openness in government decision making at all levels.[106] Court-watch groups regularly monitor court proceedings and attempt to document and often publicize inadequacies. They frequently focus on the handling of indigents, fairness in the scheduling of cases for trial, unnecessary court delays, the reduction of waiting time, the treatment of witnesses and jurors, and the adequacy of rights advisements for defendants throughout judicial proceedings.

The statistical measurement of court performance is another area that is receiving increased attention. Research has looked at the efficiency with which prosecutors schedule cases for trial, the speed with which judges resolve issues, the amount of time judges spend on the bench, and the economic and other costs to defendants, witnesses, and communities involved in the judicial process.[107] Statistical studies of this type often attempt to measure elements of court performance as diverse as sentence variation, charging accuracy, fairness in plea bargaining, evenhandedness, delays, and attitudes toward the court by lay participants. Visit **http://www.justicestudies.com/pubs/tcps.pdf** for more information on standards and measures in court performance.

CJ | ISSUES
Courtrooms of the Future

In the mid-1990s, the College of William and Mary, in conjunction with the National Center for State Courts (NCSC), unveiled Courtroom 21. At the time, it was the most technologically advanced courtroom in the United States. Courtroom 21, which has since changed its name to the Center for Legal and Court Technology (CLCT), is located in the McGlothlin Courtroom of the College of William and Mary. It offers a glimpse at what American courtrooms might be like in the mid-twenty-first century. The CLCT includes the following integrated capabilities:

1. *Automatic video recording of the proceedings, using ceiling-mounted cameras with voice-initiated switching.* A sophisticated voice-activation system directs cameras to record the person speaking and to record evidence as it is being presented.
2. *Recorded and televised evidence display with optical disk storage.* Documentary or real evidence can be presented to the judge and the jury through the use of a video "presenter," which also makes a video record of the evidence as it is being presented, so it can be used later.
3. *Remote two-way television.* The two-way television arrangement allows video and audio signals to be sent from the judge's bench to areas throughout the courtroom, including the jury box.
4. *Text-, graphics-, and video-capable jury computers.* The CLCT's jury box contains computers for information display and animation so that jury members can easily view documents, live or prerecorded video, and graphics, such as charts, diagrams, and pictures. Video-capable jury computers also allow for the remote appearance of witnesses and for the display of crime scene reenactments via computer animation.
5. *Access to online legal research databases for the judge and for counsel on both sides.* Available databases contain an extensive selection of state and federal statutes, case law, and other precedents.
6. *Built-in video playback facilities for out-of-court testimony.* Video depositions can be played on courtroom monitors to present expert witness testimony or to impeach a witness.
7. *Information storage with software search capabilities.* Integrated software programs provide text-searching capabilities for courtroom participants.

The technology demonstrated by the CLCT suggests many possibilities. For one thing, attorneys could use court video equipment for filing remote motions and for other types of hearings. As one of the CLCT designers puts it, "Imagine the productivity gains if lawyers no longer need to travel across a city or county for a ten-minute appearance."

An even more intriguing vision of courtrooms of the future is offered by the Technology of Justice Task Force in its draft report to the Pennsylvania Futures Commission on Justice in the 21st Century. The task force predicted that by the year 2020 "there will be 'virtual courtrooms,' where appropriate, to provide hearings without the need for people to come to a physical courthouse." The task force envisions trials via teleconferencing, public Internet access to many court documents, and payment of fines by credit card. Visit the Center for Legal and Court Technology on the Web at **http://www.legaltechcenter.net**.

Discussion Questions

1. Do you think that technologies like those discussed in this box might affect the outcome of criminal trials? Explain.
2. Are there any types of criminal trials in which the use of high-technology courtrooms might not be appropriate? If so, describe them.

Reference: National Center for State Courts website, http://www.ncsc.us (accessed October 11, 2007), from which some of the material in this box is taken; and Courtroom 21 website, http://www.courtroom21.net (accessed October 11, 2007).

Gary C. Knapp/AP Wide World Photos

Fred Lederer, director of the Center for Legal and Court Technology (formerly the Courtroom 21 Project) at the College of William and Mary Law School in Williamsburg, Virginia, acting as a bailiff as he swears in a witness via the Internet. What limits do you think might be applied to "virtual courtrooms" of the future?

CJ | ISSUES
The Bilingual Courtroom

One of the central multicultural issues facing the criminal justice system today is the need for clear communication with recent immigrants and subcultural groups that have not been fully acculturated. Many such groups hold to traditions and values that differ from those held by the majority of Americans. Such differences influence the interpretation of things seen and heard. Even more basic, however, are language differences that might prevent effective communication with criminal justice system personnel.

Techniques that law enforcement officers can use in overcoming language differences were discussed in Chapter 8. This box focuses on the use of courtroom interpreters to facilitate effective and accurate communication. The role of the courtroom interpreter is to present neutral verbatim, or word-for-word, translations. Interpreters must provide true, accurate, and complete interpretation of the exact statements made by non-English-speaking defendants, victims, and witnesses—whether on the stand, in writing, or in court-related conferences. The Court Interpreters and Translators Association also requires, through its code of professional ethics, that translators remember their "absolute responsibility to keep all oral and written information gained completely confidential."

Although most court interpreters are actually present in the courtroom at the time of the trial, telephone interpreting provides an alternative for courts that have trouble locating qualified interpreters. Today, state court administrative offices in Florida, Idaho, New Jersey, and Washington sponsor programs through which qualified interpreters in metropolitan counties are made available to courts in rural counties by telephone.

The federal Court Interpreters Act of 1978[1] specifically provides for the use of interpreters in federal courts. It applies to both criminal and civil trials and hearings. The act reads, in part, as follows:[2]

> The presiding judicial officers . . . shall utilize [an interpreter] . . . in judicial proceedings instituted by the United States, if the presiding judicial officer determines on such officer's own motion or on the motion of a party that such party (including the defendant in a criminal case), or a witness who may present testimony in such judicial proceedings—
>
> (A) speaks only or primarily a language other than English; or
>
> (B) suffers from a hearing impairment . . . so as to inhibit such party's comprehension of the proceedings or communication with counsel or the presiding officer, or so as to inhibit such witness's comprehension of questions and the presentation of such testimony.

As this extract from the statute shows, translators are also required for individuals with hearing impairments who communicate primarily through American Sign Language. The act does not require that an interpreter be appointed when a person has a speech impairment that is not accompanied by a hearing impairment. A court is not prohibited, however, from providing assistance to that person if it will aid in the efficient administration of justice.

Because it is a federal law, the Court Interpreters Act does not apply to state courts. Nonetheless, most states have enacted similar legislation. A few states are starting to introduce high-standard testing for court interpreters, although most states currently conduct little or no interpreter screening. The federal government and states with high standards for court interpreters generally require interpreter certification. To become certified, an interpreter must pass an oral examination, such as the federal court interpreter's examination or an examination administered by a state court or by a recognized international agency, such as the United Nations.

There is growing recognition among professional court interpreters of the need for standardized interstate testing and certification programs. To meet that need, the National Center for State Courts created the Consortium for State Court Interpreter Certification. The consortium works to pool state resources for developing and administering court interpreter testing and training programs. The consortium's founding states were Minnesota, New Jersey, Oregon, and Washington, and many other states have since joined.

Because certified interpreters are not always available, even by telephone, most states have created a special category of "language-skilled interpreters." To qualify as a language-skilled interpreter, a person must demonstrate to the court's satisfaction his or her ability to interpret court proceedings from English to a designated language and from that language to English. Many states require sign language interpreters to hold a Legal Specialist Certificate, or its equivalent, from the Registry of Interpreters for the Deaf, showing that they are certified in American Sign Language. Learn more about language interpretation in the courts from the National Association of Judiciary Interpreters and Translators via **http://www.najit.org**.

[1] U.S. Code, Title 28, Section 1827.

[2] Ibid., at Section 1827(d)(1).

Sources: The National Association of Judiciary Interpreters and Translators website, http://www.najit.org (accessed October 11, 2007); Madelynn Herman and Anne Endress Skove, "State Court Rules for Language Interpreters," memorandum no. IS 99.1242, National Center for State Courts, Knowledge Management Office, September 8, 1999; Madelynn Herman and Dot Bryant, "Language Interpreting in the Courts," National Center for State Courts, http://www.ncsc.dni.us/KMO/Projects/Trends/99-00/articles/CtInterpreters.htm (accessed October 11, 2007); and National Crime Prevention Council, *Building and Crossing Bridges: Refugees and Law Enforcement Working Together* (Washington, DC: NCPC, 1994).

SUMMARY

- This chapter describes the criminal trial process and the court-related activities that take place before the trial begins. Pretrial activities include the first appearance, which involves appointment of counsel for indigent defendants and consideration of pretrial release; the preliminary hearing to determine whether there is probable cause to hold the defendant; the filing of an information by the prosecutor or the return of an indictment by the grand jury; and arraignment, at which the defendant may enter a plea. Guilty pleas, when they are made, are often not as straightforward as they might seem and are typically arrived at only after complex negotiations known as *plea bargaining*.

- The criminal trial involves an adversarial process that pits the prosecution against the defense. Trials are peer-based fact-finding processes intended to protect the rights of the accused while disputed issues of guilt or innocence are resolved. The primary purpose of a criminal trial is to determine whether a defendant, through his or her behavior, violated the criminal law of the jurisdiction in which the court has authority.
- A criminal trial has eight stages: trial initiation, jury selection, opening statements, the presentation of evidence, closing arguments, the judge's charge to the jury, jury deliberations, and the verdict. Each is described in detail in this chapter. At least a few experts have suggested the training and use of a cadre of professional jurors, versed in the law and in trial practice, who could insulate themselves from media portrayals of famous defendants and who would resolve questions of guilt or innocence more on the basis of reason than emotion.
- The American court system has been called into question by some well-publicized trials of the last two decades, which have demonstrated apparent weaknesses in the trial process. Some people suggest that court unification might help address a number of today's problems by reducing the number of jurisdictions, resulting in more uniform procedures.

KEY TERMS

adversarial system, 320
bail bond, 312
circumstantial evidence, 326
closing argument, 330
competent to stand trial, 316
conditional release, 314
danger law, 314
direct evidence, 326
evidence, 326
first appearance, 310
hearsay, 329
hearsay rule, 329
jury selection, 323
***nolo contendere*, 316**
opening statement, 325
peremptory challenge, 323
perjury, 328
plea, 316
plea bargaining, 317
pretrial release, 312
probative value, 326
property bond, 313
real evidence, 326
reasonable doubt, 330
reasonable doubt standard, 330
release on recognizance (ROR), 313
rules of evidence, 320
scientific jury selection, 323
sequestered jury, 324
Speedy Trial Act, 322
testimony, 327
verdict, 332

KEY CASES

***County of Riverside* v. *McLaughlin*, 311**
***Coy* v. *Iowa*, 329**
***Doggett* v. *U.S.*, 322**
***Edmonson* v. *Leesville Concrete Co., Inc.*, 324**
***Fex* v. *Michigan*, 322**
***Georgia* v. *McCollum*, 325**
***Idaho* v. *Wright*, 329**
***Maryland* v. *Craig*, 329**
***McNabb* v. *U.S.*, 310**
***Michigan* v. *Lucas*, 326**
***Miller-El* v. *Cockrell*, 325**
***Mu'Min* v. *Virginia*, 323**
***Powers* v. *Ohio*, 324**
***U.S.* v. *Montalvo-Murillo*, 315**
***White* v. *Illinois*, 329**

QUESTIONS FOR REVIEW

1. What activities are typically undertaken during the pretrial period (that is, before the start of a criminal trial)?
2. What is the purpose of a criminal trial? What is the difference between factual guilt and legal guilt? What do we mean by the term *adversarial system*?
3. What are the various stages of a criminal trial? Describe each one.
4. How might the adjudication process be improved?

QUESTIONS FOR REFLECTION

1. Before trial, courts may act to shield the accused from the punitive power of the state through the use of pretrial release. In doing so, how can they balance the rights of the defendant against the potential for future harm that he or she may represent?
2. A significant issue facing pretrial decision makers is how to ensure that all defendants, rich and poor, black and white, male and female, are afforded the same degree of protection from unfair processing by the criminal justice system. How can that be achieved?
3. What is plea bargaining, and what is its function? To what kinds of cases is it most suited?
4. What purpose does plea bargaining serve for the defense? For the prosecution? Given the criticisms leveled against plea bargaining, do you believe that it's an acceptable practice? Explain.
5. Might recent advances in technology, such as DNA fingerprinting, possibly supplant the role of advocacy in the fact-finding process that is today regarded as central to criminal trials? If so, how? If not, why not?
6. What exceptions to the hearsay rule have courts recognized? Describe the reasoning behind these exceptions.
7. Do you think the present jury system is outmoded? Why? How might a professional jury system be more effective than the present system of peer jurors?

NOTES

1. Michelle Washington, "Five Things to Get You Up to Speed in Jodi Arias Trial," *USA Today*, May 6, 2013, http://m.usatoday.com/article/news/nation/2138823 (accessed July 8, 2013).
2. *Arraignment* is another term used to describe an initial appearance, although we will reserve use of that word to describe a later court appearance following the defendant's indictment by a grand jury or the filing of an information by the prosecutor.
3. *McNabb* v. *U.S.*, 318 U.S. 332 (1943).
4. This is the case because such arrests do not involve judicial determination of probable cause.
5. *County of Riverside* v. *McLaughlin*, 500 U.S. 44 (1991).
6. *White* v. *Maryland*, 373 U.S. 59 (1963).

7. *Rothgery* v. *Gillespie County, Texas*, 554 U.S. 191 (2008).
8. Much of the information in this section comes from Barry Mahoney et al., *Pretrial Services Programs: Responsibilities and Potential* (Washington, DC: National Institute of Justice, 2001).
9. *Taylor* v. *Taintor*, 83 U.S. 66 (1873).
10. National Advisory Commission on Criminal Justice Standards and Goals, *The Courts* (Washington, DC: U.S. Government Printing Office, 1973), p. 37.
11. C. Ares, A. Rankin, and H. Sturz, "The Manhattan Bail Project: An Interim Report on the Use of Pre-trial Parole," *New York University Law Review*, Vol. 38 (January 1963), pp. 68–95.
12. H. Zeisel, "Bail Revisited," *American Bar Foundation Research Journal*, Vol. 4 (1979), pp. 769–789.
13. Ibid.
14. "Twelve Percent of Those Freed on Low Bail Fail to Appear," *New York Times*, December 2, 1983, p. 1.
15. Bureau of Justice Statistics (BJS), *Report to the Nation on Crime and Justice*, 2nd ed. (Washington, DC: U.S. Dept. of Justice, 1988), p. 76.
16. See Tracey Kyckelhahn and Thomas H. Cohen, *Felony Defendants in Large Urban Counties, 2004* (Washington, DC: Bureau of Justice Statistics, 2008), p. iv.
17. John Scalia, *Federal Pretrial Release and Detention, 1996* (Washington, DC: Bureau of Justice Statistics, 1999), p. 1, http://www.ojp.usdoj.gov/bjs/pub/pdf/fprd96.pdf (accessed January 25, 2007).
18. Donald E. Pryor and Walter F. Smith, "Significant Research Findings Concerning Pretrial Release," *Pretrial Issues*, Vol. 4, No. 1 (Washington, DC: Pretrial Services Resource Center, February 1982). See also the Pretrial Services Resource Center website at http://www.pretrial.org/mainpage.htm (accessed July 15, 2009).
19. BJS, *Report to the Nation on Crime and Justice*, p. 77.
20. According to Joseph B. Vaughn and Victor E. Kappeler, the first such legislation was the 1970 District of Columbia Court Reform and Criminal Procedure Act. See Vaughn and Kappeler, "The Denial of Bail: Pre-Trial Preventive Detention," *Criminal Justice Research Bulletin*, Vol. 3, No. 6 (Huntsville, TX: Sam Houston State University, 1987), p. 1.
21. Ibid.
22. Bail Reform Act of 1984, U.S. Code, Title 18, Section 3142(e).
23. *U.S.* v. *Montalvo-Murillo*, 495 U.S. 711 (1990).
24. Ibid., syllabus.
25. *U.S.* v. *Hazzard*, 35 CrL. 2217 (1984).
26. See, for example, *U.S.* v. *Motamedi*, 37 CrL. 2394, CA 9 (1985).
27. A few states now have laws that permit the defendant to appear before the grand jury.
28. John M. Scheb and John M. Scheb II, *American Criminal Law* (St. Paul, MN: West, 1996), p. 31.
29. Ibid.
30. The information in this paragraph is adapted from Linda Greenhouse, "Supreme Court Limits Forced Medication of Some for Trial," *New York Times*, June 16, 2003, http://www.nytimes.com/2003/06/17/politics/17DRUG.html (accessed June 17, 2005).
31. *Sell* v. *U.S.*, 539 U.S. 166 (2003).
32. Federal Rules of Criminal Procedure, 5.1(a).
33. Scheb and Scheb, *American Criminal Law*, p. 32.
34. Gary Fields and John R. Emshwiller, "Federal Guilty Pleas Soar as Bargains Trump Trials," *Wall Street Journal*, September 23, 2012, http://online.wsj.com/article/SB10000872396390443589304577637610097206808.html (accessed April 1, 2013).
35. Ibid.
36. *Kercheval* v. *U.S.*, 274 U.S. 220, 223, 47 S.Ct. 582, 583 (1927); *Boykin* v. *Alabama*, 395 U.S. 238 (1969); and *Dickerson* v. *New Banner Institute, Inc.*, 460 U.S. 103 (1983).
37. Ronald F. Wright and Paul Hofer, analysis of Bureau of Justice Statistics data from: Erica Goode, "Stronger Hand for Judges in the 'Bazaar' of Plea Deals," *New York Times*, March 22, 2012, http://www.nytimes.com/2012/03/23/us/stronger-hand-for-judges-after-rulings-on-plea-deals.html?_r=2&ref=us (accessed March 23, 2012).
38. Barbara Boland et al., *The Prosecution of Felony Arrests, 1987* (Washington, DC: U.S. Government Printing Office, 1990).
39. *Santobello* v. *New York*, 404 U.S. 257 (1971).
40. *Mabry* v. *Johnson*, 467 U.S. 504 (1984).
41. *U.S.* v. *Baldacchino*, 762 F.2d 170 (1st Cir. 1985); *U.S.* v. *Reardon*, 787 F.2d 512 (10th Cir. 1986); and *U.S.* v. *Donahey*, 529 F.2d 831 (11th Cir. 1976).
42. *Missouri* v. *Frye*, U.S. Supreme Court, No. 10-444 (decided March 21, 2012), and *Lafler* v. *Cooper*, U.S. Supreme Court, No. 10-209 (decided March 21, 2012).
43. For a classic discussion of such considerations, see David Sudnow, "Normal Crimes: Sociological Features of the Penal Code in a Public Defender Office," *Social Problems*, Vol. 123, No. 3 (winter 1965), p. 255.
44. Federal Rules of Criminal Procedure, No. 11.
45. Marc G. Gertz and Edmond J. True, "Social Scientists in the Courtroom: The Frustrations of Two Expert Witnesses," in Susette M. Talarico, ed., *Courts and Criminal Justice: Emerging Issues* (Beverly Hills, CA: Sage, 1985), pp. 81–91.
46. Dotson was the first person convicted of a crime (rape) to be exonerated by DNA evidence. Kirk Bloodsworth, whose case is discussed in a "CJ News" box in the next chapter, was the first death row inmate to be exonerated through the use of DNA analysis. Richard Buckland, a 17-year-old English teenager with learning disabilities, was likely the first person whose innocence was demonstrated through the use of DNA analysis. Although Buckland was a suspect in two rape cases, he had not been convicted at the time DNA evidence proved his innocence.
47. Samuel R. Gross et al., "Exonerations in the United States, 1989 through 2003," April 4, 2004, http://www.mindfully.org/Reform/2004/Prison-Exonerations-Gross19apr04.htm (accessed May 28, 2009).
48. Ibid.
49. *Klopfer* v. *North Carolina*, 386 U.S. 213 (1967).
50. *Barker* v. *Wingo*, 407 U.S. 514 (1972).
51. *Strunk* v. *U.S.*, 412 U.S. 434 (1973).
52. Speedy Trial Act, U.S. Code, Title 18, Section 3161 (1974).
53. *U.S.* v. *Taylor*, 487 U.S. 326, 108 S.Ct. 2413, 101 L.Ed.2d 297 (1988).
54. *Fex* v. *Michigan*, 113 S.Ct. 1085, 122 L.Ed.2d 406 (1993).
55. *Doggett* v. *U.S.*, 112 S.Ct. 2686 (1992).
56. William U. McCormack, "Supreme Court Cases: 1991–1992 Term," *FBI Law Enforcement Bulletin*, November 1992, pp. 28–29.
57. *Padilla* v. *Hanft*, No. 05-533, cert. denied.
58. Ibid.
59. See, for example, the U.S. Supreme Court's decision in the case of *Murphy* v. *Florida*, 410 U.S. 525 (1973).
60. *Witherspoon* v. *Illinois*, 391 U.S. 510 (1968).
61. *Mu'Min* v. *Virginia*, 500 U.S. 415 (1991).
62. Federal Rules of Criminal Procedure, Rule 24(6).
63. Although the words *argument* and *statement* are sometimes used interchangeably to refer to opening remarks, defense attorneys are enjoined from drawing conclusions or "arguing" to the jury at this stage in the trial. Their task, as described in the section that follows, is simply to explain to the jury how the defense will be conducted.

64. Learn more about shadow juries from Molly McDonough, "Me and My Shadow: Shadow Juries Are Helping Litigators Shape Their Cases during Trial," *National Law Journal*, May 17, 2001.
65. Supreme Court majority opinion in *Powers* v. *Ohio*, 499 U.S. 400 (1991), citing *Strauder* v. *West Virginia*, 100 U.S. 303 (1880).
66. *Swain* v. *Alabama*, 380 U.S. 202 (1965).
67. *Batson* v. *Kentucky*, 476 U.S. 79 (1986).
68. *Ford* v. *Georgia*, 498 U.S. 411 (1991), footnote 2.
69. *Powers* v. *Ohio*, 499 U.S. 400 (1991).
70. *Edmonson* v. *Leesville Concrete Co., Inc.*, 500 U.S. 614 (1991).
71. *Georgia* v. *McCollum*, 505 U.S. 42 (1992).
72. *J.E.B.* v. *Alabama*, ex rel. T. B., 511 U.S. 127 (1994).
73. See, for example, *Davis* v. *Minnesota*, 511 U.S. 1115 (1994).
74. Michael Kirkland, "Court Rejects Fat Jurors Case," United Press International, January 8, 1996. The case was *Santiago-Martinez* v. *U.S.*, No. 95-567 (1996).
75. *Campbell* v. *Louisiana*, 523 U.S. 392 (1998).
76. *Miller-El* v. *Cockrell*, 537 U.S. 322 (2003).
77. Ibid., syllabus.
78. *Miller-El* v. *Dretke*, 545 U.S. 231 (2005).
79. *Snyder* v. *Louisiana*, 552 U.S. 472 (2008).
80. *U.S.* v. *Dinitz*, 424 U.S. 600, 612 (1976).
81. *Michigan* v. *Lucas*, 500 U.S. 145 (1991).
82. Associated Press, "Suit Settlement Ends Bryant Saga," March 3, 2005, http://msnbc.msn.com/id/7019659 (accessed July 12, 2010).
83. *Kotteakos* v. *U.S.*, 328 U.S. 750 (1946); *Brecht* v. *Abrahamson*, 113 S.Ct. 1710, 123 L.Ed.2d 353 (1993); and *Arizona* v. *Fulminante*, 111 S.Ct. 1246 (1991).
84. The Court, citing *Kotteakos* v. *U.S.* (1946), in *Brecht* v. *Abrahamson*, 113 S.Ct. 1710, 123 L.Ed.2d 353 (1993).
85. *Sullivan* v. *Louisiana*, 113 S.Ct. 2078, 124 L.Ed.2d 182 (1993).
86. *Griffin* v. *California*, 380 U.S. 609 (1965).
87. *Ohio* v. *Reiner*, 123 S.Ct. 1252, 532 U.S. 17 (2001).
88. Leading questions may, in fact, be permitted for certain purposes, including refreshing a witness's memory, impeaching a hostile witness, introducing undisputed material, and helping a witness with impaired faculties.
89. *In re Oliver*, 333 U.S. 257 (1948).
90. *Coy* v. *Iowa*, 487 U.S. 1012 (1988).
91. *Maryland* v. *Craig*, 497 U.S. 836, 845-847 (1990).
92. *Idaho* v. *Wright*, 497 U.S. 805 (1990).
93. *White* v. *Illinois*, 112 S.Ct. 736 (1992).
94. *Crawford* v. *Washington*, 541 U.S. 36 (2004).
95. *Davis* v. *Washington*, 547 U.S. 813 (2006). See also *Hammon* v. *Indiana*, U.S. Supreme Court, 547 U.S. 813 (2006).
96. *Davis* v. *Washington*, syllabus.
97. Federal Rules of Criminal Procedure, Rule 29.1.
98. See *Johnson* v. *Louisiana*, 406 U.S. 356 (1972); and *Apodaca* v. *Oregon*, 406 U.S. 404 (1972).
99. *Allen* v. *U.S.*, 164 U.S. 492 (1896).
100. Judge Harold J. Rothwax, *Guilty: The Collapse of Criminal Justice* (New York: Random House, 1996).
101. Amiram Elwork, Bruce D. Sales, and James Alfini, *Making Jury Instructions Understandable* (Charlottesville, VA: Michie, 1982).
102. "King Jury Lives in Fear from Unpopular Verdict," *Fayetteville (NC) Observer-Times*, May 10, 1992.
103. "Los Angeles Trials Spark Debate over Anonymous Juries," *Criminal Justice Newsletter*, February 16, 1993, pp. 3–4.
104. Some states have centralized offices called Administrative Offices of the Courts or something similar. Such offices, however, are often primarily data-gathering agencies with little or no authority over the day-to-day functioning of state or local courts.
105. See, for example, Larry Berkson and Susan Carbon, *Court Unification: Its History, Politics, and Implementation* (Washington, DC: U.S. Government Printing Office, 1978); and Thomas Henderson et al., *The Significance of Judicial Structure: The Effect of Unification on Trial Court Operators* (Alexandria, VA: Institute for Economic and Policy Studies, 1984).
106. See, for example, Thomas J. Cook et al., *Basic Issues in Court Performance* (Washington, DC: National Institute of Justice, 1982).
107. See, for example, Sorrel Wildhorn et al., *Indicators of Justice: Measuring the Performance of Prosecutors, Defense, and Court Agencies Involved in Felony Proceedings* (Lexington, MA: Lexington Books, 1977).
108. Irving Stone, *Clarence Darrow for the Defense* (New York: Doubleday, 1941).
109. *Victor* v. *Nebraska*, 114 S.Ct. 1239, 127 L.Ed.2d 583 (1994).
110. As found in the California jury instructions.

Rich Legg/Getty Images

11 SENTENCING

OUTLINE

- Introduction
- The Philosophy and Goals of Criminal Sentencing
- Indeterminate Sentencing
- Structured Sentencing
- Innovations in Sentencing
- The Presentence Investigation
- The Victim—Forgotten No Longer
- Modern Sentencing Options
- Death: The Ultimate Sanction
- Opposition to Capital Punishment

LEARNING OBJECTIVES

After reading this chapter, you should be able to

- Describe the five goals of contemporary criminal sentencing.
- Define *indeterminate sentencing*, including its purpose.
- Describe the structured sentencing models in use today.
- Describe alternative sentences, fines, diversion, and offender registries.
- Explain the purpose of presentence investigations, presentence investigation reports, and presentencing hearings.
- Describe the history of victims' rights and services, including the growing role of the victim in criminal justice proceedings today.
- List the four traditional sentencing options.
- State the arguments for and against capital punishment.

Excessive bail shall not be required, nor excessive fines imposed, nor cruel and unusual punishments inflicted.

EIGHTH AMENDMENT TO THE U.S. CONSTITUTION

sentencing The imposition of a criminal sanction by a judicial authority.

Follow the author's tweets about the latest crime and justice news @schmalleger.

Introduction

On June 25, 2013, Oregon became the third state to adopt racial impact legislation.[1] The other two states with similar laws are Connecticut and Iowa. Racial impact laws require policymakers to conduct racial-impact studies and to prepare racial-impact statements for any proposed policy changes affecting criminal **sentencing**, probation, or parole. Oregon's law was passed after research showed that black Oregonians make up only 2% of the state's population, yet constitute 9% of its prisoners. About the same time as the Oregon legislation became law, however, North Carolina, which had been one of the first states to require racial-impact studies, repealed its Racial Justice Act, noting that an unintended consequence of the legislation had been to effectively block executions in the state.[2]

Marc Mauer, head of the Washington, D.C.–based Sentencing Project, says, "The premise behind racial impact statements is that policies often have unintended consequences that would be best addressed prior to adoption of new initiatives."[3] One example Mauer gives is that of enhanced criminal penalties associated with drug sales near school grounds—a law, he says, more likely to be violated by minorities because they tend to live in areas with greater proximity to schools. Studies of the racial impact of sentencing practices, Mauer says, force us to examine twin problems in the justice system: (1) the need for policies and practices that can work effectively to promote public safety, and (2) the need to reduce disproportionate rates of minority incarceration when feasible. "These are not competing goals," says Mauer. "If we are successful in addressing crime in a proactive way, we will be able to reduce high imprisonment rates; conversely, by promoting racial justice we will increase confidence in the criminal justice system and thereby aid public safety efforts."

Under an organized system of criminal justice, sentencing is the imposition of a penalty on a person convicted of a crime. Sentencing follows what is intended to be an impartial judicial proceeding during which criminal responsibility is ascertained. Most sentencing decisions are made by judges, although in some cases, especially where a death sentence is possible, juries may be involved in a special sentencing phase of courtroom proceedings. The sentencing decision is one of the most difficult made by any judge or jury. Not only does it affect the future of the defendant—and at times it is a decision about his or her life or death—but society looks to sentencing to achieve a diversity of goals, some of which are not fully compatible with others.

Sentencing is the imposition of a penalty on a person convicted of a crime.

This chapter examines sentencing in terms of both philosophy and practice. We will describe the goals of sentencing as well as the historical development of various sentencing models in the United States. This chapter also contains a detailed overview of victimization and victims' rights in general, especially as they relate to courtroom procedure and to sentencing practice. Federal sentencing guidelines and the significance of presentence investigations are also described. For an overview of sentencing issues, visit the Sentencing Project via **http://www.sentencingproject.org**.

The Philosophy and Goals of Criminal Sentencing

Traditional sentencing options have included imprisonment, fines, probation, and—for very serious offenses—death. Limits on the range of options available to sentencing authorities are generally specified by law. Historically, those limits have shifted as understandings of crime and the goals of sentencing have changed. Sentencing philosophies, or the justifications on which various sentencing strategies are based, are manifestly intertwined with issues of religion, morals, values, and emotions.[4] Philosophies that gained ascendancy at a particular point in history usually reflected more deeply held social values. Centuries ago, for example, it was thought that crime was due to sin and that suffering was the culprit's due. Judges were expected to be harsh. Capital punishment, torture, and painful physical penalties served this view of criminal behavior.

Sentencing philosophies are intertwined with issues of religion, morals, values, and emotions.

An emphasis on equitable punishments became prevalent around the time of the American and French Revolutions, brought about in part by Enlightenment philosophies. Offenders came to be seen as highly rational beings who intentionally and somewhat carefully chose their course of action. Sentencing philosophies of the period stressed the need for sanctions that outweighed the benefits to be derived from criminal activity. The severity of punishment became less important than quick and certain penalties.

Recent thinking has emphasized the need to limit offenders' potential for future harm by separating them from society. We also still believe that offenders deserve to be punished, and we have not entirely abandoned hope for their rehabilitation. Modern sentencing practices are influenced by five goals, which

retribution The act of taking revenge on a criminal perpetrator.
just deserts A model of criminal sentencing that holds that criminal offenders deserve the punishment they receive at the hands of the law and that punishments should be appropriate to the type and severity of the crime committed.
incapacitation The use of imprisonment or other means to reduce the likelihood that an offender will commit future offenses.

Dana Verkouteren/AP Wide World Photos

A courtroom drawing showing Rosemary Dillard, whose husband was killed on September 11, 2001, speaking to Zacarias Moussaoui, as family members of other 9/11 victims listen. The scene took place in U.S. District Court in Alexandria, Virginia, during the sentencing hearing for the convicted al-Qaeda conspirator. On May 4, 2006, federal Judge Leonie M. Brinkema sentenced Moussaoui to life in prison with no possibility of release. What was Moussaoui's crime? Do you think that his sentence was just and fair? Might it deter other would-be terrorists?

TABLE 11-1 | Sentencing—Goals and Purposes

SENTENCING GOAL	PURPOSE
Retribution	A just deserts perspective that emphasizes taking revenge on a criminal perpetrator or group of offenders.
Incapacitation	The use of imprisonment or other means to reduce the likelihood that a particular offender will commit more crime.
Deterrence	A sentencing rationale that seeks to inhibit criminal behavior through punishment or the fear of punishment.
General deterrence	Seeks to prevent future crimes like the one for which the sentence is being imposed.
Specific deterrence	Seeks to prevent a *particular* offender from engaging in repeat criminality.
Rehabilitation	The attempt to reform a criminal offender.
Restoration	A goal of sentencing that seeks to make the victim "whole again."

weave their way through widely disseminated professional and legal models, continuing public calls for sentencing reform, and everyday sentencing practice. Each goal represents a quasi-independent sentencing philosophy, as each makes distinctive assumptions about human nature and holds implications for sentencing practice. Table 11-1 shows the five general goals of contemporary sentencing.

Retribution

Retribution is a call for punishment based on a perceived need for vengeance. Retribution is the earliest known rationale for punishment. Most early societies punished all offenders who were caught. Early punishments were immediate—often without the benefit of a hearing—and they were often extreme, with little thought given to whether the punishment "fit" the crime. Death and exile, for example, were commonly imposed, even for relatively minor offenses. The Old Testament dictum of "an eye for an eye, a tooth for a tooth"—often cited as an ancient justification for retribution—was actually intended to reduce the severity of punishment for relatively minor crimes.

Today, retribution corresponds to the **just deserts** model of sentencing, which holds that offenders are responsible for their crimes. When they are convicted and punished, they are said to have gotten their "just deserts." Retribution sees punishment as deserved, justified, and even required[5] by the offender's behavior. The primary sentencing tool of the just deserts model is imprisonment, but in extreme cases capital punishment (that is, death) becomes the ultimate retribution. Both in the public's view and in political policymaking, retribution is still a primary goal of criminal sentencing.

Incapacitation

Incapacitation, the second goal of criminal sentencing, seeks to protect innocent members of society from offenders who might harm them if not prevented from doing so. In ancient times, mutilation and amputation of the extremities were sometimes used to

deterrence A goal of criminal sentencing that seeks to inhibit criminal behavior through the fear of punishment.
general deterrence A goal of criminal sentencing that seeks to prevent others from committing crimes similar to the one for which a particular offender is being sentenced by making an example of the person sentenced.
specific deterrence A goal of criminal sentencing that seeks to prevent a particular offender from engaging in repeat criminality.
rehabilitation The attempt to reform a criminal offender. Also, the state in which a reformed offender is said to be.

restoration A goal of criminal sentencing that attempts to make the victim "whole again."

prevent offenders from repeating their crimes. Modern incapacitation strategies separate offenders from the community to reduce opportunities for further criminality. Incapacitation, sometimes called the "lock 'em up approach," forms the basis for the modern movement toward prison "warehousing." Unlike retribution, incapacitation requires only restraint—and not punishment.

Deterrence

Deterrence uses the example or threat of punishment to convince people that criminal activity is not worthwhile. Its overall goal is crime prevention. **Specific deterrence** seeks to reduce the likelihood of recidivism (repeat offenses) by convicted offenders, whereas **general deterrence** strives to influence the future behavior of people who have not yet been arrested and who may be tempted to turn to crime. Deterrence is one of the more "rational" goals of sentencing because it is an easily articulated goal and because it is possible to investigate objectively the amount of punishment required to deter.

Deterrence is compatible with the goal of incapacitation, as at least specific deterrence can be achieved through incapacitating offenders. Tufts University Professor Hugo Adam Bedau, however, points to significant differences between retribution and deterrence.[6] Retribution is oriented toward the past, says Bedau. It seeks to redress wrongs already committed. Deterrence, in contrast, is a strategy for the future. It aims to prevent new crimes.

Rehabilitation

Rehabilitation seeks to bring about fundamental changes in offenders and their behavior. As in the case of deterrence, the ultimate goal of rehabilitation is a reduction in the number of criminal offenses. Whereas deterrence depends on a fear of the consequences of violating the law, rehabilitation generally works through education and psychological treatment to reduce the likelihood of future criminality.

> The ultimate goal of rehabilitation is a reduction in the number of criminal offenses.

The term *rehabilitation*, however, is a misnomer for the kinds of changes that its supporters seek. Rehabilitation literally means to return a person to his or her previous condition; however, it is likely that in most cases restoring criminals to their previous state will result in nothing but a more youthful type of criminality.

In the late 1970s, the rehabilitative goal in sentencing fell victim to the "nothing-works doctrine." The nothing-works doctrine was based on studies of recidivism rates that consistently showed that rehabilitation was more an ideal than a reality.[7] With as many as 90% of former convicted offenders returning to lives of crime following release from prison-based treatment programs, public sentiments in favor of incapacitation grew. Although the rehabilitation ideal has clearly suffered in the public arena, emerging evidence has begun to suggest that effective treatment programs do exist and may be growing in number.[8]

Restoration

Victims of crime and their families are frequently traumatized by their experiences. Some victims are killed, and others receive lasting physical or emotional injuries. For many, the world is never the same. The victimized may live in constant fear, be reduced in personal vigor, and be unable to form trusting relationships. **Restoration** is a sentencing goal that seeks to

© Drew Crawford/The Image Works

Female inmates being trained to work with fiber optics at the Federal Correctional Institution in Danbury, Connecticut. Skills acquired through such prison programs might translate into productive, noncriminal careers for ex-convicts. Rehabilitation is an important, but infrequently voiced, goal of modern sentencing practices. What are some other sentencing goals identified in this chapter?

restorative justice (RJ) A sentencing model that builds on restitution and community participation in an attempt to make the victim "whole again."

address this damage by making the victim and the community "whole again."

A U.S. Department of Justice report explains restoration this way: "Crime was once defined as a 'violation of the State.' This remains the case today, but we now recognize that crime is far more. It is—among other things—a violation of one person by another. While retributive justice may address the first type of violation adequately, restorative justice is required to effectively address the latter. . . . Thus [through restorative justice] we seek to attain a balance between the legitimate needs of the community, the . . . offender, and the victim."[9] The "healing" of all parties has many aspects, ranging from victims' assistance initiatives to legislation supporting victims' compensation.

Restorative justice (RJ) is also referred to as *balanced and restorative justice.* Conceptually, "balance" is achieved by giving equal consideration to community safety and offender accountability. Restorative justice focuses on "crime as harm, and justice as repairing the harm."[10] The community safety dimension of the RJ philosophy recognizes that the justice system has a responsibility to protect the public from crime and from offenders.[11] It also recognizes that the community can participate in ensuring its own safety. The accountability element defines criminal conduct in terms of obligations incurred by the offender, both to the victim and to the community.[12] RJ also has what some describe as a competency development element, which holds that offenders who enter the justice system should leave it more capable of participating successfully in the wider society than when they entered. In essence, RJ is community-focused; its primary goal is improving the quality of life for all members of the community. See Table 11-2 for a comparison of retributive and restorative justice.

In essence, restorative justice is community-focused.

Sentencing options that seek to restore the victim have focused primarily on restitution payments that offenders are ordered to make, either to their victims or to a general fund, which may then reimburse victims for suffering, lost wages, and medical expenses. In support of these goals, the 1984 Federal Comprehensive Crime Control Act specifically requires that "[i]f sentenced to probation, the defendant must also be ordered to pay a fine, make restitution, and/or work in community service."[13]

Some advocates of the restoration philosophy of sentencing point out that restitution payments and work programs that benefit the victim can also have the added benefit of rehabilitating the offender. The hope is that such sentences will teach offenders personal responsibility through structured financial obligations, job requirements, and regularly scheduled payments. Learn more about restorative justice by visiting **http://www.ojjdp.gov/pubs/implementing**.

TABLE 11-2 | Differences between Retributive and Restorative Justice

RETRIBUTIVE JUSTICE	RESTORATIVE JUSTICE
Crime is an act against the state, a violation of a law, an abstract idea.	Crime is an act against another person or the community.
The criminal justice system controls crime.	Crime control lies primarily with the community.
Offender accountability is defined as taking punishment.	Offender accountability is defined as assuming responsibility and taking action to repair harm.
Crime is an individual act with individual responsibility.	Crime has both individual and social dimensions of responsibility.
Victims are peripheral to the process of resolving a crime.	Victims are central to the process of resolving a crime.
The offender is defined by deficits.	The offender is defined by the capacity to make reparation.
The emphasis is on adversarial relationships.	The emphasis is on dialogue and negotiation.
Pain is imposed to punish, deter, and prevent.	Restitution is a means of restoring both parties; the goal is reconciliation.
The community is on the sidelines, represented abstractly by the state.	The community is the facilitator in the restorative process.
The response is focused on the offender's past behavior.	The response is focused on harmful consequences of the offender's behavior; the emphasis is on the future and on reparation.
There is dependence on proxy professionals.	Both the offender and the victim are directly involved.

Source: Adapted from Gordon Bazemore and Mark S. Umbreit, *Balanced and Restorative Justice: Program Summary* (Washington, DC: Office of Juvenile Justice and Delinquency Prevention, 1994), p. 7.

■ **indeterminate sentencing** A model of criminal punishment that encourages rehabilitation through the use of general and relatively unspecific sentences (such as a term of imprisonment of from one to ten years).
■ **gain time** The amount of time deducted from time to be served in prison on a given sentence as a consequence of participation in special projects or programs.
■ **good time** The amount of time deducted from time to be served in prison on a given sentence as a consequence of good behavior.

Indeterminate Sentencing

Whereas the *philosophy* of criminal sentencing is reflected in the goals of sentencing we have just discussed, different sentencing *practices* have been linked to each goal. During most of the twentieth century, for example, the rehabilitation goal was influential. Because rehabilitation requires that individual offenders' personal characteristics be closely considered in defining effective treatment strategies, judges were generally permitted wide discretion in choosing from among sentencing options. Although incapacitation is increasingly becoming the sentencing strategy of choice today, many state criminal codes still allow judges to impose fines, probation, or widely varying prison terms, all for the same offense. These sentencing practices, characterized primarily by vast judicial choice, constitute an **indeterminate sentencing** model.

Indeterminate sentencing has both a historical and a philosophical basis in the belief that convicted offenders are more likely to participate in their own rehabilitation if participation will reduce the amount of time they have to spend in prison. Inmates exhibiting good behavior will be released early, while recalcitrant inmates will remain in prison until the end of their terms. For that reason, parole generally plays a significant role in states that employ the indeterminate sentencing model.

Indeterminate sentencing relies heavily on judges' discretion to choose among types of sanctions and to set upper and lower limits on the length of prison stays. Indeterminate sentences are typically imposed with wording like this: "The defendant shall serve not less than five and not more than twenty-five years in the state's prison, under the supervision of the state department of correction." Judicial discretion under the indeterminate model also extends to the imposition of concurrent or consecutive sentences when the offender is convicted on more than one charge. Consecutive sentences are served one after the other, whereas concurrent sentences expire simultaneously.

Indeterminate sentencing relies heavily on judges' discretion.

The indeterminate model was also created to take into consideration detailed differences in degrees of guilt. Under this model, judges can weigh minute differences among cases, situations, and offenders. Under the indeterminate sentencing model, the inmate's behavior while incarcerated is the primary determinant of the amount of time served. State parole boards wield great discretion under this model, acting as the final arbiters of the actual sentence served.

A few states employ a partially indeterminate sentencing model. They allow judges to specify only the maximum amount of time to be served. Some minimum is generally implied by law but is not under the control of the sentencing authority. General practice is to set one year as a minimum for all felonies, although a few jurisdictions assume no minimum time at all, making offenders eligible for immediate parole.

Critiques of Indeterminate Sentencing

Indeterminate sentencing is still the rule in many jurisdictions, including Georgia, Hawaii, Iowa, Kentucky, Massachusetts, Michigan, Nevada, New York, North Dakota, Oklahoma, Rhode Island, South Carolina, South Dakota, Texas, Utah, Vermont, West Virginia, and Wyoming.[14] Since the 1970s, however, the model has come under fire for contributing to inequality in sentencing. Critics claim that the indeterminate model allows judges' personalities and personal philosophies to produce too wide a range of sentencing practices, from very lenient to very strict. The indeterminate model is also criticized for perpetuating a system under which offenders might be sentenced, at least by some judges, more on the basis of personal and social characteristics, such as race, gender, and social class, than on culpability.

Because of the personal nature of judicial decisions under the indeterminate model, offenders often depend on the advice and ploys of their attorneys to appear before a judge who is thought to be a good sentencing risk. Requests for delays are a common defense strategy in indeterminate sentencing states, where they are used to try to manipulate the selection of the judge involved in the sentencing decision.

Another charge leveled against indeterminate sentencing is that it tends to produce "dishonesty" in sentencing. Because of sentence cutbacks for good behavior and involvement in work and study programs, time served in prison is generally far less than sentences would seem to indicate. An inmate sentenced to five to ten years, for example, might actually be released in a couple of years after all **gain time**, **good time**, and other special

■ **proportionality** A sentencing principle that holds that the severity of sanctions should bear a direct relationship to the seriousness of the crime committed.

■ **equity** A sentencing principle, based on concerns with social equality, that holds that similar crimes should be punished with the same degree of severity, regardless of the social or personal characteristics of the offenders.

■ **social debt** A sentencing principle that holds that an offender's criminal history should objectively be taken into account in sentencing decisions.

■ **structured sentencing** A model of criminal punishment that includes determinate and commission-created presumptive sentencing schemes, as well as voluntary/advisory sentencing guidelines.

■ **determinate sentencing** A model of criminal punishment in which an offender is given a fixed term of imprisonment that may be reduced by good time or gain time. Under the model, for example, all offenders convicted of the same degree of burglary would be sentenced to the same length of time behind bars.

TABLE 11-3 | Percentage of Sentence Served in State Prison by Offense and Race

OFFENSE TYPE	PERCENTAGE OF SENTENCE SERVED	
	WHITE INMATES	BLACK INMATES
Violent	57.3	60.9
Property	37.0	41.5
Drug	31.7	36.1
Public-order	40.4	49.0
Average for all offenses	42.6	48.5

Source: Thomas P. Bonczar, "First Releases from State Prison, 2009: Sentence Length and Time Served in Prison, by Offense and Race," National Corrections Reporting Program, 2011, http://bjs.ojp.usdoj.gov/content/data/ncrpt09.zip (accessed October 25, 2013).

allowances have been calculated. (Some of the same charges can be leveled against determinate sentencing schemes under which corrections officials can administratively reduce the time served by an inmate.) A survey by the Bureau of Justice Statistics found that even violent offenders released from state prisons during the study period had served, on average, only 51% of the sentences they originally received.[15] Nonviolent offenders had served even smaller portions of their sentences. Table 11-3 shows the percentage of an imposed sentence that an offender released from state prison had actually served.

To ensure long prison terms in indeterminate jurisdictions, some court officials have gone to extremes. In 1994, for example, Oklahoma Judge Dan Owens sentenced convicted child molester Charles Scott Robinson to 30,000 years in prison.[16] Judge Owens, complying with the jury's efforts to ensure that Robinson would spend the rest of his life behind bars, sentenced him to serve six consecutive 5,000-year sentences. Robinson had 14 previous felony convictions.

Structured Sentencing

Until the 1970s, all 50 states used some form of indeterminate (or partially indeterminate) sentencing. Eventually, however, calls for equity and proportionality in sentencing, heightened by claims of racial disparity in the sentencing practices of some judges,[17] led many states to move toward greater control over their sentencing systems.

Critics of the indeterminate model called for the recognition of three fundamental sentencing principles: **proportionality**, **equity**, and **social debt**. Proportionality refers to the belief that the severity of sanctions should bear a direct relationship to the seriousness of the crime committed. Equity means that similar crimes should be punished with the same degree of severity, regardless of the social or personal characteristics of offenders. According to the principle of equity, for example, two bank robbers in different parts of the country, who use the same techniques and weapons, with the same degree of implied threat, should receive roughly the same sentence even though they are tried under separate circumstances and in different jurisdictions. The equity principle needs to be balanced, however, against the notion of social debt. In the case of the bank robbers, the offender who has a prior criminal record can be said to have a higher level of social debt than the first-time robber, where all else is equal. Greater social debt, of course, suggests a more severe punishment or a greater need for treatment.

Beginning in the 1970s, a number of states addressed these concerns by developing a different model of sentencing, known as **structured sentencing**. One form of structured sentencing, called **determinate sentencing**, requires that a convicted offender be sentenced to a fixed term that may be reduced by good time (time off for good behavior) or earned time (time off in recognition of special efforts on the part of the inmate). Determinate sentencing states eliminated the use of parole and created explicit standards to specify the amount of punishment appropriate for a given offense. Determinate sentencing practices also specify an anticipated release date for each sentenced offender.

In a report that traced the historical development of determinate sentencing, the National Council on Crime and Delinquency (NCCD) observed that "the term 'determinate sentencing' is generally used to refer to the sentencing reforms of the late 1970s." At that time, the legislatures of California, Illinois, Indiana, and Maine abolished the parole release decision and replaced indeterminate penalties with fixed (or flat) sentences that could be reduced by good-time provisions.

■ **voluntary/advisory sentencing guidelines** Recommended sentencing policies that are not required by law.

■ **presumptive sentencing** A model of criminal punishment that meets the following conditions: (1) The appropriate sentence for an offender convicted of a specific charge is presumed to fall within a range of sentences authorized by sentencing guidelines that are adopted by a legislatively created sentencing body, usually a sentencing commission. (2) Sentencing judges are expected to sentence within the range or to provide written justification for failing to do so. (3) There is a mechanism for review, usually appellate, of any departure from the guidelines.

■ **aggravating circumstances** Circumstances relating to the commission of a crime that make it more grave than the average instance of that crime.

■ **mitigating circumstances** Circumstances relating to the commission of a crime that may be considered to reduce the blameworthiness of the defendant.

In response to the then-growing determinate sentencing movement, a few states developed **voluntary/advisory sentencing guidelines** during the 1980s. These guidelines consist of recommended sentencing policies that are not required by law and serve as guides to judges. Voluntary/advisory sentencing guidelines are usually based on past sentencing practices and may build on either determinate or indeterminate sentencing structures. Florida, Maryland, Massachusetts, Michigan, Rhode Island, Utah, and Wisconsin all experimented with voluntary/advisory guidelines during the 1980s. Voluntary/advisory guidelines constitute a second form of structured sentencing.

A third model of structured sentencing employs what the NCCD calls "commission-based presumptive sentencing guidelines." **Presumptive sentencing** became common in the 1980s as states began to experiment with sentencing guidelines developed by sentencing commissions. These models differed from both determinate and voluntary/advisory guidelines in three respects. First, presumptive sentencing guidelines were not developed by the state legislature but by a sentencing commission that often represented a diverse array of criminal justice and sometimes private interests. Second, presumptive sentencing guidelines were explicit and highly structured, typically relying on a quantitative scoring instrument to classify the offense for which a person was to be sentenced. Third, the guidelines were not voluntary in that judges had to adhere to the sentencing system or provide a written rationale for departing from it.

By 2010, the federal government and 16 states had established commission-created sentencing guidelines. Ten of the 16 states used presumptive sentencing guidelines; the remaining 6 relied on voluntary/advisory guidelines. As a consequence, sentencing guidelines authored by legislatively created sentencing commissions have become the most popular form of structured sentencing.

Guideline jurisdictions, which specified a presumptive sentence for a given offense, generally allowed for "aggravating" or "mitigating" circumstances—indicating a greater or lesser degree of culpability—which judges could take into consideration when imposing a sentence somewhat at variance from the presumptive term. **Aggravating circumstances** call for a tougher sentence and may include especially heinous behavior, cruelty, injury to more than one person, and so on. **Mitigating circumstances**, which indicate that a lesser sentence is called for, are generally similar to legal defenses, although in this case they only reduce criminal responsibility, not eliminate it. Mitigating circumstances include such things as cooperation with the investigating authority, surrender, and good character. Common aggravating and mitigating circumstances are listed in the "CJ Issues" box.

Federal Sentencing Guidelines

In 1984, with the passage of the Comprehensive Crime Control Act, the federal government adopted presumptive sentencing for nearly all federal offenders.[18] The act also addressed the issue of **truth in sentencing**. Under the old federal system, on average, good-time credits and parole reduced time served to about one-third of the actual sentence.[19] At the time, the sentencing practices of most states reflected the federal model. Although sentence reductions may have benefited offenders, they often outraged victims, who felt betrayed by the sentencing process. The 1984 act nearly eliminated good-time credits[20] and began the process of phasing out federal parole and eliminating the U.S. Parole Commission (read more about the commission in Chapter 12).[21] The emphasis on truth in sentencing created, in effect, a sentencing environment of "what you get is what you serve." Truth in sentencing, described as "a close correspondence between the sentence imposed upon those sent to prison and the time actually served prior to prison release,"[22] has become an important policy focus of many state legislatures and the U.S. Congress. The Violent Crime Control and Law Enforcement Act of 1994 set aside $4 billion in federal prison construction funds (called Truth in Sentencing Incentive Funds) for states that adopt truth-in-sentencing laws and are able to guarantee that certain violent offenders will serve 85% of their sentences.

Title II of the Comprehensive Crime Control Act, called the Sentencing Reform Act of 1984,[23] established the nine-member U.S. Sentencing Commission. The commission, which continues to function today, comprises presidential appointees, including three

■ **truth in sentencing** A close correspondence between the sentence imposed on an offender and the time actually served in prison.[i]

CJ | ISSUES
Aggravating and Mitigating Circumstances

Listed here are typical aggravating and mitigating circumstances that judges may consider in arriving at sentencing decisions in presumptive sentencing jurisdictions.

Aggravating Circumstances

- The defendant induced others to participate in the commission of the offense.
- The offense was especially heinous, atrocious, or cruel.
- The defendant was armed with or used a deadly weapon during the crime.
- The defendant committed the offense to avoid or prevent a lawful arrest or to escape from custody.
- The offense was committed for hire.
- The offense was committed against a current or former law enforcement or corrections officer while engaged in the performance of official duties or because of the past exercise of official duties.
- The defendant took advantage of a position of trust or confidence to commit the offense.

Mitigating Circumstances

- The defendant has no record of criminal convictions punishable by more than 60 days of imprisonment.
- The defendant has made substantial or full restitution.
- The defendant has been a person of good character or has had a good reputation in the community.
- The defendant aided in the apprehension of another felon or testified truthfully on behalf of the prosecution.
- The defendant acted under strong provocation, or the victim was a voluntary participant in the criminal activity or otherwise consented to it.
- The offense was committed under duress, coercion, threat, or compulsion that was insufficient to constitute a defense but that significantly reduced the defendant's culpability.
- At the time of the offense, the defendant was suffering from a mental or physical condition that was insufficient to constitute a defense but that significantly reduced the defendant's culpability.

Note: Recent U.S. Supreme Court rulings have held that facts influencing sentencing enhancements, other than prior record or admissions made by a defendant, must be determined by a jury, not by a judge.

federal judges. The Sentencing Reform Act limited the discretion of federal judges by mandating the creation of federal sentencing guidelines, which federal judges were required to follow. The sentencing commission was given the task of developing structured sentencing guidelines to reduce disparity, promote consistency and uniformity, and increase fairness and equity in sentencing.

The guidelines established by the commission took effect in November 1987 but quickly became embroiled in a series of legal disputes, some of which challenged Congress's authority to form the Sentencing Commission. In January 1989, in the case of ***Mistretta* v. *U.S.***,[24] the U.S. Supreme Court held that Congress had acted appropriately in establishing the Sentencing Commission and that the guidelines developed by the commission could be applied in federal cases nationwide. The federal Sentencing Commission continues to meet at least once a year to review the effectiveness of the guidelines it created. Visit the U.S. Sentencing Commission via **http://www.ussc.gov**.

Federal Guideline Provisions

As originally established, federal sentencing guidelines specified a sentencing range from which judges had to choose. If a particular case had "atypical features," judges were allowed to depart from the guidelines. Departures were generally expected only in the presence of aggravating or mitigating circumstances—a number of which are specified in the guidelines.[25] Aggravating circumstances may include the possession of a weapon during the commission of a crime, the degree of criminal involvement (whether the defendant was a leader or a follower in the criminal activity), and extreme psychological injury to the victim. Punishments also increase when a defendant violates a position of public or private trust, uses special skills to commit or conceal offenses, or has a criminal history. Defendants who express remorse, cooperate with authorities, or willingly make restitution may have their sentences reduced under the guidelines. Any departure from the guidelines may, however, become the basis for appellate review concerning the reasonableness of the sentence imposed, and judges who deviate from the guidelines were originally required to provide written reasons for doing so.

Federal sentencing guidelines are built around a table containing 43 rows, each corresponding to one offense level.

Federal sentencing guidelines are built around a table containing 43 rows, each corresponding to one offense level. The penalties associated with each level overlap those of the levels above and below to discourage unnecessary litigation. A person convicted of a crime involving $11,000, for example, and sentenced under the guidelines, is unlikely to receive a penalty substantially greater than if the amount had been somewhat less than $10,000. A change of six levels roughly doubles the sentence imposed under the guidelines, regardless of the level at which one starts. Because of their matrix-like quality, federal sentencing provisions have been referred to as *structured*. The federal sentencing table is available at **http://www.justicestudies.com/pubs/sentable.pdf**.

The sentencing table also contains six rows corresponding to the criminal history category into which an offender falls. Criminal history categories are determined on a point basis. Offenders earn points for previous convictions. Each prior sentence of imprisonment for more than one year and one month counts as three points. Two points are assigned for each prior prison sentence over six months or if the defendant committed the offense while on probation, parole, or work release. The system also assigns points for other types of previous convictions and for offenses committed less than two years after release from imprisonment. Points are added to determine the criminal history category into which an offender falls. Thirteen points or more are required for the highest category. At each offense level, sentences in the highest criminal history category are generally two to three times as severe as for the lowest category. The types of offenses for which federal offenders are sentenced, and how the proportion of those types have changed over time, can be seen in Figure 11-1.

Defendants may also move into the highest criminal history category by virtue of being designated a career offender. Under the sentencing guidelines, a defendant is a career offender if "(1) the defendant was at least 18 years old at the time of the . . . offense, (2) the . . . offense is a crime of violence or trafficking in a controlled substance, and (3) the defendant has at least two prior felony convictions of either a crime of violence or a controlled substance offense."[26]

According to the U.S. Supreme Court, an offender may be adjudged a career offender in a single hearing, even when previous convictions are lacking.

Plea Bargaining under the Guidelines

Plea bargaining plays a major role in the federal judicial system. Approximately 90% of all federal sentences are the result of guilty pleas,[27] and the large majority of those stem from plea negotiations. In the words of former Sentencing Commission Chairman William W. Wilkins, Jr., "With respect to plea bargaining, the Commission has proceeded cautiously. . . . The Commission did not believe it wise to stand the federal criminal justice system on its head by making too drastic and too sudden a change in these practices."[28]

Plea bargaining plays a major role in the federal judicial system.

Although the commission allowed plea bargaining to continue, it required that the agreement (1) be fully disclosed in the record of the court (unless there is an overriding and demonstrable reason why it should not be) and (2) detail the actual conduct of the offense. Under these requirements,

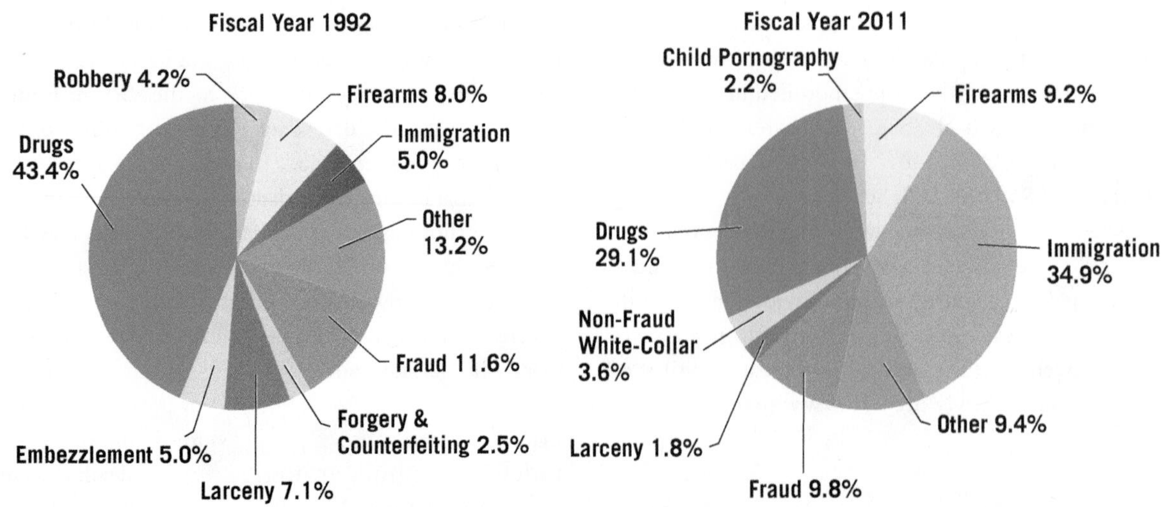

FIGURE 11-1 | Distribution of Federal Offenders in Each Primary Offense Category, Fiscal Years 1992 and 2011

Sources: U.S. Sentencing Commission, 2011 Datafile, USSC FY11; and the 1992 Datafile, USSC FY92.

defendants are unable to hide the actual nature of their offense behind a substitute plea. Information on the decision-making process itself is available to victims, the media, and the public.

In 1996, in the case of *Melendez* v. *U.S.*,[29] the U.S. Supreme Court held that a government motion requesting that a trial judge deviate from the federal sentencing guidelines as part of a cooperative plea agreement does not permit imposition of a sentence below a statutory minimum specified by law. In other words, under *Melendez*, although federal judges could depart from the guidelines, they could not accept plea bargains that would have resulted in sentences lower than the minimum required by law for a particular type of offense.

The Legal Environment of Structured Sentencing

A crucial critique of aggravating factors and their use in presumptive sentencing schemes was offered by the U.S. Supreme Court in 2000 in the case of *Apprendi* v. *New Jersey*.[30] In *Apprendi*, the Court questioned the fact-finding authority of judges in making sentencing decisions, ruling that other than the fact of a prior conviction, any fact that increases the penalty for a crime beyond the prescribed statutory *maximum* is, in effect, an element of the crime, which must be submitted to a jury and proved beyond a reasonable doubt. The case involved Charles Apprendi, a New Jersey defendant who pleaded guilty to unlawfully possessing a firearm—an offense that carried a prison term of five to ten years under state law. Before sentence was imposed, however, the judge found that Apprendi had fired a number of shots into the home of an African American family living in his neighborhood and concluded that he had done so to frighten the family and convince them to move. The judge held that statements made by Apprendi allowed the offense to be classified as a hate crime, which required a longer prison term under the sentencing enhancement provision of New Jersey's hate-crime statute than did the weapons offense to which Apprendi had confessed. The Supreme Court, in overturning the judge's finding and sentence, took issue with the fact that after Apprendi pleaded guilty, an enhanced sentence was imposed without the benefit of a jury-based fact-finding process. The high court ruled that "under the Due Process Clause of the Fifth Amendment and the notice and jury trial guarantees of the Sixth Amendment, any fact (other than prior conviction) that increases the maximum penalty for a crime must be charged in an indictment, submitted to a jury, and proven beyond a reasonable doubt."

In *Apprendi*, the Court questioned the fact-finding authority of judges in making sentencing decisions.

The *Apprendi* case essentially says that *requiring* sentencing judges to consider facts not proven to a jury violates the federal Constitution. It raised the question of whether judges anywhere could legitimately deviate from established sentencing guidelines or apply sentence enhancements based solely on judicial determinations of aggravating factors—especially when such determinations involve findings of fact that might otherwise be made by a jury.[31]

Since *Apprendi*, the Court has expanded the number and types of facts that must be decided by a jury. In 2010, for example, in the case of *U.S.* v. *O'Brien*,[32] the Court held that a determination that a firearm was a machinegun, as described by relevant law, is an element to be proved to a jury beyond a reasonable doubt, not a sentencing factor to be proved to a sentencing judge. The finding impacted a sentencing requirement that a 30-year minimum term of imprisonment be imposed for convictions involving the use of a fully automatic firearm during the commission of a crime.

The *O'Brien* case built upon the important 2004 case of ***Blakely* v. *Washington***,[33] in which the U.S. Supreme Court effectively invalidated any state sentencing schema that allows judges rather than juries to determine any factor that increases a criminal sentence, except for prior convictions. The Court found that because the facts supporting Blakely's increased sentence were neither admitted by the defendant himself nor found by a jury, the sentence violated the Sixth Amendment right to trial by jury. The *Blakely* decision required that the sentencing laws of eight states be rewritten. Washington state legislators responded quickly and created a model law for other legislatures to emulate. The Washington law mandates that "the facts supporting aggravating circumstances shall be proved to a jury beyond a reasonable doubt," or, "if a jury is waived, proof shall be to the court beyond a reasonable doubt."

In 2007, in the case of *Cunningham* v. *California*,[34] the Supreme Court applied its reasoning in *Blakely* to California's determinate sentencing law, finding the law invalid because it placed sentence-elevating fact-finding within the judge's purview. As in *Blakely*, the California law was found to violate a defendant's Sixth Amendment right to trial by jury.

In 2005, in the combined cases of ***U.S.* v. *Booker***[35] and *U.S.* v. *Fanfan*,[36] attention turned to the constitutionality of federal sentencing practices that relied on extra-verdict determinations of fact in the application of sentencing enhancements. In *Booker*, the U.S. Supreme Court issued what some have called an "extraordinary opinion,"[37] which actually encompasses two separate decisions. The combined cases brought two issues before the Court: (1) whether fact-finding done by judges under federal sentencing guidelines violates the Sixth Amendment right to trial by jury; and (2) if so, whether the guidelines are themselves unconstitutional. As in the preceding cases discussed in this section, the Court found that, on the first question, defendant Freddie Booker's drug-trafficking sentence had been improperly enhanced under the guidelines on the basis of facts found solely by a judge. In the view of the Court, the Sixth Amendment right to trial by jury is violated where, under a mandatory guidelines system, a sentence is increased because of an enhancement based on facts found by the judge that were not found by a jury nor admitted by the defendant.[38] Consequently, Booker's sentence was ruled unconstitutional and invalidated. On the second question, the Court reached a compromise and did not strike down the federal guidelines as many thought it would. Instead, it held that the guidelines could be *considered* by federal judges during sentencing but that they were no longer mandatory.

In effect, the decision in *Booker* and *Fanfan* turned the federal sentencing guidelines on their head, making them merely advisory and giving federal judges wide latitude in imposing punishments. While federal judges must still take the guidelines into consideration in reaching sentencing decisions, they do not have to follow them.

In 2007, in a continued clarification of *Booker*, the Supreme Court ruled that federal appeals courts that hear challenges from defendants about prison time may presume that federal criminal sentences are reasonable if they fall within U.S. Sentencing Guidelines. In that case, *Rita* v. *U.S.*,[39] the Court held that "even if the presumption increases the likelihood that the judge, not the jury, will find 'sentencing facts,' it does not violate the Sixth Amendment." The justices reasoned that "a nonbinding appellate reasonableness presumption for Guidelines sentences does not *require* the sentencing judge to impose a Guidelines sentence."

In another 2007 case, *Gall* v. *United States*,[40] the Court clarified its position on appellate review of sentencing decisions by lower courts when it held that "because the Guidelines are now advisory, appellate review of sentencing decisions is limited to determining whether they are 'reasonable.'"

In 2009, in what appeared to be a loosening of prohibitions on judges' sentencing authority, the U.S. Supreme Court found that the Constitution does not prohibit judges from imposing consecutive sentences based on facts not found by a jury. Writing for a slim 5–4 majority in *Oregon* v. *Ice*,[41] Justice Ruth Bader Ginsburg said, "In light of historical practice and the States' authority over administration of their criminal justice systems, the Sixth Amendment does not inhibit states from assigning to judges, rather than to juries, the finding of facts necessary to the imposition of consecutive, rather than concurrent, sentences for multiple offenses."

In 2013, in the case of *Alleyne* v. *U.S.*, the Court ruled that any fact that increases the mandatory minimum sentence is an "element" that must be submitted to the jury.[42] In this case, a federal judge had increased an offender's sentence after investigating his prior convictions and finding that he had been convicted of multiple crimes.[43] The *Alleyne* court held that "*Apprendi*'s principle applies with equal force to facts increasing the mandatory minimum, for a fact triggering a mandatory minimum alters the prescribed range of sentences to which a criminal defendant is exposed." The justices also wrote, however, that: "This ruling does not mean that any fact that influences judicial discretion must be found by a jury." Nonetheless, the *Alleyne* decision makes it more difficult for the government to use the fact of a defendant's prior conviction to enhance a federal criminal sentence.

A 2013 report submitted to Congress by the U.S. Sentencing Commission found that "the sentencing guidelines remain the essential starting point for determining all federal sentences and continue to exert significant influence on federal sentencing trends over time."[44] The commission found that "the rate at which courts impose sentences within the applicable guideline range [stood] at 53.9 percent during the most recent time period studied."[45]

In light of the Court's decisions, it is now up to Congress to reconsider federal sentencing law following *Booker*—a process that has been under way for the past few years. In 2011, the U.S. Sentencing Commission called upon Congress "to exercise its power to direct sentencing policy by enacting [new] mandatory minimum penalties" in modified format.[46] Read the Commission's 2013 congressional report about the impact of *U.S.* v. *Booker* on federal sentencing at **http://www.justicestudies.com/pdf/sentencing2013.pdf**.

Three Strikes Laws

In the spring of 1994, California legislators passed the state's now-famous "three strikes and you're out" bill. Amid much fanfare, Governor Pete Wilson signed the "three-strikes" measure into law, calling it "the toughest and most sweeping crime bill in California history."[47]

California's original three-strikes law, which was retroactive in that it counts offenses committed before the date the legislation was signed, required a sentence of 25 years to life for three-time felons with convictions for two or more serious or violent prior offenses. Criminal offenders facing a "second strike" could receive up to double the normal sentence for their most recent offense. Parole consideration was not available until at least 80% of the sentence has been served.

■ **mandatory sentencing** A structured sentencing scheme that allows no leeway in the nature of the sentence required and under which clearly enumerated punishments are mandated for specific offenses or for habitual offenders convicted of a series of crimes.

Today, about half of the states have passed three-strikes legislation. At the federal level, the Violent Crime Control and Law Enforcement Act of 1994 contains a three-strikes provision that mandates life imprisonment for federal criminals convicted of three violent felonies or drug offenses.

Questions remain, however, about the effectiveness of three-strikes legislation, and many people are concerned about its impact on the justice system. A 2001 study of the original California legislation and its consequences concluded that three-strikes laws are overrated.[48] According to the study, which was conducted by the Washington, D.C.–based Sentencing Project, "California's three-strikes law has increased the number and severity of sentences for nonviolent offenders—and contributed to the aging of the prison population—but has had no significant effect on the state's decline in crime."

A 2012 review of three-strikes legislation found that 16 states have recently modified such laws in response to difficult economic conditions; this means that the high cost of imprisonment is leading legislatures to rethink long prison terms. Modifications have included giving judges more discretion in sentencing and narrowing the types of crimes that count as a "strike."

Practically speaking, California's three-strikes law has had a dramatic impact on the state's criminal justice system. "'Three strikes and you're out' sounds great to a lot of people," says Alan Schuman, president of the American Probation and Parole Association. "But no one will cop a plea when it gets to the third time around. We will have more trials, and this whole country works on plea bargaining and pleading guilty, not jury trials," Schuman said at a meeting of the association.[49] In an early study conducted by RAND, it was estimated that full enforcement of the law could cost as much as $5.5 billion annually—or $300 per California taxpayer per year.

In 2003, however, in two separate cases, the U.S. Supreme Court upheld the three-strikes California convictions of Gary Ewing and Leandro Andrade in California.[50] Ewing, who had four prior felony convictions, had received a 25-years-to-life sentence following his conviction for felony grand theft of three golf clubs. Andrade, who also had a long record, was sentenced to 50 years in prison for two petty theft convictions.[51] In writing for the Court in the *Ewing* case, Justice Sandra Day O'Connor noted that states should be able to decide when repeat offenders "must be isolated from society . . . to protect the public safety," even when nonserious crimes trigger the lengthy sentence. In deciding these two cases, both of which were based on Eighth Amendment claims, the Court found that it is not cruel and unusual punishment to impose a possible life term for a nonviolent felony when the defendant has a history of serious or violent convictions.

In November, 2012, California voters overwhelmingly approved a change to their state's three-strikes law.[52] The changes mean that now only two categories of offenders can be sentenced as three-strikers: (1) those who commit new "serious or violent" felonies as their third offense, and (2) previously released murderers, rapists, or child molesters who are convicted of a new third strike, even if it is not a "serious or violent" felony. Under the new legislation, inmates sentenced under earlier versions of the law are allowed to petition for early release. Estimates are that around 3,000 such inmates may soon be released.

In an unanticipated consequence of the recent changes to California's law, however, newly released three-strike inmates are reentering society with only $200 in prison "gate money" and the clothes they were wearing at the time of release. Reentry services, housing or food subsidies, and other forms of assistance are not available to these former prisoners due to the fact that they are not eligible for parole supervision, causing many to fear an upsurge in crime as these former inmates try to eke out a subsistence living.[53]

Mandatory Sentencing

Mandatory sentencing, another form of structured sentencing, deserves special mention.[54] Mandatory sentencing is just what its name implies: a structured sentencing scheme that mandates clearly enumerated punishments for specific offenses or for habitual offenders convicted of a series of crimes. Mandatory sentencing, because it is truly *mandatory*, differs from presumptive sentencing, which allows at least a limited amount of judicial discretion within ranges established by published guidelines. Some mandatory sentencing laws require only modest mandatory prison terms (for example, three years for armed robbery), whereas others are much more far-reaching.

Typical of far-reaching mandatory sentencing schemes are the "three-strikes" laws just described. Three-strikes laws (and, in some jurisdictions, two-strikes laws) require mandatory sentences (sometimes life in prison without the possibility of parole) for offenders convicted of a third (or second) serious felony. Such mandatory sentencing enhancements are aimed at

Three-strikes laws require mandatory sentences for offenders convicted of a third serious felony.

■ **diversion** The official suspension of criminal or juvenile proceedings against an alleged offender at any point after a recorded justice system intake, but before the entering of a judgment, and referral of that person to a treatment or care program administered by a nonjustice or private agency. Also, release without referral.

Leila Cutler/Alamy

Noise offenders in Fort Lupton, Colorado, were recently ordered to endure an hour of unpopular music. The music, selected by a judge who wanted to punish them for disturbing the tranquility of the community, included songs by Bing Crosby and Willie Nelson. Will alternative sentences like this deter others from committing similar offenses?

deterring known and potentially violent offenders and are intended to incapacitate convicted criminals through long-term incarceration.

Three-strikes laws impose longer prison terms than most earlier mandatory minimum sentencing laws. California's three-strikes law, for example, requires that offenders who are convicted of a violent crime and who have had two prior convictions serve a minimum of 25 years in prison. The law doubled prison terms for offenders convicted of a second violent felony.[55] Three-strikes laws also vary in breadth. The laws of some jurisdictions stipulate that both of the prior convictions and the current one be for violent felonies; others require only that the prior convictions be for violent felonies. Some three-strikes laws count only prior adult convictions, whereas others permit consideration of juvenile crimes. As noted, California's 2012 revisions of its three-strikes laws reduce their application to only two categories of offenders.

By passing mandatory sentencing laws, legislators convey the message that certain crimes are deemed especially grave and that people who commit them deserve, and should expect, harsh sanctions. These laws are sometimes passed in response to public outcries following heinous or well-publicized crimes.

Research findings on the impact of mandatory sentencing laws on the criminal justice system have been summarized by British criminologist Michael Tonry.[56] Tonry found that under mandatory sentencing, officials tend to make earlier and more selective arrest, charging, and **diversion** decisions. They also tend to bargain less and to bring more cases to trial.

In an analysis of federal sentencing guidelines, other researchers found that blacks received longer sentences than whites, not because they received differential treatment by judges but because they constitute the large majority of those convicted of trafficking in crack cocaine (versus powdered cocaine)[57]—a crime that Congress had at one time singled out for especially harsh mandatory penalties. In 2006, for example, 82% of those sentenced under federal crack cocaine laws were black, and only 8.8% were white, even though more than two-thirds of people who used crack cocaine were white.[58] This seeming disparity led the U.S. Congress to eliminate the distinction between crack and regular cocaine for purposes of sentencing, and in 2010 President Barack Obama signed the federal Fair Sentencing Act (FSA)[59] into law. The act reduced a previous disparity in the amounts of powder cocaine and crack cocaine specified by the federal sentencing guidelines and eliminated what had been a mandatory minimum sentence under federal law for simple possession of crack cocaine. As a result of the FSA, a first conviction for simple possession of any amount of crack cocaine, like simple possession of powder cocaine, is subject to a penalty range of zero to one year of imprisonment regardless of quantity.

■ **alternative sentencing** The use of court-ordered community service, home detention, day reporting, drug treatment, psychological counseling, victim–offender programming, or intensive supervision in lieu of other, more traditional sanctions such as imprisonment and fines.

■ **justice reinvestment** A concept that prioritizes the use of alternatives to incarceration for persons convicted of eligible nonviolent offenses, standardizes the use of risk assessments instruments in pretrial detention, authorizes the use of early-release mechanisms for prisoners who meet eligibility requirements, and reinvests savings from such initiatives into effective crime-prevention programs.

The FSA's provisions do not apply, however, to people who were sentenced for a federal crack offense prior to August 3, 2010.[60] Consequently, in late 2011 another bill, the Fair Sentencing Clarification Act (FSCA), was introduced in the U.S. House of Representatives in an effort to make the FSA's changes to federal crack cocaine apply to people who had already been sentenced.[61] Although it failed to pass, it was reintroduced in 2013. The research arm of the U.S. Sentencing Commission estimates that 12,835 offenders now in federal prisons would be eligible to receive a reduced sentence under the FSCA, should it become law.[62]

In 2013, in an effort to modernize drug sentencing policy and to focus the resources of the criminal justice system squarely on violent offenders and public safety risks, Senator Dick Durbin (R-Illinois) introduced legislation in the U.S. Senate called the Smarter Sentencing Act. If passed into law, the act would increase federal judges' discretion at sentencing and eliminate mandatory minimum sentences for nonviolent drug offenders.[63]

Innovations in Sentencing

In an ever-growing number of cases, innovative judges in certain jurisdictions are using discretionary sentencing to impose truly unique punishments. A few years ago, for example, more than two dozen young people who broke into the former home of Pulitzer Prize–winning poet Robert Frost to hold a beer party were required to take classes in Frost's poetry as part of their punishment.[64] Also in 2008, a Florida judge ordered two young men who had thrown 32-ounce cups of soda and ice at a Taco Bell window-server during a "fire-in-the-hole" incident to post a recorded apology on the video-sharing website YouTube.[65]

Faced with prison overcrowding, high incarceration costs, and public calls for retribution, other judges have used shaming strategies to deter wrongdoers. At least one Florida court ordered those convicted of drunk driving to put a "Convicted DUI" sticker on their license plates. Similarly, a few years ago, Boston courts began ordering men convicted of sexual solicitation to spend time sweeping streets in Chinatown, an area known for prostitution. The public was invited to watch men sentenced to the city's "John Sweep" program clean up streets and alleyways littered with used condoms and sexual paraphernalia. In still other examples, an Arkansas judge made shoplifters walk in front of the stores they stole from, carrying signs describing their crimes, and in California, a purse snatcher was ordered to wear noisy tap dancing shoes whenever he went out in public.[66]

There is considerable support in criminal justice literature for shaming as a crime-reduction strategy. Australian criminologist John Braithwaite, for example, found shaming to be a particularly effective strategy because, he said, it holds the potential to enhance moral awareness among offenders, thereby building conscience and increasing inner control.[67] Dan Kahan, a professor at the University of Chicago Law School, points out that "shame supplies the main motive why people obey the law, not so much because they're afraid of formal sanctions, but because they care what people think about them."[68]

Whether public shaming will grow in popularity as an **alternative sentencing** strategy is unclear. What is clear, however, is that the American public and an ever-growing number of judicial officials are now looking for workable alternatives to traditional sentencing options.

Questions about Alternative Sanctions

Alternative sanctions include the use of court-ordered community service, home detention, day reporting, drug treatment, psychological counseling, victim–offender programming, or intensive supervision in lieu of other, more traditional, sanctions like imprisonment and fines. Many of these strategies are discussed in more detail in the next chapter.

It is important to note here, however, that a new framework, known as justice reinvestment, is starting to make a significant impact on sentencing authorities. **Justice reinvestment** is a concept that prioritizes the use of alternatives to incarceration for persons convicted of eligible nonviolent offenses, standardizes the use of risk assessments instruments in pretrial detention, authorizes the use of early-release mechanisms for prisoners who meet eligibility requirements, and reinvests savings from such initiatives into effective crime-prevention programs.[69] In general, justice reinvestment strategies included efforts to scale back certain harsh sentencing provisions and to reduce returns to prison for probation and parole violators.

> Justice reinvestment prioritizes the use of alternatives to incarceration for persons convicted of eligible nonviolent offenses.

As the term itself indicates, some recent legislative measures associated with the strategy also include statutory mechanisms

presentence investigation (PSI) The examination of a convicted offender's background prior to sentencing. Presentence examinations are generally conducted by probation or parole officers and are submitted to sentencing authorities.

for reinvesting savings that have been achieved through reducing prison populations into other aspects of the criminal justice system—including evidence-based in-prison treatment programs and local law enforcement efforts designed to deter crime.[70] One of those legislative initiatives, North Carolina's 2011 Justice Reinvestment Act, expands post-release supervision to all felons and limits the authority of parole officials and judges to revoke post-release supervision. The law also requires supervision agencies to concentrate resources on high-risk individuals and empowers probation officers to employ sanctions to increase accountability in a manner that is both cost-effective and proven to have a greater impact on reducing recidivism.[71] Finally, the North Carolina law ensures that treatment programs are targeted to people who have the greatest treatment needs and are most likely to reoffend.

A report by the Sentencing Project identified Georgia, Hawaii, Kansas, Missouri, Oklahoma, and Pennsylvania as leaders in the justice reinvestment movement.[72] Texas might be added to the list, as a 2013 study by the Council of State Governments determined, for example, that Texas saved almost $2 billion over five years by focusing on justice reinvestment efforts, including savings of $1.5 billion on prison constructions and more than $340 million in averted annual operations costs of confinement facilities. By 2013, more than half of the states had implemented comprehensive justice reinvestment programs designed to shift resources from incarceration toward treatment and prevention.

As prison populations continue to rise, alternative strategies are likely to become even more attractive. A number of questions must be answered, however, before most alternative sanctions can be employed with confidence, including whether alternative sentencing programs increase the threat to public safety, whether alternative sanctions are cost-effective, and how program outcomes should be judged.[73] Learn more about the Justice Reinvestment Initiative, a project of the Council of State Governments and the Bureau of Justice Assistance, at **http://www.justicereinvestment.org**.

The Presentence Investigation

Before imposing sentence, a judge may request information on the background of a convicted defendant. This is especially true in indeterminate sentencing jurisdictions, where judges retain considerable discretion in selecting sanctions. One of the drivers behind many sentencing decisions today is offender risk and needs assessment (RNA). In a 2011 report, the National Center for State Courts identified certain factors that increase the likelihood of reoffending, the presence of which suggest that prison terms and removal from the community are better sentencing options than probation.[74] High-risk factors identified include (1) antisocial personality patterns (impulsiveness, pleasure seeking, aggressive and irritable traits), (2) procriminal attitudes (negative attitudes toward the law), (3) social supports for crime (criminal friends), (4) substance abuse, (5) family and marital problems, (6) poor school or work performance, and (7) a lack of involvement in prosocial recreational and leisure activities.[75] Factors that are likely to increase the chances for rehabilitation, and which might indicate that probation or reduced prison terms are appropriate, include a good job record, satisfactory educational attainment, strong family ties, church attendance, no prior arrests for violent offenses, and psychological stability.

Information about a defendant's background often comes to the judge in the form of a **presentence investigation (PSI)** report. The task of preparing presentence reports usually falls to a probation or parole office. Presentence reports take one of three forms: (1) a detailed written report on the defendant's personal and criminal history, including an assessment of present conditions in the defendant's life (often called the *long form*); (2) an abbreviated written report summarizing the information most likely to be useful in a sentencing decision (the *short form*); and (3) a verbal report to the court made by the investigating officer based on field notes but structured according to established categories. A presentence report is much like a résumé, except that it focuses on what might be regarded as negative as well as positive life experiences.

Information about a defendant's background often comes to the judge in the form of a presentence investigation.

The data on which a presentence report is based come from a variety of sources. The Federal Bureau of Investigation's National Crime Information Center (NCIC), begun in 1967, contains computerized information on people wanted for criminal offenses throughout the United States. Individual jurisdictions also maintain criminal records repositories that can provide comprehensive files on the criminal history of those who have been processed by the justice system.

Sometimes the defendant provides much of the information in the presentence report. In this case, efforts must be made to corroborate the defendant's information. Unconfirmed data are generally marked on the report as "defendant-supplied data" or simply "unconfirmed."

In a presentence report, almost all third-party data are subject to ethical and legal considerations. The official records of almost all agencies and organizations, though often an ideal source of information, are protected by state and federal privacy requirements. In particular, the federal Privacy Act of 1974[76] may limit access to these records. Investigators must first check on the legal availability of all records before requesting them and must receive in writing the defendant's permission to access the records. Other public laws, among them the federal Freedom of Information Act,[77] may make the presentence report available to the defendant, although courts and court officers have generally been held to be exempt from the provision of such statutes.

The final section of a presentence report is usually devoted to the investigating officer's recommendations. A recommendation may be made in favor of probation, split sentencing, a term of imprisonment, or any other sentencing option available in the jurisdiction. Participation in community service programs or in drug- or substance-abuse programs may be recommended for probationers. Most judges are willing to accept the report writer's recommendation because they recognize the professionalism of the presentence investigator and because they know that the investigator may be assigned to supervise the defendant if he or she is sentenced to a community alternative.

Jurisdictions vary in their use of presentence reports. Federal law mandates presentence reports in federal criminal courts and specifies 15 topical areas that each report must cover. The 1984 federal Determinate Sentencing Act directs report writers to include information on the classification of the offense and of the defendant under the offense-level and criminal history categories established by the statute. Some states require presentence reports only in felony cases, and others require them in cases where the defendant faces the possibility of incarceration for six months or more. Other states have no requirement for presentence reports beyond those ordered by a judge.

Report writing, rarely anyone's favorite task, may seriously tax the limited resources of probation agencies. In September 2004, officers from the New York City Department of Probation wrote 2,414 presentence investigation reports for adult offenders and 461 reports for juvenile offenders, averaging about 10 reports per probation officer per month.[78]

The Victim—Forgotten No Longer

Thanks to a grassroots resurgence of concern for the plight of victims that began in this country in the early 1970s, the sentencing process now frequently includes consideration of the needs of victims and their survivors.[79] In times past, although victims might testify at trial, the criminal justice system frequently downplayed a victim's experience, including the psychological trauma engendered both by having been a victim and by having to endure the criminal proceedings that bring the criminal to justice. That changed in 1982, when the President's Task Force on Victims of Crime gave focus to a burgeoning victims' rights movement and urged the widespread expansion of victims' assistance programs during what was then their formative period.[80] Victims' assistance programs today offer services in the areas of crisis intervention and follow-up counseling and help victims secure their rights under the law.[81] Following successful prosecution, some victims' assistance programs also advise victims in the filing of civil suits to recoup financial losses directly from the offender.

About the same time, voters in California approved Proposition 8, a resolution that called for changes in the state's constitution to reflect concern for victims. A continuing goal of victims' advocacy groups is an amendment to the U.S. Constitution, which such groups say is needed to provide the same kind of fairness to victims that is routinely accorded to defendants. In the past, for

A continuing goal of victims' advocacy groups is an amendment to the U.S. Constitution.

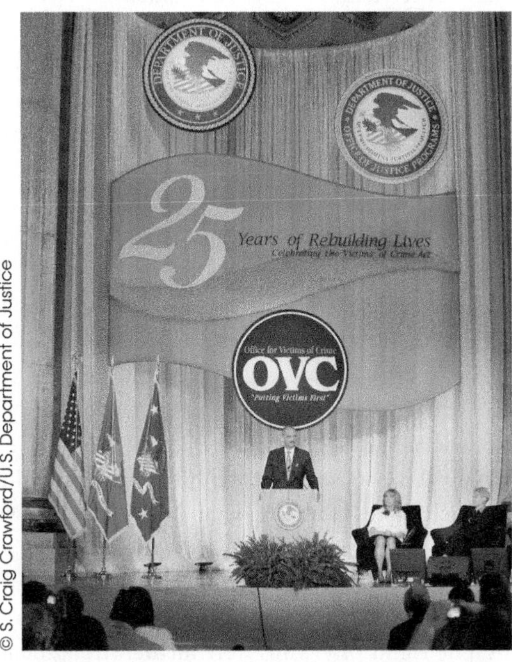

© S. Craig Crawford/U.S. Department of Justice

U.S. Attorney General Eric H. Holder, Jr., speaking at the 2009 Office for Victims of Crime Candlelight Ceremony. What more can the justice system do for crime victims? What more *should* it do?

example, the National Victims' Constitutional Amendment Passage (NVCAP) has sought to add a phrase to the Sixth Amendment: "likewise, the victim, in every criminal prosecution, shall have the right to be present and to be heard at all critical stages of judicial proceedings." The NVCAP now advocates the addition of a new amendment to the U.S. Constitution. Visit the NVCAP via **http://www.nvcap.org**.

In September 1996, a victims' rights constitutional amendment—Senate Joint Resolution 65—was proposed by a bipartisan committee in the U.S. Congress,[82] but problems of wording and terminology prevented its passage. A revised amendment was proposed in 1998,[83] but its wording was too restrictive for it to gain endorsement from victims' organizations.[84] The next year, a new amendment was proposed by the Senate Judiciary Committee's Subcommittee on the Constitution, Federalism, and Property, but it did not make it to the Senate floor. The U.S. Department of Justice, which had previously supported the measure, reversed its position due to a provision in the proposed amendment that gives crime victims the right to be notified of any state or federal grant of clemency. The U.S. attorney general apparently believed that the provision would impede the power of the president. The legislation also lacked the support of then-President Bill Clinton and was officially withdrawn by its sponsors in 2000.

Although a victims' rights amendment to the federal Constitution may not yet be a reality, more than 30 states have passed their own victims' rights amendments.[85] According to the NVCAP, California Proposition 9, or the Victims' Rights and Protection Act of 2008 (also known as Marsy's Law), is the most comprehensive victims' bill of rights of any state in the nation.[86] Proposition 9, which appeared on the November 4, 2008, ballot in California, passed with 53.8% of the vote. It amended the California Constitution by adding new provisions that provide victims in California with a number of specifically enforceable rights (see the "CJ Issues" box).

At the federal level, the 1982 Victim and Witness Protection Act (VWPA)[87] requires judges to consider victim-impact statements at federal sentencing hearings and places responsibility for their creation on federal probation officers. In 1984, the federal Victims of Crime Act (VOCA) was enacted with substantial bipartisan support. VOCA authorized federal funding to help states establish victims' assistance and victims' compensation programs. Under VOCA, the U.S. Department of Justice's Office for Victims of Crime provides a significant source of both funding and information for victims' assistance programs. The rights of victims were further strengthened under the Violent Crime Control and Law Enforcement Act of 1994, which created a federal right of allocution, or right to speak, for victims of violent and sex crimes. This gave victims the right to speak at the sentencing of their assailants. The 1994 law also requires sex offenders and child molesters convicted under federal law to pay restitution to their victims and prohibits the diversion of federal victims' funds to other programs. Other provisions of the 1994 law provide civil rights remedies for victims of felonies motivated by gender bias and extend "rape shield law" protections to civil cases and to all criminal cases, prohibiting inquiries into a victim's sexual history. A significant feature of the 1994 law can be found in a subsection titled the Violence against Women Act (VAWA). The VAWA, which provides financial support for police, prosecutors, and victims' services in cases involving sexual violence or domestic abuse, is discussed in greater detail in Chapter 2.

Much of the philosophical basis of today's victims' movement can be found in the restorative justice model, which was discussed briefly earlier in this chapter. Restorative justice emphasizes offender accountability and victim reparation. Restorative justice also provides the basis for victims' compensation programs, which are another means of recognizing the needs of crime victims. Today, all 50 states have passed legislation providing for monetary payments to victims of crime. Such payments are primarily designed to compensate victims for medical expenses and lost wages. All existing programs require that applicants meet certain eligibility criteria, and most set limits on the maximum amount of compensation that can be received. Generally disallowed are claims from victims who are significantly responsible for their own victimization, such as those who are injured in fights they provoke. In 2002, California's victims' compensation program, the largest in the nation, provided $117 million to more than 50,000 victims for crime-related expenses.

Today, all 50 states have passed legislation providing for monetary payments to victims of crime.

In 2001, the USA PATRIOT Act amended the Victims of Crime Act of 1984 to make victims of terrorism and their families eligible for victims' compensation payments.[88] It also created an antiterrorism emergency reserve fund to help provide compensation to victims of terrorism. A year earlier, in November 2000, the federal Office for Victims of Crime (OVC) created the Terrorism and International Victims Unit (TIVU) to develop and manage programs and initiatives that help victims of domestic and international terrorism, mass violence, and crimes that have transnational dimensions.[89]

In 2004, the U.S. Senate passed the Crime Victims' Rights Act[90] as part of the Justice for All Act. Some saw the legislation as at least a partial statutory alternative to a constitutional

CJ | ISSUES
Victims' Rights in California

In order to preserve and protect a victim's rights to justice and due process, a victim shall be entitled to the following rights:

1. To be treated with fairness and respect for his or her privacy and dignity, and to be free from intimidation, harassment, and abuse, throughout the criminal or juvenile justice process.
2. To be reasonably protected from the defendant and persons acting on behalf of the defendant.
3. To have the safety of the victim and the victim's family considered in fixing the amount of bail and release conditions for the defendant.
4. To prevent the disclosure of confidential information or records to the defendant, the defendant's attorney, or any other person acting on behalf of the defendant, which could be used to locate or harass the victim or the victim's family or which disclose confidential communications made in the course of medical or counseling treatment, or which are otherwise privileged or confidential by law.
5. To refuse an interview, deposition, or discovery request by the defendant, the defendant's attorney, or any other person acting on behalf of the defendant, and to set reasonable conditions on the conduct of any such interview to which the victim consents.
6. To reasonable notice of and to reasonably confer with the prosecuting agency, upon request, regarding the arrest of the defendant if known by the prosecutor, the charges filed, the determination whether to extradite the defendant, and, upon request, to be notified of and informed before any pretrial disposition of the case.
7. To reasonable notice of all public proceedings, including delinquency proceedings, upon request, at which the defendant and the prosecutor are entitled to be present and of all parole or other post-conviction release proceedings, and to be present at all such proceedings.
8. To be heard, upon request, at any proceeding, including any delinquency proceeding, involving a post-arrest release decision, plea, sentencing, post-conviction release decision, or any proceeding in which a right of the victim is at issue.
9. To a speedy trial and a prompt and final conclusion of the case and any related post-judgment proceedings.
10. To provide information to a probation department official conducting a pre-sentence investigation concerning the impact of the offense on the victim and the victim's family and any sentencing recommendations before the sentencing of the defendant.
11. To receive, upon request, the pre-sentence report when available to the defendant, except for those portions made confidential by law.
12. To be informed, upon request, of the conviction, sentence, place and time of incarceration, or other disposition of the defendant, the scheduled release date of the defendant, and the release of or the escape by the defendant from custody.
13. To restitution.
14. To the prompt return of property when no longer needed as evidence.
15. To be informed of all parole procedures, to participate in the parole process, to provide information to the parole authority to be considered before the parole of the offender, and to be notified, upon request, of the parole or other release of the offender.
16. To have the safety of the victim, the victim's family, and the general public considered before any parole or other post-judgment release decision is made.
17. To be informed of the rights enumerated in paragraphs (1) through (16).

Reference: Section 28(e) of Article I of the California Constitution.

victims' rights amendment. The Crime Victims' Rights Act establishes statutory rights for victims of federal crimes and gives them the necessary legal authority to assert those rights in federal court. The act grants the following rights to victims of federal crimes:[91]

1. The right to be reasonably protected from the accused
2. The right to reasonable, accurate, and timely notice of any public proceeding involving the crime or of any release or escape of the accused
3. The right to be included in any such public proceeding
4. The right to be reasonably heard at any public proceeding involving release, plea, or sentencing
5. The right to confer with the federal prosecutor handling the case
6. The right to full and timely restitution as provided by law
7. The right to proceedings free from unreasonable delay
8. The right to be treated with fairness and with respect for the victim's dignity and privacy

In addition to establishing these rights, the legislation expressly requires federal courts to ensure that they are afforded to victims. In like manner, federal law enforcement officials are required to make their "best efforts to see that crime victims are notified of, and accorded," these rights. To teach citizens about the rights of victims of crime, the federal government created a website that you can access via **http://www.crimevictims.gov**. It includes an online directory of crime victims' services, which can be searched locally, nationally, and internationally.

■ **victim-impact statement** The in-court use of victim- or survivor-supplied information by sentencing authorities seeking to make an informed sentencing decision.

A user-friendly database of victims' rights laws can be found online at **http://www.victimlaw.info**.

Victim-Impact Statements

Another consequence of the national victims' rights movement has been a call for the use of **victim-impact statements** before sentencing. A victim-impact statement is generally a written document describing the losses, suffering, and trauma experienced by the crime victim or by the victim's survivors. Judges are expected to consider such statements in arriving at an appropriate sanction for the offender.

The drive to mandate inclusion of victim-impact statements in sentencing decisions, already required in federal courts by the 1982 Victim and Witness Protection Act, was substantially enhanced by the "right-of-allocution" provision of the Violent Crime Control and Law Enforcement Act of 1994. Victim-impact statements played a prominent role in the sentencing of Timothy McVeigh, who was convicted of the 1995 bombing of the Murrah Federal Building in Oklahoma City and was executed in 2001. Some states, however, have gone further than the federal government. In 1984, the state of California, for example, passed legislation giving victims a right to attend and participate in sentencing and parole hearings.[92] Approximately 20 states now have laws requiring citizen involvement in sentencing, and all 50 states and the District of Columbia "allow for some form of submission of a victim-impact statement either at the time of sentencing or to be contained in the presentence investigation reports" made by court officers.[93] Where written victim-impact statements are not available, courts may invite the victim to testify directly at sentencing.

An alternative to written impact statements and to the appearance of victims at sentencing hearings is the victim-impact video. Some contemporary victim-impact videos display photo montages of the victim and are set to music and narrated. In 2008, for example, the U.S. Supreme Court rejected an appeal from a death row inmate wanting to exclude just such a digitized narrative set to music by Enya that had been played to the jury during the sentencing phase of his trial.[94]

One study of the efficacy of victim-impact statements found that sentencing decisions are rarely affected by them. The authors concluded that victim-impact statements have little effect on courts because judges and other officials "have established ways of making decisions which do not call for explicit information about the impact of crime on victims."[95] Learn more about the rights of crime victims and the history of the victims' movement at **http://www.justicestudies.com/pubs/victimrights.pdf**. You can read the 2013 Office for Victims of Crime report, *Vision 21: Transforming Victim Services*, at **http://www.justicestudies.com/pubs/vision21.pdf.** The thrust of the report is that victim services should be based on evidence of what works and what doesn't.[96]

Modern Sentencing Options

Sentencing is fundamentally a risk-management strategy designed to protect the public while serving the ends of retribution, incapacitation, deterrence, rehabilitation, and restoration. Because the goals of sentencing are difficult to agree on, so too are sanctions. Lengthy prison terms do little for rehabilitation, and community-release programs can hardly protect the innocent from offenders bent on continuing criminality.

Assorted sentencing philosophies continue to permeate state-level judicial systems. Each state has its own sentencing laws, and frequent revisions of those statutes are not uncommon. Because of huge variation from one state to another in the laws and procedures that control the imposition of criminal sanctions, sentencing has been called "the most diversified part of the Nation's criminal justice process."[97]

There is at least one common ground, however. It can be found in the four traditional sanctions that continue to dominate the thinking of most legislators and judges: fines, probation, imprisonment, and death. Fines and the death penalty are discussed in this chapter, probation is described in Chapter 12, and imprisonment is covered in Chapters 13 and 14.

In jurisdictions that employ indeterminate sentencing, fines, probation, and imprisonment are widely available to judges. The option selected generally depends on the severity of the offense and the judge's best guess as to the likelihood of the defendant's future criminal involvement. Sometimes two or more options are combined, such as when an offender is fined and sentenced to prison or placed on probation and fined in support of restitution payments.

Jurisdictions that operate under presumptive sentencing guidelines generally limit the judge's choice to only one option and often specify the extent to which that option can be applied. Dollar amounts of fines, for example, are rigidly set, and prison terms are specified for each type of offense. The death penalty remains an option in a fair number of jurisdictions, but only for a highly select group of offenders.

A recent report by the Bureau of Justice Statistics on the sentencing practices of trial courts found that state courts convicted 1,132,000 felons in 2006.[98] Another 66,518 felony convictions occurred in federal courts. The report also found the following for offenders convicted of felonies in state courts (Figure 11-2):

- About 41% were sentenced to active prison terms; another 28% received jail sentences involving less than one year's confinement.
- The average sentence length for those sent to state prisons has decreased since 1990 (from 6 years to 4 years and 11 months).
- Felons sentenced in 2006 were likely to serve more of their sentence before release (50%) than those sentenced in 1990 (33%).
- Of the total, 27% were sentenced to probation, with no jail or prison time to serve.
- The average probation sentence was 38 months.
- The largest category for which state felons were sent to prison was drug offenses.

Although the percentage of felons who receive active sentences may seem low, the number of criminal defendants receiving active prison time has increased dramatically. Figure 11-3 shows that the number of court-ordered prison commitments has increased nearly eightfold in the past 40 years. *The Justice Atlas of Sentencing and Corrections*, an interactive online tool showing the residential distribution of people sent to prison, reentering communities, and the populations of people under probation and parole supervision, can be found at **http://www.justiceatlas.org**.

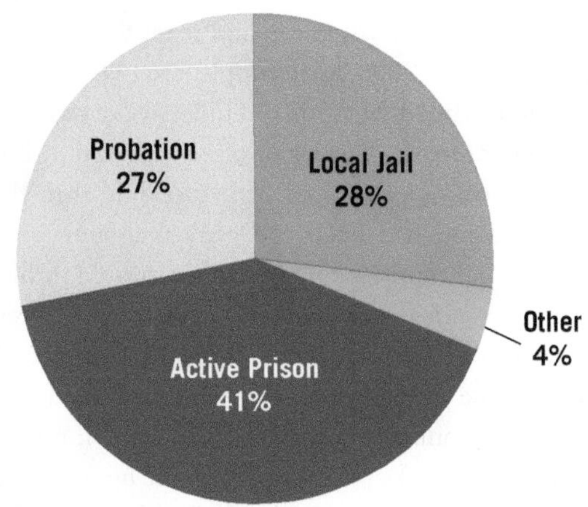

FIGURE 11-2 | The Sentencing of Convicted Felons in State Courts, by Type of Sentence

Source: Data from Sean Rosenmerkel, Matthew Durose, and Donald Farole, Jr., *Felony Sentences in State Courts, 2006* (Washington, DC: Bureau of Justice Statistics, December 2009).

Fines

Although the fine is one of the oldest forms of punishment, the use of fines as criminal sanctions suffers from built-in inequities and a widespread failure to collect them. Inequities arise when offenders with vastly different financial resources are fined similar amounts. A fine of $100, for example, can place a painful economic burden on a poor defendant but is negligible when imposed on a wealthy offender.

Nonetheless, fines are once again receiving attention as a serious sentencing alternative. One reason for the renewed interest is the stress placed on state resources by burgeoning prison populations. The extensive imposition of fines not only results in less crowded prisons but can contribute to state and local coffers and can lower the tax burden of law-abiding citizens. There are other advantages:

- Fines can deprive offenders of the proceeds of criminal activity.
- Fines can promote rehabilitation by enforcing economic responsibility.
- Fines can be collected by existing criminal justice agencies and are relatively inexpensive to administer.
- Fines can be made proportionate to both the severity of the offense and the ability of the offender to pay.

A National Institute of Justice (NIJ) survey found that an average of 86% of convicted defendants in courts of limited jurisdiction receive fines as sentences, some in combination with another penalty.[99] Fines are also widely used in courts of general jurisdiction, where the NIJ study found judges imposing fines in 42% of all cases that came before them for sentencing. Some studies estimate that more than $1 billion in fines are collected nationwide each year.[100]

Fines are often imposed for relatively minor law violations, such as driving while intoxicated, reckless driving, disturbing the peace, disorderly conduct, public drunkenness, and vandalism. Judges in many courts, however, report the use of fines for relatively serious violations of the law, including assault, auto theft, embezzlement, fraud, and the sale and possession of various controlled substances. Fines are most likely to be imposed where the offender has both a clean record and the ability to pay.[101]

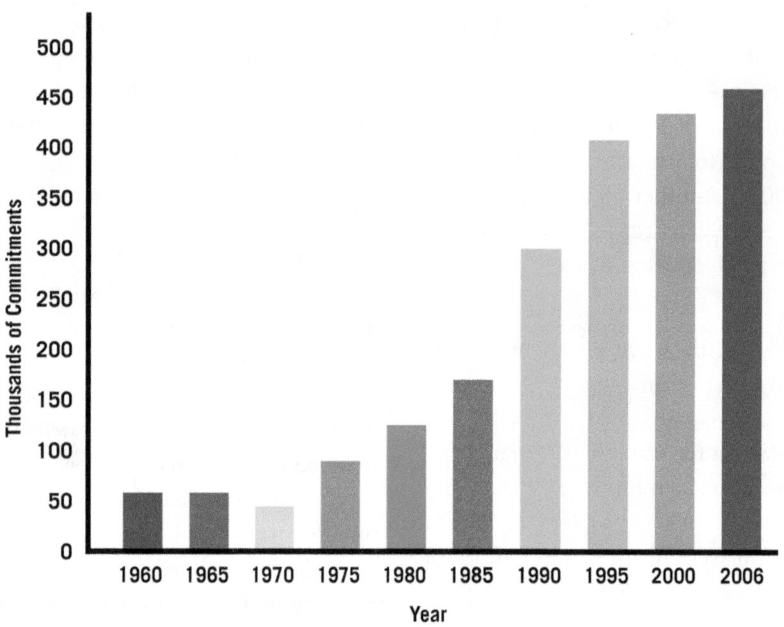

FIGURE 11-3 | Court-Ordered Prison Commitments, 1960–2006

Source: Data from Sean Rosenmerkel, Matthew Durose, and Donald Farole, Jr., *Felony Sentences in State Courts, 2006* (Washington, DC: Bureau of Justice Statistics, December 2009) and other years.

Studies have found that courts of limited jurisdiction, which are the most likely to impose fines, are also the least likely to have adequate information on offenders' financial status.[102] Perhaps as a consequence, judges are sometimes reluctant to impose fines. Two of the most widely cited objections by judges to the use of fines are (1) that fines allow more affluent offenders to "buy their way out" and (2) that poor offenders cannot pay fines.[103]

A solution to both objections can be found in the Scandinavian system of day fines. The day-fine system is based on the idea that fines should be proportionate to the severity of the offense but also need to take into account the financial resources of the offender. Day fines are computed by first assessing the seriousness of the offense, the defendant's degree of culpability, and his or her prior record as measured in "days." The use of days as a benchmark of seriousness is related to the fact that, without fines, the offender could be sentenced to a number of days (or months or years) in jail or prison. The number of days an offender is assessed is then multiplied by the daily wages that person earns. Hence, if two people are sentenced to a five-day fine, but one earns only $20 per day and the other $200 per day, the first would pay a $100 fine and the second $1,000.

In 2010, a Swiss court fined a multimillionaire, whose name was not released to the press, $290,000 for driving his Ferrari through a 35-mph speed limit zone at 85 mph.[104] The court calculated the fine based on the speeder's wealth (said to total $22.7 million) and his record of past offenses.

Death: The Ultimate Sanction

Some crimes are especially heinous and seem to cry out for extreme punishment. In 2008, for example, a 28-year-old grocery store stock clerk named Kevin Ray Underwood was sentenced to death in the atrocious murder of a ten-year-old girl in what authorities said was an elaborate plan to cannibalize the girl's flesh.[105] Underwood had been the girl's neighbor in Purcell, Oklahoma, and her mutilated body was discovered in his apartment covered with deep saw marks. Investigators told reporters that Underwood had sexually assaulted the little girl and planned to eat her corpse using the meat tenderizer and barbecue skewers that they confiscated from his kitchen. "In my 24 years as a prosecutor, this ranks as one of the most heinous and atrocious cases I've ever been involved with," said McClain County Prosecutor Tim Kuykendall.

In another shocking crime, Austin Reed Sigg, 17, called Colorado 9-1-1 dispatchers in 2012 to tell them that he had kidnapped and killed ten-year-old Jessica Ridgeway near Denver.

■ **Discuss** What factors help determine whether someone deserves the death penalty? What assumptions about mental or physical disabilities might affect the application of the death penalty?

■ **capital punishment** The death penalty. Capital punishment is the most extreme of all sentencing options.
■ **capital offense** A criminal offense punishable by death.

paying for it

Cost-Efficient Corrections and Sentencing

Since the early 1970s, the use of incarceration as a criminal sentencing option had been growing steadily, primarily as a result of the enactment of "get-tough-on-crime" legislation, like two- and three-strikes laws, and the war on drugs, which accounted for a huge number of our nation's prisoners—especially at the federal level. Faced, however, with severe budget shortfalls and rapidly rising prison populations, states were forced to find ways to save money and began looking at alternative sentencing practices and programs to lower the cost of handling convicted felons.

Four types of sentencing reforms, instituted in various ways by 28 states, have helped to lower justice systems costs by lowering prison populations in a number of jurisdictions over the past few years: (1) sentence modifications, (2) drug-law reform, (3) probation revocation reforms, and (4) reforms in juvenile sentencing.

The first of these reforms, sentence modifications, effectively diverts many nonviolent offenders from prison, makes wider use of alternative sentencing options, and shifts inmates who would normally be incarcerated in state facilities to local jails or privately run facilities. The second, drug-law reform, makes wider use of drug courts and drug treatment as alternatives to imprisonment, and has also resulted in the reformation of drug statutes, shortening periods of confinement and making wider use of supervised early release into the community. The third strategy, probation revocation reforms, allows selected probation violators to remain free in the community under more intense supervision, and subsequently requires additional rule violation for probation revocation. Depending on the offense, some probation violators are now deemed ineligible for imprisonment through changes in the law, but face tougher lifestyle restrictions if they violate the conditions of their probation. Finally, reforms in juvenile sentencing give judges greater leeway in the handling of delinquents and mean that fewer young people will spend time confined in state-run facilities.

The use of local jails to hold inmates who would otherwise be sent to state facilities and contracts with private correctional services companies to house inmates needing confinement are other ways that states are attempting to lower the cost of confinement. In Tennessee, for example, the cost to house an inmate in a county jail averages around $35 per day, and moving that inmate to a state-run facility ups the cost to almost $65 per day. Private companies, which bid for state contracts, can often be more efficient than state-run departments of corrections, at least in dealing with certain types of inmates, resulting in significant cost savings. Some government officials also claim that private prisons shelter states from at least some forms of civil liability that may arise from lawsuits brought by prisoners. Finally, one way of alleviating the high cost of incarceration is being tried in Riverside, California, where county officials have begun charging jail inmates $142.42 for every night they spend locked up.

References: Steve Ahillen, "Explore Cost-Effective Alternatives to Prison," *Tennessee News Sentinel*, March 10, 2012, http://www.politifact.com/tennessee/promises/haslam-o-meter/promise/1072/explore-cost-effective-alternatives-to-prison (accessed May 30, 2013); Nicole D. Porter, *The State of Sentencing, 2011: Developments in Policy and Practice* (Washington, DC: The Sentencing Project, 2013); and Jennifer Medina, "In California, a Plan to Charge Inmates for Their Stay," *New York Times*, December 11, 2011.

Sigg allegedly kidnapped and killed the young girl, and hid her remains in a crawl space at his mother's home.

Many states today have statutory provisions that provide for a sentence of **capital punishment** for especially repugnant crimes (known as **capital offenses**). Estimates are that more than 18,800 legal executions have been carried out in the United States since 1608, when records began to be kept on capital punishment.[106] Although capital punishment was widely used throughout the eighteenth and nineteenth centuries, the mid-twentieth century offered a brief respite in the number of offenders legally executed in this country. Between 1930 and 1967, the year when the U.S. Supreme Court ordered a nationwide stay of pending executions, nearly 3,800 people were put to death. The peak years were 1935 and 1936, with nearly 200 legal killings each year. Executions declined substantially every year thereafter. Between 1967 and 1977, a *de facto* moratorium existed, with no executions carried out in any U.S. jurisdiction. Following the lifting of the moratorium, executions resumed (Figure 11-4). In 1983, only 5 offenders were put to death, whereas 43 were executed nationwide in 2012.[107] A modern record for executions was set in 1999, with 98 executions—35 in Texas alone.[108]

Today, the federal government and 33 of the 50 states[109] permit execution for first-degree murder, and treason, kidnapping, aggravated rape, the murder of a police or corrections officer, and murder while under a life sentence are punishable by death in some jurisdictions.[110] Illinois, which up until recently was among states with a death penalty, repealed its capital punishment statute in 2011, replacing it with a sentence of life in prison without possibility of parole. In 2012, Connecticut took capital punishment off of its books, although the 11 men on death row at the time of repeal are still slated to be executed. The latest state to abolish the death penalty is Maryland, which repealed its death penalty statute in 2013.

Austin Reed Sigg. Sigg was 17 at the time that he allegedly kidnapped and killed 10-year-old Jessica Ridgeway near Denver, Colorado in 2012. Sigg later called 9-1-1 dispatchers, telling them that he had kidnapped and killed a girl and hid her remains in a crawl space at his mother's home. If Sigg is sentenced as an adult, what might an appropriate sentence be?

The United States is not the only country to make use of capital punishment. On April 2, 2013, for example, Kuwait executed three men for murder,[111] and Saudi Arabia beheaded 29 people in the first three months of 2013, including 7 for armed robbery.[112] Japan hung 3 criminals in the first two months of 2013,[113] and China, the world's most populous country, is reported to routinely execute more than 1,700 people annually—meaning that more people are executed in China than in the rest of the world combined. According to Amnesty International, at least 1,923 people were known to have been sentenced to death in 63 countries in 2011, down from 2,024 in 2010. According to that group, at least 18,750 people were under sentence of death worldwide at the end of 2011, including 8,300 people in Pakistan.[114]

The list of crimes punishable by death under federal jurisdiction in the United States increased dramatically with passage of the Violent Crime Control and Law Enforcement Act of 1994 and was expanded still further by the 2001 USA PATRIOT Act. The list now includes a total of about 60 offenses. State legislators have also worked to expand the types of crimes for which a death sentence can be imposed. In 1997, for example, the Louisiana Supreme Court upheld the state's year-old child rape statute, which allows for the imposition of a capital sentence when the victim is younger than 12 years of age. The case involved an AIDS-infected father who raped his three daughters, ages five, eight, and nine. In upholding the father's death sentence, the Louisiana court ruled that child rape is "like no other crime."[115] In 2008, however, in the case of *Kennedy* v. *Louisiana*, the U.S. Supreme Court ruled that the Eighth Amendment bars Louisiana (and other states) from imposing the death penalty for the rape of a child where the crime did not result, and was not intended to result, in the victim's death.[116]

A total of 3,146 offenders were under sentence of death throughout the United States on October 1, 2012.[117] The latest statistics show that 98.2% of those on death row are male, approximately 43.9% are white, 13.2% are Hispanic, 41.7% are African American, and the remainder consists of other races (mostly Native American and Pacific Islander).[118] Statistics on race have been less

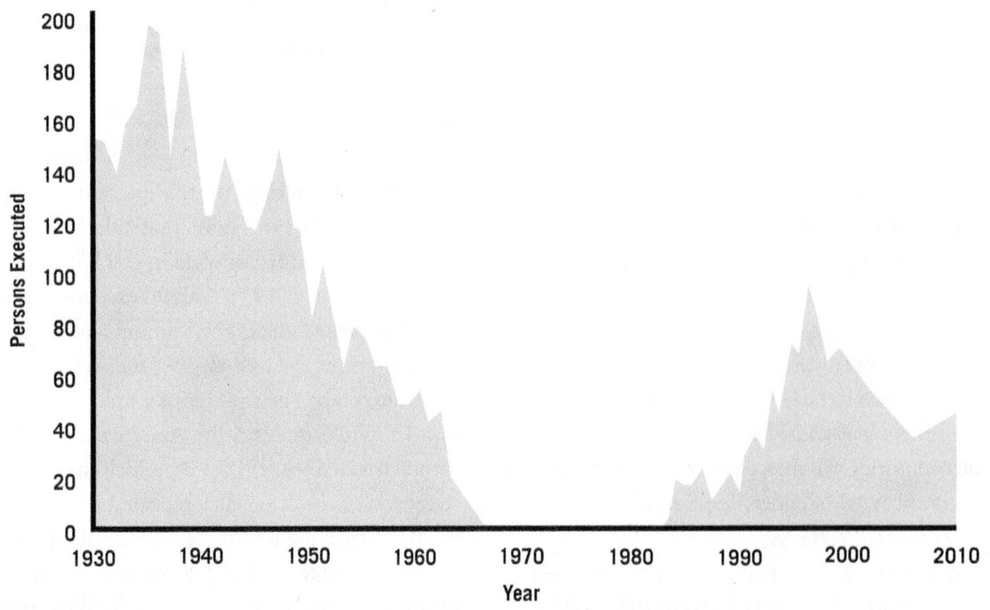

FIGURE 11-4 | Court-Ordered Executions Carried Out in the United States, 1930–2010

Note: Excludes executions ordered by military authority.

Sources: Tracy L. Snell, *Capital Punishment, 2010—Statistical Tables* (Washington, DC: Bureau of Justice Statistics, December 2011); and Death Penalty Information Center, "State-by-State Death Penalty Information," http://www.deathpenaltyinfo.org/FactSheet.pdf (accessed July 11, 2013).

■ **writ of *habeas corpus*** A writ that directs the person detaining a prisoner to bring him or her before a judicial officer to determine the lawfulness of the imprisonment.

meaningful recently, as classification depends on self-reports, and individuals may report being of more than one race.

Methods of imposing death vary by state. The majority of death penalty states authorize execution through lethal injection. Electrocution is the second most common means, whereas hanging, the gas chamber, and firing squads have survived, at least as options available to the condemned, in a few states. For the most current statistical information on capital punishment, visit the Death Penalty Information Center via **http://www.deathpenaltyinfo.org**.

Habeas Corpus Review

The legal process through which a capital sentence is carried to conclusion is fraught with problems. One serious difficulty centers on the fact that automatic review of all death sentences by appellate courts and constant legal maneuvering by defense counsel often lead to a dramatic delay between the time the sentence is handed down and the time it is carried out. Today, an average of 12 years and 9 months passes between the imposition of a death sentence and execution.[119] Such lengthy delays, compounded by uncertainty over whether an execution will ever occur, directly contravene the generally accepted notion that punishment should be swift and certain.

Even death row inmates can undergo life-altering changes. When that happens, long-delayed executions can become highly questionable events. The case of Stanley "Tookie" Williams, who was executed at California's San Quentin Prison in 2005 at age 51, is illustrative.[120] Williams, self-described cofounder of the infamous Crips street gang in the early 1970s, was sentenced to die for the brutal shotgun murders of four people during a robbery 26 years earlier. In 1993, however, he experienced what he called a "reawakening" and began working from prison as an antigang crusader. Williams found a sympathetic publisher and wrote a series of children's books titled *Tookie Speaks Out against Gang Violence*. The series was intended to help urban youth reject the lure of gang membership and embrace traditional values. He also wrote *Life in Prison*, an autobiography describing the isolation and despair experienced by death row inmates. In his final years, Williams worked with his editor, Barbara Cottman Becnel, to create the Internet Project for Street Peace, a demonstration project linking teens from the rough-and-tumble streets of Richmond, California, to peers in Switzerland in an effort to help them avoid street violence. In 2001, Williams was nominated for the Nobel Peace Prize by a member of the Swiss Parliament and for the Nobel Prize in Literature by a number of college professors. Pleas to spare his life, which came from Jesse Jackson, anti–death penalty activist Sister Helen Prejean, the National Association for the Advancement of Colored People (NAACP), and others, were rejected by Governor Arnold Schwarzenegger who said that "there is no reason to second-guess the jury's decision of guilt or raise significant doubts or serious reservations about Williams' convictions and death sentence."[121]

In a speech before the American Bar Association in 1989, then-Chief Justice William Rehnquist called for reforms of the federal *habeas corpus* system, which, at the time, allowed condemned prisoners virtually limitless opportunities for appeal. **Writs of *habeas corpus*** (Latin for "you have the body"), which require that a prisoner be brought into court to determine if he or she is being legally held, form the basis for many federal appeals made by prisoners on state death rows. In 1968, Chief Justice Earl Warren called the right to file *habeas* petitions, as guaranteed under the U.S. Constitution, the "symbol and guardian of individual liberty." Twenty years later, however, Rehnquist claimed that writs of *habeas corpus* were being used indiscriminately by death row inmates seeking to delay executions even where grounds for delay did not exist. "The capital defendant does not need to prevail on the merits in order to accomplish his purpose," said Rehnquist. "He wins temporary victories by postponing a final adjudication."[122]

> Chief Justice Earl Warren called the right to file *habeas* petitions the "symbol and guardian of individual liberty."

In a move to reduce delays in the conduct of executions, the U.S. Supreme Court, in the case of ***McCleskey* v. *Zant*** (1991),[123] limited the number of appeals a condemned person may lodge with the courts. Saying that repeated filing for the sole purpose of delay promotes "disrespect for the finality of convictions" and "disparages the entire criminal justice system," the Court established a two-pronged criterion for future appeals. According to *McCleskey*, in any petition beyond the first filed with the federal court, a capital defendant must (1) demonstrate good cause why the claim now being made was not included in the first filing and (2) explain how the absence of that claim may have harmed the petitioner's ability to mount an effective defense. Two months later, the Court reinforced *McCleskey* when it ruled, in ***Coleman* v. *Thompson*** (1991),[124] that state prisoners could not cite "procedural default," such as a defense attorney's failure to meet a state's filing deadline for appeals, as the basis for an appeal to federal court.

In 1995, in the case of ***Schlup* v. *Delo***,[125] the Court continued to define standards for further appeals from death-row inmates, ruling that before appeals based on claims of new evidence could be heard, "a petitioner must show that, in light of the new evidence, it is more likely than not that no reasonable juror would have found him guilty beyond a reasonable doubt." A "reasonable juror" was defined as one who "would consider fairly all of the evidence presented and would conscientiously obey the trial court's instructions requiring proof beyond a reasonable doubt."

Opportunities for federal appeals by death row inmates were further limited by the Antiterrorism and Effective Death Penalty Act (AEDPA) of 1996,[126] which sets a one-year postconviction deadline for state inmates filing federal *habeas corpus* appeals. The deadline is six months for state death-row inmates who were provided a lawyer for *habeas* appeals at the state level. The act also requires federal courts to presume that the factual findings of state courts are correct, does not permit the claim of state court misinterpretations of the U.S. Constitution as a basis for *habeas* relief unless those misinterpretations are "unreasonable," and requires that all petitioners must show, prior to obtaining a hearing, facts sufficient to establish by clear and convincing evidence that but for constitutional error, no reasonable fact-finder would have found the petitioner guilty. The act also requires approval by a three-judge panel before an inmate can file a second federal appeal raising newly discovered evidence of innocence. In 1996, in the case of *Felker* v. *Turpin*,[127] the U.S. Supreme Court ruled that limitations on the authority of federal courts to consider successive *habeas corpus* petitions imposed by AEDPA are permissible since they do not deprive the U.S. Supreme Court of its original jurisdiction over such petitions. Finally, in the 2013 case of *McQuiggin* v. *Perkins*, the Court held that actual innocence, if proved, "serves as a gateway through which a petitioner may pass whether the impediment is a procedural bar. . . . or expiration of the AEDPA statute of limitations." In *McQuiggin*, the justices wrote, a "fundamental miscarriage of justice exception" creates a "sensitivity to the injustice of incarcerating an innocent individual."[128]

Some recent statements by Supreme Court justices have indicated that long delays caused by the government in carrying out executions may render the punishment unconstitutionally cruel and unusual. One example comes from the 1998 case of *Elledge* v. *Florida*,[129] where the execution of William D. Elledge had been delayed for 23 years. Although the full Court refused to hear the case, Justice Stephen Breyer observed that "[t]wenty-three years under sentence of death is unusual—whether one takes as a measuring rod current practice or the practice in this country and in England at the time our Constitution was written." Moreover, wrote Breyer, execution after such a long delay could be considered cruel because Elledge "has experienced that delay because of the State's own faulty procedures and not because of frivolous appeals on his own part." Elledge died on death row at the Union Correctional Institution in Florida in 2008. He had been under sentence of death for 34 years; at the time of his death from asthma, he was 57 years old.

Long delays caused by the government in carrying out executions may render the punishment unconstitutionally cruel and unusual.

Opposition to Capital Punishment

Thirty years ago, David Magris, who was celebrating his 21st birthday with a crime spree, shot Dennis Tapp in the back during a holdup, leaving Tapp a paraplegic. Tapp had been working a late-night shift, tending his father's quick-serve gas station. Magris went on to commit more robberies that night, killing 20-year-old Steven Tompkins in a similar crime. Although Magris was sentenced to death by a California court, the U.S. Supreme Court overturned the state's death-penalty law in 1972, opening the door for Magris to be paroled in 1985. Long before Magris was freed from prison, however, Tapp had already forgiven him. A few minutes after the shooting happened, Tapp regained consciousness, dragged himself to a telephone, and called for help. The next thing he did was ask "God to forgive the man who did this to me."[130] Today, the men—both staunch death penalty opponents—are friends, and Magris is president of the Northern California Coalition to Abolish the Death Penalty. "Don't get me wrong," says Tapp, "What [David] did was wrong. . . . He did something stupid and he paid for it."[131]

Because the death penalty is such an emotional issue, attempts have been made to abolish capital punishment since the founding of the United States. The first recorded effort to eliminate the death penalty occurred at the home of Benjamin Franklin in 1787.[132] At a meeting there on March 9 of that year, Dr. Benjamin Rush, a signer of the Declaration of Independence and a leading medical pioneer, read a paper against capital punishment to a small but influential audience. Although his immediate efforts came to naught, his arguments laid the groundwork for many debates that followed. Michigan, widely regarded as the first abolitionist state, joined the Union in 1837 without a death penalty. A number of other states, including Alaska, Hawaii, Massachusetts, Minnesota, New York, New Jersey, New Mexico, West Virginia, and Wisconsin, have since spurned death as a possible sanction for criminal acts. As noted earlier, capital punishment remains a viable sentencing option in 33 of the states and in all federal jurisdictions, while arguments continue to rage over its value.

Today, six main rationales for abolishing capital punishment are heard, as shown in Table 11-4.

TABLE 11-4 | Capital Punishment: Retentionist and Abolitionist Rationales

REASONS TO ABOLISH	REASONS TO KEEP
Innocent People Have Been Executed Claim: The death penalty can be and has been inflicted on innocent people. Counterclaim: Although it has been shown that some innocent people have been condemned to death, and although it can be assumed that a number of innocent people remain on death row, it has not been demonstrated that innocent people have actually been executed.	**Just Deserts** Claim: Some people deserve to die for what they have done. Death is justly deserved; anything less cannot suffice as a sanction for the most heinous crimes. Counterclaim: Capital punishment is a holdover from primitive times; contemporary standards of human decency mandate alternatives such as life imprisonment.
Lack of Proven Deterrence Claim: The death penalty is not an effective deterrent, and numerous studies have shown the truth of that assertion. Counterclaim: If capital punishment were imposed with both certainty and swiftness, then it would be effective as a deterrent. It is our system of appeals and lengthy delays that make it ineffective.	**Revenge/Retribution** Claim: Capital punishment can be seen as revenge for the pain and suffering that the criminal inflicted on the victim. In *Gregg* v. *Georgia*, the justices of the U.S. Supreme Court wrote that "[t]he instinct for retribution is part of the nature of man." Hence, sentencing a capital offender to death can provide closure to a victim's family members. Counterclaim: Forgiveness and rehabilitation are higher goals than revenge and retribution.
Arbitrariness Claim: The imposition of the death penalty is, by the very nature of our legal system, arbitrary. Effective legal representation and access to the courts is differentially available to people with varying financial and other resources. Counterclaim: Many safeguards exist at all levels of criminal justice processing to protect the innocent and to ensure that only the guilty are actually put to death.	**Protection** Claim: Executed offenders cannot commit further crimes; and execution serves as an example to other would-be wrongdoers of the fate that awaits them. Moreover, society has a duty to act in defense of others, and to protect its innocent members. Counterclaim: Societal interests in protection can be met in other ways, such as incarceration or life imprisonment.
Discrimination Claim: The death penalty discriminates against certain ethnic and racial groups. Counterclaim: Any examination of disproportionality must go beyond simple comparisons and must measure both frequency and seriousness of capital crimes between and within racial groups. The Supreme Court, in the 1987 case of *McCleskey* v. *Kemp*, held that a simple showing of racial discrepancies in the application of the death penalty does not constitute a constitutional violation. Members of underrepresented groups were more likely to be sentenced to death, but only because they were more likely to be arrested on facts that could support a capital charge, not because the justice system acts in a discriminatory fashion.	
Expense Claim: Because of all the appeals involved in death penalty cases, the cost to a state can run into the millions of dollars for each execution. Counterclaim: Although official costs associated with capital punishment are high, no cost is *too* high if it achieves justice.	
Human Life Is Sacred Claim: Killing at the hands of the state is not a righteous act but instead lowers all of us to the same moral level as the crimes committed by the condemned. Counterclaim: If life is sacred, then the taking of life demands revenge.	
For additional perspectives: The National Coalition to Abolish the Death Penalty, http://www.ncadp.org.	*For additional perspectives:* Pro-Death Penalty.com, http://www.prodeathpenalty.com.

freedom OR safety? YOU decide

What Are the Limits of Genetic Privacy?

By mid-2013, 28 states and the federal government had enacted arrestee DNA collection laws, which authorize the collection of suspect DNA following arrest or charging. The federal law, the DNA Fingerprint Act of 2005, requires that any adult arrested for a federal crime must provide a DNA sample. The law also mandates DNA collection from persons detained under the authority of the United States who are not U.S. citizens or are not lawfully in the country. Some states, however, limit preconviction DNA collection to violent offenses or sex crimes, whereas other states include all felonies, and some extend the requirement to misdemeanors as well. Figure 11-5 shows states that have enacted arrestee DNA collection laws. In 2013, in the case of *Maryland* v. *King*, the U.S. Supreme Court upheld Maryland's practice of collecting and testing DNA from arrested felons without the use of a warrant.[137] Writing for the majority in that case, Justice Kennedy said, "When officers make an arrest supported by probable cause to hold for a serious offense and bring the suspect to the station to be detained in custody, taking and analyzing a cheek swab of the arrestee's DNA is, like fingerprinting and photographing, a legitimate police booking procedure that is reasonable under the Fourth Amendment."

Forensic DNA can be a powerful tool in the hands of investigators. In 2005, for example, police in Truro, Massachusetts, charged Christopher M. McCowen, a garbageman with a long rap sheet, with the murder of 46-year-old Christa Worthington, a fashion writer who had been raped and stabbed to death in the kitchen of her isolated home in 2002. The case, which had baffled authorities for three years, drew national interest when Truro authorities asked the town's 790 male residents to voluntarily submit saliva-swab DNA samples for analysis. Investigators were hoping to use genetic testing to match semen recovered from the murder scene to the killer. "We're trying to find the person who has something to hide," said Sergeant David Perry of the Truro Police Department. Although McCowen voluntarily submitted a DNA sample from a cheek swab in early 2004, it took the state crime lab more than a year to analyze it.

DNA profiling has been used in criminal investigations for only about 20 years. The first well-known DNA forensic analysis occurred in 1986, when British police sought the help of Alec Jeffreys, a geneticist at the University of Leicester who is widely regarded as the father of "DNA fingerprinting." The police were trying to solve the vicious rape and murder of two young schoolgirls. At the center of their investigation was a young man who worked at a mental institution close to where the girls' bodies had been found. Soon after he was questioned, the man confessed to the crimes and was arrested, but police

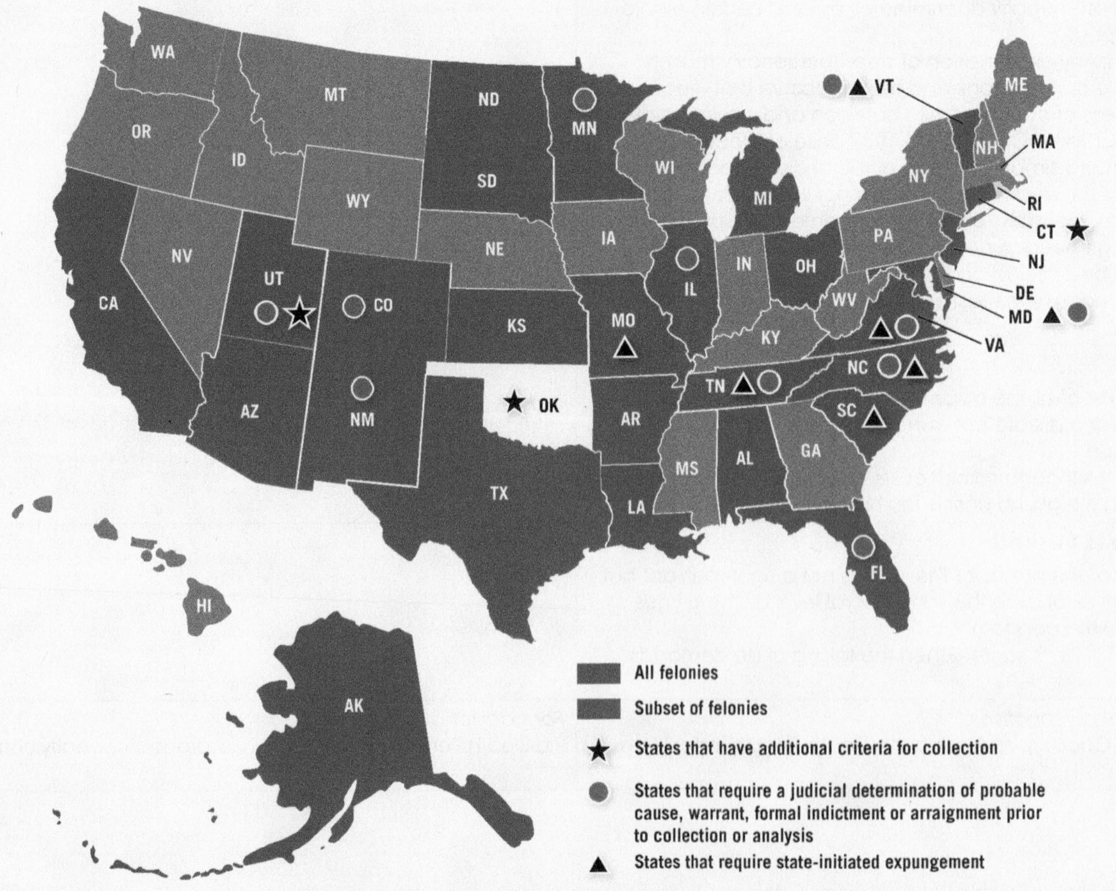

FIGURE 11-5 | States That Have Enacted Arrestee DNA Collection Laws

Source: National Institute of Justice, "DNA Sample Collection from Arrestees," http://nij.gov/topics/forensics/evidence/dna/collection-from-arrestees.htm (accessed June 1, 2013).

were uncertain of the suspect's state of mind and wanted to be sure that they had the right person.

Jeffreys compared the suspect's DNA to DNA taken from semen samples found on the victims. The samples did not match, leading to a wider police investigation. Lacking any clear leads, the authorities requested that all males living in the area of the killings voluntarily submit to DNA testing so that they might be excluded as suspects. By the fall of 1987, the number of men tested had exceeded 4,500, but the murderer still hadn't been found. Then, however, investigators received an unexpected tip. They learned that a local baker named Colin Pitchfork had convinced another man to provide a DNA sample in his place. Pitchfork was picked up and questioned. He soon confessed, providing details about the crime that only the perpetrator could know. Pitchfork became the 4,583rd man to undergo DNA testing, and his DNA proved a perfect match with that of the killer.

In the last 20 years, the use of DNA testing by police departments has come a long way. Today, the Combined DNA Index System (CODIS) database of the Federal Bureau of Investigation (FBI) makes use of computerized records to match the DNA of individuals previously convicted of certain crimes with forensic samples gathered at crime scenes across the country. A recent federal law allows the FBI and other federal law enforcement agencies to include preconviction DNA in their databases. Fifteen states also allow the collection of DNA samples from people awaiting trial.

Advocates of genetic privacy, however, question whether anyone—even those convicted of crimes—should be sampled against their wishes and have their genetic profiles added to government databases. The *Truro* case, in which the American Civil Liberties Union (ACLU) sent letters to the town's police chief and Cape Cod prosecutor calling for an end to the "DNA dragnet," highlights what many fear—especially when local police announced that they would pay close attention to those who refused to cooperate. One commentator noted that it's "a very old trap" to say, "If you have nothing to hide, then why not cooperate?"

European courts, it would seem, agree. In 2008, the European Court of Human Rights ruled unanimously that British officials had to destroy nearly 1 million DNA samples and fingerprints taken from people without criminal records. Keeping the samples, the court said, was a violation of the right to privacy established under the European Human Rights Convention, to which the United Kingdom is a signatory.

You Decide

What degree of "genetic privacy" should an individual be entitled to? Should the government require routine genetic testing of nonoffenders for identification purposes? Should it require it of arrestees who have not been convicted? How might such information be used in the event of a terrorist attack?

References: Paisley Dodds, "European Court Makes Landmark Ruling on DNA Rights," AP Worldstream, December 5, 2008; Anna Gorman, "U.S. to Collect DNA Samples of Arrested Immigrants," *Los Angeles Times*, January 9, 2009; "Man Charged with 2002 Murder of Cape Cod Writer," *USA Today*, April 15, 2005, http://www.usatoday.com/news/nation/2005-04-15-cape-cod-murder_x.htm (accessed July 4, 2006); "ACLU Slams Mass DNA Collection," CBSNews.com, January 10, 2005, http://www.cbsnews.com/stories/2005/01/10/national/main665938.shtml (accessed July 4, 2006); and Howard C. Coleman and Eric D. Swenson, *DNA in the Courtroom: A Trial Watcher's Guide* (Seattle: Genelex Corporation, 2000), http://www.genelex.com/paternitytesting/paternitybook.html (accessed July 4, 2008).

The Death Penalty and Innocent People

The Death Penalty Information Center claims that 142 people in 26 states were freed from death row between 1973 and late 2012 after it was determined that they were innocent of the capital crimes of which they had been convicted (Figure 11-6).[133] One study of felony convictions that used analysis of DNA to provide postconviction evidence of guilt or innocence found 28 cases in which defendants had been wrongly convicted and sentenced to lengthy prison terms. The study, *Convicted by Juries, Exonerated by Science*, effectively demonstrated that the judicial process can be flawed.[134] DNA testing can play a critical role in identifying wrongful convictions because, as Barry Scheck and Peter Neufeld, cofounders of the Innocence Project at the Benjamin N. Cardozo School of Law, point out, "Unlike witnesses who disappear or whose recollections fade over time, DNA in biological samples can be reliably extracted decades after the commission of the crime. The results of such testing have invariably been found to have a scientific certainty that easily outweighs the eyewitness identification testimony or other direct or circumstantial proof that led to the original conviction."[135] "Very simply," say Scheck and Neufeld, "DNA testing has demonstrated that far more wrongful convictions occur than even the most cynical and jaded scholars had suspected."[136]

A 2000 study by Columbia Law School Professor James Liebman and colleagues examined 4,578 death penalty cases in state and federal courts from 1973 to 1995.[138] They found that appellate courts overturned the conviction or reduced the sentence in 68% of the cases examined. In 82% of the successful appeals, defendants were found to be deserving of a lesser sentence, and convictions were overturned in 7% of such appeals. According to the study's authors, "Our 23 years worth of findings reveal a capital punishment system collapsing under the weight of its own mistakes." You can read the Liebman report in its entirety at **http://www.justicestudies.com/pubs/liebman.pdf**.

A 2013 NIJ-funded study found 10 factors that can lead to a wrongful conviction of an innocent defendant instead of a dismal or acquittal.[139] Those factors are shown in Figure 11-7. The NIJ study also distinguished between cases in which erroneous convictions are returned and near misses, or cases in which innocent defendants came close to being convicted but were eventually acquitted. Cases that lead to erroneous convictions and those that lead to near misses were found to share many of the same characteristics, including false confession, official misconduct, eyewitness misidentification, or an incorrect tip to the police. Factors that lead to an erroneous conviction included a punitive state culture (a just deserts mind-set

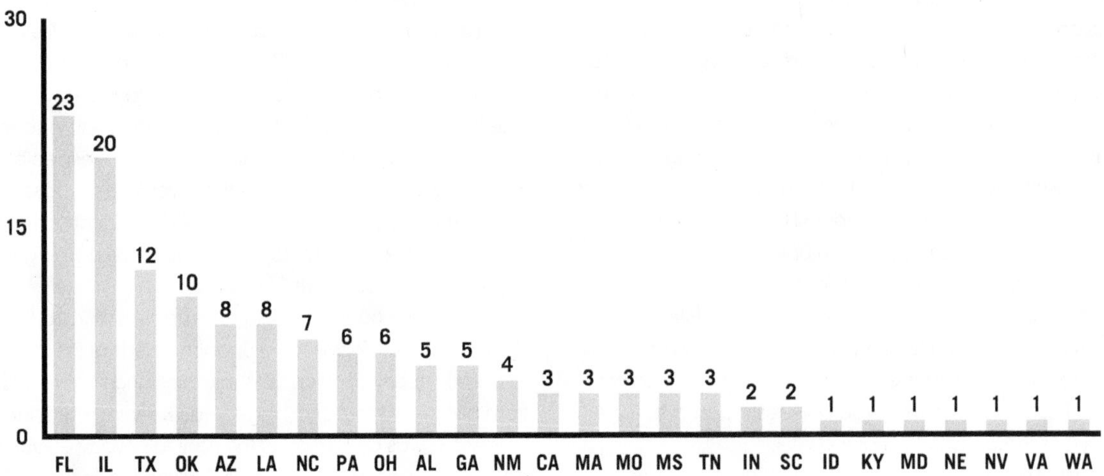

FIGURE 11-6 | Exonerations by State, 1988–2012

in which prosecutors seek convictions at all costs), forensic error (either incorrect or failed crime scene or crime laboratory analysis), weak facts still pressed by the prosecution, or a mistaken or lying eyewitness. Factors that led to a near miss included, but were not limited to, an older defendant with no criminal history, a strong defense, or prosecutorial disclosure of critical evidence.

Claims of innocence are being partially addressed today by recently passed state laws that mandate DNA testing of all death row inmates in situations where DNA testing might help establish guilt or innocence (that is, in cases where blood or semen from the perpetrator is available for testing).[140]

In 2004, in recognition of the potential of DNA testing to exonerate the innocent, President George W. Bush signed the Innocence Protection Act[141] into law. The Innocence Protection Act provides federal funds to eliminate the backlog of unanalyzed DNA samples in the nation's crime laboratories[142] and sets aside money to improve the capacity of federal,

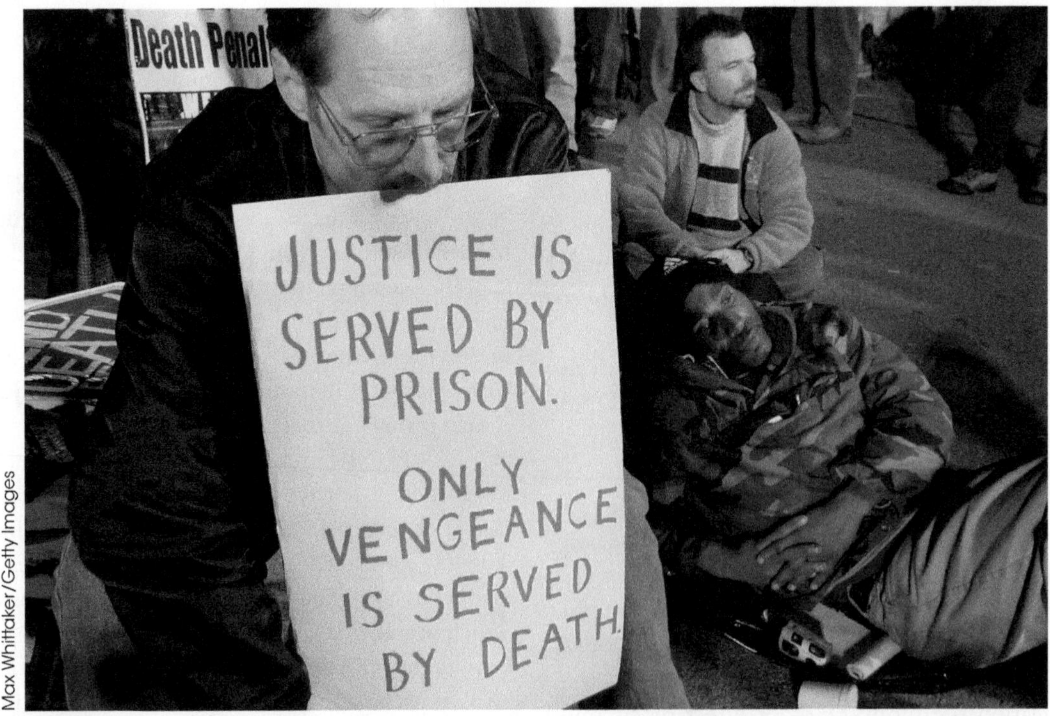

Max Whittaker/Getty Images

Death penalty opponent Mark Bherand sitting outside San Quentin Prison holding a sign as he awaits the execution of convicted killer Stanley "Tookie" Williams on December 13, 2005. Williams, reputed cofounder of the Crips street gang, had been convicted of four murders that occurred in 1979. He was denied clemency by California's then-Governor Arnold Schwartzenegger. What arguments can be made in favor of and against capital punishment? Which arguments do you find most compelling?

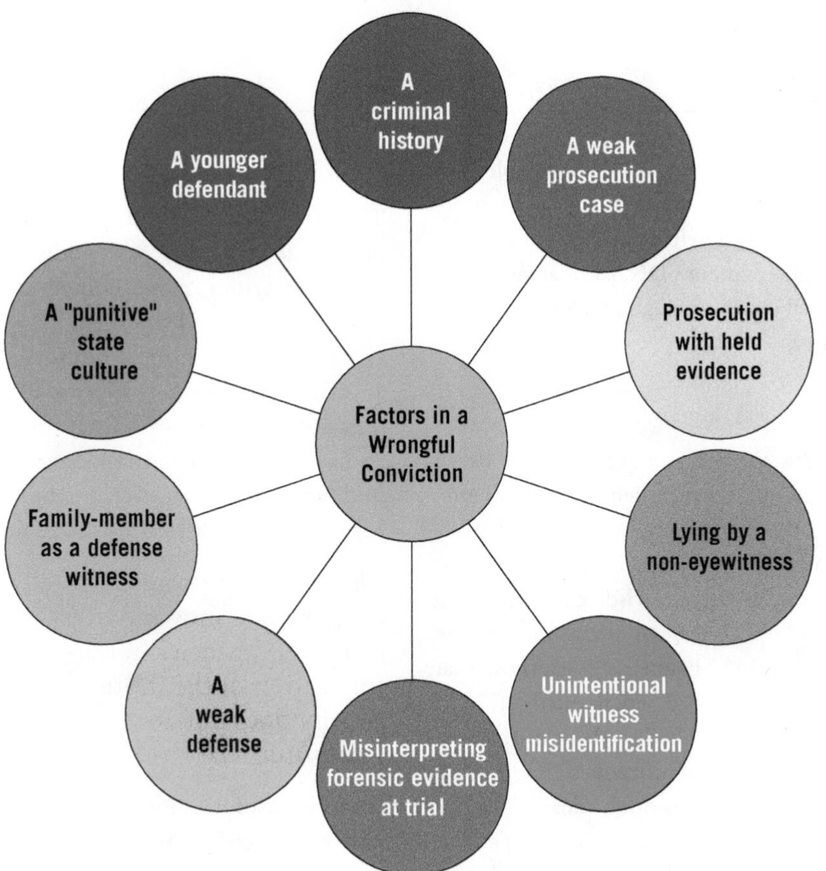

FIGURE 11-7 | Ten Factors that Can Lead to a Wrongful Conviction

Source: Adapted from Jon B. Gould, Julia Carrano, Richard Leo, and Joseph Young, "Predicting Erroneous Convictions: A Social Science Approach to Miscarriages of Justice—Final Report to the National Institute of Justice, February 2013," https://www.ncjrs.gov/pdffiles1/nij/grants/241389.pdf.

state, and local crime laboratories to conduct DNA analyses.[143] The act also facilitates access to postconviction DNA testing for those serving time in state[144] or federal prisons or on death row and sets forth conditions under which a federal prisoner asserting innocence may obtain postconviction DNA testing of specific evidence. Similarly, the legislation requires the preservation of biological evidence by federal law enforcement agencies for any defendant under a sentence of imprisonment or death.

In 2006, in the only state action of its kind to date, the North Carolina General Assembly established the North Carolina Innocence Inquiry Commission, and charged it with investigating and evaluating postconviction claims of factual innocence.[145] The commission, which comprises eight members selected by the chief justice of the North Carolina Supreme Court and the chief judge of the North Carolina Court of Appeals, examines only new evidence that was not considered at trial. As of mid-2010, the commission had considered 756 cases, resulting in one exoneration.[146] By mid-2012, 44 states had innocence projects, many of them private initiatives based at law schools or universities, devoted to helping identify and release innocent prisoners.[147]

Not all claims of innocence are supported by DNA tests or by other forms of inquiry, however. In 2006, for example, DNA test results confirmed the guilt of Roger Keith Coleman, a Virginia coal miner who had steadfastly maintained his innocence until he was executed in 1992. Coleman, executed for the 1981 rape and murder of his sister-in-law, Wanda McCoy, died declaring his innocence and proclaiming that he would one day be exonerated. His case became a cause célèbre for death penalty opponents, who convinced Virginia Governor Mark Warner to order DNA tests on surviving evidence. Coleman's supporters claimed that the tests would provide the first scientific proof that an innocent man had been executed in the United States. Results from the tests, however, conclusively showed that blood and semen found at the crime scene had come from Coleman. Recent studies have confirmed the convictions of about 42% of inmates whose cases are selected for DNA testing through the Innocence Project.[148] About 43% are exonerated by the tests. Because strong doubts about guilt already exist in cases where inmates are selected for testing, however, the percentage of confirmed convictions seems surprising.

Finally, in 2010 the U.S. Supreme Court ruled, in the case of *District Attorney's Office* v. *Osborne*,[149] that there is no fundamental constitutional right to access DNA-testable evidence long after a criminal conviction is final. Learn more about DNA testing and how it can help determine guilt or innocence from the federal government's DNA Initiative, whose motto is "advancing criminal justice through DNA technology," via **http://www.dna.gov**.

The Death Penalty and Deterrence

During the 1970s and 1980s, the deterrent effect of the death penalty became a favorite subject for debate in academic circles.[150] Studies of states that had eliminated the death penalty failed to show any increase in homicide rates.[151] Similar studies of neighboring states, in which jurisdictions retaining capital punishment were compared with those that had abandoned it, also failed to demonstrate any significant differences.[152] Although death penalty advocates remain numerous, few still argue for the penalty based on its deterrent effects. One study that has found support for use of the death penalty as a deterrent was reported in 2001 by Hashem Dezhbakhsh and his colleagues at Emory University.[153] According to the researchers, "Our results suggest that capital punishment has a strong deterrent effect. . . . In particular, each execution results, on average, in 18 fewer murders."[154] They note that most other studies in the area have not only been methodologically flawed but have failed to consider the fact that a number of states sentence select offenders to death but do not carry out executions. They write, "If criminals know that the justice system issues many death sentences but the executions are not carried out, then they may not be deterred by an increase in probability of a death sentence."[155]

> Although death penalty advocates remain numerous, few argue for the penalty based on its deterrent effects.

In 2012, however, in a succinct summary of studies on the deterrent effect of the death penalty, the Committee on Law and Justice of the National Academy of Sciences released *Deterrence and the Death Penalty,* a publication that included a detailed analysis of previous death penalty research.[156] The committee found that "research to date is not informative about whether capital punishment decreases, increases, or has no effect on homicide rates." It concluded that "claims that research demonstrates that capital punishment decreases or increases the homicide rate or has no effect on it should not influence policy judgments about capital punishment." Read the entire National Academy of Sciences report at **http://www.justicestudies.com/pdf/deathpenaltynas.pdf**.

The Death Penalty and Discrimination

The claim that the death penalty is discriminatory is hard to investigate. Although past evidence suggests that blacks and other minorities in the United States have been disproportionately sentenced to death,[157] more recent evidence is not as clear. At first glance, disproportionality seems apparent: 45 of the 98 prisoners executed between January 1977 and May 1988 were African American or Hispanic, and 84 of the 98 had been convicted of killing whites.[158] A 1996 Kentucky study found that blacks accused of killing whites in that state between 1976 and 1991 had a higher-than-average probability of being charged with a capital crime and of being sentenced to die than did homicide offenders of other races.[159] For an accurate appraisal to be made, however, any claims of disproportionality must go beyond simple comparisons with racial representation in the larger population and must somehow measure both frequency and seriousness of capital crimes between and within racial groups. Following that line of reasoning, the Supreme Court, in the 1987 case of *McCleskey* v. *Kemp*,[160] held that a simple showing of racial discrepancies in the application of the death penalty does not constitute a constitutional violation. A 2001 study of racial and ethnic fairness in federal capital punishment sentences attempted to go beyond mere percentages in its analysis of the role played by race and ethnicity in capital punishment sentencing decisions.[161] Although the study, which closely reviewed 950 capital punishment cases, found that approximately 80% of federal death row inmates are African American, researchers found "no intentional racial or ethnic bias in how capital punishment was administered in federal cases."[162] Underrepresented groups were more likely to be sentenced to death, "but only because they are more likely to be arrested on facts that could support a capital charge, not because the justice system acts in a discriminatory fashion," the report said.[163] Read the entire report at **http://www.justice.gov/dag/pubdoc/deathpenaltystudy.htm**.

> *McCleskey v. Kemp* held that a simple showing of racial discrepancies in the application of the death penalty does not constitute a constitutional violation.

Another 2001 study, this one by New Jersey Supreme Court Special Master David Baime, found no evidence of bias against African American defendants in capital cases in New Jersey during the period studied (August 1982 through May 2000). The study concluded, "Simply stated, we discern no sound basis from the statistical evidence to conclude that the race or ethnicity of the defendant is a factor in determining

CJ | NEWS

High Costs Lead to Reconsideration of Death Penalty

Judges, prosecutors, and legislators are reconsidering use of the death penalty, and the crippling cost of obtaining such convictions is a key factor.

"Death by execution is excessively expensive," wrote Florida Judge Charles M. Harris in an April 2012 opinion piece. "Most people who support the death penalty believe it is more cost-effective than life in prison. Perhaps at one time, when executions were swift and sure, this may have been the case. It is not now."

Countless studies support this argument. The state of Indiana, for example, found that the average death penalty case cost ten times more than a case involving a sentence of life without parole. Similarly, a recent Urban Institute study determined that the average capital case in Maryland cost almost $1 million more than a comparable non-death-penalty case.

Much of the cost goes into preparing for trial. The prosecution of Scott Peterson, the Californian accused of murdering his pregnant wife, Laci, for example, required more than 20,000 hours of staff time, costing $3.2 million. Peterson was sentenced to death in 2005, but he is appealing, usually a long process that takes even longer in California. The California Supreme Court spends more than half its time reviewing death penalty cases.

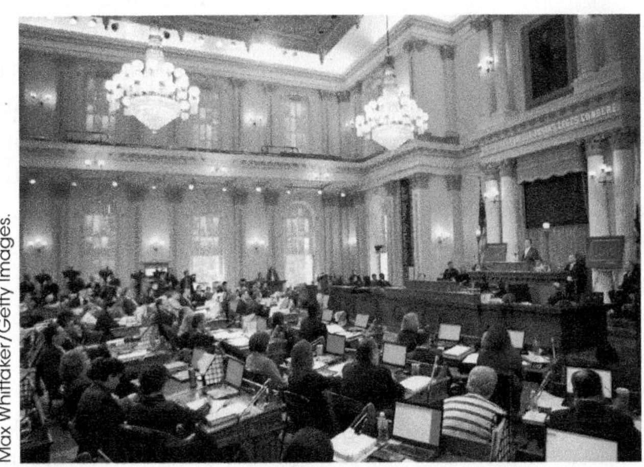

Max Whittaker/Getty Images.

A session of the California legislature. States like California are considering the cost of capital punishment, along with public sentiment and moral aspects of court-ordered executions, in weighing the future of the death penalty in their states. What role, if any, should cost play in capital punishment decisions?

The extra expenses can be traced back to a U.S. Supreme Court decision in 1976, four years after the High Court reinstated the death penalty, requiring additional precautions in death penalty cases. Jury selection, for example, takes three to four weeks longer and costs $200,000 more than in life-without-parole cases, according to a California study.

In the sentencing phase of a death penalty case, defendants have the right to present mitigating factors, requiring expensive expert testimony. After conviction, it can take years to exhaust appeals, which adds to both court and incarceration costs. According to a 2011 report, California death row inmates require solitary cells and extra guards, costing the state $100,663 more per inmate per year than regular confinement.

County governments typically pick up the tab for criminal trials, resulting in tax increases or service cuts. The Peterson trial, for example, forced Stanislaus County to redistribute legal cases and cut its consumer fraud protection unit. And counties can't easily avoid this obligation. When commissioners of Lincoln County, Georgia, for example, refused to allocate funds for a new trial ordered for death row inmate Johnny Lee Jones, they were put in jail.

But despite punishing costs, the expansive legal rights of defendants facing death have not been rolled back—perhaps in part due to disturbing reports of wrongful convictions exposed by DNA evidence, recanted testimony, and other factors. "When innocent people are executed, those mistakes cannot be remedied," observes the ACLU.

Whatever the reason, Americans seem to be losing interest in execution. According to Gallup polls, support for the death penalty has fallen from a high of 80% in 1994 to 61% in 2011. The number of death sentences handed out nationwide declined from 284 in 1999 to 111 in 2008, according to the Associated Press.

For states struggling with crippling deficits, savings from abolishing capital punishment are very tempting. North Carolina estimated potential savings at $11 million per year, Florida estimated $51 million in savings per year, and a California study said the state could immediately save $1 billion by eliminating the death penalty.

Currently 15 states have no death penalty. The latest to join the list is Maryland, which ended the death penalty in 2012.

Resources: "Fight against Death Penalty Gains Momentum in States," *Los Angeles Times*, April 14, 2012, http://articles.latimes.com/2012/apr/14/nation/la-na-death-penalty-20120415; "Just or Not, Cost of Death Penalty Is a Killer for State Budgets," Fox News, March 27, 2012, http://www.foxnews.com/us/2010/03/27/just-cost-death-penalty-killer-state-budgets/; and "Death Penalty Costs California $184 Million a Year, Study Says," *Los Angeles Times*, June 20, 2011, http://articles.latimes.com/2011/jun/20/local/la-me-adv-death-penalty-costs-20110620.

---

which cases advance to a penalty trial and which defendants are ultimately sentenced to death. The statistical evidence abounds the other way—it strongly suggests that there are no racial or ethnic disparities in capital murder prosecution and death sentencing rates."[164]

Evidence of socioeconomic discrimination in the imposition of the death penalty in Nebraska between 1973 and 1999 was found in a 2001 study of more than 700 homicide cases in that state. The study, which had been mandated by the state legislature, found that whereas race did not appear to influence death penalty decisions, killers of victims with high socioeconomic status received the death penalty four times as often as would otherwise be expected. According to the study, "The data document significant statewide disparities in charging and sentencing outcomes based on the socio-economic status of the victim."[165]

Justifications for Capital Punishment

On February 11, 2004, 47-year-old Edward Lewis Lagrone was executed by lethal injection in Huntsville, Texas, for the murder of three people in their home. Earlier, Lagrone had molested and impregnated one of the victims, a ten-year-old child, whom he shot in the head as she was trying to protect her 19-month-old sister.[166] Lagrone also killed two of the child's great-aunts who were in the house at the time of the attack. One of the women, 76-year-old Caola Lloyd, was deaf, blind, and bedridden with cancer. Prior to the killings, Lagrone had served 7 years of a 20-year prison sentence for another murder and was on parole. "He's a poster child to justify the death penalty," said David Montague, the Tarrant County assistant district attorney who prosecuted Lagrone.

Like many others today, Montague feels that "cold-blooded murder" justifies a sentence of death. Justifications for the death penalty are collectively referred to as the *retentionist position*. The three retentionist arguments are (1) just deserts, (2) revenge, and (3) protection.

The just deserts argument makes the claim that some people deserve to die for what they have done.

The just deserts argument makes the simple and straightforward claim that some people deserve to die for what they have done. Death is justly deserved; anything less cannot suffice as a sanction for the most heinous crimes. As U.S. Supreme Court Justice Potter Stewart once wrote, "The decision that capital punishment may be the appropriate sanction in extreme cases is an expression of the community's belief that certain crimes are themselves so grievous an affront to humanity that the only adequate response may be the penalty of death."[167]

Those who justify capital punishment as revenge attempt to appeal to the idea that survivors, victims, and the state are entitled to "closure." Only after execution of the criminal perpetrator, they say, can the psychological and social wounds engendered by the offense begin to heal.

The retentionist claim of protection asserts that offenders, once executed, can commit no further crimes. Clearly the least emotional of the retentionist claims, the protectionist argument may also be the weakest, as societal interests in protection can also be met in other ways, such as incarceration. In addition, various studies have shown that there is little likelihood of repeat offenses among people convicted of murder and later released.[168] One reason for such results, however, may be that murderers generally serve lengthy prison sentences prior to release and may have lost whatever youthful propensity for criminality they previously possessed. For an intriguing debate over the constitutionality of the death penalty, see **http://debatepedia.idebate.org/en/index.php/Debate:_Death_penalty**.

The Courts and the Death Penalty

The U.S. Supreme Court has for some time served as a sounding board for issues surrounding the death penalty. One of the Court's earliest cases in this area was ***Wilkerson* v. *Utah*** (1878),[169] which questioned shooting as a method of execution and raised Eighth Amendment claims that firing squads constituted a form of cruel and unusual punishment. The Court disagreed, however, contrasting the relatively civilized nature of firing squads with the various forms of torture often associated with capital punishment around the time the Bill of Rights was written.

Similarly, the Court supported electrocution as a permissible form of execution in ***In re Kemmler*** (1890).[170] In *Kemmler*, the Court defined cruel and unusual methods of execution as follows: "Punishments are cruel when they involve torture or a lingering death; but the punishment of death is not cruel, within the meaning of that word as used in the Constitution. It implies there is something inhuman and barbarous, something more than the mere extinguishing of life."[171] Almost 60 years later, the Court ruled that a second attempt at the electrocution of a convicted person, when the first did not work, did not violate the Eighth Amendment.[172] The Court reasoned that the initial failure was the consequence of accident or unforeseen circumstances and not the result of an effort on the part of executioners to be intentionally cruel.

The Supreme Court supported electrocution as a permissible form of execution in *In re Kemmler*.

It was not until 1972, however, in the landmark case of ***Furman* v. *Georgia***,[173] that the Court recognized "evolving standards of decency"[174] that might necessitate a reconsideration of Eighth Amendment guarantees. In a 5–4 ruling, the *Furman* decision invalidated Georgia's death penalty statute on the basis that it allowed a jury unguided discretion in the imposition of a capital sentence. The majority of justices concluded that the Georgia statute, which permitted a jury to decide issues of guilt or innocence while it weighed sentencing options, allowed for an arbitrary and capricious application of the death penalty.

Many other states with statutes similar to Georgia's were affected by the *Furman* ruling but moved quickly to modify their procedures. What evolved was the two-step procedure used today in capital cases. In the first stage, guilt or innocence is decided; if the defendant is convicted of a crime for which execution is possible or if he pleads guilty to such an offense, a second (or penalty) phase ensues. The penalty phase, a kind of mini-trial, generally permits the introduction of new evidence that may have been irrelevant to the question of guilt but that may be relevant to punishment, such as drug use or childhood abuse. In most death penalty jurisdictions, juries determine the punishment. However, in Arizona, Idaho, Montana, and Nebraska, the trial judge sets the sentence in the second phase of capital murder trials, and Alabama, Delaware, Florida, and Indiana allow juries only to recommend a sentence to the judge. The Supreme Court formally approved the two-step trial procedure in ***Gregg* v. *Georgia*** (1976).[175] Post-*Gregg* decisions set limits on the use of death as a penalty for all but the most severe crimes. Other important U.S. Supreme Court decisions of relevance to the death penalty are shown in Table 11-5.

Following *Apprendi* v. *New Jersey* (discussed earlier in this chapter), attorneys for an Arizona death row inmate successfully challenged that state's practice of allowing judges, sitting without a jury, to make factual determinations necessary for imposition of the death penalty. In ***Ring* v. *Arizona*** (2002),[176] a jury had found Timothy Stuart Ring guilty of felony murder occurring in the course of an armed robbery for the killing of an armored car driver in 1994, but it deadlocked on the charge of premeditated murder. Under Arizona law, Ring could not be sentenced to death, the

Matt York/AP Wide World Photos

Timothy Ring, the Arizona death row inmate who won a 2002 U.S. Supreme Court case that could potentially invalidate the death sentences of at least 150 other prisoners. In that case, *Ring* v. *Arizona*, the Court held that defendants have a Sixth Amendment right to have a jury, and not just a judge, determine the existence of aggravating factors justifying the death penalty. What other decisions made by the Court since then have further refined the *Ring* ruling?

TABLE 11-5 | The Courts and the Death Penalty

YEAR	U.S. SUPREME COURT CASE	RULING
2008	*Kennedy* v. *Louisiana*	The Eighth Amendment bars states from imposing the death penalty for the rape of a child where the crime did not result, and was not intended to result, in the victim's death.
2008	*Baze* v. *Rees*	The capital punishment protocol of lethal injection involving a three-drug "cocktail" used by Kentucky does not violate the Eighth Amendment because it does not create a substantial risk of wanton and unnecessary infliction of pain, torture, or lingering death.
2005	*Deck* v. *Missouri*	The Constitution forbids the use of visible shackles during a capital trial's penalty phase, as it does during the guilt phase, unless that use is "justified by an essential state interest"—such as courtroom security—specific to the defendant on trial.
2005	*Roper* v. *Simmons*	The Eighth and Fourteenth Amendments forbid imposition of the death penalty on offenders who were under the age of 18 when their crimes were committed.
2004	*Schriro* v. *Summerlin*	The rule established in *Apprendi* and *Ring* cannot be applied retroactively to sentences already imposed because it is merely a new procedural rule and not a substantive change.
2002	*Atkins* v. *Virginia*	Executing mentally retarded people violates the Constitution's ban on cruel and unusual punishments.
2002	*Ring* v. *Arizona*	Juries—not judges—must decide the facts, including those relating to aggravating circumstances that may lead to a death sentence.
1977	*Coker* v. *Georgia*	Struck down a Georgia law imposing the death penalty for the rape of an adult woman; the Court concluded that capital punishment under such circumstances is "grossly disproportionate" to the crime.
1976	*Gregg* v. *Georgia*	Upheld a new two-stage (bifurcated) procedural requirement of Georgia's revised capital punishment statute. The law requires guilt or innocence to be determined in the first stage of a bifurcated trial. Upon a guilty verdict, a presentencing hearing is held where the judge or jury hears additional aggravating and mitigating evidence. At least 1 of 10 specified aggravating circumstances must be found to exist beyond a reasonable doubt before a death sentence can be imposed.
1976	*Woodson* v. *North Carolina*	A state law requiring mandatory application of the death penalty for all first-degree murders was found to be unconstitutional.
1972	*Furman* v. *Georgia*	Recognized "evolving standards of decency" in invalidating Georgia's death penalty statute because it allowed a jury unguided discretion in the imposition of a capital sentence. The Georgia statute, which permitted a jury to decide issues of guilt or innocence while simultaneously weighing sentencing options, was found to allow for an arbitrary and capricious application of the death penalty.

statutory maximum penalty for first-degree murder, unless a judge made further findings in a separate sentencing hearing. The death penalty could be imposed only if the judge found the existence of at least one aggravating circumstance specified by law that was not offset by mitigating circumstances. During such a hearing, the judge listened to an accomplice who said that Ring planned the robbery and shot the guard. The judge then determined that Ring was the actual killer and found that the killing was committed for financial gain (an aggravating factor). Following the hearing, Ring was sentenced to death. His attorneys appealed, claiming that, by the standards set forth in *Apprendi*, Arizona's sentencing scheme violated the Sixth Amendment's guarantee of a jury trial because it entrusted a judge with fact-finding powers that allowed Ring's sentence to be raised above what would otherwise have been the statutory maximum. The U.S. Supreme Court agreed and overturned Ring's sentence, finding that "Arizona's enumerated aggravating factors operate as the functional equivalent of an element of a greater offense." *Ring* established that juries, not judges, must decide the facts that lead to a death sentence. The *Ring* ruling called into question at least 150 judge-imposed death sentences[177] in at least five states (Arizona, Colorado, Idaho, Montana, and Nebraska).[178]

Ring v. *Arizona* established that juries, not judges, must decide the facts that lead to a death sentence.

Although questions may arise about sentencing practices, the majority of justices on today's High Court seem largely convinced of the fundamental constitutionality of a sentence of death. Open to debate, however, is the constitutionality of *methods* for execution. In a 1993 hearing, *Poyner* v. *Murray*,[179] the U.S. Supreme Court hinted at the possibility of revisiting questions first raised in *Kemmler*. The case challenged Virginia's use of the electric chair, calling it a form of cruel and unusual punishment. Syvasky Lafayette Poyner, who originally brought the case before the Court, lost his bid for a stay of execution and was electrocuted in March 1993. Nonetheless, in *Poyner*, Justices David H. Souter, Harry A. Blackmun, and John Paul Stevens wrote, "The Court has not spoken squarely on the underlying issue since *In re Kemmler* . . . and the holding of that case does not constitute a dispositive response to litigation of the issue in light of modern knowledge about the method of execution in question."

In a still more recent ruling, members of the Court questioned the constitutionality of hanging, suggesting that it too may be a form of cruel and unusual punishment. In that case, *Campbell* v. *Wood* (1994),[180] the defendant, Charles Campbell, raped a woman, was released from prison at the completion of his sentence, and then went back and murdered her. His request for a stay of execution was denied since the law of Washington State, where the murder occurred, offered Campbell a choice of various methods of execution and therefore an alternative to hanging. Similarly, in 1996, the Court upheld California's death penalty statute, which provides for lethal injection as the primary method of capital punishment in that state.[181] The constitutionality of the statute had been challenged by two death row inmates who claimed that a provision in the law that permitted condemned prisoners the choice of lethal gas in lieu of injection brought the statute within the realm of allowing cruel and unusual punishments.

Questions about the constitutionality of electrocution as a means of execution again came to the fore in 1997, when flames shot from the head and the leather mask covering the face of Pedro Medina during his Florida execution. Similarly, in 1999, blood poured from behind the mask covering Allen Lee "Tiny" Davis's face as he was put to death in Florida's electric chair. State officials claimed that the 344-pound Davis suffered a nosebleed brought on by hypertension and the blood-thinning medication that he had been taking. Photographs of Davis taken during and immediately after the execution showed him grimacing while bleeding profusely onto his chest and neck. In 2001, the Georgia Supreme Court declared electrocution to be unconstitutional, ending its use in that state.[182] The Georgia court cited testimony from lower-court records showing that electrocution may not result in a quick death or in an immediate cessation of consciousness. By the time of the court's decision, however, the Georgia legislature had already passed a law establishing lethal injection as the state's sole method of punishment for capital crimes.[183]

In 2006, questions were raised about lethal injections as constituting cruel and unusual punishment. Those questions originated with eyewitness accounts, postmortem blood testing, and execution logs that seemed to show that some of those executed remained conscious but paralyzed and experienced excruciating pain before dying.[184] Such claims focused on the composition of the chemical cocktail used in executions, which contains one drug (sodium thiopental, a short-acting barbiturate) to induce sleep, another (pancuronium bromide) to paralyze the muscles (but which does not cause unconsciousness), and a third (potassium chloride) to stop the heart. If the first chemical is improperly administered, the condemned person remains conscious, and the procedure can cause severe pain and discomfort.

Complicating matters is the fact that the ethical codes of most professional medical organizations forbid medical practitioners to take life—meaning that although the codes are not legally binding, medical professionals are largely excluded from taking part in executions, other than to verify the fact that death has occurred. To counter

Medical professionals are largely excluded from taking part in executions, other than to verify the fact that death has occurred.

fears that lethal injections cause pain, some states have begun using medical monitoring devices that show brain activity and can ensure that sleep is occurring.[185]

In 2008, the Court took up this issue in the case of *Baze* v. *Rees*,[186] which had been brought by prisoners on Kentucky's death row. The Court held that the capital punishment protocol used by Kentucky does not violate the Eighth Amendment because it does not create a substantial risk of wanton and unnecessary infliction of pain, torture, or lingering death. "Because some risk of pain is inherent in even the most humane execution method," wrote the justices, "the Constitution does not demand the avoidance of all risk of pain."

The Future of the Death Penalty

Support for the death penalty varies considerably from state to state and from one region of the country to another. In 2007, New Jersey repealed its capital punishment legislation, and in 2009, New Mexico Governor Bill Richardson signed legislation ending capital punishment in that state. Short of renewed Supreme Court intervention, the future of capital punishment may depend more on popular opinion. A 2013 USA Today/Gallup national poll of registered voters found that 63% were in favor of capital punishment for murder.[187] Although the 63% figure is higher than in other recent years, support for the death penalty has, for the most part, consistently declined since 1994, when 80% were in favor of the punishment. Support has increased, however, for death penalty alternatives, including life with no possibility of parole, or life with the possibility of parole.

Ultimately, public opinion about the death penalty may turn on the issue of whether innocent people have been executed.

Ultimately, public opinion about the death penalty may turn on the issue of whether innocent people have been executed.

According to a number of recent studies, Americans from all walks of life are less likely to support capital punishment if they believe that innocent people have been put to death at the hands of the justice system or if they think that the death penalty is being applied unfairly.[188] One recent study found that support for the death penalty among Americans varies by race, with African Americans less likely to support capital punishment than whites.[189] The study concluded that much of the difference is explained by differing beliefs between the races about the number of executed innocents and perceived fairness in application of capital sanctions. Consequently, execution of the innocent is at the center of today's debate concerning the legitimacy of capital punishment, and it is likely to determine the future of the death penalty in individual states as local legislatures move to mandate procedural enhancements meant to guarantee fairness.

In 2002, a special commission appointed by Governor George Ryan to examine the imposition of capital punishment in Illinois made its report, saying that the system through which capital sentences are imposed should be modified to encompass a number of procedural safeguards. Safeguards that were recommended included (1) tighter controls on how the police investigate cases, including a requirement that investigators "continue to pursue all reasonable lines of inquiry, whether these point toward or away from the suspect"; (2) controls on the potential fallibility of eyewitness testimony, including lineups where the person in charge is not aware of which person in the lineup is the suspect (to preclude him or her from unconsciously identifying the suspect); and (3) statutory reform so that the death penalty cannot be applied based solely on the testimony of any single accomplice or eyewitness without further corroboration.[190] In April 2003, incoming Illinois Governor Rod R. Blagojevich said that because of his concerns over executing innocent people, he would not lift his state's ban on executions even if the state's legislature passed a bill aimed at improving the system.[191] Blagojevich was impeached by the Illinois state senate in 2009 and removed from office. In 2011, Pat Quinn, the state's new governor, signed a law abolishing capital punishment in Illinois, and commuted the sentences of all 15 men on death row, meaning that they will serve life in prison without possibility of parole.[192]

CJ | NEWS

Death-Row Exonerations Based on DNA Expose Flaws in Legal System

At last count, DNA testing has exonerated almost 60 people convicted of murder, and 17 of them were death row inmates, according to the Innocence Project.

The group, dedicated to freeing wrongly accused prisoners, says DNA testing has "opened a window into wrongful convictions so that we may study the causes and propose remedies that may minimize the chances that more innocent people are convicted."

Miscarriages of justice exposed by DNA testing include erroneous reports by witnesses, misidentification of evidence, biased jailhouse informants, and false confessions obtained by overzealous prosecutors.

Kirk Bloodsworth was the first death row inmate exonerated by DNA. He was found guilty in 1985 of raping and strangling a nine-year-old girl in Rosedale, Maryland, based on the testimony of five eyewitnesses. After learning that DNA testing was used to convict a man for murder, Bloodsworth asked to use it to un-convict him. The $15,000 test, which his attorney financed out-of-pocket, ruled him out, and he was released in 1993.

Speaking in 2013, to an audience of anti-capital-punishment supporters, Bloodsworth said "I was accused of the most brutal murder in Maryland history. . . . It [only] took the jury two and a half hours to send me to the gas chamber."

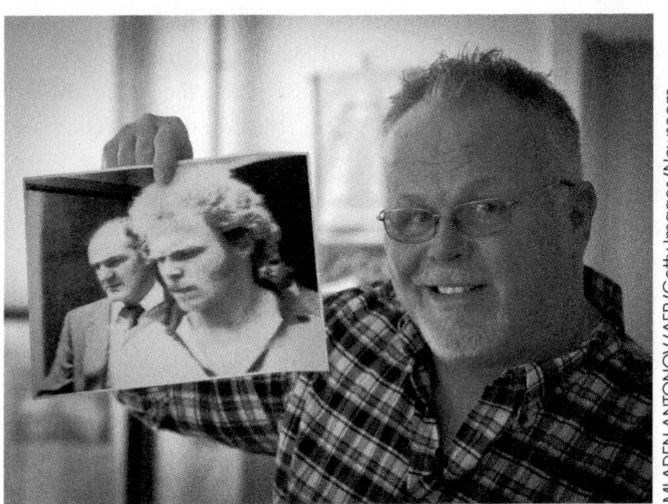

MLADEN ANTONOV/AFP/Getty Images/Newscom

Kirk Bloodsworth, the first death row inmate exonerated through the use of DNA evidence. Bloodsworth had been found guilty in 1985 of raping and strangling a nine-year-old Rosedale, Maryland, girl based on the testimony of five eyewitnesses. Later DNA testing absolved him of guilt, and he was released in 1993.

In an even more serious miscarriage of justice, Claude Jones was executed in Texas in 2000 for murdering the owner of a Texas liquor store. Jones's conviction was largely based on a strand of hair at the crime scene that purportedly was his. But DNA tests ten years after the execution showed that it actually belonged to the storeowner.

In another example of the power of DNA testing, Michael Blair had a prior sex crime conviction on his record when he was picked up in 1993 for the murder of a seven-year-old girl in Plano, Texas. Three eyewitnesses said they saw him near the crime scene, even though the police had found him 17 miles away that day. Hairs in Blair's car were falsely linked to the victim. Blair was sentenced to death for the crime, but DNA testing eight years later excluded him and identified two other men. He was released.

Although Juan Rivera was never sentenced to death, he was convicted three times for the 1992 rape and murder of an 11-year-old babysitter in Waukegan, Illinois. On the night of the murder, he had been confined to his home by an electronic leg monitor for stealing a car stereo, but after many hours of interrogation he confessed to the crime. His confession allegedly contained details that only the killer would know, and three jailhouse informants also implicated him.

Before Rivera's third trial, tests showed his DNA did not match semen from the crime scene, but the prosecutor argued it could have come from an unidentified lover of the 11-year-old. "We don't quaver because somebody holds up three letters: DNA," he said. And Rivera was found guilty again. But in December 2011, an appeals court reversed the conviction and barred any more retrials, saying the evidence had been insufficient to convince any "rational trier of fact" of Rivera's guilt. Rivera was freed after spending nearly 20 years in prison.

The Innocence Project, founded in 1992 at the Cardozo School of Law at Yeshiva University in New York City, receives 3,000 requests for help every year and is evaluating 6,000 to 8,000 potential cases at any given time. It now has 61 affiliated chapters across the country.

A similar group, the Center on Wrongful Convictions at Northwestern University Law School in Chicago, Illinois, has been instrumental in 48 exonerations, including cases pursued by its lawyers before the center was founded. Thirteen of those prisoners had been sentenced to death, and 26 of the cases involved DNA testing.

In addition, the Death Penalty Information Center in Washington, D.C., provides analysis and information on issues about capital punishment, including wrongful convictions.

Resources: "230 Exonerated in U.S. by DNA Testing, 17 Were Sentenced to Die," The Innocence Project http://www.dadychery.org/2012/02/01/230-exonerated-by-dna-17-were-sentenced-to-die/; "1st Death Row Inmate Exonerated by DNA to Speak at UM," *The Missoulian*, October 11, 2011, http://missoulian.com/news/local/article_1c836748-f3b2-11e0-b14b-001cc4c002e0.html; "'Never Think a Person in Prison Is Lost,' Juan Rivera Tells Law Students," The Chicago Tribune, April 4, 2012, http://www.chicagotribune.com/news/local/ct-met-juan-rivera-judge-20120404,0,1540689.story; and Scott Shane, "A Death Penalty Fight Comes Home," *New York Times*, February 5, 2013, http://www.nytimes.com/2013/02/06/us/exonerated-inmate-seeks-end-to-maryland-death-penalty.html?_r=0.

SUMMARY

- The goals of criminal sentencing include retribution, incapacitation, deterrence, rehabilitation, and restoration. Retribution corresponds to the just deserts model of sentencing, which holds that offenders are responsible for their crimes. Incapacitation seeks to protect innocent members of society from offenders who might harm them if not prevented from doing so. The goal of deterrence is to prevent future criminal activity through the example or threat of punishment. Rehabilitation seeks to bring about fundamental changes in offenders and their behavior to reduce the likelihood of future criminality. Restoration seeks to address the damage done by crime by making the victim and the community "whole again."
- The indeterminate sentencing model is characterized primarily by vast judicial choice. It builds on the belief that convicted offenders are more likely to participate in their own rehabilitation if such participation will reduce the amount of time that they have to spend in prison.
- Structured sentencing is largely a child of the just deserts philosophy. It grew out of concerns with proportionality, equity, and social debt—all of which this chapter discusses. Numerous different types of structured sentencing models have been created, including determinate sentencing, which requires that a convicted offender be sentenced to a fixed term that may be reduced by good time or gain time, and a voluntary/advisory sentencing model under which guidelines consist of recommended sentencing policies that are not required by law, are usually based on past sentencing practices, and are meant to serve as guides to judges. Mandatory sentencing, another form of structured sentencing, mandates clearly enumerated punishments for specific offenses or for habitual offenders convicted of a series of crimes. The applicability of structured sentencing guidelines has been called into question by recent U.S. Supreme Court decisions.
- Alternative sanctions include the use of court-ordered community service, home detention, day reporting, drug treatment, psychological counseling, victim–offender mediation, and intensive supervision in lieu of other, more traditional sanctions such as imprisonment and fines. Numerous questions have been raised about alternative sentences, including questions about their impact on public safety, the cost-effectiveness of such sanctions, and the long-term effects of community sanctions on people assigned to alternative programs.
- Probation and parole officers routinely conduct background investigations to provide information that judges may use in deciding on the appropriate kind or length of sentence for convicted offenders.
- Historically, criminal courts have often allowed victims to testify at trial but have otherwise downplayed the experience of victimization and the suffering it causes. A new interest in the experience of victims, beginning in the 1970s in this country, has led to a greater legal recognition of victims' rights, including a right to allocution (the right to be heard during criminal proceedings). Many states have passed victims' rights amendments to their constitutions, although a federal victims' rights amendment has yet to be enacted. The Crime Victims' Rights Act of 2004 established statutory rights for victims of federal crimes and gives them the necessary legal authority to assert those rights in federal court.
- The four traditional sentencing options identified in this chapter are fines, probation, imprisonment, and—in cases of especially horrific offenses—death. The appropriateness of each sentencing option for various kinds of crimes was discussed, and the pros and cons of each were examined.
- Arguments for capital punishment identified in this chapter include revenge, just deserts, and the protection of society. The revenge argument builds upon the need for personal and communal closure. The just deserts argument makes the straightforward claim that some people deserve to die for what they have done. Societal protection is couched in terms of deterrence, as those who are executed cannot commit future crimes, and execution serves as an example to other would-be criminals. Arguments against capital punishment include findings that death sentences have been imposed on innocent people, that the death penalty has not been found to be an effective deterrent, that it is often arbitrarily imposed, that it tends to discriminate against powerless groups and individuals, and that it is very expensive because of the numerous court appeals involved. Opponents also argue that the state should recognize the sanctity of human life.

KEY TERMS

aggravating circumstances, 346
alternative sentencing, 353
capital offense, 361
capital punishment, 361
determinate sentencing, 345
deterrence, 342
diversion, 352
equity, 345
gain time, 344
general deterrence, 342
good time, 344
incapacitation, 341
indeterminate sentencing, 344
just deserts, 341
justice reinvestment, 353
mandatory sentencing, 351
mitigating circumstances, 346
presentence investigation (PSI), 354
presumptive sentencing, 346
proportionality, 345
rehabilitation, 342
restoration, 342
restorative justice (RJ), 343
retribution, 341
sentencing, 340
social debt, 345
specific deterrence, 342
structured sentencing, 345
truth in sentencing, 347
victim-impact statement, 358
voluntary/advisory sentencing guidelines, 346
writ of *habeas corpus*, 363

KEY CASES

Apprendi v. *New Jersey*, 349
Blakely v. *Washington*, 349
Coleman v. *Thompson*, 363
Furman v. *Georgia*, 372
Gregg v. *Georgia*, 373
In re Kemmler, 372
McCleskey v. *Zant*, 363
Mistretta v. *U.S.*, 347
Ring v. *Arizona*, 373
Schlup v. *Delo*, 363
U.S. v. *Booker*, 349
Wilkerson v. *Utah*, 372

QUESTIONS FOR REVIEW

1. Describe the five goals of contemporary criminal sentencing discussed in this chapter. Which of these goals do you think ought to be the primary goal of sentencing? How might your choice vary with the type of offense committed? In what circumstances might your choice be less acceptable?
2. Illustrate the nature of indeterminate sentencing, and explain its positive aspects. What led some states to abandon indeterminate sentencing?
3. What is structured sentencing? What structured sentencing models are in use today? Which model holds the best promise for long-term crime reduction? Why?
4. What are alternative sanctions? Give some examples of alternative sanctions, and offer an assessment of how effective they might be.
5. What is a presentence investigation? How do presentence investigations contribute to the contents of presentence reports? How are presentence reports used?
6. Describe the history of victims' rights and services in this country. What role does the victim play in criminal justice proceedings today?
7. What are the four traditional sentencing options? Under what circumstances might each be appropriate?
8. Do you support or oppose capital punishment? Outline the arguments on both sides of the issue.

QUESTIONS FOR REFLECTION

1. Of the different kinds of sentencing practices described in this chapter, which do you think makes the most sense? Why?
2. If you could set sentencing practices in your state and had to choose between a determinate and an indeterminate scheme, which would you select? Why?
3. What is truth in sentencing? Do you agree that it is an important concept? Why or why not?
4. Explain the development of federal sentencing guidelines. What have recent court decisions said about the applicability of those guidelines?
5. In your opinion, is the return to just deserts consistent with structured sentencing?

NOTES

i. "The Crime Bust," *U.S. News and World Report*, May 25, 1998.

1. The Sentencing Project, "Oregon Passes Racial Impact Statement Legislation," *Race and Justice News*, June 28, 2013.
2. Matt Smith, "'Racial Justice Act' Repealed in North Carolina," CNN, June 21, 2013, http://www.cnn.com/2013/06/20/justice/north-carolina-death-penalty (accessed August 2, 2013).
3. Marc Mauer, "Racial Impact Statements: Changing Policies to Address Disparities," *Criminal Justice*, Vol. 23, No. 4 (winter 2009).
4. For a thorough discussion of the philosophy of punishment and sentencing, see David Garland, *Punishment and Modern Society: A Study in Social Theory* (Chicago: University of Chicago Press, 1990). See also Ralph D. Ellis and Carol S. Ellis, *Theories of Criminal Justice: A Critical Reappraisal* (Wolfeboro, NH: Longwood Academic, 1989); and Colin Summer, *Censure, Politics, and Criminal Justice* (Bristol, PA: Open University Press, 1990).
5. Punishment is said to be required because social order (and the laws that represent it) could not exist for long if transgressions went unsanctioned.
6. Hugo Adam Bedau, "Retributivism and the Theory of Punishment," *Journal of Philosophy*, Vol. 75 (November 1978), pp. 601–620.
7. The definitive study during this period was Douglas Lipton, Robert Martinson, and J. Woks, *The Effectiveness of Correctional Treatment: A Survey of Treatment Valuation Studies* (New York: Praeger Press, 1975).
8. See, for example, Lawrence W. Sherman et al., *Preventing Crime: What Works, What Doesn't, What's Promising* (Washington, DC: National Institute of Justice, 1997).
9. Gordon Bazemore and Mark S. Umbreit, foreword to *Balanced and Restorative Justice: Program Summary* (Washington, DC: Office of Juvenile Justice and Delinquency Prevention, 1994).
10. Shay Bilchik, *Balanced and Restorative Justice for Juveniles: A Framework for Juvenile Justice in the 21st Century* (Washington, DC: Office of Juvenile Justice and Delinquency Prevention, 1997), p. ii.
11. Ibid., p. 14.
12. Ibid.
13. U.S. Code, Title 18, Section 3563(a)(2).
14. Donna Hunzeker, "State Sentencing Systems and 'Truth in Sentencing,'" *State Legislative Report*, Vol. 20, No. 3 (Denver, CO: National Conference of State Legislatures, 1995).
15. Paula M. Ditton and Doris James Wilson, *Truth in Sentencing in State Prisons* (Washington, DC: Bureau of Justice Statistics, 1999).
16. "Oklahoma Rapist Gets 30,000 Years," *United Press International*, southwest edition, December 23, 1994.
17. For a historical consideration of alleged disparities, see G. Kleck, "Racial Discrimination in Criminal Sentencing: A Critical Evaluation of the Evidence with Additional Evidence on the Death Penalty," *American Sociological Review*, No. 46 (1981), pp. 783–805; and G. Kleck, "Life Support for Ailing Hypotheses: Modes of Summarizing the Evidence for Racial Discrimination in Sentencing," *Law and Human Behavior*, No. 9 (1985), pp. 271–285.
18. As discussed later in this chapter, federal sentencing guidelines did not become effective until 1987 and still had to meet many court challenges.
19. U.S. Sentencing Commission, *Federal Sentencing Guidelines Manual* (Washington, DC: U.S. Government Printing Office, 1987), p. 2.

20. Inmates can still earn a maximum of 54 days per year of good-time credit.
21. The Parole Commission Phaseout Act of 1996 requires the attorney general to report to Congress yearly as to whether it is cost-effective for the U.S. Parole Commission to remain a separate agency or whether its functions (and personnel) should be assigned elsewhere. Under the law, if the attorney general recommends assigning the commission's functions to another component of the Department of Justice, federal parole will continue as long as necessary.
22. Lawrence A. Greenfeld, *Prison Sentences and Time Served for Violence* (Washington, DC: Bureau of Justice Statistics, April 1995).
23. For an excellent review of the act and its implications, see Gregory D. Lee, "U.S. Sentencing Guidelines: Their Impact on Federal Drug Offenders," *FBI Law Enforcement Bulletin*, May 1995, pp. 17–21.
24. *Mistretta* v. *U.S.*, 488 U.S. 361, 371 (1989).
25. For an engaging overview of how mitigating factors might be applied under the guidelines, see *Koon* v. *U.S.*, 116 S.Ct. 2035, 135 L.Ed.2d 392 (1996).
26. U.S. Sentencing Commission, *Federal Sentencing Guidelines Manual*, p. 207.
27. Ibid., p. 8.
28. National Institute of Justice, *Sentencing Commission Chairman Wilkins Answers Questions on the Guidelines*, National Institute of Justice Research in Action Series (Washington, DC: NIJ, 1987), p. 7.
29. *Melendez* v. *U.S.*, 117 S.Ct. 383, 136 L.Ed.2d 301 (1996).
30. *Apprendi* v. *New Jersey*, 120 S.Ct. 2348 (2000).
31. See, for example, Alexandra A. E. Shapiro and Jonathan P. Bach, "Applying 'Apprendi' to Federal Sentencing Rules," *New York Law Journal*, March 23, 2001, http://www.lw.com/pubs/articles/pdf/applyingApprendi.pdf (accessed June 30, 2008); and Freya Russell, "Limiting the Use of Acquitted and Uncharged Conduct at Sentencing: *Apprendi* v. *New Jersey* and Its Effect on the Relevant Conduct Provision of the United States Sentencing Guidelines," *California Law Review*, Vol. 89 (July 2001), p. 1199.
32. *U.S.* v. *O'Brien*, U.S. Supreme Court, No. 08-1569 (decided May 24, 2010).
33. *Blakely* v. *Washington*, 542 U.S. 296 (2004).
34. *Cunningham* v. *California*, 549 U.S. 270 (2007).
35. *U.S.* v. *Booker*, 543 U.S. 220 (2005).
36. Combined with *U.S.* v. *Booker* (2005).
37. Stanley E. Adelman, "Supreme Court Invalidates Federal Sentencing Guidelines . . . to an Extent," *On the Line, the Newsletter of the American Correctional Association*, May 2005, p. 1.
38. See *United States* v. *Rodriguez*, 398 F.3d 1291, 1297 (11th Cir. 2005).
39. *Rita* v. *U.S.*, 551 U.S. 338 (2007).
40. *Gall* v. *U.S.*, 552 U.S. 38 (2007).
41. *Oregon* v. *Ice*, U.S. Supreme Court, No. 07-901 (decided January 14, 2009).
42. *Alleyne* v. *U.S.*, U.S. Supreme Court, No. 11-9335 (decided June 17, 2013).
43. The *Alleyne* case overturned the Court's earlier ruling in *Harris* v. *U.S.* (2002), which held that "judicial factfinding that increases the mandatory minimum sentence for a crime is permissible under the Sixth Amendment."
44. U.S. Sentencing Commission, News Release, "Sentencing Commission Issues Comprehensive Report on the Continuing Impact of *United States* v. *Booker* on Federal Sentencing," January 30, 2013.
45. Ibid.
46. United States Sentencing Commission, "Report to Congress: Mandatory Minimum Penalties in the Federal Criminal Justice System," October 2011, http://www.ussc.gov/Legislative_and_Public_Affairs/Congressional_Testimony_and_Reports/Mandatory_Minimum_Penalties/20111031_RtC_Mandatory_Minimum.cfm (accessed November 24, 2011).
47. Michael Miller, "California Gets 'Three Strikes' Anti-Crime Bill," Reuters, March 7, 1994.
48. Tamar Lewin, "Three-Strikes Law Is Overrated in California, Study Finds," *New York Times*, August 23, 2001, http://query.nytimes.com/gst/fullpage.html?res59505E7DB1531F930A1575BC0A9679C8B63 (accessed September 2, 2009).
49. Ryan S. King and Marc Mauer, *Aging behind Bars: "Three Strikes" Seven Years Later* (Washington, DC: Sentencing Project, August 2001).
50. *Ewing* v. *California*, 538 U.S. 11 (2003); and *Lockyer* v. *Andrade*, 538 U.S. 63 (2003).
51. Under California law, a person who commits petty theft can be charged with a felony if he or she has prior felony convictions. The charge is known as "petty theft with prior convictions." Andrade's actual sentence was two 25-year prison terms to be served consecutively.
52. Tracey Kaplan, "Proposition 36: Voters Overwhelmingly Ease Three Strikes Law," *Mercury News*, November 7, 2012.
53. Tracey Kaplan, "Newly Released California 'Three-Strikers' Face New Challenges," January 20, 2013, http://www.contracostatimes.com/breaking-news/ci_22404586/newly-released-three-strikers-face-new-challenges (accessed May 1, 2013).
54. Much of the material in this section is derived from Dale Parent et al., *Mandatory Sentencing,* National Institute of Justice Research in Action Series (Washington, DC: NIJ, 1997).
55. In mid-1996, the California Supreme Court ruled the state's three-strikes law an undue intrusion on judges' sentencing discretion, and California judges now use their own discretion in evaluating which offenses "fit" within the meaning of the law.
56. Michael Tonry, *Sentencing Reform Impacts* (Washington, DC: National Institute of Justice, 1987).
57. D. C. McDonald and K. E. Carlson, *Sentencing in the Courts: Does Race Matter? The Transition to Sentencing Guidelines, 1986–90* (Washington, DC: Bureau of Justice Statistics, 1993).
58. U.S. Sentencing Commission, *Special Report to Congress: Cocaine and Federal Sentencing Policy* (Washington, DC: U.S. Sentencing Commission, May 2007).
59. Fair Sentencing Act of 2010, Pub. L. 111-22.
60. In 2012, however, the U.S. Supreme Court, in the case of *Dorsey* v. *United States*, held that the FSA's sentencing provisions applied to crack offenders who committed their crimes before the statute's effective date of August 3, 2010, but who were sentenced after that date.
61. A similar bill with the same name had also been introduced a year earlier.
62. U.S. Sentencing Commission, Office of Research and Data, "Memorandum: Analysis of the Impact of Amendment to the Statutory Penalties for Crack Cocaine Offenses Made by the Fair Sentencing Act of 2010," January 28, 2011.
63. Senator Dick Durbin, "Durbin and Lee Introduce Smarter Sentencing Act," http://www.durbin.senate.gov/public/index.cfm/pressreleases?ID=be68ad86-a0a4-4486-853f-f8ef7b99e736 (accessed August 2, 2013).
64. Michelle Healy, "Frost House Vandals Do Time Studying Poet," *USA Today*, June 3, 2008, p. 6D.
65. Keyonna Summers, "Teens Must Post Apology on YouTube," *USA Today*, June 9, 2008, 3A.

66. Richard Willing, "Thief Challenges Dose of Shame as Punishment," *USA Today*, August 18, 2004, p. 3A.
67. John Braithwaite, *Crime, Shame, and Reintegration* (Cambridge, England: Cambridge University Press, 1989).
68. Such evidence does, in fact, exist. See, for example, Harold G. Grasmick, Robert J. Bursik, Jr., and Bruce J. Arneklev, "Reduction in Drunk Driving as a Response to Increased Threats of Shame, Embarrassment, and Legal Sanctions," *Criminology*, Vol. 31, No. 1 (1993), pp. 41–67.
69. Council of State Governments, Lessons from the States, *Reducing Recidivism and Curbing Corrections Costs through Justice Reinvestment* (Council of State Governments, 2013).
70. Ibid.
71. Ibid., p. 4, from which some of the wording in these sentences is adapted.
72. Nicole D. Porter, *The State of Sentencing 2012* (Washington, DC: The Sentencing Project, 2013).
73. Joan Petersilia, *House Arrest*, National Institute of Justice Crime File Study Guide (Washington, DC: NIJ, 1988).
74. The Center adapted a number of these principles from James Andrews and D. A. Bonta, "Risk-Need-Responsivity Model for Offender Assessment and Rehabilitation," www.publicsafety.gc.ca/res/cor/rep/_fl/Risk_Need_2007-06_e.pdf (accessed March 2, 2013).
75. Pamela M. Casey, Roger K. Warren, and Jennifer K. Elek, *Using Offender Risk and Needs Assessment Information at Sentencing: Guidance for Courts from a National Working Group* (National Center for State Courts, 2011).
76. Privacy Act of 1974, 5 U.S.C.A. 522a, 88 Statute 1897, Pub. L. 93-579, December 31, 1974.
77. Freedom of Information Act, U.S. Code, Title 5, Section 522, and amendments. The status of presentence investigative reports has not yet been clarified under this act to the satisfaction of all legal scholars.
78. City of New York, Citywide Accountability Program, S.T.A.R.S. (Statistical Tracking, Analysis, and Reporting System), http://www.nyc.gov/html/prob/pdf/stars_92005.pdf (accessed May 13, 2007).
79. For a good review of the issues involved, see Robert C. Davis, Arthur J. Lurigio, and Wesley G. Skogan, *Victims of Crime*, 2nd ed. (Thousand Oaks, CA: Sage, 1997); and Leslie Sebba, *Third Parties: Victims and the Criminal Justice System* (Columbus: Ohio State University Press, 1996).
80. President's Task Force on Victims of Crime, *Final Report* (Washington, DC: U.S. Government Printing Office, 1982).
81. Peter Finn and Beverly N. W. Lee, *Establishing and Expanding Victim-Witness Assistance Programs* (Washington, DC: National Institute of Justice, 1988).
82. Senate Joint Resolution (SJR) 65 is a major revision of an initial proposal, SJR 52, which Senators Kyl and Feinstein introduced on April 22, 1996. Representative Henry Hyde introduced House Joint Resolution 174, a companion to SJR 52, and a similar proposal, House Joint Resolution 173, on April 22, 1996.
83. Senate Joint Resolution 44, 105th Congress.
84. See the National Center for Victims of Crime's critique of the 1998 amendment at http://www.ncvc.org/law/Ncvca.htm (accessed January 10, 2000).
85. See the National Victims' Constitutional Amendment Network news page, http://www.nvcan.org/news.htm (accessed January 10, 2007).
86. National Victims' Constitutional Amendment Passage, http://www.nvcap.org (accessed June 9, 2009).
87. Pub. L. 97-291.
88. USA PATRIOT Act of 2001, Section 624.
89. Office for Victims of Crime, *Report to the Nation, 2003* (Washington, DC: OVC, 2003).
90. 18 U.S.C. § 3771.
91. U.S. Senate, Republican Policy Committee, Legislative Notice No. 63, April 22, 2004.
92. Proposition 8, California's Victim's Bill of Rights.
93. National Victim Center, Mothers against Drunk Driving, and American Prosecutors Research Institute, *Impact Statements: A Victim's Right to Speak; A Nation's Responsibility to Listen* (Washington, DC: Office for Victims of Crime, July 1994).
94. *Kelly* v. *California*, 555 U.S. 1020 (2008).
95. Robert C. Davis and Barbara E. Smith, "The Effects of Victim Impact Statements on Sentencing Decisions: A Test in an Urban Setting," *Justice Quarterly*, Vol. 11, No. 3 (September 1994), pp. 453–469.
96. Office for Victims of Crime, *Vision 21: Transforming Victim Services—Final Report* (Washington, DC: USDOJ, May 2013).
97. Bureau of Justice Statistics, *Report to the Nation on Crime and Justice*, 2nd ed. (Washington, DC: U.S. Government Printing Office, 1988), p. 90.
98. Sean Rosenmerkel, Matthew Durose, and Donald Farole, Jr., *Felony Sentences in State Courts, 2006* (Washington, DC: Bureau of Justice Statistics, December 2009). Data for 1990 come from Matthew R. Durose, David J. Levin, and Patrick A. Langan, *Felony Sentences in State Courts, 1998* (Washington, DC: Bureau of Justice Statistics, 2001).
99. Matthew R. Durose and Patrick A. Langan, *Felony Sentences in State Courts, 2002* (Washington, DC: Bureau of Justice Statistics, 2004), p. 2.
100. Sally T. Hillsman, Joyce L. Sichel, and Barry Mahoney, *Fines in Sentencing* (New York: Vera Institute of Justice, 1983).
101. Ibid., p. 2.
102. Ibid., p. 4.
103. Ibid.
104. "Swiss Speeder Fined a Record $290,000," *USA Today*, January 7, 2010, http://content.usatoday.com/communities/ondeadline/post/2010/01/swiss-speeder-fined-a-record-290000/1 (accessed July 5, 2010).
105. James S. Tyree and Tony Thornton, "Judge Sentences Underwood to Die," *Oklahoman*, April 3, 2008, http://newsok.com/article/3224954/1207252268 (accessed May 28, 2009).
106. Death Penalty Information Center, "State-by-State Death Penalty Information," http://www.deathpenaltyinfo.org/FactSheet.pdf (accessed July 12, 2009).
107. Death Penalty Information Center, "Executions by Year," http://www.deathpenaltyinfo.org/executions-year (accessed May 20, 2013).
108. Statistics in this paragraph from "State-by-State Death Penalty Information."
109. Death Penalty Information Center, "States with and without the Death Penalty," http://www.deathpenaltyinfo.org/states-and-without-death-penalty (accessed April 2, 2013).
110. Tracy L. Snell, *Capital Punishment, 2010* (Washington, DC: Bureau of Justice Statistics, 2012).
111. Amnesty International, "Kuwait: Deplorable Resumption of Executions," http://www.amnesty.org/en/news/kuwait-deplorable-resumption-executions-2013-04-02 (accessed April 3, 2013).
112. Drishya Nair, "Saudi Arabia Beheads Man Convicted of Murder, Deports Thousands of Yemeni Labourers," *International Business Times*, April 2, 2013, http://www.ibtimes.co.uk/articles/452511/20130402/saudi-arabia-beheading-execution-yemeni-labourers-deportation.htm (accessed April 3, 2013); and "Saudi Arabia: Seven Men Executed in Act of Sheer Brutality,"

Amnesty International, March 13, 2013, http://www.amnesty.org/en/news/saudi-arabia-seven-men-executed-act-sheer-brutality-2013-03-13 (accessed April 4, 2013).

113. Justin McCurry, "Japan Executions Resume with Three Hangings," *The Guardian*, http://www.guardian.co.uk/world/2013/feb/21/japan-executions-resume-three-hangings (accessed April 4, 2013).
114. AlJazeera, "Report Shows Surge in Worldwide Executions," March 27, 2012, http://www.aljazeera.com/news/middleeast/2012/03/201232733426626915.html (accessed May 18, 2013).
115. Richard Willing, "Expansion of Death Penalty to Nonmurders Faces Challenges," *USA Today*, May 14, 1997.
116. *Kennedy* v. *Louisiana*, 554 U.S. 407(2008).
117. Death Penalty Information Center, "Death Row Inmates by State," http://www.deathpenaltyinfo.org/death-row-inmates-state-and-size-death-row-year (accessed April 20, 2013).
118. Tracy L. Snell, *Capital Punishment, 2010—Statistical Tables* (Washington, DC: Bureau of Justice Statistics, December 2011).
119. Ibid., Table 11.
120. Details for this story come from Jenifer Warren and Maura Dolan, "Tookie Williams Is Executed," *Los Angeles Times*, December 13, 2005, http://www.latimes.com/news/local/la-me-execution13dec13,0,799154.story?coll=la-home-headlines (accessed May 20, 2006).
121. "Warden: Williams Frustrated at End," CNN.com, December 13, 2005, http://www.cnn.com/2005/LAW/12/13/williams.execution (accessed July 2, 2006).
122. "Chief Justice Calls for Limits on Death Row Habeas Appeals," *Criminal Justice Newsletter*, February 15, 1989, pp. 6–7.
123. *McCleskey* v. *Zant*, 499 U.S. 467, 493–494 (1991).
124. *Coleman* v. *Thompson*, 501 U.S. 722 (1991).
125. *Schlup* v. *Delo*, 115 S.Ct. 851, 130 L.Ed.2d 808 (1995).
126. Pub. L. 103-322.
127. *Felker* v. *Turpin*, 117 S.Ct. 30, 135 L.Ed.2d 1123 (1996).
128. *McQuiggin* v. *Perkins*, U.S. Supreme Court, No. 12-126 (decided May 28, 2013).
129. *Elledge* v. *Florida*, 525 U.S. 944 (1998).
130. Michelle Locke, "Victim Forgives," Associated Press wire service, May 19, 1996.
131. Ibid.
132. Arthur Koestler, *Reflections on Hanging* (New York: Macmillan, 1956), p. xii.
133. Death Penalty Information Center, "Innocence: List of Those Freed from Death Row," http://www.deathpenaltyinfo.org/innocence-list-those-freed-death-row (accessed July 1, 2013).
134. Edward Connors et al., *Convicted by Juries, Exonerated by Science: Case Studies in the Use of DNA Evidence to Establish Innocence after Trial* (Washington, DC: National Institute of Justice, 1996).
135. Barry Scheck and Peter Neufeld, "DNA and Innocence Scholarship," in Saundra D. Westervelt and John A. Humphrey, *Wrongly Convicted: Perspectives on Failed Justice* (New Brunswick, NJ: Rutgers University Press, 2001), pp. 248–249.
136. Ibid., p. 246.
137. *Maryland* v. *King*, U.S. Supreme Court, No. 12-207 (decided June 3, 2013).
138. James S. Liebman, Jeffrey Fagan, and Simon H. Rifkind, *A Broken System: Error Rates in Capital Cases, 1973–1995* (New York: Columbia University School of Law, 2000), http://justice.policy.net/jpreport/finrep.PDF (accessed March 3, 2008).
139. Jon B. Gould, Julia Carrano, Richard Leo, and Joseph Young, "Predicting Erroneous Convictions: A Social Science Approach to Miscarriages of Justice—Final Report to the National Institute of Justice, February 2013," https://www.ncjrs.gov/pdffiles1/nij/grants/241389.pdf.
140. See, for example, Jim Yardley, "Texas Retooling Criminal Justice in Wake of Furor on Death Penalty," *New York Times*, June 1, 2001.
141. Title IV of the Justice for All Act of 2004.
142. At the time the legislation was enacted, Congress estimated that 300,000 rape kits remained unanalyzed in police department evidence lockers across the country.
143. The act also provides funding for the DNA Sexual Assault Justice Act (Title III of the Justice for All Act of 2004) and the Rape Kits and DNA Evidence Backlog Elimination Act of 2000 (U.S. Code, Title 42, Section 14135), authorizing more than $500 million for programs to improve the capacity of crime labs to conduct DNA analysis, reduce non-DNA backlogs, train evidence examiners, support sexual assault forensic examiner programs, and promote the use of DNA to identify missing persons.
144. In those states that accept federal monies under the legislation.
145. See N.C. G.S. § 15A-1460-75.
146. North Carolina Innocence Inquiry Commission, "Case Statistics," http://www.innocencecommission-nc.gov/statistics.htm (accessed June 20, 2010).
147. The Innocence Project, "Other Projects around the World," http://www.innocenceproject.org/about/Other-Projects.php (accessed April 30, 2012).
148. Laura Bauer, "DNA Tests on Inmates Sometimes Proved They Were Guilty," *Kansas City Star*, April 7, 2009.
149. *District Attorney's Office* v. *Osborne*, 129 S.Ct. 2308 (2009).
150. Studies include S. Decker and C. Kohfeld, "A Deterrence Study of the Death Penalty in Illinois: 1933–1980," *Journal of Criminal Justice*, Vol. 12, No. 4 (1984), pp. 367–379; and S. Decker and C. Kohfeld, "An Empirical Analysis of the Effect of the Death Penalty in Missouri," *Journal of Crime and Justice*, Vol. 10, No. 1 (1987), pp. 23–46.
151. See, especially, W. C. Bailey, "Deterrence and the Death Penalty for Murders in Utah: A Time Series Analysis," *Journal of Contemporary Law*, Vol. 5, No. 1 (1978), pp. 1–20; and W. C. Bailey, "An Analysis of the Deterrent Effect of the Death Penalty for Murder in California," *Southern California Law Review*, Vol. 52, No. 3 (1979), pp. 743–764.
152. B. E. Forst, "The Deterrent Effect of Capital Punishment: A Cross-State Analysis of the 1960's," *Minnesota Law Review*, Vol. 61, No. 5 (1977), pp. 743–767.
153. Hashem Dezhbakhsh, Paul Rubin, and Joanna Mehlhop Shepherd, "Does Capital Punishment Have a Deterrent Effect? New Evidence from Post-Moratorium Panel Data," Emory University, January 2001, http://userwww.service.emory.edu/~cozden/Dezhbakhsh_01_01_paper.pdf (accessed November 13, 2001).
154. Ibid., abstract.
155. Ibid., p. 19.
156. Committee on Law and Justice, *Deterrence and the Death Penalty* (Washington, DC: National Academy of Sciences, 2012).
157. As some of the evidence presented before the Supreme Court in *Furman* v. *Georgia*, 408 U.S. 238 (1972), suggested.
158. *USA Today*, April 27, 1989.
159. Thomas J. Keil and Gennaro F. Vito, "Race and the Death Penalty in Kentucky Murder Trials: 1976–1991," *American Journal of Criminal Justice*, Vol. 20, No. 1 (1995), pp. 17–36.
160. McCleskey v. Kemp, 481 U.S. 279, 107 S.Ct. 1756, 95 L.Ed.2d 262 (1987).
161. Department of Justice, *The Federal Death Penalty System: Supplementary Data, Analysis and Revised Protocols for Capital Case Review* (Washington, DC: Department of Justice, 2001).

162. David Stout, "Attorney General Says Report Shows No Racial and Ethnic Bias in Federal Death Sentences," *New York Times*, June 7, 2001, http://college1.nytimes.com/guests/articles/2001/06/07/850513.xml (accessed May 20, 2007).
163. "Expanded Study Shows No Bias in Death Penalty, Ashcroft Says," *Criminal Justice Newsletter*, Vol. 31, No. 13 (June 18, 2001), p. 4.
164. Mary P. Gallagher, "Race Found to Have No Effect on Capital Sentencing in New Jersey," *New Jersey Law Journal* (August 21, 2001), p. 1.
165. "Nebraska Death Penalty System Given Mixed Review in a State Study," *Criminal Justice Newsletter*, Vol. 31, No. 16 (August 2001), pp. 4–5.
166. Details for this story come from Michael Graczyk, "Killer of Pregnant Ten-Year-Old Set to Die Tonight," Associated Press, February 10, 2004; and Texas Execution Information Center, "Edward Lagrone," http://www.txexecutions.org/reports/318.asp (accessed May 15, 2004).
167. Justice Potter Stewart, as quoted in *USA Today*, April 27, 1989, p. 12A.
168. Koestler, *Reflections on Hanging*, pp. 147–148; and Gennaro F. Vito and Deborah G. Wilson, "Back from the Dead: Tracking the Progress of Kentucky's Furman-Commuted Death Row Population," *Justice Quarterly*, Vol. 5, No. 1 (1988), pp. 101–111.
169. *Wilkerson* v. *Utah*, 99 U.S. 130 (1878).
170. *In re Kemmler*, 136 U.S. 436 (1890).
171. Ibid., p. 447.
172. *Louisiana ex rel. Francis* v. *Resweber*, 329 U.S. 459 (1947).
173. *Furman* v. *Georgia*, 408 U.S. 238 (1972).
174. A position first adopted in *Trop* v. *Dulles*, 356 U.S. 86 (1958).
175. *Gregg* v. *Georgia*, 428 U.S. 153 (1976).
176. *Ring* v. *Arizona*, 536 U.S. 584 (2002).
177. "Dozens of Death Sentences Overturned," Associated Press, June 24, 2002.
178. The ruling could also affect Florida, Alabama, Indiana, and Delaware, where juries recommend sentences in capital cases but judges have the final say.
179. *Poyner* v. *Murray*, 113 S.Ct. 1573, 123 L.Ed.2d 142 (1993).
180. *Campbell* v. *Wood*, 114 S.Ct. 1337, 127 L.Ed.2d 685 (1994).
181. *Director Gomez, et al.* v. *Fierro and Ruiz*, 117 S.Ct. 285 (1996).
182. The court issued its decision after reviewing two cases: *Dawson* v. *State* and *Moore* v. *State*.
183. "Georgia Court Finds Electrocution Unconstitutional," *Criminal Justice Newsletter*, Vol. 31, No. 18 (October 15, 2001), pp. 3–4.
184. Adam Liptak, "Judges Set Hurdles for Lethal Injection," *New York Times*, April 12, 2006.
185. "North Carolina, Using Medical Monitoring Device, Executes Killer," Associated Press, April 22, 2006.
186. *Baze* v. *Rees*, 553 U.S. 35 (2008).
187. Lydia Saad, "U.S. Death Penalty Support Stable at 63%," Gallup, January 11, 2013, http://www.gallup.com/poll/159770/death-penalty-support-stable.aspx (accessed January 15, 2013).
188. James D. Unnever and Francis T. Cullen, "Executing the Innocent and Support for Capital Punishment," *Criminology and Public Policy*, Vol. 4, No. 1 (2005), p. 3.
189. Death Penalty Information Center, *Crisis of Confidence: Americans' Doubts about the Death Penalty* (Washington, DC: DPIC, June 9, 2007).
190. "Illinois Commission Calls for Restrictions on Death Penalty," *Criminal Justice Newsletter*, Vol. 32, No. 7 (April 2002), pp. 1–3.
191. "Death Penalty Freeze to Remain in Illinois," *USA Today*, April 25, 2003.
192. Christopher Wills, "Illinois Gov. Pat Quinn Abolishes Death Penalty, Clears Death Row," *Washington Post*, March 9, 2011, http://www.washingtonpost.com/wp-dyn/content/article/2011/03/09/AR2011030900319.html (accessed August 1, 2013).

PART

4

CORRECTIONS

RIGHTS OF THE CONVICTED AND IMPRISONED

The convicted and imprisoned have these common law, constitutional, statutory, and humanitarian rights:

- A right against cruel or unusual punishment
- A right to protection from physical harm
- A right to sanitary and healthy conditions of confinement
- A limited right to legal assistance while imprisoned
- A limited right to religious freedom while imprisoned
- A limited right to freedom of speech while imprisoned
- A limited right to due process prior to denial of privileges

These individual rights must be effectively balanced against these public-order concerns:

- Punishment of the guilty
- Safe communities
- The reduction of recidivism
- Secure prisons
- Control over convicts
- The prevention of escape
- Rehabilitation
- Affordable prisons

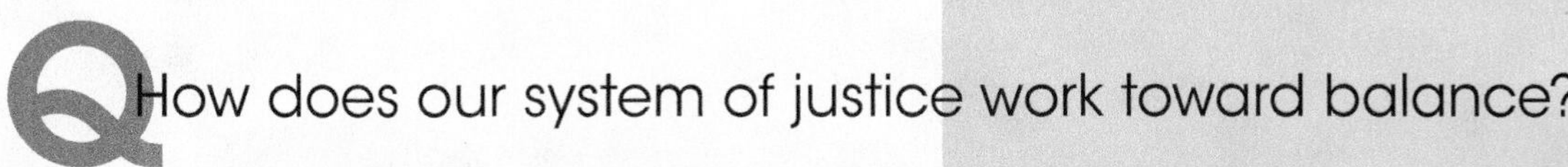

Q How does our system of justice work toward balance?

Punishment—Justice for the Unjust?

The great Christian writer C. S. Lewis (1898–1963) once remarked that if satisfying justice is to be the ultimate goal of Western criminal justice, then the fate of offenders cannot be dictated merely by practical considerations. "The concept of just desert is the only connecting link between punishment and justice," Lewis wrote. "It is only as deserved or undeserved that a sentence can be just or unjust," he concluded.

Once a person has been arrested, tried, and sentenced, the correctional process begins. Unlike Lewis's exhortation, however, the contemporary American correctional system—which includes probation, parole, jails, prisons, capital punishment, and a variety of innovative alternatives to traditional sentences—is tasked with far more than merely carrying out sentences. We also ask of our correctional system that it ensure the safety of law-abiding citizens, that it select the best alternative from among the many available for handling each offender, that it protect those under its charge, and that it guarantee fairness in the handling of all with whom it comes into contact.

This section of *Criminal Justice Today* details the development of probation, parole, community corrections, and imprisonment as corrections philosophies; describes the nuances of prison and jail life; discusses special issues in contemporary corrections (including AIDS, geriatric offenders, and female inmates); and summarizes the legal environment that both surrounds and infuses the modern-day practice of corrections. Characteristic of today's corrections emphasis is a society-wide push for harsher punishments. The culmination of that strategy, however, is significantly overcrowded correctional institutions, the problems of which are also described. As you read through this section, encountering descriptions of various kinds of criminal sanctions, you might ask yourself, "When would a punishment of this sort be deserved?" In doing so, remember to couple that thought with another question: "What are the ultimate consequences (for society and for the offender) of the kind of correctional program we are discussing here?" Unlike Lewis, you may also want to ask, "Can we afford it?"

Newscom

12 PROBATION, PAROLE, AND INTERMEDIATE SANCTIONS

OUTLINE

- Introduction
- What Is Probation?
- What Is Parole?
- Probation and Parole: The Pluses and Minuses
- The Legal Environment
- The Job of Probation and Parole Officers
- Intermediate Sanctions
- The Future of Probation and Parole

LEARNING OBJECTIVES

After reading this chapter, you should be able to

- Describe the history, purpose, and characteristics of probation.
- Describe the history, purpose, and characteristics of parole.
- Compare the advantages and disadvantages of probation and parole.
- Identify significant court cases affecting probation and parole.
- Compare and contrast the work of probation officers and parole officers.
- Describe various intermediate sanctions.
- Describe the likely future of probation and parole.

The responsibility for community treatment and supervision has been entrusted mainly to probation and parole services.

PRESIDENT'S COMMISSION ON LAW ENFORCEMENT AND ADMINISTRATION OF JUSTICE.[1]

■ **community corrections** The use of a variety of officially ordered program-based sanctions that permit convicted offenders to remain in the community under conditional supervision as an alternative to an active prison sentence.

■ **probation** A sentence of imprisonment that is suspended. Also, the conditional freedom granted by a judicial officer to a convicted offender, as long as the person meets certain conditions of behavior.

Introduction

In March 2013, Tom Clements, the chief of Colorado's corrections department, was gunned down and killed when he opened the door of his residence to a man whom he believed to be a pizza-deliverer. Clements was shot in the chest by Evan Ebel, a 28-year-old former inmate who had spent most of his eight-year prison sentence in administrative segregation for being a troublemaker. "Evil Ebel," as he was known to other inmates, had threatened to kill a female correctional officer, and was a member of a white supremacist prison gang. While in prison, Ebel was disciplined ten times for verbal abuse, twice for disobeying staff orders, four times for assault, and three times for fighting. Not long before being freed, Ebel had been described as a "very high risk" by correctional case managers, and was held in solitary confinement up until the day he was set free.[2] However, because Colorado uses a form of mandatory parole, which requires that an inmate be set free after his or her entire sentence has been served, authorities were unable to prevent Ebel's release on January 28, 2013, regardless of the danger he represented.[3]

Two years earlier, in a case that also involved parole-related issues, 75 Massachusetts police chiefs and several state senators gathered at police headquarters in the city of Woburn to demand that the state's parole board suspend all parole release hearings.[4] The demand came after police officer John B. Maguire was gunned down during an attempted robbery one day after Christmas in 2010 by 57-year-old Domenic Cinelli. Cinelli, a career criminal, had been sentenced to life in prison, but was released on parole less than two years before the shooting.

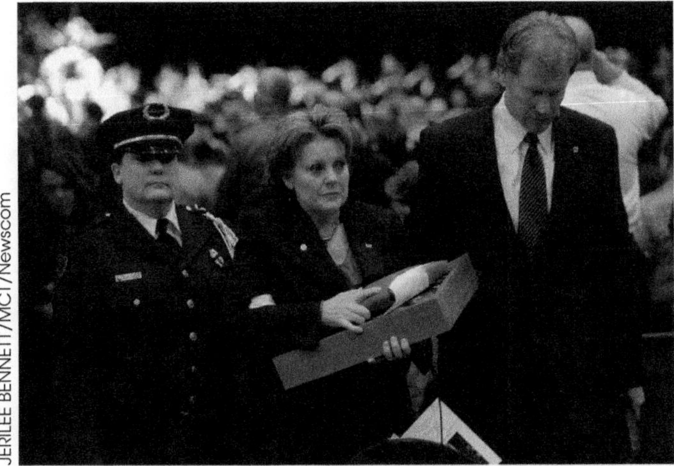

JERILEE BENNETT/MCT/Newscom

Lisa Clements, the wife of Tom Clements, the Colorado prison chief who was gunned down at his front door by parolee Evan Ebel in 2013, leaves a memorial service for her husband. What do cases like Ebel's say about the proper supervision of parolees?

Stories like these appear all too frequently in the media and cast a harsh light on the early release and poor supervision of criminal offenders. This chapter takes a close look at the realities behind the practice of what we call **community corrections**. Community corrections, also termed *community-based corrections*, is a sentencing style that depends less on traditional confinement options and more on correctional resources available in the community. Community corrections includes a wide variety of sentencing options, such as probation, parole, home confinement, the electronic monitoring of offenders, and other new and developing programs—all of which are covered in this chapter. Learn more about community corrections by visiting the International Community Corrections Association via **http://www.iccaweb.org**.

What Is Probation?

Probation, one aspect of community corrections, is "a sentence served while under supervision in the community."[5] Like other sentencing options, probation is a court-ordered sanction. Its goal is to retain some control over criminal offenders while using community programs to help rehabilitate them. Most of the alternative sanctions discussed later in this chapter are, in fact, predicated on probationary sentences in which the offender is ordered to abide by certain conditions—such as participation in a specified program—while remaining free in the community. Although the court in many jurisdictions can impose probation directly, most probationers are sentenced first to confinement but then immediately have their sentences suspended and are remanded into the custody of an officer of the court—the probation officer.

Probation has a long history. By the fourteenth century, English courts had established the practice of "binding over for good behavior,"[6] in which offenders could be entrusted into the custody of willing citizens. American John Augustus (1784–1859) is generally recognized as the world's first probation officer.

American John Augustus (1784–1859) is generally recognized as the world's first probation officer.

Augustus, a Boston shoemaker, attended sessions of criminal court in the 1850s and offered to take carefully selected offenders into his home as an alternative to imprisonment.[7] At first, he supervised only drunkards, but by 1857 Augustus was accepting many kinds of offenders and was devoting all his time to the service of the court.[8] Augustus died in 1859, having bailed out more than 2,000 convicts. In 1878, the Massachusetts legislature enacted a statute that authorized the city of Boston to hire a salaried probation officer. Missouri followed suit in 1897, along with Vermont (1898) and Rhode Island (1899).[9] Before the end of the nineteenth century, probation had become an accepted and widely used form of community-based supervision. By 1925, all 48 states had adopted probation legislation. In that same year, the federal government enacted legislation enabling federal district court judges to appoint paid probation officers and to impose probationary terms.[10]

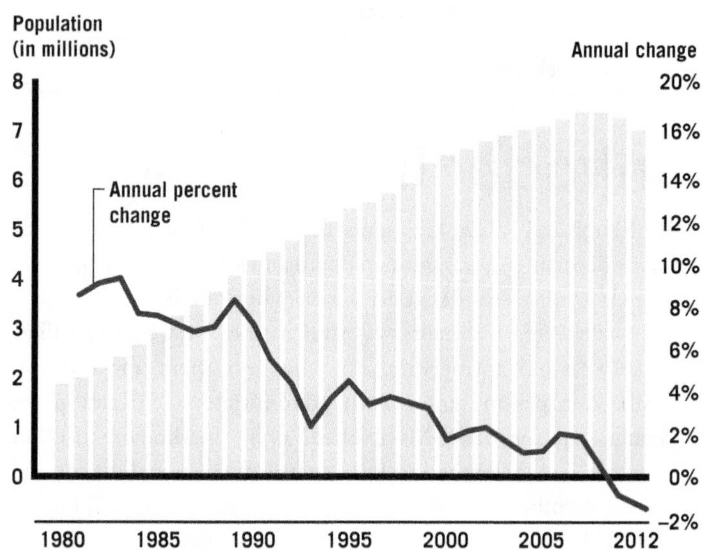

FIGURE 12-2 | **Estimated Number of Adults Under Some Form of Correctional Supervision and Annual Percent Change, 1980–2012**

Source: Lauren E. Glaze and Erika Parks, *Correctional Populations in the United States, 2011* (Washington, DC: Bureau of Justice Statistics, November 2012), p. 1.

The Extent of Probation

Today, probation is the most common form of criminal sentencing in the United States. Between 20% and 60% of those found guilty of crimes are sentenced to some form of probation. Figure 12-1 shows that 57% of all offenders under correctional supervision in the United States as of January 1, 2012, were on probation.[11] The rest were either in jail, in prison, or on parole, or under some other form of supervised or unsupervised release. Figure 12-2 shows that the number of offenders under any type of correctional supervision increased dramatically between 1980 and 2012, but that the annual rate of increase has been steadily falling during that period, and has finally turned negative. In terms of absolute numbers, persons supervised yearly on probation has increased from slightly more than 1 million in 1980 to around 5 million today—a 500% increase.[12]

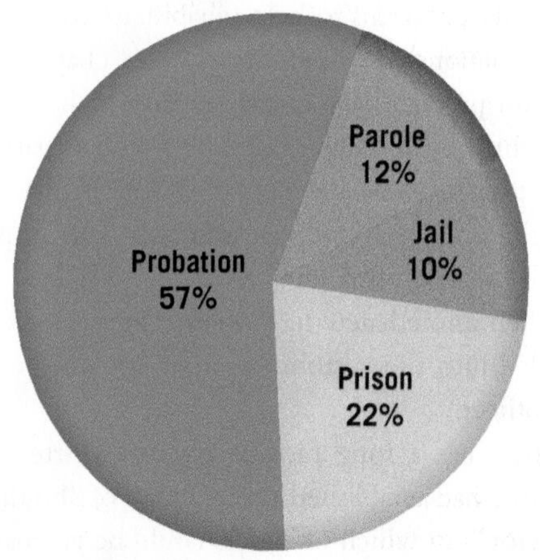

FIGURE 12-1 | **Offenders Under Correctional Supervision in the United States, by Type of Supervision**

Source: Bureau of Justice Statistics, Correctional Surveys.

Even violent offenders stand about a one in five chance of receiving a probationary term. A Bureau of Justice Statistics study of felony sentences found that 5% of people convicted of homicide were placed on probation, as were 21% of convicted sex offenders.[13] Twelve percent of convicted robbers and 30% of those committing aggravated assault were similarly sentenced to probation rather than active prison time. In one example, 47-year-old Carrie Mote of Vernon, Connecticut, was sentenced to probation for shooting her fiancé in the chest with a .38-caliber handgun after he called off their wedding.[14] Mote, who faced a maximum of 20 years in prison, claimed to be suffering from diminished psychological capacity at the time of the shooting because of the emotional stress brought on by the canceled wedding.

At the beginning of 2012, a total of 4,814,200 adults were on probation throughout the nation.[15] Individual states, however, make greater or lesser use of probation. North Dakota authorities, with the smallest probationary population, supervise only 4,339 people, while Texas reports 418,479 offenders

probation revocation A court order taking away a convicted offender's probationary status and usually withdrawing the conditional freedom associated with that status in response to a violation of the conditions of probation.

Follow the author's tweets about the latest crime and justice news @schmalleger.

on probation. Sixty-six percent of the almost 2.3 million adults discharged from probation in 2011 had successfully met the conditions of their supervision. Approximately 16% of those discharged from supervision, however, were incarcerated because of a rule violation or because they committed a new offense. Another 2% absconded, and 9% had their probation sentence revoked without being ordered to serve time.[16]

Probation Conditions

Those sentenced to probation must agree to abide by court-mandated conditions of probation. A violation of conditions can lead to **probation revocation**. Conditions are of two types: general and specific. General conditions apply to all probationers in a given jurisdiction and usually require that the probationer obey all laws, maintain employment, remain within the jurisdiction of the court, possess no firearms, allow the probation officer to visit at home or at work, and so forth. As a general condition of probation, many probationers are also required to pay a fine to the court, usually in a series of installments. The fine is designed to reimburse victims for damages and to pay lawyers' fees and other court costs.

A violation of conditions can lead to probation revocation.

Special conditions may be mandated by a judge who feels that the probationer is in need of particular guidance or control. Depending on the nature of the offense, a judge may require that the offender surrender his or her driver's license; submit at reasonable times to warrantless and unannounced searches by a probation officer; supply breath, urine, or blood samples as needed for drug or alcohol testing; complete a specified number of hours of community service; or pass the general equivalency diploma (GED) test within a specified time. The judge may also dictate special conditions tailored to the probationer's situation. Such individualized conditions may prohibit the offender from associating with named others (a codefendant, for example), they may require that the probationer be at home after dark, or they may demand that the offender complete a particular treatment program within a set time.

Federal Probation

The federal probation system is more than 80 years old.[17] In 1916, in the *Killets* case,[18] the U.S. Supreme Court ruled that federal judges did not have the authority to suspend sentences and to order probation. After a vigorous campaign by the National Probation Association, Congress passed the National Probation Act in 1925, authorizing the use of probation in federal courts. The bill came just in time to save a burgeoning federal prison

freedom OR safety? YOU decide

Special Conditions of Probation

In 2008, Texas judge Charlie Baird sentenced 22-year-old Felicia Salazar to a probationary term of ten years for injury to a child. Salazar's offense was actually one of omission, because she had failed to protect her 19-month-old child from a brutal beating by the child's father. The judge found especially problematic the fact that Salazar had failed to seek medical care for the child after the beating, even though the child had suffered a number of broken bones. In a surprising move, Judge Baird added an unusual condition to the other, more ordinary probation conditions that he imposed on Salazar: She was ordered not to conceive and bear a child during the probationary period. Following Judge Baird's probation order, some people questioned whether the special condition he imposed on Salazar unconstitutionally infringed on her fundamental right to procreate.

A similar story comes from Wisconsin, where Circuit Court Judge Tim Boyle ordered 44-year-old Corey Curtis to stop procreating until he can support his nine children whom he had fathered with six different women. The judge imposed the requirement on Curtis in 2012 as a condition of a three-year probationary term, citing the fact that he owed more than $90,000 in back child support.

Critics of both the *Salazar* and *Curtis* cases point to the 1942 case of *Skinner* v. *Oklahoma*, which overturned Oklahoma's Habitual Criminal Sterilization Act and established procreation as a fundamental constitutional right.

You Decide

Did Judge Baird go too far in requiring that Salazar not become pregnant while on probation? What other special conditions of probation might he have imposed on Salazar that might have been more acceptable to critics?

References: *Skinner* v. *Oklahoma*, 316 U.S. 535 (1942); Sherry F. Colb, "A Judge Orders a Woman Not to Have Children while on Probation: Did He Violate Her Rights?" FindLaw, November 26, 2008, http://writ.lp.findlaw.com/colb/20081126.html?=features (accessed May 25, 2013); and "Wisconsin Judge Orders Deadbeat Dad of Nine (with Six Women) to Stop Procreating," The Smoking Gun, http://www.thesmokinggun.com/buster/wisconsin/judicial-procreation-ban-647901 (accessed June 2, 2013).

■ **parole** The status of a convicted offender who has been conditionally released from prison by a paroling authority before the expiration of his or her sentence, is placed under the supervision of a parole agency, and is required to observe the conditions of parole.

■ **reentry** The managed return to the community of an individual released from prison. Also, the successful transitioning of a released inmate back into the community.

■ **parole board** A state paroling authority. Most states have parole boards that decide when an incarcerated offender is ready for conditional release. Some boards also function as revocation hearing panels.

■ **discretionary release** The release of an inmate from prison to supervision that is decided by a parole board or other authority.

system from serious overcrowding. The prostitution-fighting Mann Act, Prohibition legislation, and the growth of organized crime all led to increased arrests and a dramatic growth in the number of federal probationers in the early years of the system.

Although the 1925 act authorized one probation officer per federal judge, it allocated only a total of $25,000 for officers' salaries. As a consequence, only eight officers were hired to serve 132 judges, and the system came to rely heavily on voluntary probation officers. Some sources indicate that as many as 40,000 probationers were under the supervision of volunteers at the peak of the system.[19] By 1930, however, Congress provided adequate funding, and a corps of salaried professionals began to provide probation services to the U.S. courts. Today, approximately 7,750 federal probation officers (also known as *community corrections officers*), whose services are administered through the Administrative Office of the U.S. Courts, serve the 94 federal judicial districts in more than 500 locations across the country.[20] At any given time, they supervise approximately 151,000 offenders—a number that has increased annually throughout the past decade.

Federal probation and pretrial services officers are federal law enforcement officers. They have statutory authority to arrest or detain individuals suspected or convicted of federal offenses, as well as the authority to arrest probationers for a violation of the conditions of probation. Under existing policy, however, they are encouraged to obtain an arrest warrant from a court, and the warrant is to be executed by the U.S. Marshals Service. Most federal probation officers may carry a firearm for defensive purposes while on duty. Before doing so, however, they must complete rigorous training and certification requirements, provide objective justification for doing so, and be approved to do so on an individual basis. Some federal districts do not allow any probation officers to carry firearms in the performance of their official duties; these include the Eastern and Western districts of Wisconsin, Eastern Virginia, Eastern Virgin Islands, Middle Tennessee, Massachusetts, Connecticut, and Central California.[21]

Federal officials are close to completing the technical infrastructure needed to implement a results-based management and decision-making framework for the federal probation and pretrial services system. The Probation and Pretrial Services Automated Case Tracking System (PACTS) collects records from the electronic files of thousands of probation officers in all 94 federal districts and stores those records in a single data warehouse called the National PACTS Reporting (NPR) System.[22] The data are then fed into the federal Decision Support System (DSS), which combines data from NPR with data from other judiciary systems, the United States Sentencing Commission, the Federal Bureau of Investigation (FBI), the Federal Bureau of Prisons, and the Bureau of the Census. Because of how it works, DSS provides a valuable evidence-based initiative at the federal level, and federal probation officials have recently started using it to test underlying assumptions about the relationship between probation supervision practices and supervision outcomes.

What Is Parole?

Parole is the supervised early release of inmates from correctional confinement. It is a prisoner **reentry** strategy that differs from probation in both purpose and implementation. Whereas probationers generally avoid serving time in prison, parolees have already been incarcerated. Although probation is a sentencing option available to a judge who determines the form probation will take, parole results from an administrative decision by a legally designated paroling authority. Probation is a sentencing strategy, but parole is a corrections strategy whose primary purpose is to return offenders gradually to productive lives. By making early release possible, parole can also act as a stimulus for positive behavioral change.

Parole was a much-heralded tool of nineteenth-century corrections. Its advocates had been looking for a behavioral incentive to motivate youthful offenders to reform. Parole, through its promise of earned early release, seemed the ideal innovation. The use of parole in this country began with New York's Elmira Reformatory in 1876. Indeterminate sentences were then a key part of the rehabilitation philosophy, and they remain so today.

States differ as to the type of parole decision-making mechanism they use, as well as the level at which it operates. Two major models prevail: (1) **Parole boards** grant parole based on their judgment and assessment. The parole board's decisions are termed *discretionary parole*. (2) Statutory decrees produce *mandatory parole*, with release dates usually set near the completion of the inmate's prison sentence, minus time off for good behavior and other special considerations. Fifteen states have entirely abolished **discretionary release** from prison by a parole board

■ **medical parole** An early-release option under which an inmate who is deemed "low risk" due to a serious physical or mental health condition is released from prison earlier than he or she might have been under normal circumstances.

■ **mandatory release** The release of an inmate from prison that is determined by statute or sentencing guidelines and is not decided by a parole board or other authority.

■ **parole (probation) violation** An act or a failure to act by a parolee (or a probationer) that does not conform to the conditions of his or her parole (or probation).

■ **conditions of parole (probation)** The general and special limits imposed on an offender who is released on parole (or probation). General conditions tend to be fixed by state statute, whereas special conditions are mandated by the sentencing authority (court or board) and take into consideration the background of the offender and the circumstances of the offense.

for all offenders. Another five states have abolished discretionary parole for certain violent offenses or other crimes against a person. As a result of the movement away from release by parole boards, statutory release, usually involving a brief mandatory period of post-release supervision, has become the most common method of release from prison.[23]

One form of discretionary parole that *is* on the increase, it should be noted, is medical parole. **Medical parole** is an early release option available in some states under which an inmate who is deemed "low risk" due to a serious physical or mental health condition is released from prison earlier than he or she might have been under normal circumstances.[24]

States that do not utilize discretionary parole can still have substantial reentry populations, and everyone who is released from prison faces the challenges of reentering society. California, for example, one of the states that no longer uses parole boards for most release decisions, has traditionally had one of the largest reentry population in the country.[25] Although it does not have a parole board, California has a Board of Parole Hearings (BPH), which determines when the state's most serious offenders are ready for release from prison. California's 2011 Criminal Justice Realignment Act,[26] however, shifted the supervision of most parolees under what the state calls the Post-Release Community Supervision program, from state parole officers to county probation officers. The BPH continues to hold parole hearings for persons sentenced to life in prison, persons applying for medical parole, mentally disordered offenders, and sexually violent predators held at the state level.[27] Other inmates, sentenced after the realignment legislation went into effect, must be released without any restrictions or supervision, meaning that California has effectively eliminated parole supervision for all but its most serious offenders.

The Extent of Parole

Parolees make up one of the smallest of the correctional categories shown in Figure 12-1. The growing reluctance to use parole today seems to be due to the realization that correctional routines have generally been ineffective at producing any substantial reformation among many offenders before their release back into the community. The abandonment of the rehabilitation goal, combined with a return to determinate sentencing in many jurisdictions—including the federal judicial system—has substantially reduced the amount of time the average corrections client spends on supervised parole.

Although discretionary parole releases are far less common than they used to be, about 25% of inmates who are freed from prison are still paroled by a paroling authority, such as a parole board.[28] States operating under determinate sentencing guidelines, however, often require that inmates serve a short period of time, such as 90 days, on what some jurisdictions term *reentry parole*—a form of supervised **mandatory release**. Mandatory parole releases have increased 91% since 1990,[29] even though they typically involve either a very small amount of time on parole or no time at all. As a result, determinate sentencing schemes have changed the face of parole in America, resulting in a dramatic reduction in the average time spent under postprison supervision. They have, however, had little or no impact on the actual number of offenders released from prison.

At the beginning of 2012, approximately 853,900 people were under parole supervision throughout the United States.[30] As with probation, states vary considerably in the use they make of parole, influenced as they are by the legislative requirements of sentencing schemes. For example, on January 1, 2012, Maine, a state that is phasing out parole, reported only 32 people under parole supervision (the lowest of all the states), and North Dakota had only 428. California (the highest of all) had a parole population in excess of 105,134, and Texas officials were busy supervising almost 104,763 parolees.

Nationwide, approximately 52% of parolees successfully complete parole, whereas about 13% are returned to prison for **parole violations**, and another 5% go back to prison for new offenses during their parole period. (Others may be transferred to new jurisdictions, may abscond and not be caught, or may die—bringing the total to 100%.)[31] An interesting parole decision-making tool is available on the Web at: **http://www.insideprison.com/parole_decision_making.asp#.UWr9O6t4bYg.**

Parole Conditions

In those jurisdictions that retain discretionary parole, the **conditions of parole** remain very similar to the conditions agreed to by probationers. General conditions of parole usually include agreement not to leave the state as well as to obey extradition requests from other jurisdictions. Parolees must also periodically report to parole officers, and parole officers may visit parolees at their homes and places of business, often arriving unannounced.

parole revocation The administrative action of a paroling authority removing a person from parole status in response to a violation of lawfully required conditions of parole, including the prohibition against committing a new offense. Parole revocation usually results in the offender's return to prison.

restitution A court requirement that an accused or convicted offender pay money or provide services to the victim of the crime or provide services to the community.

CJ | ISSUES
Culturally Skilled Probation Officers

A recent article by Robert Shearer and Patricia King in the journal *Federal Probation* describes the characteristics of "good therapeutic relationships" in probation work and says that "one of the major impediments to building an effective relationship may be found in cross-cultural barriers."

According to Shearer and King, probation officers who work with immigrants or with those whose cultures differ substantially from that of mainstream America must realize that a client's culture has to be taken into consideration. Doing so can make officers far more effective as both counselors and supervisors.

That's because differences in culture can lead to difficulties in developing the rapport that is necessary to build a helping relationship between an offender and a probation officer. Consequently, effective probation officers work to understand the values, norms, lifestyles, roles, and methods of communicating that characterize their clients.

Culturally skilled probation officers, say the authors, are aware of and sensitive to their own cultural heritage, and they value and respect differences as long as they do not lead to continued law violation. Culturally skilled officers are also aware of their own preconceived notions, biases, prejudicial attitudes, feelings, and beliefs. They avoid stereotyping and labeling. Skilled officers are comfortable with the cultural differences that exist between themselves and their clients, and they willingly refer clients to someone who may be better qualified to help.

Developing multicultural awareness is the first step to becoming culturally skilled, say Shearer and King. Developing awareness is an ongoing process that culminates in cultural empathy—the ability to understand a client's worldview.

According to the authors, developing cultural empathy involves six steps:

- The counselor must understand and accept the context of family and community for clients from different cultural backgrounds. This is especially important when working with Hispanic clients, who highly value relationships within the extended family.
- Counselors should incorporate indigenous healing practices from the client's culture whenever they can. For example, this might be possible when working with Native Americans.
- Counselors must become knowledgeable about the historical and sociopolitical background of clients, especially when clients have fled from repressive regimes in their home countries and might still fear authority figures.
- They must become knowledgeable of the psychosocial adjustment that must be made by clients who have moved from one environment to another. This includes the sense of loneliness and separation that some immigrants feel on arrival in their adopted country.
- They must be sensitive to the oppression, discrimination, and racism previously encountered by many clients, such as the Kurdish people who suffered discrimination and experienced genocide under Saddam Hussein.
- Counselors must facilitate empowerment for those clients who feel underprivileged and devalued (for example, immigrants who may feel forced to accept menial jobs even though they worked in prestigious occupations in their native countries).

Shearer and King conclude that developing cultural awareness provides the probation officer with an effective approach that actively draws the probationer into the therapeutic relationship and that increases the likelihood of a successful outcome.

Reference: Robert A. Shearer and Patricia Ann King, "Multicultural Competencies in Probation: Issues and Challenges," *Federal Probation*, Vol. 68, No. 1 (June 2004).

The successful and continued employment of parolees is one of the major concerns of parole boards and their officers, and studies have found that successful employment is a major factor in reducing the likelihood of repeat offenses.[32] Hence, the importance of continued employment is typically stressed on parole agreement forms, with the condition that failure to find employment within 30 days may result in **parole revocation**. As with probationers, parolees who are working can be ordered to pay fines and penalties. A provision for making **restitution** payments is also frequently included as a condition of parole.

As with probation, special parole conditions may be added by the judge and might require the parolee to pay a "parole supervisory fee" (often around $15 to $20 per month). This relatively new innovation shifts some of the expense of community corrections to the offender.

Federal Parole

Federal parole decisions are made by the U.S. Parole Commission (USPC).

Federal parole decisions are made by the U.S. Parole Commission (USPC), located in Chevy Chase, Maryland. The Commission uses hearing examiners to visit federal prisons. Examiners typically ask inmates to describe why, in their opinion, they are ready for parole. The inmate's job readiness, home plans, past record, accomplishments while in prison, good behavior, and previous experiences on probation or parole form the basis for the examiners' report to the parole commission. The 1984 Comprehensive Crime Control Act, which mandated federal fixed sentencing and abolished parole for offenses committed after November 1, 1978, began a planned phaseout of the U.S. Parole Commission. Under the act, the commission was to be abolished by 1992. Various federal legislation has since extended the life of the commission, and it continues to have jurisdiction over all federal offenders who committed their crimes before November 1, 1987, state probationers and parolees in the Federal Witness Protection Program, persons sentenced under the criminal code of the District of Columbia, and U.S. citizens convicted in foreign countries who have elected to serve their sentences in this country. The federal budget for fiscal year 2013 included a total of $12.8 million, for 85 positions, including 7 attorneys, at the USPC.[33] Visit the commission's website via **http://www.justice.gov/uspc**.

Probation and Parole: The Pluses and Minuses

Probation is used to meet the needs of offenders who require some correctional supervision short of imprisonment while providing a reasonable degree of security to the community. Parole, which is essentially a reentry program, fulfills a similar purpose for offenders released from prison.

Advantages of Probation and Parole

Both probation and parole provide a number of advantages over imprisonment.

Both probation and parole provide a number of advantages over imprisonment, including these:

- *Lower cost.* Imprisonment is expensive. Incarcerating a single offender in Georgia, for example, costs approximately $39,501 per year, whereas the cost of intensive probation is as little as $1,321 per probationer.[34] The expense of imprisonment in some other states may be more than three times as high as it is in Georgia.
- *Increased employment.* Few people in prison have the opportunity for productive employment. Work-release programs, correctional industries, and inmate labor programs operate in most states, but they usually provide only low-paying jobs and require few skills. At best, such programs include only a small portion of the inmates in any given facility. Probation and parole, on the other hand, make it possible for offenders under correctional supervision to work full-time at jobs in the "free" economy. Offenders can contribute to their own and their families' support, stimulate the local economy by spending their wages, and support the government through the taxes they pay.
- *Restitution.* Offenders who are able to work are candidates for court-ordered restitution. Society's interest in restitution may be better served by a probationary sentence or parole than by imprisonment. Restitution payments to victims may help restore their standard of living and personal confidence while teaching the offender responsibility.
- *Community support.* The decision to release a prisoner on parole or to sentence a convicted offender to probation is often partially based on considerations of family and other social ties. Such decisions are made in the belief that offenders will be more subject to control in the community if they participate in a web of positive social relationships. An advantage of both probation and parole is that they allow the offender to continue personal and social relationships. Probation avoids splitting up families, and parole may reunite family members separated from each other by a prison sentence.
- *Reduced risk of criminal socialization.* Criminal values permeate prisons; prison has been called a "school in crime." Probation insulates adjudicated offenders, at least to some degree, from these kinds of values. Parole, by virtue of the fact that it follows time served in prison, is less successful than probation in reducing the risk of criminal socialization.
- *Increased use of community services.* Probationers and parolees can take advantage of services offered through the community, including psychological therapy, substance-abuse counseling, financial services, support groups, church outreach programs, and social services. Although a few similar opportunities may be available in prison, the community environment itself can enhance the effectiveness of treatment programs by reducing the stigmatization of the offender and by allowing the offender to participate in a more "normal" environment.
- *Increased opportunity for rehabilitation.* Probation and parole can both be useful behavioral management tools. They reward cooperative offenders with freedom and allow for the opportunity to shape the behavior of offenders who may be difficult to reach through other programs.

revocation hearing A hearing held before a legally constituted hearing body (such as a parole board) to determine whether a parolee or probationer has violated the conditions and requirements of his or her parole or probation.

Disadvantages of Probation and Parole

Any honest appraisal of probation and parole must recognize that they share a number of strategic drawbacks, including these:

- *Relative lack of punishment.* The just deserts model of criminal sentencing insists that punishment should be a central theme of the justice process. Although rehabilitation and treatment are recognized as worthwhile goals, the model suggests that punishment serves both society's need for protection and the victim's need for revenge. Many view probation, however, as practically no punishment at all, and it is coming under increasing criticism as a sentencing strategy. Parole is likewise accused of unhinging the scales of justice because (1) it releases some offenders early, even when they have been convicted of serious crimes, while some relatively minor offenders remain in prison, and (2) it is dishonest because it does not require completion of the offender's entire sentence behind bars.
- *Increased risk to the community.* Probation and parole are strategies designed to deal with convicted criminal offenders. The release into the community of such offenders increases the risk that they will commit additional offenses. Community supervision can never be so complete as to eliminate such a possibility, and evaluations of parole have pointed out that an accurate assessment of offender dangerousness is beyond our present capability.[35]
- *Increased social costs.* Some offenders placed on probation and parole will effectively and responsibly discharge their obligations. Others, however, will become social liabilities. In addition to the increased risk of new crimes, probation and parole increase the chance that added expenses will accrue to the community in the form of child support, welfare costs, housing expenses, legal aid, indigent health care, and the like.
- *Discriminatory and unequal effects.* Some experts argue that reentry programs are unfair to women because female inmates undergoing the reentry experience find themselves qualitatively disadvantaged in their search for jobs and shelter, in reobtaining custody of their children, in successfully finding programs to help them abstain from drugs, and so on.[36] Some say, for example, that a man leaving prison "has better opportunities for securing a sufficient income-producing and legal job by virtue of his gender alone."[37]

The Legal Environment

Eleven especially significant U.S. Supreme Court decisions provide the legal framework for probation and parole supervision. Among those cases, that of *Griffin* v. *Wisconsin* (1987)[38] may be the most significant. In *Griffin*, the Supreme Court ruled that probation officers may conduct searches of a probationer's residence without either a search warrant or probable cause. According to the Court, "A probationer's home, like anyone else's, is protected by the Fourth Amendment's requirement that searches be 'reasonable.'" However, "[a] State's operation of a probation system . . . presents 'special needs' beyond normal law enforcement that may justify departures from the usual warrant and probable cause requirements." Probation, the Court concluded, is similar to imprisonment because it is a "form of criminal sanction imposed upon an offender after a determination of guilt." Similarly, in the 1998 case of *Pennsylvania Board of Probation and Parole* v. *Scott*,[39] the Court declined to extend the exclusionary rule to apply to searches by parole officers, even where such searches yield evidence of parole violations. See Table 12-1 for an overview of these and other significant cases in the field of probation and parole.

Other court cases focus on the conduct of parole or probation **revocation hearings**. Revocation is a common procedure. Annually, about 21% of adults on parole as well as 20% of those on probation throughout the United States have their **conditional release** revoked.[40] The supervising officer may request that probation or parole be revoked if a client has violated the conditions of community release or has committed a new crime. The most frequent violations for which revocation occurs are (1) failure to report as required to a probation or parole officer, (2) failure to participate in a stipulated treatment

Annually, about 21% of adults on parole as well as 20% of those on probation throughout the United States have their conditional release revoked.

conditional release The release of an inmate from prison to community supervision under a set of conditions for remaining on parole. If a condition is violated, the individual might be returned to prison or might face another sanction in the community.[i]

TABLE 12-1 | **U.S. Supreme Court Decisions of Special Significance for Probation and Parole**

IN THIS CASE	THE COURT HELD THAT
Samson v. *California* (2006)	Police officers may conduct a warrantless search of a person who is subject to a parole search condition, even when there is no suspicion of criminal wrongdoing and even when the sole reason for the search is that the person is on parole.
U.S. v. *Knights* (2001)	The warrantless search authority normally reserved for probation and parole officers extends to police officers when supported by reasonable suspicion and authorized by the conditions of probation.
Pennsylvania Board of Probation and Parole v. *Scott* (1998)	The exclusionary rule does not apply to searches by parole officers, even where such searches yield evidence of parole violations.
Griffin v. *Wisconsin* (1987)	Probation officers may conduct searches of a probationer's residence without the need for a search warrant or probable cause.
Minnesota v. *Murphy* (1984)	A probationer's incriminating statements to a probation officer may be used as evidence against him or her if the probationer does not specifically claim a right against self-incrimination.
Bearden v. *Georgia* (1983)	Probation cannot be revoked for failure to pay a fine and make restitution if it can't be shown that the defendant was responsible for the failure. Moreover, if a defendant lacks the capacity to pay a fine or make restitution, then the hearing authority must consider any viable alternatives to incarceration before imposing a prison sentence.
Greenholtz v. *Nebraska Penal Inmates* (1979)	Parole boards do not have to specify the evidence or reasoning used in deciding to deny parole.
Gagnon v. *Scarpelli* (1973)	The safeguards identified in *Morrissey* v. *Brewer* were extended to probationers.
Morrissey v. *Brewer* (1972)	Procedural safeguards are necessary in revocation hearings involving parolees. They include (a) written notice of the claimed violations of parole; (b) disclosure to the parolee of evidence against him or her; (c) opportunity to be heard in person and to present witnesses and documentary evidence; (d) the right to confront and cross-examine adverse witnesses (unless the hearing officer specifically finds good cause for not allowing confrontation); (e) a "neutral and detached" hearing body such as a traditional parole board, members of which need not be judicial officers or lawyers; and (f) a written statement.
Mempa v. *Rhay* (1967)	Both notice and a hearing are required before probation revocation, and the probationer should have the opportunity for representation by counsel before a deferred prison sentence is imposed.
Escoe v. *Zerbst* (1935)	Probation "comes as an act of grace to one convicted of a crime" and the revocation of probation without hearing or notice to the probationer is permissible. This decision has since been greatly modified by other decisions in this table.

program, and (3) alcohol or drug abuse while under supervision.[41] Revocation hearings may result in an order that a probationer's suspended sentence be made "active" or that a parolee return to prison to complete his or her sentence in confinement.

In 2010 a new law went into effect in California authorizing the placement of parolees into non-revocable parole (NRP).[42] Widely regarded as a correctional innovation, NRP is an effort to safely reduce state prison populations. NRP prohibits the California Department of Corrections and Rehabilitation (CDCR) from returning certain parolees to prison, placing a parole hold on those parolees, or reporting those parolees to the Board of Parole Hearings for a violation of parole. Sex offenders, validated gang members, serious felons, and prisoners found guilty of serious disciplinary offenses are not eligible for NRP. Furthermore, only persons evaluated by the CDCR using a risk assessment tool and not determined to pose a high risk of reoffending can be assigned to NRP. The parole period under NRP generally lasts for one year, during which time parolees are not required to report to a parole officer. They are, however, subject to being searched by any law enforcement officer at any time.

Another important legal issue today surrounds the potential liability of probation officers and parole boards for the criminal actions of offenders they supervise or whom they have released. Some courts have held that officers are generally immune from suit because they are performing a judicial function on behalf of the state.[43] Other courts, however, have indicated that parole board members who do not carefully consider mandated criteria for judging parole eligibility could be liable for injurious actions committed by parolees.[44] In general, however, most experts agree that parole board members cannot be successfully sued unless release decisions are made in a grossly negligent or wantonly reckless manner.[45] Discretionary decisions of individual probation and parole officers that result in harm to members of the public, however, may be more actionable under civil law, especially where their decisions were not reviewed by judicial authority.[46]

Roth Stock/Alamy

Hotel heiress Paris Hilton arriving at Pure Nightclub in Las Vegas for her sister Nicky's 25th birthday party on October 4, 2008. One year earlier, Paris pleaded "no contest" to an alcohol-related reckless driving offense in Los Angeles and was sentenced to three years' probation. She was also fined $1,500 plus court costs and ordered to participate in an alcohol education program. In 2010, she was arrested for possession of a controlled substance after cocaine was found in her purse by Las Vegas police during a vehicle stop. Apparently probation wasn't enough to deter Paris. Why not?

The Job of Probation and Parole Officers

The tasks performed by probation and parole officers are often quite similar. Some jurisdictions combine the roles of both into one job. This section describes the duties of probation and parole officers, whether separate or performed by the same individuals. Probation/parole work consists primarily of four functions: (1) presentence investigations, (2) other intake procedures, (3) diagnosis and needs assessment, and (4) client supervision.

Supervision of sentenced probationers or released parolees is the most active stage of the probation/parole process.

Where probation is a possibility, intake procedures may include a presentence investigation, which examines the offender's background to provide the sentencing judge with facts needed to make an informed sentencing decision. Intake procedures may also involve a dispute-settlement process during which the probation officer works with the defendant and the victim to resolve the complaint before sentencing. Intake duties tend to be more common for juvenile offenders than they are for adults, but all officers may eventually have to recommend to the judge the best sentencing alternative for a particular case.

Diagnosis, the psychological inventorying of the probation or parole client, may be done either formally with written tests administered by certified psychologists or through informal arrangements, which typically depend on the observational skills of the officer. Needs assessment, another area of officer responsibility, extends beyond the psychological needs of the client to a cataloging of the services necessary for a successful experience on probation or parole. Supervision of sentenced probationers or released parolees is the most active stage of the probation/parole process, involving months (and sometimes years) of periodic meetings between the officer and the client and an ongoing assessment of the success of the probation/parole endeavor in each case.

All probation and parole officers must keep confidential the details of the presentence investigation, including psychological tests, needs assessment, conversations between the officer and the client, and so on. On the other hand, courts have generally held that communications between the officer and the client are not privileged, as they might be between a doctor and a patient or between a social worker and his or her client.[47] Hence officers can share with the appropriate authorities any incriminating evidence that a client relates.

The Challenges of the Job

One of the biggest challenges that probation and parole officers face is the need to balance two conflicting sets of duties—one

■ **caseload** The number of probation or parole clients assigned to one probation or parole officer for supervision.

Steven Hirsch/Newscom

Kelly Sott, 33, girlfriend of Cameron Douglas (son of actor Michael Douglas) is photographed at federal court in Manhattan immediately after leaving a federal lockup, where she spent seven months for attempting to smuggle heroin packed in an electric toothbrush to Cameron while he was under house arrest for drug dealing. How might court-ordered community supervision benefit Sott?

of which is to provide quasi–social work services and the other is to handle custodial responsibilities. In effect, two inconsistent models of the officer's role coexist. The social work model stresses an officer's service role and views probationers and parolees as clients. In this model, officers are caregivers whose goals are to accurately assess the needs of their clients and to match clients with community resources, such as job placement, indigent medical care, family therapy, and psychological and substance-abuse counseling. The social work model depicts probation/parole as a "helping profession" wherein officers assist their clients in meeting the conditions imposed on them by their sentence. The other model for officers is correctional. In this model, probation and parole clients are "wards" whom officers are expected to control. This model emphasizes community protection, which officers are supposed to achieve through careful and close supervision. Custodial supervision means that officers will periodically visit their charges at work and at home, often arriving unannounced. It also means that they must be willing to report clients for new offenses and for violations of the conditions of their release.

Most officers, by virtue of their personalities and experiences, identify more with one model than with the other. They consider themselves primarily caregivers or corrections officers. Regardless of the emphasis that each individual officer chooses, however, the demands of the job are bound to generate role conflict at one time or another.

A second challenge of probation and parole work is large **caseloads**. Back in 1973, the President's Commission on Law Enforcement and Administration of Justice recommended that probation and parole caseloads average around 35 clients per officer.[48] However, caseloads of 250 clients are common in some jurisdictions today, and Internet-facilitated remote supervision (discussed in a box in this chapter) can lead to higher caseloads still. Large caseloads combined with limited training and the time constraints imposed by administrative demands culminate in stopgap supervisory measures. "Postcard probation," in which clients mail in a letter or card once a month to report on their

Mark Humphrey/AP Wide World Photos

Georgia probation officers preparing to excavate a site at the Tri-State Crematory in Noble, Georgia, in 2002. Officials found the remains of hundreds of corpses on the crematory's 16-acre grounds. The crematory's operator, Ray Brent Marsh, was charged with 787 felony counts, including theft by deception, abuse of a corpse, and burial service fraud. He was also charged with 47 counts of making false statements to authorities. Convicted on many of the charges, he was sentenced to 12 years in prison in 2005. A probation officer's job can involve a wide variety of duties. What are the usual duties of a probation officer?

CJ | CAREERS
Probation Officer

Name. Stephanie Drury

Position. Probation officer, Pontiac, Michigan

College attended. Wayne State University (BS, criminal justice; MS, criminal justice)

Year hired. 2009

Please give a brief description of your job. I am a probation officer for approximately 110 men. The Adult Treatment Court is a specialty court for offenders with severe substance-abuse problems, and many of them also have a mental health diagnosis. My role there is to provide intensive supervision. I attend court with them every two weeks to inform the judge of their progress. Additionally, I see each of them at least once a week in order to ensure they are complying with all conditions of the program and maintaining their sobriety.

What appealed to you most about the position when you applied for it? I completed an internship with the federal probation department in Detroit and thoroughly enjoyed probation work, so I applied for the state probation job. The Adult Treatment Court position was appealing because I work directly with the judge and am able to provide intensive supervision to my probationers.

How would you describe the interview process? The interview consisted of a panel of three members of the Michigan Department of Corrections followed by a written test. Questions were based on my academic experience, along with any professional experience I had that would make me a perfect candidate. Also, real-life situations and scenarios were discussed in order to show the panel how I might deal with a particular situation.

What is a typical day like? I monitor the daily development of the females of the Adult Treatment Court, which includes probation supervision and making sure they are taking their medication, going to therapy, and attending programs such as Narcotics Anonymous. With the men on general supervision, I complete presentence investigations, field work, jail visits, and court appearances.

What qualities/characteristics are most helpful for this job? You have to be strong and in control at all times. If you don't have a backbone, the offenders will walk all over you and not take you seriously. It is a demanding job, and you have to be very organized to successfully supervise so many individuals on your caseload. You can exercise a lot of discretion and be your own boss, yet you also have a supervisor who will assist you in times of need.

What is a typical starting salary? $16.54 per hour, with benefits.

What is the salary potential as you move up into higher-level jobs? A probation officer with six years or more of experience will earn approximately $28.00 per hour or more, depending on his or her classification.

What advice would you give someone in college beginning studies in criminal justice? Find internships to gain experience in specific areas in the field of criminal justice. Engage yourself in as much real-life experience as possible, and network with as many professionals as possible, as these two methods will set you apart from other job candidates.

Source: Reprinted with permission of Stephanie Drury. Photo courtesy of Stephanie Drury.

whereabouts and circumstances, is an example of one stopgap measure that harried agencies with large caseloads use to keep track of their wards. A 2006 comprehensive review of state parole practices in California found that 65% of the state's parolees saw their parole officer no more than twice every three months, and 23% saw their officers only once every three months. Parolees with the highest level of supervision, including high-risk sex offenders, averaged two face-to-face meetings with their parole officer each month.[49]

Another difficulty with probation and parole work is the frequent lack of opportunity for career mobility within the profession. Probation and parole officers are generally assigned to small agencies serving limited geographic areas, under the leadership of one or two chief probation officers. Unless retirement or death claims a supervisor, there is little chance for other officers to advance.

A recent report by the National Institute of Justice (NIJ) found that, like law enforcement officers, probation and parole officers experienced a lot of stress.[50] The major sources of stress for probation and parole officers were found to be high caseloads, excess paperwork, and pressures associated with deadlines. Stress levels have also increased in recent years because offenders who are sentenced to probation and released on parole today have committed more serious crimes than in the past, and more offenders have serious drug-abuse histories and show less hesitation in using violence.[51] The NIJ study found that officers typically cope by requesting transfers, retiring early, or taking "mental health days" off from work. The report says, however, that "physical exercise is the method of choice for coping with the stress."[52] Learn more about working as a probation or parole officer at the

■ **intermediate sanctions** The use of split sentencing, shock probation or parole, shock incarceration, community service, intensive supervision, or home confinement in lieu of other, more traditional sanctions such as imprisonment and fines.

American Probation and Parole Association's website via **http://www.appa-net.org/eweb**.

Intermediate Sanctions

As noted in Chapter 11, significant new alternative sentencing options have become available to judges during the past few decades. Many such options are called **intermediate sanctions** because they employ sentencing alternatives that fall somewhere between outright imprisonment and simple probationary release back into the community. They are also sometimes termed *alternative sentencing strategies*. Michael J. Russell, former director of the National Institute of Justice, says that "intermediate punishments are intended to provide prosecutors, judges, and corrections officials with sentencing options that permit them to apply appropriate punishments to convicted offenders while not being constrained by the traditional choice between prison and probation. Rather than substituting for prison or probation, however, these sanctions, which include intensive supervision, house arrest with electronic monitoring (also referred to as *remote location monitoring*), and shock incarceration—programs that stress a highly structured and regimented routine, considerable physical work and exercise, and at times intensive substance-abuse treatment—bridge the gap between those options and provide innovative ways to ensure swift and certain punishment."[53]

Numerous citizen groups and special-interest organizations are working to widen the use of sentencing alternatives. One organization of special note is the Sentencing Project. The organization, based in Washington, D.C., is dedicated to promoting a greater use of alternatives to incarceration. It provides technical assistance to public defenders, court officials, and other community organizations.

The Sentencing Project and other groups like it have contributed to the development of more than 100 locally based alternative sentencing service programs. Most alternative sentencing services work in conjunction with defense attorneys to develop written sentencing plans. Such plans are basically well-considered citizen suggestions as to appropriate sentencing in a given instance. Plans are often quite detailed and may include letters of support from employers, family members, the defendant, and even victims. Sentencing plans may be used in plea bargaining sessions or may be presented to judges following trial and conviction. More than a decade ago, for example, lawyers for country-and-western singer Willie Nelson successfully proposed to tax court officials an alternative option that allowed the singer to pay huge past tax liabilities by performing in concerts for that purpose. Lacking such an alternative, the tax court might have seized Nelson's property or even ordered the singer to be confined to a federal facility. More recently, NBA player DeShawn Stevenson was sentenced to two years of probation in 2002 and was ordered to perform 100 hours of community service for the statutory rape of a 14-year-old girl whom he had plied with brandy.[54] Stevenson, who played for the Utah Jazz at the time of the offense, fulfilled the terms of his sentence by delivering motivational speeches at boys' clubs in California and New York.

The basic philosophy behind intermediate sanctions is this: When judges are offered well-planned alternatives to imprisonment for offenders who appear to represent little or no continuing threat to the community, the likelihood of a prison sentence is reduced. An analysis of alternative sentencing plans like those sponsored by the Sentencing Project shows that judges accept them in up to 80% of the cases in which they are recommended and that as many as two-thirds of offenders who receive intermediate sentences successfully complete them.[55]

Intermediate sanctions have three distinct advantages: (1) They are less expensive to operate per offender than imprisonment; (2) they are "socially cost-effective" because they keep the offender in the community, thus avoiding both the breakup of the family and the stigmatization that accompanies imprisonment; and (3) they provide flexibility in terms of resources, time of involvement, and place of service.[56] Some of these new sentencing options are described in the paragraphs that follow.

Split Sentencing

In jurisdictions where **split sentences** are an option, judges may impose a combination of a brief period of imprisonment and probation. Defendants who are given split sentences are often ordered to serve time in a local jail rather than in a long-term confinement facility. Ninety days in jail, followed by two years of supervised probation, is a typical split sentence. Split sentences

■ **split sentence** A sentence explicitly requiring the convicted offender to serve a period of confinement in a local, state, or federal facility, followed by a period of probation.

■ **shock probation** The practice of sentencing offenders to prison, allowing them to apply for probationary release, and surprisingly permitting such release. Offenders who receive shock probation may not be aware that they will be released on probation and may expect to spend a much longer time behind bars.

■ **shock incarceration** A sentencing option that makes use of "boot camp"–type prisons to impress on convicted offenders the realities of prison life.

are frequently given to minor drug offenders and serve notice that continued law violations may result in imprisonment for much longer periods.

Shock Probation and Shock Parole

Shock probation strongly resembles split sentencing. The offender serves a relatively short period of time in custody (usually in a prison rather than a jail) and is released on probation by court order. The difference is that shock probation clients must *apply* for probationary release from confinement and cannot be certain of the judge's decision. In shock probation, the court in effect makes a resentencing decision. Probation is only a statutory possibility and often little more than an aspiration for the offender as imprisonment begins. If probationary release is ordered, it may well come as a "shock" to the offender. The hope is that the unexpected reprieve will cause the offender to steer clear of future criminal involvement. Shock probation was begun in Ohio in 1965[57] and is used today in about half of the United States.[58] Shock probation lowers the cost of confinement, maintains community and family ties, and may be an effective rehabilitative tool.[59]

Shock parole is similar to shock probation. Whereas shock probation is ordered by judicial authority, shock parole is an administrative decision made by a paroling authority. Parole boards or their representatives may order an inmate's early release, hoping that the brief exposure to prison has reoriented the offender's life in a positive direction.

Shock Incarceration

Shock incarceration programs, which became popular during the 1990s, utilized military-style "boot camp" prison settings to provide highly regimented environments involving strict discipline, physical training, and hard labor.[60] Shock incarceration programs were designed primarily for young first offenders and are of short duration, generally lasting for only 90 to 180 days. Offenders who successfully completed these programs were typically returned to the community under some form of supervision. Program "failures" were usually moved into the general prison population for longer terms of confinement.

Vladimir Chaloupka/Las Cruces Sun-News/AP Wide World Photos

A New Mexico boot camp staff member conducting a push-up drill with young offenders. Boot camps use military-style discipline in an attempt to lessen the likelihood of recidivism among young and first-time offenders. How successful have boot camps been in reducing recidivism?

Georgia established the first shock incarceration program in 1983.[61] Following Georgia's lead, more than 30 other states began their own programs.[62] About half of the states provided for voluntary entry into the program, and a few allowed inmates to voluntarily quit the program.

One of the most comprehensive studies of boot camp prison programs that was ever conducted focused on eight states: Florida, Georgia, Illinois, Louisiana, New York, Oklahoma, South Carolina, and Texas. The report found that boot camp programs have been popular because "they are . . . perceived as being tough on crime" and "have been enthusiastically embraced as a viable correctional option."[63] The report concluded, however, that "the impact of boot camp programs on offender recidivism is at best negligible."

In recent years, boot camp programs have fallen into disfavor and have largely been discontinued. In 2005, the Bureau of

mixed sentence A sentence that requires that a convicted offender serve weekends (or other specified periods of time) in a confinement facility (usually a jail) while undergoing probationary supervision in the community.

community service A sentencing alternative that requires offenders to spend at least part of their time working for a community agency.

intensive probation supervision (IPS) A form of probation supervision involving frequent face-to-face contact between the probationer and the probation officer.

Prisons announced plans to eliminate its boot camp programs (known as "intensive confinement"), hoping to save more than $1 million a year on programs that hadn't proven their worth;[64] and in 2006, Florida Governor Jeb Bush signed legislation ending state-run boot camps in that state following the death of a 14-year-old participant. Two of the last states to continue to operate boot camps are Wyoming and Nevada. Nevada runs a "program of regimental discipline" at its Three Lakes Valley facility. The facility has a capacity of 75 youthful detainees, and accepts only nonviolent offenders who have committed relatively minor crimes.[65] The Wyoming Boot Camp, which can house up to 56 inmates, is located in the Wyoming Honor Conservation Camp at Newcastle, Wyoming.[66] It accepts young offenders under the age of 25 who have been court recommended, and sessions last for 180 days.

Mixed Sentencing and Community Service

Some **mixed sentences** require that offenders serve weekends in jail and receive probation supervision during the week. Other types of mixed sentencing require offenders to participate in treatment or community-service programs while on probation. Community-service programs began in Minnesota in 1972 with the Minnesota Restitution Program, which gave property offenders the opportunity to work and turn over part of their pay as restitution to their victims.[67] Courts throughout the nation quickly adopted the idea and began to build restitution orders into suspended-sentence agreements.

Community service is more an adjunct to, rather than a type of, correctional sentence. Community service is compatible with most other forms of innovation in probation and parole. Even with home confinement (discussed later in the chapter), offenders can be sentenced to community-service activities that are performed in the home or at a job site during the hours they are permitted to be away from their homes. Washing police cars, cleaning school buses, refurbishing public facilities, and assisting in local government offices are typical forms of community service. Some authors have linked the development of community-service sentences to the notion that work and service to others are good for the spirit.[68] Community-service participants are usually minor criminals, drunk drivers, and youthful offenders.

One problem with community-service sentences is that authorities rarely agree on what they are supposed to accomplish.

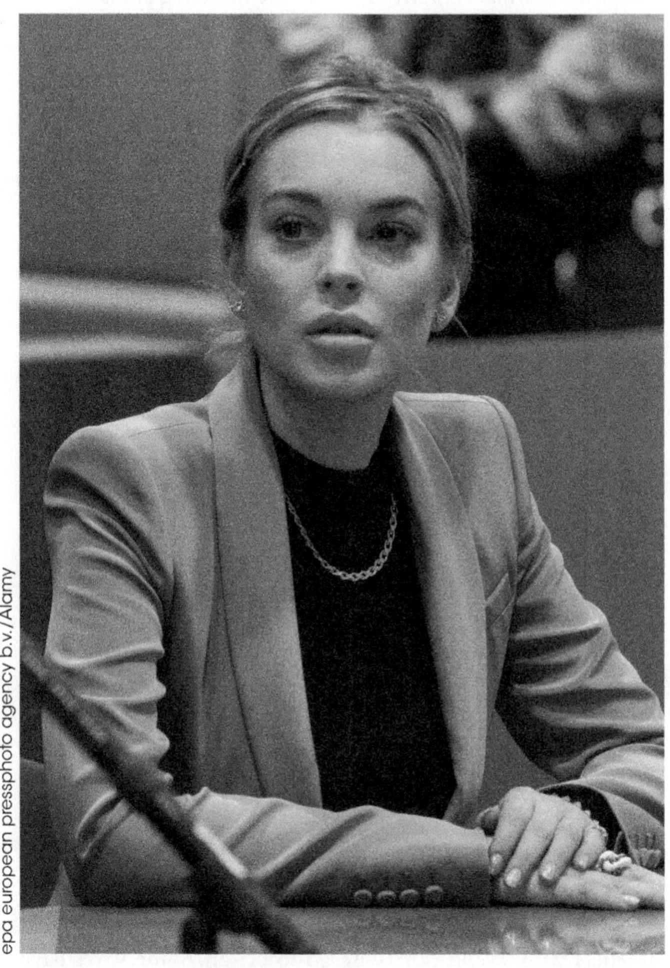

Actress Lindsay Lohan listens to the judge during a probation hearing in Los Angeles, California, on March 29, 2012. In May 2011, following a plea deal on charges of felony grand theft involving a $2,500 necklace stolen from a jewelry store, Lohan was placed under house arrest and ordered to wear an electronic monitor on her ankle. Why is remote location monitoring becoming a popular alternative to imprisonment?

Most people admit that offenders who work in the community are able to reduce the costs of their own supervision. There is little agreement, however, on whether such sentences reduce recidivism, act as a deterrent, or serve to rehabilitate offenders.

Intensive Probation Supervision

Intensive probation supervision (IPS) has been described as the "strictest form of probation for adults in the United States."[69] IPS is designed to achieve control in a community setting over

home confinement House arrest. Individuals ordered confined to their homes are sometimes monitored electronically to ensure they do not leave during the hours of confinement. Absence from the home during working hours is often permitted.

remote location monitoring A supervision strategy that uses electronic technology to track offenders who have been sentenced to house arrest or who have been ordered to limit their movements while completing a sentence involving probation or parole.

ethics and professionalism

American Probation and Parole Association Code of Ethics

- I will render professional service to the justice system and the community at large in effecting the social adjustment of the offender.
- I will uphold the law with dignity, displaying an awareness of my responsibility to offenders while recognizing the right of the public to be safeguarded from criminal activity.
- I will strive to be objective in the performance of my duties, recognizing the inalienable right of all persons, appreciating the inherent worth of the individual, and respecting those confidences which can be reposed in me.
- I will conduct my personal life with decorum, neither accepting nor granting favors in connection with my office.
- I will cooperate with my co-workers and related agencies and will continually strive to improve my professional competence through the seeking and sharing of knowledge and understanding.
- I will distinguish clearly, in public, between my statements and actions as an individual and as a representative of my profession.
- I will encourage policy, procedures and personnel practices, which will enable others to conduct themselves in accordance with the values, goals and objectives of the American Probation and Parole Association.
- I recognize my office as a symbol of public faith and I accept it as a public trust to be held as long as I am true to the ethics of the American Probation and Parole Association.
- I will constantly strive to achieve these objectives and ideals, dedicating myself to my chosen profession.

Thinking About Ethics

1. Which of the ethical principles enumerated here might also apply to corrections officers working in prisons and jails?
2. Which might apply to law enforcement officers?
3. Which might apply to prosecutors and criminal defense attorneys?

Source: American Probation and Parole Association. Reprinted with permission.

offenders who would otherwise go to prison. Some states have extended intensive supervision to parolees, allowing the early release of some who would otherwise serve longer prison terms.

Georgia was the first state to implement IPS, beginning its program in 1982. The Georgia program involves a minimum of five face-to-face contacts between the probationer and the supervising officer per week, mandatory curfew, required employment, a weekly check of local arrest records, routine and unannounced alcohol and drug testing, 132 hours of community service, and automatic notification of probation officers via the State Crime Information Network when an IPS client is arrested.[70] The caseloads of probation officers involved in IPS are much lower than the national average. Georgia officers work as a team, with one probation officer and two surveillance officers supervising about 40 probationers.[71]

A study published in 2000 shows that IPS programs can be effective at reducing recidivism, especially if the programs are well planned and fully implemented.[72] The study, which examined programs in California's Contra Costa and Ventura Counties, found that the programs worked because, among other things, they used team approaches in their supervision activities and had clear missions and goals.

Home Confinement and Remote Location Monitoring

Home confinement, also referred to as *house arrest*, can be defined as "a sentence imposed by the court in which offenders are legally ordered to remain confined in their own residences."[73] Home confinement usually makes use of a system of **remote location monitoring**. Remote location monitoring is typically performed via a computerized system of electronic bracelets. Participants wear a waterproof, shock-resistant transmitting device around the ankle 24 hours a day. The transmitter continuously emits a radio-frequency signal, which is detected by a receiving unit connected to the home telephone. Older systems use random telephone calls that require the offender to insert a computer chip worn in a wristband into a specially installed modem in the home, verifying his or her presence. Some use voice recognition technology and require the offender to verify his or her presence in the home by answering computerized calls. Modern electronic monitoring systems alert the officer when a participant leaves a specific location or tampers with the electronic monitoring equipment, and some systems even make it possible to record the time a supervised person enters or leaves the home.

Much of the electronic monitoring equipment in use today indicates only when participants enter or leave the equipment's range—not where they have gone or how far they have traveled. Newer satellite-supported systems, however, are capable of continuously monitoring the location of offenders and tracking them as they move from place to place (Figure 12-3). Satellite-based systems can alert the officer when participants venture into geographically excluded locations or when they fail to present themselves at required locations at specific times.[74]

Most remotely monitored offenders on home confinement may leave home only to go to their jobs, attend to medical emergencies, or buy household essentials. Because of the strict limits it imposes on offender movements, house arrest has been cited as offering a valuable alternative to prison for offenders with special needs. Pregnant women, geriatric convicts, offenders with disabilities, seriously or terminally ill offenders, and offenders who have intellectual disabilities may all be better supervised through home confinement than through traditional incarceration.

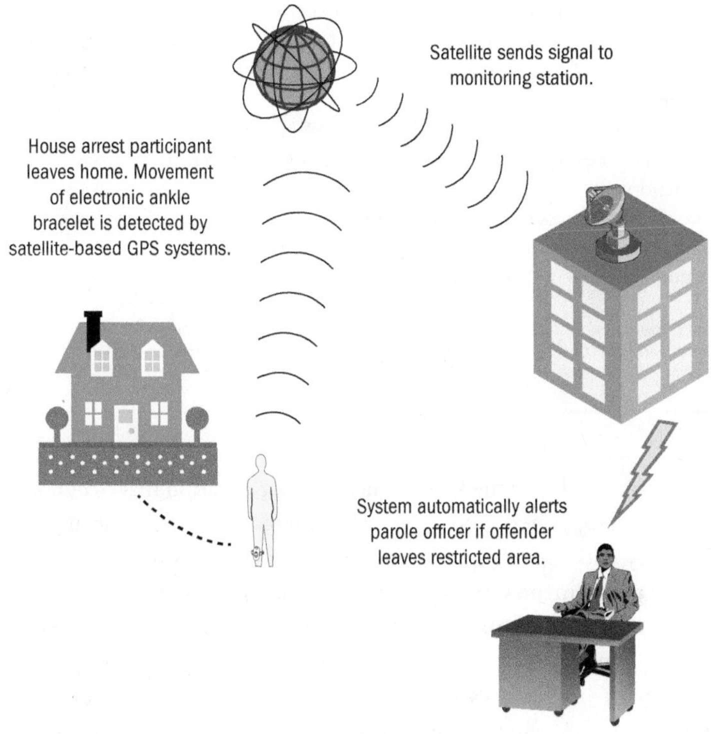

FIGURE 12-3 | Remote Location Monitoring—How It Works

One of the best-known people to be placed recently under house arrest using a remote location monitoring system was actress Lindsay Lohan. In 2011 Lohan was placed under house arrest and ordered to wear an electronic monitor on her ankle following a plea of no contest to charges that she had stolen an expensive necklace from a Los Angeles jewelry store.[75]

The Community Justice Assistance Division of the Texas Department of Criminal Justice runs one of the most ambitious home confinement programs in the country. In 1997, nearly 3.5% of the state's probationers were being electronically monitored on probation.[76] By 2006, parole offices throughout the state had adopted electronic monitoring, and 1,056 electronic monitoring units were available for use with parolees.[77]

The electronic monitoring of offenders has substantially increased across the nation during the past 20 years.

The electronic monitoring of offenders has substantially increased across the nation during the past 20 years. A survey by the National Institute of Justice in 1987, as the use of electronic monitoring was just beginning, showed only 826 offenders being monitored electronically nationwide.[78] By 2000, however, more than 16,000 defendants and offenders under the supervision of U.S. probation and pretrial services officers were on home confinement—most under electronic monitoring programs.[79] A 2012 estimate put the number of persons in the United States under electronic monitoring at up to 200,000—including 27,000 people awaiting deportation.[80]

In 1999, South Carolina became one of the first states to use satellites to track felons recently freed from state prisons. The satellite-tracking plan, which made use of 21 satellites in the global positioning system (GPS), allowed the state's Probation and Parole Department to track every move made by convicts wearing electronic bracelets.[81] The system, which also notified law enforcement officers when a bracelet-wearing offender left his or her assigned area, could electronically alert anyone holding a restraining order whenever the offender came within two miles of them. Over the past 15 years, GPS tracking of parolees has become commonplace and is now used across the country.

The home confinement program in the federal court system has three components, or levels of restriction.[82] *Curfew* requires program participants to remain at home every day during certain times, usually in the evening. With *home detention*, the participant remains at home at all times except for preapproved and scheduled absences, such as for work, school, treatment, church, attorney's appointments, court appearances, and other court-ordered obligations. *Home incarceration*, the highest level of restriction, calls for 24-hour-a-day "lockdown" at home, except for medical appointments, court appearances, and other activities that the court specifically approves.

Many states and the federal government view house arrest as a cost-effective response to the high cost of imprisonment. Georgia, for example, estimates that home confinement costs

CJ | NEWS

How GPS Bracelets Keep Track of Sex Offenders

Paul Bersebach/Newscom

An ankle bracelet with a built-in global positioning system (GPS). The bracelet can be placed on parolees and used by parole officers to monitor individuals under house arrest, or to follow the movements of those permitted by the court to move throughout the community while under supervision. What do you see as the advantages and disadvantages of this technology? How would individual-rights and public-safety advocates see GPS technology when used this way?

In 2006, when 23 states had adopted global positioning systems (GPSs) to monitor sex offenders, the approach was hailed as a promising technique to control habitual predators.

GPS monitors, strapped to the ankle, were seen as a less costly way to protect against sex offenders than prison or frequent parole officer visits. Advocates of home confinement thought that the use of monitors might even discourage recidivism, because offenders would be aware that authorities were watching their every move.

Today, however, the number of participating states has reportedly not grown and authorities seem less enthusiastic. "GPS technology is far more limited than anticipated and should be viewed as a tool rather than depended upon as a control mechanism," says Gaylene Armstrong, a professor of criminal justice at Sam Houston State University.

In a two-year study of GPS monitoring of sex offenders in Phoenix, published in the *Journal of Criminal Justice* in 2011, Armstrong discovered that considerable numbers of alerts from the devices were due to harmless events such as equipment failure. Research on whether GPS monitors deter crimes has also been inconclusive, and many offenders have been cutting off the devices or trying to find other ways of fooling them.

False alerts are a particular problem because they obscure actual trouble spots. The 274 parole officers working GPS caseloads in California, the largest user of GPS monitors for sex offenders, received almost a million alerts in 2009, according to a state report. Each alert shows up as a dot on a computer screen. "We are just drowning in dots," said Robert Coombs, chair of the state's Sex Offender Management Board. "What happens is the more broadly we use it, the more difficult it becomes in identifying the meaningful data."

California's information overload has led to some colossal failures. One paroled sex offender in the state's GPS program was Phillip Garrido, who kidnapped 11-year-old Jaycee Lee Dugard and was keeping her in a shed behind his house for 18 years. After Garrido was arrested in 2009, a state inquiry determined officers failed to respond to hundreds of alerts from his monitor, and the state subsequently paid Dugard $20 million in a settlement. Garrido, who fathered two children with Dugard, is now serving a 431-year sentence.

Some states, however, are less overwhelmed. In Washington, each parole officer is assigned between 20 and 30 offenders, and tracks each offender's GPS movements several times a day. Michigan has created a central monitoring center to weed out false alarms, and Florida has hired a private company to sort through alerts.

But effective monitoring can be costly. The reported cost of monitoring one person ranges from $5 to as much as $33 per day, and California spent $60 million to track just 6,500 parolees in 2010. Also, when parole officers devote a lot of time to GPS monitoring, it means less face-to-face and telephone time with parolees—alternative supervision strategies that are considered to be more effective.

GPS may be useful in locating an offender when a child is missing, but many law enforcement officials now say the chief advantage of GPS tracking is not stopping a crime, but gathering evidence after a crime has been committed. "Essentially, a GPS bracelet allows you to make a case after the fact," said Gerard Leone, a Massachusetts district attorney. "And that is why I stress it is not an appropriate substitution for incarceration."

Six states have authorized lifetime GPS tracking for sex offenders, extending beyond parole. Critics say this is a violation of the Fourth Amendment ban on search and seizure and of the *ex post facto* clause prohibiting retroactively adding punishment to an offender's sentence. However, the North Carolina Supreme Court rejected the *ex post facto* argument in 2010. It is yet to be tested in federal court.

Resources: "GPS Monitoring of Sex Offenders Should Be Used as Tool, Not Control Mechanism, Researchers Find," Science Daily, August 8, 2011, http://www.sciencedaily.com/releases/2011/08/110808152417.htm; "Calif. to Change Sex-Offender Tracking," Associated Press, May 26, 2011, http://abcnews.go.com/US/wireStory?id=13696574#.T5lkxRxvYzA; "Tracking Sex Offenders Is No Easy Fix," *The Bay Citizen*, July 20, 2010, http://www.baycitizen.org/crime/story/gps-tracking-sex-offenders-imperfect/.

> Many states and the federal government view house arrest as a cost-effective response to the high cost of imprisonment.

approximately $1,130 per year per supervised probationer and $2,190 per supervised parolee.[83] Incarceration costs are much higher, running around $18,100 per year per Georgia inmate, with another $43,756 needed to build each cell.[84] Advocates of house arrest argue that it is also socially cost-effective[85] because it substantially decreases the opportunity for the kinds of negative socialization that occur in prison. Opponents, however, have pointed out that house arrest may endanger the public and that it may provide little or no actual punishment. Critics of Michael Vick's home confinement, for example, complained that the sentence was more of a reward than a punishment. Vick's home, a five-bedroom, 3,538-square-foot brick house, lacks few amenities, and the conditions imposed on Vick allowed him to do pretty much as he pleased while in the house.

A large study funded by the National Institute of Justice (NIJ) of more than 5,000 Florida offenders placed on GPS monitoring found that electronic monitoring significantly reduced the likelihood of failure under community supervision.[86] The risk of failure was found to be about 31% less than that of offenders placed on other forms of community supervision. Similarly, a 2012 NIJ study that compared a group of GPS-monitored California sex offenders over a one-year period found that "a clear pattern" success for those being monitored versus a control group who received traditional parole supervision.[87] Study authors noted that the chance for both parole revocation and any return-to-custody event was about 38% higher among the subjects who received traditional parole supervision. The NIJ study also examined costs and benefits associated with electronic monitoring, and concluded that "the GPS program costs roughly $35.96 per day per parolee, while the cost of traditional supervision is $27.45 per day per parolee—a difference of $8.51. However, the results favor the GPS group in terms of both noncompliance and recidivism. In other words, the GPS monitoring program is more expensive but more effective."

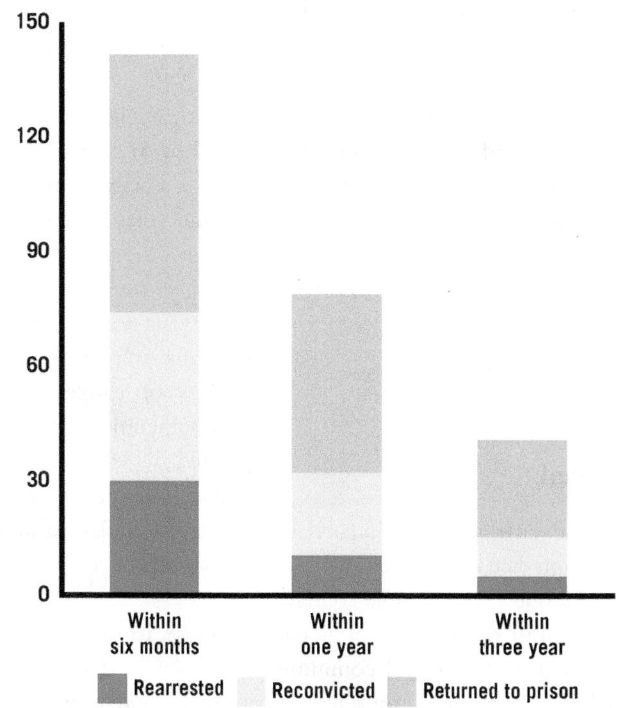

FIGURE 12-4 | Recidivism Rates of Prisoners Released from Prison in 15 States

Source: Jeremy Travis, Ronald Davis, and Sarah Lawrence, *Exploring the Role of the Police in Prisoner Reentry,* New Perspectives in Policing Bulletin (Washington, DC: U.S. Department of Justice, National Institute of Justice, 2012).

The Future of Probation and Parole

Parole was widely criticized during the 1980s and 1990s by citizen groups that claimed that it unfairly reduces prison sentences imposed on serious offenders. Official attacks on parole came from some powerful corners. Senator Edward Kennedy called for the abolition of parole, as did former Attorney General Griffin Bell and former U.S. Bureau of Prisons Director Norman Carlson.[88] Academics chimed in, alleging that parole programs provide no assurance that criminals will not commit further crimes. The media joined the fray, condemning parole for its failure to curb recidivism and highlighting the so-called revolving prison door as representative of the failure of parole.

These criticisms are not without value. Today, around 688,000 former prisoners—almost 2,000 per day—are released annually from state and federal prisons and returned to society, most of them on some form of supervised release.[89] Although statistics on the 2010 cohort are not yet fully available, estimates are that over half of them will have been reincarcerated within three years (and some of them will have successfully completed parole prior to their return to prison).[90] Figure 12-4 shows recidivism rates for released prisoners in 15 states.

Parole violators account for more than half of prison admissions in many states, and 70% of parole violators sent to in prison were arrested or were convicted of a new offense *while* on parole.[91] Many of these offenses involved drugs. In 2013, for example, a study by the Kentucky-based Council of State Governments found that one in five arrests in four of California's largest cities involved individuals under probation or parole supervision at the time of their arrest.[92] The study also found that persons under supervision were involved in one in six arrests for violent crime and one in three of all arrests for drug crime. Had the study also sought to identify persons arrested who had *previously* been on probation or parole, as well as those *currently* being supervised, the results would likely have been much higher.

Parole violators account for more than half of prison admissions in many states.

Critics say that numbers like these are indicative of poor reintegration of prisoners into the community and are associated with wide-ranging social costs, including decreased public safety and weakened family and community ties.[93] Adequate reintegration efforts have also suffered in the face of today's budget shortfalls. In California, for example, the 2011 Realignment Legislation mentioned earlier in this chapter stipulated that any parolee (other than those originally sentenced to life in prison) whose parole is revoked will serve a term no longer than 180 days in the county jail.[94] The bill also provides that parolees who do not incur any infractions will be released from parole supervision in six months. Under the law, California's Board of Parole Hearings discontinued parole revocation hearings in mid-2013, and that responsibility was moved to local criminal court judges. Although thorough assessments of California's experiment with realignment have yet to be made, a late-2012 report by a Los Angeles County advisory board found that responsibility for a large number of high-risk offenders, many with mental illness, has been shifted to counties that may be ill-prepared to deal adequately with those offenders.[95]

Some prisoners have challenged the fairness of parole, saying it is sometimes arbitrarily granted.

Even some prisoners have challenged the fairness of parole, saying it is sometimes arbitrarily granted, which creates an undue amount of uncertainty and frustration for inmates. Parolees have complained about the unpredictable nature of the parole experience, citing their powerlessness in the parole contract.

Against the pressure of attacks like these, parole advocates struggled to clarify and communicate the value of supervised release in the corrections process. As more and more states moved toward the elimination of parole, advocates called for moderation. One report by the American Probation and Parole Association (APPA), for example, concluded that states that have eliminated parole "have jeopardized public safety and wasted tax dollars." The researchers wrote, "Getting rid of parole dismantles an accountable system of releasing prisoners back into the community and replaces it with a system that bases release decisions solely on whether a prison term has been completed."[96]

Changes in Reentry Policies

By the close of the twentieth century, criticisms of parole had begun to wane, and numerous reports supported well-considered offender reentry and post-release supervision programs. In 2005, for example, the Re-entry Policy Council, a bipartisan assembly of almost 100 leading elected officials, policymakers, corrections leaders, and practitioners from community-based organizations around the country, released a report on offender reentry titled *Charting the Safe and Successful Return of Prisoners to the Community*. The 500-page document pointed out that virtually every person incarcerated in a jail in this country, as well as 97% of those incarcerated in prisons, will eventually be released back into society. This, said the report, results in nearly 650,000 people being released from prisons, and more than 7 million individuals being released from jails throughout the United States each year—many of them without any form of post-release supervision.[97]

As the report noted, almost two out of every three people released from prison are rearrested within three years of their release.[98] Report authors also noted that although the number of people reentering society has increased fourfold in the past 20 years, and spending on corrections has increased nearly sevenfold during that time, the likelihood of a former prisoner succeeding in the community upon release has not improved.

A host of complex issues create barriers to successful reentry. Three-quarters of those released from prison and jail, for example, have a history of substance abuse; two-thirds have no high school diploma; nearly half of those leaving jail earned less than $600 per month immediately prior to their incarceration; and they leave jail with significantly diminished opportunities for employment. Moreover, said the report, more than a third of jail inmates are saddled with a physical or mental disability, and the rate of serious mental illness among released inmates is at least three times higher than the rate of mental illness among the general population.[99]

According to the report, "the multi-faceted—and costly—needs of people returning to their families and communities require a re-inventing of reentry akin to the reinvention of welfare in the 90s." It requires, the report continued, "a multi-system, collaborative approach that takes into account all aspects of [the] problem." In other words, "the problems faced by re-entering adults are not merely the problems of corrections or community corrections, but also of public health workers, housing providers, state legislators, workforce development staff, and others."

To guide states and local jurisdictions in the creation of successful offender reentry programs, the report provides 35 policy statements, each of which is supported by a series of research highlights. The report can be read in its entirety at **http://www.reentrypolicy.org/publications/1694;file**.

In 2003, the U.S. Department of Justice, in conjunction with other federal agencies, initiated funding for 89 reentry sites across the country under the Serious and Violent Offender Reentry Initiative (SVORI).[100] SVORI programs were geared toward serious and violent offenders, particularly adults released from prison, as well as juveniles released from correctional facilities. The goal of the SVORI initiative was to reduce the likelihood of reincarceration by providing tailored supervision and services to improve the odds for a successful transition to the community. SVORI services included employment assistance, education and skills training, substance-abuse counseling, and help with post-release housing.

SVORI programs also tried to reduce criminality by closely monitoring participant noncompliance, reoffending, rearrest, reconviction, and reincarceration. The initiative's priorities included providing services both to those adults and juveniles who were most likely to pose a risk to the community upon release and to those who faced multiple challenges upon returning to the community. SVORI funding supported the creation of a three-phase continuum of services that (1) begins

■ **reentry courts** "Specialized courts that help reduce recidivism and improve public safety through the use of judicial oversight to apply graduated sanctions and positive reinforcement, to marshal resources to support the prisoner's reintegration, and to promote positive behavior by the returning prisoners."[ii] Also, specialized courts that are based on the drug-court model, and which function to rapidly place drug-affected defendants into appropriate treatment programs with close supervision by a single judge familiar with both the treatment and the offenders.

in prison, (2) moves to a structured reentry phase before and during the early months of release, and (3) continues for several years as released prisoners take on increasingly productive roles in the community.[101]

In 2012, after SVORI funding ended, the NIJ published a 560-page final report evaluating results of the SVORI program.[102] The study found encouraging results for the effect of the SVORI program participation on arrest and, to a lesser extent, incarceration outcomes. The effect of SVORI program participation was found to have been associated with longer times to arrest and with fewer arrests during followup periods. Results were weaker for the effects of the SVORI program on post-release reincarceration, however. For adult males, SVORI program participation was associated with a longer time to reincarceration and also fewer reincarcerations. For the adult females, the results were mixed and not significant. The final SVORI report can be read in its entirety at **http://www.justicestudies.com/pubs/final_svori.pdf.**

In response to the high post-release failure rates and the overwhelming needs of individuals returning from incarceration, many reentry-type programs designed to facilitate the transition from incarceration to the community have been implemented over the past several decades.[103] Not all of them fall under the SVORI model. Among the most significant alternatives are **reentry courts** (also discussed in Chapter 9), which combine intensive judicial oversight with rehabilitative services, and arose as part of a broader national movement toward the development and implementation of specialized "problem-solving courts," such as drug, mental health, domestic violence, and community courts, as an approach for addressing specific problems among criminal justice populations.

Many reentry-type programs designed to facilitate the transition from incarceration to the community have been implemented over the past several decades.

Reentry courts are mostly based on the drug-court model, begun in Miami in 1989, which functions to rapidly place drug-affected defendants into appropriate treatment programs with close supervision by a single judge familiar with both the treatment and the offenders.[104] Similarly, under the reentry court concept, reentry court judges oversee an offender's supervised release into the community.[105] Hence, reentry courts address the critical needs of returning prisoners—particularly in the period immediately following release—through the combination of judicial oversight and a collaborative case management process. According to the Bureau of Justice Assistance, "the underlying goal of reentry courts is to establish a seamless system of offender accountability and support services throughout the reentry process."[106]

Reentry courts are mostly based on the drug-court model.

The typical reentry court offers an array of reintegration services to which participants can be referred and provides continual oversight using a preestablished set of graduated sanctions and rewards. Throughout the reentry period, a reentry case-management team makes continual recommendations to the reentry court judge.

The National Reentry Resource Center—a joint effort by the Urban Institute, the American Probation and Parole Association, the Center of Juvenile Justice Reform at Georgetown University, the Association of State Correctional Administrators, and the Council of State Governments' Justice Center—can be visited on the Web at **http://www.nationalreentryresourcecenter.org**. Read a 2013 NIJ-sponsored study of the effectiveness of reentry courts at **http://www.justicestudies.com/pubs/reentrycourts.pdf.**

In March 2008, in an effort to help the more than 600,000 people leaving prison each year, the U.S. Congress passed the Second Chance Act.[107] The bill was signed into law by President George W. Bush shortly afterward. The law's purpose is to reduce the number of people being returned to prison after parole release due to state-run "hair-trigger" parole systems that send large numbers of people back to prison not for new crimes, but for technical violations or other relatively minor reasons.

The act authorized the expenditure of approximately $400 million in federal funds to "break the cycle of criminal recidivism [by assisting] offenders reentering the community from incarceration to establish a self-sustaining and law-abiding life."[108] The legislation funds prison-to-community transition services and programs through grants to nonprofit organizations. Such services and programs include the following:

The Second Chance Act was intended to break the cycle of criminal recidivism by assisting offenders reentering the community from incarceration to establish a self-sustaining and law-abiding life.

- Reentry courts
- Education and job training while in prison
- Mentoring programs for adults and juveniles leaving confinement
- Drug treatment (including family-based treatment) for incarcerated parents during and after incarceration

- Alternatives to incarceration for parents convicted of nonviolent drug offenses
- Supportive programming for children of incarcerated parents
- Early release for certain elderly prisoners convicted of nonviolent offenses
- Reentry research through research awards to study parole and postsupervision revocation and related community safety issues

The legislation also allocates funding for Federal Bureau of Prisons programs that do the following:

1. Provide prisoners nearing the completion of their sentences with information concerning health care, nutrition, employment opportunities, money management, and availability of government assistance
2. Allow certain nonviolent prisoners over 60 years of age to be placed in home detention for the duration of their sentences
3. Educate juvenile offenders on the consequences of drug use and criminal activity

The Second Chance Act seems to be having its desired effect, as a nationwide study of 500,000 parolees who left supervision showed that only 32% were sent back to confinement in 2011 versus a 36% recidivism rate in 2008.[109]

The Reinvention of Probation and Evidence-Based Practices

Although probation has generally fared better than parole, it too has its critics. The primary purpose of probation has always been rehabilitation. Probation is a powerful rehabilitative tool because, at least in theory, it allows the resources of a community to be focused on the offender. Unfortunately for advocates of probation, however, the rehabilitative ideal is far less popular today than it has been in the past. The contemporary demand for just deserts appears to have reduced society's tolerance for even relatively minor offenders. Also, because it has been too frequently and inappropriately used with repeat or relatively serious offenders, the image of probation has been tarnished. Probation advocates have been forced to admit that it is not a very powerful deterrent because it is far less punishing than a term of imprisonment.

In a series of reports issued in 1999 and 2000, the Reinventing Probation Council, a project of New York's Manhattan

Nick Ut/AP Wide World Photos

David Duke, the former Ku Klux Klan leader whose case raised eyebrows when he was released on federal parole in 2004. Duke, who served a year in federal prison on fraud charges, was released to a halfway house in Baton Rouge, Louisiana, and met the work requirements of his release by performing duties for the "white civil rights group" that he heads. Might a more suitable placement have been found for Duke?

CJ | ISSUES

Remote Reporting Probation

Recently, a number of Internet-based interactive probation services, including ProbationComm (created by Circle Seven Software) and PoCheck software, have been adopted by states seeking to lower the costs of probation supervision. Both ProbationComm and PoCheck, along with similar other services, allow low-risk probationers to keep in touch with their probation officers through an Internet reporting service. These online services allow for easy communication between client and officers through e-mail, Web-based forms, and instant messaging. Probationers participating in Internet supervision can access the service from home, or through public computers such as those available at local libraries. Clients are generally assessed a small fee, usually in the range of $10 to $20, for participation in the program.

Remote reporting systems typically allow probation officers to send mass e-mailings to their entire caseload of clients, or to target individual probationers in their communications. Through the use of easy-to-complete online forms, clients are able to report changes in status (such as changes in jobs, hiring, or health issues) to the probation officer, and the system notifies officers of upcoming events, such as pending discharges from supervision. It can also flag probationers who report losing jobs, changing marital status, or a change in place of residence. With links to law enforcement agencies and automated databases, Internet-based systems alerts probation officers of arrests, citations, and other law enforcement contacts with clients.

One major advantage of remote reporting programs is that they allow significantly increased caseloads. A Texas study, for example, showed that Internet reporting makes it possible for one probation officer to supervise up to 500 probationers—more than twice the normal number—without increasing the number of hours of work required over traditional supervision. This significant increase in supervisory capacity can be very important for jurisdictions seeking to make the most efficient use of limited resources.

Although Web-hosted interactive probation services are relatively new (the first went online in 2002), some jurisdictions still use interactive probation kiosks, similar to ATM machines. In 1997, for example, probation authorities in New York City began the use of probation kiosks designed to lower probation officer caseloads. Fifteen electronic kiosks, similar in design to ATMs, were scattered throughout the city, allowing probationers to check in with probation officers by placing their palms on a specially designed surface and by answering questions presented on a flashing screen.

The kiosks, which some jurisdictions still use, identify probationers by the shape and size of their hands, which were previously scanned into the system. Probationers using the kiosk system are prompted to press "yes" or "no" in response to questions like these: "Have you moved recently?" "Have you been arrested again?" "Do you need to see a probation officer?" Meetings with officers can be scheduled directly from the kiosk. By analyzing data submitted through kiosks, probation officers can zero in on individual probationers who are having problems, prompting more personal attention.

Some jurisdictions, however, may have been too quick to jump on the remote reporting bandwagon. In 2005, for example, Dallas, Texas, temporarily suspended the use of kiosks after finding that not all program participants had been properly screened. Although participation in the program required an assessment for readiness through face-to-face meetings with probation officers, some participants had undetected problems, including drug dependence and mental illness. As one critic of the Dallas program pointed out, "Inappropriate use of probation automation risks saving money in the short run while increasing long-term costs through higher recidivism rates."

Critics charge that high-tech supervision of probationers, whether online or through the use of kiosks, Internet services, or dial-in telephone numbers, carries unacceptable risk. Without personal supervision, those critics say, probationers are more likely to reoffend—an assertion that is essentially untested. Other opponents say remote reporting services are far removed from meaningful "punishment," and that offenders deserve stricter treatment. Supporters, on the other hand, say that high-tech probation supervision will have to become commonplace as probation and parole budges are strained. "New York City had no choice; it had to do something like that," says Todd Clear, professor of criminal justice at New York's John Jay College. Clear assisted the city in restructuring its probation program. "No one wants probationers reporting to kiosks, but the alternative was even more unthinkable—a system in which nobody receives quality service," said Clear.

References: PoCheck, "Probation and Parole Report-in System," http://www.pocheck.com; ProbationComm, "Introducing ProbationComm," http://www.probationcomm.com/docs/ProbationComm_Introduction.pdf (accessed March 1, 2013); and Marc A. Levin, "Salvation in Probation Automation?" *Conservative Voice*, September 27, 2005, http://www.theconservativevoice.com/articles/article.html?id=8585 (accessed May 1, 2007).

Institute, called for the "reinvention of probation."[110] Probation is currently in the midst of a crisis, said the council, because probationers are not being held to even simple standards of behavior and because the field of probation lacks leadership. According to the council, "probation will be reinvented when the probation profession places public safety first, and works with and in the community." Read the council's full reports at **http://www.manhattan-institute.org/html/cr_7.htm** and **http://www.manhattan-institute.org/html/broken_windows.htm**.

In late 2008, the Public Safety Performance Project of the Pew Center on the States released a report outlining strategies for successful probation supervision and parole reentry. The report, titled *Putting Public Safety First*, outlined 13 strategies that the center says "can reduce recidivism and hold offenders accountable for their actions while also cutting substance abuse and unemployment, and restoring family bonds."[111] Primary among the strategies is defining the success of probation and parole in terms of recidivism reduction. The entire report can be accessed at **http://www.pewtrusts.org/our_work_report_detail.aspx?id=46570**.

About a year later, in an effort to assess the degree to which the Pew Center's 13 strategies were being implemented, the Justice Policy Center of the Urban Institute published a lengthy review of parole practices across the country.[112] While the review found that few agencies were using all of the 13 strategies, it did find that most agencies are moving in the direction of implementing many of them. Although 93% of survey respondents reported that their offices have the goal of reducing recidivism, only 75% said that recidivism rates of current paroles were being tracked; and an amazingly low 13% of offices said that they continued to track recidivism rates of parolees who have completed parole. Moreover, definitions of recidivism varied considerably between agencies, and included "reincarceration," "reconviction," "new arrest," and "technical violation."[113] One positive result from the survey showed that awareness and use of evidence-based practices among parole agencies has become relatively widespread. This, say the report's authors, "suggests that a consensus on the value of the general concept is emerging." Nonetheless, the review also found that "there is considerable uncertainty on what evidence-based practice means in parole."[114] Nonetheless, the evidence-based movement in probation and parole is gaining steam, and in 2009, the California legislature enacted a law creating the California Community Corrections Performance Incentive Program, which promotes the use of evidence-based strategies for reducing the rate of failure on probation.[115]

Finally, in 2011, the National Institute of Corrections published a report showing that, among programs studied, treatment-oriented intense supervision of offenders in the community had the largest impact on reducing recidivism (Figure 12-5).[116] That report, entitled "Evidence-Based Policy, Practice and Decision-making," can be accessed at **http://www.justicestudies.com/pubs/ppdecisionmaking.pdf.**

Finally, in 2012, the NIJ funded studies of Hawaii's HOPE program, a highly successful probation initiative that addresses probation violations in a swift, certain, and proportionate manner. HOPE, which stands for Hawaii's Opportunity Probation with Enforcement, when compared with traditional probation programs results in (1) a 55% reduction in arrests for new crimes, (2) a 72% reduction in the likelihood of drug use, (3) a 61% reduction in skipped appointments with probation supervisors, and (4) a 53% reduction in probation revocation.[117]

HOPE begins with a direct, formal warning delivered by a judge in court to offenders enrolled in the program. The warning explicitly states that any future probation violations will result in an immediate, brief jail stay. Probationers with drug issues are assigned a color code at the warning hearing and are required to call the HOPE hotline each weekday morning to find out which color has been chosen for that day. Probationers whose color is selected must appear at the probation office before 2 p.m. the same day for a drug test. Non-drug-involved offenders must comply with their conditions of probation and may be required to attend treatment.

When probationers violate the conditions of probation, they are arrested or an arrest warrant is issued. As soon as a probation officer detects a violation, he or she completes a "Motion to Modify Probation" form and sends it to the judge, who promptly holds a violation hearing. A probationer found to have violated the terms of probation is sentenced to a short jail stay. Upon release, the probationer reports to his or her probation officer and resumes participation in HOPE. Each successive violation is met with an escalated response (i.e., longer jail stays). Learn more about the HOPE program at **http://www.justicestudies.com/pubs/hope.pdf.**

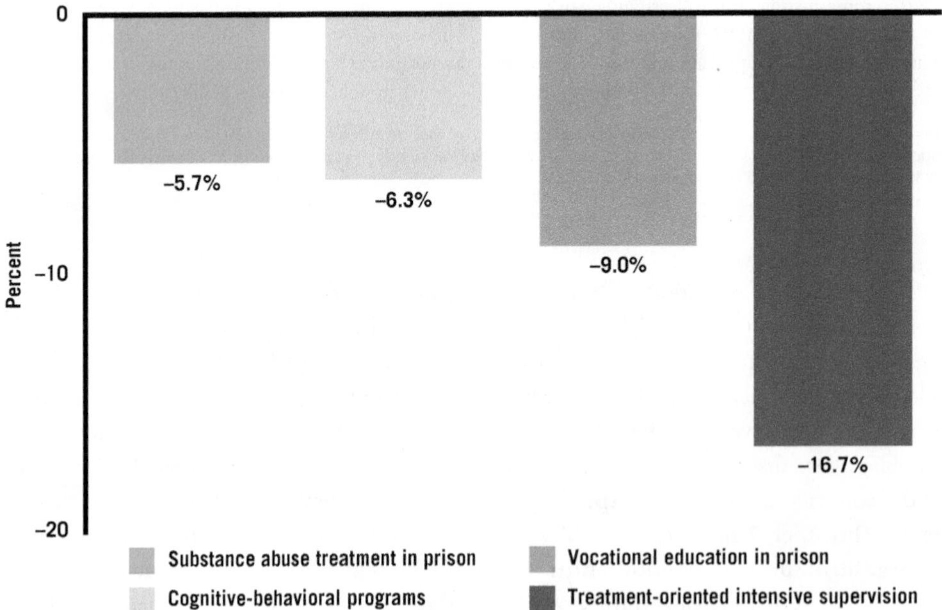

FIGURE 12-5 | Reduction in Recidivism among Released Offenders, by Program Type

Source: National Institute of Corrections, *Evidence-Based Policy, Practice, and Decisionmaking: Implications for Paroling Authorities* (Washington, DC: U.S. Department of Justice, 2011).

SUMMARY

- Probation, simply put, is a sentence of imprisonment that is suspended. Its goal is to retain some control over criminal offenders while using community programs to help rehabilitate them. Probation, a court-ordered sanction, is one form of community corrections (also termed *community-based corrections*)—that is, a sentencing style that depends less on traditional confinement options and more on correctional resources available in the community. John Augustus, a Boston shoemaker, is generally recognized as the world's first probation officer. By 1925, all 48 states had adopted probation legislation. In that same year, the federal government enacted legislation enabling federal district court judges to appoint paid probation officers and to impose probationary terms.
- Parole is the conditional early release of a convicted offender from prison. It is a corrections strategy with a primary purpose of returning offenders gradually to productive lives. Parole differs from probation in that parolees, unlike probationers, have been incarcerated. Parole supported the concept of indeterminate sentencing, which held that a prisoner could earn early release through good behavior and self-improvement.
- Both probation and parole provide opportunities for the reintegration of offenders into the community through the use of resources not readily available in institutional settings. They are far less expensive than imprisonment, lead to increased employment among program participants, make possible restitution payments, and increase opportunities for rehabilitation. Unfortunately, however, increased freedom for criminal offenders also means some degree of increased risk for other members of society and increased social costs. Until and unless we solve the problems of inaccurate risk assessment, increased recidivism, and inadequate supervision, probation and parole will continue to be viewed with suspicion by a public that has become intolerant of crime and criminal offenders.
- Eleven especially significant U.S. Supreme Court decisions, each of which was discussed in this chapter, provide the legal framework for probation and parole supervision. The 1987 case of *Griffin* v. *Wisconsin* may be the most significant. In *Griffin*, the Supreme Court ruled that probation officers may conduct searches of a probationer's residence without either a search warrant or probable cause. Other important court decisions include the 1998 case of *Pennsylvania Board of Probation and Parole* v. *Scott*, in which the Court declined to extend the exclusionary rule to apply to searches by parole officers, and the 2001 case of *U.S.* v. *Knights*, which expanded the search authority normally reserved for probation and parole officers to police officers under certain circumstances.
- Probation/parole work consists primarily of four functions: (1) presentence investigations, (2) other intake procedures, (3) diagnosis and needs assessment, and (4) client supervision. The tasks performed by probation and parole officers are often quite similar, and some jurisdictions combine the roles of both into one job.
- Intermediate sanctions, which are sometimes termed *alternative sentencing strategies*, employ sentencing alternatives that fall somewhere between outright imprisonment and simple probationary release back into the community. These sanctions include shock incarceration, intensive supervision, and home confinement with electronic monitoring (also referred to as *remote location monitoring*). Intermediate sanctions have three distinct advantages: (1) They are less expensive than imprisonment; (2) they are "socially cost-effective" because they keep the offender in the community; and (3) they provide flexibility in terms of resources, time of involvement, and place of service.
- In recent years, parole and sometimes probation have been criticized for increasing the risk of community victimization by known offenders. In response, many states have eliminated or significantly curtailed parole opportunities. The future of parole may lie in an emerging concept of reentry that envisions successfully transitioning released inmates into the community using a variety of resources, including institutional and community programs.

KEY TERMS

caseload, 396
community corrections, 385
community service, 399
conditional release, 393
conditions of parole (probation), 389
discretionary release, 388
home confinement, 400
intensive probation supervision (IPS), 399
intermediate sanctions, 397
mandatory release, 389
medical parole, 389
mixed sentence, 399
parole, 388
parole board, 388
parole (probation) violation, 389
parole revocation, 390
probation, 385
probation revocation, 387
reentry, 388
reentry courts, 405
remote location monitoring, 400
restitution, 390
revocation hearing, 392
shock incarceration, 398
shock probation, 398
split sentence, 398

KEY CASES

***Bearden* v. *Georgia*, 393**
***Escoe* v. *Zerbst*, 393**
***Gagnon* v. *Scarpelli*, 393**
***Greenholtz* v. *Nebraska Penal Inmates*, 393**
***Griffin* v. *Wisconsin*, 393**
***Mempa* v. *Rhay*, 393**
***Minnesota* v. *Murphy*, 393**
***Morrissey* v. *Brewer*, 393**
***Pennsylvania Board of Probation and Parole* v. *Scott*, 392**
***Samson* v. *California*, 393**
***U.S.* v. *Knights*, 393**

QUESTIONS FOR REVIEW

1. What is probation? How did it develop? What purpose does it serve?
2. What is parole? How do probation and parole differ? How are they alike?
3. List and explain the advantages and disadvantages of probation and parole.
4. Describe significant court cases that have had an impact on the practice of probation and parole.
5. What do probation and parole officers do? What role do probation officers play in the sentencing of convicted offenders?
6. What are intermediate sanctions? How do they differ from more traditional forms of sentencing? What advantages do they offer?
7. How are probation and parole changing? What does the future hold for them?

QUESTIONS FOR REFLECTION

1. What significance does the contemporary concept of prisoner reentry hold for today's corrections administrators? For society? How do the terms *reentry* and *parole* differ?
2. What corrections philosophy originally supported the idea of indeterminate sentencing and parole? Does that philosophy still have merit today? Why or why not?
3. Do you believe, as some do, that traditional parole has been a failure? Explain.

NOTES

i. Jeremy Travis and Sarah Lawrence, *Beyond the Prison Gates: The State of Parole in America* (Washington, DC: Urban Institute Press, 2002), p. 3.
ii. Debbie Dawes, *The National Institute of Justice's Evaluation of Second Chance Act Adult Reentry Courts: Program Characteristics and Preliminary Themes from Year 1* (Washington, DC: Bureau of Justice Assistance, 2013).

1. President's Commission on Law Enforcement and Administration of Justice, *The Challenge of Crime in A Free Society* (Washington, DC: 1967, USGPO), p. 164.
2. Daniel Chacon, "Case Manager Predicted Ebel Would Reoffend," *Colorado Springs Gazette*, March 28, 2013, http://www.gazette.com/articles/known-152842-manager-arrived.html (accessed March 29, 2013).
3. Kirk Mitchell, Lynn Bartels, and Kurtis Lee, "Evan Ebel Out of Prison Early Thanks to 2011 Colorado Law," *Denver Post*, http://www.denverpost.com/breakingnews/ci_22896714/evan-ebel-out-prison-early-thanks-2011-colorado (accessed March 29, 2013).
4. "Sentiment Mounts to Halt Parole Hearings," *The Boston Globe*, January 7, 2011, http://www.boston.com/news/local/massachusetts/articles/2011/01/07/officers_death_brings_call_for_a_halt_in_parole_hearings (accessed June 1, 2011).
5. James M. Byrne, *Probation*, National Institute of Justice Crime File Series Study Guide (Washington, DC: NIJ, 1988), p. 1.
6. Alexander B. Smith and Louis Berlin, *Introduction to Probation and Parole* (St. Paul, MN: West, 1976), p. 75.
7. John Augustus, *First Probation Officer: John Augustus' Original Report on His Labors—1852* (Montclair, NJ: Patterson-Smith, 1972).
8. Smith and Berlin, *Introduction to Probation and Parole*, p. 77.
9. Ibid., p. 80.
10. George C. Killinger, Hazel B. Kerper, and Paul F. Cromwell, Jr., *Probation and Parole in the Criminal Justice System* (St. Paul, MN: West, 1976), p. 25.
11. Laura M. Maruschak and Erika Parks, *Probation and Parole in the United States, 2011* (Washington, DC: Bureau of Justice Statistics, November 2012).
12. Ibid.
13. Jodi M. Brown and Patrick A. Langan, *Felony Sentences in the United States, 1996* (Washington, DC: Bureau of Justice Statistics, 1999).
14. "Woman Gets Probation for Shooting Fiancé," Associated Press, April 16, 1992, p. 9A.
15. Maruschak and Parks, *Probation and Parole in the United States, 2011*.
16. Laura M. Maruschak and Erika Parks, *Probation and Parole in the United States, 2011* (Washington, DC: Bureau of Justice Statistics, November, 2012), http://www.bjs.gov/content/pub/pdf/ppus11.pdf (accessed August 10, 2013), p. 6.
17. This section owes much to Sanford Bates, "The Establishment and Early Years of the Federal Probation System," *Federal Probation* (June 1987), pp. 4–9.
18. *Ex parte United States*, 242 U.S. 27 (1916).
19. Bates, "The Establishment and Early Years of the Federal Probation System," p. 6.
20. U.S. Probation and Pretrial Services System, *Year-in-Review Report: Fiscal Year 2004* (Washington, DC: U.S. Probation and Pretrial Services System, 2005).
21. See Brian A. Reaves and Timothy C. Hart, *Federal Law Enforcement Officers, 2000* (Washington, DC: Bureau of Justice Statistics, 2002), p. 4, from which some of the wording in this paragraph has been adapted.
22. John M. Hughes, "We're Back on Track: Preparing for the Next 50 Years," *Federal Probation*, Vol. 75, No. 2 (September 2011), http://www.uscourts.gov/uscourts/FederalCourts/PPS/Fedprob/2011-09/back_on_track.html (accessed August 28, 2013).
23. Adapted from Timothy A. Hughes, Doris James Wilson, and Allen J. Beck, *Trends in State Parole, 1990–2000* (Washington, DC: Bureau of Justice Statistics, 2001), p. 1.
24. Justice Policy Institute, "How to Safely Reduce Prison Populations and Support People Returning to their Communities," June 2010, p. 4.
25. Hughes, Wilson, and Beck, *Trends in State Parole, 1990–2000*.
26. California Assembly Bill 109.
27. California Department of Corrections and Rehabilitation, "Parole Revocations," http://www.cdcr.ca.gov/realignment/Parole-Revocations.html (accessed April 5, 2013).
28. Ibid.
29. Ibid.
30. Maruschak and Parks, *Probation and Parole in the United States, 2011*.
31. Ibid., Table 14.
32. "The Effectiveness of Felony Probation: Results from an Eastern State," *Justice Quarterly* (December 1991), pp. 525–543.
33. United States Parole Commission, *FY 2013 Performance Budget* (Washington, DC: USPC, February 2012).

34. State of Georgia, Board of Pardons and Paroles, "Adult Offender Sanction Costs for Fiscal Year 2001," http://www.pap.state.ga.us/otisweb/corrcost.html (accessed March 1, 2004).
35. See Andrew von Hirsch and Kathleen J. Hanrahan, *Abolish Parole?* (Washington, DC: Law Enforcement Assistance Administration, 1978).
36. Theresa A. Severance, "Preparing for Re-entry: Challenges and Strategies," *Women, Girls & Criminal Justice*, Vol. 8, No. 3 (April/May 2007), p. 1.
37. P. O'Brien, *Making It in the "Free World": Women in Transition from Prison* (Albany: State University of New York Press, 2001).
38. *Griffin* v. *Wisconsin*, 483 U.S. 868, 107 S.Ct. 3164 (1987).
39. *Pennsylvania Board of Probation and Parole* v. *Scott*, 524 U.S. 357 (1998).
40. Maruschak and Parks, *Probation and Parole in the United States, 2011*, Table 7.
41. Robyn L. Cohen, *Probation and Parole Violators in State Prison, 1991* (Washington, DC: Bureau of Justice Statistics, 1995).
42. California Department of Corrections and Rehabilitation, Division of Adult Parole Operations, "Non-Revocable Parole," http://www.cdcr.ca.gov/Parole/Non_Revocable_Parole/index.html (accessed June 5, 2011).
43. *Harlow* v. *Clatterbuick*, 30 CrL. 2364 (VA S.Ct. 1986); *Santangelo* v. *State*, 426 N.Y.S.2d 931 (1980); *Welch* v. *State*, 424 N.Y.S.2d 774 (1980); and *Thompson* v. *County of Alameda*, 614 P.2d 728 (1980).
44. *Tarter* v. *State of New York*, 38 CrL. 2364 (NY S.Ct. 1986); *Grimm* v. *Arizona Board of Pardons and Paroles*, 115 Arizona 260, 564 P.2d 1227 (1977); and *Payton* v. *U.S.*, 636 F.2d 132 (5th Cir. 1981).
45. Rolando del Carmen, *Potential Liabilities of Probation and Parole Officers* (Cincinnati, OH: Anderson, 1986), p. 89.
46. See, for example, *Semler* v. *Psychiatric Institute*, 538 F.2d 121 (4th Cir. 1976).
47. *Minnesota* v. *Murphy*, 465 U.S. 420 (1984).
48. National Advisory Commission on Criminal Justice Standards and Goals, *Task Force Report: Corrections* (Washington, DC: U.S. Government Printing Office, 1973).
49. Council of State Governments Justice Center, *The Impact of Probation and Parole Populations on Arrests in Four California Cities* (New York, 2013).
50. National Institute of Justice, *Stress among Probation and Parole Officers and What Can Be Done about It* (Washington, DC: NIJ, 2005).
51. Ibid., p. 1.
52. Ibid., p. ii.
53. From the introduction to James Austin, Michael Jones, and Melissa Bolyard, *The Growing Use of Jail Boot Camps: The Current State of the Art* (Washington, DC: National Institute of Justice, 1993), p. 1.
54. Michael McCarthy and Jodi Upton, "Athletes Lightly Punished after Their Day in Court," *USA Today*, May 4, 2006.
55. Sentencing Project, *Changing the Terms of Sentencing: Defense Counsel and Alternative Sentencing Services* (Washington, DC: Sentencing Project, no date).
56. Joan Petersilia, *Expanding Options for Criminal Sentencing* (Santa Monica, CA: RAND Corporation, 1987).
57. Ohio Revised Code, Section 2946.06.1 (July 1965).
58. Lawrence Greenfeld, *Probation and Parole, 1984* (Washington, DC: U.S. Government Printing Office, 1986).
59. Harry Allen et al., *Probation and Parole in America* (New York: Free Press, 1985), p. 88.
60. For a good overview of such programs, especially as they apply to juvenile corrections, see Doris Layton MacKenzie et al., *A National Study Comparing the Environments of Boot Camps with Traditional Facilities for Juvenile Offenders* (Washington, DC: National Institute of Justice, 2001).
61. Doris Layton MacKenzie and Deanna Bellew Ballow, "Shock Incarceration Programs in State Correctional Jurisdictions—An Update," *NIJ Reports* (May/June 1989), pp. 9–10.
62. "Shock Incarceration Marks a Decade of Expansion," *Corrections Compendium* (September 1996), pp. 10–28.
63. National Institute of Justice, *Multisite Evaluation of Shock Incarceration* (Washington, DC: NIJ, 1995).
64. Richard Willing, "U.S. Prisons to End Boot-Camp Program," *USA Today*, February 3, 2005, http://usatoday30.usatoday.com/news/nation/2005-02-03-boot-camps_x.htm (accessed July 1, 2013).
65. See, Nevada Department of Corrections, "Three Lakes Valley Boot Camp," http://www.doc.nv.gov/?q=node/36 (accessed July 5, 2013).
66. Wyoming Department of Corrections, "Youthful Offender Program (Wyoming Boot Camp), http://doc.state.wy.us/institutions/whcc/boot_camp_whcc.html (accessed July 4, 2013).
67. Douglas C. McDonald, *Restitution and Community Service*, National Institute of Justice Crime File Series Study Guide (Washington, DC: NIJ, 1988).
68. Richard J. Maher and Henry E. Dufour, "Experimenting with Community Service: A Punitive Alternative to Imprisonment," *Federal Probation* (September 1987), pp. 22–27.
69. James P. Levine, Michael C. Musheno, and Dennis J. Palumbo, *Criminal Justice in America: Law in Action* (New York: John Wiley, 1986), p. 549.
70. Billie S. Erwin and Lawrence A. Bennett, "New Dimensions in Probation: Georgia's Experience with Intensive Probation Supervision," National Institute of Justice Research in Brief (Washington, DC: NIJ, 1987).
71. Probation Division, State of Georgia, "Intensive and Specialized Probation Supervision," http://www.dcor.state.ga.us/Probation-Division/html (accessed March 2, 2009).
72. Crystal A. Garcia, "Using Palmer's Global Approach to Evaluate Intensive Supervision Programs: Implications for Practice," *Corrections Management Quarterly*, Vol. 4, No. 4 (2000), pp. 60–69.
73. Joan Petersilia, *House Arrest*, National Institute of Justice Crime File Series Study Guide (Washington, DC: NIJ, 1988).
74. Darren Gowen, "Remote Location Monitoring: A Supervision Strategy to Enhance Risk Control," *Federal Probation*, Vol. 65, No. 2 (September 2001), p. 39.
75. Alan Duke, "Lindsay Lohan Sentenced in Theft Case," CNN, May 11, 2011, http://edition.cnn.com/2011/SHOWBIZ/celebrity.news.gossip/05/11/lohan.sentence (Accessed June 1, 2011).
76. *Electronic Monitoring*, TDCJ-CJAD Agency Brief (Austin: Texas Department of Criminal Justice, March 1999).
77. Texas Department of Criminal Justice, Parole Division, "Contract Information: Electronic Monitoring," http://www.tdcj.state.tx.us/parole/parole-contracts/parolecont-em.htm (accessed September 28, 2010).
78. Marc Renzema and David T. Skelton, *The Use of Electronic Monitoring by Criminal Justice Agencies, 1989* (Washington, DC: National Institute of Justice, 1990).
79. U.S. Probation and Pretrial Services, *Court and Community* (Washington, DC: Administrative Office of the U.S. Courts, 2000).
80. James Kilgore, "The Rise of Electronic Monitoring in Criminal Justice," *Counter Punch*, April 30, 2012 (accessed August 3, 2013).
81. "Satellites Tracking People on Parole," Associated Press, April 13, 1999.

82. U.S. Probation and Pretrial Services, "Home Confinement," http://www.uscourts.gov/misc/cchome.pdf (accessed March 22, 2009).

83. State of Georgia Board of Pardons and Paroles, "Adult Offender Sanction Costs for Fiscal Year 2001," http://www.pap.state.ga.us/otisweb/corrcost.html (accessed September 20, 2002).

84. Construction costs are for cells classified as "medium security."

85. "BI Home Escort: Electronic Monitoring System," advertising brochure (Boulder, CO: BI Inc., no date).

86. William Bales, et al., *A Quantitative and Qualitative Assessment of Electronic Monitoring* (Washington, DC: National Institute of Justice, U.S. Department of Justice, May 2010), http://www.ncjrs.gov/pdffiles1/nij/grants/230530.pdf (accessed May 20, 2013).

87. Stephen V. Gies, et al., *Monitoring High-Risk Sex Offenders with GPS Technology: An Evaluation of the California Supervision Program, Final Report* (Washington, DC: National Institute of Justice, 2012).

88. James A. Inciardi, *Criminal Justice*, 2nd ed. (New York: Harcourt Brace Jovanovich, 1987), p. 664.

89. E. Ann Carson and William J. Sabol, *Prisoners in 2011* (Washington, DC: Bureau of Justice Statistics, 2012), p. 2.

90. Patrick A. Langan and David J. Levin, *National Recidivism Study of Released Prisoners: Recidivism of Prisoners Released in 1994* (Washington, DC: Bureau of Justice Statistics, 2002).

91. Bureau of Justice Statistics, "Forty-Two Percent of State Parole Discharges Were Successful," October 3, 2001, http://www.ojp.usdoj.gov/newsroom/2001/bjs01181.html (accessed July 3, 2007).

92. Council of States Government Justice Center, *The Impact of Probation and Parole Populations on Arrests in Four California Cities* (Lexington, KY: CSG, 2013).

93. Urban Institute and RTI International, *National Portrait of SVORI* (Washington, DC: Urban Institute Press, 2004).

94. California Assembly Bill 109.

95. Abby Sewell, "L.A. County Seeing High-Risk Offenders Entering Its Probation System," *Los Angeles Times*, November 30, 2012, http://articles.latimes.com/2012/nov/30/local/la-me-realignment-20121130 (accessed May 26, 2013).

96. American Probation and Parole Association and the Association of Paroling Authorities International, *Abolishing Parole: Why the Emperor Has No Clothes* (Lexington, KY: APPA, 1995).

97. Much of this information is taken from Re-entry Policy Council, *Report of the Re-entry Policy Council: Charting the Safe and Successful Return of Prisoners to the Community—Executive Summary* (New York: Council of State Governments, 2005), http://www.reentrypolicy.org/executivesummary.html (accessed July 10, 2009).

98. Langan and Levin, *National Recidivism Study of Released Prisoners*; and *Does Parole Work? Analyzing the Impact of Postprison Supervision on Rearrest Outcomes* (Washington, DC: Urban Institute, 2005).

99. Esther Griswold, Jessica Pearson, and Lanae Davis, *Testing a Modification Process for Incarcerated Parents* (Denver, CO: Center for Policy Research), pp. 11–12.

100. Urban Institute and RTI International, *National Portrait of SVORI*, from which some of the wording in this section is adapted.

101. See Laura Winterfield and Susan Brumbaugh, *The Multi-site Evaluation of the Serious and Violent Offender Reentry Initiative* (Washington, DC: Urban Institute Press, 2005).

102. Pamela K. Lattimore, et al., *Prisoner Reentry Services: What Worked for SVORI Evaluation Participants?* (Washington, DC: National Institute of Justice, 2012).

103. Wording in this paragraph is adapted from Debbie Dawes, *The National Institute of Justice's Evaluation of Second Chance Act Adult Reentry Courts: Program Characteristics and Preliminary Themes from Year 1* (Washington, DC: Bureau of Justice Assistance, 2013).

104. Lane County (Oregon) Circuit Court, "Drug Court," http://www.ojd.state.or.us/lan/drugcrt/index.htm (accessed May 29, 2009).

105. See, for example, Jeremy Travis, *But They All Come Back: Facing the Challenges of Prisoner Reentry* (Washington, DC: Urban Institute Press, 2005).

106. Bureau of Justice Assistance, *Second Chance Act State, Local, and Tribal Reentry Courts FY2010 Competitive Grant Announcement* (Washington, DC: U.S. Department of Justice, Office of Justice Programs, 2010), http://www.ojp.usdoj.gov/BJA/grant/10SecondChanceCourtsSol.pdf (accessed May 3, 2013).

107. Public Law 110-199.

108. Congressional Budget Office, "Cost Estimate: S. 1060, Second Chance Act of 2007," p. 4, http://www.cbo.gov/ftpdocs/86xx/doc8620/s1060.pdf (accessed August 28, 2008).

109. See, "Keeping Parolees Out of Prison," *New York Times*, December 28, 2012, http://www.nytimes.com/2012/12/29/opinion/keeping-parolees-out-of-prison.html (accessed June 1, 2013).

110. Reinventing Probation Council, *"Broken Windows" Probation: The Next Step in Fighting Crime* (New York: Manhattan Institute, 1999); and Reinventing Probation Council, *Transforming Probation through Leadership: The "Broken Windows" Model* (New York: Center for Civic Innovation at the Manhattan Institute, 2000), from which some of the quoted material in these paragraphs comes.

111. Public Safety Performance Project, *Putting Public Safety First: 13 Strategies for Successful Supervision and Reentry* (Washington, DC: Pew Center on the States, 2008).

112. Jesse Jannetta, Brian Elderbroom, Amy Solomon, Megan Cahill, and Barbara Parthasarthy, *An Evolving Field: Findings from the 2008 Parole Practices Survey* (Washington, DC: Urban Institute, 2009).

113. Ibid., p. 22.

114. Ibid., p. 2.

115. California Senate Bill 678 (2009).

116. National Institute of Corrections, *Evidence-Based Policy, Practice, and Decisionmaking: Implications for Paroling Authorities* (Washington, DC: U.S. Department of Justice, 2011).

117. Kevin McEvoy, "Hope: A Swift and Certain Process for Probationers," *National Institute of Justice Journal*, No. 269 (March 2012), pp. 16–17, from which some of the wording in the next two paragraphs is taken.

© Kletr/Fotolia

13 PRISONS AND JAILS

OUTLINE

- Introduction
- Early Punishments
- The Emergence of Prisons
- Prisons Today
- Jails
- Private Prisons

LEARNING OBJECTIVES

After reading this chapter, you should be able to

- Describe the history of punishment, concluding with its impact on the modern philosophy of corrections.
- List major milestones in the historical development of prisons.
- Describe the purpose and major characteristics of today's prisons.
- Summarize the role jails currently play in American corrections and issues jail administrators face.
- Describe the current and likely future roles of private prisons.

Everybody wants to send people to prison, (but) nobody wants to pay for it.

CALIFORNIA GOVERNOR JERRY BROWN, Speaking in 2013[1]

■ **prison** A state or federal confinement facility that has custodial authority over adults sentenced to confinement.

■ ***lex talionis*** The law of retaliation, often expressed as "an eye for an eye" or "like for like."

Introduction

In 2011, a two-person panel of the California Board of Parole Hearings denied medical parole to 42-year-old Steven Martinez, a convicted rapist.[2] Martinez, a quadriplegic, was the first inmate to be considered for medical parole under a new law intended to save the state money by releasing inmates who are permanently incapacitated. Paralyzed during a prison knife attack that severed his spinal cord ten years ago, Martinez was serving a 157-year sentence for numerous felonies that he committed during the violent rape of a woman in 1998. The medical care he needs had been costing the state $625,000 per year.[3] In deciding to deny Martinez's parole, parole commissioner John Peck stated, "This panel finds that he is a violent person who can use other people to carry out threats and would be a public safety threat to those attending to him outside prison walls." Even so, more than a year later, the U.S. Court of Appeals for the Fourth Circuit ordered that Martinez be released. His parents, who are still living, agreed to care for him in their San Diego home.[4]

Martinez's case illustrates the tension that exists today between the need to cut correctional costs and the concern over public safety. The fact that Martinez was denied parole seemed especially surprising to some observers because the denial came almost immediately after the U.S. Supreme Court found that California's prisons are dangerously overcrowded and upheld an earlier order by a three-judge federal panel that state officials must find a way to reduce the current 143,335-inmate population by roughly 33,000.[5] That order, originally issued in 2001, was based on a determination that overcrowding in California's prisons had led to conditions so egregious that they violate the Constitution's Eighth Amendment ban on cruel and unusual punishment.[6] In 2011, the High Court agreed that prison overcrowding left the state unable to deliver minimal care to prisoners with serious medical and mental health problems and produced "needless suffering and death." The court gave California officials two years to comply with the order to reduce prison populations. In 2013, California Governor Jerry Brown said that the state had diverted a significant number of newly sentenced low-level felons from prison and into county jails and local probation programs, and declared that federal oversight of the California prison must come to an end. Federal courts are still reviewing his request as this book goes to press.[7]

Early Punishments

The use of **prisons** as places where convicted offenders serve time as punishment for breaking the law is a relatively new development in the handling of offenders. In fact, the emphasis on *time served* as the essence of criminal punishment is scarcely 200 years old.

Before the development of prisons, early punishments were often cruel and torturous. An example is the graphic and unsettling description of a man broken on the rack in 1721, which is provided by Camden Pelham in his *Chronicles of Crime*.[8] The offender, Nathaniel Hawes, a domestic servant in the household of a wealthy nobleman, had stolen a sheep. When the overseer of the household discovered the offense, Hawes "shot him dead." This is Pelham's description of what happened next: "For these offences, of course, he was sentenced to be broken alive upon the rack, without the benefit of the *coup de grâce*, or mercy-stroke. Informed of the dreadful sentence, he composedly laid himself down upon his back on a strong cross, on which, with his arms and legs extended, he was fastened by ropes. The executioner, having by now with a hatchet chopped off his left hand, next took up a heavy iron bar, with which, by repeated blows, he broke his bones to shivers, till the marrow, blood, and splinters flew about the field; but the prisoner never uttered a groan nor a sigh! The ropes being next unlashed, I imagined him dead . . . till . . . he writhed himself from the cross. When he fell on the grass . . . he rested his head on part of the timbar, and asked the by-standers for a pipe of tobacco, which was infamously answered by kicking and spitting on him. He then begged his head might be chopped off, but to no purpose." Pelham goes on to relate how the condemned man then engaged in conversation with onlookers, recounting details of his trial. At one point he asked one of those present to repay money he had loaned him, saying, "Don't you perceive, I am to be kept alive." After six hours, Pelham says, Hawes was put out of his misery by a soldier assigned to guard the proceedings. "He was knocked on the head by the . . . sentinel; and having been raised upon a gallows, the vultures were busy picking out the eyes of the mangled corpse, in the skull of which was clearly discernible the mark of the soldier's musket."

This gruesome tale may seem foreign to modern readers—as though it describes an event that happened in a barbarous time long ago or in a place far away. However, a mere 200 years ago, before the emergence of imprisonment, convicted offenders were routinely subjected to physical punishment that often resulted in death. Although fines were sometimes levied, corporal punishments were the most common form of criminal punishment and generally fit the doctrine of ***lex talionis*** (the law of retaliation). Under *lex talionis*, the convicted offender was sentenced to suffer a punishment that closely approximated the original injury. This rule of "an eye for an eye, a tooth for a tooth," generally duplicated the offense. Hence, if a person blinded another, he was blinded in return. Murderers were executed, sometimes in a way tailored to approximate the method they had used in committing the crime.

Follow the author's tweets about the latest crime and justice news @schmalleger.

workhouse An early form of imprisonment whose purpose was to instill habits of industry in the idle.

Flogging

Historically, the most widely used of physical punishment was flogging.[9] The Bible mentions instances of whipping, and Christ himself was scourged. Whipping was widely used in England throughout the Middle Ages, and some offenders were said to have been beaten as they ran through the streets, hands tied behind their backs. American colonists carried the practice of flogging with them to the New World.

The last officially sanctioned flogging of a criminal offender in the United States was in Delaware on June 16, 1952, when a burglar received 20 lashes,[10] but the practice of whipping continues in other parts of the world. Amnesty International reports its use in various countries for political and other prisoners. In 1994, the flogging in Singapore of Michael Fay, an American teenager convicted of spray-painting parked cars, caused an international outcry from opponents of corporal punishment. But in parts of the United States some people reacted in just the opposite way. After the Fay flogging (called *caning* in Singapore because it was carried out with a bamboo rod), eight states entertained legislation to endorse whipping or paddling as a criminal sanction. For example, Mississippi legislators proposed paddling graffitists and petty thieves; Tennessee lawmakers considered punishing vandals and burglars by public caning on courthouse steps; and Louisiana looked into the possibility of ordering parents (or a corrections officer if the parents refused) to spank their children in judicial chambers.[11] None of the proposals made it into law.

Mutilation

Whereas flogging is a painful punishment whose memory might deter repeat offenses, mutilation is primarily a strategy of specific deterrence that makes it difficult or impossible for individuals to commit future crimes. Throughout history, various societies have amputated the hands of thieves and robbers, blinded spies, and castrated rapists. Blasphemers had their tongues ripped out, and pickpockets suffered broken fingers. Extensive mutilation, which included cutting off the ears and ripping out the tongue, was instituted in eleventh-century Britain and imposed on hunters who poached on royal lands.[12]

Today, some countries in the Arab world, including Iran and Saudi Arabia, still rely on a limited use of mutilation as a penalty to incapacitate selected offenders. Mutilation also creates a general deterrent by providing potential offenders with walking examples of the consequences of crime.

Branding

Before modern technology and the advent of mechanized record keeping, branding was used to readily identify convicted offenders and to warn others with whom they might come in contact of their dangerous potential.

The Romans, Greeks, French, British, and many others have all used branding at one time or another. Harry Barnes and Negley Teeters, early writers on the history of the criminal justice system, report that branding in the American colonies was customary for certain crimes, with first offenders being branded on the hand and repeat offenders receiving an identifying mark on the forehead.[13] Women were rarely marked physically, although they may have been shamed and forced to wear marked clothing. Nathaniel Hawthorne's *The Scarlet Letter* is a report on that practice, where the central figure is required to wear a red letter *A* embroidered on her dress, signifying adultery.

Public Humiliation

Many early punishments were designed to humiliate offenders in public and to allow members of the community an opportunity for vengeance. The stocks and pillory were two such punishments. The pillory closed over the head and hands and held the offender in a standing position, while the stocks kept the person sitting with the head free. A few hundred years ago, each European town had its own stocks or pillory, usually located in some central square or alongside a major thoroughfare.

Offenders sent to the stocks or pillory could expect to be heckled and spit on by passersby. Other citizens might gather to throw tomatoes or rotten eggs. On occasion, citizens who were particularly outraged by the magnitude or nature of the offense would throw rocks at the offender, ending his life. Retribution remained a community prerogative, and citizens wielded the power of final sentencing. The pillory was still used in Delaware as late as 1905.[14]

The ducking stool, used in colonial times to punish gossips, provided another form of public humiliation. The offender was tied to it and lowered into a river or lake, turning nearly upside down like a duck searching for food underwater.

Workhouses

Sixteenth-century Europe suffered severe economic upheaval, caused partly by wars and partly by the approach of the Industrial Revolution, which was soon to sweep the continent. By 1550, thousands of unemployed and vagrant people were scouring towns and villages seeking food and shelter. It was not long before they depleted the economic reserves of churches, which were the primary social relief agencies of the time.

In the belief that poverty was caused by laziness, governments were quick to create **workhouses** designed to instill "habits of industry" in the unemployed. The first workhouse in Europe opened in 1557 and taught work habits, not specific

FARZANEH KHADEMIAN/KRT/Newscom

A man undergoing public punishment for a transgression of the Islamic code in Tehran, Iran. Other than the death penalty, corporal punishment for crime has been abolished in the United States, but it remains common in some Muslim nations. Might similar corporal punishments ever again have a place in Western criminal justice? Why or why not?

skills. Inmates were made to fashion their own furniture, build additions to the facility, and raise gardens. When the number of inmates exceeded the volume of useful work to be done, make-work projects, including treadmills and cranks, were invented to keep them busy.

Workhouses were judged successful, if only because they were constantly filled. By 1576, Parliament decreed that every county in England should build a workhouse. Although workhouses were forerunners of our modern prisons, they did not incarcerate criminal offenders—only vagrants and the destitute. Nor were they designed to punish, but served instead to reinforce the value of hard work.

Exile

Many societies have banished criminals. The French sent criminal offenders to Devil's Island, and the Russians used Siberia for centuries for the same purpose. England sent convicts to the American colonies beginning in 1618. The British program of exile, known as *transportation*, served the dual purpose of providing a captive labor force for development of the colonies while assuaging growing English sentiments opposing corporal punishments. In 1776, however, the American Revolution forced the practice to end, and British penology shifted to the use of aging ships, called *hulks*, as temporary prisons. Hulks were anchored in harbors throughout England and served as floating confinement facilities even after transportation (to other parts of the globe) resumed.

In 1787, only 17 years after Captain Cook had discovered the continent, Australia became the new port of call for English prisoners. The name of Captain William Bligh, governor of the New South Wales penal colony, survives today as a symbol of the difficult conditions and the rough men and women of those times.

The Emergence of Prisons

The identity of the world's first true prison is unknown, but at some point, penalties for crime came to include incarceration. During the Middle Ages, "punitive imprisonment appears to have been introduced into Europe . . . by the Christian Church in the incarceration of certain offenders against canon law."[15] Similarly, debtors' prisons existed throughout Europe during the fifteenth and sixteenth centuries, although they housed inmates who had violated the civil law rather than criminals. John Howard,

■ **Pennsylvania system** A form of imprisonment developed by the Pennsylvania Quakers around 1790 as an alternative to corporal punishments. This style of imprisonment made use of solitary confinement and encouraged rehabilitation.

an early prison reformer, mentions prisons housing criminal offenders in Hamburg, Germany; Bern, Switzerland; and Florence, Italy, in his 1777 book, *State of Prisons*.[16] Early efforts to imprison offenders led to the founding of the Hospice of San Michele, a papal prison that opened in 1704, and the Maison de Force, begun at Ghent, Belgium, in 1773. The Hospice was actually a residential school for delinquent boys and housed 60 youngsters at its opening. Both facilities stressed reformation over punishment and became early alternatives to the use of physical and public punishments.

Near the end of the eighteenth century, the concept of imprisonment as punishment for crime reached its fullest expression in the United States. Imprisonment *as* punishment differs significantly from the concept of imprisonment *for* punishment, and embodiment of this concept in American penal institutions represented the beginning of a new chapter in corrections reform. Soon after they opened, U.S. prisons came to serve as models for European reformers searching for ways to humanize criminal punishment. For that reason, and to better appreciate how today's prisons operate, it is important to understand the historical development of the prison movement in the United States. Figure 13-1 depicts the stages through which American prisons progressed following the introduction around 1790 of the concept of incarceration as a punishment for crime. Each historical era is discussed in the pages that follow.

The Penitentiary Era (1790–1825)

In 1790, Philadelphia's Walnut Street Jail was converted into a penitentiary by the Pennsylvania Quakers. The Quakers viewed incarceration as an opportunity for penance and saw prisons as places wherein offenders might make amends with society and accept responsibility for their misdeeds. The philosophy of imprisonment begun by the Quakers, heavily imbued with elements of rehabilitation and deterrence, carries over to the present day.[17]

Inmates of the Philadelphia Penitentiary were expected to wrestle alone with the evils they harbored. Penance was the primary vehicle through which rehabilitation was anticipated, and a study of the Bible was strongly encouraged. Solitary confinement was the rule, and the penitentiary was architecturally designed to minimize contact between inmates and between inmates and staff. Exercise was allowed in small high-walled yards attached to

MPI/Getty Images

The Walnut Street Jail, America's first "true" prison, circa 1800. What philosophical principles were behind the Quaker penitentiary concept?

each cell. Eventually, handicrafts were introduced into the prison setting, permitting prisoners to work in their cells.

Fashioned after the Philadelphia model, the Western Penitentiary opened in Pittsburgh in 1826, and the Eastern Penitentiary opened in Cherry Hill, Pennsylvania, three years later. Solitary confinement and individual cells, supported by a massive physical structure with impenetrable walls, became synonymous with the Pennsylvania system of imprisonment. Supporters heralded the **Pennsylvania system** as one that was humane and provided inmates with the opportunity for rehabilitation. Many well-known figures of the day spoke out in support of the Pennsylvania system, among them Benjamin Franklin and Benjamin Rush—both of whom were influential members of the Philadelphia Society for Alleviating the Miseries of Public Prisons.[18]

The Mass Prison Era (1825–1876)

Vermont, Massachusetts, Maryland, and New York all built institutions modeled after Pennsylvania's penitentiaries. As prison populations began to grow, however, solitary confinement became prohibitively expensive. One of the first large prisons to abandon the Pennsylvania model was the New York State Prison at Auburn. Auburn introduced the congregate but silent system, under which inmates lived, ate, and worked together in enforced silence. This

Prison Era

	The Penitentiary Era	The Mass (Congregate) Prison Era	The Reformatory Era	The Industrial Era	The Punitive Era	The Treatment Era	The Community-based (Decarceration) Era	The Warehousing Era	The Just Deserts Era	The Evidence-Based Era
Year	1790	1825	1876	1890	1935	1945	1967	1980	1995	2012
Philosophy	Rehabilitation, Deterrence	Incapacitation, Deterrence	Rehabilitation	Incapacitation, Restoration	Retribution	Rehabilitation	Restoration, Rehabilitation	Incapacitation	Retribution, Incapacitation, Deterrence	Cost-Effective Workable Solutions
Representative Institutions	Philadelphia Penitentiary Eastern Penitentiary (Cherry Hill, PA) Western Penitentiary (Pittsburgh)	New York State Prison (Auburn, NY)	Elmira Reformatory (Elmira, NY)	Auburn (NY) Sing Sing (NY) Stateville (IL) San Quentin (CA) Attica (NY)	Alcatraz (CA)	Marion (IL)	Massachusetts Youth Services Halfway Houses	Many state and federal prisons	Continues to influence many prisons today	A new and growing emphasis in an era of economic retrenchment

FIGURE 13-1 | Stages of Prison Development in the United States

■ **Auburn system** A form of imprisonment developed in New York State around 1820 that depended on mass prisons, where prisoners were held in congregate fashion and required to remain silent. This style of imprisonment was a primary competitor with the Pennsylvania system.

■ **reformatory style** A late-nineteenth-century correctional model based on the use of the indeterminate sentence and a belief in the possibility of rehabilitation, especially for youthful offenders. The reformatory concept faded with the emergence of industrial prisons around the start of the twentieth century.

style of imprisonment, which came to be known as the **Auburn system**, featured group workshops rather than solitary handicrafts and reintroduced corporal punishments into the handling of offenders. Whereas isolation and enforced idleness were inherent punishments under the early Pennsylvania system, Auburn depended on whipping and hard labor to maintain the rule of silence.[19]

The Auburn prison was the site of an experiment in solitary confinement, which was the basis of the Pennsylvania system. Eighty-three men were placed in small solitary cells on Christmas Day of 1821 and were released in 1823 and 1824. Five of the 83 died, one went insane, another attempted suicide, and the others became "seriously demoralized."[20] Although the Auburn experiment did not accurately simulate the conditions in Pennsylvania (it allowed for no exercise, placed prisoners in tiny cells, and shunned handicrafts—which had been introduced into Pennsylvania's prisons by the time the experiment began), it did provide an effective basis for condemnation of the Pennsylvania system. Partly as a result of the experiment, the Reverend Louis Dwight, an influential prison reformer of the time and the leader of the prestigious Prison Discipline Society of Boston, became an advocate of the Auburn system, citing its lower cost[21] and more humane conditions.[22] The lower cost resulted from the simpler facilities required by mass imprisonment and from group workshops that provided economies of scale unachievable under solitary confinement. Dwight also believed that the Pennsylvania style of imprisonment was unconscionable and inhumane. As a consequence of criticisms fielded by Dwight and others, most American prisons built after 1825 followed the Auburn architectural style and system of prison discipline.

About the same time, however, a number of European governments sent representatives to study the virtues of the two American systems. Interestingly, most concluded that the Pennsylvania system was more conducive to reformation than the Auburn system, and many European prisons adopted a strict separation of inmates. Two French visitors, Gustave de Beaumont and Alexis de Tocqueville, stressed the dangers of what they called "contamination," whereby prisoners housed in Auburn-like prisons could negatively influence one another.[23]

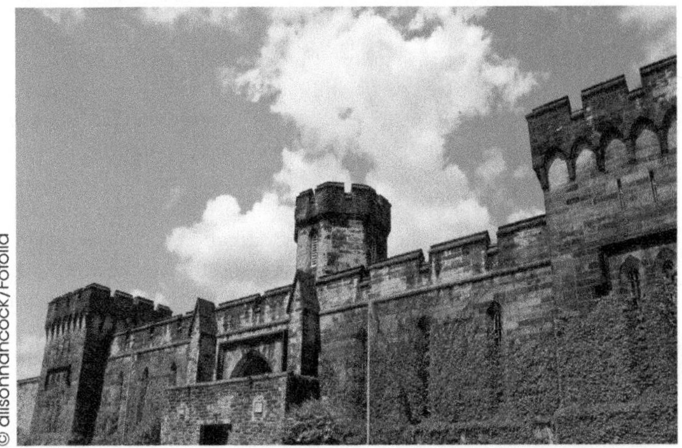

Eastern State Penitentiary in Philadelphia. Built in the 1820s, construction costs totaled $780,000, making it the most expensive public building at that time. Although the penitentiary building today serves only as a tourist attraction, its early-nineteenth-century builders hoped that just the sight of its 30-foot-high, 12-foot-thick walls would be enough to instill fear in the hearts of would-be lawbreakers. Did they achieve their goal?

The Reformatory Era (1876–1890)

With the tension between the Auburn and Pennsylvania systems, American penology existed in an unsettled state for a half century. That tension was resolved in 1876 with the emergence of the **reformatory style**, which grew out of practices innovated by two especially noteworthy corrections leaders of the mid-1880s: Captain Alexander Maconochie and Sir Walter Crofton.

Captain Alexander Maconochie and Norfolk Island

During the early 1840s, Captain Alexander Maconochie served as the warden of Norfolk Island, a prison off the coast of Australia for "doubly condemned" inmates. English prisoners sent to Australia who committed other crimes while there were taken to Norfolk to be segregated from less recalcitrant offenders. Prior to Maconochie's arrival, conditions at Norfolk had been atrocious. Disease and unsanitary conditions were rampant on the island, fights among inmates left many dead and more injured, and the physical facilities were not conducive to good supervision. Maconochie immediately set out to reform the island prison by providing incentives for prisoners to participate in their own reformation.

Maconochie developed a system of marks through which prisoners could earn enough credits to buy their freedom. Bad behavior removed marks from the inmate's ledger, and acceptable behavior added marks. The mark system made possible early

CJ | ISSUES

Chaplain James Finley's Letter from the Ohio Penitentiary, 1850

It is true, there are yet two systems of prison discipline still in use, but both claim to have the two parties—the criminal and society—equally in view. The congregate system, going on the supposition that habits of labor and moral character are the chief desiderata among this class of men, set them to work at those trades for which their physical and mental powers, together with the consideration of their former occupations, may more especially adapt them; religious instruction is also given them by men appointed expressly for the purpose; and they are permitted to labor in large communities, where they can see but not converse with each other, as the friends of this system imagine that social intercourse, of some kind and to some extent, is almost as necessary to man as food. The separate system, on the other hand, looking upon all intercourse between criminals as only evil in its tendency, by which one rogue becomes the instructor or accomplice of another, secludes the convicts from each other but, to atone for this defect, it encourages the visits of good men to the cells of the prisoners; and the officers of these prisons make it a particular point of duty to visit the inmates very frequently themselves. The physical habits of the imprisoned are provided for by such trades as can be carried on by individual industry; a teacher is employed to lead them on in the study of useful branches of education; while the Gospel is regularly taught them, not only by sermons on the Sabbath, but by private efforts of the chaplain in his daily rounds.

Source: James Finley, *Memorials of Prison Life* (Cincinnati: Swormstedt and Poe, 1855).

release and led to a recognition of the indeterminate sentence as a useful tool in the reformation of offenders. Before Maconochie, inmates had been sentenced to determinate sentences specifying a fixed number of years they had to serve before release. The mark system placed responsibility for winning an early release squarely on the inmate. Because of the system's similarity to the later practice of parole, it won for Maconochie the title "father of parole."

Opinion leaders in England, however, saw Maconochie's methods as too lenient. Many pointed out that the indeterminate sentence made possible new lives for criminals in a world of vast opportunity (the Australian continent) at the expense of the British Empire. Amid charges that he coddled inmates, Maconochie was relieved of his duties as warden in 1844.

Sir Walter Crofton and the Irish System

Maconochie's innovations soon came to the attention of Sir Walter Crofton, head of the Irish prison system. Crofton adapted the idea of early release to his program of progressive stages. Inmates who entered Irish prisons had to work their way through four stages. The first, or entry level, involved solitary confinement and dull work. Most prisoners in the first level were housed at Mountjoy Prison in Dublin. The second stage assigned prisoners to Spike Island, where they worked on fortifications. The third stage placed prisoners in field units, which worked directly in the community on public-service projects. Unarmed guards supervised the prisoners. The fourth stage depended on what Crofton called the "ticket of leave." The ticket of leave allowed prisoners to live and work in the community under the occasional supervision of a "moral instructor." It could be revoked at any time up until the expiration of the offender's original sentence.

Crofton was convinced that convicts could not be rehabilitated without successful reintegration into the community. His innovations were closely watched by reformers across Europe. But in 1862, a wave of violent robberies swept England and led to the passage of the 1863 Garotters Act, which mandated whipping for robberies involving violence and longer prison sentences for many other crimes, effectively rolling back the clock on Crofton's innovations, at least in Europe.

The Elmira Reformatory and the Birth of Parole in the United States

In 1865, Gaylord B. Hubbell, warden of Sing Sing Prison in New York, visited Great Britain and studied prisons there. He returned to the United States greatly impressed by the Irish system and recommended that indeterminate sentences be used in American prisons. The New York Prison Association supported Hubbell and called for the creation of a "reformatory" based on the concept of an earned early release if the inmate reformed himself.

When the new National Prison Association held its first conference in 1870 in Cincinnati, it adopted a 37-paragraph Declaration of Principles that called for reformation to replace punishment as the goal of imprisonment. The most significant result of the conference, however, was the move to embody those principles in a reformatory built on American soil.

■ **industrial prison** A correctional model intended to capitalize on the labor of convicts sentenced to confinement.

CJ | ISSUES
An Early Texas Prison

In 1860, an unknown writer described conditions in the Texas Penitentiary at Huntsville as follows:

> By a special enactment of the Legislature, the front of the cell of any prisoner sentenced to solitary confinement for life, is painted black, and his name and sentence distinctly marked thereon. The object would seem to be to infuse a salutary dread into the minds of the other prisoners. Upon the only black-painted cell in the prison was the following inscription, in distinct white letters: William Brown, aged twenty-four years, convicted for murder in Grimes County, spring term, 1858, for which he is now suffering solitary confinement for life. Brown himself, however, was in fact at work in the factory with the other convicts! He entered the Penitentiary in May, 1859, and had been kept in close confinement in his cell, without labor, never being permitted to leave it for any purpose, until about the first of October, when his health was found to have suffered so much that, to preserve his life, he was, under a discretionary power vested in the Directors, released from the rigor of his sentence, and subjected to only the ordinary confinement of the prison. His health has since greatly improved. It is not to be wondered at that his health should decline under the strict enforcement of such a sentence. The cell in which he was confined was the same as to size, ventilation, and light as the rest; and being one of the lower tier of cells, the top of the doorway was some feet below the lower edge of the window upon the opposite side of the corridor in the outside wall. He had even less chance for fresh air than if his cell had been in almost any other location. It is the sight and knowledge of such instances of solitary unemployed confinement as this, and a willful neglect or refusal to inform themselves upon, and recognize, the very wide distinction between the terms separate and solitary, that renders many persons so violently prejudiced against, and opposed to the "Separate System."

Source: *The Journal of Prison Discipline and Philanthropy*, Vol. 15, No. 1 (January 1860), pp. 7–17.

Because reformation was thought most likely among younger people, the Elmira Reformatory accepted only first offenders between the ages of 16 and 30.

In 1876, the Elmira Reformatory opened in Elmira, New York, under the direction of Zebulon Brockway, a leading advocate of indeterminate sentencing and the former superintendent of the Detroit House of Correction. The state of New York had passed an indeterminate sentencing bill that made possible early release for inmates who earned it. However, because reformation was thought most likely among younger people, the Elmira Reformatory accepted only first offenders between the ages of 16 and 30. A system of graded stages required inmates to meet educational, behavioral, and other goals. Schooling was mandatory, and trade training was available in telegraphy, tailoring, plumbing, carpentry, and other areas.

Unfortunately, the reformatory "proved a relative failure and disappointment."[24] Many inmates reentered lives of crime following their release, which called the success of the reformatory ideal into question. Some authors attributed the failure of the reformatory to "the ever-present jailing psychosis"[25] of the prison staff or to an overemphasis on confinement and institutional security rather than reformation, which made it difficult to implement many of the ideals on which the reformatory had been based.

Even though the reformatory was not a success, the principles it established remain important today. Thus, indeterminate sentencing, parole, trade training, education, and the primacy of reformation over punishment all serve as a foundation for ongoing debates about the purpose of imprisonment.

The Industrial Era (1890–1935)

With the failure of the reformatory style of prison, concerns over security and discipline became dominant in American prisons. Inmate populations rose, costs soared, and states began to study practical alternatives. An especially attractive option was found in the potential profitability of inmate labor, and the era of the **industrial prison** in America was born.

Industrial prisons in the northern United States were characterized by thick, high walls; stone or brick buildings; guard towers; and smokestacks rising from within the walls. These prisons smelted steel, manufactured cabinets, molded tires, and turned out many other goods for the open market. Prisons in the South, which had been devastated by the Civil War, tended more toward farm labor and public-works projects. The South, with its labor-intensive agricultural practices, used inmates to replace slaves who had been freed during the war.

The following six systems of inmate labor were in use by the early twentieth century:[26]

- *Contract system.* Private businesses paid to use inmate labor. They provided the raw materials and supervised the manufacturing process inside prison facilities.
- *Piece-price system.* Goods were produced for private businesses under the supervision of prison authorities. Prisons were paid according to the number and quality of the goods manufactured.
- *Lease system.* Prisoners were taken to the work site under the supervision of armed guards. Once there, they were turned over to the private contractor, who employed them and maintained discipline.

■ **state-use system** A form of inmate labor in which items produced by inmates may be sold by or to only state offices. Items that only the state can sell include such things as license plates and hunting licenses, while items sold only to state offices include furniture and cleaning supplies.

■ **Ashurst-Sumners Act** Federal legislation of 1935 that effectively ended the industrial prison era by restricting interstate commerce in prison-made goods.

- *Public-account system.* This system eliminated the use of private contractors. Industries were entirely prison owned, and prison authorities managed the manufacturing process from beginning to end. Goods were sold on the free market.
- ***State-use system*.** Prisoners manufactured only goods that could be sold by or to other state offices, or they provided labor to assist other state agencies.
- *Public-works system.* Prisoners maintained roads and highways, cleaned public parks and recreational facilities, and maintained and restored public buildings.

Large prisons that were built or converted to industrialization included San Quentin in California, Sing Sing and Auburn in New York, and the Illinois State Penitentiary at Stateville. Many prison industries were quite profitable and contributed significantly to state treasuries. Reports from 1932 show that 82,276 prisoners were involved in various forms of prison labor that year, producing products with a total value of $75,369,471—a huge amount considering the worth of the dollar 80 years ago.[27] Beginning as early as the 1830s, however, workers began to complain of being forced to compete with cheap prison labor. In 1834, mechanics in New York filed a petition with the state legislature asking that prison industries paying extremely low wages be eliminated. Labor unions became very well organized and powerful by the early part of the twentieth century, and the Great Depression of the 1930s, during which jobs were scarce, brought with it a call for an end to prison industries.

In 1929, union influence led Congress to pass the Hawes-Cooper Act, which required prison-made goods to conform to the regulations of the states through which they were shipped. Hence states that outlawed the manufacture of free-market goods in their own prisons were effectively protected from prison-made goods that might be imported from other states. The death blow to prison industries, however, came in 1935 with the passage of the **Ashurst-Sumners Act**, which specifically prohibited the interstate transportation and sale of prison goods where state laws forbade them. In consort with the Ashurst-Sumners legislation, and because of economic pressures brought on by the Depression, most states soon passed statutes that curtailed prison manufacturing within their borders, and the industrial era in American corrections came to a close.

Prison Industries Today

Although still hampered by some federal and state laws, prison industries began making a comeback in the latter part of the twentieth century. Under the state-use philosophy, most states still permit the prison manufacture of goods that will be used exclusively by the prison system itself or by other state agencies or that only the state can legitimately sell on the open market. An example of the latter is license plates, the sale of which is a state monopoly. North Carolina provides a good example of a modern state-use system. Its Correction Enterprises operates around 20 inmate-staffed businesses, each of which is self-supporting. North Carolina inmates manufacture prison clothing; raise vegetables and farm animals to feed inmates throughout the state; operate an oil refinery, a forestry service, and a cannery; and manufacture soap, license plates, and some office furniture. All manufactured goods other than license plates are for use within the prison system or by other state agencies. North Carolina's Correction Enterprises pays 5% of its profits to the state's crime victims' compensation fund.[28]

Under the state-use philosophy, most states still permit the prison manufacture of goods that will be used exclusively by the prison system itself or by other state agencies or that only the state can legitimately sell on the open market.

The federal government also operates a kind of state-use system in its institutions through a government-owned corporation called Federal Prison Industries, Inc. (also called UNICOR).[29] The corporation was established in 1934 to retain some employment programs for federal inmates in anticipation of the elimination of free-market prison industries. Critics of UNICOR charge that inmates are paid very low wages and are trained for jobs that do not exist in the free economy.[30] Even so, a long-term study published in 1994 found that federal inmates who participated in UNICOR "showed better adjustment, were less likely to be revoked at the end of their first year back in the community, and were more likely to find employment in the halfway house and community."[31] The study also found that inmates "earned slightly more money in the community than inmates who had similar background characteristics, but who did not participate in work and vocational training programs."

Free-market moneymaking prison industries also staged a comeback in the late 1990s and into the early years of the twenty-first century. Some were funded by private-sector investment. In 1981, under the Prison Rehabilitative Industries and Diversified Enterprises, Inc., legislation, commonly called the PRIDE Act, Florida became the first state to experiment

Picture History/Newscom

Warden T. M. Osborne and correctional officers stand in a cellblock at Sing Sing Prison at Ossining, New York, in 1915. How have prisons changed in the last 100 years?

with the wholesale transfer of its correctional industry program from public to private control.[32] PRIDE industries include sugarcane processing, construction, and automotive repair. Other states followed suit.

Today, the Prison Industry Enhancement Certification Program (PIECP),[33] administered by the Bureau of Justice Assistance (BJA), exempts certified state and local departments of corrections from normal federal restrictions on the sale of inmate-made goods in interstate commerce.[34] In addition, the program lifts restrictions on certified corrections departments, permitting them to sell inmate-made goods to the federal government in amounts exceeding the $10,000 maximum normally imposed on such transactions. The PIECP also allows private industry to establish joint ventures with state and local correctional agencies to produce goods using inmate labor. As of March 31, 2013, 45 correctional industry programs were certified to operate under the PIECP and employed 4,666 inmates.[35]

Today, however, some local community leaders fear that inmate jobs will lower employment opportunities for citizens of small towns and cities that are close to correctional facilities. The economically lean times brought about by the Great Recession of the early part of the twenty-first century have led to cost cutting by prison administrators who are sensitive to both their own budgetary needs and to the needs of civilian workers whose jobs might be threatened by inmate labor programs.[36] Learn more about the history of federal prison industries at **http://www.justicestudies.com/pubs/fedindust.pdf**. Visit the National Correctional Industries Association at **http://www.nationalcia.org** to see additional information about the PIECP.

The Punitive Era (1935–1945)

The moratorium on free-market prison industries initiated by the Ashurst-Sumners Act was to last for more than half a century. Prison administrators, left with few ready alternatives, seized on custody and institutional security as the long-lost central purposes of the correctional enterprise. The punitive era that resulted was characterized by the belief that prisoners owed a debt to society that only a rigorous period of confinement could repay. Writers of the period termed such beliefs the *convict bogey* and the *lock psychosis*,[37] referring to the fact that convicts were to be both shunned and securely locked away from society.

medical model A therapeutic perspective on correctional treatment that applies the diagnostic perspective of medical science to the handling of criminal offenders.

© Bill Perry/Fotolia

Alcatraz Federal Penitentiary. The island prison closed in 1963, a victim of changing attitudes toward corrections. It survives today as a San Francisco tourist attraction. What security levels characterize most American prisons today?

Large maximum-security institutions flourished, and the prisoner's daily routine became one of monotony and frustration. The punitive era was a lackluster time in American corrections. Innovations were rare, and a philosophy of "out of sight, out of mind" characterized American attitudes toward inmates. The term *stir-crazy* grew out of the experience of many prisoners with the punitive era's lack of educational, treatment, and work programs. In response, inmates created their own diversions, frequently attempting to escape or inciting riots. One especially secure and still notorious facility of the punitive era was the federal penitentiary on Alcatraz Island, which is described in some detail at **http://www.alcatrazhistory.com/rs2.htm**.

The Treatment Era (1945–1967)

In the late 1940s, the mood of the nation was euphoric. Memories of World War II were dimming, industries were productive beyond the best hopes of most economic forecasters, and America's position of world leadership was fundamentally unchallenged. Nothing seemed impossible. Amid the bounty of a postwar boom economy, politicians and the public accorded themselves the luxury of restructuring the nation's prisons. A new interest in "corrections" and reformation, combined with the latest in behavioral techniques, ushered in a new era. The treatment era was based on a **medical model** of corrections—one that implied that the offender was sick and that rehabilitation was only a matter of finding the right treatment. Inmates came to be seen more as "clients" or "patients" than as offenders, and terms like *resident* and *group member* replaced *inmate*.

Therapy during the period took a number of forms, many of which are still used today. Most therapeutic models assumed that inmates needed help to mature psychologically and had to be taught to assume responsibility for their lives. Prisons built their programs around both individual treatment and group therapy approaches. In individual treatment, the offender and the therapist develop a face-to-face relationship. Group therapy relies on the sharing of insights, gleaned by members of the therapeutic group, to facilitate the growth process, often by first making clear to offenders the emotional basis of their criminal behavior. Other forms of therapy used in prisons have included behavior therapy, drug therapy, neurosurgery, sensory deprivation, and aversion therapy.

Inmates have not always been happy with the treatment model. In 1972, a group of prisoners at the Marion, Illinois,

■ **work release** A prison program through which inmates are temporarily released into the community to meet job responsibilities.

federal prison joined together and demanded a right to refuse treatment.[38] The National Prison Project of the American Civil Liberties Union (ACLU) supported the inmates' right to refuse personality-altering treatment techniques.[39] Other suits followed. Worried about potential liability, the Law Enforcement Assistance Administration (LEAA) banned the expenditure of LEAA funds to support any prison programs utilizing psychosurgery, medical research, chemotherapy, or behavior modification.[40]

The treatment era also suffered from attacks on the medical model on which it was based. Academics and legal scholars pointed to a lack of evidence in support of the model[41] and began to stress individual responsibility rather than treatment in the handling of offenders. Indeterminate sentencing statutes, designed to reward inmates for improved behavior, fell before the swelling drive to replace treatment with punishment.

Any honest evaluation of the treatment era would conclude that, in practice, treatment was more an ideal than a reality. Many treatment programs existed, some of them quite intensive. Unfortunately, the correctional system in America was never capable of providing any consistent or widespread treatment because the majority of its guards and administrators were oriented primarily toward custody and were not trained to provide treatment. However, although we have identified 1967 as the end of the treatment era, many correctional rehabilitation programs survive to the present day, and new ones are continually being developed.

The Community-Based Era (1967–1980)

Beginning in the 1960s, the realities of prison overcrowding combined with a renewed faith in humanity and the treatment era's belief in the possibility of behavioral change to inspire a movement away from institutionalized corrections and toward the creation of opportunities for reformation within local communities. The transition to community corrections (also called *deinstitutionalization*, *diversion*, and *decarceration*) was based on the premise that rehabilitation could not occur in isolation from the free social world to which inmates must eventually return.[42] Advocates of community corrections portrayed prisons as dehumanizing, claiming that they further victimized offenders who had already been negatively labeled by society. Some states strongly embraced the movement toward decarceration. In 1972, for example, Massachusetts drew national attention when it closed all of its reform schools and replaced them with group homes.[43]

Advocates of community corrections portrayed prisons as dehumanizing, claiming that they further victimized offenders who had already been negatively labeled by society.

Decarceration, which built on many of the intermediate sanctions discussed in the previous chapter, used a variety of programs to keep offenders in contact with the community and out of prison. Among them were halfway houses, work-release programs, and open institutions. Halfway houses have sometimes been called *halfway-in* or *halfway-out houses*, depending on whether offenders were being given a second chance before incarceration or were in the process of gradual release from prison. Boston had halfway houses as early as the 1920s, but they operated for only a few years.[44] It was not until 1961 that the Federal Bureau of Prisons opened a few experimental residential centers in support of its new prerelease programs focusing on juveniles and youthful offenders. Called *prerelease guidance centers*, the first of these facilities were based in Los Angeles and Chicago.[45]

Halfway houses and work-release programs still operate in many parts of the country. A typical residential treatment facility today houses 15 to 20 residents and operates under the supervision of a director, supported by a handful of counselors. The environment is nonthreatening, and residents are generally free to come and go during the workday. The building looks more like a motel or a house than it does a prison. Fences and walls are nonexistent. Transportation is provided to and from work or educational sites, and the facility retains a portion of the resident's wages to pay the costs of room and board. Residents are expected to return to the facility after work, and some group therapy may be provided.

Today's work-release programs house offenders in traditional correctional environments—usually minimum-security prisons—but permit them to work at jobs in the community during the day and to return to the prison at night. Inmates are usually required to pay a token amount for their room and board in the institution. The first work-release law was passed by Wisconsin in 1913, but it was not until 1957 that a comprehensive program created by North Carolina spurred the development of work-release programs nationwide.[46] **Work release** for federal prisoners was authorized by the federal Prisoner Rehabilitation Act of 1965.[47] As work-release programs grew, study release—whereby inmates attend local colleges and technical schools—was initiated in most jurisdictions as an adjunct to work release.

Work-release programs are still very much a part of modern corrections. Almost all states have them, and many inmates work in the community as they approach the end of their sentence. Unfortunately, work-release programs are not without

■ **warehousing** An imprisonment strategy that is based on the desire to prevent recurrent crime and that has abandoned all hope of rehabilitation.

■ **nothing-works doctrine** The belief, popularized by Robert Martinson in the 1970s, that correctional treatment programs have had little success in rehabilitating offenders.

their social costs. Some inmates commit new crimes while in the community, and others use the opportunity to escape.

The community-based format led to innovations in the use of volunteers and to the extension of inmate privileges. "Open institutions" routinely provided inmates with a number of opportunities for community involvement and encouraged the community to participate in the prison environment. Some open institutions allowed weekend passes or extended visits by family members and friends, while a few experimented with conjugal visitation and with prisons that housed both men and women ("coeducational incarceration"). In 1968, the California Correctional Institute at Tehachapi initiated conjugal visits, in which inmates who were about to begin parole were permitted to live with their families for three days per month in apartments on the prison grounds. By the late 1960s, conjugal visitation was under consideration in many other states, and the National Advisory Commission on Criminal Justice Standards and Goals recommended that correctional authorities should make "provisions for family visits in private surroundings conducive to maintaining and strengthening family ties."[48] In 1995, however, California, which then allowed about 26,000 conjugal visits a year, eliminated this privilege for those sentenced to death or to life without parole and for those without a parole date. Rapists, sex offenders, and recently disciplined inmates were also denied conjugal privileges.

The Warehousing Era (1980–1995)

In the history of criminal justice, the three decades from 1980 to 2010 will likely be remembered as a time of mass imprisonment. In the 1980s, as concerns with community protection reached a near crescendo, and as stiff drug laws and strict repeat offender statutes put more and more people behind bars, rates of imprisonment reached previously unheralded levels.

About the same time, public disappointment in our nation's corrections system resulted at least partially from media reports of high recidivism,[49] coupled with descriptions of institutions where inmates lounged in relative luxury, enjoyed regular visits from spouses and lovers, and took frequent weekend passes—all of which created the image of "prison country clubs." The failure of the rehabilitative ideal in community-based corrections, however, was due as much to changes in the individual sentencing decisions of judges as it was to citizen outrage and restrictive legislative action. Evidence shows that many judges came to regard rehabilitation programs as failures and decided to implement the just deserts model[50] of criminal sentencing. The just deserts model, discussed earlier, built on a renewed belief that offenders should "get what's coming to them." It quickly led to a policy of **warehousing** serious offenders for the avowed purpose of protecting society—and led also to a rapid decline of the decarceration initiative.

Recidivism rates were widely quoted in support of the drive to warehouse offenders. One study, for example, showed that nearly 70% of young adults paroled from prison in 22 states during 1978 were rearrested for serious crimes one or more times within six years of their release.[51] The study group was estimated to have committed 36,000 new felonies within the six years following their release, including 324 murders, 231 rapes, 2,291 robberies, and 3,053 violent assaults.[52] Worse still, observed the study's authors, was the fact that 46% of recidivists would have been in prison at the time of their readmission to prison if they had served the maximum term to which they had originally been sentenced.[53]

The failure of the rehabilitative model in corrections had already been proclaimed emphatically by Robert Martinson in 1974.[54] Martinson and his colleagues had surveyed 231 research studies conducted to evaluate correctional treatments between 1945 and 1967. They were unable to identify any treatment program that substantially reduced recidivism. Although Martinson argued for fixed sentences, a portion of which would be served in the community, his findings were often interpreted to mean that lengthy prison terms were necessary to incapacitate offenders who could not be reformed. About the same time, the prestigious National Academy of Sciences released a report in support of Martinson, saying, "We do not now know of any program or method of rehabilitation that could be guaranteed to reduce the criminal activity of released offenders."[55] This combined attack on the treatment model led to the **nothing-works doctrine**, which, beginning in the late 1970s, cast a pall of doubt over the previously dominant treatment philosophy.

The nothing-works philosophy contributed to new sentencing schemes, such as mandatory minimum sentencing provisions and truth-in-sentencing requirements. Together with the growing popularity of "three-strikes-and-you're-out" laws, these sentencing rules affected prison populations by substantially increasing the average time served by offenders before release. In the 1990s, prison populations continued to grow substantially because of a rise in the number of parole violators returned to prison; a drop in the annual release rates of inmates; a small number of inmates who would serve long terms or who would never be released; and enhanced punishments for drug offenders.[56] Average time served continues to increase. In 1990, for example, murderers served, on average, 92 months before release. Today, a person convicted of murder can expect to serve 106 months in prison before being released—a 15% increase. During the same period, actual time served in prison for the crime of rape increased 27%, and drug offenders spent 35% more time behind bars.[57]

American prison populations grew dramatically during the warehousing era (Figures 13-2 and 13-3)—and the increase is only now beginning to drop off. Between 1980 and 2012, state and federal prison populations more than quadrupled, from 329,000 inmates to around 1.6 million.[58] Much of the rise in prison populations can be attributed directly to changes in

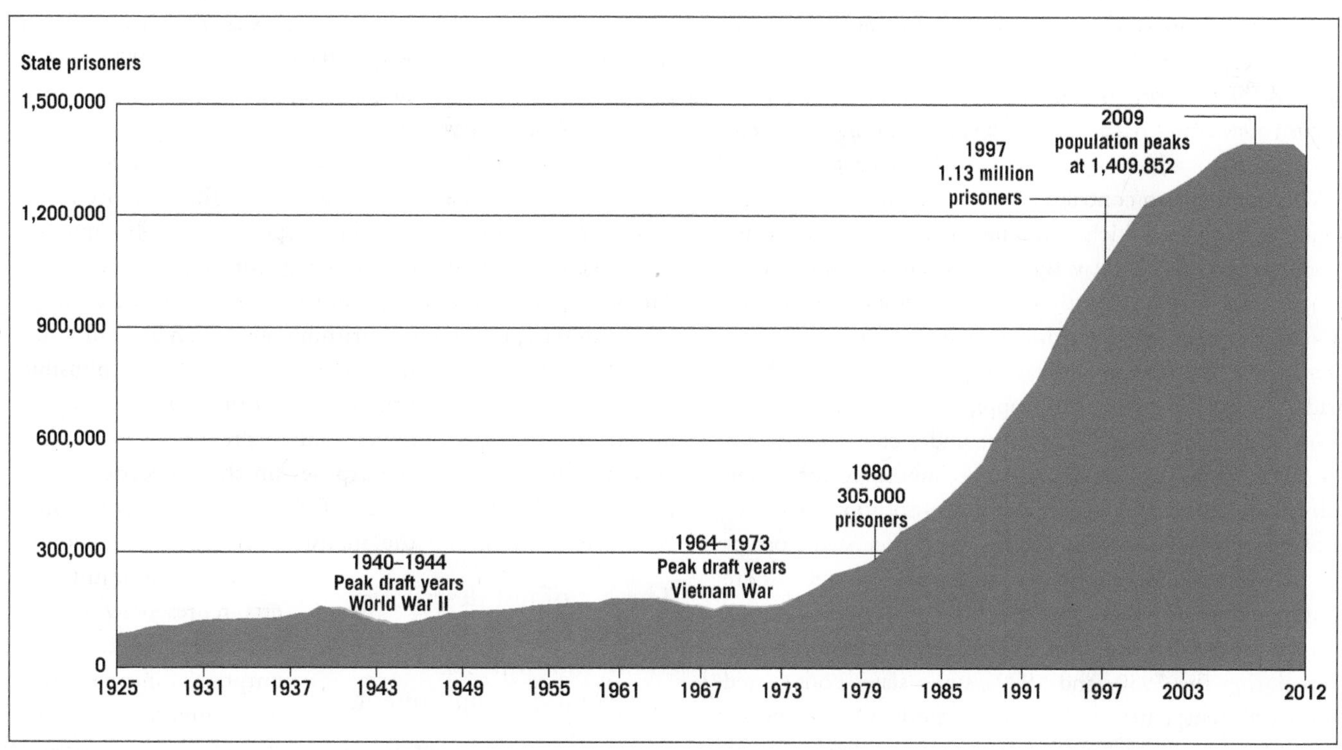

FIGURE 13-2 | State Prison Populations, 1925–2012

Note: Numbers may not reflect the actual number of persons sentenced to incarceration because some states, like California, have begun to house substantial numbers of inmates in local jails rather than in state prison facilities.

Source: Bureau of Justice Statistics, *Crime and Justice Atlas 2000* (Washington, DC: BJS, 2001), pp. 42–43; and Bureau of Justice Statistics, *Prisoners in 2012* (Washington, DC: BJS, 2013); and other years.

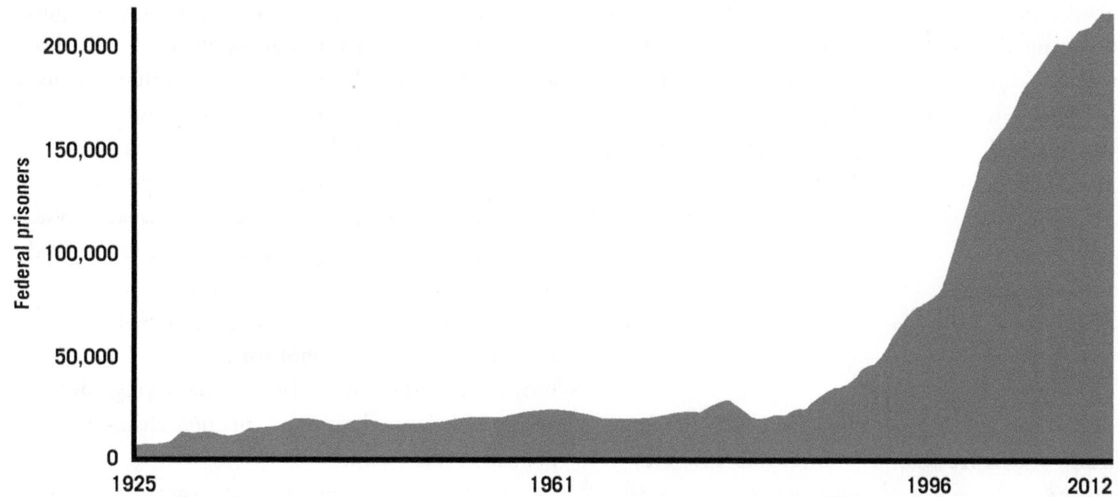

FIGURE 13-3 | Federal Prison Populations, 1925–2012

Source: Bureau of Justice Statistics and the Federal Bureau of Prisons.

■ **justice model** A contemporary model of imprisonment based on the principle of just deserts.

sentencing laws aimed at taking drug offenders off the streets and to the resulting rapid growth in the number of incarcerated drug felons and, more recently, immigration law violators. A warehousing era report by the American Bar Association, for example, directly attributed the huge growth in the number of inmates to what it saw as a system-wide overemphasis on drug-related offenses—an emphasis that tended to imprison mostly poor, undereducated African American youths who were rarely dangerous.[59] The report pointed out that while the per capita *rate of reported crime* dropped 2.2% across the nation during the 1980s, "the *incarceration rate* increased more than 110 percent."[60]

Warehousing also contributed to numerous administrative difficulties, many of which continue to affect prison systems throughout the nation today. By 1992, when the warehousing era was in full swing, institutions in 40 states and the District of Columbia were operating under court orders to alleviate overcrowding.[61] Entire prison systems in nine states—Alaska, Florida, Kansas, Louisiana, Mississippi, Nevada, Rhode Island, South Carolina, and Texas—had come under court control because overcrowded conditions made it impossible for prison administrators to meet court-supported constitutional requirements related to inmate safety. Today, even more state corrections systems have become subject to federal oversight or are operating under federal consent decrees.[62]

To meet the housing needs of burgeoning prison populations during the 1980s and 1990s, some states constructed "temporary" tent cities within prison yards. Others moved more beds into already packed dormitories, often stacking prisoners three high in triple bunk beds. A few states declared a policy of early release for less dangerous inmates and instituted mandatory diversion programs for first-time nonviolent offenders. Others used sentence rollbacks to reduce the sentences of selected inmates by a fixed amount, usually 90 days. Early parole was similarly employed by numerous states to reduce overcrowded conditions. Most states shifted some of their correctional burden to local jails, and by 2000, 34 states, the District of Columbia, and the federal government were sending some prisoners to jails because of overcrowding at their own long-term institutions.[63]

The Just Deserts Era (1995–2012)

Warehousing and prison overcrowding were primarily the result of both public and official frustration with rehabilitative efforts. In a sense, however, they were also consequences of a strategy without a clear-cut philosophy. Because rehabilitation didn't seem to work, early advocates of warehousing—not knowing what else to do—assumed a pragmatic stance and advocated separating criminals from society by keeping them locked up for as long as possible. Their avowed goal was the protection of law-abiding citizens. Consequently, by the early 2000s, prison populations approached the breaking point, requiring the construction of many new facilities.

Warehousing and prison overcrowding were primarily the result of both public and official frustration with rehabilitative efforts.

In the midst of a prison construction boom, a new philosophy based on the second prong of the **justice model**—that is, an emphasis on individual responsibility—became the operative principle underlying many correctional initiatives. The new philosophy was grounded squarely on the concept of just deserts, in which imprisonment is seen as a fully deserved and proper consequence of criminal and irresponsible behavior rather than just the end result of a bankrupt system unable to reform its charges. Unlike previous correctional eras, which layered other purposes on the correctional experience (the reformatory era, for example, was concerned with reformation, and the industrial era sought economic gain), the era of just deserts represented a kind of return to the root purpose of incarceration: punishment.

The era of just deserts represented a kind of return to the root purpose of incarceration: punishment.

At the start of the just deserts era, state legislatures, encouraged in large part by their constituencies, scrambled to limit inmate privileges and to increase the pains of imprisonment. As with any other era, the exact beginning of the just deserts era is difficult to pinpoint. Noted corrections expert Jeanne Stinchcomb says, "The justice model gained momentum throughout the 1980s and 1990s, fueled by political conservatism, media sensationalism, an all-out 'war on drugs,' and public attitudes expressed in 'zero-tolerance' terms."[64] It is safe to say, however, that the just deserts model of criminal punishments was firmly in place by 1995. In that year, Alabama became the first state in modern times to reestablish chain gangs.[65] Under the Alabama system, shotgun-armed guards oversaw prisoners who were chained together by the ankles while they worked the state's roadsides—picking up trash, clearing brush, and filling ditches. The system, intended primarily for parole violators, was tough and unforgiving. Inmates served up to 90 days on chain gangs, during which they worked 12-hour shifts and remained chained even while using portable toilet facilities.

A few months later, Arizona became the second state to field prison chain gangs. Florida jumped on the chain gang bandwagon soon afterward.[66] Alabama chain gangs, which had expanded to include female prisoners, were discontinued in 1996 following a lawsuit against the state, and other state departments of correction have discontinued their use. The few chain gangs that still exist today are run mostly by county sheriffs and are populated by jail inmates. Brevard County, Florida, for example, operates jail chain gangs, and Arizona sheriff Joe Arpaio instituted chain gangs for both male and female inmates in the jail facilities in his jurisdiction.[67]

In another example of the move toward greater punishment indicative of the just deserts era, Virginia abolished parole in 1995, increased sentences for certain violent crimes by as much as 700%, and announced that it would build a dozen new prisons.[68] Changes in Virginia law were intended to move the state further in the direction of truth in sentencing and to appease the state's voters, who—reflecting public opinion nationwide—demanded a "get-tough" stance toward criminals.

"Get-tough" initiatives were reflected in the "three-strikes-and-you're-out" laws that swept through state legislatures in the late 1990s.[69] Three-strikes legislation, which is discussed in more detail in Chapter 11, generally mandates lengthy prison terms for criminal offenders convicted of a third violent crime or felony. Three-strikes laws have been enacted in almost 30 states and by the federal government. Critics of such laws, however, say that they do not prevent crime.[70] Jerome Skolnick, of the University of California at Berkeley, for example, criticizes three-strikes legislation because, he says, such practices almost certainly do not reduce the risk of victimization—especially the risk of becoming a victim of random violence. That is so, says Skolnick, because most violent crimes are committed by young men between the ages of 13 and 23. "It follows," according to Skolnick, "that if we jail them for life after their third conviction, we will get them in the twilight of their careers, and other young offenders will take their place."[71]

Criticisms of three-strikes laws, however, failed to appreciate the sentiments supporting the just deserts era. Proponents of "get-tough" policies, although no doubt interested in personal safety, lower crime rates, and balanced state and federal budgets, were keenly focused on retribution. And where retribution fuels a correctional policy, deterrence, reformation, and economic considerations play only secondary roles. As more and more states enacted three-strikes and other "get-tough" legislation, prison populations across the nation continued to swell, eclipsing those of the warehousing era. The impact of the just deserts era remains with us today, leaving the United States with one of the highest rates of imprisonment in the world.[72] Learn more about the impact of the just deserts model on corrections via **http://www.sentencingproject.org/doc/publications/inc_lessonsofgettough.pdf.**

The Evidence-Based Era (2012–Present)

Although the just deserts philosophy provided what became for many an acceptable rationale for continued prison expansion, it soon ran up against the very practical fiscal needs imposed by the Great Recession of the early twenty-first century. The recession made it necessary for states to save money and to cut their budgets, leading to an end of the just deserts era around 2012. In the grip of newfound motivation predicated upon forced financial austerity, many state legislatures began to question the wisdom of locking up nonviolent, elderly, and seriously ill offenders for long periods of time, and prison populations started to finally decline. The new era in corrections, the evidence-based era, is built around the need to employ cost-effective solutions to correctional issues. Learn more about evidence-based practices in corrections in the "CJ Issues" box that follows.

Prisons Today

There are approximately 1,720 state prisons and 119 federal prisons in operation across the country today.[73] Recently, however, the rate of new prison construction has slowed—and even stopped in many states—as budget issues at both the state and federal level have led to a new fiscal conservatism. Likewise, the growth of America's prison population has recently been slowing, and numbers in some states (most notably California) have begun to show a decrease as state budgetary concerns have led to fiscal conservatism (see the "CJ Issues" box discussing California's Public Safety Realignment program).

On January 1, 2013, the nation's state and federal prisons held 1,571,013 inmates, of which 1,512,391 were serving sentences of a year or more.[74] Slightly more than 7% (or 108,866) of those imprisoned were women.[75] The incarceration rate for state and federal prisoners sentenced to more than a year stood at 480 prisoners for every 100,000 U.S. residents in 2012. In that year, males had an imprisonment rate (910 per 100,000 U.S. residents) that was 14 times higher than the rate for females (63 per 100,000).[76] Even if today's incarceration rates remain unchanged, 6.6% of U.S. residents born in 2001 will go to prison at some point during their lifetime.[77]

Statistics tell us quite a bit about those in our prisons (Figures 13-5 and 13-6). Most people sentenced to state prisons are convicted of violent crimes (52.6%), whereas property crimes (18.4%) and drug crimes (18.2%) are nearly tied as the second most common type of offenses for which offenders are imprisoned.[78] In contrast, prisoners sentenced for drug-law violations are the single largest group of federal inmates

CJ | ISSUES
Evidence-Based Corrections

The National Institute of Corrections (NIC) says that "in corrections, evidence-based practice is the breadth of research and knowledge around processes and tools which can improve correctional outcomes, such as reduced recidivism."[1] The NIC has been promoting the use of evidence-based practice (EBP) for a number of years, and in June 2008 the NIC partnered with the Center for Effective Public Policy to build an EBP framework that is intended to be relevant to the entire criminal justice system. The system-wide framework that the NIC is developing focuses on justice system events from arrest through final disposition and discharge. When fully implemented, the framework should result in more collaborative evidence-based decision making throughout the criminal justice system nationwide. According to the NIC, the purpose of the EBP decision-making initiative "is to equip criminal justice policymakers in local communities with the information, processes, and tools that will result in measurable reductions of pretrial misconduct and post-conviction reoffending."

There are three phases in the NIC initiative. Phase I, which has already been completed, produced the framework itself, which is outlined in the NIC publication *A Framework for Evidence-Based Decision Making in Local Criminal Justice Systems*. That publication, available at the NIC website (http://nicic.gov), describes key criminal justice decision points and provides an overview of evidence-based knowledge about effective justice practices. It defines risk and harm reduction as key goals of the criminal justice system and lays out practical local-level strategies for applying these principles and techniques.

In the second phase of its initiative, the NIC—along with its collaborating partner, the federal Office of Justice Programs (OJP)—selected seven seed sites from across the country that were interested in piloting principles included within the framework. Fifty key representatives from the selected seed sites attended a kickoff workshop in Bethesda, Maryland, in October 2010. The workshop clarified expectations for Phase II implementation, and established a working network among the selected sites.

Seed sites are now participating in an initiative evaluation, which is being administered by the Urban Institute and is designed to assess each site's readiness to implement the full framework in Phase III. During Phase III, selected sites will be expected to fully implement the NIC-established framework and to participate in a long-term outcome evaluation to measure the impact of implementing the principles contained within the framework.

[1]National Institute of Corrections, "Evidence-Based Practices," http://nicic.gov/EvidenceBasedPractices (accessed June 3, 2013).

Sources: National Institute of Corrections, "Evidence-Based Practices," http://nicic.gov/EvidenceBasedPractices (accessed June 3, 2011); and National Institute of Corrections, "Evidence-Based Decision Making," http://nicic.gov/EBDM (accessed June 3, 2013).

(47%), and the increase in the imprisonment of drug offenders accounts for more than three-quarters of the total growth in the number of federal inmates since 1980.[79] Immigration offenders now account for 12% of all federal prisoners, and their numbers are rising.[80]

An examination of imprisonment statistics by race highlights the huge disparity between blacks and whites in prison. Whereas only an estimated 1,001 white men are imprisoned in the United States for every 100,000 white men in their late 20s, figures show an incarceration rate of 6,927 black men for every 100,000 black men of the same age—seven times greater than the figure for whites.[81] Almost 17% of adult black men in the United States have served time in prison—a rate over twice as high as that for adult Hispanic males (7.7%) and over six times as high as that for adult white males (2.6%).[82] According to the Bureau of Justice Statistics (BJS), a black male living in America today has a 32.3% lifetime chance of going to prison, and a black female has a 5.6% lifetime chance of imprisonment. That contrasts sharply with the lifetime chances of imprisonment for white males (5.9%) and white females (0.9%).[83]

The use of imprisonment varies considerably between states. Although the average rate of imprisonment in the United States at the start of 2012 was 480 per every 100,000 people in the population,[84] some state rates were nearly double that figure.[85] Louisiana, for example, was holding 865 out of every 100,000 of its citizens in prison at the start of 2012, while Mississippi was second with an incarceration rate of 690 per 100,000 citizens. Texas, a state with traditionally high rates of imprisonment, held 633 prisoners per every 100,000 people. Maine had the lowest rate of imprisonment of all the states (147); other states with low rates were Rhode Island (197), Minnesota (183), and New Hampshire (198). As the "CJ News" and "CJ Issues" boxes in this chapter show, however, some states, particularly California, have found novel ways of reducing the official count of prisoners being held at the state level. In California's case, a strategy of realignment has been implemented to shift selected nonviolent prisoners out of state-run prisons and into county lockups. Consequently, when comparing state incarceration rates and when examining national statistics on imprisonment, it may make more sense to talk about the number of criminal offenders

CJ | NEWS

California's Governor Wants Federal Oversight of Prisons to End

© Paul Kitagaki Jr/ZUMA Press/Corbis

The exterior of Folsom prison in Folsom, California. The institution was immortalized in a 1955 Johnny Cash song, "Folsom Prison Blues." In 2011, the U.S. Supreme Court agreed that California prisons are dangerously overcrowded. On what did the Court base its decision?

California's broken and overcrowded prison system shows what can happen when the public demands tough sentencing provisions but not enough cells are built to deal with the ensuing flood of inmates.

A few years ago, federal judges assumed oversight of the beleaguered California prison system, ordering the state to significantly reduce its inmate population to a specified target by June 2013. But Governor Jerry Brown, grappling with a tight state budget, says the target will be too costly to meet. In January 2013, he filed a court challenge to regain state control of the prison system.

"Let those judges give us our prisons back," Brown declared. "We can run our own prisons." This messy standoff can be traced back to the 1980s and 1990s, an era of high crime rates, when Californians clamored for strict sentencing laws to lock up felons and, in some cases, actually throw away the key. In 1994, voters passed the three-strikes law, requiring a life sentence after three felony convictions. From 1982 to 2000, California's prison population swelled five-fold and the state built 23 new prisons.

In the 2000s, however, circumstances changed. Crime rates plummeted, state funds contracted, and California could no longer afford new prisons or even adequate space and health care for the inmates it already had. Tough sentencing laws, however, were still on the books, and flooding the prisons with new inmates at a cost to the state of $55,500 per prisoner per year.

With conditions deteriorating, California's inmates were being packed into three-tier bunks in prison gymnasiums and classrooms. That's when federal judges took action and found that prison overcrowding in California was so extensive that it violated the U.S. Constitution's ban on cruel and unusual punishment.

In 2006, the judges seized control of the prison health-care system and turned it over to an independent agency, which led to an increase in state spending. And in 2009, all three judges ordered the state to cut the number of inmates to a targeted level and set June 2013 as the deadline.

The state appealed the judges' order to the U.S. Supreme Court, but it lost in May 2011. To meet the mandate, more than 30,000 inmates were removed from the system through the state's "realignment initiative"—which meant shifting low-level offenders to county jails and sending some inmates to private prisons in other states. Although the state will help counties offset the cost of housing convicted offenders, estimates show that the state will save $486 million annually by sharing the burden for housing less serious offenders in county jails. Meanwhile, counties will be left holding at least some the bill for expanding their jails. One year after realignment began, some California counties, including Kern, Fresno, Sierra, and Yolo, saw their jail populations more than double—and more inmates are expected to keep coming.

In April 2012, prison officials reported that they had run out of new ways to significantly reduce the prison population, short of letting felons back out on the streets, which they vowed not to do. Predicting it would fall short of the 2013 target, the state asked the judges to lower the target level, and in exchange it would improve rehabilitative and health-care services.

But the judges refused, which prompted Brown to file his court challenge, which has yet to be resolved as this book goes to press. In the meantime, Californians have lost their zeal for the tough sentencing laws that overcrowded their prisons in the first place.

In a proposition on the November 2012 ballot, California voters opted to pare back the three-strikes law by ending the life-in-prison requirement for third-strike offenders who haven't committed serious and violent crimes. Experts said that this change in the law could lead to the release of as many as 2,800 third-strike inmates from the state's overcrowded prisons.

Resources: Howard Mintz, "Governor: Drop California Prisons from Court Orders to Shed Inmates," *Mercury News*, January 8, 2013, http://www.mercurynews.com/crime-courts/ci_22331595/governor-argues-california-prisons-should-be-removed-from; Mac Taylor, "Providing Constitutional and Cost-Effective Inmate Medical Care," Legislative Analyst's Office, April 19, 2012, http://www.lao.ca.gov/reports/2012/crim/inmate-medical-care/inmate-medical-care-041912.pdf; Solomon Moore, "Court Orders California to Cut Prison Population," *New York Times*, February 9, 2009, http://www.nytimes.com/2009/02/10/us/10prison.html; and Matthew Green, "Shouldering the Burden: California's New Jail Boom," KQED, http://blogs.kqed.org/lowdown/2012/08/16/shouldering-the-burden-californias-new-jail-boom-interactive-map/ (accessed March 2, 2013).

---

sentenced to confinement, rather than merely counting those held in state prisons.

The size of prison facilities varies greatly. One out of every four state institutions is a large maximum-security prison, with a population approaching 1,000 inmates. A few exceed that figure, but the typical state prison is small, with an inmate population of less than 500. Community-based facilities average around 50 residents. The typical prison system in relatively populous states consists of[86]

- One high-security prison for long-term, high-risk offenders
- One or more medium-security institutions for offenders who are not high risks

CJ | ISSUES

California's Public Safety Realignment (PSR) Program

In 2011, the California legislature passed the Criminal Justice Realignment Act and initiated the state's Public Safety Realignment (PSR) program. The program, which was implemented in response to a federal court order that required California to reduce overcrowding, places offenders convicted of less serious crimes in local jails rather than in state prisons (see the "CJ News" box earlier in the chapter).

California's PSR legislation has been called the most significant change in the California Penal Code since the state's Determinate Sentencing Law was passed in 1977. The most important aspect of the new law is that it shifts control over thousands of prisoners from the state to the county level. Specifically, the new law does three things. First, it mandates that low-level felons sentenced to one to a few years in prison (who in the past would normally have served their time in state-run prisons) will now be sent to county jails instead. Second, the supervision of most parolees will become the responsibility of county probation officials instead of state parole officers. Third, parolees supervised at the county level and who have their parole revoked will serve time for violations in county jails instead of state prisons, and the amount of time they serve will be limited to 180 days.

The PSR program effectively divides the state's felon population into two categories: (1) those legally defined as violent, serious, and/or sex offenders (who continue to be sent to state prison and who are supervised by state parole officers upon release), and (2) lower-level offenders who were formerly housed in state prisons or managed by the state parole system (but who are now being managed by local justice systems and are housed in county jails or managed by county probation officers).

The bill also provides that parolees who do not incur any infractions will be released from parole supervision in six months. Under the law, California's Board of Parole Hearings discontinued parole revocation hearings in mid-2013, and that responsibility was moved to local trial court judges.

California's realignment legislation effectively shifts much of the burden of paying for correctional services from the state to the counties. Serious questions, however, remain about the adequacy of funding and local capacity to manage the changes mandated by the law. The realignment statute provides a one-time appropriation to cover costs associated with hiring and training new personnel and the costs of construction of needed facilities. A dedicated and permanent revenue stream is intended to flow to the counties through allocation of a portion of both state vehicle license fees and the state sales tax (which was raised in 2012 through a state-wide referendum). It is still too early to tell whether the shift of resources between state and county levels will be sufficient to sustain the dual goals of safety and rehabilitation in California corrections. Figure 13-4 shows the projected impact of realignment on California's budget through 2016.

Consequently, although the imprisonment rate in states like California may appear to be falling when reported in national statistics, realignment strategies merely shift the responsibility for housing state prisoners to county governments and tend to disguise the actual number of people being confined. Seventy percent of the nationwide decrease in prison populations that was reported by the Bureau of Justice Statistics during 2011, for example, was due to California's Public Safety Realignment program.

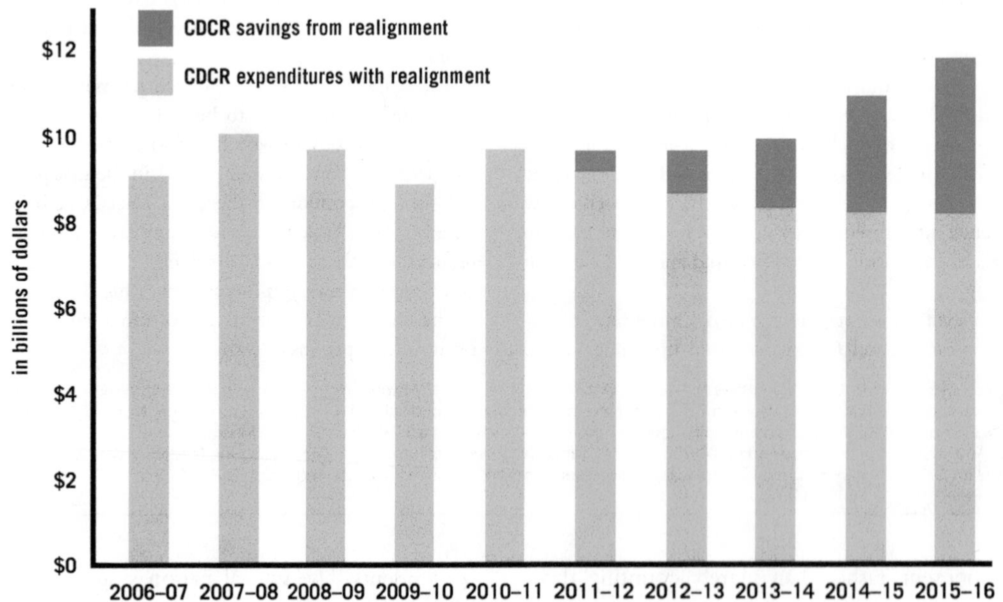

FIGURE 13-4 | Impact of Realignment on the Budget of California's Department of Corrections and Rehabilitation, 2006–2016

Source: California Department of Corrections and Rehabilitation, "The Future of California Corrections," http://www.cdcr.ca.gov/2012plan/docs/plan/complete.pdf (accessed May 3, 2013).

Who's in Prison and Why?

In federal prisons, nearly half (48%) of all inmates are serving time for drug offenses, whereas slightly more than a third (35%) are incarcerated for public-order crimes.

In state prisons, approximately 53% of prisoners are serving time for violent offenses, 18% are serving sentences for property offenses, and 17% are serving sentences for drug crimes. Eleven percent are convicted of public-order crimes.

Robbery is the most common violent crime for which males are imprisoned (14%), followed by murder (12%) and assault (11%).

Males comprise 93% of people in prison; 7% are female.

The percentage of females serving time for murder (10% of all sentenced females) is similar to that of males (12%).

Of federal prisoners, 39% are age 40 or older.

Most inmates (38%) are black; 32% are white and 22% are Hispanic.

Black and Hispanic prisoners are both younger and imprisoned at higher rates than white inmates.

The incarceration rate for black women is 2.9 times higher than the rate for white women; the rate for Hispanic women is 1.5 times higher than for white women.

Immigration offenders now account for 12% of all federal prisoners, and their numbers are rising.

Only 73.5% of federal prisoners are U.S. citizens, and more than 18% of persons confined in federal prisons hold Mexican citizenship,

Federal prisons have custody of 30% of all non-U.S. citizen inmates, and California, Florida, and Texas incarcerate 35% of prisoners who are non-U.S. citizens.

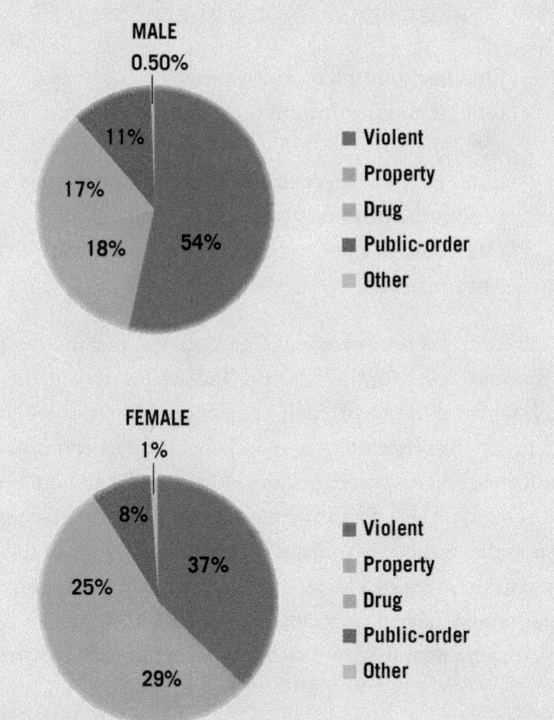

FIGURE 13-5 | State Prisoners by Gender and Type of Crime, 2012

Source: E. Ann Carson and William J. Sabol, *Prisoners in 2011* (Washington, DC: Bureau of Justice Statistics, December 2012), and E. Ann Carson and Daniela Golinelli, *Prisoners in 2012—Advance Counts* (Washington, DC: Bureau of Justice Statistics, 2013).

How Many People Are in Prison?

At the start of 2013, the number of state and federal prisoners sentenced to more than one year totaled 1,512,391.

At the start of 2013, 480 out of every 100,000 U.S. residents were sentenced to more than one year in prison.

The U.S. incarceration rate is among the highest in the world.*

The number of people incarcerated in state and federal prisons increased by 15% from 1,316,333 to 1,518,104 between 2000 and 2010.

For the first time in more than 40 years, prison populations declined in 2011 by nearly 1% over the previous year.

Seventy percent of the nationwide decrease in prison populations was due to California's Public Safety Realignment program, which shifted the responsibility for confining most lower-level offenders to the state's counties.

The percentage of all prisoners housed in private prison facilities is 8.2%, with states housing 6.7% of inmates in private facilities and the Federal Bureau of Prisons holding 17.8% of its population in private facilities.

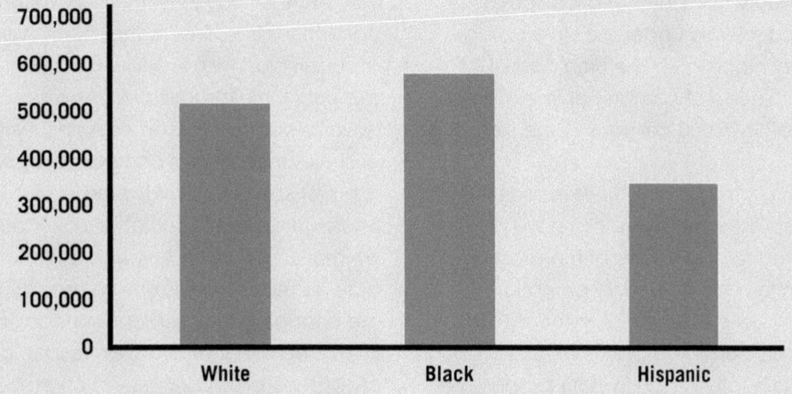

FIGURE 13-6 | Numbers of State and Federal Prisoners by Race, 2012

Source: E. Ann Carson and Daniela Golinelli, *Prisoners in 2012—Advance Counts* (Washington, DC: 2013).

*International comparisons are based on the number of people held in prisons *and* jails.

Sources: Federal Bureau of Prisons, "Quick Facts about the Bureau of Prisons," December 29, 2012, http://www.bop.gov/news/quick.jsp#4 (accessed June 3, 2013); and Roy Walmsley, *World Prison Population List*, 9th ed. (Essex University: International Center for Prison Studies, 2013).

- One institution for adult women
- One or two institutions for young adults (generally under age 25)
- One or two specialized mental-hospital-type security prisons for prisoners who are mentally ill
- One or more open-type institutions for low-risk, nonviolent inmates

Incarceration costs average around $62 per inmate per day at the state level, and $77.50 per inmate per day at the federal level, when all types of adult correctional facilities are averaged together.[87] Imprisonment is especially costly in some states, like California, where citizens pay over $150 per day to house each inmate (Figure 13-7). Prison systems across the nation face spiraling costs as the number of inmates grows and as the age of the inmate population increases. The cost of running the nation's correctional facilities and related programs exceeded $80 billion in 2012, of which more than half, or $48 billion, went to run state prisons.[88]

Overcrowding

The just deserts philosophy led to substantial and continued increases in the American prison population even as crime rates were dropping. In 1990, for example, the U.S. rate of imprisonment stood at 292 prisoners per every 100,000 residents. By 1995, it had reached 399, and by 2012 it was 480. Beginning in 2009, however, the rate of growth finally began to decline, at least in prisons run by the states.[89]

Even though many new prisons have been built throughout the nation during the past 20 years to accommodate the growing number of inmates, prison overcrowding is still a reality in many jurisdictions (Figure 13-8). Some of the most crowded prisons are those in the federal system: The crowding rate in federal prisons (which are not included in Figure 13-8) recently stood at 39% over capacity.[90] A 2012 report by the Government Accounting Office (GAO) found that "from fiscal years 2006 through 2011, the inmate population in BOP [Bureau of Prisons] run facilities grew 9.5%, while capacity grew less than 7%. As a result, BOP's overall crowding increased during this period from 36% to 39%."[91] The GAO concluded its report by noting

A. Ramey/PhotoEdit Inc.

Inmates making collect phone calls at the Davidson County Prison in Tennessee. There are approximately 1,325 state prisons and 84 federal prisons in operation across the country today. Together they hold over 1.6 million inmates. The prison shown here is run by Corrections Corporation of America. Are we likely to see a greater use of privately run correctional facilities in the future? Why or why not?

paying for it

California's Public Safety Realignment

This chapter began with the story of a paralyzed California inmate who had been denied release under the state's medical parole program. That story highlighted the high cost of confining prisoners who are in need of comprehensive medical care—in this case at a cost of $625,000 per year to the state's taxpayers.

In an effort to address budget shortfalls, however, some states have embraced cost-savings measures that have resulted in fewer people being confined to prison. One of the most significant of those measures, in terms of its impact on national prison statistics, is California's Public Safety Realignment (PSR) initiative, under which offenders convicted of less serious offenses are confined in local jails rather than in state prisons. The PSR program is discussed in the "CJ News" and "CJ Issues" boxes in this chapter.

Another way to reduce costs and to achieve savings in corrections is to ensure that offenders receive only the degree of supervision that they need in order to protect society and to facilitate their rehabilitation. As a consequence, states today have begun using risk-measuring instruments (questionnaires or survey instruments completed by prison staff, probation officers, or specially designated evaluators) to assess the potential future risk posed to society by offenders facing sentencing, and by imprisoned offenders who might otherwise be released. In order to make the maximum use of such a strategy, many states are changing their sentencing standards in order to allow those convicted of minor offenses—especially those with no history of violence or sex crimes—to be placed on probation or to be confined under living arrangements that provide alternatives to imprisonment, such as home confinement or halfway houses.

Resources: Barry Krisberg and Eleanor Taylor-Nicholson, *Criminal Justice Realignment: A Bold New Era in California Corrections* (Berkeley, CA: University of California, Berkeley Law School, 2011); and California Department of Corrections and Rehabilitation, "Funding of Realignment," http://www.cdcr.ca.gov/realignment/Funding-Realignment.html (accessed March 3, 2013).

■ **prison capacity** The size of the correctional population an institution can effectively hold.[i] There are three types of prison capacity: rated, operational, and design.

■ **rated capacity** The number of inmates a prison can handle according to the judgment of experts.

■ **operational capacity** The number of inmates a prison can effectively accommodate based on management considerations.

Approximate Annual Costs to Incarcerate an Inmate in Prison

Type of Expenditure	2010–11 (Actual)	2011–12 (Estimated)	2012–13 (Projected)
Security	**$ 24,150**	**$ 22,899**	**$ 25,627**
Inmate Health Care	**$ 14,427**	**$ 14,351**	**$ 16,222**
Medical care	$ 9,348	$ 10,101	$ 10,789
Psychiatric services	2,587	2,243	2,605
Pharmaceuticals	1,493	917	1,537
Dental care	1,000	1,090	1,291
Operations	**$ 3,517**	**$ 4,498**	**$ 4,904**
Facility operations (maintenance, utilities, etc.)	$ 1,251	$ 1,752	$ 1,785
Classification services	1,202	1,456	1,659
Maintenance of inmate records	746	904	1,030
Reception, testing, assignment	299	366	407
Transportation	19	21	24
Administration	**$ 3,026**	**$ 2,930**	**$ 3,355**
Inmate Support	**$ 2,836**	**$ 3,447**	**$ 3,927**
Food	$ 1,778	$ 2,155	$ 2,455
Inmate activities	473	573	653
Inmate employment and canteen	356	431	491
Clothing	153	195	222
Religious activities	76	92	105
Rehabilitation Programs	**$ 940**	**$ 1,253**	**$ 1,498**
Academic education	$ 632	$ 726	$ 859
Vocational training	163	227	253
Substance abuse programs	145	300	387
Miscellaneous	**$ 30**	**$ 9**	**$ 18**
Total	**$ 48,926**	**$ 49,387**	**$ 55,551**
Reflects Governor's 2012–13 Budget Proposal as of January 2012			
Totals do not include in-state and out-of-state contracted facilities.			

FIGURE 13-7 | Annual Costs to Incarcerate an Inmate in Prison in California, 2010-2013

Source: The California Legislative Analyst's Office.

that "BOP projects an additional 15% increase in its inmate population by 2020."

Prison overcrowding can be measured along a number of dimensions, including these:[92]

- Space available per inmate (such as square feet of floor space)
- How long inmates are confined in cells or housing units (versus time spent in recreation and other activities)
- Living arrangements (for example, single versus double bunks)
- Type of housing (such as use of segregation facilities, tents, and so on in place of general housing)

Further complicating the picture is the fact that prison officials have developed three definitions of **prison capacity**. **Rated capacity** refers to the size of the inmate population that a facility can handle according to the judgment of experts. **Operational capacity** is the number of inmates that a facility

■ **design capacity** The number of inmates a prison was intended to hold when it was built or modified.

■ **selective incapacitation** A policy that seeks to protect society by incarcerating individuals deemed to be the most dangerous.

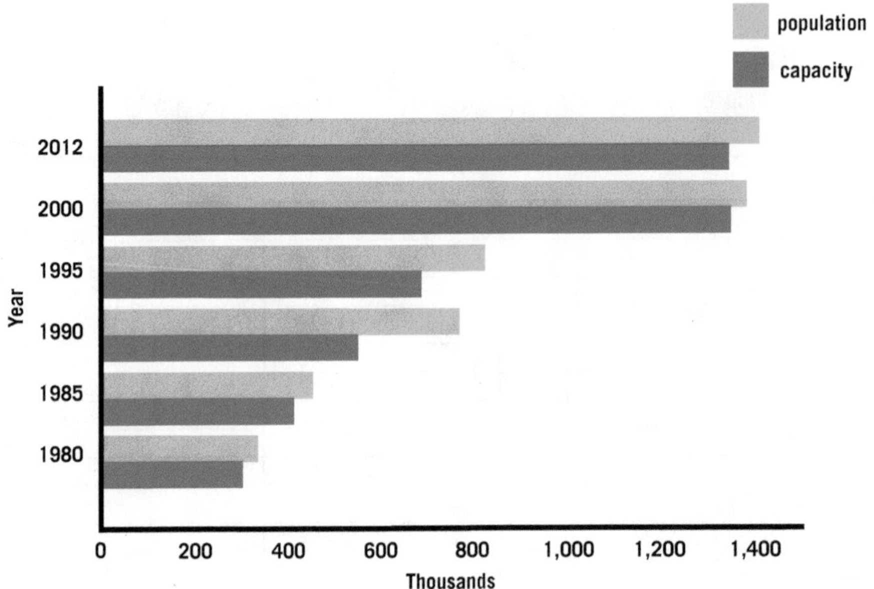

FIGURE 13-8 | State Prison Populations, Inmates versus Capacity, 1980–2012

Source: Bureau of Justice Statistics, *Correctional Populations in the United States* (Washington, DC: BJS, various years).

can effectively accommodate based on an appraisal of the institution's staff, programs, and services. **Design capacity** refers to the inmate population that the institution was originally built to handle. Rated capacity estimates usually yield the largest inmate capacities, whereas design capacity (on which observations in this chapter are based) typically shows the highest amount of overcrowding.

Overcrowding by itself is not cruel and unusual punishment, according to the U.S. Supreme Court in *Rhodes* v. *Chapman* (1981),[93] which considered the issue of double bunking along with other alleged forms of "deprivation" at the Southern Ohio Correctional Facility. The Court, reasoning that overcrowding is not necessarily dangerous if other prison services are adequate, held that prison housing conditions may be "restrictive and even harsh," for they are part of the penalty that offenders pay for their crimes.

Overcrowding by itself is not cruel and unusual punishment, according to the U.S. Supreme Court in *Rhodes* v. *Chapman* (1981).

However, overcrowding combined with other negative conditions may lead to a finding against the prison system, as was the case with the 2011 U.S. Supreme Court case of *Brown* v. *Plata*, with which this chapter opened. The American Correctional Association (ACA) notes that a totality-of-conditions approach has led courts to assess the overall quality of prison life while viewing overcrowded conditions in combination with

- the prison's ability to meet basic human needs,
- the adequacy of the facility's staff,
- the program opportunities available to inmates, and
- the quality and strength of the prison management.

Selective Incapacitation: A Contemporary Strategy to Reduce Prison Populations

Some authors have identified the central issue of imprisonment as one of collective versus **selective incapacitation**.[94] Collective incapacitation, a strategy that would imprison almost all serious offenders, is still found in jurisdictions that rely largely on predetermined, or fixed, sentences for given offenses or for a series of specified kinds of offenses (as in the case of some forms of three-strikes legislation). Collective incapacitation is, however, prohibitively expensive as well as unnecessary, in the opinion of many experts. Not all offenders need to be imprisoned because not all represent a continuing threat to society, but those who do are difficult to identify.[95]

Selective incapacitation seeks to identify the most dangerous criminals, with the goal of removing them from society. Consequently, the assessment of dangerousness (see Chapter 3) is central to today's contemporary strategy of selective incapacitation. Repeat offenders

Selective incapacitation seeks to identify the most dangerous criminals, with the goal of removing them from society.

with records of serious and violent crimes are the most likely candidates for imprisonment—as are those who will probably commit violent crimes in the future, even though they have no records.

In support of selective incapacitation, many states have enacted career-offender statutes that attempt to identify potentially dangerous offenders out of known criminal populations. Selective incapacitation efforts, however, have been criticized for yielding a rate of "false positives" of over 60%,[96] and some authors have called selective incapacitation a "strategy of failure."[97] Nevertheless, in an analysis of recidivism studies, Canadians Paul Gendreau, Tracy Little, and Claire Goggin found that criminal history, a history of preadult antisocial behavior, and "criminogenic needs"—which were defined as measurable antisocial thoughts, values, and behaviors—were all dependable predictors of recidivism.[98]

Many states today, facing budgetary challenges, have had to scramble in an attempt to implement selective incarceration principles. A recent report by the Sentencing Project, for example, found that four states—Kansas, Michigan, New Jersey, and New York—announced the closing of a combined number of 20 prisons in 2012, reducing prison capacity by over 14,100 beds.[99] The Project also reported that 13 states eliminated 15,500 additional prison beds in 2011. Savings due to the 2012 closing were estimated to total more than $337 million. The largest of the closures is the planned shuttering of the California Rehabilitation Center at Norco by June 2016. California expects to eliminate 3,900 beds and to save $125 million annually in operating costs.[100]

The state reductions came about by limiting the length of mandatory minimum sentences for drug offenses, diverting defendants with low-level convictions from incarceration, enhancing release programs, and reducing parole revocations. Recently, for example, Connecticut Governor Dannel P. Malloy signed into law a hotly debated piece of legislation that gave inmates in that state sentence-reduction credits if they participate in various kinds of prison-run self-improvement programs. Connecticut House Majority Leader Brendan Sharkey explained the new law this way: "If this is about being soft on crime, I say 'baloney.' This is about being smart on crime."[101]

As state budget problems continue, the just deserts model has relinquished ground to selective incapacitation. As more and more states embrace the evidence-based correctional model, it is likely that we will see the continued sentencing of violent criminals to lengthy prison stays, combined with the early release of offenders deemed unlikely to reoffend, and the increased use of less expensive alternative sanctions and diversion for minor offenders.

Security Levels

Maximum-custody (or maximum-security) prisons tend to be massive old buildings with large inmate populations. However, some, like Central Prison in Raleigh, North Carolina, are much newer and incorporate advances in prison architecture to provide tight security without sacrificing building aesthetics. Such institutions provide a high level of security characterized by tall fences, thick walls, secure cells, gun towers, and armed prison guards. Maximum-custody prisons tend to locate cells and other inmate living facilities at the center of the institution and place a variety of barriers between the living area and the institution's outer perimeter. Technological innovations, such as electric perimeters, laser motion detectors, electronic and pneumatic locking systems, metal detectors, X-ray machines, television surveillance, radio communications, and computer information systems, are frequently used today to reinforce the more traditional maximum-security strategies. These technologies have helped lower the cost of new prison construction. However, some people argue that prisons may rely too heavily on electronic detection devices that have not yet been adequately tested.[102] Death row inmates are all maximum-security prisoners, although the level of security on death row exceeds even that experienced by most prisoners held in maximum custody. Prisoners on death row must spend much of the day in single cells and are often permitted a brief shower only once a week under close supervision.

Most states today have one large, centrally located maximum-security institution. Some of these prisons combine more than one custody level and may be both maximum- and medium-security facilities. Medium security is a custody level that in many ways resembles maximum security. Medium-security prisoners are generally permitted more freedom to associate with one another and can go to the prison yard, exercise room, library, and shower and bathroom facilities under less intense supervision. An important security tool in medium-security prisons is the count, which is a head count of inmates taken at regular intervals. Counts may be taken four times a day and usually require inmates to report to designated areas to be counted. Until the count has been "cleared," all other inmate activity must cease. Medium-security prisons tend to be smaller than maximum-security institutions and often have barbed-wire-topped chain-link fences instead of the more secure stone or concrete block walls found in many of the older maximum-security facilities. Cells and living quarters tend to have more windows and are often located closer to the perimeter of the institution than in maximum-security facilities. Dormitory-style housing, where prisoners live together in wardlike arrangements, is sometimes found in medium-security

classification system A system used by prison administrators to assign inmates to custody levels based on offense history, assessed dangerousness, perceived risk of escape, and other factors.

facilities. There are generally more opportunities for inmates to participate in recreational and other prison programs than in maximum-custody facilities.

In minimum-security institutions, inmates are generally housed in dormitory-like settings and are free to walk the yard and to visit most of the prison facilities. Some newer prisons provide minimum-security inmates with private rooms, which they can decorate (within limits) according to their tastes. Inmates usually have free access to a canteen that sells items like cigarettes, toothpaste, and candy bars. Minimum-security inmates often wear uniforms of a different color from those of inmates in higher custody levels, and in some institutions they may wear civilian clothes. They work under only general supervision and usually have access to recreational, educational, and skills-training programs on the prison grounds. Guards are unarmed, gun towers do not exist, and fences, if they are present at all, are usually low and gates are sometimes even unlocked. Many minimum-security prisoners participate in some sort of work- or study-release program, and some have extensive visitation and furlough privileges. Counts may be taken, although most minimum- security institutions keep track of inmates through daily administrative work schedules. The primary "force" holding inmates in minimum-security institutions is their own restraint. Inmates live with the knowledge that minimum-security institutions are one step removed from close correctional supervision and that if they fail to meet the expectations of administrators, they will be transferred into more secure institutions, which will probably delay their release. Inmates returning from assignments in the community may be frisked for contraband, but body-cavity searches are rare in minimum custody, being reserved primarily for inmates suspected of smuggling.

The typical American prison today is medium or minimum custody. Some states have as many as 80 or 90 small institutions, which may originally have been located in every county to serve the needs of public works and highway maintenance. Medium- and minimum-security institutions house the bulk of the country's prison population and offer a number of programs and services designed to assist with the rehabilitation of offenders and to create the conditions necessary for the successful reentry of the inmate into society. Most prisons offer psychiatric services, academic education, vocational education, substance-abuse treatment, health care, counseling, recreation, library services, religious programs, and industrial and agricultural training.[103] Learn more about all aspects of contemporary prisons from the Corrections Connection via **http://www.corrections.com**.

Prison Classification Systems

Most states use a **classification system** to assign new prisoners to initial custody levels based on their perceived dangerousness,

Damian Dovarganes/AP Wide World Photos

Inmates flashing gang signs for the camera. If you were a warden, what changes would you make to improve the management of a prison like this one?

escape risk, and type of offense. A prisoner might be assigned to a minimum-, medium-, or maximum-custody institution. Inmates move through custody levels according to the progress they are judged to have made in self-control and demonstrated responsibility. Serious violent criminals who begin their prison careers with lengthy sentences in maximum custody have the opportunity in most states to work their way up to minimum security, although the process usually takes a number of years. Those who represent continual disciplinary problems are returned to closer custody levels. Minimum-security prisons, as a result, house inmates convicted of all types of criminal offenses.

Once an inmate has been assigned to a custody level, he or she may be reassessed for living and work assignments within the institution. Just as initial (or external) custody classification systems determine security levels, internal classification systems are designed to help determine appropriate housing plans and program interventions within a particular facility for inmates who share a common custody level. In short, initial classification determines the institution in which an inmate is placed, and internal classification determines placement and program assignment within that institution.[104]

Objective prison classification systems were adopted by many states in the 1980s, but it wasn't until the late 1990s that such systems were refined and validated. Fueled by litigation and overcrowding, classification systems are now viewed as the principal management tool for allocating scarce prison resources efficiently and for minimizing the potential for violence or escape. Classification systems are also expected to provide greater accountability and to forecast future prison bed-space needs. A properly functioning classification system is the "brain" of prison management, governing and influencing many important decisions, including such fiscal matters as staffing levels, bed space, and programming.[105]

ADMAX Administrative maximum. The term is used by the federal government to denote ultra-high-security prisons.

One of the best-known internal classification systems in use today is the adult internal management system (AIMS). AIMS was developed more than 20 years ago to reduce institutional predatory behavior by identifying potential predators and separating them from vulnerable inmates. AIMS assesses an inmate's predatory potential by quantifying aspects of his or her (1) record of misconduct, (2) ability to follow staff directions, and (3) level of aggression toward other inmates.

It is important to recognize that the criteria used to classify prisoners must be relevant to the legitimate security needs of the institution.

Before concluding this discussion of classification, it is important to recognize that the criteria used to classify prisoners must be relevant to the legitimate security needs of the institution. In 2005, for example, the U.S. Supreme Court, in the case of *Johnson* v. *California*,[106] invalidated the California Department of Corrections and Rehabilitation's (CDCR) unwritten policy of racially segregating prisoners in double cells for up to 60 days each time they entered a new correctional facility. The policy had been based on a claim that it prevented violence caused by racial gangs. The Court, however, held that the California policy was "immediately suspect" as an "express racial classification" and found that the CDCR was unable to demonstrate that the practice served a compelling state interest.

The Federal Prison System

In 1895, the federal government opened a prison at Leavenworth, Kansas, for civilians convicted of violating federal law. Leavenworth had been a military prison, and control over the facility was transferred from the Department of the Army to the Department of Justice. By 1906, the Leavenworth facility had been expanded to a capacity of 1,200 inmates, and another federal prison—in Atlanta, Georgia—was built. McNeil Island Prison in Washington State was also functioning by the early 1900s. The first federal prison for women opened in 1927 in Alderson, West Virginia. With the increasing complexity of the federal criminal code, the number of federal prisoners grew.[107]

On May 14, 1930, the Federal Bureau of Prisons (BOP) was created under the direction of Sanford Bates. The BOP was charged with providing progressive and humane care for federal inmates, professionalizing the federal prison service, and ensuring consistent and centralized administration of the 11 federal prisons in operation at the time.[108] The bureau inherited a system that was dramatically overcrowded. Many federal prisoners were among the most notorious criminals in the nation, and ideals of humane treatment and rehabilitation were all but lacking in the facilities of the 1920s. Bates began a program of improvements to relieve overcrowding and to increase the treatment capacity of the system. In 1933, the Medical Center for Federal Prisoners opened in Springfield, Missouri, with a capacity of around 1,000 inmates. Alcatraz Island began operations in 1934. Following Bates, James V. Bennett ran the BOP from 1937–1964, and worked to humanize prison conditions in the federal system. Because of his long tenure, Bennett left a mark on the system that remains today in its striving to set a standard for well-run institutions.

Most of the federal prison system's growth since the mid-1980s has been the result of the Sentencing Reform Act of 1984 (which established determinate sentencing, abolished parole, and reduced good time) and federal mandatory-minimum-sentencing laws enacted in 1986, 1988, and 1990. From 1980 to 1989, the federal inmate population more than doubled, from just over 24,000 to almost 58,000. During the 1990s, the population more than doubled again, and it continued to grow throughout the early years of the twenty-first century, reaching approximately 217,800 prisoners (or 40% over capacity) by May 2012.[109] According to the Washington, D.C.–based Urban Institute, "the increase in expected time served by drug offenders was the single greatest contributor to growth in the federal prison population between 1998 and 2010 (Figure 13-9).[110]

Today, the federal prison system consists of 119 institutions, six regional offices, the Central Office (headquarters), two staff-training centers, and 22 residential reentry management offices (which were previously known as community corrections offices).[111] The regional offices and the Central Office provide administrative oversight and support to the institutions and to the residential reentry management offices, which oversee community corrections centers and home-confinement programs. The federal correctional workforce is one of the fastest growing in the country, and at mid-2013, the BOP employed about 39,000 people.[112]

The BOP classifies its institutions according to five security levels: (1) administrative maximum (**ADMAX**), (2) high security, (3) medium security, (4) low security, and (5) minimum security. High-security facilities are called *U.S. penitentiaries* (USPs), medium- and low-security institutions are both called *federal correctional institutions* (FCIs), and minimum-security prisons are termed *federal prison camps* (FPCs).[113] Minimum-security facilities (e.g., Eglin Air Force Base, Florida, and Maxwell Air Force Base, Alabama) are essentially honor-type camps with barracks-type housing and no fencing. Low-security facilities in the federal prison system are surrounded by double chain-link fencing and employ vehicle patrols around their perimeters to enhance

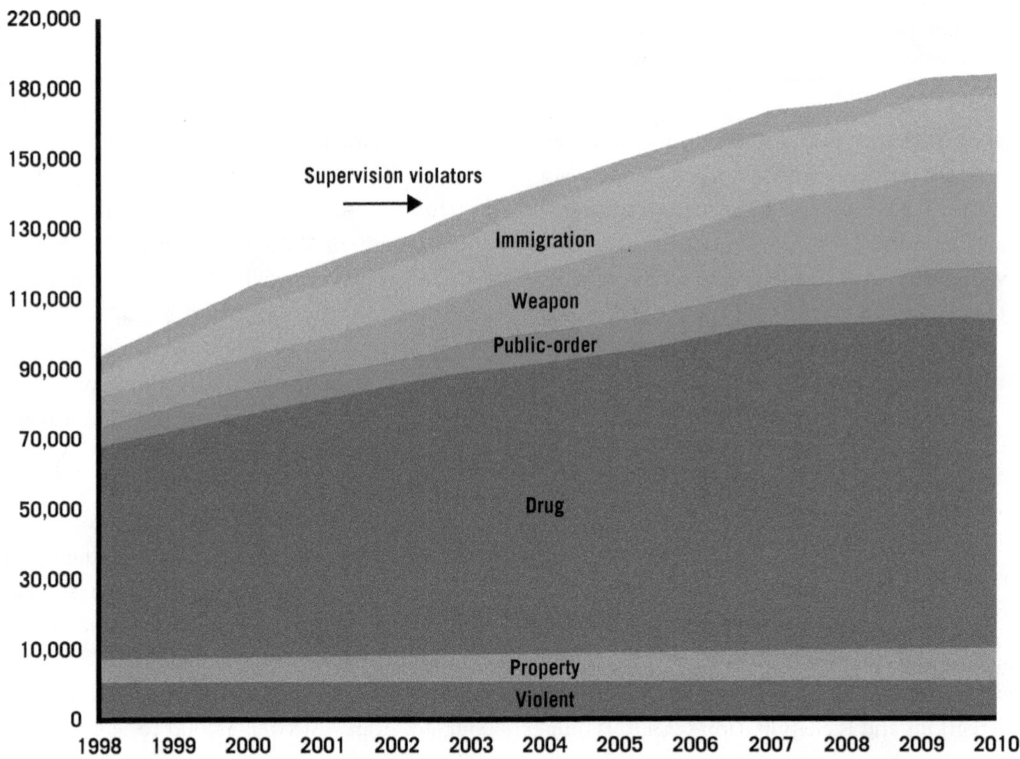

FIGURE 13-9 | Federal Prisons Populations at Yearend, by Offense, 1998–2010

Source: Bureau of Justice Statistics, Correctional Reporting Program.

security. Medium-security facilities (like those in Terminal Island, California; Lompoc, California; and Seagoville, Texas) make use of similar fencing and patrols but supplement them with electronic monitoring of the grounds and perimeter areas. High-security facilities (USPs like those in Atlanta, Georgia; Lewisburg, Pennsylvania; Terre Haute, Indiana; and Leavenworth, Kansas) are architecturally designed to prevent escapes and to contain disturbances. They also make use of armed patrols and intense electronic surveillance. Combination facilities within the BOP, which include institutions with different missions and security levels, are called Federal Correctional Complexes (FCCs).

A separate federal prison category is that of administrative facilities, consisting of institutions with special missions that are designed to house all types of inmates. Most administrative facilities are metropolitan detention centers (MDCs). MDCs, which are generally located in large cities close to federal courthouses, are the jails of the federal correctional system and hold defendants awaiting trial in federal court. Another five administrative facilities, medical centers for federal prisoners (MCFPs), function as hospitals.

Most administrative facilities are metropolitan detention centers (MDCs).

Federal correctional facilities exist either as single institutions or as federal correctional complexes—that is, sites consisting of more than one type of correctional institution (Figure 13-10). The federal correctional complex at Allenwood, Pennsylvania, for example, consists of a U.S. penitentiary, a federal prison camp, and two federal correctional institutions (one low and one medium security), each with its own warden. Federal institutions can be classified by type as follows: 55 are federal prison camps (holding 35% of all federal prisoners), 17 are low-security facilities (28%), 26 are medium-security facilities (23%), eight are high-security prisons (13%), and one is an ADMAX facility (1%).

The federal system's only ADMAX unit, the $60 million ultra-high-security prison at Florence, Colorado, is a relatively recent addition to the federal system. Dubbed "the Alcatraz of the Rockies," the 575-bed facility was designed to be the most secure prison ever built by the government.[114] Opened in 1995, it holds mob bosses, spies, terrorists, murderers, and escape artists. Dangerous inmates are confined to their cells 23 hours per day and are not allowed to see or associate with other inmates. Electronically controlled doors throughout the institution channel inmates to individual exercise sessions, and educational courses, religious services, and administrative matters are conducted via closed-circuit television piped directly into the prisoners' cells. Remote-controlled heavy steel doors within the prison allow correctional staff to section off the institution in the event of rioting, and the system can be controlled from outside if the entire prison is compromised.

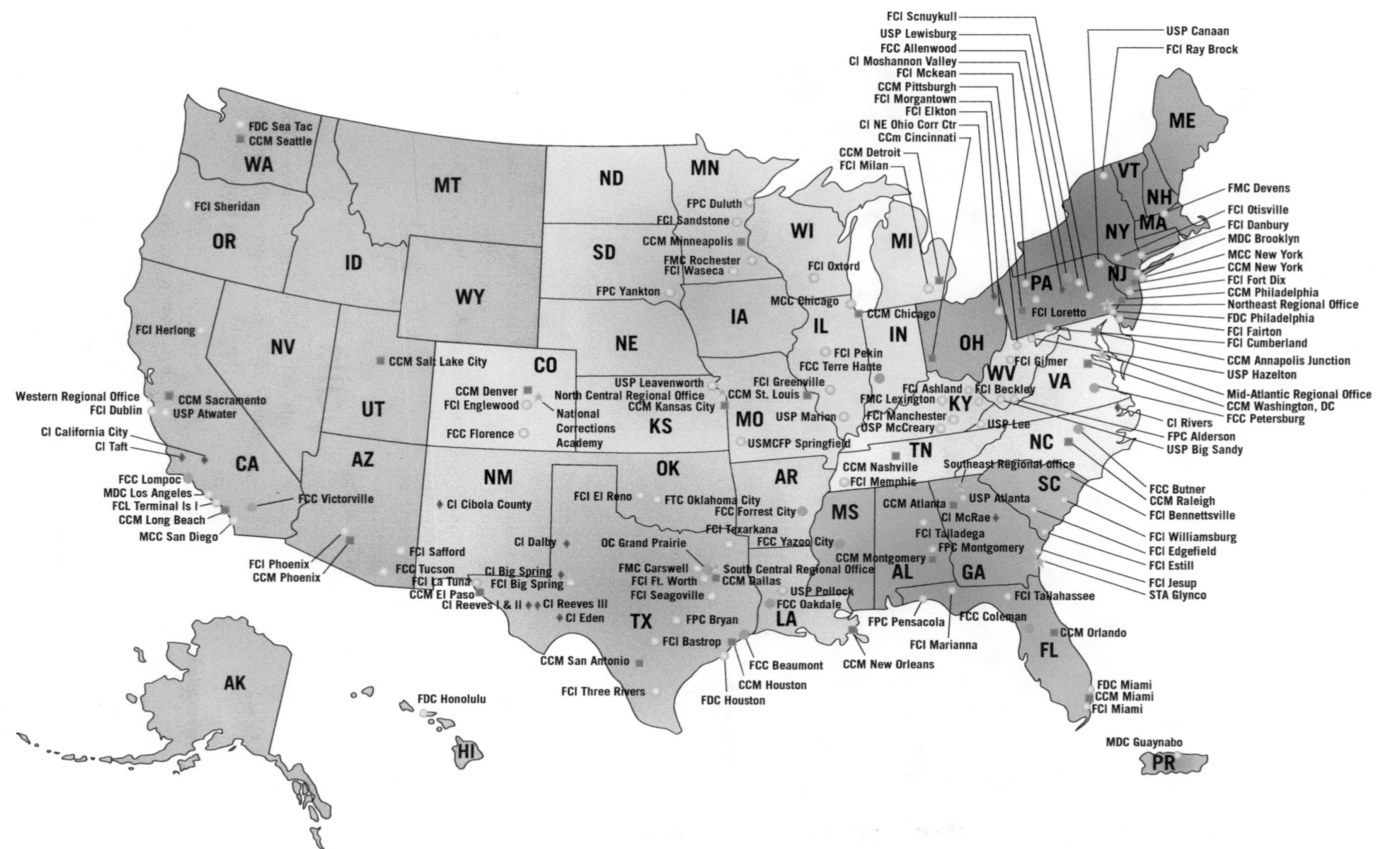

FIGURE 13-10 | Federal Bureau of Prisons Facilities by Region

Source: Federal Bureau of Prisons, http://www.bop.gov/locations/locationmap.jsp.

jail A confinement facility administered by an agency of local government, typically a law enforcement agency, intended for adults but sometimes also containing juveniles, which holds people detained pending adjudication or committed after adjudication, usually those sentenced to a year or less.

Bob Daemmrich/Agence France Presse/Getty Images

The Federal Bureau of Prisons ADMAX facility in Florence, Colorado, which opened in 1995. It is the only ultra-high-security institution in the federal system. What kinds of inmates are held here?

In an effort to combat rising expenses associated with a rapidly growing federal prison population, the U.S. Congress passed legislation in 1992 that imposes a "user fee" on federal inmates who are able to pay the costs associated with their incarceration.[115] Under the law, inmates may be assessed a dollar amount up to the cost of a year's incarceration—currently around $22,600.[116] The statute, which was designed so as not to impose hardships on poor offenders or their dependents, directs that collected funds, estimated to total $48 million per year, are to be used to improve alcohol- and drug-abuse programs within federal prisons. Visit the Federal Bureau of Prisons website at **http://www.bop.gov**.

Recent Improvements

In the midst of frequent lawsuits, court-ordered changes in prison administration, and overcrowded conditions, outstanding prison facilities are being recognized through the accreditation program of the American Correctional Association (ACA). The ACA Commission on Accreditation has developed a set of standards that correctional institutions can use for conducting self-evaluations. Institutions that meet the standards can apply for accreditation under the program.

Another avenue toward improvement of the nation's prisons can be found in the National Academy of Corrections, the training arm of the National Institute of Corrections. The academy, located in Boulder, Colorado, offers seminars, videoconferencing, and training sessions for state and local corrections managers, trainers, personnel directors, sheriffs, and state legislators.[117] Issues covered include strategies to control overcrowding, community corrections program management, prison programs, gangs and disturbances, security, and public and media relations.[118]

Jails

Jails are locally operated short-term confinement facilities originally built to hold suspects following arrest and pending trial. Today's jails also serve these purposes:[119]

- They receive individuals pending arraignment and hold them awaiting trial, conviction, or sentencing.
- They readmit probation, parole, and bail-bond violators and absconders.
- They temporarily detain juveniles, inmates who are mentally ill, and others pending transfer to appropriate facilities.
- They hold individuals for the military, for protective custody, for contempt, and for the courts as witnesses.

- They release convicted inmates to the community upon completion of their sentence.
- They transfer inmates to federal, state, or other authorities.
- They house inmates for federal, state, or other authorities because of overcrowding in their facilities.
- They operate community-based programs with day reporting, home detention, electronic monitoring, and other types of supervision.
- They hold inmates sentenced to short terms (generally less than one year).

A recent report by the Bureau of Justice Statistics (BJS) found that the nation's jails held 744,524 inmates—15% of whom were women.[120] Juveniles held in local jails numbered around 5,900.[121] More than half of jail inmates have been convicted of a crime, a quarter are being detained while awaiting arraignment or trial, and a sixth are being held on a prior sentence but are also awaiting arraignment or trial on a new charge.[122] Jail authorities also supervised an additional 62,816 men and women in the community under programs that included the following: electronic monitoring (11,950), home detention without electronic monitoring (809), day reporting (5,200), community service (11,680), and weekend programs (11,369).[123]

A total of 3,283 jails operate throughout the United States, staffed by approximately 234,000 jail employees—the equivalent of about one employee for every three jail inmates.[124] Overall, the nation's jail budget is huge, and facilities are overflowing. State and local governments spend $10 billion every year to operate the nation's jails,[125] with more than $1 billion in additional monies earmarked for new jail construction and for renovation. On average, the housing of one jail inmate costs more than $14,500 per year.[126]

Approximately 12 million people are admitted (or readmitted) to the nation's jails each year.[127] Some jail inmates stay for as little as one day, whereas others serve extended periods of time. Significantly, one of the fastest-growing sectors of today's jail population consists of sentenced offenders serving time in local jails because overcrowded prisons cannot accept them.

Most people processed through the country's jails are members of minority groups (55%), with 38% of jail inmates classifying themselves as African American, 15% as Hispanic, and 1.9% as other minorities. Less than 1% report being of more than one race, and 45% of jail inmates classify themselves as white. Slightly more than 87% are male.[128] The typical jail inmate is an unmarried black male between 25 and 34 years of age who reports having had some high school education. Typical charges include drug trafficking (12.1%), assault (11.7%), drug possession (10.8%), and larceny (7%).[129]

A. Ramey/PhotoEdit Inc.

Los Angeles County's largest jail. The $373 million jail, officially known as the Twin Towers Correctional Facility, opened in 1997 and is one of the world's largest jails. What are the differences between a prison and a jail?

According to the BJS, about 6% of jail facilities house more than half of all jail inmates in the nation.[130] So, although most jails are small—many were built to house 50 or fewer inmates—most people who spend time in jail do so in larger institutions. Across the country, a handful of "megajails" house thousands of inmates each. The largest such facilities are in Los Angeles; New York City; Cook County, Illinois; Harris County, Texas; and Maricopa County, Arizona. Los Angeles County's 4,000-bed Twin Towers Correctional Facility cost $373 million to build and opened in 1997.[131] The city of Los Angeles' 512-bed Metropolitan Detention Center, although not nearly as large, opened in 2011 and cost the city $84 million to build. The largest employer among huge jails is Cook County's, with more than 1,200 personnel on its payroll.[132] The nation's 50 largest jail jurisdictions hold 29.5% of all jail inmates.[133] The two jurisdictions with the most jail inmates, Los Angeles County and New York City, together hold approximately 31,085 inmates, or 4.2% of the national total.[134]

Women and Jail

Although women number only 15% of the country's jail population, they are the largest growth group in jails nationwide.[135] Jailed women face a number of special problems. Only 25.7% of the nation's jails report having a classification system specifically designed to evaluate female inmates,[136] and although many jurisdictions have plans "to build facilities geared to the female offender,"[137]

Although women number only 15% of the country's jail population, they are the largest growth group in jails nationwide.

not all jurisdictions today even provide separate housing areas for women. Educational levels are very low among jailed women, and fewer than half are high school graduates.[138] Drug abuse is another significant source of difficulty for jailed women. More than 30% of women who are admitted to jail have a substance-abuse problem at the time of admission, and in some parts of the country, that figure may be as high as 70%.[139]

Pregnancy is another problem. Nationally, 4% of female inmates are pregnant when they enter jail,[140] but in urban areas, as much as 10% of the female jail population is reported to be pregnant on any given day.[141] As a consequence, a few hundred children are born in jails each year. However, substantive medical programs for female inmates, such as obstetrics and gynecological care, are often lacking. In planning future medical services for female inmates, some writers have advised jail administrators to expect to see an increasingly common kind of inmate: "an opiate-addicted female who is pregnant with no prior prenatal care having one or more sexually transmitted diseases, and fitting a high-risk category for AIDS (prostitution, IV drug use)."[142]

Not only are jailed mothers separated from their children, but they may have to pay for their support. Twelve percent of all jails in one study reported requiring employed female inmates to contribute to the support of their dependent children.

When we consider women and jails, female inmates are only half the story. Women who work in corrections are the other half. In one study, Linda Zupan, a member of a new generation of jail scholars, found that women made up 22% of the corrections officer force in jails across the nation.[143] The deployment of female personnel, however, was disproportionately skewed toward jobs in the lower ranks. Although 60% of all support staff (secretaries, cooks, and janitors) were women, only one in every ten chief administrators was female. Even so, Zupan did find that female corrections employees

freedom OR **safety?** YOU **decide**

To What Degree Should the Personal Values of Workers in the Criminal Justice System Influence Job Performance?

In 2009, a "conscience-protection rule" was published in the Federal Register—having been enacted by the administration of George W. Bush just before he left office. The rule, meant mainly to apply to the health-care industry, gives doctors, hospitals, receptionists, and other workers and volunteers the right to refuse to participate in any medical care that they find morally objectionable. In particular, the rule "protects the rights of medical providers to care for their patients in accord with their conscience," said outgoing Health and Human Services Secretary Mike Leavitt.

The rule came too late to apply to a 2007 incident in which a 21-year-old college student who was visiting Tampa, Florida, was attacked and raped while walking back to her car. The story of the woman, who was attending the annual Gasparilla festival, a pirate-themed parade, took an interesting twist. Investigating officers first took her to a nearby rape crisis center, where she was physically examined and given an initial emergency post-coital contraception pill, also known as a *morning-after pill*, to prevent unwanted pregnancy.

Officers then drove the victim through the area where the attack allegedly took place in an effort to find the rapist and to pinpoint the scene of the crime. As they drove, officers entered the woman's identifying information into their car's computer system and discovered that a juvenile warrant that had been issued against her in 2003 for unpaid restitution in a theft case was still outstanding. Once they discovered the warrant, officers promptly arrested, booked, and jailed the woman. She remained behind bars for two days until her family was able to hire an attorney who arranged for her release.

During the time she was jailed, the victim said, a jail health-care worker refused to administer a second—and required—dose of the morning-after medication. The medicine's manufacturer specifies that two doses, administered 20 hours apart, are needed to prevent pregnancy. Some members of the local media, which accused the police department of insensitivity to the needs of crime victims, reported that the jail worker felt compelled to deny the woman the medication due to personal religious beliefs against use of the pill.

Vic Moore, the jailed woman's attorney, told reporters that he was "Shocked. Stunned. Outraged. I don't have words to describe it," he said. "She is not a victim of any one person. She is a victim of the system. There's just got to be some humanity involved when it's a victim of rape."

The Tampa Police Department, which was stung by media reports in the case, has since initiated a policy advising officers not to arrest a crime victim who has suffered injury or mental trauma whenever reasonably possible.

You Decide

To what extent (if at all) should the values of workers within the criminal justice system be allowed to influence their performance of job-related tasks? Do you feel that the jail worker referenced in this story was within her "rights" by denying a second dose of the morning-after pill to the victim of an alleged rape? Why or why not?

References: David G. Savage, "Health Providers' 'Conscience' Rule to Take Effect," *Los Angeles Times*, December 19, 2008; and Phil Davis, "Rape Victim Is Jailed on Old Warrant," Associated Press, January 31, 2007.

were significantly committed to their careers and that the attitudes of male workers toward female coworkers in jails were generally positive. Zupan's study uncovered 626 jails in which over 50% of the corrections officer force consisted of women. However, 954 of the nation's 3,316 jails operating at the time of the study had no female officers.[144] Zupan noted that "an obvious problem associated with the lack of female officers in jails housing females concerns the potential for abuse and exploitation of women inmates by male staff."[145]

Jails that do hire women generally accord them equal footing with male staffers. Although cross-gender privacy is a potential area of legal liability, in three-quarters of the jails studied by Zupan, female officers were assigned to supervise male housing areas. Only one in four jails that employed women restricted their access to unscreened shower and toilet facilities used by men or to other areas, such as sexual offender units.

The Growth of Jails

Jails have been called the "shame of the criminal justice system." Many are old, poorly funded, scantily staffed by underpaid and poorly trained employees, and given low priority in local budgets. By the end of the 1980s, many of our nation's jails had become seriously overcrowded, and court-ordered caps were sometimes placed on jail populations. One of the first such caps was imposed on the Harris County Jail in Houston, Texas, in 1990. In that year, the jail was forced to release 250 inmates after missing a deadline for reducing its resident population of 6,100 people.[146] A nationwide survey by the Bureau of Justice Statistics, undertaken around the same time, found that 46% of all jails had been built more than 25 years earlier, and of that percentage, over half were more than 50 years old.[147]

A 1983 national census revealed that jails were operating at 85% of their rated capacity (Table 13-1).[148] In 1990, however, the nation's jails were running at 104% of capacity, and new jails could be found on drawing boards and under construction across the country. By 2012, jail capacity had increased substantially, and overall jail occupancy was reported at 83% of rated capacity. Some individual facilities, however, were still desperately overcrowded.[149] Jail jurisdictions with the largest average daily populations also reported the highest occupancy rates.

Although jail overcrowding is not the issue it was a decade or two ago, it is still a problem. Overcrowded prisons have taken a toll on jails. At the start of 2012, for example, approximately 82,000 inmates were being held in local jails because of overcrowding in state and federal prisons.[150] Also, the practice of giving jail sentences to offenders who are unable or unwilling to make restitution, alimony, or child-support payments has added to jail occupancy and has made the local lockup, at least partially, a debtors' prison. Symptomatic of problems brought on by huge jail populations, 314 suicides were reported in jails across the nation during a recent year.[151] Jail deaths from all causes total about 980 annually. Other factors conspire to keep jail populations high, including the inability of jail inmates to make bond, delays between arrest and case disposition, an overburdened criminal justice system, and what some have called "unproductive statutes" requiring that specified nonviolent offenders be jailed.[152]

Some innovative jurisdictions have successfully contained the growth of jail populations by diverting arrestees to community-based programs. San Diego, California, for example, uses a privately operated detoxification reception program to divert many inebriates from the "drunk tank."[153] Officials in Galveston County, Texas, routinely divert arrestees who are mentally ill directly to a mental health facility.[154] Other areas use pretrial services and magistrates' offices, which are open 24 hours a day, for setting bail, making release possible.

New-Generation Jails

Some suggest that the problems found in many jails stem from "mismanagement, lack of fiscal support, heterogeneous inmate populations, overuse and misuse of detention, overemphasis

TABLE 13-1 | Jail Facts

	1983	1988	1993	2000	2012
Number of jails	3,338	3,316	3,304	3,365	3,283[a]
Number of jail inmates	223,551	343,569	459,804	621,149	744,524
Rated capacity of jails	261,556	339,949	475,224	677,787	877,302
Percentage of capacity occupied	85%	101%	97%	92%	83%

[a]Estimate based on earlier data.
Sources: Todd D. Minton, *Jail Inmates at Midyear 2012—Statistical Tables* (Washington, DC: Bureau of Justice Statistics, 2013).

■ **new-generation jail** A temporary confinement facility that eliminates many of the traditional barriers between inmates and correctional personnel. Also called *podular jail, direct-supervision jail,* and *indirect-supervision jail.*

on custodial goals, and political and public apathy."[155] Others propose that environmental and organizational aspects of traditional jail architecture and staffing have led to many difficulties.[156] Traditional jails, say these observers, were built on the assumption that inmates are inherently violent and potentially destructive. Through the use of thick walls, bars, and other architectural barriers, jails were constructed to give staff maximum control and to restrict inmates' movements. Such institutions, however, also limit the correctional staff's visibility and access to confinement areas. As a consequence, they tend to encourage just the kinds of inmate behavior that jails were meant to control. Today, efficient hallway patrols and expensive video technology help in overcoming the limits that old jail architecture places on supervision.

In an effort to solve many of the problems that dogged jails in the past, a new jail-management strategy emerged during the 1970s. Prison architects developed a new style of jail architecture in which modern designs were used to improve communications between inmates and staff, allowing for enhanced supervision. These **new-generation jails**, also known as podular jails, allow for continuous observation of inmates. New-generation jails are of two types: direct-supervision and indirect-supervision jails.[157] *Direct-supervision jails* cluster cells around a central living area or "pod," which contains tables, chairs, and televisions. A correctional officer is stationed within each pod and is able to observe inmate interaction and can relate to inmates on a personal level. During the day, inmates stay in the open area (dayroom) and are typically are not permitted to go to their rooms except with permission of the officer in charge. *Indirect-supervision jails* are similar in construction to direct-supervision facilities, but they place the correctional officer's station inside of a secure room. Officers are able to communicate with inmates through the use of microphones, and speakers with built-in microphones are placed inside living areas.

New-generation jails help eliminate the old physical barriers that separated staff and inmates in traditional facilities. In a number of new-generation jails, large reinforced Plexiglas panels supplanted walls and serve to separate activity areas, such as classrooms and dining halls, from one another. Soft furniture is the rule throughout such institutions, and individual rooms take the place of cells, allowing inmates at least a modicum of personal privacy. In today's new-generation jails, 16 to 46 inmates typically live in one pod, with correctional staffers present among the inmate population around the clock.

New-generation jails have been touted for their tendency to reduce inmate dissatisfaction and for their ability to deter rape and violence among the inmate population. By eliminating many architectural barriers to staff–inmate interaction, new-generation facilities are said to place officers back in control of institutions. Numerous studies have demonstrated the success of such jails in reducing the likelihood of inmate victimization. One such study also found that staff morale in direct-supervision jails was far higher than in traditional institutions, that inmates reported reduced stress levels, and that fewer inmate-on-inmate and inmate-on-staff assaults occurred.[158] Similarly, sexual assault, jail rape, suicide, and escape have all been found to occur far less frequently in direct-supervision facilities than in traditional institutions.[159] Significantly, new-generation jails appear to be substantially less susceptible to lawsuits brought by inmates and to adverse court-ordered judgments against jail administrators.

Jails and the Future

In contrast to more visible issues confronting the justice system—such as the death penalty, gun control, the war on drugs, terrorism, and big-city gangs—jails have received relatively little attention from the media and have generally escaped close public scrutiny.[160] National efforts are under way, however, to improve the quality of jail life. Some changes involve adding crucial programs for inmates. An American Jail Association (AJA) study of drug-treatment programs in jails, for example, found that "a small fraction (perhaps fewer than 10%) of inmates needing drug treatment actually receive these services."[161]

Jail industries are another growing programmatic area. The best of them serve the community while training inmates in marketable skills.[162] In an exemplary effort to humanize its megajails, for example, the Los Angeles County Sheriff's Department opened an inmate telephone-answering service.[163] Many callers contact the sheriff's department daily, requesting information about the county's 22,000 jail inmates. These requests for information were becoming increasingly difficult to handle due to the growing fiscal constraints facing local government. To handle the huge number of calls effectively without tying up sworn law enforcement personnel, the department began using inmates specially trained to handle incoming calls. Eighty inmates were assigned to the project, with groups of different sizes covering shifts throughout the day. Each inmate staffer went through a training program to learn proper telephone procedures and how to run computer terminals containing routine data on the department's inmates. The system now handles 4,000 telephone inquiries a day. The time needed to answer a call and to begin to provide information

■ **regional jail** A jail that is built and run using the combined resources of a variety of local jurisdictions.

Damian Dovarganes/AP Wide World Photos

Inmates playing cards at the Los Angeles North County Correctional Facility in Saugus, California. The Los Angeles County jail system is the largest in the world, housing more than 20,000 inmates on a given day. What are direct-supervision jails?

has dropped from 30 minutes under the old system to a remarkable 10 seconds today.

Capturing much recent attention are **regional jails**—that is, jails that are built and run using the combined resources of a variety of local jurisdictions. Regional jails have begun to replace smaller and often antiquated local jails in at least a few locations. One example of a regional jail is the Western Tidewater Regional Jail, serving the cities of Suffolk and Franklin and the county of Isle of Wright in Virginia.[164] Regional jails, which are just beginning to come into their own, may develop quickly in Virginia, where the state, recognizing the economies of consolidation, offers to reimburse localities up to 50% of the cost of building regional jails.

The emergence of state standards has become an increasingly important area in jail management. Thirty-two states have set standards for municipal and county jails.[165] In 25 states, those standards are mandatory. The purpose of jail standards is to identify basic minimum conditions necessary for inmate health and safety. On the national level, the Commission on Accreditation for Corrections, operated jointly by the American Correctional Association and the federal government, has developed its own set of jail standards,[166] as has the National Sheriff's Association. Both sets of standards are designed to ensure a minimal level of comfort and safety in local lockups. Increased standards, though, are costly. Local jurisdictions, already hard-pressed to meet other budgetary demands, will probably be slow to upgrade their jails to meet such external guidelines unless forced to do so. In a study of 61 jails that was designed to test compliance with the National Sheriff's Association guidelines, Ken Kerle discovered that in many standards areas—especially those of tool control, armory planning, community resources, release preparation, and riot planning—the majority of jails were badly out of compliance.[167] Lack of a written plan was the most commonly cited reason for failing to meet the standards.

One final element in the unfolding saga of jail development should be mentioned: the expansion of jails throughout California to accommodate inmates who have been reassigned under that state's realignment strategy (discussed earlier in this chapter). According to the California Board of State and Community Corrections, the state's jail population has been rising significantly as more and more inmates are sent to jail in lieu of state prison, and jail administrators are looking to increase jail capacity.[168] In Fresno County, for example, jail floors that had been closed have now been reopened, and the county is looking for additional places to house inmates.[169] Learn more about jails by visiting the American Jail Association via **http://www.aja.org**.

Private Prisons

State-run prison systems have always contracted with private industries for food, psychological testing, training, and recreational and other services, and it is estimated that more than

■ **privatization** The movement toward the wider use of private prisons.
■ **private prison** A correctional institution operated by a private firm on behalf of a local or state government.

three dozen states today rely on private businesses to serve a variety of correctional needs. It follows, then, that states have now turned to private industry for the provision of prison space. The **privatization** movement, which began in the early 1980s, was slow to catch on, but it has since grown at a rapid pace. In 1986, only 2,620 prisoners could be found in privately run confinement facilities.[170] But by 2012, privately operated correctional facilities serving as prisons and jails held over 130,900 state and federal prisoners across 31 states and the District of Columbia.[171] The largest growth came in the federal sector, with a 784% increase in the number of federal inmates held in privately run facilities between 1999 and 2010 (from 3,828 to 33,830).[172]

Private prisons held 8.2% of all state prisoners and 17.8% of federal prisoners at the start of 2012. New Mexico is the state that uses private prisons the most, with 41% of its inmates held there. One source says that the overall growth rate of the private prison industry has been around 35% annually[173]—comparable to the highest growth rates anywhere in the corporate sector.

Privately run prisons are operated by Corrections Corporation of America (CCA), GEO Group (formerly, Wackenhut Corrections Corporation), Management & Training, LCS Correctional Services, Emerald Corrections, and numerous other smaller companies. The CCA, the largest of the private prison contractors, houses more than 75,000 inmates at 66 facilities.[174] Most states that use private firms to supplement their prison resources contract with such companies to provide a full range of custodial and other correctional services. State corrections administrators use private companies to reduce overcrowding, lower operating expenses, and avoid lawsuits targeted at state officials and employees.[175] But some studies have shown that private prisons may not bring the kinds of cost savings that had been anticipated.[176] One study by the U.S. General Accounting Office,[177] for example, found "neither cost savings nor substantial differences in the quality of services" between private and publicly run prisons.[178] Similar findings emerged in a 2001 report by the Bureau of Justice Assistance. That report, titled *Emerging Issues on Privatized Prisons*, found that "private prisons offer only modest cost savings, which are basically a result of moderate reductions in staffing patterns, fringe benefits, and other labor-related costs."[179]

Many hurdles remain before the privatization movement can effectively provide large-scale custodial supervision. Among the most significant barriers to privatization are old state laws that prohibit private involvement in correctional management. Other practical hurdles exist as well. States that do contract with private firms may face the specter of strikes by corrections officers who do not come under state laws restricting the ability of public employees to strike. Moreover, because responsibility for the protection of inmate rights still lies with the states, their liability will not transfer to private corrections.[180] In today's legal climate, it is unclear whether a state can shield itself or its employees through private prison contracting, but it appears that the courts are unlikely to recognize such shielding. To limit their own liability, states will probably have to oversee private operations as well as set standards for training and custody. In 1997, in the case of *Richardson* v. *McKnight*,[181] the U.S. Supreme Court made it clear that corrections officers employed by a private firm are not entitled to qualified immunity from suits by prisoners charging a violation of Section 1983 of Title 42 of the U.S. Code. (See Chapter 8 for more information on Section 1983 lawsuits.) However, in the 2011 case of *Minneci* v. *Pollard*, the Court held that a *Bivens* action (a liability action directed specifically at federal officials or enforcement agents) against employees of a privately run federal prison in California could not proceed because state tort law already "authorizes adequate alternative damages actions."[182] In 2001, in the case of *Correctional Services Corporation* v. *Malesko*,[183] the Court found that private corporations acting under color of federal law cannot be held responsible in a *Bivens* action because the purpose of *Bivens* (which was discussed in Chapter 8) "is to deter individual federal officers from committing Constitutional violations."[184]

Perhaps the most serious legal issues confront states that contract to hold inmates outside of their own jurisdiction. More than a decade ago, for example, two inmates escaped from a 240-man sex-offender unit run by the Corrections Corporation of America (CCA) under contract with the state of Oregon. Problems immediately arose because the CCA unit was located near Houston, Texas—not in Oregon, where the men had originally been sentenced to confinement. Following the escape, Texas officials were unsure whether they even had arrest power over the former prisoners, as their escape was not a crime in Texas. Although prison escape *is* a crime under Texas law, the law applies to only state-run facilities, not to private facilities where correctional personnel are not employed by the state or empowered in any official capacity by state law. Harris County (Texas) Prosecutor John Holmes explained the situation this way: "They have not committed the offense of escape under Texas law . . . and the only reason at all that they're subject to being arrested and were arrested was because during their leaving the

ethics and professionalism

American Jail Association Code of Ethics for Jail Officers

As an officer employed in a detention/correctional capacity, I swear (or affirm) to be a good citizen and a credit to my community, state, and nation at all times. I will abstain from all questionable behavior which might bring disrepute to the agency for which I work, my family, my community, and my associates. My lifestyle will be above and beyond reproach and I will constantly strive to set an example of a professional who performs his/her duties according to the laws of our country, state, and community and the policies, procedures, written and verbal orders, and regulations of the agency for which I work.

On the job I promise to:

Keep	The institution secure so as to safeguard my community and the lives of the staff, inmates, and visitors on the premises.
Work	With each individual firmly and fairly without regard to rank, status, or condition.
Maintain	A positive demeanor when confronted with stressful situations of scorn, ridicule, danger, and/or chaos.
Report	Either in writing or by word of mouth to the proper authorities those things which should be reported, and keep silent about matters which are to remain confidential according to the laws and rules of the agency and government.
Manage	And supervise the inmates in an even-handed and courteous manner.
Refrain	At all times from becoming personally involved in the lives of the inmates and their families.
Treat	All visitors to the jail with politeness and respect and do my utmost to ensure that they observe the jail regulations.
Take	Advantage of all education and training opportunities designed to assist me to become a more competent officer.
Communicate	With people in or outside of the jail, whether by phone, written word, or word of mouth, in such a way so as not to reflect in a negative manner upon my agency.
Contribute	To a jail environment which will keep the inmate involved in activities designed to improve his/her attitude and character.
Support	All activities of a professional nature through membership and participation that will continue to elevate the status of those who operate our nation's jails. Do my best through word and deed to present an image to the public at large of a jail professional, committed to progress for an improved and enlightened criminal justice system.

Do my best through word and deed to present an image to the public at large of a jail professional, committed to progress for an improved and enlightened criminal justice system.

Thinking About Ethics

1. Why does this code of ethics require jail officers to "take advantage of all education and training opportunities designed to assist [them] to become a more competent officer"? What does education have to do with ethics?
2. Are there any elements that you might add to this code? Are there any that you might delete?

Source: American Jail Association, *Code of Ethics for Jail Officers*, adopted January 10, 1991. Revised May 19, 1993. Web available: https://members.aja.org/ethics.aspx.

facility, they assaulted a guard and took his motor vehicle. That we can charge them with and have."[185]

Opponents of the movement toward privatization cite these and many other issues. They claim that, aside from legal concerns, cost reductions via the use of private facilities can be achieved only by lowering standards. They fear a return to the inhumane conditions of early jails, as private firms seek to turn prisons into profit-making operations. For states that do choose to contract with private firms, the National Institute of Justice (NIJ) recommends a "regular and systematic sampling" of former inmates to appraise prison conditions, as well as annual on-site inspections of each privately run institution. State personnel serving as monitors should be stationed in large facilities, says the NIJ, and a "meticulous review" of all services should be conducted before the contract renewal date.[186] Finally, some fear that private prisons skim prisoners who are the "best of the worst" and leave the "worst of the worst" in public-run institutions, making *those* populations even more difficult to manage.

CJ | ISSUES

Arguments for and against the Privatization of Prisons

Reasons to Privatize

1. Private operators can provide construction financing options that allow the government to pay only for capacity as needed in lieu of assuming long-term debt.
2. Private companies offer state-of-the-art correctional facility designs that are efficient to operate and that are based on cost–benefit considerations.
3. Private operators typically design and construct a new correctional facility in half the time it takes to build a comparable government project.
4. Private companies provide government with the convenience and accountability of one entity for all compliance issues.
5. Private companies can mobilize rapidly and specialize in unique facility missions.
6. Private companies provide economic development opportunities by hiring and purchasing locally.
7. Government can reduce or share its liability exposure by contracting with private corrections companies.
8. Government can retain flexibility by limiting the contract's duration and by specifying the facility's mission.
9. The addition of alternative service providers injects competition among both public and private organizations.

Reasons Not to Privatize

1. There are certain responsibilities that only the government should meet, such as public safety. The government has legal, political, and moral obligations to provide incarceration. Constitutional issues underlie both public and private corrections and involve deprivation of liberty, discipline, and preservation of the rights of inmates. Related issues include use of force, equitable hiring practices, and segregation.
2. Few private companies are available from which to choose.
3. Private operators may be inexperienced with key corrections issues.
4. A private operator may become a monopoly through political ingratiation, favoritism, and so on.
5. Government may, over time, lose the capability to perform the corrections function.
6. The profit motive will inhibit the proper performance of corrections duties. Private companies have financial incentives to cut corners.
7. The procurement process is slow, inefficient, and open to risks.
8. Creating a good, clear contract is a daunting task.
9. The lack of enforcement remedies in contracts leaves only termination or lawsuits as recourse.

Source: Dennis Cunningham, "Public Strategies for Private Prisons," paper presented at the Private Prison Workshop at the Institute on Criminal Justice, University of Minnesota Law School, January 29–30, 1999.

Reed Saxon/AP Wide World Photos

The 2,300-bed California City Correctional Center in the Mojave Desert town of California City. The facility, which opened in December 1999, was built by the Corrections Corporation of America (CCA) to provide medium-security correctional services under a contract with the Federal Bureau of Prisons. The Nashville-based CCA says that it can run prisons as efficiently as the government, and its supporters claim that private prisons are the way of the future. Do you agree? Why or why not?

SUMMARY

- Before the development of prisons in the late eighteenth and early nineteenth centuries, early criminal punishments were frequently cruel and torturous. Flogging, mutilation, branding, and public humiliation were some of the physical punishments imposed on offenders before the development of prisons.
- In an important historical development, around the year 1800, imprisonment *as* punishment replaced the notion of imprisonment *for* punishment. The state of today's prisons is largely the result of historical efforts to humanize the treatment of offenders, coupled with recent attempts to have the prison experience reflect prevailing social attitudes toward crime and punishment. Early workhouses, which flourished in Europe a few hundred years ago and housed the noncriminal poor and destitute, provided a model for efforts to institutionalize those whom society perceived as burdensome. Imprisonment in the United States began with the penitentiary philosophy of the Pennsylvania Quakers, who believed that solitary confinement and meditation on one's transgressions could lead to reformation. Soon, however, the mass-prison philosophy, represented by prisons like Auburn Prison in New York, won the day, and the contemporary system of imprisonment—in which relatively large numbers of people are confined together and often allowed to interact closely—emerged.
- Prisons today are largely classified according to security level, such as maximum, medium, and minimum security. Most contemporary American correctional facilities are medium or minimum security. Although the goals of recidivism and deterrence are still important in the minds of corrections administrators, today's prisons tend to warehouse inmates awaiting release. Public disappointment with high rates of recidivism has produced a prison system today that is focused on the concept of just deserts and that is only beginning to emerge from the strong influence of the nothing-works doctrine discussed in this chapter. Overcrowded facilities are still the norm in many jurisdictions, although a prison-building boom over the last decade has alleviated some of the extremely overcrowded conditions that had previously existed.
- In contrast to prisons, which are long-time confinement facilities designed to hold those who have been sentenced to serve time for committing crime, jails are short-term confinement facilities whose traditional purpose has been to hold those awaiting trial or sentencing. Inmates who have been tried and sentenced may also be held at jails until their transfer to a prison facility, and today's jails sometimes hold inmates serving short sentences of confinement. Recently, the emergence of direct-supervision jails, in which traditional barriers between inmates and staff have been mostly eliminated, seems to have reduced the incidence of jail violence and can be credited with improving the conditions of jailed inmates in jurisdictions where such facilities operate.
- Privately run correctional facilities, or private prisons, have grown in number over the past few decades as the movement toward the privatization of correctional facilities has gained steam. Private prisons, operated by for-profit corporations, hold inmates on behalf of state governments or the federal government and provide for their care and security. A number of questions remain as to the role such facilities will play in the future, including whether they can be cost-effective and whether they can somehow reduce the legal liability of state governments and government employees that is often associated with confinement.

KEY TERMS

ADMAX, 439
Ashurst-Sumners Act, 422
Auburn system, 419
classification system, 438
design capacity, 436
industrial prison, 421
jail, 442
justice model, 428
***lex talionis*, 414**
medical model, 424
new-generation jail, 446
nothing-works doctrine, 426
operational capacity, 435
Pennsylvania system, 417
prison, 414
prison capacity, 435
private prison, 448
privatization, 448
rated capacity, 435
reformatory style, 419
regional jail, 447
selective incapacitation, 436
state-use system, 422
warehousing, 426
work release, 425
workhouse, 415

KEY NAMES

Zebulon Brockway, 421
Sir Walter Crofton, 419
Alexander Maconochie, 419
Robert Martinson, 426
Alexis de Tocqueville, 419

QUESTIONS FOR REVIEW

1. What types of criminal punishments were used before the advent of imprisonment as a criminal sanction? How have early punishments influenced modern correctional philosophy?
2. Trace the historical development of prisons in the United States, beginning with the Pennsylvania system. How has correctional practice in America changed over time? What changes do you predict for the future?
3. What are today's prisons like? What purposes do they serve?
4. What role do jails play in American corrections? What are some of the issues that jail administrators currently face?
5. What is the role of private prisons today?

QUESTIONS FOR REFLECTION

1. What are the demographics (social characteristics) of today's prisoners? What gender and racial disparities, if any, exist in today's prison population?
2. What is the just deserts model of corrections? Explain the pros and cons of this model. How has it led to an increased use of imprisonment and to prison overcrowding?
3. What is the relationship, if any, between changes in the rate of criminal offending and changes in the rate of imprisonment in America during the last decade? What is the reason for that relationship?
4. What will be the state of private prisons two or three decades from now?

NOTES

i. Bureau of Justice Statistics, *Prisoners in 1998* (Washington, DC: BJS, 1999), p. 7.

1. Dan Walters, "With California Prison Overcrowding, Jerry Brown Still Traversing a Minefield," *The Sacramento Bee*, January 9, 2013, http://www.sacbee.com/2013/01/09/5101509/dan-walters-with-california-prison.html#storylink=cpy (accessed March 3, 2013).
2. "Steven Martinez, Quadriplegic Rapist, Will be Freed from California Prison," *Huffington Post*, http://www.huffingtonpost.com/2012/11/16/steven-martinez-quadriplegic-rapist-_n_2145339.html (accessed October 15, 2013).
3. Rob Quinn, "Quadriplegic Rapist Denied Parole," *Newser*, May 25, 2011, http://www.newser.com/story/119382/quadriplegic-rapist-denied-parole.html (accessed June 1, 2011).
4. Lauren Steussy and Chris Chan, "Quadriplegic Rapist to Be Released from Prison," NBC San Diego, http://www.nbcsandiego.com/news/local/Quadriplegic-Rapist-to-be-Released-from-Prison-179722421.html (accessed March 3, 2013).
5. *Brown* v. *Plata*, 563 U.S. _______ (2011).
6. David G. Savage and Patrick McGreevy, "U.S. Supreme Court Orders Massive Inmate Release to Relieve California's Crowded Prisons," *Los Angeles Times*, May 24, 2011, http://articles.latimes.com/2011/may/24/local/la-me-court-prisons-20110524 (accessed June 1, 2011).
7. Walters, op. cit.
8. Camden Pelham, *Chronicles of Crime: A Series of Memoirs and Anecdotes of Notorious Characters* (London: T. Miles, 1887), pp. 28–30.
9. This section owes much to Harry Elmer Barnes and Negley K. Teeters, *New Horizons in Criminology*, 3rd ed. (Upper Saddle River, NJ: Prentice Hall, 1959).
10. Ibid., p. 290.
11. Ann O'Hanlon, "New Interest in Corporal Punishment: Several States Weigh Get-Tough Measures," *Washington Post* wire service, March 5, 1995.
12. Barnes and Teeters, *New Horizons in Criminology*, p. 292.
13. Ibid.
14. Ibid., p. 293.
15. Arthur Evans Wood and John Barker Waite, *Crime and Its Treatment: Social and Legal Aspects of Criminology* (New York: American Book Company, 1941), p. 488.
16. John Howard, *State of Prisons* (London, 1777; reprint, New York: E. P. Dutton, 1929).
17. Although some writers hold that the Quakers originated the concept of solitary confinement for prisoners, there is evidence that the practice already existed in England before 1789. John Howard, for example, described solitary confinement in use at Reading Bridewell in the 1780s.
18. Vergil L. Williams, *Dictionary of American Penology: An Introduction* (Westport, CT: Greenwood Press, 1979), p. 200.
19. Barnes and Teeters, *New Horizons in Criminology*, p. 348.
20. Williams, *Dictionary of American Penology*, p. 29.
21. With regard to cost, supporters of the Pennsylvania system argued that it was actually less expensive than the Auburn style of imprisonment because it led more quickly to reformation.
22. Williams, *Dictionary of American Penology*, p. 30.
23. Gustave de Beaumont and Alexis de Tocqueville, *On the Penitentiary System in the United States, and Its Application in France* (Philadelphia: Carey, Lea and Blanchard, 1833).
24. Barnes and Teeters, *New Horizons in Criminology*, p. 428.
25. Ibid.
26. Ibid.
27. Wood and Waite, *Crime and Its Treatment*, p. 555, citing U.S. Bureau of Labor Statistics.
28. See North Carolina Department of Corrections, Correction Enterprises website, http://www.doc.state.nc.us/eprise (accessed October 20, 2011).
29. See U.S. Department of Justice, Federal Prison Industries, Inc., website, http://www.unicor.gov.
30. Robert Mintz, "Federal Prison Industry—The Green Monster, Part One: History and Background," *Crime and Social Justice*, Vol. 6 (fall/winter 1976), pp. 41–48.
31. William G. Saylor and Gerald G. Gaes, "PREP Study Links UNICOR Work Experience with Successful Post-Release Outcome," *Corrections Compendium* (October 1994), pp. 5–6, 8.
32. Criminal Justice Associates, *Private Sector Involvement in Prison-Based Businesses: A National Assessment* (Washington, DC: U.S. Government Printing Office, 1985). See also National Institute of Justice, *Corrections and the Private Sector* (Washington, DC: U.S. Government Printing Office, 1985).
33. The PIECP was first authorized under the Justice System Improvement Act of 1979 (Public Law 96-157, Sec. 827) and later expanded under the Justice Assistance Act of 1984 (Public Law 98-473, Sec. 819). The Crime Control Act of 1990 (Public Law 101-647) authorizes continuation of the program indefinitely.
34. Domingo S. Herraiz, *Prison Industry Enhancement Certification Program* (Washington, DC: Bureau of Justice Assistance, 2004).
35. National Correctional Industries Association, "PIECP: First Quarter 2013 Statistical Data Report," http://www.nationalcia.org/wp-content/uploads/Quarter-1-2013-Statistical-Report.pdf (accessed September 4, 2013).
36. Kevin Pieper, "States Stop Funding Prison Work Crews," *USA Today*, September 14, 2011, p. 3A.
37. Barnes and Teeters, *New Horizons in Criminology*, p. 355.
38. Williams, *Dictionary of American Penology*, p. 225.
39. Ibid., p. 64.
40. Ibid., p. 227.
41. Donal E. J. MacNamara, "Medical Model in Corrections: Requiescat in Pacis," in Fred Montanino, ed., *Incarceration: The Sociology of Imprisonment* (Beverly Hills, CA: Sage, 1978).
42. For a description of the community-based format in its heyday, see Andrew T. Scull, *Decarceration: Community Treatment and the Deviant—A Radical View* (Upper Saddle River, NJ: Prentice Hall, 1977).
43. Ibid., p. 51.
44. Williams, *Dictionary of American Penology*, p. 45.

45. Ibid.
46. Clemens Bartollas, *Introduction to Corrections* (New York: Harper and Row, 1981), pp. 166–167.
47. The act also established home furloughs and community treatment centers.
48. National Advisory Commission on Criminal Justice Standards and Goals, Standard 2.17, Part 2c.
49. *Recidivism* can be defined in various ways according to the purpose the term is intended to serve in a particular study or report. Recidivism is usually defined as rearrest (versus reconviction) and generally includes a time span of five years, although some Bureau of Justice Statistics studies have used six years, and other studies one or two years, as definitional criteria.
50. Various advocates of the just deserts, or justice, model can be identified. For a detailed description of rehabilitation and just deserts, see Michael A. Pizzi, Jr., "The Medical Model and the 100 Years War," *Law Enforcement News,* July 7, 1986, pp. 8, 13; and MacNamara, "Medical Model in Corrections."
51. Bureau of Justice Statistics, *Annual Report, 1987* (Washington, DC: BJS, 1988), p. 70.
52. Ibid.
53. Ibid.
54. Robert Martinson, "What Works: Questions and Answers about Prison Reform," *Public Interest,* No. 35 (1974), pp. 22–54. See also Douglas Lipton, Robert M. Martinson, and Judith Wilkes, *The Effectiveness of Correctional Treatment: A Survey of Treatment Evaluation Studies* (New York: Praeger, 1975).
55. L. Sechrest, S. White, and E. Brown, eds., *The Rehabilitation of Criminal Offenders: Problems and Prospects* (Washington, DC: National Academy of Sciences, 1979).
56. U.S. Department of Justice, *Office of Justice Programs Fiscal Year 2000 Program Plan: Resources for the Field* (Washington, DC: Office of Juvenile Justice and Delinquency Prevention, 1999).
57. Timothy A. Hughes, Doris James Wilson, and Allen J. Beck, *Trends in State Parole, 1990–2000* (Washington, DC: Bureau of Justice Statistics, 2001).
58. E. Ann Carson and Daniela Golinelli, *Prisoners in 2012—Advance Counts* (Washington, DC: Bureau of Justice Statistics, July 2013), p. 1.
59. Lynn S. Branham, *The Use of Incarceration in the United States: A Look at the Present and the Future* (Washington, DC: American Bar Association, 1992).
60. "Reliance on Prisons Is Costly But Ineffective, ABA Panel Says," *Criminal Justice Newsletter,* April 15, 1992, p. 7.
61. *Criminal Justice Newsletter,* February 3, 1992, p. 8.
62. American Correctional Association, *Vital Statistics in Corrections* (Laurel, MD: ACA, 2000).
63. Allen J. Beck and Paige M. Harrison, *Prisoners in 2004* (Washington, DC: Bureau of Justice Statistics, 2005).
64. Jeanne B. Stinchcomb, "From Rehabilitation to Retribution: Examining Public Policy Paradigms and Personnel Education Patterns in Corrections," *American Journal of Criminal Justice,* Vol. 27, No. 1 (2002), p. 3.
65. Although many other states require inmates to work on road maintenance, and although the inmates are typically supervised by armed guards, Alabama became the first state in modern times to shackle prisoners on work crews.
66. See "Back on the Chain Gang: Florida Becomes Third State to Resurrect Forced Labor," Associated Press wire service, November 22, 1995.
67. Andrew Ford, "Brevard County Sheriff Chain Gang," *USA Today,* May 2, 2013, http://www.usatoday.com/story/news/nation/2013/05/02/brevard-county-sheriff-chain-gang/2130335/ (accessed August 9, 2013).
68. See Debra L. Dailey, "Summary of the 1998 Annual Conference of the National Association of Sentencing Commissions," http://www.ussc.gov/states/dailefsr.pdf (accessed October 30, 2006).
69. The state of Washington is generally credited with having been the first state to pass a three-strikes law by voter initiative (in 1993).
70. For a good overview of the topic, see David Shichor and Dale K. Sechrest, *Three Strikes and You're Out: Vengeance as Public Policy* (Thousand Oaks, CA: Sage, 1996).
71. David S. Broder, "When Tough Isn't Smart," *Washington Post* wire service, March 24, 1994.
72. Roy Walmsley, *World Prison Population List* (Essex, England: International Center for Prison Studies, 2013).
73. James J. Stephan, *Census of State and Federal Correctional Facilities, 2005* (Washington, DC: Bureau of Justice Statistics, 2008).
74. Carson and Golinelli, *Prisoners in 2012,* p. 2. All other statistics in this section refer to inmates sentenced to a year or more in prison.
75. Ibid., p. 2.
76. Ibid.
77. Thomas P. Bonczar, *Prevalence of Imprisonment in the U.S. Population, 1974–2001* (Washington, DC: Bureau of Justice Statistics, 2003), p. 1.
78. Carson and Sabol, *Prisoners in 2011.*
79. Federal Bureau of Prisons, "Quick Facts," http://www.bop.gov/news/quick.jsp#3 (accessed July 6, 2009); and Bureau of Justice Statistics, *National Corrections Reporting Program, 1998* (Ann Arbor, MI: Interuniversity Consortium for Political and Social Research, 2001).
80. Federal Bureau of Prisons, "Quick Facts about the Bureau of Prisons," December 29, 2012 http://www.bop.gov/news/quick.jsp#4 (accessed June 3, 2013).
81. Carson and Sabol, *Prisoners in 2011.*
82. Bonczar, *Prevalence of Imprisonment in the U.S. Population, 1974–2001,* p. 1.
83. Ibid., p. 8.
84. Carson and Golinelli, *Prisoners in 2012.*
85. Ibid.
86. Robert M. Carter, Richard A. McGee, and E. Kim Nelson, *Corrections in America* (Philadelphia: J. B. Lippincott, 1975), pp. 122–123.
87. James J. Stephan, *State Prison Expenditures, 2001* (Washington, DC: Bureau of Justice Statistics, 2004); and Administrative Office of the United States Courts, "Newly Available: Costs of Incarceration and Supervision in FY 2010," June 23, 2011, http://www.uscourts.gov/News/NewsView/11-06-23/Newly_Available_Costs_of_Incarceration_and_Supervision_in_FY_2010.aspx (accessed May 21, 2012).
88. Tracey Kyckelhahn, *Justice Expenditures and Employment Extracts Program 2010,* (Washington, DC: Bureau of Justice Statistics, July 2013).
89. Carson and Sabol, *Prisoners in 2011.* Much of the decline in state prison populations, however, can be accounted for the way in which incarcerated felons are counted—especially in the state of California, where a strategy of realignment has shifted state prisoners to county jails.
90. Ibid., p. 37.
91. United States Government Accountability Office, Bureau of Prisons: *Growing Inmate Crowding Negatively Affects Inmates, Staff, and Infrastructure* (Washington, DC: GAO, September 2012).
92. Carson and Sabol, *Prisoners in 2011,* p. 31.
93. *Rhodes* v. *Chapman,* 452 U.S. 337 (1981).

94. D. Greenberg, "The Incapacitative Effect of Imprisonment, Some Estimates," *Law and Society Review,* Vol. 9 (1975), pp. 541–580. See also Jacqueline Cohen, "Incapacitating Criminals: Recent Research Findings," National Institute of Justice, *Research in Brief* (Washington, DC: NIJ, December 1983).
95. For information on identifying dangerous repeat offenders, see M. Chaiken and J. Chaiken, *Selecting Career Criminals for Priority Prosecution,* final report (Cambridge, MA: Abt Associates, 1987).
96. J. Monahan, *Predicting Violent Behavior: An Assessment of Clinical Techniques* (Beverly Hills, CA: Sage, 1981).
97. S. Van Dine, J. P. Conrad, and S. Dinitz, *Restraining the Wicked: The Incapacitation of the Dangerous Offender* (Lexington, MA: Lexington Books, 1979).
98. Paul Gendreau, Tracy Little, and Claire Goggin, "A Meta-analysis of the Predictors of Adult Offender Recidivism: What Works!" *Criminology,* Vol. 34, No. 4 (November 1996), pp. 575–607.
99. Nicole D. Porter, *On the Chopping Block 2012: State Prison Closings* (Washington, DC: The Sentencing Project, December 2012).
100. California Department of Corrections and Rehabilitation, *The Future of California Corrections* (Sacramento, CA: California Department of Corrections and Rehabilitation, 2012), http://www.cdcr.ca.gov/2012plan/docs/plan/complete.pdf (accessed March 3, 2013).
101. Jon Lender, "Prisoner Release Bill Wins Final Approval," *The Hartford Courant,* May 31, 2001, http://www.ctnow.com/news/hc-house-prisoners-program-0601-20110531,0,6846758.story (accessed June 4, 2011).
102. George Camp and Camille Camp, "Stopping Escapes: Perimeter Security," *Prison Construction Bulletin* (Washington, DC: National Institute of Justice, 1987).
103. Adapted from G. A. Grizzle and A. D. Witte, "Efficiency in Collections Agencies," in Gordon P. Whitaker and Charles D. Phillips, eds., *Evaluating the Performance of Criminal Justice Agencies* (Washington, DC: National Institute of Justice, 1983).
104. Patricia L. Hardyman et al., *Internal Prison Classification Systems: Case Studies in Their Development and Implementation* (Washington, DC: National Institute of Corrections, 2002), from which some of the wording in this section is taken.
105. Ibid.
106. *Johnson* v. *California,* 543 U.S. 499 (2005).
107. U.S. Bureau of Prisons, "Facilities," http://www.bop.gov/map.html (accessed February 2, 2005).
108. Some of the information in this section is derived from Federal Bureau of Prisons, *About the Federal Bureau of Prisons* (Washington, DC: BOP, 2001).
109. Federal Bureau of Prisons, *Monday Morning Highlights,* May 30, 2013.
110. Kamala Malli-Kane, Barbara Parthasarathy, and William Adams, *Examining Growth in the Federal Prison Population, 1998 to 2010* (Washington, DC: Urban Institute, 2012), p. 3.
111. Federal Bureau of Prisons, "About the Bureau of Prisons," http://www.bop.gov/about/index.jsp (accessed July 5, 2013).
112. Federal Bureau of Prisons, "Quick Facts," http://www.bop.gov/about/facts.jsp (accessed July 5, 2013).
113. Ibid.
114. For additional information, see Dennis Cauchon, "The Alcatraz of the Rockies," *USA Today,* November 16, 1994.
115. "Congress OKs Inmate Fees to Offset Costs of Prison," *Criminal Justice Newsletter,* October 15, 1992, p. 6.
116. Stephan, *State Prison Expenditures, 2001,* p. 3.
117. National Institute of Corrections website, http://www.nicic.org (accessed March 2, 2009).
118. Ibid.
119. Doris J. James, *Profile of Jail Inmates, 2002* (Washington, DC: Bureau of Justice Statistics, 2004), p. 2.
120. Todd D. Minton *Jail Inmates at Midyear 2012—Statistical Tables* (Washington, DC: Bureau of Justice Statistics, 2013), p. 1.
121. Ibid., p. 7.
122. James, *Profile of Jail Inmates, 2002,* p. 1.
123. BJS, *Jail Inmates at Midyear 2011,* p. 12.
124. James Stephan, *Census of Jail Facilities, 2006* (Washington, DC: Bureau of Justice Statistics, 2011), p. 1.
125. Ibid.
126. Ibid.
127. BJS, *Jail Inmates at Midyear 2011,* p. 3.
128. BJS, *Jail Inmates at Midyear 2011,* p. 8.
129. James, *Profile of Jail Inmates, 2002,* p. 2.
130. Stephan, *Census of Jails, 1999.*
131. See Gale Holland, "L.A. Jail Makes Delayed Debut," *USA Today,* January 27, 1997, p. 3A.
132. See Dale Stockton, "Cook County Illinois Sheriff's Office," *Police,* October 1996, pp. 40–43. The Cook County Department of Correction operates ten separate jails, which house approximately 9,000 inmates. The department employs more than 2,800 correctional officers.
133. William J. Sabol and Todd D. Minton, *Jail Inmates at Midyear 2007* (Washington, DC: Bureau of Justice Statistics, 2008), p. 3.
134. Todd D. Minton, *Jail Inmates at Midyear 2012* (Washington, DC: Bureau of Justice Statistics, 2013), p. 10.
135. Ibid., p. 7.
136. William Reginald Mills and Heather Barrett, "Meeting the Special Challenge of Providing Health Care to Women Inmates in the '90's," *American Jails,* Vol. 4, No. 3 (September/October 1990), p. 55.
137. Ibid., p. 21.
138. Ibid.
139. Ibid., p. 55.
140. American Correctional Association, *Vital Statistics in Corrections.*
141. Mills and Barrett, "Providing Health Care to Women Inmates," p. 55.
142. Ibid.
143. Linda L. Zupan, "Women Corrections Officers in the Nation's Largest Jails," *American Jails* (January/February 1991), pp. 59–62.
144. Linda L. Zupan, "Women Corrections Officers in Local Jails," paper presented at the annual meeting of the Academy of Criminal Justice Sciences, Nashville, TN, March 1991.
145. Ibid., p. 6.
146. "Jail Overcrowding in Houston Results in Release of Inmates," *Criminal Justice Newsletter,* October 15, 1990, p. 5.
147. Bureau of Justice Statistics, *Census of Local Jails, 1988* (Washington, DC: BJS, 1991), p. 31.
148. Kathleen Maguire and Ann L. Pastore, *Sourcebook of Criminal Justice Statistics, 1994* (Washington, DC: U.S. Government Printing Office, 1995).
149. BJS, *Jail Inmates at Midyear 2011,* p. 3.
150. Carson and Sabol, *Prisoners in 2011,* p. 32.
151. Christopher J. Mumola, *Suicide and Homicide in State Prisons and Local Jails* (Washington, DC: Bureau of Justice Statistics, 2005), p. 1.
152. George P. Wilson and Harvey L. McMurray, "System Assessment of Jail Overcrowding Assumptions," paper presented at the annual meeting of the Academy of Criminal Justice Sciences, Nashville, TN, March 1991.
153. Andy Hall, *Systemwide Strategies to Alleviate Jail Crowding* (Washington, DC: National Institute of Justice, 1987).
154. Ibid.

155. Linda L. Zupan and Ben A. Menke, "The New Generation Jail: An Overview," in Joel A. Thompson and G. Larry Mays, eds., *American Jails: Public Policy Issues* (Chicago: Nelson-Hall, 1991), p. 180.
156. Ibid.
157. Herbert R. Sigurdson, Billy Wayson, and Gail Funke, "Empowering Middle Managers of Direct Supervision Jails," *American Jails* (winter 1990), p. 52.
158. Byron Johnson, "Exploring Direct Supervision: A Research Note," *American Jails* (March/April 1994), pp. 63–64.
159. H. Sigurdson, *The Manhattan House of Detention: A Study of Podular Direct Supervision* (Washington, DC: National Institute of Corrections, 1985). For similar conclusions, see Robert Conroy, Wantland J. Smith, and Linda L. Zupan, "Officer Stress in the Direct Supervision Jail: A Preliminary Case Study," *American Jails* (November/December 1991), p. 36.
160. For a good review of the future of American jails, see Ron Carroll, "Jails and the Criminal Justice System in the Twenty-First Century," *American Jails* (March/April 1997), pp. 26–31.
161. Robert L. May II, Roger H. Peters, and William D. Kearns, "The Extent of Drug Treatment Programs in Jails: A Summary Report," *American Jails* (September/October 1990), pp. 32–34.
162. See, for example, John W. Dietler, "Jail Industries: The Best Thing That Can Happen to a Sheriff," *American Jails* (July/August 1990), pp. 80–83.
163. Robert Osborne, "Los Angeles County Sheriff Opens New Inmate Answering Service," *American Jails* (July/August 1990), pp. 61–62.
164. See J. R. Dewan, "Regional Jail—The New Kid on the Block," *American Jails* (May/June 1995), pp. 70–72.
165. Tom Rosazza, "Jail Standards: Focus on Change," *American Jails* (November/December 1990), pp. 84–87.
166. American Correctional Association, *Manual of Standards for Adult Local Detention Facilities,* 3rd ed. (College Park, MD: ACA, 1991).
167. Ken Kerle, "National Sheriff's Association Jail Audit Review," *American Jails* (spring 1987), pp. 13–21.
168. Norimitsu Onishi, "In California, County Jails Face Bigger Loads," *New York Times*, August 5, 2012, http://www.nytimes.com/2012/08/06/us/in-california-prison-overhaul-county-jails-face-bigger-load.html (accessed March 3, 2013).
169. Ibid.
170. Beck and Harrison, *Prisoners in 2000,* p. 7.
171. Carson and Sabol, *Prisoners in 2011,* p. 32.
172. Cody Mason, *Too Good to Be True: Private Prisons in America* (Washington, DC: The Sentencing Project, 2012).
173. Eric Bates, "Private Prisons: Over the Next Five Years Analysts Expect the Private Share of the Prison 'Market' to More Than Double," *The Nation,* Vol. 266, No. 1 (1998), pp. 11–18.
174. Mason, *Too Good to Be True*, p. 2.
175. Gary Fields, "Privatized Prisons Pose Problems," *USA Today,* November 11, 1996, p. 3A.
176. Dale K. Sechrest and David Shichor, "Private Jails: Locking Down the Issues," *American Jails,* March/April 1997, pp. 9–18.
177. U.S. General Accounting Office, *Private and Public Prisons: Studies Comparing Operational Costs and/or Quality of Service* (Washington, DC: U.S. Government Printing Office, 1996).
178. Sechrest and Shichor, "Private Jails," p. 10.
179. James Austin and Garry Coventry, *Emerging Issues on Privatized Prisons* (Washington, DC: Bureau of Justice Statistics, 2001), p. ix.
180. For a more detailed discussion of this issue, see Austin and Coventry, *Emerging Issues on Privatized Prisons*.
181. *Richardson* v. *McKnight,* 117 S.Ct. 2100, 138 L.Ed.2d 540 (1997).
182. *Minneci* v. *Pollard*, U.S. Supreme Court, No. 10-1104 (decided January 2012).
183. *Correctional Services Corporation* v. *Malesko,* 122 S.Ct. 515 (2001).
184. Ibid.
185. Quoted in Bates, "Private Prisons."
186. Judith C. Hackett et al., "Contracting for the Operation of Prisons and Jails," National Institute of Justice Research in Brief (Washington, DC: NIJ, June 1987), p. 6.

© Image Source/Alamy.

14 PRISON LIFE

OUTLINE

- Introduction
- The Male Inmate's World
- The Female Inmate's World
- The Staff World
- Prison Riots
- Prisoners' Rights
- Issues Facing Prisons Today

LEARNING OBJECTIVES

After reading this chapter, you should be able to

- Describe the realities of prison life and prison subculture from the inmate's point of view.
- Differentiate between men's and women's prisons.
- Describe prison life from the corrections officer's point of view.
- Summarize the causes and stages of prison riots.
- Discuss the legal aspects of prisoners' rights, including the consequences of related precedent-setting U.S. Supreme Court cases.
- Describe the major issues that prisons face today.

Prison walls do not form a barrier separating prison inmates from the protections of the Constitution.

TURNER v. *SAFLEY*, 482 U.S. 78 (1987)

■ **total institution** An enclosed facility separated from society both socially and physically, where the inhabitants share all aspects of their daily lives.

■ **Follow the author's tweets about the latest crime and justice news @schmalleger.**

Introduction

Recently, 23-year-old Laura Kaeppeler, Miss America 2012, dedicated the year of her reign to the theme "Circles of Support: Mentoring Children of Incarcerated Parents."[1] Kaeppeler said, "It's everyday life for millions of children, and it allows me to connect with people on a level they don't expect a pageant contestant to connect with them. This is a real problem people can relate to." Kaeppeler's father had been imprisoned when she was 17 for a white-collar crime.

For many years, prisons and prison life could be described by the phrase "out of sight, out of mind." Very few citizens cared about prison conditions, and those unfortunate enough to be locked away were regarded as lost to the world. By the mid-twentieth century, however, this attitude started to change. Concerned citizens began to offer their services to prison administrators, neighborhoods began accepting work-release prisoners and halfway houses, and social scientists initiated a serious study of prison life. Today, as shows like *Prison Break* make clear, prisons and prison life have entered the American mainstream. Part of the reason for this is that prisons today hold more people than ever before, and incarceration impacts not only those imprisoned but also family members, friends, and victims on the outside.

This chapter describes the realities of prison life today, including prisoner lifestyles, prison subcultures, sexuality in prison, prison violence, and prisoners' rights and grievance procedures. We will discuss both the inmate world and the staff world. A separate section on women in prison details the social structure of women's prisons, daily life in those facilities, and the various types of female inmates. We begin with a brief overview of early research on prison life.

James Atoa/Alamy

Laura Kaeppeler, Miss America 2012. Kaeppeler dedicated the year of her reign to mentoring the children of incarcerated parents. What do most Americans think of prisons and prisoners?

Research on Prison Life—Total Institutions

In 1935, Hans Reimer, who was then chair of the Department of Sociology at Indiana University, set the tone for studies of prison life when he voluntarily served three months in prison as an incognito participant-observer.[2] Reimer reported the results of his studies to the American Prison Association, stimulating many other, albeit less spectacular, efforts to examine prison life. Other early studies include Donald Clemmer's *The Prison Community* (1940),[3] Gresham Sykes's *The Society of Captives* (1958),[4] Richard Cloward and Donald Cressey's *Theoretical Studies in Social Organization of the Prison* (1960),[5] and Cressey's edited volume, *The Prison* (1961).[6]

These studies and others focused primarily on maximum-security prisons for men. They treated correctional institutions as formal or complex organizations and employed the analytic techniques of organizational sociology, industrial psychology, and administrative science.[7] As modern writers on prisons have observed, "The prison was compared to a primitive society, isolated from the outside world, functionally integrated by a delicate system of mechanisms, which kept it precariously balanced between anarchy and accommodation."[8]

Another approach to the study of prison life was developed by Erving Goffman, who coined the term **total institution** in a 1961 study of prisons and mental hospitals.[9] Goffman described total institutions as places where the same people work, recreate, worship, eat, and sleep together daily. Such places include prisons, concentration camps, mental hospitals, seminaries, and other facilities in which residents are cut off from the larger society either forcibly or willingly. Total institutions are small societies. They evolve their own distinctive values and styles of life and pressure residents to fulfill rigidly prescribed behavioral roles.

prison subculture The values and behavioral patterns characteristic of prison inmates. Prison subculture has been found to be surprisingly consistent across the country.

prisonization The process whereby newly institutionalized offenders come to accept prison lifestyles and criminal values. Although many inmates begin their prison experience with only a few values that support criminal behavior, the socialization experience they undergo while incarcerated leads to a much greater acceptance of such values.

Generally speaking, the work of prison researchers built on findings of other social scientists who discovered that any group with similar characteristics confined in the same place at the same time develops its own subculture. Prison subcultures, described in the next section, also provide the medium through which prison values are communicated and expectations are made known.

The Male Inmate's World

Two social realities coexist in prison settings. One is the official structure of rules and procedures put in place by the wider society and enforced by prison staff. The other is the more informal but decidedly more powerful inmate world.[10] The inmate world, best described by how closely it touches the lives of inmates, is controlled by **prison subculture**. The realities of prison life—including a large and often densely packed inmate population that must look to the prison environment for all its needs—mean that prison subculture develops independently of the plans of prison administrators and is not easily subjected to the control of prison authorities.

Inmates entering prison discover a whole new social world in which they must participate or face consequences ranging from dangerous ostracism to physical violence and homicide.[11] The socialization of new inmates into the prison subculture has been described as a process of **prisonization**[12]—the new prisoner's learning of convict values, attitudes, roles, and even language. By the time this process is complete, new inmates have become "cons." Gresham Sykes and Sheldon Messinger recognized five elements of the prison code in 1960:[13]

1. Don't interfere with the interests of other inmates. Never rat on a con.
2. Don't lose your head. Play it cool and do your own time.
3. Don't exploit inmates. Don't steal. Don't break your word. Be right.

Halfdark/Getty Images

A corrections officer escorts a prison inmate through a high-security area. Custody and control remain the primary concerns of prison staff throughout the country. Is the emphasis on custody and control justified?

■ **prison argot** The slang characteristic of prison subcultures and prison life.

4. Don't whine. Be a man.
5. Don't be a sucker. Don't trust the guards or staff.

Some criminologists have suggested that the prison code is simply a reflection of general criminal values. If so, these values are brought to the institution rather than created there. Either way, the power and pervasiveness of the prison code require convicts to conform to the worldview held by the majority of prisoners.

Stanton Wheeler, Ford Foundation Professor of Law and Social Sciences at the University of Washington, closely examined the concept of prisonization in an early study of the Washington State Reformatory.[14] Wheeler found that the degree of prisonization experienced by inmates tends to vary over time. He described changing levels of inmate commitment to prison norms and values by way of a U-shaped curve. When an inmate first enters prison, Wheeler said, the conventional values of outside society are of paramount importance. As time passes, inmates adopt the lifestyle of the prison. However, within the half year prior to release, most inmates begin to demonstrate a renewed appreciation of conventional values.

Different prisons share aspects of a common inmate culture.[15] **Prison argot**, or language, provides one example of how widespread prison subculture can be. The terms used to describe inmate roles in one institution are generally understood in others. The word *rat*, for example, is prison slang for an informer. Popularized by crime movies of the 1950s, the term is understood today by members of the wider society. Recent research into prison language suggests that argot in prison reflects and reinforces "the organization, language, and status hierarchy of . . . prison subculture."[16] Researchers suggest that correctional administrators and staff must learn the language of prison in order to maximize staff efficiency, and to ensure the safety of staff and inmates.[17] Words common to prison argot are shown in the nearby "CJ Issues" box.

The Evolution of Prison Subcultures

Prison subcultures change constantly. Like any other American subculture, they evolve to reflect the concerns and experiences of the wider culture, reacting to new crime-control strategies and embracing novel opportunities for crime. The AIDS epidemic of the 1970s and 1980s, for example, brought about changes in prison sexual behavior, at least for a segment of the inmate population, and the emergence of a high-tech criminal group has further differentiated convict types. Because of such changes, John Irwin, as he was completing his classic study titled *The Felon*[18] (1970), expressed worry that his book was already obsolete.[19] *The Felon*, for all its insights into prison subcultures, follows in the descriptive tradition of works by Clemmer and Reimer. Irwin recognized that by 1970, prison subcultures had begun to reflect the cultural changes sweeping America. A decade later, other investigators of prison subcultures were able to write, "It was no longer meaningful to speak of a single inmate culture or even subculture. By the time we began our field research . . . it was clear that the unified, oppositional convict culture, found in the sociological literature on prisons, no longer existed."[20]

Charles Stastny and Gabrielle Tyrnauer, describing prison life at Washington State Penitentiary in 1982, discovered four clearly distinguishable subcultures: (1) official, (2) traditional, (3) reform, and (4) revolutionary.[21] Official culture was promoted by the staff and by the administrative rules of the institution. Enthusiastic participants in official culture were mostly corrections officers and other staff members, although inmates were also well aware of the normative expectations that official culture imposed on them. Official culture affected the lives of inmates primarily through the creation of a prisoner hierarchy based on sentence length, prison jobs, and the "perks" that cooperation with the dictates of official culture could produce. Traditional prison culture, described by early writers on the subject, still existed, but its participants spent much of their time lamenting the decline of the convict code among younger prisoners. Reform culture was unique at Washington State Penitentiary. It was the result of a brief experiment with inmate self-government during the early 1970s. Some elements of prison life that evolved during the experimental period survived the termination of self-government and were eventually institutionalized in what Stastny and Tyrnauer called "reform culture." They included inmate participation in civic-style clubs, citizen involvement in the daily activities of the prison, banquets, and inmate speaking tours. Revolutionary culture built on the radical political rhetoric of the disenfranchised and found a ready audience among minority prisoners who saw themselves as victims of society's basic unfairness. Although they did not participate in it, revolutionary inmates understood traditional prison culture and generally avoided running afoul of its rules.

The Functions of Prison Subcultures

How do social scientists and criminologists explain the existence of prison subcultures? Although people around the world live in groups and create their own cultures, in few cases does the intensity of human interaction approach the level found in prisons. As we discussed in Chapter 13, many of today's prisons are densely crowded places where inmates can find no retreat from the constant demands of staff and the pressures of fellow prisoners. Prison subcultures, according to some authors, are fundamentally an adaptation to deprivation and confinement. In *The Society of Captives*, Sykes called these deprivations the "pains of imprisonment."[22] The pains of imprisonment—the frustrations induced by the rigors of confinement—form the nexus of a deprivation model of prison subculture. Sykes said that prisoners are deprived of (1) liberty, (2) goods and services, (3) heterosexual relationships, (4) autonomy, and (5) personal security—and that these deprivations lead to the development of subcultures intended to ameliorate the personal pains that accompany deprivation.

Prison subcultures, according to some authors, are fundamentally an adaptation to deprivation and confinement.

In contrast to the deprivation model, the importation model of prison subculture suggests that inmates bring with them values, roles, and behavior patterns from the outside world. Such external values, second nature as they are to career offenders, depend substantially on the criminal worldview. When offenders are confined, these external elements shape the social world of inmates.

The social structure of the prison—the accepted and relatively permanent social arrangements—is another element that shapes prison subculture. Clemmer's early prison study recognized nine structural dimensions of inmate society. He said that prison society could be described in terms of the following:[23]

- Prisoner–staff dichotomy
- Three general classes of prisoners
- Work gangs and cell-house groups
- Racial groups
- Type of offense
- Power of inmate "politicians"
- Degree of sexual abnormality
- Record of repeat offenses
- Personality differences due to preprison socialization

Clemmer's nine structural dimensions still describe prison life today. When applied to individuals, they designate an inmate's position in the prison "pecking order" and create expectations of the appropriate role for that person. Prison roles serve to satisfy the needs of inmates for power, sexual performance, material possessions, individuality, and personal pleasure and to define the status of one prisoner relative to another. For example, inmate leaders, sometimes referred to as "real men" or "toughs" by prisoners in early studies, offer protection to those who live by the rules. They also provide for a redistribution of wealth inside prison and see to it that the rules of the complex prison-derived economic system—based on barter, gambling, and sexual favors—are observed. For an intimate multimedia portrait of life behind bars, visit **http://www.npr.org/programs/atc/prisondiaries**.

Prison roles serve to satisfy the needs of inmates for power, sexual performance, material possessions, individuality, and personal pleasure and to define the status of one prisoner relative to another.

Prison Lifestyles and Inmate Types

Prison society is strict and often unforgiving. Even so, inmates are able to express some individuality through the choice of a prison lifestyle. John Irwin viewed these lifestyles (like the subcultures of which they are a part) as adaptations to the prison environment.[24] Other writers have since elaborated on these coping mechanisms. Following are some of the types of prisoners that researchers have described.

- *The mean dude.* Some inmates adjust to prison by being violent. Other inmates know that these prisoners are best left alone. The mean dude is frequently written up and spends much time in solitary confinement. This role is most common in male institutions and in maximum-security prisons. For some prisoners, the role of mean dude in prison is similar to the role they played in their life prior to being incarcerated. Certain personality types, such as the psychopath, may feel a natural attraction to this role. Prison culture supports violence in two ways: (1) by expecting inmates to be tough and (2) through the prevalence of the idea that only the strong survive inside prison.
- *The hedonist.* Some inmates build their lives around the limited pleasures available within the confines of prison.

CJ | ISSUES

Prison Argot: The Language of Confinement

Writers who have studied prison life often comment on prisoners' use of a special language or slang termed *prison argot*. This language generally describes prison activities and the roles assigned by prison culture to types of inmates. This box lists a few of the many words and phrases identified in studies by different authors. The first group includes words that are characteristic of men's prisons; the second group includes words used in women's prisons.

Men's Prison Slang

Ace duce: A best friend

Badge (or bull, hack, the man, or screw): A corrections officer

Banger (or burner, shank, or sticker): A knife

Billy: A white man

Boneyard: The conjugal visiting area

Cat-J (or J-cat): A prisoner in need of psychological or psychiatric therapy or medication

Cellie: A cell mate

Chester: A child molester

Dog: A homeboy or friend

Fag: A male inmate who is believed to be a "natural" or "born" homosexual

Featherwood: A white prisoner's woman

Fish: A newly arrived inmate

Gorilla: An inmate who uses force to take what he wants from others

Homeboy: A prisoner from one's hometown or neighborhood

Ink: Tattoos

Lemon squeezer: An inmate who masturbates frequently

Man walking: A phrase used to signal that a guard is coming

Merchant (or peddler): One who sells when he should give

Peckerwood (or wood): A white prisoner

Punk: A male inmate who is forced into a submissive role during homosexual relations

Rat (or snitch): An inmate who squeals (provides information about other inmates to the prison administration)

Schooled: Knowledgeable in the ways of prison life

Shakedown: A search of a cell or of a work area

Teddy bear: Nonaggressive wolves

Tree jumper: A rapist

Turn out: To rape or make into a punk

Wolf: A male inmate who assumes the dominant role during homosexual relations

Women's Prison Slang

Cherry (or cherrie): A female inmate who has not yet been introduced to lesbian activities

Fay broad: A white female inmate

Femme (or mommy): A female inmate who plays the female role during lesbian relations

Safe: The vagina, especially when used for hiding contraband

Stud broad (or daddy): A female inmate who assumes the male role during lesbian relations

References: Gresham Sykes, *The Society of Captives* (Princeton, NJ: Princeton University Press, 1958); Rose Giallombardo, *Society of Women: A Study of a Woman's Prison* (New York: John Wiley, 1966); and Richard A. Cloward et al., *Theoretical Studies in Social Organization of the Prison* (New York: Social Science Research Council, 1960). For a more contemporary listing of prison slang terms, see Reinhold Aman, *Hillary Clinton's Pen Pal: A Guide to Life and Lingo in Federal Prison* (Santa Rosa, CA: Maledicta Press, 1996); Jerome Washington, *Iron House: Stories from the Yard* (Ann Arbor, MI: QED Press, 1994); Morrie Camhi, *The Prison Experience* (Boston: Charles Tuttle, 1989); and Harold Long, *Survival in Prison* (Port Townsend, WA: Loompanics, 1990).

The smuggling of contraband, homosexuality, gambling, drug running, and other officially condemned activities provide the center of interest for prison hedonists. Hedonists generally have an abbreviated view of the future, living only for the "now."

- *The opportunist.* The opportunist takes advantage of the positive experiences prison has to offer. Schooling, trade training, counseling, and other self-improvement activities are the focal points of the opportunist's life in prison. Opportunists are generally well liked by prison staff, but other prisoners shun and mistrust them because they come closest to accepting the role that the staff defines as "model prisoner."
- *The retreatist.* Prison life is rigorous and demanding. Badgering by the staff and actual or feared assaults by other inmates may cause some prisoners to attempt psychological retreat from the realities of imprisonment. Such inmates may experience neurotic or psychotic episodes, become heavily involved in drug and alcohol abuse through the illicit prison economy, or even attempt suicide. Depression and mental illness are the hallmarks of the retreatist personality in prison.
- *The legalist.* The legalist is the "jailhouse lawyer." Convicts facing long sentences, with little possibility for early release through the correctional system, are most likely to turn to the courts in their battle against confinement.
- *The radical.* Radical inmates view themselves as political prisoners. They see society and the successful conformists who populate it as oppressors who have forced criminality on many "good people" through the creation of a system that distributes wealth and power inequitably. The inmate who takes on the radical role is unlikely to receive much sympathy from prison staff.
- *The colonizer.* Some inmates think of prison as their home and don't look forward to leaving. They "know the ropes," have many "friends" inside, and may feel more

comfortable institutionalized than on the streets. They typically hold positions of power or respect among the inmate population. Once released, some colonizers commit new crimes to return to prison.

- *The religious.* Some prisoners profess a strong religious faith. They may be born-again Christians, committed Muslims, or even Satanists or witches. Religious inmates frequently attend services, may form prayer groups, and sometimes ask the prison administration to allocate meeting facilities or to create special diets to accommodate their claimed spiritual needs. Although it is certainly true that some inmates have a strong religious faith, staff members are apt to be suspicious of the overly religious prisoner.
- *The gang-banger.* Gang-bangers are affiliated with prison gangs and depend upon the gang for defense and protection. They display gang signs, sport gang-related tattoos, and use their gang membership as a channel for the procurement of desired goods and services both inside and outside of prison.
- *The realist.* The realist sees confinement as a natural consequence of criminal activity and as an unfortunate cost of doing business. This stoic attitude toward incarceration generally leads the realist to "pull his (or her) own time" and to make the best of it. Realists tend to know the inmate code, are able to avoid trouble, and continue in lives of crime once released.

Homosexuality and Sexual Victimization in Prison

Sexual behavior inside prisons is both constrained and encouraged by prison subculture. Sykes's early study of prison argot found many words describing homosexual activity. Among them were the terms *wolf*, *punk*, and *fag*. Wolves were aggressive men who assumed the masculine role in homosexual relations. Punks were forced into submitting to the female role. The term *fag* described a special category of men who had a natural proclivity toward homosexual activity and effeminate mannerisms. Whereas both wolves and punks were fiercely committed to their heterosexual identity and participated in homosexuality only because of prison conditions, fags generally engaged in homosexual lifestyles before their entry into prison and continued to emulate feminine mannerisms and styles of dress once incarcerated.

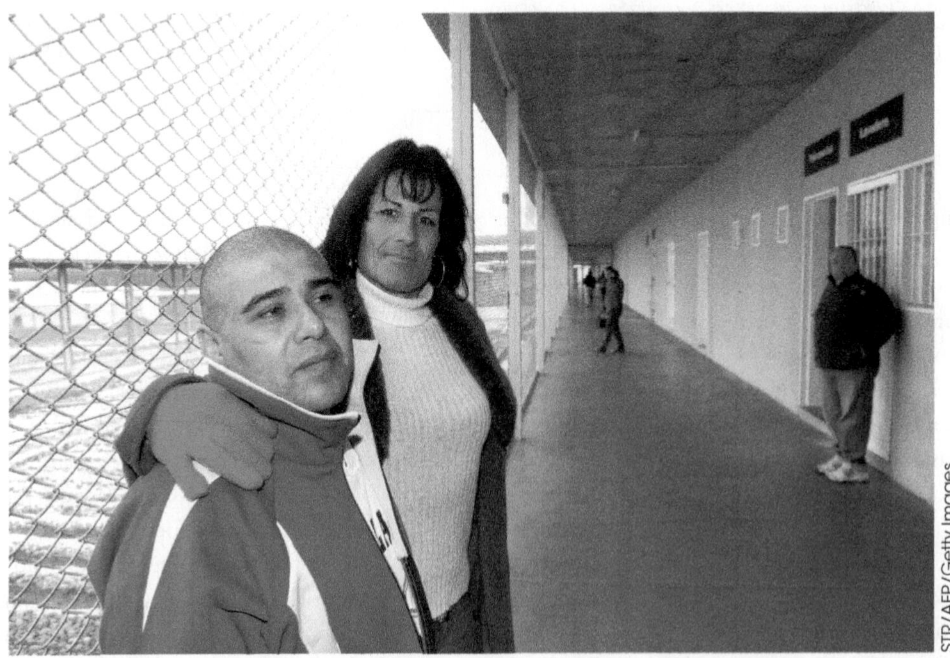
STR/AFP/Getty Images

Transvestite and ex-inmate Diana Acuna Talquenca (R) and prison inmate Osvaldo Martin Torres, shown on the day of their marriage at Almafuerte prison in Argentina. Homosexuality is common in both men's and women's prisons. How does it differ between the two? Why do Talquenca and Torres provide an exception to the "rule" of male prison homosexuality?

Prison homosexuality depends to a considerable degree on the naiveté of young inmates experiencing prison for the first time. Even when newly arrived inmates are protected from fights, older prisoners looking for homosexual liaisons may ingratiate themselves by offering cigarettes, money, drugs, food, or protection. At some future time, these "loans" will be called in, with payoffs demanded in sexual favors. Because the inmate code requires the repayment of favors, the "fish" who tries to resist may quickly find himself face to face with the brute force of inmate society.

Prison rape, which is generally considered to involve physical assault, represents a special category of sexual victimization behind bars. In 2003, Congress mandated the collection of statistics on prison rape as part of the Prison Rape Elimination Act (PREA).[25] The PREA requires the Bureau of Justice Statistics (BJS) to collect data in federal and state prisons, county and city jails, and juvenile institutions, with the U.S. Census Bureau acting as the official repository for collected data.

In 2013, the BJS published the results of its third annual National Inmate Survey (NIS).[26] The survey was conducted in 233 state and federal prisons, 358 local jails, and 15 special confinement facilities operated by Immigration and Customs Enforcement (ICE). A total of 92,449 inmates participated. The survey was also administered to 527 juveniles ages 16 to 17 held in state prisons and 1,211 juveniles of the same age held in local jails. Among the findings:

- An estimated 4.0% of state and federal prison inmates and 3.2% of jail inmates reported experiencing one or more incidents of sexual victimization by another inmate or facility staff in the past 12 months.
- Among state and federal prison inmates, 2.0% (or an estimated 29,300 prisoners) reported an incident involving another inmate, 2.4% (34,100) reported an incident involving facility staff, and 0.4% (5,500) reported both an incident by another inmate and staff.
- About 1.6% of jail inmates (11,900) reported an incident with another inmate, 1.8% (13,200) reported an incident with staff, and 0.2% (2,400) reported both an incident by another inmate and staff.
- An estimated 1.8% of juveniles ages 16 to 17 held in adult prisons and jails reported being victimized by another inmate, compared to 2.0% of adults in prisons and 1.6% of adults in jails; an estimated 3.2% of juveniles ages 16 to 17 held in adult prisons and jails reported experiencing staff sexual misconduct.
- Inmates who reported their sexual orientation as gay, lesbian, bisexual, or other were among those with the highest rates of sexual victimization. Among non-heterosexual inmates, 12.2% of prisoners and 8.5% of jail inmates reported being sexually victimized by another inmate; 5.4% of prisoners and 4.3% of jail inmates reported being victimized by staff.

The PREA survey is only a first step in understanding and eliminating prison rape. As the BJS notes, "Due to fear of reprisal from perpetrators, a code of silence among inmates, personal embarrassment, and lack of trust in staff, victims are often reluctant to report incidents to correctional authorities."[27] Learn more about the PREA and read new survey results as they become available via **http://nicic.gov/prea**.

Humbolt State University sociologist Lee H. Bowker, reviewing studies of sexual violence in prison, provides the following summary observations:[28]

- Most sexual aggressors do not consider themselves homosexuals.
- Sexual release is not the primary motivation for sexual attack.
- Many aggressors must continue to participate in gang rapes to avoid becoming victims themselves.
- The aggressors have themselves suffered much damage to their masculinity in the past.

As in cases of heterosexual rape, sexual assaults in prison are likely to leave psychological scars on the victim long after the physical event is over.[29] Victims of prison rape live in fear, may feel constantly threatened, and can turn to self-destructive activities.[30] Many victims question their masculinity and undergo a personal devaluation. Some victims of prison sexual assault become violent, attacking and sometimes killing the person who raped them. The Human Rights Watch researchers found that prisoners "fitting any part of the following description" are more likely to become rape victims: "young, small in size, physically weak, white, gay, first offender, possessing 'feminine' characteristics such as long hair or a high voice; being unassertive, unaggressive, shy, intellectual, not street-smart, or 'passive'; or having been convicted of a sexual offense against a minor." The researchers also noted that "prisoners with several overlapping characteristics are much more likely than other prisoners to be targeted for abuse."

The report concluded that to reduce the incidence of prison rape, "prison officials should take considerably more care in matching cell mates, and that, as a general rule, double-celling should be avoided."

The Female Inmate's World

As Chapter 13 showed, more than 108,800 women were imprisoned in state and federal correctional institutions throughout the United States at the start of 2013, accounting for about 7% of all prison inmates.[31] Texas had the largest number of female prisoners (13,549), exceeded only by the federal government (at 14,049).[32] Figure 14-1 provides a breakdown of the total American prison population by gender and ethnicity. While there are still far more men imprisoned across the nation than women (approximately 14 men for every woman), the number of female inmates is rising.[33] In 1981, women made up only 4% of the nation's overall prison population, but the number of female inmates nearly tripled during the 1980s and is continuing to grow at a rate greater than that of male inmates.

In 2003, the National Institute of Corrections (NIC) published the results of its three-year project on female offenders in adult correctional settings.[34] Findings from the study produced the national profile of incarcerated women that is shown in Table 14-1. Figures 14-2 and 14-3 provide additional details. The NIC says that "women involved in the criminal justice system represent a population marginalized by race, class, and gender."[35] Black women, for example, are overrepresented in correctional populations. Although they constitute only 13% of women in the United States, nearly 50% of women in prison are black, and black women are eight times more likely than white women to be incarcerated.

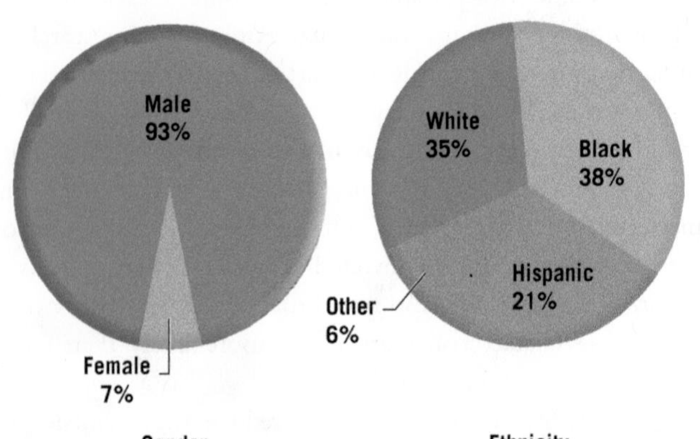

FIGURE 14-1 | **Prison Inmates by Gender and Ethnicity in State and Federal Prisons, 2012**

Source: E. Ann Carson and Daniela Golinelli, *Prisoners in 2012* (Washington, DC: Bureau of Justice Statistics, July 2013).

TABLE 14-1 | **National Profile of Female Offenders**

A profile based on national data for female offenders reveals the following characteristics:

- Disproportionately women of color
- In their early to mid-30s
- Most likely to have been convicted of a drug-related offense
- From fragmented families that include other family members who have been involved with the criminal justice system
- Survivors of physical and/or sexual abuse as children and adults
- Individuals with significant substance-abuse problems
- Individuals with multiple physical and mental health problems
- Unmarried mothers of minor children
- Individuals with a high school or general equivalency diploma (GED) but limited vocational training and sporadic work histories

Source: Barbara Bloom, Barbara Owen, and Stephanie Covington, *Gender-Responsive Strategies: Research, Practice, and Guiding Principles for Women Offenders* (Washington, DC: National Institute of Corrections, 2003).

According to the NIC, women face life circumstances that tend to be specific to their gender, such as sexual abuse, sexual assault, domestic violence, and the responsibility of being the primary caregiver for dependent children. Research shows that female offenders differ significantly from their male counterparts regarding personal histories and pathways to crime.[36] A female offender, for example, is more likely to have been the primary caretaker of young children at the time of her arrest, more likely to have experienced physical and/or sexual abuse, and more likely to have distinctive physical and mental health needs. Women's most common pathways to crime, said the NIC, involve survival strategies that result from physical and sexual abuse, poverty, and substance abuse (Figure 14-4).

Parents in Prison

Eighty percent of women entering prison are mothers, and 85% of those women had custody of their children at the time of admission. Approximately 70% of all women under correctional supervision have at least one child younger than age 18. Two-thirds of incarcerated women have minor children; about two-thirds of women in state prisons and half of women in federal prisons had lived with their young children before entering prison. One out of four women entering prison

Statistically speaking, 1 out of every 43 American children has a parent in prison today, and ethnic variation in the numbers is striking.

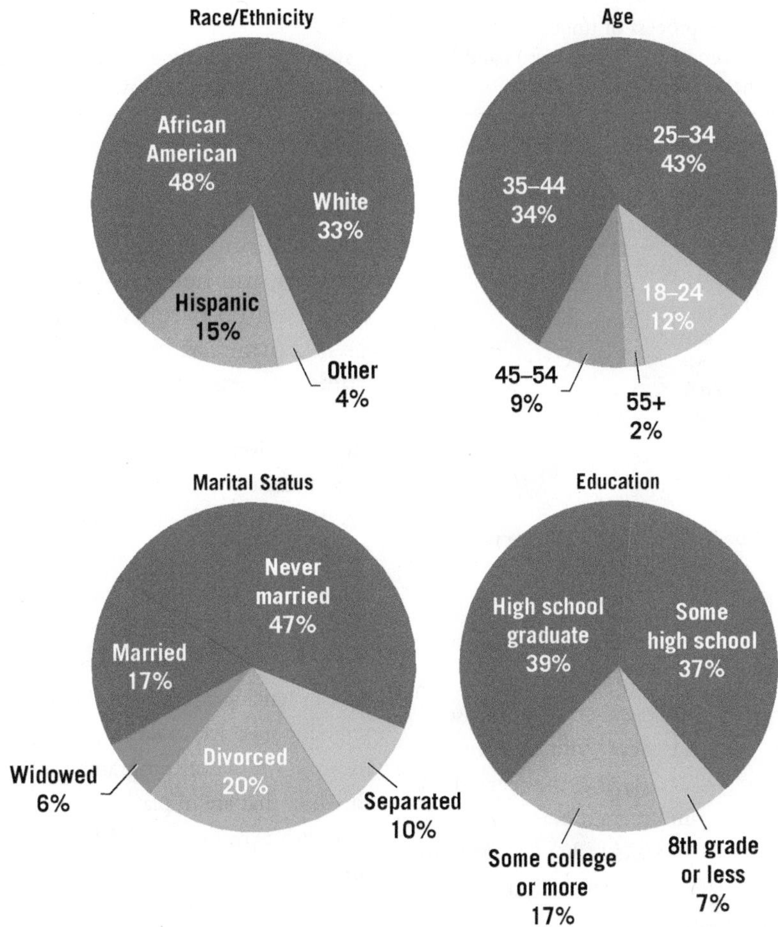

FIGURE 14-2 | Women State Prison Inmates: Features and Characteristics

Source: Lawrence A. Greenfeld and Tracy L. Snell, *Women Offenders* (Washington, DC: Bureau of Justice Statistics, October 2000).

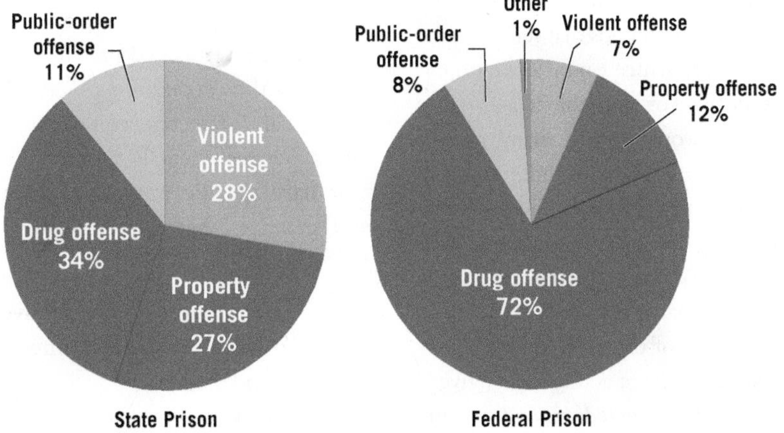

FIGURE 14-3 | Most Serious Offenses of Women in State and Federal Prisons

Source: Lawrence A. Greenfeld and Tracy L. Snell, *Women Offenders* (Washington, DC: Bureau of Justice Statistics, October 2000).

has either recently given birth or is pregnant. Pregnant inmates, many of whom are drug users, malnourished, or sick, often receive little prenatal care—a situation that risks additional complications.

More than 1.7 million American children have a parent in prison.[37] The number of mothers who are incarcerated has more than doubled, from 29,500 in 1991 to 65,600 in 2007. Statistically speaking, 1 out of every 43 American children has a parent in prison today, and ethnic variation in the numbers is striking. Whereas only 1 out of every 111 white children has experienced the imprisonment of a parent, 1 out of every 15 black children has had that experience.

■ **gender responsiveness** The process of understanding and taking into account the differences in characteristics and life experiences that women and men bring to the criminal justice system, and adjusting strategies and practices in ways that appropriately respond to those conditions.

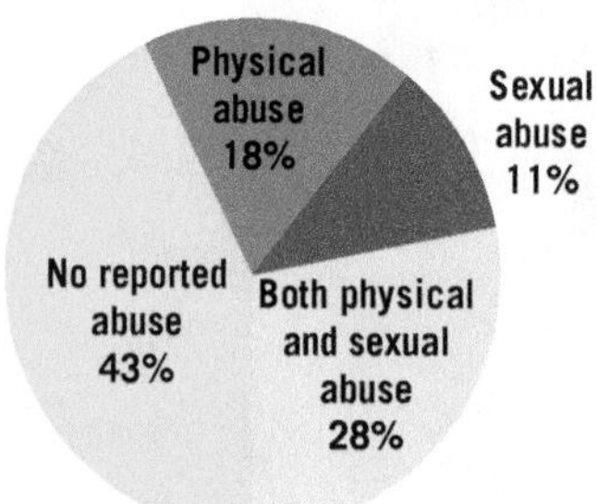

FIGURE 14-4 | Women State Prison Inmates: Physical and Sexual Abuse History

Source: Lawrence A. Greenfeld and Tracy L. Snell, *Women Offenders* (Washington, DC: Bureau of Justice Statistics, October 2000).

More than half of the children of female prisoners never visit their mothers during the period of incarceration.

More than half of the children of female prisoners never visit their mothers during the period of incarceration.[38] The lack of visits is due primarily to the remote location of prisons, a lack of transportation, and the inability of caregivers to arrange visitation.

According to one report on the children of incarcerated parents, "The pain of losing a parent to a prison sentence matches, in many respects, the trauma of losing a parent to death or divorce."[39] That report, *Children on the Outside*, prepared by Brooklyn-based Justice Strategies, recommends that states reduce what the report's authors see as overreliance on incarceration as a crime-fighting strategy—especially for nonviolent and many drug offenders. Such a reduction would return many parents to the community and reunite them with their children. Until such a policy is more fully implemented, however, the organization recommends (1) improving the sense of stability and safety that the children of imprisoned parents experience through individual counseling and educational workshops in schools; (2) enhancing the economic security of those children by providing financial support to relatives who are acting as caregivers; (3) supporting the children's sense of connectedness and worthiness by facilitating their ability to maintain regular contact with their incarcerated parent; (4) facilitating those children's social attachment and ability to trust by developing stable and consistent alternative home environments into which they can be placed; and (5) fostering a strong sense of having an important place in the world among those children through supportive counseling and prioritized placement of children with family members.

Separation from their children is a significant deprivation for many parents, and helping incarcerated parents is just as important as helping their children. Consequently, some states offer parenting classes for female inmates with children. In a national survey of prisons for women, 36 states responded that they provide parenting programs that deal with caretaking, reducing violence toward children, visitation problems, and related issues.[40] Some offer play areas furnished with toys, whereas others attempt to alleviate difficulties in mother–child visits. The typical program studied meets for two hours per week and lasts from four to nine weeks.

Separation from their children is a significant deprivation for many parents, and helping incarcerated parents is just as important as helping their children.

Gender Responsiveness

Critics have long charged that female inmates face a prison system designed for male inmates and run by men. Consequently, meaningful prison programs for women are often lacking, and the ones that are in place were originally adapted from programs in men's prisons or were based on traditional views of female roles that leave little room for employment opportunities in the contemporary world. Many trade-training programs still emphasize low-paying jobs, such as cook, beautician, or laundry machine operator, and classes in homemaking are not uncommon.

Gender responsiveness means "understanding and taking account of the differences in characteristics and life experiences that women and men bring to the criminal justice system, and adjusting strategies and practices in ways that appropriately respond to those conditions."[41] A recent NIC report concluded with a call for recognition of the behavioral and social differences between female and male offenders—especially those that have specific implications for gender-responsive policies and practices. Among the report's recommendations are the following:[42]

- The creation of an effective system for female offenders that is structured differently from a system for male offenders
- The development of gender-responsive policies and practices targeting women's pathways to criminality in order to provide effective interventions that address the intersecting issues of substance abuse, trauma, mental health needs, and economic marginality
- The modification of criminal justice sanctions and interventions to recognize the low risk to public safety represented by the typical female offender
- The consideration of women's relationships, especially those with their children, and women's roles in the community in deciding appropriate correctional sanctions

The NIC study concluded that gender-responsive correctional practices can improve outcomes for female offenders by considering their histories, behaviors, and life circumstances. It also suggested that investments in gender-responsive policy and procedures will likely produce long-term dividends for the criminal justice system and the community as well as for female offenders and their families.

One example of gender responsiveness can be found in a relatively new program in operation at the Decatur (Illinois) Correctional Center. The program allows newborn infants to live with their mothers in a special wing called the Mom and Babies Unit, where each mother has her own room and access to large, brightly colored dayrooms decorated with painted murals. The dayrooms are equipped with toys and children's books, and lead to outdoor patios that provide additional play space for the children. The wing looks much like a typical day-care center. The Decatur program is designed to facilitate the needs of women who are likely to be released by the time their children reach two years of age. The success of the program, which has been in operation for a few years, can be measured in reduced recidivism. "Of the 25 offenders that have gone through this program none . . . have returned to . . . prison," says Michael Randle, director of the Illinois Department of Corrections.[43]

Institutions for Women

Most female inmates are housed in centralized state facilities known as women's prisons, which are dedicated exclusively to incarcerating female felons. Some states, however, particularly those with small populations, continue to keep female prisoners in special wings of what are otherwise institutions for men. Although there is not a typical prison for women, the American Correctional Association's 1990 report by the Task Force on the Female Offender found that the institutions that house female inmates could be generally described as follows:[44]

- Most prisons for women are located in towns with fewer than 25,000 inhabitants.
- Significant numbers of facilities were not designed to house female inmates.
- Some facilities that house female inmates also house men.
- Few facilities for women have programs especially designed for female offenders.
- Few major disturbances or escapes are reported among female inmates.
- Substance abuse among female inmates is very high.
- Few work assignments are available to female inmates.

Social Structure in Women's Prisons

"Aside from sharing the experience of being incarcerated," says Professor Marsha Clowers of the John Jay College of Criminal Justice, "female prisoners have much in common."[45] Because so many female inmates share social characteristics such as a lack of education and a history of abuse, they often also share similar values and behaviors. Early prison researchers found that many female inmates construct organized pseudofamilies. Typical of such studies are D. Ward and G. Kassebaum's *Women's Prison* (1966),[46] Esther Heffernan's *Making It in Prison* (1972),[47] and Rose Giallombardo's *Society of Women* (1966).[48]

Giallombardo, for example, examined the Federal Reformatory for Women at Alderson, West Virginia, spending a year gathering data in the early 1960s. Focusing closely on the social formation of families among female inmates, she titled one of her chapters "The Homosexual Alliance as a Marriage Unit." In it she described in great detail the sexual identities assumed by women at Alderson and the symbols they chose to communicate those roles. Hairstyle, dress, language, and mannerisms were all used to signify "maleness" or "femaleness." Giallombardo detailed "the anatomy of the marriage relationship from courtship to 'fall out,' that is, from inception to the parting of the ways, or divorce."[49] Romantic love at Alderson was of central importance to any relationship between inmates, and all homosexual relationships were described as voluntary. Through marriage, the "stud broad" became the husband and the "femme" the wife.

Studies attempting to document how many inmates are part of prison "families" have produced varying results. Some found as many as 71% of female prisoners involved in the phenomenon, while others found none.[50] The kinship systems described by Giallombardo and others, however, extend beyond simple "family" ties to the formation of large, intricately related groups that include many nonsexual relationships. In these groups, the roles of "children," "in-laws," "grandparents," and so on may be explicitly recognized. Even "birth order" within a family can become an issue for kinship groups.[51] Kinship groups sometimes occupy a common household—usually a prison cottage or a dormitory area. The descriptions of women's prisons provided by authors like Giallombardo show a closed society in which all aspects of social interaction—including expectations, normative forms of behavior, and emotional ties—are regulated by an inventive system of artificial relationships that mirror those of the outside world.

Many studies of female prisoners have shown that incarcerated women suffer intensely from the loss of affectional relationships once they enter prison and that they form homosexual liaisons to compensate for such losses.[52] Those liaisons then become the foundation of prison social organization.

A decade ago, Barbara Owen, professor of criminology at California State University, Fresno, conducted a study of female inmates at the Central California Women's Facility (the largest prison for women in the world). Her book, *"In the Mix": Struggle and Survival in a Women's Prison*,[53] describes the daily life of the inmates, with an emphasis on prison social structure. Owen found that prison culture for women is tied directly to the roles that women normally assume in free society as well as to other factors shaped by the conditions of women's lives in prison and in the free world. Like Heffernan's work, *"In the Mix"* describes the lives of women before prison and suggests that those lifestyles shape women's adaptation to prison culture. Owen found that preexisting economic marginalization, self-destructive behaviors, and personal histories of physical, sexual, and substance abuse may be important defining features of inmates' lives before they enter prison.[54] She also discovered that the sentences that women have to serve, along with their work and housing assignments, effectively pattern their daily lives and relationships. Owen describes "the mix" as that aspect of prison culture that supports the rule-breaking behavior that propels women into crime and causes them to enter prison. Owen concludes that prison subcultures for women are very different from the violent and predatory structure of contemporary male prisons.[55] Like men, women experience "pains of imprisonment," but their prison culture offers them other ways to survive and adapt to these deprivations.

A study of a women's correctional facility in the southeastern United States found that female inmates asked about their preincarceration sexual orientation gave answers that were quite different than when they were asked about their sexual orientation while incarcerated.[56] In general, before being incarcerated, 64% of inmates interviewed reported being exclusively heterosexual, 28% said they were bisexual, and 8% said that they were lesbians. In contrast, while incarcerated, these same women reported sexual orientations of 55% heterosexual, 31% bisexual, and 13% lesbian. Researchers found that same-sex sexual behavior within the institution was more likely to occur in the lives of young inmates who had had such experiences before entering prison. The study also found that female inmates tended to take part in lesbian behavior the longer they were incarcerated.

Finally, a significant aspect of sexual activity far more commonly found in women's prisons than in men's prisons is sexual misconduct between staff and inmates. Although a fair amount of such behavior is attributed to the exploitation of female inmates by male corrections officers acting from positions of power, some studies suggest that female inmates may sometimes attempt to manipulate unsuspecting male officers into illicit relationships in order to gain favors.[57]

bikeriderlondon/Shutterstock

A female inmate in a segregation unit. The number of women in prison is growing steadily. Why?

Types of Female Inmates

As in institutions for men, the subculture of women's prisons is multidimensional. Esther Heffernan, for example, found that three terms used by the female prisoners she studied—the *square*, the *cool*, and the *life*—were indicative of three styles of adaptation to prison life.[58] Square inmates had few early experiences with criminal lifestyles and tended to sympathize with the values and attitudes of conventional society. Cool prisoners were more likely to be career offenders. They tended to keep to themselves and generally supported inmate values. Women who participated in the life subculture were quite familiar with lives of crime. Many had been arrested repeatedly for prostitution, drug use, theft, and so on. They were full participants in the economic, social, and familial arrangements of the prison. Heffernan believed that the life offered an alternative lifestyle to women who had experienced early consistent rejection by conventional society. Within the life, women could establish relationships, achieve status, and find meaning in their lives. The square, the cool, and the life represented subcultures to Heffernan because individuals with similar adaptive choices tended to relate closely to one another and to support the lifestyle characteristic of that type.

The social structure of women's prisons was altered about 20 years ago by the arrival of cocaine-addicted "crack kids," as they were called in prison argot. Crack kids, whose existence highlighted generational differences among female offenders,

Jack Kurtz/The Image Works

Female inmates in Sheriff Joe Arpaio's "equal opportunity jail" in Maricopa County, Arizona, being inspected by a corrections officer before leaving for chain gang duty. Not all states make use of chain gangs, and only a few use female inmates on chain gangs. Should jail chain gangs be more widely used?

were streetwise young women with little respect for traditional prison values, for their elders, or even for their own children. Known for frequent fights and for their lack of even simple domestic skills, these young women quickly estranged many older inmates, some of whom call them "animalescents."

Violence in Women's Prisons

Some authors suggest that violence in women's prisons is less frequent than it is in institutions for men. Lee Bowker observes that "except for the behavior of a few 'guerrillas,' it appears that violence is only used in women's prisons to settle questions of dominance and subordination when other manipulative strategies fail to achieve the desired effect."[59] It appears that few homosexual liaisons are forced, perhaps representing a general aversion among women to such victimization in wider society. At least one study, however, has shown the use of sexual violence in women's prisons as a form of revenge against inmates who are overly vocal in their condemnation of lesbian practices among other prisoners.[60]

To address the problems of imprisoned women, including violence, the Task Force on the Female Offender recommended a number of changes in the administration of prisons for women.[61] Among those recommendations were:

- Substance-abuse programs should be available to female inmates.
- Female inmates need to acquire greater literacy skills, and literacy programs should form the basis on which other programs are built.
- Female offenders should be housed in buildings without male inmates.
- Institutions for women should develop programs for keeping children in the facility in order to "fortify the bond between mother and child."
- To ensure equal access to assistance, institutions should be built to accommodate programs for female offenders.

The Staff World

The flip side of inmate society can be found in the world of the prison staff, which includes many people working in various professions. Staff roles encompass those of warden, psychologist, counselor, area supervisor, program director, instructor, corrections officer, and—in some large prisons—physician and therapist.

According to the federal government, approximately 748,000 people are employed in corrections,[62] with the majority performing direct custodial tasks in state institutions: 62% of corrections employees work for state governments, followed by 33% at the local level and 5% at the federal level.[63] On a per capita basis, the District of Columbia has the most state and local corrections employees (53.3 per every 10,000 residents), followed by Texas (43.8).[64] Across the nation, 70% of corrections officers are Caucasian, 22% are African American, and slightly more than 5% are Hispanic.[65] Women account for 20% of all corrections officers, with the proportion of female officers increasing at around 19% per year. The American Correctional Association (ACA) encourages correctional agencies to "ensure that recruitment, selection, and promotion opportunities are open to women."[66]

Corrections officers, generally considered to be at the bottom of the staff hierarchy, may be divided into cell-block guards and tower guards; others are assigned to administrative offices, where they perform clerical tasks. The inmate-to-staff ratio in state prisons averages around 4.1 inmates for each corrections officer.[67]

Like prisoners, corrections officers undergo a socialization process that helps them function by the official and unofficial rules of staff society. In a classic study, Lucien Lombardo described the process by which officers are socialized into the prison work world.[68] Lombardo interviewed 359 corrections personnel at New York's Auburn Prison and found that rookie officers quickly had to abandon preconceptions of both inmates and other staff members. According to Lombardo, new officers learn that inmates are not the "monsters" much of the public

© Marmaduke St. John / Alamy

A correctional official oversees the segregation unit for violent prisoners at a California facility. The job of a corrections officer centers largely on the custody and control of inmates, but growing professionalism is enhancing both personal opportunities and job satisfaction among officers. Why is professionalism important to job satisfaction?

makes them out to be. On the other hand, rookies may be seriously disappointed in their experienced colleagues when they realize that the ideals of professionalism, often emphasized during early training, rarely translate into reality. The pressures of the institutional work environment, however, soon force most corrections personnel to adopt a united front when relating to inmates.

One of the leading formative influences on staff culture is the potential threat that inmates pose. Inmates far outnumber corrections personnel in every institution, and the hostility they feel for guards is only barely hidden even at the best of times. Corrections personnel know that however friendly inmates may appear, a sudden change in the institutional climate—from a simple disturbance in the yard to a full-blown riot—can quickly and violently unmask deep-rooted feelings of mistrust and hatred.

As in years past, prison staffers are still most concerned with custody and control. Society, especially under the just deserts philosophy of criminal sentencing, expects corrections staff to keep inmates in custody; this is the basic prerequisite of successful job performance. Custody is necessary before any other correctional activities, such as instruction or counseling, can be undertaken. Control, the other major staff concern, ensures order, and an orderly prison is thought to be safe and secure. In routine daily activities, control over almost all aspects of inmate behavior becomes paramount in the minds of most corrections officers. It is the twin interests of custody and control that lead to institutionalized procedures for ensuring security in most facilities. The enforcement of strict rules; body and cell searches; counts; unannounced shakedowns; the control of dangerous items, materials, and contraband; and the extensive use of bars, locks, fencing, cameras, and alarms all support the staff's vigilance in maintaining security.

The Professionalization of Corrections Officers

Corrections officers have generally been accorded low occupational status. Historically, the role of prison guard required minimal formal education and held few opportunities for professional growth and career advancement. Such jobs were typically low paying, frustrating, and often boring. Growing problems in our nation's prisons, including emerging issues of legal liability, however, increasingly require a well-trained and adequately equipped force of professionals. As corrections personnel have become better trained and more proficient, the old concept of guard has been supplanted by that of corrections officer. The ACA's code of ethics for correctional officers is reproduced in the "Ethics and Professionalism" box in this chapter.

Many states and a growing number of large-city correctional systems try to eliminate individuals with potentially harmful personality characteristics from corrections officer applicant pools. New Jersey, New York, Ohio, Pennsylvania, and Rhode Island, for example, have all used some form of psychological screening in assessing candidates for prison jobs.[69]

Although only a few states utilize psychological screening, all have training programs intended to prepare successful applicants for prison work. New York, for example, requires trainees to complete six weeks of classroom-based instruction, 40 hours of rifle range practice, and six weeks of on-the-job training. Training days begin around 5 a.m. with a mile run and conclude after dark with study halls for students who need extra help. To keep pace with rising inmate populations, the state has often had to run a number of simultaneous training academies.[70] Anyone interested in working in the field of corrections should visit the website Discover Corrections. Funded by the Bureau of Justice Assistance, an arm of the U.S. Department of Justice, the site can be reached at **http://www.discovercorrections.com.**

Prison Riots

On February 19, 2012, a riot broke out in a desperately overcrowded Mexican prison in the town of Apodaca, close to the Mexican city of Monterrey.[71] By the time the fighting was over, 44 inmates had been killed and the prison was in shambles. Officials called the riot a "feud" between members of rival drug cartels, and claimed that all of the deaths had occurred at the hands of other inmates. Only a month earlier, 30 inmates died in a similar altercation in a prison in Tamaulipas, located just across the border from the U.S. city of Brownsville, Texas.

Unlike prisons in Mexico, today's American prisons are relatively calm, but the ten years between 1970 and 1980 have been called the "explosive decade" of prison riots.[72] The decade began with a massive uprising at Attica Prison in New York State in September 1971, which resulted in 43 deaths and left more than 80 men wounded. The decade ended in 1980 in Santa Fe, New Mexico. There, in a riot at the New Mexico Penitentiary, 33 inmates died, the victims of vengeful prisoners out to eliminate rats and informants. Many of the deaths involved mutilation and torture. More than 200 other inmates were beaten and sexually assaulted, and the prison was virtually destroyed.

Although the number of prison riots decreased after the 1970s, they did continue. For 11 days in 1987, the federal penitentiary in Atlanta, Georgia, was under the control of inmates. The institution was heavily damaged, and inmates had to be temporarily relocated while it was rebuilt. The Atlanta riot followed on the heels of a similar, but less intense, disturbance at the federal detention center in Oakdale, Louisiana. Both outbreaks were attributed to the dissatisfaction of Cuban inmates, most of whom had arrived in the mass exodus known as the *Mariel boatlift*.[73]

Easter Sunday 1993 marked the beginning of an 11-day rebellion at the 1,800-inmate Southern Ohio Correctional Facility in Lucasville, Ohio—one of the country's toughest maximum-security prisons. When the riot ended, 9 inmates and 1 corrections officer were dead. The officer had been hung.[74]

Riots related to inmate grievances over perceived disparities in federal drug-sentencing policies and the possible loss of weight-lifting equipment occurred throughout the federal prison system in October 1995. Within a few days, the unrest led to a nationwide lockdown of 73 federal prisons. Although fires were set and a number of inmates and guards were injured, no deaths resulted. In February 2000, a riot between 200 black and Hispanic prisoners in California's Pelican Bay State Prison resulted in the death of one inmate. Fifteen other inmates were wounded. Then, in November 2000, 32 inmates took a dozen corrections officers hostage at the privately run Torrance County Detention Facility in Estancia, New Mexico. Two of the officers were stabbed and seriously injured, while another eight were beaten. The riot was finally quelled after an emergency-response team threw tear-gas canisters into the area where the prisoners had barricaded themselves.[75]

Tom Hood/AP Wide World Photos.

The Arizona State Prison Complex at Lewis, where two inmates held two corrections officers hostage in a watchtower in 2004. One officer, a female, was raped. On April 30, 2004, inmate Steven Coy was sentenced to seven consecutive life sentences for his part in the hostage crisis. How can the safety of corrections workers be improved?

ethics and professionalism

American Correctional Association Code of Ethics

Preamble

The American Correctional Association expects of its members unfailing honesty, respect for the dignity and individuality of human beings, and a commitment to professional and compassionate service. To this end, we subscribe to the following principles:

- Members shall respect and protect the civil and legal rights of all individuals.
- Members shall treat every professional situation with concern for the welfare of the individuals involved and with no intent to personal gain.
- Members shall maintain relationships with colleagues to promote mutual respect within the profession and improve the quality of service.
- Members shall make public criticisms of their colleagues or their agencies only when warranted, verifiable, and constructive.
- Members shall respect the importance of all disciplines within the criminal justice system and work to improve cooperation with each segment.
- Members shall honor the public's right to information and share information with the public to the extent permitted by law subject to individuals' right to privacy.
- Members shall respect and protect the right of the public to be safeguarded from criminal activity.
- Members shall refrain from using their positions to secure personal privileges or advantages.
- Members shall refrain from allowing personal interest to impair objectivity in the performance of duty while acting in an official capacity.
- Members shall refrain from entering into any formal or informal activity or agreement which presents a conflict of interest or is inconsistent with the conscientious performance of duties.
- Members shall refrain from accepting any gifts, service, or favor that is or appears to be improper or implies an obligation inconsistent with the free and objective exercise of professional duties.
- Members shall clearly differentiate between personal views/statements and views/statements/positions made on behalf of the agency or association.
- Members shall report to appropriate authorities any corrupt or unethical behaviors in which there is sufficient evidence to justify review.
- Members shall refrain from discriminating against any individual because of race, gender, creed, national origin, religious affiliation, age, disability, or any other type of prohibited discrimination.
- Members shall preserve the integrity of private information; they shall refrain from seeking information on individuals beyond that which is necessary to implement responsibilities and perform their duties; members shall refrain from revealing nonpublic information unless expressly authorized to do so.
- Members shall make all appointments, promotions, and dismissals in accordance with established civil service rules, applicable contract agreements, and individual merit, and not in furtherance of partisan interests.
- Members shall respect, promote, and contribute to a workplace that is safe, healthy, and free of harassment in any form.

Adopted August 1975 at the 105th Congress of Correction. Revised August 1990 at the 120th Congress of Correction. Revised August 1994 at the 124th Congress of Correction.

Thinking About Ethics

1. How does the American Correctional Association's Code of Ethics differ from the American Jail Association's Code of Ethics found in Chapter 13? How is it similar?
2. Do you think that one code of ethics should cover corrections officers working in both jails and prisons? Why or why not?

Source: American Correctional Association. Reprinted with permission. Visit the American Correctional Association at http://www.aca.org.

In 2004, a disturbance took place at the medium- to high-security Arizona State Prison Complex at Lewis. Two corrections officers and a staff member were injured in a fight that broke out during breakfast preparations, and two other officers were captured and held hostage for 15 days in a watchtower. Officials were able to keep disorder from spreading to the rest of the facility, and the incident ended when inmates released the officers and surrendered.

In 2005, 42 inmates were injured when a ruckus broke out during breakfast between Hispanic and white prisoners at California's San Quentin State Prison. The riot occurred in a section of the prison housing about 900 inmates who were under lockdown because of previous fighting between the groups.[76] In 2008, the federal correctional institution in Three Rivers, Texas, was locked down following two gang-related fights that killed 1 inmate and injured 22.[77]

■ **security threat group (STG)** An inmate group, gang, or organization whose members act together to pose a threat to the safety of corrections staff or the public, who prey upon other inmates, or who threaten the secure and orderly operation of a correctional institution.

AP Photo/Houston Chronicle, Cody Duty

Assistant Attorney General Lanny Breuer speaks to media representatives in Houston, Texas, announcing the arrest of dozens of alleged members of the white supremacist Aryan Brotherhood of Texas security threat group in 2013 on federal racketeering and other charges. The gang is suspected of involvement in the shooting deaths of Tom Clements, the head of Colorado prisons, and two Texas prosecutors.

In 2009, 4 prisoners were hospitalized and about 700 had to be relocated after inmates set fire to the medium-security Northpoint Training Center in Kentucky.[78] About the same time, 200 inmates were injured in a riot at the California Institution for Men in Chino, California, when rioting at the institution left at least one building ablaze.[79] The Chino facility is home to more than 5,900 inmates, many of whom are housed in old military-style barracks.

Causes of Riots

Researchers have suggested a variety of causes for prison riots.[80] Among them are these:

- An insensitive prison administration that neglects inmates' demands. Calls for "fairness" in disciplinary hearings, better food, more recreational opportunities, and the like may lead to riots when ignored.
- The lifestyles most inmates are familiar with on the streets. It should be no surprise that prisoners use organized violence when many of them are violent people.
- Dehumanizing prison conditions. Overcrowded facilities, the lack of opportunity for individual expression, and other aspects of total institutions culminate in explosive situations, including riots.
- A desire to regulate inmate society and redistribute power balances among inmate groups. Riots provide the opportunity to "cleanse" the prison population of informers and rats and to resolve struggles among power brokers and ethnic groups within the institution.
- "Power vacuums" created by changes in prison administration, the transfer of influential inmates, or court-ordered injunctions that significantly alter the informal social control mechanisms of the institution.

Although riots are difficult to predict in specific institutions, some state prison systems appear ripe for disorder. The Texas prison system, for example, is home to a number of gangs—referred to by corrections personnel as **security threat groups (STGs)**—among whom turf violations can easily lead to widespread disorder. Gang membership among inmates in the Texas prison system, practically nonexistent in 1983, was estimated at more than 1,200 just nine years later.[81] The Texas Syndicate, the Aryan Brotherhood of Texas, and the Mexican Mafia (sometimes known as *La Eme*, Spanish for the letter *M*) are thought to be the largest gangs functioning in the Texas prison system today. Each has around 300 members.[82] Other gangs known to operate in some Texas prisons include the 211 Crew, Aryan Warriors, Black Gangster Disciples (mostly in midwestern Texas), the Black Guerrilla Family, the Confederate Knights of America, and Nuestra Familia, an organization of Hispanic prisoners.

Gangs in Texas grew rapidly in part because of the power vacuum created when a court ruling ended the "building tender" system.

Gangs in Texas grew rapidly in part because of the power vacuum created when a court ruling ended the "building tender" system.[83] Building tenders were tough inmates who were given almost free rein by prison administrators in keeping other inmates in line, especially in many of the state's worst prisons. The end of the building tender system dramatically increased demands on the Texas Department of Criminal Justice for increased abilities and professionalism among its guards and other prison staff. Today, prison gangs have developed into criminal organizations whose reach may extend far beyond prison walls. In 2013, for example, Colorado prison chief Tom Clements was gunned down by a former inmate and gang member as he answered the front door of his home. Authorities believe that the killing was ordered by imprisoned gang leaders known as *shot callers*. Similar killings of two district attorneys in 2013 may have been related to security threat groups in Texas prisons. Terry Pelz, a former Texas prison warden, observes that "The gangs [have gone] from protecting themselves in prison on racial lines to evolving into criminal enterprises."[84]

paying for it

The Cost-Benefit Knowledge Bank for Criminal Justice

Throughout this book, we've provided a number of boxes like this one—all of which examine criminal justice system costs and raise questions about providing cost-effective services in the justice arena. We've explored the issue of cost-efficiency in policing, courts, and corrections.

In this final box, we take a look at the Cost-Benefit Knowledge Bank for Criminal Justice (CBKB), a recently developed online resource sponsored by the Vera Institute of Justice with funding from the federal Bureau of Justice Assistance. The CBKB, which can be reached at cbkb.org, works to "help practitioners and jurisdictions build their capacity to conduct cost-benefit studies and apply cost-benefit analysis to policymaking." It supports practitioners in building the "capacity to promote, use, and interpret cost-benefit analysis in criminal justice settings."

The CBKB website offers webinars on topics such as budget and finance in criminal justice, victim costs, reading cost-benefit reports, and step-by-step guides to cost-benefit analysis for justice policy. New webinars are added continuously, and an archive of past webinars enables interested parties to review those that have already been conducted.

The site also offers a library of cost-benefit studies relative to the justice area. Topics of some of the available documents include "evidence-based programs," "a cost-benefit analysis of county diversion programs," and "can drug courts save money?" CBKB materials are available in the areas of courts, crime prevention, information technology, law enforcement, probation and parole, reentry, sentencing and corrections, substance use and mental health, and victimization.

Finally, the CBKB website offers its New Perspectives Tool, which allows justice planners and program administrators to capture the costs and benefits of anticipated and ongoing programs from the point of view of multiple affected parties. The tool provides methods to quantify costs to (1) taxpayers, (2) crime victims (including tangible and intangible costs), (3) program participants, (4) justice agencies and personnel, and (5) businesses and neighborhoods. In the reentry area, for example, the tool encourages planners to examine both benefits (such as conferring skills on participants that result in better-paying jobs and wider work prospects) and costs (such as staff salaries, transportation expenses, and lost wages that might have been earned if participants were employed instead of enrolled in the program). The tool also encourages the consideration of benefits to the children of offenders reentering society and to businesses and neighborhoods that can benefit from increased commercial activities as well as increased property values resulting from reduced crime. "Which perspectives are included in—or excluded from—a CBA [cost-benefit analysis] can affect the bottom line," says the CBKB. Table 14-2 provides an example of the kinds of useful information available through the CBKB.

The CBKB is available on Facebook (http://www.facebook.com/costbenefit) and on Twitter (@CBKBank). It also has its own YouTube channel (http://www.youtube.com/user/CBKBank). Perhaps the best way to keep up with activities and sponsored events at the CBKB, however, is through its blog at http://cbkb.org/blog. You can also subscribe to an email newsletter that will keep you updated on CBKB activities.

TABLE 14-2 | Financial Benefits of Programs for Adult Offenders

PROGRAMS FOR ADULT OFFENDERS	PERCENT CHANGE IN CRIME	TO CRIME VICTIMS	TO TAXPAYER	PROGRAM COSTS PER PARTICIPANT	COST/BENEFIT PER PARTICIPANT[a]
Vocational education in prison	−9.0	$8,114	$6,806	$1,182	$13,738
Intensive supervision: treatment-oriented programs	−16.7	9,318	9,369	7,124	11,563
General education in prison (basic education or postsecondary)	−7.0	6,325	5,306	962	10,669
Cognitive-behavioral therapy in prison or community	−6.3	5,658	4,764	105	10,299
Drug treatment in community	−9.3	5,133	5,495	574	10,054
Correctional industries in prison	−5.9	5,360	4,496	417	9,439
Drug treatment in prison (therapeutic communities or outpatient)	−5.7	5,133	4,306	1,604	7,835
Employment and job training in the community	−4.3	2,373	2,386	400	4,359

[a]Positive numbers indicate system savings.
Source: National Institute of Corrections, *Evidence-Based Policy, Practice, and Decisionmaking: Implications for Paroling Authorities* (Washington, D.C.: NIC, 2011; updated 2013).

References: Cost-Benefit Knowledge Bank for Criminal Justice, "Featured Content," http://cbkb.org (accessed August 21, 2013).

■ **hands-off doctrine** A policy of nonintervention with regard to prison management that U.S. courts tended to follow until the late 1960s. For the past 40 years, the doctrine has languished as judicial intervention in prison administration dramatically increased, although there is now some evidence that a new hands-off era is approaching.

■ **civil death** The legal status of prisoners in some jurisdictions who are denied the opportunity to vote, hold public office, marry, or enter into contracts by virtue of their status as incarcerated felons. Although civil death is primarily of historical interest, some jurisdictions still limit the contractual opportunities available to inmates.

Prisoners' Rights

In May 1995, Limestone Prison inmate Larry Hope was handcuffed to a hitching post after arguing with another inmate while working on a chain gang near an interstate highway in Alabama.[85] Hope was released two hours later, after a supervising officer determined that Hope had not instigated the altercation. During the two hours that he was coupled to the post, Hope was periodically offered drinking water and bathroom breaks, and his responses to those offers were recorded on an activity log. Because of the height of the hitching post, however, his arms grew tired, and it was later determined that whenever he tried moving his arms to improve his circulation, the handcuffs cut into his wrists, causing pain.

One month later, Hope was punished more severely after he had taken a nap during the morning bus ride to the chain gang's work site. When the bus arrived, he was slow in responding to an order to exit the vehicle. A shouting match soon led to a scuffle with an officer, and four other guards intervened and subdued Hope, handcuffing him and placing him in leg irons for transportation back to the prison. When he arrived at the facility, officers made him take off his shirt and again put him on the hitching post. He stood in the sun for approximately seven hours, sustaining a sunburn. Hope was given water only once or twice during that time and was provided with no bathroom breaks. At one point, an officer taunted him about his thirst. According to Hope: "[The guard] first gave water to some dogs, then brought the water cooler closer to me, removed its lid, and kicked the cooler over, spilling the water onto the ground."

Eventually, Hope filed a civil suit against three officers, claiming that he experienced "unnecessary pain" and that the "wanton infliction of pain . . . constitutes cruel and unusual punishment forbidden by the Eighth Amendment." His case eventually reached the U.S. Supreme Court, and on June 27, 2002, the Court found that Hope's treatment was "totally without penological justification" and constituted an Eighth Amendment violation. The Court ruled that "Despite the clear lack of emergency, respondents knowingly subjected [Hope] to a substantial risk of physical harm, unnecessary pain, unnecessary exposure to the sun, prolonged thirst and taunting, and a deprivation of bathroom breaks that created a risk of particular discomfort and humiliation."

In deciding the *Hope* case, the Court built on almost 40 years of precedent-setting decisions in the area of prisoners' rights. Before the 1960s, American courts had taken a neutral approach—commonly called the **hands-off doctrine**—toward the running of prisons. Judges assumed that prison administrators were sufficiently professional in the performance of their duties to balance institutional needs with humane considerations. The hands-off doctrine rested on the belief that defendants lost most of their rights upon conviction, suffering a kind of **civil death**. Many states defined the concept of civil death through legislation that denied inmates the right to vote, to hold public office, and even to marry. Some states made incarceration for a felony a basis for uncontested divorce at the request of the noncriminal spouse. Aspects of the old notion of civil death are still a reality in a number of jurisdictions today, and the Sentencing Project says that 3.9 million American citizens across the nation are barred from voting because of previous felony convictions.[86]

Although the concept of civil death has not entirely disappeared, the hands-off doctrine ended in 1970, when a federal court declared the entire Arkansas prison system to be unconstitutional after hearing arguments that it represented a form of cruel and unusual punishment.[87] The court's decision resulted from what it judged to be pervasive overcrowding and primitive living conditions. Longtime inmates claimed that over the years, a number of inmates had been beaten or shot to death by guards and buried in unmarked graves on prison property. An investigation did unearth some skeletons in old graves, but their origin was never determined.

Detailed media coverage of the Arkansas prison system gave rise to suspicions about correctional institutions everywhere. Within a few years, federal courts intervened in the running of prisons in Florida, Louisiana, Mississippi, New York City, and Virginia.[88] In 1975, in a precedent-setting decision, U.S. District Court Judge Frank M. Johnson issued an order banning the Alabama Board of Corrections from accepting any more inmates. Citing a population that was more than double the capacity of the state's system, Judge Johnson enumerated 44 standards to be met before additional inmates could be admitted to prison. Included in the requirements were specific guidelines on living space, staff-to-inmate ratios, visiting privileges, the racial makeup of staff, and food-service modifications.[89]

■ **balancing test** A principle, developed by the courts and applied to the corrections arena by *Pell* v. *Procunier* (1974), that attempts to weigh the rights of an individual, as guaranteed by the Constitution, against the authority of states to make laws or to otherwise restrict a person's freedom in order to protect the state's interests and its citizens.

The Legal Basis of Prisoners' Rights

In 1974, the U.S. Supreme Court case of *Pell* v. *Procunier*[90] established a "balancing test" that, although originally addressing only First Amendment rights, eventually served as a general guideline for all prison operations. In *Pell*, the Court ruled that the "prison inmate retains those First Amendment rights that are not inconsistent with his status as a prisoner or with the legitimate penological objectives of the corrections system."[91] In other words, inmates have rights, much the same as people who are not incarcerated, provided that the legitimate needs of the prison for security, custody, and safety are not compromised. Other courts have declared that order maintenance, security, and rehabilitation are all legitimate concerns of prison administration but that financial exigency and convenience are not. As the **balancing test** makes clear, we see reflected in prisoners' rights a microcosm of the dilemma of "individual rights versus public order" found in wider society.

Further enforcing the legal rights of prisoners is the Civil Rights of Institutionalized Persons Act (CRIPA) of 1980.[92] The law, which has been amended over time, applies to all adult and juvenile state and local jails, detention centers, prisons, mental hospitals, and other care facilities (such as those operated by a state, county, or city for individuals who are physically disabled or chronically ill). Another federal law, the Religious Land Use and Institutionalized Persons Act of 2000 (RLUIPA), has particular relevance to prison programs and activities that are at least partially supported with federal monies. RLUIPA states:

> No government shall impose a substantial burden on the religious exercise of a person residing in or confined to an institution even if the burden results from a rule of general applicability, unless the government demonstrates that imposition of the burden on that person (1) is in furtherance of a compelling governmental interest; and (2) is the least restrictive means of furthering that compelling governmental interest.

Significantly, the most recent version of CRIPA states:[93]

> No action shall be brought with respect to prison conditions under section 1983 of this title, or any other Federal law, by a prisoner confined in any jail, prison, or other correctional facility until such administrative remedies as are available are exhausted.

Prisoners' rights, because they are constrained by the legitimate needs of imprisonment, can be thought of as conditional rights rather than absolute rights. The Second Amendment to the U.S. Constitution, for example, grants citizens the right to bear arms. The right to arms is, however, necessarily compromised by the need for order and security in prison, and we would not expect a court to rule that inmates have a right to weapons. Prisoners' rights must be balanced against the security, order-maintenance, and treatment needs of correctional institutions.

Prisoners' rights must be balanced against the security, order-maintenance, and treatment needs of correctional institutions.

Conditional rights, because they are subject to the exigencies of imprisonment, bear a strong resemblance to privileges, which is not surprising because "privileges" were all that inmates officially had until the modern era. The practical difference between a privilege and a conditional right is that privileges exist only at the convenience of granting institutions and can be revoked at any time for any reason. The rights of prisoners, on the other hand, have a basis in the Constitution and in law external to the institution. Although the institution may restrict such rights for legitimate correctional reasons, those rights may not be infringed without cause that can be demonstrated in a court of law. Mere institutional convenience does not provide a sufficient legal basis for the denial of rights.

The past few decades have seen many lawsuits brought by prisoners challenging the constitutionality of some aspect of confinement. As mentioned in Chapter 11, suits filed by prisoners with the courts are generally called writs of *habeas*

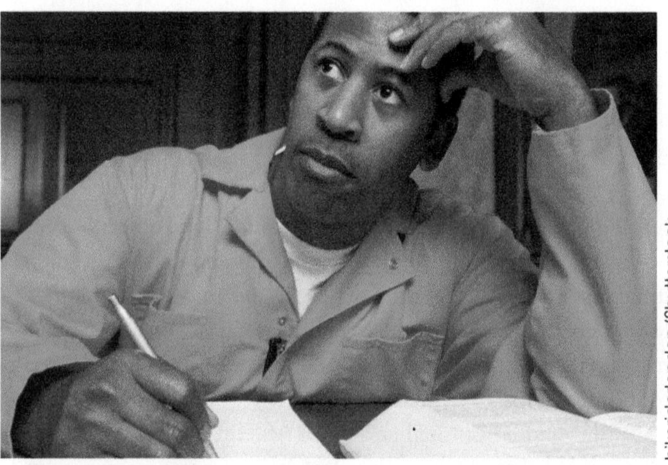

bikeriderlondon/Shutterstock

A "jailhouse lawyer" works in a prison law library. Such inmates, although they rarely have any formal legal training, help other inmates prepare legal writs and represent them in in-house disciplinary actions. Why are jailhouse lawyers important to today's prisons?

■ **grievance procedure** A formalized arrangement, usually involving a neutral hearing board, whereby institutionalized individuals have the opportunity to register complaints about the conditions of their confinement.

corpus and formally request that the person detaining a prisoner bring him or her before a judicial officer to determine the lawfulness of the imprisonment. The American Correctional Association says that most prisoner lawsuits are based on "1. the Eighth Amendment prohibition against cruel and unusual punishment; 2. the Fourteenth Amendment prohibition against the taking of life, liberty, or property without due process of law; and 3. the Fourteenth Amendment provision requiring equal protection of the laws."[94] Aside from appeals by inmates that question the propriety of their convictions and sentences, such constitutional challenges represent the bulk of legal action initiated by the imprisoned. State statutes and federal legislation, however, including Section 1983 of the Civil Rights Act of 1871, provide other bases for challenges to the legality of specific prison conditions and procedures. The U.S. Supreme Court has not yet spoken with finality on a number of prisoners' rights questions. Nonetheless, High Court decisions of the last few decades and a number of lower-court findings can be interpreted to identify the existing conditional rights of prisoners, as shown in Table 14-3. Table 14-4 shows a number of important U.S. Supreme Court cases involving prisoners' rights claims.

Grievance Procedures

Today, all sizable prisons have established **grievance procedures** whereby an inmate files a complaint with local authorities and receives a mandated response. Modern grievance procedures range from the use of a hearing board composed of staff members and inmates to a single staff appointee charged with the resolution of complaints. Inmates who are dissatisfied with the handling of their grievance can generally appeal beyond the local prison.

Disciplinary actions by prison authorities may also require a formalized hearing process, especially when staff members bring charges of rule violations against inmates that might result in some form of punishment being imposed on them. In a precedent-setting decision in the case of *Wolff* v. *McDonnell* (1974),[95] the Supreme Court decided that sanctions could not be levied against inmates without appropriate due process. The *Wolff* case involved an inmate who had been deprived of previously earned good-time credits because of misbehavior. The Court established that good-time credits were a form of "state-created right(s)," which, once created, could not be "arbitrarily abrogated."[96] *Wolff* was especially significant because it began an era of court scrutiny into what came to be called *state-created liberty interests*. State-created liberty interests were based on the language used in published prison regulations and were held, in effect, to confer due process guarantees on

TABLE 14-3 | The Conditional Rights of Inmates[a]

Communications and Visitation

A right to receive publications directly from the publisher
A right to meet with members of the press[b]
A right to communicate with nonprisoners

Religious Freedom

A right of assembly for religious services and groups
A right to attend services of other religious groups
A right to receive visits from ministers
A right to correspond with religious leaders
A right to observe religious dietary laws
A right to wear religious insignia

Access to the Courts and Legal Assistance

A right to have access to the courts[c]
A right to visits from attorneys
A right to have mail communications with lawyers[d]
A right to communicate with legal assistance organizations
A right to consult jailhouse lawyers[e]
A right to assistance in filing legal papers, which should include one of the following:

- Access to an adequate law library
- Paid attorneys
- Paralegal personnel or law students

Medical Care

A right to sanitary and healthy conditions
A right to medical attention for serious physical problems
A right to required medications
A right to treatment in accordance with "doctor's orders"

Protection from Harm

A right to food, water, and shelter
A right to protection from foreseeable attack
A right to protection from predictable sexual abuse
A right to protection against suicide

Institutional Punishment and Discipline

An absolute right against corporal punishments (unless sentenced to such punishments)
A limited right to due process before punishment, including the following:

- A notice of charges
- A fair and impartial hearing
- An opportunity for defense
- A right to present witnesses
- A written decision

[a]All "rights" listed are provisional in that they may be constrained by the legitimate needs of imprisonment.
[b]But not beyond the opportunities afforded for inmates to meet with members of the general public.
[c]As restricted by the Prison Litigation Reform Act of 1996.
[d]Mail communications are generally designated as privileged or nonprivileged. Privileged communications include those between inmates and their lawyers or court officials and cannot legitimately be read by prison officials. Nonprivileged communications include most other written communications.
[e]Jailhouse lawyers are inmates with experience in the law, usually gained from filing legal briefs on their own behalf or on the behalf of others. Consultation with jailhouse lawyers was ruled permissible in the Supreme Court case of *Johnson* v. *Avery*, 393 U.S. 483 (1968), unless inmates are provided with paid legal assistance.

TABLE 14-4 | Important U.S. Supreme Court Cases Involving Prisoners' Rights Claims, by Year of Decision

CASE NAME	YEAR DECIDED	CONSTITUTIONAL BASIS	FINDING
Howes v. *Fields*	2012	Fifth Amendment	Inmates facing questioning by law enforcement officers while incarcerated need not be advised of their *Miranda* rights.
Florence v. *Burlington County*	2012	Fourth Amendment	Officials may strip search those arrested for any offense, including minor ones, before admitting them to jail.
Brown v. *Plata*	2011	Eighth Amendment	Overcrowded conditions in California's prisons were so egregious that the state was unable to deliver minimal care to prisoners with serious medical and mental health problems, requiring a forced reduction in prison populations.
U.S. v. *Georgia*	2006		Under the Americans with Disabilities Act, a state may be liable for rights deprivations suffered by inmates held in its prisons who are disabled.
Johnson v. *California*	2005		A California Department of Corrections and Rehabilitation's unwritten policy of racially segregating prisoners in double cells each time they entered a new correctional facility was invalidated.
Wilkinson v. *Austin*	2005		Upheld an Ohio policy allowing the most dangerous offenders to be held in "supermax" cells following several levels of review prior to transfer.
Overton v. *Bazzetta*	2003		A visitation regulation that denies most visits to prisoners who commit two substance-abuse violations while incarcerated was upheld.
Porter v. *Nussle*	2002	Eighth Amendment	The Prison Litigation Reform Act of 1995 (PLRA) "exhaustion requirement" applies to all inmate suits about prison life, whether they involve general circumstances or particular episodes and whether they allege excessive force or some other wrong.
Hope v. *Pelzer*	2002	Eighth Amendment	The Court found a constitutional violation in the case of a prisoner who was subjected to unnecessary pain, humiliation, and risk of physical harm.
Booth v. *Churner*	2001	Eighth Amendment	The Prison Litigation Reform Act's requirement that state inmates must "exhaust such administrative remedies as are available" before filing a suit over prison conditions was upheld.
Lewis v. *Casey*	1996		Inmates need not be given the wherewithal to file any and every type of legal claim. All that is required is "that they be provided with the tools to attack their sentences."
Sandin v. *Conner*	1995	Fourteenth Amendment	Rejected the argument that disciplining inmates is a deprivation of constitutional due process rights.
Helling v. *McKinney*	1993	Eighth Amendment	Environmental conditions of prison life, including secondhand cigarette smoke, that pose a threat to inmate health have to be corrected.
Wilson v. *Seiter*	1991	Eighth Amendment	Clarified the totality of conditions concept by holding that some conditions of confinement, taken "in combination," may violate prisoners' rights when each would not do so alone.
Washington v. *Harper*	1990	Eighth Amendment	A mentally ill inmate who is a danger to self or others may be forcibly treated with psychoactive drugs.
Turner v. *Safley*	1987	First Amendment	A ban on correspondence between Missouri inmates was upheld as "reasonably related to legitimate penological interests."
O'Lone v. *Estate of Shabazz*	1987	First Amendment	An inmate's right to religious practice was not violated by prison officials who refused to alter his work schedule so that he could attend Friday afternoon services.

TABLE 14-4 | *(continued)*

CASE NAME	YEAR DECIDED	CONSTITUTIONAL BASIS	FINDING
Whitley v. *Albers*	1986	Eighth Amendment	The shooting and wounding of an inmate was not a violation of that inmate's rights, because "the shooting was part and parcel of a good-faith effort to restore prison security."
Ponte v. *Real*	1985		Inmates are entitled to certain rights in disciplinary hearings.
Hudson v. *Palmer*	1984	Fourth Amendment	Prisoners have no reasonable expectation of privacy in their prison cells and no protections against what would otherwise be "unreasonable searches."
Block v. *Rutherford*	1984	First Amendment	State regulations may prohibit meetings of inmate unions as well as the use of the mail to deliver union information within the prison; also, prisoners do not have a right to be present during cell searches.
Rhodes v. *Chapman*	1981	Eighth Amendment	Double-celling of inmates is not in itself cruel and unusual punishment.
Ruiz v. *Estelle*	1980	Eighth Amendment	Unconstitutional conditions were found to exist within the Texas prison system—including overcrowding, understaffing, brutality, and substandard medical care.
Cooper v. *Morin*	1980		Neither inconvenience nor cost is an acceptable excuse for treating female inmates differently from male inmates.
Bell v. *Wolfish*	1979	Fourth Amendment	Pretrial detainees and other prisoners may be strip searched, to include body-cavity searches, as needed, regardless of the reason for their incarceration.
Jones v. *North Carolina Prisoners' Labor Union, Inc.*	1977	First Amendment	Inmates have no inherent right to publish newspapers or newsletters for use by other inmates.
Bounds v. *Smith*	1977		Resulted in the creation of law libraries in many prisons.
Estelle v. *Gamble*	1976	Eighth Amendment	Prison officials have a duty to provide proper inmate medical care.
Ruiz v. *Estelle*	1975	Eighth Amendment	Conditions of confinement within the Texas prison system were found to be unconstitutional.
Wolff v. *McDonnell*	1974	Fourteenth Amendment	Sanctions cannot be levied against inmates without appropriate due process.
Procunier v. *Martinez*	1974	First Amendment	Censorship of inmate mail is acceptable only when necessary to protect legitimate governmental interests.
Pell v. *Procunier*	1974	First Amendment	Inmates retain First Amendment rights that are not inconsistent with their status as prisoners or with the legitimate penological objectives of the corrections system.
U.S. v. *Hitchcock*	1972	Fourth Amendment	A warrantless cell search is not unreasonable.
Cruz v. *Beto*	1972	First Amendment	Inmates have to be given a "reasonable opportunity" to pursue their religious faiths; also, visits can be banned if such visits constitute threats to security.
Johnson v. *Avery*	1968		Inmates have a right to consult "jailhouse lawyers" when trained legal assistance is not available.
Monroe v. *Pape*	1961		Inmates have a right to bring action in federal court when deprived of their rights by state officers acting under color of state law.

© ZUMA Press, Inc./Alamy

New Port Richey, Florida, USA—A group of inmates pray during a jailhouse bible study at the New Port Richey jail. Faith-based prison programs are sponsored by religious organizations and supplement government-sponsored training and rehabilitation programs. What special roles might such programs play?

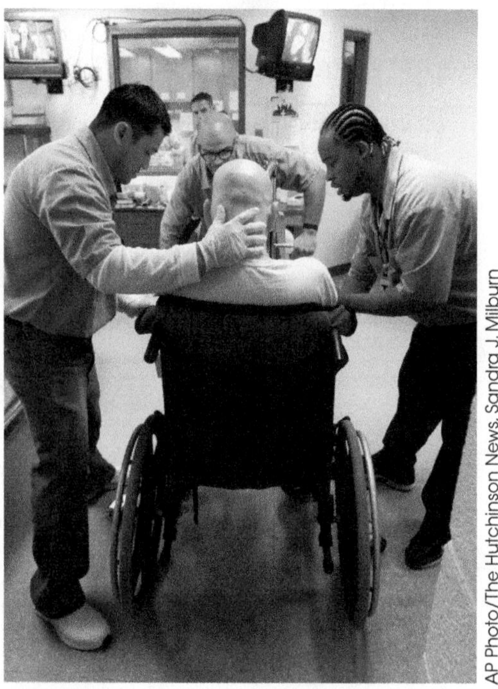

AP Photo/The Hutchinson News, Sandra J. Milburn

Hutchinson Correctional Facility (Kansas) inmate hospice volunteers Carlos Ballesteros, left, Chad Engro, and Robert Shanklin, right, help a patient in the prison's infirmary. Court decisions over the years have established a firm set of inmate rights. Among them is the right to necessary health care. What other rights do inmates have?

prisoners. Hence, if a prison regulation said that a disciplinary hearing should be held before a prisoner could be sent to solitary confinement and that the hearing should permit a discussion of the evidence for and against the prisoner, courts interpreted that regulation to mean that the prisoner had a state-created right to a hearing and that sending him or her to solitary confinement in violation of the regulation was a violation of a state-created liberty interest. In later court decisions, state-created rights and privileges were called *protected liberties* and were interpreted to include any significant change in a prisoner's status.

In the interest of due process, and especially where written prison regulations governing the hearing process exist, courts have generally held that inmates going before disciplinary hearing boards are entitled to (1) a notice of the charges brought against them, (2) the chance to organize a defense, (3) an impartial hearing, and (4) the opportunity to present witnesses and evidence in their behalf. A written statement of the hearing board's conclusions should be provided to the inmate.[97] In the case of *Ponte* v. *Real* (1985),[98] the Supreme Court held that prison officials must provide an explanation to inmates who are denied the opportunity to have a desired witness at their hearing. The case of *Vitek* v. *Jones* (1980)[99] extended the requirement of due process to inmates about to be transferred from prisons to mental hospitals.

So that inmates will know what is expected of them as they enter prison, the American Correctional Association recommends that "a rulebook that contains all chargeable offenses, ranges of penalties and disciplinary procedures [be] posted in a conspicuous and accessible area; [and] a copy . . . given to each inmate and staff member."[100]

freedom OR safety? YOU decide

Should Prison Libraries Limit Access to Potentially Inflammatory Literature?

In mid-2007, the Federal Bureau of Prisons (BOP) ordered chaplains at BOP facilities nationwide to remove potentially inflammatory literature from the shelves of chapel libraries. The move came in response to a report by the U.S. Justice Department's Office of the Inspector General, which recommended that prisons take steps to avoid becoming recruiting grounds for militant Islamists and other radical groups.

Thousands of books were soon removed under what the BOP called the Standardized Chapel Library Project, which it admitted was an effort to bar inmate access to literature that the BOP felt could "discriminate, disparage, advocate violence or radicalize." In identifying materials for removal, the BOP relied on the advice of experts who were asked to identify up to 150 book titles and 150 multimedia resources for each of 20 religious categories ranging from Bahaism to Yoruba. Prayer books were explicitly excluded from the list of materials targeted for removal.

Soon after the project was made public, however, members of Congress and a number of religious leaders urged the BOP to reverse its stance and return the books to chapel shelves.

In fall 2007, the Republican Study Committee, a group of conservative Republicans in the House of Representatives, sent a letter to BOP Director Harley G. Lappin saying, "We must ensure that in America the federal government is not the undue arbiter of what may or may not be read by our citizens."

Representative Jeb Hensarling of Texas, who heads the Republican Study Committee, explained that "anything that impinges upon the religious liberties of American citizens, be they incarcerated or not, is something that's going to cause . . . great concern." For its part, the BOP countered that it has a legitimate interest in screening out and removing items from inside of its facilities that could incite violence.

The controversy appeared to have ended in 2008 with passage of the Second Chance Act (Public Law 110-199), federal legislation that funded a number of reentry initiatives for people leaving prison and that required the director of the BOP "to discontinue the Standardized Chapel Library project or any other project that limits prisoner access to reading and other educational material." (The Second Chance Act is discussed in more detail in Chapter 12.) In 2009, however, the BOP revived its plan to limit prison chapel books and proposed a rule that would exclude materials from chapel libraries "that could incite, promote, or otherwise suggest the commission of violence or criminal activity." The proposed new rule targeted only literature encouraging violence, but critics said that it would still result in the banning of many religious texts.

You Decide

Should prison libraries be permitted to limit access to library literature that might incite violence or endanger the safety of inmates and staff? Would it matter if that literature is religious in nature? How might the Bureau of Prisons meet the concerns of the Republican Study Committee, religious leaders, and authors of the Second Chance Act while still accomplishing its objective of removing literature that it believes might incite violence?

References: Solomon Moore, "Plan Would Limit Prison Chapel Books," *New York Times*, March 18, 2009; Laurie Goodstein, "Prisons Purging Books on Faith from Libraries," *New York Times*, September 10, 2007; Laurie Goodstein, "Critics Right and Left Protest Book Removals," *New York Times*, September 21, 2007; and Neela Banerjee, "Prisons to Restore Purged Religious Books," *New York Times*, September 27, 2007.

A Return to the Hands-Off Doctrine?

Many state-created rights and protected liberties may soon be a thing of the past. In June 1991, an increasingly conservative U.S. Supreme Court signaled what seemed like the beginning of a new hands-off era. The case, *Wilson* v. *Seiter et al.*,[101] involved a Section 1983 suit brought against Richard P. Seiter, director of the Ohio Department of Rehabilitation and Correction, and Carl Humphreys, warden of the Hocking Correctional Facility (HCF) in Nelsonville, Ohio. In the suit, Pearly L. Wilson, a felon incarcerated at HCF, alleged that a number of the conditions of his confinement constituted cruel and unusual punishment in violation of the Eighth and Fourteenth Amendments. Specifically, Wilson cited overcrowding, excessive noise, insufficient locker storage space, inadequate heating and cooling, improper ventilation, unclean and inadequate restrooms, unsanitary dining facilities and food preparation, and housing with mentally and physically ill inmates. Wilson asked for a change in prison conditions and sought $900,000 from prison officials in compensatory and punitive damages.

deliberate indifference A wanton disregard by corrections personnel for the well-being of inmates. Deliberate indifference requires both actual knowledge that a harm is occurring and disregard of the risk of harm. A prison official may be held liable under the Eighth Amendment for acting with deliberate indifference to inmate health or safety only if he or she knows that inmates face a substantial risk of serious harm and disregards that risk by failing to take reasonable measures to abate it.

Both the federal district court in which Wilson first filed affidavits and the Sixth Circuit Court of Appeals held that no constitutional violations existed because the conditions cited by Wilson were not the result of malicious intent on the part of officials. The U.S. Supreme Court agreed, noting that the **deliberate indifference** standard applied in *Estelle* v. *Gamble* (1976)[102] to claims involving medical care is similarly applicable to other cases in which prisoners challenge the conditions of their confinement. In effect, the Court created a standard that effectively means that all future challenges to prison conditions by inmates, which are brought under the Eighth Amendment, must show deliberate indifference by the officials responsible for the existence of those conditions before the Court will hear the complaint.

The written opinion of the Court in *Wilson* v. *Seiter* is telling. Writing for the majority, Justice Antonin Scalia observed that "if a prison boiler malfunctions accidentally during a cold winter, an inmate would have no basis for an Eighth Amendment claim, even if he suffers objectively significant harm. If a guard accidentally stepped on a prisoner's toe and broke it, this would not be punishment in anything remotely like the accepted meaning of the word." At the time that the *Wilson* decision was handed down, critics voiced concerns that the decision could effectively excuse prison authorities from the need to improve living conditions within institutions on the basis of simple budgetary constraints.

In the 1995 case of *Sandin* v. *Conner*,[103] the U.S. Supreme Court took a much more definitive stance in favor of a new type of hands-off doctrine and voted 5 to 4 to reject the argument that any state action taken for a punitive reason encroaches on a prisoner's constitutional due process right to be free from the deprivation of liberty. In *Sandin*, Demont Conner, an inmate at the Halawa Correctional Facility in Hawaii, was serving an indeterminate sentence of 30 years to life for numerous crimes, including murder, kidnapping, robbery, and burglary. In a lawsuit in federal court, Conner alleged that prison officials had deprived him of procedural due process when a hearing committee refused to allow him to present witnesses during a disciplinary hearing and then sentenced him to segregation for alleged misconduct. An appellate court agreed with Conner, concluding that an existing prison regulation that instructed the hearing committee to find guilt in cases where a misconduct charge is supported by substantial evidence meant that the committee could not impose segregation if it did not look at all the evidence available to it.

The Supreme Court, however, reversed the decision of the appellate court, holding that while "such a conclusion may be entirely sensible in the ordinary task of construing a statute defining rights and remedies available to the general public, [i]t is a good deal less sensible in the case of a prison regulation primarily designed to guide correctional officials in the administration of a prison." The Court concluded that "such regulations [are] not designed to confer rights on inmates" but are meant only to provide guidelines to prison staff members.

In *Sandin*, the Court effectively set aside substantial portions of earlier decisions, such as *Wolff* v. *McDonnell* (1974)[104] and *Hewitt* v. *Helms* (1983),[105] which, wrote the justices, focused more on procedural issues than on those of "real substance." As a consequence, the majority opinion held, past cases like these have "impermissibly shifted the focus" away from the nature of a due process deprivation to one based on the language of a particular state or prison regulation. "The *Hewitt* approach," wrote the majority in *Sandin*, "has run counter to the view expressed in several of our cases that federal courts ought to afford appropriate deference and flexibility to state officials trying to manage a volatile environment. . . . The time has come," said the Court, "to return to those due process principles that were correctly established and applied" in earlier times. In short, *Sandin* made it much more difficult for inmates to effectively challenge the administrative regulations and procedures imposed on them by prison officials, even when stated procedures are not explicitly followed.

A more recent case whose findings support the action of federal corrections officers is that of *Ali* v. *Federal Bureau of Prisons*. The case, decided by the U.S. Supreme Court in 2008,[106] involved a federal prisoner, Abdus-Shahid M. S. Ali, who claimed that some of his personal belongings disappeared when he was transferred from one federal prison to another. The missing items, which were to have been shipped in two duffle bags belonging to Ali, included copies of the Koran, a prayer rug, and a number of religious magazines. Ali filed suit against the BOP under the Federal Tort Claims Act (FTCA),[107] which authorizes "claims against the United States for money damages . . . for injury or loss of property . . . caused by the negligent or wrongful act or omission of any employee in the government while acting within the scope of his office or employment." In denying Ali's claim, the Court found that the law specifically provides immunity for federal law enforcement officers and determined that federal corrections personnel are "law enforcement officers" within the meaning of the law.

Similarly, in 2013, in the case of *Millbrook* v. *United States*, the court again found that the FTCA excepts "law enforcement officers' [including correctional officers] acts or omissions that arise within the scope of their employment, regardless of whether the officers are engaged in investigative or law enforcement activity, or are executing a search, seizing evidence, or making an arrest."[108]

Finally, in two cases from 2012, the U.S. Supreme Court ruled firmly in favor of correctional officials in limiting the rights of inmates. In the first case, *Howes* v. *Fields* (2012), the Court found that inmates who face questioning by law enforcement officers while they are incarcerated need not be advised of their *Miranda* rights prior to the start of interrogation.[109] In the second case, *Florence* v. *Burlington County* (2012), the Court ruled that officials had the power to strip search persons who had been arrested prior to admission to a jail or other detention facility, even if the offense for which they were arrested was a minor one.[110] In that case, Justice Kennedy, writing for the majority, noted that "maintaining safety and order at detention centers requires the expertise of correctional officials, who must have substantial discretion to devise reasonable solutions to problems." He went on to write that "the term 'jail' is used here in a broad sense to include prisons and other detention facilities."

The Prison Litigation Reform Act of 1996

Only about 2,000 petitions per year concerning inmate problems were filed with the courts in 1961, but by 1975 the number of filings had increased to around 17,000, and in 1996 prisoners filed 68,235 civil rights lawsuits in federal courts nationwide.[111] Some inmate-originated suits seemed patently ludicrous and became the subject of much media coverage in the mid-1990s. One such suit involved Robert Procup, a Florida State Prison inmate serving time for the murder of his business partner. Procup repeatedly sued Florida prison officials—once because he got only one roll with his dinner, again because he didn't get a luncheon salad, a third time because prison-provided TV dinners didn't come with a drink, and a fourth time because his cell had no television. Two other well-publicized cases involved an inmate who went to court asking to be allowed to exercise religious freedom by attending prison chapel services in the nude and an inmate who, thinking he could become pregnant via homosexual relations, sued prison doctors who wouldn't provide him with birth-control pills. An infamous example of seemingly frivolous inmate lawsuits was one brought by inmates claiming religious freedoms and demanding that members of the Church of the New Song, or CONS, be provided steak and Harvey's Bristol Cream every Friday in order to celebrate communion. The CONS suit stayed in various courts for ten years before finally being thrown out.[112]

The huge number of inmate-originated lawsuits in the mid-1990s created a backlog of cases in many federal courts and was targeted by the media and by some citizens' groups as an unnecessary waste of taxpayers' money. The National Association of Attorneys General, which supports efforts to restrict frivolous inmate lawsuits, estimated that lawsuits filed by prisoners cost states more than $81 million a year in legal fees alone.[113]

The PLRA was a legislative effort to restrict inmate filings to worthwhile cases and to reduce the number of suits brought by state prisoners in federal courts.

In 1996, the federal Prison Litigation Reform Act (PLRA) became law.[114] The PLRA was a legislative effort to restrict inmate filings to worthwhile cases and to reduce the number of suits brought by state prisoners in federal courts. The PLRA

- Requires inmates to exhaust their prison's grievance procedure before filing a lawsuit.
- Requires judges to screen all inmate complaints against the federal government and to immediately dismiss those deemed frivolous or without merit.
- Prohibits prisoners from filing a lawsuit for mental or emotional injury unless they can also show there has been physical injury.
- Requires inmates to pay court filing fees. Prisoners who don't have the needed funds can pay the filing fee over a period of time through deductions from their prison commissary accounts.
- Limits the award of attorneys' fees in successful lawsuits brought by inmates.
- Revokes the credits earned by federal prisoners toward early release if they file a malicious lawsuit.
- Mandates that court orders affecting prison administration cannot go any further than necessary to correct a violation of a particular inmate's civil rights.
- Makes it possible for state officials to have court orders lifted after two years unless there is a new finding of a continuing violation of federally guaranteed civil rights.
- Mandates that any court order requiring the release of prisoners due to overcrowding be approved by a three-member court before it can become effective.

The U.S. Supreme Court has upheld provisions of the PLRA on a number of occasions. According to one BJS study, the PLRA has been effective in reducing the number of frivolous lawsuits filed by inmates alleging unconstitutional prison conditions.[115] The study found that the filing rate of inmates' civil rights petitions in federal courts had been cut in half four years after passage of the act. A similar study by the National Center for State Courts, whose results were published in 2004, found that the act "produced a statistically significant decrease in both the

According to one BJS study, the PLRA has been effective in reducing the number of frivolous lawsuits filed by inmates alleging unconstitutional prison conditions.

volume and trend of lawsuits . . . nationally and in every [federal court] circuit."[116]

Opponents of the PLRA fear that it is stifling the filing of meritorious suits by inmates facing real deprivations. According to the American Civil Liberties Union (ACLU), for example, "The Prison Litigation Reform Act . . . attempts to slam the courthouse door on society's most vulnerable members. It seeks to strip the federal courts of much of their power to correct even the most egregious prison conditions by altering the basic rules which have always governed prison reform litigation. The PLRA also makes it difficult to settle prison cases by consent decree, and limits the life span of any court judgment."[117]

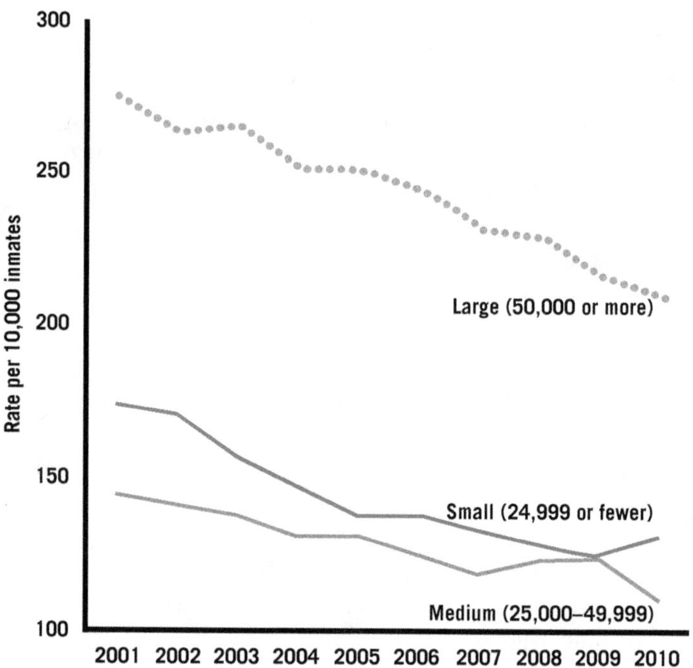

FIGURE 14-5 | Rate of HIV/AIDS Cases per 10,000 Inmates, by Size of State Prison Custody Population, 2001–2010

Source: Laura M. Maruschak, *HIV in Prisons, 2001–2010* (Washington, DC: Bureau of Justice Statistics, September 2012), p. 2.

Issues Facing Prisons Today

Prisons are society's answer to a number of social problems. They house outcasts, misfits, and some highly dangerous people. Although prisons provide a part of the answer to the question of crime control, they also face problems of their own. A few of those special problems are described here.

AIDS

Chapter 8 discussed the steps that police agencies are taking to deal with health threats from acquired immunodeficiency syndrome (AIDS). In 2012, the Bureau of Justice Statistics (BJS) reported finding that 20,093 state and federal inmates were infected with HIV (human immunodeficiency virus), the virus that causes AIDS.[118] The BJS report found that the rate of HIV/AIDS among state and federal prison inmates declined from 194 cases per 10,000 inmates in 2001 to 146 per 10,000 at year-end 2010. The size of the decline is shown in Figure 14-5.

California, Florida, New York, and Texas each hold more than 1,000 inmates with HIV/AIDS; in combination, these states hold 51% (9,492) of all state prisoners with HIV/AIDS. Among state and federal inmates with HIV/AIDS at yearend 2010, 18,337 were male and 1,756 were female.

Some years ago, AIDS was the leading cause of death among prison inmates.[119] Today, however, the number of inmates who die from AIDS (or, more precisely, from AIDS-related complications like pneumonia or Kaposi's sarcoma) is much lower. The introduction of drugs like protease inhibitors and useful combinations of antiretroviral therapies have significantly reduced inmate deaths from AIDS.[120] The BJS reported that AIDS-related deaths among all state and federal prison inmates declined by an average of 16% per year between 2001 and 2010, from 24 deaths per 100,000 inmates in 2001 to 5 per 100,000 in 2010.

Most infected inmates brought the HIV virus into prison with them, and one study found that fewer than 10% of HIV-positive inmates acquired the virus while in prison.[121] Nonetheless, the virus can be spread behind bars through homosexual activity (including rape), intravenous drug use, and the sharing of tainted tattoo and hypodermic needles. Inmates who were infected before entering prison are likely to have had histories of high-risk behavior, especially intravenous drug use.

A report by the National Institute of Justice (NIJ) suggests that corrections administrators can use two types of strategies to reduce the transmission of AIDS.[122] One strategy relies on medical technology to identify seropositive inmates and to segregate them from the rest of the prison population. Mass screening and inmate segregation, however, may be prohibitively expensive. They may also be illegal. Some states specifically prohibit HIV-antibody testing without the informed consent of the person tested.[123] The related issue of confidentiality may be difficult to manage, especially when the purpose of testing is to segregate infected inmates from others. In addition, civil liability may result if inmates are falsely labeled as infected or if inmates known to be infected are not prevented from spreading the disease. Only Alabama and South Carolina still segregate all known HIV-infected inmates,[124] but more limited forms of separation are practiced elsewhere. Many state prison systems have denied HIV-positive inmates jobs, educational opportunities, visitation privileges, conjugal visits, and home furloughs, causing some researchers to conclude that "inmates with HIV and AIDS are routinely discriminated against and denied equal treatment in ways that have no accepted medical basis."[125] In 1994, for example, a federal appeals court upheld a California prison policy that bars HIV-positive inmates from working in food-service jobs.[126] In contrast, in 2001, the Mississippi Department of Correction ended its policy of segregating HIV-positive prisoners from other inmates in educational and vocational programs.

The second strategy is prevention through education. Educational programs teach both inmates and staff members about the dangers of high-risk behavior and suggest ways to avoid HIV infection. An NIJ model program recommends the use of simple, straightforward messages presented by knowledgeable and approachable trainers.[127] Alarmism, says the NIJ, should be avoided. One survey found that 98% of state and federal prisons provide some form of AIDS/HIV education and that 90% of jails do as well—although most such training is oriented toward corrections staff rather than inmates.[128] Learn more about HIV in prisons at **http://www.justicestudies.com/pubs/hiv.pdf**.

Geriatric Offenders

In 2013, 89-year-old Anthony Marshall, the frail and wheelchair-bound son of the late philanthropist and socialite Brooke Astor, became the oldest person ever sent to a New York prison for a nonviolent crime.[129] Marshall, who depends on an oxygen tank to breathe, had been convicted of plundering his mother's huge fortune and was sentenced to one to three years behind bars.

Crimes committed by elderly people, especially violent crimes, have recently been on the decline. Nonetheless, the significant expansion of America's retiree population has led to an increase in the number of elderly people who are behind bars. In fact, crimes of violence are what bring most older people into the correctional system. According to one early study, 52% of inmates who were over the age of 50 when they entered prison had committed violent crimes, compared with 41% of younger inmates.[130] An ACLU survey found that there were 8,853 state and federal prisoners age 55 and older scattered throughout America's prisons in 1981.[131] Today, that number stands at 124,900, and experts project that by 2030 there will be over 400,000 such inmates. Thus, it is expected that the elderly prison population United States will increase by 4,400% over this 50-year span. Similarly, the per capita rate of incarceration for inmates age 55 and over now stands at more than 230 per 100,000 U.S. residents of like age.[132]

Not all of today's elderly inmates were old when they entered prison. Because of harsh sentencing laws passed throughout the country in the 1990s, a small but growing number of inmates (10%) will serve 20 years or more in prison, and 5% will never be released.[133] This means that many inmates who enter prison when they are young will grow old behind bars. The "graying" of America's prison population has a number of causes: "(1) the general aging of the American population, which is reflected inside prisons; (2) new sentencing policies such as 'three strikes,' 'truth in sentencing,' and 'mandatory minimum' laws that send more criminals to prison for longer stretches; (3) a massive prison building boom that took place in the 1980s and 1990s, and which has provided space for more inmates, reducing the need to release prisoners to alleviate overcrowding; and (4) significant changes in parole philosophies and practices,"[134] with state and federal authorities phasing out or canceling parole programs, thereby forcing jailers to hold inmates with life sentences until they die.

Long-termers and geriatric inmates have special needs. They tend to suffer from physical disabilities and illnesses not generally encountered among their more youthful counterparts. Unfortunately, few prisons are equipped to deal adequately with the medical needs of aging offenders. Some large facilities have begun to set aside special sections to care for elderly inmates with "typical" disorders, such as Alzheimer's disease, cancer, or heart disease. Unfortunately, such efforts have barely kept pace with the problems that geriatric offenders present. The number of inmates requiring around-the-clock care is expected to increase dramatically during the next two decades.[135]

Unfortunately, few prisons are equipped to deal adequately with the medical needs of aging offenders.

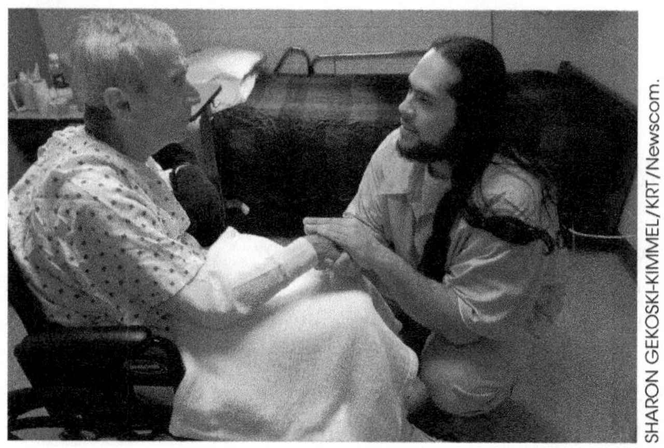

Salvatore LoGiudice, left, 78, is assisted by fellow inmate Dennis Galan, in the hospice section at South Woods State Prison in Bridgeton, New Jersey. Why is the proportion of geriatric inmates increasing? What special needs do they have?

Incarcerating people into old age is costly and may be counterproductive. Research has consistently shown that "by age 50 most people have significantly outlived the years in which they are most likely to commit crimes."[136] Moreover, most aging prisoners are not incarcerated for serious or violent offenses, and could probably be allowed to reenter the community with little danger to others. In Texas, for example, 65% of elderly prisoners are confined for nonviolent drug crimes, property crimes, and other nonviolent offenses. Because of rising medical expenses, the costs of confining a prisoner over age 50 jumps to an average of $68,270, whereas housing and other associated costs of keeping an inmate below that age behind bars is only $34,135.[137]

Finally the idea of rehabilitation takes on a new meaning where geriatric offenders are concerned. What kinds of programs are most useful in providing older inmates with the tools needed for success on the outside? Which counseling strategies hold the greatest promise for introducing socially acceptable behavior patterns into the long-established lifestyles of elderly offenders about to be released? There are few easy answers to such questions.

Inmates with Mental Illness and Intellectual Disabilities

Inmates with mental illness make up another group with special needs. Some of these inmates are neurotic or have personality problems, which increases tensions in prison. Others have serious psychological disorders that may have escaped diagnosis at trial or that did not provide a legal basis for the reduction of criminal responsibility. Other offenders develop psychiatric symptoms while in prison.

Inmates suffering from significant mental illnesses account for a substantial number of those imprisoned. A 2006 study by the BJS found that the nation's prisons and jails hold an estimated 1.25 million inmates with mental illness (56% of those confined) and that more incarcerated women (73%) than men (55%) are mentally ill.[138] A second government study found that 40% of these inmates receive no treatment at all.

One 2000 Bureau of Justice Statistics survey of public and private state-level adult correctional facilities (excluding jails) found that 51% of such institutions provide 24-hour mental health care, and 71% provide therapy and counseling by trained mental health professionals as needed.[139] A large majority of prisons distribute psychotropic medications (when such medications are ordered by a physician), and 66% have programs to help released inmates obtain community mental health services. According to BJS, 13% of state prisoners were receiving some type of mental health therapy at the time of the survey, and 10% were receiving psychotropic medications, including antidepressants, stimulants, sedatives, and tranquilizers.

Unfortunately, few state-run correctional institutions have any substantial capacity for the in-depth psychiatric treatment of inmates who have serious mental illnesses. Numerous states, however, do operate facilities that specialize in psychiatric confinement of convicted criminals. The BJS reports that state governments throughout the nation operate 12 facilities devoted exclusively to the care of inmates with mental illness and that another 143 prisons report psychiatric confinement as one specialty among other functions that they perform. As mentioned previously, the U.S. Supreme Court has ruled that inmates who are mentally ill can be required to take antipsychotic drugs, even against their wishes.[140]

Inmates with intellectual disabilities constitute still another group with special needs. Some studies estimate the proportion of these inmates at about 10%.[141] Inmates with low IQs are less likely than other inmates to complete training and rehabilitative programs successfully. They also evidence difficulty in adjusting to the routines of prison life. As a consequence, they are likely to exceed the averages in proportion of sentence served.[142] Only seven states report special facilities or programs for inmates with intellectual disabilities.[143] Other state systems "mainstream" such inmates, making them participate in regular activities with other inmates.

Terrorism and Corrections

Today's antiterrorism efforts have brought to light the important role that corrections personnel can play in preventing future attacks against America and in averting crises that could arise in correctional institutions as a result of terrorist action. Some years after the attacks of 911, former New York City Police Commissioner Bernard B. Kerik told participants at the ACA's winter conference that corrections officers can help in the fight against terrorism through effective intelligence gathering and intelligence sharing. "Intelligence—that's the key to the success of this battle," Kerik said.[144] "You have to be part of that, because when we take the people off the streets in this country that go to jail, they communicate and they talk, they work with other criminals, organized gangs, organized units. You've got to collect that information, you have to get it back to the authorities that need it."

Prison administrators must also be concerned about the potential impact of outside terrorist activity on their facility's inmate and staff populations. Of particular concern to today's prison administrators is the possibility of bioterrorism. A concentrated population like that of a prison or jail is highly susceptible to the rapid transmission of biological agents.[145]

The threat of a terrorist act being undertaken by inmates within a prison or jail can be an important consideration in facility planning and management, especially because inmates may be particularly vulnerable to recruitment by terrorist organizations. According to Chip Ellis, research and program coordinator for the National Memorial Institute for the Prevention of Terrorism, "Prisoners are a captive audience, and they usually have a diminished sense of self or a need for identity and protection. They're usually a disenchanted or disenfranchised group of people, [and] terrorists can sometimes capitalize on that situation."[146] Inmates can be radicalized in many ways, including exposure to other radical inmates, the distribution of extremist literature, and anti-U.S. sermons heard during religious services.

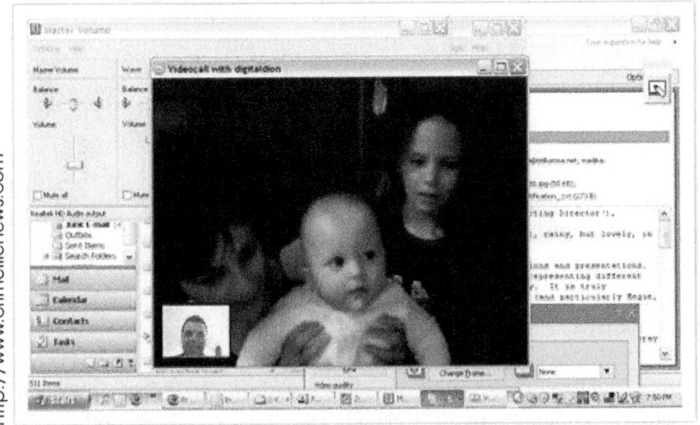

http://www.crimefilenews.com

The family of a prison inmate is shown on the screen of a prison computer during a Skype teleconference. The inmate can be seen at the bottom left corner of the image. What are the benefits of such video conferencing? Are there any hidden costs or risks?

Recently, the Institute for the Study of Violent Groups (ISVG), located at Sam Houston State University, charged that the most radical form of Islam, Wahhabism, was being spread in American prisons by clerics approved by the Islamic Society of North America, one of two organizations chosen by the Federal Bureau of Prisons to select prison chaplains.[147] "Proselytizing in prisons," said the ISVG, "can produce new recruits with American citizenship." An example of such activity can be found in the story of accused terrorist Kevin James, 32, who was sentenced in federal court in Santa Ana, California, in 2009 to 16 years in prison. James had pleaded guilty in 2007 to conspiracy to wage war against the United States[148] and was accused of plotting terrorist attacks on Jewish and military targets throughout California while imprisoned. Among his targets were the Los Angeles International Airport, the Israeli Consulate, and U.S. Army recruiting centers (Read more about James in the CJ Issues box in this chapter.).

In response to the terrorist threat, the BOP implemented a number of practices, and today it coordinates with other federal agencies to share intelligence information about suspected or known terrorists in its inmate population. The BOP closely tracks inmates with known or suspected terrorist ties and monitors their correspondence and other communications. The BOP also trains staff members to recognize terrorist-related activity and to effectively manage convicted terrorists within the correctional environment. A BOP program to counter radicalization efforts among inmates has been in place for the past nine years.[149] Learn more about prison radicalization from the Federal Bureau of Investigation (FBI) at **http://www.justicestudies.com/pubs/racial.pdf**, and read more about prison issues of all kinds from the Prison Policy Initiative via **http://www.prisonpolicy.org**.

The BOP closely tracks inmates with known or suspected terrorist ties and monitors their correspondence and other communications.

CJ | ISSUES
Technocorrections

The technological forces that have made cell phones commonplace are beginning to converge with the ongoing efforts of correctional administrators to create what some have called *technocorrections*. Members of the correctional establishment—the managers of the jail, prison, probation, and parole systems and their sponsors in elected office—are seeking more cost-effective ways to increase public safety and to meet the needs of correctional administrators as the number of people under correctional supervision continues to grow. Technocorrections is an emerging field being defined by a correctional establishment that seeks to take advantage of the potential offered by new technologies to reduce the costs of supervising criminal offenders and to minimize the risk they pose to society.

Emerging technologies in four areas will soon be central elements of technocorrections: electronic tracking and location systems, pharmacological treatments, genetic and neurobiological risk assessments, and enhanced communications both inside and outside of correctional facilities. Although these technologies may significantly increase public safety and lessen the pains of imprisonment, we must also be mindful of the threats they pose to democratic principles. The critical challenge will be to learn how to take advantage of new technological opportunities applicable to the corrections field while minimizing their threats.

Tracking and Location Systems

Electronic tracking and location systems are the technology that is perhaps most familiar to correctional practitioners today. Most states use electronic monitoring—either with the older bracelets that communicate through a device connected to telephone lines or with more modern versions based on cellular or satellite tracking.

Tiny cameras might also be integrated into tracking devices to provide live video of offenders' locations and activities. Miniature electronic devices implanted in the body to signal the location of offenders at all times, to create unique identifiers that trigger alarms, and to monitor key bodily functions that affect unwanted behaviors are under development and are close to becoming reality.[1]

Pharmacological Treatments

Pharmacological breakthroughs—new "wonder drugs" being developed to control behavior in correctional and noncorrectional settings—will also be a part of technocorrections. Corrections officials are already familiar with some of these drugs, which are currently used to treat offenders who are mentally ill. Yet these drugs could also be used to control mental conditions affecting undesirable behaviors even for offenders who are not mentally ill.

It is only a matter of time before research findings in this area lead to the development of drugs to control neurobiological processes. These drugs could become correctional tools to manage violent offenders and perhaps even to prevent violence. Such advances are related to the third area of technology that will affect corrections: genetic and neurobiological risk-assessment technologies.

Risk-Assessment Technologies

Corrections officials today are familiar with the DNA profiling of offenders, particularly sex offenders. This is just the beginning of the correctional application of gene-related technologies, however. The Human Genome Project, supported by the National Institutes of Health and the Department of Energy, began in 1990 and was completed in 2003. The goal of the Human Genome Project was to create a map of the 3 billion chemical bases that make up human DNA. The map was constructed by high-powered "sequencer" machines that can analyze human DNA faster than any human researcher can.[2] Emerging as a powerhouse of the high-tech economy, the biotechnology industry will drive developments in DNA-based risk assessment.

Neurobiological research is taking the same path, although thus far no neurobiological patterns specific enough to be reliable biological markers for violent behavior have been uncovered. Is it possible that breakthroughs in these areas will lead to the development of risk-assessment tools that use genetic or neurobiological profiles to identify children who have a propensity toward addiction or violence? We may soon be able to link genetic and neurobiological traits with social and environmental factors to reliably predict who is at risk for addiction, sex offending, violent behavior, or crime in general.

Attempts will surely be made to develop genetic or neurobiological tests for assessing risks posed by individuals. This is already done for the risk of contracting certain diseases. Demand for risk assessments of individuals will come from corrections officials under pressure to prevent violent recidivism.

"Preventive incarceration" is already a reality for some convicted sex offenders. More than a dozen states commit certain sex offenders to special "civil commitment" facilities after they have served their prison sentences because of a behavioral or mental abnormality that makes them dangerous.[3] This happens today with no clear understanding of the nature of the abnormality. It is not difficult to imagine what might be done to justify preventive incarceration if this "abnormal" or criminal behavior could be explained and predicted by genetic or neurobiological profiling.

Enhanced Communications

In 2012, a Sentencing Project study of video visitation programs found that "at least 20 states already have video capability or have plans to adopt the technology."[4] The Project noted that the benefits of video visitation for correctional facilities include reducing the risk of contraband entering facilities, cost savings associated with fewer staff needed to oversee visits, and increased revenues from fees paid by inmates or virtual visitors. The Project also said that video visitation could be of significant benefit to the children of incarcerated parents, who might not otherwise have an opportunity for face-to-face communication with their parent.

[1] "Microchip Implants Closer to Reality," *Futurist*, Vol. 33, No. 8 (October 1999), p. 9.

[2] Walter Isaacson, "The Biotech Century," *Time*, January 11, 1999, p. 42; and Michael D. Lemonick and Dick Thompson, "Racing to Map Our DNA," *Time*, January 11, 1999, p. 44.

[3] See *Kansas* v. *Hendricks*, 521 U.S. 346 (1997), in which the Court approved such a practice. In the case of *Kansas* v. *Crane* (122 S.Ct. 867 [2002]), however, the U.S. Supreme Court ruled that the Constitution does not permit commitment of certain types of dangerous sexual offenders without a "lack-of-control determination."

[4] Susan D. Phillips, *Video Visits for Children Whose Parents are Incarcerated: In Whose Best Interests?* (Washington, DC: The Sentencing Project, 2012), p. 3.

Sources: Adapted from Tony Fabelo, *"Technocorrections": The Promises, the Uncertain Threats* (Washington, DC: National Institute of Justice, 2000); and U.S. Department of Energy, "Human Genome Project Information," http://www.ornl.gov/TechResources/Human_Genome/home.html (accessed July 30, 2010).

CJ | NEWS

Radical Islam, Terrorism, and U.S. Prisons

Even though thousands of U.S. prisoners convert to Islam each year, fears that they would commit terrorism after their release have not materialized. In the few cases where prisoners have plotted terrorism, they were not connected to groups like al-Qaeda and their plans were foiled.

"The claim that U.S. prisons will generate scores of terrorists spilling out onto the streets of our cities appears to be false or, at least, much overstated," Bert Useem, PhD, a sociology professor at Purdue University, told a U.S. House panel studying the matter in June 2011. Useem noted that of 178 Muslim Americans involved in terrorism-related violence, only 12 showed any connection to radicalization behind bars.

Experts attribute this positive outcome, more than a decade after the September 11, 2001, terrorist attacks, as much to U.S. prisoners' lack of interest in Middle Eastern causes as to the steps prison authorities have taken to make sure inmates do not go down this path. The federal Bureau of Prisons and state systems have improved monitoring of Muslim prisoners and reduced their access to radical Islamist literature, and authorities such as the FBI have kept track of some prisoners after release.

Stephan Savoia/AP Wide World Photos

Muslim inmate Christopher McCullon, with his prayer rug draped over his shoulder, talking with Muslim corrections officer Umar Abdullah after weekly worship in a room used as a mosque at Rikers Island Correctional Institution, located in New York City. How might corrections officers help in the nation's fight against terrorism?

In a country that is less than 1% Muslim, reportedly 10% of U.S. prisoners have embraced Islam. "The primary motivation I found was spiritual 'searching'— seeking religious meaning to interpret and resolve discontent," wrote Mark Hamm, PhD, a professor of criminology at Indiana State University. His two-year study of prisoner radicalization appeared in the *National Institute of Justice Journal* in October 2008.

Although that spiritual quest is quite different from the path to jihad, Hamm warned that "the potential for ideologically inspired criminality" still exists. He noted that a few terrorist plots had been uncovered in Florida and California prisons. In California's New Folsom Prison in 2005, several Muslim convicts led by Kevin James plotted terrorist acts against the National Guard, synagogues, and the Israeli consulate. When several members of the group were paroled, they committed a string of bank heists to finance their plan, but they were caught before they could commit it.

Middle Eastern interests have reached out to U.S. prisons. In 2003, the *Wall Street Journal* reported that Saudi Arabia "ships out hundreds of copies of the Quran each month, as well as religious pamphlets and videos, to prison chaplains and Islamic groups who then pass them along to inmates."

Many U.S. prisoners and their Islamic chaplains have embraced the Saudis' Wahhabi Salafist sect, with its Islamic-supremacist interpretation of the Quran. Warith Deen Umar, a Wahhabi Salafist who was head Muslim chaplain of the New York prisons until 2000, told the *Wall Street Journal* that prison "is the perfect recruitment and training grounds for radicalism and the Islamic religion."

The *Wall Street Journal*'s revelations prompted a review by the Office of the Inspector General (OIG) of the use of Muslim chaplains and Islamic literature in the Bureau of Prisons. The OIG's 2004 report issued 16 recommendations, including requiring imams (Muslim religious leaders) to work closely with security staff, closely monitoring volunteer imams, and screening prayer books. Many state prisons took up the recommendations as well.

In addition, longstanding prohibitions against using the Internet have barred prisoners' access to radical sites, although some have smuggled in smartphones. As a further precaution, the Bureau of Prisons in 2006 began isolating a few dozen radical Islamist prisoners in two communication management units (CMUs) that severely restrict visitation rights and monitor all telephone calls and mail. The CMU at the U.S. Penitentiary in Marion, Illinois, houses 18 Muslims, including Kevin James.

Resources: Bert Useem, "Testimony for the Committee on Homeland Security," June 15, 2011, http://homeland.house.gov/sites/homeland.house.gov/files/Testimony%20Useem.pdf; "Imams Reject Talk That Islam Radicalizes Inmates," *New York Times*, May 23, 2009, http://www.nytimes.com/2009/05/24/nyregion/24convert.html?_r=1&ref=us; and "Prisoner Radicalization: Assessing the Threat in U.S. Correctional Institutions," *National Institute of Justice Journal*, October 2008, http://www.nij.gov/journals/261/prisoner-radicalization.htm.

freedom OR safety? YOU decide

Censoring Prison Communications

While concerns over the terrorist attacks of 911 were still high, NBC News announced that it had learned that Arab terrorists in federal maximum-security prisons had been sending letters to extremists on the outside, exhorting them to attack Western interests. The terrorists included Mohammed Salameh, a follower of radical sheik Omar Abdel-Rahman. Salameh had been sentenced to more than 100 years in prison for his part in the 1993 bombing attack on New York's World Trade Center. That attack, which killed 6 and injured more than 1,000, blew a huge hole in the basement parking garage of one of the towers but failed to topple the buildings.

NBC News revealed that the men, while being held in the federal ADMAX facility in Florence, Colorado—the country's most secure federal prison—sent at least 14 letters to a Spanish terror cell, praised Osama bin Laden in Arabic newspapers, and advocated additional terror attacks. In July 2002, Salameh, a Palestinian with a degree in Islamic law from a Jordanian university, sent a letter to the Al-Quds Arabic daily newspaper proclaiming that "Osama Bin Laden is my hero of this generation."

Andy McCarthy, a former federal prosecutor who worked to send the terrorists to prison, said that Salameh's letters were "exhorting acts of terrorism and helping recruit would-be terrorists for the *Jihad*." Michael Macko, who lost his father in the Trade Center bombing, posed this question: "If they are encouraging acts of terrorism internationally, how do we know they're not encouraging acts of terrorism right here on U.S. soil?"

Prison officials told reporters that communications involving the imprisoned bombers had not been closely censored because the men hadn't been considered very dangerous. The letters didn't contain any plans for attacks, nor did they name any specific targets. One Justice Department official said that Salameh was "a low level guy" who was not under any special restrictions and that his letters were seen as "generic stuff" and "no cause for concern."

Rights advocates suggested that inmates should have the right to free speech—even those imprisoned for acts of terrorism—and that advocating terrorism is not the same thing as planning it or carrying it out. After all, they said, calls for a holy war, however repugnant they may be in the current international context, are merely political statements—and politics is not against the law.

You Decide

What kinds of prison communications, if any, should be monitored or restricted (letters, telephone calls, e-mail)? Do you believe that communications containing statements like those described here should be confiscated? What kinds of political statements, if any, should be permitted?

References: Lisa Myers, "Imprisoned Terrorists Still Advocating Terror," NBC Nightly News, February 28, 2005, http://www.msnbc.msn.com/id/7046691 (accessed August 28, 2005); and Lisa Myers, "Bureau of Prisons under Fire for Jihad Letters," MSNBC.com, March 1, 2005, http://www.msnbc.msn.com/id/7053165 (accessed August 28, 2005).

SUMMARY

- Prisons are small, self-contained societies that are sometimes described as *total institutions*. Studies of prison life have detailed the existence of prison subcultures, or inmate worlds, replete with inmate values, social roles, and lifestyles. New inmates who are socialized into prison subculture are said to undergo the process of prisonization. Prison subcultures are very influential, and both inmates and staff must reckon with them. Today's prisons are miniature societies, reflecting the problems and challenges that exist in the larger society of which they are a part.
- Female inmates represent a small but growing proportion of the nation's prison population. Many female inmates have histories of physical and sexual abuse. Although they are likely to have dependent children, their parenting skills may be limited. Most female inmates are housed in centralized state facilities known as women's prisons, which are dedicated exclusively to incarcerating female felons. Some states, however, particularly those with small populations, continue to keep female prisoners in special wings of what are otherwise institutions for men. Few facilities for women have programs especially designed for female offenders.
- Like prisoners, corrections officers undergo a socialization process that helps them function by the official and unofficial rules of staff society. Prison staffers are most concerned with custody and control. The enforcement of strict rules; body and cell searches; counts; unannounced shakedowns; the control of dangerous items, materials, and contraband; and the extensive use of bars, locks, fencing, cameras, and alarms all support the staff's vigilance in maintaining security. Although concerns with security still command center stage, professionalism is playing an increasing role in corrections today, and today's corrections personnel are better trained and more proficient than ever before.

- As this chapter discusses, the causes of prison riots are diverse. They include (1) unmet inmate needs, (2) the violent tendencies of some inmates, (3) the dehumanizing conditions of imprisonment, (4) a desire to regulate inmate society and redistribute power, and (5) power vacuums created by changes in prison administration, the transfer of influential inmates, or court-ordered injunctions. Riots, when they do occur, typically pass through five phases: (1) explosion, (2) organization into inmate-led groups, (3) confrontation with authority, (4) termination through negotiation or physical confrontation, and (5) reaction and explanation, usually by investigative commissions.
- For many years, courts throughout the nation assumed a hands-off approach to prisons, rarely intervening in the day-to-day administration of prison facilities. That changed in the late 1960s, when the U.S. Supreme Court began to identify inmates' rights mandated by the Constitution. Rights identified by the Court include the right to physical integrity, an absolute right to be free from unwarranted corporal punishments, certain religious rights, and procedural rights, such as those involving access to attorneys and to the courts. The conditional rights of prisoners, which have repeatedly been supported by the Court, mandate professionalism among prison administrators and require vigilance in the provision of correctional services. High Court decisions have generally established that prison inmates retain those constitutional rights that are not inconsistent with their status as prisoners or with the legitimate penological objectives of the correctional system. In other words, inmates have rights, much the same as people who are not incarcerated, provided that the legitimate needs of the prison for security, custody, and safety are not compromised. The era of prisoners' rights was sharply curtailed in 1996 with the passage of the Prison Litigation Reform Act, spurred on by a growing recognition of the legal morass resulting from the unregulated access to federal courts by inmates across the nation.
- The major problems and issues facing prisons today include (1) threats from infectious diseases, including AIDS; (2) the need to deal with a growing geriatric offender population, which is the result of longer sentences and the aging of the American population; (3) a sizable number of inmates who are mentally ill and have intellectual disabilities; and (4) a concern over inmates with terrorist leanings and those who have been incarcerated for terrorism-related crimes.

KEY TERMS

balancing test, 476
civil death, 475
deliberate indifference, 482
gender responsiveness, 466
grievance procedure, 477
hands-off doctrine, 475
prison argot, 459
prison subculture, 458
prisonization, 458
security threat group (STG), 473
total institution, 457

KEY CASES

***Block* v. *Rutherford*, 479**
***Brown* v. *Plata*, 478**
***Bounds* v. *Smith*, 479**
***Cruz* v. *Beto*, 479**
***Estelle* v. *Gamble*, 482**
***Helling* v. *McKinney*, 478**
***Hudson* v. *Palmer*, 479**
***Johnson* v. *Avery*, 479**
***Jones* v. *North Carolina Prisoners' Labor Union*, 479**
***Overton* v. *Bazzetta*, 478**
***Pell* v. *Procunier*, 479**
***Ruiz* v. *Estelle*, 479**
***Sandin* v. *Conner*, 478**
***Wolff* v. *McDonnell*, 479**

QUESTIONS FOR REVIEW

1. What are prison subcultures, and how do they influence prison life? How do they develop, and what purpose do they serve?
2. How do women's prisons differ from men's? Why have women's prisons been studied less often than institutions for men?
3. What are the primary concerns of prison staff? What other goals do staff members focus on?
4. What causes prison riots? Through what stages do most riots progress? How might riots be prevented?
5. What are the commonly accepted rights of prisoners in the United States today? Where do these rights come from? What U.S. Supreme Court cases are especially significant in the area of prisoners' rights?
6. What are some of the major issues that prisons face today? What new issues might the future bring?

QUESTIONS FOR REFLECTION

1. What does *prisonization* mean? Describe the U-shaped curve developed by Stanton Wheeler to illustrate the concept of prisonization. How can an understanding of Wheeler's U-shaped curve help prevent recidivism?
2. What is the hands-off doctrine? What is the status of that doctrine today? What is its likely future?
3. Explain the balancing test established by the Supreme Court in deciding issues of prisoners' rights. How might such a test apply to the emerging area of inmate privacy?
4. What does the term *state-created rights* mean within the context of corrections? What do you predict for the future of state-created rights?

NOTES

1. "Miss Wisconsin Makes Father's Prison Time a Miss America Platform," CBS News, January 15, 2012, http://www.cbsnews.com/8301-31749_162-57359505-10391698/miss-wisconsin-makes-fathers-prison-time-a-miss-america-platform (accessed May 18, 2012).
2. Hans Reimer, "Socialization in the Prison Community," *Proceedings of the American Prison Association, 1937* (New York: American Prison Association, 1937), pp. 151–155.

3. Donald Clemmer, *The Prison Community* (Boston: Holt, Rinehart and Winston, 1940).
4. Gresham M. Sykes, *The Society of Captives: A Study of a Maximum Security Prison* (Princeton, NJ: Princeton University Press, 1958).
5. Richard A. Cloward et al., *Theoretical Studies in Social Organization of the Prison* (New York: Social Science Research Council, 1960).
6. Donald R. Cressey, ed., *The Prison: Studies in Institutional Organization and Change* (New York: Holt, Rinehart and Winston, 1961).
7. Lawrence Hazelrigg, ed., *Prison within Society: A Reader in Penology* (Garden City, NY: Anchor, 1969), preface.
8. Charles Stastny and Gabrielle Tyrnauer, *Who Rules the Joint? The Changing Political Culture of Maximum-Security Prisons in America* (Lexington, MA: Lexington Books, 1982), p. 131.
9. Erving Goffman, *Asylums: Essays on the Social Situation of Mental Patients and Other Inmates* (Garden City, NY: Anchor, 1961).
10. For a firsthand account of the prison experience, see Victor Hassine, *Life without Parole: Living in Prison Today* (Los Angeles: Roxbury, 1996); and W. Rideau and R. Wikberg, *Life Sentences: Rage and Survival behind Prison Bars* (New York: Times Books, 1992).
11. Gresham M. Sykes and Sheldon L. Messinger, "The Inmate Social System," in Richard A. Cloward et al., eds., *Theoretical Studies in Social Organization of the Prison* (New York: Social Science Research Council, 1960), pp. 5–19.
12. The concept of prisonization is generally attributed to Clemmer, *The Prison Community*, although Quaker penologists of the late eighteenth century were actively concerned with preventing "contamination" (the spread of criminal values) among prisoners.
13. Sykes and Messinger, "The Inmate Social System," p. 5.
14. Stanton Wheeler, "Socialization in Correctional Communities," *American Sociological Review*, Vol. 26 (October 1961), pp. 697–712.
15. Sykes, *The Society of Captives*, p. xiii.
16. Christopher Hensley, Jeremy Wright, Richard Tewksbury, and Tammy Castle, "The Evolving Nature of Prison Argot and Sexual Hierarchies," *The Prison Journal*, Vol. 83 (2003), pp. 289–300.
17. Ibid., p. 298.
18. John Irwin, *The Felon* (Upper Saddle River, NJ: Prentice Hall, 1970).
19. Stastny and Tyrnauer, *Who Rules the Joint?* p. 135.
20. Ibid.
21. Ibid.
22. Sykes, *The Society of Captives*.
23. Clemmer, *The Prison Community*, pp. 294–296.
24. Irwin, *The Felon*.
25. Public Law 108-79.
26. Office of Justice Programs, *PREA Data Collection Activities, 2013* (Washington, DC: Bureau of Justice Statistics, June 2013).
27. Halley, "The Prison Rape Elimination Act of 2003," p. 2.
28. Lee H. Bowker, *Prison Victimization* (New York: Elsevier, 1980), p. 42.
29. Halley, p. 1.
30. Hans Toch, *Living in Prison: The Ecology of Survival* (New York: Free Press, 1977), p. 151.
31. E. Ann Carson and Daniela Golinelli, *Prisoners in 2012*, (Washington, DC: Bureau of Justice Statistics, July 2013).
32. Ibid., p.18.
33. Some of the information in this section comes from the American Correctional Association (ACA) Task Force on the Female Offender, *The Female Offender: What Does the Future Hold?* (Washington, DC: St. Mary's Press, 1990); and "The View from behind Bars," *Time* (fall 1990, special issue), pp. 20–22.
34. Much of the information and some of the wording in this section come from Barbara Bloom, Barbara Owen, and Stephanie Covington, *Gender-Responsive Strategies: Research, Practice, and Guiding Principles for Women Offenders* (Washington, DC: National Institute of Corrections, 2003).
35. Ibid.
36. Joanne Belknap, *The Invisible Woman: Gender, Crime, and Justice* (Belmont, CA: Wadsworth, 2001).
37. Data in this paragraph come from L. E. Glaze and L. M. Maruschak, *Parents in Prison and Their Minor Children* (Washington, DC: Bureau of Justice Statistics, 2008).
38. B. Bloom and D. Steinhart, *Why Punish the Children? A Reappraisal of the Children of Incarcerated Mothers in America* (San Francisco: National Council on Crime and Delinquency, 1993).
39. Patricia Allard and Judith Greene, *Children on the Outside: Voicing the Pain and Human Costs of Parental Incarceration* (New York: Justice Strategies, 2011), pp. 4–5.
40. Mary Jeanette Clement, "National Survey of Programs for Incarcerated Women," paper presented at the annual meeting of the Academy of Criminal Justice Sciences, Nashville, TN, March 1991, pp. 8–9.
41. Barbara Bloom, Barbara Owen and Stephanie Covington, *Gender-Responsive Strategies: Research, Practice, and Guiding Principles for Women Offenders* (National Institute of Corrections, 2002)
42. Barbara Bloom and Stephanie Covington, *Research, Practice, and Guiding Principles for Women Offenders* (Washington, DC: U.S. Department of Justice, 2003).
43. Huey Freeman, "Illinois Program Guides New Mothers," *Pantagraph*, April 12, 2010, http://www.pantagraph.com/news/state-and-regional/illinois/article_ab1d5106-4631-11df-97d4-001cc4c002e0.html (accessed June 7, 2011).
44. American Correctional Association, *The Female Offender*.
45. Marsha Clowers, "Dykes, Gangs, and Danger: Debunking Popular Myths about Maximum Security Life," *Journal of Criminal Justice and Popular Culture*, Vol. 9, No. 1 (2001), pp. 22–30.
46. D. Ward and G. Kassebaum, *Women's Prison: Sex and Social Structure* (London: Weidenfeld and Nicolson, 1966).
47. Esther Heffernan, *Making It in Prison: The Square, the Cool, and the Life* (London: Wiley-Interscience, 1972).
48. Rose Giallombardo, *Society of Women: A Study of Women's Prisons* (New York: John Wiley, 1966).
49. Ibid., p. 136.
50. For a summary of such studies (including some previously unpublished), see Lee H. Bowker, *Prisoner Subcultures* (Lexington, MA: Lexington Books, 1977), p. 86.
51. Giallombardo, *Society of Women*, p. 162.
52. David Ward and Gene Kassebaum, *Women's Prison: Sex and Social Structure* (Piscataway, NJ: Aldine Transaction, 2008).
53. Barbara Owen, *"In the Mix": Struggle and Survival in a Women's Prison* (Albany: State University of New York Press, 1998).
54. Barbara Owen, "Prisons: Prisons for Women—Prison Subcultures," available online at http://law.jrank.org/pages/1802/Prisons-Prisons-Women-Prison-subcultures.html.
55. See Joanne Belknap, book review of Barbara Owen's *"In the Mix": Struggle and Survival in a Women's Prison*, in *Western Criminology Review* (1999), http://wcr.sonoma.edu/v1n2/belknap.html (accessed April 11, 2009).
56. Mary Koscheski and Christopher Hensley, "Inmate Homosexual Behavior in a Southern Female Correctional Facility," *American Journal of Criminal Justice*, Vol. 25, No. 2 (2001), pp. 269–277.

57. See, for example, Margie J. Phelps, "Sexual Misconduct between Staff and Inmates," *Corrections Technology and Management*, Vol. 12 (1999).
58. Heffernan, *Making It in Prison*.
59. Bowker, *Prison Victimization*, p. 53.
60. Giallombardo, *Society of Women*.
61. American Correctional Association, *The Female Offender*, p. 39.
62. Kristen A. Hughes, *Justice Expenditure and Employment in the United States, 2003* (Washington, DC: Bureau of Justice Statistics, 2006), p. 7.
63. Ibid., p. 6.
64. Ibid., Table 5: "Justice System Employment and Percent Distribution of Full-Time Equivalent Employment, by State and Types of Government."
65. American Correctional Association, "Correctional Officers in Adult Systems," in *Vital Statistics in Corrections* (Laurel, MD: ACA, 2000). "Other" minorities round out the percentages to a total of 100%.
66. Ibid.
67. American Correctional Association, "Correctional Officers in Adult Systems."
68. Lucien X. Lombardo, *Guards Imprisoned: Correctional Officers at Work* (New York: Elsevier, 1981), pp. 22–36.
69. Leonard Morgenbesser, "NY State Law Prescribes Psychological Screening for CO Job Applicants," *Correctional Training* (winter 1983), p. 1.
70. "A Sophisticated Approach to Training Prison Guards," *Newsday*, August 12, 1982.
71. Jose de Cordoba, "Mexico Prison Riot Leaves 44 Dead," *Wall Street Journal*, February 20, 2012, online.wsj.com/article/SB10001424052970203358704577233192848519360.html (accessed April 4, 2012).
72. Stastny and Tyrnauer, *Who Rules the Joint?* p. 1.
73. See Frederick Talbott, "Reporting from behind the Walls: Do It before the Siren Wails," *Quill* (February 1988), pp. 16–21.
74. "Ohio Prison Rebellion Is Ended," *USA Today*, April 22, 1993.
75. "Guards Hurt in Prison Riot," Associated Press, November 11, 2000.
76. "San Quentin Prison Riot Leaves 42 Injured," *USA Today*, August 9, 2005.
77. Ralph Blumenthal, "Gang Fights in Prison Injure 22 and Kill One," *New York Times*, March 29, 2008.
78. Jeffrey McMurray, "Four Kentucky Inmates Still Hospitalized after Prison Riot," Associated Press, August 22, 2009, http://news.yahoo.com/s/ap/20090822/ap_on_re_us/us_ky_prison_melee (accessed September 4, 2009).
79. John Asbury, "Chino Prison Rioting Spurs Call for Changes," The Press Enterprise, August 9, 2009, http://www.pe.com/localnews/sbcounty/stories/PE_News_Local_S_riot10.2abdafb.html (accessed September 5, 2009).
80. See, for example, Reid H. Montgomery and Gordon A. Crews, *A History of Correctional Violence: An Examination of Reported Causes of Riots and Disturbances* (Lanham, MD: American Correctional Association, 1998); Bert Useem and Peter Kimball, *States of Siege: U.S. Prison Riots, 1971–1986* (New York: Oxford University Press, 1991); and Michael Braswell et al., *Prison Violence in America*, 2nd ed. (Cincinnati, OH: Anderson, 1994).
81. Robert S. Fong, Ronald E. Vogel, and S. Buentello, "Prison Gang Dynamics: A Look inside the Texas Department of Corrections," in A.V. Merlo and P. Menekos, eds., *Dilemmas and Directions in Corrections* (Cincinnati, OH: Anderson, 1992).
82. Ibid.
83. *Ruiz* v. *Estelle*, 503 F. Supp. 1265 (S.D. Tex., 1980).
84. Alan Greenblatt, "Experts: Prison Gang Reach Increasingly Extends into Streets," NPR, April 5, 2013, http://www.npr.org/2013/04/02/176035798/experts-prison-gang-reach-increasingly-extends-into-streets (accessed April 10, 2013).
85. The facts in this story are taken from *Hope* v. *Pelzer*, 122 S.Ct. 2508, 153 L.Ed.2d 666 (2002).
86. "Convictions Bar 3.9 Million from Voting," Associated Press wire service, September 22, 2000.
87. *Holt* v. *Sarver*, 309 F.Supp. 362 (E.D. Ark. 1970).
88. Vergil L. Williams, *Dictionary of American Penology: An Introduction* (Westport, CT: Greenwood Press, 1979), pp. 6–7.
89. Joint order issued in *McCray* v. *Sullivan*, Civ. Action 5620-69-H; *McCray* v. *Sullivan*, Civ. Action 6091-70-H; *White* v. *Commissioner of Alabama Board of Corrections*, Civ. Action 7094-72-H; *Pugh* v. *Sullivan, et al.*, Civ. Action 74-57N; and *James* v. *Wallace, et al.*, Civ. Action 74-203-N.
90. *Pell* v. *Procunier*, 417 U.S. 817, 822 (1974).
91. Ibid.
92. Title 42 U.S.C.A. 1997, Public Law 104-150.
93. Section 1997e.
94. American Correctional Association, *Legal Responsibility and Authority of Correctional Officers: A Handbook on Courts, Judicial Decisions and Constitutional Requirements* (College Park, MD: ACA, 1987), p. 8.
95. *Wolff* v. *McDonnell*, 94 S.Ct. 2963 (1974).
96. Ibid.
97. Ibid.
98. *Ponte* v. *Real*, 471 U.S. 491, 105 S.Ct. 2192, 85 L.Ed.2d 553 (1985).
99. *Vitek* v. *Jones*, 445 U.S. 480 (1980).
100. American Correctional Association, Standard 2-4346. See ACA, *Legal Responsibility and Authority of Correctional Officers*, p. 49.
101. *Wilson* v. *Seiter et al.*, 501 U.S. 294 (1991).
102. *Estelle* v. *Gamble*, 429 U.S. 97, 106 (1976).
103. *Sandin* v. *Conner*, 63 U.S.L.W. 4601 (1995).
104. *Wolff* v. *McDonnell*, 94 S.Ct. 2963 (1974).
105. *Hewitt* v. *Helms*, 459 U.S. 460 (1983).
106. *Ali* v. *Federal Bureau of Prisons*, 552 U.S. 214 (2008).
107. 28 U.S.C. Section 1346(b)(1).
108. *Milbrook* v. *U.S.*, U.S. Supreme Court (decided March 27, 2013).
109. *Howes* v. *Fields*, 566 U.S. ____ (2012).
110. *Florence* v. *Burlington County*, 566 U.S. _____ (2012).
111. Laurie Asseo, "Inmate Lawsuits," Associated Press wire service, May 24, 1996; and Bureau of Justice Statistics, "State and Federal Prisoners Filed 68,235 Petitions in U.S. Courts in 1996," press release, October 29, 1997.
112. *Theriault* v. *Carlson*, 495 F.2d 390.
113. Asseo, "Inmate Lawsuits."
114. Public Law 104-134. Although the PLRA was signed into law on April 26, 1996, and is frequently referred to as the Prison Litigation Reform Act of 1996, the official name of the act is the Prison Litigation Reform Act of 1995.
115. John Scalia, *Prisoner Petitions Filed in U.S. District Courts, 2000, with Trends, 1980–2000* (Washington, DC: Bureau of Justice Statistics, 2002).
116. F. Cheesman, R. Hanson, and B. Ostrom, *A Tale of Two Laws Revisited: Investigating the Impact of the Prison Litigation Reform Act and the Antiterrorism and Effective Death Penalty Act* (Williamsburg, VA: National Center for State Courts, 2004).

117. ACLU, "ACLU Position Paper: Prisoners' Rights," 1999, http://www.aclu.org/files/FilesPDFs/prisonerrights.pdf (accessed August 11, 2013); see also ACLU, "Prisoners' Rights," http://www.aclu.org/prisoners-rights (accessed August 11, 2013).
118. Laura M. Maruschak, *HIV in Prisons, 2001–2010* (Washington, DC: Bureau of Justice Statistics, 2012), p. 1.
119. Dennis Cauchon, "AIDS in Prison: Locked Up and Locked Out," *USA Today*, March 31, 1995, p. 6A.
120. Laura M. Maruschak, *HIV in Prisons, 2005* (Washington, DC: Bureau of Justice Statistics, 2007), p. 16.
121. Centers for Disease Control and Prevention, "HIV Transmission among Male Inmates in a State Prison System: Georgia, 1992–2005," *Morbidity and Mortality Weekly Report*, Vol. 55, No. 15 (April 21, 2006), pp. 421–426.
122. Theodore M. Hammett, *AIDS in Correctional Facilities: Issues and Options*, 3rd ed. (Washington, DC: National Institute of Justice, 1988), p. 37.
123. At the time of this writing, California, Massachusetts, New York, Wisconsin, and the District of Columbia were among those jurisdictions.
124. "Mississippi Eases Policy of Separating Inmates with HIV," *Corrections Journal*, Vol. 5, No. 6 (2001), p. 5.
125. Cauchon, "AIDS in Prison."
126. See "Court Allows Restriction on HIV-Positive Inmates," *Criminal Justice Newsletter*, Vol. 25, No. 23 (December 1, 1994), pp. 2–3.
127. Ibid.
128. Darrell Bryan, "Inmates, HIV, and the Constitutional Right to Privacy: AIDS in Prison Facilities," *Corrections Compendium*, Vol. 19, No. 9 (September 1994), pp. 1–3.
129. "Anthony Marshall Surrenders, Sent to Prison in Astor Theft Case," Associated Press, June 21, 2013, http://www.nypost.com/p/news/local/manhattan/anthony_marshall_surrenders_sent_KWMFREobNwOfPdnXZSV74I (accessed August 11, 2013).
130. Lincoln J. Fry, "The Older Prison Inmate: A Profile," *Justice Professional*, Vol. 2, No. 1 (spring 1987), pp. 1–12.
131. American Civil Liberties Union, *The Mass Incarceration of the Elderly* (New York: ACLU, June 2012).
132. E. Ann Carson and William J. Sabol, *Prisoners in 2011* (Washington, DC: Bureau of Justice Statistics, December 2012).
133. Bureau of Justice Statistics, "The Nation's Prison Population Grew by 60,000 Inmates Last Year," press release, August 15, 1999.
134. Jim Krane, "Demographic Revolution Rocks U.S. Prisons," APB Online, April 12, 1999, http://www.apbonline.com/safestreets/oldprisoners/mainpris0412.html (accessed January 5, 2006).
135. Ronald Wikbert and Burk Foster, "The Long-Termers: Louisiana's Longest Serving Inmates and Why They've Stayed So Long," paper presented at the annual meeting of the Academy of Criminal Justice Sciences, Washington, DC, 1989, p. 51.
136. American Civil Liberties Union, *The Mass Incarceration of the Elderly*, p. vi.
137. Ibid., p. vii.
138. Doris J. James and Lauren E. Glaze, *Mental Health Problems of Prison and Jail Inmates* (Washington, DC: Bureau of Justice Statistics, 2006).
139. Allen J. Beck and Laura M. Maruschak, *Mental Health Treatment in State Prisons, 2000*, Bureau of Justice Statistics Special Report (Washington, DC: BJS, 2001), p. 1, from which most of the information in this paragraph and the next is derived.
140. *Washington* v. *Harper*, 494 U.S. 210 (1990).
141. Robert O. Lampert, "The Mentally Retarded Offender in Prison," *Justice Professional*, Vol. 2, No. 1 (spring 1987), p. 61.
142. Ibid., p. 64.
143. George C. Denkowski and Kathryn M. Denkowski, "The Mentally Retarded Offender in the State Prison System: Identification, Prevalence, Adjustment, and Rehabilitation," *Criminal Justice and Behavior*, Vol. 12 (1985), pp. 55–75.
144. "Opening Session: Kerik Emphasizes the Importance of Corrections' Protective Role for the Country," http://www.aca.org/conferences/Winter05/updates05.asp (accessed July 22, 2008).
145. Keith Martin, "Corrections Prepares for Terrorism," Corrections Connection News Network, January 21, 2002, http://www.corrections.com (accessed June 15, 2010).
146. Quoted in Meghan Mandeville, "Information Sharing Becomes Crucial to Battling Terrorism behind Bars," Corrections.com, December 8, 2003, http://database.corrections.com/news/results2.asp?ID_8988 (accessed July 11, 2005).
147. Institute for the Study of Violent Groups, "Land of Wahhabism," *Crime and Justice International*, March/April 2005, p. 43.
148. "Man behind U.S. Terrorism Plot Gets 16 Years," *International Herald Tribune*, March 6, 2009, http://www.iht.com/articles/ap/2009/03/06/america/NA-US-Terrorism-Probe.php (accessed March 27, 2011).
149. Federal Bureau of Prisons, *State of the Bureau, 2004* (Washington, DC: BOP, 2005).

PART 5 SPECIAL ISSUES

ISSUES FOR THE FUTURE

The accused has these common law, constitutional, statutory, and humanitarian rights that may be threatened by technological advances and other developments:

- A right to privacy
- A right to be assumed innocent
- A right against self-incrimination
- A right to equal protection of the laws
- A right against cruel and unusual punishment

These individual rights must be effectively balanced against these present and emerging community concerns:

- Continuing drug abuse among youth
- The threat of juvenile crime
- Urban gang violence
- High-technology, computer, and Internet crime (cybercrime)
- Terrorism and narcoterrorism
- Occupational and white-collar crime

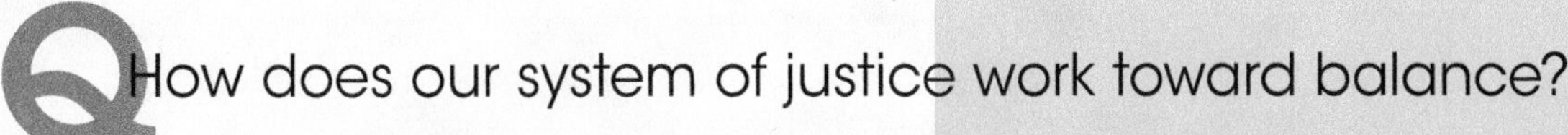

Q How does our system of justice work toward balance?

The Future Comes One Day at a Time

No one can truly say what the future holds. Will the supporters of individual rights or the advocates of public order ultimately claim the day? We cannot say for sure. This much is certain, however: Things change. The future system of American criminal justice will not be quite the same system we know today. Many of the coming changes, however, are now discernible—and hints of what is to come appear on the horizon with increasing frequency and growing clarity. Some of the more obvious of the coming changes are already upon us. They include (1) a restructuring of the juvenile justice system in the face of growing knowledge about human development and concerns about cost efficiency; (2) the increased bankruptcy of a war against drugs whose promises seem increasingly hollow; (3) a growing recognition of America's international role as both victim and purveyor of worldwide criminal activity; (4) the "war on terrorism," including its substantial potential consequences for individual rights in America; and (5) the quickly unfolding potential of cybercrimes, those that both employ high technology in their commission and target the fruits of such technology.

This last part of *Criminal Justice Today* discusses each of these issues in the chapters that follow. It also draws your attention back to the bedrock underlying the American system of justice: the Constitution, the Bill of Rights, and the demands of due process, all of which will continue to structure the American justice system well into the future.

AP Wide World Photos

15 JUVENILE JUSTICE

OUTLINE

LEARNING OBJECTIVES

After reading this chapter, you should be able to

- Describe how the juvenile justice system has evolved in the Western world.
- Describe important U.S. Supreme Court decisions relating to juvenile justice, including their impact on the handling of juveniles by the system.
- Compare juvenile and adult legal rights and their respective systems of justice.
- Briefly describe possible future directions in juvenile justice.

It is with young people that prevention efforts are most needed and hold the greatest promise.

President's Commission on Law Enforcement and Administration of Justice[1]

■ **Follow the author's tweets about the latest crime and justice news @schmalleger.**

Introduction

Serious crimes committed by juveniles and preteens seem commonplace. In 2012, for example, 18-year-old Alyssa Bustamante pleaded guilty in Jefferson City, Missouri, to second-degree murder in the 2009 slaying of a 9-year-old girl.[2] Bustamante, who was 15 years old at the time of the murder, said that she strangled, cut, and stabbed the young girl because she wanted to know how it felt to kill someone. During her sentencing hearing, prosecutors read from her personal diary, in which she described the killing as "ahmazing" and "pretty enjoyable."[3] Bustamante avoided facing life in detention without parole because of her guilty plea, and the judge sentenced her to life imprisonment *with* the possibility of parole.

A key finding of the Office of Juvenile Justice and Delinquency Prevention's Study Group on Serious and Violent Juvenile Offenders is that most chronic juvenile offenders begin their delinquency careers before age 12, and some as early as age 10.[4] The most recent national data show that in 2012 police arrested 67,723 children ages 12 and younger.[5] These very young offenders (known as *child delinquents*) represent almost 7% of the total number of juvenile arrestees (those up to age 18).

Although states vary as to the age at which a person legally enters adulthood, statistics on crime make it clear that young people are disproportionately involved in certain offenses. A recent report, for example, found that nearly 16% of all violent crimes and 26% of all property crimes are committed by people younger than 18, although this age group makes up only 26% of the population of the United States.[6] On average, about 17% of all arrests in any year are of juveniles,[7] and people younger than 18 have a higher likelihood of being arrested for robbery and other property crimes than do people in any other age group. Figure 15-1 shows Uniform Crime Report/NIBRS statistics on juvenile arrests for selected offense categories.

The Office of Juvenile Justice and Delinquency Prevention (OJJDP) is a primary source of information on juvenile justice in the United States. A sweeping OJJDP overview of juvenile crime and the juvenile justice system in America reveals the following:[8]

- About one million juveniles (under 18) are arrested annually in America.
- Violent crime by juveniles is decreasing.
- Younger juveniles account for a substantial proportion of juvenile arrests and the juvenile court caseload.
- Relative to male delinquency, female delinquency has grown substantially.
- Greater percentages of females than males are in placement for status offenses and assaults.

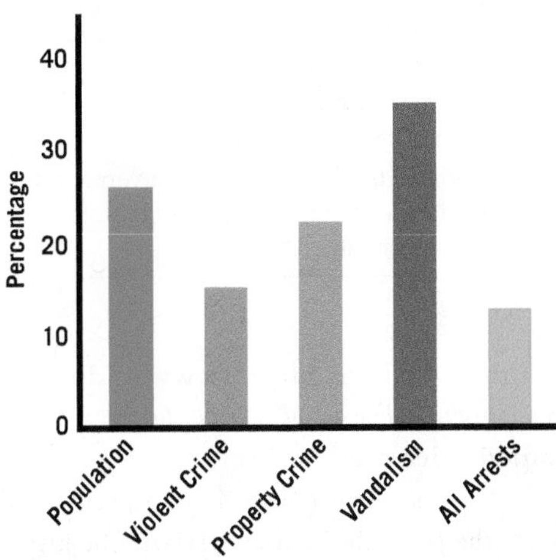

FIGURE 15-1 | **Juvenile Involvement in Crime versus System Totals, 2012**

Note: The term *juvenile* refers to people younger than 18 years of age.
Source: Federal Bureau of Investigation, *Crime in the United States, 2012* (Washington, DC: U.S. Dept. of Justice, 2013).

- Both girls and boys who are in the juvenile justice system usually have problems at home and school that have put them at risk for delinquency—including maltreatment, poverty, or both—and these factors also may have a negative impact on their adjustment to young adulthood.
- Minority juveniles are greatly overrepresented in the custody population.
- Crowding is a serious problem in juvenile facilities.

In 2011, data from a seven-year collaborative, multidisciplinary project called the Pathways to Desistance Study revealed that:[9]

- Most youth who commit felonies greatly reduce their offending over time, regardless of the intervention or treatment they receive.
- Longer stays in juvenile institutions do not reduce recidivism.
- Community-based supervision as a component of aftercare is effective for youth who have committed serious.
- Substance-abuse treatment reduces both substance use and criminal offending.

The Pathways to Desistance Study, funded by the OJJDP, followed 1,354 serious juvenile offenders ages 14 through 18 for seven years after their conviction. The study looked at the factors that lead youth who have committed serious offenses to continue or to desist from offending, including individual maturation, life changes, and involvement with the criminal justice system. Learn

■ **juvenile justice system** The aggregate of the government agencies that function to investigate, supervise, adjudicate, care for, or confine youthful offenders and other children subject to the jurisdiction of the juvenile court.

■ **delinquency** In the broadest usage, juvenile actions or conduct in violation of criminal law, juvenile status offenses, and other juvenile misbehavior.

■ ***parens patriae*** A common law principle that allows the state to assume a parental role and to take custody of a child when he or she becomes delinquent, is abandoned, or is in need of care that the natural parents are unable or unwilling to provide.

more about the OJJDP via **http://www.ojjdp.gov**, and read its recently launched *Journal of Juvenile Justice* at **http://www.journalofjuvjustice.org**.

This chapter has four purposes. First, we will briefly look at the history of the **juvenile justice system**. The juvenile justice system has its roots in the adult system. In the juvenile system, however, we find a more uniform philosophical base and a generally clear agreement about the system's purpose. These differences may be due to the system's relative newness and to the fact that society generally agrees that young people who have gone wrong are worth salvaging. However, the philosophy that underlies the juvenile justice system in America is increasingly being questioned by "get-tough" advocates of law and order, many of whom are fed up with violent juvenile crime.

The philosophy that underlies the juvenile justice system in America is being questioned by "get-tough" advocates of law and order, many of whom are fed up with violent juvenile crime.

Our second purpose is to compare the juvenile and adult systems as they currently operate. The reasoning behind the juvenile justice system has led to administrative and other procedures that, in many jurisdictions, are not found in the adult system. The juvenile justice process, for example, is frequently not as open as the adult system. Hearings may be held in secret, the names of offenders are not published, and records of juvenile proceedings may later be destroyed.[10]

Our third purpose is to describe the agencies, processes, and problems of the juvenile justice system itself. Although each state may have variations, they all share a common system structure.

Near the end of this chapter, we will turn to our fourth focus and will consider some of the issues raised by critics of the current system. As conservative attitudes brought changes in the adult criminal justice system over the past few decades, the juvenile justice system remained relatively unchanged. Based on premises quite different from those of the adult system, juvenile justice has long been a separate decision-making arena in which the best interests of the child have been accorded great importance. As we will see, substantial changes are now afoot.

Juvenile Justice Throughout History

Before the modern era, children who committed crimes in the Western world received no preferential treatment because of their youth. They were adjudicated and punished alongside adults, and a number of recorded cases have come down through history of children as young as six being hung or burned at the stake.[11]

Earliest Times

Similarly, little distinction was made between criminality and **delinquency** or other kinds of undesirable behavior.

Early philosophy in dealing with juveniles derived from a Roman principle called *patria potestas*. Under Roman law (circa 753 B.C.), children were members of their family, but the father had absolute control over children, and they in turn had an absolute responsibility to obey his wishes. Roman understanding of the social role of children strongly influenced English culture and eventually led to the development of the legal principle of ***parens patriae*** in Western law, which allowed the king, or the English state, to take the place of parents in dealing with children who broke the law.

By the end of the eighteenth century, social conditions in Europe and America had begun to change, and the Enlightenment, a highly significant intellectual and social movement, emphasized human potential. In this new age, children were recognized as the only true heirs to the future, and society became increasingly concerned about their well-being.

By the middle of the nineteenth century, large-scale immigration to America was under way. Unfortunately, some immigrant families fell victims of the cities that drew them, settling in squalor in hastily formed ghettos. Many children, abandoned by families that were unable to support them, were forced into lives on the streets, where they formed tattered gangs—surviving off the refuse of the cities. An 1823 report by the Society for the Prevention of Pauperism in the city of New York called for the development of "houses of refuge" to save children

Jefferson County Sheriff's Department/Getty Images

Columbine (Colorado) High School shooters Eric Harris (left) and Dylan Klebold examining a sawed-off shotgun in a still image taken from a videotape made at a makeshift shooting range in 1999. About six weeks after the video was made, Klebold (17) and Harris (18) shot and killed 15 people and injured 20 more at the school. How might such disasters be averted in the future?

from lives of crime and poverty, and in 1824, the first house of refuge opened in New York City.[12] It sheltered mostly young thieves, vagrants, and runaways. Other children, especially those with more severe delinquency problems, were placed in adult prisons and jails. Houses of refuge became popular in New York, and other cities quickly copied them. It was not long, however, before they became overcrowded and living conditions deteriorated.

Not long afterward, the American child-savers movement began. Child savers espoused a philosophy of productivity and eschewed idleness and unprincipled behavior.

One product of the child-savers movement was the reform school—a place for delinquent juveniles that embodied the atmosphere of a Christian home. By the middle of the nineteenth century, the reform school approach to handling juveniles led to the creation of the Chicago Reform School, which opened in the 1860s. Reform schools focused primarily on predelinquent youth who showed tendencies toward more serious criminal involvement, and attempted to emulate wholesome family environments.

One product of the child-savers movement was the reform school—a place for delinquent juveniles that embodied the atmosphere of a Christian home.

The Juvenile Court Era

In 1870, an expanding recognition of children's needs led Massachusetts to enact legislation that required separate hearings for juveniles.[13] New York followed with a similar law in 1877,[14] which also prohibited contact between juvenile and adult offenders. Rhode Island enacted juvenile court legislation in 1898, and in 1899 the Colorado School Law became the first comprehensive legislation designed to address the adjudication of problem children.[15] It was, however, the 1899 codification of Illinois juvenile law that became the model for juvenile court statutes throughout the nation.

The Illinois Juvenile Court Act created a juvenile court, separate in form and function from adult criminal courts. To avoid the lasting stigma of criminality, the law applied the term *delinquent* rather than *criminal* to young adjudicated offenders. The act specified that the best interests of the child were to guide juvenile court judges in their deliberations. In effect, judges were to serve as advocates for juveniles, guiding their development.

■ **delinquent child** A child who has engaged in activity that would be considered a crime if the child were an adult. The term *delinquent* is used to avoid the stigma associated with the term *criminal*.

■ **undisciplined child** A child who is beyond parental control, as evidenced by his or her refusal to obey legitimate authorities, such as school officials and teachers.

■ **dependent child** A child who has no parents or whose parents are unable to care for him or her.

■ **neglected child** A child who is not receiving the proper level of physical or psychological care from his or her parents or guardians or who has been placed up for adoption in violation of the law.

■ **abused child** A child who has been physically, sexually, or mentally abused. Most states also consider a child who is forced into delinquent activity by a parent or guardian to be abused.

■ **status offender** A child who commits an act that is contrary to the law by virtue of the offender's status as a child. Purchasing cigarettes, buying alcohol, and being truant are examples of such behavior.

Determining guilt or innocence took second place to the betterment of the child. The law abandoned a strict adherence to the due process requirements of adult prosecutions, allowing informal procedures designed to scrutinize the child's situation. By sheltering the juvenile from the punishment philosophy of the adult system, the Illinois Juvenile Court emphasized reformation in place of retribution.[16]

In 1938, the federal government passed the Juvenile Court Act, which embodied many of the features of the Illinois statute. By 1945, every state had enacted special legislation focusing on the handling of juveniles, and the juvenile court movement became well established.[17]

The juvenile court movement was based on five philosophical principles that can be summarized as follows:[18]

- The state is the "higher or ultimate parent" of all the children within its borders.
- Children are worth saving, and nonpunitive procedures should be used to save the child.
- Children should be nurtured. While the nurturing process is under way, they should be protected from the stigmatizing impact of formal adjudicatory procedures.
- To accomplish the goal of reformation, justice needs to be individualized; that is, each child is different, and the needs, aspirations, living conditions, and so on of each child must be known in their individual particulars if the court is to be helpful.
- Noncriminal procedures are necessary to give primary consideration to the needs of the child. The denial of due process can be justified in the face of constitutional challenges because the court acts not to punish, but to help.

Learn more about the history of juvenile justice and the juvenile court at **http://www.justicestudies.com/pubs/juvenile.pdf**.

Scott Griessel/Fotolia.

A small group of teenagers. American juveniles have many opportunities but also face numerous challenges. What are the six categories of children that state juvenile justice statutes usually describe as subject to juvenile court jurisdiction?

Categories of Children in the Juvenile Justice System

By the time of the Great Depression, most states had expanded juvenile statutes to include the following six categories of children. These categories are still used today in most jurisdictions to describe the variety of children subject to juvenile court jurisdiction.

- **Delinquent children** are those who violate the criminal law. If they were adults, the word *criminal* would be applied to them.
- **Undisciplined children** are said to be beyond parental control, as evidenced by their refusal to obey legitimate authorities, such as school officials and teachers. They need state protection.
- **Dependent children** typically have no parents or guardians to care for them. Their parents are deceased, they were placed for adoption, or they were abandoned in violation of the law.
- **Neglected children** are those who do not receive proper care from their parents or guardians. They may suffer from malnutrition or may not be provided with adequate shelter.
- **Abused children** are those who suffer physical abuse at the hands of their custodians. This category was later expanded to include emotional and sexual abuse.
- **Status offender** is a special category that embraces children who violate laws written only for them. In some states, status offenders are referred to as persons in need of supervision (PINS).

■ **status offense** An act or conduct that is declared by statute to be an offense, but only when committed by or engaged in by a juvenile, and that can be adjudicated only by a juvenile court.

Status offenses include behavior such as truancy, vagrancy, running away from home, and incorrigibility. The youthful "status" of juveniles is a necessary element in such offenses. Adults, for example, may "run away from home" and not violate any law. Runaway children, however, are subject to apprehension and juvenile court processing because state laws require that they be subject to parental control.

Status offenses were a natural outgrowth of juvenile court philosophy. As a consequence, however, juveniles in need of help often faced procedural dispositions that treated them as though they were delinquent. Rather than lowering the rate of juvenile incarceration, the juvenile court movement led to its increase. Critics of the juvenile court movement quickly focused on the abandonment of due process rights, especially in the case of status offenders, as a major

Status offenses include behavior such as truancy, vagrancy, running away from home, and incorrigibility.

CJ | NEWS

Schools Are Taking Bullying Seriously

AlexandreNunes/Shutterstock

A younger boy being physically threatened and bullied by an older one. What can be done to prevent bullying in schools? In the community?

Bullying in schools, once thought to be just part of growing up, is now widely seen as a root cause of poor learning, school violence, and suicide—a revised view that has set off an avalanche of state anti-bullying laws and major adjustments in school policies.

Experts say anywhere from 20% to 50% of students are bullied at some point, and 10% are regularly victimized. The harmful effects have been documented in several U.S. studies. Some 160,000 children stay home from school each day to avoid bullying, and 4.1% of victims have brought weapons to school in response. Victims are 5.6 times more likely to contemplate suicide.

But until recently, many school authorities did nothing. The National Association of School Psychologists reports that nearly 25% of teachers do not believe intervention in bullying is necessary.

In an age when students socialize online, bad behavior has moved from the stairwell and locker room to Facebook and Twitter. This so-called cyberbullying complicates the issue because it doesn't occur on school grounds, and many parents and teachers aren't involved in social media.

States passed the first state anti-bullying laws after the 1999 shootings at Columbine High School in suburban Denver, which were blamed in part on bullying. Suicides of some taunted students, often outed for being gay, also prompted these laws. By March 2012, every state except Montana had an anti-bullying statute.

The laws vary widely, but in general, they include requiring schools to establish anti-bullying policies, track incidents, create training and prevention programs for teachers and students, and establish sanctions such as suspension, reassignment, or expulsion. In addition, states have amended laws to cover cyberbullying and subtler kinds of harassment, such as ostracizing.

So far, the laws have stood up in the courts. When a West Virginia high school senior was suspended from school for creating a fake Internet profile of another student, calling here a "slut who had herpes," her parents sued the school on free speech grounds, but a federal appeals court threw out their lawsuit.

Even revered high school athletics programs aren't immune from angry parents citing the new laws. In 2010, three stars of the Carmel, Indiana, high school basketball team were suspended for five days for bullying two freshmen team members on the bus ride home from a game.

In many cases, however, the laws are spottily enforced. In Georgia, the first state to pass an anti-bullying law in 1999, Atlanta area schools reported more than 1,900 bullying incidents in the 2009–2010 school year, but only 30 expulsions or reassignments as a result, and a whole suburban county reported no incidents at all.

Furthermore, school policies may not deter bullying. A Massachusetts school with a suicide due to bullying had an anti-bullying policy in place.

There is a lot of bad behavior in schools, but what constitutes bullying? The test, one New York judge wrote, is whether the conduct is "sufficiently severe, persistent or pervasive that it creates a hostile environment" that "deprives a student of substantial educational opportunities."

Resources: "Schools, Parents Try to Keep Pace with Cyber-bullying Tactics," *Baltimore Sun*, April 22 2012, http://articles.baltimoresun.com/2012-04-22/news/bs-md-ho-cyber-reader-20120422_1_cyber-bullying-anti-bullying-laws-rutgers-university-freshman; "Analysis of State Bullying Laws and Policies," U.S. Department of Education, December 2011, http://www2.ed.gov/rschstat/eval/bullying/state-bullying-laws/state-bullying-laws.pdf; and "Law Firmer against Bullies," *Atlanta Journal-Constitution*, November 20, 2010, http://www.ajc.com/news/atlanta/law-firmer-against-bullies-748057.html.

source of problems. Detention and incarceration, they argued, were inappropriate options where children had not committed crimes.

The Legal Environment

Throughout the first half of the twentieth century, the U.S. Supreme Court followed a hands-off approach to juvenile justice, much like its early approach to prisons

Throughout the first half of the twentieth century, the U.S. Supreme Court followed a hands-off approach to juvenile justice, much like its early approach to prisons (see Chapter 14). The adjudication and further processing of juveniles by the system were left mostly to specialized juvenile courts or to local appeals courts. Although one or two early Supreme Court decisions[19] dealt with issues of juvenile justice, it was not until the 1960s that the Court began close legal scrutiny of the principles underlying the system itself. Some of the most important U.S. Supreme Court cases relating to juvenile justice are shown in Figure 15-2.

In the 1967 case known as *In re Gault,* the U.S. Supreme Court held, in part, as follows:[20]

> [T]he Juvenile Court Judge's exercise of the power of the state as *parens patriae* [is] not unlimited. . . . Notice, to comply with due process requirements, must be given sufficiently in advance of scheduled court proceedings so that reasonable opportunity to prepare will be afforded. . . . The probation officer cannot act as counsel for the child. His role in the adjudicatory hearing, by statute and in fact, is as arresting officer and witness against the child. There is no material difference in this respect between adult and juvenile proceedings of the sort here involved. . . . A proceeding where the issue is whether the child will be found to be "delinquent" and subjected to the loss of his liberty for years is comparable in seriousness to a felony prosecution. The juvenile needs the assistance of counsel to cope with the problems of law, to make skilled inquiry into the facts, to insist upon regularity of the proceedings, and to ascertain whether he has a defense and to prepare and submit it.

In that 1967 case, however, the Court did not agree with another contention of Gault's lawyers: that transcripts of juvenile hearings should be maintained. Transcripts are not necessary, the Court said, because (1) there is no constitutional right to a transcript, and (2) no transcripts are produced in the trials of most adult misdemeanants.

Today, the impact of *Gault* is widely felt throughout the juvenile justice system. Juveniles are now guaranteed many of the same procedural rights as adults. Most precedent-setting Supreme Court decisions that followed *Gault* further clarified the rights of juveniles, focusing primarily on those few issues of due process that it had not explicitly addressed. One of these was the 1970 case of *In re Winship,* which centered on the standard of evidence needed in juvenile hearings. Winship's attorney had argued that the guilt of a juvenile facing a hearing should have to be proved beyond a reasonable doubt—the evidentiary standard of adult criminal trials. In its ruling the Court agreed, saying:[21]

Juveniles are now guaranteed many of the same procedural rights as adults.

> The constitutional safeguard of proof beyond a reasonable doubt is as much required during the adjudicatory stage of a delinquency proceeding as are those constitutional guards applied in *Gault*. . . . We therefore hold . . . that where a 12 year old child is charged with an act of stealing which renders him liable to confinement for as long as six years, then, as a matter of due process . . . the case against him must be proved beyond a reasonable doubt.

As a consequence of *Winship*, allegations of delinquency today must be established beyond a reasonable doubt. The Court

1966	1967	1970	1971	1975
Kent* v. *United States	***In re Gault***	***In re Winship***	***Mckeiver* v. *Pennsylvania***	***Breed* v. *Jones***
Courts must provide the "essentials of due process" in juvenile proceedings. This important case signaled the beginning of systematic U.S. Supreme Court review of lower-court practices in delinquency hearings.	In hearings that could result in commitment to an institution juveniles have four basic rights: Notice of charges Right to counsel Right to confront and to cross-examine witnesses Protection against self-incrimination	In delinquency matters the state must prove its case beyond a reasonable doubt. Prior to Winship, a lower standard of evidence had been required by juvenile courts in some states–a mere preponderance of the evidence.	Jury trials are not constitutionally required in juvenile cases. At the same time the Court established that jury trials are not prohibited for juveniles. Today, 12 states allow for jury trials in serious cases involving juveniles.	Severely restricted the conditions under which transfers from juvenile to adult courts may occur. In this case Jones was adjudicated delinquent in juvenile court and then transferred to adult court resulting in double jeopardy. Today, transfers to adult court, if they are to occur, must be made before an adjudicatory hearing in juvenile court.

FIGURE 15-2 | The Legal Environment of Juvenile Justice

allowed, however, the continued use of the lower evidentiary standard in adjudicating juveniles charged with status offenses. Even though both standards continue to exist, most jurisdictions have chosen to use the stricter burden-of-proof requirement for all delinquency proceedings.

Cases like *Winship* and *Gault* have not extended all adult procedural rights to juveniles charged with delinquency. The 1971 case of *McKeiver* v. *Pennsylvania*,[22] for example, reiterated what earlier cases had established—specifically that juveniles do not have the constitutional right to trial by a jury of their peers. It is important to note, however, that the *McKeiver* decision did not specifically prohibit jury trials for juveniles. As a consequence, approximately 12 states today allow the option of jury trials for juveniles.

In 1975, in the case of *Breed* v. *Jones,* the Court severely restricted the conditions under which transfers from juvenile to adult courts may occur by mandating that such transfers that do occur must be made before any adjudicatory hearing in juvenile court. In 1984, in the case of *Schall* v. *Martin*, the U.S. Supreme Court upheld the constitutionality of a New York state statute, ruling that pretrial detention of juveniles based on "serious risk" does not violate the principle of fundamental fairness required by due process.[23] In so holding, the Court recognized that states have a legitimate interest in preventing future delinquency by juveniles thought to be dangerous.

Although the *Schall* decision upheld the practice of preventive detention, the Court seized on the opportunity provided by the case to impose procedural requirements on the detaining authority. Consequently, preventive detention today cannot be imposed without (1) prior notice, (2) an equitable detention hearing, and (3) a statement by the judge setting forth the reason or reasons for detention.

In 1988, in the case of *Thompson* v. *Oklahoma*,[24] the U.S. Supreme Court determined that national standards of decency did not permit the execution of any offender who was under age 16 at the time of the crime. In 2005, in the case of *Roper* v. *Simmons*,[25] the Court set a new standard when it ruled that age *is* a bar to execution when the offender commits a capital crime when younger than 18. The *Roper* case involved Christopher Simmons, a high school junior who, at 17, planned and committed a callous capital murder of a woman whom he bound with duct tape and electrical wire, terrorized, and threw off a bridge. About nine months later, after he had turned 18, he was tried and sentenced to death. Regardless of the heinous nature of Simmons's crime, the justices reasoned that "juveniles' susceptibility to immature and irresponsible behavior means their irresponsible conduct is not as morally reprehensible as that of an adult . . . [and] their own vulnerability and comparative lack of control over their immediate surroundings mean juveniles have a greater claim than adults to be forgiven for failing to escape negative influences in their whole environment." The fact, said the Court, "that juveniles still struggle to define their identity means it is less supportable to conclude that even a heinous crime committed by a juvenile is evidence of irretrievably depraved character." The *Roper* ruling invalidated the capital sentences of 72 death row inmates in 12 states.[26]

In 2010, the Court, in the case of *Graham* v. *Florida*,[27] interpreted the cruel and unusual punishment clause of the U.S. Constitution to mean that a juvenile offender cannot be sentenced to life in prison without parole for a crime not involving homicide. Its ruling, said the Court, "gives the juvenile offender a chance to demonstrate maturity and reform." Finally, in 2012, in *Miller* v. *Alabama*, the Court held that *mandatory* life-without-parole sentences for individuals 17 or younger convicted of homicide violate the Eighth Amendment.

Legislation Concerning Juveniles and Justice

In response to the rapidly increasing crime rates of the late 1960s, Congress passed the Omnibus Crime Control and Safe Streets Act of 1968. The act provided money and technical assistance

1984	1988-1989	2005	2010	2012
Schall* v. *Martin	***Thompson* v. *Oklahoma* and *Stanford* v. *Kentucky***	***Roper* v. *Simmons***	***Graham* v. *Florida***	***Miller* v. *Alabama***
The Court overturned lower court decisions banning the pretrial detention of juveniles, and held that such detention may be necessary for the protection of the child and of others.	Minimum age for the death penalty is set at 16.	The U.S.Supreme Court ruled that age is a bar to execution when the offender commits a capital crime when he is younger than age 18. The Court held that "even a heinous crime committed by a juvenile" is not "evidence of irretrievably depraved character." Roper invalidated the capital sentences of 72 death-row inmates in 12 states.	The Eighth Amendment's ban on cruel and unusual punishments prohibits the imprisonment of a juvenile for life without the possibility of parole as punishment for a crime not involving homicide.	Mandatory life-without-parole sentences for individuals 17 or younger convicted of homicide violate the Eighth Amendment.

for states and municipalities seeking to modernize their justice systems. The Safe Streets Act provided funding for youth services bureaus, which had been recommended by the 1967 presidential commission report *The Challenge of Crime in a Free Society*. These bureaus were available to police, juvenile courts, and probation departments and acted as a centralized community resource for handling delinquents and status offenders. Youth services bureaus also handled juveniles referred by schools and young people who referred themselves. Unfortunately, within a decade after their establishment, most youth services bureaus succumbed to a lack of continued federal funding.

In 1974, recognizing the special needs of juveniles, Congress passed the Juvenile Justice and Delinquency Prevention (JJDP) Act. Employing much the same strategy as the 1968 law, the JJDP Act provided federal grants to states and cities seeking to improve their handling and disposition of delinquents and status offenders. Nearly all the states chose to accept federal funds through the JJDP Act. Participating states had to meet two conditions within five years:

- They had to agree to a "sight and sound separation mandate," under which juveniles would not be held in institutions where they might come into regular contact with adult prisoners.
- Status offenders had to be deinstitutionalized, with most being released into the community or placed in foster homes.

Within a few years, institutional populations were cut by more than half, and community alternatives to juvenile institutionalization were rapidly being developed. Jailed juveniles were housed in separate wings of adult facilities or were removed from adult jails entirely.

When the JJDP Act was reauthorized for funding in 1980, the separation mandate was expanded to require that separate juvenile jails be constructed by the states. Studies supporting reauthorization of the JJDP Act in 1984 and 1988, however, found that nearly half the states had failed to come into "substantial compliance" with the new jail and lockup mandate. As a consequence, Congress modified the requirements of the act, continuing funding for states making "meaningful progress" toward removing juveniles from adult jails.[28] The 1988 reauthorizing legislation added a "disproportionate minority confinement" (DMC) requirement under which states seeking federal monies in support of their juvenile justice systems had to agree to ameliorate conditions leading to the disproportionate confinement of minority juveniles.[29]

In 1996, in the face of pressures toward punishment and away from treatment for violent juvenile offenders, the Office of Juvenile Justice and Delinquency Prevention proposed new rules for jailing juveniles. The new rules allow an adjudicated delinquent to be detained for up to 12 hours in an adult jail before a court appearance and make it easier for states to house juveniles in separate wings of adult jails.[30] The most recent JJDP Act reauthorization occurred in 2002[31] and expanded the DMC concept to include all aspects of the juvenile justice process. Consequently, DMC has come to mean "disproportionate minority contact" under today's law.[32] By 2005, 56 of 57 eligible states and U.S. territories had agreed to all of the act's requirements and were receiving federal funding under the legislation.[33]

In 2003, Congress passed child-protection legislation in what is commonly called the "Amber Alert" law. Officially known as the PROTECT Act of 2003 (Prosecutorial Remedies and Other Tools to End the Exploitation of Children Today), the law provides federal funding to the states to ensure the creation of a national Amber network (America's Missing: Broadcast Emergency Response) to facilitate rapid law enforcement and community response to kidnapped or abducted children. The law also established the position of a federal Amber Alert coordinator and set uniform standards for the use of Amber Alerts across our country. Another provision of the law provides for the prosecution of anyone engaged in pandering of child pornography, and it contains an extraterritorial clause that makes possible the federal prosecution of U.S. citizens who travel outside of the country to engage in child sex tourism.[34] The federal government's Amber Alert website can be accessed via **http://www.amberalert.gov**.

The Legal Rights of Juveniles

Most jurisdictions today have statutes designed to extend the *Miranda* provisions to juveniles. Many police officers routinely offer *Miranda* warnings to juveniles in their custody before questioning them. It is unclear, however, whether juveniles can legally waive their *Miranda* rights. A 1979 U.S. Supreme Court ruling held that juveniles should be accorded the opportunity for a knowing waiver when they are old enough and sufficiently educated to understand the consequences of a waiver.[35] A later High Court ruling upheld the murder conviction of a juvenile who had been advised of his rights and waived them in the presence of his mother.[36]

One important area of juvenile rights centers on investigative procedures. In 1985, for example, the U.S. Supreme Court ruled in *New Jersey* v. *T.L.O.*[37] that schoolchildren have a reasonable expectation of privacy in their personal property. The case involved a 14-year-old girl who was accused of violating school rules by smoking in a high school bathroom. A vice principal searched the girl's purse and found evidence of marijuana use. Juvenile officers were called, and the girl was eventually adjudicated in juvenile court and found delinquent.

On appeal to the New Jersey Supreme Court, the girl's lawyers were successful in having her conviction reversed on the grounds that the search of her purse, as an item of personal property, had been unreasonable. The state's appeal to the U.S. Supreme Court resulted in a ruling that prohibited school officials from engaging in unreasonable searches of students or their property. A reading of the Court's decision leads to the conclusion that a search could be considered reasonable if it (1) is based on a logical suspicion of rule-breaking actions; (2) is required to maintain order, discipline, and safety among students; and (3) does not exceed the scope of the original suspicion.

Finally, in 2011, the U.S. Supreme Court held that the age of suspects must be considered when determining whether they would feel free not to respond to police questioning. In writing for the majority in *J.D.B.* v. *North Carolina,*[38] Justice Sonia Sotomayor wrote "It is beyond dispute that children will often feel bound to submit to police questioning when an adult in the same circumstances would feel free to leave."

The Juvenile Justice Process Today

Juvenile court jurisdiction rests on the offender's age and conduct. The majority of states today define a child subject to juvenile court jurisdiction as a person who has not yet turned 18. A few states set the age at 16, and several use 17. Figure 15-3 shows the upper ages of children subject to juvenile court jurisdiction in delinquency matters, by state. When they reach their 18th birthday, children in most states become subject to the jurisdiction of adult criminal courts.

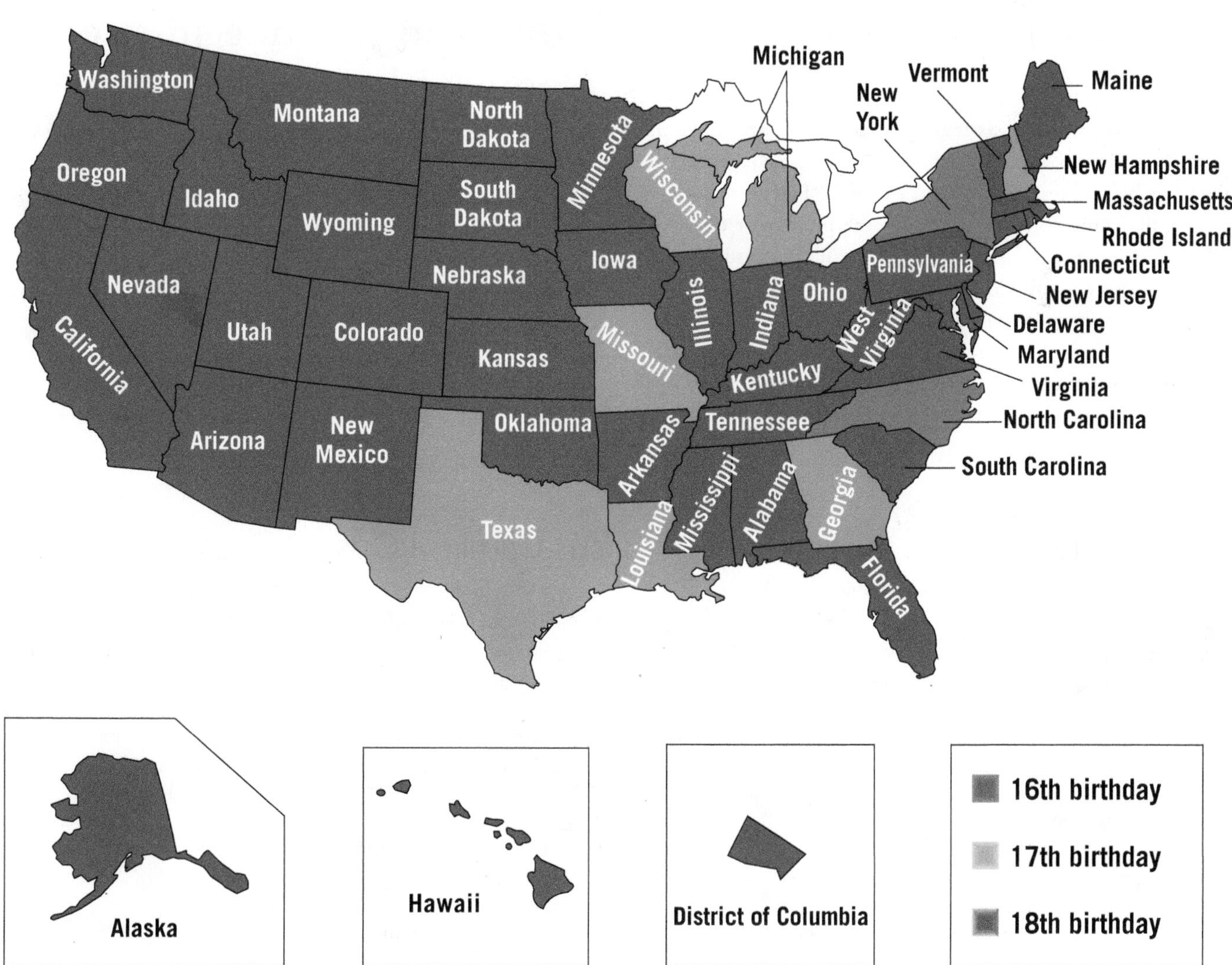

FIGURE 15-3 | **Limit of Juvenile Court Jurisdiction over Young Offenders, by State**

Note: Wisconsin places 17-year-olds in juvenile courts for misdemeanor charges, but in adult criminal courts for felony charges.

Source: Office of Juvenile Justice and Delinquency Prevention.

In 2013, the OJJDP reported that U.S. courts with juvenile jurisdiction annually handle slightly more than 1.7 million delinquency cases.[39] Depending on the laws of the state and the behavior involved, the jurisdiction of the juvenile court may be exclusive. *Exclusive jurisdiction* applies when the juvenile court is the only court that has statutory authority to deal with children for specified infractions. For example, status offenses such as truancy normally fall within the exclusive jurisdiction of juvenile courts. Delinquency, which involves violation of the criminal law, however, is often not within the juvenile court's exclusive jurisdiction. All 50 states, the District of Columbia, and the federal government have provisions that allow juveniles who commit serious crimes to be bound over to criminal court. Forty-six states give juvenile court judges the power to waive jurisdiction over cases involving juveniles so that they can be transferred to criminal court.[40] Fifteen states have "direct file" provisions that authorize the prosecutor to decide whether to file certain kinds of cases in juvenile or criminal court. Juveniles who commit violent crimes or who have prior records are among the most likely to be transferred to adult courts.[41]

The majority of states today define a child subject to juvenile court jurisdiction as a person who has not yet turned 18.

Where juvenile court authority is not exclusive, the jurisdiction of the court may be original or concurrent. Original jurisdiction means that a particular offense must originate, or begin, with juvenile court authorities. Juvenile courts have original jurisdiction over most delinquency petitions and all status offenses. Concurrent jurisdiction exists where other courts have equal statutory authority to originate proceedings. If a juvenile has committed a homicide, rape, or other serious crime, for example, an arrest warrant may be issued by the adult court.

Some states specify that juvenile courts have no jurisdiction over certain excluded offenses. Delaware, Louisiana, and Nevada, for example, allow no juvenile court jurisdiction over children charged with first-degree murder. Twenty-nine states have statutes that exclude certain serious, violent, or repeat offenders from the juvenile court's jurisdiction.

Adult and Juvenile Justice Compared

The court cases of relevance to the juvenile justice system that we have identified in this chapter have two common characteristics: They all turn on due process guarantees specified by the Bill of Rights, and they all make the claim that adult due process should serve as a model for juvenile proceedings. Due process guarantees, as interpreted by the U.S. Supreme Court, are clearly designed to ensure that juvenile proceedings are fair and that the interests of juveniles are protected. However, the Court's interpretations do not offer any pretense of providing juveniles with the same kinds of protections guaranteed to adult defendants.

CJ | ISSUES
The Juvenile Justice System versus Criminal Case Processing

Criminal Proceedings	Juvenile Proceedings
Focus on criminality	Focus on delinquency and a special category of "status offenses"
Comprehensive rights against unreasonable searches of person, home, and possessions	Limited rights against unreasonable searches
A right against self-incrimination; a knowing waiver is possible	A right against self-incrimination; waivers are questionable
Assumed innocent until proven guilty	Guilt and innocence are not primary issues; the system focuses on the interests of the child
Adversarial setting	Helping context
Arrest warrants form the basis for most arrests	Petitions or complaints legitimize apprehension
Right to an attorney	Right to an attorney
Public trial	Closed hearing; no right to a jury trial
System goals are punishment and reformation	System goals are protection and treatment
No right to treatment	Specific right to treatment
Possibility of bail or release on recognizance	Release into parental custody
Public record of trial and judgment	Sealed records; sometimes destroyed by a specified age
Possible incarceration in adult correctional facility	Separate facilities at all levels

■ **juvenile petition** A document filed in juvenile court alleging that a juvenile is a delinquent, a status offender, or a dependent and asking that the court assume jurisdiction over the juvenile or that an alleged delinquent be transferred to a criminal court for prosecution as an adult.

Although the High Court has tended to agree that juveniles are entitled to due process protection, it has refrained from declaring that juveniles have a right to all the aspects of due process afforded adult defendants.

Juvenile court philosophy brings with it other differences from the adult system. Among them are (1) a reduced concern with legal issues of guilt or innocence and an emphasis on the child's best interests; (2) an emphasis on treatment rather than punishment; (3) privacy and protection from public scrutiny through the use of sealed records, laws against publishing the names of juvenile offenders, and so forth; (4) the use of the techniques of social science in dispositional decision making rather than sentences determined by a perceived need for punishment; (5) no long-term confinement, with most juveniles being released from institutions by their 21st birthday, regardless of offense; (6) separate facilities for juveniles; and (7) broad discretionary alternatives at all points in the process.[42] This combination of court philosophy and due process requirements has created a unique justice system for juveniles that takes into consideration the special needs of young people while attempting to offer reasonable protection to society. The juvenile justice system is diagrammed in Figure 15-4.

How the System Works

The juvenile justice system can be viewed as a process that, when carried to completion, moves through four stages: intake, adjudication, disposition, and postadjudicatory review. Although organizationally similar to the adult criminal justice process, the juvenile system is far more likely to maximize the use of discretion and to employ diversion from further formal processing at every point in the process. Each stage is discussed in the pages that follow.

Intake and Detention Hearings

Delinquent juveniles may come to the attention of the police or juvenile court authorities either through arrest or through the filing of a **juvenile petition** by an aggrieved party. Juvenile petitions are much like criminal complaints in that they allege illegal behavior. They are most often filed by teachers, school administrators, neighbors, store managers, or others who have frequent contact with juveniles. Parents who are unable to control the behavior of their teenage children are the source of many other petitions. Crimes in progress bring other juveniles to the attention of the police; three-quarters of all referrals to juvenile court come directly from law enforcement authorities.[43]

Many police departments have juvenile officers who are specially trained in dealing with juveniles. Because of the emphasis on rehabilitation that characterizes the juvenile justice process, juvenile officers can usually choose from a number of discretionary alternatives in the form of special programs, especially in the handling of nonviolent offenders. In Delaware County, Pennsylvania, for example, police departments participate in "youth aid panels." These panels are composed of private citizens who volunteer their services to provide an alternative to the formal juvenile court process. Youngsters who are referred to a panel and agree to abide by the decision of the group are diverted from the juvenile court.

Real justice conferencing (RJC) is another example of a diversionary program. Started in Bethlehem, Pennsylvania, in 1995, RJC is said to be a cost-effective approach to juvenile crime, school misconduct, and violence prevention. The Bethlehem program has served as a model for programs in other cities. It makes use of family group conferences (sometimes called *community conferences*) in lieu of school disciplinary or judicial processes or as a supplement to them. The family group conference, built around a restorative justice model, allows young offenders to tell what they did, to hear from those they affected, and to help decide how to repair the harm their actions caused. Successful RJC participants avoid the more formal mechanisms of the juvenile justice process.

However, even youth who are eventually diverted from the system may spend some time in custody. One juvenile case in five involves detention before adjudication.[44] Unlike the adult system, where jail is seen as the primary custodial alternative for people awaiting a first appearance, the use of secure detention for juveniles is acceptable only as a last resort. Detention hearings investigate whether candidates for confinement represent a "clear and immediate danger to themselves and/or to others." This judgment is normally rendered within 24 hours of apprehension. Runaways, because they are

Unlike the adult system, where jail is seen as the primary custodial alternative for people awaiting a first appearance, the use of secure detention for juveniles is acceptable only as a last resort.

THE JUVENILE JUSTICE SYSTEM

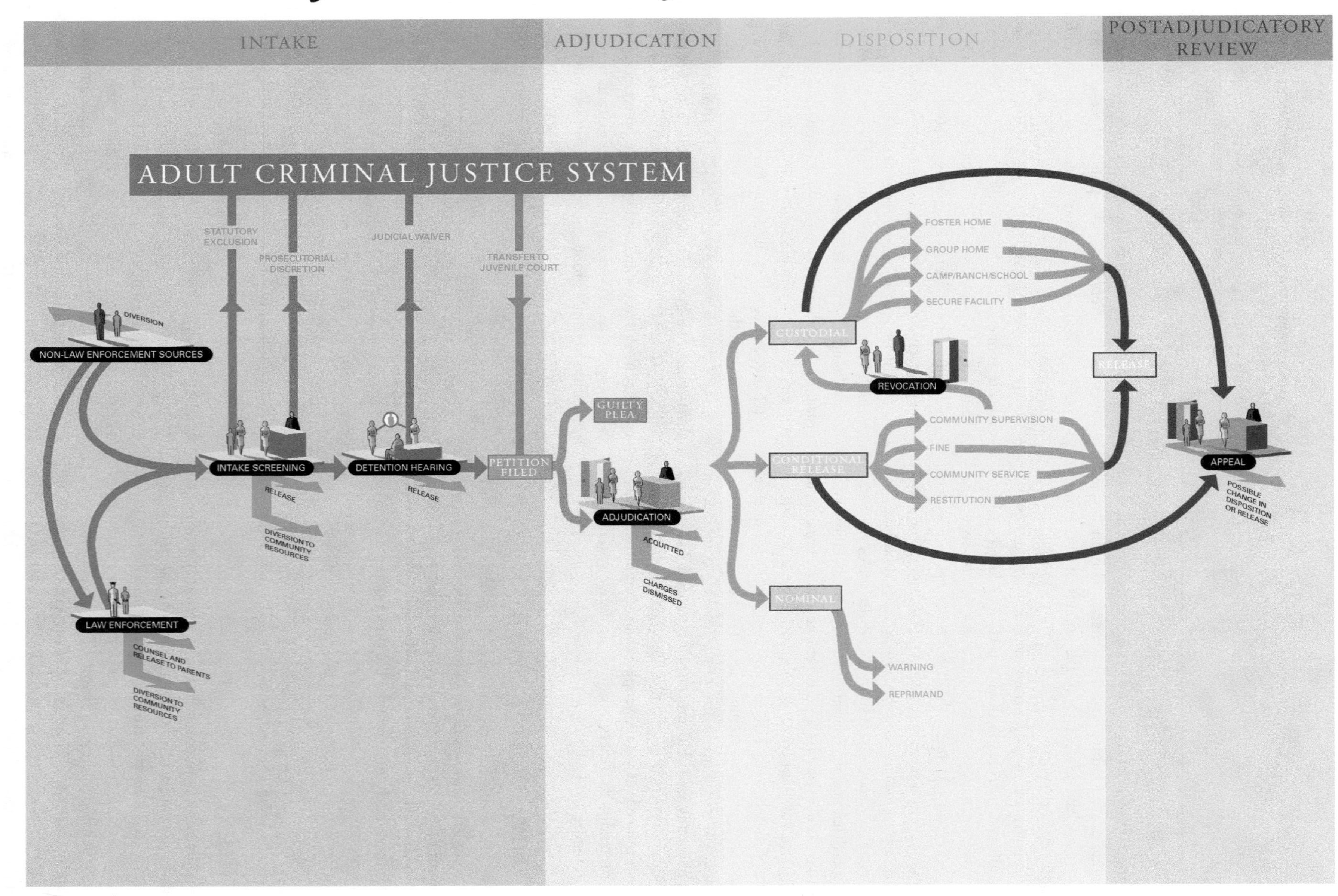

FIGURE 15-4 | The Juvenile Justice System

■ **intake** The first step in decision making regarding a juvenile whose behavior or alleged behavior is in violation of the law or could otherwise cause a juvenile court to assume jurisdiction.

often not dangerous, are especially difficult to confine. Juveniles who are not detained are generally released into the custody of their parents or guardians or into a supervised temporary shelter, such as a group home.

Detention Hearing Detention hearings are conducted by the juvenile court judge or by an officer of the court, such as a juvenile probation officer who has been given the authority to make **intake** decisions. Intake officers, like their police counterparts, have substantial discretion. Along with detention, they can choose diversion and outright dismissal of some or all of the charges against the juvenile. Diverted juveniles may be sent to job-training programs, mental health facilities, drug-treatment programs, educational counseling, or other community service agencies. When caring parents are present who can afford private counseling or therapy, intake officers may release the juvenile into their custody with the understanding that they will provide for treatment. The National Center for Juvenile Justice estimates that more than half of all juvenile cases disposed of at intake are handled informally, without a petition, and are dismissed or diverted to a social service agency.[45]

Preliminary Hearing A preliminary hearing may be held in conjunction with the detention hearing. The purpose of the preliminary hearing is to determine whether there is probable cause to believe that the juvenile committed the alleged act. At the hearing, the juvenile, along with the child's parents or guardians, will be advised of his or her rights as established by state legislation and court precedent. If probable cause is established, the juvenile may still be offered diversionary options, such as an "improvement period" or "probation with adjudication." These alternatives usually provide a one-year period during which the juvenile must avoid legal difficulties, attend school, and obey his or her parents. Charges may be dropped at the end of this informal probationary period if the juvenile has met the conditions specified.

Transfer Hearing When a serious offense is involved, statutory provisions may allow for transfer of the case to adult court at the prosecuting attorney's request. Transfer hearings are held in juvenile court and focus on (1) the applicability of transfer statutes to the case under consideration and (2) whether the juvenile is amenable to treatment through the resources available to the juvenile justice system. Exceptions exist where statutes mandate transfer (as is sometimes the case with first-degree murder).

Colleen Cahill/Design Pics Inc./Alamy

Juvenile court in action. Juvenile courts are expected to act in the best interests of the children who come before them. Should that rule apply to all juveniles who come before the court, regardless of their offense?

■ **adjudicatory hearing** The fact-finding process by which the juvenile court determines whether there is sufficient evidence to sustain the allegations in a petition.

■ **teen court** An alternative approach to juvenile justice in which alleged offenders are judged and sentenced by a jury of their peers.

■ **dispositional hearing** The final stage in the processing of adjudicated juveniles in which a decision is made on the form of treatment or penalty that should be imposed on the child.

Adjudication

Adjudicatory hearings for juveniles are similar to adult trials, with some notable exceptions. Similarities derive from the fact that the due process rights of children and adults are essentially the same. Differences include the following:

- *Emphasis on privacy.* An important distinctive characteristic of the juvenile system is its concern with privacy. Juvenile hearings are not open to the public or to the media. Witnesses are permitted to be present only to offer testimony and may not stay for the rest of the hearing. No transcript of the proceedings is created. One purpose of the emphasis on privacy is to prevent juveniles from being negatively labeled by the community.
- *Informality.* Whereas the adult criminal trial is highly structured, the juvenile hearing is more informal and less adversarial. The juvenile court judge takes an active role in the fact-finding process rather than serving as arbitrator between prosecution and defense.
- *Speed.* Informality, the lack of a jury, and the absence of an adversarial environment promote speed. Whereas the adult trial may run into weeks or even months, the juvenile hearing is normally completed in a matter of hours or days.
- *Evidentiary standard.* On completion of the hearing, the juvenile court judge must weigh the evidence. If the charge involves a status offense, the judge may adjudicate the juvenile as a status offender upon finding that a preponderance of the evidence supports this finding. A preponderance of the evidence exists when evidence of an offense is more convincing than evidence offered to the contrary. If the charge involves a criminal-type offense, the evidentiary standard rises to the level of reasonable doubt.
- *Philosophy of the court.* Even in the face of strong evidence pointing to the offender's guilt, the judge may decide that it is not in the juvenile's best interests to be adjudicated delinquent. The judge also has the power, even after the evidence is presented, to divert the juvenile from the system. Juvenile court statistics indicate that only about half of all cases disposed of by juvenile courts are processed formally.[46] Formal processing involves the filing of a petition requesting an adjudicatory or transfer hearing. Informal cases, on the other hand, are handled without a petition. Among informally handled (nonpetitioned) delinquency cases, almost half were dismissed by the court. Most of the remainder resulted in voluntary probation (33%) or other dispositions (27%), but a small number (less than 1%) involved voluntary out-of-home placements.[47] Residential treatment was ordered 27% of the time in cases where the youth was adjudicated delinquent.[48]
- *No right to trial by jury.* As referred to earlier, the U.S. Supreme Court case of *McKeiver* v. *Pennsylvania*,[49] juveniles do not have a constitutional right to trial by jury, and most states do not provide juveniles with a statutory opportunity for jury trial.[50]

Some jurisdictions, however, allow juveniles to be tried by their peers. The juvenile court in Columbus County, Georgia, for example, began experimenting with peer juries in 1980.[51] In Georgia, peer juries are composed of youths under the age of 17 who receive special training by the court. Jurors are required to be successful in school and may not be under the supervision of the court or have juvenile petitions pending against them. Training consists of classroom exposure to the philosophy of the juvenile court system, Georgia's juvenile code, and Supreme Court decisions affecting juvenile justice.[52] The county's youthful jurors are used only in the dispositional (or sentencing) stage of the court process, and then only when adjudicated youths volunteer to go before the jury.

Today, hundreds of **teen court** programs are in operation across the country. The OJJDP notes that teen courts are "an effective intervention in many jurisdictions where enforcement of misdemeanor charges is sometimes given low priority because of heavy caseloads and the need to focus on more serious offenders."[53] Teen courts, says the OJJDP, "present communities with opportunities to teach young people valuable life and coping skills and promote positive peer influence for youth who are defendants and for volunteer youth who play a variety of roles in the teen court process." Learn more about teen courts via **http://www.justicestudies.com/pubs/teencourts.pdf**.

Disposition

Once a juvenile has been found delinquent, the judge will set a **dispositional hearing**, which is similar to an adult sentencing hearing. Dispositional hearings are used to decide what action the court should take relative to the juvenile. As in adult courts, the judge may order a presentence investigation before making a dispositional decision. These investigations are conducted by special court personnel, sometimes called *juvenile court counselors*, who are, in effect, juvenile probation officers. Attorneys on both sides of the issue will also have the opportunity to make recommendations concerning dispositional alternatives.

juvenile disposition The decision of a juvenile court, concluding a dispositional hearing, that an adjudicated juvenile be committed to a juvenile correctional facility; be placed in a juvenile residence, shelter, or care or treatment program; be required to meet certain standards of conduct; or be released.

CJ | ISSUES
Juvenile Courts versus Adult Courts

The language used in juvenile courts is less harsh than that used in adult courts. For example, juvenile courts

- Accept "petitions of delinquency" rather than criminal complaints
- Conduct "hearings," not trials
- "Adjudicate" juveniles to be "delinquent" rather than find them guilty of a crime
- Order one of a number of available "dispositions" rather than sentences

© Mikael Karlsson/Alamy

A young in-custody female being led to a detention holding cell by a female deputy sheriff in Saline County, Nebraska. Although institutionalized juveniles are housed separately from adult offenders, juvenile institutions share many of the problems of adult facilities. What changes have recently occurred in the handling of juvenile offenders?

The juvenile justice system typically gives the judge a much wider range of sentencing alternatives than does the adult system. Two major classes of **juvenile disposition** exist to confine or not to confine. Because rehabilitation is still the primary objective of the juvenile court, the judge is likely to select the least restrictive alternative that meets the needs of the juvenile while recognizing the legitimate concerns of society for protection.

Most judges decide not to confine juveniles. Statistics indicate that in nearly two-thirds (60%) of all adjudicated delinquency cases, juveniles are placed on formal probation.[54] Probationary disposition usually means that juveniles will be released into the custody of a parent or guardian and ordered to undergo some form of training, education, or counseling. As in the adult system, juveniles placed on probation may be ordered to pay fines or to make restitution. In 18% of adjudicated delinquency cases, courts order juveniles to pay restitution or a fine, to participate in some form of community service, or to enter a treatment or counseling program—dispositions that require minimal continuing supervision by probation staff.[55] Because juveniles rarely have financial resources or jobs, most economic sanctions take the form of court-ordered work programs, as in refurbishing schools or cleaning school buses.

Of course, not all juveniles who are adjudicated delinquent receive probation. Nearly one-quarter (22%) of adjudicated cases in 2009 resulted in the youth being placed outside the home in a residential facility. In a relatively small number of cases (4%), the juvenile was adjudicated delinquent, but the case was then dismissed or the youth was otherwise released.[56]

Secure Institutions for Juveniles Juveniles who demonstrate the potential for serious new offenses may be ordered to participate in rehabilitative programs within a secure environment, such as a youth center or a training school. As of January 2010, approximately 70,792 young people were being held under custodial supervision in the United States.[57] Of these, 37% were being held for personal crimes like murder, rape, or robbery; 24% were being held for property crimes; 7% were locked up for drug offenses; 11% were held for public-order offenses (including weapons offenses); 16% were held for technical violations of the conditions of their release, and 4% were held for status offenses.[58]

Most confined juveniles are held in semisecure facilities designed to look less like prisons and more like residential high school campuses. Most states, however, operate at least one secure facility for juveniles that is intended as a home for the most recalcitrant youthful offenders. Halfway houses, "boot camps,"[59] ranches, forestry camps, wilderness programs, group homes, and state-hired private facilities also hold some of the juveniles reported to be under confinement. Children placed in group homes continue to attend school and live in a family-like environment in the company of other adjudicated children, shepherded by "house parents." Learn more about the juvenile justice systems of each state from the National Center for Juvenile Justice's State Juvenile Justice Profiles via **http://www.ncjj.org/Research_Resources/State_Profiles.aspx**.

The operative philosophy of custodial programs for juveniles focuses squarely on the rehabilitative ideal. Juveniles are usually committed to secure facilities for indeterminate periods of time, with the typical stay being less than one year. Release is often timed to coincide with the beginning or the end of the school year.

Most juvenile facilities are small, with 80% designed to hold 40 residents or fewer.[60] Many institutionalized juveniles are held in the thousand or so homelike facilities across the nation that are limited to ten residents or fewer.[61] At the other end of the scale are the nation's 70 large juvenile institutions, each designed to hold more than 200 hard-core delinquents.[62] Residential facilities for juveniles are intensively staffed. One study found that staff members outnumber residents ten to nine on the average in state-run institutions, and by an even greater ratio in privately run facilities.[63]

Jurisdictions vary widely in their use of secure detention for juveniles. In 2010, juvenile custody populations ranged from a low of 6 in Vermont to a high of 6,561 in California.[64] This variance reflects population differences as well as economic realities and philosophical beliefs. Some jurisdictions, like California, expect rehabilitative costs to be borne by the state rather than by families or local government agencies. Hence, California shows a higher rate of institutionalization than many other states. Similarly, some states have more firmly embraced the reformation ideal and are more likely to use diversionary options for juveniles.

Characteristics of Juveniles in Confinement Institutionalized juveniles are a small but special category of young people with serious problems. A recent report on institutionalized youth by the Bureau of Justice Statistics found five striking characteristics:[65]

- 87.8% were male.
- 41.1% were black, 34.8% were white, and 21.1% were Hispanic.
- 4% were institutionalized for having committed a status offense, such as being truant, running away, or violating curfew.
- 61% were in residential facilities for a serious personal or property offense.
- 1.3% were charged with homicide.

Overcrowding in Juvenile Facilities As in adult prisons, overcrowding exists in many juvenile institutions. In one recent government survey, 31% of facilities surveyed said that the number of residents they held put them at or over capacity.[66]

A national study of the conditions of confinement in juvenile detention facilities conducted by the OJJDP found that "there are several areas in which problems in juvenile facilities are substantial and widespread—most notably living space, health care, security, and control of suicidal behavior."[67] Using a variety of evaluative criteria, the study found that 47% of juveniles were confined in facilities whose populations exceeded their reported design capacity and that 33% of residents had to sleep "in rooms that were smaller than required by nationally recognized standards." To address the problem, the authors of the study recommended the use of alternative placement options so that only juveniles judged to be the most dangerous to their communities would be confined in secure facilities. Similarly, because it found that injuries to residents were most likely to occur within large dormitory-like settings, the OJJDP study recommended that "large dormitories be eliminated from juvenile facilities." Finally, the study recommended that "all juveniles be screened for risk of suicidal behavior immediately upon their admission to confinement" and that initial health screenings be "carried out promptly at admission." Other problems that the OJJDP found "important enough to warrant attention" included education and treatment services. Further study of both areas is needed, the OJJDP said.

Numerous states use private facilities. A survey found that 13 states contract with 328 private facilities—most of which were classified as halfway houses—for the custody of adjudicated juveniles.[68] In the past few years, admissions to private facilities (comprised primarily of halfway houses, group homes, shelters, ranches, camps, and farms) have increased by more than 100%, compared with an increase of only about 10% for public facilities (mostly detention centers and training schools).[69] The fastest-growing category of detained juveniles is drug and alcohol offenders. Approximately 7.4% of all juvenile detainees are being held because of alcohol- and drug-related offenses.[70] Reflecting widespread socioeconomic disparities, an OJJDP report found that "a juvenile held in a public facility . . . was most likely to be black, male, between 14 and 17 years of age, and held for a delinquent offense such as a property crime or a crime against a person. On the other hand, a juvenile held in custody in a private facility . . . was most likely to be white, male, 14 to 17 years of age, and held for a nondelinquent offense such as running away, truancy, or incorrigibility."[71] The report also noted that "juvenile corrections has become increasingly privatized."

Postadjudicatory Review

The detrimental effects of institutionalization on young offenders may make the opportunity for appellate review more critical for juveniles than it is for adults. However, federal court precedents have yet to establish a clear right to appeal from juvenile court. Even so, most states do have statutory provisions that make such appeals possible.[72]

CJ | NEWS
Delinquent Girls

In the 1990s, a surge of girls' arrests brought female juvenile crime to the country's attention. Girls' rates of arrest for some crimes increased faster than boys' rates of arrest. By 2004, girls accounted for 30% of all juvenile arrests, but delinquency experts did not know whether these trends reflected changes in girls' behavior or changes in arrest patterns. The juvenile justice field struggled to understand how best to respond to the needs of the girls entering the system.

Consequently, in 2004, the OJJDP convened the Girls Study Group (GSG) to establish a research-based foundation to guide the development, testing, and dissemination of strategies to reduce or prevent girls' involvement in delinquency and violence. Fiscal year 2008 saw the beginning of the OJJDP's dissemination of the GSG's findings. The study group sponsored a one-day preconference session at the March 2008 Blueprints for Violence Prevention conference in Denver, Colorado. The focus of the preconference session was to convey findings and discuss the evidence base for girls' programming and needs. In addition, GSG members presented some of the group's findings to the Coordinating Council on Juvenile Justice and Delinquency Prevention.

In June 2008, the OJJDP launched a Girls' Delinquency web page and began producing a series of bulletins that present the study group's findings on such issues as patterns of offending among adolescents and how they differ for girls and boys; risk and protective factors associated with delinquency, including gender differences; and the causes and correlates of girls' delinquency.

Finally, in 2012, the Georgetown Center on Poverty, Inequality, and Public Policy released a report on improving the juvenile justice system for girls. The report noted that the existing juvenile justice system was originally designed for delinquent boys, and doesn't adequately recognize the needs of girls. The Center also examined the challenges facing girls in the juvenile justice system and offered suggestions for gender-responsive reform at the local, state, and federal levels. In the words of the report:

> The typical girl in the system is a non-violent offender, who is very often low-risk, but high-need, meaning the girl poses little risk to the public but she enters the system with significant and pressing personal needs. The set of challenges that girls often face as they enter the juvenile justice system include trauma, violence, neglect, mental and physical problems, family conflict, pregnancy, residential and academic instability, and school failure. The juvenile justice system only exacerbates these problems by failing to provide girls with services at the time when they need them most.

The Center concluded its report with a number of policy recommendations that it hopes will be enacted at the federal level. They include:

- Conduct research on programs for girls, particularly regarding best practices in gender-responsive programming, and conditions of confinement for girls.
- Mandate a comprehensive effort by the U.S. Department of Justice to improve training and technical assistance for better recognition of the unique needs of marginalized girls among judges, law enforcement, and juvenile justice staff.
- Allocate federal funding and encourage states to apply for federal funding for gender-specific programming.
- Close the loophole that currently allows states to detain youths for technical violations of court orders—a practice that has a disproportionate impact on girls.
- Encourage the development of national standards for gender-responsive programming.
- Promote policies to keep girls out of the adult criminal justice system.

See the Girls' Delinquency page at the Office of Juvenile Justice and Delinquency Prevention at **http://www.ojjdp.gov/programs/girlsdelinquency.html**.

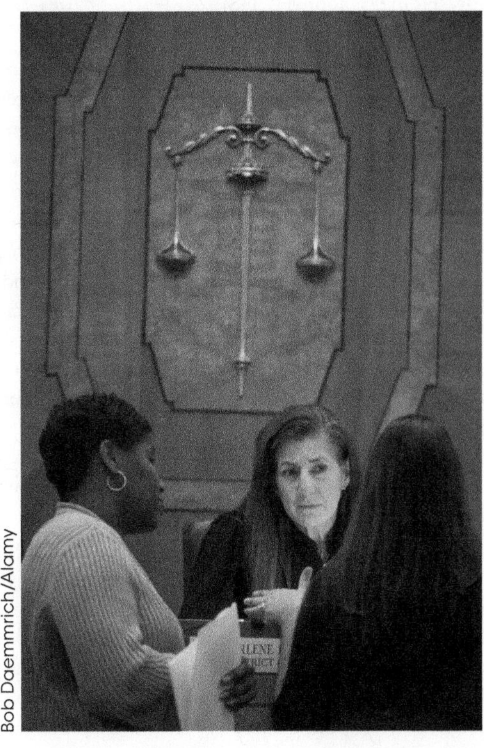

Bob Daemmrich/Alamy

A female delinquent appears before a judge in juvenile court. How does the delinquency of girls differ from that of boys?

Note: Detailed information about the GSG can be found at the Girls Study Group website at http://www.girlsstudygroup.rti.org.

Sources: *Girls Study Group: Understanding and Responding to Girls' Delinquency* (Washington, DC: OJJDP, 2010); and Liz Watson and Peter Edelman, *Improving the Juvenile Justice System for Girls: Lessons from the States* (Washington, DC: Georgetown Center on Poverty, Inequality and Public Policy, October 2012).

From a practical point of view, however, juvenile appeals may not be as consequential as are appeals of adult criminal convictions. Most juvenile complaints are handled informally, and only relatively low numbers of adjudicated delinquents are placed outside the family. Moreover, because sentence lengths are short for most confined juveniles, appellate courts hardly have time to complete the review process before the juvenile is released.

> Most juvenile complaints are handled informally, and only relatively low numbers of adjudicated delinquents are placed outside the family.

CAREER | PROFILE

Juvenile Justice Professional

Name. Fred Bryan

Position. Director, Juvenile Service Division, Hennepin County Department of Community Corrections and Rehabilitation

Colleges attended. University of Northern Iowa (BA)

Majors. Social Work; Corrections minor

Year hired. 1984–1990 Juvenile Correctional Officer, 1990–1991 Juvenile Corrections Supervisor, 1991–1997 Juvenile Probation (JP) Officer, 1997–2002 JP Unit Supervisor, 2002–2006 JP Administrative Manager, 2006–2007 (Acting) Superintendent Juvenile Detention Center, 2007–2009 Assistant Superintendent Hennepin County Home School, 2009–2012 Superintendent Hennepin County Home School (HCHS), 2012–present Area Director Juvenile Services

Please give a brief description of your job. As the Area Director of Juvenile Services, I am responsible for oversight of our three juvenile services areas—our Juvenile Probation Department, our Juvenile Detention Center, and our juvenile residential treatment center (Hennepin County Home School)

What appealed to you most about the position when you applied for it? In Hennepin County we have committed ourselves to providing juvenile services that are evidenced-based practices and to making decisions regarding program changes based on data collected internally and from other jurisdictions. Thus, I was at a point in my career where I wanted to be in a position that afforded me the opportunity to make policy decisions involving the implementation of evidenced-based programs that have system-wide impacts. By being in this position, I am able to work with system stakeholders and partners to implement program changes that affect how we deal with youth on a county-wide level.

How would you describe the interview process? Interviewing for a job at this level requires knowledge of not only the intricacies of the specific areas in juvenile services that are reporting to me, but also required knowledge and understanding of how juvenile services fit into the larger picture of our department as well as the structure of the county as a whole. During the interview process, I had to articulate how I would be able to work with system partners and stakeholders such as the County Board and Administration, the Juvenile Court, the Human Services Department, and community stakeholders in such a manner that addressed the needs of youth while being able to foresee how a decision in the juvenile services area may impact another aspect of our department or the community at large.

What is a typical day like? A typical day for me may require that I spend time in each area of juvenile services addressing such needs as programming, budget, staffing, or disciplinary issues. Each area has a manager who is responsible for the day-to-day operations, and these managers and I work closely together to ensure each area has the resources and support needed to continue to provide effective evidenced-based practices for youth. I am also part of our department's administrative team, which requires me to work with our other Area Directors and Department Directors to address department-wide issues. Additionally, on any given day I may be working with our juvenile judges, County Administration, the Human Services Department, or community-based organizations.

What qualities/characteristics are most helpful for this job? The ability to work with a broad range of professionals who all may have their own agenda is essential. Political acumen is also a highly useful skill, as often the decisions made or not made have impact on other areas within the broader system or may be in conflict with the status quo. This job also requires the ability to assimilate a broad range of information and apply what is relevant.

What is a typical starting salary? The salary range is $95,000–$131,000 per year.

What is the salary potential as you move up into higher-level jobs? The highest step in our department would be the Department Director, which has a salary range of $117,000–$176,000 per year.

What career advice would you give someone in college beginning studies in criminal justice? My advice would be to focus on what the research is saying in regard to the relevant and effective current practices in criminal justice. For example, in the juvenile justice field the research tells us that only the high-risk juveniles should be removed from the community and placed out of their homes—that low- to moderate-risk youth are better served with a community-based approach and that to remove these youth from their homes and communities unnecessarily will in fact make them worse. Additionally, spend time researching or volunteering in different areas within the criminal justice field that interest you. You will acquire a broader perspective, which will aid you in determining an eventual career path.

The Post-Juvenile Court Era

In the late twentieth century, and extending into the early years of the twenty-first, cases of serious juvenile offending, like that of Alyssa Bustamante, with which this chapter opened, combined with extensive media coverage of violent juvenile crime across the United States to fuel public misperceptions that violence committed by teenagers had reached epidemic proportions and that no community was immune to random acts of youth violence. At the same time, the apparent "professionalization" of delinquency, the hallmark of which is the repeated and often violent criminal involvement of juveniles in drug-related gang activity, came to be viewed as a major challenge to the idealism of the juvenile justice system. Consequently, by the turn of the twenty-first century, the issue of youth violence was at or near the top of nearly every state's agenda. Most states took some form of legislative or executive action to stem what was seen as an escalating level of dangerous crime by juveniles. As the OJJDP observed, "This level of [legislative and executive] activity has occurred only three other times in our nation's history: at the outset of the juvenile court

■ **blended sentence** A juvenile court disposition that imposes both a juvenile sanction and an adult criminal sentence upon an adjudicated delinquent. The adult sentence is suspended if the juvenile offender successfully completes the term of the juvenile disposition and refrains from committing any new offense.[i]

movement at the turn of the [twentieth] century; following the U.S. Supreme Court's *Gault* decision in 1967; and with the enactment of the Juvenile Justice and Delinquency Prevention Act in 1974."[73] The OJJDP identified five significant developments that took place in many states between 1990 and 2005:[74]

1. *Transfer provisions.* New transfer provisions made it easier to move juvenile offenders from the juvenile justice system to the criminal justice system.
2. *Sentencing authority.* New laws on sentencing gave criminal and juvenile courts the authority to use expanded sentencing options such as the **blended sentence** (the combination of a juvenile disposition followed by a suspended adult sentence if the former is carried out successfully) in cases involving juveniles.
3. *Confidentiality changes.* Modifications were made to laws containing court confidentiality provisions in order to make juvenile records and proceedings more open.
4. *Victims' rights.* Laws were passed that increased the role of victims of juvenile crime in the juvenile justice process.
5. *Correctional programming.* New correctional programs in adult and juvenile facilities were developed to handle juveniles sentenced as adults or as violent juvenile offenders.

Changes like these prompted juvenile justice experts Jeffrey Butts and Ojmarrh Mitchell, members of the Program on Law and Behavior at the Urban Institute in Washington, D.C., to say that "policymakers throughout the United States have greatly dissolved the border between juvenile and criminal justice."[75] As evidence, they noted that juvenile courts across the United States are becoming increasingly similar to criminal courts in the methods they use to reach conclusions and to process cases, as well as in the general atmosphere that characterizes them.

Following these changes, some claimed that many states had substantially "criminalized" juvenile courts. In March 2000, for example, California voters endorsed sweeping changes in the state's juvenile justice system by passing Proposition 21, the Gang Violence and Juvenile Crime Prevention Act. The law reduced confidentiality in the juvenile court, limited the use of probation for young offenders, and increased the power of prosecutors to send juveniles to adult court and to put them in adult prisons. Public support for the measure was undiminished by projections that it would increase operational costs in the California juvenile justice system by $500 million annually.[76] Because of laws like California's Proposition 21, a leading expert on juvenile justice noted that "the similarities of juvenile and adult courts are becoming greater than the differences between them."[77]

Because of laws like California's Proposition 21, leading experts on juvenile justice note that the similarities of juvenile and adult courts are becoming greater than the differences between them.

Cindy Lederman, presiding judge of the Miami-Dade Juvenile Court, referred to such changes as the "adultification" of the juvenile justice system.[78] The juvenile court, said Lederman, has undergone significant change since it was created. In the early twentieth century, the juvenile court focused on social welfare and was primarily concerned with acting in a child's best interest. By the mid-twentieth century, it had seized on the issue of children's due process rights as an important guiding principle. By the start of the twenty-first century, said Lederman, it had turned its focus to accountability and punishment.

At the federal level, the Department of Justice Authorization Act for Fiscal Year 2003[79] set dramatic new accountability standards for federally funded programs for juveniles who violate the law.[80] The law built on the premise that young people who violate criminal laws should be held accountable for their offenses through the swift and consistent application of sanctions that are proportionate to the offense.[81] Lawmakers made it clear that it was their belief that enhanced accountability and swift sanctions were both a matter of basic justice and a way to combat delinquency and improve the quality of life in our nation's communities.

It now seems, however, that in recent years the pendulum has begun to swing back toward the original principles of the juvenile court. In an age of shrinking state budgets and lack of faith in the ability of residential placement to accomplish reformation, a number of states are moving to reestablish such principles. In 2011, for example, Texas—a state normally known for its conservative approach to criminal and juvenile justice—enacted legislation consolidating the former Texas Youth Commission with the Texas Juvenile Probation Commission into one agency: the Texas Juvenile Justice Department.[82] The legislation tasks the newly created Texas Juvenile Justice Department with evaluating the effectiveness of county and state programs and services for youth, and with developing outcome measures appropriate to such an evaluation. The department was also directed to make full use of community-based programs as alternatives to residential placement. The Texas legislature closed 3 of 10 youth prisons in the states, and shifted a substantial amount of state money to local rehabilitation programs. One important feature of the new approach in Texas is the funding of county probation departments throughout Texas to provide mental health services for juvenile offenders kept in the community.[83] Similarly, in 2007, the Rhode Island General Assembly reversed the governor's recommendation to decrease the age of juvenile jurisdiction from 18 to 17, and restored the age of juvenile jurisdiction to 18; and that same year, Connecticut raised the age of juvenile court jurisdiction from 16 to 18.[84] In 2010, Virginia allowed juveniles transferred to or charged in criminal courts to remain in juvenile, rather than adult, detention facilities.[85]

By 2012 the National Conference on State Legislatures was able to note that research distinguishing adolescents from adults is contributing to an important and growing trend among states to re-establish boundaries between the adult and juvenile justice systems. One of the more prominent shifts in juvenile justice policy, said the Conference, has been the focus on juveniles' developmental needs.[86] In keeping with that focus, a recent report by the National Academy of Sciences (NAS) found that "adolescents differ from adults and children in three important ways that contribute to differences in behavior."[87] NAS researchers found that, because of significant differences in developing adolescent brains, young people (1) have less capacity for self-regulation in emotionally charged contexts; (2) have a heightened sensitivity to proximal external influences, such as peer pressure and immediate incentives; and (3) show less ability than adults to make judgments and decisions that require future orientation. According to the NAS report, "the combination of these three cognitive patterns accounts for the tendency of adolescents to prefer and engage in risky behaviors that have a high probability of immediate reward but can have harmful consequences."[88]

In 2013, as further evidence of a move away from severe punishments for juveniles, the Washington, D.C.–based Justice Policy Institute (JPI) reported findings from five states that showed a significant move away from the use of juvenile confinement.[89] Those states, Connecticut, Tennessee, Louisiana, Minnesota, and Arizona, achieved a greater than 50% drop in juvenile residential placement populations between the years 2001 and 2010.[90] The experience in the states studied was similar to that of the nation as a whole, where juvenile incarceration rates declined from 335 per 100,000 in 2001 to 225 by 2010.[91] For all states and the District of Columbia, the number of youth in residential placement dropped steadily from its high of 107,493 in 1999 to 70,792 in 2010 (Figure 15-5).[92] Declines in residential populations were mostly the result of decreases in confinement for property offenses, and a move away from holding youth for drug offenses. In the states studied, the JPI found that "state leaders recommitted their systems to a holistic juvenile justice ideal that acknowledges that youthful behavior is inherently different than adult behavior and that it requires different interventions and services."[93]

Proposals for further change abound. In 2011, New York's John Jay College of Criminal Justice released a comprehensive study of strategies for changing the juvenile justice system.[94] The study's authors noted that "Placing youth in large, group confinement facilities does not seem to be justified from the perspective of treatment effectiveness or the prevention of future recidivism." According to the study, recent models for reform adopted by a number of states can be categorized into three groups according to the kinds of influences that have led to their development. The three models are: (1) *resolution strategies* (involving direct managerial changes brought about by the efforts of administrators, policymakers, and elected officials), (2) *reinvestment strategies* (the use of financial incentives to encourage state and local governments to reduce spending on confinement and to invest in community-based programs), and (3) *realignment strategies* (permanent organizational and structural modifications intended to alter the juvenile justice system, including the closing of facilities and the elimination of agencies). The study found that "reform strategies in juvenile justice are sustainable when they cannot be easily reversed by future policymakers facing different budgetary conditions and changing political environments." Consequently, the study authors noted that realignment strategies may be the best choice for sustaining reform over the long term. Access the John Jay report at **http://tinyurl.com/6bpx98x**.

Finally, in 2012, the state of California moved to complete a strategy of juvenile justice "realignment." Under the strategy, the state's counties will assume full responsibility for managing all of the state's juvenile offenders. Even before the implementation of the realignment strategy, California law allowed only juveniles who had been adjudicated for a serious, violent, or sex offense to be sent to state facilities. Consequently, 99% of the state's juvenile offenders were housed or supervised in county-run facilities by the middle of 2012.[95] To finalize the realignment strategy, California Governor Jerry Brown announced that he would stop new admissions to the state's Division of Juvenile Justice (DJJ) facilities

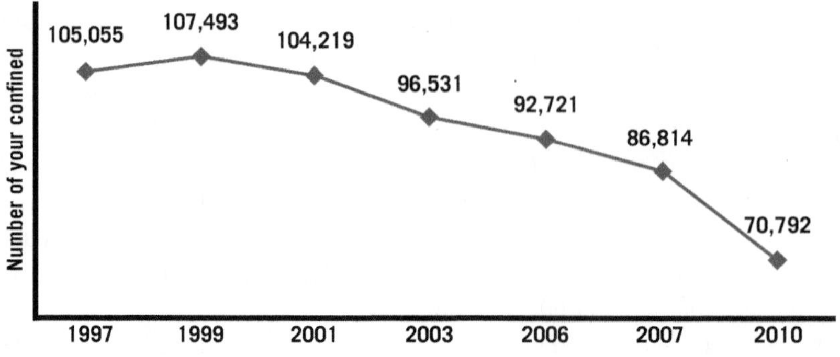

FIGURE 15-5 | Number of Youth Held in Secure Confinement in the United States, 1997–2010

Source: Office of Juvenile Justice and Delinquency Prevention, "Easy Access to the Census of Juveniles in Residential Placement," http://www.ojjdp.gov/ojstatbb/ezacjrp.

as of January 1, 2013. Governor Brown offered to provide counties with the funding needed to manage juvenile offenders at the local level. The realignment strategy was proposed as an effort to offer correctional intervention "at the point where the offender is most likely to return."[96] Even so, the strategy was largely based on economic necessity. As a report by the California-based Center on Juvenile and Criminal Justice noted, "the state of California can no longer afford to operate a dual juvenile justice system."[97]

Today, evidence-based practices in the juvenile justice arena (see the CJ Issues box in this chapter) are helping to establish a set of best-practice guidelines, providing state policymakers and juvenile justice administrators insight into what works best to control juvenile crime and to rehabilitate youthful offenders. In 2010, for example, the National Center for Youth in Custody (NC4YC) was launched by the Office of Juvenile Justice and Delinquency Prevention (OJJDP) to support, improve, and reform youth detention and correction facilities and adult facilities housing youthful offenders. The objectives of NC4YC are to advance the field of juvenile justice by providing training and technical assistance and by disseminating effective practices and approaches to the justice community. The center will strive to serve the range of facilities in which juveniles are placed, including adult facilities that confine juvenile offenders. The center emphasizes the rehabilitative goals of the juvenile justice system and has four central objectives:

- To deliver strategic, targeted, and measurable training and technical assistance directly to facilities that detain or confine youth.
- To identify, document, and promote effective, evidence-based approaches to working with youth in custody.
- To expand the knowledge base and research on juvenile justice and best practices in detaining and confining youth.
- To create a resource community for juvenile justice practitioners, youth in custody, and families.

Necessitated by budgetary concerns at both the state and federal level, the tide is now shifting to evidence-based models that demonstrate effectiveness in the handling of juvenile offenders. Consequently, the flood of recent federal and state legislation, mandated by surging public demand for greater responsibility among adolescents, has come up against recent implementation of the evidence-based cost-saving model. As a result, the juvenile justice system of the mid-twenty-first century may in many respects be quite different than the one we have known.

CJ | ISSUES

Evidence-Based Juvenile Justice

Evidence-based research permits the identification of effective strategies through the evaluation and analysis of ongoing programs. In 2012, the Committee on Assessing Juvenile Justice Reform of the National Academies of Sciences released a report on reforming juvenile justice.[1] The Committee found that "a harsh system of punishing troubled youth can make things worse, while a scientifically based juvenile justice system can make an enduring difference in the lives of many youth who most need the structure and services it can provide." The Committee recommended that the goals, design, and operation of the juvenile justice system "should be informed by the growing body of knowledge about adolescent development. If designed and implemented in a developmentally informed way," the Committee said, "procedures for holding adolescents accountable for their offending, and the services provided to them, can promote positive legal socialization, reinforce a prosocial identity, and reduce reoffending." The Committee warned, however, that "if the goals, design, and operation of the juvenile justice system are not informed by this growing body of knowledge, the outcome is likely to be negative interactions between youth and justice system officials, increased disrespect for the law and legal authority, and the reinforcement of a deviant identity and social disaffection."

Two of today's best-known evidence-based initiatives in the area of juvenile justice are (1) the Blueprints for Violence Prevention program developed by the Center for the Study and Prevention of Violence (CSPV) at the University of Colorado–Boulder, and (2) the OJJDP's Model Programs Guide (MPG). The Blueprints study, one of the earliest research efforts to focus on evidence-based delinquency programs, began as an effort to identify model violence-prevention initiatives and implement them within the state of Colorado.[2] The OJJDP soon became an active supporter of the Blueprints project and provided additional funding to the CSPV to sponsor and evaluate program replications in sites across the United States. As a result, Blueprints has evolved into a large-scale prevention initiative, both identifying model programs and providing technical support to help sites choose and implement those programs that have been proven to be effective. After reviewing more than 600 programs to date, the Blueprints study has identified 11 model programs and 21 promising programs that prevent violence and drug use and treat youth with problem behaviors.[3]

The MPG, also developed with support from the OJJDP, is intended to assist communities in implementing evidence-based prevention and intervention programs that can make a difference in the lives of children.[4] The MPG database consists of over 200 evidence-based programs that cover the continuum of youth services, from prevention through sanctions to reentry. It is used by juvenile justice practitioners, administrators, and researchers to initiate programs that have already proven their ability to enhance accountability, ensure public safety, and reduce recidivism. The OJJDP offers the MPG in the form of an easy-to-use online database that address a range of issues, including substance abuse, mental health, and education programs. The MPG database contains summary information on many evidence-based delinquency programs. Programs are categorized into exemplary, effective, and promising, based on an established set of methodological criteria and the strength of the findings. The MPG database can be queried through an online search tool at http://www.ojjdp.gov/mpg/search.aspx.

[1]National Research Council, *Reforming Juvenile Justice: A Developmental Approach*, Committee on Assessing Juvenile Justice Reform, Richard J. Bonnie, Robert L. Johnson, Betty M. Chemers, and Julie A. Schuck, eds. Committee on Law and Justice, Division of Behavioral and Social Sciences and Education (Washington, DC: The National Academies Press, 2012).

[2]Sharon Mihalic, Abigail Fagan, Katherine Irwin, Diane Ballard, and Delbert Elliott, *Blueprints for Violence Prevention* (Washington, DC: OJJDP, July 2004).

[3]Ibid.

[4]OJJDP, "OJJDP Model Programs Guide," http://www.ojjdp.gov/mpg/Default.aspx (accessed March 10, 2013).

SUMMARY

- Under today's laws, children occupy a special status that is tied closely to cultural advances that occurred in the Western world during the past 200 years. Before the modern era, children who committed crimes received no preferential treatment. They were adjudicated, punished, and imprisoned alongside adults. Beginning a few hundred years ago, England, from which we derive many of our legal traditions, adapted the principle of *parens patriae*. That principle allowed the government to take the place of parents in dealing with children who broke the law. Around the middle of the nineteenth century, the child-savers movement began in the United States. Child savers espoused a philosophy of productivity and eschewed idleness and unprincipled behavior. Not long afterward, the 1899 codification of Illinois juvenile law became the model for juvenile court statutes throughout the United States. It created a juvenile court separate in form and function from adult criminal courts and based on the principle of *parens patriae*. To avoid the lasting stigma of criminality, the term *delinquent*, rather than *criminal*, began to be applied to young adjudicated offenders. Soon, juvenile courts across the country focused primarily on the best interests of the child as a guide in their deliberations.
- Important U.S. Supreme Court decisions of special relevance to the handling of juveniles by the justice system include (1) *Kent* v. *U.S.* (1966), which established minimal due process standards for juvenile hearings; (2) *In re Gault* (1967), in which the Court found that a child has many of the same due process rights as an adult; (3) *In re Winship* (1970), which held that the constitutional safeguard of proof beyond a reasonable doubt is required during the adjudicatory stage of a delinquency proceeding; (4) *McKeiver* v. *Pennsylvania* (1971), which held that jury trials were not required in delinquency cases; (5) *Breed* v. *Jones* (1975), which restricted the conditions under which transfers from juvenile to adult court may occur; (6) *Schall* v. *Martin* (1984), in which the Court held that pretrial detention of juveniles based on "serious risk" does not violate due process, although prior notice, an equitable detention hearing, and a statement by the juvenile court judge explaining the reasons for detention are required; (7) *Roper* v. *Simmons* (2005), which held that age *is* a bar to capital punishment when the offender commits a capital crime when he or she is younger than 18; (8) *Graham* v. *Florida* (2010), in which the Court found that the Constitution does not permit a juvenile offender to be sentenced to life in prison without parole for a nonhomicide crime; and (9) *Miller* v. *Alabama* (2012), in which the Court held that *mandatory* life-without-parole sentences for individuals 17 or younger convicted of homicide violate the Eighth Amendment.
- Due process guarantees, as interpreted by the U.S. Supreme Court, are designed to ensure that juvenile proceedings are fair and that the interests of juveniles are protected. Although the Court has established that juveniles are entitled to fundamental due process protections, it has refrained from declaring that juveniles have a right to all aspects of due process afforded adult defendants. The juvenile justice system differs in other ways from the adult system. For example, the juvenile system (1) is less concerned with legal issues of guilt or innocence and focuses on the child's best interests; (2) emphasizes treatment rather than punishment; (3) ensures privacy and protection from public scrutiny through the use of sealed records and laws against publishing the names of juvenile offenders; (4) uses the techniques of social science in dispositional decision making rather than sentences determined by a perceived need for punishment; (5) does not order long-term confinement, with most juveniles being released from institutions by their 21st birthday; (6) has separate facilities for juveniles; and (7) allows broad discretionary alternatives at all points in the process.
- The "professionalization" of delinquency, the hallmark of which is the repeated and often violent criminal involvement of juveniles in drug-related gang activity, presented a major challenge to the idealism of the juvenile justice system in the latter part of the twentieth century. Consequently, the juvenile justice system's commitment to a philosophy of protection and restoration, expressed in the juvenile court movement of the late nineteenth and early twentieth centuries began to dissipate. However, necessitated by budgetary concerns at both the state and federal level, the tide is now shifting to evidence-based models that demonstrate effectiveness in the handling of juvenile offenders. The present juvenile justice system, for the most part, continues to differ substantially from the adult system in the multitude of opportunities it provides for diversion and in the emphasis it places on rehabilitation rather than punishment.

KEY TERMS

abused child, 500
adjudicatory hearing, 510
blended sentence, 515
delinquency, 498
delinquent child, 500
dependent child, 500
dispositional hearing, 510
intake, 509
juvenile disposition, 511
juvenile justice system, 498
juvenile petition, 507
neglected child, 500
***parens patriae*, 498**
status offender, 500
status offense, 501
teen court, 510
undisciplined child, 500

KEY CASES

***Breed* v. *Jones*, 503**
***Graham* v. *Florida*, 503**
***In re Gault*, 502**
***In re Winship*, 502**
***Kent* v. *U.S.*, 518**
***McKeiver* v. *Pennsylvania*, 503**
***Miller* v. *Alabama*, 503**
***Roper* v. *Simmons*, 503**
***Schall* v. *Martin*, 503**

QUESTIONS FOR REVIEW

1. Describe the history and evolution of the juvenile justice system in the Western world, and list the six categories of children recognized by the laws of most states.
2. What was the impact of the *Gault* decision on juvenile justice in America? What adult rights were not accorded to juveniles by *Gault*? What other U.S. Supreme Court decisions have had a substantial impact on the handling of juvenile offenders by the justice system?
3. What are the major similarities and differences between the juvenile and adult justice systems?
4. In your opinion, should juveniles continue to receive what many regard as preferential treatment from the courts? Why or why not?

QUESTIONS FOR REFLECTION

1. This chapter pointed out that substantial changes are now afoot in the area of juvenile justice. What are some of those changes? With which of those changes do you agree? Are there any with which you don't agree? Explain.
2. This chapter discussed California's Proposition 21, which voters in that state passed in 2000. What was the intent of Proposition 21? Were the changes that it brought about needed, or do you think that the state would have been better off if the proposition had failed to pass? Why?
3. What is meant by the "adultification" of the juvenile justice system? Is adultification a good idea? Explain.

NOTES

i. Howard N. Snyder and Melissa Sickmund, *Juvenile Offenders and Victims: 2006 National Report* (Washington, DC: Office of Juvenile Justice and Delinquency Prevention, 2006).

1. President's Commission on Law Enforcement and Administration of Justice, *The Challenge of Crime in A Free Society* (Washington, DC: 1967, USGPO), p. 58.
2. "MO. Teen Gets Life with Possible Parole in Killing," *USA Today*, February 7, 2012, http://www.usatoday.com/news/nation/story/2012-02-07/teen-killer-missouri/53004116/1 (accessed April 4, 2012).
3. Michael Winter, "Mo. Teen's Journal Says Killing Girl was 'Pretty Enjoyable,'" *USA Today*, February 6, 2012, http://content.usatoday.com/communities/ondeadline/post/2012/02/in-journal-mo-teen-says-killing-girl-was-pretty-exciting/1#.T3zRir9YuKJ (accessed May 20, 2012).
4. Office of Juvenile Justice and Delinquency Prevention, *OJJDP Research, 2000* (Washington, DC: OJJDP, 2001).
5. Federal Bureau of Investigation, *Crime in the United States, 2012* (Washington, DC: U.S. Dept. of Justice, 2013).
6. Ibid.; and U.S. Census Bureau, *Age, 2000: A Census 2000 Brief* (Washington, DC: U.S. Census Bureau, 2001), http://www.census.gov/prod/2001pubs/c2kbr01-12.pdf (accessed January 2, 2011).
7. The term *juvenile* refers to people younger than 18 years of age.
8. H. Snyder, C. Puzzanchera, and W. Kang, *Easy Access to FBI Arrest Statistics, 1994–2002* (Washington, DC: Office of Juvenile Justice and Delinquency Prevention, 2005), http://ojjdp.ncjrs.org/ojstatbb/ezaucr (accessed November 11, 2012); Andrea J. Sedlak and Carol Bruce, *Youth's Characteristics and Backgrounds: Findings from the Survey of Youth in Residential Placement* (Washington, DC: OJJDP, 2010); and C. L. Bright, et al., "Young Adult Outcomes of Girls Involved in the Juvenile Justice System: Distinct Patterns of Risk and Protection," *Corrections and Mental Health*, Vol. 1, No. 3 (2013).
9. Edward P. Mulvey, *Highlights from Pathways to Desistance: A Longitudinal Study of Serious Adolescent Offenders* (Washington, DC: OJJDP).
10. A reform movement, now under way, may soon lead to changes in the way juvenile records are handled.
11. For an excellent review of the handling of juveniles throughout history, see Wiley B. Sanders, ed., *Juvenile Offenders for a Thousand Years* (Chapel Hill: University of North Carolina Press, 1970).
12. See Sanford Fox, "Juvenile Justice Reform: An Historical Perspective," in Sanford Fox, ed., *Modern Juvenile Justice: Cases and Materials* (St. Paul, MN: West, 1972), pp. 15–48.
13. Johnson, *Introduction to the Juvenile Justice System*, p. 3.
14. Ibid.
15. Ibid.
16. Fox, "Juvenile Justice Reform," p. 47.
17. Ibid., p. 5.
18. Principles adapted from Robert G. Caldwell, "The Juvenile Court: Its Development and Some Major Problems," in Rose Giallombardo, ed., *Juvenile Delinquency: A Book of Readings* (New York: John Wiley, 1966), p. 358.
19. See, for example, *Haley* v. *Ohio*, 332 U.S. 596 (1948).
20. *In re Gault*, 387 U.S. 1 (1967).
21. *In re Winship*, 397 U.S. 358 (1970).
22. *McKeiver* v. *Pennsylvania*, 403 U.S. 528 (1971).
23. *Schall* v. *Martin*, 467 U.S. 253 (1984).
24. *Thompson* v. *Oklahoma*, 487 U.S. 815, 818–838 (1988).
25. *Roper* v. *Simmons*, 543 U.S. 551 (2005).
26. Death Penalty Information Center, "Juvenile Offenders Currently on Death Row, or Executed, by State," http://www.deathpenaltyinfo.org/article.php?scid527&did5882 (accessed September 10, 2011).
27. *Graham* v. *Florida*, No. 08–7412. Decided May 17, 2010.
28. "Drug Bill Includes Extension of OJJDP, with Many Changes," *Criminal Justice Newsletter*, Vol. 19, No. 22 (November 15, 1988), p. 4.
29. The Formula Grants Program supports state and local delinquency prevention and intervention efforts and juvenile justice system improvements. Through this program, the OJJDP provides funds directly to states, territories, and the District of Columbia to help them implement comprehensive state juvenile justice plans based on detailed studies of needs in their jurisdictions. The Formula Grants Program is authorized under the JJDP Act of 2002 (U.S. Code, Title 42, Section 5601, *et seq.*).
30. See "OJJDP Eases Rules on Juvenile Confinement," *Corrections Compendium* (November 1996), p. 25.
31. The Juvenile Justice and Delinquency Prevention Act of 2002 (Public Law 107-273).
32. Howard N. Snyder and Melissa Sickmund, *Juvenile Offenders and Victims: 2006 National Report* (Washington, DC: Office of Juvenile Justice and Delinquency Prevention, 2006).

33. Ibid., p. 97.
34. See, for example, *United States* v. *Williams,* U.S. Supreme Court, 2008 (No. 06-694), which upheld the law's provision criminalizing the possession and distribution of material pandered as child pornography; and U.S. Department of State, *Trafficking in Persons Report* (Washington, DC: U.S. Department of State, June 2007), p. 72.
35. *Fare* v. *Michael C.*, 442 U.S. 707 (1979).
36. *California* v. *Prysock*, 453 U.S. 355 (1981).
37. *New Jersey* v. *T.L.O.*, 105 S.Ct. 733 (1985).
38. *J.D.B.* v. *North Carolina,* U.S. Supreme Court, No. 09-11121 (decided June 16, 2011).
39. Office of Juvenile Justice and Delinquency Prevention, "Juvenile Court Cases," *Statistical Briefing Book*, http://ojjdp.ncjrs.gov/ojstatbb/court/qa06201.asp (accessed August 12, 2013).
40. National Center for Juvenile Justice, "State Juvenile Justice Profiles," http://www.ncjj.org/stateprofiles (accessed August 10, 2011).
41. Charles M. Puzzanchera, *Delinquency Cases Waived to Criminal Court, 1990–1999* (Washington, DC: Office of Juvenile Justice and Delinquency Prevention, 2003).
42. Adapted from Peter Greenwood, *Juvenile Offenders*, National Institute of Justice Crime File Series Study Guide (Washington, DC: NIJ, n.d.).
43. Bureau of Justice Statistics, *Report to the Nation on Crime and Justice*, 2nd ed. (Washington, DC: U.S. Government Printing Office, 1988), p. 78.
44. Ibid.
45. Ibid.
46. Charles Puzzanchera et al., *Juvenile Court Statistics, 2009* (Pittsburgh, PA: National Center for Juvenile Justice, 2012).
47. Ibid.
48. Ibid., p.
49. *McKeiver* v. *Pennsylvania*, 403 U.S. 528 (1971).
50. Some states, such as West Virginia, do provide juveniles with a statutory right to trial.
51. Other early peer juries in juvenile courts began operating in Denver, Colorado; Duluth, Minnesota; Deerfield, Illinois; Thompkins County, New York; and Spanish Fork City, Utah, at about the same time. See Philip Reichel and Carole Seyfrit, "A Peer Jury in the Juvenile Court," *Crime and Delinquency*, Vol. 30, No. 3 (July 1984), pp. 423–438.
52. Ibid.
53. Tracy M. Godwin, *A Guide for Implementing Teen Court Programs* (Washington, DC: Office of Juvenile Justice and Delinquency Prevention, 1996).
54. Sarah Livsey, *Juvenile Delinquency Probation Caseload, 2005* (Washington, DC: Office of Juvenile Justice and Delinquency Prevention, 2009), p. 1.
55. Livsey, *Juvenile Delinquency Probation Caseload*, 2005, p. 1.
56. Benjamin Adams and Sean Addie, *Delinquency Cases Waived to Criminal Court, 2009*, p. 1.
57. Office of Juvenile Justice and Delinquency Prevention, "Easy Access to the Census of Juveniles in Residential Placement," http://www.ojjdp.gov/ojstatbb/ezacjrp (accessed August 12, 2013).
58. Melissa Sickmund, T. J. Sladky, Wei Kang, and C. Puzzanchera, "Easy Access to the Census of Juveniles in Residential Placement," 2010, http://ojjdp.ncjrs.gov/ojstatbb/ezacjrp (accessed June 6, 2013).
59. See, for example, Blair B. Bourque et al., *Boot Camps for Juvenile Offenders: An Implementation Evaluation of Three Demonstration Programs*, National Institute of Justice Research in Brief (Washington, DC: NIJ, 1996).
60. Sarah Hockenberry, *Juvenile in Residential Placement, 2010* (Washington, DC: Office of Juvenile Justice and Delinquency Prevention, 2013).
61. Ibid.
62. Ibid.
63. Ibid.
64. M. Sickmund, T. J. Sladky, W. Kang, and C. Puzzanchera, "Easy Access to the Census of Juveniles in Residential Placement," 2011, http://www.ojjdp.gov/ojstatbb/ezacjrp/
65. Ibid.
66. Sarah Hockenberry, Melissa Sickmund, and Anthony Sladky, *Juvenile Residential Facility Census, 2006* (Washington, DC: OJJDP, 2009).
67. Dale G. Parent et al., *Conditions of Confinement: Juvenile Detention and Corrections Facilities* (Washington, DC: Office of Juvenile Justice and Delinquency Prevention, 1994).
68. *Corrections Compendium* (December 1993), p. 14.
69. Ibid.
70. Sickmund et al., "Easy Access to the Census of Juveniles in Residential Placement," 2011, http://www.ojjdp.gov/ojstatbb/ezacjrp/.
71. Office of Juvenile Justice and Delinquency Prevention, *National Juvenile Custody Trends, 1978–1989* (Washington, DC: U.S. Dept. of Justice, 1992), p. 2.
72. Section 59 of the Uniform Juvenile Court Act recommends the granting of a right to appeal for juveniles (National Conference of Commissioners on Uniform State Laws, Uniform Juvenile Court Act, 1968).
73. Patricia Torbet et al., *State Responses to Serious and Violent Juvenile Crime* (Washington, DC: Office of Juvenile Justice and Delinquency Prevention, 1996).
74. Snyder and Sickmund, *Juvenile Offenders and Victims: 2006 National Report*, pp. 96–97.
75. Jeffrey A. Butts and Ojmarrh Mitchell, "Brick by Brick: Dismantling the Border between Juvenile and Adult Justice," in Phyllis McDonald and Janice Munsterman, eds., *Criminal Justice 2000, Vol. 2: Boundary Changes in Criminal Justice Organizations* (Washington, DC: National Institute of Justice, 2000), p. 207.
76. Ibid., pp. 167–213.
77. Barry C. Feld, "Abolish the Juvenile Court: Youthfulness, Criminal Responsibility, and Sentencing Policy," *Journal of Criminal Law and Criminology* (winter 1998).
78. Cindy S. Lederman, "The Juvenile Court: Putting Research to Work for Prevention," *Juvenile Justice Bulletin*, Vol. 6, No. 2 (Washington, DC: Office of Juvenile Justice and Delinquency Prevention, 1999), p. 23.
79. Public Law 107-273.
80. Activities funded under the legislation fall under Juvenile Accountability Block Grants (JABG) program.
81. See Cheryl Andrews and Lynn Marble, "Changes to OJJDP's Juvenile Accountability Program," *Juvenile Justice Bulletin* (Washington, DC: Office of Juvenile Justice and Delinquency Prevention, 2003).
82. SB 653.
83. Patricia Kilday Hart, "Lawmakers in Lockstep on Juvenile-Justice Bills," *The Houston Chronicle*, May 21, 2011, http://www.chron.com/disp/story.mpl/metropolitan/7575646.html (accessed June 7, 2011).
84. Sarah Alice Brown, *Trends in Juvenile Justice State Legislation: 2001–2011* (Washington, DC: National Conference of State Legislatures, 2012).
85. Ibid.
86. Ibid., p. 3.
87. Richard J. Bonnie, et al, *Reforming Juvenile Justice: A Developmental Approach* (Washington, DC: National Academies Press, 2012).
88. Ibid.

89. Justice Policy Institute, "Common Ground: Lessons Learned from Five States That Reduced Juvenile Confinement by More Than Half," February 2013, http://www.justicepolicy.org/uploads/justicepolicy/documents/commonground_online.pdf (accessed May 10, 2013).
90. Part of the decline in juvenile justice populations held in detention in Connecticut came about as a result of that state's raising its age of juvenile court jurisdiction to include people who are 17 years old.
91. Sickmund et al., "Easy Access to the Census of Juveniles in Residential Placement," http://www.ojjdp.gov/ojstatbb/ezacjrp/.
92. Ibid., p. 8.
93. Ibid., p. 12
94. Jeffrey A. Butts and Douglas N. Evans, *Resolution, Reinvestment, and Realignment: Three Strategies for Changing Juvenile Justice* (New York: John College of Criminal Justice, 2011).
95. Legislative Analyst's Office, "The 2012–13 Budget: Completing Juvenile Justice Realignment," February 15, 2002, http://www.lao.ca.gov/analysis/2012/crim_justice/juvenile-justice-021512.aspx (accessed May 3, 2012).
96. Brian Heller de Leon and Selena Teji, "Juvenile Justice Realignment in 2012," a Center on Juvenile and Criminal Justice Policy Brief, January 12, 2012.
97. Ibid.

© berc/Fotolia

16 DRUGS AND CRIME

OUTLINE

- Introduction
- What Is a Drug?
- A History of Drug Abuse in America
- The Most Common Drugs—And Who Is Using Them
- The Costs of Abuse
- Solving the Drug Problem

LEARNING OBJECTIVES

After reading this chapter, you should be able to

- Explain the nature of illegal drugs and the role social convention plays in deciding what constitutes an illegal drug.
- Discuss the history of drug abuse and antidrug legislation in America.
- Describe the categories and effects of each major type of illegal and abused drugs.
- Explain the link between drugs and other social problems.
- Summarize various efforts to respond to the drug problem, including your assessment of each effort's effectiveness.

This Administration remains committed to a balanced public health and public safety approach to drug policy. This approach is based on science, not ideology—and scientific research suggests that we have made real progress.

PRESIDENT BARACK OBAMA[1]

■ **Follow the author's tweets about the latest crime and justice news @schmalleger**

■ **drug abuse** Illicit drug use that results in social, economic, psychological, or legal problems for the user.[i]

Introduction

In 2013, the Chicago Crime Commission named Joaquin "El Chapo" Guzman as its first "public enemy number one" since Al Capone held that title back in the 1930s. Guzman is the leader of the powerful Sinaloa drug cartel, which federal agents believe supplies the bulk of narcotics that are sold in Chicago and other American cities. Jack Riley, head of the Drug Enforcement Administration's Chicago office, says that Guzman's cartel uses Chicago as a distribution hub for the rest of the United States. "This is where Guzman turns his drugs into money," he said.[2] The federal government has offered a $5 million reward for Guzman's capture, and *Forbes* magazine estimates that the drug lord controls a personal fortune worth over $1 billion. Guzman is also Mexico's most-wanted man.[3]

PUBLIC ENEMY NUMBER ONE
Joaquín Guzmán Loera
"El Chapo"
ALIASES: El Chapo, Chapo Guzman, El Rapido
DOB: April 4, 1957
ALT. DOB: December 25, 1954
POB: Sinaloa, Mexico
NATIONALITY: Mexican
CITIZENSHIP: Mexico
HEIGHT: 5 feet 8 inches
WEIGHT: 165 pounds
HAIR COLOR: Black
EYE COLOR: Brown
Joaquin Archivaldo Guzmán Loera, aka "El Chapo", is wanted in Chicago on charges for participating in international drug trafficking conspiracies in collaboration with 35 other defendants. El Chapo is the leader of the notorious Sinaloa drug cartel, and had helped manage part of his operation in Chicago, where allegedly 1,500 to 2,000 kilograms of cocaine were handled per month. The Northern District of Illinois seeks the forfeiture of more than $1.8 billion in cash proceeds in the indictments against him. He is known to be frequently travelling throughout Mexico to evade capture with the help of the members of the notorious Sinaloa Cartel.

AP Photo/M. Spencer Green

Drug lord Joaquin Guzman, aka "El Chapo," shown in a 2013 wanted poster displayed by the Chicago Crime Commission. El Chapo was named as Chicago's "Public Enemy Number 1" because of allegations that he controls much of the cocaine flowing into the city from Mexico. How would you address America's drug problems?

Kelley McCall/AP Wide World Photos

A package of K2, which has been described as "a concoction of dried herbs sprayed with chemicals." In 2011 the federal government outlawed five chemicals used in herbal blends and sold over the Internet to a growing number of teens and young adults. Do you agree that people who buy and sell substances like K2 should be subject to criminal sanctions?

Drug Abuse: More Than an Individual Choice

Drug abuse is pervasive in American society. A recent Police Foundation survey of 300 police chiefs across the country found that drug abuse is the most serious law enforcement problem facing communities today.[4] Sixty-three percent of the chiefs, who represented cities and towns of all sizes, cited drug abuse as an "extremely serious" or "very serious" problem. Other serious problems that the chiefs identified were domestic violence (50%), property crime (48%), violent crime (18%), and the threat of terrorism (17%).

The resulting impact of drug crimes on the American criminal justice system over the past four or five decades has been nothing less than phenomenal. In some parts of the country, court dockets became so clogged with drug cases that criminal case processing almost ground to a halt. Prison populations also reflect the huge increase in drug crimes (Table 16-1). Three-quarters of the growth in the number of federal prison inmates between 1980 and 2010 was due to drug crimes,[5] and about 47% of all offenders in federal prisons today are serving drug sentences.[6] This is also true of 85% of the noncitizens and 66% of women who are imprisoned. Yet drug offenders are rarely violent. More than half (55.7%) of federal prisoners sentenced for a drug offense fall into the lowest criminal history category of the federal sentencing guidelines, and in 87% of cases no weapon was involved in their crime.[7]

Although drug crimes account for only about 20% of state prison populations, the number of men held in state prisons as a result of drug crimes has increased by almost 50% since 1990, whereas the number of women incarcerated for drug crimes has risen by almost 200%.[8] Even though state governments are making efforts to reduce prison populations and to divert nonviolent

■ **controlled substance** A specifically defined bioactive or psychoactive chemical substance proscribed by law.

TABLE 16-1 | Federal Prisoners, by Type of Offense

OFFENSE TYPE	NUMBER OF PRISONERS	PERCENTAGE OF INMATE POPULATION
Drug Offenses	90,245	47.3
Weapons, Explosives, Arson	30,893	16.2
Immigration	22,526	11.9
Robbery	7,927	4.2
Burglary, Larceny, Property Offenses	7,650	4.0
Extortion, Fraud, Bribery	10,994	5.8
Homicide, Aggravated Assault, and Kidnapping Offenses	5,667	3.0
Miscellaneous	1,572	0.8
Sex Offenses	11,385	6.0
Banking and Insurance, Counterfeit, Embezzlement	818	0.4
Courts or Corrections	619	0.3
Continuing Criminal Enterprise	494	0.3
National Security	85	0.0

Note: Data calculated only for those with offense-specific information available.
Sources: Federal Bureau of Prisons, "Quick Facts," http://www.bop.gov/news/quick.jsp#3 (accessed July 2, 2013).

offenders from lengthy prison stays, the number of drug offenders still confined remains astonishingly high—due in large part to antiquated laws, long sentences that were handed out in the past, and repeat offending by those attracted to illicit drugs.

Drug Crime

Whereas in many textbooks drug-related crime is looked at briefly as one of several social-order or victimless crimes, in this book we take an in-depth look at drug crime because of its pervasive and far-reaching impact, not only on the criminal justice system but on all aspects of society. Drug abuse accounts for a large proportion of present-day law violations. It contributes to other types of criminal activity, such as smuggling, theft, robbery, and murder, and leads to a huge number of arrests, clogged courtrooms, and overcrowded prisons. As a consequence, drug abuse places tremendous strain on the criminal justice system, and the fight against it is one of the most expensive activities ever undertaken by federal, state, and local governments.

Because drug abuse is one of a great number of social-order offenses, it shares many characteristics with "victimless" crimes, such as prostitution and gambling. A hallmark of such crimes is that they involve willing participants. In the case of drug-law violations, buyers, sellers, and users willingly purchase, sell, and consume illegal drugs. They do not complain to the authorities of criminal injuries to themselves or to others resulting from the illegal use of drugs. Few so-called victimless crimes, however, are truly without an injured party. Even where the criminal participant does not perceive an immediate or personal injury, the behavior frequently affects the legitimate interests of nonparticipants. In many so-called victimless crimes, it is society that is the ultimate victim. Prostitution, for example, lowers property values in areas where it regularly occurs, degrades the status of women, and may victimize the customers and their families through the spread of AIDS and other sexually transmitted diseases.

Drug abuse has many of its own destructive consequences, including lost productivity, an inequitable distribution of economic resources among the poorest members of society, disease, wasted human potential, fragmented families, violence, and other crimes. Some evidence has also linked drug trafficking to international terrorism and to efforts to overthrow the democratic governments of the West. Each of these consequences will be discussed in some detail in this chapter. We begin now with an analysis of what constitutes a drug, explore the history of drug abuse in America, and then describe the various categories of major **controlled substances**. Finally, we will look at the link between drugs and other forms of crime and will describe possible solutions to the problem of drug abuse. See **http://www.justicestudies.com/pubs/drugabuse.pdf** to learn more about drugs and crime.

■ **drug** Any chemical substance defined by social convention as bioactive or psychoactive.
■ **recreational drug user** A person who uses drugs relatively infrequently, primarily with friends, and in social contexts that define drug use as pleasurable. Most addicts begin as recreational users.
■ **psychoactive substance** A chemical substance that affects cognition, feeling, or awareness.

What Is a Drug?

Before we begin any comprehensive discussion of drugs, we must first grapple with the concept of what a drug is. In common usage, a **drug** may be any ingestible substance that has a noticeable effect on the mind or body. Drugs may enter the body via injection, inhalation, swallowing, or even direct absorption through the skin or mucous membranes. Some drugs, like penicillin and tranquilizers, are useful in medical treatment, whereas others, like heroin and cocaine, are attractive almost exclusively to **recreational drug users**[9] or to those who are addicted to them.[10]

In determining which substances should be called "drugs," it is important to recognize the role that social definitions of any phenomenon play in our understanding of it. Hence what Americans today consider to be a drug depends more on social convention or agreed-on definitions than it does on any inherent property of the substance itself. The history of marijuana provides a case in point. Before the early twentieth century, marijuana was freely available in the United States. Although alcohol was the recreational drug of choice at the time, marijuana found a following among some artists and musicians. Marijuana was also occasionally used for medical purposes to "calm the nerves" and to treat hysteria. Howard Becker, in his classic study of the early Federal Bureau of Narcotics (forerunner of the Drug Enforcement Administration, or DEA), demonstrates how federal agencies worked to outlaw marijuana in order to increase their power.[11] Federally funded publications voiced calls for laws against the substance, and movies like *Reefer Madness* led the drive toward classifying marijuana as a dangerous drug. The 1939 Marijuana Tax Act was the result, and marijuana has been thought of as a drug worthy of federal and local enforcement efforts ever since.

Both the law and social convention make strong distinctions between drugs that are socially acceptable and those that are not. Some substances with profound effects on the mind and body are not even thought of as drugs. Gasoline fumes, chemical vapors of many kinds, perfumes, certain vitamins, sugar-rich foods, and toxic chemicals may all have profound effects. Even so, most people do not think of these substances as drugs, and they are rarely regulated by criminal law.

Changing social awareness has reclassified alcohol, caffeine, and nicotine as "drugs," although before the 1960s it is doubtful that most Americans would have applied that word to these three substances. Even today, alcohol, caffeine, and nicotine are readily available throughout the country, with only minimal controls on their manufacture and distribution. As a result, these three drugs continue to enjoy favored status in both our law and culture. Nonetheless, alcohol abuse and addiction are commonplace in American society, and anyone who has tried to quit smoking knows the power that nicotine can wield.

Occupying a middle ground on the continuum between acceptability and illegality are substances that have a legitimate medical use and are usually available only with a prescription. Antibiotics, diet pills, and, in particular, tranquilizers, stimulants, and mood-altering chemicals (like the popular drug Prozac) are culturally acceptable but typically can be attained legally only with a physician's prescription. The majority of Americans clearly recognize these substances as drugs, albeit useful ones.

Powerful drugs, those with the ability to produce substantially altered states of consciousness and with a high potential for addiction, occupy the forefront in social and legal condemnation. Among them are **psychoactive substances** like heroin, peyote, mescaline, LSD, and cocaine. Even here, however, legitimate uses for such drugs may exist. Cocaine is used in the treatment of certain medical conditions and can be applied as a topical anesthetic during medical interventions. LSD has been employed experimentally to investigate the nature of human consciousness, and peyote and mescaline may be used legally by members of the Native American Church in religious services. Even heroin has been advocated as beneficial in relieving the suffering associated with some forms of terminal illness. Hence, answers to the question of "What is a drug?" depend to a large extent on the social definitions and conventions operating at a given time and in a given place. Some of the clearest definitional statements relating to controlled substances can be found in the law, although informal strictures and definitions guide much of everyday drug use.

Alcohol Abuse

Although the abuse of alcohol is rarely described in the same terms as the illegal use of controlled substances, alcohol misuse can lead to serious problems with grim consequences. Fifteen years ago, for example, a pickup truck driven by Gallardo

Bermudes, 35, rear-ended a car carrying 11 people—two adults and nine children—near Beaumont, California.[12] Most of the children in the car were the sons and daughters of Jose Luis Rodriquez and Mercedes Diaz. Eight of the children burned to death when the car flipped over and caught fire after being hit. Bermudes, who fled from the scene, had been convicted of drunk driving on three previous occasions. He later told police investigators that he had consumed 10 to 15 beers before the crash.

Most states define a blood-alcohol level of 0.08% as intoxication and hold that anyone who drives with that amount of alcohol in his or her blood is driving under the influence (DUI) of alcohol;[13] and in October 2000, an amendment to a federal highway construction bill[14] required that states lower their blood-alcohol limits for drunk driving to 0.08% or lose a substantial percentage of the federal highway construction funds allocated to them.[15]

Drunk driving has been a major social concern for some time. Groups like Mothers Against Drunk Driving (MADD) and Remove Intoxicated Drivers (RID) have given impetus to enforcement efforts to curb drunk drivers. Today, approximately 1.2 million drunk-driving arrests are made annually—more than for any offense other than drug abuse.[16] The average driver arrested for DUI is substantially impaired. Studies show that he or she has consumed an average of six ounces of pure alcohol (the equivalent of a dozen bottles of beer) in the four hours preceding arrest.[17] Twenty-six percent of arrestees have consumed nearly twice that amount Approximately 22% of all vehicle crashes resulting in death are alcohol related.[18] The National Highway Traffic Safety Administration estimates that alcohol causes around 12,000 trafficfatalities annually.[19]

Another offense directly related to alcohol consumption is public drunkenness. During the late 1960s and early 1970s, some groups fought to decriminalize drunkenness and to treat it as a health problem. Although the number of arrests for public drunkenness reached more than 530,000 in 2012,[20] law enforcement officers retain a great deal of discretion in handling these offenders. Many people who are drunk in public, unless they are assaultive or involved in other crimes, are likely to receive an "official escort" home rather than face arrest.

The use of alcohol may also lead to the commission of other, very serious crimes. Some experts have found that alcohol use lowers inhibitions and increases the likelihood of aggression.[21] A report by the National Institute of Justice (NIJ) concluded that "of all psychoactive substances, alcohol is the only one whose consumption has been shown to commonly increase aggression."[22] Approximately 37% of offenders consume alcohol immediately before committing a crime.[23] In cases of violent crime, the percentage of offenders under the influence of alcohol at the time of the crime jumps to 42%—and is highest for murder (44.6%).[24]

Approximately 37% of offenders consume alcohol immediately before committing a crime.

Lawmakers appear willing to deal with the problems caused by alcohol only indirectly. The American experience with Prohibition is not one that legislators are anxious to repeat. In all likelihood, future efforts to reduce the damaging effects of alcohol will continue to take the form of educational programs, legislation to raise the drinking age, and enforcement efforts designed to deter the most visible forms of abuse. Struggles in other areas may also have some impact. For example, lawsuits claiming civil damages are now being brought against some liquor companies and taverns on behalf of accident victims, cirrhosis patients, and others. We can anticipate, however, that although concern over alcohol abuse will continue, few sweeping changes in either law or social custom will occur anytime soon.

A History of Drug Abuse in America

Alcohol is but one example of the many conflicting images of drug use prevalent in contemporary American society. The "war on drugs," initiated during the latter part of the twentieth century, portrayed an America fighting for its very existence against the scourge of drug abuse. Although many of the negative images of drugs that emanated from the "war" period may be correct, they have not always been a part of the American worldview.

Opium and its derivatives, for example, were widely available in patent medicines of the nineteenth and early twentieth centuries. Corner drugstores stocked mixtures of opium and alcohol, and traveling road shows extolled the virtues of these magical curatives. These elixirs, purported to offer relief from almost every malady, did indeed bring about feelings of well-being in most users. Although no one is certain just how widespread opium use was in the United States a hundred years ago, some authors have observed that baby formulas containing opium were fed to infants born to addicted mothers.[25]

Opium was also widely used by Chinese immigrants who came to the West Coast in the nineteenth century, often to work on the railroads. Opium dens—in which the drug was smoked—flourished, and the use of opium quickly spread to other ethnic groups throughout the West. Some of the more affluent denizens of West Coast cities ate the substance, and avant-garde poetry was written extolling the virtues of the drug.

Morphine, an opium derivative, has a similar history. Although it was legally available in this country almost since its invention, its use as a painkiller on the battlefields of the Civil War dramatically heightened public awareness of the drug.[26] In the late nineteenth century, morphine was widely prescribed by physicians and dentists, many of whom abused the substance themselves. By 1896, per capita morphine consumption peaked, and addiction to the substance throughout the United States was apparently widespread.[27]

Heroin, the most potent derivative of opium ever created, was invented as a substitute for morphine in 1874.

Heroin, the most potent derivative of opium ever created, was invented as a substitute for morphine in 1874. It was commercially marketed as a new pain remedy and cough suppressant beginning in 1898.[28] When it was first introduced, heroin's addictive properties were unknown, and it was said to be useful in treating morphine addiction.[29]

Marijuana, which is considerably less potent than heroin, has a relatively short history in this country. Imported by Mexican immigrants around the turn of the twentieth century, the drug quickly became associated with nonmainstream groups. By 1930, most of the states in the Southwest had passed legislation outlawing marijuana, and some authors have suggested that antimarijuana laws were primarily targeted at Spanish-speaking immigrants who were beginning to challenge whites in the economic sector.[30] As mentioned earlier, other writers have suggested that the rapidly growing use of marijuana throughout the 1920s and 1930s provided a rationale for the development of drug legislation and the concomitant expansion of drug enforcement agencies.[31] By the 1960s, public attitudes regarding marijuana had begun to change. The hippie generation popularized the drug, touting its "mellowing" effects on users. In a short time, marijuana use became epidemic across the country, and books on marijuana cultivation and preparation flourished.

Another drug that found adherents among some youthful idealists of the 1960s and 1970s was LSD. LSD, whose chemical name is lysergic acid diethylamide, was first synthesized in Switzerland in 1938 and was used occasionally in this country in the 1950s for the treatment of psychiatric disorders.

Many drugs, when first "discovered," were touted for their powerful analgesic or therapeutic effects. Cocaine was one of them. An early leading proponent of cocaine use, for example, was Sigmund Freud, who prescribed it for a variety of psychological disorders. Freud was himself a user and wrote a book, *The Cocaine Papers*, describing the many benefits of the drug. The cocaine bandwagon reached the United States in the late nineteenth century, and various medicines and beverages containing cocaine were offered to the American public. Prominent among them was Coca-Cola, which combined seltzer water, sugar, and cocaine in a new soft drink advertised as providing a real "pick-me-up." Cocaine was removed from Coca-Cola in 1910 but continued to be used by jazz musicians and artists. Beginning in the 1970s, cocaine became associated with exclusive parties, the well-to-do, and the jet set. It was not long before an extensive drug underworld developed, catering to the demands of affluent users. Crack cocaine, a derivative of powdered cocaine that is smoked, became popular in the 1980s and is sold today in the form of "rocks," "cookies," or "biscuits" (large pieces of crack).

Tito Herrera/AP Wide World Photos

U.S. Coast Guard officers guard 19.4 metric tons of cocaine confiscated from the cargo ship *Gatun* on March 22, 2007. The seizure proved to be one of the biggest maritime cocaine hauls on record. What other kinds of crime are linked to drug crime?

Drug Use and Social Awareness

Although drugs have long been a part of American society, there have been dramatic changes during the last century in the form drug use takes and in the social consequences associated with

■ **Harrison Narcotics Act** The first major piece of federal antidrug legislation, passed in 1914.

drug involvement. Specifically, six elements have emerged that today cast drug use in a far different light than in the past:

- The conceptualization of addiction as a physical condition
- The understanding that drug use is associated with other kinds of criminal activity
- Generally widespread social condemnation of drug use as a waste of economic resources and human lives
- Comprehensive and detailed federal and state laws regulating the use or availability of drugs
- A large and perhaps still-growing involvement with illicit drugs among the urban poor and the socially disenfranchised, both as an escape from the conditions of life and as a path to monetary gain
- The view that drug abuse is a law enforcement issue rather than primarily a medical problem

In an insightful work that clarifies the ideational basis of modern antidrug sentiments, criminologists Franklin Zimring and Gordon Hawkins examine three schools of thought that, they say, form the basis for current drug policy in the United States.[32] The first is "public health generalism," a perspective that holds that all controlled substances are potentially harmful and that drug abusers are victimized by the disease of addiction. This approach views drugs as medically harmful and argues that effective drug control is necessary as a matter of public health. The second approach, "cost–benefit specifism," proposes that drug policy be built around a balancing of the social costs of drug abuse (crime, broken families, drug-related killings, and so on) with the costs of enforcement. The third approach, the "legalist," suggests that drug-control policies are necessary to prevent the collapse of public order and of society itself. Advocates of the legalist perspective say that drug use is "defiance of lawful authority that threatens the social fabric."[33] According to Zimring and Hawkins, all recent and contemporary antidrug policies have been based on one of these three schools of thought. Unfortunately, say these authors, it may not be possible to base successful antidrug policy on such beliefs because they do not necessarily recognize the everyday realities of drug use. Nonetheless, antidrug legislation and activities undertaken in the United States today are accorded political and ideational legitimacy via all three perspectives. Learn more about addiction from the National Institute of Drug Abuse at **http://www.nida.nih.gov/scienceofaddiction/sciofaddiction.pdf**.

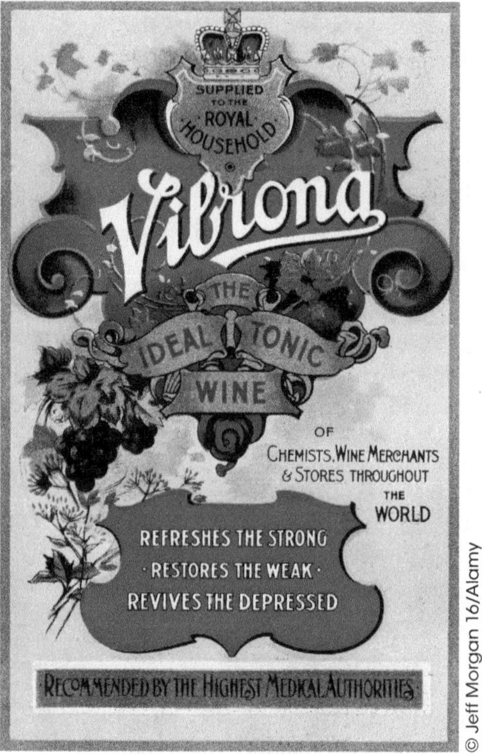

© Jeff Morgan 16/Alamy

A 1907 advertisement for cocaine-laced wine. Cocaine, a controlled substance today, was commonly found in late-nineteenth-century medicines and consumer products. Why did the federal government enact legislation outlawing the use of psychoactive substances like marijuana and cocaine?

Antidrug Legislation

Antidrug legislation in the United States dates back to around 1875, when the city of San Francisco enacted a statute prohibiting the smoking of opium.[34] A number of western states quickly followed the city's lead. The San Francisco law and many that followed it, however, clearly targeted Chinese immigrants and were rarely applied to other ethnic groups involved in the practice.

The first major piece of federal antidrug legislation came in 1914, with the enactment of the **Harrison Narcotics Act**. The Harrison Act required anyone dealing in opium, morphine, heroin, cocaine, and specified derivatives of these drugs to register with the federal government and to pay a tax of $1 per year. The only people permitted to register were physicians, pharmacists, and other members of the medical profession. Nonregistered drug traffickers faced a maximum fine of $2,000 and up to five years in prison.

Because the Harrison Act allowed physicians to prescribe controlled drugs for the purpose of medical treatment, heroin addicts and other drug users could still legally purchase the drugs they needed. All the law required was a physician's prescription. By 1920, however, court rulings had established

■ **Controlled Substances Act (CSA)** Title II of the Comprehensive Drug Abuse Prevention and Control Act of 1970, which established schedules classifying psychoactive drugs according to their degree of psychoactivity.

■ **psychological dependence** A craving for a specific drug that results from long-term substance abuse. Psychological dependence on drugs is marked by the belief that drugs are needed to achieve a feeling of well-being.[ii]

■ **physical dependence** A biologically based craving for a specific drug that results from frequent use of the substance. Physical dependence on drugs is marked by a growing tolerance of a drug's effects, so that increased amounts of the drug are needed to obtain the desired effect, and by the onset of withdrawal symptoms over periods of prolonged abstinence.[iii]

that drug "maintenance" only prolonged addiction and did not qualify as "treatment."[35] The era of legally available heroin had ended.

Marijuana was not included in the Harrison Act because it was not considered a dangerous drug.[36] By the 1930s, however, government attention became riveted on marijuana. At the urging of the Federal Bureau of Narcotics, Congress passed the Marijuana Tax Act in 1937. As the title of the law indicates, the act simply placed a tax of $100 per ounce on cannabis. Those who did not pay the tax were subject to prosecution. With the passage of the Boggs Act in 1951, however, marijuana, along with a number of other drugs, entered the class of federally prohibited controlled substances. The Boggs Act also removed heroin from the list of medically useful substances and required the removal, within 120 days, of any medicines containing heroin from pharmacies across the country.[37]

The Narcotic Control Act of 1956 increased penalties for drug trafficking and possession and made the sale of heroin to anyone under age 18 a capital offense. However, on the eve of the massive explosion in drug use that was to begin in the mid-1960s, the Kennedy administration began a shift in emphasis from the strict punishment of drug traffickers and users to rehabilitation. A 1963 presidential commission recommended the elimination of the Federal Bureau of Narcotics, recommended shorter prison terms for drug offenders, and stressed the need for research and social programs in dealing with the drug problem.[38]

The Comprehensive Drug Abuse Prevention and Control Act of 1970

By 1970, America's drug problem was clear, and legislators were anxious to return to a more punitive approach to controlling drug abuse. Under President Richard Nixon, legislation designed to encompass all aspects of drug abuse and to permit federal intervention at all levels of use was enacted. Termed the Comprehensive Drug Abuse Prevention and Control Act of 1970, the legislation still forms the basis of federal enforcement efforts today. Title II of the law is the **Controlled Substances Act (CSA)**. The CSA sets up five schedules that classify psychoactive drugs according to their degree of psychoactivity and abuse potential:[39]

- Schedule I controlled substances have no established medical usage, cannot be used safely, and have great potential for abuse.[40] Federal law requires that any research employing Schedule I substances be fully documented and that the substances themselves be stored in secure vaults. Included under this category are heroin, LSD, mescaline, peyote, methaqualone (Quaaludes), psilocybin, marijuana,[41] and hashish, as well as other specified hallucinogens. Penalties for first-offense possession and sale of Schedule I controlled substances under the federal Narcotic Penalties and Enforcement Act of 1986 include up to life imprisonment and a $10 million fine. Penalties increase for subsequent offenses.
- Schedule II controlled substances are drugs with high abuse potential for which there is a currently accepted pharmacological or medical use. Most Schedule II substances are also considered to be addictive.[42] Drugs that fall into this category include opium, morphine, codeine, cocaine, phencyclidine (PCP), and their derivatives. Certain other stimulants, such as methylphenidate (Ritalin) and phenmetrazine (Preludin), and a few barbiturates with high abuse potential also come under Schedule II. Legal access to Schedule II substances requires written nonrefillable prescriptions, vault storage, and thorough record keeping by vendors. Penalties for first-offense possession and sale of Schedule II controlled substances include up to 20 years' imprisonment and a $5 million fine under the federal Narcotic Penalties and Enforcement Act. Penalties increase for subsequent offenses.
- Schedule III controlled substances have lower abuse potential than do those in Schedules I and II. They are drugs with an accepted medical use but that may lead to a high level of **psychological dependence** or to moderate or low **physical dependence**.[43] Schedule III substances include many of the drugs found in Schedule II but in derivative or diluted form. Common low-dosage antidiarrheals, such as opium-containing paregoric, and cold medicines and pain relievers with low concentrations of codeine fall into this category. Anabolic steroids, whose abuse by professional athletes has been subject to scrutiny, were added to the list of

Schedule III controlled substances in 1991. Legitimate access to Schedule III drugs is through a doctor's prescription (written or oral), with refills authorized in the same manner. Maximum penalties associated with first-offense possession and sale of Schedule III controlled substances under federal law include five years' imprisonment and fines of up to $1 million.

- Schedule IV controlled substances have a relatively low potential for abuse (when compared to those in higher schedules), are useful in established medical treatments, and involve only a limited risk of psychological or physical dependence.[44] Depressants and minor tranquilizers such as Valium, Librium, and Equanil fall into this category, as do some stimulants. Schedule IV substances are medically available in the same fashion as Schedule III drugs. Maximum penalties associated with first-offense possession and sale of Schedule IV substances under federal law include three years in prison and fines of up to $1 million.
- Schedule V controlled substances are prescription drugs with a low potential for abuse and with only a very limited possibility of psychological or physical dependence.[45] Cough medicines (antitussives) and antidiarrheals containing small amounts of opium, morphine, or codeine are found in Schedule V. A number of Schedule V medicines may be purchased through retail vendors with only minimal controls or upon the signature of the buyer (with some form of identification required). Maximum federal penalties for first-offense possession and sale of Schedule V substances include one year in prison and a $250,000 fine.

Pharmacologists, chemists, and botanists regularly create new drugs. Likewise, street-corner "chemists" in clandestine laboratories churn out inexpensive designer drugs—laboratory-created psychoactive substances with widely varying effects and abuse potential. Designer drugs include substances with names like Ecstasy (MDMA), GHB (gamma-hydroxybutyrate), K2, ketamine, MDPV (methylenedioxypyrovalerone), and meth (methamphetamine), which will be discussed in greater detail later in this chapter. The Controlled Substances Act (CSA) includes provisions for determining which new drugs should be controlled and into which schedule they should be placed (Table 16-2). Under the CSA, criteria for assigning a new drug

© Aflo Foto Agency/Alamy

Cyclist Lance Armstrong, who was forced to give up seven Tour de France titles after he admitted to "doping." Anabolic steroids were added to the list of Schedule III controlled substances in 1991. Why did the federal government outlaw the nonmedical use of most steroidal compounds?

■ **drug czar** The popular name for the head of the Office of National Drug Control Policy (ONDCP), a federal position that was created during the Reagan presidency to organize federal drug-fighting efforts.

TABLE 16-2 | Major Controlled Substances Under the Federal Controlled Substances Act

SCHEDULE	DESCRIPTION OF SCHEDULE	DRUGS IN SCHEDULE	STREET NAMES
I	• high potential for abuse • no currently accepted medical use in the United States • lacks accepted safety standards for use under medical supervision	marijuana, heroin, opioids, hallucinogenic substances, peyote, mescaline, gamma-hydroxybutyric acid (GHB), and others	pot, weed, grass, reefer, joint, angel dust, horse
II	• high potential for abuse • currently accepted for medical use • may lead to severe psychological or physical dependence	cocaine, opium, oxycodone, methadone, morphine, Seconal, methamphetamine, and other amphetamines	snow, crack, coke, meth, speed, uppers
III	• potential for abuse less than the drugs or other substances in Schedules I and II • currently accepted for medical use • may lead to moderate or low physical dependence or high psychological dependence	anabolic steroids, ketamine, hydrocodone, and a number of barbiturates and sedatives	downers, goof balls, yellow jackets
IV	• lower potential for abuse relative to the drugs or other substances in Schedule III • currently accepted for medical use • may lead to limited physical dependence or psychological dependence relative to the drugs or other substances in Schedule III	some antidiarrheal drugs; some partial opioid analgesics; some sleeping pills such as Zolpidem; long-acting barbiturates; and benzodiazepines such as Xanax, Librium, and Valium	blues, peaches, bars, zombie pills, no-go pills, A-minus
V	• low potential for abuse relative to the drugs or other substances in Schedule IV • currently accepted for medical use • may lead to limited physical dependence or psychological dependence relative to the drugs or other substances in Schedule IV	some cough suppressants, anticonvulsants, and selected prescription pain pills	

to one of the existing schedules include (1) the drug's actual or relative potential for abuse; (2) scientific evidence of the drug's pharmacological effects; (3) the state of current scientific knowledge regarding the substance; (4) its history and current pattern of abuse; (5) the scope, duration, and significance of abuse; (6) risk, if any, to the public health; (7) the drug's psychic or physiological dependence liability; and (8) whether the substance is an immediate precursor of a substance already controlled.[46] Proceedings to add a new chemical substance to the list of those controlled by law or to delete or change the schedule of an existing drug may be initiated by the chief administrator of the Drug Enforcement Administration, by the Department of Health and Human Services, or by a petition from any interested party, including manufacturers, medical societies, or public-interest groups.[47] Read the text of the CSA at **http://www.justice.gov/dea/pubs/csa.html**.

The Anti-Drug Abuse Act of 1988

In 1988, the country's Republican leadership, under President Ronald Reagan, capitalized on the public's frustration with rampant drug abuse and stepped up the "war on drugs." The president created a new cabinet-level post, naming a **drug czar** to be in charge of federal drug-fighting initiatives through the Office of National Drug Control Policy (ONDCP). William Bennett, a former secretary of education, was appointed to fill the post. At the same time, Congress passed the Anti-Drug Abuse Act. The overly optimistic tenor of the act is clear from its preamble, which reads, "It is the declared policy of the United States

Government to create a Drug-Free America by 1995."[48] That goal, which reflected far more political rhetoric than realistic planning, was incredibly naïve.

Even so, the Anti-Drug Abuse Act of 1988 carries much weight. Under the law, penalties for "recreational" drug users increased substantially,[49] and weapons purchases by suspected drug dealers became more difficult. The law also denies federal benefits, ranging from loans (including student loans) to contracts and licenses, to convicted drug offenders.[50] Earned benefits, such as Social Security, retirement, and health and disability benefits, are not affected by the legislation, nor are welfare payments or existing public-housing arrangements (although separate legislation does provide for termination of public-housing tenancy for drug offenses[51]). Under the law, civil penalties of up to $10,000 may be assessed against convicted "recreational" users for possession of even small amounts of drugs.

Under the Anti-Drug Abuse Act of 1988, penalties for "recreational" drug users increased substantially.

The legislation also allows capital punishment for drug-related murders. The killing of a police officer by an offender seeking to avoid apprehension or prosecution is specifically cited as carrying a possible sentence of death, although other murders by major drug dealers also fall under the capital punishment provision.[52] In May 1991, 37-year-old David Chandler, an Alabama marijuana kingpin, became the first person to be sentenced to die under the law.[53] Chandler was convicted of ordering the murder of a police informant in 1990.

One especially interesting aspect of the Anti-Drug Abuse Act is its provision for designating selected areas as high-intensity drug-trafficking areas (HIDTAs), making them eligible for federal drug-fighting assistance so that joint interagency operations can be implemented to reduce drug problems. Using the law, former drug czar William Bennett declared Washington, D.C., a "drug zone" in 1989. His designation was based in part on what was then the city's reputation as the murder capital of the country. At the time of the declaration, more than 60% of Washington's murders were said to be drug related,[54] and legislators and tourists were clamoring for action. Bennett's plan called for more federal investigators and prosecutors and for specially built prisons to handle convicted drug dealers. Visit ONDCP at **http://www.whitehousedrugpolicy.gov.**

Other Federal Antidrug Legislation

Other significant federal antidrug legislation exists in the form of the Crime Control Act of 1990, the Violent Crime Control and Law Enforcement Act of 1994, the Drug-Free Communities Act of 1997, and the reauthorization of the USA PATRIOT Act in 2006.[55] The Crime Control Act of 1990 (1) doubled the appropriations authorized for drug-law enforcement grants to states and local communities; (2) enhanced drug-control and drug-education programs aimed at the nation's schools; (3) expanded specific drug enforcement assistance to rural states; (4) expanded regulation of precursor chemicals used in the manufacture of illegal drugs; (5) sanctioned anabolic steroids under the Controlled Substances Act; (6) included provisions to enhance control over international money laundering; (7) created "drug-free school zones" by enhancing penalties for drug offenses occurring in proximity to schools; and (8) enhanced the ability of federal agents to seize property used in drug transactions or purchased with drug proceeds.

The Violent Crime Control and Law Enforcement Act of 1994 provided $245 million for rural anticrime and antidrug efforts; set aside $1.6 billion for direct funding to localities around the country for anticrime efforts, including drug-treatment programs; budgeted $383 million for drug-treatment programs for state and federal prisoners; created a treatment schedule for all drug-addicted federal prisoners; required post-conviction drug testing of all federal prisoners upon release; allocated $1 billion for drug-court programs for nonviolent offenders with substance-abuse problems; and mandated new stiff penalties for drug crimes committed by gangs. The act also tripled penalties for using children to deal drugs and enhanced penalties for drug dealing in drug-free zones near playgrounds, schoolyards, video arcades, and youth centers. Finally, the law also expanded the federal death penalty to cover offenders involved in large-scale drug trafficking and mandated life imprisonment for criminals convicted of three violent felonies or drug offenses.

The Drug-Free Communities Act of 1997 provided support to local communities to reduce substance abuse among youth. It helped enhance broad-based community antidrug coalitions, which were previously shown to be successful at driving down casual drug use. Under the law, neighborhoods with successful anti-drug programs became eligible to apply for federal grants to assist in their continued development.

More recently, the congressional reauthorization of the USA PATRIOT Act in 2006 led to enactment of a provision in that legislation known as the Combat Methamphetamine Epidemic Act. That legislation makes it harder to obtain pseudoephedrine, ephedrine, and phenylpropanolamine—ingredients in some over-the-counter cold medicines that can be used in the manufacture of methamphetamine.[56] The legislation requires medicines containing these chemicals to be kept behind store counters or in locked cabinets and limits the amount of those substances that a person can

The 2006 Combat Methamphetamine Epidemic Act made it harder to obtain pseudoephedrine, ephedrine, and phenylpropanolamine—ingredients in some over-the-counter cold medicines that can be used in the manufacture of methamphetamine.

curtilage In legal usage, the area surrounding a residence that can reasonably be said to be a part of the residence for Fourth Amendment purposes.

purchase to 3.6 grams per day, or up to 9 grams per month. Under the legislation, customers purchasing pseudoephedrine, ephedrine, or phenylpropanolamine are required to show photo identification and to sign a store log. The PATRIOT Act renewal also authorized $99 million per year for the federal Meth Hot Spots program, which was intended to train state and local law enforcement officers in how to investigate methamphetamine offenses and to provide personnel and equipment for enforcement and prosecution.

The Investigation of Drug Abuse and Manufacturing

Investigation of the illegal production, transportation, sale, and use of controlled substances is a major police activity. Investigation of drug-manufacturing activities has given rise to an area of case law that supplements the plain-view doctrine discussed in Chapter 7. Two legal concepts, abandonment and curtilage, have taken on special significance in drug investigations.

Abandonment refers to the fact that property, once it has been clearly thrown away or discarded, ceases to fall under Fourth Amendment protections against unreasonable search and seizure. The U.S. Supreme Court case of *California* v. *Greenwood* (1988)[57] began when Officer Jenny Stracner of the Laguna Beach (California) Police Department arranged with a neighborhood trash collector to receive garbage collected at a suspect's residence. The refuse was later found to include items "indicative of narcotics use."[58] Based on this evidence, Stracner applied for a search warrant, which was used in a search of the defendant's home. The search uncovered controlled substances, including cocaine and hashish. The defendant, Billy Greenwood, was arrested. Upon conviction, Greenwood appealed, arguing that the trash had been placed in opaque bags and could reasonably be expected to remain unopened until it was collected and disposed of. His appeal emphasized his right to privacy with respect to his trash.

The Supreme Court disagreed, saying that "[a]n expectation of privacy does not give rise to Fourth Amendment protection unless society is prepared to accept that expectation as objectively reasonable. . . . [I]t is common knowledge that plastic garbage bags left on or at the side of a public street are readily accessible to animals, children, scavengers, snoops, and other members of the public." Hence, the Court concluded, the property in question had been abandoned, and no reasonable expectation of privacy can attach to trash left for collection "in an area accessible to the public." The concept of abandonment extends beyond trash that is actively discarded. In *Abel* v. *U.S.* (1960),[59] for example, the Court found that the warrantless search of a motel room by an Federal Bureau of Investigation (FBI) agent immediately after it had been vacated was acceptable.

Curtilage, a concept that the Supreme Court clearly recognized in the case of *Oliver* v. *U.S.* (1984),[60] refers to the fact that household activity generally extends beyond the walls of a residence. People living in a house, for example, spend some of their time in their yard. Property within the curtilage of a residence has generally been accorded the same Fourth Amendment guarantees against search and seizure as areas within the walls of a house or an apartment. But just how far does the curtilage of a residence extend? Does it vary according to the type or location of the residence? Is it necessary for an area to be fenced for it to fall within residential curtilage?

A collateral area of concern is that of activity conducted in fields. The open-fields doctrine began with the case of *Hester* v. *U.S.* (1924),[61] in which the Supreme Court held that law enforcement officers could search an open field without a warrant. The *Oliver* case extended that authorityto include secluded and fenced fields posted with "No Trespassing" signs.

In *U.S.* v. *Dunn* (1987),[62] the U.S. Supreme Court considered a Houston-area defendant's claim that the space surrounding a barn, which was located approximately 50 yards from the edge of a fence surrounding a farmhouse, was protected against intrusion by the Fourth Amendment. The Court rejected the defendant's arguments and concluded that even though an area may be fenced, it is not within the curtilage of a residence if it is sufficiently distant from the area of household activity that attends the residence.

Other related decisions have supported seizures based on warrantless aerial observation of marijuana plants growing in the backyard of a defendant's home[63] and those based on naked-eye sightings from helicopters of the contents of a greenhouse.[64] The Court's reasoning in such cases is that flights within navigable airspace are common. Where no comprehensive efforts to secure privacy have been made, there can be no reasonable expectation of privacy—even within

According to the courts, where no comprehensive efforts to secure privacy have been made, there can be no reasonable expectation of privacy.

areas that might normally be considered curtilage. Were sophisticated surveillance techniques to be employed by law enforcement authorities, however—such as the use of drone aircraft, satellite, or infrared photography—the Court's decision would be in doubt because such devices extend beyond the realm of "normal flight."

The Most Common Drugs—And Who Is Using Them

The *National Survey on Drug Use and Health* (NSDUH), an annual publication of the federal Substance Abuse and Mental Health Services Administration (SAMHSA), estimates that 22.5 million Americans age 12 and older are "current" users of illegal drugs—defined as those who have used an illicit drug in the month preceding the survey[65] (Figure 16-1). Nearly 18.4 million people are estimated to be using marijuana, and an estimated 1.4 million people are current cocaine users. Hallucinogens are used by more than one million people, including 695,000 users of Ecstasy. There are an estimated 439,000 current methamphetamine users and 620,000 current heroin users. An estimated 6.1 million Americans are current nonmedical users of prescription-type psychotherapeutic drugs. This includes 5.1 million using pain relievers, 2.2 million using tranquilizers, 1.1 million using stimulants, and nearly 374,000 using sedatives.

These figures represent a considerable decline from 1979, the year in which the highest levels of drug abuse in the United States were reported, although figures for recent years have shown a gradual increase in drug use (especially "occasional use"). As the Office of National Drug Control Policy (ONDCP) points out, however, federal studies typically underestimate the number of hard-core drug abusers in the country because they fail to survey the homeless, prisoners, people living at colleges, active-duty military personnel, and those in mental and other institutions. ONDCP estimates that there are 2.1 million hard-core cocaine addicts and up to 1 million heroin addicts in the country[66]—figures well above those reported by the survey.

Rates of drug use show substantial variation by age. In 2011, for example, 3.3% of American youths age 12 or 13 reported current illicit drug use compared with 9.2% of youths age 14 or 15 and 17.2% of youths age 16 or 17 (Figure 16-2). As in other years, illicit drug use in 2011 tended to increase with age among young people, peaking among 18- to 20-year-olds (23.8%) and declining steadily after that point with increasing age. Current employment status is also highly correlated with

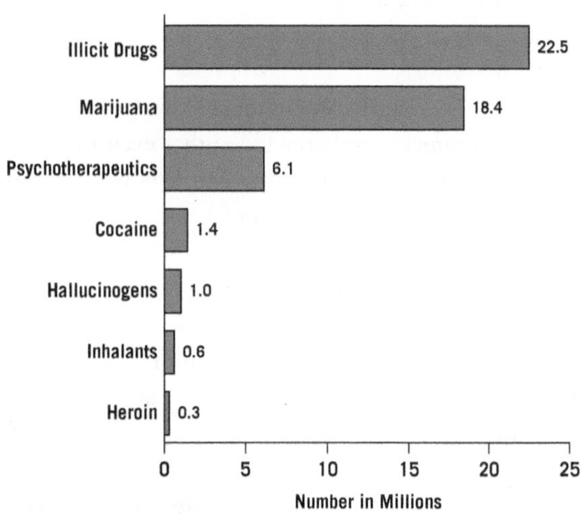

FIGURE 16-1 | Current Illicit Drug Use among Persons Aged 12 or Older in the United States, 2011

Source: Substance Abuse and Mental Health Services Administration, *National Survey on Drug Use and Health* (Rockville, MD: Office of Applied Studies, NHSDA, 2012).

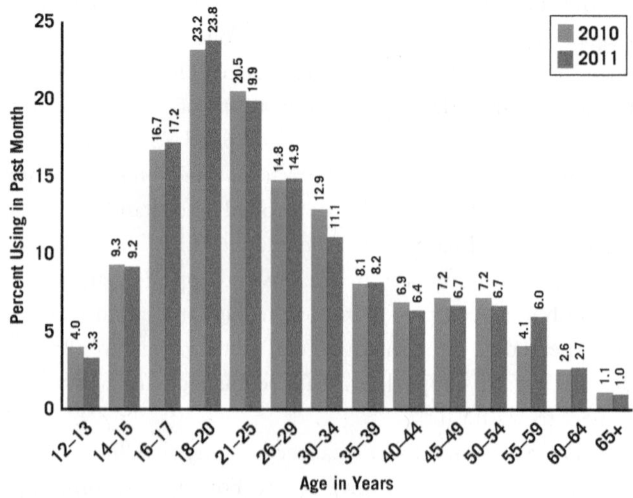

FIGURE 16-2 | Current Illicit Drug Use by Age in the United States, 2010 and 2011

Source: Substance Abuse and Mental Health Services Administration, *National Survey on Drug Use and Health* (Rockville, MD: Office of Applied Studies, NHSDA, 2012).

Of the 20.2 million illicit drug users age 18 or older in 2011, 13.1 million were employed either full- or part-time.

rates of current illicit drug use. An estimated 17.2% of unemployed adults age 18 or older were current illicit drug users in the United States in 2011, compared with 8.0% of those employed full-time and 11.6% of those employed part-time. Although the rate of drug use was higher among the unemployed compared with those from other employment groups, most drug users were employed. Of the 20.2 million illicit drug users age 18 or older in 2011, 13.1 million were employed either full- or part-time. The use of drugs is also more prevalent in some parts of the country than in others. Read a summary of the latest findings from the National Survey on Drug Use and Health at **http://oas.samhsa.gov/nsduhLatest.htm**.

freedom OR safety? YOU decide

Drug-Related Criminal Activity and Public Housing

Seventy-nine-year-old Herman Walker lives in a public-housing development in Oakland, California. Walker, who suffers from severe arthritis and complications from a stroke he suffered five years ago, is facing eviction from his apartment because federal housing authority officials determined that his full-time caretaker had hidden crack pipes in his home. Authorities admit that Walker likely had no knowledge of his caretaker's illegal actions, but they say that Walker's eviction will serve notice to other residents that they must carefully oversee the activities of people who live with them.

Walker's problems stem from federal law[1] and from a rule based on that law that was adopted by the Department of Housing and Urban Development (HUD) in 1991. Both the law and the HUD rule were upheld by a unanimous U.S. Supreme Court decision in 2002.[2] The rule provides that "any drug-related criminal activity on or off [federally assisted low-income housing] premises, engaged in by a public housing tenant, any member of the tenant's household, or any guest or other person under the tenant's control, shall be cause for termination of tenancy." The decision opened the door for the eviction of poor, elderly, and sick public-housing residents for drug use of which they had no personal knowledge. Tenants' rights advocates condemned the ruling, saying that it allows harsh punishments to be imposed on the innocent. Supporters of the Court's decision saw it as an affirmation of their belief that drug-free public housing is an important priority.

In a related issue, the U.S. Supreme Court upheld a Richmond, Virginia, public-housing trespass law in 2003.[3] The law makes it illegal for nonresidents to be on public-housing premises without a legitimate reason. The case grew out of efforts by the Richmond Redevelopment and Housing Authority (RRHA) to combat "rampant crime and drug dealing" at its Whitcomb Court development, where "open-air drug markets" had been commonplace.

The RRHA closed the streets of the development to nonresidents and posted "No Trespassing" signs, warning that "unauthorized persons will be subject to arrest and prosecution." Police were authorized to arrest any nonresidents who refused to leave or who returned after being warned that they were trespassing. Critics charged that housing authority streets were public avenues and that members of the public should have access to them.[4]

Finally, in 2011, the U.S. Department of Housing and Urban Development issued a memorandum reinforcing a position that it had previously announced on the use of medical marijuana in public housing. The memorandum stated that "any state law purporting to legalize the use of medical marijuana in public or other assisted housing would conflict with the admission termination standards" of the agency.[5]

You Decide

In your opinion, does the goal of reducing drug-related criminal activity in public housing justify evicting residents who have no knowledge of such activities in their homes? Does it justify restricting access to public housing and criminalizing the acts of nonresident trespassers? Should HUD officials permit the use of medical marijuana in federal public housing, when the drug is prescribed by a practicing licensed physician?

[1] U.S. Code, Title 42, Section 1437d(l)(6). Also, see the Public and Assisted Housing Drug Elimination Act of 1990 and the Public and Assisted Housing Drug Elimination Program Amendments of 1998.

[2] *Department of Housing and Urban Development* v. *Rucker*, 122 S.Ct. 1230, 152 L.Ed.2d 258 (2002).

[3] *Virginia* v. *Hicks*, 539 U.S. 113 (2003).

[4] The argument before the Court was actually more complex. The RRHA, which had assumed control of the Whitcomb Court development from the city of Richmond some years previously, is not regarded as a public agency. Lawyers representing nonresidents argued that the area's streets had served as a "traditional public forum," although from a strict legal viewpoint they may no longer be public.

[5] U.S. Department of Housing and Urban Development, Memorandum: "Medical Use of Marijuana and Reasonable Accommodation in Federal Public and Assisted Housing," January 20, 2011, http://www.scribd.com/doc/47657807/HUD-policy-Memo-on-Medical-Marijuana-in-Public-Housing.

References: Evelyn Nieves, "Drug Ruling Worries Some in Public Housing," *New York Times*, March 28, 2002; Tom Schoenberg, "Supremes Examine Trespassing Policy," Law.com, May 1, 2003; and "U.S. Supreme Court Upholds Public Housing Trespass Law," *Criminal Justice Newsletter*, July 1, 2003, p. 4.

drug trafficking Trading or dealing in controlled substances, including the transporting, storage, importing, exporting, or sale of a controlled substance.

CJ | ISSUES
Drugs: What's in a Name?

Drug names have been a source of confusion for many people who have attempted to grapple with the drug problem. A single drug may have a dozen or more names. Drugs may be identified according to brand name, generic name, street name, or psychoactive category.

Brand Name

The name given to a chemical substance by its manufacturer is the brand name. Brand names are registered and are often associated with trademarks. They identify a drug in the pharmaceutical marketplace and may not be used by other manufacturers. Psychoactive substances with no known medical application or experimental use are not produced by legitimate companies and have no brand name.

Generic Name

The chemical or other identifying name of a drug is the generic name. Generic names are often used by physicians in writing prescriptions because generic drugs are often less costly than brand-name drugs. Generic names are also used in most drug-abuse legislation at the federal and state levels to specify controlled substances. Generic names are sometimes applicable only to the psychoactive chemical substances in drugs and not to the drugs themselves. With marijuana, for example, the chemical tetrahydrocannabinol, or THC, is the active substance.

Street Name

Street names are slang terms. Many of them originated with the pop culture of the 1960s, and others continue to be produced by modern-day drug subculture. For example, street names for cocaine include coke, flake, and snow; heroin is known as horse, smack, or H.

Psychoactive Category

Psychoactive drugs are categorized according to the effects they produce on the human mind. Narcotics, stimulants, depressants, and hallucinogens are typical psychoactive categories.

An Example

PCP and angel dust are the street names for a veterinary anesthetic marketed under the brand name Sernylan. Sernylan contains the psychoactive chemical phencyclidine, which is classified as a depressant under the Controlled Substances Act.

Drug Trafficking

A number of agencies report on the amount and types of illicit drugs that enter the country or are produced here. The federal General Counterdrug Intelligence Plan,[67] implemented in February 2000, designated the National Drug Intelligence Center (NDIC) as the nation's principal center for strategic domestic counterdrug intelligence and planning.[68] Prior to 2012, when the office was closed, the NDIC published the National Drug Threat Assessment, a comprehensive annual report on **drug trafficking** and abuse trends within the United States. The assessment identified the most serious drug threats, monitored fluctuations in national consumption levels, tracked drug availability by geographic area, and analyzed trafficking and distribution patterns. The report also included information on illicit drug availability, demand, production, cultivation, transportation, and distribution, as well as the effects of particular drugs on abusers and society as a whole. With the NDIC's closure, responsibility for gathering and disseminating data on drug trafficking was transferred to the DEA. Learn more about the DEA via **http://www.justice.gov/dea**.

Marijuana

Marijuana, whose botanical name is *Cannabis sativa* L., grows wild throughout most of the tropic and temperate regions of the world.[69] Marijuana commonly comes in loose form, as the ground leaves and seeds of the hemp plant. Also available to street-level users are stronger forms of the drug, such as sinsemilla (the flowers and the leaves of the female cannabis plant), hashish (the resinous secretions of the hemp plant), and hash oil (a chemically concentrated form of delta-9-tetrahydrocannabinol, or THC, the psychotropic agent in marijuana).

Marijuana is usually smoked, although it may be eaten or made into a "tea." Low doses of marijuana create restlessness and an increasing sense of well-being, followed by dreamy relaxation and a frequent craving for sweets. Sensory perceptions may be heightened by the drug, whereas memory and rational thought are impaired. Marijuana's effects begin within a few minutes following use and may last for two to three hours.

Although marijuana has no officially sanctioned medical use, it may sometimes serve as a supplemental medication in cases of ongoing chemotherapy (where it often reduces nausea), glaucoma (where it may reduce pressure within the eye), anorexia and "AIDS wasting" (where it may increase appetite and lead to weight gain), and sleep disorders.[70] To support such use, voters in California and Arizona passed ballot initiatives in 1996 legalizing the use of marijuana for medical purposes when approved or prescribed by a doctor. California's medical marijuana law was overturned, however, by a unanimous U.S. Supreme

Court in the 2001 case of *U.S. v. Oakland Cannabis Buyers' Cooperative*.[71] In that case, the Court found that the activities of the Oakland (California) Cannabis Buyers' Cooperative, which distributed marijuana to qualified patients for medical purposes, were in violation of the U.S. Controlled Substances Act—regardless of what state law said. The Court also held that there is no medical necessity exception to the federal act's prohibitions on manufacturing and distributing marijuana.[72] In 2005, in the case of *Gonzales v. Raich*,[73] the Court reinforced its earlier holding, ruling that Congress holds the final authority, under the commerce clause of the U.S. Constitution, to prohibit the cultivation and use of marijuana. Even so, outgoing White House drug czar Gil Kerlikowske announced in 2009 that federal authorities would no longer raid medical-marijuana providers in the 13 states where voters have made medical marijuana legal.[74]

Most illicit marijuana users, however, do not use cannabis for medical purposes. The majority of users are young people, many younger than 20 years old. In 2011, for example, the National Institute on Drug Abuse reported that past-year use of marijuana was 13.7% for 8th graders, 27.5% for 10h graders, and 34.8% for 12th graders.[75]

Intelligence shows that domestic production accounts for about 19% of all marijuana in the United States.

Intelligence shows that domestic production accounts for about 19% of all marijuana in the United States. Most marijuana brought into the United States comes from Mexico, Jamaica, and Colombia.[76] Of all the marijuana entering the country or produced domestically, approximately one-quarter, or 4,000 metric tons, is seized or lost in transit.[77]

Cocaine

Cocaine (cocaine hydrochloride [HCL]) is the most potent central nervous system stimulant of natural origin.[78] Cocaine is extracted from the leaves of the coca plant (whose botanical name is *Erythroxylon coca*). Since ancient times, the drug has been used by native Indians throughout the highlands of Central and South America, who chew the leaves of the coca plant to overcome altitude sickness and to sustain the high levels of physical energy needed for strenuous mountain farming.

Cocaine has some medical value as a topical anesthetic for use on sensitive tissues, such as the eyes and mucous membranes. Throughout the early twentieth century, physicians valued cocaine for its ability to anesthetize tissue while simultaneously constricting blood vessels and reducing bleeding. Recently, more effective products have replaced cocaine in many medical applications.

A report by the ONDCP classifies cocaine users into three groups: "(1) the younger, often minority crack user; (2) the older injector who is combining cocaine HCL with heroin in a speedball; and (3) the older, more affluent user who is snorting cocaine HCL."[79] Cocaine generally reaches the United States in the form of a much-processed white crystalline powder. It is often diluted with a variety of other ingredients, including sugar and anesthetics like lidocaine. Dilution allows sellers to reap high profits from small amounts of the drug.

Cocaine is often diluted with a variety of other ingredients, allowing sellers to reap high profits from small amounts of the drug.

Cocaine produces intense psychological effects, including a sense of exhilaration, superabundant energy, hyperactivity, and extended wakefulness.[80] Irritability and apprehension may be unwanted side effects. Excessive doses may cause seizures and death from heart failure, cerebral hemorrhage, and respiratory collapse. Some studies show that repeated use of cocaine may heighten sensitivity to these toxic side effects of the drug.[81]

Federal data indicate that cocaine has become the country's most dangerous commonly used drug. During a recent year, nearly 100,000 hospital emergencies involving cocaine abuse were reported across the country.[82] The Federal Drug Seizure System reported the seizure of around 137,000 pounds of cocaine throughout the United States in 2010.[83]

Most cocaine enters the United States from Peru, Bolivia, or Colombia. Together, these three countries have an estimated annual production capability of around 555 tons of pure cocaine.[84] During the 1980s, most cocaine coming into the United States was controlled by the Medellín Cartel, based in Medellín, Colombia. Multinational counterdrug efforts had crippled the cartel by the start of the 1990s, however, and the Cali Cartel (based in Cali, Colombia), a loose organization of five semi-independent trafficking organizations, took over as the major illegal supplier of cocaine to this country. Arrests of the Cali Cartel's top leaders, Gilberto Rodriguez and his brother, Miguel, however, sounded the death knell for what may have been the world's most successful drug-trafficking organization ever.[85] By 2013, however, Mexican drug gangs had largely replaced Columbian cartels as major drug suppliers to the United States and Canada. In that same year, Mexican officials announced the arrest of Miguel Angel Trevino Morales, one of Mexico's most-wanted drug lords and leader of the Zetas cartel, and Mario Armando Ramirez Trevino, a top leader of the Gulf Cartel.[86]

Heroin

Classified as a narcotic, heroin is a derivative of opium—itself the product of the milky fluid found in the flowering poppy plant (*Papaver somniferum*). Opium poppies have been grown in the Mediterranean region since 300 B.C.[87] and are now produced in many other parts of the world as well. Although heroin is not used medicinally in this country, many of the substances to which it is chemically related—such as morphine, codeine, hydrocodone, naloxone, and oxymorphone—do have important medical uses as pain relievers.

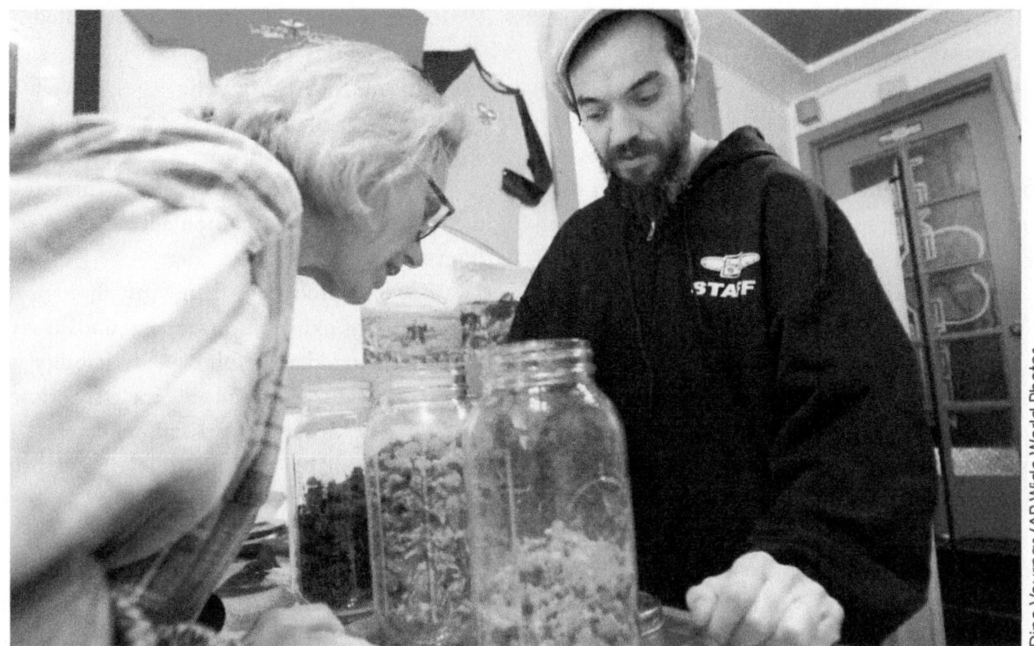

Dino Vournas/AP Wide World Photos

An unidentified medical marijuana patient smells different offerings at the Love Shack medicinal cannabis shop in the Mission District of San Francisco. In 1996, voters in California and Arizona passed ballot initiatives legalizing the use of marijuana for medical purposes when approved or prescribed by a doctor. In 2010, New Jersey enacted similar legislation. In 2001 and again in 2005, however, the U.S. Supreme Court effectively invalidated California's Compassionate Use Act when it held that Congress has the authority to prohibit marijuana cultivation and use nationwide. What is the current legal status of medical marijuana in the United States?

Heroin is a highly seductive and addictive drug that produces euphoria when smoked, injected underneath the skin ("skin popping"), or shot directly into the bloodstream ("mainlining"). Because tolerance for the drug increases with use, larger and larger doses of heroin must be taken to achieve the pleasurable effects desired by addicts. Heroin deprivation causes withdrawal symptoms that initially include watery eyes, runny nose, yawning, and perspiration. Further deprivation results in restlessness, irritability, insomnia, tremors, nausea, and vomiting. Stomach cramps, diarrhea, chills, and other flulike symptoms are also common. Most withdrawal symptoms disappear within seven to ten days[88] or when the drug is readministered.

Street-level heroin varies widely in purity. It is often cut with powdered milk, food coloring, cocoa, or brown sugar. Most heroin sold in the United States is only 5% pure.[89] Because of dosage uncertainties, overdosing is common. Mild overdoses produce lethargy and stupor, whereas larger doses may cause convulsions, coma, and death. Other risks, including infectious hepatitis and AIDS, are associated with using contaminated needles from other users. The Centers for Disease Control and Prevention (CDC) estimates that almost one-third of AIDS cases are associated with intravenous drug use.[90]

Heroin abuse has remained fairly constant during the past few decades. Some indicators point to an increased availability of heroin in the last few years.[91] Street-level heroin prices have declined in recent years, and nationwide heroin-related emergency room admissions have reached almost 40,000 per year.

Most heroin in the United States comes from South America, Southwest Asia (Afghanistan, Pakistan, and Iran), Southeast Asia (Burma, Laos, and Thailand), and Mexico. According to data from the Heroin Signature Program (HSP), which uses chemical analysis of the trace elements in heroin supplies to identify source countries, 65% of all heroin entering the United States comes from South America.[92] The Federal Drug Seizure System reports the seizure of approximately 5,510 pounds of heroin throughout the United States annually.[93]

Evidence indicates that the heroin abuse picture is changing. Although older users still dominate heroin markets in all parts of the country,[94] increasing numbers of non-inner-city young users (under 30 years of age) are turning to the drug. Additionally, because high-purity powdered heroin is widely available in most parts of the country, new users seem to be experimenting with heroin inhalation, which often appears to lead to injection as addiction progresses. Treatment programs report that the typical heroin user is male, is over 30 years old, and has been in treatment previously.[95] Alcohol, cocaine, and marijuana remain concurrent problems for heroin users in treatment.

Methamphetamine

Known on the street as speed, chalk, meth, ice, crystal, and glass, methamphetamine is a stimulant drug chemically related to other amphetamines (like MDMA) but with stronger effects on the central nervous system. Methamphetamine is taken in pill form or is used in powdered form by snorting or injecting.[96] Crystallized methamphetamine (known as ice, crystal, or glass) is a smokable and even more powerful form of the drug. Effects

■ **club drug** A synthetic psychoactive substance often found at nightclubs, bars, "raves," and dance parties. Club drugs include MDMA (Ecstasy), ketamine, methamphetamine (meth), GBL, PCP, GHB, and Rohypnol.

Tahir Safi/Xinhua/Photoshot/Newscom

An Afghan farmer works in a poppy field in Nangarhar province of eastern Afghanistan. Despite U.S. efforts to curtail poppy cultivation in the country, Afghanistan remains the world's largest producer of heroin. Much of the money that's spent on heroin comes from the United States, where the sale of illicit drugs constitutes a multibillion-dollar industry. Why haven't U.S. efforts to stop poppy cultivation worked?

of methamphetamine use include increased heart rate and blood pressure, increased wakefulness, insomnia, increased physical activity, decreased appetite, and anxiety, paranoia, or violent behavior. The drug is easily made in simple home "laboratories" ("meth labs") from readily available chemicals, and recipes describing how to produce the substance circulate on the Internet. Methamphetamine appeals to the abuser because it increases the body's metabolism, produces euphoria and alertness, and gives the user a sense of increased energy. An increasingly popular drug at raves, it is not physically addictive but can be psychologically addictive. High doses or chronic use of the drug increases nervousness, irritability, and paranoia.

Methamphetamine use increases the release of very high levels of the neurotransmitter dopamine, which stimulates brain cells, enhancing mood and body movement.[97] Chronic methamphetamine abuse significantly changes how the brain functions. Animal research going back more than 30 years shows that high doses of methamphetamine can damage neuron cell endings. Dopamine- and serotonin-containing neurons do not die after methamphetamine use, but their nerve endings ("terminals") are stunted, and regrowth appears to be limited. Noninvasive human-brain-imaging studies have shown alterations in the activity of the dopamine system with regular methamphetamine use. These alterations are associated with reduced motor speed and impaired verbal learning. Recent studies in chronic methamphetamine abusers have also revealed significant structural and functional changes in areas of the brain associated with emotion and memory, which may account for many of the emotional and cognitive problems observed in chronic methamphetamine abusers.

Recently, the DEA reported the emergence of candy-flavored methamphetamine around the country, leading to fears that methamphetamine manufacturers were targeting especially young users. Police departments in Nevada, California, Washington, Idaho, Texas, and New Mexico reported finding bags of what users call "Strawberry Quick"—a flavored form of methamphetamine meant to be snorted or sold illegally as a powerful energy drink.[98]

Club Drugs

In 1997, DEA officials recommended that the "date rape drug" Rohypnol (also discussed in Chapters 2 and 4) be added to the list of Schedule I controlled substances. Rohypnol is a powerful sedative manufactured by Hoffmann-LaRoche Pharmaceuticals.[99] Rohypnol is among the "club drugs" that became popular in the mid- to late 1990s. **Club drug** is a general term used to refer primarily to synthetic psychoactive substances often found at nightclubs, bars, and "raves" (all-night dance parties). In addition to Rohypnol, club drugs include GHB, GBL (gamma-butyrolactone), MDMA (Ecstasy), ketamine, methamphetamine (meth), and PCP.

A few years ago, the growing use of Rohypnol at fraternity parties, raves, bars, and dance clubs gave rise to the phrase *chemically assisted date rape*, a term now applied to rapes in which sexual predators use drugs to incapacitate unsuspecting victims. Rohypnol (a brand name for flunitrazepam) is a member of the benzodiazepine family of depressants and is legally prescribed in 64 countries for insomnia and as a preoperative anesthetic. Seven to ten times more powerful than Valium, Rohypnol has become popular with some college students and with "young men [who] put doses of Rohypnol in women's drinks without

CJ | NEWS

New "Bath Salts" Drugs: Very Potent, Hard to Target

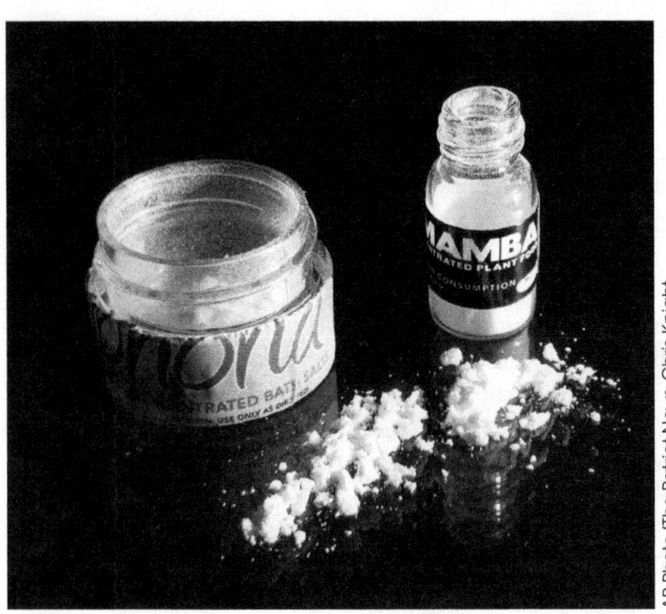

AP Photo/The Patriot-News, Chris Knight

Bath salts displayed on a store counter in Pennsylvania. Bath salts are synthetic stimulants that mimic the effects of traditional drugs like cocaine and methamphetamine, but a recent law banned more than two dozen of the most common chemicals used to make the drugs.

When a naked Florida man tried to chew off the face of a homeless man in May 2012, police initially reported he was high on "bath salts." It turned out the rampaging man—shot dead by police—only had marijuana in his system. But his bizarre behavior seemed to fit the profile of people high on bath salts, a relatively cheap but extremely potent new drug.

After initially giving users a quick high, bath salts can plunge them into agitation, paranoia, hallucinations, extreme violence, and suicide. An emergency room doctor reported that one user had been running for more than 24 hours, convinced that the devil was chasing him with an ax.

Bath salts have little in common with soap, although they come in a powder that resembles Epsom salts—a non-drug that is put into bathwater to relieve aches and pains. Rather than being one specific drug, this new narcotic is actually a family of drugs, first developed in makeshift laboratories about a decade ago.

After bath salts overran Europe, U.S. poison control centers began registering overdoses from them in 2009. The drugs, often imported from China or India, proved to be particularly popular in the American South. When they were initially not outlawed in the United States, they were openly sold in head shops, adult book shops, and convenience stores for as little as $15 a packet. Each packet, wrapped in foil or plastic, holds 200 to 500 milligrams of powder.

These potent packets have been sold as fake plant food, stain remover, toilet bowl cleaner, and hookah cleaner, in addition to bath salts. They are usually labeled "Not for Human Consumption," in an attempt to protect purveyors from prosecution. When a drug is not specifically outlawed, federal law stipulates that law enforcement officials must show it was intended for human use before targeting purveyors.

The enforcement situation changed in October 2011, however, when the U.S. Food and Drug Administration (FDA) took action. Citing an "imminent threat to public safety," the FDA placed a temporary federal ban on three of the most common drugs used for bath salts: mephedrone, methylenedioxypyrovalerone (MDPV), and methylone.

By 2011, several states had also banned the drug. West Virginia, for instance, made it a misdemeanor to sell, buy, or possess the drug, with a maximum sentence of six months in jail and a $1,000 fine.

In 2012, the federal ban became permanent and was widened to more than two dozen of the most common bath salt drugs. But even with the full federal ban, bath salts remain difficult for law enforcement to identify. Many of these substances are too new to show up on standard drug tests, and new variations come out constantly. According to the United Nations Office of Drugs and Crime, 42% of testing laboratories in 48 countries reported new substances in 2011 alone.

Enforcement will continue to be difficult, because the changing chemistry of the drugs will require new laws to ban them and changes in standard drug tests to identify them. "The moment you start to regulate one of them, they'll come out with a variant that sometimes is even more potent," said Dr. Nora Volkow, director of the National Institute on Drug Abuse.

Resources: Matthew Perrone, "Bath Salts Laws: Officials Struggle to Regulate New Recipes for Synthetic Drugs," Associated Press, July 25, 2012, http://www.huffingtonpost.com/2012/07/25/bath-salts-laws_n_1701339.html; United Nations Office of Drugs and Crime, "Tracking Designer Drugs, Legal Highs and Bath Salts, November 1, 2012, https://www.unodc.org/unodc/en/frontpage/2012/November/tracking-designer-drugs-legal-highs-and-bath-salts.html; Matt McMillan,"'Bath Salts' Drug Trend: Expert Q&A," WebMD, no date, http://www.webmd.com/mental-health/features/bath-salts-drug-dangers.

their consent in order to lower their inhibitions."[100] Available on the black market, it dissolves easily in drinks and can leave anyone who unknowingly consumes it unconscious for hours, making them vulnerable to sexual assault. The drug is variously known as roples, roche, ruffles, roofies, and rophies on the street.

Penalties for trafficking in flunitrazepam were increased under the Drug-Induced Rape Prevention and Punishment Act of 1996,[101] effectively placing it into a Schedule I category for sentencing purposes. Under the act, it is a crime to give someone a controlled substance without the person's knowledge and with intent to commit a violent crime.

GHB, another "date rape drug," has effects similar to those of Rohypnol. GHB, a central nervous system depressant, is now designated as a Schedule I drug but was once sold in health food stores as a performance enhancer for use by bodybuilders. Rumors that GHB stimulates muscle growth were never proven. The intoxicating effects of GHB, however, soon became obvious. In 1990, the Food and Drug Administration (FDA) banned the use of GHB except under the supervision of a physician. In 2001, federal sentencing guideline changes removed the upper limit, or cap, on GHB sentences in cases where large amounts of the drug were sold or distributed.[102]

■ **pharmaceutical diversion** The transfer of prescription medicines controlled by the Controlled Substances Act by theft, deception, and/or fraudulent means for other than their intended legitimate therapeutic purposes.

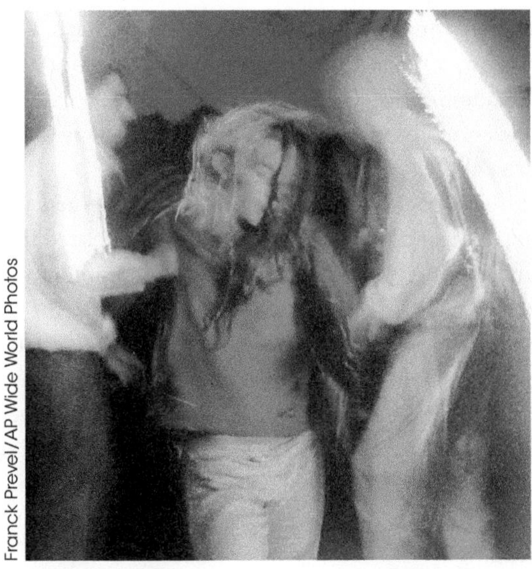

Franck Prevel/AP Wide World Photos

A fire juggler lighting up the night at a rave attended by thousands in the French village of Paule. Raves typically involve abundant drugs, particularly the designer drug Ecstasy. What are some other club drugs?

GBL is a chemical used in many industrial cleaners and is the precursor chemical for the manufacture of GHB. Several Internet businesses offer kits that contain GBL and the proper amount of sodium hydroxide or potassium hydroxide, along with litmus paper and directions for the manufacture of GHB. The process is quite simple and does not require complex laboratory equipment. Like GHB, GBL can be added to water and is nearly undetectable. GBL is synthesized by the body to produce GHB. As a consequence, some users drink small quantities of unmodified GBL. This often causes a severe physical reaction, usually vomiting. GBL increases the effects of alcohol and can cause respiratory distress, seizure, coma, and death.

MDMA (Ecstasy), the most popular of the club drugs, is primarily manufactured in and trafficked from Europe. DEA reports indicate widespread abuse of this drug within virtually every city in the United States. Estimates from the Drug Abuse Warning Network (DAWN) show that hospital emergency department mentions for MDMA quadrupled over three years, from 1,143 in 1998 to 4,511 in 2000.[103] A redesigned DAWN survey, known as the New DAWN, found that 21,836 MDMA-related emergency department visits were reported in 2010.[104] Although MDMA is primarily found in urban settings, abuse of this substance has also been noted in rural communities. Prices in the United States generally range from $20 to $30 per dosage unit; however, prices as high as $50 per dosage unit have been reported in Miami. MDMA (3, 4-methylenedioxymethamphetamine) is a synthetic psychoactive substance possessing stimulant and mild hallucinogenic properties. Known as the "hug drug" or the "feel-good drug," it reduces inhibitions, produces feelings of empathy for others, eliminates anxiety, and produces extreme relaxation. In addition to chemical stimulation, the drug reportedly suppresses the need to eat, drink, or sleep. This enables club goers to endure all-night and sometimes two- to three-day parties. MDMA is taken orally, usually in tablet form, and its effects last approximately four to six hours. Often taken in conjunction with alcohol, the drug destroys both dopamine and serotonin cells in the brain. When taken at raves, the drug often leads to severe dehydration and heatstroke, as it has the effect of "short-circuiting" the body's temperature signals to the brain. An MDMA overdose is characterized by a rapid heartbeat, high blood pressure, faintness, muscle cramping, panic attacks, and, in more severe cases, seizures or loss of consciousness. Side effects of the drug are jaw muscle tension and teeth grinding. As a consequence, MDMA users will often use pacifiers to help relieve the tension. The most critical life-threatening response to MDMA is hyperthermia, or excessive body heat. Many rave clubs now have cooling centers or cold showers designed to allow participants to lower their body temperatures. MDMA is a Schedule I drug under the Controlled Substances Act.

The Ecstasy Anti-Proliferation Act of 2000[105] directed the U.S. Sentencing Commission to increase penalties for the manufacture, importation, exportation, and trafficking of MDMA. Under resulting emergency amendments to the U.S. sentencing guidelines, MDMA trafficking became a crime with serious consequences. As a result of this penalty enhancement, which became permanent in 2001, a violator convicted of trafficking 200 grams of MDMA (approximately 800 tablets) can receive a five-year prison sentence.

Ketamine (known as K, special K, and cat Valium) produces effects that include mild intoxication, hallucinations, delirium, catatonia, and amnesia. Low doses of the drug create an experience called K-Land, a mellow, colorful "wonder world." Higher doses produce an effect referred to as K-Hole, an "out-of-body" or "near-death" experience. Use of the drug can cause delirium, amnesia, depression, long-term memory and cognitive difficulties, and fatal respiratory problems.[106]

Marketed as a dissociative general anesthetic for human and veterinary use, the only known street source of ketamine is **pharmaceutical diversion**. Significant numbers of veterinary clinics have been robbed specifically for their ketamine stock.

Ketamine liquid can be injected, applied to smokable material, or consumed in drinks. The powdered form is made by allowing the solvent to evaporate, leaving a white or slightly off-white powder that, once pulverized, looks very similar to cocaine. The powder can be put into drinks, smoked, or injected. Pharmaceutical diversion and illicit Internet pharmacies are major sources of supply for pharming parties, which have been called "the newest venue for teenage prescription-drug abuse."[107]

Finally, in 2011, the DEA used its emergency scheduling authority to temporarily control methylenedioxypyrovalerone and two other synthetic stimulants, mephedrone and methylone.[108] The drugs, which can be snorted or taken orally, are also known as psychoactive bath salts (PBAs), and go by names such as Ivory Wave and Vanilla Sky. They act as central nervous system stimulants.

The Costs of Abuse

The societal costs of drug abuse can be categorized as direct and indirect. Direct costs are those costs immediately associated with drug crimes themselves, such as the dollar losses incurred by a homeowner from a burglary committed to support a drug habit. The value of stolen property, damage to the dwelling, and the costs of cleanup and repair figure into any calculation of direct costs. Indirect costs, which are harder to measure, include such things as the homeowner's lost wages from time off at work needed to deal with the burglary's aftermath, the value of time spent filling out police reports, going to court, and so on. Other indirect costs, such as the mental stress and feelings of violation and personal insecurity that often linger in the wake of criminal victimization are much harder to measure.

The Indirect Costs of Abuse

A recent report by the U.S. Department of Justice's National Drug Intelligence Center (NDIC), entitled *The Economic Impact of Illicit Drug Use on American Society*[109] placed the annual national cost of illicit drug use in the United States at a staggering $193 billion. That total includes costs from three areas: (1) justice system expenditures needed to deal with the consequences of illegal drug use, (2) health care, and (3) lost productivity.

The first area, justice system expenditures, includes three component costs: criminal justice–system costs (estimated to be $56,373,000), direct costs to crime victims ($1,455,000), and a catchall category of other crime costs ($3,547,885). The three subcategories together total $61,376,694. Justice system–related expenses include money spent on incarcerating drug offenders, on state and local drug abuse–related police protection, on jails for holding drug offenders prior to trial, and on the adjudication of drug offenders. Much of the justice system cost comes in the form of private legal defense attributable to drug abuse.

Health-care costs include money spent on emergency room care, ongoing medical treatment for drug abuse–related illnesses and dependence, psychiatric institutionalization, and hospitalization. A major component of health-care costs related to drug abuse consists of spending on care for HIV/AIDS patients and hepatitis patients whose infections are directly attributable to drug-related activities (for example, the sharing of needles). Also included are expenses stemming from the annual estimated 23,500 drug-related deaths from overdose, poisoning, and homicide. The costs associated with this second category total $11,416,232.

Finally, costs of lost productivity include six components: labor participation costs ($49,237,777), specialty treatment costs for services provided at the state level ($2,828,207), specialty treatment costs for services provided at the federal level ($44,830), hospitalization costs ($287,260), costs of incarceration ($48,121,949), and premature mortality costs ($16,005,008). These categories total $120,304,004.

As the NDIC report points out, the largest proportion of indirect costs comes from lost worker productivity. In contrast to the other indirect costs of drug abuse (which entail expenditures for goods and services), this value reflects a loss of potential—specifically, lost work in the labor market and in household production that was never performed but could reasonably be expected to have been performed in the absence of drug abuse. Estimates of lost worker productivity are based on premature death from drug use, lost time at work due to criminal victimization, and institutionalization for drug treatment and dependence also enter the totals. Other studies have found that the legitimate U.S. economy loses about 1 million person years of effort every 12 months as the result of drug-related crimes.[110]

Drug-Related Crime

The direct costs of drug-related crime have at least three dimensions: (1) economic losses from crimes committed by drug users to obtain money for drugs or from crimes committed by users whose judgment is altered by drugs; (2) the costs associated with drug transactions themselves (for example, what people spend to buy drugs); and (3) economic losses due to organized criminal activities in support of the drug trade (including money laundering).

The Office of National Drug Control Policy says that about 382,000 individuals suffer drug abuse–attributable violent crimes every year and that about 5.2% of all homicides are related to narcotic drug-law violations.[111] Additionally, an estimated 5 million property offenses are committed annually in order to pay for illicit drugs. The ONDCP estimates that more than a quarter of the total number of property offenses in any given year are directly attributable to drug abuse.[112] Other crimes committed by those seeking to pay for drugs include prostitution, identity theft, fraud, and robbery. As Figure 16-3 shows, approximately 1.53 million people were arrested for drug-law violations (excluding alcohol) in the United States in 2011.[113]

Crimes committed by drug-dependent offenders can run the gamut from serious to relatively minor. A National Institute of Justice study of 201 heroin users in Central and East Harlem (New York City), for example, found that each daily user committed on average about 1,400 crimes per year. Of these offenses, 1,116 were directly drug related, involving primarily drug sales and use.[114] Another 75 were relatively minor crimes, such as shoplifting, but the remaining 209 offenses committed by each user involved relatively serious violations of the law, such as robbery, burglary, theft, forgery, fraud, and the fencing of stolen goods. Another study, which examined the daily activities of 354 Baltimore heroin addicts over a nine-year period, found that they had committed a total of nearly 750,000 criminal offenses.[115] Learn more about the dynamics of the drug–crime relationship at **http://www.justicestudies.com/pubs/dynamics.pdf**, and see a summary of national findings from the 2012 National Survey on Drug Use and Health at **http://tinyurl.com/kforc7f.**

The sale of illegal drugs is a $57 billion industry in the United States; that's the amount that the ONDCP estimates that Americans spend annually on illicit drugs.[116] Some perspective on this figure can be gained by recognizing that each year Americans spend approximately $44 billion on alcohol products and another $37 billion on tobacco products.[117]

Organized criminal activities in support of the drug trade represent a third area of direct costs. Cash can flow into the

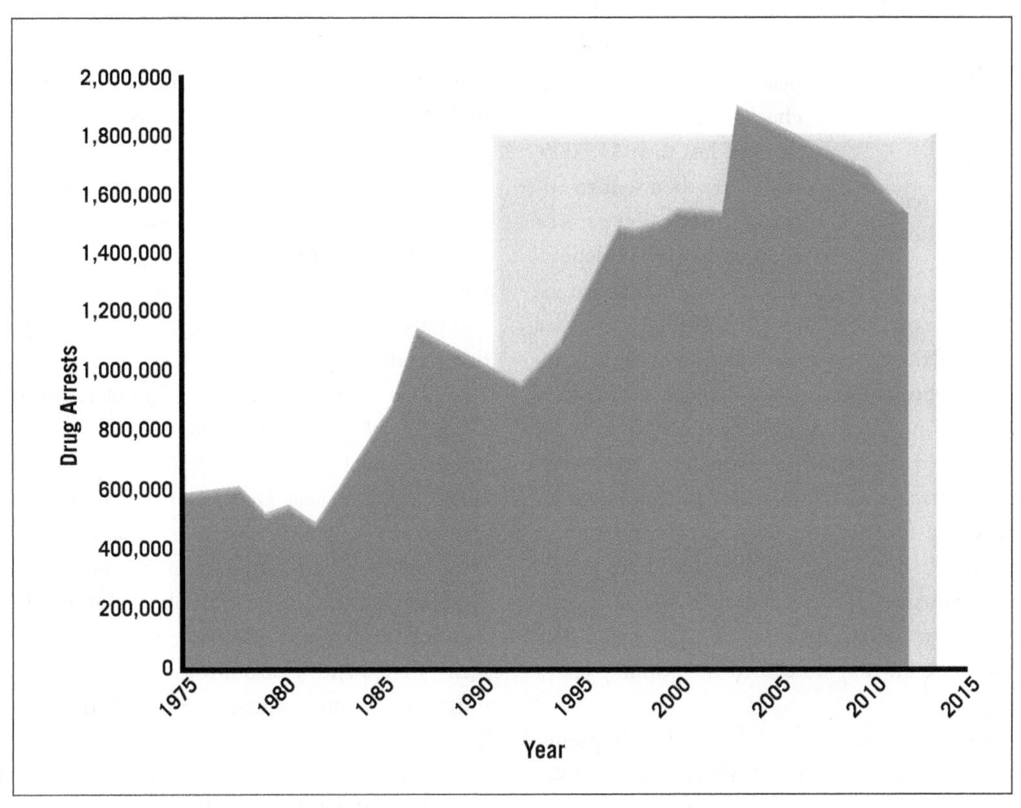

FIGURE 16-3 | Drug Arrests in the United States, 1975–2012

Source: Federal Bureau of Investigation, *Crime in the United States*, various years.

money laundering The process by which criminals or criminal organizations seek to disguise the illicit nature of their proceeds by introducing them into the stream of legitimate commerce and finance.[iv]

hands of dealers in such huge amounts that it can be difficult for them to spend it. Few people buy houses, cars, and other big-ticket items with cash, and cash transactions arouse suspicion. **Money laundering** is the name given to the process used by drug dealers to hide the source of their revenues, to avoid taxes, and to disguise the financial evidence of drug dealing. Drug profits are laundered by converting them into other assets, such as real estate, stocks and bonds, racehorses, jewels, gold, and other valuables. The Bureau of Justice Statistics says that many millions of dollars in drug money are laundered through commercial banks and other financial institutions each year.[118] Under the federal Money Laundering Strategy Act of 1998,[119] particular regions have been designated as high-intensity financial crimes areas (HIFCAs). HIFCAs can be found in Chicago, New York, New Jersey, San Juan, Los Angeles, San Francisco, and the southwestern border region, including Arizona and Texas. During 2001, more than 1,400 defendants were charged in U.S. district courts with money laundering as their most serious offense.[120]

In an effort to catch money launderers, U.S. banking law requires financial institutions to report deposits in excess of $10,000.[121] Traffickers attempt to avoid the law through two techniques known as smurfing and structuring.[122] Smurfers repeatedly purchase bank checks in denominations of less than $10,000, which are then sent to accomplices in other parts of the country, who deposit them in existing accounts. Once the checks have cleared, the funds are transferred to other banks or moved out of the country. Structuring is very similar and involves cash deposits to bank accounts in amounts of less than $10,000 at a time. After accounts are established, the money is withdrawn and deposited in increments elsewhere, making it difficult to trace. Countries that have secrecy laws protecting depositors are favorites for drug traffickers. Among them are Switzerland, Panama, Hong Kong, the United Arab Emirates, and the Bahamas.[123] Recent action by the U.S. government, however, has forced Swiss banks to reveal the identities of American depositors who may have used the country's laws to avoid scrutiny.[124]

In an effort to catch money launderers, U.S. banking law requires financial institutions to report deposits in excess of $10,000.

In 1994, in the case of *Ratzlaf* v. *U.S.*,[125] the U.S. Supreme Court made the task of catching money launderers more difficult. The Court ruled that no one can be convicted of trying to evade bank-reporting requirements unless authorities can prove that offenders knew they were violating the law.

In 2001, in an effort to enhance the amount of information received by federal regulators from banks about potential money-laundering activities, Congress passed the International Money Laundering Abatement and Anti-Terrorist Financing Act of 2001, which is Title III of the USA PATRIOT Act.[126] The law requires banks to make considerable effort in determining the source of money held in individual overseas accounts and provides for sanctions to be placed on nations that hinder this reporting.

Although federal law prohibits the laundering of money, relatively few states have had strict laws against the practice. As a consequence, many local enforcement agencies were reluctant to investigate money-laundering activities in their jurisdictions. To counteract this reluctance and to facilitate interagency cooperation, the federal government created the Financial Crimes Enforcement Network (FINCEN). Partially as a result of FINCEN leadership, 36 states have adopted money-laundering legislation, and more are likely to do so.[127] You can access the FINCEN website via **http://www.fincen.gov**.

Solving the Drug Problem

American drug-control strategies seem caught in a kind of limbo between conservative approaches, advocating supply reduction through strict enforcement and interdiction, and innovative strategies, proposing demand reduction through education, treatment, and counseling. In 2013, the Office of Control Policy (ONDCP) released its annual publication, *National Drug Control Strategy*,[128] offering a balanced public-health and public-safety approach to drug policy. Strategy authors said that the document represented a new approach to drug control "based on science, not ideology." In fact, the 2013 *National Drug Control Strategy* recognizes that substance-use disorders "are not just a criminal justice issue, but also a major public health concern." The *National Drug Control Strategy* recognizes that "the United States cannot arrest or incarcerate its way out of the drug problem," and emphasizes prevention over incarceration. Significantly, the publication also acknowledges that "drug issues are a truly global challenge requiring shared solutions," and seeks to expand global drug-prevention and drug-treatment initiatives through cooperation with other countries and the United Nations.

In developing the 2013 *National Drug Control Strategy*, officials at the ONDCP drew upon the *Principles of Modern Drug Policy* that were released at the Third World Forum Against Drugs, a gathering of international drug policy leaders hosted in Stockholm by the government of Sweden. The *Principles* document addresses the drug problem as a shared responsibility among nations, reaffirming support for the three United Nations drug conventions and calling for international cooperation to counter transnational organized crime and protect citizen security. Among the ten principles identified by the international conference, a number are especially important because they inform the ONDCP's 2013 strategy. They include:

1. *Ensure Balanced, Compassionate, and Humane Drug Policies.* Modern drug policies must acknowledge that drug addiction is a chronic disease of the brain that can be prevented and treated. Public health and public safety initiatives are complementary and equally vital to achieving reductions in drug use and its consequences. The challenge lies in combining cost-effective, evidence-based approaches that protect public health and safety.
2. *Integrate Prevention, Treatment, and Recovery Support Services into Public-Health Systems.* Public-health approaches, such as evidenced-based prevention, screening, and brief interventions in health-care settings, drug treatment programs, and recovery support services, are vital components of an effective drug-control strategy.
3. *Protect Human Rights.* Respect for human rights is an integral part of drug policy. Citizens, especially children, have the right to be safe from illegal drug use and associated crime, violence, and other consequences—whether in their family or the community. Drug-involved offenders who have contact with the criminal justice system deserve to be supervised with respect for their basic human rights and to be provided with services to treat their underlying substance-use disorder.
4. *Support and Expand Access to Medication-Assisted Therapies.* Recent innovations in medication-assisted therapies have demonstrated increasing effectiveness in reducing drug use and its consequences. These medications should be further studied to identify new therapies and best practices in program implementation.
5. *Reform Criminal Justice Systems to Support Both Public Health and Public Safety.* Criminal justice systems play a vital role in breaking the cycle of drug use, crime, incarceration, and rearrest. Although individuals should be held responsible for breaking the law, the criminal justice system should help bring them into contact with treatment services if they are suffering from a substance-use disorder. This includes providing treatment services in correctional facilities, providing alternatives to incarceration such as drug courts for nonviolent drug-involved offenders, and using monitoring, drug testing, and other means to ensure recovery from illegal drug use.
6. *Disrupt Drug Trafficking.* Transnational criminal organizations should be targeted, with a focus on the arrest, prosecution, and incarceration of drug traffickers; the seizure of illegal assets; the disruption of drug production networks; the control of precursor chemicals; and the eradication of illegal drug crops. International cooperation on information exchange, extradition, and training and technical assistance should be strengthened to eliminate safe harbors for transnational criminal organizations.
7. *Address the Drug Problem as a Shared Responsibility.* Drug use, production, and trafficking are increasingly globalized problems and pose challenges to all nations. Because of the global nature of today's drug markets, international cooperation is essential to protect public health and safety.[129]

Read the 2013 *National Drug Control Strategy* in its entirety at **http://justicestudies.com/pubs/ndcs_2013.pdf.**

Politics aside, six general types of strategies can be identified among the many methods proposed for attacking the drug problem: (1) strict law enforcement, (2) asset forfeiture, (3) interdiction, (4) domestic and international crop control, (5) prevention and treatment, and (6) legalization and decriminalization. Each of these strategies is discussed in the following pages, and the amount of money spent by the federal government on enforcement, prevention, treatment, interdiction is shown in Figure 16-4.

Strict Law Enforcement

Trafficking in controlled substances is, of course, an illegal activity in the United States—and has been for a long time. Conservative politicians generally opt for a strict program of antidrug law enforcement and costly drug sentences, with the goal of removing dealers from the streets, disrupting supply lines, and eliminating sources of supply. Unfortunately, legal prohibitions appear to have done little to discourage widespread drug abuse. Those who look to strict law enforcement as a primary drug-control strategy usually stress the need for secure borders, drug testing to

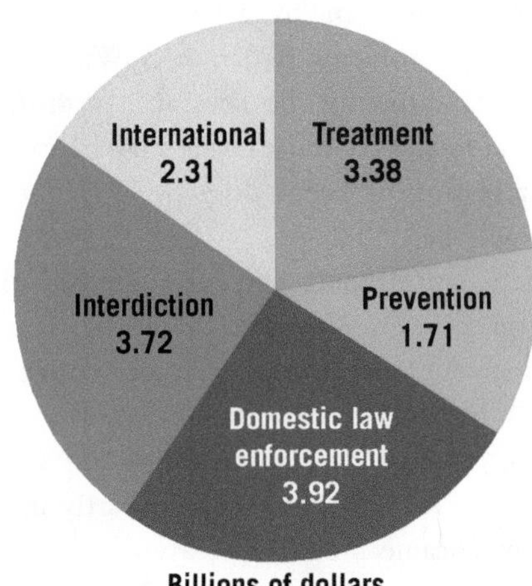

FIGURE 16-4 | Federal Drug Control Spending, 2012

Source: Office of National Drug Control Policy, *National Drug Control Budget, FY 2013.*

■ **forfeiture** The authorized seizure of money, negotiable instruments, securities, or other things of value. Under federal antidrug laws, judicial representatives are authorized to seize all cash, negotiable instruments, securities, or other things of value furnished or intended to be furnished by any person in exchange for a controlled substance, as well as all proceeds traceable to such an exchange.

■ **Racketeer Influenced and Corrupt Organizations (RICO)** A federal statute that allows for the federal seizure of assets derived from illegal enterprise.

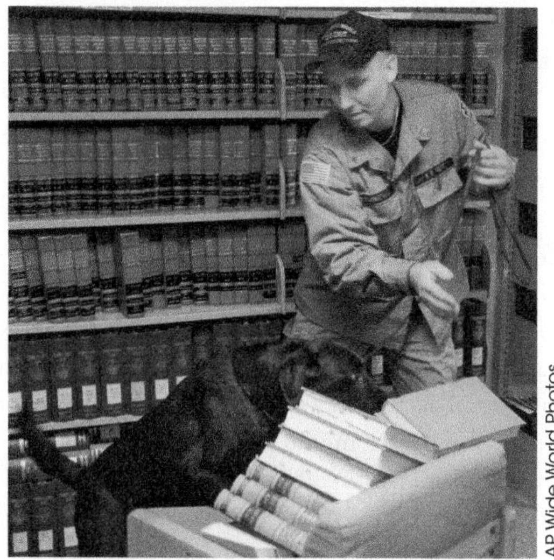
AP Wide World Photos

Sergeant Jeff Yurkiewicz of the Pennsylvania State Police K-9 Unit leading his dog, Jake, through a search for drugs and contraband at the Allegheny County Jail in Pittsburgh. More than 20 dogs were brought in to search the entire jail for drugs. Strict enforcement of antidrug laws is one of six strategies discussed in this chapter for attacking the drug problem. What are the other five?

identify users, and stiff penalties to discourage others from drug involvement. The U.S. Coast Guard policy of "zero tolerance," for example, which was highly touted in the late 1980s, led to widely publicized seizures of multimillion-dollar vessels when even small amounts of drugs (probably carried aboard by members of the crew) were found.

But strict enforcement measures may eventually lead to greater long-term problems. As James Q. Wilson observes, "It is not clear that enforcing the laws against drug use would reduce crime. On the contrary, crime may be caused by such enforcement because it keeps drug prices higher than they would otherwise be."[130]

Some U.S. enforcement strategies attempt to enlist the help of foreign officials. However, because drug exports represent extremely lucrative sources of revenue and may even be thought of as valuable "foreign trade" by the governments of some nations, effective international antidrug cooperation is hard to come by. In 1991, for example, partly in response to pressures from cocaine-producing cartels within the country, Colombia outlawed the extradition of Colombian citizens for any purpose—making the extradition and trial of Colombian cocaine kingpins impossible.

A number of international drug-control treaties do, however, exist. In 2005, in actions supported by such treaties, the DEA announced that its Operation Cyber Chase, which had targeted Internet traffickers who used more than 200 websites to illicitly distribute pharmaceutical controlled substances, had led to more than 20 arrests in the United States, Australia, Costa Rica, and India.[131] Among the substances being sold by the cybertraffickers through illegal pharmaceutical websites were the drugs Vicodin, Xanax, and OxyContin. International cooperation resulted in the forfeiture of 41 bank accounts that were linked to the storefronts and worth over $6 million.[132] One important group concerned with ensuring compliance with United Nations drug-control conventions is the International Narcotics Control Board (INCB). Visit the INCB via **http://www.incb.org.**

Asset Forfeiture

Forfeiture, an enforcement strategy that federal statutes and some state laws support, bears special mention. Antidrug forfeiture statutes authorize judges to seize "all monies, negotiable instruments, securities, or other things of value furnished or intended to be furnished by any person in exchange for a controlled substance . . . [and] all proceeds traceable to such an exchange."[133] Forfeiture statutes are based on the relation-back doctrine. This doctrine assumes that because the government's right to illicit proceeds relates back to the time they are generated, anything acquired through the expenditure of those proceeds also belongs to the government.[134]

The first federal laws to authorize forfeiture as a criminal sanction were passed in 1970. They were the Continuing Criminal Enterprise (CCE) statute and the Organized Crime Control Act. A section of the Organized Crime Control Act known as the **Racketeer Influenced and Corrupt Organizations (RICO)** statute was designed to prevent criminal infiltration of legitimate businesses and has been extensively applied in federal drug-smuggling cases. In 1978, Congress authorized civil forfeiture of any assets acquired through narcotics trafficking in violation of federal law. Many states modeled their own legislation after federal law and now have similar statutes.

The newer civil statutes have the advantage of being relatively easy to enforce. Civil forfeiture requires proof only by a preponderance of the evidence, rather than proof beyond a reasonable doubt, as in criminal prosecution. In civil proceedings based on federal statutes, there is no need to trace the proceeds in question to a particular narcotics transaction. It is enough to

In a single investigation involving two brothers convicted of heroin smuggling, the federal government seized a shopping center, three gasoline stations, and seven homes worth more than $20 million in New York City.

link them to narcotics trafficking generally.[135]

Forfeiture amounts can be huge. In one 15-month period, for example, the South Florida–Caribbean Task Force, composed of police agencies from the federal, state, and local levels, seized $47 million in airplanes, vehicles, weapons, cash, and real estate.[136] In a single investigation involving two brothers convicted of heroin smuggling, the federal government seized a shopping center, three gasoline stations, and seven homes worth more than $20 million in New York City.[137]

Although all states now have forfeiture statutes, prosecutions built on them have met with less success than prosecutions based on federal law. The Police Executive Research Forum (PERF) attributes the difference to three causes: (1) the fact that federal law is more favorable to prosecutors than most state laws are (2) the greater resources of the federal government, and (3) the difficulties imposed by statutory requirements that illegal proceeds be traced to narcotics trafficking.[138]

In 1993, in *U.S.* v. *92 Buena Vista Ave.*,[139] the U.S. Supreme Court established an "innocent owner defense" in forfeiture cases, whereby the government is prohibited from seizing drug-transaction assets that were later acquired by a new and innocent owner. In the same year, in the case of *Austin* v. *U.S.*,[140] the Court placed limits on the government's authority to use forfeiture laws against drug criminals, finding that seizures of property must not be excessive when compared to the seriousness of the offense charged. Otherwise, the justices wrote, the Eighth Amendment's ban on excessive fines could be contravened. The justices, however, refused to establish a rule by which excessive fines could be judged. The *Austin* ruling was supported by two other 1993 cases, *Alexander* v. *U.S.* and *U.S.* v. *James Daniel Good Real Property*.[141] In *Alexander*, the Court found that forfeitures under the RICO statute must be limited according to the rules established in *Austin*, and in *Good*, the Court held that "absent exigent circumstances, the Due Process Clause requires the Government to afford notice and a meaningful opportunity to be heard before seizing real property subject to civil forfeiture."

In 1996, the U.S. Supreme Court upheld the seizure of private property used in the commission of a crime, even though the property belonged to an innocent owner not involved in the crime. The case, *Bennis* v. *Michigan*,[142] involved the government's taking of a car that had been used by the owner's husband when procuring the services of a prostitute. In effect, the justices ruled, an innocent owner is not protected from property forfeiture related to criminal conviction.

Also in 1996, in the case of *U.S.* v. *Ursery*,[143] the Supreme Court rejected claims that civil forfeiture laws constitute a form of double jeopardy. In *Ursery*, the defendant's house had been seized by federal officials who claimed that it had been used to facilitate drug transactions. The government later seized other personal items owned by Guy Jerome Ursery, saying that they had been purchased with the proceeds of drug sales and that Ursery had engaged in money-laundering activities to hide the source of his illegal income. The court of appeals, however, reversed Ursery's drug conviction and the forfeiture judgment, holding that the double jeopardy clause of the U.S. Constitution prohibits the government from both punishing a defendant for a criminal offense and forfeiting his or her property for that same offense in a separate civil proceeding. In reaffirming Ursery's conviction, however, the U.S. Supreme Court concluded that "civil forfeitures are neither 'punishment' nor criminal for purposes of the Double Jeopardy Clause." In distinguishing civil forfeitures and criminal punishments, the majority opinion held that "Congress has long authorized the Government to bring parallel criminal actions and . . . civil forfeiture proceedings based upon the same underlying events . . . , and this Court consistently has concluded that the Double Jeopardy Clause does not apply to such forfeitures because they do not impose punishment."

Civil forfeiture laws have come under considerable fire recently as being fundamentally unfair. More than 200 forfeiture laws have been enacted across the country in recent years, many requiring only mere suspicion before items of value can be seized by government agents. Once property has been seized, getting it back can be a nightmare, even when no crime was committed. A few years ago, U.S. Representative Henry Hyde of Illinois reported that 80% of people whose property was seized by the federal government under drug laws were never formally charged with any crime.[144]

To address problems with federal forfeiture provisions, Congress passed the Civil Asset Forfeiture Reform Act of 2000. Under the law, federal prosecutors must meet a burden-of-proof standard in forfeiture cases. They are required to establish by a preponderance of the evidence that the property in question was subject to forfeiture. The property owner has five years in which to make a claim on the property after the government has claimed it, but a claimant's status as a fugitive from justice is grounds for dismissal of the case contesting the forfeiture of the property. Under the new law, it is a crime to remove or destroy property to prevent seizure for forfeiture.

interdiction The interception of drug traffic at the nation's borders. Interdiction is one of the many strategies used to stem the flow of illegal drugs into the United States.

© Tim Rue/Corbis

U.S. Customs and Border Protection canine officer Steve Fischer works with his dog, Hex, while examining a cargo container looking for illegal drugs at the Port of Long Beach, California. Where do most illegal drugs come from?

Interdiction

Annual seizures of cocaine in the United States total about 140 tons. In 2007, however, officials were surprised at the amount of cocaine seized when the U.S. Coast Guard cutter *Sherman* stopped the Panamanian cargo ship *Gatun* about 20 miles off the California coast.[145] Twenty tons of cocaine, with an estimated street value of $600 million, was discovered and transported to the Coast Guard facility in Alameda to be destroyed. The 14 crew members aboard the *Gatun* were Panamanians and Mexicans who were not armed and offered no resistance when stopped. It was not immediately clear if any of them knew what cargo they were carrying. Prior to the 2007 Coast Guard seizure, other large caches had vied for size records, including 9 tons of cocaine found in a house in Harlingen, Texas; 6 tons discovered on a ship in the Gulf of Mexico; and more than 5 tons hidden in barrels of lye in New York City.[146] A 2001 seizure by the Coast Guard of 13 tons of cocaine aboard a Belize-registered fishing boat south of San Diego, California, had held the previous record as the biggest cocaine seizure in U.S. maritime history.[147]

Interdiction involves efforts aimed at stopping drugs from entering the United States. The Coast Guard, the Border Patrol, and U.S. Customs agents have played the most visible roles in interdiction efforts during the last few decades. Interdiction strategies in the fight against drugs, however, are almost doomed to failure by the sheer size of the task. Although most enforcement efforts are focused on international airports and major harbors, the international boundary of the United States extends over 12,000 miles. Rough coastline, sparsely populated desert, and dense forests provide natural barriers to easy observation and make detection of controlled substances entering the country very difficult. Add to this the fact that more than 420 billion tons of goods and more than 270 million people cross over the American border annually, and the job of interdiction becomes more complicated still.[148] Because most drugs can be highly potent in even minute quantities, the interdiction strategy suffers from the proverbial "needle in the haystack" predicament.

Interdiction strategies in the fight against drugs are almost doomed to failure by the sheer size of the task.

Crop Control

Crop control strategies attempt to limit the amount of drugs available for the illicit market by targeting foreign producers. Crop control in source countries generally takes one of two forms. In the first, government subsidies (often with U.S. support) are made available to farmers to induce them to grow other kinds of crops. Sometimes illegal crops are bought and destroyed. The second form of control involves aerial spraying or ground-level crop destruction.

Source country crop control suffers from two major drawbacks.[149] First, the potentially large profits that can be made from illegal acreage encourage farmers in unaffected areas to take up the production of crops that have been destroyed elsewhere. Second, it can be difficult to get foreign governments to cooperate in eradication efforts. In some parts of the world, opium and coca are major cash crops, and local governments are reluctant to undertake any action directed against them.

Prevention and Treatment

As the population of incarcerated drug offenders swelled, state legislatures began to question the necessity of imprisoning nonviolent substance abusers who were not involved in drug sale or distribution. In 1996, as a consequence of such thinking, Arizona voters approved Proposition 200, the Drug Medicalization, Prevention, and Control Act. A central purpose of the act was to expand drug-treatment and drug-education services for drug offenders and to utilize probation for nonviolent drug offenders, thereby potentially diverting many arrested drug abusers from prison. To fund the program, the Arizona law established the state's Drug Treatment and Education Fund, administered by Arizona's Office of the Courts; the fund draws revenues from the state's luxury tax on liquor.

A study by Arizona's Administrative Office of the Courts concluded that the Arizona law is "resulting in safer communities

Frank Schmalleger

French customs officers check the luggage of a passenger arriving from Istanbul, Turkey. Drug interdiction, which involves efforts aimed at stopping drugs from entering a country illegally, is an international strategy. Are U.S. interdiction efforts working?

and more substance abusing probationers in recovery."[150] Moreover, said the report, the law has saved the state millions of dollars and has helped more than 75% of program participants to remain drug free.[151] In 2000, the state of California followed Arizona's lead when voters approved Proposition 36 (the California Substance Abuse and Crime Prevention Act of 2000), a sweeping initiative requiring treatment instead of imprisonment for nonviolent drug users throughout the state.[152] Similar legislation became law in Kansas in 2003 when Governor Kathleen Sebelius signed Senate Bill 123, the First Time Non-Violent Drug Offenders Act. The law requires Kansas judges to place nonviolent offenders convicted of nothing more than drug possession in community-based or faith-based drug-treatment programs for up to 18 months.[153]

Many different kinds of prevention and treatment programs are available for drug offenders. Michael Goodstadt of the Addiction Research Foundation groups drug-prevention and drug-treatment programs into three categories: (1) those that provide factual information about drugs; (2) those that address feelings, values, and attitudes; and (3) those that focus directly on behavior.[154] Most modern programs contain elements of all three approaches, and most experts agree that drug-prevention programs, if they are to be successful, must include a wide array of programs including components for individuals, families, schools, the media, health-care providers, law enforcement officials, and other community agencies and organizations.[155]

Most experts agree that drug-prevention programs, if they are to be successful, must include a wide array of programs, including components for individuals, families, schools, the media, health-care providers, law enforcement officials, and other community agencies and organizations.

Antidrug education programs can be found in schools, churches, and youth groups and may be provided by police departments, social service agencies, hospitals, and private citizens' groups. Project DARE (the Drug Abuse Resistance Education program) falls into Goodstadt's second category. DARE, which for many years had been the nation's most visible school-based antidrug education program, began as a cooperative effort between the Los Angeles Police Department and the Los Angeles Unified School District in 1983. Using uniformed law enforcement officers to conduct classes in elementary schools, the program focused on decision-making skills, peer pressure, and alternatives to drug use.

A 1994 study cast the effectiveness of the DARE program into doubt, and officials in the Clinton administration were charged with refusing to recognize the study's results. The study, published in the *American Journal of Public Health*, reviewed DARE programs in six states and British Columbia and found that "the popular drug prevention program does not work well and is less effective than other drug prevention efforts targeted at students."[156] Defending the DARE program, Justice Department officials questioned the study's methodology and published their own version of the study's results, which showed that "user satisfaction" with the DARE program is high. The study, according to Justice Department interpreters, found substantial grassroots support for the DARE program and led to the conclusion that DARE "has been extremely successful at placing substance abuse education in the nation's schools."[157]

Later studies again questioned DARE's effectiveness. A 1997 review of numerous DARE studies concluded that the program's "effects on drug use, except for tobacco use, are nonsignificant."[158] A 1999 University of Kentucky study tracked more than 1,000 midwestern students who participated in Project DARE in the sixth grade in order to see if the level of drug abuse among them differed from those who had not been exposed to the program.[159] The study found no difference in actual drug use immediately following exposure to the program or ten years later, when most of the former students were 20 years old. In 2001, the U.S. Surgeon General categorized DARE programs as "ineffective," and in 2007 the DARE program appeared on a list of treatments that have the potential to harm clients published by the Association for Psychological Science.[160] Even so, the program survives into the present day and has grown internationally—with programs in Europe as well as the United States.

drug court A special state, county, or municipal court that offers first-time substance-abuse offenders judicially mandated and court-supervised treatment alternatives to prison.

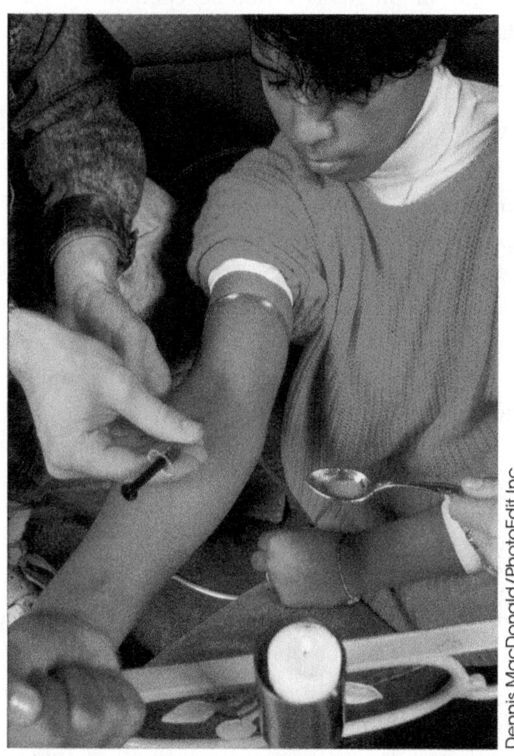
Dennis MacDonald/PhotoEdit Inc.

A young woman shooting up with help from friends. Drug abuse extends to all social groups and can be found among all ages. Why does illicit drug use persist in the United States after decades of efforts to curtail it?

Other studies also show that there is little evidence to support the belief that school-based antisubstance-abuse education will produce the desired effect on problem drug users or those at risk of beginning drug use.[161] Studies analyzing state-by-state spending on school-based drug education, for example, show little relationship between the amount of money spent on drug education and the number of hard-core cocaine users.[162] To be effective, programs will probably have to acknowledge the perceived positive aspects of the drug experience, as well as cultural messages that encourage drug use.[163] Until they do, many participants in today's antidrug programs may discount them as conflicting with personal experience.

Other kinds of drug-education programs may be effective, however. A study by the RAND Corporation's Drug Policy Research Center (DPRC), for example, found education to be the most efficacious alternative for dealing with drug abuse.[164] DPRC researchers focused on the use of alternative strategies for reducing cocaine abuse. Visit RAND's DPRC via **http://www.rand.org/multi/dprc.**

Drug Courts

One of the most widely accepted antidrug programs operating today is the **drug court**. Drug courts focus on promoting public safety and employ a nonadversarial approach that provides defendants with easy access to a range of alcohol-, drug-, and other related treatment and rehabilitation services. Drug courts also monitor abstinence from the use of drugs on an individual basis through frequent alcohol and other drug testing. Failing to comply with court-ordered treatment, or returning to drug use, may result in harsher punishments, including imprisonment.

Modern drug courts are modeled after a Dade County, Florida, innovation that became known as the Miami Drug Court model. An early evaluation of Miami's drug court found a high rate of success: Few clients were rearrested, incarceration rates were lowered, and the burden on the criminal justice system was lessened.[165] The success of the drug-court model led to $1 billion worth of funding under the Violent Crime Control and Law Enforcement Act of 1994 for the establishment of similar courts throughout the nation. Since then, the growth in the number of drug courts serving the nation has been huge. In 2013, the National Association of Drug Court Professionals (NADCP) reported that more than 2,700 drug courts were operating in the United States.[166]

A recent NIJ Multisite Adult Drug Court Evaluation[167] found that drug-court participants reported less criminal activity (40% vs. 53%) and had fewer rearrests (52% vs. 62%) than comparable offenders who were not handled by specialized courts. The study also found that drug-court participants reported less drug use (56% vs. 76%) and were less likely to test positive (29% vs. 46%) than comparable offenders. Finally, the study found that treatment investment costs were higher for participants, but because of lowered recidivism, drug courts averaged an overall savings of $5,680 to $6,208 per offender.

There are special drug courts for juveniles and for drunk drivers (sometimes called DUI courts). The National Drug Court Institute, in conjunction with the NADCP, provides training for judges and professional courtroom staff interested in today's drug-court movement. Learn more about drug courts via **http://www.ndci.org/ndci-home**.

Legalization and Decriminalization

According to the 2011 report by the Global Commission on Drug Policy, with which this chapter opened, "political leaders and public figures should have the courage to articulate publicly what many of them acknowledge privately: that the evidence overwhelmingly demonstrates that repressive strategies will not solve the drug problem."[168]

Two years before that report was issued, Gil Kerlikowske, the then-newly appointed Obama administration director of the Office of National Drug Control Policy, said that he wanted to

■ **legalization** Elimination of the laws and criminal penalties associated with certain behaviors—usually the production, sale, distribution, and possession of a controlled substance.

■ **decriminalization** The redefinition of certain previously criminal behaviors into regulated activities that become "ticketable" rather than "arrestable."

AFP PHOTO/Jaime Razuri/Getty Images

Cher Fisher (left) of England and Henny Fou of Holland posing before the start of the sixth annual beauty pageant for inmates at the Santa Monica Women's Prison in Lima, Peru. Most women incarcerated at the Peruvian penitentiary worked as drug "mules" and were caught trying to smuggle cocaine out of Peru. How can we solve the drug problem?

scrap the idea that the United States is fighting "a war on drugs," noting that the war analogy has created an unnecessary barrier to dealing with real problems. "Regardless of how you try to explain to people it's a 'war on drugs' or a 'war on a product,' people see a war as a war on them," Kerlikowske said. "We're not at war with people in this country."[169]

Also, in mid-2011, the Global Commission on Drug Policy, a prestigious group of internationally recognized political and scientific leaders, released a detailed report calling the war on drugs a failure. The commission recommended ending "the criminalization, marginalization, and stigmatization of people who use drugs but who do no harm to others." It also encouraged governments around the world to regulate drugs without unnecessary criminalization, and to undermine the power of organized crime groups that depend upon drug moneys to threaten the social order in many parts of the world. The commission explained that it wanted to "bring to the international level an informed, science-based discussion about humane and effective ways to reduce the harm caused by drugs to people and societies." The full report, *War on Drugs: Report of the Global Commission on Drug Policy*, is available for viewing at the commission's website (**http://www.globalcommissionondrugs.org**).

In mid-2011, the Global Commission on Drug Policy recommended ending "the criminalization, marginalization, and stigmatization of people who use drugs but who do no harm to others."

Realizations like those reached by former Drug Czar Gil Kerlikowske and the Global Commission on Drug Policy have led a number of well-meaning people to question the wisdom of current laws and to seek alternatives to existing U.S. drug-control policies. For them, it has become clear that the fight against drug abuse through the application of strict criminal justice sanctions is bound to fail. Arrest, incarceration, and a national prison system filled with drug-law violators do not seem to hold the answer to winning the drug-control battle.

More than one-third (37%) of the police chiefs who participated in the Police Foundation survey mentioned near the start of this chapter say that our nation's drug policy needs a fundamental overhaul, and 47% think that it needs major changes. Only 2% of responding chiefs said that they would maintain the status quo.[170]

Often regarded as the most "radical" approach to solving the drug problem, legalization and decriminalization have been proposed repeatedly, and in recent years, these ideas seem to be gaining at least a modicum of respectability. Although the words *legalization* and *decriminalization* are often used interchangeably, there is a significant difference. **Legalization** refers to the removal of all legal strictures from the use or possession of the drug in question. Manufacture and distribution might still be regulated. **Decriminalization**, on the other hand, substantially reduces penalties associated with drug use but may not eliminate them entirely. States like Oregon, which have decriminalized marijuana possession, for example, treat simple possession of small amounts of the substance as a ticketable offense similar to jaywalking or improper parking.[171] Hence decriminalization of a controlled substance might mean that the drug "would remain illegal but the offense of possession would be treated like a traffic violation, with no loss of liberty involved for the transgressor."[172] Other states, like Colorado and Washington, recently legalized possession of small amounts of marijuana for personal use, although laws in those jurisdictions bar public use of the drug, and driving while using marijuana still violates DUI laws.[173] In response to state action, in 2013 the U.S. Department of Justice issued a memorandum to all federal prosecutors providing guidance on enforcement of the Controlled Substances Act in those jurisdictions. The memorandum took a "hands-off" approach and established federal enforcement priorities with regard to marijuana distribution and use in states that have legalized the drug. Those priorities include preventing the distribution of marijuana to minors and

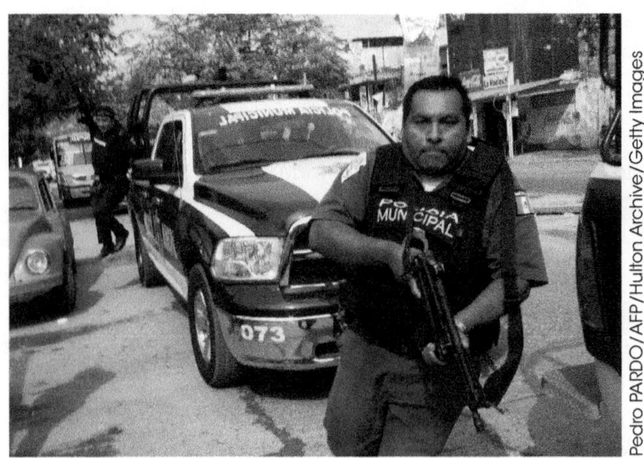

Pedro PARDO/AFP/Hulton Archive/Getty Images

A Mexican police officer responds to street violence initiated by drug gangs in Acapulco. Earlier, 15 decapitated bodies were discovered in front of a popular shopping area. Is the legalization or decriminalization of controlled substances a realistic option for Mexico? For the United States?

preventing marijuana sales revenue from going to criminal enterprises and cartels.[174]

Various arguments have been offered in support of both legalization and decriminalization. They say that if drugs were legal or decriminalized, they:[175]

- would be easy to track and control. The involvement of organized criminal cartels in the drug-distribution network could be substantially curtailed.
- could be taxed, generating huge revenues.
- would be cheap, significantly reducing the number of drug-related crimes committed to feed expensive drug habits.
- might decline in attractiveness, as some people find excitement in violating the law.
- would enhance civil liberties and reduce political turmoil.

Advocates of legalization are primarily motivated by cost–benefit considerations, weighing the social costs of prohibition against its results.[176] The results, they say, have been meager at best, whereas the costs have been almost more than society can bear.

Opponents of legalization argue from both a moral and a practical stance. Some, like former New York City Mayor Rudolph Giuliani, believe that legalization would only condone a behavior that is fundamentally immoral.[177] Others argue that under legalization, drug use would increase, causing more widespread drug-related social problems than exist today. Robert DuPont, former head of the National Institute on Drug Abuse, for example, estimates that up to ten times the number of people who now use cocaine would turn to the substance if it were legal.[178]

A compromise approach has been suggested in what some writers call the limitation model. The limitation model "would make drugs legally available, but with clearly defined limits as to which institutions and professions could distribute the drugs."[179] Hence, under such a model, doctors, pharmacists, and perhaps licensed drug counselors could prescribe controlled substances under appropriate circumstances, and the drugs themselves might be taxed. Some claim that a more extreme form of the limitation model might be workable. Under that model, drugs would be sold through designated "drugstores" with distribution systems structured much like those of liquor stores today. Controlled substances would be sold to those of suitable age but taxed substantially, and the use of such substances under certain circumstances (when driving, for example) might still be illegal. The regulation and taxation of controlled substances would correspond to today's handling of alcoholic beverages.

Another example of the limitation model, already tried in some countries, is the two-market system.[180] The two-market approach would allow inexpensive and legitimate access to controlled substances for registered addicts. Only maintenance amounts (the amounts needed to forestall symptoms of drug withdrawal) of the needed drugs, however, would be available. The two-market approach would purportedly reduce the massive profits available to criminal drug cartels while simultaneously discouraging new drug use among those who are not addicted. Great Britain provides an example of the two-market system. During the 1960s and 1970s, British heroin addicts who registered with the government received prescriptions for limited amounts of heroin, which was dispensed through medical clinics. Because of concern about system abuses, clinics in the late 1970s began to dispense reduced amounts of heroin, hoping to wean addicts away from the drug.[181] By 1980, heroin was replaced by methadone,[182] a synthetic drug designed to prevent the physical symptoms of heroin withdrawal. Methadone, in amounts sufficient to prevent withdrawal, does not produce a heroin-like high. Recent studies, however, show that methadone can build up in the body to a toxic level if taken too often.[183]

It is doubtful that the two-market system will be adopted in the United States anytime soon. American cultural condemnation of major mind-altering drugs has created a reluctance to accept the legitimacy of drug treatment using controlled substances. In addition, cocaine is much more of a problem in the United States than heroin is. The large number of drug abusers in the country, combined with the difficulty of defining and measuring addiction to drugs like cocaine, would make any maintenance program impractical.

One group advocating for a change in current drug laws, including the possible decriminalization of some controlled substances, is Law Enforcement Against Prohibition (LEAP). LEAP, whose members are current and former law enforcement officers, describes itself as "an organization made up of former drug warriors speaking out about the excesses and abuses of current drug policy and the utter failure of the war on drugs." The group originated with Peter Christ, a retired police captain living in New York City. Christ believed that an organization like LEAP would catch the attention of the media and appeal to other law enforcement officers. Visit LEAP at **http://www.leap.cc.**

SUMMARY

- In determining which substances should be called drugs, it is important to recognize the role of social convention. Hence, what Americans today consider to be a drug depends more on agreed-on understandings than it does on any inherent property of the chemical substance itself. Powerful drugs, those with the ability to produce substantially altered states of consciousness and with a high potential for addiction, occupy the forefront in social and legal condemnation. Among them are psychoactive substances like heroin, peyote, mescaline, LSD, and cocaine. Changes in thinking that took place during the 1960s and 1970s led to the inclusion of far less powerful substances, such as alcohol and nicotine, in the "drug" category.
- Many of today's controlled substances were once unregulated by law. Even heroin, cocaine, opium, and marijuana were once freely available and contained in widely used medicines. The first major piece of federal antidrug legislation was the Harrison Narcotics Act of 1914. It required anyone dealing in opium, morphine, heroin, cocaine, and specified derivatives of these drugs to register with the federal government and to pay a tax. In 1937, Congress passed the Marijuana Tax Act, which simply placed a tax on cannabis; those who did not pay the tax were subject to prosecution. The passage of the Boggs Act in 1951 made marijuana, along with a number of other drugs, a federally prohibited controlled substance. The Narcotic Control Act of 1956 increased penalties for drug trafficking and possession and made the sale of heroin to anyone under age 18 a capital offense. The Comprehensive Drug Abuse Prevention and Control Act, passed in 1970, is the basis of federal enforcement efforts today. Title II of the law is the Controlled Substances Act (CSA). The CSA sets up five schedules that classify psychoactive drugs according to their degree of psychoactivity and abuse potential. The Anti-Drug Abuse Act of 1988 increased penalties for "recreational" drug users and made weapons purchases by suspected drug dealers more difficult. The law also denies federal benefits, ranging from loans to contracts and licenses, to convicted drug offenders and allows capital punishment for drug-related murders.
- The use of illicit drugs is rather widespread in the United States. One of the best sources of data on the use of illegal drugs and the characteristics of drug users is the federal *National Survey on Drug Use and Health* (NSDUH), an annual publication of the Substance Abuse and Mental Health Services Administration. NSDUH data for 2011 showed that 22.5 million Americans age 12 and older were "current" users of illegal drugs. Nearly 18.4 million people were estimated to be using marijuana, and an estimated 1.4 million people were current cocaine users. An estimated 6.1 million Americans were current nonmedical users of prescription-type psychotherapeutic drugs. Although the numbers may seem large, these figures represent a considerable decline from 1979, the year in which the highest levels of drug abuse in the United States were reported. Nonetheless, figures for recent years show a gradual increase in drug use (especially "occasional use"). As this chapter points out, rates of drug use vary considerably by age, and adolescents and people in their 20s tend to show the highest rates of illicit drug use.
- Drug crimes and drug-related crimes account for a substantial proportion of all crimes committed in this country. Although the manufacture, importation, sale, and use of illegal drugs account for many law violations, many others are also linked to drug use. Among them are thefts of all kinds, burglary, assault, and murder. Similarly, many criminal enterprises are supported by the street-level demand for drugs. The high cost of drugs forces many users, some of whom have little legitimate income, to commit property crimes to make money to continue their drug habit. On the other hand, users of illicit drugs who have substantial legitimate incomes may indirectly shift the cost of drug use to society through lowered job productivity, psychological or family problems, and medical expenses.
- Six general types of strategies are among the many methods proposed for attacking the drug problem: (1) strict law enforcement, (2) asset forfeiture, (3) interdiction, (4) crop

control, (5) prevention and treatment, and (6) legalization and decriminalization. Recently, some states, including Colorado and Washington, have legalized the possession and use of small amounts of marijuana for private recreational purposes. It remains to be seen whether the federal government will aggressively enforce its own antidrug policies in those jurisdictions.

KEY TERMS

club drug, 539
controlled substance, 524
Controlled Substances Act (CSA), 529
curtilage, 533
decriminalization, 551
drug, 525
drug abuse, 523
drug court, 550
drug czar, 531
drug trafficking, 536
forfeiture, 546
Harrison Narcotics Act, 528
interdiction, 548
legalization, 551
money laundering, 544
pharmaceutical diversion, 541
physical dependence, 529
psychoactive substance, 525
psychological dependence, 529
Racketeer Influenced and Corrupt Organizations (RICO), 546
recreational drug user, 525

KEY CASES

***Alexander* v. *U.S.*, 547**
***Austin* v. *U.S.*, 547**
***California* v. *Greenwood*, 533**
***Oliver* v. *U.S.*, 533**
***Ratzlaf* v. *U.S.*, 544**
***U.S.* v. *Dunn*, 533**
***U.S.* v. *92 Buena Vista Ave.*, 547**
***U.S.* v. *Oakland Cannabis Buyers' Cooperative*, 537**
***U.S.* v. *Ursery*, 547**

QUESTIONS FOR REVIEW

1. What constitutes a drug for purposes of the criminal law? What role does social convention play in deciding what constitutes a controlled substance?
2. How long have substances that today would be considered illicit been used in the United States? For what purposes? List and describe some of the most important pieces of federal drug-control legislation.
3. What are the major types of drugs that are illegally used in this country? Describe the effects and legal classification of each.
4. What is the relationship between drug use and other social problems? What kinds of crimes might be linked to drug use?
5. What strategies have been used or suggested as ways of responding to the drug problem? Which of these strategies seem to hold the most potential?

QUESTIONS FOR REFLECTION

1. How successful have government efforts to curtail illicit drug use been? Why haven't they met with greater success?
2. What is meant by the decriminalization of illicit drugs? How does decriminalization differ from legalization?
3. Would you be in favor of the decriminalization of any drugs that are currently considered to be federally controlled substances? Legalization? If so, which ones and why?

NOTES

i. Bureau of Justice Statistics, *Drugs, Crime, and the Justice System* (Washington, DC: BJS, 1992), p. 20.
ii. Ibid., p. 21.
iii. Ibid.
iv. U.S. Department of Treasury, *2000–2005 Strategic Plan* (Washington, DC: U.S. Government Printing Office, 2000), p. 1.

1. Office of National Drug Control Policy, *Fact Sheet: A 21st Century Drug Policy* (Washington, DC: ONDCP, 2013), p. 1.
2. Michael Tarm, "Chicago Gets First 'Public Enemy No. 1' Since Al Capone: Mexican Cartel Kingpin," NBCnews.com, February 14, 2013, usnews.nbcnews.com/_news/2013/02/14/16961063-chicago-gets-first-public-enemy-no-1-since-al-capone-mexican-cartel-kingpin (accessed May 2, 2013).
3. "The World's Most Powerful People," *Forbes*, http://www.forbes.com/lists/2009/20/power-09_Joaquin-Guzman_NQB6.html (accessed May 20, 2013).
4. Peter D. Hart Research Associates, *Drugs and Crime across America: Police Chiefs Speak Out—A National Survey among Chiefs of Police* (Washington, DC: Police Foundation, December 2004).
5. National Association of Drug Court Professionals, *The Facts: Facts on Drug Courts* (Alexandria, VA: NADCP, 2001).
6. Federal Bureau of Prisons, "Quick Facts," http://www.bop.gov/news/quick.jsp#3 (accessed July 6, 2013).
7. Sentencing Project, *The Federal Prison Population: A Statistical Analysis* (Washington, DC: Sentencing Project, 2005).
8. Bureau of Justice Statistics, "Data Analysis Tool," http://www.bjs.gov/content/dtdata.cfm#corrections (accessed May 30, 2013).
9. The term *recreational user* is well established in the literature of drug abuse. Unfortunately, it tends to minimize the seriousness of drug abuse by according the abuse of even hard drugs the status of a hobby.
10. Cocaine has some legitimate medical uses, and can be a valuable anesthetic and vasoconstricting agent.
11. Howard Becker, *Outsiders: Studies in the Sociology of Deviance* (New York: Free Press, 1963).
12. Jay Tokasz, "Eight of 11 People in Car Die in Crash," *USA Today*, June 20, 1995.
13. In most states, individuals may also be arrested for driving under the influence of other drugs and controlled substances, including prescription medicines.
14. Fiscal year 2001 Transportation Appropriations Bill (H.R. 4475), signed by the president on October 23, 2000.
15. "Drunk Driving Limit Lowered," *Lawyers Weekly USA*, October 16, 2000.
16. Federal Bureau of Investigation, *Crime in the United States, 2012* (Washington, DC: U.S. Dept. of Justice, 2013).
17. James B. Jacobs, *Drinking and Crime, National Institute of Justice Crime File Series Study Guide* (Washington, DC: NIJ, n.d.).
18. *Traffic Safety Facts: 2008 Data* (Washington, DC: National Highway Traffic Safety Administration, 2008), http://www-nrd.nhtsa.dot.gov/Pubs/811155.PDF (accessed October 10, 2011).
19. National Highway Traffic Safety Administration, http://www.nhtsa.gov (accessed May 20, 2013)
20. FBI, *Crime in the United States, 2012*.
21. Bureau of Justice Statistics, *Report to the Nation on Crime and Justice*, 2nd ed. (Washington, DC: U.S. Government Printing Office, 1988), p. 50.

22. Jeffrey A. Roth, "Psychoactive Substances and Violence," *National Institute of Justice Research in Brief* (Washington, DC: NIJ, February 1994), p. 1.
23. Christopher J. Mumola, *Substance Abuse and Treatment, State and Federal Prisoners, 1997* (Washington, DC: Bureau of Justice Statistics, 1999).
24. Ibid.
25. Howard Abadinsky, *Drug Abuse: An Introduction* (Chicago: Nelson-Hall, 1989), p. 32.
26. Charles E. Terry and Mildred Pellens, *The Opium Problem* (New York: Committee on Drug Addiction, 1928).
27. Ibid.
28. Office of National Drug Control Policy, *Heroin, ONDCP Fact Sheet* (Washington, DC: ONDCP, 2003), p. 1.
29. Terry and Pellens, *The Opium Problem*, p. 76.
30. David Musto, *The American Disease: Origins of Narcotic Control* (New Haven, CT: Yale University Press, 1973).
31. Becker, Outsiders.
32. Franklin E. Zimring and Gordon Hawkins, *The Search for Rational Drug Control* (New York: Cambridge University Press, 1992).
33. Ibid., p. 9.
34. President's Commission on Organized Crime, *Organized Crime Today* (Washington, DC: U.S. Government Printing Office, 1986).
35. *Webb* v. *U.S.*, 249 U.S. 96 (1919).
36. Michael D. Lyman and Gary W. Potter, *Drugs in Society: Causes, Concepts, and Control* (Cincinnati, OH: Anderson, 1991), p. 359.
37. Drug Enforcement Administration, *Drug Enforcement: The Early Years* (Washington, DC: DEA, 1980), p. 41.
38. White House Conference on Drug Abuse, *Commission Report* (Washington, DC: U.S. Government Printing Office, 1963).
39. For a good summary of the law, see Drug Enforcement Administration, *Drugs of Abuse* (Washington, DC: U.S. Government Printing Office, 1997).
40. Drug Enforcement Administration, *Drug Enforcement Briefing Book* (Washington, DC: DEA, n.d.), p. 3.
41. A number of states now recognize that marijuana may be useful in the treatment of nausea associated with cancer chemotherapy, glaucoma, and other medical conditions.
42. DEA, *Drug Enforcement Briefing Book*, p. 3.
43. Ibid.
44. Ibid., p. 4.
45. Ibid.
46. DEA, *Drugs of Abuse*.
47. Ibid.
48. Anti-Drug Abuse Act of 1988, Public Law 100-690, Section 5251.
49. This provision became effective on September 1, 1989.
50. "Congress Gives Final OK to Major Antidrug Bill," *Criminal Justice Newsletter*, Vol. 19, No. 21 (November 1, 1988), pp. 1–4.
51. The U.S. Supreme Court upheld that legislation in the 2002 case of *Department of Housing and Urban Development* v. *Rucker*, 122 S.Ct. 1230, 152 L.Ed.2d 258 (2002).
52. "Congress Gives Final OK to Major Antidrug Bill," p. 2.
53. "Drug Lord Sentenced to Death," *USA Today*, May 15, 1991, p. 3A.
54. Ibid.
55. Public Laws 101–647, 103–322, 105–20, and 109–177.
56. USA PATRIOT Improvement and Reauthorization Act of 2005 (Public Law 109–177). The act was signed into law by President George W. Bush on March 9, 2006.
57. *California* v. *Greenwood*, 486 U.S. 35 (1988).
58. Ibid.
59. *Abel* v. *U.S.*, 363 U.S. 217 (1960).
60. *Oliver* v. *U.S.*, 466 U.S. 170 (1984).
61. *Hester* v. *U.S.*, 265 U.S. 57 (1924).
62. *U.S.* v. *Dunn*, 480 U.S. 294 (1987).
63. *California* v. *Ciraolo*, 476 U.S. 207 (1986).
64. *Florida* v. *Riley*, 488 U.S. 445, (1989).
65. Substance Abuse and Mental Health Services Administration, *National Survey on Drug Use and Health* (Rockville, MD: Office of Applied Studies, NHSDA, 2012).
66. ONDCP, *Heroin*, p. 1.
67. Office of National Drug Control Policy, *General Counterdrug Intelligence Plan* (Washington, DC: ONDCP, 2000), http://www.fas.org/irp/ops/le/docs/gcip/index.html.
68. Information in this section comes from the National Drug Intelligence Center, http://www.usdoj.gov/ndic.
69. Office of National Drug Control Policy, *Pulse Check: National Trends in Drug Abuse—Marijuana* (Washington, DC: ONDCP, 2002), http://www.whitehousedrugpolicy.gov/publications/drugfact/pulsechk/nov02/marijuana.html (accessed August 4, 2003).
70. See Anita Manning and Andrea Stone, "How States Will Face Regulating Marijuana as Medicine," *USA Today*, November 7, 1996.
71. *U.S.* v. *Oakland Cannabis Buyers' Cooperative*, 532 U.S. 483 (2001).
72. Ibid., syllabus.
73. *Gonzales* v. *Raich*, 545 U.S. 1 (2005).
74. Gary Fields, "White House Czar Calls for End to 'War on Drugs,'" *Wall Street Journal*, May 14, 2009, http://online.wsj.com/article/SB124225891527617397.html (accessed June 5, 2011).
75. National Institute on Drug Abuse, *Monitoring the Future: National Results on Adolescent Drug Use* (Ann Arbor, MI: Institute for Social Research, 2011), Table 6.
76. National Narcotics Intelligence Consumers Committee, *The NNICC Report, 1998* (Washington, DC: Drug Enforcement Administration, 2000), preface.
77. Ibid.
78. Ibid.
79. ONDCP, *Pulse Check*.
80. NNICC, *The NNICC Report, 1998*.
81. Ibid.
82. Ibid.
83. U.S. Census Bureau, "Federal Drug Arrests and Seizures by Type of Drug," http://www.census.gov/compendia/statab/2012/tables/12s0328.xls (accessed August 10, 2013).
84. NNICC, *The NNICC Report, 1998*.
85. Sam Vincent Meddis, "Arrests 'Last Rites' for Cali Cartel," *USA Today*, August 7, 1995.
86. Jessica King, "Mexico Arrests Alleged Leader of Gulf Cartel Near U.S. Border," CNN, August 20, 2013, http://www.cnn.com/2013/08/18/world/americas/mexico-cartel-arrest (accessed August 21, 2013).
87. DEA, *Drugs of Abuse*, p. 14.
88. Ibid., p. 12.
89. Ibid., p. 15.
90. Office of National Drug Control Policy, *The National Drug Control Strategy: Executive Summary* (Washington, DC: ONDCP, 1995), p. 13.
91. DEA, *Drugs of Abuse*.
92. NNICC, *The NNICC Report, 1998*.
93. U.S. Drug Enforcement Administration, *Drug Trafficking in the United States* (Washington, DC: DEA, 2004), http://www.policyalmanac.org/crime/archive/drug_trafficking.shtml (accessed December 3, 2011).
94. ONDCP, *Pulse Check*.

95. Ibid.
96. Much of the information in this section comes from the National Institute on Drug Abuse's website at http://www.nida.nih.gov (accessed July 4, 2011).
97. National Institute on Drug Abuse, "NIDA InfoFacts: Methamphetamine," http://www.nida.nih.gov/Infofacts/methamphetamine.html (accessed May 9, 2011).
98. Donna Leinwand, "DEA Sees Flavored Meth Use," *USA Today*, March 26, 2007.
99. Much of the information on club drugs in this section comes from Drug Enforcement Administration, "An Overview of Club Drugs," *Drug Intelligence Brief*, February 2000, http://www.usdoj.gov/dea/pubs/intel/20005intellbrief.pdf (accessed March 2, 2010).
100. "'Rophies' Reported Spreading Quickly throughout the South," *Drug Enforcement Report*, June 23, 1995, pp. 1–5.
101. Public Law 104-305.
102. Sentencing enhancement information in this section comes from the congressional testimony of Asa Hutchinson, administrator of the Drug Enforcement Agency, before the Senate Caucus on International Narcotics Control, December 4, 2001, http://www.usdoj.gov/dea/pubs/cngrtest/ct120401.html (accessed February 3, 2009).
103. Substance Abuse and Mental Health Services Administration, *The DAWN Report*, http://www.samhsa.gov/oas/dawn.htm (accessed March 10, 2010).
104. Substance Abuse and Mental Health Services Administration, *Drug Abuse Warning Network, 2010: National Estimates of Drug-Related Emergency Department Visits* (Washington, DC: U.S. Dept. of Health and Human Services, September, 2012), http://www.samhsa.gov/data/2k13/DAWN2k10ED/DAWN2k10ED.htm (accessed August 11, 2013).
105. Public Law 106-310.
106. DEA, "An Overview of Club Drugs," from which some of the wording in this section is taken.
107. Carolyn Banta, "Trading for a High: An Inside Look at a 'Pharming Party,'" *Time*, August 1, 2005, p. 35.
108. Fran Lowry, "DEA Moves to Make 'Bath Salts' Illegal as Overdoses Rise," *Medscape Medical News*, September 7, 2011.
109. National Drug Intelligence Center, *The Economic Impact of Illicit Drug Use on American Society* (Washington, DC: U.S. Department of Justice, 2011).
110. Office of National Drug Control Policy, *The Economic Costs of Drug Abuse in the United States, 1992–2002* (Washington, DC: ONDCP, December 2004).
111. Office of National Drug Control Policy, *The National Drug Control Strategy 2003: Executive Summary* (Washington, DC: ONDCP, 2003), p. 12.
112. Material in this paragraph is taken from ONDCP, *The Economic Costs of Drug Abuse in the United States, 1992–2002*, pp. iii–18.
113. FBI, *Crime in the United States*, 2011 Washington, DC: U.S. Dept. of Justice, 2012).
114. Bernard A. Gropper, "Probing the Links between Drugs and Crime," *National Institute of Justice Research in Brief* (Washington, DC: NIJ, February 1985), p. 4.
115. J. C. Ball, J. W. Shaffer, and D. N. Nurco, *Day to Day Criminality of Heroin Addicts in Baltimore: A Study in the Continuity of Offense Rates* (Washington, DC: National Institute of Justice, 1983).
116. "ONDCP Finds Americans Spent $57 Billion in One Year on Illegal Drugs," Office of National Drug Control Policy press release, 1997.
117. Office of National Drug Control Policy, *What America's Users Spend on Illegal Drugs* (Washington, DC: ONDCP, 1991), p. 4.
118. Mark Motivans, *Money Laundering Offenders, 1994–2001* (Washington, DC: Bureau of Justice Statistics, 2003).
119. Public Law 105-310.
120. Motivans, *Money Laundering Offenders*, p. 1.
121. U.S. Code, Title 18, Section 1957.
122. NNICC, *The NNICC Report, 1998.*
123. Ibid.
124. "Swiss Banking," Swissprivacy.com, http://www.swissprivacy.com/swiss-banking (accessed August 20, 2013).
125. *Ratzlaf* v. *U.S.*, 114 S.Ct. 655, 126 L.Ed.2d 615 (1994).
126. Public Law 107-56.
127. Motivans, *Money Laundering Offenders*, p. 10.
128. ONDCP, *The National Drug Control Strategy, 2013.*
129. Office of National Drug Control Policy, "Principles of Modern Drug Policy," http://www.whitehouse.gov/ondcp/policy-and-research/principles-of-modern-drug-policy (accessed August 20, 2013).
130. James Q. Wilson, "Drugs and Crime," in Michael Tonry and James Q. Wilson, eds., *Drugs and Crime* (Chicago: University of Chicago Press, 1990), p. 522.
131. Drug Enforcement Administration, "DEA Announces Major Takedown of Online Drug Dealers," April 20, 2005, http://www.pushingback.com/archives/042005_2.html (accessed July 4, 2007).
132. "Twenty Arrested in Crackdown on Internet Pharmacies," CNN.com, April 20, 2005, http://www.cnn.com/2005/LAW/04/20/internet.drugs.ap (accessed July 4, 2007).
133. U.S. Code, Title 21, Section 881(a)(6).
134. Michael Goldsmith, *Civil Forfeiture: Tracing the Proceeds of Narcotics Trafficking* (Washington, DC: Police Executive Research Forum, 1988), p. 3.
135. *U.S.* v. *$4,255,625.39 in Currency*, 762 F.2d 895, 904 (1982).
136. Bureau of Justice Assistance, *Asset Forfeiture Bulletin*, October 1988, p. 2.
137. Ibid.
138. Goldsmith, *Civil Forfeiture.*
139. *U.S.* v. *92 Buena Vista Ave.*, 113 S.Ct. 1126, 122 L.Ed.2d 469 (1993).
140. *Austin* v. *U.S.*, 113 S.Ct. 2801, 15 L.Ed.2d 448 (1993).
141. *Alexander* v. *U.S.*, 113 S.Ct. 2766, 125 L.Ed.2d 441 (1993); and *U.S.* v. *James Daniel Good Real Property*, 114 S.Ct. 492, 126 L.Ed.2d 490 (1993).
142. *Bennis* v. *Michigan*, 116 S.Ct. 1560, 134 L.Ed.2d 661 (1996).
143. *U.S.* v. *Ursery*, 116 S.Ct. 2135, 135 L.Ed.2d 549 (1996).
144. Statement by the Honorable Henry J. Hyde, "Civil Asset Forfeiture Reform Act," http://www.house.gov/judiciary/161.htm (accessed March 10, 2010).
145. National Briefing: "Largest Drug Seizure at Sea," *New York Times*, April 24, 2007, http://query.nytimes.com/gst/fullpage.html?res59801EEDD143EF937A15757C0A9619C8B63 (accessed May 10, 2010).
146. "Cocaine Found Packed in Toxic Chemical Drums," *Fayetteville (NC) Observer-Times*, November 5, 1989.
147. "Raid on Boat in Pacific Seizes 13 Tons of Cocaine," Associated Press, May 15, 2001.
148. Mark Moore, *Drug Trafficking, National Institute of Justice Crime File Series Study Guide* (Washington, DC: NIJ, 1988), p. 3.
149. Ibid.
150. Ibid.
151. Ibid.
152. In 2003, a California appellate court ruled that Proposition 36 does not apply to inmates in the state's correctional system. See *People* v. *Ponce*, Court of Appeals of California, First Appellate District, Division Five, No. A096707, March 7, 2003.

153. "Governor Signs Final Round of Bills," Kansas Governor's Office, April 21, 2003, http://www.ksgovernor.org/news/docs/news_rel042103.html (accessed August 3, 2006).
154. Michael S. Goodstadt, *Drug Education, National Institute of Justice Crime File Series Study Guide* (Washington, DC: NIJ, n.d.), p. 1.
155. See Federal Advisory Committee, *Methamphetamine Interagency Task Force: Final Report* (Washington, DC: Office of National Drug Control Policy, 2000), p. 5, from which some of the wording in this paragraph is adapted.
156. "DARE Not Effective in Reducing Drug Abuse, Study Finds," *Criminal Justice Newsletter*, October 3, 1994, pp. 6–7.
157. The government version of the study was first reported as *The DARE Program: A Review of Prevalence, User Satisfaction, and Effectiveness, National Institute of Justice Update* (Washington, DC: NIJ, October 1994). The full study, as published by the NIJ, is Christopher L. Ringwalt et al., *Past and Future Directions of the DARE Program: An Evaluation Review* (Washington, DC: National Institute of Justice, 1995).
158. Fox Butterfield, no headline, *New York Times* wire service, April 16, 1997, citing Office of Justice Programs, *Preventing Crime: What Works, What Doesn't, What's Promising* (Washington, DC: U.S. Dept. of Justice, 1997).
159. Donald R. Lynam et al., "Project DARE: No Effects at Ten-Year Follow-Up," *Journal of Consulting and Clinical Psychology*, Vol. 67, No. 4 (1999).
160. S. O. Lilienfeld, "Psychological Treatments That Cause Harm," *Perspectives on Psychological Science*, Vol. *2* (2007), pp. 53–70.
161. Goodstadt, *Drug Education*, p. 3.
162. *USA Today*, September 6, 1990, citing a report by the U.S. Senate Judiciary Committee.
163. Ibid.
164. RAND Corporation, *Drug Policy Research Center: Are Mandatory Minimum Drug Sentences Cost-Effective?* (Santa Monica, CA: RAND, 1997).
165. John S. Goldkamp and Doris Weiland, "Assessing the Impact of Dade County's Felony Drug Court," *National Institute of Justice Research in Brief* (Washington, DC: NIJ, December 1993).
166. National Institute of Justice, *Drug Courts* (Washington, DC: NIJ, April 2013).
167. National Institute of Justice, "Multisite Adult Drug Court Evaluation," http://www.nij.gov/nij/topics/courts/drug-courts/madce.htm (accessed August 20, 2013).
168. The Global Commission on Drug Policy, "War on Drugs: Report of the Global Commission on Drug Policy," 2011, http://www.globalcommissionondrugs.org/Report (accessed June 8, 2013), p. 10.
169. Fields, "White House Czar Calls for End to 'War on Drugs.'"
170. Peter D. Hart Research Associates, *Drugs and Crime across America*, p. 5.
171. Paul H. Blachy, "Effects of Decriminalization of Marijuana in Oregon," *Annals of the New York Academy of Sciences*, Vol. 282 (1976), pp. 405–415. For more information on the decriminalization of marijuana, see James A. Inciardi, "Marijuana Decriminalization Research: A Perspective and Commentary," *Criminology*, Vol. 19, No. 1 (May 1981), pp. 145–159.
172. Arnold S. Trebach, "Thinking through Models of Drug Legalization," *Drug Policy Letter* (July/August 1994), p. 10.
173. In mid-2013, Colorado lawmakers sets limits on levels of delta-9-tetrahydrocannabinol, or THC, at five nanograms or more per milliliter of blood, for drivers. Those found with THC at that amount or more are considered to be under the influence by juries during court proceedings.
174. U.S. Dept. of Justice, Memorandum for all United States Attorneys, "Guidance Regarding Marijuana Enforcement," August 29, 2013.
175. For a more thorough discussion of some of these arguments, see Ronald Hamowy, ed., *Dealing with Drugs: Consequences of Government Control* (Lexington, MA: Lexington Books, 1987).
176. "Should Drugs Be Legal?" *Newsweek*, May 30, 1988, p. 36.
177. Ibid., p. 37.
178. Ibid., pp. 37–38.
179. Trebach, "Thinking through Models of Drug Legalization," p. 10.
180. For a more detailed discussion of the two-market system, see John Kaplan, *Heroin, National Institute of Justice Crime File Series Study Guide* (Washington, DC: NIJ, n.d.).
181. Ibid., p. 3.
182. Ibid., p. 4.
183. Donna Leinwand, "Deadly Abuse of Methadone Tops Other Prescription Drugs," *USA Today*, February 13, 2007, citing a representative of the Food and Drug Administration.

Stephen Chernin/Getty Images

17 TERRORISM AND MULTINATIONAL CRIMINAL JUSTICE

OUTLINE

- Introduction
- Islamic Criminal Justice
- International Criminal Justice Organizations
- Globalization and Crime
- Human Smuggling and Trafficking
- Terrorism

LEARNING OBJECTIVES

After reading this chapter, you should be able to

- Describe the principles that form the basis of Islamic law.
- List five important international criminal justice organizations, and summarize their collective role in fighting international crime.
- Explain globalization and its possible relationship to crime and terrorism.
- Distinguish between human smuggling and human trafficking, and describe the extent of both problems today.
- Define two major types of terrorism.

In the 21st century, Americans have come to appreciate that they are part of a global society and that criminal transgressions within and beyond our Nation's borders have worldwide ramifications.

OFFICE FOR VICTIMS OF CRIME[1]

■ **Follow the author's tweets about the latest crime and justice news @schmalleger.**

■ **comparative criminologist** One who studies crime and criminal justice on a cross-national level.

Introduction

In 2013, Quazi Mohammad Rezwanul Ahsan Nafis, a Bangladeshi citizen, pled guilty in federal court to terrorism charges for attempting to blow up the Federal Reserve Bank of New York, located in Lower Manhattan.[2] Nafis, 21, had been tracked by undercover agents after they had learned that he wanted to attack an important financial center in an effort to destroy the American economy. In earlier recorded conversations with undercover agents, Nafis said, "I just want something big. Something very big. Very very very very big, that will shake the whole country." Prosecutors said that Nafis had travelled to the United States on a student visa in order to carry out the attack. He attended Southeast Missouri State University during the spring semester of 2012, pursuing a bachelor's degree in cybersecurity.[3] In October of that year, Nafis built a 1,000-pound bomb in a New York City warehouse, using fake explosives supplied by undercover agents. After the device was assembled, Nafis placed it in a van and drove it to the Federal Reserve Bank, intending to set it off with a detonator that was to be triggered by a cell phone call. Agents arrested him in a nearby hotel room as he tried to explode the bomb.

AFP/Getty Images/Newscom

Twenty-one-year-old Quazi Mohammad Rezwanul Ahsan Nafis, convicted in 2013 of terrorism charges in New York City. Nafis, who came to America from Bangladesh, is alleged to have planned to blow up the city's Federal Reserve Bank building using a 1,000 pound bomb. Are Americans likely to see more terrorism attacks in the future, or fewer?

The terrorism-related case of Quazi Nafis is not unusual. In 2013, a south Florida imam, Hafiz Muhammed Sher Ali Khan, was convicted on multiple terrorism charges for financially supporting an al-Qaeda branch in his native Pakistan.[4] The imam, a Pakistani national with U.S. citizenship, had served as the leader of a Miami mosque. Not long before Ali Khan went to prison, a New York City man, 24-year-old Betim Kaziu, was sentenced to serve 27 years behind bars by a federal judge in New York City for traveling to the Middle East in a failed effort to join al-Qaeda and kill American troops.[5] Finally, in 2013, three young British Muslims were convicted of plotting terrorist bombings in the English industrial city of Birmingham. A British jury found Irfan Naseer, 31, and Irfan Khalid and Ashik Ali, both 27, guilty of conspiracy in the foiled plot to explode backpack bombs in crowded public areas.[6]

These stories, which span the globe, show how vital it is for American criminal justice and other government organizations to appreciate the ideology, culture, and means of communications linking criminals and potential terrorists in this country to those overseas and around the world.

Criminologists who study crime and criminal justice on a cross-national level are referred to as **comparative criminologists**, and their field is called *comparative criminal justice, comparative criminology*, or *cross-national criminal justice*. Comparative criminal justice is becoming increasingly valued for the insights it provides. By contrasting native institutions of justice with similar institutions in other countries, procedures and problems in one system can be reevaluated in the light of world experience. As technological advances effectively "shrink" the world, we are able to learn firsthand about the criminal justice systems of other countries and to use that information to improve our own.

This chapter explains the value of comparative criminal justice, points to the problems that arise in comparing data from different nations, and explains international terrorism within the context of cross-national crime. By way of example, this chapter also briefly examines criminal justice systems based on Islamic principles. International police agencies are described, and the role of the United Nations (UN) in the worldwide fight against crime and terrorism is discussed. Additional information on the justice systems of many countries can be found in the *World Factbook of Criminal Justice Systems*, available at **http://bjs.ojp.usdoj.gov/content/pub/html/wfcj.cfm**. Another place to visit for international criminal justice information is the National Institute of Justice's International Center, which is accessible via **http://www.nij.gov/international**.

ethnocentric Holding a belief in the superiority of one's own social or ethnic group and culture.

Karim Kadim/AP Wide World Photos

An Iraqi man holding a picture of top Shiite cleric Ayatollah Ali Sistani during a protest in support of an Islamic constitution. The traditions and legal systems of many Middle Eastern countries are strongly influenced by Islamic law, which is based on the teachings of the Koran and the sayings of the Prophet Muhammad. How does Islamic law differ from the laws of most Western nations?

Ethnocentrism and the Study of Criminal Justice

The study of criminal justice in the United States has been largely **ethnocentric**. Because people are socialized from birth into a particular culture, they tend to prefer their own culture's way of doing things over that of any other. Native patterns of behavior are seen as somehow "natural" and therefore better than foreign ones. The same is true for values, beliefs, and customs. People tend to think that their religion holds a spiritual edge over other religions, that their values and ethical sense are superior to those of others, and that the fashions they wear, the language they speak, and the rituals of daily life in which they participate are somehow better than comparable practices elsewhere. Ethnocentric individuals do not consider that people elsewhere in the world cling to their own values, beliefs, and standards of behavior with just as much fervor as they do.

Only in recent years have American students of criminal justice begun to examine the justice systems of other cultures. Unfortunately, not all societies are equally open, and it is not always easy to explore them. In some societies, even the *study* of criminal justice is taboo. As a result, data-gathering strategies taken for granted in Western societies may not be well received elsewhere. One author, for example, has observed that in China, "the seeking of criminal justice information through face-to-face questioning takes on a different meaning in Chinese officialdom than it does generally in the Western world. While we accept this method of inquiry because we prize thinking on our feet and quick answers, it is rather offensive in China because it shows lack of respect and appreciation for the information given through the preferred means of prepared questions and formal briefings."[7] Hence, most of the information available about Chinese criminal justice comes by way of bureaucracy, and routine Western social science practices like door-to-door interviews, participant observation, and random surveys would produce substantial problems for researchers who attempt to use these techniques in China.

Problems with Data

Similar difficulties arise in the comparison of crime rates from one country to another. The crime rates of different nations are difficult to compare because of (1) differences in the way a specific crime is defined, (2) diverse crime reporting practices, and

(3) political and other influences on the reporting of statistics to international agencies.[8]

Definitional differences create what may be the biggest problem. For cross-national comparisons of crime data to be meaningful, it is essential that the reported data share conceptual similarities. Unfortunately, that is rarely the case. Nations report offenses according to the legal criteria by which arrests are made and under which prosecution can occur. Switzerland, for example, includes bicycle thefts in its reported data on what we call "auto theft" because Swiss data gathering focuses more on the concept of personal transportation than it does on the type of vehicle stolen. The Netherlands has no crime category for robberies, counting them as thefts. Japan classifies an assault that results in death as an assault or an aggravated assault, not as a homicide. Greek rape statistics include crimes of sodomy, "lewdness," seduction of a child, incest, and prostitution. China reports only robberies and thefts that involve the property of citizens; crimes against state-owned property fall into a separate category.

For cross-national comparisons of crime data to be meaningful, it is essential that the reported data share conceptual similarities.

Social, cultural, and economic differences among countries compound these difficulties. Auto theft statistics, for example, when compared between countries like the United States and China, need to be placed in an economic as well as demographic context. Whereas the United States has two automobiles for every 3 people, Bangladesh has only one car per every 2,600 of its citizens.[9] For the auto theft rate in Bangladesh to equal that of the United States, every automobile in the country would have to be stolen over 100 times each year!

Reporting practices vary substantially between nations. The International Criminal Police Organization (Interpol) and the UN are the only international organizations that regularly collect crime statistics from a large number of countries.[10] Both agencies can only request data and have no way of checking on the accuracy of the data reported to them. Many countries do not disclose the requested information, and those that do often make only partial reports. In general, small countries are more likely to report than are large ones, and nonsocialist countries are more likely to report than are socialist countries.[11]

International reports of crime are often delayed. Complete up-to-date data are rare because the information made available to agencies like the UN and Interpol is reported at different times and according to schedules that vary from nation to nation. In addition, official UN world crime surveys are conducted infrequently. To date, only ten such surveys have been undertaken.[12]

Crime statistics also reflect political biases and national values. Some nations do not accurately admit to the frequency of certain kinds of culturally reprehensible crimes. Communist countries, for example, appear loathe to report crimes like theft, burglary, and robbery because the very existence of such offenses demonstrates felt inequities within the communist system. After the breakup of the Soviet Union, Alexander Larin, a criminal justice scholar who worked as a Russian investigator during the 1950s and 1960s, revealed that "inside the state security bureaucracy, where statistics were collected and circulated, falsification of crime figures was the rule, not the exception. The practice was self-perpetuating. . . . Supervisors in the provinces were under pressure to provide Moscow with declining crime rates. And no self-respecting investigator wanted to look worse than his neighbor. . . . From the top to the bottom, the bosses depended on their employees not to make them look bad with high crime statistics."[13]

On the other hand, observers in democratic societies showed similar biases in their interpretation of statistics following the end of the cold war. Some Western analysts, for example, reporting on declines in the prison populations of Eastern and Central Europe during that period, attributed the decline to lessened frustration and lowered crime rates brought about by democratization. In one country, Hungary, prison populations declined from 240 inmates per 100,000 residents in 1986 to 130 per 100,000 in 1993, with similar decreases in other nations.[14] The more likely explanation, however, is the wholesale post-Soviet release of political dissidents from prisons formerly run by communist regimes. Learn more about world crime via the UN's *Global Report on Crime and Justice*, which is available at **http://www.uncjin.org/Special/GlobalReport.html**.

Islamic Criminal Justice

Islamic law has been the subject of much discussion in the United States since the September 11, 2001, terrorist attacks on the World Trade Center and the Pentagon. It is important

Hadi Misban/AP Wide World Photos

Iraqi Shiite Muslims flagellating themselves during a procession in Karbala, Iraq, on March 20, 2006. Islamic law, which is based on the teachings of Islam, underpins the legal systems of many nations in the Middle East and elsewhere. What kinds of offenses does it prohibit? What punishments does it specify?

for American students of criminal justice to recognize, however, that Islamic law refers to legal ideas (and sometimes entire legal systems) based on the teachings of Islam and that it bears no intrinsic relationship to acts of terrorism committed by misguided zealots with Islamic backgrounds. Similarly, Islamic law is by no means the same thing as jihad (Islamic holy war) or Islamic fundamentalism. Although Americans are now much better informed about the concept of Islamic law than they were in the past, some may not be aware that various interpretations of Islam still form the basis of laws in many countries and that the entire legal systems of some nations are based on Islamic principles. Islamic law holds considerable sway in a large number of countries, including Syria, Iran, Iraq (where a new constitution was voted on and approved in 2005), Pakistan, Afghanistan, Yemen, Saudi Arabia, Kuwait, the United Arab Emirates, Bahrain, Algeria, Jordan, Lebanon, Libya, Ethiopia, Gambia, Nigeria, Oman, Qatar, Senegal, Tunisia, Tajikistan, Uzbekistan, and Turkey (which practices official separation of church and state).

Islamic law descends directly from the teachings of the Prophet Muhammad, whom the *Cambridge Encyclopedia of Islam* describes as a "prophet-lawyer."[15] Muhammad rose to fame in the city of Mecca (in what is now Saudi Arabia) as a religious reformer. Later, however, he traveled to Medina, where he became the ruler and lawgiver of a newly formed religious society. In his role as lawgiver, Muhammad enacted legislation whose aim was to teach men what to do and how to behave in order to achieve salvation. As a consequence, Islamic law today is a system of duties and rituals founded on legal and moral obligations—all of which are ultimately sanctioned by the authority of a religious leader (or leaders) who may issue commands (known as *fatwas* or *fatwahs*) that the faithful are bound to obey.

Criminal justice professor Sam Souryal and his coauthors describe four aspects of justice in Arab philosophy and religion. Islamic justice, they say, means the following:[16]

- A sacred trust, a duty imposed on humans to be discharged sincerely and honestly. As such, these authors say, "justice is the quality of being morally responsible and merciful in giving everyone his or her due."
- A mutual respect of one human being by another. From this perspective, a just society is one that offers equal respect for individuals through social arrangements made in the common interest of all members.
- An aspect of the social bond that holds society together and transforms it into a brotherhood in which everyone becomes a keeper of everyone else and each is held accountable for the welfare of all.
- A command from God. Whoever violates God's commands should be subject to strict punishments according to Islamic tradition and belief.

Islamic law A system of laws, operative in some Arab countries, based on the Muslim religion and especially the holy book of Islam, the Koran.

***Hudud* crime** A serious violation of Islamic law that is regarded as an offense against God. *Hudud* crimes include such behavior as theft, adultery, sodomy, alcohol consumption, and robbery.

- "The third and fourth meanings of justice are probably the ones most commonly invoked in Islamic jurisprudence" and form the basis of criminal justice practice in many Middle Eastern countries.

The *Hudud* Crimes

Islamic law forms the basis of theocratic judicial systems in Kuwait, Saudi Arabia, the Sudan, Iran, and Algeria. Other Arabic nations, such as Egypt, Syria, and Jordan, recognize substantial elements of Islamic law in their criminal justice systems but also make wide use of Western and nontheocratic legal principles. Islamic law is based on four sources. In order of importance, these sources are (1) the Koran (also spelled *Quran* and *Qur'an*), or Holy Book of Islam, which Muslims believe is the word of God, or Allah; (2) the teachings of the Prophet Muhammad; (3) a consensus of the clergy in cases where neither the Koran nor the prophet directly addresses an issue; and (4) reason or logic, which should be used when no solution can be found in the other three sources.[17]

Islamic law is sometimes also referred to as *Sharia* law (or *Shari'ah* in Arabic). The Arabic word *Sharia* means "path of God" and can be more fully described as "a process through which Muslim scholars and jurists determine God's will and moral guidance as they apply to every aspect of a Muslim's life."[18]

Islamic law recognizes seven ***Hudud* crimes**—or crimes based on religious strictures. *Hudud* (sometimes called *Hodood* or *Huddud*) crimes are essentially violations of "natural law" as interpreted by Arab culture. Divine displeasure is thought to be the basis of crimes defined as *Hudud*, and *Hudud* crimes are often said to be crimes against God (or, more specifically, God's rights). The Koran specifies punishments for four of the seven *Hudud* crimes: (1) making war on Allah and His messengers, (2) theft, (3) adultery or fornication, and (4) false accusation of fornication or adultery. The three other *Hudud* offenses are mentioned by the Koran, but no punishment is specified: (1) "corruption on earth," (2) drinking alcohol, and (3) highway robbery—and the punishments for these crimes are determined by tradition.[19] The *Hudud* offenses and associated typical punishments are shown in Table 17-1. "Corruption on earth" is a general category of religious offense, not well understood in the West, that includes activities such as embezzlement, revolution against lawful authority, fraud, and "weakening the society of God." In 2011, for example, American pastor Terry Jones was sentenced to death by an Egyptian court for his role in burning the Koran shown in an anti-Islamic film.[20] Jones, the head of the Dove World Outreach church in Florida, was tried and sentenced in absentia, but authorities have warned that he could be executed if he ever sets foot in to Egypt.

Islamic law mandates strict punishment of moral failure. Sexual offenders, even those who engage in what would be considered essentially victimless crimes in Western societies, are subject to especially harsh treatment. The Islamic penalty for sexual intercourse outside of marriage, for example, is 100 lashes. Men

TABLE 17-1 | Crime and Punishment in Islamic Law

Islamic law looks to the Koran and to the teachings of the Prophet Muhammad to determine which acts should be classified as crimes. The Koran and tradition specify punishments to be applied to designated offenses, as the following verse from the Koran demonstrates: "The only reward of those who make war upon Allah and His messenger and strive after corruption in the land will be that they will be killed or crucified, or have their hands and feet on alternate sides cut off, or will be expelled out of the land" (*Surah* V, Verse 33). Other crimes and punishments include the following:

OFFENSE	PUNISHMENT
Theft	Amputation of the hand
Adultery	Stoning to death
Fornication	One hundred lashes
False accusation (of fornication or adultery)	Eighty lashes
Corruption on earth	Death by the sword or by burning
Drinking alcohol	Eighty lashes; death if repeated three times
Robbery	Cutting off of hands and feet on alternate sides, exile, or execution

Sources: For more information, see Sam S. Souryal, Dennis W. Potts, and Abdullah I. Alobied, "The Penalty of Hand Amputation for Theft in Islamic Justice," *Journal of Criminal Justice*, Vol. 22, No. 3 (1994), pp. 249–265; and Parviz Saney, "Iran," in Elmer H. Johnson, ed., *International Handbook of Contemporary Developments in Criminology* (Westport, CT: Greenwood Press, 1983), pp. 356–369.

■ *Tazir* crime A minor violation of Islamic law that is regarded as an offense against society, not God.

The Islamic penalty for sexual intercourse outside of marriage is 100 lashes; adultery carries a much more severe penalty: flogging and stoning to death.

are stripped to the waist, women have their clothes bound tightly, and flogging is carried out with a leather whip. Adultery carries a much more severe penalty: flogging and stoning to death.

Under Islamic law, even property crimes are firmly punished. Thieves who are undeterred by less serious punishments may eventually suffer amputation of the right hand. In a reputedly humane move, Iranian officials recently began to use an electric guillotine, specially made for the purpose, which can sever a hand at the wrist in one-tenth of a second. For amputation to be imposed, the item stolen must have value in Islam. Pork and alcohol, for example, are regarded as being without value, and their theft is not subject to punishment. Islamic legal codes also establish a minimum value for stolen items that could result in a sentence of amputation. Likewise, offenders who have stolen because they are hungry or are in need are exempt from the punishment of amputation and receive fines or prison terms.

Slander and the consumption of alcohol are both punished by 80 lashes. Legal codes in strict Islamic nations also specify whipping for the crimes of pimping, lesbianism, kissing by an unmarried couple, cursing, and failure of a woman to wear a veil. Islamic law provides for the execution, sometimes through crucifixion, of robbers. Laws stipulate that anyone who survives three days on the cross may be spared. Depending on the circumstances of the robbery, however, the offender may suffer the amputation of opposite hands and feet or may be exiled.

Rebellion, or revolt against a legitimate political leader or established economic order, which is considered an aspect of "corruption on earth," is punishable by death. The offender may be killed outright in a military or police action or, later, by sentence of the court. The last of the *Hudud* crimes is rejection of Islam. The penalty, once again, is death and can be imposed for denying the existence of God or angels, denying any of the prophets of Islam, or rejecting any part of the Koran.

Souryal and coauthors observe that *Hudud* crimes can be severely punished because "punishment serves a three-tiered obligation: (1) the fulfillment of worship, (2) the purification of society, and (3) the redemption of the individual." However, they add, the interests of the individual are the least valuable component of this triad and may have to be sacrificed "for the wholesomeness and integrity of the encompassing justice system."[21]

The *Tazir* Crimes

All crimes other than *Hudud* crimes fall into an offense category called *tazirat*. ***Tazir* crimes** are regarded as any actions not considered acceptable in a spiritual society. They include crimes against society and against individuals, but not against God. *Tazir* crimes may call for *quesas* (retribution) or *diya* (compensation or fines). Crimes requiring *quesas* are based on the Arabic principle of "an eye for an eye" and generally require physical punishments up to and including death. *Quesas* offenses may include murder, manslaughter, assault, and maiming. Under Islamic law, such crimes may require the victim or his representative to serve as prosecutor. The state plays a role only in providing the forum for the trial and in imposing punishment. Sometimes victims' representatives dole out punishment. In 1997, for example, 28-year-old taxi driver Ali Reza Khoshruy, nicknamed "The Vampire" because he stalked, raped, and killed women at night after picking them up in his cab, was hung from a yellow crane in the middle of Tehran, the Iranian capital.[22] Before the hanging, prison officials and male relatives of the victims cursed Khoshruy and whipped him with thick leather belts as he lay tied to a metal bed. The whipping was part of a 214-lash sentence.

Unlike statutory law in the West, Islamic law is not codified—meaning that judges are empowered to interpret the law based on their readings of the holy texts, precedent, and their own personal judgment. In some countries governed by Sharia law, however, the law of criminal procedure can be found in written form, similar to its counterpart in the West.

Islamic Courts

Islamic courts typically exist on three levels.[23] The first level hears cases involving the potential for serious punishments, including death, amputation, and exile. The second level deals with relatively minor matters, such as traffic offenses and violations of city ordinances. Special courts, especially in Iran, may hear cases involving crimes against the government, narcotics offenses, state security, and corruption. Appeals within the Islamic court system are only possible under rare circumstances and are by no means routine. A decision rendered by second-level courts will generally stand without intervention by higher judicial authorities.

Under Islamic law, men and women are treated very differently. Testimony provided by a man, for example, can be heard in court. The same evidence, however, can be provided only by two virtuous women; one female witness is not sufficient.

Although Islamic law may seem archaic or even barbaric to many Westerners, Islamic officials defend their system by pointing to low crime rates at home and by pointing to what they consider near anarchy in Western nations. An early criticism of Islamic law, however, was offered by Max Weber at the start of the twentieth century.[24] Weber said that Islamic justice is based more on the moral conceptions of individual judges than on any rational and

Weber said that Islamic justice is based more on the moral conceptions of individual judges than on any rational and predictable code of laws.

predictable code of laws. He found that the personality of each judge, what he called "charisma," was more important in reaching a final legal result than was the written law. Weber's conclusion was that a modern society could not develop under Islamic law because enforcement of the law was too unpredictable. Complex social organizations, he argued, could only be based on a rational and codified law that is relatively unchanging from place to place and over time.[25]

More recent observers have agreed that "Islamic justice is based on philosophical principles that are considered alien, if not unconscionable, to the Western observer." However, these same writers note, strict punishments such as hand amputation "may not be inconsistent with the fundamentals of natural law or Judeo-Christian doctrine. The imposition of the penalty in specific cases and under rigorous rules of evidence—as the principle requires—may be indeed justifiable, and even necessary, in the Islamic context of sustaining a spiritual . . . society."[26]

International Criminal Justice Organizations

The first international conference on criminology and criminal justice met in London in 1872.[27] It evolved out of emerging humanitarian concerns about the treatment of prisoners. Human rights, the elimination of corporal punishment, and debates over capital punishment occupied the conference participants. Although other meetings were held from time to time, little agreement could be reached among the international community on criminal etiology, justice paradigms, or the philosophical and practical bases for criminal punishment and rehabilitation. Finally, in 1938, the International Society for Criminology (ISC) was formed to bring together people from diverse cultural backgrounds who shared an interest in social policies relating to crime and justice. In its early years, membership in the ISC consisted mostly of national officials and academics with close government ties.[28] As a consequence, many of the first conferences (called *international congresses*) sponsored by the ISC strongly supported the status quo and were devoid of any significant recommendations for change or growth.

Throughout the 1960s and 1970s, the ISC was strongly influenced by a growing worldwide awareness of human rights. About the same time, a number of international organizations began to press for an understanding of the political and legal processes through which deviance and crime come to be defined. Among them were the Scandinavian Research Council for Criminology (formed in 1962), the Criminological Research Council (created in 1962 by the Council of Europe), and other regional associations concerned with justice issues.

Many contemporary organizations and publications continue to focus world attention on criminal justice issues. Perhaps the best-known modern center for the academic study of cross-national criminal justice is the International Center of Comparative Criminology at the University of Montreal. Established in 1969, the center serves as a locus of study for criminal justice professionals from around the world and maintains an excellent library of international criminal justice information. The International Police Executive Symposium (IPES) was founded in 1994 to bring international police researchers and practitioners together and to facilitate cross-cultural and international exchanges between criminal justice experts around the world. The IPES, which is associated with the Human Rights and Law Enforcement Institute (HRALEI) at the State University of New York at Plattsburg, publishes *Police Practice and Research: An International Journal*. The Office of International Criminal Justice (OICJ), at the University of New Haven in West Haven, Connecticut, has also become a well-known contributor to the study of comparative criminal justice. Similarly, Sam Houston State University's Criminal Justice Center (in Huntsville, Texas) publishes the magazine *Crime and Justice International* and sponsors study tours of various nations.

In 1995, Mitre Corporation in McLean, Virginia, began an Internet service that provides information about the UN Crime Prevention Branch. The UN Crime and Justice Information Network (UNCJIN) holds much promise as an online provider of international criminal justice information. Visit the UNCJIN via **http://www.uncjin.org**. Finally, the UN Center for International Crime Prevention, in conjunction with the World Society of Victimology, sponsors the International Victimology website, available at **http://www.worldsocietyofvictimology.org**.

The Role of the United Nations in Criminal Justice

The United Nations, composed of 185 member states and based in New York City, is the largest and most inclusive international body in the world. From its inception in 1945, the UN has been very interested in international crime prevention and world criminal justice systems. A UN resolution titled the International Bill of Human Rights supports the rights and dignity of everyone who comes into contact with a criminal justice system.

One of the best-known specific UN recommendations on criminal justice is its Standard Minimum Rules for the Treatment of Prisoners. The rules call for the fair treatment of prisoners, including recognition of the basic humanity of all inmates, and set specific standards for housing, nutrition, exercise, and medical care. Follow-up surveys conducted by the UN have shown that the rules have had a considerable influence on national legislation and prison regulations throughout the world.[29] Although the rules do not have the weight of law unless adopted and enacted into local legislation, they carry the strong weight of tradition, and at least one expert claims that "there are indeed those who argue that the rules have entered the *corpus* of generally customary human rights law, or that they are binding . . . as an authoritative interpretation of the human rights provisions of the UN charter."[30]

A more recent and potentially significant set of recommendations can be found in the UN Code of Conduct for Law Enforcement Officials. The code calls on law enforcement officers throughout the world to be cognizant of human rights in the performance of their duties. It specifically proscribes the use of torture and other abuses.

The UN World Crime Surveys, which report official crime statistics from nearly 100 countries, provide a global portrait of criminal activity. Seen historically, the surveys have shown that crimes against property are most characteristic of nations with developed economies (where they constitute approximately 82% of all reported crime), whereas crimes against the person occur much more frequently in developing countries (where they account for 43% of all crime).[31] Complementing the official statistics of the World Crime Surveys are data from the International Crime Victim Survey (ICVS), which is conducted in approximately 50 countries. To date, five surveys have been conducted—in 1989, 1992, 1996–1997, 2000, and 2005. A sixth round of surveys is under way as this book goes to press.

Through its Office for Drug Control and Crime Prevention (ODCCP), the UN continues to advance the cause of crime prevention and to disseminate useful criminal justice information. The program provides forums for ongoing discussions of justice practices around the world. It has regional links throughout the world, sponsored by supportive national governments that have agreed to fund the program's work. The European Institute for Crime Prevention and Control (HEUNI), for example, provides the program's regional European link in a network of institutes operating throughout the world. Other network components include the UN Interregional Crime and Justice Research Institute (UNICRI) in Rome; an Asian regional institute (UNAFEI) in Tokyo; ILANUE, based in San Jose, Costa Rica, which focuses on crime problems in Latin America and the Caribbean; an African institute (UNAFRI) in Kampala, Uganda; Australia's AIC in Canberra; an Arabic institute (ASSTC) in Riyadh, Saudi Arabia; and other centers in Siracusa, Italy, and in Vancouver and Montreal, Canada.[32] Visit the UN Office for Drug Control and Crime Prevention via **http://www.unodc.org**.

Young Vietnamese prostitutes detained by Cambodian police during a brothel raid in Phnom Penh. The 2003 federal Trafficking Victims Protection Reauthorization Act focuses on the illegal practice of sex trafficking and on the illegal "obtaining of a person for labor services." How common is human trafficking? In what parts of the world is it most prevalent?

Gary Way/AFP/Getty Image

In 1995, the United States signed an agreement with the UN Crime Prevention and Criminal Justice Branch that is intended to facilitate the international sharing of information and research findings.[33] Under the agreement, the National Institute of Justice joined 11 other criminal justice research organizations throughout the world as an associate UN institute.

Continuing a tradition begun in 1885 by the former International Penal and Penitentiary Commission, the UN holds an international congress on crime every five years. The first UN crime congress, the 1955 Congress on the Prevention of Crime and the Treatment of Offenders, met in Geneva, Switzerland. Crime congresses provide a forum through which member states can exchange information and experiences, compare criminal justice practices between countries, find solutions to crime, and take action at an international level. The 12th UN crime congress was held in Brazil in 2010. That meeting highlighted the important role of the criminal justice system in economic development and called for recognition of the rule of law in every part of the globe. The 13th Congress is planned for 2015 in Qatar. A summary of declarations that were agreed upon at the 12th Congress can be read at **https://www.unodc.org/documents/crime-congress/12th-Crime-Congress/Documents/Salvador_Declaration/Salvador_Declaration_E.pdf**.

UN Crime Congresses frequently encourage international enforcement of the UN Protocol to Prevent, Suppress and Punish Trafficking in Persons, Especially Women and Children, which was created in 2000, and supplements the UN Convention against Transnational Organized Crime (TOC).[34] Nations that are parties to the protocol must criminalize the offense of human trafficking, prevent trafficking, protect and assist victims of trafficking, and promote international cooperation to combat the problem of trafficking.[35] The UN reports that by 2008, 63% of the 155 countries that responded to a survey had adopted a statute specifically criminalizing trafficking in persons at least for the purposes of sexual exploitation and forced labor (Figure 17-1). Seventeen percent of responding countries said that they had a less-specific law that could be applied to trafficking n persons. Twenty percent of the countries covered, however, did not have a specific offense of

International Criminal Police Organization (Interpol) An international law enforcement support organization that began operations in 1946 and today has 182 member nations.

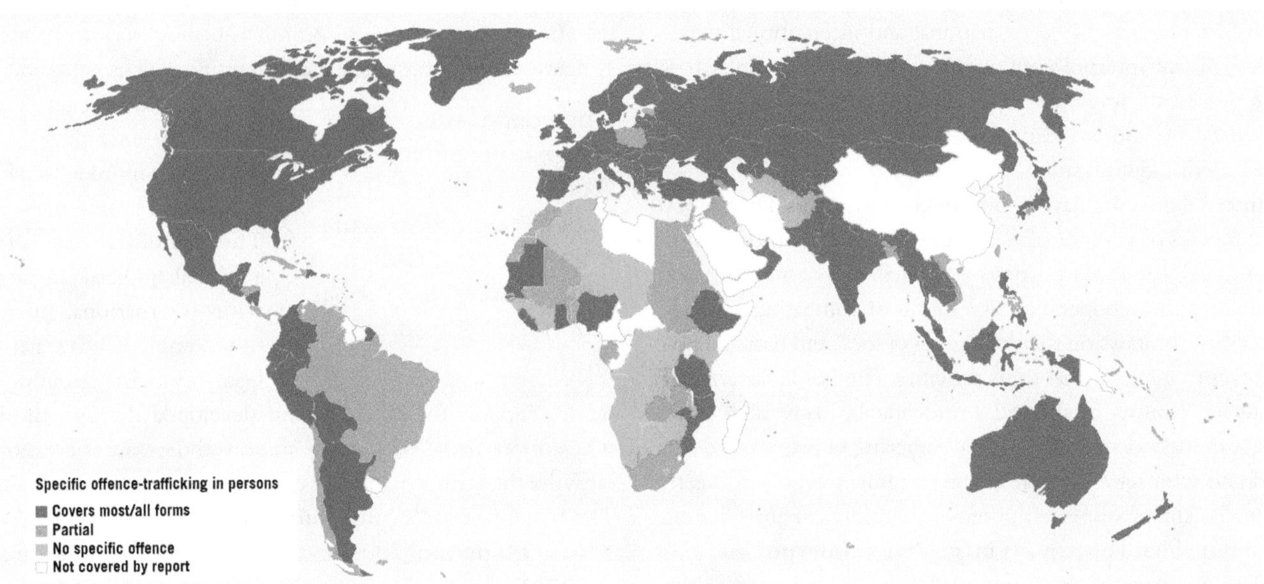

FIGURE 17-1 | Trafficking in Persons: Status of National Legislation, by Country

Source: United Nations Office on Drugs and Crime.

trafficking in persons in their legislation. Read the U.S. Department of State's 2011 *Trafficking in Persons Report* at **http://www.justicestudies.com/tip2011.pdf**.

Interpol and Europol

The **International Criminal Police Organization (Interpol)**, headquartered in Lyons, France, traces its origins back to the first International Criminal Police Congress of 1914, which met in Monaco.[36] The theme of that meeting was international cooperation in the investigation of crimes and the apprehension of fugitives. Interpol, however, did not officially begin operations until 1946, when the end of World War II brought about a new spirit of international harmony.

Today, 190 nations belong to Interpol.[37] The U.S. Interpol unit is called the U.S. National Central Bureau (USNCB) and is a separate agency within the U.S. Department of Justice. USNCB is staffed with personnel from 12 federal agencies, including the Drug Enforcement Administration, the Secret Service, and the Federal Bureau of Investigation. Through the USNCB, Interpol is linked to all major U.S. computerized criminal records repositories, including the FBI's National Crime Information Index, the State Department's Advanced Visa Lookout System, and the Department of Homeland Security's Master Index.

Interpol's primary purpose is to act as a clearinghouse for information on offenses and suspects who are believed to operate across national boundaries. The organization is committed to promoting "the widest possible mutual assistance between all criminal police authorities within the limits of laws existing in . . . different countries and in the spirit of the Universal Declaration of Human Rights."[38] Historically, Interpol pledged itself not to intervene in religious, political, military, or racial disagreements in participant nations. As a consequence, numerous bombings and hostage situations that were related to these types of disagreements were not officially investigated until 1984, when Interpol officially entered the fight against international terrorism.

Laurent Cipriani/AP Wide World Photos

The entrance hall of Interpol headquarters in Lyon, France. What does Interpol do?

At Interpol's Eighty-First General Assembly, held in Rome, Italy, in 2012, senior law enforcement officials from around the world discussed critical challenges facing police agencies in

■ **European Police Office (Europol)** The integrated police intelligence-gathering and dissemination arm of the member nations of the European Union.

responding to current and developing criminal phenomena, and shared best practices based on national and international experience.[39] Today, Interpol continues to expand its activities. It is in the process of developing a centralized international forensic DNA database and is creating an international framework for disaster victim identification.[40]

Interpol does not have its own field investigators. The agency has no powers of arrest or of search and seizure in member countries. Instead, Interpol's purpose is to facilitate, coordinate, and encourage police cooperation as a means of combating international crime. It draws on the willingness of local and national police forces to lend support to its activities. The headquarters staff of Interpol consists of about 250 individuals, many with prior police experience, who direct data-gathering efforts around the world and who serve to alert law enforcement organizations to the movement of suspected offenders within their jurisdiction. Visit Interpol headquarters via **http://www.interpol.int**.

The members of the European Union (EU) agreed to the establishment of the **European Police Office (Europol)** in the Maastricht Treaty of February 7, 1992. Based in The Hague, the Netherlands, Europol started limited operations in 1994 in the form of the Europol Drugs Unit. Over time, other important law enforcement activities were added to the Europol agenda. The Europol Convention was ratified by all member states in 1998, and Europol commenced full operations the next year. Europol's mission is to improve the effectiveness and cooperation of law enforcement agencies within the member states of the EU with the ultimate goal of preventing and combating terrorism, illegal drug trafficking, illicit trafficking in radioactive and nuclear substances, illegal money laundering, trafficking in human beings, and other serious forms of international organized crime. Europol is sometimes described as the "European Union police clearing house."[41] Following the July 2005 London underground and bus bombings, in which more than 50 people died and hundreds were injured, German Interior Minister Otto Schilly asked his EU counterparts meeting in Brussels to give Europol executive powers to conduct EU-wide investigations.[42]

Europol and Interpol work together to develop information on international terrorism, drug trafficking, and trafficking in human beings.[43] Visit Europol on the Web at **http://www.europol.europa.eu**.

The International Criminal Court

On April 12, 2000, the International Criminal Court (ICC) was created under the auspices of the United Nations. The ICC is intended to be a permanent criminal court for trying individuals (not countries) who commit the most serious crimes of concern to the international community, such as genocide, war crimes, and crimes against humanity—including the wholesale murder of civilians, torture, and mass rape. The goal of the ICC is to be a global judicial institution with international jurisdiction complementing national legal systems around the world. Support for the ICC was developed through the UN, where more than 70 countries approved the court's creation by ratifying the Rome Statute of the International Criminal Court. The ICC's first prosecutor, Luis Moreno Ocampo of Argentina, was elected in April 2003, and was still serving in that capacity in 2013.[44]

The goal of the International Criminal Court is to be a global judicial institution with international jurisdiction complementing national legal systems around the world.

The ICC initiative began after World War II, with unsuccessful efforts to establish an international tribunal to try individuals accused of genocide and other war crimes.[45] In lieu of such a court, military tribunals were held in Nuremberg, Germany, and Tokyo, Japan, to try those accused of war crimes. Although the 1948 UN Genocide Convention[46] called for the creation of an international criminal court to punish genocide-related offenses, efforts to establish a permanent court were delayed for decades by the cold war and by the refusal of some national governments to accept the court's proposed international legal jurisdiction.

In December 1948, the UN General Assembly adopted the Universal Declaration of Human Rights and the Convention on the Prevention and Punishment of the Crime of Genocide. It also called for criminals to be tried "by such international penal tribunals as may have jurisdiction." A number of member states soon asked the UN International Law Commission (ILC) to study the possibility of establishing an international criminal court.

Development of the ICC was delayed by the cold war that took place between the world's superpowers, which were not willing to subject their military personnel or commanders to international criminal jurisdiction in the event of a "hot" war. In 1981, however, the UN General Assembly asked the International Law Commission to consider creating an international Code of Crimes.

The 1992 war in Bosnia-Herzegovina, which involved clear violations of the Genocide and Geneva Conventions, heightened world interest in the establishment of a permanent ICC. A few years later, 160 countries participated in the

■ **globalization** The internationalization of trade, services, investment, information, and other forms of human social activity.

Conference of Plenipotentiaries on the Establishment of an International Criminal Court,[47] which was held in Rome. At the end of that conference, member states voted overwhelmingly in favor of the Rome Statute,[48] calling for establishment of an ICC.

In 2012, in the first verdict ever reached by the ICC, judges found Thomas Lubanga, a rebel leader in eastern Congo, guilty of conscripting child soldiers.

In 2012, in the first verdict ever reached by the ICC, judges found Thomas Lubanga, a rebel leader in eastern Congo, guilty of conscripting child soldiers.[49] Learn more about this case and other activities of the ICC by visiting the Coalition for an International Criminal Court via **http://www.iccnow.org**.

Before the ICC came into existence, Belgium made its courts available to the rest of the world for the prosecution of alleged crimes against humanity.[50] The country's legal system, in essence, took on the role of global prosecutor for these kinds of crimes. Under a 1993 Belgian law, which is regarded by many as the world's most expansive statute against genocide and other crimes against humanity, Belgian justices were called on to enforce substantial portions of the country's criminal laws on a global scale. Belgian courts also focused on enforcing the 1949 Geneva Convention governing the conduct of war and the treatment of refugees. Belgian law specifically provides for the criminal prosecution of individuals who are not Belgian citizens, and it provides no immunity to prosecution for foreign leaders. In 2001, for example, a Brussels jury convicted four people, including two Catholic nuns, of contributing to ethnic violence in the central African nation of Rwanda in 1994.

DPI/E. Schneider/United Nations Photo Library

Kofi Annan, who was secretary general of the United Nations at the time of this photo, speaking in Rome at opening ceremonies that marked the signing of the Treaty on Establishment of the International Criminal Court in 1998. What is the jurisdiction of the International Criminal Court?

Belgian authorities have investigated more than a dozen complaints involving current and former state officials, including Ariel Sharon (former prime minister of Israel), Saddam Hussein (former Iraqi leader), Hissene Habre (former dictator of Chad), Hashemi Rafsanjani (former president of Iran), Driss Basri (former interior minister of Morocco), Denis Sassou Nguesso (president of Congo-Brazzaville), and Fidel Castro (former leader of Cuba). In the case of the Cuban leader, Cuban exiles charged Castro in Brussels's criminal court in October 2001 with false imprisonment, murder, torture, and other crimes against humanity. As a result of such investigations, Belgium has experienced strained relationships with a number of countries, and some in the nation have questioned the wisdom of charging sitting heads of state with violations of the criminal law.

Globalization and Crime

Globalization refers to the internationalization of trade, services, investments, information, and other forms of human social activity, including crime. The process of globalization is fed by modern systems of transportation and communication, including air travel, television, and the Internet. Globalization contributes to growing similarities in the way people do things and in the beliefs and values that they hold. The lessening of differences brought about by globalization is highlighted by a definition from one authoritative source, which says that globalization is "a process of social homogenization by which the experiences of everyday life, marked by the diffusion of commodities and ideas, can foster a standardization of cultural expressions around the world."[51] The adoption of English as the *de facto* standard language on the Internet and of the global software community, for example, has exposed many around the world to literature and ideas that they might not otherwise have encountered and has influenced the way they think. Consequently, globalization is opposed in many parts of the world by those who would hold to traditional ways of thinking and acting. Instead of inevitably uniting humanity, as some had hoped, globalization has also made people aware of differences—and has led many people to reject cultures and ideas dissimilar to their own.

Instead of inevitably uniting humanity, globalization has also made people aware of differences—and has led many people to reject cultures and ideas dissimilar to their own.

transnational crime Unlawful activity undertaken and supported by organized criminal groups operating across national boundaries.

The first steps toward globalization occurred long before the modern era and were taken by nation-states seeking to expand their spheres of influence. The banner of globalization today is carried by multinational corporations whose operations span the globe. The synergistic effects of rapid travel, instantaneous communication, and national economies that are tied closely to one another have led to an increasingly rapid pace of the globalization process, which some refer to as *hyperglobalization*. Criminal entrepreneurs and terrorists are among those with a global vision, and at least some of them think and plan like the CEOs of multinational businesses. Today's international criminal community consists of terrorists, drug traffickers, pornography peddlers, identity thieves, copyright violators, and those who traffic in human beings, body parts, genetic material, and military weapons.

Transnational Crime

In 2006, Cheng Chui Ping, known to her associates as the Snakehead Queen, was sentenced in U.S. District Court to 35 years in prison for having smuggled as many as 3,000 illegal immigrants into the United States from her native China. "Snakeheads" are human smugglers, and, prior to her arrest, Ping may have been the most active human smuggler in New York City. Her fees, which were partially determined by an immigrant's ability to pay, ranged up to $40,000 per person, and the Federal Bureau of Investigation (FBI) says that her illegal transnational activities may have netted her as much as $40 million.[52]

Transnational crime and the internationally organized criminal groups that support it are partly the result of an ongoing process of globalization. Transnational crime is unlawful activity undertaken and supported by organized criminal groups operating across national boundaries, and it promises to become one of the most pressing challenges of the twenty-first century for criminal justice professionals. In a recent conference in Seoul, Korea, then-U.S. Attorney General Laurie Robinson addressed the issue of transnational crime, saying, "The United States recognizes that we cannot confront crime in isolation. . . . It is clear crime does not respect international boundaries. It is clear crime is global. As recent economic trends demonstrate, what happens in one part of the world impacts all the rest. And crime problems and trends are no different."[53]

According to the United Nations, an offense can be considered transnational in nature if any of the following conditions are met:[54]

1. It is committed in more than one country.
2. It is committed in one country but a substantial part of its preparation, planning, direction, or control takes place in another country.
3. It is committed in one country but involves an organized criminal group that engages in criminal activities in more than one country.
4. It is committed in one country but has substantial effects in another country.

According to Robert Gelbard, U.S. assistant secretary for international narcotics and law enforcement affairs, "The main threat now is transnational organized crime. It comes in many forms: drug trafficking, money laundering, terrorism, alien smuggling, trafficking in weapons of mass destruction, [human trafficking, often involving forced prostitution], fraud and other forms of corruption. These problems all have one critical element in common." Gelbard continues, "They threaten the national security of all states and governments—from our closest allies to those that we find most repugnant. No country is safe. International criminal organizations all seek to establish pliant governments that can be manipulated through bribery and intimidation. They respect no national boundaries and already act with virtual impunity in many parts of the world."[55]

According to the National Institute of Justice (NIJ), transnational crime groups have profited more from globalization than have legitimate businesses, which are subject to domestic and host country laws and regulations. The NIJ points out that transnational crime syndicates and networks, abetted by official corruption, blackmail, and intimidation, can use open markets and open societies to their full advantage.[56]

Worse still, entire nations may become rogue countries, or quasi-criminal regimes where criminal activity runs rampant and wields considerable influence over the national government (Figure 17-2). Russia, for example, may be approaching this status through an intertwining of the goals of organized criminal groups and official interests that run to the top levels of government. The number of organized criminal groups operating in Russia is estimated to be more than 12,000.[57] Emilio Viano, professor of criminology at American University and an expert on Russian organized crime, notes that "what we have is an immense country practically controlled by organized crime. These groups are getting stronger and stronger and using Russia as a base for their global ventures—taking over everything from drugs and prostitution to currency exchange and stealing World Bank and IMF [International Monetary Fund] loans."[58] Not long ago, for example, Russian organized crime hit men shot and killed Andrei Kozlov, the top deputy chairman of the Russian Central Bank.[59] Kozlov, who was gunned down as he left a soccer match in Moscow, had worked for four years to fight criminality and money

The number of organized criminal groups operating in Russia is estimated to be more than 12,000.

■ **extradition** The surrender by one state or jurisdiction to another of an individual accused or convicted of an offense in the second state or jurisdiction.

■ **sex trafficking** The recruitment, harboring, transportation, provision, or obtaining of a person for the purpose of a commercial sex act.

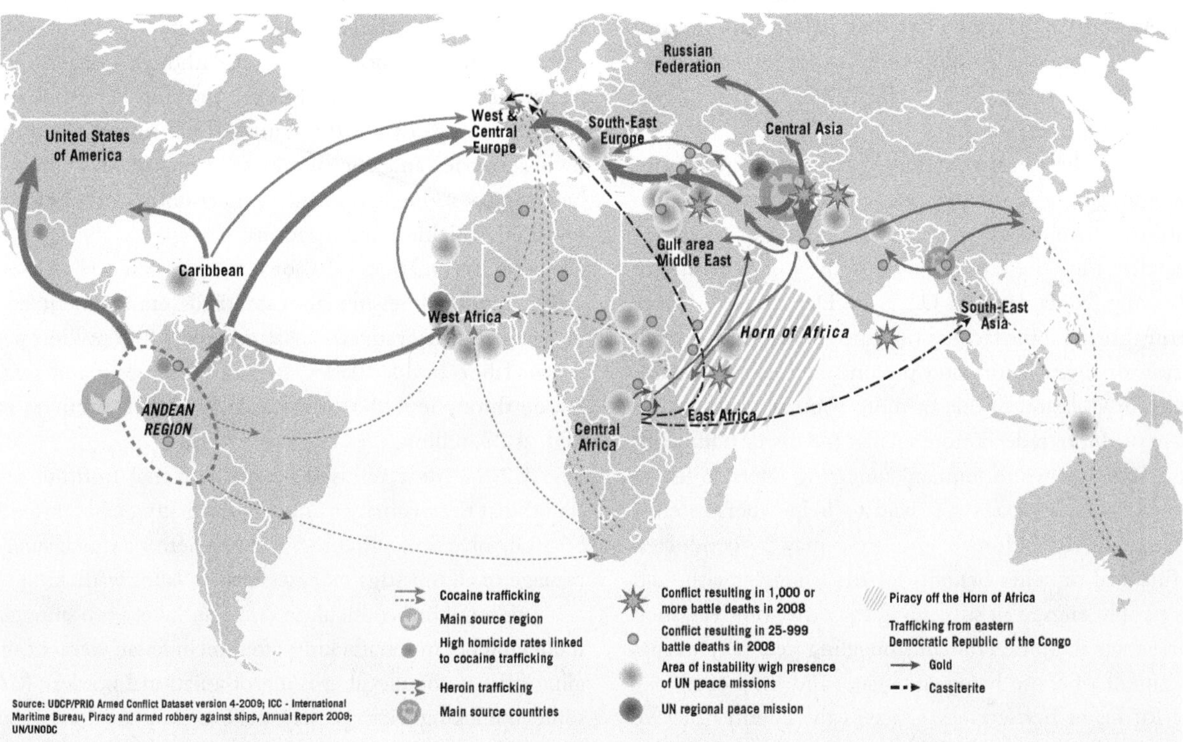

FIGURE 17-2 | Transnational Organized Crime and Political Instability

Source: United Nations Office on Drugs and Crime.

laundering in Russia's banking system in an effort to draw foreign investments into the country.

One tool in the fight against transnational crime is **extradition**. Not all countries, however, are willing to extradite suspects wanted in the United States. Consequently, as Kevin Ryan of Vermont's Norwich University observes, "The globalization of United States law enforcement policy has also entailed the abduction of fugitives from abroad to stand trial when an asylum nation refuses an extradition request."[60] Although certainly not a common practice, the forcible removal of criminal suspects from foreign jurisdictions appears more likely with suspected terrorists than with other types of criminals. A special report on transnational organized crime and its impact on the United States is available at **http://justicestudies.com/pubs/toc2011.pdf**.

Human Smuggling and Trafficking

The recent globalization of crime and terrorism, which is sometimes called the *globalization of insecurity*, has necessitated enhanced coordination of law enforcement efforts in different parts of the world as well as the expansion of American law enforcement activities beyond national borders. In 2000, for example, the U.S. Congress passed the Trafficking Victims Protection Act (TVPA).[61] Trafficking offenses under the law, which is aimed primarily at international offenders, include (1) **sex trafficking**, in which a commercial sex act is induced by force, fraud, or coercion or in which the person induced to perform such act has not attained 18 years of age;[62] and (2) the recruitment, harboring, transportation, provision, or obtaining of a person for labor services, through the use of force, fraud, or coercion, for the purpose of subjection to involuntary servitude, peonage, debt bondage, or slavery. The TVPA also provides funds for training U.S. law enforcement personnel at international police academies, and U.S. police agencies routinely send agents to assist law enforcement officers in other countries who are involved in transnational investigations.

Under the TVPA, human trafficking does not require the crossing of an international border, nor does it even require the transportation of victims from one locale to another. That's because victims of severe forms of trafficking are not always illegal aliens; they may be U.S. citizens, legal residents, or visitors. Victims do not have to be women or children—they may also be

■ **human smuggling** Illegal immigration in which an agent is paid to help a person cross a border clandestinely.

■ **trafficking in persons (TIP)** The exploitation of unwilling or unwitting people through force, coercion, threat, or deception.

adult males. The Trafficking Victims Protection Reauthorization Act (TVPRA) of 2003[63] added a new initiative to the original law to collect foreign data on trafficking investigations, prosecutions, convictions, and sentences. The TVPA was authorized again in 2005, 2008, and 2013.[64]

According to the United Nations,[65] trafficking in persons and human smuggling are some of the fastest-growing areas of international criminal activity today. There are important distinctions that must be made between these two forms of crime. Following federal law, the U.S. State Department defines **human smuggling** as "the facilitation, transportation, attempted transportation or illegal entry of a person(s) across an international border, in violation of one or more country's laws, either clandestinely or through deception, such as the use of fraudulent documents." In other words, human smuggling refers to illegal immigration in which an agent is paid to help a person cross a border clandestinely.[66] Human smuggling may be conducted to obtain financial or other benefits for the smuggler, although sometimes people engage in smuggling for other motives, such as to reunite their families. Human smuggling generally occurs with the consent of those being smuggled, and they often pay a smuggler for his or her services. Once in the country they've paid to enter, smuggled individuals rarely remain in contact with the smuggler. The State Department notes that the vast majority of people who are assisted in illegally entering the United States annually are smuggled, rather than trafficked.

Although smuggling might not involve active coercion, it can be deadly. In January 2007, for example, truck driver Tyrone Williams, 36, a Jamaican citizen living in Schenectady, New York, was sentenced to life in prison for causing the deaths of 19 illegal immigrants in the nation's deadliest known human smuggling attempt.[67] Williams locked more than 70 immigrants in a container truck during a 2003 trip from South Texas to Houston but abandoned the truck about 100 miles from its destination. The victims died from dehydration, overheating, and suffocation in the Texas heat before the truck was discovered and its doors opened.

In contrast to smuggling, **trafficking in persons (TIP)** can be compared to a modern-day form of slavery, prompting former Secretary of State Condoleezza Rice to say that "defeating human trafficking is a great moral calling of our day."[68] Trafficking involves the exploitation of unwilling or unwitting people through force, coercion, threat, or deception and includes human rights abuses such as debt bondage, deprivation of liberty, or lack of control over freedom and labor. Trafficking is often undertaken for purposes of sexual or labor exploitation.

U.S. government officials estimate that 800,000 to 900,000 victims are trafficked globally each year and that 17,500 to 18,500 are trafficked into the United States.[69] Women and children comprise the largest group of victims, and they are often physically and emotionally abused. Although TIP is often an international crime that involves the crossing of borders, it is important to note that TIP victims can be trafficked within their own countries and communities. Traffickers can move victims between locations within the same country and often sell them to other trafficking organizations.

The International Labor Organization, the UN agency charged with addressing labor standards, employment, and social protection issues, estimates that there are 12.3 million people in forced labor, bonded labor, forced child labor, and sexual servitude throughout the world today.[70] Other estimates range as high as 27 million.[71]

A 2012 study released by the National Institute of Justice found that the majority of human trafficking cases in the United States involve sex trafficking (85%), whereas a much smaller percentage of all investigated cases involve labor trafficking (11%).[72]

It is sometimes difficult to distinguish between smuggling and trafficking because trafficking often includes an element of smuggling (that is, the illegal crossing of a national border). Moreover, some trafficking victims may believe they are being smuggled when they are really being trafficked. This happens, for example, when women trafficked for sexual exploitation believe they are agreeing to work in legitimate industries for decent wages—part of which they may have agreed to pay to the trafficker who smuggled them. They didn't know that upon arrival the traffickers would keep them in bondage, subject them to physical force or sexual violence, force them to work in the sex trade, and take most or all of their income. United Nations literature notes that Chinese syndicates are notorious for continuing to control the lives of migrants at their destination and that they discipline them by force and extract heavy payment for smuggling services—holding "their clients as virtual hostages until the fees have been paid."[73]

The U.S. Department of State's *Trafficking in Persons* report says that "human trafficking is a multi-dimensional threat. It deprives people of their human rights and freedoms, it increases global health risks, and it fuels the growth of organized crime."[74] At the individual level, the report notes, "human trafficking has a devastating impact on individual victims, who often suffer physical and emotional abuse, rape, threats against self and family, document theft, and even death."

The distinction between smuggling and trafficking is sometimes very subtle, but key components that generally distinguish trafficking from smuggling are the elements of fraud, force, or coercion. However, under U.S. law, if the person is under 18 and induced to perform a commercial sex act, then it is considered

■ **terrorism** A violent act or an act dangerous to human life, in violation of the criminal laws of the United States or of any state, that is committed to intimidate or coerce a government, the civilian population, or any segment thereof, in furtherance of political or social objectives.[i]

TABLE 17-2 | **Distinguishing between Human Trafficking and Smuggling**

TRAFFICKING	SMUGGLING
Must contain an element of force, fraud, or coercion (actual, perceived, or implied), unless victim under 18 years of age is involved in commercial sex acts.	The person being smuggled is generally cooperating.
Involves forced labor and/or exploitation.	Involves no forced labor or other exploitation.
Persons trafficked are victims.	Persons smuggled are violating the law. They are not victims.
Victims are enslaved, are subjected to limited movement or isolation, or have had documents confiscated.	Smuggled individuals are free to leave, change jobs, etc.
Need not involve the actual movement of the victim.	Facilitates the illegal entry of people from one country into another.
May or may not cross an international border.	Always crosses an international border.
Victim must be involved in labor/services or commercial sex acts (that is, must be "working").	Person must only be in country or attempting entry illegally.

Note: This table is meant to be conceptual and is not intended to provide precise legal distinctions between smuggling and trafficking.
Source: Adapted from U.S. Department of State, Bureau for International Narcotics and Law Enforcement Affairs, Human Smuggling and Trafficking Center, *Distinctions between Human Smuggling and Human Trafficking* (Washington, DC: January 1, 2005).

trafficking, regardless of whether fraud, force, or coercion is involved. Table 17-2 provides a guide to distinguishing human trafficking from smuggling.

According to the United Nations, human smuggling and trafficking have become a worldwide industry that "employs" millions of people and leads to the annual turnover of billions of dollars.[75] The UN also says that many of the routes used by smugglers have become well established and are widely known. Routes from Mexico and Central America to the United States, for example; from West Asia through Greece and Turkey to Western Europe; and within East and Southeast Asia are regularly traveled. More often than not, the UN says, the ongoing existence of flourishing smuggling routes is facilitated by weak legislation, lax border controls, corrupt officials, and the power and influence of organized crime.

Although there are significant differences between TIP and human smuggling, the underlying conditions that give rise to both of these illegal activities are often similar. Extreme poverty, lack of economic opportunity, civil unrest, and political uncertainty are all factors that contribute to social environments in which human smuggling and trafficking in persons occurs.

Section 7202 of the Intelligence Reform and Terrorism Prevention Act of 2004 established the Human Smuggling and Trafficking Center within the U.S. State Department. The secretary of state, the secretary of homeland security, the attorney general, and members of the national intelligence community oversee the center. The center was created to achieve greater integration and overall effectiveness in the U.S. government's enforcement of issues related to human smuggling, trafficking in persons, and criminal support of clandestine terrorist travel. Visit the Human Smuggling and Trafficking Center via **http://www.state.gov/m/ds/hstcenter**. Learn more about the characteristics of suspected human trafficking incidents at **http://www.justicestudies.com/pubs/humtraffick.pdf**, and about human sex trafficking at **http://www.justicestudies.com/pubs/sextraffick.pdf**. Also, you can examine the 2013–2017 *Federal Strategic Action Plan on Services for Victims of Human Trafficking in the United States* at **http://www.justicestudies.com/pubs/antitrafficking_plan.pdf**.

Terrorism

Terrorism as a criminal activity and the prevention of further acts of terrorism became primary concerns of American political leaders and justice system officials following the September 11, 2001, terrorist attacks on the United States. There is, however, no single uniformly accepted definition of terrorism that is applicable to all places and all circumstances. Some definitions are statutory in nature, whereas others were created for such practical purposes as gauging success in the fight against terrorism. Still others relate to specific forms of terrorism, such as cyberterrorism (discussed later in this section), and many legislative sources speak only of "acts of terrorism" or "terrorist activity" rather than terrorism itself because the nature of Western jurisprudence is to legislate against acts rather than against concepts.

A widely accepted definition of the term can be found in the federal Foreign Relations Authorization Act,[76] which defines

CJ | ISSUES

How Do People Become Violent Jihadists?

In 2013, the Congressional Research Service (CRS) of the United States released a report on combating American jihadist terrorism. Edited excerpts from the report are included in this box.

"Homegrown" is a term that describes terrorist activity or plots perpetrated within the United States or abroad by American citizens, legal permanent residents, or visitors radicalized largely within the United States. "Radicalization" describes the process of acquiring and holding extremist, or jihadist beliefs. The term "jihadist" describes radicalized individuals using Islam as an ideological and/or religious justification for their belief in the establishment of a global caliphate, or jurisdiction governed by a Muslim civil and religious leader known as a caliph.

The CRS estimated that there have been 63 homegrown violent jihadist plots or attacks in the United States between September 11, 2001 (9/11) and January 1, 2013. The report did not include the April 2013 bombings at the Boston Marathon, as it was released a few months prior to that incident.

The report, however, does reveal that the activities of homegrown terrorists expanded considerably beginning in May 2009, and resulted in 42 arrests to thwart "homegrown," jihadist-inspired terrorist plots by American citizens or legal permanent residents of the United States through January 2013. Two arrests resulted from actual attacks that took place, whereas arrests were made in the other incidents before attacks could be carried out. Most of the increase in homegrown plots between 2009–2013 likely reflects a trend in jihadist terrorist activity away from schemes directed by core members of significant terrorist groups such as al-Qaeda.

Individuals can become jihadist terrorists by radicalizing and then adopting violence as a tactic. "Radicalization" which, as mentioned, describes the process of "acquiring and holding extremist or jihadist beliefs," is not necessarily illegal because American law and values guarantee both free speech and free thought. Actions undertaken in violation of the law, however, are another matter. "Violent extremism" describes violent action taken on the basis of radical or extremist beliefs. For many, "violent extremism" is synonymous with "violent jihadist" and "jihadist terrorist." In other words, when someone moves from simply believing in jihad to illegally pursuing it via violent methods, he or she becomes a terrorist. Because the move from belief to violence is so individualized, there is no single path that individuals follow to become full-fledged terrorists.

Intermediaries, social networks, the Internet, and prisons have been cited as playing key roles in the radicalization process. Intermediaries—who are often charismatic individuals—frequently help persuade previously law-abiding citizens to radicalize or even become violent jihadists. Social networks, virtual or actual, support and reinforce the decisions individuals make as they embrace violent jihad, as does perusal of online materials. Although there has been much discussion regarding the powerful influence online jihadist material may have on the formation of terrorists, no consensus has emerged regarding the Web and terrorism. Prisons, seen by some as potential hotbeds of radicalization, have not yet played a large role in producing homegrown jihadists.

To counter violent jihadist plots, U.S. law enforcement has employed at least one tactic that uses "agent provocateurs." In agent provocateur cases—often called sting operations—government undercover agents befriend suspects and offer to facilitate their activities. The use of these techniques has generated considerable public controversy and illustrates an issue facing law enforcement today. Enforcement agencies are expected to prevent homegrown terrorism, but their use of preemptive techniques spawns concern among community members and civil libertarians. In cases where sting operations are used, law enforcement officials must be careful to avoid enticing the terrorist plotter to engage in activities that he or she might not otherwise have undertaken. Should that happen, the plotter, if arrested and charged, might be acquitted under an entrapment defense (see Chapter 3).

Reference: Jerome P. Bjelopera, *American Jihadist Terrorism: Combating a Complex Threat* (Washington, DC: Congressional Research Service, 2013).

---

terrorism in terms of four primary elements. The act says that terrorism is (1) premeditated, (2) politically motivated, (3) violence, (4) committed against noncombatant targets.[77] The FBI offers a nonstatutory working definition of terrorism as "a violent act or an act dangerous to human life in violation of the criminal laws of the United States or of any state to intimidate or coerce a government, the civilian population, or any segment thereof, in furtherance of political or social objectives."[78] Among the laws that define certain forms of human *activity* as terrorism, the Immigration and Nationality Act provides one of the most comprehensive and widely used definitions. That definition is shown in the "CJ Issues" box.

According to criminologist Gwynn Nettler, all forms of terrorism share six characteristics:[79]

- *No rules.* There are no moral limitations on the type or degree of violence that terrorists can use.
- *No innocents.* No distinctions are made between soldiers and civilians. Children can be killed as well as adults.
- *Economy.* Kill one, frighten 10,000.
- *Publicity.* Terrorists seek publicity, and publicity encourages terrorism.
- *Meaning.* Terrorist acts give meaning and significance to the lives of terrorists.
- *No clarity.* Beyond the immediate aim of destructive acts, the long-term goals of terrorists are likely to be poorly conceived or impossible to implement.

Moreover, notes Nettler, "Terrorism that succeeds escalates."[80]

Types of Terrorism

It is important to distinguish between two major forms of terrorism: domestic and international. Distinctions between the two forms are made in terms of the origin, base of operations,

domestic terrorism The unlawful use of force or violence by an individual or a group that is based and operates entirely within the United States and its territories, acts without foreign direction, and directs its activities against elements of the U.S. government or population.[ii]

and objectives of a terrorist organization. In the United States, *domestic terrorism* refers to the unlawful use of force or violence by an individual or a group that is based in and operates entirely within this country and its territories without foreign direction and whose acts are directed against elements of the U.S. government or population.[81] *International terrorism,* in contrast, is the unlawful use of force or violence by an individual or a group that has some connection to a foreign power, or whose activities transcend national boundaries, against people or property in order to intimidate or coerce a government, the civilian population, or any segment thereof, in furtherance of political or social objectives.[82] International terrorism is sometimes mistakenly called *foreign terrorism*, a term that, strictly speaking, refers only to acts of terrorism that occur outside of the United States.

It is important to distinguish between two major forms of terrorism: domestic and international.

Domestic Terrorism

Throughout the 1960s and 1970s, **domestic terrorism** in the United States required the expenditure of considerable criminal justice resources. The Weathermen, Students for a Democratic Society, the Symbionese Liberation Army, the Black Panthers, and other radical groups routinely challenged the authority of federal and local governments. Bombings, kidnappings, and shoot-outs peppered the national scene. As overt acts of domestic terrorism declined in frequency in the 1980s, international terrorism took their place. The war in Lebanon; terrorism in Israel; bombings in France, Italy, and Germany; and the many violent offshoots of the Iran-Iraq war and the first Gulf War occupied the attention of the media and of much of the rest of the world. Vigilance by the FBI, the Central Intelligence Agency (CIA), and other agencies largely prevented the spread of terrorism to the United States.

Worrisome today are domestic underground survivalist and separatist groups and potentially violent special-interest groups, each with its own vision of a future America. In 1993, for example, a confrontation between David Koresh's Branch Davidian followers and federal agents left 72 Davidians (including Koresh) and four federal agents dead in Waco, Texas.

Worrisome today are domestic underground survivalist and separatist groups and potentially violent special-interest groups, each with its own vision of a future America.

Exactly two years to the day after the Davidian standoff ended in a horrific fire that destroyed the compound, a powerful truck bomb devastated the Alfred P. Murrah Federal Building in downtown Oklahoma City. One hundred sixty-eight people died, and hundreds more were wounded. The targeted nine-story building had housed offices of the Social Security Administration; the Drug Enforcement Administration; the Secret Service; the Bureau of Alcohol, Tobacco, Firearms and Explosives; and a day-care center called America's Kids. The fertilizer-and-diesel-fuel device used in the terrorist attack was estimated to have weighed about 1,200 pounds and had been left in a rental truck on the Fifth Street side of the building. The blast, which left a crater 30 feet wide and 8 feet deep and spread debris over a ten-block area, demonstrated just how vulnerable the United States is to terrorist attack.

In 1997, a federal jury found 29-year-old Timothy McVeigh guilty of 11 counts, ranging from conspiracy to first-degree murder, in the Oklahoma City bombing. Jurors concluded that McVeigh had conspired with Terry Nichols, a friend he had met in the U.S. Army, and with unknown others to destroy the Murrah Building. Prosecutors made clear their belief that the attack was intended to revenge the 1993 assault on the Branch Davidian compound. McVeigh was sentenced to death and was executed by lethal injection at the U.S. penitentiary in Terre Haute, Indiana, in 2001.[83] McVeigh was the first person under federal jurisdiction to be put to death since 1963. In 2004, Terry Nichols was convicted of 161 counts of first-degree murder by an Oklahoma jury and was sentenced to 161 life terms for his role in the bombings.[84] He had previously been convicted of various federal charges.

In 2005, 38-year-old Eric Robert Rudolph pleaded guilty to a string of bombing attacks in Alabama and Georgia, including a blast at Atlanta's Centennial Park during the 1996 Olympics in which 1 person died and 111 were injured.[85] Rudolph, an antiabortion and antigay extremist, was sentenced to life in prison without the possibility of parole after having eluded law enforcement officers for years.

Active fringe groups include the Sovereign Citizens (discussed in Chapter 1) and those espousing a nationwide "common law movement," under which the legitimacy of elected government officials is not recognized. An example is the Republic of Texas separatists who took neighbors hostage near Fort Davis, Texas, in 1997 to draw attention to their claims that Texas was illegally annexed by the United States in 1845. Although not necessarily bent on terrorism, such special-interest groups may turn to violence if thwarted in attempts to reach their goals.

Sometimes individuals can be as dangerous as organized groups. In 1996, for example, 52-year-old Theodore Kaczynski, a Lincoln, Montana, antitechnology recluse, was arrested and charged in the Unabomber case. The Unabomber (so called

CJ | ISSUES
What Is Terrorist Activity?

Federal law enforcement efforts directed against agents of foreign terrorist organizations derive their primary authority from the Immigration and Nationality Act, found in Title 8 of the U.S. Code. The act defines *terrorist activity* as follows:

(ii) "Terrorist activity" defined

As used in this chapter, the term "terrorist activity" means any activity which is unlawful under the laws of the place where it is committed (or which, if committed in the United States, would be unlawful under the laws of the United States or any State) and which involves any of the following:

(I) The hijacking or sabotage of any conveyance (including an aircraft, vessel, or vehicle).
(II) The seizing or detaining, and threatening to kill, injure, or continue to detain, another individual in order to compel a third person (including a governmental organization) to do or abstain from doing any act as an explicit or implicit condition for the release of the individual seized or detained.
(III) A violent attack upon an internationally protected person (as defined in section 1116(b)(4) of title 18) or upon the liberty of such a person.
(IV) An assassination.
(V) The use of any—
(a) biological agent, chemical agent, or nuclear weapon or device, or
(b) explosive or firearm (other than for mere personal monetary gain), with intent to endanger, directly or indirectly, the safety of one or more individuals or to cause substantial damage to property.
(VI) A threat, attempt, or conspiracy to do any of the foregoing.

(iii) "Engage in terrorist activity" defined

As used in this chapter, the term "engage in terrorist activity" means to commit, in an individual capacity or as a member of an organization, an act of terrorist activity or an act which the actor knows, or reasonably should know, affords material support to any individual, organization, or government in conducting a terrorist activity at any time, including any of the following acts:

(I) The preparation or planning of a terrorist activity.
(II) The gathering of information on potential targets for terrorist activity.
(III) The providing of any type of material support, including a safe house, transportation, communications, funds, false documentation or identification, weapons, explosives, or training, to any individual the actor knows or has reason to believe has committed or plans to commit a terrorist activity.
(IV) The soliciting of funds or other things of value for terrorist activity or for any terrorist organization.
(V) The solicitation of any individual for membership in a terrorist organization, terrorist government, or to engage in a terrorist activity.

Crowds gather at the Boston Marathon bombing memorial on Boylston Street in Boston, Massachusetts in May, 2013, three weeks after the attacks. How does federal law define "terrorist activity"?

■ **international terrorism** The unlawful use of force or violence by an individual or a group that has some connection to a foreign power, or whose activities transcend national boundaries, against people or property in order to intimidate or coerce a government, the civilian population, or any segment thereof, in furtherance of political or social objectives.[iii]

■ **cyberterrorism** A form of terrorism that makes use of high technology, especially computers and the Internet, in the planning and carrying out of terrorist attacks.

Ron Edmonds/AP Wide World Photos

President Barack Obama speaks in the East Room of the White House on May 29, 2009, about the need to secure America's digital infrastructure. What kinds of criminal opportunities does cyberspace provide?

because the bomber's original targets were universities and airlines) had led police and FBI agents on a 17-year-long manhunt through a series of incidents that involved as many as 16 bombings, resulting in three deaths and 23 injuries. Kaczynski pleaded guilty to federal charges in 1998 and was sentenced to life in prison without possibility of parole.

International Terrorism

In 1988, Pan American's London–New York Flight 103 was destroyed over Scotland by a powerful two-stage bomb as it reached its cruising altitude of 30,000 feet, killing all of the 259 passengers and crew members aboard. Another 11 people on the ground were killed and many others injured as flaming debris from the airplane crashed down on the Scottish town of Lockerbie. It was the first time Americans were clearly the target of **international terrorism**. Any doubts that terrorists were targeting U.S. citizens were dispelled by the 1996 truck bomb attack on U.S. military barracks in Dhahran, Saudi Arabia. Nineteen U.S. Air Force personnel were killed and more than 250 others were injured in the blast, which destroyed the Khobar Towers housing complex.

The 1993 bombing of the World Trade Center in New York City and the 1995 conviction of Sheik Omar Abdel-Rahman and eight other Islamic fundamentalists on charges of plotting to start a holy war and of conspiring to commit assassinations and bomb the United Nations[86] indicated to many that the threat of international terrorism could soon become a part of daily life in America. According to some terrorism experts, the 1993 explosion at the World Trade Center, which killed four people and created a 100-foot hole through four subfloors of concrete, ushered in an era of international terrorist activity in the United States. In 1999, the Second U.S. Circuit Court of Appeals upheld the convictions of the sheik and his co-conspirators. They remain in federal prison.

In 2001, Islamic terrorist Osama bin Laden showed the world how terrorists can successfully strike at American interests on U.S. soil when members of his organization attacked the World Trade Center and the Pentagon using commandeered airliners, killing approximately 3,000 people. Earlier, in 1998, bin Laden's agents struck American embassies in Nairobi, Kenya, and Dares Salaam, Tanzania, killing 257 people, including 12 Americans. In 2003, a coordinated attack by Islamic extremists on a residential compound for foreigners in Riyadh, Saudi Arabia, killed 34 people (nine attackers died), including eight Americans, and wounded many more.[88] Similar attacks are continuing in the Middle East and elsewhere.

Some believe that the wars in Afghanistan and Iraq, as well as a coordinated international effort against al-Qaeda, may have substantially weakened that organization's ability to carry out future strikes outside of the Middle East. Those who study international terrorism, however, note that jihadism, or the Islamic holy war movement, survives independent of any one organization and appears to be gaining strength around the world.[89] Jihadist principles continue to serve as the organizing rationale for extremist groups in much of the Muslim world. In 2012, Brian Michael Jenkins, of the RAND Corporation, told Congress that jihadism is difficult to defeat because it "is many things at once—an ideology of violent jihad, a universe of like-minded fanatics, a global terrorist enterprise—and it operates on a number of fronts in both the physical and virtual worlds."[90] Learn more about the global threat from Islamic fundamentalism at **http://justicestudies.com/pubs/al_qae.da.pdf**, and about how terrorism has evolved since 9/11 at **http://justicestudies.com/pubs/since911.pdf**.

Cyberterrorism

A relatively new kind of terrorism, called **cyberterrorism**, makes use of high technology, especially computers and the Internet, in

■ **infrastructure** The basic facilities, services, and installations that a country needs to function. Transportation and communications systems, water and power lines, and institutions that serve the public, including banks, schools, post offices, and prisons, are all part of a country's infrastructure.[iv]

CJ | NEWS

American Woman Embraces Islam on the Internet, Becomes "Jihad Jane"

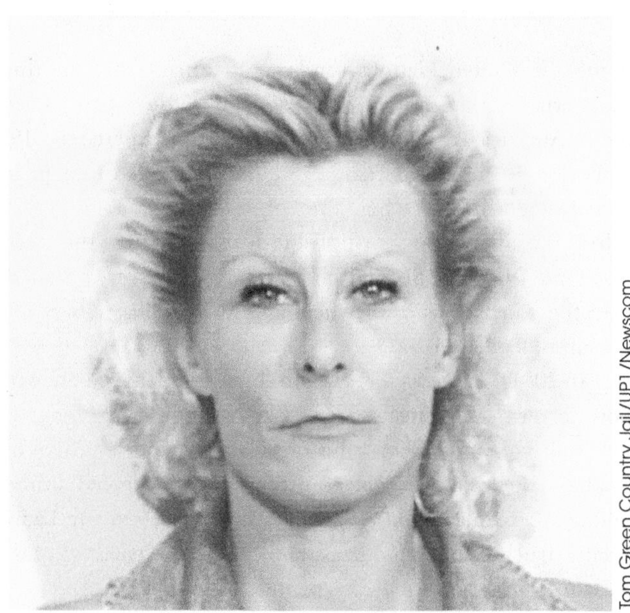

Tom Green Country Jail/UPI/Newscom

Colleen LaRose, aka "Jihad Jane." LaRose, an American woman who aided Islamic terrorists plotting to kill a Swedish cartoonist, pleaded guilty in federal court in 2011 to charges of conspiracy to murder a foreign target, conspiracy to support terrorists, and lying to the FBI. How can the justice system help in the fight against international terrorism?

In 2014, 50-year-old Colleen LaRose was sentenced in federal court to 10 years in prison for conspiracy to murder a foreign target, conspiracy to support terrorists, and lying to the FBI.[87] LaRose, aka "Jihad Jane," is an American woman who aided a small group of Islamic terrorists who were plotting to kill Swedish cartoonist Lars Vilks. Vilks had been marked for death by radical Muslims after he drew a cartoon showing the Prophet Muhammad's head on the body of a dog. Prior to her arrest, LaRose had posted a YouTube video expressing her hatred of what she called Zionists, and saying that she was "desperate to do something somehow to help" Muslims whom she saw as suffering around the world. Following a series of Internet contacts with people who became co-conspirators, LaRose flew to Europe, apparently in preparation for an attempt on Vilks's life. The plan, however, was never carried out, and she was arrested at the Philadelphia International Airport upon her return to the United States. The arrest of LaRose, who was born in Michigan and raised in Texas, got the attention of enforcement agencies throughout the United States because it demonstrated how native-born American citizens could become radicalized and participate in terrorist ideology independently of organized leadership.

LaRose is not like most Americans who join extreme Muslim causes. She has no Muslim background and apparently had no interest in the religion until she went on the Internet and assumed the cyber-personality of "Jihad Jane." LaRose grew up in Texas. Divorced twice at a young age, she was moving from city to city when, at age 41, she became romantically involved with Kurt Gorman, a businessman visiting from Pennsylvania. In 2004, he took her back to his hometown outside Philadelphia, where she helped take care of his elderly father.

While Gorman went to work each day, LaRose developed an obsession with the Internet and became a secret advocate for Muslim causes. According to federal prosecutors, LaRose "worked obsessively on her computer to communicate with, recruit and incite other jihadists."

On the same day that LaRose's arrest was announced, five of her alleged co-conspirators were arrested in Ireland. One of them was Jamie Paulin-Ramirez, a Coloradan who was a lot like LaRose. Known on the Internet as "Jihad Jamie," she went to Ireland and married an Algerian man she had never met before, apparently as a cover for the alleged plot. Paulin-Ramirez was later charged as a co-defendant with LaRose.

Assistant U.S. Attorney General David Kris said LaRose's alleged co-conspirators saw her American looks and U.S. citizenship as a way to operate without attracting attention. "Today's guilty plea, by a woman from suburban America who plotted with others to commit murder overseas and to provide material support to terrorists, underscores the evolving nature of the threat we face," he said in an announcement.

Resources: "Jihad Jane, Colleen LaRose, Recruited Terrorists and Plotted Murder, Prosecutors Say," *Huffington Post*, May 9, 2010, http://www.huffingtonpost.com/2010/03/09/jihad-jane-colleen-larose_n_492586.html; "'Jihad Jane' Pleads Guilty to Murder Attempt on Swedish Cartoonist," *The Guardian*, February 1, 2011, http://www.guardian.co.uk/world/2011/feb/02/jihad-jane-pleads-guilty-cartoonist-murder; and "'Jihad Jane' Admits to Conspiracy to Support Terrorists, Murder," *Christian Science Monitor*, February 1, 2011, http://www.csmonitor.com/USA/Latest-News-Wires/2011/0201/Jihad-Jane-admits-to-conspiracy-to-support-terrorists-murder.

the planning and carrying out of terrorist attacks. The term was coined in the 1980s by Barry Collin, a senior research fellow at the Institute for Security and Intelligence in California, who used it to refer to the convergence of cyberspace and terrorism.[91] It was later popularized by a 1996 RAND report that warned of an emerging "new terrorism" distinguished by how terrorist groups organize and by how they use technology. The report warned of a coming "netwar" or "infowar" consisting of coordinated cyberattacks on our nation's economic, business, and military **infrastructure**.[92] A year later, FBI agent Mark Pollitt offered a working definition of *cyberterrorism*, saying that it is "the premeditated, politically motivated attack against information, computer systems, computer programs, and data which results in violence against noncombatant targets by subnational groups or clandestine agents."[93]

Scenarios describing cyberterrorism possibilities are imaginative and diverse. Some have suggested that a successful

■ **narcoterrorism** A political alliance between terrorist organizations and drug-supplying cartels. The cartels provide financing for the terrorists, who in turn provide quasi-military protection to the drug dealers.

cyber-terrorist attack on the nation's air traffic control system might cause airplanes to collide in midair or that an attack on food- and cereal-processing plants that drastically altered the levels of certain nutritional supplements might sicken or kill a large number of our nation's children. Other such attacks might cause the country's power grid to collapse or could muddle the records and transactions of banks and stock exchanges. Possible targets in such attacks are almost endless.

In 1998, the Critical Infrastructure Assurance Office (CIAO) was created by a presidential directive to coordinate the federal government's initiatives on critical infrastructure protection and to provide a national focus for cyberspace security. In 2001, the White House formed the President's Critical Infrastructure Protection Board (PCIPB) and tasked it with recommending policies in support of critical infrastructure protection.[94] In February 2003, the PCIPB released an important document titled *The National Strategy to Secure Cyberspace*,[95] which is available at **http://www.justicestudies.com/pubs/cyberstrategy.pdf**.

In 2003, CIAO functions were transferred to the National Cyber Security Division (NCSD) of the Directorate of Information Analysis and Infrastructure Protection within the Department of Homeland Security (DHS). According to DHS, the creation of the NCSD improved protection of critical cyberassets by "maximizing and leveraging the resources" of previously separate offices.[96] The NCSD coordinates its activities with the U.S. Computer Emergency Response Team (US-CERT), which runs a National Cyber Alert System. Visit US-CERT, which is also a part of the Department of Homeland Security, at **http://www.us-cert.gov**. Another group, the Secret Service National Threat Assessment Center (NTAC), developed its Critical Systems Protection Initiative to offer advanced cybersecurity prevention and response capabilities to the nation's business community. Visit the NTAC at **http://www.secretservice.gov/ntac_ssi.shtml**.

In 2009, President Obama announced the creation of a new White House position: security "czar" for cyberspace. The president's announcement followed news that the Pentagon would create a new cybercommand in an effort to improve the protection of military computer networks and to coordinate both offensive and defensive cybermissions.[97] Today, Michael Daniels, former research assistant at the Southern Center for International Studies, heads the White House's office of cybersecurity. Visit the U.S. Army's cybercommand at **http://www.arcyber.army.mil**.

Narcoterrorism

Some authors have identified a link between major drug traffickers and terrorist groups.[98] In mid-2005, for example, Afghan drug lord Bashir Noorzai was arrested in New York and held without bond on charges that he tried to smuggle more than $50 million worth of heroin into the United States.[99] Noorzai, who was on the Drug Enforcement Administration's (DEA's) list of most wanted drug kingpins, had apparently operated with impunity under the protection of the Taliban between 1990 and 2004. According to the DEA, Noorzai's organization "provided demolitions, weapons and manpower to the Taliban." In exchange, the Taliban was said to have protected Noorzai's opium crops and transit routes through Afghanistan and Pakistan.

The link between drug traffickers and insurgents has been termed **narcoterrorism**.[100] Narcoterrorism, simply defined, is the involvement of terrorist organizations and insurgent groups in the trafficking of narcotics.[101] The relationship that exists between terrorist organizations and drug traffickers is mutually beneficial. Insurgents derive financial benefits from their supporting role in drug trafficking, and the traffickers receive protection and benefit from the use of terrorist tactics against foes and competitors.

The first documented instance of an insurgent force financed at least in part with drug money came to light during an investigation of the virulent anti-Castro Omega 7 group in the early 1980s.[102] Clear-cut evidence of modern narcoterrorism, however, is difficult to obtain. Contemporary insurgent organizations with links to drug dealers probably include the 19th of April Movement (M-19) operating in Colombia, Sendero Luminoso (Shining Path) of Peru, the Revolutionary Armed Forces of Colombia, and the large Farabundo Marti National Liberation Front, which has long sought to overthrow the elected government of El Salvador.[103]

Narcoterrorism raises a number of questions. Drug researcher James Inciardi summarizes them as follows:[104]

- What is the full threat posed by narcoterrorism?
- How should narcoterrorism be dealt with?
- Is narcoterrorism a law enforcement problem or a military one?
- How might narcoterrorism be affected by changes in official U.S. policy toward drugs and drug use?
- Is the international drug trade being used as a tool by anti-U.S. and other interests to undermine Western democracies in a calculated way?

Unfortunately, in the opinion of some experts, the United States is ill prepared to combat this type of international organized crime. Testifying before the Senate's Foreign Relations

Subcommittee on Terrorism, Narcotics, and International Operations, William J. Olson, a senior fellow at the National Strategy Information Center, told Congress that more than $1 trillion (equivalent to one-sixth of the U.S. gross national product) is generated yearly by organized criminal activities like those associated with narcoterrorism. "We must recognize that the rules of the crime game have changed," said Olson. "International criminal organizations are challenging governments, permeating societies. They're running roughshod over weak institutions and exploiting gaps in the U.S. and international response. They have the upper hand at the moment and they know it," he added.[105] Other experts testified that a comprehensive national strategy—one that goes far beyond law enforcement and criminal prosecution to include diplomacy and organized international efforts—is needed to combat international organized criminal enterprises before they can co-opt global markets and worldwide financial institutions.[106]

Even more potentially damaging are efforts being made by some criminal groups to wrest control of political institutions in various parts of the world. As transnational organized crime expert Emilio Viano points out, "Powerful drug constituencies influence the electoral process more and more, seeking to gain actual political representation and consequently weaken the rule of law in a number of countries."[107]

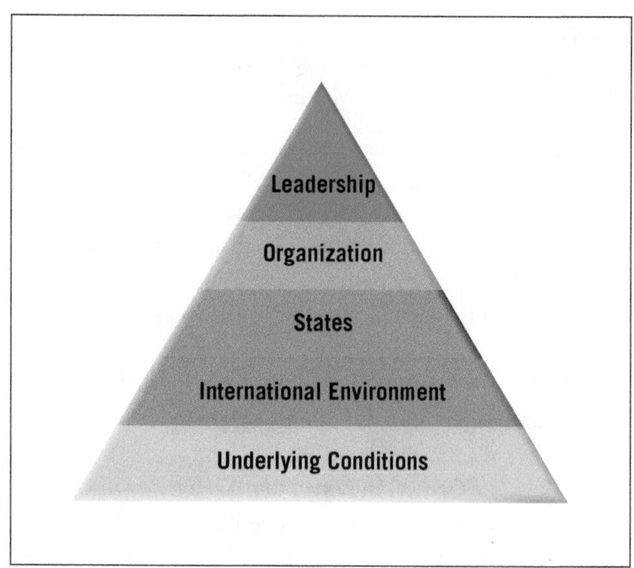

FIGURE 17-3 | The Building Process for International Terrorist Organizations

Source: *National Strategy for Combating Terrorism* (Washington, DC: White House, 2003), p. 6.

Causes of Terrorism

According to the U.S. government,[108] international terrorist organizations build on a process shown in Figure 17-3. The federal government's *National Strategy for Counterterrorism*[109] says that the *underlying conditions* that lead to terrorism include poverty, political corruption, religious and ideational conflict, and ethnic strife. Such conditions provide terrorists with the opportunity to legitimize their cause and to justify their actions. Feeding on the social disorganization fostered by these conditions, terrorists position themselves to demand political change.

The second level in Figure 17-3, the *international environment*, refers to the geopolitical boundaries within which terrorist organizations form and through which they operate. If international borders are free and open, then terrorist groups can readily establish safe havens, hone their capabilities, practice their techniques, and provide support and funding to distant members and collaborators. Either knowingly or unwittingly, nations (*states*) can provide the physical assets and bases needed for the terrorist *organization* to grow and function. Finally, the terrorist *leadership*, at the top of the pyramid, provides the overall direction and strategy that give life to the organization's terror campaign.

Combating Terrorism

Terrorism represents a difficult challenge to all societies. The open societies of the Western world, however, are potentially more vulnerable than are totalitarian regimes such as dictatorships. Western democratic ideals restrict police surveillance of likely terrorist groups and curtail luggage, vehicle, and airport searches. Press coverage of acts of terrorism encourage copycat activities by other fringe groups and communicate information on workable techniques. Laws designed to limit terrorist access to technology, information, and physical locations are stopgap measures at best. The federal Terrorist Firearms Detection Act of 1988 is an example. Designed to prevent the development of plastic firearms by requiring handguns to contain at least 3.7 ounces of detectable metal,[110] it applies only to weapons manufactured within U.S. borders.

In 1996, the Antiterrorism and Effective Death Penalty Act (AEDPA) became law. The act includes a number of provisions:

- It bans fundraising and financial support within the United States for international terrorist organizations.
- It provides $1 billion for enhanced terrorism-fighting measures by federal and state authorities.
- It allows foreign terrorism suspects to be deported or to be kept out of the United States without the disclosure of classified evidence against them.
- It permits a death sentence to be imposed on anyone committing an international terrorist attack in the United States in which a death occurs.
- It makes it a federal crime to use the United States as a base for planning terrorist attacks overseas.
- It orders identifying chemical markers known as *taggants* to be added to plastic explosives during manufacture.
- It orders a feasibility study on marking other explosives (except gunpowder).

More than a year before the events of September 11, 2001, the National Commission on Terrorism released a report titled

Countering the Changing Threat of International Terrorism.[111] The commission, created by House and Senate leaders in 1998 in response to the bombings of the U.S. embassies in Kenya and Tanzania, was led by former U.S. Ambassador-at-Large for Counter-Terrorism L. Paul Bremer. The commission's report, which we now see presaged the 2001 attacks on the World Trade Center and the Pentagon, began with these words: "International terrorism poses an increasingly dangerous and difficult threat to America." The report identified Afghanistan, Iran, Iraq, Sudan, and Syria as among state sponsors of terrorism and concluded that "the government must immediately take steps to reinvigorate the collection of intelligence about terrorists' plans, use all available legal avenues to disrupt and prosecute terrorist activities and private sources of support, convince other nations to cease all support for terrorists, and ensure that federal, state, and local officials are prepared for attacks that may result in mass casualties." A number of the commission's recommendations were implemented only *after* the terrorist attacks of 2001.

Following the 2001 attacks, Congress enacted and the president signed the USA PATRIOT Act. The act, which is discussed in detail in other chapters and which was reauthorized in 2006 with some amendments, and had certain expiring provisions extended again in 2011, created a number of new crimes, such as terrorist attacks against mass transportation and harboring or concealing terrorists. Those crimes were set forth in Title VIII of the act, titled "Strengthening the Criminal Laws against Terrorism." Excerpts from Title VIII can be found in the "CJ Issues" box.

Following the 2001 attacks, Congress enacted and the president signed the USA PATRIOT Act.

Antiterrorism Committees and Reports

Numerous important antiterrorism reports and studies have been released during the last seven or eight years by various groups, including the Advisory Panel to Assess Domestic Response Capabilities for Terrorism Involving Weapons of Mass Destruction (also known as the Gilmore Commission), the National Commission on Terrorism, the U.S. Commission on National Security in the Twenty-First Century, the New York–based Council on Foreign Relations (CFR), and the National Commission on Terrorist Attacks upon the United States (aka the *9/11 Commission*).

Some pre–September 11, 2001, reports offered valuable suggestions that, if followed, might have helped prevent the events that took place on that day. Some of the subsequent reports have been voices of reason in the rush to strengthen the nation's antiterrorism defenses at potentially high costs to individual freedoms. The 2002 CFR report, for example, notes that "systems such as those used in the aviation sector, which start from the assumption that every passenger and every bag of luggage poses an equal risk, must give way to more intelligence-driven and layered security approaches that emphasize prescreening and monitoring based on risk criteria."

The report of the 9/11 Commission, released on July 22, 2004, which many saw as especially valuable, said that the September 11, 2001, attacks should have come as no surprise because the U.S. government had received clear warnings that Islamic terrorists

Murad Sezer/AP Wide World Photos

Palestinian boys holding toy rifles as a girl displays a poster of Osama bin Laden in Gaza City during a demonstration at Al Azhar University to honor suicide bombers. The school was organized by members of the Islamic Jihad. The 9/11 Commission report, released in 2004, pointed to the radical ideology underpinning international Islamic terrorism today and bemoaned the fact that too many Middle Eastern children are being socialized into a culture of terrorism. How can radical ideologies be combated?

CJ | ISSUES

The USA PATRIOT Act of 2001 (as Amended and Reauthorized in 2006)

Title VIII of the USA PATRIOT Act created two new federal crimes of terrorist activity: (1) terrorist attacks against mass transportation systems and (2) harboring or concealing terrorists. The following excerpts from the act describe these offenses.

Title VIII—Strengthening the Criminal Laws Against Terrorism

Sec. 801. Terrorist Attacks and Other Acts of Violence Against Mass Transportation Systems Chapter 97 of title 18, United States Code, is amended by adding at the end the following:

§ 1993. Terrorist attacks and other acts of violence against mass transportation systems

(a) GENERAL PROHIBITIONS.—Whoever willfully—

(1) wrecks, derails, sets fire to, or disables a mass transportation vehicle or ferry;

(2) places or causes to be placed any biological agent or toxin for use as a weapon, destructive substance, or destructive device in, upon, or near a mass transportation vehicle or ferry, without previously obtaining the permission of the mass transportation provider, and with intent to endanger the safety of any passenger or employee of the mass transportation provider, or with a reckless disregard for the safety of human life;

(3) sets fire to, or places any biological agent or toxin for use as a weapon, destructive substance, or destructive device in, upon, or near any garage, terminal, structure, supply, or facility used in the operation of, or in support of the operation of, a mass transportation vehicle or ferry, without previously obtaining the permission of the mass transportation provider, and knowing or having reason to know such activity would likely derail, disable, or wreck a mass transportation vehicle or ferry used, operated, or employed by the mass transportation provider;

(4) removes appurtenances from, damages, or otherwise impairs the operation of a mass transportation signal system, including a train control system, centralized dispatching system, or rail grade crossing warning signal without authorization from the mass transportation provider;

(5) interferes with, disables, or incapacitates any dispatcher, driver, captain, or person while they are employed in dispatching, operating, or maintaining a mass transportation vehicle or ferry, with intent to endanger the safety of any passenger or employee of the mass transportation provider, or with a reckless disregard for the safety of human life;

(6) commits an act, including the use of a dangerous weapon, with the intent to cause death or serious bodily injury to an employee or passenger of a mass transportation provider or any other person while any of the foregoing are on the property of a mass transportation provider;

(7) conveys or causes to be conveyed false information, knowing the information to be false, concerning an attempt or alleged attempt being made or to be made, to do any act which would be a crime prohibited by this subsection; or

(8) attempts, threatens, or conspires to do any of the aforesaid acts, shall be fined under this title or imprisoned not more than twenty years, or both, if such act is committed, or in the case of a threat or conspiracy such act would be committed, on, against, or affecting a mass transportation provider engaged in or affecting interstate or foreign commerce, or if in the course of committing such act, that person travels or communicates across a State line in order to commit such act, or transports materials across a State line in aid of the commission of such act.

(b) AGGRAVATED OFFENSE.—Whoever commits an offense under subsection (a) in a circumstance in which—

(1) the mass transportation vehicle or ferry was carrying a passenger at the time of the offense; or

(2) the offense has resulted in the death of any person, shall be guilty of an aggravated form of the offense and shall be fined under this title or imprisoned for a term of years or for life, or both. Sec. 803. Prohibition Against Harboring Terrorists

(a) IN GENERAL.—Chapter 113B of title 18, United States Code, is amended by adding after section 2338 the following new section:

§ 2339. Harboring or concealing terrorists

(a) Whoever harbors or conceals any person who he knows, or has reasonable grounds to believe, has committed, or is about to commit, an offense under section 32 (relating to destruction of aircraft or aircraft facilities), section 175 (relating to biological weapons), section 229 (relating to chemical weapons), section 831 (relating to nuclear materials), paragraph (2) or (3) of section 844(f) (relating to arson and bombing of government property risking or causing injury or death), section 1366(a) (relating to the destruction of an energy facility), section 2280 (relating to violence against maritime navigation), section 2332a (relating to weapons of mass destruction), or section 2332b (relating to acts of terrorism transcending national boundaries) of this title, section 236(a) (relating to sabotage of nuclear facilities or fuel) of the Atomic Energy Act of 1954 (42 U.S.C. 2284(a)), or section 46502 (relating to aircraft piracy) of title 49, shall be fined under this title or imprisoned not more than ten years, or both.

(b) A violation of this section may be prosecuted in any Federal judicial district in which the underlying offense was committed, or in any other Federal judicial district as provided by law.

(c) TECHNICAL AMENDMENT.—The chapter analysis for chapter 113B of title 18, United States Code, is amended by inserting after the item for section 2338 the following: "2339. Harboring or concealing terrorists."

Note: The USA PATRIOT Act was reauthorized by Congress in March 2006. Some subsections that had been subject to sunset provisions were extended in 2011.

---

were planning to strike at targets within the United States. The report also said that the United States is still not properly prepared to deal adequately with terrorist threats and called for the creation of a new federal intelligence-gathering center to unify the more than a dozen federal agencies currently gathering terrorism-related intelligence at home and abroad. In December 2005, members of the 9/11 Commission held a final news conference in which they lambasted the lack of progress made by federal officials charged with implementing safeguards to prevent future terrorist attacks within the United States. Former Commission Chair Thomas Kean called it "shocking" that the nation remained so vulnerable. "We shouldn't need another wake-up call," said Kean. "We believe that the terrorists will strike again."[112]

In 2010, the Bipartisan Policy Center's National Security Preparedness Group released a wide-ranging report on the evolving nature of terrorism. The report, *Assessing the Terrorist Threat*, made clear that the biggest threat to American national security may no longer come from large international terrorist organizations—but may come instead from small groups of homegrown terrorists, or even loners, who have bought into the ideology of terrorism.[113]

Finally, in 2012, Brian Michael Jenkins, a senior advisor to the president of the RAND Corporation, testified before the U.S. Senate's Homeland Security and Governmental Affairs Committee, telling its members that "Al Qaeda finds fertile ground in failed or failing states where it can attach itself to local insurgencies. It may provide only modest material assistance and operational advice, but the diffusion of al Qaeda-affiliated and connected movements in the region demonstrates that its brand name still carries prestige."[114] Jenkins's testimony followed the "Arab Spring" uprisings of 2010–2013, in which a wave of antigovernment demonstrations, protests, and civil wars broke out in North African and Middle Eastern countries and led to the overthrow of a number of political leaders who were in power at the time.

Although it is impossible to discuss each of the reports mentioned here in detail in this chapter, most of them are available in their entirety at **http://justicestudies.com/terror_reports**.

The Department of Homeland Security

The Homeland Security Act of 2002, enacted to protect America against terrorism, created the federal Department of Homeland Security (DHS), which is charged with protecting the nation's critical infrastructure against terrorist attack. The department began operations on March 1, 2003, with former Pennsylvania Governor Tom Ridge as its first director. The director, whose official title is secretary of homeland security, is a member of the president's cabinet. On January 21, 2009, Janet Napolitano became the third secretary of homeland security, and continues to serve in that capacity as this book goes to press. A former Arizona governor, Napolitano also served as the U.S. attorney who led the investigation into the Oklahoma City bombing.

Experts say that the creation of DHS is the most significant transformation of the U.S. government since 1947, when President Harry S. Truman merged the various branches of the armed forces into the Department of Defense in an effort to better coordinate the nation's defense against military threats.[115] DHS coordinates the activities of 22 disparate domestic agencies, the largest of which are (1) U.S. Customs and Border Protection (CBP), (2) U.S. Citizenship and Immigration Services (CIS), (3) the U.S. Coast Guard (USCG), (4) the Federal Emergency Management Agency (FEMA), (5) U.S. Immigration and Customs Enforcement (ICE), (6) the U.S. Secret Service (USSS), and (7) the Transportation Security Administration (TSA).

The *Bureau of Immigration and Customs Enforcement (ICE),* also known as U.S. Immigration and Customs Enforcement, is the largest investigative arm of the Department of Homeland Security. The ICE is responsible for identifying and eliminating vulnerabilities in the nation's border, economic, transportation, and infrastructure security. The *Bureau of Customs and Border Protection (CBP)* is the unified border-control agency of the United States, and has as its mission the protection of our country's borders and the American people. The *Bureau of Citizenship and Immigration Services (CIS),* also known as U.S. Citizenship and Immigration Services, or USCIS, dedicates its energies to providing efficient immigration services and easing the transition to American citizenship.

Immigration law enforcement is a major function of DHS and its component agencies. In the words of a 2013 DHS report, the department "continues the Administration's unprecedented focus on border security, travel and trade by supporting 21,370 Border Patrol agents and 21,186 CBP Officers at our ports of entry as well the continued deployment of proven, effective surveillance technology along the highest trafficked areas of the Southwest Border."[116] The total federal budget for DHS in 2013 was $59 billion, with immigration services receiving much of that money. In 2012, spending for the two main immigration enforcement agencies, the CBP and the ICE exceeded $17.9 billion.[117] The U.S. Coast Guard, which also plays an important role in securing the nation's ports of call, received more than $10 billion to fund continuing operations. Border apprehensions reached a peak in 2000, with 1.7 million arrests.[118] By 2011, the number of arrests for border violations had declined to 340,252,[119] largely as the result of declining economic conditions in the United States that led to fewer attempts to gain access to the country by undocumented aliens.

The DHS organizational chart is shown in Figure 17-4, and you can visit DHS on the Web via **http://www.dhs.gov**.

The National Counterterrorism Strategy

In 2011, the White House released its official *National Strategy for Counterterrorism.*[120] The strategy maintained a focus on deterring Islamic-inspired terrorism and promised to pressure "al-Qa'ida's core while emphasizing the need to build foreign partnerships and capacity . . . to strengthen our resilience." The authors of the strategy noted that it "augments our focus on confronting the al-Qa'ida-linked threats that continue to emerge from beyond its core safehaven in South Asia." The strategy makes it clear that "The preeminent security threat to the United States continues to be from *al-Qa'ida and its affiliate and adherents.*" The avowed goals of the *National Strategy* are as follows:

- Protect the American People, Homeland, and American Interests.
- Disrupt, Degrade, Dismantle, and Defeat al-Qa'ida and Its Affiliates and Adherents.
- Prevent Terrorist Development, Acquisition, and Use of Weapons of Mass Destruction.
- Eliminate Safehavens.
- Build Enduring Counterterrorism Partnerships and Capabilities.
- Degrade Links between al-Qa'ida and its Affiliates and Adherents.
- Counter al-Qa'ida Ideology and Its Resonance and Diminish the Specific Drivers of Violence that al-Qa'ida Exploits.
- Deprive Terrorists of their Enabling Means.

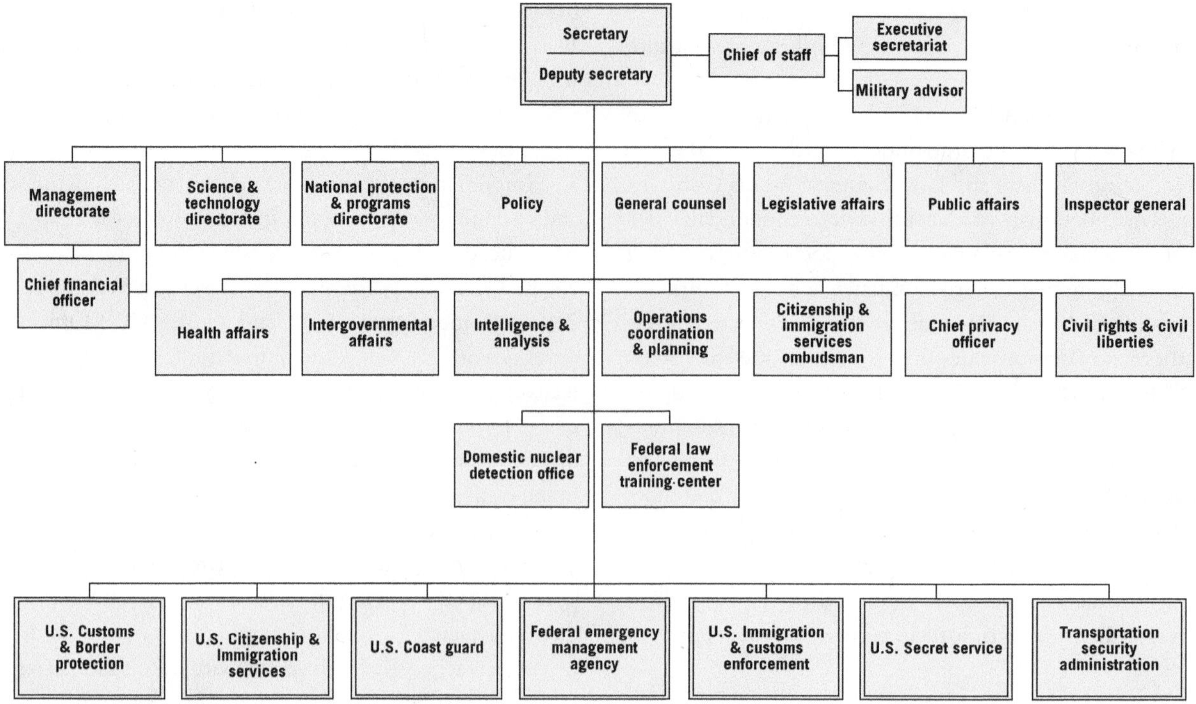

FIGURE 17-4 | Organizational Chart of the Department of Homeland Security

Source: Department of Homeland Security.

The national strategy in the fight against terrorism includes a two-pronged approach: (1) reduce the scope of operations of terrorist organizations, and (2) reduce their capability (Figure 17-5). The July 2004 report of the 9/11 Commission proposed sweeping changes within the U.S. intelligence community, including the creation of the position of national intelligence director (NID). Soon afterward, the Intelligence Reform and Terrorism Prevention Act of 2004 facilitated the creation of the National Counterterrorism Center (NCTC) under the newly created position of NID.[121] The NID acts as the principal advisor to the president, the National Security Council, and the Homeland Security Council for intelligence matters related to national security. The NCTC serves as the primary organization in the U.S. government for integrating and analyzing all intelligence pertaining to terrorism and counterterrorism and for conducting strategic counterterrorism operational planning. Today's NCTC intelligence analysts have access to dozens of networks and information systems from across the intelligence, law enforcement, military, and homeland security communities. These systems provide foreign and domestic information pertaining to international terrorism and sensitive law enforcement activities.[122] The

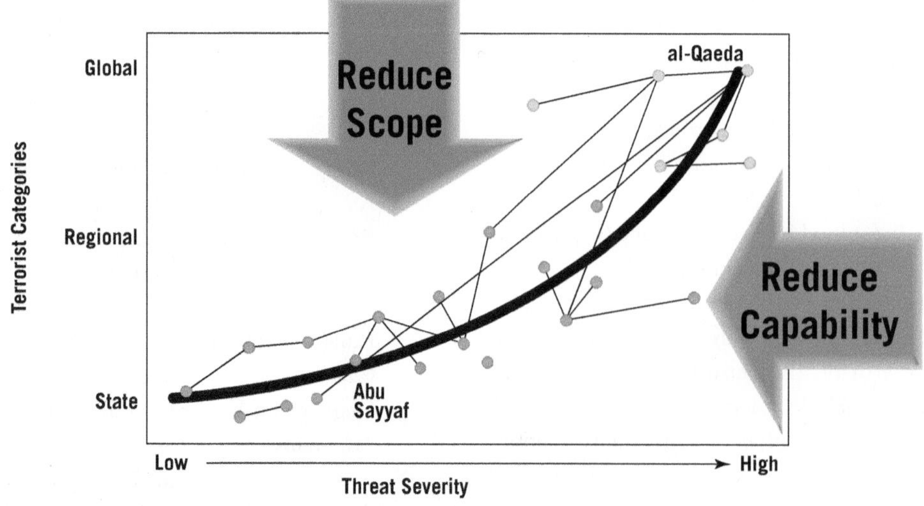

FIGURE 17-5 | Reducing the Scope and Capability of Terrorist Organizations

Source: *National Strategy for Combating Terrorism* (Washington, DC: White House, 2003) p. 13.

foreign terrorist organization (FTO) A foreign organization that engages in terrorist activity that threatens the security of U.S. nationals or the national security of the United States and that is so designated by the U.S. secretary of state.

© Heide Benser/Corbis/Glow Image

An air traveler being screened by Transportation Security Administration employees in Chicago's O'Hare International Airport. The hijackings of four airplanes by Islamic terrorists on September 11, 2001, led to tightened security controls over air travel nationwide and abroad. How did the hijackings reduce freedoms that Americans had previously taken for granted?

National Strategy is available in its entirety at **http://www.justicestudies.com/pubs/counterterrorismstrategy.pdf**. Visit the National Counterterrorism Center at **http://www.nctc.gov**.

Foreign Terrorist Organizations

The Immigration and Nationality Act[123] and the Intelligence Reform and Terrorism Prevention Act of 2004[124] provide the U.S. Department of State with the authority to designate any group outside the United States as a **foreign terrorist organization (FTO)**. The process involves an exhaustive interagency review process in which all evidence of a group's activity, from both classified and open sources, is scrutinized. The State Department, working closely with the Justice and Treasury Departments and the intelligence community, prepares a detailed "administrative record" that documents the organization's terrorist activity.

Federal law requires that any organization considered for FTO designation must meet three criteria: (1) It must be foreign; (2) it must engage in terrorist activity as defined in Section 212 (a)(3)(B) of the Immigration and Nationality Act;[125] and (3) the organization's activities must threaten the security of U.S. nationals or the national security (national defense, foreign relations, or economic interests) of the United States. Table 17-3 lists 52 FTOs, as designated by the U.S. Department

TABLE 17-3 | Designated Foreign Terrorist Organizations as of Mid-2013

Foreign terrorist organizations (FTOs) are foreign organizations that are designated by the secretary of state in accordance with Section 219 of the Immigration and Nationality Act (INA), as amended. FTO designations play a critical role in the fight against terrorism and are an effective means of curtailing support for terrorist activities and pressuring groups to get out of the terrorism business.

Abu Nidal Organization (ANO)	Kata'ib Hizballah (KH)
Abu Sayyaf Group (ASG)	Kurdistan Workers' Party (PKK)
Al-Aqsa Martyrs Brigade (AAMB)	Lashkar e-Tayyiba (LT)
Ansar al-Islam (AAI)	Lashkar i Jhangvi (LJ)
Ansar Dine (AD)	Liberation Tigers of Tamil Eelam (LTTE)
Army of Islam (AOI)	Libyan Islamic Fighting Group (LIFG)
Asbat al-Ansar (AAA)	Moroccan Islamic Combatant Group (GICM)
Aum Shinrikyo (AUM)	Mujahadin-e Khalq Organization (MEK)
Basque Fatherland and Liberty (ETA)	National Liberation Army (ELN)
Communist Party of Philippines/New People's Army (CPP/NPA)	Palestine Islamic Jihad—Shaqaqi Faction (PIJ)
	Palestine Liberation Front—Abu Abbas Faction (PLF)
Continuity Irish Republican Army (CIRA)	Popular Front for the Liberation of Palestine (PFLP)
Gama'a al-Islamiyya (IG)	Popular Front for the Liberation of Palestine-General Command (PFLP-GC)
Hamas	
Haqqani Network	Al-Qa'ida (AQ)
Harakat ul-Jihad-i-Islami (HUJI)	Al-Qa'ida in the Arabian Peninsula (AQAP)
Harakat ul-Jihad-i-Islami/Bangladesh (HUJI-B)	Al-Qa'ida in Iraq (AQI)
Harakat ul-Mujahideen (HUM)	Al-Qa'ida in the Islamic Maghreb (AQIM)
Hizballah	Real IRA (RIRA)
Indian Mujahideen (IM)	Revolutionary Armed Forces of Colombia (FARC)
Islamic Jihad Union (IJU)	Revolutionary Organization 17 November (17N)
Islamic Movement of Uzbekistan (IMU)	Revolutionary People's Liberation Party/Front (DHKP/C)
Jabhat al-Nusra	Revolutionary Struggle (RS)
Jaish-e-Mohammed (JEM)	Al-Shabaab (AS)
Jemaah Islamiya (JI)	Shining Path (SL)
Jundallah	Tehrik-e Taliban Pakistan (TTP)
Kahane Chai	United Self-Defense Forces of Colombia (AUC)

Source: U.S. Department of State, Office of the Coordinator for Counterterrorism. Current as of May 19, 2013.

aL-QAEDA
Global
ACTIVITIES
Funding, planning, and conducting terrorism
MEMBERS
Unknown
Founded by Osama bin Laden in the 1980s, al-Qaeda first supported the *mujahidin* fighting Soviets in Afghanistan. Today the group wages war on the world, through a global Islamist insurgency.

1. UNITED SELF-DEFENSE FORCES OF COLOMBIA
Colombia
ACTIVITIES
Massacres, narcotics
MEMBERS
12,000 to 15,000
This right-wing coalition of paramilitaries was formed to fight leftist insurgents but often targets civilians.

1. REVOLUTIONARY ARMED FORCES OF COLOMBIA (FARC)
Colombia
ACTIVITIES
Bombing, kidnapping, narcotics
MEMBERS
15,000 to 18,000
These communist insurgents use kidnapping and mass murder in their fight to overthrow the Colombian government and redistribute wealth.

1. NATIONAL LIBERATION ARMY (ELN)
Colombia
ACTIVITIES
Kidnapping, bombing, extortion
MEMBERS
3,000
This leftist group is one of the leading practitioners of kidnapping for ransom. It also attacks government oil pipelines and energy infrastructure.

2. ■ SALAFIST GROUP FOR CALL AND COMBAT
Algeria
ACTIVITIES
Attacks on government and military
MEMBERS
Several hundred
This newly powerful Islamist group aims to topple Algeria's secular government, expel foreign influences, and advance al-Qaeda's agenda in Africa and Europe.

3. ■ MOROCCAN ISLAMIC COMBATANT GROUP
Morocco
ACTIVITIES
Bombing, arms, forgery
MEMBERS
Unknown
This Moroccan Islamist group, reportedly linked to al-Qaeda, is accused of recent mass-casualty bombings in Madrid and Casablanca.

HOT SPOT
COLOMBIA

As communist insurgents battle right-wing militias—and each other—for territory and drug profits, locals are caught in the crossfire. The government is now fighting to regain control of the countryside.

HOT SPOT
ISRAEL & THE OCCUPIED TERRITORIES

Fueled by nationalism and mistrust, the cycle continues: Palestinian insurgents use terrorism against Israeli troops, settlers, and civilians in the occupied territories and Israel—while Israeli forces target militants, often inflicting civilian casualties.

The latest wave of international terrorism has focused the world's attention on a tactic that uses death and destruction as political tools. But terrorism itself, with roots deep in history and geography, is hardly new.

6. ISLAMIC RESISTANCE MOVEMENT (HAMAS)
Israel, West Bank, Gaza Strip
ACTIVITIES
Suicide attacks
MEMBERS
Several thousand
Seeking to destroy Israel and extend Muslim rule across the Middle East, Hamas has mounted dozens of suicide attacks against Israeli civilians.

6. PALESTINE ISLAMIC JIHAD
Israel, West Bank, Gaza Strip
ACTIVITIES
Suicide attacks
MEMBERS
Several dozen
Led by operatives based in Lebanon and Syria, this radical group aims to replace Israel with a Palestinian Islamic state.

6. AL AQSA MARTYRS' BRIGADES
Israel, West Bank, Gaza Strip
ACTIVITIES
Shootings, suicide attacks
MEMBERS
Unknown
This group, linked to Palestinian leader Yasser Arafat's Fatah movement, arose during a Palestinian intifada in 2000.

6. KACH AND KAHANE CHAI
Israel, West Bank
ACTIVITIES
Shootings, assaults
MEMBERS
Several dozen
Outlawed since the massacre of 29 Muslims at Hebron in 1994, these groups seek to expand Israel by driving Palestinians from the West Bank and Gaza Strip.

6. HEZBOLLAH
Lebanon
ACTIVITIES
Bombing, hijacking, suicide attacks
MEMBERS
Several hundred
Formed in 1982 after the Israeli invasion of Lebanon, this Iran-backed group claimed victory when Israel pulled out in 2000. Its goal: destruction of the Jewish state.

6. ■ ASBAT AL ANSAR
Lebanon
ACTIVITIES
Assassination, bombing
MEMBERS
About 300
These al-Qaeda-linked extremists attack both domestic and international targets within Lebanon.

FIGURE 17-6 | International Terrorist Groups and Areas of Operation

Source: Walter Laqueur, "World of Terror" (National Geographic Maps), *National Geographic*, November 2004, pp. 72–74. Reprinted by permission.

WHERE THEY ARE

This map shows a sample of the many groups that use terror to achieve their goals, attracting an array of nationalists, political ideologues, and religious zealots. Some groups are multifaceted, incorporating politics and social programs along with violence; others are purely brutal. Today one type of group—related to a movement called Islamism—has earned an especially high profile for its drive to impose theocracy on Muslim lands and excise "impure" Western influences. According to the CIA, the deadliest of these groups—al-Qaeda—operates in 68 countries worldwide.

4. BASQUE FATHERLAND AND LIBERTY (ETA)
Spain, France
ACTIVITIES
Assassination, bombing, extortion
MEMBERS
Dozens
Founded in 1959, this group has targeted Spanish officials and security forces in its fight for an independent Basque state in northern Spain and southwestern France.

5. REAL IRA
Northern Ireland
ACTIVITIES
Assassination, bombing, robbery
MEMBERS
100 to 200
An offshoot that formed after the Irish Republican Army declared a cease-fire in 1997, the RIRA has killed dozens in its fight for a united Ireland, free from British rule.

HOT SPOT
INDIA & PAKISTAN

Nuclear rivals India and Pakistan duel over the region of Kashmir, a flash point for conflict between Indian troops and Pakistan-based terrorist groups. Attacks against the pro-U.S. government of Pakistan are also on the rise.

5. ULSTER DEFENCE ASSOCIATION
Northern Ireland
ACTIVITIES
Bombing, narcotics, shootings, intimidation
MEMBERS
Several hundred
Largest of the Protestant paramilitary groups that favor retaining British rule. Though bound by a cease-fire, the group often engages in violence against Catholics.

8. KURDISTAN WORKERS' PARTY (PKK)
Turkey
ACTIVITIES
Assassination, bombing
MEMBERS
More than 5,000
Also known as Kongra-Gel, this separatist group operates from northern Iraq and targets Turkish security forces and civilians in its fight for an independent Kurdish state.

9. ■ CHECHEN SEPARATISTS
Russia
ACTIVITIES
Bombing, kidnapping, murder
MEMBERS
Several thousand
Seeking independence from Russia, rebels have killed Moscow-backed Chechen officials, including Chechnya's president, and killed and kidnapped Russian civilians.

9. ■ ISLAMIC MOVEMENT OF UZBEKISTAN
Central Asia
ACTIVITIES
Bombing, kidnapping
MEMBERS
More than 1,000
This homegrown Islamist coalition seeks to replace Uzbekistan's secular regime and advance the regional goals of al-Qaeda.

10. ■ LASHKAR E-JHANGVI
Pakistan
ACTIVITIES
Massacres, bombing
MEMBERS
Fewer than a hundred
A small but brutally effective Sunni group, LEJ has attacked Shiite mosques and foreigners in a bid to destabilize Pakistan. Also linked to the 2002 murder of journalist Daniel Pearl.

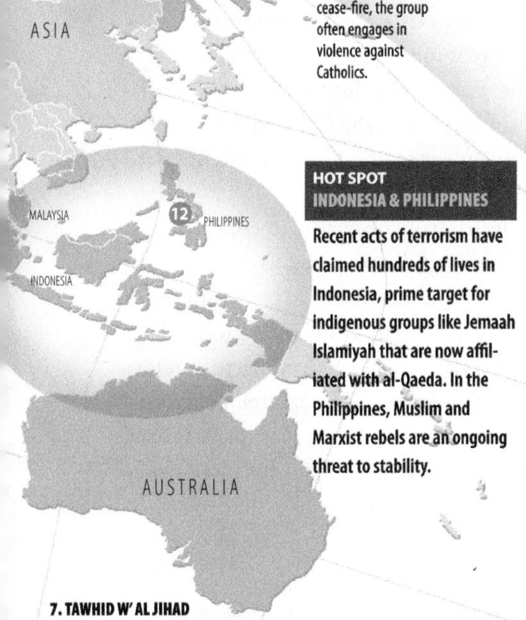

HOT SPOT
INDONESIA & PHILIPPINES

Recent acts of terrorism have claimed hundreds of lives in Indonesia, prime target for indigenous groups like Jemaah Islamiyah that are now affiliated with al-Qaeda. In the Philippines, Muslim and Marxist rebels are an ongoing threat to stability.

10. ■ JAISH-E-MOHAMMED
Pakistan
ACTIVITIES
Massacres, bombing
MEMBERS
Several hundred
This Islamist group is blamed for the bombing of an Indian state legislature in Kashmir that killed 38. Now split into two factions, this group, like others, fights to make predominantly Muslim Kashmir part of Pakistan.

10. LASHKAR E-TAIBA
Pakistan
ACTIVITIES
Massacres, bombing
MEMBERS
Several hundred
With training camps in Afghanistan, LET specializes in daredevil missions with devastating results, directed mainly against Indian troops and civilians in Kashmir.

11. LIBERATION TIGERS OF TAMIL EELAM
Sri Lanka
ACTIVITIES
Assassination, bombing
MEMBERS
10,000 to 15,000
Favoring suicide attacks, members seek an independent Tamil state in Sri Lanka. A precarious cease-fire is now in place.

12. ■ JEMAAH ISLAMIYAH
Southeast Asia
ACTIVITIES
Bombing
MEMBERS
Unknown
Responsible for a series of deadly bombings across Southeast Asia—including the Bali nightclub attacks in 2002—al-Qaeda's local partner seeks an Islamic superstate spanning the region.

7. TAWHID W' AL JIHAD
Iraq
ACTIVITIES
Kidnapping, bombing
MEMBERS
Unknown
Jordanian Abu Musab al Zarqawi leads this loose network of jihadists, most of whom are Iraqi. Their common goal: to expel U.S. forces and create a Sunni Islamic state in Iraq. Many of its fighters are veterans of an older group, Ansar al Islam.

12. ABU SAYYAF
Philippines
ACTIVITIES
Kidnapping, bombing, piracy
MEMBERS
300 to 500
High-profile kidnappings of foreigners for ransom keep this group well financed—though the profit motive may be clouding Abu Sayyaf's founding vision of an Islamic state in the southern Philippines.

12. ■ MORO ISLAMIC LIBERATION FRONT
Philippines
ACTIVITIES
Bombing
MEMBERS
Around 12,000
Though it officially disavows terrorism, this insurgent group is linked to attacks on Philippine cities through its support for Jemaah Islamiyah. Now in peace talks with the government, the MILF aims for ethnic autonomy.

LEGEND

- **Countries where al-Qaeda cells are known to be operating**
- **Countries where al-Qaeda cells may be operating**
- **■ Group affiliated with al-Qaeda**

of State. The most recent organization to be added to the list is the Mali-based Ansar Dine, which was placed on the list in early 2013.[126] For more detailed descriptions of these organizations, see the latest State Department *Country Reports on Terrorism*, which can be accessed at **http://www.state.gov/j/ct/rls/crt/2011.**

Under federal law, FTO designations are subject to judicial review. In the event of a challenge to a group's FTO designation in federal court, the U.S. government relies on the administrative record to defend the designation decision. These administrative records contain intelligence information and are therefore classified. FTO designations expire in two years unless renewed.

Once an organization has been designated as an FTO, specific legal consequences follow. First, it becomes unlawful for a person in the United States or subject to the jurisdiction of the United States to provide funds or other material support to a designated FTO. Second, representatives and certain members of a designated FTO, if they are aliens, can be denied visas or kept from entering the United States. Finally, U.S. financial institutions must block funds of designated FTOs and their agents and must report the blockage to the Office of Foreign Assets Control within the U.S. Department of the Treasury.

The State Department also has the authority to designate selected foreign governments as state sponsors of international terrorism. In mid-2007, Cuba, Iran, North Korea, Sudan, and Syria were designated as state sponsors of international terrorism. The situation in Syria has changed since the Arab spring that began in 2010; however, Iran remains the most active state sponsor of terrorism, according to the State Department.[127] The State Department says that the Iranian government provides continuing support to numerous terrorist groups, including the Lebanese Hizballah, Hamas, and the Palestinian Islamic Jihad, all of which seek to undermine the Middle East peace process through the use of terrorism.

Cuba, however, continues to provide safe haven to several terrorists and U.S. fugitives and maintains ties to other state sponsors of terrorism and to Latin American insurgents. North Korea harbored several hijackers of a Japanese Airlines flight to North Korea in the 1970s and maintains links to terrorist groups. It also continues to sell ballistic missile technology to countries designated by the United States as state sponsors of terrorism.

Finally, Sudan continues to provide a safe haven for members of various terrorist groups, including the Lebanese Hizballah, Gama'a al-Islamiyya, Egyptian Islamic Jihad, the Palestinian Islamic Jihad, and Hamas, although it has been engaged in a counterterrorism dialogue with the United States since mid-2000.

The Future of International Terrorism

Terrorist groups are active throughout the world (Figure 17-6), and the United States is not their only target. Terrorist groups operate in South America, Africa, the Middle East, Latin America, the Philippines, Japan, India, England, Nepal, and some of the now independent states of the former Soviet Union. The Central Intelligence Agency reports that by "2015 terrorist tactics will become increasingly sophisticated and designed to achieve mass casualties."[128] The CIA also notes that nations "with poor governance; ethnic, cultural, or religious tensions; weak economies; and porous borders will be prime breeding grounds for terrorism."[129] In the area of Islamic terrorism, the CIA expects that "by 2020 Al-Qaeda will have been superseded by similarly inspired but more diffuse Islamic extremist groups."[130]

The current situation leads many observers to conclude that the American justice system is not fully prepared to deal with the threat represented by domestic and international terrorism. Prior intelligence-gathering efforts that focused on such groups have largely failed or were not quickly acted on, leading to military intervention in places like Afghanistan and Iraq. Intelligence failures are at least partially understandable, given that many terrorist organizations are tight-knit and very difficult for intelligence operatives to penetrate.

SUMMARY

- Islamic law descends directly from the teachings of the Prophet Muhammad and looks to the Koran to determine which acts should be classified as crimes. Today's Islamic law is a system of duties and rituals founded on legal and moral obligations—all of which are ultimately sanctioned by the authority of religious leaders who may issue commands known as *fatwas*. Islamic law recognizes seven *Hudud* crimes—or crimes based on religious strictures. In Middle Eastern countries today, punishments for *Hudud* offenses are often physical and may include lashing, flogging, or even stoning. All other crimes fall into an offense category called *tazirat*. *Tazir* crimes are regarded as any actions not considered acceptable in a spiritual society. They include crimes against society and against individuals, but not those against God.
- The United Nations is the largest and most inclusive international body in the world. Since its inception in 1945, it has concerned itself with international crime prevention and world criminal justice systems, as illustrated by a number of important resolutions and documents, including the International Bill of Human Rights, which supports the rights and dignity of everyone who comes into contact with a criminal justice system; the Standard Minimum Rules for the Treatment of Prisoners; and the UN Code of Conduct for Law Enforcement Officials, which calls on law enforcement officers

throughout the world to be cognizant of human rights in the performance of their duties. The World Crime Surveys, which report official crime statistics from nearly 100 countries, provide a periodic global portrait of criminal activity. Other significant international criminal justice organizations are the International Criminal Police Organization (Interpol), which acts as a clearinghouse for information on offenses and suspects who are believed to operate across national boundaries, and the European Police Office (Europol), which aims to improve the effectiveness and cooperation of law enforcement agencies within the member states of the European Union. Finally, the International Criminal Court (ICC) was created in 2000 under the auspices of the United Nations. The ICC is intended to be a permanent criminal court for trying individuals who commit the most serious crimes of concern to the international community, such as genocide, war crimes, and crimes against humanity—including the wholesale murder of civilians, torture, and mass rape.

- Globalization—the internationalization of trade, services, investment, information, and other forms of human social activity—has been occurring for a long time but has recently increased in pace due largely to advances in technology, such as new modes of transportation and communication. Transnational crime, which may be one of the most significant challenges of the twenty-first century, is a negative consequence of globalization. Transnational crime is unlawful activity undertaken and supported by organized criminal groups operating across national boundaries. Criminal opportunities for transnational groups have come about in part by globalization of the world's economy and by advances in communications, transportation, and other technologies. Today's organized international criminal cartels recognize no boundaries and engage in activities like drug trafficking, money laundering, human trafficking, counterfeiting of branded goods, and weapons smuggling.
- In 2000, the U.S. Congress passed the Trafficking Victims Protection Act (TVPA). Trafficking offenses under the law include (1) sex trafficking and (2) other forms of trafficking, defined as the recruitment, harboring, transportation, provision, or obtaining of a person for labor services, through the use of force, fraud, or coercion, for the purpose of subjection to involuntary servitude, peonage, debt bondage, or slavery. There are important legal differences between human trafficking and human smuggling. Under federal law human smuggling refers to illegal immigration in which an agent is paid to help a person cross a border clandestinely. Human smuggling generally occurs with the consent of those being smuggled, and they often pay a smuggler for his or her services.
- This chapter defines *terrorism* as a violent act or an act dangerous to human life, in violation of the criminal laws of the United States or of any state, that is committed to intimidate or coerce a government, the civilian population, or any segment thereof, in furtherance of political or social objectives. Terrorism, which today is the focus of significant criminal justice activity, brings with it the threat of massive destruction and large numbers of casualties. Domestic and international terrorism are the two main forms of terrorism with which law enforcement organizations concern themselves today. Specific forms of terrorist activity, such as cyberterrorism and attacks on information-management segments of our nation's critical infrastructure, could theoretically shut down or disable important infrastructure services such as electricity, food processing, military activity, and even state and federal governments. The vigilance required to prevent terrorism, both domestic and international, consumes a significant amount of law enforcement resources and has resulted in new laws that restrict a number of freedoms that many Americans have previously taken for granted.

KEY TERMS

comparative criminologist, 559
cyberterrorism, 577
domestic terrorism, 575
ethnocentric, 560
European Police Office (Europol), 568
extradition, 571
foreign terrorist organization (FTO), 585
globalization, 569
***Hudud* crime, 563**
human smuggling, 572
infrastructure, 578
International Criminal Police Organization (Interpol), 567
international terrorism, 577
Islamic law, 563
narcoterrorism, 579
sex trafficking, 571
***Tazir* crime, 564**
terrorism, 573
trafficking in persons (TIP), 572
transnational crime, 570

QUESTIONS FOR REVIEW

1. What are the principles that inform Islamic law? How do these principles contribute to the structure and activities of the criminal justice systems of Muslim nations that follow Islamic law?
2. What important international criminal justice organizations does this chapter discuss? Describe the role of each in fighting international crime.
3. What is globalization, and how does it relate to transnational crime? What relationships might exist between transnational crime and terrorism?
4. What is human smuggling? Human trafficking? How do the two differ under the law?
5. What is terrorism? What are the two major types of terrorism discussed in this chapter?

QUESTIONS FOR REFLECTION

1. Why is terrorism a law enforcement concern? How is terrorism a crime? What can the American criminal justice system do to better prepare for future terrorist crimes?

2. What are the causes of terrorism? What efforts is the U.S. government making to prevent and control the spread of domestic terrorism and international terrorism?
3. What are the benefits of studying criminal justice systems in other countries? What problems are inherent in such study?

NOTES

i. Federal Bureau of Investigation, Counterterrorism Section, *Terrorism in the United States, 1987* (Washington, DC: FBI, 1987).
ii. Adapted from Federal Bureau of Investigation, "FBI Policy and Guidelines: Counterterrorism," http://www.fbi.gov/contact/fo/jackson/cntrterr.htm (accessed March 4, 2011).
iii. Ibid.
iv. Adapted from Dictionary.com, http://dictionary.reference.com/search?q5infrastructure (accessed January 10, 2011).

1. Office for Victims of Crime, *Report to the Nation, 2003* (Washington, DC: OVC, 2003), p. 83.
2. Mosi Secret, "Bangladeshi Admits Trying to Blow Up Federal Bank," *New York Times*, February 7, 2013.
3. Farid Hossain, "Quazi Mohammad Rezwanul Ahsan Nafis: Federal Reserve Terror Plot Shocks Family," *Huffington Post*, October 18, 2012, http://www.huffingtonpost.com/2012/10/18/quazi-mohammad-rezwanul-ashan-nafis-federal-reserve-terror-shocks-family_n_1978596.html (accessed June 12, 2013).
4. Judicial Watch, "MSM Ignores Fla. Imam Terrorism Conviction," March 5, 2013, http://www.judicialwatch.org/blog/2013/03/msm-ignores-fla-imam-terrorism-conviction (accessed July 4, 2013).
5. Tom Hays, "Betim Kaziu Gets 27 Years in Homegrown Terror Case," MEXH 2, 2012, http://www.huffingtonpost.com/2012/03/03/betim-kaziu-gets-27-years_n_1318288.html (accessed July 4, 2013).
6. Jill Lawless, "3 British Men Convicted in Terrorist Bomb Plot," *USA Today*, February 21, 2013, http://www.usatoday.com/story/news/world/2013/02/21/terrorism-bomb-britain-uk/1935177 (accessed July 4, 2013).
7. Robert Lilly, "Forks and Chopsticks: Understanding Criminal Justice in the PRC," *Criminal Justice International* (March/April 1986), p. 15.
8. Adapted from Carol B. Kalish, *International Crime Rates, Bureau of Justice Statistics Special Report* (Washington, DC: BJS, 1988).
9. "Which Country Has the Fewest Cars," Big Site of Amazing Facts, http://www.bigsiteofamazingfacts.com/which-country-has-the-fewest-cars (accessed July 2, 2013).
10. Kalish, *International Crime Rates*.
11. Ibid.
12. For information about the latest survey, see *The Twelfth United Nations Survey on Crime Trends and the Operations of Criminal Justice* (New York: United Nations, 2012), http://www.unodc.org/unodc/en/data-and-analysis/crimedata.html (accessed December 9, 2011).
13. As quoted in Lee Hockstader, "Russia's War on Crime: A Lopsided, Losing Battle," Washington Post wire service, February 27, 1995.
14. Roy Walmsley, *Developments in the Prison Systems of Central and Eastern Europe*, HEUNI papers No. 4 (Helsinki, 1995).
15. J. Schact, "Law and Justice," *The Cambridge Encyclopedia of Islam*, Vol. 2, p. 539, from which most of the information in this paragraph comes. Available at http://www.fordham.edu/halsall/med/schacht.html (accessed July 1, 2011).
16. Sam S. Souryal, Dennis W. Potts, and Abdullah I. Alobied, "The Penalty of Hand Amputation for Theft in Islamic Justice," *Journal of Criminal Justice*, Vol. 22, No. 3 (1994), pp. 249–265.
17. Parviz Saney, "Iran," in Elmer H. Johnson, ed., *International Handbook of Contemporary Developments in Criminology* (Westport, CT: Greenwood Press, 1983), p. 359.
18. Amy Sullivan, "Sharia Myth Sweeps America," *USA Today*, June 13, 2011, p. 11A.
19. This section owes much to Matthew Lippman, "Iran: A Question of Justice?" *Criminal Justice International*, 1987, pp. 6–7.
20. Sarah El Deeb, "Terry Jones, Florida Pastor, Sentenced to Death in Egypt over Anti-Islam Film along with 7 Coptic Christians," *Huffington Post*, November 28, 2012 (accessed July 4, 2013).
21. Souryal, Potts, and Alobied, "The Penalty of Hand Amputation."
22. Afshin Valinejad, "Iran Flogs, Hangs Serial Killer Known as 'The Vampire,'" *USA Today*, August 14, 1997, p. 11A.
23. For additional information on Islamic law, see Adel Mohammed el Fikey, "Crimes and Penalties in Islamic Criminal Legislation," *Criminal Justice International*, 1986, pp. 13–14; and Sam S. Souryal, "Shariah Law in Saudi Arabia," *Journal for the Scientific Study of Religion*, Vol. 26, No. 4 (1987), pp. 429–449.
24. Max Weber, in Max Rheinstein, ed., *On Law in Economy and Society* (New York: Simon and Schuster, 1967), translated from the 1925 German edition.
25. Ibid.
26. Souryal, Potts, and Alobied, "The Penalty of Hand Amputation."
27. Paul Friday, "International Organization: An Introduction," in Elmer H. Johnson, ed., *International Handbook of Contemporary Developments in Criminology* (Westport, CT: Greenwood Press, 1983), p. 31.
28. Ibid., p. 32.
29. Gerhard O. W. Mueller, "The United Nations and Criminology," in Elmer H. Johnson, ed., *International Handbook of Contemporary Developments in Criminology* (Westport, CT: Greenwood Press, 1983), pp. 74–75.
30. Roger S. Clark, *The United Nations Crime Prevention and Criminal Justice Program: Formulation of Standards and Efforts at Their Implementation* (Philadelphia: University of Pennsylvania Press, 1994).
31. Ibid., pp. 71–72.
32. "International News," *Corrections Compendium*, June 1995, p. 25.
33. Khaled Dawoud, "U.N. Crime Meeting Wants Independent Jail Checks," Reuters, May 6, 1995.
34. "Protocol to Prevent, Suppress and Punish Trafficking in Persons, Especially Women and Children, Supplementing the United Nations Convention against Transnational Organized Crime," Report of the Ad Hoc Committee on the Elaboration of a Convention against Transnational Organized Crime on the Work of Its First to Eleventh Sessions, U.N. GAOR, 55th Sess., Agenda Item 105, U.N. Document Number A/55/383 (2000), Annex II.
35. For additional information, see Mohamed Y. Mattar, "Trafficking in Persons, Especially Women and Children, in Countries of the Middle East: The Scope of the Problem and the Appropriate Legislative Response," *Fordham International Law Journal*, Vol. 26 (March 2003), p. 721, http://209.190.246.239/article.pdf (accessed August 2, 2006).
36. See "Interpol: Extending Law Enforcement's Reach around the World," *FBI Law Enforcement Bulletin* (December 1998), pp. 10–16.
37. Interpol, "Member Countries," http://www.interpol.int/Member-countries/World (accessed April 21, 2013).
38. "Interpol at Forty," *Criminal Justice International*, November/December 1986, pp. 1, 22.

39. Interpol, "81st INTERPOL General Assembly," http://www.interpol.int/News-and-media/Events/2012/81st-INTERPOL-General-Assembly2/81st-INTERPOL-General-Assembly (accessed July 4, 2013).
40. Interpol General Secretariat, *Interpol at Work: 2003 Activity Report* (Lyons, France, 2004).
41. Marc Champion, Jeanne Whalen, and Jay Solomon, "Terror in London: Police Make One Arrest after Raids in North England," *Wall Street Journal*, July 12, 2005, http://online.wsj.com/article/0,SB112116092902883194,00.html?mod5djemTAR (accessed August 15, 2007).
42. Ibid.
43. ICPO-Interpol General Assembly Resolution No. AG-2001-RES-07.
44. See the Coalition for an International Criminal Court, "Building the Court," http://www.iccnow.org/buildingthecourt.html (accessed July 30, 2011).
45. Much of the information and some of the wording in this section are adapted from "The ICC International Criminal Court Home Page," http://www.icc-cpi.int/Menus/ICC (accessed July 4, 2011); and the ICC "Timeline," http://www.iccnow.org/html/timeline.htm (accessed April 12, 2009).
46. Convention on the Prevention and Punishment of the Crime of Genocide, adopted by Resolution 260 (III) A of the U.N. General Assembly on December 9, 1948, http://www.prevent-genocide.org/law/convention/text.htm (accessed July 4, 2011).
47. Plenipotentiary is another word for "diplomat."
48. Rome Statute of the International Criminal Court, United Nations Diplomatic Conference of Plenipotentiaries on the Establishment of an International Criminal Court, Rome, Italy, June 15–July 16, 1998 U.N. Document Number A/CONF.183/9 (1998), art. 7, http://www.un.org/law/icc/statutw/romefra.htm (accessed July 4, 2009).
49. Roy Gutman, "Is International Criminal Court the Best Way to Stop War Crimes?" *McClatchy Newspapers*, April 27, 2012, http://www.kentucky.com/2012/04/26/2164351/is-international-criminal-court.html (accessed August 12, 2012).
50. Much of the information in this paragraph and the next comes from David J. Lynch, "Belgium Plays Global Prosecutor," *USA Today*, July 16, 2001; and Katie Nguyen, "Cubans Use Belgian Law to File Case against Castro," Reuters, October 4, 2001.
51. Adapted from "Globalization," *Encyclopedia Britannica*, http://www.britannica.com/eb/article?eu5369857 (accessed July 28, 2011).
52. Federal Bureau of Investigation, "The Case of the Snakehead Queen: Chinese Human Smuggler Gets 35 Years," March 17, 2006, http://www.fbi.gov/page2/march06/sisterping031706.htm (accessed May 11, 2009).
53. Laurie Robinson, address given at the Twelfth International Congress on Criminology, Seoul, Korea, August 28, 1998.
54. National Institute of Justice, *Asian Transnational Organized Crime and Its Impact on the United States* (Washington, DC: NIJ, 2007), p. 1.
55. Robert S. Gelbard, "Foreign Policy after the Cold War: The New Threat—Transnational Crime," address at St. Mary's University, San Antonio, TX, April 2, 1996.
56. NIJ, *Asian Transnational Organized Crime*, p. 1.
57. Barbara Starr, "A Gangster's Paradise," ABC News Online, September 14, 1998, http://more.abcnews.go.com/sections/world/dailynews/russiacrime980914.html (accessed January 24, 2004).
58. As quoted in Starr, "A Gangster's Paradise."
59. Raymond Bonner and Timothy L. O'Brien, "Activity at Bank Raises Suspicions of Russia Mob Tie," *New York Times*, August 19, 1999.
60. Kevin F. Ryan, "Globalizing the Problem: The United States and International Drug Control," in Eric L. Jensen and Jurg Gerber, eds., *The New War on Drugs: Symbolic Politics and Criminal Justice Policy* (Cincinnati, OH: Anderson, 1997).
61. Trafficking Victims Protection Act of 2000, Div. A of Public Law 106-386, Section 108, as amended.
62. Sex trafficking is defined separately under U.S. Code, Title 22, Section 7102 (8); (9); (14) as "the recruitment, harboring, transportation, provision, or obtaining of a person for the purpose of a commercial sex act."
63. Public Law 108-193.
64. President Obama signed into law the Trafficking Victims Protection Reauthorization Act (TVPRA) of 2005 on January 10, 2006, and the Trafficking Victims Protection Reauthorization Act of 2013 was part of the Violence Against Women Reauthorization Act of 2013.
65. Bureau for International Narcotics and Law Enforcement Affairs, Human Smuggling and Trafficking Center, *Distinctions between Human Smuggling and Human Trafficking* (Washington, DC: January 1, 2005).
66. Raimo Väyrynen, "Illegal Immigration, Human Trafficking, and Organized Crime," United Nations University/World Institute for Development Economics Research, Discussion Paper No. 2003/72 (October 2003), p. 16.
67. Details for this story come from "Immigrant Smuggler Faulted in 19 Deaths Sentenced to Life in Prison," Associated Press, January 18, 2007, http://www.usatoday.com/news/nation/2007-01-18-smuggler_x.htm (accessed September 9, 2009).
68. Office of the Under Secretary for Democracy and Global Affairs, *Trafficking in Persons Report* (Washington, DC: U.S. Dept. of State, June 2007).
69. Ibid., p. 8.
70. Ibid.
71. Ibid.
72. Amy Farrell, Jack McDevitt, Rebecca Pfeffer, Stephanie Fahy, Colleen Owens, Meredith Dank, and William Adams, *Identifying Challenges to Improve the Investigation and Prosecution of State and Local Human Trafficking Cases: Executive Summary* (Washington, DC: National Institute of Justice, 2012), p. 3.
73. Bureau for International Narcotics and Law Enforcement Affairs, *Human Smuggling and Trafficking Center, Distinctions between Human Smuggling and Human Trafficking*, p. 16.
74. Office of the Under Secretary for Democracy and Global Affairs, *Trafficking in Persons Report*, p. 5.
75. Ibid.
76. Foreign Relations Authorization Act, U.S. Code, Title 22, Section 2656 f(d)(2).
77. In the words of the act: "The term 'terrorism' means premeditated, politically motivated violence perpetrated against noncombatant targets by subnational groups or clandestine agents" U.S. Code, Title 22, Section 2656 f(d)(2).
78. Federal Bureau of Investigation, Counterterrorism Section, *Terrorism in the United States, 1987* (Washington, DC: FBI, 1987), in which the full definition offered here can be found. See also "FBI Policy and Guidelines: Counterterrorism," http://www.fbi.gov/contact/fo/jackson/cntrterr.htm (accessed January 15, 2008), which offers a somewhat less formal definition of the term.
79. Gwynn Nettler, *Killing One Another* (Cincinnati, OH: Anderson, 1982).
80. Ibid., p. 253.

81. Adapted from "FBI Policy and Guidelines."
82. Ibid.
83. The death penalty was imposed for the first-degree murders of eight federal law enforcement agents who were at work in the Murrah Building at the time of the bombing. Although all of the killings violated Oklahoma law, only the killings of the federal agents fell under federal law, which makes such murders capital offenses.
84. "Terry Nichols Receives Life Sentences for Each of 161 Victims in 1995 Oklahoma City Bombing," Associated Press, August 9, 2004.
85. "Rudolph Agrees to Plea Agreement," CNN Law Center, April 12, 2005, http://www.cnn.com/2005/LAW/04/08/rudolph.plea (accessed May 21, 2007).
86. Bruce Frankel, "Sheik Guilty in Terror Plot," *USA Today*, October 2, 1995, p. 1A. Sheik Abdel-Rahman and codefendant El Sayyid Nosair were both sentenced to life in prison. Other defendants received sentences of between 25 and 57 years in prison. See Sascha Brodsky, "Terror Verdicts Denounced," United Press International, January 17, 1996.
87. Maryclaire Dale, "'Jihad Jane' Admits to Conspiracy to Support Terrorists, Murder," *The Christian Science Monitor*, February 1, 2011, http://www.csmonitor.com/USA/Latest-News-Wires/2011/0201/Jihad-Jane-admits-to-conspiracy-to-support-terrorists-murder (accessed June 9, 2011).
88. "Qaeda Suspect Dead, Suicide Eyed," CBSNews.com, July 3, 2003, http://www.cbsnews.com/stories/2003/06/26/world/main560618.shtml (accessed July 10, 2003).
89. Philip Stephens, "All Nostalgia Is Futile at the Beginning of History," *Financial Times*, May 27, 2005, p. 13.
90. Brian Michael Jenkins, *New Challenges to U.S. Counterrorism Efforts: An Assessment of the Current Terrorist Threat*, testimony before the Committee on Homeland security and Governmental Affairs of the United States Senate, July 11, 2012 (Santa Monica, CA: Rand Corporation, 2012), http://www.rand.org/pubs/testimonies/CT377.html (accessed May 1, 2013).
91. See Barry Collin, "The Future of Cyberterrorism," *Crime and Justice International,* March 1997, pp. 15–18.
92. John Arquilla and David Ronfeldt, *The Advent of Netwar* (Santa Monica, CA: RAND Corporation, 1996).
93. Mark M. Pollitt, "Cyberterrorism: Fact or Fancy?" *Proceedings of the Twentieth National Information Systems Security Conference,* October 1997, pp. 285–289.
94. The White House Office of the Press Secretary, "Executive Order on Critical Infrastructure Protection," October 16, 2001, http://www.whitehouse.gov/news/releases/2001/10/20011016-12.html (accessed May 21, 2007).
95. President's Critical Infrastructure Protection Board, *The National Strategy to Secure Cyberspace* (Washington, DC: U.S. Government Printing Office, September 18, 2002).
96. Department of Homeland Security, "Ridge Creates New Division to Combat Cyber Threats," press release, June 6, 2003, http://www.dhs.gov/dhspublic/display?content5916 (accessed May 28, 2007).
97. Lolita C. Baldor and John Andrew Prime, "Obama Announces Cyber Security Office," Associated Press, http://www.shreveporttimes.com/article/20090530/NEWS01/905300321/1060/NEWS01 (accessed July 3, 2009).
98. Daniel Boyce, "Narco-terrorism," *FBI Law Enforcement Bulletin* (October 1987), p. 24; and James A. Inciardi, "Narcoterrorism: A Perspective and Commentary," in Robert O. Slater and Grant Wardlaw, eds., *International Narcotics* (London: Macmillan/St. Martins, 1989).
99. Details for this story come from "Alleged Afghan Drug Kingpin Arrested," *USA Today*, April 26, 2005.
100. The term narcoterrorism was reportedly invented by former Peruvian President Fernando Belaunde Terry; see James A. Inciardi, "Narcoterrorism," paper presented at the 1988 annual meeting of the Academy of Criminal Justice Sciences, San Francisco, CA, p. 8.
101. Boyce, "Narco-terrorism," p. 24.
102. Ibid., p. 25.
103. U.S. Department of State, *Terrorist Group Profiles* (Washington, DC: U.S. Government Printing Office, 1989).
104. Inciardi, "Narcoterrorism."
105. "U.S. Government Lacks Strategy to Neutralize International Crime," *Criminal Justice International*, Vol. 10, No. 5 (September/October 1994), p. 5.
106. *National Strategy for Combating Terrorism* (Washington, DC: White House, 2003).
107. Emilio C. Viano, Jose Magallanes, and Laurent Bridel, "Transnational Organized Crime: Myth, Power, and Profit," *Crime and Justice International*, May/June 2005, p. 23.
108. *National Strategy for Combating Terrorism,* p. 6.
109. *National Strategy for Counterterrorism* (Washington, DC: White House, 2011).
110. The actual language of the act sets a standard for metal detectors through the use of a "security exemplar" made of 3.7 ounces of stainless steel in the shape of a handgun. Weapons made of other substances might still pass the test provided that they could be detected by metal detectors adjusted to that level of sensitivity. See "Bill Is Signed Barring Sale or Manufacture of Plastic Guns," *Criminal Justice Newsletter*, Vol. 19, No. 23 (December 1, 1988), pp. 4–5.
111. National Commission on Terrorism, *Countering the Changing Threat of International Terrorism* (Washington, DC: U.S. Dept. of State, 2000).
112. Mimi Hall, "Report: USA Left Open to Attack," *USA Today*, December 6, 2005, p. 1A.
113. Peter Bergen and Bruce Hoffman, *Assessing the Terrorist Threat* (Washington, DC: National Security Preparedness Group, 2010).
114. Brian Michael Jenkins, *New Challenges to U.S. Counterterrorism Efforts.*
115. U.S. Department of Homeland Security, "DHS Organization: Building a Secure Homeland," http://www.dhs.gov/dhspublic/theme_home1.jsp (accessed August 28, 2007).
116. U.S. Department of Homeland Security, *Fiscal Year 2013, Budget in Brief* (Washington, DC: DHS, 2013), http://www.dhs.gov/xlibrary/assets/mgmt/dhs-budget-in-brief-fy2013.pdf (accessed May 15, 2013).
117. Ibid.
118. Doris Meissner, Donald M. Kerwin, Muzaffar Chishti, and Claire Bergeron, *Immigration Enforcement in the United States: The Rise of a Formidable Machinery* (Washington, DC: Migration Policy Institute, 2013).
119. Ibid, p. 3.
120. *National Strategy for Counterterrorism.*
121. The NCTC was established by executive order in 2004, although Congress codified the NCTC in the Intelligence Reform and Terrorism Prevention Act of 2004 and placed the NCTC within the Office of the Director of National Intelligence.
122. National Counterterrorism Center, *NCTC and Information Sharing* (Washington, DC: NCTC, 2006), p. i, from which some of the wording in this paragraph is taken.
123. U.S. Code, Title 8, Section 1-1599.

124. Public Law 108-408.
125. U.S. Code, Title 8, Section 219.
126. Declan Walsh and Eric Schmitt, "U.S. Blacklists Militant Haqqani Network," *New York Times*, September 7, 2012, http://www.nytimes.com/2012/09/08/world/asia/state-department-blacklists-militant-haqqani-network.html (accessed May 25, 2013).
127. Information in this paragraph comes from U.S. Department of State, "Patterns of Global Terrorism, 2002," http://www.state.gov/s/ct/rls/pgtrpt/2002/ (accessed August 2, 2007); and U.S. Department of State, "State Sponsors of Terrorism," http://www.state.gov/s/ct/c14151.htm (accessed July 2, 2008).
128. Central Intelligence Agency, *National Foreign Intelligence Council, Global Trends, 2015: A Dialogue about the Future with Nongovernment Experts* (Washington, DC: U.S. Government Printing Office, 2000).
129. Ibid.
130. Central Intelligence Agency, *National Foreign Intelligence Council, Mapping the Global Future: Report of the National Intelligence Council's 2020 Project* (Washington, DC: U.S. Government Printing Office, 2005).

COLUMBIA PICTURES/Album/Newscom.

18 THE FUTURE OF CRIMINAL JUSTICE

OUTLINE

- Introduction
- Technology and Crime
- Technology and Crime Control
- Criminalistics: Past, Present, and Future

LEARNING OBJECTIVES

After reading this chapter, you should be able to

- Describe the historical relationship between technological advances and criminal activity.
- Describe the current and likely future roles of technology in both crime and in the fight against crime.
- Describe the field of criminalistics, including the contribution of evolving technology.

The rise of a new kind of America requires a new kind of law enforcement system.

ALVIN TOFFLER

Introduction

In 2013, a cyberterrorist organization calling itself Izz ad-Din al-Qassam Cyber Fighters released an anonymous statement on the Internet saying that it was attacking U.S. banks to protest anti-Islmaic films that had been posted online. Although the attacks were very effective and resulted in hundreds of hours of downtime on financial servers throughout the United States, bank officials downplayed the seriousness of the incidents in order not to alarm their customers. In one report by CNBC, however, newscasters noted that "even with advance notice, the biggest financial institutions in the world can't seem to stop them."[1] Rodney Joffe, a senior technologist at Neustar, an Internet infrastructure security company, analyzed the attacks and concluded: "The bad guys here are using just enough of their firepower to achieve their objectives and not more. They are creating a disruption to the banking industry. . . . We already know if they wanted to make it [a] bigger attack, they could."[2]

Just as police departments are making use of new technologies, so too are modern-day criminals who use the Internet and other communications technologies because they provide novel criminal opportunities. Recently, for example, Phoenix police investigators discovered a DVD inside a suspect's car containing personal information about a number of undercover officers taken from Facebook and other websites. Phoenix authorities were forced to issue a "security alert," telling officers that they were being "targeted" on Facebook, and warning them that posting photographs and other personal information on social media sites "may create serious officer safety consequences."[3] Similarly, one gang expert recently discovered that gang members were using cameras in their cell phones to provide real-time "surveillance" of police activities.

Because technology is one of the most important instruments of change in the modern world, this chapter focuses on the opportunities and threats that contemporary technology presents to the justice system.

Technology and Crime

Rapid advances in the biological sciences and electronic technologies during the past few decades, including genetic mapping, nanotechnology, computer networking, the Internet,

Boston Private Bank & Trust company in Boston, Massachusetts. In 2013, a cyberterrorist organization effectively attacked computers at many U.S. banks to protest American anti-Islmaic films that had been posted online. How does the attack illustrate the changing nature of criminal activity?

■ **technocrime** A criminal offense that employs advanced or emerging technology in its commission.

■ **Follow the author's tweets about the latest crime and justice news @schmalleger.**

■ **biocrime** A criminal offense perpetrated through the use of biologically active substances, including chemicals and toxins, disease-causing organisms, altered genetic material, and organic tissues and organs. Biocrimes unlawfully affect the metabolic, biochemical, genetic, physiological, or anatomical status of living organisms.

Rapid advances in the biological sciences and electronic technologies during the past few decades have ushered in a wealth of new criminal opportunities.

wireless services of all kinds, artificial intelligence (AI), and global positioning system (GPS) devices, have ushered in a wealth of new criminal opportunities. Crimes that employ advanced or emerging technologies in their commission are referred to as **technocrimes**.

New York State Police Captain and law enforcement visionary Thomas Cowper says that "it is important for police officers and their agencies to understand emerging technologies" for three reasons:[4] (1) to anticipate their use by terrorists and criminals and thereby thwart their use against our nation and citizens, (2) to incorporate their use into police operations when necessary, and (3) to deal effectively with the social changes and cultural impact that inevitably result from technological advances. According to Cowper, "Continued police apathy and ignorance of nanotech, biotech and AI, and the potential changes they will bring to our communities and way of life, will only add to the turmoil, making law enforcement a part of the problem and not part of the solution."[5]

Biocrime

In 2005, the World Health Organization raised alarms when it said that some samples of a potentially dangerous influenza virus that had been sent to thousands of laboratories in 18 countries had been lost and could not be located. Bio-kits containing the influenza A (H2N2) virus, which caused the flu pandemic of 1957–1958, were sent to 4,614 laboratories for use in testing the labs' ability to identify flu viruses. Meridian Bioscience Inc. of Cleveland, Ohio, sent the kits on behalf of the College of American Pathologists and three other U.S. organizations that set testing standards for laboratories. Although most of the laboratories were in the United States, some were in Latin America, and a few were in the Arab world—raising fears that Islamic terrorists might use the viral material, against which most people living today have no immunity, to create a pandemic. The H2N2 scare ended on May 2, 2005, when the U.S. Centers for Disease Control and Prevention (CDC) issued a press release saying that the last remaining sample of the virus outside the United States had been found and destroyed at the American University of Beirut in Lebanon.[6] The Lebanese sample had been misplaced by a local delivery service but was discovered in a warehouse at the Beirut airport. Although the incident came to a successful conclusion, it heightened concerns about the spread of highly pathogenic avian influenza viruses and the possible appropriation by criminals of reverse-genetics research on the 1918 pandemic flu virus that killed millions worldwide.

Biological crime, or **biocrime**, is a criminal offense perpetrated through the use of biologically active substances, including chemicals and toxins, disease-causing organisms, altered genetic material, and organic tissues and organs. Biocrimes unlawfully affect the metabolic, biochemical, genetic, physiological, or anatomical status of living organisms. A major change in such status can, of course, produce death.

Biocrimes can be committed with simple poisons, but the biocrimes of special concern today involve technologically sophisticated delivery and dispersal systems and include the use of substances that have been bioengineered to produce the desired effect. Biocrime becomes a high-technology offense when it involves the use of purposefully altered genetic material or advanced bioscientific techniques.

Biocrime is a high-technology offense that involves the use of purposefully altered genetic material or advanced bioscientific techniques.

Although many people are aware of the dangers of terrorist-related biocrimes, including biological attacks on agricultural plants and animals (agroterrorism) and on human beings, many other kinds of potential biocrimes lurk on the horizon. They include the illegal harvesting of human organs for medical transplantation, human cloning, and the direct alteration of the DNA of living beings to produce a mixing of traits between species. Stem cell harvesting, another area that faces possible criminalization, is currently the subject of hot debate. The situation in the United States with regard to stem cell harvesting is one of funding restrictions, not legal or criminal restrictions. Although the federal government has yet to enact comprehensive legislation curtailing, regulating, or forbidding many of the kinds of activities mentioned here, there are a number of special interest groups that continue to lobby for such laws.

In 2004, Korean scientists became the first to announce that they had successfully cloned a human embryo and had extracted embryonic stem cells from it.[7] In 2005, those same scientists used the process to make stem cells tailored to match an individual patient, meaning that medical treatments for diseases like diabetes might be possible without fear of cellular rejection. Similarly, in 2005, British scientists working at Newcastle University in England disclosed that they had created a cloned human embryo. Cloning is a cellular reproductive process that does not require

■ **hacker** A computer hobbyist or professional, generally with advanced programming skills. Today, the term *hacker* has taken on a sinister connotation, referring to hobbyists who are bent on illegally accessing the computers of others or who attempt to demonstrate their technological prowess through computerized acts of vandalism.

the joining of a sperm and an egg; it occurs when the nucleus of an egg is replaced with the nucleus of another cell.

President George W. Bush favored a ban on all research into human cloning in the United States[8] and threatened to veto proposed federal legislation in 2005 that would have provided federal support for cloning research.[9] Similarly, in 2003, the U.S. House of Representatives voted to criminalize all human cloning activities and research.[10] The proposed legislation, known as the Human Cloning Research Prohibition Act, would have made it a crime to transfer the nucleus of an ordinary human cell into an unfertilized human egg whose own nucleus had been removed.[11] It also would have made it a crime to "receive or import a cloned human embryo or any product derived from a cloned human embryo." The scientific technique targeted by the bill, known as *nuclear transfer*, is the process that was used to clone Dolly the sheep in 1996.[12] A similar bill, known as the Human Cloning Prohibition Act of 2005, was introduced by Senator Sam Brownback, a Republican from Kansas.[13] Although it didn't become law, the Human Cloning Prohibition Act of 2009, a similar bill, died in the House.[14] If passed, the bills would have prohibited both reproductive cloning and the use of cloning technology to derive stem cells. In other words, the legislation aimed to thwart not just reproductive cloning, in which a copy of a living organism might be made, but also therapeutic cloning.[15]

Therapeutic cloning is a healing technique in which a person's own cells are used to grow a new organ, such as a heart, liver, or lungs, to replace a diseased or damaged organ. Opponents feared that the proposed legislation, which specified punishments of up to a $1 million fine and ten years in prison, would have significantly retarded biomedical progress in the United States, relegating America to a kind of technological backwater in the world's burgeoning biotechnology industry.[16] In 2009, President Obama, in what many saw as an important step forward for the American scientific community, signed a presidential directive lifting restrictions on federal funding for embryonic stem cell research, but promised that the U.S. government would "never open the door" to human cloning.[17]

Cybercrime

The dark side of new technologies, as far as the justice system is concerned, is the potential they create for committing old crimes in new ways or for committing new crimes never before imagined. In 2013, for example, two sophisticated operations involving people in more than two dozen countries acting in close coordination hacked their way into a database of prepaid debit cards and then used the card numbers to drain $45 million in cash from ATM machines around the world. Seven people were arrested in the United States, some with backpacks stuffed with hundred dollar bills, and charged with using bogus magnetic swipe cards at teller machines in Japan, Russia, Romania, Egypt, Colombia, the U.K., and Canada.[18]

Similarly, a few years ago, technologically savvy scam artists replicated the website of the Massachusetts State Lottery Commission.[19] The scammers, believed to be operating out of Nigeria, sent thousands of e-mails and cell phone text messages telling people that they had won $30,000 in the Massachusetts State Lottery. People who received the messages were told to sign on to an official-looking website to claim their prize. The site required that users enter their Social Security and credit card numbers and pay a $100 processing fee before the winnings could be distributed.

A person's online activities occur in a virtual world comprised of bits and bytes. That's why we said in Chapter 2 that "true" computer criminals engage in behavior that goes beyond the theft of hardware. Cybercrime, or computer crime, focuses on the information stored in electronic media, which is why it is sometimes referred to as *information technology crime* or *infocrime*. Two decades ago, for example, the activities of computer expert Kevin Mitnick, then known as the Federal Bureau of Investigation's (FBI's) "most wanted **hacker**,"[20] alarmed security experts because of the potential for harm that Mitnick's electronic intrusions represented. The 31-year-old Mitnick broke into an Internet service provider's computer system and stole more than 20,000 credit card numbers. Tsutoma Shimomura, whose home computer Mitnick had also attacked, helped FBI experts track Mitnick through telephone lines and computer networks to the computer in his Raleigh, North Carolina, apartment, where he was arrested. In March 1999, Mitnick pleaded guilty to seven federal counts of computer and wire fraud. He was sentenced to 46 months in prison but was released on parole in January 2000. Under the terms of his release, Mitnick was barred from access to computer hardware and software and from any form of wireless communication for a period of three years.[21] In an interview after his release, Mitnick pointed out that "malicious hackers don't need to use stealth computer techniques to break into a network. . . . Often they just trick someone into giving them passwords and other information."[22] According to Mitnick, "People are the weakest link. . . . You can have the best technology, firewalls, intrusion-detection systems, biometric devices . . . and somebody can call an unsuspecting employee . . . [and] they [get] everything."

■ **social engineering** A nontechnical kind of cyberintrusion that relies heavily on human interaction and often involves tricking people into breaking normal security procedures.

Neil Barrett, a digital crime expert at International Risk Management, a London-based security consultancy, agrees. "The most likely way for bad guys to break into the system is through **social engineering**. This involves persuading administrators or telephonists to give details of passwords or other things by pretending to be staff, suppliers or trusted individuals—even police officers. They could be even masquerading as a computer repair man to get access to the premises."[23] Social engineering is a devastating security threat, says Barrett, because it targets and exploits a computer network's most vulnerable aspect—people.

Transnational Cybercrime

An especially important characteristic of cybercrime is that it can easily be cross-jurisdictional or transnational. A cybercriminal sitting at a keyboard in Australia, for example, can steal money from a bank in Russia and then transfer the digital cash to an account in Chile. For investigators, the question may be "What laws were broken?" Complicating matters is the fact that Australia and Chile have fragmented cybercrime laws, and Russia[24] has laws that are particularly ineffective.

According to researchers at McConnell International, a consulting firm based in Washington, D.C., of 52 developing countries surveyed in 2000, only the Philippines had effective cybercrime legislation in effect.[25] The Philippines enacted a new cybercrime law in 2000 after the creator of the highly damaging "Love Bug" computer virus, a 23-year-old Filipino student named Onel de Guzman, could not be prosecuted under the country's existing cybercrime laws.[26] De Guzman was finally charged with theft and violation of a law that had been enacted to deter credit card fraud. The country's new cybercrime law could not be applied to him retroactively.

In an effort to enhance similarities in the cybercrime laws of different countries and to provide a model for national lawmaking bodies concerned with controlling cybercrimes, the 43-nation Council of Europe approved a cybercrime treaty in November 2001.[27] The treaty outlaws specific online activities, including fraud and child pornography, and outlines what law enforcement officials in member nations may and may not do in enforcing cybercrime laws. The goal of the treaty is to standardize both legal understandings of cybercrime and cybercrime laws in member nations. It also allows police officers to detain suspects wanted in other countries for cybercrimes and facilitates the gathering of information on such crimes across national borders. In addition to the council's member states, the treaty was also signed by the United States, Canada, Japan, and South Africa.[28]

Types of Cybercrime

In 2005, a novel form of cybercrime made its appearance in the form of computer ransomware that installs itself on users' computers through an insecure Internet connection and then encrypts the users' data files.[29] When the machines' owners try to access their own information, they are presented with a message telling them to provide their charge card number to a remote server, which then sends them an unlock code. According to the FBI, this high-tech form of extortion is still rare but on the rise. Particularly targeted are financial institutions and other businesses that stand to lose large amounts of money if their data is corrupted or irretrievable.[30]

In 2005, a novel form of cybercrime made its appearance in the form of computer ransomware that installs itself on users' computers through an insecure Internet connection and then encrypts the users' data files.

Peter Grabosky of the Australian Institute of Criminology suggests that most cybercrimes fall into one of the following broad categories:[31] (1) theft of services, such as telephone or long-distance access; (2) communications in furtherance of criminal conspiracies—for example, the e-mail communications said to have taken place between members of Osama bin Laden's al-Qaeda terrorist network;[32] (3) information piracy and forgery—that is, the stealing of trade secrets or copyrighted information; (4) the dissemination of offensive materials such as child pornography, high volumes of unwanted commercial material such as bulk e-mail (spam), or extortion threats like those made against financial institutions by hackers claiming the ability to destroy a company's electronic records; (5) electronic money laundering and tax evasion (through electronic funds transfers that conceal the origin of financial proceeds); (6) electronic vandalism and terrorism, including computer viruses, worms, Trojan horses, and cyberterrorism (see Chapter 17); (7) telemarketing fraud (including investment fraud and illegitimate electronic auctions); (8) illegal interception of telecommunications—that is, illegal eavesdropping; and (9) fraud involving electronic funds transfer (specifically, the illegal interception and diversion of legitimate transactions).

The 2010/2011 Computer Crime and Security Survey, conducted by the Computer Security Institute (CSI) and the FBI, found that the most expensive computer security incidents were those involving financial fraud.[33] Forty-six percent of the 351 information security professionals responding to the survey reported that their companies or organizations had been subjected to at least one targeted attack during the survey period (July 2009 to June 2010). "Targeted attacks" were defined as malware attacks aimed exclusively at the respondent's organization. Eighteen percent of respondents stated that they notified individuals whose personal information was breached. Sixteen percent said that as a result of attacks they provided new security

■ **computer virus** A computer program designed to secretly invade systems and either modify the way in which they operate or alter the information they store. Viruses are destructive software programs that may effectively vandalize computers of all types and sizes.

services to users or customers. An overview of the Computer Security Institute's survey results can be found online at **http://gocsi.com/survey**.

In 2008, the Bureau of Justice Statistics (BJS) published results from its fifth (and most recent) National Computer Security Survey (NCSS).[34] Sixty-seven percent of the 7,818 businesses that responded to the NCSS reported that they had detected at least one cybercrime in 2005. Nearly 60% reported one or more types of cyberattack, 11% report cyberthefts, and 24% of the businesses and agencies responding reported other types of computer security incidents. Overall, respondents said they detected more than 22 million incidents of cybercrime. The vast majority of reported cybercrimes (20 million incidents) were primarily spyware, adware, phishing, and spoofing incidents. There were nearly 1.5 million computer virus infections reported, along with 126,000 cyberfraud incidents. Ninety-one percent of businesses providing information sustained system downtime, direct monetary loss, or both. Reported direct monetary losses totaled $867 million, and cybertheft accounted for more than half of the loss ($450 million). Cyberattacks cost businesses $314 million, and system downtime caused by cyberattacks and other computer security incidents totaled 323,900 hours among the businesses reporting. Computer viruses accounted for 193,000 downtime hours, and other computer security incidents resulted in more than 100,000 hours of system downtime. As might be expected, telecommunications businesses, computer system design businesses, and manufacturers of durable goods had the highest prevalence of cybercrime during the period covered by the survey.

Another source of data on Internet crime is the Internet Crime Complaint Center (IC3), a partnership between the FBI, BJA, and the White Collar Crime Center. In 2012, the IC3 published its *2011 Internet Crime Report*—the 11th annual compilation of information on complaints received and/or referred to the IC3 by law enforcement agencies for appropriate action.[35] In 2011, the IC3 received 314,246 complaints involving financial losses of more than $485 million. Nondelivery of merchandise ordered over the Internet, identity theft, overpayment fraud, advance-fee fraud, and fraudulent FBI-related scams (in which an individual poses as an FBI agent in an effort to defraud victims) were among the top types of fraud reported. The 2011 IC3 report, which provides a snapshot of the prevalence and impact of Internet fraud cases and describes the kinds of complaints that were filed, is available at **http://ic3report.nw3c.gov**.

Computer Viruses, Worms, and Trojan Horses

Computer viruses are a special concern of computer users everywhere. Computer viruses were first brought to public attention in 1988, when the Pakistani virus (or Pakistani brain virus) became widespread in personal and office computers across the United States.[36] The Pakistani virus was created by Amjad Farooq Alvi and his brother, Basit Farooq Alvi, two cut-rate computer software dealers in Lahore, Pakistan. The Alvi brothers made copies of costly software products and sold them at low prices, mostly to Western shoppers looking for a bargain. Motivated by convoluted logic, the brothers hid a virus on each disk they sold to punish buyers for seeking to evade copyright laws.

AP Photo/Nick Ut

Luis Mijangos, 32, of Santa Ana, California. Mijangos was sentenced to six years in prison in 2011 for sextortion (digital extortion) after he pleaded guilty to computer hacking and wiretapping. Mijangos used file-sharing networks to infect the computers of women and teenage girls, searching them for sexually explicit pictures. He'd then contact the victims demanding that they provide more photos or videos, or he'd post what he had on the Web. In some cases he was also able to turn on victims' computer microphones and cameras to record their personal activities. How can you tell if your computer is immune to attacks like those perpetrated by Mijangos?

■ **malware** Malicious computer programs such as viruses, worms, and Trojan horses.

■ **software piracy** The unauthorized duplication of software or the illegal transfer of data from one storage medium to another. Software piracy is one of the most prevalent cybercrimes in the world.

A more serious virus incident later that year affected sensitive machines in National Aeronautics and Space Administration (NASA) nuclear weapons labs, federal research centers, and universities across the United States.[37] The virus did not destroy data. Instead, it made copies of itself and multiplied so rapidly that it clogged and effectively shut down computers within hours after invading them. Robert Morris, creator of the virus, was sentenced in 1990 to 400 hours of community service, three years' probation, and a fine of $10,000.[38] Since then, many other virus attacks have made headlines, including the infamous Michelangelo virus in 1992; the intentional distribution of infected software on an AIDS-related research CD-ROM distributed about the same time; the Kournikova virus in 2000; and the later Sircam, Nimda, W32, NastyBrew, Berbew, Mydoom, and Code Red worms.

Technically speaking, most of today's malicious software falls under the category of worms or Trojan horses—called **malware** by technophiles. Malware (also called *crimeware*) has become increasingly sophisticated. Although early viruses were relatively easy to detect with hardware or software scanning devices that looked for virus "signatures," new malicious software using stealth and polymorphic computer codes changes form with each new "infection" and is much more difficult to locate and remove. Moreover, whereas older viruses infected only executable programs, or those that could be run, newer malware (such as the Word for Windows Macro virus, also called the *Concept virus*) attaches itself to word-processing documents and to computer codes that are routinely distributed via the World Wide Web (including Java and Active-X components used by Web browsers). In 1998, the world's first HTML virus was discovered. The virus, named HTML Internal, infects computers whose users are merely viewing Web pages.[39] Later that year, the first Java-based malware, named Strange Brew, made its appearance,[40] and in 2004 malware capable of infecting digital images using the Joint Photographic Experts Group (JPEG) format was discovered.[41] Evolving forms of malware are even able to infect cell phones and other wireless-enabled handheld devices.

Phishing is a relatively new form of high-technology fraud that uses official-looking e-mail messages to elicit responses from victims, directing them to phony websites.

Phishing One form of cybercrime that relies primarily on social engineering to succeed is *phishing* (pronounced "fishing"). Phishing is a relatively new form of high-technology fraud that uses official-looking e-mail messages to elicit responses from victims, directing them to phony websites. Microsoft Corporation says that phishing is "the fastest-growing form of online fraud in the world today."[42] Phishing e-mails typically instruct recipients to validate or update account information before their accounts are canceled. Phishing schemes, which have targeted most major banks, the Federal Deposit Insurance Corporation, IBM, eBay, PayPal, and some major health-care providers, are designed to steal valuable information like credit card numbers, Social Security numbers, user IDs, and passwords. In 2004, Gartner Inc., a leading provider of research and analysis on the global information technology industry, released a report estimating that some 57 million adult Americans received phishing e-mails during the spring of 2004 and that 11 million recipients clicked on the link contained in the messages.[43] Gartner estimated that 1.78 million recipients actually provided personal information to the thieves behind the phishing schemes.

Software Piracy Another form of cybercrime, the unauthorized copying of software programs, also called **software piracy**, appears to be rampant. According to the Software and Information Industry Association (SIIA), global losses from software piracy total nearly $12.2 billion annually.[44] The SIIA says that 38% of all software in use in the world today has been copied illegally. Some countries have especially high rates of illegal use. Of all the computer software in use in Vietnam, for example, the SIIA estimates that 97% has been illegally copied, whereas 95% of the software used in China and 92% of the software used in Russia are thought to be pirated—resulting in a substantial loss in manufacturers' revenue.

Software pirates seem to be especially adept at evading today's copy-protection schemes, including those that involve software "keys" and Internet authentication. Similar to software piracy, peer-to-peer Internet file-sharing services (which directly connect users' computers with one another via the Internet) have been criticized for allowing users to download copyright-protected e-music and digital video files free of charge. Lawsuits involving the music-sharing service Napster resulted in the site's near closure, and similar websites, such as KaZaA, Morpheus, and Grokster, are the targets of ongoing music industry lawsuits. In 2003, however, a U.S. district court in New York held that many music-swapping services and their operators could not be held accountable for the actions of their users, although individual users who download copyrighted materials *can* be held liable for copyright infringements.[45] That same year, a federal judge in Los Angeles ruled that peer-to-peer network software providers Grokster and StreamCast Networks could not be held liable for the copyright infringements of their users.[46] In 2004, the 9th U.S. Circuit Court of Appeals upheld that ruling,[47] but in 2005,

■ **spam** Unsolicited commercial bulk e-mail whose primary purpose is the advertisement or promotion of a commercial product or service.

■ **weapon of mass destruction (WMD)** A chemical, biological, or nuclear weapon that has the potential to cause mass casualties.

in the landmark case of *MGM* v. *Grokster*,[48] the U.S. Supreme Court found that online file-sharing services may be held liable for copyright infringement if they promote their services explicitly as a way for users to download copyrighted music and other content. The *Grokster* decision contrasts with the 1984 case of *Sony Corporation of America* v. *Universal City Studios, Inc.*, in which the Court held that a distributor/operator of a copying tool cannot be held liable for users' copyright infringements so long as the tool in question is capable of substantial noninfringing uses.[49]

Spam Nearly a decade ago, federal legislators acted to criminalize the sending of unsolicited commercial e-mail, or **spam**. The federal CAN-SPAM Act (Controlling the Assault of Non-Solicited Pornography and Marketing), which took effect on January 1, 2004, regulates the sending of "commercial electronic mail messages."[50] The law, which applies equally to mass mailings and to individual e-mail messages, defines commercial electronic mail messages as electronic mail whose *primary purpose* is the "commercial advertisement or promotion of a commercial product or service." The CAN-SPAM law requires that a commercial e-mail message include the following three features: (1) a clear and conspicuous identification that the message is an advertisement or solicitation, (2) an opt-out feature, allowing recipients to opt out of future mailings, and (3) a valid physical address identifying the sender.

Some experts estimate that 80% of all e-mail today is spam,[51] and many states have enacted their own antispam laws. Virginia's 2003 antispam statute,[52] for example, imposes criminal penalties of from one to five years for anyone convicted of falsifying electronic mail transmission information or other routing information during the sending of unsolicited commercial bulk e-mail (UCBE). The law applies to anyone sending more than 10,000 UCBEsin a 24-hour period and to anyone who generates more than $1,000 in revenue from a UCBE transmission. The law also applies to anyone who uses fraudulent practices to send bulk e-mail to or from Virginia, a state that is home to a number of large Internet service providers, including America Online. In 2005, in the nation's first felony prosecution of a spammer, Jeremy Jaynes, age 30, one of the world's most active spammers, received a nine-year prison sentence under Virginia's law after he was convicted of using false Internet addresses and aliases to send mass e-mailings to America Online subscribers. Prosecutors were able to prove that Jaynes, a Raleigh, North Carolina, resident, earned as much as $750,000 a month by sending as many as 10 million illegal messages a day using computers operating in Virginia.[53]

Terrorism and Technology

The technological sophistication of state-sponsored terrorist organizations is rapidly increasing. Handguns and even larger weapons are now being manufactured out of plastic polymers and ceramics. Capable of firing Teflon-coated armor-piercing hardened ceramic bullets, such weapons are extremely powerful and impossible to uncover with metal detectors. Some people have also raised concerns over the new technology represented by 3-D printers, capable of cranking out complex shapes that could be assembled into weapons—including handguns and other weapons; and in 2013 the State Department ordered the removal of what are believed to be the world's first printable gun blueprints from a Website called Defense Distributed.[54] The do-it-yourself instructions had already been downloaded more than 100,000 times before the site was able to take them down.

Evidence points to the black market availability of other sinister items, including liquid metal embrittlement (LME), a chemical that slowly weakens any metal it contacts. LME could easily be applied with a felt-tipped pen to fuselage components in domestic aircraft, causing delayed structural failure.[55] Backpack-type electromagnetic pulse generators may soon be available to terrorists. Such devices could be carried into major cities, set up next to important computer installations, and activated to wipe out billions of items of financial, military, or other information now stored on magnetic media. International terrorists, along with the general public, have easy access to maps and other information that could be used to cripple the nation. The approximately 500 extremely-high-voltage (EHV) transformers on which the nation's electric grid depends, for example, are largely undefended and until recently were specified with extreme accuracy on easily available Web-based power network maps.

It is now clear that at least some terrorist organizations are seeking to obtain **weapons of mass destruction (WMDs)**, involving possible chemical, biological, radiological, and nuclear threats. A Central Intelligence Agency (CIA) report recently made public warned that al-Qaeda's "end goal" is to use WMDs. The CIA noted that the group had "openly expressed its desire to produce nuclear weapons" and that sketches and documents recovered from an al-Qaeda facility in Afghanistan contained plans for a crude nuclear device.[56]

The collapse of the Soviet Union in the late 1980s led to very loose internal control over nuclear weapons and weapons-grade fissionable materials held in the former Soviet republics. Evidence of this continues to surface. In 2003, for example, a cab driver in the Eastern European nation of Georgia was arrested

■ **bioterrorism** The intentional or threatened use of viruses, bacteria, fungi, or toxins from living organisms to produce death or disease in humans, animals, or plants.[i]

while transporting containers of cesium-137 and strontium-90, materials that could be used to make a "dirty" bomb (a radiological dispersal device, or RDD)[57] that would use conventional explosives to spread nuclear contamination over a wide area.[58] A month later, officials arrested a traveler in Bangkok, Thailand, who had a canister of cesium-137 in his possession. Although the Thai traveler told police that he had acquired the cesium in Laos, scientists were able to determine that it had originated in Russia.

A study by Harvard University researchers found that the United States and other countries were moving too slowly in efforts to help Russia and other former Soviet-bloc nations destroy poorly protected nuclear material and warheads left over from the cold war.[59] The study also warned that most civilian nuclear reactors in Eastern Europe are "dangerously insecure." Experts say the amount of plutonium needed to make one bomb can be smuggled out of a supposedly secure area in a briefcase or even in the pocket of an overcoat.

Biological weapons were banned by the 1975 international Biological Weapons Convention,[60] but biological terrorism (or bioterrorism), which seeks to disperse destructive or disease-producing biologically active agents among civilian or military populations, is of considerable concern today. **Bioterrorism**, one form of biocrime, is defined by the Centers for Disease Control and Prevention as the "intentional or threatened use of viruses, bacteria, fungi, or toxins from living organisms to produce death or disease in humans, animals, or plants."[61] The infamous anthrax letters mailed to at least four people in the United States in 2001 provide an example of a bioterrorism incident intended to create widespread fear among Americans. Five people, including mail handlers, died, and 23 others were infected.[62] Other possible bioterror agents include botulism toxin, brucellosis, cholera, glanders, plague, ricin, smallpox, tularemia Q fever, and a number of viral agents capable of producing diseases such as viral hemorrhagic fever and severe acute respiratory syndrome (SARS). As mentioned earlier, experts fear that technologically savvy terrorists could create their own novel bioweapons through bioengineering, a process that uses snippets of made-to-order DNA, the molecular code on which life is based.[63] Visit the Institute for Biosecurity at **http://www.bioterrorism.slu.edu**, and read the CDC's overview of bioterrorism at **http://www.justicestudies.com/pubs/biochemcdc.pdf**.

Technology and Crime Control

Technology, although it has increased criminal opportunity, has also been a boon to police investigators and other justice system personnel. In one example from 2013, the Omaha Police Department hosted the eighth Social Media Internet Law Enforcement (SMILE) national conference (also known as SMILECon 8) at Omaha's Old Market District. Conference organizers noted that police departments can both benefit as well as suffer from recent developments in social networking, and said that the adoption of social media by law enforcement agencies "is in a stage of exponential growth."[64]

In a practical example of the use of social media in policing, the Bergen County (New Jersey) Sheriff's Office launched "FaceCrook" in 2012, which includes public information on outstanding warrants tied to a Google Maps app, including an anonymous tip feature that allows people to provide anonymous tips via computer and telephone (**http://www.facecrook.net**).[65]

In another example, the Dunwoody, Georgia, Police Department recently experimented with using Twitter to help the city's 46,000 residents better understand the nature of police work. For 24 hours the department tweeted about each significant activity undertaken by its officers—beginning with an early morning traffic stop and concluding the next morning with a 6 a.m. report of a suspicious person.

Other police departments are jumping on board the social media bandwagon. In 2011, for example, the California Highway Patrol created Twitter pages—one for each of its divisions; and the Modesto, California, Police Department set up an active Twitter account to notify followers about major incidents and to provide links to ongoing investigations and newsworthy events. The department also uses Twitter to steer people away from accident sites, to coordinate the activities of searchers during Amber Alerts, and to warn people to stay inside during potentially dangerous situations. "It's a valuable tool that allows us to get our message out," says Stanislaus County Sheriff's Department spokesperson Deputy Luke Schwartz.[66] "You're going to see a lot more law enforcement agencies get on board with social networking sites like Twitter and Facebook," says Schwartz.

Schwartz points out, however, that social networking technologies don't always benefit the police. "The element of surprise is everything, and social media is taking away the element of surprise that we need to keep people safe when we have tactical situations," Schwartz said.[67]

One of the best examples of the use of social media in law enforcement today is TheDailyOfficer. Follow TheDailyOfficer on Twitter **@DailyOfficer**, from which you can access an ever-changing compilation of current police news and blogs from around the world. Concerned citizens can provide tips to law enforcement agencies via the Web-based Crime Stoppers International tipline at **http://www.facebook.com/CSIWorld**.

Another website, Connected Cops, describes itself as "law enforcement's partner on the social web," and can be visited at **http://connectedcops.net**. Connected Cops is international in scope, and provides a blog populated with messages from law enforcement social media visionaries on how to leverage technology in the service of law enforcement.

Similarly, access by law enforcement to high-technology investigative tools has produced enormous amounts of information on crimes and suspects, and the use of innovative investigative tools like DNA fingerprinting, keystroke captures, laser and night-vision technologies, digital imaging, and thermography are beginning to shape many of the practical aspects of the twenty-first-century criminal justice system. Today, some laptop computers and vehicles are programmed to contact police when they are stolen and provide satellite-based tracking information so authorities can determine their whereabouts. Many rental car companies, for example, now have cars equipped with systems that can send and receive from a central location. Security employees at those companies can send instructions to vehicles to prevent the car from starting and thus being stolen. The system can also track the car as it moves. Likewise, some police departments are using high-technology "bait cars" to catch auto thieves.[68] Bait cars can signal when stolen, send digitized images of perpetrators to investigators, radio their position to officers, be remotely immobilized, and lock their doors on command, trapping thieves inside.

Today, some laptop computers and vehicles are programmed to contact police when they are stolen and provide satellite-based tracking information so authorities can determine their whereabouts.

Another crime-fighting technology making headway in the identification of stolen vehicles is automatic plate recognition (APR) technology. In December 2004, for example, the Ohio State Highway Patrol completed a four-month evaluation of an APR system using infrared cameras mounted at strategic points along the state's highways and connected to computers to alert troopers to the possible presence of stolen vehicles or wanted persons. During the four-month test period, the system led to the apprehension of 23 criminal suspects and the recovery of 24 stolen vehicles.[69]

Car thieves, however, have made some technological advances of their own, including the "laundering" of vehicle identification numbers (VINs), which allows stolen cars to be sold as legitimate vehicles.[70] Stolen cars with "cloned" VINs are usually not discovered until an insurance claim is filed and investigators learn that there are two or more vehicles registered with the same VIN to people in different locations. As these stories indicate, the future will no doubt see a race between technologically sophisticated offenders and law enforcement authorities to determine who can wield the most advanced technical skills in the age-old battle between crime and justice.[71] Have a look at how the FBI sees crime fighting's future at **http://www.justicestudies.com/pubs/futuretech.pdf**.

Jason DeCrow/AP Wide World Photos

The New York City Police Department's Real Time Crime Center, where police work can seem like science fiction. At the center, where about a dozen analysts work, information on suspects is displayed on huge screens and can be relayed to detectives' laptops instantly. What do you imagine the future of police work will be like?

One of the best examples of the use of contemporary technologies in the service of crime fighting can be found at New York City's Real Time Crime Center. The center is staffed by specially trained data analysts who pore over enormous multiple-screen monitors that feed streams of information to them from video cameras, human intelligence gatherers, detectives and police officers, and computer programs searching for links between diverse bits of information. The center has been described as "a round-the-clock computer-data warehouse that can digitally track down information, from a perpetrator's mug shot to his second former mother-in-law's address." Kenneth Mekeel, a former captain of detectives, now runs the center. "It used to take us days to find a number or an address," Mekeel says. "Now we send stuff to detectives who are literally standing [at the crime scene]."[72]

Leading Technological Organizations in Criminal Justice

The National Law Enforcement and Corrections Technology Center (NLECTC) performs yearly assessments of key technological needs and opportunities facing the justice system. The center is responsible for helping identify, develop, manufacture, and adopt new products and technologies designed for law enforcement, corrections, and other criminal justice applications.[73] The NLECTC concentrates on four areas of advancing technology: (1) communications and electronics, (2) forensic science, (3) transportation and weapons, and (4) protective equipment.[74] Once NLECTC researchers have identified opportunities for improvement in any area, they make referrals to the Law Enforcement Standards Laboratory—a part of the National Bureau of Standards—for the testing of available hardware. The Justice Technology Information Network (JUSTNET), a service of the NLECTC, acts as an information gateway for law enforcement, corrections, and criminal justice technology and notifies the justice community of the latest technological advances. JUSTNET, accessible on the Web, lists the websites of technology providers and makes them easy to access. Visit the NLECTC at **justnet.org.**

Also, in 2013, the U.S. Department of Justice in conjunction with the National Institute of Standards and Technology (NIST) established the National Commission on Forensic Science as part of a new initiative to strengthen and enhance the practice of forensic science (which is discussed in more detail in the section that follows).[75] The commission provides guidance for federal, state, and local forensic science laboratories and works to coordinate technical advances in forensic sciences across federal, state, and local department and agencies. It is also working to create uniform codes for professional responsibility and requirements for training and certification in the area of forensic sciences.

Another important organization is the Society of Police Futurists International (PFI). PFI members are a highly select group of forward-thinking international police professionals. The group employs prediction techniques developed by other futures researchers to make reasonable forecasts about the likely role of the criminal justice system in the future. Recently, the PFI and the FBI collaborated to form a futures working group (FWG) to examine and promote innovation in policing. Consisting of approximately 15 members from the PFI and staff members from the FBI Academy, the FWG has implemented a variety of projects in collaboration with other organizations and academic institutions engaged in futures research. The group intends to continue to pursue opportunities for further cooperative efforts between American and international law enforcement agencies and organizations like the Foresight Institute (a British-based futures think tank).

Keep abreast of technological, cultural, and other changes affecting justice systems worldwide by visiting the Society of Police Futurists International via **http://www.police-futurists.org** and the Foresight Institute at **http://www.foresight.org**.

Criminalistics: Past, Present, and Future

Technological advances throughout history have signaled both threats and opportunities for the justice field. By the turn of the twentieth century, for example, police call boxes were standard features in many cities, utilizing the new technology of telephonic communications to pass along information on crimes in progress or to describe suspects and their activities. A few years later, police departments across the nation adapted to the rapid growth in the number of private automobiles and the laws governing their use. Over the years, motorized patrol, VASCAR speed-measuring devices, radar, laser speed detectors, and police helicopters and aircraft were all called into service to meet the need for a rapid response to criminal activity. Today's citizens band radios, often monitored by local police and highway patrol agencies, and cell phones with direct numbers to police dispatchers are continuing the trend of adapting advances in communications technology to police purposes. In-field computers

■ **criminalistics** The use of technology in the service of criminal investigation; the application of scientific techniques to the detection and evaluation of criminal evidence.

■ **criminalist** A police crime-scene analyst or laboratory worker versed in criminalistics.

(that is, laptop or handheld computers typically found in police vehicles) are commonplace, and many local police departments provide their officers with access to computer databases from the field.

The use of technology in the service of criminal investigation is a subfield of criminal justice referred to as **criminalistics**. Criminalistics applies scientific techniques to the detection and evaluation of criminal evidence. Police crime-scene analysts and laboratory personnel who use these techniques are referred to as **criminalists**. Modern criminalistics began with the need for the certain identification of individuals. Early methods of personal identification were notoriously inaccurate. In the nineteenth century, for instance, one day of the week was generally dedicated to a "parade" of newly arrested offenders; experienced investigators from distant jurisdictions would scrutinize the convicts, looking for recognizable faces.[76] By the 1840s, the Quetelet system of anthropometry was gaining in popularity.[77] The Quetelet system depended on precise measurements of various parts of the body to give an overall "picture" of a person for use in later identification.

The first "modern" system of personal identification was created by Alphonse Bertillon.[78] Bertillon was the director of the Bureau of Criminal Identification of the Paris Police Department during the late nineteenth century. The Bertillon system of identification was based on the idea that certain physical characteristics, such as eye color, skeletal size and shape, and ear form, did not change substantially after physical maturity. The system combined physical measurements with the emerging technology of photography. Although photography had been used previously in criminal identification, Bertillon standardized the technique by positioning measuring guides beside suspects so that their physical dimensions could be calculated from their photographs and by taking both front views and profiles.

Fingerprints, produced by contact with the ridge patterns in the skin on the fingertips, became the subject of intense scientific study in the mid-1840s. Although their importance in criminal investigation today seems obvious, it was not until the 1880s that scientists began to realize that each person's fingerprints are unique and unchangeable over a lifetime. Both discoveries appear to have come from the Englishmen William Herschel and Henry Faulds, who were working in Asia.[79] Some writers, observing that Asian lore about finger ridges and their significance extends back to antiquity, suggest that Herschel and Faulds must have been privy to such information.[80] As early as the Tang Dynasty (A.D. 618–906), inked fingerprints were being used in China as personal seals on important documents, and there is some evidence that the Chinese had classified patterns of the loops and whorls found in fingerprints and were using them for the identification of criminals as far back as 1,000 years ago.[81]

The use of fingerprints in identifying offenders was popularized by Sir Francis Galton[82] and was officially adopted by Scotland Yard in 1901. By the 1920s, fingerprint identification was being used in police departments everywhere, having quickly replaced Bertillon's anthropometric system. Suspects were fingerprinted, and their prints were compared with those lifted from a crime scene. Those comparisons typically required a great deal of time and a bit of luck to produce a match.

Over time, as fingerprint inventories in the United States grew huge, including those of everyone in the armed services and in certain branches of federal employment, researchers looked for a rapid and efficient way to compare large numbers of prints. Until the 1980s, most effective comparison schemes depended on manual classification methods that automatically eliminated large numbers of prints from consideration. As late as 1974, one author lamented, "Considering present levels of technology in other sciences . . . [the] classification of fingerprints has profited little by technological advancements, particularly in the computer sciences. [Fingerprint comparisons are] limited by the laborious inspection by skilled technicians required to accurately classify and interpret prints. Automation of the classification and comparison process would open up fingerprinting to its fullest potential."[83]

Within a decade, advances in computer hardware and software made possible CAL-ID, the automated fingerprint identification system (AFIS) of the California Department of Justice. The system used optical scanning and software pattern matching to compare suspects' fingerprints. Such computerized systems have grown rapidly in capability, and links between systems operated by different agencies are now routine. Modern technology employs proprietary electro-optical scanning systems that digitize live fingerprints, eliminating the need for traditional inking and rolling techniques.[84] Other advances in fingerprint identification and matching are also being made. The use of lasers in fingerprint lifting, for example, allowed the FBI to detect a 50-year-old fingerprint of a Nazi war criminal on a postcard.[85] Other advances, including a process known as surface-enhanced Raman spectroscopy (SERS), now make it possible, in at least some cases, to lift latent fingerprints from the skin of crime victims and even from bodies that have been submerged underwater for considerable periods of time.[86]

■ **biometrics** The science of recognizing people by physical characteristics and personal traits.

■ **ballistics** The analysis of firearms, ammunition, projectiles, bombs, and explosives.

■ **forensic entomology** The study of insects to determine such matters as a person's time of death.

■ **forensic anthropology** The use of anthropological principles and techniques in criminal investigation.

Computerization and digitization have improved accuracy and reduced the incidence of "false positives" in fingerprint comparisons.[87] The Los Angeles Police Department (LAPD), which uses an automated fingerprint identification system, estimates that fingerprint comparisons that in the past would have taken as long as 60 years can now be performed in a single day or less.[88] Computerized fingerprint identification systems took a giant step forward in 1986 with the introduction of a new electronic standard for fingerprint data exchange.[89] This standard makes it possible to exchange data between different automated fingerprint identification systems. Before its invention, the comparison of fingerprint data among AFISs was often difficult or impossible. Using the standard, cities across the nation can share and compare fingerprint information over the Internet or over secure networks linking their AFISs.[90]

Some years ago, the FBI developed the Integrated Automated Fingerprint Identification System (IAFIS) as part of the National Crime Information Center (NCIC) (see Chapter 5). The IAFIS integrates state fingerprint databases and automates search requests from police agencies throughout the country. A few years ago, use of IAFIS led to the arrest of a convicted murderer who was on parole in Reno, Nevada, and resulted in his being charged with a beating death that took place in Escondido, California, in 1977.[91] A smudged fingerprint found at the scene of the 1977 killing couldn't be matched with suspects at the time of the murder, but a cross-check of state databases undertaken by a cold case squad more than 30 years later took only 16 minutes to return a match. The suspect in the case was extradited to San Diego, where he pleaded guilty to charges in the 1977 crime. Learn more about IAFIS at **http://www.fbi.gov/hq/cjisd/iafis.htm**.

Fingerprinting provides an example of an early form of biometric technology used to positively identify individuals. Modern **biometrics** typically employs hardware and software to provide identity verification for specific purposes. Today's biometric devices include retinal and iris scanners, facial recognition systems, keyboard rhythm recognition units, voice authentication systems, hand geometry and digital fingerprint readers, facial thermography, and body odor sniffers. Some universities are now using hand geometry units to allow resident access to secure dormitories. In a significant adaptation of biometric technology, the Liberian International Ship and Corporate Registry, one of the largest shipping registries in the world, announced in 2003 that it was implementing a digital fingerprint recognition system to prevent known terrorists from infiltrating the cargo ship industry.[92] Multimodal biometric systems utilize more than one physiological or behavioral characteristic for identification (preventing, for example, the use of a severed finger to gain access to a controlled area).

Modern criminalistics also depend heavily on **ballistics** to analyze weapons, ammunition, and projectiles; medical pathology to determine the cause of injury or death; **forensic anthropology** to reconstruct the likeness of a decomposed or dismembered body; **forensic entomology** to determine issues such as the time of death; forensic dentistry to help identify deceased victims and offenders; the photography of crime scenes (now often done with video or digital cameras); plaster and polymer castings of tire tracks, boot prints, and marks made by implements; polygraph (the "lie detector") and voiceprint identification (used by the Central Intelligence Agency and the National Security Agency to authenticate voice recordings made by known terrorists); as well as a plethora of other techniques. Many criminal investigative practices have been thoroughly tested and are now accepted by most courts for the evidence they offer. Polygraph[93] and voiceprint identification techniques are still being refined, however, and have not won the wide acceptance of the other techniques mentioned.

New Technologies in Criminalistics

New and emerging law enforcement technologies include the following:

- DNA profiling and new serological/tissue identification techniques, many of which have already received widespread acceptability
- Online databases for the sharing of in-depth and timely criminal justice information
- Computer-aided investigations
- Computer-based training

Brief descriptions of these technologies, including their current state of development and the implications they hold for the future, are provided in the paragraphs that follow.

DNA Identification

In March 2000, a man known only by his genetic makeup was indicted and charged with a series of sexual assaults in Manhattan.[94] Authorities said that it was the first indictment based solely

CJ | NEWS

Kim Dotcom of Megaupload Arrested for Online Piracy

Max Gilbert/dpa/picture-alliance/Newscom

Megaupload founder Kim Dotcom poses in front of his New Zealand Mansion. Dotcom, whose given name is Kim Schmitz, was arrested in 2012 and charged with criminal copyright infringement for allegedly digitizing and stealing $500 million worth of music, film, and TV shows and making them available on his servers. Might Dotcom have avoided arrest if he lived in another country?

At 6-foot-6 and 322 pounds, Web entrepreneur Kim Dotcom has made a career of being larger than life, and his spectacular arrest on January 20, 2012, in his sprawling mansion in New Zealand lived up to that image.

New Zealand police cut through a series of locks to get to the 38-year-old native German, whose given name is Kim Schmitz. Though there were reports he had a shotgun handy, Dotcom, who had holed up in a safe room at his mansion when police arrived, surrendered peacefully.

Concurrent with the arrest, authorities in nine countries shut down worldwide operations of Megaupload, Dotcom's hugely popular file-sharing website. Executing 20 warrants, they seized hundreds of servers and closed 18 domain names.

U.S. prosecutors orchestrated the entire operation, executing an indictment against Dotcom and others at Megaupload for criminal copyright infringement. The company is accused of stealing $500 million worth of copyrighted material from music, film, and television rights holders over five years of operation.

The film and recording industries pushed to prosecute Dotcom, pointing to a disturbing erosion of their royalty income through unauthorized use on the Internet. The criminal investigation, begun two years prior to the arrest, was based on a lawsuit filed by the Motion Picture Association of America against the Megaupload website.

The indictment points to a new, gloves-off stage in the battle against unauthorized use of copyrighted material on the Internet. A decade ago, when copyright holders sued the file-sharing service Napster and shut it down, no criminal charges were filed, no one was arrested, and no one went to prison.

In addition to criminal copyright violations, Dotcom and his associates were charged with money laundering and racketeering, which alone could bring ten years in prison. Dotcom asserts that his site, Megaupload, is no different than YouTube, which escaped infringement charges in 2010. But Dotcom, who started his career as a hacker, had been previously convicted of insider trading and computer hacking in Germany.

Megaupload made its money by serving as a "digital locker" that stored users' files, which then could be accessed by anyone entering the site. At its peak, the site logged 50 million visits daily, making up 4% of all Internet traffic.

The company gave payments to locker-users whose content generated high traffic. Prosecutors allege this content was often pirated. For example, one copyright infringer allegedly uploaded nearly 17,000 videos to the site, which gleaned 334 million views as a result of that content.

Under the federal Digital Millennium Copyright Act, websites are protected from prosecution if they are unaware of pirated content and take down content when copyright holders inform them of violations. But prosecutors charge that Megaupload staff knew full well they were harboring pirated content and did not completely take down content when requested, leaving hundreds of copies still on the site, in some cases.

But some experts think prosecutors may be overreaching. James Grimmelmann of New York Law School said he hopes Dotcom is found guilty, but added that many of the activities in the indictment appear to be legitimate business strategies for Internet sites, such as offering premium subscriptions, running ads, and rewarding active users.

Jennifer Granick, an attorney blogging for Stanford's Center for Internet and Society, said it's going to be hard to win infringement charges based on users' content, rather than content directly pirated by Megaupload. She added that some legal arguments in the case are based on civil copyright law, which is not applicable to criminal copyright law.

New Zealand authorities were squeamish about cooperating too closely with U.S. officials. Over U.S. objections, a New Zealand judge granted Dotcom bail, requiring that he remain in the area and not use the Internet. U.S. officials will argue for his extradition in a hearing scheduled for around the time that this book goes to press.

In 2013, however, Dotcom opened a new file-sharing site called Mega, which was still running on servers in New Zealand as he awaits the completion of extradition proceedings.

Resources: "Megaupload Founder Launches New Sharing Site," *USA Today*, January 22, 2013, p. B1; "MegaUpload File Sharing Site Shut Down for Piracy by Feds, *Los Angeles Times*, January 19, 2012, http://latimesblogs.latimes.com/entertainmentnewsbuzz/2012/01/file-sharing-megaupload-shut-down-for-piracy-by-feds.html; "Why the Feds Smashed Megaupload," *Ars Technica*, February 8, 2012, http://arstechnica.com/tech-policy/news/2012/01/why-the-feds-smashed-megaupload.ars; and "Kim Dotcom's Wild Ride Hits Digital Piracy Wall," *Newsday*, February 27, 2012, http://www.newsday.com/business/technology/kim-dotcom-s-wild-ride-hits-digital-piracy-wall-1.3560434.

---

on a DNA profile. The man, dubbed the "East Side Rapist" and named in the indictment as "John Doe, an unidentified male," followed by his DNA profile, was charged with two sexual assaults in 1995 and one in 1997. He is alleged to have sexually attacked 16 women since 1994. No arrest has yet been made.

Three years later, New York City Mayor Michael Bloomberg announced that his city would begin using DNA to seek hundreds of indictments in unsolved sexual attacks.[95] Bloomberg said that the DNA-based indictments would effectively "stop the clock" on the state's ten-year statute of limitations, which bars

■ **DNA profiling** The use of biological residue, found at the scene of a crime, for genetic comparisons in aiding in the identification of criminal suspects.

Dan Loh/AP Wide World Photos

Forensic anthropologist Frank Bender explaining how he makes forensic models at his studio in Philadelphia. Bender, who describes himself as "the recomposer of the decomposed," has helped police identify dozens of murder victims and, in some cases, find their killers. Would you consider working as a forensic anthropologist?

prosecution of even known felons if they have not been charged with the crime within ten years of its commission.

DNA analysis is nearly infallible from a scientific point of view and is increasingly preferred by criminal justice experts as a method of identification.

DNA analysis (also discussed in Chapter 11) is nearly infallible from a scientific point of view and is increasingly preferred by criminal justice experts as a method of identification. It can prove innocence as well as demonstrate guilt. In December 2001, for example, Marvin Lamond Anderson, a Virginia parolee, was cleared of rape charges stemming from a 1982 crime for which he had served 15 years in prison.[96] Anderson received assistance from the Innocence Project, a volunteer organization specializing in the use of DNA technology to investigate and challenge what it regards as dubious convictions. A Virginia law passed in 2000, which allows felons to seek exoneration and expungement of their convictions on the basis of modern DNA testing, helped Anderson prove that he could not have committed the crime of which he had been convicted. DNA taken from a 19-year-old cotton swab was compared to the state's DNA database of more than 100,000 convicted felons and conclusively demonstrated that Anderson had not committed the crime. Learn more about the Innocence Project via **http://www.innocenceproject.org**.

The federal DNA Fingerprint Act of 2005[97] repealed an earlier provision found in the DNA Identification Act of 1994 that had prohibited including in the National DNA Index System (CODIS) any DNA profiles taken from arrestees who had not been charged with a crime. The 2005 law also requires the director of the FBI to expunge the DNA analysis record of a person from the system if the attorney general receives a certified copy of a final court order establishing that each charge serving as the basis on which the analysis was included has been dismissed, has resulted in an acquittal, or has not been filed within the applicable period. However, the law amended the DNA Analysis Background Elimination Act of 2000 to authorize the U.S. attorney general's office to (1) collect DNA samples from individuals who are arrested, or from non-U.S. residents who are detained under U.S. authority, and (2) to authorize any other federal agency that arrests or detains individuals or supervises individuals facing charges to collect DNA samples.[98]

The U.S. Department of Justice notes that "DNA evidence is playing a larger role than ever before in criminal cases throughout the country, both to convict the guilty and to exonerate those wrongly accused or convicted."[99] **DNA profiling**, also termed *DNA fingerprinting*, makes use of human DNA for purposes of identification. DNA (deoxyribonucleic acid) is a nucleic acid found in the center of cells. It is the principal component of chromosomes, the structures that transmit hereditary characteristics between generations. Each DNA molecule is a long two-stranded chain made up of subunits called *nucleotides,* coiled in the form of a double helix. Because genetic material is unique to each individual (except in the case of identical twins or clones), it can provide a highly reliable source of suspect identification. DNA profiling was originally used as a test for determining paternity.

DNA profiling requires only a few human cells for comparison. One drop of blood, a few hairs, a small amount of skin, or a trace of semen usually provides sufficient genetic material. Because the DNA molecule is very stable, genetic tests can be conducted on evidence taken from crime scenes long after fingerprints have disappeared. The process, diagrammed in Figure 18-1, involves the use of a highly technical procedure called *electrophoresis*. All 50 states and the Federal Bureau of Investigation now collect DNA samples from convicted offenders and retain the profiles generated from those samples in databases.[100]

All 50 states and the Federal Bureau of Investigation now collect DNA samples from convicted offenders and retain the profiles generated from those samples in databases.

Forensic use of DNA technology in criminal cases began in 1986 when British police asked Dr. Alec Jeffreys (who coined the term *DNA fingerprint*)[101] of Leicester University to verify a suspect's confession that he was responsible for two rape-murders in the English Midlands. DNA tests proved that the suspect could not have committed the crimes. Police then began obtaining blood samples from several thousand male inhabitants in the area in an attempt to identify a new suspect.[102]

In another British case the next year, 32-year-old Robert Melias became the first person ever convicted of a crime on the basis of DNA evidence.[103] Melias was convicted of raping a 43-year-old disabled woman, and the conviction came after genetic tests of semen left on the woman's clothes positively identified him as the perpetrator.[104]

In 1994, the DNA Identification Act[105] provided substantial funding to improve the quality and availability of DNA analyses for law enforcement identification. The act also provided for the establishment of the Combined DNA Index System (CODIS) for law enforcement purposes (see Chapter 5 for more information). The index, which held 1 million profiles by mid-2002,[106] allows investigators to produce quick matches with DNA samples already on file. The law limits accessibility of DNA samples to investigators, court officials, and personnel authorized to evaluate such samples for the purposes of criminal prosecution and defense.

In 1998, in an effort to enhance the use of DNA evidence as a law enforcement tool, the U.S. attorney general established the National Commission on the Future of DNA Evidence. The task of the commission was to submit recommendations to the U.S. Department of Justice to help ensure more effective use of DNA as a crime-fighting tool and to foster its use throughout the criminal justice system. The commission addressed issues in five specific areas: (1) the use of DNA in post-conviction relief cases; (2) legal concerns, including *Daubert* challenges (see Chapter 9) and the scope of discovery in DNA cases; (3) criteria for training and technical assistance for criminal justice professionals involved in the identification, collection, and preservation of DNA evidence at the crime scene; (4) essential laboratory capabilities in the face of emerging technologies; and (5) the impact of future technological developments on the use of DNA in the criminal justice system. Each topic became the focus of in-depth analysis by separate working groups comprised of prominent professionals. The work of the commission culminated in the National Law Enforcement Summit on DNA Technology, held in Washington, D.C., on July 27–28, 2000. The proceedings of the summit, as well as transcripts of commission meetings, are available via **http://www.nij.gov/nij/topics/forensics/evidence/dna/commission/welcome.html**.

The commission's work led the White House to sponsor an *Advancing Justice through DNA Technology* initiative. The initiative culminated in passage of federal legislation designed to take advantage of the opportunities offered by DNA testing. That legislation, the DNA Sexual Assault Justice Act of 2004 and the Innocence Protection Act of 2004 (also discussed in Chapter 11)—both of which are parts of the Justice for All Act of 2004[107]—was signed into law by President George W. Bush on October 30, 2004. The Innocence Protection Act established new procedures for applications for DNA testing by inmates in the federal prison system. Those new procedures require a court to order DNA testing if (1) the inmate applicant asserts that he or she is actually innocent of a qualifying offense, (2) the proposed DNA testing would produce new material evidence that would support such an assertion, and (3) it would create a reasonable probability that the applicant did not commit the offense. The court must grant the applicant's motion for a new trial or resentencing if DNA testing indicates that a new trial would likely result in acquittal. The act also seeks to preserve DNA evidence by prohibiting the destruction of biological evidence in a federal criminal case while a defendant remains incarcerated. The law established the Kirk Bloodsworth Post-Conviction DNA Testing Program, which provides millions of dollars in grants to states for post-conviction DNA testing. It also provided money for states to train prosecutors in the appropriate use of DNA evidence and to train defense counsel to ensure effective representation in capital cases. A provision of the Innocence Protection Act increased the maximum amount of damages an individual may be awarded for being wrongfully imprisoned in the federal system from $5,000 to $50,000 per year in noncapital cases and $100,000 per year in capital cases.

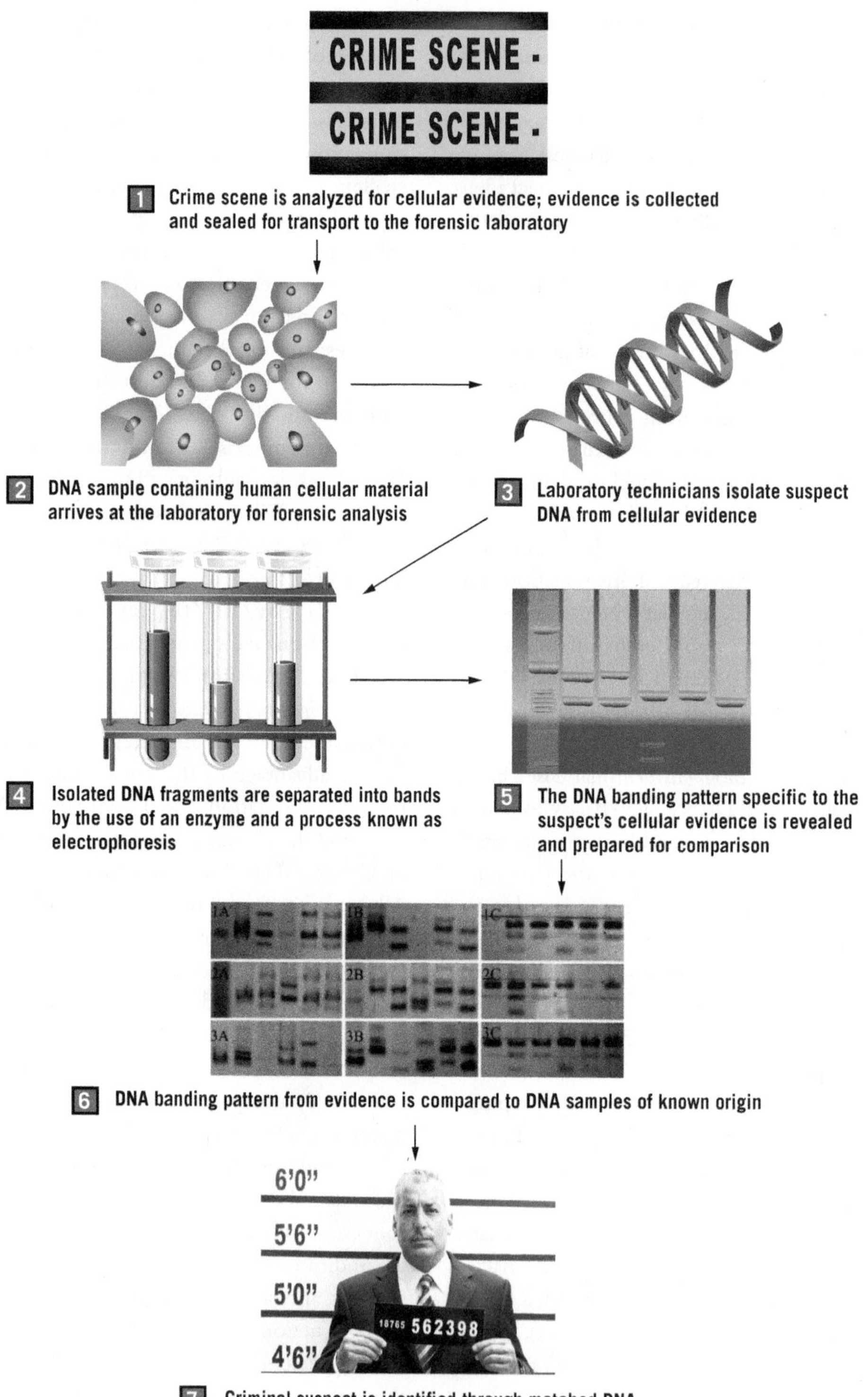
CRIME SCENE -
CRIME SCENE -
1 Crime scene is analyzed for cellular evidence; evidence is collected and sealed for transport to the forensic laboratory
2 DNA sample containing human cellular material arrives at the laboratory for forensic analysis
3 Laboratory technicians isolate suspect DNA from cellular evidence
4 Isolated DNA fragments are separated into bands by the use of an enzyme and a process known as electrophoresis
5 The DNA banding pattern specific to the suspect's cellular evidence is revealed and prepared for comparison
1A
1B
1C
2A
2B
2C
3A
3B
3C
6 DNA banding pattern from evidence is compared to DNA samples of known origin
6'0"
5'6"
5'0"
4'6"
562398
7 Criminal suspect is identified through matched DNA

FIGURE 18-1 | The DNA Fingerprinting Process.

The DNA Sexual Assault Justice Act authorized (1) $10 million per year for five years for grants to states and local governments to eliminate forensic science backlogs; (2) $12.5 million per year for five years to provide grants for training and education relating to the identification, collection, preservation, and analysis of DNA evidence for law enforcement officers, correctional personnel, and court officers; (3) $42.1 million in additional funds for the FBI to enhance its DNA programs, including the Combined DNA Index System; (4) $30 million per year for five years to create a grant program to provide training, technical assistance, education,

■ **expert system** Computer hardware and software that attempt to duplicate the decision-making processes used by skilled investigators in the analysis of evidence and in the recognition of patterns that such evidence might represent.

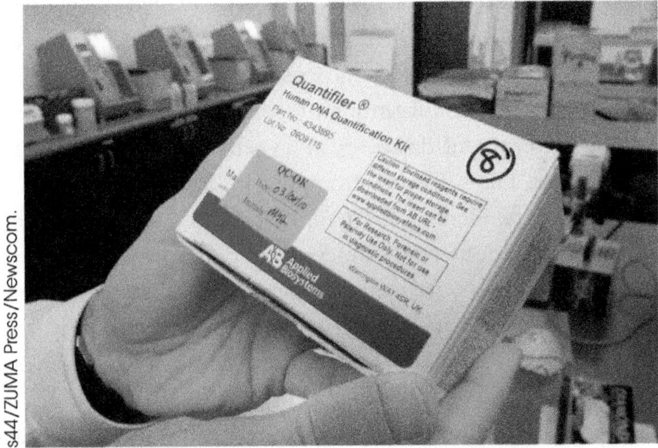

s44/ZUMA Press/Newscom.

A Human DNA Quantification Kit made by Applied Biosystems for use by law enforcement officers. What benefits can on-the-scene DNA collection and analysis provide to police agencies?

equipment, and information to medical personnel relating to the identification, collection, preservation, analysis, and use of DNA evidence; and (5) $15 million per year for five years to establish a National Forensic Science Commission to be appointed by the attorney general to provide recommendations for maximizing the use of forensic science technology in the criminal justice system.

The Justice for All Act also amended the federal statute of limitations[108] by adding the following words to existing law: "In a case in which DNA testing implicates an identified person in the commission of a felony . . . no statute of limitations that would otherwise preclude prosecution of the offense shall preclude such prosecution until a period of time following the implication of the person by DNA testing has elapsed that is equal to the otherwise applicable limitation period." The wording allows for prosecutions where DNA analysis reveals the identity of "cold case" perpetrators in investigations that might have otherwise been abandoned.

The 2013 U.S. Supreme Court case of *Maryland* v. *King* upheld state and federal laws that permit law enforcement agencies to collect DNA samples from criminal suspects following arrest for serious offenses.

Finally, as mentioned in a previous chapter, the 2013 U.S. Supreme Court case of *Maryland* v. *King* upheld state and federal laws that permit law enforcement agencies to collect DNA samples from criminal suspects following arrest for serious offenses.[109] Learn more about the impact of forensic DNA on American criminal justice from the National Academy of Sciences via its recent report, *Strengthening Forensic Science in the United States: A Path Forward*, at **http://www.justicestudies.com/pubs/forensics.pdf**.

Online Databases

Computerized information systems and the personnel who operate them are an integral part of most police departments today. Police department computers assist with such routine tasks as word processing, filing, record keeping, report printing, and personnel, equipment, and facilities scheduling. Computers that serve as investigative tools, however, have the greatest potential to affect criminal justice in the near future. The automated fingerprint technology discussed earlier is but one example of information-based systems designed to help in identifying offenders and solving crimes. Others include the nationwide National Crime Information Center and the Violent Criminal Apprehension Program (ViCAP) databases; state-operated police identification networks; specialized services like METAPOL, an information-sharing network run by the Police Executive Research Forum; and the FBI's CODIS, which allows law enforcement agencies to compare DNA profiles in their possession with other DNA profiles that have been entered into local, state, and national databases in order to identify a suspect or to link serial crimes. NCIC and police information networks furnish a 24-hour channel with information on suspects, stolen vehicles, and other data that can be accessed through computers installed in patrol cars.

Increasingly, law enforcement agencies are making criminal database information available to the public via the Internet. Among the most common forms of information available are sex-offender registries, although the FBI's Most Wanted list and the Most Wanted lists of various states can also be viewed online. In 1998, Texas became the first state to make its entire criminal convictions database available on the Internet.[110] See the FBI's Most Wanted list via **http://www.fbi.gov/wanted/topten**.

Computer-Aided Investigations

Some police agencies use large computer databases that can cross-reference specific information about crimes to determine patterns and to identify suspects. One of the earliest of these programs was HITMAN, developed by the Hollywood (California) Police Department in 1985. HITMAN has since evolved into a department-wide database that helps detectives in the Los Angeles Police Department solve violent crimes. The LAPD uses a similar computer program to track a target population of approximately 60,000 gang members.[111]

The developing field of artificial intelligence uses computers to make inferences based on available information and to draw conclusions or to make recommendations to the system's operators. **Expert systems**, as these computer models are often called, depend on three components: (1) a user interface or terminal, (2) a knowledge base containing information on what is already known in the area of investigation, and (3) a computer program known as an *inference engine* that compares user input and stored information according to established decision-making rules.

Numerous expert systems exist today. One is used by the FBI's National Center for the Analysis of Violent Crime (NCAVC) in a project designed to profile violent serial criminals. The NCAVC system depends on computer models of criminal profiling to provide a theoretical basis for the development of investigative strategies. Other systems have been developed as well, including some that focus on serological (blood serum) analysis, narcotics interdiction, serial murder and rape, and counterterrorism.[112]

Similar to expert systems are relational databases, which permit fast and easy sorting of large numbers of records. Perhaps the best-known early criminal justice database of this sort was called Big Floyd. It was developed in the 1980s by the FBI in conjunction with the Institute for Defense Analyses. Big Floyd was designed to access the more than 3 million records in the FBI's Organized Crime Information System and to allow investigators to decide which federal statutes apply in a given situation and whether investigators have enough evidence for a successful prosecution.[113] In the years since Big Floyd, other "bad-guy" relational databases targeting malfeasants of various types have been created, including computer systems to track deadbeat parents and quack physicians. In 1996, President Bill Clinton ordered the Department of Justice to create a computerized national registry of sex offenders.[114] The national sex-offender registry, developed as part of an overhaul of the FBI's computer systems, went online in 1999. It provides a database of registered sex offenders that is available only to law enforcement personnel. A publically available resource, the Dru Sjodin National Sex Offender Public Website (NSOPW), which is named in memory of a 22-year-old college student who was kidnapped and murdered by a registered sex offender, provides information on thousands of sex offenders under the Sex Offender Registration and Notification Act (SORNA). It can be found on the Web at **http://www.nsopw.gov.**

Some systems are even more problem specific. For example, ImAger, a product of Face Software, Inc., uses computer technology to artificially age photographs of missing children. The program has been used successfully to identify and recover a number of children. One of them was only six months old when he disappeared and was found after ImAger created a photo of what the child would look like at age five. The child was recognized by viewers who called police after the image was broadcast on television.[115] Another composite-imaging program, Compusketch by Visatex Corporation, is used by police artists to create simulated photographs of criminal suspects.[116]

The most advanced computer-aided investigation systems are being touted by agencies like NASA and the Defense Advanced Research Projects Agency (DARPA) as having the ability to prevent crime. DARPA, for example, announced its new Total Information Awareness (TIA) Program in 2003.[117] The five-year development project used information-sorting and pattern-matching software to sift through vast numbers of existing business and government databases in an effort to identify possible terror threats. The software attempted to detect suspicious patterns of activity, identify the people involved, and locate them so that investigations could be conducted. Suspected insurgents might be identified with similar software when it detects a series of credit card, bank, and official transactions that form a pattern that resembles preparations for an insurgency attack. The process, which is known as *data mining,* generates computer models in an attempt to predict terrorists' actions. Privacy advocates have raised concerns about the DARPA software, but the agency has tried to defuse concerns by assuring the public that the project "is not an attempt to build a supercomputer to snoop into the private lives or track the everyday activities of American citizens." The agency claims that "all TIA research complies with all privacy laws, without exception."

Another DARPA project that could meet the needs of American law enforcement agencies but is currently being developed for military use overseas is called Combat Zones That See (CZTS).[118] The CZTS program will build a huge surveillance system by networking existing cameras from department stores, subway platforms, banks, airports, parking lots, and other points of surveillance and by feeding images to supercomputer-like processors capable of recognizing suspects by face, gait, and mannerisms as they move from one place to another. The data can be fed via satellite to remote locations across the globe, allowing the agency to track suspects on the move—either within cities or between countries. Vehicles could also be tracked. CZTS is being introduced gradually in selected locations, beginning with areas in and around American military bases. Recently, General Electric announced development of an advanced behavior recognition system for use in crowded environments that uses computer software to analyze the images sent from surveillance cameras to interpret and predict the behavior of individuals and groups in social settings. The software, a form of intelligent video, can, for example, alert human operators to assaults from the moment they begin, and identify individuals whose behavior might indicate they are casing a retail establishment for criminal opportunities.[119] Future implementations of CZTS may involve nanocameras equipped with microminiaturized transmitters that can be spread over a city like grains of dust but that have the power to communicate relatively detailed

Future implementations of CZTS may involve nanocameras equipped with microminiaturized transmitters that can be spread over a city like grains of dust.

information to local cellular-like installations for entry into the CZTS network. The civil rights implications of local adaptations of DARPA's TIA and CZTS technology within the United States must be explored by any law enforcement agency considering the use of similar kinds of technologies.

Computer-Based Training

Computers provide an ideal training medium for criminal justice agencies. They allow users to work at their own pace, and they can be made available around the clock to provide off-site instruction to personnel whose job requirements make other kinds of training difficult to implement. Computer-based training (CBT) is already well established as a management training tool and is used extensively in law enforcement. CBT has the added advantage of familiarizing personnel with computers so that they will be better able to use them in other tasks.

Some of the more widely used computer-training programs include shoot/no-shoot decision-based software and police-pursuit driving simulators. The Atari Mobile Operations Simulator, firearms training simulation, and Robbec's JUST (Judgment under Stress Training) are just a few of the products available to police-training divisions. Recent innovations in the field of virtual reality (a kind of high-tech-based illusion) have led to the creation of realistic computer-based virtual environments in which law enforcement agents can test their skills.[120] Ever more advanced training tools are being developed for use in the criminal justice area. Recently, for example, the Law Enforcement Innovation Center at the University of Tennessee announced availability of a virtual reality simulator for training forensic investigators. Visit the simulator's home page at **http://leic.tennessee.edu/online/ivr.html.**

We have looked at just some of the most prominent uses of technology in criminal justice. Laser fingerprint-lifting devices, space-age photography, video camera–equipped patrol cars, satellite and computerized mapping,[121] field DNA-analysis kits, advanced chemical analysis techniques, chemical sniffers, and hair and fiber identification are all contemporary crime-fighting techniques based on new and emerging technologies. Field test kits for drug analysis, chemical sobriety checkers, and handheld ticket-issuing computers have also made the transition from costly high technology to widespread and relatively inexpensive use. As one expert has observed, "Police agencies throughout the world are entering an era in which high technology is not only desirable but necessary in order to combat crime effectively."[122]

On the Horizon

At the end of 2012, the Department of Homeland Security (DHS) submitted its semiannual report to Congress.[123] The report, which is available in its entirety at **http://justicestudies**

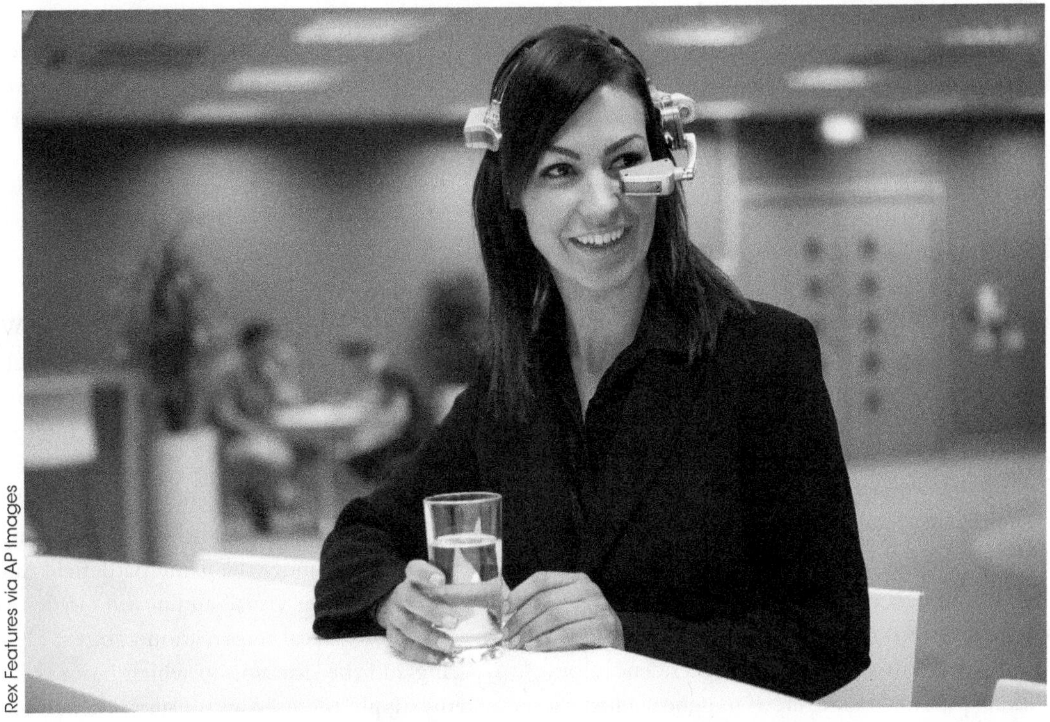

A model demonstrates use of the Golden-i headset computer. The wearable computer lets police see through walls using proprietary infrared technology and promises to give officers access to vital information without the need to use their hands or a keyboard. How can such technology enhance law enforcement capabilities?

■ **augmented reality (AR)** The real-time and accurate overlay of digital information on a user's real-world experience, through visual, aural, and/or tactile interfaces.[ii] The computer readouts superimposed on the visual fields of the fictional cyborgs in the *RoboCop* and *Terminator* movies provide an example.

.com/pubs/DHS2012.pdf, provides insight into some of the intrusion-detection technologies being used to help secure the nation's borders.

Various DHS semiannual reports have acknowledged concerns that weapons of mass destruction and other contraband of use to terrorists might enter the country through our nation's seaports. Shipping containers are too numerous for each to be opened and visually inspected. Millions of such containers enter the country every year from ports around the world. The DHS notes that shipping containers are "highly vulnerable to exploitation by terrorists" and has begun to focus on the need to enhance container-inspection efforts.

Since the terrorist attacks of September 11, 2001, border security has expanded to include the use of high-technology equipment to search for radioactive materials, explosives, toxic chemicals, and dangerous biological materials. These pieces of equipment—which include various vehicle and rail X-ray systems, radiation-detection units, trace-detection devices, video systems, and the like—permit officers to inspect cargo and conveyances for contraband without having to perform the costly and time-consuming process of unloading cargo or drilling through or dismantling containers.

Trace-detection technology, which focuses on cargo, luggage, packages, containers, and vehicles, gathers and analyzes the minute amounts of vapors given off and the microscopic particles left behind when narcotics and explosives contraband are packaged and handled. Current technology provides security screeners with nonintrusive search capabilities.

Radiation-detection equipment is used at the nation's ports and border crossings to detect attempts to smuggle radioactive materials into the United States. Detection devices range from personal radiation detectors, which are somewhat limited in capability and not very costly, to more sophisticated, capable, and expensive portable radiation-detection systems.

Passengers, cargo handlers, seamen, and flight crews must also be screened to determine the level of risk they represent. The DHS notes that Customs and Border Protection routinely processes more than 1.1 million arriving passengers for entry into the United States at 324 air, land, and seaports every day. The Advance Passenger Information System (APIS) is a border enforcement tool used at our nation's airports to identify and detain high-risk travelers on flights bound for the United States. The system is intended to collect biographical information such as name, date of birth, and country of residence from international airline passengers and crew members entering the United States at airports around the country. Before arrival, travelers are matched against law enforcement databases to identify people who should be detained and examined for violation of U.S. law. All airlines serving the United States are required to provide APIS information to the Department of Homeland Security.

A police surveillance drone in operation. What other new police technologies can you envision?

The Remote Video Inspection System (RVIS) used at border crossings is designed to expedite the clearance of low-risk travelers and to enhance security at remote border areas, including parts of the U.S.–Canadian border. The RVIS transmits images of a driver, vehicle, documents, and passengers to an inspector located miles away at a main port of entry that is monitored 24 hours a day.

Other security technologies now being employed sound like science fiction. For example, NASA is developing "noninvasive neuro-electric sensors," or brain-monitoring devices, that can receive and analyze brain-wave and heartbeat patterns from a distance.[124] The data are fed into a computer, which scrutinizes the information in order to "detect passengers who potentially might pose a threat."[125]

Especially intriguing technological advances can be found in the field of **augmented reality (AR)**.[126] Whereas virtual-reality systems generate audio and visual stimuli predicated on fictional scenarios and usually experienced by relatively passive viewers in situations not requiring interpersonal interaction, AR technology provides users with real-time fact-based information that can be accessed in the midst of real-world activity. Wearable AR systems, like those being developed by the U.S. military under the name Battlefield Augmented Reality System, provide visual, audio, and tactile overlays that can give the user critical information about the people he or she is facing and the situation in which he or she is involved. AR systems supply the user with data presented in a fashion similar to the science fiction visual readouts shown in *Terminator* films. There, the main character's computer-like brain automatically and continuously computes threat assessments by accessing stored databases and displays them in the character's visual field as easy-to-read schematics that are overlaid on the immediate surroundings. It is predicted that AR systems will soon be available that will provide "wired" officers with capabilities like these:

- Real-time intelligence about crime and criminals in the surrounding area
- Facial, voiceprint, and other biometric recognition data of known criminals, allowing for instantaneous identification
- Automated scans for chemical, biological, and explosive threats in the immediate area
- Real-time language translation to assist interaction with non-English-speaking people
- Three-dimensional maps, complete with building floor plans, sewer system schematics, and possible access and escape routes
- Advanced optics, including digital zoom and audio amplification for seeing and hearing at a distance
- Friend-or-foe identification technology to allow immediate recognition of "good guys"
- Coordinated deployment of robots and unmanned aerial vehicles (UAVs), including the ability to "see" and "hear" what the robots or UAVs encounter

Augmented-reality systems incorporating at least some of the features mentioned here are already a reality in police work. Xybernaut Corporation, for example, a leading provider of wearable computers, has teamed up with ZNQ3, a company that specializes in secure communications and dynamic identification, to provide wearable computers that enhance tactical awareness. According to Jeffrey Stutzman, founder and CEO of ZNQ3, "The secure communications and point-of-task computing power afforded by the joint Xybernaut/ZNQ3 solution allow first responders complete access to information providing critical situational awareness during a crisis."[127]

Thomas Cowper, whom we mentioned earlier in this chapter, poses some important questions about the practicality of augmented-reality applications in police work. How would "wired" officers be accepted by the public, given that their appearance would differ substantially from that of other officers? How cost-effective would AR technology be in police work? Who will pay for such systems, especially in smaller agencies? How can the accuracy of AR databases be ensured? What legal issues might arise?

Nanotechnology, or engineering and creating useful products on a molecular level, is another cutting-edge technology whose application to policing and the justice system is still largely in the realm of science fiction. Nonetheless, the National Science Foundation predicts that the field will grow into a $1 trillion industry annually by 2015. Nanotechnology may produce practical investigative applications in the near future. Microscopic cameras, motors, solar cells, recording devices, and high-frequency transmitters built with nanotechnology may have already resulted in the production of classified spy hardware such as a maneuverable mechanical mosquito able to fly into buildings and vehicles, providing its controllers with "fly-on-the-wall" observation capabilities.[128] Super sensors on such ultraminiaturized devices are said to be able to literally read over a person's shoulder and transmit visual, audio, global positioning system (GPS), infrared, and other data to remote recording and viewing devices, all the while remaining nearly invisible to those being targeted. The Institute of Nanotechnology says that miniaturized machines will soon be used to enhance tamper-prevention devices; bolster anticounterfeiting efforts; provide labs on a chip (sometimes called *dipstick technology*) for drug, food, explosives, and DNA testing; permit easy product tracking; and contribute to futuristic intruder-detection and intruder-identification systems.[129]

The Japanese news agency Kyodo reports that Hitachi Corporation is involved in talks with the European Central Bank to control counterfeiting and money laundering by embedding radio tags much smaller than a grain of sand in European bank notes (Euros).

A few years ago, the Japanese news agency Kyodo reported that Hitachi Corporation is involved in talks with the European Central Bank to control counterfeiting and money laundering by embedding radio tags much smaller than a grain of sand in European bank notes (Euros).[130] Radio-frequency identification (RFID) tags built with nanotechnology cannot be seen with the naked eye or felt by fingertips. The devices, called Mu-Chips, can authenticate bank notes that carry them and can even record details about the transactions in which they have been involved. RFID devices, which act much like digital watermarks, are queried by radio and use the energy of the incoming signal to generate a reply. Applicability of the technology was demonstrated at Japan's 2005 International Expo—an event that used RFID-tagged admission tickets. The Expo, which ran for five months, involved participants from 125 countries and drew nearly 15 million visitors.[131]

When agencies of the justice system use cutting-edge technology, it inevitably provokes fears of a future in which citizens' rights are abrogated in favor of advancing technology. Individual rights, equal treatment under the law, and due process issues all require constant reinterpretation as technology improves.

Criminal Justice in 2040

At a recent symposium sponsored by the National institute of Justice (NIJ), three experts offered their views of what American criminal justice will look like in 2040.[132] The three were Bryan J. Vila, former chief of the NIJ's Crime Control and Prevention Research Division; Christopher E. Stone, professor of the practice of criminal justice at Harvard University's John F. Kennedy School of Government; and David Weisburd, professor of criminology at the University of Maryland.

Vila said that he believes that future crime fighters will need to more accurately understand what he calls the *coevolution* of crime commission and crime fighting. Technological advances, he says, will have a great influence on crime fighting. Developments in surveillance, biometrics, DNA analysis, and RFID microchips will enhance crime prevention and crime solving. Increasingly sophisticated intelligence databases will likely be used not only by police officers and analysts but by the general public—as is now common with sex-offender registries. The future, says Vila, will also bring improvements in systems that allow officials to talk electronically to one another, particularly during emergencies. He concludes that better connections among people and agencies will lead to a decrease in criminal opportunities.

Stone pointed to what he sees as an emerging professional culture around the globe that will influence the world's criminal justice systems in the decades to come. He believes that a new culture is spreading professionalism through justice systems worldwide in these areas:

- The bilateral transfer of information between countries
- The global dissemination of justice products, such as court management computer systems, consulting services, and prison design
- Comparative empirical evidence about what works, what doesn't, and why

Weisburd says that the nature of criminal justice in 2040 will depend in large part on the primary research methodology that we employ between now and then. Is the criminal justice community better served, he asks, by relying on the experiences and opinions of practitioners (which he calls the *clinical experience model*) or by research that tests programs and measures outcomes (the *evidence-based model*)?

The clinical experience model is currently the research path most frequently followed, Weisburd says. As a consequence, today's policies and technologies are based primarily on reports from practitioners about what they have found to work or not work. The drawback to this model, says Weisburd, is that a program may be widely adopted before scientific research demonstrates its efficacy in more than one place. In contrast, under the evidence-based model, a new program undergoes systematic research and evaluation before it is widely adopted. But the evidence-based model also has shortcomings, says Weisburd. Effective research requires a large investment of time and money, and many practitioners would rather spend resources implementing an innovation than wait for confirming research. Weisburd, a proponent of the evidence-based model, proposes making the evidence-based model "more realistic." He believes this can be done by streamlining the process of developing evidence and conducting evaluations and by building an infrastructure to ensure that studies do not reinvent the wheel.

All three experts emphasized the need to find new ways to work with practitioners around the globe. Ultimately, Vila, Stone, and Weisburd agreed that the world of criminal justice in 2040 will have a more shared culture due to trends like globalization, mobility, and integrated communications. Within this context, they say, the priority over the next three decades should be to develop policies and technologies that will help policymakers and citizens realize a criminal justice system that is fair, equitable, and respectful for all.

The priority over the next three decades should be to develop policies and technologies that will help policymakers and citizens realize a criminal justice system that is fair, equitable, and respectful for all.

Finally, in 2012, the Washington, D.C.–based Sentencing Project released a 68-page report on the future of the American criminal justice system. Entitled *To Build a Better Criminal Justice System: 25 Experts Envision the Next 25 Years of Reform*,[133] the report pointed to twin threads that have shaped the justice system over the past few decades: (1) a policy climate in which "punishment has been exalted in ways unimaginable not very long ago," resulting in huge numbers of incarcerated individuals, and (2) the steep drop in crime in recent years accompanied by the "broad acceptance of the need for reentry programming and increasing support for the concept of justice reinvestment." The 25 experts who contributed to the volume make a number of predictions about what the American system of criminal justice will be like in the future. They include:

- An end to the mass prison era as fiscal imperatives cause policymakers to focus their attention on evidence-based approaches to fighting crime, leading to a system built on facts and reason, not political whims or sensational headlines
- Partnerships between criminal justice and mental health professionals that will grow increasingly strong as the nation seeks to grapple with contemporary forms of serious offending, including mass shootings and individual acts of terrorism
- A justice system that will produce more socially desirable results—including greater safety, less fear, less suffering, greater respect for the rule of law, and less injustice
- The development of a more humane criminal justice system that recognizes the humanity of those victimized by crime, those arrested and convicted of crime, and others who experience the ripple effects of crime and our justice system, leading to a system that truly provides "equal justice" for all

- The development of strategies that address particular issues, such as excessive sentences, race discrimination, wretched prison conditions, and disenfranchisement (the loss of voting and other civil rights by the convicted)
- A greater emphasis on the strategic role of race in addressing criminal justice policy
- A focus on issues specific to women, leading to more gender-responsive strategies throughout the justice system
- A wholesale reconsideration of national drug policy in order to reverse the harmful impacts of recent decades, including the nation's disastrous "war on drugs"
- A juvenile justice policy that will be reformed under a "my child test" that promotes compassionate and effective treatment for all

Although many of these changes may come about, the American criminal justice system of the future will likely remain recognizable through its backbone of subsystems: the police, the courts, and corrections. It will continue to rest on constitutional mandates and be responsive to court precedent. New issues will arise, but most of them will be resolved within the context of the question that has guided American criminal justice since its inception: How do we ensure public order and safety while guaranteeing individual rights and social justice in a free society? Learn more about what the American criminal justice system of the future may be like at **http://www.justicestudies.com/pubs/bjafuture.pdf**.

SUMMARY

- Old concepts of crime and criminality have undergone significant revision as a result of emerging technologies. Science fiction–like products that are now readily available either legally or on the black market have brought with them a plethora of possibilities for new high-stakes crimes. The well-equipped, technologically advanced offender in tomorrow's world will be capable of attempting crimes involving dollar amounts undreamed of only a few decades ago, and the potential for crime-caused human suffering will rise astronomically. Some of these crimes, like the theft of funds from electronic repositories or the ready availability of illegal goods and services, are much like traditional offenses, except that they use new communications technologies in their commission. The relentless advance of globalization is now combining with powerful emerging technologies to produce a new world of challenges for criminal justice agencies. Domestic and international terrorism, highly organized transnational criminal cartels, and changing social values are having a synergistic effect that is creating a complex tangle of legal, technological, and social issues.
- In response to new forms of crime and new technologies of crime commission, the crime-fighting abilities of police agencies will need to be substantially enhanced by cutting-edge surveillance and enforcement technologies and by international and interagency cooperation. A massive infusion of funds will be needed to support the adoption of new crime-fighting technologies such as laser and night-vision technologies, digital imaging, wearable computers, and thermography. Similarly, sophisticated personnel capable of operating in multicultural environments must be hired and trained to allow tomorrow's enforcement agencies to compete with the global reach of technologically adept criminals.
- Criminalistics refers to the use of technology in the service of criminal investigation and the application of scientific techniques to the detection and evaluation of criminal evidence. Law enforcement practitioners of the future will be aided in their work by a number of technologies, some of which are still in their infancy. These technologies include (1) DNA profiling and new serological/tissue identification techniques, many of which have already received widespread acceptability; (2) online databases for sharing digitized criminal justice information; (3) computer-aided investigations; and (4) computer-based training.

KEY TERMS

augmented reality (AR), 614
ballistics, 606
biocrime, 596
biometrics, 606
bioterrorism, 602
computer virus, 599
criminalist, 605
criminalistics, 605
DNA profiling, 608
expert system, 611
forensic anthropology, 606
forensic entomology, 606
hacker, 597
malware, 600
social engineering, 598
software piracy, 600
spam, 601
technocrime, 596
weapon of mass destruction (WMD), 601

QUESTIONS FOR REVIEW

1. Historically speaking, how have advances in technology affected society and criminal activity? What new kinds of crimes have technological advances made possible? Distinguish between new types of crimes produced by advancing technology and new ways of committing "old crimes" that have been facilitated by emerging technologies.
2. What role does technology play in the fight against crime? What new crime-fighting technologies hold the most promise for combating high-technology crimes?

3. What is criminalistics? Explain the interplay between advancing technology and methods used to gather evidence in the fight against crime.

QUESTIONS FOR REFLECTION

1. How has technology affected the practice of criminal justice in America during the past century? How has it affected the criminal law?
2. Why do criminal laws have to change to keep up with changes in technology? What modifications in current laws defining criminal activity might soon be necessary to meet the criminal possibilities inherent in new technologies?
3. What threats to individual rights might advanced technology create? Will our standards as to what constitutes admissible evidence, what is reasonable privacy, and so on undergo a significant reevaluation as a result of emerging technologies?

NOTES

i. Centers for Disease Control and Prevention, "Bioterrorism: An Overview," http://www.bt.cdc.gov/documents/PPTResponse/laboverview.pdf (accessed July 5, 2011).
ii. Thomas J. Cowper and Michael E. Buerger, *Improving Our View of the World: Police and Augmented Reality Technology* (Washington, DC: Federal Bureau of Investigation, 2003), http://www.fbi.gov/publications/realitytech/realitytech.pdf (accessed October 7, 2009).

1. Bob Sullivan, "Hackers Besiege Banks as Global Cyber War Ramps Up," CNBC, April 3, 2013, http://finance.yahoo.com/news/hackers-besiege-banks-global-cyber-175523351.html (accessed April 3, 2013).
2. Ibid.
3. Levine, "Officials Warn Facebook and Twitter Increase Police Vulnerability."
4. Thomas J. Cowper, "Foresight Update 49," http://www.foresight.org/Updates/Update49/Update49.4.html (accessed August 5, 2011).
5. Ibid.
6. University of Minnesota Center for Infectious Disease Research and Policy, "All H2N2 Flu Virus Samples Destroyed, CDC Says," May 3, 2005, http://www.cidrap.umn.edu/cidrap/content/influenza/general/news/may0305h2n2.html (accessed July 10, 2008).
7. "Stem Cells Extracted from Human Clone," MSNBC News, February 12, 2004, http://www.msnbc.msn.com/id/4244988 (accessed July 8, 2006).
8. "President Bush Calls on Senate to Back Human Cloning Ban," White House press release, April 10, 2002.
9. "Bush Condemns Embryonic Cloning," Fox News, May 21, 2005, http://www.foxnews.com/story/0,2933,157163,00.html (accessed July 18, 2007).
10. H.R. 222, Human Cloning Research Prohibition Act.
11. Many other countries, such as England, permit therapeutic cloning, although they often criminalize or severely restrict human cloning efforts.
12. Dolly was euthanized in 2003 after falling ill with lung disease.
13. S. 658, Human Cloning Prohibition Act of 2005.
14. H.R. 1050, Human Cloning Prohibition Act of 2009.
15. House Committee on Energy and Commerce, Subcommittee on Health, "Prepared Witness Testimony," June 20, 2001, http://energycommerce.house.gov/107/hearins/06202001Hearing291/Allen449.htm (accessed August 15, 2006).
16. "Bush Backs Total Ban on Human Cloning: Declares Life Is a 'Creation, Not a Commodity,'" April 10, 2002, http://usgovinfo.about.com/library/weekly/aa041102a.htm (accessed August 10, 2006).
17. "Obama Says Government Will Not Open the Door for Human Cloning," Fox News, March 9, 2009, http://www.foxnews.com/politics/2009/03/09/obama-says-government-open-door-human-cloning/ (accessed April 3, 2013).
18. "Feds in NYC: Hackers Stole $45 Million in ATM Card Breach," *Wall Street Journal*, May 9, 2013, http://online.wsj.com/article/APb7e60868bda84f45ae5f13909616bde7.html?KEYWORDS=two+dozen+countries (accessed May 10, 2013); and Marc Santora, "In Hours, Thieves Took $45 Million in A.T.M. Scheme," *New York Times*, http://www.nytimes.com/2013/05/10/nyregion/eight-charged-in-45-million-global-cyber-bank-thefts.html?hp&_r=1& (accessed May 10, 2013).
19. Linda Rosencrance, "Cyberscam Strikes Massachusetts State Lottery," *Computerworld*, July 24, 2003.
20. "Are You Vulnerable to Cybercrime?" *USA Today*, February 20, 1995.
21. "Most Wanted Hacker Released from Prison," *USA Today*, January 21, 2000, http://www.usatoday.com/news/ndsfri02.htm (accessed January 28, 2006).
22. Elinor Abreu, "Kevin Mitnick Bares All," *Industry Standard*, September 28, 2000, http://www.nwfusion.com/news/2000/0928mitnick.html (accessed January 26, 2002).
23. Pia Turunen, "Hack Attack: How You Might Be a Target," CNN.com, April 12, 2002, http://www.cnn.com/2002/TECH/ptech/04/12/hack.dangers (accessed August 3, 2006).
24. Nikola Krastev, "East: Many Nations Lack Effective Computer Crime Laws," *Radio Free Europe*, December 19, 2000, http://www.rferl.org/nca/features/2000/12/15122000153858.asp (accessed April 28, 2006).
25. Ibid.
26. "'Love Bug' Prompts New Philippine Law," *USA Today*, June 14, 2000.
27. "Cybercrime Treaty Gets Green Light," BBC News Online, November 12, 2001.
28. Details for this section come from the Council of Europe, Convention on Cybercrime signatories website, http://conventions.coe.int (accessed April 8, 2011).
29. Susan Schaibly, "Files for Ransom," *Network World*, September 26, 2005, http://www.networkworld.com/buzz/2005/092605-ransom.html (accessed May 12, 2007).
30. Ibid.
31. Peter Grabosky, "Computer Crime: A Criminological Overview," paper presented at the Workshop on Crimes Related to the Computer Network, Tenth United Nations Congress on the Prevention of Crime and the Treatment of Offenders, Vienna, Austria, April 15, 2000, http://www.aic.gov.au/conferences/other/compcrime/computercrime.pdf (accessed January 12, 2007).
32. Kevin Johnson, "Hijackers' E-Mails Sifted for Clues," *USA Today*, October 11, 2001.

33. Robert Richardson, *CSI Computer Crime & Security Survey 2010/2011* (New York: Computer Security Institute, 2011), http://gocsi.com/survey (accessed June 5, 2011).
34. Ramona R. Rantala, *Cybercrime against Businesses, 2005* (Washington, DC: Bureau of Justice Statistics, 2008).
35. Internet Crime Complaint Center, *2011 Internet Crime Report* (Washington, DC: Bureau of Justice Assistance, 2012), http://www.ic3.gov/media/annualreport/2011_IC3Report.pdf (accessed July 20, 2013).
36. "Invasion of the Data Snatchers!" *Time*, September 26, 1988, pp. 62–67.
37. "Virus Infects NASA, Defense, University Computer Systems," *Fayetteville (NC) Observer-Times*, November 4, 1988, p. 19A.
38. Barbara E. McMullin and John F. McMullin, "Hacker Morris Sentenced," Newsbytes News Network, May 4, 1990, http://findarticles.com/p/articles/mi_m0NEW/is_1990_May_8/ai_9831055 (accessed June 23, 2007).
39. "First HTML Virus Detected," Andover News Network, http://www.andovernews.com/cgi-bin/news_story.pl?95529/topstories (accessed January 16, 2006).
40. Sophos Antivirus, "The First JAVA Virus," http://www.sophos.com/virusinfo/articles/java.html (accessed January 5, 2006).
41. Net IQ, "Virus Protection," http://marshal.netiq.com/0195/solutions_virusprotection.html (accessed August 1, 2010).
42. Gregg Keizer, "Microsoft Says Phishing Bad, Offers Little New for Defense," *TechWeb News*, March 15, 2005, http://www.techweb.com/wire/159900391 (accessed July 7, 2007).
43. Avivah Litan, "Phishing Victims Likely Will Suffer Identity Theft Fraud," Gartner, Inc., May 14, 2004, http://www.gartner.com/DisplayDocument?ref5g_search&id544811 (accessed July 6, 2007).
44. Software Information Industry Association, "Report on Global Software Piracy, 2000," http://www.siia.net/piracy/pubs/piracy2000.pdf (accessed August 1, 2007).
45. See the music industry's reaction to the court's decision at http://www.nmpa.org/pr/NMPAPressRelease.doc (accessed August 1, 2008).
46. *Metro-Goldwyn-Mayer Studios, Inc.* v. *Grokster, Ltd.*, 259 F.Supp.2d 1029 (C.D. Cal. 2003).
47. Motion to dismiss denied, 243 F.Supp.2d 1073 (C.D. Cal. 2003).
48. *MGM* v. *Grokster*, 545 U.S. 913 (2005).
49. *Sony Corporation of America* v. *Universal City Studios, Inc.*, 464 U.S. 417 (1984).
50. Public Law 108-187.
51. Peter Firstbrook, "META Trend Update: The Changing Threat Landscape," Meta Group, March 24, 2005, http://www.meta-group.com/us/displayArticle.do?oid551768 (accessed July 5, 2007).
52. Virginia Statutes, Section 18.2-152.3:1.
53. Jack McCarthy, "Spammer Sentenced to Nine Years in Prison," *InfoWorld*, April 11, 2005.
54. "Printable-Gun Instructions Spread Online after State Dept. Orders Their Removal," *New York Times*, May 10, 2013, http://thelede.blogs.nytimes.com/2013/05/10/printable-gun-instructions-spread-online-after-state-dept-orders-their-removal/?src=recg (accessed May 12, 2013).
55. Some of the technological devices described in this section are discussed in G. Gordon Liddy, "Rules of the Game," *Omni*, January 1989, pp. 43–47, 78–80.
56. Central Intelligence Agency Directorate of Intelligence, *Terrorist CBRN: Materials and Effects* (Washington, DC: CIA, 2003).
57. Radiological Weapons Working Group, Harvard Project on Managing the Atom.
58. The information in this paragraph comes from a June 30, 2003, General Accounting Office report. See "Continuing Radioactive Materials Seizures," Nuclear Threat Initiative website, http://www.nti.org/e_research/cnwm/overview/cnwm_home.asp (accessed August 1, 2003).
59. Matthew Bunn, Anthony Wier, and John P. Holden, *Controlling Nuclear Warheads and Materials: A Report Card and Action Plan* (Cambridge, MA: Nuclear Threat Initiative and Harvard University, 2003).
60. *Fact Sheet: The Biological Weapons Convention* (Washington, DC: Bureau of Arms Control, 2002), http://www.state.gov/t/ac/rls/fs/10401.htm (accessed August 8, 2010).
61. Ali S. Kahn et al., *Biological and Chemical Terrorism: Strategic Plan for Preparedness and Response* (Atlanta, GA: Centers for Disease Control and Prevention, April 21, 2000), http://www.cdc.gov/mmwr/preview/mmwrhtml/rr4904a1.htm (accessed August 2, 2007).
62. Council on Foreign Relations, "Terrorism: Questions and Answers—The Anthrax Letters," http://www.terrorismanswers.com/weapons/anthraxletters.html (accessed August 23, 2009).
63. See Rick Weiss, "DNA by Mail: A Terror Risk," *Washington Post*, July 18, 2002.
64. SMILE, "Smile Conference, 2013," http://smileconference.com (accessed April 4, 2013).
65. "Inmates Provide Anonymous Tips with FaceCrook," *TechBeat*, Winter 2013.
66. Rosalio Ahumada, "California Police Use Twitter as Public Info Tool," *The Modesto Bee*, February 7, 2011.
67. Mike Levine, "Officials Warn Facebook and Twitter Increase Police Vulnerability," FoxNews.com, May 10, 2011, http://www.foxnews.com/scitech/2011/05/10/officials-warn-facebook-twitter-increase-police-vulnerability/#ixzz1Otq6y5F0 (accessed June 10, 2011).
68. Peter Eisler, "High-Tech 'Bait Cars' Catch Unsuspecting Auto Thieves," *USA Today*, November 29, 2004, p. 1A.
69. See, for example, Paul McClellan, "Automatic Plate Recognition Evaluation Ends with Positive Results," Ohio State Highway Patrol, December 22, 2004, http://www.statepatrol.ohio.gov/colcolumn/2004/AutoScanner-2.htm (accessed July 9, 2005).
70. Toni Locy, "Thieves Target Auto Identification," *USA Today*, May 20, 2005, p. 1A.
71. For an excellent overview of technology in criminal justice, see Laura J. Moriarty and David L. Carter, eds., *Criminal Justice Technology in the Twenty-First Century* (Springfield, IL: Charles C. Thomas, 1998).
72. Alan Feuer, "Where Police Work Has a Tinge of Sci-Fi," *New York Times*, January 1, 2009, http://www.nytimes.com/2009/01/01/nyregion/01roomsmet.html (accessed June 4, 2009).
73. National Law Enforcement and Corrections Technology Center, electronic press release, April 7, 1995.
74. Lester D. Shubin, *Research, Testing, Upgrading Criminal Justice Technology*, National Institute of Justice Reports (Washington, DC: U.S. Government Printing Office, 1984), pp. 2–5.
75. U.S. Department of Justice press release, "Department of Justice and National Institute of Standards and Technology Announce Launch of National Commission on Forensic Science," February 15, 2013, http://www.justice.gov/opa/pr/2013/February/13-dag-203.html (accessed April 23, 2013).

76. Harry Soderman and John J. O'Connell, *Modern Criminal Investigation* (New York: Funk and Wagnalls, 1945), p. 41.
77. The system was invented by Lambert Adolphe Jacques Quetelet (1796–1874), a Belgian astronomer and statistician.
78. For more on Bertillon's system, see Alphonse Bertillon, *Signaletic Instructions* (New York: Werner, 1896).
79. Robert D. Foote, "Fingerprint Identification: A Survey of Present Technology, Automated Applications, and Potential for Future Development," *Criminal Justice Monograph Series*, Vol. 5, No. 2 (Huntsville, TX: Sam Houston State University Press, 1974), pp. 3–4.
80. Soderman and O'Connell, *Modern Criminal Investigation*, p. 57.
81. Ibid.
82. Francis Galton, *Finger Prints* (London: Macmillan, 1892).
83. Foote, "Fingerprint Identification," p. 1.
84. Office of Technology Assessment, *Criminal Justice: New Technologies and the Constitution: A Special Report* (Washington, DC: U.S. Government Printing Office, 1988), p. 18. Electro-optical systems for live fingerprint scanning were developed by Fingermatric, Inc., of White Plains, New York.
85. T. F. Wilson and P. L. Woodard, *Automated Fingerprint Identification Systems—Technology and Policy Issues* (Washington, DC: U.S. Dept. of Justice, 1987), p. 5.
86. Kristi Gulick, "Latent Prints from Human Skin," *Law and Order Magazine,* http://www.lawandordermag.com/magazine/current/latentprints.html.htm (accessed September 26, 2001); and "Murder Victims Finger Their Killer," *New Scientist*, May 10, 2008, p. 27.
87. Los Angeles Police Department, *Annual Report, 1985–1986*, p. 26.
88. Ibid., p. 27.
89. American National Standards Institute, *American National Standard for Information Systems—Fingerprint Identification—Data Format for Information Interchange* (New York: ANSI, 1986). Originally developed as the Proposed American National Standard Data Format for the Interchange of Fingerprint Information by the National Bureau of Standards (Washington, DC: NBS, 1986).
90. Dennis G. Kurre, "On-Line Exchange of Fingerprint Identification Data," *FBI Law Enforcement Bulletin*, December 1987, pp. 14–16.
91. Federal Bureau of Investigation, "30-Year-Old Murder Solved by the 'Hit of the Year,'" May 8, 2009, http://www.fbi.gov/page2/may09/iafis_050809.html (accessed May 9, 2009).
92. Jon Swartz, "Ins and Outs of Biometrics," *USA Today*, January 27, 2003, p. 3B.
93. In 1998, ruling for the first time on polygraph examinations, the U.S. Supreme Court upheld the military's ban on the use of polygraph tests in criminal trials. In refusing to hear a case, Justice Clarence Thomas wrote, "[T]he aura of infallibility attending polygraph evidence can lead jurors to abandon their duty to assess credibility and guilt."
94. Details for this story come from *USA Today*, Nationline, March 16, 2000.
95. "NYC Seeks to Indict Rapists by DNA Alone," *USA Today*, August 5, 2003.
96. Francis X. Clines, "DNA Clears Virginia Man of 1982 Assault," *New York Times*, December 10, 2001.
97. Public Law No. 109-162, Title X, Sec. 1002 (2005).
98. Public Law No. 109-162, Title X, Sec. 1004 (2005).
99. U.S. Department of Justice, *Understanding DNA Evidence: A Guide for Victim Service Providers* (Washington, DC: DOJ, 2001).
100. Seth Axelrad, "Survey of State DNA Database Statutes," http://www.aslme.org/dna_04/grid/guide.pdf (accessed July 4, 2007).
101. See Alec J. Jeffreys, Victoria Wilson, and Swee Lay Thein, "Hypervariable 'Minisatellite' Regions in Human Nature," *Nature*, No. 314 (1985), p. 67; and "Individual-Specific 'Fingerprints' of Human DNA," *Nature*, No. 316 (1985), p. 76.
102. Peter Gill, Alec J. Jeffreys, and David J. Werrett, "Forensic Application of DNA Fingerprints," *Nature*, No. 318 (1985), p. 577. See also Craig Seton, "Life for Sex Killer Who Sent Decoy to Take Genetic Test," *London Times*, January 23, 1988, p. 3. A popular account of this case, *The Blooding*, was written by crime novelist Joseph Wambaugh (New York: William Morrow, 1989).
103. Bureau of Justice Statistics, *Forensic DNA Analysis: Issues* (Washington, DC: BJS, 1991).
104. "Genetic Fingerprinting Convicts Rapist in U.K.," *Globe and Mail*, November 14, 1987.
105. Violent Crime Control and Law Enforcement Act of 1994, Section 210301.
106. "National DNA Index System Reaches 1,000,000 Profiles," FBI press release, June 14, 2002.
107. Public Law 108-405.
108. U.S. Code, Title 18, Chapter 213, Section 3297.
109. *Maryland* v. *King*, U.S. Supreme Court, No. 12-207 (decided June 3, 2013).
110. "Time Line '98," *Yahoo! Internet Life*, January 1999, p. 90. To access the database, visit http://www.publicdata.com.
111. William S. Sessions, "Criminal Justice Information Services: Gearing Up for the Future," *FBI Law Enforcement Bulletin*, February 1993, pp. 181–188.
112. OTA, *Criminal Justice*, p. 29.
113. Ibid.
114. For more on the system, see Craig Stedman, "Feds to Track Sex Offenders with Database," *Computerworld*, September 2, 1996, p. 24.
115. "Saving Face," *PC Computing*, December 1988, p. 60.
116. See Dawn E. McQuiston and Roy S. Malpass, "Use of Facial Composite Systems in U.S. Law Enforcement Agencies," http://eyewitness.utep.edu/Documents/McQuiston%20APLS%202000.pdf (accessed March 25, 2007).
117. "Security or Privacy? DARPA's Total Information Awareness Program Tests the Boundaries," InformationWeek.com, http://www.informationweek.com/story/showArticle.jhtml?articleID510000184 (accessed August 2, 2008).
118. Information in this paragraph comes from "U.S. Sensors Could Track Any Car, All Passengers in Foreign Cities," WorldTribune.com, July 30, 2003, http://www.worldtribune.com/worldtribune/breaking_8.html (accessed August 5, 2007).
119. Ming-Ching Chang, Weina Ge, Nils Krahnstoever, Ting Yu, Ser Nam Lim, and Xiaoming Liu, *Advanced Behavior Recognition in Crowded Environments* (Niskayuna, NY: GE Global Research, 2013).
120. See, for example, Jeffrey S. Hormann, "Virtual Reality: The Future of Law Enforcement Training," *FBI Law Enforcement Bulletin*, July 1995, pp. 7–12.
121. See, for example, Thomas F. Rich, *The Use of Computerized Mapping Crime Control and Prevention Programs* (Washington, DC: National Institute of Justice, 1995).
122. Matt L. Rodriguez, "The Acquisition of High Technology Systems by Law Enforcement," *FBI Law Enforcement Bulletin* (December 1988), p. 10.
123. Office of the Inspector General, Department of Homeland Security, *Semiannual Report to the Congress* (Washington, DC: DHS, 2011).

124. Frank J. Murray, "NASA Plans to Read Terrorists' Minds at Airports," *Washington Times*, August 17, 2002.
125. Ibid.
126. The information in this section comes from Thomas J. Cowper and Michael E. Buerger, *Improving Our View of the World: Police and Augmented Reality Technology* (Washington, DC: Federal Bureau of Investigation, 2003), http://www.fbi.gov/publications/realitytech/realitytech.pdf (accessed October 27, 2006).
127. "Xybernaut and ZNQ3, Inc. Team to Deliver Secure Mobile Wearable Computing Solutions to State and Local Governments," *Business Wire*, July 29, 2003.
128. See the fictional discussion of such an advanced device in Dan Brown, *Deception Point* (New York: Simon and Schuster, 2002).
129. See "Nanotechnology in Crime Prevention and Detection," Institute of Nanotechnology, http://www.nano.org.uk/crime2.htm (accessed August 5, 2007).
130. Winston Chai, "Radio ID Chips May Track Banknotes," CNET News.com, May 23, 2003, http://news.com.com/2100-1019-1009155.html (accessed August 12, 2005).
131. The 2005 World Exposition website, http://www1.expo2005.or.jp/en/whatexpo/index.html (accessed August 3, 2005).
132. The material in this section is adapted from Nancy M. Ritter, "Preparing for the Future: Criminal Justice in 2040," *NIJ Journal*, No. 255 (November 2006).
133. Marc Mauer and Kate Epstein, eds., *To Build a Better Criminal Justice System: 25 Experts Envision the Next 25 Years of Reform* (Washington, DC: The Sentencing Project, 2012).

List of Acronyms

ABA	American Bar Association
ACA	American Correctional Association
ACJS	Academy of Criminal Justice Sciences
ACLU	American Civil Liberties Union
ADA	Americans with Disabilities Act (1990)
ADAM	Arrestee Drug Abuse Monitoring
ADMAX	administrative maximum
AEDPA	Antiterrorism and Effective Death Penalty Act (1996)
AFDA	Association of Federal Defense Attorneys
AFIS	automated fingerprint identification system
AI	artificial intelligence
AIDS	acquired immunodeficiency syndrome
AIMS	adult internal management system
AJA	American Jail Association
ALI	American Law Institute
AOUSC	Administrative Office of the United States Courts
APIS	Advance Passenger Information System
APPA	American Probation and Parole Association
AR	augmented reality
ASC	American Society of Criminology
ASIS	ASIS International (formerly the American Society for Industrial Security)
ASLET	American Society for Law Enforcement Training
ATF	Bureau of Alcohol, Tobacco, Firearms and Explosives
AWDWWITK	assault with a deadly weapon with intent to kill
BJA	Bureau of Justice Assistance
BJS	Bureau of Justice Statistics
BOP	Bureau of Prisons
BSEBP	British Society of Evidence-Based Policing
BTS	Border and Transportation Security
BWS	battered women's syndrome
CAD	computer-assisted dispatch
CAFA	Class Action Fairness Act
CALEA	Commission on Accreditation for Law Enforcement Agencies
CAN-SPAM	Controlling the Assault of Non-Solicited Pornography and Marketing
CAPS	Chicago's Alternative Policing Strategy
CAT	computer-aided transcription
CBT	computer-based training
CCA	Corrections Corporation of America
CCE	Continuing Criminal Enterprise (statute) (1970)
CCIPS	Computer Crime and Intellectual Property Section
CDA	Communications Decency Act (1996)
CDC	Centers for Disease Control and Prevention
CFAA	Computer Fraud and Abuse Act (1986)
CFR	Council on Foreign Relations
CIA	Central Intelligence Agency
CIAO	Critical Infrastructure Assurance Office
CJA	Criminal Justice Act (England)
CJIS	Criminal Justice Information Services (FBI)
CLET	Certified Law Enforcement Trainer
CMEA	Combat Methamphetamine Epidemic Act (2005)
CODIS	Combined DNA Index System (FBI)
COPS	Community Oriented Policing Services
CPO	Certified Protection Officer
CPP	Certified Protection Professional
CPTED	crime prevention through environmental design
CRIPA	Civil Rights of Institutionalized Persons Act (1980)
CRIPP	Courts Regimented Intensive Probation Program (Texas)
CSA	Controlled Substances Act (1970)
CSC	Correctional Services Corporation
CZTS	Combat Zones That See
DARE	Drug Abuse Resistance Education
DARPA	Defense Advanced Research Projects Agency
DAWN	Drug Abuse Warning Network
DEA	Drug Enforcement Administration
DHS	Department of Homeland Security
DNA	deoxyribonucleic acid
DOJ	United States Department of Justice
DPIC	Death Penalty Information Center
DPRC	Drug Policy Research Center (RAND Corporation)
DUI	driving under the influence (of alcohol or drugs)
DWI	driving while intoxicated
EBP	evidence-based policing
ECPA	Electronic Communications Privacy Act (1986)
EPR	Emergency Preparedness and Response
Europol	European Police Office
FBI	Federal Bureau of Investigation
FCC	federal correctional complex
FCI	federal correctional institution
FDA	Food and Drug Administration
FINCEN	Financial Crimes Enforcement Network
FLETC	Federal Law Enforcement Training Center
FLIR	forward-looking infrared
FOP	Fraternal Order of Police
FPC	federal prison camp
FTCA	Federal Tort Claims Act
FTO	foreign terrorist organization
FWG	futures working group
GBL	gamma-butyrolactone
GBMI	guilty but mentally ill
GED	general equivalency diploma
GHB	gamma hydroxybutyric acid
HEUNI	European Institute for Crime Prevention and Control
HIDTA	high-intensity drug-trafficking area
HIFCA	high-intensity financial crimes area

HIV	human immunodeficiency virus
HRALEI	Human Rights and Law Enforcement Institute
HSP	Heroin Signature Program
IACP	International Association of Chiefs of Police
IAD	internal affairs division
IAFIS	Integrated Automated Fingerprint Identification System (FBI)
IAIP	Information Analysis and Infrastructure Protection
ICC	International Criminal Court
ICE	Bureau of Immigration and Customs Enforcement
IDRA	Insanity Defense Reform Act (1984)
ILC	International Law Commission
ILEA	International Law Enforcement Academy
ILP	intelligence-led policing
INCB	International Narcotics Control Board
Interpol	International Criminal Police Organization
IPES	International Police Executive Symposium
IPS	intensive probation supervision
IRTPA	Intelligence Reform and Terrorism Prevention Act (2004)
ISC	International Society for Criminology
IVS	International Victim Survey (UN)
JIC	Justice Information Center
JJDP	Juvenile Justice and Delinquency Prevention [Act] (1974)
JTTF	Joint Terrorism Task Force
JUST	Judgment under Stress Training
JUSTNET	Justice Technology Information Network
LAPD	Los Angeles Police Department
LASD	Los Angeles County Sheriff's Department
LEAA	Law Enforcement Assistance Administration
LEAP	law enforcement availability pay
M-19	19th of April Movement
MADD	Mothers Against Drunk Driving
MATRIX	Multistate Anti-Terrorism Information Exchange
MCFP	medical center for federal prisoners
MDC	metropolitan detention center
MPC	Model Penal Code
MROP	Mentally Retarded Offender Program (Texas)
MTF	Monitoring the Future (survey)
NAACP	National Association for the Advancement of Colored People
NACDL	National Association of Criminal Defense Lawyers
NADCP	National Association of Drug Court Professionals
NADDIS	Narcotics and Dangerous Drugs Information System
NCAVC	National Center for the Analysis of Violent Crime (FBI)
NCCD	National Council on Crime and Delinquency
NCCS	National Computer Crime Squad (FBI)
NCEA	National Center on Elder Abuse
NCIC	National Crime Information Center (FBI)
NCISP	National Criminal Intelligence Sharing Plan
NCJRS	National Criminal Justice Reference Service
NCSC	National Center for State Courts
NCTC	National Counterterrorism Center
NCVC	National Center for Victims of Crime
NCVS	National Crime Victimization Survey
NCWP	National Center for Women and Policing
NDAA	National District Attorneys Association
NDIC	National Drug Intelligence Center
NDIS	National DNA Index System (FBI)
NETA	No Electronic Theft Act (1997)
NGCRC	National Gang Crime Research Center
NIBRS	National Incident-Based Reporting System (FBI)
NIDA	National Institute on Drug Abuse
NIJ	National Institute of Justice
NIPC	National Infrastructure Protection Center
NISMART	National Incidence Studies of Missing, Abducted, Runaway, and Thrownaway Children
NLADA	National Legal Aid and Defender Association
NLECTC	National Law Enforcement and Corrections Technology Center
NLETS	International Justice and Public Safety Information Sharing Network
NNICC	National Narcotics Intelligence Consumers Committee
NOBLE	National Organization of Black Law Enforcement Executives
NRA	National Rifle Association
NSA	National Security Agency
NSA	National Sheriffs' Association
NSDUH	National Survey on Drug Use and Health
NVAWS	National Violence against Women Survey
NW3C	National White Collar Crime Center
NYGC	National Youth Gang Center
NYPD	New York City Police Department
ODCCP	Office for Drug Control and Crime Prevention (UN)
OICJ	Office of International Criminal Justice
OIG	Office of the Inspector General (DOJ)
OJARS	Office of Justice Assistance, Research, and Statistics
OJJDP	Office of Juvenile Justice and Delinquency Prevention
ONDCP	Office of National Drug Control Policy
PCIPB	President's Critical Infrastructure Protection Board
PCP	phencyclidine
PCR	police–community relations
PDS	podular/direct supervision
PERF	Police Executive Research Forum
PFI	Police Futurists International
PHDCN	Project on Human Development in Chicago Neighborhoods
PLRA	Prison Litigation Reform Act (1996)
PORAC	Peace Officers Research Association of California
POST	peace officer standards and training
PREA	Prison Rape Elimination Act (2003)
PSI	presentence investigation
RFID	radio-frequency identification

RICO	Racketeer Influenced and Corrupt Organizations (statute) (1970)
RID	Remove Intoxicated Drivers
RISE	Reintegrative Shaming Experiments (Australian Institute of Criminology)
RJC	real justice conferencing (Pennsylvania)
RLUIPA	Religious Land Use and Institutionalized Persons Act (2000)
ROR	release on recognizance
RTTF	Regional Terrorism Task Force
RVIS	Remote Video Inspection System
SAMHSA	Substance Abuse and Mental Health Services Administration
SARA	scanning, analysis, response, and assessment
SARS	severe acute respiratory syndrome
SBI	State Bureau of Investigation
SCU	Street Crimes Unit
SEARCH	National Consortium for Justice Information and Statistics
SIIA	Software and Information Industry Association
SLATT	State and Local Anti-Terrorism Training Program
STG	security threat group
SVORI	Serious and Violent Offender Reentry Initiative
SWAT	special weapons and tactics
TFJJR	Task Force on Juvenile Justice Reform
TIA	Total Information Awareness
TIP	trafficking in persons
TIVU	Terrorism and International Victims Unit (Office for Victims of Crime)
TVPA	Trafficking Victims Protection Act (2000)
TVPRA	Trafficking Victims Protection Reauthorization Act (2003)
TWGECSI	Technical Working Group for Electronic Crime Scene Investigation
TWGEDE	Technical Working Group for the Examination of Digital Evidence
U.S.C.	United States Code
UAV	unmanned aerial vehicle
UCBE	unsolicited commercial bulk e-mail
UCR	Uniform Crime Reports
UN	United Nations
UNCJIN	United Nations Crime and Justice Information Network
UNICRI	United Nations Interregional Crime and Justice Research Institute
USCG	United States Coast Guard
USCIS	United States Citizenship and Immigration Services
USNCB	United States National Central Bureau (Interpol)
USP	United States penitentiary
USSC	United States Sentencing Commission
VAWA	Violence against Women Act (1994)
ViCAP	Violent Criminal Apprehension Program (FBI)
VOCA	Victims of Crime Act (1984)
VWPA	Victim and Witness Protection Act (1982)
WJIN	World Justice Information Network
WMD	weapon of mass destruction

Glossary

The 18 chapters of *Criminal Justice Today* contain hundreds of terms commonly used in the field of criminal justice. This glossary contains many more. The terms in this glossary are explained whenever possible according to definitions provided by the Bureau of Justice Statistics under a mandate of the Justice System Improvement Act. That mandate was to create a consistent terminology set for use by criminal justice students, practitioners, and planners. It found its most complete expression in the *Dictionary of Criminal Justice Data Terminology*,[1] the second edition of which provides many of our definitions. Others (especially those in Chapter 2) are derived from the Uniform Crime Reporting (UCR) Program of the Federal Bureau of Investigation (FBI) and are taken from the most recent edition of the agency's *Uniform Crime Reporting Handbook*.[2]

Standardization of terminology is important because American criminal justice agencies, justice practitioners, and involved citizens now routinely communicate between and among themselves, often over considerable distances, about the criminal justice system and about justice-related issues. For communications to be meaningful and efficient, a shared terminology is necessary. Standardization, however desirable, is not easy to achieve—sometimes because of legal and technical distinctions between jurisdictions or because of variations in customary usage. In the words of the Bureau of Justice Statistics, "It is not possible to construct a single national standard criminal justice data terminology where every term always means the same thing in all of its appearances. However, it is possible and necessary to standardize the language that represents basic categorical distinctions."[3] Although this glossary should be especially valuable to the student who will one day work in the criminal justice system, it should also prove beneficial to anyone seeking a greater insight into that system.

1983 lawsuit A civil suit brought under Title 42, Section 1983, of the U.S. Code against anyone who denies others their constitutional right to life, liberty, or property without due process of law.

abused child A child who has been physically, sexually, or mentally abused. Most states also consider a child who is forced into delinquent activity by a parent or guardian to be abused.

acquittal The judgment of a court, based on a verdict of a jury or a judicial officer, that the defendant is not guilty of the offense or offenses for which he or she was tried.

actus reus An act in violation of the law. Also, a guilty act.

adjudication The process by which a court arrives at a decision regarding a case. Also, the resultant decision.

adjudicatory hearing The fact-finding process by which the juvenile court determines whether there is sufficient evidence to sustain the allegations in a petition.

ADMAX Administrative maximum. The term is used by the federal government to denote ultra-high-security prisons.

administration of justice The performance of any of the following activities: detection, apprehension, detention, pretrial release, post-trial release, prosecution, adjudication, correctional supervision, or rehabilitation of accused persons or criminal offenders.[4]

admission In corrections, the entry of an offender into the legal jurisdiction of a correctional agency or into the physical custody of a correctional facility.

adult A person who is within the original jurisdiction of a criminal court, rather than a juvenile court, because his or her age at the time of an alleged criminal act was above a statutorily specified limit.

adversarial system The two-sided structure under which American criminal trial courts operate. The adversarial system pits the prosecution against the defense. In theory, justice is done when the most effective adversary is able to convince the judge or jury that his or her perspective on the case is the correct one.

aftercare In juvenile justice usage, the status or program membership of a juvenile who has been committed to a treatment or confinement facility, conditionally released from the facility, and placed in a supervisory or treatment program.

aggravated assault The unlawful, intentional inflicting, or attempted or threatened inflicting, of serious injury upon the person of another. Although *aggravated assault* and *simple assault* are standard terms for reporting purposes, most state penal codes use labels like *first-degree* and *second-degree assault* to make such distinctions.

aggravating circumstances Circumstances relating to the commission of a crime that make it more grave than the average instance of that crime. See also **mitigating circumstances**.

alias Any name used for an official purpose that is different from a person's legal name.

alibi A statement or contention by an individual charged with a crime that he or she was so distant when the crime was committed, or so engaged in other provable activities, that his or her participation in the commission of that crime was impossible.

alter ego rule In some jurisdictions, a rule of law that holds that a person can defend a third party only under circumstances and only to the degree that the third party could legally act on his or her own behalf.

alternative sanctions See **intermediate sanctions**.

alternative sentencing The use of court-ordered community service, home detention, day reporting, drug treatment, psychological counseling, victim–offender programming, or intensive supervision in lieu of other, more traditional sanctions, such as imprisonment and fines.

anomie A socially pervasive condition of normlessness. Also, a disjunction between approved goals and means.

anticipatory warrant A search warrant issued on the basis of probable cause to believe that evidence of a crime, although not presently at the place described, will likely be there when the warrant is executed.

Antiterrorism Act See **USA PATRIOT Act.**

appeal Generally, the request that a court with appellate jurisdiction review the judgment, decision, or order of a lower court and set it aside (reverse it) or modify it.

appearance (court) The act of coming into a court and submitting to its authority.

appellant The person who contests the correctness of a court order, judgment, or other decision and who seeks review and relief in a court having appellate jurisdiction. Also, the person on whose behalf this is done.

appellate court A court whose primary function is to review the judgments of other courts and of administrative agencies.

appellate jurisdiction The lawful authority of a court to review a decision made by a lower court.

arraignment Strictly, the hearing before a court having jurisdiction in a criminal case in which the identity of the defendant is established, the defendant is informed of the charge and of his or her rights, and the defendant is required to enter a plea. Also, in some usages, any appearance in criminal court before trial.

arrest The act of taking an adult or juvenile into physical custody by authority of law for the purpose of charging the person with a criminal offense, a delinquent act, or a status offense, terminating with the recording of a specific offense. Technically, an arrest occurs whenever a law enforcement officer curtails a person's freedom to leave.

arrest (UCR/NIBRS) Each separate instance in which a person is taken into physical custody or is notified or cited by a law enforcement officer or agency, except those incidents relating to minor traffic violations.

arrest rate The number of arrests reported for each unit of population.

arrest warrant A document issued by a judicial officer that directs a law enforcement officer to arrest an identified person who has been accused of a specific offense.

arson (UCR/NIBRS) Any willful or malicious burning or attempting to burn, with or without intent to defraud, a dwelling house, public building, motor vehicle or aircraft, personal property of another, and so on. Some instances of arson result from malicious mischief, some involve attempts to claim insurance money, and some are committed in an effort to disguise other crimes, such as murder, burglary, or larceny.

Ashurst-Sumners Act Federal legislation of 1935 that effectively ended the industrial prison era by restricting interstate commerce in prison-made goods.

assault (UCR/NIBRS) An unlawful attack by one person upon another. Historically, *assault* meant only the attempt to inflict injury on another person; a completed act constituted the separate offense of battery. Under modern statistical usage, however, attempted and completed acts are grouped together under the generic term *assault*.

assault on a law enforcement officer A simple or aggravated assault in which the victim is a law enforcement officer engaged in the performance of his or her duties.

atavism A condition characterized by the existence of features thought to be common in earlier stages of human evolution.

attendant circumstances The facts surrounding an event.

attorney A person trained in the law, admitted to practice before the bar of a given jurisdiction, and authorized to advise, represent, and act for others in legal proceedings. Also called *lawyer; legal counsel*.

Auburn system A form of imprisonment developed in New York State around 1820 that depended on mass prisons, where prisoners were held in congregate fashion and required to remain silent. This style of imprisonment was a primary competitor with the Pennsylvania system.

augmented reality (AR) The real-time and accurate overlay of digital information on a user's real-world experience, through visual, aural, and/or tactile interfaces.[5] The computer readouts superimposed on the visual fields of the fictional cyborgs in the *RoboCop* and *Terminator* movies provide an example.

backlog (court) The number of cases awaiting disposition in a court that exceeds the court's capacity for disposing of them within the period of time considered appropriate.

bail The money or property pledged to the court or actually deposited with the court to effect the release of a person from legal custody.

bail bond A document guaranteeing the appearance of a defendant in court as required and recording the pledge of money or property to be paid to the court if he or she does not appear, which is signed by the person to be released and anyone else acting on his or her behalf.

bail bond agent A person, usually licensed, whose business it is to effect release on bail for people charged with offenses and held in custody, by pledging to pay a sum of money if the defendant fails to appear in court as required.

bailiff The court officer whose duties are to keep order in the courtroom and to maintain physical custody of the jury.

bail revocation A court decision withdrawing the status of release on bail that was previously conferred on a defendant.

balancing test A principle, developed by the courts and applied to the corrections arena by *Pell* v. *Procunier* (1974), that attempts to weigh the rights of an individual, as guaranteed by the Constitution, against the authority of states to make laws or to otherwise restrict a person's freedom in order to protect the state's interests and its citizens.

ballistics The analysis of firearms, ammunition, projectiles, bombs, and explosives.

battered women's syndrome (BWS) 1. A series of common characteristics that appear in women who are abused physically and psychologically over an extended period of time by the dominant male figure in their lives. 2. A pattern of psychological symptoms that develops after somebody has lived in a battering relationship. 3. A pattern of responses and perceptions presumed to be characteristic of women who have been subjected to continuous physical abuse by their mates.[6]

behavioral conditioning A psychological principle that holds that the frequency of any behavior can be increased or decreased through reward, punishment, and association with other stimuli.

bench warrant A document issued by a court directing that a law enforcement officer bring a specified person before the court. A bench warrant is usually issued for a person who has failed to obey a court order or a notice to appear.

bias crime See **hate crime**.

Bill of Rights The popular name given to the first ten amendments to the U.S. Constitution, which are considered especially important in the processing of criminal defendants.

bind over To require by judicial authority that a person promise to appear for trial, appear in court as a witness, or keep the peace. Also, the decision by a court of limited jurisdiction requiring that a person charged with a felony appear for trial on that charge in a court of general jurisdiction, as the result of a finding of probable cause at a preliminary hearing held in the court of limited jurisdiction.

biocrime A criminal offense perpetrated through the use of biologically active substances, including chemicals and toxins, disease-causing organisms, altered genetic material, and organic tissues and organs. Biocrimes unlawfully affect the metabolic, biochemical, genetic, physiological, or anatomical status of living organisms.

Biological School A perspective on criminological thought that holds that criminal behavior has a physiological basis.

biological weapon A biological agent used to threaten human life (for example, anthrax, smallpox, or any infectious disease).[7]

biometrics The science of recognizing people by physical characteristics and personal traits.

biosocial criminology A theoretical perspective that sees the interaction between biology and the physical and social environments as key to understanding human behavior, including criminality.

bioterrorism The intentional or threatened use of viruses, bacteria, fungi, or toxins from living organisms to produce death or disease in humans, animals, or plants.[8]

***Bivens* action** A civil suit, based on the case of *Bivens* v. *Six Unknown Federal Agents*, brought against federal government officials for denying the constitutional rights of others.

blended sentence A juvenile court disposition that imposes both a juvenile sanction and an adult criminal sentence upon an adjudicated delinquent. The adult sentence is suspended if the juvenile offender successfully completes the term of the juvenile disposition and refrains from committing any new offense.[9]

bobbies The popular British name given to members of Sir Robert (Bob) Peel's Metropolitan Police Force.

booking A law enforcement or correctional administrative process officially recording an entry into detention after arrest and identifying the person, the place, the time, the reason for the arrest, and the arresting authority.

Bow Street Runners An early English police unit formed under the leadership of Henry Fielding, magistrate of the Bow Street region of London.

broken windows theory A perspective on crime causation that holds that the physical deterioration of an area leads to higher crime rates and an increased concern for personal safety among residents.

Bureau of Justice Statistics (BJS) A U.S. Department of Justice agency responsible for the collection of criminal justice data, including the annual National Crime Victimization Survey.

burglary By the narrowest and oldest definition, the trespassory breaking and entering of the dwelling house of another in the nighttime with the intent to commit a felony.

burglary (UCR/NIBRS) The unlawful entry of a structure to commit a felony or a theft (excludes tents, trailers, and other mobile units used for recreational purposes). For the UCR/NIBRS Program, the crime of burglary can be reported if (1) an unlawful entry of an unlocked structure has occurred, (2) a breaking and entering (of a secured structure) has taken place, or (3) a burglary has been attempted.

capacity (legal) The legal ability of a person to commit a criminal act. Also, the mental and physical ability to act with purpose and to be aware of the certain, probable, or possible results of one's conduct.

capacity (prison) See **prison capacity**.

capital offense A criminal offense punishable by death.

capital punishment The death penalty. Capital punishment is the most extreme of all sentencing options.

career criminal In prosecutorial and law enforcement usage, a person who has a past record of multiple arrests or convictions for serious crimes or who has an unusually large number of arrests or convictions for crimes of varying degrees of seriousness. Also called *professional criminal.*

carnal knowledge Sexual intercourse, coitus, sexual copulation. Carnal knowledge is accomplished "if there is the slightest penetration of the sexual organ of the female by the sexual organ of the male."[10]

case law The body of judicial precedent, historically built on legal reasoning and past interpretations of statutory laws, that serves as a guide to decision making, especially in the courts.

caseload The number of probation or parole clients assigned to one probation or parole officer for supervision.

caseload (corrections) The total number of clients registered with a correctional agency or agent on a given date or during a specified time period, often divided into active supervisory cases and inactive cases, thus distinguishing between clients with whom contact is regular and those with whom it is not.

caseload (court) The number of cases requiring judicial action at a certain time. Also, the number of cases acted on in a given court during a given period.

certiorari See **writ of *certiorari***.

chain of command The unbroken line of authority that extends through all levels of an organization, from the highest to the lowest.

change of venue The movement of a trial or lawsuit from one jurisdiction to another or from one location to another within the same jurisdiction. A change of venue may be made in a criminal case to ensure that the defendant receives a fair trial.

charge An allegation that a specified person has committed a specific offense, recorded in a functional document such as a record of an arrest, a complaint, an information or indictment, or a judgment of conviction. Also called *count.*

Chicago School A sociological approach that emphasizes demographics (the characteristics of population groups) and geographics (the mapped location of such groups relative to one another) and that sees the social disorganization that characterizes delinquency areas as a major cause of criminality and victimization.

child abuse The illegal physical, emotional, or sexual mistreatment of a child by his or her parent or guardian.

child neglect The illegal failure by a parent or guardian to provide proper nourishment or care to a child.

chromosomes Bundles of genes.

circumstantial evidence Evidence that requires interpretation or that requires a judge or jury to reach a conclusion based on what the evidence indicates. From the proximity of the defendant to a smoking gun, for example, the jury might conclude that he or she pulled the trigger.

citation (to appear) A written order issued by a law enforcement officer directing an alleged offender to appear in a specific court at a specified time to answer a criminal charge and not permitting forfeit of bail as an alternative to court appearance.

citizen's arrest The taking of a person into physical custody by a witness to a crime other than a law enforcement officer for the purpose of delivering him or her to the physical custody of a law enforcement officer or agency.

civil death The legal status of prisoners in some jurisdictions who are denied the opportunity to vote, hold public office, marry, or enter into contracts by virtue of their status as incarcerated felons. Although civil death is primarily of historical interest, some jurisdictions still limit the contractual opportunities available to inmates.

civil justice The civil law, the law of civil procedure, and the array of procedures and activities having to do with private rights and remedies sought by civil action. Civil justice cannot be separated from social justice because the justice enacted in our nation's civil courts reflects basic American understandings of right and wrong.

civil law The branch of modern law that governs relationships between parties.

civil liability Potential responsibility for payment of damages or other court-ordered enforcement as a result of a ruling in a lawsuit. Civil liability is not the same as criminal liability, which means "open to punishment for a crime."[11]

class-action lawsuit A lawsuit filed by one or more people on behalf of themselves and a larger group of people "who are similarly situated."[12]

Classical School An eighteenth-century approach to crime causation and criminal responsibility that grew out of the Enlightenment and that emphasized the role of free will and reasonable punishments. Classical thinkers believed that punishment, if it is to be an effective deterrent, has to outweigh the potential pleasure derived from criminal behavior.

classification system A system used by prison administrators to assign inmates to custody levels based on offense history, assessed dangerousness, perceived risk of escape, and other factors.

clearance (UCR/NIBRS) The event in which a known occurrence of a Part I offense is followed by an arrest or another decision that indicates that the crime has been solved.

clearance rate A traditional measure of investigative effectiveness that compares the number of crimes reported or discovered to the number of crimes solved through arrest or other means (such as the death of the suspect).

clemency An executive or legislative action in which the severity of punishment of a single person or a group of people is reduced, the punishment is stopped, or the person or group is exempted from prosecution for certain actions.

closing argument An oral summation of a case presented to a judge, or to a judge and jury, by the prosecution or by the defense in a criminal trial.

club drug A synthetic psychoactive substance often found at nightclubs, bars, "raves," and dance parties. Club drugs include MDMA (Ecstasy), ketamine, methamphetamine (meth), GBL, PCP, GHB, and Rohypnol.

codification The act or process of rendering laws in written form.

cohort A group of individuals sharing similarities of age, place of birth, and residence. Cohort analysis is a social science technique that tracks cohorts over time to identify the unique and observable behavioral traits that characterize them.

comes stabuli A nonuniformed mounted law enforcement officer of medieval England. Early police forces were small and relatively unorganized but made effective use of local resources in the formation of posses, the pursuit of offenders, and the like.

commitment The action of a judicial officer in ordering that a person subject to judicial proceedings be placed in a particular kind of confinement or residential facility for a specific reason authorized by law. Also, the result of the action—that is, the admission to the facility.

common law Law originating from usage and custom rather than from written statutes. The term refers to an unwritten body of judicial opinion, originally developed by English courts, that is based on nonstatutory customs, traditions, and precedents that help guide judicial decision making.

community-based corrections See **community corrections**.

community corrections The use of a variety of officially ordered program-based sanctions that permit convicted offenders to remain in the community under conditional supervision as an alternative to an active prison sentence. Also called *community-based corrections*.

community court A low-level court that focuses on quality-of-life crimes that erode a neighborhood's morale. Community courts emphasize problem solving rather than punishment and build on restorative principles like community service and restitution.

community policing "A collaborative effort between the police and the community that identifies problems of crime and disorder and involves all elements of the community in the search for solutions to these problems."[13]

community service A sentencing alternative that requires offenders to spend at least part of their time working for a community agency.

comparative criminologist One who studies crime and criminal justice on a cross-national level.

compelling interest A legal concept that provides a basis for suspicionless searches when public safety is at stake. (Urinalysis tests of train engineers are an example.) It is the concept on which the U.S. Supreme Court cases of *Skinner* v. *Railway Labor Executives' Association* (1989) and *National Treasury Employees Union* v. *Von Raab* (1989) turned. In those cases, the Court held that public safety may sometimes provide a sufficiently compelling interest to justify limiting an individual's right to privacy.

compensatory damages Damages recovered in payment for an actual injury or economic loss.

competent to stand trial A finding by a court that the defendant has sufficient present ability to consult with his or her attorney with a reasonable degree of rational understanding and that the defendant has a rational as well as factual understanding of the proceedings against him or her.

complaint Generally, any accusation that a person has committed an offense, received by or originating from a law enforcement or prosecutorial agency or received by a court. Also, in judicial process usage, a formal document submitted to the court by a prosecutor, law enforcement officer, or other person, alleging that a specified person has committed a specific offense and requesting prosecution.

CompStat A crime-analysis and police-management process, built on crime mapping, that was developed by the New York City Police Department in the mid-1990s.

computer crime See **cybercrime**.

computer virus A computer program designed to secretly invade systems and either modify the way in which they operate or alter the information they store. Viruses are destructive software programs that may effectively vandalize computers of all types and sizes.

concurrence The coexistence of (1) an act in violation of the law and (2) a culpable mental state.

concurrent sentence One of two or more sentences imposed at the same time, after conviction for more than one offense, and served at the same time. Also, a new sentence for a new conviction, imposed upon a person already under sentence for a previous offense, served at the same time as the previous sentence.

concurring opinion An opinion written by a judge who agrees with the conclusion reached by the majority of judges hearing a case but whose reasons for reaching that conclusion differ. Concurring opinions, which typically stem from an appellate review, are written to identify issues of precedent, logic, or emphasis that are important to the concurring judge but that were not identified by the court's majority opinion.

conditional release The release by executive decision of a prisoner from a federal or state correctional facility who has not served his or her full sentence and whose freedom is contingent on obeying specified rules of behavior.

conditions of parole (probation) The general and special limits imposed on an offender who is released on parole (or probation). General conditions tend to be fixed by state statute, whereas special conditions are mandated by the sentencing authority (court or board) and take into consideration the background of the offender and the circumstances of the offense.

confinement In corrections, the physical restriction of a person to a clearly defined area from which he or she is lawfully forbidden to depart and from which departure is usually constrained by architectural barriers, guards or other custodians, or both.

conflict model A criminal justice perspective that assumes that the system's components function primarily to serve their own interests. According to this theoretical framework, justice is more a product of conflicts among agencies within the system than it is the result of cooperation among component agencies.

conflict perspective A theoretical approach that holds that crime is the natural consequence of economic and other social inequities. Conflict theorists highlight the stresses that arise among and within social groups as they compete with one another for resources and for survival. The social forces that result are viewed as major determinants of group and individual behavior, including crime.

consecutive sentence One of two or more sentences imposed at the same time, after conviction for more than one offense, and served in sequence with the other sentence. Also, a new sentence for a new conviction, imposed upon a person already under sentence for a previous offense, which is added to the previous sentence, thus increasing the maximum time the offender may be confined or under supervision.

consensus model A criminal justice perspective that assumes that the system's components work together harmoniously to achieve the social product we call *justice*.

constitutive criminology The study of the process by which human beings create an ideology of crime that sustains the notion of crime as a concrete reality.

containment The aspects of the social bond and of the personality that act to prevent individuals from committing crimes and engaging in deviance.

contempt of court Intentionally obstructing a court in the administration of justice, acting in a way calculated to lessen the court's authority or dignity, or failing to obey the court's lawful orders.

controlled substance A specifically defined bioactive or psychoactive chemical substance proscribed by law.

Controlled Substances Act (CSA) Title II of the Comprehensive Drug Abuse Prevention and Control Act of 1970, which established schedules classifying psychoactive drugs according to their degree of psychoactivity.

conviction The judgment of a court, based on the verdict of a jury or judicial officer or on the guilty plea or *nolo contendere* plea of the defendant, that the defendant is guilty of the offense with which he or she has been charged.

corporate crime A violation of a criminal statute by a corporate entity or by its executives, employees, or agents acting on behalf of and for the benefit of the corporation, partnership, or other form of business entity.[14]

corpus delicti The facts that show that a crime has occurred. The term literally means "the body of the crime."

correctional agency A federal, state, or local criminal or juvenile justice agency, under a single administrative authority, whose principal functions are the intake screening, supervision, custody, confinement, treatment, or presentencing or predisposition investigation of alleged or adjudicated adult offenders, youthful offenders, delinquents, or status offenders.

corrections A generic term that includes all government agencies, facilities, programs, procedures, personnel, and techniques concerned with the intake, custody, confinement, supervision, treatment, and presentencing and predisposition investigation of alleged or adjudicated adult offenders, youthful offenders, delinquents, and status offenders.

corruption See **police corruption**.

Cosa Nostra A secret criminal organization of Sicilian origin. Also called *Mafia*.

counsel (legal) See **attorney**.

count (offense) See **charge**.

court An agency or unit of the judicial branch of government, authorized or established by statute or constitution and consisting of one or more judicial officers, which has the authority to decide cases, controversies in law, and disputed matters of fact brought before it.

court calendar The court schedule; the list of events comprising the daily or weekly work of a court, including the assignment of the time and place for each hearing or other item of business or the list of matters that will be taken up in a given court term. Also called *docket*.

court clerk An elected or appointed court officer responsible for maintaining the written records of the court and for supervising or performing the clerical tasks necessary for conducting judicial business. Also, any employee of a court whose principal duties are to assist the court clerk in performing the clerical tasks necessary for conducting judicial business.

court disposition 1. For statistical reporting purposes, generally, the judicial decision terminating proceedings in a case before judgment is reached. 2. The judgment. 3. The outcome of judicial proceedings and the manner in which the outcome was arrived at.

court-martial A military court convened by senior commanders under the authority of the Uniform Code of Military Justice for the purpose of trying a member of the armed forces accused of a violation of the code.

court of last resort The court authorized by law to hear the final appeal on a matter.

court of record A court in which a complete and permanent record of all proceedings or specified types of proceedings is kept.

court order A mandate, command, or direction issued by a judicial officer in the exercise of his or her judicial authority.

court probation A criminal court requirement that an offender fulfill specified conditions of behavior in lieu of a sentence to confinement, but without assignment to a probation agency's supervisory caseload.

court reporter A person present during judicial proceedings who records all testimony and other oral statements made during the proceedings.

courtroom work group The professional courtroom actors, including judges, prosecuting attorneys, defense attorneys, public defenders, and others who earn a living serving the court.

credit card fraud The use or attempted use of a credit card to obtain goods or services with the intent to avoid payment.

crime Conduct in violation of the criminal laws of a state, the federal government, or a local jurisdiction, for which there is no legally acceptable justification or excuse.

crime-control model A criminal justice perspective that emphasizes the efficient arrest and conviction of criminal offenders.

Crime Index A now defunct but once inclusive measure of the UCR Program's violent and property crime categories, or what are called *Part I offenses*. The Crime Index, long featured in the FBI's publication *Crime in the United States*, was discontinued in 2004. The index had been intended as a tool for geographic (state-to-state) and historical (year-to-year) comparisons via the use of crime rates (the number of crimes per unit of population). However, criticism that the index was misleading arose after researchers found that the largest of the index's crime categories, larceny-theft, carried undue weight and led to an underappreciation of changes in the rates of more violent and serious crimes.

crime prevention The anticipation, recognition, and appraisal of a crime risk and the initiation of action to eliminate or reduce it.

crime rate The number of offenses reported for each unit of population.

crime scene The physical area in which a crime is thought to have occurred and in which evidence of the crime is thought to reside.

crime scene investigator An expert trained in the use of forensics techniques, such as gathering DNA evidence, collecting fingerprints, photographing the scene, sketching, and interviewing witnesses.

crime typology A classification of crimes along a particular dimension, such as legal categories, offender motivation, victim behavior, or the characteristics of individual offenders.

criminal homicide (UCR/NIBRS) The act of causing the death of another person without legal justification or excuse.

criminal incident In National Crime Victimization Survey terminology, a criminal event involving one or more victims and one or more offenders.

criminal intelligence Information compiled, analyzed, or disseminated in an effort to anticipate, prevent, or monitor criminal activity.[15]

criminal investigation "The process of discovering, collecting, preparing, identifying, and presenting evidence to determine *what happened and who is responsible*"[16] when a crime has occurred.

criminal justice In the strictest sense, the criminal (penal) law, the law of criminal procedure, and the array of procedures and activities having to do with the enforcement of this body of law. Criminal justice cannot be separated from social justice because the justice enacted in our nation's criminal courts reflects basic American understandings of right and wrong.

criminal justice system The aggregate of all operating and administrative or technical support agencies that perform criminal justice functions. The basic divisions of the operational aspects of criminal justice are law enforcement, courts, and corrections.

criminal law The body of rules and regulations that define and specify the nature of and punishments for offenses of a public nature or for wrongs committed against the state or society. Also called *penal law*.

criminal negligence Behavior in which a person fails to reasonably perceive substantial and unjustifiable risks of dangerous consequences.

criminalist A police crime scene analyst or laboratory worker versed in criminalistics.

criminalistics The use of technology in the service of criminal investigation; the application of scientific techniques to the detection and evaluation of criminal evidence.

criminal proceedings The regular and orderly steps, as directed or authorized by statute or a court of law, taken to determine whether an adult accused of a crime is guilty or not guilty.

criminology The scientific study of the causes and prevention of crime and the rehabilitation and punishment of offenders.

cruel and unusual punishment Punishment involving torture or a lingering death or the infliction of unnecessary and wanton pain.

culpability Blameworthiness; responsibility in some sense for an event or situation deserving of moral blame. Also, in Model Penal Code usage, a state of mind on the part of one who is committing an act that makes him or her potentially subject to prosecution for that act.

cultural defense A defense to a criminal charge in which the defendant's culture is taken into account in judging his or her culpability.

cultural pluralism See **multiculturalism**.

curtilage In legal usage, the area surrounding a residence that can reasonably be said to be a part of the residence for Fourth Amendment purposes.

custody The legal or physical control of a person or a thing. Also, the legal, supervisory, or physical responsibility for a person or a thing.

cybercrime Any crime perpetrated through the use of computer technology. Also, any violation of a federal or state cybercrime statute. Also called *computer crime*.

cyberstalking The use of the Internet, e-mail, and other electronic communication technologies to stalk another person.[17]

cyberterrorism A form of terrorism that makes use of high technology, especially computers and the Internet, in the planning and carrying out of terrorist attacks.

danger law A law intended to prevent the pretrial release of criminal defendants judged to represent a danger to others in the community.

dangerousness The likelihood that a given individual will later harm society or others. Dangerousness is often measured in terms of recidivism, or the likelihood that an individual will commit another crime within five years following arrest or release from confinement.

dark figure of crime Crime that is not reported to the police and that remains unknown to officials.

data encryption The encoding of computerized information.

date rape Unlawful forced sexual intercourse that occurs within the context of a dating relationship. Date rape, or acquaintance rape, is a subcategory of rape that is of special concern today.

Daubert standard A test of scientific acceptability applicable to the gathering of evidence in criminal cases.

deadly force Force likely to cause death or great bodily harm. Also, "the intentional use of a firearm or other instrument resulting in a high probability of death."[18]

deadly weapon An instrument that is designed to inflict serious bodily injury or death or that is capable of being used for such a purpose.

deconstructionist theory One of the emerging approaches that challenges existing criminological perspectives to debunk them and that works toward replacing them with concepts more applicable to the postmodern era.

decriminalization The redefinition of certain previously criminal behaviors into regulated activities that become "ticketable" rather than "arrestable."

defendant A person formally accused of an offense by the filing in court of a charging document.

defense (to a criminal charge) Evidence and arguments offered by a defendant and his or her attorney to show why the defendant should not be held liable for a criminal charge.

defense attorney See **defense counsel**.

defense counsel A licensed trial lawyer hired or appointed to conduct the legal defense of a person accused of a crime and to represent him or her before a court of law. Also called *defense attorney*.

defensible space theory The belief that an area's physical features may be modified and structured so as to reduce crime rates in that area and to lower the fear of victimization that residents experience.

deliberate indifference A wanton disregard by correctional personnel for the well-being of inmates. Deliberate indifference requires both actual knowledge that a harm is occurring and disregard of the risk of harm. A prison official may be held liable under the Eighth Amendment for acting with deliberate indifference to inmate health or safety only if he or she knows that inmates face a substantial risk of serious harm and disregards that risk by failing to take reasonable measures to abate it.

delinquency In the broadest usage, juvenile actions or conduct in violation of criminal law, juvenile status offenses, and other juvenile misbehavior.

delinquent A juvenile who has been adjudged by a judicial officer of a juvenile court to have committed a delinquent act.

delinquent act An act committed by a juvenile for which an adult could be prosecuted in a criminal court but for which a juvenile can be adjudicated in a juvenile court or prosecuted in a court having criminal jurisdiction if the juvenile court transfers jurisdiction. Generally, a felony- or misdemeanor-level offense in states employing those terms.

delinquent child A child who has engaged in activity that would be considered a crime if the child were an adult. The term *delinquent* is used to avoid the stigma associated with the term *criminal*.

dependent child A child who has no parents or whose parents are unable to care for him or her.

design capacity The number of inmates a prison was intended to hold when it was built or modified. Also called *bed capacity*.

detainee Usually, a person held in local short-term confinement while awaiting consideration for pretrial release or a first appearance for arraignment.

detention The legally authorized confinement of a person subject to criminal or juvenile court proceedings, until the point of commitment to a correctional facility or until release.

detention hearing In juvenile justice usage, a hearing by a judicial officer of a juvenile court to determine whether a juvenile is to be detained, is to continue to be detained, or is to be released while juvenile proceedings are pending.

determinate sentencing A model of criminal punishment in which an offender is given a fixed term of imprisonment that may be reduced by good time or gain time. Under the model, for example, all offenders convicted of the same degree of burglary would be sentenced to the same length of time behind bars. Also called *fixed sentencing*.

deterrence A goal of criminal sentencing that seeks to inhibit criminal behavior through the fear of punishment.

deviance A violation of social norms defining appropriate or proper behavior under a particular set of circumstances. Deviance often includes criminal acts. Also called *deviant behavior*.

digital criminal forensics The lawful seizure, acquisition, analysis, reporting, and safeguarding of data from digital devices that may contain information of evidentiary value to the trier of fact in criminal events.[19]

diminished capacity A defense based on claims of a mental condition that may be insufficient to exonerate the defendant of guilt but that may be relevant to specific mental elements of certain crimes or degrees of crime. Also called *diminished responsibility*.

direct evidence Evidence that, if believed, directly proves a fact. Eyewitness testimony and videotaped documentation account for the majority of all direct evidence heard in the criminal courtroom.

directed patrol A police-management strategy designed to increase the productivity of patrol officers through the scientific analysis and evaluation of patrol techniques.

discharge To release from confinement or supervision or to release from a legal status imposing an obligation upon the subject person.

discretion See **police discretion**.

discretionary release The release of an inmate from prison to supervision that is decided by a parole board or other authority.

disposition The action by a criminal or juvenile justice agency that signifies that a portion of the justice process is complete and that jurisdiction is terminated or transferred to another agency or that signifies that a decision has been reached on one aspect of a case and a different aspect comes under consideration, requiring a different kind of decision.

dispositional hearing The final stage in the processing of adjudicated juveniles in which a decision is made on the form of treatment or penalty that should be imposed on the child.

dispute-resolution center An informal hearing place designed to mediate interpersonal disputes without resorting to the more formal arrangements of a criminal trial court.

district attorney (DA) See **prosecutor**.

diversion The official suspension of criminal or juvenile proceedings against an alleged offender at any point after a recorded justice system intake, but before the entering of a judgment, and referral of that person to a treatment or care program administered by a nonjustice or private agency. Also, release without referral.

DNA profiling The use of biological residue, found at the scene of a crime, for genetic comparisons in aiding in the identification of criminal suspects.

docket See **court calendar**.

domestic terrorism The unlawful use of force or violence by an individual or a group that is based and operates entirely within the United States and its territories, acts without foreign direction, and directs its activities against elements of the U.S. government or population.[20]

double jeopardy A common law and constitutional prohibition against a second trial for the same offense.

drug Any chemical substance defined by social convention as bioactive or psychoactive.

drug abuse Illicit drug use that results in social, economic, psychological, or legal problems for the user.[21]

drug court A special state, county, or municipal court that offers first-time substance-abuse offenders judicially mandated and court-supervised treatment alternatives to prison.

drug czar The popular name for the head of the Office of National Drug Control Policy (ONDCP), a federal position that was created during the Reagan presidency to organize federal drug-fighting efforts.

drug-law violation The unlawful sale, purchase, distribution, manufacture, cultivation, transport, possession, or use of a controlled or prohibited drug. Also, the attempt to commit one of these acts.

drug trafficking Trading or dealing in controlled substances, including the transporting, storage, importing, exporting, or sale of a controlled substance.

due process A right guaranteed by the Fourth, Fifth, Sixth, and Fourteenth Amendments of the U.S. Constitution and generally understood, in legal contexts, to mean the due course of legal proceedings according to the rules and forms established for the protection of individual rights. In criminal proceedings, due process of law is generally understood to include the following basic elements: a law creating and defining the offense, an impartial tribunal having jurisdictional authority over the case, accusation in proper form, notice and opportunity to defend, trial according to established procedure, and discharge from all restraints or obligations unless convicted.

due process model A criminal justice perspective that emphasizes individual rights at all stages of justice system processing.

Electronic Communications Privacy Act (ECPA) A law passed by Congress in 1986 establishing the due process requirements that law enforcement officers must meet in order to legally intercept wire communications.

electronic evidence Information and data of investigative value that are stored in or transmitted by an electronic device.[22]

element (of a crime) In a specific crime, one of the essential features of that crime, as specified by law or statute.

embezzlement The misappropriation, or illegal disposal, of legally entrusted property by the person to whom it was entrusted, with the intent to defraud the legal owner or the intended beneficiary.

emergency search A search conducted by the police without a warrant, which is justified on the basis of some immediate and overriding need, such as public safety, the likely escape of a dangerous suspect, or the removal or destruction of evidence.

entrapment An improper or illegal inducement to crime by agents of law enforcement. Also, a defense that may be raised when such inducements have occurred.

equity A sentencing principle, based on concerns with social equality, that holds that similar crimes should be punished with the same degree of severity, regardless of the social or personal characteristics of the offenders.

espionage The "gathering, transmitting, or losing"[23] of information related to the national defense in such a manner that the information becomes available to enemies of the United States and may be used to their advantage.

ethnocentric Holding a belief in the superiority of one's own social or ethnic group and culture.

ethnocentrism The phenomenon of "culture-centeredness" by which one uses one's own culture as a benchmark against which to judge all other patterns of behavior.

European Police Office (Europol) The integrated police intelligence-gathering and intelligence-dissemination arm of the member nations of the European Union.

evidence Anything useful to a judge or jury in deciding the facts of a case. Evidence may take the form of witness testimony, written documents, videotapes, magnetic media, photographs, physical objects, and so on.

evidence-based policing (EBP) The use of the best available research on the outcomes of police work to implement guidelines and evaluate agencies, units, and officers.[24]

evidence-based practice Crime-fighting strategies that have been scientifically tested and are based on social science research.

ex post facto Latin for "after the fact." The Constitution prohibits the enactment of *ex post facto* laws, which make acts committed before the laws in question were passed punishable as crimes.

excessive force The application of an amount and/or frequency of force greater than that required to compel compliance from a willing or unwilling subject.[25]

exclusionary rule The understanding, based on U.S. Supreme Court precedent, that incriminating information must be seized according to constitutional specifications of due process or it will not be allowed as evidence in a criminal trial.

exculpatory evidence Any information having a tendency to clear a person of guilt or blame.

excuse A legal defense in which the defendant claims that some personal condition or circumstance at the time of the act was such that he or she should not be held accountable under the criminal law.

exemplary damages See **punitive damages**.

expert system Computer hardware and software that attempt to duplicate the decision-making processes used by skilled investigators in the analysis of evidence and in the recognition of patterns that such evidence might represent.

expert witness A person who has special knowledge and skills recognized by the court as relevant to the determination of guilt or innocence. Unlike lay witnesses, expert witnesses may express opinions or draw conclusions in their testimony.

extradition The surrender by one state or jurisdiction to another of an individual accused or convicted of an offense in the second state or jurisdiction.

federal court system The three-tiered structure of federal courts, comprising U.S. district courts, U.S. courts of appeal, and the U.S. Supreme Court.

federal law enforcement agency A U.S. government agency or office whose primary functional responsibility is to enforce federal criminal laws.

felony A criminal offense punishable by death or by incarceration in a prison facility for at least one year.

feminist criminology A developing intellectual approach that emphasizes gender issues in criminology.

filing The initiation of a criminal case by formal submission to the court of a charging document, alleging that a named person has committed a specified criminal offense.

fine The penalty imposed on a convicted person by a court, requiring that he or she pay a specified sum of money to the court.

first appearance An appearance before a magistrate during which the legality of the defendant's arrest is initially assessed and the defendant is informed of the charges on which he or she is being held. At this stage in the criminal justice process, bail may be set or pretrial release arranged. Also called *initial appearance*.

first plea See **initial plea**.

fixed sentencing See **determinate sentencing**.

fleeting-targets exception An exception to the exclusionary rule that permits law enforcement officers to search a motor vehicle based on probable cause and without a warrant. The fleeting-targets exception is predicated on the fact that vehicles can quickly leave the jurisdiction of a law enforcement agency.

force See **police use of force**.

forcible rape (UCR/NIBRS) The carnal knowledge of a person, forcibly and against his or her will. More specifically, penetration, no matter how slight, of the vagina or anus with any body part or object, or oral penetration by a sex organ of another person, without the consent of the victim. Statutory rape differs from forcible rape in that it generally involves nonforcible sexual intercourse with a minor. See also **carnal knowledge; rape**.

foreign terrorist organization (FTO) A foreign organization that engages in terrorist activity that threatens the security of U.S. nationals or the national security of the United States and that is so designated by the U.S. secretary of state.

forensic anthropology The use of anthropological principles and techniques in criminal investigation.

forensic entomology The study of insects to determine such matters as a person's time of death.

forfeiture The authorized seizure of money, negotiable instruments, securities, or other things of value. Under federal antidrug laws, judicial representatives are authorized to seize all cash, negotiable instruments, securities, or other things of value furnished or intended to be furnished by any person in exchange for a controlled substance, as well as all proceeds traceable to such an exchange. Also called *asset forfeiture*.

forgery The creation or alteration of a written or printed document, which if validly executed would constitute a record of a legally binding transaction, with the intent to defraud by affirming it to be the act of an unknowing second person. Also, the creation of an art object with intent to misrepresent the identity of the creator.

fraud An offense involving deceit or intentional misrepresentation of fact, with the intent of unlawfully depriving a person of his or her property or legal rights.

frivolous suit A lawsuit with no foundation in fact. Frivolous suits are generally brought by lawyers and plaintiffs for reasons of publicity, politics, or other non-law-related issues and may result in fines against plaintiffs and their counsel.

fruit of the poisonous tree doctrine A legal principle that excludes from introduction at trial any evidence later developed as a result of an illegal search or seizure.

gain time The amount of time deducted from time to be served in prison on a given sentence as a consequence of participation in special projects or programs.

gender ratio problem The need for an explanation of the fact that the number of crimes committed by men routinely far exceeds the number of crimes committed by women in almost all categories.

gender responsiveness The process of understanding and taking into account the differences in characteristics and life experiences that women and men bring to the criminal justice system, and adjusting strategies and practices in ways that appropriately respond to those conditions.

general deterrence A goal of criminal sentencing that seeks to prevent others from committing crimes similar to the one for which a particular offender is being sentenced by making an example of the person sentenced.

genes Distinct portions of a cell's DNA that carry coded instructions for making everything the body needs.

globalization The internationalization of trade, services, investment, information, and other forms of human social activity. Also, a process of social homogenization by which the experiences of everyday life, marked by the diffusion of commodities and ideas, can foster a standardization of cultural expressions around the world.[26]

good-faith exception An exception to the exclusionary rule. Law enforcement officers who conduct a search or who seize evidence on the basis of good faith (that is, when they believe they are operating according to the dictates of the law) and who later discover that a mistake was made (perhaps in the format of the application for a search warrant) may still provide evidence that can be used in court.

good time The amount of time deducted from time to be served in prison on a given sentence as a consequence of good behavior.

grand jury A group of jurors who have been selected according to law and have been sworn to hear the evidence and to determine whether there is sufficient evidence to bring the accused person to trial, to investigate criminal activity generally, or to investigate the conduct of a public agency or official.

grievance procedure A formalized arrangement, usually involving a neutral hearing board, whereby institutionalized individuals have the opportunity to register complaints about the conditions of their confinement.

gross negligence The intentional failure to perform a manifest duty in reckless disregard of the consequences as affecting the life or property of another.[27]

guilty but mentally ill (GBMI) A verdict, equivalent to a finding of "guilty," that establishes that the defendant, although mentally ill, was in sufficient possession of his or her faculties to be morally blameworthy for his or her acts.

guilty plea A defendant's formal answer in court to the charge or charges contained in a complaint, information, or indictment, claiming that he or she did commit the offense or offenses listed.

guilty verdict See **verdict**.

habeas corpus See **writ of *habeas corpus***.

habitual offender A person sentenced under the provisions of a statute declaring that people convicted of a given offense and shown to have previously been convicted of another specified offense shall receive a more severe penalty than that for the current offense alone.

hacker A computer hobbyist or professional, generally with advanced programming skills. Today, the term *hacker* has taken on a sinister connotation, referring to hobbyists who are bent on illegally accessing the computers of others or who attempt to demonstrate their technological prowess through computerized acts of vandalism.

hands-off doctrine A policy of nonintervention with regard to prison management that U.S. courts tended to follow until the late 1960s. For the past 50 years, the doctrine has languished as judicial intervention in prison administration dramatically increased, although there is now some evidence that a new hands-off era is approaching.

Harrison Narcotics Act The first major piece of federal antidrug legislation, passed in 1914.

hate crime (UCR/NIBRS) A criminal offense committed against a person, property, or society that is motivated, in whole or in part, by the offender's bias against a race, religion, disability, sexual orientation, or ethnicity/national origin. Also called *bias crime*.

hearing A proceeding in which arguments, witnesses, or evidence is heard by a judicial officer or an administrative body.

hearsay Something that is not based on the personal knowledge of a witness. Witnesses who testify about something they have heard, for example, are offering hearsay by repeating information about a matter of which they have no direct knowledge.

hearsay rule The long-standing precedent that hearsay cannot be used in American courtrooms. Rather than accepting testimony based on hearsay, the court will ask that the person who was the original source of the hearsay information be brought in to be questioned and cross-examined. Exceptions to the hearsay rule may occur when the person with direct knowledge is dead or is otherwise unable to testify.

heritability A statistical construct that estimates the amount of variation in the traits of a population that is attributable to genetic factors.

hierarchy rule A pre-NIBRS Uniform Crime Reporting Program scoring practice in which only the most serious offense was counted in a multiple-offense incident.

high-technology crime Violations of the criminal law whose commission depends on, makes use of, and often targets sophisticated and advanced technology. See also **cybercrime**.

home confinement House arrest. Individuals ordered confined to their homes are sometimes monitored electronically to ensure they do not leave during the hours of confinement. Absence from the home during working hours is often permitted.

homicide See **criminal homicide**.

***Hudud* crime** A serious violation of Islamic law that is regarded as an offense against God.

Hudud crimes include such behavior as theft, adultery, sodomy, alcohol consumption, and robbery.

human smuggling Illegal immigration in which an agent is paid to help a person cross a border clandestinely.

hung jury A jury that, after long deliberation, is so irreconcilably divided in opinion that it is unable to reach any verdict.

hypothesis An explanation that accounts for a set of facts and that can be tested by further investigation. Also, something that is taken to be true for the purpose of argument or investigation.[28]

identity management The comprehensive management and administration of a user's individual profile information, permissions, and privileges across a variety of social settings.[29]

identity theft A crime in which an impostor obtains key pieces of information, such as Social Security and driver's license numbers, to obtain credit, merchandise, and services in the name of the victim. The victim is often left with a ruined credit history and the time-consuming and complicated task of repairing the financial damage.[30]

illegally seized evidence Evidence seized without regard to the principles of due process as described by the Bill of Rights. Most illegally seized evidence is the result of police searches conducted without a proper warrant or of improperly conducted interrogations.

illegal search and seizure An act in violation of the Fourth Amendment of the U.S. Constitution, which reads, "The right of the people to be secure in their persons, houses, papers, and effects, against unreasonable searches and seizures, shall not be violated, and no Warrants shall issue, but upon probable cause, supported by Oath or affirmation, and particularly describing the place to be searched, and the persons or things to be seized."

incapacitation The use of imprisonment or other means to reduce the likelihood that an offender will commit future offenses.

inchoate offense An offense not yet completed. Also, an offense that consists of an action or conduct that is a step toward the intended commission of another offense.

incident-based reporting Compared with summary reporting, a less restrictive and more expansive method of collecting crime data in which all of the analytical elements associated with an offense or arrest are compiled by a central collection agency on an incident-by-incident basis.

included offense An offense that is made up of elements that are a subset of the elements of another offense having a greater statutory penalty, the occurrence of which is established by the same evidence or by some portion of the evidence that has been offered to establish the occurrence of the greater offense.

incompetent to stand trial In criminal proceedings, a finding by a court that, as a result of mental illness, defect, or disability, a defendant is incapable of understanding the nature of the charges and proceedings against him or her, of consulting with an attorney, and of aiding in his or her own defense.

indeterminate sentence A type of sentence imposed on a convicted criminal that is meant to encourage rehabilitation through the use of relatively unspecific punishments (such as a term of imprisonment of from one to ten years).

indeterminate sentencing A model of criminal punishment that encourages rehabilitation through the use of general and relatively unspecific sentences (such as a term of imprisonment of from one to ten years).

index crime See **Crime Index**.

indictment A formal, written accusation submitted to the court by a grand jury, alleging that a specified person has committed a specified offense, usually a felony.

individual rights The rights guaranteed to all members of American society by the U.S. Constitution (especially those found in the first ten amendments to the Constitution, known as the *Bill of Rights*). These rights are particularly important to criminal defendants facing formal processing by the criminal justice system.

individual-rights advocate One who seeks to protect personal freedoms within the process of criminal justice.

industrial prison A correctional model intended to capitalize on the labor of convicts sentenced to confinement.

information A formal, written accusation submitted to the court by a prosecutor, alleging that a specified person has committed a specific offense.

infraction A minor violation of state statute or local ordinance punishable by a fine or other penalty or by a specified, usually limited, term of incarceration.

infrastructure The basic facilities, services, and installations that a country needs to function. Transportation and communications systems, water and power lines, and institutions that serve the public, including banks, schools, post offices, and prisons, are all part of a country's infrastructure.[31]

inherent coercion The tactics used by police interviewers that fall short of physical abuse but that nonetheless pressure suspects to divulge information.

initial appearance See **first appearance**.

initial plea The first plea to a given charge entered in the court record by or for the defendant. The acceptance of an initial plea by the court unambiguously indicates that the arraignment process has been completed. Also called *first plea*.

insanity defense A legal defense based on claims of mental illness or mental incapacity.

institutional capacity The official number of inmates that a confinement or residential facility is housing or was intended to house.

intake The first step in decision making regarding a juvenile whose behavior or alleged behavior is in violation of the law or could otherwise cause a juvenile court to assume jurisdiction.

intelligence-led policing (ILP) The collection and analysis of information to produce an intelligence end product designed to inform police decision making at both the tactical and strategic levels.[32]

intensive probation supervision (IPS) A form of probation supervision involving frequent face-to-face contact between the probationer and the probation officer.

intent The state of mind or attitude with which an act is carried out. Also, the design, resolve, or determination with which a person acts to achieve a certain result.

interdiction The interception of drug traffic at the nation's borders. Interdiction is one of the many strategies used to stem the flow of illegal drugs into the United States.

interdisciplinary theory An approach that integrates a variety of theoretical viewpoints in an attempt to explain something, such as crime and violence.

intermediate appellate court An appellate court whose primary function is to review the judgments of trial courts and the decisions of administrative agencies and whose decisions are, in turn, usually reviewable by a higher appellate court in the same state.

intermediate sanctions The use of split sentencing, shock probation or parole, shock incarceration, community service, intensive supervision, or home confinement in lieu of other, more traditional, sanctions, such as imprisonment and fines. Also called *alternative sanctions*.

internal affairs The branch of a police organization tasked with investigating charges of wrongdoing involving members of the department.

International Criminal Police Organization (Interpol) An international law enforcement support organization that began operations in 1946 and today has 182 member nations.

international terrorism The unlawful use of force or violence by an individual or a group that has some connection to a foreign power, or whose activities transcend national boundaries, against people or property in order to intimidate or coerce a government, the civilian population, or any segment thereof, in furtherance of political or social objectives.[33]

interrogation The information-gathering activity of police officers that involves the direct questioning of suspects.

Islamic law A system of laws, operative in some Arab countries, based on the Muslim religion and especially the holy book of Islam, the Koran.

jail A confinement facility administered by an agency of local government, typically a law enforcement agency, intended for adults but sometimes also containing juveniles, which holds people detained pending adjudication or committed after adjudication, usually those sentenced to a year or less.

jail commitment A sentence of commitment to the jurisdiction of a confinement facility system for adults that is administered by an agency of local government and whose custodial authority is usually limited to people sentenced to a year or less of confinement.

judge An elected or appointed public official who presides over a court of law and who is authorized to hear and sometimes to decide cases and to conduct trials.

judgment The statement of the decision of a court that the defendant is acquitted or convicted of the offense or offenses charged.

judgment suspending sentence A court-ordered sentencing alternative that results in the convicted offender being placed on probation.

judicial officer Any person authorized by statute, constitutional provision, or court rule to exercise the powers reserved to the judicial branch of government.

judicial review The power of a court to review actions and decisions made by other agencies of government.

jural postulates Propositions developed by the famous jurist Roscoe Pound that hold that the law reflects shared needs without which members of society could not coexist. Pound's jural postulates are often linked to the idea that the law can be used to engineer the social structure to ensure certain kinds of outcomes. In capitalist societies, for example, the law of theft protects property rights.

jurisdiction The territory, subject matter, or people over which a court or other justice agency may exercise lawful authority, as determined by statute or constitution. See also **venue**.

jurisprudence The philosophy of law. Also, the science and study of the law.

juror A member of a trial or grand jury who has been selected for jury duty and is required to serve as an arbiter of the facts in a court of law. Jurors are expected to render verdicts of "guilty" or "not guilty" as to the charges brought against the accused, although they sometimes fail to do so (as in the case of a hung jury).

jury panel The group of people summoned to appear in court as potential jurors for a particular trial. Also, the people selected from the group of potential jurors to sit in the jury box, from which those acceptable to the prosecution and the defense are finally chosen as the jury.

jury selection The process whereby, according to law and precedent, members of a trial jury are chosen.

just deserts A model of criminal sentencing that holds that criminal offenders deserve the punishment they receive at the hands of the law and that punishments should be appropriate to the type and severity of the crime committed.

justice The principle of fairness; the ideal of moral equity.

justice model A contemporary model of imprisonment based on the principle of just deserts.

justice reinvestement A concept that prioritizes the use of alternatives to incarceration for persons convicted of eligible nonviolent offenses, standardizes the use of risk assessments instruments in pretrial detention, authorizes the use of early-release mechanisms for prisoners who meet eligibility requirements, and reinvests savings from such initiatives into effective crime-prevention programs.

justification A legal defense in which the defendant admits to committing the act in question but claims it was necessary in order to avoid some greater evil.

juvenile A person subject to juvenile court proceedings because a statutorily defined event or condition caused by or affecting that person was alleged to have occurred while his or her age was below the statutorily specified age limit of original jurisdiction of the juvenile court.

juvenile court A court that has, as all or part of its authority, original jurisdiction over matters concerning people statutorily defined as juveniles.

juvenile court judgment The juvenile court decision, terminating an adjudicatory hearing, that the juvenile is a delinquent, a status offender, or a dependent or that the allegations in the petition are not sustained.

juvenile disposition The decision of a juvenile court, concluding a dispositional hearing, that an adjudicated juvenile be committed to a juvenile correctional facility; be placed in a juvenile residence, shelter, or care or treatment program; be required to meet certain standards of conduct; or be released.

juvenile justice The policies and activities of law enforcement and the courts in handling law violations by youths under the age of criminal jurisdiction.[34]

juvenile justice agency A government agency, or subunit thereof, whose functions are the investigation, supervision, adjudication, care, or confinement of juvenile offenders and nonoffenders subject to the jurisdiction of a juvenile court. Also, in some usages, a private agency providing care and treatment.

juvenile justice system The aggregate of the government agencies that function to investigate, supervise, adjudicate, care for, or confine youthful offenders and other children subject to the jurisdiction of the juvenile court.

juvenile petition A document filed in juvenile court alleging that a juvenile is a delinquent, a status offender, or a dependent and asking that the court assume jurisdiction over the juvenile or that an alleged delinquent be transferred to a criminal court for prosecution as an adult.

Kansas City experiment The first large-scale scientific study of law enforcement practices. Sponsored by the Police Foundation, it focused on the practice of preventive patrol.

kidnapping The transportation or confinement of a person without authority of law and without his or her consent or without the consent of his or her guardian, if a minor.

Knapp Commission A committee that investigated police corruption in New York City in the early 1970s.

labeling theory A social process perspective that sees continued crime as a consequence of the limited opportunities for acceptable behavior that follow from the negative responses of society to those defined as offenders.

landmark case A precedent-setting court decision that produces substantial changes in both the understanding of the requirements of due process and in the practical day-to-day operations of the justice system.

larceny-theft (UCR/NIBRS) The unlawful taking or attempted taking, carrying, leading, or riding away of property, from the possession or constructive possession of another. Motor vehicles are excluded. Larceny is the most common of the eight major offenses, although probably only a small percentage of all larcenies are actually reported to the police because of the small dollar amounts involved.

latent evidence Evidence of relevance to a criminal investigation that is not readily seen by the unaided eye.

law A rule of conduct, generally found enacted in the form of a statute, that proscribes or mandates certain forms of behavior. Statutory law is often the result of moral enterprise by interest groups that, through the exercise of political power, are successful in seeing their valued perspectives enacted into law.

law enforcement The generic name for the activities of the agencies responsible for maintaining public order and enforcing the law, particularly the activities of preventing, detecting, and investigating crime and apprehending criminals.

law enforcement agency A federal, state, or local criminal justice agency or identifiable subunit whose principal functions are the prevention, detection, and investigation of crime and the apprehension of alleged offenders.

Law Enforcement Assistance Administration (LEAA) A now-defunct federal agency established under Title I of the Omnibus Crime Control and Safe Streets Act of 1968 to funnel federal funding to state and local law enforcement agencies.

law enforcement intelligence See **criminal intelligence**.

law enforcement officer An officer employed by a law enforcement agency who is sworn to carry out law enforcement duties.

lawyer See **attorney**.

lay witness An eyewitness, character witness, or other person called on to testify who is not considered an expert. Lay witnesses must testify to facts only and may not draw conclusions or express opinions.

learning organization "An organization skilled at creating, acquiring, and transferring knowledge and at modifying its behavior to reflect new knowledge and insights."[35]

legal cause A legally recognizable cause. A legal cause must be demonstrated in court in order to hold an individual criminally liable for causing harm.

legal counsel See **attorney**.

legalistic style A style of policing marked by a strict concern with enforcing the precise letter of the law. Legalistic departments may take a hands-off approach to disruptive or problematic behavior that does not violate the criminal law.

legalization Elimination of the laws and associated criminal penalties associated with certain behaviors—usually the production, sale, distribution, and possession of a controlled substance.

less-lethal weapon A weapon that is designed to disable, capture, or immobilize—but not kill—a suspect. Occasional deaths do result from the use of such weapons, however.

lex talionis The law of retaliation, often expressed as "an eye for an eye" or "like for like."

life course perspective An approach to explaining crime and deviance that investigates developments and turning points in the course of a person's life.

line operations In police organizations, the field activities or supervisory activities directly related to day-to-day police work.

Mafia See **Cosa Nostra**.

major crimes See **Part I offenses**.

mala in se Acts that are regarded, by tradition and convention, as wrong in themselves.

mala prohibita Acts that are considered wrong only because there is a law against them.

malware Malicious computer programs like viruses, worms, and Trojan horses.

mandatory release The release of an inmate from prison that is determined by statute or sentencing guidelines and is not decided by a parole board or other authority.

mandatory sentence A statutorily required penalty that must be set and carried out in all cases upon conviction for a specified offense or series of offenses.

mandatory sentencing A structured sentencing scheme that allows no leeway in the nature of the sentence required and under which clearly enumerated punishments are mandated for specific offenses or for habitual offenders convicted of a series of crimes.

MATRIX An acronym for the Multistate Anti-Terrorism Information Exchange, an Internet-based proof-of-concept pilot program funded by the Department of Justice and the Department of Homeland Security to increase and enhance the exchange of sensitive information about terrorism and other criminal activity between enforcement agencies at the local, state, and federal levels.

maximum sentence In legal usage, the maximum penalty provided by law for a given criminal offense, usually stated as a maximum term of imprisonment or a maximum fine. Also, in corrections usage in relation to a given offender, any of several quantities (expressed in days, months, or years) that vary according to whether calculated at the point of sentencing or at a later point in the correctional process and according to whether the time period referred to is the term of confinement or the total period under correctional jurisdiction.

medical model A therapeutic perspective on correctional treatment that applies the diagnostic perspective of medical science to the handling of criminal offenders.

medical parole An early release option under which an inmate who is deemed "low risk" due to a serious physical or mental health condition is released from prison earlier than he or she might have been under normal circumstances.

mens rea The state of mind that accompanies a criminal act. Also, a guilty mind.

***Miranda* rights** The set of rights that a person accused or suspected of having committed a specific offense has during interrogation and of which he or she must be informed prior to questioning, as stated by the U.S. Supreme Court in deciding *Miranda* v. *Arizona* (1966) and related cases.

***Miranda* triggers** The dual principles of custody and interrogation, both of which are necessary before an advisement of rights is required.

***Miranda* warnings** The advisement of rights due criminal suspects by the police before questioning begins. *Miranda* warnings were first set forth by the U.S. Supreme Court in the 1966 case of *Miranda* v. *Arizona*.

misdemeanor An offense punishable by incarceration, usually in a local confinement facility, for a period whose upper limit is prescribed by statute in a given jurisdiction, typically one year or less.

mistrial A trial that has been terminated and declared invalid by the court because of some circumstance that created a substantial and uncorrectable prejudice to the conduct of a fair trial or that made it impossible to continue the trial in accordance with prescribed procedures.

mitigating circumstances Circumstances relating to the commission of a crime that may be considered to reduce the blameworthiness of the defendant. See also **aggravating circumstances**.

mixed sentence A sentence that requires that a convicted offender serve weekends (or other specified periods of time) in a confinement facility (usually a jail) while undergoing probationary supervision in the community.

M'Naghten rule A rule for determining insanity, which asks whether the defendant knew what he or she was doing or whether the defendant knew that what he or she was doing was wrong.

Model Penal Code (MPC) A generalized modern codification considered basic to criminal law, published by the American Law Institute in 1962.

money laundering The process by which criminals or criminal organizations seek to disguise the illicit nature of their proceeds by introducing them into the stream of legitimate commerce and finance.[36]

moral enterprise The process undertaken by an advocacy group to have its values legitimated and embodied in law.

motion An oral or written request made to a court at any time before, during, or after court proceedings, asking the court to make a specified finding, decision, or order.

motive A person's reason for committing a crime.

motor vehicle theft (UCR/NIBRS) The theft or attempted theft of a motor vehicle. A *motor vehicle* is defined as a self-propelled road vehicle that runs on land surface and not on rails. The stealing of trains, planes, boats, construction equipment, and most farm machinery is classified as larceny under the UCR/NIBRS Program, not as motor vehicle theft.

multiculturalism The existence within one society of diverse groups that maintain unique cultural identities while frequently accepting and participating in the larger society's legal and political systems.[37] *Multiculturalism* is often used in conjunction with the term *diversity* to identify many distinctions of social significance. Also called *cultural pluralism*.

municipal police department A city- or town-based law enforcement agency. Also known as *local police*.

murder The unlawful killing of a human being. *Murder* is a generic term that in common usage may include first- and second-degree murder, manslaughter, involuntary manslaughter, and other similar offenses.

murder and nonnegligent manslaughter (UCR/NIBRS) Intentionally causing the death of another without legal justification or excuse. Also, causing the death of another while committing or attempting to commit another crime.

narcoterrorism A political alliance between terrorist organizations and drug-supplying cartels. The cartels provide financing for the terrorists, who in turn provide quasi-military protection to the drug dealers.

National Crime Victimization Survey (NCVS) An annual survey of selected American households conducted by the Bureau of Justice Statistics to determine the extent of criminal victimization—especially unreported victimization—in the United States.

National Incident-Based Reporting System (NIBRS) An incident-based reporting system that collects data on every single crime occurrence. NIBRS data will soon supersede the kinds of summary data that have traditionally been provided by the FBI's Uniform Crime Reporting Program.

natural law Rules of conduct inherent in human nature and in the natural order that are thought to be knowable through intuition, inspiration, and the exercise of reason, without the need for reference to created laws.

NCVS See **National Crime Victimization Survey**.

neglected child A child who is not receiving the proper level of physical or psychological care from his or her parents or guardians or who has been placed up for adoption in violation of the law.

negligence In legal usage, generally, a state of mind accompanying a person's conduct such that he or she is not aware, though a reasonable person should be aware, that there is a risk that the conduct might cause a particular harmful result.

negligent manslaughter (UCR/NIBRS) Causing the death of another by recklessness or gross negligence.

neoclassical criminology A **contemporary** version of classical criminology that emphasizes deterrence and retribution and that holds that human beings are essentially free to make choices in favor of crime and deviance or conformity to the law.

new-generation jail A temporary confinement facility that eliminates many of the traditional barriers between inmates and correctional personnel. Also called *podular jail*, *direct-supervision jail*, and *indirect-supervision jail*.

new police A police force formed in 1829 under the command of Sir Robert Peel. It became the model for modern-day police forces throughout the Western world. Also called *Metropolitan Police Force*.

night watch An early form of police patrol in English cities and towns.

NLETS The International Justice and Public Safety Information Sharing Network.

nolle prosequi A formal entry in the record of the court indicating that the prosecutor declares that he or she will proceed no further in the action. The prosecutor's decision not to pursue the case requires the approval of the court in some jurisdictions.

nolo contendere A plea of "no contest." A no-contest plea is used when the defendant does not wish to contest conviction. Because the plea does not admit guilt, however, it cannot provide the basis for later civil suits that might follow a criminal conviction.

not guilty by reason of insanity The plea of a defendant or the verdict of a jury or judge in a criminal proceeding that the defendant is not guilty of the offense charged because at the time the crime was committed, the defendant did not have the mental capacity to be held criminally responsible for his or her actions.

nothing-works doctrine The belief, popularized by Robert Martinson in the 1970s, that correctional treatment programs have had little success in rehabilitating offenders.

no true bill The decision by a grand jury that it will not return an indictment against the person accused of a crime on the basis of the allegations and evidence presented by the prosecutor.

occupational crime Any act punishable by law that is committed through opportunity created in the course of a legitimate occupation.

offender An adult who has been convicted of a criminal offense.

offense A violation of the criminal law. Also, in some jurisdictions, a minor crime, such as jaywalking, that is sometimes described as *ticketable*.

offenses known to police (UCR/NIBRS) Reported occurrences of offenses that have been verified at the police level.

opening statement The initial statement of the prosecutor or the defense attorney, made in a court of law to a judge or jury, describing the facts that he or she intends to present during trial to prove the case.

operational capacity The number of inmates a prison can effectively accommodate based on management considerations.

opinion The official announcement of a decision of a court, together with the reasons for that decision.

opportunity theory A perspective that sees delinquency as the result of limited legitimate opportunities for success available to most lower-class youth.

organized crime The unlawful activities of the members of a highly organized, disciplined association engaged in supplying illegal goods or services, including gambling, prostitution, loan-sharking, narcotics, and labor racketeering, and in other unlawful activities.[38]

original jurisdiction The lawful authority of a court to hear or to act on a case from its beginning and to pass judgment on the law and the facts. The authority may be over a specific geographic area or over particular types of cases.

parens patriae A common law principle that allows the state to assume a parental role and to take custody of a child when he or she becomes delinquent, is abandoned, or is in need of care that the natural parents are unable or unwilling to provide.

Parliament The British legislature, the highest law-making body of the United Kingdom.

parole The status of a convicted offender who has been conditionally released from prison by a paroling authority before the expiration of his or her sentence, is placed under the supervision of a parole agency, and is required to observe the conditions of parole.

parole board A state paroling authority. Most states have parole boards that decide when an incarcerated offender is ready for conditional release. Some boards also function as revocation hearing panels. Also called *parole commission.*

parolee A person who has been conditionally released by a paroling authority from a prison prior to the expiration of his or her sentence, is placed under the supervision of a parole agency, and is required to observe conditions of parole.

parole (probation) violation An act or a failure to act by a parolee (or a probationer) that does not conform to the conditions of his or her parole (or probation).

parole revocation The administrative action of a paroling authority removing a person from parole status in response to a violation of lawfully required conditions of parole, including the prohibition against committing a new offense. Parole revocation usually results in the offender's return to prison.

parole supervision Guidance, treatment, or regulation of the behavior of a convicted adult who is obligated to fulfill conditions of parole or conditional release. Parole supervision is authorized and required by statute, is performed by a parole agency, and occurs after a period of prison confinement.

parole supervisory caseload The total number of clients registered with a parole agency or officer on a given date or during a specified time period.

paroling authority A board or commission that has the authority to release on parole adults committed to prison, to revoke parole or other conditional release, and to discharge from parole or other conditional release status.

Part I offenses A UCR/NIBRS offense group used to report murder, rape, robbery, aggravated assault, burglary, larceny-theft, motor vehicle theft, and arson, as defined under the FBI's UCR/NIBRS Program. Also called *major crimes.*

Part II offenses A UCR/NIBRS offense group used to report arrests for less serious offenses. Agencies are limited to reporting only arrest information for Part II offenses, with the exception of simple assault.

PATRIOT Act See **USA PATRIOT Act**.

peace officer standards and training (POST) program The official program of a state or legislative jurisdiction that sets standards for the training of law enforcement officers. All states set such standards, although not all use the term *POST.*

peacemaking criminology A perspective that holds that crime-control agencies and the citizens they serve should work together to alleviate social problems and human suffering and thus reduce crime.

penal code The written, organized, and compiled form of the criminal laws of a jurisdiction.

penal law See **criminal law**.

penitentiary A prison. See also **Pennsylvania system**.

Pennsylvania system A form of imprisonment developed by the Pennsylvania Quakers around 1790 as an alternative to corporal punishments. This style of imprisonment made use of solitary confinement and encouraged rehabilitation.

peremptory challenge The right to challenge a potential juror without disclosing the reason for the challenge. Prosecutors and defense attorneys routinely use peremptory challenges to eliminate from juries individuals who, although they express no obvious bias, are thought to be capable of swaying the jury in an undesirable direction.

perjury The intentional making of a false statement as part of the testimony by a sworn witness in a judicial proceeding on a matter relevant to the case at hand.

perpetrator The chief actor in the commission of a crime; that is, the person who directly commits the criminal act.

personality The relatively stable characteristic patterns of thoughts, feelings and behaviors that make a person unique, and which influences that person's behavior.

petition A written request made to a court asking for the exercise of its judicial powers or asking for permission to perform some act that requires the authorization of a court.

petit jury See **trial jury**.

pharmaceutical diversion The transfer of prescription medicines controlled by the Controlled Substance Act by theft, deception, and or fraudulent means for other than their intended legitimate therapeutic purposes.

phrenology The study of the shape of the head to determine anatomical correlates of human behavior.

physical dependence A biologically based craving for a specific drug that results from frequent use of the substance. Physical dependence on drugs is marked by a growing tolerance of a drug's effects, so that increased amounts of the drug are needed to obtain the desired effect, and by the onset of withdrawal symptoms over periods of prolonged abstinence.[39] Also called *physical addiction.*

piracy See **software piracy**.

plaintiff A person who initiates a court action.

plain view A legal term describing the ready visibility of objects that might be seized as evidence during a search by police in the absence of a search warrant specifying the seizure of those objects. To lawfully seize evidence in plain view, officers must have a legal right to be in the viewing area and must have cause to believe that the evidence is somehow associated with criminal activity.

plea In criminal proceedings, the defendant's formal answer in court to the charge contained in a complaint, information, or indictment that he or she is guilty of the offense charged, is not guilty of the offense charged, or does not contest the charge.

plea bargaining The process of negotiating an agreement among the defendant, the prosecutor, and the court as to an appropriate plea and associated sentence in a given case. Plea bargaining circumvents the trial process and dramatically reduces the time required for the resolution of a criminal case.

police–community relations (PCR) An area of police activity that recognizes the need for the community and the police to work together effectively. PCR is based on the notion that the police derive their legitimacy from the community they serve. Many police agencies began to explore PCR in the 1960s and 1970s.

police corruption The abuse of police authority for personal or organizational gain.[40]

police discretion The opportunity for police officers to exercise choice in their enforcement activities.

police ethics The special responsibility to adhere to moral duty and obligation that is inherent in police work.

police management The administrative activities of controlling, directing, and coordinating police personnel, resources, and activities in the service of preventing crime, apprehending criminals, recovering stolen property, and performing regulatory and helping services.[41]

police professionalism The increasing formalization of police work and the accompanying rise in public acceptance of the police.

police subculture A particular set of values, beliefs, and acceptable forms of behavior characteristic of American police. Socialization into the police subculture begins with recruit training and continues thereafter. Also called *police culture*.

police use of force The use of physical restraint by a police officer when dealing with a member of the public.[42]

police working personality All aspects of the traditional values and patterns of behavior evidenced by police officers who have been effectively socialized into the police subculture. Characteristics of the police personality often extend to the personal lives of law enforcement personnel.

political defense An innovative defense to a criminal charge that claims that the defendant's actions stemmed from adherence to a set of political beliefs and standards significantly different from those on which the American style of government is based. A political defense questions the legitimacy and purpose of all criminal proceedings against the defendant.

Positivist School An approach theory that stresses the application of scientific techniques to the study of crime and criminals.

POST See **peace officer standards and training (POST) program**.

postconviction remedy The procedure or set of procedures by which a person who has been convicted of a crime can challenge in court the lawfulness of a judgment of conviction, a penalty, or a correctional agency action and thus obtain relief in situations where this cannot be done by a direct appeal.

postmodern criminology A branch of criminology that developed after World War II and that builds on the tenets of postmodern social thought.

precedent A legal principle that ensures that previous judicial decisions are authoritatively considered and incorporated into future cases.

preliminary hearing A proceeding before a judicial officer in which three matters must be decided: (1) whether a crime was committed, (2) whether the crime occurred within the territorial jurisdiction of the court, and (3) whether there are reasonable grounds to believe that the defendant committed the crime.

preliminary investigation All of the activities undertaken by a police officer who responds to the scene of a crime, including determining whether a crime has occurred, securing the crime scene, and preserving evidence.

presentence investigation (PSI) The examination of a convicted offender's background prior to sentencing. Presentence examinations are generally conducted by probation or parole officers and are submitted to sentencing authorities.

presentment Historically, unsolicited written notice of an offense provided to a court by a grand jury from their own knowledge or observation. In current usage, any of several presentations of alleged facts and charges to a court or a grand jury by a prosecutor.

presumptive sentencing A model of criminal punishment that meets the following conditions: (1) The appropriate sentence for an offender convicted of a specific charge is presumed to fall within a range of sentences authorized by sentencing guidelines that are adopted by a legislatively created sentencing body, usually a sentencing commission. (2) Sentencing judges are expected to sentence within the range or to provide written justification for failing to do so. (3) There is a mechanism for review, usually appellate, of any departure from the guidelines.

pretrial detention Confinement occurring between the time of arrest or of being held to answer a charge and the conclusion of prosecution.[43]

pretrial discovery In criminal proceedings, disclosure by the prosecution or the defense prior to trial of evidence or other information that is intended to be used in the trial.

pretrial release The release of an accused person from custody, for all or part of the time before or during prosecution, on his or her promise to appear in court when required.

prison A state or federal confinement facility that has custodial authority over adults sentenced to confinement.

prison argot The slang characteristic of prison subcultures and prison life.

prison capacity The size of the correctional population an institution can effectively hold.[44] There are three types of prison capacity: rated, operational, and design.

prison commitment A sentence of commitment to the jurisdiction of a state or federal confinement facility system for adults whose custodial authority extends to offenders sentenced to more than a year of confinement, to a term expressed in years or for life, or to await execution of a death sentence.

prison subculture The values and behavioral patterns characteristic of prison inmates. Prison subculture has been found to be surprisingly consistent across the country.

prisoner A person in physical custody in a state or federal confinement facility or in the personal physical custody of a criminal justice official while being transported to or between confinement facilities.

prisoner reentry See **reentry**.

prisonization The process whereby newly institutionalized offenders come to accept prison lifestyles and criminal values. Although many inmates begin their prison experience with only a few values that support criminal behavior, the socialization experience they undergo while incarcerated leads to a much greater acceptance of such values.

private prison A correctional institution operated by a private firm on behalf of a local or state government.

private protective service An independent or proprietary commercial organization that provides protective services to employers on a contractual basis.

private security Self-employed individuals and privately funded business entities and organizations that provide security-related services to specific clientele for a fee, for the individual or entity that retains or employs them or for themselves, in order to protect people, private property, or interests from various hazards.[45]

private security agency See **private protective service**.

privatization The movement toward the wider use of private prisons.

probable cause A set of facts and circumstances that would induce a reasonably intelligent and prudent person to believe that a specified person has committed a specified crime. Also, reasonable grounds to make or believe an accusation. Probable cause refers to the necessary level of belief that would allow for police seizures (arrests) of individuals and full searches of dwellings, vehicles, and possessions.

probation A sentence of imprisonment that is suspended. Also, the conditional freedom granted by a judicial officer to a convicted offender, as long as the person meets certain conditions of behavior.

probation revocation A court order taking away a convicted offender's probationary status and usually withdrawing the conditional freedom associated with that status in response to a violation of the conditions of probation.

probation termination The ending of the probation status of a given person by routine expiration of the probationary period, by special early termination by the court, or by revocation of probation.

probation violation An act or a failure to act by a probationer that does not conform to the conditions of his or her probation.

probation workload The total set of activities required to carry out the probation agency functions of intake screening of juvenile cases, referral of cases to other service agencies, investigation of juveniles and adults for the purpose of preparing predisposition or presentence reports, supervision or treatment of juveniles and adults granted probation, assistance in the enforcement of court orders concerning family problems, such as abandonment and nonsupport cases, and other such functions assigned by statute or court order.

probative value The degree to which a particular item of evidence is useful in, and relevant to, proving something important in a trial.

problem police officer A law enforcement officer who exhibits problem behavior, as indicated by high rates of citizen complaints and use-of-force incidents and by other evidence.[46]

problem-solving policing A type of policing that assumes that crimes can be controlled by uncovering and effectively addressing the underlying social problems that cause crime. Problem-solving policing makes use of community resources, such as counseling centers, welfare programs, and job-training facilities. It also attempts to involve citizens in crime prevention through education, negotiation, and conflict management. Also called *problem-oriented policing*.

procedural defense A defense that claims that the defendant was in some significant way discriminated against in the justice process or that some important aspect of official procedure was not properly followed in the investigation or prosecution of the crime charged.

procedural law The part of the law that specifies the methods to be used in enforcing substantive law.

profession An organized undertaking characterized by a body of specialized knowledge acquired through extensive education and by a well-considered set of internal standards and ethical guidelines that hold members of the profession accountable to one another and to society.

professional criminal See **career criminal**.

property bond The setting of bail in the form of land, houses, stocks, or other tangible property. In the event that the defendant absconds prior to trial, the bond becomes the property of the court.

property crime A UCR/NIBRS summary offense category that includes burglary, larceny-theft, motor vehicle theft, and arson.

proportionality A sentencing principle that holds that the severity of sanctions should bear a direct relationship to the seriousness of the crime committed.

prosecution agency A federal, state, or local criminal justice agency or subunit whose principal function is the prosecution of alleged offenders.

prosecutor An attorney whose official duty is to conduct criminal proceedings on behalf of the state or the people against those accused of having committed criminal offenses. Also called *county attorney; district attorney (DA); state's attorney; U.S. attorney*.

prosecutorial discretion The decision-making power of prosecutors, based on the wide range of choices available to them, in the handling of criminal defendants, the scheduling of cases for trial, the acceptance of negotiated pleas, and so on. The most important form of prosecutorial discretion lies in the power to charge, or not to charge, a person with an offense.

prostitution The act of offering or agreeing to engage in, or engaging in, a sex act with another in return for a fee.

psychoactive substance A chemical substance that affects cognition, feeling, or awareness.

psychoanalysis A theory of human behavior, based on the writings of Sigmund Freud, that sees personality as a complex composite of interacting mental entities.

psychological dependence A craving for a specific drug that results from long-term substance abuse. Psychological dependence on drugs is marked by the belief that drugs are needed to achieve a feeling of well-being.[47] Also called *psychological addiction*.

psychological manipulation Manipulative actions by police interviewers that are designed to pressure suspects to divulge information and that are based on subtle forms of intimidation and control.

psychological profiling The attempt to categorize, understand, and predict the behavior of certain types of offenders based on behavioral clues they provide.

Psychological School A perspective on criminological thought that views offensive and deviant behavior as the product of dysfunctional personality. Psychological thinkers identify the conscious, and especially the subconscious, contents of the human psyche as major determinants of behavior.

psychopath A person with a personality disorder, especially one manifested in aggressively antisocial behavior, which is often said to be the result of a poorly developed superego. Also called *sociopath*.

psychopathology The study of pathological mental conditions—that is, mental illness.

psychosis A form of mental illness in which sufferers are said to be out of touch with reality.

public defender An attorney employed by a government agency or subagency, or by a private organization under contract to a government body, for the purpose of providing defense services to indigents, or an attorney who has volunteered such service.

public-defender agency A federal, state, or local criminal justice agency or subunit whose principal function is to represent in court people accused or convicted of a crime who are unable to hire private counsel.

public-order advocate One who believes that under certain circumstances involving a criminal threat to public safety, the interests of society should take precedence over individual rights.

public-safety department A state or local agency that incorporates various law enforcement and emergency service functions.

punitive damages Damages requested or awarded in a civil lawsuit when the defendant's willful acts were malicious, violent, oppressive, fraudulent, wanton, or grossly reckless.[48] Also called *exemplary damages*.

quality-of-life offense A minor violation of the law (sometimes called a *petty crime*) that demoralizes community residents and businesspeople. Quality-of-life offenses involve acts that create physical disorder (for example, excessive noise or vandalism) or that reflect social decay (for example, panhandling and prostitution).

racial profiling "Any police-initiated action that relies on the race, ethnicity, or national origin, rather than [1] the behavior of an individual, or [2] . . . information that leads the police to a particular individual who has been identified as being, or having been, engaged in criminal activity."[49]

Racketeer Influenced and Corrupt Organizations (RICO) A federal statute that allows for the federal seizure of assets derived from illegal enterprise.

radical criminology A conflict perspective that sees crime as engendered by the unequal distribution of wealth, power, and other resources, which adherents believe is especially characteristic of capitalist societies. Also called *critical criminology; Marxist criminology*.

rape Unlawful sexual intercourse achieved through force and without consent. Broadly speaking, the term *rape* has been applied to a wide variety of sexual attacks and may include same-sex rape and the rape of a male by a female. Some jurisdictions refer to same-sex rape as *sexual battery*. See also **forcible rape; sexual battery**.

rated capacity The number of inmates a prison can handle according to the judgment of experts.

rational choice theory A perspective on crime causation that holds that criminality is the result of conscious choice. Rational choice theory predicts that individuals will choose to commit crime when the benefits of doing so outweigh the costs of disobeying the law.

reaction formation The process whereby a person openly rejects that which he or she wants or aspires to but cannot obtain or achieve.

real evidence Evidence that consists of physical material or traces of physical activity.

reasonable doubt In legal proceedings, an actual and substantial doubt arising from the evidence, from the facts or circumstances shown by the evidence, or from the lack of evidence.[50] Also, the state of a case such that, after the comparison and consideration of all the evidence, jurors cannot say they feel an abiding conviction of the truth of the charge.[51]

reasonable doubt standard The standard of proof necessary for conviction in criminal trials.

reasonable force A degree of force that is appropriate in a given situation and is not excessive. Also, the minimum degree of force necessary to protect oneself, one's property, a third party, or the property of another in the face of a substantial threat.

reasonable suspicion The level of suspicion that would justify an officer in making further inquiry or in conducting further investigation. Reasonable suspicion may permit stopping a person for questioning or for a simple pat-down search. Also, a belief, based on a consideration of the facts at hand and on reasonable inferences drawn from those facts, that would induce an ordinarily prudent and cautious person under the same circumstances to conclude that criminal activity is taking place or that criminal activity has recently occurred. Reasonable suspicion is a *general* and reasonable belief that a crime is in progress or has occurred, whereas probable cause is a reasonable belief that a *particular* person has committed a *specific* crime. See also **probable cause**.

recidivism The repetition of criminal behavior. In statistical practice, a recidivism rate may be any of a number of possible counts or instances of arrest, conviction, correctional commitment, or correctional status change related to repetitions of these events within a given period of time.

recidivist A person who has been convicted of one or more crimes and who is alleged or found to have subsequently committed another crime or series of crimes.

reckless behavior Activity that increases the risk of harm.

recreational drug user A person who uses drugs relatively infrequently, primarily with friends, and in social contexts that define drug use as pleasurable. Most addicts begin as recreational users.

reentry The managed return to the community of an individual released from prison. Also, the successful transitioning of a released inmate back into the community. Also called *prisoner reentry*.

reentry courts "Specialized courts that help reduce recidivism and improve public safety through the use of judicial oversight to apply graduated sanctions and positive reinforcement, to marshal resources to support the prisoner's reintegration, and to promote positive behavior by the returning prisoners."[52]

reformatory style A late-nineteenth-century correctional model based on the use of the indeterminate sentence and a belief in the possibility of rehabilitation, especially for youthful offenders. The reformatory concept faded with the emergence of industrial prisons around the start of the twentieth century.

regional jail A jail that is built and run using the combined resources of a variety of local jurisdictions.

rehabilitation The attempt to reform a criminal offender. Also, the state in which a reformed offender is said to be.

release on recognizance (ROR) The pretrial release of a criminal defendant on his or her written promise to appear in court as required. No cash or property bond is required.

remote location monitoring A supervision strategy that uses electronic technology to track offenders who have been sentenced to house arrest or who have been ordered to limit their movements while completing a sentence involving probation or parole.

reprieve An executive act temporarily suspending the execution of a sentence, usually a death sentence. A reprieve differs from other suspensions of sentence not only in that it almost always applies to the temporary withdrawing of a death sentence, but also in that it is usually an act of clemency intended to provide the prisoner with time to secure amelioration of the sentence.

research The use of standardized, systematic procedures in the search for knowledge.

resident A person required, by official action or by his or her acceptance of placement, to reside in a public or private facility established for purposes of confinement, supervision, or care.

residential commitment A sentence of commitment to a correctional facility for adults in which the offender is required to reside at night but from which he or she is regularly permitted to depart during the day, unaccompanied by any official.

response time A measure of the time that it takes for police officers to respond to calls for service.

restitution A court requirement that an accused or convicted offender pay money or provide services to the victim of the crime or provide services to the community.

restoration A goal of criminal sentencing that attempts to make the victim "whole again."

restorative justice (RJ) A sentencing model that builds on restitution and community participation in an attempt to make the victim "whole again."

retribution The act of taking revenge on a criminal perpetrator.

revocation hearing A hearing held before a legally constituted hearing body (such as a parole board) to determine whether a parolee or probationer has violated the conditions and requirements of his or her parole or probation.

rights of defendant The powers and privileges that are constitutionally guaranteed to every defendant.

robbery (UCR/NIBRS) The unlawful taking or attempted taking of property that is in the immediate possession of another by force or violence and/or by putting the victim in fear. Armed robbery differs from unarmed, or strong-arm, robbery in that it involves a weapon. Contrary to popular conceptions, highway robbery does not necessarily occur on a street—and rarely in a vehicle. The term *highway robbery* applies to any form of robbery that occurs outdoors in a public place.

routine activities theory (RAT) A neoclassical perspective that suggests that lifestyles contribute significantly to both the amount and the type of crime found in any society.

rule of law The maxim that an orderly society must be governed by established principles and known codes that are applied uniformly and fairly to all of its members.

rules of evidence Court rules that govern the admissibility of evidence at criminal hearings and trials.

runaway A juvenile who has been adjudicated by a judicial officer of juvenile court as having committed the status offense of leaving the custody and home of his or her parents, guardians, or custodians without permission and of failing to return within a reasonable length of time.

schizophrenic A mentally ill individual who suffers from disjointed thinking and possibly from delusions and hallucinations.

scientific jury selection The use of correlational techniques from the social sciences to gauge the likelihood that potential jurors will vote for conviction or for acquittal.

scientific police management The application of social science techniques to the study of police administration for the purpose of increasing effectiveness, reducing the frequency of citizen complaints, and enhancing the efficient use of available resources.

search incident to an arrest A warrantless search of an arrested individual conducted to ensure the safety of the arresting officer. Because individuals placed under arrest may be in possession of weapons, courts have recognized the need for arresting officers to protect themselves by conducting an immediate search of arrestees without obtaining a warrant.

search warrant A document issued by a judicial officer that directs a law enforcement officer to conduct a search at a specific location for specified property or a specific person relating to a crime, to seize the property or person if found, and to account for the results of the search to the issuing judicial officer.

security The restriction of inmate movement within a correctional facility, usually divided into maximum, medium, and minimum levels.

security threat group (STG) An inmate group, gang, or organization whose members act together to pose a threat to the safety of corrections staff or the public, who prey upon other inmates, or who threaten the secure and orderly operation of a correctional institution.

selective incapacitation A policy that seeks to protect society by incarcerating individuals deemed to be the most dangerous.

self-defense The protection of oneself or of one's property from unlawful injury or from the immediate risk of unlawful injury. Also, the justification that the person who committed an act that would otherwise constitute an offense reasonably believed that the act was necessary to protect self or property from immediate danger.

self-reports Crime measures based on surveys that ask respondents to reveal any illegal activity in which they have been involved.

sentence 1. The penalty imposed by a court on a person convicted of a crime. 2. The court judgment specifying the penalty imposed on a person convicted of a crime. 3. Any disposition of a defendant resulting from a conviction, including the court decision to suspend execution of a sentence.

sentencing The imposition of a criminal sanction by a judicial authority.

sentencing disposition 1. A court disposition of a defendant after a judgment of conviction, expressed as a penalty, such as imprisonment or payment of a fine. 2. Any of a number of alternatives to actually executed penalties, such as a suspended sentence, a grant of probation, or an order to perform restitution. 3. Various combinations of the foregoing.

sentencing hearing In criminal proceedings, a hearing during which the court or jury considers relevant information, such as evidence concerning aggravating or mitigating circumstances, for the purpose of determining a sentencing disposition for a person convicted of an offense.

sequestered jury A jury that is isolated from the public during the course of a trial and throughout the deliberation process.

service style A style of policing marked by a concern with helping rather than strict enforcement. Service-oriented police agencies are more likely to use community resources, such as drug-treatment programs, to supplement traditional law enforcement activities than are other types of agencies.

sex offense In current statistical usage, any of a broad category of varying offenses, usually consisting of all offenses having a sexual element except forcible rape and commercial sex offenses. The category includes all unlawful sexual intercourse, unlawful sexual contact, and other unlawful behavior intended to result in sexual gratification or profit from sexual activity.

sex offense (UCR/NIBRS) Any of various "offenses against chastity, common decency, morals, and the like," except forcible rape, prostitution, and commercialized vice.

sex trafficking The recruitment, harboring, transportation, provision, or obtaining of a person for the purpose of a commercial sex act.

sexual battery Intentional and wrongful physical contact with a person, without his or her consent, that entails a sexual component or purpose.

sheriff The elected chief officer of a county law enforcement agency. The sheriff is usually responsible for law enforcement in unincorporated areas and for the operation of the county jail.

sheriff's department A local law enforcement agency, directed by a sheriff, that exercises its law enforcement functions at the county level, usually within unincorporated areas, and that operates the county jail in most jurisdictions.

shock incarceration A sentencing option that makes use of "boot camp"—type prisons to impress on convicted offenders the realities of prison life.

shock probation The practice of sentencing offenders to prison, allowing them to apply for probationary release, and surprisingly permitting such release. Offenders who receive shock probation may not be aware that they will be released on probation and may expect to spend a much longer time behind bars.

simple assault (UCR/NIBRS) The unlawful threatening, attempted inflicting, or inflicting of less-than-serious bodily injury, without a deadly weapon.

smuggling The unlawful movement of goods across a national frontier or state boundary or into or out of a correctional facility.

sneak-and-peek search A search that occurs in the suspect's absence and without his or her prior knowledge. Also known as *delayed notification search*.

social control The use of sanctions and rewards within a group to influence and shape the behavior of individual members of that group. Social control is a primary concern of social groups and communities, and it is their interest in the exercise of social control that leads to the creation of both criminal and civil statutes.

social debt A sentencing principle that holds that an offender's criminal history should objectively be taken into account in sentencing decisions.

social development theory An integrated view of human development that points to the process of interaction among and between individuals and society as the root cause of criminal behavior.

social disorganization A condition said to exist when a group is faced with social change, uneven development of culture, maladaptiveness, disharmony, conflict, and lack of consensus.

social ecology A criminological approach that focuses on the misbehavior of lower-class youth and sees delinquency primarily as the result of social disorganization.

social engineering A nontechnical kind of cyberintrusion that relies heavily on human interaction and often involves tricking people into breaking normal security procedures.

social justice An ideal that embraces all aspects of civilized life and that is linked to fundamental notions of fairness and to cultural beliefs about right and wrong.

social learning theory A psychological perspective that says that people learn how to behave by modeling themselves after others whom they have the opportunity to observe.

social order The condition of a society characterized by social integration, consensus, smooth functioning, and lack of interpersonal and institutional conflict. Also, a lack of social disorganization.

social process theory A perspective on criminological thought that highlights the process of interaction between individuals and society. Most social process theories highlight the role of social learning.

social-psychological theory A perspective on criminological thought that highlights the role played in crime causation by weakened self-esteem and meaningless social roles. Social-psychological thinkers stress the relationship of the individual to the social group as the underlying cause of behavior.

sociopath See **psychopath**.

software piracy The unauthorized duplication of software or the illegal transfer of data from one storage medium to another. Software piracy is one of the most prevalent cybercrimes in the world.

solvability factor Information about a crime that forms the basis for determining the perpetrator's identity.

somatotyping The classification of human beings into types according to body build and other physical characteristics.

spam Unsolicited commercial bulk e-mail whose primary purpose is the advertisement or promotion of a commercial product or service.

span of control The number of police personnel or the number of units supervised by a particular commander.

specific deterrence A goal of criminal sentencing that seeks to prevent a particular offender from engaging in repeat criminality.

speedy trial A trial that is held in a timely manner. The right of a defendant to have a prompt trial is guaranteed by the Sixth Amendment of the U.S. Constitution, which begins, "In all criminal prosecutions, the accused shall enjoy the right to a speedy and public trial."

Speedy Trial Act A 1974 federal law requiring that proceedings against a defendant in a federal criminal case begin within a specified period of time, such as 70 working days after indictment. Some states also have speedy trial requirements.

split sentence A sentence explicitly requiring the convicted offender to serve a period of confinement in a local, state, or federal facility, followed by a period of probation.

staff operations In police organizations, activities (such as administration and training) that provide support for line operations.

stalking Repeated harassing and threatening behavior by one individual against another, aspects of which may be planned or carried out in secret. Stalking might involve following a person, appearing at a person's home or place of business, making harassing phone calls, leaving written messages or objects, or vandalizing a person's property. Most stalking laws require that the perpetrator make a credible threat of violence against the victim or members of the victim's immediate family.

stare decisis A legal principle that requires that, in subsequent cases on similar issues of law and fact, courts be bound by their own earlier decisions and by those of higher courts having jurisdiction over them. The term literally means "standing by decided matters."

state-action doctrine The traditional legal principle that only government officials or their representatives in the criminal justice process can be held accountable for the violation of an individual's constitutional civil rights.

state court administrator A coordinator who assists with case-flow management, operating funds budgeting, and court docket administration.

state court system A state judicial structure. Most states have at least three court levels: trial courts, appellate courts, and a state supreme court.

state highway patrol A state law enforcement agency whose principal functions are preventing, detecting, and investigating motor vehicle offenses and apprehending traffic offenders.

state police A state law enforcement agency whose principal functions usually include maintaining statewide police communications, aiding local police in criminal investigations, training police, and guarding state property. The state police may include the highway patrol.

state-use system A form of inmate labor in which items produced by inmates may only be sold by or to state offices. Items that only the state can sell include such things as license plates and hunting licenses, whereas items sold only to state offices include furniture and cleaning supplies.

status offender A child who commits an act that is contrary to the law by virtue of the offender's status as a child. Purchasing cigarettes, buying alcohol, and being truant are examples of such behavior.

status offense An act or conduct that is declared by statute to be an offense, but only when committed by or engaged in by a juvenile, and that can be adjudicated only by a juvenile court.

Statute of Winchester A law, written in 1285, that created a watch and ward system in English cities and towns and that codified early police practices.

statutory law Written or codified law; the "law on the books," as enacted by a government body or agency having the power to make laws.

statutory rape Sexual intercourse with a person who is under the legal age of consent.

stay of execution The stopping by a court of the implementation of a judgment—that is, of a court order previously issued.

stolen property offense The unlawful receiving, buying, distributing, selling, transporting, concealing, or possessing of the property of another by a person who knows that the property has been unlawfully obtained from the owner or other lawful possessor.

stop and frisk The detaining of a person by a law enforcement officer for the purpose of investigation, accompanied by a superficial examination by the officer of the person's body surface or clothing to discover weapons, contraband, or other objects relating to criminal activity.

stranger violence Seemingly random violence perpetrated by assailants who were previously unknown to their victims. Stranger violence often results from rage, opportunity, or insanity.

strategic policing A type of policing that retains the traditional police goal of professional crime fighting but enlarges the enforcement target to include nontraditional kinds of criminals, such as serial offenders, gangs and criminal associations, drug-distribution networks, and sophisticated white-collar and computer criminals. Strategic policing generally makes use of innovative enforcement techniques, including intelligence operations, undercover stings, electronic surveillance, and sophisticated forensic methods.

street crime A class of offenses, sometimes defined with some degree of formality as those that occur in public locations and are visible and assaultive, that are a special risk to the public and a special target of law enforcement preventive efforts and prosecutorial attention.

strict liability Liability without fault or intention. Strict liability offenses do not require *mens rea*.

structured sentencing A model of criminal punishment that includes determinate and commission-created presumptive sentencing schemes, as well as voluntary/advisory sentencing guidelines.

subculture of violence A cultural setting in which violence is a traditional and often accepted method of dispute resolution.

subpoena A written order issued by a judicial officer or grand jury requiring an individual to appear in court and to give testimony or to bring material to be used as evidence. Some subpoenas mandate that books, papers, and other items be surrendered to the court.

substantive criminal law The part of the law that defines crimes and specifies punishments.

supermale A human male displaying the XYY chromosome structure.

superpredator A juvenile who is coming of age in actual and "moral poverty" without the benefits of parents, teachers, coaches, and clergy to teach right from wrong[53] and who turns to criminal activity. The term is often applied to inner-city youths, socialized in violent settings without the benefit of wholesome life experiences, who hold considerable potential for violence.

supervised probation Guidance, treatment, or regulation by a probation agency of the behavior of a person who is subject to adjudication or who has been convicted of an offense, resulting from a formal court order or a probation agency decision.

suspect An adult or a juvenile who has not been arrested or charged but whom a criminal justice agency believes may be the person responsible for a specific criminal offense.

suspended sentence The court decision to delay imposing or executing a penalty for a specified or unspecified period. Also, a court disposition of a convicted person pronouncing a penalty of a fine or a commitment to confinement but unconditionally discharging the defendant or holding execution of the penalty in abeyance upon good behavior. Also called *sentence withheld*.

suspicionless search A search conducted by law enforcement personnel without a warrant and without suspicion. Suspicionless searches are permissible only if based on an overriding concern for public safety.

sustainable justice Criminal laws and criminal justice institutions, policies, and practices that achieve justice in the present without compromising the ability of future generations to have the benefits of a just society.[54]

sworn officer A law enforcement officer who is trained and empowered to perform full police duties, such as making arrests, conducting investigations, and carrying firearms.[55]

***Tazir* crime** A minor violation of Islamic law that is regarded as an offense against society, not God.

team policing The reorganization of conventional patrol strategies into "an integrated and versatile police team assigned to a fixed district."[56]

technocrime A criminal offense that employs advanced or emerging technology in its commission.

teen court An alternative approach to juvenile justice in which alleged offenders are judged and sentenced by a jury of their peers.

TEMPEST A standard developed by the federal government that requires that electromagnetic emanations from computers designated as "secure" be below levels that would allow radio receiving equipment to "read" the data being computed.

terrorism A violent act or an act dangerous to human life, in violation of the criminal laws of the United States or of any state, that is committed to intimidate or coerce a government, the civilian population, or any segment thereof, in furtherance of political or social objectives.[57]

testimony Oral evidence offered by a sworn witness on the witness stand during a criminal trial.

theft Generally, any taking of the property of another with intent to permanently deprive the rightful owner of possession.

theory A set of interrelated propositions that attempt to describe, explain, predict, and ultimately control some class of events. A theory is strengthened by its logical consistency and is "tested" by how well it describes and predicts reality.

three-strikes laws Statutes that require mandatory sentences (sometimes life in prison without the possibility of parole) for offenders convicted of a third felony. Such mandatory sentencing enhancements are aimed at deterring known and potentially violent offenders and are intended to incapacitate convicted criminals through long-term incarceration.

tort A wrongful act, damage, or injury not involving a breach of contract. Also, a private or civil wrong or injury.

total institution An enclosed facility separated from society both socially and physically, where the inhabitants share all aspects of their daily lives.

trafficking in persons (TIP) The exploitation of unwilling or unwitting people through force, coercion, threat, or deception.

traits stable personality patterns that tend to endure throughout the life course and across social and cultural contexts.

transfer to adult court The decision by a juvenile court, resulting from a transfer hearing, that jurisdiction over an alleged delinquent will be waived and that he or she should be prosecuted as an adult in a criminal court.

transnational organized crime Unlawful activity undertaken and supported by organized criminal groups operating across national boundaries. Also called *transnational crime*.

treason A U.S. citizen's actions to help a foreign government overthrow, make war against, or seriously injure the United States.[58] Also, the attempt to overthrow the government of the society of which one is a member.

trial In criminal proceedings, the examination in court of the issues of fact and relevant law in a case for the purpose of convicting or acquitting the defendant.

trial *de novo* Literally, "new trial." The term is applied to cases that are retried on appeal, as opposed to those that are simply reviewed on the record.

trial judge A judicial officer who is authorized to conduct jury and nonjury trials but who may not be authorized to hear appellate cases. Also, the judicial officer who conducts a particular trial.

trial jury A statutorily defined number of people selected according to law and sworn to determine, in accordance with the law as instructed by the court, certain matters of fact based on evidence presented in a trial and to render a verdict. Also called *petit jury*.

truth in sentencing A close correspondence between the sentence imposed on an offender and the time actually served in prison.[59]

UCR See **Uniform Crime Reporting Program (UCR)**.

unconditional release The final release of an offender from the jurisdiction of a correctional agency. Also, a final release from the jurisdiction of a court.

undisciplined child A child who is beyond parental control, as evidenced by his or her refusal to obey legitimate authorities, such as school officials and teachers.

Uniform Crime Reporting (UCR) Program A statistical reporting program run by the FBI's Criminal Justice Information Services (CJIS) division. The UCR Program publishes *Crime in the United States*, which provides an annual summation of the incidence and rate of reported crimes throughout the United States.

USA PATRIOT Act A federal law (Public Law 107–56) enacted in response to terrorist attacks on the World Trade Center and the Pentagon on September 11, 2001. The law, officially titled the Uniting and Strengthening America by Providing Appropriate Tools Required to Intercept and Obstruct Terrorism Act, substantially broadened the investigative authority of law enforcement agencies throughout America and is applicable to many crimes other than terrorism. The law was slightly revised and reauthorized by Congress in 2006. Also called *Antiterrorism Act*.

use of force See **police use of force**.

vagrancy (UCR/NIBRS) An offense related to being a suspicious person, including vagrancy, begging, loitering, and vagabondage.

vandalism (UCR/NIBRS) The destroying or damaging of public property or the property of another without the owner's consent, or the attempt to destroy or damage such property. This definition of vandalism does not include burning.

venue The particular geographic area in which a court may hear or try a case. Also, the locality within which a particular crime was committed. See also **jurisdiction**.

verdict The decision of the jury in a jury trial or of a judicial officer in a nonjury trial.

victim A person who has suffered death, physical or mental anguish, or loss of property as the result of an actual or attempted criminal offense committed by another person.

victim-impact statement The in-court use of victim- or survivor-supplied information by sentencing authorities seeking to make an informed sentencing decision.

victimization In National Crime Victimization Survey terminology, the harming of any single victim in a criminal incident.

victimology The scientific study of crime victims and the victimization process. Victimology is a subfield of criminology.

victims' assistance program An organized program that offers services to victims of crime in the areas of crisis intervention and follow-up counseling and that helps victims secure their rights under the law.

vigilantism The act of taking the law into one's own hands.

violation 1. The performance of an act forbidden by a statute or the failure to perform an act commanded by a statute. 2. An act contrary to a local government ordinance. 3. An offense punishable by a fine or other penalty but not by incarceration. 4. An act prohibited by the terms and conditions of probation or parole.

violent crime A UCR/NIBRS summary offense category that includes murder, rape, robbery, and aggravated assault.

voluntary/advisory sentencing guidelines Recommended sentencing policies that are not required by law.

warden The official in charge of the operation of a prison, the chief administrator of a prison, or the prison superintendent.

warehousing An imprisonment strategy that is based on the desire to prevent recurrent crime and that has abandoned all hope of rehabilitation.

warrant In criminal proceedings, a writ issued by a judicial officer directing a law enforcement officer to perform a specified act and affording the officer protection from damages if he or she performs it.

watchman style A style of policing marked by a concern for order maintenance. Watchman policing is characteristic of lower-class communities where police intervene informally into the lives of residents to keep the peace.

weapon of mass destruction (WMD) A chemical, biological, or nuclear weapon that has the potential to cause mass casualties.

weapons offense The unlawful sale, distribution, manufacture, alteration, transportation, possession, or use, or the attempted unlawful sale, distribution, manufacture, alteration, transportation, possession, or use, of a deadly or dangerous weapon or accessory.

white-collar crime Violations of the criminal law committed by a person of respectability and high social status in the course of his or her occupation. Also, nonviolent crime for financial gain utilizing deception and committed by anyone who has special technical or professional knowledge of business or government, irrespective of the person's occupation.

Wickersham Commission The National Commission on Law Observance and Enforcement. In 1931, the commission issued a report stating that Prohibition was unenforceable and carried a great potential for police corruption.

witness Generally, a person who has knowledge of the circumstances of a case. Also, in court usage, one who testifies as to what he or she has seen, heard, or otherwise observed or who has expert knowledge.

work release A prison program through which inmates are temporarily released into the community to meet job responsibilities.

workhouse An early form of imprisonment whose purpose was to instill habits of industry in the idle. Also called *bridewell*.

writ A document issued by a judicial officer ordering or forbidding the performance of a specified act.

writ of *certiorari* A writ issued from an appellate court for the purpose of obtaining from a lower court the record of its proceedings in a particular case. In some states, this writ is the mechanism for discretionary review. A request for review is made by petitioning for a writ of *certiorari*, and the granting of review is indicated by the issuance of the writ.

writ of *habeas corpus* A writ that directs the person detaining a prisoner to bring him or her before a judicial officer to determine the lawfulness of the imprisonment.

youthful offender A person, adjudicated in criminal court, who may be above the statutory age limit for juveniles but is below a specified upper age limit, for whom special correctional commitments and special record-sealing procedures are made available by statute.

NOTES

1. Bureau of Justice Statistics, *Dictionary of Criminal Justice Data Terminology*, 2nd ed. (Washington, DC: U.S. Government Printing Office, 1982).
2. Federal Bureau of Investigation, *Uniform Crime Reporting Handbook, 2004* (Washington, DC: U.S. Dept. of Justice, 2005).
3. BJS, *Dictionary of Criminal Justice Data Terminology*, p. 5.
4. Adapted from U.S. Code, Title 28, Section 20.3 (2[d]). Title 28 of the U.S. Code defines the term *administration of criminal justice*.
5. Thomas J. Cowper and Michael E. Buerger, *Improving Our View of the World: Police and Augmented Reality Technology* (Washington, DC: Federal Bureau of Investigation, 2003), http://www.fbi.gov/publications/realitytech/realitytech.pdf (accessed October 7, 2007).
6. *People* v. *Romero*, 8 Cal. 4th 728, 735 (1994).
7. Technical Working Group on Crime Scene Investigation, *Crime Scene Investigation: A Guide for Law Enforcement* (Washington, DC: National Institute of Justice, 2000), p. 12.
8. Centers for Disease Control and Prevention, "Bioterrorism: An Overview," http://www.bt.cdc.gov/bioterrorism/overview.asp (accessed August 15, 2007).
9. Howard N. Snyder and Melissa Sickmund, *Juvenile Offenders and Victims: 2006 National Report* (Washington, DC: Office of Juvenile Justice and Delinquency Prevention, 2006).
10. *State* v. *Cross*, 200 S.E.2d 27, 29 (1973).
11. Adapted from Gerald Hill and Kathleen Hill, "The Real Life Dictionary of the Law," http://www.law.com (accessed June 11, 2007).
12. Hill and Hill, "The Real Life Dictionary of the Law" (accessed February 27, 2007).
13. Community Policing Consortium, *What Is Community Policing?* (Washington, DC: Community Policing Consortium, 1995).
14. Michael L. Benson, Francis T. Cullen, and William J. Maakestad, *Local Prosecutors and Corporate Crime* (Washington, DC: National Institute of Justice, 1992), p. 1.
15. Office of Justice Programs, *The National Criminal Intelligence Sharing Plan* (Washington, DC: U.S. Dept. of Justice, 2005), p. 27.
16. Wayne W. Bennett and Karen M. Hess, *Criminal Investigation*, 6th ed. (Belmont, CA: Wadsworth, 2001), p. 3 (italics in original).
17. Violence against Women Office, *Stalking and Domestic Violence: Report to Congress* (Washington, DC: U.S. Dept. of Justice, 2001), p. 5.
18. Sam W. Lathrop, "Reviewing Use of Force: A Systematic Approach," *FBI Law Enforcement Bulletin*, October 2000, p. 18.
19. Adapted from Larry R. Leibrock, "Overview and Impact on 21st Century Legal Practice: Digital Forensics and Electronic Discovery," http://www.courtroom21.net/FDIC.pps (accessed July 15, 2007).
20. Adapted from Federal Bureau of Investigation, "FBI Policy and Guidelines: Counterterrorism," http://jackson.fbi.gov/cntrterr.htm (accessed March 24, 2007).
21. Bureau of Justice Statistics, *Drugs, Crime, and the Justice System* (Washington, DC: BJS, 1992), p. 20.
22. Adapted from Technical Working Group for Electronic Crime Scene Investigation, *Electronic Crime Scene Investigation: A Guide for First Responders* (Washington, DC: National Institute of Justice, 2001), p. 2.
23. Henry Campbell Black, Joseph R. Nolan, and Jacqueline M. Nolan-Haley, *Black's Law Dictionary*, 6th ed. (St. Paul, MN: West, 1990), p. 24.
24. Lawrence W. Sherman, *Evidence-Based Policing* (Washington, DC: Police Foundation, 1998), p. 3.
25. International Association of Chiefs of Police, *Police Use of Force in America, 2001* (Alexandria, VA: IACP, 2001), p. 1.
26. Adapted from "Globalization," Encyclopedia Britannica, 2003, http://www.britannica.com/eb/article?eu5369857 (accessed July 23, 2003).
27. Black et al., *Black's Law Dictionary*, p. 1003.
28. *The American Heritage Dictionary and Electronic Thesaurus on CD-ROM* (Boston: Houghton Mifflin, 1987).
29. Adapted from Entrust, Inc., "Secure Identity Management: Challenges, Needs, and Solutions," p. 1, http://www.entrust.com (accessed August 5, 2007).
30. Identity Theft Resource Center website, http://www.idtheftcenter.org (accessed April 24, 2007).
31. Adapted from Dictionary.com, http://dictionary.reference.com/search?q5infrastructure (accessed January 10, 2007).
32. Angus Smith, ed., *Intelligence-Led Policing* (Richmond, VA: International Association of Law Enforcement Intelligence Analysts, 1997), p. 1.
33. Adapted from FBI, "FBI Policy and Guidelines: Counterterrorism."
34. Jeffrey A. Butts and Ojmarrh Mitchell, "Brick by Brick: Dismantling the Border between Juvenile and Adult Justice," in Phyllis McDonald and Janice Munsterman, eds., *Boundary Changes in Criminal Justice Organizations*, Vol. 2 of *Criminal Justice 2000* (Washington, DC: National Institute of Justice, 2000), p. 207.
35. David A. Garvin, "Building a Learning Organization," *Harvard Business Review* (1993), pp. 78–91.
36. U.S. Department of Treasury, *2000–2005 Strategic Plan* (Washington, DC: U.S. Government Printing Office, 2000), p. 1.
37. Adapted from Robert M. Shusta et al., *Multicultural Law Enforcement*, 2nd ed. (Upper Saddle River, NJ: Prentice Hall, 2002), p. 443.
38. The Organized Crime Control Act of 1970 (Public Law 91-451).
39. BJS, *Drugs, Crime, and the Justice System*, p. 20.
40. Carl B. Klockars et al., *The Measurement of Police Integrity*, National Institute of Justice Research in Brief (Washington, DC: NIJ, 2000), p. 1.

41. This definition draws on the classic work by O.W.Wilson, *Police Administration* (New York: McGraw-Hill, 1950), pp. 2–3.
42. National Institute of Justice, *Use of Force by Police: Overview of National and Local Data* (Washington, DC: NIJ, 1999).
43. National Council on Crime and Delinquency, *National Assessment of Structured Sentencing* (Washington, DC: Bureau of Justice Statistics, 1996), p. xii.
44. Bureau of Justice Statistics, *Prisoners in 1998* (Washington, DC: BJS, 1999), p. 7.
45. *Private Security: Report of the Task Force on Private Security* (Washington, DC: U.S. Government Printing Office, 1976), p. 4.
46. Samuel Walker, Geoffrey P. Albert, and Dennis J. Kenney, *Responding to the Problem Police Officer: A National Study of Early Warning Systems* (Washington, DC: National Institute of Justice, 2000).
47. BJS, *Drugs, Crime, and the Justice System*, p. 21.
48. Gerald Hill and Kathleen Hill, *The Real Life Dictionary of the Law* (Santa Monica, CA: General Publishing Group, 2000), http://dictionary.law.com/lookup2.asp (accessed February 28, 2007).
49. Deborah Ramierz, Jack McDevitt, and Amy Farrell, *A Resource Guide on Racial Profiling Data Collection Systems: Promising Practices and Lessons Learned* (Washington, DC: U.S. Dept. of Justice, 2000), p. 3.
50. *Victor* v. *Nebraska*, 114 S.Ct. 1239, 127 L.Ed.2d 583 (1994).
51. As found in the California jury instructions.
52. Debbie Dawes, *The National Institute of Justice's Evaluation of Second Chance Act Adult Reentry Courts: Program Characteristics and Preliminary Themes from Year 1* (Washington, DC: Bureau of Justice Assistance, 2013).
53. The term *superpredator* is generally attributed to John J. DiIulio, Jr. See John J. DiIulio, Jr., "The Question of Black Crime," *Public Interest* (fall 1994), pp. 3–12.
54. Melissa Hickman Barlow, "Sustainable Justice: 2012 Presidential Address to the Academy of Criminal Justice Sciences, *Justice Quarterly*, Vol. 30, No. 1 (2013), pp. 1–17.
55. Adapted from Darl H. Champion and Michael K. Hooper, *Introduction to American Policing* (New York: McGraw-Hill, 2003), p. 166.
56. Sam S. Souryal, *Police Administration and Management* (St. Paul, MN: West, 1977), p. 261.
57. Federal Bureau of Investigation, Counterterrorism Section, *Terrorism in the United States, 1987* (Washington, DC: FBI, 1987).
58. Daniel Oran, *Oran's Dictionary of the Law* (St. Paul, MN: West, 1983), p. 306.
59. Lawrence A. Greenfeld, *Prison Sentences and Time Served for Violence*, Bureau of Justice Statistics Selected Findings, No. 4 (Washington, DC: Bureau of Justice Statistics, April 1995).

Case Index

Name Index

J

K

L

M

U

V

W

Y

Z

Subject Index

E

J

K

L

M

N

O

S

T

U

V

W

Y

20°E
40°E
60°E
80°E
100°E
120°E
140°E
160°E
180°
80°N
ARCTIC OCEAN
URAL MTS.
Ob
Volga
60°N
EUROPE
ALPS
GOBI DESERT
ASIA
40°N
HINDU KUSH
HIMALAYA MTS.
Indus
Ganges
Yangzi
SYRIAN DESERT
SAHARA
Tropic of Cancer
20°N
Nile
DECCAN PLATEAU
AFRICA
PACIFIC OCEAN
0°
INDIAN OCEAN
GREAT SANDY DESERT
20°S
NAMIB DESERT
KALAHARI DESERT
Tropic of Capricorn
AUSTRALIA
Cape of Good Hope
0
1000
2000
3000 Km.
0
1000
2000
3000 Mi.
60°S
Antarctic Circle
ANTARCTICA
80°S
180°

The Earth and Its Peoples

A Global History

The Earth and Its Peoples

A Global History

THIRD EDITION

Richard W. Bulliet
Columbia University

Pamela Kyle Crossley
Dartmouth College

Daniel R. Headrick
Roosevelt University

Steven W. Hirsch
Tufts University

Lyman L. Johnson
University of North Carolina–Charlotte

David Northrup
Boston College

Houghton Mifflin Company   Boston   New York

Publisher: Charles Hartford
Editor-in-Chief: Jean L. Woy
Senior Sponsoring Editor: Nancy Blaine
Senior Development Editor: Jennifer Sutherland
Editorial Associate: Annette Fantasia
Senior Project Editor: Carol Newman
Editorial Assistant: Trinity Peacock-Broyles
Senior Design Coordinator: Jill Haber
Senior Designer: Henry Rachlin
Manufacturing Manager: Florence Cadran
Senior Marketing Manager: Sandra McGuire

Cover illustration: *New Year's Festival* (woodcut) by Utagawa Kunisada (1786–1864) Victoria and Albert Museum, London, UK / Bridgeman Art Library International, Ltd.

Part opener credits

Pt. 1, p. 1: Gian Berto Vanni/Corbis; Pt. 2, p. 115: © Corbis; Pt. 3, p. 205: Tokyo National Museum/DNP Archives; Pt. 4, p. 333: Bibliothèque nationale de France; Pt. 5, p. 445: Library of Congress; Pt. 6, p. 577: © Hulton-Deutsch/Corbis; Pt. 7, p. 719: Charles O'Rear/Corbis; Pt. 8, p. 857 © Corbis.

Chapter opener credits

Ch. 1, p. 4: David Coulson/Robert Estall Photo Agency; Ch. 2, p. 27: Giraudon/Art Resource, NY; Ch. 3, p. 55: Courtesy of the Trustees of the British Museum; Ch. 4, p. 81: Woodfin Camp & Associates; Ch. 5, p. 118: Biblioteque nationale de France; Ch. 6, p. 150: © Dennis Cox/ChinaStock; Ch. 7, p. 178: Dinodia Photo Library; Ch. 8, p. 208: Allan Eaton/Ancient Art & Architecture; Ch. 9, p. 229: Suleymaniye Library, Istanbul. Courtesy, Karen Pinto, History Department, Columbia University; Ch. 10, p. 249: Musée de Bayeaux/Michael Holford; Ch. 11, p. 280 Fujita Art Museum; Ch. 12, p. 305: Justin Kerr; Ch. 13, p. 336: Imperial Household Agency/International Society for Educational Information, Japan; Ch. 14, p. 366: Imperial Household Collection, Kyoto; Ch. 15, p. 391: Copyright Brussels, Royal Library of Belgium; Ch. 16, p. 417: G. Dagli Orti/The Art Archive; Ch. 17, p. 448: Kunsthistorisches Museum, Vienna/The Bridgeman Art Library, New York and London; Ch. 18, p. 473: Archivo General de la Nación, Buenos Aires; Ch. 19, p. 499: From William Clark, *Ten Views in the Islands of Antigua,* 1823. British Library; Ch. 20, p. 525: V&A Picture Library; Ch. 21, p. 550: Novosti; Ch. 22, p. 580: Jean-Loup Charmet/ The Bridgeman Art Library; Ch. 23, p. 608: Science & Society Picture Library; Ch. 24, p. 632: *Estación de Orizaba,* 1877. From Casimiro Castro, *Album del Ferro-Carril Mexicano: Coleccion de Vista Pintadas* (Victor Debray and Company, 1877); Ch. 25, p. 663: Eyre and Hobbs House Art Gallery; Ch. 26, p. 690: Mary Evans Picture Library; Ch. 27, p. 722: The Metropolitan Museum of Art, gift of Lincoln Kirstein, 1959 (JP 3346). Photograph by Otto E. Nelson. Photograph © 1986 The Metropolitan Museum of Art; Ch. 28, p. 748: Bildarchiv Preussischer Kulturbesitz; Ch. 29, p. 775: Imperial War Museum/The Art Archive; Ch. 30, p. 804: akg-images; Ch. 31, p. 831: Genevieve Naylor, photographer/ Reznikoff Artistic Partnership, NY; Ch. 32, p. 860: Bettmann/Corbis; Ch. 33, p. 887: Paul Chesley/Getty Images; Ch. 34, p. 918: AFP Photo/Doug Kanter/Getty Images.

Printed in U.S.A.

Library of Congress Catalog Card Number: 2003115591

ISBN: 0-618-40334-5

1 2 3 4 5 6 7 8 9—VH—2008 2007 2006 2005 2004

Brief Contents

PART SEVEN
Global Diversity and Dominance, 1850–1945 719

PART EIGHT
Perils and Promises of a Global Community, 1945 to the Present 857

Contents

PART THREE
Growth and Interaction of Cultural Communities, 300 B.C.E.–1200 C.E.
205

Maps

Environment and Technology

Diversity and Dominance

Issues in World History

Preface

Reaching the point of preparing the third edition of a textbook is particularly gratifying for its authors. The sustained appeal of their writing tells them that they have done something good and useful. But that in turn prompts them to ponder what they can do to make their book still better. Fortunately, feedback from teachers and students provides a regular stream of helpful suggestions. We have tried to respond to the most frequent and constructive of these suggestions in preparing the third edition.

Our overall goal remains unchanged: to produce a textbook that not only speaks for the past but speaks to today's student and today's teacher. Students and instructors alike should take away from this text a broad vision of human societies beginning as sparse and disconnected communities reacting creatively to local circumstances; experiencing ever more intensive stages of contact, interpenetration, and cultural expansion and amalgamation; and arriving at a twenty-first century world in which people increasingly visualize a single global community.

Process, not progress, is the keynote of this book: a steady process of change over time, at first differently experienced in various regions, but eventually connecting peoples and traditions from all parts of the globe. Students should come away from this book with a sense that the problems and promises of their world are rooted in a past in which people of every sort, in every part of the world, confronted problems of a similar character and coped with them as best they could. We believe that our efforts will help students see where their world has come from and learn thereby something useful for their own lives.

Central Themes

We subtitled *The Earth and Its Peoples* "A Global History" because the book explores the common challenges and experiences that unite the human past. Although the dispersal of early humans to every livable environment resulted in a myriad of different economic, social, political, and cultural systems, all societies displayed analogous patterns in meeting their needs and exploiting their environments. Our challenge was to select the particular data and episodes that would best illuminate these global patterns of human experience.

To meet this challenge, we adopted two themes to serve as the spinal cord of our history: "technology and the environment" and "diversity and dominance." The first theme represents the commonplace material bases of all human societies at all times. It grants no special favor to any cultural group even as it embraces subjects of the broadest topical, chronological, and geographical range. The second theme expresses the reality that every human society has constructed or inherited structures of domination. We examine practices and institutions of many sorts: military, economic, social, political, religious, and cultural, as well as those based on kinship, gender, and literacy. Simultaneously we recognize that alternative ways of life and visions of societal organization continually manifest themselves both within and in dialogue with every structure of domination.

With respect to the first theme, it is vital for students to understand that technology, in the broad sense of experience-based knowledge of the physical world, underlies all human activity. Writing is a technology, but so is oral transmission from generation to generation of lore about medicinal or poisonous plants. The magnetic compass is a navigational technology, but so is Polynesian mariners' hard-won knowledge of winds, currents, and tides that made possible the settlement of the Pacific islands.

All technological development has come about in interaction with environments, both physical and human, and has, in turn, affected those environments. The story of how humanity has changed the face of the globe is an integral part of our first theme. Yet technology and the environment do not explain or underlie all important episodes of human experience. The theme of "diversity and dominance" informs all our discussions of politics, culture, and society. Thus when narrating the histories of empires, we describe a range of human experiences within and beyond the imperial frontiers without assuming that imperial institutions are a more fit topic for discussion than the economic and social organization of pastoral nomads or the lives of peasant women. When religion and culture occupy our narrative, we focus not only on the dominant tradition but also on the diversity of alternative beliefs and practices.

Changes in the Third Edition

A reader comparing the second and third editions will notice changes in both structure and coverage. Most apparent among the structural changes are two new features. In each chapter a two-page primary source feature, "Diversity and Dominance," has replaced the brief "Society and Culture" excerpts of the previous edition. The new feature fills two needs. First, it gives students extended documentary selections on which to hone their analytical skills. This, we believe, will serve well the desire of many teachers to expose their students to the raw material with which historians work. Second, it provides a focus for students to consider the many forms of dominance that have developed over time and the many ways in which human diversity has continued to express itself regardless of these forms of dominance. The topics covered under "Diversity and Dominance" range from "Hierarchy and Conduct in the Analects of Confucius" (Chapter 3) and "Archbishop Adalbert of Hamburg and the Christianization of the Scandinavians and Slavs" (Chapter 10) to "The Afro-Brazilian Experience, 1828" (Chapter 24) and "Women, Family Values, and the Russian Revolution" (Chapter 30).

"Issues in World History," the second new feature, comprises original essays that appear at the end of Parts One through Seven. As we surveyed the burgeoning field of global history, we became aware of issues of such broad significance, often involving new kinds of historical evidence, that they could not easily be discussed in a chapter concentrating on a specific time and place. We therefore highlight seven of these issues in part-ending essays: "Animal Domestication," "Oral Societies and the Consequences of Literacy," "Religious Conversion," "Climate and Population, to 1500," "The Little Ice Age," "State Power, the Census, and the Question of Identity," and "Famines and Politics." We believe that teachers and students will be stimulated to see the great reach and exciting potential of the field of global history and be encouraged to pose broader questions of their own.

We sifted through a mass of helpful suggestions on how to revise and reorganize the content itself. Along with hundreds of minor revisions and clarifications, we effected a number of major changes:

- Chapters 3 and 4 have been rethought and reorganized: Chapter 3 now deals with several civilizations that emerged independently in different parts of the world in the second and first millennia B.C.E., while Chapter 4 focuses on the same time period in Western Asia and the Mediterranean, giving greater stress to continuity and interaction in that region.
- Chapter 10, on early medieval Europe, has been reorganized so that it opens with Byzantium and proceeds from there to western Europe. Two new maps have been added—one on German kingdoms, c. 530, and the other on Kievan Russia and the Byzantine Empire in the eleventh century.
- We greatly increased the coverage of Russian history, including expanded discussions in Chapters 10 and 21 and an entirely new section in Chapter 26.
- The history and impact of the Mongols are now covered in a single chapter, Chapter 13, "Mongol Eurasia and Its Aftermath, 1200–1500." Combining previously separated materials allowed us to make more evident the parallels and contrasts between the impact of the Mongols in the west and in the east.
- Chapter 17, on early modern Europe, has been reorganized and streamlined.
- Coverage of the United States in the late nineteenth century, previously in two separate chapters, has been reorganized and consolidated in Chapter 24.
- Chapter 26 now includes an extended discussion of the beginnings of European impact on Egypt.
- Discussions of the modernization of Japan in the late nineteenth century have been combined in Chapter 27. The discussion of nationalism now includes coverage of the unification of Italy as well as two new maps on the unifications of Italy and Germany.
- Chapter 33 brings the account of threats and strains to the global environment up to the present, including a new map showing stresses on the world's fresh water supplies.
- The final chapter, Chapter 34, "Globalization at the Turn of the Millennium," has been entirely rewritten to reflect current developments in global politics, the global economy, and global culture. New maps have been added showing regional trade associations and the unequal distribution of wealth around the world. The terrorist attacks of September 11 and the responses to them receive special attention.
- Suggested Reading lists were updated with important recent scholarship.

Organization

The Earth and Its Peoples uses eight broad chronological divisions to define its conceptual scheme of global historical development. In **Part One: The Emergence of Human Communities, to 500 B.C.E.,** we examine important patterns of human communal organization in both the Eastern and Western Hemispheres. Small, dispersed human communities living by foraging spread to most parts of the world over tens of thousands of years. They responded to enormously diverse environmental conditions, at different times in different ways, discovering how to cultivate plants and utilize the products of domestic animals. On the basis of these new modes of sustenance, population grew, permanent towns appeared, and political and religious authority, based on collection and control of agricultural surpluses, spread over extensive areas.

Part Two: The Formation of New Cultural Communities, 1000 B.C.E.–400 C.E., introduces the concept of a "cultural community," in the sense of a coherent pattern of activities and symbols pertaining to a specific human community. While all human communities develop distinctive cultures, including those discussed in Part One, historical development in this stage of global history prolonged and magnified the impact of some cultures more than others. In the geographically contiguous African-Eurasian land mass, the cultures that proved to have the most enduring influence traced their roots to the second and first millennia B.C.E.

Part Three: Growth and Interaction of Cultural Communities, 300 B.C.E.–1200 C.E., deals with early episodes of technological, social, and cultural exchange and interaction on a continental scale both within and beyond the framework of imperial expansion. These are so different from earlier interactions arising from more limited conquests or extensions of political boundaries that they constitute a distinct era in world history, an era that set the world on the path of increasing global interaction and interdependence that it has been following ever since.

In Part Four: Interregional Patterns of Culture and Contact, 1200–1550, we look at the world during the three and a half centuries that saw both intensified cultural and commercial contact and increasingly confident self-definition of cultural communities in Europe, Asia, and Africa. The Mongol conquest of a vast empire extending from the Pacific Ocean to eastern Europe greatly stimulated trade and interaction. In the West, strengthened European kingdoms began maritime expansion in the Atlantic, forging direct ties with sub-Saharan Africa and beginning the conquest of the civilizations of the Western Hemisphere.

Part Five: The Globe Encompassed, 1500–1750, treats a period dominated by the global effects of European expansion and continued economic growth. European ships took over, expanded, and extended the maritime trade of the Indian Ocean, coastal Africa, and the Asian rim of the Pacific Ocean. This maritime commercial enterprise had its counterpart in European colonial empires in the Americas and a new Atlantic trading system. The contrasting capacities and fortunes of traditional land empires and new maritime empires, along with the exchange of domestic plants and animals between the hemispheres, underline the technological and environmental dimensions of this first era of complete global interaction.

In Part Six: Revolutions Reshape the World, 1750–1870, the word *revolution* is used in several senses: in the political sense of governmental overthrow, as in France and the Americas; in the metaphorical sense of radical transformative change, as in the Industrial Revolution; and in the broadest sense of a perception of a profound change in circumstances and worldview. Technology and environment lie at the core of these developments. With the rapid ascendancy of the Western belief that science and technology could overcome all challenges—environmental or otherwise—technology became an instrument not only of transformation but also of domination, to the point of threatening the integrity and autonomy of cultural traditions in nonindustrial lands.

Part Seven: Global Diversity and Dominance, 1850–1945, examines the development of a world arena in which people conceived of events on a global scale. Imperialism, world war, international economic connections, and world-encompassing ideological tendencies, such as nationalism and socialism, present the picture of a globe becoming increasingly interconnected. European dominance took on a worldwide dimension, seeming at times to threaten the diversity of human cultural experience with permanent subordination to European values and philosophies, while at other times triggering strong political or cultural resistance.

For Part Eight: Perils and Promises of a Global Community, 1945 to the Present, we divided the last half of the twentieth century into three time periods: 1945–1975, 1975–1991, and 1991 to the present. The challenges of the Cold War and post-colonial nation building dominated most of the period and unleashed global economic, technological, and political forces that became increasingly important in all aspects of human life. Technology plays a central role in Part Eight, because of its integral role in the growth of a global community and because its many benefits in improving the quality of life seem clouded by real and potential negative impacts on the environment.

Formats

To accommodate different academic calendars and approaches to the course, *The Earth and Its Peoples* is available in three formats. There is a one-volume hardcover version containing all 34 chapters, along with a two-volume paperback edition: Volume I: *To 1550* (Chapters 1–16) and Volume II: *Since 1500* (Chapters 16–34). For readers at institutions with the quarter system, we offer a three-volume paperback version: Volume A: *To 1200* (Chapters 1–12); Volume B: *From 1200 to 1870* (Chapters 12–26); and Volume C: *Since 1750* (Chapters 22–34). Volume II includes an Introduction that surveys the main developments set out in Volume I and provides a groundwork for students studying only the period since 1500.

Supplements

We have assembled an array of supplements to aid students in learning and instructors in teaching. These supplements, including our new *History Companion*, a *Study Guide*, an *Instructor's Resource Manual*, *Test Items*, *Blackboard* and *Web CT* course cartridges, and *Map Transparencies* provide a tightly integrated program of teaching and learning.

In keeping with Houghton Mifflin's goal of being your primary source for history, we are proud to announce the *History Companion*, your new primary source for history technology solutions. History instructors have enough to do without having to master new software or download the latest plug-in to gain access to primary sources, maps, and other tools of the trade. The *History Companion* provides hundreds of resources with only a few clicks of your mouse. The *History Companion* has three components:

The *Instructor Companion* is an easily searchable CD-ROM that makes hundreds of historical images and maps instantly accessible in PowerPoint format. Each image is accompanied by notes that place it in its proper historical context and tips for ways it can be presented in the classroom. This CD is free to instructors with the adoption of this or any Houghton Mifflin history textbook. In addition to visual presentation materials, the CD includes our *HM Testing* program; a computerized version of the *Test Items* to enable instructors to alter, replace, or add questions; as well as resources from the *Instructor's Resource Manual*.

The *Student Research Companion* is a free Internet-based tool with 100 interactive maps and 500 primary sources. The primary sources include headnotes that provide pertinent background information and questions that students can answer and email to their instructors.

The *Student Study Companion* is a free online study guide that contains ACE self-tests, which feature 25 to 30 multiple-choice questions per chapter with feedback, an audio pronunciation guide, web-based flashcards, chapter chronologies, and web links. In addition, *History WIRED: Web Intensive Research Exercises and Documents*, updated by John Reisbord (Ph.D. Northwestern University), offers text-specific links to visual and written sources on the World Wide Web, along with exercises to enhance learning. These study tools will help make your students succeed in the classroom.

The *Study Guide*, authored by Michele G. Scott James of MiraCosta College, contains learning objectives, chapter outlines (with space for students' notes on particular sections), key-term identifications, multiple-choice questions, short-answer and essay questions, and map exercises. Included too are distinctive "comparison charts" to help students organize the range of information about different cultures and events discussed in each chapter. The *Study Guide* is published in two volumes, to correspond to Volumes I and II of the textbook: Volume I contains Chapters 1–16; Volume II, Chapters 16–34.

The *Instructor's Resource Manual*, thoroughly revised by John Reisbord (Ph.D. Northwestern University), provides useful teaching strategies for the global history course and tips for getting the most out of the text. Each chapter contains instructional objectives, a detailed chapter outline, discussion questions, in-depth learning projects, and audio-visual resources.

Our *Test Items*, prepared by Jane Scimeca of Brookdale Community College, offers 20 to 25 key-term identifications, 5 to 10 essay questions with answer guidelines, 35 to 40 multiple-choice questions, and 2 to 3 history and geography exercises.

We have designed *Blackboard* and *WebCT* course cartridges for institutions using these platforms, so that students and instructors can access a wealth of resources including learning objectives, chapter outlines, and Internet assignments, in addition to our testing and quizzing programs.

Finally, a set of transparencies of all the maps in the textbook is available on adoption.

Acknowledgments

In preparing the third edition, we benefited from the critical readings of many colleagues. Our sincere thanks go in particular to the following instructors: Joseph Adams, Walton High School, Cobb County, Georgia; William H. Alexander, Norfolk State University; Corinne Blake, Rowan University; Olwyn M. Blouet, Virginia State University; Eric Bobo, Hinds Community College; James Boyden, Tulane University; Craige B.

Champion, Syracuse University; Eleanor A. Congdon, Youngstown State University; Philip Daileader, The College of William and Mary; Donald M. Fisher, Niagara County Community College; Nancy Fitch, California State University, Fullerton; Jay Harmon, Catholic High School, Baton Rouge, Louisiana; Carol A. Keller, San Antonio College; Susan Maneck, Jackson State University; Laurie S. Mannino, Magruder High School, North Potomac, Maryland; Margaret Malamud, New Mexico State University; Randall McGowen, University of Oregon; Diethelm Prowe, Carleton College; Michael D. Richards, Sweet Briar College; William Schell, Jr., Murray State University; Jeffrey M. Shumway, Brigham Young University; Jonathan Skaff, Shippensburg University of Pennsylvania; Tracy L. Steele, Sam Houston State University; and Peter von Sivers, University of Utah.

When textbook authors set out on a project, they are inclined to believe that 90 percent of the effort will be theirs and 10 percent that of various editors and production specialists employed by their publisher. How very naïve. This book would never have seen the light of day had it not been for the unstinting labors of the great team of professionals who turned the authors' words into beautifully presented print. Our debt to the staff of Houghton Mifflin remains undiminished in the third edition. Nancy Blaine, Senior Sponsoring Editor, has offered us firm but sympathetic guidance throughout the revision process. Jennifer Sutherland, Senior Development Editor, offered astute and sympathetic assistance as the authors worked to incorporate many new ideas and subjects into the text. Carol Newman, Senior Project Editor, moved the work through the production stages to meet what had initially seemed like an unachievable schedule. Carole Frolich did an outstanding job of art and photo research. Jill Haber, Senior Production Design Coordinator, dealt with many of the technological issues that arise in producing a text of this size. We also recognize the invaluable contributions of Senior Designer Henry Rachlin, who created the book's elegant new design, Editorial Associate Annette Fantasia, who oversaw the review process and the preparation of supplemental material, and Florence Cadran, Manufacturing Manager, who saw to it that the text was printed on schedule.

We thank also the many students whose questions and concerns, expressed directly or through their instructors, shaped much of this revision. We continue to welcome all readers' suggestions, queries, and criticisms. Please contact us at our respective institutions or at this e-mail address: history@hmco.com

About the Authors

Richard W. Bulliet Professor of Middle Eastern History at Columbia University, Richard W. Bulliet received his Ph.D. from Harvard University. He has written scholarly works on a number of topics: the social history of medieval Iran *(The Patricians of Nishapur)*, the historical competition between pack camels and wheeled transport *(The Camel and the Wheel)*, the process of conversion to Islam *(Conversion to Islam in the Medieval Period)*, and the overall course of Islamic social history *(Islam: The View from the Edge)*. He is the editor of the *Columbia History of the Twentieth Century*. He has published four novels, co-edited *The Encyclopedia of the Modern Middle East*, and hosted an educational television series on the Middle East. He was awarded a fellowship by the John Simon Guggenheim Memorial Foundation.

Pamela Kyle Crossley Pamela Kyle Crossley received her Ph.D. in Modern Chinese History from Yale University. She is Professor of History and Rosenwald Research Professor in the Arts and Sciences at Dartmouth College. Her books include *A Translucent Mirror: History and Identity in Qing Imperial Ideology; The Manchus; Orphan Warriors: Three Manchu Generations and the End of the Qing World;* and (with Lynn Hollen Lees and John W. Servos) *Global Society: The World Since 1900*. Her research, which concentrates on the cultural history of China, Inner Asia, and Central Asia, has been supported by the John Simon Guggenheim Memorial Foundation and the National Endowment for the Humanities.

Daniel R. Headrick Daniel R. Headrick received his Ph.D. in History from Princeton University. Professor of History and Social Science at Roosevelt University in Chicago, he is the author of several books on the history of technology, imperialism, and international relations, including *The Tools of Empire: Technology and European Imperialism in the Nineteenth Century; The Tentacles of Progress: Technology Transfer in the Age of Imperialism; The Invisible Weapon: Telecommunications and International Politics;* and *When Information Came of Age: Technologies of Knowledge in the Age of Reason and Revolution, 1700–1850*. His articles have appeared in the *Journal of World History* and the *Journal of Modern History*, and he has been awarded fellowships by the National Endowment for the Humanities, the John Simon Guggenheim Memorial Foundation, and the Alfred P. Sloan Foundation.

Steven W. Hirsch Steven W. Hirsch holds a Ph.D. in Classics from Stanford University and is currently Associate Professor Classics and History at Tufts University. He has received grants from the National Endowment for the Humanities and the Massachusetts Foundation for Humanities and Public Policy. His research and publications include *The Friendship of the Barbarians: Xenophon and the Persian Empire*, as well as articles and reviews in the *Classical Journal*, the *American Journal of Philology*, and the *Journal of Interdisciplinary History*. He is currently working on a comparative study of ancient Mediterranean and Chinese civilizations.

Lyman L. Johnson Professor of History at the University of North Carolina at Charlotte, Lyman L. Johnson earned his Ph.D. in Latin American History from the University of Connecticut. A two-time Senior Fulbright-Hays Lecturer, he also has received fellowships from the Tinker Foundation, the Social Science Research Council, the National Endowment for the Humanities, and the American Philosophical Society. His recent books include *Death, Dismemberment, and Memory; The Faces of Honor* (with Sonya Lipsett-Rivera); *The Problem of Order in Changing Societies; Essays on the Price History of Eighteenth-Century Latin America* (with Enrique Tandeter); and *Colonial Latin America* (with Mark A. Burkholder). He also has published in journals, including the *Hispanic American Historical Review*, the *Journal of Latin American Studies*, the *International Review of Social History, Social History*, and *Desarrollo Económico*. He recently served as president of the Conference on Latin American History.

David Northrup Professor of History at Boston College, David Northrup earned his Ph.D. in African and European History from the University of California at Los Angeles. He earlier taught in Nigeria with the Peace Corps and at Tuskegee Institute. Research supported by the Fulbright-Hays Commission, the National Endowment for the Humanities, and the Social Science Research Council led to publications concerning pre-colonial Nigeria, the Congo (1870–1940), the Atlantic slave trade, and Asian, African, and Pacific Islander indentured labor in the nineteenth century. A contributor to the *Oxford History of the British Empire* and *Blacks in the British Empire*, his latest book is *Africa's Discovery of Europe, 1450–1850*. For 2004 and 2005 he serves as president of the World History Association.

Note on Spelling and Usage

Where necessary for clarity, dates are followed by the letters C.E. or B.C.E. The abbreviation C.E. stands for "Common Era" and is equivalent to A.D. (*anno Domini,* Latin for "in the year of the Lord"). The abbreviation B.C.E stands for "before the Common Era" and means the same as B.C. ("before Christ"). In keeping with our goal of approaching world history without special concentration on one culture or another, we chose these neutral abbreviations as appropriate to our enterprise. Because many readers will be more familiar with English than with metric measurements, however, units of measure are generally given in the English system, with metric equivalents following in parentheses.

In general, Chinese has been romanized according to the *pinyin* method. Exceptions include proper names well established in English (e.g., Canton, Chiang Kai-shek) and a few English words borrowed from Chinese (e.g., kowtow). Spellings of Arabic, Ottoman Turkish, Persian, Mongolian, Manchu, Japanese, and Korean names and terms avoid special diacritical marks for letters that are pronounced only slightly differently in English. An apostrophe is used to indicate when two Chinese syllables are pronounced separately (e.g., Chang'an).

For words transliterated from languages that use the Arabic script—Arabic, Ottoman Turkish, Perisan, Urdu—the apostrophe indicating separately pronounced syllables may represent either of two special consonants, the *hamza* or the *ain*. Because most English-speakers do not hear the distinction between these two, they have not been distinguished in transliteration and are not indicated when they occur at the beginning or end of a word. As with Chinese, some words and commonly used place-names from these languages are given familiar English spellings (e.g., Quran instead of Qur'an, Cairo instead of al-Qahira). Arabic romanization has normally been used for terms relating to Islam, even where the context justifies slightly different Turkish or Persian forms, again for ease of comprehension.

Before 1492 the inhabitants of the Western Hemisphere had no single name for themselves. They had neither a racial consciousness nor a racial identity. Identity was derived from kin groups, language, cultural practices, and political structures. There was no sense that physical similarities created a shared identity. America's original inhabitants had racial consciousness and racial identity imposed on them by conquest and the occupation of their lands by Europeans after 1492. All of the collective terms for these first American peoples are tainted by this history. *Indians, Native Americans, Amerindians, First Peoples, and Indigenous Peoples* are among the terms in common usage. In this book the names of individual cultures and states are used wherever possible. *Amerindian* and other terms that suggest transcultural identity and experience are used most commonly for the period after 1492.

There is an ongoing debate about how best to render Amerindian words in English. It has been common for authors writing in English to follow Mexican usage for Nahuatl and Yucatec Maya words and place-names. In this style, for example, the capital of the Aztec state is spelled Tenochtitlán, and the important late Maya city-state is spelled Chichén Itzá. Although these forms are still common even in the specialist literature, we have chosen to follow the scholarship that sees these accents as unnecessary. The exceptions are modern place-names, such as Mérida and Yucatán, which are accented. A similar problem exists for the spelling of Quechua and Aymara words from the Andean region of South America. Although there is significant disagreement among scholars, we follow the emerging consensus and use the spellings khipu (not quipu), Tiwanaku (not Tiahuanaco), and Wari (not Huari). However, we keep Inca (not Inka) and Cuzco (not Cusco), since these spellings are expected by most of our potential readers and we hope to avoid confusion.

The Earth and Its Peoples

A Global History

PART ONE

The Emergence of Human Communities, to 500 B.C.E.

Human beings evolved over several million years from primates in Africa. Differing from other primates in their ability to walk upright on two legs and their possession of large brains, hands with opposable thumbs, and the capacity for speech, early humans used teamwork and created tools that enabled them to survive in diverse environments. They spread relatively quickly to almost every habitable area of the world, sustaining themselves by hunting and by gathering wild plant products. Then, around 10,000 years ago, some human groups began to cultivate plants, domesticate animals, and make pottery vessels for storage. One consequence of this shift to agriculture was the emergence of permanent settlements—at first small villages but eventually larger towns as well.

The earliest complex societies arose in the great river valleys of Asia and Africa, around 3100 B.C.E. in the valley between the Tigris and Euphrates Rivers in Mesopotamia and along the Nile River in Egypt, somewhat later in the valley of the Indus River in Pakistan, and on the floodplain of the Yellow River in China. In these arid regions, agriculture depended on irrigation with river water, and centers of political power arose to organize the massive human labor required to dig and maintain channels to carry water to the fields.

Kings and priests dominated these early societies. Kings controlled the military forces; priests managed the temples and the wealth of the gods. Within the urban centers—in the midst of palaces, temples, fortification walls, and other monumental buildings—lived administrators, soldiers, priests, merchants, craftsmen, and others with specialized skills. The production of surplus food grown on rural estates by a dependent peasantry sustained the activities of these groups. Professional scribes kept administrative and financial records and preserved their civilization's religious and scientific knowledge.

Over time, certain centers extended their influence and came to dominate broad expanses of territory. The rulers of these early empires were motivated primarily by the need to secure access to raw materials, especially tin and copper, from which to make bronze. A similar motive accounts for the development of long-distance trade and diplomatic relations between major powers. Fueling long-distance trade was the desire for bronze, which had both practical and symbolic importance. From bronze, artisans made weapons, tools and utensils, and ritual objects. Ownership of bronze items was a sign of wealth and power. Trade and diplomacy helped spread culture and technology from the core river-valley areas to neighboring regions, such as southern China, Nubia, Syria-Palestine, Anatolia, and the Aegean.

In the Western Hemisphere, different geographical circumstances called forth distinctive patterns of technological and cultural response in the early civilizations of the Olmec in southern Mexico and Chavín in the Andean region of South America. Nevertheless, the challenges of organizing agriculture and trade led to many of the same features of complex societies—social stratification, specialization of labor, urbanization, monumental building, technological development, and artistic achievement.

	8000 B.C.E.	7000 B.C.E.	6000 B.C.E.	5000 B.C.E.
Americas		• **7000** Incipient plant domestication in Peru		• **5000** Maize, beans, and squash domestication in Mesoamerica
Europe	Spread of Indo-European languages		• **6000** Farming in southern Europe	
Africa	• **8000** Farming in eastern Sahara		• **5500** Farming in Egypt	
Middle East	• **8000** Domestication of plants and animals in Fertile Crescent			• **5000** Irrigation in Mesopotamia
Asia and Oceania		• **6500** Rice cultivation in China		• **5000** Farming in India

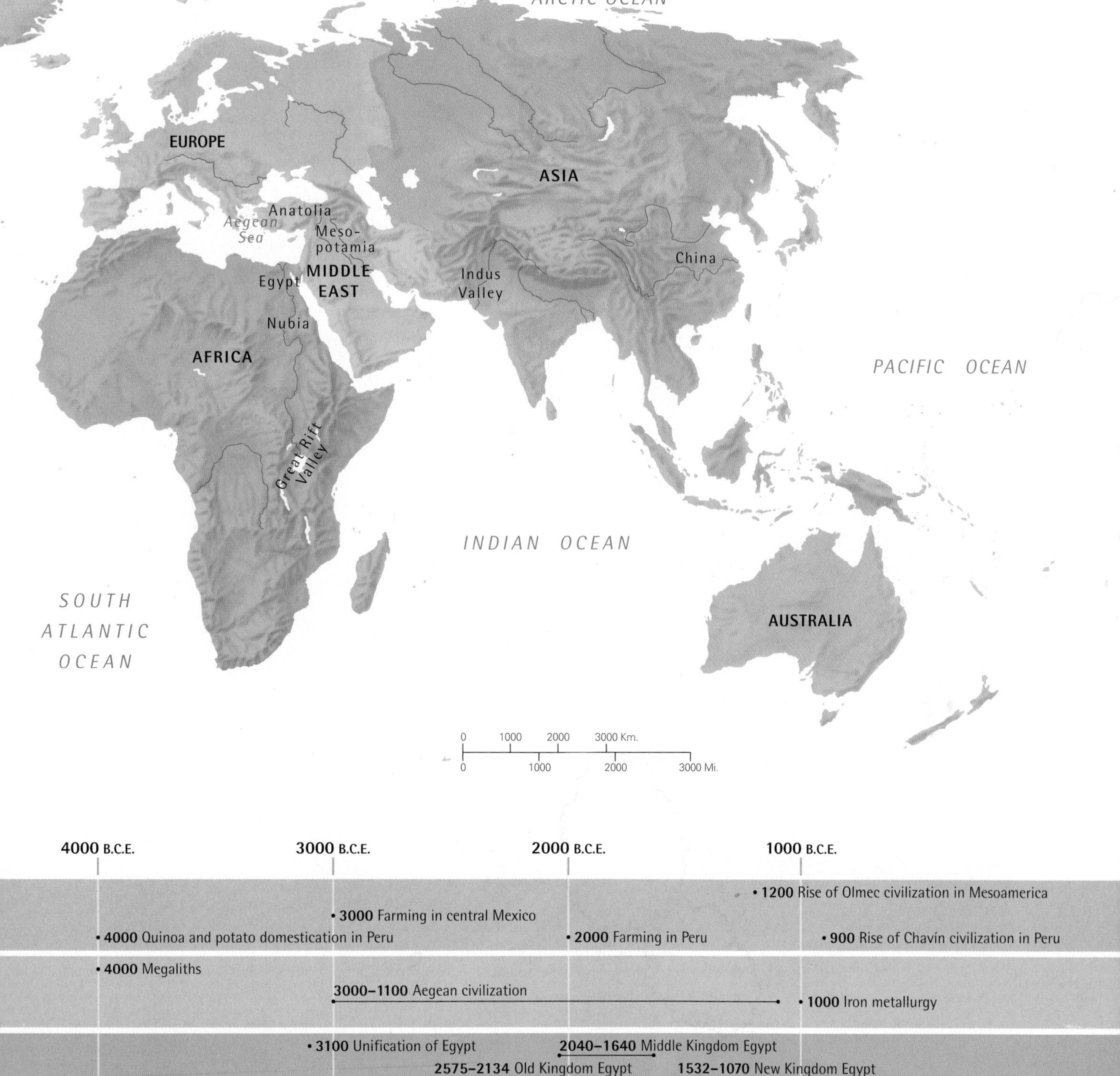

4000 B.C.E. | **3000** B.C.E. | **2000** B.C.E. | **1000** B.C.E.

- **1200** Rise of Olmec civilization in Mesoamerica
- **3000** Farming in central Mexico
- **4000** Quinoa and potato domestication in Peru
- **2000** Farming in Peru
- **900** Rise of Chavín civilization in Peru

- **4000** Megaliths
- **3000–1100** Aegean civilization
- **1000** Iron metallurgy

- **3100** Unification of Egypt
- **2040–1640** Middle Kingdom Egypt
- **2575–2134** Old Kingdom Egypt
- **1532–1070** New Kingdom Egypt
- **2000** Rise of Kush in Nubia
- **800** Rise of Nubian kingdom at Napata

- **3100** Mesopotamian civilization
- **1750** Hammurabi's law code
- **911** Rise of Neo-Assyrian Empire
- Advent of horses in western Asia **2000**
- **1700–1200** Hittites dominant in Anatolia
- **2350** Akkadian kingdom

- Bronze metallurgy in China **2000**
- **1600–1027** Shang kingdom in China
- **2600–1900** Indus Valley civilization
- **1027–221** Zhou kingdom in China

1 Nature, Humanity, and History to 3500 B.C.E.

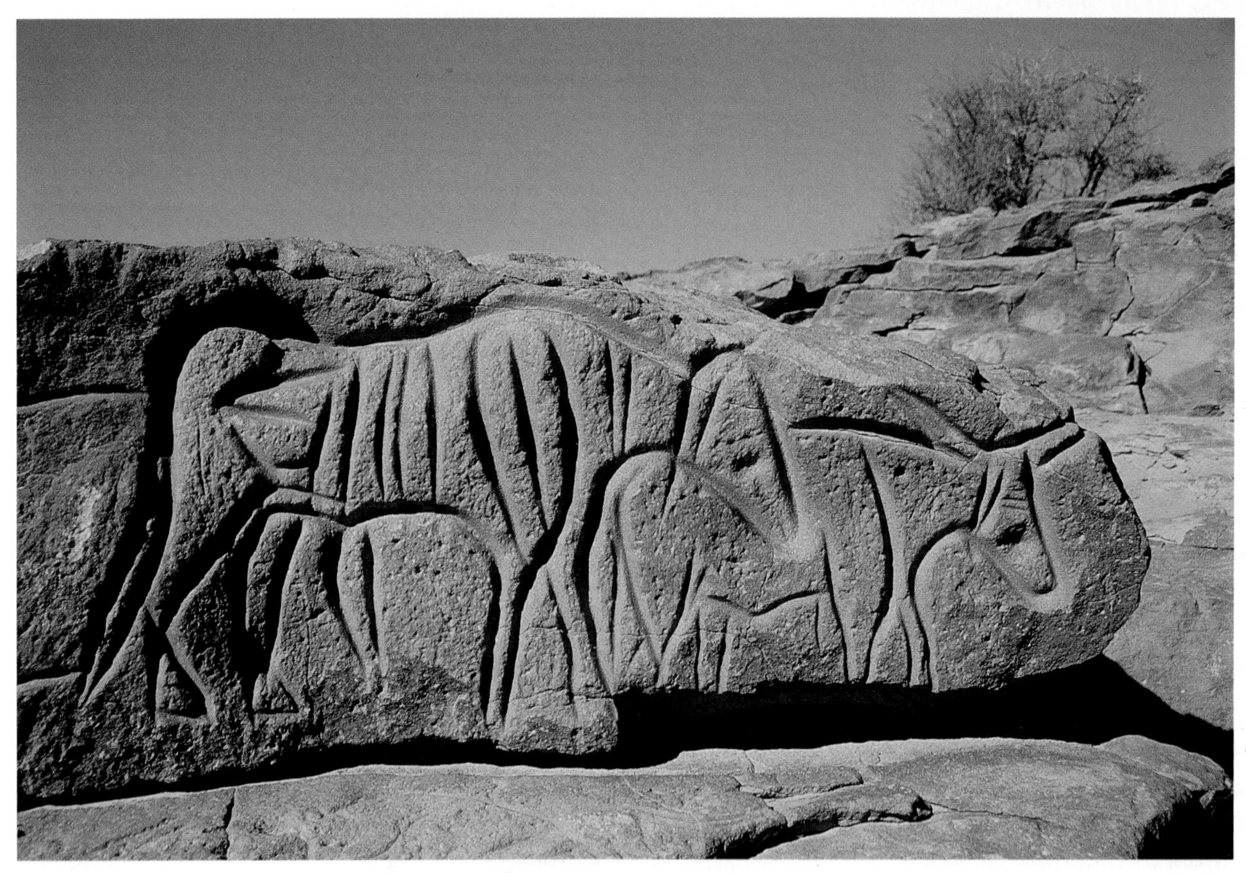

Cattle in the Sahara, ca. 5000 B.C.E.
During a rainy era when grass grew in what is now desert unknown artists enscribed rock outcroppings with images of the herds that roamed there.

CHAPTER OUTLINE

According to a story handed down by the Yoruba° people of West Africa, at one time there was only water below the sky. Then the divine Owner of the Sky let down a chain by which his son Oduduwa° descended along with sixteen male companions. Oduduwa scattered a handful of soil across the water and set down a chicken that scratched the soil into the shape of the land. A palm nut that he planted in the soil grew to become the bountiful forest that is the home of the Yoruba people. Oduduwa was their first king.

At some point in their history most human societies began telling similar stories about their origins. Some related that the first humans came down from the sky, others that they emerged out of a hole in the ground. Historical accuracy was not the point of such creation myths. Like the story of Adam and Eve in the Hebrew Bible, their primary purpose was to define the moral principles that people thought should govern their dealings with the supernatural world, with each other, and with the rest of nature. In addition, they provided an explanation of how a people's way of life, social divisions, and cultural system arose.

In the nineteenth century evidence started to accumulate that human beings had quite different origins. Natural scientists were finding remains of early humans who resembled apes rather than gods. Other evidence suggested that the familiar ways of life based on farming and herding did not arise within a generation or two of creation, as the myths suggested, but tens of thousands of years after humans first appeared. Although such evidence has long stirred controversy, a careful questioning of it reveals insights into human identity that may be as meaningful as those propounded by the creation myths.

As you read this chapter, ask yourself the following questions:

- What is the significance of the fact that humans evolved as part of the natural world, subject to its laws?
- How did the physical and mental abilities that humans gradually evolved give them a unique capacity to adapt to new environments by altering their way of life rather than by evolving physically as other species did?
- After nearly 2 million years of physical and cultural development, how did human communities in different parts of the world learn how to manipulate the natural world, domesticating plants and animals for their food and use? In short, how did people's relationship with their environments change?

African Genesis

The discovery in the mid-nineteenth century of the remains of ancient creatures that were at once humanlike and apelike generated both excitement and controversy. The evidence upset many people because it challenged accepted beliefs about human origins. Others welcomed the new evidence as proof of what some researchers had long suspected: the physical characteristics of modern humans, like those of all other creatures, had evolved over incredibly long periods of time. Until recently, the evidence was too fragmentary to be convincing.

Interpreting the Evidence

In 1856 in the Neander Valley of what is now Germany, laborers discovered fossilized bones of a creature with a body much like that of modern humans but with a face that, like the faces of apes, had heavy brow ridges and a low forehead. Although we now know these "Neanderthals" were a type of human common in Europe some 40,000 years ago, in the mid-nineteenth century the idea that humans so different in appearance from modern people could have existed was so novel that some of the scholars who first examined them thought they must be deformed individuals from recent times.

Three years after the Neanderthal finds, Charles Darwin, a young English naturalist (student of natural history), published *On the Origin of Species.* In this work he argued that the time frame for all biological life was far longer than most persons had supposed. Darwin based his conclusion on pioneering naturalists' research and on his own investigations of fossils and living plant and animal species in Latin America. He proposed that the great diversity of living species and the profound changes in them over time could be explained by **evolution,** the process by which biological variations that enhance a population's ability to survive became dominant in that species. He theorized that, over very long periods

Yoruba (yoh-roo-bah) **Oduduwa** (oh-DOO-doo-wah)

Fossilized Footprints Archaeologist Mary Leakey (shown at top) found these remarkable footprints of a hominid adult and child at Laetoli, Tanzania. The pair had walked through fresh volcanic ash that solidified after being buried by a new volcanic eruption. Dated to 3.5 million years ago, the footprints are the oldest evidence of bipedalism yet found. (John Reader/Photo Researchers, Inc.)

of time, the changes brought about by evolution could lead to distinct new species.

Turning to the sensitive subject of human evolution in *The Descent of Man* (1871), Darwin summarized the growing consensus among naturalists that human beings had also come into existence through the same process of natural selection. Because humans shared so many physical similarities with African apes, he proposed that Africa must have been the home of the first humans, even though there was no fossil evidence at the time to support his hypothesis.

Instead, the next major discoveries pointed to Asia, rather than Africa, as the original human home. On the Southeast Asian island of Java in 1891 Eugene Dubois uncovered an ancient skullcap of what was soon called "Java man," a find that has since been dated to 1.8 million years ago. In 1929 near Peking (Beijing°), China, W. C. Pei discovered a similar skullcap of what became known as "Peking man."

By then, even older fossils had been found in southern Africa. In 1924, while examining fossils from a lime quarry, Raymond Dart found the skull of an ancient creature that he named *Australopithecus africanus*° (African southern ape), which he argued was transitional between apes and early humans. For many years most specialists disputed Dart's idea, because, although *Australopithecus africanus* walked upright like a human, its brain was ape-size. Such an idea went against their expectations that large brains would have evolved first and that Asia, not Africa, was the first home of humans.

Since 1950, Louis and Mary Leakey and their son Richard, along with many others, have discovered a wealth of early human fossils in the exposed sediments of the Great Rift Valley of eastern Africa. These finds are strong evidence for Dart's hypothesis and for Darwin's guess that the tropical habitat of the African apes was the cradle of humanity.

The development of precise archaeological techniques has enhanced the quantity of evidence currently available. Rather than collect isolated bones, modern researchers literally sift the neighboring soils to extract the remains of other creatures existing at the time, locating fossilized seeds and even pollen by which to document the environment in which the humans lived. They can also measure the age of most finds by the rate of molecular change in potassium, in minerals in lava flows, or in carbon from wood and bone.

By combining that evidence with the growing understanding of how other species adapt to their natural environments, scientists can describe with some precision when, where, and how human beings evolved and how they lived. As the result of this new work, it is now possible to trace the evolutionary changes that produced modern humans during a period of 4 million years. As Darwin suspected, the earliest transitional creatures have been found only in Africa; the later human species (including Java man and Peking man) had wider global distribution.

Human Evolution

Evidence that humans evolved gradually over millions of years caused much debate about how species should be defined. Biologists now classify **australopithecines**° and humans as members of a fam-

Beijing (bay-jeeng) ***Australopithecus africanus*** (aw-strah-loh-PITH-uh-kuhs ah-frih-KAH-nuhs) **Australopithecine** (aw-strah-loh-PITH-uh-seen)

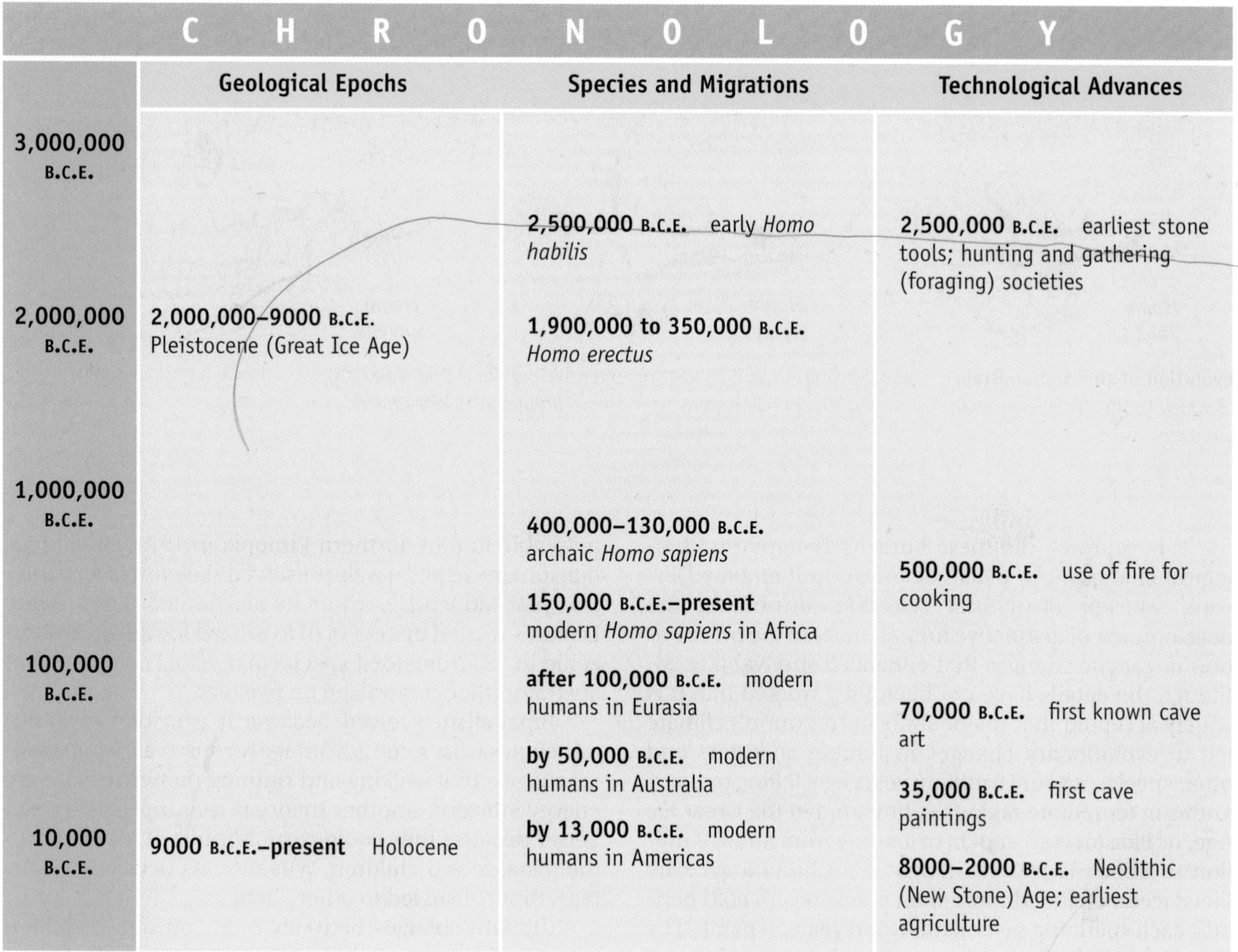

CHRONOLOGY

	Geological Epochs	Species and Migrations	Technological Advances
3,000,000 B.C.E.			
		2,500,000 B.C.E. early *Homo habilis*	**2,500,000 B.C.E.** earliest stone tools; hunting and gathering (foraging) societies
2,000,000 B.C.E.	**2,000,000–9000 B.C.E.** Pleistocene (Great Ice Age)	**1,900,000 to 350,000 B.C.E.** *Homo erectus*	
1,000,000 B.C.E.		**400,000–130,000 B.C.E.** archaic *Homo sapiens* **150,000 B.C.E.–present** modern *Homo sapiens* in Africa	**500,000 B.C.E.** use of fire for cooking
100,000 B.C.E.		**after 100,000 B.C.E.** modern humans in Eurasia **by 50,000 B.C.E.** modern humans in Australia	**70,000 B.C.E.** first known cave art **35,000 B.C.E.** first cave paintings
10,000 B.C.E.	**9000 B.C.E.–present** Holocene	**by 13,000 B.C.E.** modern humans in Americas	**8000–2000 B.C.E.** Neolithic (New Stone) Age; earliest agriculture

ily of primates known as **hominids°.** Primates are members of a family of warm-blooded, four-limbed, social animals known as mammals that first appeared about 65 million years ago. The first hominids date to about 7 million years ago.

Within the primate kingdom modern humans are most closely related to the African apes—chimpanzees and gorillas. Since Darwin's time it has been popular (and controversial) to say that we are descended from apes. Modern research has found that over 98 percent of human DNA, the basic genetic blueprint, is identical to that of the great apes.

But three traits distinguish humans from apes and other primates. As Dart's australopithecines demonstrated, the earliest of these traits to appear was **bipedalism** (walking upright on two legs). This frees the forelimbs from any necessary role in locomotion and enhances an older primate trait: a hand that has a long thumb that can work with the fingers to manipulate objects skillfully. Modern humans' second distinctive trait was a very large brain. Besides enabling humans to think abstractly, experience profound emotions, and construct complex social relationships, this larger brain controls the fine motor movements of the hand and of the tongue, increasing humans' tool-using capacity and facilitating the development of speech. The physical possibility of language, however, depends on a third distinctive human trait: the location of the human larynx (voice box). It lies much lower in the neck than does the larynx of any other primate. This trait is associated with many other changes in the face and neck.

---

hominid (HOM-uh-nid)

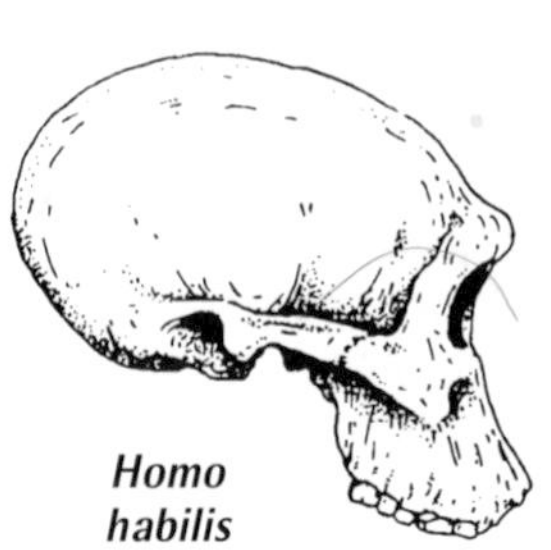

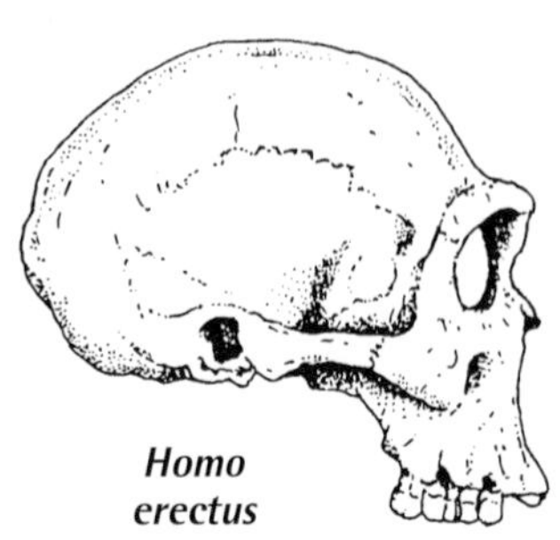

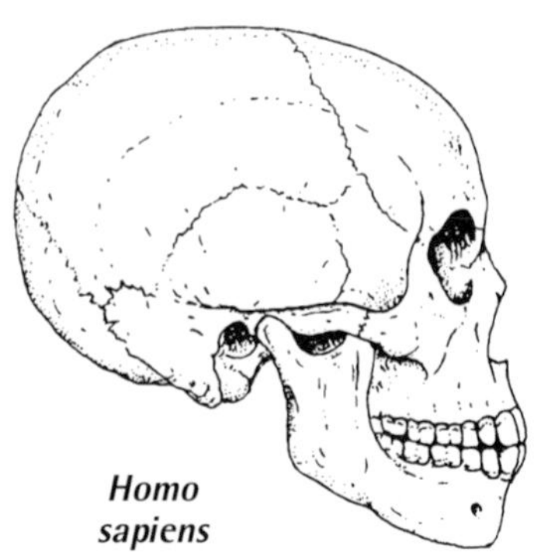

Evolution of the Human Brain These drawings of skulls show the extensive cranial changes associated with the increase in brain size during the 3 million years from *Homo habilis* to *Homo sapiens sapiens.*

How and why did these immensely important biological changes take place? Scientists still employ Darwin's concept of natural selection, attributing the development of distinctive human traits to the preservation of genetic changes that enhanced survivability. Although the details have not been fully worked out, it is widely accepted that major shifts in the world's climate led to evolutionary changes in human ancestors and other species. About 10 million years ago, falling temperatures in temperate regions culminated in the **Great Ice Age,** or Pleistocene° epoch, extending from about 2 million to about 11,000 years ago (see Chronology). The Pleistocene included more than a dozen very cold periods, each spanning several thousand years, separated by warmer periods. These temperature changes and the altered rainfall and vegetation that accompanied them imposed great strains on existing plant and animal species. As a result, large numbers of new species evolved.

During the Pleistocene, massive glaciers of frozen water spread out from the poles and mountains. At their peak such glaciers covered a third of the earth's surface and contained so much frozen water that ocean levels were lowered by over 450 feet (140 meters), exposing land bridges between many places now isolated by water (see Map 1.1).

Although the glaciers did not extend beyond the arctic and temperate zones, the equatorial regions of the world probably also experienced altered climates during the Pleistocene epoch. Between 3 million and 4 million years ago, several new species of bipedal australopithecines evolved in southern and eastern Africa. In a remarkable find in northern Ethiopia in 1974, Donald Johanson unearthed a well-preserved skeleton of a twenty-five-year-old female, whom he nicknamed "Lucy." Mary Leakey's related discovery of fossilized footprints in Tanzania in 1977 provided spectacular visual evidence that australopithecines walked on two legs.

Bipedalism evolved because it provided australopithecines with some advantage for survival. Some studies suggest that walking and running on two legs is very energy efficient. Another theory is that bipeds survived better because they could carry armfuls of food back to their mates and children. Whatever its decisive advantage, bipedalism led to other changes.

Climate changes between 2 million and 3 million years ago led to the evolution of a new species, the first to be classified in the same genus (*Homo*) with modern humans. At Olduvai° Gorge in northern Tanzania in the early 1960s, Louis Leakey discovered the first fossilized remains of this creature, which he named ***Homo habilis***° (handy human). What most distinguished *Homo habilis* from the australopithecines was a brain that was nearly 50 percent larger. A larger brain would have added to the new species' intelligence. What was happening in this period that favored greater mental capacity? Some scientists believe that the answer had to do with food. Greater intelligence enabled *Homo habilis* to locate a vast number of different kinds of things to eat throughout the seasons of the year. They point to seeds and other fossilized remains in ancient *Homo habilis* camps that indicate that the new species ate a greater variety of more nutritious seasonal foods than did the australopithecines.

Pleistocene (PLY-stuh-seen)

Olduvai (ol-DOO-vy) ***Homo habilis*** (HOH-moh HAB-uh-luhs)

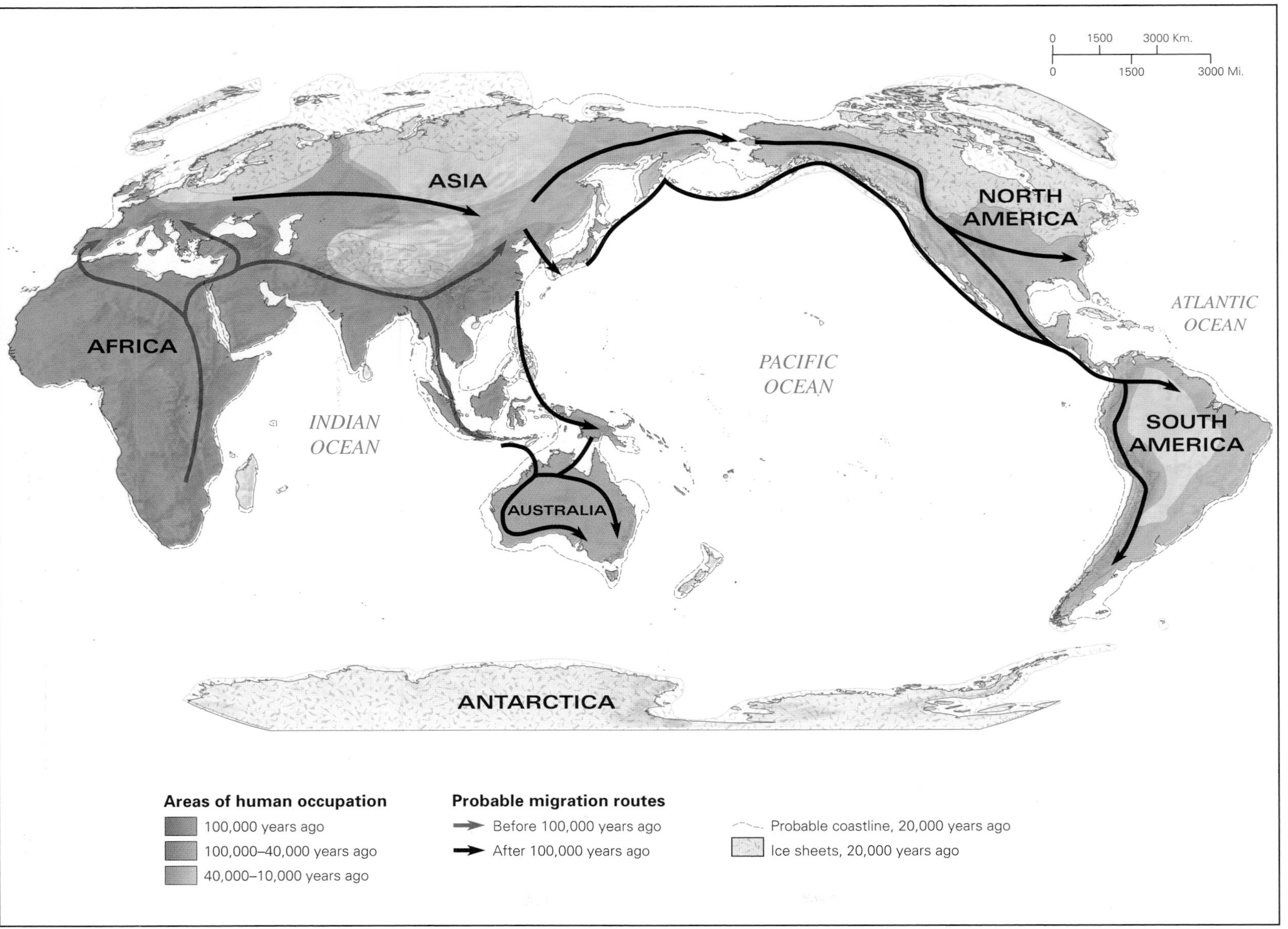

Map 1.1 Human Dispersal to 10,000 Years Ago Early migrations from Africa into southern Eurasia were followed by treks across land bridges during cold spells, when giant ice sheets had lowered ocean levels. Boats may also have been employed.

By 1 million years ago *Homo habilis* and all the australopithecines had become extinct. In their habitat lived a new hominid, ***Homo erectus***° (upright human), which had first appeared in eastern Africa about 1.9 million years ago. These creatures possessed brains a third larger than those of *Homo habilis,* which presumably accounted for their better survivability. A nearly complete skeleton of a twelve-year-old male of the species discovered by Richard Leakey in 1984 on the shores of Lake Turkana in Kenya shows that *Homo erectus* closely resembled modern people from the neck down. *Homo erectus* was very successful in dealing with different environments and underwent hardly any biological changes over a million years.

However, by a long, imperfectly understood evolutionary process between 400,000 and 130,000 years ago, a new human species emerged: ***Homo sapiens***° (wise human). The brains of *Homo sapiens* were a third larger than those of *Homo erectus,* whom they gradually superseded. Indeed, these brains were more than three times the size one would expect in another primate of comparable body size and gave *Homo sapiens* tremendous capacity for speech.

This slow but remarkable process of physical evolution, which distinguished humans by a small but significant degree from other primates, was one part of what was happening. Equally remarkable was the way in which humans were extending their habitat.

Migrations from Africa

Early humans first expanded their range in eastern and southern Africa. Then they ventured out of Africa, perhaps following migrating herds of animals or searching for more abundant food supplies in a time of drought. The reasons are uncertain, but the end results are vividly clear: Humans successfully colonized environments, including deserts and arctic lands (see Map 1.1). This dispersal demonstrates early humans' talent for adaptation.

Homo erectus was the first human species to inhabit all parts of Africa and the first to be found outside Africa. Java Man and Peking Man were members of this species. By migrating overland from Africa across southern Asia, *Homo erectus* reached Java as early as 1.8 million years ago. At that time, because of the great volume of water trapped in ice-age glaciers, sea levels were so low that Java was not an island but was part of the Southeast Asian mainland. Java's climate would have been no colder than East Africa's. The harsh winters of northern Europe and northern China, where *Homo erectus* settled between 700,000 and 300,000 years ago, posed a greater challenge.

DNA and fossil evidence suggest that *Homo sapiens* spread outward from an African homeland, although some scientists hold that *Homo sapiens* may have evolved separately from *Homo erectus* populations in Africa, Europe, China, and Southeast Asia. Their migrations to the rest of the world would have been made easier by a wet period that transformed the normally arid Sahara and Middle East into fertile grasslands until about 40,000 years ago. The abundance of plant and animal food during this wet period would have promoted an increase in human populations.

By the end of the wet period, further evolutionary changes had produced fully modern humans (*Homo sapiens sapiens*). This new species displaced older human populations, such as the Neanderthals in Europe, and penetrated for the first time into the Americas, Australia, and the Arctic.

During glacial periods when sea levels were low, hunters would have been able to cross a land bridge from northeastern Asia into North America. Recently a hypothesis has been advanced that some early colonizers of the Americas may also have come by boat along the Pacific coast. As these pioneers from East Asia and later migrants moved southward (penetrating southern South America by at least 12,500 years ago), they passed through lands teeming with life, including easily hunted large animal species. Meanwhile, traveling by boat from Java, other modern humans colonized New Guinea and Australia when both were part of a single landmass, and they crossed the land bridge then existing between the Asian mainland and Japan. Australia was reached by about 50,000 years ago. For a time, new waves of migrants entered the Americas and Australia. Then, when the glaciers melted, the seas rose and the lands underwent a long period of isolation from the rest of humanity.

As populations migrated, they may have undergone some minor evolutionary changes that helped them adapt to extreme environments. One such change was in skin color. The deeply pigmented skin of today's indigenous inhabitants of the tropics (and presumably of all early humans who evolved there) is an adaptation that reduces the harmful effects of the harsh tropical sun. At some point, possibly as recently as 5,000 years ago, especially pale skin became characteristic of Europeans living in northern latitudes that had far less sunshine, especially during winter months. The loss of pigment enabled their skin to produce more vitamin D from sunshine, though it exposed Europeans to a greater risk of sunburn and skin cancer in sunnier climates. This was not the only possible way to adapt to the arctic. Eskimos

Homo erectus (HOH-moh ee-REK-tuhs)
Homo sapiens (HOH-moh SAY-pee-enz)

who began moving into northern latitudes of North America no more than 5,000 years ago retain the deeper pigmentation of their Asian ancestors but are able to gain sufficient vitamin D from eating fish and sea mammals.

As distinctive as skin color seems, it represents a very minor biological change. What is far more remarkable is that these widely dispersed populations vary so little. Instead of needing to evolve physically like other species in order to adapt to new environments, modern humans have been able to change their eating habits and devise new forms of clothing and shelter. As a result, human communities have become culturally diverse while remaining physically homogeneous.

History and Culture in the Ice Age

Evidence of early humans' splendid creative abilities first came to light in 1940 near Lascaux in southern France. Examining a newly uprooted tree, youths discovered the entrance to a vast underground cavern. Once inside, they found that its walls were covered with paintings of animals, including many that had been extinct for thousands of years. Other cave paintings have been found in Spain and elsewhere in southern France.

Modern observers have been struck by the artistic quality of these ancient cave paintings. To even the most skeptical person, such rich finds are awesome demonstrations of richly developed imagination and skill. The ancient cave art is vivid evidence that the biologically modern people who made such art were intellectually modern as well (see Diversity and Dominance: Cave Art, page 16).

These ancient people's specialized tools and complex social relations may be less striking visually, but they also display uniquely human talents. The production of similar art and tools over wide areas and long periods of time demonstrates that skills and ideas were not simply bursts of individual genius but were deliberately passed along within societies. These learned patterns of action and expression constitute **culture.** Culture includes both material objects, such as dwellings, clothing, tools, and crafts, and nonmaterial values, beliefs, and languages.

Although it is true that some animals also learn new ways, their activities are determined primarily by inherited instincts. Among humans the proportions are reversed: instincts are less important than the cultural traditions that each generation learns from its elders. All living creatures are part of natural history, which traces biological development, but only human communities display profound cultural developments over time. The development, transmission, and transformation of cultural practices and events are the subject of **history.**

Food Gathering and Stone Tools

When archaeologists examine the remains of ancient human sites, the first thing that jumps out at them is the abundant evidence of human toolmaking—the first recognizable cultural activity. Because the tools that survive are made of stone, the extensive period of history from the appearance of the first fabricated stone tools around 2 million years ago until the appearance of metal tools around 4 thousand years ago has been called the **Stone Age.**

Making Stone Tools About 35,000 years ago the manufacture of stone tools became highly specialized. Small blades chipped from a rock core were mounted in a bone or wooden handle. Not only were such composite tools more varied than earlier all-purpose hand axes, but the small blades required fewer rock cores—an important consideration in areas where suitable rocks were scarce. (From Jacques Bordaz, *Tools of the Old and New Stone Age*. Copyright 1970 by Jacques Bordaz. Redrawn by the permission of Addison-Wesley Educational Publishers, Inc.)

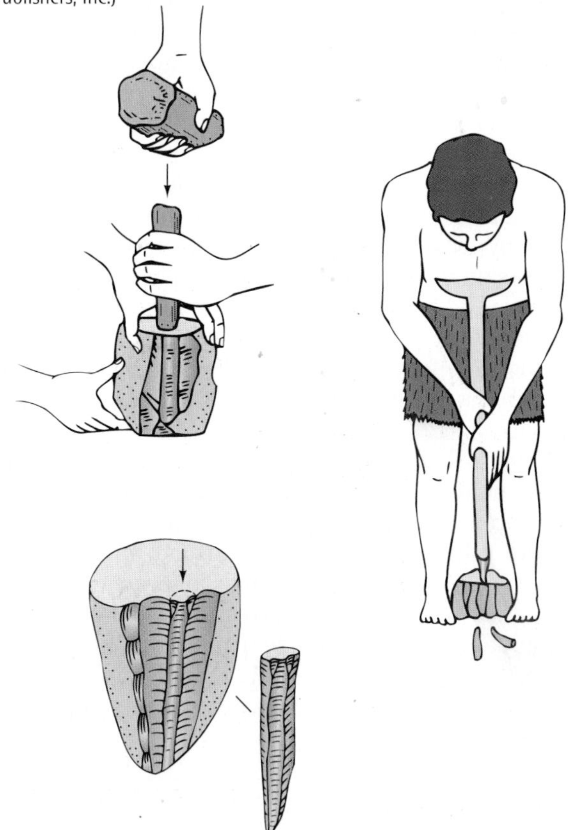

The name can be misleading. In the first place, not all tools were made of stone. Early humans would also have made useful objects and tools out of bone, skin, wood, and other natural materials less likely than stone to survive the ravages of time. In the second place, this period of nearly 2 million years contains many distinct periods and cultures. Early students recognized two distinct periods in the Stone Age: the **Paleolithic**° (Old Stone Age) down to 10,000 years ago and the **Neolithic**° (New Stone Age) associated with agriculture. Modern scientists have found evidence for many more subdivisions.

Most early human activity centered on gathering food. Like the australopithecines, early humans depended heavily on vegetable foods such as leaves, seeds, and grasses, but one of the changes evident in the Ice Age is the growing consumption of highly nutritious animal flesh. Moreover, unlike australopithecines, humans regularly made tools. These two changes—increased meat eating and toolmaking—appear to be closely linked.

The first crude tools made their appearance with *Homo habilis.* Most stone tools made by *Homo habilis* have been found in the Great Rift Valley of eastern Africa, whose sides expose sediments laid down over millions of years. One branch of this valley, the Olduvai Gorge in Tanzania, explored by Louis and Mary Leakey, has yielded evidence that *Homo habilis* made tools by chipping flakes off the edges of volcanic stones. Modern experiments show that the razor-sharp edges of such flakes are highly effective for skinning and butchering wild animals. Later human species made much more sophisticated tools.

Lacking the skill to hunt and kill large animals, small-brained *Homo habilis* probably obtained animal protein by scavenging meat from kills made by animal predators or resulting from accidents. There is evidence that they used large stone "choppers" for cracking open bones to get at the nutritious marrow. The fact that many such tools are found together far from the outcrops of volcanic rock suggests that people carried them long distances for use at kill sites and camps.

Homo erectus were also scavengers, but their larger brains would have made them cleverer at it—capable, for example, of finding and stealing the kills that leopards and other large predators dragged up into trees. They also made more effective tools for butchering large animals, although the stone flakes and choppers of earlier eras continued to be made. The stone tool most associated with *Homo erectus* was a hand ax formed by removing chips from both sides of a stone to produce a sharp outer edge.

Paleolithic (pay-lee-oh-LITH-ik) **Neolithic** (nee-oh-LITH-ik)

Modern experiments show the hand ax to be an efficient multipurpose tool, suitable for skinning and butchering animals, for scraping skins clean for use as clothing and mats, for sharpening wooden tools, and for digging up edible roots. Since a hand ax can also be hurled accurately for nearly 100 feet (30 meters), it might also have been used as a projectile to fell animals. From sites in Spain there is evidence that *Homo erectus* even butchered elephants, which then ranged across southern Europe, by driving them into swamps where they became trapped and died.

Homo sapiens were far more skillful hunters. They tracked and killed large animals (such as mastodons, mammoths, and bison) throughout the world. Their success reflected their superior intelligence and use of an array of finely made tools. Sharp stone flakes chipped from carefully prepared rock cores were often used in combination with other materials. Attaching a stone point to a wooden shaft made a spear. Embedding several sharp stone flakes in a bone handle produced a sawing tool.

Indeed, *Homo sapiens* were so skillful and successful as hunters that they may have caused or contributed to a series of ecological crises. Between 40,000 and 13,000 years ago the giant mastodons and mammoths gradually disappeared, first from Africa and Southeast Asia and then from northern Europe. In North America the sudden disappearance around 11,000 years ago of highly successful large-animal hunters known as the Clovis people was almost simultaneous with the extinction of three-fourths of the large mammals in the Americas, including giant bison, camels, ground sloths, stag-moose, giant cats, mastodons, and mammoths. In Australia there was a similar event. Since these extinctions occurred during the last series of severe cold spells at the end of the Ice Age, it is difficult to measure which effects were the work of global and regional climate changes and which resulted from the excesses of human predators.

Finds of fossilized animal bones bearing the marks of butchering tools clearly attest to the scavenging and hunting activities of Stone Age peoples, but anthropologists do not believe that early humans depended primarily on meat for their food. Modern **foragers** (hunting and food-gathering peoples) in the Kalahari Desert of southern Africa and the Ituri Forest of central Africa derive the bulk of their day-to-day nourishment from wild vegetable foods; meat is the food of feasts. It is likely that the same was true for Stone Age peoples, even though the tools and equipment for gathering and processing vegetable foods have left few traces because they were made of materials unable to survive for thousands of years.

Like modern foragers, ancient humans would have used skins and mats woven from leaves for collecting fruits, berries, and wild seeds. They would have dug edible roots out of the ground with wooden sticks. Archaeologists believe that donut-shaped stones often found at Stone Age sites may have been weights placed on wooden digging sticks to increase their effectiveness.

Both meat and vegetables become tastier and easier to digest when they are cooked. The first cooked foods were probably found by accident after wildfires, but there is new evidence from East and South Africa that humans may have been setting fires deliberately between 1 million and 1.5 million years ago. The wooden spits and hot rocks that they would have used for roasting, frying, or baking are not distinctive enough to stand out in an archaeological site. Only with the appearance of clay cooking pots some 12,500 years ago in East Asia is there hard evidence of cooking.

Gender Roles and Social Life

Some researchers have studied the organization of nonhuman primates for clues about very early human society. Gorillas and chimpanzees live in groups consisting of several adult males and females and their offspring. Status varies with age and sex, and a dominant male usually heads the group. Sexual unions between males and females generally do not result in long-term pairing. Instead, the strongest ties are those between a female and her children and among siblings. Adult males are often recruited from neighboring bands.

Very early human groups likely shared some of these primate traits, but by the time of modern *Homo sapiens* the two-parent family would have been characteristic. How this change from a mother-centered family to a two-parent family developed over the intervening millennia can only be guessed at, but it is likely that physical and social evolution were linked. Larger brain size was a contributing factor. Big-headed humans have to be born in a less mature state than other mammals so they can pass through the narrow birth canal. Other large mammals are mature at two or three years of age; humans are not able to care for themselves until the age of twelve to fifteen. Human infants' and children's need for much longer nurturing makes care by mothers, fathers, and other family members a biological imperative.

The human reproductive cycle also became unique at some point. In other species sexual contact is biologically restricted to a special mating season of the year or to the fertile part of the female's menstrual cycle. As well, among other primates the choice of mate is usually not a matter for long deliberation. To a female baboon in heat (estrus) any male will do, and to a male baboon any receptive female is a suitable sexual partner. In contrast, adult humans can mate at any time and are much choosier about their partners. Once they mate, frequent sexual contact promotes deep emotional ties and long-term bonding.

An enduring bond between human parents made it much easier for vulnerable offspring to receive the care they needed during the long period of their childhood. Working together, mothers and fathers could nurture dependent children of different ages at the same time, unlike other large mammals whose females must raise their offspring nearly to maturity before beginning another reproductive cycle. Spacing births close together also ensured offspring a high rate of survival and would have enabled humans to multiply more rapidly than other large mammals.

Other researchers have studied the few surviving present-day foragers for models of what such early societies could have been like. They infer that Ice Age women would have done most of the gathering and cooking (which they could do while caring for small children). Older women past childbearing age would have been the most knowledgeable and productive food gatherers. Men, with stronger arms and shoulders, would have been more suited than women to hunting, particularly for large animals. Some early cave art shows males in hunting activities.

Other aspects of social life in the Ice Age are suggested by studies of modern peoples. All recent hunter-gatherers have lived in small groups or bands. The community had to have enough members to defend itself from predators and to divide responsibility for the collection and preparation of animal and vegetable foods. However, if it had too many members, it risked exhausting the food available in its immediate vicinity. Even a band of optimal size had to move at regular intervals to follow migrating animals and take advantage of seasonally ripening plants in different places. Archaeological evidence from Ice Age campsites suggests early humans, too, lived in highly mobile bands.

Hearths and Cultural Expressions

Because frequent moves were necessary to keep close to migrating herds and ripening plants, early hunting and gathering peoples usually did not lavish much time on housing. Natural shelters under overhanging rocks or in caves in southern Africa and southern France are known to have been favorite camping places to which bands returned at regular intervals.

Where the climate was severe or where natural shelters did not exist, people erected huts of branches, stones, bones, skins, and leaves as seasonal camps. More elaborate dwellings were common in areas where protection against harsh weather was necessary.

An interesting camp dating to 15,000 years ago has been excavated in the Ukraine southeast of Kiev. Its communal dwellings were framed with the bones of elephant-like mammoths, then covered with hides. Each oblong structure, measuring 15 to 20 feet (4.5 to 6 meters) by 40 to 50 feet (12 to 15 meters), was capable of holding fifty people and would have taken several days to construct. The camp had five such dwellings, making it a large settlement for a foraging community. Large, solid structures were common in fishing villages that grew up along riverbanks and lakeshores, where the abundance of fish permitted people to occupy the same site year-round.

Making clothing was another necessary technology in the Stone Age. Animal skins were an early form of clothing, and the oldest evidence of fibers woven into cloth dates from about 26,000 years ago. An "Iceman" from 5,300 years ago, whose frozen remains were found in the European Alps in 1991, was wearing many different garments made of animal skins sewn together with cord fashioned from vegetable fibers and rawhide (see Environment and Technology: The Iceman).

Although accidents, erratic weather, and disease took a heavy toll on a foraging band, there is no reason to believe that day-to-day existence was particularly hard or unpleasant. Some studies suggest that, under the conditions operating on the African savannas and in other game-rich areas, securing necessary food, clothing, and shelter would have occupied only from three to five hours a day. This would have left a great deal of time for artistic endeavors as well as for toolmaking and social life.

The foundations of what later ages called science, art, and religion were also built during the Stone Age. Basic to human survival was extensive and precise knowledge about the natural environment. Gatherers needed to know which local plants were best for food and the seasons when they were available. Successful hunting required intimate knowledge of the habits of game animals. People learned how to use plant and animal parts for clothing, twine, and building materials, as well as

Interior of a Neolithic House This stone structure from the Orkney Islands off Scotland shows a double hearth for cooking and a small window in the center, along with stone partitions. Elsewhere, few Neolithic houses were made of stone, but wood was scarce in the Orkneys. (Ronald Sheridan/Ancient Art & Architecture)

ENVIRONMENT + TECHNOLOGY

The Iceman

The discovery of the well-preserved remains of a man at the edge of a melting glacier in the European Alps in 1991 provides unusually detailed information about everyday technologies of the fourth millennium B.C.E. Not just the body of this "Iceman" was well preserved. His clothing, his tools, and even the food in his stomach survived in remarkably good condition.

Dressed from head to toe for the cold weather of the mountains, the fifty-year-old man was wearing a fur hat fastened under the chin with a strap, a tailored vest of different colored deerskins, leather leggings and loincloth, and a padded cloak made of grasses. On his feet were calfskin shoes also padded with grass for warmth and comfort. The articles of clothing had been sewn together with fiber and leather cords. He carried a birch-bark drinking cup.

Most of his tools were those of the late Stone Age. In a sort of leather fanny pack he carried small flint tools for cutting, scraping, and punching holes, as well as some tinder for making a fire. He also carried a leather quiver with flint-tipped arrows, but his 6-foot (1.8-meter) bow was unfinished, lacking a bowstring. In addition he had a flint knife and a tool for sharpening flints. His most sophisticated tool was of the age of metals that was just dawning: a copper-bladed ax with a wooden handle.

Further investigations of the body have revealed that a small arrowhead lodged in his shoulder caused the Iceman's death. In his stomach, researchers found the remains of the meat-rich meal he had eaten not long before he died.

The Iceman This is an artist's rendition of what the Iceman might have looked like. Notice his tools, remarkable evidence of the technology of his day. (Weislav Smetek/STERN)

which natural substances were effective for medicine, consciousness altering, dyeing, and other purposes. Knowledge of the natural world included identifying minerals suitable for paints, stones for making the best tools, and so forth. Given humans' physical capacity for speech, it is likely that the transmission of such prescientific knowledge involved verbal communication, even though direct evidence for language appears only in later periods.

Early music and dance have left no traces, but there is abundant evidence of painting and drawing (see Diversity and Dominance: Cave Art). The oldest known cave paintings in Europe and North Africa date to 32,000 years ago, and there are many others from later times in other parts of the world. Because many cave paintings feature wild animals such as oxen, reindeer, and horses that were hunted for food, some believe that the art was meant to record hunting scenes or that it formed part of

DIVERSITY AND DOMINANCE

CAVE ART

Were the people who lived tens of thousands of years ago different from people today? Biologically, *Homo sapiens sapiens* seem not to have become more diverse over time. But what were prehistoric people like inside—in their thoughts, imaginations, and emotions? Did their eyes see beauty, their ears hear music, and their imaginations wonder at the meaning of the world and the celestial bodies above them?

Very little evidence exists to answer these important questions except in one form: cave paintings. First discovered in France in the late nineteenth century, such art immediately suggested that those who drew it were sophisticated modern people like ourselves. Just as the skeletal remains of *Homo sapiens* of a hundred thousand years ago show they had modern bodies, the art they made suggests they had modern minds.

The oldest cave paintings discovered in southeastern France date from 30,000 years ago—a very long time measured in human lifetimes, but a small part of human existence. The oldest recognizable human art, a carefully crosshatched bone from Blombos Cave east of Cape Town, South Africa, dates from over 70,000 years ago. Even as the temporal distance from us increases, the evidence supports the conclusion that these early people had minds and imaginations no different from those of people today.

We may sense these cave artists' common humanity with ourselves, but it is not easy to understand the cultural context of their work. Why did they draw what they did? And why in caves? In his book *From Black Land to Fifth Sun* (1998), archaeologist Brian Fagan suggests three approaches to bridging the gap, based on his own examination of cave paintings.

His first suggestion is that the context in which the art was made tells us a great deal. Throughout the world, early artists drew, carved, and painted on many surfaces, many fairly inaccessible. The decision to work inside dark caves that the artists could illuminate only with crude torches was not an accident. The fact that the hidden caves protected and preserved their art for tens of thousands of years could not have been part of their plan. Rather, Fagan suggests, the artists went deep underground "to feel the power of the earth." Unlike contemporary urban people who have lost a sense of nature's spiritual power, the cave painters would have believed that the wild animals and the earth itself were full of spiritual energy. The dark and enclosed caves would have heightened the sense of nature's mystery and power with which they informed their paintings. It is thus likely that the artists were already the spiritual guides of their communities.

As for the art itself, one should begin with the cautionary remark that even today's art conveys many messages. Still, Fagan believes, since the artists and original viewers were part of a community, it is likely that the common culture they shared enabled them to understand art in the same ways. He cites the example of the rock art traditions of the San artists of southern Africa that continued into the twentieth century to suggest that other cave art concerned the mystical relationship of humans with the animals they hunted. The form of the paintings and the ingredients that went into them meant that humans could absorb something of the power of the bears, antelope, bison, or other animals depicted in the caves by viewing or touching them.

Finally, Fagan says, we need to consider what these caves were used for and why cave artists returned over many generations, filling the walls and ceilings with their works. In

magical and religious rites to ensure successful hunting. However, a newly discovered cave at Vallon Pont-d'Arc° in southern France features rhinoceros, panthers, bears, owls, and a hyena, which probably were not the objects of hunting. Still other drawings include people dressed in animal skins and smeared with paint. In many caves there are stencils of human hands. Are these the signatures of the artists or the world's oldest graffiti? Some scholars suspect that other marks in cave paintings and

Vallon Pont-d'Arc (vah-LON pon-DAHRK)

The Lion Panel in Chauvet Cave, France (Jean Cottes/Ministere de la Culture/Corbis)

some places, later artists even painted over earlier works. Fagan compares the decorated caverns of remote antiquity with the Sistine Chapel in the Vatican, beautifully decorated by the artist Michelangelo, where many religious ceremonies are staged, including the election of the pope. The decorated caverns were not galleries where people went to view art, but holy places where religious ceremonies were performed and where those present would have had powerful religious experiences.

The scenes reproduced here from the large tableau of animal drawings known as the "Lion Panel" show the skill techniques and the variety of art in the Chauvet Cave. From the right come a band of female lions on the hunt, approaching a herd of bison, who turn to regard them. Across a cleft in the rock the panel resumes with a herd of rhinoceroses and another group of lions at the far left of the panel.

QUESTIONS FOR ANALYSIS

1. **Is there anything in the depiction of the animals that suggests whether the artists were in awe of them, felt superior to them, or felt at one with them?**
2. **Are all the animals ones that people hunted to eat? How persuasive are Fagan's explanations?**

on bones from this period may represent efforts at counting or writing.

Newer theories suggest that cave and rock art represent concerns with fertility, efforts to educate the young, or elaborate mechanisms for time reckoning. Another approach to understanding such art draws on the traditions of peoples like the San—hunters, gatherers, and artists in southern Africa since time immemorial.

Some cave art suggests that Stone Age people had well-developed religions, but without written religious texts it is difficult to know exactly what they believed. Sites of deliberate human burials from about 100,000 years ago give some hints. The fact that an adult was often buried with stone implements, food, clothing, and red-ochre powder suggests that early people revered their leaders enough to honor them after death and may imply a belief in an afterlife.

Today we recognize that the Stone Age, whose existence was scarcely dreamed of two centuries ago, was a formative period. Important in its own right, it also laid the basis for major changes ahead as human communities passed from being food gatherers to being food producers. Future discoveries are likely to add substantially to our understanding of these events.

THE AGRICULTURAL REVOLUTIONS

For most of history people ate only wild plants and animals. But around 10,000 years ago global climate changes seem to have induced some societies to enhance their food supplies with domesticated plants and animals. More and more people became food producers over the next millennium. Although hunting and gathering did not disappear, this transition from foraging to food production was one of the great turning points in history because it fostered a rapid increase in population and greatly altered humans' relationship to nature (see Map 1.2).

What should this historic transformation be called? Because agriculture arose in combination with new kinds of stone tools, archaeologists called the period the "Neolithic" and the rise of agriculture the "Neolithic Revolution." But that name can be misleading: first, stone tools were not its essential component, and second, it was not a single event but a series of separate transformations in different parts of the world. A better term is **Agricultural Revolutions,** which emphasizes that the central change was in food production and indicates that agriculture arose independently in many different places. In most cases agriculture included the domestication of animals for food as well as the cultivation of new food crops.

The Transition to Plant Cultivation

Food gathering gave way to food production in stages spread over hundreds of generations. The process may have begun when forager bands returning year after year to the same seasonal camps took measures to encourage the nearby growth of the foods they liked. They deliberately scattered the seeds of desirable plants in locations where they would thrive, and they discouraged the growth of competing plants by clearing them away. Such techniques of semicultivation could have supplemented food gathering for many generations. Families choosing to concentrate their energies on food production, however, would have had to settle permanently near their fields.

Settled agriculture required new, specialized tools. Indeed, it was the presence of new tools that first alerted archaeologists to the beginning of a food production revolution. Many specialized stone tools were developed or improved for agricultural use, including polished or ground stone heads to work the soil, sharp stone chips embedded in bone or wooden handles to cut grain, and stone mortars to pulverize grain. However, stone axes were not very efficient for clearing away shrubs and trees. To do that, farmers used a much older technology: fire. Fires got rid of unwanted undergrowth, and the ashes were a natural fertilizer. After the burn-off farmers could use blades and axes to cut away new growth.

Also fundamental to the success of agriculture was selecting the highest-yielding strains of wild plants, which led to the development of valuable new domesticated varieties over time. As the principal gatherers of wild plant foods, women probably played a major role in this transition to plant cultivation, but the heavy work of clearing the fields would have fallen to the men.

The transition to agriculture occurred first in the Middle East. By 8000 B.C.E. human intervention transformed certain wild grasses into higher-yielding domesticated grains, now known as emmer wheat and barley. Farmers there also discovered that alternating the cultivation of grains and pulses (plants yielding edible seeds such as lentils and peas) helped maintain soil fertility.

Plants domesticated in the Middle East spread to adjacent lands. Farmers in Greece were cultivating wheat and barley as early as 6000 B.C.E. Shortly after 4000 B.C.E. farming developed in the light-soiled plains of Central Europe and along the Danube River. As forests receded because of climate changes and human clearing efforts, agriculture spread to other parts of Europe over the next millennium.

Early farmers in Europe and elsewhere practiced shifting cultivation, also known as swidden agriculture. After a few growing seasons, the fields were left fallow (abandoned to natural vegetation), and new fields were cleared nearby. In the Danube Valley of Central Europe between 4000 and 3000 B.C.E., for example, communities of from forty to sixty people supported themselves on about 500 acres (200 hectares) of farmland, cultivating a third or less each year while leaving the rest fallow to restore its fertility. From around 2600 B.C.E. people in Central Europe began using ox-drawn wooden plows to till heavier and richer soils.

Although the lands around the Mediterranean seem

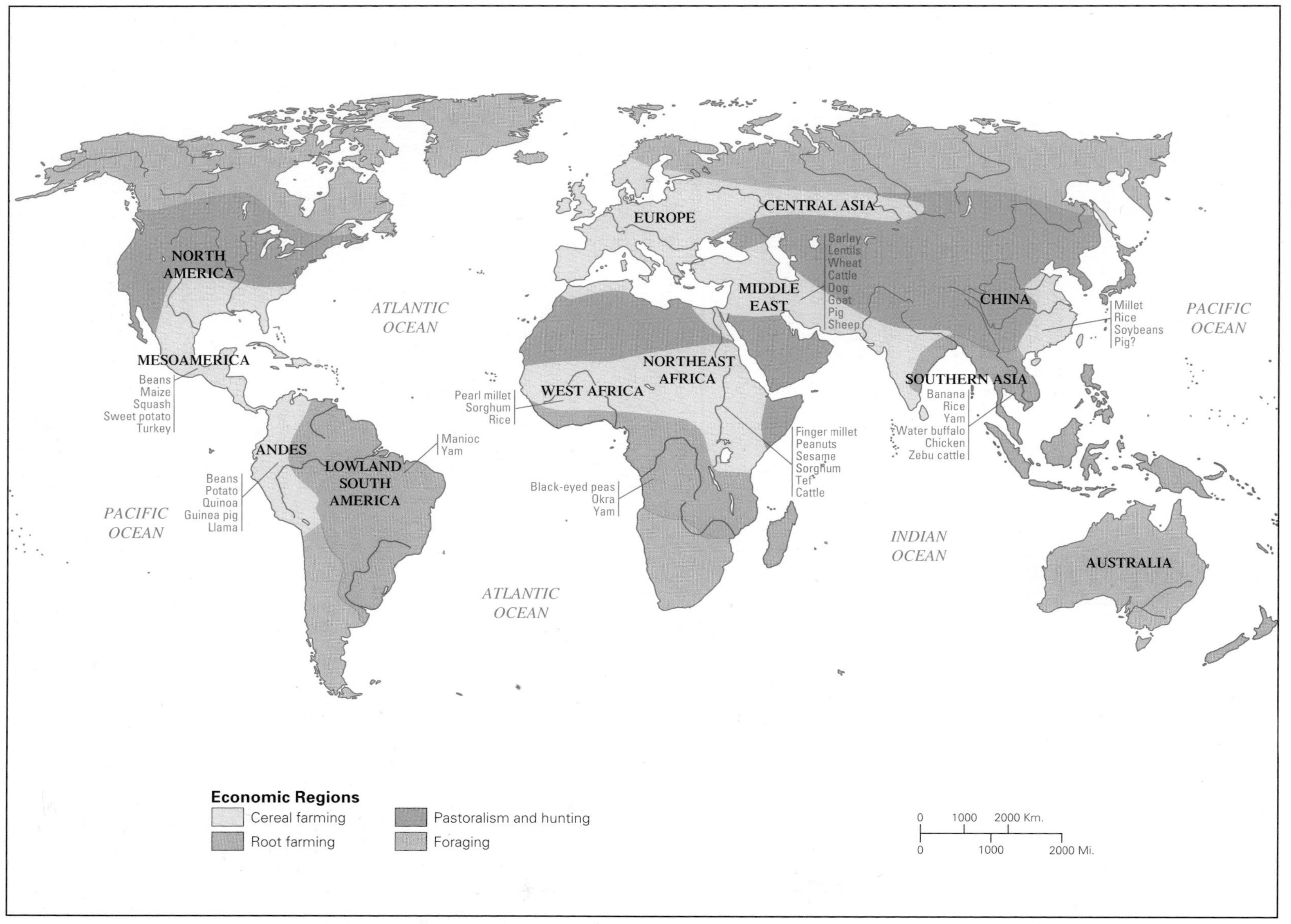

Map 1.2 Early Centers of Plant and Animal Domestication Many different parts of the world made original contributions to domestication during the Agricultural Revolutions that began about 10,000 years ago. Later interactions helped spread these domesticated animals and plants to new locations. In lands less suitable for crop cultivation, pastoralism and hunting remained more important for supplying food.

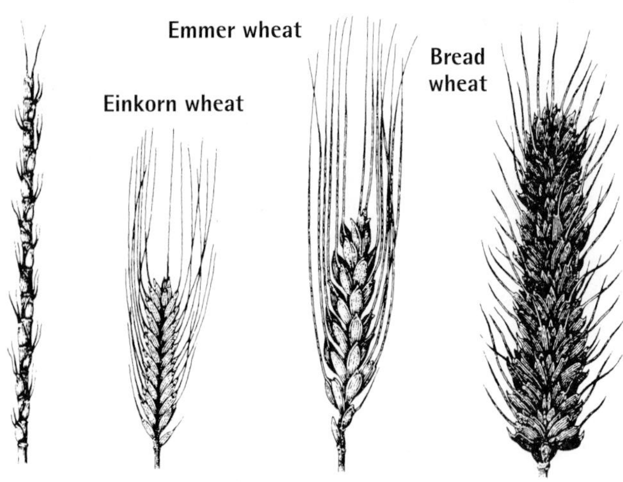

Domestication of Wheat Through selection of the largest seeds of this wild grass, early farmers in the Middle East were able to develop varieties with larger edible kernels. Bread wheat was grown in the Nile Valley by 5000 B.C.E. (From Iris Barn, *Discovering Archaeology*, © 1981)

to have shared a complex of crops and farming techniques, wheat and barley could not spread farther south because the rainfall patterns in most of the rest of Africa were unsuited to the growth of these grains. Instead, separate agricultural revolutions took place in Saharan and sub-Saharan Africa, beginning almost as early as in the Middle East. During a particularly wet period after 8000 B.C.E. people in what is now the eastern Sahara began to cultivate sorghum, a grain they derived from wild grasses they had previously gathered. Over the next 3,000 years the Saharan farmers domesticated pearl millet, black-eyed peas, a kind of peanut, sesame, and gourds. In the Ethiopian highlands farmers domesticated finger millet and a grain called tef. The return of drier conditions about 5000 B.C.E. led many Saharan farmers to move to the Nile Valley, where the annual flooding of the Nile River provided moisture for cereal farming. In the rain forests of equatorial West Africa there is early evidence of indigenous domestication of yams and rice.

Eastern and southern Asia were also major centers of plant domestication, although the details are not as clearly documented as in the Middle East. Rice was first domesticated in southern China, the northern half of Southeast Asia, or northern India, possibly as early as 10,000 B.C.E. but more likely closer to 5000 B.C.E. Rice cultivation thrived in the warm and wet conditions of southern China. In India several pulses (including hyacinth beans, green grams, and black grams) domesticated about 2000 B.C.E. were cultivated along with rice.

While food production was spreading in Eurasia and Africa, the inhabitants of the isolated American continents were creating other major centers of crop domestication. Recent evidence dates the cultivation of several important food crops to about 5000 B.C.E.: maize° (corn) in the Tabasco area of eastern Mexico, manioc in Panama, and beans and squash in Mesoamerica. It seems likely that the domestication of maize occurred earlier in western Mexico and manioc originated from Brazil. By 4000 B.C.E., the inhabitants of Peru were developing a food production system based on potatoes and quinoa°, a protein-rich seed grain. In so far as their climates and soils permitted, other farming communities throughout the Americas adopted such crops as these, along with tomatoes and peppers.

The fact that people in Asia, the Americas, and Africa developed their own domesticated plants in isolation from outside influences added to the variety of cultivated plants. After 1500 C.E. many of these crops became important foods throughout the world.

Domesticated Animals and Pastoralism

The domestication of animals also expanded rapidly during these same millennia. The first domesticated animal was probably the dog, tamed to help early hunters track game. Later animals were domesticated to provide meat, milk, and energy. Like the domestication of plants, this process is best known in the Middle East.

Refuse heaps outside some Middle East villages show fewer and fewer wild gazelle bones during the centuries after 7000 B.C.E. This probably reflects the depletion of such wild animals through overhunting by the local farming communities, but meat eating did not decline. The deposits show that sheep and goat bones gradually replaced gazelle bones. It seems likely that as wild sheep and goats scavenged for food scraps around agricultural villages, the tamer animals accepted human control and protection in exchange for a ready supply of food. Differences between the bones of wild and newly tamed species are too slight to date domestication precisely. However, selective breeding for desirable characteristics such as high milk production and long wooly coat eventually led to clearly distinct breeds of sheep and goats.

maize (mayz) **quinoa** (kee-NOH-uh)

Elsewhere, other animal species were domesticated during the centuries before 3000 B.C.E. Wild cattle were domesticated in northern Africa or the Middle East; donkeys in northern Africa; water buffalo in China; and humped-back Zebu° cattle in India. As in the case of food plants, varieties of domesticated animals spread from one region to another. Zebu cattle, for example, grew important in sub-Saharan Africa after about 2,000 years ago.

Once cattle became tame enough to be yoked to plows, they became essential to successful grain production. In addition, animal droppings provided valuable fertilizer. These developments and the widespread use of wool and milk from domesticated animals occurred much later than initial domestication. However, there were two notable deviations from the pattern of mixed agriculture and animal husbandry. One variation was in the Americas. There, comparatively few species of wild animals were suitable for domestication, and domesticated animals could not be borrowed from elsewhere because the land bridge to Asia had submerged as melting glaciers raised sea levels. Domesticated llamas provided transport and wool, while guinea pigs and turkeys furnished meat. Hunting remained the most important source of meat for Amerindians.

The other notable variation from mixed farming occurred in the more arid parts of Africa and Central Asia. There, pastoralism, a way of life dependent on large herds of small and large stock, predominated. As the Sahara approached its maximum dryness around 2500 B.C.E., pastoralists replaced farmers who migrated southward (see Chapter 8). Moving their herds to new pastures and watering places throughout the year made pastoralists almost as mobile as foragers and discouraged accumulation of bulky possessions and construction of substantial dwellings. Like modern pastoralists, early cattle-keeping people probably relied more heavily on milk than on meat, since killing animals diminished the size of their herds. During wet seasons, they may also have done some hasty crop cultivation or bartered meat and skins for plant foods with nearby farming communities.

Agriculture and Ecological Crisis

Why did the Agricultural Revolutions occur? Some theories assume that people were drawn to food production by its obvious advantages. For example, it has recently been suggested that people in the Middle East might have settled down so they could grow enough grains to ensure themselves a ready supply of beer. Beer drinking is frequently depicted in ancient Middle Eastern art and can be dated to as early as 3500 B.C.E.

However, most researchers today believe that climate change drove people to abandon hunting and gathering in favor of agriculture or pastoralism. Temperatures warmed so much at the end of the Great Ice Age that geologists give the era since about 9000 B.C.E. a new name: the **Holocene°.** There is evidence that temperate lands were exceptionally warm between 6000 and 2000 B.C.E., the era when people in many parts of the world adopted agriculture. The precise nature of the crisis probably varied. Shortages of wild food in the Middle East caused by a dry spell or population growth may have prodded people to take up food production. Elsewhere, a warmer, wetter climate could turn grasslands into forest, thereby reducing supplies of game and wild grains.

Additional support for an ecological explanation comes from the fact that in many drier parts of the world, where wild food remained abundant, people did not take up agriculture. The inhabitants of Australia continued to rely exclusively on foraging until recent centuries, as did some peoples on all the other continents. Many Amerindians in the arid grasslands from Alaska to the Gulf of Mexico hunted bison, while in the Pacific Northwest others took up salmon-fishing. Abundant supplies of fish, shellfish, and aquatic animals permitted food gatherers east of the Mississippi River to become increasingly sedentary. In Africa conditions favored retention of the older ways in the equatorial rain forest and in the southern part of the continent. The reindeer-based societies of northern Eurasia were also unaffected by the spread of farming.

Whatever the causes, the gradual adoption of food production transformed most parts of the world. A hundred thousand years ago there were fewer than 2 million people, and their range was largely confined to the temperate and tropical regions of Africa and Eurasia. The population may have fallen even lower during the last glacial epoch, between 32,000 and 13,000 years ago. Then, as the glaciers retreated and people took up agriculture, their numbers rose. World population may have reached 10 million by 5000 B.C.E. and then mushroomed to between 50 million and 100 million by 1000 B.C.E.[1] This increase led to important changes to social and cultural life.

Zebu (ZEE-boo)

Holocene (HAWL-oh-seen)

LIFE IN NEOLITHIC COMMUNITIES

Evidence that an ecological crisis may have driven people to food production has prompted a reexamination of the assumption that farmers enjoyed better lives than foragers. Modern studies demonstrate that food producers have to work much harder and for much longer periods than do food gatherers. Long days spent clearing and cultivating the land yielded meager harvests. Guarding herds from wild predators, guiding them to fresh pastures, and tending to their many needs imposed similar burdens.

Early farmers were less likely to starve because they could store food between harvests to tide people over seasonal changes and short-term droughts, but their diet was less varied and nutritious than that of foragers. Skeletal remains show that Neolithic farmers were shorter on average than earlier food-gathering peoples. Farmers were also more likely to die at an earlier age because people in permanent settlements were more exposed to diseases. Their water was contaminated by human waste; disease-bearing vermin and insects infested their bodies and homes; and they could catch new diseases from their domesticated animals (especially pigs and cattle).

So how did farmers displace foragers? Some researchers have envisioned a violent struggle between practitioners of the two ways of life; others have argued for a more peaceful transition. Some violence was likely, especially as the amount of cleared land reduced the wild foods available to foragers. Conflicts among farmers for control of the best land must also have occurred. In most cases, however, farmers seem to have displaced foragers by gradual infiltration rather than by conquest.

The key to the food producers' expansion may have been the simple fact that their small surpluses gave them a long-term advantage in population growth by ensuring slightly higher survival rates during times of drought or other crisis. The respected archaeologist Colin Renfrew argues, for example, that over a few centuries farming-population densities in Europe could have increased by a factor of fifty to one hundred. In his view, as population densities rose, individuals who had to farm at a great distance from their native village would have formed a new farming settlement on the outskirts. A steady, nonviolent expansion of only 12 to 19 miles (20 to 30 kilometers) a generation could have repopulated the whole of Europe from Greece to Britain between 6500 and 3500 B.C.E.[2] The process would have been so gradual that it need not have provoked any sharp conflicts with existing foragers, who simply could have stayed clear of the agricultural frontier or gradually adopted agriculture themselves. New studies that map genetic changes also support the hypothesis of a gradual spread of agricultural people across Europe from southeast to northwest.[3]

Like forager bands, the expanding farming communities were organized around kinship and marriage. Nuclear families (parents and their children) probably lived in separate households, but felt great solidarity with all those who were related to them by descent from common ancestors several generations back. These kinship units, known as lineages° or clans, acted together to defend their common interests and land.

Even if one assumes stable marriage patterns, tracing descent is a complex matter. Because each person has two parents, four grandparents, eight great-grandparents, and so on, each individual has a bewildering number of ancestors. Some societies trace descent equally through both parents, but most give greater importance to descent through either the mother (matrilineal° societies) or the father (patrilineal° societies).

Some scholars have argued that very ancient peoples traced descent through women and may have been ruled by women. For example, the traditions of Kikuyu° farmers on Mount Kenya in East Africa relate that women ruled until the Kikuyu men conspired to get all the women pregnant at once and then overthrew them while the women were unable to fight back. No evidence exists to prove or disprove legends such as this, but it is important not to confuse tracing descent through women (matrilineality) with the rule of women (matriarchy°).

Cultural Expressions

Kinship systems influenced early agricultural people's outlook on the world. When old persons died, their burials might be occasions for elaborate ceremonies that expressed their descendants' group solidarity. Plastered skulls found in the ancient city of Jericho° (see Map 2.1) may be evidence of such early ancestor reverence or worship.

A society's religious beliefs tend to reflect relations to nature. The religions of food gatherers tended to center on sacred groves, springs, and wild animals. Pastoralists tended to worship the Sky God who controlled the rains and guided their migrations. In contrast, the religious activities of many farming communities centered

lineage (LIN-ee-ij) **matrilineal** (mat-ruh-LIN-ee-uhl) **patrilineal** (pat-ruh-LIN-ee-uhl) **Kikuyu** (ki-KOO-yoo) **matriarchy** (MAY-tree-ahr-key) **Jericho** (JER-ih-koh)

Stonehenge, in Southern England This view from the center of the megalithic circle looks through an arch to the Heel Stone, which marks the precise place where the sun rises on the horizon on the summer solstice, the beginning of summer. The changing of the seasons was an important part of religion in Neolithic Europe. (© Mick Sharp)

on the Earth Mother, a female deity believed to be the source of all new life, and on other gods and goddesses representing fire, wind, and rain.

The story in an ancient Hindu text about the burning of a large forest near modern India's capital, New Delhi°, may preserve a memory of the conflict between old and new beliefs. In the story the gods Krishna° and Arjuna° are picnicking in the forest when Agni, the fire-god, appears in disguise and asks them to satisfy his hunger by burning the forest and every creature in it. As interpreted by some scholars, this story portrays both the clearing of the land for cultivation and the destruction of the wildlife on which food gatherers depended.[4]

The worship of ancestors, gods of the heavens, and earthly nature and fertility deities varied from place to place, and many societies combined the different elements in their religious practices. A recently discovered complex of stone structures in the Egyptian desert that was in use by 5000 B.C.E. includes burial chambers presumably for ancestors, a calendar circle, and pairs of upright stones that frame the rising sun on the summer solstice. The calendar and the structure aligned with the solstice reflect a strong devotion to the cycle of the seasons and knowledge of how they were linked to the movement of heavenly bodies. Other **megaliths** (meaning "big stones") were erected elsewhere. Observation and worship of the sun is evident at the famous Stonehenge monolithic site in England constructed about 2000 B.C.E. Megalithic burial chambers dating from 4000 B.C.E. are evidence of ancestor rituals in western and southern Europe. The early ones appear to have been communal burial chambers, which descent groups may have erected to mark their claims to farmland. In the Middle East, the Americas, and other parts of the world, giant earth burial mounds may have served similar functions.

Another fundamental cultural contribution of the Neolithic period was the dissemination of the large language families that form the basis of most languages spoken today. The root language of the giant Indo-European language family (from which the Germanic, Romance, and Celtic languages are derived) arose around 5000 B.C.E. Its westward spread across Europe may have been the work of pioneering agriculturalists. In the course of this very gradual expansion, Celtic, Germanic, Slavic, and Romance languages developed. Similarly, the Afro-Asiatic language family of the Middle East and northern Africa may have been the result of the food producers' expansion, as might the spread of the Sino-Tibetan family in East and Southeast Asia.

Delhi (DEL-ee) **Krishna** (KRISH-nuh) **Arjuna** (AHR-joo-nuh)

Early Towns and Specialists

Most early farmers lived in small villages, but in some geographically favored parts of the world a few villages grew into towns, which were centers of trade and specialized crafts. These towns had elaborate dwellings and ceremonial buildings, as well as many large structures for storing surplus food until the next harvest. Baskets and other woven containers held dry foods; pottery jugs, jars, and pots stored liquids. Residents could make most of these structures and objects in their spare time, but in large communities some craft specialists devoted their full time to making products of unusual complexity or beauty.

Two towns in the Middle East that have been extensively excavated are Jericho on the west bank of the Jordan River and Çatal Hüyük° in central Anatolia (modern Turkey). (Map 2.1 shows their locations.) The excavations at Jericho revealed an unusually large and elaborate early agricultural settlement. The round, mud-brick dwellings characteristic of Jericho around 8000 B.C.E. may have been modeled on the tents of hunters who once had camped near Jericho's natural spring. A millennium later, rectangular rooms with finely plastered walls and floors and wide doorways opened onto central courtyards. A massive stone wall surrounding the 10-acre (4-hectare) settlement helped defend it against attacks.

The ruins of Çatal Hüyük, an even larger Neolithic town, date to between 7000 and 5000 B.C.E. and cover 32 acres (13 hectares). Its residents also occupied plastered mud-brick rooms with elaborate decorations, but Çatal Hüyük had no defensive wall. Instead, the outer walls of the town's houses formed a continuous barrier without doors or large windows, so invaders would have found it difficult to break in. Residents entered their house by means of ladders through holes in the roof.

Çatal Hüyük prospered from long-distance trade in obsidian, a hard volcanic rock that craftspeople skillfully chipped, ground, and polished into tools, weapons, mirrors, and ornaments. Other residents made fine pottery, wove baskets and woolen cloth, made stone and shell beads, and worked leather and wood. House sizes varied, but there is no evidence that Çatal Hüyük had a dominant class or a centralized political structure.

Agriculture was the basis of Çatal Hüyük's existence. Fields around the town produced crops of barley and emmer wheat, as well as legumes° and other vegetables. Pigs were kept along with goats and sheep. Yet wild foods still featured prominently in the diet of the town's residents. Archaeologists have dug up remains of acorns, wild grains, and wild game animals.

Neolithic Goddess Many versions of a well-nourished and pregnant female figure were found at Çatal Hüyük. Here she is supported by twin leopards whose tails curve over her shoulders. To those who inhabited the city some 8,000 years ago the figure likely represented fertility and power over nature. (C. M. Dixon)

Representational art at Çatal Hüyük makes it clear that hunting retained a powerful hold on people's minds. Elaborate wall paintings of hunting scenes are remarkably similar to earlier cave paintings. Scenes depict men or women adorned with the skins of wild leopards. Also, men were buried with weapons of war and hunting, not with the tools of farming.

Perhaps the most striking finds at Çatal Hüyük are those that reveal religious practices. There is a religious shrine for every two houses. At least forty rooms contained shrines with depictions of horned wild bulls, female breasts, goddesses, leopards, and handprints. Rituals involved burning grains, legumes, and meat as offerings, but there is no evidence of live animal sacrifice. Statues of plump female deities far outnumber statues of male deities, suggesting that the inhabitants

Çatal Hüyük (cha-TAHL hoo-YOOK) **legume** (LEG-yoom)

venerated a goddess as their principal deity. The site's principal excavator believed that, although male priests existed, "It seems extremely likely that the cult of the goddess was administered mainly by women."[5]

Metalworking became an important specialized occupation in the late Neolithic period. At Çatal Hüyük objects of copper and lead—metals that occur naturally in a fairly pure form—can be dated to about 6400 B.C.E. In many parts of the world silver and gold were also worked at an early date. Because of their rarity and their softness, those metals did not replace stone tools and weapons but instead were used primarily to make decorative or ceremonial objects. The discovery of many such objects in graves suggests they were symbols of status and power.

Towns, specialized crafts, and elaborate religious shrines added to the workload of agriculturalists. Extra food had to be produced for nonfarmers, such as priests and artisans. Added labor was needed to build permanent houses, town walls, and towers, not to mention megalithic monuments. Stonehenge, for example, may have taken 30,000 person-hours to build. It is not known whether these tasks were performed freely or coerced.

Conclusion

This chapter covers a far longer period than do all the chapters in the rest of the book combined. The reason for including so much time is that the rate of change was much slower during this era and the number of people on earth was much smaller than would be true in later times. Compressing so long a period into a single chapter also highlights the evolution of the fundamental relationships between humans and their natural environment that still underlie all human history.

In the first stage of human existence, hominids had to evolve physically to survive changing environments. Next, early humans began to use their distinctive physical and mental abilities to adapt culturally to many different natural environments. Societies passed down and slowly improved their tools, techniques, and specialized technical knowledge. By the late Paleolithic period all hominid species had become extinct except one: *Homo sapiens sapiens.* They were the least varied biologically of any living organism, yet they were earth's most widely dispersed mammals. Cultural diversity permitted humans to thrive in all the habitable continents.

Environmental forces still played a powerful role. To survive the climate changes that began the Holocene, humans in several different parts of the world successfully made the complex technological change from food collection to food production. In turn, the spread of agriculture greatly modified the natural environment and led to great new cultural changes.

Agriculture brought many toils and hardships, but it enabled people to manipulate plants, animals, and the surface of the planet and to greatly increase their own numbers. Besides bringing still greater changes in technology, farming and settled life led to increased social and cultural diversity. The patterns of language and belief, of diet, dress, and dwelling that emerged in the Neolithic period shaped the next several millennia. As Chapters 2 and 3 detail, specialization made possible by settled life also gave rise to significant advances in architecture and metallurgy, to artistic achievements, and to the growth of complex religious and political systems.

Key Terms

evolution
australopithecine
hominid
bipedalism
Great Ice Age
Homo habilis
Homo erectus
Homo sapiens
culture
history
Stone Age
Paleolithic
Neolithic
forager
Agricultural Revolutions
Holocene
megalith

Suggested Reading

Useful reference works for this period are the *Encyclopedia of Human Evolution and Prehistory* (1988) and the *Cambridge Encyclopedia of Human Evolution* (1992). Reliable textbooks are Brian Fagan's *People of the Earth: An Introduction to World Prehistory,* 9th ed. (1997), and Robert J. Wenke, *Patterns in Prehistory: Humankind's First Three Million Years,* 4th ed. (1999).

Accounts of the discoveries of early human remains written for nonspecialists by eminent researchers include Brian Fagan, *The Journey from Eden* (1990), Donald Johanson, Leorna Johanson, and Blake Edgar, *In Search of Human Origins* (1994), based on the *Nova* television series of the same name; and Richard Leakey and Roger Lewin, *Origins Reconsidered: In Search of What Makes Us Human* (1992). Other useful books that deal with this subject include George D. Brown, Jr., *Human Evolution* (1995), for a precise biological and geological perspective; Adam Kuper, *The Chosen Primate: Human Nature and Cultural Diversity* (1994), for an anthropological analysis; Glyn Daniel and Colin Renfrew, *The Idea of Prehistory,* 2d ed. (1988), detailing the development of the discipline and relying primarily on European examples; and Robert Foley, *Another Unique Species: Patterns in Human Evolutionary Ecology* (1987), a thoughtful and readable attempt to bring together archaeological evidence and biological processes.

More analytical overviews of the evolutionary evidence are James L. Newman, *The Peopling of Africa: A Geographical Interpretation* (1995); L. Luca Cavalli-Sforza and Francesco Cavalli-Sforza, *The Great Human Diasporas: The History of Diversity and Evolution* (1995), for genetic evidence; Richard G. Klein, *The Human Career: Human Biological and Cultural Origins* (1989); and Paul Mellars, ed., *The Emergence of Modern Humans* (1991). Thoughtful explorations of key issues are Colin Renfrew, *Archaeology and Language: The Puzzle of Indo-European Origins* (1988); and Marija Gimbutas, *The Civilization of the Goddess: The World of Old Europe* (1991). Margaret Ehrenberg, *Women in Prehistory* (1989), and M. Kay Martin and Barbara Voorhies, *Female of the Species* (1975), provide interesting, though necessarily speculative, discussions of women's history.

Cave and rock art and their implications are the subjects of many works. A broad, global introduction is Hans-Georg Bandi, *The Art of the Stone Age: Forty Thousand Years of Rock Art* (1961). Ann Sieveking, *The Cave Artists* (1979), provides a brief overview of the major European finds. Other specialized studies are Robert R. R. Brooks and Vishnu S. Wakankar, *Stone Age Painting in India* (1976); R. Townley Johnson, *Major Rock Paintings of Southern Africa* (1979); J. D. Lewis-Williams, *Believing and Seeing* (1981) and *Discovering Southern African Rock Art* (1990); Mario Ruspoli, *The Cave Art of Lascaux* (1986); and Jean-Marie Chauvet, Eliette Brunel Deschamps, and Christian Hillaire, *Dawn of Art: The Chauvet Cave, the Oldest Known Paintings in the World* (1996).

For the transition to food production see Jared Diamond, *Guns, Germs, and Steel: The Fates of Human Societies* (1997), and Allen W. Johnson and Timothy Earle, *The Evolution of Human Societies: From Foraging Group to Agrarian State* (1987). Jean-Pierre Mohen, *The World of Megaliths* (1990), analyzes early monumental architecture. James Mellaart, the principal excavator of Çatal Hüyük, has written an account of the town for the general reader: *Çatal Hüyük: A Neolithic Town in Anatolia* (1967). A pioneering work on human ecology, the early sections of which are about this period, is Madhav Gadgil and Ramachandra Guha, *This Fissured Land: An Ecological History of India* (1992).

Notes

1. Colin McEvedy and Richard Jones, *Atlas of World Population History* (New York: Penguin Books, 1978), 13–15.
2. Colin Renfrew, *Archaeology and Language: The Puzzle of Indo-European Origins* (New York: Cambridge University Press, 1988), 125, 150.
3. Luigi Cavalli-Sforza, L. Luca, Paolo Menozzi, and Alberto Piazza, *The History and Geography of Human Genes* (Princeton, NJ: Princeton University Press, 1994).
4. Madhav Gadgil and Ramachandra Guha, *This Fissured Land: An Ecological History of India* (Berkeley: University of California Press, 1992), 79.
5. James Mellaart, *Çatal Hüyük: A Neolithic Town in Anatolia* (New York: McGraw-Hill, 1967), 202.

2

The First River-Valley Civilizations, 3500–1500 B.C.E.

Painted Wooden Models from the Tomb of an Egyptian Nobleman, ca. 2000 B.C.E.
Meketre, seated at right, oversees inspection of his cattle with the help of herdsmen and other servants.

CHAPTER OUTLINE

One of the oldest surviving works of literature, the *Epic of Gilgamesh*, whose roots date to before 2000 B.C.E., provides a definition of *civilization* as the people of ancient Mesopotamia (present-day Iraq) understood it. Gilgamesh, an early king, sends a temple-prostitute to tame Enkidu°, a wild man who lives like an animal in the grasslands. After using her sexual charms to win Enkidu's trust, the temple-prostitute tells him:

> Come with me to the city, to Uruk°,
> to the temple of Anu and the goddess Ishtar . . .
> to Uruk, where the processions are and music,
> let us go together through the dancing
> to the palace hall where Gilgamesh presides.[1]

She then clothes Enkidu and teaches him to eat cooked food, drink brewed beer, and bathe and oil his body. By her words and actions she indicates some of the behavior that ancient Mesopotamians associated with civilized life.

The tendency of the Mesopotamians, like other peoples throughout history, to equate civilization with their own way of life should serve as a caution for us. What assumptions are hiding behind the frequently made claim that the "first" civilizations, or the first "advanced" or "high" civilizations, arose in western Asia and northeastern Africa sometime before 3000 B.C.E.? *Civilization* is a loaded and ambiguous concept, and the idea that the first civilizations emerged in ancient Mesopotamia and Egypt needs to be carefully explained.

Scholars agree that the following political, social, economic, and technological phenomena are indicators of **civilization:** (1) cities that served as administrative centers, (2) a political system based on control of a defined territory rather than on kinship connections, (3) a significant number of people engaged in specialized, non-food-producing activities, (4) status distinctions, usually linked to the accumulation of substantial wealth by some groups, (5) monumental building, (6) a system for keeping permanent records, (7) long-distance trade, and (8) major advances in science and the arts. The earliest societies in which those features are apparent developed in the floodplains of great rivers in Asia and Africa: the Tigris° and Euphrates° in Iraq, the Indus in Pakistan, the Yellow (Huang He°) in China, and the Nile in Egypt (see Map 2.1). The periodic flooding of the rivers brought benefits—deposits of fertile silt and water for agriculture—but also threatened lives and property. To protect themselves and channel these powerful forces of nature, people living near the rivers created new technologies and forms of political and social organization.

In this chapter we trace the rise of complex societies in Mesopotamia, Egypt, and the Indus River Valley from approximately 3500 to 1500 B.C.E. Our starting point roughly coincides with the origins of writing, so we can observe aspects of human experience that scholars cannot deduce from archaeological evidence alone. Because the independent emergence of civilization based on river floods and irrigation occurred somewhat later in China than in Mesopotamia, Egypt, and the Indus Valley, early China is taken up in the next chapter.

As you read this chapter, ask yourself the following questions:

- Why did the earliest civilizations arise in such challenging environments?
- How did the need to organize labor resources shape the political and social structures of these societies?
- To what degree did new technologies, such as metallurgy, writing, and monumental construction, contribute to the power and wealth of elite groups?
- How is the interaction of these societies with the environment reflected in their religious beliefs and worldviews?

Enkidu (EN-kee-doo) **Uruk** (OO-rook)

Tigris (TIE-gris) **Euphrates** (you-FRAY-teez)
Huang He (hwang huh)

CHRONOLOGY

	Mesopotamia	Egypt	Indus Valley
3500 B.C.E.			
3000 B.C.E.	**3000–2350 B.C.E.** Early Dynastic (Sumerian)	**3100–2575 B.C.E.** Early Dynastic	
2500 B.C.E.		**2575–2134 B.C.E.** Old Kingdom	**2600 B.C.E.** Beginning of Indus Valley civilization
	2350–2230 B.C.E. Akkadian (Semitic)	**2134–2040 B.C.E.** First Intermediate Period	
2000 B.C.E.	**2112–2004 B.C.E.** Third Dynasty of Ur (Sumerian)	**2040–1640 B.C.E.** Middle Kingdom	
	1900–1600 B.C.E. Old Babylonian (Semitic)	**1640–1532 B.C.E.** Second Intermediate Period	**1900 B.C.E.** End of Indus Valley civilization
1500 B.C.E.	**1500–1150 B.C.E.** Kassite	**1532–1070 B.C.E.** New Kingdom	

MESOPOTAMIA

Because of the unpredictable nature of the Tigris and Euphrates Rivers and the weather, the peoples of ancient Mesopotamia saw the world as a hazardous place where human beings were at the mercy of gods who embodied the forces of nature. One of their explanations for the origins and characteristics of their world is what we know as the Babylonian Creation Epic (see Diversity and Dominance: Violence and Order in the Babylonian New Year's Festival—**Babylon** was the most important city in southern Mesopotamia in the second and first millennia B.C.E.). The high point of the myth is a cosmic battle between Marduk, the chief god of Babylon, and Tiamat°, a female figure who personifies the salt sea. Marduk cuts up Tiamat and from her body fashions the earth and sky. He then creates the divisions of time, the celestial bodies, rivers, and weather phenomena, and from the blood of a defeated rebel god he creates human beings. Creation myths of this sort provided the ancient inhabitants of Mesopotamia with a satisfactory explanation for the environment in which they were living.

Settled Agriculture in an Unstable Landscape

Mesopotamia is a Greek word meaning "land between the rivers." It reflects the centrality of the Euphrates and Tigris Rivers to the way of life in this region (see Map 2.2). Mesopotamian civilization developed in the plain along and between the rivers, which originate in the mountains of eastern Anatolia (modern Turkey) and empty into the Persian Gulf. This is an alluvial plain—a flat, fertile expanse built up over many millennia by silt that the rivers deposited.

Mesopotamia lies mostly within modern Iraq. To the north and east, an arc of mountains extends from northern Syria and southeastern Anatolia to the Zagros° Mountains, which separate the plain from the Iranian Plateau. The Syrian and Arabian deserts lie to the west and southwest, and the Persian Gulf is in the southeast.

Tiamat (TEE-ah-mat)

Zagros (ZAG-ruhs)

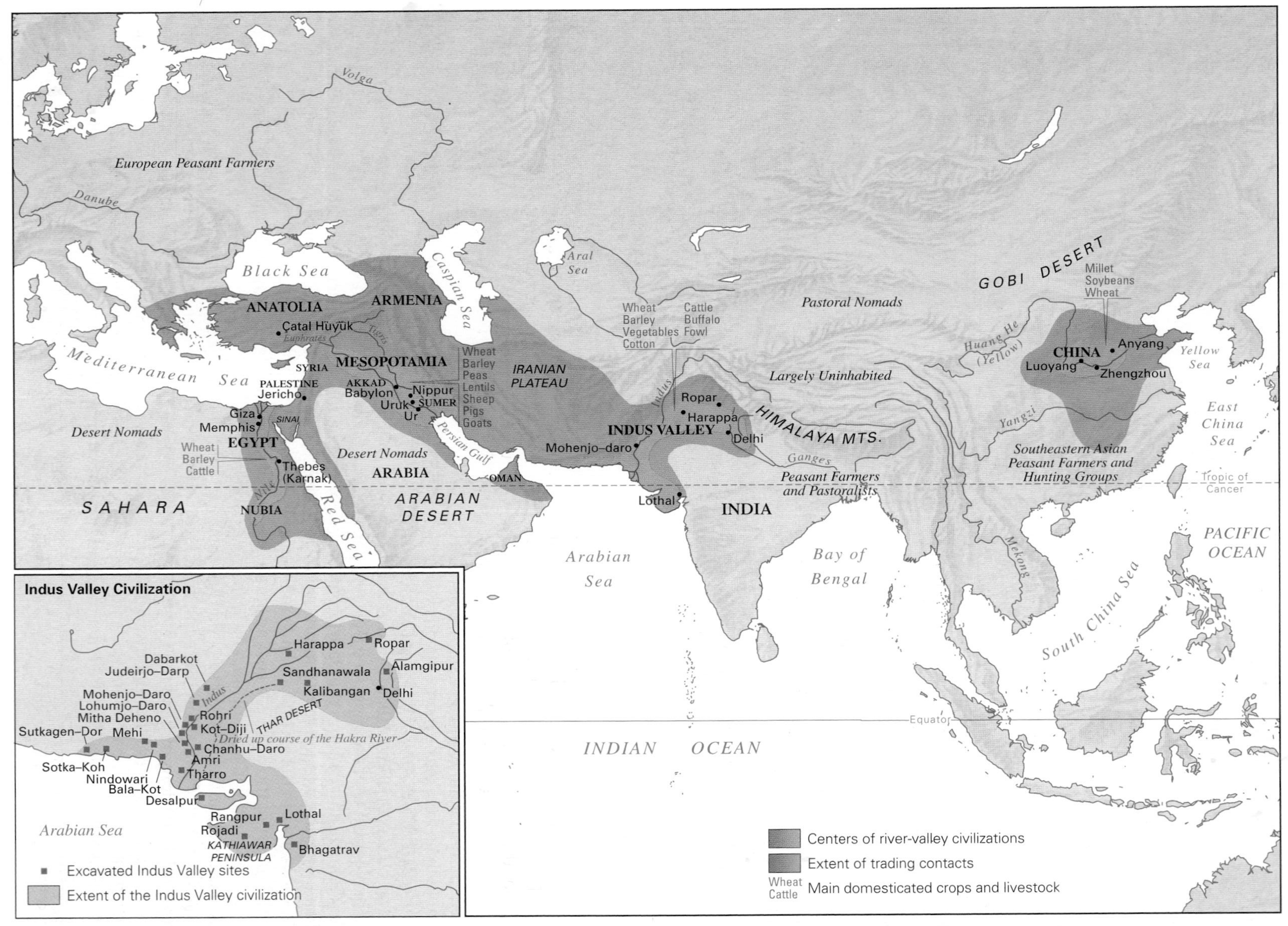

Map 2.1 River-Valley Civilizations, 3500–1500 B.C.E. The earliest complex societies arose in the floodplains of large rivers: in the fourth millennium B.C.E. in the valley of the Tigris and Euphrates Rivers in Mesopotamia and the Nile River in Egypt, in the third millennium B.C.E. in the valley of the Indus River in Pakistan, and in the second millennium B.C.E. in the valley of the Yellow River in China.

Floods can be sudden and violent and tend to come at the wrong time for grain agriculture—in the spring when the crop is ripening in the field. The floods sometimes cause the rivers to suddenly change course, cutting off fields and population centers from supplies of water and avenues of communication.

The first domestication of plants and animals took place in the "Fertile Crescent" region of northern Syria and southeastern Anatolia around 8000 B.C.E. Agriculture did not come to Mesopotamia until approximately 5000 B.C.E. Since agriculture requires annual rainfall of at least 8 inches (20 centimeters), it depended on irrigation—the artificial provision of water to crops—in hot, dry southern Mesopotamia. At first, people probably took advantage of the occasional flooding of the rivers into nearby fields, but shortly after 3000 B.C.E. they learned to construct canals to carry water to more distant parcels of land.

By 4000 B.C.E. farmers were using plows pulled by cattle to turn over the earth. A funnel attached to the plow dropped a carefully measured amount of seed. Barley was the main cereal crop in southern Mesopotamia because of its ability to tolerate hot, dry conditions and withstand the salt drawn to the surface when the fields were flooded. Fields were left fallow (unplanted) every other year to replenish the nutrients in the soil. Date palms provided food, fibers, and some wood. Small garden plots produced vegetables. Reed plants, which grew on the river banks and in the marshy southern delta, could be woven into mats, baskets, huts, and boats. Fish from the rivers and marshes were an important part of people's diet. Herds of sheep and goats, which grazed on the fallow land and beyond the zone of cultivation, provided wool and milk. Cattle and donkeys carried or pulled burdens; in the second millennium B.C.E. they were joined by newly introduced camels and horses.

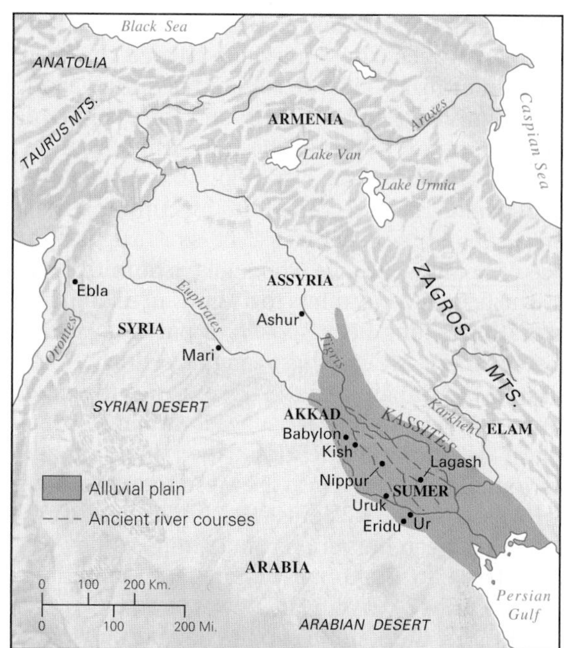

Map 2.2 Mesopotamia The Sumerians of southern Mesopotamia developed new technologies, complex political and social institutions, and distinctive cultural practices, responding to the need to organize labor resources to create and maintain an irrigation network in the Tigris-Euphrates Valley, a land of little rain.

The earliest people living in Mesopotamia in the "historical period"—the period for which we have written evidence—are the **Sumerians.** Archaeological evidence

Reed Huts in the Marshes of Southern Iraq Reeds growing along the riverbanks or in the swampy lands at the head of the Persian Gulf were used in antiquity—and continue to be used today—for a variety of purposes, including baskets and small watercraft as well as dwellings. (Courtesy, Dominique Collon)

places them in southern Mesopotamia by 5000 B.C.E. and perhaps even earlier. The Sumerians created the main framework of civilization in Mesopotamia during a long period of dominance in the fourth and third millennia B.C.E. However, they were not the only ethnic and linguistic group inhabiting the Tigris-Euphrates Valley. The names of individuals recorded in inscriptions from northerly cities from as early as 2900 B.C.E. suggest the presence of Semites, people who spoke a **Semitic**° language. (The term *Semitic* refers to a family of related languages that have long been spoken in parts of western Asia and northern Africa. These languages include ancient Hebrew, Aramaic°, and Phoenician°; the most widespread modern Semitic language is Arabic.) Historians believe that these Semites descended from nomadic peoples who had migrated into the Mesopotamian plain from the western desert. There is little indication of ethnic conflict between Sumerians and Semites. The Semites assimilated to Sumerian culture and sometimes achieved positions of wealth and power.

By 2000 B.C.E. the Semitic peoples had become politically dominant, and from this time forward the Semitic language Akkadian° took precedence over Sumerian, although the Sumerian cultural legacy was preserved. Sumerian-Akkadian dictionaries were compiled and Sumerian literature was translated. The characteristics and adventures of the Semitic gods borrow heavily from Sumerian precedents. This cultural synthesis parallels a biological merging of Sumerians and Semites through intermarriage. Other ethnic groups, including mountain peoples such as the Kassites° as well as Elamites° and Persians from Iran, played a part in Mesopotamian history. But not until the arrival of Greeks in the late fourth century B.C.E. was the Sumerian/Semitic cultural heritage of Mesopotamia fundamentally altered.

Cities, Kings, and Trade

Mesopotamia was a land of villages and cities. Groups of farming families banded together in villages to protect each other, share tools and facilities such as barns and threshing floors, and help each other at key times in the agricultural cycle. Villages also provided companionship as well as a pool of potential marriage partners.

Most cities evolved from villages. When a successful village grew, small satellite villages developed nearby, and eventually the main village and its satellites coalesced into an urban center. Cities and villages were dependent upon one another. Cities depended on agriculture. The earliest known urban centers in the Middle East, such as Jericho° and Çatal Hüyük°, sprang up shortly after the first appearance of agriculture (see Chapter 1), and many early Mesopotamian city dwellers went out each day to labor in nearby fields. In villages almost everyone engaged in the basic tasks of subsistence, gathering or growing enough food to feed themselves and their families. In cities, on the other hand, some urban residents did not engage in food production but instead specialized in such activities as metallurgy (creating useful objects from metal), crafts, administration, and serving the gods, and they depended on the surplus food production of the villagers. Mesopotamian cities controlled the agricultural land and collected crop surpluses from the villages in their vicinity. In return, the city provided rural districts with military protection against bandits and raiders and a market where villagers could trade surplus products for manufactured goods produced by urban specialists.

The term **city-state** refers to an independent urban center and the agricultural territories it controlled. Stretches of open and uncultivated land, either desert or swamp, served as buffers between the many small city-states of early Mesopotamia. However, disputes over land, water rights, and movable property often sparked hostilities between neighboring cities and prompted most to build protective walls of sun-dried mud bricks. Cities also cooperated in various ways, sharing water and allowing safe passage of trade goods through their territories.

Mesopotamians opened new land to agriculture by building and maintaining an extensive irrigation network. Canals brought water to fields far away from the rivers. Dams raised the water level of the river so that gravity would cause the water to flow into the irrigation canals. Drainage ditches carried water away from flooded fields before evaporation could draw salt and minerals harmful to crops to the surface of the soil. Dikes protected young plants in fields near the riverbanks from floods. A machine with counterweights was invented to lift heavy buckets of water—for example, up from the river and over the dike to the land beyond. Because the rivers carried so much silt, channels got clogged and needed constant dredging.

Successful operation of this sophisticated irrigation system depended on leaders capable of compelling and

Semitic (suh-MIT-ik) **Aramaic** (ar-uh-MAY-ik)
Phoenician (fi-NEE-shuhn) **Akkadian** (uh-KAY-dee-uhn)
Kassite (KAS-ite) **Elamite** (EE-luh-mite)

Jericho (JER-ih-koe) **Çatal Hüyük** (cha-TAHL hoo-YOOK)

organizing large numbers of people to work together. Other projects also required cooperation: the harvest, sheep shearing, the erection of fortification walls, the construction of large public buildings, and warfare. Little is known about the political institutions of early Mesopotamian city-states, although there are traces of some sort of citizens' assembly that may have evolved from the traditional village council. The two centers of power for which there are written records are the temple and the palace of the king.

Each Mesopotamian city had one or more centrally located temples that housed the cult (a set of religious practices) of the deity or deities who watched over the community. The temples owned extensive tracts of agricultural land and stored the gifts that worshipers donated. The importance of cults is confirmed by the central location of the temple buildings. The leading priests, who controlled the shrine and managed the deity's considerable wealth, appear to have been the most prominent political and economic forces in early Mesopotamian communities.

In the third millennium B.C.E. the *lugal*°, or "big man"—we would call him a king—emerged in Sumerian cities. How this position evolved is not clear, but it may have been related to an increase in the frequency and scale of warfare as ever-larger communities quarreled over land, water, and raw materials. According to one plausible theory, certain men chosen by the community to lead the armies in time of war extended their authority in peacetime and assumed key judicial and ritual functions. The position of lugal was not automatically hereditary, but capable sons could succeed their fathers. The location of the temple in the city's heart and the less prominent location of the king's palace symbolize the later emergence of royalty. The king's power grew at the expense of the priesthood because the army backed him. The priests and temples retained influence because of their wealth and religious mystique, but they gradually became dependent on the palace. Some Mesopotamian kings claimed divinity, but this concept did not take root. Normally, the king portrayed himself as the deity's earthly representative and assumed responsibility for the upkeep and building of temples and the proper performance of ritual. Other key royal responsibilities included maintenance of the city walls and defenses, upkeep and extension of the irrigation channels, preservation of property rights, and protection of the people from outside attackers and from perversions of justice at home.

lugal (LOO-gahl)

The *Epic of Gilgamesh* provides glimpses of both the restless ambition and the value to the community of this new breed of ruler. Gilgamesh, who was probably based on a historical king of Uruk, is depicted as the strongest man in his community. He stirs resentment by exercising the royal prerogative to have sex with new brides, but his subjects depend on his wisdom and courage to protect them. In his quest for everlasting glory, Gilgamesh builds magnificent walls around the city and stamps his name on all the bricks. His journey to the distant Cedar Mountains reflects the king's role in bringing valuable resources to the community.

Over time some political centers became powerful enough to extend their control over other city-states. Sargon°, ruler of the city of Akkad° around 2350 B.C.E., was the first to unite many cities under the control of one king and capital. His title, "King of Sumer and Akkad," symbolized his claim to universal dominion. Sargon and the four members of his family who succeeded him over a period of 120 years secured their power in a number of ways. They razed the walls of conquered cities and installed governors backed by garrisons of Akkadian troops. They gave land to soldiers to ensure their loyalty. Because Sargon and his people were of Semitic stock, the cuneiform° system of writing used for Sumerian (discussed later in the chapter) was adapted to express their language. A uniform system of weights and measures and standardized formats for official documents facilitated tasks of administration such as the assessment and collection of taxes, recruitment of soldiers, and organization of large labor projects.

For reasons that are not completely clear, the Akkadian state fell around 2230 B.C.E. The Sumerian language and culture were dominant again in the cities of the southern plain under the Third Dynasty of Ur (2112–2004 B.C.E.). Based on a combination of campaigns of conquest and alliances cemented by marriage, the dynasty encompassed five kings who ruled for a century. This state did not control territories as extensive as those of its Akkadian predecessor, but a rapidly expanding bureaucracy of administrators led to tight government control of a wide range of activities and obsessive record-keeping. A corps of messengers and well-maintained road stations facilitated rapid communication, and an official calendar, standardized weights and measures, and uniform writing practices enhanced the effectiveness of the central administration. As the southern plain came under increasing pressure from Semitic Amorites°

Sargon (SAHR-gone) **Akkad** (AH-kahd)
cuneiform (kyoo-NEE-uh-form) **Amorite** (AM-uh-rite)

in the northwest, the kings erected a great wall 125 miles (201 kilometers) in length to keep out the nomadic invaders. In the end, though, the Third Dynasty of Ur succumbed to the combined pressure of nomadic incursions and an Elamite attack from the southeast.

The Amorites founded a new city at Babylon, not far from Akkad. Toward the end of a long reign, **Hammurabi**° (r. 1792–1750 B.C.E.) initiated a series of aggressive military campaigns, and Babylon became the capital of what historians have named the "Old Babylonian" state, which stretched beyond Sumer and Akkad into the north and northwest from 1900 to 1600 B.C.E. Hammurabi is best known for his Law Code, inscribed on a polished black stone pillar. The Code provides a fascinating window on the activities of everyday life, anticipating a wide range of problems that might need to be resolved: false accusations, bad judicial decisions, crimes, physical injury, property damage, debt, inheritance, ransom of prisoners-of-war, real estate, business deals, wages and prices, marriage, adoption, sexual misconduct, medical malpractice, shoddy construction, and shipwreck. Though probably not a comprehensive list of all the laws of the time, Hammurabi's Code provided judges with a lengthy set of examples illustrating principles to use in deciding cases. Some call for severe physical punishments and, not infrequently, the death penalty. These Amorite principles of justice differed from the monetary penalties prescribed in earlier codes from Ur.

The far-reaching conquests of some Mesopotamian states were motivated, at least in part, by the need to obtain vital resources. The alternative was to trade for raw materials, and long-distance commerce did flourish in most periods. Evidence of boats used in sea trade goes back as far as the fifth millennium B.C.E. Wool, cloth, barley, and oil were exported in exchange for wood from cedar forests in Lebanon and Syria, silver from Anatolia, gold from Egypt, copper from the eastern Mediterranean and Oman (on the Arabian peninsula), and tin from Afghanistan (in south-central Asia). Chlorite, a greenish stone from which bowls were carved, came from the Iranian Plateau, and for jewelry and carved figurines, black diorite was imported from the Persian Gulf, blue lapis lazuli° from eastern Iran and Afghanistan, and reddish carnelian from Pakistan.

In the third millennium B.C.E. merchants were primarily in the employ of the palace or temple, which were the only two institutions with the financial resources and long-distance connections to organize the collection, transport, and protection of goods. Merchants exchanged the surplus from the agricultural estates of kings or priests for vital raw materials and luxury goods. In the second millennium B.C.E. more commerce came into the hands of independent merchants, and merchant guilds became powerful forces.

Modern scholars do not know whether the most important commercial activities took place in the area just inside the city gates or in the vicinity of the docks. Wherever they occurred, commercial activity was accomplished without the benefit of money. Coins—pieces of metal whose value the state guarantees—were not invented until the sixth century B.C.E. and did not reach Mesopotamia until several centuries later. For most of Mesopotamian history, items could be bartered—traded for one another—or valued in relation to fixed weights of precious metal, primarily silver, or measures of grain.

Mesopotamian Society

A persistent feature of urbanized civilizations is the development of social divisions—that is, obvious variations in the status and privileges of different groups of people due to differences in wealth, social functions, and legal and political rights. The rise of cities, specialization of function, centralization of power, and use of written records enabled some groups to amass wealth on an unprecedented scale. Mesopotamian temple leaders and kings controlled large agricultural estates, and the palace administration collected various taxes from subjects. Mesopotamians who made up what we might call an elite class acquired large holdings of land. Debtors who could not pay what they owed forfeited their land, and soldiers and religious officials received plots of land in return for their services.

The Law Code of Hammurabi in eighteenth century B.C.E. Babylonia reflects social divisions that may have been valid for other places and times. Society was divided into three classes: (1) the free, landowning class, which included royalty, high-ranking officials, warriors, priests, merchants, and some artisans and shopkeepers; (2) the class of dependent farmers and artisans, who were legally attached to land that belonged to king, temple, or elite families and made up the primary rural work force; and (3) the class of slaves, primarily employed in domestic service. Penalties for crimes prescribed in the Law Code depended on the class of the offender. The most severe punishments were reserved for the lower orders.

Slavery was not as prevalent and fundamental to the economy as it would be in the later societies of Greece and Rome (see Chapters 5 and 6). Many slaves came from mountain tribes and had either been captured in

Hammurabi (HAM-uh-rah-bee) **lapis lazuli** (LAP-is LAZ-uh-lee)

war or sold by slave traders. There was a separate category of slavery for people who were unable to pay their debts. Under normal circumstances, slaves were not chained or otherwise constrained, but they had to wear a distinctive hair style. If they were given their freedom, a barber shaved off the telltale mark. In the surviving documents it is often hard to distinguish slaves or dependent workers from free laborers because all were compensated with commodities such as food and oil in quantities proportional to their age, gender, and tasks. In the Old Babylonian period, as the class of people who were not dependent on the great institutions of temple or palace grew in numbers and importance, the amount of land and other property in private hands increased, and there was a greater tendency to hire free laborers.

It is difficult to reconstruct the life experiences of ordinary Mesopotamians, especially those who lived in villages or on large estates in the countryside, because they left few archaeological or literary traces. Rural peasants built their houses out of materials such as mud brick and reed, which quickly disintegrate, and they possessed little in the way of metals. Being illiterate, they were not able to write about their lives. It is particularly difficult to discover much about the experiences of women. The written sources are the product of male **scribes**—trained professionals who applied their reading and writing skills to tasks of administration—and for the most part reflect elite male activities. Archaeological remains provide only limited insight into women's status and activities and attitudes toward them.

Anthropologists theorize that women lost social standing and freedom in societies where agriculture superseded hunting and gathering (see Chapter 1). In hunting-and-gathering societies women provided most of the community's food from their gathering activities, and this work was highly valued. But in Mesopotamia the provision of food required dragging around a plow and digging irrigation channels, and that sort of hard physical labor usually was done by men. Food surpluses permitted families to have more children, and bearing and rearing children became the primary occupation of many women, preventing most from acquiring the specialized skills of the scribe or artisan.

Women had no political role, but they were able to own property, maintain control of their dowries (sums of money given by the woman's father to support her in her husband's household), and even engage in trade. Some worked outside the household in textile factories and breweries or as prostitutes, tavern keepers, bakers, or fortunetellers. Nonelite women who stayed at home

Mesopotamian Cylinder Seal Seals indicated the identity of an individual and were impressed into wet clay or wax to "sign" legal documents or to mark ownership of an object. This seal, produced in the period of the Akkadian Empire, depicts Ea (second from right), the god of underground waters, symbolized by the stream with fish emanating from his shoulders; Ishtar, whose attributes of fertility and war are indicated by the date cluster in her hand and the pointed weapons showing above her wings; and the sun-god Shamash, cutting his way out of the mountains with a jagged knife, an evocation of sunrise. (Courtesy of the Trustees of the British Museum)

must have engaged in tasks other than child care, such as helping with the harvest, planting vegetable gardens, cooking and baking, cleaning the house, fetching water, tending the household fire, and weaving baskets and textiles.

The standing of women seems to have declined further in the second millennium B.C.E. This development may have been linked to the rise of an urbanized middle class and an increase in private wealth. The husband became more dominant in the household and marriage and divorce laws favored his rights. Although Mesopotamian society was generally monogamous, a man could take a second wife if the first gave him no children, and in later Mesopotamian history kings and others who could afford to do so had several wives. Marriages that were arranged for the purpose of creating alliances between families made women instruments for preserving and increasing family wealth. Or a family could decide to avoid a daughter's marriage—and the resulting loss of a dowry—by dedicating the girl to the service of a deity as "god's bride." Some scholars believe that the constraints on women that eventually became part of the Islamic tradition, such as the expectation that they confine themselves to the household and wear veils in public (see Chapter 9), may have originated in the second millennium B.C.E.

Gods, Priests, and Temples

The Sumerian gods embodied the forces of nature: Anu was the sky, Enlil the air, Enki the water, Utu the sun, and Nanna the moon. The emotional impulses of sexual attraction and violence were the domain of the goddess Inanna. When the Semitic peoples became dominant, they equated their deities with those of the Sumerians. For example, Nanna and Utu became the Semitic Sin and Shamash, and Inanna became Ishtar. The myths of the Sumerian deities were transferred to their Semitic counterparts, and many of the same rituals continued to be practiced.

People believed the gods were anthropomorphic°—like humans in form and conduct. They thought the gods had bodies and senses, sought nourishment from sacrifice, enjoyed the worship and obedience of humanity, and were driven by lust, love, hate, anger, and all the other emotions that motivated human beings. The Mesopotamians feared their gods. They believed the gods were responsible for the natural disasters that occurred without warning in the landscape in which they lived, and they sought to appease the deities by any means.

The public, state-organized religion is most visible in the archaeological record. Each city built temples and showed devotion to one or more patron divinities who protected the community. All the peoples of Sumer venerated Nippur (see Map 2.2) as a religious center because of its temple of the air-god Enlil. The temple was considered the residence of the god, and the cult statue in a special interior shrine was believed to embody the deity's life-force. Priests tried to anticipate and meet every need of this physical image of the divinity in a daily cycle of waking, bathing, dressing, feeding, moving around, entertaining, soothing, and revering. These efforts reflected the emphatic claim of the Babylonian Creation Myth that humankind had been created to serve the gods. Several thousand priests may have staffed a large temple like that of the chief god Marduk at Babylon.

The office of priest was hereditary; fathers passed along sacred lore to their sons. Priests were paid in food raised on the deity's estates. The amount depended on an individual's rank within a complicated hierarchy of status and specialized function. The high priest performed the central acts in the great rituals. Certain priests made music to please the gods. Others exorcised evil spirits. Still others interpreted dreams and divined the future by examining the organs of sacrificed animals, reading patterns in the rising incense smoke, or casting dice.

A high wall surrounded the temple precinct, which included the shrine of the chief deity; open-air plazas; chapels for lesser gods; housing, dining facilities, and offices for the priests and other members of the temple staff; and craft shops, storerooms, and service buildings. The most visible part of the temple compound was the **ziggurat°**, a multistory, mud-brick, pyramid-shaped tower approached by ramps and stairs. Modern scholars are not certain of the ziggurat's function and symbolic meaning.

Even harder to determine are the everyday beliefs and religious practices of the common people. Modern scholars do not know how accessible the temple buildings were to the general public. Individuals placed votive statues in the sanctuaries. They believed that these miniature replicas of themselves could continually beseech and seek the favor of the deity. The survival of many **amulets** (small charms meant to protect the bearer from evil) and representations of a host of demons suggest widespread belief in magic—the use of special words and rituals to manipulate and control the

anthropomorphic (an-thruh-puh-MORE-fik)

ziggurat (ZIG-uh-rat)

forces of nature. A headache, for example, was believed to be caused by a demon that could be driven out of the ailing body. Lamashtu, who was held responsible for miscarriages, could be frightened off if a pregnant woman wore an amulet with the likeness of the hideous but beneficent demon Pazuzu. In return for an appropriate gift or sacrifice, a god or goddess might be persuaded to reveal information about the future. The elite and the ordinary people came together in great festivals such as the twelve-day New Year's Festival held each spring in Babylon to mark the beginning of a new agricultural cycle (see Diversity and Dominance: Violence and Order in the Babylonian New Year's Festival).

Technology and Science

The term *technology* comes from the Greek word *techne,* meaning "skill" or "specialized knowledge." It normally refers to the tools and machinery that humans use to manipulate the physical world. Many scholars now use the term more broadly to encompass any specialized knowledge that is used to transform the natural environment and human society. Ancient Mesopotamian use of irrigation techniques that expanded agricultural production fit the first definition; priests' belief that they could enhance prosperity through prayers and rituals the second.

A particularly important example of the broader type of technology is writing, which first appeared in Mesopotamia before 3300 B.C.E. The earliest inscribed tablets, found in the chief temple at Uruk, date from a time when the temple was the most important economic institution in the community. According to a plausible recent theory, writing originated from a system of tokens used to keep track of property—such as sheep, cattle, or wagon wheels—when increases in the amount of accumulated wealth and the volume and complexity of commercial transactions strained people's memories. The tokens, made in the shape of the commodity, were inserted and sealed in clay envelopes, and pictures of the tokens were incised on the outside of the envelopes as a reminder of what was inside. Eventually, people realized that the incised pictures were an adequate record of the transaction and that the tokens inside the clay envelope were redundant. These pictures were the first written symbols. The earliest symbols represented various objects, and they also could stand for the sound of the word for an object if the sound was part of a longer word. For example, the symbols *shu* for "hand" and *mu* for "water" could be combined to form *shumu,* the word for "name."

The most common method of writing involved pressing the point of a sharpened reed into a moist clay tablet. Because the reed made wedge-shaped impressions, the early pictures were increasingly stylized into a combination of strokes and wedges that evolved into **cuneiform** (Latin for "wedge-shaped") writing. Mastering this system required years of training and practice. Several hundred signs were in use at any one time, as compared to the twenty-five or so signs required for an alphabetic system. In the "tablet-house," which may have been attached to a temple or palace, students were taught writing and mathematics by a stern headmaster and were tutored and bullied by older students called "big brothers." The prestige and regular employment that went with their position may have made scribes reluctant to simplify the cuneiform system. In the Old Babylonian period, the growth of the private commercial sector was accompanied by an increase in the number of people who could read and write, but only a small percentage of the population was literate.

Cuneiform is not a language but rather a system of writing. Developed originally for the Sumerian language, it was later adapted to the Akkadian language of the Mesopotamian Semites as well as other languages of western Asia such as Hittite, Elamite, and Persian. The remains of the ancient city of Ebla° in northern Syria (see Map 2.2) illustrate the Mesopotamian influence on other parts of western Asia. Ebla's buildings and artifacts follow Mesopotamian models, and thousands of tablets are inscribed with cuneiform symbols in Sumerian and the local Semitic dialect. The high point of Ebla's wealth and power occurred from 2400 to 2250 B.C.E., roughly contemporary with the Akkadian Empire. Ebla controlled extensive territory and derived wealth from agriculture, manufacture of woolen cloth, and trade with Mesopotamia and the Mediterranean.

The earliest Mesopotamian documents are economic, but cuneiform came to have wide-ranging uses beyond its initial purpose. In the early period, legal acts had been validated by the recitation of oral formulas and the performance of symbolic actions. After the development of cuneiform, written documents marked with the seal of the participants became the primary proof of legitimacy. Cuneiform also served political, literary, religious, and scientific purposes.

Other technologies enabled the Mesopotamians to meet the challenges of their physical environment. Irrigation, indispensable to agriculture, called for the construction and maintenance of canals, dams, and dikes. Carts and sledges drawn by cattle were a common means of transportation in some locations. In the south,

---

Ebla (EH-bluh)

파운드폭탄 4발 투하… 두 아들과 함께 사망
이틀째 시가戰
령이 대중 앞에 나타나거나 애국심
을 고취하는 노래만을 내보내던 방
송마저 중단됐다.

Diversity and Dominance

Violence and Order in the Babylonian New Year's Festival

The twelve-day Babylonian New Year's Festival was one of the grandest and most important religious celebrations in ancient Mesopotamia. Complex rituals, both private and public, were performed in accordance with detailed formulas. Fragmentary Babylonian documents of the third century B.C.E. *(fifteen hundred years after Hammurabi) provide most of our information about the festival, but because of the continuity of culture over several millennia, the later Babylonian New Year's Festival is likely to preserve many of the beliefs and practices of earlier epochs.*

In the first days of the festival, most of the activity took place in inner chambers of the temple of Marduk, patron deity of Babylon, attended only by ranking members of the priesthood. A particularly interesting ceremony was a ritualized humiliation of the king, followed by a renewal of the institution of divinely sanctioned kingship:

On the fifth day of the month Nisannu . . . they shall bring water for washing the king's hands and then shall accompany him to the temple Esagil. The *urigallu*-priest shall leave the sanctuary and take away the scepter, the circle, and the sword from the king. He shall bring them before the god Bel [Marduk] and place them on a chair. He shall leave the sanctuary and strike the king's cheek. He shall accompany the king into the presence of the god Bel. He shall drag him by the ears and make him bow to the ground. The king shall speak the following only once: "I did not sin, lord of the countries. I was not neglectful of the requirements of your godship. I did not destroy Babylon. The temple Esagil, I did not forget its rites. I did not rain blows on the cheek of a subordinate." . . . [The *urigallu*-priest responds:] "The god Bel will listen to your prayer. He will exalt your kingship. The god Bel will bless you forever. He will destroy your enemy, fell your adversary." After the *urigallu*-priest says this, the king shall regain his composure. The scepter, circle, and sword shall be restored to the king.

Also in the early days of the festival, in conjunction with rituals of purification and invocations to Marduk, a priest recited the entire text of the Babylonian Creation Epic to the image of the god. After relating the origins of the gods from the mating of two primordial creatures, Tiamat, the female embodiment of the salt sea, and Apsu, the male embodiment of fresh water, the myth tells how Tiamat gathered an army of old gods and monsters to destroy the younger generation of gods.

When her labor of creation was ended, against her children Tiamat began preparations of war . . . all the Anunnaki [the younger gods], the host of gods gathered into that place tongue-tied; they sat with mouths shut for they thought, "What other god can make war on Tiamat? No one else can face her and come back" . . . Lord Marduk exulted, . . . with racing spirits he said to the father of gods, "Creator of the gods who decides their destiny, if I must be your avenger, defeating Tiamat, saving your lives, call the Assembly, give me precedence over all the rest; . . . now and for ever let my word be law; I, not you, will decide the world's nature, the things to come. My decrees shall never be altered, never be annulled, but my creation endures to the ends of the world" . . . He took his route towards the rising sound of Tiamat's rage, and all the gods besides, the fathers of the gods pressed in around him, and the lord approached Tiamat. . . . When Tiamat heard him her wits scattered, she was possessed and shrieked aloud, her legs shook from the crotch down, she gabbled spells, muttered maledictions, while the gods of war sharpened their weapons. . . . The lord shot his net to entangle Tiamat, and the pursuing tumid wind, Imhullu, came from behind and beat in her face. When the mouth gaped open to suck him down he drove Imhullu in, so that the mouth would not shut but wind raged through her belly; her carcass blown up, tumescent. She gaped. And now he shot the arrow that split the belly, that pierced the gut and cut the womb.

Now that the Lord had conquered Tiamat he ended her life, he flung her down and straddled the carcass; the leader was killed, Tiamat was dead her rout was shattered, her band dispersed. . . . The lord rested; he gazed at the huge body, pondering how to use it, what to create from the dead carcass. He split it apart like a cockle-shell; with the upper half he constructed the arc of sky, he pulled down the bar and set a watch on the waters, so they should never escape. . . . He projected positions for the Great Gods conspicuous in the sky, he gave them a starry aspect as constellations; he measured the year, gave it a beginning and an end, and to each month of the twelve three rising stars. . . . Through her ribs he opened gates in the east and west, and gave them strong bolts on the right and left; and high in the belly of Tiamat he set the zenith. He gave the moon the luster of a jewel, he gave him all the night, to mark off days, to watch by night each month the circle of a waxing waning light. . . . When Marduk had sent out the moon, he took the sun and set him to complete the cycle from this one to the next New Year. . . .

Then Marduk considered Tiamat. He skimmed spume from the bitter sea, heaped up the clouds, spindrift of wet and wind and cooling rain, the spittle of Tiamat. With his own hands from the steaming mist he spread the clouds. He pressed hard down the head of water, heaping mountains over it, opening springs to flow: Euphrates and Tigris rose from her eyes, but he closed the nostrils and held back their springhead. He piled huge mountains on her paps and through them drove water-holes to channel the deep sources; and high overhead he arched her tail, locked-in to the wheel of heaven; the pit was under his feet, between was the crotch, the sky's fulcrum. Now the earth had foundations and the sky its mantle. . . . When it was done, when they had made Marduk their king, they pronounced peace and happiness for him, "Over our houses you keep unceasing watch, and all you wish from us, that will be done."

Marduk considered and began to speak to the gods assembled in his presence. This is what he said, "In the former time you inhabited the void above the abyss, but I have made Earth as the mirror of Heaven, I have consolidated the soil for the foundations, and there I will build my city, my beloved home. A holy precinct shall be established with sacred halls for the presence of the king. When you come up from the deep to join the Synod you will find lodging and sleep by night. When others from heaven descend to the Assembly, you too will find lodging and sleep by night. It shall be BABYLON the home of the gods. The masters of all crafts shall build it according to my plan". . . . Now that Marduk has heard what it is the gods are saying, he is moved with desire to create a work of consummate art. He told Ea the deep thought in his heart.

"Blood to blood
I join,
blood to bone
I form
an original thing,
its name is MAN,
aboriginal man
is mine in making.

"All his occupations
are faithful service . . ."

Ea answered with carefully chosen words, completing the plan for the gods' comfort. He said to Marduk, "Let one of the kindred be taken; only one need die for the new creation. Bring the gods together in the Great Assembly; there let the guilty die, so the rest may live."

Marduk called the Great Gods to the Synod; he presided courteously, he gave instructions and all of them listened with grave attention. The king speaks to the rebel gods, "Declare on your oath if ever before you spoke the truth, who instigated rebellion? Who stirred up Tiamat? Who led the battle? Let the instigator of war be handed over; guilt and retribution are on him, and peace will be yours for ever."

The great Gods answered the Lord of the Universe, the king and counselor of gods, "It was Kingu who instigated rebellion, he stirred up that sea of bitterness and led the battle for her." They declared him guilty, they bound and held him down in front of Ea, they cut his arteries and from his blood they created man; and Ea imposed his servitude. . . .

Much of the subsequent activity of the festival, which took place in the temple courtyard and streets, was a reenactment of the events of the Creation Myth. The festival occurred at the beginning of spring, when the grain shoots were beginning to emerge, and the essential symbolism of the event concerns the return of natural life to the world. The Babylonians believed that time moved in a circular path and that the natural world had a life cycle consisting of birth, growth, maturity, and death. In winter the cycle drew to a close, and there was no guarantee that it would repeat and that life would return to the world. Babylonians hoped that the New Year's Festival would encourage the gods to grant a renewal of time and life, in essence to recreate the world.

QUESTIONS FOR ANALYSIS

1. **According to the Creation Epic, how did the present order of the universe come into being? What does the violent nature of this creation tell us about the Mesopotamian view of the physical world and the gods?**
2. **How did the symbolism of the events of the New Year's Festival, with its ritual reading and recreation of the story of the Creation Myth, validate such concepts as kingship, the primacy of Babylon, and mankind's relationship to the gods?**
3. **What is the significance of the distinction between the "private" ceremonies celebrated in the temple precincts and the "public" ceremonies that took place in the streets of the city? What does the festival tell us about the relationship of different social groups to the gods?**

Source: Adapted from James B. Pritchard, ed., *Ancient Near Eastern Texts Relating to the Old Testament*, 3d ed. (Princeton, NJ: Princeton University Press, 1969), 332–334.

Plaque Showing Harpist, ca. 2000–1600 B.C.E. This image can be attributed to the Old Babylonian period by the style of fringed robe and cap worn by the performer, but harps existed in Mesopotamia and Egypt thousands of years earlier. Clay plaques such as this were mass-produced from a mold. (Courtesy of the Oriental Institute, University of Chicago)

where numerous water channels cut up the landscape, boats and barges were used. In northern Mesopotamia, donkeys were the chief pack animals for overland caravans in the centuries before the advent of the camel (see Chapter 8).

The Mesopotamians had to import raw metal ore, but they became skilled in metallurgy, refining ores composed of copper and arsenic or copper and tin to make **bronze,** which is more malleable than stone. Liquid bronze can be poured into molds, and hardened bronze takes a sharper edge than stone, is less likely to break, and is more easily repaired. Stone implements continued to be produced for the poorest members of the population, who usually could not afford bronze.

Resource-poor Mesopotamians possessed one commodity in abundance: clay. Mud bricks, dried in the sun or baked in an oven for greater durability, were the primary building material. Construction of city walls, temples, and palaces required practical knowledge of architecture and engineering. For example, the reed mats that Mesopotamian builders laid between the mud-brick layers of ziggurats served the same stabilizing purpose as girders in modern high-rise construction. Because of the abundance of good clay, pottery was the most common material for dishware and storage vessels. The potter's wheel, a revolving platform that made possible the rapid production of vessels with precise and complex shapes, was in use by 4000 B.C.E.

In the military sphere, there were innovative developments in organization, tactics, and weapons and other machinery of warfare. Early military forces were militias made up of able-bodied members of the community called up for short periods when needed. The powerful states of the later third and second millennia B.C.E. built up armies of well-trained and well-paid full-time soldiers. In the early second millennium B.C.E. horses appeared in western Asia, and the horse-drawn chariot came into vogue. Infantry found themselves at the mercy of swift chariots carrying a driver and an archer who could get close and unleash a volley of arrows. Using increasingly effective siege machinery, Mesopotamian soldiers could climb over, undermine, or knock down the walls protecting the cities of their enemies.

In other ways, too, the Mesopotamians sought to control their physical environment. They used a base-60 number system (the origin of the seconds and minutes we use today), in which numbers were expressed as fractions or multiples of 60 (in contrast to our base-10 system). Advances in mathematics and careful observation of the skies made the Mesopotamians sophisticated practitioners of astronomy. Mesopotamian priests compiled lists of omens or unusual sightings on earth and in the heavens, together with a record of the events that coincided with them. They consulted these texts at critical times, for they believed that the recurrence of such phenomena could provide clues to future developments. The underlying premise was that the elements of the material universe, from the microscopic to the macrocosmic, were interconnected in mysterious but undeniable ways.

EGYPT

No place exhibits the impact of the natural environment on the history and culture of a society better than ancient Egypt. Located at the intersection of Asia and Africa, Egypt was protected by surrounding barriers of desert and a harborless, marshy seacoast. Where Mesopotamia was open to migration or invasion and was dependent on imported resources, Egypt's natural isolation and essential self-sufficiency fostered a unique culture that for long periods had relatively little to do with other civilizations.

The Land of Egypt: "Gift of the Nile"

The fundamental geographical feature of Egypt is the Nile River. The world's longest river, the Nile originates from Lake Victoria and from several large tributaries in the highlands of tropical Africa and flows northward, carving a narrow valley between the chain of hills on either side, until it reaches the Mediterranean Sea (see Map 2.3). The land through which it flows is mostly desert, but the river makes green a narrow strip on its banks. About 100 miles (160 kilometers) from the Mediterranean the Nile divides into channels to form a triangular delta. Nearly the entire population of the region lives in that twisting, green ribbon alongside the river or in the Nile Delta. The rest of the country, 90 percent or more, is a bleak and inhospitable desert of mountains, rocks, and dunes. The ancient Egyptians recognized the stark dichotomy between the low-lying, life-sustaining soil of the "Black Land" along the river and the elevated, deadly "Red Land" of the desert. With justification and insight the fifth-century B.C.E. Greek traveler Herodotus° called Egypt the "gift of the Nile."

The river was the main means of travel and communication, and the most important cities were located considerably upstream. Because the river flows from south to north, the Egyptians called the southern part of the country "Upper Egypt" and the northern delta "Lower Egypt." In most periods the southern boundary of Egypt was the First Cataract of the Nile, the northernmost of a series of impassable rocks and rapids below Aswan° (about 500 miles [800 kilometers] south of the Mediterranean). At times Egyptian control extended farther south into what was called "Kush" (later Nubia, the southern part of the modern state of Egypt and northern Sudan). The Egyptians also settled a number of large oases, green and habitable "islands" in the midst of the desert, some distance west of the river.

While the hot, sunny climate favored agriculture, rain rarely falls south of the delta, and agriculture was entirely dependent on river water. Throughout Egyptian history irrigation channels were dug to carry water out into the desert to increase the amount of land suitable for planting. Drainage techniques reduced the size of Lake Faiyum°, a large depression west of the Nile, allowing more land to be reclaimed for agriculture.

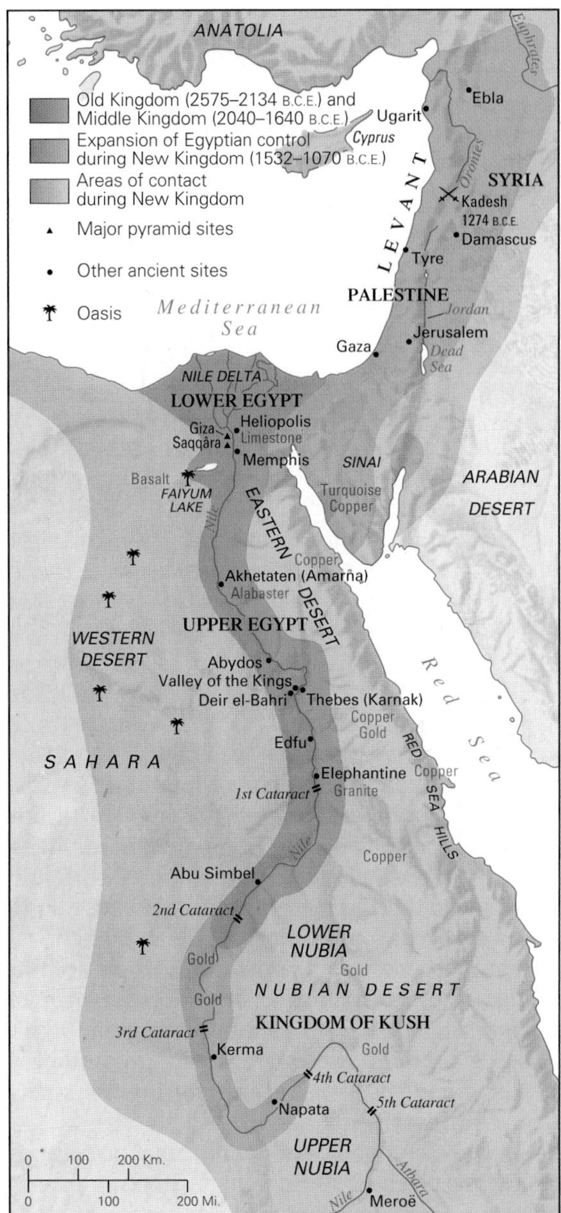

Map 2.3 Ancient Egypt The Nile River, flowing south to north, carved out of the surrounding desert a narrow green valley that became heavily settled in antiquity.

Herodotus (he-ROD-uh-tuhs) **Aswan** (AS-wahn)

Faiyum (fie-YOOM)

Model of Egyptian River Boat, ca. 1985 B.C.E. This model was buried in the tomb of a Middle Kingdom official, Meketre, who is shown in the cabin being entertained by musicians. The captain stands in front of the cabin, the helmsman on the left steers the boat with the rudder, while the lookout on the right lets out a weighted line to determine the river's depth. The vessel is being rowed downstream (northward); the white post in the middle would support a mast and sail when traveling upstream. (The Metropolitan Museum of Art, Rogers Fund and Edward S. Harkness Gift, 1920 (20.3.1). Photograph © 1992 The Metropolitan Museum of Art.

Each September the river overflowed its banks, spreading water into the bordering depressed basins. Unlike the Mesopotamians, the Egyptians did not need to construct dams to lift river water to channels and fields. And unlike the Tigris and Euphrates, whose flood came at a disadvantageous time, the Nile flooded at exactly the right time for grain agriculture. When the waters receded, they left behind a moist, fertile layer of mineral-rich silt, where farmers could easily plant their crops. The Egyptians' many creation myths commonly featured the emergence of a life-supporting mound of earth from a primeval swamp.

The level of the flood's crest determined the abundance of the next harvest. "Nilometers," stone staircases with incised units of measure, were placed along the river's edge to gauge the flood surge. When the flood was too high, dikes protecting inhabited areas were washed out, and much damage resulted. When the floods were too low for several years, less land could be cultivated, and the country experienced famine and decline. The ebb and flow of successful and failed regimes seems to have been linked to the cycle of floods. Nevertheless, remarkable stability characterized most eras, and Egyptians viewed the universe as an orderly and beneficent place.

Egypt was well endowed with natural resources. Egyptians used reeds that grew in marshy areas and along the banks of the river to make sails, ropes, and a kind of paper. Hunters pursued the wild animals and birds that abounded in the marshes and on the edge of the desert, and fishermen netted fish from the river. Building stone could be quarried and floated downstream from a number of locations in southern Egypt. Clay for mud bricks and pottery could be found almost everywhere. Copper and turquoise deposits in the Sinai desert to the east and gold from Nubia to the south were within reach, and the state organized armed expeditions and mustered forced labor to exploit these resources. Thus Egypt was considerably more self-sufficient than Mesopotamia.

The farming villages that appeared in Egypt as early as 5500 B.C.E. relied on domesticated plant and animal species that had emerged several millennia earlier in western Asia. However, Egypt's emergence as a focal point of civilization was due, at least in part, to a climate change that took place gradually from the fifth to the third millennium B.C.E. Until then, the Sahara, the vast region that is now the world's largest desert, had a relatively mild and wet climate, and its lakes and grasslands supported a variety of plant and animal species as well as populations of hunter-gatherers (see Chapter 8). As the climate changed and the Sahara began to dry up and become a desert, displaced groups migrated into the Nile Valley, where they developed a sedentary way of life.

Divine Kingship

The increase in population produced new, more complex levels of political organization, including a form of local kingship. Later generations of Egyptians saw the conquest of these smaller units and the unification of all Egypt by Menes°, a ruler from the south, as a pivotal event. Although some scholars question whether Menes was a historical or a mythical figure, many authorities equate Menes with Narmer, a historical ruler around 3100 B.C.E., who is shown on a decorated slate palette exulting over defeated enemies. Later kings of Egypt were referred to as "Rulers of the Two Lands"—Upper and Lower Egypt—and were depicted with two crowns and implements symbolizing the unification of the country. In contrast to Mesopotamia, Egypt was unified early in its history.

The system that historians use to organize Egyptian history is based on thirty dynasties (sequences of kings from the same family) identified by Manetho, an Egyptian from the third century B.C.E. The rise and fall of dynasties often reflects the dominance of different parts of the country. At a broader level of generalization, scholars refer to the "Old," "Middle," and "New Kingdoms," each a period of centralized political power and brilliant cultural achievement, punctuated by "Intermediate Periods" of political fragmentation and cultural decline. Although experts disagree about specific dates for these periods, the chronology (on page 29) reflects current opinion.

The central figure in the Egyptian state was the king (often known as the **pharaoh,** from an Egyptian phrase meaning "palace," which began to be used in the New Kingdom). From the time of the Old Kingdom, if not earlier, Egyptians considered the king to be a god come to earth, the incarnation of Horus and the son of the sun-god Re°. They believed that their king had been placed on earth by the gods to maintain **ma'at°,** the divinely authorized order of the universe. He was the indispensable link between his people and the gods, and his benevolent rule ensured the welfare and prosperity of the country. The Egyptians' conception of a divine king who was the source of law and justice may explain the apparent absence in Egypt of an impersonal code of law comparable to Hammurabi's Code in Mesopotamia.

So much depended on the king that his death evoked elaborate efforts to ensure the well-being of his spirit on its perilous journey to rejoin the gods. Massive resources were poured into the construction of royal tombs, the celebration of elaborate funerary rites, and the sustenance of kings' spirits in the afterlife by perpetual offerings in funerary chapels attached to the royal tombs. Early rulers were buried in flat-topped, rectangular tombs made of mud brick. Around 2630 B.C.E. Djoser°, a Third Dynasty king, ordered the construction of a spectacular stepped **pyramid** consisting of a series of stone platforms laid one on top of the other for himself at Saqqara°, near Memphis. Rulers in the Fourth Dynasty filled in the steps to create the smooth-sided, limestone pyramids that have become the most memorable symbol of ancient Egypt. Between 2550 and 2490 B.C.E. the pharaohs Khufu° and Khefren° erected huge pyramids at Giza, several miles north of Saqqara, the largest stone structures ever built by human hands. Khufu's pyramid originally reached a height of 480 feet (146 meters).

Egyptians accomplished this construction with stone tools (bronze was still expensive and rare) and no machinery other than simple levers, pulleys, and rollers. What made it possible was almost unlimited human muscle power. Calculations of the human resources needed to build a pyramid within the lifetime of the ruler suggest that large numbers of people must have been pressed into service for part of each year, probably during the flood season when no agricultural work could be done. Although this labor was compulsory, the Egyptian masses probably regarded it as a kind of religious service that helped ensure prosperity. Most of the country's surplus resources went into the construction of these artificial mountains of stone. The age of the great pyramids lasted only about a century, although pyramids continued to be built on a smaller scale for two millennia.

Administration and Communication

Ruling dynasties usually placed their capitals in the area of their original power base. **Memphis,** on the Lower Nile near the apex of the delta (close to Cairo, the modern capital), held this central position during the Old Kingdom. **Thebes,** far to the south, came to prominence during much of the Middle and New Kingdom periods (see Map 2.3).

A complex bureaucracy kept detailed records of the resources of the country. The extensive administrative apparatus began at the village level and progressed to the districts into which the country was divided and, finally, to the central government based in the capital city. Bureaucrats in the central administration kept track of

Menes (MEH-neez) **Re** (ray) **ma'at** (muh-AHT)

Djoser (JO-sur) **Saqqara** (suh-KAHR-uh) **Khufu** (KOO-foo) **Khefren** (KEF-ren)

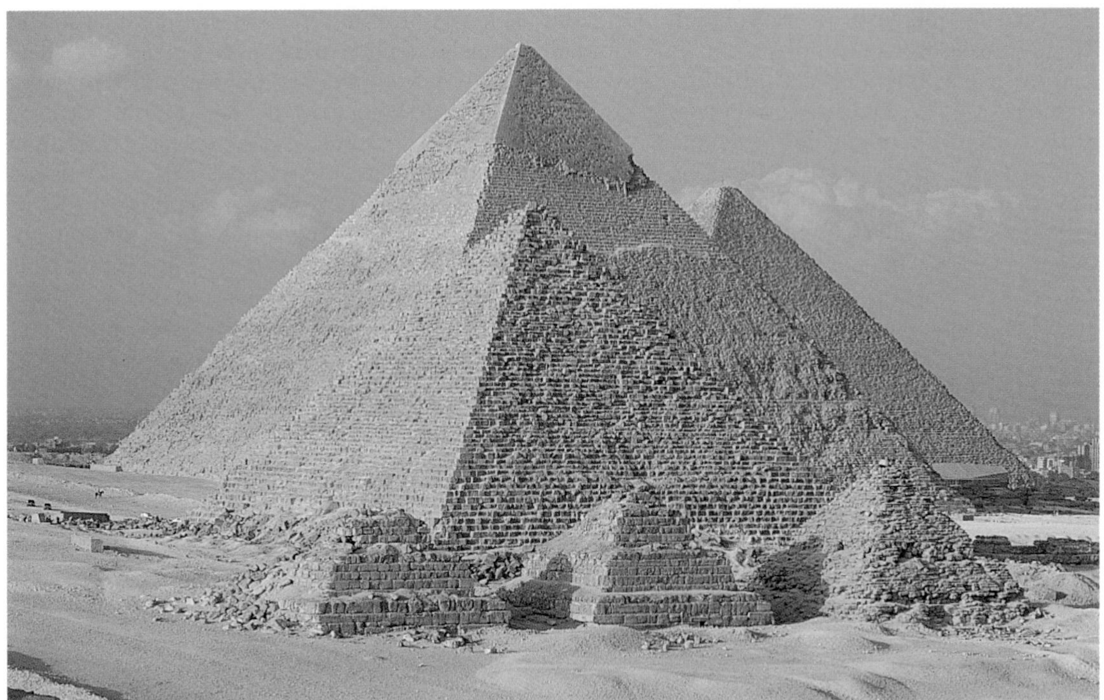

Pyramids of Menkaure, Khafre, and Khufu at Giza, ca. 2500 B.C.E. With a width of 755 feet (230 meters) and a height of 480 feet (146 meters), the Great Pyramid of Khufu is the largest stone structure ever built. The construction of these massive edifices depended on relatively simple techniques of stonecutting, transport (the stones were floated downriver on boats and rolled to the site on sledges), and lifting (the stones were dragged up the face of the pyramid on mud-brick ramps). However, the surveying and engineering skills required to level the platform, lay out the measurements, and securely position the blocks were very sophisticated and have withstood the test of time. (Carolyn Clarke/Spectrum Colour Library)

land, labor, products, and people, extracting a substantial portion of the country's annual revenues—at times as much as 50 percent—in taxes. The income subsidized the palace, bureaucracy, and army, built and maintained temples, and raised great monuments celebrating the ruler's reign. The government maintained a monopoly over key sectors of the economy and controlled long-distance trade. This was quite different from Mesopotamia, where commerce increasingly fell into the hands of an acquisitive urban middle class.

The hallmark of the administrative class was literacy. A system of writing had been developed by the beginning of the Early Dynastic period. **Hieroglyphics°**, the earliest form of this writing system, were picture symbols standing for words, syllables, or individual sounds. Our ability to read ancient Egyptian writing is due to the decipherment, in the early nineteenth century C.E., of the Rosetta Stone, a document from the second century B.C.E. with hieroglyphic and Greek versions of the same text.

Hieroglyphic writing long continued to be used on monuments and ornamental inscriptions. By 2500 B.C.E., however, a cursive script, in which the original pictorial nature of the symbol was less readily apparent, had been developed for the everyday needs of administrators and copyists. They worked with ink on a writing material called **papyrus°**, after the reed from which it was made. The stems of the papyrus reed were laid out in a vertical and horizontal grid pattern and then pounded with a soft mallet until the moist fibers formed a sheet of writing material. The plant grew only in Egypt but was in demand throughout the ancient world and was exported in large quantities. Indeed, the word *paper* is derived from Greek and Roman words for papyrus.

hieroglyphics (high-ruh-GLIF-iks)

papyrus (puh-PIE-ruhs)

The Egyptians used writing for many purposes other than administrative recordkeeping. Their written literature included tales of adventure and magic, love poetry, religious hymns, and manuals of instruction on technical subjects. Scribes in workshops attached to the temples made copies of traditional texts.

When the monarchy was strong, officials were appointed and promoted on the basis of merit and accomplishment. They received grants of land from the king and were supported by dependent peasants who worked the land. Low-level officials were assigned to villages and district capitals; high-ranking officials served in the royal capital. When Old Kingdom officials died, they were buried in tombs around the monumental tomb of the king so that they could serve him in death as they had done in life.

Throughout Egyptian history there was an underlying tension between the centralizing power of the monarchy and the decentralizing tendencies of the Egyptian bureaucracy. One sign of the breakdown of centralized power in the late Old Kingdom and First Intermediate Period was the placement of officials' tombs in their home districts, where they spent much of their time and exercised power more or less independently, rather than near the royal tomb. Another sign was the tendency of administrative posts to become hereditary. The early monarchs of the Middle Kingdom responded to the fragmentation of the preceding period by reducing the power and prerogatives of the old elite and creating a new middle class of administrators.

Egypt has often been called a land of villages without real cities because the political capitals were primarily extensions of the palace and central administration. In comparison with Mesopotamia, a far larger percentage of Egyptians lived in rural villages and engaged in agriculture, and the essential wealth of Egypt resided to a higher degree in the land and its products. But there were towns and cities in ancient Egypt, although they were less crucial to the economic and cultural dynamism of the country than were Mesopotamian urban centers. Unfortunately, archaeologists have been unable to excavate many ancient urban sites in Egypt because they have been continuously inhabited and lie beneath modern communities.

During the Old and Middle Kingdoms, Egypt's foreign policy was essentially isolationist. Technically, all foreigners were considered to be enemies. When necessary, local militia units backed up a small standing army of professional soldiers. Nomadic tribes living in the eastern and western deserts and Libyans living in the northwest were a nuisance rather than a real danger and were readily handled by the Egyptian military. The king maintained limited contact with the other advanced civilizations of the region. Egypt's interests abroad focused primarily on maintaining access to valuable resources rather than on acquiring territory. Trade with the coastal towns of the Levant° (modern Israel, the Palestinian territories, Lebanon, and Syria) brought in cedar wood. In return, Egypt exported grain, papyrus, and gold.

In all periods the Egyptians had a particularly strong interest in goods that came from the south. Nubia had rich sources of gold (Chapter 3 examines the rise of a civilization in Nubia that, though considerably influenced by Egypt, created a vital and original culture that lasted for more than two thousand years), and the southern course of the Nile offered the only easily passable corridor to sub-Saharan Africa.

In the Old Kingdom, Egyptian noblemen living at Aswan on the southern border led donkey caravans south to trade for gold, incense, and products of tropical Africa such as ivory, dark ebony wood, and exotic jungle animals. A line of forts along the southern border protected Egypt from attack. In the early second millennium B.C.E. Egyptian forces struck south into Nubia, extending the Egyptian border as far as the Third Cataract of the Nile and taking possession of the gold fields. Still farther to the south, perhaps in the coastal region of present-day Sudan or Eritrea, lay the fabled land of Punt°, source of the fragrant myrrh resin that priests burned on the altars of the Egyptian gods.

The People of Egypt

The million to million and a half inhabitants of Egypt included various physical types, ranging from dark-skinned people related to the populations of sub-Saharan Africa to lighter-skinned people akin to the populations of North Africa and western Asia. Although Egypt did not experience the large-scale migrations and invasions common in Mesopotamia, settlers periodically trickled into the Nile Valley and assimilated with the people already living there.

Although some Egyptians had higher status and more wealth and power than others, in contrast to Mesopotamia no formal class structure emerged. At the top of the social hierarchy were the king and high-ranking officials. In the middle were lower-level officials, local leaders, priests and other professionals, artisans, and well-to-do farmers. At the bottom were peasants, who made up the vast majority of the population.

Levant (luh-VANT) **Punt** (poont)

Peasants lived in rural villages, where they engaged in the seasonally changing tasks of agriculture: plowing, sowing, tending emerging shoots, reaping, threshing, and storing grain or other products of the soil. The irrigation network of channels, basins, and dikes had to be maintained, improved, and extended. Domesticated animals—cattle, sheep, goats, and fowl—and fish supplemented a diet based on wheat or barley, beer, and garden vegetables. Villagers probably shared implements, work animals, and storage facilities and helped one another at peak times in the agricultural cycle and in the construction of houses and other buildings. They prayed and feasted together at festivals to the local gods and other public celebrations. Periodically they were required to contribute labor to state projects, such as construction of the pyramids. If taxation or compulsory service was too great a burden, flight into the desert was the only escape.

This account of the lives of ordinary Egyptians is largely conjectural; the villages of ancient Egypt, like those of Mesopotamia, left few traces in the archaeological or literary record. Tomb paintings of the elite sometimes depict common people. The artists employed pictorial conventions to indicate status, such as obesity for the possessors of wealth and comfort, and baldness and deformity for members of the working classes. Egyptian poets frequently used metaphors of farming and hunting, and legal documents on papyrus preserved in the hot, dry sands tell of property transactions and legal disputes among ordinary people.

Slavery existed on a limited scale but was of little economic significance. Prisoners of war, condemned criminals, and debtors could be found on the country estates or in the households of the king and wealthy families. Treatment of slaves was relatively humane, and they could be freed.

Some information is available about the lives of women of the upper classes, but it is filtered through the brushes and pens of male artists and scribes. Tomb paintings show women of the royal family and elite classes accompanying their husbands and engaging in typical domestic activities. They are depicted with dignity and affection, though they are clearly subordinate to the men. The artistic convention of depicting men with a dark red and women with a yellow flesh tone implies that the elite woman's proper sphere was indoors, away from the searing sun. In the beautiful love poetry of the New Kingdom, lovers address each other in terms of apparent equality and express emotions akin to our own ideal of romantic love. We cannot be sure how accurately this poetry represents the prevalent attitude of other periods of Egyptian history or among groups other than the educated elite.

Legal documents show that Egyptian women could own property, inherit from their parents, and will their property to whomever they wished. Marriage, usually monogamous, was not confirmed by any legal or religious ceremony and essentially constituted a decision by a man and woman to establish a household together. Either party could dissolve the relationship, and the divorced woman retained rights over her dowry. At certain times queens and queen-mothers played significant behind-the-scenes roles in the politics of the royal court, and priestesses sometimes supervised the cults of female deities. In general, the limited evidence suggests that women in ancient Egypt were treated more respectfully and had more legal rights and social freedom than women in Mesopotamia and other ancient societies.

Belief and Knowledge

The religion of the Egyptians was rooted in the landscape of the Nile Valley and in the vision of cosmic order that this environment evoked. The consistency of their environment—the sun rose every day in a clear and cloudless sky, and the river flooded on schedule every year, ensuring a bounteous harvest—persuaded the Egyptians that the natural world was a place of recurrent cycles and periodic renewal. The sky was imagined to be a great ocean surrounding the inhabited world. The sun-god Re traversed this blue waterway in a boat by day, then returned through the Underworld at night, fighting off the attacks of demonic serpents so that he could be born anew in the morning. In one especially popular story Osiris°, a god who once ruled Egypt, was slain by his jealous brother Seth, who then scattered the dismembered pieces. Isis, Osiris's devoted sister and wife, found and reconstructed the remnants, and Horus, his son, took revenge on Seth. Osiris was restored to life and installed as king of the Underworld, and his example gave people hope of a new life in a world beyond this one.

The king, who was seen as Horus (son of Osiris) and as the son of Re, was thus associated with both the return of the dead to life and the life-giving and self-renewing symbolism of the sun-god. He was the chief priest of Egypt, intervening with the gods on behalf of his land and people. When a town attained special significance as the capital of a ruling dynasty, the chief god of that town became prominent across the land. Thus did Ptah° of Memphis, Re of Heliopolis°, and Amon° of Thebes be-

Osiris (oh-SIGH-ris) **Ptah** (puh-TAH)
Heliopolis (he-lee-OP-uh-lis) **Amon** (AH-muhn)

Scene from the Egyptian Book of the Dead, ca. 1300 B.C.E. The mummy of a royal scribe named Hunefar is approached by members of his household before being placed in the tomb. Behind Hunefar is jackel-headed Anubis, the god who will conduct the spirit of the deceased to the afterlife. The Book of the Dead provided Egyptians with the instructions they needed to complete this arduous journey and gain a blessed existence in the afterlife. (Courtesy of the Trustees of the British Museum)

come gods of all Egypt, serving to unify the country and strengthen the monarchy.

Egyptian rulers were especially interested in building new temples, refurbishing old ones, and making lavish gifts to the gods, as well as overseeing the construction of their own monumental tombs. A considerable portion of the wealth of Egypt was used in a ceaseless effort to win the gods' favor, maintain the continuity of divine kingship, and ensure the renewal of the life-giving forces that sustained the world.

The many gods of ancient Egypt were diverse in origin and nature. Some were normally depicted with animal heads; others were always given human form. Few myths about the origins and adventures of the gods have survived, but there must have been a rich oral tradition. Many towns had temples in which locally prominent deities were thought to reside. The fluidity of the metaphysical realm allowed local deities to be viewed as manifestations of the great gods, and gods could be merged to form hybrids, such as Amon-Re. Cult activities were carried out in the private inner reaches of the temples, off limits to all but the priests who served the needs of the deity by attending to his or her statue. Food offered to the image was later distributed to temple staff. As in Mesopotamia, some temples possessed extensive landholdings worked by dependent peasants, and the priests who administered the deity's wealth were influential locally and sometimes even throughout the land.

During great festivals, the priests paraded a boat-shaped litter carrying the shrouded statue and cult items of the deity. Such occasions brought large numbers of people into contact with the deity in an outpouring of devotion and celebration. Little is known about the day-to-day beliefs and practices of the common people. In the household family members revered and made small offerings to Bes, the grotesque god of marriage and domestic happiness, to local deities, and to the family's ancestors. Amulets and depictions of demonic figures were supposed to protect the bearer and ward off evil forces. In later times Greeks and Romans commented that the devotion to magic was especially strong in Egypt.

Egyptians believed in the afterlife, and they made extensive preparations for safe passage to the next world and a comfortable existence once they arrived there. One common belief was that death was a journey beset with hazards. The Egyptian Book of the Dead, present in many excavated tombs, contained rituals and spells to protect the journeying spirit. The final and most important challenge was the weighing of the deceased's heart (believed to be the source of personality, intellect, and emotion) in the presence of the judges of the Underworld to determine whether the person had led a good life and deserved to reach the ultimate blessed destination.

Obsession with the afterlife produced great concern about the physical condition of the cadaver. Egyptians perfected techniques of mummification to preserve the dead body. The idea probably grew out of the early practice of burying the dead in the hot, dry sand on the edge of the desert, where bodies decomposed slowly. The elite classes utilized the most expensive kind of mummification. Vital organs were removed, preserved, and stored in stone jars laid out around the corpse. Body cavities were filled with various packing materials. The cadaver was immersed for long periods in dehydrating and preserving chemicals and eventually was wrapped in linen. The **mummy** was then placed in one or more decorated wooden caskets and was deposited in a tomb.

The tombs, which usually were built at the edge of the desert so as not to tie up valuable farmland, were filled with pictures, food, and the objects of everyday life so that the deceased would have whatever he or she might need in the next life. Archaeologists and historians have gleaned much of what is now known about ancient Egyptian life from this practice of stocking tombs with utilitarian and luxury household objects. Small figurines called shawabtis° were included to play the part of servants and to take the place of the deceased in case the regimen of the afterlife included periodic calls for compulsory labor. The elite classes ordered chapels attached to their tombs and left endowments to subsidize the daily attendance of a priest and offerings of foodstuffs to sustain their spirits for all eternity.

The form of a tomb also reflected the wealth and status of the deceased. Common people had to make do with simple pit graves or small mud-brick chambers. Members of the privileged classes built larger tombs and covered the walls with pictures and inscriptions. Kings erected pyramids and other grand edifices, employing subterfuge to hide the sealed chamber containing the body and treasures, as well as curses and other magical precautions to foil tomb robbers. Rarely did they succeed, however. Archaeologists have seldom discovered an undisturbed royal tomb.

The ancient Egyptians made remarkable advances in many areas of knowledge and developed an array of advantageous technologies. They learned about chemistry through experiments on preserving dead bodies. The process of mummification also provided opportunities to learn about human anatomy, and Egyptian doctors were in demand in the courts of western Asia because of their relatively advanced medical knowledge and techniques.

The Egyptians sought ways to control and profit from the Nile flood and worked hard at constructing, maintaining, and expanding the network of irrigation channels and holding basins. They needed mathematics to survey and measure the dimensions of fields and calculate the quantity of agricultural produce owed to the state. By careful observation of the stars they constructed the most accurate calendar in the world, and they knew that the appearance of the star Sirius on the horizon shortly before sunrise meant that the Nile flood surge was imminent.

Pyramids, temple complexes, and other monumental building projects called for great skill in engineering and architecture. Vast quantities of earth had to be moved to make the construction sites level. Large stones had to be quarried, dragged on rollers, floated downstream on barges, lifted into place along ramps of packed earth, and then carved to the exact size needed and made smooth. Long underground passageways were excavated to connect mortuary temples by the river with tombs near the desert's edge. On several occasions Egyptian kings dredged out a canal more than 50 miles (80 kilometers) long in order to join the Nile Valley to the Red Sea and expedite the transport of goods.

Relatively simple technologies facilitated the transportation of goods and people. River barges were used to carry stones from quarries to construction sites. Lightweight ships equipped with sails and oars were well suited for travel on the peaceful Nile and sometimes were used for voyages on the Mediterranean and Red Seas. Carts and sledges pulled by draft animals were of limited use in a landscape interrupted by canals and flooded basins. Archaeologists recently discovered an 8-mile (13-kilometer) road made of slabs of sandstone and limestone connecting a rock quarry with Faiyum Lake. Dating to the second half of the third millennium B.C.E., it is the oldest known paved road in the world.

THE INDUS VALLEY CIVILIZATION

Civilization arose almost as early in South Asia as in Mesopotamia and Egypt. Just as each of the Middle Eastern civilizations was centered on a great river valley, so civilization in the Indian subcontinent originated on a fertile floodplain. In the valley of the Indus River, settled

---

shawabtis (shuh-WAB-tees)

farming created the agricultural surplus essential to urbanized society.

Natural Environment

A plain of more than 1 million acres (400,000 hectares) stretches from the mountains of western Pakistan east to the Thar° Desert in the central portion of the Indus Valley, the Sind° region of modern Pakistan (see Map 2.1). Over many centuries silt carried downstream and deposited on the land by the Indus River has elevated the riverbed and its containing banks above the plain. Twice a year the river overflows its banks and spreads as far as 10 miles (16 kilometers). In March and April melting snow feeds the river's sources in the Pamir° and Himalaya° mountain ranges. Then in August, the great monsoon (seasonal wind) blowing off the ocean to the southwest brings rains that swell the streams flowing into the Indus. As a result, farmers in this region of little rainfall are able to plant and harvest two crops a year. In ancient times the Hakra° River (sometimes referred to as the Saraswati), which has since dried up, ran parallel to the Indus about 25 miles (40 kilometers) to the east and provided a second area suitable for intensive cultivation.

Adjacent regions shared many cultural traits with this core area. To the northeast is the Punjab, where five rivers converge to form the main course of the Indus. Lying beneath the shelter of the towering Himalaya range, the Punjab receives considerably more rainfall than the central plain but is less prone to flooding. From there settlements spread as far as Delhi° in northwest India. Settlement also extended south into the great delta where the Indus empties into the Arabian Sea, and southeast into India's hook-shaped Kathiawar° Peninsula, an area of alluvial plains and coastal marshes. The territory covered by the Indus Valley civilization is roughly equivalent in size to modern France—much larger than the zone of Mesopotamian civilization.

Material Culture

The Indus Valley civilization flourished from approximately 2600 to 1900 B.C.E. Although archaeologists have located several hundred sites, the culture is best known from the archaeological remains of two great cities first discovered eighty years ago. The ancient names of these cities are unknown, so they are referred to by modern names: **Harappa** and **Mohenjo-Daro°.** Unfortunately, the high water table at these sites makes excavation of the earliest levels of settlement nearly impossible.

Bronze Statue from the Indus Valley Found in a house in Mohenjo-Daro, this small statue represents a young woman whose only apparel is a necklace and an armful of bracelets. Appearing relaxed and confident, she has been identified by some scholars as a dancer. (National Museum, New Delhi)

Scholars once assumed that the people who created this civilization were related to speakers of the Dravidian° languages whose descendants were driven into central and southern India by invading Indo-European herders around 1500 B.C.E. Skeletal evidence, however, indicates that the population of the Indus Valley remained stable from ancient times to the present, and it is now believed that settled agriculture in this part of the world dates back to at least 5000 B.C.E. The precise relationship between the Indus Valley civilization and earlier

Thar (tahr) **Sind** (sinned) **Pamir** (pah-MEER)
Himalaya (him-uh-LAY-uh) **Hakra** (HAK-ruh) **Delhi** (DEL-ee)
Kathiawar (kah-tee-uh-WAHR)

Mohenjo-Daro (moe-hen-joe–DAHR-oh)
Dravidian (druh-VID-ee-uhn)

cultural complexes in the Indus Valley and in the hilly lands to the west is unclear. Also unclear are the forces that gave rise to urbanization, population increase, and technological advances in the mid-third millennium B.C.E. Nevertheless, the case for continuity with the earlier cultures seems stronger than the case for a sudden transformation due to the movement of new peoples into the valley.

Like the Mesopotamians and Egyptians, the people of the Indus Valley had a system of writing. They used more than four hundred signs to represent syllables and words. Archaeologists have recovered thousands of inscribed seal stones and copper tablets. Unfortunately, no one has been able to decipher these documents.

This society produced major urban centers. Harappa was 3.5 miles (5.6 kilometers) in circumference and may have housed a population of 35,000. Mohenjo-Daro was several times larger. High, thick brick walls surrounded each city. The streets were laid out in a rectangular grid pattern. Covered drainpipes carried away waste. The regular size of the streets and length of the city blocks and the uniformity of the mud bricks used in construction have been taken as evidence of a strong central authority. The seat of this authority may have been the citadel—an elevated, enclosed compound containing large buildings. Nearby were well-ventilated structures that scholars think were storehouses of grain for feeding the urban population and for export. The presence of barracks may point to some regimentation of the skilled artisans.

It is often assumed that these urban centers controlled the rural farmlands around them, though there is no proof that they did. Various factors may account for the location of the chief centers, and different centers may have had different functions. Mohenjo-Daro seems to dominate the great floodplain of the Indus. Harappa, which is nearly 500 miles (805 kilometers) from Mohenjo-Daro, is on a frontier between farmland and herding land, and no other settlements have been found west of it. Harappa may have served as a "gateway" to the copper, tin, and precious stones of the northwest. Coastal towns to the south also would have had commercial functions, gathering fish and highly prized seashells and expediting seaborne trade with the Persian Gulf.

Mohenjo-Daro and Harappa have been extensively excavated, and published accounts on the Indus Valley civilization tend to treat them as the norm. Most people, however, lived in smaller settlements, which exhibit the same artifacts and the same standardization of styles and shapes as the large cities. Some scholars attribute this standardization to extensive exchange and trading of goods within the zone of Indus Valley civilization, rather than to a strong and authoritarian central government.

There is a greater abundance of metal in the Indus Valley than in Mesopotamia and Egypt, and most of the metal objects that archaeologists have found are utilitarian tools and other everyday objects. In contrast, more jewelry and other decorative metal objects have been unearthed in Mesopotamia and Egypt. Moreover, metal objects were available to a large cross-section of the population in the Indus Valley, while they were primarily reserved for the elite in the Middle East.

The civilization of the Indus Valley possessed impressive technological capabilities. The people were adept in the technology of irrigation, used the potter's wheel, and laid the foundations of large public buildings with mud bricks baked in kilns (sun-dried bricks would have dissolved quickly in floodwaters). Smiths worked with gold, silver, copper, and tin. The varying ratios of tin to copper in their bronze objects suggest that they were acutely aware of the hardness of different mixtures and used the smallest amount possible of the relatively rare tin, making, for example, axes harder than knives.

The people of the Indus Valley had widespread trading contacts. Utilizing passes through the mountains in the northwest, they had ready access to the valuable resources of eastern Iran and Afghanistan as well as to ore deposits in western India. These resources included metals (such as copper and tin), precious stones (lapis lazuli, jade, and turquoise), building stone, and timber. Goods were moved on rivers within the zone of Indus Valley culture. It has been suggested that the undeciphered writing on seal stones may represent the names of merchants who stamped their wares.

The inhabitants of the Indus Valley and of Mesopotamia obtained raw materials from some of the same sources. Indus Valley seal stones have been found in the Tigris-Euphrates Valley, and some scholars believe that Indus Valley merchants served as middlemen in the long-distance trade, obtaining raw materials from the lands of west-central Asia and shipping them to the Persian Gulf.

Little is known about the political, social, economic, and religious structures of Indus Valley society. Attempts to link artifacts and images to cultural features characteristic of later periods of Indian history (see Chapter 7)—including sociopolitical institutions (a system of hereditary occupational groups, the predominant role of priests), architectural forms (bathing tanks like those later found in Hindu temples, private interior courtyards in houses), and religious beliefs and practices (depictions of gods and sacred animals on the seal stones, a cult of the mother-goddess)—are highly speculative.

Environmental Stress in the Indus Valley

The three river-valley civilizations discussed in this chapter were located in arid or semiarid regions. Such regions are particularly vulnerable to changes in the environment. Scholars' debates about the existence and impact of changes in the climate and landscape of the Indus Valley illuminate some of the possible factors at work, as well as the difficulties of verifying and interpreting such long-ago changes.

One of the points at issue is climatic change. An earlier generation of scholars believed that the climate of the Indus Valley was considerably wetter during the height of that civilization than it is now. As evidence, they cited the enormous quantities of timber, cut from extensive forests, that would have been needed to bake the millions of mud bricks used to construct the cities (see photo), the distribution of human settlements on land that is now unfavorable for agriculture, and the representation of jungle and marsh animals on decorated seals. This approach assumes that the growth of population, prosperity, and complexity in the Indus Valley in the third millennium B.C.E. required wet conditions, and it concludes that the change to a drier climate in the early second millennium B.C.E. pushed this civilization into decline.

Other experts, skeptical about radical climate change, countered with alternative calculations of the amount of timber needed and evidence of plant remains—particularly barley, a grain that is tolerant of dry conditions. However, recent studies of the stabilization of sand dunes, which occurs in periods of heavy rainfall, and analysis of the sediment deposited by rivers and winds have been used to strengthen the claim that the Indus Valley used to be wetter and that in the early- to mid-second millennium B.C.E. it entered a period of relatively dry conditions that have persisted to the present.

A much clearer case can be made for changes in the landscape caused by shifts in the courses of rivers. These shifts are due, in many cases, to tectonic forces such as earthquakes. Dry channels, whether detected in satellite photographs or by on-the-ground inspection, reveal the location of old riverbeds, and it appears that a second major river system, the Hakra, once ran parallel to the Indus some distance to the east. The Hakra, with teeming towns and fertile fields along its banks, appears to have been a second axis of this civilization. Either the Sutlej, which now feeds into the Indus, or the Yamuna, which now pours into the Ganges, may have been the main source of water for this long-gone system before undergoing a change of course. The consequences of the drying-up of this major waterway must have been immense—the loss of huge amounts of arable land and the food that it produced, the abandonment of cities and villages and consequent migration of their populations, shifts in the trade routes, and desperate competition for shrinking resources.

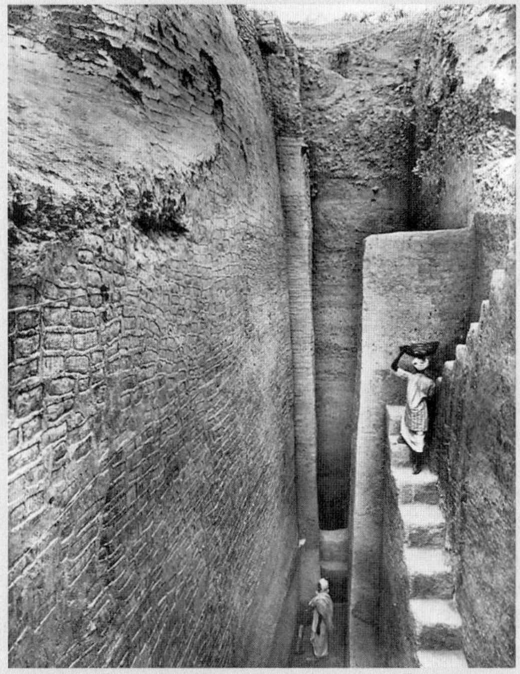

Mud-Brick Fortification Wall of the Citadel at Harappa Built upon a high platform, this massive and towering construction required large numbers of bricks and enormous man-hours of labor. *The Cambridge History of India: The Indus Civilization,* 3d ed. (1968), by Sir Mortimer Wheeler. With permission of the Syndics of the Cambridge University Press.

As for the Indus itself, the present-day course of the lower reaches of the river has shifted 100 miles (161 kilometers) to the west since the arrival of the Greek conqueror Alexander the Great in the late fourth century B.C.E., and the deposit of massive volumes of silt has pushed the mouth of the river 50 miles (80 kilometers) farther south. Such a shift of the river bed and buildup of alluvial deposits also may have occurred in the third and second millennia B.C.E.

A recent study concludes: "It is obvious that ecological stresses, caused both climatically and technically, played an important role in the life and decay" of the Indus civilization.

Source: Quotation from D. P. Agarwal and R. K. Sood in Gregory L. Possehl, ed., *Harappan Civilization: A Contemporary Perspective* (Warminster, England: Aris and Phillips, 1982), 229.

Further knowledge about this society awaits additional archaeological finds and the deciphering of the Indus Valley script.

Transformation of the Indus Valley Civilization

The Indus Valley cities were abandoned sometime after 1900 B.C.E. Archaeologists once thought that invaders destroyed them, but now they believe that the civilization suffered "systems failure"—the breakdown of the fragile interrelationship of the political, social, and economic systems that sustained order and prosperity. The cause may have been one or more natural disasters, such as an earthquake or massive flooding. Gradual ecological changes may also have played a role as the Hakra river system dried up and salinization (an increase in the amount of salt in the soil, inhibiting plant growth) and erosion increased (see Environment and Technology: Environmental Stress in the Indus Valley).

When towns were no longer on the river, ports were separated from the sea by silt deposits in the deltas, and regions lost fertile soil and water, large numbers of people would have had to relocate, and those who remained would need new ways of making a living. The causes, patterns, and pace of change probably varied in different areas. Urbanization is likely to have persisted longer in some regions than in others. But in the end, the urban centers could not be sustained, and village-based farming and herding took their place. As the interaction between regions lessened, distinct regional variations replaced the standardization of technology and style of the previous era.

Historians can do little more than speculate about the causes behind the changes and the experiences of the people who lived in the Indus Valley around 1900 B.C.E. It is important to keep two tendencies in mind. In most cases like this, the majority of the population adjusts to the new circumstances. But members of the political and social elite, who depended on the urban centers and complex political and economic structures, lose the source of their authority and are merged with the population as a whole.

CONCLUSION

It is surely no accident that the first civilizations to develop high levels of political centralization, urbanization, and technology were situated in river valleys where rainfall was insufficient for dependable agriculture. Dependent as they were on river water to irrigate the cultivated land that fed their populations, Mesopotamia, Egypt, and the Indus Valley civilization channeled significant human resources into the construction and maintenance of canals, dams, and dikes. This work required expertise in engineering, mathematics, and metallurgy, as well as the formation of political centers that could organize the necessary labor force.

The unpredictable and violent floods in the Tigris-Euphrates Basin were a constant source of alarm for the people of Mesopotamia. In contrast, the predictable, opportune, and gradual Nile floods were eagerly anticipated events in Egypt. The relationship with nature stamped the worldview of both peoples. Mesopotamians nervously tried to appease their harsh deities so as to survive in a perverse world. Egyptians largely trusted in and nurtured the supernatural powers that, they believed, guaranteed orderliness and prosperity.

In both Egypt and Mesopotamia, kingship emerged as the dominant political form. The Egyptian king's divine origins and symbolic association with the forces of renewal made him central to the welfare of the entire country and gave him a religious monopoly superseding the authority of the temples and priests. Egyptian monarchs lavished much of the country's wealth on their tombs, believing that a proper burial would ensure the continuity of kingship and the attendant blessings that it brought to the land and people. Mesopotamian rulers, who were not normally regarded as divine, built new cities, towering walls, splendid palaces, and religious edifices as lasting testaments to their power.

The religious outlook of both cultures included a hierarchy of gods, ranging from protective demons and local deities to the gods of the state, whose importance rose or fell with the power of the political centers with which they were associated. Cheered by the essential stability of their environment, the Egyptians tended to have a more positive conception of the gods' designs for humankind. The Egyptians believed that although the journey to the next world was beset with hazards, the righteous spirit that overcame them could look forward to a blessed existence. In contrast, Gilgamesh, the hero of the Mesopotamian epic, is tormented by terrifying visions of the afterlife: disembodied spirits of the dead stumbling around in the darkness of the Underworld for all eternity, eating dust and clay, and slaving for the heartless gods of that realm.

Although the populations of Egypt and Mesopotamia were ethnically heterogeneous, both regions experienced a remarkable degree of cultural continuity. New immigrants readily assimilated to the dominant language, belief system, and lifestyles of the civilization. People were identified by culture, not physical appearance. Mesopotamian women's apparent loss of freedom and legal privilege in the second millennium B.C.E. may have been related to the higher degree of urbanization and class stratification in this society. In contrast, Egyptian pictorial documents, love poems, and legal records indicate respect and greater equality for women in the valley of the Nile.

In the second millennium B.C.E., as the societies of Mesopotamia and Egypt consolidated their cultural achievements and entered new phases of political expansion, and as the Indus Valley centers went into irreversible decline, a new and distinctive civilization, based likewise on the exploitation of the agricultural potential of a floodplain, was emerging in the valley of the Yellow River in eastern China. We turn our attention to that area in Chapter 3.

Key Terms

civilization
Babylon
Sumerians
Semitic
city-state
Hammurabi
scribe
ziggurat
amulet
cuneiform
bronze
pharaoh
ma'at
pyramid
Memphis
Thebes
hieroglyphics
papyrus
mummy
Harappa
Mohenjo-Daro

Suggested Reading

Jack M. Sasson, ed., *Civilizations of the Ancient Near East,* 4 vols. (1993), contains up-to-date articles and bibliography on a wide range of topics. An excellent starting point for geography, chronology, and basic institutions and cultural concepts in ancient western Asia is Michael Roaf, *Cultural Atlas of Mesopotamia and the Ancient Near East* (1990). Amelie Kuhrt, *The Ancient Near East, c. 3000–330 B.C.*, 2 vols. (1995), is the best and most up-to-date introduction to the historical development of western Asia and Egypt, offering a clear and concise historical outline and a balanced presentation of continuing controversies. Other general historical introductions can be found in A. Bernard Knapp, *The History and Culture of Ancient Western Asia and Egypt* (1988); Hans J. Nissen, *The Early History of the Ancient Near East, 9000–2000 B.C.* (1988); and H. W. F. Saggs, *Civilization Before Greece and Rome* (1989).

Georges Roux, *Ancient Iraq,* 3d ed. (1992), traces the long history of ancient Mesopotamia, while Joan Oates, *Babylon* (1979), focuses on the most important of all the Mesopotamian cities. J. N. Postgate, *Early Mesopotamia: Society and Economy at the Dawn of History* (1992), offers deep insights into the political, social, and economic dynamics of Mesopotamian society. Susan Pollock, *Ancient Mesopotamia: The Eden That Never Was* (1999), applies anthropological theory and models to early Mesopotamia. Marc van de Mierop, *The Ancient Mesopotamian City* (1997), explores the political, social, and economic dimensions of Mesopotamian urbanism. Daniel C. Snell, *Life in the Ancient Near East 3100–322 B.C.E.* (1997), emphasizes social and economic matters for those already familiar with the main outlines of ancient Near Eastern history. Stephanie Dalley, ed., *The Legacy of Mesopotamia* (1998), explores the interactions of the Mesopotamians with other peoples of the ancient world.

The most direct and exciting introduction to the world of early Mesopotamians is through the *Epic of Gilgamesh,* in the attractive translation of David Ferry, *Gilgamesh: A New Rendering in English Verse* (1992). Thorkild Jacobsen, *The Treasures of Darkness: A History of Mesopotamian Religion* (1976), is a classic study of the evolving mentality of Mesopotamian religion. Stephanie Dalley, *Myths from Mesopotamia* (1989), and Henrietta McCall, *Mesopotamian Myths* (1990), deal with the mythical literature. Jeremy Black and Anthony Green, *Gods, Demons and Symbols of Ancient Mesopotamia* (1992), is a handy illustrated encyclopedia of myth, religion, and religious symbolism. Pierre Amiet, *Art of the Ancient Near East* (1980), offers a richly illustrated introduction to a wide spectrum of artistic media. Dominique Collon, *First Impressions: Cylinder Seals in the Ancient Near East* (1988), explores a class of common objects that reveal much about art and daily life.

C. B. F. Walker, *Cuneiform* (1987), is a concise guide to the Mesopotamian system of writing. James B. Pritchard, *Ancient Near Eastern Texts Relating to the Old Testament,* 3d ed. (1969), contains an extensive collection of translated documents and texts from western Asia and Egypt. Karen Rhea Nemet-Nejat, *Daily Life in Ancient Mesopotamia* (1998), is an introduction to social history. Attitudes, roles, and the treatment of women are taken up by Karen Rhea Nemet-Nejat, "Women in Ancient Mesopotamia," in Bella Vivante, ed., *Women's Roles in Ancient Civilizations: A Reference Guide* (1999), and Barbara Lesko, "Women of Egypt and the Ancient Near East," in *Becoming Visible: Women in European History,* 2d ed., ed. Renata Bridenthal, Claudia Koonz, and Susan Stuard (1994). The significance of ancient Syria as a region with its own cultural vitality as well as indebtedness to Mesopotamia is taken up in Harvey Weiss, ed., *Ebla to Damascus: Art and Archaeology of Ancient Syria* (1985), and Giovanni Pettinato, *Ebla: A New Look at History* (1991).

A fine and lavishly illustrated introduction to the many facets of ancient Egyptian civilization is David P. Silverman, ed., *Ancient Egypt* (1997). John Baines and Jaromir Malek, *Atlas of Ancient Egypt* (1980), and T. G. H. James, *Ancient Egypt: The Land and Its Legacy* (1988), are primarily organized around the sites of ancient Egypt and provide general introductions to Egyptian civilization. Donald B. Redford, ed., *The Oxford Encyclopedia of Ancient Egypt,* 3 vols. (2001), and Kathryn A. Bard, ed.,

Encyclopedia of the Archaeology of Ancient Egypt (1999), are comprehensive reference tools. Historical treatments include B. G. Trigger, B. J. Kemp, D. O'Connor, and A. B. Lloyd, *Ancient Egypt: A Social History* (1983); Barry J. Kemp, *Ancient Egypt: Anatomy of a Civilization* (1989); Nicholas-Cristophe Grimal, *A History of Ancient Egypt* (1992); Erik Hornung, *History of Ancient Egypt: An Introduction* (1999); and Ian Shaw, ed., *The Oxford History of Ancient Egypt* (2000). John Romer, *People of the Nile: Everyday Life in Ancient Egypt* (1982); Miriam Stead, *Egyptian Life* (1986); Eugen Strouhal, *Life of the Ancient Egyptians* (1992); and Lionel Casson, *Everyday Life in Ancient Egypt* (2001), emphasize social history. For women see the article by Lesko cited above; Barbara Watterson, *Women in Ancient Egypt* (1991); Gay Robins, *Women in Ancient Egypt* (1993); and the articles and museum exhibition catalogue in Anne K. Capel and Glenn E. Markoe, eds., *Mistress of the House, Mistress of Heaven: Women in Ancient Egypt* (1996).

Stephen Quirke, *Ancient Egyptian Religion* (1990), is a highly regarded treatment of a complex subject. Erik Hornung and Betsy M. Bryan, eds., *The Quest for Immortality: Treasures of Ancient Egypt* (2002), is the lavishly illustrated and annotated catalogue of an exhibition that focused on Egyptian funerary practices and beliefs about the afterlife. George Hart, *Egyptian Myths* (1990), gathers the limited written evidence for what must have been a thriving oral tradition. Maria C. Betro, *Hieroglyphics: The Writings of Ancient Egypt* (1996), introduces the complex and alluring writing system. Pritchard's collection, cited above, and Miriam Lichtheim, *Ancient Egyptian Literature: A Book of Readings, vol. 1, The Old and Middle Kingdoms* (1973), provide translated original texts and documents. William Stevenson Smith, *The Art and Architecture of Ancient Egypt* (1998); Gay Robins, *The Art of Ancient Egypt* (1997); Jaromir Malek, *Egyptian Art* (1999); and Dieter Arnold, *The Encyclopedia of Ancient Egyptian Architecture* (2003), are introductions to the visual record.

For the Indus Valley civilization there is a brief treatment in Stanley Wolpert, *A New History of India*, 3d ed. (1989). Mortimer Wheeler's *Civilizations of the Indus Valley and Beyond* (1966) and *The Indus Civilization*, 3d ed. (1968), though still useful, are now largely superseded by Jonathan Mark Kenoyer, *Ancient Cities of the Indus Valley Civilization* (1998); Jane McIntosh, *A Peaceful Realm: The Rise and Fall of the Indus Civilization* (2002); and Gregory L. Possehl, *The Indus Civilization: A Contemporary Perspective* (2002). Possehl also has edited two collections of articles by Indus Valley scholars: *Ancient Cities of the Indus* (1979) and *Harappan Civilization: A Contemporary Perspective* (1982).

Notes

1. David Ferry, *Gilgamesh: A New Rendering in English Verse* (New York: Noonday Press, 1992).

3 New Civilizations in the Eastern and Western Hemispheres, 2200–250 B.C.E.

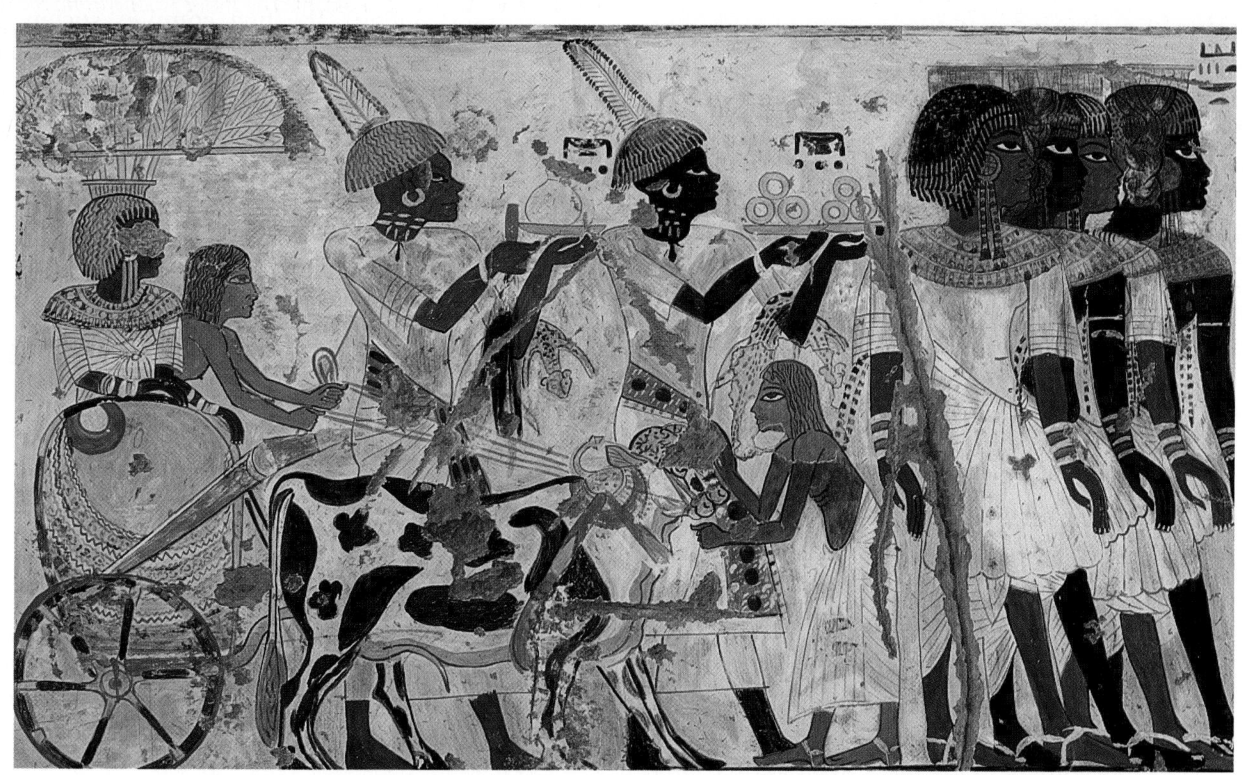

Wall Painting of Nubians Arriving in Egypt with Rings and Bags of Gold, Fourteenth Century B.C.E.
This image decorated the tomb of an Egyptian administrator in Nubia.

CHAPTER OUTLINE

Early China, 2000–221 B.C.E.

Nubia, 3100 B.C.E.–350 C.E.

Celtic Europe, 1000–50 B.C.E.

First Civilizations of the Americas: The Olmec and Chavín, 1200–250 B.C.E.

ENVIRONMENT AND TECHNOLOGY: Divination in Ancient Societies

DIVERSITY AND DOMINANCE: Hierarchy and Conduct in the Analects of Confucius

Around 2200 B.C.E. an Egyptian official named Harkhuf°, who lived at Aswan° on the southern boundary of Egypt, set out for a place called Yam, far to the south in the land that later came to be called Nubia. He had made this trek three times before, so he was familiar with the route and skillful in dealing with various Nubian chieftains along the way. He brought gifts from the Egyptian pharaoh for the ruler of Yam, and he returned home with three hundred donkeys loaded with incense, dark ebony wood, ivory, panthers, and other exotic products from tropical Africa. While this exchange was couched in the diplomatic fiction of gifts, we should probably regard it as a form of trade and Harkhuf as a brave and enterprising caravan leader. On this particular trip he returned with something so special that the eight-year-old boy pharaoh, Pepi II, could not contain his excitement. He wrote:

> Come north to the residence at once! Hurry and bring with you this pygmy whom you brought from the land of the horizon-dwellers live, hale, and healthy, for the dances of the god, to gladden the heart, to delight the heart of king Neferkare [Pepi] who lives forever! When he goes down with you into the ship, get worthy men to be around him on deck, lest he fall into the water! When he lies down at night, get worthy men to lie around him in his tent. Inspect ten times at night! My majesty desires to see this pygmy more than the gifts of the mine-land and of Punt![1]

Although the precise location of Yam is uncertain, scholars are beginning to identify it with Kerma, later the capital of the kingdom of Nubia, on the upper Nile in modern Sudan. From the Egyptian point of view, Nubia was a wild and dangerous place. Yet we can see that it was developing features of more complex political organization, and that the burgeoning trade between Nubia and Egypt was important to both societies.

In contrast to the river-valley civilizations of Mesopotamia, Egypt, and the Indus Valley surveyed in the previous chapter, the complex societies examined in this chapter subsequently emerged in ecological conditions quite a bit more diverse, sometimes independently, sometimes under the influence of the older centers. Whereas the river-valley civilizations were originally largely self-sufficient, each of the new civilizations discussed in this chapter and the next was shaped by the development of networks of long-distance trade.

In the second millennium B.C.E. a civilization based on irrigation agriculture arose along the valley of the Yellow River and its tributaries in northern China. In the same epoch, in Nubia (southern Egypt and northern Sudan), the first complex society in tropical Africa continued to develop from the roots observed earlier by Harkhuf. The first millennium B.C.E. witnessed the spread of Celtic peoples across much of continental Europe, as well as the flourishing of the earliest complex societies of the Western Hemisphere, the Olmec of Mesoamerica and the Chavín culture on the flanks of the Andes Mountains in South America. These societies had no contact with one another, and they represent a variety of responses to different environmental and historical circumstances. Thus, their stories will necessarily be separate. However, as we shall see, they have certain features in common and collectively point to a distinct stage in the development of human societies.

As you read this chapter, ask yourself the following questions:

- How did the peoples of early China, Nubia, Celtic Europe, and the Olmec and Chavín civilizations each develop distinctive political and social institutions, cultural patterns, and technologies in response to the challenges of the environment?
- What was the basis of the status, power, and wealth of elite groups in each society, and how did they dominate the rest of the population?
- In the case of Nubia and the Celts, how did the technological and cultural influences of older centers affect the formation of the new civilizations?
- Why did societies in the Eastern and Western Hemispheres acquire complex organizations and potent technologies at different times and in different sequences?

Harkhuf (HAHR-koof) **Aswan** (AS- wahn)

CHRONOLOGY

	China	Nubia	Celtic Europe	Americas
	8000–2000 B.C.E. Neolithic cultures	**4500 B.C.E.** Early agriculture in Nubia		**3500 B.C.E.** Early agriculture in Mesoamerica and Andes
2500 B.C.E.		**2200 B.C.E.** Harkhuf's expeditions to Yam		**2600 B.C.E.** Rise of Caral
2000 B.C.E.	**2000 B.C.E.** Bronze metallurgy			
	1750–1027 B.C.E. Shang dynasty	**1750 B.C.E.** Rise of kingdom of Kush based on Kerma		
1500 B.C.E.		**1500 B.C.E.** Egyptian conquest of Nubia		
	1027–221 B.C.E. Zhou dynasty			**1200–900 B.C.E.** Rise of Olmec civilization, centered on San Lorenzo
1000 B.C.E.		**1000 B.C.E.** Decline of Egyptian control in Nubia	**1000 B.C.E.** Origin of Celtic culture in Central Europe	**900–600 B.C.E.** La Venta, the dominant Olmec center
		750 B.C.E. Rise of kingdom based on Napata		**900–250 B.C.E.** Chavín civilization in the Andes
	600 B.C.E. Iron Metallurgy	**712–660 B.C.E.** Nubian kings rule Egypt	**500 B.C.E.** Celtic elites trade for Mediterranean goods	**600–400 B.C.E.** Ascendancy of Tres Zapotes and Olmec decline
500 B.C.E		**300 B.C.E.–350 C.E.** Kingdom of Meroë	**500–300 B.C.E.** Migrations across Europe	**500 B.C.E.** Early metallurgy in Andes
			390 B.C.E. Celts sack Rome	

EARLY CHINA, 2000–221 B.C.E.

On the eastern edge of the great Eurasian landmass, Neolithic cultures developed as early as 8000 B.C.E. A more complex civilization evolved in the second millennium B.C.E. Under the Shang and Zhou monarchs many of the institutions and values of classical Chinese civilization emerged and spread south and west. As in Mesopotamia, Egypt, and the Indus Valley, the rise of cities, specialization of labor, bureaucratic government, writing, and other advanced technologies depended on the exploitation of a great river system—the Yellow River (Huang He°) and its tributaries—to support intensive agriculture. Although there is archaeological evidence of some movement of goods and ideas between western and eastern Asia, developments in China were largely independent of the complex societies in the Middle East and the Indus Valley.

Geography and Resources

China is isolated from the rest of the Eastern Hemisphere by formidable natural barriers: the Himalaya° mountain range on the southwest; the Pamir° and Tian° mountains and the Takla Makan° Desert on the west; the Gobi° Desert and the treeless and grassy hills and plains of the Mongolian steppe on the northwest (see Map 3.1). To the east lies the Pacific Ocean. Although China's separation was not total—trade goods, people, and ideas moved back and forth between China, India, and Central Asia— in many respects its development was distinctive.

Most of East Asia is covered with mountains, making overland travel, transport, and communications difficult and slow. The great river systems of eastern China, however—the Yellow and the Yangzi° Rivers and their tributaries—facilitate east-west movement. In the eastern river valleys dense populations could practice intensive agriculture; on the steppe lands of Mongolia, the deserts and oases of Xinjiang°, and the high plateau of Tibet sparser populations engaged in different forms of livelihood. The climate zones of East Asia range from the dry, subarctic reaches of Manchuria in the north to the lush, subtropical forests of the south, and support a rich variety of plant and animal life adapted to these zones.

Within the eastern agricultural zone, the north and the south have strikingly different environments. Each zone produced distinctive patterns for the use of the land, the kinds of crops that could flourish, and the organization of agricultural labor. The monsoons that affect India and Southeast Asia (see Chapter 2) drench southern China with heavy rainfall in the summer, the most beneficial time for agriculture. Northern China, in contrast, where rainfall is much more erratic, receives less moisture. As in Mesopotamia and the Indus Valley, where technological and social developments unfolded in relatively adverse conditions, China's early history unfolded on the northern plains, a demanding environment that stimulated important technologies and political traditions as well as the philosophical and religious views that became hallmarks of Chinese civilization. By the third century C.E., however, the gradual flow of population toward the warmer southern lands caused the political and intellectual center to move south.

The eastern river valleys and North China Plain contained timber, stone, scattered deposits of metals, and, above all, potentially productive land. Since prehistoric times, winds blowing from Central Asia have deposited a yellowish-brown dust called **loess**° (these particles suspended in the water give the Yellow River its distinctive hue and name). Over the ages a thick mantle of soil has accumulated that is extremely fertile and soft enough to be worked with wooden digging sticks. The lack of compactness of this soil accounts for the severity of earthquake damage in this region.

In this landscape, agriculture demanded the coordinated efforts of large groups of people. In parts of northern China forests had to be cleared. Recurrent floods on the Yellow River necessitated the construction of earthen dikes and channels to carry off the overflow. To cope with the periodic droughts, catch basins (reservoirs) were dug to store river water and rainfall. As the population grew, people built retaining walls to partition the hillsides into tiers of flat arable terraces.

The staple crops in the northern region were millet, a grain indigenous to China, and wheat, which had spread to East Asia from the Middle East. Rice requires a warmer climate and prospered in the south. The cultivation of rice in the Yangzi River Valley and the south required a great outlay of labor. Rice paddies—the fields where rice is grown—must be absolutely flat and surrounded by water channels to bring and lead away water according to a precise schedule. Seedlings sprout in a nursery, and are transplanted one by one to the paddy, which is then flooded. Flooding eliminates weeds and rival plants and supports microscopic organisms that keep the soil fertile. When the crop is ripe, the paddy is drained; the rice stalks are harvested with a sickle; and

Huang He (hwahng-HUH) **Himalaya** (him-uh-LAY-uh)
Pamir (pah-MEER) **Tian** (tee-en)
Takla Makan (TAH-kluh muh-KAHN) **Gobi** (GO-bee)
Yangzi (yang-zuh) **Xinjiang** (shin-jyahng)

loess (less)

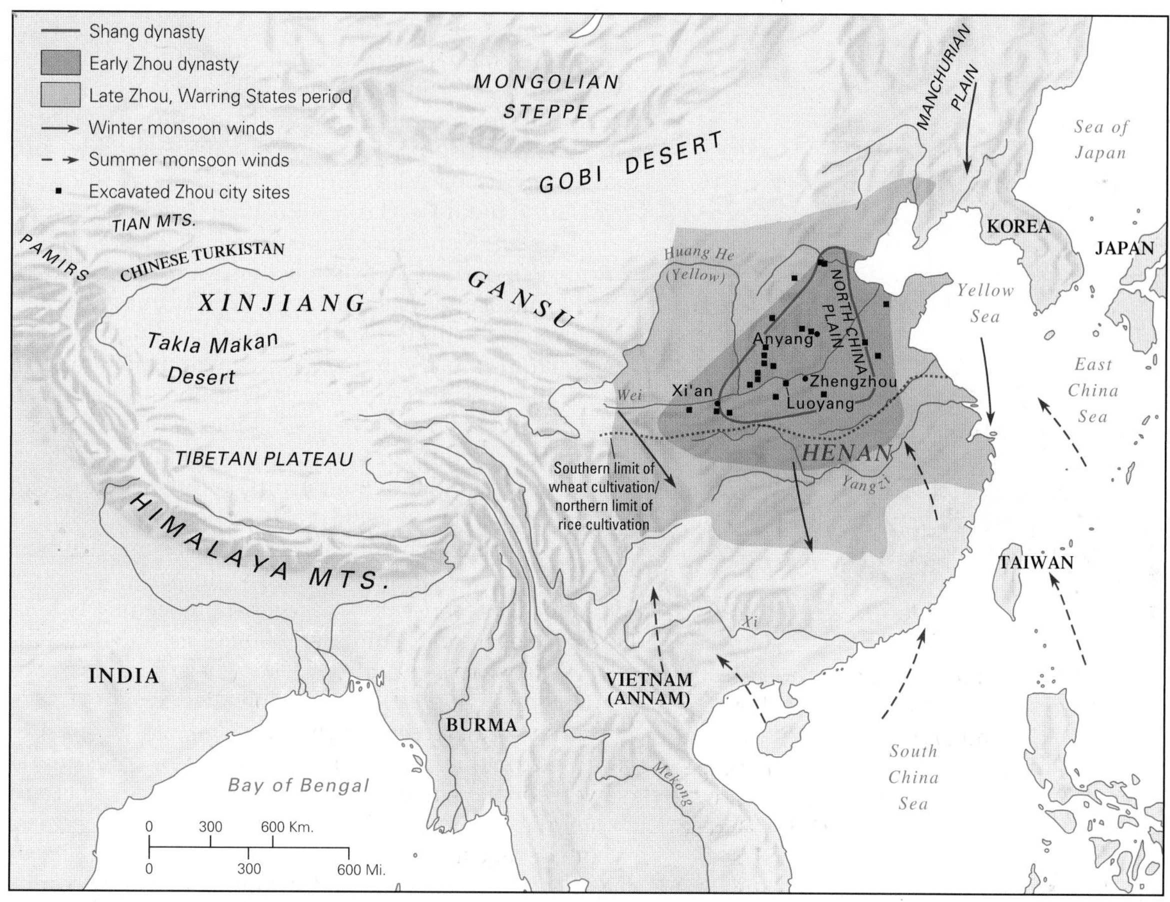

Map 3.1 China in the Shang and Zhou Periods, 1750–221 B.C.E. The Shang dynasty arose in the second millennium B.C.E. in the floodplain of the Yellow River. While southern China benefits from the monsoon rains, northern China depends on irrigation. As population increased, the Han Chinese migrated from their eastern homeland to other parts of China, carrying their technologies and cultural practices. Other ethnic groups predominated in more outlying regions, and the nomadic peoples of the northwest constantly challenged Chinese authority.

the edible kernels are separated out. The reward for this effort is a spectacular yield. Rice can feed more people per cultivated acre than any other grain, which explains why the south eventually became more populous and important than the north.

The Shang Period, 1750–1027 B.C.E.

Archaeologists have identified several Neolithic cultural complexes in China, primarily on the basis of styles of pottery and forms of burial. These early populations grew millet, raised pigs and chickens, and used stone tools. They made pottery on a wheel and fired it in high-temperature kilns. They pioneered the production of silk cloth, first raising silkworms on mulberry trees, then carefully unraveling their cocoons to produce silk thread. The early Chinese built walls of pounded earth by hammering the soil inside temporary wooden frames until it became hard as cement. By 2000 B.C.E. they had begun to make bronze (roughly a thousand years after the beginnings of bronze-working in the Middle East).

Later generations of Chinese told stories about the ancient dynasty of the Xia, said to have ruled the core region of the Yellow River Valley. The validity of those stories is difficult to gauge, though some archaeologists identify the Xia with the Neolithic Longshan cultural complex in the centuries before and after 2000 B.C.E. Chinese history proper begins with the rise to power of the Shang clans, which coincides with the earliest written records anywhere in China.

Bronze Vessel from the Shang Period, 13th–11th Century B.C.E. Vessels such as this large wine jar were used in rituals that allowed members of the Shang ruling class to make contact with their ancestors. Signifying both the source and the proof of the elite's authority, these vessels were often buried in Shang tombs. The complex shapes and elaborate decorations testify to the artisans' skill. (Tokyo National Museum Image: TNM Image)

The **Shang°** originated in the part of the Yellow River Valley that lies in the present-day province of Henan°. After 1750 B.C.E. they extended their control north into Mongolia, west as far as Gansu°, and south to the Yangzi River Valley. Shang society was dominated by a warrior aristocracy whose greatest pleasures were warfare, hunting (for recreation and to fine-tune skills required for war), exchanging gifts, feasting, and wine-filled revelry.

The king and his court ruled the core area of the Shang state directly. Aristocrats served as generals, ambassadors, and supervisors of public projects. Other members of the royal family and high-ranking nobility governed outlying provinces. The most distant regions were governed by native rulers who swore allegiance to the Shang king. The king was often on the road, traveling to the courts of his subordinates to reinforce their loyalty.

Frequent military campaigns provided the warrior aristocracy with a theater for brave achievements and yielded considerable plunder. The nomadic peoples who occupied the steppe and desert regions to the north and west were periodically rolled back and given a demonstration of Shang power. (Chinese sources refer to these peoples as "barbarians." Modern readers should be wary of the Chinese claim that these nomads were culturally backward and morally inferior to the Chinese.) Large numbers of prisoners of war were taken in these campaigns and used as slaves in the Shang capital.

Various cities served as the capital of the Shang kingdom. The last and most important was near modern Anyang° (see Map 3.1). Shang cities were centers of political control and religion. Surrounded by massive walls of pounded earth, they contained palaces, administrative buildings and storehouses, royal tombs, shrines of gods and ancestors, and houses of the nobility. The common people lived in agricultural villages outside these centers. Because stone was in short supply, buildings were set on foundation platforms of pounded earth and constructed with wooden posts and dried mud. These cities, which were laid out on a grid plan aligned with the north polar star and had gates opening to the cardinal directions, are an early manifestation of the Chinese concern with the orientation of buildings known as *feng shui*,° and they symbolized the order imposed by gods and monarchs.

A key to effective administration was the form of writing developed in this era. Pictograms (pictures representing objects and concepts) and phonetic symbols representing the sounds of syllables were combined to form a complex system of hundreds of signs. Only a small, educated elite had the time to master this system. Despite substantial changes through the ages, the fundamental principles of the Chinese system still endure today. As a result, people speaking essentially different languages, such as Mandarin and Cantonese, can read and understand the same text. In contrast, the cuneiform of Mesopotamia and the hieroglyphics of Egypt were eventually replaced by simpler alphabetic scripts.

The Shang ideology of kingship glorified the king as the indispensable intermediary between the people and the gods. The Shang royal family and aristocracy worshiped the spirits of their male ancestors. They believed that these ancestors were intensely interested in the fortunes of their descendants and had special influence with the gods. Before taking any action, the Shang rulers used **divination** to determine the will of the gods (see Environment and Technology: Divination in Ancient Societies). They made ritual sacrifices to their gods and ancestors in order to win divine favor. Burials of kings also entailed sacrifices, not only of animals but also of humans, including noble officials of the court, women, servants, soldiers, and prisoners of war.

Possession of bronze objects was a sign of authority

Shang (shahng) **Henan** (heh-nahn) **Gansu** (gahn-soo)

Anyang (ahn-yahng) **feng shui** (fung shway)

Women Beating Chimes This scene, from a bronze vessel of the Zhou era, illustrates the important role of music in festivals, religious rituals, and court ceremonials. During the politically fragmented later (Eastern) Zhou era, many small states marked their independence by having their own musical scales and distinctive arrangements of orchestral instruments. (Courtesy, Sichuan Museum)

and nobility. Bronze weapons allowed the state to assert its authority, and bronze vessels were used in rituals seeking the support of ancestors and gods. The quantity of bronze objects found in Shang tombs is impressive. The relatively modest tomb of one queen contained 450 bronze articles (ritual vessels, bells, weapons, and mirrors)—remarkable because copper and tin, the principal ingredients of bronze, were not plentiful in northern China. (Also found in the same tomb were numerous objects in jade, bone, ivory, and stone; seven thousand cowrie shells; sixteen sacrificed men, women, and children; and six dogs!) The Shang elite expended huge effort to find and mine deposits of copper and tin, refine them into pure metal, transport the ingots to the capital, and commission the creation of weapons and beautifully decorated objects.

Artisans worked in foundries outside the main cities. They poured the molten bronze into clay molds, and joined together the hardened pieces as necessary. Shang artisans made weapons, chariot fittings, musical instruments, and the ritual vessels used in religious ceremonies. Many of these elegant vessels were vividly decorated with stylized depictions of real and imaginary animals.

Far-reaching networks of trade sprang up across China, bringing the Shang valued commodities such as jade, ivory, and mother of pearl (a hard, shiny substance from the interior of mollusk shells) used for jewelry, carved figurines, and decorative inlays. Some evidence suggests that Shang China may have exchanged goods and ideas with distant Mesopotamia. The horse-drawn chariot, which the Shang may have adopted from Western Asia, was a formidable instrument of war.

The Zhou Period, 1027–221 B.C.E.

Shang domination of central and northern China lasted more than six centuries. In the eleventh century B.C.E. the last Shang king was defeated by Wu, the ruler of **Zhou**°, a dependent state in the Wei° River Valley. The Zhou line of kings (ca. 1027–221 B.C.E.) was the longest lasting and most revered of all dynasties in Chinese history. Just as the Semitic peoples in Mesopotamia had adopted and adapted the Sumerian legacy (see Chapter 2), the Zhou preserved the essentials of Shang culture and added new elements of ideology and technology.

The positive image of Zhou rule was skillfully constructed by propagandists for the new regime. The early Zhou monarchs had to justify their seizure of power to the restive remnants of the Shang clans. The chief deity was now referred to as "Heaven"; the monarch was called the "Son of Heaven"; and his rule was called the "**Mandate of Heaven.**" According to the new theory, the ruler had been chosen by the supreme deity and would retain his backing as long as he served as a wise, principled, and energetic guardian of his people. The proof of divine favor was the prosperity and the stability of the kingdom. If the ruler misbehaved, as the last Shang ruler had done, his right to rule could be withdrawn. Corruption, violence, arrogance, and insurrection, such as had occurred under the last Shang king, were signs of divine displeasure and validated the ruler's replacement by a new dynasty that was committed to just rule.

The Zhou kings continued some of the Shang ritu-

Zhou (joe) **Wei** (way)

ENVIRONMENT + TECHNOLOGY

Divination in Ancient Societies

The ancient inhabitants of China, the Middle East, Europe, and the Americas, as well as many other peoples throughout history, believed that the gods controlled the forces of nature and shaped destinies. Starting from this premise, they practiced various techniques of divination—the effort to interpret phenomena in the natural world as signs of the gods' will and intentions. Through divination the ancients sought to communicate with the gods and thereby anticipate—even influence—the future.

The Shang ruling class in China frequently sought information from shamans, individuals who claimed the ability to make direct contact with ancestors and other higher powers. The Shang monarch himself often functioned as a shaman. Chief among the tools of divination used by a shaman were oracle bones. The shaman touched a tortoiseshell or the shoulder bone of an animal (sometimes holes had been drilled in it ahead of time) with the heated point of a stick. The shell or bone would crack, and the cracks were "read" as a message from the spirit world.

Tens of thousands of oracle bones survive. They are a major source of information about Shang life; usually the question, the resulting answer, and often confirmation of the accuracy of the prediction were inscribed on the back of the shell or bone. The rulers asked about the proper performance of ritual, the likely outcome of wars or hunting expeditions, the prospects for rainfall and the harvest, and the meaning of strange occurrences.

In Mesopotamia in the third and second millennia B.C.E. the most important divination involved the close inspection of the form, size, and markings of the organs of sacrificed animals. Archaeologists have found models of sheep's livers accompanied by written explanations of the meaning of various features. Two other techniques of divination were following the trail of smoke from burning incense and examining the patterns that resulted when oil was thrown on water.

From about 2000 B.C.E. Mesopotamian diviners foretold the future from their observation of the movements of the sun, moon, planets, stars, and constellations. In the centuries after 1000 B.C.E. celestial omens were the most important source of predictions about the future, and specialists maintained precise records of astronomical events. Mesopotamian mathematics, essential for calculations of the movements of celestial bodies, was the most sophisticated in the ancient Middle East. Astrology, with its division of the sky into the twelve segments of the zodiac and its use of the position of the stars and planets to predict an individual's destiny, developed out of long-standing Mesopotamian attention to the movements of celestial objects. Horoscopes—charts with calculations and predictions based on an individual's date of birth—have been found from shortly before 400 B.C.E. In the Hellenistic period (323–30 B.C.E.), Greek settlers flooding into western Asia built on this Mesopotamian foundation and greatly advanced the study of astrology.

Greek and Roman sources make occasional references to practices of divination among the Celts. Prediction of the future is one of the many religious functions attributed to the Druids, but certain sources distinguish a specialized group of "seers." Among their methods were careful observation of the patterns of flight of birds through the sky and the ap-

als, but there was a marked decline in the practice of divination and in extravagant and bloody sacrifices and burials. The priestly power of the ruling class, the only ones who had been able to make contact with the spirits of ancestors during the Shang period, faded away. The resulting separation of religion and government promoted the development of important philosophical and mystical systems in the Zhou period. The bronze vessels that had been sacred implements in the Shang period now became family treasures.

The early period of Zhou rule, the eleventh through ninth centuries B.C.E., is sometimes called the Western Zhou era because of the location of the capitals in the western part of the kingdom. These centuries saw the development of a sophisticated administrative apparatus. The Zhou built a series of capital cities with pounded-earth foundations and walls. The major buildings all faced south, in keeping with an already ancient concern to orient structures so that they would be in a harmonious relationship with the terrain, the forces of wind, water, and sunlight, and the invisible energy perceived to be flowing through the natural world. All gov-

pearance of sacrificial offerings. In Ireland a ritual specialist ate the meat of a freshly-killed bull, lay down to sleep on the bull's hide, then had prophetic dreams. The most startling form of Celtic divination is described by the geographer Strabo:

> *The Romans put a stop to [the] customs . . . connected with sacrifice and divination, as they were in conflict with our own ways: for example, they would strike a man who had been consecrated for sacrifice in the back with a sword, and make prophecies based on his death-spasms.*

Reports about this and other Celtic practices, such as human sacrifice and the display of heads of conquered enemies, were used by the Romans to justify the conquest of Celtic peoples in order to "civilize" them.

Little is known for certain about the divinatory practices of early American peoples. The Olmec produced polished stone mirrors whose concave surfaces gave off reflected images that were thought to emanate from a supernatural realm. Painted basins found in Olmec households have been compared to those attested for later Mesoamerican groups. In the latter, women threw maize kernels onto the surface of water-filled basins and noted the patterns by which they floated or sank, in order to ascertain information useful to the family, such as the cause and cure of illness, the right time for agricultural tasks or marriage, and propitious names for newborn children.

It may seem surprising that divination is being treated here as a form of technology. Most modern people would regard such interpretations of patterns in everyday phenomena as mere superstition. However, within the context of the laws of nature as understood by ancient societies (the gods control and direct events in the natural world), divination involved the application of principles of causation to the socially beneficial task of acquiring information about what would happen in the future. These techniques were usually known only to a class of experts whose special training and knowledge gave them high status in their society.

Chinese Divination Shell After inscribing questions on a bone or shell, the diviner applied a red-hot point and interpreted the resulting cracks as a divine response. (Institute of History and Philology, Academia Sinica)

ernment officials, including the king, were supposed to be models of morality, fairness, and concern for the welfare of the people.

Like the Shang, the Zhou regime was highly decentralized. Members and allies of the royal family ruled more than a hundred largely autonomous territories. The court was the scene of elaborate ceremonials, embellished by music and dance, that impressed on observers the glory of Zhou rule and reinforced the bonds of obligation between rulers and ruled.

Around 800 B.C.E. Zhou power began to wane. Ambitious local rulers operated ever more independently and waged war on one another, while nomadic peoples attacked the northwest frontiers (see Map 3.1). The following five hundred years are sometimes referred to as the Eastern Zhou era. In 771 B.C.E. members of the Zhou lineage relocated to a new, more secure, eastern capital near Luoyang°, where they continued to hold the royal title and received at least nominal homage from the real power

Luoyang (LWOE-yahng)

brokers of the age. This was a time of political fragmentation, rapidly shifting centers of power, and fierce competition and warfare among numerous small and independent states. Historians conventionally divide Eastern Zhou into the "Spring and Autumn Period," from 771 to 481 B.C.E., after a collection of chronicles that give annual entries for those two seasons, and the "Warring States Period," from 480 to the unification of China in 221 B.C.E.

The many states of the Eastern Zhou era contended with one another for leadership. Cities, some of them quite large, spread across the Chinese landscape. Long walls of pounded earth, the ancestors of the Great Wall of China, protected the kingdoms from each other and from northern nomads. The Chinese also learned from the steppe nomads to put fighters on horseback. By 600 B.C.E. iron began to replace bronze as the primary metal for tools and weapons. There is mounting evidence that ironworking came to China from the nomadic peoples of the northwest. Subsequently, metalworkers in southern China, which had limited access to copper and tin for making bronze, were the first in the world to forge steel by removing carbon during the iron-smelting process.

In many of the states, bureaucrats expanded in number and function. Codes of law were written down. Governments collected taxes from the peasants directly, imposed standardized money, and managed large-scale public works projects. The wealth and power of the state and its demands for obedience were justified by an authoritarian political philosophy that came to be called **Legalism.** Legalist thinkers maintained that human nature is essentially wicked and that people behave in an orderly fashion only if compelled by strict laws and harsh punishments. Legalists believed that every aspect of human society ought to be controlled and personal freedom sacrificed for the good of the state.

Confucianism, Daoism, and Chinese Society

The governments of the major Zhou states took over many of the traditional functions of the aristocracy. To maintain their influence, aristocrats sought a new role as advisers to the rulers. One who lived through the political flux and social change of this anxious time was Kongzi (551–479 B.C.E.)— known in the West by the Latin form of his name, **Confucius.** Coming from one of the smaller states, he had not been particularly successful in obtaining administrative posts. His doctrine of duty and public service, initially aimed at fellow aristocrats, was to become a central influence in Chinese thought (see Diversity and Dominance: Hierarchy and Conduct in the Analects of Confucius).

Many elements in Confucius's teaching had roots in earlier Chinese belief, including folk religion and the rites of the Zhou royal family, such as the veneration of ancestors and elders and worship of the deity Heaven. Confucius drew a parallel between the family and the state. Just as the family is a hierarchy, with the father at its top, sons next, then wives and daughters in order of age, so too the state is a hierarchy, with the ruler at the top, the public officials as the sons, and the common people as the women.

Confucius took a traditional term for the feelings between family members (*ren*) and expanded it into a universal ideal of benevolence toward all humanity, which he believed was the foundation of moral government. Government exists, he said, to serve the people, and the administrator or ruler gains respect and authority by displaying fairness and integrity. Confucian teachings emphasized benevolence, avoidance of violence, justice, rationalism, loyalty, and dignity. Confucius, who held a far more optimistic view of the basic goodness of human nature than the adherents of Legalism, sought to affirm and maintain the political and social order by improving it.

It is ironic that Confucius, whose ideas were to become so important in Chinese thought, actually had little influence in his own time. His later follower Mencius (Mengzi, 371–289 B.C.E.), who opposed despotism and argued against the authoritarian political ideology of the Legalists, made Confucius's teachings much better known. In the era of the early emperors, Confucianism became the dominant political philosophy and the core of the educational system for government officials (see Chapter 6).

The Warring States Period also saw the rise of the school of thought known as **Daoism°.** According to tradition, Laozi°, the originator of Daoism (believed to have lived in the sixth century B.C.E., though some scholars doubt his existence), sought to stop the warfare of the age by urging humanity to follow the *Dao*, or "path." Daoists accept the world as they find it, avoiding useless struggles and adhering to the "path" of nature. They avoid violence if at all possible and take the minimal action necessary for a task. Rather than fight the current of a stream, a wise man allows the onrushing waters to pass around him. This passivity arises from the Daoist's sense that the world is always changing and lacks any absolute morality or meaning. In the end, Daoists believe, all that matters is the individual's fundamental understanding of the "path."

The original Daoist philosophy was greatly expanded in subsequent centuries to incorporate popular

Daoism (DOW-izm) **Laozi** (low-zuh)

beliefs, magic, and mysticism. Daoism represented an important stream of thought throughout Chinese history. By idealizing individuals who find their own "path" to right conduct, it offered an alternative to the Confucian emphasis on hierarchy and duty and to the Legalist approval of force.

Social organization also changed in this period. The kinship structures of the Shang and early Zhou periods, based on the clan (a relatively large group of related families), gave way to the three-generation family of grandparents, parents, and children as the fundamental social unit. A related development was the emergence of the concept of private property. Land was considered to belong to the men of the family and was divided equally among the sons when the father died.

Little is known about the conditions of life for women in early China. Some scholars believe that women may have acted as shamans, entering into trances to communicate with supernatural forces, making requests on behalf of their communities, and receiving predictions of the future. By the time written records begin to illuminate our knowledge of women's experiences, they show women in a subordinate position in the strongly patriarchal family.

Confucian thought codified this male-female hierarchy. Only men could conduct rituals and make offerings to the ancestors, though women could help maintain the household's ancestral shrines. Fathers held authority over the women and children, arranged marriages for their offspring, and could sell the labor of family members. A man was limited to one wife but was permitted additional sexual partners, who had the lower status of concubines. The elite classes used marriage to create political alliances, and it was common for the groom's family to offer a substantial "bride-gift," a proof of the wealth and standing of his family, to the family of the prospective bride. A man whose wife died had a duty to remarry in order to produce male heirs to keep alive the cult of the ancestors.

These differences in male and female activities were explained by the concept of **yin** and **yang,** the complementary nature of male and female roles in the natural order. The male principle (yin) was equated with the sun, active, bright, and shining; the female principle (yang) corresponded to the moon, passive, shaded, and reflective. Male toughness was balanced by female gentleness, male action and initiative by female endurance and need for completion, and male leadership by female supportiveness. In its earliest form, the theory considered yin and yang as equal and alternately dominant, like day and night, creating balance in the world. However, as a result of the changing role of women in the Zhou period and the pervasive influence of Confucian ideology, the male principle came to be seen as superior to the female.

The classical Chinese patterns of family, property, and bureaucracy took shape during the long centuries of Zhou rule and the competition among small states. At the end of this period the state of Qin°, whose aggressive and disciplined policies made it the premier power among the warring states, defeated all rivals and unified China (see Chapter 6).

Nubia, 3100 B.C.E.–350 C.E.

Since the first century B.C.E. the name *Nubia* has been applied to a thousand-mile (1,600-kilometer) stretch of the Nile Valley lying between Aswan and Khartoum° and straddling the southern part of the modern nation of Egypt and the northern part of Sudan (see Map 3.2). The ancient Egyptians called it Ta-sety, meaning "Land of the Bow," after the favorite weapon of its warriors. Nubia is the only continuously inhabited stretch of territory connecting sub-Saharan Africa (the lands south of the vast Sahara Desert) with North Africa. For thousands of years it has served as a corridor for trade between tropical Africa and the Mediterranean. Nubia was richly endowed with natural resources such as gold, copper, and semiprecious stones.

Nubia's location and natural wealth, along with Egypt's quest for Nubian gold, explain the early rise of a civilization with a complex political organization, social stratification, metallurgy, monumental building, and writing. Nubia traditionally was considered a periphery, or outlying region, of Egypt, and its culture was regarded as derivative. Now, however, most scholars emphasize the interactions between Egypt and Nubia and the mutually beneficial borrowings and syntheses that took place, and there is growing evidence that Nubian culture drew on influences from sub-Saharan Africa.

Early Cultures and Egyptian Domination, 2300–1100 B.C.E.

The central geographical feature of Nubia, as of Egypt, is the Nile River. This part of the Nile flows through a landscape of rocky desert, grassland, and fertile plain. River irrigation

Qin (chin) **Khartoum** (kahr-TOOM)

Diversity and Dominance

Hierarchy and Conduct in the Analects of Confucius

The Analects are a collection of sayings of Confucius, probably compiled and written down several generations after he lived, though some elements may have been added even later. They cover a wide range of matters, including ethics, government, education, music, and rituals. Taken as a whole, they are a guide to living a proper, honorable, virtuous, useful, and satisfying life. While subject to reinterpretation according to the circumstances of the times, Confucian principles have had a great influence on Chinese values and behavior ever since.

Chinese society in Confucius's time was very attuned to distinctions of status. Confucius assumed that hierarchy is innate in the order of the universe and that human society should echo and harmonize with the natural world. Each person has a role to play, with prescribed rules of conduct and proper ceremonial behavior, in order to maintain the social order. The following selections illuminate the particular attention paid by Confucius to the important status categories in his society, the proper way for individuals to treat others, and the necessity of hierarchy and inequality.

1:6 Confucius said: "A young man should serve his parents at home and be respectful to elders outside his home. He should be earnest and truthful, loving all, but become intimate with *ren* [an inner capacity, possessed by all human beings, to do good]. After doing this, if he has energy to spare, he can study literature and the arts."

4:18 Confucius said: "When you serve your mother and father it is okay to try to correct them once in a while. But if you see that they are not going to listen to you, keep your respect for them and don't distance yourself from them. Work without complaining."

2:5 Meng Yi Zi asked about the meaning of filial piety. Confucius said, "It means 'not diverging (from your parents).'" Later, when Fan Chi was driving him, Confucius told Fan Chi, "Meng asked me about the meaning of filial piety, and I told him 'not diverging.'" Fan Chi said, "What did you mean by that?" Confucius said, "When your parents are alive, serve them with propriety; when they die, bury them with propriety, and then worship them with propriety."

1:2 Master You said: "There are few who have developed themselves filially and fraternally who enjoy offending their superiors. Those who do not enjoy offending superiors are never troublemakers. The Superior Man concerns himself with the fundamentals. Once the fundamentals are established, the proper way (*dao*) appears. Are not filial piety and obedience to elders fundamental to the enactment of *ren*?"

1:8 Confucius said: "If the Superior Man is not 'heavy,' then he will not inspire awe in others. If he is not learned, then he will not be on firm ground. He takes loyalty and good faith to be of primary importance, and has no friends who are not of equal (moral) caliber. When he makes a mistake, he doesn't hesitate to correct it."

4:5 Confucius said, "Riches and honors are what all men desire. But if they cannot be attained in accordance with the *dao* they should not be kept. Poverty and low status are what all men hate. But if they cannot be avoided while staying in accordance with the *dao*, you should not avoid them. If a Superior Man departs from *ren*, how can he be worthy of that name? A Superior Man never leaves *ren* for even the time of a single meal. In moments of haste he acts according to it. In times of difficulty or confusion he acts according to it."

15:20 Confucius said: "The Superior Man seeks within himself. The inferior man seeks within others."

16:8 Confucius said: "The Superior Man stands in awe of three things:

(1) He is in awe of the decree of Heaven.
(2) He is in awe of great men.
(3) He is in awe of the words of the sages.

The inferior man does not know the decree of Heaven; takes great men lightly and laughs at the words of the sages."

4:14 Confucius said: "I don't worry about not having a good position; I worry about the means I use to gain position. I don't worry about being unknown; I seek to be known in the right way."

7:15 Confucius said: "I can live with coarse rice to eat, water for drink and my arm as a pillow and still be happy. Wealth and honors that one possesses in the midst of injustice are like floating clouds."

4:17 Confucius said: "When you see a good person, think of becoming like her/him. When you see someone not so good, reflect on your own weak points."

13:6 Confucius said: "When you have gotten your own life straightened out, things will go well without your giving orders. But if your own life isn't straightened out, even if you give orders, no one will follow them."

12:2 Zhonggong asked about the meaning of *ren.* The Master said: "Go out of your home as if you were receiving an important guest. Employ the people as if you were assisting at a great ceremony. What you don't want done to yourself, don't do to others. Live in your town without stirring up resentments, and live in your household without stirring up resentments."

1:5 Confucius said: "If you would govern a state of a thousand chariots (a small-to-middle-size state), you must pay strict attention to business, be true to your word, be economical in expenditure and love the people. You should use them according to the seasons."

2:3 Confucius said: "If you govern the people legalistically and control them by punishment, they will avoid crime, but have no personal sense of shame. If you govern them by means of virtue and control them with propriety, they will gain their own sense of shame, and thus correct themselves."

12:7 Zigong asked about government.

The Master said, "Enough food, enough weapons and the confidence of the people."

Zigong said, "Suppose you had no alternative but to give up one of these three, which one would be let go of first?"

The Master said, "Weapons."

Zigong said "What if you had to give up one of the remaining two which one would it be?"

The Master said, "Food. From ancient times, death has come to all men, but a people without confidence in its rulers will not stand."

12:19 Ji Kang Zi asked Confucius about government saying: "Suppose I were to kill the unjust, in order to advance the just. Would that be all right?"

Confucius replied: "In doing government, what is the need of killing? If you desire good, the people will be good. The nature of the Superior Man is like the wind, the nature of the inferior man is like the grass. When the wind blows over the grass, it always bends."

2:19 The Duke of Ai asked: "How can I make the people follow me?" Confucius replied: "Advance the upright and set aside the crooked, and the people will follow you. Advance the crooked and set aside the upright, and the people will not follow you."

2:20 Ji Kang Zi asked: "How can I make the people reverent and loyal, so they will work positively for me?" Confucius said, "Approach them with dignity, and they will be reverent. Be filial and compassionate and they will be loyal. Promote the able and teach the incompetent, and they will work positively for you."

QUESTIONS FOR ANALYSIS

1. **What are the important social categories and status distinctions in early China? What kinds of behaviors are expected of individuals in particular social categories toward individuals in other categories?**
2. **How does Confucius explain and justify the inequalities among people? Why is it important for people to behave in appropriate ways toward others?**
3. **How does the experience of family life prepare an individual to conduct himself or herself properly in the wider spheres of community and state?**
4. **Which personal qualities and kinds of actions will allow a ruler to govern successfully? Why might Confucius's passionate concern for ethical behavior on the part of officials and rulers arise at a time when the size and power of governments was growing?**

Source: From "Hierarchy and Conduct in the Analects of Confucius," translated by Charles Muller, as seen at http://www.human.toyogakuen-u.ac.jp/~acmuller/contao/analects.htm.

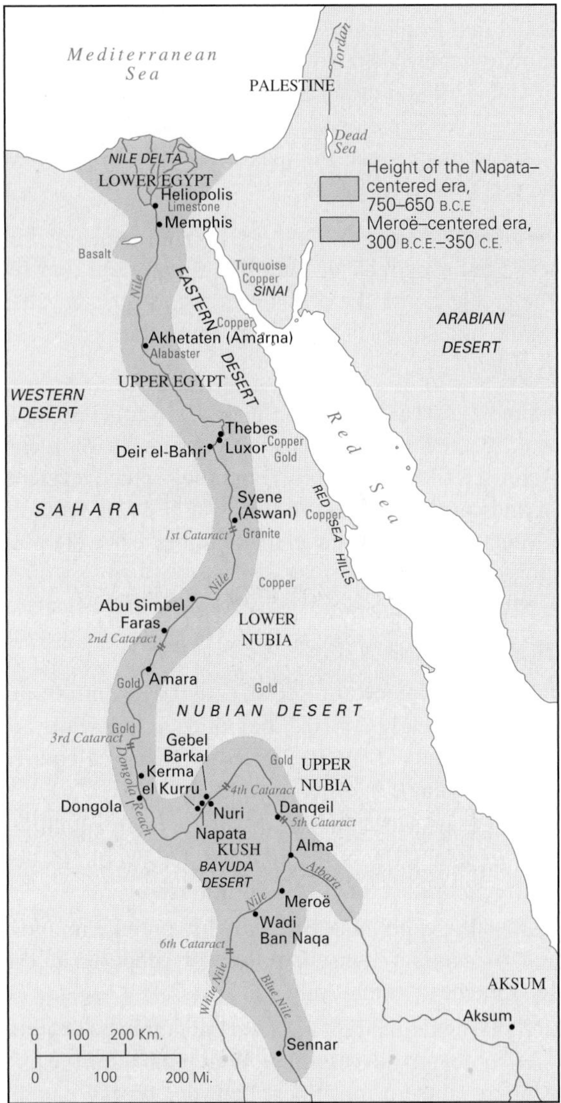

Map 3.2 Ancient Nubia The land route alongside the Nile River as it flows through Nubia has long served as a corridor connecting sub-Saharan Africa with North Africa. The centuries of Egyptian occupation, as well as time spent in Egypt by Nubian hostages, mercenaries, and merchants, led to a marked Egyptian cultural influence in Nubia. (Based on Map 15 from *The Historical Atlas of Africa*, ed. by J. F. Ajyi and Michael Crowder. Reprinted by permission of Addison Wesley Longman Ltd.)

was essential for agriculture in a climate that was severely hot and, in the north, nearly without rainfall. Six cataracts, barriers formed by large boulders and rapids, obstructed boat traffic. Commerce and travel were achieved by boats operating between the cataracts and by caravan tracks alongside the river or across the desert.

In the fourth millennium B.C.E. bands of people in northern Nubia made the transition from seminomadic hunting and gathering to a settled life based on grain agriculture and cattle herding. From this time on, the majority of the population lived in agricultural villages alongside the river. Even before 3000 B.C.E. Nubia served as a corridor for long-distance commerce. Egyptian craftsmen of the period were working in ivory and in ebony wood—products of tropical Africa that had to have come through Nubia.

Nubia enters the historical record around 2300 B.C.E. in Old Kingdom Egyptian accounts of trade missions to southern lands. At that time Aswan, just north of the First Cataract, was the southern limit of Egyptian control. As we saw with the journey of Harkhuf at the beginning of this chapter, Egyptian noblemen stationed there led donkey caravans south in search of gold, incense, ebony, ivory, slaves, and exotic animals from tropical Africa. This was dangerous work, requiring delicate negotiations with local Nubian chiefs in order to secure protection, but it brought substantial rewards to those who succeeded.

During the Middle Kingdom (ca. 2040–1640 B.C.E.), Egypt adopted a more aggressive stance toward Nubia. Egyptian rulers sought to control the gold mines in the desert east of the Nile and to cut out the Nubian middlemen who drove up the cost of luxury goods from the tropics. The Egyptians erected a string of mud-brick forts on islands and riverbanks south of the Second Cataract. The forts protected the southern frontier of Egypt against Nubians and nomadic raiders from the desert, and regulated the flow of commerce. There seem to have been peaceable relations but little interaction between the Egyptian garrisons and the indigenous population of northern Nubia, which continued to practice its age-old farming and herding ways.

Farther south, where the Nile makes a great U-shaped turn in the fertile plain of the Dongola Reach (see Map 3.2), a more complex political entity was evolving from the chiefdoms of the third millennium B.C.E. The Egyptians gave the name **Kush** to the kingdom whose capital was located at Kerma, one of the earliest urbanized centers in tropical Africa. Beginning around 1750 B.C.E. the kings of Kush marshaled a labor force to build monumental walls and structures of mud brick. The dozens or even hundreds of servants and wives sacrificed for burial with the kings, as well as the rich objects found in their tombs, testify to the wealth and power of the rulers of Kush and suggest a belief in some sort of afterlife in which attendants and possessions would be useful. Kushite craftsmen were skilled in metalworking, whether for weapons or jewelry, and their pottery surpassed anything produced in Egypt.

Temple of the Lion-Headed God Apedemak at Naqa in Nubia, First Century C.E. Queen Amanitore (right) and her husband, Natakamani, are shown slaying their enemies. The architectural forms are Egyptian, but the deity is Nubian. The costumes of the monarchs and the important role of the queen also reflect the trend in the Meroitic era to draw upon sub-Saharan cultural practices. (P. L. Shinnie)

During the expansionist New Kingdom (ca. 1532–1070 B.C.E.) the Egyptians penetrated more deeply into Nubia (see Chapter 4). They destroyed Kush and its capital and extended their frontier to the Fourth Cataract. A high-ranking Egyptian official called "Overseer of Southern Lands" or "King's Son of Kush" ruled Nubia from a new administrative center at Napata°, near Gebel Barkal°, the "Holy Mountain," believed to be the home of a local god. In an era of intense commerce among the states of the Middle East, when everyone was looking to Egypt as the prime source of gold, Egypt exploited the mines of Nubia at considerable human cost. Fatalities were high among native workers in the brutal desert climate, and the army had to ward off attacks from desert nomads.

Five hundred years of Egyptian domination in Nubia left many marks. The Egyptian government imposed Egyptian culture on the native population. Children from elite families were brought to the Egyptian royal court to guarantee the good behavior of their relatives in Nubia; they absorbed Egyptian language, culture, and religion, which they later carried home with them. Other Nubians served as archers in the Egyptian armed forces. The manufactured goods that they brought back to Nubia have been found in their graves. The Nubians built towns on the Egyptian model and erected stone temples to Egyptian gods, particularly Amon. The frequent depiction of Amon with the head of a ram may reflect a blending of the chief Egyptian god with a Nubian ram deity.

The Kingdom of Meroë, 800 B.C.E.–350 C.E.

Egypt's weakness after 1200 B.C.E. led to the collapse of its authority in Nubia. In the eighth century B.C.E. a powerful new native kingdom emerged in southern Nubia. The story of this civilization, which lasted for over a thousand years, can be divided into two parts. During the early period, between the eighth and fourth centuries B.C.E., Napata, the former Egyptian headquarters, was the primary center. During the later period, from the fourth century B.C.E. to the fourth century C.E., the center was farther south, at **Meroë°,** near the Sixth Cataract.

For half a century, from around 712 to 660 B.C.E., the kings of Nubia ruled all of Egypt as the Twenty-fifth Dynasty. They conducted themselves in the age-old manner of Egyptian rulers. They were addressed by royal titles, depicted in traditional costume, and buried ac-

Napata (nah-PAH-tuh) **Gebel Barkal** (JEB-uhl BAHR-kahl)

Meroë (MER-oh-ee)

cording to Egyptian custom. However, they kept their Nubian names and were depicted with physical features suggesting peoples of sub-Saharan Africa. They inaugurated an artistic and cultural renaissance, building on a monumental scale for the first time in centuries and reinvigorating Egyptian art, architecture, and religion. The Nubian kings resided at Memphis, the Old Kingdom capital, while Thebes, the New Kingdom capital, was the residence of a celibate female member of the king's family who was titled "God's Wife of Amon."

The Nubian dynasty made a disastrous mistake in 701 B.C.E. when it offered help to local rulers in Palestine who were struggling against the Assyrian Empire. The Assyrians retaliated by invading Egypt and driving the Nubian monarchs back to their southern domain by 660 B.C.E. Napata again became the chief royal residence and religious center of the kingdom. Egyptian cultural influences remained strong. Court documents continued to be written in Egyptian hieroglyphs, and the mummified remains of the rulers were buried in modestly sized sandstone pyramids along with hundreds of shawabti° figurines.

By the fourth century B.C.E. the center of gravity had shifted south to Meroë, perhaps because Meroë was better situated for agriculture and trade, the economic mainstays of the Nubian kingdom. As a result, sub-Saharan cultural patterns gradually replaced Egyptian ones. Egyptian hieroglyphs gave way to a new set of symbols, still essentially undeciphered, for writing the Meroitic language. People continued to worship Amon as well as Isis, an Egyptian goddess connected to fertility and sexuality. But those deities had to share the stage with Nubian deities like the lion-god Apedemak, and elephants had some religious significance. Meroitic art combined Egyptian, Greco-Roman, and indigenous traditions.

Women of the royal family played an important role in Meroitic politics, another reflection of the influence of sub-Saharan Africa. The Nubians employed a matrilineal system in which the king was succeeded by the son of his sister. Nubian queens sometimes ruled by themselves and sometimes in partnership with their husbands. Greek, Roman, and biblical sources refer to a queen of Nubia named Candace. Since these sources relate to different times, *Candace* was probably a title rather than a proper name. At least seven queens ruled between 284 B.C.E. and 115 C.E. They played a part in warfare, diplomacy, and the building of temples and pyramid tombs. They are depicted in scenes reserved for male rulers in Egyptian imagery, smiting enemies in battle and being suckled by the mother-goddess Isis. Roman sources marvel at the fierce resistance put up by a one-eyed warrior-queen.

Meroë was a huge city for its time, more than a square mile in area, overlooking fertile grasslands and dominating converging trade routes. Much of the city is still buried under the sand. In 2002 archaeologists using a magnetometer to detect buried structures discovered a large palace and will soon begin excavation. Great reservoirs were dug to catch precious rainfall. The city was a major center for iron smelting (after 1000 B.C.E. iron had replaced bronze as the primary metal for tools and weapons). The Temple of Amon was approached by an avenue of stone rams, and the enclosed "Royal City" was filled with palaces, temples, and administrative buildings. The ruler, who may have been regarded as divine, was assisted by a professional class of officials, priests, and army officers.

Meroë collapsed in the early fourth century C.E. It may have been overrun by nomads from the western desert who had become more mobile because of the arrival of the camel in North Africa. Meroë had already been weakened when profitable commerce with the Roman Empire was diverted to the Red Sea and to the rising kingdom of Aksum° (in present-day Ethiopia). In any case, the end of the Meroitic kingdom, and of this phase of civilization in Nubia, was as closely linked to Nubia's role in long-distance commerce as had been its beginning.

CELTIC EUROPE, 1000–50 B.C.E.

The southern peninsulas of Europe—present-day Spain, Italy, and Greece—are surrounded on three sides by the Mediterranean Sea, share in the relatively mild climate of all the Mediterranean lands, and are separated from "continental" Europe to the north by high mountains (the Pyrenees and Alps). For all these reasons, the history of southern Europe in antiquity is primarily connected to that of the Middle East, at least until the Roman conquests north of the Alps (see Chapters 4, 5, and 6).

Continental Europe (including the modern nations of France, Germany, Switzerland, Austria, the Czech Republic, Slovakia, Hungary, Poland, and Romania—see Map 3.3) is well-suited to agriculture and herding. It contains broad plains with good soil and has a temperate climate with cold winters, warm summers, and ample rainfall. It is well-endowed with natural resources, such as timber and metals, and large, navigable rivers

shawabti (shuh-WAB-tee)

Aksum (AHK-soom)

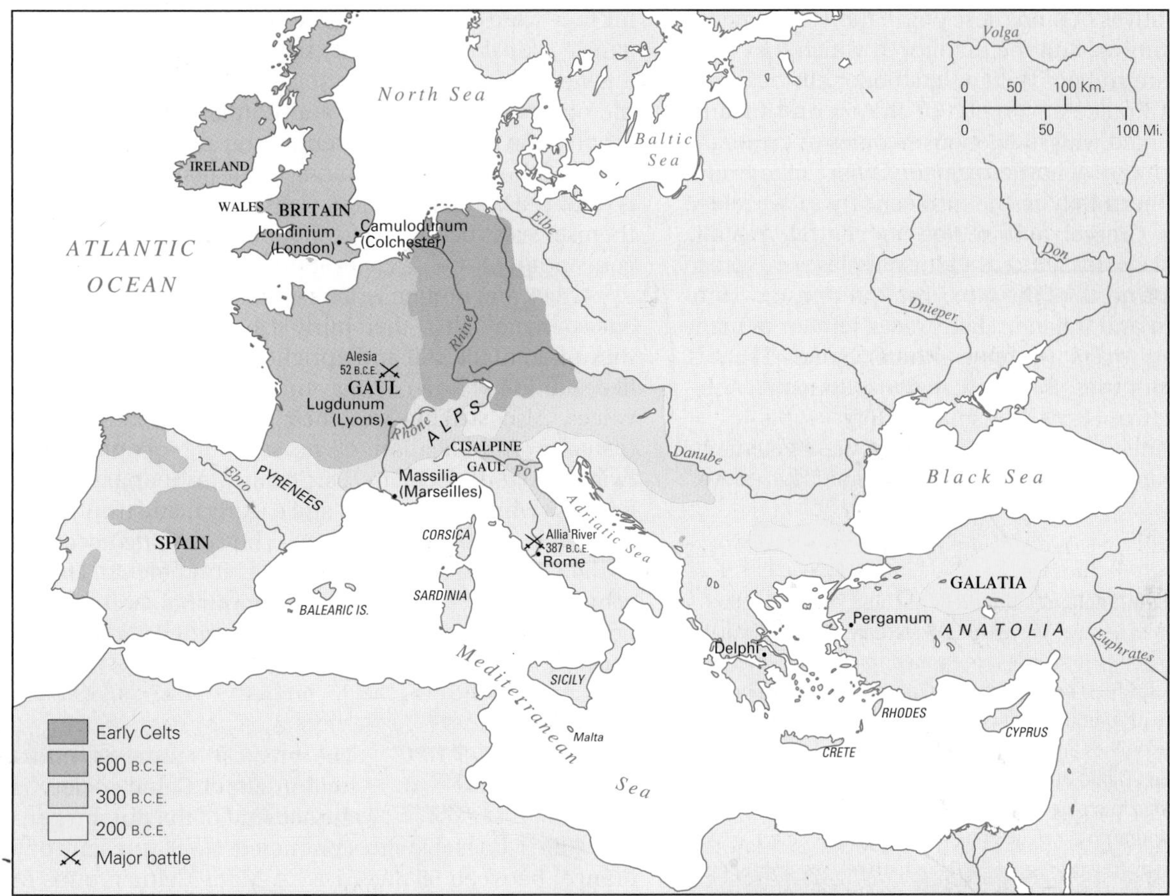

Map 3.3 The Celtic Peoples Celtic civilization originated in Central Europe in the early part of the first millennium B.C.E. Around 500 B.C.E. Celtic peoples began to migrate, making Celtic civilization the dominant cultural style in Europe north of the Alps. The Celts' interactions with the peoples of the Mediterranean, including Greeks and Romans, encompassed both warfare and trade. (From *Atlas of Classical History*, Fifth Edition, by Michael Grant. Copyright © 1994 by Michael Grant. Used by permission of Oxford University Press, Inc.)

(the Rhone, Rhine, and Danube) facilitate travel and trade.

Humans were living in this part of Europe for many thousands of years (see Chapter 1), but their lack of any system of writing severely limits our knowledge of the earliest inhabitants. Around 500 B.C.E. Celtic peoples spread across a substantial portion of Europe and, by coming into contact with the literate societies of the Mediterranean, entered the historical record. Information about the early **Celts**° comes from the archaeological record, the accounts of Greek and Roman travelers and conquerors, and the Celtic literature of Wales and Ireland that originated in oral traditions and was written down during the European Middle Ages.

Celts (kelts)

The Spread of the Celts

The term *Celtic* is a linguistic designation, referring to a branch of the Indo-European family of languages found throughout Europe and in west and south Asia. Scholars link the Celtic language group to archaeological remains first appearing in parts of present-day Germany, Austria, and the Czech Republic after 1000 B.C.E. (see Map 3.3). Many early Celts lived in or near hill-forts—lofty natural locations made more defensible by earthwork fortifications. By 500 B.C.E. Celtic elites were trading with Mediterranean societies for crafted goods and wine. This contact may have stimulated the new styles of Celtic manufacture and art that appeared at this time.

These new cultural features coincided with a period in which Celtic groups migrated to many parts of Europe. The motives behind these population movements, the precise timing, and the manner in which they were carried out are still not well understood. Celts occupied nearly all of France and much of Britain and Ireland, and they merged with indigenous peoples to create the Celtiberian culture of northern Spain. Other Celtic groups overran northern Italy in the fifth century B.C.E., raided into central Greece, and settled in central Anatolia (modern Turkey). By 300 B.C.E. Celtic peoples were spread across Europe north of the Alps, from present-day Hungary to Spain and Ireland. Their traces remain in many place names: rivers (Danube, Rhine, Seine, Thames, Shannon); countries (Belgium); regions (Bohemia, Aquitaine); and towns (Paris, Bologna, Leiden).

These widely diffused Celtic groups shared elements of language and culture, but there was no Celtic "state," for they were divided into hundreds of small, loosely organized kinship groups. In the past scholars built up a generic picture of Celtic society derived largely from the observations of Greek and Roman writers. Current scholarship is focusing attention on the differences as much as the similarities among Celtic peoples. Indeed, it is doubtful whether ancient Celts would have identified themselves as belonging to anything akin to our modern conception of "Celtic civilization."

Greek and Roman writers were struck by the appearance of male Celts—their burly size, long red hair (which they often made stiff and upright by applying a cement-like solution of lime), shaggy mustaches, and loud, deep voices. Also striking was their strange apparel: pants (usually an indication of horse-riding peoples) and twisted gold neck collars. Particularly terrifying were the warriors who fought naked and eagerly made trophies of the heads of defeated enemies. The surviving accounts of the Celts describe them as wildly fond of war, courageous, childishly impulsive and emotional, and fond of boasting and exaggeration, yet quick-witted and eager to learn.

Celtic Hill-Fort in England Hundreds of these fortresses have been found across Europe. They served as centers of administration, gathering points for Celtic armies, manufacturing centers, storage depots for food and trade goods, and places of refuge. The natural defense offered by a hill could be improved, as here, by the construction of ditches and earthwork walls. Particularly effective was the so-called Gallic Wall, made of a combination of earth, stone, and timber to create both strength and enough flexibility to absorb the pounding from siege engines. (English Heritage)

Celtic Society

The greatest source of information about Celtic society is the account of the Roman general Julius Caesar, who conquered Gaul (present-day France) between 58 and 51 B.C.E. Many Celtic groups in Gaul had once been ruled by kings, but by about 60 B.C.E. they periodically chose public officials, perhaps under Greek and Roman influence.

Celtic society, according to Greek and Roman commentators, was divided into an elite class of warriors, professional groups of priests and bards (singers of poems about glorious deeds of the past), and commoners (the largest group of all). The warriors owned land and flocks of cattle and sheep and monopolized both wealth and power. The common people labored on their land. The Celts built houses (usually round in Britain, rectangular in France) out of wattle and daub—a wooden framework filled in with clay and straw—with thatched straw roofs. An enclosure containing several such houses belonging to related families might be surrounded by a wooden fence to protect people and domestic animals from wild animals.

The warriors of Welsh and Irish legend reflect a stage of political and social development less complex than that of the Celts in Gaul. They raided one another's flocks, reveled in drunken feasts, and engaged in contests of strength and wit. At banquets warriors would fight to the death just to claim the choicest cut of the meat, the "hero's portion."

The Gundestrup Cauldron This silver vessel was found in a peat bog in Denmark, but must have come from elsewhere. It is usually dated to the second or first century B.C.E. On the inside left are Celtic warriors on horse and on foot, with lozenge-shaped shields and long battle-horns. On the inside right is a horned deity, possibly Cernunnos. (The National Museum of Denmark)

Druids, the Celtic priests in Gaul and Britain, formed a well-organized fraternity that performed religious, judicial, and educational functions. Trainees spent years memorizing prayers, secret rituals, legal precedents, and other traditions. The priesthood was the one Celtic institution that crossed tribal lines. The Druids sometimes headed off warfare between feuding groups and served as judges in cases involving Celts from different groups. In the first century C.E. the Roman government attempted to stamp out the Druids, probably because of concern that they might serve as a rallying point for Celtic opposition to Roman rule, as well as because of their involvement in human sacrifices.

The Celts were successful farmers, able to support large populations by tilling the heavy but fertile soils of continental Europe. Their metallurgical skills probably surpassed those of the Mediterranean peoples. Celts living on the Atlantic shore of France built sturdy ships that braved ocean conditions, and they developed extensive trade networks along Europe's large, navigable rivers. One lucrative commodity was tin, which Celtic traders from southwest England brought to Greek buyers in southern France. By the first century B.C.E some hill-forts were evolving into urban centers.

Women's lives were focused on child rearing, food production, and some crafts. Celtic women did not have true equality with men, but their situation was superior to that of women in the Middle East and in the Greek and Roman Mediterranean. Greek and Roman sources depict Celtic women as strong and proud. Welsh and Irish tales portray self-assured women who sat at banquets with their husbands, engaged in witty conversation, and provided ingenious solutions to vexing problems. Marriage was a partnership to which both parties contributed property. Each party had the right to inherit the estate if the other died. Celtic women also had greater freedom in their sexual relations than did their southern counterparts.

Tombs of elite women have yielded rich collections of clothing, jewelry, and furniture for use in the next world. Daughters of the elite were married to leading members of other tribes to create alliances. When the Romans invaded Celtic Britain in the first century C.E., they sometimes were opposed by Celtic tribes headed by queens, although some experts see this as an abnormal circumstance created by the Roman invasion itself.

Belief and Knowledge

Historians know the names of more than four hundred Celtic gods and goddesses, mostly associated with particular localities or kinship groups. More widely revered deities included Lug°, the god of light, crafts, and inventions; the horse-goddess Epona°; and the horned god Cernunnos°. "The Mothers," three goddesses depicted together holding symbols of abundance, probably played a part in a fertility cult. Halloween and May Day preserve the

Lug (loog) **Epona** (eh-POH-nuh) **Cernunnos** (KURN-you-nuhs)

ancient Celtic holidays of Samhain° and Beltaine° respectively, which took place at key moments in the agricultural cycle.

The early Celts did not build temples, but instead worshipped wherever they felt the presence of divinity—at springs, groves, and hilltops. At the sources of the Seine and Marne Rivers in France, archaeologists have found huge caches of Celtic wooden statues thrown into the water by worshippers.

The burial of elite members of early Celtic society in wagons filled with extensive grave goods suggests belief in some sort of afterlife. In Irish and Welsh legends, heroes and gods pass back and forth between the natural and supernatural worlds much more readily than in the mythology of other cultures, and magical occurrences are commonplace. Celtic priests set forth a doctrine of reincarnation—the rebirth of the soul in a new body. In contrast, other ancient peoples in Europe and western Asia believed that the barrier separating life from death could not be crossed.

The Roman conquest from the second century B.C.E. to the first century C.E. of Spain, southern Britain, France, and parts of Central Europe curtailed the evolution of Celtic society. The peoples in these lands were largely assimilated to Roman ways (see Chapter 6). That is why the inhabitants of modern Spain and France speak languages that are descended from Latin. From the third century C.E. on, Germanic invaders diminished the Celts still further, and the English language has a Germanic base. Only on the western fringes of the European continent—in Brittany (northwest France), Wales, Scotland, and Ireland—did Celtic peoples maintain their language, art, and culture into modern times.

FIRST CIVILIZATIONS OF THE AMERICAS: THE OLMEC AND CHAVÍN, 1200–250 B.C.E.

Humans reached the Western Hemisphere through a series of migrations from Asia (see Chapter 1). Some scholars believe that the first migrations occurred as early as 35,000 to 25,000 B.C.E., but most accept a later date of 20,000 to 13,000 B.C.E. Although some limited contacts with other cultures—for example, with Polynesians—may have occurred later, the peoples in the Western Hemisphere were virtually isolated from the rest of the world for at least fifteen thousand years. The duration and comprehensiveness of their isolation distinguishes the Americas from the world's other major cultural regions. While technological innovations passed back and forth among the civilizations of Asia, Africa, and Europe, the peoples of the Americas faced the challenges of the natural environment on their own.

Over thousands of years the population of the Americas grew and spread throughout the hemisphere, responding to environments that included frozen regions of the polar extremes, tropical rain forests, and high mountain ranges as well as deserts, woodlands, and prairies. Two of the hemisphere's most impressive cultural traditions developed in Mesoamerica (Mexico and northern Central America) and in the mountainous Andean region of South America. Well before 1000 B.C.E. the domestication of new plant varieties, the introduction of new technologies, and a limited development of trade led to greater social stratification and the beginnings of urbanization in both regions. Cultural elites associated with these changes used their increased political and religious authority to organize great numbers of laborers to construct large-scale irrigation and drainage works, to clear forests, and to unleash the productive potential of floodplains and steeply pitched hillsides. These transformed environments provided the economic platform for the construction of urban centers dominated by monumental structures devoted to religious purposes and to housing for members of the elite. By 1000 B.C.E. the major urban centers of Mesoamerica and the Andes had begun to project their political and cultural power over broad territories: they had become civilizations. The cultural legacies of the two most important of these early civilizations, the Olmec of Mesoamerica and Chavín of the Andes, would persist for more than a thousand years.

The Mesoamerican Olmec, 1200–400 B.C.E.

Mesoamerica is a region of great geographic and climatic diversity. It is extremely active geologically, experiencing both earthquakes and volcanic eruptions. Mountain ranges break the region into micro environments, including the temperate climates of the Valley of Mexico and the Guatemalan highlands, the tropical forests of the Peten and Gulf of Mexico coast, the rain forest of the southern Yucatán and Belize, and the drier scrub forest of the northern Yucatán (see Map 3.4).

Within these ecological niches, Amerindian peoples developed specialized technologies that exploited indigenous plants and animals, as well as minerals like obsidian, quartz, and jade. Eventually, contacts across these environmental boundaries led to trade and cultural ex-

Samhain (SAH-win) **Beltaine** (BEHL-tayn)

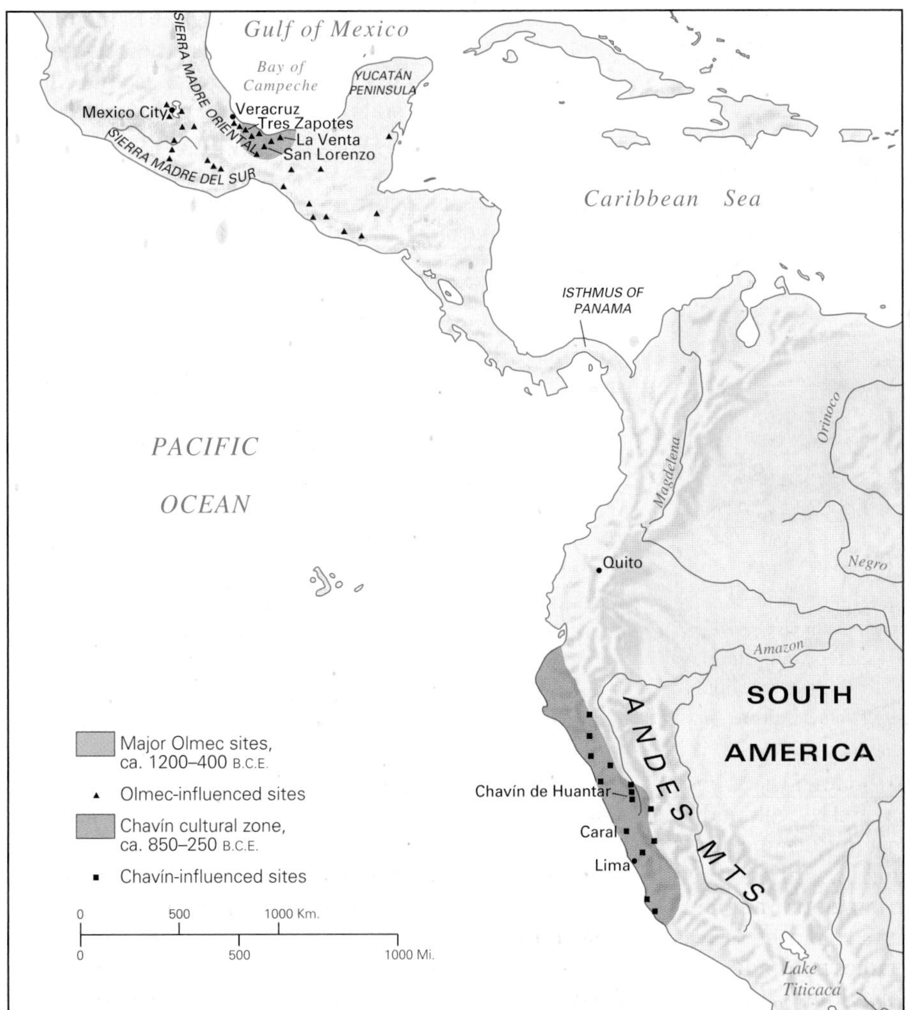

Map 3.4 Olmec and Chavín Civilizations The regions of Mesoamerica (most of modern Mexico and Central America) and the Andean highlands of South America have hosted impressive civilizations since early times. The civilizations of the Olmec and Chavín were the originating civilizations of these two regions, providing the foundations of architecture, city planning, and religion.

change. Enhanced trade, increasing agricultural productivity, and rising population led, in turn, to urbanization and the gradual appearance of powerful political and religious elites. Although a number of militarily powerful civilizations developed in Mesoamerica, the region was never unified politically. All Mesoamerican civilizations, however, shared fundamental elements of material culture, technology, religious belief and ritual, political organization, art, architecture, and sports.

The most influential early Mesoamerican civilization was the **Olmec,** flourishing between 1200 and 400 B.C.E. (see Map 3.4). The center of Olmec civilization was located near the tropical Atlantic coast of what are now the Mexican states of Veracruz and Tabasco. Olmec cultural influence reached as far as the Pacific coast of Central America and the Central Plateau of Mexico.

Olmec urban development was made possible by earlier advances in agriculture. Original settlements depended on the region's rich plant diversity and on fishing. Later, by 3500 B.C.E or earlier, the staples of the Mesoamerican diet—corn, beans, and squash—were domesticated. Recent research indicates that manioc, a calorie-rich root crop, was also grown in the floodplains of the region, multiplying food resources. The ability of farmers to produce dependable surpluses of these products permitted the first stages of craft specialization and social stratification. As religious and political elites emerged, they used their prestige and authority to organize the population to dig irrigation and drainage canals, develop raised fields in wetlands that could be farmed more intensively, and construct the large-scale religious and civic buildings that became the cultural signature of Olmec civilization.

The cultural core of the early Olmec civilization was located at San Lorenzo but included smaller centers

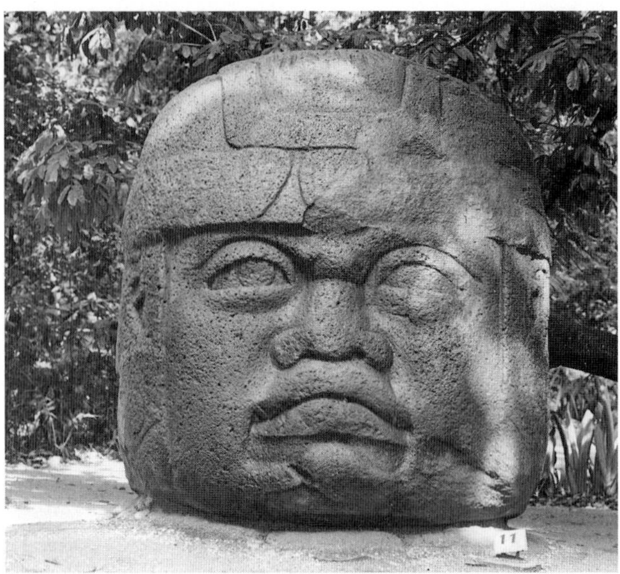

Olmec Head Giant heads sculpted from basalt are a widely recognized legacy of Olmec culture. Sixteen heads have been found, the largest approximately 11 feet (3.4 meters) tall. Experts in Olmec archaeology believe the heads are portraits of individual rulers, warriors, or ballplayers. (Georg Gerster/Photo Researchers, Inc.)

nearby (1200–900 B.C.E.). La Venta°, which developed at about the same time, became the most important Olmec center after 900 B.C.E. when San Lorenzo was abandoned or destroyed. Tres Zapotes° was the last dominant center, rising to prominence after La Venta collapsed or was destroyed around 600 B.C.E. The relationship among these centers is unclear. Scholars have found little evidence to suggest that they were either rival city states or dependent centers of a centralized political authority. It appears that each center developed independently to exploit and exchange specialized products like salt, cacao (chocolate beans), clay for ceramics, and limestone. Each major Olmec center was eventually abandoned, its monuments defaced and buried and its buildings destroyed. Archaeologists interpret these events differently; some see them as evidence of internal upheavals or military defeat by neighboring peoples, and others suggest that they were rituals associated with the death of a ruler.

Large artificial platforms and mounds of packed earth dominated Olmec urban centers and served to frame the collective ritual and political activities that brought the rural population to the cities at special times in the year. Some of the platforms also served as foundations for elite residences, in effect lifting the elite above the masses. The Olmec laid out their cities in alignment with the paths of certain stars, reflecting their strong belief in the significance of astronomical events. Since these centers had small permanent populations, the scale of construction suggests that the Olmec elite was able to require and direct the labor of thousands of men and women from surrounding settlements and dispersed family plots in the region. This labor pool was used primarily for low-skill tasks like moving dirt and stone construction materials. Skilled artisans who lived in or near the urban core decorated the buildings with carvings and sculptures. They also produced the high-quality crafts, such as exquisite carved jade figurines, necklaces, and ceremonial knives and axes, that distinguished Olmec culture. Archaeological evidence suggests the existence of a class of merchants who traded with distant peoples for obsidian, jade, and pottery.

Little is known about Olmec political structure, but it seems likely that the rise of major urban centers coincided with the appearance of a form of kingship that combined religious and secular roles. Finely crafted objects decorated the households of the elite and distinguished their dress from that of the commoners who lived in dispersed small structures constructed of sticks and mud. The authority of the rulers and their kin groups is suggested by a series of colossal carved stone heads, some as large as 11 feet (3.4 meters) high. Since each head is unique and suggestive of individual personality, most archaeologists believe they were carved to memorialize individual rulers. This theory is reinforced by the location of the heads close to the major urban centers, especially San Lorenzo. These remarkable stone sculptures are the best-known monuments of Olmec culture.

The organization of collective labor by the Olmec elites benefited the commoners by increasing food production and making it more reliable. People also enjoyed a more diverse diet. Ceramic products such as utilitarian pots and small figurines as well as small stone carvings associated with religious belief have been found in commoner households. This suggests that at least some advantages gained from urbanization and growing elite power were shared broadly in the society.

The Olmec elite used elaborate religious rituals to control this complex society. Thousands of commoners were drawn from the countryside to attend awe-inspiring ceremonies at the centers. The elevated platforms and mounds with carved stone veneers served as potent backdrops for these rituals. Rulers and their close kin came to be associated with the gods through bloodletting and human sacrifice, evidence of which is found in all the urban centers. The Olmec were polytheistic, and most of their deities had dual (male and female) natures. Human and animal characteristics were also blended.

La Venta (LA BEN-tah) **Tres Zapotes** (TRACE zah-POE-tace)

Surviving representations of jaguars, crocodiles, snakes, and sharks suggest that these powerful animals provided the most enduring images used in Olmec religious representation. The ability of humans to transform themselves into these animals is a common decorative motif. Rulers were especially associated with the jaguar.

An important class of shamans and healers attached to the elite organized religious life and provided practical advice about the periodic rains essential to agricultural life. They directed the planning of urban centers to reflect astronomical observations and were responsible for developing a form of writing that may have influenced later innovations among the Maya (see Chapter 12). From their close observation of the stars, they produced a calendar that was used to organize ritual life and agriculture. The Olmec were also the likely originators of a ritual ball game that became an enduring part of Mesoamerican ceremonial life.

There is little evidence for the existence of an Olmec empire. Given the limited technological and agricultural base of the society, it is unlikely that the power of the Olmecs could have been projected over significant distances militarily. However, the discovery of Olmec products and images, such as jade carvings decorated with the jaguar-god, as far away as central Mexico provides evidence that the Olmec did exercise cultural influence over a wide area. This influence would endure for centuries.

Early South American Civilization: Chavín, 900–250 B.C.E.

Geography played an important role in the development of human society in the Andes. The region's diverse environment—a mountainous core, arid coastal plain, and dense interior jungles—challenged human populations, encouraging the development of specialized regional production as well as complex social institutions and cultural values that facilitated interregional exchanges and shared labor responsibilities. These adaptations to environmental challenge became enduring features of Andean civilization.

The earliest urban centers in the Andean region were villages of a few hundred people built along the coastal plain or in the foothills near the coast. The abundance of fish and mollusks along the coast of Peru provided a dependable supply of food that helped make the development of early cities possible. The coastal populations traded these products as well as decorative shells for corn, other foods, and eventually textiles produced in the foothills. The two regions also exchanged ceremonial practices, religious motifs, and aesthetic ideas. Recent discoveries demonstrate that as early as 2600 B.C.E. the vast site called Caral in the Supe Valley had developed many of the characteristics now viewed as the hallmarks of later Andean civilization, including ceremonial plazas, pyramids, elevated platforms and mounds, and extensive irrigation works. The scale of the public works in Caral suggests a population of thousands and a political structure capable of organizing the production and distribution of maritime and agricultural products over a broad area.

Chavín, one of the most impressive of South America's early urban civilizations (see Map 3.4), inherited many of the cultural and economic characteristics of Caral. Its capital, Chavín de Huantar°, was located at 10,300 feet (3,139 meters) in the eastern range of the Andes north of the modern city of Lima. Between 900 and 250 B.C.E., a period roughly coinciding with Olmec civilization in Mesoamerica, Chavín dominated a densely populated region that included large areas of the Peruvian coastal plain and Andean foothills. Chavín de Huantar's location at the intersection of trade routes connecting the coast with populous mountain valleys and the tropical lowlands on the eastern flank of the Andes allowed the city's rulers to control trade among these distinct ecological zones and gain an important economic advantage over regional rivals.

Chavín's dominance as a ceremonial and commercial center depended on earlier developments in agriculture and trade, including the introduction of maize cultivation from Mesoamerica. Maize increased the food supplies of the coast and interior foothills, allowing greater levels of urbanization. As Chavín grew, its trade linked the coastal economy with the producers of quinoa (a local grain), potatoes, and llamas in the high mountain valleys and, to a lesser extent, with Amazonian producers of coca (the leaves were chewed, producing a mild narcotic effect) and fruits.

These developments were accompanied by the evolution of reciprocal labor obligations that permitted the construction and maintenance of roads, bridges, temples, palaces, and large irrigation and drainage projects as well as textile production. The exact nature of these reciprocal labor obligations at Chavín is unknown. In later times groups of related families who held land communally and claimed descent from a common ancestor organized these labor obligations. Group members thought of each other as brothers and sisters and were obligated to aid each other, providing a model for the organization of labor and the distribution of goods at every level of Andean society.

The increased use of **llamas** to move goods from one ecological zone to another promoted specialization of

---

Chavín de Huantar (cha-BEAN day WAHN-tar)

production and increased trade. Llamas were the only domesticated beasts of burden in the Americas, and they played an important role in the integration of the Andean region. They were first domesticated in the mountainous interior of Peru and were crucial to Chavín's development, not unlike the camel in the evolution of trans-Saharan trade (see Chapter 8). Llamas provided meat and wool and decreased the labor needed to transport goods. A single driver could control ten to thirty animals, each carrying up to 70 pounds (32 kilograms); a human porter could carry only about 50 pounds (22.5 kilograms).

The enormous scale of the capital and the dispersal of Chavín's pottery styles, religious motifs, and architectural forms over a wide area suggest that Chavín imposed some form of political integration and trade dependency on its neighbors that may have relied in part on military force. Most modern scholars believe that, as in the case of the Olmec civilization, Chavín's influence depended more on the development of an attractive and convincing religious belief system and related rituals. Chavín's most potent religious symbol, a jaguar deity, was dispersed over a broad area, and archaeological evidence suggests that Chavín de Huantar served as a pilgrimage site.

The architectural signature of Chavín was a large complex of multilevel platforms made of packed earth or rubble and faced with cut stone or adobe (sun-dried brick made of clay and straw). Small buildings used for ritual purposes or as elite residences were built on these platforms. Nearly all the buildings were decorated with relief carvings of serpents, condors, jaguars, or human forms. The largest building at Chavín de Huantar measured 250 feet (76 meters) on each side and rose to a height of 50 feet (15 meters). About one-third of its interior is hollow, containing narrow galleries and small rooms that may have housed the remains of royal ancestors.

American metallurgy was first developed in the Andean region. The later introduction of metallurgy in Mesoamerica, like the appearance of maize agriculture in the Andes, suggests sustained trade and cultural contacts between the two regions. Archaeological investigations of Chavín de Huantar and smaller centers have revealed remarkable three-dimensional silver, gold, and gold alloy ornaments that represent a clear advance over earlier technologies. Improvements in both the manufacture and the decoration of textiles are also associated with the rise of Chavín. The quality of these products, probably used only by the elite or in religious rituals, added to the reputation and prestige of the culture and aided in the projection of its power and influence. The most common decorative motif in sculpture, pottery, and textiles was a jaguar-man similar in conception to the Olmec symbol. In both civilizations and in many other cultures in the Americas, this powerful predator provided an enduring image of religious authority and a vehicle through which the gods could act in the world of men and women.

Class distinctions appear to have increased during this period of expansion. A class of priests directed religious life. Modern scholars also see evidence that both local chiefs and a more powerful chief or king dominated Chavín's politics. Excavations of graves reveal that superior-quality textiles as well as gold crowns, breastplates, and jewelry distinguished rulers from commoners. These rich objects, the quality and abundance of pottery, and the monumental architecture of the major centers all suggest the presence of highly skilled artisans as well.

There is no convincing evidence, like defaced buildings or broken images, that the eclipse of Chavín (unlike the Olmec centers) was associated with conquest or rebellion. However, recent investigations have suggested that increased warfare throughout the region around 200 B.C.E. disrupted Chavín's trade and undermined the authority of the governing elite. Regardless of what caused the collapse of this powerful culture, the technologies, material culture, statecraft, architecture, and urban planning associated with Chavín influenced the Andean region for centuries.

CONCLUSION

The civilizations of early China, Nubia, the Celts, the Olmec, and Chavín emerged in very different ecological contexts in widely separated parts of the globe, and the patterns of organization, technology, behavior, and belief that they developed were, in large part, responses to the challenges and opportunities of those environments.

In the north China plain, as in the river-valley civilizations of Mesopotamia and Egypt, the presence of great, flood-prone rivers and the lack of dependable rainfall led to the formation of powerful institutions capable of organizing large numbers of people to dig and maintain irrigation channels and build dikes. An authoritarian central government has been a recurring feature of Chinese history, beginning with the Shang monarchy and warrior elite.

In Nubia, the initial impetus for the formation of a strong state was the need for protection from desert nomads and from the Egyptian rulers who coveted Nubian gold and other resources. Control of these resources and of the trade route between sub-Saharan Africa and the north, as well as the agricultural surplus to feed administrators and specialists in the urban centers, made the rulers of Kush, Napata, and Meroë wealthy and formidable.

The Celtic peoples of continental Europe never developed a strong state. They occupied fertile lands with adequate rainfall for agriculture, grazing territory for flocks, and timber for fuel and construction. Kinship groups dominated by warrior elites and controlling compact territories were the usual form of organization.

While the ecological zones in Mesoamerica and South America in which the Olmec and Chavín cultures emerged were quite different, both societies created networks that brought together the resources and products of disparate regions. Little is known about the political and social organization of these societies, but archaeological evidence makes clear the existence of ruling elites that gathered wealth and organized labor for the construction of monumental centers.

In most complex societies small groups achieve a level of wealth and prestige that allows them to dominate the majority. It is important to understand how these elite groups maintain and justify their position.

Among both the early Chinese and the Celts a warrior aristocracy, with wealth based on land and flocks, controlled significant numbers of human laborers. When the Zhou overthrew the Shang, they curtailed the power of the warrior elite, and over time a new elite of educated government officials evolved. Much less is known about the emergence of elite groups in Nubia and the states of the Olmec and Chavín. However, it is likely that they played key roles in the organization of trade and the construction of the irrigation networks that greatly increased the food supply available to their communities.

In the Eastern Hemisphere, the production of metal tools, weapons, and luxury and ceremonial implements were vital to the success of elite groups. Bronze metallurgy began at different times—in western Asia around 2500 B.C.E., in East Asia around 2000 B.C.E., in northeastern Africa around 1500 B.C.E. Possession of bronze weapons with hard, sharp edges enabled the warriors of Shang and Zhou China, like the royal armies of Egypt and Mesopotamia, to dominate the peasant masses. In Shang China bronze was also used to craft the vessels that played a vital role in the rituals of contact with the spirits of ancestors.

Throughout history, elites have used religion to bolster their position. The Shang rulers of China were indispensable intermediaries between their kingdom and powerful and protective gods and ancestors. Their Zhou successors developed the concept of the ruler as divine Son of Heaven who ruled in accord with the Mandate of Heaven. The rulers of Nubia, drawing on Egyptian concepts, claimed to be gods on earth. In the Olmec and Chavín zones there is some evidence of religious rituals performed to affirm the position of the ruling class. Human sacrifice was practiced among the Celts and in Shang China, Nubia, and Olmec Mesoamerica. This, too, was a mechanism by which ruling elites inspired fear and obedience in their subjects.

The construction and use of "urban" centers and monumental spaces and structures for dramatic religious rituals and colorful political events also propagated the ideologies of power. Ceremonies involving impressive pageantry communicated a message of the "superiority" of the elite and the desirability of being associated with them. In early China and the Olmec and Chavín civilizations, the centers appear to have been the sites of palaces, shrines, and the dwellings of the elite.

Scholars have debated why powerful civilizations appeared many centuries later in the Western Hemisphere than in the Eastern Hemisphere. Recent theories have focused on environmental differences. The Eastern Hemisphere was home to a far larger number of wild plant and animal species that were particularly well suited to domestication. In addition, the natural east-west axis of the huge landmass of Europe and Asia allowed for the relatively rapid spread of domesticated plants and animals to climatically similar zones along the same latitudes. Settled agriculture led to population growth, more complex political and social organization, and increased technological sophistication. In the Americas, by contrast, there were fewer wild plant and animal species that could be domesticated, and the north-south axis of the continents made it more difficult for domesticated species to spread because of variations in climate at different latitudes. As a result, the processes that foster the development of complex societies evolved somewhat more slowly.

The comparison of the two hemispheres leads to another important realization. The complex societies of the Western Hemisphere did not necessarily develop technologies in the same sequence as their Eastern Hemisphere counterparts. The Olmec and Chavín peoples did not possess large draft animals, wheeled vehicles, or metal weapons and tools. Nevertheless, they created sophisticated political, social, and economic institutions that rivaled those developed in the Eastern Hemisphere in the third and second millennia B.C.E.

Key Terms

loess	**Confucius**	**Celts**
Shang	**Daoism**	**Druids**
divination	**yin/yang**	**Olmec**
Zhou	**Kush**	**Chavín**
Mandate of Heaven	**Meroë**	**llama**
Legalism		

Suggested Reading

Caroline Blunden and Mark Elvin, *Cultural Atlas of China* (1983), contains general geographic, ethnographic, and historical information about China through the ages, as well as many maps and illustrations. Conrad Schirokauer, *A Brief History of Chinese Civilization* (1991), and John King Fairbank, *China: A New History* (1992), offer useful chapters on early China. Edward L. Shaughnessy and Michael Loewe, eds., *The Cambridge History of Ancient China* (1998), approaches the subject in far greater depth. Nicola Di Cosmo, *Ancient China and Its Enemies: The Rise of Nomadic Power in East Asian History* (2002), sets the development of Chinese civilization in the broader context of interactions with nomadic neighbors. Jessica Rawson, *Ancient China: Art and Archaeology* (1980), Kwang-chih Chang, *The Archaeology of Ancient China*, 4th ed. (1986), and Ronald G. Knapp, *China's Walled Cities* (2000), emphasize archaeological evidence. W. Thomas Chase, *Ancient Chinese Bronze Art: Casting the Precious Sacral Vessel* (1991), contains a brief but useful discussion of the importance of bronzes in ancient China, as well as a detailed discussion of bronze-casting techniques. Robert Temple, *The Genius of China: 3,000 Years of Science, Discovery, and Invention* (1986), explores many aspects of Chinese technology, using a division into general topics such as agriculture, engineering, and medicine. Anne Behnke Kinney, "Women in Ancient China," in *Women's Roles in Ancient Civilizations: A Reference Guide*, ed. Bella Vivante (1999), and Patricia Ebrey, "Women, Marriage, and the Family in Chinese History," in *Heritage of China: Contemporary Perspectives on Chinese Civilization*, ed. Paul S. Ropp (1990), address the very limited evidence for women in early China. Michael Loewe and Carmen Blacker, *Oracles and Divination* (1981), addresses practices in China and other ancient civilizations. Simon Leys, *The Analects of Confucius* (1997), provides a translation of and a commentary on this fundamental text. Benjamin I. Schwartz, *The World of Thought in Ancient China* (1985), is a broad introduction to early Chinese ethical and spiritual concepts.

After a long period of scholarly neglect, with an occasional exception such as Bruce G. Trigger, *Nubia Under the Pharaohs* (1976), the study of ancient Nubia is now receiving considerable attention. David O'Connor, *Ancient Nubia: Egypt's Rival in Africa* (1993); Joyce L. Haynes, *Nubia: Ancient Kingdoms of Africa* (1992); Karl-Heinz Priese, *The Gold of Meroë* (1993); P. L. Shinnie, *Ancient Nubia* (1996); Derek A. Welsby, *The Kingdom of Kush: The Napatan and Meroitic Empires* (1996); and Timothy Kendall, *Kerma and the Kingdom of Kush, 2500-1500 B.C.: The Archaeological Discovery of an Ancient Nubian Empire* (1997), all reflect the new interest of major museums in the art and artifacts of this society. Robert Morkot, "Egypt and Nubia," in *Empires: Perspectives from Archaeology and History*, ed. Susan E. Alcock (2001), examines the political dimension of Egyptian domination, while John H. Taylor, *Egypt and Nubia* (1991), also emphasizes the fruitful interaction of the Egyptian and Nubian cultures.

Simon James, *The World of the Celts* (1993), is a concise, well-illustrated introduction to Celtic civilization. Fuller treatments can be found in Barry W. Cunliffe, *The Ancient Celts* (1997), and Peter Ellis, *The Celtic Empire: The First Millennium of Celtic History, c. 1000 B.C.–51 A.D.* (1990). Miranda J. Green, *The Celtic World* (1995), is a large and comprehensive collection of articles on many aspects of Celtic civilization. Philip Freeman, *War, Women, and Druids: Eyewitness Accounts and Early Reports on the Ancient Celts* (2002), collects the ancient textual evidence. John Haywood, *Atlas of the Celtic World* (2001), is a useful reference. Simon James, *The Atlantic Celts: Ancient People or Modern Invention* (1999), reflects the current scholarly emphasis on articulating the important differences between Celtic groups and deconstructing the modern "myth" of a monolithic Celtic identity. On Celtic religion and mythology see Bernhard Maier, *Dictionary of Celtic Religion and Culture* (1997); James MacKillop, *Dictionary of Celtic Mythology* (1998); Proinsias Mac Cana, *Celtic Mythology* (1983); Paul R. Lonigan, *The Druids: Priests of the Ancient Celts* (1996); and two books by Miranda Green: *The Gods of the Celts* (1986) and *Celtic Myths* (1993). Peter Ellis, *Celtic Women: Women in Celtic Society and Literature* (1996), collects and evaluates the evidence for women's roles. Celtic art is covered by Ruth and Vincent Megaw, *Celtic Art: From Its Beginnings to the Book of Kells* (1989), and I. M. Stead, *Celtic Art* (1985). For translations and brief discussion of Celtic legends see Patrick K. Ford, *The Mabinogi and Other Medieval Welsh Tales* (1977), and Jeffrey Gantz, *Early Irish Myths and Sagas* (1981).

A number of useful books provide an introduction to the early Americas. In *Prehistory of the Americas* (1987) Stuart Fiedel provides an excellent summary of the early history of the Western Hemisphere. *Early Man in the New World*, ed. Richard Shutler, Jr. (1983), is also a useful general work. *Atlas of Ancient America* (1986), by Michael Coe, Elizabeth P. Benson, and Dean R. Snow, offers a compendium of maps and information. George Kubler, *The Art and Architecture of Ancient America: The Mexican, Maya, and Andean Peoples* (1984), is an essential tool, though dated.

For the Olmecs see Jacques Soustelle, *The Olmecs: The Oldest Civilization in Mexico* (1984). More reliable is Michael Coe, *The Olmec World* (1996). Richard W. Keatinge, ed., *Peruvian Prehistory* (1988), provides a helpful introduction to the scholarship on Andean societies. The most useful summary of recent research on Chavín is Richard L. Burger, *Chavín and the Origins of Andean Civilization* (1992).

Jared Diamond, *Guns, Germs, and Steel: The Fates of Human Societies* (1997), tackles the difficult question of why technological development occurred at different times and took different paths of development in the Eastern and Western Hemispheres.

Notes

1. Quoted in Miriam Lichtheim, ed., *Ancient Egyptian Literature: A Book of Readings* (Berkeley: University of California Press 1978).

4 The Mediterranean and Middle East, 2000–500 B.C.E.

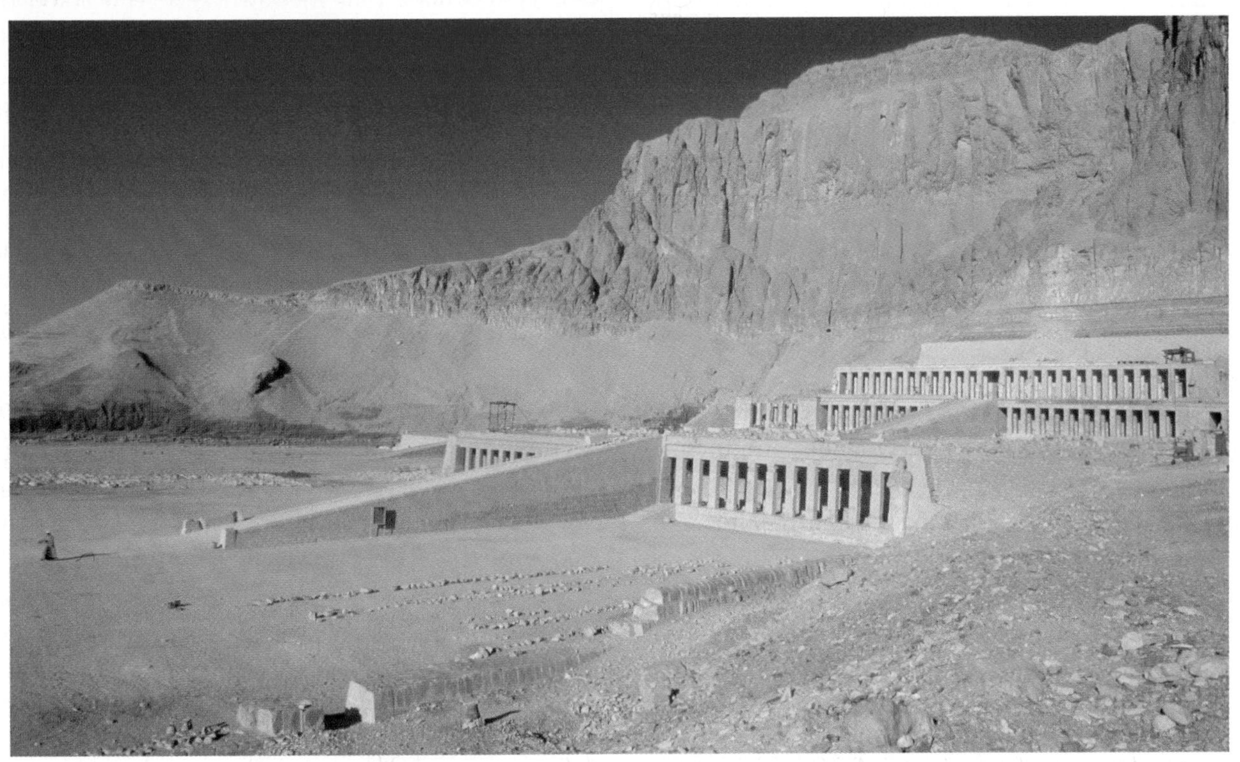

The Mortuary Temple of Queen Hatshepsut at Deir el-Bahri, Egypt, ca. 1460 B.C.E. This beautiful complex of terraces, ramps, and colonnades featured relief sculptures and texts commemorating the famous expedition to Punt.

CHAPTER OUTLINE

Ancient peoples' stories—even those that are not historically accurate—provide valuable insights into how people thought about their origins and identity. One famous story concerned the city of Carthage° in present-day Tunisia, which for centuries dominated the commerce of the western Mediterranean. Tradition held that Dido, a member of the royal family of the Phoenician city-state of Tyre° in southern Lebanon, fled with her supporters to the western Mediterranean after her husband was murdered by her brother, the king of Tyre. Landing on the North African coast, the refugees made friendly contact with local people, who agreed to give them as much land as a cow's hide could cover. By cleverly cutting the hide into narrow strips, they were able to mark out a substantial piece of territory for Kart Khadasht, the "New City" (called *Carthago* by their Roman enemies). Later, faithful to the memory of her dead husband, Dido committed suicide rather than marry a local chieftain.

This story highlights the spread of cultural patterns from older centers to new regions, and the migration and resettlement of Late Bronze Age and Early Iron Age peoples in the Mediterranean lands and western Asia. Just as Egyptian cultural influences helped transform Nubian society, influences from the older centers in Mesopotamia and Egypt penetrated throughout western Asia and the Mediterranean. Far-flung trade, diplomatic contacts, military conquests, and the relocation of large numbers of people spread knowledge, beliefs, practices, and technologies.

By the end of the second millennium B.C.E. many of the societies of the Eastern Hemisphere had entered the **Iron Age:** they had begun to use iron instead of bronze for tools and weapons. Iron offered several advantages. It was a single metal rather than an alloy and thus was simpler to obtain; and there were many potential sources of iron ore. Once the technology of iron making had been mastered—iron has to be heated to a higher temperature than bronze, and its hardness depends on the amount of carbon added during the forging process—iron tools were found to have harder, sharper edges than bronze tools.

These advantages were not discovered all at once. The Hittites of iron-rich Anatolia had learned to make iron implements by 1500 B.C.E. but did not share their knowledge. Some scholars believe that, in the disrupted period after 1200 B.C.E., blacksmiths from the Hittite core area migrated and spread the technology. Others speculate that metalworkers who could not obtain copper and tin turned to dumps of slag (the byproduct of bronze production) containing iron residue and found that they could create useful objects from it. As its usefulness became recognized and techniques were perfected, iron came to be used on an ever wider scale, though bronze also continued to be used.

The first part of this chapter resumes the story of Mesopotamia and Egypt in the Late Bronze Age, the second millennium B.C.E.: their complex relations with neighboring peoples, the development of a prosperous, "cosmopolitan" network of states in the Middle East, and the period of destruction and decline that set in around 1200 B.C.E. We also look at how the Minoan and Mycenaean civilizations of the Aegean Sea were inspired by the technologies and cultural patterns of the older Middle Eastern centers and prospered from participation in long-distance networks of trade. The remainder of the chapter examines the resurgence of this region in the early Iron Age, from 1000 to 500 B.C.E. The focus is on three societies: the Assyrians of northern Mesopotamia; the Israelites of Israel; and the Phoenicians of Lebanon and Syria and their colonies in the western Mediterranean, mainly Carthage. After the decline or demise of the ancient centers dominant throughout the third and second millennia B.C.E., these societies evolved into new political, cultural, and commercial centers.

As you read this chapter, ask yourself the following questions:

- What environmental, technological, political, and cultural factors led these societies to develop their distinctive institutions and values?

Carthage (KAHR-thuhj) **Tyre** (tire)

C H R O N O L O G Y

	Western Asia	Egypt	Syria–Palestine	Mediterranean
2000 B.C.E.	**2000 B.C.E.** Horses in use **1700–1200 B.C.E.** Hittites dominant in Anatolia	**2040–1640 B.C.E.** Middle Kingdom **1640–1532 B.C.E.** Hyksos dominate northern Egypt **1532 B.C.E.** Beginning of New Kingdom		**2000 B.C.E.** Rise of Minoan civilization on Crete; early Greeks arrive in Greece **1600 B.C.E.** Rise of Mycenaean civilization in Greece
1500 B.C.E.	**1500 B.C.E.** Hittites develop iron metallurgy **1460 B.C.E.** Kassites assume control of southern Mesopotamia **1200 B.C.E.** Destruction of Hittite kingdom	**1470 B.C.E.** Queen Hatshepsut dispatches expedition to Punt **1353 B.C.E.** Akhenaten launches reforms **1200–1150 B.C.E.** Sea Peoples attack Egypt **1070 B.C.E.** End of New Kingdom	**1500 B.C.E.** Early “alphabetic” script developed at Ugarit **1250–1200 B.C.E.** Israelite occupation of Canaan **1150 B.C.E.** Philistines settle southern coast of Israel	**1450 B.C.E.** Destruction of Minoan palaces in Crete **1200–1150 B.C.E.** Destruction of Mycenaean centers in Greece
1000 B.C.E.	**1000 B.C.E.** Iron metalurgy begins **911 B.C.E.** Rise of Neo-Assyrian Empire **744–727 B.C.E.** Reforms of Tiglath-pileser **668–627 B.C.E.** Reign of Ashurbanipal **626–539 B.C.E.** Neo-Babylonian kingdom **612 B.C.E.** Fall of Assyria	**750 B.C.E.** Kings of Kush control Egypt **671 B.C.E.** Assyrian conquest of Egypt	**1000 B.C.E.** David establishes Jerusalem as Israelite capital **969 B.C.E.** Hiram of Tyre comes to power **960 B.C.E.** Solomon builds First Temple **920 B.C.E.** Division into two kingdoms of Israel and Judah **721 B.C.E.** Assyrian conquest of northern kingdom **701 B.C.E.** Assyrian humiliation of Tyre **587 B.C.E.** Neo-Babylonian capture of Jerusalem	**1000 B.C.E.** Iron metallurgy **814 B.C.E.** Foundation of Carthage
600 B.C.E.			**515 B.C.E.** Deportees from Babylon return to Jerusalem **450 B.C.E.** Completion of Hebrew Bible; Hanno the Phoenician explores West Africa	**550–300 B.C.E.** Rivalry of Carthaginians and Greeks in western Mediterranean

- In what ways were the societies of this era more interconnected and interdependent than before, and what were the consequences—positive and negative—of these connections?
- What were the causes and consequences of large-scale movements of peoples to new homes during this era?
- Why were certain cultures destroyed or assimilated while others survived?

THE COSMOPOLITAN MIDDLE EAST, 1700–1100 B.C.E.

Both Mesopotamia and Egypt succumbed to outside invaders in the seventeenth century B.C.E. (see Chapter 2). Eventually the outsiders were either ejected or assimilated, and conditions of stability and prosperity were restored. Between 1500 and 1200 B.C.E. a number of large territorial states dominated the Middle East (see Map 4.1). These centers of power controlled the smaller city-states, kingdoms, and kinship groups as they competed with, and sometimes fought against, one another for control of valuable commodities and trade routes.

Historians have called the Late Bronze Age in the Middle East a "cosmopolitan" era, meaning a time of widely shared cultures and lifestyles. Extensive diplomatic relations and commercial contacts between states fostered the flow of goods and ideas, and elite groups shared similar values and enjoyed a relatively high standard of living. The peasants in the countryside who comprised the majority of the population may have seen some improvement in their standard of living, but they reaped far fewer benefits from the increasing contacts and trade.

Western Asia

By 1500 B.C.E. Mesopotamia was divided into two distinct political zones: Babylonia in the south and Assyria in the north (see Map 4.1). The city of Babylon had gained political and cultural ascendancy over the southern plain under the dynasty of Hammurabi in the eighteenth and seventeenth centuries B.C.E. Subsequently there was a persistent inflow of Kassites°, peoples from the Zagros° Mountains to the east who spoke a non-Semitic language, and by 1460 B.C.E a Kassite dynasty had come to power in Babylon. The Kassites retained names in their native language but otherwise embraced Babylonian language and culture and intermarried with the native population. During their 250 years in power, the Kassite lords of Babylonia defended their core area and traded for raw materials, but they did not pursue territorial conquest.

The Assyrians of the north had more ambitious designs. As early as the twentieth century B.C.E. the city of Ashur,° the leading urban center on the northern Tigris, anchored a busy trade route across the northern Mesopotamian plain and onto the Anatolian Plateau. Representatives of Assyrian merchant families maintained settlements outside the walls of important Anatolian cities. The Assyrians exported textiles and tin, used since about 2500 B.C.E. to make bronze, which they exchanged for silver from Anatolia. In the eighteenth century B.C.E. an Assyrian dynasty briefly gained control of the upper Euphrates River near the present-day border of Syria and Iraq. This "Old Assyrian" kingdom, as it is now called, illustrates the importance of the trade routes connecting Mesopotamia to Anatolia and the Syria-Palestine coast. After 1400 B.C.E. a resurgent "Middle Assyrian" kingdom again engaged in campaigns of conquest and expansion of its economic interests.

Other ambitious states emerged on the periphery of the Mesopotamian heartland, including Elam in southwest Iran and Mitanni° in the broad plain between the upper Euphrates and Tigris Rivers. Most formidable of all were the **Hittites°**, speakers of an Indo-European language, who became the foremost power in Anatolia from around 1700 to 1200 B.C.E. From their capital at Hattusha°, near present-day Ankara° in central Turkey, they deployed the fearsome new technology of horse-drawn war chariots. The Hittites exploited Anatolia's rich deposits of copper, silver, and iron to play an indispensable role in international commerce. Many historians believe that the Hittites were the first to develop a technique for making tools and weapons of iron. They heated the ore until it was soft enough to shape, pounded it to remove impurities, and then plunged it into cold water to harden. The Hittites were anxious to keep knowledge of this process secret since it provided both military and economic advantages.

During the second millennium B.C.E. Mesopotamian political and cultural concepts spread across much of western Asia. Akkadian° became the language of diplo-

Kassite (KAS-ite) **Zagros** (ZAH-groes)

Ashur (AH-shoor) **Mitanni** (mih-TAH-nee) **Hittite** (HIT-ite) **Hattusha** (haht-tush-SHAH) **Ankara** (ANG-kuh-ruh) **Akkadian** (uh-KAY-dee-uhn)

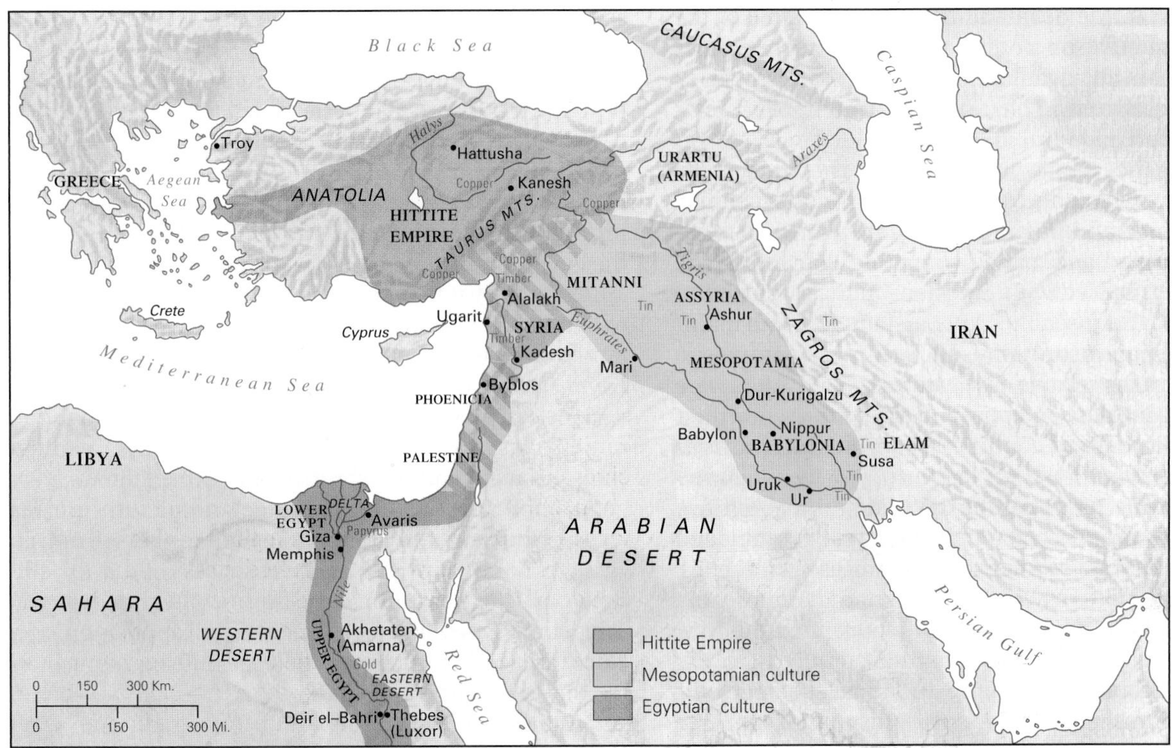

Map 4.1 The Middle East in the Second Millennium B.C.E. Although warfare was not uncommon, treaties, diplomatic missions, and correspondence in Akkadian cuneiform fostered cooperative relationships between states. All were tied together by extensive networks of exchange centering on the trade in metals, and peripheral regions, such as Nubia and the Aegean Sea, were drawn into the web of commerce.

macy and correspondence between governments. The Elamites° and Hittites, among others, adapted the cuneiform system to write their own languages. In the Syrian coastal city of Ugarit° thirty cuneiform symbols were used to write consonant sounds, an early use of the alphabetic principle and a considerable advance over the hundreds of signs required in conventional cuneiform and hieroglyphic writing. Mesopotamian myths and legends and styles of art and architecture were widely imitated. Newcomers who had learned and improved on the lessons of Mesopotamian civilization often put pressure on the old core area. The small, fractious city-states of the third millennium B.C.E. had been concerned only with their immediate neighbors in southern Mesopotamia. In contrast, the larger states of the second millennium B.C.E. interacted politically, militarily, and economically in a geopolitical sphere encompassing all of western Asia.

New Kingdom Egypt

After flourishing for nearly four hundred years (see Chapter 2), the Egyptian Middle Kingdom declined in the seventeenth century B.C.E. As high-level officials in the countryside became increasingly independent and new groups migrated into the Nile Delta, central authority broke down, and Egypt entered a period of political fragmentation and economic decline. Around 1640 B.C.E. Egypt came under foreign rule for the first time, at the hands of the Hyksos°, or "Princes of Foreign Lands."

Historians are uncertain about who the Hyksos were and how they came to power. Semitic peoples had been migrating from the Syria-Palestine region (sometimes called the Levant, present-day Syria, Lebanon, Israel, and the Palestinian territories) into the eastern Nile Delta for centuries. In the chaotic conditions of this time, other peoples may have joined them and established

Elamite (EE-luh-mite) **Ugarit** (OO-guh-reet)

Hyksos (HICK-soes)

control, first in the delta and then in the middle of the country. The Hyksos possessed military technologies that gave them an advantage over the Egyptians, such as the horse-drawn war chariot and a composite bow, made of wood and horn, that had greater range and velocity than the simple wooden bow. The process by which the Hyksos came to dominate much of Egypt may not have been far different from that by which the Kassites first settled and gained control in Babylonia. The Hyksos intermarried with Egyptians and assimilated to native ways. They used the Egyptian language and maintained Egyptian institutions and culture. Nevertheless, in contrast to the relative ease with which outsiders were assimilated in Mesopotamia, the Egyptians, with their strong ethnic identity, continued to regard the Hyksos as "foreigners."

As with the formation of the Middle Kingdom five hundred years earlier, the reunification of Egypt under a native dynasty was accomplished by princes from Thebes. After three decades of warfare, Kamose° and Ahmose° expelled the Hyksos from Egypt and inaugurated the New Kingdom, which lasted from about 1532 to 1070 B.C.E.

A century of foreign domination had shaken Egyptian pride and shattered the isolationist mindset of earlier eras. New Kingdom Egypt was an aggressive and expansionist state, extending its territorial control north into Syria-Palestine and south into Nubia and winning access to timber, gold, and copper (bronze metallurgy took hold in Egypt around 1500 B.C.E.) as well as taxes and tribute (payments from the territories it had conquered). The occupied territories provided a buffer zone, protecting Egypt from attack. In Nubia, Egypt imposed direct control and pressed the native population to adopt Egyptian language and culture. In the Syria-Palestine region, in contrast, the Egyptians stationed garrisons at strategically placed forts and supported local rulers willing to collaborate.

The New Kingdom was a period of innovation. Egypt fully participated in the diplomatic and commercial networks that linked the states of western Asia. Egyptian soldiers, administrators, diplomats, and merchants traveled widely, exposing Egypt to exotic fruits and vegetables, new musical instruments, and new technologies, such as an improved potter's wheel and weaver's loom.

At least one woman held the throne of New Kingdom Egypt. When Pharaoh Tuthmosis° II died, his queen, **Hatshepsut°**, served as regent for her young stepson and soon claimed the royal title for herself (r. 1473–1458 B.C.E.). In inscriptions she often used the male pronoun to refer to herself, and drawings and sculptures show her wearing the long, conical beard of the ruler of Egypt.

Around 1460 B.C.E. Hatshepsut sent a naval expedition down the Red Sea to the fabled land that the Egyptians called "Punt°." Historians believe that Punt may have been near the coast of eastern Sudan or Eritrea. Hatshepsut was seeking the source of myrrh°, a reddish-brown resin from the hardened sap of a local tree, which the Egyptians burned on the altars of their gods and used as an ingredient in medicines and cosmetics. She hoped to bypass the middlemen who drove up the price exorbitantly, and establish direct trade between Punt and Egypt. When the expedition returned with myrrh and various sub-Saharan luxury goods—ebony and other rare woods, ivory, cosmetics, live monkeys, panther skins—Hatshepsut celebrated the achievement in a great public display and in words and pictures on the walls of the mortuary temple she built for herself at Deir el-Bahri°. She may have used the success of this expedition to bolster her claim to the throne. After her death, in a reaction that reflected some official opposition to a woman ruler, her image was defaced and her name blotted out wherever it appeared.

Another ruler who departed from traditional ways ascended the throne as Amenhotep° IV. He soon began to refer to himself as **Akhenaten°** (r. 1353–1335 B.C.E.), meaning "beneficial to the Aten°" (the disk of the sun). Changing his name was one of the ways in which he sought to spread his belief in Aten as the supreme deity. He closed the temples of other gods, challenging the age-old supremacy of the chief god Amon° and the power and influence of the priests of Amon.

Some scholars have credited Akhenaten with the invention of monotheism—the belief in one exclusive god. It is likely, however, that Akhenaten was attempting to reassert the superiority of the king over the priests and to renew belief in the king's divinity. Worship of Aten was confined to the royal family: the people of Egypt were pressed to revere the divine ruler.

Akhenaten built a new capital at modern-day Amarna°, halfway between Memphis and Thebes (see Map 4.1). He transplanted thousands of Egyptians to construct the site and serve the ruling elite. Akhenaten and his artists created a new style that broke with the conventions of earlier art: the king, his wife Nefertiti°, and their daughters were depicted in fluid, natural poses with strangely elongated heads and limbs and swelling abdomens.

Kamose (KAH-mose) **Ahmose** (AH-mose)
Tuthmosis (tuth_MOE-sis) **Hatshepsut** (hat-SHEP-soot)

Punt (poont) **myrrh** (murr) **Deir el-Bahri** (DARE uhl–BAH-ree)
Amenhotep (ah-muhn-HOE-tep) **Akhenaten** (ah-ken-AHT-n)
Aten (AHT-n) **Amon** (AH-muhn) **Amarna** (uh-MAHR-nuh)
Nefertiti (nef-uhr-TEE-tee)

Colossal Statues of Ramesses II at Abu Simbel Strategically placed at a bend in the Nile River so as to face the southern frontier, this monument was an advertisement of Egyptian power. A temple was carved into the cliff behind the gigantic statues of the pharaoh. Within the temple, a corridor decorated with reliefs of military victories leads to an inner shrine containing images of the divine ruler seated alongside three of the major gods. In a modern marvel of engineering, the monument was moved to higher ground in the 1960s C.E. to protect it from rising waters when a dam was constructed upriver. (Susan Lapides/Woodfin Camp & Associates)

Akhenaten's reforms were strongly resented by government officials, priests, and others whose privileges and wealth were linked to the traditional system. After his death the temples were reopened; Amon was reinstated as chief god; the capital returned to Thebes; and the institution of kingship was weakened to the advantage of the priests. The boy-king Tutankhamun° (r. 1333–1323 B.C.E.), one of the immediate successors of Akhenaten and famous solely because his was the only royal tomb found by archaeologists that had not been pillaged by tomb robbers, reveals both in his name (meaning "beautiful in life is Amon") and in his insignificant reign the ultimate failure of Akhenaten's revolution.

In 1323 B.C.E. the general Haremhab seized the throne and established a new dynasty, the Ramessides°. The rulers of this line renewed the policy of conquest and expansion that Akhenaten had neglected. The greatest of these monarchs, **Ramesses° II**—sometimes called Ramesses the Great—ruled for sixty-six years (r. 1290–1224 B.C.E.) and dominated his age. Ramesses looms large in the archaeological record because he undertook monumental building projects all over Egypt. Living into his nineties, he had many wives and concubines and may have fathered more than a hundred children. Since 1990 archaeologists have been excavating a network of more than a hundred corridors and chambers carved deep into a hillside in the Valley of the Kings where many sons of Ramesses were buried.

Commerce and Communication

Early in his reign Ramesses II fought a major battle against the Hittites at Kadesh in northern Syria (1285 B.C.E.). Although Egyptian scribes presented this encounter as a great victory, the lack of territorial gains suggests that it

Tutankhamun (tuht-uhnk-AH-muhn) **Ramesside** (RAM-ih-side) **Ramesses** (RAM-ih-seez)

was essentially a draw. In subsequent years Egyptian and Hittite diplomats negotiated a treaty, which was strengthened by Ramesses' marriage to a Hittite princess. At issue was control of Syria-Palestine, strategically located at a crossroads between the great powers of the Middle East and at the end of the east-west trade route across Asia. The inland cities of Syria-Palestine—such as Mari° on the upper Euphrates and Alalakh° in western Syria—were active centers of international trade. The coastal towns—particularly Ugarit and the Phoenician towns of the Lebanese seaboard—served as transshipment points for trade to and from the lands ringing the Mediterranean Sea.

In the eastern Mediterranean, northeastern Africa, and western Asia in the Late Bronze Age, any state that wanted to project its power needed metal to make tools and weapons. Commerce in metals energized the long-distance trade of the time. We have seen the Assyrian traffic in silver from Anatolia and the Egyptian passion for Nubian gold (see Chapter 3). Copper came from Anatolia and Cyprus, tin from Afghanistan and possibly the British Isles. Both ores had to be carried long distances and pass through a number of hands before reaching their final destinations.

New modes of transportation expedited communications and commerce across great distances and inhospitable landscapes. Horses arrived in western Asia around 2000 B.C.E. Domesticated by nomadic peoples in Central Asia, they were brought into Mesopotamia through the Zagros mountains and reached Egypt by 1600 B.C.E. The speed of travel and communication made possible by horses contributed to the creation of large states and empires. Soldiers and government agents could cover great distances quickly, and swift, maneuverable horse-drawn chariots became the premier instrument of war. The team of driver and archer could ride forward and unleash a volley of arrows or trample terrified foot soldiers.

Sometime after 1500 B.C.E in western Asia, but not for another thousand years in Egypt, people began to make common use of camels, though the animal may have been domesticated a millennium earlier in southern Arabia. Thanks to their strength and ability to go long distances without water, camels were able to travel across barren terrain. Their physical qualities eventually led to the emergence of a new kind of desert nomad and the creation of cross-desert trade routes (see Chapter 8).

Mari (MAH-ree) **Alalakh** (UH-luh-luhk)

THE AEGEAN WORLD, 2000–1100 B.C.E.

In this era of far-flung trade and communication, the influence of Mesopotamia and Egypt was felt as far away as the Aegean Sea, a gulf of the eastern Mediterranean. The emergence of the Minoan° civilization on the island of Crete and the Mycenaean° civilization of Greece is another manifestation of the fertilizing influence of older centers on outlying lands and peoples, who then struck out on their own unique paths of cultural evolution

The landscape of southern Greece and the Aegean islands is mostly rocky and arid, with small plains lying between ranges of hills. The limited arable land is suitable for grains, grapevines, and olive trees. Flocks of sheep and goats graze the slopes. Sharply indented coastlines, natural harbors, and small islands within sight of one another made the sea the fastest and least costly mode of travel and transport. With few deposits of metals and little timber, Aegean peoples had to import these commodities, as well as food, from abroad. As a result, the rise, success, and eventual fall of the Minoan and Mycenaean societies were closely tied to their commercial and political relations with other peoples in the region.

Minoan Crete

By 2000 B.C.E. the island of Crete (see Map 4.2) housed the first European civilization to have complex political and social structures and advanced technologies like those found in western Asia and northeastern Africa. The **Minoan** civilization had centralized government, monumental building, bronze metallurgy, writing, and recordkeeping. Archaeologists named this civilization after Greek legends about King Minos, who was said to have ruled a vast naval empire, including the southern Greek mainland, and to have kept the monstrous Minotaur° (half-man, half-bull) beneath his palace in a mazelike labyrinth built by the ingenious inventor Daedalus°. Thus later Greeks recollected a time when Crete was home to many ships and skilled craftsmen.

The ethnicity of the Minoans is uncertain, and their writing has not been deciphered. But their sprawling

Minoan (mih-NO-uhn) **Mycenaean** (my-suh-NEE-uhn)
Minotaur (MIN-uh-tor) **Daedalus** (DED-ih-luhs)

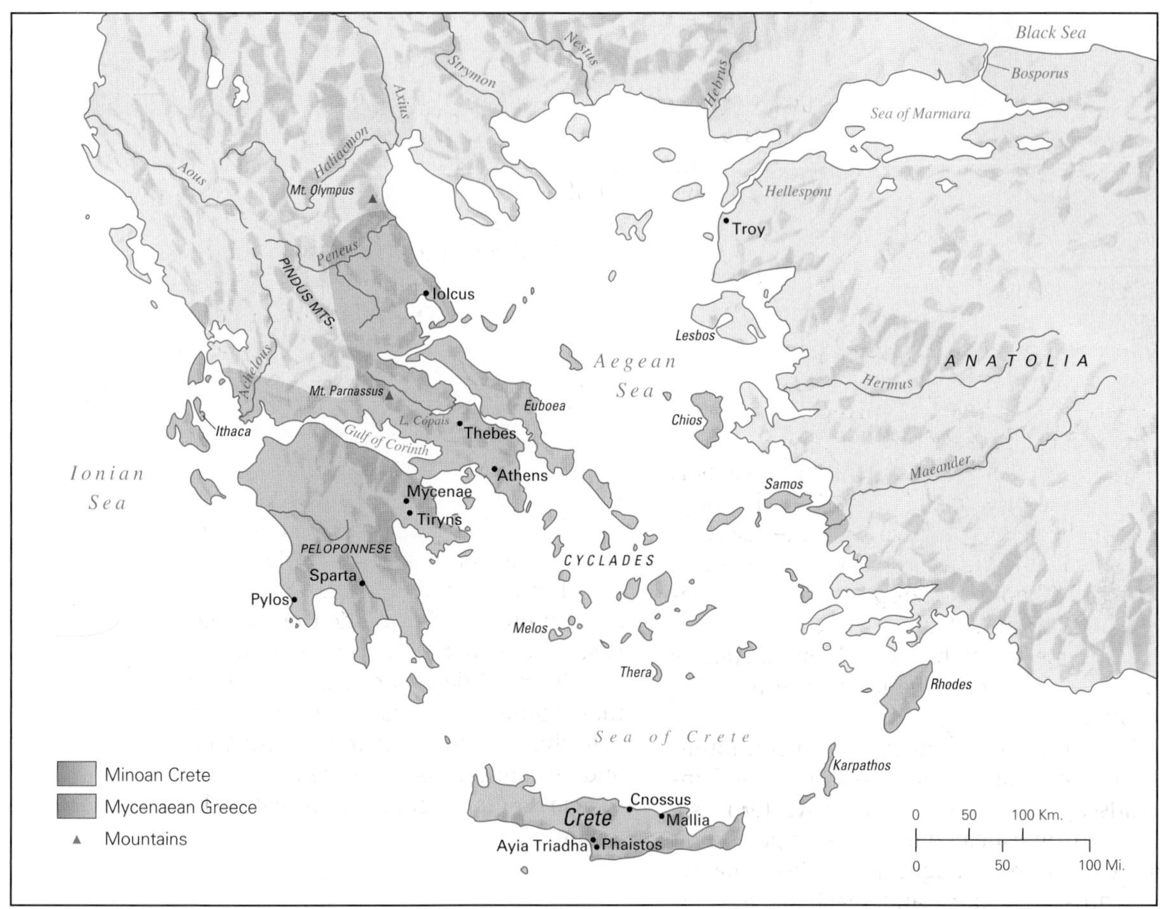

Map 4.2 Minoan and Mycenaean Civilizations of the Aegean The earliest complex civilizations in Europe arose in the Aegean Sea. The Minoan civilization on the island of Crete evolved in the later third millennium B.C.E. and had a major cultural influence on the Mycenaean Greeks. Palaces decorated with fresco paintings, a centrally controlled economy, and the use of a system of writing for recordkeeping are some of the most conspicuous features of these societies.

palace complexes at Cnossus°, Phaistos°, and Mallia° and the distribution of Cretan pottery and other artifacts around the Mediterranean and Middle East testify to widespread trading connections. Egyptian, Syrian, and Mesopotamian influences can be seen in the design of the Minoan palaces, centralized government, and system of writing. The absence of identifiable representations of Cretan rulers, however, contrasts sharply with the grandiose depictions of kings in the Middle East and suggests a different conception of authority. Also noteworthy is the absence of fortifications at the palace sites and the presence of high-quality indoor plumbing.

Statuettes of women with elaborate headdresses and serpents coiling around their limbs may represent fertility goddesses. Colorful frescoes (paintings done on a moist plaster surface) on the walls of Cretan palaces portray groups of women in frilly, layered skirts engaged in conversation or watching rituals or entertainment. We do not know whether pictures of young acrobats vaulting over the horns and back of an onrushing bull show a religious activity or mere sport. Scenes of servants carrying jars and fishermen throwing nets and hooks from their boats suggest a joyful attitude toward work, but this portrayal may say more about the tastes of the elite than about the reality of daily toil. The stylized depictions of plants and animals on Minoan vases—plants with swaying leaves and playful octopuses whose tentacles wind around the surface of the vase—seem to reflect a delight in the beauty and order of the natural world.

Cnossus (NOSS-suhs) **Phaistos** (FIE-stuhs) **Mallia** (mahl-YAH)

Fresco from the Aegean Island of Thera, ca. 1650 B.C.E. This picture, originally painted on wet plaster, depicts the arrival of a fleet in a harbor as people watch from the walls of the town. The Minoan civilization of Crete was famous in later legend for its naval power. The fresco reveals the appearance and design of ships in the Bronze Age Aegean. In the seventeenth century B.C.E., the island of Thera was devastated by a massive volcanic explosion, thought by many to be the origin of the myth of Atlantis sinking beneath the sea. (Archaeological Receipts Fund, Athens)

All the Cretan palaces except Cnossus, along with the houses of the elite and peasants in the countryside, were deliberately destroyed around 1450 B.C.E. Because Mycenaean Greeks took over at Cnossus, most historians regard them as the likely culprits.

Mycenaean Greece

Most historians believe that speakers of an Indo-European language ancestral to Greek migrated into the Greek peninsula around 2000 B.C.E., although some argue for earlier and later dates. Through intermarriage, blending of languages, and melding of cultural practices, the indigenous population and the newcomers created the first Greek culture. For centuries this society remained simple and static. Farmers and shepherds lived in Stone Age conditions, wringing a bare living from the land. Then, sometime around 1600 B.C.E., life changed relatively suddenly.

More than a century ago a German businessman, Heinrich Schliemann°, set out to prove that the *Iliad* and the *Odyssey* were true. These epics attributed to the poet Homer, who probably lived shortly before 700 B.C.E., spoke of Agamemnon°, the king of **Mycenae**° in southern Greece. In 1876 Schliemann stunned the scholarly world by discovering at Mycenae a circle of graves at the base of deep, rectangular shafts. These **shaft graves** contained the bodies of men, women, and children and were filled with gold jewelry and ornaments, weapons, and utensils. Clearly, some people in this society had acquired wealth, authority, and the capacity to mobilize human labor. Subsequent excavation uncovered a large

Schliemann (SHLEE-muhn) **Agamemnon** (ag-uh-MEM-non) **Mycenae** (my-SEE-nee)

palace complex, massive walls, more shaft graves, and other evidence of a rich and technologically advanced civilization that lasted from around 1600 to 1150 B.C.E.

How can the sudden rise of Mycenae and other centers in mainland Greece be explained? Despite legends about the power of King Minos of Crete, there is no archaeological evidence of Cretan political control of the Greek mainland. But Crete exerted a powerful cultural influence. The Mycenaeans borrowed the Minoan idea of the palace, centralized economy, and administrative bureaucracy, as well as the Minoan writing system. They adopted Minoan styles and techniques of architecture, pottery making, and fresco and vase painting. This explains where the Mycenaean Greeks got their technology. But how did they suddenly accumulate power and wealth? Most historians look to the profits from trade and piracy and perhaps also to the pay and booty brought back by mercenaries (soldiers who served for pay in foreign lands).

The first advanced civilization in Greece is called "Mycenaean" largely because Mycenae was the first site excavated. Excavations at other centers have revealed that Mycenae exemplifies the common pattern of these citadels: built at a commanding location on a hilltop and surrounded by high, thick fortification walls made of stones so large that later Greeks believed that the giant, one-eyed Cyclopes° of legend had lifted them into place. The fortified enclosure provided a place of refuge for the entire community in time of danger and contained the palace and administrative complex. The large central hall with an open hearth and columned porch was surrounded by courtyards, living quarters for the royal family and their retainers, and offices, storerooms, and workshops. The palace walls were covered with brightly painted frescoes depicting scenes of war, the hunt, and daily life, as well as decorative motifs from nature.

Nearby lay the tombs of the rulers and leading families: shaft graves at first; later, grand beehive-shaped structures made of stone and covered with a mound of earth. Large houses, probably belonging to the aristocracy, lay just outside the walls. The peasants lived on the lower slopes and in the plain below, close to the land they worked.

Additional information about Mycenaean life is provided by over four thousand baked clay tablets written in a script now called **Linear B.** Like its predecessor, the undeciphered Minoan script called Linear A, Linear B uses pictorial signs to represent syllables, but it is recognizably an early form of Greek. The extensive palace bureaucracy kept track of people, animals, and objects in

Cyclopes (SIGH-kloe-pees)

Lion Gate at Mycenae View over the massive fortification wall encircling the citadel. Above the entrance a large stone depicts a Minoan-style column with lions on either side, thought to signify royal power. Just inside the gate on the right is one of the shaft grave circles containing the treasure-filled tombs of the elite. (Dimitrios Harissiadis/Benaki Museum)

exhaustive detail and exercised a high degree of control over the economy of the kingdom. The tablets list everything from the number of chariot wheels in palace storerooms, the rations paid to textile workers, and the gifts dedicated to various gods, to the ships stationed along the coasts.

The government organized and coordinated grain production and controlled the wool industry from raw material to finished product. Scribes kept track of the flocks in the field, the sheared wool, the allocation of raw wool to spinners and weavers, and the production, storage, and distribution of cloth articles.

The tablets say almost nothing about individual people—not even the name of a single Mycenaean king—and very little about the political and legal systems, social structures, gender relations, and religious beliefs. They tell nothing about particular historical events and relations with other Mycenaean centers or peoples overseas.

The evidence for a broad political organization of Greece in this period is contradictory. In Homer's *Iliad,* Agamemnon, the king of Mycenae, leads a great expedition of Greeks from different regions against the city of Troy in northwest Anatolia. To this can be added the cultural uniformity of all the Mycenaean centers: a remarkable similarity in the shapes, decorative styles, and production techniques of buildings, tombs, utensils, tools, clothing, and works of art. Some scholars argue that such cultural uniformity could have occurred only in a context of political unity. The plot of the *Iliad,* however, revolves around the difficulties Agamemnon has in asserting control over other Greek leaders. Moreover, the archaeological remains and the Linear B tablets give strong indications of independent centers of power at Mycenae, Pylos°, and elsewhere. Cultural uniformity might simply have resulted from extensive contacts and commerce between the various Greek kingdoms.

Long-distance contact and trade were made possible by the seafaring skill of Minoans and Mycenaeans. Commercial vessels depended primarily on wind and sail. In general, ancient sailors preferred to sail in daylight hours and keep the land in sight. Their light, wooden vessels had little storage area and decking, so the crew had to go ashore to eat and sleep every night. With their low keels the ships could run up onto the beach.

Cretan and Greek pottery and crafted goods are found not only in the Aegean but also in other parts of the Mediterranean and Middle East. At certain sites the quantity and range of artifacts suggest settlements of Aegean peoples. The oldest artifacts are Minoan; then Minoan and Mycenaean objects are found side by side; and eventually Greek wares replace Cretan goods altogether. Such evidence indicates that Cretan merchants pioneered trade routes and established trading posts and then admitted Mycenaean traders, who eventually supplanted them in the fifteenth century B.C.E.

What commodities formed the basis of this widespread commercial activity? The numerous Aegean pots found throughout the Mediterranean and Middle East must once have contained such products as wine and olive oil. Other possible exports include weapons and other crafted goods, as well as slaves and mercenary soldiers. Minoan and Mycenaean sailors also may have made tidy profits by transporting the trade goods of other peoples.

As for imports, amber (a hard, translucent, yellowish-brown fossil resin used for jewelry) from northern Europe and ivory carved in Syria have been discovered at Aegean sites, and the large population of southwest Greece and other regions probably relied on imports of grain. Above all, the Aegean lands needed metals, both the gold prized by rulers and the copper and tin needed to make bronze. A number of sunken ships carrying copper ingots have been found on the floor of the Mediterranean. Scholars believe that these ships were transporting metals from Cyprus to the Aegean (see Map 4.2). As in early China, the elite classes were practically the only people who owned metal goods, which may have been symbols of their superior status. The bronze tripods piled up in the storerooms of the Greek heroes in Homer's epic poems bring to mind the bronze vessels buried in Shang tombs.

In this era, trade and piracy were closely linked. Mycenaeans were tough, warlike, and acquisitive. They traded with those who were strong and took from those who were weak. This may have led to conflict with the Hittite kings of Anatolia in the fourteenth and thirteenth centuries B.C.E. Documents found in the archives at Hattusha, the Hittite capital, refer to the king and land of Ahhijawa°, most likely a Hittite rendering of *Achaeans*°, the term used most frequently by Homer for the Greeks. The documents indicate that relations were sometimes friendly, sometimes strained, and that the people of Ahhijawa were aggressive and tried to take advantage of Hittite preoccupation or weakness. The *Iliad,* Homer's tale of the Achaeans' ten-year siege and eventual destruction of Troy, a city on the fringes of Hittite territory that controlled the sea route between the Mediterranean and Black Seas, should be seen against this backdrop of Mycenaean belligerence and opportunism. Archaeology has confirmed a destruction at Troy around 1200 B.C.E.

The Fall of Late Bronze Age Civilizations

Hittite difficulties with Ahhijawa and the Greek attack on Troy foreshadowed the troubles that culminated in the destruction of many of the old centers of the Middle East and Mediterranean around 1200 B.C.E. In this period, for reasons that historians do not completely understand, large numbers of people were on the move. As migrants swarmed into one region, they displaced other peoples, who then joined the tide of refugees.

Around 1200 B.C.E. unidentified invaders destroyed Hattusha, and the Hittite kingdom in Anatolia came crashing down. The tide of destruction moved south into Syria, and the great coastal city of Ugarit was swept away.

Pylos (PIE-lohs)

Ahhijawa (uh-key-YAW-wuh) **Achaeans** (uh-KEY-uhns)

Egypt managed to beat back two attacks. Around 1220 B.C.E., Merneptah°, the son and successor of Ramesses II, repulsed an assault on the Nile Delta. His official account identified the attackers as "Libyans and Northerners coming from all lands." About thirty years later Ramesses III checked a major invasion of Palestine by the "Sea Peoples." Although he claimed to have won a great victory, the Philistines° were able to occupy the coast of Palestine. Egypt soon surrendered all its territory in Syria-Palestine and lost contact with the rest of western Asia. The Egyptians also lost their foothold in Nubia, opening the way for the emergence of the native kingdom centered on Napata (see Chapter 3).

Among the invaders listed in the Egyptian inscriptions are the Ekwesh°, who could be Achaeans—that is, Greeks. In this time of troubles it is easy to imagine opportunistic Mycenaeans taking a prominent role. Whether or not the Mycenaeans participated in the destructions elsewhere, their own centers collapsed in the first half of the twelfth century B.C.E. The rulers had seen trouble coming; at some sites they began to build more extensive fortifications and took steps to guarantee the water supply of the citadels. But their efforts were in vain, and nearly all the palaces were destroyed. The Linear B tablets survive only because they were baked hard in the fires that consumed the palaces.

Scholars are not in agreement about how these events came about. The archaeological record contains no trace of foreign invaders. An attractive explanation combines external and internal factors, since it is likely to be more than coincidence that the collapse of Mycenaean civilization occurred at roughly the same time as the fall of other great civilizations in the region. Since the Mycenaean ruling class depended on the import of vital commodities and the profits from trade, the destruction of major trading partners and disruption of trade routes would have weakened their position. Competition for limited resources may have led to internal unrest and, ultimately, political collapse.

The end of Mycenaean civilization illustrates the interdependence of the major centers of the Late Bronze Age. It also serves as a case study of the consequences of political and economic collapse. The destruction of the palaces ended the domination of the ruling class. The massive administrative apparatus revealed in the Linear B tablets disappeared, and the technique of writing was forgotten, since it had been known only to a few palace officials and was no longer useful. Archaeological studies indicate the depopulation of some regions of Greece and an inflow of people to other regions that had escaped destruction. The Greek language persisted, and a thousand years later people were still worshiping gods mentioned in the Linear B tablets. People also continued to make the vessels and implements that they were familiar with, although there was a marked decline in artistic and technical skill in the new, much poorer society. The cultural uniformity of the Mycenaean Age gave way to regional variations in shapes, styles, and techniques, reflecting increased isolation of different parts of Greece.

Thus perished the cosmopolitan world of the Late Bronze Age in the Mediterranean and Middle East. Societies that had long prospered through complex links of trade, diplomacy, and shared technologies now collapsed in the face of external violence and internal weakness, and the peoples of the region entered a centuries-long "Dark Age" of poverty, isolation, and loss of knowledge.

THE ASSYRIAN EMPIRE, 911–612 B.C.E.

A number of new centers emerged in western Asia and the eastern Mediterranean in the centuries after 1000 B.C.E. The chief force for change was the powerful and aggressive **Neo-Assyrian Empire** (911–612 B.C.E.). Although historians sometimes apply the term *empire* to earlier regional powers, the Assyrians of this era were the first to rule over far-flung lands and diverse peoples (see Map 4.3).

The Assyrian homeland in northern Mesopotamia differs in essential respects from the flat expanse of Sumer and Akkad to the south. It is hillier, has a more temperate climate and greater rainfall, and is more exposed to raiders from the mountains to the east and north and from the arid plain to the west. Peasant farmers, accustomed to defending themselves against marauders, provided the foot-soldiers for the revival of Assyrian power in the ninth century B.C.E. The rulers of the Neo-Assyrian Empire struck out in a ceaseless series of campaigns: westward across the steppe and desert as far as the Mediterranean, north into mountainous Urartu° (modern Armenia), east across the Zagros range onto the Iranian Plateau, and south along the Tigris River to Babylonia.

These campaigns largely followed the most important long-distance trade routes in western Asia and

Merneptah (mehr-NEH-ptuh) **Philistine** (FIH-luh-steen)
Ekwesh (ECK-wesh)

Urartu (ur-RAHR-too)

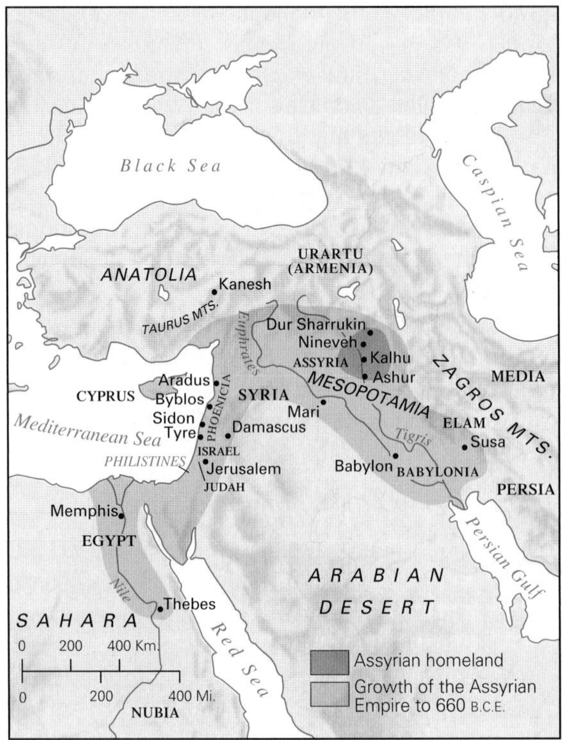

Map 4.3 The Assyrian Empire From the tenth to the seventh century B.C.E. the Assyrians of northern Mesopotamia created the largest empire the world had yet seen, extending from the Iranian Plateau to the eastern shore of the Mediterranean and containing a diverse array of peoples.

provided immediate booty and the prospect of tribute and taxes. They also secured access to vital resources such as iron and silver and brought the Assyrians control of international commerce. As noted earlier in this chapter, Assyria already had a long tradition of commercial and political interests in Syria and Anatolia. What started out as an aggressive program of self-defense and reestablishment of old claims soon became far more ambitious. Driven by pride, greed, and religious conviction, the Assyrians defeated all the great kingdoms of the day—Elam (southwest Iran), Urartu, Babylon, and Egypt. At its peak their empire stretched from Anatolia, Syria-Palestine, and Egypt in the west, across Armenia and Mesopotamia, as far as western Iran. The Assyrians created a new kind of empire, larger in extent than anything seen before and dedicated to the enrichment of the imperial center at the expense of the subjugated periphery.

God and King

The king was literally and symbolically the center of the Assyrian universe. All the land belonged to him, and all the people, even the highest-ranking officials, were his servants. Assyrians believed that the gods chose the king to rule as their earthly representative. Normally the king chose one of his sons to be his successor, and his choice was confirmed by divine oracles and the Assyrian elite. In the revered ancient city of Ashur the high priest anointed the new king by sprinkling his head with oil and gave him the insignia of kingship: a crown and scepter. The kings were buried in Ashur.

Every day messengers and spies brought the king information from every corner of the empire. He made decisions, appointed officials, and heard complaints. He dictated his correspondence to an army of scribes and received and entertained foreign envoys and high-ranking government figures. He was the military leader, responsible for planning campaigns, and he often was away from the capital commanding operations in the field.

Among the king's chief responsibilities was supervision of the state religion. He devoted much of his time to elaborate public and private rituals and to overseeing the upkeep of the temples. He made no decisions of state without consulting the gods through elaborate rituals. All state actions were carried out in the name of Ashur, the chief god. Military victories were cited as proof of Ashur's superiority over the gods of the conquered peoples.

Relentless government propaganda secured popular support for military campaigns that mostly benefited the king and the nobility. Royal inscriptions posted throughout the empire catalogued recent military victories, extolled the charisma and relentless will of the king, and promised ruthless punishments to anyone who resisted him. Art, too, served the Assyrian state. Relief sculptures depicting hunts, battles, sieges, executions, and deportations covered the walls of the royal palaces at Kalhu° and Nineveh°. Looming over most scenes was the king, larger than anyone else, muscular and fierce, with the appearance of a god. Few visitors to the Assyrian court could fail to be awed—and intimidated.

Conquest and Control

The Assyrians' unprecedented conquests were made possible by their superior military organization and technology. Early Assyrian armies consisted of men who served in return for grants of land, and peasants and slaves whose service was contributed by large landowners. Later, King Tig-

Kalhu (KAL-oo) **Nineveh** (NIN-uh-vuh)

Section of Balawat Gates Bronze bands with images of military campaigns and court life were affixed to the cedarwood gates of a palace built by the Assyrian king Shalmaneser III (r. 858–824 B.C.E.). (British Museum/Michael Holford)

lathpileser° (r. 744–727 B.C.E.) created a core army of professional soldiers made up of Assyrians and the most formidable subject peoples. At its peak the Assyrian state could mobilize a half-million troops, including light-armed bowmen and slingers who launched stone projectiles, armored spearmen, cavalry equipped with bows or spears, and four-man chariots.

Iron weapons gave Assyrian soldiers an advantage over many opponents, and cavalry provided unprecedented speed and mobility. Assyrian engineers developed machinery and tactics for besieging fortified towns. They dug tunnels under the walls, built mobile towers for their archers, and applied battering rams to weak points. The Assyrians destroyed some of the best-fortified cities of the Middle East—Babylon, Thebes in Egypt, Tyre in Phoenicia, and Susa in Elam (see Map 4.3). Couriers and signal fires provided long-distance communication, while a network of spies gathered intelligence.

The Assyrians used terror tactics to discourage resistance and rebellion, inflicting swift and harsh retribution and publicizing their brutality: civilians were thrown into fires, prisoners were skinned alive, and the severed heads of defeated rulers hung on city walls. **Mass deportation**—forcibly uprooting entire communities and resettling them elsewhere—broke the spirit of rebellious peoples. This tactic had a long history in the ancient Middle East—in Sumer, Babylon, Urartu, Egypt, and the Hittite Empire—but the Neo-Assyrian monarchs used it on an unprecedented scale. Surviving documents record the relocation of over 1 million people, and historians estimate that the true figure exceeds 4 million. Deportation also shifted human resources from the periphery to the center, where the deportees worked on royal and noble estates, opened new lands for agriculture, and built new palaces and cities. Deportees who were craftsmen and soldiers could be assigned to the Assyrian army.

To control their empire the Assyrians had to contend with vast distances, diverse landscapes, and an array of peoples with different languages, customs, religions, and political organization. The Assyrians never found a single, enduring method of governing an empire that included nomadic and sedentary kinship groups, temple-states, city-states, and kingdoms. Control tended to be tight and effective at the center and in lands closest to the core area, and less so farther away. The Assyrian kings waged many campaigns to reimpose control on territories subdued in previous wars.

Tiglathpileser (TIG-lath-pih-LEE-zuhr)

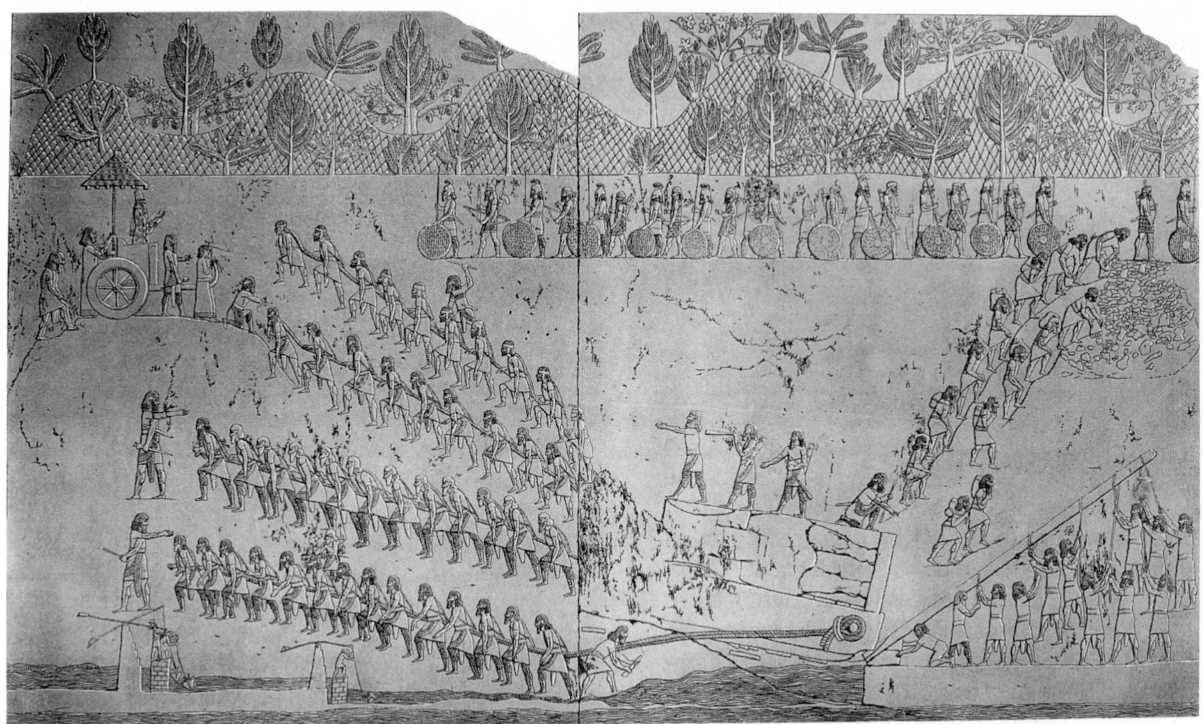

Wall Relief from the Palace of Sennacherib at Nineveh Against a backdrop of wooded hills representing the landscape of Assyria, workers are hauling a huge stone sculpture from the riverbank to the palace under the watchful eyes of officials and soldiers. They accomplish this task with simple equipment—a lever, a sledge, and thick ropes—and a lot of human muscle power. (Courtesy of the Trustees of the British Museum)

Assyrian provincial officials oversaw the payment of tribute and taxes, maintained law and order, raised troops, undertook public works, and provisioned armies and administrators that were passing through their territory. Provincial governors were subject to frequent inspections by royal overseers.

The elite class was bound to the monarch by oaths of obedience, fear of punishment, and the expectation of rewards, such as land grants or shares of booty and taxes. Skilled professionals—priests, diviners, scribes, doctors, and artisans—were similarly bound.

The Assyrians ruthlessly exploited the wealth and resources of their subjects. Military campaigns and administration had to be funded by plunder and tribute. Wealth from the periphery was funneled to the center, where the king and nobility grew rich. Proud kings used their riches to expand the ancestral capital and religious center at Ashur and to build magnificent new royal cities encircled by high walls and containing ornate palaces and temples. Dur Sharrukin°, the "Fortress of Sargon," was completed in a mere ten years, thanks to a massive labor force composed of prisoners of war and Assyrian citizens who owed periodic service to the state.

Nevertheless, the Assyrian Empire was not simply parasitic. There is some evidence of royal investment in provincial infrastructure. The cities and merchant classes thrived on expanded long-distance commerce, and some subject populations were surprisingly loyal to their Assyrian rulers.

Assyrian Society and Culture

Surviving sources shed light on the deeds of kings, victories of armies, and workings of government. A few things are known about the lives and activities of the millions of Assyrian subjects. In the core area people belonged to the same three classes that had existed in Hammurabi's Babylon a millennium before (see Chapter 2): (1) free, landowning citizens, (2) farmers and artisans attached to the estates of the king or other rich landholders, and (3) slaves. Slaves—debtors and prisoners of war—had le-

Dur Sharrukin (DOOR SHAH-roo-keen)

gal rights and, if sufficiently talented, could rise to positions of influence.

The government normally did not distinguish between native Assyrians and the increasingly large number of immigrants and deportees residing in the Assyrian homeland. All were referred to as "human beings," entitled to the same legal protections and liable for the same labor and military service. Over time the inflow of outsiders changed the ethnic makeup of the core area.

The vast majority of subjects worked on the land. The agricultural surpluses they produced allowed substantial numbers of people—the standing army, government officials, religious experts, merchants, artisans, and all manner of professionals in the towns and cities—to engage in specialized activities.

Individual artisans and small workshops in the towns manufactured pottery, tools, and clothing, and most trade took place at the local level. The state fostered long-distance trade, since imported luxury goods—metals, fine textiles, dyes, gems, and ivory—brought in substantial customs revenues and found their way to the royal family and elite classes. Silver was the basic medium of exchange, weighed out for each transaction in a time before the invention of coins.

Building on the achievements of their Mesopotamian ancestors, Assyrian scholars created and preserved lists of plant and animal names, geographic terms, and astronomical occurrences, and made original contributions in mathematics and astronomy. Their assumption that gods or demons caused disease obstructed the investigation of natural causes, but in addition to exorcists trained to expel demons, another type of physician experimented with medicines and surgical treatments to relieve symptoms.

Some Assyrian temples may have had libraries. When archaeologists excavated the palace of Ashurbanipal° (r. 668–627 B.C.E.), one of the last Assyrian kings, at Nineveh, they discovered more than twenty-five thousand tablets or fragments of tablets. The **Library of Ashurbanipal** contained official documents as well as literary and scientific texts. Some were originals that had been brought to the capital; others were copies made at the king's request. Ashurbanipal was an avid collector of the literary and scientific heritage of Mesopotamia, and the "House of Knowledge" referred to in some of the documents may have been an academy that attracted learned men to the imperial center. Much of what we know about Mesopotamian art, literature, and science and earlier Mesopotamian history comes from discoveries at Assyrian sites.

Ashurbanipal (ah-shur-BAH-nee-pahl)

Israel, 2000–500 B.C.E.

On the western edge of the Assyrian Empire lived a people who probably seemed of no great significance to the masters of western Asia but were destined to play an important role in world history. The history of ancient Israel is marked by two grand and interconnected dramas that played out from around 2000 to 500 B.C.E. First, a loose collection of nomadic kinship groups engaged in herding and caravan traffic became a sedentary, agricultural people, developed complex political and social institutions, and became integrated into the commercial and diplomatic networks of the Middle East. Second, these people transformed the austere cult of a desert god into the concept of a single, all-powerful, and all-knowing deity, in the process creating the ethical and intellectual traditions that underlie the beliefs and values of Judaism and Christianity.

The land and the people at the heart of this story have gone by various names: Canaan, Israel, Palestine; Hebrews, Israelites, Jews. For the sake of consistency, the people are referred to here as *Israelites*, the land they occupied in antiquity as **Israel.**

Israel is a crossroads, linking Anatolia, Egypt, Arabia, and Mesopotamia (see Map 4.4). Its location has given Israel an importance in history out of all proportion to its size. Its natural resources are few. The Negev Desert and the vast wasteland of the Sinai° lie to the south. The Mediterranean coastal plain was usually in the hands of others, particularly the Philistines, throughout much of this period. At the center are the rock-strewn hills of the Shephelah°. Galilee to the north, with its sea of the same name, was a relatively fertile land of grassy hills and small plains. The narrow ribbon of the Jordan River runs down the eastern side of the region into the Dead Sea, so named because its high salt content is toxic to life.

Origins, Exodus, and Settlement

Information about ancient Israel comes partly from archaeological excavations and references in contemporary documents such as the royal annals of Egypt and Assyria. However, the fundamental source is the collection of writings preserved in the **Hebrew Bible** (called the Old Testament by Christians). The Hebrew Bible is a compilation of several collections of materials that originated with different groups, employed distinctive vocabularies, and advocated particular interpretations of past events.

Sinai (SIE-nie) **Shephelah** (sheh-FEH-luh)

Map 4.4 Phoenicia and Israel The lands along the eastern shore of the Mediterranean Sea—sometimes called the Levant or Syria-Palestine—have always been a crossroads, traversed by migrants, nomads, merchants, and armies moving between Egypt, Arabia, Mesopotamia, and Anatolia.

Traditions about the Israelites' early days were long transmitted orally. Not until the tenth century B.C.E. were they written down in a script borrowed from the Phoenicians. The text that we have today dates from the fifth century B.C.E., with a few later additions, and reflects the point of view of the priests who controlled the Temple in Jerusalem. Historians disagree about how accurately this document represents Israelite history. In the absence of other written sources, however, it provides a foundation to be used critically and modified in light of archaeological discoveries.

The Hebrew language of the Bible reflects the speech of the Israelites until about 500 B.C.E. It is a Semitic language, most closely related to Phoenician and Aramaic (which later supplanted Hebrew in Israel), more distantly related to Arabic and the Akkadian language of the Assyrians. This linguistic affinity probably parallels the Israelites' ethnic relationship to the neighboring peoples.

In some respects the history of ancient Israel is unique, but it also reflects a familiar pattern in the ancient Middle East, a story of nomadic pastoralists who occupied marginal land between the inhospitable desert and settled agricultural areas. Early on, these nomads raided the farms and villages of settled peoples, but eventually they settled down to an agricultural way of life and later developed a unified state.

The Hebrew Bible tells the story of the family of Abraham. Born in the city of Ur in southern Mesopotamia, Abraham rejected the traditional idol worship of his homeland and migrated with his family and livestock across the Syrian desert. Eventually he arrived in the land of Israel, which, according to the biblical account, had been promised to him and his descendants as part of a "covenant," or pact, with the Israelite god, Yahweh.

These "recollections" of the journey of Abraham (who, if he was a real person, probably lived in the twentieth century B.C.E.) may compress the experiences of generations of pastoralists who migrated from the grazing lands between the upper reaches of the Tigris and Euphrates Rivers to the Mediterranean coastal plain. Abraham, his family, and his companions were following the usual pattern in this part of the world. They camped by a permanent water source in the dry season, then drove herds of domesticated animals (sheep, cattle, donkeys) to a well-established sequence of grazing areas during the rest of the year. The animals provided them with milk, cheese, meat, and cloth.

The early Israelites and the settled peoples of the region were suspicious of one another. This friction between nomadic herders and settled farmers, as well as the Israelites' view of their ancestors as having been nomads, comes through in the story of the innocent shepherd Abel, who was killed by his farmer brother Cain, and in the story of Sodom° and Gomorrah°, two cities that Yahweh destroyed because of their wickedness.

Abraham's son Isaac and then his grandson Jacob became the leaders of this wandering group of herders. In the next generation the squabbling sons of Jacob's several wives sold their brother Joseph as a slave to passing merchants heading for Egypt. According to the biblical account, through luck and ability Joseph became a high official at Pharaoh's court. Thus he was in a position to help his people when drought struck Israel and forced the Israelites to migrate to Egypt. The sophisticated Egyptians feared and looked down on these rough herders and eventually reduced the Israelites to slaves, putting them to work on the grand building projects of the pharaoh.

Sodom (SOE-duhm) **Gomorrah** (guh-MORE-uh)

That is the version of events given in the Hebrew Bible. Several points need to be made about it. First, the biblical account glosses over the period from 1700 to 1500 B.C.E., when Egypt was dominated by the Hyksos. Since the Hyksos are thought to have been Semitic groups that infiltrated the Nile Delta from the northeast, the Israelite migration to Egypt and later enslavement could have been connected to the Hyksos' rise and fall. Second, although the surviving Egyptian sources do not refer to Israelite slaves, they do complain about Apiru°, a derogatory term applied to caravan drivers, outcasts, bandits, and other marginal groups. The word seems to designate a class of people rather than a particular ethnic group, but some scholars believe there may be a connection between the similar-sounding terms *Apiru* and *Hebrew*. Third, the period of alleged Israelite slavery coincided with the era of ambitious building programs launched by several New Kingdom pharaohs. However, there is little archaeological evidence of an Israelite presence in Egypt.

According to the Hebrew Bible, the Israelites were led out of captivity by Moses, an Israelite with connections to the Egyptian royal family. The narrative of their departure, the Exodus, is overlaid with folktale motifs, including the ten plagues that Yahweh inflicted on Egypt to persuade the pharaoh to release the Israelites and the miraculous parting of the waters of the Red Sea that enabled the refugees to escape. It is possible that oral tradition may have preserved memories of a real emigration from Egypt followed by years of wandering in the wilderness of Sinai.

During their reported forty years in the desert, the Israelites became devoted to a stern and warlike god. According to the Hebrew Bible, Yahweh made a covenant with the Israelites: they would be his "Chosen People" if they promised to worship him exclusively. This pact was confirmed by tablets that Moses brought down from the top of Mount Sinai. Written on the tablets were the Ten Commandments, which set out the basic tenets of Jewish belief and practice. The Commandments prohibited murder, adultery, theft, lying, and envy, and demanded respect for parents and rest from work on the Sabbath, the seventh day of the week.

The biblical account tells how Joshua, Moses's successor, led the Israelites from the east side of the Jordan River into the land of Canaan° (modern Israel and the Palestinian territories). They attacked and destroyed Jericho° and other Canaanite° cities. Archaeological evidence confirms the destruction of some Canaanite towns between 1250 and 1200 B.C.E., though not precisely the towns mentioned in the biblical account. Shortly thereafter, lowland sites were resettled and new sites were established in the hills, thanks to the development of cisterns carved into nonporous rock to hold rainwater and the construction of leveled terraces on the slopes to expand the cultivable area. The material culture of the new settlers was cruder but continued Canaanite patterns.

Most scholars doubt that Canaan was conquered by a unified Israelite army. In a time of widespread disruption, movements of peoples, and decline and destruction of cities throughout this region, it is more likely that Israelite migrants took advantage of the disorder and were joined by other loosely organized groups and even refugees from the Canaanite cities.

In a pattern common throughout history, the new coalition of peoples invented a common ancestry. The "Children of Israel," as they called themselves, were divided into twelve tribes supposedly descended from the sons of Jacob and Joseph. Each tribe installed itself in a different part of the country and was led by one or more chiefs. Such leaders usually had limited power and were primarily responsible for mediating disputes and seeing to the welfare and protection of the group. Certain charismatic figures, famed for their daring in war or genius in arbitration, were called "Judges" and enjoyed a special standing that transcended tribal boundaries. The tribes also shared access to a shrine in the hill country at Shiloh°, which housed the Ark of the Covenant, a sacred chest containing the tablets that Yahweh had given Moses.

Rise of the Monarchy

The time of troubles that struck the eastern Mediterranean around 1200 B.C.E. also brought the Philistines to Israel. Possibly related to the pre-Greek population of the Aegean Sea region and likely participants in the Sea People's attack on Egypt, the Philistines occupied the coastal plain of Israel and came into frequent conflict with the Israelites. Their wars were memorialized in Bible stories about the long-haired strongman Samson, who toppled a Philistine temple, and the shepherd boy David, whose slingshot felled the towering warrior Goliath.

A religious leader named Samuel recognized the need for a stronger central authority to lead the Israelites against the Philistine city-states and anointed Saul as the first king of Israel around 1020 B.C.E. When Saul perished in battle, the throne passed to David (r. ca. 1000–960 B.C.E.).

Apiru (uh-PEE-roo) **Canaan** (KAY-nuhn) **Jericho** (JEH-rih-koe) **Canaanite** (KAY-nuh-nite)

Shiloh (SHIE-loe)

Artist's Rendering of Solomon's Jerusalem Strategically located in the middle of lands occupied by the Israelite tribes and on a high plateau overlooking the central hills and the Judaean desert, Jerusalem was captured around 1000 B.C.E. by King David, who made it his capital (the City of David is at left, the citadel and palace complex at center). The next king, Solomon, built the First Temple to serve as the center of worship of the Israelite god, Yahweh. Solomon's Temple (at upper right) was destroyed during the Neo-Babylonian sack of the city in 587 B.C.E. The modest structure soon built to take its place was replaced by the magnificent Second Temple, erected by King Herod in the last decades of the first century B.C.E. and destroyed by the Romans in 70 C.E. (Ritmeyer Archaeological Design, London)

A gifted musician, warrior, and politician, David oversaw Israel's transition from a tribal confederacy to a unified monarchy. He strengthened royal authority by making the captured hill city of Jerusalem, which lay outside tribal boundaries, his capital. Soon after, David brought the Ark to Jerusalem, making the city the religious as well as the political center of the kingdom. A census was taken to facilitate the collection of taxes, and a standing army, with soldiers paid by and loyal to the king, was instituted. These innovations enabled David to win a string of military victories and expand Israel's borders.

The reign of David's son Solomon (r. ca. 960–920 B.C.E.) marked the high point of the Israelite monarchy. Alliances and trade linked Israel with near and distant lands. Solomon and Hiram, the king of Phoenician Tyre, together commissioned a fleet that sailed into the Red Sea and brought back gold, ivory, jewels, sandalwood, and exotic animals. The story of the visit to Solomon by the queen of Sheba, who brought gold, precious stones, and spices, may be mythical, but it reflects the reality of trade with Saba° in south Arabia (present-day Yemen) or the Horn of Africa (present-day Somalia). Such wealth supported a lavish court life, a sizeable bureaucracy, and an intimidating chariot army that made Israel a regional power. Solomon undertook an ambitious building program employing slaves and the compulsory labor of citizens. To strengthen the link between religious and secular authority, he built the **First Temple** in Jerusalem. The Israelites now had a central shrine and an impressive set of rituals that could compete with other religions in the area.

The Temple priests became a powerful and wealthy class, receiving a share of the annual harvest in return for making animal sacrifices to Yahweh on behalf of the community. The expansion of Jerusalem, new commercial op-

Saba (SUH-buh)

portunities, and the increasing prestige of the Temple hierarchy changed the social composition of Israelite society. A gap between urban and rural, rich and poor, polarized a people that previously had been relatively homogeneous. Fiery prophets, claiming revelation from Yahweh, accused the monarchs and aristocracy of corruption, impiety, and neglect of the poor (see Diversity and Dominance: An Israelite Prophet Chastizes the Ruling Class).

The Israelites lived in extended families, several generations residing together under the authority of the eldest male. Marriage, usually arranged between families, was an important economic as well as social institution. When the groom, in order to prove his financial worthiness, gave a substantial gift to the father of the bride, her entire family participated in the ceremonial weighing out of silver or gold. The wife's dowry often included a slave girl who attended her for life.

Male heirs were of paramount importance, and firstborn sons received a double share of the inheritance. If a couple had no son, they could adopt one, or the husband could have a child by the wife's slave attendant. If a man died childless, his brother was expected to marry his widow and sire an heir.

In early Israel women provided a vital portion of the goods and services that sustained the family. As a result, women were respected and enjoyed relative equality with their husbands. Unlike men, however, they could not inherit property or initiate divorce, and a woman caught in extramarital relations could be put to death. Working-class women labored with other family members in agriculture or herding in addition to caring for the house and children. As the society became urbanized, some women worked outside the home as cooks, bakers, perfumers, wet nurses (usually a recent mother, still producing milk, hired to provide nourishment to another person's child), prostitutes, and singers of laments at funerals. A few women reached positions of influence, such as Deborah the Judge, who led troops in battle against the Canaanites. Women known collectively as "wise women" appear to have composed sacred texts in poetry and prose. This reality has been obscured, in part by the male bias of the Hebrew Bible, in part because the status of women declined as Israelite society became more urbanized.

Fragmentation and Dispersal

After Solomon's death around 920 B.C.E., resentment over royal demands and the neglect of tribal prerogatives split the monarchy into two kingdoms: Israel in the north, with its capital at Samaria°; and Judah° in the southern territory around Jerusalem (see Map 4.4). The two were sometimes at war, sometimes allied.

This period saw the final formulation of **monotheism,** the absolute belief in Yahweh as the one and only god. Nevertheless, religious leaders still had to contend with cults professing polytheism (the belief in multiple gods). The ecstatic rituals of the Canaanite storm-god Baal° and the fertility goddess Astarte° attracted many Israelites. Prophets condemned the adoption of foreign ritual and threatened that Yahweh would punish Israel severely.

The small states of Syria and the two Israelite kingdoms laid aside their rivalries to mount a joint resistance to the Neo-Assyrian Empire, but to no avail. In 721 B.C.E. the Assyrians destroyed the northern kingdom of Israel and deported much of its population to the east. New settlers were brought in from Syria, Babylon, and Iran, changing the area's ethnic, cultural, and religious character and removing it from the mainstream of Jewish history. The kingdom of Judah survived for more than a century longer, sometimes rebelling, sometimes paying tribute to the Assyrians or the Neo-Babylonian kingdom (626–539 B.C.E.) that succeeded them. When the Neo-Babylonian monarch Nebuchadnezzar° captured Jerusalem in 587 B.C.E., he destroyed the Temple and deported to Babylon the royal family, the aristocracy, and many skilled workers such as blacksmiths and scribes.

The deportees prospered so well in their new home "by the waters of Babylon" that half a century later most of their descendants refused the offer of the Persian monarch Cyrus (see Chapter 5) to return to their homeland. This was the origin of the **Diaspora**°—a Greek word meaning "dispersion" or "scattering." This dispersion outside the homeland of many Jews—as we may now call these people, since an independent Israel no longer existed—continues to this day. To maintain their religion and culture outside the homeland, the Diaspora communities developed institutions like the synagogue (Greek for "bringing together"), a communal meeting place that served religious, educational, and social functions.

Several groups of Babylonian Jews did make the long trek back to Judah, where they met with a cold reception from the local population. Persevering, they rebuilt the Temple in modest form and drafted the Deuteronomic° Code (*deuteronomic* is Greek for "second set of laws") of law and conduct. The fifth century B.C.E. also saw the

Samaria (suh-MAH-ree-yuh) **Judah** (JOO-duh)

Baal (BAHL) **Astarte** (uh-STAHR-tee)
Nebuchadnezzar (NAB-oo-kuhd-nez-uhr)
Diaspora (die-ASS-peh-rah)
Deuteronomic (doo-tuhr-uh-NAHM-ik)

Diversity and Dominance

An Israelite Prophet Chastizes the Ruling Class

Israelite society underwent profound changes in the period of the monarchy. A loosely organized society of village-based farmers and herders was transformed relatively rapidly into a centrally controlled state with urban centers, a standing army, an administrative bureaucracy supported by taxation, and involvement in long-distance trade networks. A central religious shrine emerged with a hierarchy of priests and other religious specialists maintained at public expense. The new opportunities for some to acquire considerable wealth led to greater disparities between rich and poor.

Throughout this period a series of prophets publicly challenged the behavior of the Israelite ruling elite. They denounced the changes in Israelite society as corrupting people and separating them from the religious devotion and moral rectitude of an earlier, better time. The prophets often spoke out on behalf of the uneducated, inarticulate, illiterate, and powerless lower classes, and thus provide valuable information about the experiences of different social groups. Theirs was not objective reporting, but rather the angry, anguished, visions of unconventional individuals.

The following excerpts from the Hebrew Bible are taken from the book of Amos. A herdsman from the southern kingdom of Judah (in the era of the divided monarchy), Amos was active in the northern kingdom of Israel in the mid-eighth century B.C.E., when Assyria threatened the Syria-Palestine region.

1:1 The following is a record of what Amos prophesied. He was one of the herdsmen from Tekoa. These prophecies about Israel were revealed to him during the time of King Uzziah of Judah and King Jeroboam son of Joash of Israel, two years before the earthquake. . . .

3:1 Listen, you Israelites, to this message which the Lord is proclaiming against you. This message is for the entire clan I brought up from the land of Egypt: 3:2 "I have chosen you alone from all the clans of the earth. Therefore I will punish you for all your sins" . . .

3:9 Make this announcement in the fortresses of Ashdod and in the fortresses in the land of Egypt. Say this: "Gather on the hills around Samaria! [capital of the northern kingdom] Observe the many acts of violence taking place within the city, the oppressive deeds occurring in it."

3:10 "They do not know how to do what is right. They store up the spoils of destructive violence in their fortresses."

3:11 Therefore," says the sovereign Lord, "an enemy will encircle the land. Your power, Samaria, will be taken away; your fortresses will be looted."

3:12 This is what the Lord says: "Just as a shepherd salvages from the lion's mouth a couple of leg bones or a piece of an ear, so the Israelites who live in Samaria will be salvaged. They will be left with just a corner of a bed, and a part of a couch" . . .

3:14 "Certainly when I punish Israel for their treaty violations, I will destroy Bethel's altars. The horns of the altars will be cut off and fall to the ground.

3:15 I will destroy both the winter and summer houses. The houses filled with ivory will be ruined, the great houses will be swept away." The Lord is speaking!

4:1 Listen to this message, you "cows of Bashan" who live on Mount Samaria! You oppress the poor; you crush the needy. You say to your husbands, "Bring us more to drink so we can party!"

4:2 The sovereign Lord confirms this oath by his own holy character: "Certainly the time is approaching! You will be carried away in baskets, every last one of you in fishermen's pots.

4:3 Each of you will go straight through the gaps in the walls; you will be thrown out toward Harmon" . . .

5:10 The Israelites hate anyone who arbitrates at the city gate; they despise anyone who speaks honestly.

5:11 Therefore, because you make the poor pay taxes on their crops and exact a grain tax from them, you will not live in the houses you built with chiseled stone, nor will you drink the wine from the fine vineyards you planted.

5:12 Certainly I am aware of your many rebellious acts and your numerous sins. You torment the innocent, you take bribes, and you deny justice to the needy at the city gate.

5:13 For this reason whoever is smart keeps quiet in such a time, for it is an evil time.

5:15 Hate what is wrong, love what is right! Promote justice at the city gate! Maybe the Lord, the God who leads armies, will have mercy on those who are left from Joseph [the Israelites] . . .
5:21 "I absolutely despise your festivals. I get no pleasure from your religious assemblies.
5:22 Even if you offer me burnt and grain offerings, I will not be satisfied; I will not look with favor on the fattened calves you offer in peace.
5:23 Take away from me your noisy songs; I don't want to hear the music of your stringed instruments.
5:24 Justice must flow like water, right actions like a stream that never dries up . . ."

6:3 You refuse to believe a day of disaster will come, but you establish a reign of violence.
6:4 They lie around on beds decorated with ivory, and sprawl out on their couches. They eat lambs from the flock, and calves from the middle of the pen.
6:5 They sing to the tune of stringed instruments; like David they invent musical instruments.
6:6 They drink wine from sacrificial bowls, and pour the very best oils on themselves.
6:7 Therefore they will now be the first to go into exile, and the religious banquets where they sprawl out on couches will end.

7:10 Amaziah the priest of Bethel sent this message to King Jeroboam of Israel: "Amos is conspiring against you in the very heart of the kingdom of Israel! The land cannot endure all his prophecies.
7:11 As a matter of fact, Amos is saying this: 'Jeroboam will die by the sword and Israel will certainly be carried into exile away from its land.'"
7:12 Amaziah then said to Amos, "Leave, you visionary! Run away to the land of Judah! Earn money and prophesy there!
7:13 Don't prophesy at Bethel any longer, for a royal temple and palace are here!"
7:14 Amos replied to Amaziah, "I was not a prophet by profession. No, I was a herdsman who also took care of sycamore fig trees.
7:15 Then the Lord took me from tending flocks and gave me this commission, 'Go! Prophesy to my people Israel!'
7:16 So now listen to the Lord's message! You say, 'Don't prophesy against Israel! Don't preach against the family of Isaac!'
7:17 "Therefore this is what the Lord says: 'Your wife will become a prostitute in the streets and your sons and daughters will die violently. Your land will be given to others and you will die in a foreign land. Israel will certainly be carried into exile away from its land.'"

8:4 Listen to this, you who trample the needy, and get rid of the destitute in the land.
8:5 You say, "When will the new moon festival be over, so we can sell grain? When will the Sabbath end, so we can open up the grain bins? We're eager to sell less for a higher price, and to cheat the buyer with rigged scales.
8:6 We're eager to trade silver for the poor, a pair of sandals for the needy. We want to mix in some chaff with the grain."
8:7 The Lord confirms this oath by the arrogance of Jacob: "I swear I will never forget all you have done!
8:8 Because of this the earth will quake, and all who live in it will mourn. The whole earth will rise like the River Nile, it will surge upward and then grow calm, like the Nile in Egypt.
8:9 In that day," says the sovereign Lord, "I will make the sun set at noon, and make the earth dark in the middle of the day.
8:10 I will turn your festivals into funerals, and all your songs into funeral dirges. I will make everyone wear funeral clothes and cause every head to be shaved bald. I will make you mourn as if you had lost your only son; when it ends it will indeed have been a bitter day.
8:11 Be certain of this, the time is coming," says the sovereign Lord, "when I will send a famine through the land. I'm not talking about a shortage of food or water, but an end to divine revelation.
8:12 People will stagger from sea to sea, and from the north around to the east. They will wander around looking for a revelation from the Lord, but they will not find any . . ."

9:8 "Look, the sovereign Lord is watching the sinful nation, and I will destroy it from the face of the earth. But I will not completely destroy the family of Jacob," says the Lord.
9:9 "For look, I am giving a command and I will shake the family of Israel together with all the nations. It will resemble a sieve being shaken, when not even a pebble falls to the ground.
9:10 All the sinners among my people will die by the sword, the ones who say, 'Disaster will not come near, it will not confront us.'
9:11 In that day I will rebuild the collapsing hut of David. I will seal its gaps, repair its ruins, and restore it to what it was like in days gone by."

QUESTIONS FOR ANALYSIS

1. **For whom is Amos's message primarily intended? How does the ruling class react to Amos's prophetic activity, and how does he respond to their tactics?**
2. **What does Amos see as wrong in Israelite society, and who is at fault? Why are even the religious practices of the elite criticized?**
3. **What will be the means by which God punishes Israel, and why does God punish them this way? What grounds for hope remain?**

Source: http://www.netbible.com. Reprinted courtesy of Biblical Studies Press, L.L.C.

compilation of much of the Hebrew Bible in roughly its present form.

The loss of political autonomy and the experience of exile had sharpened Jewish identity, with an unyielding monotheism as the core belief. Jews lived by a rigid set of rules. Dietary restrictions forbade the eating of pork and shellfish and mandated that meat and dairy products not be consumed together. Ritual baths were used to achieve spiritual purity, and women were required to take ritual baths after menstruation. The Jews venerated the Sabbath (Saturday, the seventh day of the week) by refraining from work and from fighting, following the example of Yahweh, who, according to the Bible, rested on the seventh day after creating the world (this is the origin of the concept of the weekend). These strictures and others, including a ban on marrying non-Jews, tended to isolate the Jews from other peoples, but they also fostered a powerful sense of community and the belief that they were protected by a watchful and beneficent deity.

PHOENICIA AND THE MEDITERRANEAN, 1200–500 B.C.E.

While the Israelite tribes were being forged into a united kingdom, the people who occupied the coast of the Mediterranean to the north were developing their own distinctive civilization. Historians refer to a major element of the ancient population of Syria-Palestine as **Phoenicians°**, though they referred to themselves as "Can'ani"—Canaanites. Despite the sparse written record and the disturbance of the archaeological record by frequent migrations and invasions, enough of their history survives to reveal major transformations.

The Phoenician City-States

When the eastern Mediterranean entered a period of violent upheaval and mass migrations around 1200 B.C.E. (discussed earlier), many Canaanite settlements were destroyed. Aramaeans°—nomadic pastoralists similar to the early Israelites—migrated into the interior portions of Syria. Farther south, Israelites settled in the interior of present-day Israel as herders and farmers. At the same time, the Philistines occupied the coast and introduced iron-based metallurgy to this part of the world.

By 1100 B.C.E. Canaanite territory had shrunk to a narrow strip of present-day Lebanon between the mountains and the sea (see Map 4.4). The inhabitants of this densely populated area adopted new political forms and turned to seaborne commerce and new kinds of manufacture for their survival. Sometime after 1000 B.C.E. the Canaanites encountered the Greeks, who referred to them as *Phoinikes*, or Phoenicians. The term may mean "red men" and refer to the color of their skin, or it may refer to the highly valued purple dye they extracted from the murex snail (see Environment and Technology: Ancient Textiles and Dyes).

Rivers and rocky spurs of Mount Lebanon sliced the coastal plain into a series of small city-states, chief among them Byblos°, Berytus°, Sidon°, and Tyre. A thriving trade in raw materials (cedar and pine, metals, incense, papyrus), foodstuffs (wine, spices, salted fish), and crafted luxury goods (textiles, carved ivory, glass) brought considerable wealth to the Phoenician city-states and gave them an important role in international politics.

The Phoenicians developed earlier Canaanite models into an "alphabetic" system of writing with about two dozen symbols, in which each symbol represented a sound. (The Phoenicians represented only consonants, leaving the vowel sounds to be inferred by the reader. The Greeks added symbols for vowel sounds, thereby creating the first truly alphabetic system of writing—see Chapter 5.) Little Phoenician writing survives, however, probably because scribes used perishable papyrus. Some information in Greek and Roman documents may be based on Phoenician sources

Before 1000 B.C.E. Byblos had been the most important Phoenician city-state. It was a distribution center for cedar timber from the slopes of Mount Lebanon and for papyrus from Egypt. The English word *bible* comes from the Greek *biblion*, meaning "book written on papyrus from Byblos." After 1000 B.C.E. Tyre, in southern Lebanon, surpassed Byblos. King Hiram, who came to power in 969 B.C.E., was responsible for Tyre's rise to prominence. According to the Bible, he formed a close alliance with the Israelite king Solomon and provided skilled Phoenician craftsmen and cedar wood for building the Temple in Jerusalem. In return, Tyre gained access to silver, food, and trade routes to the east and south. In the 800s B.C.E. Tyre took control of nearby Sidon and monopolized the Mediterranean coastal trade.

Located on an offshore island, Tyre was practically impregnable. It had two harbors, one facing north, the other south, connected by a canal. The city boasted a large

Phoenician (fi-NEE-shun) **Aramaean** (ah-ruh-MAY-uhn)

Byblos (BIB-loss) **Berytus** (buh-RIE-tuhs) **Sidon** (SIE-duhn)

ENVIRONMENT + TECHNOLOGY

Ancient Textiles and Dyes

Throughout human history the production of textiles—cloth for clothing, blankets, carpets, and coverings of various sorts—may have required an expenditure of human labor second only to the amount of work necessary to provide food. Nevertheless, textile production in antiquity has left few traces in the archaeological record. The plant fibers and animal hair used for cloth are organic and quickly decompose except in rare and special circumstances. Some textile remains have been found in the hot, dry conditions of Egypt, the cool, arid Andes of South America, and the peat bogs of northern Europe. But most of our knowledge of ancient textiles depends on the discovery of equipment used in textile production—such as spindles, loom weights, and dyeing vats—and on pictorial representations and descriptions in texts.

Ancient Peruvian Textiles The weaving of Chavín was famous for its color and symbolic imagery. Artisans both wove designs into the fabric and used paint or dyes to decorate plain fabric. This early Chavín painted fabric was used in a burial. Notice how the face suggests a jaguar and the headdress includes the image of a serpent. (Private collection)

The production of cloth usually has been the work of women for a simple but important reason. Responsibility for child rearing limits women's ability to participate in other activities but does not consume all their time and energy. In many societies textile production has been complementary to child-rearing activities, for it can be done in the home, is relatively safe, does not require great concentration, and can be interrupted without consequence. For many thousands of years cloth production has been one of the great common experiences of women around the globe. The growing and harvesting of plants such as cotton or flax (from which linen is made) and the shearing of wool from sheep and, in the Andes, llamas are outdoor activities, but the subsequent stages of production can be carried out inside the home. The basic methods of textile production did not change much from early antiquity until the late eighteenth century C.E., when the fabrication of textiles was transferred to mills and mass production began.

When textile production has been considered "women's work," most of the output has been for household consumption. One exception was in the early civilizations of Peru, where women weavers developed new raw materials, new techniques, and new decorative motifs around three thousand years ago. They began to use the wool of llamas and alpacas in addition to cotton. Three women worked side by side and passed the weft from hand to hand in order to overcome limitations to the width of woven fabric imposed by the back-strap loom. Women weavers also introduced embroidery, and they decorated garments with new religious motifs, such as the jaguar-god of Chavín. Their high-quality textiles were given as tribute to the elite and were used in trade to acquire luxury goods as well as dyes and metals.

More typically, men dominated commercial production. In ancient Phoenicia, fine textiles with bright, permanent colors became a major export product. These striking colors were produced by dyes derived from several species of snail. Most prized was the red-purple known as Tyrian purple because Tyre was the major source. Persian and Hellenistic kings wore robes dyed this color, and a white toga with a purple border was the sign of a Roman senator.

The production of Tyrian purple was an exceedingly laborious process. The spiny dye-murex snail lives on the sandy Mediterranean bottom at depths ranging from 30 to 500 feet (10 to 150 meters). Nine thousand snails were needed to produce 1 gram (0.035 ounce) of dye. The dye was made from a colorless liquid in the snail's hypobranchial gland. The gland sacs were removed, crushed, soaked with salt, and exposed to sunlight and air for some days; then they were subject to controlled boiling and heating.

Huge mounds of broken shells on the Phoenician coast are testimony to the ancient industry. It is likely that the snail was rendered nearly extinct at many locations, and some scholars have speculated that Phoenician colonization in the Mediterranean may have been motivated in part by the search for new sources of snails.

Phoenician Scarab Representing a Sea Deity This carved gemstone, made of green jasper and mounted on a gold hoop, would have been pressed into clay or wax to impress the owner's seal, the ancient equivalent of a signature. Made in Phoenicia but showing influences from Greek art, it depicts a bearded sea deity holding a conical cup and wreath accompanied by a dolphin or fish. (Bibliotheque Nationale de France)

marketplace, a magnificent palace complex with treasury and archives, and temples to the gods Melqart° and Astarte. Some of its thirty thousand or more inhabitants lived in suburbs on the mainland. Its one weakness was its dependence on the mainland for food and fresh water.

Little is known about the internal affairs of Tyre and other Phoenician cities. The names of a series of kings are preserved, and the scant evidence suggests that the political arena was dominated by leading merchant families. Between the ninth and seventh centuries B.C.E. the Phoenician city-states contended with Assyrian aggression, followed in the sixth century B.C.E. by the expansion of the Neo-Babylonian kingdom and later the Persian Empire (see Chapter 5). The Phoenician city-states preserved their autonomy by playing the great powers off against one another when possible and accepting a subordinate relationship to a distant master when necessary.

Expansion into the Mediterranean

After 900 B.C.E. Tyre began to turn its attention westward, establishing colonies on Cyprus, a copper-rich island 100 miles (161 kilometers) from the Syrian coast (see Map 4.4) that was strategically located on a major trade route. Phoenician merchants sailing into the Aegean Sea are mentioned in Homer's *Iliad* and *Odyssey* around 700 B.C.E. By that time a string of settlements in the western Mediterranean formed a "Phoenician triangle" composed of the North African coast from western Libya to Morocco; the south and southeast coast of Spain, including Gades° (modern Cadiz°) on the Strait of Gibraltar, controlling passage between the Mediterranean and the Atlantic Ocean; and the islands of Sardinia, Sicily, and Malta off the coast of Italy (see Map 4.5). Many of these new settlements were situated on promontories or offshore islands in imitation of Tyre. The Phoenician trading network spanned the entire Mediterranean.

State enterprise and private initiative made Tyrian expansion possible. Frequent and destructive Assyrian invasions of Syria-Palestine and the lack of arable land to feed a swelling population probably made it necessary. Overseas settlement provided an outlet for excess population, new sources of trade goods, and new trading partners. Tyre maintained its autonomy until 701 B.C.E. by paying tribute to the Assyrian kings. In that year it finally fell to an Assyrian army that stripped it of much of its territory and population, allowing Sidon to become the leading city in Phoenicia.

The Phoenicians' activities in the western Mediterranean often brought them into conflict with the Greeks, who were also expanding trade and establishing colonies.

Melqart (MEL-kahrt)

Gades (GAH-days) **Cadiz** (kuh-DEEZ)

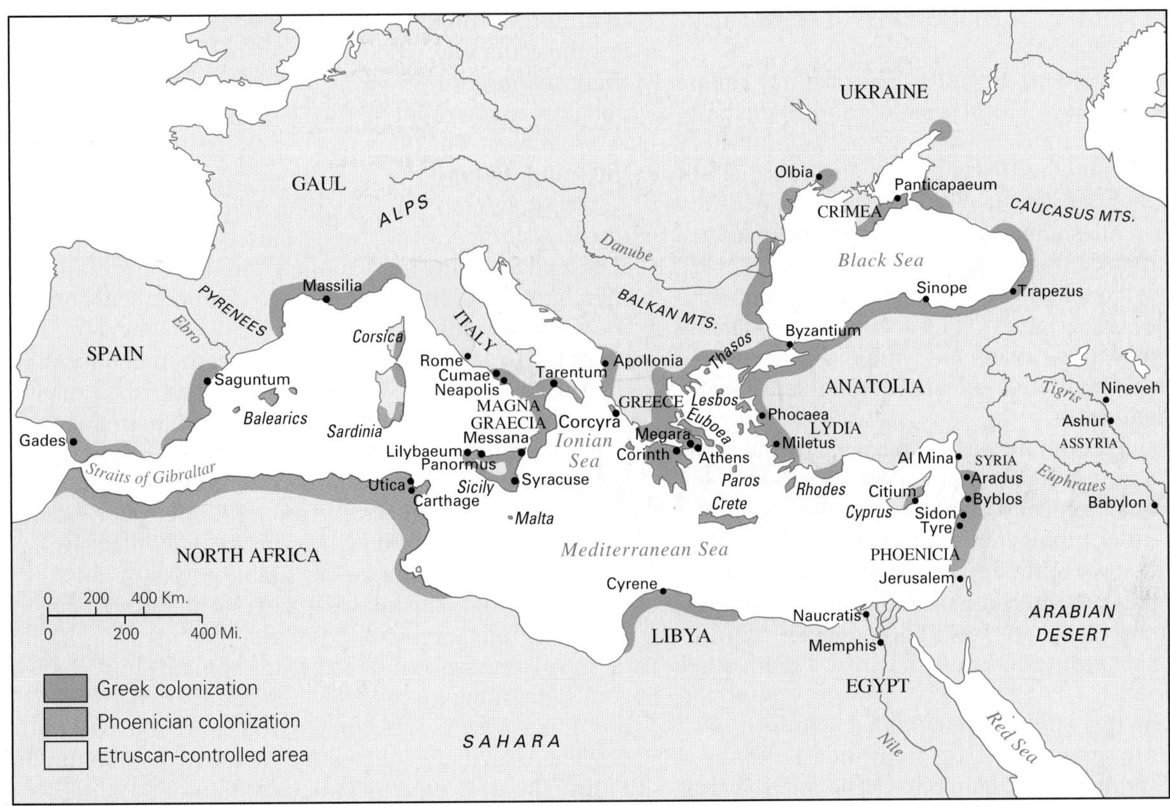

Map 4.5 Colonization of the Mediterranean In the ninth century B.C.E., the Phoenicians of Lebanon began to explore and colonize parts of the western Mediterranean, including the coast of North Africa, southern and eastern Spain, and the islands of Sicily and Sardinia. The Phoenicians were primarily interested in access to valuable raw materials and trading opportunities.

The focal point of this rivalry was Sicily. Phoenicians occupied the western end of the island, Greeks its eastern and central parts. For centuries Greeks and Phoenicians fought for control of Sicily in some of the most savage wars in the history of the ancient Mediterranean. Surviving accounts tell of atrocities, massacres, wholesale enslavements, and mass deportations. The high level of brutality suggests that each side believed its survival to be at stake. Both communities survived, but the Phoenician colony of Carthage in Tunisia, which led the coalition of Phoenician communities in the western Mediterranean, controlled all of Sicily by the mid-third century B.C.E.

Carthage's Commercial Empire

Historians know far more about **Carthage** and the other Phoenician colonies than they do about the Phoenician homeland. Much of this knowledge comes from Greek and Roman reports of their wars with the western Phoenician communities. For example, the account of the origins of Carthage that begins this chapter comes from Roman sources (most famously Virgil's epic poem *The Aeneid*) but probably is based on a Carthaginian original. Archaeological excavation has roughly confirmed the city's traditional foundation date of 814 B.C.E. Just outside the present-day city of Tunis in Tunisia, Carthage controlled the middle portion of the Mediterranean where Europe comes closest to Africa. The new settlement grew rapidly and soon dominated other Phoenician colonies in the west.

Located on a narrow promontory jutting into the Mediterranean, Carthage stretched between Byrsa°, the original hilltop citadel of the community, and a double harbor. The inner harbor could accommodate up to 220 warships. A watchtower allowed surveillance of the surrounding area, and high walls made it impossible to see in from the outside. The outer commercial harbor was filled with docks for merchant ships and shipyards. In

Byrsa (BURR-suh)

case of attack, the harbor could be closed off by a huge iron chain.

Government offices ringed a large central square where magistrates heard legal cases outdoors. The inner city was a maze of narrow, winding streets, multistory apartment buildings, and sacred enclosures. Farther out was a sprawling suburban district where the wealthy built spacious villas amid fields and vegetable gardens. This entire urban complex was enclosed by a wall 22 miles (35 kilometers) in length. At the most critical point—the 2½-mile-wide (4-kilometer-wide) isthmus connecting the promontory to the mainland—the wall was over 40 feet (13 meters) high and 30 feet (10 meters) thick and had high watchtowers.

With a population of roughly 400,000, Carthage was one of the largest cities in the world by 500 B.C.E. The population was ethnically diverse, including people of Phoenician stock, indigenous peoples likely to have been the ancestors of modern-day Berbers, and immigrants from other Mediterranean lands and sub-Saharan Africa. Contrary to the story of Dido's reluctance to remarry, Phoenicians intermarried quite readily with other peoples.

Each year two "judges" were elected from upper-class families to serve as heads of state and carry out administrative and judicial functions. The real seat of power was the Senate, where members of the leading merchant families, who sat for life, formulated policy and directed the affairs of the state. An inner circle of thirty or so senators made the crucial decisions. From time to time the leadership convened an Assembly of the citizens to elect public officials or vote on important issues, particularly when the leaders were divided or wanted to stir up popular enthusiasm for some venture.

There is little evidence at Carthage of the kind of social and political unrest that later plagued Greece and Rome (see Chapters 5 and 6). This perception may be due in part to the limited information in existing sources about internal affairs at Carthage. However, a merchant aristocracy (unlike an aristocracy of birth) was not a closed circle, and a climate of economic and social mobility allowed newly successful families and individuals to push their way into the circle of politically influential citizens. The ruling class also made sure that everyone benefited from the riches of empire, and the masses were usually ready to defer to those who made prosperity possible.

Carthaginian power rested on its navy, which dominated the western Mediterranean for centuries. Phoenician towns provided a chain of friendly ports. The Carthaginian fleet consisted of fast, maneuverable galleys—oared warships. A galley had a sturdy, pointed ram in front that could pierce the hull of an enemy vessel below the water line, while marines (soldiers aboard a ship) fired weapons. Innovations in the placement of benches and oars made room for 30, 50, and eventually as many as 170 rowers. The Phoenicians and their Greek rivals set the standard for naval technology in this era.

Carthaginian foreign policy reflected its economic interests. Protection of the sea lanes, access to raw materials, and fostering trade mattered most to the dominant merchant class. Indeed, Carthage claimed the waters of the western Mediterranean as its own. Foreign merchants were free to sail to Carthage to market their goods, but if they tried to operate on their own, they risked having their ships sunk by the Carthaginian navy. Treaties between Carthage and other states included formal recognition of this maritime commercial monopoly.

The archaeological record provides few clues about the commodities traded by the Carthaginians. Commerce may have included perishable goods—foodstuffs, textiles, animal skins, slaves—and raw metals such as silver, lead, iron, and tin, whose Carthaginian origin would not be evident. We know that Carthaginian ships carried goods manufactured elsewhere and that products brought to Carthage by foreign traders were reexported.

There is also evidence for trade with sub-Saharan Africa. Hanno°, a Carthaginian captain of the fifth century B.C.E., claimed to have sailed through the Strait of Gibraltar into the Atlantic Ocean and to have explored the West African coast (see Map 4.5). His report includes vivid descriptions of ferocious savages, drums in the night, and rivers of fire. Scholars have had difficulty matching up Hanno's topographic descriptions and distances with the geography of West Africa, and some regard his account as outright fiction. Others believe that he misstated distances and exaggerated the dangers to deter other explorers from following his route and competing for the trade in West African gold. Other Carthaginians explored the Atlantic coast of Spain and France and secured control of an important source of tin in the "Tin Islands," probably Cornwall in southwestern England.

War and Religion

Unlike Assyria, Carthage did not directly rule a large amount of territory. A belt of fertile land in northeastern Tunisia, owned by Carthaginians but worked by native peasants and imported slaves, provided a secure food supply. Beyond this core area the Carthaginians ruled most of their "empire" indirectly,

Hanno (HA-noe)

The Tophet of Carthage Here, from the seventh to second centuries B.C.E., the cremated bodies of sacrificed children were buried. Archaeological excavation has confirmed the claim in ancient sources that the Carthaginians sacrificed children to their gods at times of crisis. Stone markers, decorated with magical signs and symbols of divinities as well as family names, were placed over ceramic urns containing the ashes and charred bones of one or more infants or, occasionally, older children. (Martha Cooper/Peter Arnold, Inc.)

and allowed other Phoenician communities in the western Mediterranean to remain independent. These Phoenician communities looked to Carthage for military protection and followed its lead in foreign policy. Only Sardinia and southern Spain were put under the direct control of a Carthaginian governor and garrison, presumably to safeguard their agricultural, metal, and manpower resources.

Carthage's focus on trade may explain the unusual fact that citizens were not required to serve in the army: they were of more value in other capacities, such as trading activities and the navy. Since the indigenous North African population was not politically or militarily well organized, Carthage had little to fear from potential enemies close to home. When Carthage was drawn into a series of wars with the Greeks and Romans from the fifth through third centuries B.C.E., it relied on mercenaries from the most warlike peoples in its dominions or from neighboring areas—Numidians from North Africa, Iberians from Spain, Gauls from France, and various Italian peoples. These well-paid mercenaries were under the command of Carthaginian officers.

Another sign that war was not the primary business of the state was the separation of military command from civilian government. Generals were chosen by the Senate and kept in office for as long as they were needed. In contrast, the kings of Assyria and the other major states of the ancient Middle East normally led military campaigns.

Carthaginian religion fascinated Greek and Roman writers. Like the deities of Mesopotamia (see Chapter 2), the gods of the Carthaginians—chief among them Baal Hammon°, a male storm-god, and Tanit°, a female fertility figure—were powerful and capricious entities who had to be appeased by anxious worshipers. Roman sources report that members of the Carthaginian elite would sacrifice their own male children in times of crisis. Excavations at Carthage and other western Phoenician towns have turned up *tophets*°—walled enclosures where thousands of small, sealed urns containing the burned bones of children lay buried. Although some

Baal Hammon (BAHL ha-MOHN) **Tanit** (TAH-nit)
tophet (TOE-fet)

scholars argue that these were infants born prematurely or taken by childhood illnesses, most maintain that the western Phoenicians practiced child sacrifice on a more or less regular basis. Originally practiced by the upper classes, child sacrifice seems to have become more common and to have involved broader elements of the population after 400 B.C.E.

Plutarch°, a Greek who lived around 100 C.E., long after the demise of Carthage, wrote the following on the basis of earlier sources:

> The Carthaginians are a hard and gloomy people, submissive to their rulers and harsh to their subjects, running to extremes of cowardice in times of fear and of cruelty in times of anger; they keep obstinately to their decisions, are austere, and care little for amusement or the graces of life.[1]

We should not take the hostile opinions of Greek and Roman sources at face value. Still, it is clear that the Carthaginians were perceived as different and that cultural barriers, leading to misunderstanding and prejudice, played a significant role in the conflicts among these peoples of the ancient Mediterranean. In Chapter 6 we follow the protracted and bloody struggle between Rome and Carthage for control of the western Mediterranean.

Failure and Transformation, 750–550 B.C.E.

The extension of Assyrian power over the entire Middle East had enormous consequences for all the peoples of this region and caused the stories of Mesopotamia, Israel, and Phoenicia to converge. In 721 B.C.E. the Assyrians destroyed the northern kingdom of Israel and deported a substantial portion of the population, and for over a century the southern kingdom of Judah was exposed to relentless pressure. Assyrian threats and demands for tribute spurred the Phoenicians to colonize and exploit the western Mediterranean. Tyre's fall to the Assyrians in 701 B.C.E. accelerated the decline of the Phoenician homeland, but the western colonies, especially Carthage, lying far beyond Assyrian reach, flourished.

Even Egypt, for so long impregnable behind its desert barriers, fell to Assyrian invaders in the mid-seventh century B.C.E. Thebes, its ancient capital, never recovered. The southern plains of Sumer and Akkad, the birthplace of Mesopotamian civilization, were reduced to a protectorate, while Babylon was alternately razed and rebuilt by Assyrian kings of differing dispositions. Urartu and Elam, Assyria's great-power rivals close to home, were destroyed.

By 650 B.C.E. Assyria stood unchallenged in western Asia. But the arms race with Urartu, the frequent expensive campaigns, and the protection of lengthy borders had sapped Assyrian resources. Assyrian brutality and exploitation aroused the hatred of conquered peoples. At the same time, changes in the ethnic composition of the army and the population of the homeland had reduced popular support for the Assyrian state.

Two new political entities spearheaded resistance to Assyria. First, Babylonia had been revived by the Neo-Babylonian, or Chaldaean°, dynasty (the Chaldaeans had infiltrated southern Mesopotamia around 1000 B.C.E.). Second, the Medes°, an Iranian people, were extending their kingdom eastward across the Iranian Plateau in the seventh century B.C.E. The two powers launched a series of attacks on the Assyrian homeland that destroyed the chief cities by 612 B.C.E.

The rapidity of the Assyrian fall is stunning. The destruction systematically carried out by the victorious attackers led to the depopulation of northern Mesopotamia. Two centuries later, when a corps of Greek mercenaries passed by mounds that concealed the ruins of the Assyrian capitals, the Athenian chronicler Xenophon° had no inkling that their empire had ever existed.

The Medes took over the Assyrian homeland and the northern steppe as far as eastern Anatolia, but most of the territory of the old empire fell to the **Neo-Babylonian kingdom** (626–539 B.C.E.), thanks to the energetic campaigns of kings Nabopolassar° (r. 625–605 B.C.E.) and Nebuchadnezzar (r. 604–562 B.C.E.). Babylonia underwent a cultural renaissance. The city of Babylon was enlarged and adorned, becoming the greatest metropolis of the world in the sixth century B.C.E. Old cults were revived, temples rebuilt, festivals resurrected. The related pursuits of mathematics, astronomy, and astrology reached new heights.

Conclusion

This chapter traces developments in the Middle East and the Mediterranean from 2000 to 500 B.C.E. The patterns of culture that originated in the river-valley civilizations of Egypt and Mesopotamia persisted into this era. Peoples such as the Amorites, Kassites, and Chal-

Plutarch (PLOO-tawrk)

Chaldaean (chal-DEE-uhn) **Mede** (MEED)
Xenophon (ZEN-uh-fahn) **Nabopolassar** (NAB-oh-poe-lass-uhr)

daeans, who migrated into the Tigris-Euphrates plain, were largely assimilated into the Sumerian-Semitic cultural tradition, adopting the language, religious beliefs, political and social institutions, and forms of artistic expression. Similarly, the Hyksos, who migrated into the Nile Delta and controlled much of Egypt for a time, adopted the ancient ways of Egypt. When the founders of the New Kingdom finally ended Hyksos domination, they reinstituted the united monarchy and the religious and cultural traditions of earlier eras.

Yet the Middle East was in many important respects a different place after 2000 B.C.E. New centers of political and economic power had emerged—the Elamites in southwest Iran, the Assyrians in northern Mesopotamia, Urartu in present-day Armenia, the Hittites of Anatolia, and the Minoan and Mycenaean peoples of the Aegean Sea. These new centers often borrowed heavily from the technologies and cultural practices of Mesopotamia and Egypt, creating dynamic syntheses of imported and indigenous elements. The entire Middle East was drawn together by networks of trade and diplomacy, a situation that provided general stability and raised the standard of living for many. Ultimately, though, the very interdependence of these societies made them vulnerable to the destructions and disorder of the decades around 1200 B.C.E. The entire region slipped into a "Dark Age" of isolation, stagnation, and decline that lasted several centuries.

The early centuries after 1000 B.C.E. saw a resurgence of political organization and international commerce, and the spread of technologies and ideas. The Neo-Assyrian Empire, the great power of the time, represented a continuation of the Mesopotamian tradition, though the center of empire moved to the north. Israel and Phoenicia, on the other hand, reflected the influence of Mesopotamia and Egypt but also evolved distinctive cultural traditions.

Throughout this era people were on the move, sometimes voluntarily and sometimes under compulsion. The Assyrians deported large numbers of prisoners of war from outlying subject territories to the core area in northern Mesopotamia. The Phoenicians left their overpopulated homeland to establish new settlements in North Africa, Spain, and islands off the coast of Italy. In their new homes the Phoenician colonists tried to duplicate familiar ways of life from the old country. In contrast, the Israelites who settled in Canaan and, at a later time, emigrated to the Diaspora underwent significant political, social, and cultural transformations as they adapted to new zones of settlement.

It is no accident that several of the peoples featured in this and the previous chapters who settled outside their places of origin had long and distinguished destinies ahead of them. Diasporas proved to be fertile sources of innovation and helped preserve culture. The Carthaginian enterprise eventually was cut short by the Romans, but Jews and Greeks survive into our own time. Ironically, the Assyrians, the most powerful of all these societies, suffered the most complete termination of their way of life. Because Assyrians did not settle outside their homeland in significant numbers, when their state was toppled in the late seventh century B.C.E. their culture all but perished.

The Neo-Babylonian kingdom that arose on the ashes of the Neo-Assyrian Empire would be the last revival of the ancient Sumerian and Semitic cultural legacy in western Asia. The next chapter relates how the destinies of the peoples of the Mediterranean and the Middle East became enmeshed in the new forms of political and social organization emerging from Iran and Greece.

Key Terms

Iron Age	**mass deportation**
Hittites	**Library of Ashurbanipal**
Hatshepsut	**Israel**
Akhenaten	**Hebrew Bible**
Ramesses II	**First Temple**
Minoan	**monotheism**
Mycenae	**Diaspora**
shaft graves	**Phoenicians**
Linear B	**Carthage**
Neo-Assyrian Empire	**Neo-Babylonian kingdom**

Suggested Reading

Fundamental for all periods in the ancient Middle East is Jack M. Sasson, ed., *Civilizations of the Ancient Near East*, 4 vols. (1995), containing nearly two hundred articles by contemporary experts and bibliography on a wide range of topics. John Boardman, I. E. S. Edwards, N. G. L. Hammond, and E. Sollberger, *The Cambridge Ancient History*, 2d ed., vols. 3.1–3.3 (1982–1991), provides extremely detailed historical coverage of the entire Mediterranean and western Asia. Barbara Lesko, ed., *Women's Earliest Records: From Ancient Egypt and Western Asia* (1989), is a collection of papers on the experiences of women in the ancient Middle East.

Many of the books recommended in the Suggested Reading list for Chapter 2 are useful for Mesopotamia, Syria, and Egypt in the Late Bronze Age. In addition see Miriam Lichtheim, *Ancient Egyptian Literature: A Book of Readings*, vol. 2, *The New Kingdom* (1978); Donald B. Redford, *Egypt, Canaan, and Israel in Ancient Times* (1992), which explores the relations of Egypt with the Syria-Palestine region in this period; Erik Hornung, *Akhenaten and the Religion of Light* (1999), which, while focusing on the religious innovations, deals with many facets of the reign of Akhenaten; Karol Mysliwiec, *The Twilight of Ancient Egypt: First Millennium B.C.E.* (2000), which traces the story of Egyptian civilization after the New Kingdom; and H. W. F. Saggs, *Babylonians* (1995), which devotes several chapters to this more thinly documented epoch in the history of southern Mesopotamia. The most up-to-date treatment of the Hittites can be found in Trevor Boyce, *The Kingdom of the Hittites* (1998) and *Life and Society in the Hittite World* (2002). Also useful are O. R. Gurney, *The Hittites*, 2d ed., rev. (1990), and J. G. Macqueen, *The Hittites and Their Contemporaries in Asia Minor* (1975).

R. A. Higgins, *The Archaeology of Minoan Crete* (1973) and *Minoan and Mycenaean Art,* new rev. ed. (1997); Rodney Castleden, *Minoans: Life in Bronze Age Crete* (1990); J. Walter Graham, *The Palaces of Crete* (1987); O. Krzyszkowska and L. Nixon, *Minoan Society* (1983); and N. Marinatos, *Minoan Religion* (1993), examine the archaeological evidence for the Minoan civilization. The brief discussion of M. I. Finley, *Early Greece: The Bronze and Archaic Ages* (1970), and the much fuller accounts of Emily Vermeule, *Greece in the Bronze Age* (1972), and J. T. Hooker, *Mycenaean Greece* (1976), are still useful treatments of Mycenaean Greece, based primarily on archaeological evidence. Robert Drews, *The Coming of the Greeks: Indo-European Conquests in the Aegean and the Near East* (1988), examines the evidence for the earliest Greeks. For the Linear B tablets see John Chadwick, *Linear B and Related Scripts* (1987) and *The Mycenaean World* (1976). J. V. Luce, *Homer and the Heroic Age* (1975), and Carol G. Thomas, *Myth Becomes History: Pre-Classical Greece* (1993), examine the usefulness of the Homeric poems for reconstructing the Greek past. For the disruptions and destructions of the Late Bronze Age in the eastern Mediterranean, see N. K. Sandars, *The Sea Peoples: Warriors of the Ancient Mediterranean* (1978), and Trude Dothan and Moshe Dothan, *People of the Sea: The Search for the Philistines* (1992).

For general history and cultural information about the Neo-Assyrian Empire, Mesopotamia, and western Asia in the first half of the first millennium B.C.E. see Michael Roaf, *Cultural Atlas of Mesopotamia and the Ancient Near East* (1990); Amelie Kuhrt, *The Ancient Near East, c. 3000–300 B.C.* (1995); H. W. F. Saggs, *Civilization Before Greece and Rome* (1989); and A. Bernard Knapp, *The History and Culture of Ancient Western Asia and Egypt* (1988). H. W. F. Saggs, *Babylonians* (1995), has coverage of the fate of the old centers in southern Mesopotamia during this era in which the north attained dominance. Primary texts in translation for Assyria and other parts of western Asia can be found in James B. Pritchard, ed., *Ancient Near Eastern Texts Relating to the Old Testament,* 3d ed. (1969). Jeremy Black and Anthony Green, *Gods, Demons and Symbols of Ancient Mesopotamia: An Illustrated Dictionary* (1992), is valuable for religious concepts, institutions, and mythology. Julian Reade, *Assyrian Sculpture* (1983), provides a succinct introduction to the informative relief sculptures from the Assyrian palaces. J. E. Curtis and J. E. Reade, eds., *Art and Empire: Treasures from Assyria in the British Museum* (1995), relates the art to many facets of Assyrian life. Andre Parrot, *The Arts of Assyria* (1961), provides full coverage of all artistic media.

For general historical introductions to ancient Israel see Michael Grant, *The History of Israel* (1984); J. Maxwell Miller and John H. Hayes, *A History of Ancient Israel and Judah* (1986); and J. Alberto Soggin, *A History of Israel: From the Beginnings to the Bar Kochba Revolt, A.D. 135* (1984). Amnon Ben-Tor, *The Archaeology of Ancient Israel* (1991), and Amihai Mazar, *Archaeology of the Land of the Bible, 10,000–586 B.C.E.* (1990), provide overviews of the discoveries of archaeological excavation in Israel. William G. Dever, *What Did the Biblical Writers Know, and When Did They Know It? What Archaeology Can Tell Us About the Reality of Ancient Israel* (2001), and B. J. S. Isserlin, *The Israelites* (2001), both review the archaeological evidence and take moderate positions in the heated debate about the value of the biblical text for reconstructing the history of Israel. Hershel Shanks, *Jerusalem, an Archaeological Biography* (1995), explores the long and colorful history of the city. For social and economic issues see Shunya Bendor, *The Social Structure of Ancient Israel: The Institution of the Family (beit 'ab) from the Settlement to the End of the Monarchy* (1996), and Moses Aberbach, *Labor, Crafts and Commerce in Ancient Israel* (1994). Carol Meyers, *Discovering Eve: Ancient Israelite Women in Context* (1998), carefully sifts through literary and archaeological evidence to reach a balanced assessment of the position of women in the period before the monarchy. Victor H. Matthews, *The Social World of the Hebrew Prophets* (2001), provides social and historical contexts for all the prophets. For the Philistines see Trude Dothan, *The Philistines and Their Material Culture* (1982).

Glenn Markoe, *Phoenicians* (2000), Sabatino Moscati, *The Phoenicians* (1988), and Gerhard Herm, *The Phoenicians: The Purple Empire of the Ancient World* (1975), are general introductions to the Phoenicians in their homeland. Maria Eugenia Aubet, *The Phoenicians and the West: Politics, Colonies and Trade* (2001), is an insightful investigation of the dynamics of Phoenician expansion into the western Mediterranean. Lionel Casson, *The Ancient Mariners: Seafarers and Sea Fighters of the Mediterranean in Ancient Times,* 2d ed. (1991), 75–79, discusses the design of warships and merchant vessels. For Carthage see Serge Lancel, *Carthage: A History* (1995), and David Soren, Aicha Ben Abed Ben Khader, and Hedi Slim, *Carthage: Uncovering the Mysteries and Splendors of Ancient Tunisia* (1990). Aicha Ben Abed Ben Khader and David Soren, *Carthage: A Mosaic of Ancient Tunisia* (1987), includes articles by American and Tunisian scholars as well as the catalog of a museum exhibition. R. C. C. Law, "North Africa in the Period of Phoenician and Greek Colonization, c. 800 to 323 B.C.," Chapter 2 in *The Cambridge History of Africa,* vol. 2 (1978), places the history of Carthage in an African perspective.

Elizabeth Wayland Barber, *Women's Work: The First 20,000 Years: Women, Cloth, and Society in Early Times* (1994), is an intriguing account of textile manufacture in antiquity, with emphasis on the social implications and primary role of women. I. Irving Ziderman, "Seashells and Ancient Purple Dyeing," *Biblical Archaeologist* 53 (June 1990): 98–101, is a convenient summary of Phoenician purple-dyeing technology.

Notes

1. Plutarch, *Moralia,* 799 D, trans. B. H. Warmington, *Carthage* (Harmondsworth, England: Penguin 1960), 163.

Animal Domestication

The earliest domestication of plants and animals took place long before the existence of written records. For this reason, we cannot be sure how and when humans first learned to plant crops and certain animals became tame enough to live among humans. Anthropologists and historians usually link the two processes as part of a Neolithic Revolution, but they were not necessarily connected.

The domestication of plants is much better understood than the domestication of animals. Foraging bands of preagricultural humans gained much of their sustenance from seeds, fruits, and tubers collected from wild plants. Humans may have planted seeds and tubers many times without lasting effect. In a few instances, however, their plantings accidentally included a higher proportion of one naturally occurring variety of a wild species. After repeated planting cycles, this variety, which was rare in the wild, became common. When a new variety suited human needs, usually by having more food value or being easier to grow or process, people stopped collecting the wild types and relied on farming and further developing their new domestic type. In some seemingly wild forest areas of Southeast Asia and Central America, a higher than normal frequency of certain fruit trees indicates that people deliberately planted them sometime in the distant past.

In the case of animals, the question of selection to suit human needs is hard to judge. Archaeologists and anthropologists looking at ancient bones and images interpret changes in hair color, horn shape, and other visible features as indicators of domestication. But these visible changes did not generally serve human purposes. As for the uses that are most commonly associated with domestic animals, some of the most important, such as milking cows, shearing sheep, and harnessing oxen and horses to plows and vehicles, first appeared hundreds and even thousands of years after domestication.

Anthropologists and archaeologists usually assume that animals were domesticated as meat producers, but even this is questionable. Dogs, which became domestic tens of thousands of years before any other species, seem not to have been eaten in most cultures, and cats, which became domestic much later, were eaten even less often.

Cattle, sheep, and goats became domestic around ten thousand years ago in the Middle East and North Africa. Coincidentally, wheat and barley were being domesticated at roughly the same time in the same general area. This is the main reason historians generally conclude that plant and animal domestication are closely related. Yet other major meat animals, such as chickens, which originated as jungle fowl in Southeast Asia, and pigs, which probably became domestic separately in several parts of North Africa, Europe, and Asia, have no agreed-upon association with early plant domestication. Nor is plant domestication connected with the horses and camels that became domestic in western Asia and the donkeys that became domestic in the Sahara region around six thousand years ago. Though the wild forebears of these species were probably eaten, the domestic forms were usually not used for meat.

In the Middle East humans may have originally kept wild sheep, goats, and cattle for food, though wild cattle were large and dangerous and must have been hard to control. It is questionable whether keeping these or other wild animals captive for food would have been more productive, in the earliest stages, than hunting. It is even more questionable whether the humans who kept animals for this purpose had any reason to anticipate that life in captivity would cause them to become domestic.

The human motivations for the domestication of animals can be better assessed after a consideration of the physical changes involved in going from wild to domestic. Genetically transmitted tameness, defined as the ability to live with and accept handling by humans, lies at the core of the domestication process. In separate experiments with wild rats and foxes in the twentieth century, scientists found that wild individuals with strong fight-or-flight tendencies reproduce poorly in captivity. Individual animals with the lowest adrenaline levels have the most offspring in captivity. In the wild, the same low level of excitability would have made these individuals vulnerable to predators and kept their reproduction rate down. Human selection probably reinforced the natural tendency for the least excitable animals to reproduce best in captivity. In other words, humans probably preferred the animals that seemed the tamest, and destroyed those that were most wild. In the rat and fox experiments, after twenty generations or so, the surviving animals were born with much smaller adrenal glands and greatly reduced fight-or-flight reactions. Since adrenaline production normally increases in the transition to adulthood, many of the low-adrenaline animals also retained juvenile characteristics, such as floppy ears and pushed-in snouts, both indicators of domestication. This tendency of certain domestic species to preserve immature characteristics is called *neoteny*.

It is quite probable that animal domestication was not a deliberate process but rather the unanticipated outcome of keeping animals for other purposes. Since a twenty-generation time span for wild cattle and other large quadrupeds would have amounted to several human lifetimes, it is highly unlikely that the people who ended up with domestic cows had any recollection of how the process started. This seems to rule out the possibility that people who had unwittingly domesticated one species would have attempted to repeat the process with other species. Since they probably did not know what they had done to produce genetically transmitted tameness, they would not have known how to duplicate the process.

Historians disagree on this matter. Some assume that domestication was an understood and reproducible process and conclude that through a series of domestication attempts, humans domesticated every species that could be domesticated. This is unlikely. It is probable that more species could be domesticated over time. Twentieth-century efforts to domesticate bison, eland, and elk have not fully succeeded, but they have generally not been maintained for as long as twenty generations. Rats and foxes have more rapid reproduction rates, and the experiments with them succeeded. In looking at the impact of animal domestication on different parts of the world, it is unwarranted to assume that some regions were luckier than others in being home to species that were ripe for domestication, or that some human societies were cleverer than others in figuring out how to make animals genetically tame.

Rather than being treated as a process once known to early human societies and subsequently forgotten, animal domestication is best studied on a case-by-case basis as an unintended result of other processes. In some instances, sacrifice probably played a key role. Religious traditions of animal sacrifice rarely utilize, and sometimes prohibit, the ritual killing of wild animals. It is reasonable to suppose that the practice of capturing wild animals and holding them for sacrifice sometimes eventually led to the appearance of genetically transmitted tameness as an unplanned result.

Horses and camels were domesticated relatively late, and most likely not for meat consumption. The societies within which these animals first appeared as domestic species already had domestic sheep, goats, and cattle and used oxen to carry loads and pull plows and carts. Horses, camels, and later reindeer may represent successful experiments with substituting one draft animal for another, with genetically transmitted tameness an unexpected consequence of separating animals trained for riding or pulling carts from their wilder kin.

Once human societies had developed the full range of uses of domestic animals—meat, eggs, milk, fiber, labor, transport—the likelihood of domesticating more species diminished. In the absence of concrete knowledge of how domestication had occurred, it was usually easier for people to move domestic livestock to new locations than to attempt to develop new domestic species. Domestic animals accompanied human groups wherever they ventured, and this practice triggered enormous environmental changes as domestic animals, and their human keepers, competed with wild species for food and living space.

PART TWO

The Formation of New Cultural Communities, 1000 B.C.E.–400 C.E.

The fourteen centuries from 1000 B.C.E. to 400 C.E. mark a new chapter in the story of humanity. Important changes in the ways of life established in the river-valley civilizations in the two previous millennia occurred, and the scale of human institutions and activities increased.

The political and social structure of the earliest river-valley centers reflected the importance of irrigation for agriculture. Powerful kings, hereditary priesthoods, dependent laborers, limited availability of metals, and very restricted literacy are hallmarks of the complex societies described in Part One. In the first millennium B.C.E., new centers arose, in lands watered by rainfall and worked by a free peasantry, on the shores of the Mediterranean, in Iran, India, Southeast Asia, and in Central and South America. Shaped by the natural environments in which they arose, they developed new patterns of political and social organization and economic activity, and moved in new intellectual, artistic, and spiritual directions, though under the influence of the older centers.

The rulers of the empires of this era took steps intended to control and tax their subjects: they constructed extensive networks of roads and promoted urbanization. These measures brought incidental benefits: more rapid communication, the transport of trade goods over greater distances, and the broad diffusion of religious ideas, artistic styles, and technologies. Large cultural zones unified by common traditions emerged. A number of these cultural traditions—Iranian, Hellenistic, Roman—were to exercise substantial influence on subsequent ages. The influence of some—Hindu and Chinese—persists into our own time.

The expansion of agriculture and trade and improvements in technology led to population increases, the spread of cities, and the growth of a comfortable middle class. In many parts of the world iron replaced bronze as the preferred metal for weapons, tools, and utensils. People using iron tools cleared extensive forests around the Mediterranean, in India, and in eastern China. Iron weapons gave an advantage to the armies of Greece, Rome, and imperial China. Metal, still an important item of long-distance trade, was available to more people than it had been in the preceding age. Metal coinage, which originated in Anatolia, was adopted by many peoples. Metal coins facilitated commercial transactions and the acquisition of wealth.

New systems of writing also developed. Because these systems were more easily and rapidly learned, writing moved out of the control of specialists. The vast majority of people remained illiterate, but writing became an increasingly important medium for preserving and transmitting cultural knowledge. The spread of literacy gave birth to new ways of thinking, new genres of literature, and new types of scientific endeavor.

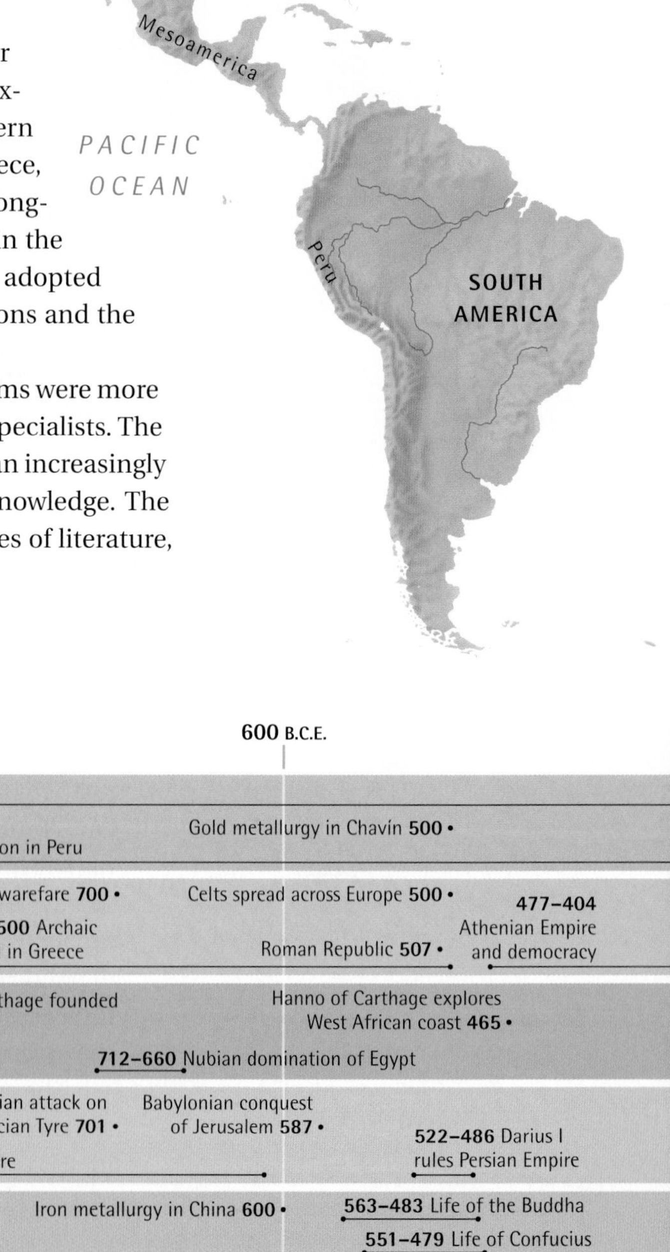

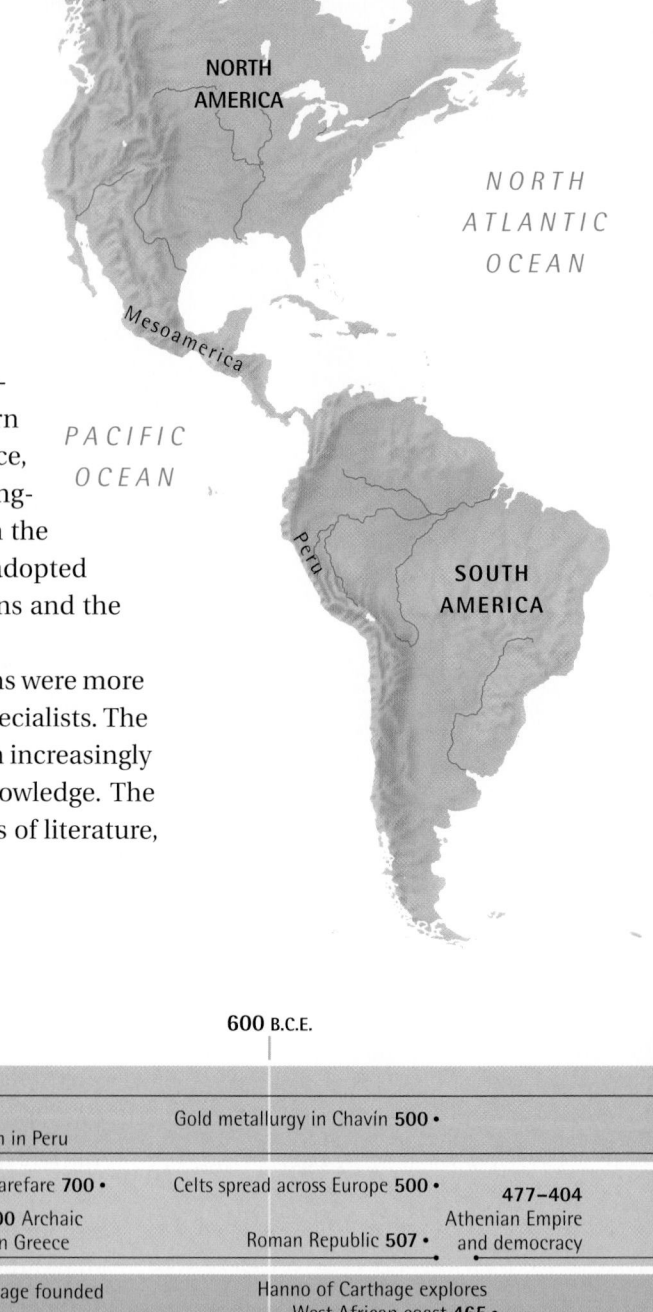

	1000 B.C.E.	800 B.C.E.	600 B.C.E.
Americas	**1200–400** Olmec civilization in Mesoamerica; **900–250** Chavín civilization in Peru		Gold metallurgy in Chavín **500**
Europe	**1000** Iron metallurgy	Hoplite warefare **700**; **800–500** Archaic period in Greece	Celts spread across Europe **500**; Roman Republic **507**; **477–404** Athenian Empire and democracy
Africa	Rise of Nubian kingdom at Napata **800**	**814** Carthage founded; **712–660** Nubian domination of Egypt	Hanno of Carthage explores West African coast **465**
Middle East	**1000** David establishes Jerusalem as capital of Israel; **911–612** Neo-Assyrian Empire	Assyrian attack on Phoenician Tyre **701**	Babylonian conquest of Jerusalem **587**; **522–486** Darius I rules Persian Empire
Asia and Oceania	**1000** Aryans settle Ganges Plain; **1027–221** Zhou kingdom in China		Iron metallurgy in China **600**; **563–483** Life of the Buddha; **551–479** Life of Confucius

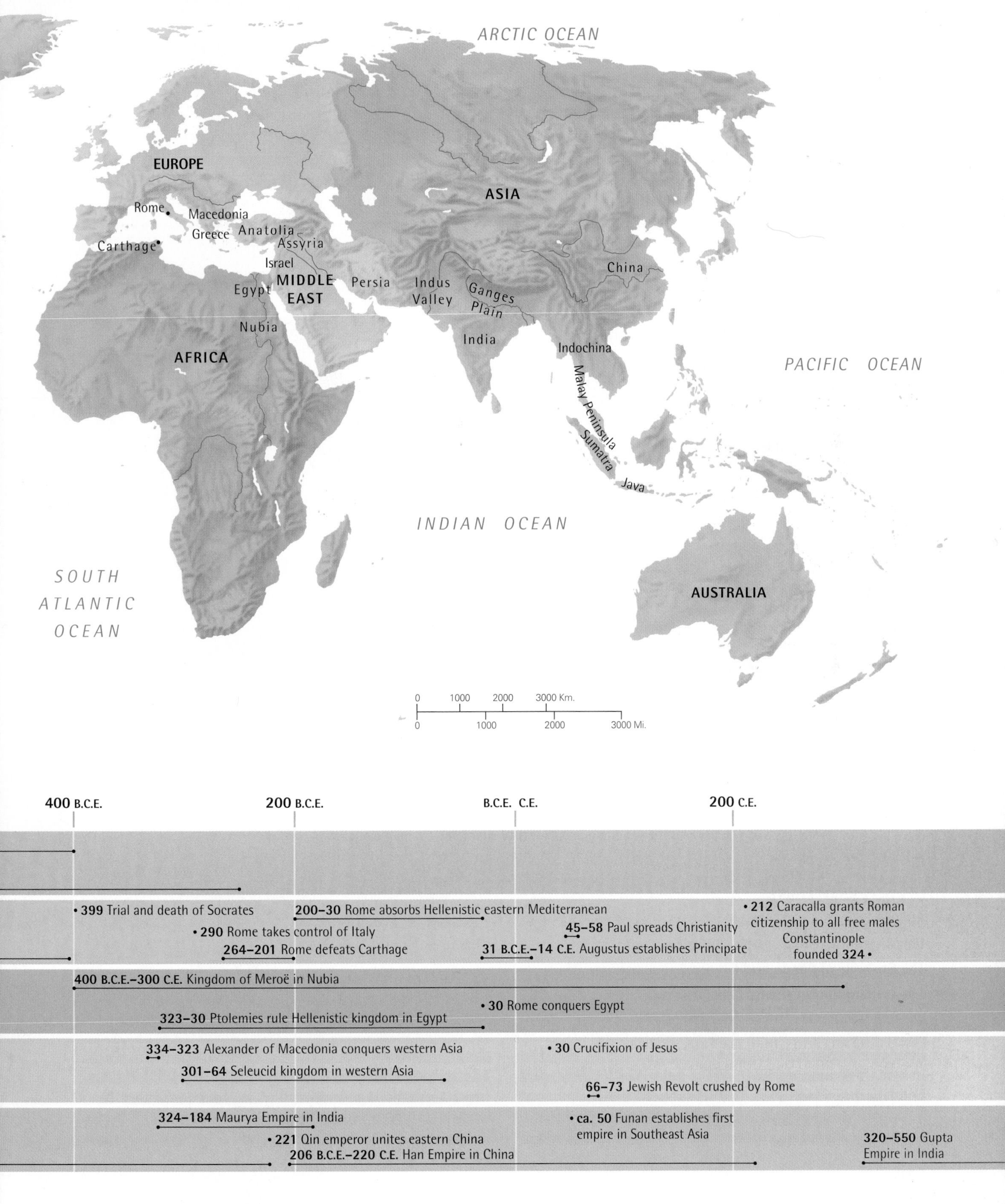
ARCTIC OCEAN
EUROPE
ASIA
Rome
Macedonia
Greece
Anatolia
Carthage
Assyria
Israel
MIDDLE EAST
Egypt
Persia
Indus Valley
Ganges Plain
China
Nubia
India
Indochina
AFRICA
Malay Peninsula
Sumatra
Java
PACIFIC OCEAN
INDIAN OCEAN
SOUTH ATLANTIC OCEAN
AUSTRALIA
0 1000 2000 3000 Km.
0 1000 2000 3000 Mi.
400 B.C.E.
200 B.C.E.
B.C.E. C.E.
200 C.E.
• 399 Trial and death of Socrates
200–30 Rome absorbs Hellenistic eastern Mediterranean
• 212 Caracalla grants Roman citizenship to all free males
• 290 Rome takes control of Italy
45–58 Paul spreads Christianity
Constantinople founded 324 •
264–201 Rome defeats Carthage
31 B.C.E.–14 C.E. Augustus establishes Principate
400 B.C.E.–300 C.E. Kingdom of Meroë in Nubia
• 30 Rome conquers Egypt
323–30 Ptolemies rule Hellenistic kingdom in Egypt
334–323 Alexander of Macedonia conquers western Asia
• 30 Crucifixion of Jesus
301–64 Seleucid kingdom in western Asia
66–73 Jewish Revolt crushed by Rome
324–184 Maurya Empire in India
• ca. 50 Funan establishes first empire in Southeast Asia
• 221 Qin emperor unites eastern China
320–550 Gupta Empire in India
206 B.C.E.–220 C.E. Han Empire in China

5 Greece and Iran, 1000–30 B.C.E.

Painted Cup of Arcesilas of Cyrene The ruler of this Greek community in North Africa supervises the weighing and export of silphium, a valuable medicinal plant.

CHAPTER OUTLINE

Ancient Iran, 1000–500 B.C.E.

The Rise of the Greeks, 1000–500 B.C.E.

The Struggle of Persia and Greece, 546–323 B.C.E.

The Hellenistic Synthesis, 323–30 B.C.E.

DIVERSITY AND DOMINANCE: The Persian Idea of Kingship

ENVIRONMENT AND TECHNOLOGY: The Farmer's Year

The Greek historian Herodotus° (ca. 485–425 B.C.E.), chronicler of the struggles of the city-states of Greece with the Persian Empire in the sixth and fifth centuries B.C.E., teaches a lesson about cultural differences. The Persian king Darius° I, whose vast empire stretched from eastern Europe to Pakistan, summoned the Greek and Indian wise men who served him at court. He first asked the Greeks whether under any circumstances they would be willing to eat the bodies of their deceased fathers. The Greeks, who cremated their dead, recoiled at the impiety of such an act. Darius then asked the Indians whether they would be prepared to burn the bodies of their dead parents. The Indians were repulsed; their practice was to ritually partake of the bodies of the dead. The point, as Herodotus noted, was that different peoples have very different practices, but each regards its own way as "natural" and superior.

Distinguishing between what was natural and what was cultural convention created much discomfort among Greeks in Herodotus's lifetime, for it called into question the validity of their fundamental beliefs. Herodotus's story also reminds us that the Persian Empire (and the Hellenistic Greek kingdoms that succeeded it) brought together, in eastern Europe, western Asia, and northwest Africa, peoples and cultural systems that previously had known little direct contact, and that this new cross-cultural interaction could be alarming even while it stimulated new and exciting cultural syntheses.

In this chapter we look at the eastern Mediterranean and western Asia in the first millennium B.C.E., emphasizing the experiences of the Persians and Greeks. The rivalry and wars of Greeks and Persians from the sixth to fourth centuries B.C.E. are traditionally seen as the first act of a drama that has continued intermittently ever since: the clash of the civilizations of East and West, of two peoples and two ways of life that were fundamentally different and thus almost certain to come into conflict. Some see recent tensions between the United States and Middle Eastern states such as Iran and Iraq as the latest manifestation of this age-old conflict.

Ironically, Greeks and Persians had far more in common than they realized. Both spoke in tongues belonging to the same Indo-European family of languages found throughout Europe and western and southern Asia. Many scholars believe that all the ancient peoples who spoke languages belonging to this family inherited fundamental cultural traits, forms of social organization, and religious outlooks from their shared past.

As you read this chapter, ask yourself the following questions:

- How did geography, environment, and contacts with other peoples shape the institutions and values of Persians and Greeks?
- What brought the Greek city-states and the Persian Empire into conflict, and which factors dictated the outcome of their rivalry?
- In what ways were the lands and peoples of the eastern Mediterranean and western Asia influenced—culturally, economically, and politically—by the domination of the Persian Empire and the Greek kingdoms that succeeded it?

Ancient Iran 1000–500 B.C.E.

Iran, the "land of the Aryans," links western Asia and southern and Central Asia, and its history has been marked by this mediating position (see Map 5.1). In the sixth century B.C.E. the vigorous Persians of southwest Iran created the largest empire the world had yet seen. Heirs to the long legacy of Mesopotamian history and culture, they introduced distinctly Iranian elements and developed new forms of political and economic organization in western Asia.

Relatively little written material from within the Persian Empire has survived, so we are forced to view it mostly through the eyes of the ancient Greeks—outsiders who were ignorant at best, usually hostile, and interested primarily in events that affected themselves. (Iranian groups and individuals are known in the western world by Greek approximations of their names; thus these familiar forms are used here, with the original Iranian

Herodotus (heh-ROD-uh-tuhs) **Darius** (duh-RIE-uhs)

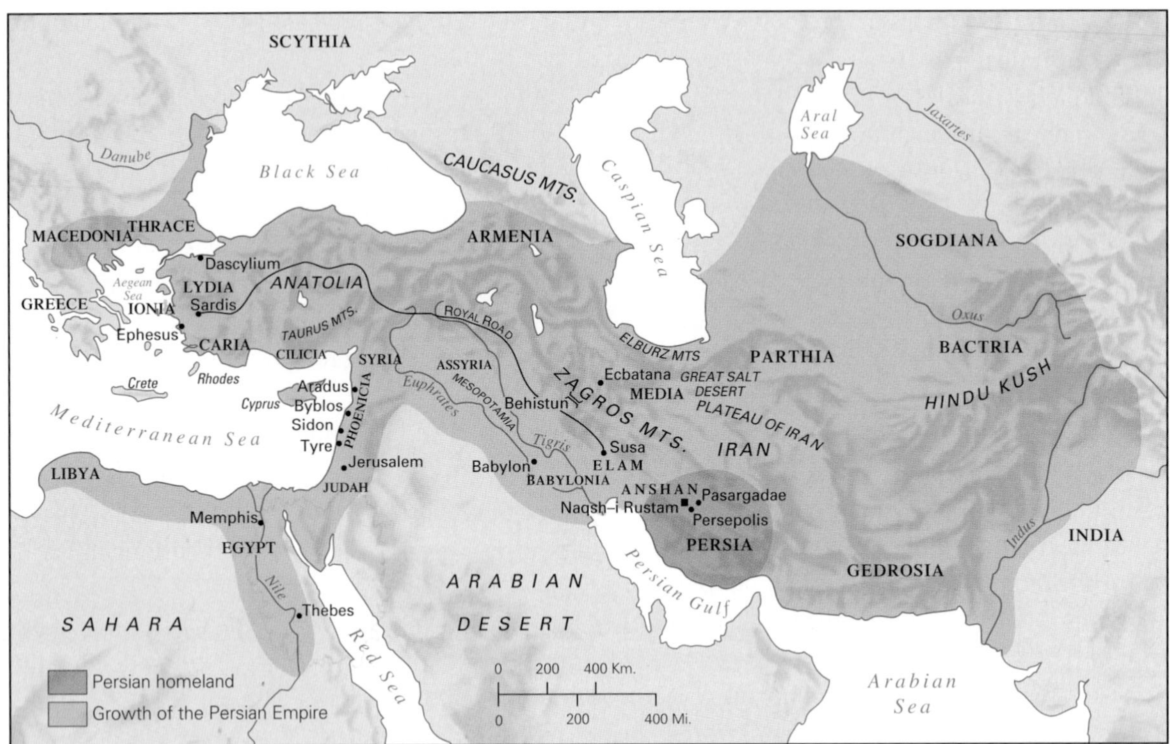

Map 5.1 The Persian Empire Between 550 and 522 B.C.E., the Persians of southwest Iran, under their first two kings, Cyrus and Cambyses, conquered each of the major states of western Asia—Media, Babylonia, Lydia, and Egypt. The third king, Darius I, extended the boundaries as far as the Indus Valley to the east and the European shore of the Black Sea to the west. The first major setback came when the fourth king, Xerxes, failed in his invasion of Greece in 480 B.C.E. The Persian Empire was considerably larger than its recent predecessor, the Assyrian Empire. For their empire, the Persian rulers developed a system of provinces, governors, regular tribute, and communication by means of royal roads and couriers that allowed for efficient operations for almost two centuries.

names given in parentheses.) This Greek perspective leaves us unaware of developments in the central and eastern portions of the Persian Empire. Nevertheless, recent archaeological discoveries and close analysis of the limited written material from within the empire can supplement and correct the perspective of the Greek sources.

Geography and Resources

Iran is bounded by the Zagros° Mountains to the west, the Caucasus° Mountains and Caspian Sea to the northwest and north, the mountains of Afghanistan and the desert of Baluchistan° to the east and southeast, and the Persian Gulf to the southwest. The northeast is less protected by natural boundaries, and from that direction Iran was open to attacks by the nomads of Central Asia.

The fundamental topographical features of Iran are high mountains at the edges, salt deserts in the interior depressions, and mountain streams crossing a sloping plateau and draining into seas or interior salt lakes and marshes. Humans trying to survive in these harsh lands had to find ways to exploit limited water resources. Unlike the valleys of the Nile, Tigris-Euphrates, Ganges, and Yellow Rivers, ancient Iran never had a dense population. The best-watered and most populous parts of the country lie to the north and west; aridity increases and population decreases as one moves south and east. On the interior plateau, oasis settlements sprang up beside streams or springs. The Great Salt Desert, which covers most of eastern Iran, and Baluchistan in the southeast corner were extremely inhospitable. Scattered settlements in the narrow plains beside the Persian Gulf were cut off from the interior plateau by mountain barriers.

Zagros (ZUHG-roes) **Caucasus** (KAW-kuh-suhs)
Baluchistan (buh-loo-chi-STAN)

CHRONOLOGY

	Greece and the Hellenistic World	Persian Empire
1000 B.C.E.	**1150–800 B.C.E.** Greece's "Dark Age"	**ca. 1000 B.C.E.** Persians settle in southwest Iran
800 B.C.E.	**ca. 800 B.C.E.** Resumption of Greek contact with eastern Mediterranean	
	800–480 B.C.E. Greece's Archaic Period	
	ca. 750–550 B.C.E. Era of colonization	
	ca. 700 B.C.E. Beginning of hoplite warfare	
	ca. 650–500 B.C.E. Era of tyrants	
600 B.C.E.	**594 B.C.E.** Solon reforms laws at Athens	
		550 B.C.E. Cyrus overthrows Medes
	546–510 B.C.E. Pisistratus and sons hold tyranny at Athens	**550–530 B.C.E.** Reign of Cyrus
		546 B.C.E. Cyrus conquers Lydia
		539 B.C.E. Cyrus takes control of Babylonia
		530–522 B.C.E. Reign of Cambyses; Conquest of Egypt
		522–486 B.C.E. Reign of Darius
500 B.C.E.	**499–494 B.C.E.** Ionian Greeks rebel against Persia	
	490 B.C.E. Athenians check Persian punitive expedition at Marathon	
	480–323 B.C.E. Greece's classical period	**480–479 B.C.E.** Xerxes' invasion of Greece
	477 B.C.E. Athens becomes leader of Delian League	
	461–429 B.C.E. Pericles dominant at Athens; Athens completes evolution to democracy	
400 B.C.E.	**431–404 B.C.E.** Peloponnesian War	
	399 B.C.E. Trial and execution of Socrates	**387 B.C.E.** King's Peace makes Persia arbiter of Greek affairs
	359 B.C.E. Philip II becomes king of Macedonia	
	338 B.C.E. Philip takes control of Greece	**334–323 B.C.E.** Alexander the Great defeats Persia and creates huge empire
		323–30 B.C.E. Hellenistic period
	317 B.C.E. End of democracy in Athens	
300 B.C.E.	**ca. 300 B.C.E.** Foundation of the Museum in Alexandria	
	200 B.C.E. First Roman intervention in the Hellenistic East	
100 B.C.E.		
	30 B.C.E. Roman annexation of Egypt, the last Hellenistic kingdom	

In the first millennium B.C.E. irrigation enabled people to move down from the mountain valleys and open the plains to agriculture. To prevent evaporation of precious water in the hot, dry climate, they devised underground irrigation channels. Constructing and maintaining these subterranean channels and the vertical shafts that provided access to them was labor-intensive. Normally, local leaders oversaw the expansion of the network in each district. Activity accelerated when a strong central authority was able to organize large numbers of laborers. The connection between royal authority and prosperity is evident in the ideology of the first Persian Empire (discussed below). Even so, human survival depended on a delicate ecological balance, and a buildup of salt in the soil or a falling water table sometimes forced the abandonment of settlements.

Iran's mineral resources—copper, tin, iron, gold, and silver—were exploited on a limited scale in antiquity. Mountain slopes, more heavily wooded than they are now, provided fuel and materials for building and crafts. Because this austere land could not generate much of an agricultural surplus, objects of trade tended to be minerals and crafted goods such as textiles and carpets.

The Rise of the Persian Empire

In antiquity many groups of people, whom historians refer to collectively as "Iranians" because they spoke related languages and shared certain cultural features, spread out across western and Central Asia—an area comprising not only the modern state of Iran but also Turkmenistan, Afghanistan, and Pakistan. Several of these groups arrived in western Iran near the end of the second millennium B.C.E. The first to achieve a complex level of political organization was the Medes (Mada in Iranian). They settled in the northwest and came under the influence of the ancient centers in Mesopotamia and Urartu (modern Armenia and northeast Turkey). The Medes played a major role in the destruction of the Assyrian Empire in the late seventh century B.C.E. and extended their control westward across Assyria into Anatolia (modern Turkey). They also projected their power southeast toward the Persian Gulf, a region occupied by another Iranian people, the Persians (Parsa).

The Persian rulers—now called Achaemenids° because they traced their lineage back to an ancestor named Achaemenes—cemented their relationship with the Median court through marriage. **Cyrus** (Kurush), the son of a Persian chieftain and a Median princess, united the various Persian tribes and overthrew the Median monarch sometime around 550 B.C.E. His victory should perhaps be seen less as a conquest than as an alteration of the relations between groups, for Cyrus placed both Medes and Persians in positions of responsibility and retained the framework of Median rule. The differences between these two Iranian peoples—principally differences in the dialects they spoke and the way they dressed—were not great. The Greeks could not readily tell the two apart.

Gold Plaque from the Eastern Achaemenid Empire, fifth-fourth century B.C.E. Part of the Oxus Treasure, a cache of gold and silver objects discovered in Tajikistan. A Median magus (religious expert), armed with a short sword and wearing pants, boots, tunic, and cloth headdress, holds a sheaf of twigs for use in a sacrificial ceremony. (Courtesy of the Trustees of the British Museum)

Like most Indo-European peoples, the early inhabitants of western Iran had a patriarchal family organization: the male head of the household had nearly absolute authority over family members. Society was divided into three social and occupational classes: warriors, priests, and peasants. Warriors were the dominant element. A landowning aristocracy, they took pleasure in hunting,

Achaemenid (a-KEY-muh-nid)

fighting, and gardening. The king was the most illustrious member of this group. The priests, or Magi (*magush*), were ritual specialists who supervised the proper performance of sacrifices. The common people—peasants—were primarily village-based farmers and shepherds.

Over the course of two decades the energetic Cyrus (r. 550–530 B.C.E.) redrew the map of western Asia. In 546 B.C.E. he prevailed in a cavalry battle outside the gates of Sardis, the capital of the kingdom of Lydia in western Anatolia, reportedly because the smell of his camels caused a panic among his opponents' horses. All Anatolia, including the Greek city-states on the western coast, came under Persian control. In 539 B.C.E. he swept into Mesopotamia, where the Neo-Babylonian dynasty had ruled since the collapse of Assyrian power (see Chapter 4). Cyrus made a deal with disaffected elements within Babylon, and when he and his army approached, the gates of the city were thrown open to him without a struggle. A skillful propagandist, Cyrus showed respect to the Babylonian priesthood and had his son crowned king in accordance with native traditions.

After Cyrus lost his life in 530 B.C.E. while campaigning against a coalition of nomadic Iranians in the northeast, his son Cambyses° (Kambujiya, r. 530–522 B.C.E.) set his sights on Egypt, the last of the great ancient kingdoms of the Middle East. The Persians prevailed over the Egyptians in a series of bloody battles; then they sent exploratory expeditions south to Nubia and west to Libya. Greek sources depict Cambyses as a cruel and impious madman, but contemporary documents from Egypt show him operating in the same practical vein as his father, cultivating local priests and notables and respecting native traditions.

When Cambyses died in 522 B.C.E., **Darius I** (Darayavaush) seized the throne. His success in crushing many early challenges to his rule was a testimony to his skill, energy, and ruthlessness. From this reign forward, Medes played a lesser role, and the most important posts went to members of leading Persian families. Darius (r. 522–486 B.C.E.) extended Persian control eastward as far as the Indus Valley and westward into Europe, where he bridged the Danube River and chased the nomadic Scythian° peoples north of the Black Sea. The Persians erected a string of forts in Thrace (modern-day northeast Greece and Bulgaria) and by 500 B.C.E. were on the doorstep of Greece. Darius also promoted the development of maritime routes. He dispatched a fleet to explore the waters from the Indus Delta to the Red Sea, and he completed a canal linking the Red Sea with the Nile.

Cambyses (kam-BIE-sees) **Scythian** (SITH-ee-uhn)

Imperial Organization and Ideology

The empire of Darius I was the largest the world had yet seen (see Map 5.1). Stretching from eastern Europe to Pakistan, from southern Russia to Sudan, it encompassed a multitude of ethnic groups and many forms of social and political organization, from nomadic kinship group to subordinate kingdom to city-state. Darius can rightly be considered a second founder of the Persian Empire, after Cyrus, because he created a new organizational structure that was maintained throughout the remaining two centuries of the empire's existence.

Darius divided the empire into twenty provinces. Each was under the supervision of a Persian **satrap°**, or governor, who was likely to be related or connected by marriage to the royal family. The satrap's court was a miniature version of the royal court. The tendency for the position of satrap to become hereditary meant that satraps' families lived in the province governed by their head, acquired a fund of knowledge about local conditions, and formed connections with the local native elite. The farther a province was from the center of the empire, the more autonomy the satrap had, because slow communications made it impractical to refer most matters to the central administration. This system of administration brought significant numbers of Persians and other peoples from the center of the empire to the provinces, resulting in intermarriage and cultural and technological exchanges. For example, recent archaeological work at a site in the western desert of Egypt has shown the use of underground water channels of Iranian design to serve a new agricultural settlement.

One of the satrap's most important duties was to collect and send tribute to the king. Darius prescribed how much precious metal each province was to contribute annually. This amount was forwarded to the central treasury. Some of it was disbursed for necessary expenditures, but most was hoarded. As more and more precious metal was taken out of circulation, the price of gold and silver rose, and provinces found it increasingly difficult to meet their quotas. Evidence from Babylonia indicates a gradual economic decline setting in by the fourth century B.C.E. The increasing burden of taxation and official corruption may have inadvertently caused the economic downturn.

Well-maintained and patrolled royal roads connected the outlying provinces to the heart of the empire. Way stations were built at intervals to receive important travelers and couriers carrying official correspondence. At

satrap (SAY-trap)

strategic points, such as mountain passes, river crossings, and important urban centers, garrisons controlled people's movements. The administrative center of the empire was Susa, the ancient capital of Elam, in southwest Iran near the present-day border with Iraq. It was to Susa that Greeks and others went with requests and messages for the king. It took a party of Greek ambassadors at least three months to make the journey. Altogether, travel time, time spent waiting for an audience with the Persian king, delays due to weather, and the duration of the return trip probably kept the ambassadors away from home a year or more.

The king lived and traveled with his numerous wives and children. The little information that we have about the lives of Persian royal women comes from foreign sources and is thus suspect. The Book of Esther in the Hebrew Bible tells a romantic story of how King Ahasuerus° (Xerxes° to the Greeks) picked the beautiful Jewish woman Esther to be one of his wives and how the courageous and clever queen later saved the Jewish people from a plot to massacre them. Greek sources show women of the royal family being used as pawns in the struggle for power. Darius strengthened his claim to the throne by marrying a daughter of Cyrus, and later the Greek conqueror Alexander the Great married a daughter of the last Persian king. Greek sources portray Persian queens as vicious intriguers, poisoning rival wives and plotting to win the throne for their sons. However, a recent study suggests that the Greek stereotype misrepresents the important role played by Persian women in protecting family members and mediating conflicts. Both Greek sources and documents within the empire reveal that Persian elite women were politically influential, possessed substantial property, traveled, and were prominent on public occasions.

Besides the royal family, the king's large entourage included several other groups: (1) the sons of Persian aristocrats, who were educated at court and also served as hostages for their parents' good behavior; (2) many noblemen, who were expected to attend the king when they were not otherwise engaged; (3) the central administration, including officials and employees of the treasury, secretariat, and archives; (4) the royal bodyguard; and (5) countless courtiers and slaves. Long gone were the simple days when the king hunted and caroused with his warrior companions. Inspired by Mesopotamian conceptions of monarchy, the king of Persia had become an aloof figure of majesty and splendor: "The Great King, King of Kings, King in Persia, King of countries." He referred to everyone, even the Persian nobility, as "my slaves," and anyone who approached him had to bow down before him.

The king owned vast tracts of land throughout the empire. Some of it he gave to his supporters. Donations called "bow land," "horse land," and "chariot land" in Babylonian documents obliged the recipient to provide military service. Scattered around the empire were gardens, orchards, and hunting preserves belonging to the king and the high nobility. The *paradayadam* (meaning "walled enclosure"—the term has come into English as *paradise*), a green oasis in an arid landscape, advertised the prosperity that the king could bring to those who loyally served him.

Surviving administrative records from the Persian homeland give us a glimpse of how the complex tasks of administration were managed. The **Persepolis**° Treasury and Fortification Texts, inscribed in Elamite cuneiform on baked clay tablets, show that government officials distributed food and other essential commodities to large numbers of workers of many different nationalities. Some of these workers may have been prisoners of war brought to the center of the empire to work on construction projects, maintain and expand the irrigation network, and farm the royal estates. Workers were divided into groups of men, women, and children. Women received less than men of equivalent status, but pregnant women and women with babies received more. Men and women performing skilled jobs received more than their unskilled counterparts.

Tradition remembered Darius as a lawgiver who created a body of "laws of the King" and a system of royal judges operating throughout the empire, as well as encouraging the codification and publication of the laws of the various subject peoples. In a manner that typifies the decentralized character of the Persian Empire, he allowed each people to live in accordance with its own traditions and ordinances.

The central administration was based not in the Persian homeland (present-day Fars, directly north of the Persian Gulf) but farther west in Elam and Mesopotamia. Closer to the geographical center of the empire, this location allowed the kings to employ the trained administrators and scribes of those ancient civilizations. However, on certain occasions the kings returned to one special place back in the homeland. Darius began construction of a ceremonial capital at Persepolis (Parsa). An artificial platform was erected, and on it were built a series of palaces, audience halls, treasury buildings, and barracks. Here, too, Darius and his son Xerxes, who completed the project, were inspired by Mesopotamian

Ahasuerus (uh-HAZZ-yoo-ear-uhs) **Xerxes** (ZERK-sees)

Persepolis (Per-SEH-poe-lis)

View of the East Front of the Apadana (Audience Hall) at Persepolis, ca. 500 B.C.E. To the right lies the Gateway of Xerxes. Persepolis, in the Persian homeland, was built by Darius I and his son Xerxes, and it was used for ceremonies of special importance to the Persian king and people—coronations, royal weddings, funerals, and the New Year's festival. The stone foundations, walls, and stairways of Persepolis are filled with sculpted images of members of the court and embassies bringing gifts, offering a vision of the grandeur and harmony of the Persian Empire. (Courtesy of the Oriental Institute, University of Chicago)

traditions, for the great Assyrian kings had created new fortress-cities as advertisements of wealth and power.

Darius's approach to governing can be seen in the luxuriant relief sculpture that covers the foundations, walls, and stairwells of the buildings at Persepolis. Representatives of all the peoples of the empire—recognizable by their distinctive hair, beards, dress, hats, and footwear—are depicted in the act of bringing gifts to the king. Historians used to think that the sculpture represented a real event that transpired each year at Persepolis, but now they see it as an exercise in what today we would call public relations or propaganda. It is Darius's carefully crafted vision of an empire of vast extent and abundant resources in which all the subject peoples willingly cooperate. In one telling sculptural example, Darius subtly contrasted the character of his rule with that of the Assyrian Empire, the Persians' predecessors in these lands (see Chapter 4). Where Assyrian kings had gloried in their power and depicted subjects staggering under the weight of a giant platform that supported the throne, Darius's artists showed erect subjects shouldering the burden willingly and without strain.

What actually took place at Persepolis? This opulent retreat in the homeland probably was the scene of events of special significance for the king and his people: the New Year's Festival, coronation, marriage, death, and burial. The kings from Darius on were buried in elaborate tombs cut into the cliffs at nearby Naqsh-i Rustam°.

Another perspective on what the Persian monarchy claimed to stand for is provided by the several dozen inscriptions that have survived (see Diversity and Dominance: The Persian Idea of Kingship). At Naqsh-i Rustam, Darius makes the following claim:

> Ahuramazda° [a Persian deity], when he saw this earth in commotion, thereafter bestowed it upon me, made me king. . . . By the favor of Ahuramazda I put it down in its place. . . . I am of such a sort that I am a friend to right, I am not a friend to wrong. It is not my desire that the weak man should have wrong done to him by the mighty; nor is that my desire, that the mighty man should have wrong done to him by the weak.[1]

Naqsh-i Rustam (NUHK-shee ROOS-tuhm)
Ahuramazda (ah-HOOR-uh-MAZZ-duh)

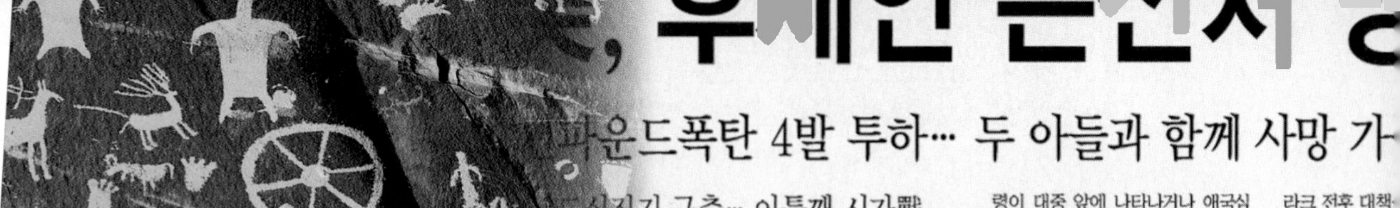
운드폭탄 4발 투하… 두 아들과 함께 사망
진지 구축… 이틀째 시가戰
령이 대중 앞에 나타나거나 애국심
을 고취하는 노래만을 내보내던 방
송마저 중단됐다.
의에서는 전후

Diversity and Dominance

The Persian Idea of Kingship

Our most important internal source of information about the Persian Empire is a group of inscriptions commissioned by several kings. The most extensive and informative of these is the inscription that Darius had carved into a cliff face at Behistun (Beh-HISS-toon), high above the road leading from Mesopotamia to northwest Iran through a pass in the Zagros mountain range. It is written in three versions—Old Persian, the language of the ruling people (quite possibly being put into written form for the first time); Elamite, the language native to the ancient kingdom lying between southern Mesopotamia and the Persian homeland and used in Persia for local administrative documents; and Akkadian, the language of Babylonia, widely used for administrative purposes throughout western Asia. The multilingual inscription accompanied a monumental relief representing Darius looming over a line of bound prisoners, the leaders of the many forces he had to defeat in order to secure the throne after the death of Cambyses in 522 B.C.E.

I am Darius, the great king, king of kings, the king of Persia, the king of countries, the son of Hystaspes, the grandson of Arsames, the Achaemenid . . . from antiquity we have been noble; from antiquity has our dynasty been royal . . .

King Darius says: By the grace of Ahuramazda am I king; Ahuramazda has granted me the kingdom.

King Darius says: These are the countries which are subject unto me, and by the grace of Ahuramazda I became king of them: Persia, Elam, Babylonia, Assyria, Arabia, Egypt, the countries by the Sea, Lydia, the Greeks, Media, Armenia, Cappadocia, Parthia, Drangiana, Aria, Chorasmia, Bactria, Sogdiana, Gandara, Scythia, Sattagydia, Arachosia and Maka; twenty-three lands in all.

King Darius says: These are the countries which are subject to me; by the grace of Ahuramazda they became subject to me; they brought tribute unto me. Whatsoever commands have been laid on them by me, by night or by day, have been performed by them.

King Darius says: Within these lands, whosoever was a friend, him have I surely protected; whosoever was hostile, him have I utterly destroyed. By the grace of Ahuramazda these lands have conformed to my decrees; as it was commanded unto them by me, so was it done.

King Darius says: Ahuramazda has granted unto me this empire. Ahuramazda brought me help, until I gained this empire; by the grace of Ahuramazda do I hold this empire.

King Darius says: The following is what was done by me after I became king.

A lengthy description of the many battles Darius and his supporters fought against a series of other claimants to power follows.

King Darius says: This is what I have done. By the grace of Ahuramazda have I always acted. After I became king, I fought nineteen battles in a single year and by the grace of Ahuramazda I overthrew nine kings and I made them captive . . .

King Darius Says: As to these provinces which revolted, lies made them revolt, so that they deceived the people. Then Ahuramazda delivered them into my hand; and I did unto them according to my will.

King Darius says: You who shall be king hereafter, protect yourself vigorously from lies; punish the liars well, if thus you shall think, 'May my country be secure!' . . .

King Darius says: On this account Ahuramazda brought me help, and all the other gods, all that there are, because I was not wicked, nor was I a liar, nor was I a tyrant, neither I nor any of my family. I have ruled according to righteousness. Neither to the weak nor to the powerful did I do wrong. Whosoever helped by house, him I favored; he who was hostile, him I destroyed . . .

King Darius says: By the grace of Ahuramazda this is the inscription which I have made. Besides, it was in Aryan script, and it was composed on clay tablets and on parchment. Besides, a sculptured figure of myself I made. Besides, I made my lineage. And it was inscribed and was read off before me. Afterwards this inscription I sent off everywhere among the provinces. The people unitedly worked upon it.

This is an extremely important historical document. For all practical purposes, it is the only version we have of the circumstances by which Darius, who was not a member of the family of Cyrus, took over the Persian throne and established a new dynasty. The account of these events given by the Greek historian Herodotus, for all its additional (and often suspect) detail, is clearly based, however indirectly, on Darius' own account. While scholars have doubted the truthfulness of Darius's claims, the inscription is a resounding example of how the victors often get to impose their version of events on the historical record.

The Behistun inscription is certainly propaganda, but that does not mean that it lacks value. To be effective propaganda must be predicated on the moral values, political principles, and religious beliefs that are familiar and acceptable in a society, and thus it can provide us with a window on those views. The Behistun inscription also allows us to glimpse something of the personality of Darius and how he wished to be perceived.

Another document, found at Persepolis, the magnificent ceremonial center built by Darius and his son Xerxes, expands on the qualities of an exemplary ruler. While it purports to be the words of Xerxes, it is almost an exact copy of an inscription of Darius from nearby Naqsh-i Rustam, where Darius and subsequent kings were buried in monumental tombs carved into the sheer cliff. This shows the continuity of concepts through several reigns.

A great god is Ahuramazda, who created this excellent thing which is seen, who created happiness for man, who set wisdom and capability down upon King Xerxes.

Proclaims Xerxes the King: By the will of Ahuramazda I am of such a sort, I am a friend of the right, of wrong I am not a friend. It is not my wish that the weak should have harm done him by the strong, nor is it my wish that the strong should have harm done him by the weak.

The right, that is my desire. To the man who is a follower of the lie I am no friend. I am not hot-tempered. Whatever befalls me in battle, I hold firmly. I am ruling firmly my own will.

The man who is cooperative, according to his cooperation thus I reward him. Who does harm, him according to the harm I punish. It is not my wish that a man should do harm; nor indeed is it my wish that if he does harm he should not be punished.

What a man says against a man, that does not persuade me, until I hear the sworn statements of both.

What a man does or performs, according to his ability, by that I become satisfied with him, and it is much to my desire, and I am well pleased, and I give much to loyal men.

Of such a sort are my understanding and my judgment: if what has been done by me you see or hear of, both in the palace and in the expeditionary camp, this is my capability over will and understanding.

This indeed my capability: that my body is strong. As a fighter of battles I am a good fighter of battles. When ever with my judgment in a place I determine whether I behold or do not behold an enemy, both with understanding and with judgment, then I think prior to panic, when I see an enemy as when I do not see one.

I am skilled both in hands and in feet. A horseman, I am a good horseman. A bowman, I am a good bowman, both on foot and on horseback. A spearman, I am a good spearman, both on foot and on horseback.

These skills that Ahuramazda set down upon me, and which I am strong enough to bear, by the will of Ahuramazda, what was done by me, with these skills I did, which Ahuramazda set down upon me.

May Ahuramazda protect me and what was done by me.

QUESTIONS FOR ANALYSIS

1. **How does Darius justify his assumption of power in the Behistun inscription? What is his relationship to Ahuramazda, the Zoroastrian god, and what role does divinity play in human affairs?**
2. **How does Darius conceptualize his empire (look at a map and follow the order in which he lists the provinces) and what are the expectations and obligations that he places on his subjects? What does his characterization of his opponents as "Lie-followers" tell us about his view of human nature?**
3. **Looking at the document of Xerxes from Persepolis, what qualities (physical, mental, and moral) are desirable in a ruler? What is the Persian concept of justice?**
4. **To what audiences are Darius and Xerxes directing their messages, and in what media are they being disseminated? Given that Darius himself is, in all likelihood, illiterate, and that so are most of his subjects, what is the effect of the often repeated phrase: "Darius the King says"?**

Sources: Behistun inscription translated by L. W. King and R. C. Thompson, *The Sculptures and Inscription of Darius the Great on the Rock of Behistun in Persia*, London, 1907 (http://www.livius.org/be-bm/behistun03.html); document from Nagsh-i Rustam (http://www.livius.org/x/xerxes/xerxes_texts.htm#daeva)

As this inscription makes clear, behind Darius and the empire stands the will of god. Ahuramazda made Darius king and gave him a mandate to bring order to a world in turmoil, and, despite his reasonable and just disposition, the king will brook no opposition. Ahuramazda is the great god of a religion called **Zoroastrianism°**, and it is nearly certain that Darius and his successors were Zoroastrians.

The origins of this religion are shrouded in uncertainty. The Gathas, hymns in an archaic Iranian dialect, are said to be the work of Zoroaster° (Zarathushtra). The dialect and physical setting of the hymns indicate that Zoroaster lived in eastern Iran. Scholarly guesses about when he lived range from 1700 to 500 B.C.E. He revealed that the world had been created by Ahuramazda, "the wise lord," and was threatened by Angra Mainyu°, "the hostile spirit," backed by a host of demons. In this dualistic universe, the struggle between good and evil plays out over twelve thousand years, after which good is destined to prevail, and the world will return to the pure state of creation. In the meantime, humanity is a participant in the cosmic struggle, and individuals are rewarded or punished in the afterlife for their actions.

In addition to Zoroastrianism, the Persians drew on moral and metaphysical conceptions with deep roots in the Iranian past. They were sensitive to the beauties of nature and venerated beneficent elements, such as water, which was not to be sullied, and fire, which was worshiped at fire altars. They were greatly concerned about the purity of the body. Corpses were exposed to wild beasts and the elements to prevent them from putrefying in the earth or tainting the sanctity of fire. The Persians still revered major deities from the polytheist past, such as Mithra, associated with the sun and defender of oaths and compacts. They were expected to keep promises and tell the truth. In his inscriptions at Persepolis, Darius castigated evildoers as followers of "the Lie."

Zoroastrianism was one of the great religions of the ancient world. It preached belief in one supreme deity, held humans to a high ethical standard, and promised salvation. It traveled across western Asia with the advance of the Persian Empire, and it may have exerted a major influence on Judaism and thus, indirectly, on Christianity. God and the Devil, Heaven and Hell, reward and punishment, the Messiah and the End of Time all appear to be legacies of this profound belief system. Because of the accidents of history—the fall of the Achaemenid Persian Empire in the later fourth century B.C.E. and the Islamic conquest of Iran in the seventh century C.E. (see Chapter 9)—Zoroastrianism has all but disappeared (except among a relatively small number of Parsees, as Zoroastrians are now called, in Iran and India).

Zoroastrianism (zo-roe-ASS-tree-uh-niz-uhm)
Zoroaster (zo-roe-ASS-ter)
Angra Mainyu (ANG-ruh MINE-yoo)

THE RISE OF THE GREEKS, 1000–500 B.C.E.

Because Greece was a relatively resource-poor region, the cultural features that emerged there in the first millennium B.C.E. came into being only because the Greeks had access to foreign sources of raw materials and to markets abroad. Greeks were in contact with other peoples, and Greek merchants and mercenaries brought home not only raw materials and crafted goods but also ideas. Under the pressure of population, poverty, war, or political crisis, Greeks moved to other parts of the Mediterranean and western Asia, bringing their language and culture and exerting a powerful influence on other societies. Encounters with the different practices and beliefs of other peoples stimulated the formation of a Greek identity and sparked interest in geography, ethnography, and history. A two-century-long rivalry with the Persian Empire also played a large part in shaping the destinies of the Greek city-states.

Geography and Resources

Greece is part of a large ecological zone that encompasses the Mediterranean Sea and the lands surrounding it (see Map 4.5). This zone is bounded by the Atlantic Ocean to the west, the several ranges of the Alps to the north, the Syrian desert to the east, and the Sahara to the south. The lands lying within this zone have a roughly uniform climate, experience a similar sequence of seasons, and are home to similar plants and animals. In the summer a weather front stalls near the entrance of the Mediterranean, impeding the passage of storms from the Atlantic and allowing hot, dry air from the Sahara to creep up over the region. In winter the front dissolves and the ocean storms roll in, bringing waves, wind, and cold. It was relatively easy for people to migrate to new homes within this ecological zone without having to alter familiar cultural practices and means of livelihood.

Greek civilization arose in the lands bordering the Aegean Sea: the Greek mainland, the islands of the Aegean, and the western coast of Anatolia (see Map 5.2). As we saw in Chapter 4, southern Greece is a dry and

Map 5.2 Ancient Greece By the early first millennium B.C.E. Greek-speaking peoples were dispersed throughout the Aegean region, occupying the Greek mainland, most of the islands, and the western coast of Anatolia. The rough landscape of central and southern Greece, with small plains separated by ranges of mountains, and the many islands in the Aegean favored the rise of hundreds of small, independent communities. The presence of adequate rainfall meant that agriculture was organized on the basis of self-sufficient family farms. As a result of the limited natural resources of this region, the Greeks had to resort to sea travel and trade with other lands in the Mediterranean to acquire metals and other vital raw materials.

ENVIRONMENT + TECHNOLOGY

The Farmer's Year

Perhaps the first Greek we can get to know as an individual is Hesiod (HEE-see-uhd). Hesiod lived near a village in Boeotia, in central Greece, around 700 B.C.E. In his poem *Works and Days*, we learn about his work as a farmer and about his relationships with family members and neighbors. The poem is presented as advice to his good-for-nothing brother, stressing the necessity of hard and perpetual work in order to survive. Much of the poem is a kind of farmer's almanac, describing the annual cycle of tasks on a Greek farm.

As Hesiod makes clear, it was very important for farmers to perform work at the right time. How did Greeks of the Archaic period, with no clocks, calendars, or newspapers, know where they were in the cycle of the year? They oriented themselves by acute observation of natural phenomena such as the flowering of plants and trees and the behavior of animals, the migration of birds and changes in the weather, and the movements of planets, stars, and constellations in the night sky.

Hesiod gives the following advice for determining the proper times for planting and harvesting grain:

Pleiades rising in the dawning sky,
Harvest is nigh.
Pleiades setting in the waning night,
Plowing is right.

The Pleiades (PLEE-uh-dees) is a cluster of seven stars visible to the naked eye. In Greek mythology, the Pleiades were seven sisters whom the gods placed in the sky to help them escape from the hunter Orion. The ancient Greeks observed that individual stars and constellations (groups of stars perceived by the human eye to form images in the sky) moved from east to west during the night and appeared in different parts of the sky at different times of the year. (In fact, the apparent movement of the stars is due to the earth's rotation on its axis and orbit around the sun against a background of unmoving stars. To earthly observers, however, the stars appear to move.) Hesiod is telling his audience that, when the Pleiades appear above the eastern horizon just before the light of the rising sun makes all the other stars invisible (in May on the modern calendar), a sensible farmer will cut down his grain crop. Some months later (in our September), when the Pleiades dip below the western horizon just before sunrise, it is time to plow the fields and plant seeds for the next year's harvest.

Other events in nature provide similar indicators:

Mind now, when you hear the call of the crane
Coming from the clouds, as it does year by year:
That's the sign for plowing . . .

rocky land with small plains carved up by low mountain ranges. No navigable rivers ease travel or the transport of commodities across this difficult terrain. The small islands dotting the Aegean were inhabited from early times. People could cross the water from Greece to Anatolia almost without losing sight of land. From about 1000 B.C.E. Greeks began to settle on the western edge of Anatolia. Rivers that formed broad and fertile plains near the coast made Ionia, as the ancient Greeks called this region, a comfortable place. The interior of Anatolia is rugged plateau, and the Greeks of the coast were in much closer contact with their fellows across the Aegean than with the native peoples of the interior. The sea was always a connector, not a barrier.

Without large rivers, Greek farmers on the mainland depended entirely on rainfall to water their crops (see Environment and Technology: The Farmer's Year). The limited arable land, thin topsoil, and sparse rainfall in the south could not sustain large populations. In the historical period farmers usually planted grain (mostly barley, which was hardier than wheat) in the flat plain, olive trees at the edge of the plain, and grapevines on the terraced lower slopes of the foothills. Sheep and goats grazed in the hills during the growing season. In northern Greece, where the rainfall is greater and the land opens out into broad plains, cattle and horses were more abundant. These Greek lands had few metal deposits and little timber, although both building stone, includ-

And even the stern Hesiod allows himself a break at the height of summer:

But when the thistle's in bloom, and the cicada
Chirps from its perch in a branch, pouring down
Shrill song from its wings in the withering heat,
Then goats are plumpest, wine at its best, women
Most lustful, but men at their feeblest, since Sirius
Scorches head and knees, and skin shrivels up. . . .
Time to drink sparkling wine
Sitting in the shade, heart satisfied with food,
Face turned toward the cooling West Wind . . .

Sirius (SIH-ree-uhs), the brightest star in the sky, rose with the sun in late July. The ancients believed that the addition of its heat to the heat already provided by the sun accounted for sizzling temperatures at this time of year. (The ancient Egyptians connected the rising of Sirius with the beginning of the Nile flood.)

It is clear to any reader of Hesiod's poem that he and his fellow Greek farmers were intimately attuned to their environment. Their extensive knowledge of the natural world provided them with information vital for survival.

Source: From *Hesiod: Works and Days and Theogony,* translated by Stanley Lombardo (Indianapolis/Cambridge: Hackett Publishing, 1993) Reprinted by permission of Hacket Publishing Company, Inc.

Black-Figure Vase from Athens, Late Sixth Century B.C.E. In this rare depiction of the activities of the working class, one man is up in an olive tree shaking the branches, two others knock olives down with sticks, while a fourth picks them off the ground. Olives were an important agricultural product, not only for eating, but also for the oil that was used for lamps, cooking, and cleaning and moisturizing the skin. Olive oil was a major export product at Athens. (Courtesy of the Trustees of the British Museum)

ing some fine marble, and clay for the potter were abundant.

A glance at a map of Greece reveals a deeply pitted coastline with many natural harbors. A combination of circumstances—the difficulty of overland transport, the availability of good anchorages, and the need to import metals, timber, and grain—drew the Greeks to the sea. They obtained timber from the northern Aegean, gold and iron from Anatolia, copper from Cyprus, tin from the western Mediterranean, and grain from the Black Sea, Egypt, and Sicily. Sea transport was much cheaper and faster than overland transport. Thus, though never comfortable with "the wine-dark sea," as the poet Homer called it, the Greeks had no choice but to embark upon it in their small, frail ships, hugging the coastline or island-hopping where possible.

The Emergence of the Polis

The first flowering of Greek culture in the Mycenaean civilization of the second millennium B.C.E. is described in Chapter 4. This was largely an adaptation of the imported institutions of Middle Eastern palace-dominated states to the Greek terrain. For several centuries after the destruction of the Mycenaean palace-states, Greece lapsed into a "Dark Age" (ca. 1150–800 B.C.E.): for those who lived through it, dark because of depopulation, poverty, and backwardness; for us, dark because it left few traces in the archaeological record. During the Dark Age, Greece and the whole Aegean region were largely isolated from the rest of the world. The importation of raw materials, especially metals, had been the chief source of Mycenaean prosperity. Lack of access to vital resources lay behind the poverty of the Dark Age.

Within Greece, regions that had little contact with one another developed distinctive local styles in pottery and other crafts. With fewer people to feed, the land was largely given over to grazing flocks of sheep, goats, and cattle. While there was continuity of language, religion, and other aspects of culture, there was a sharp break with the authoritarian Mycenaean political structure and centralized control of the economy. This would open the way for the development of new political, social, and economic forms rooted in the Greek environment.

The isolation of Greece ended around 800 B.C.E. when Phoenician ships began to visit the Aegean (see Chapter 4). The Phoenician city-states were dominated by a merchant class that was making ever more distant voyages west in search of valuable commodities and trading partners. By reestablishing contact between the Aegean and the Middle East, the Phoenicians gave Greek civilization an important push and inaugurated what scholars now term the "Archaic" period of Greek history (ca. 800–480 B.C.E.). Soon Greek ships were also plying the waters of the Mediterranean in search of raw materials, trade opportunities, and fertile farmland.

Various evidence reveals the influx of new ideas from the east, such as the appearance of naturalistic human and animal figures and imaginative mythical beasts on painted Greek pottery. The most auspicious gift of the Phoenicians was a writing system. The Phoenicians used a set of twenty-two symbols to represent the consonants in their language, leaving the vowel sounds to be inferred by the reader. To represent Greek vowel sounds, the Greeks utilized some of the Phoenician symbols for which there were no equivalent sounds in the Greek language. This was the first true alphabet, a system of writing that fully represents the sounds of spoken language. An alphabet offers tremendous advantages over systems of writing such as cuneiform and hieroglyphics, whose signs represent entire words or syllables. Because cuneiform and hieroglyphics required years of training and the memorization of several hundred signs, they remained the preserve of a scribal class whose elevated social position stemmed from their mastery of the technology. An alphabet opens the door for more widespread literacy. Because only a few dozen signs are required to represent all the possible statements in a language, people can learn an alphabet in a relatively short period of time.

There is controversy about the earliest uses of the Greek alphabet. Some scholars maintain that the Greeks first used it for economic purposes, such as to keep inventories of a merchant's wares. Others propose that it originated as a vehicle for preserving the oral poetic epics so important to the Greeks. Whatever its first use, the Greeks soon came to employ the new technology to produce new forms of literature, law codes, religious dedications, and epitaphs on gravestones. This does not mean, however, that Greek society immediately became literate in the modern sense. For many centuries, Greece remained a primarily oral culture: people used storytelling, rituals, and performances to preserve and transmit information. Many of the distinctive intellectual and artistic creations of Greek civilization, such as theatrical drama, philosophical dialogues, and political and courtroom oratory, are products of the dynamic interaction of speaking and writing.

One indicator of the powerful new forces at work in the Archaic period was a veritable explosion of population. Studies of cemeteries in the vicinity of Athens show that there was a dramatic population increase (perhaps as much as fivefold or sevenfold) during the eighth century B.C.E. Its causes are not fully understood but probably include the more intensive use of land as farming replaced herding and independent farmers and their families began to work previously unused land on the margins of the plains. The accompanying shift to a diet based on bread and vegetables rather than meat may have increased fertility and life span. A second factor was increasing prosperity based on the importation of food and raw materials. Rising population density led villages to merge and become urban centers. It also created the potential for specialization of labor: freed from agricultural tasks, some members of the society were able to develop skills in other areas, such as crafts and commerce.

Greece at this time consisted of hundreds of independent political entities, reflecting the facts of Greek geography—small plains separated from each other by mountain barriers. The Greek **polis**° (usually translated "city-state") consisted of an urban center and the rural territory that it controlled. City-states came in various sizes, with populations as small as several thousand or as large as several hundred thousand in the case of Athens.

Most urban centers had certain characteristic features. A hilltop *acropolis*° ("top of the city") offered a place of refuge in an emergency. The town spread out around the base of this fortified high point. An *agora*° ("gathering place") was an open area where citizens came together to ratify the decisions of their leaders or to line up with their weapons before military ventures.

---

polis (POE-lis) **acropolis** (uh-KRAW-poe-lis) **agora** (ah-go-RAH)

The Acropolis at Athens This steep, defensible plateau jutting up from the Attic Plain served as a Mycenaean fortress in the second millennium B.C.E., and the site of Athens has been continuously occupied since that time. In the mid-sixth century B.C.E. the tyrant Pisistratus built a temple to Athena, the patron goddess of the community. It was destroyed by the Persians when they invaded Greece in 480 B.C.E. The Acropolis was left in ruins for three decades as a reminder of what the Athenians sacrificed in defense of Greek freedom, but in the 440s B.C.E. Pericles initiated a building program, using funds from the naval empire that Athens headed. These construction projects, including a new temple to Athena—the Parthenon—brought glory to the city and popularity to Pericles and to the new democracy that he championed. (Robert Harding Picture Library)

Government buildings were located there, but the agora soon developed into a marketplace as well (vendors everywhere are eager to set out their wares wherever crowds gather). Fortified walls surrounded the urban center; but as the population expanded, new buildings went up beyond the perimeter.

City and country were not as sharply distinguished as they are today. The urban center depended on its agricultural hinterland to provide food, and many of the people living within the walls of the city went out to work on nearby farms during the day. Unlike the dependent workers on the estates of early Mesopotamia, the rural populations of the Greek city-states were free members of the community.

Each polis was fiercely jealous of its independence and suspicious of its neighbors, and this state of mind led to frequent conflict. By the early seventh century B.C.E. the Greeks had developed a new kind of warfare, waged by **hoplites**°—heavily armored infantrymen who fought in close formation. Protected by a helmet, a breastplate, and leg guards, each hoplite held a round shield over his own left side and the right side of the man next to him and brandished a thrusting spear, keeping a sword in reserve. In this style of combat, the key to victory was maintaining the cohesion of one's own formation while breaking open the enemy's line. Most of the casualties were suffered by the defeated army in flight.

Recent studies have emphasized the close relationship of hoplite warfare to the agricultural basis of Greek society. Greek states were defended by armies of private citizens—mostly farmers—called up for brief periods of crisis, rather than by a professional class of soldiers. Although this kind of fighting called for strength to bear the weapons and armor, and courage to stand one's ground in battle, no special training was needed by the citizen-soldiers. Campaigns took place when farmers were available, in the windows of time between major tasks in the agricultural cycle. When a hoplite army marched into the fields of another community, the enraged farmers of that community, who had expended a

hoplite (HAWP-lite)

lot of hard labor on their land and buildings, could not fail to meet the challenge. Though brutal and terrifying, the clash of two hoplite lines did offer a quick decision. Battles rarely lasted more than a few hours, and the survivors could promptly return home to tend their farms.

The expanding population soon surpassed the capacity of the small plains, and many communities sent excess population abroad to establish independent "colonies" in distant lands. Not every colonist left willingly. Sources tell of people being chosen by lot and forbidden to return on pain of death. Others, seeing an opportunity to escape from poverty, avoid the constraints of family, or find adventure, voluntarily set out to seek their fortunes on the frontier. After obtaining the approval of the god Apollo from his sanctuary at Delphi, the colonists departed, carrying fire from the communal hearth of the "mother-city," a symbol of the kinship and religious ties that would connect the two communities. They settled by the sea in the vicinity of a hill or other natural refuge. The "founder," a prominent member of the mother-city, allotted parcels of land and drafted laws for the new community. In some cases the indigenous population was driven away or reduced to a semiservile status; in other cases there was intermarriage and mixing between colonists and natives.

A wave of colonization from the mid-eighth through mid-sixth centuries B.C.E. spread Greek culture far beyond the land of its origins. New settlements sprang up in the northern Aegean area, around the Black Sea, and on the Libyan coast of North Africa. In southern Italy and on the island of Sicily (see Map 4.5) another Greek core area was established. Although the creation of new homes, farms, and communities undoubtedly posed many challenges for the Greek settlers, they were able to transplant their entire way of life, mostly because of the general similarity in climate and ecology in the Mediterranean lands.

Greeks began to use the term *Hellenes*° (*Graeci* is what the Romans later called them) to distinguish themselves from *barbaroi* (the root of the English word *barbarian*). Interaction with new peoples and exposure to their different practices made the Greeks aware of the factors that bound them together: their language, religion, and lifestyle. It also introduced them to new ideas and technologies. Developments first appearing in the colonial world traveled back to the Greek homeland—urban planning, new forms of political organization, and, as we shall see shortly, new intellectual currents.

Another significant development was the invention of coins in the early sixth century B.C.E., probably in Lydia (western Anatolia). They soon spread throughout the Greek world and beyond. In the ancient world a coin was a piece of metal whose weight and purity, and thus value, were guaranteed by the state. Silver, gold, bronze, and other metals were attractive choices for a medium of exchange: sufficiently rare to be valuable, relatively lightweight and portable (at least in the quantities available to most individuals), seemingly indestructible and therefore permanent, yet easily divided. (Other items with similar qualities have been used as money in various historical societies, including beads, hard-shelled beans, and cowrie shells.) Prior to the invention of coinage, people in the lands of the eastern Mediterranean and western Asia weighed out quantities of gold, silver, or bronze in exchange for the items they wanted to buy. Coinage allowed for more rapid exchanges of goods as well as for more efficient recordkeeping and storage of wealth. It stimulated trade and increased the total wealth of the society. Even so, international commerce could still be confusing because different states used different weight standards that had to be reconciled, just as people have to exchange currencies when traveling today.

By reducing surplus population, colonization helped relieve pressures within the Archaic Greek world. Nevertheless, this was an era of political instability. Kings ruled the Dark Age societies depicted in Homer's *Iliad* and *Odyssey*, but at some point councils composed of the heads of noble families superseded the kings. This aristocracy derived its wealth and power from ownership of large tracts of land. Peasant families worked this land; they were allowed to occupy a plot and keep a portion of what they grew. Debt-slaves, too, worked the land. They were people who had borrowed money or seed from the lord and lost their freedom when they were unable to repay the loan. Also living in a typical community were free peasants, who owned small farms, and urban-based craftsmen and merchants, who began to constitute a "middle class."

In the mid-seventh and sixth centuries B.C.E. in one city-state after another, an individual **tyrant**—a person who seized and held power in violation of the normal political institutions and traditions of the community—gained control. Greek tyrants were often disgruntled or ambitious members of the aristocracy, backed by the emerging middle class. New opportunities for economic advancement and the declining cost of metals meant that more and more men could acquire arms. These individuals, who already played an important role as hoplite soldiers in the local militias, must have demanded some political rights as the price of their support for their local tyrant.

Ultimately, the tyrants of this age were unwitting catalysts in an evolving political process. Some were able

Hellenes (HELL-leans)

Vase Painting Depicting a Sacrifice to the God Apollo, ca. 440 B.C.E. For the Greeks, who believed in a multitude of gods who looked and behaved like humans, the central act of worship was the sacrifice, the ritualized offering of a gift. Sacrifice created a relationship between the human worshiper and the deity and raised expectations that the god would bestow favors in return. Here we see a number of male devotees, wearing their finest clothing and garlands in their hair, near a sacred outdoor altar and statue of Apollo. The god is shown at the far right, standing on a pedestal and holding his characteristic bow and laurel branch. The first worshiper offers the god bones wrapped in fat. All of the worshipers will feast on the meat carried by the boy. (Museum für Vor-und. Frühgeschichte, Frankfurt)

to pass their positions on to their sons, but eventually the tyrant-family was ejected. Authority in the community developed along one of two lines: toward oligarchy°, the exercise of political privilege by the wealthier members of society, or toward **democracy,** the exercise of political power by all free adult males. In any case, the absence of a professional military class in the early Greek states was essential to broadening the base of political participation.

Greek religion encompassed a wide range of cults and beliefs. The ancestors of the Greeks brought a collection of sky-gods with them when they entered the Greek peninsula at the end of the third millennium B.C.E. Male gods predominated, but several female deities had important roles. Some of the gods represented forces in nature: for example, Zeus sent storms and lightning, and Poseidon was master of the sea and earthquakes. The two great epic poems, the *Iliad* and *Odyssey,* which Greek schoolboys memorized and professional performers recited, put a distinctive stamp on the personalities and characters of these deities. The gods that Homer portrayed were anthropomorphic°—that is, conceived as humanlike in appearance (though they were taller, more beautiful, and more powerful than mere mortals and had a supernatural radiance) and humanlike in their displays of emotion. Indeed, the chief difference between them and human beings was humans' mortality.

The worship of the gods at state-sponsored festivals was as much an expression of civic identity as of personal piety. **Sacrifice,** the central ritual of Greek religion, was performed at altars in front of the temples that the Greeks built to be the gods' places of residence. Greeks gave their gods gifts, often as humble as a small cake or a cup of wine poured on the ground, in the hope that the gods would favor and protect them. In more spectacular forms of sacrifice, a group of people would kill one or more animals, spray the altar with the victim's blood, burn parts of its body so that the aroma would ascend to the gods on high, and enjoy a rare feast of meat. In this way the Greeks created a sense of community out of shared participation in the taking of life.

Greek individuals and communities sought information, advice, or predictions about the future from oracles—sacred sites where they believed the gods communicated with humans. Especially prestigious was the oracle of Apollo at Delphi in central Greece. Petitioners left gifts in the treasuries, and the god responded to their questions through his priestess, the Pythia°, who gave forth obscure, ecstatic utterances. Because most Greeks were farmers, fertility cults, whose members worshiped and sought to enhance the productive forces in nature (usually conceived as female), were popular, though often hidden from modern view because of our dependence on literary texts expressing the values of an educated, urban elite.

New Intellectual Currents

The material changes taking place in Greece in the Archaic period—new technologies, increasing prosperity, and social

oligarchy (OLL-ih-gahr-key)
anthropomorphic (an-thruh-puh-MORE-fik)

Pythia (PITH-ee-uh)

and political development—led to innovations in intellectual outlook and artistic expression. One distinctive feature of the Archaic period was a growing emphasis on the individual. In early Greek communities the family enveloped the individual, and land belonged collectively to the family, including ancestors and descendants. Ripped out of this communal network and forced to establish new lives on a distant frontier, the colonist became a model of rugged individualism, as did the tyrant who seized power for himself alone. These new patterns led toward the concept of humanism—a valuing of the uniqueness, talents, and rights of the individual—which remains a central tenet of Western civilization.

We see clear signs of individualism in the new lyric poetry—short verses in which the subject matter is intensely personal, drawn from the experience of the poet and expressing his or her feelings and views. Archilochus°, a soldier and poet living in the first half of the seventh century B.C.E., made a surprising admission:

> Some barbarian is waving my shield, since I was obliged to
> leave that perfectly good piece of equipment behind
> under a bush. But I got away, so what does it matter?
> Let the shield go; I can buy another one equally good.[2]

Here Archilochus is poking fun at the heroic ideal that scorned a soldier who ran away from the enemy. In challenging traditional values and exploiting the medium to express personal feeling and opinion, lyric poets paved the way for the modern Western conception of poetry.

There were also challenges to traditional religion from thinkers now known as pre-Socratic philosophers (the term *pre-Socratic* refers to philosophers before Socrates, who in the later fifth century B.C.E. shifted the focus of philosophy to ethical questions). In the sixth century B.C.E. Xenophanes° called into question the kind of gods that Homer had popularized.

> But if cattle and horses or lions had hands, or were able to draw with their hands and do the works that men can do, horses would draw the forms of the gods like horses, and cattle like cattle, and they would make their bodies such as they each had themselves.[3]

The pre-Socratic philosophers rejected traditional religious explanations of the origins and nature of the world and sought rational explanations. They were primarily concerned with learning how the world was created, what it is made of, and why changes occur. Some pre-Socratic thinkers postulated various combinations of earth, air, fire, and water as the primal elements that combine or dissolve to form the numerous substances found in nature. One advanced the theory that the world is composed of microscopic *atoms* (from a Greek word meaning "indivisible") that move through the void of space, colliding randomly and combining in various ways to form the many substances of the natural world. In some respects startlingly similar to modern atomic theory, this model was essentially a lucky intuition, but it is a testament to the sophistication of these thinkers. It is probably no coincidence that most of them came from Ionia and southern Italy, two zones in which Greeks were in close contact with non-Greek peoples. The shock of encountering people with very different ideas may have stimulated new lines of inquiry.

Another important intellectual development also took place in Ionia in the sixth century B.C.E. A group of men later referred to as logographers° ("writers of prose accounts"), taking full advantage of the nearly infinite capacity of writing to store information, began gathering data on a wide range of topics, including ethnography (description of a people's physical characteristics and cultural practices), the geography of Mediterranean lands, the foundation stories of important cities, and the origins of famous Greek families. They were the first to write in prose—the language of everyday speech—rather than poetry, which had long facilitated the memorization essential to an oral society. *Historia,* "investigation/research," was the name they gave to the method they used to collect, sort, and select information. In the mid-fifth century B.C.E. **Herodotus** (ca. 485–425 B.C.E.), from Halicarnassus in southwest Anatolia, published his *Histories.* Early parts of the work are filled with the geographic and ethnographic reports, legends, folktales, and marvels dear to the logographers, but in later sections Herodotus focuses on the great event of the previous generation: the wars between the Greeks and the Persian Empire.

Herodotus declared his new conception of his mission in the first lines of the book:

> I, Herodotus of Halicarnassus, am here setting forth my history, that time may not draw the color from what man has brought into being, nor those great and wonderful deeds, manifested by both Greeks and barbarians, fail of their report, and, together with all this, the reason why they fought one another.[4]

In stating that he wants to find out *why* Greeks and Persians came to blows, he reveals that he has become a historian seeking the causes behind historical events.

Archilochus (ahr-KIL-uh-kuhs)
Xenophanes (zeh-NOFF-uh-nees)
logographer (loe-GOG-ruff-er)

Herodotus directed the all-purpose techniques of *historia* to the service of *history* in the modern sense of the term, thereby narrowing the meaning of the word. For this achievement he is known as the "father of history."

Athens and Sparta

The two preeminent Greek city-states of the late Archaic and Classical periods were Athens and Sparta. The different character of these two communities underscores the potential for diversity in the evolution of human societies, even those arising in similar environmental and cultural contexts.

The ancestors of the Spartans migrated into the Peloponnese°, the southernmost part of the Greek mainland, around 1000 B.C.E. For a time Sparta followed a typical path of development, participating in trade and fostering the arts. Then in the seventh century B.C.E. something happened to alter the destiny of the Spartan state. Like many other parts of Greece, the Spartan community was feeling the effects of increasing population and a shortage of arable land. However, instead of sending out colonists, the Spartans crossed their mountainous western frontier and invaded the fertile plain of Messenia (see Map 5.2). Hoplite tactics may have given the Spartans the edge they needed to prevail over fierce Messenian resistance. The result was the takeover of Messenia and the domination of the native population, who descended to the status of helots°, the most abused and exploited population on the Greek mainland.

Fear of a helot uprising led to the evolution of the unique Spartan way of life. The Spartan state became a military camp in a permanent state of preparedness. Territory in Messenia and Laconia (the Spartan homeland) was divided into several thousand lots, which were assigned to Spartan citizens. Helots worked the land and turned over a portion of what they grew to their Spartan masters, who were thereby freed from food production and able to spend their lives in military training and service.

The professional Spartan soldier was the best in Greece, and the Spartan army was superior to all others, since the other Greek states relied on citizen militias called out only in time of crisis. The Spartans, however, paid a huge personal price for their military readiness. At age seven, boys were taken from their families and put into barracks, where they were toughened by a severe regimen of discipline, beatings, and deprivation. A Spartan male's whole life was subordinated to the demands of the state. Sparta essentially stopped the clock, declining to participate in the economic, political, and cultural renaissance taking place in the Archaic Greek world. There were no longer any poets or artists at Sparta. In an attempt to maintain equality among citizens, precious metals and coinage were banned, and Spartans were forbidden to engage in commerce. The fifth-century B.C.E. historian Thucydides°, a native of Athens, remarked that in his day Sparta appeared to be little more than a large village and that no future observer of the ruins of the site would be able to guess its power.

The Spartans purposefully cultivated a mystique by rarely putting their reputation to the test, practicing a foreign policy that was cautious and isolationist. Reluctant to march far from home for fear of a helot uprising, the Spartans sought to maintain peace in the Peloponnese through the Peloponnesian League, a system of alliances between Sparta and its neighbors.

Athens followed a different path. In comparison with other Greek city-states, it possessed an unusually large and populous territory: the entire region of Attica. Attica contained a number of moderately fertile plains and was ideally suited for cultivation of olive trees. In addition to the urban center of Athens, located some 5 miles (8 kilometers) from the sea where the sheer-sided Acropolis towered above the Attic Plain, the peninsula was dotted with villages and a few larger towns.

Attica's large land area provided a buffer against the initial stresses of the Archaic period, but by the early sixth century B.C.E. things had reached a critical point. In 594 B.C.E. Solon was appointed lawgiver and was granted extraordinary powers to avert a civil war. He divided Athenian citizens into four classes based on the annual yield of their farms. Those in the top three classes could hold state offices. Members of the lowest class, who had little or no property, could not hold office but were allowed to participate in meetings of the Assembly. This arrangement, which made rights and privileges a function of wealth, was far from democratic. But it broke the absolute monopoly on power of a small circle of aristocratic families, and it allowed for social and political mobility. By abolishing the practice of enslaving individuals for failure to repay their debts, Solon guaranteed the freedom of Athenian citizens.

Despite Solon's efforts to defuse the crisis, political turmoil continued until 546 B.C.E., when an aristocrat named Pisistratus° seized power. To strengthen his position and weaken the aristocracy, the tyrant Pisistratus tried to shift the allegiance of the still largely rural population to the urban center of Athens, where he was the dominant figure. He undertook a number of monumental

Peloponnese (PELL-uh-puh-neze) **helot** (HELL-ut)

Thucydides (thoo-SID-ih-dees) **Pisistratus** (pie-SIS-truh-tuhs)

building projects, including a Temple of Athena on the Acropolis. He also instituted or expanded several major festivals that drew people to Athens for religious processions, performances of plays, and athletic and poetic competitions.

Pisistratus passed the tyranny on to his sons, but with Spartan assistance the Athenians turned the tyrant-family out in the last decade of the sixth century B.C.E. In the 460s and 450s B.C.E. **Pericles**° and his political allies took the last steps in the evolution of Athenian democracy, transferring all power to popular organs of government: the Assembly, Council of 500, and People's Courts. From that time on, men of moderate or little means could hold office and participate in the political process. Men were selected by lot to fill even the highest offices, and they were paid for public service so they could afford to take time off from their work. The focal point of Athenian political life became the Assembly of all citizens. Several times a month proposals were debated there; decisions were openly made, and any citizen could speak to the issues of the day.

During this century and a half of internal political evolution, Athens's economic clout and international reputation rose steadily. From the time of Pisistratus, Athenian pottery is increasingly prominent in the archaeological record at sites all around the Mediterranean, crowding out the products of former Greek commercial powerhouses such as Corinth and Aegina (see Map 5.2). These pots often contained olive oil, Athens's chief export, but elegant painted vases were desirable luxury commodities in their own right. Extensive trade increased the numbers and wealth of the middle class and helps explain why Athens took the path of increasing democratization.

THE STRUGGLE OF PERSIA AND GREECE, 546–323 B.C.E.

For the Greeks of the fifth and fourth centuries B.C.E., Persia was the great enemy and the wars with Persia were the decisive historical event. The Persians probably were more concerned about developments farther east and did not regard the wars with the Greeks as so consequential. Nevertheless, the encounter with the Greeks over a period of two centuries was of profound importance for the history of the eastern Mediterranean and western Asia.

Early Encounters

Cyrus's conquest of Lydia in 546 B.C.E. led to the subjugation of the Greek cities on the Anatolian seacoast. In the years that followed, these cities were ruled by local groups or individuals who collaborated with the Persian government so as to maintain themselves in power and allow their cities to operate with minimal Persian interference. All this changed when the Ionian Revolt, a great uprising of Greeks and other subject peoples on the western frontier, broke out in 499 B.C.E. The Persians needed five years and a massive infusion of troops and resources to stamp out the insurrection.

The failed revolt led to the **Persian Wars**—two Persian attacks on Greece in the early fifth century B.C.E. In 490 B.C.E. Darius dispatched a naval fleet to punish Eretria° and Athens, two states on the Greek mainland that had given assistance to the Ionian rebels, and to warn others about the foolhardiness of crossing the Persian king. Eretria was betrayed to the Persians by several of its own citizens, and the survivors were marched off to permanent exile in southwest Iran. In this, as in many things, the Persians took over the practices of their Assyrian predecessors, although they resorted to mass deportation less often and were more reticent about advertising it. Next on the Persians' list were the Athenians, who probably would have suffered a similar fate if their hoplites had not defeated the lighter-armed Persian troops in a short, sharp engagement at Marathon, 26 miles (42 kilometers) from Athens.

Xerxes (Khshayarsha, r. 486–465 B.C.E.) succeeded his father on the Persian throne and soon turned his attention to the troublesome Greeks. In 480 B.C.E. he set out with a huge invasionary force consisting of the Persian army, contingents summoned from all the peoples of the Persian Empire, and a large fleet of ships drawn from maritime subjects. Crossing the Hellespont (the narrow strait at the edge of the Aegean separating Europe and Asia), Persian forces descended into central and southern Greece (see Map 5.2). Xerxes sent messengers ahead to most of the Greek states, bidding them to offer up "earth and water"—tokens of submission.

Many Greek communities acknowledged Persian overlordship. But in southern Greece an alliance of states bent on resistance was formed under the leadership of the Spartans. This Hellenic League, as modern historians call it, initially failed to halt the Persian advance. At the pass of Thermopylae° in central Greece, three hundred Spartans and their king gave their lives to buy time for their fellows to escape. However, after seizing and sacking the city of Athens in 480 B.C.E., the Persians allowed their navy to be lured into the narrow straits of nearby

Pericles (PER-eh-kleez)

Eretria (er-EH-tree-uh) **Thermopylae** (thuhr-MOP-uh-lee)

Salamis°, where they lost their advantage in numbers and maneuverability and suffered a devastating defeat. The following spring (479 B.C.E.), the Persian land army was routed at Plataea°, and the immediate threat to Greece receded. A number of factors account for the outcome: the Persians' difficulty in supplying their very large army in a distant land; the Persian high command's tactical error in allowing naval forces to be drawn into the narrow waters off Salamis; and the superiority of heavily armed Greek hoplite soldiers over lighter-armed Asiatic infantry.

The collapse of the threat to the Greek mainland did not mean an end to war. The Greeks went on the offensive. Athens's stubborn refusal to submit to the Persian king, even after the city was sacked twice in two successive years, and the vital role played by the Athenian navy, which made up fully half of the allied Greek fleet, earned the city a large measure of respect. The next phase of the war, designed to drive the Persians away from the Aegean and liberate Greek states still under Persian control, was naval. Thus Athens replaced land-based, isolationist Sparta as leader of the campaign against Persia.

In 477 B.C.E. the Delian° League was formed. It was initially a voluntary alliance of Greek states eager to prosecute the war against Persia. In less than twenty years, League forces led by Athenian generals swept the Persians from the waters of the eastern Mediterranean and freed all Greek communities except those in distant Cyprus (see Map 4.5).

The Height of Athenian Power

By scholarly convention, the Classical period of Greek history (480–323 B.C.E.) begins with the successful defense of the Greek homeland against the forces of the Persian Empire. Ironically, the Athenians, who had played such a crucial role, exploited these events to become an imperial power. A string of successful campaigns and the passage of time led many of their Greek allies to grow complacent and contribute money instead of military forces. The Athenians used the money to build up and staff their navy. Eventually they saw the other members of the Delian League as their subjects and demanded annual contributions and other signs of submission from them. States that tried to leave the League were brought back by force, stripped of their defenses, and rendered subordinate to Athens.

Athens's mastery of naval technology transformed Greek warfare and politics and brought power and wealth to Athens itself. Unlike commercial ships, whose stable, round-bodied hulls were propelled by a single square sail, military vessels could not risk depending on the wind. By the late sixth century B.C.E. the **trireme°**, a sleek, fast vessel powered by 170 rowers, had become the premier warship. The design of the trireme has long been a puzzle, but the unearthing of the slips where these vessels were moored at Athens and recent experiments with a full-scale replica manned by international volunteers have revealed much about the trireme's design and the battle tactics it made possible. Rowers using oars of different lengths and carefully positioned on three levels so as not to run afoul of one another were able to achieve short bursts of speed of up to 7 knots. Athenian crews, by constant practice, became the best in the eastern Mediterranean.

The effectiveness of the new Athenian navy had significant consequences both at home and abroad. The emergence at Athens of a democratic system in which each male citizen had, at least in principle, an equal voice is connected to the new primacy of the fleet. Hoplites were members of the middle and upper classes (they had to provide their own protective gear and weapons). Rowers, in contrast, came from the lower classes, but because they were providing the chief protection for the community and were the source of its power, they could insist on full rights.

Possession of a navy allowed Athens to project its power farther than it could have done with a citizen militia (which could be kept in arms for only short periods of time). In previous Greek wars, the victorious state had little capability to occupy a defeated neighbor permanently (with the exception, as we have seen, of Sparta's takeover of Messenia). Usually the victor was satisfied with booty and, perhaps, minor adjustments to boundary lines. Athens was able to continually dominate and exploit other, weaker communities in an unprecedented way.

Athens did not hesitate to use military and political power to promote its commercial interests. Athens's port, Piraeus°, grew into the most important commercial center in the eastern Mediterranean. The money collected each year from the subject states helped subsidize the increasingly expensive Athenian democracy as well as underwrite the construction costs of the beautiful buildings on the Acropolis, including the majestic new temple of Athena, the Parthenon. Many Athenians worked on the construction and decoration of these monuments. Indeed, the building program was a means by which the Athenian leader Pericles redistributed the profits of em-

Salamis (SAH-lah-miss) **Plataea** (pluh-TEE-uh)
Delian (DEE-lih-yuhn)

trireme (TRY-reem) **Piraeus** (pih-RAY-uhs)

Replica of Ancient Greek Trireme Greek warships had a metal-tipped ram in front to pierce the hulls of enemy vessels and a pair of steering rudders in the rear. Though equipped with masts and sails, in battle these warships were propelled by 170 rowers. This modern, full-size replica represents one solution to the puzzle of how three tiers of oars could operate simultaneously without becoming entangled. Volunteer crews are helping scholars to determine attainable speeds and maneuvering techniques. (Courtesy, the Trireme Trust)

pire to the Athenian people and gained extraordinary popularity.

In other ways as well, Athens's cultural achievements were dependent on the profits of empire. The economic advantages that empire brought to Athens indirectly subsidized the festivals at which the great dramatic tragedies of Aeschylus, Sophocles, and Euripides and the comedies of Aristophanes° were performed. Money is a prerequisite for support of the arts and sciences, and the brightest and most creative artists and thinkers in the Greek world were drawn to Athens. Traveling teachers called Sophists ("wise men") provided instruction in logic and public speaking to pupils who could afford their fees. The new discipline of rhetoric—the construction of attractive and persuasive arguments—gave those with training and quick wits a great advantage in politics and the courts. The Greek masses became connoisseurs of oratory, eagerly listening for each innovation, yet so aware of the power of words that *sophist* came to mean one who uses cleverness to distort and manipulate reality.

Aristophanes (ah-ruh-STOFF-eh-neze)

These new intellectual currents came together in 399 B.C.E. when the philosopher **Socrates** (ca. 470–399 B.C.E.) was brought to trial. A sculptor by trade, Socrates spent most of his time in the company of young men who enjoyed conversing with him and observing him deflate the pretensions of those who thought themselves wise. He wryly commented that he knew one more thing than everyone else: that he knew nothing. At his trial, Socrates was easily able to dispose of the charges of corrupting the youth of Athens and not believing in the gods of the city. He argued that the real basis of the hostility he faced was twofold: (1) He was being held responsible for the actions of several of his aristocratic students who had tried to overthrow the Athenian democracy. (2) He was being blamed unfairly for the controversial teachings of the Sophists, which were widely believed to be contrary to traditional religious beliefs and to undermine morality. In Athenian trials, juries of hundreds of citizens decided guilt and punishment, often motivated more by emotion than by legal principles. The vote that found Socrates guilty was fairly close. But his lack of contrition in the penalty phase—he proposed that he be rewarded for his services to the state—led the jury to condemn him to death by drinking hemlock. Socrates' disciples regarded his execution as a martyrdom, and smart young men such as Plato withdrew from public life and dedicated themselves to the philosophical pursuit of knowledge and truth.

This period encompasses the last stage in Greece of the transition from orality to literacy. Socrates himself wrote nothing, preferring to converse with people he met in the street. His disciple Plato (ca. 428–347 B.C.E.) may represent the first generation to be truly literate. He gained much of his knowledge from books and habitually wrote down his thoughts. On the outskirts of Athens, Plato founded the Academy, a school where young men could pursue a course of higher education. Yet even Plato retained traces of the orality of the world in which he had grown up. He wrote dialogues—an oral form—in which his protagonist, Socrates, uses the "Socratic method" of question and answer to reach a deeper understanding of the meaning of values such as justice, excellence, and wisdom. Plato refused to write down the most advanced stages of the philosophical and spiritual training that took place at his Academy. He believed that full apprehension of a higher reality, of which our own sensible world is but a pale reflection, could be entrusted only to "initiates" who had completed the earlier stages.

The third of the great classical philosophers, Aristotle (384–322 B.C.E.), came from Stagira, a community on the Thracian coast. After several decades of study at Plato's Academy in Athens, he was chosen by the king of Macedonia, Philip II, who had a high regard for Greek culture, to be the tutor of his son Alexander. Later, Aristotle returned to Athens to found his own school, the Lyceum. Of a very different temperament than Plato, who had been drawn to mysticism and metaphysical speculation, Aristotle sought to collect and categorize a vast array of knowledge. He lectured and wrote about politics, philosophy, ethics, logic, poetry, rhetoric, physics, astronomy, meteorology, zoology, and psychology, laying the foundations for many modern disciplines.

Inequality in Classical Greece

Athenian democracy, the inspiration for the concept of democracy in the Western tradition, was a democracy only for the relatively small percentage of the inhabitants of Attica who were truly citizens—free adult males of pure Athenian ancestry. Excluding women, children, slaves, and foreigners, this group amounted to 30,000 or 40,000 people out of a total population of approximately 300,000—only 10 or 15 percent.

Vase Painting Depicting Women at an Athenian Fountain House, ca. 520 B.C.E. Paintings on Greek vases provide the most vivid pictorial record of ancient Greek life. The subject matter usually reflects the interests of the aristocratic males who purchased the vases—warfare, athletics, mythology, drinking parties—but sometimes we are given glimpses into the lives of women and the working classes. These women are presumably domestic servants sent to fetch water for the household from the public fountain. The large water jars they are filling are like the one on which this scene is depicted. (William Francis Warden Fund, Courtesy, Museum of Fine Arts Boston)

Slaves, mostly of foreign origin, constituted perhaps one-third of the population of Attica in the fifth and fourth centuries B.C.E., and the average Athenian family owned one or more. Slaves were needed to run the shop or work on the farm while the master was attending meetings of the Assembly or serving on one of the boards that oversaw the day-to-day activities of the state. The slave was a "living piece of property," required to do any work, submit to any sexual acts, and receive any punishments that the owner ordained. In the absence of huge estates, there were no rural slave gangs, and most Greek slaves were domestic servants, often working on the same tasks as the master or mistress. Close daily contact between owners and slaves meant, in many cases, that a relationship developed, making it hard for Greek slave owners to deny the essential humanity of their slaves. Still, Greek thinkers rationalized the institution of slavery by arguing that barbaroi (non-Greeks) lacked the capacity to reason and thus were better off under the direction of rational Greek owners.

The position of women varied across Greek communities. The women of Sparta, who were expected to bear and raise strong children, were encouraged to exercise, and they enjoyed a level of public visibility and outspokenness that shocked other Greeks. Athens may have been at the opposite extreme as regards the confinement and suppression of women. Ironically, the exploitation of women in Athens, as of slaves, is linked to the high degree of freedom enjoyed by Athenian men in the democratic state.

Athenian marriages were unequal affairs. A new husband might be thirty, reasonably well educated, a veteran of war, and experienced in business and politics. Under law he had nearly absolute authority over the members of his household. He arranged his marriage with the parents of his prospective wife, who was likely to be a teenager brought up with no formal education and only minimal training in weaving, cooking, and household management. Coming into the home of a husband she hardly knew, she had no political rights and limited legal protection. Given the differences in age, social experience, and authority, the relationship between husband and wife was in many ways similar to that of father and daughter.

The primary function of marriage was to produce children, preferably male. It is impossible to prove the extent of infanticide—the killing through exposure of unwanted children—because the ancients were sufficiently ashamed to say little about it. But it is likely that more girls than boys were abandoned.

Husbands and wives had limited daily contact. The man spent the day outdoors attending to work or political responsibilities; he dined with male friends at night; and usually he slept alone in the men's quarters. The woman stayed home to cook, clean, raise the children, and supervise the servants. The closest relationship in the family was likely to be between the wife and her slave attendant. These women, often roughly the same age, spent enormous amounts of time together. The servant could be sent into town on errands. The wife stayed in the house, except to attend funerals and certain festivals and to make discreet visits to the houses of female relatives. Greek men justified the confinement of women by claiming that they were naturally promiscuous and likely to introduce other men's children into the household—an action that would threaten the family property and violate the strict regulation of citizenship rights.

Without any documents written by women in this period, we cannot tell the extent to which Athenian women resented their situation or accepted it because they knew little else. Women's festivals provided rare opportunities for women to get out. During the three-day Thesmophoria° festival, the women of Athens lived together and managed their own affairs in a great encampment, carrying out mysterious rituals meant to enhance the fertility of the land. The appearance of bold and self-assertive women on the Athenian stage is also suggestive: the defiant Antigone° of Sophocles' play who buried her brother despite the prohibition of the king; and the wives in Aristophanes' comedy *Lysistrata*° who refused to have sex with their husbands until the men ended a war. Although these plays were written by men and probably reflect a male fear of strong women, the playwrights must have had models in their mothers, sisters, and wives.

The inequality of men and women posed obstacles to creating a "meaningful" relationship between the sexes. To find his intellectual and emotional equal, a man often looked to other men. Bisexuality was common in ancient Greece, as much a product of the social structure as of biological inclinations. A common pattern was that of an older man serving as admirer, pursuer, and mentor of a youth. Bisexuality became part of a system by which young men were educated and initiated into the community of adult males. At least this was true of the elite intellectual groups that loom large in the written sources. It is hard to say how prevalent bisexuality and the confinement of women were among the Athenian masses.

Failure of the City-State and Triumph of the Macedonians

The emergence of Athens as an imperial power in the half-century after the Persian invasion aroused the suspicions of other Greek states and led to open hostilities between former allies. In 431 B.C.E. the **Peloponnesian War** broke out. This nightmarish struggle for survival between the Athenian and Spartan alliance systems encompassed most of the Greek world. It was a war unlike any previous Greek war because the Athenians used their naval power to insulate themselves from the dangers of an attack by land. In midcentury they had built three long walls connecting the city with the port of Piraeus and the adjacent shoreline. At the start of the war, Pericles formulated an unprecedented strategy, refusing to engage the Spartan-

Thesmophoria (thes-moe-FOE-ree-uh)
Antigone (an-TIG-uh-nee) **Lysistrata** (lis-uh-STRAH-tuh)

led armies that invaded Attica each year. Pericles knew that, as long as Athens controlled the sea lanes and was able to provision itself, the enemy hoplites must soon return to their farms and the city could not be starved into submission by a land-based siege. Thus, instead of culminating in a short, decisive battle like most Greek hoplite warfare, the Peloponnesian War dragged on for nearly three decades with great loss of life and squandering of resources. It sapped the morale of all of Greece and ended only with the defeat of Athens in a naval battle in 404 B.C.E. The Persian Empire had bankrolled the construction of ships by the Spartan alliance, so Sparta finally was able to take the conflict into Athens's own element, the sea.

The victorious Spartans, who had entered the war championing "the freedom of the Greeks," took over Athens's overseas empire until their own increasingly highhanded behavior aroused the opposition of other city-states. Indeed, the fourth century B.C.E. was a time of nearly continuous skirmishing among Greek states. One can make the case that the independent polis, from one point of view the glory of Greek culture, was also the fundamental structural flaw because it fostered rivalry, fear, and mistrust among neighboring communities.

Internal conflict in the Greek world allowed the Persians to recoup old losses. By the terms of the King's Peace of 387 B.C.E., to which most of the states of war-weary Greece subscribed, all of western Asia, including the Greek communities of the Anatolian seacoast, were conceded to Persia. The Persian king became the guarantor of a status quo that kept the Greeks divided and weak. Luckily for the Greeks, rebellions in Egypt, Cyprus, and Phoenicia as well as trouble with some of the satraps in the western provinces diverted Persian attention from thoughts of another Greek invasion.

Meanwhile, in northern Greece developments were taking place that would irrevocably alter the balance of power in the eastern Mediterranean and western Asia. Philip II (r. 359–336 B.C.E.) was transforming his previously backward kingdom of Macedonia into the premier military power in the Greek world. (Although southern Greeks had long doubted the "Greekness" of the rough and rowdy Macedonians, modern scholarship is inclined to regard their language and culture as Greek at base, though much influenced by contact with non-Greek neighbors.) Philip had made a number of improvements to the traditional hoplite formation. He increased the striking power and mobility of his force by equipping soldiers with longer thrusting spears and less armor. Because horses thrived in the broad, grassy plains of the north, he experimented with the coordinated use of infantry and cavalry. His engineers had also developed new kinds of siege equipment, including the first catapults—machines using the power of twisted cords that, when released, hurled arrows or stones great distances. For the first time it became possible to storm a fortified city rather than wait for starvation to take effect.

In 338 B.C.E. Philip defeated a coalition of southern states and established the Confederacy of Corinth as an instrument for controlling the Greek city-states. Philip had himself appointed military commander for a planned all-Greek campaign against Persia, and his generals established a bridgehead on the Asiatic side of the Hellespont. It appears that Philip was following the advice of Greek thinkers who had pondered the lessons of the Persian Wars of the fifth century B.C.E. and had urged a crusade against the national enemy as a means of unifying their quarrelsome countrymen.

We will never know how far Philip's ambitions extended, for an assassin killed him in 336 B.C.E. When **Alexander** (356–323 B.C.E.), his son and heir, crossed over into Asia in 334 B.C.E., his avowed purpose was to exact revenge for Xerxes' invasion a century and half before. He defeated the Persian forces of King Darius III (r. 336–330 B.C.E.) in three pitched battles in Anatolia and Mesopotamia, and ultimately campaigned as far as the Punjab region of modern Pakistan.

Alexander the Great, as he came to be called, maintained the framework of Persian administration in the lands he conquered. He realized that it was well adapted to local circumstances and familiar to the subject peoples. At first, however, he replaced Persian officials with his own Macedonian and Greek comrades. To control strategic points in his expanding empire, he established a series of Greek-style cities, beginning with Alexandria in Egypt, and he settled wounded and aged former soldiers in them. After his decisive victory at Gaugamela in northern Mesopotamia (331 B.C.E.), he began to experiment with leaving cooperative Persian officials in place. He also admitted some Persians and other Iranians into his army and into the circle of his courtiers, and he adopted elements of Persian dress and court ceremonial. Finally, he married several Iranian women who had useful royal or aristocratic connections, and he pressed his leading subordinates to do the same.

Scholars have reached widely varying conclusions about why Alexander adopted these policies, which were unexpected and fiercely resented by the Macedonian nobility. It is probably wisest to see Alexander as operating from a combination of motives, both pragmatic and idealistic. He set off on his Asian campaign with visions of glory, booty, and revenge. But the farther east he traveled, the more he began to see himself as the legitimate successor of the Persian king (a claim facilitated by the death of Darius III at the hands of subordinates). Alexander may have recognized that he had responsibilities to all the diverse peoples who fell under his control. He also

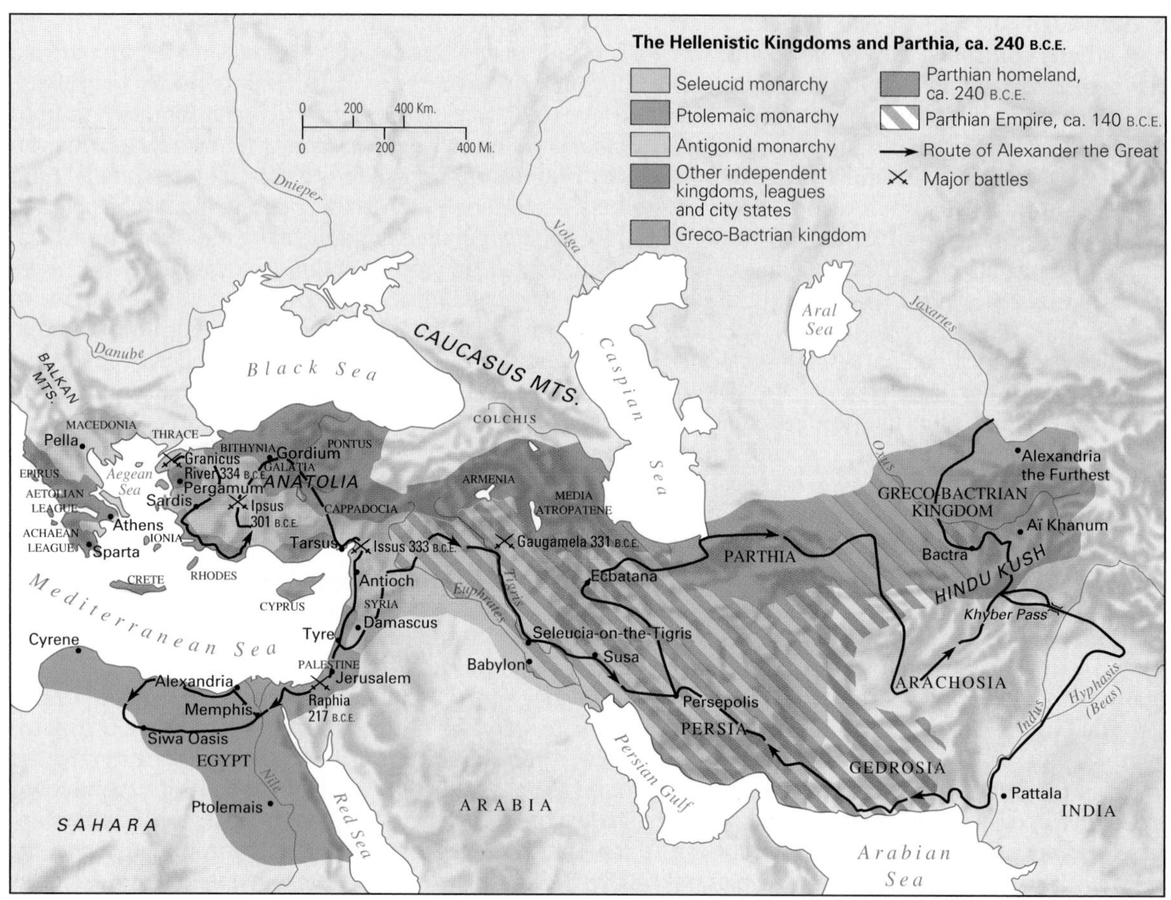

Map 5.3 Hellenistic Civilization After the death of Alexander the Great in 323 B.C.E., his vast empire soon split apart into a number of large and small political entities. A Macedonian dynasty was established on each continent: the Antigonids ruled the Macedonian homeland and tried with varying success to extend their control over southern Greece: the Ptolemies ruled Egypt; and the Seleucids inherited the majority of Alexander's conquests in Asia, though they lost control of the eastern portions because of the rise of the Parthians of Iran in the second century B.C.E. This period saw Greeks migrating in large numbers from their overcrowded homeland to serve as a privleged class of soldiers and administrators on the new frontiers, where they replicated the lifestyle of the city-state.

may have realized the difficulty of holding down so vast an empire by brute force and without the cooperation of important elements among the conquered peoples. In this, he was following the example of the Achaemenids.

THE HELLENISTIC SYNTHESIS, 323–30 B.C.E.

At the time of his sudden death in 323 B.C.E. at the age of thirty-two, Alexander apparently had made no plans for the succession. Thus his death ushered in a half-century of chaos as the most ambitious and ruthless of his officers struggled for control of the vast empire. When the dust cleared, the empire had been broken up into three major kingdoms, each ruled by a Macedonian dynasty—the Seleucid°, Ptolemaic°, and Antigonid° kingdoms (see Map 5.3). Each major kingdom faced a unique set of problems, and although the three frequently were at odds with one another, a rough balance of power prevented any one from gaining the upper hand and enabled smaller states to survive by playing off the great powers.

Historians call the epoch ushered in by the conquests of Alexander the **"Hellenistic Age"** (323–30 B.C.E.)

Seleucid (sih-LOO-sid) **Ptolemaic** (tawl-uh-MAY-ik) **Antigonid** (an-TIG-uh-nid)

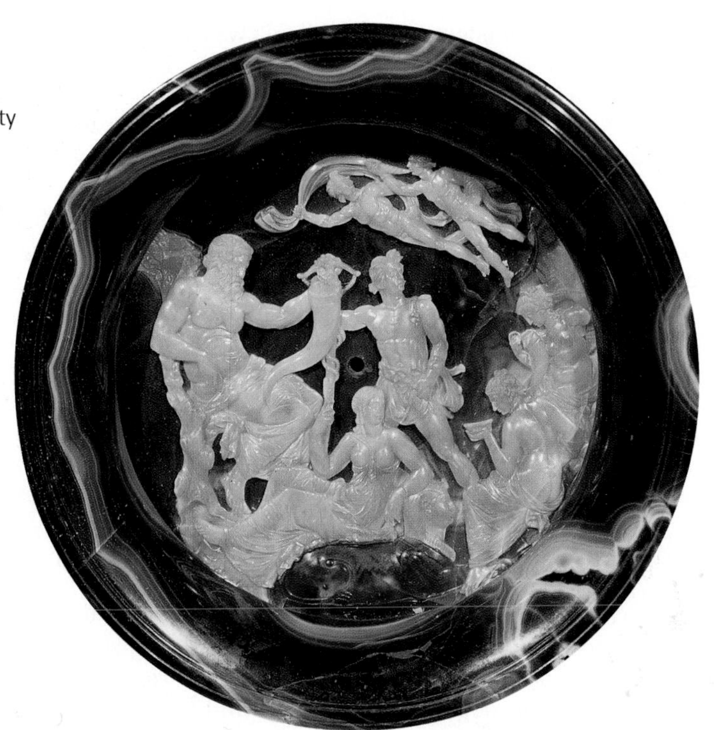

Hellenistic Cameo, Second Century B.C.E. This sardonyx cameo is an allegory of the prosperity of Ptolemaic Egypt. At left, the bearded river-god Nile holds a horn of plenty while his wife, seated on a sphinx and dressed like the Egyptian goddess Isis, raises a stalk of grain. Their son, at center, carries a seed bag and the shaft of a plow. The Seasons are seated at right. Two wind-gods float overhead. The style is entirely Greek, but the motifs are a blending of Greek and Egyptian elements. (G. Dagli-Orti, Paris)

because the lands in northeastern Africa and western Asia that came under Greek rule tended to be "Hellenized"—that is, powerfully influenced by Greek culture. This was a period of large kingdoms with heterogeneous populations, great cities, powerful rulers, pervasive bureaucracies, and vast disparities in wealth—a far cry from the small, homogeneous, independent city-states of Archaic and Classical Greece. It was a cosmopolitan age of long-distance trade and communications, which saw the rise of new institutions like libraries and universities, new kinds of scholarship and science, and the cultivation of sophisticated tastes in art and literature. In many respects, in comparison with the preceding Classical era, it was a world much more like our own.

Of all the successor states, the kingdom of the Seleucids, who took over the bulk of Alexander's conquests, faced the greatest challenges. The Indus Valley and Afghanistan soon split off, and over the course of the third and second centuries B.C.E. Iran was lost to the Parthians. What remained for the Seleucids was a core in Mesopotamia, Syria, and parts of Anatolia, which the Seleucid monarchs ruled from their capital at Syrian Antioch°. Their sprawling territories were open to attack from many directions, and, like the Persians before them, they had to administer lands inhabited by many different ethnic groups organized under various political and social forms. In the countryside, where most of the native peoples resided, the Seleucids maintained an administrative structure modeled on the Persian system. They also continued Alexander's policy of founding Greek-style cities throughout their domains. These cities served as administrative centers and were also the lure that the Seleucids used to attract colonists from Greece. The Seleucids desperately needed Greek soldiers, engineers, administrators, and other professionals.

The dynasty of the **Ptolemies**° ruled Egypt and sometimes laid claim to adjacent Syria-Palestine. The people of Egypt belonged to only one ethnic group and were fairly easily controlled because the vast majority of them were farmers living in villages alongside the Nile. The Ptolemies were able to take over much of the administrative structure of the pharaohs and to extract the surplus wealth of this populous and productive land. The Egyptian economy was centrally planned and highly controlled. Vast revenues poured into the royal treasury from rents (the king owned most of the land), taxes of all sorts, and royal monopolies on olive oil, salt, papyrus, and other key commodities.

The Ptolemies ruled from **Alexandria,** the first of the new cities laid out by Alexander himself. The orientation and status of this city says much about Ptolemaic policies and attitudes. Memphis and Thebes, the capitals of

---

Antioch (AN-tee-awk)

Ptolemies (TAWL-uh-meze)

ancient Egypt, had been located upriver. Alexandria was situated near to where the westernmost branch of the Nile runs into the Mediterranean Sea and clearly was meant to be a link between Egypt and the Mediterranean world. In the language of the Ptolemaic bureaucracy, Alexandria was technically "beside Egypt" rather than in it, as if to emphasize the gulf between rulers and subjects.

Like the Seleucids, the Ptolemies actively encouraged the immigration of Greeks from the homeland and, in return for their skills and collaboration in the military or civil administration, gave them land and a privileged position in the new society. But the Ptolemies did not seek to plant Greek-style cities throughout the Egyptian countryside, and they made no effort to encourage the native population to adopt the Greek language or ways. In fact, so separate was the Greek ruling class from the subject population that only the last Ptolemy, Queen Cleopatra (r. 51–30 B.C.E.), even bothered to learn the language of the Egyptians. For the Egyptian peasant population laboring on the land, life was little changed by the advent of new masters. Yet from the early second century B.C.E., periodic native insurrections in the countryside, which government forces in cooperation with Greek and Hellenized settlers quickly stamped out, were signs of Egyptians' growing resentment of the Greeks' exploitation and arrogance.

In Europe, the Antigonid dynasty ruled the Macedonian homeland and adjacent parts of northern Greece. This was a compact and ethnically homogeneous kingdom, so there was little of the hostility and occasional resistance that the Seleucid and Ptolemaic ruling classes faced. Macedonian garrisons at strongpoints gave the Antigonids a toehold in central and southern Greece, and the shadow of Macedonian intervention always hung over the south. The southern states met the threat by banding together into confederations, such as the Achaean° League in the Peloponnese, in which the member-states maintained local autonomy but pooled resources and military power.

Athens and Sparta, the two leading cities of the Classical period, stood out from these confederations. The Spartans never quite abandoned the myth of their own invincibility and made a number of heroic but futile stands against Macedonian armies. Athens, which held a special place in the hearts of all Greeks because of the artistic and literary accomplishments of the fifth century B.C.E., pursued a policy of neutrality. The city became a large museum, filled with the relics and memories of a glorious past, as well as a university town that attracted the children of the well-to-do from all over the Mediterranean and western Asia.

In an age of cities, the greatest city of all was Alexandria, with a population of nearly half a million. At the heart of this city was the royal compound, containing the palace and administrative buildings for the ruling dynasty and its massive bureaucracy. The centerpiece was the magnificent Mausoleum of Alexander. The first Ptolemy had stolen the body of Alexander while it was being brought back to Macedonia for burial. The theft was aimed at gaining legitimacy for Ptolemaic rule by claiming the blessing of the great conqueror, who was declared to be a god. Two harbors served the needs of the many trading ventures that linked the commerce of the Mediterranean with the Red Sea and Indian Ocean. A great lighthouse—the first of its kind, a multistory tower with a fiery beacon visible at a distance of 30 miles (48 kilometers)—was one of the wonders of the ancient world.

Alexandria gained further luster from its famous Library, which had several hundred thousand volumes, and from its Museum, or "House of the Muses" (divinities who presided over the arts and sciences), a research institution that supported the work of the greatest poets, philosophers, doctors, and scientists of the day. The existence of such well-funded institutions made possible significant advances in science, both in the systematization and extension of earlier work. Some of the greatest achievements were in mathematics and astronomy. The mathematical writings of Euclid° (ca. 276–194 B.C.E.) and the astronomical text of Claudius Ptolemy (second century C.E.), each a grand synthesis of Greek accomplishments in these areas, were highly influential in Europe and the Islamic world into early modern times. Aristarchus° (ca. 310–230 B.C.E.) calculated the distances and relative sizes of the moon and sun. He also argued against the prevailing notion that the earth was the center of the universe, asserting that the earth and other planets revolved around the sun, a view that would not be accepted for another 1,800 years. Eratosthenes° (ca. 276–194 B.C.E.) made a surprisingly accurate calculation of the circumference of the earth. While the claim is often made that the Greeks had a strong predilection for abstract theorizing rather than experimental verification and practical application, experience was put to use in some fields. Archimedes° (ca. 287–211 B.C.E.) invented many mechanical devices, including the screw pump for extracting underground water, and developed a tech-

Achaean (uh-KEY-uhn)

Euclid (YOO-klid) **Aristarchus** (ah-ris-TAWR-kiss)
Eratosthenes (eh-ruh-TOSS-thih-nees)
Archimedes (ahr-kih-MEE-dees)

nique for determining the volume of an object. Galen° (ca. 129–210 C.E.), a Greek physician of the Roman era, conveyed the legacy of Greek medical knowledge to subsequent ages.

Greek residents of Alexandria enjoyed citizenship in a Greek-style polis with an Assembly, a Council, and officials who dealt with purely local affairs, and they took advantage of public works and institutions that signified the Greek way of life. Public baths and shaded arcades were places to relax and socialize with friends. Ancient plays were revived in the theaters, and musical performances and demonstrations of oratory took place in the concert halls. Gymnasiums offered facilities for exercise and fitness and were places where young men of the privileged classes were schooled in athletics, music, and literature. Jews had their own civic corporation, officials, and courts and predominated in two of the five main residential districts. Other quarters were filled with the sights, sounds, and smells of ethnic groups from Syria, Anatolia, and the Egyptian countryside.

In all the Hellenistic states, ambitious members of the indigenous populations learned the Greek language and adopted elements of the Greek way of life, because doing so put them in a position to become part of the privileged and wealthy ruling class. For the ancient Greeks, to be Greek was primarily a matter of language and lifestyle rather than physical traits. In the Hellenistic Age there was a spontaneous synthesis of Greek and indigenous ways. Egyptians migrated to Alexandria, and Greeks and Egyptians intermarried in the villages of the countryside. Greeks living amid the monuments and descendants of the ancient civilizations of Egypt and western Asia were exposed to the mathematical and astronomical wisdom of Mesopotamia, the elaborate mortuary rituals of Egypt, and the many attractions of foreign religious cults. With little official planning or blessing, stemming for the most part from the day-to-day experiences and actions of ordinary people, a great multicultural experiment unfolded as Greek and Middle Eastern cultural traits clashed and merged.

Conclusion

Profound changes took place in the lands of the eastern Mediterranean and western Asia in the first millennium B.C.E. Persians and Greeks played pivotal roles. Let us compare the impacts of these two peoples and assess the broad significance of these centuries.

Galen (GAY-luhn)

The empire of the Achaemenid Persians was the largest empire yet to appear in the world. It was also a new kind of empire because it encompassed such a wide variety of landscapes, peoples, and social, political, and economic systems. How did the Persians manage to hold together this diverse collection of lands for more than two centuries?

The answer did not lie entirely in brute force. The Persians lacked the manpower to install garrisons everywhere, and communication between the central administration and provincial officials was sporadic and slow. They managed to co-opt leaders among the subject peoples who were willing to collaborate in return for being allowed to retain their power and influence. The Persian government demonstrated flexibility and tolerance in its handling of the laws, customs, and beliefs of subject peoples. Persian administration, superimposed on top of local structures, left a considerable role for local institutions.

The Persians also displayed a flair for public relations. The Zoroastrian religion underlined the authority of the king as the appointee of god and upholder of world order. In their art and inscriptions, the Persian kings broadcast an image of a benevolent empire in which the dependent peoples contributed to the welfare of the realm. Certain peoples with long and proud traditions, such as the Egyptians and Babylonians, revolted from time to time. But most subjects found the Persians to be decent enough masters and a great improvement over earlier Middle Eastern empires such as that of the Assyrians.

Western Asia underwent significant changes in the period of Persian supremacy. First, the early Persian kings put an end to the ancient centers of power in Mesopotamia, Anatolia, and Egypt. Then, by imposing a uniform system of law and administration and by providing security and stability, the Persian government fostered commerce and prosperity, at least for some. Some historians have argued that this period was a turning point in the economic history of western Asia. The Achaemenid government possessed an unprecedented capacity to organize labor on a large scale to construct an expanded water distribution network and work the extensive estates of the Persian royal family and nobility. The Persian "paradise" was not only the symbol but also the proof of the connection between political authority and the productivity of the earth.

Most difficult to assess is the cultural impact of Persian rule. The long-dominant culture of Mesopotamia fused with some Iranian elements. The resulting new synthesis is most visible in the art, architecture, and inscriptions of the Persian monarchs. The lands east of the Zagros Mountains as far as northwest India were brought within this cultural sphere. It has been suggested that the Zoroastrian religion spread across the empire and influenced other religious traditions, such as Judaism, but Zoroastrianism does not appear to have had broad, popular appeal. The Persian administration relied heavily on the scribes and written languages of its Mesopotamian, Syrian, and Egyptian subjects, and literacy remained the preserve of a small, professional class. Thus the Persian language does not seem to have been widely adopted by inhabitants of the empire. Even if there was a greater degree of Persianization in the provinces than is suggested by the extant evidence, it was so thoroughly swamped by Hellenism in the succeeding era that few traces are left.

Nearly two centuries of trouble with the Greeks on their western frontier vexed the Persians but was probably not their first priority. It appears that Persian kings were always more concerned about the security of their eastern and northeastern frontiers, where they were vulnerable to attack by the nomads of Central Asia. The technological differences between Greece and Persia were not great. The only difference that seems to have been of significance was a set of arms and a military formation used by the Greeks that often allowed them to prevail over the Persians. The Persian king's response in the later fifth and fourth centuries B.C.E. was to hire Greek mercenaries to use hoplite tactics for his benefit. The claim is sometimes made that the Persian Empire was weak and crumbling by the time Alexander invaded, but there is little evidence to support this, and no one could have anticipated the charismatic leadership and boundless ambition of Alexander of Macedonia.

The shadow of Persia loomed large over the affairs of the Greek city-states for more than two centuries, and even after the repulse of Xerxes' great expeditionary force there was perpetual fear of another Persian invasion. The victories in 480 and 479 B.C.E. did allow the Greek city-states to continue to evolve politically and culturally at a critical time. Athens, in particular, vaulted into power, wealth, and intense cultural creativity as a result of its role in the Greek victory. It evolved into a new kind of Greek state, upsetting the rough equilibrium of the Archaic period by threatening the autonomy of other city-states and changing the rules of war. The result was the Peloponnesian War, which squandered lives and resources for a generation, raised serious doubts about the viability of the city-state, and diminished many people's allegiance to it.

Alexander's conquests brought changes to the Greek world almost as radical as those suffered by the Persians. Greeks spilled out into the sprawling new frontiers in northeastern Africa and western Asia, and the independent city-state became inconsequential in a world of large kingdoms. The centuries of Greek domination had a far more pervasive cultural impact on the Middle East than did the Persian period. Alexander had been inclined to preserve the Persian administrative apparatus, leaving native institutions and personnel in place. His successors relied almost exclusively on a privileged class of Greek soldiers, officers, and administrators.

Equally significant were the foundation of Greek-style cities, which exerted a powerful cultural influence on important elements of the native populations, and a system of easily learned alphabetic Greek writing, which led to more widespread literacy and far more effective dissemination of information. The result was that the Greeks had a profound impact on the peoples and lands of the Middle East, and Hellenism persisted as a cultural force for a thousand years. As we shall see in the next chapter, the Romans who arrived in the eastern Mediterranean in the second century B.C.E. were greatly influenced by the cultural and political practices of the Hellenistic kingdoms.

Key Terms

Cyrus	**Herodotus**
Darius I	**Pericles**
satrap	**Persian Wars**
Persepolis	**trireme**
Zoroastrianism	**Socrates**
polis	**Peloponnesian War**
hoplite	**Alexander**
tyrant	**Hellenistic Age**
democracy	**Ptolemies**
sacrifice	**Alexandria**

Suggested Reading

The most up-to-date treatment of ancient Persia is Pierre Briant, *From Cyrus to Alexander: A History of the Persian Empire* (2002). Also useful is J. M. Cook, *The Persian Empire* (1983). Josef Wiesehofer, *Ancient Persia: From 550 B.C. to 650 A.D.* (1996); Richard N. Frye, *The History of Ancient Iran* (1984); and volume 2 of *The Cambridge History of Iran*, ed. Ilya Gershevitch (1985), are written by Iranian specialists and have abundant bibliographies. John Curtis, *Ancient Persia* (1989), emphasizes the archaeological record. Roland G. Kent, *Old Persian: Grammar, Texts, Lexicon*, 2d ed. (1953), contains translations of the royal inscriptions.

Maria Brosius, *Women in Ancient Persia, 559–331 B.C.* (1996), gathers and evaluates the scattered evidence. William W. Malandra, *An Introduction to Ancient Iranian Religion: Readings from the Avesta and Achaemenid Inscriptions* (1983), contains documents in translation pertaining to religious subjects. Vesta

Sarkhosh Curtis, *Persian Myths* (1993), is a concise, illustrated introduction to Iranian myths and legends. John Boardman, *Persia and the West: An Archaeological Investigation of the Genesis of Achaemenid Persian Art* (2000), explores the complex question of Greek influence on Persian art and architecture.

The fullest treatment of Greek history and civilization in this period is in *The Cambridge Ancient History,* 3d ed., vols. 3–7 (1970–). Sarah B. Pomeroy, Stanley M. Burstein, Walter Donlan, and Jennifer Tolbert Roberts, *Ancient Greece: A Political, Social, and Cultural History* (1999), is a fine one-volume treatment of Greek civilization. Bella Vivante, ed., *Events That Changed Ancient* Greece (2002), contains an overview, interpretative essay, and up-to-date bibliography for each period of Greek history. Other general treatments include J. B. Bury and Russell Meiggs, *A History of Greece* (1975), and Nancy Demand, *A History of Ancient Greece (*1996*)*. For the Archaic period see Oswyn Murray, *Early Greece,* 2d ed. (1993), and Robin Osborne, *Greece in the Making, 1200–479 B.C.* (1996).

Social history is emphasized by Frank J. Frost, *Greek Society,* 3d ed. (1987). Robert Morkot, *The Penguin Historical Atlas of Ancient Greece* (1996), and Peter Levi, *Atlas of the Greek World* (1980), are filled with maps, pictures, and general information about Greek civilization, as is Lesley Adkins and Roy A. Adkins, *Handbook to Life in Ancient Greece* (1997). Michael Grant and Rachel Kitzinger, eds., *Civilization of the Ancient Mediterranean* (1987), is a three-volume collection of essays by contemporary experts on nearly every aspect of ancient Greco-Roman civilization and includes select bibliographies.

We are fortunate to have an abundant written literature from ancient Greece, and the testimony of the ancients themselves should be the starting point for any inquiry. Herodotus, Thucydides, and Xenophon chronicled the history of the Greeks and their Middle Eastern neighbors from the sixth through fourth centuries B.C.E. Arrian, who lived in the second century C.E., provides the most useful account of the career of Alexander the Great. Among the many collections of documents in translation, see Michael Crawford and David Whitehead, eds., *Archaic and Classical Greece: A Selection of Ancient Sources in Translation* (1983). David G. Rice and John E. Stambaugh, eds., *Sources for the Study of Greek Religion* (1979); Mary R. Lefkowitz and Maureen B. Fant, eds., *Women's Life in Greece and Rome: A Source Book in Translation* (1982); Thomas Wiedemann, ed., *Greek and Roman Slavery* (1981); Michael M. Sage, *Warfare in Ancient Greece: A Sourcebook* (1996), and Michael Gagarin and Paul Woodruff, *Early Greek Political Thought from Homer to the Sophists* (1995), are specialized collections. The Perseus Project (*www.perseus.tufts.edu*) is a remarkable internet site containing hundreds of ancient texts, thousands of photographs of artifacts and sites, maps, encyclopedias, dictionaries, and other resources for the study of Greek (and Roman) civilization.

Victor Davis Hanson, *The Other Greeks: The Family Farm and the Agrarian Roots of Western Civilization* (1995), emphasizes the centrality of farming to the development of Greek institutions and values. Eric A. Havelock, *The Muse Learns to Write: Reflections on Orality and Literacy from Antiquity to the Present* (1986), and Rosalind Thomas, *Literacy and Orality in Ancient* Greece (1992), explore the profound effects of alphabetic literacy on the Greek mind.

Valuable treatments of other key topics include Elaine Fantham, Helene Peet Foley, Natalie Boymel Kampen, Sarah B. Pomeroy, and H. Alan Shapiro, *Women in the Classical World* (1994); Cynthia Patterson, *The Family in Greek History* (1998); Yvon Garlan, *Slavery in Ancient Greece* (1988); Walter Burkert, *Greek Religion* (1985); Victor Davis Hanson, *The Western Way of War: Infantry Battle in Classical Greece* (1989); Lionel Casson, *The Ancient Mariners: Seafarers and Sea Fighters of the Mediterranean in Ancient Times,* 2d ed. (1991); Michail Yu Treister, *The Role of Metals in Ancient Greek History* (1996); Joint Association of Classical Teachers, *The World of Athens: An Introduction to Classical Athenian Culture* (1984); N. G. L. Hammond, *The Macedonian State: The Origins, Institutions and History* (1989); Joseph Roisman, ed., *Alexander the Great: Ancient and Modern Perspectives* (1995); and William R. Biers, *The Archaeology of Greece: An Introduction* (1990). Mary R. Lefkowitz and Guy MacLean Rogers, *Black Athena Revisited* (1996), explores the controversies surrounding the Greek cultural obligation to Egypt and western Asia. For the Hellenistic world see F. W. Walbank, *The Hellenistic World,* rev. ed. (1993), and Michael Grant, *From Alexander to Cleopatra: The Hellenistic World* (1982). M. M. Austin, ed., *The Hellenistic World from Alexander to the Roman Conquest: A Selection of Ancient Sources in Translation* (1981), provides sources in translation. Jean-Yves Empereur, *Alexandria Rediscovered* (1998), summarizes exciting new finds from the palace precinct in the waters off Alexandria.

Notes

1. Quoted in Roland G. Kent, *Old Persian: Grammar, Texts, Lexicon,* 2d ed. (New Haven, CT: American Oriental Society, 1953), 138, 140.
2. Richmond Lattimore, *Greek Lyrics,* 2d ed. (Chicago: University of Chicago Press, 1960), 2.
3. G. S. Kirk and J. E. Raven, *The Presocratic Philosophers: A Critical History with a Selection of Texts* (Cambridge, England: Cambridge University Press, 1957), 169.
4. Herodotus, *The History,* trans. David Grene (Chicago: University of Chicago Press, 1988), 33. (Herodotus 1.1)

6 An Age of Empires: Rome and Han China, 753 B.C.E.–330 C.E.

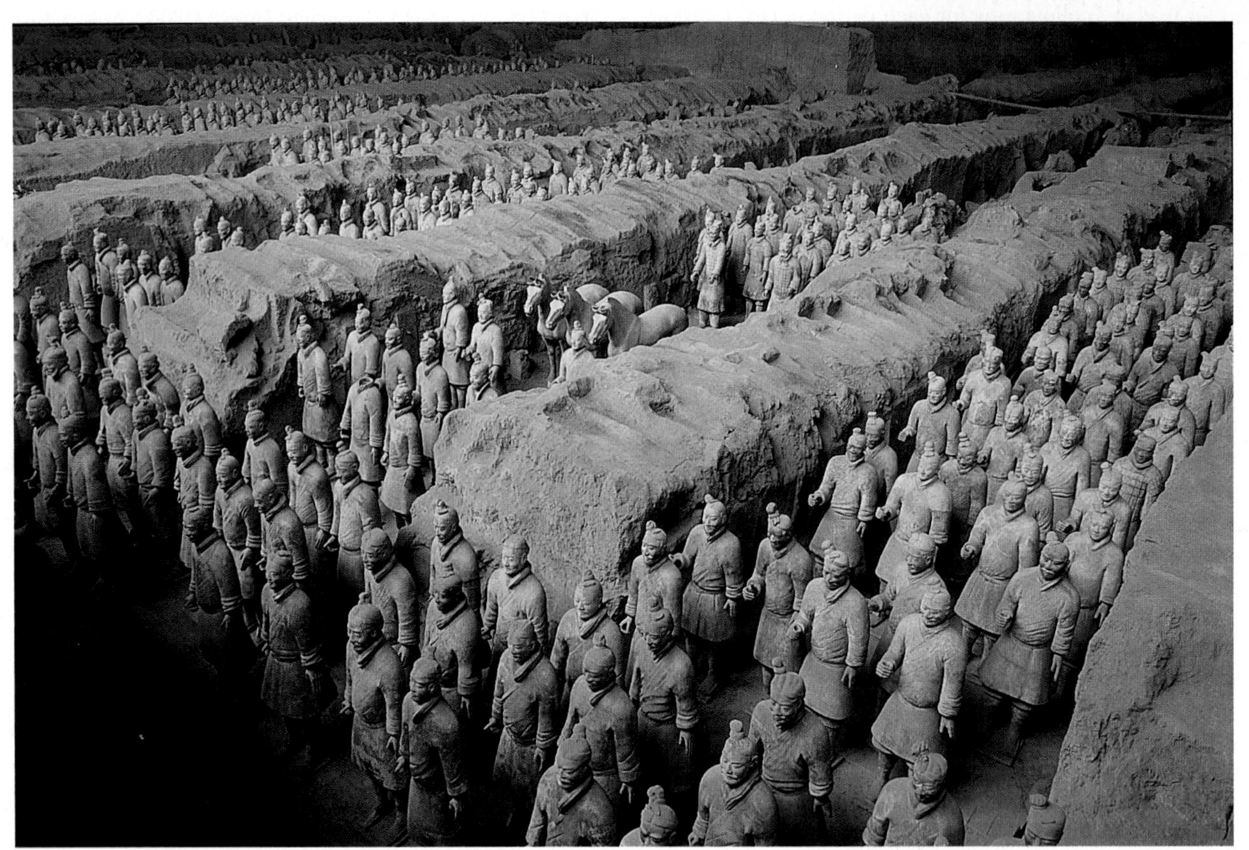

Terracotta Soldiers from the Tomb of Shi Huangdi, "First Emperor" of China Thousands of these life-size, baked-clay figures—each with distinctive features—have been unearthed.

CHAPTER OUTLINE

According to Chinese sources, in the year 166 C.E. a group of travelers identifying themselves as delegates from Andun, the king of distant Da Qin, arrived at the court of the Chinese emperor Huan, one of the Han rulers. Andun was Marcus Aurelius Antoninus, the emperor of Rome. As far as we know, these travelers were the first "Romans" to reach China, although they probably were residents of one of the eastern provinces of the Roman Empire, perhaps Egypt or Syria, and they may have stretched the truth in claiming to be official representatives of the Roman emperor. More likely they were merchants hoping to set up a profitable trading arrangement at the source of the silk so highly prized in the West. Chinese officials, however, were in no position to disprove their claim, since there was no direct contact between the Roman and Chinese Empires.

We do not know what became of these travelers, and their mission apparently did not lead to more direct or regular contact between the empires. Even so, the episode raises some interesting points. First, in the early centuries C.E. Rome and China were linked by far-flung international trading networks encompassing the entire Eastern Hemisphere, and were dimly aware of each other's existence. Second, the last centuries B.C.E. and the first centuries C.E. saw the emergence of two manifestations of a new kind of empire.

The Roman Empire encompassed all the lands surrounding the Mediterranean Sea as well as substantial portions of continental Europe and the Middle East. The Han Empire stretched from the Pacific Ocean to the oases of Central Asia. The largest empires the world had yet seen, they managed to centralize control to a greater degree than earlier empires; their cultural impact on the lands and peoples they dominated was more pervasive; and they were remarkably stable and lasted for many centuries.

Thousands of miles separated Rome and Han China; neither influenced the other. Why did two such unprecedented political entities flourish at the same time? Historians have put forth theories stressing supposedly common factors—such as climate change and the pressure of nomadic peoples from Central Asia on the Roman and Chinese frontiers—but no theory has won the support of most scholars.

As you read this chapter, ask yourself the following questions:

- How did the Roman and Han Empires come into being?
- What were the sources of their stability or instability?
- What benefits and liabilities did these empires bring to the rulers and their subjects?
- What were the most important similarities and differences between these two empires, and what do the similarities and differences tell us about the circumstances and the character of each?

Rome's Creation of a Mediterranean Empire, 753 B.C.E.–330 C.E.

Rome's central location contributed to its success in unifying Italy and then all the lands ringing the Mediterranean Sea (see Map 6.1). The middle of three peninsulas that jut from the European landmass into the Mediterranean, the boot-shaped Italian peninsula and the large island of Sicily constitute a natural bridge almost linking Europe and North Africa. Italy was a crossroads in the Mediterranean, and Rome was a crossroads within Italy. Rome lay at the midpoint of the peninsula, about 15 miles (24 kilometers) from the western coast, where a north-south road intersected an east-west river route. The Tiber River on one side and a double ring of seven hills on the other afforded natural protection to the site.

Italy is a land of hills and mountains. The Apennine range runs along its length like a spine, separating the eastern and western coastal plains, while the arc of the Alps shields it on the north. Many of Italy's rivers are navigable, and passes through the Apennines and through the snowcapped Alps allowed merchants and armies to travel overland. The mild Mediterranean climate affords a long growing season and conditions suitable for a wide variety of crops. The hillsides, largely denuded of cover today, were well forested in ancient times, providing tim-

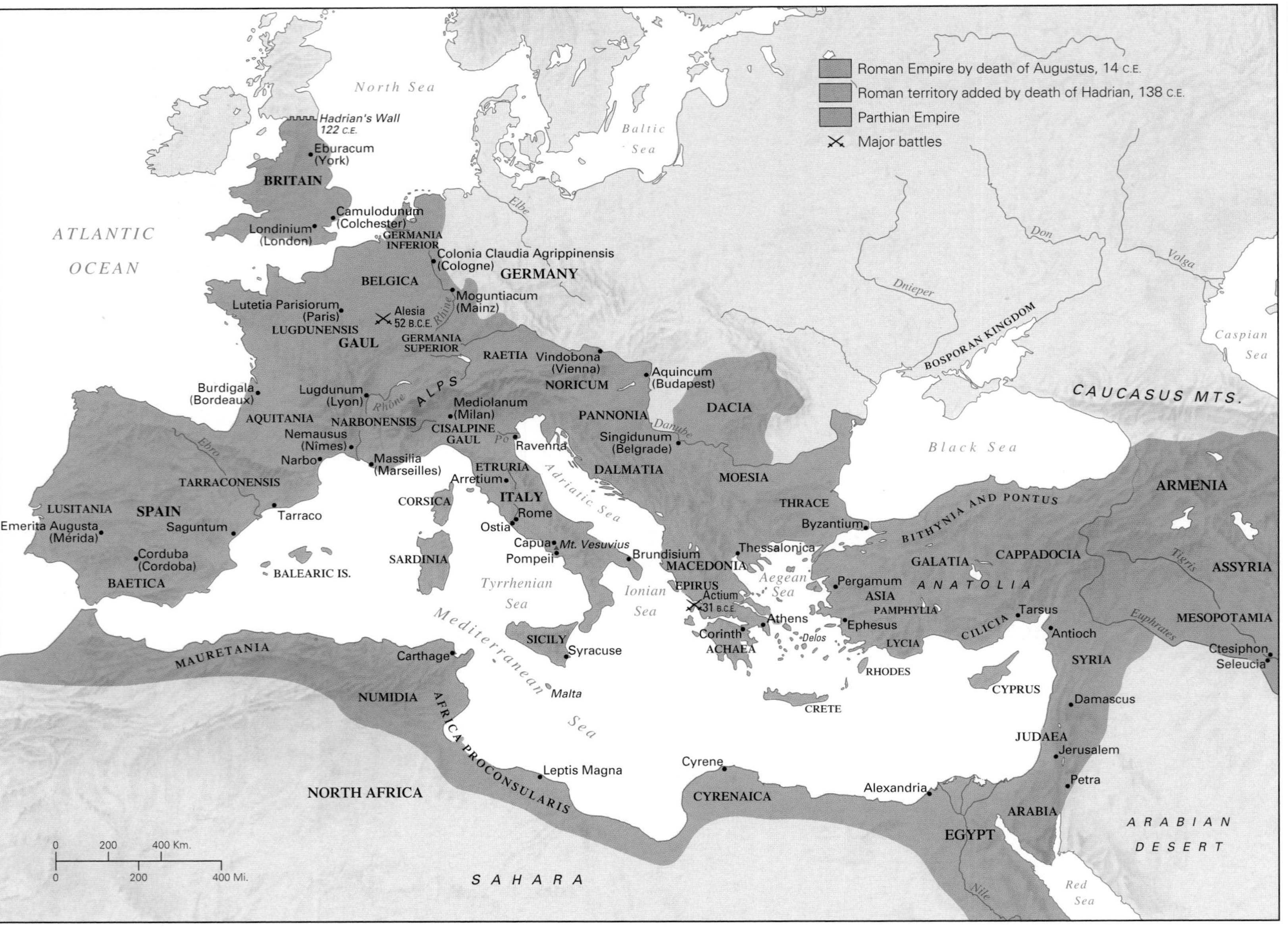

Map 6.1 The Roman Empire The Roman Empire came to encompass all the lands surrounding the Mediterranean Sea, as well as parts of continental Europe. When Augustus died in 14 C.E., he left instructions to his successors not to expand beyond the limits he had set, but Claudius invaded southern Britain in the mid-first century and the soldier-emperor Trajan added Romania early in the second century. Deserts and seas provided solid natural boundaries, but the long and vulnerable river border in central and eastern Europe would eventually prove expensive to defend and vulnerable to invasion by Germanic and Central Asian peoples.

CHRONOLOGY

	Rome	China
1000 B.C.E.	**1000 B.C.E.** First settlement on site of Rome	
500 B.C.E.	**507 B.C.E.** Establishment of the Republic	**480–221 B.C.E.** Warring States Period
300 B.C.E.	**290 B.C.E.** Defeat of tribes of Samnium gives Romans control of Italy **264–202 B.C.E.** Wars against Carthage guarantee Roman control of western Mediterranean	**221 B.C.E.** Qin emperor unites eastern China **206 B.C.E.** Han dynasty succeeds Qin
200 B.C.E.	**200–146 B.C.E.** Wars against Hellenistic kingdoms lead to control of eastern Mediterranean	**140–87 B.C.E.** Emperor Wu expands the Han Empire
100 B.C.E.	**88–31 B.C.E.** Civil wars and failure of the Republic **31 B.C.E.–14 C.E.** Augustus establishes the Principate	
50 C.E.	**45–58 C.E.** Paul spreads Christianity in the eastern Mediterranean	**23 C.E.** Han capital transfered from Chang'an to Luoyang
200 C.E.	**235–284 C.E.** Third-century crisis	**220 C.E.** Fall of Han Empire
300 C.E.	**324 C.E.** Constantine moves capital to Constantinople	

ber for construction and fuel. The region of Etruria in the northwest was rich in iron and other metals.

Even though as much as 75 percent of the total area of the Italian peninsula is hilly, there is still ample arable land in the coastal plains and river valleys. Much of this land has extremely fertile volcanic soil and sustained a much larger population than was possible in Greece. While expanding within Italy, the Roman state created effective mechanisms for tapping the human resources of the countryside.

A Republic of Farmers, 753–31 B.C.E.

According to popular legend, Romulus, who was cast adrift on the Tiber River as a baby and was nursed by a she-wolf, founded the city of Rome in 753 B.C.E. Archaeological research, however, shows that the Palatine Hill—one of the seven hills on the site of Rome—was occupied as early as 1000 B.C.E. The merging of several hilltop communities to form an urban nucleus, made possible by the draining of a swamp on the

Statue of a Roman Carrying Busts of His Ancestors, First Century B.C.E. Roman society was extremely conscious of status, and the status of an elite Roman family was determined in large part by the public achievements of ancestors and living members. A visitor to a Roman home found portraits of distinguished ancestors in the entry hall, along with labels listing the offices they held. Portrait heads were carried in funeral processions. (Alinari/Art Resource, NY)

site of the future Roman Forum (civic center), took place shortly before 600 B.C.E. The Latin speech and cultural patterns of the original inhabitants of the site were typical of the indigenous population of most of the peninsula. However, tradition remembered Etruscan immigrants arriving in the seventh century B.C.E., and Rome came to pride itself on offering hospitality to exiles and outcasts.

Agriculture was the essential economic activity in the early Roman state, and land was the basis of wealth. As a consequence, social status, political privilege, and fundamental values were related to landownership. The vast majority of early Romans were self-sufficient independent farmers who owned small plots of land. A relatively small number of families managed to acquire large tracts of land. The heads of these wealthy families were members of the Senate—a "Council of Elders" that played a dominant role in the politics of the Roman state. According to tradition, there were seven kings of Rome between 753 and 507 B.C.E. The first was Romulus; the last was the tyrannical Tarquinius Superbus. In 507 B.C.E. members of the senatorial class, led by Brutus "the Liberator," deposed Tarquinius Superbus and instituted a *res publica*, a "public possession," or republic.

The **Roman Republic,** which lasted from 507 to 31 B.C.E., was not a democracy. Sovereign power resided in several assemblies, and while male citizens were eligible to attend, the votes of the wealthy classes counted for more than the votes of poor citizens. A slate of civic officials was elected each year, and a hierarchy of state offices evolved. The culmination of a political career was to be selected as one of the two consuls who presided over meetings of the Senate and assemblies and commanded the army on military campaigns.

The real center of power was the **Roman Senate.** Technically an advisory council, first to the kings and later to the annually changing Republican officials, the Senate increasingly made policy and governed. Senators nominated their sons for public offices and filled Senate vacancies from the ranks of former officials. This self-perpetuating body, whose members served for life, brought together the state's wealth, influence, and political and military experience.

The inequalities in Roman society led to periodic unrest and conflict between the elite (called 'patricians°') and the majority of the population (called 'plebeians°'), a struggle known as the Conflict of the Orders. On a number of occasions the plebeians refused to work or fight, and even physically withdrew from the city, in order to pressure the elite to make political concessions. One result was publication of the laws on twelve stone tablets ca. 450 B.C.E., a check on arbitrary decisions by judicial officials. Another important reform was the creation of new officials, the tribunes°, who were drawn from and elected by the lower classes, and who had the power to veto, or block, any action of the Assembly or patrician officials that they deemed to be against the inter-

---

patrician (puh-TRISH-uhn) **plebeian** (pluh-BEE-uhn)
tribune (TRIH-byoon)

ests of the lower orders. The elite, though forced to give in on key points, found ways to blunt the reforms, in large part by bringing the plebeian leadership into an expanded elite.

The basic unit of Roman society was the family, made up of several generations of family members plus domestic slaves. The oldest living male, the *paterfamilias*, exercised absolute authority over other family members. The important male members of the society possessed *auctoritas*, the quality that enabled them to inspire and demand obedience from their inferiors.

Complex ties of obligation, such as the **patron/client relationship,** bound together individuals and families. Clients sought the help and protection of patrons, men of wealth and influence. A senator might have dozens or even hundreds of clients, to whom he provided legal advice and representation, physical protection, and loans of money in tough times. In turn, the client was expected to follow his patron into battle, support him in the political arena, work on his land, and even contribute toward the dowry of his daughter. Throngs of clients awaited their patrons in the morning and accompanied them to the Forum for the day's business. Especially large retinues brought great prestige. Middle-class clients of aristocrats might be patrons of poorer men. In Rome inequality was accepted, institutionalized, and turned into a system of mutual benefits and obligations.

Historical sources do not often report on the activities of Roman women, largely because they played no public role. Nearly all our information about Roman women pertains to those in the upper classes. In early Rome, a woman never ceased to be a child in the eyes of the law. She started out under the absolute authority of her paterfamilias. When she married, she came under the jurisdiction of the paterfamilias of her husband's family. Unable to own property or represent herself in legal proceedings, she had to depend on a male guardian to advocate her interests.

Despite the limitations put on them, Roman women seem to have been less constrained than their counterparts in the Greek world (see Chapter 5). Over time they gained greater personal protection and economic freedom: for instance, some took advantage of a form of marriage that left a woman under the jurisdiction of her father and independent after his death. There are many stories of strong women who had great influence on their husbands or sons and thereby helped shape Roman history. Roman poets confess their love for women who appear to have been educated and outspoken, and the accounts of the careers of the early emperors are filled with tales of self-assured and assertive queen-mothers and consorts.

Like other Italian peoples, early Romans believed in invisible, shapeless forces known as *numina*. Vesta, the living, pulsating energy of fire, dwelled in the hearth. Janus guarded the door. The Penates watched over food stored in the cupboard. Other deities resided in nearby hills, caves, grottoes, and springs. Romans made small offerings of cakes and liquids to win the favor of these spirits. Certain gods had larger spheres of operation—for example, Jupiter was the god of the sky, and Mars initially was a god of agriculture as well as of war.

The Romans tried to maintain the *pax deorum* ("peace of the gods"), a covenant between the gods and the Roman state. Boards of priests drawn from the aristocracy performed sacrifices and other rituals to win the gods' favor. In return, the gods were expected to bring success to the undertakings of the Roman state. When the Romans came into contact with the Greeks of southern Italy (see Chapter 5), they equated their major deities with gods from the Greek pantheon, such as Zeus (Jupiter) and Ares (Mars), and they took over the myths attached to those gods.

Expansion in Italy and the Mediterranean

At the dawn of the Roman Republic, around 500 B.C.E., Rome was a relatively insignificant city-state among many in the region of central Italy called Latium. Three-and-a-half centuries later, Rome was the center of a huge empire encompassing virtually all the lands surrounding the Mediterranean Sea. Expansion began slowly, then picked up momentum, reaching a peak in the third and second centuries B.C.E. Some scholars attribute this expansion to the greed and aggressiveness of a people fond of war. Others observe that the structure of the Roman state encouraged war, because the two consuls had only one year in office in which to gain military glory. The Romans invariably claimed that they were only defending themselves. It is possible that, as fear drove the Romans to expand the territory under their control in order to provide a buffer against attack, each new conquest became vulnerable and a sense of insecurity led to further expansion. Yet the Romans were also quick to seize opportunities as they appeared.

The chief instrument of Roman expansion was the army. All male citizens who owned a specified amount of land were subject to service. The Roman soldiers' equipment—body armor, shield, spear, and sword—was not far different from that of Greek hoplites, but the Roman battle line was more flexible than the phalanx, being subdivided into units that could maneuver independently. Roman armies were famous for their training and discipline. One observer noted that, whereas a Greek army would minimize its exertions by finding a hill or some other naturally defended location to camp for the night, a Roman army would go to the trouble of fortifying an identical camp in the plain on every occasion.

Rome's conquest of Italy was sparked by ongoing friction between the pastoral hill tribes of the Apennines, whose livelihood depended on driving their herds to seasonal grazing grounds, and the farmers of the coastal plains. In the fifth century B.C.E. Rome rose to a position of leadership within a league of central Italian cities organized for defense against the hill tribes. On several occasions in the fourth century B.C.E. the Romans were asked to defend the wealthy and sophisticated cities of Campania, the region on the Bay of Naples possessing the richest farmland in the peninsula. By 290 B.C.E., in the course of three wars with the tribes of Samnium in central Italy, the Romans had extended their "protection" over nearly the entire peninsula.

Unlike the Greeks, who were reluctant to share the privileges of citizenship with outsiders (see Chapter 5), the Romans granted the political, legal, and economic privileges of Roman citizenship to conquered populations. In essence, they co-opted the most influential elements within the conquered communities and made Rome's interests their interests. Rome demanded soldiers from its Italian subjects, and a seemingly inexhaustible reservoir of manpower was a key element of its military success. In a number of crucial wars, Rome was able to endure higher casualties than the enemy and to prevail by sheer numbers.

Between 264 and 202 B.C.E. Rome fought two protracted and bloody wars against the Carthaginians, those energetic descendants of Phoenicians from Lebanon who had settled in present-day Tunisia and dominated the commerce of the western Mediterranean (see Chapter 4). The Roman state emerged as the unchallenged master of the western Mediterranean and acquired its first overseas provinces in Sicily, Sardinia, and Spain (see Map 6.1). Between 200 and 146 B.C.E. a series of wars pitted the Roman state against the major Hellenistic kingdoms in the eastern Mediterranean. The Romans were at first reluctant to occupy such distant territories and withdrew their troops at the conclusion of several wars. But when the settlements that they imposed failed to take root, the frustrated Roman government took over direct administration of the turbulent lands. The conquest of the Celtic peoples of Gaul (modern France; see Chapter 3) by Rome's most brilliant general, Gaius Julius Caesar, between 59 and 51 B.C.E. led to its first territorial acquisitions in Europe's heartland.

At first the Romans resisted extending their system of governance and citizenship rights to the distant provinces. Indigenous elite groups willing to collaborate with the Roman authorities were given considerable autonomy, including responsibility for local administration and tax collection. Every year a senator, usually someone who recently had held a high public post, was dispatched to each province to serve as governor. The governor, accompanied by a surprisingly small retinue of friends and relations who served as advisers and deputies, was primarily responsible for defending the province against outside attack and internal disruption, overseeing the collection of taxes and other revenues due Rome, and deciding legal cases.

Over time, this system of provincial administration proved inadequate. Officials were chosen because of their political connections and often lacked competence or experience. Yearly changes of governor meant that incumbents had little time to gain experience or make local contacts. Although many governors were honest, some were notoriously unscrupulous and extorted huge sums of money from the provincial populace. While governing an ever-larger Mediterranean empire, the Romans were still relying on the institutions and attitudes that had developed when Rome was merely a city-state.

The Failure of the Republic

Rome's success in creating a vast empire unleashed forces that eventually destroyed the Republican system of government. As a result of the frequent wars and territorial expansion of the third and second centuries B.C.E., profound changes were taking place in the Italian landscape. Italian peasant farmers were away from home on military service for long periods of time, and while they were away, it was easy for investors to take possession of their farms by purchase, deception, or intimidation. Most of the wealth generated by the conquest and control of new provinces ended up in the hands of the upper classes, who used it to purchase Italian land. As a result, the small, self-sufficient farms of the Italian countryside, whose peasant owners had been the backbone of the Roman legions (units of 6,000 soldiers), were replaced by *latifundia*, literally "broad estates," or ranches.

The owners of these large estates found it more lucrative to graze herds of cattle or to grow crops—such as grapes for wine—that brought in big profits than to grow wheat, the staple food of ancient Italy. Large segments of the population of Italy, especially in the burgeoning cities, became dependent on expensive imported grain. Meanwhile, the cheap slave labor provided by prisoners of war (see Diversity and Dominance: The Treatment of Slaves in Rome and China) made it hard for peasants who had lost their farms to find work in the countryside. When they moved to Rome and other cities, they found

Scene from Trajan's Column, Rome, ca. 113 C.E. The Roman emperor Trajan erected a marble column 125 feet (38 meters) in height to commemorate his triumphant campaign in Dacia (modern Romania). The relief carving, which snakes around the column for 656 feet (200 meters), illustrates numerous episodes of the conquest and provides a detailed pictorial record of the equipment and practices of the Roman army in the field. This panel depicts soldiers building a fort. (Peter Rockwell, Rome)

no work there either, and they lived in dire poverty. The growing urban masses, idle and prone to riot, would play a major role in the political struggles of the late Republic.

One consequence of the decline of peasant farmers in Italy was a shortage of men who owned the minimum amount of property required for military service. During a war in North Africa at the end of the second century B.C.E. Gaius Marius—a "new man," as the Romans called politically active individuals who did not belong to the traditional ruling class—achieved political prominence by accepting into the Roman legions poor, propertyless men to whom he promised farms upon retirement from military service. These troops became devoted to Marius and helped him get elected to an unprecedented (and illegal) six consulships.

Between 88 and 31 B.C.E., a series of ambitious individuals—Sulla, Pompey, Julius Caesar, Mark Antony, and Octavian—commanded armies that were more loyal to them than to the state. Their use of Roman troops to increase their personal power and influence led to bloody civil wars between military factions. The city of Rome itself was taken by force on several occasions, and victorious commanders executed political opponents and exercised dictatorial control of the state.

The Roman Principate, 31 B.C.E.–330 C.E.

Julius Caesar's grandnephew and heir, Octavian (63 B.C.E.–14 C.E.), eliminated all rivals by 31 B.C.E. and painstakingly set about refashioning the Roman system of government. He was careful to maintain the forms of the Republic—the offices, honors, and social prerogatives of the senatorial class—but fundamentally altered the realities of power. A military dictator in fact, he never called himself king or emperor, claiming merely to be *princeps*, "first among equals," in a restored Republic. For this reason, the period following the Roman Republic is called the **Roman Principate.**

Augustus, one of the many honorific titles that the Roman Senate gave Octavian, connotes prosperity and piety, and it became the name by which he is best known to posterity. Augustus's ruthlessness, patience, and intuitive grasp of psychology enabled him to manipulate all the groups that made up Roman society. When he died in 14 C.E., after forty-five years of carefully veiled rule, almost no one could remember the Republic. During his reign Egypt and parts of the Middle East and Central Europe were added to the empire, leaving only the southern half of Britain and modern Romania to be added later.

Augustus had allied himself with the ***equites,***° the class of well-to-do Italian merchants and landowners second in wealth and social status only to the senatorial class. This body of competent and self-assured individuals became the core of a new civil service that helped run the Roman Empire. At last Rome had an administrative bureaucracy up to the task of managing a large empire with considerable honesty, consistency, and efficiency.

So popular was Augustus when he died that four members of his family succeeded to the position of "emperor" (as we call it) despite their serious personal and political shortcomings. However, due to Augustus's calculated ambiguity about his role, the position of emperor was never automatically regarded as hereditary, and after the mid-first century C.E. other families obtained the post. In theory the early emperors were affirmed by the Senate; in reality they were chosen by the armies. By the second century C.E. a series of very capable emperors instituted a

equites (EH-kwee-tays)

Diversity and Dominance

The Treatment of Slaves in Rome and China

Although slaves were found in most ancient societies, Rome was one of the few in which slave labor became the indispensable foundation of the economy. In the course of the frequent wars of the second century B.C.E., *large numbers of prisoners were carried into slavery. The prices of such slaves were low, and landowners and manufacturers found they could compel slaves to work longer and harder than hired laborers. Periodically, the harsh working and living conditions resulted in slave revolts.*

The following excerpt, from one of several surviving manuals on agriculture, gives advice about controlling and efficiently exploiting slaves:

When the head of a household arrives at his estate, after he has prayed to the family god, he must go round his farm on a tour of inspection on the very same day, if that is possible, if not, then on the next day. When he has found out how his farm has been cultivated and which jobs have been done and which have not been done, then on the next day after that he must call in his manager and ask him which are the jobs that have been done and which remain, and whether they were done on time, and whether what still has to be done can be done, and how much wine and grain and anything else has been produced. When he has found this out, he must make a calculation of the labor and the time taken. If the work doesn't seem to him to be sufficient, and the manager starts to say how hard he tried, but the slaves weren't any good, and the weather was awful, and the slaves ran away, and he was required to carry out some public works, then when he has finished mentioning these and all sorts of other excuses, you must draw his attention to your calculation of the labor employed and time taken. If he claims that it rained all the time, there are all sorts of jobs that can be done in rainy weather—washing wine-jars, coating them with pitch, cleaning the house, storing grain, shifting muck, digging a manure pit, cleaning seed, mending ropes or making new ones; the slaves ought to have been mending their patchwork cloaks and their hoods. On festival days they would have been able to clean out old ditches, work on the public highway, prune back brambles, dig up the garden, clear a meadow, tie up bundles of sticks, remove thorns, grind barley and get on with cleaning. If he claims that the slaves have been ill, they needn't have been given such large rations. When you have found out about all these things to your satisfaction, make sure that all the work that remains to be done will be carried out... The head of the household [on his tour of inspection] should examine his herds and arrange a sale; he should sell the oil if the price makes it worthwhile, and any wine and rain that is surplus to needs; he should sell any old oxen, cattle or sheep that are not up to standard, wool and hides, an old cart or old tools, an old slave, a sick slave—anything else that is surplus to requirements. The head of a household ought to sell, and not to buy. (Cato the Elder, *Concerning Agriculture*, bk. 2, second century B.C.E.)

Cato, the Roman author of that excerpt, was notorious for his stern manner and hard-edged traditionalism, and he expresses a point of view that Roman society found acceptable. In reality, the treatment of slaves by Roman masters varied widely.

Slavery was far less prominent in ancient China. During the Warring States Period, dependent peasants as well as slaves worked the large holdings of the landowning aristocracy. The Qin government sought to abolish slavery, but the institution persisted into the Han period, although it involved only a small fraction of the population and was not a central component of the economy. The relatives of criminals could be seized and enslaved, and poor families sometimes sold unwanted children into slavery. In China slaves, whether they belonged to the state or to individuals, generally performed domestic tasks, as can be seen in the following text:

Wang Ziyuan of Shu Commandery went to the Jian River on business, and went up to the home of the widow Yang Hui, who had a male slave named Bianliao. Wang Ziyuan requested him to go and buy some wine. Picking up a big stick, Bianliao climbed to the top of the grave mound and said: "When my master bought me, Bianliao, he only contracted for me to care for the grave and did not contract for me to buy wine for some other gentleman."

Wang Ziyuan was furious and said to the widow: "Wouldn't you prefer to sell this slave?"

Yang Hui said: "The slave's father offered him to people, but no one wanted him."

Wang Ziyuan immediately settled on the sale contract.

The slave again said: "Enter in the contract everything you wish to order me to do. I, Bianliao, will not do anything not in the contract."

Wang Ziyuan said: "Agreed."

The text of the contract said:

Third year of Shenjiao , the first month, the fifteenth day, the gentleman Wang Ziyuan, of Zizhong, purchases from the lady Yang Hui of Anzhi village in Zhengdu, the bearded male slave, Bianliao, of her husband's household. The fixed sale [price] is 15,000 [cash]. The slave shall obey orders about all kinds of work and may not argue.

He shall rise at dawn and do an early sweeping. After eating he shall wash up. Ordinarily he should pound the grain mortar, tie up broom straws, carve bowls and bore wells, scoop out ditches, tie up fallen fences, hoe the garden, trim up paths and dike up plots of land, cut big flails, bend bamboos to make rakes, and scrape and fix the well pulley. In going and coming he may not ride horseback or in the cart, [nor may he] sit crosslegged or make a hubbub. When he gets out of bed he shall shake his head [to wake up], fish, cut forage, plait reeds and card hemp, draw water for gruel, and help in making zumo [drink]. He shall weave shoes and make [other] coarse things . . .

In the second month at the vernal equinox he shall bank the dikes and repair the boundary walls [of the fields]; prune the mulberry trees, skin the palm trees, plant melons to make gourd [utensils], select eggplant [seeds for planting], and transplant onion sets; burn plant remains to generate the fields, pile up refuse and break up lumps [in the soil]. At midday he shall dry out things in the sun. At cockcrow he shall rise and pound grain in the mortar, exercise and curry the horses, the donkeys, and likewise the mules . . . [The list of tasks continues for two-and-a-half pages.]

He shall be industrious and quick-working, and he may not idle and loaf. When the slave is old and his strength spent, he shall plant marsh grass and weave mats. When his work is over and he wishes to rest he should pound a picul [of grain]. Late at night when there is no work he shall wash clothes really white. If he has private savings they shall be the master's gift, or from guests. The slave may not have evil secrets; affairs should be open and reported. If the slave does not heed instructions, he shall be whipped a hundred strokes.

The reading of the text of the contract came to an end. The slave was speechless and his lips were tied. Wildly he beat his head on the ground, and beat himself with his hands; from his eyes the tears streamed down, and the drivel from his nose hung a foot long.

He said: "If it is to be exactly as master Wang says, I would rather return soon along the yellow-soil road, with the grave worms boring through my head. Had I known before I would have bought the wine for master Wang. I would not have dared to do that wrong." (Wang Bao, first century B.C.E.)

This story shows that Chinese slaves could be forced to work hard and engaged in many of the same menial tasks as their Roman counterparts. However, it is hard to imagine a Roman slave daring to refuse a request and arguing publicly with a nobleman, for fear of severe punishment. It also appears that slaves in China had legal protections provided by contracts specifying and limiting what could be demanded of them.

QUESTIONS FOR ANALYSIS

1. **Why might slavery have been less important in Han China than in the Roman Empire? Why would the treatment of slaves have been less harsh in China than in Rome?**
2. **In what ways were slaves treated like other forms of property, such as animals and tools? In what ways was a slave's "humanity" taken into account?**
3. **What are some of the passive-resistance tactics that slaves resorted to, and what did they achieve by these actions?**

Source: First selection from Thomas Wiedemann, *Greek and Roman Slavery,* (Baltimore: Johns Hopkins University Press (1981), 183–184. Reprinted with the permission of Thomas Publishing Services. Second selection reprinted with permission of Scribner, an imprint of Simon and Schuster Adult Publishing Group, from *Slavery in China During the Former Han Dynasty, 206 B.C.–A.D. 25* by Clarence Martin Wilbur (New York: Russell & Russell, 1967).

new mechanism of succession: each adopted a mature man of proven ability as his son, designated him as his successor, and shared offices and privileges with him.

While Augustus had felt it important to appeal to Republican traditions and conceal the source and extent of his power, this became less necessary over time, and later emperors exercised their authority more overtly. In imitation of Alexander the Great and the Hellenistic kings, many Roman emperors were officially deified (regarded as gods) after death. A cult of worship of the living emperor developed as a useful way to commemorate and increase the loyalty of subjects.

During the Republic a body of laws had developed, starting with the terse Law of the Twelve Tables ca. 450 B.C.E., supplemented by decrees of the Senate, bills passed in the Assembly, and the annual proclamations of the praetors,° elected public officials responsible for hearing cases and administering the law. In the later Republic a relatively small group of legal experts began to emerge who analyzed laws and legal procedures to determine the underlying principles, then applied these principles to the creation of new laws required by a changing society. These experts were less lawyers in the modern sense than teachers, though they were sometimes consulted by magistrates or the parties to legal actions.

During the Principate the emperor became a major source of new laws. In this period the law was studied and codified with a new intensity by the class of legal experts, and their opinions and interpretations often were given the force of law. The basic divisions of Roman law—persons, things, and actions—reveal the importance of property and the rights of individuals in Roman eyes. The separation of the class of jurists from the government, at least before the later second century C.E., gave Roman Law a unique independence and flexibility. The culmination of this long process of development and interpretation of the law was the sixth-century C.E. Digest of Justinian. Roman law has remained the foundation of European law to this day.

An Urban Empire

The Roman Empire of the first three centuries C.E. was an "urban" empire. This does not mean that most people were living in cities and towns. Perhaps 80 percent of the 50 to 60 million people living within the borders of the empire engaged in agriculture and lived in villages or on isolated farms in the countryside. The empire, however, was administered through a network of towns and cities, and the urban populace benefited most.

Numerous towns had several thousand inhabitants. A handful of major cities—Alexandria in Egypt, Antioch in Syria, and Carthage—had populations of several hundred thousand. Rome itself had approximately a million residents. The largest cities strained the limited technological capabilities of the ancients; providing adequate food and water and removing sewage were always problems.

In Rome the upper classes lived in elegant townhouses on one or another of the seven hills. Such a house was centered around an *atrium*, a rectangular courtyard with an open skylight that let in light and rainwater for drinking and washing. Surrounding the atrium were a large dining room for dinner and drinking parties, an interior garden, a kitchen, and possibly a private bath. Bedrooms were on the upper level. The floors were decorated with pebble mosaics, and the walls and ceilings were covered with frescoes (paintings done directly on wet plaster) of mythological scenes or outdoor vistas, giving a sense of openness in the absence of windows. The typical aristocrat also owned a number of villas in the Italian countryside to which the family could retreat to escape the pressures of city life.

The poor lived in crowded slums in the low-lying parts of the city. Damp, dark, and smelly, with few furnishings, their wooden tenements were susceptible to frequent fires. Fortunately, Romans could spend much of the year outdoors.

The cities, towns, and even the ramshackle settlements that sprang up on the edge of frontier forts were miniature replicas of the capital city in political organization, physical layout, and appearance. A town council and two annually elected officials drawn from prosperous members of the community maintained law and order and collected both urban and rural taxes. In return for the privilege of running local affairs with considerable autonomy and in appreciation of the state's protection of their wealth and position, this "municipal aristocracy" served Rome loyally. In their desire to imitate the manners and values of Roman senators, they endowed cities and towns, which had very little revenue of their own, with attractive elements of Roman urban life—a forum (an open plaza that served as a civic center), government buildings, temples, gardens, baths, theaters, amphitheaters, and games and public entertainments of all sorts. These amenities made the situation of the urban poor superior to that of the rural poor. Poor people living in a city could pass time at the baths, seek refuge from the elements amid the colonnades, and attend the games.

In the countryside hard work and drudgery were relieved by occasional holidays and village festivals and by the everyday pleasures of sex, family, and social exchange. Rural people had to fend for themselves in deal-

praetor (PRAY-tuhr)

Roman Shop Selling Food and Drink
The bustling town of Pompeii on the Bay of Naples was buried in ash by the eruption of Mt. Vesuvius in 79 C.E. Archaeologists have unearthed the streets, stores, and houses of this typical Roman town. Shops such as this sold hot food and drink served from clay vessels set into the counter. Shelves and niches behind the counter contained other items. In the background can be seen a well-paved street and a public fountain where the inhabitants could fetch water. (Courtesy, Leo C. Curran)

ing with bandits, wild animals, and other hazards of country life. People living away from urban centers had little direct contact with the Roman government other than occasional run-ins with bullying soldiers and the dreaded arrival of the tax collector.

The concentration of ownership of the land in ever fewer hands was temporarily reversed during the civil wars that brought an end to the Roman Republic, but it resumed in the era of the emperors. However, after the era of conquest ended in the early second century C.E., slaves were no longer plentiful or inexpensive, and landowners needed a new source of labor. Over time, the independent farmers were replaced by "tenant farmers" who were allowed to live on and cultivate plots of land in return for a portion of their crops. The landowners still lived in the cities and hired foremen to manage their estates. Thus wealth was concentrated in the cities but was based on the productivity of rural agricultural laborers.

Some urban dwellers got rich from manufacture and trade. Commerce was greatly enhanced by the ***pax romana*** ("Roman peace"), the safety and stability guaranteed by Roman might. Grain, meat, vegetables, and other bulk foodstuffs usually could be exchanged only locally because transportation was expensive and many products spoiled quickly. However, the city of Rome depended on the import of massive quantities of grain from Sicily and Egypt to feed its huge population, and special naval squadrons performed this vital task.

Glass, metalwork, delicate pottery, and other fine manufactured products were exported throughout the empire. The centers of production, first located in Italy, moved into the provinces as knowledge of the necessary skills spread. Roman armies stationed on the frontiers were a large market, and their presence promoted the prosperity of border provinces. Other merchants traded in luxury items from far beyond the boundaries of the empire, especially silk from China and spices from India and Arabia.

The system of taxes and other revenues collected by the central government produced a transfer of wealth. Funds from the rich interior provinces like Gaul (France) and Egypt flowed to Rome to support the emperor and the central government, then were dispatched to the frontier provinces to subsidize the armies.

Romanization—the spread of the Latin language and Roman way of life—was one of the most enduring consequences of empire, primarily in the western provinces. Greek language and culture, a legacy of the Hellenistic kingdoms, continued to dominate the eastern Mediterranean (see Chapter 5). Portuguese, Spanish, French, Italian, and Romanian evolved from the Latin language, proving that the language of the conquerors spread among the common people as well as the elite.

The Roman government did not force Romanization. The inhabitants of the provinces chose to switch to Latin and adopt the cultural habits that went with it. There were advantages to speaking Latin and wearing a *toga* (the traditional cloak worn by Roman male citizens), just as people in today's developing nations see advantages in moving to the city, learning English, and putting on a suit and tie. Latin facilitated dealings with the Roman administration and helped merchants get contracts to supply the military. Many also must have been drawn to the aura of success surrounding the language and culture of a people who had created so vast an empire.

As towns sprang up and acquired the features of Roman urban life, they served as magnets for ambitious members of the indigenous populations. The empire gradually and reluctantly granted Roman citizenship, with its attendant privileges, legal protections, and exemptions from some types of taxation, to people living outside Italy. Men who completed a twenty-six-year term of service in the native military units that backed up the Roman legions were granted citizenship and could pass this coveted status on to their descendants. Emperors made grants of citizenship to individuals or entire communities as rewards for good service. In 212 C.E. the emperor Caracalla granted citizenship to all free, adult, male inhabitants of the empire.

The gradual extension of citizenship mirrored the empire's transformation from an Italian dominion over Mediterranean lands into a commonwealth of peoples. As early as the first century C.E. some of the leading literary and intellectual figures came from the provinces. By the second century even the emperors hailed from Spain, Gaul, and North Africa.

The Rise of Christianity

During this same period of general peace and prosperity, at the eastern end of the Mediterranean events were taking place that, though little noted at the moment, would prove to be of great historical significance. The Jewish homeland of Judaea (see Chapter 4), roughly equivalent to present-day Israel, was put under direct Roman rule in 6 C.E. Over the next half-century Roman governors insensitive to the Jewish belief in one god managed to increase tensions, and various kinds of opposition to Roman rule sprang up. Many waited for the arrival of the Messiah, the "Anointed One," presumed to be a military leader who would liberate the Jewish people and drive the Romans out of the land.

It is in this context that we must see the career of **Jesus,** a young carpenter from the Galilee region in northern Israel. While scholars largely agree that the portrait of Jesus found in the New Testament reflects the viewpoint of followers a half-century after his death, it is difficult to determine the motives and teachings of the historical Jesus. Some experts believe that he was essentially a rabbi, or teacher, and that, offended by what he perceived as Jewish religious and political leaders' excessive concern with money and power and by the perfunctory nature of mainstream Jewish religious practice in his time, he prescribed a return to the personal faith and spirituality of an earlier age. Others stress his connections to the apocalyptic fervor found in certain circles of Judaism, such as John the Baptist and the community that authored the Dead Sea Scrolls. They view Jesus as a fiery prophet who urged people to prepare themselves for the imminent end of the world and God's ushering in of a blessed new age. Still others see him as a political revolutionary, upset by the downtrodden condition of the peasants in the countryside and the poor in the cities, who determined to drive out the Roman occupiers and their collaborators among the Jewish elite. Whatever the real nature of his mission may have been, the charismatic Jesus eventually attracted the attention of the Jewish authorities in Jerusalem, who regarded popular reformers as potential troublemakers. They turned him over to the Roman governor, Pontius Pilate. Jesus was imprisoned, condemned, and executed by crucifixion, a punishment usually reserved for common criminals. His followers, the Apostles, carried on after his death and sought to spread his teachings and their belief that he was the Messiah and had been resurrected (returned from death to life) among their fellow Jews.

Paul, a Jew from the Greek city of Tarsus in southeast Anatolia, converted to the new creed. Between 45 and 58 C.E. he threw his enormous talent and energy into spreading the word. Traveling throughout Syria-Palestine, Anatolia, and Greece, he became increasingly frustrated with the refusal of most Jews to accept his claim that Jesus was the Messiah and had ushered in a new age. Many Jews, on the other hand, were appalled by the failure of the followers of Jesus to maintain traditional Jewish practices. Discovering a spiritual hunger among many non-Jews (sometimes called "gentiles"), Paul redirected his efforts toward them and set up a string of Christian (from the Greek name *christos*, meaning "anointed one," given to Jesus by his followers) communities in the eastern Mediterranean. Paul's career exemplifies the cosmopolitan nature of the Roman Empire. Speaking both Greek and Aramaic, he moved comfortably between the Greco-Roman and Jewish worlds. He used Roman roads, depended on the peace guaranteed by Roman arms, called on his Roman citizenship to protect him from the arbitrary action of local authorities, and moved from city to city in his quest for converts. In 66 C.E. long-building tensions in Roman Judaea erupted into a full-scale revolt that lasted until 73. One of the casualties of the Roman reconquest of Judaea was the Jerusalem-based Christian community, which focused on converting the Jews. This left the field clear for Paul's non-Jewish converts, and Christianity began to diverge more and more from its Jewish roots.

For more than two centuries, the sect grew slowly but steadily. Many of the first converts were from disenfranchised groups—women, slaves, the urban poor. They hoped to receive respect not accorded them in the larger society and to obtain positions of responsibility when the members of early Christian communities democratically elected their leaders. However, as the religious movement grew and prospered, it developed a hierarchy of priests and bishops and became subject to bitter disputes over theological doctrine (see Chapter 10).

As monotheists forbidden to worship other gods, early Christians were persecuted by Roman officials who regarded their refusal to worship the emperor as a sign of disloyalty. Despite occasional government-sponsored attempts at suppression and spontaneous mob attacks, or perhaps because of them, the young Christian movement continued to gain strength and attract converts. By the late third century C.E. its adherents were a sizable minority within the Roman Empire and included many educated and prosperous people with posts in the local and imperial governments.

The expansion of Christianity should be seen as part of a broader religious tendency. By the Greek Classical period a number of "mystery" cults had gained popularity by claiming to provide secret information about the nature of life and death and promising a blessed afterlife to their adherents. In the Hellenistic and Roman periods, a number of cults making similar promises arose in the eastern Mediterranean and spread throughout the Greco-Roman lands, presumably in response to a growing spiritual and intellectual hunger not satisfied by traditional pagan practices. These included the worship of the mother-goddess Cybele in Anatolia, the Egyptian goddess Isis, and the Iranian sun-god Mithra. As we shall see, the ultimate victory of Christianity over these rivals had as much to do with historical circumstances as with its spiritual appeal.

Technology and Transformation

The relative ease and safety of travel brought by Roman arms and engineering enabled merchants to sell their wares and helped the early Christians spread their faith. Surviving remnants of roads, fortification walls, aqueducts, and buildings testify to the engineering expertise of the ancient Romans. Some of the best engineers served with the army, building bridges, siege works, and ballistic weapons that hurled stones and shafts. In peacetime soldiers were often put to work on construction projects. **Aqueducts**—long elevated or underground conduits—carried water from a source to an urban center, using only the force of gravity (see Environment and Technology: Water Engineering in Rome and China). The Romans were pioneers in the use of arches, which allow the even distribution of great weights without thick supporting walls. The invention of concrete—a mixture of lime powder, sand, and water that could be poured into molds—allowed the Romans to create vast vaulted and domed interior spaces unlike the rectilinear pillar-and-post designs of the Greeks.

Defending borders that stretched for thousands of miles was a great challenge. In a document released after his death, Augustus advised against expanding the empire because the costs of administering and defending subsequent acquisitions would be greater than the revenues. The Roman army was reorganized and redeployed to reflect the shift from an offensive to a defensive strategy. At most points the empire was protected by mountains, deserts, and seas. But the lengthy Rhine and Danube river frontiers in Germany and Central Europe were vulnerable. They were guarded by a string of forts with relatively small garrisons adequate for dealing with raiders. On particularly desolate frontiers, such as in Britain and North Africa, the Romans built long walls to keep out the peoples who lived beyond.

Most of Rome's neighbors were less technologically advanced and more loosely organized, and they did not pose a serious threat to the security of the empire. The one exception was the Parthian kingdom, heir to the Mesopotamian and Persian Empires, which controlled the lands on the eastern frontier (today's Iran and Iraq). For centuries Rome and Parthia engaged in a rivalry that sapped both sides without any significant territorial gain by either party.

The Roman state prospered for two-and-a-half centuries after Augustus stabilized the internal political situation and addressed the needs of the empire with an ambitious program of reforms. In the third century C.E. cracks in the edifice became visible. Historians use the expression **"third-century crisis"** to refer to the period from 235 to 284 C.E., when political, military, and economic problems beset and nearly destroyed the Roman Empire. The most visible symptom of the crisis was the frequent change of rulers. Twenty or more men claimed the office of emperor during this period. Most reigned for only a few months or years before being overthrown by rivals or killed by their own troops. Germanic tribesmen on the Rhine/Danube frontier took advantage of the frequent civil wars and periods of anarchy to raid deep into the empire. For the first time in centuries, Roman cities began to erect walls for protection. Several regions, feeling that the central government was not adequately protecting them, turned power over to a man on the spot who promised to put their interests first.

The political and military emergencies had a devastating impact on the empire's economy. Buying the loyalty of the army and paying to defend the increasingly permeable frontiers drained the treasury. The unending demands of the central government for more tax revenues from the provinces, as well as the interruption of commerce by fighting, eroded the towns' prosperity. Shortsighted emperors, desperate for cash, secretly reduced the amount of precious metal in Roman coins and pocketed the excess. The public quickly caught on, and the devalued coinage became less and less acceptable in the marketplace. The empire reverted to a barter economy, a far less efficient system that further curtailed large-scale and long-distance commerce.

The municipal aristocracy, once the most vital and public-spirited class in the empire, was slowly crushed out of existence. As town councilors, its members were personally liable for shortfalls in taxes owed to the state. The decline in trade eroded their wealth, which often was based on manufacture and commerce, and many began to evade their civic duties and even went into hiding.

Population shifted out of the cities and into the countryside. Many people sought employment and protection from both raiders and government officials on the estates of wealthy and powerful country landowners. The shrinking of cities and movement of the population to the country estates were the first steps in a demographic shift toward the social and economic structures of the European Middle Ages—roughly seven hundred years during which wealthy rural lords dominated a peasant population tied to the land (see Chapter 10).

Roman Aqueduct Near Tarragona, Spain How to provide an adequate supply of water was a problem posed by the growth of Roman towns and cities. Aqueducts channeled water from a source, sometimes many miles away, to an urban complex, using only the force of gravity. To bring an aqueduct from high ground into the city, Roman engineers designed long, continuous rows of arches that maintained a steady downhill slope. Roman troops were often used in such large-scale construction projects. Scholars sometimes can roughly estimate the population of an ancient city by calculating the amount of water that was available to it. (Robert Frerck/Woodfin Camp & Associates)

ENVIRONMENT + TECHNOLOGY

Water Engineering in Rome and China

People needed water to drink; it was vital for agriculture; and it provided a rapid and economical means for transporting people and goods. Some of the most impressive technological achievements of ancient Rome and China involved hydraulic (water) engineering.

Roman cities, with their large populations, required abundant and reliable sources of water. One way to obtain it was to build aqueducts—stone channels to bring water from distant lakes and streams to the cities. The water flowing in these conduits was moved only by the force of gravity. Surveyors measured the land's elevation and plotted a course that very gradually moved downhill.

Some conduits were elevated atop walls or bridges, which made it difficult for unauthorized parties to tap the water line for their own use. Portions of some aqueducts were built underground. Still-standing aboveground segments indicate that the Roman aqueducts were well-built structures made of large cut stones closely fitted and held together by a cement-like mortar. Construction of the aqueducts was labor-intensive, and often both design and construction were carried out by military personnel. This was one of the ways in which the Roman government could keep large numbers of soldiers busy in peacetime.

Sections of aqueduct that crossed rivers presented the same construction challenges as bridges. Roman engineers lowered prefabricated wooden cofferdams—large, hollow cylinders—into the riverbed and pumped out the water so workers could descend and construct cement piers to support the arched segments of the bridge and the water channel itself. This technique is still used for construction in water.

When an aqueduct reached the outskirts of a city, the water flowed into a reservoir, where it was stored. Pipes connected the reservoir to different parts of the city. Even within the city, gravity provided the motive force until the water reached the public fountains used by the poor and the private storage tanks of individuals wealthy enough to have plumbing in their houses.

In ancient China, rivers running generally in an east-west direction were the main thoroughfares. The earliest development of complex societies centered on the Yellow River Valley, but by the beginning of the Qin Empire the Yangzi River Valley and regions farther south were becoming increasingly important to China's political and economic vitality. In this era the Chinese began to build canals connecting the northern and southern zones, at first for military purposes but eventually for transporting commercial goods as well. In later periods, with the acquisition of more advanced engineering skills, an extensive network of canals was built, including the 1,100-mile-long (1,771-kilometer-long) Grand Canal.

One of the earliest efforts was the construction of the Magic Canal. A Chinese historian tells us that the Qin emperor Shi Huangdi ordered his engineers to join two rivers by a 20-mile-long (32.2-kilometer-long) canal so that he could more easily supply his armies of conquest in the south. Construction of the canal posed a difficult engineering challenge, because the rivers Hsiang and Li, though coming within 3 miles (4.8 kilometers) of one another, flowed in opposite directions and with a strong current.

The engineers took advantage of a low point in the chain of hills between the rivers to maintain a relatively level grade. The final element of the solution was to build a snout-shaped mound to divide the waters of the Hsiang, funneling part of that river into an artificial channel. Several spillways further reduced the volume of water flowing into the canal, which was 15 feet wide and 3 feet deep (about 4.5 meters wide and 1 meter deep). The joining of the two rivers completed a network of waterways that permitted continuous inland water transport of goods between the latitudes of Beijing and Guangzhou (Canton), a distance of 1,250 miles (2,012 kilometers). Modifications were made in later centuries, but the Magic Canal is still in use.

The Magic Canal Engineers of Shi Huangdi, "First Emperor" of China, exploited the contours of the landscape to connect the river systems of northern and southern China. (From Robert Temple, *The Genius of China* [1986]. Photographer: Robert Temple)

Just when things looked bleakest, one man pulled the empire back from the brink of self-destruction. Like many of the rulers of that age, Diocletian came from one of the eastern European provinces most vulnerable to invasion. A commoner by birth, he had risen through the ranks of the army and gained power in 284. His success is indicated by the fact that he ruled for more than twenty years and died in bed.

Diocletian implemented radical reforms that saved the Roman state by transforming it. To halt inflation (the process by which prices rise as money becomes worth less), Diocletian issued an edict that specified the maximum prices that could be charged for various commodities and services. To ensure an adequate supply of workers in vital services, he froze many people into their professions and required them to train their sons to succeed them. This unprecedented government regulation of prices and vocations had unforeseen consequences. A "black market" arose among buyers and sellers who chose to ignore the government's price controls and establish their own prices for goods and services. Many inhabitants of the empire began to see the government as an oppressive entity that no longer deserved their loyalty.

When Diocletian resigned in 305, the old divisiveness reemerged as various claimants battled for the throne. The eventual winner was **Constantine** (r. 306–337), who reunited the entire empire under his sole rule by 324.

In 312 Constantine won a key battle at the Milvian Bridge over the Tiber River near Rome. He later claimed that he had seen a cross (the sign of the Christian God) superimposed on the sun before this battle. Believing that the Christian God had helped him achieve the victory, in the following year Constantine issued the so-called Edict of Milan, ending the persecution of Christianity and guaranteeing freedom of worship to Christians and all others. Throughout his reign he supported the Christian church, although he tolerated other beliefs as well. Historians disagree about whether Constantine was spiritually motivated or was pragmatically seeking to unify the peoples of the empire under a single religion. In either case his embrace of Christianity was of tremendous historical significance. Large numbers of people began to convert when they saw that Christians seeking political office or favors from the government had clear advantages over non-Christians.

In 324 Constantine transferred the imperial capital from Rome to Byzantium, an ancient Greek city on the Bosporus° strait leading from the Mediterranean into the Black Sea. The city was renamed Constantinople°, "City of Constantine." This move both reflected and accelerated changes already taking place. Constantinople was closer than Rome to the most-threatened borders in eastern Europe (see Map 6.1). The urban centers and prosperous middle class in the eastern half of the empire had better withstood the third-century crisis than had those in the western half. In addition, more educated people and more Christians were living in the eastern provinces (see Chapter 10).

The conversion of Constantine and the transfer of the imperial capital away from Rome often have been seen as marking the end of Roman history. But many of the important changes that culminated during Constantine's reign had their roots in events of the previous two centuries, and the Roman Empire as a whole survived for at least another century. The eastern, or Byzantine, portion of the empire (discussed in Chapter 10) survived Constantine by more than a thousand years. Nevertheless, the Roman Empire of the fourth century was fundamentally different from the earlier empire, and for that reason it is convenient to see Constantine's reign as the beginning of a new epoch.

THE ORIGINS OF IMPERIAL CHINA, 221 B.C.E.–220 C.E.

The early history of China (described in Chapter 3) was characterized by the fragmentation that geography seemed to dictate. The Shang (ca. 1750–1027 B.C.E.) and Zhou (1027–221 B.C.E.) dynasties ruled over a relatively compact zone in northeastern China. The last few centuries of nominal Zhou rule—the Warring States Period—saw rivalry and belligerence among a group of small states with somewhat different languages and cultures. As in the contemporary Greek city-states (see Chapter 5), competition and conflict gave rise to many distinctive elements of a national culture.

In the second half of the third century B.C.E. one of the warring states—the **Qin**° state of the Wei° Valley—rapidly conquered its rivals and created China's first empire (221–206 B.C.E.). Built at a great cost in human lives and labor, the Qin Empire barely survived the death of its founder, **Shi Huangdi°**. Power soon passed to a new dynasty, the **Han**, which ruled China from 206 B.C.E. to 220 C.E. (see Map 6.2). Thus began the long history of imperial China—a tradition of political and cultural unity and continuity that lasted into the early twentieth century

Bosporus (BAHS-puhr-uhs)
Constantinople (cahn-stan-tih-NO-pul)

Qin (chin) **Wei** (way) **Shi Huangdi** (Shee wahng-dee)

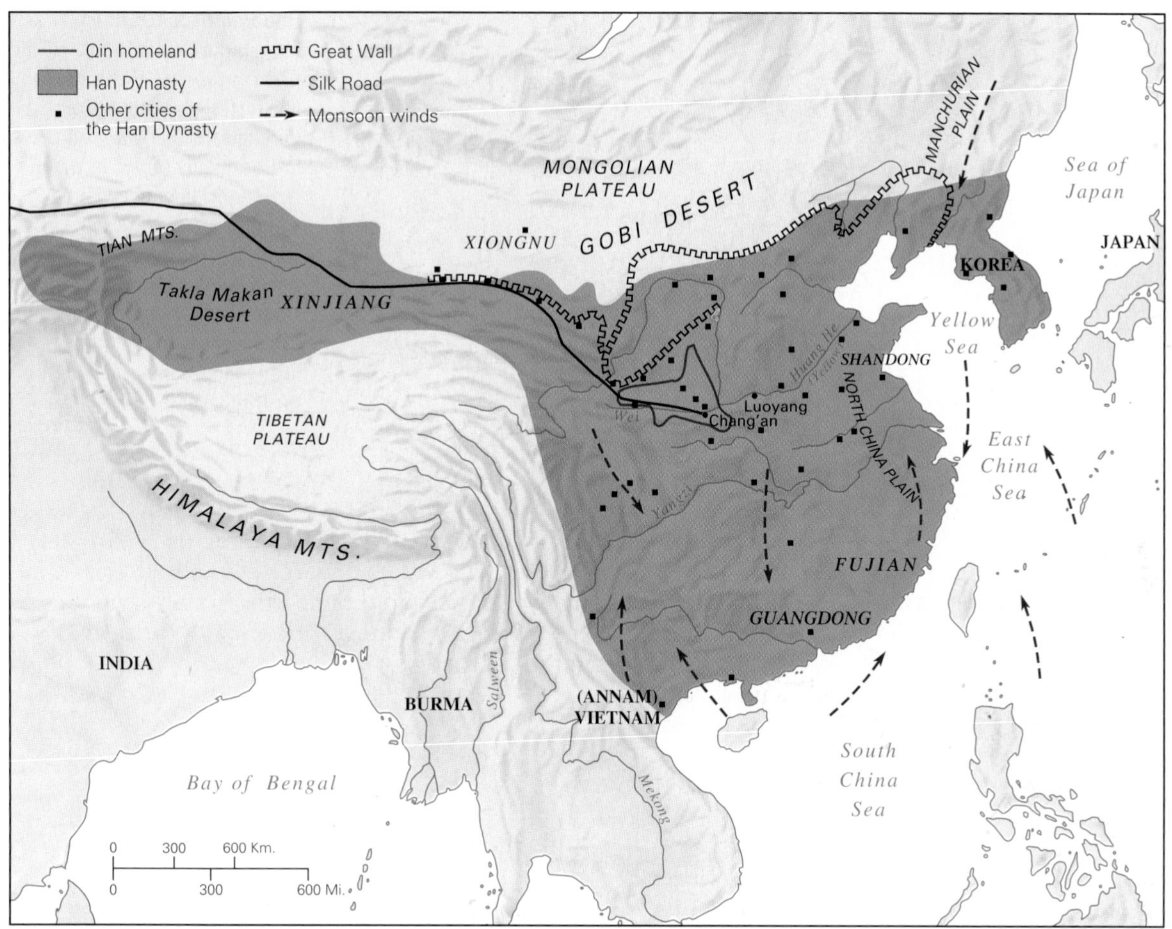

Map 6.2 Han China The Qin and Han rulers of northeast China extended their control over all of eastern China and extensive territories to the west. A series of walls in the north and northwest, built to check the incursions of nomadic peoples from the steppes, were joined together to form the ancestor of the present-day Great Wall of China. An extensive network of roads connecting towns, cities, and frontier forts promoted rapid communication and facilitated trade. The Silk Road carried China's most treasured product to Central, South, and West Asia and the Mediterranean lands.

and still has meaning for the very different China of our own time.

Resources and Population

An imperial state in East Asia controlling lands of extremely diverse topography, climate, plant and animal life, and human population faced greater obstacles to long-distance communications and to a uniform way of life than did the Roman Empire. The climates and agricultural potentials of Rome's territories were, for the most part, roughly similar, and the Mediterranean Sea facilitated relatively rapid and inexpensive travel and transport of commodities. What resources, technologies, institutions, and values made possible the creation and maintenance of a Chinese empire?

Agriculture produced the wealth and taxes that supported the institutions of imperial China. The main tax, a percentage of the annual harvest, funded government activities ranging from the luxurious lifestyle of the royal court to the daily tasks of officials and military units throughout the country and on the frontiers. Large populations in China's capital cities, first Chang'an° and later Luoyang°, had to be fed. As intensive agriculture spread in the Yangzi River Valley, the need to transport southern crops to the north spurred the construction of canals to connect the Yangzi with the Yellow River (see

Chang'an (chahng-ahn) **Luoyang** (LWOE-yahng)

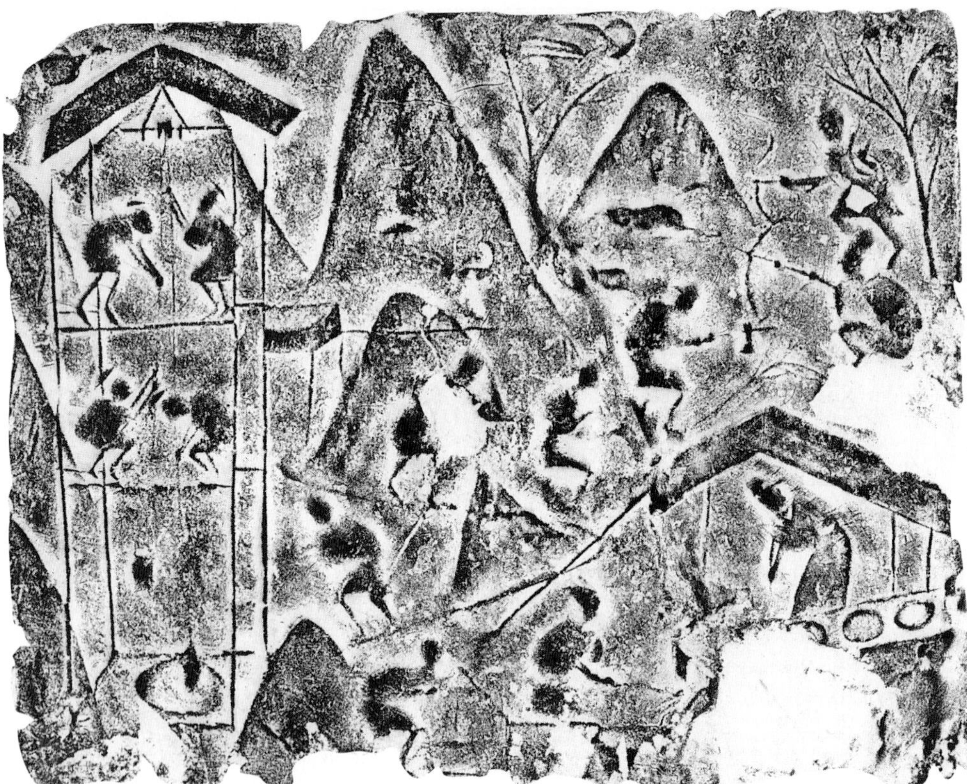

Rubbing of Salt Mining Found in a Chinese tomb of the first century C.E., this rubbing illustrates a procedure for mining salt. The tower on the left originally served as a derrick for drilling a deep hole through dirt and rock. In this scene workers are hauling up buckets full of brine (saltwater) from underground deposits. In the background are hunters in the mountains. (Courtesy of the Trustees of the British Museum)

Environment and Technology: Water Engineering in Rome and China). During prosperous times, the government also collected and stored surplus grain that could be sold at reasonable prices in times of shortage.

Human labor was the other fundamental commodity. The government periodically conducted a census of inhabitants, and the results for 2 C.E. and 140 C.E. are available today. The earlier survey counted approximately 12 million households and 60 million people; the later, not quite 10 million households and 49 million people. The average household contained 5 persons. Then, as now, the vast majority of the people lived in the eastern portion of the country, the river-valley regions where intensive agriculture could support a dense population. At first the largest concentration was in the Yellow River Valley and North China Plain, but by early Han times the demographic center had begun to shift to the Yangzi River Valley.

In the intervals between seasonal agricultural tasks, every able-bodied man donated one month of labor a year to public works projects—building palaces, temples, fortifications, and roads; transporting goods; excavating and maintaining canal channels; laboring on imperial estates; or working in the mines. The state also required two years of military service. On the frontiers, young conscripts built walls and forts, kept an eye on barbarian neighbors, fought when necessary, and grew crops to support themselves. Annually updated registers of land and households enabled imperial officials to keep track of money and services due. Like the Romans, the Chinese government depended on a large population of free peasants to contribute taxes and services to the state.

The Han Chinese gradually but persistently expanded at the expense of other ethnic groups. Population growth in the core regions and a shortage of good, arable land spurred pioneers to push into new areas. Sometimes the government organized new settlements, at militarily strategic sites and on the frontiers, for example. Neighboring kingdoms also invited Chinese settlers so as to exploit their skills and learn their technologies.

Han people preferred regions suitable for the kind of agriculture they had practiced in the eastern river valleys. They took over land on the northern frontier, pushing back nomadic populations. They also expanded into the tropical forests of southern China and settled in the western oases. In places not suitable for their preferred kind of agriculture, particularly the steppe and the desert, Han Chinese did not displace other groups.

Hierarchy, Obedience, and Belief

As the Han Chinese expanded into new regions, they took along their social organization, values, language, and other cultural practices. The basic unit of Chinese society was the family, which included not only the living generations but also all the previous generations—the ancestors. The Chinese believed that their ancestors maintained an ongoing interest in the fortunes of living family members, so they consulted, appeased, and venerated them in order to maintain their favor. The family was viewed as a living, self-renewing organism, and each generation was required to have sons to perpetuate the family and maintain the ancestor cult that provided a kind of immortality to the deceased.

The doctrine of Confucius (Kongzi), which had its origins in the sixth century B.C.E. (see Chapter 3) became very influential in the imperial period. Confucianism regarded hierarchy as a natural aspect of human society and laid down rules of appropriate conduct. People saw themselves as part of an interdependent unit rather than as individual agents. Each person had a place and responsibilities within the family hierarchy, based on his or her gender, age, and relationship to other family members. Absolute authority rested with the father, who was an intermediary between the living members and the ancestors, presiding over the rituals of ancestor worship.

The same concepts operated in society as a whole. Peasants, soldiers, administrators, and rulers all made distinctive and necessary contributions to the welfare of society. Confucianism optimistically maintained that people could be guided to the right path through education, imitation of proper role models, and self-improvement. The family inculcated the basic values of Chinese society: loyalty, obedience to authority, respect for elders and ancestors, and concern for honor and appropriate conduct. Because the hierarchy in the state mirrored the hierarchy in the family, these same attitudes carried over into the relationship between individuals and the state.

The experiences of women in ancient Chinese society are hard to pinpoint because, as elsewhere, contemporary written sources are largely silent on the subject. Confucian ethics stressed the impropriety of women participating in public life. Traditional wisdom about conduct appropriate for women is preserved in an account of the life of the mother of the Confucian philosopher Mencius (Mengzi):

> A woman's duties are to cook the five grains, heat the wine, look after her parents-in-law, make clothes, and that is all! . . . [She] has no ambition to manage affairs outside the house. . . . She must follow the "three submissions." When she is young, she must submit to her parents. After her marriage, she must submit to her husband. When she is widowed, she must submit to her son.[1]

That is an ideal perpetuated by males of the upper classes, the social stratum that is the source of most of the written texts. Upper-class females were under considerable pressure to conform to those expectations. Women of the lower classes, less affected by Confucian ways of thinking, may have been less constrained than their more "privileged" counterparts.

After her parents arranged her marriage, a young bride went to live with her husband's family, where she was a stranger who had to prove herself. Ability and force of personality—as well as the capacity to produce sons—could make a difference. Dissension between the wife and her mother-in-law and sisters-in-law grew out of competition for influence with husbands, sons, and brothers and for a larger share of the family's economic resources.

Like the early Romans, the ancient Chinese believed that divinity resided within nature rather than outside and above it, and they worshiped and tried to appease the forces of nature. The state erected and maintained shrines to the lords of rain and winds as well as to certain great rivers and high mountains. Gathering at mounds or altars where the local spirit of the soil was thought to reside, people sacrificed sheep and pigs and beat drums loudly to promote the fertility of the earth. Strange or disastrous natural phenomena, such as eclipses or heavy rains, called for symbolic restraint of the deity by tying a red cord around the sacred spot. Because it was believed that supernatural forces flowed through the landscape, bringing good and evil fortune, experts in *feng shui*, meaning "earth divination," were consulted to determine the most favorable location and orientation for buildings and graves. The faithful learned to adapt their lives to the complex rhythms they perceived in nature.

Some people tried to cheat death by taking life-enhancing drugs or building ostentatious tombs flanked by towers or covered by mounds of earth and filled with things they believed would allow them to maintain the quality of life they had enjoyed on earth. The objects in these tombs have provided archaeologists with a wealth of knowledge about Han society.

The First Chinese Empire, 221–207 B.C.E.

For centuries eastern China was divided among rival states whose frequent hostilities gave rise to the label "Warring States Period" (480–221 B.C.E.). In the second half of the third century B.C.E. the state of the Qin suddenly burst forth and took over the other states one by one. By 221 B.C.E., the first emperor had united the northern plain and the Yangzi River Valley under one rule, marking the creation of China and the inauguration of the imperial age. Many scholars maintain that the name "China," by which this land has been known in the Western world, is derived from "Qin."

Several factors account for the meteoric rise of the Qin. The Qin ruler, who took the title *Shi Huangdi* ("First Emperor"), and his adviser and prime minister Li Si° were able and ruthless men who exploited the exhaustion resulting from the long centuries of interstate rivalry. The Qin homeland in the valley of the Wei, a tributary of the Yellow River, was less urbanized and commercialized than the kingdoms farther east, with a large pool of sturdy peasants to serve in the army. Moreover, long experience in mobilizing manpower for the construction of irrigation and flood-control works had strengthened the authority of the Qin king at the expense of the nobles and endowed his government with superior organizational skills.

Shi Huangdi and Li Si created a totalitarian structure that subordinated the individual to the needs of the state. By publicly burning large numbers of books, they symbolically expressed a radical break with the past. They cracked down on Confucianism, regarding its demands for benevolent and nonviolent conduct from rulers to be a check on the absolute power they sought. They instead drew from a stream of political thought known as Legalism (see Chapter 3). Developing earlier Legalist thinking, Li Si insisted that the will of the ruler was supreme, and that it was necessary to impose discipline and obedience on the subjects through the rigid application of rewards and punishments.

The new regime was determined to eliminate rival centers of authority. Its first target was the landowning aristocracy of the conquered rival states and the system on which aristocratic wealth and power had been based. Because primogeniture—the right of the eldest son to inherit all the landed property—allowed a small number of individuals to accumulate vast tracts of land, the Qin government abolished it, instead requiring estates to be broken up and passed on to several heirs.

The large estates of the aristocracy had been worked by slaves (see Diversity and Dominance: The Treatment of Slaves in Rome and China) and peasant serfs, who gave their landlords a substantial portion of their harvest. The Qin abolished slavery and took steps to create a free peasantry who paid taxes and provided labor, as well as military service, to the state.

The Qin government's commitment to standardization helped create a unified Chinese civilization. During the Warring States Period, small states found many ways to emphasize their independence. For example, states had their own forms of music, with different scales, systems of notation, and instruments. The Qin imposed standard weights, measures, and coinage, a uniform law code, a common system of writing, and even regulations governing the axle length of carts so as to leave just one set of ruts on the roads.

The Qin built thousands of miles of roads—comparable in scale to the roads of the Roman Empire—to connect the parts of the empire and to move Qin armies quickly. They also built canals connecting the river systems of northern and southern China (see Environment and Technology: Water Engineering in Rome and China). The frontier walls of the old states began to be linked into a continuous barricade, the precursor of the Great Wall (see Chapter 11), to protect cultivated lands from raids by northern nomads. Large numbers of people were forced to donate their labor and often their lives to build the walls and roads. So oppressive were the financial exploitation and demands for forced labor that a series of rebellions broke out when Shi Huangdi died in 210 B.C.E., bringing down the Qin dynasty.

The Long Reign of the Han, 206 B.C.E.–220 C.E.

When the dust cleared, Liu Bang°, who may have been born a peasant, had outlasted his rivals and established a new dynasty, the Han (206 B.C.E.–220 C.E.). The new emperor promised to reject the excesses and mistakes of the Qin and to restore the institutions of a venerable past. To sustain and protect a large empire, however, the Han administration maintained much of Qin's structure and Legalist ideology, though with less fanatical zeal. The Han tempered Legalist government with a Confucianism revised to serve a large, centralized political entity. This Confucianism emphasized the government's benevolence and the appropriateness of particular rituals and behaviors in a manifestly hierarchical society. The Han system of administration became the standard for later ages, and the Chinese people today refer to themselves ethnically as "Han."

After eighty years of imperial consolidation, Emperor Wu (r. 140–87 B.C.E.) launched a period of military expansion, south into Fujian, Guangdong, and present-day north Vietnam, and north into Manchuria and present-day North Korea. Han armies also went west to inner Mongolia and Xinjiang° to secure the lucrative Silk

Li Si (luh suh)

Lui Bang (le-oo bahng) **Xinjiang** (SHIN-jyahng)

Road (see Chapter 8). Controlling the newly acquired territories was expensive, however, so Wu's successors curtailed further expansion.

The Han Empire endured, with a brief interruption between 9 and 23 C.E., for more than four hundred years. From 202 B.C.E. to 8 C.E.—the period of the Early, or Western, Han—the capital was at Chang'an, in the Wei Valley, an ancient seat of power from which the Zhou and Qin dynasties had emerged. From 23 to 220 C.E. the Later, or Eastern, Han established its base farther east, in the more centrally located Luoyang.

Protected by a ring of hills but with ready access to the fertile plain, **Chang'an** was surrounded by a wall of pounded earth and brick 15 miles (24 kilometers) in circumference. Contemporaries described it as a bustling place, filled with courtiers, officials, soldiers, merchants, craftsmen, and foreign visitors. In 2 C.E. its population was 246,000. Part of the city was carefully planned. Broad thoroughfares running north and south intersected with others running east and west. High walls protected the palaces, administrative offices, barracks, and storehouses of the imperial compound, and access was restricted. Temples and marketplaces were scattered about the civic center. Chang'an became a model of urban planning, and its main features were imitated in the cities and towns that sprang up throughout the Han Empire.

Moralizing writers who criticized the elite provide glimpses of their private lives. Living in multistory houses, wearing fine silks, traveling about Chang'an in ornate horse-drawn carriages, well-to-do officials and merchants devoted their leisure time to art and literature, occult religious practices, elegant banquets, and various entertainments—music and dance, juggling and acrobatics, dog and horse races, cock and tiger fights. In stark contrast, the common people inhabited a sprawling warren of alleys, living in dwellings packed "as closely as the teeth of a comb," as one poet put it.

As in the Zhou monarchy (see Chapter 3), the emperor was the "Son of Heaven," chosen to rule in accordance with the Mandate of Heaven. He stood at the center of government and society. As the father held authority in the family and was a link between the living generations and the ancestors, so was the emperor supreme in the state. He brought the support of powerful imperial ancestors and guaranteed the harmonious interaction of heaven and earth. To a much greater degree than his Roman counterpart, he was regarded as a divinity and his word was law.

Living in seclusion within the walled palace compound, surrounded by his many wives, children, servants, courtiers, and officials, the emperor presided over unceasing pomp and ritual emphasizing the worship of Heaven and imperial ancestors as well as the practical business of government. The royal compound was also a hive of intrigue, no more so than when the emperor died and his chief widow chose his heir from among the male members of the ruling clan.

Clay Figurine of a Storyteller Found in a tomb of the later Han period, this performer, who has bare feet and a bare chest and is holding a drum and stick, clearly relates his tales in a dramatic and humorous manner. Storytelling was a popular form of entertainment in this era. (The National Museum of Chinese History)

The central government was run by a prime minister, a civil service director, and nine ministers with military, economic, legal, and religious responsibilities. Like the imperial Romans, the Han depended on local officials for day-to-day administration of their far-flung territories. Local people collected taxes and dispatched revenues to the central government, regulated conscription for the army and for labor projects, provided protection, and settled disputes. The remote central government rarely impinged on the lives of most citizens.

As part of their strategy to weaken the rural aristocrats and exclude them from political posts, the Qin and Han emperors allied themselves with the **gentry**—the class next in wealth below the aristocrats. To serve as local officials the central government chose members of this class of moderately prosperous landowners, usually men with education and valued expertise who resembled the Roman equites favored by Augustus and his successors. These officials were a privileged and respected group within Chinese society, and they made the government more efficient and responsive than it had been in the past.

The guiding philosophy of the new gentry class of officials was a modified Confucianism that provided a system for training officials to be intellectually capable and morally worthy of their role and set forth a code of conduct for measuring their performance. According to Chinese tradition, an imperial university with as many as thirty thousand students was located outside Chang'an, and provincial centers of learning were established. (Some scholars doubt that such a complex institution existed this early.) Students from these centers were chosen to enter various levels of government service.

In theory, young men from any class could rise in the state hierarchy. In practice, sons of the gentry had an advantage because they were most likely to receive the necessary training in the Confucian classics. As civil servants advanced in the bureaucracy, they received distinctive emblems and privileges of rank, including preferential treatment in the legal system and exemption from military service. Over time, the gentry became a new aristocracy of sorts, banding together in cliques and family alliances that had considerable clout and worked to advance the careers of group members.

Daoism, which also had its origins in the Warring States Period (see Chapter 3), took deeper root, becoming popular with the common people. Daoism emphasized the search for the *Dao*, or "path," of nature and the value of harmonizing with the cycles and patterns of the natural world. Enlightenment was achieved not so much by education as by solitary contemplation and physical and mental discipline. Daoism was skeptical, questioning age-old beliefs and values and rejecting the hierarchy, rules, and rituals of the Confucianism of the elite classes. It urged passive acceptance of the disorder of the world, denial of ambition, contentment with simple pleasures, and trusting one's own instincts.

Technology and Trade

China was the home of many important inventions, and what the Chinese did not invent they improved. Chinese tradition seems to have recognized the importance of technology for the success and spread of Chinese civilization,

Han-Era (First Century B.C.E.) Stone Rubbing of a Horse-Drawn Carriage The "trace harness," a strap running across the horse's chest, was a Chinese invention that allowed horses to pull far heavier loads than were possible with the constricting throat harness used in Europe. In the Han period, officials, professionals, and soldiers who served the regime enjoyed a lifestyle made pleasant by fine clothing, comfortable transportation, servants, and delightful pastimes, but at the same time they were guided by a Confucian emphasis on duty, honesty, and appropriate behavior. (From Wu family shrine, Jiaxiang, Shantung. From *Chin-shih-so* [Jinshisuo])

crediting legendary rulers of the distant past with the introduction of major new technologies.

The advent of bronze tools around 1500 B.C.E. helped clear the forests and open land for agriculture on the North China Plain. Almost a thousand years later iron arrived. The Qin may have been among the first to take full advantage of the new iron technology. Chinese metallurgists employed more advanced techniques than did their counterparts elsewhere in the hemisphere. Whereas Roman blacksmiths produced wrought-iron tools and weapons by hammering heated iron, the Chinese hammered ores with a higher carbon content to produce steel, and they mastered the technique of liquefying iron and pouring it into molds. The resulting steel and cast-iron tools and weapons were considerably stronger.

In the succeeding centuries, the crossbow and use of cavalry helped the Chinese military repel nomads from the steppe regions. The watermill, which harnessed the power of running water to turn a grindstone, was used in China long before it appeared in Europe. The development of a horse collar that did not constrict the animal's breathing allowed Chinese horses to pull much heavier loads than European horses could. The Chinese also were the first to make paper, perhaps as early as the second century B.C.E. They pounded soaked plant fibers and bark with a mallet, then poured the mixture through a porous mat. Once the residue left on the mat surface dried out, it provided a relatively smooth, lightweight medium for writing on with ink.

The Qin began and the Han rulers continued an extensive program of road building. Roads enabled rapid movement of military forces and supplies. The network of couriers that carried messages to and from the central administration used horses, boats, and even footpaths, and they found food and shelter at relay stations. The network of navigable rivers was improved and connected by canals (see Environment and Technology: Water Engineering in Rome and China).

Population growth and increasing trade gave rise to local market centers. These thriving towns grew to become county seats from which imperial officials operated. Between 10 and 30 percent of the population lived in Han towns and cities.

China's most important export commodity was silk. For a long time the fact that silk cocoons are secreted onto the leaves of mulberry trees by silkworms was a closely guarded secret that gave the Chinese a monopoly on the manufacture of silk. As silk was carried on a perilous journey westward through the Central Asian oases to the Middle East, India, and the Mediterranean, it passed through the hands of middlemen who raised the price to make a profit. The value of a beautiful textile may have increased a hundredfold by the time it reached its destination. The Chinese government sought to control the Silk Road by launching periodic campaigns into Central Asia. Garrisons were installed, and colonies of Chinese settlers were sent out to occupy the oases.

Decline of the Han Empire

For the Han government, as for the Romans, maintaining the security of the frontiers—particularly the north and northwest frontiers—was a primary concern. In general, the Han Empire successfully controlled lands occupied by farming peoples, but met resistance from nomadic groups whose livelihood depended on their horses and herds. The different ways of life of farmers and herders gave rise to insulting stereotypes on both sides. The settled Chinese thought of nomads as "barbarians"—rough, uncivilized peoples—much as the inhabitants of the Roman Empire looked down on the Germanic tribes living beyond their frontier.

Along the boundary, the closeness of the herders and farmers often led to significant commercial activity. The nomadic herders sought the food and crafted goods produced by the farmers and townsfolk, and the settled farmers depended on the nomads for horses and other herd animals and products. Sometimes, however, nomads raided the settled lands and took what they needed or wanted. Tough and warlike because of the demands of their way of life, mounted nomads could strike swiftly and just as swiftly disappear.

Although nomadic groups tended to be relatively small and often fought with one another, from time to time circumstances and a charismatic leader could create a large coalition. The major external threat to Chinese civilization in the Han period came from the **Xiongnu°**, a great confederacy of Turkic peoples. For centuries the Chinese succeeded in containing the Xiongnu. In order to mount periodic campaigns onto the steppe, they developed cavalry forces that could match the mobility of the nomads, and access to good stocks of horses and pasturing of herds on northern grasslands became a state priority. Other strategies included maintaining colonies of soldier-farmers and garrisons on the frontier; settling compliant nomadic groups inside the borders to serve as a buffer against warlike groups; paying bribes to promote dissension among the nomad leadership; and paying protection money. One frequently successful approach was a "tributary system" in which nomad rulers nominally accepted Chinese su-

---

Xiongnu (SHE-OONG-noo)

premacy and paid tribute, for which they were rewarded with marriages to Chinese princesses, dazzling receptions at court, and gifts from the Han emperor that exceeded the value of the tribute.

In the end, continuous military vigilance along the frontier burdened Han finances and worsened the economic troubles of later Han times. Despite the earnest efforts of Qin and Early Han emperors to reduce the power and wealth of the aristocracy and to turn land over to a free peasantry, by the end of the first century B.C.E. nobles and successful merchants again controlled huge tracts of land, and many peasants sought their protection against the demands of the imperial government. Over the next two centuries strongmen who were largely independent of imperial control emerged, and the central government was deprived of tax revenues and manpower. The system of military conscription broke down, forcing the government to hire more and more foreign soldiers and officers. These men were willing to serve for pay, but they were not very loyal to the Han state.

Several factors contributed to the fall of the Han dynasty in 220 C.E.: factional intrigues within the ruling clan, official corruption and inefficiency, uprisings of desperate and hungry peasants, the spread of banditry, attacks by nomadic groups on the northwest frontier, and the ambitions of rural warlords. China entered a period of political fragmentation and economic and cultural regression that lasted until the rise of the Sui° and Tang° dynasties in the late sixth and early seventh centuries C.E., a story we take up in Chapter 11.

Imperial Parallels

The similarities between the Roman and Han Empires begin at the level of the family. In both cultures the family comprised the living generations and was headed by an all-powerful patriarch. Strong loyalties and obligations bound family members. Values first learned in the family—obedience, respect for superiors, piety, and a strong sense of duty and honor—created a pervasive social cohesion.

Agriculture was the fundamental economic activity and source of wealth in both civilizations. Government revenues were primarily derived from a percentage of the annual harvest. Both empires depended on free peasantry—sturdy farmers who could be pressed into military service or other forms of compulsory labor. Conflicts over who owned the land and how it was to be used were at the heart of the political and social turmoil in both places. The autocratic rulers of the Roman and Chinese states secured their positions by breaking the power of the old aristocratic families, seizing their excess land, and giving land to small farmers (as well as keeping extensive tracts for themselves). They veiled the revolutionary nature of these changes by claiming to restore the institutions of a venerable past. The later reversal of this process, when wealthy noblemen once again gained control of vast tracts of land and reduced the peasants to dependent tenant farmers, signaled the erosion of the authority of the state.

Both empires spread out from an ethnically homogeneous core to encompass widespread territories containing diverse ecosystems, populations, and ways of life. Both brought those regions a cultural unity that has persisted, at least in part, to the present day. This development involved far more than military conquest and political domination. The skill of Roman and Chinese farmers and the high yields that they produced led to a dynamic expansion of population. As the population of the core areas outstripped the available resources, Italian and Han settlers moved into new regions, bringing their languages, beliefs, customs, and technologies with them. Many people in the conquered lands were attracted to the culture of the ruler nation and chose to adopt these practices and attach themselves to a "winning cause." Both empires found similar solutions to the problems of administering far-flung territories and large populations in an age when men on horseback or on foot carried messages. The central government had to delegate considerable autonomy to local officials. These local elites identified their own interests with the central government they loyally served. In both empires a kind of civil service developed, staffed by educated and capable members of a prosperous middle class.

Technologies that facilitated imperial control also fostered cultural unification and improvements in the general standard of living. Roads built to expedite the movement of troops became the highways of commerce and the thoroughfares by which imperial culture spread. A network of cities and towns served as the nerve center of each empire, providing local administrative bases, further promoting commerce, and radiating imperial culture out into the surrounding countryside.

Cities and towns modeled themselves on the capital cities of Rome and Chang'an. Travelers could find the same types and styles of buildings and public spaces, as well as other attractive features of urban life, in outlying

Sui (sway) **Tang** (tahng)

regions that they had seen in the capital. The majority of the population still resided in the countryside, but most of the advantages of empire were enjoyed by people living in urban centers.

The empires of Rome and Han China faced similar problems of defense: long borders located far from the administrative center and aggressive neighbors who coveted the prosperity of the empire. Both empires had to build walls and maintain a chain of forts and garrisons to protect against incursions. The cost of frontier defense was staggering and eventually eroded the economic prosperity of the two empires. Rough neighbors gradually learned the skills that had given the empires an initial advantage and were able to close the "technology gap." As the imperial governments became ever more beholden to the military and demanded more taxes and services from the hard-pressed civilian population, they lost the loyalty of their own people, many of whom sought protection on the estates of powerful rural landowners. Eventually, both empires were so weakened that their borders were overrun and their central governments collapsed. Ironically, the newly dominant immigrant groups had been so deeply influenced by imperial culture that they maintained it to the best of their abilities.

In referring to the eventual failure of these two empires, we are brought up against the different long-term consequences of their respective demises. In China the imperial model was revived in subsequent eras, but the lands of the Roman Empire never again achieved the same level of unification. Several interrelated factors help account for the different outcomes.

First, these cultures had different attitudes about the relationship of individuals to the state. In China the individual was deeply embedded in the larger social group. The Chinese family, with its emphasis on a precisely defined hierarchy, unquestioning obedience, and solemn rituals of deference to elders and ancestors, served as the model for society and the state. Respect for authority was (and remains) deeply seated. The architects of Qin Legalism largely got their way, and the emperor's word was regarded as law. Moreover, Confucianism, which sanctified hierarchy and provided a code of conduct for professionals and public officials, had arisen long before the imperial system and could be revived and tailored to fit subsequent political circumstances. Although the Roman family had its own hierarchy and traditions of obedience, the cult of ancestors was not as strong as among the Chinese, and the family was not the organizational model for Roman society and the Roman state. Also, there was no Roman equivalent of Confucianism—no ideology of political organization and social conduct that could survive the dissolution of the Roman state.

It is probably also fair to say that economic and social mobility, which allows some people to rise dramatically in wealth and status, enhances a society's sense of the significance of the individual. Opportunities for individuals to improve their economic status were more limited in ancient China than in the Roman Empire, and the merchant class in China was frequently disparaged and constrained by the government. The greater importance of commerce in the Roman Empire and the absence of government interference resulted in greater economic mobility. Roman law gave great weight to the sanctity of property and the rights of the individual. To a much greater extent than the Chinese emperor, the Roman emperor had to resort to persuasion, threats, and promises in order to forge a consensus for his initiatives.

Although Roman emperors tried to create an ideology to bolster their position, they were hampered by the persistence of Republican traditions and the ambiguities about the position of emperor deliberately cultivated by Augustus. As a result, Roman rulers were likely to be chosen by the army or by the Senate; the dynastic principle never took deep root; and the cult of the emperor had little spiritual content. This stands in sharp contrast to the clear-cut Chinese belief that the emperor was the divine Son of Heaven with privileged access to the beneficent power of the royal ancestors. Thus, in the lands that had once comprised the western part of the Roman Empire, there was no compelling basis for reviving the position of emperor and the territorial claims of empire in later ages.

Finally, Christianity, with its insistence on monotheism and one doctrine of truth, negated the Roman emperor's pretensions to divinity and was essentially unwilling to come to terms with pagan beliefs. The spread of Christianity through the provinces during the Late Roman Empire, and the decline of the western half of the empire in the fifth century C.E. (see Chapter 10), constituted an irreversible break with the past. On the other hand, Buddhism, which came to China in the early centuries C.E. and flourished in the post-Han era (see Chapter 11), was more easily reconciled with traditional Chinese values and beliefs.

Conclusion

Both the Roman Empire and the first Chinese empire arose from relatively small states that, because of their discipline and military toughness, were initially able to subdue small and quarreling neighbors. Ultimately they unified widespread territories under strong central governments.

In China the Qin Empire emerged rapidly, in the reign of a single ruler, because many of the elements for unification were already in place. The "First Emperor" looked back to the precedents of the Shang and Zhou states, which had controlled large core areas in the North China Plain. He drew upon the preexisting concept of the Mandate of Heaven, a claim to divine backing for the ruler who was himself the Son of Heaven; and the Legalist political philosophy justified authoritarian measures. The harshness of the new order generated discontent and resistance that soon brought down the Qin dynasty, but Han successors were able to moderate and build on Qin structures to create a durable imperial regime.

The early Roman state had no such precedents to draw upon. The creation of the Roman Empire was a much slower process in which solutions were discovered by trial and error. The Republican form of government, developed to meet the needs of an Italian city-state, proved inadequate to the demands of empire, and Rome's military success led to social and economic disruption and an acute political struggle. Out of this crisis emerged the Principate, which persevered for several centuries. Even so, the Roman emperors were never able to develop an effective ideology of rule.

In both empires, large and efficient professional armies maintained social order and defended the frontiers. An administrative bureaucracy staffed by educated civil servants kept records and collected taxes to support the military and government. Roads, cities, standardized systems of money and measurement, and widely understood languages facilitated travel, commerce, and communication. The culture of the imperial center spread throughout the lands under its control, and this shared culture, as well as shared self-interest, bonded local elites to the empire's ruling class.

For long periods these stabilizing forces, which brought peace, prosperity, and an improved standard of living to many, were stronger than the weaknesses inherent in these two great empires. Over time, however, the costs of defending lengthy frontiers drained imperial treasuries and imposed greater burdens of taxation on the subjects. As hard-pressed subjects sought the protection of rural landowners, cities became depopulated, commerce was disrupted, and the central government was less able to compel payment of taxes and find recruits for the armed forces.

In the end, both empires succumbed to a combination of external pressures and internal divisions. In China the imperial tradition and the class structure and value system that maintained it were eventually revived (see Chapters 11 and 14), and they survived with remarkable continuity into the twentieth century C.E. In Europe, North Africa, and the Middle East, in contrast, there was no restoration of the Roman Empire, and the later history of those lands was marked by great political changes and cultural diversity.

Key Terms

Roman Republic
Roman Senate
patron/client relationship
Roman Principate
Augustus
equites
pax romana
Romanization
Jesus
Paul
aqueduct
third-century crisis
Constantine
Qin
Shi Huangdi
Han
Chang'an
gentry
Xiongnu

Suggested Reading

Tim Cornell and John Matthews, *Atlas of the Roman World* (1982), offers a general introduction, pictures, and maps to illustrate many aspects of Roman civilization. Michael Grant and Rachel Kitzinger, eds., *Civilization of the Ancient Mediterranean,* 3 vols. (1988), is an invaluable collection of essays with bibliographies by specialists on every major facet of life in the Greek and Roman worlds. Among the many good surveys of Roman history are Michael Grant, *History of Rome* (1978), and M. Cary and H. H. Scullard, *A History of Rome Down to the Reign of Constantine* (1975). Naphtali Lewis and Meyer Reinhold, eds., *Roman Civilization,* 2 vols. (1951), contains extensive ancient sources in translation.

For Roman political and legal institutions, attitudes, and values see J. A. Crook, *Law and Life of Rome: 90 B.C.–A.D. 212* (1967). Michael Crawford, *The Roman Republic,* 2d ed. (1993), and Chester G. Starr, *The Roman Empire, 27 B.C.–A.D. 476: A Study in Survival* (1982), assess the evolution of the Roman state during the Republic and Principate. Fergus Millar, *The Emperor in the Roman World (31 B.C.–A.D. 337)* (1977), is a comprehensive study of the position of the princeps. Barbara Levick, *The Government of the Roman Empire: A Sourcebook* (2000), presents original texts in translation.

For Roman military expansion and defense of the frontiers see W. V. Harris, *War and Imperialism in Republican Rome* (1979), and Stephen L. Dyson, *The Creation of the Roman Frontier* (1985). For military technology see M. C. Bishop, *Roman Military Equipment: From the Punic Wars to the Fall of Rome* (1993). David Macaulay, *City: A Story of Roman Planning and Construction* (1974), uses copious illustrations to reveal the wonders of Roman engineering; more depth and detail are found in K. D.

White, *Greek and Roman Technology* (1984). The characteristics of Roman urban centers are highlighted in John E. Stambaugh, *The Ancient Roman City* (1988).

Kevin Greene, *The Archaeology of the Roman Economy* (1986), showcases new approaches to social and economic history. Suzanne Dickson, *The Roman Family* (1992) explores this most basic social group. Lionel Casson, *Everyday Life in Ancient Rome* (1998), and U. E. Paoli, *Rome: Its People, Life and Customs* (1983), look at the features that typified daily life. Jo-Ann Shelton, ed., *As the Romans Did: A Sourcebook in Roman Social History* (1998), offers a selection of translated ancient sources. Elaine Fantham, Helene Peet Foley, Natalie Boymel Kampen, Sarah B. Pomeroy, and H. Alan Shapiro, *Women in the Classical World: Image and Text* (1994), provides an up-to-date discussion of women in the Roman world. Many of the ancient sources on Roman women can be found in Mary R. Lefkowitz and Maureen B. Fant, eds., *Women's Life in Greece and Rome: A Source Book in Translation* (1982). Thomas Wiedemann, ed., *Greek and Roman Slavery* (1981), contains the ancient sources in translation. Donald G. Kyle, *Spectacles of Death in Ancient Rome* (1998), explores the nature and significance of blood sports in the arena.

A number of the chapters in John Boardman, Jasper Griffin, and Oswyn Murray, eds., *The Roman World* (1988), survey the intellectual and literary achievements of the Romans. Ronald Mellor, ed., *The Historians of Ancient Rome* (1998), provides context for reading the historical sources. Michael von Albrecht, *History of Roman Literature: From Livius Andronicus to Boethius: With Special Regard to Its Influence on World Literature* (1997), Michael Grant, *Art in the Roman Empire* (1995), and Nancy H. Ramage and Andrew Ramage, *The Cambridge Illustrated History of Roman Art* (1991) are surveys of Roman creative arts. Robert Turcan, *The Gods of Ancient Rome: Religion in Everyday Life from Archaic to Imperial Times* (2000), and R. M. Ogilvie, *The Romans and Their Gods in the Age of Augustus* (1969), are accessible introductions to Roman religion in its public and private manifestations. Michael Grant, *The Jews in the Roman World* (1973), and Erich S. Gruen, *Diaspora: Jews Amidst Greeks and Romans* (2002), explore the complicated situation of Jews in the Roman Empire. Joseph F. Kelly, *The World of the Early Christians* (1997), W. H. C. Frend, *The Rise of Christianity* (1984), and R. A. Markus, *Christianity in the Roman World* (1974), investigate the rise of Christianity. Everett Ferguson, ed., *Encyclopedia of Early Christianity* (2d ed., 1998), contains articles and bibliographies on a wide range of topics.

For the geography and demography of China see the well-illustrated *Cultural Atlas of China* (1983) by Caroline Blunden and Mark Elvin. Valerie Hansen, *The Open Empire: A History of China to 1600* (2000), emphasizes social history and China's interactions with other societies. Other basic surveys of Chinese history include Jacques Gernet, *A History of Chinese Civilization* (1982), and John K. Fairbank, *China: A New History* (1992). In greater depth for the ancient period is Edward L. Shaughnessy and Michael Loewe, eds., *The Cambridge History of Ancient China* (1998); Denis Twitchett and Michael Loewe, eds., *The Cambridge History of China,* vol. 1, *The Ch'in and Han Empires, 221 B.C.–A.D. 220* (1986); and Michele Pirazzoli-t'Serstevens, *The Han Dynasty* (1982). Nicola Di Cosmo, *Ancient China and Its Enemies: The Rise of Nomadic Power in East Asian History* (2002), explores the interactions of Chinese and nomads on the northern frontier. Kwang-chih Chang, *The Archaeology of Ancient China,* 4th ed. (1986), emphasizes the archaeological record. Patricia Buckley Ebrey, *Chinese Civilization: A Sourcebook* (2d ed., 1993), and W. de Bary, W. Chan, and B. Watson, eds., *Sources of Chinese Tradition* (1960), are collections of sources in translation. Sima Qian, *Historical Records* (1994), translated by Raymond Dawson, provides a very readable selection of varied material pertaining to the Qin dynasty compiled by the premier historian of the Han period.

For social history see Michael Loewe, *Everyday Life in Early Imperial China During the Han Period, 202 B.C.–A.D. 220* (1988), and Anne Behnke Kinney, "Women in Ancient China," in Bella Vivante, ed., *Women's Roles in Ancient Civilizations: A Reference Guide* (1999). For economic history and foreign relations see Xinru Liu, *Ancient India and Ancient China: Trade and Religious Exchanges, A.D. 1–600* (1994), and Ying-shih Yu, *Trade and Expansion in Han China* (1967). For scientific and technological achievements see Robert Temple, *The Genius of China: 3,000 Years of Science, Discovery, and Invention* (1986).

Benjamin I. Schwartz addresses intellectual history in *The World of Thought in Ancient China* (1985). Spiritual matters are taken up by Laurence G. Thompson, *Chinese Religion: An Introduction,* 3d ed. (1979). For art see Michael Sullivan, *A Short History of Chinese Art,* rev. ed. (1970), and Jessica Rawson, *Ancient China: Art and Archaeology* (1980).

For a stimulating comparison of the Roman and Han Empires that emphasizes the differences, see the first chapter of S. A. M. Adshead, *China in World History,* 2d ed. (1995).

Notes

1. Patricia Buckley Ebrey, ed., *Chinese Civilization and Society: A Sourcebook* (New York: Free Press, 1981), 33–34.

7 India and Southeast Asia, 1500 B.C.E.–1025 C.E.

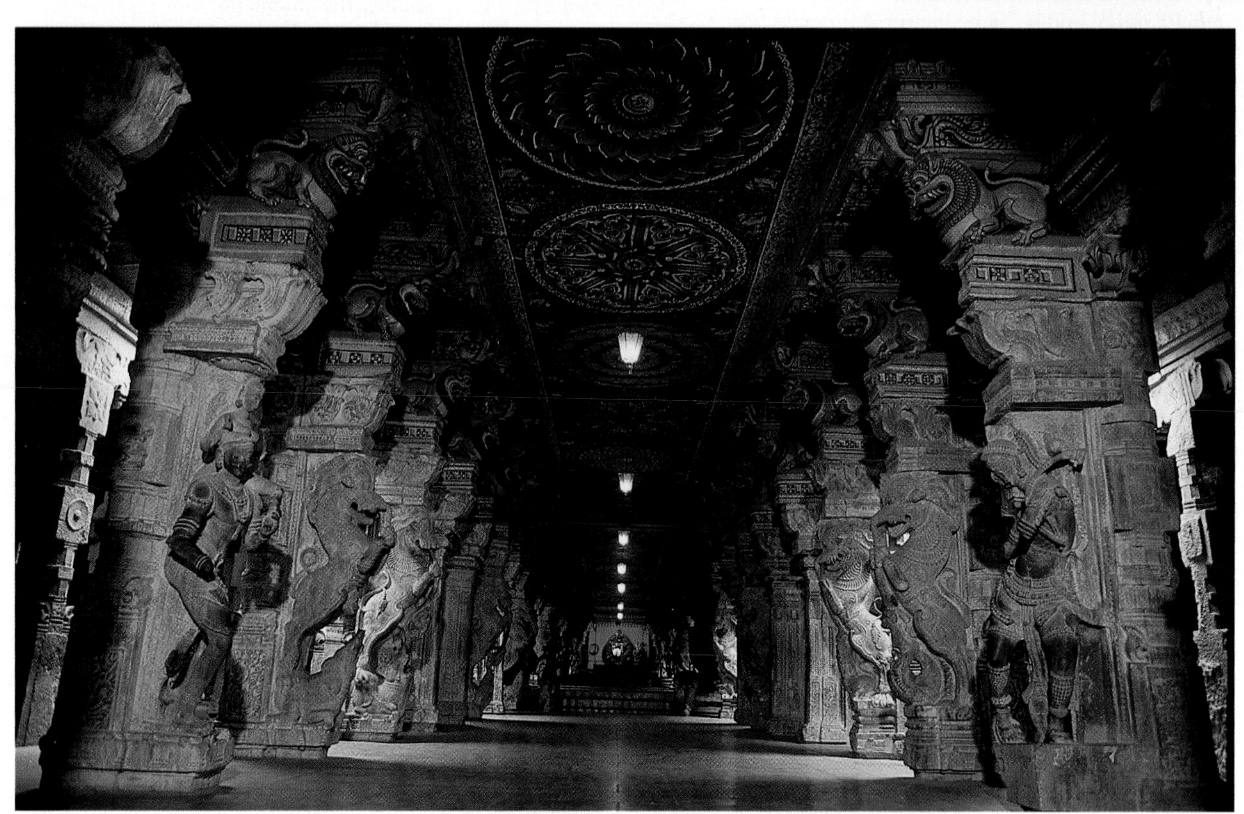

The Thousand Pillared Hall in the Temple of Minakshi at Madurai
At the annual Chittarai Festival, the citizens of this city in south India celebrate the wedding of their patron goddess, Minakshi, to Shiva.

CHAPTER OUTLINE

In the *Bhagavad-Gita*°, the most renowned of all Indian sacred texts, Arjuna°, the greatest warrior of Indian legend, rides out in his chariot to the open space between two armies preparing for battle. Torn between his social duty to fight for his family's claim to the throne and his conscience, which balks at the prospect of killing the relatives, friends, and former teachers who are in the enemy camp, Arjuna slumps down in his chariot and refuses to fight. But his chariot driver, the god Krishna° in disguise, persuades him, in a carefully structured dialogue, both of the necessity to fulfill his duty as a warrior and of the proper frame of mind for performing these acts. In the climactic moment of the dialogue Krishna endows Arjuna with a "divine eye" and permits him to see the true appearance of god:

> It was a multiform, wondrous vision,
> with countless mouths and eyes
> and celestial ornaments,
> Everywhere was boundless divinity
> containing all astonishing things,
> wearing divine garlands and garments,
> anointed with divine perfume.
> If the light of a thousand suns
> were to rise in the sky at once,
> it would be like the light
> of that great spirit.
> Arjuna saw all the universe
> in its many ways and parts,
> standing as one in the body
> of the god of gods.[1]

In all of world literature, this is one of the most compelling attempts to depict the nature of deity. Graphic images emphasize the vastness, diversity, and multiplicity of the god, but in the end we learn that Krishna is the organizing principle behind all creation, that behind diversity and multiplicity lies a higher unity.

This is an apt metaphor for Indian civilization. If one word can characterize India in both ancient and modern times, it is *diversity.* The enormous variety of the Indian landscape is mirrored in the patchwork of ethnic and linguistic groups that occupy it, the political fragmentation that has marked most of Indian history, the elaborate hierarchy of social groups into which the Indian population is divided, and the thousands of deities who are worshiped at the innumerable holy places that dot the subcontinent. Yet, in the end, one can speak of an Indian civilization that is united by a set of shared views and values.

In this chapter we survey the history of South and Southeast Asia from approximately 1500 B.C.E. to 1025 C.E., focusing on the evolution of defining features of Indian civilization. Considerable attention is given to Indian religious conceptions. This coverage is due, in part, to religion's profound role in shaping Indian society. It is also a consequence of the sources of information available to historians. Lengthy epic poems, such as the *Mahabharata*° and *Ramayana*°, preserve useful information about early Indian society, but most of the earliest texts are religious documents—such as the *Vedas*°, *Upanishads*°, and Buddhist dialogues and stories—that were preserved and transmitted orally long before they were written down. In addition, Indian civilization held a conception of vast expanses of time during which creatures were repeatedly reincarnated and lived many lives. This belief may be why ancient Indians did not develop a historical consciousness like that of their Israelite and Greek contemporaries and took little interest in recording specific historical events: such events seemed relatively insignificant when set against the long cycles of time and lives.

As you read this chapter, ask yourself the following questions:

- What historical forces led to the development of complex social groupings in ancient India?
- Why did Indian civilization develop religious traditions with such distinctive conceptions of space, time, gods, and the life cycle, and how did these beliefs shape nearly every aspect of South Asian culture?

Bhagavad-Gita (BUH-guh-vahd GEE-tuh)
Arjuna (AHR-joo-nuh) **Krishna** (KRISH-nuh)

Mahabharata (muh-huh-BAH-ruh-tuh)
Ramayana (ruh-muh-YAH-nuh) ***Vedas*** (VAY-duhs)
Upanishads (oo-PAHN-ih-shahds)

- How, in the face of powerful forces that tended to keep India fragmented, did two great empires—the Mauryan° Empire of the fourth to second centuries B.C.E. and the Gupta° Empire of the fourth to sixth centuries C.E.—succeed in unifying much of India?
- How did a number of states in Southeast Asia become wealthy and powerful by exploiting their position on the trade routes between China and India?

FOUNDATIONS OF INDIAN CIVILIZATION, 1500 B.C.E.–300 C.E.

India is called a *subcontinent* because it is a large—roughly 2,000 miles (3,200 kilometers) in both length and breadth—and physically isolated landmass within the continent of Asia. It is set off from the rest of Asia by the Himalayas°, the highest mountains on the planet, to the north, and by the Indian Ocean on its eastern, southern, and western sides (see Map 7.1). The most permeable frontier, and the one used by a long series of invaders and migrating peoples, lies to the northwest. But people using this corridor must cross over the mountain barrier of the Hindu Kush° (via the Khyber° Pass) and the Thar° Desert east of the Indus River.

The Indian Subcontinent

The subcontinent—which encompasses the modern nations of Pakistan, Nepal, Bhutan, Bangladesh, India, and the adjacent island of Sri Lanka—can be divided into three distinct topographical zones. The mountainous northern zone takes in the heavily forested foothills and high meadows on the edge of the Hindu Kush and Himalaya ranges. Next come the great basins of the Indus and Ganges° Rivers. Originating in the ice of the Tibetan mountains to the north, these rivers have repeatedly overflowed their banks and deposited layer on layer of silt, creating large alluvial plains. Northern India is divided from the third zone, the peninsula proper, by the Vindhya range and the Deccan°, an arid, rocky plateau that brings to mind parts of the American southwest. The tropical coastal strip of Kerala (Malabar) in the west, the Coromandel Coast in the east with its web of rivers descending from the central plateau, the flatlands of Tamil Nadu on the southern tip of the peninsula, and the island of Sri Lanka often have followed paths of political and cultural development separate from those of northern India.

The rim of mountains looming above India's northern frontier shelters the subcontinent from cold Arctic winds and gives it a subtropical climate. The most dramatic source of moisture is the **monsoon** (seasonal wind). The Indian Ocean is slow to warm or cool, and the vast landmass of Asia swings rapidly between seasonal extremes of heat and cold. The temperature difference between the water and the land acts like a bellows, producing a great wind in this and adjoining parts of the globe. The southwest monsoon begins in June. It picks up huge amounts of moisture from the Indian Ocean and drops it over a swath of India that encompasses the rain-forest belt on the western coast and the Ganges Basin. Three harvests a year are possible in some places. Rice is grown in the moist, flat Ganges Delta (the modern region of Bengal). Elsewhere the staples are wheat, barley, and millet. The Indus Valley, in contrast, gets little precipitation (see Chapter 2). In this arid region agriculture depends on extensive irrigation. Moreover, the volume of water in the Indus is irregular, and the river has changed course from time to time.

Although invasions and migrations usually came by land through the northwest corridor, the ocean surrounding the peninsula has not been a barrier to travel and trade. Indian Ocean mariners learned to ride the monsoon winds across open waters from northeast to southwest in January and to make the return voyage in July. Ships made their way west across the Arabian Sea to the Persian Gulf, the southern coast of Arabia, and East Africa, and east across the Bay of Bengal to Indochina and Indonesia (see Chapter 8).

It is tempting to trace many of the characteristic features of later Indian civilization back to the Indus Valley civilization of the third and early second millennia B.C.E., but proof is hard to come by because the writing from that period has not yet been deciphered. That society, which responded to the challenge of an arid terrain by developing high levels of social organization and technology, seems to have succumbed around 1900 B.C.E. to some kind of environmental crisis (see Chapter 2).

The Vedic Age

Historians call the period from 1500 to 500 B.C.E. the "Vedic Age," after the ***Vedas,*** religious texts that are our main source of information about the period. The foundations for Indian civilization were laid

Mauryan (MORE-yuhn) **Gupta** (GOOP-tuh)
Himalayas (him-uh-LAY-uhs) **Hindu Kush** (HIHN-doo KOOSH)
Khyber (KIE-ber) **Thar** (tahr) **Ganges** (GAHN-jeez)
Deccan (de-KAN)

CHRONOLOGY

	India	Southeast Asia
2000 B.C.E.		ca. 2000 B.C.E. Swidden agriculture
		ca. 1600 B.C.E. Beginning of migrations from mainland Southeast Asia to islands in Pacific and Indian Oceans
1500 B.C.E.	ca. 1500 B.C.E. Migration of Indo-European peoples into northwest India	
1000 B.C.E.	ca. 1000 B.C.E. Indo-European groups move into the Ganges Plain	
500 B.C.E.	ca. 500 B.C.E. Siddhartha Gautama founds Buddhism; Mahavira founds Jainism	
	324 B.C.E. Chandragupta Maurya becomes king of Magadha and lays foundation for Mauryan Empire	
	184 B.C.E. Fall of Mauryan Empire	
1 C.E.		
	320 C.E. Chandra Gupta establishes Gupta Empire	ca. 50–560 B.C.E. Funan dominates southern Indochina and the Isthmus of Kra
500 C.E.		
	550 C.E. Collapse of Gupta Empire	ca. 500 B.C.E. Trade route develops through Strait of Malacca
	606–647 B.C.E. Reign of Harsha Vardhana	
		683 C.E. Rise of Srivijaya in Sumatra
1000 C.E.		770–825 C.E. Construction of Borobodur in Java
		1025 C.E. Chola attack on Palembang and decline of Srivijaya

in the Vedic Age. Most historians believe that new groups of people—nomadic warriors speaking Indo-European languages—migrated into northwest India around 1500 B.C.E. Some argue for a much earlier Indo-European presence in this region in conjunction with the spread of agriculture. In any case, in the mid-second millennium B.C.E. northern India entered a new historical period associated with the dominance of Indo-European groups.

After the collapse of the Indus Valley civilization there was no central authority to direct irrigation efforts. The region became home to kinship groups that depended mostly on their herds of cattle for sustenance and perhaps supplemented their diet by doing some gardening. These societies, like those of other Indo-European peoples—Celts, Greeks, Iranians, Romans—were patriarchal. The father dominated the family as the king ruled the tribe. Members of the warrior class boasted of their martial skill and courage, relished combat, celebrated with lavish feasts of beef and rounds of heavy drinking, and filled their leisure time with chariot racing and gambling.

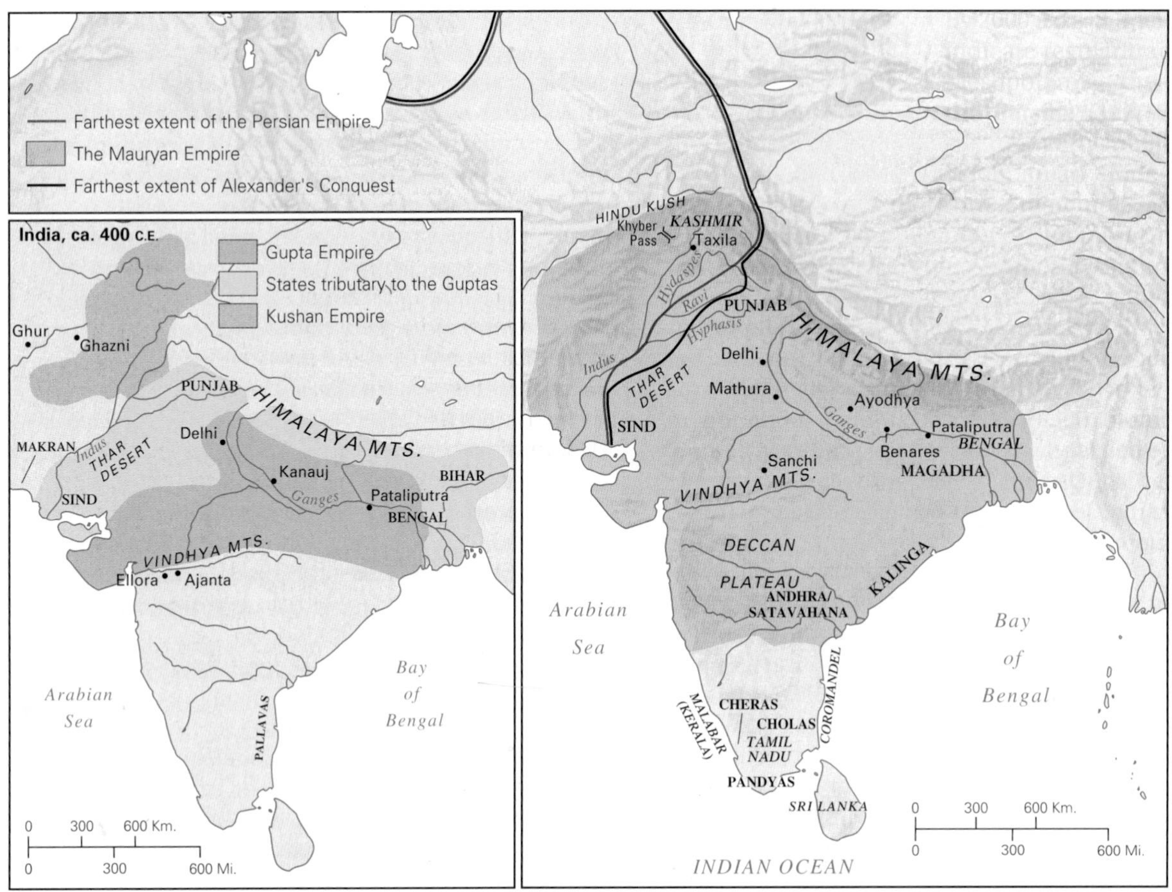

Map 7.1 Ancient India Mountains and ocean largely separate the Indian subcontinent from the rest of Asia. Migrations and invasions usually came through the Khyber Pass in the northwest. Seaborne commerce with western Asia, Southeast Asia, and East Asia often flourished. Peoples speaking Indo-European languages migrated into the broad valleys of the Indus and Ganges Rivers in the north. Dravidian-speaking peoples remained the dominant population in the south. The diversity of the Indian landscape, the multiplicity of ethnic groups, and the primary identification of people with their class and caste lie behind the division into many small states that has characterized much of Indian political history.

After 1000 B.C.E. some of these groups began to push east into the Ganges Plain. New technologies made this advance possible. Iron tools—harder than bronze and able to hold a sharper edge—allowed settlers to fell trees and work the newly cleared land with plows pulled by oxen. The soil of the Ganges Plain was fertile, well watered by the annual monsoon, and able to sustain two or three crops a year. As in Greece at roughly the same time (see Chapter 5), the use of iron tools to open new land for agriculture must have led to a significant increase in population.

Stories about this era, not written down until much later but long preserved by memorization and oral recitation, speak of bitter rivalry and warfare between two groups of people: the Aryas, relatively light-skinned speakers of Indo-European languages, and the Dasas, dark-skinned speakers of Dravidian languages. Some scholars contend that some Dasas were absorbed into Arya populations and elites from both groups merged. For the most part, however, Aryas pushed the Dasas south into central and southern India, where their descendants still live. Signaling the ultimate success of the Aryas is the fact that Indo-European languages are primarily spoken in northern India today. Dravidian speech prevails in the south.

Skin color has been a persistent concern of Indian society and is one of the bases for its historically sharp internal divisions. Over time there evolved a system of **varna**—literally "color," though the word came to indicate something akin to "class." Individuals were born into one of four classes: *Brahmin,* the group comprising priests and scholars; *Kshatriya*°, warriors and officials; *Vaishya*°, merchants, artisans, and landowners; or *Shudra*°, peasants and laborers. The designation *Shudra* originally may have been reserved for Dasas, who were given the menial jobs in society. Indeed, the very term *dasa* came to mean "slave." Eventually a fifth group was marked off: the Untouchables. They were excluded from the class system, and members of the other groups literally avoided them because of the demeaning or polluting work to which they were relegated—such as leather tanning, which involved touching dead animals, and sweeping away ashes after cremations.

People at the top of the social pyramid in ancient India could explain why this hierarchy existed. According to one creation myth, a primordial creature named Purusha allowed itself to be sacrificed. From its mouth sprang the class of Brahmin priests, the embodiment of intellect and knowledge. From its arms came the Kshatriya warrior class, from its thighs the Vaishya landowners and merchants, and from its feet the Shudra workers.

The varna system was just one of the mechanisms that Indian society developed to regulate relations between different groups. Within the broad class divisions, the population was further subdivided into numerous **jati,** or birth groups (sometimes called *castes,* from a Portuguese term meaning "breed"). Each jati had its proper occupation, duties, and rituals. Individuals who belonged to a given jati lived with members of their group, married within the group, and ate only with members of the group. Elaborate rules governed their interactions with members of other groups. Members of higher-status groups feared pollution from contact with lower-caste individuals and had to undergo elaborate rituals of purification to remove any taint.

The class and caste systems came to be connected to a widespread belief in reincarnation. The Brahmin priests taught that every living creature had an immortal essence: the *atman,* or "breath." Separated from the body at death, the atman was later reborn in another body. Whether the new body was that of an insect, an animal, or a human depended on the **karma,** or deeds, of the atman in its previous incarnations. People who lived exemplary lives would be reborn into the higher classes. Those who misbehaved would be punished in the next life by being relegated to a lower class or even a lower life form. The underlying message was: You are where you deserve to be, and the only way to improve your lot in the next cycle of existence is to accept your current station and its attendant duties.

The dominant deities in Vedic religion were male and were associated with the heavens. To release the dawn, Indra, god of war and master of the thunderbolt, daily slew the demon encasing the universe. Varuna, lord of the sky, maintained universal order and dispensed justice. Agni, the force of fire, consumed the sacrifice and bridged the spheres of gods and humans.

Sacrifice—the dedication to a god of a valued possession, often a living creature—was the essential ritual. The purpose of these offerings was to invigorate the gods and thereby sustain their creative powers and promote stability in the world.

Brahmin priests controlled the technology of sacrifice, for only they knew the rituals and prayers. The *Rig Veda,* a collection of more than a thousand poetic hymns to various deities, and the *Brahmanas,* detailed prose descriptions of procedures for ritual and sacrifice, were collections of priestly lore couched in the Sanskrit language of the Arya upper classes. This information was handed down orally from one generation of priests to the next. Some scholars have hypothesized that the Brahmins opposed the introduction of writing. Such opposition would explain why this technology did not come into widespread use in India until the Gupta period (320–550 C.E.), long after it had begun to play a conspicuous role in other societies of equivalent complexity. The priests' "knowledge" (the term *veda* means just that) was the basis of their economic well-being. They were amply rewarded for officiating at sacrifices, and their knowledge gave them social and political power because they were the indispensable intermediaries between gods and humans.

As in nearly all ancient societies, it is difficult to uncover the experiences of women in ancient India. Limited evidence indicates that women in the Vedic period studied sacred lore, composed religious hymns, and participated in the sacrificial ritual. They had the opportunity to own property and usually were not married until they reached their middle or late teens. A number of strong and resourceful women appear in the epic poem *Mahabharata.* One of them, the beautiful and educated Draupadi, married—by her own choice—the five royal Pandava brothers. This probably should not be taken as evidence of the regular practice of polyandry (having more than one husband). In India, as in Greece, legendary figures had their own rules.

The sharp internal divisions of Indian society, the complex hierarchy of groups, and the claims of some to superior virtue and purity served important social functions. They provided each individual with a clear identity

---

Kshatriya (kshuh-TREE-yuh) **Vaishya** (VIESH-yuh)
Shudra (SHOOD-ra)

Carved Stone Gateway Leading to the Great Stupa at Sanchi Pilgrims traveled long distances to visit stupas, mounds containing relics of the Buddha. The complex at Sanchi, in central India, was begun by Ashoka in the third century B.C.E., though the gates probably date to the first century C.E. This relief shows a royal procession bringing the remains of the Buddha to the city of Kushinagara. (Dinodia Photo Library)

and role and offered the benefits of group solidarity and support. There is evidence that groups sometimes were able to upgrade their status. Thus the elaborate system of divisions was not static and provided a mechanism for working out social tensions. Many of these features persisted into modern times.

Challenges to the Old Order: Jainism and Buddhism

After 700 B.C.E. various forms of reaction against Brahmin power and privilege emerged. People who objected to the rigid hierarchy of classes and castes or the community's demands on the individual could retreat to the forest. Despite the clearing of extensive tracts of land for agriculture, much of ancient India was covered with forest. Never very far from civilized areas, these wild places served as a refuge and symbolized freedom from societal constraints.

Certain charismatic individuals who abandoned their town or village and moved to the forest attracted bands of followers. Calling into question the priests' exclusive claims to wisdom and the necessity of Vedic chants and sacrifices, they offered an alternate path to salvation: the individual pursuit of insight into the nature of the self and the universe through physical and mental discipline (*yoga*), special dietary practices, and meditation. They taught that by distancing oneself from desire for the things of this world, one could achieve **moksha,** or "liberation." This release from the cycle of reincarnations and union with the divine force that animates the universe sometimes was likened to "a deep, dreamless sleep." The *Upanishads*—a collection of more than one hundred mystical dialogues between teachers and disciples—reflect this questioning of the foundations of Vedic religion.

The most serious threat to Vedic religion and to the prerogatives of the Brahmin priestly class came from two new religions that emerged around this time: Jainism° and Buddhism. Mahavira (540–468 B.C.E.) was known to his followers as Jina, "the Conqueror," from which is derived *Jainism,* the name of the belief system that he established. Emphasizing the holiness of the life force that animates all living creatures, Mahavira and his followers practiced strict nonviolence. They wore masks to prevent themselves from accidentally inhaling small insects, and they carefully brushed off a seat before sitting down. Those who gave themselves over completely to Jainism practiced extreme asceticism and nudity, ate only what they were given by others, and eventually starved themselves to death. Less zealous Jainists, restricted from agricultural work by the injunction against killing, tended to be city dwellers engaged in commerce and banking.

Of far greater significance for Indian and world history was the rise of Buddhism. So many stories have been told about Siddhartha Gautama (563–483 B.C.E.), known as the **Buddha,** "the Enlightened One," that it is difficult to separate fact from legend. He came from a Kshatriya family of the Sakyas, a people in the foothills of the Himalayas. As a young man he enjoyed the princely lifestyle to which he had been born, but at some point he experienced a change of heart and gave up family and privilege to become a wandering ascetic. After six years of self-deprivation, he came to regard asceticism as no more likely than the luxury of his previous life to produce spiritual insight, and he decided to adhere to a "Middle

---

Jainism (JINE-iz-uhm)

Sculpture of the Buddha, Second or Third Century C.E. This depiction of the Buddha, showing the effects of a protracted fast before he abandoned asceticism for the path of moderation, is from Gandhara in the northwest. It displays the influence of Greek artistic styles emanating from Greek settlements established in that region by Alexander the Great in the late fourth century B.C.E. (Robert Fisher)

Path" of moderation. Sitting under a tree in a deer park near Benares on the Ganges River, he gained a sudden and profound insight into the true nature of reality, which he set forth as "Four Noble Truths": (1) life is suffering; (2) suffering arises from desire; (3) the solution to suffering lies in curbing desire; and (4) desire can be curbed if a person follows the "Eightfold Path" of right views, aspirations, speech, conduct, livelihood, effort, mindfulness, and meditation. Rising up, the Buddha preached his First Sermon, a central text of Buddhism, and set into motion the "Wheel of the Law." He soon attracted followers, some of whom took vows of celibacy, nonviolence, and poverty.

In its original form, Buddhism centered on the individual. Although it did not quite reject the existence of gods, it denied their usefulness to a person seeking enlightenment. What mattered was living one's life with moderation, in order to minimize desire and suffering, and searching for spiritual truth through self-discipline and meditation. The ultimate reward was *nirvana,* literally "snuffing out the flame." With nirvana came release from the cycle of reincarnations and achievement of a state of perpetual tranquility. The Vedic tradition emphasized the eternal survival of the atman, the "breath" or nonmaterial essence of the individual. In contrast, Buddhism regarded the individual as a composite without any soul-like component that survived upon entering nirvana.

When the Buddha died, he left no final instructions, instead urging his disciples to "be their own lamp." As the Buddha's message—contained in philosophical discourses memorized by his followers—spread throughout India and into Central, Southeast, and East Asia, its very success began to subvert the individualistic and essentially atheistic tenets of the founder. Buddhist monasteries were established, and a hierarchy of Buddhist monks and nuns came into being. Worshipers erected *stupas*° (large earthen mounds that symbolized the universe) over relics of the cremated founder and walked around them in a clockwise direction. Believers began to worship the Buddha himself as a god. Many Buddhists also revered *bodhisattvas*°, men and women who had achieved enlightenment and were on the threshold of nirvana but chose to be reborn into mortal bodies to help others along the path to salvation.

The makers of early pictorial images had refused to show the Buddha as a living person and represented him only indirectly, through symbols such as his footprints, his begging bowl, or the tree under which he achieved enlightenment, as if to emphasize his achievement of a state of nonexistence. From the second century C.E., however, statues of the Buddha and bodhisattvas began to proliferate, done in native sculptural styles and in a style that showed the influence of the Greek settlements established in Bactria (modern Afghanistan) by Alexander the Great (see Chapter 5). A schism emerged within Buddhism. Devotees of **Mahayana**° ("Great Vehicle") **Buddhism** embraced the popular new features, while practitioners of **Theravada**° ("Teachings of the Elders") **Buddhism** followed most of the original teachings of the founder.

The Rise of Hinduism

Challenged by new, spiritually satisfying, and egalitarian movements, Vedic religion made important adjustments, evolving into **Hinduism,** the religion of hundreds of millions of people in South Asia today. (The term *Hinduism,* how-

stupa (STOO-puh) **bodhisattva** (boe-dih-SUT-vuh)
Mahayana (mah-huh-YAH-nuh) **Theravada** (there-uh-VAH-duh)

Hindu Temple at Khajuraho This sandstone temple of the Hindu deity Shiva, representing the celestial mountain of the gods, was erected at Khajuraho, in central India, around 1000 C.E., but it reflects the architectural symbolism of Hindu temples developed in the Gupta period. Worshipers made their way through several rooms to the image of the deity, located in the innermost "womb-chamber" directly beneath the tallest tower. (Jean-Louis Nou)

ever, was imposed from outside. Islamic invaders who reached India in the eleventh century C.E. labeled the diverse range of practices they saw there as Hinduism: "what the Indians do.") The foundation of Hinduism is the Vedic religion of the Arya peoples of northern India. But Hinduism also incorporated elements drawn from the Dravidian cultures of the south, such as an emphasis on intense devotion to the deity and the prominence of fertility rituals and symbolism. Also present are elements of Buddhism.

The process by which Vedic religion was transformed into Hinduism by the fourth century C.E. is largely hidden from us. The Brahmin priests maintained their high social status and influence. But sacrifice, though still part of traditional worship, was less central, and there was much more opportunity for direct contact between gods and individual worshipers.

The gods were altered, both in identity and in their relationships with humanity. Two formerly minor deities, Vishnu° and Shiva°, assumed preeminent positions in the Hindu pantheon. Hinduism emphasized the worshiper's personal devotion to a particular deity, usually Vishnu, Shiva, or Devi° ("the Goddess"). Both Shiva and Devi appear to be derived from the Dravidian tradition, in which a fertility cult and female deities played a prominent role. Their Dravidian origin is a telling example of how Arya and non-Arya cultures fused to form classic Hindu civilization. It is interesting to note that Vishnu, who has a clear Arya pedigree, remains more popular in northern India, while Shiva is dominant in the Dravidian south. These gods can appear in many guises. They are identified by various cult names and are represented by a complex symbolism of stories, companion animals, birds, and objects.

Vishnu, the preserver, is a benevolent deity who helps his devotees in time of need. Hindus believe that whenever demonic forces threaten the cosmic order, Vishnu appears on earth in one of a series of *avataras,* or incarnations. Among his incarnations are the legendary hero Rama, the popular cowherd-god Krishna, and the Buddha (a clear attempt to co-opt the rival religion's founder). Shiva, who lives in ascetic isolation on Mount Kailasa in

Vishnu (VIHSH-noo) **Shiva** (SHEE-vuh)

Devi (DEH-vee)

the Himalayas, is a more ambivalent figure. He represents both creation and destruction, for both are part of a single, cyclical process. He often is represented performing dance steps that symbolize the acts of creation and destruction. Devi manifests herself in various ways—as a full-bodied mother-goddess who promotes fertility and procreation, as the docile and loving wife Parvati, and as the frightening deity who, under the name Kali or Durga, lets loose a torrent of violence and destruction.

The multiplicity of gods (330 million according to one tradition), sects, and local practices within Hinduism is dazzling, reflecting the ethnic, linguistic, and cultural diversity of India. Yet within this variety there is unity. A worshiper's devotion to one god or goddess does not entail denial of the other main deities or the host of lesser divinities and spirits. Ultimately, all are seen as manifestations of a single divine force that pervades the universe. This sense of underlying unity is expressed in texts, such as the passage from the Bhagavad-Gita quoted at the beginning of this chapter; in the different potentials of women represented in the various manifestations of Devi; and in composite statues that are split down the middle—half Shiva, half Vishnu—as if to say that they are complementary aspects of one cosmic principle.

Hinduism offers the worshiper a variety of ways to approach god and obtain divine favor—through special knowledge of sacred truths, mental and physical discipline, or extraordinary devotion to the deity. Worship centers on the temples, which range from humble village shrines to magnificent, richly decorated stone edifices built under royal patronage. Beautifully proportioned statues beckon the deity to take up temporary residence within the image, to be reached and beseeched by eager worshipers. A common form of worship is *puja,* service to the deity, which can take the form of bathing, clothing, or feeding the statue. Potent blessings are conferred on the man or woman who glimpses the divine image.

Pilgrimage to famous shrines and attendance at festivals offer worshipers additional opportunities to show devotion. The entire Indian subcontinent is dotted with sacred places where a worshiper can directly sense and benefit from the inherent power of divinity. Mountains, caves, and certain trees, plants, and rocks are enveloped in an aura of mystery and sanctity. The literal meaning of *tirthayatra,* the term for a pilgrimage site, is "journey to a river-crossing," pointing out the frequent association of Hindu sacred places with flowing water. Hindus consider the Ganges River to be especially sacred, and each year millions of devoted worshipers travel to its banks to bathe and receive the restorative and purifying power of its waters. The habit of pilgrimage to the major shrines has promoted contact and the exchange of ideas among people from different parts of India and has helped create a broad Hindu identity and the concept of India as a single civilization, despite enduring political fragmentation.

Stone Relief Depicting Vishnu Asleep and Dreaming on the Ocean Floor, Fifth Century C.E. In this relief from a temple at Deogarh, in central India, Vishnu reclines on the coiled body of a giant multiheaded serpent that he subdued. The beneficent god of preservation, Vishnu appears in a new incarnation whenever demonic forces threaten the world. The Indian view of the vastness of time is embodied in this mythic image, which conceives of Vishnu as creating and destroying universes as he exhales and inhales. (John C. Huntington)

Religious duties may vary, depending not only on the worshiper's social standing and gender but also on his or her stage of life. A young man from one of the three highest classes (Brahmin, Kshatriya, or Vaishya) undergoes a ritual rebirth through the ceremony of the sacred thread, marking the attainment of manhood and readiness to receive religious knowledge. From this point, the ideal life cycle passes through four stages: (1) the young man becomes a student and studies the sacred texts; (2) he then becomes a householder, marries, has children, and acquires material wealth; (3) when his grandchildren are born, he gives up home and family and becomes a forest dweller, meditating on the nature and meaning of existence; (4) he abandons his personal identity altogether and becomes a wandering ascetic awaiting death. In the course of a virtuous life he has fulfilled first his duties to society and then his duties to himself, so that by the end of his life he is so disconnected from the world that he can achieve moksha (liberation).

The successful transformation of a religion based on Vedic antecedents and the ultimate victory of Hinduism over Buddhism—Buddhism was driven from the land of its birth, though it maintains deep roots in Central, East, and Southeast Asia (see Chapters 8 and 11)—are remarkable phenomena. Hinduism responded to the needs of people for personal deities with whom they could establish direct connections. The austerity of Buddhism in its most authentic form, its denial of the importance of gods, and its expectation that individuals find their own path to enlightenment may have demanded too much of ordinary people. The very features that made Mahayana Buddhism more accessible to the populace—gods, saints, and myths—also made it more easily absorbed into the vast social and cultural fabric of Hinduism.

IMPERIAL EXPANSION AND COLLAPSE, 324 B.C.E.–650 C.E.

Political unity in India, on those rare occasions when it has been achieved, has not lasted long. A number of factors have contributed to India's habitual political fragmentation. Different terrains—mountains, foothills, plains, forests, steppes, deserts—called forth different forms of organization and economic activity, and peoples occupying topographically diverse zones differed from one another in language and cultural practices. Perhaps the most significant barrier to political unity lay in the complex social hierarchy. Individuals identified themselves primarily in terms of their class and caste (birth group); allegiance to a higher political authority was of secondary concern.

Despite these divisive factors, two empires arose in the Ganges Plain: the Mauryan Empire of the fourth to second centuries B.C.E. and the Gupta Empire of the fourth to sixth centuries C.E. Each extended political control over a substantial portion of the subcontinent and fostered the formation of a common Indian civilization.

The Mauryan Empire, 324–184 B.C.E.

Around 600 B.C.E. separate kinship groups and independent states dotted the landscape of north India. The kingdom of Magadha, in eastern India south of the Ganges (see Map 7.1), began to play an increasingly influential role, however, thanks to wealth based on agriculture, iron mines, and its strategic location astride the trade routes of the eastern Ganges Basin. In the late fourth century B.C.E. Chandragupta Maurya°, a young man who may have belonged to the Vaishya or Shudra class, gained control of the kingdom of Magadha and expanded it into the **Mauryan Empire**—India's first centralized empire. He may have been inspired by the example of Alexander the Great, who had followed up his conquest of the Persian Empire with a foray into the Punjab (northern Pakistan) in 326 B.C.E. (see Chapter 5). Indeed, Greek tradition claimed that Alexander met a young Indian native by the name of "Sandracottus," an apparent corruption of "Chandragupta."

The collapse of Greek rule in the Punjab after the death of Alexander created a power vacuum in the northwest. Chandragupta (r. 324–301 B.C.E.) and his successors Bindusara (r. 301–269 B.C.E.) and Ashoka (r. 269–232 B.C.E.) extended Mauryan control over the entire subcontinent except for the southern tip of the peninsula. Not until the height of the Mughal Empire of the seventeenth century C.E. and then the advent of British rule in the nineteenth century was so much of India again under the control of a single government.

Tradition holds that Kautilya, a crafty elderly Brahmin, guided Chandragupta in his conquests and consolidation of power. Kautilya is said to have written a surviving treatise on government, the *Arthashastra*°. Although recent studies have shown that the *Arthashastra* in its present form is a product of the third century C.E., its core text may well go back to Kautilya. This coldly pragmatic guide to political success and survival advocates the so-called *mandala*° (circle) theory of foreign policy: "My enemy's enemy is my friend." It also relates a long list of schemes for enforcing and increasing the collection of tax revenues, and it prescribes the use of spies to keep watch on everyone in the kingdom.

A tax equivalent to one-fourth the value of the harvest supported the Mauryan kings and government. Close relatives and associates of the king governed administrative districts based on traditional ethnic boundaries. A large imperial army—with infantry, cavalry, chariot, and elephant divisions—and royal control of mines, shipbuilding, and the manufacture of armaments further secured power. Standard coinage issued throughout the empire fostered support for the government and military and promoted trade.

The Mauryan capital was at Pataliputra (modern Patna), where five tributaries join the Ganges. Several extant descriptions of the city composed by foreign visitors provide valuable information and testify to the international connections of the Indian monarchs. Surrounded

Maurya (MORE-yuh) **Arthashastra** (ahr-thuh-SHAHS-truh) **mandala** (man-DAH-luh)

by a timber wall and moat, the city extended along the river for 8 miles (13 kilometers). It was governed by six committees with responsibility for features of urban life such as manufacturing, trade, sales, taxes, the welfare of foreigners, and the registration of births and deaths.

Ashoka, Chandragupta's grandson, is an outstanding figure in early Indian history. At the beginning of his reign he engaged in military campaigns that extended the boundaries of the empire. During his conquest of Kalinga (modern Orissa, a coastal region southeast of Magadha), hundreds of thousands of people were killed, wounded, or deported. Overwhelmed by the brutality of this victory, the young monarch became a convert to Buddhism and preached nonviolence, morality, moderation, and religious tolerance in both government and private life.

Ashoka publicized this program by inscribing edicts on great rocks and polished pillars of sandstone scattered throughout his enormous empire. Among the inscriptions that have survived—they constitute the earliest decipherable Indian writing—is the following:

> For a long time in the past, for many hundreds of years have increased the sacrificial slaughter of animals, violence toward creatures, unfilial conduct toward kinsmen, improper conduct toward Brahmins and ascetics. Now with the practice of morality by King [Ashoka], the sound of war drums has become the call to morality . . . You [government officials] are appointed to rule over thousands of human beings in the expectation that you will win the affection of all men. All men are my children. Just as I desire that my children will fare well and be happy in this world and the next, I desire the same for all men . . . King [Ashoka] . . . desires that there should be the growth of the essential spirit of morality or holiness among all sects . . . There should not be glorification of one's own sect and denunciation of the sect of others for little or no reason. For all the sects are worthy of reverence for one reason or another.[2]

Ashoka, however, was not naive. Despite his commitment to employing peaceful means whenever possible, he hastened to remind potential transgressors that "the king, remorseful as he is, has the strength to punish the wrongdoers who do not repent."

Commerce and Culture in an Era of Political Fragmentation

The Mauryan Empire prospered for a time after Ashoka's death in 232 B.C.E. Then, weakened by dynastic disputes, it collapsed from the pressure of attacks in the northwest in 184 B.C.E. Five hundred years passed before another indigenous state was able to extend its control over northern India.

In the meantime, a series of foreign powers dominated the northwest, present-day Afghanistan and Pakistan, and extended their influence east and south. The first was the Greco-Bactrian kingdom (180–50 B.C.E.), descended from troops and settlers left in Afghanistan by Alexander the Great. Greek influence is especially evident in the art of this period and in the designs of coins. Occupation by two nomadic peoples from Central Asia followed, resulting from large-scale movements of peoples set off by the pressure of Han Chinese forces on the Xiongnu (see Chapter 6). The Shakas, an Iranian people known as Scythians in the Mediterranean world, driven southwest along the edge of the mountain barrier of the Pamirs and Himalayas, were dominant from 50 B.C.E. to 50 C.E. They were followed by the Kushans°, originally from Xinjiang in northwest China, who were preeminent from 50 to 240 C.E. At its height the Kushan kingdom controlled much of present-day Uzbekistan, Afghanistan, Pakistan, and northwest India, fostering trade and prosperity by connecting to both the overland Silk Road and Arabian seaports (see Chapter 8). Several foreign kings—most notably the Greco-Bactrian Milinda (Menander in Greek) and the Kushan Kanishka—were converts to Buddhism, a logical choice because of the lack of an easy mechanism for working foreigners into the Hindu system of class and caste. The eastern Ganges region reverted to a patchwork of small principalities, as it had been before the Mauryan era.

Despite the political fragmentation of India in the five centuries after the collapse of the Mauryan Empire, there were many signs of economic, cultural, and intellectual development. The network of roads and towns that had sprung up under the Mauryans fostered lively commerce within the subcontinent, and India was at the heart of international land and sea trade routes that linked China, Southeast Asia, Central Asia, the Middle East, East Africa, and the lands of the Mediterranean. In the absence of a strong central authority, guilds of merchants and artisans became politically powerful in the Indian towns. Their wealth enabled them to serve as patrons of culture and to endow the religious sects to which they adhered—particularly Buddhism and Jainism—with richly decorated temples and monuments.

During the last centuries B.C.E. and first centuries C.E. the two greatest Indian epics, the *Ramayana* and the *Mahabharata,* based on oral predecessors dating back many centuries, achieved their final form. The events that both epics describe are said to have occurred several million years in the past, but the political forms, social organization, and other elements of cultural context—proud kings,

Kushan (KOO-shahn)

beautiful queens, wars among kinship groups, heroic conduct, and chivalric values—seem to reflect the conditions of the early Vedic period, when Arya warrior societies were moving onto the Ganges Plain.

The *Ramayana* relates the exploits of Rama, a heroic prince, who is an incarnation of the god Vishnu. When his beautiful wife is kidnapped, aided by his loyal brother and the king of the monkeys, he defeats and destroys the chief of the demons and his evil horde. The vast pageant of the ***Mahabharata*** (it is eight times the length of the Greek *Iliad* and *Odyssey* combined) tells the story of two sets of cousins, the Pandavas and Kauravas, whose quarrel over succession to the throne leads them to a cataclysmic battle at the field of Kurukshetra. The battle is so destructive on all sides that the eventual winner, Yudhishthira, is reluctant to accept the fruits of so tragic a victory.

The ***Bhagavad-Gita,*** quoted at the beginning of this chapter, is a self-contained (and perhaps originally separate) episode set in the midst of those events. The great hero Arjuna, at first reluctant to fight his own kinsmen, is tutored by the god Krishna and learns the necessity of fulfilling his duty as a warrior. Death means nothing in a universe in which souls will be reborn again and again. The climactic moment comes when Krishna reveals his true appearance—awesome and overwhelmingly powerful—and his identity as time itself, the force behind all creation and destruction. The Bhagavad-Gita offers an attractive resolution to the tension in Indian civilization between duty to society and duty to one's own soul. Disciplined action—that is, action taken without regard for any personal benefits that might derive from it—is a form of service to the gods and will be rewarded by release from the cycle of rebirths.

This era also saw significant advances in science and technology. Indian doctors had a wide knowledge of herbal remedies and were in demand in the courts of western and southern Asia. Indian scholars made impressive strides in linguistics. Panini (late fourth century B.C.E.) undertook a detailed analysis of Sanskrit word forms and grammar. The work of Panini and later linguists led to the standardization of Sanskrit, which arrested its natural development and turned it into a formal, literary language. Prakrits—popular dialects—emerged to become the ancestors of the modern Indo-European languages of northern and central India.

This period of political fragmentation in the north also saw the rise of important states in central India, particularly the Andhra dynasty in the Deccan Plateau (from the second century B.C.E. to the second century C.E.), and the three **Tamil kingdoms** of Cholas, Pandyas, and Cheras in southern India (see Map 7.1). The three Tamil kingdoms were in frequent conflict with one another and experienced periods of ascendancy and decline, but they persisted in one form or another for over two thousand years. Historians regard the period from the third century B.C.E. to the third century C.E. as a "classical" period of great literary and artistic productivity in Tamil society. Under the patronage of the Pandya kings and the intellectual leadership of an academy of five hundred authors, works of literature on a wide range of topics—grammatical treatises, collections of ethical proverbs, epics, and short poems about love, war, wealth, and the beauty of nature—were produced, and music, dance, and drama were performed.

The Gupta Empire, 320–550 C.E.

In the early fourth century C.E. a new imperial entity took shape in northern India. Like its Mauryan predecessor, the **Gupta Empire** grew out of the kingdom of Magadha on the Ganges Plain and had its capital at Pataliputra. Clear proof that the founder of this empire consciously modeled himself on the Mauryans is the fact that he called himself Chandra Gupta (r. 320–335), borrowing the very name of the Mauryan founder. A claim to wide dominion was embodied in the title that the monarchs of this dynasty assumed—"Great King of Kings"—although they never controlled territories as extensive as those of the Mauryans. Nevertheless, over the fifteen-year reign of Chandra Gupta and the forty-year reigns of his three successors—Samudra Gupta, Chandra Gupta II, and Kumara Gupta—Gupta power and influence reached across northern and central India, west to Punjab and east to Bengal, north to Kashmir, and south into the Deccan Plateau (see Map 7.1).

This new empire enjoyed the same strategic advantages as its Mauryan predecessor, sitting astride important trade routes, exploiting the agricultural productivity of the Ganges Plain, and controlling nearby iron deposits. It adopted similar methods for raising revenue and administering broad territories. The chief source of revenue was a 25 percent tax on agriculture. Those who used the irrigation network also had to pay for the service, and there were special taxes on particular commodities. The state maintained monopolies in key areas such as the mining of metals and salt. The state also owned extensive tracts of farmland and demanded a specified number of days of labor annually from the subjects for the construction and upkeep of roads, wells, and the irrigation network.

Gupta control, however, was never as effectively centralized as Mauryan authority. The Gupta administrative bureaucracy and intelligence network were smaller and less pervasive. A powerful army maintained tight control and taxation in the core of the empire, but governors had a free hand in organizing the outlying areas. The position of governor offered tempting opportunities to exploit the populace. It often was hereditary, passed from father to son in families of high-ranking members of the civil and military administrations. Distant subordinate kingdoms and areas inhabited by kinship groups were expected to make annual donations of tribute, and garrisons were stationed at certain key frontier points to keep open the lines of trade and expedite the collection of customs duties.

Limited in its ability to enforce its will on outlying areas, the empire found ways to "persuade" others to follow its lead. One medium of persuasion was the splendor, beauty, and orderliness of life at the capital and royal court. A constant round of solemn rituals, dramatic ceremonies, and exciting cultural events were such a potent advertisement for the benefits of association with the empire that modern historians point to the Gupta Empire as a good example of a **"theater-state."** The relationship of ruler and subjects in a theater-state also has an economic base. The center collects luxury goods and profits from trade and redistributes them to its dependents through the exchange of gifts and other means. Subordinate princes gained prestige by emulating the Gupta center on whatever scale they could manage, and maintained close ties through visits, gifts, and marriages to the Gupta royal family.

Astronomers, mathematicians, and other scientists received royal Gupta support. Indian mathematicians invented the concept of zero and developed the "Arabic" numerals and system of place-value notation that are in use in most parts of the world today (see Environment and Technology: Indian Mathematics).

Because the moist climate of the Ganges Plain does not favor the preservation of buildings and artifacts, there is relatively little archaeological data for the Gupta era. An eyewitness account, however, provides valuable information about the Gupta kingdom and Pataliputra, its capital city. A Chinese Buddhist monk named Faxian° made a pilgrimage to the homeland of his faith around 400 C.E. and left a record of his journey:

> The royal palace and halls in the midst of the city, which exist now as of old, were all made by spirits which [King Ashoka] employed, and which piled up the stones, reared the walls and gates, and executed the elegant carving and inlaid sculpture-work—in a way which no human hands of this world could accomplish . . . By the side of the stupa of Ashoka, there has been made a Mahayana [Buddhist] monastery, very grand and beautiful; there is also a Hinayana [Theravada] one; the two together containing six hundred or seven hundred monks. The rules of demeanor and the scholastic arrangements in them are worthy of observation . . . The cities and towns of this country are the greatest of all in the Middle Kingdom. The inhabitants are rich and prosperous, and vie with one another in the practice of benevolence and righteousness . . . The heads of the Vaishya families in them establish in the cities houses for dispensing charity and medicines. All the poor and destitute in the country, orphans, widowers, and childless men, maimed people and cripples, and all who are diseased, go to those houses, and are provided with every kind of help.[3]

Various kinds of evidence point to a decline in the status of women in this period (see Diversity and Dominance: The Situation of Women in the *Kama Sutra*). In all likelihood, this was similar to developments in Mesopotamia from the second millennium B.C.E., in Archaic and Classical Greece, and in China from the first millennium B.C.E. In those civilizations, several factors—urbanization, the formation of increasingly complex political and social structures, and the emergence of a nonagricultural middle class that placed high value on the acquisition and inheritance of property—led to a loss of women's rights and an increase in male control over women's behavior.

Over time, women in India lost the right to own or inherit property. They were barred from studying sacred texts and participating in the sacrificial ritual. In many respects, they were treated as equivalent to the lowest class, the Shudra. As in Confucian China, a woman was expected to obey first her father, then her husband, and finally her sons (see Chapter 6). Indian girls were married at an increasingly early age, sometimes as young as six or seven. This practice meant that the prospective husband could be sure of his wife's virginity and, by bringing her up in his own household, could train and shape her to suit his purposes. The most extreme form of control of women's conduct took place in parts of India where a widow was expected to cremate herself on her husband's funeral pyre. This ritual, called *sati*°, was seen as a way of keeping a woman "pure." Women who declined to make this ultimate gesture of devotion were forbidden to remarry, shunned socially, and given little opportunity to earn a living.

Some women escaped these instruments of male control. One way to do so was by entering a Jainist or Buddhist religious community. Status also gave women more freedom. Women who belonged to powerful families and courtesans who were trained in poetry and music as well as in ways of providing sexual pleasure had high social standing and sometimes gave money for the erection of Buddhist stupas and other shrines.

Faxian (fah-shee-en)

sati (suh-TEE)

ENVIRONMENT + TECHNOLOGY

Indian Mathematics

The so-called Arabic numerals used in most parts of the world today were developed in India. The Indian system of place-value notation was far more efficient than the unwieldy numerical systems of Egyptians, Greeks, and Romans, and the invention of zero was a profound intellectual achievement. Indeed, it has to be ranked as one of the most important and influential discoveries in human history. This system is used even more widely than the alphabet derived from the Phoenicians (see Chapter 4) and is, in one sense, the only truly global language.

In its fully developed form the Indian method of arithmetic notation employed a base-10 system. It had separate columns for ones, tens, hundreds, and so forth, as well as a zero sign to indicate the absence of units in a given column. This system makes possible the economical expression of even very large numbers. And it allows for the performance of calculations not possible in a system like the numerals of the Romans, where any real calculation had to be done mentally or on a counting board.

A series of early Indian inscriptions using the numerals from 1 to 9 are deeds of property given to religious institutions by kings or other wealthy individuals. They were incised in the Sanskrit language on copper plates (see below). The earliest known example has a date equivalent to 595 C.E. A sign for zero is attested by the eighth century. Other textual evidence leads to the inference that a place-value system and the zero concept were already known in the fifth century.

This Indian system spread to the Middle East, Southeast Asia, and East Asia by the seventh century. Other peoples quickly recognized its capabilities and adopted it, sometimes using indigenous symbols. Europe received the new technology somewhat later. Gerbert of Aurillac, a French Christian monk, spent time in Spain between 967 and 970, where he was exposed to the mathematics of the Arabs. A great scholar and teacher who eventually became Pope Sylvester II (r. 999–1003), he spread word of the "Arabic" system in the Christian West.

Knowledge of the Indian system of mathematical notation eventually spread throughout Europe, in part through the use of a mechanical calculating device—an improved version of the Roman counting board, with counters inscribed with variants of the Indian numeral forms. Because the counters could be turned sideways or upside down, at first there was considerable variation in the forms. But by the twelfth century they had become standardized into forms close to those in use today. As the capabilities of the place-value system for written calculations became clear, the counting board fell into disuse. The abandonment of this device led to the adoption of the zero sign—not necessary on the counting board, where a column could be left empty—by the twelfth century. Leonardo Fibonacci, a thirteenth century C.E. Italian who learned algebra in Muslim North Africa and employed the Arabic numeral system in his mathematical treatise, gave additional impetus to the movement to discard the traditional system of Roman numerals.

Why was this marvelous system of mathematical notation invented in ancient India? The answer may lie in the way in which its range and versatility correspond to elements of Indian cosmology. The Indians conceived of immense spans of time—trillions of years (far exceeding current scientific estimates of the age of the universe as approximately 14 billion years old)—during which innumerable universes like our own were created, existed for a finite time, then were destroyed. In one popular creation myth, Vishnu is slumbering on the coils of a giant serpent at the bottom of the ocean, and worlds are being created and destroyed as he exhales and inhales. In Indian thought our world, like others, has existed for a series of epochs lasting more than 4 million years, yet the period of its existence is but a brief and insignificant moment in the vast sweep of time. The Indians developed a number system that allowed them to express concepts of this magnitude.

Copper Plate with Indian Numerals
This property deed from western India shows an early form of the symbol system for numbers that spread to the Middle East and Europe, and today is used all over the world. (Facsimile by Georges Ifrah. Reproduced by permission of Georges Ifrah.)

Wall Painting from the Caves at Ajanta, Fifth or Sixth Century C.E During and after the Gupta period, natural caves in the Deccan were turned into complexes of shrines decorated with sculpture and painting. This painting depicts one of the earlier lives of the Buddha, a king named Mahajanaka who lost and regained his kingdom, here listening to his queen, Sivali. While representing scenes from the earlier lives of the Buddha, the artists also give us a glimpse of life at the royal court in their own times. (Benoy K. Behl)

The Mauryans had been Buddhists, but the Gupta monarchs were Hindus. They revived ancient Vedic practices to bring an aura of sanctity to their position. This period also saw a reassertion of the importance of class and caste and the influence of Brahmin priests. Nevertheless, it was an era of religious tolerance. The Gupta kings were patrons for Hindu, Buddhist, and Jain endeavors. Buddhist monasteries with hundreds or even thousands of monks and nuns in residence flourished in the cities. Northern India was the destination of Buddhist pilgrims from Southeast and East Asia, traveling to visit the birthplace of their faith.

The classic form of the Hindu temple evolved during the Gupta era. Sitting atop a raised platform surmounted by high towers, the temple was patterned on the sacred mountain or palace in which the gods of mythology resided, and it represented the inherent order of the universe. From an exterior courtyard worshipers approached the central shrine, where the statue of the deity stood. Paintings or sculptured depictions of gods and mythical events covered the walls of the best-endowed sanctuaries. Cave-temples carved out of rock were also richly adorned with frescoes or with sculpture.

During the period of political fragmentation between the eclipse of the Mauryan Empire and the rise of the Guptas, extensive networks of trade within India, as well as land and sea routes to foreign lands, developed. This vibrant commerce continued into the Gupta period. Coined money served as the medium of exchange, and artisan guilds played an influential role in the economic, political, and religious life of the towns. The Guptas sought control of the ports on the Arabian Sea but saw a decline in trade with the weakened Roman Empire. In compensation, trade with Southeast and East Asia was on the rise. Adventurous merchants from the ports of eastern and southern India made the sea voyage to the Malay° Peninsula and islands of Indonesia in order to exchange Indian cotton cloth, ivory, metalwork, and exotic animals for Chinese silk or Indonesian spices. The overland Silk Road from China was also in operation but was vulnerable to disruption by Central Asian nomads (see Chapter 8).

By the later fifth century C.E. the Gupta Empire was coming under pressure from the Huns. These nomadic invaders from the steppes of Central Asia poured into the northwest corridor. Defense of this distant frontier region eventually exhausted the imperial treasury, and the empire collapsed by 550.

The early seventh century saw a brief but glorious revival of imperial unity. Harsha Vardhana (r. 606–647), ruler of the region around Delhi, extended his power over the northern plain and moved his capital to Kanauj on the Ganges River. We have an account of the life and long reign of this fervent Buddhist, poet, patron of artists,

Malay (muh-LAY)

DIVERSITY AND DOMINANCE

THE SITUATION OF WOMEN IN THE *KAMA SUTRA*

The ancient Indians articulated three broad areas of human concern: Dharma—the realm of religious and moral behavior; Artha—the acquisition of wealth and property; and Kama—the pursuit of pleasure. The Kama Sutra, *which means "Treatise on Pleasure," while best known in the West for its detailed descriptions of erotic activities, is actually far more than a sex manual. It addresses, in a very broad sense, the relations between women and men in ancient Indian society, providing valuable information about the character and activities of men and women, the psychology of relationships, the forms of courtship and marriage, the household responsibilities of married women, appropriate behavior, and much more. The author of this text, Vatsyayana, lived in the third century* C.E. *He claims to be abridging and sharpening a series of earlier texts on the subject.*

When a girl of the same caste, and a virgin, is married in accordance with the precepts of Holy Writ, the results of such a union are the acquisition of Dharma and Artha, offspring, affinity, increase of friends, and untarnished love. For this reason a man should fix his affections upon a girl who is of good family, whose parents are alive, and who is three years or more younger than himself. She should be born of a highly respectable family, possessed of wealth, well connected, and with many relations and friends. She should also be beautiful, of a good disposition, with lucky marks on her body, and with good hair, nails, teeth, ears, eyes and breasts, neither more nor less than they ought to be, and no one of them entirely wanting, and not troubled with a sickly body. The man should, of course, also possess these qualities himself. But at all events, says Ghotakamukha [an earlier writer], a girl who has been already joined with others (i.e. no longer a maiden) should never be loved, for it would be reproachable to do such a thing.

Now in order to bring about a marriage with such a girl as described above, the parents and relations of the man should exert themselves, as also such friends on both sides as may be desired to assist in the matter. These friends should bring to the notice of the girl's parents the faults, both present and future, of all the other men that may wish to marry her, and should at the same time extol even to exaggeration all the excellencies, ancestral, and paternal, of their friend, so as to endear him to them, and particularly to those that may be liked by the girl's mother. One of the friends should also disguise himself as an astrologer, and declare the future good fortune and wealth of his friend by showing the existence of all the lucky omens and signs, the good influence of planets, the auspicious entrance of the sun into a sign of the Zodiac, propitious stars and fortunate marks on his body. Others again should rouse the jealousy of the girl's mother by telling her that their friend has a chance of getting from some other quarter even a better girl than hers.

A girl should be taken as a wife, as also given in marriage, when fortune, signs, omens, and the words of others are favourable, for, says Ghotakamukha, a man should not marry at any time he likes. A girl who is asleep, crying, or gone out of the house when sought in marriage, or who is betrothed to another, should not be married. The following also should be avoided:

- One who is kept concealed
- One who has an ill-sounding name
- One who has her nose depressed
- One who has her nostril turned up
- One who is formed like a male
- One who is bent down
- One who has crooked thighs
- One who has a projecting forehead
- One who has a bald head
- One who does not like purity
- One who has been polluted by another
- One who is affected with the Gulma [glandular enlargement]
- One who is disfigured in any way
- One who has fully arrived at puberty
- One who is a friend
- One who is a younger sister
- One who is a Varshakari [prone to extreme perspiration]

In the same way a girl who is called by the name of one of the twenty-seven stars, or by the name of a tree, or of a river, is considered worthless, as also a girl whose name ends in "r" or "l." But some authors say that prosperity is gained only by marrying that girl to whom one becomes attached, and that therefore no other girl but the one who is loved should be married by anyone.

When a girl becomes marriageable her parents should dress her smartly, and should place her where she can be easily seen by all. Every afternoon, having dressed her and decorated her in a becoming manner, they should send her with her female companions to sports, sacrifices, and marriage ceremonies, and thus show her to advantage in society, because she is a kind of merchandise. They should also receive with kind words and signs of friendliness those of an auspicious appearance who may come accompanied by their friends and relations for the purpose of marrying their daughter, and under some pretext or other having first dressed her becomingly, should then present her to them. . . .

When a girl, possessed of good qualities and well-bred, though born in a humble family, or destitute of wealth, and not therefore desired by her equals, or an orphan girl, or one deprived of her parents, but observing the rules of her family and caste, should wish to bring about her own marriage when she comes of age, such a girl should endeavour to gain over a strong and good looking young man, or a person whom she thinks would marry her on account of the weakness of his mind, and even without the consent of his parents. She should do this by such means as would endear her to the said person, as well as by frequently seeing and meeting him. Her mother also should constantly cause them to meet by means of her female friends, and the daughter of her nurse. The girl herself should try to get alone with her beloved in some quiet place, and at odd times should give him flowers, betel nut, betel leaves and perfumes. She should also show her skill in the practice of the arts, in shampooing, in scratching and in pressing with the nails. She should also talk to him on the subjects he likes best, and discuss with him the ways and means of gaining over and winning the affections of a girl . . .

To the girl also she [the daughter of the girl's nurse, essentially a friend of the same age serving as a go-between] should speak about the excellent qualities of the man, especially of those qualities which she knows are pleasing to the girl. She should, moreover, speak with disparagement of the other lovers of the girl, and talk about the avarice and indiscretion of their parents, and the fickleness of their relations. She should also quote samples of many girls of ancient times, such as Sakoontala and others, who, having united themselves with lovers of their own caste and their own choice, were ever happy afterwards in their society. And she should also tell of other girls who married into great families, and being troubled by rival wives, became wretched and miserable, and were finally abandoned. She should further speak of the good fortune, the continual happiness, the chastity, obedience, and affection of the man, and if the girl gets amorous about him, she should endeavour to allay her shame and her fear as well as her suspicions about any disaster that might result from her marriage. In a word, she should act the whole part of a female messenger by telling the girl all about the man's affection for her, the places he frequented, and the endeavours he made to meet her, and by frequently repeating, "It will be all right if the man will take you away forcibly and unexpectedly." . . .

A virtuous woman, who has affection for her husband, should act in conformity with his wishes as if he were a divine being, and with his consent should take upon herself the whole care of his family. She should keep the whole house well cleaned, and arrange flowers of various kinds in different parts of it, and make the floor smooth and polished so as to give the whole a neat and becoming appearance. She should surround the house with a garden, and place ready in it all the materials required for the morning, noon and evening sacrifices. Moreover she should herself revere the sanctuary of the Household Gods, for, says Gonardiya [another earlier writer], "nothing so much attracts the heart of a householder to his wife as a careful observance of the things mentioned above." . . .

The wife should always avoid the company of female beggars, female Buddhist mendicants, unchaste and roguish women, female fortune tellers and witches. As regards meals, she should always consider what her husband likes and dislikes and what things are good for him, and what are injurious to him. When she hears the sounds of his footsteps coming home she should at once get up and be ready to do whatever he may command her, and either order her female servant to wash his feet, or wash them herself. When going anywhere with her husband, she should put on her ornaments, and without his consent she should not either give or accept invitations, or attend marriages and sacrifices, or sit in the company of female friends, or visit the temples of the Gods. And if she wants to engage in any kind of games or sports, she should not do it against his will. In the same way she should always sit down after him, and get up before him, and should never awaken him when he is asleep.

QUESTIONS FOR ANALYSIS

1. **In what ways are women given essentially equal treatment to men in these excerpts? In what ways are they treated unequally?**
2. **On what bases do men and women choose spouses and lovers?**
3. **What were the most important household responsibilities of ancient Indian women? What social, intellectual, and cultural activities did they engage in?**
4. **In light of the treatise's prescriptions for how a married woman should treat her husband, what do you think was the nature of the emotional relationship of husband and wife? How might this differ from marriages in our society?**

Source: Sir Richard Burton and F. F. Arbuthnot, *The Kama Sutra of Vatsyayana* (1883), sections III.1, III.4, III.5, IV.1, found at http://www.sacred-texts.com/sex/kama/index.htm.

and dynamic warrior, written by the courtier Bana. In addition, the Chinese Buddhist pilgrim Xuanzang° (600–664) left an account of his travels in India during Harsha's reign. After Harsha's death, northern India reverted to its customary state of political fragmentation and remained divided until the Islamic invasions of the eleventh and twelfth centuries (see Chapter 14).

During the centuries of Gupta ascendancy and decline in the north, the Deccan Plateau and the southern part of the peninsula followed an independent path. In this region, where the landscape is segmented by mountains, rocky plateaus, tropical forests, and sharply cut river courses, there were many small centers of power. Later, from the seventh to twelfth centuries, the Pallavas, Cholas, and other warrior dynasties collected tribute and plundered as far as their strength permitted, storing their wealth in urban fortresses. These rulers sought legitimacy and fame as patrons of religion and culture, and much of the distinguished art and architecture of the period was produced in the kingdoms of the south. These kingdoms served as the conduit through which Indian religion and culture reached Southeast Asia.

Southeast Asia, 50–1025 c.e.

Southeast Asia consists of three geographical zones: the Indochina mainland, the Malay Peninsula, and thousands of islands extending on an east-west axis far out into the Pacific Ocean (see Map 7.2). Encompassing a vast area of land and water, this region is now occupied by the countries of Myanmar° (Burma), Thailand, Laos, Cambodia, Vietnam, Malaysia, Singapore, Indonesia, Brunei°, and the Philippines. Poised between the ancient centers of China and India, Southeast Asia has been influenced by the cultures of both civilizations. The region first rose to prominence and prosperity because of its intermediate role in the trade exchanges between southern and eastern Asia.

The strategic importance of Southeast Asia is enhanced by the region's natural resources. This is a geologically active zone; the islands are the tops of a chain of volcanoes. Lying along the equator, Southeast Asia has a tropical climate. The temperature hovers around 80 degrees Fahrenheit (30 degrees Celsius), and the monsoon winds provide dependable rainfall throughout the year. Thanks to several growing cycles each year, the region is capable of supporting a large human population. The most fertile agricultural lands lie along the floodplains of the largest silt-bearing rivers or contain rich volcanic soil deposited by ancient eruptions.

Early Civilization

Rain forest covers much of Southeast Asia. Rain-forest ecosystems are particularly fragile because of the great local variation of plant forms within them and because of the vulnerability of their soil to loss of fertility if the protective forest canopy is removed. As early as 2000 b.c.e. people in this region were clearing land for farming by cutting and burning the vegetation growing on it. The cleared land, known as swidden, was farmed for several growing seasons. When the soil was exhausted, the farmers abandoned the patch, allowing the forest to reclaim it before they cleared it again for agriculture. In the meantime, they cleared and cultivated other nearby fields in similar fashion.

A number of plant and animal species spread from Southeast Asia to other regions. Among them were wet rice (rice cultivated in deliberately flooded fields), soybeans, sugar cane, yams, bananas, coconuts, cocoyams, chickens, and pigs. Rice was the staple food product, for even though rice cultivation is labor-intensive (see Chapter 3), it can support a large population.

Historians believe that the **Malay peoples** who became the dominant population in this region were the product of several waves of migration from southern China beginning around 3000 b.c.e. In some cases the indigenous peoples merged with the Malay newcomers; in other cases they retreated to remote mountain and forest zones. Subsequently, rising population and disputes within communities prompted streams of people to leave the Southeast Asian mainland in the longest-lasting colonization movement in human history. By the first millennium b.c.e. the inhabitants of Southeast Asia had developed impressive navigational skills. They knew how to ride the monsoon winds and interpret the patterns of swells, winds, clouds, and bird and sea life. Over a period of several thousand years groups of Malay peoples in large, double outrigger canoes spread out across the Pacific and Indian Oceans—half the circumference of the earth—to settle thousands of islands.

The inhabitants of Southeast Asia tended to cluster along riverbanks or in fertile volcanic plains. Their fields and villages were never far from the rain forest, with its wild animals and numerous plant species. Forest trees provided fruit, wood, and spices. The shallow waters surrounding the islands teemed with fish. This region was also an early center of metallurgy, particularly bronze. Metalsmiths heated copper and tin ore to the right tem-

Xuanzang (shoo-wen-zahng) **Myanmar** (myahn-MAH) **Brunei** (broo-NIE)

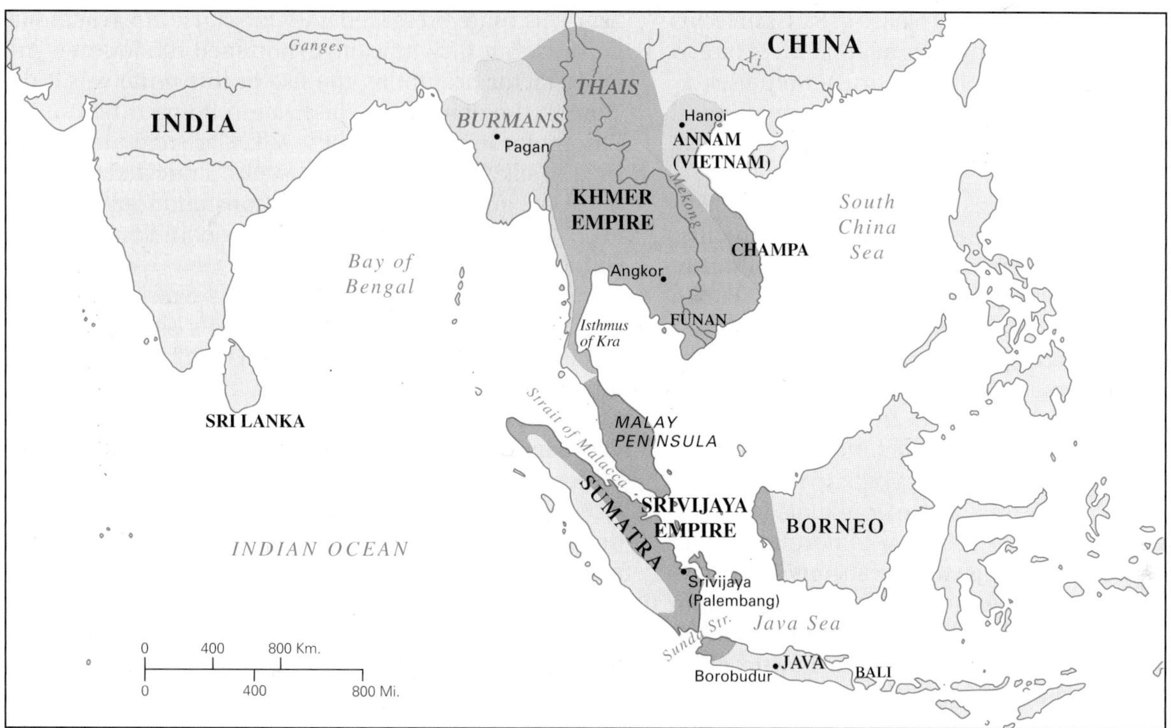

Map 7.2 Southeast Asia Southeast Asia's position between the ancient centers of civilization in India and China had a major impact on its history. In the first millennium C.E. a series of powerful and wealthy states arose in the region by gaining control of major trade routes: first Funan, based in southern Vietnam, Cambodia, and the Malay Peninsula, then Srivijaya on the island of Sumatra, then smaller states on the island of Java. Shifting trade routes led to the demise of one and the rise of others.

perature for producing and shaping bronze implements by using hollow bamboo tubes to funnel a stream of oxygen to the furnace.

The first political units were small. The size of the fundamental unit reflected the number of people who drew water from the same source. Water resource "boards," whose members were representatives of the leading families of the different villages involved, met periodically to allocate and schedule the use of this critical resource.

Northern Indochina, by its geographic proximity, was particularly vulnerable to Chinese pressure and cultural influences, and was under Chinese political control for a thousand years (111 B.C.E.–939 C.E.). Farther south, larger states emerged in the early centuries C.E. in response to two powerful forces: commerce and Hindu-Buddhist culture. Southeast Asia was strategically situated along a new trade route that merchants used to carry Chinese silk westward to India and the Mediterranean. The movements of nomadic peoples had disrupted the old land route across Central Asia. But in India demand for silk was increasing—both for domestic use and for transshipment to the Arabian Gulf and Red Sea to satisfy the fast-growing luxury market in the Roman Empire. At first, a route developed across the South China Sea, by land over the Isthmus of Kra on the Malay peninsula, and across the Bay of Bengal to India (see Map 7.2). Over time, merchants extended this exchange network to include not only silk but also goods from Southeast Asia, such as aromatic woods, resins, and cinnamon, pepper, cloves, nutmeg, and other spices. By serving this trade network and controlling key points, Southeast Asian centers rose to prominence.

The other force leading to the rise of larger political entities was the influence of Hindu-Buddhist culture imported from India. Commerce brought Indian merchants and sailors into the ports of Southeast Asia. As Buddhism spread, Southeast Asia became a way station for Indian missionaries and East Asian pilgrims going to and coming from the birthplace of their faith. Indian cosmology, rituals, art, and statecraft constituted a rich treasury of knowledge and a source of prestige and legitimacy for local rulers who adopted them. The use of Sanskrit terms such as *maharaja*° (great king), the adaptation of Indian ceremonial practices and forms of artistic representation, and the employment of scribes skilled in writing all proved invaluable to the most ambitious and capable Southeast Asian rulers.

The first major Southeast Asian center, called **"Funan°"** by Chinese visitors, flourished between the first and sixth centuries C.E. (see Map 7.2). Its capital was at the modern site of Oc-Eo in southern Vietnam. Funan occupied the delta of the Mekong° River, a "rice bowl" capable of supporting a large population. The rulers mobilized large numbers of laborers to dig irrigation channels and prevent destructive floods. By extending its control over most of southern Indochina and the Malay Peninsula, Funan was able to dominate the Isthmus of Kra—a key point on the trade route from India to China. Seaborne merchants from the ports of northeast India found that offloading their goods from ships and carrying them across the narrow strip of land was safer than making the 1,000-mile (1,600-kilometer) voyage around the Malay Peninsula—a dangerous trip marked by treacherous currents, rocky shoals, and pirates. Once the portage across the isthmus was finished, the merchants needed food and lodging while they waited for the monsoon winds to shift so that they could make the last leg of the voyage to China by sea. Funan stockpiled food and provided security for those engaged in this trade—in return, most probably, for customs duties and other fees.

According to one legend (a sure indicator of the influence of Indian culture in this region), the kingdom of Funan arose out of the marriage of an Indian Brahmin and a local princess. Chinese observers have left reports of the prosperity and sophistication of Funan, emphasizing the presence of walled cities, palaces, archives, systems of taxation, and state-organized agriculture. Nevertheless, for reasons not yet clear to modern historians, Funan declined in the sixth century. The most likely explanation is that international trade routes changed and Funan no longer held a strategic position.

The Srivijayan Kingdom

By the sixth century a new, all-sea route had developed. Merchants and travelers from south India and Sri Lanka sailed through the Strait of Malacca (lying between the west side of the Malay Peninsula and the northeast coast of the large island of Sumatra) and into the South China Sea. This route presented both human and navigational hazards, but it significantly shortened the journey. Another factor promoting the use of this route was a decline in the demand of the Eastern Roman (Byzantine) Empire for imported Chinese silk. Christian monks had hidden silkworms in bamboo stalks, smuggled them out of China, and brought them to Constantinople, thereby exposing the secret of silk production and breaking the Chinese monopoly.

A new center of power, **Srivijaya**°—Sanskrit for "Great Conquest"—was dominating the new southerly route by 683 C.E. The capital of the Srivijayan kingdom was at modern-day Palembang, 50 miles (80 kilometers) up the Musi River from the southeastern coast of Sumatra. Srivijaya had a good natural harbor on a broad and navigable river and a productive agricultural hinterland. The kingdom was well situated to control the southern part of the Malay Peninsula, Sumatra, parts of Java and Borneo, and the Malacca° and Sunda straits—vital passageways for shipping (see Map 7.2).

The Srivijayan capital, one of several thriving Sumatran river ports, gained ascendancy over its rivals and assumed control of the international trade route by fusing four distinct ecological zones into an interdependent network. The core area was the productive agricultural plain along the Musi River. The king and his clerks, scribes, judges, and tax collectors controlled this zone directly. Less direct was the king's control of the second zone, the upland regions of Sumatra's interior, which were the source of commercially valuable forest products. The local rulers of this area were bound to the center in a dependent relationship held together by oaths of loyalty, elaborate court ceremonies, and the sharing of profits from trade. The third zone consisted of river ports that had been Srivijaya's main rivals. They were conquered and controlled thanks to an alliance between Srivijaya and neighboring sea nomads, pirates who served as a Srivijayan navy as long as the king guaranteed them a steady income.

The fourth zone was a fertile "rice bowl" on the central plain of the nearby island of Java—a region so productive, because of its volcanic soil, that it houses and feeds the majority of the population of present-day Indonesia. Srivijayan monarchs maintained alliances with several ruling dynasties that controlled this region. The alliances were cemented by intermarriage, and the Srivijayan kings even claimed descent from the main Javanese dynasty. These arrangements gave Srivijaya easy access to the large quantities of foodstuffs that people living in the capital and merchants and sailors visiting the various ports needed.

maharaja (mah-huh-RAH-juh) **Funan** (FOO-nahn) **Mekong** (MAY-kawng)

Srivijaya (sree-vih-JUH-yuh) **Malacca** (muh-LAH-kuh)

The kings of Srivijaya who constructed and maintained this complex network of social, political, and economic relationships were men of extraordinary energy and skill. Although their authority depended in part on force, it owed more to diplomatic and even theatrical talents. Like the Gupta monarchy, Srivijaya should be seen as a theater-state, securing its position of prominence and binding dependents by its sheer splendor and its ability to attract labor, talent, and luxury products. According to one tradition, the Srivijayan monarch was so wealthy that he deposited bricks of gold in the river estuary to appease the local gods, and a hillside near town was said to be covered with silver and gold images of the Buddha to which devotees brought lotus-shaped vessels of gold. The gold originated in East or West Africa and came to Southeast Asia through trade with the Muslim world (see Chapter 8).

The Srivijayan king drew upon Buddhist conceptions to present himself as a bodhisattva, one who had achieved enlightenment and sought to share his precious insights for the betterment of his subjects. The king was believed to have great magical powers. He mediated between the spiritually potent realms of the mountains and the sea, and he embodied powerful forces of fertility associated with the rivers in flood. His capital and court were the scene of ceremonies designed to dazzle observers and reinforce his image of wealth, power, and sanctity. Subjects and visitors wanted to be associated with his success. Subordinate rulers took oaths of loyalty that carried dire threats of punishment for violations, and in their own home locales they imitated the splendid ceremonials of the capital.

The kings built and patronized Buddhist monasteries and schools. In central Java local dynasties allied with Srivijaya built magnificent temple complexes to advertise their glory. The most famous of these, **Borobodur**°, built between 770 C.E. and 825 C.E., was the largest human construction in the Southern Hemisphere. The winding ascent through the ten tiers of this mountain of volcanic stone is a Buddhist allegory for the progressive stages of enlightenment. Numerous sculptured reliefs depicting Buddhist legends provide modern viewers with glimpses of daily life in early Java.

In all of this, the cultural influence of India was paramount. Shrewd Malay rulers looked to Indian traditions to supply conceptual rationales for kingship and social order. They utilized Indian models of bureaucracy and the Sanskrit system of writing to expedite government business. Their special connection to powerful gods and higher knowledge raised them above their rivals. Southeast Asia's central position on long-distance trade and pilgrimage routes guaranteed the presence of foreigners with useful skills to serve as priests, scribes, and administrators. Hindu beliefs and social structures have survived to this day on the island of Bali, east of Java. Even more influential was Buddhism because of the flow of Buddhist pilgrims and missionaries between East Asia and India. (Islam, the dominant religion in modern-day Indonesia, was not introduced until the thirteenth century.)

Stone Image of Durga, a Fierce Manifestation of the Goddess, Slaying the Buffalo-Demon, from Java, Thirteenth Century C.E. The Goddess, one of the three major Hindu divinities, appeared in a number of complementary manifestations. The most dramatic is Durga, a murderous warrior equipped with multiple divine weapons. That the same divine figure could, in its other manifestations, represent life-bringing fertility and docile wifely duties in the household shows how attuned Indian thought was to the interconnectedness of different aspects of life. (Eliot Elisofon Collection, Harry Ransom Humanities Center, University of Texas, Austin)

The Southeast Asian kingdoms, however, were not just passive recipients of Indian culture. They took what was useful to them and synthesized it with indigenous beliefs, values, and institutions—for example, local concepts of chiefship, ancestor worship, and forms of oaths. Moreover, they trained their own people in the new ways, so that the bureaucracy contained both foreign experts and native disciples. The whole process amounted

Borobodur (booh-roe-boe-DOOR)

View of the Buddhist Monument at Borobodur, Java The great monument was more than 300 feet (90 meters) in length and over 100 feet (30 meters) high. Pilgrims made a three-mile-long (nearly 5-kilometer-long) winding ascent through ten levels intended to represent the ideal Buddhist journey from ignorance to enlightenment. (Josephine Powell, Rome)

to a cultural dialogue between India and Southeast Asia, in which both were active participants.

The kings of Srivijaya carried out this marvelous balancing act for centuries. But the system they erected was vulnerable to shifts in the pattern of international trade. Some such change must have contributed to the decline of Srivijaya in the eleventh century, even though the immediate cause was a destructive raid on the Srivijayan capital by forces of the Chola kingdom of southeast India in 1025 C.E.

After the decline of Srivijaya, the leading role passed to new, vigorous kingdoms on the eastern end of Java, and the maritime realm of Southeast Asia remained prosperous and connected to the international network of trade. A few Europeans were aware of this region as a source of spices and other luxury items. Some four centuries after the decline of Srivijaya, an Italian navigator serving under the flag of Spain—Christopher Columbus—embarked on a westward course across the Atlantic Ocean, seeking to establish a direct route to the fabled "Indies" from which the spices came.

CONCLUSION

This chapter traces the emergence of complex societies in India and Southeast Asia between the second millennium B.C.E. and the first millennium C.E. Because of migrations, trade, and the spread of belief systems, an Indian style of civilization spread throughout the subcontinent and adjoining regions and eventually made its way to the mainland and island chains of Southeast Asia. In this period were laid cultural foundations that in large measure still endure.

The development and spread of belief systems—Vedism, Buddhism, Jainism, and Hinduism—have a central place in this chapter because nearly all the sources are religious. A visitor to a museum who examines artifacts from ancient Mesopotamia, Egypt, the Greco-Roman Mediterranean, China, and India will find that a prominent part of the collection consists of objects from religious shrines or with cultic function. Only the Indian artifacts, however, will be almost exclusively from the religious sphere.

The prolific use of writing came later to India than to other parts of the Eastern Hemisphere, for reasons particular to the Indian situation. Like Indian artifacts, most of the ancient Indian texts are of a religious nature. Ancient Indians did not generate historiographic texts of the kind written elsewhere in the ancient world, primarily because they held a strikingly different view of time. Mesopotamian scribes compiled lists of political and military events and the strange celestial and earthly phenomena that coincided with them. They were inspired by a cyclical conception of time and believed that the recurrence of an omen at some future date potentially signaled a repetition of the historical event associated with it. Greek and Roman historians described and analyzed the progress of wars and the character of rulers. They believed that these accounts would prove useful because of the essential constancy of human nature and the value of understanding the past as a sequence of causally linked events. Chinese annalists set down the deeds and conduct of rulers as inspirational models of right conduct and cautionary tales of the consequences of impropriety. In contrast, the distinctive Indian view of time—as vast epochs in which universes are created and destroyed again and again and the essential spirit of living creatures is reincarnated repeatedly—made the particulars of any brief moment seem relatively unilluminating.

The tension between divisive and unifying forces can be seen in many aspects of Indian life. Political and social division has been the norm throughout much of the history of India. It is a consequence of the topographical and environmental diversity of the subcontinent and the complex mix of ethnic and linguistic groups inhabiting it. The elaborate structure of classes and castes was a response to this diversity—an attempt to organize the population and position individuals within an accepted hierarchy, as well as to regulate group interactions. Strong central governments, such as those of the Mauryan and Gupta kings, gained ascendancy for a time and promoted prosperity and development. They rose to dominance by gaining control of metal resources and important trade routes, developing effective military and administrative institutions, and creating cultural forms that inspired admiration and emulation. However, as in Archaic Greece and Warring States China, the periods of fragmentation and multiple small centers of power seemed as economically and intellectually fertile and dynamic as the periods of unity.

India possessed many of the advanced technologies available elsewhere in the ancient world—agriculture, irrigation, metallurgy, textile manufacture, monumental construction, military technology, writing, and systems of administration. But of all the ancient societies, India made the most profound contribution to mathematics, devising the so-called Arabic numerals and place-value notation.

Many distinctive social and intellectual features of Indian civilization—the class and caste system, models of kingship and statecraft, and Vedic, Jainist, and Buddhist belief systems—originated in the great river valleys of the north, where descendants of Indo-European immigrants came to dominate. Hinduism embraced elements drawn from the Dravidian cultures of the south as well as from Buddhism. Hindu beliefs and practices are less fixed and circumscribed than the beliefs and practices of Judaism, Christianity, and Islam, which rely on clearly defined textual and organizational sources of authority. The capacity of the Hindu tradition to assimilate a wide range of popular beliefs facilitated the spread of elements of a common Indian civilization across the subcontinent, although there was, and is, considerable variation from one region to another.

This same malleable quality also came into play as the pace of international commerce quickened in the first millennium C.E. and Indian merchants embarking by sea for East Asia passed through Funan, Srivijaya, and other commercial centers in Southeast Asia. Indigenous elites in Southeast Asia came into contact with Indian merchants, sailors, and pilgrims. Involvement in the lucrative long-distance commerce and adoption of Indian political and religious ideas and methods brought wealth, power, and prestige to able and ambitious leaders. Finding elements of Indian civilization attractive and useful, they fused it with their own traditions to create a culture unique to Southeast Asia. Chapter 8 describes how the networks of long-distance trade and communication established in the Eastern Hemisphere in antiquity continued to expand and foster technological and cultural development in the subsequent era.

Key Terms

monsoon
Vedas
varna
jati
karma
moksha
Buddha
Mahayana Buddhism
Theravada Buddhism
Hinduism
Mauryan Empire
Ashoka
Mahabharata
Bhagavad-Gita
Tamil kingdoms
Gupta Empire
theater-state
Malay peoples
Funan
Srivijaya
Borobodur

Suggested Reading

A useful starting point for the Indian subcontinent is Karl J. Schmidt, *An Atlas and Survey of South Asian History* (1995), with maps and facing text illustrating geographic, environmental, cultural, and historical features of South Asian civilization. Concise discussions of the history of ancient India can be found in Stanley Wolpert, *A New History of India,* 3d ed. (1989), and Romila Thapar, *A History of India,* vol. 1 (1966). D. D. Kosambi, *Ancient India: A History of Its Culture and Civilization* (1965), and Paul Masson-Oursel, *Ancient India and Indian Civilization* (1998), are fuller presentations.

Ainslie T. Embree, *Sources of Indian Tradition,* vol. 1, 2d ed. (1988), contains translations of primary texts, with the emphasis almost entirely on religion and few materials from southern India. Barbara Stoler Miller, *The Bhagavad-Gita: Krishna's Counsel in Time of War* (1986), is a readable translation of this ancient classic with a useful introduction and notes. An abbreviated version of the greatest Indian epic can be found in R. K. Narayan, *The Mahabharata: A Shortened Modern Prose Version of the Indian Epic* (1978). The filmed version of Peter Brook's stage production of *The Mahabharata* (3 videos, 1989) generated much controversy because of its British director and multicultural cast, but it is a painless introduction to the plot and main characters. Robert Goldman, *The Ramayana of Valmiki: An Epic of Ancient India* (1984), makes available the other Indian epic. To sample the fascinating document on state building supposedly composed by the adviser to the founder of the Mauryan Empire, see T. N. Ramaswamy, *Essentials of Indian Statecraft: Kautilya's Arthasastra for Contemporary Readers* (1962). James Legge, *The Travels of Fa-hien [Faxian]: Fa-hien's Record of Buddhistic Kingdoms* (1971), and John W. McCrindle, *Ancient India as Described by Megasthenes and Arrian* (1877), provide translations of reports of foreign visitors to ancient India.

A number of works explore political institutions and ideas in ancient India: Charles Drekmeier, *Kingship and Community in Early India* (1962); John W. Spellman, *Political Theory of Ancient India: A Study of Kingship from the Earliest Times to Circa A.D. 300* (1964); and R. S. Sharma, *Aspects of Political Ideas and Institutions in Ancient India,* 2d ed. (1968). Romila Thapar, *Asoka and the Decline of the Mauryas* (1963), is a detailed study of the most interesting and important Maurya king.

For fundamental Indian social and religious conceptions see David R. Kinsley, *Hinduism: A Cultural Perspective* (1982). See also David G. Mandelbaum, *Society in India,* 2 vols. (1970), who provides essential insights into the complex relationship of class and caste. Kevin Trainor, ed., *Buddhism: The Illustrated Guide* (2001), devotes several chapters to Buddhism in Ancient India. Jacob Pandian, *The Making of India and Indian Tradition* (1995), contains much revealing historical material, with particular attention to often neglected regions such as southern India, in its effort to explain the diversity of contemporary India. The chapter on ancient India by Karen Lang in Bella Vivante, ed., *Women's Roles in Ancient Civilizations: A Reference Guide* (1999), provides an up-to-date overview and bibliography. Stephanie W. Jamison, *Sacrificed Wife/Sacrificer's Wife: Women, Ritual, and Hospitality in Ancient India* (1996), deals with the roles early Indian women filled in ritual practices and the creation and maintenance of social relations, including several forms of marriage. Stella Kramrisch, *The Hindu Temple,* 2 vols. (1946), and Surinder M. Bhardwaj, *Hindu Places of Pilgrimage in India: A Study in Cultural Geography* (1973), examine important elements of worship in the Hindu tradition.

Roy C. Craven, *Indian Art* (1976), is a clear, historically organized treatment of its subject. Mario Bussagli and Calembus Sivaramamurti, *5000 Years of the Art of India* (1971), is lavishly illustrated. For the uniqueness and decisive historical impact of Indian mathematics see Georges Ifrah, *From One to Zero: A Universal History of Numbers* (1985).

Kameshwar Prasad, *Cities, Crafts, and Commerce under the Kusanas* (1984), discusses the dynamic, multicultural domain of the Kushans. Jean W. Sedlar, *India and the Greek World: A Study in the Transmission of Culture* (1980), relates the interaction of Greek and Indian civilizations. Lionel Casson, *The Periplus Maris Erythraei: Text with Introduction, Translation and Commentary* (1989), explicates a fascinating mariner's guide to the ports, trade goods, and human and navigational hazards of Indian Ocean commerce in the Roman era. Xinru Liu, *Ancient India and Ancient China: Trade and Religious Exchanges, A.D. 1–600* (1994), covers interactions with East Asia.

Richard Ulack and Gyula Pauer, *Atlas of Southeast Asia* (1989), provides a very brief introduction and maps for the environment and early history of Southeast Asia. Nicholas Tarling, ed., *The Cambridge History of Southeast Asia,* vol. 1 (1999); D. R. SarDeSai, *Southeast Asia: Past and Present,* 3d ed. (1994); and Milton E. Osborne, *Southeast Asia: An Introductory History* (1995), provide general accounts of Southeast Asian history. Lynda Shaffer, *Maritime Southeast Asia to 1500* (1996), focuses on early Southeast Asian history in a world historical context. Also useful is Kenneth R. Hall, *Maritime Trade and State Development in Early Southeast Asia* (1985).

The art of Southeast Asia is taken up by M. C. S. Diskul, *The Art of Srivijaya* (1980); Maud Girard-Geslan et al., *Art of Southeast Asia* (1998); and Daigoro Chihara, *Hindu-Buddhist Architecture in Southeast Asia* (1996).

Notes

1. Barbara Stoler Miller, *The Bhagavad-Gita: Krishna's Counsel in Time of War* (New York: Bantam, 1986), 98–99.
2. B. G. Gokhale, *Asoka Maurya* (New York: Twayne, 1966), 152–153, 156–157, 160.
3. James Legge, *The Travels of Fa-hien: Fa-hien's Record of Buddhistic Kingdoms* (Delhi: Oriental Publishers, 1971), 77–79.

ISSUES IN WORLD HISTORY

Oral Societies and the Consequences of Literacy

The availability of written documents is one of the key factors historians use to divide human prehistory from history. When we can read what the people of the past thought and said about their lives, we can begin to understand their cultures, institutions, values, and beliefs in ways that are not possible based only on the material remains unearthed by archaeologists.

There are profound differences between nonliterate and literate societies. However, literacy and nonliteracy are not absolute alternatives. Personal literacy ranges from illiteracy through many shades of partial literacy (the ability to write one's name or to read simple texts with difficulty) to the fluent ability to read that is possessed by anyone reading this textbook. And there are degrees of societal literacy, ranging from nonliteracy through so-called craft literacy—in which a small specialized elite uses writing for limited purposes, such as administrative record-keeping—and a spectrum of conditions in which more and more people use writing for more and more purposes, up to the near-universal literacy and the use of writing for innumerable purposes that is the norm in the developed world in our times.

The vast majority of human beings of the last five to six thousand years living in societies that possessed the technology of writing were not themselves literate. If most people in a society rely on the spoken word and memory, that culture is essentially "oral" even if some members know how to write. The differences between oral and literate cultures are immense, affecting not only the kinds of knowledge that are valued and the forms in which information is preserved, but the very use of language, the categories for conceptualizing the world, and ultimately the hard-wiring of the individual human brain (now recognized by neuroscientists to be strongly influenced by individual experience and mental activity).

Ancient Greece of the Archaic and Classical periods (ca. 800–323 B.C.E.) offers a particularly instructive case study because we can observe the process by which writing was introduced into an oral society as well as the far-reaching consequences. The Greeks of the Dark Age and early Archaic Period lived in a purely oral society; all knowledge was preserved in human memory and passed on by telling it to others. The *Iliad* and the *Odyssey* (ca. 700 B.C.E.), Homer's epic poems, reflect this state of affairs. Scholars recognize that the creator of these poems was an oral poet, almost certainly not literate, who had heard and memorized the poems of predecessors and retold them his own way. The poems are treasuries of information that this society regarded as useful—events of the past; the conduct expected of warriors, kings, noblewomen, and servants; how to perform a sacrifice, build a raft, put on armor, and entertain guests; and much more.

Embedding this information in a story and using the colorful language, fixed phrases, and predictable rhythm of poetry made it easier for poet and audience to remember vast amounts of material. The early Greek poets, drawing on their strong memories, skill with words, and talent for dramatic performance, developed highly specialized techniques to assist them in memorizing and presenting their tales. They played a vital role in the preservation and transmission of information and thus enjoyed a relatively high social standing and comfortable standard of living. Analogous groups can be found in many other oral cultures of the past, including the bards of medieval Celtic lands, Norse *skalds,* west African *griots,* and the tribal historians of Native American peoples.

Nevertheless, human memory, however cleverly trained and well-practiced, can only do so much. Oral societies must be extremely selective about what information to preserve in the limited storage medium of human memory, and they are slow to give up old information to make way for new.

Sometime in the eighth century B.C.E. the Greeks borrowed the system of writing used by the Phoenicians of Lebanon and, in adapting it to their language, created the first purely alphabetic writing, employing several dozen symbols to express the sounds of speech. The Greek alphabet, although relatively simple to learn as compared to the large and cumbersome sets of symbols in such craft-literacy systems as cuneiform, hieroglyphics, or Linear B, was probably known at first only to a small number of people and used for restricted purposes. Scholars believe that it may have taken three or four centuries for knowledge of reading and writing to spread to large numbers of Greeks and for the written word to became the primary storage medium for the accumulated knowledge of Greek civilization. Throughout that time Greece was still primarily an oral society, even though some Greeks, mostly highly educated members of the upper classes, were beginning to write down poems, scientific speculations, stories about the past, philosophic musings, and the laws of their communities.

It is no accident that some of the most important intellectual and artistic achievements of the Greeks, including early science, history, drama, and rhetoric, developed in the period when oral and literate ways existed side-by-side. Scholars have persuasively argued that writing, by opening up a virtually limitless capacity to store information, released the human mind from the hard discipline of memorization and ended the need to be so painfully selective about what was preserved. This made previously unimaginable innovation and experimentation possible. The Greeks began to organize and categorize information in linear ways, perhaps inspired by the linear sequence of the alphabet; and they began to engage in abstract thinking now that it was no longer necessary to put everything in a story format. We can observe changes in the Greek language as it developed a vocabulary full of abstract nouns, accompanied by increasing complex sentence structure now that the reader had time to go back over the text.

Nevertheless, all the developments associated with literacy were shaped by the deeply rooted oral habits of Greek culture. It is often said that Plato (ca. 429–347 B.C.E.) and his contemporaries of the later Classical period may have been the first generation of Greeks who learned much of what they knew from books. Even so, Plato was a disciple of the philosopher Socrates, who wrote nothing, and Plato employed the oral form of the dialogue, a dramatized sequence of questions and answers, to convey his ideas in written form.

The transition from orality to literacy met stiff resistance in some quarters. Groups whose position in the oral culture was based on the special knowledge only they possessed—members of the elite who judged disputes, priests who knew the time-honored formulas and rituals for appeasing the gods, oral poets who preserved and performed the stories of a heroic past—resented the consequences of literacy. They did what they could to inflame the common people's suspicions of the impiety of literate men who sought scientific explanations for phenomena, such as lightning and eclipses, that had traditionally been attributed to the will and action of the gods. They attacked the so-called Sophists, or "wise men," who charged fees to teach what they claimed were the skills necessary for success, accusing them of subverting traditional morals and corrupting the young.

Other societies, ancient and modern, offer parallel examples of these processes. Oral "specialists" in antiquity, including the Brahmin priests of India and the Celtic Druids, preserved in memory valuable religious information about how to win the favor of the gods. These groups jealously guarded their knowledge because it was the basis of their livelihood and social standing. They resisted committing it to writing even after that technology was available, in their determination to select and to maintain control over those who received it from them. The ways in which oral authorities feel threatened by writing and resist it can be seen in the following quotation from a twentieth century C.E. "griot," an oral rememberer and teller of the past in Mali in West Africa:

> *We griots are depositories of the knowledge of the past . . . Other peoples use writing to record the past, but this invention has killed the faculty of memory among them. They do not feel the past anymore, for writing lacks the warmth of the human voice. With them everybody thinks he knows, whereas learning should be a secret . . . What paltry learning is that which is congealed in dumb books! . . . For generations we have passed on the history of kings from father to son. The narrative was passed on to me without alteration, for I received it free from all untruth.*[1]

This point of view is hard for us to grasp, living as we do in an intensely literate society in which the written word is often felt to be more authoritative and objective than the spoken word. It is important, in striving to understand societies of the past, not to superimpose our assumptions on them, and to appreciate the complex interplay of oral and literate patterns in many of them.

Notes

1. D. T. Niane, *Sundiata: An Epic of Old Mali.* (Harlow U.K.: Longman, 1986), 41.

PART THREE

Growth and Interaction of Cultural Communities, 300 B.C.E.–1200 C.E.

In 300 B.C.E., societies still had only limited contacts beyond their frontiers. Fifteen centuries later, by 1200 C.E., this situation had changed dramatically. Trade, folk migrations, and religious missionary work had created a world of pervasive interconnections among peoples. Three long-distance trade routes fostered the exchange of products and technologies: the Silk Road across Inner Asia, trans-Saharan caravan routes linking northern and sub-Saharan Africa, and a variety of maritime routes connecting the coastal lands of the Indian Ocean.

In Africa, the spread of the Bantu peoples from West Africa brought iron implements and new techniques of food production to most of sub-Saharan Africa and helped foster a distinctive African cultural pattern. In the Middle East, the Arabs of the Arabian peninsula, under the inspiration of the Prophet Muhammad, conquered an empire that stretched from Spain to India, implanting their faith, their cultural values, and an urban-based style of life.

In Asia, Buddhism drew on the energies of missionaries and pilgrims as it spread by land and sea from India to Sri Lanka, Tibet, Southeast Asia, China, Korea, and Japan. In each of these lands, the new faith interacted with older philosophies and religious outlooks to produce distinctive patterns of social interaction. At about the same time, the expansion of the Tang Empire resulted in the dissemination of Chinese culture and technologies throughout Inner and East Asia.

In Europe, monks and missionaries labored to convert the Celtic, Germanic, and Slavic peoples to Christianity. Christian beliefs became wedded to new political and social structures: a struggle between royal and church authority in western Europe; a combining of religious and imperial authority in the Byzantine East; and distinctive Christian kingdoms in Armenia, Kievan Russia, and Ethiopia. The Crusades opened new contacts between western Europe and lands to the east after centuries of near isolation.

Unexplored seas still separated the Eastern and Western Hemispheres, but the development of urban, agricultural civilizations in the Andes, the Yucatán lowlands, and the central plateau of Mexico climaxed during this period in the Aztec and Inca Empires and, somewhat earlier, in the flourishing of the Maya. All of the aspects of long-distance cultural exchange and interaction that mark this era in Eurasia and Africa have their counterparts in the Western Hemisphere.

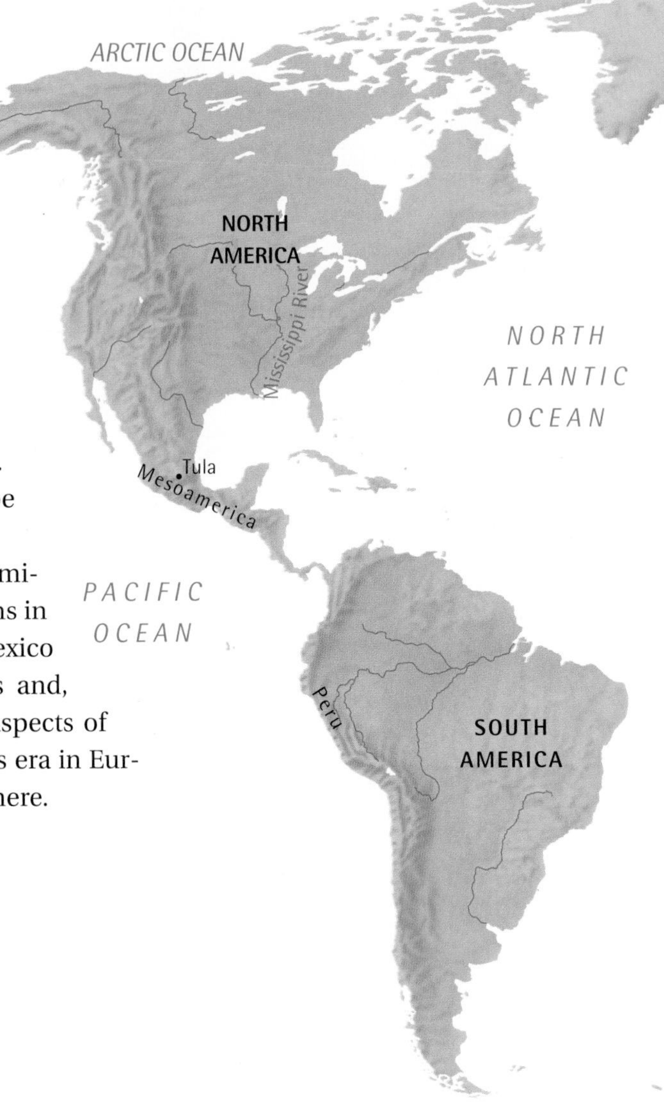

	300 B.C.E. — B.C.E. C.E. — 300 C.E.
Americas	• **300** Migrants from Mesoamerica bring irrigation farming to Arizona; • **100** Teotihuacan founded; **250–900** Classic period of Maya civilization; **200–700** Moche culture in coastal Peru
Europe	• **146** Rome destroys Carthage, begins direct control of territories ouside Europe; Council of Nicaea **325** •; Reign of Roman emperor Diocletian **284–305**; Fall of Roman Empire in West **476** •
Africa	First Christian bishop in Ethiopia **ca. 330** •; Bananas and yams reach Africa from Southeast Asia **ca. 100** •; • **ca. 300** Camel use spreads in southern Sahara; **500 B.C.E.–1000 C.E.** Bantu migrations
Middle East	• **300** Petra flourishes as caravan city in Jordan; **248 B.C.E–226 C.E** Kingdom of Parthia in Iran; • **276** Prophet Mani martyred; **226–650** Sasanid Empire in Iraq and Iran
Asia and Oceania	• **128** Chinese general Zhang Jian explores Silk Road; • **ca. 100** Stirrup developed in Afghanistan; **206 B.C.E–220 C.E** Han Empire in China; **200–400** Rice introduced to Japan from Korea

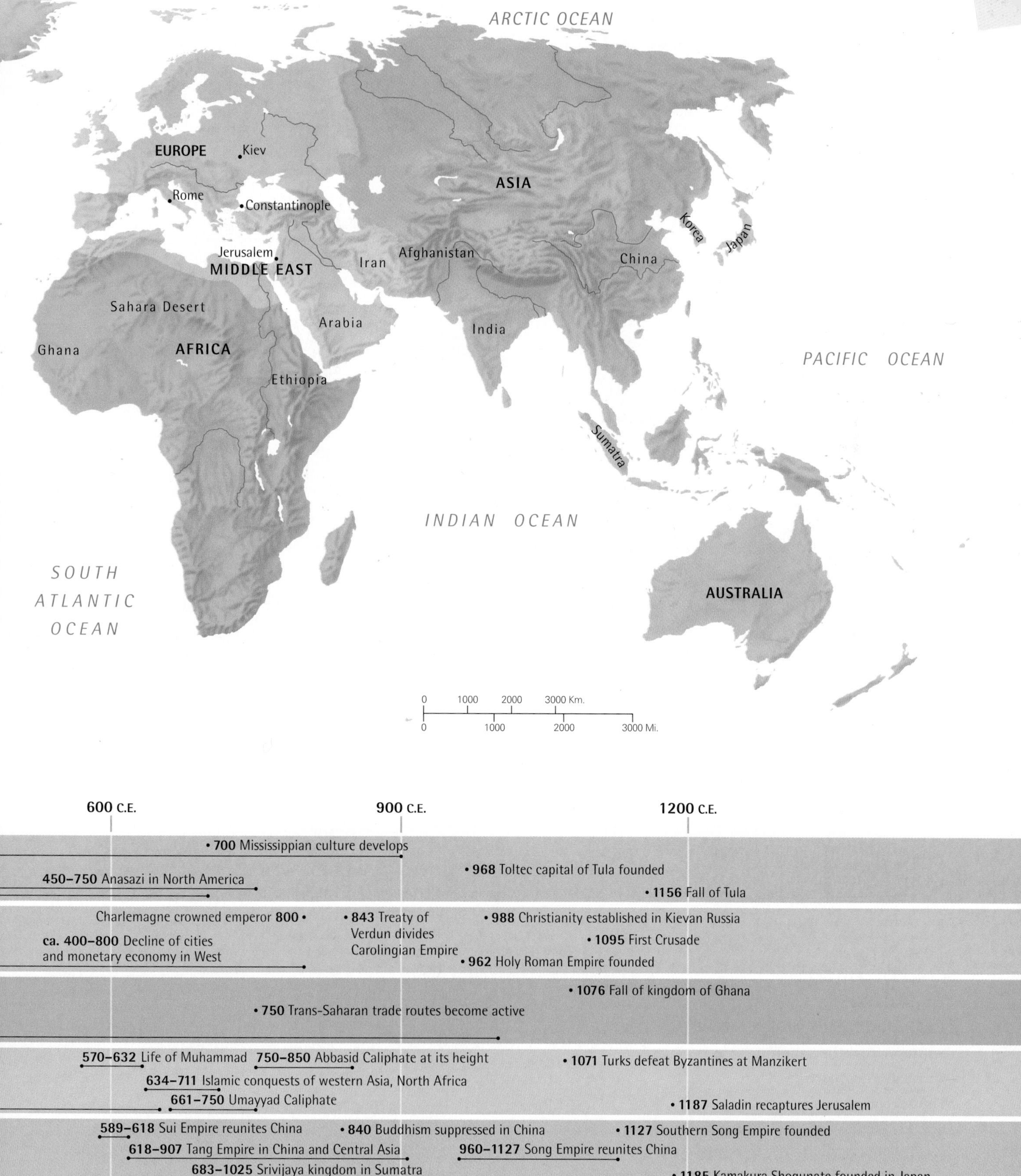
ARCTIC OCEAN
EUROPE
Kiev
Rome
Constantinople
ASIA
Korea
Japan
Jerusalem
MIDDLE EAST
Iran
Afghanistan
China
Sahara Desert
Arabia
India
Ghana
AFRICA
Ethiopia
PACIFIC OCEAN
Sumatra
INDIAN OCEAN
SOUTH ATLANTIC OCEAN
AUSTRALIA
0 1000 2000 3000 Km.
0 1000 2000 3000 Mi.
600 C.E.
900 C.E.
1200 C.E.
• 700 Mississippian culture develops
• 968 Toltec capital of Tula founded
450–750 Anasazi in North America
• 1156 Fall of Tula
Charlemagne crowned emperor 800 •
• 843 Treaty of Verdun divides Carolingian Empire
• 988 Christianity established in Kievan Russia
ca. 400–800 Decline of cities and monetary economy in West
• 1095 First Crusade
• 962 Holy Roman Empire founded
• 1076 Fall of kingdom of Ghana
• 750 Trans-Saharan trade routes become active
570–632 Life of Muhammad
750–850 Abbasid Caliphate at its height
• 1071 Turks defeat Byzantines at Manzikert
634–711 Islamic conquests of western Asia, North Africa
661–750 Umayyad Caliphate
• 1187 Saladin recaptures Jerusalem
589–618 Sui Empire reunites China
• 840 Buddhism suppressed in China
• 1127 Southern Song Empire founded
618–907 Tang Empire in China and Central Asia
960–1127 Song Empire reunites China
683–1025 Srivijaya kingdom in Sumatra
• 1185 Kamakura Shogunate founded in Japan

8 Networks of Communication and Exchange, 300 B.C.E.–1100 C.E.

Indian Ocean Sailing Vessel Ships like this one, in a rock carving on the Buddhist temple of Borobodur in Java, probably carried colonists from Indonesia to Madagascar.

CHAPTER OUTLINE

Around the year 800 C.E., a Chinese poet named Po Zhuyi° nostalgically wrote:

> Iranian whirling girl, Iranian whirling girl—
> Her heart answers to the strings,
> Her hands answer to the drums.
> At the sound of the strings and drums, she raises her arms,
> Like whirling snowflakes tossed about, she turns in her twirling dance.
> Iranian whirling girl,
> You came from Sogdiana°.
> In vain did you labor to come east more than ten thousand tricents.
> For in the central plains there were already some who could do the Iranian whirl,
> And in a contest of wonderful abilities, you would not be their equal.[1]

The western part of Central Asia, the region around Samarkand° and Bukhara° known in the eighth century C.E. as Sogdiana, was 2,500 miles (4,000 kilometers) from the Chinese capital of Chang'an°. Caravans took more than four months to trek across the mostly unsettled deserts, mountains, and grasslands.

The Silk Road connecting China and the Middle East across Central Asia fostered the exchange of agricultural goods, manufactured products, and ideas. Musicians and dancing girls traveled, too—as did camel pullers, merchants, monks, and pilgrims. The Silk Road was not just a means of bringing peoples and parts of the world into contact; it was a social system. This and similar trading networks that have had a deep impact on world history deserve special scrutiny.

With every expansion of territory, the growing wealth of temples, kings, and emperors enticed traders to venture ever farther afield for precious goods. For the most part, the customers were wealthy elites. But the new products, agricultural and industrial processes, and foreign ideas and customs these long-distance traders brought with them sometimes affected an entire society.

Travelers and traders seldom owned much land or wielded political power. Socially isolated (sometimes by law) and secretive because any talk about markets, products, routes, and travel conditions could help their competitors, they nevertheless contributed more to drawing the world together than did all but a few kings and emperors.

This chapter examines the social systems and historical impact of exchange networks that developed between 300 B.C.E. and 1100 C.E. in Europe, Asia, and Africa. The Silk Road, the Indian Ocean maritime system, and the trans-Saharan caravan routes in Africa illustrate the nature of long-distance trade in this era.

Trading networks were not the only medium for the spread of new ideas, products, and customs. Chapter 3 discussed the migration into Europe of people speaking Celtic languages. This chapter compares folk migration with developments along trade routes by looking at the rise of trans-Saharan caravan commerce and the simultaneous spread of Bantu-speaking peoples within sub-Saharan Africa. Chapter 6 discussed a third pattern of cultural contact and exchange, that taking place with the beginning of Christian missionary activity in Europe. This chapter further explores the process by examining the spread of Buddhism in Asia and Christianity in Africa and Asia.

As you read this chapter, ask yourself the following questions:

- What role does technology play in long-distance trade?
- How does geography affect trade patterns?
- How do human groups affect communication between regions?
- Why do some goods and ideas travel more easily than others?
- How do the three modes of cultural contact and exchange affect patterns of dominance and diversity?

The Silk Road

Archaeology and linguistic studies show that the peoples of Central Asia engaged in long-distance movement and exchange from at least 1500 B.C.E. In Roman times Europeans became captivated by the idea of a trade route linking the lands of the Mediterranean with China by way of Mesopotamia, Iran, and Central Asia. The **Silk Road,** as it came to be called in modern times,

Po Zhuyi (boh joo-yee) **Sogdiana** (sog-dee-A-nuh) **Samarkand** (SAM-mar-kand) **Bukhara** (boo-CAR-ruh) **Chang'an** (chahng-ahn)

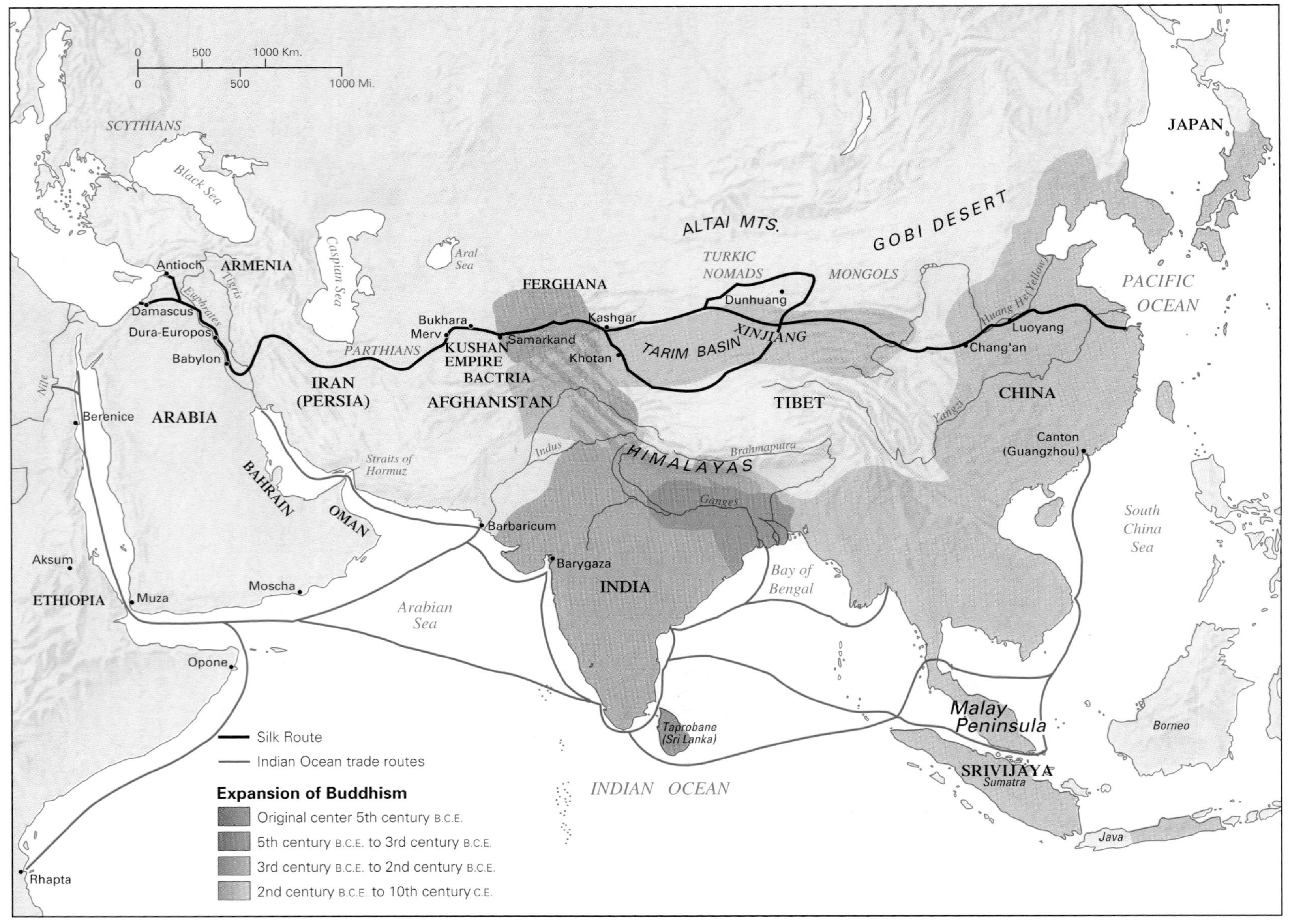

Map 8.1 Asian Trade and Communication Routes The overland Silk Road was vulnerable to political disruption, but was much shorter than the maritime route from the South China Sea to the Red Sea, and ships were more expensive than pack animals. Moreover, China's political centers were in the north.

CHRONOLOGY

	Silk Road	Indian Ocean Trade	Saharan Trade
			500 B.C.E.–ca. 1000 C.E. Bantu migrations
300 B.C.E.	**247 B.C.E.** Parthian rule begins in Iran **128 B.C.E.** General Zhang Jian reaches Ferghana		**ca. 200 B.C.E.** Camel nomads in southern Sahara **46 B.C.E.** First mention of camels in northern Sahara
1 C.E.	**100 B.C.E.–300 C.E.** Kushans rule northern Afghanistan and Sogdiana	**1st cent. C.E.** *Periplus of the Erythraean Sea;* Indonesian migration to Madagascar	
300 C.E.	**ca. 400** Buddhist pilgrim Faxian travels Silk Road		**ca. 300** Beginning of camel nomadism in northern Sahara
600 C.E.	**ca. 630** Buddhist pilgrim Xuanzang travels Silk Road	**683–1025** Srivijaya trading kingdom in Southeast Asia **711** Arabs conquer lower Indus Valley partially by sea	**6th cent.** Kingdom of Ghana begins **639–42** Arabs conquer Egypt **711** Berbers and Arabs conquer Spain **740** Berber revolts; independent states in North Africa; trade develops across Sahara
900 C.E.	**907** Collapse of Tang Empire	**ca. 900** Arab and Persian merchants in Canton	**1076** Almoravids defeat ruler of Ghana

experienced several periods of heavy use (see Map 8.1). The first extended from approximately 100 B.C.E. to 907 C.E., when the collapse of the Tang° Empire in China led to disruption at its eastern end (see Chapter 11). Another period of heavy use began with the Mongol invasions in the thirteenth century C.E. and lasted until the seventeenth century (see Chapter 13).

Origins and Operations

The Seleucid kings who succeeded to the eastern parts of Alexander the Great's empire in the third century B.C.E. focused their energies on Mesopotamia and Syria, their most prosperous and densely populated provinces, allowing an Iranian nomadic leader to establish an independent kingdom in northeastern Iran. The **Parthians,** named after their homeland east of the Caspian Sea, had become a major force by 247 B.C.E. They left few written sources, and recurring wars between the Parthians and the Seleucids, and later between the Parthians and the Romans, prevented travelers from the Mediterranean region from gaining firm knowledge of the Parthian kingdom. It seems likely, however, that their place of origin on the threshold of Central Asia and the lifestyle they had in common with nomadic pastoral groups farther to the east helped foster the Silk Road.

In 128 B.C.E. a Chinese general named Zhang Jian° made his first exploratory journey westward across the trackless deserts and mountains of Central Asia on be-

Tang (tahng)

Zhang Jian (jahng jee-en)

Hybrid Camel Breeding This small breeding herd is one of the last remnants of the once widespread practice of crossing one-humped and two-humped camels to produce very strong and cold resistant animals for Silk Road caravans. The two-humped male is accompanied by several one-humped females. The two animals on the left have the depressed area toward the front of the long hump and the long neck wool that marks them as bukhts, or hybrids. (Courtesy, Mike Bonine, photographer)

half of Emperor Wu of the Han dynasty. After crossing the broad and desolate Tarim Basin north of Tibet, he reached the fertile valley of Ferghana° and for the first time encountered westward-flowing rivers. There he found horse breeders whose animals far outclassed any horses he had seen.

Later Chinese historians looked on General Zhang, who ultimately led eighteen expeditions, as the originator of overland trade with the western lands, and they credited him with personally introducing a whole garden of new plants and trees to China. Zhang's own account, however, proves that the people of Ferghana were already familiar with goods produced in China, though they probably learned of them by way of India.

Long-distance travel was more familiar to the Central Asians than to the Chinese. Kin to the trouser-wearing, horse-riding Parthians in language and customs, the populations of Ferghana and neighboring regions included many nomads who followed their herds. Their migrations had little to do with trade. The trading demands that brought the Silk Road into being were Chinese eagerness for western products, especially horses, and on the western end, the organized Parthian state, which controlled the flourishing markets of Mesopotamia and linked them culturally to the pastoralists of Central Asia. These nomads provided pack animals and controlled transit across their lands. Caravan cities that supported the trade and organized relations with the nomads were an equally important intermediate factor.

Once the route was fully functioning, around 100 B.C.E., Greeks could buy Chinese silk from Parthian traders in Mesopotamian border entrepôts. Yet caravans also bought and sold goods along the way in prosperous Central Asian cities like Samarkand and Bukhara. These cities grew and flourished, often under the rule of local princes.

General Zhang definitely seems to have brought two plants to China: alfalfa and wine grapes. The former provided the best fodder for the growing Chinese herds of Ferghana horses. In addition, Chinese farmers adopted pistachios, walnuts, pomegranates, sesame, coriander, spinach, and other new crops. Chinese artisans and physicians made good use of other trade products, such as jasmine oil, oak galls (used in tanning animal hides, dyeing, and making ink), sal ammoniac (for medicines), copper oxides, zinc, and precious stones.

Caravan traders going west from China carried new fruits such as peaches and apricots, which the Romans mistakenly attributed to other eastern lands, calling them Persian plums and Armenia plums, respectively. They also carried cinnamon, ginger, and other spices that could not be grown in the West. Manufactured goods—particularly silk, pottery, and paper—were eventually adopted or imitated in western lands, starting with Iran.

Ferghana (fer-GAH-nuh)

Iranian Musicians from Silk Road This three-color glazed pottery figurine, 23 inches (58.4 centimeters) high, comes from a northern Chinese tomb of the Tang era (sixth to ninth centuries C.E.) The musicians playing Iranian instruments confirm the migration of Iranian culture across the Silk Road. At the same time, dishes decorated by the Chinese three-color glaze technique were in vogue in northern Iran. (The National Museum of Chinese History)

The Impact of the Silk Road

As trade became a more important part of Central Asian life, the Iranian-speaking peoples increasingly settled in trading cities, which remained comparatively small, and surrounding farm villages. This allowed nomads originally from the Altai Mountains farther east to spread across the steppes and become the dominant pastoral group. These peoples, who spoke Turkic languages unrelated to the Iranian tongues, were well in evidence by the sixth century C.E. The prosperity that trade created affected not only the ethnic mix of the region but also its cultural values. The nomads continued to live in the round, portable felt huts called yurts that can still occasionally be seen in Central Asia, but prosperous merchants and landholders built stately homes decorated with brightly colored wall paintings. The paintings show the merchants and landholders wearing Chinese silks and Iranian brocades and riding on richly outfitted horses and camels. They also give evidence of an avid interest in Buddhism, which competed with Christianity, Manichaeism, Zoroastrianism, and—eventually—Islam in a lively and inquiring intellectual milieu.

Religion (discussed later in this chapter) exemplifies the impact of foreign customs and beliefs on the Central Asian peoples, but Central Asian practices in turn affected surrounding areas. For example, Central Asian military techniques had a profound impact on both East and West. Chariot warfare and the use of mounted bowmen originated in Central Asia and spread eastward and westward through military campaigns and folk migrations that began in the second millennium B.C.E. and recurred throughout the period of the Silk Road.

Evidence of the **stirrup,** one of the most important inventions, comes first from the Kushan people who ruled northern Afghanistan in approximately the first century C.E. At first a solid bar, then a loop of leather to support the rider's big toe, and finally a device of leather and metal or wood supporting the instep, the stirrup gave riders far greater stability in the saddle—which itself was in all likelihood an earlier Central Asian invention.

Using stirrups, a mounted warrior could supplement his bow and arrow with a long lance and charge his enemy at a gallop without fear that the impact of his attack would push him off his mount. Far to the west, the stirrup made possible the armored knights who dominated the battlefields of Europe (see Chapter 10), and it contributed to the superiority of the Tang cavalry in China (see Chapter 11).

The Indian Ocean Maritime System

A multilingual, multiethnic society of seafarers established the **Indian Ocean Maritime System,** a trade network across the Indian Ocean and the South China Sea. These people left few records and seldom played a visible part in the rise and fall of kingdoms and empires, but they forged increasingly strong economic and social ties between the coastal lands of East Africa, southern Arabia, the Persian Gulf, India, Southeast Asia, and southern China.

This trade took place in three distinct regions: (1) In the South China Sea, Chinese and Malays (including Indonesians) dominated trade. (2) From the east coast of India to the islands of Southeast Asia, Indians and Malays were the main traders. (3) From the west coast of India to the Persian Gulf and the east coast of Africa, merchants and sailors were predominantly Persians and Arabs. However, Chinese and Malay sailors could and did voyage to East Africa, and Arab and Persian traders reached southern China.

From the time of Herodotus in the fifth century B.C.E., Greek writers regaled their readers with stories of marvelous voyages down the Red Sea into the Indian Ocean and around Africa from the west. Most often, they attributed such trips to the Phoenicians, the most fearless of Mediterranean seafarers. Occasionally a Greek appears. One such was Hippalus, a Greek ship's pilot who was said to have discovered the seasonal monsoon winds that facilitate sailing across the Indian Ocean (see Diversity and Dominance: The Indian Ocean Trading World).

Of course, the regular, seasonal alternation of steady winds could not have remained unnoticed for thousands of years, waiting for an alert Greek to happen along. The great voyages and discoveries made before written records became common should surely be attributed to the peoples who lived around the Indian Ocean rather than to interlopers from the Mediterranean Sea. The story of Hippalus resembles the Chinese story of General Zhang Jian, whose role in opening trade with Central Asia overshadows the anonymous contributions made by the indigenous peoples. The Chinese may indeed have learned from General Zhang and the Greeks from Hippalus, but other people played important roles anonymously.

Mediterranean sailors of the time of Alexander used square sails and long banks of oars to maneuver among the sea's many islands and small harbors. Indian Ocean vessels relied on roughly triangular lateen sails and normally did without oars in running before the wind on long ocean stretches. Mediterranean shipbuilders nailed their vessels together. The planks of Indian Ocean ships were pierced, tied together with palm fiber, and caulked with bitumen. Mediterranean sailors rarely ventured out of sight of land. Indian Ocean sailors, thanks to the monsoon winds, could cover long reaches entirely at sea.

These technological differences prove that the world of the Indian Ocean developed differently from the world of the Mediterranean Sea, where the Phoenicians and Greeks established colonies that maintained contact with their home cities (see Chapters 4 and 5). The traders of the Indian Ocean, where distances were greater and contacts less frequent, seldom retained political ties with their homelands. The colonies they established were sometimes socially distinctive but rarely independent of the local political powers. War, so common in the Mediterranean, seldom beset the Indian Ocean maritime system prior to the arrival of European explorers at the end of the fifteenth century C.E.

Origins of Contact and Trade

By 2000 B.C.E. Sumerian records indicate regular trade between Mesopotamia, the islands of the Persian Gulf, Oman, and the Indus Valley. However, this early trading contact broke off, and later Mesopotamian trade references mention East Africa more often than India.

A similarly early chapter in Indian Ocean history concerns migrations from Southeast Asia to Madagascar, the world's fourth largest island, situated off the southeastern coast of Africa. About two thousand years ago, people from one of the many Indonesian islands of Southeast Asia established themselves in that forested, mountainous land 6,000 miles (9,500 kilometers) from home. They could not possibly have carried enough supplies for a direct voyage across the Indian Ocean, so their route must have touched the coasts of India and southern Arabia. No physical remains of their journeys have been discovered, however.

Apparently, the sailing canoes of these people plied the seas along the increasingly familiar route for several hundred years. Settlers farmed the new land and entered into relations with Africans who found their way across the 250-mile-wide (400-kilometer-wide) Mozambique° Channel around the fifth century C.E. Descendants of the seafarers preserved the language of their homeland and some of its culture, such as the cultivation of bananas, yams, and other native Southeast Asian plants. These food crops spread to mainland Africa. But the memory of their distant origins gradually faded, not to be recovered until modern times, when scholars established the linguistic link between the two lands.

The Impact of Indian Ocean Trade

The only extensive written account of trade in the Indian Ocean before the rise of Islam in the seventh century C.E. is an anonymous work by a Greco-Egyptian of the first century C.E. *The Periplus of the Erythraean° Sea* (that is, the Indian Ocean). It describes ports of call along the Red Sea and down the East African coast to somewhere south of the island of Zanzibar. Then it describes the ports of southern Arabia and the Persian Gulf before continuing eastward to India, mentioning ports all the way around the subcontinent to the mouth of the Ganges River. Though the geographer Ptolemy, who lived slightly later, had heard of ports as far away as Southeast Asia, the author of the *Periplus* had obviously voyaged to the places he mentions. What he describes is unquestionably a trading *system* and is clear evidence of

Mozambique (moe-zam-BEEK) **Erythraean** (eh-RITH-ree-an)

Asklepios, the Greek God of Medicine This representation, found in the sea off the coast of Bahrain in the Persian Gulf, reflects the extension of Greek culture along sea routes into distant lands. Greek medical knowledge and principles became known as far away as India. The crude craftsmanship of this effigy indicates that it was locally made and not imported from Greece. (Courtesy, Bahrain National Museum)

the steady growth of interconnections during the preceding centuries.

The demand for products from the coastal lands inspired mariners to persist in their long ocean voyages. Africa produced exotic animals, wood, and ivory. Since ivory also came from India, Mesopotamia, and North Africa, the extent of African ivory exports cannot be determined. The highlands of northern Somalia and southern Arabia grew the scrubby trees whose aromatic resins were valued as frankincense and myrrh. Pearls abounded in the Persian Gulf, and evidence of ancient copper mines has been found in Oman in southeastern Arabia. India shipped spices and manufactured goods, and more spices came from Southeast Asia, along with manufactured items, particularly pottery, obtained in trade with China. In sum, the Indian Ocean trading region had a great variety of highly valued products. Given the long distances and the comparative lack of islands, however, the volume of trade there was undoubtedly much lower than in the Mediterranean Sea.

Furthermore, the culture of the Indian Ocean ports was often isolated from the hinterlands, particularly in the west. The coasts of the Arabian peninsula, the African side of the Red Sea, southern Iran, and northern India (today's Pakistan) were mostly barren desert. Ports in all these areas tended to be small, and many suffered from meager supplies of fresh water. Farther south in India, the monsoon provided ample water, but steep mountains cut off the coastal plain from the interior of the country. Thus few ports between Zanzibar and Sri Lanka had substantial inland populations within easy reach. The head of the Persian Gulf was one exception: shipborne trade was possible from the port of Apologus (later called Ubulla, the precursor of modern Basra) as far north as Babylon and, from the eighth century C.E., nearby Baghdad.

By contrast, eastern India, the Malay Peninsula, and Indonesia afforded more hospitable and densely populated shores with easier access to inland populations. Though the fishers, sailors, and traders of the western Indian Ocean system supplied a long series of kingdoms and empires, none of these consumer societies became primarily maritime in orientation, as the Greeks and Phoenicians did in the Mediterranean. In the east, in contrast, sea-borne trade and influence seem to have been important even to the earliest states of Southeast Asia (see Chapter 7).

In coastal areas throughout the Indian Ocean system, small groups of seafarers sometimes had a significant social impact despite their usual lack of political power. Women seldom accompanied the men on long sea voyages, so sailors and merchants often married local women in port cities. The families thus established were bilingual and bicultural. As in many other situations in world history, women played a crucial though not well-documented role as mediators between cultures. Not only did they raise their children to be more cosmopolitan than children from inland regions, but they also introduced the men to customs and attitudes that they carried with them when they returned to sea. As a consequence, the designation of specific seafarers as Persian, Arab, Indian, or Malay often conceals mixed heritages and a rich cultural diversity.

ROUTES ACROSS THE SAHARA

The windswept Sahara, a desert stretching from the Red Sea to the Atlantic Ocean and broken only by the Nile River, isolates sub-Saharan Africa from the Mediterranean world (see Map 8.2). The current dryness of the Sahara dates only to about 2500 B.C.E. The period of drying out that preceded that date lasted twenty-five centuries and encompassed several cultural changes. During that time, travel between a slowly shrinking number of

Diversity and Dominance

The Indian Ocean Trading World

*The most revealing description of ancient trade in the Indian Ocean and of the diversity and economic forces shaping the Indian Ocean trading system, "The Periplus of the Erythraean Sea," a sailing itinerary (*periplus *in Greek), was composed in the first century* C.E. *by an unknown Greco-Egyptian merchant. It highlights the diversity of peoples and products from the Red Sea to the Bay of Bengal and illustrates the comparative absence of a dominating political force in the Indian Ocean trading system. Historians believe that the descriptions of market towns were based on first-hand experience. Information on more remote regions was probably hearsay (see Map 8.1).*

Of the designated ports on the Erythraean Sea [Indian Ocean], and the market-towns around it, the first is the Egyptian port of Mussel Harbor. To those sailing down from that place, on the right hand . . . there is Berenice. The harbors of both are at the boundary of Egypt. . . .

On the right-hand coast next below Berenice is the country of the Berbers. Along the shore are the Fish-Eaters, living in scattered caves in the narrow valleys. Further inland are the Berbers, and beyond them the Wild-flesh-Eaters and Calf-Eaters, each tribe governed by its chief; and behind them, further inland, in the country towards the west, there lies a city called Meroe.

Below the Calf-Eaters there is a little market-town on the shore . . . called Ptolemais of the Hunts, from which the hunters started for the interior under the dynasty of the Ptolemies . . . But the place has no harbor and is reached only by small boats . . . .

Beyond this place, the coast trending toward the south, there is the Market and Cape of Spices, an abrupt promontory, at the very end of the Berber coast toward the east. . . . A sign of an approaching storm . . . is that the deep water becomes more turbid and changes its color. When this happens they all run to a large promontory called Tabae, which offers safe shelter. . . .

Beyond Tabae [lies] . . . another market-town called Opone . . . [I]n it the greatest quantity of cinnamon is produced . . . and slaves of the better sort, which are brought to Egypt in increasing numbers. . . .

[Ships also come] from the places across this sea, from . . . Barygaza, bringing to these . . . market-towns the products of their own places; wheat, rice, clarified butter, sesame oil, cotton cloth . . . and honey from the reed called sacchari [sugar cane]. Some make the voyage especially to these market-towns, and others exchange their cargoes while sailing along the coast. This country is not subject to a King, but each market-town is ruled by its separate chief.

Beyond Opone, the shore trending more toward the south . . . this coast [the Somali region of Azania, or East Africa] is destitute of harbors . . . until the Pyralax islands [Zanzibar] . . . . [A] little to the south of south-west . . . is the island Menuthias [Madagascar], about three hundred stadia from the mainland, low and wooded, in which there are rivers and many kinds of birds and the mountain-tortoise. There are no wild beasts except the crocodiles; but there they do not attack men. In this place there are sewed boats, and canoes hollowed from single logs. . . .

Two days' sail beyond, there lies the very last market-town of the continent of Azania, which is called Rhapta [Dar es-Salaam]; which has its name from the sewed boats (*rhapton ploiarion*) . . . ; in which there is ivory in great quantity, and tortoise-shell. Along this coast live men of piratical habits, very great in stature, and under separate chiefs for each place. [One] chief governs it under some ancient right that subjects it to the sovereignty of the state that is become first in Arabia. And the people of Muza [Mocha in Yemen] now hold it under his authority, and send thither many large ships; using Arab captains and agents, who are familiar with the natives and intermarry with them, and who know the whole coast and understand the language.

There are imported into these markets the lances made at Muza especially for this trade, and hatchets and daggers and awls, and various kinds of glass; and at some places a little wine, and wheat, not for trade, but to serve for getting the good-will of the savages. There are exported from these places a great quantity of ivory . . . and rhinoceros-horn. . . .

And these markets of Azania are the very last of the continent that stretches down on the right hand from Berenice; for beyond these places the unexplored ocean curves around toward the west, and running along by the regions to the south of Aethiopia and Libya and Africa, it mingles with the western sea....

Beyond the harbor of Moscha [Musqat in Oman] ... a mountain range runs along the shore; at the end of which, in a row, lie seven islands.... Beyond these there is a barbarous region which is no longer of the same Kingdom, but now belongs to Persia. Sailing along this coast well out at sea ... there meets you an island called Sarapis.... It is about two hundred stadia wide and six hundred long, inhabited by three settlements of Fish-Eaters, a villainous lot, who use the Arabian language and wear girdles of palm-leaves....

[T]here follows not far beyond, the mouth of the Persian Gulf, where there is much diving for the pearl-mussel.... At the upper end of this Gulf there is a market-town designated by law called Apologus, situated near ... the River Euphrates.

Sailing [southeast] through the mouth of the Gulf, after a six-days' course there is another market-town of Persia called Ommana .... [L]arge vessels are regularly sent from Barygaza, loaded with copper and sandalwood and timbers of teakwood and logs of blackwood and ebony....

Beyond this region ... there follows the coast district of Scythia, which lies above toward the north; the whole marshy; from which flows down the river Sinthus [Indus], the greatest of all the rivers that flow into the Erythraean Sea, bringing down an enormous volume of water.... This river has seven mouths, very shallow and marshy, so that they are not navigable, except the one in the middle; at which by the shore, is the market-town, Barbaricum.... [I]nland behind it is the metropolis of Scythia ... it is subject to Parthian princes who are constantly driving each other out.

Now the whole country of India has very many rivers, and very great ebb and flow of the tides.... But about Barygaza [Broach] it is much greater, so that the bottom is suddenly seen, and now parts of the dry land are sea, and now it is dry where ships were sailing just before; and the rivers, under the inrush of the flood tide, when the whole force of the sea is directed against them, are driven upwards more strongly against their natural current....

The country inland from Barygaza is inhabited by numerous tribes.... Above these is the very warlike nation of the Bactrians, who are under their own king. And Alexander, setting out from these parts, penetrated to the Ganges.... [T]o the present day ancient drachmae are current in Barygaza, coming from this country, bearing inscriptions in Greek letters, and the devices of those who reigned after Alexander....

Inland from this place and to the east, is the city called Ozene [Ujjain].... [F]rom this place are brought down all things needed for the welfare of the country about Barygaza, and many things for our trade: agate and carnelian, Indian muslins ....

There are imported into this market-town, wine, Italian preferred, also Laodicean and Arabian; copper, tin, and lead; coral and topaz; thin clothing and inferior sorts of all kinds ... gold and silver coin, on which there is a profit when exchanged for the money of the country.... And for the King there are brought into those places very costly vessels of silver, singing boys, beautiful maidens for the harem, fine wines, thin clothing of the finest weaves, and the choicest ointments. There are exported from these places [spices], ivory, agate and carnelian ... cotton cloth of all kinds, silk cloth....

Beyond Barygaza the adjoining coast extends in a straight line from north to south.... The inland country back from the coast toward the east comprises many desert regions and great mountains; and all kinds of wild beasts—leopards, tigers, elephants, enormous serpents, hyenas, and baboons of many sorts; and many populous nations, as far as the Ganges....

This whole voyage as above described ... they used to make in small vessels, sailing close around the shores of the gulfs; and Hippalus was the pilot who by observing the location of the ports and the conditions of the sea, first discovered how to lay his course straight across the ocean....

About the following region, the course trending toward the east, lying out at sea toward the west is the island Palaesimundu, called by the ancients Taprobane [Sri Lanka].... It produces pearls, transparent stones, muslins, and tortoise-shell....

Beyond this, the course trending toward the north, there are many barbarous tribes, among whom are the Cirrhadae, a race of men with flattened noses, very savage; another tribe, the Bargysi; and the Horse-faces and the Long-faces, who are said to be cannibals.

After these, the course turns toward the east again, and sailing with the ocean to the right and the shore remaining beyond to the left, Ganges comes into view.... And just opposite this river there is an island in the ocean, the last part of the inhabited world toward the east, under the rising sun itself; it is called Chryse; and it has the best tortoise-shell of all the places on the Erythraean Sea.

After this region under the very north, the sea outside ending in a land called This, there is a very great inland city called Thinae, from which raw silk and silk yarn and silk cloth are brought on foot.... But the land of This is not easy of access; few men come from there, and seldom.

QUESTIONS FOR ANALYSIS

1. **Of what importance were political organization and ethnicity to a traveling merchant?**
2. **How might a manual like this have been used?**
3. **To what extent can the observations of a Greco-Egyptian merchant be taken as evidence for understanding how merchants from other lands saw the trade in the Indian Ocean?**

Source: Excerpts from W. H. Schoff (tr. & ed.), *The Periplus of the Erythraean Sea: Travel and Trade in the Indian Ocean by a Merchant of the First Century* (London, Bombay & Calcutta, 1912).

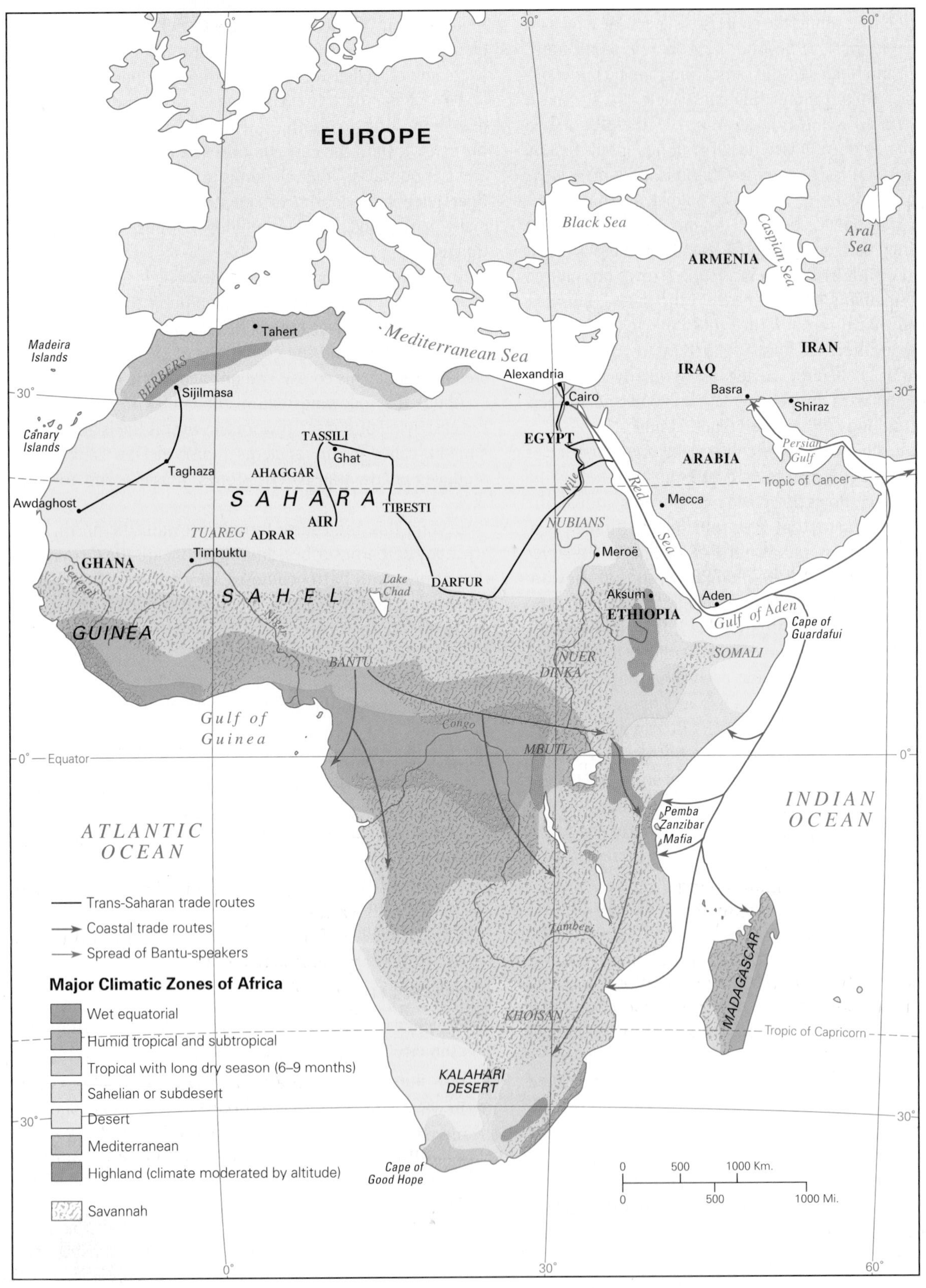
EUROPE
Black Sea
Caspian Sea
Aral Sea
ARMENIA
IRAN
IRAQ
Basra
Shiraz
ARABIA
Persian Gulf
Tropic of Cancer
Mecca
Red Sea
Aden
Gulf of Aden
Cape of Guardafui
SOMALI
Mediterranean Sea
Alexandria
Cairo
EGYPT
Nile
NUBIANS
Meroë
Aksum
ETHIOPIA
Madeira Islands
Tahert
BERBERS
Sijilmasa
Canary Islands
TASSILI
Ghat
Taghaza
AHAGGAR
Awdaghost
S A H A R A
TIBESTI
AIR
TUAREG
ADRAR
Timbuktu
GHANA
Senegal
S A H E L
Lake Chad
DARFUR
GUINEA
Niger
BANTU
NUER
DINKA
Gulf of Guinea
Congo
MBUTI
Equator
INDIAN OCEAN
Pemba
Zanzibar
Mafia
ATLANTIC OCEAN
Zambezi
MADAGASCAR
KHOISAN
Tropic of Capricorn
KALAHARI DESERT
Cape of Good Hope
0 500 1000 Km.
0 500 1000 Mi.
Trans-Saharan trade routes
Coastal trade routes
Spread of Bantu-speakers
Major Climatic Zones of Africa
Wet equatorial
Humid tropical and subtropical
Tropical with long dry season (6–9 months)
Sahelian or subdesert
Desert
Mediterranean
Highland (climate moderated by altitude)
Savannah

Cattle Herders in Saharan Rock Art These paintings represent the most artistically accomplished type of Saharan art. Herding societies of modern times living in the Sahel region south of the Sahara strongly resemble the society depicted here. (Henri Lhote)

grassy areas was comparatively easy. However, by 300 B.C.E., scarcity of water was restricting travel to a few difficult routes initially known only to desert nomads. Trade over **trans-Saharan caravan routes,** at first only a trickle, eventually expanded into a significant stream.

Early Saharan Cultures

Sprawling sand dunes, sandy plains, and vast expanses of exposed rock make up most of the great desert. Stark and rugged mountain and highland areas separate its northern and southern portions. The cliffs and caves of these highlands, the last spots where water and grassland could be found as the climate changed, preserve rock paintings and engravings that constitute the primary evidence for early Saharan history.

Though dating is difficult, what appear to be the earliest images, left by hunters in much wetter times, include elephants, giraffes, rhinoceros, crocodiles, and other animals that have long been extinct in the region. Overlaps in the artwork indicate that the hunting societies were gradually joined by new cultures based on cattle breeding and well adapted to the sparse grazing that remained. Domestic cattle may have originated in western Asia or in North Africa. They certainly reached the Sahara before it became completely dry. The beautiful paintings of cattle and scenes of daily life seen in the Saharan rock art depict pastoral societies that bear little similarity to any in western Asia. The people seem physically akin to today's West Africans, and the customs depicted, such as dancing and wearing masks, as well as the breeds of cattle, particularly those with piebald coloring (splotches of black and white), strongly suggest later societies to the south of the Sahara. These factors support the hypothesis that some southern cultural patterns originated in the Sahara.

Map 8.2 Africa and the Trans-Saharan Trade Routes The Sahara and the surrounding oceans isolated most of Africa from foreign contact before 1000 C.E. The Nile Valley, a few trading points on the east coast, and limited transdesert trade provided exceptions to this rule; but the dominant forms of sub-Saharan African culture originated far to the west, north of the Gulf of Guinea.

Overlaps in artwork also show that horse herders succeeded the cattle herders. The rock art changes dramatically in style, from the superb realism of the cattle pictures to sketchier images that are often strongly geometric. Moreover, the horses are frequently shown drawing light chariots. According to the most common theory, intrepid charioteers from the Mediterranean shore drove their flimsy vehicles across the desert and established societies in the few remaining grassy areas of the central Saharan highlands. Some scholars suggest possible chariot routes that refugees from the collapse of the Mycenaean and Minoan civilizations of Greece and Crete (see Chapter 4) might have followed deep into the desert around the twelfth century B.C.E. However, no archaeological evidence of actual chariot use in the Sahara has been discovered, and it is difficult to imagine large numbers of refugees from the politically chaotic Mediterranean region driving chariots into a waterless, trackless desert in search of a new homeland somewhere to the south.

As with the cattle herders, therefore, the identity of the Saharan horse breeders and the source of their passion for drawing chariots remain a mystery. Only with the coming of the camel is it possible to make firm connections with the Saharan nomads of today through the depiction of objects and geometric patterns still used by the veiled, blue-robed Tuareg° people of the highlands in southern Algeria, Niger, and Mali.

Some historians maintain that the Romans inaugurated an important trans-Saharan trade, but they lack firm archaeological evidence. More plausibly, Saharan trade relates to the spread of camel domestication. Supporting evidence comes from rock art, where overlaps of images imply that camel riders in desert costume constitute the latest Saharan population. The camel-oriented images are decidedly the crudest to be found in the region.

First mention of camels in North Africa comes in a Latin text of 46 B.C.E. Since the native camels of Africa probably died out before the era of domestication, the domestic animals probably reached the Sahara from Arabia, probably by way of Egypt in the first millennium B.C.E. They could have been adopted by peoples farther and farther to the west, from one central Saharan highland to the next, only much later spreading northward and coming to the attention of the Romans (see Environment and Technology: Camel Saddles). Camel herding made it easier for people to move away from the Saharan highlands and roam the deep desert. Through contacts made by far-ranging camel herders, the people north of the Sahara finally gained access to the camel, though they exploited it primarily as a work animal, even developing harnesses for attaching camels to plows and carts. These practices, entirely unknown in the southern Sahara, persist in Tunisia° today.

Trade Across the Sahara

Linkage between two different trading systems, one in the south, the other in the north, developed slowly. Southern traders concentrated on supplying salt from large deposits in the southern desert to the peoples of sub-Saharan Africa. Traders from the equatorial forest zone brought forest products, such as kola nuts (a condiment and source of caffeine) and edible palm oil, to trading centers near the desert's southern fringe. Each received the products they needed in their homelands from the other, or from the farming peoples of the **Sahel**°—literally "the coast" in Arabic, the southern borderlands of the Sahara (see Map 8.2). Middlemen who were native to the Sahel played an important role in this trade, but precise historical details are lacking.

In the north, Roman colonists supplied Italy with agricultural products, primarily wheat and olives. Surviving mosaic pavements depicting scenes from daily life show that people living on the farms and in the towns of the interior consumed Roman manufactured goods and shared Roman styles. This northern pattern began to change in the third century C.E. with the decline of the Roman Empire, the abandonment of many Roman farms, the growth of nomadism, and a lessening of trade across the Mediterranean. After the Arabs invaded North Africa in the middle of the seventh century C.E., the direction of trade shifted to the Middle East, the center of Arab rule. Since the Arab conquests were inspired by the new religion of Islam (see Chapter 9) and the Christian lands of Europe constituted enemy territory, trans-Mediterranean trade diminished still further. The Arabs, many of them from camel-breeding societies, felt a cultural kinship with those Berber-speakers who had taken up camel pastoralism during the preceding centuries. Like the Parthians involved in opening the Silk Road, they related better to the peoples of the interior than had the previous Carthaginian and Roman regimes.

A series of Berber revolts against Arab rule from 740 onward led to the appearance of several small principalities on the northern fringe of the Sahara. The Islamic beliefs of their rulers, which differed somewhat from those of the Arab rulers to the east, may have interfered with their east-west overland trade and led them to look for new possibilities elsewhere. It appears that these city-states, Sijilmasa° and Tahert°, developed the first significant and regular trading contact with the south in the ninth century. Most of their populations being Berber, they already knew that nomads speaking closely related languages inhabited the central and southern reaches of the desert.

Once traders looked south, they discovered that the already existing trade in the south sometimes involved exchanging gold dust for salt. The gold came from deposits along the Niger and other West African rivers (see Map 8.2). The people who panned for the gold did not value it nearly as highly as did the traders from Sijilmasa. They readily provided the nomads of the southern desert, who controlled the salt sources but had little use for gold, with products not available from the south, such as copper and certain manufactured goods. Thus everyone benefited from the creation of the new trade

Tuareg (TWAH-reg) **Tunisia** (too-NEE-zhee-uh)

Sahel (SAH-hel) **Sijilmasa** (sih-jil-MAS-suh) **Tahert** (TAH-hert)

ENVIRONMENT + TECHNOLOGY

Camel Saddles

As seemingly simple a technology as saddle design can indicate a society's economic structure. The South Arabian saddle, a Tunisian example of which is shown to the right, was good for riding, and baggage could easily be tied to the wooden arches at its front. It was militarily inefficient, however, because the rider knelt on the cushion behind the camel's hump, which made it difficult to use weapons.

The North Arabian saddle was a significant improvement that came into use in the first centuries B.C.E. The two arches anchoring the front end of the South Arabian saddle were separated and greatly enlarged, one arch going in front of the hump and the other behind. This formed a solid wooden framework to which loads could easily be attached, but the placement of the prominent front and back arches seated the rider on top of the camel's hump instead of behind it and thereby gave warriors a solid seat and the advantage of height over enemy horsemen. Arabs in northern Arabia used these saddles to take control of the caravan trade through their lands.

The lightest and most efficient riding saddles, shown below, come from the southern Sahara, where personal travel and warfare took priority over trade. These excellent war saddles could not be used for baggage because they did not offer a convenient place to tie bundles.

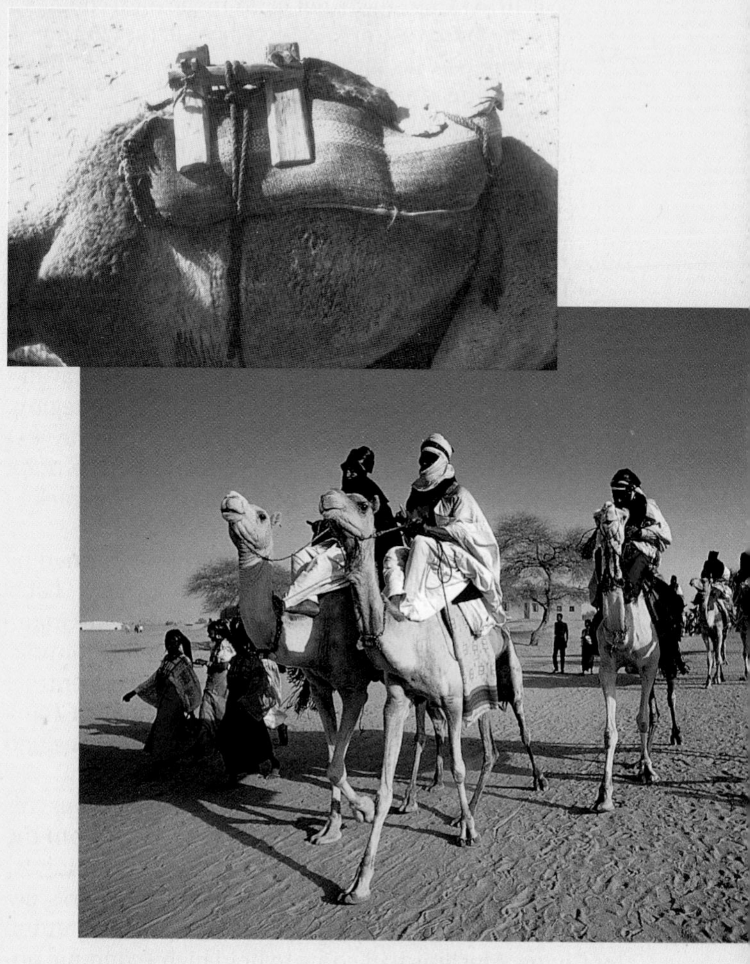

Camel Saddles The militarily inefficient south Arabian saddle (above) seats the rider behind the animal's hump atop its hindquarters. The rider controls his mount by tapping its neck with a long camelstick. The Tuareg saddle (below) seats the rider over the animal's withers, leaving his hands free to wield a sword and letting him control his mount with his toes. (above: Private collection; below: Fred Bavendam/Peter Arnold, Inc.)

link. Sijilmasa and Tahert became wealthy cities, the former minting gold coins that circulated as far away as Egypt and Syria.

The Kingdom of Ghana

The earliest known sub-Saharan beneficiary of the new exchange system was the kingdom of **Ghana°**. Its first appearance is in an Arabic text of the late eighth century as the "land of gold." Few details survive about the early years of this realm, which was established by the Soninke° people and covered parts of Mali, Mauritania, and Senegal. In the mid-eleventh century the Arab geographer al-Bakri (d. 1094) described it as follows:

> The city of Ghana consists of two towns situated on a plain. One of these towns is inhabited by Muslims. It is large and possesses a dozen mosques, one being for the Friday prayer, and each having imams [prayer leaders], muezzins [people to make the call to prayer], and salaried reciters of the Quran. There are jurisconsults [legal specialists] and scholars. Around the town

Ghana (GAH-nuh)

Soninke (soh-NIN-kay)

are sweet wells, which they use for drinking and for cultivating vegetables. The royal city, called al-Ghaba ["the grove"], is six miles away, and the area between the two towns is covered with habitations. Their houses are constructed of stone and acacia wood. The king has a palace with conical huts, surrounded by a fence like a wall. In the king's town, not far from the royal court, is a mosque for the use of Muslims who visit the king on missions. . . . The interpreters of the king are Muslims, as are his treasurer and the majority of his ministers.

Their religion is paganism, and the worship of idols. . . . Around the royal town are domed dwellings, woods and copses where live their sorcerers, those in charge of their religious cults. There are also their idols and their kings' tombs.[2]

The king of Ghana required the sons of vassal kings to attend his court. He meted out justice and controlled trade, collecting taxes on the salt and copper coming from the north. His large army of bowmen and cavalry made Ghana the dominant power in the entire region. By the end of the tenth century, the king's sway extended even to Awdaghost°, the Arab and Berber trade entrepôt in the desert at the southern end of the track to Sijilmasa.

After 1076 Ghana fell prey to a new state formed by Muslim desert nomads known as Almoravids°. Later Muslim historians assert that many people in Ghana converted to Islam during the decade of nomad domination before the Almoravids withdrew to concentrate their attentions on Morocco and Spain. Although Ghana regained its independence, many former provinces had fallen away, and it never recovered its greatness.

Prior to the arrival of the religiously zealous Almoravids, the traders who had reached Ghana from the north had not been overly insistent on propagating Islam. Over the three centuries separating al-Bakri's account in the eleventh century from the earliest mention of Ghana, Muslims had come to hold high economic positions, and the kings tolerated their religious practices. But in general, the people of Ghana had not converted to Islam. Widespread adoption of the Islamic religion, with consequent impact on the way of life of the Sahel peoples, came under later kingdoms.

SUB-SAHARAN AFRICA

The Indian Ocean network and later trade across the Sahara provided **sub-Saharan Africa,** the portion of Africa south of the Sahara, with a few external contacts. The most important African network of cultural exchange from 300 B.C.E. to 1100 C.E., however, arose within the region and took the form of folk migration. These migrations and exchanges put in place enduring characteristics of African culture.

A Challenging Geography

Many geographic obstacles impede access to and movement within sub-Saharan Africa (see Map 8.2). The Sahara, the Atlantic and Indian Oceans, and the Red Sea form the boundaries of the region. With the exception of the Nile, a ribbon of green traversing the Sahara from south to north, the major river systems empty into the Atlantic, in the case of the Senegal, Niger, and Zaire° Rivers, or into the Mozambique Channel of the Indian Ocean, in the case of the Zambezi. Rapids limit the use of these rivers for navigation.

Stretching over 50 degrees of latitude, sub-Saharan Africa encompasses dramatically different environments. A 4,000-mile (6,500-kilometer) trek from the southern edge of the Sahara to the Cape of Good Hope would take a traveler from the flat, semiarid **steppes** of the Sahel region to tropical **savanna** covered by long grasses and scattered forest, and then to **tropical rain forest** on the lower Niger and in the Zaire Basin. The rain forest gives way to another broad expanse of savanna, followed by more steppe and desert, and finally by a region of temperate highlands at the southern extremity, located as far south of the equator as Greece and Sicily are to its north. East-west travel is comparatively easy in the steppe and savanna regions—a caravan from Senegal to the Red Sea would have traversed a distance comparable to that of the Silk Road—but difficult in the equatorial rain-forest belt and across the mountains and deep rift valleys that abut the rain forest to the east and separate East from West Africa.

The Development of Cultural Unity

Cultural heritages shared by the educated elites within each region—heritages that some anthropologists call "**great traditions**"—typically include a written language, common legal and belief systems, ethical codes, and other intellectual attitudes. They loom large in written records as traditions that rise above the diversity of local customs and beliefs commonly distinguished as "**small traditions.**"

By the year 1 C.E. sub-Saharan Africa had become a distinct cultural region, though one not shaped by impe-

Awdaghost (OW-duh-gost) **Almoravid** (al-moe-RAH-vid)

Zaire (zah-EER)

rial conquest or characterized by a shared elite culture, a "great tradition." The cultural unity of sub-Saharan Africa rested on similar characteristics shared to varying degrees by many popular cultures, or "small traditions." These had developed during the region's long period of isolation from the rest of the world and had been refined, renewed, and interwoven by repeated episodes of migration and social interaction. Historians know little about this complex prehistory. Thus, to a greater degree than in other regions, they call on anthropological descriptions, oral history, and comparatively late records of various "small traditions" to reconstruct the broad outlines of cultural formation.

Sub-Saharan Africa's cultural unity is less immediately apparent than its diversity. By one estimate, Africa is home to two thousand distinct languages, many corresponding to social and belief systems endowed with distinctive rituals and cosmologies. There are likewise numerous food production systems, ranging from hunting and gathering—very differently carried out by the Mbuti° Pygmies of the equatorial rain forest and the Khoisan° peoples of the southwestern deserts—to the cultivation of bananas, yams, and other root crops in forest clearings and of sorghum and other grains in the savanna lands. Pastoral societies, particularly those depending on cattle, display somewhat less diversity across the Sahel and savanna belt from Senegal to Kenya.

Sub-Saharan Africa covered a larger and more diverse area than any other cultural region of the first millennium C.E. and had a lower overall population density. Thus societies and polities had ample room to form and reform, and a substantial amount of space separated different groups. The contacts that did occur did not last long enough to produce rigid cultural uniformity.

In addition, for centuries external conquerors could not penetrate the region's natural barriers and impose a uniform culture. The Egyptians occupied Nubia, and some traces of Egyptian influence appear in Saharan rock art farther west, but the Nile cataracts and the vast swampland in the Nile's upper reaches blocked movement farther south. The Romans sent expeditions against pastoral peoples living in the Libyan Sahara but could not incorporate them into the Roman world. Not until the nineteenth century did outsiders gain control of the continent and begin the process of establishing an elite culture—that of European imperialism.

African Cultural Characteristics

European travelers who got to know the sub-Saharan region well in the nineteenth and twentieth centuries observed broad commonalties underlying African life and culture. In agriculture, the common technique was cultivation by hoe and digging stick. Musically, different groups of Africans played many instruments, especially types of drums, but common features, particularly in rhythm, gave African music as a whole a distinctive character. Music played an important role in social rituals, as did dancing and wearing masks, which often showed great artistry in their design.

African kingdoms varied, but kingship displayed common features, most notably the ritual isolation of the king himself (see Diversity and Dominance: Personal Styles of Rule in India and Mali in Chapter 14). Fixed social categories—age groupings, kinship divisions, distinct gender roles and relations, and occupational groupings—also show resemblances from one region to another, even in societies too small to organize themselves into kingdoms. Though not hierarchical, these categories played a role similar to the divisions between noble, commoner, and slave prevalent where kings ruled. Such indications of underlying cultural unity have led modern observers to identify a common African quality throughout most of the region, even though most sub-Saharan Africans themselves did not perceive it. An eminent Belgian anthropologist, Jacques Maquet, has called this quality "Africanity."

Some historians hypothesize that this cultural unity emanated from the peoples who once occupied the southern Sahara. In Paleolithic times, periods of dryness alternated with periods of wetness as the Ice Age that locked up much of the world's fresh water in glaciers and icecaps came and went. When European glaciers receded with the waning of the Ice Age, a storm belt brought increased wetness to the Saharan region. Rushing rivers scoured deep canyons. Now filled with fine sand, those canyons are easily visible on flights over the southern parts of the desert. As the glaciers receded farther, the storm belt moved northward to Europe, and dryness set in after 5000 B.C.E. As a consequence, runs the hypothesis, the region's population migrated southward, becoming increasingly concentrated in the Sahel, which may have been the initial incubation center for Pan-African cultural patterns.

Increasing dryness and the resulting difficulty in supporting the population would have driven some people out of this core into more sparsely settled lands to the east, west, and south. In a parallel development farther to the east, migration away from the growing aridity of the desert seems to have contributed to the settling of the Nile Valley and the emergence of the Old Kingdom of Egypt (see Chapter 2).

Mbuti (m-BOO-tee) **Khoisan** (KOI-sahn)

The Advent of Iron and the Bantu Migrations

Archaeology confirms that agriculture had become common between the equator and the Sahara by the early second millennium B.C.E. It then spread southward, displacing hunting and gathering as a way of life. Moreover, botanical evidence indicates that banana trees, probably introduced to southeastern Africa from Southeast Asia, made their way north and west, retracing in the opposite direction the presumed migration routes of the first agriculturists.

Archaeology has also uncovered traces of copper mining in the Sahara from the early first millennium B.C.E. Copper appears in the Niger Valley somewhat later, and in the Central African copper belt between 400 and 900 C.E. Gold was mined in Zimbabwe by the eighth and ninth centuries C.E. Most important of all, iron smelting began in northern sub-Saharan Africa in the early first millennium C.E. and spread southward from there, becoming firmly established in southern Africa by 800.

Many historians believe that the secret of smelting iron, which requires very high temperatures, was discovered only once, by the Hittites of Anatolia (modern Turkey) around 1500 B.C.E. (see Chapter 4). If that is the case, it is hard to explain how iron smelting reached sub-Saharan Africa. The earliest evidence of ironworking from the kingdom of Meroë, situated on the upper Nile and in cultural contact with Egypt, is no earlier than the evidence from West Africa (northern Nigeria). Even less plausible than the Nile Valley as a route of technological diffusion is the idea of a spread southward from Phoenician settlements in North Africa, since archaeological evidence has failed to substantiate the vague Greek and Latin accounts of Phoenician excursions to the south.

A more plausible scenario focuses on Africans' discovering for themselves how to smelt iron. Some historians suggest that they might have done so while firing pottery in kilns. No firm evidence exists to prove or disprove this theory.

Linguistic analysis provides the strongest evidence of extensive contacts among sub-Saharan Africans in the first millennium C.E.—and offers suggestions about the spread of iron. More than three hundred languages spoken south of the equator belong to the branch of the Niger-Congo family known as **Bantu,** after the word meaning "people" in most of the languages.

The distribution of the Bantu languages both north and south of the equator is consistent with a divergence beginning in the first millennium B.C.E. By comparing core words common to most of the languages, linguists have drawn some conclusions about the original Bantu-speakers, whom they call "proto-Bantu." These people engaged in fishing, using canoes, nets, lines, and hooks. They lived in permanent villages on the edge of the rain forest, where they grew yams and grains and harvested wild palm nuts from which they pressed oil. They possessed domesticated goats, dogs, and perhaps other animals. They made pottery and cloth. Linguists surmise that the proto-Bantu homeland was near the modern boundary of Nigeria and Cameroon. Although dates for their dispersal are scarce, Bantu-speaking people appear in East Africa by the eighth century C.E.

Because the presumed home of the proto-Bantu lies near the known sites of early iron smelting, migration by Bantu-speakers seems a likely mechanism for the southward spread of iron. The migrants probably used iron axes and hoes to hack out forest clearings and plant crops. According to this scenario, their actions would have established an economic basis for new societies capable of sustaining much denser populations than could earlier societies dependent on hunting and gathering alone. Thus the period from 500 B.C.E. to 1000 C.E. saw a massive transfer of Bantu traditions and practices southward, eastward, and westward and their transformation, through intermingling with preexisting societies, into Pan-African traditions and practices.

THE SPREAD OF IDEAS

Ideas, like social customs, religious attitudes, and artistic styles, can spread along trade routes and through folk migrations. In both cases, documenting the dissemination of ideas, particularly in preliterate societies, poses a difficult historical problem.

Ideas and Material Evidence

Historians know about some ideas only through the survival of written sources. Other ideas do not depend on writing but are inherent in material objects studied by archaeologists and anthropologists. Customs surrounding the eating of pork are a case in point. Scholars disagree about whether pigs became domestic in only one place, from which the practice of pig keeping spread elsewhere, or whether several peoples hit on the same idea at different times and in different places.

Southeast Asia was an important early center of pig domestication. Anthropological studies tell us that the eating of pork became highly ritualized in this area and that it was sometimes allowed only on ceremonial occasions. On the other side of the Indian Ocean, wild swine were common in the Nile swamps of ancient Egypt. There, too, pigs took on a sacred role, being associated with the evil god Set, and eating them was prohibited. The biblical prohibition on the Israelites' eating pork, echoed later by the Muslims, probably came from Egypt in the second millennium B.C.E.

In a third locale in eastern Iran, an archaeological site dating from the third millennium B.C.E. provides evidence of another religious taboo relating to pork. Although the area around the site was swampy and home to many wild pigs, not a single pig bone has been found. Yet small pig figurines seem to have been used as symbolic religious offerings, and the later Iranian religion associates the boar with an important god.

What accounts for the apparent connection between domestic pigs and religion in these far-flung areas? There is no way of knowing. It has been hypothesized that pigs were first domesticated in Southeast Asia by people who had no herd animals—sheep, goats, cattle, or horses—and who relied on fish for most of their animal protein. The pig therefore became a special animal to them. The practice of pig herding, along with religious beliefs and rituals associated with the consumption of pork, could conceivably have spread from Southeast Asia along the maritime routes of the Indian Ocean, eventually reaching Iran and Egypt. But no evidence survives to support this hypothesis. In this case, therefore, material evidence can only hint at the spread of religious ideas, leaving the door open for other explanations.

A more certain example of objects' indicating the spread of an idea is the practice of hammering a carved die onto a piece of precious metal and using the resulting coin as a medium of exchange. From its origin in the Lydian kingdom in Anatolia in the first millennium B.C.E. (see Chapter 5), the idea of trading by means of struck coinage spread rapidly to Europe, North Africa, and India. Was the low-value copper coinage of China, made by pouring molten metal into a mold, also inspired by this practice from far away? It may have been, but it might also derive from indigenous Chinese metalworking. There is no way to be sure. Theoretically, all that is needed for an idea to spread is a single returning traveler telling about some wonder that he or she saw abroad.

Statue of a Bodhisattva at Bamian This is one of two monumental Buddhist sculptures near the top of a high mountain pass connecting Kabul, Afghanistan, with the northern parts of the country. Carved into the side of a cliff in the sixth or seventh century, C.E., the sculptures were surrounded by cave dwellings of monks and rock sanctuaries, some dating to the first century B.C.E. This statue and the one alongside it were blown to pieces by the intolerant Taliban regime in Afghanistan in 2001. (Ian Griffiths/Robert Harding Picture Library)

The Spread of Buddhism

While material objects associated with religious beliefs and rituals are important indicators of the spread of spiritual ideas, written sources deal with the spread of today's major religions. Buddhism grew to become, with Christianity and Islam (see Chapter 9), one of the most popular and widespread religions in the world. In all three cases, the religious ideas spread without dependency on a single ethnic or kinship group.

King Ashoka, the Maurya ruler of India, and Kanishka, the greatest king of the Kushans of northern Afghanistan, promoted Buddhism between the third century B.C.E. and the second century C.E. However, monks, missionaries, and pilgrims who crisscrossed India, followed the Silk Road, or took ships on the Indian Ocean brought the Buddha's teachings to Southeast Asia, China, Korea, and ultimately Japan (see Map 8.1).

The Chinese pilgrims Faxian° (died between 418 and 423 C.E.) and Xuanzang° (600–664 C.E.) left written accounts of their travels. Both followed the Silk Road, through which Buddhism had arrived in China. Along the way they encountered Buddhist communities and monasteries that previous generations of missionaries and pilgrims had established.

Faxian began his trip in the company of a Chinese envoy to an unspecified ruler or people in Central Asia. After traveling from one Buddhist site to another across Afghanistan and India, he reached Sri Lanka, a Buddhist land, where he lived for two years. He then embarked for China on a merchant ship with two hundred men aboard. A storm drove the ship to Java, which he chose not to describe since it was Hindu rather than Buddhist. After five months ashore, Faxian finally reached China on another ship. The narrative of Xuanzang's journey two centuries later is quite similar, though he returned to China the way he had come, along the Silk Road.

Less reliable accounts make reference to missionaries traveling to Syria, Egypt, and Macedonia, as well as to Southeast Asia. One of Ashoka's sons allegedly led a band of missionaries to Sri Lanka. Later, his sister brought a company of nuns there, along with a branch of the sacred Bo tree under which the Buddha had received enlightenment. At the same time, there are reports of other monks traveling to Burma, Thailand, and Sumatra. Ashoka's missionaries may also have reached Tibet by way of trade routes across the Himalayas. A firmer tradition maintains that in 622 C.E. a minister of the Tibetan king traveled to India to study Buddhism and on his return introduced writing to his homeland.

The different lands that received the story and teachings of the Buddha preserved or adapted them in different ways. Theravada Buddhism, "Teachings of the Elder," was centered in Sri Lanka. Holding closely to the Buddha's earliest teachings, it maintained that the goal of religion, available only to monks, is *nirvana,* the total absence of suffering and the end of the cycle of rebirth (see Chapter 7). This teaching contrasted with Mahayana, or "Great Vehicle" Buddhism, which stressed the goal of becoming a *bodhisattva,* a person who attains nirvana but chooses to remain in human company to help and guide others.

An offshoot of Mahayana Buddhism stressing ritual prayer and personal guidance by "perfected ones" became dominant in Tibet after the eighth century C.E. In China another offshoot, Chan (called Zen in its Japanese form), focused on meditation and sudden enlightenment. It became one of the dominant sects in China, Korea, and Japan (see Chapter 11).

Faxian (fah-shee-en) **Xuanzang** (shoo-wen-zahng)

The Spread of Christianity

The post-Roman development of Christianity in Europe is discussed in Chapter 10. The Christian faith enjoyed an earlier spread in Asia and Africa before its confrontation with Islam (described in Chapter 9). Jerusalem in Palestine, Antioch in Syria, and Alexandria in Egypt became centers of Christian authority soon after the crucifixion, but the spread of Christianity to Armenia and Ethiopia illustrates the connections between religion, trade, and imperial politics.

Situated in eastern Anatolia (modern Turkey), **Armenia** served recurrently as a battleground between Iranian states to the south and east and Mediterranean states to the west. Each imperial power wanted to control this region so close to the frontier where Silk Road traders met their Mediterranean counterparts. In Parthian times, Armenia's kings favored Zoroastrianism. Armenian not then being a written language, Christianity was known to "only those who were to some degree acquainted with Greek or Syriac learning" and thus able to obtain "some partial inkling of it."[3]

The invention of an Armenian alphabet in the early fifth century opened the way to a wider spread of Christianity. The Iranians did not give up domination easily, but within a century the Armenian Apostolic Church had become the center of Armenian cultural life.

Far to the south Christians similarly sought to outflank Iran. The Christian emperors in Constantinople (see Chapter 10) sent missionaries along the Red Sea trade route to seek converts in Yemen and **Ethiopia.** In the fourth century C.E. a Syrian philosopher traveling with two young relatives sailed to India. On the way back the ship docked at a Red Sea port occupied by Ethiopians from the prosperous kingdom of Aksum. Being then at odds with the Romans, the Ethiopians killed everyone on board except the two boys, Aedisius—who later narrated this story—and Frumentius. Impressed by their learning, the king made the former his cupbearer and the latter his treasurer and secretary.

When the king died, his wife urged Frumentius to govern Aksum on her behalf and that of her infant son, Ezana. As regent Frumentius sought out Roman Christians among the merchants who visited the country and helped them establish Christian communities. When he became king, Ezana, who may have become a Christian, permitted Aedisius and Frumentius to return to Syria. The patriarch of Alexandria, on learning about the progress of Christianity in Aksum, elevated Frumentius to the rank of bishop, though he had not previously been a clergyman, and sent him back to Ethiopia as the first leader of its church.

Stele of Aksum This 70-foot (21-meter) stone is the tallest remnant of a field of stelae, or standing stones, marking the tombs of Aksumite kings. The carvings of doors, windows, and beam ends imitate common features of Aksumite architecture, suggesting that each stele symbolized a multistory royal palace. The largest stelae date from the fourth century C.E. (J. Allan Cash)

The patriarch of Alexandria continues today to appoint the head of the Ethiopian Church, but the spread of Christianity into Nubia, the land south of Egypt along the Nile River, proceeded from Ethiopia rather than Egypt. Politically and economically, Ethiopia became a power at the western end of the Indian Ocean trading system, occasionally even extending its influence across the Red Sea and asserting itself in Yemen (see Map 8.2).

Ethiopian Christianity developed its own unique features. One popular belief, perhaps deriving from the Ethiopian Jewish community, was that the Ark of the Covenant, the most sacred object of the ancient Hebrews (see Chapter 4), had been transferred from Jerusalem to the Ethiopian church of Our Lady of Zion. Another tradition maintains that Christ miraculously dried up a lake to serve as the site for this church, which became the place of coronation for Ethiopia's rulers.

CONCLUSION

Exchange facilitated by the early long-distance trading systems differed in many ways from the ebb and flow of culture, language, and custom that folk migrations brought about. Transportable goods and livestock and ideas about new technologies and agricultural products sometimes worked great changes on the landscape and in people's lives. But nothing resembling the Africanity observed south of the Sahara can be attributed to the societies involved in the Silk Road, Indian Ocean, or trans-Saharan exchanges. Not only were few people directly involved in these complex social systems of travel and trade compared with the populations with whom they were brought into contact, but their lifestyles as pastoral nomads or seafarers isolated them still more. Communities of traders contributed to this isolation by their reluctance to share knowledge with people who might become commercial competitors.

The Bantu, however, if current theories are correct, spread far and wide in sub-Saharan Africa with the deliberate intent of settling and implanting a lifestyle based on iron implements and agriculture. The metallurgical skills and agricultural techniques they brought with them permitted much denser habitation and helped ensure that the languages of the immigrants would supplant those of their hunting and gathering predecessors. Where the trading systems encouraged diversity by introducing new products and ideas, the Bantu migrations brought a degree of cultural dominance that strongly affected later African history.

An apparent exception to the generalization that trading systems have less impact than folk migrations on patterns of dominance lies in the intangible area of ideas. Christianity, Buddhism, and Islam all spread along trade routes, at least to some degree. Each instance of spread, however, gave rise to new forms of cultural diversity even as overall doctrinal unity made these religions dominant. As "great traditions," the new faiths based on conversion linked priests, monks, nuns, and religious scholars across vast distances. The masses of believers, however, seldom considered their spiritual lives in such broad contexts. Missionary religions imported through long-distance trading networks merged with myriad "small traditions" to provide for the social and spiritual needs of peoples living in many lands under widely varying circumstances.

Key Terms

Silk Road
Parthians
stirrup
Indian Ocean Maritime System
trans-Saharan caravan routes
Sahel
Ghana
sub-Saharan Africa
steppes
savanna
tropical rain forest
"great traditions"
"small traditions"
Bantu
Armenia
Ethiopia

Suggested Reading

For broad and suggestive overviews on cross-cultural exchange see Philip D. Curtin, *Cross-Cultural Trade in World History* (1985), and C. G. F. Simkin, *The Traditional Trade of Asia* (1968).

Readable overviews of the Silk Road include Luce Boulnois, *The Silk Road* (1966), and Irene M. Franck and David M. Brownstone, *The Silk Road: A History* (1986). For products traded across Central Asia based on an eighth-century Japanese collection, see Ryoichi Hayashi, *The Silk Road and the Shoso-in* (1975). Xinru Liu, *Silk and Religion* (1996), covers one specific product. Owen Lattimore gives a first-person account of traveling by camel caravan in *The Desert Road to Turkestan* (1928). More generally on Central Asia, see Denis Sinor, *Inner Asia, History-Civilization-Languages: A Syllabus* (1987), and Karl Jettmar, *Art of the Steppes,* rev. ed. (1967). Richard Foltz, *Religions of the Silk Road* (1999), is an excellent brief introduction.

For a readable but sketchy historical overview see August Toussaint, *History of the Indian Ocean* (1966). Alan Villiers recounts what it was like to sail dhows between East Africa and the Persian Gulf in *Sons of Sinbad* (1940).

On a more scholarly plane, see K. N. Chaudhuri's *Trade and Civilization in the Indian Ocean: An Economic History from the Rise of Islam to 1750* (1985). Archaeologist Pierre Vérin treats the special problem of Madagascar in *The History of Civilisation in North Madagascar* (1986). For Rome and India see E. H. Warmington's *The Commerce Between the Roman Empire and India* (1974); J. Innes Miller's *The Spice Trade of the Roman Empire, 29 B.C. to A.D. 641* (1969); and Vimala Begley and Richard Daniel De Puma's edited collection of articles, *Rome and India: The Ancient Sea Trade* (1991), along with the primary source *The Periplus Maris Erythraei: Text with Introduction, Translation, and Commentary* (1989) edited and translated by Lionel Casson. George F. Hourani's brief *Arab Seafaring in the Indian Ocean in Ancient and Early Medieval Times* (1975) covers materials in Arabic sources.

Nicholas Tarling, ed., *The Cambridge History of Southeast Asia,* vol. 1 (1992); D. R. SarDesai, *Southeast Asia: Past and Present,* 3d ed. (1994); and Milton E. Osborne, *Southeast Asia: An Introductory History* (1995), provide general accounts of Southeast Asian history. Lynda Shaffer, *Maritime Southeast Asia to 1500* (1996), focuses on the world historical context. Also useful is Kenneth R. Hall, *Maritime Trade and State Development in Early Southeast Asia* (1985).

On art see M. C. S. Diskul, *The Art of Srivijaya* (1980); Maud Girard-Geslan et al., *Art of Southeast Asia* (1998); and Daigoro Chihara, *Hindu-Buddhist Architecture in Southeast Asia* (1996).

Richard W. Bulliet's *The Camel and the Wheel* (1975) deals with camel use in the Middle East, along the Silk Road, and in North Africa and the Sahara. For a well-illustrated account of Saharan rock art see Henri Lhote, *The Search for the Tassili Frescoes: The Story of the Prehistoric Rock-Paintings of the Sahara* (1959). Additional views on Saharan trade and politics appear in E. Ann McDougall, "The Sahara Reconsidered: Pastoralism, Politics and Salt from the Ninth Through the Twelfth Centuries," *History in Africa 12* (1983): 263–286, and Nehemia Levtzion, *Ancient Ghana and Mali,* 2d ed. (1980). For translated texts see J. F. P. Hopkins and Nehemia Levtzion, eds., *Corpus of Early Arabic Sources for West African History* (1981).

J. F. A. Ajayi and Michael Crowder, *A History of West Africa,* vol. 1 (1976), and G. Mokhtar, ed., *General History of Africa II: Ancient Civilizations of Africa* (1981), include many articles by numerous authors; the latter work specifically treats ironworking and the Bantu migrations. On African cultural unity see Jacques Maquet, *Africanity: The Cultural Unity of Black Africa* (1972).

Of special importance on Christianity in Asia and Africa is Garth Fowden, *Empire to Commonwealth: Consequences of Monotheism in Late Antiquity* (1993). For specific topics treated in this chapter see Stuart Munro-Hay, *Aksum: An African Civilisation of Late Antiquity* (1991); Xinru Liu, *Ancient India and Ancient China: Trade and Religious Exchanges, A.D. 1–600* (1998); Rolf A. Stein, *Tibetan Civilization* (1972); Tilak Hettiarachchy, *History of Kingship in Ceylon up to the Fourth Century A.D.* (1972); and Yoneo Ishii, *Sangha, State, and Society: Thai Buddhism in History* (1986). The Chinese travelers' accounts cited are Fa-hsien [Faxian], *The Travels of Fahsien (399–414 A.D.), or, Record of the Buddhistic Kingdoms,* trans. H. A. Giles (1923; reprint, 1981), and Hiuen Tsiang [Xuanzang], *Si-Yu-Ki: Buddhist Records of the Western World,* trans. Samuel Beal (1884; reprint, 1981).

Notes

1. Victor H. Mair, ed., *The Columbia Anthology of Traditional Chinese Literature* (New York: Columbia University Press, 1994), 485; translated by Victor H. Mair.
2. J. F. A. Ajayi and Michael Crowder, eds., *History of West Africa,* vol. 1 (New York: Columbia University Press, 1976), 120–121.
3. Pawstos Busand, *Epic Histories* (late fifth century), quoted in Garth Fowden, *Empire to Commonwealth* (Princeton NJ: Princeton University Press, 1993), 105.

9

The Sasanid Empire and the Rise of Islam, 200–1200

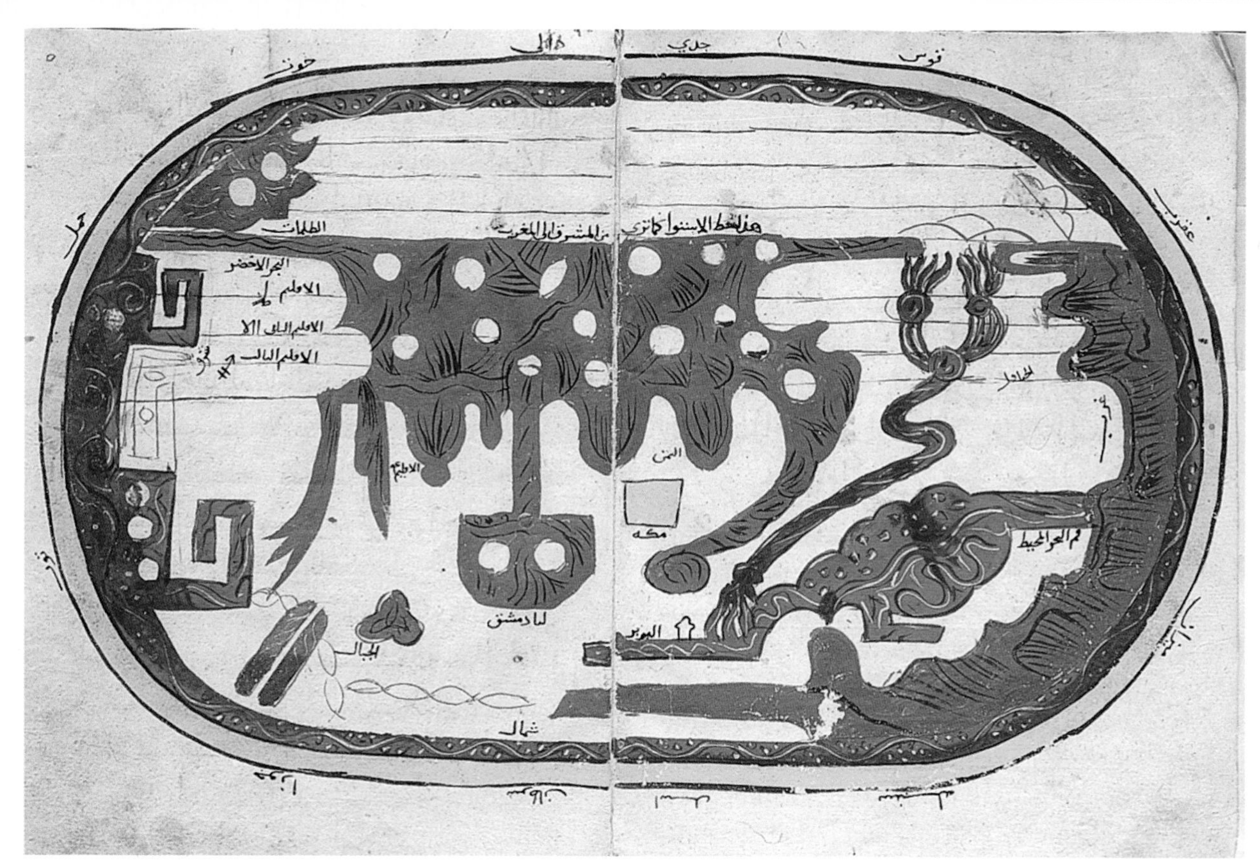

Islamic World Map Oriented with south at the top, this copy of a tenth-century original was probably made in the fourteenth century.

CHAPTER OUTLINE

The Sasanid Empire, 224–651

The Origins of Islam

The Rise and Fall of the Caliphate, 632–1258

Islamic Civilization

DIVERSITY AND DOMINANCE: Beggars, Con Men, and Singing-girls

ENVIRONMENT AND TECHNOLOGY: Automata

The story is told that in the early days of Islam, at the time of the Prophet Muhammad's last pilgrimage to Mecca in 630, a dispute over distribution of booty arose between his daughter's husband, Ali, who was also Muhammad's first cousin, and some troops Ali commanded. Muhammad quelled the grumbling and later on the same journey, at a place named Ghadir al-Khumm°, drew his followers together, took Ali's hand, and declared: "Am I not nearer to the believers than their own selves? Whomever I am nearest to, so likewise is Ali. O God, be the friend of him who is his friend, and the foe of him who is his foe."

Written narratives of Muhammad's praise of Ali, like all stories of Muhammad's life, date to well over a century after the event. By that time, Ali had served as leader of Muhammad's community for a brief time and had then been defeated in a civil war and assassinated. Subsequently, his son Husayn, along with his family, died in a hopelessly lopsided battle while trying to claim leadership as the Prophet's grandson.

Out of these events grew a division in the Islamic community: some believers, called **Shi'ites°,** from the Arabic term *Shi'at Ali* ("Party of Ali"), thought that religious leadership rightfully belonged to Ali and his descendants; others, eventually called **Sunnis°**, followers of the sunna, or "tradition" of the community, felt that the community should choose its leaders more broadly. Sunnis and Shi'ites agreed that Muhammad commended Ali at Ghadir al-Khumm. But the Sunnis considered his remarks to relate only to the distribution of the booty, and the Shi'ites understood them to be Muhammad's formal and public declaration of Ali's special and elevated position, and hence of his right to rule.

Shi'ite rulers rarely achieved power, but those who ruled from Cairo between 969 and 1171 made the commemoration of Ghadir al-Khumm a major festival. At the beginning of every year, Shi'ites everywhere also engaged in public mourning over the deaths of Husayn and his family. Sunni rulers, in contrast, sometimes ordered that Ali be cursed in public prayers.

Muhammad's Arab followers conquered an enormous territory in the seventh century. In the name of Islam, they created an empire that encompassed many peoples speaking many languages and worshiping in many ways. Its immediate forerunners, the realms of the Byzantine emperors (see Chapter 10) and Iran's Sasanid° shahs, closely linked religion with imperial politics.

Although urbanism, science, manufacturing, trade, and architecture flourished in the lands of Islam while medieval Europe was enduring hardship and economic contraction, religion shaped both societies. Just as the medieval Christian calendar revolved around Easter and Christmas, Islamic fasts, pilgrimages, and political religious observances like Ghadir al-Khumm marked the yearly cycle in the lands of Muhammad's followers.

As you read this chapter, ask yourself the following questions:

- How did social and political developments under the Sasanid Empire pave the way for the spread of Islam?
- How did the Arab conquests grow out of the career of Muhammad?
- Why did the caliphate break up?
- How did Muslim societies differ from region to region?
- What was the relationship between urbanization and the development of Islamic culture?

The Sasanid Empire, 224–651

The rise in the third century of a new Iranian state, the **Sasanid Empire,** continued the old rivalry between Rome and the Parthians along the Euphrates frontier. However, behind this façade of continuity, a social and economic transformation took place that set the stage for a new and powerful religio-political movement: Islam.

Ghadir al-Khumm (ga-DEER al-KUM) **Shi'ite** (SHE-ite) **Sunni** (SUN-nee)

Sasanid (SAH-suh-nid)

CHRONOLOGY

	The Arab Lands	Iran and Central Asia
200		**224–651** Sasanid Empire
600	**570–632** Life of the Prophet Muhammad **634** Conquests of Iraq and Syria commence **639–42** Conquest of Egypt by Arabs **656–61** Ali caliph; first civil war **661–750** Umayyad Caliphate rules from Damascus	
700	**711** Berbers and Arabs invade Spain from North Africa **750** Beginning of Abbasid Caliphate **755** Umayyad state established in Spain **776–809** Caliphate of Hurun al-Rashid	**711** Arabs capture Sind in India **747** Abbasid revolt begins in Khurasan
800	**835–92** Abbasid capital moved from Baghdad to Samarra	**875** Independent Samanid state founded in Bukhara
900	**909** Fatimids seize North Africa, found Shi'ite Caliphate **929** Abd al-Rahman III declares himself caliph in Cordoba **945** Shi'ite Buyids take control in Baghdad **969** Fatimids conquer Egypt	**945** Buyids from northern Iran take control of Abbasid Caliphate
1000	**1055** Seljuk Turks take control in Baghdad **1099** First Crusade captures Jerusalem **1171** Fall of Fatimid Egypt **1187** Saladin recaptures Jerusalem **1250** Mamluks control Egypt **1258** Mongols sack Baghdad and end Abbasid Caliphate **1260** Mamluks defeat Mongols at Ain Jalut	**1036** Beginning of Turkish Seljuk rule in Khurasan

Politics and Society

Ardashir, whose dynasty takes its name from an ancestor named Sasan, defeated the Parthians around 224 and established the Sasanid kingdom. To the west, the new rulers confronted the Romans, whom later historians frequently refer to as the Byzantines after about 330. Along their desert Euphrates frontier, the Sasanids subsidized nomadic Arab chieftains to protect their empire from invasion (the Byzantines did the same with Arabs on their Jordanian desert frontier). Arab pastoralists farther to the south remained isolated and independent. The rival empires launched numerous attacks on each other across that frontier between the 340s and 628. In

Sasanid Silver Vase The Sasanid aristocracy, based in the countryside, invested part of its wealth in silver plates and vessels. The image is of the fertility goddess Anahita, a deity acceptable to the Zoroastrian faith. One inscription in Pahlavi (a Middle Persian language) gives the weight, 116.9 grams in modern terms, while another in Sogdian, a language common along the Silk Road, gives the owner's name, Mithrak. (The State Heritage Museum, St Petersburg)

times of peace, however, exchange between the empires flourished, allowing goods transported over the Silk Road to enter the zone of Mediterranean trade.

The Arab pastoralists inhabiting the desert between Syria and Mesopotamia supplied camels and guides and played a significant role as merchants and organizers of caravans. The militarily efficient North Arabian camel saddle (see Chapter 8, Environment and Technology: Camel Saddles), developed around the third century B.C.E., provided another key to Arab prosperity. The Arabs used it to take control of the caravan trade in their territories and thereby became so important as suppliers of animal power even in agricultural districts that wheeled vehicles—mostly ox carts and horse-drawn chariots—had all but disappeared by the sixth century C.E.

The mountains and plateaus of Iran proper formed the Sasanids' political hinterland, often ruled by the cousins of the shah (king) or by powerful nobles. Cities there were small walled communities that served more as military strongpoints than as centers of population and production. Society revolved around a local aristocracy that lived on rural estates and cultivated the arts of hunting, feasting, and war just like the noble warriors described in the sagas of ancient kings and heroes sung at their banquets.

Despite the dominance of powerful aristocratic families, long-lasting political fragmentation of the medieval European variety did not develop (see Chapter 10). Also, although many nomads lived in the mountain and desert regions, no folk migration took place comparable to that of the Germanic peoples who defeated Roman armies and established kingdoms in formerly Roman territory from about the third century C.E. onward. The Sasanid and Byzantine Empires successfully maintained central control of imperial finances and military power and found effective ways of integrating frontier peoples as mercenaries or caravaneers.

The Silk Road brought new products to Mesopotamia, some of which became part of the agricultural landscape. Sasanid farmers pioneered in planting cotton, sugar cane, rice, citrus trees, eggplants, and other crops adopted from India and China. Although the acreage devoted to new crops increased slowly, these products became important consumption and trade items during the succeeding Islamic period.

Religion and Empire

The Sasanids established their Zoroastrian faith (see Chapter 5), which the Parthians had not particularly stressed, as a state religion similar to Christianity in the Byzantine Empire (see Chapter 10). The proclamation of Christianity and Zoroastrianism as official faiths marked the fresh emergence of religion as an instrument of politics both within and between the empires, setting a precedent for the subsequent rise of Islam as the focus of a political empire.

Both Zoroastrianism and Christianity practiced intolerance. A late-third-century inscription in Iran boasts of the persecutions of Christians, Jews, and Buddhists carried out by the Zoroastrian high priest. Yet sizable Christian and Jewish communities remained, especially in Mesopotamia. Similarly, from the fourth century onward, councils of Christian bishops declared many theological beliefs heretical—so unacceptable that they were un-Christian.

Christians became pawns in the political rivalry with the Byzantines and were sometimes persecuted, sometimes patronized by the Sasanid kings. In 431 a council of bishops called by the Byzantine emperor declared the Nestorian Christians heretics for overemphasizing the humanness of Christ. The Nestorians believed that human characteristics and divinity coexisted in Jesus and that Mary was not the mother of God, as many other Christians maintained, but the mother of the human Jesus. After the bishops' ruling, the Nestorians sought refuge under the Sasanid shah and eventually extended their missionary activities along the Central Asian trade routes.

In the third century a preacher named Mani had founded a new religion in Mesopotamia: Manichaeism. He preached a dualist faith—a struggle between Good and Evil—theologically derived from Zoroastrianism. Although at first Mani enjoyed the favor of the shah, he and many of his followers were martyred in 276. His religion survived and spread widely. Nestorian missionaries in Central Asia competed with Manichaean missionaries for converts. In later centuries, the term *Manichaean* was applied to all sorts of beliefs about a cosmic struggle between Good and Evil.

The Arabs became enmeshed in this web of religious conflict. The border protectors subsidized by the Byzantines adopted a Monophysite theology, which emphasized Christ's divine nature; the allies of the Sasanids, the Nestorian faith. Through them, knowledge of Christianity penetrated deeper into the Arabian peninsula during the fifth and sixth centuries.

Religion permeated all aspects of community life. Most subjects of the Byzantine emperors and Sasanid shahs identified themselves first and foremost as members of a religious community. Their schools and law courts were religious. They looked on priests, monks, rabbis, and the Zoroastrian mobads as moral guides in daily life. Most books discussed religious subjects. In some areas, religious leaders represented their flocks even in such secular matters as tax collection.

The Origins of Islam

The Arabs who lived beyond the frontiers of the Sasanid Empire seldom interested the Sasanid rulers. But it was precisely in the interior of Arabia, far from the gaze and political reach of the Sasanid and Byzantine Empires, that the religion of Islam took form and inspired a movement that would humble the proud emperors.

The Arabian Peninsula Before Muhammad

Throughout history more people living on the Arabian peninsula have lived in settled communities than as pastoral nomads. The highlands of Yemen, fertile and abundantly watered by the spring monsoon, and the interior mountains farther east in southern Arabia have supported farming and village life. Small inlets along the southern coast favored occasional fishing or trading communities. However, the enormous sea of sand known as the "Empty Quarter" isolated these southern regions from the Arabian interior. In the seventh century, most people in southern Arabia knew more about Africa, India, and the Persian Gulf (see Chapter 8, Diversity and Dominance: "The Indian Ocean Trading World") than about the forbidding interior and the scattered camel- and sheep-herding nomads who lived there.

Exceptions to this pattern mostly involved caravan trading. Several kingdoms rose and fell in Yemen, leaving stone ruins and stone-cut inscriptions to testify to their bygone prosperity. From these commercial entrepôts came the aromatic resins frankincense and myrrh. Nomads derived income from providing camels, guides, and safe passage to merchants wanting to transport incense northward, where the fragrant substances had long been burned in religious rituals. Return caravans brought manufactured products from Mesopotamia and the Mediterranean.

Just as the Silk Road enabled small towns in Central Asia to become major trading centers, so the trans-Arabian trade gave rise to desert caravan cities. The earliest and most prosperous, Petra in southern Jordan and Palmyra in northern Syria, were swallowed up by Rome. This, coupled with an early Christian distaste for incense, which seemed too much a feature of pagan worship, contributed to a slackening of trade in Sasanid times. Nevertheless, trade across the desert did not lapse altogether. Camels, leather, and gold and other minerals mined in the mountains of western Arabia took the place of frankincense and myrrh as exports. This reduced trade kept alive the relations between the Arabs and the settled farming regions to the north, and it familiarized the Arabs who accompanied the caravans with the cultures and lifestyles of the Sasanid and Byzantine Empires.

In the desert, Semitic polytheism, with its worship of natural forces and celestial bodies, began to encounter other religions. Christianity, as practiced by Arabs in Jordan and southern Mesopotamia, and Judaism, possibly carried by refugees from the Roman expulsion of the Jews from their homeland in the first century C.E., made inroads on polytheism.

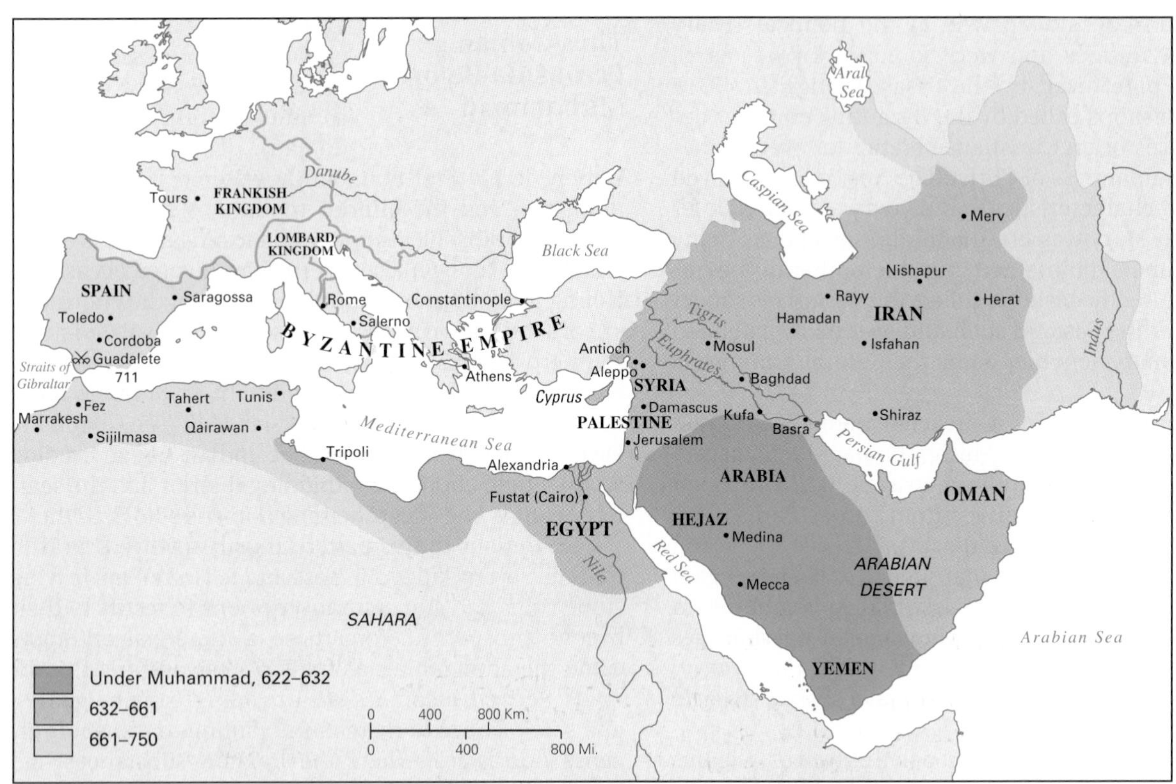

Map 9.1 Early Expansion of Muslim Rule Arab conquests of the first Islamic century brought vast territory under Muslim rule, but conversion to Islam proceeded slowly. In most areas outside the Arabian peninsula, the only region where Arabic was then spoken, conversion did not accelerate until the third century after the conquest.

Mecca, a late-blooming caravan city, lies in a barren mountain valley halfway between Yemen and Syria and a short way inland from the Red Sea coast of Arabia (see Map 9.1). A nomadic kin group known as the Quraysh° settled in Mecca in the fifth century and assumed control of trade. Mecca rapidly achieved a measure of prosperity, partly because it was too far from Byzantine Syria, Sasanid Iraq, and Ethiopian-controlled Yemen for them to attack it.

A cubical shrine called the Ka'ba°, containing idols, a holy well called Zamzam, and a sacred precinct surrounding the two wherein killing was prohibited, contributed to the emergence of Mecca as a pilgrimage site. Some Meccans associated the shrine with stories known to Jews and Christians. They regarded Abraham (Ibrahim in Arabic) as the builder of the Ka'ba, and they identified a site outside Mecca as the location where God asked Abraham to sacrifice his son. The son was not Isaac (Ishaq in Arabic), the son of Sarah, but Ishmael (Isma'il in Arabic), the son of Hagar, cited in the Bible as the forefather of the Arabs.

Muhammad in Mecca

Born in Mecca in 570, **Muhammad** grew up an orphan in the house of his uncle. He engaged in trade and married a Quraysh widow named Khadija°, whose caravan interests he superintended. Their son died in childhood, but several daughters survived. Around 610 Muhammad began meditating at night in the mountainous terrain around Mecca. During one night vigil, known to later tradition as the "Night of Power and Excellence," a being whom Muhammad later understood to be the angel Gabriel (Jibra'il in Arabic) spoke to him:

Quraysh (koo-RYYSH) **Ka'ba** (KAH-buh)

Khadija (kah-DEE-juh)

Proclaim! In the name of your Lord who created.
Created man from a clot of congealed blood.
Proclaim! And your Lord is the Most Bountiful.
He who has taught by the pen.
Taught man that which he knew not.[1]

For three years he shared this and subsequent revelations only with close friends and family members. This period culminated in Muhammad's conviction that he was hearing the words of God (Allah° in Arabic). Khadija, his uncle's son Ali, his friend Abu Bakr°, and others close to him shared this conviction. The revelations continued until Muhammad's death in 632.

Like most people of the time, including Christians and Jews, the Arabs believed in unseen spirits: gods, desert spirits called *jinns,* demonic *shaitans,* and others. They further believed that certain individuals had contact with the spirit world, notably seers and poets, who were thought to be possessed by jinns. Therefore, when Muhammad began to recite his rhymed revelations in public, many people believed he was inspired by an unseen spirit even if it was not, as Muhammad asserted, the one true god.

Muhammad's earliest revelations called on people to witness that one god had created the universe and everything in it, including themselves. At the end of time, their souls would be judged, their sins balanced against their good deeds. The blameless would go to paradise; the sinful would taste hellfire:

By the night as it conceals the light;
By the day as it appears in glory;
By the mystery of the creation of male and female;
Verily, the ends ye strive for are diverse.
So he who gives in charity and fears God,
And in all sincerity testifies to the best,
We will indeed make smooth for him the path to Bliss.
But he who is a greedy miser and thinks himself
self-sufficient,
And gives the lie to the best,
We will indeed make smooth for him the path to
misery.[2]

The revelation called all people to submit to God and accept Muhammad as the last of his messengers. Doing so made one a **muslim,** meaning one who makes "submission," **Islam,** to the will of God.

Because earlier messengers mentioned in the revelations included Noah, Moses, and Jesus, Muhammad's hearers felt that his message resembled the Judaism and Christianity they were already somewhat familiar with. Yet his revelations charged the Jews and Christians with being negligent in preserving God's revealed word. Thus, even though they identified Abraham/Ibrahim, whom Muslims consider the first Muslim, as the builder of the Ka'ba, which superseded Jerusalem as the focus of Muslim prayer in 624, Muhammad's followers considered his revelation more perfect than the Bible because it had not gone through an editing process.

Some non-Muslim scholars maintain that Muhammad's revelations appealed especially to people distressed over wealth replacing kinship as the most important aspect of social relations. They see verses criticizing taking pride in money and neglecting obligations to orphans and other powerless people as conveying a message of social reform. Other scholars, along with most Muslims, put less emphasis on a social message and stress the power and beauty of Muhammad's revelations. Forceful rhetoric and poetic vision, coming in the Muslim view directly from God, go far to explain Muhammad's early success.

The Formation of the Umma

Mecca's leaders feared that accepting Muhammad as the sole agent of the one true God would threaten their power and prosperity. They pressured his kin to disavow him and persecuted the weakest of his followers. Stymied by this hostility, Muhammad and his followers fled Mecca in 622 to take up residence in the agricultural community of **Medina** 215 miles (346 kilometers) to the north. This hijra° marks the beginning of the Muslim calendar.

Prior to the hijra, Medinan representatives had met with Muhammad and agreed to accept and protect him and his followers because they saw him as an inspired leader who could calm their perpetual feuding. Together, the Meccan migrants and major groups in Medina bound themselves into a single **umma°**, a community defined solely by acceptance of Islam and of Muhammad as the "Messenger of God," his most common title. Three Jewish kin groups chose to retain their own faith, thus contributing to the Muslims' changing the direction of their prayer toward the Ka'ba, now thought of as the "House of God."

During the last decade of his life, Muhammad took active responsibility for his umma. Having left their Meccan kin groups, the immigrants in Medina felt vulnerable. Fresh revelations provided a framework for regulating social and legal affairs and stirred the Muslims to fight against the still-unbelieving city of Mecca. Sporadic war, largely conducted by raiding and negotiation with

Allah (AH-luh) **Abu Bakr** (ah-boo BAK-uhr)

hijra (HIJ-ruh) **umma** (UM-muh)

desert nomads, sapped Mecca's strength and convinced many Meccans that God favored Muhammad. In 630 Mecca surrendered. Muhammad and his followers made the pilgrimage to the Ka'ba unhindered.

Muhammad did not return to Mecca again. Medina had grown into a bustling city-state. He had charged the Jewish kin groups with disloyalty at various points during the war and had expelled or eliminated them. Delegations from all over Arabia came to meet Muhammad, and he sent emissaries back with them to teach about Islam and collect their alms. Muhammad's mission to bring God's message to humanity had brought him unchallenged control of a state that was coming to dominate the Arabian peninsula. But the supremacy of the Medinan state, unlike preceding short-lived nomadic kingdoms, depended not on kinship but on a common faith in a single god.

In 632, after a brief illness, Muhammad died. Within twenty-four hours a group of Medinan leaders, along with three of Muhammad's close friends, determined that Abu Bakr, one of the earliest believers and the father of Muhammad's favorite wife A'isha°, should succeed him. They called him the *khalifa*°, or "successor," the English version of which is *caliph*. But calling Abu Bakr a successor did not clarify his powers. Everyone knew that neither Abu Bakr nor anyone else could receive revelations, and they likewise knew that Muhammad's revelations made no provision for succession or for any government purpose beyond maintaining the umma. Indeed, some people thought the world would soon end because God's last messenger was dead.

Abu Bakr continued and confirmed Muhammad's religious practices, notably the so-called Five Pillars of Islam: (1) avowal that there is only one god and Muhammad is his messenger, (2) prayer five times a day, (3) fasting during the lunar month of Ramadan, (4) paying alms, and (5) making the pilgrimage to Mecca at least once during one's lifetime. He also reestablished and expanded Muslim authority over Arabia's nomadic and settled communities. After Muhammad's death, some had abandoned their allegiance to Medina or followed various would-be prophets. Muslim armies fought hard to confirm the authority of the newborn **caliphate.** In the process, some fighting spilled over into non-Arab areas in Iraq.

Abu Bakr ordered those who had acted as secretaries for Muhammad to organize the Prophet's revelations into a book. Hitherto written haphazardly on pieces of leather or bone, the verses of revelation became a single document gathered into chapters. This resulting book, which Muslims believe acquired its final form around the year 650, was called the **Quran**°, or the Recitation. Muslims regard it not as the words of Muhammad but as the unalterable word of God. As such, it compares not so much to the Bible, a book written by many hands over many centuries, as to the person of Jesus Christ, whom Christians consider a human manifestation of God.

Though united in its acceptance of God's will, the umma soon disagreed over the succession to the caliphate. The first civil war in Islam followed the assassination of the third caliph, Uthman°, in 656. To succeed him, his assassins, rebels from the army, nominated Ali, Muhammad's first cousin and the husband of his daughter Fatima. Ali had been passed over three times previously, even though many people considered him to be the Prophet's natural heir. As mentioned previously, Ali and his supporters felt that Muhammad had indicated as much at Ghadir al-Khumm.

When Ali accepted the nomination to be caliph, two of Muhammad's close companions and his favorite wife A'isha challenged him. Ali defeated them in the Battle of the Camel (656), so called because the fighting raged around the camel on which A'isha was seated in an enclosed woman's saddle.

After the battle, the governor of Syria, Mu'awiya°, a kinsman of the slain Uthman from the Umayya clan of the Quraysh, renewed the challenge. Inconclusive battle gave way to arbitration. The arbitrators decided that Uthman, whom his assassins considered corrupt, had not deserved death and that Ali had erred in accepting the nomination. Ali rejected the arbitrators' findings, but before he could resume fighting, one of his own supporters killed him for agreeing to the arbitration. Mu'awiya then offered Ali's son Hasan a dignified retirement and thus emerged as caliph in 661.

Mu'awiya chose his own son, Yazid, to succeed him, thereby instituting the **Umayyad° Caliphate.** When Hasan's brother Husayn revolted in 680 to reestablish the right of Ali's family to rule, Yazid ordered Husayn and his family killed. Sympathy for Husayn's martyrdom helped transform Shi'ism from a political movement into a religious sect.

Several variations in Shi'ite belief developed, but Shi'ites have always agreed that Ali was the rightful successor to Muhammad and that God's choice as Imam, leader of the Muslim community, has always been one or another of Ali's descendants. They see the office of caliph as more secular than religious. Because the Shi'ites seldom held power, their religious feelings came to focus on

A'isha (AH-ee-shah) **khalifa** (kah-LEE-fuh)

Quran (kuh-RAHN) **Uthman** (ooth-MAHN)
Mu'awiya (moo-AH-we-yuh) **Umayyad** (oo-MY-ad)

outpourings of sympathy for Husayn and other martyrs and on messianic dreams that one of their Imams would someday triumph.

Those Muslims who supported the first three caliphs gradually came to be called "People of Tradition and Community"—in Arabic, *Ahl al-Sunna wa'l-Jama'a,* Sunnis for short. Sunnis consider the caliphs to be Imams. As for Ali's followers who had abhorred his acceptance of arbitration, they evolved into small and rebellious Kharijite sects (from *kharaja* meaning "to secede or rebel") claiming righteousness for themselves alone. These three divisions of Islam, the last now quite minor, still survive. Today the umma numbers more than a billion people.

The Rise and Fall of the Caliphate, 632–1258

The Islamic caliphate built on the conquests the Arabs carried out after Muhammad's death gave birth to a dynamic and creative religious society. By the late 800s, however, one piece after another of this huge realm broke away. Yet the idea of a caliphate, however unrealistic it became, remained a touchstone of Sunni belief in the unity of the umma.

Sunni Islam never gave a single person the power to define true belief, expel heretics, and discipline clergy. Thus, unlike Christian popes and patriarchs, the caliphs had little basis for reestablishing their universal authority once they lost political and military power.

The Islamic Conquests, 634–711

Arab conquests outside Arabia began under the second caliph, Umar (r. 634–644), possibly prompted by earlier forays into Iraq. Arab armies wrenched Syria (636) and Egypt (639–642) away from the Byzantine Empire and defeated the last Sasanid shah, Yazdigird III (r. 632–651) (see Map. 9.1). After a decade-long lull, expansion began again. Tunisia fell and became the governing center from which was organized, in 711, the conquest of Spain by an Arab-led army mostly composed of Berbers from North Africa. In the same year, Sind—the southern Indus Valley and westernmost region of India—succumbed to partially seaborne invaders from Iraq. The Muslim dominion remained roughly stable for the next three centuries. In the eleventh century, conquest began anew in India, Anatolia, and sub-Saharan Africa. Islam also expanded peacefully by trade in these and other areas both before and after the year 1000.

The speed and political cohesiveness of the Arab campaigns distinguishes them from the piecemeal incursions of the Germanic peoples into the Roman Empire (see Chapter 10). The close Meccan companions of the Prophet, men of political and economic sophistication inspired by his charisma, guided the conquests. The social structure and hardy nature of Arab society lent itself to flexible military operations; and the authority of Medina, reconfirmed during the caliphate of Abu Bakr, ensured obedience.

The decision made during Umar's caliphate to prohibit Arabs from taking over conquered territory for their own use proved important. Umar tied army service, with its regular pay and occasional windfalls of booty, to residence in large military camps—two in Iraq (Kufa and Basra), one in Egypt (Fustat), and one in Tunisia (Qairawan). East of Iraq, Arabs settled around small garrison towns at strategic locations and in one large garrison at Marv in present-day Turkmenistan. Down to the early eighth century, this policy kept the armies together and ready for action and preserved life in the countryside, where some three-fourths of the population lived, virtually unchanged. Most people who became subjects of the caliphate by conquest probably never saw an Arab, and only a tiny proportion in Syria, Egypt, and Iraq understood the Arabic language.

The million or so Arabs who participated in the conquests over several generations constituted a small, self-isolated ruling minority living on the taxes paid by a vastly larger non-Arab, non-Muslim subject population. The Arabs had little material incentive to encourage conversion, and there is no evidence of coherent missionary efforts to spread Islam during the conquest period.

The Umayyad and Early Abbasid Caliphates, 661–850

The Umayyad caliphs presided over an ethnically defined Arab realm rather than a religious empire. Ruling from Damascus, their armies consisted almost entirely of Muslim Arabs. They adopted and adapted the administrative practices of their Sasanid and Byzantine predecessors, as had the caliphs who preceded them. Only gradually did they replace non-Muslim secretaries and tax officials with Muslims and introduce Arabic as the language of government. The introduction of distinctively Muslim silver and gold coins early in the eighth century symbolized the new order. From that time on, silver dirhams and gold dinars bearing Arabic religious phrases circulated in monetary exchanges from Morocco to the frontiers of China.

The Umayyad dynasty fell in 750 after a decade of growing unrest. Converts to Islam, by that date no more than 10 percent of the indigenous population, were numerically significant because of the comparatively small number of Arab warriors. They resented not achieving equal status with the Arabs. The Arabs of Iraq and elsewhere envied the Syrian Arab influence in caliphal affairs. Pious Muslims looked askance at the secular and even irreligious behavior of the caliphs. Shi'ites and Kharijites attacked the Umayyad family's legitimacy as rulers, launching a number of rebellions.

In 750 one such rebellion, in the region of Khurasan° in what is today northeastern Iran, Turkmenistan, and northwestern Afghanistan, overthrew the last Umayyad caliph, though one family member escaped to Spain and founded an Umayyad principality there in 755. Many Shi'ites supported the rebellion, thinking they were fighting for the family of Ali. As it turned out, the family of Abbas, one of Muhammad's uncles, controlled the secret organization that coordinated the revolt. Upon victory they established the **Abbasid° Caliphate.** Some of the Abbasid caliphs who ruled after 750 befriended their relatives in Ali's family, and one even flirted with transferring the caliphate to them. The Abbasid family, however, held on to the caliphate until 1258, when Mongol invaders killed the last of them in Baghdad (see Chapter 13).

At its outset the Abbasid dynasty made a fine show of leadership and concern for Islam. Theology and religious law became preoccupations at court and among a growing community of scholars, along with interpretation of the Quran, collecting the sayings of the Prophet, and Arabic grammar. (In recent years, some western scholars have maintained that the Quran, the sayings of the Prophet, and the biography of the Prophet were all composed around this time and do not reflect historical fact. This radical reinterpretation of Islamic origins has not been generally accepted in either the scholarly community or among Muslims.) Some caliphs fought on the Byzantine frontier to extend Islam. Others sponsored ambitious projects to translate the great works of Greek, Persian, and Indian thought into Arabic.

At the same time, the new dynasty, with its roots among the semi-Persianized Arabs of Khurasan, gradually adopted the ceremonies and customs of the Sasanid shahs. Government grew increasingly complex in Baghdad, the newly built capital city on the Tigris River. As more and more non-Arabs converted to Islam, the ruling elite became more cosmopolitan. Greek, Iranian, Central Asian, and African cultural currents met in the capital and gave rise to an abundance of literary works, a process facilitated by the introduction of papermaking from China. Arab poets neglected the traditional odes extolling life in the desert and wrote instead wine songs (despite Islam's prohibition of alcohol) or poems in praise of their patrons.

The translation of Aristotle into Arabic, the founding of the main currents of theology and law, and the splendor of the Abbasid court—reflected in stories of *The Arabian Nights* set in the time of the caliph Harun al-Rashid° (r. 776–809)—in some respects warrant calling the early Abbasid period a "golden age." Yet the refinement of Baghdad culture only slowly made its way into the provinces. Egypt remained predominantly Christian and Coptic-speaking in the early Abbasid period. Iran never adopted Arabic as a spoken tongue. Berber-speaking North Africa freed itself almost entirely of caliphal rule: Morocco and Algeria through Kharijite revolts in 740, Tunisia after 800 by agreeing to pay regular tribute to Baghdad.

Gradual conversion to Islam among the conquered population accelerated in the second quarter of the ninth century. Social discrimination against non-Arab converts gradually faded, and the Arabs themselves—at least those living in cosmopolitan urban settings—lost their previously strong attachment to kinship and ethnic identity.

Political Fragmentation, 850–1050

Abbasid decline became evident in the second half of the ninth century as the conversion to Islam accelerated (see Map 9.2). No government ruling an empire stretching almost a quarter of the way around the world could hold power easily. Caravans traveled only 20 miles (32 kilometers) a day, and the couriers of the caliphal post system usually did not exceed 100 miles (160 kilometers) a day. News of frontier revolts took weeks to reach Baghdad. Military responses might take months. Administrators struggled to centralize tax payments, often made in grain or other produce rather than cash, and ensure that provincial governors forwarded the proper amounts to Baghdad.

The first Arab garrisons had been strung like beads across territory populated mostly by non-Muslims; revolts against Arab rule had been a concern. Members of the Muslim umma had had every reason to cling together, despite the long distances. But with the growing conversion of the population to Islam, the idea that Islam might disappear faded. Muslims became an over-

Khurasan (kor-uh-SAHN) **Abbasid** (ah-BASS-id)

Harun al-Rashid (hah-ROON al–rah-SHEED)

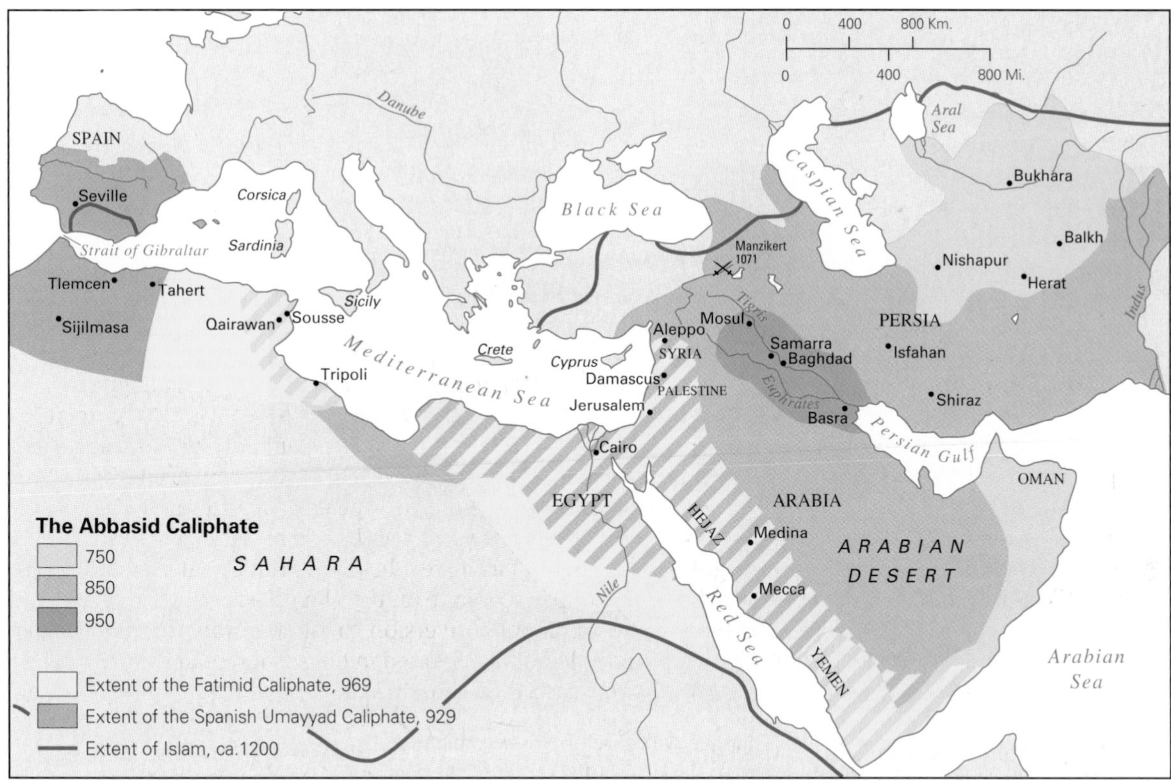

Map 9.2 Rise and Fall of the Abbasid Caliphate Though Abbasid rulers occupied the caliphal seat in Iraq from 750 to 1258, when Mongol armies destroyed Baghdad, real political power waned sharply and steadily after 850. The rival caliphates of the Fatimids (909–1171) and Spanish Umayyads (929–976) were comparatively short-lived.

whelming majority and gradually realized that a highly centralized empire with a rich and splendid capital did not necessarily serve the interests of all the people.

Eighth-century revolts had often targeted Arab or Muslim domination. By the middle of the ninth century, this type of rebellion gave way to movements within the Islamic community that concentrated on seizure of territory and formation of principalities. None of the states carved out of the Abbasid Caliphate after 850 repudiated or even threatened Islam. They did, however, prevent tax revenues from flowing to Baghdad, thereby increasing local prosperity. Local Muslim communities either supported such rebels or remained neutral.

Increasingly starved for funds by breakaway provinces and by an unexplained fall in revenues from Iraq itself, the caliphate experienced a crisis in the late ninth century. Distrusting generals and troops from outlying areas, the caliphs purchased Turkic slaves, **mamluks°**, from Central Asia and established them as a standing army. Well trained and hardy, the Turks proved an effective but expensive military force. When the government could not pay them, the mamluks took it on themselves to seat and unseat caliphs, a process made easier by the construction of a new capital at Samarra, north of Baghdad on the Tigris River.

The Turks dominated Samarra without interference from an unruly Baghdad populace that regarded them as rude and highhanded. However, the money and effort that went into the huge city, which was occupied only from 835 to 892, further sapped the caliphs' financial strength and deflected labor from more productive pursuits.

In 945, after several attempts to find a strongman to reform government administration and restore military power, the Abbasid Caliphate fell under the control of rude mountain warriors from the province of Daylam in northern Iran. Led by the Shi'ite Buyid° family, they

mamluk (MAM-luke)

Buyid (BOO-yid)

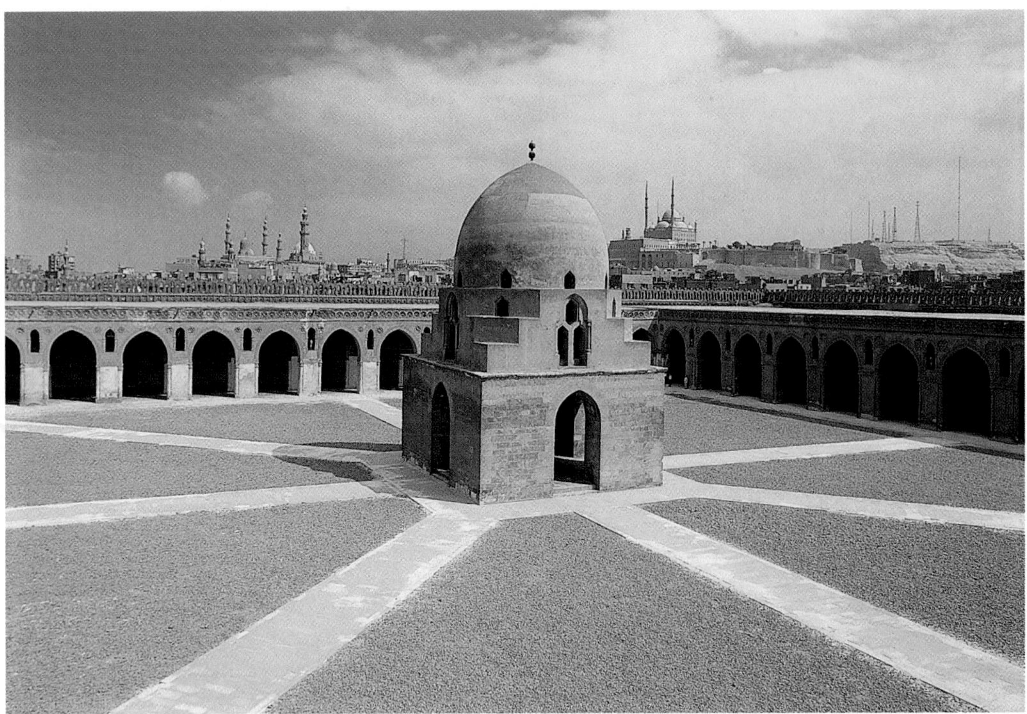

Mosque of Ibn Tulun in Fustat Completed in 877, this mosque symbolized Egypt becoming for the first time a quasi-independent province under its governor. The kiosk in the center of the courtyard contains fountains for washing before prayer. Before its restoration in the thirteenth century, the mosque had a spiral minaret and a door to an adjoining governor's palace.
(Ellen Rooney/Robert Harding Picture Library)

conquered western Iran as well as Iraq. Each Buyid commander ruled his own principality. After almost two centuries of glory, the sun began to set on Baghdad. The Abbasid caliph remained, but the Buyid princes controlled him. Being Shi'ites, the Buyids had no special reverence for the Sunni caliph. According to their particular Shi'ite sect, the twelfth and last divinely appointed Imam had disappeared around 873 and would return as a messiah only at the end of the world. Thus they had no Shi'ite Imam to defer to and retained the caliph only to help control their predominantly Sunni subjects.

Dynamic growth in outlying provinces paralleled the caliphate's gradual loss of temporal power. In the east in 875, the dynasty of the Samanids°, one of several Iranian families to achieve independence, established a glittering court in Bukhara, a major city on the Silk Road (see Map 9.2). Samanid princes patronized literature and learning, but the language they favored was Persian written in Arabic letters. For the first time, a non-Arabic literature rose to challenge the eminence of Arabic within the Islamic world. The new Persian poetry and prose foreshadowed the situation today, in which Iran sharply distinguishes itself from the Arab world.

In Egypt a Shi'ite ruler established himself as a rival caliph in 969, culminating a sixty-year struggle by his family, the Fatimids°, to extend their power beyond an initial base in Tunisia. His governing complex outside the old conquest-era garrison city of Fustat° was named Cairo. For the first time Egypt became a major cultural, intellectual, and political center of Islam (see Map 9.2). The al-Azhar Mosque built at this time remains a paramount religious and educational center to this day. Shi'ite religious influence in Sunni Egypt remained slight even after two centuries of Fatimid rule. Nevertheless, the abundance of Fatimid gold coinage, derived from West African sources, made them an economic power in the Mediterranean.

Samanid (sah-MAN-id)

Fatimid (FAT-uh-mid) **Fustat** (fuss-TAHT)

Cut off from the rest of the Islamic world by the Strait of Gibraltar and, from 740 onward, by independent city-states in Morocco and Algeria, Umayyad Spain developed a distinctive Islamic culture blending Roman, Germanic, and Jewish traditions with those of the Arabs and Berbers (see Map 9.1). Historians disagree on how rapidly and completely the Spanish population converted to Islam. If we assume a process similar to that in the eastern regions, it seems likely that the most rapid surge in Islamization occurred in the middle of the tenth century.

As in the east, governing cities symbolized the Islamic presence in al-Andalus, as the Muslims called their Iberian territories. Cordoba, Seville, Toledo, and other cities grew substantially, becoming much larger and richer than contemporary cities in neighboring France. Converts to Islam and their descendants, unconverted Arabic-speaking Christians, and Jews joined with the comparatively few descendants of Arab settlers to create new architectural and literary styles. In the countryside, where the Berbers preferred to settle, a fusion of preexisting agricultural technologies with new crops, notably citrus fruits, and irrigation techniques from the east gave Spain the most diverse and sophisticated agricultural economy in Europe.

The rulers of al-Andalus took the title *caliph* only in 929, when Abd al-Rahman° III (r. 912–961) did so in response to a similar declaration by the newly established (909) Fatimid ruler in Tunisia. By the century's end, however, this caliphate encountered challenges from breakaway movements that eventually splintered al-Andalus into a number of small states. Political decay did not impede cultural growth. Some of the greatest writers and thinkers in Jewish history worked in Muslim Spain in the eleventh and twelfth centuries, sometimes writing in Arabic, sometimes in Hebrew. Judah Halevi (1075–1141) composed exquisite poetry and explored questions of religious philosophy. Maimonides (1135–1204) made a major compilation of Judaic law and expounded on Aristotelian philosophy. At the same time, Islamic thought in Spain attained its loftiest peaks in Ibn Hazm's (994–1064) treatises on love and other subjects, the Aristotelian philosophical writings of Ibn Rushd° (1126–1198, known in Latin as Averroës°) and Ibn Tufayl° (d. 1185), and the mystic speculations of Ibn al-Arabi° (1165–1240). Christians, too, shared in the intellectual and cultural dynamism of al-Andalus. Translations from Arabic to Latin made during this period had a profound effect on the later intellectual development of western Europe (see Chapter 10).

Abd al-Rahman (AHB-d al–ruh-MAHN) **Ibn Rushd** (IB-uhn RUSHED) **Averroës** (uh-VERR-oh-eez) **Ibn Tufayl** (IB-uhn too-FILE) **Ibn al-Arabi** (IB-uhn ahl-AH-rah-bee)

Tomb of the Samanids in Bukhara This early-tenth-century structure has the basic layout of a Zoroastrian fire temple: a dome on top of a cube. However, geometic ornamentation in baked brick marks it as an early masterpiece of Islamic architecture. The Samanid family achieved independence as rulers of northeastern Iran and western Central Asia in the tenth century. (Art Resource, NY)

The Samanids, Fatimids, and Spanish Umayyads, three of many regional principalities, represent the political diversity and awakening of local awareness that coincided with Abbasid decline. Yet drawing and redrawing political boundaries did not result in the rigid division of the Islamic world into kingdoms, as was then occurring in Europe. Religious and cultural developments, particularly the rise in cities of a social group of religious scholars known as the **ulama**°—Arabic for "people with (religious) knowledge"—worked against any permanent division of the Islamic umma.

Assault from Within and Without, 1050–1258

The role played by Turkish mamluks in the decline of Abbasid power established an enduring stereotype of the Turk as a ferocious warrior little interested in religion or urban

ulama (oo-leh-MAH)

Spanish Muslim Textile of the Twelfth Century This fragment of woven silk, featuring peacocks and Arabic writing, is one of the finest examples of Islamic weaving. The cotton industry flourished in the early Islamic centuries, but silk remained a highly valued product. Some fabrics were treasured in Christian Europe. (Victoria & Albert Museum)

sophistication. This image gained strength in the 1030s when the Seljuk° family established a Turkish Muslim state based on nomadic power. Taking the Arabic title *Sultan,* meaning "power," and the revived Persian title *Shahan-shah,* or King of Kings, the Seljuk ruler Tughril° Beg created a kingdom that stretched from northern Afghanistan to Baghdad, which he occupied in 1055. After a century under the thumb of the Shi'ite Buyids, the Abbasid caliph breathed easier under the slightly lighter thumb of the Sunni Turks. The Seljuks pressed on into Syria and Anatolia, administering a lethal blow to Byzantine power at the Battle of Manzikert° in 1071. The Byzantine army fell back on Constantinople, leaving Anatolia open to Turkish occupation.

Under Turkish rule, cities shrank as pastoralists overran their agricultural hinterlands, already short on labor because of migration to the cities. Irrigation works suffered from lack of maintenance in the unsettled countryside. Tax revenues fell. Twelfth-century Seljuk princes contesting for power fought over cities, but few Turks participated in urban cultural and religious life. The gulf between a religiously based urban society and the culture and personnel of the government deepened. When factional riots broke out between Sunnis and Shi'ites, or between rival schools of Sunni law, rulers generally remained aloof, even as destruction and loss of life mounted. Similarly, when princes fought for the title *sultan,* religious leaders advised citizens to remain neutral.

By the early twelfth century, unrepaired damage from floods, fires, and civil disorder had reduced old Baghdad on the west side of the Tigris to ruins. The caliphs took advantage of fighting among the Seljuks to regain some power locally and built a wall around the palace precinct on the east side of the river. Nevertheless, the heart of the city died, not to regain prosperity until the twentieth century. The withering of Baghdad reflected a broader environmental problem: the collapse of the canal system on which agriculture in the Tigris and Euphrates Valley depended. For millennia a center of world civilization, Mesopotamia underwent substantial population loss and never again regained its geographical importance.

The Turks alone cannot be blamed for the demographic and economic misfortunes of Iran and Iraq. Too-robust urbanization had strained food resources, and political fragmentation had dissipated revenues. The growing practice of using land grants to pay soldiers and courtiers also played a role. When absentee grant holders used agents to collect taxes, the agents tended to gouge villagers and take little interest in improving production, all of which weakened the agricultural base of the economy.

The Seljuk Empire was beset by internal quarrels when the first crusading armies of Christians reached the Holy Land. The First Crusade captured Jerusalem in 1099 (see Chapter 10). Though charged with the stuff of romance, the Crusades had little lasting impact on the Islamic lands. The four crusader principalities of Edessa, Antioch, Tripoli, and Jerusalem simply became pawns in the shifting pattern of politics already in place. Newly arrived knights eagerly attacked the Muslim enemy, whom they called "Saracens°;" but veteran crusaders, including

Seljuk (sel-JOOK) **Tughril** (TUUG-ruhl)
Manzikert (MANZ-ih-kuhrt)

Saracen (SAR-uh-suhn)

the religious orders of the Knights of the Temple (Templars) and the Knights of the Hospital of St. John (Hospitallers), recognized that diplomacy and seeking partners of convenience among rival Muslim princes offered a sounder strategy.

The Muslims finally unified to face the European enemy in the mid-twelfth century. Nur al-Din ibn Zangi° established a strong state based in Damascus and sent an army to terminate the Fatimid Caliphate in Egypt. A nephew of the Kurdish commander of that expedition, Salah-al-Din, known in the West as Saladin, took advantage of Nur al-Din's timely death to seize power and unify Egypt and Syria. The Fatimid dynasty fell in 1171. In 1187 Saladin recaptured Jerusalem from the Europeans.

Saladin's descendants fought off subsequent Crusades. After one such battle, however, in 1250, Turkish mamluk troops seized control of the government in Cairo, ending Saladin's dynasty. In 1260 these mamluks rode east to confront a new invading force. At the Battle of Ain Jalut° (Spring of Goliath) in Syria, they met and defeated an army of Mongols from Central Asia (see Chapter 13), thus stemming an invasion that had begun several decades before and legitimizing their claim to dominion over Egypt and Syria.

A succession of Mamluk sultans ruled Egypt and Syria until 1517. In Abbasid times, *mamluk* was a term used for military slaves; the Mamluks who established an empire in Egypt and Syria in 1250 used the name "Mamluk" for their regime and their ruling class. Fear of new Mongol attacks receded after 1300, but by then the new ruling system had become fixed. Young Turkish or Circassian slaves, the latter from Georgia and other parts of the Caucasus region, were imported from non-Muslim lands, raised in military training barracks, and converted to Islam. Owing loyalty to the Mamluk officers who purchased them and also to their barracks mates, they formed a military ruling class that was socially disconnected from the Arabic-speaking native population.

The Mongol invasions, especially their destruction of the Abbasid Caliphate in Baghdad in 1258, shocked the world of Islam. The Mamluk sultan placed a relative of the last Baghdad caliph on a caliphal throne in Cairo, but the Egyptian Abbasids were never more than puppets serving Mamluk interests. In the Muslim lands from Iraq eastward, non-Muslim rule lasted for much of the thirteenth century. Although the Mongols left few ethnic or linguistic traces in these lands, their initial destruction of cities and slaughter of civilian populations, their diversion of Silk Road trade from the traditional route terminating in Baghdad to more northerly routes ending at ports on the Black Sea, and their casual disregard, even after their conversion to Islam, of Muslim religious life and urban culture, hastened currents of change already under way.

Nur al-Din ibn Zangi (NOOR-al-DEEN ib-uhn ZAN-gee)
Ain Jalut (ine jah-LOOT)

Islamic Civilization

Though increasingly unsettled in its political dimension and subject to economic disruptions caused by war, the ever-expanding Islamic world underwent a fruitful evolution in law, social structure, and religious expression. Religious conversion and urbanization reinforced each other to create a distinct Islamic civilization. The immense geographical and human diversity of the Muslim lands allowed many "small traditions" to coexist with the developing "great tradition" of Islam.

Law and Dogma

The Shari'a, the law of Islam, provides the foundation of Islamic civilization. Yet aside from certain Quranic verses conveying specific divine ordinances—most pertaining to personal and family matters—Islam had no legal system in the time of Muhammad. Arab custom and the Prophet's own authority offered the only guidance. After Muhammad died, the umma tried to follow his example. This became harder and harder to do, however, as those who knew Muhammad best passed away, and many Arabs found themselves living in far-off lands. Non-Arab converts to Islam, who at first tried to follow Arab customs they had little familiarity with, had an even harder time.

Islam slowly developed laws to govern social and religious life. The full sense of Islamic civilization, however, goes well beyond the basic Five Pillars mentioned earlier. Some Muslim thinkers felt that the reasoned consideration of a mature man—women had little voice in religious matters—offered the best resolution of issues not covered by Quranic revelation. Others argued for the sunna, or tradition, of the Prophet as the best guide. To understand that sunna they collected and studied the thousands of reports, called **hadith°**, purporting to convey the precise words or deeds of Muhammad. It gradually became customary to precede each hadith with a statement indicating whom the speaker had heard it from, whom that person had heard it from, and so on, back to the Prophet personally.

hadith (hah-DEETH)

Scholarly Life in Medieval Islam Books being scarce and expensive, teachers dictated to their students, as shown on the right. Notice that the student is writing on a single sheet of paper while the scholar in the center holds an entire book. On the left, an author presents his work to a wealthy patron. (Bibliothèque nationale de France)

Many hadith dealt with ritual matters, such as how to wash before prayer. Others provided answers to legal questions not covered by Quranic revelation or suggested principles for deciding such matters. By the eleventh century most legal thinkers had accepted the idea that Muhammad's personal behavior provided the best model for Muslim behavior, and that the hadith constituted the most authoritative basis for Islamic law after the Quran itself.

Yet the hadith themselves posed a problem because the tens of thousands of anecdotes included not only genuine reports about the Prophet but also invented ones, politically motivated ones, and stories derived from non-Muslim religious traditions. Only a specialist could hope to separate a sound from a weak tradition. As the hadith grew in importance, so did the branch of learning devoted to their analysis. Scholars discarded thousands for having weak chains of authority. The most reliable they collected into books that gradually achieved authoritative status. Sunnis placed six books in this category; Shi'ites, four. The Shari'a grew over centuries, incorporating the ideas of many legal scholars as well as the implications of thousands of hadith.

The Shari'a embodies a vision of an umma in which all Muslims subscribe to the same moral values. In this vision, political or ethnic divisions lose importance, for the Shari'a expects every Muslim ruler to abide by and enforce the religious law. In practice, this expectation often lost out in the hurly-burly of political life. Even so, it proved an important basis for an urban lifestyle that varied surprisingly little from Morocco to India.

Converts and Cities

Conversion to Islam, more the outcome of people's learning about the new rulers' religion than an escape from the tax on non-Muslims, as some scholars have suggested, helped spur urbanization. Conversion did not require extensive knowledge of the faith. To become a Muslim, a person recited, in the presence of a Muslim, the profession of faith in Arabic: "There is no God but God, and Muhammad is the Messenger of God."

Few converts knew Arabic, and fewer could read the Quran. Many converts knew no more of the Quran than the verses necessary for their daily prayers. Muhammad had established no priesthood to define and spread the faith. Thus new converts, whether Arab or non-Arab, faced the problem of finding out for themselves what Islam was about and how they should act as Muslims.

Spending time with Muslims, learning their language, and imitating their behavior proved the best way to solve this problem. In many areas, this meant migrating to an Arab governing center. The alternative, converting to Islam but remaining in one's home community, posed a problem. Before the emergence of Islam, religion had developed into the main component of social identity in the Byzantine and Sasanid Empires. Converts to Islam thus encountered discrimination if they went on living within their Christian, Jewish, or Zoroastrian communities. Again, migration afforded a solution, and the economic opportunities opened up by tax revenues flowing into the Arab governing centers made it more attractive.

The large Arab military settlements of Kufa and Basra in Iraq blossomed into cities and became important centers for Muslim cultural activities. As conversion rapidly spread in the mid-ninth century, urbanization also increased in other regions, most visibly in Iran, where most cities previously had been quite small. Nishapur in the northeast grew from fewer than 10,000 pre-Islamic inhabitants to between 100,000 and 200,000 by the year 1000. Other Iranian cities experienced similar growth. In Iraq, Baghdad and Mosul joined Kufa and Basra as major cities. In Syria, Aleppo and Damascus flourished under Muslim rule. New districts added to Fustat—the final one in 969 named Cairo—created one of the largest and greatest of the Islamic cities. The primarily Christian patriarchal cities of Jerusalem, Antioch, and Alexandria, not being Muslim governing centers, shrank and stagnated.

The cities became heavily Muslim before the countryside. Muhammad and his first followers had lived in a commercial city, and Islam acquired a peculiarly urban character very different from that of medieval European Christendom. Mosques in large cities served both as ritual centers and as places for learning and social activities.

Islam colored all aspects of urban social life (see Diversity and Dominance: Beggars, Con Men, and Singing-girls). Without religious officials to instruct them, the new Muslims imitated Arab dress and customs and emulated people they regarded as particularly pious. Inevitably, in the absence of a central religious authority comparable to a pope, local variations developed in the way people practiced Islam and in the hadith they attributed to the Prophet. This gave the rapidly growing religion the flexibility to accommodate many different social situations. Since the profession of faith called only for the acknowledgment of God's unity and Muhammad's prophethood, Islam escaped most of the severe conflicts over heresy that beset Christianity at a comparable stage of development.

By the tenth century, urban growth was affecting the countryside by expanding the consumer market. Citrus fruits, rice, and sugar cane increased in acreage and spread to new areas. Cotton became a major crop in Iran and elsewhere and supplied a diverse and profitable textile industry. Irrigation works expanded. Diet diversified. Abundant coinage made for a lively economy. Intercity and long-distance trade flourished, providing regular links between isolated districts and integrating the pastoral nomads, who provided pack animals, into the region's economy. Manufacturing expanded as well, particularly the production of cloth, metal goods, and pottery. Urban economies grew under the strong influence of Islamic ethics and law, overseen by religiously sanctioned market inspectors.

Science and technology also flourished (see Environment and Technology: Automata). Building on Hellenistic traditions and their own observations and experience, Muslim doctors and astronomers developed skills and theories far in advance of their European counterparts. Working in Egypt in the eleventh century, the mathematician and physicist Ibn al-Haytham° wrote more than a hundred works. Among other things, he determined that the Milky Way lies far beyond earth's atmosphere, proved that light travels from a seen object to the eye and not the reverse, and explained why the sun and moon appear larger on the horizon than overhead.

Islam, Women, and Slaves

Women seldom traveled. Those living in rural areas worked in the fields and tended animals. Urban women, particularly members of the elite, lived in seclusion and did not leave their homes without covering themselves completely. Seclusion of women in their houses and veiling in public already existed in Byzantine and Sasanid times. Through interpretation of specific verses from the Quran, these practices now became fixtures of Muslim social life. Although women sometimes studied and became literate, they did so away from the gaze of men who were not related to them. Although women played influential roles within the family, any public role had to be indirect, through their husbands. Only slave women could perform before unrelated men as musicians and dancers. A man could have sexual relations with as many slave concubines as he pleased, in addition to marrying as many as four wives.

Muslim women fared better legally under Islamic law than did Christian and Jewish women under their respective religious codes. Muslim women could own property and retain it in marriage. They could remarry if their husbands divorced them, and they received a cash payment upon divorce. Although a man could divorce his wife without stating a cause, a woman could initiate

Ibn al-Haytham (IB-uhn al–HY-tham)

Diversity and Dominance

Beggars, Con Men, and Singing-girls

Though rulers, warriors, and religious scholars dominate the traditional narratives, the society that developed over the early centuries of Islam was remarkably diverse. Beggars, tricksters, and street performers belonged to a single loose fraternity: the Banu Sasan, or Tribe of Sasan. Tales of their tricks and exploits amused staid, pious Muslims, who often encountered them in cities and on their scholarly travels. The tenth-century poet Abu Dulaf al-Khazraji, who lived in Iran, studied the jargon of the Banu Sasan and their way of life and composed a long poem in which he cast himself as one of the group. However, he added a commentary to each verse to explain the jargon words that his sophisticated court audience would have found unfamiliar.

We are the beggars' brotherhood, and no one can deny
us our lofty pride . . .
And of our number if the feigned madman and mad
woman, with metal charms strung from their [sic] necks.
And the ones with ornaments drooping from their ears,
and with collars of leather or brass round their necks . . .
And the one who simulates a festering internal wound,
and the people with false bandages round their heads
and sickly, jaundiced faces.
And the one who slashes himself, alleging that he has
been mutilated by assailants, or the one who darkens
his skin artificially pretending that he has been
beaten up and wounded . . .
And the one who practices as a manipulator and quack
dentist, or who escapes from chains wound round his
body, or the one who uses almost invisible silk thread
mysteriously to draw off rings . . .
And of our number are those who claim to be refugees
from the Byzantine frontier regions, those who go
round begging on pretext of having left behind captive families . . .
And the one who feigns an internal discharge, or who
showers the passers-by with his urine, or who farts in
the mosque and makes a nuisance of himself, thus
wheedling money out of people . . .
And of our number are the ones who purvey objects of
veneration made from clay, and those who have their
beards smeared with red dye.
And the one who brings up secret writing by immersing it
in what looks like water, and the one who similarly
brings up the writing by exposing it to burning embers.

One of the greatest masters of Arabic prose, Jahiz (776–869), was a famously ugly man—his name means "Pop-eyed"—of Abyssinian family origin. Spending part of his life in his native Basra, in southern Iraq, and part in Baghdad, the Abbasid capital, he wrote voluminously on subjects ranging from theology to zoology to miserliness. These excerpts come from his book devoted to the business of training slave girls as musicians, a lucrative practice of suspect morality but great popularity among men of wealth. He pretends that he is not the author, but merely writing down the views of the owners of singing-girls.

Now I will describe for you the definition of the passion of love, so that you may understand what exactly it is. It is a malady which smites the spirit, and affects the body as well by contagion: just as physical weakness impairs the spirit and low spirits in a man make him emaciated . . . The stronger the constituent causes of the malady are, the more inveterate it is, and the slower to clear up . . .

Passion for singing-girls is dangerous, in view of their manifold excellences and the satisfaction one's soul finds in them. . . . The singing-girl is hardly ever sincere in her passion, or wholehearted in her affection. For both by training and by innate instinct her nature is to set up snares and traps for the victims, in order that they may fall into her toils. As soon as the observer notices her, she exchanges provocative glances with him, gives him playful smiles, dallies with him in verses set to music, falls in with his suggestions, is eager to drink when he drinks, expresses her fervent desire for him to stay a long while, her yearning for his prompt return, and her sorrow at his departure. Then when she perceives that her sorcery has worked on him and that he has become entangled in the net, she redoubles the wiles she had used at first, and leads him to suppose that she is more in love than he is . . .

But it sometimes happens that this pretence leads her on to turning it into reality, and she in fact shares her lover's torments . . . Sometimes she may renounce her craft, in order for her to be cheaper for him [to buy], and makes a show of illness and is sullen towards her guardians and asks the owners to sell her . . . specially if she finds [her lover] to be sweet-tempered, clever in expressing himself, pleasant-tongued, with a fine apprehension and delicate sensibility, and light-hearted; while if he can compose and quote poetry or warble a tune, that gives him all the more favour in her eyes . . .

How indeed could a singing-girl be saved from falling prey to temptation, and how is it possible for her to be chaste? It is in the very place where she is brought up that she acquires unbridled desires, and learns her modes of speech and behaviour. From cradle to grave she is nourished by such idle talk, and all sorts of frivolous and impure conversation, as must hinder her from recollection of God; among abandoned and dissolute persons, who never utter a serious word, from whom she could never look for any trustworthiness, religion, or safe-guarding of decent standards.

An accomplished singing-girl has a repertoire of upwards of four thousands songs, each of them two to four verses long, so that the total amount . . . comes to ten thousand verses, in which there is not one mention of God (except by inadvertence). . . . They are all founded on references to fornication, pimping, passion, yearning, desire, and lust. Later on she continues to study her profession assiduously, learning from music teachers whose lessons are all flirting and whose directives are a seduction . . .

Among the advantages enjoyed by each man among us [i.e., speaking as a keeper of singing-girls] is that other men seek him out eagerly in his abode, just as one eagerly seeks out caliphs and great folk; is visited without having the trouble of visiting; receives gifts and is not compelled to give; has presents made to him and none required from him. Eyes remain wakeful, tears flow, minds are agitated, emotions lacerated, and hopes fixed—all on the property which he has under his control: which is something that does not occur with anything [else] that is sold or bought. . . . [F]or who could reach anything like the price fetched by an Abyssinian girl, the slave of Awn, namely 120,000 dinars [i.e., gold coins]?

The owner of singing-girls . . . takes the substance and gives the appearance, gets the real thing and gives the shadow, and sells the gusty wind for solid ore and pieces of silver and gold. Between the suitors and what they desire lies the thorniest of obstacles. For the owner, were he not to abstain from granting the dupe his desire for motives of purity and decency, would at any rate do so out of sharp-wittedness and wiliness, and to safeguard his trade and defend the sanctity of his estate. For when the lover once possesses himself of the beloved, nine-tenths of his ardour disappear, and his liberality and contributions [to the owner] diminish on the same scale. What is there, consequently, to induce the owner of the singing-girls to give you his girl, spiting his own face and causing himself to be no longer sought after?

If he were not a past-master in this splendid and noble profession, why is it that he abandons jealous surveillance of the girls (though choosing his spies well), accepts the room rent, pretends to doze off before supper, takes no notice of winkings, is indulgent to a kiss, ignores signs [passing between the pair of lovers], turns a blind eye to the exchange of billets-doux, affects to forget all about the girl on the day of the visit, does not scold her for retiring to a private place, does not pry into her secrets or cross-examine her about how she passed the night, and does not bother to lock the doors and draw close the curtains? He reckons up each victim's income separately, and knows how much money he is good for; just as the trader sorts out his various kinds of merchandise and prices them according to their value . . . When he has an influential customer, he takes advantage of his influence and makes requests from him; if the customer is rich but not influential, he borrows money from him without interest. If he is a person connected with the authorities, such a one can be used as a shield against the unfriendly attentions of the police; and when such a one comes on a visit, drums and hautbois [i.e., double-reed pipes] are sounded.

Both of these passages fall into the category of Arabic literature known as adab, *or belles-lettres. The purpose of adab was to entertain and instruct through a succession of short anecdotes, verses, and expository discussions. It attracted the finest writers of the Abbasid era and affords one of the richest sources for looking at everyday life, always keeping in mind that the intended readers were a restricted class of educated men, including merchants, court and government officials, and even men of religion.*

QUESTIONS FOR ANALYSIS

1. **What do the authors' portrayals of beggars, con men, singing-girls, and keepers of singing-girls indicate about the diversity of life in the city?**
2. **Taken together, what do these passages indicate about the conventional portrayal of religious laws and moral teachings dominating everyday life?**
3. **In the discussion of singing-girls, what do you see as the importance of the practices of veiling and seclusion among urban, free-born, Muslim women?**
4. **In evaluating these as historical sources, is it necessary to take the tastes of the intended audience into account?**

Sources: First selection excerpts from Clifford Edmund Bosworth, *The Mediaeval Islamic Underworld: The Banu Sasan in Arabic Society and Literature* (Leiden: E. I. Brill, 1976), 191–199. Second selection excerpts from Jahiz, *The Epistle on Singing-Girls*, tr. and ed. A. F. L. Beeston (Warminster: Aris and Phillips, 1980), 28–37.

ENVIRONMENT + TECHNOLOGY

Automata

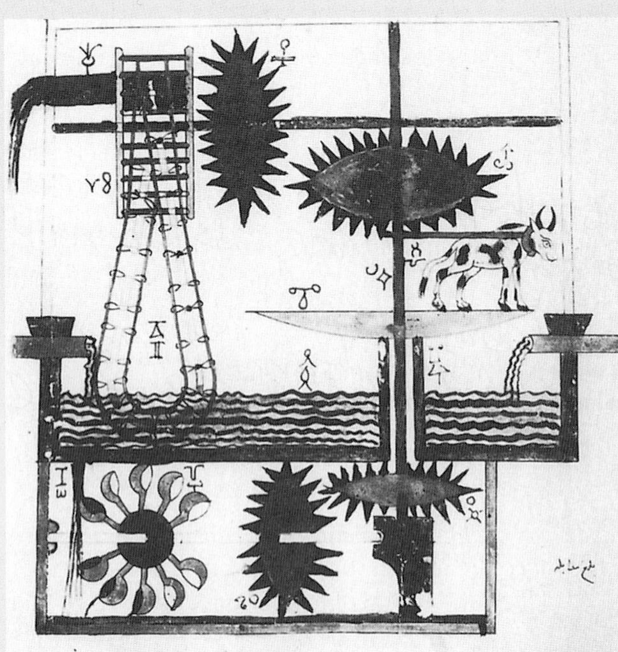

Model of a Water-Lifting Device The artist's effort to render a three-dimensional construction in two dimensions shows a talent for schematic drawing. (Widener Library Photographic Services)

Muslim scientists made discoveries and advances in almost every field, from mathematics and astronomy to chemistry and optics. Many worked under the patronage of rulers who paid for translations from Greek and other languages into Arabic and built libraries and observatories to facilitate their work. Fascination with science and technology also manifested itself in designs for elaborate mechanical devices—automata—intended for the entertainment of rulers and amazement of court visitors. In this example, a conventional-looking device for drawing water from a well, known as a saqiya (suh-KEY-yuh) and still in use from Morocco to Afghanistan, appears to be powered by a wooden cow that actually is moved by the force of the beam it is attached to rather than providing the motion itself.

A saqiya is a chain of buckets descending to a water source from a spoked drum attached to interlocking gears. In real life, an animal walks in a circle turning the first gear above it and thereby setting the drum in motion by way of a connecting gear that turns horizontal rotation into vertical rotation. In this automaton, real power comes from a water wheel with cups on its arms and hidden beneath the pool of water and connected by gears to the platform the wooden cow is standing on. The water flowing into the pond at left and right provides the hydraulic pressure needed to keep the apparatus in motion, causing the gears above to operate the chain of buckets lifting water to the outlet trough on the upper left.

divorce under specified conditions. Women could practice birth control. They could testify in court, although their testimony counted as half that of a man. They could go on pilgrimage. Nevertheless, a misogynistic tone sometimes appears in Islamic writings. One saying attributed to the Prophet observed: "I was raised up to heaven and saw that most of its denizens were poor people; I was raised into the hellfire and saw that most of its denizens were women."[3]

In the absence of writings by women about women from this period, the status of women must be deduced from the writings of men. Two episodes involving the Prophet's wife A'isha, the daughter of Abu Bakr, provide examples of how Muslim men appraised women in society. Only eighteen when Muhammad died, A'isha lived for another fifty years. Early reports stress her status as Muhammad's favorite, the only virgin he married and the only wife to see the angel Gabriel. These reports emanate from A'isha herself, who was an abundant source of hadith. As a fourteen-year-old she had become separated from a caravan and rejoined it only after traveling through the night with a man who found her alone in the desert. Gossips accused her of being untrue to the Prophet, but a revelation from God proved her innocence. The second event was her participation in the Battle of the Camel, fought to derail Ali's caliphate. These two episodes came to epitomize what Muslim men feared most about women: sexual infidelity and med-

Women Playing Chess in Muslim Spain As shown in this thirteenth-century miniature, women in their own quarters, without men present, wore whatever clothes and jewels they liked. Notice the henna decorating the hands of the woman in the middle. The woman on the left, probably a slave, plays an oud. (Institute Amatller d'Art Hispanic. © Patrimonio Nacional, Madrid)

dling in politics. Even though the earliest literature dealing with A'isha stresses her position as Muhammad's favorite, his first wife, Khadija, and his daughter, Ali's wife Fatima, eventually surpassed A'isha as ideal women. Both appear as model wives and mothers with no suspicion of sexual irregularity or political manipulation.

As the seclusion of women became commonplace in urban Muslim society, some writers extolled homosexual relationships, partly because a male lover could appear in public or go on a journey. Although Islam deplored homosexuality, one ruler wrote a book advising his son to follow moderation in all things and thus share his affections equally between men and women. Another ruler and his slave-boy became models of perfect love in the verses of mystic poets.

Islam allowed slavery but forbade Muslims from enslaving other Muslims or so-called People of the Book—Jews, Christians, and Zoroastrians, who revered holy books respected by the Muslims—who were living under Muslim protection. Being enslaved as a prisoner of war constituted an exception. Later centuries saw a constant flow of slaves into Islamic territory from Africa and Central Asia. A hereditary slave society, however, did not develop. Usually slaves converted to Islam, and many masters then freed them as an act of piety. The offspring of slave women and Muslim men were born free.

The Recentering of Islam

Early Islam centered on the caliphate, the political expression of the unity of the umma. No formal organization or hierarchy, however, directed the process of conversion. Thus there emerged a multitude of local Islamic communities so disconnected from each other that numerous competing interpretations of the developing religion arose. Inevitably, the centrality of the caliphate diminished (see Map 9.2). The appearance of rival caliphates in Tunisia and Cordoba accentuated the problem of decentralization just as Abbasid temporal power waned.

The rise of the ulama as community leaders did not prevent growing fragmentation because the ulama themselves divided into contentious factions. During the twelfth century factionalism began to abate, and new socioreligious institutions emerged to provide the umma with a different sort of religious center. These new developments stemmed in part from an exodus of religious scholars from Iran in response to economic and political disintegration during the late eleventh and twelfth centuries.

The flow of Iranians to the Arab lands and to newly conquered territories in India and Anatolia increased after the Mongol invasion. Fully versed in Arabic as well as their native Persian, immigrant scholars were warmly received. They brought with them a view of religion devel-

Quran Page Printed from a Woodblock Printing from woodblocks or tin plates existed in Islamic lands between approximately 800 and 1400. Most prints were narrow amulets designed to be rolled and worn around the neck in cylindrical cases. Less valued than handwritten amulets, many prints came from Banu Sasan con men. Why blockprinting had so little effect on society in general and eventually disappeared is unknown. (Cambridge University Library)

oped in Iran's urban centers. A type of religious college, the *madrasa*°, gained sudden popularity outside Iran, where madrasas had been known since the tenth century. Scores of madrasas, many founded by local rulers, appeared throughout the Islamic world.

Iranians also contributed to the growth of mystic groups known as *Sufi* brotherhoods in the twelfth and thirteenth centuries. The doctrines and rituals of certain Sufis spread from city to city, giving rise to the first geographically extensive Islamic religious organizations. Sufi doctrines varied, but a quest for a sense of union with God through rituals and training was a common denominator. Sufism had begun in early Islamic times and had doubtless benefited from the ideas and beliefs of people from religions with mystic traditions who converted to Islam.

The early Sufis had been saintly individuals given to ecstatic and poetic utterances and wonderworking. They attracted disciples but did not try to organize them. The growth of brotherhoods, a less ecstatic form of Sufism, set a tone for society in general. It soon became common for most Muslim men, particularly in the cities, to belong to at least one brotherhood.

A sense of the social climate the Sufi brotherhoods fostered can be gained from a twelfth-century manual:

> Every limb has its own special ethics. . . . The ethics of the tongue. The tongue should always be busy in reciting God's names (*dhikr*) and in saying good things of the brethren, praying for them, and giving them counsel. . . . The ethics of hearing. One should not listen to indecencies and slander. . . . The ethics of sight. One should lower one's eyes in order not to see forbidden things. . . . The ethics of the hands: to give charity and serve the brethren and not use them in acts of disobedience.[4]

Special dispensations allowed people who merely wanted to emulate the Sufis and enjoy their company to follow less demanding rules:

> It is allowed by way of dispensation to possess an estate or to rely on a regular income. The Sufis' rule in this matter is that one should not use all of it for himself, but should dedicate this to public charities and should take from it only enough for one year for himself and his family. . . .
>
> There is a dispensation allowing one to be occupied in business; this dispensation is granted to him who has to support a family. But this should not keep him away from the regular performance of prayers. . . .
>
> There is a dispensation allowing one to watch all kinds of amusement. This is, however, limited by the rule: What you are forbidden from doing, you are also forbidden from watching.[5]

Some Sufi brotherhoods spread in the countryside. Local shrines and pilgrimages to the tombs of Muhammad's descendants and saintly Sufis became popular. The pilgrimage to Mecca, too, received new prominence as a religious duty. The end of the Abbasid Caliphate enhanced the religious centrality of Mecca, which eventually became an important center of madrasa education.

---

madrasa (MAH-dras-uh)

Conclusion

The Sasanid empire that held sway in Iran and Iraq from the third to the seventh century strongly resembled the contemporary realm of the eastern Roman emperors ruling from Constantinople. Both states forged strong relations between the ruler and the dominant religion, Zoroastrianism in the former empire, Christianity in the latter. Priestly hierarchies paralleled state administrative structures, and the citizenry came to think of themselves more as members of a faith community than as subjects of a ruler. This gave rise to conflict among religious sects and also raised the possibility of the founder of a new religion commanding both political and religious loyalty on an unprecedented scale. This possibility was realized in the career of the prophet Muhammad in the seventh century.

Islam culminated the trend toward identity based on religion. The concept of the umma united all Muslims in a universal community embracing enormous diversity of language, appearance, and social custom. Though Muslim communities adapted to local "small traditions," by the twelfth century a religious scholar could travel anywhere in the Islamic world and blend easily into the local Muslim community.

By the ninth century, the forces of conversion and urbanization fostered social and religious experimentation in urban settings. From the eleventh century onward, political disruption and the spread of pastoral nomadism slowed this early economic and technological dynamism. The Muslim community then turned to new religious institutions, such as the madrasas and Sufi brotherhoods, to create the flexible and durable community structures that carried Islam into new regions and protected ordinary believers from capricious political rule.

Key Terms

Shi'ites
Sunnis
Sasanid Empire
Mecca
Muhammad
muslim
Islam
Medina
umma
caliphate
Quran
Umayyad Caliphate
Abbasid Caliphate
mamluks
ulama
hadith

Suggested Reading

For Sasanid history see Josef Wiesehöfer, *Ancient Persia* (2001). Ehsan Yarshater, ed., *The Cambridge History of Iran,* vol. 3 (pts. 1–2), *The Seleucid, Parthian and Sasanian Periods* (1983) contains up-to-date articles on Iranian history just prior to Islam.

Ira M. Lapidus, *A History of Islamic Societies* (1988), focuses on social developments and includes the histories of Islam in India, Southeast Asia, sub-Saharan Africa, and other parts of the world. Marshall G. S. Hodgson, *The Venture of Islam,* 3 vols. (1974), critiques traditional ways of studying the Islamic Middle East while offering an alternative interpretation. Bernard Lewis's *The Middle East: A Brief History of the Last 2,000 Years* (1995) provides a lively narration from the time of Christ.

For a shorter survey see J. J. Saunders, *History of Medieval Islam* (1965; reprint, 1990). Richard W. Bulliet, *Islam: The View from the Edge* (1993), offers, in brief form, an approach that concentrates on the lives of converts to Islam and local religious notables.

Muslims regard the Quran as untranslatable because they consider the Arabic in which it is couched to be inseparable from God's message. Most "interpretations" in English adhere reasonably closely to the Arabic text.

Martin Lings, *Muhammad: His Life Based on the Earliest Sources,* rev. ed. (1991), offers a readable biography reflecting Muslim viewpoints. Standard Western treatments include W. Montgomery Watt's *Muhammad at Mecca* (1953) and *Muhammad at Medina* (1956; reprint, 1981); and the one-volume summary: *Muhammad, Prophet and Statesman* (1974). Michael A. Cook, *Muhammad* (1983), intelligently discusses historiographical problems and source difficulties. Karen Armstrong's *Muhammad: A Biography of the Prophet* (1993) achieves a sympathetic balance.

For information on the new school of thought that rejects the traditional accounts of Muhammad's life and of the origins of the Quran, see Patricia Crone and Michael Cook, *Hagarism* (1977), Patricia Crone, *Meccan Trade and the Rise of Islam* (1987), and Fred Donner, *Narratives of Islamic Origins* (1998).

Wilfred Madelung's *The Succession to Muhammad: A Study of the Early Caliphate* (1997) gives an interpretation unusually sympathetic to Shi'ite viewpoints. G. R. Hawting, *The First Dynasty of Islam: The Umayyad Caliphate,* A.D. *661–750* (1987), offers a more conventional and easily readable history of a crucial century.

Western historians have debated the beginnings of the Abbasid Caliphate. Moshe Sharon, *Black Banners from the East: The Establishment of the 'Abbasid State—Incubation of a Revolt* (1983), and Jacob Lassner, *Islamic Revolution and Historical Memory: An Inquiry into the Art of Abbasid Apologetics* (1987), give differing accounts based on newly utilized sources. For a broader history that puts the first three centuries of Abbasid rule into the context of the earlier periods, see Hugh N. Kennedy, *The Prophet and the Age of the Caliphates: The Islamic Near East from the Sixth to the Eleventh Century* (1986). Harold

Bowen, *The Life and Times of Ali ibn Isa "The Good Vizier"* (1928; reprint, 1975), supplements Kennedy's narrative superbly with a detailed study of corrupt caliphal politics in the tumultuous early tenth century.

Articles in Michael Gervers and Ramzi Jibran Bikhazi, eds., *Conversion and Continuity: Indigenous Christian Communities in Islamic Lands, Eighth to Eighteenth Centuries* (1990), detail Christian responses to Islam. For a Zoroastrian perspective see Jamsheed K. Choksy, *Conflict and Cooperation: Zoroastrian Subalterns and Muslim Elites in Medieval Iranian Society* (1997). Jacob Lassner summarizes S. D. Goitein's definitive multivolume study of the Jews of medieval Egypt in *A Mediterranean Society: An Abridgement in One Volume* (1999). On the process of conversion see the work in quantitative history of Richard W. Bulliet, *Conversion to Islam in the Medieval Period* (1979).

With the fragmentation of the Abbasid Caliphate beginning in the ninth century, studies of separate areas become more useful than general histories. Richard N. Frye, *The Golden Age of Persia: The Arabs in the East* (1975), skillfully evokes the complicated world of early Islamic Iran and the survival and revival of Persian national identity. Thomas F. Glick, *Islamic and Christian Spain in the Early Middle Ages* (1979) and *From Muslim Fortress to Christian Castle: Social and Cultural Change in Medieval Spain* (1995), questions standard ideas about Christians and Muslims in Spain from a geographical and technological standpoint. For North Africa, Charles-André Julien, *History of North Africa: Tunisia, Algeria, Morocco, from the Arab Conquest to 1830* (1970), summarizes a literature primarily written in French. This same French historiographical tradition is challenged and revised by Abdallah Laroui, *The History of the Maghrib: An Interpretive Essay* (1977). For a detailed primary source, see the English translation of the most important chronicle of early Islamic history, *The History of al-Tabari*, published in thirty-eight volumes under the general editorship of Ehsan Yarshater.

Roy P. Mottahedeh, *Loyalty and Leadership in an Early Islamic Society* (1980); Richard W. Bulliet, *The Patricians of Nishapur* (1972); and Ira Marvin Lapidus, *Muslim Cities in the Later Middle Ages* (1984), discuss social history in tenth-century Iran, eleventh-century Iran, and fourteenth-century Syria, respectively. Jonathan Berkey, *The Transmission of Knowledge in Medieval Cairo: A Social History of Islamic Education* (1992), and Michael Chamberlain, *Knowledge and Social Practice in Medieval Damascus, 1190–1350* (1994), put forward competing assessments of education and the ulama. For urban geography see Paul Wheatley, *The Places Where Men Pray Together* (2001).

Ahmad Y. al-Hassan and Donald R. Hill, *Islamic Technology: An Illustrated History* (1986), introduces a little-studied field. For a more crafts-oriented look see Hans E. Wulff, *The Traditional Crafts of Persia: Their Development, Technology, and Influence on Eastern and Western Civilizations* (1966). Jonathan Bloom's *Paper Before Print* (2001) details the great impact of papermaking in many cultural areas.

Denise Spellberg, *Politics, Gender, and the Islamic Past: The Legacy of A'isha bint Abi Bakr* (1994), provides pathbreaking guidance on women's history. Basim Musallam, *Sex and Society in Islamic Civilization* (1983), treats the social, medical, and legal history of birth control. On race and slavery see Bernard Lewis, *Race and Slavery in the Middle East: A Historical Enquiry* (1992).

Among the numerous introductory books on Islam as a religion, a reliable starting point is David Waines, *An Introduction to Islam* (1995). For more advanced work, Fazlur Rahman, *Islam*, 2d ed. (1979), skillfully discusses some of the subject's difficulties. Islamic law is well covered in Noel J. Coulson, *A History of Islamic Law* (1979). For Sufism see Annemarie Schimmel, *Mystical Dimensions of Islam* (1975).

Two religious texts available in translation are Abu Hamid al-Ghazali, *The Faith and Practice of al-Ghazali*, trans. W. Montgomery Watt (1967; reprint, 1982), and Abu al-Najib al-Suhrawardi, *A Sufi Rule for Novices*, trans. Menahem Milson (1975).

For detailed and abundant maps see William C. Brice, ed., *An Historical Atlas of Islam* (1981). The most complete reference work for people working in Islamic studies is *The Encyclopedia of Islam*, new ed. (Leiden: E. J. Brill, 1960–), now available in CD-ROM format. For encyclopedia-type articles on pre-Islamic topics see G.W. Bowersock, Peter Brown, and Oleg Grabar *Late Antiquity: A Guide to the Postclassical World* (1999). On Iran see the excellent but still unfinished *Encyclopedia Iranica*, edited by Ehsan Yarshater.

Notes

1. Quran. Sura 96, verses 1–5.
2. Quran. Sura 92, verses 1–10.
3. Richard W. Bulliet, *Islam: The View from the Edge* (New York: Columbia University Press, 1994), 87.
4. Abu Najib al-Suhrawardi, *A Sufi Rule for Novices*, trans. Menahem Milson (Cambridge, MA: Harvard University Press, 1975), 45–58.
5. Ibid., 73–82.

10
Christian Europe Emerges, 300–1200

Boatbuilding Scene from the Bayeaux Tapestry Eleventh-century shipwrights prepare vessels for William of Normandy's invasion of England.

CHAPTER OUTLINE

Christmas Day in 800 found Charles, king of the Franks, in Rome instead of at his palace at Aachen in northwestern Germany. At six-foot-three, Charles towered over the average man of his time, and his royal career had been equally gargantuan. Crowned king in his mid-twenties in 768, he had crisscrossed Europe for three decades, waging war on Muslim invaders from Spain, Avar° invaders from Hungary, and a number of German princes.

Charles had subdued many enemies and had become protector of the papacy. So not all historians believe the eyewitness report of his secretary and biographer that Charles was surprised when, as the king rose from his prayers, Pope Leo III placed a new crown on his head. "Life and victory to Charles the August, crowned by God the great and pacific Emperor of the Romans," proclaimed the pope.[1] Then, amid the cheers of the crowd, he humbly knelt before the new emperor.

Charlemagne° (from Latin *Carolus magnus*, "Charles the Great") was the first in western Europe to bear the title *emperor* in over three hundred years. Rome's decline and Charlemagne's rise marked a shift of focus for Europe—away from the Mediterranean and toward the north and west. German custom and Christian piety transformed the Roman heritage to create a new civilization. Irish monks preaching in Latin became important intellectual influences in some parts of Europe, while the memory of Greek and Roman philosophy faded. Urban life continued the decline that began in the later days of the Roman Empire. Historians originally called this era "**medieval,**" literally "middle age," because it comes between the era of Greco-Roman civilization and the intellectual, artistic, and economic changes of the Renaissance in the fourteenth century; but research has uncovered many aspects of medieval culture that are as rich and creative as those that came earlier and later.

Charlemagne was not the only ruler in Europe to claim the title emperor. Another emperor held sway in the Greek-speaking east, where Rome's political and legal heritage continued. The Eastern Roman Empire was often called the **Byzantine Empire** after the seventh century, and was known to the Muslims as Rum. Western Europeans lived amid the ruins of empire, while the Byzantines maintained and reinterpreted Roman traditions. The authority of the Byzantine emperors blended with the influence of the Christian church to form a cultural synthesis that helped shape the emerging kingdom of **Kievan Russia.** Byzantium's centuries-long conflict with Islam helped spur the crusading passion that overtook western Europe in the eleventh century.

The comparison between western and eastern Europe appears paradoxical. Byzantium inherited a robust and self-confident late Roman society and economy, while western Europe could not achieve political unity and suffered severe economic decline. Yet by 1200 western Europe was showing renewed vitality and flexing its military muscles, while Byzantium was showing signs of decline and military weakness. As we explore the causes and consequences of these different historical paths, we must remember that the emergence of Christian Europe included both developments.

As you read this chapter, ask yourself the following questions:

- What role did Christianity play in reshaping European society in east and west?
- How did the Roman heritage differently affect the east and the west?
- How can one compare Kievan Russia's resemblances to western Europe and to the Byzantine Empire?
- How did Mediterranean trade and the Crusades help revive western Europe?

The Byzantine Empire, 300–1200

The Byzantine emperors established Christianity as their official religion, but they also represented a continuation of Roman imperial rule and tradition that was largely absent in the kingdoms that succeeded Rome in the west. They inherited imperial law intact; only provincial forms of Roman law survived in the west. Combining the imperial role with political oversight over the Christian church, they made a comfortable transition into the role of all-powerful Christian monarchs. The Byzantine drama, however, played on a steadily shrinking stage. Territorial losses and almost constant military pressure from north and south deprived the empire of long periods of peace.

Avar (ah-vahr) **Charlemagne** (SHAHR-leh-mane)

CHRONOLOGY

	Western Europe	Eastern Europe
300		
		325 Constantine convenes Council of Nicaea; Arian heresy condemned
		392 Emperor Theodosius bans paganism in Byzantine Empire
	432 Saint Patrick begins missionary work in Ireland	
	476 Deposing of the last Roman emperor in the West	
500		
	ca. 547 Death of Saint Benedict	**527–565** Justinian and Theodora rule Byzantine Empire; imperial edicts collected in single law code
		634–650 Muslims conquer Byzantine provinces of Syria, Egypt, and Tunisia
	711 Muslim conquest of Spain	
	732 Battle of Tours	
800	**800** Coronation of Charlemagne	
	843 Treaty of Verdun divides Carolingian Empire among Charlemagne's grandsons	
	910 Monastery of Cluny founded	**882** Varangians take control of Kiev
	962 Beginning of Holy Roman Empire	
1000		**980** Vladimir becomes grand prince of Kievan Russia
	1054 Formal schism between Latin and Orthodox Churches	
	1066 Normans under William the Conqueror invade England	
	1077 Climax of investiture controversy	
	1095 Pope Urban II preaches First Crusade	**1081–1118** Alexius Comnenus rules Byzantine Empire, calls for western military aid against Muslims
1200		
		1204 Western knights sack Constantinople in Fourth Crusade

Church and State

In 324, in the nineteenth year of his reign, the emperor Constantine (r. 306–337) led a procession marking the expanded limits of the city he had selected as his new capital: the millennium-old Greek city of Byzantium, located on a long, narrow inlet at the entrance to the Bosporus strait (see Chapter 6). In the forum of the new Constantinople°, he erected a 120-foot-tall (36-meter) column topped with a statue of Apollo, and he retained the old Roman title *pontifex maximus*° (chief priest). Nevertheless, he leaned toward Christianity—historians disagree on when he embraced it fully—and he and his mother studded both his capital and the Christian centers of Jerusalem and Rome with important churches.

Constantinople (cahn-stan-tih-NO-pul)

pontifex maximus (PAHN-tih-fex MAX-ih-muhs)

Constantine appointed the patriarch of Constantinople and involved himself in doctrinal disputes over which beliefs constituted heresy. In 325 he called hundreds of bishops to a council at the city of Nicaea° (modern Iznik in northwestern Turkey) to resolve disputes over religious doctrine. The bishops rejected the views of a priest from Alexandria named Arius, who maintained that Jesus was of lesser importance than God the Father. The Arian doctrine enjoyed greatest popularity among the Germanic peoples then migrating along the Danube frontier and into the western Roman lands. An Arian bishop named Ulfilas (ca. 311–383), himself belonging to the Germanic people known as Goths, translated the Bible into Gothic, reportedly using an alphabet of his own devising. This set the Arians apart from Christians who relied on scriptures written in Latin or Greek.

Following the Arian controversy, disputes over theology and quarrels among the patriarchs of Constantinople, Alexandria, and Antioch continued to tear at the Byzantine Empire. Literature of the period shows widespread concern for religious affairs, which deeply permeated society. A fourth-century bishop reported: "Everything is full of those who are speaking of unintelligible things. . . . I wish to know the price of bread; one answers, 'The Father is greater than the Son.' I inquire whether my bath is ready; one says, 'The Son has been made out of nothing.'"[2]

Early Christians had established communities in many cities (see Map 10.1). The most prominent were in Jerusalem, Antioch, Alexandria, and Rome, and their bishops became recognized as patriarchs and paramount leaders. Other important theologians, like St. Augustine (354–430), the bishop of Hippo in North Africa, were not patriarchs. Constantine made Constantinople a fifth patriarchate°. The patriarchs appointed bishops throughout their regions, and each bishop consecrated priests within his area of jurisdiction, called a diocese. Church rules set by the patriarch or by councils of bishops guided priests in serving ordinary believers.

Priests commemorated Christ's sacrifice on the cross in the consumption of bread and wine in the Mass, or church service, and performed ceremonies relating to birth, marriage, and death. But church leaders differed on the precise form of rituals and on which should be considered sacred mysteries, or sacraments. Before baptism became standardized as a ritual for newborns, for example, it was sometimes postponed until late in life so that the person could benefit from the forgiveness of sin that it conveyed.

The church hierarchy strove for consistency in Christian belief throughout the Christian community, but disagreement arose here as well. One area of disagreement centered on Jesus' relationship to God the Father and to the Holy Spirit. The bishops gathered for the Council of Nicaea agreed that, contrary to the view of the Arians, the three formed a divine Trinity in which three aspects or manifestations of God somehow came together. But they did not all understand the Trinity in the same way. They also disagreed on whether Mary was the mother of God, or the mother of a man named Jesus. Some Christians thought that images of God or Jesus or Mary, called icons, were proper objects to pray before because they stimulated pious thoughts; others, known as iconoclasts, or image-breakers, condemned the practice as too much like praying to pagan statues.

For some four centuries after 300, disagreements like these led to charges and countercharges of heresy, beliefs or practices so unacceptable as to be un-Christian. Charges of heresy touched ordinary people, even when they involved hard-to-understand theological issues, because they involved salvation. They also threatened the unity of the Christian church at a time of rapidly increasing political fragmentation.

The most severe disagreements arose in North Africa and the lands of the eastern Mediterranean and resulted in **schism**°—a formal division resulting from disagreements about doctrine. Monophysite° (Greek for "one nature") doctrine, for example, emphasized the divinity of Jesus Christ and minimized his human characteristics. Finding abhorrent the idea that Christ suffered like an ordinary human on the cross, some Monophysites maintained that another man had been substituted for him. Versions of Monophysitism persist to this day in Egyptian, Ethiopian, and Armenian churches. Commonly, a council of bishops, like that at Nicaea, deliberated and declared a particular doctrine true or false. In the east, the Byzantine emperor claimed the authority to call such conferences.

In the Byzantine world, as in the western Roman lands, Christianity progressed most rapidly in urban centers. Though the country folk (Latin *pagani,* whence the word *pagan* used as a negative label for polytheists) long retained customs deriving from worship of the old gods, the emperor Julian (r. 361–363) tried in vain to restore the old polytheism as the state cult. When a blind Christian addressed Julian by the pejorative term "apostate" (renegade from Christianity), which later historians commonly attached to his name, calling him Julian the Apostate, the emperor said, "You are blind, and your God will not cure you." To this the Christian replied, "I thank God for my blindness, since it prevents me from behold-

Nicaea (nye-SEE-uh) **patriarchate** (PAY-tree-ar-kayt)

schism (SKIZ-uhm) **Monophysite** (muh-NAH-fi-site)

Map 10.1 The Spread of Christianity By the early eighth century, Christian areas around the southern Mediterranean from northern Syria to northern Spain, accounting for most of the Christian population, had fallen under Muslim rule; the slow process of conversion to Islam had begun. This accentuated the importance of the patriarchs of Constantinople, the popes in Rome, and the later converting regions of northern and eastern Europe.

ing your impiety."[3] In 392 the emperor Theodosius banned all pagan ceremonies. The following year he terminated the eleven-hundred-year-old tradition of the Olympic Games, which had originated as religious rites but had become increasingly professionalized in Roman times.

Having a single ruler endowed with supreme legal and religious authority prevented the breakup of the Eastern Empire into petty principalities, but a series of territorial losses sapped the empire's strength. A strong emperor might temporarily recover lost ground, as Justinian (r. 527–565) did in seizing Tunisia from Germanic Vandal rulers and reasserting Byzantine control along the east coast of Italy, but military pressures seldom abated. A new Iranian empire ruled by the Sasanid family (see Chapter 9) threatened from the east in the fourth century. Various enemies including the Germanic Goths and the nomadic Huns of Central Asia threatened from the north at different periods. Bribes, diplomacy, and occasional military victories usually persuaded the Goths and Huns to settle peacefully or move on and attack western Europe. War with the Sasanids, however, flared up repeatedly for almost three hundred years. Finally, a new enemy appeared from the Arabian peninsula: followers of the Arab prophet Muhammad. Between 634 and 650, Arab armies destroyed the Sasanid Empire and captured Byzantine Egypt, Syria, and Tunisia. By the end of the twelfth century, at least

Byzantine Church from a Twelfth-Century Manuscript
The upper portion shows the church façade and domes. The lower portion shows the interior with a mosaic of Christ enthroned at the altar end. (Bibliothèque nationale de France)

two-thirds of the Christians in these former Byzantine territories had adopted the Muslim faith.

The loss of such populous and prosperous provinces shook the empire and reduced its power. Although the empire had largely recovered and reorganized militarily by the tenth century, it never regained the lost lands and eventually succumbed to Muslim conquest in 1453. The later Byzantine emperors faced new enemies in the north and south. Following the wave of Germanic migrations, Slavic and Turkic peoples appeared on the northern frontiers as part of centuries-long and poorly understood population migrations in Eurasian steppe lands. Other Turks led by the Seljuk family became the primary foe in the south (see Chapter 9).

At the same time, relations with the popes and princes of western Europe steadily worsened. In the mid-ninth century the patriarchs of Constantinople had challenged the territorial jurisdiction of the popes of Rome and some of the practices of the Latin Church. These arguments worsened over time and in 1054 culminated in a formal schism between the Latin Church and the Orthodox Church—a break that has been only partially mended.

Society and Urban Life

Imperial authority and urban prosperity in the eastern provinces of the old Roman Empire initially sheltered Byzantium from many of the economic reverses and population losses suffered by western Europe from the third century on. The two regions shared a common demographic crisis during a sixth-century epidemic of bubonic plague known as "the plague of Justinian." A similar though gradual and less pronounced social transformation set in around the seventh century, possibly sparked by the loss of Egypt and Syria to the Muslims. Narrative histories tell us little, but popular narratives of saints' lives show a transition from stories about educated saints hailing from cities to stories about saints who originated as peasants. In many areas, barter replaced money transactions; some cities declined in population and wealth; and the traditional class of local urban notables nearly disappeared.

As the urban elite class shrank, the importance of high-ranking aristocrats at the imperial court and of rural landowners increased. Power organized by family began to rival power from class-based officeholding. By the end of the eleventh century, a family-based military aristocracy had emerged. Of Byzantine emperor Alexius Comnenus° (r. 1081–1118) it was said: "He considered himself not a ruler, but a lord, conceiving and calling the empire his own house."[4]

The situation of women changed, too. Although earlier Roman family life was centered on a legally all-powerful father, women enjoyed comparative freedom in public. After the seventh century women increasingly found themselves confined to the home. Some sources indicate that when they went out, they concealed their faces behind veils. The only men they socialized with were family members. Paradoxically, however, from 1028 to 1056 women ruled the Byzantine Empire alongside their husbands. These social changes and the apparent increase in the seclusion of women resemble simultaneous developments in neighboring Islamic countries, but historians have not uncovered any firm linkage between them.

Alexius Comnenus (uh-LEX-see-uhs kom-NAY-nuhs)

Economically, the Byzantine emperors continued the Late Roman inclination to set prices, organize grain shipments to the capital, and monopolize trade in luxury goods like Tyrian purple cloth. Such government intervention may have slowed technological development and economic innovation. So long as merchants and pilgrims hastened to Constantinople from all points of the compass, aristocrats could buy rare and costly goods. Just as the provisioning and physical improvement of Rome overshadowed the development of other cities at the height of the Roman Empire, so other Byzantine cities suffered from the intense focus on Constantinople. In the countryside, Byzantine farmers continued to use slow oxcarts and light scratch plows, which were efficient for many, but not all, soil types, long after farmers in western Europe had begun to adopt more efficient techniques (see below).

Because Byzantium's Roman inheritance remained so much more intact than western Europe's, few people recognized the slow deterioration. Gradually, however, pilgrims and visitors from the west saw the reality beyond the awe-inspiring, incense-filled domes of cathedrals and beneath the glitter and silken garments of the royal court. An eleventh-century French visitor wrote:

> The city itself [Constantinople] is squalid and fetid and in many places harmed by permanent darkness, for the wealthy overshadow the streets with buildings and leave these dirty, dark places to the poor and to travelers; there murders and robberies and other crimes which love the darkness are committed. Moreover, since people live lawlessly in this city, which has as many lords as rich men and almost as many thieves as poor men, a criminal knows neither fear nor shame, because crime is not punished by law and never entirely comes to light. In every respect she exceeds moderation; for, just as she surpasses other cities in wealth, so too, does she surpass them in vice.[5]

A Byzantine contemporary, Anna Comnena, the brilliant daughter of Emperor Alexius Comnenus, expressed the view from the other side. She scornfully described a prominent churchman and philosopher who happened to be from Italy: "Italos . . . was unable with his barbaric, stupid temperament to grasp the profound truths of philosophy; even in the act of learning he utterly rejected the teacher's guiding hand, and full of temerity and barbaric folly, [believed] even before study that he excelled all others."[6]

Cultural Achievements

Justinian's collection of Roman laws endured far longer than his restoration of Byzantine rule in Italy and North Africa. At his command a team of seventeen legal scholars made a systematic compilation, in Latin, of a thousand years of Roman legal tradition. The *Corpus Juris Civilis (Body of Civil Law),* as it has been called since the sixteenth century, consisted of four sections: a general introduction and survey, a digest for lawyers and judges containing specific laws and quotations from well-known commentaries, a collection of imperial decrees since the time of the emperor Hadrian (r. 117–138), and another collection of recent decrees not previously collected. In the eleventh century a legal scholar named Irnerius (ca. 1055–ca. 1130) revived the study of this code (see below) at the University of Bologna° in Italy, and it subsequently became the basis of most modern European legal systems.

Constantinople's cathedral, the Hagia Sophia° ("Sacred Wisdom"), also dates in its present form to the reign of Justinian and his influential wife, the empress Theodora. Its great dome became a hallmark of Byzantine architecture. Artistic creativity appeared in the design and ornamentation of other churches and monasteries as well. Byzantine religious art, featuring stiff but arresting images of holy figures against gold backgrounds, strongly influenced painting in western Europe down to the thirteenth century, and Byzantine musical traditions strongly affected the chanting employed in medieval Latin churches.

Other important Byzantine achievements date to the empire's long period of political decline. In the ninth century brothers named Cyril and Methodius embarked on a highly successful mission to the Slavs of Moravia (part of the modern Czech Republic). Like the Gothic bishop Ulfilas in the fourth century, they preached in the local language, and their followers perfected a writing system, called Cyrillic°, that came to be used by Slavic Christians adhering to the Orthodox—that is, Byzantine—rite. Their careers also mark the beginning of a competition between the Greek and Latin forms of Christianity for the allegiance of the Slavs. The use today of the Cyrillic alphabet among the Russians and other Slavic peoples of Orthodox Christian faith, and of the Roman alphabet among the Poles, Czechs, and Croatians, testifies to this competition (see the section below on Kievan Russia).

Bologna (boe-LOAN-yuh) **Hagia Sophia** (AH-yah SOH-fee-uh) **Cyrillic** (sih-RIL-ik)

EARLY MEDIEVAL EUROPE, 300–1000

Constantine kept the Roman Empire under his sole rule (see Chapter 6) even as he was building his new capital of Constantinople, but union did not last. Divisions between east and west that had appeared earlier became permanent in 395. Germanic peoples fleeing the Huns, a new invader from Asia, put pressure on both halves. Byzantine armies and diplomats warded off most assaults on the comparatively short Danube River frontier, persuading the bands of warriors to keep moving westward. But the Roman legions in the west could not hold. Gaul, Britain, Spain, and North Africa fell to various Germanic peoples in the early fifth century. Visigoths sacked Rome itself in 410, and the last Roman emperor was deposed in 476.

The disappearance of the imperial legal framework that had persisted to the final days of the Western Roman Empire and the rise of various kings, nobles, and chieftains changed the legal and political landscape of western Europe. In region after region, the family-based traditions of the Germanic peoples, which often fit local conditions better than previous practices, supplanted the edicts of the Roman emperors.

Fear and physical insecurity led communities to seek the protection of local strongmen. In places where looters and pillagers might appear at any moment, a local lord with a castle at which peasants could take refuge counted for more than a distant king. Dependency of weak people on strong people became a hallmark of the post-Roman period in western Europe.

From Roman Empire to Germanic Kingdoms

By 530 the Western Roman Empire had fragmented into a handful of kingdoms under Germanic rulers. The Franks held much of Gaul; the Visigoths ruled in Spain and the Ostrogoths in Italy and present-day Austria and Hungary. Saxons, Angles, and Jutes made raids across the North Sea and eventually took over most of Britain (see Map 10.2). By 600 the Lombards had replaced the Ostrogoths in northern Italy, and the Byzantine Empire had regained footholds in the south and around Ravenna along the east coast. The city of Rome had lost its political importance but retained prominence as the seat of the most influential Western churchman, the bishop of Rome. Local noble families competed for control of this position, which over several centuries acquired the title *Pope* along with supreme power in the Latin-speaking church. Greek, which had once been common in Rome and had become the religious language of the Byzantine church, became rare.

The educated few, increasingly only Christian priests and monks, still spoke and wrote a somewhat simplified form of Latin. But the Latin of the uneducated masses who had lived under Roman rule rapidly evolved into the Romance dialects that eventually became modern Portuguese, Spanish, French, Italian, and Romanian. In the north and east of the Rhine River, where Roman culture had scarcely penetrated, people spoke Germanic and related Scandinavian languages. East of the Elbe River speakers of Slavic languages formed a third major group.

In 711 a frontier raiding party of Arabs and Berbers, acting under the authority of the Umayyad caliph in

Saxon Belt Buckle from Eastern England This fine specimen of the German jeweler's art was found in the excavation of a buried ship at the site known as Sutton Hoo. The find dates from ca. 660 and shows the fascination of the Germanic peoples with patterns of interlaced animal figures. This interlace style reappears in Christian manuscripts such as the Book of Kells shown on page 268. (Courtesy of the Trustees of the Bristish Museum)

Map 10.2 Germanic Kingdoms Though German kings asserted authority over most of western Europe, German-speaking peoples were most numerous east of the Rhine River. In most other areas, Celtic languages, for example, Breton on this map, or languages derived from Latin predominated. Though the Germanic Anglo-Saxon tongue increasingly supplanted Welsh and Scottish in Britain, the absolute number of Germanic settlers seems to have been fairly limited.

Syria, crossed the Strait of Gibraltar and overturned the kingdom of the Visigoths in Spain (see Chapter 9). The disunited Europeans could not stop them from consolidating their hold on the Iberian Peninsula. After pushing the remaining Christian chieftains into the northern mountains, the Muslims moved on to France. They occupied much of the southern coast and penetrated as far north as Tours, less than 150 miles (240 kilometers) from the English Channel, before Charlemagne's grandfather, Charles Martel, stopped their most advanced raiding party in 732.

Military effectiveness was the key element in the rise of the Carolingian° family (from Latin *Carolus*, "Charles") first as protectors of the Frankish kings, then as kings themselves under Charlemagne's father Pepin (r. 751–768), and finally, under Charlemagne, as emperors. At the peak of Charlemagne's power, the Carolingian Empire encompassed all of Gaul and parts of Germany and Italy, with the pope ruling part of the latter. When Charlemagne's son, Louis the Pious, died, the Germanic tradition of splitting property among sons led to the Treaty of Verdun (843), which split the empire into three parts. French-speaking in the west (France) and middle (Burgundy), and German-speaking in the east (Germany), the three regions never reunited. Nevertheless, the Carolingian economic system based on landed wealth and a brief intellectual revival sponsored personally by Charlemagne—though he himself was illiterate—provided a common heritage.

A new threat to western Europe appeared in 793, when the Vikings, sea raiders from Scandinavia, attacked and plundered a monastery on the English coast, the first of hundreds of such raids. Local sources from France, the British Isles, and Muslim Spain attest to widespread dread of Viking warriors descending from multi-oared, dragon-prowed boats to pillage monasteries, villages,

Carolingian (kah-roe-LIN-gee-uhn)

and towns. Viking shipbuilders made versatile vessels that could brave the stormy North Atlantic and also maneuver up rivers to attack inland towns. In the ninth century raiders from Denmark and Norway harried the British and French coasts (see Diversity and Dominance: Archbishop Adalbert of Hamburg and the Christianization of the Scandinavians and Slavs) while Varangians° (Swedes) pursued raiding and trading interests, and eventually the building of kingdoms, along the rivers of eastern Europe and Russia, as we shall see. Although many Viking raiders sought booty and slaves, in the 800s and 900s Viking captains organized the settlement of Iceland, Greenland, and, around the year 1000, Vinland on the northern tip of Newfoundland.

Vikings long settled on lands they had seized in Normandy (in northwestern France) organized the most important and ambitious expeditions in terms of numbers of men and horses and long-lasting impact. William the Conqueror, the duke of Normandy, invaded England in 1066 and brought Anglo-Saxon domination of the island to an end. Other Normans (from "north men") attacked Muslim Sicily in the 1060s and, after thirty years of fighting, permanently severed it from the Muslim world.

A Self-Sufficient Economy

Archaeology and records kept by Christian monasteries and convents reveal a profound economic transformation that accompanied the new Germanic political order. The new rulers cared little for the urban-based civilization of the Romans, which accordingly shrank in importance. Though the pace of change differed from region to region, most cities lost population, in some cases becoming villages. Roman roads fell into disuse and disrepair. Small thatched houses sprang up beside abandoned villas, and public buildings made of marble became dilapidated in the absence of the laborers, money, and civic leadership needed to maintain them. Paying for purchases in coin largely gave way to bartering goods and services.

The level of trade diminished. Egyptian wheat that had once fed the multitudes of Rome went to Constantinople and after the seventh century to Mecca and Medina. In 439 an invasion by Germanic Vandals from Spain cut off Tunisia, another of Rome's breadbaskets. Trade across the Mediterranean did not entirely stop; occasional shipments from Egypt and Syria continued to reach western ports. But most of western Europe came to rely on meager local resources. These resources, moreover, underwent redistribution.

Varangians (va-RAN-gee-anz)

Roman centralization had channeled the wealth and production of the empire to the capital, which in turn radiated Roman cultural styles and tastes to the provinces. As Roman governors were replaced by Germanic territorial lords who found the riches of their own culture more appealing than those of Rome, local self-sufficiency became more important. The decline of literacy and other aspects of Roman life made room for the growth of Celtic and Germanic cultural traditions.

The diet in the northern countries featured beer, lard or butter, and bread made of barley, rye, or wheat, all supplemented by pork from herds of swine fed on forest acorns and beechnuts, and by game from the same forests. Nobles ate better than peasants, but even the peasant diet was reasonably balanced. The Roman diet based on wheat, wine, and olive oil persisted in the south. The average western European of the ninth century was probably better nourished than his or her descendants three hundred years later, when population was increasing and the nobility monopolized the resources of the forests.

In both north and south, self-sufficient farming estates known as **manors** became the primary centers of agricultural production. Wealthy Romans had commonly built country houses on their lands. From the fourth century onward, fear of attack led many common farmers in the most vulnerable regions to give their lands to large landowners in return for political and physical protection. The warfare and instability of the post-Roman centuries made unprotected country houses especially vulnerable to pillaging. Isolated by poor communications and lack of organized government, landowners depended on their own resources for survival. Many became warriors or maintained a force of armed men. Others swore allegiance to landowners who had armed forces to protect them.

A well-appointed manor possessed fields, gardens, grazing lands, fish ponds, a mill, a church, workshops for making farm and household implements, and a village where the farmers dependent on the lord of the manor lived. Depending on local conditions, protection ranged from a ditch and wooden stockade to a stone wall surrounding a fortified keep (a stone building). Fortification tended to increase until the twelfth century, when stronger monarchies made it less necessary.

Manor life reflected personal status. Nobles and their families exercised almost unlimited power over the **serfs**—agricultural workers who belonged to the manor, tilled its fields, and owed other dues and obligations. Serfs could not leave the manor where they were born and attach themselves to another lord. Most peasants in England, France, and western Germany were unfree serfs in the tenth and eleventh centuries. In Bordeaux°, Saxony, and a few other regions free peasantry survived based on the egalitarian social structure of the Germanic peoples during their period of migration. Outright slavery, the mainstay of the Roman economy (see Chapter 6), diminished as more and more peasants became serfs in return for a lord's protection. The enslavement of prisoners to serve as laborers became less important as an object of warfare.

Early Medieval Society in the West

Europe's reversion to a self-sufficient economy limited the freedom and potential for personal achievement of most people, but an emerging class of nobles reaped great benefits. During the Germanic migrations and later among the Vikings of Scandinavia, men regularly answered the call to arms issued by war chiefs, to whom they swore allegiance. All warriors shared in the booty gained from raiding. As settlement enhanced the importance of agricultural tasks, laying down the plow and picking up the sword at the chieftain's call became harder.

Those who, out of loyalty or desire for adventure, continued to join the war parties included a growing number of horsemen. Mounted warriors became the central force of the Carolingian army. At first, fighting from horseback did not make a person either a nobleman or a landowner. By the tenth century, however, nearly constant warfare to protect land rights or support the claims of a lord brought about a gradual transformation in the status of the mounted warrior, which led, at different rates in different areas, to landholding becoming almost inseparable from military service.

In trying to understand long-standing traditions of landholding and obligation, lawyers in the sixteenth century and later simplified thousands of individual agreements into a neat system they called "feudalism," from Latin *feodum* meaning a land awarded for military service. It became common to refer to medieval Europe as a "feudal society" in which kings and lords gave land to "vassals" in return for sworn military support. By analyzing original records, more recent historians have discovered this to be an oversimplification. Relations between landholders and serfs and between lords and vassals differed too much from one place to another, and from one time to another, to fit together in anything resembling a system.

Bordeaux (bore-DOE)

The German foes of the Roman legions had equipped themselves with helmets, shields, and swords, spears, or throwing axes. Some rode horses, but most fought on foot. Before the invention of the stirrup by Central Asian pastoralists in approximately the first century C.E., horsemen had gripped their mounts with their legs and fought with bows and arrows, throwing javelins, stabbing spears, and swords. Stirrups allowed a rider to stand in the saddle and absorb the impact when his lance struck an enemy at full gallop. This type of warfare required grain-fed horses that were larger and heavier than the small, grass-fed animals of the Central Asian nomads, though smaller and lighter than the draft horses bred in later times for hauling heavy loads. Thus agricultural Europe rather than the grassy steppes produced the charges of armored knights that came to dominate the battlefield.

By the eleventh century, the knight, called by different terms in different places, had emerged as the central figure in medieval warfare. He wore an open-faced helmet and a long linen shirt, or hauberk°, studded with small metal disks. A century later, knightly equipment commonly included a visored helmet that covered the head and neck and a hauberk of chain mail.

Each increase in armor for knight and horse entailed a greater financial outlay. Since land was the basis of wealth, a knight needed financial support from land revenues. Accordingly, kings began to reward armed service with grants of land from their own property. Lesser nobles with extensive properties built their own military retinues the same way.

A grant of land in return for a pledge to provide military service was often called a **fief.** At first, kings granted fiefs to their noble followers, known as **vassals,** on a temporary basis. By the tenth century, most fiefs could be inherited as long as the specified military service continued to be provided. Though patterns varied greatly, the association of landholding with military service made the medieval society of western Europe quite different from the contemporary city-based societies of the Islamic world.

Kings and lords might be able to command the service of their vassals for only part of the year. Vassals could hold land from several different lords and owe loyalty to each one. Moreover, the allegiance that a vassal owed to one lord could entail military service to that lord's master in time of need.

A "typical" medieval realm—actual practices varied between and within realms—consisted of lands directly owned by a king or a count and administered by his royal

hauberk (HAW-berk)

DIVERSITY AND DOMINANCE

ARCHBISHOP ADALBERT OF HAMBURG AND THE CHRISTIANIZATION OF THE SCANDINAVIANS AND SLAVS

Adam of Bremen's History of the Archbishops of Hamburg-Bremen, *consists of four sections. The third is devoted to the Archbishop Adalbert, whose death in 1072 stirred Adam to write. References to classical poets, the lives of saints, and royal documents show that Adam, a churchman, had a solid education and access to many sources. He also drew on living informants, in particular the Danish king Svein Estrithson, a nephew of Canute, king of England from 1015 to 1035, and father-in-law of Gottschalk, a lord over the Slavs mentioned below. The excerpts below illustrate the close connection between political and religious institutions in establishing a structure of domination in lands on the European frontier.*

Archbishop Adalbert held the see for twenty-nine years. He received the pastoral staff from the [Holy Roman] Emperor Henry, the son of Conrad, who was, counting from Caesar Augustus, the ninetieth Roman emperor to sit upon the throne . . . The archiepiscopal pallium [i.e., bishop's cloak] was brought to him . . . by legates from the Pope Benedict . . . [who] was the one hundred and forty-seventh after the Apostles in the succession of Roman pontiffs. His consecration took place in Aachen in the presence of Caesar and of the princes of the realm. Twelve bishops assisted and laid their hands on him . . .

This remarkable man may for all that be extolled with praise of every kind in that he was noble, handsome, wise, eloquent, chaste, temperate. All these qualities he comprised in himself and others besides, such as one is wont to attach to the outer man: that he was rich, that he was successful, that he was glorious, that he was influential. All these things were his in abundance. Moreover, in respect of the mission to the heathen, which is the first duty of the Church at Hamburg, no one so vigorous could ever be found . . . Although he was such in the beginning, he seemed to fail toward the end. Not being well on his guard against any defect in his virtue, the man met with ruin as much through his own negligence as through the driving malice of others . . .

Keen and well trained of mind, he was skillful in many arts. In things divine and human he was possessed of great prudence and was well known for retaining in memory and setting forth with matchless eloquence what he had acquired by hearing or by study. Then, besides, although handsome in physical form, he was a lover of chastity. His generosity was of a kind that made him regard asking favors as unworthy, that made him slow and humble in accepting them but prompt and cheerful in giving, often generously, to those who had not asked. His humility appears doubtful in that he exhibited it only in respect of the servants of God, the poor, and pilgrims, and it went to such lengths that before retiring he often would on bended knees personally wash the feet of thirty or more beggars. To the princes of the world, however, and to his peers he would in no way stoop. Toward them he even broke out at times with a vehemence that at last spared no one he thought outstanding. Some he upbraided for luxury, others for greed, still others for infidelity . . .

On seeing that the basilica [i.e., cathedral] which had lately been started was an immense structure requiring very great resources, he with too precipitate judgment immediately had the city wall, begun by his predecessors, pulled down, as if it were not at all necessary, and ordered its stones built into the temple. Even the beautiful tower, . . . fitted out with seven chambers, was then razed to its foundations . . . Alebrand before him had begun [the cathedral] in the style of the church at Cologne [in western Germany], but he planned to carry it out in the manner of the cathedral at Benevento [in southern Italy] . . .

And because the great prelate saw that his Church and bishopric . . . was troubled again by the iniquitous might of the dukes, he made a supreme effort to restore to that Church its former freedom, that thus neither the duke nor the count nor any person of judicial position would have any right or power in his diocese. But this objective could not be attained without incurring hatred, since the wrath of the princes, rebuked for their wickedness, would be further inflamed. And they say that Duke Bernhard, who held the archbishop under suspicion because of his nobility and wisdom, often said that Adalbert had been stationed in this country like a spy, to betray the weaknesses of the land to the aliens and to Caesar. Consequently the duke declared that as long as he or any of his sons lived, the bishop should not have a happy day in the bishopric . . .

As soon as the metropolitan [i.e., Archbishop Adalbert] had entered upon his episcopate, he sent legates to the kings of the north in the interest of friendship. There were also dispersed throughout all Denmark and Norway and Sweden and to the ends of the earth admonitory letters in which he exhorted the bishops and priests living in those parts . . . fearlessly to forward the conversion of the pagans . . . [Svein, the Danish king who died after invading England in 1013 and left his throne to his son Canute] forgot the heavenly King as things prospered with him and married a blood relative from Sweden. This mightily displeased the lord archbishop, who sent legates to the rash king, rebuking him severely for his sin, and who stated finally that if he did not come to his senses, he would have to be cut off with the sword of excommunication. Beside himself with rage, the king then threatened to ravage and destroy the whole diocese of Hamburg. Unperturbed by these threats, our archbishop, reproving and entreating, remained firm, until at length the Danish tyrant was prevailed upon by letters from the pope to give his cousin a bill of divorce. Still the king would not give ear to the admonitions of the priests. Soon after he had put aside his cousin he took to himself other wives and concubines, and again still others . . .

While these events were taking place there, the most Christian king of the Swedes, James, departed this world, and his brother, Edmund the Bad, succeeded him. He was born of a concubine by Olaf [the Lapp King] and, although he had been baptized, took little heed of our religion. He had with him a certain bishop named Osmund, of irregular status, whom the bishop of the Norwegians, Sigefrid, had once commended to the school at Bremen for instruction. But later he forgot these kindnesses and went to Rome for consecration. When he was rejected there, he wandered about through many parts and so finally secured consecration from a Polish archbishop. Going to Sweden then, he boasted that he had been consecrated archbishop for those parts. But when our archbishop sent his legates to King [Edmund], they found this same vagabond Osmund there, having the cross borne before him after the manner of an archbishop. They also heard that he had by his unsound teaching of our faith corrupted the barbarians, who were still neophytes [i.e., beginners] . . .

In Norway . . . King Harold surpassed all the madness of tyrants in his savage wildness. Many churches were destroyed by that man; many Christians were tortured to death by him. But he was a mighty man and renowned for the victories he had previously won in many wars with barbarians in Greece and in the Scythian regions [i.e., while assisting the Byzantine empress Zoë fight the Seljuk Turks]. After he came into his fatherland, however, he never ceased from warfare; he was the thunderbolt of the north . . . And so, as he ruled over many nations, he was odious to all on account of his greed and cruelty. He also gave himself up to the magic arts and, wretched man that he was, did not heed the fact that his most saintly brother [i.e., Saint Olaf, one of Harold's predecessors] had eradicated such illusions from the realm and striven even unto death for the adoption of the precepts of Christianity . . .

Across the Elbe [i.e., east of the river Hamburg is on] and in Slavia our affairs were still meeting with great success. For Gottschalk . . . married a daughter of the Danish king and so thoroughly subdued the Slavs that they feared him like a king, offered to pay tribute, and asked for peace with subjection. Under these circumstances our Church at Hamburg enjoyed peace, and Slavia abounded in priests and churches . . . Gottschalk is said to have been inflamed with such ardent zeal for the faith that, forgetting his station, he frequently made discourse in church in exhortation of the people—in church because he wished to make clearer in the Slavic speech what was abstrusely preached by the bishops or priests. Countless was the number of those who were converted every day; so much so that he sent into every province for priests. In the several cities were then also founded monasteries for holy men who lived according to canonical rule . . .

I have also heard the most veracious king of the Danes say . . . that the Slavic peoples without doubt could easily have been converted to Christianity long ago but for the avarice of the Saxons. "They are," he said, "more intent on the payment of tribute than on the conversion of the heathen." Nor do these wretched people realize with what great danger they will have to atone for their cupidity, they who through their avarice in the first place threw Christianity in Slavia into disorder, in the second place have by their cruelty forced their subjects to rebel, and who now by their desire only for money hold in contempt the salvation of a people who wish to believe" . . .

QUESTIONS FOR ANALYSIS

1. **Using this work as a historical source, what would you consider the main concerns of the church in northern Germany?**
2. **How does Adam distinguish Christians from pagans in his descriptive passages?**
3. **What appears to be the relationship between ecclesiastical lords like the archbishop and the secular kings and dukes?**

Source: Excerpts from *History of the Archbishops of Hamburg-Bremen*, tr. Francis J. Tschan (New York: Columbia University Press, 1959 [new ed. 2002]), 114–133.

Noblewoman Directing Construction of a Church This picture of Berthe, wife of Girat de Rouissillion, acting as mistress of the works comes from a tenth-century manuscript that shows a scene from the ninth century. Wheelbarrows rarely appear in medieval building scenes. (Copyright Brussels, Royal Library of Belgium)

officers. The king's or count's major vassals held and administered other lands, often the greater portion, in return for military service. These vassals, in turn, granted land to their own vassals.

The lord of a manor provided governance and justice, direct royal government being quite limited. The king had few financial resources and seldom exercised legal jurisdiction at a local level. Members of the clergy, as well as the extensive agricultural lands owned by monasteries and nunneries, fell under the jurisdiction of the church, which further limited the reach and authority of the monarch.

Noblewomen became enmeshed in this tangle of obligations as heiresses and as candidates for marriage. A man who married the widow or daughter of a lord with no sons could gain control of that lord's property. Marriage alliances affected entire kingdoms. Noble daughters and sons had little say in marriage matters; issues of land, power, and military service took precedence. Noblemen guarded the women in their families as closely as their other valuables.

Nevertheless, women could own land. A noblewoman sometimes administered her husband's estates when he was away at war. Nonnoble women usually worked alongside their menfolk, performing agricultural tasks such as raking and stacking hay, shearing sheep, and picking vegetables. As artisans, women spun, wove, and sewed clothing. The Bayeux° Tapestry, a piece of embroidery 230 feet (70 meters) long and 20 inches (51 centimeters) wide depicting William the Conqueror's invasion of England in 1066, was designed and executed entirely by women, though historians do not agree on who those women were.

THE WESTERN CHURCH

Just as the Christian populations in eastern Europe followed the religious guidance of the patriarch of Constantinople appointed by the Byzantine emperor, so the pope commanded similar authority over church affairs in western Europe. And just as missionaries in the east spread Christianity among the Slavs, so missionaries in

Bayeux (bay-YUH)

the west added territory to Christendom with forays into the British Isles and the lands of the Germans. Throughout the period covered by this chapter Christian society was emerging and changing in both areas.

In the west Roman nobles lost control of the **papacy**—the office of the pope—and it became a more powerful international office after the tenth century. Councils of bishops—which normally set rules, called canons, to regulate the priests and laypeople (men and women who were not members of the clergy) under their jurisdiction—became increasingly responsive to papal direction.

Nevertheless, regional disagreements over church regulations, shortages of educated and trained clergy, difficult communications, political disorder, and the general insecurity of the period posed formidable obstacles to unifying church standards and practices. Clerics in some parts of western Europe were still issuing prohibitions against the worship of rivers, trees, and mountains as late as the eleventh century. Church problems included lingering polytheism, lax enforcement of prohibitions against marriage of clergy, nepotism (giving preferment to one's close kin), and simony (selling ecclesiastical appointments, often to people who were not members of the clergy). The persistence of the papacy in asserting its legal jurisdiction over clergy, combating polytheism and heretical beliefs, and calling on secular rulers to recognize the pope's authority, including unpopular rulings like a ban on first-cousin marriage, constituted a rare force for unity and order in a time of disunity and chaos.

Politics and the Church

In politically fragmented western Europe, the pope needed allies. Like his son, Charlemagne's father Pepin was a strong supporter of the papacy. The relationship between kings and popes was tense, however, since both thought of themselves as ultimate authorities. In 962 the pope crowned the first "Holy Roman Emperor" (Charlemagne never held this full title). This designation of a secular political authority as the guardian of general Christian interests proved more apparent then real. Essentially a loose confederation of German princes who named one of their own to the highest office, the **Holy Roman Empire** had little influence west of the Rhine River.

Although the pope crowned the early Holy Roman emperors, this did not signify political superiority. The law of the church (known as canon law because each law was called a canon) gave the pope exclusive legal jurisdiction over all clergy and church property wherever located. But bishops who held land as vassals owed military support or other services and dues to kings and princes. The secular rulers argued that they should have the power to appoint those bishops because that was the only way to guarantee fulfillment of their duties as vassals. The popes disagreed.

In the eleventh century, this conflict over the control of ecclesiastical appointments came to a head. Hildebrand°, an Italian monk, capped a career of reorganizing church finances when the cardinals (a group of senior bishops) meeting in Rome selected him to be Pope Gregory VII in 1073. His personal notion of the papacy (preserved among his letters) represented an extreme position, stating among other claims, that

§ The pope can be judged by no one;
§ The Roman church has never erred and never will err till the end of time;
§ The pope alone can depose and restore bishops;
§ He alone can call general councils and authorize canon law;
§ He can depose emperors;
§ He can absolve subjects from their allegiance;
§ All princes should kiss his feet.[7]

Such claims antagonized lords and monarchs, who had become accustomed to *investing*—that is, conferring a ring and a staff as symbols of authority on bishops and abbots in their domains. Historians apply the term **investiture controversy** to the medieval struggle between the church and the lay lords to control ecclesiastical appointments; the term also refers to the broader conflict of popes versus emperors and kings. When Holy Roman Emperor Henry IV defied Gregory's reforms, Gregory excommunicated him in 1076, thereby cutting him off from church rituals. Stung by the resulting decline in his influence, Henry stood barefoot in the snow for three days outside a castle in northern Italy waiting for Gregory, a guest there, to receive him. Henry's formal act of penance induced Gregory to forgive him and restore him to the church; but the reconciliation, an apparent victory for the pope, did not last. In 1078 Gregory declared Henry deposed. The emperor then forced Gregory to flee from Rome to Salerno, where he died two years later.

The struggle between the popes and emperors continued until 1122, when a compromise was reached at Worms, a town in Germany. In the Concordat of Worms, Emperor Henry V renounced his right to choose bishops and abbots or bestow spiritual symbols upon them. In return, Pope Calixtus II permitted the emperor to invest papally appointed bishops and abbots with any lay rights or obligations before their spiritual consecration.

Hildebrand (HILL-de-brand)

Such compromises did not fully solve the problem, but they reduced tensions between the two sides.

Assertions of royal authority triggered other conflicts as well. Though barely twenty when he became king of England in 1154, Henry II, a great-grandson of William the Conqueror, instituted reforms designed to strengthen the power of the Crown and weaken the nobility. He appointed traveling justices to enforce his laws. He made juries, a holdover from traditional Germanic law, into powerful legal instruments. He established the principle that criminal acts violated the "king's peace" and should be tried and punished in accordance with charges brought by the Crown instead of in response to charges brought by victims.

Henry had a harder time controlling the church. His closest friend and chancellor, or chief administrator, Thomas à Becket (ca. 1118–1170), lived the grand and luxurious life of a courtier. In 1162 Henry persuaded Becket to become a priest and assume the position of archbishop of Canterbury, the highest church office in England. Becket agreed but cautioned that from then on he would act solely in the interest of the church if it came into conflict with the Crown. When Henry sought to try clerics accused of crimes in royal instead of ecclesiastical courts, Archbishop Thomas, now leading an austere and pious life, resisted.

In 1170 four of Henry's knights, knowing that the king desired Becket's death, murdered the archbishop in Canterbury Cathedral. Their crime backfired, and an outpouring of sympathy caused Canterbury to become a major pilgrimage center. In 1173 the pope declared the martyred Becket a saint. Henry allowed himself to be publicly whipped twice in penance for the crime, but his authority had been badly damaged.

Henry II's conflict with Thomas à Becket, like the Concordat of Worms, yielded no clear victor. The problem of competing legal traditions made political life in western Europe more complicated than in Byzantium or the lands of Islam (see Chapter 9). Feudal law, rooted in Germanic custom, gave supreme power to the king. Canon law, based on Roman precedent, visualized a single hierarchical legal institution with jurisdiction over all of Western Christendom. In the eleventh century Roman civil law, contained in the *Corpus Juris Civilis*, added a third tradition.

Illuminated Manuscript from Monastic Library This page from the Book of Kells, written around 800 in Ireland, contains the Greek letters chi and rho, or CR, a monogram for Jesus Christ. The intricate interwoven forms that fill the background derive from pagan design traditions that featured intertangled dragons, snakes, and other beasts. (The Board of Trinity College, Dublin)

Monasticism

Monasticism featured prominently in the religious life of almost all medieval Christian lands. The origins of group monasticism lay in the eastern lands of the Roman Empire. Pre-Christian practices such as celibacy, continual devotion to prayer, and living apart from society (alone or in small groups) came together in Christian form in Egypt. A fourth-century account portrays Anthony, the most important solitary monk, as a pious desert hermit continually tempted by Satan. On one occasion, "when he was weaving palm leaves . . . that he might make baskets to give as gifts to people who were continually coming to visit him . . . he saw an animal which had the following form: from its head to its side it was like a man, and its legs and feet were those of an ass."[8] As was his custom, Anthony prayed to God upon seeing this sight, and Satan left him alone. Exaggerated stories like these are common in the popular accounts of saints' lives. In reality, saintly hermits gave strong moral leadership to their pious admirers.

The most important form of monasticism in western Europe involved groups of monks or nuns living together in a single community. An Egyptian monk named Pachomius had begun this practice in Egypt, but the person most responsible for introducing it in the Latin west was Benedict of Nursia (ca. 480–547) in Italy. Benedict began his pious career as a hermit in a cave but eventually organized several monasteries, each headed by an abbot. The Rule he wrote to govern the monks' behavior envisions a balanced life of devotion and work, along with obligations of celibacy, poverty, and obedience to the abbot. Those who lived by this or other monastic rules became *regular clergy,* in contrast to *secular clergy,* priests who lived in society instead of in seclusion and did not follow a formal code of regulations. The Rule of Benedict was the starting point for most forms of western European monastic life and remains in force today in Benedictine monasteries.

Though monks and nuns, women who lived by monastic rules in convents, made up a small percentage of the total population, their secluded way of life reinforced the separation of religious affairs from ordinary politics and economics. Monasteries followed Jesus' axiom to "render unto Caesar what is Caesar's and unto God what is God's" better than the many town-based bishops who behaved like lords.

Monasteries preserved literacy and learning in the early medieval period, although some rulers, like Charlemagne, encouraged scholarship at court. Many illiterate lay nobles interested themselves only in warfare and hunting. Monks (but seldom nuns) saw copying manuscripts and even writing books as a religious calling. Monastic scribes preserved many ancient Latin works that would otherwise have disappeared. The survival of Greek works depended more on Byzantine and Muslim scribes in the east.

Monasteries and convents served other functions as well (see Environment and Technology: Cathederal Organs). A few planted Christianity in new lands, as Irish monks did in parts of Germany. Most serviced the needs of travelers, organized agricultural production on their lands, and took in infants abandoned by their parents. Convents provided refuge for widows and other women who lacked male protection in the harsh medieval world or who desired a spiritual life. These religious houses presented problems of oversight to the church, however. A bishop might have authority over an abbot or abbess (head of a convent), but he could not exercise constant vigilance over what went on behind monastery walls.

The failure of some abbots to maintain monastic discipline led to the growth of a reform movement centered on the Benedictine abbey of Cluny° in eastern France. Founded in 910 by William the Pious, the first duke of Aquitaine, who completely freed it of lay authority, Cluny gained similar freedom from the local bishop a century later. Its abbots pursued a vigorous campaign, eventually in alliance with reforming popes like Gregory VII, to improve monastic discipline and administration. A magnificent new abbey church symbolized Cluny's claims to eminence. With later additions, it became the largest church in the world.

At the peak of Cluny's influence, nearly a thousand Benedictine abbeys and priories (lower-level monastic houses) in various countries accepted the authority of its abbot. The Benedictine Rule had presumed that each monastery would be independent; the Cluniac reformers stipulated that every abbot and every prior (head of a priory) be appointed by the abbot of Cluny and have personal experience of the religious life of Cluny. Monastic reform gained new impetus in the second half of the twelfth century with the rapid rise of the Cistercian order, which emphasized a life of asceticism and poverty. These movements set the pattern for the monasteries, cathedral clergy, and preaching friars that would dominate ecclesiastical life in the thirteenth century.

Cluny (KLOO-nee)

Kievan Russia, 900–1200

Though Latin and Orthodox Christendom followed different paths in later centuries, which had a more promising future was not apparent in 900. The Poles and other Slavic peoples living in the north eventually accepted the Christianity of Rome as taught by German priests and missionaries (see Diversity and Dominance: Archbishop Adalbert of Hamburg and the Christianization of Scandinavians and Slavs). The Serbs and other southern Slavs took their faith from Constantinople.

The conversion of Kievan Russia, farther to the east, shows how economics, politics, and religious life were closely intertwined. The choice of orthodoxy over Catholicism had important consequences for later European history.

The Rise of the Kievan State

The territory between the Black and Caspian Seas in the south and the Baltic and White Seas in the north divides into a series of east-west zones. Frozen tundra in the far north gives way to a cold forest zone, then to a more temperate forest, then to a mix of forest and steppe grasslands, and

ENVIRONMENT + TECHNOLOGY

Cathedral Organs

The Christian church directly encouraged musical development. Pope Gregory I (d. 604) is traditionally credited with making a standard collection of chants then in use. Later, a special school in Rome trained choir directors who were sent out to teach the chants in cathedrals and monasteries. Organ accompaniment, initially in the form of long, sustained bass notes, came into common use by the end of the seventh century. The organ worked by directing a current of air to a set of pipes of different lengths that could be opened or closed at one end. Each pipe sounded a tone as long as the air was flowing past its open end.

A monk named Wulstan (d. 963) described the organ installed in Winchester Cathedral in England:

> *Twice six bellows above are ranged in a row, and fourteen lie below. These, by alternate blasts, supply an immense quantity of wind, and are worked by 70 strong men, laboring with their arms, covered with perspiration, each inciting his companions to drive the wind up with all his strength, that the full-bosomed box may speak with its 400 pipes, which the hand of the organist governs. Some when closed he opens, others when open he closes, as the individual nature of the varied sound requires. Two brethren of concordant spirit sit at the instrument . . . Like thunder their tones batter the ear, so that it may receive no sound but that alone. To such an amount does it reverberate, echoing in every direction, that everyone stops with his hand his gaping ears, being in no wise able to draw near and bear the sound, which so many combinations produce.*

A century later huge levers or keys came into use for opening and closing the pipes. Each was several inches in width, one or two inches thick, and up to three feet in length. So much muscle was required to operate the keys that organists were called "organ pounders." Over time, organs became smaller and capable of playing magnificent music.

Cathedral Organ Note the unhappy faces on the men assigned the dreary and noisy job of pumping the bellows for an organ. Note also the ping-pong paddle shaped keys that are more appropriate to pounding with a fist than pressing with a finger.
(St. John's College Library, Cambridge Manuscript, B.18)

Source: Alexander Russell, "Organ," *The International Cyclopedia of Music and Musicians*, ed. Oscar Thompson (New York: Dodd, Mead, 1943), 1315.

finally to grassland only. Several navigable rivers, including the Volga, the Dnieper°, and the Don, run from north to south across these zones.

Early historical sources reflect repeated linguistic and territorial changes, seemingly under pressure from poorly understood population migrations. Most of the Germanic peoples, along with some Iranian and west Slavic peoples, migrated into eastern Europe from Ukraine and Russia in Roman times. The peoples who remained behind spoke eastern Slavic languages, except in the far north and south: Finns and related peoples lived in the former region, Turkic-speakers in the latter.

Forest dwellers, farmers, and steppe nomads complemented each other economically. Nomads traded an-

Dnieper (d-NYEP-er)

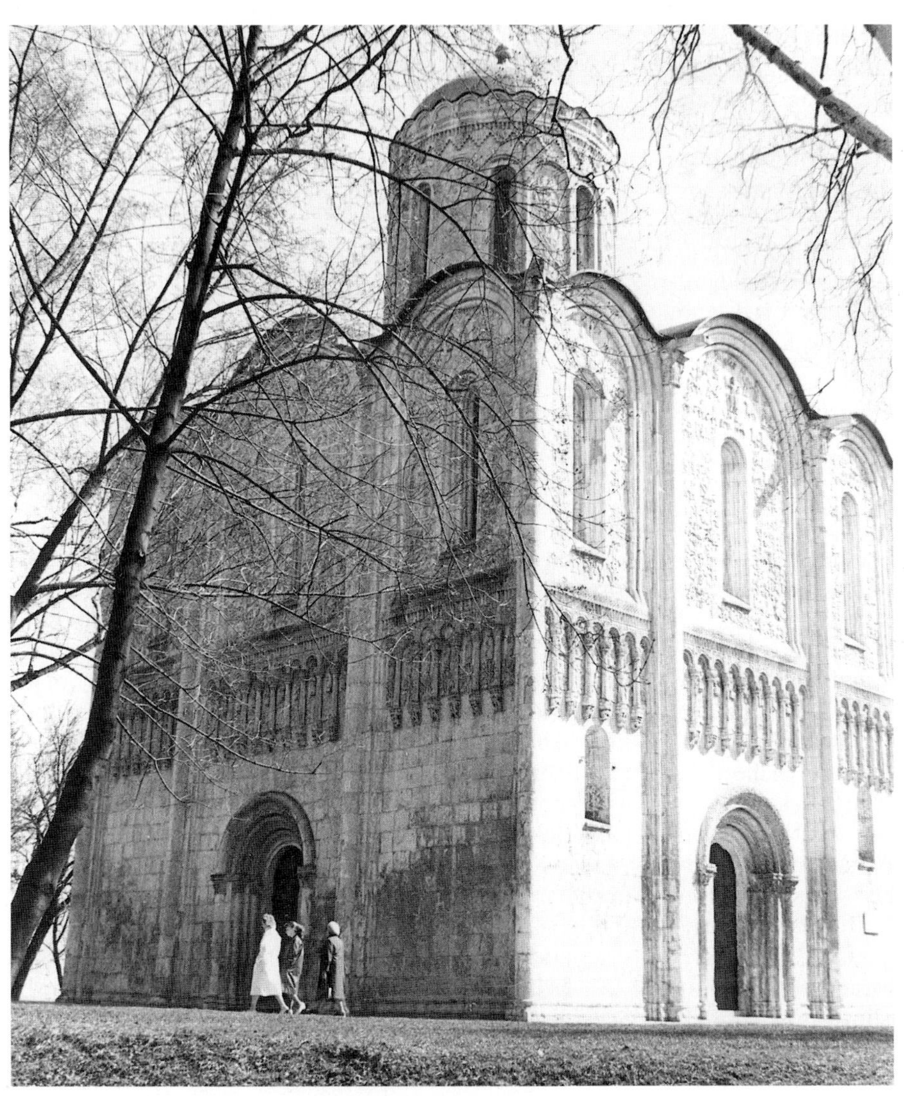

Cathedral of Saint Dmitry in Vladimir Built between 1193 and 1197, this Russian Orthodox cathedral shows Byzantine influence. The three-arch façade, small dome, and symmetrical Greek-cross floor plan strongly resemble features of the Byzantine church shown on page 258. (Sovfoto)

imals for the farmers' grain; and honey, wax, and furs from the forest became important exchange items. Traders could travel east and west by steppe caravan (see Chapters 8 and 13), or they could use boats on the rivers to move north and south.

Hoards containing thousands of Byzantine and Islamic coins buried in Poland and on islands in the Baltic Sea where fairs were held attest to the trading activity of Varangians (Swedish Vikings) who sailed across the Baltic and down Russia's rivers. They exchanged forest products and slaves for manufactured goods and coins, which they may have used as jewelry rather than as money, at markets controlled by the Khazar Turks. The powerful Khazar kingdom centered around the mouth of the Volga River.

Historians debate the early meaning of the word *Rus* (from which *Russia* is derived), but at some point it came to refer to Slavic-speaking peoples ruled by Varangians. Unlike western European lords, the Varangian princes and their *druzhina* (military retainers) lived in cities, while the Slavs farmed. The princes occupied themselves with trade and fending off enemies. The Rus of the city of Kiev° controlled trade on the Dnieper River and dealt more with Byzantium than with the Muslim world because the Dnieper flows into the Black Sea. The Rus of Novgorod° played the same role on the Volga. The semi-legendary account of the Kievan Rus conversion to Christianity must be seen against this background.

In 980 Vladimir° I, a ruler of Novgorod who had fallen from power, returned from exile to Kiev with a band of

---

Kiev (KEE-yev) **Novgorod** (NOHV-goh-rod)
Vladimir (VLAD-ih-mir)

Varangians and made himself the grand prince of Kievan Russia (see Map 10.3). Though his grandmother Olga had been a Christian, Vladimir built a temple on Kiev's heights and placed there the statues of the six gods his Slavic subjects worshipped. The earliest Russian chronicle reports that Vladimir and his advisers decided against Islam as the official religion because of its ban on alcohol, rejected Judaism (the religion to which the Khazars had converted) because they thought that a truly powerful god would not have let the ancient Jewish kingdom be destroyed, and even spoke with German emissaries advocating Latin Christianity. Why Vladimir chose Orthodox Christianity over the Latin version is not precisely known. The magnificence of Constantinople seems to have been a consideration. After visiting Byzantine churches, his agents reported: "We knew not whether we were in heaven or on earth, for on earth there is no such splendor of [sic] such beauty, and we are at a loss how to describe it. We know only that God dwells there among men, and their service is finer than the ceremonies of other nations."[9]

After choosing a reluctant bride from the Byzantine imperial family, Vladimir converted to Orthodox Christianity, probably in 988, and opened his lands to Orthodox clerics and missionaries. The patriarch of Constantinople appointed a metropolitan (chief bishop) at Kiev to govern ecclesiastical affairs. Churches arose in Kiev, one of them on the ruins of Vladimir's earlier hilltop temple. Writing was introduced, using the Cyrillic alphabet devised earlier for the western Slavs. This extension of Orthodox Christendom northward provided a barrier against the eastward expansion of Latin Christianity. Kiev became firmly oriented toward trade with Byzantium and turned its back on the Muslim world, though the Volga trade continued through Novgorod.

Struggles within the ruling family and with other enemies, most notably the steppe peoples of the south, marked the later political history of Kievan Russia. But down to the time of the Mongols in the thirteenth century (see Chapter 13), the state remained and served as an instrument for the Christianization of the eastern Slavs.

Society and Culture

In Kievan Russia political power derived from trade rather than from landholding, so the manorial agricultural system of western Europe never developed. Farmers practiced shifting cultivation of their own lands. They would burn a section of forest, then lightly scratch the ash-strewn surface with a plow. When fertility waned, they would move to another section of forest. Poor land and a short growing season in the most northerly latitudes made food scarce. Living on their own estates, the druzhina evolved from infantry into cavalry and focused their efforts more on horse breeding than on agriculture.

Large cities like Kiev and Novgorod may have reached thirty thousand or fifty thousand people—roughly the size of contemporary London or Paris, but far smaller than Constantinople or major Muslim metropolises like Baghdad and Nishapur. Many cities amounted to little more than fortified trading posts. Yet they served as centers for the development of crafts, some, such as glassmaking, based on skills imported from Byzantium. Artisans enjoyed higher status in society than peasant farmers. Construction relied on wood from the forests, although Christianity brought the building of stone cathedrals and churches on the Byzantine model.

Christianity penetrated the general population slowly. Several polytheist uprisings occurred in the eleventh century, particularly in times of famine. Passive resistance led some groups to reject Christian burial and persist in cremating the dead and keeping the bones of the deceased in urns. Women continued to use polytheist designs on their clothing and bracelets, and as late as the twelfth century they were still turning to polytheist priests for charms to cure sick children. Traditional Slavic marriage practices involving casual and polygamous relations particularly scandalized the clergy.

Christianity eventually triumphed, and its success led to increasing church engagement in political and economic affairs. In the twelfth century, Christian clergy became involved in government administration, some of them collecting fees and taxes related to trade. Direct and indirect revenue from trade provided the rulers with the money they needed to pay their soldiers. The rule of law also spread as Kievan Russia experienced its peak of culture and prosperity in the century before the Mongol invasion of 1237.

Map 10.3 Kievan Russia and the Byzantine Empire in the Eleventh Century By the mid-eleventh century, the princes of Kievan Russia had brought all the eastern Slavs under their rule. The loss of Egypt, Syria, and Tunisia to Arab invaders in the seventh to eighth century had turned Byzantium from a far-flung empire into a fairly compact state. From then on the Byzantine rulers looked to the Balkans and Kievan Russia as the primary arena for extending their political and religious influence.

URAL MTS.
FINNS
ESTS
Novgorod
Volga
Suzdal
VOLGA
BULGARS
Moscow
Baltic Sea
W. Dvina
Smolensk
LITHUANIANS
PRUSSIANS
Minsk
KIEVAN
RUSSIA
POLAND
Chernigov
Kiev
KHAZARS
Volga
Cracow
Dnieper
Don
CARPATHIAN MOUNTAINS
PECHENEGS
Caspian
Sea
HUNGARY
Kaffa
Cherson
CAUCASUS MTS
Black Sea
Danube
Adriatic Sea
Sinope
Trebizond
Adrianople
Constantinople
BYZANTINE EMPIRE
Bari
Brindisi
Nicaea
Ancyra
Aegean
Sea
Athens
Antioch
Crete
Cyprus
Mediterranean Sea
0
250
500 Km.
0
250
500 Mi.

WESTERN EUROPE REVIVES, 1000–1200

Between 1000 and 1200 western Europe slowly emerged from nearly seven centuries of subsistence economy—in which most people who worked on the land could meet only their basic needs for food, clothing, and shelter. Population and agricultural production climbed, and a growing food surplus found its way to town markets, speeding the return of a money-based economy and providing support for larger numbers of craftspeople, construction workers, and traders.

Historians have attributed western Europe's revival to population growth spurred by new technologies and to the appearance in Italy and Flanders, on the coast of the North Sea, of self-governing cities devoted primarily to seaborne trade. For monarchs, the changes facilitated improvements in central administration, greater control over vassals, and consolidation of realms on the way to becoming stronger kingdoms.

The Role of Technology

A lack of concrete evidence confirming the spread of technological innovations frustrates efforts to relate the exact course of Europe's revival to technological change. Nevertheless, most historians agree that technology played a significant role in the near doubling of the population of western Europe between 1000 and 1200. The population of England seems to have risen from 1.1 million in 1086 to 1.9 million in 1200, and the population of the territory of modern France seems to have risen from 5.2 million to 9.2 million over the same period.

Examples that illustrate the difficulty of drawing historical conclusions from scattered evidence of technological change were a new type of plow and the use of efficient draft harnesses for pulling wagons. The Roman plow, which farmers in southern Europe and Byzantium continued to use, scratched shallow grooves, as was appropriate for loose, dry Mediterranean soils. The new plow cut deep into the soil with a knife-like blade, while a curved board mounted behind the blade lifted the cut layer and turned it over. This made it possible to farm the heavy, wet clays of the northern river valleys. Pulling the new plow took more energy, which could mean harnessing several teams of oxen or horses.

Horses plowed faster than oxen but were more delicate. Iron horseshoes, which were widely adopted in this period, helped protect their feet, but like the plow itself, they added to the farmer's expenses. Roman horse harnesses, inefficiently modeled on the yoke used for oxen, put such pressure on the animal's neck that a horse pulling a heavy load risked strangulation. A mystery surrounds the adoption of more efficient designs. The **horse collar,** which moves the point of traction from the animal's throat to its shoulders, first appeared around 800 in a miniature painting, and it is shown clearly as a harness for plow horses in the Bayeux Tapestry, embroidered after 1066. The breast-strap harness, which is not as well adapted for the heaviest work but was preferred in southern Europe, seems to have appeared around 500. In both cases, linguists have tried to trace key technical terms to Chinese or Turko-Mongol words and have argued for technological diffusion across Eurasia. Yet third-century Roman farmers in Tunisia and Libya used both types of harness to hitch horses and camels to plows and carts. This technology, which is still employed in Tunisia, appears clearly on Roman bas-reliefs and lamps; but there is no more evidence of its movement northward into Europe than there is of similar harnessing moving across Asia. Thus the question of where efficient harnessing came from and whether it began in 500 or in 800, or was known even earlier but not extensively used, cannot be easily resolved.

Hinging on this problem is the question of when and why landowners in northern Europe began to use teams of horses to pull plows through moist, fertile river-valley soils that were too heavy for teams of oxen. Stronger and faster than oxen, horses increased productivity by reducing the time needed for plowing, but they cost more to feed and equip. Thus, while agricultural surpluses did grow and better plowing did play a role in this growth, areas that continued to use oxen and even old-style plows seem to have shared in the general population growth of the period.

Cities and the Rebirth of Trade

Independent cities governed and defended by communes appeared first in Italy and Flanders and then elsewhere. Communes were groups of leading citizens who banded together to defend their cities and demand the privilege of self-government from their lay or ecclesiastical lord. Lords who granted such privileges benefited from the commune's economic dynamism. Lacking extensive farmlands, these cities turned to manufacturing and trade, which they encouraged through the laws they enacted. Laws making serfs free once they came into the city, for example, attracted many workers from the countryside. Cities in Italy that had shrunk within walls built by the Romans now pressed against those walls, forcing the construction of new ones. Pisa built a new wall in 1000 and

Vertical Two-Beam Loom These women weavers set up their loom out-of-doors. The vertical strands are the warp threads around which the weft is interwoven. The pole across the bottom of the loom holds the warp threads taut. The kneeling weaver holds a beater to compact the weft at the loom's bottom. In Europe, horizontal looms were more common and paved the way for the mechanization of weaving. (Courtesy, Master and Fellows of Trinity College, Cambridge, Ms. R17.I.f.260 [detail])

expanded it in 1156. Other twelfth-century cities that built new walls include Florence, Brescia°, Pavia, and Siena°.

Settlers on a group of islands at the northern end of the Adriatic Sea that had been largely uninhabited in Roman times organized themselves into the city of Venice. In the eleventh century it became the dominant sea power in the Adriatic. Venice competed with Pisa and Genoa, its rivals on the western side of Italy, for leadership in the trade with Muslim ports in North Africa and the eastern Mediterranean. A somewhat later merchant's list mentions trade in some three thousand "spices" (including dyestuffs, textile fibers, and raw materials), some of them products of Muslim lands and some coming via the Silk Road or the Indian Ocean trading system (see Chapter 8). Among them were eleven types of alum (for dyeing), eleven types of wax, eight types of cotton, four types of indigo, five types of ginger, four types of paper, and fifteen types of sugar, along with cloves, caraway, tamarind, and fresh oranges. By the time of the Crusades (see below), maritime commerce throughout the Mediterranean had come to depend heavily on ships from Genoa, Venice, and Pisa.

Ghent, Bruges°, and Ypres° in Flanders rivaled the Italian cities in prosperity, trade, and industry. Enjoying comparable independence based on privileges granted by the counts of Flanders, these cities centralized the fishing and wool trades of the North Sea region. Around 1200 raw wool from England began to be woven into woolen cloth for a very large market.

More abundant coinage also signaled the upturn in economic activity. In the ninth and tenth centuries most gold coins had come from Muslim lands and the Byzantine Empire. Being worth too much for most trading purposes, they seldom reached Germany, France, and England. The widely imitated Carolingian silver penny sufficed. With the economic revival of the twelfth century, minting of silver coins began in Scandinavia, Poland, and other outlying regions. In the following century the reinvigoration of Mediterranean trade made possible a new and abundant gold coinage.

The Crusades, 1095–1204

Western European revival coincided with and contributed to the **Crusades,** a series of religiously inspired Christian military campaigns against Muslims in the eastern Mediterranean that dominated the politics of Europe from 1095 to 1204 (see Chapter 9 and Map 10.4). Four great expeditions, the last redirected against the Byzantines and resulting in the Latin capture of Constantinople, constituted the region's largest military undertakings since the fall of Rome. The cultural impact of the Crusades upon western Europe resulted in noble courts and burgeoning cities consuming more goods from the east. This set the stage for the later adoption of

Brescia (BREH-shee-uh) **Siena** (see-EN-uh) **Bruges** (broozh) **Ypres** (EEP-r)

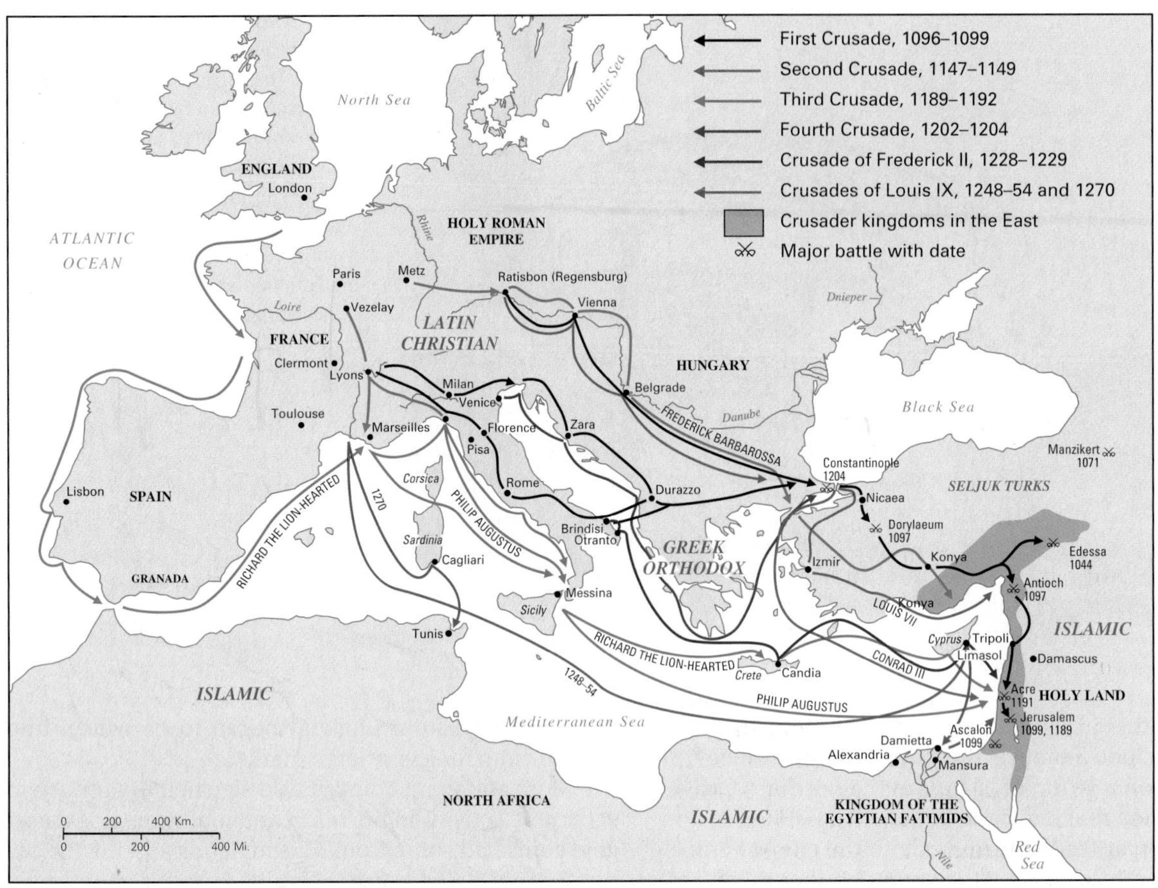

Map 10.4 The Crusades The first two Crusades proceeded overland through Byzantine territory. The Third Crusade included contingents under the French and English kings, Philip Augustus and Richard the Lion-Hearted, that traveled by sea, and a contingent under the Holy Roman Emperor Frederick Barbarossa that took the overland route. Frederick died in southern Anatolia. Later Crusades were mostly seaborne, with Sicily, Crete, and Cyprus playing important roles.

ideas, artistic styles, and industrial processes from Byzantium and the lands of Islam.

The Roots of the Crusades

Several social and economic currents of the eleventh century contributed to the Crusades. First, reforming leaders of the Latin Church, seeking to soften the warlike tone of society, popularized the Truce of God. This movement limited fighting between Christian lords by specifying times of truce, such as during Lent (the forty days before Easter) and on Sundays. Many knights welcomed a religiously approved alternative to fighting other Christians. Second, ambitious rulers, like the Norman chieftains who invaded England and Sicily, were looking for new lands to conquer. Nobles, particularly younger sons in areas where the oldest son inherited everything, were hungry for land and titles to maintain their status. Third, Italian merchants wanted to increase trade in the eastern Mediterranean and acquire trading posts in Muslim territory. However, without the rivalry between popes and kings already discussed, and without the desire of the church to demonstrate political authority over western Christendom, the Crusades might never have occurred.

Several factors focused attention on the Holy Land, which had been under Muslim rule for four centuries. **Pilgrimages** played an important role in European religious life. In western Europe, pilgrims traveled under royal protection, a few actually being tramps, thieves, beggars, peddlers, and merchants for whom pilgrimage was a safe way of traveling. Genuinely pious pilgrims often journeyed to visit the old churches and sacred relics preserved in Rome or Constantinople. The most intrepid went to Jerusalem, Antioch, and other cities under Muslim control to fulfill a vow or to atone for a sin.

Knights who followed a popular pilgrimage route across northern Spain to pray at the shrine of Santiago de Compostela learned of the expanding efforts of Christian kings to dislodge the Muslims. The Umayyad Caliphate in al-Andalus had broken up in the eleventh century, leaving its smaller successor states prey to Christian attacks from the north (see Chapter 9). This was the beginning of a movement of reconquest that culminated in 1492 with the surrender of the last Muslim kingdom. The word *crusade*, taken from Latin *crux* for "cross," was first used in Spain. Stories also circulated of the war conducted by seafaring Normans against the Muslims in Sicily, whom they finally defeated in the 1090s after thirty years of fighting.

The tales of pilgrims returning from Palestine further induced both churchmen and nobles to consider the Muslims a proper target for Christian militancy. Muslim rulers, who had controlled Jerusalem, Antioch, and Alexandria since the seventh century, generally tolerated and protected Christian pilgrims. But after 1071, when a Seljuk army defeated the Byzantine emperor at the Battle of Manzikert (see Chapter 9), Turkish nomads spread throughout the region, and security along the pilgrimage route through Anatolia, already none too good, deteriorated further. The decline of Byzantine power threatened ancient centers of Christianity, such as Ephesus in Anatolia, previously under imperial control.

Despite the theological differences between the Orthodox and Roman churches, the Byzantine emperor Alexius Comnenus asked the pope and western European rulers to help him confront the Muslim threat and reconquer what the Christians termed the Holy Land, the early centers of Christianity in Palestine and Syria. Pope Urban II responded at the Council of Clermont in 1095. He addressed a huge crowd of people gathered in a field and called on them, as Christians, to stop fighting one another and go to the Holy Land to fight Muslims.

"God wills it!" exclaimed voices in the crowd. People cut cloth into crosses and sewed them on their shirts to symbolize their willingness to march on Jerusalem. Thus began the holy war now known as the "First Crusade." People at the time more often used the word *peregrinatio*, "pilgrimage." Urban promised to free crusaders who had committed sins from their normal penance, or acts of atonement, the usual reward for peaceful pilgrims to Jerusalem.

The First Crusade captured Jerusalem in 1099 and established four crusader principalities, the most important being the Latin Kingdom of Jerusalem. The next two expeditions strove with diminishing success to protect these gains. Muslim forces retook Jerusalem in 1187. By the time of the Fourth Crusade in 1204, the original religious ardor had so diminished that the commanders agreed, at the urging of the Venetians, to sack Constantinople first to help pay the cost of transporting the army by ship.

Armored Knights in Battle This painting from around 1135 shows the armament of knights at the time of the Crusades. Chain mail, a helmet, and a shield carried on the left side protect the rider. The lance carried underarm and the sword are the primary weapons. Notice that riders about to make contact with lances have their legs straight and braced in the stirrups, while riders with swords and in flight have bent legs. (Pierpont Morgan Library/Art Resource, NY)

The Impact of the Crusades

Exposure to Muslim culture in Spain, Sicily, and the crusader principalities established in the Holy Land made many Europeans aware of things lacking in their own lives. Borrowings from Muslim society occurred gradually and are not always easy to date, but Europeans eventually learned how to manufacture hard soap, pasta, paper, refined sugar, colored glass, and many other items that had formerly been imported. Arabic translations of and commentaries on Greek philosophical and scientific works, and equally important original works by Arabs and Iranians, provided a vital stimulus to European thought.

Some works were brought directly into the Latin world through the conquests of Sicily, parts of Spain and the Holy Land, and Constantinople (for Greek texts). Others were rendered into Latin by translators who worked in parts of Spain that continued under Muslim rule. Generations passed before all these works were studied and understood, but they eventually transformed the intellectual world of the western Europeans, who previously had little familiarity with Greek writings. The works of Aristotle and the Muslim commentaries on them were of particular importance to theologians, but Muslim writers like Avicenna (980–1037) were of parallel importance in medicine.

Changes affecting the lifestyle of the nobles took place more quickly. Eleanor of Aquitaine (1122?–1204), one of the most influential women of the crusading era, accompanied her husband, King Louis VII of France, on the Second Crusade (1147–1149). The court life of her uncle Raymond, ruler of the crusader principality of Antioch, particularly appealed to her. After her return to France, a lack of male offspring led to an annulment of her marriage with Louis, and she married Henry of Anjou in 1151. He inherited the throne of England as Henry II three years later. Eleanor's sons Richard Lion-Heart, famed in romance as the chivalrous foe of Saladin during the Third Crusade (1189–1192), and John rebelled against their father but eventually succeeded him as kings of England.

In Aquitaine, a powerful duchy in southern France, Eleanor maintained her own court for a time. The poet-singers called troubadours who enjoyed her favor made her court a center for new music based on the idea of "courtly love," an idealization of feminine beauty and grace that influenced later European ideas of romance. Thousands of troubadour melodies survive in manuscripts, and some show the influence of the poetry styles then current in Muslim Spain. The favorite troubadour instrument, moreover, was the lute, a guitar-like instrument with a bulging shape whose design and name (Arabic *al-ud*) come from Muslim Spain. In centuries to come the lute would become the mainstay of Renaissance music in Italy.

Conclusion

The collapse of imperial Rome was not unique. China's Han dynasty (see Chapter 6) and the Abbasid Caliphate (see Chapter 9) both dissolved into successor states. Although western Europe endured chaos, disunity, and economic regression, cultural vitality emerged from the centuries of disorder. Similarly, the Tang Empire, which emerged in China in the seventh century C.E. (see Chapter 11), had a distinctive and lively culture based only in part on survivals from the Han era. In the Middle East the emergence of a distinctive society based on the Islamic religion largely followed the collapse of the central Islamic state in the tenth century (see Chapter 9). The dynamic development of Islam after this political collapse parallels the powerful influence gained by Christianity in western Europe by the end of the twelfth century.

However, the competition between the Orthodox and Catholic forms of Christianity complicated the role of religion in the emergence of medieval European society and culture. The Byzantine Empire, constructed on a Roman political and legal heritage that had largely passed away in the west, was more prosperous than the Germanic kingdoms of western Europe, and its arts and culture were initially more sophisticated. Furthermore, Byzantine society became deeply Christian well before a comparable degree of Christianization had been reached in western Europe. Yet despite their success in transmitting their versions of Christianity and imperial rule to Kievan Russia, and in the process erecting a barrier between the Russians and the Catholic Slavs to their west, the Byzantines failed to demonstrate the dynamism and ferment that characterized both the Europeans to their west and the Muslims to their south. Byzantine armies played only a supporting role in the Crusades, and the emperors lost their capital and at least temporarily lost their power to western crusaders in 1204.

Technology and commerce deepened the political and religious gulf between the two Christian zones. Changes in military techniques in western Europe increased battlefield effectiveness, while new agricultural technologies led to population increases that revitalized urban life and contributed to the crusading movement by making the nobility hunger for new lands. At the same time, the need to import food for growing urban populations contributed to the growth of maritime commerce in the Mediterranean and North Seas. Culture and manufacturing benefited greatly from the increased pace of communication and exchange. Lacking parallel developments of a similar scale, the Byzantine Empire steadily lost the dynamism of its early centuries and by the end of the period had clearly fallen behind western Europe in prosperity and cultural innovation.

Key Terms

Charlemagne	**serf**	**investiture controversy**
medieval	**fief**	**monasticism**
Byzantine Empire	**vassal**	**horse collar**
Kievan Russia	**papacy**	**Crusades**
schism	**Holy Roman Empire**	**pilgrimage**
manor		

Suggested Reading

Standard Byzantine histories include Dimitri Obolensky, *The Byzantine Commonwealth* (1971); and Warren Treadgold, *A History of Byzantine State and Society* (1997). Cyril Mango's *Byzantium: The Empire of New Rome* (1980) emphasizes cultural matters. For later Byzantine history see A. P. Kazhdan and Ann Wharton Epstein in *Change in Byzantine Culture in the Eleventh and Twelfth Centuries* (1985), which stresses social and economic issues; and D. M. Nicol, *Byzantium and Venice* (1988).

Roger Collins's *Early Medieval Europe, 300–1000* (1991), surveys institutional and political developments, while Robert Merrill Bartlett, *The Making of Europe* (1994), emphasizes frontiers. For the later part of the period see Susan Reynolds, *Kingdoms and Communities in Western Europe, 900–1300*, 2d ed. (1997). Jacques Le Goff, *Medieval Civilization, 400–1500* (1989), stresses questions of social structure. Among many books on religious matters see Richard W. Southern, *Western Society and the Church in the Middle Ages* (1970) and Richard Fletcher, *The Barbarian Conversion* (1997). Susan Reynolds makes the case for avoiding the term *feudalism* in *Fiefs and Vassals* (1994).

More specialized economic and technological studies begin with the classic Lynn White, Jr., *Medieval Technology and Social Change* (1962). See also Michael McCormick, *Origins of the European Economy: Communications and Commerce, AD 300–900* (2002); C. M. Cipolla, *Money, Prices and Civilization in the Mediterranean World, Fifth to Seventeenth Century* (1956); and Georges Duby, *Rural Economy and Country Life in the Medieval West* (1990), which includes translated documents. J. C. Russell, *The Control of Late Ancient and Medieval Population* (1985), analyzes demographic history and the problems of data.

On France see the numerous works of Rosamond McKitterick, including *The Frankish Kingdoms Under the Carolingians, 751–987* (1983). On England see Peter Hunter Blair, *An Introduction to Anglo-Saxon England* (1977), and Christopher Brooke, *The Saxon and Norman Kings* 3d ed. (2001). On Italy see Chris Wickham, *Early Medieval Italy: Central Power and Local Society, 400–1000* (1981), and Edward Burman, *Emperor to Emperor: Italy Before the Renaissance* (1991). On Germany and the Holy Roman Empire see Timothy Reuter, *Germany in the Early Middle Ages, c. 800–1056* (1991). On Spain see J. F. O'Callaghan, *A History of Medieval Spain* (1975), and R. Collins, *Early Medieval Spain: Unity and Diversity 400–1000* (1983). On Viking Scandinavia see John Haywood's illustrated *Encyclopaedia of the Viking age* (2000).

Amy Keller's popularly written *Eleanor of Aquitaine and the Four Kings* (1950), tells the story of an extraordinary woman. Dhuoda, *Handbook for William: A Carolingian Woman's Counsel for Her Son*, trans. Carol Neel (1991), offers a firsthand look at a Carolingian noblewoman. More general works include Margaret Wade's *A Small Sound of the Trumpet: Women in Medieval Life* (1986), and Bonnie S. Anderson and Judith P. Zinsser's *A History of Their Own: Women in Europe from Prehistory to the Present* (1989). In the area of religion, Caroline Bynum's *Jesus as Mother: Studies in the Spirituality of the High Middle Ages* (1982) illustrates new views about women.

On Kievan Russia see Janet Martin's *Medieval Russia, 980–1584* (1995); Simon Franklin and Jonathan Shepard, *The Emergence of Rus: 750–1200* (1996); and Thomas S. Noonan, *The Islamic World, Russia and the Vikings, 750–900: The Numismatic Evidence* (1998).

Jonathan Riley-Smith, *The Crusades: A Short History* (1987), is a standard work. He has also a more colorful version in *The Oxford Illustrated History of the Crusades* (1995). For other views see Jonathan Phillips, *The Crusades, 1095–1197* (2002), and Norman Housley, *Crusading and Warfare in Medieval and Renaissance Europe* (2001). For a masterful account with a Byzantine viewpoint, see Steven Runciman, *A History of the Crusades*, 3 vols. (1987). For accounts from the Muslim side see Carole Hillenbrand, *The Crusades: Islamic Perspectives* (1999).

Henri Pirenne, *Medieval Cities: Their Origins and the Revival of Trade* (1952), and Robert S. Lopez, *The Commercial Revolution of the Middle Ages, 950–1350* (1971), masterfully discuss the revival of trade. Lopez and Irving W. Raymond compile and translate primary documents in *Medieval Trade in the Mediterranean World: Illustrative Documents with Introductions and Notes* (1990).

Notes

1. Lewis G. M. Thorpe, *Two Lives of Charlemagne* (Harmondsworth, England: Penguin, 1969).
2. A. A. Vasiliev, *History of the Byzantine Empire, 324–1453*, vol. 1 (Madison: University of Wisconsin Press, 1978), 79–80.
3. Ibid., p 71.
4. A. P. Kazhdan and Ann Wharton Epstein, *Change in Byzantine Culture in the Eleventh and Twelfth Centuries* (Berkeley: University of California Press, 1985), 71.
5. Ibid., 248.
6. Ibid., 255.
7. R. W. Southern, *Western Society and the Church in the Middle Ages* (Harmondsworth, England: Penguin, 1970), 102.
8. Anne Fremantle, *A Treasury of Early Christianity* (New York: New American Library of World Literature, 1960), 400–401.
9. S. A. Zenkovsky, ed., *Medieval Russia's Epics, Chronicles, and Tales* (New York: New American Library, 1974), 67.

11 Inner and East Asia, 400–1200

Buddhism at a Distance The Buddhist monk Xuanzang returns to the Tang capital Chang'an from Tibet in 645, his ponies laden with Sanskrit texts.

CHAPTER OUTLINE

The powerful and expansive Tang° Empire (618–907) ended four centuries of rule by short-lived and competing states that had repeatedly brought turmoil to China after the fall of the Han Empire in 220 C.E. (see Chapter 6) but had also encouraged the spread of Buddhism. The Tang left an indelible mark on the Chinese imagination long after it too fell.

According to surviving memoirs, people could watch shadow plays and puppet shows, listen to music and scholarly lectures, or take in less edifying spectacles like wrestling and bear baiting in the entertainment quarters of the cities that flourished in southern China under the succeeding Song° Empire. Song-stories provided a novel and popular entertainment from the 1170s onward. Singer-storytellers spun long romantic narratives that alternated prose passages with sung verse.

Master Tung's *Western Chamber Romance* stood out for its literary quality. Little is known of Master Tung° beyond a report that he lived at the end of the twelfth century. In 184 prose passages and 5,263 lines of verse the narrator tells the story of a love affair between Chang, a young Confucian scholar, and Ying-ying, a ravishing damsel. Secondary characters include Ying-ying's shrewd and worldly mother, a general who practices just and efficient administration, and a fighting monk named Fa-ts'ung°. It is based on *The Story of Ying-ying* by the Tang period author Yüan Chen° (779–831).

As the tale begins, the abbot of a Buddhist monastery responds to Chang's request to rent him a study room, singing:

> Sir, you're wrong to offer me rent.
> We Buddhists and Confucians are of one family.
> As things stand, I can't give you
> A place in our dormitory,
> But you're welcome to stay
> In one of the guest apartments.

As soon as Chang spies Ying-ying, who lives there with her mother, thoughts of studying flee his mind. The course of romance takes a detour, however, when bandits attack the monastery. A prose passage explains:

> During the T'ang dynasty, troops were stationed in the P'u prefecture. The year of our story, the commander of the garrison, Marshal Hun, died. Because the second-in-command, Ting Wen-ya, did not have firm control of the troops, Flying Tiger Sun, a subordinate general, rebelled with five thousand soldiers. They pillaged and plundered the P'u area. How do I know this to be true? It is corroborated by *The Ballad of the True Story of Ying-ying.*

As the monks dither, one of them lifts his robe to reveal his "three-foot consecrated sword."

> [Prose] Who was this monk? He was none other than Fa-ts'ung. Fa-ts'ung was a descendant of a tribesman from western Shensi. When he was young he took great pleasure in archery, fencing, hunting, and often sneaked into foreign states to steal. He was fierce and courageous. When his parents died, it suddenly became clear to him that the way of the world was frivolous and trivial, so he became a monk in the Temple of Universal Salvation . . .
>
> [Song] He didn't know how to read sutras;
> He didn't know how to follow rituals;
> He was neither pure nor chaste
> But indomitably courageous . . . [1]

Amidst the love story, the ribaldry, and the derring-do, the author implants historical vignettes that mingle fact and fiction. Sophisticates of the Song era, living a life of ease, enjoyed these romanticized portrayals of Tang society.

As you read this chapter, ask yourself the following questions:

- What is the importance of Inner and Central Asia as a region of interchange during the Tang period?
- On what were new relationships among East Asian societies based after the fall of the Tang?

Tang (tahng) **Song** (soong) **Tung** (toong) **Fa-ts'ung** (fa-soong) **Yüan Chen** (you-ahn shen)

- Why do Buddhism and Confucianism play different political roles in Tang and Song China, and in Tibet, Korea, and Japan?
- What accounts for the scientific and economic advancement that contributed to the thriving urban life of Song China?

THE SUI AND TANG EMPIRES, 581–755

The reunification of China took place under the Sui° dynasty, father and son rulers who held sway from 581 until Turks from Inner Asia (the part of the Eurasian steppe east of the Pamir Mountains) defeated the son in 615. He was assassinated three years later, and the Tang filled the political vacuum.

The small kingdoms of northern China and Inner Asia that had come and gone during the centuries following the fall of the Han Empire had structured themselves around a variety of political ideas and institutions. Some favored the Chinese tradition, with an emperor, a bureaucracy using the Chinese language exclusively, and a Confucian state philosophy (see Chapter 3). Others reflected Tibetan, Turkic, or other regional cultures and depended on Buddhism to legitimate their rule. Throughout the period the relationship between northern China and the deserts and steppe of Inner Asia remained a central focus of political life, a key commercial linkage, and a source of new ideas and practices.

Reunification Under the Sui and Tang

In their brief time in power, the Sui rulers had not only reunified China but had also reestablished the Confucian system of examining candidates for bureaucratic office on the classic Confucian texts, a practice that the Tang continued. Yet Buddhism, which had gained many adherents and widespread respect during the centuries of disunity, exerted a strong political influence as well. Other religious and philosophical beliefs, including Daoism, Nestorian Christianity, and Islam, enjoyed some popularity, the latter two signaling the continuing cultural importance of communications along the Silk Road (see Chapter 8).

The Sui rulers called their new capital Chang'an° in honor of the old Han capital nearby in the Wei° River Valley (modern Shaanxi province). Though northern China constituted the Sui heartland, population centers along the Yangzi° River in the south grew steadily and pointed to what would be the future direction of Chinese expansion. To facilitate communication and trade with the south, the Sui built the 1,100-mile (1771 kilometers) **Grand Canal,** linking the Yellow River with the Yangzi, and constructed irrigation systems in the Yangzi valley. On their northern frontier, the Sui also improved the Great Wall, the barrier against nomadic incursions that had been gradually constructed by several earlier states.

Sui military ambition, which extended to Korea and Vietnam as well as Inner Asia, required high levels of organization and mustering of resources—manpower, livestock, wood, iron, and food supplies. The same is true of their massive public works projects. These burdens proved more than the Sui could sustain. Overextension compounded the political dilemma stemming from the military defeat and subsequent assassination of the second Sui emperor. This opened the way for another strong leader to establish a new state.

In 618 the powerful Li family took advantage of Sui disorder to carve out an empire of similar scale and ambition. They adopted the dynastic name Tang (Map 11.1). The brilliant emperor **Li Shimin**° (r. 627–649) extended his power primarily westward into Inner Asia. Though he and succeeding rulers of the **Tang Empire** retained many Sui governing practices, they avoided overcentralization by allowing local nobles, gentry, officials, and religious establishments to exercise significant power. (See Diversity and Dominance: Law and Society in Tang China).

The Tang emperors and nobility descended from the Turkic elites that built small states in northern China after the Han, and from Chinese officials and settlers who had settled there. They appreciated Turkic Inner Asian culture as well as Chinese traditions Some of the most impressive works of Tang ceramic sculpture, for example, are large figurines of the horses and two-humped camels used along the Silk Road, brilliantly colored with glazes devised by Chinese potters. In warfare, the Tang combined Chinese weapons—the crossbow and armored infantrymen—with Inner Asian expertise in horsemanship and the use of iron stirrups. At their peak, from about 650 to 751, when they were defeated in Central Asia (present-day Kirgizstan) by an Arab Muslim army at the Battle of the Talas River, the Tang armies were a formidable force.

Sui (sway)

Chang'an (chahng-ahn) **Wei** (way) **Yangzi** (yahng-zeh)
Li Shimin (lee shir-meen)

CHRONOLOGY

	Inner Asia	China	Northeast Asia	Japan
200		**220–589** China disunited		
	552 Turkic Empire founded			
		581–618 Sui unification		
600	**620–640** Tibetan Empire emerges under Songsam Gyampo	**618** Tang Empire founded **627–649** Li Shimin reign		
				645–655 Taika era
		690–705 Wu Zhao reign	**668** Silla victory in Korea	
	744 Uighur empire founded **751** Battle of Talas River	**755–757** An Lushan rebellion		**710–784** Nara as capital **752** "Eye-Opening" ceremony **794–1185** Heian era
800	**ca. 850** Buddhist political power secured in Tibet	**840** Suppression of Buddhism **879–881** Huang Chao rebellion **907** End of Tang Empire		
		938 Liao capital at Beijing **960** Song Empire Founded	**916** Liao Empire founded **918** Koryo founded	**ca. 950–1180** Fujiwara influence
1000		**1127–1279** Southern Song period	**1115** Jin Empire founded	**ca. 1000** *The Tale of Genji* **1185** Kamakura shogunate founded

Buddhism and the Tang Empire

The Tang rulers followed Inner Asian precedents in their political use of Buddhism. State cults based on Buddhism had flourished in Inner Asia and north China since the fall of the Han. Some interpretations of Buddhist doctrine accorded kings and emperors the spiritual function of welding humankind into a harmonious Buddhist society. Protecting spirits were to help the ruler govern and prevent harm from coming to his people.

Mahayana°, or "Great Vehicle," Buddhism predominated. Mahayana fostered faith in enlightened beings—bodhisattvas—who postpone nirvana (see Chapter 7) to help others achieve enlightenment. This permitted the absorption of local gods and goddesses into Mahayana sainthood and thereby made conversion more attractive to the common people. Mahayana also encouraged translating Buddhist scripture into local languages, and it accepted

Mahayana (mah-HAH-YAH-nah)

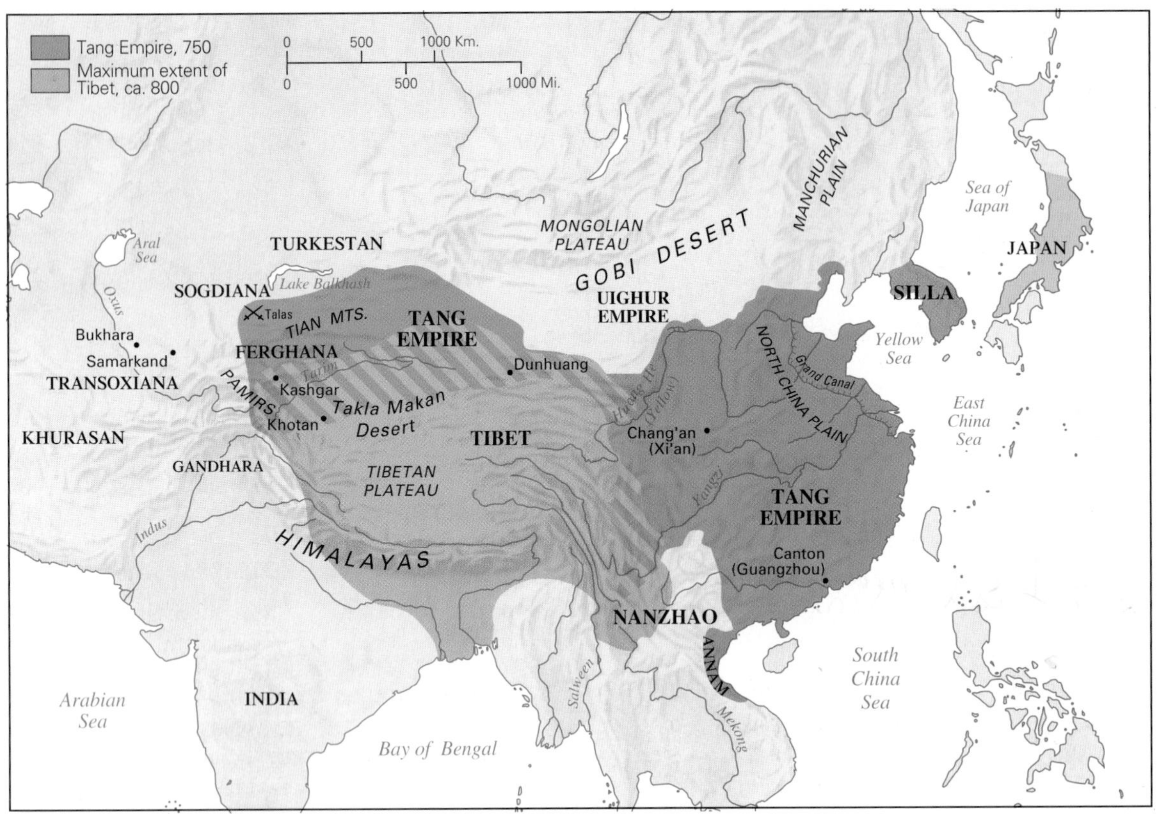

Map 11.1 The Tang Empire in Inner and Eastern Asia, 750 For over a century the Tang Empire controlled China and a very large part of Inner Asia. The defeat of Tang armies in 751 by a force of Arabs, Turks, and Tibetans at the Talas River in present-day Kirgizstan ended Tang westward expansion. To the east the Tang dominated Annam, and Japan and the Silla kingdom in Korea were leading tributary states of the Tang.

religious practices not based on written texts. The tremendous reach of Mahayana views, which proved adaptable to different societies and classes of people, invigorated travel, language learning, and cultural exchange.

Early Tang princes competing for political influence enlisted monastic leaders to pray for them, preach on their behalf, counsel aristocrats to support them, and—perhaps most important—contribute monastic wealth to their war chests. In return, the monasteries received tax exemptions, land privileges, and gifts.

As the Tang Empire expanded westward, contacts with Central Asia and India increased, and so did the complexity of Buddhist influence throughout China. Chang'an, the Tang capital, became the center of a continentwide system of communication. Central Asians, Tibetans, Vietnamese, Japanese, and Koreans regularly visited the capital and took away with them the most recent ideas and styles. Thus the Mahayana network connecting Inner Asia and China intersected a vigorous commercial world in which material goods and cultural influences mixed. Though Buddhism and Confucianism proved attractive to many different peoples, regional cultures and identities remained strong, just as regional commitments to Tibetan, Uighur, and other languages and writing systems coexisted with the widespread use of written Chinese. Textiles reflected Persian, Korean, and Vietnamese styles, while influences from every part of Asia appeared in sports, music, and painting. Many historians characterize the Tang Empire as "cosmopolitan" because of its breadth and diversity.

To Chang'an by Land and Sea

Well-maintained roads and water transport connected Chang'an, the capital and hub of Tang communications, to the coastal towns of south China, most importantly Canton (Guangzhou°). Though the Grand Canal did not reach Chang'an, it was a key component of this trans-

Guangzhou (gwahng-jo)

Iron Stirrups This bas-relief from the tomb of Li Shimin depicts the type of horse on which the Tang armies conquered China and Inner Asia. Saddles with high supports in front and back, breastplates, and cruppers (straps beneath the tail that help keep the saddle in place) point to the importance of high speeds and quick maneuvering. Central and Inner Asian horsemen had iron stirrups available from the time of the Huns (fifth century). Earlier stirrups were of leather or wood. Stirrups could support the weight of shielded and well-armed soldiers rising in the saddle to shoot arrows or use lances. (University of Pennsylvania Museum, neg. #S8-62844)

portation network. Chang'an became the center of what is often called the **tributary system,** a type of political relationship dating from Han times by which independent countries acknowledged the Chinese emperor's supremacy. Each tributary state sent regular embassies to the capital to pay tribute (see Chapter 6). As symbols of China's political supremacy, these embassies sometimes meant more to the Chinese than to the tribute-payers, who might see them more as a means of accessing the Chinese trading system.

During the Tang period, Chang'an had something over a million people, only a minority of whom lived in the central city. Most people lived in suburbs that extended beyond the main gates. Others dwelt in separate outlying towns that had special responsibilities like maintaining nearby imperial tombs or operating the imperial resort, where aristocrats relaxed in sunken tile tubs while the steamy waters of natural springs swirled around them.

Foreigners, whether merchants, students, or ambassadors, resided in special compounds in Chang'an and other entrepôts. These included living accommodations and general stores. By the end of the Tang period, West Asians in Chang'an probably numbered over 100,000.

In the main parts of the city, restaurants, inns, temples, mosques, and street stalls along the main thoroughfares kept busy every evening. At curfew, generally between eight and ten o'clock, commoners returned to their neighborhoods, which were enclosed by brick walls and wooden gates that guards locked until dawn to control crime.

Of the many routes converging on Chang'an, the Grand Canal commanded special importance with its own army patrols, boat design, canal towns, and maintenance budget. It conveyed vital supplies and contributed to the economic and cultural development of eastern China, where later capitals were built within easier reach.

The Tang consolidated Chinese control of the southern coastal region, increasing access to the Indian Ocean and facilitating the spread of Islamic and Jewish influences. A legend credits an uncle of Muhammad with erecting the Red Mosque at Canton in the mid-seventh century.

Chinese mariners and shipwrights excelled in compass design and the construction of very large oceangoing vessels. The government took direct responsibility for outfitting grain transport vessels for the Chinese coastal cities and the Grand Canal. Commercial ships, built to sail from south China to the Philippines and Southeast Asia, carried twice as much as contemporary vessels in the Mediterranean Sea or the western parts of the Indian Ocean trading system (see Chapter 8).

The sea route linking the Red Sea and Persian Gulf with Canton also brought East Asia the **bubonic plague,** called the Justinian plague because it coincided with the reign of the Byzantine emperor Justinian. Historical sources mention plague in Canton and south China in the early 600s. As in certain other parts of the world, the plague bacillus became endemic among rodent populations in parts of southwestern China and thus lingered long after its disappearance in West Asia and Europe.

DIVERSITY AND DOMINANCE

LAW AND SOCIETY IN TANG CHINA

The Tang law code, compiled in the early seventh century, served as the basis for the Tang legal system and as a model for later dynastic law codes. It combined the centralized authority of the imperial government, as visualized in the legalist tradition dating back to Han times, with Confucian concern for status distinctions and personal relationships. Like contemporary approaches to law in Christian Europe and the Islamic world, it did not fully distinguish between government as a structure of domination and law as an echo of religious and moral values.

Following a Preface, 502 articles, each with several parts, are divided into twelve books: (1) General Principles, (2) Imperial Guard and Prohibitions, (3) Administrative Regulations, (4) Household and Marriage, (5) Public Stables and Granaries, (6) Unauthorized Levies, (7) Violence and Robberies, (8) Assaults and Accusations, (9) Fraud and Counterfeiting, (10) Miscellaneous Articles, (11) Arrest and Flight, and (12) Judgment and Imprisonment. Each article contained a basic ordinance with commentary, subcommentary, and sometimes additional questions. Excerpts from a single Article from Book 1 follow.

THE TEN ABOMINATIONS

Text: The first is called plotting rebellion.

Subcommentary: The *Gongyang* [GON-gwang] *Commentary* states: "The ruler or parent has no harborers [of plots]. If he does have such harborers, he must put them to death." This means that if there are those who harbor rebellious hearts that would harm the ruler or father, he must then put them to death.

The king occupies the most honorable position and receives Heaven's precious decrees. Like Heaven and Earth, he acts to shelter and support, thus serving as the father and mother of the masses. As his children, as his subjects, they must be loyal and filial. Should they dare to cherish wickedness and have rebellious hearts, however, they will run counter to Heaven's constancy and violate human principle. Therefore this is called plotting rebellion.

Text: The second is called plotting great sedition.

Subcommentary: This type of person breaks laws and destroys order, is against traditional norms, and goes contrary to virtue . . .

Commentary: Plotting great sedition means to plot to destroy the ancestral temples, tombs, or palaces of the reigning house.

Text: The third is called plotting treason.

Subcommentary: The kindness of father and mother is like "great heaven, illimitable" . . . Let one's heart be like the *xiao* bird or the *jing* beast, and then love and respect both cease. Those whose relationship is within the five degrees of mourning are the closest of kin. For them to kill each other is the extreme abomination and the utmost in rebellion, destroying and casting aside human principles. Therefore this is called contumacy.

Commentary: Contumacy means to beat or plot to kill [without actually killing] one's paternal grandparents or parents; or to kill one's paternal uncles or their wives, or one's elder brothers or sisters, or one's maternal grandparents, or one's husband, or one's husband's paternal grandparents, or his parents . . . .

Text: The fifth is called depravity.

Subcommentary: This article describes those who are cruel and malicious and who turn their backs on morality. Therefore it is called depravity.

Commentary: Depravity means to kill three members of a single household who have not committed a capital crime, or to dismember someone . . .

Commentary: The offense also includes the making or keeping of poison or sorcery.

Subcommentary: This means to prepare the poison oneself, or to keep it, or to give it to others in order to harm people. But if the preparation of the poison is not yet completed, this offense does not come under the ten abominations. As to sorcery, there are a great many methods, not all of which can be described.

Text: The sixth is called great irreverence . . .

Commentary: Great irreverence means to steal the objects of the great sacrifices to the spirits or the carriage or possessions of the emperor.

Text: The seventh is called lack of filiality.

Subcommentary: Serving one's parents well is called filiality. Disobeying them is called lack of filiality.

Text: The ninth is called what is not right . . .

Commentary: [This] means to kill one's department head, prefect, or magistrate, or the teacher from whom one has received one's education . . .

Text: The tenth is called incest.

Subcommentary: The *Zuo Commentary* states: "The woman has her husband's house; the man has his wife's chamber; and there must be no defilement on either side." If this is changed, then there is incest. If one behaves like birds and beasts and introduces licentious associates into one's family, the rules of morality are confused. Therefore this is called incest.

Commentary: This section includes having illicit sexual intercourse with relatives who are of the fourth degree of mourning or closer . . . .

The following are the titles of 26 of the 46 articles in Book 4 of the Code entitled "The Household and Marriage.

- Omitting to File a Household Register
- Unauthorized Ordainment as a Buddhist or Daoist Priest
- Sons and Grandsons in the Male Line Are Not Permitted to Have a Separate Household Register
- Having a Child During the Period of Mourning for Parents
- Adopted Sons Who Reject Their Adoptive Parents
- Falsely Combining Households
- Possession of More than the Permitted Amount of Land
- Illegal Cultivation of Public or Private Land
- Wrongfully Laying Claim to or Selling Public or Private Land
- Officials Who Encroach Upon Private Land
- Illegal Cultivation of Other Persons' Grave Plots
- Not Allowing Rightful Exemption from Taxes and Labor Services
- Betrothal of a Daughter and Announcement of the Marriage Contract
- Wrongful Substitution by the Bride's Family in a Marriage
- Taking a Second Wife
- Making the Wife a Concubine
- Marriage During the Period of Mourning for Parents or Husband
- Marriage While Parents Are in Prison
- Marriage by Those of the Same Surname
- Marrying a Runaway Wife
- Marriage of Officials with Women Within Their Area of Jurisdiction
- Marrying Another Man's Wife by Consent
- Divorcing a Wife Who Has Not Given Any of the Seven Causes for Repudiation
- Divorce
- Slaves Who Take Commoners as Wives
- General Bondsmen Are Not Permitted to Marry Commoners
- Marriages That Violate the Code

The day-to-day realities of country life appear in the following account by a scholar living during the late 700s. Wealthy landowning families bought townhouses and engaged in conspicuous consumption while farmers, whose high rents and low pay contributed to the gentry's growing wealth, enjoyed few direct benefits.

When a farmer falls on bad times, he has to sell his field and his hut. If it is a good year, he might be able to pay his debts by selling out. But no sooner will the harvest be in than his storage bins will be empty again, and he will have to try to contract a new debt promising his labor for the next year. Each time he indentures himself he incurs higher interest rates, and soon will be destitute again.

If it is a bad year, and there is a famine, then the situation is hopeless. Families break up, parents separate, and all try to sell themselves into slavery. But in a bad year nobody will buy them.

In these circumstances land prices fall low enough that the rich buy up tens of thousands of acres, or simply seize the land of defaulted farmers. The poor then have no land, and try for places as servants, bodyguards, or enforcers for the rich families. If they manage to attach themselves to the organization of a gentry family, they can borrow seed and grain, and rent land as tenants. Then they will work themselves to death, all year round, without a day off. If they should manage to clear their debts, they live in constant anxiety about when the next bad patch will leave them destitute again.

The gentry, however, live off their rents, with no troubles and no cares. Wealth and poverty are very clearly divided.

This is how we have reached the situation where the rents from private land are much higher, and collected more ruthlessly, than the government's taxes. In areas around the capital, rents are twenty times higher than taxes. Even rents in more remote areas are ten times what the government collects in tax.

QUESTIONS FOR ANALYSIS

1. **Comparing these historical documents, what would seem to have been the relationship between law and equity under the Tang?**
2. **Did the Confucian concern for family relations and social status manifested in the law code prevent injustice?**
3. **Does the law code appear more an expression of ideals and compilation of past philosophical ideas than a practical guide to a just society?**

Sources: The first two selections are from Theodore de Bary and Irene Bloom, eds., *Sources of Chinese Tradition*, vol. 1, 2d ed. Copyright © 1999 by Columbia University Press. Reprinted with permission of the publisher. The third selection is adapted from Etienne Balazs, *Chinese Civilization and Bureaucracy: Variations on a Theme*, trans. by H. M. Wright, ed. by Arthur F. Wright. Copyright © 1964. Reprinted by permission of Yale University Press.

The disease followed trade and embassy routes to Korea, Japan, and Tibet, where initial outbreaks followed the establishment of diplomatic ties in the seventh century.

Trade and Cultural Exchange

Influences from Central Asia and the Islamic world introduced lively new motifs to ceramics, painting, and silk designs. At the other end of the Silk Road, Iranian potters imitated the glazes of Tang vessels. Clothing styles changed in north China; working people switched from robes to the pants favored by horse-riding Turks from Central Asia. Inexpensive cotton imported from Central Asia, where cotton production boomed in the early Islamic centuries, gradually replaced hemp in clothes worn by commoners. The Tang court promoted polo, a pastime from the steppes, and followed the Inner Asian tradition of allowing noblewomen to compete. Various stringed instruments reached China across the Silk Road, along with Turkic folk melodies. Grape wine from West Asia and tea, sugar, and spices from India and Southeast Asia transformed the Chinese diet.

Such changes reflected new economic and trade relationships. Silk had dominated the caravan trade across Central Asia in Han times (see Chapter 8). Now China's monopoly on silk disappeared as several centers in West Asia learned to compete. However, western Asia lost its monopoly in cotton; by the end of the Tang, China had begun to produce its own. This process of "import substitution"—the domestic production and sale of previously imported goods—also affected tea and sugar.

By about the year 1000 the magnitude of exports from Tang territories, facilitated by China's excellent transportation systems, dwarfed Chinese imports from Europe, West Asia, and South Asia. Stories of ships carrying Chinese exports outnumbering those laden with South Asian, West Asian, European, or African goods by a hundred to one cannot be relied on. Tang exports did, however, tilt the trade balance with both the Central Asia caravan cities and the lands of the Indian Ocean, causing precious metal to flow into China in return for export goods.

China remained the source of superior silks. Tang factories created more and more complex styles, partly to counter foreign competition. China became the sole supplier of porcelain—a fine, durable ceramic made from a special clay—to West Asia. As travel along the Silk Road and to the various ports of the Indian Ocean trading system increased, the economies of seaports and entrepôts involved in the trade—even distant ones—became increasingly commercialized, leading to networks of private traders devising new instruments of credit and finance. As we shall see, these networks would later contribute to the prosperity of the Song era.

Tang Women at Polo The Tang Empire, like the Sui, was strongly influenced by Inner Asian as well as Chinese traditions. As in many Inner Asian cultures, women in Tang China were likely to exercise greater influence in the management of property, in the arts, and in politics than women in Chinese society at later times. They were not excluded from public view, and noblewomen could even compete at polo. The game, widely known in various forms in Central and Inner Asia from a very early date, combined the Tang love of riding, military arts, and festive spectacles. (The Nelson-Atkins Museum of Art, Kansas City, Missouri)

RIVALS FOR POWER IN INNER ASIA AND CHINA, 600–907

Li Bo, the most renowned Tang poet and one of the greatest ever to write in the Chinese language, wrote in 751 of the seemingly endless succession of wars:

> The beacons are always alight, fighting and marching
> never stop.
> Men die in the field, slashing sword to sword;
> The horses of the conquered neigh piteously to
> Heaven.
> Crows and hawks peck for human guts,
> Carry them in their beaks and hang them on the
> branches of withered trees.

Captains and soldiers are smeared on the bushes and
grass;
The General schemed in vain.
Know therefore that the sword is a cursed thing
which the wise man uses only if he must.[2]

Between 600 and 751, when the Tang Empire was at its height, the Turkic-speaking Uighurs° and the Tibetans built large rival states in Inner Asia. The power of the former centered on the basin of the Tarim River, a largely desert area north of Tibet that formed a vital link on the Silk Road. The Tibetan empire at its peak stretched well beyond modern Tibet into northeastern India, southwestern China, and the Tarim Basin. The contest between these states and the Tang for control of the land routes west of China reached a standoff by the end of the period. Mutually beneficial trade required diplomatic accommodation more than political unity. By the mid-800s all three empires were experiencing political decay and military decline. The problems of one aggravated those of the others, since governmental collapse allowed soldiers, criminals, and freebooters to roam without hindrance into neighboring territories.

Centralization and integration being most extensively developed in Tang territory, the impact fell most heavily there. Nothing remained of Tang power but pretense by the early 800s, the period reflected in the original romance of Ying-ying described at the start of this chapter. In the provinces military governors suppressed the rebellion of General An Lushan°, a commander of Sogdian (Central Asian) and Turkic origin, which raged from 755 to 763, and then seized power for themselves.

The nomads of the steppe survived the social disorder and agricultural losses best. The caravan cities that had prospered from overland trade, and that lay at the heart of the Uighur state in the Tarim Basin, had as much to lose as China itself. Eventually, the urban and agricultural economies of Inner Asia and China recovered. In the short term, however, the debilitating contest for power with the Inner Asian states prompted a strong cultural backlash, particularly in China, where disillusionment with northern neighbors combined with social and economic anxieties to fuel an antiforeign movement.

The Uighur and Tibetan Empires

The original homeland of the Turks lay in the northern part of modern Mongolia. After the fall of the Han Empire, Turkic peoples began moving south and west, through Mongolia, then west to Central Asia, on the long migration that eventually brought them to what is today modern Turkey (see Chapter 9). In 552 a unified Turkic state had emerged, only to split internally a century later. It was this fissure that allowed the Tang Empire under Li Shimin to establish control over the Tarim Basin. Yet within a century, a new Turkic group, the **Uighurs,** had taken much of Inner Asia.

Under the Uighurs, caravan cities like Kashgar and Khotan (see Map 11.1) displayed a literate culture with strong ties to both the Islamic world and China. The Uighurs excelled as merchants and as scribes able to transact business in many languages. They adapted the syllabic script of the Sogdians, who lived to the west of them in Central Asia, to writing Turkic. Literacy made possible several innovations in Uighur government, such as changing from a tax paid in kind (with products or services) to a money tax and, later, the minting of coins. Their flourishing urban culture exhibited a cosmopolitan enthusiasm for Buddhist teachings, religious art derived from northern India, and a mixture of East Asian and Islamic tastes in dress.

Unified Uighur power collapsed after half a century, leaving only Tibet as a rival to the Tang in Inner Asia. A large, stable empire critically positioned where China, Southeast Asia, South Asia, and Central Asia meet, **Tibet**

Women of Turfan Grinding Flour Women throughout Inner and East Asia were critical to all facets of economic life. In the Turkic areas of Central and Inner Asia, women commonly headed households, owned property, and managed businesses. These small figurines, made to be placed in tombs, portray women of Turfan—an Inner Asian area crossed by the Silk Road—performing tasks in the preparation of wheat flour. (Xinjiang Uighur Autonomous District Museum)

Uighur (WEE-ger) **An Lushan** (ahn loo-shahn)

experienced a variety of cultural influences. In the seventh century Chinese Buddhists on pilgrimage to India advanced contacts between India and Tibet. The Tibetans derived their alphabet from India, as well as a variety of artistic and architectural styles. India and China both contributed to Tibetan knowledge of mathematics, astronomy, divination, farming, and milling of grain. Islam and the monarchical traditions of Iran and Rome became familiar through Central Asian trading connections. The Tibetan royal family favored Greek medicine transmitted through Iran.

Under Li Shimin, cautious friendliness had prevailed between China and Tibet. A Tang princess, called Kongjo by the Tibetans, came to Tibet in 634 to marry the Tibetan king and cement an alliance. She brought Mahayana Buddhism, which combined with the native religion to create a distinctive form of Buddhism. Tibet sent ambassadors and students to the Tang imperial capital. Regular contact and Buddhist influences consolidated the Tang-Tibet relationship for a time. The Tibetan kings encouraged Buddhist religious establishments and prided themselves on being cultural intermediaries between India and China.

Tibet also excelled at war. Horses and armor, techniques borrowed from the Turks, raised Tibetan forces to a level that startled even the Tang. By the late 600s the Tang emperor and the Tibetan king were rivals for religious leadership and political dominance in Inner Asia, and Tibetan power reached into what are now Qinghai°, Sichuan°, and Xinjiang° provinces in China. War weariness affected both empires after 751, however.

In the 800s a new king in Tibet decided to follow the Tang lead and eliminate the political and social influence of the monasteries (see below). He was assassinated by Buddhist monks, and control of the Tibetan royal family passed into the hands of religious leaders. In the centuries that followed down to modern times, monastic domination isolated Tibet from surrounding regions.

Upheavals and Repression, 750–879

The Tang elites came to see Buddhism as undermining the Confucian idea of the family as the model for the state. The Confucian scholar Han Yu (768–824) spoke powerfully for a return to traditional Confucian practices. In "Memorial on the Bone of Buddha" written to the emperor in 819 on the occasion of ceremonies to receive a bone of the Buddha in the imperial palace, he scornfully disparages the Buddha and his followers:

> Now Buddha was a man of the barbarians who did not speak the language of China and wore clothes of a different fashion. His sayings did not concern the ways of our ancient kings, nor did his manner of dress conform to their laws. He understood neither the duties that bind sovereign and subject nor the affections of father and son. If he were still alive today and came to our court by order of his ruler, Your Majesty might condescend to receive him, but . . . he would then be escorted to the borders of the state, dismissed, and not allowed to delude the masses. How then, when he has long been dead, could his rotten bones, the foul and unlucky remains of his body, be rightly admitted to the palace? Confucius said, "Respect spiritual beings, while keeping at a distance from them."[3]

Buddhism was also attacked for encouraging women in politics. Wu Zhao°, a woman who had married into the imperial family, seized control of the government in 690 and declared herself emperor. She based her legitimacy on claiming to be a bodhisattva, an enlightened soul who had chosen to remain on earth to lead others to salvation. She also favored Buddhists and Daoists over Confucianists in her court and government.

Later Confucian writers expressed contempt for Wu Zhao and other powerful women, such as the concubine Yang Guifei°. Bo Zhuyi°, in his poem "Everlasting Remorse," lamented the influence of women at the Tang court, which had caused "the hearts of fathers and mothers everywhere not to value the birth of boys, but the birth of girls."[4] Confucian elites heaped every possible charge on prominent women who offended them, accusing Emperor Wu of grotesque tortures and murders, including tossing the dismembered but still living bodies of enemies into wine vats and cauldrons. They blamed Yang Guifei for the outbreak of the An Lushan rebellion in 755.

Serious historians dismiss the stories about Wu Zhao as stereotypical characterizations of "evil" rulers. Eunuchs (castrated palace servants) charged by historians with controlling Chang'an and the Tang court and publicly executing rival bureaucrats represent a similar stereotype. In fact Wu seems to have ruled effectively and was not deposed until 705, when extreme old age (eighty-plus) incapacitated her. Nevertheless, traditional Chinese historians commonly describe unorthodox rulers and all-powerful women as evil, and the truth about Wu will never be known.

Qinghai (CHING-hie) **Sichuan** (SUH-chwahn)
Xinjiang (shin-jee-yahng)

Wu Zhao (woo jow) **Yang Guifei** (yahng gway-fay)
Bo Zhuyi (baw joo-ee)

Buddhist Cave Painting at Dunhuang Hundreds of caves dating to the period when Buddhism enjoyed popularity and government favor in China survive in Gansu province, which was beyond the reach of the Tang rulers when they turned against Buddhism. This cave, dated to the year 538/9, contains elaborate wall decorations narrating the life of the Buddha and depicting scenes from the Western Paradise, where devotees of the Pure Land sect of Buddhism hoped to be reborn. (NHK International, Inc.)

Even Chinese gentry living in safe and prosperous localities associated Buddhism with social ills. People who worried about "barbarians" ruining their society pointed to Buddhism as evidence of the foreign evil since it had such strong roots in Inner Asia and Tibet. They claimed that eradicating Buddhist influence would restore the ancient values of hierarchy and social harmony. Because Buddhism shunned earthly ties, monks and nuns severed relations with the secular world in search of enlightenment. They paid no taxes, served in no army. They deprived their families of advantageous marriage alliances and denied descendants to their ancestors. The Confucian elites saw all this as threatening to the family, and to the family estates that underlay the Tang economic and political structure.

In 840 (a year of disintegration on many fronts) the government moved to crush the monasteries. An imperial edict of 845 reports the demolition of 4,600 temples and the forcible conversion of 26,500 monks and nuns into ordinary workers. The tax exemption of monasteries had allowed them to purchase land and precious objects and to employ large numbers of serfs. Wealthy believers had given the monasteries large tracts of land, and poor people had flocked to the Buddhist institutions to work as artisans, fieldworkers, cooks, housekeepers, and guards. By the ninth century, hundreds of thousands of people had entered tax exempt Buddhist institutions. Now an enormous amount of land and 150,000 workers were returned to the tax rolls.

Though some Buddhist cultural centers, such as the cave monasteries at Dunhuang, were protected by local warlords dependent on the favor of Buddhist rulers in Inner Asia, the dissolution of the monasteries was an incalculable loss to China's cultural heritage. Some sculptures and grottoes survived only in defaced form. Wooden temples and façades sheltering great stone carvings burned to the ground. Monasteries became legal again in later times, but Buddhism never recovered the social, political, and cultural influence of early Tang times.

The End of the Tang Empire, 879–907

The Tang order succumbed to the very forces that were essential to its creation and maintenance. The campaigns of expansion in the seventh century had left the empire dependent on local military commanders and a complex tax collection system. Such reverses as the Battle of the Talas River in 751, which halted the drive westward into Central Asia, led to military demoralization and underfunding. In 755 An Lushan, a Tang general appointed as regional commander on the northeast frontier, led about 200,000 soldiers in a rebellion that forced the emperor to flee Chang'an and execute his favorite concubine, Yang Guifei, whom some accused of being An Lushan's lover. Though he was killed by his own son in 757, An Lushan's rebellion lasted for eight years and resulted in new powers and greater independence for the provincial military governors who helped suppress it. The Uighurs also helped bring the disorder to an end.

Despite continuing prosperity, political disintegration and the elite's sense of cultural decay created an unsettled environment that encouraged aspiring dictators. A disgruntled member of the gentry, Huang Chao°, led the most devastating uprising between 879 and 881. Despite ruthless and violent domination of the villages he controlled, his rebellion attracted hundreds of thousands of poor farmers and tenants who could not protect themselves from local bosses, or who sought escape from oppressive landlords or taxes, or who simply did not know what else to do in the deepening chaos. The new hatred of "barbarians" spurred the rebels to murder thousands of foreign residents in Canton and Beijing°.

Local warlords finally wiped out the rebels, using the same violent tactics. But Tang society did not find peace. Refugees, migrant workers, and homeless people became common sights in both city and country. Residents of northern China fled to the southern frontiers as groups from Inner Asia took advantage of the flight of population to move into localities in the north. Though Tang emperors continued to rule in Chang'an until their line was terminated by one of the warlords in 907, they never regained effective power after Huang Chao's rebellion.

Silk Painting Depicting Khitan Hunters Resting Their Horses The artist shows the Khitans' soft riding boots, leggings, and robes (much like those used by the Mongols) and the Khitans' patterned hairstyle, with part of the skull shaved and some of the hair worn long. Men in Inner and North Asia (including Japan) used patterned hairstyles to indicate their political allegiance. The custom was documented in the 400s (but is certainly much older) and continued up to the twentieth century. (National Palace Museum, Taipai, Taiwan, Republic of China)

THE EMERGENCE OF EAST ASIA, TO 1200

In the aftermath of the Tang, three new states emerged and competed to inherit its legacy (see Map 11.2). The Liao° Empire of the Khitan° people, pastoral nomads related to the Mongols living on the northeastern frontier, established their rule in the north. They centered their government on several cities, but the emperors preferred to spend their time in their nomad encampments. In western China, the Minyak people (closely related to the Tibetans) established a second successor state. They called themselves "Tangguts°" to show their connection with the former empire. The third state, the Chinese-speaking **Song Empire,** came into being in 960 in central China.

Competition among these states was unavoidable. They embodied the political ambitions of peoples who spoke very different languages and subscribed to different religious and philosophical systems—Mahayana Buddhism among the Liao, Tibetan Buddhism among the Tangguts, and Confucianism among the Song. The Liao and especially the Tangguts maintained some continuing relationship with Inner and Central Asia, but the Song were cut off. Instead they developed their sea connections with other states in East Asia, West Asia, and Southeast Asia. This effort led to advanced seafaring and sailing technologies. The Song elite shared the late Tang dislike of "barbaric" or "foreign" influences as they tried to cope with multiple enemies that heavily taxed their military capacities. Meanwhile, Korea and Japan strengthened political and cultural ties with China, including an appreciation of Confucianism; and some Southeast Asian states, relieved of any Tang military threat, entered into friendly relations with the Song court.

Huang Chao (wang show) **Beijing** (bay-jeeng) **Liao** (lee-OW) **Khitan** (kee-THAN) **Tanggut** (TAHNG-gut)

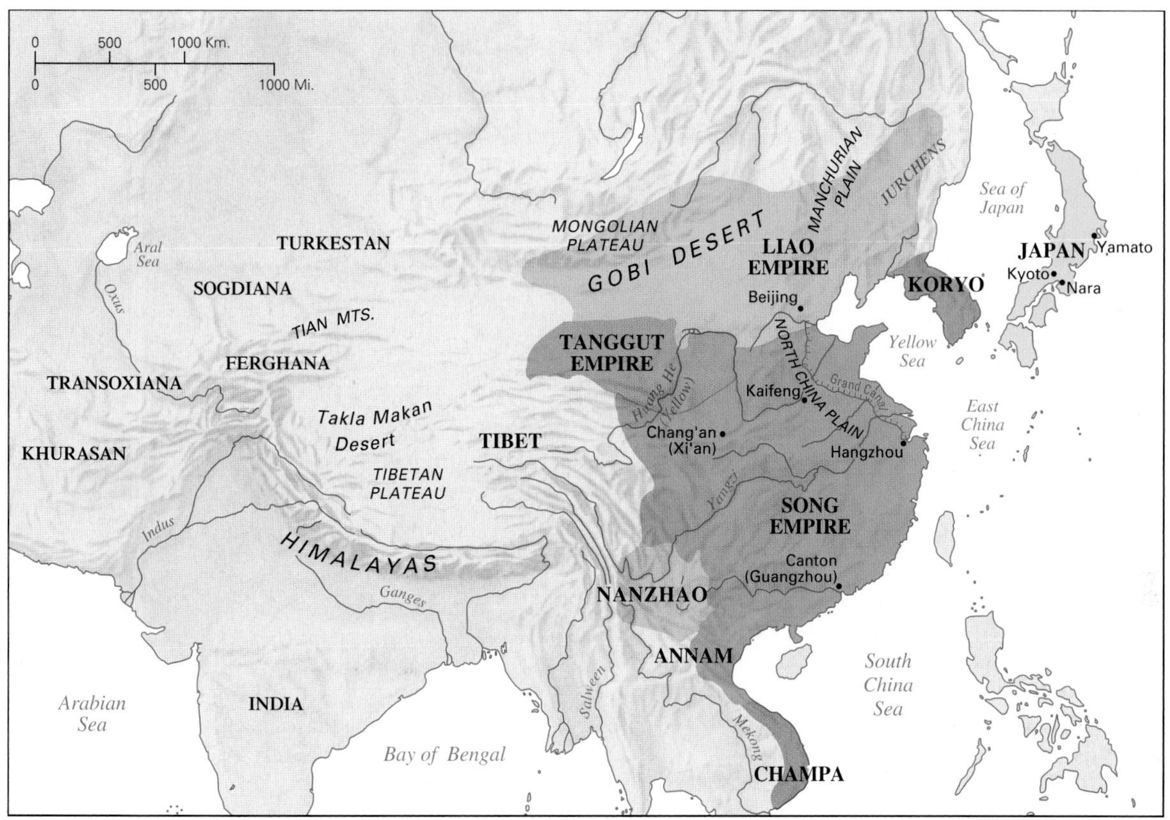

Map 11.2 Liao and Song Empires, ca. 1100 The states of Liao in the north and Song in the south generally ceased open hostilities after a treaty in 1005 stabilized the border and imposed an annual payment on Song China.

The Liao and Jin Challenge

The Liao Empire of the Khitan people extended from Siberia to Central Asia, connecting China with societies to the north and west. Variations on the Khitan name became the name for China in these distant regions: "Kitai" for the Mongols, "Khitai" for the Russians, and "Cathay" for those, like contemporaries of the Italian merchant Marco Polo, who reached China from Europe (see Chapter 13).

The Liao rulers prided themselves on their pastoral traditions, the continuing source of their military might, and made no attempt to create a single elite culture. They encouraged Chinese elites to use their own language, study their own classics, and see the emperor through Confucian eyes; and they encouraged other peoples to use their own languages and see the emperor as a champion of Buddhism or as a nomadic leader. On balance, Buddhism far outweighed Confucianism in this and other northern states, where rulers depended on their roles as bodhisattvas or as Buddhist kings to legitimate power. Liao rule lasted from 916 to 1121.

Superb horsemen and archers, the Khitans added siege machines from China and Central Asia to their armory for challenging the Song. In 1005 the Song emperor agreed to a truce that included enormous annual payments in cash and silk to the Liao. This lasted for more than a century, but eventually the Song tired of paying the annual tribute and entered into a secret alliance with the Jurchens of northeastern Asia, who were also chafing under Liao rule. In 1125 the Jurchens destroyed the Liao capital in Mongolia and proclaimed their own empire—the Jin. Then they turned against their former Song ally (Map 11.2).

The Jurchens grew rice, millet, and wheat, but they also spent a good deal of time hunting, fishing, and tending livestock. Though their language was unrelated to that of the Khitan, the Jurchens nevertheless learned much from the Khitan about the military arts and politi-

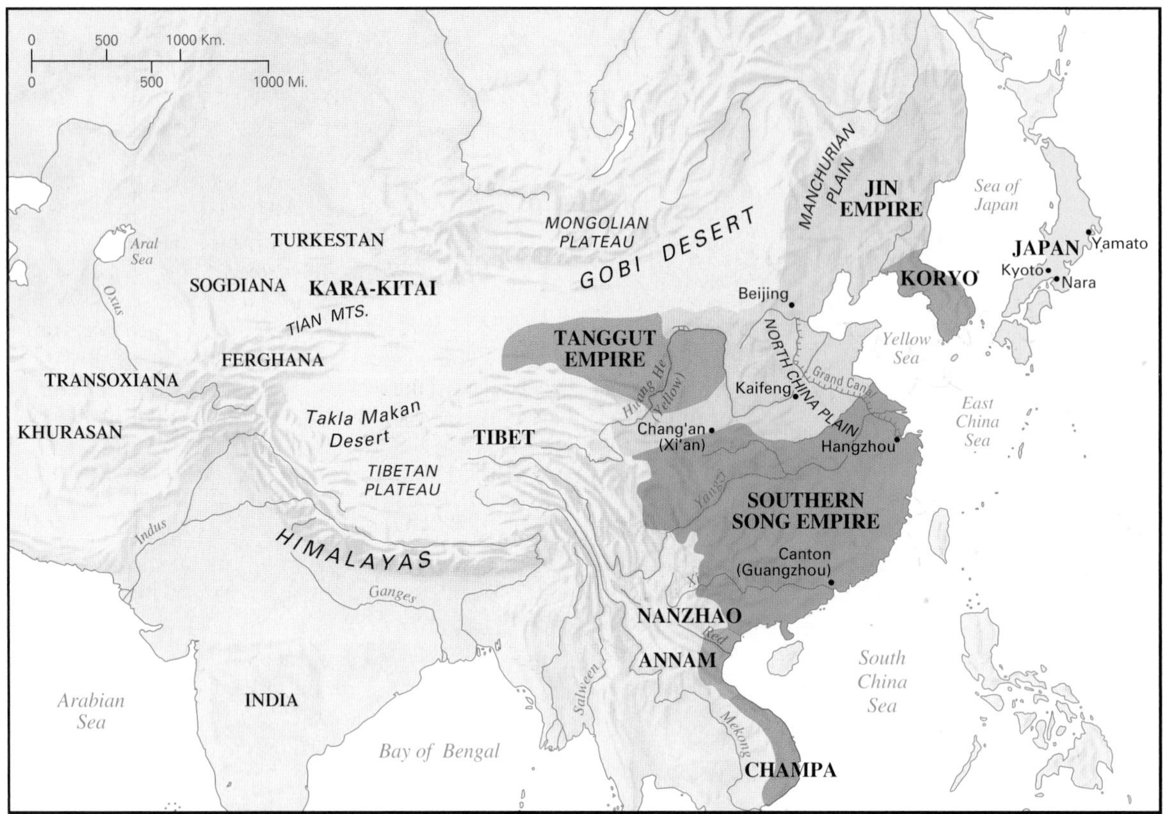

Map 11.3 Jin and Southern Song Empires, ca. 1200 After 1127 Song abandoned its northern territories to Jin. The Southern Song continued the policy of annual payments—to Jin rather than Liao—and maintained high military preparedness to prevent further invasions.

cal organization. This helped them become formidable enemies of the Song Empire, against whom they mounted an all-out campaign in 1127. They laid siege to the Song capital, Kaifeng°, and captured the Song emperor. Within a few years the Song withdrew south of the Yellow River and established a new capital at Hangzhou°, leaving central as well as northern China in Jurchen control (Map 11.3). The Song made annual payments to the Jin Empire to avoid open warfare. Historians generally refer to this period as the "Southern Song" (1127–1279).

Song Industries

Historians look upon the Southern Song as the premodern state and society that came closest to initiating an industrial revolution. Divided into three separate states from 907 to 1279, China did not exhibit the military expansionism and exploitation of far-flung networks of communication that had characterized the Tang at their height. Yet many of the advances in technology, medicine, astronomy, and mathematics for which the Song is famous derived from information that had come to China in Tang times, sometimes from very distant places. Song officials, scholars, and businessmen had the motivation and resources to adapt Tang information and technology to meet their needs, particularly in warfare, extension of agriculture, and the management of economic and social changes.

Chinese scholars made great strides in the arts of measurement and observation, drawing on the work of Indian and West Asian mathematicians and astronomers who had migrated to the Tang Empire in previous generations. Song mathematicians introduced the use of fractions, first employing them to describe the phases of the moon. From lunar observations, Song astronomers constructed a very precise calendar and, alone among the world's astronomers, noted the explosion of the Crab Nebula in 1054. Chinese scholars used their work in as-

Kaifeng (kie-fuhng) **Hangzhou** (hahng-jo)

Su Song's Astronomical Clock This gigantic clock built at Kaifeng between 1088 and 1092 combined mathematics, astronomy, and calendar-making with skillful engineering. The team overseen by Su Song placed an armillary sphere on the observation platform and linked it with chains to the water-driven central mechanism shown in the cutaway view. The water wheel also rotated the buddha statues in the multistory pagoda the spectators are looking at. Other devices displayed the time of the day, the month, and the year. (Courtesy, Joseph Needham, *Science and Civilization in China*)

tronomy and mathematics to make significant contributions to timekeeping and the development of the compass.

In 1088 the engineer Su Song constructed a gigantic mechanical celestial clock in Kaifeng. Escapement mechanisms for controlling the revolving wheels in water-powered clocks had appeared under the Tang, as had the application of water wheels to weaving and threshing. But this knowledge had not been widely applied. Su Song adapted the escapement and water wheel to his clock, which featured the first known chain-drive mechanism. The clock told the time of day and the day of the month, and it indicated the movement of the moon and certain stars and planets across the night sky. An observation deck and a mechanically rotated armillary sphere crowned the 80-foot (24-meter) structure. The clock exemplified the Song ability to integrate observational astronomy, applied mathematics, and engineering.

Song inventors drew on their knowledge of celestial coordinates, particularly the Pole Star, to refine the design of the compass. Long known in China, the magnetic compass shrank in size in Song times and gained a fixed pivot point for the needle, and sometimes even a small protective case with a glass covering. These changes made the compass suitable for seafaring, a use first attested in 1090. The Chinese compass and the Greek astrolabe, introduced later, improved navigation throughout Southeast Asia and the Indian Ocean.

Development of the seaworthy compass coincided with new techniques in building China's main oceangoing ship, the **junk.** A stern-mounted rudder improved the steering of the large ship in uneasy seas, and watertight bulkheads helped keep it afloat in emergencies. The shipwrights of the Persian Gulf soon copied these features in their ship designs.

Song innovation carried over into military affairs as well, though military pressure from the Liao and Jin Empires remained a serious challenge. The Song fielded an army four times as large as that of the Tang—about 1.25 million men (roughly the size of the present-day army of the United States)—though it occupied less than half the territory of the Tang. Song commanders were specially educated for the task, examined on military subjects, and paid regular salaries.

Because of the need for iron and steel to make weapons, the Song rulers fought their northern rivals for control of iron and coal mines in north China. The volume of Song mining and iron production, which again became a government monopoly in the eleventh century, soared. By the end of that century cast iron production reached about 125,000 tons (113,700 metric tons) annually, putting it on a par with the output of eighteenth-century Britain. Engineers became skilled at high-temperature metallurgy. They produced steel weapons of unprecedented strength by using enormous bellows, often driven by water wheels, to superheat the molten ore. Military engineers used iron to buttress defensive works because it was impervious to fire or concussion. Armorers used it in mass-produced body armor (in small, medium, and large sizes). Iron construction also appeared in bridges and small buildings. Mass-production techniques for bronze and ceramics in use in China for nearly two thousand years were adapted to iron casting and assembly.

To counter cavalry assaults, the Song experimented with **gunpowder,** which they initially used to propel clusters of flaming arrows. During the wars against the Jurchens in the 1100s the Song introduced a new and terrifying weapon. Shells launched from Song fortifications exploded in the midst of the enemy, blowing out shards of iron and dismembering men and horses. The short range of the shells limited them to defensive uses, and they had no major impact on the overall conduct of war.

Economy and Society in Song China

Despite the continuous military threats and the vigor of Song responses, Song elite culture idealized civil pursuits. Socially, the civil man outranked the military man. Private academies, designed to train young men for the official examinations and develop intellectual interests, became influential in culture and politics. New interpretations of Confucian teachings became so important and influential that the term **neo-Confucianism** is used for Song and later versions of Confucian thought.

Zhu Xi° (1130–1200), the most important early neo-Confucian thinker, wrote in reaction to the many centuries during which Buddhism and Daoism had often overshadowed the precepts of Confucius. He and others worked out a systematic approach to cosmology that focused on the central conception that human nature is moral, rational, and essentially good. To combat the Buddhist dismissal of worldly affairs as a transitory distraction, they reemphasized individual moral and social responsibility. Their human ideal was the sage, a person who could preserve mental stability and serenity while dealing conscientiously with troubling social problems. Where earlier Confucian thinkers had written about sage kings and political leaders, the neo-Confucians espoused the spiritual idea of universal sagehood, a state that could be achieved through proper study of the new Confucian principles and cosmology.

Despite the vigor and pervasiveness of neo-Confucianism, popular Buddhist sects persisted during the Song. The excerpt from a Song song-story quoted at the beginning of this chapter contained the line "We Buddhists and Confucians are of one family." While historically suitable for the time when the original version of the story of Ying-ying was written, before the Tang abolition of the Buddhist monasteries in 845, it is unlikely that the line would have pleased a Song audience if anti-Buddhist feelings had remained so ferocious. Some Buddhists elaborated upon Tang-era folk practices derived from India and Tibet. The best known, Chan Buddhism (known as **Zen** in Japan and as Son in Korea), asserted that mental discipline alone could win salvation.

Meditation, a key Chan practice, could be employed by Confucians as well as Buddhists. It could afford prospective officials relief from their preparation for civil service examinations, which continued into the Song from the Tang period. Dramatically different from the Han policy of hiring and promoting on the basis of recommendations, Song-style examinations persisted for nearly a thousand years. A large bureaucracy oversaw their design and administration. Test questions, which changed each time the examinations were given, even though they were always based on Confucian classics, often related to economic management or foreign policy.

The examinations had social implications, for hereditary class distinctions meant less than they had in Tang times, when noble lineages played a greater role in the structure of power. The new system recruited the most talented men for government service, whatever their origin. Men from wealthy families, however, succeeded most often. The tests required memorization of classics believed to date from the time of Confucius; preparation consumed so much time that peasant boys could rarely compete.

Success in the examinations brought good marriage prospects, the chance for a high salary, and enormous

Zhu Xi (jew she)

Going up the River Song cities hummed with commercial and industrial activity, much of it concentrated on the rivers and canals linking the capital Kaifeng to the provinces. This detail from *Going Upriver at the Qingming [Spring] Festival* shows a tiny portion of the scroll painting's panorama. Painted by Zhang Zeduan sometime before 1125, its depiction of daily life makes it an important source of information on working people. Before open shop fronts and tea houses a camel caravan departs, donkey carts are unloaded, a scholar rides loftily (if gingerly) on horseback, and women of wealth go by in closed sedan-chairs. (The Palace Museum, Beijing)

prestige. Failure could bankrupt a family and ruin a man both socially and psychologically. This put great pressure on candidates who spent days at a time in tiny, dim, airless examination cells, attempting to produce their answers—in beautiful calligraphy.

Changes in printing, from woodblock to an early form of **movable type,** allowed cheaper printing of many kinds of informative books and of test materials. The Song government realized that the examination system schooled millions of ambitious young men in Confucian ideals of state service—many times the number who eventually passed the tests. To promote its ideological goals, the government authorized the mass production of preparation books in the years before 1000. Though a man had to be literate to read the preparation books and basic education was still not common, some people of limited means were now able to take the examinations; and a moderate number of candidates entered the Song bureaucracy without noble, gentry, or elite backgrounds.

The availability of printed books changed country life as well, since landlords now had access to expert advice on planting and irrigation techniques, harvesting, tree cultivation, threshing, and weaving. Landlords frequently gathered their tenants and workers to show them illustrated texts and explain their meaning. This dissemination of knowledge, along with new technologies, furthered the development of new agricultural land south of the Yangzi River. Iron implements such as plows and rakes, first used in the Tang era, were adapted to wet-rice cultivation as the population moved south. Landowners and village leaders learned from books how to fight the mosquitoes that carried malaria. Control of the disease became one of the factors encouraging northerners to move south, which led to a sharp increase in population.

The increasing profitability of agriculture caught the attention of some ambitious members of the gentry. Still a frontier for Chinese settlers under the Tang, the south saw increasing concentration of land in the hands of a few wealthy families. In the process, the indigenous inhabitants of the region, related to the modern-day populations of Malaysia, Thailand, and Laos, retreated into the mountains or southward toward Vietnam.

During the 1100s the total population of the Chinese territories, spurred by prosperity, rose above 100 million. An increasing proportion lived in large towns and cities, though the leading Song cities had fewer than a million inhabitants. This still put them among the largest cities in the world.

Health and crowding posed problems in the Song capitals. Multistory wooden apartment houses fronted on narrow streets—sometimes only 4 or 5 feet (1.2 to 1.5

meters) wide—clogged by peddlers or families spending time outdoors. The crush of people called for new techniques in waste management, water supply, and firefighting. Controlling urban rodent and insect infestations improved health and usually kept the bubonic plague isolated in a few rural areas.

In Hangzhou engineers diverted the nearby river to flow through the city, flushing away waste and disease. Arab and European travelers who had firsthand experience with the Song capital, and who were sensitive to the urban crowding in their own societies, expressed amazement at the way Hangzhou city officials sheltered the densely packed population from danger so that they could enjoy the abundant pleasures of the city: restaurants, parks, bookstores, wine shops, tea houses, theaters, and the various entertainments mentioned at the start of this chapter.

The idea of credit, originating in the robust long-distance trade of the Tang period, spread widely under the Song. Intercity or interregional credit—what the Song called "flying money"—depended on the acceptance of guarantees that the paper could be redeemed for coinage at another location. The public accepted the practice because credit networks tended to be managed by families, so that brothers and cousins were usually honoring each other's certificates.

"Flying money" certificates differed from government-issued paper money, which the Song pioneered. In some years, military expenditures consumed 80 percent of the government budget. The state responded to this financial pressure by distributing paper money. But this made inflation so severe that by the beginning of the 1100s paper money was trading for only 1 percent of its face value. Eventually the government withdrew paper money and instead imposed new taxes, sold monopolies, and offered financial incentives to merchants. Privatization created opportunities for individuals with capital to engage in businesses that previously had been state monopolies.

Hard-pressed for the revenue needed to maintain the army, canals, roads, waterworks, and other state functions, the government finally resorted to tax farming, selling the rights to tax collection to private individuals. Tax farmers made their profit by collecting the maximum amount and sending an agreed upon smaller sum to the government. This meant exorbitant rates for taxable services, such as tolls, and much heavier tax burdens on the common people.

Rapid economic growth undermined the remaining government monopolies and the traditional strict regulation of business. Now merchants and artisans as well as gentry and officials could make fortunes. With land no longer the only source of wealth, the traditional social hierarchy common to an agricultural economy weakened, while cities, commerce, consumption, and the use of money and credit boomed. Urban life reflected the elite's growing taste for fine fabrics, porcelain, exotic foods, large houses, and exquisite paintings and books. Because the government and traditional elites did not control much of the new commercial and industrial development, historians sometimes describe Song China as "modern," using the term to refer to the era of private capitalism and the growth of an urban middle class in eighteenth-century Europe.

In conjunction with the backlash against Buddhism and revival of Confucianism that began under the Tang and intensified under the Song, women entered a long period of cultural subordination, legal disenfranchisement, and social restriction. Merchants spent long periods away from home, and many maintained several wives in different locations. Frequently they depended on wives to manage their homes and even their businesses in their absence. But though women took on responsibility for the management of their husbands' property, their own property rights suffered legal erosion. Under Song law, a woman's property automatically passed to her husband, and women could not remarry if their husbands divorced them or died.

The subordination of women proved compatible with Confucianism, and it became fashionable to educate girls just enough to read simplified versions of Confucian philosophy that emphasized the lowly role of women. Modest education made these young women more desirable as companions for the sons of gentry or noble families, and as literate mothers in lower ranking families aspiring to improve their status. Only rarely did a woman of extremely high station with unusual personal determination, as well as uncommon encouragement from father and husband, manage to acquire extensive education and freedom to pursue the literary arts. The poet Li Qingzhao° (1083–1141) acknowledged and made fun of her unusual status as a highly celebrated female writer:

> Although I've studied poetry for thirty years
> I try to keep my mouth shut and avoid reputation.
> Now who is this nosy gentleman talking about my
> poetry
> Like Yang Ching-chih°
> Who spoke of Hsiang Ssu° everywhere he went. [5]

Her reference is to a hermit poet of the ninth century who was continually and extravagantly praised by a court official, Yang Ching-chih.

Li Qingzhao (lee CHING-jow)
Yang Ching-chih (yahng SHING-she) **Hsiang Ssu** (sang sue)

The Players Women—often enslaved—entertained at Chinese courts from early times. Tang art often depicts women with slender figures, but Tang taste also admired more robust physiques. Song women, usually pale with willowy figures, appear as here with bound feet. The practice appeared in Tang times but was not widespread until the Song, when the image of weak, housebound women unable to work became a status symbol and pushed aside the earlier enthusiasm for healthy women who participated in family business. (The Palace Museum, Beijing)

Female footbinding first appeared among slave dancers at the Tang court, but it did not become widespread until the Song period. The bindings forced the toes under and toward the heel, so that the bones eventually broke and the woman could not walk on her own. In noble and gentry families, footbinding began between ages five and seven. In less wealthy families, girls worked until they were older, so footbinding began only in a girl's teens.

Many literate men condemned the maiming of innocent girls and the general uselessness of footbinding. Nevertheless, bound feet became a status symbol. By 1200 a woman with unbound feet had become undesirable in elite circles, and mothers of elite status, or aspiring to such status, almost without exception bound their daughters' feet. They knew that girls with unbound feet faced rejection by society, by prospective husbands, and ultimately by their own families. Working women and the indigenous peoples of the south, where northern practices took a longer time to penetrate, did not practice footbinding. As a consequence, they enjoyed considerably more mobility and economic independence than did elite Chinese women.

New Kingdoms in East Asia

With the rival states to the northeast and northwest strongly oriented toward Buddhism, the best possibilities for expanding the Confucian worldview of the Song lay with newly emerging kingdoms to the east and south. Korea, Japan, and Vietnam, like Song China, depended on agriculture. The cultivation of rice, an increasingly widespread crop, fit well with Confucian social ideas. Tending the young rice plants, irrigating the rice paddies, and managing the harvest required coordination among many village and kin groups and rewarded hierarchy, obedience, and self-discipline. Confucianism also justified using agricultural profits to support the education, safety, and comfort of the literate elite. In each of these new kingdoms Song civilization melded with indigenous cultural and historical traditions to create a distinctive synthesis.

Chinese Influences

Since Han times Confucianism had spread through East Asia with the spread of the Chinese writing system. Political ideologies in Korea, Japan, and Vietnam varied somewhat from those of Song China, however. These three East Asian neighbors had first centralized power under ruling houses in the early Tang period, and their state ideologies continued to resemble that of the early Tang, when Buddhism and Confucianism were still seen as compatible.

Government offices in Korea, Japan, and Vietnam went to noble families and did not depend on passing an elaborate set of examinations on Confucian texts. Landowning and agriculture remained the major sources of income, and landowners did not face challenges to their status from a large merchant class or an urban elite.

Nevertheless, men in Korea, Japan, and Vietnam prized literacy in classical Chinese and a good knowledge of Confucian texts. Members of the ruling and landholding elite sought to instill Confucian ideals of hierarchy and harmony among the general population through teaching by example and formal education, which was available to only a small number of people. The elite in every country learned to read Chinese and the Confucian classics, and Chinese characters contributed to locally invented writing systems (see Environment and Technology: Writing in East Asia, 400–1200).

ENVIRONMENT + TECHNOLOGY

Writing in East Asia, 400–1200

An ideographic writing system that originated in China became a communications tool throughout East Asia. Variations on this system, based more on depictions of meanings than representations of sound, spread widely by the time of the Sui and Tang Empires. Many East Asian peoples adapted ideographic techniques to writing languages unrelated to Chinese in grammar or sound.

The Vietnamese, Koreans, and Japanese often simplified Chinese characters and associated them with the sounds of their own non-Chinese languages. For instance, the Chinese character *an,* meaning "peace" (Fig. 1), was pronounced "an" in Japanese and was familiar as a Chinese character to Confucian scholars in Japan's Heian (hay-ahn) period. However, nonscholars simplified the character and used it to write the Japanese sound "a" (Fig. 2). A set of more than thirty of these syllabic symbols adapted from Chinese characters could represent the inflected forms (forms with grammatical endings) of any Japanese word. Murasaki Shikibu used such a syllabic system when she wrote *The Tale of Genji.*

In Vietnam and later in northern Asia, phonetic and ideographic elements combined in new ways. The apparent circles in some *chu nom* writing from Vietnam (Fig. 3) derive from the Chinese character for "mouth" and indicate a primary sound association for the word. The Khitans, who spoke a language related to Mongolian, developed an ideographic system of their own, inspired by Chinese characters. The Chinese character *wang* (Fig. 4), meaning "king, prince, ruler," was changed to represent the Khitan word for "emperor" by adding an upward stroke representing a "superior" ruler (Fig. 5). Because the system was ideographic, we do not know the pronunciation of this Khitan word. The Khitan character for "God" or "Heaven" adds a top stroke representing the "supreme" ruler or power to the character meaning "ruler" (Fig. 6). Though inspired by Chinese characters, Khitan writings could not be read by anyone who was not specifically educated in them.

The Khitans developed another system to represent the sounds and grammar of their language. They used small, simplified elements arranged within an imaginary frame to indicate the sounds in any word. This idea might have come from the phonetic script used by the Uighurs. Here (Fig. 7) we see the word for horse in a Khitan inscription. Fitting sound elements within a frame also occurred later in *hangul,* the Korean phonetic system introduced in the 1400s. Here (Fig. 8) we see the two words making up the country name "Korea."

The Chinese writing system served the Chinese elite well. But peoples speaking unrelated languages continually experimented with the Chinese invention to produce new ways of expressing themselves. Some of the resulting sound-based writing systems remain in common use; others are still being deciphered.

Figure 1

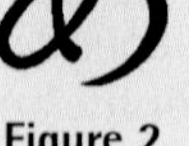

Figure 2

Figure 3

Figure 4

Figure 5

Figure 6

Figure 7

Figure 8

Korea

Written language arrived too late for these societies to record their earliest histories. Our first knowledge of Korea, Japan, and Vietnam comes from early Chinese officials and travelers. When the Qin Empire established its first colony in the Korean peninsula in the third century B.C.E., Chinese bureaucrats began documenting Korean history and customs. Han writers noted the horse breeding, strong hereditary elites, and **shamanism** (belief in the ability of certain individuals to contact ancestors and the invisible spirit world) of Korea's small kingdoms. But Korea quickly absorbed Confucianism and Buddhism.

A land of mountains, particularly in the east and north, Korea was largely covered by forest until modern times. Less than 20 percent of the land, mostly in the warmer south, is suitable for agriculture. In the early 500s the dominant landholding families made inherited status—the "bone ranks"—permanent in Silla°, a kingdom in the southeast of the peninsula. In 668 the larger Koguryo kingdom in the north came to an end after prolonged conflict with the Sui and Tang, and with Tang encouragement, Silla took control of much of the Korean peninsula. Silla could not stand by itself without Tang support, however, so after the fall of the Tang in the early 900s, the ruling house of **Koryo°**, from which the modern name "Korea" derives, united the peninsula. At constant threat from the Liao and then the Jin, Koryo pursued amicable relations with Song China. The Koryo kings supported Buddhism and made superb printed editions of Buddhist texts.

Woodblock printing exemplifies the technological exchanges that Korea enjoyed with China. The oldest surviving woodblock print in Chinese characters comes from Korea in the middle 700s. Commonly used during the Tang period, woodblock printing required great technical skill. A calligrapher would write the text on thin paper, which would then be pasted upside down on a block of wood. When the paper was wetted, the characters showed through from the back, and an artisan would carve away the wooden surface surrounding each character. A fresh block had to be carved for each printed page. Korean artisans developed their own advances in printing. By Song times, Korean experiments with movable type reached China, where further improvements led to metal or porcelain type from which texts could be cheaply printed.

Japan

Japan consists of four main islands and many smaller ones stretching in an arc from as far south as Georgia to as far north as Maine. The nearest point of contact with the Asian mainland lies 100 miles away in southern Korea. In early times Japan was even more mountainous and heavily forested than Korea, and only 11 percent of its land area was suitable for cultivation.

Japan's earliest history, like Korea's, comes from Chinese records. The first description, dating from the fourth century, tells of an island at the eastern edge of the world, divided into hundreds of small countries and ruled over by a shamaness named Himiko or Pimiko. This account describes the Japanese terrain, mountainous with small pockets and stretches of land suitable for agriculture, as influencing the social and political structures of the early period. The unification of central Japan came sometime in the fourth or fifth century C.E. How it occurred remains a question, but horse-riding warriors from Korea may have united the small countries of Japan under a central government at Yamato, on the central plain of Honshu island.

In the mid-600s the rulers based at Yamato implemented the Taika° and other reforms, giving the Yamato regime the key features of Tang government, which they knew of through embassies to Chang'an: a legal code, an official variety of Confucianism, and an official reverence for Buddhism. Within a century a centralized government with a complex system of law had emerged, as attested by a massive history in the Confucian style. The Japanese mastered Chinese building techniques so well that Nara° and Kyoto, Japan's early capitals, provide invaluable evidence of the wooden architecture long since vanished from China. During the eighth century Japan in some ways surpassed China in Buddhist studies. In 752 dignitaries from all over Mahayana Buddhist Asia gathered at the enormous Todaiji temple, near Nara, to celebrate the "eye-opening" of the "Great Buddha" statue.

Japanese admiration of Chinese culture did not extend to everything, however. Though the Japanese adopted Chinese building styles and some street plans, Japanese cities were built without walls. Unlike China, central Japan was not plagued by constant warfare. Also, the Confucian Mandate of Heaven, which justified dynastic changes, played no role in legitimating Japanese government. The *tenno*—often called "emperor" in English—belonged to a family believed to have ruled Japan since the beginning of known history. The dynasty never changed. The royal family endured because the emperors seldom wielded political power. A prime minister and the leaders of the native religion, in later times called Shinto, the "way of the gods," exercised real control.

In 794 the central government moved to Kyoto, usually called by its ancient name, Heian. Legally centralized government lasted there until 1185, though power became decentralized toward the end. Members of the **Fujiwara°** family—an ancient family of priests, bureaucrats, and warriors—controlled power and protected the emperor. Fujiwara dominance favored men of Confucian learning over the generally illiterate warriors. Noblemen of the Fujiwara period read the Chinese classics, appreciated painting and poetry, and refined their sense of wardrobe and interior decoration.

Pursuit of an aesthetic way of life prompted the Fujiwara nobles to entrust responsibility for local government, policing, and tax collection to their warriors. Though often of humble origins, a small number of warriors had achieved wealth and power by the late

Silla (SILL-ah or SHILL-ah) **Koryo** (KAW-ree-oh)

Taika (TIE-kah) **Nara** (NAH-rah) **Fujiwara** (foo-jee-WAH-rah)

1000s. By the middle 1100s the nobility had lost control, and civil war between rival warrior clans engulfed the capital.

Like other East Asian states influenced by Confucianism, the elite families of Fujiwara Japan did not encourage education for women. However, this did not prevent the exceptional woman from having a strong cultural impact. The hero of the celebrated Japanese novel *The Tale of Genji,* written around the year 1000 by the noblewoman Murasaki Shikibu, remarks: "Women should have a general knowledge of several subjects, but it gives a bad impression if they show themselves to be attached to a particular branch of learning."[6]

Fujiwara noblewomen lived in near-total isolation, generally spending their time on cultural pursuits and the study of Buddhism. To communicate with their families or among themselves, they depended on writing. The simplified syllabic script that they used represented the Japanese language in its fully inflected form (the Chinese classical script used by Fujiwara men could not do so). Loneliness, free time, and a ready instrument for expression produced an outpouring of poetry, diaries, and storytelling by women of the Fujiwara era. Their best-known achievement, however, remains Murasaki's portrait of Fujiwara court culture.

Military values acquired increasing importance during the period 1156–1185 when warfare between rival clans culminated in the establishment of the **Kamakura° shogunate,** the first of three decentralized military governments, in eastern Honshu, far from the old religious and political center at Kyoto. The standing of the Fujiwara family fell as nobles and the emperor hurried to accommodate the new warlords. *The Tale of the Heike,* an anonymously composed thirteenth-century epic account of the clan war, reflects an appreciation of the Buddhist doctrine of the impermanence of worldly things, a view that became common at that time among a new warrior class. This new class, in later times called *samurai,* eventually absorbed some of the Fujiwara aristocratic values, but the ascendancy of the nonmilitary civil elite had come to an end.

Vietnam

Vietnam had had contact with empires based in China since the third century B.C.E., but not until Tang times did the relationship become close enough for economic and cultural interchange to play an important cultural role. Occupying the coastal regions east of the mountainous spine of mainland Southeast Asia, Vietnam's economic and political life centered on two fertile river valleys, the Red River in the north and the Mekong° in the south. Agriculture was also possible in many smaller coastal areas where streams from the mountains—torrents during the monsoon season—flowed down to the sea. The rice-based agriculture of Vietnam made the region well suited for integration with southern China. As in southern China, the wet climate and hilly terrain of Vietnam demanded expertise in irrigation.

The ancestors of the Vietnamese may have preceded the Chinese in using draft animals in farming, working with metal, and making certain kinds of pots. But in Tang and Song times the elites of "Annam°"—as the Chinese called early Vietnam—adopted Confucian bureaucratic training, Mahayana Buddhism, and other aspects of Chinese culture. Annamese elites continued to rule in the Tang style after that dynasty's fall. Annam assumed the name Dai Viet° in 936 and maintained good relations with Song China as an independent country.

Champa, located largely in what is now southern Vietnam, rivaled the Dai Viet state. The cultures of India and Malaya strongly influenced Champa through the networks of trade and communication that encompassed the Indian Ocean. During the Tang period Champa had hostile relations with Dai Viet, but both kingdoms cooperated with the less threatening Song, the former as a voluntary tributary state. Among the tribute gifts brought to the Song court by Champa emissaries was **Champa rice** (originally from India). Chinese farmers soon made use of this fast-maturing variety to improve their yields of the essential crop.

Vietnam shared the Confucian interest in hierarchy that was also evident in Korea and Japan, but attitudes toward women, like those in the other two countries, differed from the Chinese model. None of the societies adopted the Chinese practice of footbinding. In Korea strong family alliances that functioned like political and economic organizations allowed women a role in negotiating and disposing of property. Before the adoption of Confucianism, Annamese women had enjoyed higher status than women in China, perhaps because both women and men participated in wet-rice cultivation. The Trung sisters of Vietnam, who lived in the second century C.E. and led local farmers in resistance against the Han Empire, still serve as national symbols in Vietnam and as local heroes in southern China. They recall a time when women played visible and active roles in community and political life.

Kamakura (kah-mah-KOO-rah)

Mekong (may-KONG) **Annam** (ahn-nahm)
Dai Viet (die vee-yet)

Conclusion

The reunification of China under the Sui and Tang triggered major changes both within China and in neighboring lands. Connections across Inner Asia and Tibet facilitated the flow of cultural and economic influences into China. Diversity within the empire produced great wealth and new ideas, and the dominant position of the Tang in the entire region led neighboring peoples in Korea, Japan, and Vietnam to imitate their practices. In time, however, internal tensions and foreign military pressure from the Uighurs and Tibetans weakened the Tang political structure and touched off rebellions that eventually doomed the empire.

The post-Tang fragmentation reduced the degree of Chinese domination in East Asia. Combining indigenous traditions and ideas borrowed from the Tang, neighboring peoples experimented with and often improved upon Tang military, architectural, and scientific technologies. The Jin, Tangguts, and Jurchens pursued these refinements on the basis of Buddhism as the state ideology. But they were not averse to adopting bureaucratic practices based on Chinese traditions and military techniques combining nomadic horsemanship and strategies with Chinese armaments and weapons. Korea, Japan, and Vietnam became much more closely wedded to Confucian models of state and society.

In Song China the spread of Tang technological knowledge resulted in the privatization of commerce, major advances in technology and industry, increased productivity in agriculture, and deeper exploration of ideas relating to time, cosmology, and mathematics. The brilliant achievements of the Song period came from mutually reinforcing developments in economy and technology. Avoiding the Tang's discouragement of innovation and competition, the Song economy, though much smaller than its predecessor, showed great productivity, circulating goods and money throughout East Asia and stimulating the economies of neighboring states. In terms of industrial specialization Song China excelled in military technology, engineering of all kinds, and production of iron and coal.

All the East Asian societies made advances in agricultural technology and productivity. All raised their literacy rates after the improvement of printing. Building on knowledge derived from Tang and Song sources, Japan went beyond China in developing advanced techniques in steel making, and Korea excelled in textiles and agriculture and produced major innovations in printing.

In the long run Song China could not maintain the equilibrium necessary to sustain its own prosperity and that of the region. Constant military challenges from the north eventually overwhelmed Song finances, and the need to buy high-quality steel from Japan caused a drain of copper coinage. When historians compare Song China with eighteenth-century Great Britain, another society that achieved unprecedented industrial production and technological innovation, they speculate about the reasons China progressed to such high levels of achievement and then tapered off while developments in Britain interacted with those in other European countries to produce an industrial revolution. No one can answer such questions conclusively, but the complex character of interrelationships among the East Asian and Inner Asian states as a whole, and the differing views of the world presented by Buddhism and neo-Confucianism surely played important roles.

Key Terms

Grand Canal
Li Shimin
Tang Empire
tributary system
bubonic plague
Uighurs
Tibet
Song Empire
junk
gunpowder
neo-Confucianism
Zen
movable type
shamanism
Koryo
Fujiwara
Kamakura shogunate
Champa rice

Suggested Reading

On Inner Asia see the bibliography for Chapter 8 relating to the Silk Road. In addition, Denis Sinor, ed., *The Cambridge History of Early Inner Asia* (1990), and M. S. Asimov and C. E. Bosworth, eds., *History of Civilizations of Central Asia: Volume IV—The Age of Achievement, A.D. 750 to the End of the Fifteenth Century—Part Two, the Achievements* (2000), contain articles on many topics. Thomas Barfield, *The Perilous Frontier: Nomadic Empires and China* (1992), is an anthropologist's view of the broad relationship between pastoralists and agriculturists in the region. Susan Whitfield's *Life Along the Silk Road* (2001) uses fictional travelers as a narrative device but is solidly based on documentary research.

Arthur F. Wright, *The Sui Dynasty* (1978), is a very readable narrative of the reunification of China in the sixth century. The Tang Empire is the topic of a huge literature, but for a variety of enduring essays see Arthur F. Wright and David Twitchett, eds., *Perspectives on the T'ang* (1973). On Tang contacts with the cultures of Central, South, and Southeast Asia see Edward Schaefer, *The Golden Peaches of Samarkand* (1963), *The Vermilion Bird* (1967), and *Pacing the Void* (1977). For an introduction to medieval Tibet see Rolf Stein, *Tibetan Civilization* (1972). On the Uighurs see Colin MacKarras, *The Uighur Empire* (1968).

There is comparatively little secondary work in English on the Inner and northern Asian empires that succeeded the Tang. But for a classic text see Karl Wittfogel and Chia-sheng Feng, *History of Chinese Society: Liao* (1949). On the Jurchen Jin, see Jin-sheng Tao, *The Jurchens in Twelfth Century China,* and on the Tangguts see Ruth Dunnell, *The State of High and White: Buddhism and the State in Eleventh-Century Xia* (1996). Morris Rossabi, ed., *China Among Equals: The Middle Kingdom and Its Neighbors, 10th–14th Centuries* (1983), deals with post-Tang relationships more broadly.

On the Song there is a large volume of material, particularly relating to technological achievements. For an introduction to the monumental work of Joseph Needham see *Science in Traditional China* (1981). A classic thesis on Song advancement (and Ming backwardness) is Mark Elvin, *The Pattern of the Chinese Past* (1973), particularly Part II. Joel Mokyr, *The Lever of Riches* (1990), is a more-recent comparative treatment. Agriculture is the special concern of Francesca Bray, *The Rice Economies: Technology and Development in Asian Societies* (1994).

For neo-Confucianism and Buddhism see W. T. de Bary, W-T Chan, and B. Watson, compilers, *Sources of Chinese Tradition,* vol. 1, 2d ed. (1999), as well as Arthur F. Wright, *Buddhism in Chinese History* (1983). On religion more broadly see Robert P. Hymes, *Way and Byway: Taoism, Local Religion, and Models of Divinity in Sung China* (2002). On social and economic history see Miyazaki Ichisada, *China's Examination Hell* (1971); Richard von Glahn, *The Land of Streams and Grottoes* (1987); and Patricia Ebery, *The Inner Quarters: Marriage and the Lives of Chinese Women in the Sung Period* (1993). On the poet Li Qingzhao see Hu Pin-ch'ing, *Li Ch'ing-chao* (1966).

On the history of Korea see Andrew C. Nahm, *Introduction to Korean History and Culture* (1993), and Ki-Baik Kim, *A New History of Korea* (1984). Yongho Ch'oe et al., eds., include excerpts from many historical works in *Sources of Korean Tradition* (2000). An excellent introduction to Japanese history is Paul H. Varley, *Japanese Culture* (1984). Selections of relevant documents may be found in David John Lu, *Sources of Japanese History,* vol. 1 (1974), and R. Tsunoda, W. T. de Bary, and D. Keene, compilers, *Sources of Japanese Tradition,* vol. 1 (1964). Ivan Morris, *The World of the Shining Prince: Court Life in Ancient Japan* (1979), is a classic introduction to the literature and culture of Fujiwara Japan at the time of the composition of Murasaki Shikibu's *The Tale of Genji.* For Vietnam see Keith Weller Taylor, *The Birth of Vietnam* (1983).

Notes

1. *Master Tung's Western Chamber Romance,* tr. Li-li Ch'en (New York: Columbia University Press, 1994), 22, 42–43, 45–46.
2. Arthur Waley, *Poetry and Career of Li Po* (London: Unwin Hyman, 1954), 35.
3. Theodore de Bary, ed., *Sources of Chinese Tradition*, vol. 1, 2d ed. (New York: Columbia University Press, 1999), 584
4. Quoted in David Lattimore, "Allusion in T'ang Poetry," in *Perspectives on the T'ang,* ed. Arthur F. Wright and David Twitchett (New Haven, CT: Yale University Press, 1973), 436.
5. Quoted at "Women's Early Music, Art, Poetry," http://music.acu.edu/www/iawm/pages/reference/tzusongs.html.
6. Quoted in Ivan Morris, *The World of the Shining Prince*: *Court Life in Ancient Japan* (New York: Penguin Books, 1979), 221–222.

12

Peoples and Civilizations of the Americas, 200–1500

Maya Scribe Mayan scribes used a complex writing system to record religious concepts and memorialize the actions of their kings. This picture of a scribe was painted on a ceramic plate.

CHAPTER OUTLINE

In late August 682 C.E. the Maya° princess Lady Wac-Chanil-Ahau° walked down the steep steps from her family's residence and mounted a sedan chair decorated with rich textiles and animal skins. As the procession exited from the urban center of Dos Pilas°, her military escort spread out through the fields and woods along its path to prevent ambush by enemies. Lady Wac-Chanil-Ahau's destination was the Maya city of Naranjo°, where she was to marry a powerful nobleman. Her marriage had been arranged to re-establish the royal dynasty that had been eliminated when Caracol, the region's major military power, had defeated Naranjo. Lady Wac-Chanil-Ahau's passage to Naranjo symbolized her father's desire to forge a military alliance that could resist Caracol. For us, the story of Lady Wac-Chanil-Ahau illustrates the importance of marriage and lineage in the politics of the classic-period Maya.

Smoking Squirrel, the son of Lady Wac-Chanil-Ahau, ascended the throne of Naranjo as a five-year-old in 693 C.E. During his long reign he proved to be a careful diplomat and formidable warrior. He was also a prodigious builder, leaving behind an expanded and beautified capital as part of his legacy. Mindful of the importance of his mother and her lineage from Dos Pilas, he erected numerous stelae (carved stone monuments) that celebrated her life.[1]

When population increased and competition for resources grew more violent, warfare and dynastic crisis convulsed the world of Wac-Chanil-Ahau. The defeat of the city-states of Tikal and Naranjo by Caracol undermined long-standing commercial and political relations in much of southern Mesoamerica and led to more than a century of conflict. Caracol, in turn, was challenged by the dynasty created at Dos Pilas by the heirs of Lady Wac-Chanil-Ahau. Despite a shared culture and religion, the great Maya cities remained divided by the dynastic ambitions of their rulers and by the competition for resources.

As the story of Lady Wac-Chanil-Ahau's marriage and her role in the development of a Maya dynasty suggests, the peoples of the Americas were in constant competition for resources. Members of hereditary elites organized their societies to meet these challenges, even as their ambition for greater power predictably ignited new conflicts. No single set of political institutions or technologies worked in every environment, and enormous cultural diversity existed in the ancient Americas. In Mesoamerica (Mexico and northern Central America) and in the Andean region of South America, Amerindian peoples developed an extraordinarily productive and diversified agriculture.[2] They also built great cities that rivaled the capitals of the Chinese and Roman Empires in size and beauty. The Olmecs of Mesoamerica and Chavín° of the Andes were among the earliest civilizations of the Americas (see Chapter 3). In the rest of the hemisphere, indigenous peoples adapted combinations of hunting and agriculture to maintain a wide variety of settlement patterns, political forms, and cultural traditions. All the cultures and civilizations of the Americas experienced cycles of expansion and contraction as they struggled with the challenges of environmental changes, population growth, social conflict, and war.

As you read this chapter, ask yourself the following questions:

- How did differing environments influence the development of Mesoamerican, Andean, and northern peoples?
- What technologies were developed to meet the challenges of these environments?
- How were the civilizations of Mesoamerica and the Andean region similar? How did they differ?
- How did religious belief and practice influence political life in the ancient Americas?

Maya (MY-ah) **Wac-Chanil-Ahau** (wac-cha-NEEL-ah-HOW)
Dos Pilas (dohs PEE-las) **Naranjo** (na-ROHN-hoe)

Chavín (cha-VEEN)

CHRONOLOGY

	Mesoamerica	Northern peoples	Andes
100	**100** Teotihuacan founded **250** Maya early clasic period begins	**100–400** Hopewell culture in Ohio River Valley	**100–600** Nazca culture **200–700** Moche culture
400			**500–1000** Tiwanaku and Wari control Peruvian highlands
700	**ca. 750** Teotihuacan destroyed **800–900** Maya centers abandoned, end of classic period **968** Toltec capital of Tula founded	**700–1200** Anasazi culture **919** Pueblo Bonito founded	
1000	**1156** Tula destroyed	**1050–1250** Cahokia reaches peak power **1150** Collapse of Anasazi centers begins	**1200** Chimu begin military expansion
1300	**1325** Aztec capital Tenochtitlan founded		**1438** Inca expansion begins **1465** Inca conquer Chimu
1500	**1502** Moctezuma II crowned Aztec ruler	**1500** Mississippian culture declines	**1500–1525** Inca conquer Ecuador

Classic-Era Culture and Society in Mesoamerica, 200–900

Between about 200 and 900 C.E. the peoples of Mesoamerica created a remarkable civilization. Despite enduring differences in language and the absence of regional political integration, Mesoamericans were unified by similarities in material culture, religious beliefs and practices, and social structures. Building on the earlier achievements of the Olmecs and others, the peoples of the area that is now Central America and south and central Mexico developed new forms of political organization, made great strides in astronomy and mathematics, and improved the productivity of their agriculture. This mix of achievements is called the classic period by archaeologists. During this period, population grew, a greater variety of products were traded over longer distances, and social hierarchies became more complex. Great cities were constructed, serving as centers of political life and as arenas of religious ritual and spiritual experience.

Classic-period civilizations built on the religious and political foundations established earlier in Olmec centers. The cities of the classic period continued to be

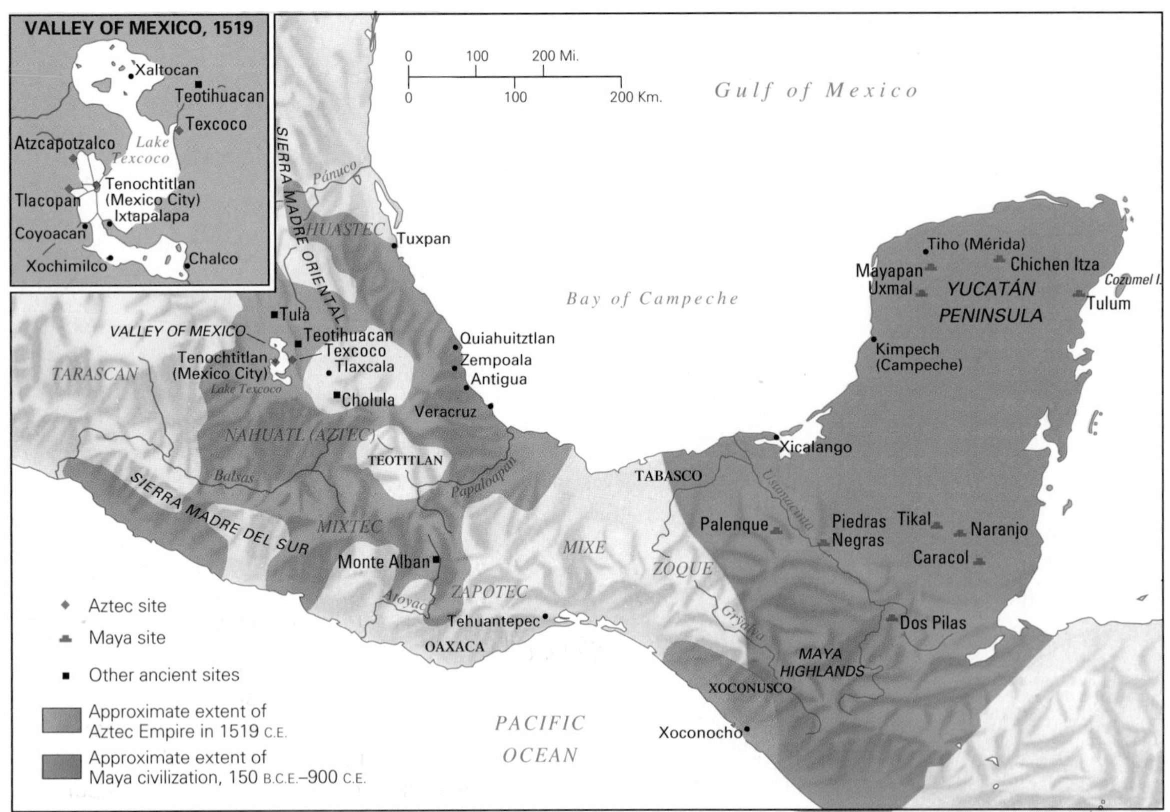

Map 12.1 Major Mesoamerican Civilizations, 1000 B.C.E.–1519 C.E. From their island capital of Tenochtitlan, the Aztecs militarily and commercially dominated a large region. Aztec achievements were built on the legacy of earlier civilizations such as the Olmecs and Maya.

dominated by platforms and pyramids devoted to religious functions, but they were more impressive and architecturally diversified. They had large full-time populations divided into classes and dominated by hereditary political and religious elites who controlled nearby towns and villages and imposed their will on the rural peasantry.

The political and cultural innovations of this period did not depend on the introduction of new technologies. The agricultural foundation of Mesoamerican civilization had been developed centuries earlier. Major innovations in agriculture such as irrigation, the draining of wetlands, and the terracing of hillsides had all been in place for more than a thousand years when great cities were developed after 200 C.E. Instead, the achievements of the classic era depended on the ability of increasingly powerful elites to organize and command growing numbers of laborers and soldiers. What had changed was the reach and power of religious and political leaders. The scale and impressive architecture found at Teotihuacan° or at the great Maya cities illustrate both Mesoamerican aesthetic achievements and the development of powerful political institutions.

Teotihuacan

Located about 30 miles (48 kilometers) northeast of modern Mexico City, **Teotihuacan** (100 B.C.E.–750 C.E.) was one of Mesoamerica's most important classic-period civilizations (see Map 12.1). At the height of its power, from 450 to 600 C.E., it was the largest city in the Americas. With between 125,000 and 200,000 inhabitants, it was larger than all but a small number of contemporary European and Asian cities.

Religious architecture rose above a city center aligned with nearby sacred mountains and reflecting the

Teotihuacan (teh-o-tee-WAH-kahn)

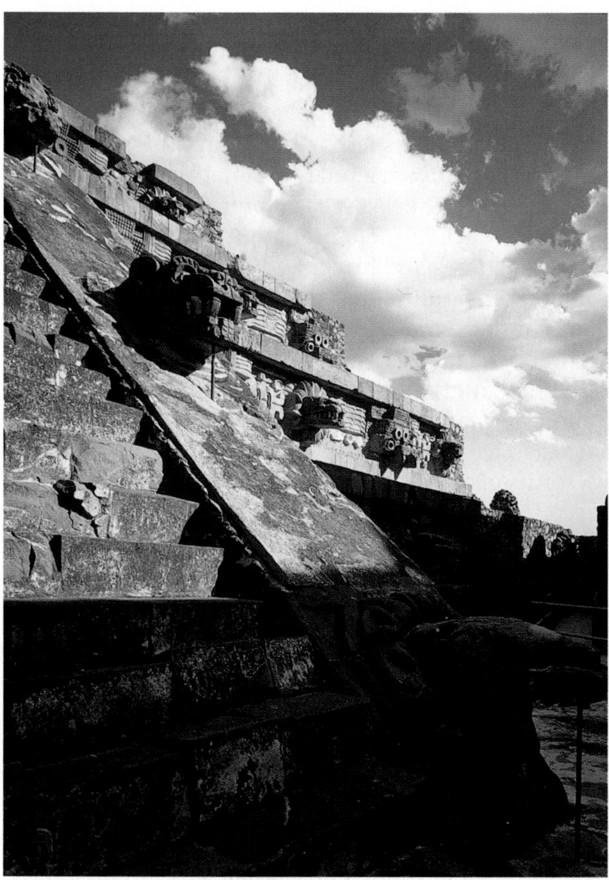

Temple of Quetzalcoatl in Teotihuacan This impressive temple was decorated with images of two gods, Quetzalcoatl and Tlaloc. Along both sides of the main temple steps are arrayed the serpent images associated with Quetzalcoatl, a culture god common to most of the Mesoamerican civilizations. Along the front of the temple the image of Quetzalcoatl is decorated with a feathered necklace. The image with the goggle-like decoration is Tlaloc, the rain or storm god. (Jean Mazenod/Citadelles & Mazenod, Paris)

movement of the stars. Enormous pyramids dedicated to the Sun and Moon and more than twenty smaller temples devoted to other gods were arranged along a central avenue. The people recognized and worshiped many gods and lesser spirits. Among the gods were the Sun, the Moon, a storm-god, and Quetzalcoatl°, the feathered serpent. Quetzalcoatl was a culture-god believed to be the originator of agriculture and the arts. Like the earlier Olmecs, people living at Teotihuacan practiced human sacrifice. More than a hundred sacrificial victims were found during the excavation of the temple of Quetzalcoatl at Teotihuacan. Sacrifice was viewed as a sacred duty toward the gods and as essential to the well-being of human society.

The rapid growth in urban population initially resulted from a series of volcanic eruptions that disrupted agriculture. Later, as the city elite increased its power, farm families from the smaller villages in the region were forced to relocate to the urban core. As a result, more than two-thirds of the city's residents retained their dependence on agriculture, walking out from urban residences to their fields. The elite of Teotihuacan used the city's growing labor resources to bring marginal lands into production. Swamps were drained, irrigation works were constructed, terraces were built into hillsides, and the use of chinampas was expanded. **Chinampas°**, sometimes called "floating gardens," were narrow artificial islands constructed along lakeshores or in marshes. They were created by heaping lake muck and waste material on beds of reeds that were then anchored to the shore by trees. Chinampas permitted year-round agriculture—because of subsurface irrigation and resistance to frost—and thus played a crucial role in sustaining the region's growing population. The productivity of the city's agriculture made possible its accomplishments in art, architecture, and trade.

As population grew, the housing of commoners underwent dramatic change. Apartment-like stone buildings were constructed for the first time. These apartment compounds were unique to Teotihuacan. They commonly housed members of a single kinship group, but some were used to house craftsmen working in the same trade. The two largest craft groups produced pottery and obsidian tools, the most important articles of long-distance trade. It appears that more than 2 percent of the urban population was engaged in making obsidian tools and weapons. The city's pottery and obsidian have been found throughout central Mexico and even in the Maya region of Guatemala.

The city's role as a religious center and commercial power provided both divine approval of and a material basis for the elite's increased wealth and status. Members of the elite controlled the state bureaucracy, tax collection, and commerce. Their prestige and wealth were reflected in their style of dress and diet and in the separate residence compounds built for aristocratic families. The central position and great prestige of the priestly class were evident in temple and palace murals. Teotihuacan's economy and religious influence drew pilgrims from as far away as Oaxaca and Veracruz. Some of them became permanent residents.

Unlike the other classic-period civilizations, the people of Teotihuacan did not concentrate power in the

Quetzalcoatl (kate-zahl-CO-ah-tal)

chinampas (chee-NAM-pahs)

hands of a single ruler. Although the ruins of their impressive housing compounds demonstrate the wealth and influence of the city's aristocracy, there is no clear evidence that individual rulers or a ruling dynasty gained overarching political power. In Teotihuacan the deeds of individual rulers were not featured in public art, nor were their images represented by statues or other monuments as in other Mesoamerican civilizations. In fact, some scholars suggest that Teotihuacan was ruled by alliances forged among elite families or by weak kings who were the puppets of these powerful families. Regardless of what form political decision making took, we know that this powerful classic-period civilization achieved regional preeminence without subordinating its political life to the personality of a powerful individual ruler or lineage.

Historians debate the role of the military in the development of Teotihuacan. The absence of walls or other defensive structures before 500 C.E. suggests that Teotihuacan enjoyed relative peace during its early development. Archaeological evidence, however, reveals that the city created a powerful military to protect long-distance trade and to compel peasant agriculturalists to transfer their surplus production to the city. The discovery of representations of soldiers in typical Teotihuacan dress in the Maya region of Guatemala suggests to some that Teotihuacan used its military to expand trade relations. Unlike later postclassic civilizations, however, Teotihuacan was not an imperial state controlled by a military elite.

It is unclear what forces brought about the collapse of Teotihuacan about 650 C.E. Weakness was evident as early as 500 C.E., when the urban population declined to about 40,000 and the city began to build defensive walls. These fortifications and pictorial evidence from murals suggest that the city's final decades were violent. Early scholars suggested that the city was overwhelmed militarily by a nearby rival city or by nomadic warrior peoples from the northern frontier. More recently, investigators have uncovered evidence of conflict within the ruling elite and the mismanagement of resources. This, they argue, led to class conflict and the breakdown of public order. As a result, most important temples in the city center were pulled down and religious images defaced. Elite palaces were also systematically burned and many of the residents killed. Regardless of the causes, the eclipse of Teotihuacan was felt throughout Mexico and into Central America.

The Maya

During Teotihuacan's ascendancy in the north, the **Maya** developed an impressive civilization in the region that today includes Guatemala, Honduras, Belize, and southern Mexico (see Map 12.1). Given the difficulties imposed by a tropical climate and fragile soils, the cultural and architectural achievements of the Maya were remarkable. Although they shared a single culture, they were never unified politically. Instead, rival kingdoms led by hereditary rulers struggled with each other for regional dominance, much like the Mycenaean-era Greeks (see Chapter 4).

Today Maya farmers prepare their fields by cutting down small trees and brush and then burning the dead vegetation to fertilize the land. Swidden agriculture (also called shifting agriculture or slash and burn agriculture) can produce high yields for a few years. However, it uses up the soil's nutrients, eventually forcing people to move to more fertile land. The high population levels of the Maya classic period (250–900 C.E.) required more intensive forms of agriculture. Maya living near the major urban centers achieved high agricultural yields by draining swamps and building elevated fields. They used irrigation in areas with long dry seasons, and they terraced hillsides in the cooler highlands. Nearly every household planted a garden to provide condiments and fruits to supplement dietary staples. Maya agriculturists also managed nearby forests, favoring the growth of the trees and shrubs that were most useful to them, as well as promoting the conservation of deer and other animals hunted for food.

During the classic period, Maya city-states proliferated. The most powerful cities controlled groups of smaller dependent cities and a broad agricultural zone by building impressive religious temples and by creating rituals that linked the power of kings to the gods. Classic-period cities, unlike earlier sites, had dense central precincts that were visually dominated by monumental architecture. These political and ceremonial centers were commonly aligned with the movements of the sun and Venus. Open plazas were surrounded by high pyramids and by elaborately decorated palaces often built on high ground or on constructed mounds. The effect was to awe the masses drawn to the centers for religious and political rituals.

The Maya loved decoration. Nearly all of their public buildings were covered with bas-relief and painted in bright colors. Religious allegories, the genealogies of rulers, and important historical events were the most common motifs. Beautifully carved altars and stone monoliths were erected near major temples. This rich legacy of monumental architecture was constructed without the aid of wheels—no pulleys, wheelbarrows, or carts—or metal tools. Masses of men and women aided only by levers and stone tools cut and carried construction materials and lifted them into place.

The Maya cosmos was divided into three layers connected along a vertical axis that traced the course of the

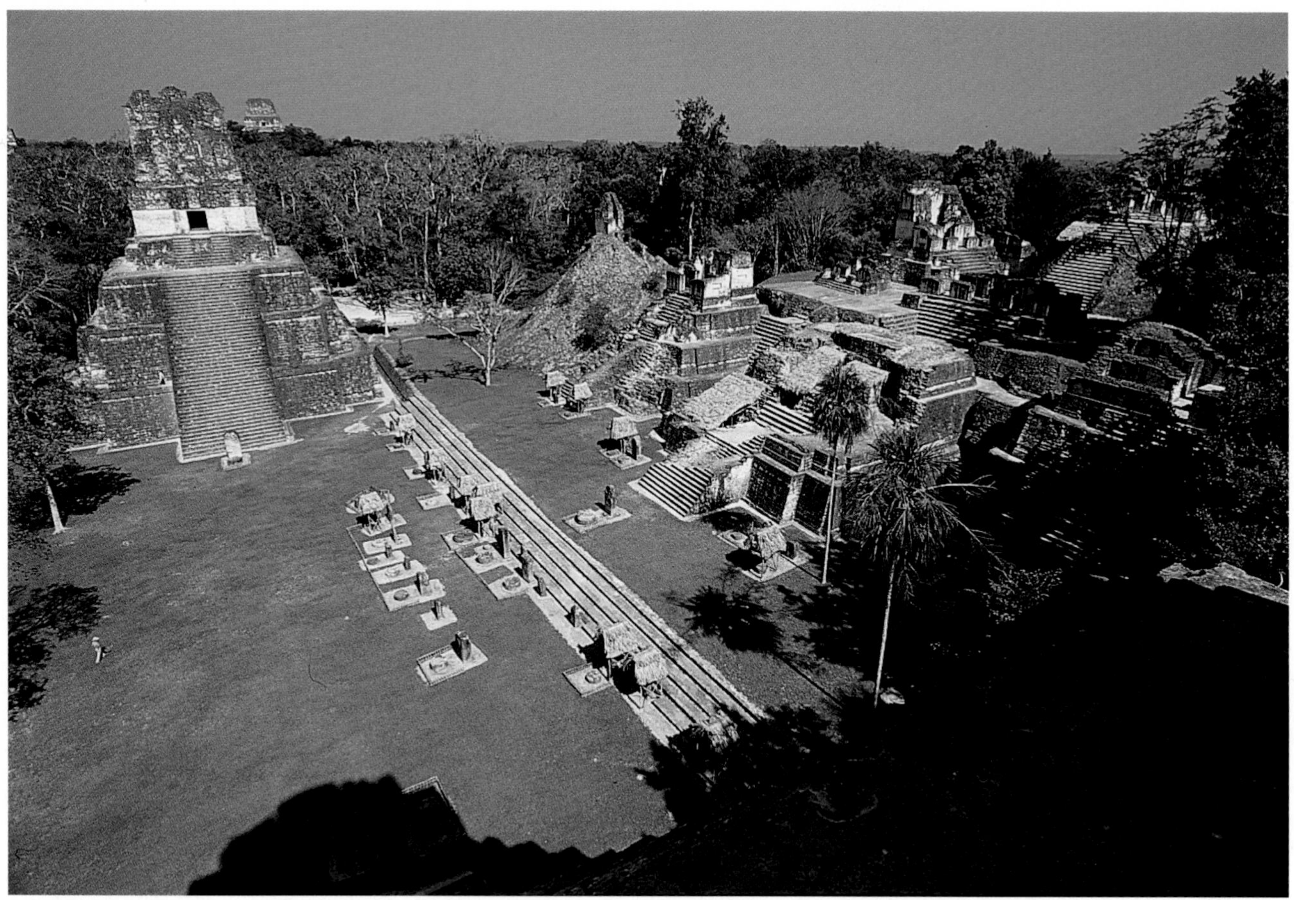

The Great Plaza at Tikal Still visible in the ruins of Tikal, in modern Guatemala, are the impressive architectural and artistic achievements of the classic-era Maya. Maya centers provided a dramatic setting for the rituals that dominated public life. Construction of Tikal began before 150 B.C.E.; the city was abandoned about 900 C.E. A ball court and residences for the elite were part of the Great Plaza. (Martha Cooper/Peter Arnold, Inc.)

sun. The earthly arena of human existence held an intermediate position between the heavens, conceptualized by the Maya as a sky-monster, and a dark underworld. A sacred tree rose through the three layers; its roots were in the underworld, and its branches reached into the heavens. The temple precincts of Maya cities physically represented essential elements of this religious cosmology. The pyramids were sacred mountains reaching to the heavens. The doorways of the pyramids were portals to the underworld.

Rulers and other members of the elite served both priestly and political functions. They decorated their bodies with paint and tattoos and wore elaborate costumes of textiles, animal skins, and feathers to project both secular power and divine sanction. Kings communicated directly with the supernatural residents of the other worlds and with deified royal ancestors through bloodletting rituals and hallucinogenic trances. Scenes of rulers drawing blood from lips, ears, and penises are common in surviving frescoes and on painted pottery.

Warfare in particular was infused with religious meaning and attached to elaborate rituals. Battle scenes and the depiction of the torture and sacrifice of captives were frequent decorative themes. Typically, Maya military forces fought to secure captives rather than territory. Days of fasting, sacred ritual, and rites of purification preceded battle. The king, his kinsmen, and other ranking nobles actively participated in war. Elite captives were nearly always sacrificed; captured commoners were more likely to be forced to labor for their captors.

Only two women are known to have ruled Maya kingdoms. Maya women of the ruling lineages did play

The Mesoamerican Ball Game From Guatemala to Arizona, archaeologists have found evidence of an ancient ball game played with a solid rubber ball on slope-sided courts shaped like a capital T. Among the Maya the game was associated with a creation myth and thus had deep religious meaning. There is evidence that some players were sacrificed. In this scene from a ceramic jar, players wearing elaborate ritual clothing—which includes heavy, protective pads around the chest and waist—play with a ball much larger than the ball actually used in such games. Some representations show balls drawn to suggest a human head. (Chrysler Museum of Art/Justin Kerr)

important political and religious roles, however. The consorts of male rulers participated in bloodletting rituals and in other important public ceremonies, and their noble blood helped legitimate the rule of their husbands. Although Maya society was patrilineal (tracing descent in the male line), there is evidence that some male rulers traced their lineages bilaterally (in both the male and the female lines). Like Lady Wac-Chanil-Ahau's son Smoking Squirrel, some rulers emphasized the female line if it held higher status. Much less is known about the lives of the women of the lower classes, but scholars believe that women played a central role in the religious rituals of the home. They were also healers and shamans. Women were essential to the household economy, maintaining essential garden plots and weaving, and in the management of family life.

Building on what the Olmecs had done, the Maya made important contributions to the development of the Mesoamerican calendar and to mathematics and writing. Their interest in time and in the cosmos was reflected in the complexity of their calendric system. Each day was identified by three separate dating systems. Like other peoples throughout Mesoamerica, the Maya had a calendar that tracked the ritual cycle (260 days divided into thirteen months of 20 days) as well as a solar calendar (365 days divided into eighteen months of 20 days, plus 5 unfavorable days at the end of the year). The concurrence of these two calendars every fifty-two years was believed to be especially ominous. Alone among Mesoamerican peoples, the Maya also maintained a continuous "long count" calendar, which began at a fixed date in the past that scholars have identified as 3114 B.C.E., a date that the Maya probably associated with creation.

Both the calendars and the astronomical observations on which they were based depended on Maya mathematics and writing. Their system of mathematics incorporated the concept of the zero and place value but had limited notational signs. Maya writing was a form of hieroglyphic inscription that signified whole words or concepts as well as phonetic cues or syllables. Aspects of public life, religious belief, and the biographies of rulers and their ancestors were recorded in deerskin and bark-paper books, on pottery, and on the stone columns and monumental buildings of the urban centers. In this sense every Maya city was a sacred text.

Between 800 and 900 C.E. many of the major urban centers of the Maya were abandoned or destroyed, although a small number of classic-period centers survived for centuries. This collapse was preceded in some areas by decades of urban population decline and increased warfare. Some scholars have proposed that epidemic disease and pestilence played a role in this catastrophe, although there is little evidence to support this argument. Other experts have contended that the earlier destruction of Teotihuacan around 650 C.E. disrupted trade, thus undermining the legitimacy of Maya rulers who had used the goods in rituals. There is growing consensus that the growing population led to environmental degradation and declining agricultural productivity. This environmental crisis, in turn, led to social conflict and increased levels of warfare as desperate elites sought to acquire additional agricultural land through conquest.

The Postclassic Period in Mesoamerica, 900–1500

The division between the classic and postclassic periods is somewhat arbitrary. Not only is there no single explanation for the collapse of Teotihuacan and many of the major Maya centers, but these events occurred over more than a century and a half. In fact, some important classic-period civilizations survived unscathed. Moreover, the essential cultural characteristics of the classic period were carried over to the postclassic. The two periods are linked by similarities in religious belief and practice, architecture, urban planning, and social organization.

There were, however, some important differences between the periods. There is evidence that the population of Mesoamerica expanded during the postclassic period. Resulting pressures led to an intensification of agricultural practices and to increased warfare. The governing elites of the major postclassic states—the Toltecs and the Aztecs—responded to these harsh realities by increasing the size of their armies and by developing political institutions that facilitated their control of large and culturally diverse territories acquired through conquest.

The Toltecs

Little is known about the **Toltecs**° prior to their arrival in central Mexico. Some scholars speculate that they were originally a satellite population that Teotihuacan had placed on the northern frontier to protect against the incursions of nomads. After their migration south, the Toltecs borrowed from the cultural legacy of Teotihuacan and created an important postclassic civilization. Memories of their military achievements and the violent imagery of their political and religious rituals dominated the Mesoamerican imagination in the late postclassic period. In the fourteenth century, the Aztecs and their contemporaries erroneously believed that the Toltecs were the source of nearly all the great cultural achievements of the Mesoamerican world. As one Aztec source later recalled:

> In truth [the Toltecs] invented all the precious and marvelous things. . . . All that now exists was their discovery. . . . And these Toltecs were very wise; they were thinkers, for they originated the year count, the day count. All their discoveries formed the book for interpreting dreams. . . . And so wise were they [that] they understood the stars which were in the heavens.[3]

In fact, all these contributions to Mesoamerican culture were in place long before the Toltecs gained control of central Mexico. The most important Toltec innovations were instead political and military.

The Toltecs created the first conquest state based largely on military power, and they extended their political influence from the area north of modern Mexico City to Central America. Established about 968 C.E., the Toltec capital of Tula° was constructed in a grand style (see Map 12.1). Its public architecture featured colonnaded patios and numerous temples. Although the population of Tula never reached the levels of classic-period Teotihuacan, the Toltec capital dominated central Mexico. Toltec decoration had a more warlike and violent character than did the decoration of earlier Mesoamerican cultures. Nearly all Toltec public buildings and temples were decorated with representations of warriors or with scenes suggesting human sacrifice.

Two chieftains or kings apparently ruled the Toltec state together. Evidence suggests that this division of responsibility eventually weakened Toltec power and led to the destruction of Tula. Sometime after 1000 C.E. a struggle between elite groups identified with rival religious cults undermined the Toltec state. According to legends that survived among the Aztecs, Topiltzin°—one of the two rulers and a priest of the cult of Quetzalcoatl—and his followers bitterly accepted exile in the east, "the land of the rising sun." These legendary events coincided with growing Toltec influence among the Maya of the Yucatán Peninsula. One of the ancient texts relates these events in the following manner:

Toltec (TOLL-tek)

Tula (TOO-la) **Topilitzin** (tow-PEELT-zeen)

> Thereupon he [Topiltzin] looked toward Tula, and then wept. . . . And when he had done these things . . . he went to reach the seacoast. Then he fashioned a raft of serpents. When he had arranged the raft, he placed himself as if it were his boat. Then he set off across the sea.[4]

After the exile of Topiltzin, the Toltec state began to decline, and around 1156 C.E. northern invaders overcame Tula itself. After its destruction, a centuries-long process of cultural and political assimilation produced a new Mesoamerican political order based on the urbanized culture and statecraft of the Toltecs. Like Semitic peoples of the third millennium B.C.E. interacting with Sumerian culture (see Chapter 2), the new Mesoamerican elites were drawn in part from the invading cultures. The Aztecs of the Valley of Mexico became the most important of these late postclassic peoples.

The Aztecs

The Mexica°, more commonly known as the **Aztecs,** were among the northern peoples who pushed into central Mexico in the wake of the collapse of Tula. At the time of their arrival they had a clan-based social organization. In their new environment they began to adopt the political and social practices that they found among the urbanized agriculturalists of the valley. At first, the Aztecs served their more powerful neighbors as serfs and mercenaries. As their strength grew, they relocated to small islands near the shore of Lake Texcoco, and around 1325 C.E. they began the construction of their twin capitals, **Tenochtitlan**° and Tlatelolco (together the foundation for modern Mexico City).

Military successes allowed the Aztecs to seize control of additional agricultural land along the lakeshore. With the increased economic independence and greater political security that resulted from this expansion, the Aztecs transformed their political organization by introducing a monarchical system similar to that found in more powerful neighboring states. The kinship-based organizations that had organized political life earlier survived to the era of Spanish conquest, but lost influence relative to monarchs and hereditary aristocrats. Aztec rulers did not have absolute power, and royal succession was not based on primogeniture. A council of powerful aristocrats selected new rulers from among male members of the ruling lineage. Once selected, the ruler was forced to renegotiate the submission of tribute dependencies and then demonstrate his divine mandate by undertaking a new round of military conquests. War was infused with religious meaning, providing the ruler with legitimacy and increasing the prestige of successful warriors.

With the growing power of the ruler and aristocracy, social divisions were accentuated. These alterations in social organization and political life were made possible by Aztec military expansion. Territorial conquest allowed the warrior elite of Aztec society to seize land and peasant labor as spoils of war (see Map 12.1). In time, the royal family and highest-ranking members of the aristocracy possessed extensive estates that were cultivated by slaves and landless commoners. The Aztec lower classes received some material rewards from imperial expansion but lost most of their ability to influence or control decisions. Some commoners were able to achieve some social mobility through success on the battlefield or by entering the priesthood, but the highest social ranks were always reserved for hereditary nobles.

The urban plan of Tenochtitlan and Tlatelolco continued to be organized around the clans, whose members maintained a common ritual life and accepted civic responsibilities such as caring for the sick and elderly. Clan members also fought together as military units. Nevertheless, the clans' historical control over common agricultural land and other scarce resources, such as fishing and hunting rights, declined. By 1500 C.E. great inequalities in wealth and privilege characterized Aztec society.

Aztec kings and aristocrats legitimated their ascendancy by creating elaborate rituals and ceremonies to distinguish themselves from commoners. One of the Spaniards who participated in the conquest of the Aztec Empire remembered his first meeting with the Aztec ruler Moctezuma° II (r. 1502–1520): "many great lords walked before the great Montezuma [Moctezuma II], sweeping the ground on which he was to tread and laying down cloaks so that his feet should not touch the earth. Not one of these chieftains dared look him in the face."[5] Commoners lived in small dwellings and ate a limited diet of staples, but members of the nobility lived in large, well-constructed two-story houses and consumed a diet rich in animal protein and flavored by condiments and expensive imports like chocolate from the Maya region to the south. Rich dress and jewelry also set apart the elite. Even in marriage customs the two groups were different. Commoners were monogamous, great nobles polygamous.

The Aztec state met the challenge of feeding an urban population of approximately 150,000 by efficiently

Mexica (meh-SHE-ca) **Tenochtitlan** (teh-noch-TIT-lan)

Moctezuma (mock-teh-ZU-ma)

Costumes of Aztec Warriors In Mesoamerican warfare individual warriors sought to gain prestige and improve their status by taking captives. This illustration from the sixteenth-century Codex Mendoza was drawn by an Amerindian artist. It shows the Aztecs' use of distinctive costumes to acknowledge the prowess of warriors. These costumes indicate the taking of two (top left) to six captives (bottom center). The individual on the bottom right shown without a weapon was a military leader. As was common in Mesoamerican illustrations of military conflict, the captives, held by their hair, are shown kneeling before the victors. (The Bodleian Library, University of Oxford, Selder. A.I. fol. 64r)

organizing the labor of the clans and additional laborers sent by defeated peoples to expand agricultural land. The construction of a dike more than 5½ miles (9 kilometers) long by 23 feet (7 meters) wide to separate the freshwater and saltwater parts of Lake Texcoco was the Aztecs' most impressive land reclamation project. The dike allowed a significant extension of irrigated fields and the construction of additional chinampas. One expert has estimated that the project consumed 4 million person-days to complete. Aztec chinampas contributed maize, fruits, and vegetables to the markets of Tenochtitlan. The imposition of a **tribute system** on conquered peoples also helped relieve some of the pressure of Tenochtitlan's growing population. Unlike the tribute system of Tang China, where tribute had a more symbolic character (see Chapter 11), one-quarter of the Aztec capital's food requirements was satisfied by tribute payments of maize, beans, and other foods sent by nearby political dependencies. The Aztecs also demanded cotton cloth, military equipment, luxury goods like jade and feathers, and sacrificial victims as tribute. Trade supplemented these supplies.

A specialized class of merchants controlled long-distance trade. Given the absence of draft animals and wheeled vehicles, this commerce was dominated by lightweight and valuable products like gold, jewels, feathered garments, cacao, and animal skins. Merchants also provided essential political and military intelligence for the Aztec elite. Operating outside the protection of Aztec military power, merchant expeditions were armed and often had to defend themselves. Although merchants became wealthy and powerful as the Aztecs expanded their empire, they were denied the privileges of the high nobility, which was jealous of its power. As a result, the merchants feared to publicly display their affluence.

Like commerce throughout the Mesoamerican world, Aztec commerce was carried on without money and credit. Barter was facilitated by the use of cacao, quills filled with gold, and cotton cloth as standard units of value to compensate for differences in the value of bartered goods. Aztec expansion facilitated the integration of producers and consumers in the central Mexican economy. As a result, the markets of Tenochtitlan and

Tlatelolco offered a rich array of goods from as far away as Central America and what is now the southwestern border of the United States. Hernán Cortés (1485–1547), the Spanish adventurer who eventually conquered the Aztecs, expressed his admiration for the abundance of the Aztec marketplace:

> One square in particular is twice as big as that of Salamanca and completely surrounded by arcades where there are daily more than sixty thousand folk buying and selling. Every kind of merchandise such as may be met with in every land is for sale. . . . There is nothing to be found in all the land which is not sold in these markets, for over and above what I have mentioned there are so many and such various things that on account of their very number . . . I cannot detail them.[6]

The Aztecs succeeded in developing a remarkable urban landscape. The combined population of Tenochtitlan and Tlatelolco and the cities and hamlets of the surrounding lakeshore was approximately 500,000 by 1500 C.E. The island capital was designed so that canals and streets intersected at right angles. Three causeways connected the city to the lakeshore.

Religious rituals dominated public life in Tenochtitlan. Like the other cultures of the Mesoamerican world, the Aztecs worshiped a large number of gods. Most of these gods had a dual nature—both male and female. The major contribution of the Aztecs to the religious life of Mesoamerica was the cult of Huitzilopochtli°, the southern hummingbird. As the Aztec state grew in power and wealth, the importance of this cult grew as well. Huitzilopochtli was originally associated with war, but eventually the Aztecs identified this god with the Sun, worshiped as a divinity throughout Mesoamerica. Huitzilopochtli, they believed, required a diet of human hearts to sustain him in his daily struggle to bring the Sun's warmth to the world. Tenochtitlan was architecturally dominated by a great twin temple devoted to Huitzilopochtli and Tlaloc, the rain god, symbolizing the two bases of the Aztec economy: war and agriculture.

War captives were the preferred sacrificial victims, but large numbers of criminals, slaves, and people provided as tribute by dependent regions were also sacrificed. Although human sacrifice had been practiced since early times in Mesoamerica, the Aztecs and other societies of the late postclassic period transformed this religious ritual by dramatically increasing its scale. There are no reliable estimates for the total number of sacrifices, but the numbers clearly reached into the thousands each year. This form of violent public ritual had political consequences and was not simply the celebration of religious belief. Some scholars have emphasized the political nature of the rising tide of sacrifice, noting that sacrifices were carried out in front of large crowds that included leaders from enemy and subject states as well as the masses of Aztec society. The political subtext must have been clear: rebellion, deviancy, and opposition were extremely dangerous.

Huitzilopochtli (wheat-zeel-oh-POSHT-lee)

Northern Peoples

By the end of the classic period in Mesoamerica, around 900 C.E., important cultural centers had appeared in the southwestern desert region and along the Ohio and Mississippi river valleys of what is now the United States. In both regions improved agricultural productivity and population growth led to increased urbanization and complex social and political structures. In the Ohio Valley Amerindian peoples who depended on locally domesticated seed crops as well as traditional hunting and gathering developed large villages with monumental earthworks. The introduction of maize, beans, and squash into this region from Mesoamerica after 1000 B.C.E. played an important role in the development of complex societies. Once established, these useful food crops were adopted throughout North America.

As growing populations came to depend on maize as a dietary staple, large-scale irrigation projects were undertaken in both the southwestern desert and the eastern river valleys. This development is a sign of increasingly centralized political power and growing social stratification. The two regions, however, evolved different political traditions. The Anasazi° and their neighbors in the southwest maintained a relatively egalitarian social structure and retained collective forms of political organization based on kinship and age. The mound builders of the eastern river valleys evolved more hierarchical political institutions: groups of small towns were subordinate to a political center ruled by a hereditary chief who wielded both secular and religious authority.

Southwestern Desert Cultures

Immigrants from Mexico introduced agriculture based on irrigation to present-day Arizona around 300 B.C.E. Because irrigation allowed the planting of two crops per year, the population grew and settled village life soon appeared.

Anasazi (ah-nah-SAH-zee)

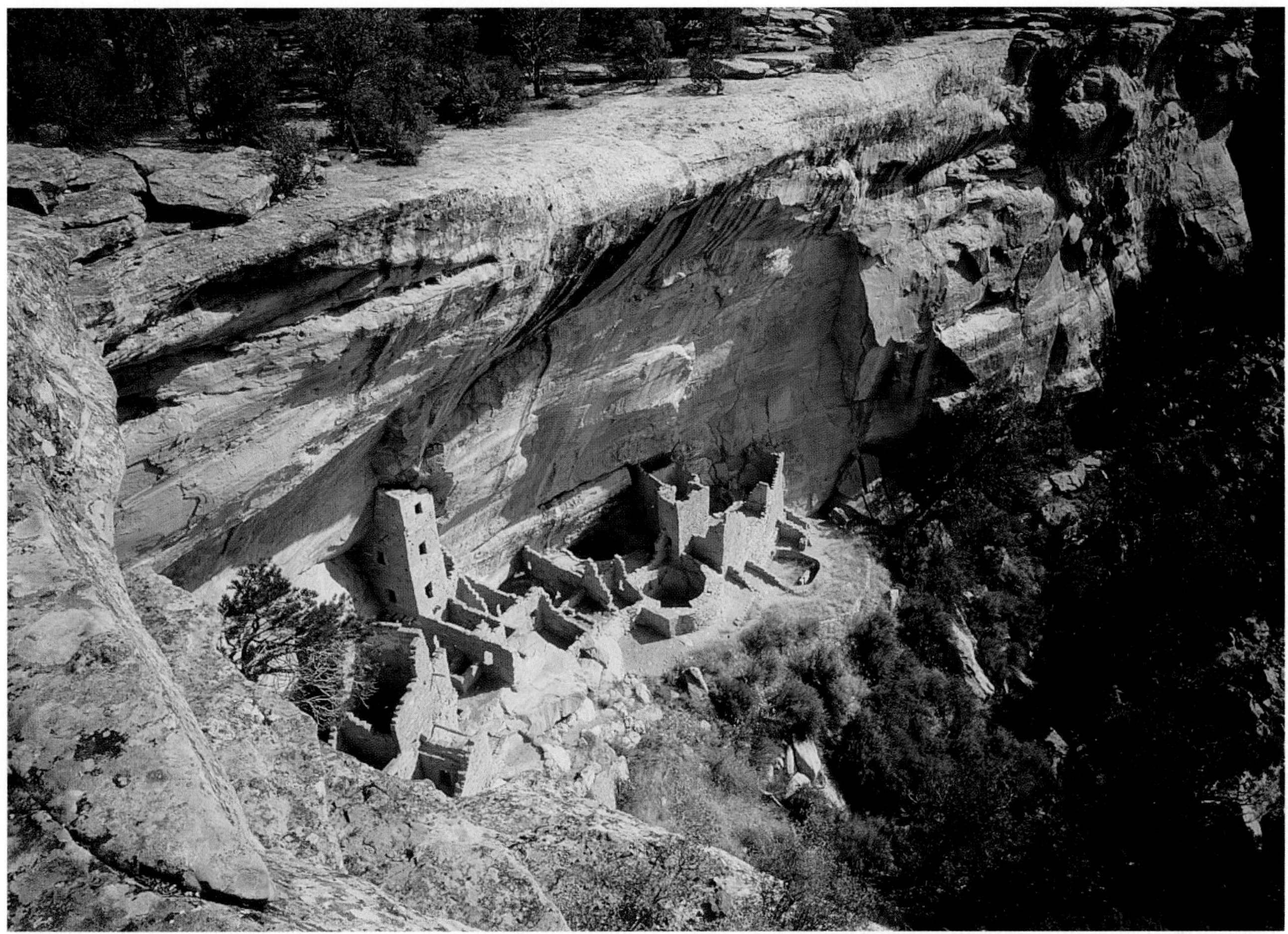

Mesa Verde Cliff Dwelling Located in southern Colorado, the Anasazi cliff dwellings of the Mesa Verde region hosted a population of about 7,000 in 1250 C.E. The construction of housing complexes and religious buildings in the area's large caves was probably prompted by increased warfare in the region. (David Muench Photography)

Of all the southwestern cultures, the Hohokam of the Salt and Gila river valleys show the strongest Mexican influence. Hohokam sites have platform mounds and ball courts similar to those of Mesoamerica. Hohokam pottery, clay figurines, cast copper bells, and turquoise mosaics also reflect Mexican influence. By 1000 C.E. the Hohokam had constructed an elaborate irrigation system that included one canal more than 18 miles (30 kilometers) in length. Hohokam agricultural and ceramic technology spread over the centuries to neighboring peoples, but it was the Anasazi to the north who left the most vivid legacy of these desert cultures.

Archaeologists use **Anasazi,** a Navajo word meaning "ancient ones," to identify a number of dispersed, though similar, desert cultures located in what is now the Four Corners region of Arizona, New Mexico, Colorado, and Utah (see Map 12.2). Between 450 and 750 C.E. the Anasazi developed an economy based on maize, beans, and squash. Their successful adaptation of these crops permitted the formation of larger villages and led to an enriched cultural life centered in underground buildings called kivas. Evidence suggests that the Anasazi may have used kivas for weaving and pottery making, as well as religious rituals. They produced pottery decorated with geometric patterns, learned to weave cotton cloth, and, after 900 C.E., began to construct large multistory residential and ritual centers.

One of the largest Anasazi communities was located in Chaco Canyon in what is now northwestern New Mexico. Eight large towns were built in the canyon and four more on surrounding mesas, suggesting a regional population of approximately 15,000. Many smaller villages were located nearby. Each town contained hundreds of rooms arranged in tiers around a central plaza. At Pueblo Bonito, the largest town, more than 650 rooms were arranged in a four-story block of residences and storage rooms. Pueblo Bonito had thirty-eight kivas, including a great kiva more than 65 feet (19 meters) in diameter. Social life and craft activities were concentrated in small open plazas or common rooms. Hunting, trade, and the need to maintain irrigation works often drew men away from the village. Women shared in agricultural tasks and were specialists in many crafts. They also were responsible for food preparation and childcare. If the practice of the modern Pueblos, cultural descendants of the Anasazi, is a guide, houses and furnishings may have belonged to the women, who formed extended families with their mothers and sisters.

At Chaco Canyon high-quality construction, the size and number of kivas, and the system of roads linking the canyon to outlying towns all suggest that Pueblo Bonito and its nearest neighbors exerted some kind of political or religious dominance over a large region. Some archaeologists have suggested that the Chaco Canyon culture originated as a colonial appendage of Mesoamerica, but the archaeological record provides little evidence for this theory. Merchants from Chaco provided Toltec-period peoples of northern Mexico with turquoise in exchange for shell jewelry, copper bells, macaws, and trumpets. But these exchanges occurred late in Chaco's development, and more important signs of Mesoamerican influence such as pyramid-shaped mounds and ball courts are not found at Chaco. Nor is there evidence from the excavation of burials and residences of clear class distinctions, a common feature of Mesoamerican culture. Instead, it appears that the Chaco Canyon culture developed from earlier societies in the region.

The abandonment of the major sites in Chaco Canyon in the twelfth century most likely resulted from a long drought that undermined the culture's fragile agricultural economy. Nevertheless, the Anasazi continued in the Four Corners region for more than a century after the abandonment of Chaco Canyon. There were major centers at Mesa Verde in present-day Colorado and at Canyon de Chelly and Kiet Siel in Arizona. Anasazi settlements on the Colorado Plateau and in Arizona were constructed in large natural caves high above valley floors. This hard-to-reach location suggests increased levels of warfare, probably provoked by population pressure on limited arable land. Elements of this cultural tradition survive today among the Pueblo peoples of the Rio Grande Valley and Arizona who still live in multistory villages and worship in kivas.

Mound Builders: The Adena, Hopewell, and Mississippian Cultures

The Adena people of the Ohio River Valley constructed large villages with monumental earthworks from about 500 B.C.E. This early mound-building culture was based on traditional hunting and gathering supplemented by limited cultivation of locally domesticated seed crops. Nearly all of the Adena mounds contained burials. Items found in these graves indicate a hierarchical society with an elite distinguished by its access to rare and valuable goods such as mica from North Carolina and copper from the Great Lakes region.

Around 100 C.E. the Adena culture blended into a successor culture now called Hopewell, also centered in the Ohio River Valley. The largest Hopewell centers appeared in present-day Ohio; but Hopewell influence, in the form of either colonies or trade dependencies, spread west to Illinois, Michigan, and Wisconsin, east to New York and Ontario, and south to Alabama, Louisiana, Mississippi, and even Florida (see Map 12.2). For the necessities of daily life Hopewell people were dependent on hunting and gathering and a limited agriculture inherited from the Adena.

Hopewell is an early example of a North American **chiefdom**—territory that had a population as large as 10,000 and was ruled by a chief, a hereditary leader with both religious and secular responsibilities. Chiefs organized periodic rituals of feasting and gift giving that established bonds among diverse kinship groups and guaranteed access to specialized crops and craft goods. They also managed long-distance trade, which provided luxury goods and additional food supplies.

The largest Hopewell towns in the Ohio River Valley served as ceremonial and political centers and had several thousand inhabitants. Villages had populations of a few hundred. Large mounds built to house elite burials and as platforms for temples and the residences of chiefs dominated major Hopewell centers. Chiefs and other members of the elite were buried in vaults surrounded by valuable goods such as river pearls, copper jewelry, and, in some cases, women and retainers who seem to have been sacrificed to accompany a dead chief into the afterlife. As was true of the earlier Olmec culture of Mexico, the abandonment of major Hopewell sites around 400 C.E. has no clear environmental or political explanation.

Map 12.2 Culture Areas of North America In each of the large ecological regions of North America, native peoples evolved distinctive cultures and technologies. Here the Anasazi of the arid southwest and the mound-building cultures of the Ohio and Mississippi river valleys are highlighted.

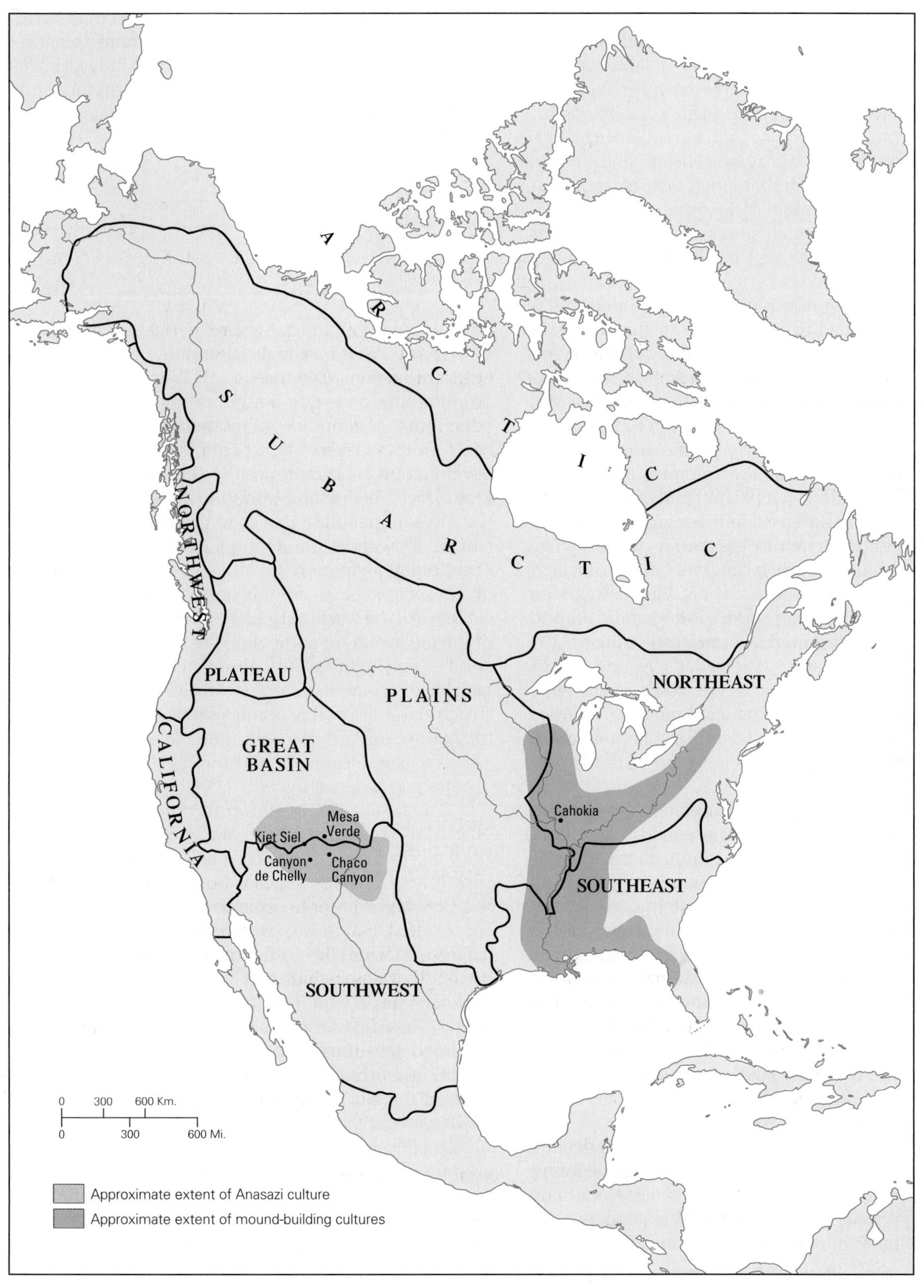
ARCTIC
SUBARCTIC
NORTHWEST
PLATEAU
PLAINS
NORTHEAST
GREAT BASIN
CALIFORNIA
SOUTHWEST
SOUTHEAST
Cahokia
Mesa Verde
Kiet Siel
Canyon de Chelly
Chaco Canyon
0 300 600 Km.
0 300 600 Mi.
Approximate extent of Anasazi culture
Approximate extent of mound-building cultures

Hopewell technology and mound building continued in smaller centers that have been linked to the development of Mississippian culture (700–1500 C.E.). As in the case of the Anasazi, some experts have suggested that contacts with Mesoamerica influenced Mississippian culture, but there is no convincing evidence to support this theory. It is true that maize, beans, and squash, all first domesticated in Mesoamerica, were closely associated with the development of the urbanized Mississippian culture. But these plants and related technologies were probably passed along through numerous intervening cultures.

The development of urbanized Mississippian chiefdoms resulted instead from the accumulated effects of small increases in agricultural productivity, the adoption of the bow and arrow, and the expansion of trade networks. An improved economy led to population growth, the building of cities, and social stratification. The largest towns shared a common urban plan based on a central plaza surrounded by large platform mounds. Major towns were trade centers where people bartered essential commodities, such as the flint used for weapons and tools.

The Mississippian culture reached its highest stage of evolution at the great urban center of Cahokia, located near the modern city of East St. Louis, Illinois (see Map 12.2). At the center of this site was the largest mound constructed in North America, a terraced structure 100 feet (30 meters) high and 1,037 by 790 feet (316 by 241 meters) at the base. Areas where commoners lived ringed the center area of elite housing and temples. At its height in about 1200 C.E., Cahokia had a population of about 20,000—about the same as some of the largest postclassic Maya cities.

Cahokia controlled surrounding agricultural lands and a number of secondary towns ruled by subchiefs. The urban center's political and economic influence depended on its location on the Missouri, Mississippi and Illinois Rivers. This location permitted canoe-based commercial exchanges as far away as the coasts of the Atlantic and the Gulf of Mexico. Sea shells, copper, mica, and flint were drawn to the city by trade and tribute from distant sources and converted into ritual goods and tools. Burial evidence suggests that the rulers of Cahokia enjoyed most of the benefits of this exalted position. In one burial more than fifty young women and retainers were apparently sacrificed to accompany a ruler on his travels after death.

As at Hopewell sites, no evidence links the decline and eventual abandonment of Cahokia, which occurred after 1250 C.E., with military defeat or civil war. Climate changes and population pressures undermined the center's vitality. Environmental degradation caused by deforestation, as more land was cleared to feed the growing population, and more intensive farming practices played roles as well. After the decline of Cahokia, smaller Mississippian centers continued to flourish in the southeast of the present-day United States until the arrival of Europeans.

ANDEAN CIVILIZATIONS, 200–1500

The Andean region of South America was an unlikely environment for the development of rich and powerful civilizations (see Map 12.3). Much of the region's mountainous zone is at altitudes that seem too high for agriculture and human habitation. Along the Pacific coast an arid climate posed a difficult challenge to the development of agriculture. To the east of the Andes Mountains, the hot and humid tropical environment of the Amazon headwaters also offered formidable obstacles to the organization of complex societies. Yet the Amerindian peoples of the Andean area produced some of the most socially complex and politically advanced societies of the Western Hemisphere. The very harshness of the environment compelled the development of productive and reliable agricultural technologies and attached them to a complex fabric of administrative structures and social relationships that became the central features of Andean civilization.

Cultural Response to Environmental Challenge

From the time of Chavín (see Chapter 3) all of the great Andean civilizations succeeded in connecting the distinctive resources of the coastal region with its abundant fisheries and irrigated maize fields to the mountainous interior with its herds of llamas and rich mix of grains and tubers. Both regions faced significant environmental challenges. The coastal region's fields were periodically overwhelmed by droughts or shifting sands that clogged irrigation works. The mountainous interior presented some of the greatest environmental challenges, averaging between 250 and 300 frosts per year.

The development of compensating technologies required an accurate calendar to time planting and harvests and the domestication of frost-resistant varieties of potatoes and grains. Native peoples learned to practice dispersed farming at different altitudes to reduce risks

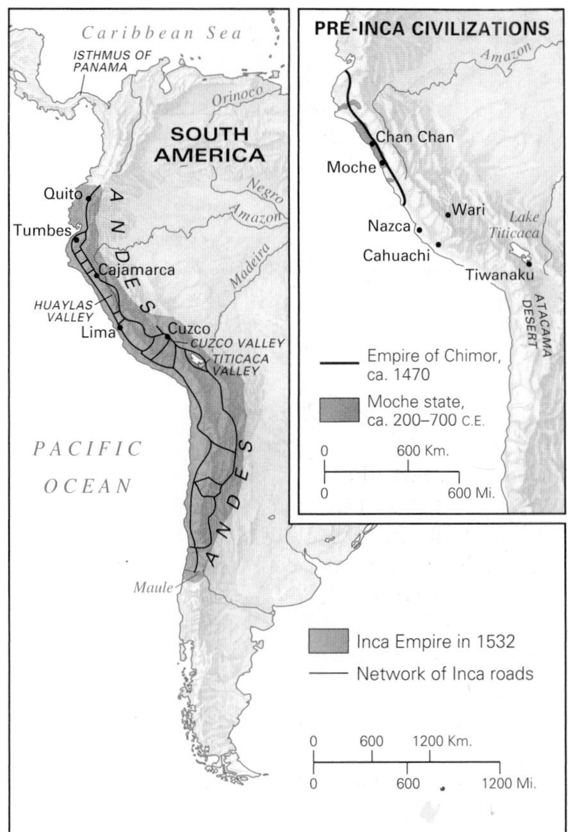

Map 12.3 Andean Civilizations, 200 B.C.E.–1532 C.E. In response to environmental challenges posed by an arid coastal plain and high interior mountain ranges, Andean peoples made complex social and technological adaptations. Irrigation systems, the domestication of the llama, metallurgy, and shared labor obligations helped provide a firm economic foundation for powerful, centralized states. In 1532 the Inca Empire's vast territory stretched from modern Chile in the south to Colombia in the north.

from frosts, and they terraced hillsides to create micro environments within a single area. They also discovered how to use the cold, dry climate to produce freeze-dried vegetable and meat products that prevented famine when crops failed. The domestication of the llama and alpaca also proved crucial, providing meat, wool, and long-distance transportation that linked coastal and mountain economies. Even though the Andean environment was harsher than that of Mesoamerica, the region's agriculture proved more dependable, and Andean peoples faced fewer famines.

The effective organization of human labor allowed the peoples of both the high mountain valleys and dry coastal plain to overcome the challenges posed by their environments. The remarkable collective achievements of Andean peoples were accomplished with a record-keeping system more limited than the one found in Mesoamerica. A system of knotted colored cords, **khipus°**, was used to aid administration and record population counts and tribute obligations. Large-scale drainage and irrigation works and the terracing of hillsides to control erosion and provide additional farmland led to an increase in agricultural production. Andean people also collectively undertook road building, urban construction, and even textile production.

The sharing of responsibilities began at the household level. But it was the clan, or **ayllu°**, that provided the foundation for Andean achievement. Members of an ayllu held land communally. Although they claimed descent from a common ancestor, they were not necessarily related. Ayllu members thought of each other as brothers and sisters and were obligated to aid each other in tasks that required more labor than a single household could provide. These reciprocal obligations provided the model for the organization of labor and the distribution of goods at every level of Andean society. Just as individuals and families were expected to provide labor to kinsmen, members of an ayllu were expected to provide labor and goods to their hereditary chief.

With the development of territorial states ruled by hereditary aristocracies and kings after 1000 B.C.E., these obligations were organized on a larger scale. The **mit'a°** was a rotational labor draft that organized members of ayllus to work the fields and care for the llama and alpaca herds owned by religious establishments, the royal court, and the aristocracy. Each ayllu contributed a set number of workers for specific tasks each year. Mit'a laborers built and maintained roads, bridges, temples, palaces, and large irrigation and drainage projects. They produced textiles and goods essential to ritual life, such as beer made from maize and coca (dried leaves chewed as a stimulant and now also the source of cocaine). The mit'a system was an essential part of the Andean world for more than a thousand years.

Work was divided along gender lines, but the work of men and women was interdependent. Hunting, military service, and government were largely reserved for men. Women had numerous responsibilities in textile production, agriculture, and the home. One early Spanish commentator described the responsibilities of Andean women in terms that sound very modern:

> [T]hey did not just perform domestic tasks, but also [labored] in the fields, in the cultivation of their lands,

khipus (KEY-pooz) **ayllu** (aye-YOU) **mit'a** (MEET-ah)

> in building houses, and carrying burdens. . . . [A]nd more than once I heard that while women were carrying these burdens, they would feel labor pains, and giving birth, they would go to a place where there was water and wash the baby and themselves. Putting the baby on top of the load they were carrying, they would then continue walking as before they gave birth. In sum, there was nothing their husbands did where their wives did not help.[7]

The ayllu was intimately tied to a uniquely Andean system of production and exchange. Because the region's mountain ranges created a multitude of small ecological areas with specialized resources, each community sought to control a variety of environments so as to guarantee access to essential goods. Coastal regions produced maize, fish, and cotton. Mountain valleys contributed quinoa (the local grain) as well as potatoes and other tubers. Higher elevations contributed the wool and meat of llamas and alpacas, and the Amazonian region provided coca and fruits. Ayllus sent out colonists to exploit the resources of these ecological niches. Colonists remained linked to their original region and kin group by marriage and ritual. Historians commonly refer to this system of controlled exchange across ecological boundaries as vertical integration, or verticality.

The historical periodization of Andean history is similar to that of Mesoamerica. Both regions developed highly integrated political and economic systems long before 1500. The pace of agricultural development, urbanization, and state formation in the Andes also approximated that in Mesoamerica. Due to the unique environmental challenges in the Andean region, however, distinctive highland and coastal cultures appeared. In the Andes, more than in Mesoamerica, geography influenced regional cultural integration and state formation.

Moche and Chimu

Around 200 C.E., some four centuries after the collapse of Chavín (see Chapter 3), the **Moche**° developed cultural and political tools that allowed them to dominate the north coastal region of Peru. Moche identity was cultural in character. They did not establish a formal empire or create unified political structures. The most powerful of the Moche urban centers, such as Cerro Blanco located near the modern Peruvian city of Trujillo (see Map 12.3), did establish hegemony over smaller towns and villages. There is also evidence that the Moche extended political and economic control over their neighbors militarily.

Moche Portrait Vase The Moche of ancient Peru were among the most accomplished ceramic artists of the Americas. Moche potters produced representations of gods and spirits, scenes of daily life, and portrait vases of important people. This man wears a headdress adorned by two birds and seashells. The stains next to the eyes of the birds represent tears. (Museo de Arqueologica y Antropologia, Lima/Lee Bolton Picture Library)

Archaeological evidence indicates that the Moche cultivated maize, quinoa, beans, manioc, and sweet potatoes with the aid of massive irrigation works. At higher elevations they also produced coca, which they used ritually. Archaeological excavations reveal the existence of complex networks of canals and aqueducts that connected fields with water sources as far away as 75 miles (121 kilometers). These hydraulic works were maintained by mit'a labor imposed on Moche commoners or on subject peoples. The Moche maintained large herds of alpacas and llamas to transport goods across the region's difficult terrain. Their wool, along with cotton provided by farmers, provided the raw material for the thriving Moche textile production. Their meat provided an important part of the diet.

Evidence from surviving murals and decorated ceramics suggests that Moche society was highly stratified and theocratic. The need to organize large numbers of laborers to construct and maintain the irrigation system helped promote class divisions. Wealth and power among the Moche was concentrated, along with political control, in the hands of priests and military leaders. Hi-

Moche (MO-che)

erarchy was further reinforced by the military conquest of neighboring regions. The residences of the elite were constructed atop large platforms at Moche ceremonial centers. The elite literally lived above the commoners. Their power was also apparent in their rich clothing and jewelry, which confirmed their divine status and set them farther apart from commoners. Moche rulers and other members of the elite wore tall headdresses. They used gold and gold alloy jewelry to mark their social position: gold plates suspended from their noses concealed the lower portion of their faces, and large gold plugs decorated their ears.

These deep social distinctions also were reflected in Moche burial practices. A recent excavation in the Lambeyeque Valley discovered the tomb of a warrior-priest who was buried with a rich treasure of gold, silver, and copper jewelry, textiles, feather ornaments, and shells (see Diversity and Dominance: Burials as Historical Texts). Retainers and servants were also buried with this powerful man to serve him in the afterlife.

Most commoners, on the other hand, devoted their time to subsistence farming and to the payment of labor dues owed to their ayllu and to the elite. Both men and women were involved in agriculture, care of llama herds, and the household economy. They lived with their families in one-room buildings clustered in the outlying areas of cities and in surrounding agricultural zones.

The high quality of Moche textiles, ceramics, and metallurgy indicates the presence of numerous skilled artisans. As had been true centuries earlier in Chavín, women had a special role in the production of textiles; even elite women devoted time to weaving. Moche culture developed a brilliant representational art. Moche craftsmen produced highly individualized portrait vases that today adorn museum collections in nearly every city of the world. Ceramics were also decorated with line drawings representing myths and rituals. The most original Moche ceramic vessels were decorated with explicit sexual acts. The Moche were also accomplished metalsmiths, producing beautiful gold and silver religious and decorative objects and items for elite adornment. Metallurgy served more practical ends as well: artisans produced a range of tools made of heavy copper and copper alloy for agricultural and military purposes.

Since we have no written sources, a detailed history of the Moche can never be written. The archaeological record makes clear that the rapid decline of the major centers coincided with a succession of natural disasters in the sixth century and with the rise of a new military power in the Andean highlands. When an earthquake altered the course of the Moche River, major flooding seriously damaged urban centers. The Moche region also was threatened by long-term climate changes. A thirty-year drought expanded the area of coastal sand dunes during the sixth century, and powerful winds pushed sand onto fragile agricultural lands, overwhelming the irrigation system. As the land dried, periodic heavy rains caused erosion that damaged fields and weakened the economy that had sustained ceremonial and residential centers. This succession of disasters undermined the authority of the religious and political leaders, whose privileges were based on their ability to control natural forces through rituals. Despite massive efforts to keep the irrigation canals open and despite the construction of new urban centers in less vulnerable valleys to the north, Moche civilization never recovered. In the eighth century, the rise of a new military power, the **Wari**°, also contributed to the disappearance of the Moche by putting pressure on trade routes that linked the coastal region with the highlands.

At the end of the Moche period the **Chimu**° developed a new and more powerful coastal civilization. Chan Chan, capital of the Empire of Chimor, was constructed around 800 C.E. near the earlier Moche cultural center. After 1200 C.E. Chimu began a period of aggressive military expansion. At the apex of its power, The Empire of Chimor controlled 625 miles (1,000 kilometers) of the Peruvian coast.

Within Chan Chan was a series of walled compounds, each one containing a burial pyramid. Scholars believe that each ruler built his own compound and was buried in it on death. Sacrifices and rich grave goods accompanied each royal burial. As did the Moche, Chimor's rulers separated themselves from the masses of society by their consumption of rare and beautiful textiles, ceramics, and precious metals as a way of suggesting the approval of the gods. Some scholars suggest that the Chimu dynasty practiced split inheritance: goods and lands of the deceased ruler went to secondary heirs or for religious sacrifices. The royal heir who inherited the throne was forced to construct his own residence compound and then undertake new conquests to fund his household. After the Inca conquered the northern coast in 1465, they borrowed from the rich rituals and court customs of the Chimu.

Tiwanaku and Wari

After 500 C.E. two powerful civilizations developed in the Andean highlands. At nearly 13,000 feet (3,962 meters) on the high treeless plain near Lake Titicaca in modern Bolivia stand the ruins of **Tiwanaku**° (see Map 12.3). Initial

Wari (WAH-ree) **Chimu** (chee-MOO)
Tiwanaku (tee-wah-NA-coo)

Diversity and Dominance

Burials as Historical Texts

Efforts to reveal the history of the Americas before the arrival of Europeans depend on the work of archaeologists. The burials of rulers and other members of elites can be viewed as historical texts that describe how textiles, precious metals, beautifully decorated ceramics, and other commodities were used to reinforce the political and cultural power of ruling lineages. In public, members of the elite were always surrounded by the most desirable and rarest products as well as by elaborate rituals and ceremonies. The effect was to create an aura of godlike power. The material elements of political and cultural power were integrated into the experience of death and burial as members of the elite were sent into the afterlife.

The first photograph is of an excavated Moche tomb in Sipán, Peru. The Moche (100 C.E.–ca. 700 C.E.) were one of the most important of the pre-Inca civilizations of the Andean region. They were masters of metallurgy, ceramics, and textiles. The excavations at Sipán revealed a "warrior/priest" buried with an amazing array of gold ornaments, jewels, textiles, and ceramics. He was also buried with two women, perhaps wives or concubines, two male servants, and a warrior. The warrior, one woman, and one man are missing feet, as if this deformation would guarantee their continued faithfulness to the deceased ruler.

The second photograph shows the excavation of a Classic-Era (250 C.E.–ca. 800 C.E.) Maya burial at Río Azul in Guatemala. Here a member of the elite was laid out on a carved wooden platform and cotton mattress; his body painted with decorations. He was covered in beautifully woven textiles and surrounded by valuable goods. Among the discoveries were a necklace of individual stones carved in the shape of heads, perhaps a symbol of his prowess in battle, high-quality ceramics, some filled with foods consumed by the elite like cacao. The careful preparation of the burial chamber had required the work of numerous artisans and laborers, as was the case in the burial of the Moche warrior/priest. In death, as in life, these early American civilizations acknowledged the high status, political power, and religious authority of their elites.

QUESTIONS FOR ANALYSIS

1. **If these burials are texts, what are stories?**
2. **Are there any visible differences in the two burials?**
3. **What questions might historians ask of these burials that cannot be answered?**
4. **Are modern burials texts in similar ways to these ancient practices?**

occupation may have occurred as early as 400 B.C.E., but significant urbanization began only after 200 C.E. Tiwanaku's expansion depended on the adoption of technologies that increased agricultural productivity. Modern excavations provide the outline of vast drainage projects that reclaimed nearly 200,000 acres (8,000 hectares) of rich lakeside marshes for agriculture. This system of raised fields and ditches permitted intensive cultivation similar to that achieved by use of chinampas in Mesoamerica. Fish from the nearby lake and llamas added protein to a diet largely dependent on potatoes and grains. Llamas were also crucial for the maintenance of long-distance trade relationships that brought in corn, coca, tropical fruits, and medicinal plants.

The urban center of Tiwanaku was distinguished by the scale of its construction and by the high quality of its stone masonry. Large stones and quarried blocks were moved many miles to construct a large terraced pyramid, walled enclosures, and a reservoir—projects that probably required the mobilization of thousands of laborers over a period of years. Despite a limited metallurgy that produced only tools of copper alloy, Tiwanaku's artisans built large structures of finely cut stone that required little mortar to fit the blocks. They also produced gigantic human statuary. The largest example, a stern figure with a military bearing, is cut from a single block of stone that measures 24 feet (7 meters) high.

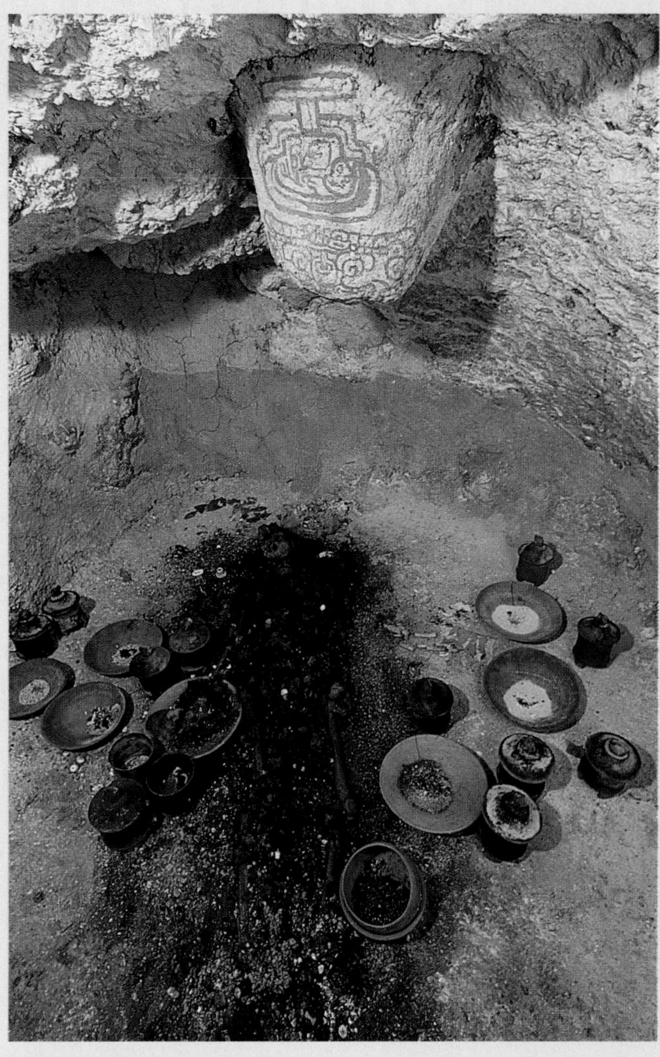

Burials Reveal Ancient Civilizations (Left) Buried around 300 C.E., this Moche warrior-priest was buried amid rich tribute at Sipán in Peru. Also, buried were the bodies of retainers or kinsmen probably sacrificed to accompany this powerful man. The body lies with the head on the right and the feet on the left. (Right) Similarly, the burial of a member of the Maya elite at Río Azul in northern Guatemala indicates the care taken to surround the powerful with fine ceramics, jewelry and other valuable goods. (*left:* Heinze Plenge/NGS Image Collection; *right:* George Mobley/NGS Image Collection)

Little is known of the social structure or daily life of this civilization. Neither surviving murals nor other decorative arts offer the suggestive guidance found in the burial goods of the Moche. Nevertheless, it is clear that Tiwanaku was a highly stratified society ruled by a hereditary elite. Most women and men devoted their time to agriculture and the care of llama herds. However, the presence of specialized artisans is evident in the high-quality construction in public buildings and in locally produced ceramics. The distribution of these ceramics to distant places suggests the presence of a specialized merchant class as well.

Many scholars portray Tiwanaku as the capital of a vast empire, a precursor to the later Inca state. It is clear that the elite controlled a large, disciplined labor force in the surrounding region. Military conquests and the establishment of colonial populations provided the highland capital with dependable supplies of products from ecologically distinct zones. Tiwanaku cultural influence extended eastward to the jungles and southward to the coastal regions and oases of the Atacama Desert in Chile. But archaeological evidence suggests that Tiwanaku, in comparison with contemporary Teotihuacan in central Mexico, had a relatively small full-time population of around 30,000. It was not a metropolis like the largest Mesoamerican cities; it was a ceremonial and political center for a large regional population.

ENVIRONMENT + TECHNOLOGY

Inca Roads

From the time of Chavín (900–250 B.C.E.), Andean peoples built roads to facilitate trade across ecological boundaries and to project political power over conquered peoples. In the fifteenth and sixteenth centuries, the Inca extended and improved the networks of roads constructed in earlier eras. Roads were crucially important to Inca efforts to collect and redistribute tribute paid in food, textiles, and chicha (corn liquor).

Two roads connected Cuzco, the Inca capital in southern Peru, to Quito, Ecudaor, in the north and to Chile farther south. One ran along the flat and arid coastal plain, the other through the mountainous interior. Shorter east-west roads connected important coastal and interior cities. Evidence suggests that administrative centers were sited along these routes to expedite rapid communication with the capital. Rest stops at convenient distances provided shelter and food to traveling officials and runners who carried messages between Cuzco and the empire's cities and towns. Warehouses were constructed along the roads to provide food and military supplies for passing Inca armies or to supply local laborers working on construction projects or cultivating the ruler's fields.

Because communication with regional administrative centers and the movement of troops were the central objectives of the Inca leadership, routes were selected to avoid natural obstacles and to reduce travel time. Mit'a laborers recruited from nearby towns and villages built and maintained the roads. Roads were commonly paved with stone or packed earth and often were bordered by stone or adobe walls to keep soldiers or pack trains of llamas from straying into farmers' fields. Whenever possible, roadbeds were made level. In mountainous terrain some roads were little more than improved paths, but in flat country three or four people could walk abreast. Care was always taken to repair damage caused by rain runoff or other drainage problems.

The achievement of Inca road builders is clearest in the mountainous terrain of the interior. They built suspension bridges across high gorges and cut roadbeds into the face of cliffs. A Spanish priest living in Peru in the seventeenth century commented that the Inca roads "were magnificent constructions, which could be compared favorably with the most superb roads of the Romans."

Source: Quotation from Father Bernabe Cobo, *History of the Inca Empire. An account of the Indians' customs and origin together with a treatise on Inca legends, history, and social institutions* (Austin: University of Texas Press, 1983), 223.

Inca Road The Inca built roads to connect distant parts of the empire to Cuzco, the Inca capital. These roads are still used in Peru. (Loren McIntyre/Woodfin Camp & Associates)

The contemporary site of Wari was located about 450 miles (751 kilometers) to the northwest of Tiwanaku, near the modern Peruvian city of Ayacucho. Wari clearly shared elements of the culture and technology of Tiwanaku, but the exact nature of this relationship remains unclear. Some scholars argue that Wari began as a dependency of Tiwanaku, while others suggest that they were joint capitals of a single empire. Recent archaeological discoveries indicate that Wari was also closely tied to Nazca, a powerful state located to the south. As was common throughout the history of the Andes, Wari benefited from its contacts and commercial exchanges with other powerful societies in the region.

Wari was larger than Tiwanaku, measuring nearly 4 square miles (10 square kilometers). The city center was surrounded by a massive wall and included a large temple. The center had numerous multifamily housing blocks. Less-concentrated housing for commoners was located in a sprawling suburban zone. Wari's development, unlike that of most other major urban centers in the Andes, appears to have occurred without central planning.

The small scale of its monumental architecture and the near absence of cut stone masonry in public and private buildings distinguish Wari from Tiwanaku. It is not clear that these characteristics resulted from the relative weakness of the elite or the absence of specialized construction crafts. There is a distinctive Wari ceramic style that has allowed experts to trace Wari's expanding power to the coastal area earlier controlled by the Moche and to the northern highlands. Wari's military expansion occurred at a time of increasing warfare throughout the Andes. As a result, roads were built to maintain communication with remote fortified dependencies. Perhaps as a consequence of military conflict, both Tiwanaku and Wari declined to insignificance by about 1000 C.E. The Inca inherited their political legacy.

The Inca

In little more than a hundred years, the **Inca** developed a vast imperial state, which they called "Land of Four Corners." By 1525 the empire had a population of more than 6 million and stretched from the Maule River in Chile to northern Ecuador and from the Pacific coast across the Andes to the upper Amazon and, in the south, into Argentina (see Map 12.3). In the early fifteenth century the Inca were one of many competing military powers in the southern highlands, an area of limited political significance after the collapse of Wari. Centered in the valley of Cuzco, the Inca were initially organized as a chiefdom based on reciprocal gift giving and the redistribution of food and textiles. Strong and resourceful leaders consolidated political authority in the 1430s and undertook an ambitious campaign of military expansion.

The Inca state, like earlier highland powers, was built on traditional Andean social customs and economic practices. Tiwanaku had relied in part on the use of colonists to provide supplies of resources from distant, ecologically distinct zones. The Inca built on this legacy by conquering additional distant territories and increasing the scale of forced exchanges. Crucial to this process was the development of a large, professional military. Unlike the peoples of Mesoamerica, who distributed specialized goods by developing markets and tribute relationships, Andean peoples used state power to broaden and expand the vertical exchange system that had permitted ayllus to exploit a range of ecological niches.

Like earlier highland civilizations, the Inca were pastoralists. Inca prosperity and military strength depended on vast herds of llamas and alpacas, which provided food and clothing as well as transport for goods. Both men and women were involved in the care of these herds. Women were primarily responsible for weaving; men were drivers in long-distance trade. This pastoral tradition provided the Inca with powerful metaphors that helped shape their political and religious beliefs. They believed that the gods and their ruler shared the obligations of the shepherd to his flock—an idea akin to references to "The Lord is my Shepherd."

Collective efforts by mit'a laborers made the Inca Empire possible. Cuzco, the imperial capital, and the provincial cities, the royal court, the imperial armies, and the state's religious cults all rested on this foundation. The mit'a system also created the material surplus that provided the bare necessities for the old, weak, and ill of Inca society. Each ayllu contributed approximately one-seventh of its adult male population to meet these collective obligations. These draft laborers served as soldiers, construction workers, craftsmen, and runners to carry messages along post roads. They also drained swamps, terraced mountainsides, filled in valley floors, built and maintained irrigation works, and built storage facilities and roads. Inca laborers constructed 13,000 miles (20,930 kilometers) of road, facilitating military troop movements, administration, and trade (see Environment and Technology: Inca Roads).

Imperial administration was similarly superimposed on existing political structures and established elite groups. The hereditary chiefs of ayllus carried out administrative and judicial functions. As the Inca expanded, they generally left local rulers in place. By leaving the rulers of defeated societies in place, the Inca risked rebellion, but they controlled these risks by means of a thinly veiled system of hostage taking and the

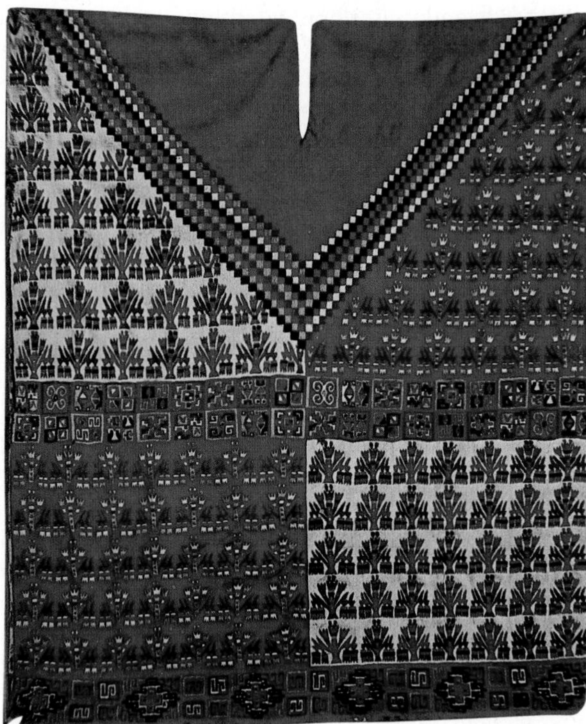

Inca Tunic Andean weavers produced beautiful textiles from cotton and from the wool of llamas and alpacas. The Inca inherited this rich craft tradition and produced some of the world's most remarkable textiles. The quality and design of each garment indicated the weaver's rank and power in this society. This tunic was an outer garment for a powerful male. (From *Textile Art of Peru.* Collection created and directed by Jose Antonio de Lavalle and Jose Alejandro Gonzalez Garcia [L. L. Editores, 1989])

use of military garrisons. The rulers of defeated regions were required to send their heirs to live at the Inca royal court in Cuzco. Inca leaders even required that representations of important local gods be brought to Cuzco and made part of the imperial pantheon. These measures promoted imperial integration while at the same time providing hostages to ensure the good behavior of subject peoples.

Conquests magnified the authority of the Inca ruler and led to the creation of an imperial bureaucracy drawn from among his kinsmen. The royal family claimed descent from the Sun, the primary Inca god. Members of the royal family lived in palaces maintained by armies of servants. The lives of the ruler and members of the royal family were dominated by political and religious rituals that helped legitimize their authority. Among the many obligations associated with kingship was the requirement to extend imperial boundaries by warfare. Thus each new ruler began his reign with conquest.

Tenochtitlan, the Aztec capital, had a population of about 150,000 in 1520. At the height of Inca power in 1530, Cuzco had a population of less than 30,000. Nevertheless, Cuzco was a remarkable place. The Inca were highly skilled stone craftsmen: their most impressive buildings were constructed of carefully cut stones fitted together without mortar. The city was laid out in the shape of a giant puma (a mountain lion). At the center were the palaces that each ruler built when he ascended to the throne, as well as the major temples. The richest was the Temple of the Sun. Its interior was lined with sheets of gold, and its patio was decorated with golden representations of llamas and corn. The ruler made every effort to awe and intimidate visitors and residents alike with a nearly continuous series of rituals, feasts, and sacrifices. Sacrifices of textiles, animals, and other goods sent as tribute dominated the city's calendar. The destruction of these valuable commodities, and a small number of human sacrifices, helped give the impression of splendor and sumptuous abundance that appeared to demonstrate the ruler's claimed descent from the Sun.

Inca cultural achievement rested on the strong foundation of earlier Andean civilizations. We know that astronomical observation was a central concern of the priestly class, as in Mesoamerica; the Inca calendar, however, is lost to us. All communication other than oral was transmitted by the khipus borrowed from earlier Andean civilizations. In weaving and metallurgy, Inca technology, building on earlier regional developments, was more advanced than in Mesoamerica. Inca craftsmen produced utilitarian tools and weapons of copper and bronze as well as decorative objects of gold and silver. Inca women produced textiles of extraordinary beauty from cotton and the wool of llamas and alpacas.

Although the Inca did not introduce new technologies, they increased economic output and added to the region's prosperity. The conquest of large populations in environmentally distinct regions allowed the Inca to multiply the yields produced by the traditional exchanges between distinct ecological niches. But the expansion of imperial economic and political power was purchased at the cost of reduced equality and diminished local autonomy. The imperial elite, living in richly decorated palaces in Cuzco and other urban centers, was increasingly cut off from the masses of Inca society. The royal court held members of the provincial nobility at arm's length, and commoners were subject to execution if they dared to look directly at the ruler's face.

After only a century of regional dominance, the Inca Empire faced a crisis in 1525. The death of the Inca ruler

Huayna Capac at the conclusion of the conquest of Ecuador initiated a bloody struggle for the throne. Powerful factions coalesced around two sons whose rivalry compelled both the professional military and the hereditary Inca elite to choose sides. Civil war was the result. The Inca state controlled a vast territory spread over more than 3,000 miles (4,830 kilometers) of mountainous terrain. Regionalism and ethnic diversity had always posed a threat to the empire. Civil war weakened imperial institutions and ignited the resentments of conquered peoples. On the eve of the arrival of Europeans, the destructive consequences of this violent conflict undermined the institutions and economy of Andean civilizations.

Conclusion

The indigenous societies of the Western Hemisphere developed unique technologies and cultural forms in mountainous regions, tropical rain forests, deserts, woodlands, and arctic regions. In Mesoamerica, North America, and the Andean region, the natural environment powerfully influenced cultural development. The Maya of southern Mexico, for example, developed agricultural technologies that compensated for the tropical cycle of heavy rains followed by long dry periods. On the coast of Peru the Moche used systems of trade and mutual labor obligation to meet the challenge of an arid climate and mountainous terrain, while the mound builders of North America expanded agricultural production by utilizing the rich floodplains of the Ohio and Mississippi Rivers. Across the Americas, hunting and gathering peoples and urbanized agricultural societies produced rich religious and aesthetic traditions as well as useful technologies and effective social institutions in response to local conditions. Once established, these cultural traditions proved very durable.

The Aztec and Inca Empires represented the culmination of a long developmental process that had begun before 1000 B.C.E. Each imperial state controlled extensive and diverse territories with populations that numbered in the millions. The capital cities of Tenochtitlan and Cuzco were great cultural and political centers that displayed some of the finest achievements of Amerindian technology, art, and architecture. Both states were based on conquests and were ruled by powerful hereditary elites who depended on the tribute of subject peoples. In both traditions religion met spiritual needs while also organizing collective life and legitimizing political authority.

The Aztec and Inca Empires were created militarily, their survival depending as much on the power of their armies as on the productivity of their economies or the wisdom of their rulers. Both empires were ethnically and environmentally diverse, but there were important differences. Elementary markets had been developed in Mesoamerica to distribute specialized regional production, although the forced payment of goods as tribute remained important. In the Andes reciprocal labor obligations and managed exchange relationships were used to allocate goods. The Aztecs used their military to force defeated peoples to provide food, textiles, and even sacrificial captives as tribute, but they left local hereditary elites in place. The Incas, in contrast, created a more centralized administrative structure managed by a trained bureaucracy.

As the Western Hemisphere's long isolation drew to a close in the late fifteenth century, both empires were challenged by powerful neighbors or by internal revolts. In earlier periods similar challenges had contributed to the decline of great civilizations in both Mesoamerica and the Andean region. In those cases, a long period of adjustment and the creation of new indigenous institutions followed the collapse of dominant powers such as the Toltecs in Mesoamerica and Tiwanaku in the Andes. With the arrival of Europeans, this cycle of crisis and adjustment would be transformed, and the future of Amerindian peoples would become linked to the cultures of the Old World.

Key Terms

Teotihuacan
chinampas
Maya
Toltecs
Aztecs
Tenochtitlan
tribute system
Anasazi
chiefdom
khipu
ayllu
mit'a
Moche
Wari
Chimu
Tiwanaku
Inca

Suggested Reading

In *Prehistory of the Americas* (1987) Stuart Fiedel provides an excellent summary of the early history of the Western Hemisphere. Alvin M. Josephy, Jr., in *The Indian Heritage of America* (1968), also provides a thorough introduction to the topic. *Canada's First Nations* (1992) by Olive Patricia Dickason is a well-written survey that traces the history of Canada's Amerindian peoples to the modern era. *Early Man in the New World,* ed. Richard Shutler, Jr. (1983), provides a helpful addition to these works. *Atlas of Ancient America* (1986) by Michael Coe, Elizabeth P. Benson, and Dean R. Snow is a useful compendium of maps and information. George Kubler, *The Art and Architecture of Ancient America* (1962), is a valuable resource, though now dated.

Eric Wolf provides an enduring synthesis of Mesoamerican history in *Sons of the Shaking Earth* (1959). A good summary of recent research on Teotihuacan is found in Esther Pasztori, *Teotihuacan* (1997). Linda Schele and David Freidel summarize the most recent research on the classic-period Maya in their excellent *A Forest of Kings* (1990). See also David Drew, *The Lost Chronicles of the Maya Kings* (1999). The best summary of Aztec history is Nigel Davies, *The Aztec Empire: The Toltec Resurgence* (1987). Jacques Soustelle, *Daily Life of the Aztecs,* trans. Patrick O'Brian (1961), is a good introduction. Though controversial in some of its analysis, Inga Clendinnen's *Aztecs* (1991) is also an important contribution.

Chaco and Hohokam (1991), ed. Patricia L. Crown and W. James Judge, is a good summary of research issues. Robert Silverberg, *Mound Builders of Ancient America* (1968), supplies a good introduction to this topic. See also *Understanding Complexity in the Prehistoric Southwest,* ed. George J. Gumerman and Murray Gell-Mann (1994).

A helpful introduction to the scholarship on early Andean societies is provided by Karen Olsen Bruhns, *Ancient South America* (1994). For the Moche see Garth Bawden, *The Moche* (1996). *The History of the Incas* (1970) by Alfred Metraux is dated but offers a useful summary. The best recent modern synthesis is María Rostworowski de Diez Canseco, *History of the Inca Realm,* trans. by Harry B. Iceland (1999). John Murra, *The Economic Organization of the Inca State* (1980), and Irene Silverblatt, *Moon, Sun, and Witches: Gender Ideologies and Class in Inca and Colonial Peru* (1987), are challenging, important works on Peru before the arrival of Columbus in the Western Hemisphere. Frederich Katz, *The Ancient Civilizations of the Americas* (1972), offers a useful comparative perspective on ancient American developments.

Notes

1. This summary closely follows the historical narrative and translation of names offered by Linda Schele and David Freidel in *A Forest of Kings: The Untold Story of the Ancient Maya* (New York: Morrow, 1990), 182–186.
2. From the Florentine Codex, quoted in Inga Clendinnen, *Aztecs* (New York: Cambridge University Press, 1991), 213.
3. Quoted in Nigel Davies, *The Toltec Heritage: From the Fall of Tula to the Rise of Tenochtitlán* (Norman: University of Oklahoma Press, 1980), 3.
4. Bernal Díaz del Castillo, *The Conquest of New Spain,* trans. J. M. Cohen (London: Penguin Books, 1963), 217.
5. Hernando Cortés, *Five Letters, 1519–1526,* trans. J. Bayard Morris (New York: Norton, 1991), 87.
6. Quoted in Irene Silverblatt, *Moon, Sun, and Witches: Gender Ideologies and Class in Inca and Colonial Peru* (Princeton, NJ: Princeton University Press, 1987), 10.
7. Quoted in Irene Silverblatt, *Moon, Sun, and Witches: Gender Ideologies and Class in Inca and Colonial Peru* (Princeton, N.J.: Princeton University Press, 1987), 10.

Religious Conversion

Religious conversion has two meanings that often get confused. The term can refer to the inner transformation an individual may feel on joining a new religious community or becoming revitalized in his or her religious belief. Conversions of this sort are often sudden and deeply emotional. In historical terms, they may be important when they transform the lives of prominent individuals.

In its other meaning, *religious conversion* refers to a change in the religious identity of an entire population, or a large portion of a population. This generally occurs slowly and is hard to trace in historical documents. As a result, historians have sometimes used superficial indicators to trace the spread of a religion. Doing so can result in misleading conclusions, such as considering the spread of the Islamic faith to be the result of forced conversion by Arab conquerors, or taking the routes traveled by Christian or Buddhist missionaries as evidence that the people they encountered adopted their spiritual message, or assuming that a king or chieftain's adherence to a new religion immediately resulted in a religious change among subjects or followers.

In addition to being difficult to document, religious conversion in the broad societal sense has followed different patterns according to changing circumstances of time and place. Historians have devised several models to explain the different conversion patterns. According to one model, religious labels in a society change quickly, through mass baptism, for example, but devotional practices remain largely the same. Evidence for this can be found in the continuation of old religious customs among people who identify themselves as belonging to a new religion. Another model sees religious change as primarily a function of economic benefit or escape from persecution. Taking this approach makes it difficult to explain the endurance of certain religious communities in the face of hardship and discrimination. Nevertheless, most historians pay attention to economic advantage in their assessments of mass conversion. A third model associates a society's religious conversion with its desire to adopt a more sophisticated way of life, by shifting, for example, from a religion that does not use written texts to one that does.

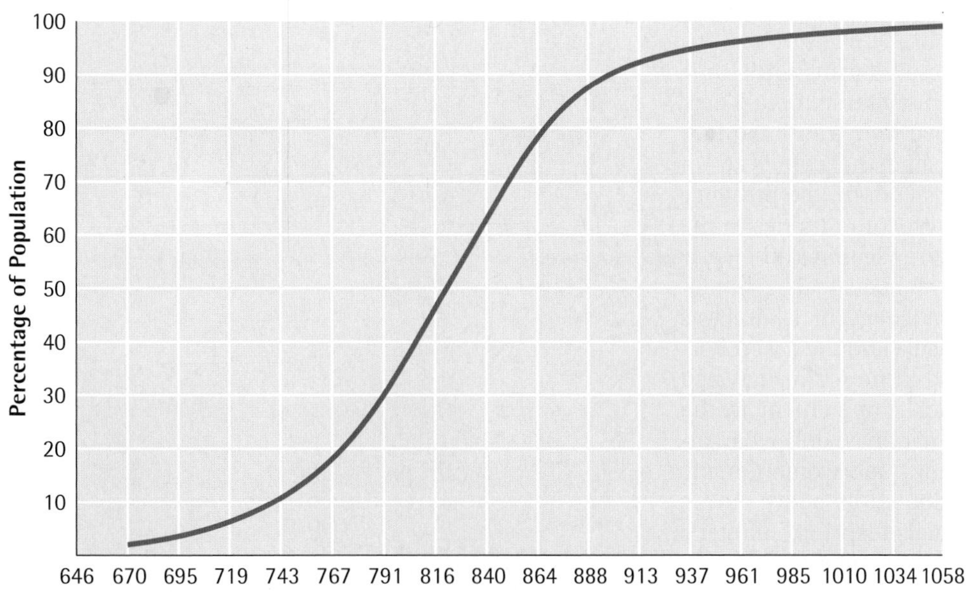

Figure 1 Conversion to Islam in Iran *Source:* Richard W. Bulliet, *Conversion to Islam in the Medieval Period,* Cambridge, MA: Harvard University Press, 1979, 23. Copyright ©1979 by the President and Fellows of Harvard College.

One final conceptual approach to explaining the process of mass religious change draws on the quantitative models of innovation diffusion that were originally developed to analyze the spread of new technologies in the twentieth century. According to this approach, new ideas, whether in the material or religious realm, depend on the spread of information. A few early adopters—missionaries, pilgrims, or conquerors, perhaps—spread word of the new faith to the people they come in contact with, some of whom follow their example and convert. Those converts in turn spread the word to others, and a chain reaction picks up speed in what might be called a bandwagon effect. The period of bandwagon conversion tapers off when the number of people who have not yet been offered an opportunity to convert diminishes. The entire process can be graphed as a *logistic* or S-shaped curve. Figure 1, the graph of conversion to Islam in Iran based on changes from Persian (non-Islamic) to Arabic (Islamic) names in family genealogies, shows such a curve over a period of almost four centuries.

In societies that were largely illiterate, like those in which Buddhism, Christianity, and Islam slowly achieved spiritual dominance, information spread primarily by word of mouth. The proponents of the new religious views did not always speak the same language as the people they hoped to bring into the faith. Under these circumstances, significant conversion, that is, conversion that involved some understanding of the new religion, as opposed to forced baptism or imposed mouthing of a profession of faith, must surely have started with fairly small numbers.

Language was crucial. Chinese pilgrims undertook lengthy travels to visit early Buddhist sites in India. There they acquired Sanskrit texts, which they translated into Chinese. These translations became the core texts of Chinese Buddhism. In early Christendom, the presence of bilingual (Greek-Aramaic) Jewish communities in the eastern parts of the Roman Empire facilitated the early spread of the religion beyond its Aramaic-speaking homeland. By contrast, Arabic, the language of Islam, was spoken only in the Arabian peninsula and the desert borderlands that extended northwards from Arabia between Syria, Jordan, and Iraq. This initial impediment to the spread of knowledge about Islam dissolved only when intermarriage with non-Muslim, non-Arab women, many of them taken captive and distributed as booty during the conquests, produced bilingual offspring. Bilingual preachers of the Christian faith were similarly needed in the Celtic, Germanic, and Slavic language areas of western and eastern Europe.

This slow process of information diffusion, which varied from region to region, made changing demands on religious leaders and institutions. When a faith was professed primarily by a ruler, his army, and his dependents, religious leaders gave the highest priority to servicing the needs of the ruling minority and perhaps discrediting, denigrating, or exterminating the practices of the majority. Once a few centuries had passed and the new faith had become the religion of the great majority of the population, religious leaders turned to establishing popular institutions and reaching out to the common people. Historical interpretation can benefit from knowing where a society is in a long-term process of conversion.

These various models reinforce the importance of distinguishing between emotional individual conversion experiences and broad changes in a society's religious identity. New converts are commonly thought of as especially zealous in their faith, and that description is often apt in instances of individual conversion experiences. It is less appropriate, however, to broader episodes of conversion. In a conversion wave that starts slowly, builds momentum in the bandwagon phase, and then tapers off, the first individuals to convert are likely to be more spiritually motivated than those who join the movement toward its end. Religious growth depends as much on making the faith attractive to late converts as to ecstatic early converts.

PART FOUR

Interregional Patterns of Culture and Contact, 1200–1550

In Eurasia, overland trade along the Silk Road, which had begun before the Roman and Han empires, reached its peak during the era of the Mongol empires. Beginning in 1206 with the rise of Genghis Khan, the Mongols tied Europe, the Middle East, Russia, and East Asia together with threads of conquest and trade centered on Central and Inner Asia. For over a century and a half, some communities thrived on the continental connections that the Mongols fostered, while others groaned under the tax burdens and physical devastation of Mongol rule. But whether for good or ill, Mongol power was based on the skills, strategies, and technologies of the overland trade and life on the steppes.

The impact of the Mongols was also felt by societies that escaped conquest. In Eastern Europe, the Mediterranean coastal areas of the Middle East, Southeast Asia, and Japan, fear of Mongol attack stimulated societies to organize more intensively in their own defense, accelerating processes of urbanization, technological development, and political centralization that in many cases were already underway.

By 1500, Mongol dominance was past, and new powers had emerged. A new Chinese empire, the Ming, was expanding its influence in Southeast

Asia. The Ottomans had captured Constantinople and overthrown the Byzantine Empire. And the Christian monarchs who had defeated the Muslims in Spain and Portugal were laying the foundations of new overseas empires. With the fall of the Mongol Empire, Central and Inner Asia were no longer at the center of Eurasian trade.

As the overland trade of Eurasia faded, merchants, soldiers, and explorers took to the seas. The most spectacular of the early state-sponsored long-distance ocean voyages were undertaken by the Chinese admiral Zheng He. The 1300s and 1400s also saw African exploration of the Atlantic and Polynesian colonization of the central and eastern Pacific. By 1500 the navigator Christopher Columbus, sailing for Spain, had reached the Americas; within twenty-five years a Portuguese ship would sail all the way around the world. New sailing technologies and a sounder knowledge of the size of the globe and the contours of its shorelines made sub-Saharan Africa, the Indian Ocean, Asia, Europe, and finally the Americas more accessible to each other than ever before.

The great overland routes of Eurasia had generated massive wealth in East Asia and a growing hunger for commerce in Europe. These factors animated the development of the sea trade, too. Exposure to the achievements, wealth, and resources of societies in the Americas, sub-Saharan Africa, and Asia enticed the emerging European monarchies to pursue further exploration and control of the seas.

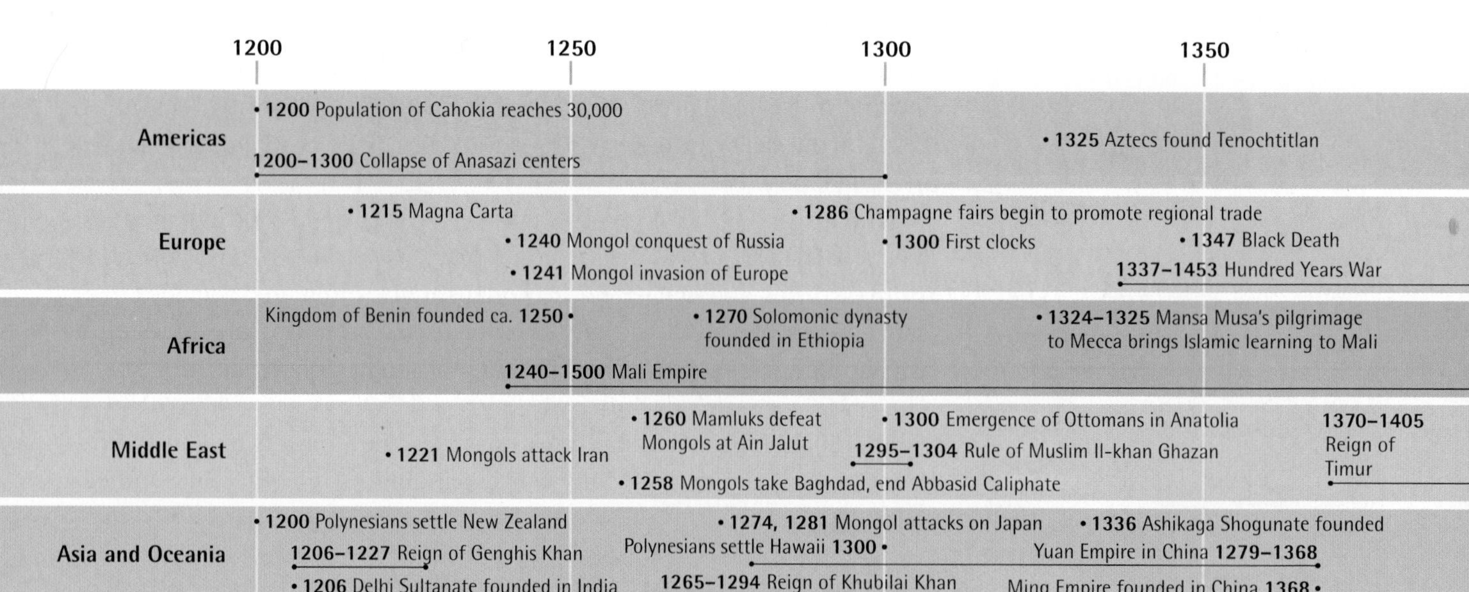
1200
1250
1300
1350
Americas
• 1200 Population of Cahokia reaches 30,000
1200–1300 Collapse of Anasazi centers
• 1325 Aztecs found Tenochtitlan
Europe
• 1215 Magna Carta
• 1240 Mongol conquest of Russia
• 1241 Mongol invasion of Europe
• 1286 Champagne fairs begin to promote regional trade
• 1300 First clocks
• 1347 Black Death
1337–1453 Hundred Years War
Africa
Kingdom of Benin founded ca. 1250 •
• 1270 Solomonic dynasty founded in Ethiopia
• 1324–1325 Mansa Musa's pilgrimage to Mecca brings Islamic learning to Mali
1240–1500 Mali Empire
Middle East
• 1221 Mongols attack Iran
• 1260 Mamluks defeat Mongols at Ain Jalut
• 1258 Mongols take Baghdad, end Abbasid Caliphate
• 1300 Emergence of Ottomans in Anatolia
1295–1304 Rule of Muslim Il-khan Ghazan
1370–1405 Reign of Timur
Asia and Oceania
• 1200 Polynesians settle New Zealand
1206–1227 Reign of Genghis Khan
• 1206 Delhi Sultanate founded in India
• 1274, 1281 Mongol attacks on Japan
Polynesians settle Hawaii 1300 •
1265–1294 Reign of Khubilai Khan
• 1336 Ashikaga Shogunate founded
Yuan Empire in China 1279–1368
Ming Empire founded in China 1368 •

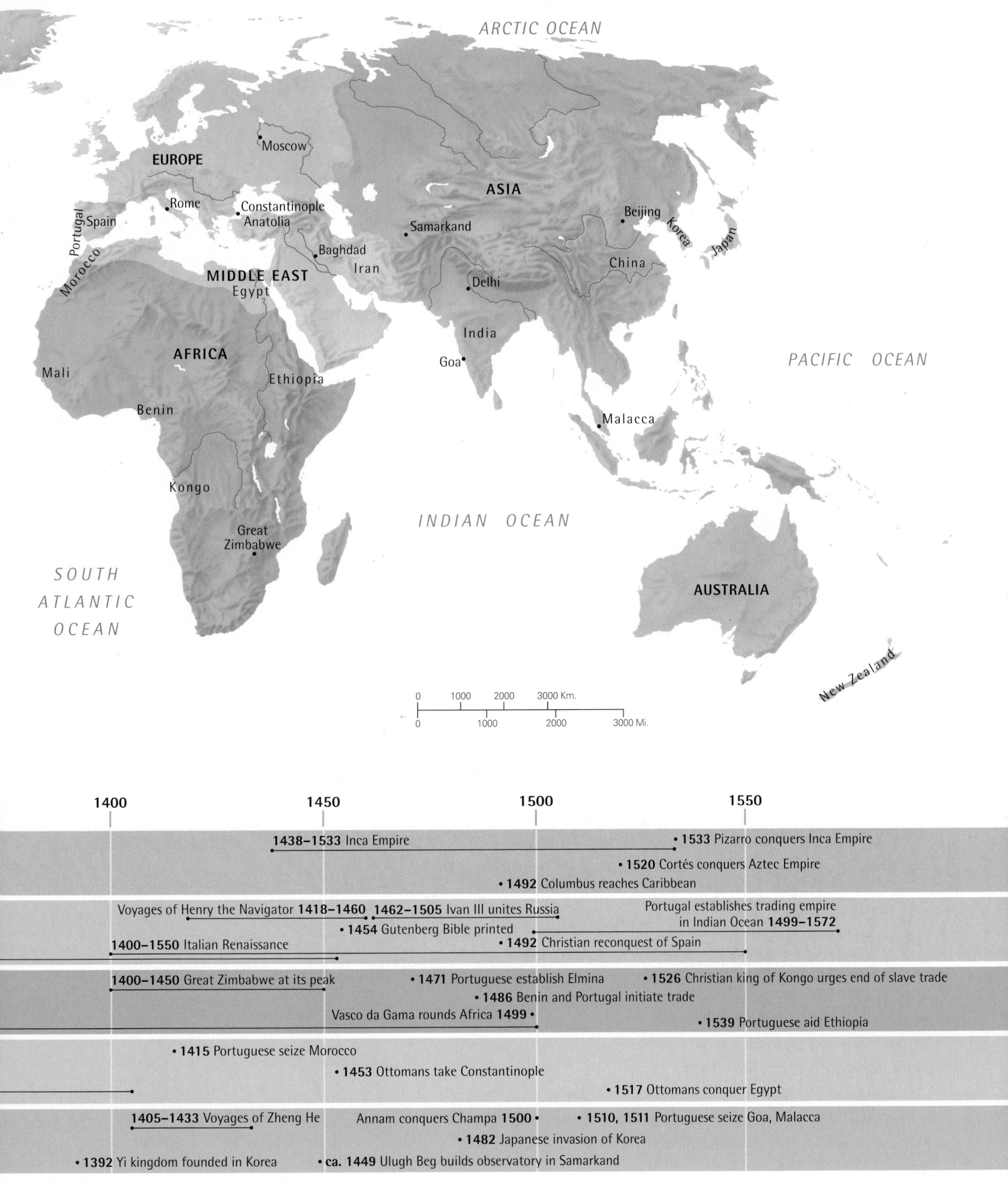
ARCTIC OCEAN
Moscow
EUROPE
ASIA
Rome
Constantinople
Anatolia
Portugal
Spain
Beijing
Korea
Japan
Samarkand
Baghdad
Iran
Morocco
MIDDLE EAST
Egypt
China
Delhi
India
Goa
PACIFIC OCEAN
AFRICA
Mali
Ethiopia
Benin
Malacca
Kongo
INDIAN OCEAN
Great Zimbabwe
SOUTH ATLANTIC OCEAN
AUSTRALIA
New Zealand
0 1000 2000 3000 Km.
0 1000 2000 3000 Mi.
1400
1450
1500
1550
1438–1533 Inca Empire
• 1533 Pizarro conquers Inca Empire
• 1520 Cortés conquers Aztec Empire
• 1492 Columbus reaches Caribbean
Voyages of Henry the Navigator 1418–1460
1462–1505 Ivan III unites Russia
Portugal establishes trading empire in Indian Ocean 1499–1572
• 1454 Gutenberg Bible printed
1400–1550 Italian Renaissance
• 1492 Christian reconquest of Spain
1400–1450 Great Zimbabwe at its peak
• 1471 Portuguese establish Elmina
• 1526 Christian king of Kongo urges end of slave trade
• 1486 Benin and Portugal initiate trade
Vasco da Gama rounds Africa 1499 •
• 1539 Portuguese aid Ethiopia
• 1415 Portuguese seize Morocco
• 1453 Ottomans take Constantinople
• 1517 Ottomans conquer Egypt
1405–1433 Voyages of Zheng He
Annam conquers Champa 1500 •
• 1510, 1511 Portuguese seize Goa, Malacca
• 1482 Japanese invasion of Korea
• 1392 Yi kingdom founded in Korea
• ca. 1449 Ulugh Beg builds observatory in Samarkand

13 Mongol Eurasia and Its Aftermath, 1200–1500

Defending Japan Japanese warriors board Mongol warships with swords to prevent the landing of the invasion force in 1281.

CHAPTER OUTLINE

When the Mongol leader Temüjin° was a boy, a rival group murdered his father. Temüjin's mother tried to shelter him (and protect him from dogs, which he feared), but she could not find a safe haven. At fifteen Temüjin sought refuge with the leader of the Keraits°, one of Mongolia's many warring confederations. The Keraits spoke Turkic and respected both Christianity and Buddhism. Gifted with strength, courage, and intelligence, Temüjin learned the importance of religious tolerance, the necessity of dealing harshly with enemies, and the variety of Central Asia's cultural and economic traditions.

In 1206 the **Mongols** and their allies acknowledged Temüjin as **Genghis Khan°**, or supreme leader. His advisers included speakers of many languages and adherents of all the major religions of the Middle East and East Asia. His deathbed speech, which cannot be literally true even though a contemporary recorded it, captures the strategy behind Mongol success: "If you want to retain your possessions and conquer your enemies, you must make your subjects submit willingly and unite your diverse energies to a single end."[1] By implementing this strategy, Genghis Khan became the most famous conqueror in history, initiating an expansion of Mongol dominion that by 1250 stretched from Poland to northern China.

Scholars today stress the immense impact Temüjin and his successors had on the later medieval world, and the positive developments that transpired under Mongol rule. European and Asian sources of the time, however, vilify the Mongols as agents of death, suffering, and conflagration, a still-common viewpoint based on reliable accounts of horrible massacres.

The tremendous extent of the Mongol Empire promoted the movement of people and ideas from one end of Eurasia to the other. Specialized skills developed in different parts of the world spread rapidly throughout the Mongol domains. Trade routes improved, markets expanded, and the demand for products grew. Trade on the Silk Road, which had declined with the fall of the Tang Empire (see Chapter 11), revived.

During their period of domination, lasting from 1218 to about 1350 in western Eurasia and to 1368 in China, the Mongols focused on specific economic and strategic interests and usually permitted local cultures to survive and continue to develop. In some regions, local reactions to Mongol domination and unification sowed seeds of regional and ethnic identity that grew extensively in the period of Mongol decline. Societies in regions as widely separated as Russia, Iran, China, Korea, and Japan benefited from the Mongol stimulation of economic and cultural exchange and also found in their opposition to the Mongols new bases for political consolidation and affirmation of cultural difference.

As you read this chapter, ask yourself the following questions:

- What accounts for the magnitude and speed of the Mongol conquests?
- What benefits resulted from the integration of Eurasia in the Mongol Empire?
- How did the effect of Mongol rule on Russia and the lands of Islam differ from its effect on East Asia?
- In what ways did the Ming Empire continue or discontinue Mongol practices?

The Rise of the Mongols, 1200–1260

The environment, economic life, cultural institutions, and political traditions of the steppes (prairies) and deserts of Central and Inner Asia contributed to the expansion and contraction of empires. The Mongol Empire owes much of its success to these long-term conditions. Yet the interplay of environment and technology, on the one hand, and specific human actions, on the other, cannot easily be determined. The way of life known as **nomadism** gives rise to imperial expansion only occasionally, and historians disagree about what triggers these episodes. In the case of the Mongols, a precise assessment of the personal contributions of Genghis Khan and his followers remains uncertain.

Temüjin (TEM-uh-jin) **Keraits** (keh-rates)
Genghis Khan (GENG-iz KAHN)

Nomadism in Central and Inner Asia

Descriptions of steppe nomads from as early as the Greek writer Herodotus in the sixth century B.C.E. portray them as superb riders, herdsmen, and hunters. Traditional accounts maintain that the Mongols put their infants on goats to accustom them to riding. Moving regularly and efficiently with flocks and herds required firm decision making, and the independence of individual Mongols and their families made this decision making public, with many voices being heard. A council with representatives from powerful families ratified the decisions of the leader, the *khan*. Yet people who disagreed with a decision could strike off on their own. Even during military campaigns, warriors moved with their families and possessions.

Menial work in camps fell to slaves—people who were either captured during warfare or who sought refuge in slavery to escape starvation. Weak groups secured land rights and protection from strong groups by providing them with slaves, livestock, weapons, silk, or cash. More powerful groups, such as Genghis Khan's extended family and descendants, lived almost entirely off tribute, so they spent less time and fewer resources on herding and more on warfare designed to secure greater tribute.

Leading families combined resources and solidified intergroup alliances through arranged marriages and other acts, a process that helped generate political federations. Marriages were arranged in childhood—in Temüjin's case, at the age of eight—and children thus became pawns of diplomacy. Women from prestigious families could wield power in negotiation and management, though they ran the risk of assassination or execution just like men (see Diversity and Dominance: Mongol Politics, Mongol Women).

Families often included believers in two or more religions, most commonly Buddhism, Christianity, or Islam. Virtually all Mongols observed the practices of traditional shamanism, rituals in which special individuals visited and influenced the supernatural world. Whatever their faith, the Mongols believed in world rulership by a khan who, with the aid of his shamans, could speak to and for an ultimate god, represented as Sky or Heaven. This universal ruler transcended particular cultures and dominated them all.

The Mongols were not unfamiliar with agriculture or unwilling to use products grown by farmers, but their ideal was self-sufficiency. Since their wanderings with their herds normally took them far from any farming region, self-sufficiency dictated foods they could provide for themselves—primarily meat and milk—and clothing made from felt, leather, and furs. Women oversaw the breeding and birthing of livestock and the preparation of furs.

Mongol dependency on settled regions related primarily to iron for bridles, stirrups, cart fittings, and weapons. They acquired iron implements in trade and reworked them to suit their purposes. As early as the 600s the Turks, a related pastoral people, had large ironworking stations south of the Altai Mountains in western Mongolia. Neighboring agricultural states tried to limit the export of iron but never succeeded. Indeed, Central Asians developed improved techniques of iron forging, which the agricultural regions then adopted. The Mongols revered iron and the secrets of ironworking. Temüjin means "blacksmith," and several of his prominent followers were the sons of blacksmiths.

Steppe nomads situated near settled areas traded wool, leather, and horses for wood, cotton and cottonseed, silk, vegetables, grain, and tea. An appreciation of the value of permanent settlements for growing grain and cotton, as well as for working iron, led some nomadic groups to establish villages at strategic points, often with the help of migrants from the agricultural regions. The frontier regions east of the Caspian Sea and in northern China thus became economically and culturally diverse. Despite their interdependence, nomads and farmers often came into conflict. On rare occasion such conflicts escalated into full-scale invasions in which the martial prowess of the nomads usually resulted in at least temporary victory.

The Mongol Conquests, 1215–1283

Shortly after his acclamation in 1206 Genghis set out to convince the kingdoms of Eurasia to pay him tribute. Two decades of Mongol aggression followed. By 1209 he had forced the Tanggut rulers of northwest China to submit, and in 1215 he captured the Jin capital of Yanjing, today known as Beijing. He began to attack the west in 1219 with a full-scale invasion of a Central Asian state centered on Khwarezm, an oasis area east of the Caspian Sea. By 1221 he had overwhelmed most of Iran. By this time his conquests had gained such momentum that Genghis did not personally participate in all campaigns, and subordinate generals sometimes led the Mongol armies, which increasingly contained non-Mongol nomads as well.

Genghis Khan died in 1227. His son and successor, the Great Khan Ögödei° (see Figure 13.1), continued to

Ögödei (ERG-uh-day)

CHRONOLOGY

	Mongolia and China	Central Asia and Middle East	Russia	Korea, Japan, and Southeast Asia
1200	**1206** Temüjin chosen Genghis Khan of the Mongols **1227** Death of Genghis Khan **1227–1241** Reign of Great Khan Ögödei **1234** Mongols conquer northern China **1271** Founding of Yuan Empire **1279** Mongol conquest of Southern Song	**1221–1223** First Mongol attacks in Iran **1250** Mamluk regime controls Egypt and Syria **1258** Mongols sack Baghdad and kill the caliph **1260** Mamluks defeat Il-khans at Ain Jalut **1295** Il-khan Ghazan converts to Islam	**1221–1223** First Mongol attacks on Russia **1240** Mongols sack Kiev **1242** Alexander Nevskii defeats Teutonic Knights **1260** War between Il-khans and Golden Horde	**1258** Mongols conquer Koryo rulers in Korea **1274, 1281** Mongols attack Japan **1283** Yuan invades Annam **1293** Yuan attacks Java
1300	**1368** Ming Empire founded	**1349** End of Il-khan rule **ca. 1350** Egypt infected by plague **1370–1405** Reign of Timur	**1346** Plague outbreak at Kaffa	**1333–1338** End of Kamakura Shogunate in Japan, beginning of Ashikaga **1392** Founding of Yi kingdom in Korea
1400	**1403–1424** Reign of Yongle **1405–1433** Voyages of Zheng He **1449** Mongol attack on Beijing	**1402** Timur defeats Ottoman sultan **1453** Ottomans capture Constantinople	**1462–1505** Ivan III establishes authority as tsar. Moscow emerges as major political center.	**1471–1500** Annam conquers Champa

Diversity and Dominance

Mongol Politics, Mongol Women

Women in nomadic societies often enjoy more freedom and wield greater influence than women in villages and towns. The wives or mothers of Mongol rulers traditionally managed state affairs during the interregnum between a ruler's death and the selection of a successor. Princes and heads of ministries treated such regents with great deference and obeyed their commands without question. Since a female regent could not herself succeed to the position of khan, her political machinations usually focused on gaining the succession for a son or other male relative.

The History of the World-Conqueror *by the Iranian historian 'Ata-Malik Juvaini, elegantly written in Persian during the 1250s, combines a glorification of the Mongol rulers with an unflinching picture of the cruelties and devastation inflicted by their conquests. As a Muslim, he explains these events as God's punishment for Muslim sins. But this religious viewpoint does not detract from his frank depiction of the instruments of Mongol domination and the fate of those who tried to resist.*

When [Qa'an, i.e., Ögödei, Genghis Khan's son and successor] was on his hunting ground someone brought him two or three water-melons. None of his attendants had any [money] or garments available, but Möge Khatun [his wife], who was present, had two pearls in her ears like the two bright stars of the Lesser Bear when rendered auspicious by conjunction with the radiant moon. Qa'an ordered these pearls to be given to the man. But as they were very precious she said: "This man does not know their worth and value: it is like giving saffron to a donkey. If he is commanded to come to the *ordu* [residence] tomorrow, he will there receive [money] and clothing." "He is a poor man," said Qa'an, "and cannot bear to wait until tomorrow. And whither should these pearls go? They too will return to us in the end. . . ."

At Qa'an's command she gave the pearls to the poor man, and he went away rejoicing and sold them for a small sum, round about two thousand dinars [Note: this is actually a very large sum]. The buyer was very pleased and thought to himself: "I have acquired two fine jewels fit for a present to the Emperor. He is rarely brought such gifts as these." He accordingly took the pearls to the Emperor, and at that time Möge Khatun was with him. Qa'an took the pearls and said: "Did we not say they would come back to us?" . . . And he distinguished the bearer with all kinds of favours. . . .

When the decree of God Almighty had been executed and the Monarch of the World . . . . Qa'an had passed away, Güyük, his eldest son, had not returned from the campaign against the Qifchaq, and therefore in accordance with precedent the dispatch of orders and the assembling of the people took place at the door of the *ordu*, or palace of his wife, Möge Khatun, who, in accordance with the Mongol custom, had come to him from his father, Chinggiz-Khan. But since Töregene Khatun was the mother of his eldest sons and was moreover shrewder and more sagacious than Möge Khatun, she sent messages to the princes, i.e. the brothers and nephews of the Qa'an, and told them of what had happened and of the death of Qa'an, and said that until a Khan was appointed by agreement someone would have to be ruler and leader in order that the business of state might not be neglected nor the affairs of the commonweal thrown into confusion; in order, too, that the army and the court might be kept under control and the interests of the people protected.

Chaghatai [another of Genghis's sons] and the other princes sent representatives to say that Töregene Khatun was the mother of the princes who had a right to the Khanate; therefore, until a *quriltai* [family council] was held, it was she that should direct the affairs of the state, and the old ministers should remain in the service of the Court, so that the old and new *yasas* [imperial decrees] might not be changed from what was the law.

Now Töregene Khatun was a very shrewd and capable woman, and her position was greatly strengthened by this unity and concord. And when Möge Khatun shortly followed in the wake of Qa'an [i.e., died], by means of finesse and cunning she obtained control of all the affairs of state and won over the hearts of her relatives by all kind of favours and kindnesses and by the sending of gifts and presents. And for the most part strangers and kindred, family and army inclined towards her, and submitted themselves obediently and gladly to her commands and prohibitions, and came under her sway. . . .

And when Güyük came to his mother, he took no part in affairs of state, and Töregene Khatun still executed the decrees of the Empire although the Khanate was settled upon her son. But when two or three months had passed and the son was somewhat estranged from his mother on account of Fatima [see below], the decree of God the Almighty and Glorious was fulfilled and Töregene passed away. . . .

And at that time there was a woman called Fatima, who had acquired great influence in the service of Töregene Khatun and to whose counsel and capability were entrusted all affairs of state. . . .

At the time of the capture of the place [Mashhad, Iran] in which there lies the Holy Shrine of 'Ali ar-Riza [the eighth Shi'ite Imam], she was carried off into captivity. It so chanced she came to Qara-Qorum [Karakorum], where she was a procuress in the market; and in the arts of shrewdness and cunning the wily Delilah could have been her pupil. During the reign of Qa'an she had constant access to the *ordu* of Töregene Khatun; and when times changed and Chinqai [a high official] withdrew from the scene, she enjoyed even greater favour, and her influence became paramount; so that she became the sharer of intimate confidences and the depository of hidden secrets, and the ministers were debarred from executing business, and she was free to issue commands and prohibitions. And from every side the grandees sought her protection, especially the grandees of Khorasan [where Mashhad is located]. And there also came to her certain of the *sayyids* [i.e., descendants of Muhammad] of the Holy Shrine [the tomb of 'Ali ar-Riza], for she claimed to be of the race of the great *sayyids*.

When Güyük succeeded to the Khanate, a certain native of Samarqand, who was said to be an 'Alid [i.e., descendant of Muhammad], one Shira . . . hinted that Fatima had bewitched Köten [another of Töregene Khatun's sons], which was why he was so indisposed. When Köten returned, the malady from which he was suffering grew worse, and he sent a messenger to his brother Güyük to say that he had been attacked by that illness because of Fatima's magic and that if anything happened to him Güyük should seek retribution from her. Following on this message there came tidings of Köten's death. Chinqai, who was now a person of authority, reminded Güyük of the message, and he sent an envoy to his mother to fetch Fatima. His mother refused to let her go saying that she would bring her herself. He sent again several times, and each time she refused him in a different way. As a result his relations with his mother became very bad, and he sent the man from Samarqand with instructions to bring Fatima by force if his mother should still delay in sending her or find some reason for refusing. It being no longer possible to excuse herself, she agreed to send Fatima; and shortly afterwards she passed away. Fatima was brought face to face with Güyük, and was kept naked, and in bonds, and hungry and thirsty for many days and nights; she was plied with all manner of violence, severity, harshness and intimidation; and at last she confessed to the calumny of the slanderous talebearer and avowed her falseness . . . She was rolled up in a sheet of felt and thrown into the river.

And everyone who was connected with her perished also. And messengers were sent to fetch certain persons who had come from the Shrine and claimed to be related to her; and they suffered many annoyances.

This was the year in which Güyük Khan went to join his father, and it was then that 'Ali Khoja of Emil accused Shira of the same crime, namely of bewitching Khoja. He was cast into bonds and chains and remained imprisoned for nearly two years, during which time by reason of all manner of questioning and punishment he despaired of the pleasure of life. And when he recognized and knew of a certainty that this was [his] punishment he resigned himself to death and surrendering his body to the will of Fate and Destiny confessed to a crime which he had not committed. He too was cast into the river, and his wives and children were put to the sword. . . .

[I]n that same year, in a happy and auspicious hour, the Khanate had been settled upon Mengü Qa'an. . . . And when Khoja was brought to the Qa'an, a messenger was sent to 'Ali Khoja, who was one of his courtiers. Some other person brought the same accusation against him, and Mengü-Qa'an ordered him to be beaten from the left and the right until all his limbs were crushed; and so he died. And his wives and children were cast into the baseness of slavery and disgraced and humiliated.

And it is not hidden from the wise and intelligent man, who looks at these matters in the light of understanding and reflects and ponders on them, that the end of treachery and the conclusion of deceit, which spring from evil ways and wicked pretensions, is shameful and the termination thereof unlucky. . . . God preserve us from the like positions and from trespassing into the region of deliberate offenses!

QUESTIONS FOR ANALYSIS

1. **How do the stories of Töregene Khatun and Fatima differ in their presentation of female roles?**
2. **What does the passage indicate concerning the respect of the Mongols for women?**
3. **What does Güyük's refusal to take over the affairs of state while his mother is still alive imply?**

Source: Reprinted by permission of the publisher from 'Ala-ad-Din 'Ata-Malik Juvaini, *The History of the World-Conqueror*, vol. 1, trans. John Andrew Boyle (Cambridge, MA: Harvard University Press, 1958), 211–212, 239–248.

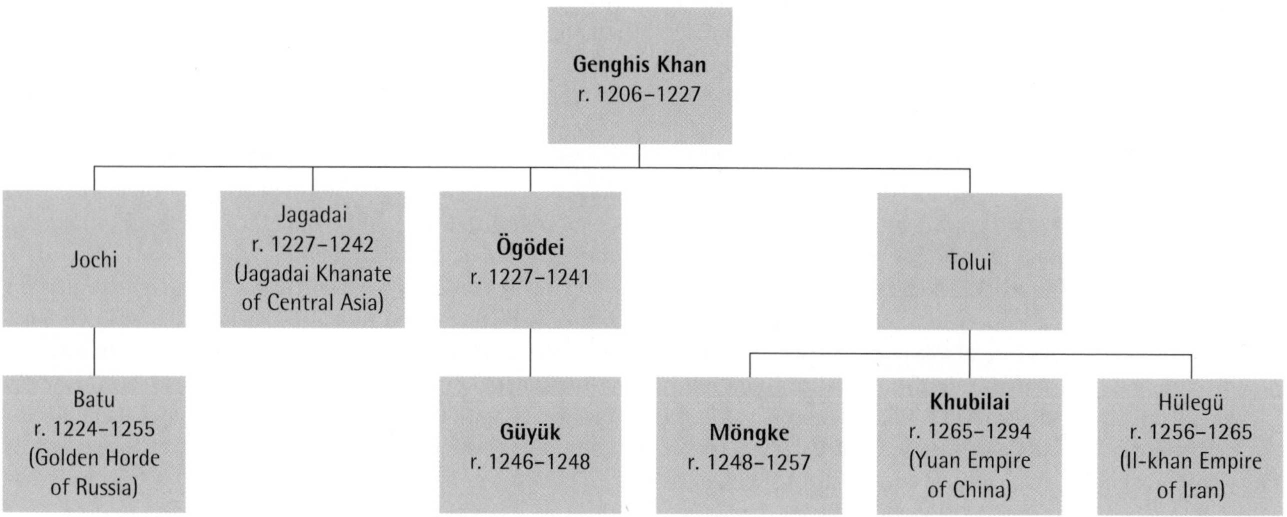

Figure 13.1 Mongol Rulers, 1206–1260 The names of the Great Khans are shown in bold type. Those who founded the regional khanates are listed with their dates of rule.

assault China. He destroyed the Tanggut and then the Jin and put their territories under Mongol governors. In 1236 Genghis's grandson Batu° (d. 1255) attacked Russian territories, took control of all the towns along the Volga° River, and within five years conquered Kievan Russia, Moscow, Poland, and Hungary. Europe would have suffered grave damage in 1241 had not the death of Ögödei compelled the Mongol forces to suspend their campaign. With Genghis's grandson Güyük° installed as the new Great Khan, the conquests resumed. By 1234 the Mongols controlled most of northern China and were threatening the Southern Song. In the Middle East they sacked Baghdad in 1258 and executed the last Abbasid caliph (see Chapter 9).

Although the Mongols' original objective may have been tribute, the scale and success of the conquests created a new historical situation. Ögödei unquestionably sought territorial rule. Between 1240 and 1260 his imperial capital at Karakorum° attracted merchants, ambassadors, missionaries, and adventurers from all over Eurasia. A European who visited in 1246 found the city isolated but well populated and cosmopolitan.

The Mongol Empire remained united until about 1265, as the Great Khan in Mongolia exercised authority over the khans of the Golden Horde in Russia, the khans of the Jagadai domains in Central Asia, and the Il-khans in Iran (see Map 13.1). After Ögödei's death in 1241 family unity began to unravel. When Khubilai° declared himself Great Khan in 1265, the descendants of Jagadai and other branches of the family refused to accept him. The destruction of Karakorum in the ensuing fighting contributed to Khubilai's transferring his court to the old Jin capital that is now Beijing. In 1271 he declared himself founder of the **Yuan Empire.**

Jagadai's descendants, who continued to dominate Central Asia, had much closer relations with Turkic-speaking nomads than did their kinsmen farther east. This, plus a continuing hatred of Khubilai and the Yuan, contributed to the strengthening of Central Asia as an independent Mongol center and to the adoption of Islam in the western territories.

After the Yuan destroyed the Southern Song (see Chapter 11) in 1279, Mongol troops crossed south of the Red River and attacked Annam—now northern Vietnam. They occupied Hanoi three times and then withdrew after arranging for the payment of tribute. In 1283 Khubilai's forces invaded Champa in what is now southern Vietnam and made it a tribute nation as well. A plan to invade Java by sea failed, as did two invasions of Japan in 1274 and 1281.

In tactical terms, the Mongols did not usually outnumber their enemies, but like all steppe nomads for many centuries, they displayed extraordinary abilities

Batu (BAH-too) **Volga** (VOHL-gah) **Güyük** (gi-yik) **Karakorum** (kah-rah-KOR-um)

Khubilai (KOO-bih-lie)

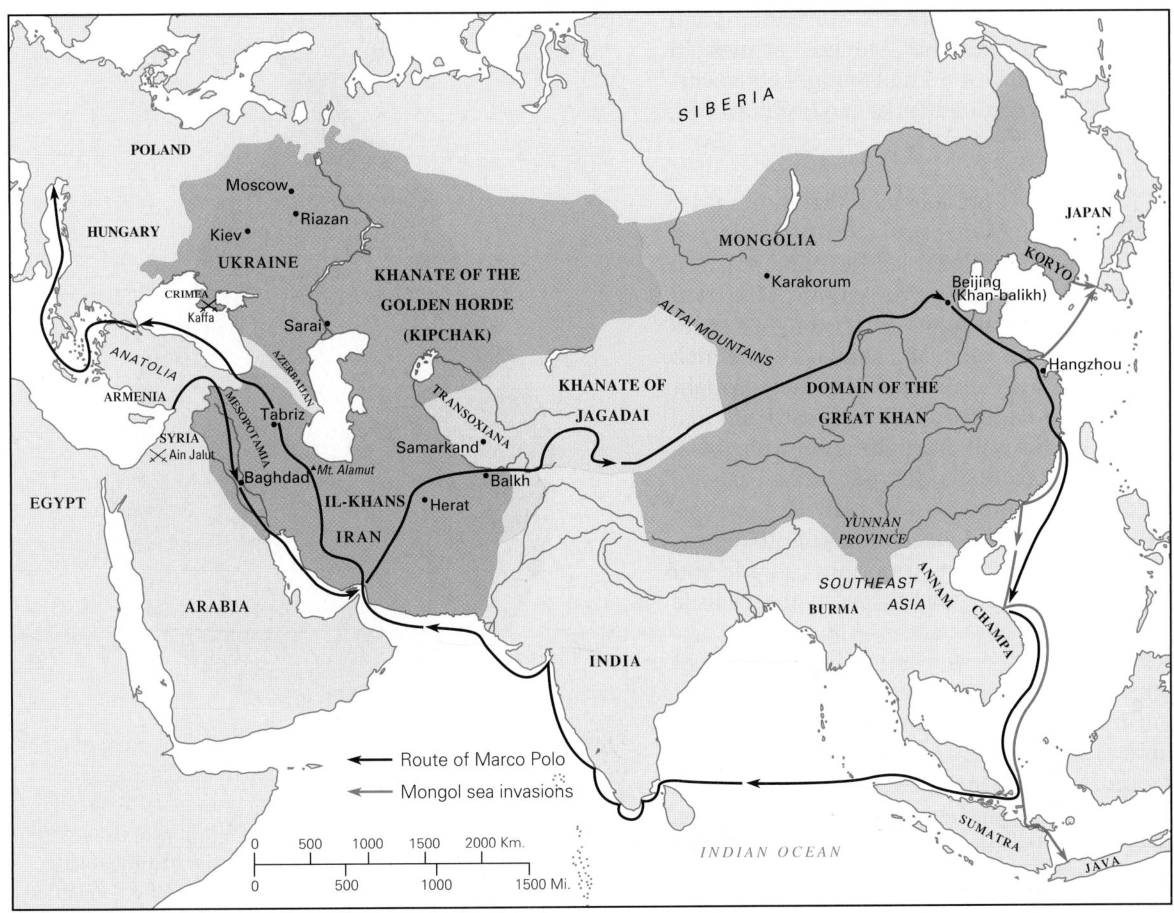

Map 13.1 The Mongol Domains in Eurasia in 1300 After the death of Genghis Khan in 1227, his empire was divided among his sons and grandsons. Son Ögödei succeeded Genghis as Great Khan. Grandson Khubilai expanded the domain of the Great Khan into southern China by 1279. Grandson Hülegü was the first Il-khan in the Middle East. Grandson Batu founded the Khanate of the Golden Horde in southern Russia. Son Jagadai ruled the Jagadai Khanate in Central Asia.

on horseback and utilized superior bows. The Central Asian bow, made strong by laminated layers of wood, leather, and bone, could shoot one-third farther (and was significantly more difficult to pull) than the bows used by their enemies in the settled lands.

Mounted Mongol archers rarely expended all of the five dozen or more arrows they carried in their quivers. As the battle opened, they shot arrows from a distance to decimate enemy marksmen. Then they galloped against the enemy's infantry to fight with sword, lance, javelin, and mace. The Mongol cavalry met its match only at the Battle of Ain Jalut°, where it confronted Mamluk forces whose war techniques shared some of the same traditions (see Chapter 9).

To penetrate fortifications, the Mongols fired flaming arrows and hurled enormous projectiles—sometimes flaming—from catapults. The first Mongol catapults, built on Chinese models, transported easily but had short range and poor accuracy. During western campaigns in Central Asia, the Mongols encountered a catapult design that was half again as powerful as the Chinese model. They used this improved weapon against the cities of Iran and Iraq.

Cities that resisted Mongol attack faced mass slaughter or starvation under siege. Timely surrender brought food, shelter, and protection. The bloodletting the Mongols inflicted on cities such as Balkh° (in present-day northern Afghanistan) spread terror and made it easier

Ain Jalut (ine jah-LOOT)

Balkh (bahlk)

for the Mongols to persuade cities to surrender. Each conquered area helped swell the "Mongol" armies. In campaigns in the Middle East a small Mongol elite oversaw armies of recently recruited Turks and Iranians.

Overland Trade and the Plague

Commercial integration under Mongol rule strongly affected both the eastern and western wings of the empire. Like their aristocratic predecessors in Inner Asia, Mongol nobles had the exclusive right to wear silk, almost all of which came from China. Trade under Mongol dominion brought new styles and huge quantities of silk westward, not just for clothing but also for wall hangings and furnishings. Abundant silk fed the luxury trade in the Middle East and Europe. Artistic motifs from Japan and Tibet reached as far as England and Morocco. Porcelain was another eastern luxury product that became important in trade and strongly influenced later cultural tastes in the Islamic world.

Traders from all over Eurasia enjoyed the benefits of Mongol control. Merchants encountered ambassadors, scholars, and missionaries over the long routes to the Mongol courts. Some of the resulting travel literature, like the account of the Venetian Marco Polo° (1254–1324), freely mixed the fantastic with the factual. Stories of fantastic wealth stimulated a European ambition to find easier routes to Asia.

Exchange also held great dangers. In southwestern China **bubonic plague** had festered in Yunnan province since the early Tang period. In the mid-thirteenth century Mongol troops established a garrison in Yunnan whose military and supply traffic provided the means for flea-infested rats to carry the plague into central China, northwestern China, and Central Asia. Marmots and other desert rodents along the routes became infected and passed the disease to dogs and people. The caravan traffic infected the oasis towns. The plague incapacitated the Mongol army during their assault on the city of Kaffa° in Crimea° in 1346. They withdrew, but the plague remained. From Kaffa rats infected by fleas reached Europe and Egypt by ship (see Chapter 15).

Typhus, influenza, and smallpox traveled with the plague. The combination of these and other diseases created what is often called the "great pandemic" of 1347–1352 and spread devastation far in excess of what the Mongols inflicted in war. Peace and trade, not conquest, gave rise to the great pandemic.

Marco Polo (mar-koe POE-loe) **Kaffa** (KAH-fah)
Crimea (cry-MEE-ah)

Passport The Mongol Empire facilitated the movement of products, merchants, and diplomats over long distances. Travelers frequently encountered new languages, laws, and customs. The *paisa* (from a Chinese word for "card" or "sign"), with its inscription in Mongolian, proclaimed that the traveler had the ruler's permission to travel through the region. Europeans later adopted the practice, thus making the *paisa* the ancestor of modern passports. (The Metropolitan Museum of Art, purchase bequest of Dorothy Graham Bennett, 1993 [1993.256]. Photograph 1997 The Metropolitan Museum of Art)

THE MONGOLS AND ISLAM, 1260–1500

From the perspective of Mongol imperial history, the issue of which branches of the family espoused Islam and which did not mostly concerns their political rivalries and their respective quests for allies. From the standpoint of the history of Islam, however, recovery from the political, religious, and physical devastation that culminated in the destruction of the Abbasid caliphate in Baghdad in 1258 attests to the vitality of the faith and the ability of Muslims to overcome adversity. Within fifty years of its darkest hour, Islam had reemerged as a potent ideological and political force.

Mongol Rivalry

By 1260 the **Il-khan°** state, established by Genghis's grandson Hülegü, controlled parts of Armenia and all of Azerbaijan, Mesopotamia, and Iran. The Mongols who had conquered southern Russia settled north of the Caspian Sea and established the capital of their Khanate of the **Golden Horde** (also called the Kipchak° Khanate) at Sarai° on the Volga River. There they established dominance over the indigenous Muslim Turkic population, both settled and pastoral.

Some members of the Mongol imperial family had professed Islam before the Mongol assault on the Middle East, and Turkic Muslims had served the family in various capacities. Indeed, Hülegü himself, though a Buddhist, had a trusted Shi'ite adviser and granted privileges to the Shi'ites. As a whole, however, the Mongols under Hülegü's command came only slowly to Islam.

The passage of time did little to reconcile Islamic doctrines with Mongol ways. Muslims abhorred the Mongols' worship of idols, a fundamental part of shamanism. Furthermore, Mongol law specified slaughtering animals without spilling blood, which involved opening the chest and stopping the heart. This horrified Muslims, who were forbidden to consume blood and slaughtered animals by slitting their throats and draining the blood.

Islam became a point of inter-Mongol tension when Batu's successor as leader of the Golden Horde declared himself a Muslim, swore to avenge the murder of the Abbasid caliph, and laid claim to the Caucasus—the region between the Black and Caspian Seas—which the Il-khans also claimed (see Map 13.2).

Some European leaders believed that if they helped the non-Muslim Il-khans repel the Golden Horde from the Caucasus, the Il-khans would help them relieve Muslim pressure on the crusader states in Syria, Lebanon, and Palestine (see Chapter 9). This resulted in a brief correspondence between the Il-khan court and Pope Nicholas IV (r. 1288–1292) and a diplomatic mission that sent two Christian Turks to western Europe as Il-khan ambassadors in the late 1200s. Many Christian crusaders enlisted in the Il-khan effort, but the pope later excommunicated some for doing so.

The Golden Horde responded by seeking an alliance with the Muslim Mamluks in Egypt (see Chapter 9) against both the crusaders and the Il-khans. These complicated efforts effectively extended the life of the crusader states; the Mamluks did not finish ejecting the crusaders until the fifteenth century.

Before the Europeans' diplomatic efforts could produce a formal alliance, however, a new Il-khan ruler, Ghazan° (1271–1304), declared himself a Muslim in 1295. Conflicting indications of Sunni and Shi'ite affiliation on such things as coins indicate that the Il-khans did not pay too much attention to theological matters. Nor is it clear whether the many Muslim Turkic nomads who served alongside the Mongols in the army were Shi'ite or Sunni.

Islam and the State

Like the Turks before them (see Chapter 9), the Il-khans gradually came to appreciate the traditional urban culture of the Muslim territories they ruled. Though nomads continued to serve in their armies, the Il-khans used tax farming, a fiscal method developed earlier in the Middle East, to extract maximum wealth from their domain. The government sold tax-collecting contracts to small partnerships, mostly consisting of merchants who might also work together to finance caravans, small industries, or military expeditions. The corporations that offered to collect the most revenue for the government won the contracts. They could use whatever methods they chose and could keep anything over the contracted amount.

Initially, the cost of collecting taxes fell, but over the long term, the exorbitant rates the tax farmers charged drove many landowners into debt and servitude. Agricultural productivity declined. The government had difficulty procuring supplies for the soldiers and resorted to taking land to grow its own grain. Like land held by religious trusts, this land paid no taxes. Thus the tax base shrank even as the demands of the army and the Mongol nobility continued to grow.

Ghazan faced many economic problems. Citing the humane values of Islam, he promised to reduce taxes, but the need for revenues kept the decrease from being permanent. He also witnessed the failure of a predecessor's experiment with the Chinese practice of using paper money. Having no previous exposure to paper money, the Il-khan's subjects responded negatively. The economy quickly sank into a depression that lasted beyond the end of the Il-khan state in 1349. High taxes caused widespread popular unrest and resentment. Mongol nobles competed fiercely among themselves for the decreasing revenues, and fighting among Mongol factions destabilized the government.

In the mid-fourteenth century Mongols from the Golden Horde moved through the Caucasus into the

Il-khan (IL-con) **Kipchak** (KIP-chahk) **Sarai** (sah-RYE)

Ghazan (haz-ZAHN)

Map 13.2 Western Eurasia in the 1300s Ghazan's conversion to Islam in 1295 upset the delicate balance of power in Mongol domains. European leaders abandoned their hope of finding an Il-khan ally against the Muslim defenders in Palestine, while an alliance between the Mamluks and the Golden Horde kept the Il-khans from advancing west. This helped the Europeans retain their lands in Palestine and Syria.

western regions of the Il-khan Empire and then into the Il-khan's central territory, Azerbaijan, briefly occupying its major cities. At the same time a new power was emerging to the east, in the Central Asian Khanate of Jagadai (see Map 13.1). The leader **Timur°**, known to Europeans as Tamerlane, skillfully maneuvered himself into command of the Jagadai forces and launched campaigns into western Eurasia, apparently seeing himself as a new Genghis Khan. By ethnic background he was a Turk with only an in-law relationship to the family of the Mongol conqueror. This prevented him from assuming the title *khan*, but not from sacking the Muslim sultanate of Delhi in northern India in 1398 or defeating the sultan of the rising Ottoman Empire in Anatolia in 1402. By that time he had subdued much of the Middle East, and he was reportedly preparing to march on China when he died in 1405. The Timurids (descendants of Timur) could not hold the empire together, but they laid the groundwork for the establishment in India of a Muslim Mongol-Turkic regime, the Mughals, in the sixteenth century.

Culture and Science in Islamic Eurasia

The Il-khans of Iran and Timurids of Central Asia presided over a brilliant cultural flowering in Iran, Afghanistan, and Central Asia based on the shar-

Timur (tem-EER)

Tomb of Timur in Samarqand The turquoise tiles that cover the dome are typical of Timurid architectural decoration. Timur's family ornamented his capital with an enormous mosque, three large religious colleges facing one another on three sides of an open plaza, and a lane of brilliantly tiled Timurid family tombs in the midst of a cemetery. Timur brought craftsmen to Samarqand from the lands he conquered to build these magnificent structures. (Sassoon/Robert Harding Picture Library)

ing of artistic trends, administrative practices, and political ideas between Iran and China, the dominant urban civilizations at opposite ends of the Silk Road. The dominant cultural tendencies of the Il-khan and Timurid periods are Muslim, however. Although Timur died before he could reunite Iran and China, his forcible concentration of Middle Eastern scholars, artists, and craftsmen in his capital, Samarkand, fostered advancement in some specific activities under his descendants.

The historian Juvaini° (d. 1283), the literary figure who noted Genghis Khan's deathbed speech, came from the city of Balkh, which the Mongols had devastated in 1221. His family switched their allegiance to the Mongols, and both Juvaini and his older brother assumed high government posts. The Il-khan Hülegü, seeking to immortalize and justify the Mongol conquest of the Middle East, enthusiastically supported Juvaini's writing. This resulted in the first comprehensive narrative of the rise of the Mongols under Genghis Khan.

Juvaini combined a florid style with historical objectivity—he often criticized the Mongols—and served as an inspiration to **Rashid al-Din°**, Ghazan's prime minister, when he attempted the first history of the world. Rashid al-Din's work included the earliest known general history of Europe, derived from conversations with European monks, and a detailed description of China based on information from an important Chinese Muslim official stationed in Iran. The miniature paintings that accompanied some copies of Rashid al-Din's work included depictions of European and Chinese people and events and reflected the artistic traditions of both cultures. The Chinese techniques of composition helped inaugurate the greatest period of Islamic miniature painting under the Timurids.

Rashid al-Din traveled widely and collaborated with administrators from other parts of the far-flung Mongol dominions. His idea that government should be in accord with the moral principles of the majority of the population buttressed Ghazan's adherence to Islam. Administratively, however, Ghazan did not restrict himself to Muslim precedents but employed financial and monetary techniques that roughly resembled those in use in Russia and China.

Under the Timurids, the tradition of the Il-khan historians continued. After conquering Damascus, Timur himself met there with the greatest historian of the age, Ibn Khaldun° (1332–1406), a Tunisian. In a scene reminiscent of Ghazan's answering Rashid al-Din's questions on the history of the Mongols, Timur and Ibn Khaldun exchanged historical, philosophical, and geographical viewpoints. Like Genghis, Timur saw himself as a world conqueror. At their capitals of Samarkand and Herat (in western Afghanistan), later Timurid rulers sponsored historical writing in both Persian and Turkish.

A Shi'ite scholar named **Nasir al-Din Tusi°** represents the beginning of Mongol interest in the scientific traditions of the Muslim lands. Nasir al-Din may have

---

Juvaini (joo-VINE-nee) **Rashid al-Din** (ra-SHEED ad-DEEN)
Ibn Khaldun (ee-bin hal-DOON)
Nasir al-Din Tusi (nah-SEER ad-DEEN TOO-si)

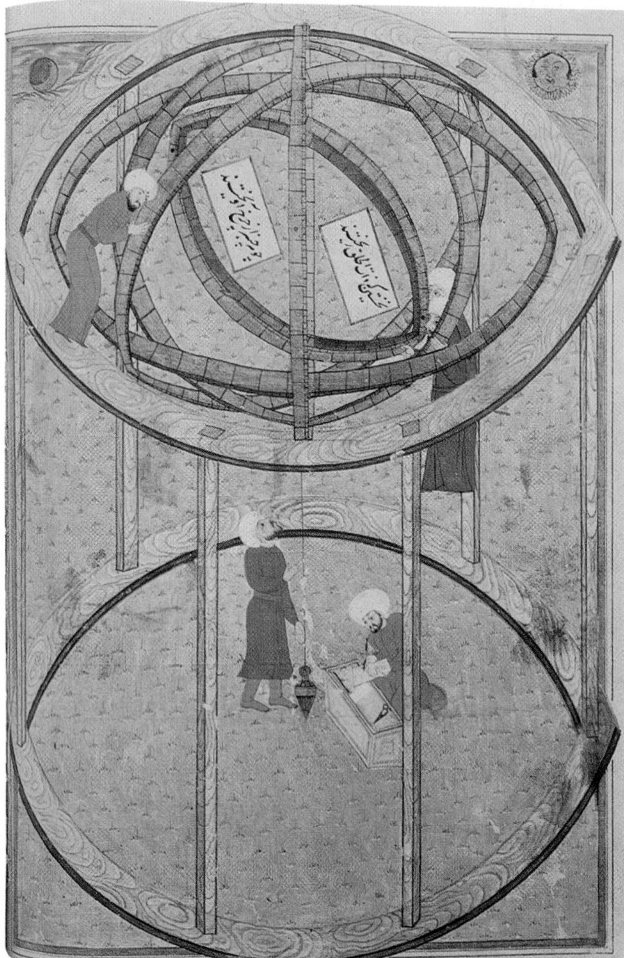

Astronomy and Engineering Observational astronomy went hand in hand not only with mathematics and calendrical science but also with engineering as the construction of platforms, instruments for celestial measurement, and armillary spheres became more sophisticated. This manual in Persian, completed in the 1500s but illustrating activities of the Il-khan period, illustrates the use of a plumb line with an enormous armillary sphere. (Istanbul University Library)

joined the entourage of Hülegü during a campaign in 1256 against the Assassins, a Shi'ite religious sect derived from the Fatimid dynasty in Egypt and at odds with his more mainstream Shi'ite views (see Chapter 9). Nasir al-Din wrote on history, poetry, ethics, and religion, but made his most outstanding contributions in mathematics and cosmology. Following Omar Khayyam° (1038?–1131), a poet and mathematician of the Seljuk° period, he laid new foundations for algebra and trigonometry. Some followers working at an observatory built for Nasir al-Din at Maragheh°, near the Il-khan capital of Tabriz, used the new mathematical techniques to solve a fundamental problem in classical cosmology.

Islamic scholars had preserved and elaborated on the insights of the Greeks in astronomy and mathematics and adopted the cosmological model of Ptolemy°, which assumed a universe with the earth at its center surrounded by the sun, moon, and planets traveling in concentric circular orbits. However, the motions of these orbiting bodies did not coincide with predictions based on circular orbits. Astronomers and mathematicians had long sought a mathematical explanation for the movements that they observed.

Nasir al-Din proposed a model based on the idea of small circles rotating within a large circle. One of his students reconciled this model with the ancient Greek idea of epicycles (small circles rotating around a point on a larger circle) to explain the movement of the moon around the earth. The mathematical tables and geometric models devised by this student somehow became known to Nicholas Copernicus (1473–1543), a Polish monk and astronomer. Copernicus adopted the lunar model as his own, virtually without revision. He then proposed the model of lunar movement developed under the Il-khans as the proper model for planetary movement as well—but with the planets circling the sun.

Sponsorship of observational astronomy and the making of calendars had engaged the interest of earlier Central Asian rulers, particularly the Uighurs° and the Seljuks. Under the Il-khans, the astronomers of Maragheh excelled in predicting lunar and solar eclipses. Astrolabes, armillary spheres, three-dimensional quadrants, and other instruments acquired new precision.

The remarkably accurate eclipse predictions and tables prepared by Il-khan and Timurid astronomers reached the hostile Mamluk lands in Arabic translation. Byzantine monks took them to Constantinople and translated them into Greek, while Christian scholars working in Muslim Spain translated them into Latin. In India the sultan of Delhi ordered them translated into Sanskrit. The Great Khan Khubilai (see below) summoned a team of Iranians to Beijing to build an observatory for him. Timur's grandson Ulugh Beg° (1394–1449), who mixed science and rule, constructed a great observatory in Samarkand and actively participated in compiling observational tables that were later translated into Latin and used by European astronomers.

Omar Khayyam (oh-mar kie-YAM) **Seljuk** (SEL-jook)

Maragheh (mah-RAH-gah) **Ptolemy** (TOHL-uh-mee)
Uigur (WEE-ger) **Ulugh Beg** (oo-loog bek)

A further advance made under Ulugh Beg came from the mathematician Ghiyas al-Din Jamshid al-Kashi°, who noted that Chinese astronomers had long used one ten-thousandth of a day as a unit in calculating the occurrence of a new moon. This seems to have inspired him to employ decimal fractions, by which quantities less than one could be represented by a marker to show place. Al-Kashi's proposed value for *pi* (π) was far more precise than any previously calculated. This innovation arrived in Europe by way of Constantinople, where a Greek translation of al-Kashi's work appeared in the fifteenth century.

Regional Responses in Western Eurasia

Safe, reliable overland trade throughout Eurasia benefited Mongol ruling centers and commercial cities along the length of the Silk Road. But the countryside, ravaged by conquest, sporadically continuing violence, and heavy taxes, suffered terribly. As Mongol control weakened, regional forces in Russia, eastern Europe, and Anatolia reasserted themselves. All were influenced by Mongol predecessors, and all had to respond to the social and economic changes of the Mongol era. Sometimes this meant collaborating with the Mongols. At other times it meant using local ethnic or religious traditions to resist or roll back Mongol influence.

Russia and Rule from Afar

The Golden Horde established by Genghis's grandson Batu after his defeat of a combined Russian and Kipchak (a Turkic people) army in 1223 started as a unified state but gradually lost its unity as some districts crystallized into smaller khanates. The White Horde, for instance, came to rule much of southeastern Russia in the fifteenth century, and the Crimean khanate on the northern shore of the Black Sea succumbed to Russian invasion only in 1783.

Trade routes east and west across the steppe and north and south along the rivers of Russia and Ukraine conferred importance on certain trading entrepôts, as they had under Kievan Russia (see Chapter 10). The Mongols of the Golden Horde settled at (Old) Sarai, just north of where the Volga flows into the Caspian Sea (see Map 13.1). They ruled their Russian domains to the north and east from afar. To facilitate their control, they granted privileges to the Orthodox Church, which then helped reconcile the Russian people to their distant masters.

The politics of language played a role in subsequent history. Old Church Slavonic, an ecclesiastical language, revived; but Russian steadily acquired greater importance and eventually became the dominant written language. Russian scholars shunned Byzantine Greek, previously the main written tongue, even after the Golden Horde permitted renewed contacts with Constantinople. The Golden Horde enlisted Russian princes to act as their agents, primarily as tax collectors and census takers. Some had to visit the court of the Great Khans at Karakorum to secure the documents upon which their authority was based.

The flow of silver and gold into Mongol hands starved the local economy of precious metal. Like the Il-khans, the khans of the Golden Horde attempted to introduce paper money as a response to the currency shortage. This had little effect in a largely nonmonetary economy, but the experiment left such a vivid memory that the Russian word for money (*denga*°) comes from the Mongolian word for the stamp (*tamga*°) used to create paper currency. But commerce depended more on direct exchange of goods than on currency transactions.

Alexander Nevskii° (ca. 1220–1263), the prince of Novgorod, persuaded some fellow princes to submit to the Mongols. In return, the Mongols favored both Novgorod and the emerging town of Moscow, ruled by Alexander's son Daniel. These towns eclipsed devastated Kiev as political, cultural, and economic centers. This, in turn, drew people northward to open new agricultural land far from the Mongol steppe lands to the southwest. Decentralization continued in the 1300s, with Moscow only very gradually becoming Russia's dominant political center (see Map 13.2).

Russia was deeply affected by the Mongol presence. Bubonic plague became endemic among rodents in the Crimea. Ukraine°, a fertile and well-populated region in the late Kievan period (1000–1230), suffered severe population loss as Mongol armies passed through on campaigns against eastern Europe and raided villages to collect taxes.

Historians debate the Mongol impact on Russia. Some see the destructiveness of the Mongol conquests and the subsequent domination of the khans as isolating

Ghiyas al-Din Jamshid al-Kashi (gee-YASS ad-DIN jam-SHEED al-KAH-shee)

denga (DENG-ah) ***tamga*** (TAHM-gah) **Nevskii** (nih-EFF-skee) **Ukraine** (you-CRANE)

Transformation of the Kremlin Like other northern Europeans, the Russians preferred to build in wood, which was easy to handle and comfortable to live in. But they fortified important political centers with stone ramparts. In the 1300s, the city of Moscow emerged as a new capital, and its old wooden palace, the Kremlin, was gradually transformed into a stone structure. (Novosti)

Russia and parts of eastern Europe from developments to the west. These historians refer to the "Mongol yoke" and hypothesize a sluggish economy and dormant culture under the Mongols.

Others point out that Kiev declined economically well before the Mongols struck and that the Kievan princes had already ceased to mint coins. Moreover, the Russian territories regularly paid their heavy taxes in silver. These payments indicate both economic surpluses and an ability to convert goods into cash. The burdensome taxes stemmed less from the Mongols than from their tax collectors, Russian princes who often exempted their own lands and shifted the load to the peasants.

As for Russia's cultural isolation, skeptics observe that before the Mongol invasion, the powerful and constructive role played by the Orthodox Church oriented Russia primarily toward Byzantium (see Chapter 10). This situation discouraged but did not eliminate contacts with western Europe, which probably would have become stronger after the fall of Constantinople to the Ottomans in 1453 regardless of Mongol influence.

The traditional structure of local government survived Mongol rule, as did the Russian princely families, who continued to battle among themselves for dominance. The Mongols merely added a new player to those struggles.

Ivan° III, the prince of Moscow (r. 1462–1505), established himself as an autocratic ruler in the late 1400s. Before Ivan, the title **tsar** (from "caesar"), of Byzantine origin, applied only to foreign rulers, whether the emperors of Byzantium or the Turkic khans of the steppe. Ivan's use of the title, which began early in his reign, probably represents an effort to establish a basis for legitimate rule with the decline of the Golden Horde and disappearance of the Byzantine Empire.

New States in Eastern Europe and Anatolia

The interplay between religion, political maneuvering, and new expressions of local identity affected Anatolia and parts of Europe confronted with the Mongol challenge as well. Raised in Sicily, the Holy Roman Emperor Frederick II (r. 1212–1250) appreciated Muslim culture and did not recoil from negotiating with Muslim rulers. When the pope threatened to excommunicate him unless he went on a crusade, Frederick nominally regained Jerusalem through a flimsy treaty with the Mamluk sultan in Egypt. This did not satisfy the pope, and the preoccupation of both pope and emperor with their quarrel left Hungary, Poland, and other parts of eastern Europe to deal with the Mongol onslaught on their own. Many princes capitulated and went to (Old) Sarai to offer their submission of Batu.

The Teutonic° Knights, however, resisted. Like the Knights Templar in the Middle East (see Chapter 9), the German-speaking Teutonic Knights had a crusading goal: to Christianize the Slavic and Kipchak populations of northern Europe, whose territories they colonized with thousands of German-speaking settlers. Having an interest in protecting Slav territory from German expansion, Alexander Nevskii cooperated in the Mongol campaigns against the Teutonic Knights and their Finnish allies. The latter suffered a catastrophic setback in 1242,

Ivan (ee-VAHN) **Teutonic** (two-TOHN-ik)

when many broke through ice on Lake Chud (see Map 13.2) and drowned. This destroyed the power of the Knights, and the northern Crusades virtually ceased.

The "Mongol" armies encountered by the Europeans were barely Mongol other than in most command positions. Mongol recruitment and conscription created an international force of Mongols, Turks, Chinese, Iranians, a few Europeans, and at least one Englishman, who had gone to the Middle East as a crusader but joined the Mongols and served in Hungary.

Initial wild theories describing the Mongols as coming from Hell or from the caves where Alexander the Great confined the monsters of antiquity gave way to more sophisticated understanding as European embassies to the Golden Horde, the Il-khan, and the Great Khan in Mongolia reported on Mongol trade routes and the internal structure of Mongol rule. In some quarters terror gave way to awe and even idealization of Mongol wealth and power. Europeans learned about diplomatic passports, coal mining, movable type, high-temperature metallurgy, higher mathematics, gunpowder, and, in the fourteenth century, the casting and use of bronze cannon. Yet with the outbreak of bubonic plague in the late 1340s (see Chapter 15), the memory of Mongol terror helped ignite religious speculation that God might be punishing the Christians of eastern and central Europe with a series of tribulations.

In the fourteenth century several regions, most notably Lithuania° (see Map 13.2), escaped the Mongol grip. When Russia fell to the Mongols and eastern Europe was first invaded, Lithuania had experienced an unprecedented centralization and military strengthening. Like Alexander Nevskii, the Lithuanian leaders maintained their independence by cooperating with the Mongols. In the late 1300s Lithuania capitalized on its privileged position to dominate its neighbors—particularly Poland—and ended the Teutonic Knights' hope of regaining power.

In the Balkans independent and well-organized kingdoms separated themselves from the chaos of the Byzantine Empire and thrived amidst the political uncertainties of the Mongol period. The Serbian king Stephen Dushan (ca. 1308–1355) proved to be the most effective leader. Seizing power from his father in 1331, he took advantage of Byzantine weakness to raise the archbishop of Serbia to the rank of an independent patriarch. In 1346 the patriarch crowned him "tsar and autocrat of the Serbs, Greeks, Bulgarians, and Albanians," a title that fairly represents the wide extent of his rule. As in the case of Timur, however, his kingdom declined after his death in 1355 and disappeared entirely after a defeat by the Ottomans at the battle of Kosovo in 1389.

The Turkic nomads from whom the rulers of the **Ottoman Empire** descended had come to Anatolia in the same wave of Turkic migrations as the Seljuks (see Chapter 9). Though centered in Iran and preoccupied with quarrels with the Golden Horde, the Il-khans exerted great influence in eastern Anatolia. However, a number of small Turkic principalities emerged farther to the west. The Ottoman principality was situated in the northwest, close to the Sea of Marmara. This not only put them in a position to cross into Europe and take part in the internal dynastic struggles of the declining Byzantine state, but it also attracted Muslim religious warriors who wished to extend the frontiers of Islam in battle with the Christians. Though the Ottoman sultan suffered defeat at the hands of Timur in 1402, this was only a temporary setback. In 1453 Sultan Mehmet II captured Constantinople and brought the Byzantine Empire to an end.

The Ottoman sultans, like the rulers of Russia, Lithuania, and Serbia, seized the political opportunity that arose with the decay of Mongol power. The new and powerful states they created put strong emphasis on religious and linguistic identity, factors that the Mongols themselves did not stress. As we shall see, Mongol rule stimulated similar reactions in the lands of east and southeast Asia.

Lithuania (lith-oo-WAY-nee-ah)

Mongol Domination in China, 1271–1368

After the Mongols conquered northern China in the 1230s, Great Khan Ögödei told a newly recruited Confucian adviser that he planned to turn the heavily populated North China Plain into a pasture for livestock. The adviser reacted calmly but argued that taxing the cities and villages would bring greater wealth. The Great Khan agreed, but he imposed the oppressive tax-farming system in use in the Il-khan Empire, rather than the fixed-rate method traditional to China.

The Chinese suffered under this system during the early years, but Mongol rule under the Yuan Empire, established by Genghis Khan's grandson Khubilai in 1271, also brought benefits: secure routes of transport and communication; exchange of experts and advisers between eastern and western Eurasia; and transmission of information, ideas, and skills.

The Yuan Empire, 1279–1368

Just as the Il-khans in Iran and the Golden Horde in Russia came to accept many aspects of Muslim and Christian culture, so the Mongols in China sought to construct a fruitful synthesis of the Mongol and Chinese religious and moral traditions. **Khubilai Khan** gave his oldest son a Chinese name and had Confucianists participate in the boy's education. In public announcements and the crafting of laws, he took Confucian conventions into consideration. Buddhist and Daoist leaders visited the Great Khan and came away believing that they had all but convinced him to accept their beliefs.

The teachings of Buddhist priests from Tibet called **lamas**° became increasingly popular with some Mongol rulers in the 1200s and 1300s. Their idea of a militant universal ruler bringing the whole world under control of the Buddha and thus pushing it nearer to salvation mirrored an ancient Central Asia idea of universal rulership.

Beijing, the Yuan capital, became the center of cultural and economic life. Where Karakorum had been remote from any major settled area, Beijing served as the eastern terminus of the caravan routes that began near Tabriz, the Il-khan capital, and (Old) Sarai, the Golden Horde capital. An imperial horseback courier system utilizing hundreds of stations maintained close communications along routes that were generally policed and safe for travelers. Ambassadors and merchants arriving in Beijing found a city that was much more Chinese in character than its predecessor in Mongolia.

Called Great Capital (Dadu) or City of the Khan (*khan-balikh*°, Marco Polo's "Cambaluc"), Khubilai's capital featured massive Chinese-style walls of rammed earth, a tiny portion of which can still be seen. Khubilai's engineers widened the streets and developed linked lakes and artificial islands at the city's northwest edge to form a closed imperial complex, the Forbidden City. For his summer retreat, Khubilai maintained the palace and parks at Shangdu°, now in Inner Mongolia. This was "Xanadu°" celebrated by the English poet Samuel Taylor Coleridge, its "stately pleasure dome" the hunting preserve where Khubilai and his courtiers practiced riding and shooting.

"China" as we think of it today did not exist before the Mongols. Before they reunified it, China had been divided into three separate states (see Chapter 11). The Tanggut and Jin empires controlled the north, the Southern Song most of the area south of the Yellow River. These states had different languages, writing systems, forms of government, and elite cultures. The Great Khans destroyed all three and encouraged the restoration or preservation of many features of Chinese government and society, thereby reuniting China in what proved to be a permanent fashion.

By law, Mongols had the highest social ranking. Below them came, in order, Central Asians and Middle Easterners, then northern Chinese, and finally southern Chinese. This apparent racial ranking also reflected a hierarchy of functions, the Mongols being the empire's warriors, the Central Asians and Middle Easterners its census takers and tax collectors. The northern Chinese outranked the southern Chinese because they had come under Mongol control almost two generations earlier.

Though Khubilai included some "Confucians" (under the Yuan, a formal and hereditary status) in government, their position compared poorly with their status as elite officeholders in pre-Mongol times. The Confucians criticized the favoring of merchants, many of whom were from the Middle East or Central Asia, and physicians. They regarded doctors as mere technicians, or even heretical practitioners of Daoist mysticism. The Yuan encouraged medicine and began the long process of integrating Chinese medical and herbal knowledge with western approaches derived from Greco-Roman and Muslim sources.

Like the Il-khan rulers in the Middle East, the Yuan rulers concentrated on counting the population and collecting taxes. They brought Persian, Arab, and Uighur administrators to China to staff the offices of taxation and finance, and Muslim scholars worked at calendar making and astronomy. For census taking and administration, the Mongols organized all of China into provinces. Central appointment of provincial governors, tax collectors, and garrison commanders marked a radical change by systematizing government control in all parts of the country.

The scarcity of contemporary records and the hostility of later Chinese writers make examination of the Yuan economy difficult. Many cities seem to have prospered: in north China by being on the caravan routes; in the interior by being on the Grand Canal; and along the coast by participation in maritime grain shipments from south China. The reintegration of East Asia (though not Japan) with the overland Eurasian trade, which had lapsed with the fall of the Tang (see Chapter 11), stimulated the urban economies.

The privileges and prestige that merchants enjoyed changed urban life and the economy of China. With only

---

lama (LAH-mah) ***khan-balikh*** (kahn-BAL-ik)
Shangdu (shahng-DOO) **Xanadu** (ZAH-nah-doo)

a limited number of government posts open to the old Chinese elite, great families that had previously spent fortunes on educating sons for government service sought other outlets. Many gentry families chose commerce, despite its lesser prestige. Corporations—investor groups that behaved as single commercial and legal units and shared the risk of doing business—handled most economic activities, starting with financing caravans and expanding into tax farming and lending money to the Mongol aristocracy. Central Asians and Middle Easterners headed most corporations in China in the early Yuan period; but as Chinese bought shares, most corporations acquired mixed membership, or even complete Chinese ownership.

The agricultural base, damaged by war, overtaxation, and the passage of armies, could not satisfy the financial needs of the Mongol aristocracy. Following earlier precedent, the imperial government issued paper money to make up the shortfall. But the massive scale of the Yuan experiment led people to doubt the value of the notes, which were unsecured. Copper coinage partially offset the failure of the paper currency. During the Song, exports of copper to Japan, where the metal was scarce, had caused a severe shortage in China, leading to a rise in value of copper in relation to silver. By cutting off trade with Japan, the Mongols intentionally or unintentionally stabilized the value of copper coins.

Gentry families that had previously prepared their sons for the state examinations moved from their traditional homes in the countryside to engage in urban commerce, and city life began to cater to the tastes of merchants instead of scholars. Specialized shops selling clothing, grape wine, furniture, and religiously butchered meats became common. Teahouses featured sing-song girls, drum singers, operas, and other entertainments previously considered coarse. Writers published works in the style of everyday speech. And the increasing influence of the northern, Mongolian-influenced Chinese language, often called Mandarin in the West, resulted in lasting linguistic change.

Cottage industries linked to the urban economies dotted the countryside, where 90 percent of the people lived. Some villages cultivated mulberry trees and cotton using dams, water wheels, and irrigation systems patterned in part on Middle Eastern models. Treatises on planting, harvesting, threshing, and butchering were published. One technological innovator, Huang Dao Po°, brought knowledge of cotton growing, spinning, and weaving from her native Hainan Island to the fertile Yangzi Delta. Some villagers came to revere such innovators as local gods.

Yet on the whole, the countryside did poorly during the Yuan period. After the initial conquests, the Mongol princes evicted many farmers and subjected the rest to brutal tax collection. As in Iran under the Il-khans, by the time the Yuan shifted to lighter taxes and encouragement of farming at the end of the 1200s, it was too late. Servitude or homelessness had overtaken many farmers. Neglect of dams and dikes caused disastrous flooding, particularly on the Yellow River.

According to Song records from before the Mongol conquest and the Ming census taken after their overthrow—each, of course, possibly subject to inaccuracy or exaggeration—China's population may have shrunk by 40 percent during eighty years of Mongol rule, with many localities in northern China losing up to five-sixths of their inhabitants. Scholars have suggested several causes, not all of them directly associated with Mongol rule: prolonged warfare, privations in the countryside causing people to resort to female infanticide, a southward movement of people fleeing the Mongols, and flooding on the Yellow River. The last helps explain why losses in the north exceeded those in the south and why the population along the Yangzi River markedly increased.

The bubonic plague and its attendant diseases, spread by the population movements, contributed as well. The Mongol incorporation of Yunnan°, a mountainous southwestern province where rodents commonly carried bubonic plague, into the centralized provincial system of government exposed the lowlands to plague (see Map 13.1). Cities seem to have managed outbreaks of disease better than rural areas as the epidemic moved from south to north in the 1300s.

Cultural and Scientific Exchange

Government officials in Yuan China maintained regular contact with their counterparts in Il-khan Iran and pursued similar economic and financial policies. While Chinese silks and porcelains affected elite tastes at the western end of the Silk Road, Il-khan engineering, astronomy, and mathematics reached China and Korea. Just as Chinese painters taught Iranian artists appealing new ways of drawing clouds, rocks, and trees, Muslims from the Middle East oversaw most of the weapons manufacture and engineering projects for

Huang Dao Po (hwahng DOW poh)

Yunnan (YOON-nahn)

Khubilai's armies. Similarly, the Il-khans imported scholars and texts that helped them understand Chinese technological advances, including stabilized sighting tubes for precisely noting the positions of astronomical objects, mechanically driven armillary spheres that showed how the sun, moon, and planets moved in relation to one another, and new techniques for measuring the movement of the moon. And Khubilai brought Iranians to Beijing to construct an observatory and an institute for astronomical studies similar to the Il-khans' facility at Maragheh. He made the state responsible for maintaining and staffing the observatory.

Muslim doctors and Persian medical texts—particularly in anatomy, pharmacology, and ophthalmology—circulated in China during the Yuan. Khubilai, who suffered from alcoholism and gout, accorded high status to doctors. New seeds and formulas from the Middle East stimulated medical practice. The traditional Chinese study of herbs, drugs, and potions came in for renewed interest and publication.

The Fall of the Yuan Empire

In the 1340s power contests broke out among the Mongol princes. Within twenty years farmer rebellions and feuds among the Mongols engulfed the land. Amidst the chaos, a charismatic Chinese leader, Zhu Yuanzhang°, mounted a campaign that destroyed the Yuan Empire and brought China under control of his new empire, the Ming, in 1368. Many Mongols—as well as the Muslims, Jews, and Christians who had come with them—remained in China, some as farmers or shepherds, some as high-ranking scholars and officials. Most of their descendants took Chinese names and became part of the diverse cultural world of China.

Many other Mongols, however, had never moved out of their home territories in Mongolia. Now they welcomed back refugees from the Yuan collapse. Though Turkic peoples were becoming predominant in the steppe region in the west of Central Asia, including territories still ruled by descendants of Genghis Khan, Mongols retained control of Inner Asia, the steppe regions bordering on Mongolia. Their reconcentration in this region fostered a renewed sense of Mongol unity. Some Mongol groups adopted Islam; others favored Tibetan Buddhism. But religious affiliation proved less important than Mongol identity.

The Ming thus fell short of dominating all the Mongols. The Mongols of Inner Asia paid tribute to the Ming only to the extent that doing so facilitated their trade. The Mongols remained a continuing threat on the northern Ming frontier.

THE EARLY MING EMPIRE, 1368–1500

The history of the **Ming Empire** raises questions about the overall impact of the Mongol era in China. Just as historians of Russia and Iran divide over whether Mongol invasion and political domination retarded or stimulated the pace and direction of political and economic change, so historians of China have differing opinions about the Mongols. Since the Ming reestablished many practices that are seen as purely Chinese, they receive praise from people who ascribe central importance to Chinese traditions. On the other hand, historians who look upon the Mongol era as a pivotal historical moment when communication across the vast interior of Eurasia served to bring east and west together sometimes see the inward-looking Ming as less dynamic and productive than the Yuan.

Ming China on a Mongol Foundation

Zhu Yuanzhang, a former monk, soldier, and bandit, had watched his parents and other family members die of famine and disease, conditions he blamed on Mongol misrule. During the Yuan Empire's chaotic last decades, he vanquished rival rebels and assumed imperial power under the name Hongwu (r. 1368–1398). He ruled a highly centralized, militarily formidable empire.

Hongwu moved the capital to Nanjing° ("southern capital") on the Yangzi River, turning away from the Mongol's Beijing ("northern capital"; see Map 13.3). Though Zhu Yuanzhang the rebel had espoused a radical Buddhist belief in a coming age of salvation, once in power he used Confucianism to depict the emperor as the champion of civilization and virtue, justified in making war on uncivilized "barbarians."

Hongwu choked off the close relations with Central Asia and the Middle East fostered by the Mongols and imposed strict limits on imports and foreign visitors. Silver replaced paper money for tax payments and commerce. These practices, illustrative of an anti-Mongol ideology, proved as economically unhealthy as some of the Yuan economic policies and did not last. Instead, the Ming government gradually came to resemble the Yuan. Ming

Zhu Yuanzhang (JOO yuwen-JAHNG)

Nanjing (nahn-JING)

Map 13.3 The Ming Empire and Its Allies, 1368–1500 The Ming Empire controlled China but had a hostile relationship with peoples in Mongolia and Inner Asia who had been under the rule of the Mongol Yuan emperors. Mongol attempts at conquest by seas were continued by the Ming mariner Zheng He. Between 1405 and 1433 he sailed to Southeast Asia and then beyond, to India, the Persian Gulf, and East Africa.

rulers retained the provincial structure and continued to observe the hereditary professional categories of the Yuan period. Muslims made calendars and astronomical calculations at a new observatory at Nanjing, a replica of Khubilai's at Beijing. The Mongol calendar continued in use.

Continuities with the Yuan became more evident after an imperial prince seized power through a coup d'état to rule as the emperor **Yongle**° (r. 1403–1424). He returned the capital to Beijing, enlarging and improving Khubilai's imperial complex. The central area—the Forbidden City—acquired its present character, with moats, orange-red outer walls, golden roofs, and marble bridges.

Yongle (yoong-LAW)

Yongle intended this combination fortress, religious site, bureaucratic center, and imperial residential park to overshadow Nanjing, and it survives today as China's most imposing traditional architectural complex.

Yongle also restored commercial links with the Middle East. Because hostile Mongols still controlled much of the caravan route, Yongle explored maritime connections. In Southeast Asia, Annam became a Ming province as the early emperors continued the Mongol program of aggression. This focus on the southern frontier helped inspire the naval expeditions of the trusted imperial eunuch **Zheng He**° from 1405 to 1433.

A Muslim whose father and grandfather had made the pilgrimage to Mecca, Zheng He had a good knowledge of the Middle East; and his religion eased relations with the states of the Indian subcontinent, where he directed his first three voyages. Subsequent expeditions reached Hormuz on the Persian Gulf, sailed the southern coast of Arabia and the Horn of Africa (modern Somalia), and possibly reached as far south as the Strait of Madagascar (see Map 13.3).

On early voyages he visited long-established Chinese merchant communities in Southeast Asia in order to cement their allegiance to the Ming Empire and to collect taxes. When a community on the island of Sumatra resisted, he slaughtered the men to set an example. By pursuing commercial relations with the Middle East and possibly Africa, he also publicized Yongle's reversal of Hongwu's opposition to foreign trade.

The expeditions added some fifty new tributary states to the Ming imperial universe, but trade did not increase as dramatically. Sporadic embassies reached Beijing from rulers in India, the Middle East, Africa, and Southeast Asia. During one visit the ruler of Brunei° died and received a grand burial at the Chinese capital. Occasional expeditions continued until the 1430s, after the death of both Yongle and Zheng He, when they stopped.

Having demonstrated such abilities at long-distance navigation, why did the Chinese not develop seafaring for commercial and military gain? Contemporaries considered the voyages a personal project of Yongle, an upstart ruler who had always sought to prove his worthiness. Building the Forbidden City in Beijing and sponsoring gigantic encyclopedia projects might be taken to reflect a similar motivation. Yongle may also have been emulating Khubilai Khan, who had sent enormous fleets against Japan and Southeast Asia. This would fit with the rumor spread by Yongle's political enemies that he was actually a Mongol.

A less speculative approach to the question starts with the fact that the new commercial opportunities fell short of expectations, despite bringing foreign nations into the Ming orbit. In the meantime, Japanese coastal piracy intensified, and Mongol threats in the north and west grew. The human and financial demands of fortifying the north, redesigning and strengthening Beijing, and outfitting military expeditions against the Mongols ultimately took priority over the quest for maritime empire.

Technology and Population

Although innovation continued in all areas of the Ming economy, advances were less frequent and less significant than under the Song, particularly in agriculture. Agricultural production peaked around the mid-1400s and remained level for more than a century.

The Ming government limited mining, partly to reinforce the value of metal coins and partly to control and tax the industry. Farmers had difficulty obtaining iron and bronze for farm implements. The peace that had followed the Mongol conquest resulted in a decline in techniques for making high-quality bronze and steel, which were especially used for weapons. Central Asian and Middle Eastern technicians rather than Chinese cast the bronze instruments for Khubilai's observatory at Beijing. Japan quickly surpassed China in the production of extremely high-quality steel swords. Copper, iron, and steel became expensive in Ming China, leading to a lessened use of metal.

After the death of Emperor Yongle in 1424, shipbuilding also declined, and few advances occurred in printing, timekeeping, and agricultural technology. New weaving techniques did appear, but technological development in this field had peaked by 1500.

Reactivation of the examination system as a way of recruiting government officials (see Chapter 11) drew large numbers of educated, ambitious men into a renewed study of the Confucian classics. This reduced the vitality of commerce, where they had previously been employed, just as population increase was creating a labor surplus. Records indicating a growth from 60 million at the end of the Yuan period in 1368 to nearly 100 million by 1400 may not be entirely reliable, but rapid population growth encouraged the production of staples—wheat, millet, and barley in the north and rice in the south—at the expense of commercial crops such as cotton that had stimulated many technological innovations under the Song. Staple crops yielded lower profits, which further discouraged capital improvements. New

---

Zheng He (JEHNG HUH) **Brunei** (broo-NIE)

Ming Porcelain Bowl High-quality Chinese blue-and-white ware commanded an international market under the Ming Empire. This piece, bearing a Portuguese inscription showing that it was made in 1541 for the Portuguese governor of Malacca, is one of the earliest examples of works made specifically for a European. (Collection, Junta de Baixo Alentago, Beja, Portugal)

foods, such as sweet potatoes, became available but were little adopted. Population growth in southern and central China caused deforestation and raised the price of wood.

The Mongols that the Ming confronted in the north fought on horseback with simple weapons. The Ming fought back with arrows, scattershot mortars, and explosive canisters. They even used a few cannon, which they knew about from contacts with the Middle East and later with Europeans (see Environment and Technology: From Gunpowder to Guns). Fearing that technological secrets would get into enemy hands, the government censored the chapters on gunpowder and guns in early Ming encyclopedias. Shipyards and ports shut down to avoid contact with Japanese pirates and to prevent Chinese from migrating to Southeast Asia.

A technology gap with Korea and Japan opened up nevertheless. When superior steel was needed, supplies came from Japan. Korea moved ahead of China in the design and production of firearms and ships, in printing techniques, and in the sciences of weather prediction and calendar making. The desire to tap the wealthy Ming market fueled some of these advances.

The Ming Achievement

In the late 1300s and the 1400s the wealth and consumerism of the early Ming stimulated high achievement in literature, the decorative arts, and painting. The Yuan period interest in plain writing had produced some of the world's earliest novels. This type of literature flourished under the Ming. *Water Margin,* which originated in the raucous drum-song performances loosely related to Chinese opera, features dashing Chinese bandits who struggle against Mongol rule, much as Robin Hood and his merry men resisted Norman rule in England. Many authors had a hand in the final print version.

Luo Guanzhong°, one of the authors of *Water Margin,* is also credited with *Romance of the Three Kingdoms,* based on a much older series of stories that in some ways resemble the Arthurian legends. It describes the attempts of an upright but doomed war leader and his followers to restore the Han Empire of ancient times and resist the power of the cynical but brilliant villain. *Romance of the Three Kingdoms* and *Water Margin* expressed much of the militant but joyous pro-China sentiment of the early Ming era and remain among the most appreciated Chinese fictional works.

Probably the best-known product of Ming technological advance was porcelain. The imperial ceramic works at Jingdezhen° experimented with new production techniques and new ways of organizing and rationalizing workers. "Ming ware," a blue-on-white style developed in the 1400s from Indian, Central Asian, and Middle Eastern motifs, became especially prized around the world. Other Ming goods in high demand included furniture, lacquered screens, and silk, all eagerly transported by Chinese and foreign merchants throughout Southeast Asia and the Pacific, India, the Middle East, and East Africa.

Luo Guanzhong (LAW GWAHB-JOONG)
Jingdezhen (JING-deh-JUHN)

From Gunpowder to Guns

Long before the invention of guns, gunpowder was used in China and Korea to excavate mines, build canals, and channel irrigation. Alchemists in China used related formulas to make noxious gas pellets to paralyze enemies and expel evil spirits. A more realistic benefit was eliminating disease-carrying insects, a critical aid to the colonization of malarial regions in China and Southeast Asia. The Mongol Empire staged fireworks displays on ceremonial occasions, delighting European visitors to Karakorum who saw them for the first time.

Anecdotal evidence in Chinese records gives credit for the introduction of gunpowder to a Sogdian Buddhist monk of the 500s. The monk described the wondrous alchemical transformation of elements produced by a combination of charcoal and saltpeter. In this connection he also mentioned sulfur. The distillation of naphtha, a light, flammable derivative of oil or coal, seems also to have been first developed in Central Asia, the earliest evidence coming from the Gandhara region (in modern Pakistan).

Launching Flaming Arrows Song soldiers used gunpowder to launch flaming arrows. (British Library)

By the eleventh century, the Chinese had developed flamethrowers powered by burning naphtha, sulfur, or gunpowder in a long tube. These weapons intimidated and injured foot soldiers and horses and also set fire to thatched roofs in hostile villages and, occasionally, the rigging of enemy ships.

In their long struggle against the Mongols, the Song learned to enrich saltpeter to increase the amount of nitrate in gunpowder. This produced forceful explosions rather than jets of fire. Launched from catapults, gunpowder-filled canisters could rupture fortifications and inflict mass casualties. Explosives hurled from a distance could sink or burn ships.

The Song also experimented with firing projectiles from metal gun barrels. The earliest gun barrels were broad and squat and were transported on special wagons to their emplacements. The mouths of the barrels projected saltpeter mixed with scattershot minerals. The Chinese and then the Koreans adapted gunpowder to shooting masses of arrows—sometimes flaming—at enemy fortifications.

In 1280 weapons makers of the Yuan Empire produced the first device featuring a projectile that completely filled the mouth of the cannon and thus concentrated the explosive force. The Yuan used cast bronze for the barrel and iron for the cannonball. The new weapon shot farther and more accurately, and was much more destructive, than the earlier Song devices.

Knowledge of the cannon and cannonball moved westward across Eurasia. By the end of the thirteenth century cannon were being produced in the Middle East. By 1327 small, squat cannon called "bombards" were being used in Europe.

Centralization and Militarism in East Asia, 1200–1500

Korea, Japan, and Annam, the other major states of East Asia, were all affected by confrontation with the Mongols, but with differing results. Japan and Annam escaped Mongol conquest but changed in response to the Mongol threat, becoming more effective and expansive regimes with enhanced commitments to independence.

As for Korea, just as the Ming stressed Chinese traditions and identity in the aftermath of Yuan rule, so Mongol domination contributed to revitalized interest in Korea's own language and history. The Mongols conquered Korea after a difficult war, and though Korea suffered socially and economically under Mongol rule, members of the elite associated closely with the Yuan Empire. After the fall of the Yuan, merchants continued the international connections established in the Mongol period, while Korean armies consolidated a new kingdom and fended off pirates.

Korea from the Mongols to the Yi, 1231–1500

In their effort to establish control over all of China, the Mongols searched for coastal areas from which to launch naval expeditions and choke off the sea trade of their adversaries. Korea offered such possibilities. When the Mongols attacked in 1231, the leader of a prominent Korean family assumed the role of military commander and protector of the king (not unlike the shoguns of Japan). His defensive war, which lasted over twenty years, left a ravaged countryside, exhausted armies, and burned treasures, including the renowned nine-story pagoda at Hwangnyong-sa° and the wooden printing blocks of the *Tripitaka*°, a ninth-century masterpiece of printing art. The commander's underlings killed him in 1258. Soon afterward the Koryo° king surrendered to the Mongols and became a subject monarch by linking his family to the Great Khan by marriage.

By the mid-1300s the Koryo kings were of mostly Mongol descent, and they favored Mongol dress, customs, and language. Many lived in Beijing. The kings, their families, and their entourages often traveled between China and Korea, thus exposing Korea to the philosophical and artistic styles of Yuan China: neo-Confucianism, Chan Buddhism (called *Sōn* in Korea), and celadon (light green) ceramics.

Mongol control was a stimulus after centuries of comparative isolation. Cotton began to be grown in southern Korea; gunpowder came into use; and the art of calendar making, including eclipse prediction and vector calculation, stimulated astronomical observation and mathematics. Celestial clocks built for the royal observatory at Seoul reflected Central Asian and Islamic influences more than Chinese. Avenues of advancement opened for Korean scholars willing to learn Mongolian, landowners willing to open their lands to falconry and grazing, and merchants servicing the new royal exchanges with Beijing. These developments contributed to the rise of a new landed and educated class.

When the Yuan Empire fell in 1368, the Koryo ruling family remained loyal to the Mongols and had to be forced to recognize the new Ming Empire. In 1392 the **Yi**° established a new kingdom with a capital in Seoul and sought to reestablish a local identity. Like Russia and China after the Mongols, the Yi regime publicly rejected the period of Mongol domination. Yet the Yi government continued to employ Mongol-style land surveys, taxation in kind, and military garrison techniques.

Like the Ming emperors, the Yi kings revived the study of the Confucian classics, an activity that required knowledge of Chinese and showed the dedication of the state to learning. This revival may have led to a key technological breakthrough in printing technology.

Koreans had begun using Chinese woodblock printing in the 700s. This technology worked well in China, where a large number of buyers wanted copies of a comparatively small number of texts. But in Korea, the comparatively few literate men had interests in a wide range of texts. Movable wooden or ceramic type appeared in Korea in the early thirteenth century and may have been invented there. But the texts were frequently inaccurate and difficult to read. In the 1400s Yi printers, working directly with the king, developed a reliable device to anchor the pieces of type to the printing plate: they replaced the old beeswax adhesive with solid copper frames. The legibility of the printed page improved, and high-volume, accurate production became possible. Combined with the phonetic *han'gul*° writing system, this printing technology laid the foundation for a high literacy rate in Korea.

Yi publications told readers how to produce and use fertilizer, transplant rice seedlings, and engineer reservoirs. Building on Eurasian knowledge imported by the Mongols and introduced under the Koryo, Yi scholars

Hwanghnyong-sa (hwahng-NEEYAHNG-sah)
Tripitaka (tri-PIH-tah-kah) **Koryo** (KAW-ree-oh)

Yi (YEE) ***han'gul*** (HAHN-goor)

Movable Type The improvement of cast bronze tiles, each showing a single character, eliminated the need to cast or carve whole pages. Individual tiles—the ones shown are Korean—could be moved from page frame to page frame and gave an even and pleasing appearance. All parts of East Asia eventually adopted this form of printing for cheap, popular books. In the mid-1400s Korea also experimented with a fully phonetic form of writing, which in combination with movable type allowed Koreans unprecedented levels of literacy and access to printed works. (Courtesy, Yushin Yoo)

developed a meteorological science of their own. They invented or redesigned instruments to measure wind speed and rainfall and perfected a calendar based on minute comparisons of the systems of China and the Islamic world.

In agriculture, farmers expanded the cultivation of cash crops, the reverse of what was happening in Ming China. Cotton, the primary crop, enjoyed such high value that the state accepted it for tax payments. The Yi army used cotton uniforms, and cotton became the favored fabric of the Korean civil elite. With cotton gins and spinning wheels powered by water, Korea advanced more rapidly than China in mechanization and began to export considerable amounts of cotton to China and Japan.

Although both the Yuan and the Ming withheld the formula for gunpowder from the Korean government, Korean officials acquired the information by subterfuge. By the later 1300s they had mounted cannon on ships that patrolled against pirates and used gunpowder-driven arrow launchers against enemy personnel and the rigging of enemy ships. Combined with skills in armoring ships, these techniques made the small Yi navy a formidable defense force.

Political Transformation in Japan, 1274–1500

Having secured Korea, the Mongols looked toward Japan, a target they could easily reach from Korea and a possible base for controlling China's southern coast. Their first thirty-thousand-man invasion force in 1274 included Mongol cavalry and archers and sailors from Korea and northeastern Asia. Its weaponry included light catapults and incendiary and explosive projectiles of Chinese manufacture. The Mongol forces landed successfully and decimated the Japanese cavalry, but a great storm on Hakata° Bay on the north side of Kyushu° Island (see Map 13.4) prevented the establishment of a beachhead and forced the Mongols to sail back to Korea.

The invasion deeply impressed Japan's leaders and hastened social and political changes that were already under way. Under the Kamakura° Shogunate established in 1185—another powerful family actually exercised control—the shogun, or military leader, distributed land and privileges to his followers. In return they paid him tribute and supplied him with soldiers. This stable, but decentralized, system depended on the balancing of power among regional warlords. Lords in the north and east of Japan's main island were remote from those in the south and west. Beyond devotion to the emperor and the shogun, little united them until the alien and terrifying Mongol threat materialized.

After the return of his fleet, Khubilai sent envoys to Japan demanding submission. Japanese leaders executed them and prepared for war. The shogun took steps to centralize his military government. The effect was to increase the influence of warlords from the south and west of Honshu (Japan's main island) and from the island of Kyushu, because this was where invasion seemed most likely, and they were the local commanders acting under the shogun's orders.

Military planners studied Mongol tactics and retrained and outfitted Japanese warriors for defense against advanced weaponry. Farm laborers drafted from all over the country constructed defensive fortifications at Hakata and other points along the Honshu and Kyushu coasts. This effort demanded, for the first time, a national system to move resources toward western points rather than toward the imperial or shogunal centers to the east.

The Mongols attacked in 1281. They brought 140,000 warriors, including many non-Mongols, as well as thousands of horses, in hundreds of ships. However, the wall the Japanese had built to cut off Hakata Bay from the mainland deprived the Mongol forces of a reliable landing point. Japanese swordsmen rowed out and boarded the Mongol ships lingering offshore. Their superb steel swords shocked the invaders. After a prolonged standoff, a typhoon struck and sank perhaps half of the Mongol ships. The remainder sailed away, never again to harass Japan. The Japanese gave thanks to the "wind of the Gods"—***kamikaze***°—for driving away the Mongols.

Nevertheless, the Mongol threat continued to influence Japanese development. Prior to his death in 1294, Khubilai had in mind a third invasion. His successors did not carry through with it, but the shoguns did not know that the Mongols had given up the idea of conquering Japan. They rebuilt coastal defenses well into the fourteenth century, helping to consolidate the social position of Japan's warrior elite and stimulating the development of a national infrastructure for trade and communication. But the Kamakura Shogunate, based on regionally collected and regionally dispersed revenues, suffered financial strain in trying to pay for centralized road and defense systems.

Between 1333 and 1338 the emperor Go-Daigo broke the centuries-old tradition of imperial seclusion and aloofness from government and tried to reclaim power from the shoguns. This ignited a civil war that destroyed the Kamakura system. In 1338, with the Mongol

Map 13.4 Korea and Japan, 1200–1500 The proximity of Korea and northern China to Japan gave the Mongols the opportunity to launch enormous fleets against the Kamakura Shogunate, which controlled most of the three islands (Honshu, Shikoku, and Kyushu) of central Japan.

Hakata (HAH-kah-tah) **Kyushu** (KYOO-shoo)
Kamakura (kah-mah-KOO-rah) ***kamikaze*** (KUM-i-kuh-zee)

Painting by Sesshu Sesshu Toyo (1420–1506) created a distinctive style of ink painting that contrasted with the Chinese styles that predominated earlier in Japan. Benefiting from growing Japanese commerce in the period of the Ashikaga Shogunate, he traveled to China as a youth and studied Chinese techniques. As he developed his style, a market for his art developed among merchant communities and other urban elites. (Collection of the Tokyo National Museum)

threat waning, the **Ashikaga Shogunate**°, took control at the imperial center of Kyoto.

Provincial warlords enjoyed renewed independence. Around their imposing castles, they sponsored the development of market towns, religious institutions, and schools. The application of technologies imported in earlier periods, including water wheels, improved plows, and Champa rice, increased agricultural productivity. Growing wealth and relative peace stimulated artistic creativity, mostly reflecting Zen Buddhist beliefs held by the warrior elite. In the simple elegance of architecture and gardens, in the contemplative landscapes of artists like Sesshu Toyo, and in the eerie, stylized performances of the No theater, the unified aesthetic code of Zen became established in the Ashikaga era.

Despite the technological advancement, artistic productivity, and rapid urbanization of this period,

Ashikaga (ah-shee-KAH-gah)

competition among warlords and their followers led to regional wars. By the later 1400s these conflicts resulted in the near destruction of the warlords. The great Onin War in 1477 left Kyoto devastated and the Ashikaga Shogunate a central government in name only. Ambitious but low-ranking warriors, some with links to trade with the continent, began to scramble for control of the provinces.

After the fall of the Yuan in 1368 Japan resumed trade with China and Korea. Japan exported raw materials as well as folding fans, invented in Japan during the period of isolation, and swords. Japan's primary imports from China were books and porcelain. The volatile political environment in Japan gave rise to partnerships between warlords and local merchants. All worked to strengthen their own towns and treasuries through overseas commerce or, sometimes, through piracy.

The Emergence of Vietnam, 1200–1500

Before the first Mongol attack in 1257, the states of Annam (northern Vietnam) and Champa (southern Vietnam) had clashed frequently. Annam (once called Dai Viet) looked toward China and had once been subject to the Tang. Chinese political ideas, social philosophies, dress, religion, and language heavily influenced its official culture. Champa related more closely to the trading networks of the Indian Ocean; its official culture was strongly influenced by Indian religion, language, architecture, and dress. Champa's relationship with China depended in part on how close its enemy Annam was to China at any particular time. During the Song period Annam was neither formally subject to China nor particularly threatening to Champa militarily, so Champa inaugurated a trade and tribute relationship with China that spread fast-ripening Champa rice throughout East Asia.

The Mongols exacted submission and tribute from both Annam and Champa until the fall of the Yuan Empire in 1368. Mongol political and military ambitions were mostly focused elsewhere, however, which minimized their impact on politics and culture. The two Vietnamese kingdoms soon resumed their warfare. When Annam moved its army to reinforce its southern border, Ming troops occupied the capital, Hanoi, and installed a puppet government. Almost thirty years elapsed before Annam regained independence and resumed a tributary status. By then the Ming were turning to meet Mongol challenges to their north. In a series of ruthless campaigns, Annam terminated Champa's independence, and by 1500 the ancestor of the modern state of Vietnam, still called Annam, had been born.

The new state still relied on Confucian bureaucratic government and an examination system, but some practices differed from those in China. The Vietnamese legal code, for example, preserved group landowning and decision making within the villages, as well as women's property rights. Both developments probably had roots in an early rural culture based on the growing of rice in wet paddies; by this time the Annamese considered them distinctive features of their own culture.

Conclusion

Despite their brutality and devastation, the Mongol conquests brought a degree of unity to the lands between China and Europe that had never before been known. Nomadic mobility and expertise in military technology contributed to communication across vast spaces and initially, at least, an often-callous disregard for the welfare of farmers, as manifested in oppressive tax policies. Trade, on the other hand, received active Mongol stimulation through the protection of routes and encouragement of industrial production. The Mongol regimes were characterized by an unprecedented openness, employing talented people irrespective of their linguistic, ethnic, or religious affiliations. As a consequence, the period of comparative Mongol unity, which lasted less than a century, saw a remarkable exchange of ideas, techniques, and products across the breadth of Eurasia. Chinese gunpowder spurred the development of Ottoman and European cannon; Muslim astronomers introduced new instruments and mathematical techniques to Chinese observatories.

However, rule over dozens of restive peoples could not endure. Where Mongol military enterprise reached its limit of expansion, it stimulated local aspirations for independence. Division and hostility among branches of Genghis Khan's family—between the Yuan in China and the Jagadai in Central Asia or between the Golden Horde in Russia and the Il-khans in Iran—provided opportunities for achieving these aspirations. The Russians gained freedom from Mongol domination in western Eurasia, and the general political disruption and uncertainty of the Mongol era assisted the emergence of the Lithuanian, Serbian, and Ottoman states. In the east, China, Korea, and Annam similarly found renewed political identity in the aftermath of Mongol rule, while Japan fought off two Mongol invasions and transformed its internal political and cultural identity in the process. In every case, the reality or threat of Mongol attack and domination encouraged centralization of government, improvement of military techniques, and renewed stress on local cultural identity. Thus, in retrospect, despite its traditional association with death and destruction, the Mongol period appears as a watershed establishing new connections between widespread parts of Eurasia and leading to the development of strong, assertive, and culturally creative regional states.

Key Terms

Mongols	**tsar**
Genghis Khan	**Ottoman Empire**
nomadism	**Khubilai Khan**
Yuan Empire	**lama**
bubonic plague	**Beijing**
Il-khan	**Ming Empire**
Golden Horde	**Yongle**
Timur	**Zheng He**
Rashid al-Din	**Yi**
Nasir al-Din Tusi	**kamikaze**
Alexander Nevskii	**Ashikaga Shogunate**

Suggested Reading

David Morgan's *The Mongols* (1986) affords an accessible introduction to the Mongol Empire. Morgan and Reuven Amitai-Preiss have also edited a valuable collection of essays, *The Mongol Empire and Its Legacy* (2000). Thomas T. Allsen has written more-specialized studies: *Mongol Imperialism: The Policies of the Grand Qan Möngke in China, Russia, and the Islamic Lands, 1251–1259* (1987); *Commodity and Exchange in the Mongol Empire: A Cultural History of Islamic Textiles* (2002); and *Culture and Conquest in Mongol Eurasia* (2001). Larry Moses and Stephen A. Halkovic, Jr., *Introduction to Mongolian History and Culture* (1985) links early and modern Mongol history and culture. Tim Severin, *In Search of Chinggis Khan* (1992), revisits the paths of Genghis's conquests.

William H. McNeill's *Plagues and Peoples* (1976) outlines the demographic effects of the Mongol conquests, and Joel Mokyr discusses their technological impact in *The Lever of Riches: Technological Creativity and Economic Progress* (1990). Connections between commercial development in Europe and Eurasian trade routes of the Mongol era within a broad theoretical framework inform Janet L. Abu-Lughod's *Before European Hegemony: The World System A.D. 1250–1350* (1989).

The only "primary" document relating to Genghis Khan, *Secret History of the Mongols,* has been reconstructed in Mongolian from Chinese script and has been variously produced in scholarly editions by Igor de Rachewilz and Francis Woodman Cleaves, among others. Paul Kahn produced a readable prose English paraphrase of the work in 1984. Biographies of Genghis Khan include Leo de Hartog, *Genghis Khan, Conqueror of the World* (1989); Michel Hoang, *Genghis Khan,* trans. Ingrid Canfield (1991); and Paul Ratchnevsky, *Genghis Khan: His Life and Legacy,* trans. and ed. Thomas Nivison Haining (1992), which is most detailed on Genghis's childhood and youth.

On Central Asia after the conquests see S. A. M. Adshead, *Central Asia in World History* (1993). The most recent scholarly study of Timur is Beatrice Manz, *The Rise and Rule of Tamerlane* (1989).

David Christian, *A History of Russia, Central Asia, and Mongolia* (1998), and Charles Halperin, *Russia and the Golden Horde: The Mongol Impact on Medieval Russian History* (1987), provide one-volume accounts of the Mongols in Russia. A more detailed study is John Lister Illingworth Fennell, *The Crisis of Medieval Russia, 1200–1304* (1983). See also Donald Ostrowski, *Muscovy and the Mongols: Cross-Cultural Influences on the Steppe Frontier* (1998). Religion forms the topic of Devin DeWeese, *Islamization and Native Religion in the Golden Horde* (1994).*The Cambridge History of Iran*: Volume 5, *The Saljuq and Mongol Periods,* ed. J. A. Boyle (1968) and Volume 6, *The Timurid and Safavid Periods,* eds. Peter Jackson and Laurence Lockhart (rprt 2001) contain detailed scholarly articles covering the period in Iran and Central Asia.

Translations from the great historians of the Il-khan period include Juvaini, 'Ala al-Din 'Ata Malek, *The History of the World-Conqueror,* trans. John Andrew Boyle (1958), and Rashid al-Din, *The Successors of Genghis Khan,* trans. John Andrew Boyle (1971). The greatest traveler of the time was Ibn Battuta; see C. Defremery and B. R. Sanguinetti, eds., *The Travels of Ibn Battuta, A.D. 1325–1354,* translated with revisions and notes from the Arabic text by H. A. R. Gibb (1994), and Ross E. Dunn, *The Adventures of Ibn Battuta, a Muslim Traveler of the 14th Century* (1986).

On Europe's Mongol encounter see James Chambers, *The Devil's Horsemen: The Mongol Invasion of Europe* (1979). Christopher Dawson, ed., *Mission to Asia* (1955; reprinted 1981), assembles some of the best-known European travel accounts. See also Marco Polo, *The Travels of Marco Polo* (many editions), and the controversial skeptical appraisal of his account in Frances Wood, *Did Marco Polo Really Go to China?* (1995). Morris Rossabi's *Visitor from Xanadu* (1992) deals with the European travels of Rabban Sauma, a Christian Turk.

For China under the Mongols see Morris Rossabi's *Khubilai Khan: His Life and Times* (1988). On the Mongol impact on economy and technology in Yuan and Ming China see Mark Elvin, *The Pattern of the Chinese Past* (1973); Joseph Needham, *Science in Traditional China* (1981). Also see the important interpretation of Ming economic achievement in Andre Gunder Frank, *ReORIENT: Global Economy in the Asian Age* (1998).

The Cambridge History of China, Vol. 8, The Ming Dynasty 1368–1644, part 2, ed. Denis Twitchett and Frederick W. Mote (1998), provides scholarly essays about a little studied period. See also Albert Chan, *The Glory and Fall of the Ming Dynasty* (1982), and Edward L. Farmer, *Early Ming Government: The Evolution of Dual Capitals* (1976).

On early Ming literature see Lo Kuan-chung, *Three Kingdoms: A Historical Novel Attributed to Luo Guanzhong,* translated and annotated by Moss Roberts (1991); Pearl Buck's translation of

Water Margin, entitled *All Men Are Brothers,* 2 vols. (1933), and a later translation by J. H. Jackson, *Water Margin, Written by Shih Nai-an* (1937); and Shelley Hsüeh-lun Chang, *History and Legend: Ideas and Images in the Ming Historical Novels* (1990).

Joseph R. Levenson, ed., *European Expansion and the Counter-Example of Asia, 1300–1600* (1967), recounts the Zheng He expeditions. Philip Snow's *The Star Raft* (1988) contains more recent scholarship, while Louise Levathes, *When China Ruled the Seas* (1993) makes for lively reading.

For a general history of Korea in this period see Andrew C. Nahm, *Introduction to Korean History and Culture* (1993); Ki-Baik Lee, *A New History of Korea* (1984); and William E. Henthorn, *Korea: The Mongol Invasions* (1963). On a more specialized topic see Joseph Needham et al., *The Hall of Heavenly Records: Korean Astronomical Instruments and Clocks, 1380–1780* (1986).

For a collection of up-to-date scholarly essays on Japan, see Kozo Yamamura, ed., *The Cambridge History of Japan, Vol. 3: Medieval Japan* (1990). See also John W. Hall and Toyoda Takeshi, eds., *Japan in the Muromachi Age* (1977); H. Paul Varley, trans., *The Onin War: History of Its Origins and Background with a Selective Translation of the Chronicle of Onin* (1967); Yamada Nakaba, *Ghenko, the Mongol Invasion of Japan, with an Introduction by Lord Armstrong* (1916); and the novel *Fûtô* by Inoue Yasushi, translated by James T. Araki as *Wind and Waves* (1989).

Notes

1. Quotation adapted from Desmond Martin, *Chingis Khan and His Conquest of North China* (Baltimore: The John Hopkins Press, 1950), 303.

14 Tropical Africa and Asia, 1200–1500

East African Pastoralists Herding large and small livestock has long been a way of life in drier parts of the tropics.

CHAPTER OUTLINE

Sultan Abu Bakr° customarily offered his personal hospitality to every distinguished visitor to his city of Mogadishu, an Indian Ocean port in northeast Africa. In 1331 he provided food and lodging for Muhammad ibn Abdullah ibn Battuta° (1304–1369), a young Muslim scholar from Morocco who had set out to explore the Islamic world. Before beginning his tour of the trading cities of the Red Sea and East Africa, Ibn Battuta had completed a pilgrimage to Mecca and had traveled throughout the Middle East. Subsequent travels took him through Central Asia and India, China and Southeast Asia, Muslim Spain, and sub-Saharan West Africa. Logging some 75,000 miles (120,000 kilometers) in twenty-nine years, Ibn Battuta became the most widely traveled man of his times. For this reason the journals he wrote about his travels provide valuable information about these lands.

Other Muslim princes and merchants welcomed Ibn Battuta as graciously as did the ruler of Mogadishu. Hospitality was a noble virtue among Muslims, and they ignored visitors' physical and cultural differences. Although the Moroccan traveler noted that Sultan Abu Bakr had skin darker than his own and spoke a different native language (Somali), that was of little consequence. They were brothers in faith when they prayed together at Friday services in the Mogadishu mosque, where the sultan greeted his foreign guest in Arabic, the common language of the Islamic world: "You are heartily welcome, and you have honored our land and given us pleasure." When Sultan Abu Bakr and his jurists heard cases after the mosque service, they decided them on the basis of the law code familiar in all the lands of Islam.

Islam was not the only thing that united the diverse peoples of Africa and southern Asia. They also shared a tropical environment itself and a network of land and sea trade routes. The variations in tropical environments led societies to develop different specialties, which stimulated trade among them. Tropical winds governed the trading patterns of the Indian Ocean. Older than Islam, these routes were important for spreading beliefs and technologies as well as goods. Ibn Battuta made his way down the coast of East Africa in merchants' ships and joined their camel caravans across the Sahara to West Africa. His path to India followed overland trade routes, and a merchant ship carried him on to China.

As you read this chapter, ask yourself the following questions:

- How did environmental differences shape cultural differences in tropical Africa and Asia?
- How did cultural and ecological differences promote trade in specialized goods from one place to another?
- How did trade and other contacts promote state growth and the spread of Islam?

Tropical Lands and Peoples

To obtain food, the people who inhabited the tropical regions of Africa and Asia used methods that had proved successful during generations of experimentation, whether at the desert's edge, in grasslands, or in tropical rain forests. Much of their success lay in learning how to blend human activities with the natural order, but their ability to modify the environment to suit their needs was also evident in irrigation works and mining.

The Tropical Environment

Because of the angle of earth's axis, the sun's rays warm the **tropics** year-round. The equator marks the center of the tropical zone, and the Tropic of Cancer and Tropic of Capricorn mark its outer limits. As Map 14.1 shows, Africa lies almost entirely within the tropics, as do southern Arabia, most of India, and all of the Southeast Asian mainland and islands.

Lacking the hot and cold seasons of temperate lands, the Afro-Asian tropics have their own cycle of rainy and dry seasons caused by changes in wind patterns across the surrounding oceans. Winds from a permanent high-pressure air mass over the South Atlantic deliver heavy rainfall to the western coast of Africa during much of the year. In December and January large

Abu Bakr (a-BOO BAK-uhr) **Ibn Battuta** (IB-uhn ba-TOO-tuh)

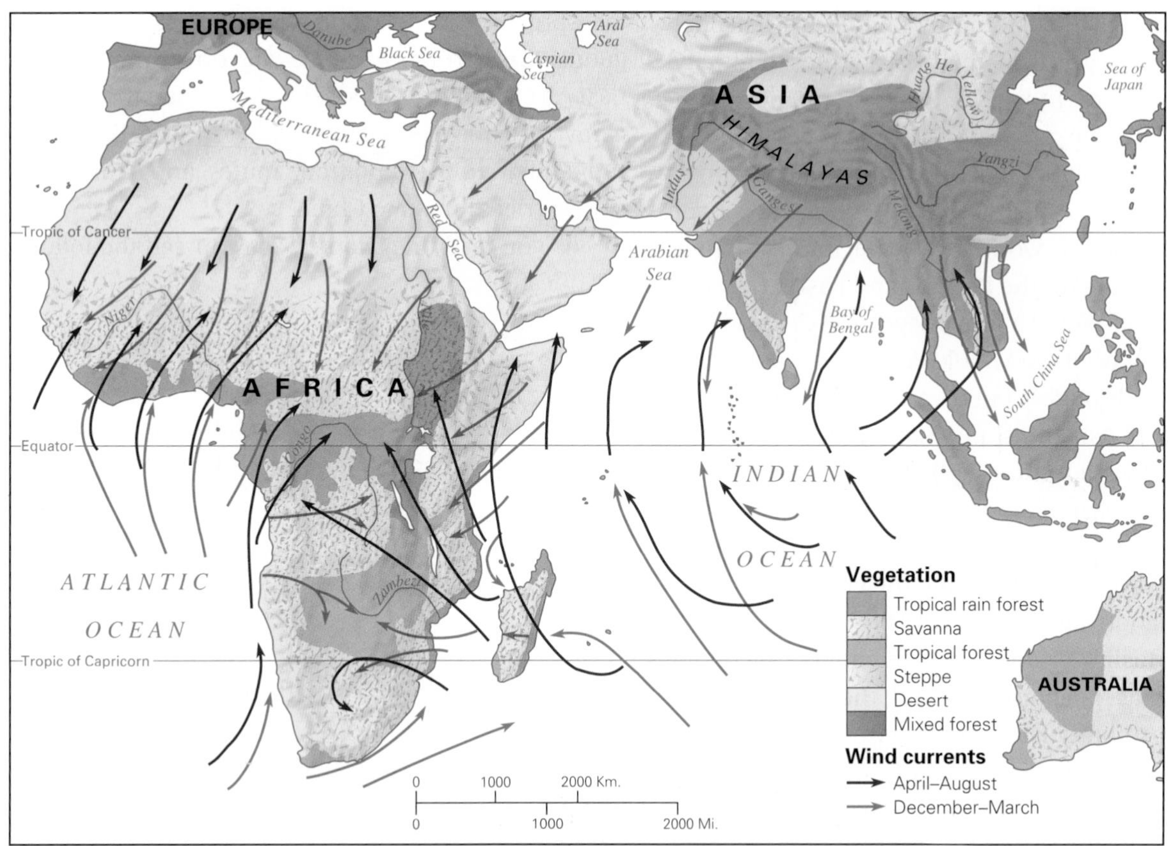

Map 14.1 Africa and the Indian Ocean Basin: Physical Characteristics Seasonal wind patterns control rainfall in the tropics and produce the different tropical vegetation zones to which human societies have adapted over thousands of years. The wind patterns also dominated sea travel in the Indian Ocean.

high-pressure zones over northern Africa and Arabia produce a southward movement of dry air that limits the inland penetration of the moist ocean winds.

In the lands around the Indian Ocean the rainy and dry seasons reflect the influence of alternating winds known as **monsoons.** A gigantic high-pressure zone over the Himalaya° Mountains that is at its peak from December to March produces a strong southward air movement (the northeast monsoon) in the western Indian Ocean. This is southern Asia's dry season. Between April and August a low-pressure zone over India creates a northward movement of air from across the ocean (the southwest monsoon) that brings southern Asia its heaviest rains. This is the wet season.

Areas with the heaviest rainfall—coastal West Africa and west-central Africa, Southeast Asia, and much of India—have dense rain forests. Lighter rains produce other tropical forests. The English word *jungle* comes from an Indian word for the tangled undergrowth in the tropical forests that once covered most of southern India.

Other parts of the tropics rarely see rain at all. The Sahara, the world's largest desert, stretches across northern Africa. This arid zone continues eastward across Arabia and into northwest India. Another desert zone occupies southwestern Africa. Most of the people of tropical India and Africa live between the deserts and the rain forests in lands that are favored with moderate amounts of moisture during the rainy seasons. These lands range from fairly wet woodlands to the much drier grasslands characteristic of much of East Africa.

Altitude produces other climatic changes. Thin atmospheres at high altitudes hold less heat than atmospheres at lower elevations. Snow covers some of the volcanic mountains of eastern Africa all or part of the year. The snowcapped Himalayas rise so high that they block cold air from moving south, thus giving northern

Himalaya (him-uh-LAY-uh)

CHRONOLOGY

	Tropical Africa	Tropical Asia
1200	**1230s** Mali Empire founded	**1206** Delhi Sultanate founded in India
	1270 Solomonic dynasty in Ethiopia founded	
1300	**1324–1325** Mansa Musa's pilgrimage to Mecca	**1298** Delhi Sultanate annexes Gujarat
1400	**1400s** Great Zimbabwe at its peak	**1398** Timur sacks Delhi, Delhi Sultanate declines
	1433 Tuareg retake Timbuktu, Mali declines	
1500		**1500** Port of Malacca at its peak

India a more tropical climate than its latitude would suggest. The many plateaus of inland Africa and the Deccan° Plateau of central India also make these regions somewhat cooler than the coastal plains.

The mighty rivers that rise in these mountains and plateaus redistribute water far from where it falls. Heavy rains in the highlands of Central Africa and Ethiopia supply the Nile's annual floods that make Egypt bloom in the desert. On its long route to the Atlantic, the Niger River of West Africa arcs northward to the Sahara's edge, providing waters to the trading cities along its banks. In like fashion, the Indus River provides nourishing waters from the Himalayas to arid northwest India. The Ganges° and its tributaries provide valuable moisture to northeastern India during the dry season. Mainland Southeast Asia's great rivers, such as the Mekong, are similarly valuable.

Human Ecosystems

Thinkers in temperate lands once imagined that surviving in the year-round warmth of the tropics was simply a matter of picking wild fruit off trees. In fact, mastering the tropics' many different environments was a long and difficult struggle. A careful observer touring the tropics in 1200 would have noticed that the many differences in societies derived from their particular ecosystems—that is, how people made use of the plants, animals, and other resources of their physical environments.

Domesticated plants and animals had been commonplace long before 1200, but people in some environments found it preferable to rely primarily on wild food that they obtained by hunting, fishing, and gathering. The small size of the ancient Pygmy° people in the dense forests of Central Africa permitted them to pursue their prey through dense undergrowth. Hunting also continued as a way of life in the upper altitudes of the Himalayas and in some desert environments. According to a Portuguese expedition in 1497, the people along the arid coast of southwestern Africa were well fed from a diet of "the flesh of seals, whales, and gazelles, and the roots of wild plants." Fishing was common along all the major lakes and rivers as well as in the oceans. The boating skills of ocean fishermen in East Africa, India, and Southeast Asia often led them to engage in ocean trade.

Tending herds of domesticated animals was common in areas too arid for agriculture. Unencumbered by bulky personal possessions and elaborate dwellings, they used their knowledge of local water and rain patterns to find adequate grazing for their animals in all but the severest droughts. Pastoralists consumed milk from their herds and traded hides and meat to neighboring farmers for grain and vegetables. The arid and semiarid lands of northeastern Africa and Arabia were home to the world's largest concentration of pastoralists. Like Ibn Battuta's host at Mogadishu, some Somali were urban dwellers, but most grazed their herds of goats and camels in the desert hinterland of the Horn of Africa. The western Sahara sustained

Deccan (de-KAN) **Ganges** (GAN-jeez)

Pygmy (PIG-mee)

herds of sheep and camels belonging to the Tuareg°, whose intimate knowledge of the desert also made them invaluable as guides to caravans, such as the one **Ibn Battuta** joined on the two-month journey across the desert. Along the Sahara's southern edge the cattle-herding Fulani° people gradually extended their range during this period. By 1500 they had spread throughout the western and central Sudan. Pastoralists in southern Africa sold meat to early Portuguese visitors.

By 1200 most Africans had been making their livelihood through agricultural for many centuries. Favorable soils and rainfall made farming even more dominant in South and Southeast Asia. High yields from intensive cultivation supported dense populations in Asia. In 1200 over 100 million people may have lived in South and Southeast Asia, more than four-fifths of them on the fertile Indian mainland. Though a little less than the population of China, this was triple the number of people living in all of Africa at that time and nearly double the number of people in Europe.

India's lush vegetation led one Middle Eastern writer to call it "the most agreeable abode on earth . . . its delightful plains resemble the garden of Paradise."[1] Rice cultivation dominated in the fertile Ganges plain of northeast India, in mainland Southeast Asia, and in southern China. Farmers in drier areas grew grains—such as wheat, sorghum, millet, and ensete—and legumes such as peas and beans, whose ripening cycle matched the pattern of the rainy and dry seasons. Tubers and tree crops characterized farming in rain-forest clearings.

Many useful domesticated plants and animals spread around the tropics. By 1200 Bantu-speaking farmers (see Chapter 8) had introduced grains and tubers from West Africa throughout the southern half of the continent. Bananas, brought to southern Africa centuries earlier by mariners from Southeast Asia, had become the staple food for people farming the rich soils around the Great Lakes of East Africa. Yams and cocoyams of Asian origin had spread across equatorial Africa. Asian cattle breeds grazed contentedly in pastures throughout Africa, and coffee of Ethiopian origin would shortly become a common drink in the Middle East.

Water Systems and Irrigation

In most parts of sub-Saharan Africa and many parts of Southeast Asia until quite recent times, the basic form of cultivation was extensive rather than intensive. Instead of enriching fields with manure and vegetable compost so they could be cultivated year after year, farmers abandoned fields every few years when the natural fertility of the soil was exhausted, and they cleared new fields. Ashes from the brush, grasses, and tree limbs that were cut down and burned gave the new fields a significant boost in fertility. Even though a great deal of work was needed to clear the fields initially, modern research suggests that such shifting cultivation was an efficient use of labor in areas where soils were not naturally rich in nutrients.

In other parts of the tropics, environmental necessity and population pressure led to the adoption of more intensive forms of agriculture. A rare area of intensive cultivation in sub-Saharan Africa was the inland delta of the Niger River, where large crops of rice were grown using the river's naturally fertilizing annual floods. The rice was probably sold to the trading cities along the Niger bend.

The uneven distribution of rainfall during the year was one of the great challenges faced by many Asian farmers. Unlike pastoralists who could move their herds to the water, they had to find ways of moving the water to their crops. Farmers in Vietnam, Java, Malaya, and Burma constructed special water-control systems to irrigate their terraced rice paddies. Villagers in southeast India built a series of stone and earthen dams across rivers to store water for gradual release through elaborate irrigation canals. Over many generations these canals were extended to irrigate more and more land. Although the dams and channels covered large areas, they were relatively simple structures that local people could keep working by routine maintenance. Other water-storage and irrigation systems were constructed in other parts of India in this period.

As had been true since the days of the first river-valley civilizations (see Chapter 2), the largest irrigation systems in the tropics were government public works projects. The **Delhi° Sultanate** (1206–1526) introduced extensive new water-control systems in northern India. Ibn Battuta commented appreciatively on one reservoir that supplied the city of Delhi with water. He reported that enterprising farmers planted sugar cane, cucumbers, and melons along the reservoir's rim as the water level fell during the dry season. A sultan in the fourteenth century built a network of irrigation canals in the Ganges plain that were not surpassed in size until the nineteenth century. These irrigation systems made it possible to grow crops throughout the year.

Since the tenth century the Indian Ocean island of Ceylon (modern Sri Lanka°) had been home to the greatest concentration of irrigation reservoirs and canals

Tuareg (TWAH-reg) **Fulani** (foo-LAH-nee)

Delhi (DEL-ee) **Sri Lanka** (sree LAHNG-kuh)

in the world. These facilities enabled the powerful Sinhalese° kingdom in arid northern Ceylon to support a large population. There was another impressive waterworks in Southeast Asia, where a system of reservoirs and canals served Cambodia's capital city Angkor°.

These complex systems were vulnerable to disruption. Between 1250 and 1400 the irrigation complex in Ceylon fell into ruin when invaders from South India disrupted the Sinhalese government. The population of Ceylon then suffered from the effects of malaria, a tropical disease spread by mosquitoes breeding in the irrigation canals. The great Cambodian system fell into ruin in the fifteenth century when the government that maintained it collapsed. Neither system was ever rebuilt.

The vulnerability of complex irrigation systems built by powerful governments suggests an instructive contrast. Although village-based irrigation systems could be damaged by invasion and natural calamity, they usually bounced back because they were the product of local initiative, not centralized direction, and they depended on simpler technologies.

Mineral Resources

Throughout the tropics people mined and refined metal-rich ores, which skilled metalworkers turned into tools, weapons, and decorative objects. The more valuable metals, copper and gold, became important in long-distance trade.

Iron was the most abundant and useful of the metals worked in the tropics. Farmers depended on iron hoes, axes, and knives to clear and cultivate their fields and to open up parts of the rain forests of coastal West Africa and Southeast Asia for farming. Iron-tipped spears and arrows improved hunting success. Needles facilitated making clothes and leather goods; nails held timbers together. Indian metalsmiths were renowned for making strong and beautiful swords. In Africa the ability of iron smelters and blacksmiths to transform metal fostered a belief in their magical powers.

Copper and its alloys were of special importance in Africa. In the Copperbelt of southeastern Africa, the refined metal was cast into large X-shaped ingots (metal castings). Local coppersmiths worked these copper ingots into wire and decorative objects. Ibn Battuta described a town in the western Sudan that produced two sizes of copper bars that were used as a currency in place of coins. Skilled artisans in West Africa cast copper and brass (an alloy of copper and zinc) statues and heads that are considered among the masterpieces of world art. These works were made by the "lost-wax" method, in which molten metal melts a thin layer of wax sandwiched between clay forms, replacing the "lost" wax with hard metal.

King and Queen of Ife This copper-alloy work shows the royal couple of the Yoruba kingdom of Ife, the oldest and most sacred of the Yoruba kingdoms of southwestern Nigeria. The casting dates to the period between 1100 and 1500, except for the reconstruction of the male's face, the original of which shattered in 1957 when the road builder who found it accidentally struck it with his pick. (Andre Held, Switzerland)

Africans exported large quantities of gold across the Sahara, the Red Sea, and the Indian Ocean. Some gold came from stream beds along the upper Niger River and farther south in modern Ghana°. In the hills south of the

Sinhalese (sin-huh-LEEZ) **Angkor** (ANG-kor)

Ghana (GAH-nuh)

Zambezi° River (in modern Zimbabwe°) archaeologists have discovered thousands of mine shafts, dating from 1200, that were sunk up to 100 feet (30 meters) into the ground to get at gold ores. Although panning for gold remained important in the streams descending from the mountains of northern India, the gold and silver mines in India seem to have been exhausted by this period. For that reason, Indians imported considerable quantities of gold from Southeast Asia and Africa for jewelry and temple decoration.

Although they are rarely given credit for it, ordinary farmers, fishermen, herders, metalworkers, and others made possible the rise of powerful states and profitable commercial systems. Caravans could not have crossed the Sahara without the skilled guidance of desert pastoralists. The seafaring skills of the coastal fishermen underlay the trade of the Indian Ocean. Cities and empires rested on the food, labors, and taxes of these unsung heroes.

NEW ISLAMIC EMPIRES

The empires of Mali in West Africa and Delhi in South Asia were the largest and richest tropical states of the period between 1200 and 1500. Both utilized Islamic administrative and military systems introduced from the Islamic heartland, but in other ways these two Muslim sultanates were very different. **Mali** was founded by an indigenous African dynasty that had earlier adopted Islam through the peaceful influence of Muslim merchants and scholars. In contrast, the Delhi Sultanate was founded and ruled by invading Turkish and Afghan Muslims. Mali's wealth depended heavily on its participation in the trans-Saharan trade, but long-distance trade played only a minor role in Delhi.

Mali in the Western Sudan

The consolidation of the Middle East and North Africa under Muslim rule during the seventh and eighth centuries (see Chapter 9) greatly stimulated exchanges along the routes that crossed the Sahara. In the centuries that followed, the faith of Muhammad gradually spread to the lands south of the desert, which the Arabs called the *bilad al-sudan*°, "land of the blacks."

The role of force in spreading Islam south of the Sahara was limited. Muslim Berbers invading out of the desert in 1076 caused the collapse of Ghana, the empire that preceded Mali in the western Sudan (see Chapter 8), but their conquest did little to spread Islam. To the east, the Muslim attacks that destroyed the Christian Nubian kingdoms on the upper Nile in the late thirteenth century opened that area to Muslim influences, but Christian Ethiopia successfully withstood Muslim advances. Instead, the usual pattern for the spread of Islam south of the Sahara was through gradual and peaceful conversion. The expansion of commercial contacts in the western Sudan and on the East African coast greatly promoted the process of conversion. African converts found the teachings of Islam meaningful, and rulers and merchants found that the administrative, legal, and economic aspects of Islamic traditions suited their interests. The first sub-Saharan African ruler to adopt the new faith was in Takrur° in the far western Sudan, about 1030.

Shortly after 1200 Takrur expanded in importance under King Sumanguru°. Then in about 1240 Sundiata°, the upstart leader of the Malinke° people, handed Sumanguru a major defeat. Even though both leaders were Muslims, the Malinke epic sagas recall their battles as the clash of two powerful magicians, suggesting how much older beliefs shaped popular thought. The sagas say that Sumanguru was able to appear and disappear at will, assume dozens of shapes, and catch arrows in midflight. Sundiata defeated Sumanguru's much larger forces through superior military maneuvers and by successfully wounding his adversary with a special arrow that robbed him of his magical powers. This victory was followed by others that created Sundiata's Mali empire (see Map 14.2).

Like Ghana before it, Mali depended on a well-developed agricultural base and control of the lucrative regional and trans-Saharan trade routes. But Mali differed from Ghana in two ways. First, it was much larger. Mali controlled not only the core trading area of the upper Niger but the gold fields of the Niger headwaters to the southwest as well. Second, from the beginning its rulers were Muslims who fostered the spread of Islam among the political and trading elite of the empire. Control of the important gold and copper trades and contacts with North African Muslim traders gave Mali and its rulers unprecedented prosperity. The pilgrimage to Mecca of the ruler **Mansa Kankan Musa**° (r. 1312–1337), in fulfillment of his personal duty as a Muslim, also gave him an opportunity to display Mali's exceptional wealth. As befitted a powerful ruler, he

Zambezi (zam-BEE-zee) **Zimbabwe** (zim-BAHB-way)
bilad al-sudan (bih-LAD uhs–soo-DAN)

Takrur (TAHK-roor) **Sumanguru** (soo-muhn-GOO-roo)
Sundiata (soon-JAH-tuh) **Malinke** (muh-LING-kay)
Mansa Kankan Musa (MAHN-suh KAHN-kahn MOO-suh)

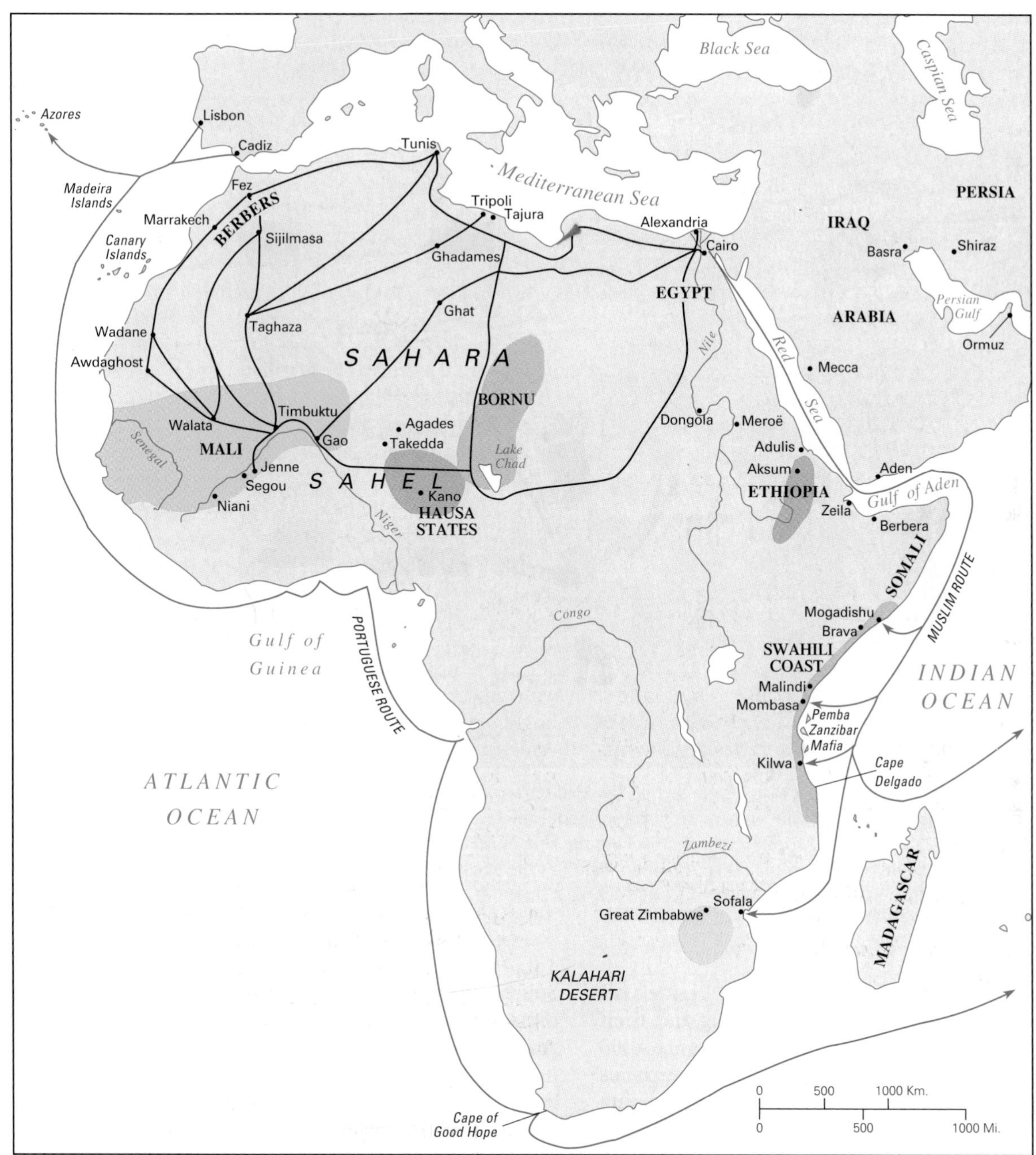

Map 14.2 Africa, 1200–1500 Many African states had beneficial links to the trade that crossed the Sahara and the Indian Ocean. Before 1500, sub-Saharan Africa's external ties were primarily with the Islamic world.

Map of the Western Sudan (1375) A Jewish geographer on the Mediterranean island of Majorca drew this lavish map in 1375, incorporating all that was known in Europe about the rest of the world. This portion of the Catalan Atlas shows a North African trader approaching the king of Mali, who holds a gold nugget in one hand and a golden scepter in the other. A caption identifies the black ruler as Mansa Musa, "the richest and noblest king in all the land." (Bibliothèque Nationale de France)

departed in 1324 with a large entourage. Besides his senior wife and 500 of her ladies in waiting and their slaves, according to one account, there were also 60,000 porters and a vast caravan of camels carrying supplies and provisions. For purchases and gifts he took eighty packages of gold each weighing 122 ounces (3.8 kilograms). In addition, 500 slaves each carried a golden staff. Mansa Musa was so lavish with his gifts when the entourage passed through Cairo that the value of gold there remained depressed for years.

After his return from the pilgrimage in 1325, Mansa Musa was eager to promote the religious and cultural influence of Islam in his empire. He built new mosques and opened Quranic schools in the cities along the Niger bend. When Ibn Battuta visited Mali from 1352 to 1354, during the reign of Mansa Musa's successor Mansa Suleiman° (r. 1341–1360), he praised the Malians for their faithful recitation of Islamic prayers and for their zeal in teaching children the Quran.

Ibn Battuta also had high praise for Mali's government. He reported that "complete and general safety" prevailed in the vast territories ruled by Suleiman and that foreign travelers had no reason to fear being robbed by thieves or having their goods confiscated if they died. (For Ibn Battuta's account of the sultan's court and his subjects' respect see Diversity and Dominance: Personal Styles of Rule in India and Mali.)

Two centuries after Sundiata founded the empire, Mali began to disintegrate. When Mansa Suleiman's successors proved to be less able rulers, rebellions broke out

---

Mansa Suleiman (MAHN-suh SOO-lay-mahn)

among the diverse peoples who had been subjected to Malinke rule. Avid for Mali's wealth, other groups attacked from without. The desert Tuareg retook their city of Timbuktu° in 1433. By 1500 the rulers of Mali had dominion over little more than the Malinke heartland.

The cities of the upper Niger survived Mali's collapse, but some of the western Sudan's former trade and intellectual life moved east to other African states in the central Sudan. Shortly after 1450 the rulers of several of the Hausa city-states adopted Islam as their official religion. The Hausa states were also able to increase their importance as manufacturing and trading centers, becoming famous for their cotton textiles and leatherworking. Also expanding in the late fifteenth century was the central Sudanic state of Kanem-Bornu°. It was descended from the ancient kingdom of Kanem, whose rulers had accepted Islam in about 1085. At its peak about 1250, Kanem had absorbed the state of Bornu south and west of Lake Chad and gained control of important trade routes crossing the Sahara. As Kanem-Bornu's armies conquered new territories in the late fifteenth century, they also spread the rule of Islam.

Salt Making in the Central Sahara For many centuries, people have extracted salt from the saline soils of places like Tegguida N'Tisent. Spring water is poured into shallow pits to dissolve the salt. The desert sun soon evaporates the water, leaving pure salt behind. (Afrique Photo, Cliché Naud, Paris)

The Delhi Sultanate in India

The arrival of Islam in India was more violent than in West Africa. Having long before lost the defensive unity of the Gupta Empire (see Chapter 7), the divided states of northwest India were subject to raids by Afghan warlords beginning in the early eleventh century. Motivated by a wish to spread their Islamic faith and by a desire for plunder, the raiders looted Hindu and Buddhist temples of their gold and jewels, kidnapped women for their harems, and slew Indian defenders by the thousands.

In the last decades of the twelfth century a new Turkish dynasty mounted a furious assault that succeeded in capturing the important northern Indian cities of Lahore and Delhi. The Muslim warriors could fire powerful crossbows from the backs of their galloping horses thanks to the use of iron stirrups. One partisan Muslim chronicler recorded, "The city [Delhi] and its vicinity was freed from idols and idol-worship, and in the sanctuaries of the images of the [Hindu] Gods, mosques were raised by the worshippers of one God."[2] The invaders' strength was bolstered by a ready supply of Turkish adventurers from Central Asia eager to follow individual leaders and by the unifying force of their common religious faith. Although Indians fought back bravely, their small states, often at war with one another, were unable to present an effective united front.

Between 1206 and 1236, the Muslim invaders extended their rule over the Hindu princes and chiefs in much of northern India. Sultan Iltutmish° (r. 1211–1236) consolidated the conquest of northern India in a series of military expeditions that made his empire the largest state in India (see Map 14.3). He also secured official recognition of the Delhi Sultanate as a Muslim state by the caliph of Baghdad. Although the looting and destruction of temples, enslavement, and massacres continued, especially on the frontiers of the empire, the Muslim invaders gradually underwent a transformation from brutal conquerors to more benign rulers. Muslim commanders accorded protection to the conquered, freeing them from persecution in return for payment of a special tax. Yet Hindus never forgot the intolerance and destruction of their first contacts with the invaders.

Timbuktu (tim-buk-TOO)
Kanem-Bornu (KAH-nuhm–BOR-noo)
Iltutmish (il-TOOT-mish)

DIVERSITY AND DOMINANCE

PERSONAL STYLES OF RULE IN INDIA AND MALI

Ibn Battuta wrote vivid descriptions of the powerful men who dominated the Muslim states he visited. Although his accounts are explicitly about the rulers, they also raise important issues about their relations with their subjects. The following account of Sultan Muhammad ibn Tughluq of Delhi may be read as a treatise on the rights and duties of rulers and ways in which individual personalities shaped diverse governing styles.

Muhammad is a man who, above all others, is fond of making presents and shedding blood. There may always be seen at his gate some poor person becoming rich, or some living one condemned to death. His generous and brave actions, and his cruel and violent deeds, have obtained notoriety among the people. In spite of this, he is the most humble of men, and the one who exhibits the greatest equity. The ceremonies of religion are dear to his ears, and he is very severe in respect of prayer and the punishment which follows its neglect. . . .

When drought prevailed throughout India and Sind, . . . the Sultan gave orders that provisions for six months should be supplied to all the inhabitants of Delhi from the royal granaries. . . . The officers of justice made registers of the people of the different streets, and these being sent up, each person received sufficient provisions to last him for six months.

The Sultan, notwithstanding all I have said about his humility, his justice, his kindness to the poor, and his boundless generosity, was much given to bloodshed. It rarely happened that the corpse of some one who had been killed was not seen at the gate of his palace. I have often seen men killed and their bodies left there. One day I went to his palace and my horse shied. I looked before me, and I saw a white heap on the ground, and when I asked what it was, one of my companions said it was the trunk of a man cut into three pieces. The sovereign punished little faults like great ones, and spared neither the learned, the religious, nor the noble. Every day hundreds of individuals were brought chained into his hall of audience; their hands tied to their necks and their feet bound together. Some of them were killed, and others were tortured, or well beaten . . . .

The Sultan has a brother named Masud Khan, [who] was one of the handsomest fellows I have even seen. The king suspected him of intending to rebel, so he questioned him, and, under fear of the torture, Masud confessed the charge. Indeed, every one who denies charges of this nature, which the Sultan brings against him, is put to the torture, and most people prefer death to being tortured. The Sultan had his brother's head cut off in the palace, and the corpse, according to custom, was left neglected for three days in the same place. The mother of Masud had been stoned two years before in the same place on a charge of debauchery or adultery. . . .

One of the most serious charges against this Sultan is that he forced all the inhabitants of Delhi to leave their homes. [After] the people of Delhi wrote letters full of insults and invectives against [him,] the Sultan . . . decided to ruin Delhi, so he purchased all the houses and inns from the inhabitants, paid them the price, and then ordered them to remove to Daulatabad. . . .

The greater part of the inhabitants departed, but [h]is slaves found two men in the streets: one was paralyzed, the other blind. They were brought before the sovereign, who ordered the paralytic to be shot away from a *manjanik* [catapult], and the blind man to be dragged from Delhi to Daulatabad, a journey of forty days' distance. The poor wretch fell to pieces during the journey, and only one of his legs reached Daulatabad. All of the inhabitants of Delhi left; they abandoned their baggage and their merchandize, and the city remained a perfect desert.

A person in whom I felt confidence assured me that the Sultan mounted one evening upon the roof of his palace, and, casting his eyes over the city of Delhi, in which there was neither fire, smoke, nor light, he said, "Now my heart is satisfied, and my feelings are appeased." . . . When we entered this capital, we found it in the state which has been described. It was empty, abandoned, and had but a small population.

In his description of Mansa Suleiman of Mali in 1353, Ibn Battuta places less emphasis on personality, a difference that may only be due to the fact that he had little personal contact with him. He stresses the huge social distance between the ruler and the ruled, between the master and the slave, and goes on to tell more of the ways in which Islam had altered life in Mali's cities as well as complaining about customs that the introduction of Islam had not changed.

The sultan of Mali is *Mansa* Suleiman, *mansa* meaning sultan, and Suleiman being his proper name. He is miserly, not a man from which one might hope for a rich present. It happened that I spent these two months without seeing him on account of my illness. Later on he held a banquet . . . to which the commanders, doctors, *qadi* and preacher were invited, and I went along with them. . . .

On certain days the sultan holds audiences in the palace yard, where there is a platform under a tree . . . carpeted with silk, [over which] is raised the umbrella, . . . surmounted by a bird in gold, about the size of a falcon. The sultan comes out of a door in a corner of the palace, carrying a bow in his hand and a quiver on his back. On his head he has a golden skullcap, bound with a gold band which has narrow ends shaped like knives, more than a span in length. His usual dress is a velvety red tunic, made of the European fabrics called *mutanfas.* The sultan is preceded by his musicians, who carry gold and silver [two-stringed guitars], and behind him come three hundred armed slaves. He walks in a leisurely fashion, affecting a very slow movement, and even stops and looks round the assembly, then ascends [the platform] in the sedate manner of a preacher ascending a mosque-pulpit. As he takes his seat, the drums, trumpets, and bugles are sounded. Three slaves go at a run to summon the sovereign's deputy and the military commanders, who enter and sit down. . . .

The blacks are of all people the most submissive to their king and the most abject in their behavior before him. They swear by his name, saying *Mansa Suleiman ki* [by Mansa Suleiman's law]. If he summons any of them while he is holding an audience in his pavilion, the person summoned takes off his clothes and puts on worn garments, removes his turban and dons a dirty skullcap and enters with his garments and trousers raised knee-high. He goes forward in an attitude of humility and dejection, and knocks the ground hard with his elbows, then stands with bowed head and bent back listening to what he says. If anyone addresses the king and receives a reply from him, he uncovers his back and throws dust over his head and back, for all the world like a bather splashing himself with water. I used to wonder how it was that they did not blind themselves.

Among the admirable qualities of these people, the following are to be noted:

1. The small number of acts of injustice that one finds there; for the blacks are of all people those who most abhor injustice. The sultan pardons no one who is guilty of it.
2. The complete and general safety one enjoys throughout the land. The traveller has no more reason than the man who stays at home to fear brigands, thieves, or ravishers.
3. The blacks do not confiscate the goods of white men [i.e., North Africans and the Middle Easterners] who die in their country, not even when these consist of big treasure, They deposit them, on the contrary, with a man of confidence among the whites until those who have a right to the goods present themselves and take possession.
4. They make all their prayers punctually; they assiduously attend their meetings of the faithful, and punish their children if these should fail in this. On Fridays, anyone who is late at the mosque will find nowhere to pray, the crowd is so great. . . .
5. The blacks wear fine white garments on Fridays. If by chance a man has no more than one shirt or a soiled tunic, at least he washes it before putting it on to go to public prayer.
6. They zealously learn the Koran by heart. Those children who are neglectful in this are put in chains until they have memorized the Koran by heart. . . .

But these people have some deplorable customs, as for example:

1. Women servants, slave women, and young girls go about quite naked, not even covering their sexual parts. I saw many like this during Ramadan. . . .
2. Women go naked in the sultan's presence, too, without even a veil; his daughters also go about naked. On the twenty-seventh night of Ramadan I saw about a hundred women slaves coming out of the sultan's palace with food and they were naked. Two daughters of the sultan were with them, and these had no veil either, although they had big breasts.
3. The blacks throw dust and cinders on their heads as a sign of good manners and respect.
4. They have buffoons who appear before the sultan when his poets are reciting their praise songs.
5. And then a good number of the blacks eat the flesh of dogs and donkeys.

QUESTIONS FOR ANALYSIS

1. **How would the actions of these rulers have enhanced their authority? To what extent do their actions reflect Islamic influences?**
2. **Although Ibn Battuta tells what the rulers did, can you imagine how one of their subjects would have described his or her perception of the same events and customs?**
3. **Which parts of Ibn Battuta's descriptions seem to be objective and believable? Which parts are more reflective of his personal values?**

Source: The first excerpt is from Henry M. Elliot, *The History of India as Told by Its Own Historians* (London: Trübner and Co., 1869–1871) 3:611–614. The second excerpt is adapted from H. A. R. Gibb, ed., *Selections from the Travels of Ibn Battuta in Asia and Africa, 1325–1354* (London: Cambridge University Press, 1929), pp. 326–328.

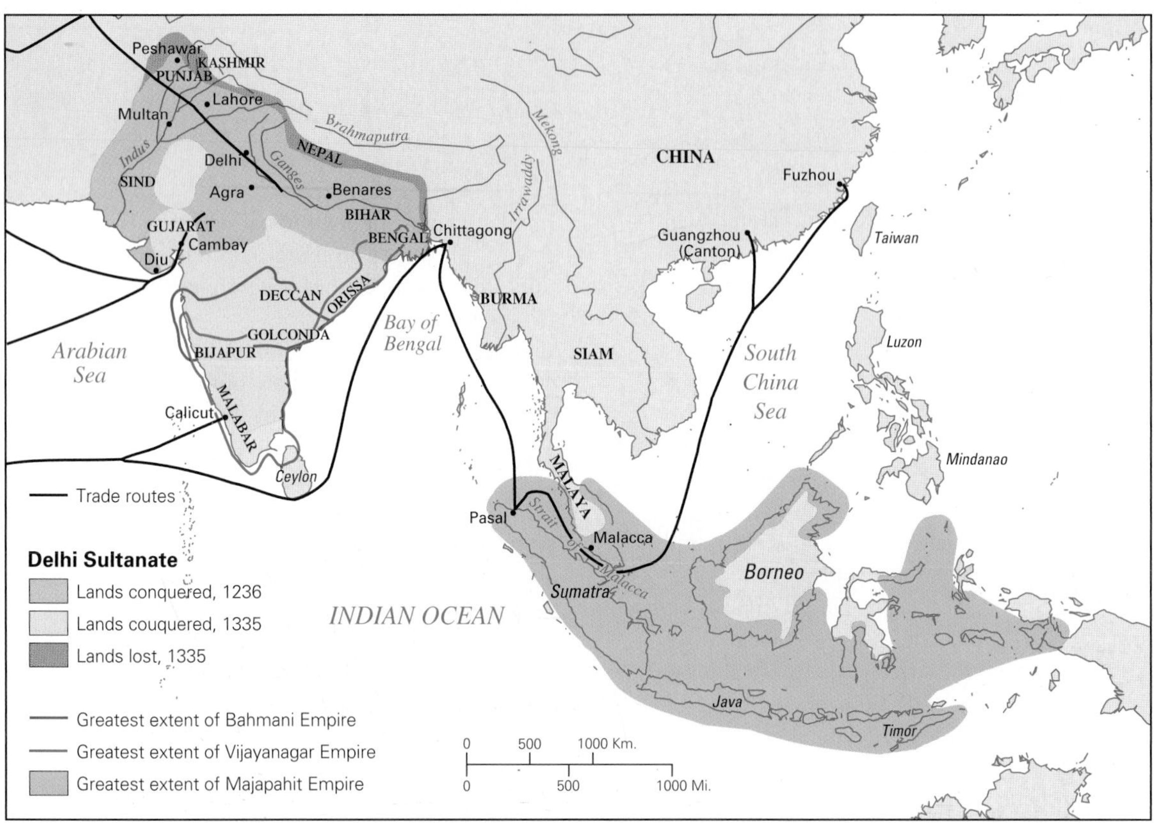

Map 14.3 South and Southeast Asia, 1200–1500 The rise of new empires and the expansion of maritime trade reshaped the lives of many tropical Asians.

To the astonishment of his ministers, Iltutmish passed over his weak and pleasure-seeking sons and designated his beloved and talented daughter Raziya° as his heir. When they questioned the unprecedented idea of a woman ruling a Muslim state, he said, "My sons are devoted to the pleasures of youth: no one of them is qualified to be king. . . . There is no one more competent to guide the State than my daughter.

In the event, her brother—whose great delight was riding his elephant through the bazaar, showering the crowds with coins—ruled ineptly for seven months before the ministers relented and put Raziya (r. 1236–1240) on the throne.

A chronicler who knew her explained why the reign of this able ruler lasted less than four years:

> Sultan Raziya was a great monarch. She was wise, just, and generous, a benefactor to her kingdom, a dispenser of justice, the protector of her subjects, and the leader of her armies. She was endowed with all the qualities befitting a king, but that she was not born of the right sex, and so in the estimation of men all these virtues were worthless. May God have mercy upon her![3]

Doing her best to prove herself a proper king, Raziya dressed like a man and rode at the head of her troops atop an elephant. Nothing, however, could overcome the prejudice against a woman ruler. In the end the Turkish chiefs imprisoned her. Soon after she escaped, she died at the hands of a robber.

After a half-century of stagnation and rebellion, the ruthless but efficient policies of Sultan Ala-ud-din Khalji° (r. 1296–1316) increased his control over the empire's outlying provinces. Successful frontier raids and high taxes kept his treasury full; wage and price controls in Delhi kept down the cost of maintaining a large army; and a network of spies stifled intrigue. When a Mongol threat from the northeast eased, Ala-ud-din's forces extended the sultanate's southern flank, seizing the rich

Raziya (rah-ZEE-uh)

Ala-ud-din Khalji (uh-LAH–uh-DEEN KAL-jee)

Meenakshi Temple, Madurai, India Some 15,000 pilgrims a day visit the large Hindu temple of Meenakshi (the fish-eyed goddess) in the ancient holy city of Madurai in India's southeastern province of Tamil Nadu. The temple complex dates from at least 1000 C.E., although the elaborately painted statues of these gopuram (gate towers) have been rebuilt and restored many times. The largest gopura rises 150 feet (46 meters) above the ground. (Jean Louis NOU/akg-images)

trading state of **Gujarat**° in 1298. Then troops drove southward, briefly seizing the southern tip of the Indian peninsula.

At the time of Ibn Battuta's visit, Delhi's ruler was Sultan Muhammad ibn Tughluq° (r. 1325–1351), who received his visitor at his palace's celebrated Hall of a Thousand Pillars. The world traveler praised the sultan's piety and generosity, but also recounted his cruelties (see Diversity and Dominance: Personal Styles of Rule in India and Mali). In keeping with these complexities, the sultan resumed a policy of aggressive expansion that enlarged the sultanate to its greatest extent. He balanced that policy with religious toleration intended to win the loyalty of Hindus and other non-Muslims. He even attended Hindu religious festivals. However, his successor Firuz Shah° (r. 1351–1388) alienated powerful Hindus by taxing the Brahmins, preferring to cultivate good relations with the Muslim elite. Muslim chroniclers praised him for constructing forty mosques, thirty colleges, and a hundred hospitals.

A small minority in a giant land, the Turkish rulers relied on terror more than on toleration to keep their subjects submissive, on harsh military reprisals to put down rebellion, and on pillage and high taxes to sustain the ruling elite in luxury and power. Though little different from most other large states of the time (including Mali) in being more a burden than a benefit to most of its subjects, the sultanate never lost the disadvantage of foreign origins and alien religious identity. Nevertheless, over time, the sultans incorporated some Hindus into their administration. Some members of the ruling elite also married women from prominent Hindu families, though the brides had to become Muslims.

Personal and religious rivalries within the Muslim elite, as well as the discontent of the Hindus, threatened the Delhi Sultanate with disintegration whenever it showed weakness and finally hastened its end. In the mid-fourteenth century Muslim nobles challenged the sultan's dominion and successfully established the

Gujarat (goo-juh-RAHT) **Tughluq** (toog-LOOK)
Firuz Shah (fuh-ROOZ shah)

Bahmani° kingdom (1347–1482), which controlled the Deccan Plateau. To defend themselves against the southward push of Bahmani armies, the Hindu states of southern India united to form the Vijayanagar° Empire (1336–1565), which at its height controlled the rich trading ports on both coasts and held Ceylon as a tributary state.

The rulers of Vijayanagar and the Bahmani turned a blind eye to religious differences when doing so favored their interests. Bahmani rulers sought to balance devotion to Muslim domination with the practical importance of incorporating the leaders of the majority Hindu population into the government, marrying Hindu wives, and appointing Brahmins to high offices. Vijayanagar rulers hired Muslim cavalry specialists and archers to strengthen their military forces, and they formed an alliance with the Muslim-ruled state of Gujarat.

By 1351, when all of South India was independent of Delhi's rule, much of north India was also in rebellion. In the east, Bengal successfully broke away from the sultanate in 1338, becoming a center of the mystical Sufi tradition of Islam (see Chapter 9). In the west, Gujarat had regained its independence by 1390. The weakening of Delhi's central authority revived Mongol interests in the area. In 1398 the Turko-Mongol leader Timur (see Chapter 13) seized the opportunity to invade and captured the city of Delhi. When his armies withdrew the next year with vast quantities of pillage and tens of thousands of captives, the largest city in southern Asia lay empty and in ruins. The Delhi Sultanate never recovered.

For all its shortcomings, the Delhi Sultanate was important in the development of centralized political authority in India. It established a bureaucracy headed by the sultan, who was aided by a prime minister and provincial governors. There were efforts to improve food production, promote trade and economic growth, and establish a common currency. Despite the many conflicts that Muslim conquest and rule provoked, Islam gradually acquired a permanent place in South Asia.

INDIAN OCEAN TRADE

The maritime network that stretched across the Indian Ocean from the Islamic heartland of Iran and Arabia to Southeast Asia connected to Europe, Africa, and China. The Indian Ocean region was the world's richest maritime trading network and an area of rapid Muslim expansion.

Bahmani (bah MAHN-ee) **Vijayanagar** (vee-juh-yah-NAH-gar)

Monsoon Mariners

The rising prosperity of Asian, European, and African states stimulated the expansion of trade in the Indian Ocean after 1200. Some of the growth was in luxuries for the wealthy—precious metals and jewels, rare spices, fine textiles, and other manufactures. The construction of larger ships also made shipments of bulk cargoes of ordinary cotton textiles, pepper, food grains (rice, wheat, barley), timber, horses, and other goods profitable. When the collapse of the Mongol Empire in the fourteenth century disrupted overland trade routes across Central Asia, the Indian Ocean routes assumed greater strategic importance in tying together the peoples of Eurasia and Africa.

Some goods were transported from one end of this trading network to the other, but few ships or crews made a complete circuit. Instead the Indian Ocean trade was divided into two legs: one from the Middle East across the Arabian Sea to India, and the other from India across the Bay of Bengal to Southeast Asia (see Map 14.4).

The characteristic cargo and passenger ship of the Arabian Sea was the **dhow**° (see Environment and Technology: The Indian Ocean Dhow). Ports on the Malabar coast of southwestern India constructed many of these vessels, which grew from an average capacity of 100 tons in 1200 to 400 tons in 1500. On a typical expedition, a dhow might sail west from India to Arabia and Africa on the northeast monsoon winds (December to March) and return on the southwest monsoons (April to August). Small dhows kept the coast in sight. Relying on the stars to guide them, skilled pilots steered large vessels by the quicker route straight across the water. A large dhow could sail from the Red Sea to mainland Southeast Asia in from two to four months, but few did so. Instead, cargoes and passengers normally sailed eastward to India in junks, which dominated travel in the Bay of Bengal and the South China Sea.

The largest, most technologically advanced, and most seaworthy vessel of this time, the junk had been developed in China. Junks were built from heavy spruce or fir planks held together with enormous nails. The space below the deck was divided into watertight compartments to minimize flooding in case of damage to the ship's hull. According to Ibn Battuta, the largest junks had twelve sails made of bamboo and carried a crew of a thousand men, of whom four hundred were soldiers. A large junk might have up to a hundred passenger cabins and could carry a cargo of over 1,000 tons. Chinese junks dominated China's foreign shipping to Southeast Asia

dhow (dow)

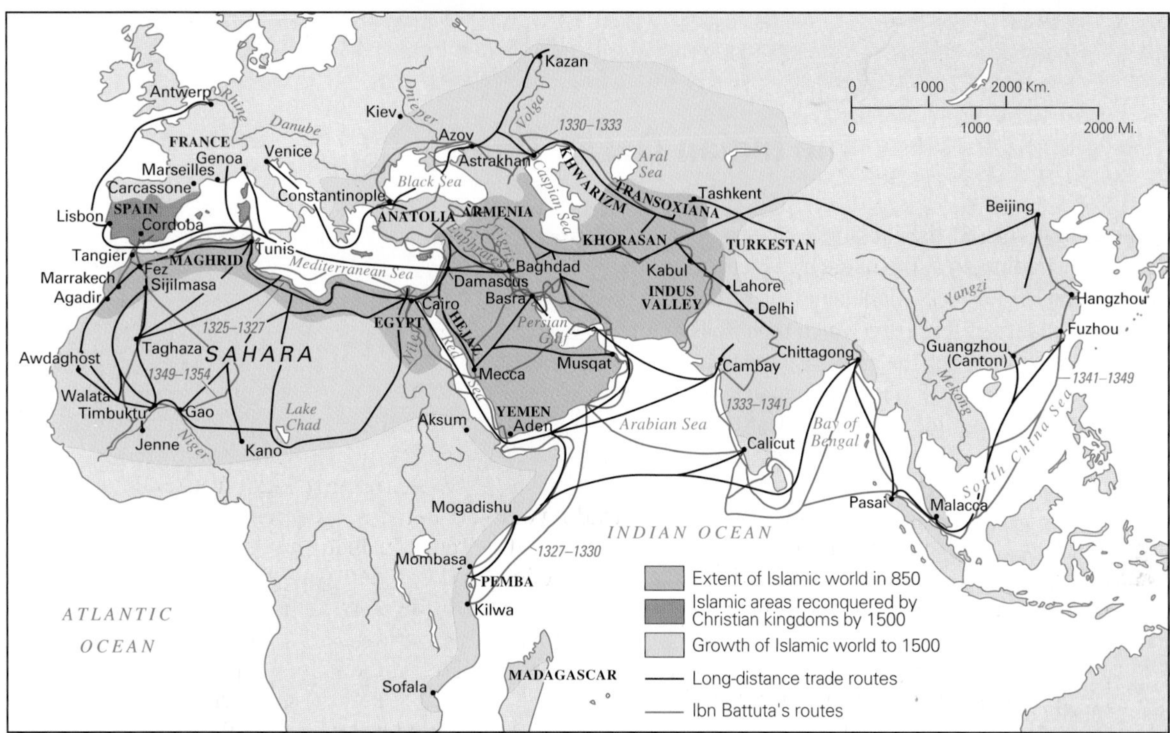

Map 14.4 Arteries of Trade and Travel in the Islamic World, to 1500 Ibn Battuta's journeys across Africa and Asia made use of land and sea routes along which Muslim traders and the Islamic faith had long traveled.

and India, but not all of the junks that plied these waters were Chinese. During the fifteenth century, vessels of this type came from shipyards in Bengal and Southeast Asia and were sailed by local crews.

The trade of the Indian Ocean was decentralized and cooperative. Commercial interests, rather than political authorities, tied several distinct regional networks together (see Map 14.4). Eastern Africa supplied gold from inland areas. Ports around the Arabian peninsula shipped horses and goods from the northern parts of the Middle East, the Mediterranean, and eastern Europe. At the center of the Indian Ocean trade, merchants in the cities of coastal India received goods from east and west, sold some locally, passed others along, and added vast quantities of Indian goods to the trade. The Strait of Malacca°, between the eastern end of the Indian Ocean and the South China Sea, was the meeting point of trade from Southeast Asia, China, and the Indian Ocean. In each region certain ports functioned as giant emporia, consolidating goods from smaller ports and inland areas for transport across the seas. The operation of this complex trading system can best be understood by looking at some of the regions and their emporia in greater detail.

Africa: The Swahili and Zimbabwe

Trade expanded steadily along the East African coast from about 1250, giving rise to between thirty and forty separate city-states by 1500. As a result of this rising prosperity, new masonry buildings, sometimes three or four stories high, replaced many of the mud and thatch African fishing villages. Archaeology reveals the growing presence of imported glass beads, Chinese porcelain, and other exotic goods. As a result of trading contacts, many loan words from Arabic and Persian enriched the language of the coastal Africans, and the first to write in it used Arabic script. The visitors called these people "Swahili,"° from the Arabic name *sawahil*° *al-sudan*, meaning "shores of the blacks," and the name stuck.

Malacca (meh-LAK-eh)

Swahili (swah-HEE-lee) ***sawahil*** (suh-WAH-hil)

ENVIRONMENT + TECHNOLOGY

The Indian Ocean Dhow

The sailing vessels that crossed the Indian Ocean shared the diversity of that trading area. The name by which we know them, *dhow*, comes from the Swahili language of the East African coast. The planks of teak from which their hulls were constructed were hewn from the tropical forests of South India and Southeast Asia. Their pilots, who navigated by stars at night, used the ancient technique that Arabs had used to find their way across the desert. Some pilots used a magnetic compass, which originated in China.

Dhows came in various sizes and designs, but all had two distinctive features in common. The first was hull construction. The hulls of dhows consisted of planks that were sewn together, not nailed. Cord made of fiber from the husk of coconuts or other materials was passed through rows of holes drilled in the planks. Because cord is weaker than nails, outsiders considered this shipbuilding technique strange. Marco Polo fancifully suggested that it indicated sailors' fear that large ocean magnets would pull any nails out of their ships. More probable explanations are that pliant sewn hulls were cheaper to build than rigid nailed hulls and were less likely to be damaged if the ships ran aground on coral reefs.

The second distinctive feature of dhows was their triangular (lateen) sails made of palm leaves or cotton. The sails were suspended from tall masts and could be turned to catch the wind.

The sewn hull and lateen sails were technologies developed centuries earlier, but there were two innovations between 1200 and 1500. First, a rudder positioned at the stern (rear end) of the ship replaced the large side oar that formerly had controlled steering. Second, shipbuilders increased the size of dhows to accommodate bulkier cargoes.

Dhow This modern model shows the vessel's main features. (National Maritime Museum, London)

Royal Enclosure, Great Zimbabwe Inside these oval stone walls the rulers of the trading state of Great Zimbabwe lived. Forced to enter the enclosure through a narrow corridor between two high walls, visitors were meant to be awestruck. (Courtesy of the Department of Information, Rhodesia)

At the time of Ibn Battuta's visit, the southern city of Kilwa had displaced Mogadishu as the **Swahili Coast's** most important commercial center. The traveler declared Kilwa "one of the most beautiful and well-constructed towns in the world." He noted that its dark-skinned inhabitants were devout and pious Muslims, and he took special pains to praise their ruler as a man rich in the traditional Muslim virtues of humility and generosity.

Swahili oral traditions associate the coast's commercial expansion with the arrival of Arab and Iranian merchants, but do not say what had attracted them. In Kilwa's case the answer is gold. By the late fifteenth century the city was exporting a ton of gold a year. The gold was mined by inland Africans much farther south. Much of it came from or passed through a powerful state on the plateau south of the Zambezi River, whose capital city is known as **Great Zimbabwe.** At its peak in about 1400, the city, which occupied 193 acres (78 hectares), may have had 18,000 inhabitants.

Between about 1250 and 1450, local African craftsmen built stone structures for Great Zimbabwe's rulers, priests, and wealthy citizens. The largest structure, a walled enclosure the size and shape of a large football stadium, served as the king's court. Its walls of unmortared stone were up to 17 feet (5 meters) thick and 32 feet (10 meters) high. Inside the walls were many buildings, including a large conical stone tower. The stone ruins of Great Zimbabwe are one of the most famous historical sites in sub-Saharan Africa.

Mixed farming and cattle-herding was Great Zimbabwe's economic base, but, as in Mali, the state's wealth came from long-distance trade. Trade began regionally with copper ingots from the upper Zambezi Valley, salt, and local manufactures. The gold exports into the Indian Ocean in the fourteenth and fifteenth centuries brought Zimbabwe to the peak of its political and economic power. However, historians suspect that the city's residents depleted nearby forests for firewood while their cattle overgrazed surrounding grasslands. The resulting ecological crisis hastened the empire's decline in the fifteenth century.

Arabia: Aden and the Red Sea

The city of **Aden**° had a double advantage in the Indian Ocean trade. Most of the rest of Arabia was desert, but monsoon winds brought Aden enough rainfall to supply drinking water to a large population and to grow grain for export. In addition, Aden's location (see Map 14.2) made it a convenient stopover for trade with India, the Persian Gulf, East Africa, and Egypt. Aden's merchants sorted out the goods from one place and sent them on to another: cotton cloth and beads from India, spices from Southeast Asia, horses from Arabia and Ethiopia, pearls from the Red Sea, luxurious manufactures from Cairo, slaves, gold, and ivory from Ethiopia, and grain, opium, and dyes from Aden's own hinterland.

After visiting Mecca in 1331, Ibn Battuta sailed down the Red Sea to Aden, probably wedged among bales of trade goods. His comments on the great wealth of Aden's leading merchants include a story about the slave of one merchant who paid the fabulous sum of 400 dinars for a ram in order to keep the slave of another merchant from buying it. Instead of punishing the slave for this extravagance, the master freed him as a reward for outdoing his rival. Ninety years later a Chinese Muslim visitor, Ma Huan, found "the country . . . rich, and the people numerous," living in stone residences several stories high.

Common commercial interests generally promoted good relations among the different religions and cultures of this region. For example, in the mid-thirteenth century a wealthy Jew from Aden named Yosef settled in Christian Ethiopia, where he acted as an adviser. South Arabia had been trading with neighboring parts of Africa since before the time of King Solomon of Israel. The dynasty that ruled Ethiopia after 1270 claimed descent from Solomon and from the South Arabian princess Sheba. Solomonic Ethiopia's consolidation was associated with a great increase in trade through the Red Sea port of Zeila°, including slaves, amber, and animal pelts, which went to Aden and on to other destinations.

Friction sometimes arose, however. In the fourteenth century the Sunni Muslim king of Yemen sent materials for the building of a large mosque in Zeila, but the local Somalis (who were Shi'ite Muslims) threw the stones into the sea. The result was a year-long embargo of Zeila ships in Aden. In the late fifteenth century Ethiopia's territorial expansion and efforts to increase control over the trade provoked conflicts with Muslims who ruled the coastal states of the Red Sea.

Aden (AY-den) **Zeila** (ZEYE-luh)

India: Gujarat and the Malabar Coast

The state of Gujarat in western India prospered as its ports shared in the expanding trade of the Arabian Sea and the rise of the Delhi Sultanate. Blessed with a rich agricultural hinterland and a long coastline, Gujarat attracted new trade after the Mongol capture of Baghdad in 1258 disrupted the northern land routes. Gujarat's forcible incorporation into the Delhi Sultanate in 1298 had mixed results. The state suffered from the violence of the initial conquest and from subsequent military crackdowns, but it also prospered from increased trade with Delhi's wealthy ruling class. Independent again after 1390, Gujarat's Muslim rulers extended their control over neighboring Hindu states and regained their preeminent position in the Indian Ocean trade.

The state derived much of its wealth from its export of cotton textiles and indigo to the Middle East and Europe, largely in return for gold and silver. Gujaratis also dominated the trade from India to the Swahili Coast, selling cotton cloth, carnelian beads, and foodstuffs in exchange for ebony, slaves, ivory, and gold. During the fifteenth century traders expanded their trade from Gujarat eastward to the Strait of Malacca. These Gujarati merchants helped spread the Islamic faith among East Indian traders, some of whom even imported specially carved gravestones from Gujarat.

Unlike Kilwa and Aden, Gujarat was important for its manufactures as well as its commerce. According to the thirteenth-century Venetian traveler Marco Polo, Gujarat's leatherworkers dressed enough skins in a year to fill several ships to Arabia and other places and also made beautiful sleeping mats for export to the Middle East "in red and blue leather, exquisitely inlaid with figures of birds and beasts, and skilfully embroidered with gold and silver wire," as well as leather cushions embroidered in gold. Later observers considered the Gujarati city of Cambay the equal of cities in Flanders and northern Italy (see Chapter 15) in the size, skill, and diversity of its textile industries.

Gujarat's cotton, linen, and silk cloth, as well as its carpets and quilts, found a large market in Europe, Africa, the Middle East, and Southeast Asia. Cambay also was famous for its polished gemstones, gold jewelry, carved ivory, stone beads, and both natural and artificial pearls. At the height of its prosperity in the fifteenth century, this substantial city's well-laid-out streets and open places boasted fine stone houses with tiled roofs. Although most of Gujarat's overseas trade was in the hands of its Muslim residents, members of its Hindu merchant caste profited so much from related commercial activities that their wealth and luxurious lives were the envy of other Indians.

More southerly cities on the Malabar Coast duplicated Gujarat's importance in trade and manufacturing. Calicut° and other coastal cities prospered from their commerce in locally made cotton textiles and locally grown grains and spices, and as clearing-houses for the long-distance trade of the Indian Ocean. The Zamorin° (ruler) of Calicut presided over a loose federation of its Hindu rulers along the Malabar Coast. As in eastern Africa and Arabia, rulers were generally tolerant of other religious and ethnic groups that were important to commercial profits. Most trading activity was in the hands of Muslims, many originally from Iran and Arabia, who intermarried with local Indian Muslims. Jewish merchants also operated from Malabar's trading cities.

Southeast Asia: The Rise of Malacca

At the eastern end of the Indian Ocean, the principal passage into the South China Sea was through the Strait of Malacca between the Malay Peninsula and the island of Sumatra (see Map 14.3). As trade increased in the fourteenth and fifteenth centuries, this commercial choke point became the object of considerable political rivalry. The mainland kingdom of Siam gained control of most of the upper Malay Peninsula, while the Java-based kingdom of Majapahit° extended its dominion over the lower Malay Peninsula and much of Sumatra. Majapahit, however, was not strong enough to suppress a nest of Chinese pirates who had gained control of the Sumatran city of Palembang° and preyed on ships sailing through the strait. In 1407 a fleet sent by the Chinese government smashed the pirates' power and took their chief back to China for trial.

Weakened by internal struggles, Majapahit was unable to take advantage of China's intervention. The chief beneficiary of the safer commerce was the newer port of **Malacca** (or Melaka), which dominated the narrowest part of the strait. Under the leadership of a prince from Palembang, Malacca had quickly grown from an obscure fishing village into an important port by means of a series of astute alliances. Nominally subject to the king of Siam, Malacca also secured an alliance with China that was sealed by the visit of the imperial fleet in 1407. The conversion of an early ruler from Hinduism to Islam helped promote trade with the Gujarati and other Muslim merchants who dominated so much of the Indian Ocean commerce. Merchants also appreciated Malacca's security and low taxes.

Malacca served as the meeting point for traders from India and China as well as an emporium for Southeast Asian trade: rubies and musk from Burma, tin from Malaya, gold from Sumatra, cloves and nutmeg from the Moluccas (or Spice Islands, as Europeans later dubbed them) to the east. Shortly after 1500, when Malacca was at its height, one resident counted eighty-four languages spoken among the merchants gathered there, who came from as far away as Turkey, Ethiopia, and the Swahili Coast. Four officials administered the large foreign merchant communities: one official for the very numerous Gujaratis, one for other Indians and Burmese, one for Southeast Asians, and one for the Chinese and Japanese. Malacca's wealth and its cosmopolitan residents set the standard for luxury in Malaya for centuries to come.

Calicut (KAL-ih-cut) **Zamorin** (ZAH-much-ruhn)
Majapahit (mah-jah-PAH-hit) **Palembang** (pah-lem-BONG)

Social and Cultural Change

State growth, commercial expansion, and the spread of Islam between 1200 and 1500 led to many changes in the social and cultural life of tropical peoples. The political and commercial elites at the top of society grew more numerous, as did the slaves who served their needs. The spread of Islamic practices and beliefs affected social and cultural life—witness words of Arabic origin like *Sahara, Sudan, Swahili,* and *monsoon*—yet local traditions remained important.

Architecture, Learning, and Religion

Social and cultural changes typically affect cities more than rural areas. As Ibn Battuta observed, wealthy merchants and the ruling elite spent lavishly on new mansions, palaces, and places of worship.

Places of worship from this period exhibit fascinating blends of older traditions and new influences. African Muslims strikingly rendered Middle Eastern mosque designs in local building materials: sun-baked clay and wood in the western Sudan, coral stone on the Swahili Coast. Hindu temple architecture influenced the design of mosques, which sometimes incorporated pieces of older structures. The congregational mosque at Cambay, built in 1325, was assembled out of pillars,

Church of Saint George, Ethiopia King Lalibela, who ruled the Christian kingdom of Ethiopia between about 1180 and 1220, had a series of churches carved out of solid volcanic rock to adorn his kingdom's new capital (also named Lalibela). The church of Saint George, excavated to a depth of 40 feet (13 meters) and hollowed out inside, has the shape of a Greek cross. (S. Sassoon/ Robert Harding Picture Library)

porches, and arches taken from sacked Hindu and Jain° temples. The culmination of a mature Hindu-Muslim architecture was the congregational mosque erected at the Gujarati capital of Ahmadabad° in 1423. It had an open courtyard typical of mosques everywhere, but the surrounding verandas incorporated many typical Gujarati details and architectural conventions.

Even more unusual than these Islamic architectural amalgams were the Christian churches of King Lalibela° of Ethiopia, constructed during the first third of the thirteenth century. As part of his new capital, Lalibela directed Ethiopian sculptors to carve eleven churches out of solid rock, each commemorating a sacred Christian site in Jerusalem. These unique structures carried on an old Ethiopian tradition of rock sculpture, though on a far grander scale.

Mosques, churches, and temples were centers of education as well as prayer. Muslims promoted literacy among their sons (and sometimes their daughters) so that they could read the religion's classic texts. Ibn Battuta reported seeing several boys in Mali who had been placed in chains until they finished memorizing passages of the Quran. In sub-Saharan Africa the spread of Islam was associated with the spread of literacy, which had previously been confined largely to Christian Ethiopia. Initially, literacy was in Arabic, but in time Arabic characters were used to write local languages.

Islam affected literacy less in India, which had an ancient heritage of writing. Arabic served primarily for religious purposes, while Persian became the language of high culture and was used at court. Eventually, **Urdu°** arose, a Persian-influenced literary form of Hindi written in Arabic characters. Muslims also introduced papermaking in India.

Advanced Muslim scholars studied Islamic law, theology, and administration, as well as works of mathematics, medicine, and science, derived in part from ancient Greek writings. By the sixteenth century in the West African city **Timbuktu,** there were over 150 Quranic

Jain (jine) **Ahmadabad** (AH-muhd-ah-bahd)
Lalibela (LAH-lee-BEL-uh)

Urdu (ER-doo)

schools, and advanced classes were held in the mosques and homes of the leading clerics. So great was the demand for books that they were the most profitable item to bring from North Africa to Timbuktu. At his death in 1536 one West African scholar, al-Hajj Ahmed of Timbuktu, possessed some seven hundred volumes, an unusually large library for that time. In Southeast Asia, Malacca became a center of Islamic learning from which scholars spread Islam throughout the region. Other important centers of learning developed in Muslim India, particularly in Delhi, the capital.

Even in conquered lands, such as India, Muslim rulers generally did not impose their religion. Example and persuasion by merchants and Sufis proved a more effective way of making converts. Many Muslims were active missionaries for their faith and worked hard to persuade others of its superiority. Islam's influence spread along regional trade routes from the Swahili Coast, in the Sudan, in coastal India, and in Southeast Asia. Commercial transactions could take place between people of different religions, but the common code of morality and law that Islam provided attracted many local merchants.

Marriage also spread Islam. Single Muslim men who journeyed along the trade routes often married local women and raised their children in the Islamic faith. Since Islam permitted a man to have up to four legal wives and many men took concubines as well, some wealthy men had dozens of children. In large elite Muslim households the many servants, both free and enslaved, were also required to be Muslims. Although such conversions were not fully voluntary, individuals could still find personal fulfillment in the Islamic faith.

In India Islamic invasions practically destroyed the last strongholds of long-declining Buddhism. In 1196 invaders overran the great Buddhist center of study at Nalanda° in Bihar° and burned its manuscripts, killing thousands of monks or driving them into exile in Nepal and Tibet. With Buddhism reduced to a minor faith in the land of its birth (see Chapter 8), Islam emerged as India's second most important religion. Hinduism was still India's dominant faith in 1500, but in most of maritime Southeast Asia Islam displaced Hinduism.

Islam also spread among the pastoral Fulani of West Africa and Somali of northeastern Africa, as well as among pastoralists in northwest India. In Bengal Muslim religious figures oversaw the conversion of jungle into farmland and thereby gained many converts among low-caste Hindus who admired the universalism of Islam.

Nalanda (nuh-LAN-duh) **Bihar** (bee-HAHR)

The spread of Islam did not simply mean the replacement of one set of beliefs by another. Islam also adapted to the cultures of the regions it penetrated, developing African, Indian, and Indonesian varieties.

Social and Gender Distinctions

The conquests and commerce brought new wealth to some and new hardships to others. The poor may not have become poorer, but a significant growth in slavery accompanied the rising prosperity of the elite. According to Islamic sources, military campaigns in India reduced hundreds of thousands of Hindu "infidels" to slavery. Delhi overflowed with slaves. Sultan Ala-ud-din owned 50,000; Firuz Shah had 180,000, including 12,000 skilled artisans. Sultan Tughluq sent 100 male slaves and 100 female slaves as a gift to the emperor of China in return for a similar gift. His successor prohibited any more exports of slaves, perhaps because of reduced supplies in the smaller empire.

Mali and Bornu sent slaves across the Sahara to North Africa, including young maidens and eunuchs (castrated males). Ethiopian expansion generated a regular supply of captives for sale to Aden traders at Zeila. About 2.5 million enslaved Africans may have crossed the Sahara and the Red Sea between 1200 and 1500. Other slaves were shipped from the Swahili Coast to India, where Africans played conspicuous roles in the navies, armies, and administrations of some Indian states, especially in the fifteenth century. A few African slaves even found their way to China, where a Chinese source dating from about 1225 says that rich families preferred gatekeepers whose bodies were "black as lacquer."

With "free" labor abundant and cheap, most slaves were trained for special purposes. In some places, skilled trades and military service were dominated by hereditary castes of slaves, some of whom were rich and powerful. Indeed, the earliest rulers of the Delhi Sultanate rose from military slaves. A slave general in the western Sudan named Askia Muhammad seized control of the Songhai Empire (Mali's successor) in 1493. Less fortunate slaves, like the men and women who mined copper in Mali, did hard menial work.

Wealthy households in Asia and Africa employed many slaves as servants. Eunuchs guarded the harems of wealthy Muslims; female slaves were in great demand as household servants, entertainers, and concubines. Some rich men aspired to have a concubine from every part of the world. One of Firuz Shah's nobles was said to have two thousand harem slaves, including women from Turkey and China.

Indian Woman Spinning, ca. 1500 This drawing of a Muslim woman by an Indian artist shows the influence of Persian styles. The spinning of cotton fiber into thread—women's work—was made much easier by the spinning wheel, which the Muslim invaders introduced. Men then wove the threads into the cotton textiles for which India was celebrated. (British Library, Oriental and Indian Office Library, Or 3299, f. 151)

Sultan Ala-ud-din's campaigns against Gujarat at the end of the thirteenth century yielded a booty of twenty thousand maidens in addition to innumerable younger children of both sexes. The supply of captives became so great that the lowest grade of horse sold for five times as much as an ordinary female slave destined for service, although beautiful young virgins destined for the harems of powerful nobles commanded far higher prices. Some decades later, when Ibn Battuta was given ten girls captured from among the "infidels," he commented: "Female captives [in Delhi] are very cheap because they are dirty and do not know civilized ways. Even the educated ones are cheap." It would seem fairer to say that such slaves were cheap because the large numbers offered for sale had made them so.

Hindu legal digests and commentaries suggest that the position of Hindu women may have improved somewhat overall. The ancient practice of sati°—in which an upper-caste widow threw herself on her husband's funeral pyre—remained a meritorious act strongly approved by social custom. But Ibn Battuta believed that sati was strictly optional, an interpretation reinforced by the Hindu commentaries that devote considerable attention to the rights of widows.

Indian parents still gave their daughters in marriage before the age of puberty, but consummation of the marriage was supposed to take place only when the young woman was ready. Wives were expected to observe far stricter rules of fidelity and chastity than were their husbands and could be abandoned for many serious breaches. But women often were punished by lighter penalties than men for offenses against law and custom.

A female's status was largely determined by the status of her male master—father, husband, or owner. Women usually were not permitted to play the kind of active roles in commerce, administration, or religion that would have given them scope for personal achievements. Even so, women possessed considerable skills within those areas of activity that social norms allotted to them.

Besides child rearing, one of the most widespread female skills was food preparation. So far, historians have paid little attention to the development of culinary skills, but preparing meals that were healthful and tasty required much training and practice, especially given the limited range of foods available in most places. One kitchen skill that has received greater attention is brewing, perhaps because men were the principal consumers. In many parts of Africa women commonly made beer from grains or bananas. These mildly alcoholic beverages, taken in moderation, were a nutritious source of vitamins and minerals. Socially they were an important part of male rituals of hospitality and relaxation.

Throughout tropical Africa and Asia women did much of the farm work. They also toted home heavy loads of food, firewood, and water for cooking, balanced on their heads. Other common female activities included making clay pots for cooking and storage and making clothing. In India the spinning wheel, introduced by the Muslim invaders, greatly reduced the cost of making yarn for weaving. Spinning was a woman's activity done in the home; the weavers were generally men. Marketing was a common activity among women, especially in West Africa, where they commonly sold agricultural products, pottery, and other craftwork in the markets.

Some free women found their status improved by becoming part of a Muslim household, while many others were forced to become servants and concubines. Adopting Islam did not require accepting all the social customs of the Arab world. Ibn Battuta was appalled that Muslim women in Mali did not completely cover their

sati (suh-TEE)

bodies and veil their faces when appearing in public. He considered their nakedness an offense to women's (and men's) modesty. In another part of Mali he berated a Muslim merchant from Morocco for permitting his wife to sit on a couch and chat with a male friend of hers. The husband replied, "The association of women with men is agreeable to us and part of good manners, to which no suspicion attaches." Ibn Battuta's shock at this "laxity" and his refusal to ever visit the merchant again reveal the patriarchal precepts that were dear to most elite Muslims. So does the fate of Sultan Raziya of Delhi.

CONCLUSION

Tropical Africa and Asia contained nearly 40 percent of the world's population and over a quarter of its habitable land. Between 1200 and 1500 commercial, political, and cultural expansion drew the region's diverse peoples closer together. The Indian Ocean became the world's most important and richest trading area. The Delhi Sultanate brought South Asia its greatest political unity since the decline of the Guptas. In the western Sudan, Mali extended the political and trading role pioneered by Ghana. This growth of trade and empires was closely connected with the enlargement of Islam's presence in the tropical world along with the introduction of greater diversity into Islamic practice.

But if change was an important theme of this period, so too was social and cultural stability. Most tropical Africans and Asians never ventured far outside the rural communities in which their families had lived for generations. Their lives followed the familiar pattern of the seasons, the cycle of religious rituals and festivals, and the stages from childhood to elder status. Custom and necessity defined occupations. Most people engaged in food production by farming, herding, and fishing; some specialized in crafts or religious leadership. Based on the accumulated wisdom about how best to deal with their environment, such village communities were remarkably hardy. They might be ravaged by natural disaster or pillaged by advancing armies, but over time most recovered. Empires and kingdoms rose and fell in these centuries, but the villages endured.

In comparison, social, political, and environmental changes taking place in the Latin West, described in the next chapter, were in many ways more profound and disruptive. They would have great implications for tropical peoples after 1500.

Key Terms

tropics	**dhow**
monsoon	**Swahili Coast**
Ibn Battuta	**Great Zimbabwe**
Delhi Sultanate	**Aden**
Mali	**Malacca**
Mansa Kankan Musa	**Urdu**
Gujarat	**Timbuktu**

Suggested Reading

The trading links among the lands around the Indian Ocean have attracted the attention of recent scholars. A fine place to begin is Patricia Risso, *Merchants and Faith: Muslim Commerce and Culture in the Indian Ocean* (1995). More ambitious but perhaps more inclined to overreach the evidence is Janet Abu-Lughod, *Before European Hegemony: The World System, A.D. 1250–1350* (1989), which may usefully be read with K. N. Chaudhuri, *Asia Before Europe: Economy and Civilization of the Indian Ocean from the Rise of Islam to 1750* (1991). Students will find clear summaries of Islam's influences in tropical Asia and Africa in Ira Lapidus, *A History of Islamic Societies,* 2d ed. (2002), part II, and of commercial relations in Philip D. Curtin, *Cross-Cultural Trade in World History* (1984).

Greater detail about tropical lands is found in regional studies. For Southeast Asia see Nicholas Tarling, ed., *The Cambridge History of Southeast Asia,* vol. 1 (1992); John F. Cady, *Southeast Asia: Its Historical Development* (1964); and G. Coedes, *The Indianized States of Southeast Asia,* ed. Walter F. Vella (1968). India is covered comprehensively by R. C. Majumdar, ed., *The History and Culture of the Indian People,* vol. 4, *The Delhi Sultanate,* 2d ed. (1967); with brevity by Stanley Wolpert, *A New History of India,* 6th ed. (1999); and from an intriguing perspective by David Ludden, *A Peasant History of South India* (1985). For advanced topics see Tapan Raychaudhuri and Irfan Habib, eds., *The Cambridge Economic History of India,* vol. 1, *c. 1200–c. 1750* (1982).

A great deal of new scholarship on Africa in this period is summarized in chapters 6 and 7 of Christopher Ehret's *The Civilizations of Africa: A History to 1800* (2002). See also the latter parts of Graham Connah's *African Civilizations: Precolonial Cities and States in Tropical Africa: An Archaeological Perspective* (1987), and, for greater depth, D. T. Niane, ed., *UNESCO General History of Africa,* vol. 4, *Africa from the Twelfth to the Sixteenth Century* (1984), and Roland Oliver, ed., *The Cambridge History of Africa,* vol. 3, *c. 1050 to c. 1600* (1977).

For accounts of slavery and the slave trade see Salim Kidwai, "Sultans, Eunuchs and Domestics: New Forms of Bondage in Medieval India," in *Chains of Servitude: Bondage and Slavery in India,* ed. Utsa Patnaik and Manjari Dingwaney (1985), and the first two chapters of Paul E. Lovejoy, *Transformations in Slavery: A History of Slavery in Africa,* 2d ed. (2000).

Three volumes of Ibn Battuta's writings have been translated by H. A. R. Gibb, *The Travels of Ibn Battuta, A.D. 1325–1354* (1958–1971). Ross E. Dunn, *The Adventures of Ibn Battuta: A Muslim of the 14th Century* (1986), provides a modern retelling of his travels with commentary. For annotated selections see Said Hamdun and Noël King, *Ibn Battuta in Black Africa* (1995).

The most accessible survey of Indian Ocean sea travel is George F. Hourani, *Arab Seafaring,* expanded ed. (1995). For a Muslim Chinese traveler's observations see Ma Huan, *Ying-yai Sheng-lan, "The Overall Survey of the Ocean's Shore" [1433],* trans. and ed. J. V. G. Mills (1970). Another valuable contemporary account of trade and navigation in the Indian Ocean is G. R. Tibbetts, *Arab Navigation in the Indian Ocean Before the Coming of the Portuguese, Being a Translation of the Kitab al-Fawa'id . . . of Ahmad b. Majidal-Najdi* (1981).

Notes

1. Tarikh-i-Wassaf, in Henry M. Elliot, *The History of India as Told by Its Own Historians,* ed. John Dowson (London: Trübner and Co., 1869–1871), 2:28.
2. Hasan Nizami, Taju-l Ma-asir, in Elliot, *The History of India as Told by Its Own Historians,* 2:219.
3. Minhaju-s Siraj, Tabakat-i Nasiri, in Elliot, *The History of India as Told by Its Own Historians,* 2:332–333.

15

The Latin West, 1200–1500

Burying Victims of the Black Death This scene from Tournai, Flanders, captures the magnitude of the plague.

CHAPTER OUTLINE

In the summer of 1454, a year after the Ottoman Turks had captured the Greek Christian city of Constantinople, Aeneas Sylvius Piccolomini° was trying to stir up support for a crusade to halt the Muslim advances that were engulfing southeastern Europe and that showed no sign of stopping. The man who in four years would become pope doubted that anyone could persuade the rulers of Christian Europe to take up arms together against the Muslims: "Christendom has no head whom all will obey;" he lamented, "neither the pope nor the emperor receives his due."

Aeneas Sylvius had good reason to believe that Latin Christians were more inclined to fight with each other than to join a common front against the Turks. French and English armies had been at war for more than a century. The German emperor presided over dozens of states that were virtually independent of his control. The numerous kingdoms and principalities of Mediterranean Europe had never achieved unity. With only slight exaggeration Aeneas Sylvius complained, "Every city has its own king, and there are as many princes as there are households."

He attributed this lack of unity to Europeans' being so preoccupied with personal welfare and material gain that they would never sacrifice themselves to stop the Turkish armies. During the century since a devastating plague had carried off a third of western Europe's population, people had become cynical about human nature and preoccupied with material things.

Yet despite all these divisions, disasters, and wars, historians now see the period from 1200 to 1500 (Europe's later Middle Ages) as a time of unusual progress. The avarice and greed Aeneas Sylvius lamented were the dark side of the material prosperity that was most evident in the splendid architecture, institutions of higher learning, and cultural achievements of the cities. Frequent wars caused havoc and destruction, but in the long run they promoted the development of more powerful weapons and more unified monarchies.

A European fifty years later would have known that the Turks did not overrun Europe, that a truce in the Anglo-French conflict would hold, and that explorers sent by Portugal and a newly united Spain would extend Europe's reach to other continents. In 1454 Aeneas Sylvius knew only what had been, and the conflicts and calamities of the past made him shudder.

Although their contemporary Muslim and Byzantine neighbors commonly called western Europeans "Franks," western Europeans ordinarily referred to themselves as "Latins." That term underscored their allegiance to the Latin rite of Christianity (and to its patriarch, the pope) as well as the use of the Latin language by their literate members. The **Latin West** deserves special attention because its achievements during this period had profound implications for the future of the world. The region was emerging from the economic and cultural shadow of its Islamic neighbors and, despite grave disruptions caused by plague and warfare, boldly setting out to extend its dominance. Some common elements promoted the Latin West's remarkable resurgence: competition, the pursuit of success, and the effective use of borrowed technology and learning.

As you read this chapter, ask yourself the following questions:

- How well did inhabitants of the Latin West deal with their natural environment?
- How did warfare help rulers in the Latin West acquire the skills, weapons, and determination that enabled them to challenge other parts of the world?
- How did superior technology in the Latin West promote excellence in business, learning, and architecture?
- How much did the region's achievements depend on its own people, and how much on things borrowed from Muslim and Byzantine neighbors?

Aeneas Sylvius Piccolomini (uh-NEE-uhs SIL-vee-uhs pee-kuh-lo-MEE-nee)

CHRONOLOGY

	Technology and Environment	Culture	Politics and Society
1200	**1200s** Use of crossbows and longbows becomes widespread; windmills in increased use	**1210s** Religious orders founded: Teutonic Knights, Franciscans, Dominicans **1225–1274** Thomas Aquinas, monk and philosopher **1265–1321** Dante Alighieri, poet **ca. 1267–1337** Giotto, painter	**1200s** Champagne fairs flourish **1204** Fourth Crusade launched **1215** Magna Carta issued
1300	**1300** First mechanical clocks in the West **1315–1317** Great Famine **1347–1351** Black Death **ca. 1350** Growing deforestation	**1300–1500** Rise of universities **1304–1374** Francesco Petrarch, humanist writer **1313–1375** Giovanni Boccaccio, humanist writer **ca. 1340–1400** Geoffrey Chaucer, poet **1389–1464** Cosimo de' Medici, banker **ca. 1390–1441** Jan van Eyck, painter	**1337** Start of Hundred Years War **1381** Wat Tyler's Rebellion
1400	**1400s** Large cannon in use in warfare; hand-held firearms become prominent **ca. 1450** First printing with movable type in the West **1454** Gutenberg Bible printed	**1449–1492** Lorenzo de' Medici, art patron **1452–1519** Leonardo da Vinci, artist **ca. 1466–1536** Erasmus of Rotterdam, humanist **1472–1564** Michelangelo, artist **1492** Explusion of Jews from Spain	**1415** Portuguese take Ceuta **1431** Joan of Arc burned as witch **1453** End of Hundred Years War; Turks take Constantinople **1469** Marriage of Ferdinand of Aragon and Isabella of Castile **1492** Fall of Muslim state of Granada

RURAL GROWTH AND CRISIS

Between 1200 and 1500 the Latin West brought more land under cultivation, adopted new farming techniques, and made greater use of machinery and mechanical forms of energy. Yet for most rural Europeans—more than nine out of ten people were rural—this period was a time of calamity and struggle. Most rural men and women worked hard for meager returns and suffered mightily from the effects of famine, epidemics, warfare, and social exploitation. After the devastation caused from 1347 to 1351 by the plague known as the Black Death, social changes speeded up by peasant revolts released many persons from serfdom and brought some improvements to rural life.

Rural French Peasants Many scenes of peasant life in winter are visible in this small painting by the Flemish Limbourg brothers from the 1410s. Above the snow-covered beehives one man chops firewood, while another drives a donkey loaded with firewood to a little village. At the lower right a woman, blowing on her frozen fingers, heads past the huddled sheep and hungry birds to join other women warming themselves in the cottage (whose outer wall the artists have cut away). (Musée Conde, Chantilly, France/Art Resource, NY)

Peasants and Population

Society was divided by class and gender. In 1200 most western Europeans were serfs, obliged to till the soil on large estates owned by the nobility and the church (see Chapter 10). Each noble household typically rested on the labors of from fifteen to thirty peasant families. The standard of life in the lord's stone castle or manor house stood in sharp contrast to that in the peasant's one-room thatched cottage containing little furniture and no luxuries. Despite numerous religious holidays, peasant cultivators labored long hours, but more than half of the fruits of their labor went to the landowner. Because of these meager returns, serfs were not motivated to introduce extensive improvements in farming practices.

Scenes of rural life show both men and women at work in the fields, although there is no reason to believe that equality of labor meant equality of decision making at home. In the peasant's hut, as elsewhere in medieval Europe, women were subordinate to men. The influential theologian Thomas Aquinas° (1225–1274) spoke for his age when he argued that, although both men and women were created in God's image, there was a sense in which "the image of God is found in man, and not in woman: for man is the beginning and end of woman; as God is the beginning and end of every creature."[1]

Rural poverty was not simply the product of inefficient farming methods and social inequality. It also re-

Aquinas (uh-KWY-nuhs)

sulted from the rapid growth of Europe's population. In 1200 China's population may have surpassed Europe's by two to one; by 1300 the population of each was about 80 million. China's population fell because of the Mongol conquest (see Chapter 13). Why Europe's more than doubled between 1100 and 1345 is uncertain. Some historians believe that the reviving economy may have stimulated the increase. Others argue that warmer-than-usual temperatures reduced the number of deaths from starvation and exposure, while the absence of severe epidemics lessened deaths from disease.

Whatever the causes, more people required more productive ways of farming and new agricultural settlements. One new technique gaining widespread acceptance in northern Europe increased the amount of farmland available for producing crops. Instead of following the custom of leaving half of their land fallow (uncultivated) every year to regain its fertility, some farmers tried a new **three-field system.** They grew crops on two-thirds of their land each year and planted the third field in oats. The oats stored nitrogen and rejuvenated the soil, and they could be used to feed plow horses. In much of Europe, however, farmers continued to let half of their land lie fallow and to use oxen (less efficient but cheaper than horses) to pull their plows.

Population growth also led to the foundation of new agricultural settlements. In the twelfth and thirteenth centuries large numbers of Germans migrated into the fertile lands east of the Elbe River and into the eastern Baltic states. Knights belonging to Latin Christian religious orders slaughtered or drove away native inhabitants who had not yet adopted Christianity. For example, during the thirteenth century, the Order of Teutonic Knights conquered, resettled, and administered a vast area along the eastern Baltic that later became Prussia (see Map 15.3). Other Latin Christians founded new settlements on lands conquered from the Muslims and Byzantines in southern Europe and on Celtic lands in the British Isles.

Draining swamps and clearing forests also brought new land under cultivation. But as population continued to rise, some people had to farm lands that had poor soils or were vulnerable to flooding, frost, or drought. As a result average crop yields declined after 1250, and more people were vulnerable to even slight changes in the food supply resulting from bad weather or the disruptions of war. According to one historian, "By 1300, almost every child born in western Europe faced the probability of extreme hunger at least once or twice during his expected 30 to 35 years of life."[2] One unusually cold spell led to the Great Famine of 1315–1317, which affected much of Europe.

The Black Death and Social Change

The **Black Death** cruelly resolved the problem of overpopulation by killing off a third of western Europeans. This terrible plague spread out of Asia and struck Mongol armies attacking the city of Kaffa° on the Black Sea in 1346 (see Chapter 13). A year later Genoese° traders in Kaffa carried the disease back to Italy and southern France. During the next two years the Black Death spread across Europe, sparing some places and carrying off two-thirds of the populace in others.

The plague's symptoms were ghastly to behold. Most victims developed boils the size of eggs in their groins and armpits, black blotches on their skin, foul body odors, and severe pain. In most cases, death came within a few days. To prevent the plague from spreading, town officials closed their gates to people from infected areas and burned victims' possessions. Such measures helped spare some communities but could not halt the advance of the disease across Europe (see Map 15.1). It is now believed that the Black Death was a combination of two diseases. One was anthrax, a disease that can spread to humans from cattle and sheep. The primary form of the Black Death was bubonic plague, a disease spread by contact with an infected person or from the bites of fleas that infest the fur of certain rats. But even if medieval Europeans had been aware of that route of infection, they could have done little to eliminate the rats, which thrived on urban refuse.

The plague left its mark on the survivors, bringing home how sudden and unexpected death could be. Some people became more religious, giving money to the church or flogging themselves with iron-tipped whips to atone for their sins. Others turned to reckless enjoyment, spending their money on fancy clothes, feasts, and drinking. Whatever their mood, most people soon resumed their daily routines.

Periodic returns of plague made recovery from population losses slow and uneven. By 1400 Europe's population regained the size it had had in 1200. Not until after 1500 did it rise above its preplague level.

In addition to its demographic and psychological effects, the Black Death triggered social changes in western Europe. Skilled and manual laborers who survived demanded higher pay for their services. At first authorities tried to freeze wages at the old levels. Seeing such repressive measures as a plot by the rich, peasants rose up against wealthy nobles and churchmen. During a widespread revolt in France in 1358 known as the Jacquerie,

Kaffa (KAH-fah) **Genoese** (JEN-oh-eez)

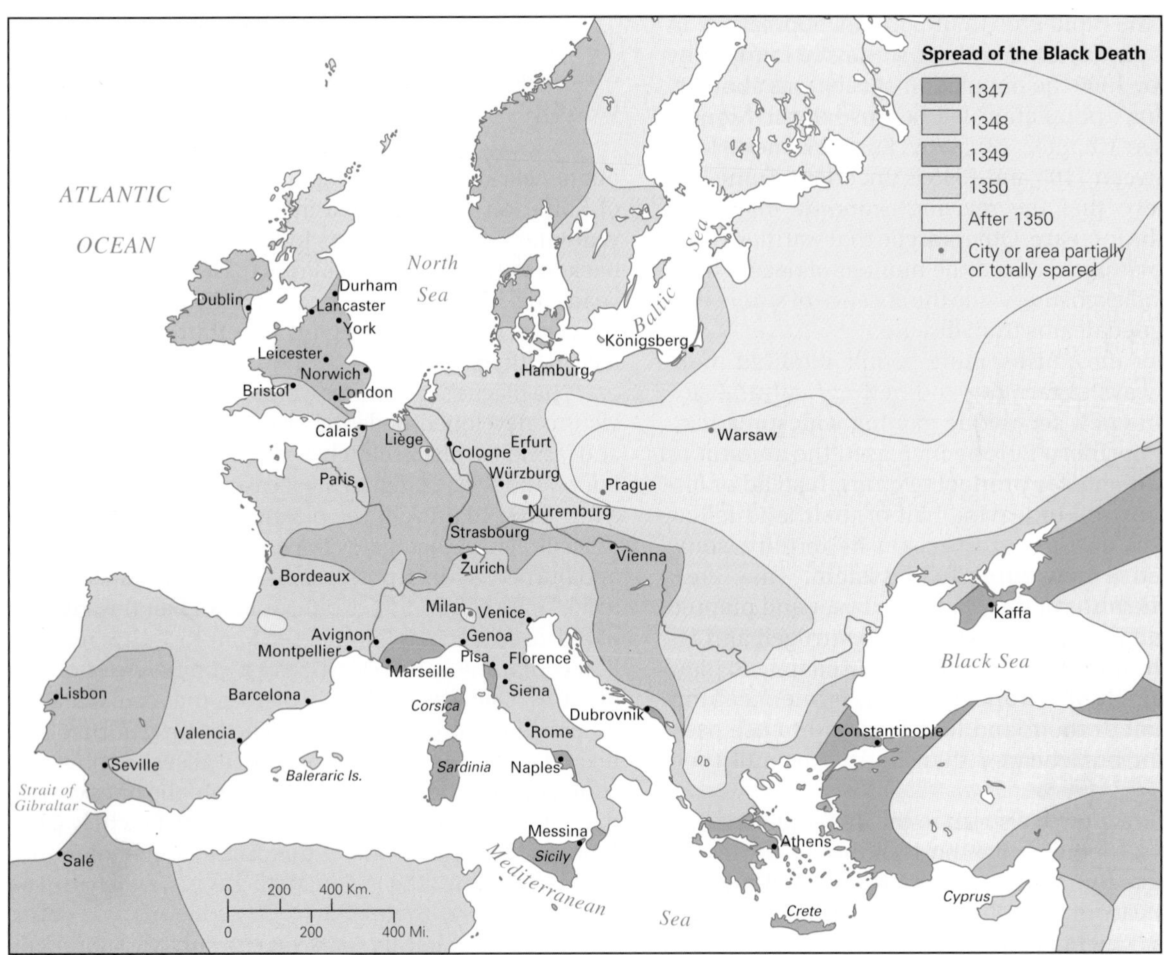

Map 15.1 The Black Death in Fourteenth-Century Europe Spreading out of southwestern China along the routes opened by Mongol expansion, the plague reached the Black Sea port of Kaffa in 1346. This map documents its deadly progress year by year from there into the Mediterranean and north and east across the face of Europe.

peasants looted castles and killed dozens of persons. Urban unrest also took place. In a large revolt led by Wat Tyler in 1381, English peasants invaded London, calling for an end to all forms of serfdom and to most kinds of manorial dues. Angry demonstrators murdered the archbishop of Canterbury and many royal officials. Authorities put down these rebellions with even greater bloodshed and cruelty, but they could not stave off the higher wages and other social changes the rebels demanded.

Serfdom practically disappeared in western Europe as peasants bought their freedom or ran away. Free agricultural laborers used their higher wages to purchase land that they could farm for themselves. Some English landowners who could no longer afford to hire enough fieldworkers used their land to pasture sheep for their wool. Others grew less-labor-intensive crops or made greater use of draft animals and labor-saving tools. Because the plague had not killed wild and domesticated animals, more meat was available for each survivor and more leather for shoes. Thus the welfare of the rural masses generally improved after the Black Death, though the gap between rich and poor remained wide.

In urban areas employers had to raise wages to attract enough workers to replace those killed by the plague. Guilds (see below) found it necessary to reduce the period of apprenticeship. Competition within crafts also became more common. Although the overall econ-

Watermills on the Seine River in Paris Sacks of grain were brought to these mills under the bridge called the Grand Pont to be ground into flour. The water wheels were turned by the river flowing under them. Gears translated the vertical motion of the wheels into the horizontal motion of the millstones. (Bibliothèque Nationale de France)

omy shrank with the decline in population, per capita production actually rose.

Mines and Mills

Mining, metalworking, and the use of mechanical energy expanded so much in the centuries before 1500 that some historians have spoken of an "industrial revolution" in medieval Europe. That may be too strong a term, but the landscape fairly bristled with mechanical devices. Mills powered by water or wind were used to grind grain and flour, saw logs into lumber, crush olives, tan leather, make paper, and perform other useful tasks.

England's many rivers had some fifty-six hundred functioning watermills in 1086. After 1200 such mills spread rapidly across the western European mainland. By the early fourteenth century entrepreneurs had crammed sixty-eight watermills into a one-mile section of the Seine° River in Paris. The flow of the river below turned the simplest **water wheels.** Greater efficiency came from channeling water over the top of the wheel. Dams ensured these wheels a steady flow of water throughout the year. Some watermills in France and England even harnessed the power of ocean tides.

Windmills were common in comparatively dry lands like Spain and in northern Europe, where ice made water wheels useless in winter. Water wheels and windmills had long been common in the Islamic world, but people in the Latin West used these devices on a much larger scale than did people elsewhere.

Wealthy individuals or monasteries built many mills, but because of the expenses involved groups of investors undertook most of the construction. Since nature furnished the energy to run them for free, mills could be very profitable, a fact that often aroused the jealousy of their neighbors. In his *Canterbury Tales* the English poet Geoffrey Chaucer (ca. 1340–1400) captured millers' unsavory reputation (not necessarily deserved) by portraying a miller as "a master-hand at stealing grain" by pushing down on the balance scale with his thumb.[3]

Waterpower also made possible such a great expansion of iron making that some historians say Europe's real Iron Age came in the later Middle Ages, not in antiquity. Water powered the stamping mills that broke up the iron, the trip hammers that pounded it, and the bellows (first documented in the West in 1323) that raised temperatures to the point where the iron was liquid enough to pour into molds. Blast furnaces capable of producing high-quality iron are documented from 1380. The finished products included everything from armor and nails to horseshoes and agricultural tools.

Iron mining expanded in many parts of Europe to meet the demand. In addition, new silver, lead, and copper mines in Austria and Hungary supplied metal for coins, church bells, cannon, and statues. Techniques of deep mining that developed in Central Europe spread farther west in the latter part of the fifteenth century. To keep up with a building boom France quarried more

Seine (sen)

stone during the eleventh, twelfth, and thirteenth centuries than ancient Egypt had done during two millennia for all of its monuments.

The rapid growth of industry changed the landscape significantly. Towns grew outward and new ones were founded; dams and canals changed the flow of rivers; and the countryside was scarred by quarry pits and mines tunneled into hillsides. Pollution sometimes became a serious problem. Urban tanneries (factories that cured and processed leather) dumped acidic wastewater back into streams, where it mixed with human waste and the runoff from slaughterhouses. The first recorded antipollution law was passed by the English Parliament in 1388, although enforcing it was difficult.

One of the most dramatic environmental changes was deforestation. Trees were cut to provide timber for buildings and for ships. Tanneries stripped bark to make acid for tanning leather. Many forests were cleared to make room for farming. The glass and iron industries consumed great quantities of charcoal, made by controlled burning of oak or other hardwood. It is estimated that a single iron furnace could consume all the trees within five-eighths of a mile (1 kilometer) in just forty days. Consequently, the later Middle Ages saw the depletion of many once-dense forests in western Europe.

Urban Revival

In the tenth century not a single town in the Latin West could compare in wealth and comfort—still less in size—with the cities in the Byzantine Empire and the Islamic caliphates. Yet by the later Middle Ages wealthy commercial centers stood all along the Mediterranean, Baltic, and Atlantic, as well as on major rivers draining into these bodies of water (see Map 15.2). The greatest cities in the East were still larger, but those in the West were undergoing greater commercial, cultural, and administrative changes. Their prosperity was visible in impressive new churches, guild halls, and residences. This urban revival is a measure of the Latin West's recovery from the economic decline that had followed the collapse of the Roman Empire (see Chapter 10) as well as an illustration of how the West's rise was aided by its ties to other parts of the world.

Trading Cities

Most urban growth in the Latin West after 1200 was a result of the continuing growth of trade and manufacturing. Most of the trade was between cities and their hinterlands, but long-distance trade also stimulated urban revival. Cities in northern Italy in particular benefited from maritime trade with the bustling port cities of the eastern Mediterranean and, through them, with the great markets of the Indian Ocean and East Asia. In northern Europe commercial cities in the County of Flanders (roughly today's Belgium) and around the Baltic Sea profited from growing regional networks and from overland and sea routes to the Mediterranean.

Venice's diversion of the Fourth Crusade into an assault in 1204 against the city of Constantinople temporarily removed an impediment to Italian commercial expansion in the eastern Mediterranean. By crippling this Greek Christian stronghold, Venetians were able to seize the strategic island of Crete in the eastern Mediterranean and expand their trading colonies around the Black Sea.

Another boon to Italian trade was the westward expansion of the Mongol Empire, which opened trade routes from the Mediterranean to China (see Chapter 13). In 1271 the young Venetian merchant Marco Polo set out to reach the Mongol court by a long overland trek across Central Asia. There he spent many years serving the emperor Khubilai Khan as an ambassador and as the governor of a Chinese province. Some scholars question the truthfulness of Polo's later account of these adventures and of his treacherous return voyage through the Indian Ocean that finally brought him back to Venice in 1295, after an absence of twenty-four years. Few in Venice could believe Polo's tales of Asian wealth.

Even after the Mongol Empire's decline disrupted the trans-Asian caravan trade in the fourteenth century, Venetian merchants continued to purchase the silks and spices that reached Constantinople, Beirut, and Alexandria. Three times a year galleys (ships powered by some sixty oarsmen each) sailed in convoys of two or three from Venice, bringing back some 2,000 tons of goods. Other merchants began to explore new overland or sea routes.

Venice was not the only Latin city whose trade expanded in the thirteenth century. The sea trade of Genoa on the west coast of northern Italy probably equaled that of Venice. Genoese merchants established colonies on the shores of the eastern Mediterranean and around the Black Sea as well as in the western Mediterranean. In northern Europe an association of trading cities known as the **Hanseatic° League** traded extensively in the Baltic, including the coasts of Prussia, newly conquered by German knights. Their merchants ranged eastward to Novgorod in Russia and westward across the North Sea to London.

Hanseatic (han-see-AT-ik)

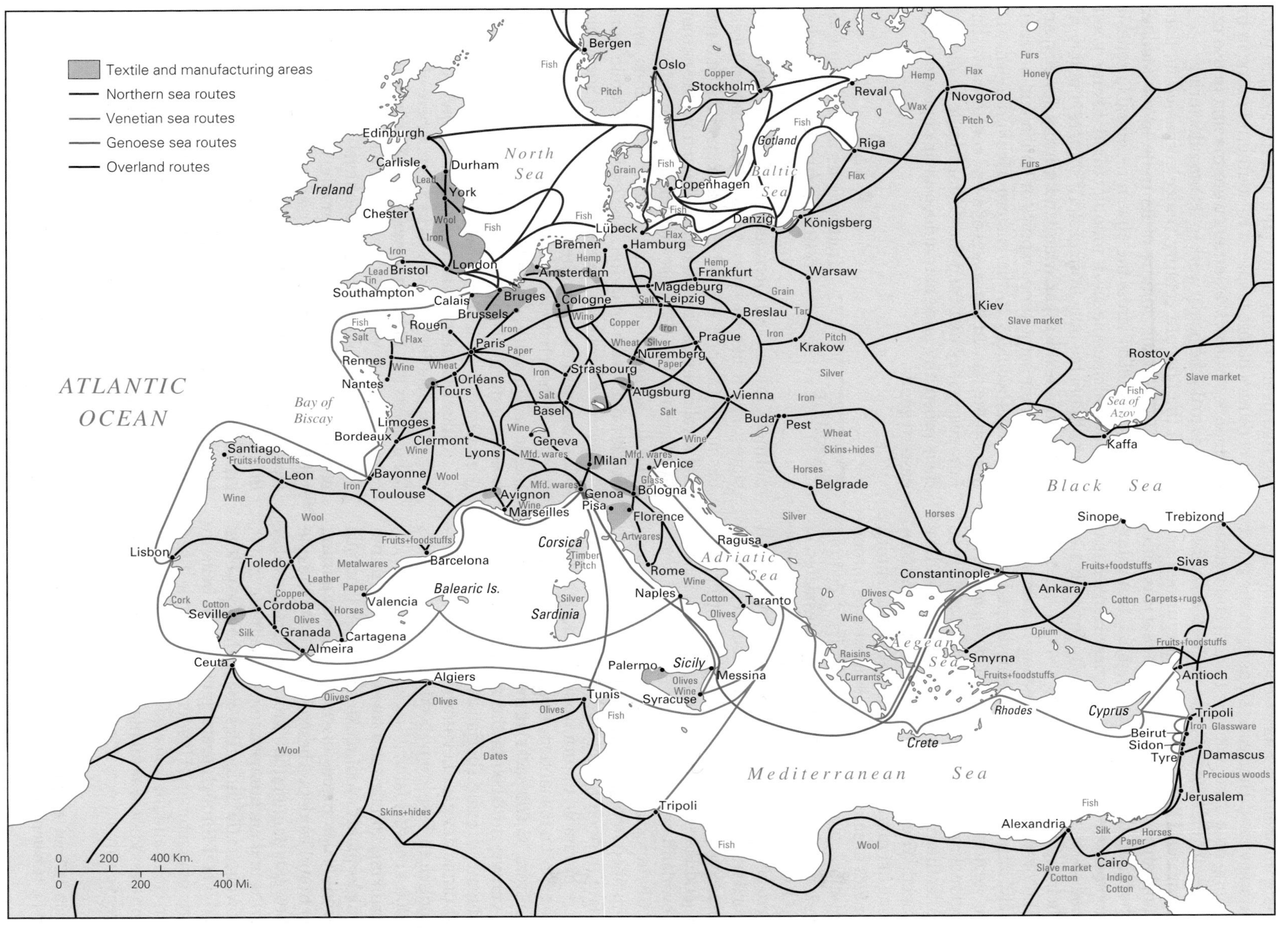

Map 15.2 Trade and Manufacturing in Later Medieval Europe The economic revival of European cities was associated with great expansion of commerce. Notice the concentration of wool and linen textile manufacturing in northern Italy, the Netherlands, and England; the importance of trade in various kinds of foodstuffs; and the slave-exporting markets in Cairo, Kiev, and Rostov.

By the late thirteenth century Genoese galleys from the Mediterranean and Hanseatic ships from the Baltic were converging on a third area, the trading and manufacturing cities in Flanders. In the Flemish towns of Bruges°, Ghent°, and Ypres° skilled artisans turned raw wool from English sheep into a fine cloth that was softer and smoother than the coarse "homespuns" from simple village looms. Dyed in vivid hues, these Flemish textiles appealed to wealthy Europeans who formerly had imported their fine textiles from Asia.

Along the overland route connecting Flanders and northern Italy, important trading fairs developed in the Champagne° region of Burgundy. The Champagne fairs began as regional markets, meeting once or twice a year, where manufactured goods, livestock, and farm produce were exchanged. When Champagne came under the control of the king of France at the end of the twelfth century, royal guarantees of safe conduct to all merchants turned the regional markets into international fairs. A century later fifteen Italian cities had permanent consulates in Champagne to represent the interests of their citizens. The fairs were also important for currency exchange and other financial transactions. During the fourteenth century the volume of trade grew so large that it became cheaper to send Flemish woolens to Italy by sea than to send them overland on pack animals. As a consequence, the fairs of Champagne lost some of their international trade but remained important regional markets.

In the late thirteenth century higher English taxes made it more profitable to turn wool into cloth in England than to export it to Flanders. Raw wool exports from England fell from 35,000 sacks at the beginning of the fourteenth century to 8,000 in the mid-fifteenth. With the aid of Flemish textile specialists and the spinning wheels and other devices they introduced, English exports of wool cloth rose from 4,000 pieces just before 1350 to 54,000 a century later.

Local banking families also turned Florence into a center for high-quality wool making. In 1338 Florence manufactured 80,000 pieces of cloth, while importing only 10,000 from Flanders. These changes in the textile industry show how competition promoted the spread of manufacturing and encouraged new specialties.

The growing textile industries channeled the power of wind and water through gears, pulleys, and belts to drive all sorts of machinery. Flanders, for example, used windmills to clean and thicken woven cloth by beating it in water, a process known as fulling. Another application of mill power was in papermaking. Although papermaking had been common in China and the Muslim world for centuries before it spread to southern Europe in the thirteenth century, Westerners were the first to use machines to do the heavy work in its manufacturing.

In the fifteenth century Venice surpassed its European rivals in the volume of its trade in the Mediterranean as well as across the Alps into Central Europe. Its skilled craftspeople also manufactured luxury goods once obtainable only from eastern sources, notably silk and cotton textiles, glassware and mirrors, jewelry, and paper. At the same time, exports of Italian and northern European woolens to the eastern Mediterranean were also on the rise. In the space of a few centuries western European cities had used the eastern trade to increase their prosperity and then reduce their dependence on eastern goods.

Civic Life

Trading cities in Europe offered people more social freedom than did rural places. Most northern Italian and German cities were independent states, much like the port cities of the Indian Ocean basin (see Chapter 14). Other European cities held special royal charters that exempted them from the authority of local nobles. Because of their autonomy, they were able to adapt to changing market conditions more quickly than were cities in China and the Islamic world that were controlled by imperial authorities. Social mobility was also easier in the Latin West because anyone who lived in a chartered city for over a year might claim freedom. Thus cities became a refuge for all sorts of ambitious individuals, whose labor and talent added to their wealth.

Cities were also home to most of Europe's Jews. The largest population of Jews was in Spain, where earlier Islamic rulers had made them welcome. Many commercial cities elsewhere welcomed Jews for their manufacturing and business skills. Despite the official protection they received from Christian rulers and the church, Jews were subject to violent religious persecutions or expulsions (see Diversity and Dominance: Persecution and Protection of Jews, 1272–1349). Persecution peaked in times of crisis, such as during the Black Death. In the Spanish kingdom of Castile violent attacks on Jews were widespread in 1391 and brought the once vibrant Jewish community in Seville to an end. Terrified Jews left or converted to Christianity, but Christian fanaticism continued to rise over the next century, leading to new attacks on Jews and Jewish converts. In the Latin West only the papal city of Rome left its Jews undisturbed throughout the centuries before 1500.

Bruges (broozh) **Ghent** (gent [hard *g* as in *get*])
Ypres (EE-pruh) **Champagne** (sham-PAIN)

Flemish Weavers, Ypres The spread of textile weaving gave employment to many people in the Netherlands. The city of Ypres in Flanders (now northern Belgium) was an important textile center in the thirteenth century. This drawing from a fourteenth-century manuscript shows a man and a woman weaving cloth on a horizontal loom, while a child makes thread on a spinning wheel. (Stedelijke Openbare Bibliotheek, Ypres)

Opportunities for individual enterprise in European cities came with many restrictions. In most towns and cities powerful associations known as guilds dominated civic life. A **guild** was an association of craft specialists, such as silversmiths, or of merchants that regulated the business practices of its members and the prices they charged. Guilds also trained apprentices and promoted members' interests with the city government. By denying membership to outsiders and all Jews, guilds perpetuated the interests of the families that already were members. Guilds also perpetuated male dominance of most skilled jobs.

Nevertheless, in a few places women were able to join guilds either on their own or as the wives, widows, or daughters of male guild members. Large numbers of poor women also toiled in nonguild jobs in urban textile industries and in the food and beverage trades, generally receiving lower wages than men. Some women advanced socially through marriage. One of Chaucer's *Canterbury Tales* concerns a woman from Bath, a city in southern England, who became wealthy by marrying a succession of old men for their money (and then two other husbands for love), "aside from other company in youth." Chaucer says she was also a skilled weaver: "In making cloth she showed so great a bent, / She bettered those of Ypres and of Ghent."

By the fifteenth century a new class of wealthy merchant-bankers operated on a vast scale and specialized in money changing, loans, and investments. The merchant-bankers handled the financial transactions of a variety of merchants as well as of ecclesiastical and secular officials. They arranged for the transmission to the pope of funds known as Peter's pence, a collection taken up annually in every church in the Latin West. Their loans supported rulers' wars and lavish courts. Some merchant-bankers even developed their own news services, gathering information on any topic that could affect business.

Florence became a center of new banking services from checking accounts and shareholding companies

DIVERSITY AND DOMINANCE

PERSECUTION AND PROTECTION OF JEWS, 1272–1349

Because they did not belong to the dominant Latin Christian faith, Jews suffered from periodic discrimination and persecution. For the most part, religious and secular authorities tried to curb such anti-Semitism. Jews, after all, were useful citizens who worshipped the same God as their Christian neighbors. Still it was hard to know where to draw the line between justifiable and unjustifiable discrimination. The famous reviser of Catholic theology, St. Thomas Aquinas, made one such distinction in his Summa Theologica *with regard to attempts at forced conversion.*

Now, the practice of the Church never held that the children of Jews should be baptized against the will of their parents. . . . Therefore, it seems dangerous to bring forward this new view, that contrary to the previously established custom of the Church, the children of Jews should be baptized against the will of their parents.

There are two reasons for this position. One stems from danger to faith. For, if children without the use of reason were to receive baptism, then after reaching maturity they could easily be persuaded by their parents to relinquish what they had received in ignorance. This would tend to do harm to the faith.

The second reason is that it is opposed to natural justice . . . it [is] a matter of natural right that a son, before he has the use of reason, is under the care of his father. Hence, it would be against natural justice for the boy, before he has the use of reason, to be removed from the care of his parents, or for anything to be arranged for him against the will of his parents.

The "new view" Aquinas opposed was much in the air, for in 1272 Pope Gregory X issued a decree condemning forced baptism. The pope's decree reviews the history of papal protection given to the Jews, starting with a quotation from Pope Gregory I dating from 598, and decrees two new protections of Jews' legal rights.

Even as it is not allowed to the Jews in their assemblies presumptuously to undertake for themselves more than that which is permitted them by law, even so they ought not to suffer any disadvantage in those [privileges] which have been granted them.

Although they prefer to persist in their stubbornness rather than to recognize the words of their prophets and the mysteries of the Scriptures, and thus to arrive at a knowledge of Christian faith and salvation; nevertheless, inasmuch as they have made an appeal for our protection and help, we therefore admit their petition and offer them the shield of our protection through the clemency of Christian piety. In so doing we follow in the footsteps of our predecessors of happy memory, the popes of Rome—Calixtus, Eugene, Alexander, Clement, Celestine, Innocent, and Honorius.

We decree moreover that no Christian shall compel them or any one of their group to come to baptism unwillingly. But if any one of them shall take refuge of his own accord with Christians, because of conviction, then, after his intention will have been made manifest, he shall be made a Christian without any intrigue. For indeed that person who is known to come to Christian baptism not freely, but unwillingly, is not believed to possess the Christian faith.

Moreover, no Christian shall presume to seize, imprison, wound, torture, mutilate, kill, or inflict violence on them; furthermore no one shall presume, except by judicial action of the authorities of the country, to change the good customs in the land where they live for the purpose of taking their money or goods from them or from others.

In addition, no one shall disturb them in any way during the celebration of their festivals, whether by day or by night, with clubs or stones or anything else. Also no one shall exact any compulsory service of them unless it be that which they have been accustomed to render in previous times.

Inasmuch as the Jews are not able to bear witness against the Christians, we decree furthermore that the testimony of Christians against Jews shall not be valid unless there is among these Christians some Jew who is there for the purpose of offering testimony.

Since it occasionally happens that some Christians lose their Christian children, the Jews are accused by their enemies of secretly carrying off and killing these same Christian children, and of making sacrifices of the heart and blood of these very children. It happens, too, that the parents of these children, or some other Christian enemies of these Jews, secretly hide these very children in order that they may be able to injure these Jews, and in order that they may be able to extort from them a certain amount of money by redeeming them from their straits.

And most falsely do these Christians claim that the Jews have secretly and furtively carried away these children and killed them, and that the Jews offer sacrifice from the heart and the blood of these children, since their law in this matter precisely and expressly forbids Jews to sacrifice, eat, or drink the blood, or eat the flesh of animals having claws. This has been demonstrated many times at our court by Jews converted to the Christian faith: nevertheless very many Jews are often seized and detained unjustly because of this.

We decree, therefore, that Christians need not be obeyed against Jews in such a case or situation of this type, and we order that Jews seized under such a silly pretext be freed from imprisonment, and that they shall not be arrested henceforth on such a miserable pretext, unless—which we do not believe—they be caught in the commission of the crime. We decree that no Christian shall stir up anything against them, but that they should be maintained in that status and position in which they were from the time of our predecessors, from antiquity till now.

We decree, in order to stop the wickedness and avarice of bad men, that no one shall dare to devastate or to destroy a cemetery of the Jews or to dig up human bodies for the sake of getting money [by holding them for ransom]. Moreover, if anyone, after having known the content of this decree, should—which we hope will not happen—attempt audaciously to act contrary to it, then let him suffer punishment in his rank and position, or let him be punished by the penalty of excommunication, unless he makes amends for his boldness by proper recompense. Moreover, we wish that only those Jews who have not attempted to contrive anything toward the destruction of the Christian faith be fortified by the support of such protection. . . .

Despite such decrees violence against Jews might burst out when fears and emotions were running high. This selection is from the official chronicles of the upper-Rhineland towns.

In the year 1349 there occurred the greatest epidemic that ever happened. Death went from one end of the earth to the other, on that side and this side of the [Mediterranean] sea, and it was greater among the Saracens [Muslims] than among the Christians. In some lands everyone died so that no one was left. Ships were also found on the sea laden with wares; the crew had all died and no one guided the ship. The Bishop of Marseilles and priests and monks and more than half of all the people there died with them. In other kingdoms and cities so many people perished that it would be horrible to describe. The pope at Avignon stopped all sessions of court, locked himself in a room, allowed no one to approach him and had a fire burning before him all the time. And from what this epidemic came, all wise teachers and physicians could only say that it was the God's will. And the plague was now here, so it was in other places, and lasted more than a whole year. This epidemic also came to Strasbourg in the summer of the above mentioned year, and it is estimated about sixteen thousand people died.

In the matter of this plague the Jews throughout the world were reviled and accused in all lands of having caused it through the poison which they are said to have put into the water and the wells—that is what they were accused of—and for this reason the Jews were burnt all the way from the Mediterranean into Germany, but not in Avignon, for the pope protected them there.

Nevertheless they tortured a number of Jews in Berne and Zofingen who admitted they had put poison into many wells, and they found the poison in the wells. Thereupon they burnt the Jews in many towns and wrote of this affair to Strasbourg, Freibourg, and Basel in order that they too should burn their Jews. . . . The deputies of the city of Strasbourg were asked what they were going to do with their Jews. They answered and said that they knew no evil of them. Then . . . there was a great indignation and clamor against the deputies from Strasbourg. So finally the Bishop and the lords and the Imperial Cities agreed to do away with the Jews. The result was that they were burnt in many cities, and wherever they were expelled they were caught by the peasants and stabbed to death or drowned. . . .

On Saturday—that was St. Valentine's Day—they burnt the Jews on a wooden platform in their cemetery. There were about two thousand people of them. Those who wanted to baptize themselves were spared. Many small children were taken out of the fire and baptized against the will of their fathers and mothers. And everything that was owed to the Jews was cancelled, and the Jews had to surrender all pledges and notes that they had taken for debts. The council, however, took the cash that the Jews possessed and divided it among the working-men proportionately. The money was indeed the thing that killed the Jews. If they had been poor and if the feudal lords had not been in debt to them, they would not have been burnt.

QUESTIONS FOR ANALYSIS

1. **Why do Aquinas and Pope Gregory oppose prejudicial actions against Jews?**
2. **Why did prejudice increase at the time of the Black Death?**
3. **What factors account for the differences between the views of Christian leaders and the Christian masses?**

---

to improved bookkeeping. In the fifteenth century the Medici° family of Florence operated banks in Italy, Flanders, and London. Medicis also controlled the government of Florence and were important patrons of the arts. By 1500 the greatest banking family in western Europe was the Fuggers° of Augsburg, who had ten times the Medici bank's lending capital. Starting out as cloth merchants under Jacob "the Rich" (1459–1525), the family branched into many other activities, including the trade in Hungarian copper, essential for casting cannon.

Christian bankers had to devise ways to profit indirectly from loans in order to get around the Latin Church's condemnation of usury (charging interest). Some borrowers agreed to repay a loan in another currency at a rate of exchange favorable to the lender. Others added a "gift" in thanks to the lender to the borrowed sum. For example, in 1501 papal officials agreed to repay a loan of 6,000 gold ducats in five months to the Fuggers along with a "gift" of 400 ducats, amounting to an effective interest rate of 16 percent a year. In fact, the return was much smaller since the church failed to repay the loan on time. Because they were not bound by church laws, Jews were important moneylenders.

Despite the money made by some, for most residents of western European cities poverty and squalor were the norm. Even for the wealthy, European cities generally lacked civic amenities, such as public baths and water supply systems, that had existed in the cities of Western antiquity and still survived in cities of the Islamic Middle East.

Strasbourg Cathedral Only one of the two spires originally planned for this Gothic cathedral was completed when work ceased in 1439. But the Strasbourg Cathedral was still the tallest masonry structure of medieval Europe. This engraving is from 1630. (Courtesy of the Trustees of the British Museum)

Gothic Cathedrals

Master builders were in great demand in the thriving cities of late medieval Europe. Cities vied to outdo one another in the magnificence of their guild halls, town halls, and other structures (see Environment and Technology: The Clock). But the architectural wonders of their times were the new **Gothic cathedrals,** which made their appearance in about 1140 in France.

The hallmark of the new cathedrals was the pointed Gothic arch, which replaced the older round Roman arch. External (flying) buttresses stabilized the high, thin stone columns below the arches. This method of construction enabled master builders to push the Gothic cathedrals to great heights and fill the outside walls with giant windows of brilliantly colored stained glass. During the next four centuries, interior heights went ever higher, towers and spires pierced the heavens, and walls dazzled worshippers with religious scenes in stained glass.

The men who designed and built the cathedrals had little or no formal education and limited understanding of the mathematical principles of modern civil engineering. Master masons sometimes miscalculated, and parts of some overly ambitious cathedrals collapsed. For instance, the record-high choir vault of Beauvais Cathedral—154 feet (47 meters) in height—came tumbling down in 1284. But as builders gained experience, they devised new ways to push their steeples heavenward. The spire of the Strasbourg cathedral reached

Medici (MED-ih-chee) **Fuggers** (FOOG-uhrz)

ENVIRONMENT + TECHNOLOGY

The Clock

Clocks were a prominent feature of the Latin West in the late medieval period. The Song-era Chinese had built elaborate mechanical clocks centuries earlier (see Chapter 11), but the West was the first part of the world where clocks became a regular part of urban life. Whether mounted in a church steeple or placed on a bridge or tower, mechanical clocks proclaimed Western people's delight with mechanical objects, concern with precision, and display of civic wealth.

The word *clock* comes from a word for bell. The first mechanical clocks that appeared around 1300 in western Europe were simply bells with an automatic mechanical device to strike the correct number of hours. The most elaborate Chinese clock had been powered by falling water, but this was impractical in cold weather. The levers, pulleys, and gears of European clocks were powered by a weight hanging from a rope wound around a cylinder. An "escapement" lever regulated the slow, steady unwinding.

Enthusiasm for building expensive clocks came from various parts of the community. For some time, monks had been using devices to mark the times for prayer. Employers welcomed chiming clocks to regulate the hours of their employees. Universities used them to mark the beginning and end of classes. Prosperous merchants readily donated money to build a splendid clock that would display their city's wealth. The city of Strasbourg, for example, built a clock in the 1350s that included statues of the Virgin, the Christ Child, and the three Magi; a mechanical rooster; the signs of the zodiac; a perpetual calendar; and an astrolabe—and it could play hymns, too!

By the 1370s and 1380s clocks were common enough for their measured hours to displace the older system that varied the length of the hour in proportion to the length of the day. Previously, for example, the London hour had varied from thirty-eight minutes in winter to eighty-two minutes in summer. By 1500 clocks had numbered faces with hour and minute hands. Small clocks for indoor use were also in vogue. Though not very accurate by today's standards, these clocks were still a great step forward. Some historians consider the clock the most important of the many technological advances of the later Middle Ages because it fostered so many changes during the following centuries.

Early Clock This weight-driven clock dates from 1454. (Bodleian Library Oxford, Ms. Laud Misc. 570, 25v.)

466 feet (142 meters) into the air—as high as a 40-story building. Such heights were unsurpassed until the twentieth century.

LEARNING, LITERATURE, AND THE RENAISSANCE

Throughout the Middle Ages people in the Latin West lived amid reminders of the achievements of the Roman Empire. They wrote and worshiped in a version of its language, traveled its roads, and obeyed some of its laws. Even the vestments and robes of medieval popes, kings, and emperors were modeled on the regalia of Roman officials. Yet early medieval Europeans lost touch with much of the learning of Greco-Roman antiquity. More vivid was the biblical world they heard about in the Hebrew and Christian scriptures.

A small revival of classical learning associated with the court of Charlemagne in the ninth century was followed by a larger renaissance (rebirth) in the twelfth century. The growing cities were home to intellectuals, artists, and universities after 1200. In the mid-fourteenth century the pace of intellectual and artistic life quickened in what is often called the **Renaissance,** which began in northern Italy and later spread to northern Europe. Some Italian authors saw the Italian Renaissance as a sharp break with an age of darkness. A more balanced view might reveal this era as the high noon of a day that had been dawning for several centuries.

Universities and Learning

Before 1100 Byzantine and Islamic scholarship generally surpassed scholarship in Latin Europe. When southern Italy was wrested from the Byzantines and Sicily and Toledo from the Muslims in the eleventh century, many manuscripts of Greek and Arabic works came into Western hands and were translated into Latin for readers eager for new ideas. These included philosophical works by Plato and Aristotle°; newly discovered Greek treatises on medicine, mathematics, and geography; and scientific and philosophical writings by medieval Muslims. Latin translations of the Iranian philosopher Ibn Sina° (980–1037), known in the West as Avicenna°, were particularly influential. Jewish scholars contributed significantly to the translation and explication of Arabic and other manuscripts.

Two new religious orders, the Dominicans and the Franciscans, contributed many talented professors to the growing number of new independent colleges after 1200. Some scholars believe that the colleges established in Paris and Oxford in the late twelfth and thirteenth centuries may have been modeled after similar places of study then spreading in the Islamic world—*madrasas,* which provided subsidized housing for poor students and paid the salaries of their teachers. The Latin West, however, was the first part of the world to establish modern **universities,** degree-granting corporations specializing in multidisciplinary research and advanced teaching.

Between 1300 and 1500 sixty new universities joined the twenty existing institutions of higher learning in the Latin West. Students banded together to found some of them; guilds of professors founded others. Teaching guilds, like the guilds overseeing manufacturing and commerce, set the standards for membership in their profession, trained apprentices and masters, and defended their professional interests.

Universities set the curriculum of study for each discipline and instituted comprehensive final examinations for degrees. Students who passed the exams at the end of their apprenticeship received a teaching diploma known as a "license." Students who completed longer training and successfully defended a scholarly treatise became "masters" or "doctors." The colleges of Paris were gradually absorbed into the city's university, but the colleges of Oxford and Cambridge remained independent, self-governing organizations.

Universally recognized degrees, well-trained professors, and exciting new texts promoted the rapid spread of universities in late medieval Europe. Because all university courses were taught in Latin, students and masters could move freely across political and linguistic lines, seeking out the university that offered the courses they wanted and that had the most interesting professors. Universities offered a variety of programs of study but generally were identified with a particular specialty. Bologna° was famous for the study of law; Montpellier and Salerno specialized in medicine; Paris and Oxford excelled in theology.

The prominence of theology partly reflected the fact that many students were destined for ecclesiastical careers, but theology was also seen as "queen of the sciences"—the central discipline that encompassed all knowledge. For this reason thirteenth-century theologians sought to synthesize the newly rediscovered philosophical works of Aristotle, as well as the commentaries of Avicenna, with the revealed truth of the Bible. Their

Aristotle (AR-ih-stah-tahl) **Ibn Sina** (IB-uhn SEE-nah)
Avicenna (av-uh-SEN-uh)

Bologna (buh-LOHN-yuh)

daring efforts to synthesize reason and faith were known as **scholasticism**°.

The most notable scholastic work was the *Summa Theologica*°, issued between 1267 and 1273 by Thomas Aquinas, a brilliant Dominican priest who was a professor of theology at the University of Paris. Although Aquinas's exposition of Christian belief organized on Aristotelian principles was later accepted as a masterly demonstration of the reasonableness of Christianity, scholasticism upset many traditional thinkers. Some church authorities even tried to ban Aristotle from the curriculum. There also was much rivalry between the leading Dominican and Franciscan theological scholars over the next two centuries. However, the considerable freedom of medieval universities from both secular and religious authorities eventually enabled the new ideas of accredited scholars to prevail over the fears of church administrators.

Humanists and Printers

The intellectual achievements of the later Middle Ages were not confined to the universities. Talented writers of this era made important contributions to literature and literary scholarship. A new technology in the fifteenth century helped bring works of literature and scholarship to a larger audience.

Dante Alighieri° (1265–1321) completed a long, elegant poem, the *Divine Comedy*, shortly before his death. This supreme expression of medieval preoccupations tells the allegorical story of Dante's journey through the nine circles of hell and the seven terraces of purgatory (a place where the souls not deserving eternal punishment were purged of their sinfulness), followed by his entry into Paradise. His guide through hell and purgatory is the Roman poet Virgil. His guide through Paradise is Beatrice, a woman whom he had loved from afar since childhood and whose death inspired him to write the poem.

The *Divine Comedy* foreshadows some of the literary fashions of the later Italian Renaissance. Like Dante, later Italian writers made use of Greco-Roman classical themes and mythology and sometimes chose to write not in Latin but in the vernacular languages spoken in their regions, in order to reach broader audiences. (Dante used the vernacular spoken in Tuscany°.)

The English poet Geoffrey Chaucer was another vernacular writer of this era. Many of his works show the influence of Dante, but he is most famous for the *Canterbury Tales*, the lengthy poem written in the last dozen years of his life. These often humorous and earthy tales, told by fictional pilgrims on their way to the shrine of Thomas à Becket in Canterbury, are cited several times in this chapter because they present a marvelous cross-section of medieval people and attitudes.

Dante also influenced the literary movement of the **humanists** that began in his native Florence in the mid-fourteenth century. The term refers to their interest in the humanities, the classical disciplines of grammar, rhetoric, poetry, history, and ethics. With the brash exaggeration characteristic of new intellectual fashions, humanist writers such as the poet Francesco Petrarch° (1304–1374) and the poet and storyteller Giovanni Boccaccio° (1313–1375) claimed that their new-found admiration for the classical values revived Greco-Roman traditions that for centuries had lain buried under the rubble of the Middle Ages. This idea of a rebirth of learning long dead overlooks the fact that scholars at the monasteries and universities had been recovering and preserving all sorts of Greco-Roman learning for many centuries. Dante (whom the humanists revered) had anticipated humanist interests by a generation.

Yet it is hard to exaggerate the beneficial influences of the humanists as educators, advisers, and reformers. Their greatest influence was in reforming secondary education. Humanists introduced a curriculum centered on the languages and literature of Greco-Roman antiquity, which they felt provided intellectual discipline, moral lessons, and refined tastes. This curriculum dominated secondary education in Europe and the Americas well into the twentieth century. Despite the humanists' influence, theology, law, medicine, and branches of philosophy other than ethics remained prominent in university education during this period. After 1500 humanist influence grew in university education.

Believing the pinnacle of learning, beauty, and wisdom had been reached in antiquity, many humanists tried to duplicate the elegance of classical Latin or Greek. Others followed Dante in composing literary works in vernacular languages. Boccaccio is most famous for his vernacular writings, especially the *Decameron*, an earthy work that has much in common with Chaucer's boisterous tales. Under Petrarch's influence, however, Boccaccio turned to writing in classical Latin, including *De mulieribus claris (Famous Women)*, a chronicle of 106

scholasticism (skoh-LAS-tih-sizm)
Summa Theologica (SOOM-uh thee-uh-LOH-jih-kuh)
Dante Alighieri (DAHN-tay ah-lee-GYEH-ree)
Tuscany (TUS-kuh-nee)

Franceso Petrarch (fran-CHES-koh PAY-trahrk)
Giovanni Boccaccio (jo-VAH-nee boh-KAH-chee-oh)

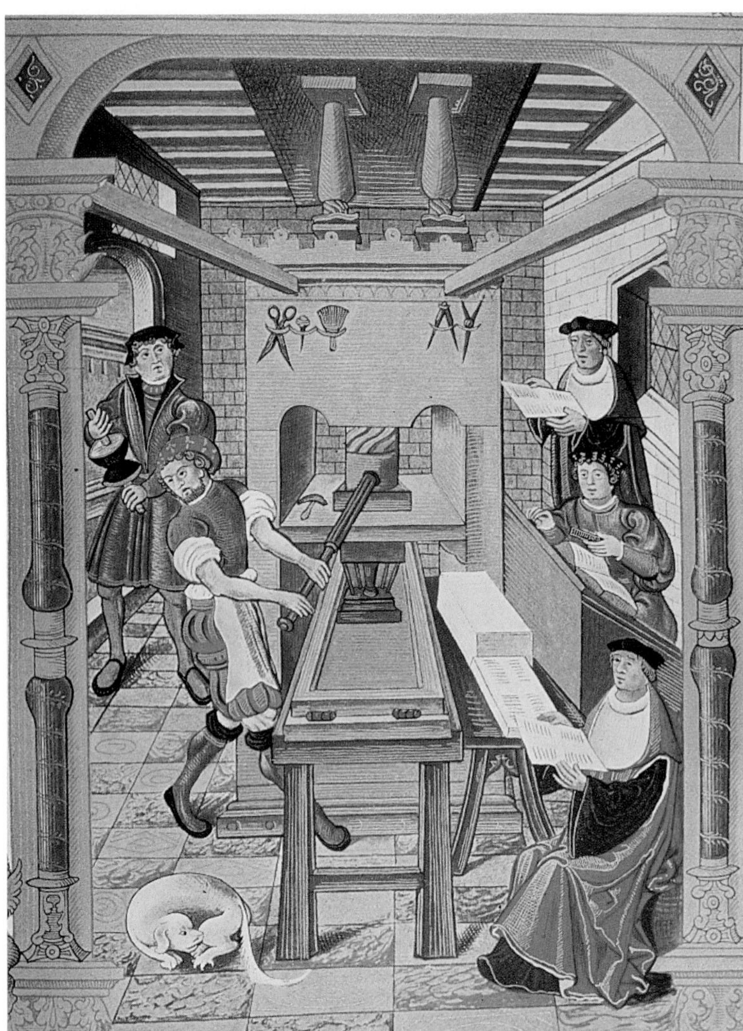

A French Printshop, 1537 A workman operates the "press," quite literally a screw device that presses the paper to the inked type. Other employees examine the printed sheets, each of which holds four pages. When folded, the sheets make a book. (Giraudon/Art Resource, NY)

famous women from Eve to his own day. It was the first collection of women's lives in Western literature.

Once they had mastered classical Latin and Greek, a number of humanist scholars of the fifteenth century worked to restore the original texts of Greco-Roman writers and of the Bible. By comparing many different manuscripts, they eliminated errors introduced by generations of copyists. To aid in this task, Pope Nicholas V (r. 1447–1455) created the Vatican Library, buying scrolls of Greco-Roman writings and paying to have accurate copies and translations made. Working independently, the respected Dutch scholar Erasmus° of Rotterdam (ca. 1466–1536) produced a critical edition of the New Testament in Greek. Erasmus was able to correct many errors and mistranslations in the Latin text that had been in general use throughout the Middle Ages. In later years this humanist priest and theologian also wrote—in classical Latin—influential moral guides including the *Enchiridion militis christiani* (*The Manual of the Christian Knight*, 1503) and *The Education of a Christian Prince* (1515).

The influence of the humanists was enhanced after 1450 because new printing technology increased the availability of their critical editions of ancient texts, literary works, and moral guides. The Chinese were the first to use carved wood blocks for printing (see Chapter 13), and block-printed playing cards from China were circulating in Europe before 1450. Then, around 1450, three technical improvements revolutionized printing: (1) mov-

Erasmus (uh-RAZ-muhs)

The Medici Family This detail of a mural painting of 1459 by Benozzo Gozzoli depicts the arrival of the Magi at the birthplace of the Christ Child, but the principal figures are important members of the wealthy Medici family of Florence and their entourage in costumes of their day. The bowman on the left suggests how common African servants and slaves became in southern Europe during the Renaissance. (Art Resource, NY)

able pieces of type consisting of individual letters, (2) new ink suitable for printing on paper, and (3) the **printing press,** a mechanical device that pressed inked type onto sheets of paper.

The man who did most to perfect printing was Johann Gutenberg° (ca. 1394–1468) of Mainz. The Gutenberg Bible of 1454, the first book in the West printed from movable type, was a beautiful and finely crafted work that bore witness to the printer's years of diligent experimentation. As printing spread to Italy and France, humanists worked closely with printers. Erasmus worked for years as an editor and proofreader for the great scholar-printer Aldo Manuzio (1449–1515), whose press in Venice published critical editions of many classical Latin and Greek texts.

By 1500 at least 10 million printed copies had issued forth from presses in 238 towns in western Europe. Though mass-produced paperbacks were still in the future, the printers and humanists had launched a revolution that was already having an effect on students, scholars, and a growing number of literate people who could gain access to ancient texts as well as to unorthodox political and religious tracts.

Johann Gutenberg (yoh-HAHN GOO-ten-burg)

Renaissance Artists

The fourteenth and fifteenth centuries were as distinguished for their masterpieces of painting, sculpture, and architecture as they were for their scholarship. Although artists continued to depict biblical subjects, the spread of Greco-Roman learning led many artists, especially in Italy, to portray Greco-Roman deities and mythical tales. Another popular trend was depicting the scenes of daily life.

However, neither daily life nor classical images were entirely new subjects. Renaissance art, like Renaissance scholarship, owed a major debt to earlier generations. The Florentine painter Giotto° (ca. 1267–1337) had a formidable influence on the major Italian painters of the fifteenth century, who credited him with single-handedly reviving the "lost art of painting." In his religious scenes Giotto replaced the stiff, staring figures of the Byzantine style, which were intended to overawe viewers, with more natural and human portraits with whose emotions of grief and love viewers could identify. Rather than floating on backgrounds of gold leaf, his saints inhabit earthly landscapes.

Giotto (JAW-toh)

Another important contribution to the early Italian Renaissance was a new painting technology from north of the Alps. The Flemish painter Jan van Eyck° (ca. 1390–1441) mixed his pigments with linseed oil instead of the diluted egg yolk of earlier centuries. Oil paints were slower drying and more versatile, and they gave pictures a superior luster. Van Eyck's use of the technique for his own masterfully realistic paintings on religious and domestic themes was quickly copied by talented painters of the Italian Renaissance.

The great Italian Leonardo da Vinci° (1452–1519), for example, used oil paints for his famous *Mona Lisa.* Renaissance artists like Leonardo were masters of many media. His other works include the fresco (painting in wet plaster) *The Last Supper*, bronze sculptures, and imaginative designs for airplanes, submarines, and tanks. Leonardo's younger contemporary Michelangelo° (1472–1564) painted frescoes of biblical scenes on the ceiling of the Sistine Chapel in the Vatican, sculpted statues of David and Moses, and designed the dome for a new Saint Peter's Basilica.

The patronage of wealthy and educated merchants and prelates did much to foster an artistic blossoming in the cities of northern Italy and Flanders. The Florentine banker Cosimo de' Medici (1389–1464), for example, spent immense sums on paintings, sculpture, and public buildings. His grandson Lorenzo (1449–1492), known as "the Magnificent," was even more lavish. The church was also an important source of artistic commissions. Seeking to restore Rome as the capital of the Latin Church, the papacy° launched a building program culminating in the construction of the new Saint Peter's Basilica and a residence for the pope.

These scholarly and artistic achievements exemplify the innovation and striving for excellence of the Late Middle Ages. The new literary themes and artistic styles of this period had lasting influence on Western culture. But the innovations in the organization of universities, in printing, and in oil painting had wider implications, for they were later adopted by cultures all over the world.

Political and Military Transformations

Stronger and more unified states and armies developed in western Europe in parallel with the economic and cultural revivals. In no case were transformations smooth and steady, and the political changes unfolded somewhat differently in each state (see Map 15.3). During and after the prolonged struggle of the Hundred Years War, French and English monarchs forged closer ties with the nobility, the church, and the merchants. The consolidation of Spain and Portugal was linked to crusades against Muslim states. In Italy and Germany, however, political power remained in the hands of small states and loose alliances.

Monarchs, Nobles, and Clergy

Thirteenth-century states still shared many features of early medieval states (see Chapter 10). Hereditary monarchs occupied the peak of the political pyramid, but their powers were limited by modest treasuries and the rights possessed by others. Below them came the powerful noblemen who controlled vast estates and whose advice and consent were often required on important matters of state. The church, jealous of its traditional rights and independence, was another powerful body within each kingdom. Towns, too, had acquired many rights and privileges. Indeed, the towns in Flanders, the Hanseatic League, and Italy were nearly independent from royal interference.

In theory, nobles were vassals of the reigning monarchs and were obliged to furnish them with armored knights in time of war. In practice, vassals sought to limit the monarch's power and protect their own rights and privileges. The nobles' privileged economic and social position rested on the large estates that had been granted to their ancestors in return for supporting and training knights in armor to serve in a royal army.

In the year 1200 knights were still the backbone of western European fighting forces, but two changes in weaponry were bringing their central military role, and thus the system of estates that supported them, into question. The first involved the humble arrow. Improved crossbows could shoot metal-tipped arrows with such force that they could pierce helmets and light body armor. Professional crossbowmen, hired for wages, became increasingly common and much feared. Indeed, a church council in 1139 outlawed the crossbow as being too deadly for use against Christians. The ban was largely ignored. The second innovation in military technology that weakened the feudal system was the firearm. This Chinese invention, using gunpowder to shoot stone or metal projectiles, further transformed the medieval army.

The church also resisted royal control. In 1302 the outraged Pope Boniface VIII (r. 1294–1303) went so far as to assert that divine law made the papacy superior to

Jan van Eyck (yahn vahn-IKE)
Leonardo da Vinci (lay-own-AHR-doh dah-VIN-chee)
Michelangelo (my-kuhl-AN-juh-low) **papacy** (PAY-puh-see)

Map 15.3 Europe in 1453 This year marked the end of the Hundred Years War between France and England and the fall of the Byzantine capital city of Constantinople to the Ottoman Turks. Muslim advances into southeastern Europe were offset by the Latin Christian reconquests of Islamic holdings in southern Italy and the Iberian Peninsula and by the conversion of Lithuania.

The Magna Carta One of four extant copies, this document shows the ravages of time, but the symbolic importance of the charter King John of England signed under duress in 1215 for English constitutional history has not been dimished. Originally a guarantee of the baron's feudal rights, it came to be seen as a limit on the monarch's authority over all subjects. (The National Archives, Public Record Office and Historical Manuscripts Commission)

"every human creature," including monarchs. This theoretical claim of superiority was challenged by force. Issuing his own claim of superiority, King Philip "the Fair" of France (r. 1285–1314) sent an army to arrest the pope. After this treatment hastened Pope Boniface's death, Philip engineered the election of a French pope who established a new papal residence at Avignon° in southern France in 1309.

With the support of the French monarchy, a succession of popes residing in Avignon improved church discipline—but at the price of compromising the papacy's neutrality in the eyes of other rulers. Papal authority was further eroded by the **Great Western Schism** (1378–1415), a period when rival papal claimants at Avignon and Rome vied for the loyalties of Latin Christians. The conflict was eventually resolved by returning the papal residence to its traditional location, the city of Rome. The papacy regained its independence, but the long crisis broke the pope's ability to challenge the rising power of the larger monarchies.

King Philip gained an important advantage at the beginning of his dispute with Pope Boniface when he persuaded a large council of French nobles to grant him the right to collect a new tax, which sustained the monarchy for some time. Earlier, by adroitly using the support of the towns, the saintly King Louis IX of France (r. 1226–1270) had been able to issue ordinances that applied throughout his kingdom without first obtaining the nobles' consent. But later kings' efforts to extend royal authority sparked prolonged resistance by the most powerful vassals.

English monarchs wielded more centralized power as a result of consolidation that had taken place after the Norman conquest of 1066. Anglo-Norman kings also extended their realm by assaults on their Celtic neighbors. Between 1200 and 1400 they incorporated Wales and reasserted control over most of Ireland. Nevertheless, English royal power was far from absolute. In the span of just three years the ambitions of King John (r. 1199–1216) were severely set back. First he was compelled to acknowledge the pope as his overlord (1213). Then he lost his bid to reassert claims to Aquitaine in southern France (1214). Finally he was forced to sign the Magna Carta ("Great Charter," 1215), which affirmed that monarchs were subject to established law, confirmed the independence of the church and the city of London, and guaranteed nobles' hereditary rights.

Separate from the challenges to royal authority by the church and the nobles were the alliances and conflicts generated by the hereditary nature of monarchial

---

Avignon (ah-vee-NYON)

rule. Monarchs and their vassals entered into strategic marriages with a view to increasing their lands and their wealth. Such marriages showed scant regard for the emotions of the wedded parties or for "national" interests. Besides unhappiness for the parties involved, these marriages often led to conflicts over far-flung inheritances. Although these dynastic struggles and shifting boundaries make European politics seem chaotic in comparison with the empires of Asia, some important changes were emerging from them. Aided by the changing technology of war, monarchs were strengthening their authority and creating more stable (but not entirely fixed) state boundaries within which the nations of western Europe would in time develop. Nobles lost autonomy and dominance on the battlefield but retained their social position and important political roles.

The Hundred Years War, 1337–1453

The long conflict between the king of France and his vassals known as the **Hundred Years War** (1337–1453) was a key example of the transformation in politics and warfare. This long conflict set the power of the French monarchy against the ambitions of his vassals, who included the kings of England (for lands that belonged to their Norman ancestors) and the heads of Flanders, Brittany, and Burgundy. In typical fashion, the conflict grew out of a marriage alliance.

Princess Isabella of France married King Edward II of England (r. 1307–1327) to ensure that this powerful vassal remained loyal to the French monarchy. However, when none of Isabella's three brothers, who served in turn as kings of France, produced a male heir, Isabella's son, King Edward III of England (r. 1327–1377), laid claim to the French throne in 1337. Edward decided to fight for his rights after French courts awarded the throne to a more distant (and more French) cousin. Other vassals joined in a series of battles for the French throne that stretched out over a century.

New military technology shaped the conflict. Early in the war, hired Italian crossbowmen reinforced the French cavalry, but arrows from another late medieval innovation, the English longbow, nearly annihilated the French force. Adopted from the Welsh, the 6-foot (1.8-meter) longbow could shoot farther and more rapidly than the crossbow. Although arrows from longbows could not pierce armor, in concentrated volleys they often found gaps in the knights' defenses or struck their less-well-protected horses. To defend against these weapons, armor became heavier and more encompassing, making it harder for a knight to move. A knight who was pulled off his steed by a foot soldier armed with a pike (hooked pole) was usually unable to get up to defend himself.

Firearms became prominent in later stages of the Hundred Years War. Early cannon were better at spooking the horses than at hitting rapidly moving targets. As cannon grew larger, they proved quite effective in blasting holes through the heavy walls of medieval castles and towns. The first use of such artillery, against the French in the Battle of Agincourt (1415), gave the English an important victory.

A young French peasant woman, Joan of Arc, brought the English gains to a halt. Believing she was acting on God's instructions, she donned a knight's armor and rallied the French troops, which defeated the English in 1429 just as they seemed close to conquering France. Shortly after this victory, Joan had the misfortune of falling into English hands. English churchmen tried her for witchcraft and burned her at the stake in 1431.

In the final battles of the Hundred Years War, French forces used large cannon to demolish the walls of once-secure castles held by the English and their allies. The truce that ended the struggle in 1453 left the French monarchy in firm control.

New Monarchies in France and England

The war proved to be a watershed in the political history of France and England. The **new monarchies** that emerged differed from their medieval predecessors in having greater centralization of power, more fixed "national" boundaries, and stronger representative institutions. English monarchs after 1453 strove to consolidate control within the British Isles, though the Scots strongly defended their independence. French monarchs worked to tame the independence of their powerful noble vassals. Holdings headed by women were especially vulnerable. Mary of Burgundy (1457–1482) was forced to surrender much of her family's vast holdings to the king. Anne of Brittany's forced marriage to the king led to the eventual incorporation of her duchy° into France.

Changes in military technology helped undermine nobles' resistance. Smaller, more mobile cannon developed in the late fifteenth century blasted through their castle walls. More powerful hand-held firearms that could pierce even the heaviest armor hastened the demise of the armored knights. New armies depended less on knights from noble vassals and more on bowmen,

duchy (DUTCH-ee)

pikemen, musketeers, and artillery units paid by the royal treasury.

The new monarchies tried several strategies to pay for their standing armies. Monarchs encouraged noble vassals to make monetary payments in place of military service and levied additional taxes in time of war. For example, Charles VII of France (r. 1422–1461) won the right to impose a land tax on his vassals that enabled him to pay the costs of the last years of war with England. This new tax sustained the royal treasury for the next 350 years.

Taxes on merchants were another important revenue source. The taxes on the English wool trade, begun by King Edward III, paid most of the costs of the Hundred Years War. Some rulers taxed Jewish merchants and extorted large contributions from wealthy towns. Individual merchants sometimes curried royal favor with loans, even though such debts could be difficult or dangerous to collect. For example, the wealthy fifteenth-century French merchant Jacques Coeur° gained many social and financial benefits for himself and his family by lending money to important members of the French court, but he was ruined when his jealous debtors accused him of murder and had his fortune confiscated.

The church was a third source of revenue. The clergy often made voluntary contributions to a war effort. English and French monarchs gained further control of church funds in the fifteenth century by gaining the right to appoint important ecclesiastical officials in their realms. Although reformers complained that this subordinated the church's spiritual mission to political and economic concerns, the monarchs often used state power to enforce religious orthodoxy in their realms more vigorously than the popes had ever been able to do.

The shift in power to the monarchs and away from the nobility and the church did not deprive nobles of social privileges and special access to high administrative and military offices. Moreover, towns, nobles, and clergy found new ways to check royal power in the representative institutions that came into existence in England and France. By 1500 Parliament had become a permanent part of English government: the House of Lords contained all the great nobles and English church officials; the House of Commons represented the towns and the leading citizens of the counties. In France a similar but less effective representative body, the Estates General, represented the church, the nobles, and the towns.

Coeur (cur)

Iberian Unification

The growth of Spain and Portugal into strong, centralized states was also shaped by struggles between kings and vassals, dynastic marriages and mergers, and warfare. But Spain and Portugal's **reconquest** of Iberia from Muslim rule was also a religious crusade. Religious zeal did not rule out personal gain. The Christian knights who gradually pushed the borders of their kingdoms southward expected material rewards. The spoils of victory included irrigated farmland, cities rich in Moorish architecture, and trading ports with access to the Mediterranean and the Atlantic. Serving God, growing rich, and living off the labor of others became a way of life for the Iberian nobility.

The reconquest advanced in waves over several centuries. Christian knights took Toledo in 1085. The Atlantic port of Lisbon fell in 1147 with the aid of English crusaders on their way to capture the Holy Land. It became the new capital of Portugal and the kingdom's leading city, displacing the older capital of Oporto, whose name (meaning "the port") is the root of the word *Portugal.* A Christian victory in 1212 broke the back of Muslim power in Iberia. During the next few decades Portuguese and Castilian forces captured the beautiful and prosperous cities of Cordova (1236) and Seville (1248) and in 1249 drove the Muslims from the southwestern corner of Iberia, known as Algarve° ("the west" in Arabic). Only the small kingdom of Granada hugging the Mediterranean coast remained in Muslim hands.

By incorporating Algarve in 1249, Portugal attained its modern territorial limits. After a long pause to colonize, Christianize, and consolidate this land, Portugal took the Christian crusade to North Africa. In 1415 Portuguese knights seized the port city of Ceuta° in Morocco, where they learned more about the trans-Saharan caravan trade in gold and slaves (see Chapter 14). During the next few decades, Portuguese mariners sailed down the Atlantic coast of Africa seeking access to this rich trade and alliances with rumored African Christians (see Chapter 16).

Although it took the other Iberian kingdoms much longer to complete the reconquest, the struggle served to bring them together and to keep their Christian religious zealotry at a high pitch. The marriage of Princess Isabella of Castile and Prince Ferdinand of Aragon in 1469 led to the permanent union of their kingdoms into Spain a decade later when they inherited their respective thrones. Their conquest of Granada in 1492 secured the final piece of Muslim territory in Iberia for the new kingdom.

Algarve (ahl-GAHRV) **Ceuta** (say-OO-tuh)

The year 1492 was also memorable because of Ferdinand and Isabella's sponsorship of the voyage led by Christopher Columbus in search of the riches of the Indian Ocean (see Chapter 16). A third event that year also reflected Spain's crusading mentality. Less than three months after Granada's fall, the monarchs ordered all Jews to be expelled from their kingdoms. Efforts to force the remaining Muslims to convert or leave led to a Muslim revolt at the end of 1499 that was not put down until 1501. Portugal also began expelling Jews in 1493, including many thousands who had fled from Spain.

Conclusion

From an ecological perspective, the later medieval history of the Latin West is a story of triumphs and disasters. Westerners excelled in harnessing the inanimate forces of nature with their windmills, water wheels, and sails. They mined and refined the mineral wealth of the earth, although localized pollution and deforestation were among the results. But their inability to improve food production and distribution as rapidly as their population grew created a demographic crisis that became a demographic calamity when the Black Death swept through Europe in the mid-fourteenth century.

From a regional perspective, the period witnessed the coming together of the basic features of the modern West. States were of moderate size but had exceptional military capacity honed by frequent wars with one another. The ruling class, convinced that economic strength and political strength were inseparable, promoted the welfare of the urban populations that specialized in trade, manufacturing, and finance—and taxed their profits. Autonomous universities fostered intellectual excellence, and printing diffused the latest advances in knowledge. Art and architecture reached peaks of design and execution that set the standard for subsequent centuries. Perhaps most fundamentally, later medieval Europeans were fascinated by tools and techniques. In commerce, warfare, and industry, new inventions and improved versions of old ones underpinned the region's continuing dynamism.

From a global perspective, these centuries marked the Latin West's change from a region dependent on cultural and commercial flows from the East to a region poised to export its culture and impose its power on other parts of the world. It is one of history's great ironies that many of the tools that the Latin West used to challenge Eastern supremacy had originally been borrowed from the East. Medieval Europe's mills, printing, firearms, and navigational devices owed much to Eastern designs, just as its agriculture, alphabet, and numerals had in earlier times. Western European success depended as much on strong motives for expansion as on adequate means. Long before the first voyages overseas, population pressure, religious zeal, economic motives, and intellectual curiosity had expanded the territory and resources of the Latin West. From the late eleventh century onward such expansion of frontiers was notable in the English conquest of Celtic lands, in the establishment of crusader and commercial outposts in the eastern Mediterranean and Black Seas, in the massive German settlement east of the Elbe River, and in the reconquest of southern Iberia from the Muslims. The early voyages into the Atlantic were an extension of similar motives in a new direction.

Key Terms

Latin West
three-field system
Black Death
water wheel
Hanseatic League
guild
Gothic cathedral
Renaissance (European)
universities
scholasticism
humanists (Renaissance)
printing press
Great Western Schism
Hundred Years War
new monarchies
reconquest

Suggested Reading

A fine guide to the Latin West (including its ties to eastern Europe, Africa, and the Middle East) is Robert Fossier, ed., *The Cambridge Illustrated History of the Middle Ages*, vol. 3, *1250–1520* (1986). George Holmes, *Europe: Hierarchy and Revolt, 1320–1450*, 2d ed. (2000), and Denys Hay, *Europe in the Fourteenth and Fifteenth Centuries,* 2d ed. (1989), are comprehensive overviews. For the West's economic revival and growth, see Robert S. Lopez, *The Commercial Revolution of the Middle Ages, 950–1350* (1976), and Harry A. Miskimin, *The Economy of Early Renaissance Europe, 1300–1460* (1975). For greater detail see *The New Cambridge Medieval History,* vol. 6, *1300–c.1415,* ed. M. Jones (1998), and vol. 7, *1415–1500,* ed. C. Allmand (1999).

For fascinating primary sources see James Bruce Ross and Mary Martin McLaughlin, eds., *The Portable Medieval Reader* (1977) and *The Portable Renaissance Reader* (1977). *The Notebooks of Leonardo da Vinci*, ed. Pamela Taylor (1960), show this versatile genius at work.

Technological change is surveyed by Arnold Pacey, *The Maze of Ingenuity: Ideas and Idealism in the Development of Technology* (1974); Jean Gimpel, *The Medieval Machine: The Industrial Revolution of the Middle Ages* (1977); and William H. McNeill, *The Pursuit of Power: Technology, Armed Force, and Society Since* A.D. *1000* (1982). For a key aspect of the environment see Roland Bechmann, *Trees and Man: The Forest in the Middle Ages* (1990).

Charles Homer Haskins, *The Rise of the Universities* (1923; reprint, 1957), is a brief, lighthearted introduction; more detailed and scholarly is Olef Pedersen, *The First Universities:* Studium Generale *and the Origins of University Education in Europe* (1998). Johan Huizinga, *The Waning of the Middle Ages* (1924), is the classic account of the "mind" of the fifteenth century. A multitude of works deal with the Renaissance, but few in any broad historical context. Lisa Jardine, *Worldly Goods: A New History of the Renaissance* (1996), is well illustrated and balanced; see also John R. Hale, *The Civilization of Europe in the Renaissance* (1995).

For social history see Georges Duby, *Rural Economy and Country Life in the Medieval West* (1990), for the earlier centuries. George Huppert, *After the Black Death: A Social History of Early Modern Europe* (1986), takes the analysis past 1500. Brief lives of individuals are found in Eileen Power, *Medieval People,* new ed. (1997), and Frances Gies and Joseph Gies, *Women in the Middle Ages* (1978). More systematic are the essays in Mary Erler and Maryanne Kowaleski, eds., *Women and Power in the Middle Ages* (1988). Vita Sackville-West, *Saint Joan of Arc* (1926; reprint, 1991), is a readable introduction to this extraordinary person.

Key events in the Anglo-French dynastic conflict are examined by Christopher Alland, *The Hundred Years War: England and France at War, ca. 1300–ca. 1450* (1988). Joseph F. O'Callaghan, *A History of Medieval Spain* (1975), provides the best one-volume coverage; for more detail see Jocelyn N. Hillgarth, *The Spanish Kingdoms,* 2 vols. (1976, 1978). Barbara W. Tuchman, *A Distant Mirror: The Calamitous 14th Century* (1978), is a popular account of the crises of that era. Norman F. Cantor, *In the Wake of the Plague: The Black Death and the World It Made* (2001), supplies a thorough introduction.

The Latin West's expansion is well treated by Robert Bartlett, *The Making of Europe: Conquest, Colonization, and Cultural Change* (1993); J. R. S. Phillips, *The Medieval Expansion of Europe,* 2d ed. (1998); and P. E. Russell, *Portugal, Spain and the African Atlantic, 1343–1492* (1998).

Francis C. Oakley, *The Western Church in the Later Middle Ages* (1985), is a reliable summary of modern scholarship. Kenneth R. Stow, *Alienated Minority: The Jews of Medieval Latin Europe* (1992), provides a fine survey up through the fourteenth century. For pioneering essays on the Latin West's external ties see Khalil I. Semaan, ed., *Islam and the Medieval West: Aspects of Intercultural Relations* (1980).

Notes

1. Quoted in Marina Warner, *Alone of All Her Sex: The Myth and Cult of the Virgin Mary* (New York: Random House, 1983), 179.
2. Harry Miskimin, *The Economy of the Early Renaissance, 1300–1460* (Englewood Cliffs, NJ: Prentice-Hall, 1969), 26–27.
3. Quotations here and later in the chapter are from Geoffrey Chaucer, *The Canterbury Tales,* trans. Nevill Coghill (New York: Penguin Books, 1952), 25, 29, 32.

16

The Maritime Revolution, to 1550

Columbus Prepares to Cross the Atlantic, 1492 This later representation shows Columbus with the ships, soldiers, priests, and seamen that were part of Spain's enterprise.

CHAPTER OUTLINE

In 1511 young Ferdinand Magellan sailed from Europe around the southern tip of Africa and eastward across the Indian Ocean as a member of the first Portuguese expedition to explore the East Indies (maritime Southeast Asia). Eight years later, this time in the service of Spain, he headed an expedition that sought to demonstrate the feasibility of reaching the East Indies by sailing westward from Europe. By the middle of 1521 Magellan's expedition had achieved its goal by sailing across the Atlantic, rounding the southern tip of South America, and crossing the Pacific Ocean—but at a high price.

One of the five ships that had set out from Spain in 1519 was wrecked on a reef, and the captain of another deserted and sailed back to Spain. The passage across the vast Pacific took much longer than anticipated, resulting in the deaths of dozens of sailors due to starvation and disease. In the Philippines, Magellan himself was killed on April 27, 1521, while aiding a local king who had promised to become a Christian. Magellan's successor met the same fate a few days later.

To consolidate their dwindling resources, the expedition's survivors burned the least seaworthy of their remaining three ships and transferred the men and supplies from that ship to the smaller *Victoria*, which continued westward across the Indian Ocean, around Africa, and back to Europe. Magellan's flagship, the *Trinidad*, tried unsuccessfully to recross the Pacific to Central America. The *Victoria*'s return to Spain on September 8, 1522, was a crowning example of Europeans' new ability and determination to make themselves masters of the oceans. A century of daring and dangerous voyages backed by the Portuguese crown had opened new routes through the South Atlantic to Africa, Brazil, and the rich trade of the Indian Ocean. Rival voyages sponsored by Spain since 1492 had opened new contacts with the American continents. Now the unexpectedly broad Pacific Ocean had been crossed as well. A maritime revolution was under way that would change the course of history.

That new maritime skill marked the end of an era in which the flow of historical influences tended to move from east to west. Before 1500 most overland and maritime expansion had come from Asia, as had the most useful technologies and the most influential systems of belief. Asia also had been home to the most powerful states and the richest trading networks. The Iberians set out on their voyages of exploration to reach Eastern markets, and their success began a new era in which the West gradually became the world's center of power, wealth, and innovation.

The maritime revolution created many new contacts, alliances, and conflicts. Some ended tragically for individuals like Magellan. Some were disastrous for entire populations: Amerindians, for instance, suffered conquest, colonization, and a rapid decline in numbers. Sometimes the results were mixed: Asians and Africans found both risks and opportunities in their new relations with the visitors from Europe.

As you read this chapter, ask yourself the following questions:

- Why did Portugal and Spain undertake voyages of exploration?
- Why do the voyages of Magellan and other Iberians mark a turning point in world history?
- What were the consequences for the different peoples of the world of the new contacts resulting from these voyages?

Global Maritime Expansion Before 1450

Since ancient times travel across the salt waters of the world's seas and oceans had been one of the great challenges to people's technological ingenuity. Ships had to be sturdy enough to survive heavy winds and waves, and pilots had to learn how to cross featureless expanses of water to reach their destinations. In time ships, sails, and navigational techniques perfected in the more protected seas were tried on the vast, open oceans.

However complex the solutions and dangerous the voyages, the rewards of sea travel made them worthwhile. Ships could move goods and people more quickly and cheaply than any form of overland travel then possible. Because of its challenges and rewards, sea travel attracted adventurers. To cross the unknown waters, find

CHRONOLOGY

	Pacific Ocean	Atlantic Ocean	Indian Ocean
	400–1300 Polynesian settlement of Pacific islands	**770–1200** Viking voyages **1300s** Settlement of Madeira, Azores, Canaries **Early 1300s** Mali voyages	
1400		**1418–1460** Voyages of Henry the Navigator **1440s** Slaves from West Africa **1482** Portuguese at Gold Coast and Kongo **1486** Portuguese at Benin **1488** Bartolomeu Dias reaches Indian Ocean **1492** Columbus reaches Caribbean **1492–1500** Spanish conquer Hispaniola **1493** Columbus returns to Caribbean (second voyage) **1498** Columbus reaches mainland of South America (third voyage)	**1405–1433** Voyages of Zheng He **1497–1498** Vasco da Gama reaches India
1500		**1500** Cabral reaches Brazil **1513** Ponce de León explores Florida	**1505** Portuguese bombard Swahili Coast cities **1510** Portuguese take Goa **1511** Portuguese take Malacca **1515** Portuguese take Hormuz
	1519–1522 Magellan expedition	**1519–1520** Cortés conquers Aztec Empire **1531–1533** Pizarro conquers Inca Empire	**1535** Portuguese take Dui **1538** Portuguese defeat Ottoman fleet **1539** Portuguese aid Ethiopia

new lands, and open up new trade or settlements was an exciting prospect. For these reasons, some men on every continent had long turned their attention to the sea.

By 1450 much had been accomplished and much remained undone. Daring mariners had discovered and settled most of the islands of the Pacific, the Atlantic, and the Indian Oceans. The greatest success was the trading system that united the peoples around the Indian Ocean. But no individual had yet crossed the Pacific in either direction. Even the narrower Atlantic was a barrier that kept the peoples of the Americas, Europe, and Africa in ignorance of each other's existence. The inhabitants of Australia were likewise completely cut off from contact with the rest of humanity. All this was about to change.

The Pacific Ocean

The voyages of Polynesian peoples out of sight of land over vast distances across the Pacific Ocean are one of the most impressive feats in maritime history before 1450 (see Map 16.1). Though they left no written records, over several thousand years

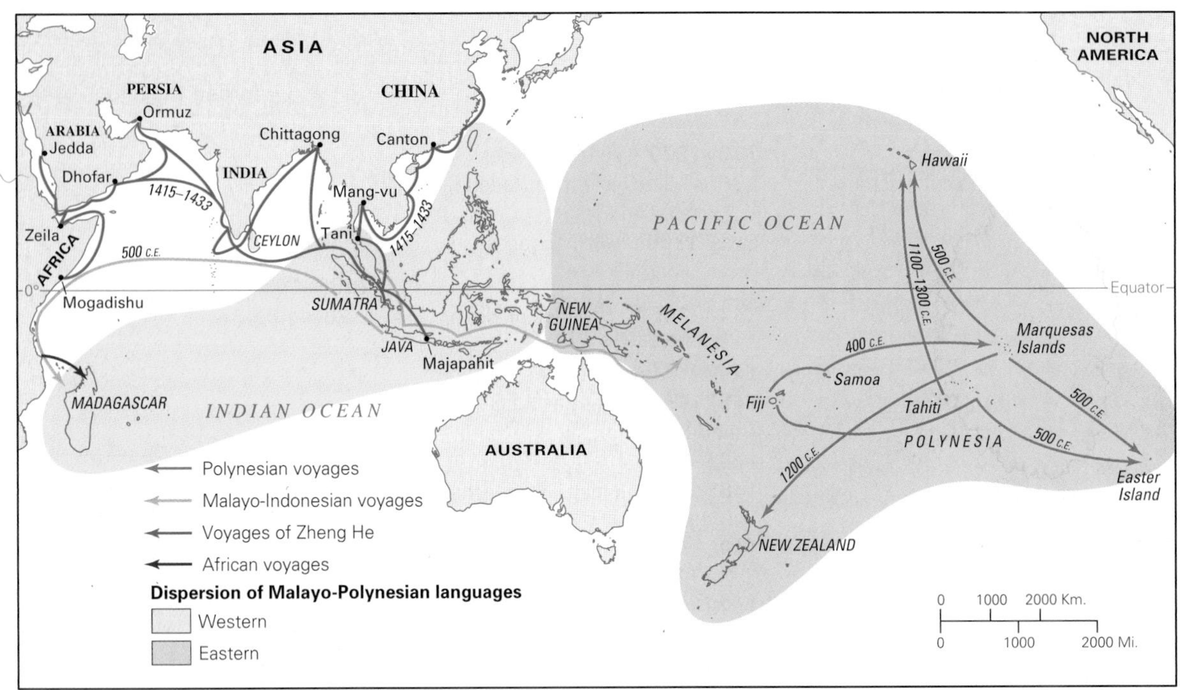

Map 16.1 Exploration and Settlement in the Indian and Pacific Oceans Before 1500 Over many centuries, mariners originating in Southeast Asia gradually colonized the islands of the Pacific and Indian Oceans. The Chinese voyages led by Zheng He in the fifteenth century were lavish official expeditions.

intrepid mariners from the Malay° Peninsula of Southeast Asia explored and settled the island chains of the East Indies and moved onto New Guinea and the smaller islands of Melanesia°. Beginning sometime before the Common Era (C.E.), a new wave of expansion from the area of Fiji brought the first humans to the islands of the central Pacific known as Polynesia. The easternmost of the Marquesas° Islands were reached about 400 C.E.; Easter Island, 2,200 miles (3,540 kilometers) off the coast of South America, was settled a century later. From the Marquesas, Polynesian sailors sailed to the Hawaiian Islands as early as 500 C.E. They settled New Zealand about 1200. Then, between 1100 and 1300, new voyages northward from Tahiti to Hawaii brought more Polynesian settlers across the more than 2,000 nautical miles (4,000 kilometers) to Hawaii.

Until recent decades some historians argued that Polynesians could have reached the eastern Pacific islands only by accident because they lacked navigational devices to plot their way. Others wondered how Polynesians could have overcome the difficulties, illustrated by Magellan's flagship, *Trinidad,* of sailing eastward across the Pacific. In 1947 one energetic amateur historian of the sea, Thor Heyerdahl°, argued that Easter Island and Hawaii were actually settled from the Americas. He sought to prove his theory by sailing his balsa-wood raft, *Kon Tiki,* westward from Peru.

Although some Amerindian voyagers did use ocean currents to travel northward from Peru to Mexico between 300 and 900 C.E., there is now considerable evidence that the settlement of the islands of the eastern Pacific was the result of planned expansion by Polynesian mariners. The first piece of evidence is the fact that the languages of these islanders are all closely related to the languages of the western Pacific and ultimately to those of Malaya. The second is the finding that accidental voyages could not have brought sufficient numbers of men and women for founding a new colony along with all the plants and domesticated animals that were basic to other Polynesian islands.

In 1976 a Polynesian crew led by Ben Finney used traditional navigational methods to sail an ocean canoe from Hawaii south to Tahiti. The *Hokulea* was a 62-foot-

Malay (May-LAY) **Melanesia** (mel-uh-NEE-zhuh)
Marquesas (mar-KAY-suhs)

Heyerdahl (HIGH-uhr-dahl)

Polynesian Canoes Pacific Ocean mariners sailing canoes such as these, shown in an eighteenth-century painting, made epic voyages of exploration and settlement. A large platform connects two canoes at the left, providing more room for the members of the expedition, and a sail supplements the paddlers. ("Tereoboo, King of Owyhee, bringing presents to Captain Cook," D. L. Ref. p. xx 2f. 35. Courtesy, The Dixon Library, State Library of New South Wales)

long (19-meter-long) double canoe patterned after old oceangoing canoes, which sometimes were as long as 120 feet (37 meters). Not only did the *Hokulea* prove seaworthy, but, powered by an inverted triangular sail and steered by paddles (not by a rudder), it was able to sail across the winds at a sharp enough angle to make the difficult voyage, just as ancient mariners must have done. Perhaps even more remarkable, the *Hokulea*'s crew was able to navigate to their destination using only their observation of the currents, stars, and evidence of land.

The Indian Ocean

While Polynesian mariners were settling Pacific islands, other Malayo-Indonesians were sailing westward across the Indian Ocean and colonizing the large island of Madagascar off the southeastern coast of Africa. These voyages continued through the fifteenth century. To this day the inhabitants of Madagascar speak Malayo-Polynesian languages. However, part of the island's population is descended from Africans who had crossed the 300 miles (500 kilometers) from the mainland to Madagascar, most likely in the centuries leading up to 1500.

Other peoples had been using the Indian Ocean for trade since ancient times. The landmasses of Southeast Asia and eastern Africa that enclose the Indian Ocean on each side, and the Indian subcontinent that juts into its middle, provided coasts that seafarers might safely follow and coves for protection. Moreover, seasonal winds known as monsoons are so predictable and steady that navigation using sailing vessels called dhows° was less difficult and dangerous in ancient times than elsewhere.

The rise of medieval Islam gave Indian Ocean trade an important boost. The great Muslim cities of the Middle East provided a demand for valuable commodities. Even more important were the networks of Muslim traders that tied the region together. Muslim traders shared a common language, ethic, and law and actively spread their religion to distant trading cities. By 1400 there were Muslim trading communities all around the Indian Ocean.

The Indian Ocean traders operated largely independently of the empires and states they served, but in East Asia imperial China's rulers were growing more and more interested in these wealthy ports of trade. In 1368

dhow (dow)

Chinese Junk This modern drawing shows how much larger one of Zheng He's ships was than one of Vasco da Gama's vessels. Watertight interior bulkheads made junks the most seaworthy large ships of the fifteenth century. Sails made of pleated bamboo matting hung from the junk's masts, and a stern rudder provided steering. European ships of exploration, though smaller, were faster and more maneuverable. (Dugald Stermer)

the Ming dynasty overthrew Mongol rule and began expansionist policies to reestablish China's predominance and prestige abroad.

Having restored Chinese dominance in East Asia, the Ming next moved to establish direct contacts with the peoples around the Indian Ocean. In choosing to send out seven imperial fleets between 1405 and 1433, the Ming may have been motivated partly by curiosity. The fact that most of the ports the fleets visited were important in the Indian Ocean trade suggests that enhancing China's commerce was also a motive. Yet because the expeditions were far larger than needed for exploration or promoting trade, their main purpose probably was to inspire awe of Ming power and achievements.

The Ming expeditions into the Indian Ocean basin were launched on a scale that reflected imperial China's resources and importance. The first consisted of sixty-two specially built "treasure ships," large Chinese junks each about 300 feet long by 150 feet wide (90 by 45 meters). There were also at least a hundred smaller vessels, most of which were larger than the flagship in which Columbus later sailed across the Atlantic. Each treasure ship had nine masts, twelve sails, many decks, and a carrying capacity of 3,000 tons (six times the capacity of Columbus's entire fleet). One expedition carried over 27,000 individuals, including infantry and cavalry troops. The ships would have been armed with small cannon, but in most Chinese sea battles arrows from highly accurate crossbows dominated the fighting.

At the command of the expeditions was Admiral **Zheng He**° (1371–1435). A Chinese Muslim with ancestral connections to the Persian Gulf, Zheng was a fitting emissary to the increasingly Muslim-dominated Indian Ocean basin. The expeditions carried other Arabic-speaking Chinese as interpreters.

One of these interpreters kept a journal recording the customs, dress, and beliefs of the people visited, along with the trade, towns, and animals of their countries. He observed exotic animals such as the black panther of Malaya and the tapir of Sumatra; beliefs in legendary "corpse headed barbarians" whose heads left their bodies at night and caused infants to die; the division of coastal Indians into five classes, which correspond to the four Hindu varna and a separate Muslim class; and the fact

Zheng He (jung huh)

that traders in the rich Indian trading port of Calicut° could perform error-free calculations by counting on their fingers and toes rather than using the Chinese abacus. After his return, the interpreter went on tour in China, telling of these exotic places and "how far the majestic virtue of [China's] imperial dynasty extended."[1]

The Chinese "treasure ships" carried rich silks, precious metals, and other valuable goods intended as gifts for distant rulers. In return those rulers sent back gifts of equal or greater value to the Chinese emperor. Although the main purpose of these exchanges was diplomatic, they also stimulated trade between China and its southern neighbors. For that reason they were welcomed by Chinese merchants and manufacturers. Yet commercial profits could not have offset the huge cost of the fleets.

Interest in new contacts was not confined to the Chinese side. In 1415–1416 at least three trading cities on the Swahili° Coast of East Africa sent delegations to China. The delegates from one of them, Malindi, presented the emperor of China with a giraffe, creating quite a stir among the normally reserved imperial officials. Such African delegations may have encouraged more contacts, for the next three of Zheng's voyages were extended to the African coast. Unfortunately, no documents record how Africans and Chinese reacted to each other during these historic meetings between 1417 and 1433. It appears that China's lavish gifts stimulated the Swahili market for silk and porcelain. An increase in Chinese imports of pepper from southern Asian lands also resulted from these expeditions.

Had the Ming court wished to promote trade for the profit of its merchants, Chinese fleets might have continued to play a dominant role in Indian Ocean trade. But some high Chinese officials opposed increased contact with peoples whom they regarded as barbarians with no real contribution to make to China. Such opposition caused a suspension in the voyages from 1424 to 1431, and after the final expedition of 1432 to 1433, no new fleets were sent out. Later Ming emperors focused their attention on internal matters in their vast empire. China's withdrawal left a power vacuum in the Indian Ocean.

The Atlantic Ocean

The greatest mariners of the Atlantic in the early Middle Ages were the Vikings. These northern European raiders and pirates used their small, open ships to attack coastal European settlements for several centuries. They also discovered and settled one island after another in the North Atlantic during these warmer than usual centuries. Like the Polynesians, the Vikings had neither maps nor navigational devices, but they managed to find their way wonderfully well using their knowledge of the heavens and the seas.

The Vikings first settled Iceland in 770. From there some moved to Greenland in 982, and by accident one group sighted North America in 986. Fifteen years later Leif Ericsson established a short-lived Viking settlement on the island of Newfoundland, which he called Vinland. When a colder climate returned after 1200, the northern settlements in Greenland went into decline, and Vinland became only a mysterious place mentioned in Norse sagas.

Some southern Europeans also used the maritime skills they had acquired in the Mediterranean and coastal Atlantic to explore the Atlantic. In 1291 two Vivaldo brothers from Genoa set out to sail through the South Atlantic and around Africa to India. They were never heard of again. Other Genoese and Portuguese expeditions into the Atlantic in the fourteenth century discovered (and settled) the islands of Madeira°, the Azores°, and the Canaries.

There is also written evidence of African voyages of exploration in the Atlantic in this period. The celebrated Syrian geographer al-Umari (1301–1349) relates that when Mansa Kankan Musa°, the ruler of the West African empire of Mali, passed through Egypt on his lavish pilgrimage to Mecca in 1324, he told of voyages to cross the Atlantic undertaken by his predecessor, Mansa Muhammad. Muhammad had sent out four hundred vessels with men and supplies, telling them, "Do not return until you have reached the other side of the ocean or if you have exhausted your food or water." After a long time one canoe returned, reporting that the others had been swept away by a "violent current in the middle of the sea." Muhammad himself then set out at the head of a second, even larger, expedition, from which no one returned.

In addition to sailing up the Pacific coast, early Amerindian voyagers from South America also colonized the West Indies. By the year 1000 Amerindians known as the **Arawak**° had moved up from the small islands of the Lesser Antilles (Barbados, Martinique, and Guadeloupe) into the Greater Antilles (Cuba, Hispaniola, Jamaica, and Puerto Rico) as well as into the Bahamas

Calicut (KAL-ih-kut) **Swahili** (swah-HEE-lee)

Madeira (muh-DEER-uh) **Azores** (A-zorz)
Mansa Kankan Musa (MAHN-suh KAHN-kahn MOO-suh)
Arawak (AR-uh-wahk)

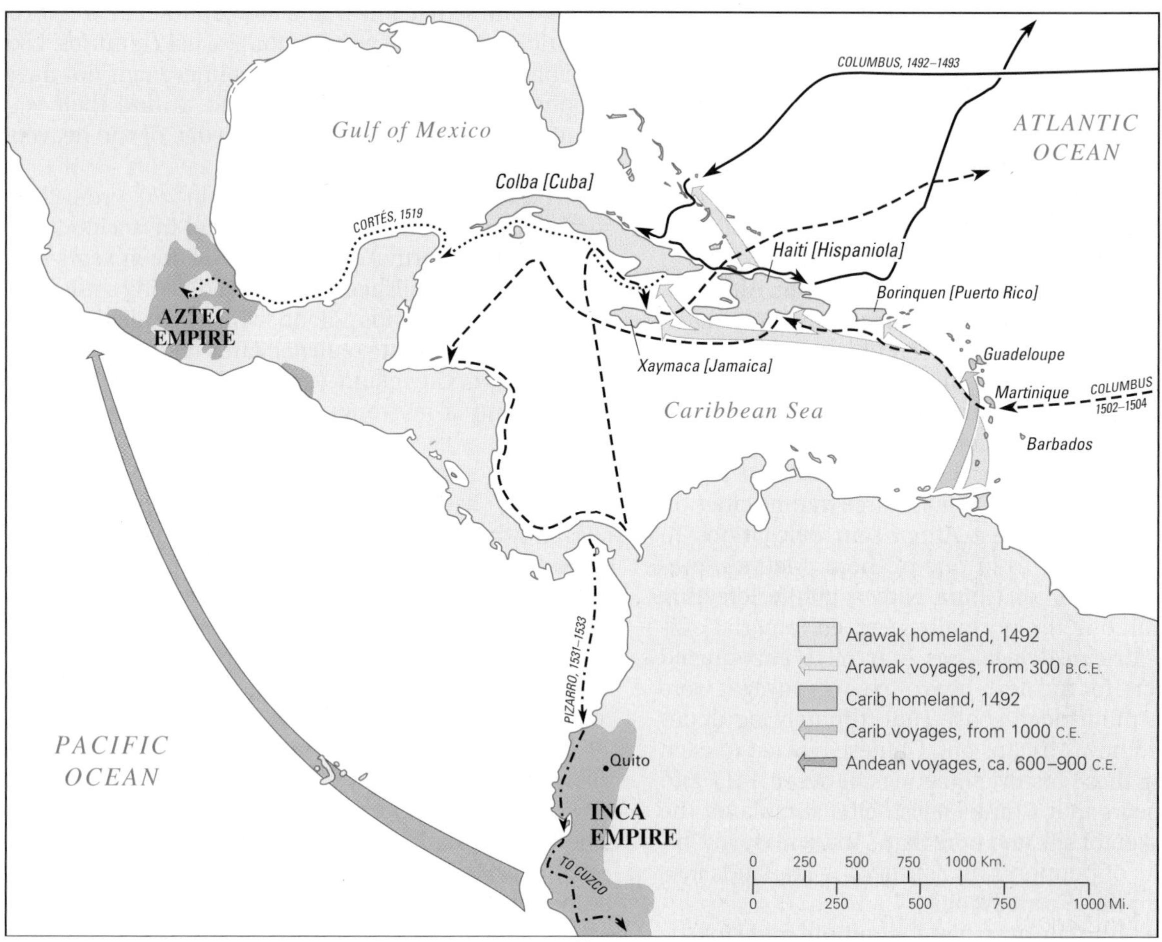

Map 16.2 Middle America to 1533 Early Amerindian voyages from South America brought new settlers to the West Indies and western Mexico. The arrival of Europeans in 1492 soon led to the conquest and depopulation of Amerindians.

(see Map 16.2). The Carib followed the same route in later centuries and by the late fifteenth century had overrun most Arawak settlements in the Lesser Antilles and were raiding parts of the Greater Antilles. From the West Indies Arawak and Carib also undertook voyages to the North American mainland.

EUROPEAN EXPANSION, 1400–1550

The preceding survey shows that maritime expansion occurred in many parts of the world before 1450. The epic sea voyages sponsored by the Iberian kingdoms of Portugal and Spain are of special interest because they began a maritime revolution that profoundly altered the course of world history. The Portuguese and Spanish expeditions ended the isolation of the Americas and increased global interaction. The influence in world affairs of the Iberians and other Europeans who followed them overseas rose steadily in the centuries after 1500.

Iberian overseas expansion was the product of two related phenomena. First, Iberian rulers had strong economic, religious, and political motives to expand their contacts and increase their dominance. Second, improvements in their maritime and military technologies gave them the means to master treacherous and unfamiliar ocean environments, seize control of existing maritime trade routes, and conquer new lands.

Motives for Exploration

Why did Iberian kingdoms decide to sponsor voyages of exploration in the fifteenth century? Part of the answer lies in the individual ambitions and adventurous personalities of these states' leaders. Another part of the answer can be found in long-term tendencies in Europe and the Mediterranean. In many ways these voyages continued four trends evident in the Latin West since about the year 1000: (1) the revival of urban life and trade, (2) a struggle with Islamic powers for dominance of the Mediterranean that mixed religious motives with the desire for trade with distant lands, (3) growing intellectual curiosity about the outside world, and (4) a peculiarly European alliance between merchants and rulers.

The city-states of northern Italy took the lead in all these developments. By 1450 they had well-established trade links to northern Europe, the Indian Ocean, and the Black Sea, and their merchant princes had also sponsored an intellectual and artistic Renaissance. But there were two reasons why Italian states did not take the lead in exploring the Atlantic, even after the expansion of the Ottoman Empire disrupted their trade to the East and led other Christian Europeans to launch new religious wars against the Ottomans in 1396 and 1444. The first was that the trading states of Venice and Genoa preferred to continue the system of alliances with the Muslims that had given their merchants privileged access to the lucrative trade from the East. The second was that the ships of the Mediterranean were ill suited to the more violent weather of the Atlantic. However, many individual Italians played leading roles in the Atlantic explorations.

In contrast, the special history and geography of the Iberian kingdoms led them in a different direction. Part of that special history was centuries of anti-Muslim warfare that dated back to the eighth century, when Muslim forces overran most of Iberia. By about 1250 the Iberian kingdoms of Portugal, Castile, and Aragon had conquered all the Muslim lands in Iberia except the southern kingdom of Granada. United by a dynastic marriage in 1469, Castile and Aragon conquered Granada in 1492. These territories were gradually amalgamated into Spain, sixteenth-century Europe's most powerful state.

Christian militancy continued to be an important motive for both Portugal and Spain in their overseas ventures. But the Iberian rulers and their adventurous subjects were also seeking material returns. With only a modest share of the Mediterranean trade, they were much more willing than the Italians to take risks to find new routes through the Atlantic to the rich trade of Africa and Asia. Moreover, both were participants in the shipbuilding changes and the gunpowder revolution that were under way in Atlantic Europe. Though not centers of Renaissance learning, both were especially open to new geographical knowledge. Finally, both states were blessed with exceptional leaders.

Portuguese Voyages

Portugal's decision to invest significant resources in new exploration rested on well-established Atlantic fishing and a history of anti-Muslim warfare. When the Muslim government of Morocco in northwestern Africa showed weakness in the fifteenth century, the Portuguese went on the attack, beginning with the city of Ceuta° in 1415. This assault combined aspects of a religious crusade, a plundering expedition, and a military tournament in which young Portuguese knights displayed their bravery. The capture of the rich North African city, whose splendid homes, they reported, made those of Portugal look like pigsties, also made the Portuguese better informed about the caravans that brought gold and slaves to Ceuta from the African states south of the Sahara. Despite the capture of several more ports along Morocco's Atlantic coast, the Portuguese were unable to push inland and gain access to the gold trade. So they sought more direct contact with the gold producers by sailing down the African coast.

The attack on Ceuta was led by young Prince Henry (1394–1460), third son of the king of Portugal. Because he devoted the rest of his life to promoting exploration of the South Atlantic, he is known as **Henry the Navigator**. His official biographer emphasized Henry's mixed motives for exploration—converting Africans to Christianity, making contact with existing Christian rulers in Africa, and launching joint crusades with them against the Ottomans. Prince Henry also wished to discover new places and hoped that such new contacts would be profitable. His initial explorations were concerned with Africa. Only later did reaching India become an explicit goal of Portuguese explorers.

Despite being called "the Navigator," Prince Henry himself never ventured much farther from home than North Africa. Instead, he founded a sort of research institute at Sagres° for studying navigation and collecting information about the lands beyond Muslim North Africa. His staff drew on the pioneering efforts of Italian merchants, especially the Genoese, who had learned some of the secrets of the trans-Saharan trade, and of fourteenth-century Jewish cartographers who used information from Arab and European sources to produce remarkably

---

Ceuta (say-OO-tuh) **Sagres** (SAH-gresh)

accurate sea charts and maps of distant places. Henry also oversaw the collection of new geographical information from sailors and travelers and sent out ships to explore the Atlantic. His ships established permanent contact with the islands of Madeira in 1418 and the Azores in 1439.

Henry devoted resources to solving the technical problems faced by mariners sailing in unknown waters and open seas. His staff studied and improved navigational instruments that had come into Europe from China and the Islamic world. These instruments included the magnetic compass, first developed in China, and the astrolabe, an instrument of Arab or Greek invention that enabled mariners to determine their location at sea by measuring the position of the sun or the stars in the night sky. Even with such instruments, however, voyages still depended on the skill and experience of the navigators.

Another achievement of Portuguese mariners was the design of vessels appropriate for the voyages of exploration. The galleys in use in the Mediterranean were powered by large numbers of oarsmen and were impractical for long ocean voyages. The square sails of the three-masted European ships of the North Atlantic were propelled by friendly winds but could not sail at much of an angle against the wind. The voyages of exploration made use of a new vessel, the **caravel°.** Caravels were small, only one-fifth the size of the largest European ships of their day and of the large Chinese junks. Their size permitted them to enter shallow coastal waters and explore upriver, but they were strong enough to weather ocean storms. When equipped with lateen sails, caravels had great maneuverability and could sail deeply into the wind; when sporting square Atlantic sails, they had great speed. The addition of small cannon made them good fighting ships as well. The caravels' economy, speed, agility, and power justified a contemporary's claim that they were "the best ships that sailed the seas."[2]

To conquer the seas, pioneering captains had to overcome crew's fears that the South Atlantic waters were boiling hot and contained ocean currents that would prevent any ship entering them from ever returning home. It took Prince Henry fourteen years—from 1420 to 1434—to coax an expedition to venture beyond southern Morocco (see Map 16.3). The crew's fears proved unfounded, but the next stretch of coast, 800 miles (1,300 kilometers) of desert, offered little of interest to the explorers. Finally, in 1444 the mariners reached the Senegal River and the well-watered and well-populated lands below the Sahara beginning at what they named "Cape Verde" (Green Cape) because of its vegetation.

In the years that followed, Henry's explorers made an important addition to the maritime revolution by learning how to return speedily to Portugal. Instead of battling the prevailing northeast trade winds and currents back up the coast, they discovered that by sailing northwest into the Atlantic to the latitude of the Azores, ships could pick up prevailing westerly winds that would blow them back to Portugal. The knowledge that ocean winds tend to form large circular patterns helped explorers discover many other ocean routes.

To pay for the research, the ships, and the expeditions during the many decades before the voyages became profitable, Prince Henry drew partly on the income of the Order of Christ, a military religious order of which he was governor. The Order of Christ had inherited the properties and crusading traditions of the Order of Knights Templar, which had disbanded in 1314. The Order of Christ received the exclusive right to promote Christianity in all the lands that were discovered, and the Portuguese emblazoned their ships' sails with the crusaders' red cross.

The first financial return from the voyages came from selling into slavery Africans captured by the Portuguese in raids on the northwest coast of Africa and the Canary Islands during the 1440s. The total number of Africans captured or purchased on voyages exceeded eighty thousand by the end of the century and rose steadily thereafter. However, the gold trade quickly became more important than the slave trade as the Portuguese made contact with the trading networks that flourished in West Africa and reached across the Sahara. By 1457 enough African gold was coming back to Portugal for the kingdom to issue a new gold coin called the *cruzado* (crusade), another reminder of how deeply the Portuguese entwined religious and secular motives.

By the time of Prince Henry's death in 1460, his explorers had established a secure base of operations in the uninhabited Cape Verde Islands and had explored 600 miles (950 kilometers) of coast beyond Cape Verde, as far as what they named Sierra Leone° (Lion Mountain). From there they knew the coast of Africa curved sharply toward the east. It had taken the Portuguese four decades to cover the 1,500 miles (2,400 kilometers) from Lisbon to Sierra Leone; it took only three decades to explore the remaining 4,000 miles (6,400 kilometers) to the southern tip of the African continent.

The Portuguese crown continued to sponsor voyages of exploration, but speedier progress resulted from the growing participation of private commercial interests. In 1469 a prominent Lisbon merchant named

---

caravel (KAR-uh-vel)

Sierra Leone (see- ER-uh lee-OWN)

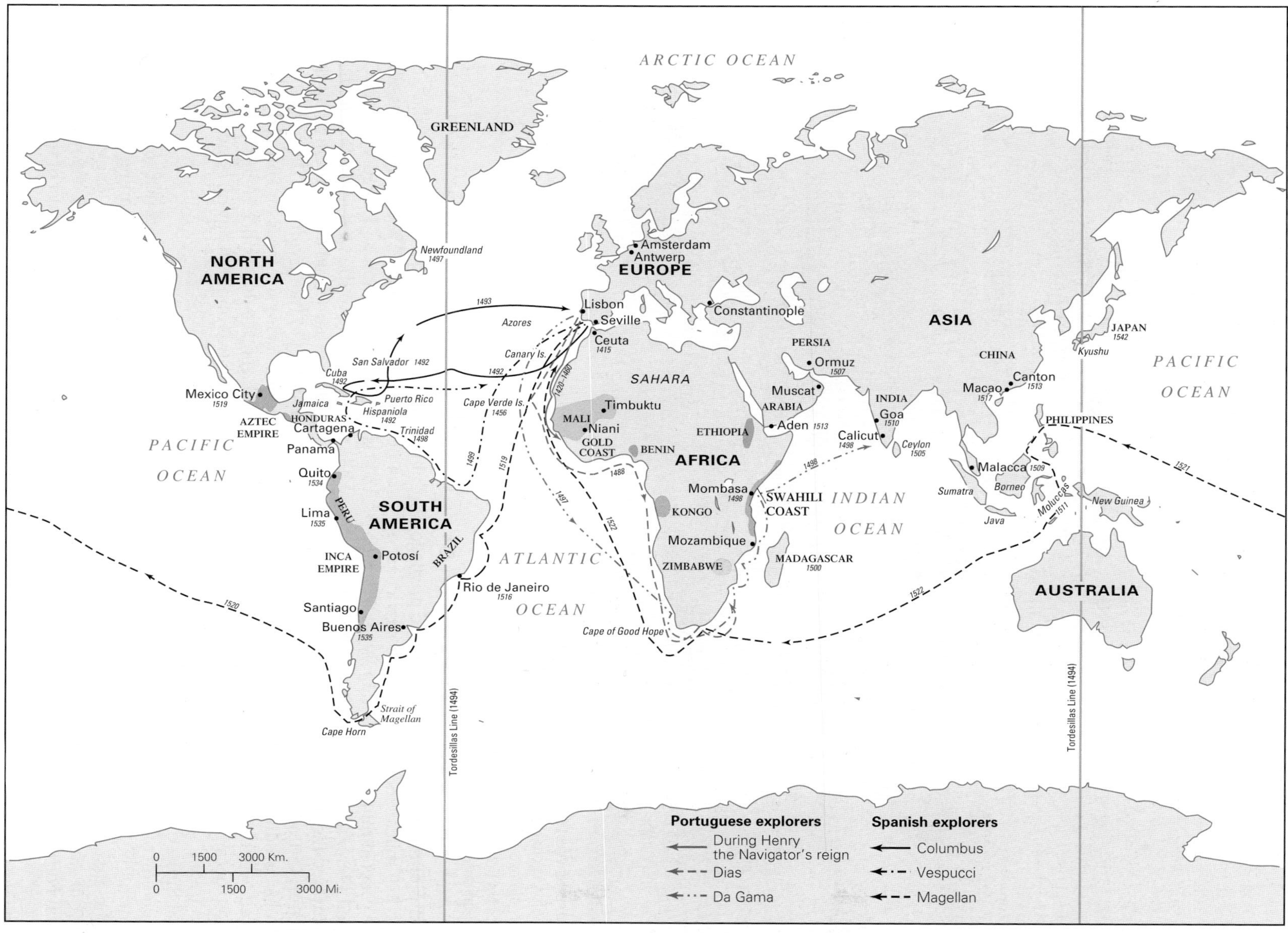

Map 16.3 European Exploration, 1420–1542 Portuguese and Spanish explorers showed the possibility and practicality of intercontinental maritime trade. Before 1540 European trade with Africa and Asia was much more important than that with the Americas, but after the Spanish conquest of the Aztec and Inca Empires transatlantic trade began to increase. Notice the Tordesillas line, which in theory separated the Spanish and Portuguese spheres of activity.

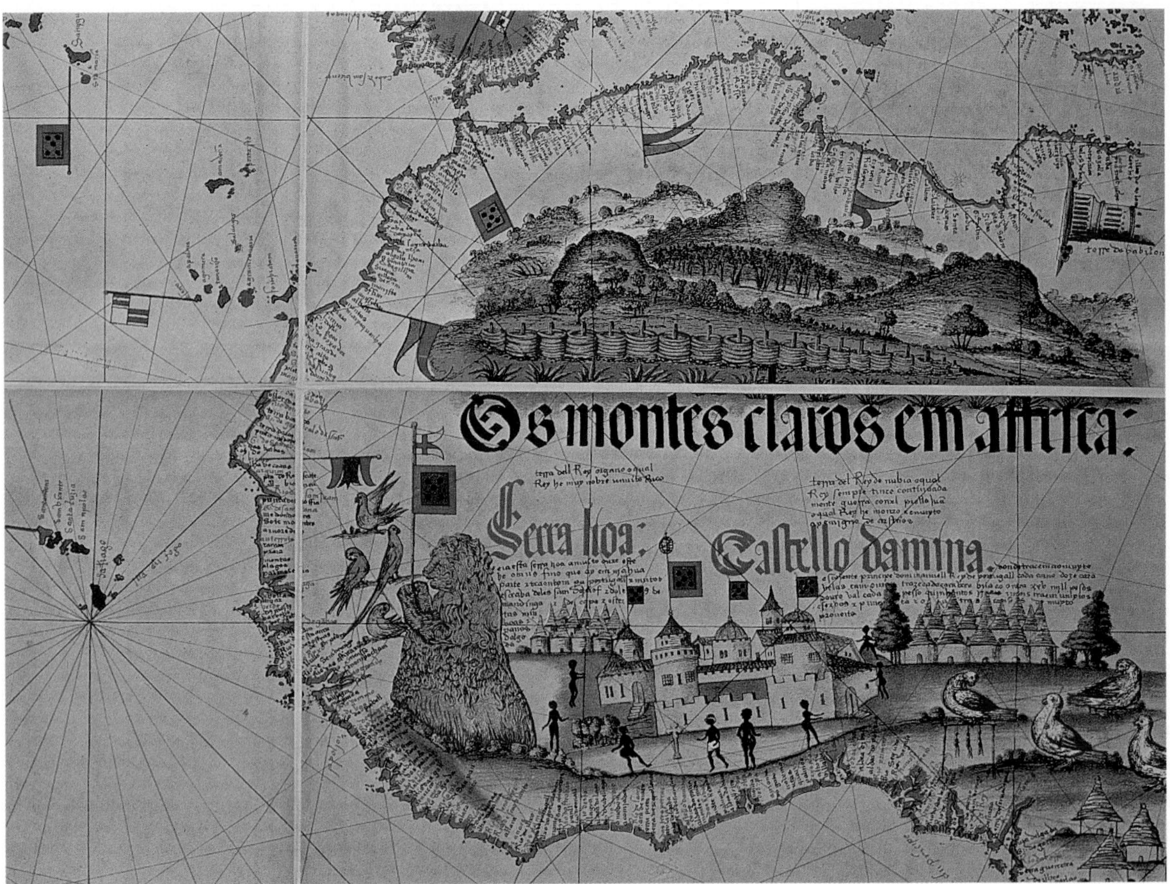

Portuguese Map of Western Africa, 1502 This map shows in great detail a section of African coastline that Portuguese explorers charted and named in the fifteenth century. The cartographer illustrated the African interior, which was almost completely unknown to Europeans, with drawings of birds and views of coastal sights: Sierra Leone (Serra lioa), named for a mountain shaped like a lion, and the Portuguese Castle of the Mine (Castello damina) on the Gold Coast. (akg-images)

Fernão Gomes purchased from the Crown the privilege of exploring 350 miles (550 kilometers) of new coast a year for five years in return for a monopoly on the trade he developed there. During the period of his contract, Gomes discovered the uninhabited island of São Tomé° on the equator; in the next century it became a major source of sugar produced with African slave labor. He also explored what later Europeans called the **Gold Coast**, which became the headquarters of Portugal's West African trade.

The final thrust down the African coast was spurred by the expectation of finding a passage around Africa to the rich trade of the Indian Ocean. In 1488 **Bartolomeu Dias** was the first Portuguese explorer to round the southern tip of Africa and enter the Indian Ocean. In 1497–1498 a Portuguese expedition led by **Vasco da Gama** sailed around Africa and reached India (see Environment and Technology: Vasco da Gama's Fleet). In 1500 ships in an expedition under Pedro Alvares Cabral°, while swinging wide to the west in the South Atlantic to catch the winds that would sweep them around southern Africa and on to India, came on the eastern coast of South America, laying the basis for Portugal's later claim to Brazil. The gamble that Prince Henry had begun eight decades earlier was about to pay off handsomely.

Spanish Voyages

In contrast to the persistence and planning behind Portugal's century-long exploration of the South Atlantic, haste and blind luck lay behind Spain's early discoveries. Throughout most of the fifteenth cen-

São Tomé (sow toh-MAY)

Cabral (kah-BRAHL)

Vasco da Gama's Fleet

The four small ships that sailed for India from Lisbon in June 1497 may seem a puny fleet compared to the sixty-two Chinese vessels that Zheng He had led into the Indian Ocean ninety-five years earlier. But given the fact that China had a hundred times as many people as Portugal, Vasco da Gama's fleet represented at least as great a commitment of resources. In any event, the Portuguese expedition had a far greater impact on the course of history. Having achieved its aim of inspiring awe at China's greatness, the Chinese throne sent out no more expeditions after 1432. Although da Gama's ships seemed more odd than awesome to Indian Ocean observers, that modest fleet began a revolution in global relations.

Portugal spared no expense in ensuring that the fleet would make it to India and back. Craftsmen built extra strength into the hulls to withstand the powerful storms that Dias had encountered in 1488 at the tip of Africa. Small enough to be able to navigate any shallow harbors and rivers they might encounter, the ships were crammed with specially strengthened casks and barrels of water, wine, oil, flour, meat, and vegetables far in excess of what was required even on a voyage that would take the better part of a year. Arms and ammunition were also in abundance.

Three of da Gama's ships were rigged with square sails on two masts for speed and a lateen sail on the third mast. The fourth vessel was a caravel with lateen sails. Each ship carried three sets of sails and plenty of extra rigging so as to be able to repair any damages due to storms. The crusaders' red crosses on the sails signaled one of the expedition's motives.

The captains and crew—Portugal's most talented and experienced—received extra pay and other rewards for their service. Yet there was no expectation that the unprecedented sums spent on this expedition would bring any immediate return. According to a contemporary chronicle, the only immediate return the Portuguese monarch received was "the knowledge that some part of Ethiopia and the beginning of Lower India had been discovered." However, the scale and care of the preparations suggest that the Portuguese expected the expedition to open up profitable trade to the Indian Ocean. And so it did.

Vasco da Gama's Flagship This vessel carried the Portuguese captain on his second expedition to India in 1505. (The Pierpont Morgan Library/Art Resource, NY)

tury, the Spanish kingdoms had been preoccupied with internal affairs: completion of the reconquest of southern Iberia; amalgamation of the various dynasties; and the conversion or expulsion of religious minorities. Only in the last decade of the century were Spanish monarchs ready to turn again to overseas exploration, by which time the Portuguese had already found a new route to the Indian Ocean.

The leader of their overseas mission was **Christopher Columbus** (1451–1506), a Genoese mariner. His four voyages between 1492 and 1502 established the existence of a vast new world across the Atlantic, whose existence few in "old world" Eurasia and Africa had ever suspected. But Columbus refused to accept that he had found unknown continents and peoples, insisting that he had succeeded in his goal of finding a shorter route to the Indian Ocean than the one the Portuguese had found.

As a younger man Columbus had gained considerable experience of the South Atlantic while participating in Portuguese explorations along the African coast, but he had become convinced there was a shorter way to reach the riches of the East than the route around Africa. By his reckoning (based on a serious misreading of a ninth-century Arab authority), the Canaries were a mere 2,400 nautical miles (4,450 kilometers) from Japan. The actual distance was five times as far.

It was not easy for Columbus to find a sponsor willing to underwrite the costs of testing his theory that one could reach Asia by sailing west. Portuguese authorities twice rejected his plan, first in 1485 following a careful study and again in 1488 after Dias had established the feasibility of a route around Africa. Columbus received a more sympathetic hearing in 1486 from Castile's able ruler, Queen Isabella, but no commitment of support. After a four-year study a Castilian commission appointed by Isabella concluded that a westward sea route to the Indies rested on many questionable geographical assumptions, but Columbus's persistence finally won over the queen and her husband, King Ferdinand of Aragon. In 1492 they agreed to fund a modest expedition. Their elation at expelling the Muslims from Granada may have put them in a favorable mood.

Columbus recorded in his log that he and his mostly Spanish crew of ninety men "departed Friday the third day of August of the year 1492," toward "the regions of India." Their mission, the royal contract stated, was "to discover and acquire certain islands and mainland in the Ocean Sea." He carried letters of introduction from the Spanish sovereigns to Eastern rulers, including one to the "Grand Khan" (meaning the Chinese emperor). Also on board was a Jewish convert to Christianity whose knowledge of Arabic was expected to facilitate communication with the peoples of eastern Asia. The expedition traveled in three small ships, the *Santa María*, the *Santa Clara* (nicknamed the *Niña*), and a third vessel now known only by its nickname, the *Pinta*. The *Niña* and the *Pinta* were caravels.

The expedition began well. Other attempts to explore the Atlantic west of the Azores had been impeded by unfavorable headwinds. But on earlier voyages along the African coast, Columbus had learned that he could find west-blowing winds in the latitudes of the Canaries, which is why he chose that southern route. After reaching the Canaries, he had the *Niña's* lateen sails replaced with square sails, for he knew that from then on speed would be more important than maneuverability.

In October 1492 the expedition reached the islands of the Caribbean. Columbus insisted on calling the inhabitants "Indians" because he believed that the islands were part of the East Indies. A second voyage to the Caribbean in 1493 did nothing to change his mind. Even when, two months after Vasco da Gama reached India in 1498, Columbus first sighted the mainland of South America on a third voyage, he stubbornly insisted it was part of Asia. But by then other Europeans were convinced that he had discovered islands and continents previously unknown to the Old World. Amerigo Vespucci's explorations, first on behalf of Spain and then for Portugal, led mapmakers to name the new continents "America" after him, rather than "Columbia" after Columbus.

To prevent disputes arising from their efforts to exploit their new discoveries and to spread Christianity among the people there, Spain and Portugal agreed to split the world between them. The Treaty of Tordesillas°, negotiated by the pope in 1494, drew an imaginary line down the middle of the North Atlantic Ocean. Lands east of the line in Africa and southern Asia could be claimed by Portugal; lands to the west in the Americas were reserved for Spain. Cabral's discovery of Brazil, however, gave Portugal a valid claim to the part of South America that bulged east of the line.

But if the Tordesillas line were extended around the earth, where would Spain's and Portugal's spheres of influence divide in the East? Given Europeans' ignorance of the earth's true size in 1494, it was not clear whether the Moluccas°, whose valuable spices had been a goal of the Iberian voyages, were on Portugal's or Spain's side of the line. The missing information concerned the size of the Pacific Ocean. By chance, in 1513 a Spanish adventurer named Vasco Núñez de Balboa° crossed the

Tordesillas (tor-duh-SEE-yuhs) **Moluccas** (muh-LOO-kuhz) **Balboa** (bal-BOH-uh)

isthmus (a narrow neck of land) of Panama from the east and sighted the Pacific Ocean on the other side. And the 1519 expedition of **Ferdinand Magellan** (ca. 1480–1521) was designed to complete Columbus's interrupted westward voyage by sailing around the Americas and across the Pacific, whose vast size no European then guessed. The Moluccas turned out to lie well within Portugal's sphere, as Spain formally acknowledged in 1529.

Magellan's voyage laid the basis for Spanish colonization of the Philippine Islands after 1564. Nor did Magellan's death prevent him from being considered the first person to encircle the globe, for a decade earlier he had sailed from Europe to the East Indies as part of an expedition sponsored by his native Portugal. His two voyages took him across the Tordesillas line, through the separate spheres claimed by Portugal and Spain—at least until other Europeans began demanding a share. Of course, in 1500 European claims were largely theoretical. Portugal and Spain had only modest settlements overseas.

Although Columbus failed to find a new route to the East, the consequences of his voyages for European expansion were momentous. Those who followed in his wake laid the basis for Spain's large colonial empires in the Americas and for the empires of other European nations. In turn, these empires promoted, among the four Atlantic continents, the growth of a major new trading network whose importance rivaled and eventually surpassed that of the Indian Ocean network. The more immediately important consequence was Portugal's entry into the Indian Ocean, which quickly led to a major European presence and profit. Both the eastward and the westward voyages of exploration marked a tremendous expansion of Europe's role in world history.

Encounters with Europe, 1450–1550

European actions alone did not determine the consequences of the new contacts that Iberian mariners had opened. The ways in which Africans, Asians, and Amerindians perceived their new visitors and interacted with them also influenced their future relations. Some welcomed the Europeans as potential allies; others viewed them as rivals or enemies. In general, Africans and Asians had little difficulty in recognizing the benefits and dangers that European contacts might bring. However, the long isolation of the Amerindians from the rest of the world added to the strangeness of their encounter with the Spanish and made them more vulnerable to the unfamiliar diseases that these explorers inadvertently introduced.

Western Africa

Many Africans along the West African coast were eager for trade with the Portuguese. It would give them new markets for their exports and access to imports cheaper than those that reached them through the middlemen of the overland routes to the Mediterranean. This reaction was evident along the Gold Coast of West Africa, first visited by the Portuguese in 1471. Miners in the hinterland had long sold their gold to African traders, who took it to the trading cities along the southern edge of the Sahara, where it was sold to traders who had crossed the desert from North Africa. Recognizing that they might get more favorable terms from the new sea visitors, coastal Africans were ready to negotiate with the royal representative of Portugal who arrived in 1482 seeking permission to erect a trading fort.

The Portuguese noble in charge and his officers (likely including the young Christopher Columbus, who had entered Portuguese service in 1476) were eager to make a proper impression. They dressed in their best clothes, erected and decorated a reception platform, celebrated a Catholic Mass, and signaled the start of negotiations with trumpets, tambourines, and drums. The African king, Caramansa, staged his entrance with equal ceremony, arriving with a large retinue of attendants and musicians. Through an African interpreter, the two leaders exchanged flowery speeches pledging goodwill and mutual benefit. Caramansa then gave his permission for a small trading fort to be built, assured, he said, by the appearance of these royal delegates that they were honorable persons, unlike the "few, foul, and vile" Portuguese visitors of the previous decade.

Neither side made a show of force, but the Africans' upper hand was evident in Caramansa's warning that if the Portuguese failed to be peaceful and honest traders, he and his people would simply move away, depriving their post of food and trade. Trade at the post of Saint George of the Mine (later called Elmina) enriched both sides. From there the Portuguese crown was soon purchasing gold equal to one-tenth of the world's production at the time. In return, Africans received large quantities of goods that Portuguese ships brought from Asia, Europe, and other parts of Africa.

After a century of aggressive expansion, the kingdom of Benin in the Niger Delta was near the peak of its power when it first encountered the Portuguese. Its oba (king) presided over an elaborate bureaucracy from a spacious palace in his large capital city, also known as Benin. In response to a Portuguese visit in 1486, the oba sent an ambassador to Portugal to learn more about the homeland of these strangers. Then he established a royal monopoly on trade with the Portuguese, selling pepper and ivory tusks (to be taken back to Portugal) as well as stone beads, textiles, and prisoners of war (to be resold at Elmina). In return, the Portuguese merchants provided Benin with copper and brass, fine textiles, glass beads, and a horse for the king's royal procession. In the early sixteenth century, as the demand for slaves for the Portuguese sugar plantations on the nearby island of São Tomé grew, the oba first raised the price of slaves and then imposed restrictions that limited their sale.

Early contacts generally involved a mixture of commercial, military, and religious interests. Some African rulers were quick to appreciate that the European firearms could be a useful addition to their spears and arrows in conflicts with their enemies. Because African religions did not presume to have a monopoly on religious knowledge, coastal rulers were also willing to test the value of Christian practices, which the Portuguese eagerly promoted. The rulers of Benin and Kongo, the two largest coastal kingdoms, invited Portuguese missionaries and soldiers to accompany them into battle to test the Christians' religion along with their muskets.

Portuguese efforts to persuade the king and nobles of Benin to accept the Catholic faith ultimately failed. Early kings showed some interest, but after 1538 the rulers declined to receive any more missionaries. They also closed the market in male slaves for the rest of the sixteenth century. Exactly why Benin chose to limit its contacts with the Portuguese is uncertain, but the rulers clearly had the power to control the amount of interaction.

Afro-Portuguese Ivory A skilled ivory carver from the kingdom of Benin probably made this saltcellar. Intended for a European market, it depicts a Portuguese ship on the cover and Portuguese nobles around the base. However European the subject, the craftsmanship is typical of Benin. (Courtesy of the Trustees of the British Museum)

Farther south, on the lower Congo River, relations between the kingdom of Kongo and the Portuguese began similarly but had a very different outcome. Like the oba of Benin, the manikongo° (king of Kongo) sent delegates to Portugal, established a royal monopoly on trade with the Portuguese, and expressed interest in missionary teachings. Deeply impressed with the new religion, the royal family made Catholicism the kingdom's official faith. But Kongo, lacking ivory and pepper, had less to trade than Benin. To acquire the goods brought by Portugal and to pay the costs of the missionaries, it had to sell more and more slaves.

Soon the manikongo began to lose his royal monopoly over the slave trade. In 1526 the Christian manikongo, Afonso I (r. 1506–ca. 1540), wrote to his royal "brother," the king of Portugal, begging for his help in stopping the trade because unauthorized Kongolese were kidnapping and selling people, even members of good families (see Diversity and Dominance: Kongo's Christian King). Alfonso's appeals for help received no reply from Portugal, whose interests had moved to the Indian Ocean. Some subjects took advantage of the manikongo's weakness to rebel against his authority. After 1540 the major part of the slave trade from this part of Africa moved farther south.

manikongo (mah-NEE-KONG-goh)

Eastern Africa

Different still were the reactions of the Muslim rulers of the trading coastal states of eastern Africa. As Vasco da Gama's fleet sailed up the coast in 1498, most rulers gave the Portuguese a cool reception, suspicious of the intentions of these visitors who painted crusaders' crosses on their sails. But the ruler of one of the ports, Malindi, saw in the Portuguese an ally who could help him expand the city's trading position and provided da Gama with a pilot to guide him to India. The suspicions of most rulers were justified seven years later when a Portuguese war fleet bombarded and looted most of the coastal cities of eastern Africa in the name of Christ and commerce, though they spared Malindi.

Another eastern African state that saw potential benefit in an alliance with the Portuguese was Christian Ethiopia. In the fourteenth and early fifteenth centuries, Ethiopia faced increasing conflicts with Muslim states along the Red Sea. Emboldened by the rise of the Ottoman Turks, who had conquered Egypt in 1517 and launched a major fleet in the Indian Ocean to counter the Portuguese, the talented warlord of the Muslim state of Adal launched a furious assault on Ethiopia. Adal's decisive victory in 1529 reduced the Christian kingdom to a precarious state. At that point Ethiopia's contacts with the Portuguese became crucial.

For decades, delegations from Portugal and Ethiopia had been exploring a possible alliance between their states based on their mutual adherence to Christianity. A key figure was Queen Helena of Ethiopia, who acted as regent for her young sons after her husband's death in 1478. In 1509 Helena sent a letter to "our very dear and well-beloved brother," the king of Portugal, along with a gift of two tiny crucifixes said to be made of wood from the cross on which Christ had died in Jerusalem. In her letter she proposed an alliance of her land army and Portugal's fleet against the Turks. No such alliance was completed by the time Helena died in 1522. But as Ethiopia's situation grew increasingly desperate, renewed appeals for help were made.

Finally, a small Portuguese force commanded by Vasco da Gama's son Christopher reached Ethiopia in 1539, at a time when what was left of the empire was being held together by another woman ruler. With Portuguese help, the queen rallied the Ethiopians to renew their struggle. Christopher da Gama was captured and tortured to death, but the Muslim forces lost heart when their leader was mortally wounded in a later battle. Portuguese aid helped the Ethiopian kingdom save itself from extinction, but a permanent alliance faltered because Ethiopian rulers refused to transfer their Christian affiliation from the patriarch of Alexandria to the Latin patriarch of Rome (the pope) as the Portuguese wanted.

As these examples illustrate, African encounters with the Portuguese before 1550 varied considerably, as much because of the strategies and leadership of particular African states as because of Portuguese policies. Africans and Portuguese might become royal brothers, bitter opponents, or partners in a mutually profitable trade, but Europeans remained a minor presence in most of Africa in 1550. By then the Portuguese had become far more interested in the Indian Ocean trade.

Indian Ocean States

Vasco da Gama's arrival on the Malabar Coast of India in May 1498 did not make a great impression on the citizens of Calicut. After more than ten months at sea, many members of the crew were in ill health. Da Gama's four small ships were far less imposing than the Chinese fleets of gigantic junks that had called at Calicut sixty-five years earlier and no larger than many of the dhows that filled the harbor of this rich and important trading city. The samorin (ruler) of Calicut and his Muslim officials showed mild interest in the Portuguese as new trading partners, but the gifts da Gama had brought for the samorin evoked derisive laughter. Twelve pieces of fairly ordinary striped cloth, four scarlet hoods, six hats, and six wash basins seemed inferior goods to those accustomed to the luxuries of the Indian Ocean trade. When da Gama tried to defend his gifts as those of an explorer, not a rich merchant, the samorin cut him short, asking whether he had come to discover men or stones: "If he had come to discover men, as he said, why had he brought nothing?"

Coastal rulers soon discovered that the Portuguese had no intention of remaining poor competitors in the rich trade of the Indian Ocean. Upon da Gama's return to Portugal in 1499, the jubilant King Manuel styled himself "Lord of the Conquest, Navigation, and Commerce of Ethiopia, Arabia, Persia, and India," setting forth the ambitious scope of his plans. Previously the Indian Ocean had been an open sea, used by merchants (and pirates) of all the surrounding coasts. Now the Portuguese crown intended to make it Portugal's sea, the private property of the Portuguese alone, which others might use only on Portuguese terms.

The ability of little Portugal to assert control over the Indian Ocean stemmed from the superiority of its ships and weapons over the smaller and lightly armed merchant dhows. In 1505 the Portuguese fleet of eighty-one ships and some seven thousand men bombarded Swahili Coast cities. Next on the list were Indian ports. Goa, on the

Portuguese in India In the sixteenth century Portuguese men moved to the Indian Ocean basin to work as administrators and traders. This Indo-Portuguese drawing from about 1540 shows a Portuguese man speaking to an Indian woman, perhaps making a proposal of marriage. (Ms. 1889, c. 97, Biblioteca Casanateunse Rome. Photo: Humberto Nicoletti Serra)

west coast of India, fell to a well-armed fleet in 1510, becoming the base from which the Portuguese menaced the trading cities of Gujarat° to the north and Calicut and other Malabar Coast cities to the south. The port of Hormuz, controlling the entry to the Persian Gulf, was taken in 1515. Aden, at the entrance to the Red Sea, used its intricate natural defenses to preserve its independence. The addition of the Gujarati port of Diu in 1535 consolidated Portuguese dominance of the western Indian Ocean.

Meanwhile, Portuguese explorers had been reconnoitering the Bay of Bengal and the waters farther east. The independent city of Malacca° on the strait between the Malay Peninsula and Sumatra became the focus of their attention. During the fifteenth century Malacca had become the main entrepôt° (a place where goods are stored or deposited and from which they are distributed) for the trade from China, Japan, India, the Southeast Asian mainland, and the Moluccas. Among the city's more than 100,000 residents an early Portuguese counted eighty-four different languages, including those of merchants from as far west as Cairo, Ethiopia, and the Swahili Coast of East Africa. Many non-Muslim residents supported letting the Portuguese join this cosmopolitan trading community, perhaps to offset the growing solidarity of Muslim traders. In 1511, however, the Portuguese seized this strategic trading center with a force of a thousand fighting men, including three hundred recruited in southern India.

Force was not always necessary. On the China coast, local officials and merchants interested in profitable new trade with the Portuguese persuaded the imperial government to allow the Portuguese to establish a trading post at Macao° in 1557. Operating from Macao, Portuguese ships nearly monopolized the trade between China and Japan.

In the Indian Ocean, the Portuguese used their control of the major port cities to enforce an even larger trading monopoly. They required all spices, as well as all goods on the major ocean routes such as between Goa

Gujarat (goo-juh-RAHT) **Malacca** (muh-LAH-kuh)
entrepôt (ON-truh-poh)

Macao (muh-COW)

and Macao, to be carried in Portuguese ships. In addition, the Portuguese also tried to control and tax other Indian Ocean trade by requiring all merchant ships entering and leaving one of their ports to carry a Portuguese passport and to pay customs duties. Portuguese patrols seized vessels that attempted to avoid these monopolies, confiscated their cargoes, and either killed the captain and crew or sentenced them to forced labor.

Reactions to this power grab varied. Like the emperors of China, the Mughal° emperors of India largely ignored Portugal's maritime intrusions, seeing their interests as maintaining control over their vast land possessions. The Ottomans responded more aggressively. From 1501 to 1509 they supported Egypt's fleet of fifteen thousand men against the Christian intruders. Then, having absorbed Egypt into their empire, the Ottomans sent another large expedition against the Portuguese in 1538. Both expeditions failed because the Ottoman galleys were no match for the faster, better-armed Portuguese vessels in the open ocean. However, the Ottomans retained the advantage in the Red Sea and Persian Gulf, where they had many ports of supply.

The smaller trading states of the region were even less capable of challenging Portuguese domination head on, since their mutual rivalry impeded the formation of any common front. Some chose to cooperate with the Portuguese to maintain their prosperity and security. Others engaged in evasion and resistance. Two examples illustrate the range of responses among Indian Ocean peoples.

The merchants of Calicut put up some of the most sustained local resistance. In retaliation, the Portuguese embargoed all trade with Aden, Calicut's principal trading partner, and centered their trade on the port of Cochin, which had once been a dependency of Calicut. Some Calicut merchants became adept at evading the patrol, but the price of resistance was the shrinking of Calicut's importance as Cochin gradually became the major pepper-exporting port on the Malabar Coast.

The traders and rulers of the state of Gujarat farther north had less success in keeping the Portuguese at bay. At first they resisted Portuguese attempts at monopoly and in 1509 joined Egypt's failed effort to sweep the Portuguese from the Arabian Sea. But in 1535, finding his state at a military disadvantage due to Mughal attacks, the ruler of Gujarat made the fateful decision to allow the Portuguese to build a fort at Diu in return for their support. Once established, the Portuguese gradually extended their control, so that by midcentury they were licensing and taxing all Gujarati ships. Even after the Mughals (who were Muslims) took control of Gujarat in 1572, the Mughal emperor Akbar permitted the Portuguese to continue their maritime monopoly in return for allowing one ship a year to carry pilgrims to Mecca without paying the Portuguese any fee.

Mughal (MOO-gahl)

The Portuguese never gained complete control of the Indian Ocean trade, but their domination of key ports and the main trade routes during the sixteenth century brought them considerable profit, which they sent back to Europe in the form of spices and other luxury goods. The effects were dramatic. The Portuguese sold the large quantities of pepper that they exported for less than the price charged by Venice and Genoa for pepper obtained through Egyptian middlemen, thus breaking the Italian cities' monopoly.

In Asia the consequences were equally startling. Asian and East African traders were at the mercy of Portuguese warships, but their individual responses affected their fates. Some were devastated. Others prospered by meeting Portuguese demands or evading their patrols. Because the Portuguese were ocean-based, they had little impact on the Asian and African mainlands, in sharp contrast to what was occurring in the Americas.

The Americas

In the Americas the Spanish established a vast territorial empire, in contrast to the trading empires the Portuguese created in Africa and Asia. This outcome had little to do with differences between the two Iberian kingdoms, except for the fact that the Spanish kingdoms had somewhat greater resources to draw on. The Spanish and Portuguese monarchies had similar motives for expansion and used identical ships and weapons. Rather, the isolation of the Amerindian peoples made their responses to outside contacts different from the responses of peoples in Africa and the Indian Ocean cities. In dealing with the small communities in the Caribbean, the first European settlers resorted to conquest and plunder rather than trade. This practice was later extended to the more powerful Amerindian kingdoms on the American mainland. The spread of deadly new diseases among the Amerindians after 1518 weakened their ability to resist.

The first Amerindians to encounter Columbus were the Arawak of Hispaniola (modern Haiti and the Dominican Republic) in the Greater Antilles and the Bahamas to the north (see Map 16.2). They cultivated maize (corn), cassava (a tuber), sweet potatoes, and hot peppers, as well as cotton and tobacco, and they met their other material needs from the sea and wild plants. Although they were skilled at mining and working gold, the Arawak did not trade gold over long distances as

Africans did, and they had no iron. The Arawak at first extended a cautious welcome to the Spanish but were unprepared to sell them large quantities of gold. Instead, they told Columbus exaggerated stories about gold in other places to persuade him to move on.

When Columbus made his second trip to Hispaniola in 1493, he brought several hundred settlers from southern Iberia who hoped to make their fortune and missionaries who were eager to persuade the Indians to accept Christianity. The settlers stole gold ornaments, confiscated food, and raped women, provoking the Hispaniola Arawak to war in 1495. In this and later conflicts, horses and body armor gave the Spaniards a great advantage. Tens of thousands of Arawak were slaughtered. Those who survived were forced to pay a heavy tax in gold, spun cotton, and food. Any who failed to meet the quotas were condemned to forced labor. Meanwhile, the cattle, pigs, and goats introduced by the settlers devoured the Arawak's food crops, causing deaths from famine and disease. A governor appointed by the Spanish crown in 1502 forced the Arawak remaining on Hispaniola to be laborers under the control of Spanish settlers.

The actions of the Spanish in the Antilles were reflections of Spanish actions and motives during the wars against the Muslims in Spain in the previous centuries: seeking to serve God by defeating nonbelievers and placing them under Christian control—and becoming rich in the process. Individual **conquistadors**° (conquerors) extended that pattern around the Caribbean. Some attacked the Bahamas to get gold and labor as both became scarce on Hispaniola. Many Arawak from the Bahamas were taken to Hispaniola as slaves. Juan Ponce de León (1460–1521), who had participated in the conquest of Muslim Spain and the seizure of Hispaniola, conquered the island of Borinquen (Puerto Rico) in 1508 and explored southeastern Florida in 1513.

An ambitious and ruthless nobleman, **Hernán Cortés**° (1485–1547), led the most audacious expedition to the mainland. Cortés left Cuba in 1519 with six hundred fighting men and most of the island's stock of weapons to assault the Mexican mainland in search of slaves and to establish trade. When the expedition learned of the rich Aztec Empire in central Mexico, Cortés brought to the American mainland, on a massive scale, the exploitation and conquest begun in the reconquest of Muslim Iberia and continued in the Greater Antilles.

The Aztecs themselves had conquered their vast empire only during the previous century, and many of the Amerindians they had subjugated were far from loyal subjects. Many resented the tribute they had to pay the

conquistador (kon-KEY-stuh-dor) **Cortés** (kor-TEZ)

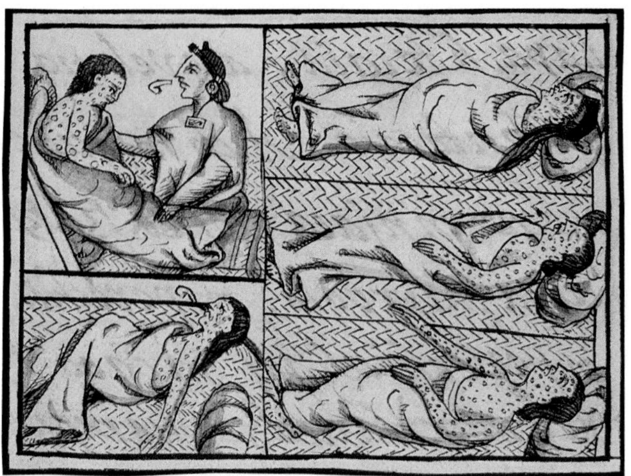

Death from Smallpox This Aztec drawing shows a healer attending smallpox victims. The little puffs coming from their mouths represent speech. (Biblioteca Medicea Laurenziana. Photo: MicroFoto, Florence)

Aztecs, the forced labor, and the large-scale human sacrifices to the Aztec gods. Many subject people saw the Spaniards as powerful human allies against the Aztecs and gave them their support. Like the Caribbean people, the Amerindians of Mexico had no precedent by which to judge these strange visitors.

Aztec accounts suggest that some believed Cortés to be the legendary ruler Quetzalcoatl°, whose return to earth had been prophesied, and treated him with great deference. Another consequence of millennia of isolation was far more significant: the lack of acquired immunity to the diseases of the Old World. Smallpox was the most deadly of the early epidemics that accompanied the Spanish conquistadors. It appeared for the first time on the island of Hispaniola late in 1518. An infected member of the Cortés expedition then transmitted smallpox to Mexico in 1519, where it spread with deadly efficiency.

From his glorious capital city Tenochtitlan°, the Aztec emperor **Moctezuma**° II (r. 1502–1520) sent messengers to greet Cortés and determine whether he was god or man, friend or foe. Cortés advanced steadily toward Tenochtitlan, overcoming Aztec opposition with cavalry charges and steel swords and gaining the support of thousands of Amerindian allies from among the unhappy subjects of the Aztecs. When the Spaniards

Quetzalcoatl (ket-zahl-COH-ah-tal)
Tenochtitlan (teh-noch-TIT-lan)
Moctezuma (mock-teh-ZOO-ma)

Coronation of Emperor Moctezuma This painting by an unnamed Aztec artist depicts the Aztec ruler's coronation. Moctezuma, his nose pierced by a bone, receives the crown from a prince in the palace at Tenochtitlan. (Oronoz)

were near, the emperor went out in a great procession, dressed in all his finery, to welcome Cortés with gifts and flower garlands.

Despite Cortés's initial promise that he came in friendship, Moctezuma quickly found himself a prisoner in his own palace. The Spanish looted his treasury and melted down its golden objects. Soon a battle was raging in and about the capital between the Spaniards (helped by their new Amerindian allies) and the Aztecs and their supporters. Briefly the Aztecs gained the upper hand. They destroyed half of the Spanish force and four thousand of the Spaniards' Amerindian allies, and they sacrificed to their gods fifty-three Spanish prisoners and four horses, displaying their severed heads in rows on pikes. In the battle Moctezuma was killed.

The Spanish survivors retreated from the city and rebuilt their strength. Their successful capture of Tenochtitlan in 1521 was greatly facilitated by the spread of smallpox, which weakened and killed more of the city's defenders than died in the fighting. One source remembered that the disease "spread over the people as a great destruction." The bodies of the afflicted were covered with oozing sores, and large numbers soon died. It is likely that many Amerindians as well as Europeans blamed the devastating spread of this disease on supernatural forces.

After the capital fell, the conquistadors took over other parts of Mexico. Then some Spaniards began eyeing the vast Inca Empire, stretching nearly 3,000 miles (5,000 kilometers) south from the equator and containing half of the population in South America. The Inca had conquered the inhabitants of the Andes Mountains and the Pacific coast of South America during the previous century, and their rule was not fully accepted by all of the peoples they had defeated.

With the vast Pacific Ocean on one side of their realm and the sparsely inhabited Amazon forests on the other, it is not surprising that Inca rulers believed they controlled most of the world worth controlling. Theirs was a great empire with highly productive agriculture, exquisite stone cities (such as the capital, Cuzco), and rich gold and silver mines. The power of the Inca emperor was sustained by beliefs that he was descended from the Sun God and by an efficient system of roads and messengers that kept him informed about major events in the empire. Yet all was not well.

At the end of the 1520s, before even a whisper of news about the Spanish reached the Inca rulers, small-

DIVERSITY AND DOMINANCE

KONGO'S CHRISTIAN KING

The new overseas voyages brought conquest to some and opportunities for fruitful borrowings and exchanges to others. The decision of the ruler of the kingdom of Kongo to adopt Christianity in 1491 added cultural diversity to Kongolese society and in some ways strengthened the hand of the king. From then on Kongolese rulers sought to introduce Christian beliefs and rituals while at the same time Africanizing Christianity to make it more intelligible to their subjects. In addition, the kings of Kongo sought a variety of more secular aid from Portugal, including schools and medicine. Trade with the Portuguese introduced new social and political tensions, especially in the case of the export trade in slaves for the Portuguese sugar plantations on the island of São Tomé to the north.

Two letters sent to King João (zhwao) III of Portugal in 1526 illustrate how King Afonso of Kongo saw his kingdom's new relationship with Portugal and the problems that resulted from it. (Afonso adopted that name when he was baptized as a young prince.) After the death of his father in 1506, Afonso successfully claimed the throne and ruled until 1542. His son Henrique became the first Catholic bishop of the Kongo in 1521.

These letters were written in Portuguese and penned by the king's secretary João Teixera (tay-SHER-uh), a Kongo Christian, who, like Afonso, had been educated by Portuguese missionaries.

6 July 1526

To the very powerful and excellent prince Dom João, our brother:

On the 20th of June just past, we received word that a trading ship from your highness had just come to our port of Sonyo. We were greatly pleased by that arrival for it had been many days since a ship had come to our kingdom, for by it we would get news of your highness, which many times we had desired to know, . . . and likewise as there was a great and dire need for wine and flour for the holy sacrament; and of this we had had no great hope for we have the same need frequently. And that, sir, arises from the great negligence of your highness's officials toward us and toward shipping us those things. . . .

Sir, your highness should know how our kingdom is being lost in so many ways that we will need to provide the needed cure, since this is caused by the excessive license given by your agents and officials to the men and merchants who come to this kingdom to set up shops with goods and many things which have been prohibited by us, and which they spread throughout our kingdoms and domains in such abundance that many of our vassals, whose submission we could once rely on, now act independently so as to get the things in greater abundance than we ourselves; whom we had formerly held content and submissive and under our vassalage and jurisdiction, so it is doing a great harm not only to the service of God, but also to the security and peace of our kingdoms and state.

And we cannot reckon how great the damage is, since every day the mentioned merchants are taking our people, sons of the land and the sons of our noblemen and vassals and our relatives, because the thieves and men of bad conscience grab them so as to have the things and wares of this kingdom that they crave; they grab them and bring them to be sold. In such a manner, sir, has been the corruption and deprivation that our land is becoming completely depopulated, and your highness should not deem this good nor in your service. And to avoid this we need from these kingdoms [of yours] no more than priests and a few people to teach in schools, and no other goods except wine and flour for the holy sacrament, which is why we beg of your highness to help and assist us in this matter. Order your agents to send here neither merchants nor wares, because it is our will that in these kingdoms there should not be any dealing in slaves nor outlet for them, for the reasons stated above. Again we beg your highness's agreement, since otherwise we cannot cure such manifest harm. May Our Lord in His mercy have your highness always under His protection and may you always do the things of His holy service. I kiss your hands many times.

From our city of Kongo. . . .

The King, Dom Afonso

18 October 1526

Very high and very powerful prince King of Portugal, our brother,

Sir, your highness has been so good as to promise us that anything we need we should ask for in our letters, and that everything will be provided. And so that there may be peace and health of our kingdoms, by God's will, in our lifetime. And as there are among us old folks and people who have lived for many days, many and different diseases happen so often that we are pushed to the ultimate extremes. And the same happens to our children, relatives, and people, because this country lacks physicians and surgeons who might know the proper cures for such diseases, as well as pharmacies and drugs to make them better. And for this reason many of those who had been already confirmed and instructed in the things of the holy faith of Our Lord Jesus Christ perish and die. And the rest of the people for the most part cure themselves with herbs and sticks and other ancient methods, so that they live putting all their faith in the these herbs and ceremonies, and die believing that they are saved; and this serves God poorly.

And to avoid such a great error, I think, and inconvenience, since it is from God and from your highness that all the good and the drugs and medicines have come to us for our salvation, we ask your merciful highness to send us two physicians and two pharmacists and one surgeon, so that they may come with their pharmacies and necessary things to be in our kingdoms, for we have extreme need of each and everyone of them. We will be very good and merciful to them, since sent by your highness, their work and coming should be for good. We ask your highness as a great favor to do this for us, because besides being good in itself it is in the service of God as we have said above.

Moreover, sir, in our kingdoms there is another great inconvenience which is of little service to God, and this is that many of our people, out of great desire for the wares and things of your kingdoms, which are brought here by your people, and in order to satisfy their disordered appetite, seize many of our people, freed and exempt men. And many times noblemen and the sons of noblemen, and our relatives are stolen, and they take them to be sold to the white men who are in our kingdoms and take them hidden or by night, so that they are not recognized. And as soon as they are taken by the white men, they are immediately ironed and branded with fire. And when they are carried off to be embarked, if they are caught by our guards, the whites allege that they have bought them and cannot say from whom, so that it is our duty to do justice and to restore to the free their freedom. And so they went away offended.

And to avoid such a great evil we passed a law so that every white man living in our kingdoms and wanting to purchase slaves by whatever means should first inform three of our noblemen and officials of our court on whom we rely in this matter, namely Dom Pedro Manipunzo and Dom Manuel Manissaba, our head bailiff, and Gonçalo Pires, our chief supplier, who should investigate if the said slaves are captives or free men, and, if cleared with them, there will be no further doubt nor embargo and they can be taken and embarked. And if they reach the opposite conclusion, they will lose the aforementioned slaves. Whatever favor and license we give them [the white men] for the sake of your highness in this case is because we know that it is in your service too that these slaves are taken from our kingdom; otherwise we should not consent to this for the reasons stated above that we make known completely to your highness so that no one could say the contrary, as they said in many other cases to your highness, so that the care and remembrance that we and this kingdom have should not be withdrawn. . . .

We kiss your hands of your highness many times.

From our city of Kongo, the 18th day of October,

The King, Dom Afonso

QUESTIONS FOR ANALYSIS

1. **What sorts of things does King Afonso desire from the Portuguese?**
2. **What is he willing and unwilling to do in return?**
3. **What problem with his own people has the slave trade created and what has King Afonso done about it?**
4. **Does King Afonso see himself as an equal to King João or his subordinate? Do you agree with that analysis?**

Source: From António Brásio, ed., *Monumenta Missionaria Africana: Africa Ocidental (1471-1531)* (Lisbon: Agência Geral do Ultramar, 1952), I:468, 470-471, 488-491. Translated by David Northrup.

pox claimed countless Amerindian lives, perhaps including the Inca emperor in 1530. Even more devastating was the threat awaiting the empire from **Francisco Pizarro**° (ca. 1478– 1541) and his motley band of 180 men, 37 horses, and two cannon.

With limited education and some military experience, Pizarro had come to the Americas in 1502 at the age of twenty-five to seek his fortune. He had participated in the conquest of Hispaniola and in Balboa's expedition across the Isthmus of Panama. By 1520 Pizarro was a wealthy landowner and official in Panama, yet he gambled his fortune on more adventures, exploring the Pacific coast to a point south of the equator, where he learned of the riches of the Inca. With a license from the king of Spain, he set out from Panama in 1531 to conquer them.

In November 1532 Pizarro arranged to meet the new Inca emperor, **Atahualpa**° (r. 1531–1533), near the Andean city of Cajamarca°. With supreme boldness and brutality, Pizarro's small band of armed men seized Atahualpa off a rich litter borne by eighty nobles as it passed through an enclosed courtyard. Though surrounded by an Inca army of at least forty thousand, the Spaniards were able to use their cannon to create confusion while their swords sliced thousands of the emperor's lightly armed retainers and servants to pieces. The strategy to replicate the earlier Spanish conquest of Mexico was working.

Noting the glee with which the Spaniards seized gold, silver, and emeralds, the captive Atahualpa offered them what he thought would satisfy even the greediest among them in exchange for his freedom: a roomful of gold and silver. But when the ransom of 13,400 pounds (6,000 kilograms) of gold and 26,000 pounds (12,000 kilograms) of silver was paid, the Spaniards gave Atahualpa a choice: he could be burned at the stake as a heathen or baptized as a Christian and then strangled. He chose the latter. His death and the Spanish occupation broke the unity of the Inca Empire.

In 1533 the Spaniards took Cuzco and from there set out to conquer and loot the rest of the empire. The defeat of a final rebellion in 1536 spelled the end of Inca rule. Five years later Pizarro himself met a violent death at the hands of Spanish rivals, but the conquest of the mainland continued. Incited by the fabulous wealth of the Aztecs and Inca, conquistadors extended Spanish conquest and exploration in South and North America, dreaming of new treasuries to loot.

Pizarro (pih-ZAHR-oh) **Atahualpa** (ah-tuh-WAHL-puh) **Cajamarca** (kah-hah-MAHR-kah)

Patterns of Dominance

Within fifty years of Columbus's first landing in 1492, the Spanish had located and occupied all of the major population centers of the Americas, and the penetration of the more thinly populated areas was well under way. In no other part of the world was European dominance so complete. Why did the peoples of the Americas suffer a fate so different from that of peoples in Africa and Asia? Why were the Spanish able to erect a vast land empire in the Americas so quickly? Three factors seem crucial.

First, long isolation from the rest of humanity made the inhabitants of the Americas vulnerable to new diseases. The unfamiliar illnesses first devastated the native inhabitants of the Caribbean islands and then spread to the mainland. Contemporaries estimated that between 25 and 50 percent of those infected with smallpox died. Repeated epidemics inhibited Amerindians' ability to regain control. Because evidence is very limited, estimates of the size of the population before Columbus's arrival vary widely, but there is no disputing the fact that the Amerindian population fell sharply during the sixteenth century. The Americas became a "widowed land," open to resettlement from across the Atlantic.

A second major factor was Spain's military superiority. Steel swords, protective armor, and horses gave the Spaniards an advantage over their Amerindian opponents in many battles. Though few in number, muskets and cannon also gave the Spaniards a significant psychological edge. However, it should not be forgotten that the Spanish conquests depended heavily on large numbers of Amerindian allies armed with the same weapons as the people they defeated. Perhaps the Spaniards' most decisive military advantage came from the no-holds-barred fighting techniques they had developed during a long history of warfare at home.

The patterns of domination previously established in reconquest of Iberia were a third factor in Spain's ability to govern its New World empire. The forced labor, forced conversion, and system for administering conquered lands all had their origins in the Iberian reconquest.

The same three factors help explain the quite different outcomes elsewhere. Because of centuries of contacts before 1500, Europeans, Africans, and Asians shared the same Old World diseases. Only small numbers of very isolated peoples in Africa and Asia suffered the demographic calamity that undercut Amerindians' ability to retain control of their lands. The Iberians enjoyed a military advantage at sea, as the conquest of the Indian Ocean trade routes showed, but on land they had no decisive advantage against more numerous indigenous people who were not weakened by disease. Everywhere, Iberian religious zeal to conquer non-Christians went hand in hand with a desire for riches. In Iberia and America conquest brought wealth. But in Africa and Asia, where existing trading networks were already well established, Iberian desire for wealth from trade restrained or negated the impulse to conquer.

Conclusion

Historians agree that the century between 1450 and 1550 was a major turning point in world history. It was the beginning of an age to which they have given various names: the "Vasco da Gama epoch," the "Columbian era," the "age of Magellan," or simply the "modern period." During those years European explorers opened new long-distance trade routes across the world's three major oceans, for the first time establishing regular contact among all the continents. By 1550 those who followed them had broadened trading contacts with sub-Saharan Africa, gained mastery of the rich trade routes of the Indian Ocean, and conquered a vast land empire in the Americas.

As dramatic and momentous as these events were, they were not completely unprecedented. The riches of the Indian Ocean trade that brought a gleam to the eye of many Europeans had been developed over many centuries by the trading peoples who inhabited the surrounding lands. European conquests of the Americas were no more rapid or brutal than the earlier Mongol conquests of Eurasia. Even the crossing of the Pacific had been done before, though in stages.

What gave this maritime revolution unprecedented importance had more to do with what happened after 1550 than with what happened earlier. Europeans' overseas empires would endure longer than the Mongols' and would continue to expand for three-and-a-half centuries after 1550. Unlike the Chinese, the Europeans did not turn their backs on the world after an initial burst of exploration. Not content with dominance in the Indian Ocean trade, Europeans opened an Atlantic maritime network that grew to rival the Indian Ocean network in the wealth of its trade. They also pioneered regular trade across the Pacific. The maritime expansion begun in the period from 1450 to 1550 marked the beginning of a new age of growing global interaction.

Key Terms

Zheng He	**Christopher Columbus**
Arawak	**Ferdinand Magellan**
Henry the Navigator	**conquistadors**
caravel	**Hernán Cortés**
Gold Coast	**Moctezuma**
Bartolomeu Dias	**Francisco Pizarro**
Vasco da Gama	**Atahualpa**

Suggested Reading

There is no single survey of the different expansions covered by this chapter, but the selections edited by Joseph R. Levenson, *European Expansion and the Counter Example of Asia, 1300–1600* (1967), remain a good introduction to Chinese expansion and Western impressions of China. Janet Abu-Lughod, *Before European Hegemony: The World System, A.D. 1250–1350* (1989), provides a stimulating speculative reassessment of the importance of the Mongols and the Indian Ocean trade in the creation of the modern world system; she summarizes her thesis in the American Historical Association booklet *The World System in the Thirteenth Century: Dead-End or Precursor?* (1993).

The Chinese account of Zheng He's voyages is Ma Huan, *Ying-yai Sheng-lan: "The Overall Survey of the Ocean's Shores"* [1433], ed. and trans. J. V. G. Mills (1970). A reliable guide to Polynesian expansion is Jesse D. Jennings, ed., *The Prehistory of Polynesia* (1979), especially the excellent chapter "Voyaging" by Ben R. Finney, which encapsulates his *Voyage of Rediscovery: A Cultural Odyssey Through Polynesia* (1994). The medieval background to European intercontinental voyages is summarized by Felipe Fernandez-Armesto, *Before Columbus: Exploration and Colonization from the Mediterranean to the Atlantic, 1229–1492* (1987). Tim Severin, *The Brendan Voyage* (2000) vividly recounts a modern retracing of even earlier Irish voyages.

A simple introduction to the technologies of European expansion is Carlo M. Cipolla, *Guns, Sails, and Empires: Technological Innovation and the Early Phases of European Expansion, 1400–1700* (1965; reprint, 1985). More advanced is Roger C. Smith, *Vanguard of Empire: Ships of Exploration in the Age of Columbus* (1993).

The European exploration is well documented and the subject of intense historical investigation. Clear general accounts based on the contemporary records are Boies Penrose, *Travel and Discovery in the Age of the Renaissance, 1420–1620* (1952); J. H. Parry, *The Age of Reconnaissance: Discovery, Exploration, and Settlement, 1450–1650* (1963); and G. V. Scammell, *The World Encompassed: The First European Maritime Empires, c. 800–1650* (1981).

An excellent general introduction to Portuguese exploration is C. R. Boxer, *The Portuguese Seaborne Empire, 1415–1825* (1969). More detail can be found in Bailey W. Diffie and George D. Winius, *Foundations of the Portuguese Empire, 1415–1580*

(1977); A. J. R. Russell-Wood, *The Portuguese Empire: A World on the Move* (1998); and Luc Cuyvers, *Into the Rising Sun: The Journey of Vasco da Gama and the Discovery of the Modern World* (1998). John William Blake, ed., *Europeans in West Africa, 1450–1560* (1942), is an excellent two-volume collection of contemporary Portuguese, Castilian, and English sources. Elaine Sanceau, *The Life of Prester John: A Chronicle of Portuguese Exploration* (1941), is a very readable account of Portuguese relations with Ethiopia. The *Summa Oriental of Tomé Pires: An Account of the East, from the Red Sea to Japan, Written in Malacca and India in 1512–1515,* trans. Armando Cortesão (1944), provides a detailed firsthand account of the Indian Ocean during the Portuguese's first two decades there.

The other Iberian kingdoms' expansion is well summarized by J. H. Parry, *The Spanish Seaborne Empire* (1967). Samuel Eliot Morison's *Admiral of the Ocean Sea: A Life of Christopher Columbus* (1942) is a fine scholarly celebration of the epic mariner, and is also available in an abridged version as *Christopher Columbus, Mariner* (1955). More focused on the shortcomings of Columbus and his Spanish peers is Tzvetan Todorov, *The Conquest of America,* trans. Richard Howard (1985). Marvin Lunenfeld, ed., *1492: Discovery, Invasion, Encounter* (1991), critically examines contemporary sources and interpretations. William D. Phillips and Carla Rhan Phillips, *The Worlds of Christopher Columbus* (1992), examines the mariner and his times in terms of modern concerns. Peggy K. Liss, *Isabel the Queen: Life and Times* (1992), is a sympathetic examination of Queen Isabella of Castile. Detailed individual biographies of all of the individuals in Pizarro's band are the subject of James Lockhart's *Men of Cajamarca: A Social and Biographical Study of the First Conquerors of Peru* (1972). A firsthand account of Magellan's expedition is Antonio Pigafetta, *Magellan's Voyage: A Narrative Account of the First Circumnavigation,* available in a two-volume edition (1969) that includes a facsimile reprint of the manuscript.

Matthew Restall, *Seven Myths of the Spanish Conquests* (2003) uses indigenous sources to challenge traditional interpretations of New World conquests. The trans-Atlantic encounters of Europe and the Americas are described by J. H. Elliott, *The Old World and the New, 1492–1650* (1970). Alfred W. Crosby, *The Columbian Voyages, the Columbian Exchange, and Their Historians* (1987), available as an American Historical Association booklet, provides a brief overview of the first encounters in the Americas and their long-term consequences. The early chapters of Mark A. Burkholder and Lyman L. Johnson, *Colonial Latin America,* 2d ed. (1994), give a clear and balanced account of the Spanish conquest.

The perceptions of the peoples European explorers encountered are not as well documented. David Northrup, *Africa's Discovery of Europe, 1450–1850* (2002) and John Thornton, *Africa and Africans in the Making of the Atlantic World, 1400–1800,* 2d ed. (1998), examine Africans' encounters with Europe and their involvement in the Atlantic economy. *The Broken Spears: The Aztec Account of the Conquest of Mexico,* ed. Miguel Leon-Portilla (1962), presents Amerindian chronicles in a readable package, as does Nathan Wachtel, *The Vision of the Vanquished: The Spanish Conquest of Peru Through Indian Eyes* (1977). Anthony Reid, *Southeast Asia in the Age of Commerce, 1450–1680,* 2 vols. (1988, 1993), deals with events in that region.

Notes

1. Ma Huan, *Ying-yai Sheng-lan: "The Overall Survey of the Ocean's Shores,"* ed. Feng Ch'eng-Chün, trans. J. V. G. Mills (Cambridge, England: Cambridge University Press, 1970), 180.
2. Alvise da Cadamosto in *The Voyages of Cadamosto and Other Documents,* ed. and trans. G. R. Crone (London: Hakluyt Society, 1937), 2.

Climate and Population, to 1500

During the millennia before 1500 human populations expanded in three momentous surges. The first occurred after 50,000 B.C.E. when humans emigrated from their African homeland to all of the inhabitable continents. After that, the global population remained steady for several millennia. During the second expansion, between about 5000 and 500 B.C.E., population rose from about 5 million to 100 million as agricultural societies spread around the world (see Figure 1). Again population growth then slowed for several centuries before a third surge took world population to over 350 million by 1200 C.E. (see Figure 2).

For a long time historians tended to attribute these population surges to cultural and technological advances. Indeed, a great many changes in culture and technology are associated with adaptation to different climates and food supplies in the first surge and with the domestication of plants and animals in the second. However, historians have not found a cultural or technological change to explain the third surge, nor can they explain why creativity would have stagnated for long periods between the surges. Something else must have been at work.

Recently historians have begun to pay more attention to the impact of long-term variations in global climate. By examining ice cores drilled out of glaciers, scientists have been able to compile records of thousands of years of climate change. The comparative width of tree rings from ancient forests has provided additional data on periods of favorable and unfavorable growth. Such evidence shows that cycles of population growth and stagnation followed changes in global climate.

Historians now believe that global temperatures were above normal for extended periods from the late 1100s to the late 1200s C.E. In the temperate lands where most of the world's people lived, above-normal temperatures meant a longer growing season, more bountiful harvests, and thus a more adequate and reliable food supply. The ways in which societies responded to the medieval warm period are as important as the climate change, but it is unlikely that human agency alone would have produced the medieval surge. One notable response was that of the Vikings, who increased the size and range of their settlements in the North Atlantic, although their raids also caused death and destruction.

Some of the complexities involved in the interaction of human agency, climate, and other natural factors are also evident in the demographic changes that followed the medieval warm period. During the 1200s the Mongol invasions caused death and disruption of agriculture across Eurasia. China's population, which had been over 100 million in 1200, declined by a third or more by 1300. The Mongol invasions did not cause harm west of Russia, but climate changes in the 1300s resulted in population losses in Europe. Unusually heavy rains caused crop failures and a prolonged famine in northern Europe from 1315 to 1319.

The freer movement of merchants within the Mongol empire also facilitated the spread of disease across Eurasia, culminating in the great pandemic known as the Black Death in Europe. The demographic recovery underway in China was reversed. The even larger population losses in Europe may have been affected by the decrease in global temperatures to their lowest point in many millennia between 1350 and 1375. Improving economic conditions enabled population to recover more rapidly in Europe after 1400 than in China, where the conditions of rural life remained harsh.

Because many other historical circumstances interact with changing weather patterns, historians have a long way to go in deciphering the role of climate in history. Nevertheless, it is a factor that can no longer be ignored.

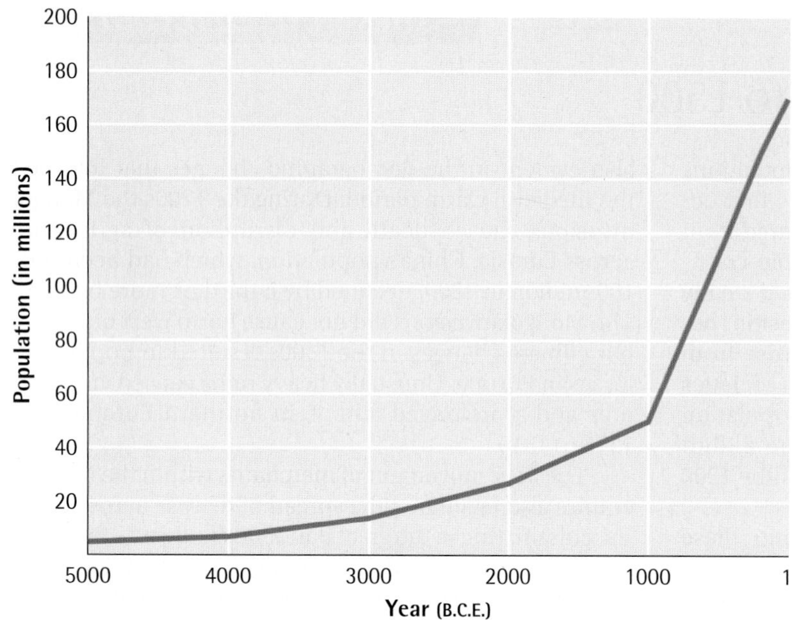

Figure 1 World Population, 5000–1 B.C.E.

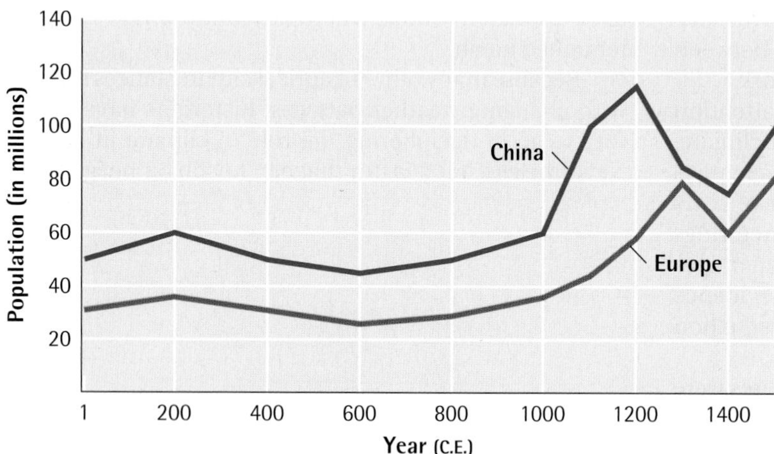

Figure 2 Population in China and Europe, 1–1500 C.E.

PART FIVE

The Globe Encompassed, 1500–1750

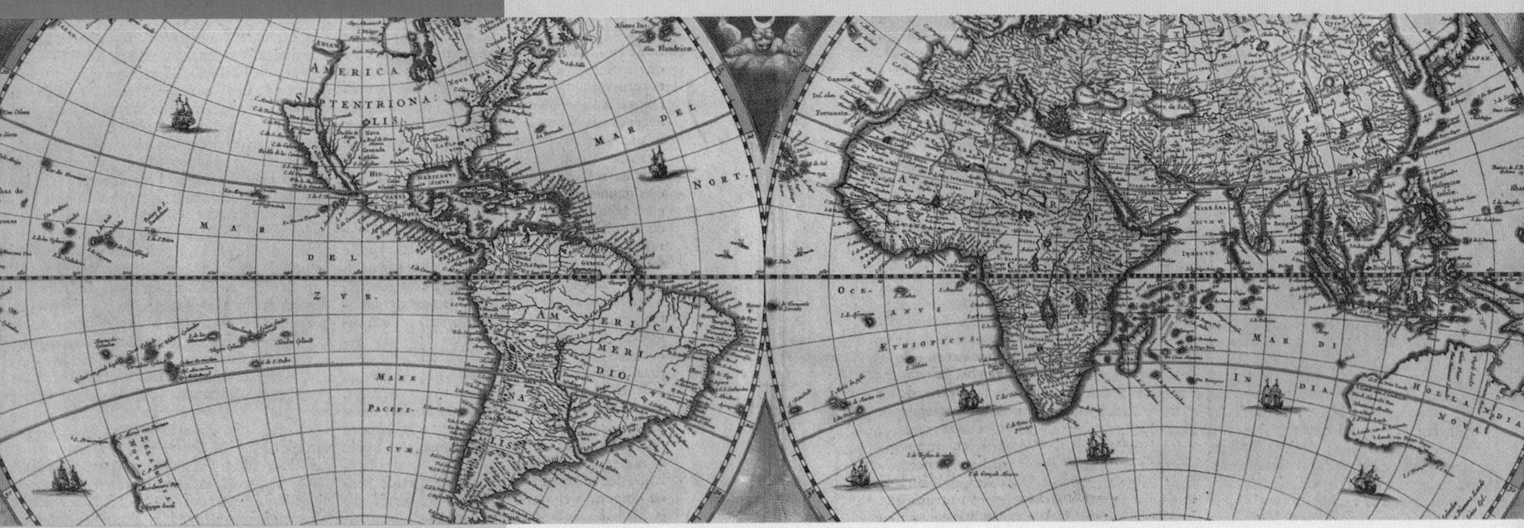

The decades between 1500 and 1750 witnessed a tremendous expansion of commercial, cultural, and biological exchanges around the world. New long-distance sea routes linked Europe with sub-Saharan Africa and the existing maritime networks of the Indian Ocean and East Asia. Spanish and Portuguese voyages ended the isolation of the Americas and created new webs of exchange in the Atlantic and Pacific. Overland expansion of Muslim, Russian, and Chinese empires also increased global interaction.

These expanding contacts had major demographic and cultural consequences. In the Americas, European diseases devastated the Amerindian population, facilitating the establishment of large Spanish, Portuguese, French, and British empires. Europeans introduced enslaved Africans to relieve the labor shortage. Immigrant Africans and Europeans brought new languages, religious practices, music, and forms of personal adornment.

In Asia and Africa, by contrast, the most important changes owed more to internal forces than to European actions. The Portuguese seized control of some important trading ports and networks in the Indian Ocean and pioneered new contacts with China and Japan. In time, the Dutch, French, and English expanded these profitable connections, but in 1750 Europeans were still primarily a maritime force. Asians and Africans generally retained control of their lands and participated freely in overseas trade.

The Islamic world saw the dramatic expansion of the Ottoman Empire in the Middle East and the establishment of the Safavid Empire in Iran and the Mughal Empire in South Asia. In northern Eurasia, Russia and China acquired vast new territories and populations, while a new national government in Japan promoted economic development and stemmed foreign influence.

Ecological change was rapid in areas of rising population and economic activity. Forests were cut down to meet the increasing need for farmland, timber, and fuel. Population growth in parts of Eurasia placed great strain on the environment. On a more positive note, domesticated animals and crops from the Old World transformed agriculture in the Americas, while Amerindian foods such as the potato became staples of the diet of the Old World.

New goods, new wealth, and new tastes from overseas transformed Europe in this period. Global and regional trade promoted urban growth, but conflict was also rife. States spent heavily on warfare in Europe and abroad. The printing press spread new religious and scientific ideas, and challenges to established values and institutions.

By 1750 the balance of power in the world had begun to shift from the East to the West. The Ottoman, Mughal, and Chinese empires had declined in relative strength compared to the much smaller but technologically more sophisticated states of northwestern Europe.

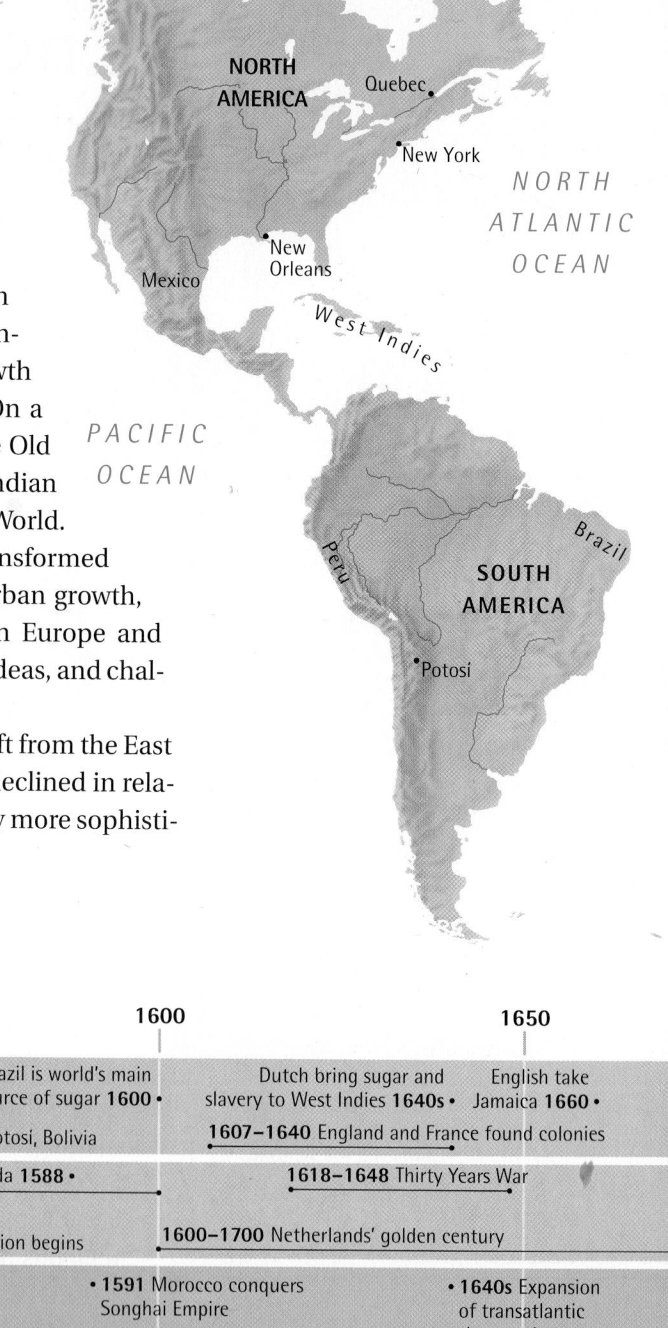
ARCTIC OCEAN
NORTH AMERICA
Quebec
New York
NORTH ATLANTIC OCEAN
New Orleans
Mexico
West Indies
PACIFIC OCEAN
Peru
Brazil
SOUTH AMERICA
Potosí

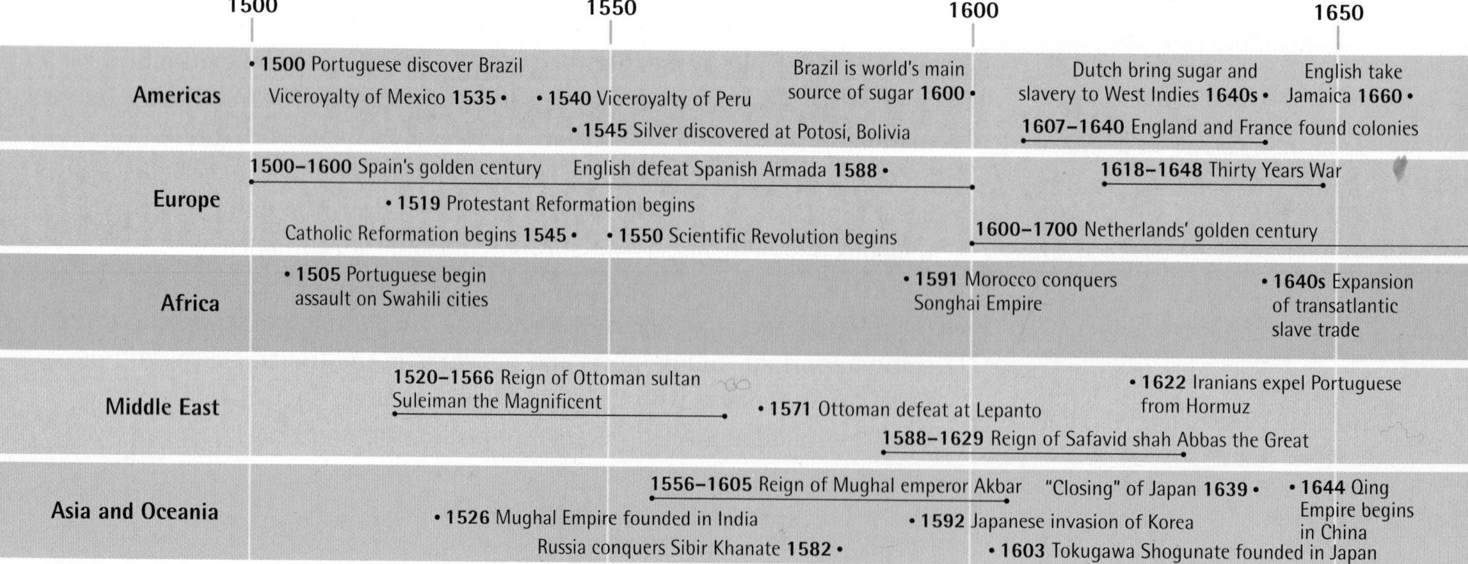
1500
1550
1600
1650
Americas
• 1500 Portuguese discover Brazil
Viceroyalty of Mexico 1535 •
• 1540 Viceroyalty of Peru
• 1545 Silver discovered at Potosí, Bolivia
Brazil is world's main source of sugar 1600 •
Dutch bring sugar and slavery to West Indies 1640s •
English take Jamaica 1660 •
1607–1640 England and France found colonies
Europe
1500–1600 Spain's golden century
English defeat Spanish Armada 1588 •
• 1519 Protestant Reformation begins
Catholic Reformation begins 1545 •
• 1550 Scientific Revolution begins
1618–1648 Thirty Years War
1600–1700 Netherlands' golden century
Africa
• 1505 Portuguese begin assault on Swahili cities
• 1591 Morocco conquers Songhai Empire
• 1640s Expansion of transatlantic slave trade
Middle East
1520–1566 Reign of Ottoman sultan Suleiman the Magnificent
• 1571 Ottoman defeat at Lepanto
• 1622 Iranians expel Portuguese from Hormuz
1588–1629 Reign of Safavid shah Abbas the Great
Asia and Oceania
1556–1605 Reign of Mughal emperor Akbar
• 1526 Mughal Empire founded in India
Russia conquers Sibir Khanate 1582 •
"Closing" of Japan 1639 •
• 1592 Japanese invasion of Korea
• 1603 Tokugawa Shogunate founded in Japan
• 1644 Qing Empire begins in China

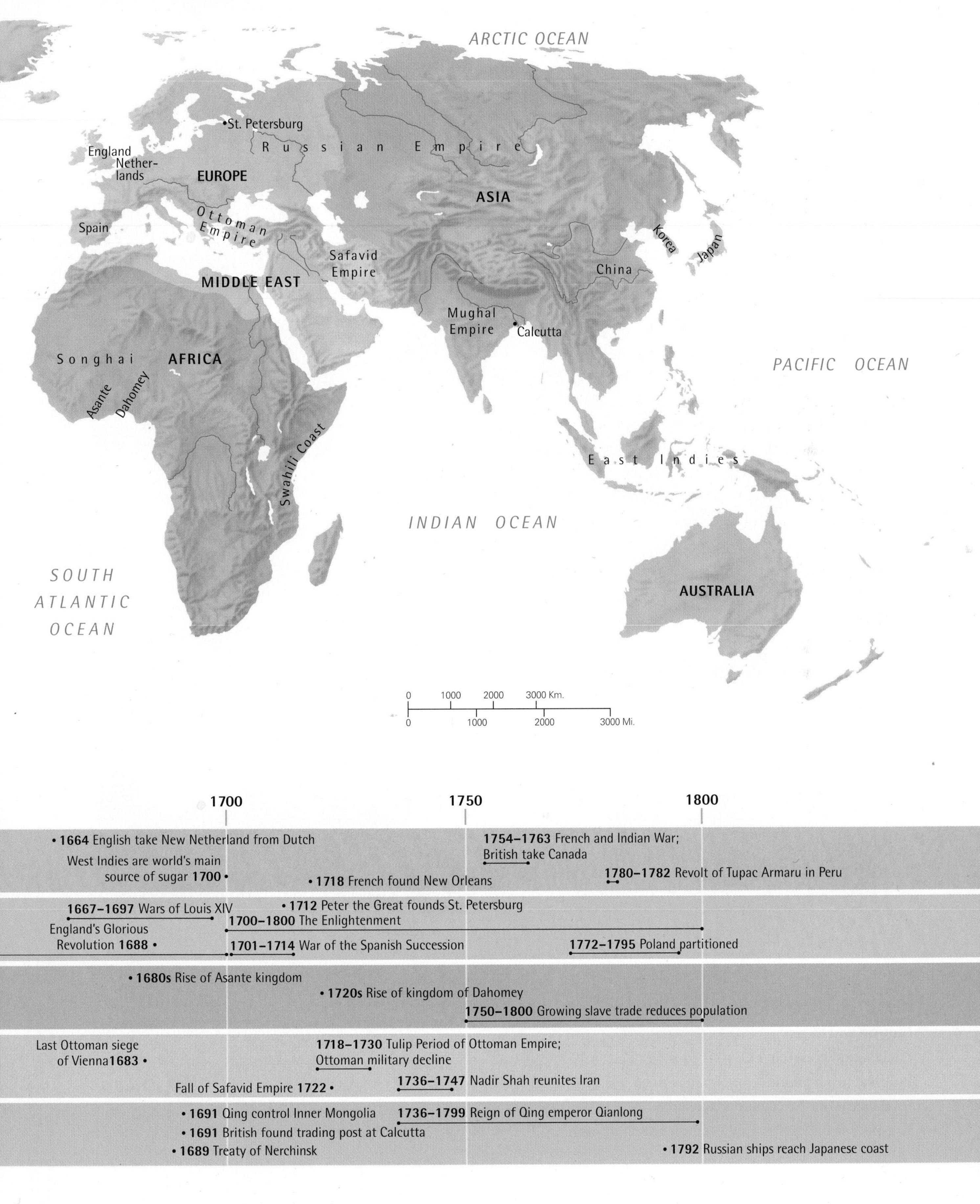

ARCTIC OCEAN
St. Petersburg
Russian Empire
England
Netherlands
EUROPE
ASIA
Spain
Ottoman Empire
Korea
Japan
Safavid Empire
China
MIDDLE EAST
Mughal Empire
Calcutta
Songhai
AFRICA
Asante
Dahomey
PACIFIC OCEAN
Swahili Coast
East Indies
INDIAN OCEAN
SOUTH ATLANTIC OCEAN
AUSTRALIA
0 1000 2000 3000 Km.
0 1000 2000 3000 Mi.
1700
1750
1800
• 1664 English take New Netherland from Dutch
West Indies are world's main source of sugar 1700 •
• 1718 French found New Orleans
1754–1763 French and Indian War; British take Canada
1780–1782 Revolt of Tupac Armaru in Peru
1667–1697 Wars of Louis XIV
• 1712 Peter the Great founds St. Petersburg
1700–1800 The Enlightenment
England's Glorious Revolution 1688 •
1701–1714 War of the Spanish Succession
1772–1795 Poland partitioned
• 1680s Rise of Asante kingdom
• 1720s Rise of kingdom of Dahomey
1750–1800 Growing slave trade reduces population
Last Ottoman siege of Vienna1683 •
1718–1730 Tulip Period of Ottoman Empire; Ottoman military decline
Fall of Safavid Empire 1722 •
1736–1747 Nadir Shah reunites Iran
• 1691 Qing control Inner Mongolia
1736–1799 Reign of Qing emperor Qianlong
• 1691 British found trading post at Calcutta
• 1689 Treaty of Nerchinsk
• 1792 Russian ships reach Japanese coast

17 Transformations in Europe, 1500–1750

Winter in Flanders, 1565 This January scene by the Flemish artist Pieter Bruegel, the Elder, shows many everyday activities.

CHAPTER OUTLINE

As he neared the end of his life in 1575, the French scholar and humanist Loys Le Roy° reflected on the times in which he lived. It was, he believed, a golden age for Europe, and he ticked off the names of more than 130 scholars and translators, writers and poets, artists and sculptors, and explorers and philosophers whose work over the preceding two centuries had restored the standards of ancient learning. Later ages would call this scholarly and artistic revival the European **Renaissance.**

In addition, Le Roy enumerated a series of technological innovations that he believed had also transformed his age: printing, the marine compass, and cannonry. He put printing first because its rapid spread across Europe had done so much to communicate the literary and scholarly revival. The marine compass had made possible the sea voyages that now connected Europe directly to Africa and Asia and had led to the discovery and conquest of the Americas.

Le Roy gave third place to firearms because they had transformed warfare. Cannon and more recently devised hand-held weapons had swept before them all older military instruments. His enthusiasm for this transformation was dampened by the demonstrated capacity of firearms to cause devastation and ruin. Among the other evils of his age Le Roy enumerated syphilis and the spread of religious heresies and sects.

Reading Loys Le Roy's analysis more than four centuries later, one is struck not only by the acuity of his judgment and the beauty and clarity of his prose, but also by the astonishing geographical and historical range of his understanding. He credits both ancient and modern Greeks and Italians for their cultural contributions, the Germans for their role in perfecting printing and cannonry, and the Spanish for their overseas voyages. But his frame of reference is not confined to Europe. He cites the mathematical skills of ancient Egyptians; the military conquests of Mongols, Turks, and Persians (Iranians); Arabs' contributions to science and medicine; and China's contributions to the development of printing.

Loys Le Roy (lwa-EES le-RWAH)

The global framework of Le Roy's analysis led him to conclude that he was living at a turning point in world history. For long centuries, he argued, the military might of the Mongols and Turks had threatened the peoples of Europe, and Safavid Iran and Mamluk Egypt had surpassed any European land in riches. Now the West was in the ascendancy. Europeans' military might equaled that of their Middle Eastern neighbors. They were amassing new wealth from Asian trade and American silver. Most of all, the explosion of learning and knowledge had given Europe intellectual equality and perhaps superiority. Le Roy noted perceptively that while printing presses were in use all across Europe, the Islamic world has closed itself off to the benefits of this new technology, refusing to allow presses to be set up and even forbidding the entry of Arabic works about their lands printed in Europe.

As you read this chapter ask yourself these questions:

- How perceptive was Loys Le Roy about his own age and its place in world history?
- How much did learning, printing, and firearms define early modern Europe? (The marine compass was considered in Chapter 16.)
- Would someone from a lower social station in Europe share Le Roy's optimism about their era?

Culture and Ideas

One place to observe the conflict and continuity of early modern Europe is in the world of ideas. Theological controversies broke the religious unity of the Latin Church and contributed to violent wars. A huge witch scare showed the power of Christian beliefs about the Devil and traditional folklore about malevolent powers. The influence of classical ideas from Greco-Roman antiquity increased among better-educated people, but some thinkers challenged the authority of the ancients. Their new models of the motion of the planets encouraged others to challenge traditional social and political systems, with important implications for the period after 1750. Each of these events has its own causes, but the technology of the printing press enhanced the impact of all.

Martin Luther This detail of a painting by Lucas Cranach (1547) shows the Reformer preaching in his hometown church at Wittenberg. (Church of St. Marien, Wittenberg, Germany/The Bridgeman Art Library, New York and London)

Religious Reformation

In 1500 the **papacy,** the central government of Latin Christianity, was simultaneously gaining stature and suffering from corruption and dissent. Larger donations and tax receipts let popes fund ambitious construction projects in Rome, their capital city. During the sixteenth century Rome gained fifty-four new churches and other buildings, which showcased the artistic Renaissance then under way. However, the church's wealth and power also attracted ambitious men, some of whose personal lives became the source of scandal.

The jewel of the building projects was the magnificent new Saint Peter's Basilica in Rome. The unprecedented size and splendor of this church were intended to glorify God, display the skill of Renaissance artists and builders, and enhance the standing of the papacy. Such a project required refined tastes and vast sums of money.

The skillful overseer of the design and financing of the new Saint Peter's was Pope Leo X (r. 1513–1521), a member of the wealthy Medici° family of Florence, famous for its patronage of the arts. Pope Leo's artistic taste was superb and his personal life free from scandal, but he was more a man of action than a spiritual leader. One technique that he used to raise funds for the basilica was to authorize an **indulgence**—a forgiveness of the punishment due for past sins, granted by church authorities as a reward for a pious act such as making a pilgrimage, saying a particular prayer, or making a donation to a religious cause.

A young professor of sacred scripture, Martin Luther (1483–1546), objected to the way the new indulgence was preached. As the result of a powerful religious experience, Luther had forsaken money and marriage for a monastic life of prayer, self-denial, and study. He found personal consolation in his own religious quest in passage in Saint Paul's Epistle to the Romans that argued that salvation came not from "doing certain things" but from religious faith. That passage also led Luther to object to the way the indulgence preachers appeared to emphasize giving money more than the faith behind the act. He wrote to Pope Leo, asking him to stop this abuse, and challenged the preachers to a debate on the theology of indulgences.

This theological dispute quickly escalated into a contest between two strong-minded men. Largely ignoring Luther's theological objections, Pope Leo regarded his letter as a challenge to papal power and moved to silence the German monk. During a debate in 1519, a papal representative led Luther into open disagreement with some church doctrines, for which the papacy condemned him. Blocked in his effort to reform the church from within, Luther burned the papal bull (document) of condemnation, rejecting the pope's authority and beginning the movement known as the **Protestant Reformation.**

Accusing those whom he called "Romanists" (Roman Catholics) of relying on "good works," Luther insisted that the only way to salvation was through faith in Jesus Christ. He further declared that Christian belief must be based on the word of God in the Bible and on Christian tradition, not on the authority of the pope, as Catholics held. Eventually his conclusions led him to abandon his monastic prayers and penances and to marry a former nun.

Today Roman Catholics and Lutherans have resolved many of their theological differences, but in the sixteenth century stubbornness on both sides made reconciliation impossible. Moreover, Luther's use of the printing press to promote his ideas won him the support

Medici (MED-ih-chee)

CHRONOLOGY

	Politics and Culture	Environment and Technology	Warfare
1500	**1500s** Spain's golden century **1519** Protestant Reformation begins **1540s** Scientific Revolution begins **1545** Catholic Reformation begins	**Mid-1500s** Improved windmills and increasing land drainage in Holland	**1526–1571** Ottoman wars **1546–1555** German Wars of Religion **1562–1598** French Wars of Religion **1566–1648** Netherlands Revolt
	Late 1500s Witch-hunts increase	**1590s** Dutch develop flyboats; Little Ice Age begins	
1600	**1600s** Holland's golden century	**1600s** Depletion of forests growing **1609** Galileo's astronomical telescope **1682** Canal du Midi completed	**1618–1648** Thirty Years War **1642–1648** English Civil War **1652–1678** Anglo-Dutch Wars **1667–1697** Wars of Louis XIV **1683–1697** Ottoman wars
1700	**1700s** The Enlightenment begins	**1750** English mine nearly 5 million tons of coal a year **1755** Lisbon earthquake	**1700–1721** Great Northern War **1701–1714** War of the Spanish Succession

of powerful Germans, who responded to his nationalist portrayal of the dispute as an effort of an Italian pope to beautify his city with German funds.

Inspired by Luther's denunciation of the ostentation and corruption of church leaders, other leaders called for a return to authentic Christian practices and beliefs. John Calvin (1509–1564), a well-educated Frenchman who turned from the study of law to theology after experiencing a religious conversion, became a highly influential Protestant leader. As a young man, Calvin published *The Institutes of the Christian Religion*, a masterful synthesis of Christian teachings, in 1535. Much of the *Institutes* was traditional medieval theology, but Calvin's teaching differed from that of Roman Catholics and Lutherans in two respects. First, while agreeing with Luther's emphasis on faith over works, Calvin denied that even human faith could merit salvation. Salvation, said Calvin, was a gift God gave to those He "predestined" for salvation. Second, Calvin went farther than Luther in curtailing the power of a clerical hierarchy and in simplifying religious rituals. Calvinist congregations elected their own governing committees and in time created regional and national synods (councils) to regulate doctrinal issues. Calvinists also displayed simplicity in dress, life, and worship. In an age of ornate garments, they wore simple black clothes, avoided ostentatious living, and worshiped in churches devoid of statues, most musical instruments, stained-glass windows, incense, and vestments.

The Reformers appealed to genuine religious sentiments, but their successes and failures were also due to political circumstances (discussed below) and the social agendas that motivated people to join them. It was no coincidence that Lutheranism had its greatest appeal to German speakers and linguistically related Scandinavians. Peasants and urban laborers sometimes defied their masters by adopting a different faith. Protestants were no more inclined than Roman Catholics to question male dominance in the church and the family, but most Protestants rejected the medieval tradition of celibate priests and nuns and advocated Christian marriage for all adults.

Shaken by the intensity of the Protestant Reformers' appeal, the Catholic Church undertook its own reforms.

Map 17.1 Religious Reformation in Europe The Reformation brought greater religious freedom but also led to religious conflict and persecution. In many places the Reformation accelerated the trend toward state control of religion and added religious differences to the motives for wars among Europeans.

Death to Witches This woodcut from 1574 depicts three women convicted of witchcraft being burned alive in Baden, Switzerland. The well dressed townsmen look on stolidly. (Zentralbibliothek Zurich)

A council that met at the city of Trent, in northern Italy, in three sessions between 1545 and 1563 painstakingly distinguished proper Catholic doctrines from Protestant "errors." The council also reaffirmed the supremacy of the pope and called for a number of reforms, including requiring each bishop to reside in his diocese and each diocese to have a theological seminary to train priests. Also important to this **Catholic Reformation** were the activities of a new religious order—the Society of Jesus, or "Jesuits," that Ignatius of Loyola (1491–1556), a Spanish nobleman, founded in 1540. Well-educated Jesuits helped stem the Protestant tide and win back some adherents by their teaching and preaching (see Map 17.1). Other Jesuits became important missionaries overseas (see Chapters 18 and 21).

Given the complexity of the issues and the intensity of the emotions that the Protestant Reformation stirred, it is not surprising that violence often flared up. Both sides persecuted and sometimes executed those of differing views. Bitter "wars of religion," fought over a mixture of religious and secular issues, continued in parts of western Europe until 1648.

Traditional Thinking and Witch-Hunts

Religious differences among Protestants and between them and Catholics continued to generate animosity long after the first generation of reformers, but from a global perspective European Christians still had much in common both in their theology and in the local folk customs and pre-Christian beliefs that remained powerful everywhere in Europe. The widespread **witch-hunts** that Protestants and Catholics undertook in early modern Europe are a dramatic illustration of those common beliefs and cultural heritage.

Prevailing European ideas about the natural world blended two distinct traditions. One was the folklore about magic and forest spirits passed down orally from pre-Christian times. The second was the biblical teachings of the Christian and Jewish scriptures, heard by all in church and read by growing numbers in vernacular translations. In the minds of most people, Christian teachings about miracles, saints, and devils mixed with folklore.

Like people in other parts of the world, most early modern Europeans believed that natural events could have supernatural causes. When crops failed or domestic animals died unexpectedly, many people blamed unseen spirits. People also attributed human triumphs and tragedies to supernatural causes. When an earthquake destroyed much of Lisbon, Portugal's capital city, in November 1755, for example, both educated and uneducated people saw the event as a punishment sent by God. A Jesuit charged it "scandalous to pretend that the earthquake was just a natural event." An English Protestant leader agreed, comparing Lisbon's fate with that of Sodom, the city that God destroyed because of the sinfulness of its citizens, according to the Hebrew Bible.

The extraordinary fear of the power of witches that swept across northern Europe in the late sixteenth and seventeenth centuries was powerful testimony to belief in the spiritual causes of natural events. It is estimated that secular and church authorities tried over a hundred thousand people—some three-fourths of them women—for practicing witchcraft. Some were acquitted; some recanted; but more than half were executed—most in Protestant lands. Torture and badgering questions persuaded many accused witches to confess to casting spells and to describe in vivid detail their encounters with the Devil and their attendance at nighttime assemblies of witches.

The trial records make it clear that both the accusers and the accused believed that it was possible for angry and jealous individuals to use evil magic and the power of the Devil to cause people and domestic animals to sicken and die or to cause crops to wither in the fields.

Researchers think that at least some of those accused in early modern Europe may really have tried to use witchcraft to harm their enemies. However, it was the Reformation's focus on the Devil—the enemy of God—as the source of evil that made such malevolence so serious a crime and may have helped revive older fears of witchcraft.

Modern historians also argue that many accusations against widows and independent-minded women drew on the widespread belief that women not directly under the control of fathers or husbands were likely to turn to evil. The fact that such women had important roles in tending animals and the sick and in childbirth also made them suspects if death occurred. In parts of the world where belief in witchcraft is still strong, witch-hunts arise at times of social stress, and people who are marginalized by poverty and by the suspicions of others often relish the celebrity that public confession brings. Self-confessed "witches" may even find release from the guilt they feel for wishing evil on their neighbors.

No single reason can explain the rise in witchcraft accusations and fears in early modern Europe, but, for both the accusers and the accused, there are plausible connections between the witch-hunts and rising social tensions, rural poverty, and environmental strains. Far from being a bizarre aberration, witch-hunts reflected the larger social climate of early modern Europe.

The Scientific Revolution

Among the educated, the writings of Greco-Roman antiquity and the Bible were more trusted guides to the natural world than was folklore. The Renaissance had recovered many manuscripts of ancient writers, some of which were printed and widely circulated. The greatest authority on physics was Aristotle, a Greek philosopher who taught that everything on earth was reducible to four elements. The surface of the earth was composed of the two heavy elements, earth and water. The atmosphere was made up of two lighter elements, air and fire, which floated above the ground. Higher still were the sun, moon, planets, and stars, which, according to Aristotelian physics, were so light and pure that they floated in crystalline spheres. This division between the ponderous, heavy earth and the airy, celestial bodies accorded perfectly with the commonsense perception that all heavenly bodies revolved around the earth.

The prevailing conception of the universe was also influenced by the tradition derived from the ancient Greek mathematician Pythagoras, who proved the validity of the famous theorem that still bears his name: in a right triangle, the square of the hypotenuse is equal to the sum of the squares of the other two sides ($a^2 + b^2 = c^2$). Pythagoreans attributed to mystical properties the ability of simple mathematical equations to describe physical objects. They attached special significance to the simplest (to them perfect) geometrical shapes: the circle (a point rotated around another point) and the sphere (a circle rotated on its axis). They believed that celestial objects were perfect spheres orbiting the earth in perfectly circular orbits.

In the sixteenth century, however, the careful observations and mathematical calculations of some daring and imaginative European investigators began to challenge these prevailing conceptions of the physical world. These pioneers of the **Scientific Revolution** demonstrated that the workings of the universe could be explained by natural causes.

Over the centuries, observers of the nighttime skies had plotted the movements of the heavenly bodies, and mathematicians had worked to fit these observations into the prevailing theories of circular orbits. To make all the evidence fit, they had come up with eighty different spheres and some ingenious theories to explain the many seemingly irregular movements. Pondering these complications, a Polish monk and mathematician named Nicholas Copernicus (1473–1543) came up with a mathematically simpler solution: switching the center of the different orbits from the earth to the sun would reduce the number of spheres that were needed.

Copernicus did not challenge the idea that the sun, moon, and planets were light, perfect spheres or that they moved in circular orbits. But his placement of the sun, not the earth, at the center of things began a revolution in understanding about the structure of the heavens and about the central place of humans in the universe. To escape the anticipated controversies, Copernicus delayed the publication of his heliocentric (sun-centered) theory until the end of his life.

Other astronomers, including the Danish Tycho Brahe (1546–1601) and his German assistant Johannes Kepler (1571–1630), strengthened and improved on Copernicus's model, showing that planets actually move in elliptical, not circular orbits. The most brilliant of the Copernicans was the Italian Galileo Galilei° (1564–1642). In 1609 Galileo built a telescope through which he took a closer look at the heavens. Able to magnify distant objects thirty times beyond the power of the naked eye, Galileo saw that heavenly bodies were not the perfectly smooth spheres of the Aristotelians. The moon, he reported in *The Starry Messenger* (1610), had mountains and valleys; the sun had spots; other planets had their own moons. In other words, the earth was not alone in being heavy and changeable.

Galileo Galilei (gal-uh-LAY-oh gal-uh-LAY-ee)

Galileo in 1624 This engraving by Ottavio Leone shows the Italian scientist in full vigor at age sixty. (British Museum)

At first, the Copernican universe found more critics than supporters because it so directly challenged not just popular ideas but also the intellectual synthesis of classical and biblical authorities. How, demanded Aristotle's defenders, could the heavy earth move without producing vibrations that would shake the planet apart? Is the Bible wrong, asked the theologians, when the Book of Joshua says that, by God's command, "the sun [not the earth] stood still . . . for about a whole day" to give the ancient Israelites victory in their conquest of Palestine? If Aristotle's physics was wrong, worried other traditionalists, would not the theological synthesis built on other parts of his philosophy be open to question?

Intellectual and religious leaders encouraged political authorities to suppress the new ideas. Most Protestant leaders, following the lead of Martin Luther, condemned the heliocentric universe as contrary to the Bible. Catholic authorities waited longer to act. After all, both Copernicus and Galileo were Roman Catholics. Copernicus had dedicated his book to the pope, and in 1582 another pope, Gregory XIII, had used the latest astronomical findings to issue a new and more accurate calendar (still used today). Galileo ingeniously argued that the conflict between scripture and science was only apparent: the word of God revealed in the Bible was expressed in the imperfect language of ordinary people, but in nature God's truth was revealed more perfectly in a language that could be learned by careful observation and scientific reasoning.

Unfortunately, Galileo also ridiculed those who were slow to accept his findings, charging that Copernican ideas were "mocked and hooted at by an infinite multitude . . . of fools." Smarting under Galileo's stinging sarcasm, some Jesuits and other critics got his ideas condemned by the Roman Inquisition in 1616, which put *The Starry Messenger* on the Index of Forbidden Books and prohibited Galileo from publishing further on the subject. (In 1992 the Catholic Church officially retracted its condemnation of Galileo.)

Despite official opposition, printed books spread the new scientific ideas among scholars across Europe. In England, Robert Boyle (1627–1691) used experimental methods and a trial-and-error approach to examine the inner workings of chemistry. Through the Royal Society, chartered in London in 1662 to promote knowledge of the natural world, Boyle and others became enthusiastic missionaries of mechanical science and fierce opponents of the Aristotelians.

Meanwhile, English mathematician Isaac Newton (1642–1727) was carrying Galileo's demonstration that the heavens and earth share a common physics to its logical conclusion. Newton formulated a set of mathematical laws that all physical objects obeyed. It was the force of gravity—not angels—that governed the elliptical orbits of heavenly bodies. It was gravitation (and the resistance of air) that caused cannonballs to fall back to earth. From 1703 until his death Newton served as president of the Royal Society, using his prestige to promote the new science that came to bear his name.

As the condemnation of Galileo demonstrates, in 1700 most religious and intellectual leaders viewed the new science with suspicion or outright hostility because of the unwanted challenge it posed to established ways of thought. Yet all the principal pioneers of the Scientific Revolution were convinced that scientific discoveries and revealed religion were not in conflict. At the peak of his fame Newton promoted a series of lectures devoted to proving the validity of Christianity. However, by showing that the Aristotelians and biblical writers held ideas about the natural world that were naive and unfactual, these pioneers opened the door to others who used reason to challenge a broader range of unquestioned traditions and superstitions. The world of ideas was forever changed.

The Early Enlightenment

The advances in scientific thought inspired a few brave souls to question the reasonableness of everything from agricultural methods to laws, religion, and social hierarchies. The belief that human reason could discover the laws that governed social behavior and were just as scientific as the laws that governed physics energized a movement known as the **Enlightenment.** Like the Scientific Revolution, this movement was the work of a few "enlightened" individuals, who often faced bitter opposition from the political, intellectual, and religious establishment. Leading Enlightenment thinkers became accustomed to having their books burned or banned and spent long periods in exile to escape being imprisoned.

Influences besides the Scientific Revolution affected the Enlightenment. The Reformation had aroused many to champion one creed or another, but partisan bickering and bloodshed led others to doubt the superiority of any theological position and to recommend toleration of all religions. The killing of suspected witches also shocked many thoughtful people. The leading French thinker Voltaire (1694–1778) declared: "No opinion is worth burning your neighbor for."

Accounts of cultures in other parts of the world also led some European thinkers to question assumptions about the superiority of European political institutions, moral standards, and religious beliefs. Reports of Amerindian life, though romanticized, led some to conclude that those whom they had called savages were in many ways nobler than European Christians. Matteo Ricci, a Jesuit missionary to China whose journals made a strong impression in Europe, contrasted the lack of territorial ambition of the Chinese with the constant warfare in the West and attributed the difference to the fact that China was wisely ruled by educated men whom he called "Philosophers."

Although many circumstances shaped "enlightened" thinking, the new scientific methods and discoveries provided the clearest model for changing European society. Voltaire posed the issues in these terms: "it would be very peculiar that all nature, all the planets, should obey eternal laws" but a human being, "in contempt of these laws, could act as he pleased solely according to his caprice." The English poet Alexander Pope (1688–1774) made a similar point in verse: "Nature and Nature's laws lay hidden in night;/God said, 'Let Newton be' and all was light."

The Enlightenment was more a frame of mind than a coherent movement. Individuals who embraced it drew inspiration from different sources and promoted different agendas. By 1750 its proponents were clearer about what they disliked than about what new institutions should be created. Some "enlightened" thinkers thought society could be made to function with the mechanical orderliness of planets spinning in their orbits. Nearly all were optimistic that—at least in the long run—human beliefs and institutions could be improved. This belief in progress would help foster political and social revolutions after 1750, as Chapter 22 recounts.

Despite the enthusiasm the Enlightenment aroused in some circles, it was decidedly unpopular with many absolutist rulers and with most clergymen. Europe in 1750 was neither enlightened nor scientific. It was a place where political and religious divisions, growing literacy, and the printing press made possible the survival of the new ideas that profoundly changed life in future centuries.

SOCIAL AND ECONOMIC LIFE

From a distance European society seemed quite rigid. At the top of the social pyramid a small number of noble families had privileged access to high offices in the church, government, and military and enjoyed many special privileges, including exemption from taxation. A big step below them were the classes of merchants and professionals, who had acquired wealth but no legal privileges. At the base of the pyramid were the masses, mostly rural peasants and landless laborers, who were exploited by everyone above them. The subordination of women to men seemed equally rigid.

This model of European society is certainly not wrong, but even contemporaries knew that it was too simple. A study of English society in 1688, for example, distinguished twenty-five different social categories and pointed up the shocking inequality among them. It argued that less than half the population contributed to increasing the wealth of the kingdom, while the rest—the majority—were too poor and unskilled to make any substantial contribution.

Some social mobility did occur, particularly in the middle. The principal engine of social change was the economy, and the places where social change occurred most readily were the cities. A secondary means of change was education—for those who could get it.

The Bourgeoisie

Europe's growing cities were the products of a changing economy. In 1500 Paris was the only northern European city with over 100,000 inhabitants. By 1700 both Paris and London had populations over 500,000, and twenty other European cities contained over 60,000 people.

The wealth of the cities came from manufacturing and finance, but especially from trade, both within Europe and overseas. The French called the urban class that dominated these activities the **bourgeoisie**° (burghers, town dwellers). Members of the bourgeoisie devoted long hours to their businesses and poured much of their profits back into them or into new ventures. Even so, they had enough money to live comfortably in large houses with many servants. In the seventeenth and eighteenth centuries wealthier urban classes could buy exotic luxuries imported from the far corners of the earth—Caribbean and Brazilian sugar and rum, Mexican chocolate, Virginia tobacco, North American furs, East Indian cotton textiles and spices, and Chinese tea.

The Netherlands provided many good examples of bourgeois enterprise in the seventeenth century. Manufacturers and skilled craftsmen turned out a variety of goods in the factories and workshops of many cities and towns in the province of Holland. The highly successful Dutch textile industry concentrated on the profitable weaving, finishing, and printing of cloth, leaving the spinning to low-paid workers elsewhere. Along with fine woolens and linens the Dutch were successfully making cheaper textiles for mass markets. Other factories in Holland refined West Indian sugar, brewed beer from Baltic grain, cut Virginia tobacco, and made imitations of Chinese ceramics (see Environment and Technology: East Asian Porcelain in Chapter 21). Free from the censorship imposed by political and religious authorities in neighboring countries, Holland's printers published books in many languages, including manuals with the latest advances in machinery, metallurgy, agriculture, and other technical areas. For a small province barely above sea level, lacking timber and other natural resources, this was a remarkable achievement.

Burgeoning from a fishing village to a metropolis of some 200,000 by 1700, Amsterdam was Holland's largest city and Europe's major port. The bourgeoisie there and in other cities had developed huge commercial fleets that dominated sea trade in Europe and overseas. Dutch ships carried over 80 percent of the trade between Spain and northern Europe, even while Spain and the Netherlands were at war. By one estimate, the Dutch conducted more than half of all the oceangoing commercial shipping in the world in the seventeenth century (for details see Chapters 20 and 21).

Amsterdam also served as Europe's financial center. Seventeenth-century Dutch banks had such a reputation for security that wealthy individuals and governments from all over western Europe entrusted them with their money. The banks in turn invested these funds in real estate, loaned money to factory owners and governments, and provided capital for big business operations overseas.

bourgeoisie (boor-zwah-ZEE)

The Fishwife, 1572 Women were essential partners in most Dutch family businesses. This scene by the Dutch artist Adriaen van Ostade shows a woman preparing fish for retail sale. (Rijksmuseum-Amsterdam)

The expansion of maritime trade led to new designs for merchant ships. In this, too, the Dutch played a dominant role. Using timber imported from northern Europe, shipyards in Dutch ports built their own vast fleets and other ships for export. Especially successful was the *fluit*, or "flyboat," a large-capacity cargo ship developed in the 1590s. It was inexpensive to build and required only a small crew. Another successful type of merchant ship, the heavily armed "East Indiaman," helped the Dutch establish their supremacy in the Indian Ocean. The Dutch also excelled at mapmaking (see Environment and Technology: Mapping the World).

Like merchants in the Islamic world, Europe's merchants relied on family and ethnic networks. In addition to families of local origin, many northern European cities contained merchant colonies from Venice, Florence, Genoa, and other Italian cities. In Amsterdam and Hamburg lived Jewish merchants who had fled religious persecution in Iberia. Other Jewish communities expanded out of eastern Europe into the German states, especially after the Thirty Years War. Armenian merchants from Iran were moving into the Mediterranean and became important in Russia in the seventeenth century.

ENVIRONMENT + TECHNOLOGY

Mapping the World

In 1602 in China the Jesuit missionary Matteo Ricci printed an elaborate map of the world. Working from maps produced in Europe and incorporating the latest knowledge gathered by European maritime explorers, Ricci introduced two changes to make the map more appealing to his Chinese hosts. He labeled it in Chinese characters, and he split his map down the middle of the Atlantic so that China lay in the center. This version pleased Chinese elite, who considered China the "Middle Kingdom" surrounded by lesser states. A copy of Ricci's map in six large panels adorned the emperor's Beijing palace.

The stunningly beautiful maps and globes of sixteenth-century Europe were the most complete, detailed, and useful representations of the earth that any society had ever produced. The best mapmaker of the century was Gerhard Kremer, who is remembered as Mercator (the merchant) because his maps were so useful to European ocean traders. By incorporating the latest discoveries and scientific measurements, Mercator could depict the outlines of the major continents in painstaking detail, even if their interiors were still largely unknown to outsiders.

To represent the spherical globe on a flat map, Mercator drew the lines of longitude as parallel lines. Because such lines actually meet at the poles, Mercator's projection greatly exaggerated the size of every landmass and body of water distant from the equator. However, Mercator's rendering offered a very practical advantage: sailors could plot their course by drawing a straight line between their point of departure and their destination. Because of this useful feature, the Mercator projection of the world remained in common use until quite recently. To some extent, its popularity came from the exaggerated size this projection gave to Europe. Like the Chinese, Europeans liked to think of themselves as at the center of things. Europeans also understood their true geographical position better than people in any other part of the world.

Dutch World Map, 1641 It is easy to see why the Chinese would not have liked to see their empire at the far right edge of this widely printed map. Besides the distortions caused by the Mercator projection, geographical ignorance exaggerates the size of North America and Antarctica. (Courtesy of the Trustees British Museum)

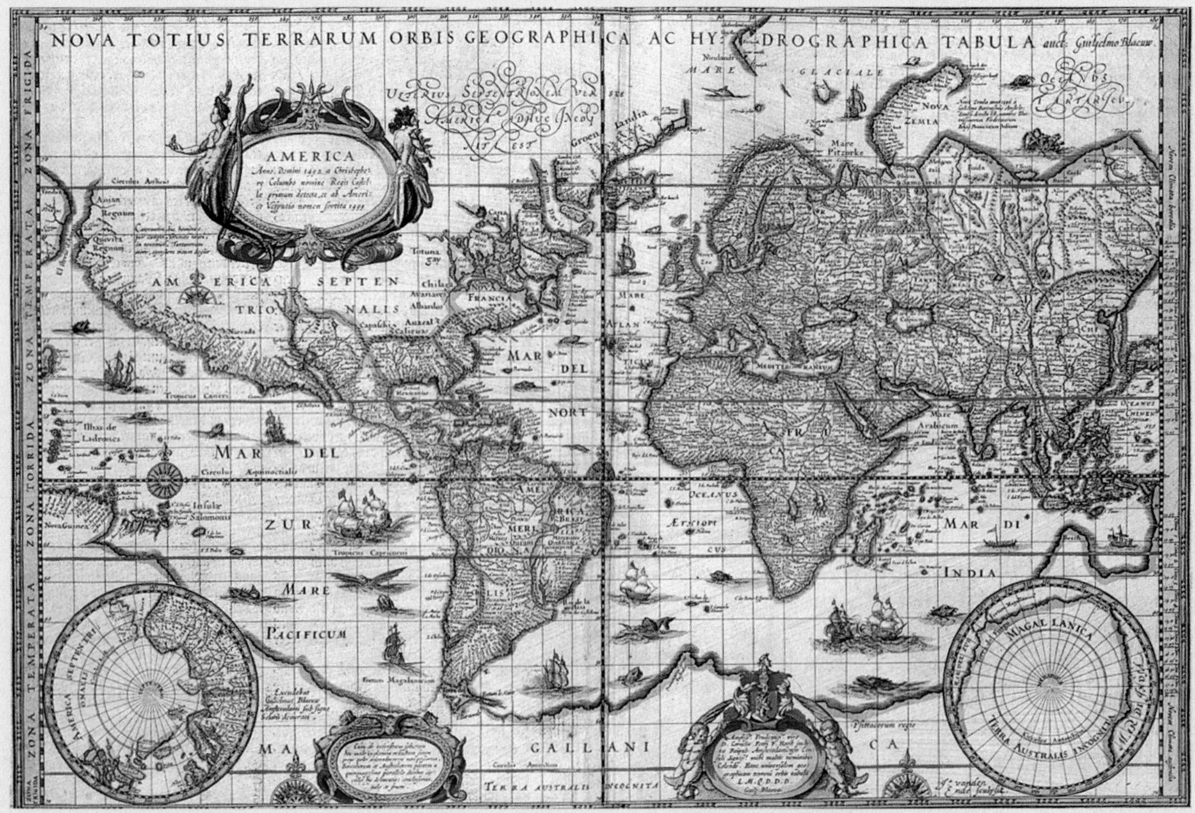

Port of Amsterdam Ships, barges, and boats of all types are visible in this busy seventeenth-century scene. The large building in the center is the Admiralty House, the headquarters of the Dutch East India Company. (Mansell TimeLife Pictures/Getty Images)

The bourgeoisie sought mutually beneficial alliances with European monarchs, who welcomed economic growth as a means of increasing state revenues. The Dutch government pioneered chartering **joint-stock companies,** giving the Dutch East and West India Companies monopolies over trade to the East and West Indies. France and England chartered companies of their own. The companies then sold shares to individuals to raise large sums for overseas enterprises while spreading the risks (and profits) among many investors (see Chapter 19). Investors could buy and sell shares in specialized financial markets called **stock exchanges,** an Italian innovation transferred to the cities of northwestern Europe in the sixteenth century. The greatest stock market in the seventeenth and eighteenth centuries was the Amsterdam Exchange, founded in 1530. Large insurance companies also emerged in this period, and insuring long voyages against loss became a standard practice after 1700.

Governments also undertook large projects to improve water transport. The Dutch built numerous canals for transport and to drain the lowlands for agriculture. Other governments also financed canals, which included elaborate systems of locks to raise barges up over hills. One of the most important was the 150-mile (240-kilometer) Canal du Midi in France, built by the French government between 1661 and 1682 to link the Atlantic and the Mediterranean. By the seventeenth century rulers sought the talents of successful businessmen as administrators. Jean Baptiste Colbert° (1619–1683), Louis XIV's able minister of finance, was a notable example.

After 1650 the Dutch faced growing competition from the English, who were developing their own close association of business and government. With government support, the English merchant fleet doubled between 1660 and 1700, and foreign trade rose by 50 percent. As a result, state revenue from customs duties tripled. In a series of wars (1652–1678) the English government used its naval might to break Dutch dominance in overseas trade and to extend England's colonial empire.

Some successful members of the bourgeoisie in England and France chose to use their wealth to raise their social status. By retiring from their businesses and buying country estates, they could become members of the **gentry.** These landowners affected the lifestyle of the old aristocracy. The gentry loaned money to impoverished peasants and to members of the nobility and in time increased their ownership of land. Some families sought aristocratic husbands for their daughters. The old nobility found such alliances attractive because of the large dowries that the bourgeoisie provided. In France a family could gain the exemption from taxation by living in gentility for three generations or, more quickly, by purchasing a title from the king.

Colbert (kohl-BEAR)

Peasants and Laborers

At the other end of society things were bad, but they had been worse. Serfdom, which bound men and women to land owned by a local lord, had been in deep decline since the great plague of the mid-fourteenth century. The institution did not return in western Europe as the population recovered, but competition for work exerted a downward pressure on wages. However, the development of large estates raising grain for the cities led to the rise of serfdom in eastern Europe for the first time. There was also a decline in slavery, which had briefly expanded in southern Europe around 1500 as the result of the Atlantic slave trade from sub-Saharan Africa. After 1600, however, Europeans shipped nearly all African slaves to the Americas.

There is much truth in the argument that western Europe continued to depend on unfree labor but kept it at a distance rather than at home. In any event, legal freedom did little to make a peasant's life safer and more secure. The techniques and efficiency of European agriculture had improved little since 1300. As a result, bad years brought famine; good ones provided only small surpluses. Indeed, the condition of the average person in western Europe may have worsened between 1500 and 1750 as the result of prolonged warfare, environmental problems, and adverse economic conditions. In addition, Europeans felt the adverse effects of a century of relatively cool climate that began in the 1590s. During this **Little Ice Age** average temperatures fell only a few degrees, but the effects were startling (see Issues in World History: The Little Ice Age).

By 1700 high-yielding new crops from the Americas were helping the rural poor avoid starvation. Once grown only as hedges against famine, potatoes and maize (corn) became staples for the rural poor in the eighteenth century. Potatoes sustained life in northeastern and Central Europe and in Ireland, while poor peasants in Italy subsisted on maize. The irony is that all of these lands were major exporters of wheat, but most of those who planted and harvested it could not afford to eat it.

Instead, the grain was put on carts, barges, and ships and carried to the cities of Western Europe. Other fleets brought wine from southern to northern Europe. Parisians downed 100,000 barrels of wine a year at the end of the seventeenth century. Some of the grain was made into beer, which the poor drank because it was cheaper than wine. In 1750 Parisian breweries brewed 23 million quarts (22 million liters) of beer for local consumption.

Other rural men made a living as miners, lumberjacks, and charcoal makers. The expanding iron industry in England provided work for all three, but the high consumption of wood fuel for this and other purposes caused serious **deforestation.** One early-seventeenth-century observer lamented: "within man's memory, it was held impossible to have any want of wood in England. But . . . at present, through the great consuming of wood . . . and the neglect of planting of woods, there is a great scarcity of wood throughout the whole kingdom."[1] The managers of the hundreds of ironworks in England tried to meet the shortages by importing timber and charcoal from more heavily forested Scandinavian countries and Russia. Eventually, the high price of wood and charcoal encouraged smelters to use coal as an alternative fuel. England's coal mining increased twelvefold from 210,000 tons in 1550 to 2,500,000 tons in 1700. From 1709 coke—coal refined to remove impurities—gradually replaced charcoal in the smelting of iron. These new demands drove English coal production to nearly 5 million tons a year by 1750.

France was much more forested than England, but increasing deforestation there prompted Colbert to predict that "France will perish for lack of wood." By the late eighteenth century deforestation had become an issue even in Sweden and Russia, where iron production had become a major industry. New laws in France and England designed to protect the forests were largely inspired by fears of shortages for naval vessels, whose keels required high-quality timbers of exceptional size and particular curvature. Although wood consumption remained high, rising prices encouraged some individuals to plant trees for future harvest.

Everywhere in Europe the rural poor felt the depletion of the forests most strongly. For centuries they had depended on woodlands for abundant supplies of wild nuts and berries, free firewood and building materials, and wild game. Modest improvements in food production in some places were overwhelmed by population growth. Rural women had long supplemented household incomes by spinning yarn. From the mid-1600s rising wages in towns led textile manufacturers to farm more and more textile weaving out to rural areas with high underemployment. This provided men and women with enough to survive on, but the piecework paid very little for long hours of tedious labor.

Throughout this period, many rural poor migrated to the towns and cities in hopes of better jobs, but only some were successful. Even in the prosperous Dutch towns, half of the population lived in acute poverty. Authorities estimated that those permanent city residents who were too poor to tax, the "deserving poor," made up 10 to 20 percent of population. That calculation did not include the large numbers of "unworthy poor"—recent migrants from impoverished rural areas, peddlers traveling from place to place, and beggars (many with horrible deformities and sores) who tried to survive on charity.

Many young women were forced into prostitution to survive. There were also many criminals, usually organized in gangs, ranging from youthful pickpockets to highway robbers.

The pervasive poverty of rural and urban Europe shocked those who were not hardened to it. In about 1580 the mayor of the French city of Bordeaux° asked a group of visiting Amerindian chiefs what impressed them most about European cities. The chiefs are said to have expressed astonishment at the disparity between the fat, well-fed people and the poor, half-starved men and women in rags. Why, the visitors wondered, did the poor not grab the rich by the throat or set fire to their homes?[2]

In fact, misery provoked many rebellions in early modern Europe. For example, in 1525 peasant rebels in the Alps attacked both nobles and clergy as representatives of the privileged and landowning classes. They had no love for merchants either, whom they denounced for lending at interest and charging high prices. Rebellions multiplied as rural conditions worsened. In southwestern France alone some 450 uprisings occurred between 1590 and 1715, many of them set off by food shortages and tax increases. The exemption of the wealthy from taxation was a frequent source of complaint. A rebellion in southern France in 1670 began when a mob of townswomen attacked the tax collector. It quickly spread to the country, where peasant leaders cried, "Death to the people's oppressors!" Authorities dealt severely with such revolts and executed or maimed their leaders.

Women and the Family

Women's status and work were closely tied to their husbands' and families'. In lands that allowed it, a woman in a royal family might inherit a throne (see Table 17.1, page 467 for examples)—in the absence of a male heir. These rare exceptions do not negate the rule that women everywhere ranked below men, but one should also not forget that her class and wealth defined a woman's position in life more than her sex. The wife or daughter of a rich man, for example, had a much better life than any poor man. In special cases, a single woman might be secure and respected, as in the case of women from good families who might head convents of nuns in Catholic countries. But unmarried women and widows were less well off than their married sisters. A good marriage was thus of great importance.

In contrast to the arranged marriages that prevailed in much of the rest of the world, young men and women in early modern Europe most often chose their own spouses. Ironically, privileged families were more inclined to control marriage plans than poor ones. Royal and noble families carefully plotted the suitability of their children's marriages in furthering the family's status. Bourgeois parents were less likely to force their children into arranged marriages, but the fact that nearly all found spouses within their social class strongly suggests that the bourgeoisie promoted marriages that furthered their business alliances.

Europeans also married later than people in other lands. The sons and daughters of craftworkers and the poor had to delay marriage until they could afford to live on their own. Young men had to serve long apprenticeships to learn trades. Young women also had to work—helping their parents, as domestic servants, or in some other capacity—to save money for the dowry they were expected to bring into the marriage. A dowry was the money and household goods—the amount varied by social class—that enabled a young couple to begin marriage independent of their parents. The typical groom in western and central Europe could not hope to marry before his late twenties, and his bride would be a few years younger—in contrast to the rest of the world, where people usually married in their teens. Marriage also came late in bourgeois families, in part to allow young men to complete their education.

Besides enabling young people to be independent of their parents, the late age of marriage in early modern Europe also held down the birthrate and thus limited family size. Even so, about one-tenth of the births in a city were to unmarried women, often servants, who generally left their infants on the doorsteps of churches, convents, or rich families. Despite efforts to raise such abandoned children, many perished. Delayed marriage also had links to the existence of public brothels, where young men could satisfy their lusts in cheap and impersonal encounters with unfortunate young women, often newly arrived from impoverished rural villages. Nevertheless, rape was a common occurrence, usually perpetrated by gangs of young men who attacked young women rumored to be free with their favors. Some historians believe that such gang rapes reflected poor young men's jealousy at older men's easier access to women.

Bourgeois parents were very concerned that their children have the education and training necessary for success. They promoted the establishment of municipal schools to provide a solid education, including Latin and perhaps Greek, for their sons, who were then sent abroad to learn modern languages or to a university to earn a law degree. Legal training was useful for conducting business and was a prerequisite for obtaining government judgeships and treasury positions. Daughters were less likely to be groomed for business careers, but

---

Bordeaux (bor-DOH)

wives often helped their husbands as bookkeepers and sometimes inherited businesses.

The fact that most schools barred female students, as did most guild and professions, explains why women were not prominent in the cultural Renaissance, the Reformation, the Scientific Revolution, and the Enlightenment. Yet from a global perspective, women in early modern Europe were more prominent in the creation of culture than were women in most other parts of the world. Recent research has brought to light the existence of a number of successful women who were painters, musicians, and writers. Indeed, the spread of learning, the stress on religious reading, and the growth of business likely meant that Europe led the world in female literacy. In a period when most men were illiterate, the number of literate women was small, and only women in wealthier families might have a good education. From the late 1600s some wealthy French women ran intellectual gatherings in their homes. Many more were prominent letter writers. Galileo's daughter, Maria Celeste Galilei, carried on a detailed correspondence with her father from the confinement of her convent, whose walls she had taken a religious vow never to leave.

POLITICAL INNOVATIONS

The monarchs of early modern Europe occupied the apex of the social order, were arbitrators of the intellectual and religious conflicts of their day, and had important influences on the economic life of their realms. For these reasons an overview of political life incorporates all the events previously described in this chapter. In addition, monarchs' political agendas introduced new elements of conflict and change.

The effort to create a European empire failed, but monarchs succeeded in achieving a higher degree of political centralization within their separate kingdoms. The frequent civil and international conflicts of this era sometimes promoted cooperation, but they often encouraged innovation. Leadership and success passed from Spain to the Netherlands and then to England and France. It is hard to avoid the conclusion that the key political technology was cannonry.

State Development

Political diversity characterized Europe. City-states and principalities abounded, either independently or bound into loose federations, of which the **Holy Roman Empire** of the German heartland was the most notable example. In western Europe the strong monarchies that had emerged were acquiring national identities. Dreams of a European empire comparable to those of Asia remained strong, although efforts to form one were frustrated.

Dynastic ambitions and historical circumstances combined to favor and then block the creation of a powerful empire in the early sixteenth century. In 1519 electors of the Holy Roman Empire chose Charles V (r. 1519–1556) to be the new emperor. Like his predecessors for three generations, Charles belonged to the powerful **Habsburg**° family of Austria, but he had recently inherited the Spanish thrones of Castile and Aragon. With the vast resources of all these offices behind him (see Map 17.2), Charles hoped to centralize his imperial power and lead a Christian coalition to halt the advance into southeastern Europe of the Ottoman Empire, whose Muslim rulers already controlled most of the Middle East and North Africa.

Charles and his Christian allies eventually halted the Ottomans at the gates of Vienna in 1529, although Ottoman attacks continued on and off until 1697. But Charles's efforts to forge his several possessions into Europe's strongest state failed. King Francis I of France, who had lost to Charles in the election for Holy Roman Emperor, openly supported the Muslim Turks to weaken his rival. In addition, the princes of the Holy Roman Empire's many member states were able to use Luther's religious Reformation to frustrate Charles's efforts to reduce their autonomy. Swayed partly by Luther's appeals to German nationalism, many German princes opposed Charles's defense of Catholic doctrine in the imperial Diet (assembly).

After decades of bitter squabbles turned to open warfare in 1546 (the German Wars of Religion), Charles V finally gave up his efforts at unification, abdicated control of his various possessions to different heirs, and retired to a monastery. By the Peace of Augsburg (1555), he recognized the princes' right to choose whether Catholicism or Lutheranism would prevail in their particular states, and he allowed them to keep the church lands they had seized before 1552. The triumph of religious diversity had derailed Charles's plan for centralizing authority in central Europe and put off German political unification for three centuries.

Meanwhile, the rulers of Spain, France, and England were building a more successful program of political unification based on political centralization and religious unity. The most successful rulers reduced the autonomy of the church and the nobility in their states, while making them part of a unified national structure

Habsburg (HABZ-berg)

Map 17.2 The European Empire of Charles V Charles was Europe's most powerful ruler from 1519 to 1556, but he failed to unify the Christian West. In addition to being the elected head of the Holy Roman Empire, he was the hereditary ruler of the Spanish realms of Castile and Aragon and the possessions of the Austrian Habsburgs in Central Europe. The map does not show his extensive holdings in the Americas and Asia.

with the monarch at its head (see Diversity and Dominance: Political Craft and Craftiness). The cooption of the church in the sixteenth century was stormy, but the outcome was clear. Bringing the nobles and other powerful interests into a centralized political system took longer and led to more diverse outcomes.

Religious Policies

The rulers of Spain and France successfully defended the Catholic tradition against Protestant challenges. Following the pattern used by his predecessors to suppress Jewish and Muslim practices, King Philip II of Spain used an ecclesiastical court, the

Diversity and Dominance

Political Craft and Craftiness

Political power was becoming more highly concentrated in early modern Europe, but absolute dominance was more a goal than a reality. Whether subject to constitutional checks or not, rulers were very concerned with creating and maintaining good relations with their more powerful subjects. Their efforts to manipulate public opinion and perceptions have much in common with the efforts of modern politicians to manage their "image."

A diplomat and civil servant in the rich and powerful Italian city-state of Florence, Niccolò Machiavelli, is best known for his book The Prince *(1532). This influential essay on the proper exercise of political power has been interpreted as cynical by some and as supremely practical and realistic by others. Because Machiavelli did not have a high opinion of the intelligence and character of most people, he urged rulers to achieve obedience by fear and deception. But he also suggested that genuine mercy, honesty, and piety may be superior to feigned virtue.*

OF CRUELTY AND CLEMENCY, AND WHETHER IT IS BETTER TO BE LOVED THAN FEARED

. . . It will naturally be answered that it would be desirable to be both the one and the other; but, as it is difficult to be both at the same time, it is much safer to be feared than to be loved, when you have to choose between the two. For it may be said of men in general that they are ungrateful and fickle, dissemblers, avoiders of danger, and greedy of gain. So long as you shower benefits on them, they are all yours; they offer you their blood, their substance, their lives, and their children, provided the necessity for it is far off; but when it is near at hand, then they revolt. And the prince who relies on their words, without having otherwise provided for his security is ruined; for friendships that are won by rewards, not by greatness and nobility of soul, although deserved, yet are not real, and cannot be depended upon in time of adversity.

Besides, men have less hesitation in offending one who makes himself beloved than one who makes himself feared; for love holds by a bond of obligation which, as mankind is bad, is broken on every occasion whenever it is for the interest of the obligated party to break it. But fear holds by the apprehension of punishment, which never leaves men. A prince, however, should make himself feared in such a manner that, if he has not won the affection of his people, he shall at least not incur their hatred. . . .

IN WHAT MANNER PRINCES SHOULD KEEP THEIR FAITH

It must be evident to every one that it is more praiseworthy for a prince always to maintain good faith, and practice integrity rather than craft and deceit. And yet the experience of our own times has shown those princes have achieved great things who made small account of good faith, and who understood by cunning to circumvent the intelligence of others; and that in the end they got the better of those whose actions were dictated by loyalty and good faith. You must know, therefore, that there are two ways of carrying on a struggle; one by law and the other by force. The first is practiced by men, and the other by animals; and as the first is often insufficient, it becomes necessary to resort to the second.

. . . If men were altogether good, this advice would be wrong; but since they are bad and will not keep faith with you, you need not keep faith with them. Nor will a prince ever be short of legitimate excuses to give color to his breaches of faith. Innumerable modern examples could be given of this; and it could easily be shown how many treaties of peace, and how many engagements, have been made null and void by the faithlessness of princes; and he who has best known how to play the fox has ever been the most successful.

But it is necessary that the prince should know how to color this nature well, and how to be a great hypocrite and dissembler. For men are so simple, and yield so much to immediate necessity, that the deceiver will never lack dupes. I will mention one of the most recent examples. [Pope] Alexander VI never did nor ever thought of anything but to deceive, and always found a reason for doing so . . . and yet he was always successful in his deceits, because he knew the weakness of men in that particular.

It is not necessary, however, for a prince to possess all the above-mentioned qualities; but it is essential that he should at least seem to have them. I will even venture to say, that to have and practice them constantly is pernicious, but to seem to have them is useful. For instance, a prince should seem to be merciful, faithful, humane, religious, and upright, and should even be so in reality; but he should have his mind so trained that, when occasion requires it, he may know how to change to the opposite. And it must be understood that a prince, and especially one who has but recently acquired his state, cannot perform all those things which cause men to be esteemed as good; he being obligated, for the sake of maintaining his state, to act contrary to humanity, charity, and religion. And therefore, it is necessary that he should have a versatile mind, capable of changing readily, according as the winds and changes of fortune bid him; and, as has been said above, not to swerve from the good if possible, but to know how to resort to evil if necessity demands it.

A prince then should be very careful never to allow anything to escape his lips that does not abound in the above-mentioned five qualities, so that to see and to hear him he may seem all charity, integrity, and humanity, all uprightness and all piety. And more than all else is it necessary for a prince to seem to possess the last quality; for mankind in general judge more by what they see than by what they feel, every one being capable of the former, and few of the latter. Everybody sees what you seem to be, but few really feel what you are; and those few dare not oppose the opinion of the many, who are protected by the majority of the state; for the actions of all men, and especially those of princes, are judged by the result, where there is no other judge to whom to appeal.

A prince should look mainly to the successful maintenance of his state. For the means which he employs for this will always be counted honorable, and will be praised by everybody; for the common people are always taken in by appearances and by results, and it is the vulgar mass that constitutes the world.

Because, as Machiavelli argued, appearances count for as much in the public arena as realities, it is difficult to judge whether rulers' statements expressed their real feelings and beliefs or what may have been the most expedient to say at the moment. An example is this speech Queen Elizabeth of England made at the end of November 1601 to Parliament after a particularly difficult year. One senior noble had led a rebellion and was subsequently executed. Parliament was pressing for extended privileges. Having gained the throne in 1558 after many difficulties (including a time in prison), the sixty-eight-year-old queen had much experience in the language and wiles of politics and was well aware of the importance of public opinion. Reprinted many times, the speech became famous as "The Golden Speech of Queen Elizabeth."

I do assure you, there is no prince that loveth his subjects better, or whose love can countervail our love. There is no jewel, be it of never so rich a price, which I set before this jewel: I mean your love. For I do esteem it more than any treasure or riches; for that we know how to prize, but love and thanks I count unvaluable.

And, though God has raised me high, yet this I count the glory of my crown, that I have reigned with your loves. This makes me that I do not so much rejoice that God hath made me to be a Queen, as to be Queen over so thankful a people.

Therefore, I have cause to wish nothing more than to content the subjects; and that is the duty I owe. Neither do I desire to live longer days than I may see your prosperity; and that is my only desire.

And as I am that person that still (yet under God) has delivered you, so I trust, by the almighty power of God, that I shall be His instrument to preserve you from every peril, dishonour, shame, tyranny, and oppression. . . .

Of myself I must say this: I was never any greedy scraping grasper, nor a straight, fast-holding prince, nor yet a waster. My heart was never set on worldly goods, but only for my subjects' good. What you bestow on me, I will not hoard it up, but receive it to bestow on you again. Yea, mine own properties I count yours, and to be expended for your good. . . .

To be a king and wear a crown is a thing more glorious to them that see it, than it is pleasing to them that bear it. For myself, I was never so much enticed with the glorious name of king, or royal authority of a queen, as delighted that God made me his instrument to maintain his truth and glory, and to defend this Kingdom (as I said) from peril, dishonour, tyranny and oppression.

There will never Queen sit in my seat with more zeal to my country, care for my subjects, and that sooner with willingness will venture her life for your good and safety than myself. For it is not my desire to live nor reign longer than my life and reign shall be for your good. And though you have had and may have many more princes more mighty and wise sitting in this state, yet you never had or shall have any that will be more careful and loving.

Shall I ascribe anything to myself and my sexly weakness? I were not worthy to live then; and of all, most unworthy of the great mercies I have had from God, who has even yet given me a heart, which never feared foreign of home enemy. I speak to give God the praise . . . That I should speak for any glory, God forbid.

QUESTIONS FOR ANALYSIS

1. **Do you find Machiavelli's advice to be cynical or realistic?**
2. **Describe how a member of Parliament might have responded to Queen Elizabeth's declarations of her concern for the welfare of her people above all else.**
3. **Can a ruler be sincere and manipulative at the same time?**

Source: From *The Historical, Political, and Diplomatic Writings of Niccolo Machiavelli*, trans. Christian E. Detmold (Boston: Houghton, Mifflin and Company, 1891), II: 54–59, and Heywood Townshend, *Historical Collections, or an Exact Account of the Proceedings of the Last Four Parliaments of Q. Elizabeth* (London: Basset, Crooke, and Cademan, 1680), 263–266.

Spanish Inquisition, to bring into line those who resisted his authority. Suspected Protestants, as well as critics of the king, found themselves accused of heresy, an offense punishable by death. Even those who were acquitted of the charge learned not to oppose the king again.

In France the Calvinist opponents of the Valois rulers gained the military advantage in the French Wars of Religion (1562–1598), but in the interest of forging lasting unity, their leader Prince Henry of Navarre then embraced the Catholic faith of the majority of his subjects. In their embrace of a union of church and state, the new Bourbon king, Henry IV, his son King Louis XIII, and his grandson King Louis XIV were as supportive of the Catholic Church as their counterparts in Spain. In 1685 Louis XIV even revoked the Edict of Nantes°, by which his grandfather had granted religious freedom to his Protestant supporters in 1598.

In England King Henry VIII had initially been a strong defender of the papacy against Lutheran criticism. But when Henry failed to obtain a papal annulment of his marriage to Catherine of Aragon, who had not furnished him with a male heir, he challenged the papacy's authority over the church in his kingdom. Henry had the English archbishop of Canterbury annul the marriage in 1533. The breach with Rome was sealed the next year when Parliament made the English monarch head of the Church of England.

Like many Protestant rulers, Henry used his authority to disband monasteries and convents and seize their lands. He gave the lands to his powerful allies and sold some to pay for his new navy. However, under Henry and his successors the new Anglican church moved away from Roman Catholicism in ritual and theology much less than was wanted by English Puritans (Calvinists who wanted to "purify" the Anglican church of Catholic practices and beliefs). In 1603 the first Stuart king, James I, dismissed a Puritan petition to eliminate bishops with the statement "No bishops, no king"—a reminder of the essential role of the church in supporting royal power.

Monarchies in England and France

Over the course of the seventeenth century, the rulers of England and France went through some very intense conflicts with their leading subjects over the limits of royal authority. Religion was never absent as an issue in these struggles, but the different constitutional outcomes they produced were of more significance in the long run.

So as to evade any check on his power, King Charles I of England (see Table 17.1) ruled for eleven years without summoning Parliament, his kingdom's representative body. Lacking Parliament's consent to new taxes, he raised funds by coercing "loans" from wealthy subjects and applying existing tax laws more broadly. Then in 1640 a rebellion in Scotland forced him to summon a Parliament to approve new taxes to pay for an army. Noblemen and churchmen sat in the House of Lords. Representatives from the towns and counties sat in the House of Commons. Before it would authorize new taxes, Parliament insisted on strict guarantees that the king would never again ignore the body's traditional rights. These King Charles refused to grant. When he ordered the arrest of his leading critics in the House of Commons in 1642, he plunged the kingdom into the **English Civil War.**

Charles suffered defeat on the battlefield, but still refused to compromise. In 1649 a "Rump" Parliament purged of his supporters ordered him executed and replaced the monarchy with a republic under the Puritan general Oliver Cromwell. During his rule, Cromwell expanded England's presence overseas and imposed firm control over Ireland and Scotland, but he was as unwilling as the Stuart kings to share power with Parliament. After his death Parliament restored the Stuart line, and for a time it was unclear which side had won the war.

However, when King James II refused to respect Parliament's rights and had his heir baptized a Roman Catholic, the leaders of Parliament forced James into exile in the bloodless Glorious Revolution of 1688. The Bill of Rights of 1689 specified that Parliament had to be called frequently and had to consent to changes in laws and to the raising of an army in peacetime. Another law reaffirmed the official status of the Church of England but extended religious toleration to the Puritans.

A similar struggle in France produced a different outcome. There the Estates General represented the traditional rights of the clergy, the nobility, and the towns (that is, the bourgeoisie). The Estates General was able to assert its rights during the sixteenth-century French Wars of Religion, when the monarchy was weak. But thereafter the Bourbon monarchs generally ruled without having to call it into session. They avoided financial crises by more efficient tax collection and by selling appointments to high government offices. In justification they claimed that the monarch had absolute authority to rule in God's name on earth.

Louis XIV's gigantic new palace at **Versailles**° symbolized the French monarch's triumph over the traditional rights of the nobility, clergy, and towns. Capable of hous-

Nantes (nahnt)

Versailles (vuhr-SIGH)

Table 17.1 Rulers in Early Modern Western Europe

Spain	France	England/Great Britain
Habsburg Dynasty	**Valois Dynasty**	**Tudor Dynasty**
Charles I (1516–1556) (Holy Roman Emperor Charles V)	Francis I (1515–1547)	Henry VIII (1509–1547)
	Henry II (1547–1559)	Edward VI (1547–1553)
Philip II (1556–1598)	Francis II (1559–1560)	Mary I (1553–1558)
	Charles IX (1560–1574)	Elizabeth I (1558–1603)
	Henry III (1574–1589)	
	Bourbon Dynasty	**Stuart Dynasty**
Philip III (1598–1621)	Henry IV (1589–1610)[a]	James I (1603–1625)
Philip IV (1621–1665)	Louis XIII (1610–1643)	Charles I (1625–1649)[a, b]
Charles II (1665–1700)	Louis XIV (1643–1715)	(Puritan Republic, 1649–1660)
		Charles II (1660–1685)
		James II (1685–1688)[b]
		William III (1689–1702) and Mary II (1689–1694)
Bourbon Dynasty		
Philip V (1700–1746)		Anne (1702–1714)
		Hanoverian Dynasty
	Louis XV (1715–1774)	George I (1714–1727)
Ferdinand VI (1746–1759)		George II (1727–1760)

[a]Died a violent death. [b]Was overthrown.

ing ten thousand people and surrounded by elaborately landscaped grounds and parks, the palace can be seen as a sort of theme park of royal absolutism. Elaborate ceremonies and banquets centered on the king kept the nobles who lived at Versailles away from plotting rebellion. According to one of them, the duke of Saint-Simon°, "no one was so clever in devising petty distractions" as the king.

The balance of powers in the English model would be widely admired in later times. Until well after 1750 most European rulers admired and imitated the centralized powers and absolutist claims of the French. Some went so far as to build imitations of the Versailles palace. The checks and balances of the English model had a less immediate effect. In his influential *Second Treatise of Civil Government* (1690), the English political philosopher John Locke (1632–1704) disputed monarchial claims to absolute authority by divine right. Rather, he argued, rulers derived their authority from the consent of the governed and, like everyone else, were subject to the law. If monarchs overstepped the law, Locke argued, citizens had not only the right but also the duty to rebel. The later consequences of this idea are considered in Chapter 22.

Saint-Simon (san see-MON)

Warfare and Diplomacy

In addition to the bitter civil wars that pounded the Holy Roman Empire, France, and England, European states engaged in numerous international conflicts. Warfare was almost constant in early modern Europe (see the Chronology at the beginning of the chapter). In their pursuit of power monarchs expended vast sums of money and caused widespread devastation and death. The worst of the international conflicts, the Thirty Years War (1618–1648), caused long-lasting depopulation and economic decline in much of the Holy Roman Empire.

However, the wars also produced dramatic improvements in the skill of European armed forces and in their weaponry that arguably made them the most powerful in the world. The numbers of men in arms increased steadily throughout the early modern period. French forces, for example grew from about 150,000 in 1630 to 400,000 by the early eighteenth century. Even smaller European states built up impressive armies. Sweden, with under a million people, had one of the finest and best-armed military forces in seventeenth-century Europe. Though the country had fewer than 2 million inhabitants in 1700, Prussia's splendid army made it one of Europe's major powers.

Versailles, 1722 This painting by P.-D. Martin shows the east expanse of buildings and courtyards that make up the palace complex built by King Louis XIV. (Giraudon/Art Resource, NY)

Larger armies required more effective command structures. In the words of a modern historian, European armies "evolved . . . the equivalent of a central nervous system, capable of activating technologically differentiated claws and teeth."[3] New signaling techniques improved control of battlefield maneuvers. Frequent marching drills trained troops to obey orders instantly and gave them a close sense of comradeship. To defend themselves cities built new fortifications able to withstand cannon bombardments. Each state tried to outdo its rivals by improvements in military hardware, but battles between evenly matched armies often ended in stalemates that prolonged the wars. Victory increasingly depended on naval superiority.

Only England did not maintain a standing army in peacetime, but England's rise as a sea power had begun under King Henry VIII, who spent heavily on ships and promoted a domestic iron-smelting industry to supply cannon. The Royal Navy also copied innovative ship designs from the Dutch in the second half of the seventeenth century. By the early eighteenth century the Royal Navy surpassed the rival French fleet in numbers. By then, England had merged with Scotland to become Great Britain, annexed Ireland, and built a North American empire.

Although France was Europe's most powerful state, Louis XIV's efforts to expand its borders and dominance were increasingly frustrated by coalitions of the other great powers. In a series of eighteenth-century wars beginning with the War of the Spanish Succession (1701–1714), the combination of Britain's naval strength and the land armies of its Austrian and Prussian allies was able to block French expansionist efforts and prevent the Bourbons from uniting the thrones of France and Spain.

This defeat of the French monarchy's empire-building efforts illustrated the principle of **balance of power** in international relations: the major European states formed

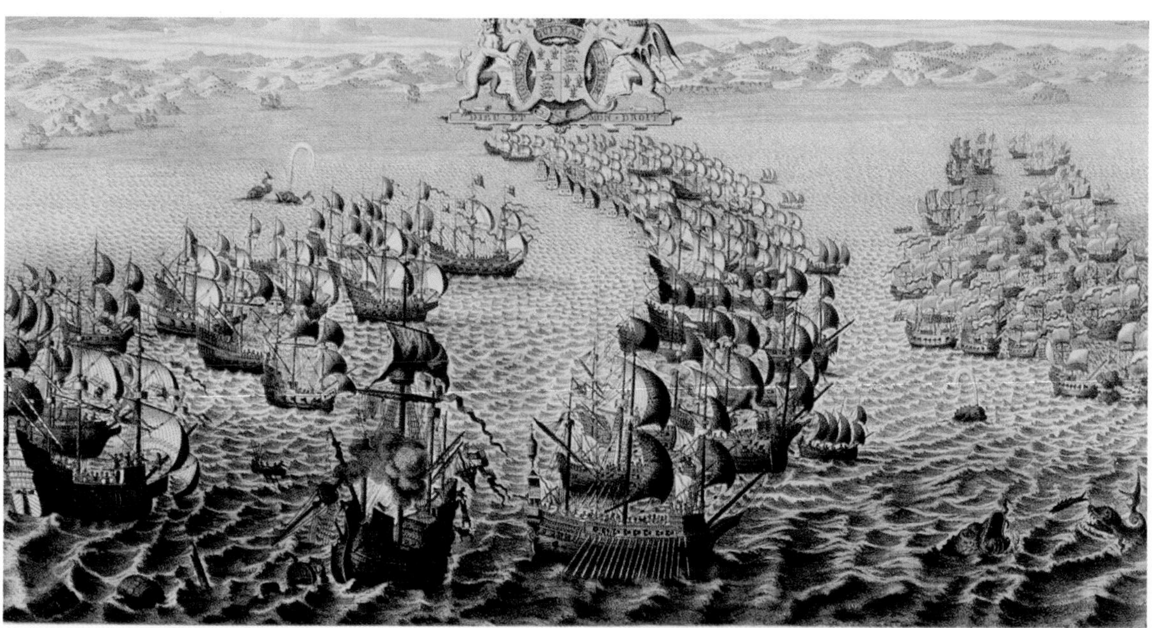

The Spanish Armada This drawing for a tapestry shows the great warships of the Spanish fleet lined up to face the smaller but faster vessels of the British navy. The ship with oars in the foreground is a galley. (Eileen Tweedy/The Art Archive)

temporary alliances to prevent any one state from becoming too powerful. Russia emerged as a major power in Europe after its modernized armies defeated Sweden in the Great Northern War (1700–1721). During the next two centuries, though adhering to four different branches of Christianity, the great powers of Europe—Catholic France, Anglican Britain, Catholic Austria, Lutheran Prussia, and Orthodox Russia (see Map 17.3)—maintained an effective balance of power in Europe by shifting their alliances for geopolitical rather than religious reasons. These pragmatic alliances were the first successful efforts at international peacekeeping.

Paying the Piper

To pay the extremely heavy military costs of their wars, European rulers had to increase their revenues. The most successful of them after 1600 promoted mutually beneficial alliances with the rising commercial elite. Both sides understood that trade thrived where government taxation and regulation were not excessive, where courts enforced contracts and collected debts, and where military power stood ready to protect overseas expansion by force when necessary.

Spain, sixteenth-century Europe's mightiest state, illustrates how the financial drains of an aggressive military policy and the failure to promote economic development could lead to decline. Expensive wars against the Ottomans, northern European Protestants, and rebellious Dutch subjects caused the treasury to default on its debts four times during the reign of King Philip II. Moreover, the Spanish rulers' concerns for religious uniformity and traditional aristocratic privilege further undermined the country's economy. In the name of religious uniformity they expelled Jewish merchants, persecuted Protestant dissenters, and forced tens of thousands of skilled farmers and artisans into exile because of their Muslim ancestry. In the name of aristocratic privilege the 3 percent of the population that controlled 97 percent of the land in 1600 was exempt from taxation, while high sales taxes discouraged manufacturing.

For a time, vast imports of silver and gold bullion from Spain's American colonies filled the government treasury. These bullion shipments also contributed to severe inflation (rising prices), worst in Spain but bad throughout the rest of western Europe as well. A Spanish saying captured the problem: American silver was like rain on the roof—it poured down and washed away. Huge debts for foreign wars drained bullion from Spain to its creditors. More wealth flowed out to purchase manufactured goods and even food in the seventeenth century.

The rise of the Netherlands as an economic power stemmed from opposite policies. The Spanish crown had acquired these resource-poor but commercially successful provinces as part of Charles V's inheritance. But King Philip II's decision to impose Spain's ruinously heavy

Map 17.3 Europe in 1740 By the middle of the eighteenth century the great powers of Europe were France, the Austrian Empire, Great Britain, Prussia, and Russia. Spain, the Holy Roman Empire, and the Ottoman Empire were far weaker in 1740 than they had been two centuries earlier.

sales tax and enforce Catholic orthodoxy drove the Dutch to revolt in 1566 and again in 1572. If successful, those measures would have discouraged business and driven away the Calvinists, Jews, and others who were essential to Dutch prosperity. The Dutch fought with skill and ingenuity, raising and training an army and a navy that were among the most effective in Europe. By 1609 Spain was forced to agree to a truce that recognized the autonomy of the northern part of the Netherlands. In 1648, after eight decades of warfare, the independence of these seven United Provinces of the Free Netherlands (their full name) became final.

Rather than being ruined by the long war, the United Netherlands emerged as the dominant commercial power in Europe and the world's greatest trading nation. During the seventeenth century, the wealth of the Netherlands multiplied. This economic success owed much to a decentralized government. During the long struggle against Spain, the provinces united around the prince of Orange, their sovereign, who served as commander-in-chief of the armed forces. But in economic matters each province was free to pursue its own interests. The maritime province of Holland grew rich by favoring commercial interests.

After 1650 the Dutch faced growing competition from the English, who were developing their own close association of business and government. In a series of wars (1652–1678) England used its naval might to break Dutch dominance in overseas trade and to extend its own colonial empire. With government support, the English merchant fleet doubled between 1660 and 1700, and foreign trade rose by 50 percent. As a result, state revenue from customs duties tripled. During the eighteenth century Britain's trading position strengthened still more.

The debts run up by the Anglo-Dutch Wars helped persuade the English monarchy to greatly enlarge the government's role in managing the economy. The outcome has been called a "financial revolution." The government increased revenues by taxing the formerly exempt landed estates of the aristocrats and by collecting taxes directly. Previously, private individuals known as tax farmers had advanced the government a fixed sum of money; in return they could keep whatever money they were able to collect from taxpayers. To secure cash quickly for warfare and other emergencies and to reduce the burden of debts from earlier wars, England also followed the Dutch lead in creating a central bank, from which the government was able to obtain long-term loans at low rates.

The French government was also developing its national economy, especially under Colbert. He streamlined tax collection, promoted French manufacturing and shipping by imposing taxes on foreign goods, and improved transportation within France itself. Yet the power of the wealthy aristocrats kept the French government from following England's lead in taxing wealthy landowners, collecting taxes directly, and securing low-cost loans. Nor did France succeed in managing its debt as efficiently as England. (The role of governments in promoting overseas trade is further discussed in Chapter 19.)

Conclusion

European historians have used the word *revolution* to describe many different changes taking place in Europe between 1500 and 1750. The expansion of trade has been called a commercial revolution, the reform of state spending a financial revolution, and the changes in weapons and warfare a military revolution. We have also encountered a scientific revolution and the religious revolution of the Reformation.

These important changes in government, economy, society, and thought were parts of a dynamic process that began in the later Middle Ages and led to even bigger industrial and political revolutions before the eighteenth century was over. Yet the years from 1500 to 1750 were not simply—perhaps not even primarily—an age of progress for Europe. For many, the ferocious competition of European armies, merchants, and ideas was a wrenching experience. The growth of powerful states extracted a terrible price in death, destruction, and misery. The Reformation brought greater individual choice in religion but widespread religious persecution as well. Individual women rose or fell with their social class, but few gained equality with men. The expanding economy benefited members of the emerging merchant elite and their political allies, but most Europeans became worse off as prices rose faster than wages. New scientific and enlightened ideas ignited new controversies long before they yielded any tangible benefits.

The historical significance of this period of European history is clearer when viewed in a global context. What stands out are the powerful and efficient European armies, economies, and governments, which larger states elsewhere in the world feared, envied, and sometimes imitated. From a global perspective, the balance of political and economic power was shifting slowly, but inexorably, in the Europeans' favor. In 1500 the Ottomans threatened Europe. By 1750, as the remaining chapters of Part Five detail, Europeans had brought the world's seas and a growing part of its land and people under their control. No single group of Europeans accomplished this. The Dutch eclipsed the pioneering Portuguese and Spanish; then the English and French bested the Dutch. Competition, too, was a factor in European success.

Other changes in Europe during this period had no great overseas significance at the time. The new ideas of the Scientific Revolution and the Enlightenment were still of minor importance. Their full effects in furthering Europeans' global dominion were felt after 1750, as Parts Six and Seven explore.

Key Terms

Renaissance (European)
papacy
indulgence
Protestant Reformation
Catholic Reformation
witch-hunt
Scientific Revolution
Enlightenment
bourgeoisie
joint-stock company
stock exchange
gentry
Little Ice Age
deforestation
Holy Roman Empire
Habsburg
English Civil War
Versailles
balance of power

Suggested Reading

Overviews of this period include Euan Cameron, ed., *Early Modern Europe* (1999); H. G. Koenigsberger, *Early Modern Europe: Fifteen Hundred to Seventeen Eighty-Nine* (1987); and Joseph Bergin, *The Short Oxford History of Europe: The Seventeenth Century* (2001). Global perspectives can be found in Fernand Braudel, *Civilization and Capitalism, 15th–18th Century*, trans. Siân Reynolds, 3 vols. (1979), and Immanuel Wallerstein, *The Modern World-System*, vol. 2, *Mercantilism and the Consolidation of the European World-Economy, 1600–1750* (1980).

Technological and environmental changes are the focus of Geoffrey Parker, *Military Revolution: Military Innovation and the Rise of the West, 1500–1800*, 2d ed. (1996); William H. McNeill, *The Pursuit of Power: Technology, Armed Force, and Society Since A.D. 1000* (1982); Robert Greenhalgh Albion, *Forests and Sea Power: The Timber Problem of the Royal Navy, 1652–1862* (1965); Emmanuel Le Roy Ladurie, *Times of Feast, Times of Famine: A History of Climate Since the Year 1000*, trans. Barbara Bray (1971); and Brian Fagan, *The Little Ice Age: How Climate Made History, 1300–1850* (1988). Robert C. Allen, *Enclosure and the Yeoman: The Agricultural Development of the South Midlands, 1450–1850* (1992), focuses on England.

Steven Stapin, *The Scientific Revolution* (1998), and Hugh Kearney, *Science and Change, 1500–1700* (1971) are accessible introductions. Thomas S. Kuhn, *The Structure of Scientific Revolution*, 3d ed. (1996), and A. R. Hall, *The Scientific Revolution, 1500–1800: The Formation of the Modern Scientific Attitude*, 2d ed. (1962), are classic studies. Carolyn Merchant, *The Death of Nature: Women, Ecology and the Scientific Revolution* (1980), tries to combine several broad perspectives. *The Sciences in Enlightened Europe*, ed. W. Clark, J. Golinski, and S. Schaffer (1999), examines particular topics in a sophisticated way. Dorinda Outram, *The Enlightenment* (1995), provides a recent summary of research.

Excellent introductions to social and economic life are George Huppert, *After the Black Death: A Social History of Early Modern Europe* (1986), and Carlo M. Cipolla, *Before the Industrial Revolution: European Society and Economy, 1000–1700*, 2d ed. (1980). Peter Burke, *Popular Culture in Early Modern Europe* (1978), offers a broad treatment of nonelite perspectives, as does Robert Jütte, *Poverty and Deviance in Early Modern Europe* (1994). For more economic detail see Robert S. DuPlessis, *Transitions to Capitalism in Early Modern Europe* (1997); Myron P. Gutmann, *Toward the Modern Economy: Early Industry in Europe, 1500–1800* (1988); and Carlo M. Cipolla, ed., *The Fontana Economic History of Europe*, vol. 2, *The Sixteenth and Seventeenth Centuries* (1974).

Topics of women's history are examined by Merry Wiesner, *Women and Gender in Early Modern Europe*, 2d ed. (2000); Bonie S. Anderson and Judith Zinsser, *A History of Their Own: Women in Europe*, vol. II, rev. ed. (2000); and Monica Chojnacka and Merry E. Wiesner-Hanks, *Ages of Woman, Ages of Man* (2002). An excellent place to begin examining the complex subject of witchcraft is Brian Levack, *The Witch-Hunt in Early Modern Europe*, 2d ed. (1995); other up-to-date perspectives can be found in J. Barry, M. Hester, and G. Roberts, eds., *Witchcraft in Early Modern Europe: Studies in Culture and Belief* (1998), and Carlo Ginzburg, *The Night Battles: Witchcraft and Agrarian Cults in the Sixteenth and Seventeenth Centuries*, trans. John and Anne Tedechi (1983).

Good single-country surveys are J. A. Sharpe, *Early Modern England: A Social History*, 2d ed. (1997); Emmanuel Le Roy Ladurie, *The Royal French State, 1460–1610* (1994), and *The Ancien Régime: A History of France, 1610–1774* (1998); Jonathan Israel, *The Dutch Republic: Its Rise, Greatness and Fall, 1477–1806* (1995); and James Casey, *Early Modern Spain: A Social History* (1999).

Notes

1. Quoted by Carlo M. Cipolla, "Introduction," *The Fontana Economic History of Europe*, vol. 2, *The Sixteenth and Seventeenth Centuries* (Glasgow: Collins/Fontana Books, 1974), 11–12.
2. Michel de Montaigne, *Essais* (1588), ch. 31, "Des Cannibales."
3. William H. McNeill, *The Pursuit of Power: Technology, Armed Force, and Society Since A.D. 1000* (Chicago: University of Chicago Press, 1982), 124.

CHRONOLOGY

	Spanish America	Brazil	British America	French America
1500	**1518** Smallpox arrives in Caribbean **1535** Creation of Viceroyalty of New Spain **1540s** Creation of Viceroyalty of Peru **1542** New Laws attempt to improve treatment of Amerindians **1545** Silver discovered at Potosí, Bolivia	**1540–1600** Era of Amerindian slavery **After 1540** Sugar begins to dominate the economy	**1583** Unsuccessful effort to establish colony on Newfoundland	**1524–1554** Jacques Cartier's voyages to explore Newfoundland and Gulf of St. Lawrence
1600	**1625** Population of Potosí reaches 120,000	**By 1620** African slave trade provides majority of plantation workers	**1607** Jamestown founded **1620** Plymouth founded **1660** Slave population in Virginia begins period of rapid growth **1664** English take New York from Dutch	**1608** Quebec founded **1699** Louisiana founded
1700	**1700** Last Habsburg ruler of Spain dies **1713** First Bourbon ruler of Spain crowned **1770s and 1780s** Amerindian revolts in Andean region	**1750–1777** Reforms of marquis de Pombal	**1754–1763** French and Indian War	**1760** English take Canada

plants, animals, and related technologies. As a result, the colonies of Spain, Portugal, England, and France became vast arenas of cultural and social experimentation.

Demographic Changes

Because of their long isolation from other continents (see Chapter 16), the peoples of the New World lacked immunity to diseases introduced from the Old World. As a result, death rates among Amerindian peoples during the epidemics of the early colonial period were very high. The lack of reliable data has frustrated efforts to measure the deadly impact of these diseases. Scholars disagree about the size of the precontact population but generally agree that, after contact, Old World diseases overwhelmed native populations. According to one estimate, in the century that followed the triumph of Hernán Cortés in 1521, the indigenous population of central Mexico fell from a high somewhere between 13 million and 25 million to approximately 700,000. In this same period nearly 75 percent of the Maya population disappeared. In the region of the Inca Empire, population fell from about 9 million to approximately 600,000. Brazil's native population was similarly ravaged, falling from 2.5 million to under a million within a century of the arrival of the Portuguese. The most conservative estimates of population loss begin with smaller precontact populations but accept that epidemics had a catastrophic effect.

Smallpox, which arrived in the Caribbean in 1518, was the most deadly of the early epidemics. In Mexico and Central America, 50 percent or more of the Amerindian population died during the first wave of smallpox epidemics. The disease then spread to South America with equally devastating effects. Measles arrived in the New World in the 1530s and was followed by diphtheria, typhus, influenza, and, perhaps, pulmonary plague. Mortality was often greatest when two or more diseases struck at the same time. Between 1520 and 1521 influenza, in combination with other ailments, attacked the Cakchiquel of Guatemala. Their chronicle recalls:

> Great was the stench of the dead. After our fathers and grandfathers succumbed, half the people fled to the fields. The dogs and vultures devoured the bodies. . . . So it was that we became orphans, oh my sons! . . . We were born to die![1]

By the mid-seventeenth century malaria and yellow fever were also present in tropical regions. The deadliest form of malaria arrived with the African slave trade. It ravaged the already reduced native populations and afflicted European immigrants as well. Most scholars believe that yellow fever was also brought from Africa, but new research suggests that the disease was present before the conquest in the tropical low country near present-day Veracruz on the Gulf of Mexico. Whatever its origins, yellow fever killed Europeans in the Caribbean Basin and in other tropical regions nearly as efficiently as smallpox had earlier extinguished Amerindians.

The development of English and French colonies in North America in the seventeenth century led to similar patterns of contagion and mortality. In 1616 and 1617 epidemics nearly exterminated many of New England's indigenous groups. French fur traders transmitted measles, smallpox, and other diseases as far as Hudson Bay and the Great Lakes. Although there is very little evidence that Europeans consciously used disease as a tool of empire, the deadly results of contact clearly undermined the ability of native peoples to resist settlement.

The Columbian Exchange After the conquest, the introduction of plants and animals from the Old World dramatically altered the American environment. Here an Amerindian woman is seen milking a cow. Livestock sometimes destroyed the fields of native peoples, but cattle, sheep, pigs, and goats also provided food, leather, and wool. (From Martinez Compañon, Trujillo del Perú, V.II, E 79. Photo: Imaging services, Harvard College Library)

Transfer of Plants and Animals

Even as epidemics swept through the indigenous population, the New and the Old Worlds were participating in a vast exchange of plants and animals that radically altered diet and lifestyles in both regions. All the staples of southern European agriculture—such as wheat, olives, grapes, and garden vegetables—were being grown in the Americas in a remarkably short time after contact. African and Asian crops—such as rice, bananas, coconuts, breadfruit, and sugar cane—were soon introduced as well. Native peoples remained loyal to their traditional staples but added many Old World plants to their diet. Citrus fruits, melons, figs, and sugar as well as onions, radishes, and salad greens all found a place in Amerindian cuisines.

In return the Americas offered the Old World an abundance of useful plants. The New World staples—maize, potatoes, and manioc—revolutionized agriculture and diet in parts of Europe, Africa, and Asia (see Environment and Technology: Amerindian Foods in Africa, in Chapter 19). Many experts assert that the rapid growth of world population after 1700 resulted in large measure from the spread of these useful crops, which provided more calories per acre than did any Old World staples other than rice. Beans, squash, tomatoes, sweet potatoes, peanuts, chilies, and chocolate also gained widespread acceptance in the Old World. In addition, the New World provided the Old with plants that provided dyes, medicinal plants, varieties of cotton, and tobacco.

The introduction of European livestock had a dramatic impact on New World environments and cultures. Faced with few natural predators, cattle, pigs, horses, and sheep, as well as pests like rats and rabbits, multiplied rapidly in the open spaces of the Americas. On the vast plains of present-day southern Brazil, Uruguay, and Argentina, herds of wild cattle and horses exceeded 50 million by 1700. Large herds of both animals also appeared in northern Mexico and what became the southwest of the United States.

Where Old World livestock spread most rapidly, environmental changes were most dramatic. Many priests and colonial officials noted the destructive impact of marauding livestock on Amerindian agriculturists. The first viceroy of Mexico, Antonio de Mendoza, wrote to the Spanish king: "May your Lordship realize that if cattle are allowed, the Indians will be destroyed." Sheep, which grazed grasses close to the ground, were also an environmental threat. Yet the viceroy's stark choice misrepresented the complex response of indigenous peoples to these new animals.

Wild cattle on the plains of South America, northern Mexico, and Texas provided indigenous peoples with abundant supplies of meat and hides. In the present-day southwestern United States, the Navajo became sheepherders and expert weavers of woolen cloth. Even in the centers of European settlement, individual Amerindians turned European animals to their own advantage by becoming muleteers, cowboys, and sheepherders.

No animal had a more striking effect on the cultures of native peoples than the horse, which increased the efficiency of hunters and the military capacity of warriors on the plains. The horse permitted the Apache, Sioux, Blackfoot, Comanche, Assiniboine, and others to more efficiently hunt the vast herds of buffalo in North America. The horse also revolutionized the cultures of the Araucanian (or Mapuche) and Pampas peoples in South America.

Spanish America and Brazil

The frontiers of conquest and settlement expanded rapidly. Within one hundred years of Columbus's first voyage to the Western Hemisphere, the Spanish Empire in America included most of the islands of the Caribbean, Mexico, the American southwest, Central America, the Caribbean and Pacific coasts of South America, the Andean highlands, and the vast plains of the Rio de la Plata region (a region that includes the modern nations of Argentina, Uruguay, and Paraguay). Portuguese settlement in the New World developed more slowly. But before the end of the sixteenth century, Portugal occupied most of the Brazilian coast.

Early settlers from Spain and Portugal sought to create colonial societies based on the institutions and customs of their homelands. They viewed society as a vertical hierarchy of estates (classes of society), as uniformly Catholic, and as an arrangement of patriarchal extended-family networks. They quickly moved to establish the religious, social, and administrative institutions that were familiar to them.

Despite the imposition of foreign institutions and the massive loss of life caused by epidemics in the sixteenth century, indigenous peoples exercised a powerful influence on the development of colonial societies. Aztec and Inca elite families sought to protect their traditional privileges and rights through marriage or less formal alliances with the Spanish settlers. They also often used colonial courts to defend their claims to land. In Spanish and Portuguese colonies, indigenous military allies and laborers proved crucial to the development of European settlements. Nearly everywhere, Amerindian religious beliefs and practices survived beneath the surface of an imposed Christianity. Amerindian languages, cuisines, medical practices, and agricultural techniques also survived the conquest and influenced the development of Latin American culture.

The African slave trade added a third cultural stream to colonial Latin American society. At first, African slaves were concentrated in plantation regions of Brazil and the Caribbean (see Chapter 19), but by the end of the colonial era, Africans and their descendants were living throughout Latin America, enriching colonial societies with their traditional agricultural practices, music, religious beliefs, cuisine, and social customs.

State and Church

The Spanish crown moved quickly to curb the independent power of the conquistadors and to establish royal authority over both the defeated native populations and the rising tide of European settlers. Created in 1524, the **Council of the Indies** in Spain supervised all government, ecclesiastical, and commercial activity in the Spanish colonies. Geography and technology, however, limited the Council's real power. Local officials could not be controlled too closely, because a ship needed more than two hundred days to make a roundtrip voyage from Spain to Veracruz,

Saint Martín de Porres (1579–1639) Martín de Porres was the illegitimate son of a Spanish nobleman and his black servant. Eventually recognized by his father, he entered the Dominican Order in Lima, Peru. Known for his generosity, he experienced visions and gained the ability to heal the sick. As was common in colonial religious art, the artist celebrates Martín de Porres's spirituality while representing him doing the type of work assumed most suitable for a person of mixed descent. (Private Collection)

Mexico, and additional months of travel were required to reach Lima, Peru.

The highest-ranking Spanish officials in the colonies, the viceroys of New Spain and Peru, enjoyed broad power because of their distance from Spain. But the two viceroyalties in their jurisdiction were also vast territories with geographic obstacles to communication. Created in 1535, the Viceroyalty of New Spain, with its capital in Mexico City, included Mexico, the southwest of what is now the United States, Central America, and the islands of the Caribbean. The Viceroyalty of Peru, with its capital in Lima, was formed in the 1540s to govern Spanish South America (see Map 18.1). Each viceroyalty was divided into a number of judicial and administrative districts. Until the seventeenth century, almost all of the officials appointed to high positions in Spain's colonial bureaucracy were born in Spain. Eventually, economic mismanagement in Spain forced the Crown to sell appointments to these positions; as a result, local-born members of the colonial elite gained many offices.

In the sixteenth century Portugal concentrated its resources and energies on Asia and Africa. Because early settlers found neither mineral wealth nor rich native empires in Brazil, the Portuguese king hesitated to set up expensive mechanisms of colonial government in the New World. Seeking to promote settlement but limit costs, the king in effect sublet administrative responsibilities in Brazil to court favorites by granting twelve hereditary captaincies in the 1530s. After mismanagement and inadequate investment doomed this experiment, the king appointed a governor-general in 1549 and made Salvador, in the northern province of Bahia, Brazil's capital. In 1720 the first viceroy of Brazil was named.

The government institutions of the Spanish and Portuguese colonies had a more uniform character and were much more extensive and costly than those later established in North America by France and Great Britain. Taxes paid in Spanish America by the silver and gold mines and in Brazil by the sugar plantations and, after 1690, gold mines funded large and intrusive colonial bureaucracies. These institutions made the colonies more responsive to the initiatives of Spain and Portugal, but they also thwarted local economic initiative and political experimentation.

In both Spanish America and Brazil the Catholic Church became the primary agent for the introduction and transmission of Christian belief as well as European language and culture. It undertook the conversion of Amerindians, ministered to the spiritual needs of European settlers, and promoted intellectual life through the introduction of the printing press and formal education.

Spain and Portugal justified their American conquests by assuming an obligation to convert native populations to Christianity. This religious objective was sometimes forgotten, and some members of the clergy were themselves exploiters of native populations. Nevertheless, the effort to convert America's native peoples expanded Christianity on a scale similar to its earlier expansion in Europe at the time of Constantine in the fourth century. In New Spain alone hundreds of thousands of conversions and baptisms were achieved within a few years of the conquest.

The Catholic clergy sought to achieve their evangelical ends by first converting members of the Amerindian elites, in the hope that they could persuade others to fol-

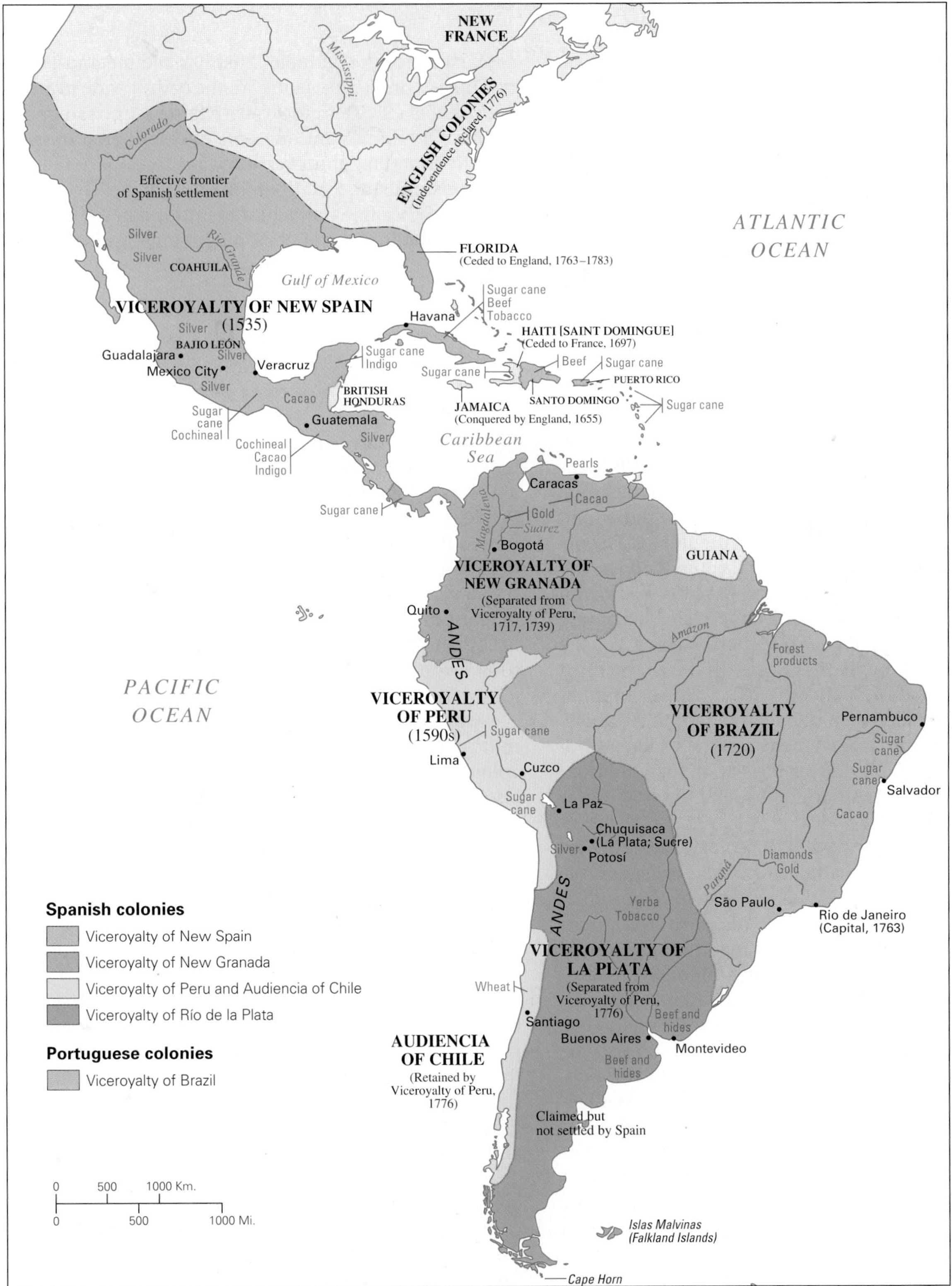

Map 18.1 Colonial Latin America in the Eighteenth Century Spain and Portugal controlled most of the Western Hemisphere in the eighteenth century. In the sixteenth century they had created new administrative jurisdictions—viceroyalties—to defend their respective colonies against European rivals. Taxes assessed on colonial products helped pay for this extension of governmental authority.

low their example. Franciscan missionaries in Mexico hoped to train members of the indigenous elite for the clergy. These idealistic efforts had to be abandoned when church authorities discovered that many converts were secretly observing old beliefs and rituals. The trial and punishment of two converted Aztec nobles for heresy in the 1530s highlighted this problem. Three decades later, Spanish clergy resorted to torture, executions, and the destruction of native manuscripts to eradicate traditional beliefs and rituals among the Maya. Repelled by these events, the church hierarchy ended both the violent repression of native religious practice and efforts to recruit an Amerindian clergy.

Despite its failures, the Catholic clergy did provide native peoples with some protections against the abuse and exploitation of Spanish settlers. The priest **Bartolomé de Las Casas** (1474–1566) was the most influential defender of the Amerindians in the early colonial period. He arrived in Hispaniola in 1502 as a settler and initially lived off the forced labor of Amerindians. Deeply moved by the deaths of so many Amerindians and by the misdeeds of the Spanish, Las Casas gave up this way of life and entered the Dominican Order, later becoming the first bishop of Chiapas, in southern Mexico. For the remainder of his long life Las Casas served as the most important advocate for native peoples, writing a number of books that detailed their mistreatment by the Spanish. His most important achievement was the enactment of the New Laws of 1542—reform legislation that outlawed the enslavement of Amerindians and limited other forms of forced labor.

European clergy arrived in the colonies with the intention of transmitting Catholic Christian belief and ritual without alteration. But the large size of Amerindian populations and their geographic dispersal over a vast landscape thwarted this objective. Linguistic and cultural differences among native peoples also inhibited missionary efforts. These problems frustrated Catholic missionaries and sometimes led to repression and cruelty. The limited success of evangelization permitted the appearance of what must be seen as an Amerindian Christianity that blended Catholic Christian beliefs with important elements of traditional native cosmology and ritual. Most commonly, indigenous beliefs and rituals came to be embedded in the celebration of saints' days or Catholic rituals associated with the Virgin Mary. The Catholic clergy and most European settlers viewed this evolving mixture as the work of the Devil or as evidence of Amerindian inferiority. Instead, it was one component of the process of cultural borrowing and innovation that contributed to a distinct and original Latin American culture.

After 1600 the terrible loss of Amerindian population caused by epidemics and growing signs of resistance to conversion led the Catholic Church to redirect most of its resources from native regions in the countryside to growing colonial cities and towns with large European populations. One important outcome of this altered mission was the founding of universities and secondary schools and the stimulation of urban intellectual life. Over time, the church became the richest institution in the Spanish colonies, controlling ranches, plantations, and vineyards as well as serving as the society's banker.

Colonial Economies

The silver mines of Peru and Mexico and the sugar plantations of Brazil dominated the economic development of colonial Latin America. The mineral wealth of the New World fueled the early development of European capitalism and funded Europe's greatly expanded trade with Asia. Profits produced in these economic centers also promoted the growth of colonial cities, concentrated scarce investment capital and labor resources, and stimulated the development of livestock raising and agriculture in neighboring rural areas (see Map 18.1). Once established, this colonial dependence on mineral and agricultural exports left an enduring social and economic legacy in Latin America.

Gold worth millions of pesos was extracted from mines in Latin America, but silver mines in the Spanish colonies generated the most wealth and therefore exercised the greatest economic influence. The first important silver strikes occurred in Mexico in the 1530s and 1540s. In 1545 the single richest silver deposit in the Americas was discovered at **Potosí°**, in what is now Bolivia, and until 1680 the silver production of Bolivia and Peru dominated the Spanish colonial economy. After this date Mexican silver production greatly surpassed that of the Andean region.

A large labor force was needed to mine silver. The metal was extracted from deep shafts, and the refining process was complex. Silver mines supported farming, livestock raising, and even textile production, which in turn promoted urbanization and the elaboration of regional commercial relations. Silver mining also greatly altered the environment.

At first, silver was extracted from ore by smelting: the ore was crushed in giant stamping mills, then packed with charcoal in a furnace and fired. Within a short time, the wasteful use of forest resources for fuel destroyed forests near the mining centers. Faced with rising fuel costs, Mexican miners developed an efficient method of chemical extraction that relied on mixing mercury with

Potosí (poh-toh-SEE)

ENVIRONMENT + TECHNOLOGY

A Silver Refinery at Potosí, Bolivia, 1700

The silver refineries of Spanish America were among the largest and most heavily capitalized industrial enterprises in the Western Hemisphere during the colonial period. By the middle of the seventeenth century the mines of Potosí, Bolivia, had attracted a population of more than 120,000.

The accompanying illustration shows a typical refinery (ingenio). Aqueducts carried water from large reservoirs on nearby mountainsides to the refineries. The water wheel shown on the right drove two sets of vertical stamps that crushed ore. Each iron-shod stamp was about the size and weight of a telephone pole. Crushed ore was sorted, dried, and mixed with mercury and other catalysts to extract the silver. The amalgam was then separated by a combination of washing and heating. The end result was a nearly pure ingot of silver that was later assayed and taxed at the mint.

Silver production carried a high environmental cost. Forests were cut to provide fuel and the timbers needed to shore up mine shafts and construct stamping mills and other machinery. Unwanted base metals produced in the refining process poisoned the soil. In addition, the need for tens of thousands of horses, mules, and oxen to drive machinery and transport material led to overgrazing and widespread erosion.

A Bolivian Silver Refinery, 1700 The silver refineries of Spanish America were among the largest industrial establishments in the Western Hemisphere. (From *In Quest of Mineral Wealth: Aboriginal and Colonial Mining and Metallurgy in Spanish America*, edited by Alan K. Craig and Robert C. West, 1994. Vol. 33 of *Geoscience and Man.* Courtesy, Geoscience Publications)

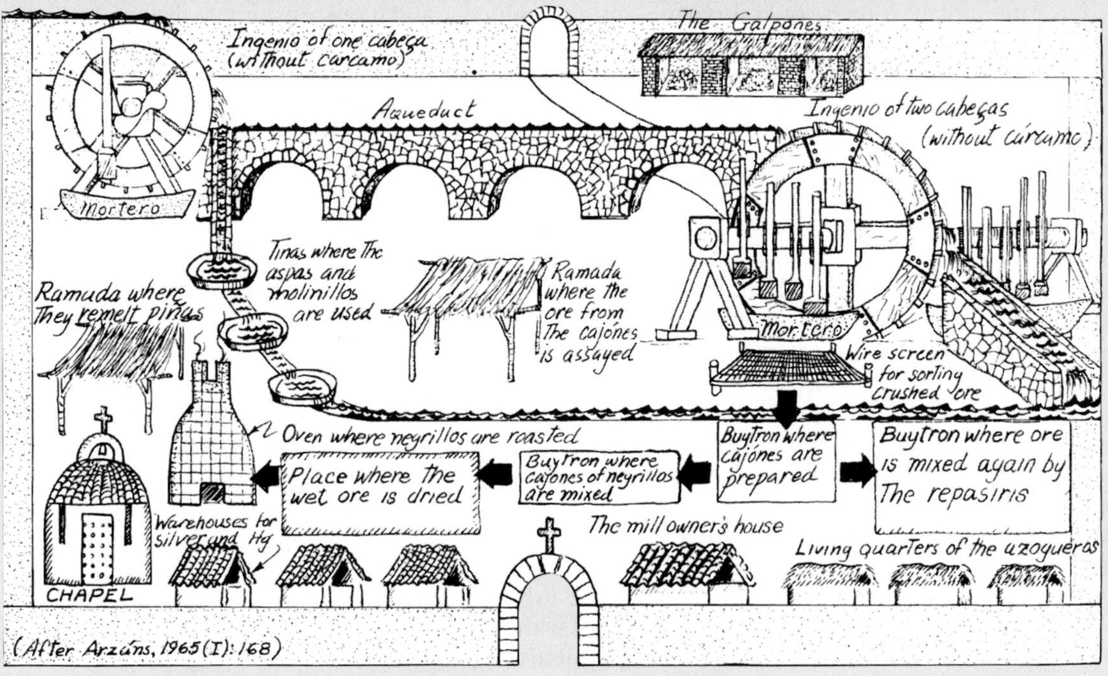

the silver ore (see Environment and Technology: The Silver Refinery at Potosí, Bolivia, 1700). Silver yields and profits increased with the use of mercury amalgamation, but this process, too, had severe environmental costs. Mercury was a poison, and its use contaminated the environment and sickened the Amerindian work force.

From the time of Columbus, indigenous populations had been compelled to provide labor for European settlers in the Americas. Until the 1540s in Spanish colonies, Amerindian peoples were divided among the settlers and were forced to provide them with labor or with textiles, food, or other goods. This form of forced labor was called the **encomienda**°. As epidemics and mistreatment led to the decline in Amerindian population, reforms such as the New Laws sought to eliminate the encomienda. The discovery of silver in both Peru and Mexico, however, led to new forms of compulsory labor. In the mining region of Mexico, Amerindian populations had been greatly reduced by epidemic diseases. Therefore, from early in the colonial period, Mexican silver miners relied on free-wage laborers. Peru's Amerindian population survived in larger numbers, allowing the Spanish to impose a form of labor called the mita°. Under this system, one-seventh of adult male Amerindians were compelled to work for six months each year in mines, farms, or textile factories. The most dangerous working conditions existed in the silver mines, where workers were forced to carry heavy bags of ore up fragile ladders to the surface.

This colonial institution was a corrupted version of the Inca-era mit'a, which had been both a labor tax that supported elites and a reciprocal labor obligation that allowed kin groups to produce surpluses of essential goods that provided for the elderly and incapacitated. In the Spanish mita, few Amerindian workers could survive on their wages. Wives and children were commonly forced to join the work force to help meet expenses. Even those who remained behind in the village were forced to send food and cash to support mita workers.

As the Amerindian population fell with each new epidemic, some of Peru's villages were forced to shorten the period between mita obligations. Instead of serving every seven years, many men were forced to return to mines after only a year or two. Unwilling to accept mita service and the other tax burdens imposed on Amerindian villages, large numbers of Amerindians abandoned traditional agriculture and moved permanently to Spanish mines and farms as wage laborers. The long-term result of these individual decisions weakened Amerindian village life and promoted the assimilation of Amerindians into Spanish-speaking Catholic colonial society.

Before the settlement of Brazil, the Portuguese had already developed sugar plantations that depended on slave labor on the Atlantic islands of Madeira, the Azores, the Cape Verdes, and São Tomé. Because of the success of these early experiences, they were able to quickly transfer this profitable form of agriculture to Brazil. After 1550 sugar production expanded rapidly in the northern provinces of Pernambuco and Bahia. By the seventeenth century, sugar dominated the Brazilian economy.

The sugar plantations of colonial Brazil always depended on slave labor. At first the Portuguese sugar planters enslaved Amerindians captured in war or seized from their villages. They used Amerindian men as field hands, although in this indigenous culture women had primary responsibility for agriculture. Any effort to resist or flee led to harsh punishments. Thousands of Amerindian slaves died during the epidemics that raged across Brazil in the sixteenth and seventeenth centuries. This terrible loss of Amerindian life and the rising profits of the sugar planters led to the development of an internal slave trade dominated by settlers from the southern region of São Paulo. To supply the rising labor needs of the sugar plantations of the northeast, slave raiders pushed into the interior, even attacking Amerindian populations in neighboring Spanish colonies. Many of the most prominent slavers were the sons of Portuguese fathers and Amerindian mothers.

Amerindian slaves remained an important source of labor and slave raiding a significant business in frontier regions into the eighteenth century. But sugar planters eventually came to rely more on African than Amerindian slaves. Although African slaves at first cost much more than Amerindian slaves, planters found them to be more productive and more resistant to disease. As profits from the plantations increased, imports of African slaves rose from an average of two thousand per year in the late sixteenth century to approximately seven thousand per year a century later, outstripping the immigration of free Portuguese settlers. Between 1650 and 1750, for example, more than three African slaves arrived in Brazil for every free immigrant from Europe.

Within Spanish America, the mining centers of Mexico and Peru eventually exercised global economic influence. American silver increased the European money supply, promoting commercial expansion and, later, industrialization. Large amounts of silver also flowed across the Pacific to the Spanish colony of the Philippines, where it was exchanged for Asian spices, silks, and pottery. Spain tried to limit this trade, but the desire for Asian goods in the colonies was so strong that there was large-scale trade in contraband goods.

The rich mines of Peru, Bolivia, and Mexico stimulated urban population growth as well as commercial links with distant agricultural and textile producers. The population of the city of Potosí, high in the Andes, reached 120,000 inhabitants by 1625. This rich mining town became the center of a vast regional market that depended on Chilean wheat, Argentine livestock, and Ecuadorian textiles.

The sugar plantations of Brazil played a similar role in integrating the economy of the south Atlantic region. The ports of Salvador and Rio de Janeiro in Brazil exchanged sugar, tobacco, and reexported slaves from

---

encomienda (in-co-mee-EN-dah) **mita** (MEE-tah)

Brazilian Sugar Plantation Sugar was the most important agricultural product exported from Europe's Western Hemisphere colonies. The African slave trade was developed in large measure to supply the labor needs of sugar plantations and refineries in the Americas. Brazil's economy was dominated by sugar and slavery in the colonial period. In this illustration slaves unload sugar cane from a cart before crushing it in the horizontal mill to extract the juice to process into molasses and sugar. (From Johann Mority Rugendas, Viagem Pitoresca Atraves di Brasil (São Paolo: Livraria Martins Editora, 1954). Harvard College Library Imaging Services)

Brazil for yerba (Paraguayan tea), hides, livestock, and silver produced in neighboring Spanish colonies. Portugal's increasing openness to British trade also allowed Brazil to become a conduit for an illegal trade between Spanish colonies and Europe. At the end of the seventeenth century the discovery of gold in Brazil helped overcome this large region's currency shortage and promoted further economic integration.

Both Spain and Portugal attempted to control the trade of their American colonies. Spain's efforts were more ambitious, granting first Seville and then Cádiz monopoly trade rights. Similar monopoly privileges were then awarded to the merchant guilds of Lima, Peru, and Mexico City. Because ships returning to Spain with silver and gold were often attacked by foreign naval forces and pirates, Spain came to rely on convoys escorted by warships to supply the colonies and return with silver and gold. By 1650 Portugal had instituted a similar system of monopoly trade and fleets. The combination of monopoly commerce and convoy systems protected shipping and facilitated the collection of taxes, but these measures also slowed the flow of European goods to the colonies and kept prices high. Frustrated by these restraints, colonial populations established illegal commercial relations with the English, French, and Dutch. By the middle of the seventeenth century a majority of European imports were arriving in Latin America illegally.

Society in Colonial Latin America

With the exception of some early viceroys, few members of Spain's great noble families came to the New World. *Hidalgos*°—lesser nobles—were well represented, as were Spanish merchants, artisans, miners, priests, and lawyers. Small numbers of criminals, beggars, and prostitutes also found their way to the colonies. This flow of immigrants from Spain was never large, and Spanish settlers were always a tiny minority in a colonial society numerically dominated by Amerindians and rapidly growing populations of Africans, **creoles** (whites born in America to European parents), and people of mixed ancestry (see Diversity and Dominance: Race and Ethnicity in the Spanish Colonies: Negotiating Hierarchy).

Conquistadors and early settlers who received from the Crown grants of labor and tribute goods (encomienda) from Amerindian communities as rewards for service to Spain dominated colonial society in early Spanish America. These encomenderos sought to create a hereditary social and political class comparable to the nobles of Europe. But their systematic abuse of Amerindian communities and the catastrophic loss of Amerindian life during the epidemics of the sixteenth century undermined their position. They also confronted the

hidalgos (ee-DAHL-goes)

Diversity and Dominance

Race and Ethnicity in the Spanish Colonies: Negotiating Hierarchy

Many European visitors to colonial Latin America were interested in the mixing of Europeans, Amerindians, and Africans in the colonies. Many also commented on the treatment of slaves. The passages that follow allow us to examine two colonial societies.

The first selection was written by two young Spanish naval officers and scientists, Jorge Juan and Antonio de Ulloa, who arrived in the colonies in 1735 as members of a scientific expedition. They visited the major cities of the Pacific coast of South America and traveled across some of the most difficult terrain in the hemisphere. In addition to their scientific chores, they described architecture, local customs, and the social order. In this section they describe the ethnic mix in Quito, now the capital of Ecuador.

The second selection was published in Lima under the pseudonym Concolorcorvo around 1776. We now know that the author was Alonso Carrío de la Vandera. Born in Spain, he traveled to the colonies as a young man. He served in many minor bureaucratic positions, one of which was the inspection of the postal route between Buenos Aires and Lima. Carrío turned his long and often uncomfortable trip into an insightful, and sometimes highly critical, examination of colonial society. The selection that follows describes Córdoba, Argentina.

Juan and Ulloa and Carrío seem perplexed by colonial efforts to create and enforce a racial taxonomy that stipulated and named every possible mixture of European, Amerindian, and African, noting the vanity and social presumptions of the dominant white population. We are fortunate to have these contemporary descriptions of the diversity of colonial society, but it is important to remember that these authors were clearly rooted in their time and confident in the superiority of Europe. Although they noted many of the abuses of Amerindian, mixed, and African populations while puncturing the pretensions of the colonial elites, they were also quick to assume the inferiority of the nonwhite population.

QUITO

This city is very populous, and has, among its inhabitants, some families of high rank and distinction; though their number is but small considering its extent, the poorer class bearing here too great a proportion. The former are the descendants either of the original conquerors, or of presidents, auditors, or other persons of character [high rank], who at different times came over from Spain invested with some lucrative post, and have still preserved their luster, both of wealth and descent, by intermarriages, without intermixing with meaner families though famous for their riches. The commonalty may be divided into four classes; Spaniards or Whites, Mestizos, Indians or Natives, and Negroes, with their progeny. These last are not proportionally so numerous as in the other parts of the Indies; occasioned by it being something inconvenient to bring Negroes to Quito, and the different kinds of agriculture being generally performed by Indians.

The name of Spaniard here has a different meaning from that of Chapitone [sic] or European, as properly signifying a person descended from a Spaniard without a mixture of blood. Many Mestizos, from the advantage of a fresh complexion, appear to be Spaniards more than those who are so in reality; and from only this fortuitous advantage are accounted as such. The Whites, according to this construction of the word, may be considered as one sixth part of the inhabitants.

The Mestizos are the descendants of Spaniards and Indians, and are to be considered here in the same different degrees between the Negroes and Whites, as before at Carthagena [sic]; but with this difference, that at Quito the degrees of Mestizos are not carried so far back; for, even in the second or third generations, when they acquire the European color, they are considered as Spaniards. The complexion of the Mestizos is swarthy and reddish, but not of that red common in the fair Mulattos. This is the first degree, or the immediate issue of a Spaniard and Indian. Some are, however, equally tawny with the Indians themselves, though they are distinguished from them by their beards: while others, on the contrary, have so fine a complexion that they might pass for Whites, were it not for some signs which betray them, when viewed attentively. Among these, the most remarkable is the lowness of the forehead, which often leaves but a small space between their hair and eye-brows; at the same time the hair grows remarkably forward on the temples, extending to the lower part of the ear. Besides, the hair itself is harsh, lank, coarse, and very black; their nose very small, thin, and has a little rising on the middle, from whence it forms a small curve, terminating in a point, bending towards the upper lip. These marks, besides some dark spots on the body, are so constant and invariable, as to make it very difficult to conceal the fallacy of their complexion. The Mestizos may be reckoned a third part of the inhabitants.

The next class is the Indians, who form about another third; and the others, who are about one sixth, are the Castes [mixed]. These four classes, according to the most authentic accounts taken from the parish register, amount to between 50 and 60,000 persons, of all ages, sexes, and ranks. If among these classes the Spaniards, as is natural to think, are the most eminent for riches, rank, and power, it must at the same time be owned, however melancholy the truth may appear, they are in proportion the most poor, miserable and distressed; for they refuse to apply themselves to any mechanic business, considering it as a disgrace to that quality they so highly value themselves upon, which consists in not being black, brown, or of a copper color. The Mestizos, whose pride is regulated by prudence, readily apply themselves to arts and trades, but chose those of the greatest repute, as painting, sculpture, and the like, leaving the meaner sort to the Indians.

CÓRDOBA

There was not a person who would give me even an estimate of the number of residents comprising this city, because neither the secular nor the ecclesiastical council has a register, and I know not how these colonists prove the ancient and distinguished nobility of which they boast; it may be that each family has its genealogical history in reserve. In my computation, there must be within the city and its limited common lands around 500 to 600 residents, but in the principal houses there are a very large number of slaves, most of them Creoles [native born] of all conceivable classes, because in this city and in all of Tucumán there is no leniency about granting freedom to any of them. They are easily supported since the principal aliment, meat, is of such moderate price, and there is a custom of dressing them only in ordinary cloth which is made at home by the slaves themselves, shoes being very rare. They aid their masters in many profitable ways and under this system do not think of freedom, thus exposing themselves to a sorrowful end, as is happening in Lima.

As I was passing through Córdoba, they were selling 2,000 Negroes, all Creoles from Temporalidades [property confiscated from the Jesuit order in 1767], from just the two farms of the [Jesuit] colleges of this city. I have seen the lists, for each one has its own, and they proceed by families numbering from two to eleven, all pure Negroes and Creoles back to the fourth generation, because the priests used to sell all of those born with a mixture of Spanish, mulatto, or Indian blood. Among this multitude of Negroes were many musicians and many of other crafts; they proceeded with the sale by families. I was assured that the nuns of Santa Teresa alone had a group of 300 slaves of both sexes, to whom they give their just ration of meat and dress in the coarse cloth which they make, while these good nuns content themselves with what is left from other ministrations. The number attached to other religious establishments is much smaller, but there is a private home which has 30 or 40, the majority of whom are engaged in various gainful activities. The result is a large number of excellent washerwomen whose accomplishments are valued so highly that they never mend their outer skirts in order that the whiteness of their undergarments may be seen. They do the laundry in the river, in water up to the waist, saying vaingloriously that she who is not soaked cannot wash well. They make ponchos [hand-woven capes], rugs, sashes, and sundries, and especially decorated leather cases which the men sell for 8 reales each, because the hides have no outlet due to the great distance to the port; the same thing happens on the banks of the Tercero and Cuarto rivers, where they are sold at 2 reales and frequently for less.

The principal men of the city wear very expensive clothes, but this is not true of the women, who are an exception in both Americas and even in the entire world, because they dress decorously in clothing of little cost. They are very tenacious in preserving the customs of their ancestors. They do not permit slaves, or even freedmen who have a mixture of Negro blood, to wear any cloth other than that made in this country, which is quite coarse. I was told recently that a certain bedecked mulatto [woman] who appeared in Córdoba was sent word by the ladies of the city that she should dress according to her station, but since she paid no attention to this reproach, they endured her negligence until one of the ladies, summoning her to her home under some other pretext, had the servants undress her, whip her, burn her finery before her eyes, and dress her in the clothes befitting her class; despite the fact that the [victim] was not lacking in persons to defend her, she disappeared lest the tragedy be repeated.

QUESTIONS FOR ANALYSIS

1. **What do the authors of these selections seem to think about the white elites of the colonies? Are there similarities in the ways that Juan and Ulloa and Carrío describe the mixed population of Quito and the slave population of Córdoba?**
2. **Are there differences in the way that the authors characterize the relationship between color and class?**
3. **What does the humiliation of the mixed-race woman in Córdoba tell us about ideas of race and class in the Spanish colony?**

Sources: Jorge Juan and Antonio de Ulloa, *A Voyage to South America*, The John Adams translation (abridged), Introduction by Irving A. Leonard (New York: Alfred A. Knopf, 1964), 135–137, copyright © 1964 by Alfred A. Knopf, Inc. Used by permission of Alfred A. Knopf, a division of Random House, Inc.; Concolorcorvo, *El Lazarillo, A Guide for Inexperienced Travelers between Buenos Aires and Lima*, 1773, translated by Walter D. Kline, (Bloomington: Indiana University Press, 1965), 78–80. Used with permission of Indiana University Press.

growing power of colonial viceroys, judges, and bishops appointed by the king.

By the end of the sixteenth century, the elite of Spanish America included both European immigrants and creoles. Europeans dominated the highest levels of the church and government as well as commerce. Creoles commonly controlled colonial agriculture and mining. Wealthy creole families with extensive holdings in land and mines often sought to increase their family prestige by arranging for their daughters to marry successful Spanish merchants and officials. Often richer in reputation than in wealth, immigrants from Spain welcomed the opportunity to forge these connections. Although tensions between Spaniards and creoles were inevitable, most elite families included members of both groups.

Before the Europeans arrived in the Americas, the native peoples were members of a large number of distinct cultural and linguistic groups. Cultural diversity and class distinctions were present even in the highly centralized Aztec and Inca empires. The loss of life provoked by the European conquest undermined this rich social and cultural complexity, and the imposition of Catholic Christianity further eroded ethnic boundaries among native peoples. Colonial administrators and settlers broadly applied the racial label "Indian," which facilitated the imposition of special taxes and labor obligations while at the same time erasing long-standing class and ethnic differences.

Amerindian elites struggled to survive in the new political and economic environments created by military defeat and European settlement. Crucial to this survival was the maintenance of hereditary land rights and continued authority over indigenous commoners. Some elite families sought to protect their positions by forging links with conquistadors and early settlers through marriage or less formal relations. As a result, indigenous and colonial elite families were often tied together by kinship, particularly in the sixteenth century. Both self-interest and a desire to protect their communities led them to quickly gain familiarity with colonial legal systems and establish political alliances with judges and other members of the colonial administrative classes. In many cases they were successful. For example, in New Spain many representatives of the indigenous elite gained both recognition of their nobility and new hereditary land rights from Spanish authorities. As this successful minority of elite families solidified their position in the new order, they became essential intermediaries between the indigenous masses and colonial administrators, collecting Spanish taxes and organizing the labor of their dependents for colonial enterprises.

Indigenous commoners suffered the heaviest burdens. Tribute payments, forced labor obligations, and the loss of traditional land rights were common. European domination dramatically changed the indigenous world. The old connections between peoples and places were weakened or, in some cases, lost. Religious life, marriage practices, diet, and material culture were altered profoundly. The survivors of these terrible shocks learned to adapt to the new colonial environment. They embraced some elements of the dominant colonial culture and its technologies. They found ways to enter the market economies of the cities. They learned to produce new products, such as raising sheep and growing wheat. Most importantly, they learned new forms of resistance, like using colonial courts to protect community lands or to resist the abuses of corrupt officials.

Thousands of blacks participated in the conquest and settlement of Spanish America. The majority were European-born Catholic slaves who came to the New World with their masters. Some free blacks immigrated voluntarily. More than four hundred blacks, most of them slaves, participated in the conquest of Peru and Chile. In the fluid social environment of the conquest era, many slaves gained their freedom. Some simply fled from their masters. Juan Valiente escaped his master in Mexico, participated in Francisco Pizarro's conquest of the Inca Empire, and later became one of the most prominent early settlers of Chile, where he was granted Amerindian laborers in an encomienda.

The status of the black population of colonial Latin America declined with the opening of a direct slave trade with Africa (for details, see Chapter 19). Africans were culturally different from the Afro-Iberian slaves and freedmen who accompanied the conquerors. Afro-Iberians commonly had deep roots in Spain or Portugal; their language was Spanish or Portuguese; and their religion was Catholicism. African slaves had different languages, religious beliefs, and cultural practices, and these differences were viewed by settlers as signs of inferiority, ultimately serving as a justification for slavery. By 1600 people with black ancestry were barred from positions in church and government as well as from many skilled crafts.

The rich mosaic of African identities was retained in colonial Latin America. Enslaved members of many cultural groups struggled to retain their languages, religious beliefs, and marriage customs. But in regions with large slave majorities, these cultural and linguistic barriers often divided slaves and made resistance more difficult. Over time, elements from many African traditions blended and mixed with European (and in some cases Amerindian) language and beliefs to forge distinct local cultures. The rapid growth of an American-born slave population accelerated this process of cultural change.

Slave resistance took many forms, including sabotage, malingering, running away, and rebellion. Although many slave rebellions occurred, colonial authorities were always able to reestablish control. Groups of runaway slaves, however, were sometimes able to defend themselves for years. In both Spanish America and Brazil, communities of runaways (called quilombos° in Brazil and palenques° in Spanish colonies) were common. The largest quilombo was Palmares, where thousands of slaves defended themselves against Brazilian authorities for sixty years until they were finally overrun in 1694.

Slaves were skilled artisans, musicians, servants, artists, cowboys, and even soldiers. However, the vast majority worked in agriculture. Conditions for slaves were worst on the sugar plantations of Brazil and the Caribbean, where harsh discipline, brutal punishments, and backbreaking labor were common. Because planters preferred to buy male slaves, there was always a gender imbalance on plantations. As a result, neither the traditional marriage and family patterns of Africa nor those of Europe developed. The disease environment of the tropics, as well as the poor housing, diet, hygiene, and medical care offered to slaves, also weakened slave families.

The colonial development of Brazil was distinguished from that of Spanish America by the absence of rich and powerful indigenous civilizations such as those of the Aztecs and Inca and by lower levels of European immigration. Nevertheless, Portuguese immigrants came to exercise the same domination in Brazil as the Spanish exercised in their colonies. The growth of cities and the creation of imperial institutions eventually duplicated in outline the social structures found in Spanish America, but with an important difference. By the early seventeenth century, Africans and their American-born descendants were the largest racial group in Brazil. As a result, Brazilian colonial society (unlike Spanish Mexico and Peru) was influenced more by African culture than by Amerindian culture.

Both Spanish and Portuguese law provided for manumission, the granting of freedom to individual slaves. The majority of those gaining their liberty had saved money and purchased their own freedom. This was easiest to do in cities, where slave artisans and market women had the opportunity to earn and save money. Only a tiny minority of owners freed slaves without demanding compensation. Household servants were the most likely beneficiaries of this form of manumission. Only about 1 percent of the slave population gained freedom each year through manumission. However, because slave women received the majority of manumissions and because children born subsequently were considered free, the free black population grew rapidly.

Painting of Castas This is an example of a common genre of colonial Spanish American painting. In the eighteenth century there was increased interest in ethnic mixing, and wealthy colonials as well as some Europeans commissioned sets of paintings that showed mixed families. The paintings commonly also indicated what the artist believed was an appropriate class setting. In this painting a richly dressed Spaniard is depicted with his Amerindian wife dressed in European clothing. Notice that the painter has the mestiza daughter look to her European father for guidance. (Private Collection. Photographer: Camilo Garza/Fotocam, Monterrey, Mexico)

Within a century of settlement, groups of mixed descent were in the majority in many regions. There were few marriages between Amerindian women and European men, but less formal relationships were common. Few European or creole fathers recognized their mixed offspring, who were called **mestizos°**. Nevertheless, this rapidly expanding group came to occupy a middle position in colonial society, dominating urban artisan trades and small-scale agriculture and ranching. In frontier regions many members of the elite were mestizos, some proudly asserting their descent from the Amerindian

quilombos (key-LOM-bos) **palenques** (pah-LEN-kays)

mestizo (mess-TEE-zoh)

elite. The African slave trade also led to the appearance of new American ethnicities. Individuals of mixed European and African descent—called **mulattos**—came to occupy intermediate position in the tropics similar to the social position of mestizos in Mesoamerica and the Andean region. In Spanish Mexico and Peru and in Brazil, mixtures of Amerindians and Africans were also common.

All these mixed-descent groups were called castas° in Spanish America. Castas dominated small-scale retailing and construction trades in cities. In the countryside, many small ranchers and farmers as well as wage laborers were castas. Members of mixed groups who gained high status or significant wealth generally spoke Spanish or Portuguese, observed the requirements of Catholicism, and, whenever possible, lived the life of Europeans in their residence, dress, and diet.

English and French Colonies in North America

The North American colonial empires of England and France and the colonies of Spain and Portugal had many characteristics in common (see Map 18.1). The governments of England and France hoped to find easily extracted forms of wealth or great indigenous empires like those of the Aztecs or Inca. Like the Spanish and Portuguese, English and French settlers responded to native peoples with a mixture of diplomacy and violence. African slaves proved crucial to the development of all four colonial economies.

Important differences, however, distinguished North American colonial development from the Latin American model. The English and French colonies were developed nearly a century after Cortés's conquest of Mexico and initial Portuguese settlement in Brazil. The intervening period witnessed significant economic and demographic growth in Europe. It also witnessed the Protestant Reformation, which helped propel English and French settlement in the Americas. By the time England and France secured a foothold in the Americas, the regions of the world were also more interconnected by trade. Distracted by ventures elsewhere and by increasing military confrontation in Europe, neither England nor France imitated the large and expensive colonial bureaucracies established by Spain and Portugal. As a result, private companies and individual proprietors played a much larger role in the development of English and French colonies. Particularly in the English colonies, this practice led to greater regional variety in economic activity, political institutions and culture, and social structure than was evident in the colonies of Spain and Portugal.

Early English Experiments

England's first efforts to gain a foothold in the Americas produced more failures than successes. The first attempt was made by a group of West Country gentry and merchants led by Sir Humphrey Gilbert. Their effort in 1583 to establish a colony in Newfoundland, off the coast of Canada, quickly failed. After Gilbert's death in 1584, his half-brother, Sir Walter Raleigh, organized private financing for a new colonization scheme. A year later 108 men attempted a settlement on Roanoke Island, off the coast of present-day North Carolina. Afflicted with poor leadership, undersupplied, and threatened by Amerindian groups, the colony was abandoned within a year. Another effort to settle Roanoke was made in 1587. Because the Spanish Armada was threatening England, no relief expedition was sent to Roanoke until 1590. When help finally arrived, there was no sign of the 117 men, women, and children who had attempted settlement. Raleigh's colonial experiment was abandoned.

In the seventeenth century England renewed its effort to establish colonies in North America. England continued to rely on private capital to finance settlement and continued to hope that the colonies would become sources of high-value products such as silk, citrus, and wine. New efforts to establish American colonies were also influenced by English experience in colonizing Ireland after 1566. In Ireland land had been confiscated, cleared of its native population, and offered for sale to English investors. The city of London, English guilds, and wealthy private investors all purchased Irish "plantations" and then recruited "settlers." By 1650 investors had sent nearly 150,000 English and Scottish immigrants to Ireland. Indeed, Ireland attracted six times as many colonists in the early seventeenth century as did New England.

The South

London investors, organized as the privately funded Virginia Company, took up the challenge of colonizing Virginia in 1606. A year later 144 settlers disembarked at Jamestown, an island 30 miles (48 kilometers) up the James River in the Chesapeake Bay region. Additional settlers arrived in 1609. The investors and settlers hoped for immediate profits, but these unrealistic dreams were soon dashed. Although the location was easily defended, it was a swampy and unhealthy

---

castas (CAZ-tahs)

place; in the first fifteen years nearly 80 percent of all settlers in Jamestown died from disease or Amerindian attacks. There was no mineral wealth, no passage to Asia, and no docile and exploitable native population. By concentrating their energies on the illusion of easy wealth, settlers failed to grow enough food and were saved on more than one occasion by the generosity of neighboring Amerindian peoples.

In 1624 the English crown was forced to dissolve the Virginia Company because of its mismanagement of the colony. Freed from the company's commitment to Jamestown's unhealthy environment, colonists pushed deeper into the interior, developing a sustainable economy based on furs, timber, and, increasingly, tobacco. The profits from tobacco soon attracted new immigrants and new capital. Along the shoreline of Chesapeake Bay and the rivers that fed it, settlers spread out, developing plantations and farms. Colonial Virginia's population remained dispersed. In Latin America large and powerful cities dominated by viceroys and royal courts and networks of secondary towns flourished. In contrast, no city of any significant size developed in colonial Virginia.

Colonists in Latin America had developed systems of forced labor to develop the region's resources. Encomienda, mita, and slavery were all imposed on indigenous peoples, and later the African slave trade compelled the migration of millions of additional forced laborers to the colonies of Spain and Portugal. The English settlement of the Chesapeake Bay region added a new system of compulsory labor to the American landscape: **indentured servants.** Ethnically indistinguishable from free settlers, indentured servants eventually accounted for approximately 80 percent of all English immigrants to Virginia and the neighboring colony of Maryland. A young man or woman unable to pay for transportation to the New World accepted an indenture (contract) that bound him or her to a term ranging from four to seven years of labor in return for passage and, at the end of the contract, a small parcel of land, some tools, and clothes.

During the seventeenth century approximately fifteen hundred indentured servants, mostly male, arrived each year (see Chapter 19 for details on the indentured labor system). Planters were less likely to lose money if they purchased the cheaper limited contracts of indentured servants instead of purchasing African slaves during the period when both groups suffered high mortality rates. As life expectancy in the colony improved, planters began to purchase more slaves. They calculated that greater profits could be secured by paying the higher initial cost of slaves owned for life than by purchasing the contracts of indentured servants bound for short periods of time. As a result, Virginia's slave population grew rapidly from 950 in 1660 to 120,000 by 1756.

By the 1660s many of the elements of the mature colony were in place in Virginia. Colonial government was administered by a Crown-appointed governor and his council, as well as by representatives of towns meeting together as the **House of Burgesses.** When these representatives began to meet alone as a deliberative body, they initiated a form of democratic representation that distinguished the English colonies of North America from the colonies of other European powers. Ironically, this expansion in colonial liberties and political rights occurred along with the dramatic increase in the colony's slave population. The intertwined evolution of American freedom and American slavery gave England's southern colonies a unique and conflicted political character that endured even after independence.

At the same time, the English colonists were expanding settlements in the South. The Carolinas at first prospered from the profits of the fur trade. Fur traders pushed into the interior, eventually threatening the French trading networks based in New Orleans and Mobile. Native peoples eventually provided over 100,000 deerskins annually to this profitable commerce. The environmental and cultural costs of the fur trade were little appreciated at the time. As Amerindian peoples hunted more intensely, the natural balance of animals and plants was disrupted in southern forests. The profits of the fur trade altered Amerindian culture as well, leading villages to place less emphasis on subsistence hunting and fishing and traditional agriculture. Amerindian life was profoundly altered by deepening dependencies on European products, including firearms, metal tools, textiles, and alcohol.

Although increasingly brought into the commerce and culture of the Carolina colony, indigenous peoples were being weakened by epidemics, alcoholism, and a rising tide of ethnic conflicts generated by competition for hunting grounds. Conflicts among indigenous peoples—who now had firearms—became more deadly. Many Amerindians captured in these wars were sold as slaves to local colonists, who used them as agricultural workers or exported them to the sugar plantations of the Caribbean islands. Dissatisfied with the terms of trade imposed by fur traders and angered by this slave trade, Amerindians launched attacks on English settlements in the early 1700s. Their defeat by colonial military forces inevitably led to new seizures of Amerindian land by European settlers.

The northern part of the Carolinas had been settled from Virginia and followed that colony's mixed economy of tobacco and forest products. Slavery expanded slowly in this region. Charleston and the interior of South Carolina followed a different path. Settled first by planters from the Caribbean island of Barbados in 1670, this colony soon developed an economy based on plantations and slavery in imitation of the colonies of the Caribbean and Brazil. In 1729 North and South Carolina became separate colonies.

Despite an unhealthy climate, the prosperous rice and indigo plantations near Charleston attracted a diverse array of immigrants and an increasing flow of African slaves. African slaves were present from the founding of Charleston. They were instrumental in introducing irrigated rice agriculture along the coastal lowlands and in developing indigo (a plant that produced a blue dye) plantations at higher elevations away from the coast. Slaves were often given significant responsibilities. As one planter sending two slaves and their families to a frontier region put it: "[They] are likely young people, well acquainted with Rice & every kind of plantation business, and in short [are] capable of the management of a plantation themselves."[2]

As profits from rice and indigo rose, the importation of African slaves created a black majority in South Carolina. African languages, as well as African religious beliefs and diet, strongly influenced this unique colonial culture. Gullah, a dialect with African and English roots, evolved as the common idiom of the Carolina coast. African slaves were more likely than American-born slaves to rebel or run away. Africans played a major role in South Carolina's largest slave uprising, the Stono Rebellion of 1739. After a group of about twenty slaves, many of them African Catholics who sought to flee south to Spanish Florida, seized firearms, about a hundred slaves from nearby plantations joined them. The colonial militia soon defeated the rebels and executed many of them, but the rebellion shocked slave owners throughout England's southern colonies and led to greater repression.

Colonial South Carolina was the most hierarchical society in British North America. Planters controlled the economy and political life. The richest families maintained impressive households in Charleston, the largest city in the southern colonies, as well as on their plantations in the countryside. Small farmers, cattlemen, artisans, merchants, and fur traders held an intermediate but clearly subordinate social position. Native peoples remained influential participants in colonial society through commercial contacts and alliances, but they were increasingly marginalized. As had occurred in colonial Latin America, the growth of a large mixed population blurred racial and cultural boundaries. On the frontier, the children of white men and Amerindian women held an important place in the fur trade. In the plantation regions and Charleston, the offspring of white men and black women often held preferred positions within the slave work force or, if they had been freed, as carpenters, blacksmiths, or in other skilled trades.

New England

The colonization of New England by two separate groups of Protestant dissenters, Pilgrims and Puritans, put the settlement of this region on a different course. The **Pilgrims,** who came first, wished to break completely with the Church of England, which they believed was still essentially Catholic. Unwilling to confront the power of the established church and the monarch, they sought an opportunity to pursue their spiritual ends in a new land. As a result, in 1620 approximately one hundred settlers—men, women, and children—established the colony of Plymouth on the coast of present-day Massachusetts. Although nearly half of the settlers died during the first winter, the colony survived. Plymouth benefited from strong leadership and the discipline and cooperative nature of the settlers. Nevertheless, this experiment in creating a church-directed community failed. The religious enthusiasm and purpose that at first sustained the Pilgrims was dissipated by new immigrants who did not share the founders' religious beliefs, and by geographic dispersal to new towns. In 1691 Plymouth was absorbed into the larger Massachusetts Bay Colony of the Puritans.

The **Puritans** wished to "purify" the Church of England, not break with it. They wanted to abolish its hierarchy of bishops and priests, free it from governmental interference, and limit membership to people who shared their beliefs. Subjected to increased discrimination in England for their efforts to transform the church, large numbers of Puritans began emigrating from England in 1630.

The Puritan leaders of the Massachusetts Bay Company—the joint-stock company that had received a royal charter to finance the Massachusetts Bay Colony—carried the company charter, which spelled out company rights and obligations as well as the direction of company government, with them from England to Massachusetts. By bringing the charter, they limited Crown efforts to control them; the Crown could revoke but not alter the terms of the charter. By 1643 more than twenty thousand Puritans had settled in the Bay Colony.

Immigration to Massachusetts differed from immigration to the Chesapeake and to South Carolina. Most newcomers to Massachusetts arrived with their families. Whereas 84 percent of Virginia's white population in 1625 was male, Massachusetts had a normal gender balance in its population almost from the beginning. It was also the healthiest of England's colonies. The result was a rapid natural increase in population. The population of Massachusetts quickly became more "American" than the population of the colonies to the south or in the Caribbean, whose survival depended on a steady flow of new English immigrants to counter high mortality rates.

The Home of Sir William Johnson, British Superintendent for Indian Affairs, Northern District As the colonial era drew to a close, the British attempted to limit the cost of colonial defense by negotiating land settlements between native peoples and settlers. These agreements were doomed by the growing tide of western migration. William Johnson (1715–1774) maintained a fragile peace along the northern frontier by building strong personal relations with influential leaders of the Mohawk and other members of the Iroquois Confederacy. His home in present-day Johnstown, New York, shows the mixed nature of the frontier—the relative opulence of the main house offset by the two defensive blockhouses built for protection. ("Johnson Hall," by E. L. Henry. Courtesy, Albany Institute of History and Art)

Massachusetts also was more homogeneous and less hierarchical than the southern colonies.

Political institutions evolved out of the terms of the company charter. A governor was elected, along with a council of magistrates drawn from the board of directors of the Massachusetts Bay Company. Disagreements between this council and elected representatives of the towns led, by 1650, to the creation of a lower legislative house that selected its own speaker and began to develop procedures and rules similar to those of the House of Commons in England. The result was greater autonomy and greater local political involvement than in the colonies of Latin America.

Economically, Massachusetts differed dramatically from the southern colonies. Agriculture met basic needs, but poor soils and harsh climate offered no opportunity to develop cash crops like tobacco or rice. To pay for imported tools, textiles, and other essentials, the colonists needed to discover some profit-making niche in the growing Atlantic market. Fur, timber and other forest products, and fish provided the initial economic foundation, but New England's economic well-being soon depended on providing commercial and shipping services in a dynamic and far-flung commercial arena that included the southern colonies, the smaller Caribbean islands, Africa, and Europe.

In Spanish and Portuguese America, heavily capitalized monopolies (companies or individuals given exclusive economic privileges) dominated international trade. In New England, by contrast, merchants survived by discovering smaller but more sustainable profits in diversified trade across the Atlantic. The colony's commercial success rested on market intelligence, flexibility, and streamlined organization. The success of this development strategy is demonstrated by urban population growth. With sixteen thousand inhabitants in 1740, Boston, the capital of Massachusetts Bay Colony, was the largest city in British North America. This coincided with the decline of New England's once-large indigenous population, which had been dramatically

Canadian Fur Trader The fur trade provided the economic foundation of early Canadian settlement. The trade depended on a mix of native and European skills and resources. Fur traders were cultural intermediaries. They transmitted European skills and resources. Fur traders were cultural intermediaries. They transmitted European technologies and products like firearms and machine-made textiles to native peoples and native technologies and products to the canoe and furs to European settlements. Many were the sons of native women and nearly all were fluent in native languages. (National Archives of Canada)

reduced by a combination of epidemics and brutal military campaigns.

Lacking a profitable agricultural export like tobacco, New England did not develop the extreme social stratification of the southern plantation colonies. Slaves and indentured servants were present, but in very small numbers. New England was ruled by the richest colonists and shared the racial attitudes of the southern colonies, but it also was the colonial society with fewest differences in wealth and status and with the most uniformly British and Protestant population in the Americas.

The Middle Atlantic Region

Much of the future success of English-speaking America was rooted in the rapid economic development and remarkable cultural diversity that appeared in the Middle Atlantic colonies. In 1624 the Dutch West India Company established the colony of New Netherland and located its capital on Manhattan Island. The colony was poorly managed and underfinanced from the start, but its location commanded the potentially profitable and strategically important Hudson River. Dutch merchants established trading relationships with the **Iroquois Confederacy**—an alliance among the Mohawk, Oneida, Onondaga, Cayuga, and Seneca peoples—and with other native peoples that gave them access to the rich fur trade of Canada. When confronted by an English military expedition in 1664, the Dutch surrendered without a fight. James, duke of York and later King James II of England, became proprietor of the colony, which was renamed New York.

New York was characterized by tumultuous politics and corrupt public administration. The colony's success was guaranteed in large measure by the development of New York City as a commercial and shipping center. Located at the mouth of the Hudson River, the city played an essential role in connecting the region's grain farmers to the booming markets of the Caribbean and southern Europe. By the early eighteenth century New York Colony had a diverse population that included English colonists; Dutch, German, and Swedish settlers; and a large slave community.

Pennsylvania began as a proprietary colony and as a refuge for Quakers, a persecuted religious minority. In 1682 William Penn secured an enormous grant of territory (nearly the size of England) because the English king Charles II was indebted to Penn's father. As proprietor (owner) of the land, Penn had sole right to establish a government, subject only to the requirement that he provide for an assembly of freemen.

Penn quickly lost control of the colony's political life, but the colony enjoyed remarkable success. By 1700 Pennsylvania had a population of more than 21,000, and Philadelphia, its capital, soon passed Boston to become the largest city in the British colonies. Healthy climate, excellent land, relatively peaceful relations with native peoples (prompted by Penn's emphasis on negotiation rather than warfare), and access through Philadelphia to good markets led to rapid economic and demographic growth in the colony.

Both Pennsylvania and South Carolina were grain-exporting colonies, but they were very different societies. South Carolina's rice plantations required large numbers of slaves. In Pennsylvania free workers, including a large number of German families, produced the bulk of the colony's grain crops on family farms. As a result, Pennsylvania's economic expansion in the late seventeenth century occurred without reproducing South Carolina's hierarchical and repressive social order. By the early eighteenth century, however, the prosperous city of Philadelphia did have a large population of black slaves and freedmen. Many were servants in the homes of wealthy merchants, but the fast-growing economy offered many opportunities in skilled trades as well.

French America

Patterns of French settlement more closely resembled those of Spain and Portugal than of England. The French were committed to missionary activity among Amerindian peoples and emphasized the extraction of natural resources—furs rather than minerals. The navigator and promoter Jacques Cartier first stirred France's interest in North America. In three voyages between 1524 and 1542, he explored the region of Newfoundland and the Gulf of St. Lawrence. A contemporary of Cortés and Pizarro, Cartier also hoped to find mineral wealth, but the stones he brought back to France turned out to be quartz and iron pyrite, "fool's gold."

The French waited more than fifty years before establishing settlements in North America. Coming to Canada after spending years in the West Indies, Samuel de Champlain founded the colony of **New France** at Quebec°, on the banks of the St. Lawrence River, in 1608. This location provided ready access to Amerindian trade routes, but it also compelled French settlers to take sides in the region's ongoing warfare. Champlain allied New France with the Huron and Algonquin peoples, traditional enemies of the powerful Iroquois Confederacy. Although French firearms and armor at first tipped the balance of power to France's native allies, the members of the Iroquois Confederacy proved to be resourceful and persistent enemies.

The European market for fur, especially beaver, fueled French settlement. Young Frenchmen were sent to live among native peoples to master their languages and customs. These **coureurs de bois°**, or runners of the woods, often began families with indigenous women, and they and their children, who were called métis°, helped direct the fur trade, guiding French expansion to the west and south. Amerindians actively participated in the trade because they quickly came to depend on the goods they received in exchange for furs—firearms, metal tools and utensils, textiles, and alcohol. This change in the material culture of the native peoples led to overhunting, which rapidly transformed the environment and led to the depletion of beaver and deer populations. It also increased competition among native peoples for hunting grounds, thus promoting warfare.

The proliferation of firearms made indigenous warfare more deadly. The Iroquois Confederacy responded to the increased military strength of France's Algonquin allies by forging commercial and military links with Dutch and later English settlements in the Hudson River Valley. Well armed by the Dutch and English, the Iroquois Confederacy nearly eradicated the Huron in 1649 and inflicted a series of humiliating defeats on the French. At the high point of their power in the early 1680s, Iroquois hunters and military forces gained control of much of the Great Lakes region and the Ohio River Valley. A large French military expedition and a relentless attack focused on Iroquois villages and agriculture finally checked Iroquois power in 1701.

Spain had effectively limited the spread of firearms in its colonies. But the fur trade, together with the growing military rivalry between Algonquin and Iroquois peoples and their respective French and English allies, led to the rapid spread of firearms in North America. Use of firearms in hunting and warfare moved west and south, reaching indigenous plains cultures that had previously adopted the horse introduced by the Spanish. This intersection of horse and gun frontiers in the early eighteenth century dramatically increased the military power and hunting efficiency of the Sioux, Comanche, Cheyenne, and other indigenous peoples, and slowed the pace of European settlement in the North American west.

In French Canada, the Jesuits led the effort to convert native peoples to Christianity. Building on earlier evangelical efforts in Brazil and Paraguay, French Catholic missionaries mastered native languages, created boarding schools for young boys and girls, and set up model agricultural communities for converted Amerindians. The Jesuits' greatest successes coincided with a destructive wave of epidemics and renewed warfare among native peoples in the 1630s. Eventually, churches were established throughout Huron and Algonquin territories. Nevertheless, local culture persisted. In 1688 a French nun who had devoted her life to instructing Amerindian girls expressed the frustration of many missionaries with the resilience of indigenous culture:

> We have observed that of a hundred that have passed through our hands we have scarcely civilized one. . . . When we are least expecting it, they clamber over our wall and go off to run with their kinsmen in the woods, finding more to please them there than in all the amenities of our French house.[3]

Quebec (kwuh-BEC) **coureurs de bois** (koo-RUHR day BWA)
métis (may-TEES)

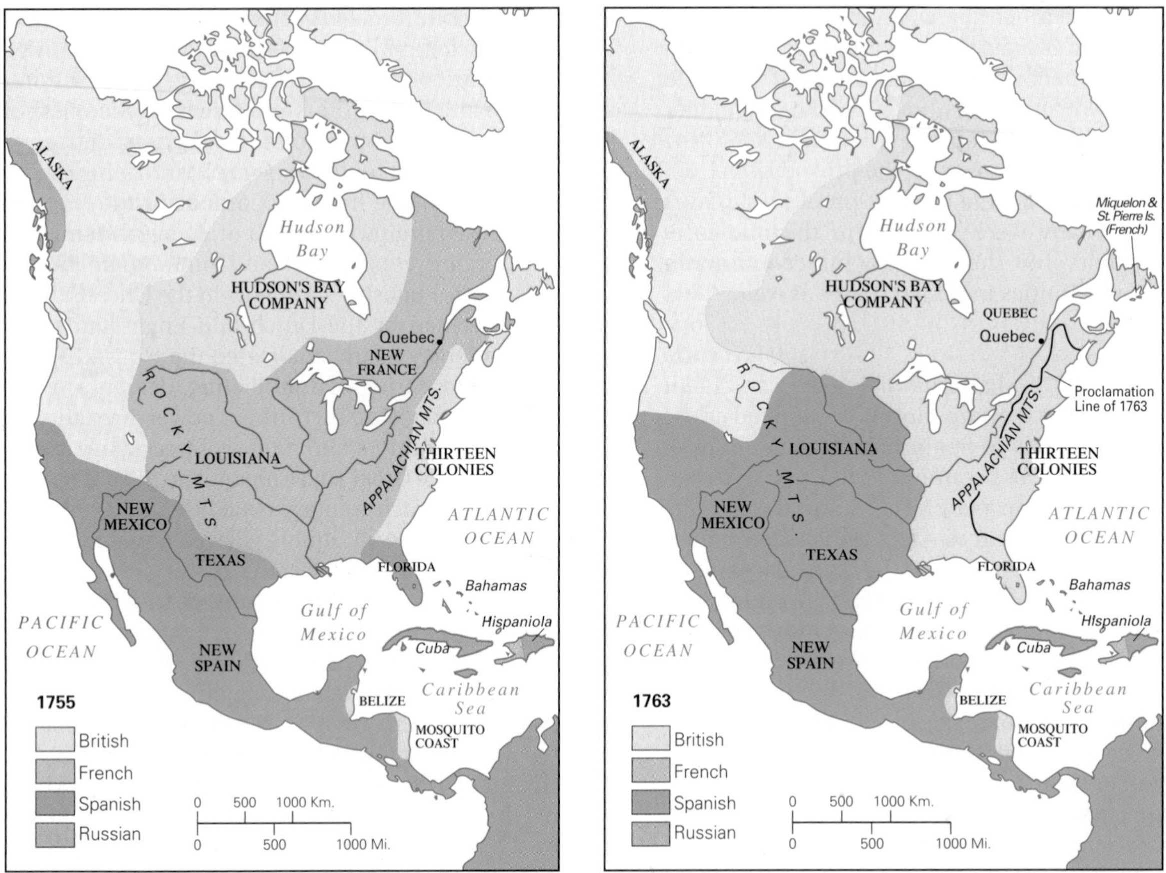

Map 18.2 European Claims in North America, 1755–1763 The results of the French and Indian War dramatically altered the map of North America. France's losses precipitated conflicts between Amerindian peoples and the rapidly expanding population of the British colonies.

As epidemics undermined conversion efforts in mission settlements and evidence of indigenous resistance to conversion mounted, the church redirected some of its resources from the evangelical effort to the larger French settlements, founding schools, hospitals, and churches.

Responsibility for finding settlers and supervising the colonial economy was first granted to a monopoly company chartered in France. Even though the fur trade flourished, population growth was slow. Founded at about the same time as French Canada, Virginia had twenty times more European residents by 1627. After the establishment of royal authority in the 1660s, Canada's French population increased but remained at only seven thousand in 1673. Although improved fiscal management and more effective colonial government did promote a limited agricultural expansion, the fur trade remained important. It is clear that Canada's small settler population and the fur trade's dependence on the voluntary participation of Amerindians allowed indigenous peoples to retain greater independence and more control over their traditional lands than was possible in the colonies of Spain, Portugal, or England. Unlike these colonial regimes, which sought to transform ancient ways of life or force the transfer of native lands, the French were compelled to treat indigenous peoples as allies and trading partners. This permitted indigenous peoples to more gradually adapt to new religious, technological, and market realities.

Despite Canada's small population, limited resources, and increasing vulnerability to attack by the English and their indigenous allies, the French aggressively expanded to the west and south. Louisiana was founded in 1699, but by 1708 there were fewer than three hundred soldiers, settlers, and slaves in the territory. Like Canada, Louisiana depended on the fur trade, exporting more than fifty thousand deerskins in 1726. Also as in Canada,

Amerindians, driven by a desire for European goods, eagerly embraced this trade. In 1753 a French official reported a Choctaw leader as saying, "[The French] were the first . . . who made [us] subject to the different needs that [we] can no longer now do without."[4]

France's North American colonies were threatened by a series of wars fought by France and England and by the population growth and increasing prosperity of neighboring English colonies. The "French and Indian War" (which led to a broader conflict, the Seven Years War, 1756–1763), however, proved to be the final contest for North American empire (see Map 18.2). England committed a larger military force to the struggle and, despite early defeats, took the French capital of Quebec in 1759. Although resistance continued briefly, French forces in Canada surrendered in 1760. The peace agreement forced France to yield Canada to the English and cede Louisiana to Spain. The differences between French and English colonial realities were suggested by the petition of one Canadian indigenous leader to a British officer after the French surrender. "[W]e learn that our lands are to be given away not only to trade thereon but also to them in full title to various [English] individuals. . . . We have always been a free nation, and now we will become slaves, which would be very difficult to accept after having enjoyed our liberty so long."[5] With the loss of Canada the French concentrated their efforts on their sugar-producing colonies in the Caribbean (see Chapter 19).

Colonial Expansion and Conflict

In the last decades of the seventeenth century, all of the European colonies in the Americas began to experience a long period of economic and demographic expansion. The imperial powers responded by strengthening their administrative and economic controls in the colonies. They also sought to force colonial populations to pay a larger share of the costs of administration and defense. These efforts at reform and restructuring coincided with a series of imperial wars fought along Atlantic trade routes and in the Americas. France's loss of its North American colonies was one of the most important results of these struggles. Equally significant, colonial populations throughout the Americas became more aware of separate national identities and more aggressive in asserting local interests against the will of distant monarchs.

Imperial Reform in Spanish America and Brazil

Spain's Habsburg dynasty ended when the Spanish king Charles II died without an heir in 1700 (see Table 17.1, page 467). After thirteen years of conflict involving the major European powers and factions within Spain, Philip of Bourbon, grandson of Louis XIV of France, gained the Spanish throne. Under Philip V and his Bourbon heirs, Spain's colonial administration and tax collection were reorganized. Spain's reliance on convoys protected by naval vessels was abolished; more colonial ports were permitted to trade with Spain; and intercolonial trade was expanded. Spain also created new commercial monopolies to produce tobacco, some alcoholic beverages, and chocolate. The Spanish navy was strengthened, and trade in contraband was more effectively policed.

For most of the Spanish Empire, the eighteenth century was a period of remarkable economic expansion associated with population growth. Amerindian populations began to recover from the early epidemics; the flow of Spanish immigrants increased; and the slave trade to the plantation colonies was expanded. Mining, the heart of the Spanish colonial economy, increased as silver production in Mexico and Peru rose steadily into the 1780s. Agricultural exports also expanded: tobacco, dyes, hides, chocolate, cotton, and sugar joined the flow of goods to Europe.

But these reforms carried unforeseen consequences that threatened the survival of the Spanish Empire. Despite expanded silver production, the economic growth of the eighteenth century was led by the previously minor agricultural and grazing economies of Cuba, the Rio de la Plata region, Venezuela, Chile, and Central America. These export economies were less able than the mining economies of Mexico and Peru to weather breaks in trade caused by imperial wars. Each such disruption forced landowning elites in Cuba and the other regions to turn to alternative, often illegal, trade with English, French, or Dutch merchants. By the 1790s the wealthiest and most influential sectors of Spain's colonial society had come to view the Spanish Empire as an impediment to prosperity and growth.

Bourbon political and fiscal reforms also contributed to a growing sense of colonial grievance by limiting creoles' access to colonial offices and by imposing new taxes and monopolies on colonial production. Consumer and producer resentment, for example, led to rioting when the Spanish established monopolies on tobacco, cacao (chocolate), and brandy. Because these reforms produced a more intrusive and expensive colonial government that interfered with established business practices,

Market in Rio de Janeiro In many of the cities of colonial Latin America female slaves and black free women dominated retail markets. In this scene from late colonial Brazil Afro-Brazilian women sell a variety of foods and crafts. (Sir Henry Chamberlain, Views and Costumes of the City and Neighborhoods of Rio de Janeiro, London, 1822)

many colonists saw the changes as an abuse of the informal constitution that had long governed the empire. Only in the Bourbon effort to expand colonial militias in the face of English threats did creoles find opportunity for improved status and greater responsibility.

In addition to tax rebellions and urban riots, colonial policies also provoked Amerindian uprisings. Most spectacular was the rebellion initiated in 1780 by the Peruvian Amerindian leader José Gabriel Condorcanqui. Once in rebellion, he took the name of his Inca ancestor Tupac Amaru°, who had been executed as a rebel in 1572. **Tupac Amaru II** was well connected in Spanish colonial society. He had been educated by the Jesuits and was actively involved in trade with the silver mines at Potosí. Despite these connections, he still resented the abuse of Amerindian villagers.

Historians still debate the objectives of this rebellion. Tupac Amaru's own pronouncements did not clearly state whether he sought to end local injustices or overthrow Spanish rule. It appears that a local Spanish judge who challenged Tupac Amaru's hereditary rights provided the initial provocation, but that Tupac Amaru was ultimately driven by the conviction that colonial authorities were oppressing the indigenous people. As thousands joined him, he dared to contemplate the overthrow of Spanish rule.

Tupac Amaru (TOO-pack a-MAH-roo)

Amerindian communities suffering under the mita and tribute obligations provided the majority of Tupac Amaru's army. He also received some support from creoles, mestizos, and slaves. After his capture, he was brutally executed, as were his wife and fifteen other family members and allies. Even after his execution, Amerindian rebels continued the struggle for more than two years. By the time Spanish authority was firmly reestablished, more than 100,000 lives had been lost and enormous amounts of property destroyed.

Brazil experienced a similar period of expansion and reform after 1700. Portugal created new administrative positions and gave monopoly companies exclusive rights to little-developed regions. Here, too, a more intrusive colonial government led to rebellions and plots, including open warfare in 1707 between "sons of the soil" and "outsiders" in São Paulo. The most aggressive period of reform occurred during the ministry of the marquis of Pombal (1750–1777). The Pombal reforms were made possible by an economic expansion fueled by the discovery of gold in the 1690s and diamonds after 1720 as well as by the development of markets for coffee and cotton. This new wealth paid for the importation of nearly 2 million African slaves. In Spanish America, a reinvigorated Crown sought to eliminate contraband trade. Portugal, however, had fallen into the economic orbit of England, and Brazil's new prosperity fueled a new wave of English imports.

Reform and Reorganization in British America

England's efforts to reform and reorganize its North American colonies began earlier than the Bourbon initiative in Spanish America. After the period of Cromwell's Puritan Republic (see Chapter 17), the restored Stuart king, Charles II, undertook an ambitious campaign to establish greater Crown control over the colonies. Between 1651 and 1673 a series of Navigation Acts sought to severely limit colonial trading and colonial production that competed directly with English manufacturers. James II also attempted to increase royal control over colonial political life. Royal governments replaced original colonial charters as in Massachusetts and proprietorships as in the Carolinas. Because the New England colonies were viewed as centers of smuggling, the king temporarily suspended their elected assemblies. At the same time, he appointed colonial governors and granted them new fiscal and legislative powers.

James II's overthrow in the Glorious Revolution of 1688 ended this confrontation, but not before colonists were provoked to resist and, in some cases, rebel. They overthrew the governors of New York and Massachusetts and removed the Catholic proprietor of Maryland. William and Mary restored relative peace, but these conflicts alerted the colonists to the potential for aggression by the English government. Colonial politics would remain confrontational until the American Revolution.

During the eighteenth century the English colonies experienced renewed economic growth and attracted a new wave of European immigration, but social divisions were increasingly evident. The colonial population in 1770 was more urban, more clearly divided by class and race, and more vulnerable to economic downturns. Crises were provoked when imperial wars with France and Spain disrupted trade in the Atlantic, increased tax burdens, forced military mobilizations, and provoked frontier conflicts with the Amerindians. On the eve of the American Revolution, England defeated France and weakened Spain. The cost, however, was great. Administrative, military, and tax policies imposed to gain empirewide victory alienated much of the American colonial population.

Conclusion

The New World colonial empires of Spain, Portugal, France, and England had many characteristics in common. All subjugated Amerindian peoples and introduced large numbers of enslaved Africans. Within all four empires forests were cut down, virgin soils were turned with the plow, and Old World animals and plants were introduced. Colonists in all four applied the technologies of the Old World to the resources of the New, producing wealth and exploiting the commercial possibilities of the emerging Atlantic market.

Each of the New World empires also reflected the distinctive cultural and institutional heritages of its colonizing power. Mineral wealth allowed Spain to develop the most centralized empire. Political and economic power was concentrated in the great capital cities of Mexico City and Lima. Portugal and France pursued objectives similar to Spain's in their colonies. However, neither Brazil's agricultural economy nor France's Canadian fur trade produced the financial resources that made possible the centralized control achieved by Spain. Nevertheless, all three of these Catholic powers were able to impose and enforce significant levels of religious and cultural uniformity, relative to the British.

Greater cultural and religious diversity characterized British North America. Colonists were drawn from throughout the British Isles and included participants in all of Britain's numerous religious traditions. They were joined by German, Swedish, Dutch, and French Protestant immigrants. British colonial government varied somewhat from colony to colony and was more responsive to local interests. Thus colonists in British North America were better able than those in the areas controlled by Spain, Portugal, and France to respond to changing economic and political circumstances. Most importantly, the British colonies attracted many more European immigrants than did the other New World colonies. Between 1580 and 1760 French colonies received 60,000 immigrants, Brazil 523,000, and the Spanish colonies 678,000. Within a shorter period—between 1600 and 1760—the British settlements welcomed 746,000. Population in British North America—free and slave combined—reached an extraordinary 2.5 million by 1775.

By the eighteenth century, colonial societies across the Americas had matured as wealth increased, populations grew, and contacts with the rest of the world became more common (see Chapter 19). Colonial elites were more confident of their ability to define and defend local interests. Colonists in general were increasingly aware of their unique and distinctive cultural identities and willing to defend American experience and practice in the face of European presumptions of superiority. Moreover, influential groups in all the colonies were drawn toward the liberating ideas of Europe's Enlightenment. In the open and less inhibited spaces of the Western Hemisphere, these ideas (as Chapter 22 examines) soon provided a potent intellectual basis for opposing the continuation of empire.

Key Terms

Columbian Exchange
Council of the Indies
Bartolomé de Las Casas
Potosí
encomienda
creoles
mestizo
mulatto
indentured servant
House of Burgesses
Pilgrims
Puritans
Iroquois Confederacy
New France
coureurs de bois
Tupac Amaru II

Suggested Reading

Alfred W. Crosby, Jr., is justifiably the best-known student of the Columbian Exchange. See his *The Columbian Exchange: Biological and Cultural Consequences of 1492* (1972) and *Ecological Imperialism* (1986). William H. McNeill, *Plagues and Peoples* (1976), puts the discussion of the American exchange in a world history context. Elinor G. K. Melville, *A Plague of Sheep: Environmental Consequences of the Spanish Conquest of Mexico* (1994), is the most important recent contribution to this field.

Colonial Latin America, 4th ed. (2001), by Mark A. Burkholder and Lyman L. Johnson, provides a good introduction to colonial Latin American history. *Early Latin America* (1983) by James Lockhart and Stuart B. Schwartz and *Spain and Portugal in the New World, 1492–1700* (1984) by Lyle N. McAlister are both useful introductions as well.

The specialized historical literature on the American colonial empires is extensive and deep. A sampling of useful works follows. For the early colonial period see Inga Clendinnen, *Ambivalent Conquests* (1987); James Lockhart, *The Nahuas After the Conquest* (1992); and John Hemming, *Red Gold: The Conquest of the Brazilian Indians* (1978). Nancy M. Farriss, *Maya Society Under Spanish Rule: The Collective Enterprise of Survival* (1984), is also one of the most important books on colonial Spanish America. For the Catholic Church see William Taylor, *Magistrates of the Sacred: Priests and Parishioners in Eighteenth-Century Mexico* (1996). Lyman L. Johnson and Sonya Lipsett-Rivera, eds., *The Faces of Honor* (1999), provides a good introduction to the culture of honor. For the place of women see Asunción Lavrin, ed., *Sexuality and Marriage in Colonial Latin America* (1989). On issues of class R. Douglas Cope, *The Limits of Racial Domination* (1994), is recommended. On the slave trade Herbert S. Klein, *The Middle Passage* (1978), and Philip D. Curtin, *The Atlantic Slave Trade: A Census* (1969), are indispensable. Frederick P. Bowser, *The African Slave in Colonial Peru, 1524–1650* (1973); Mary C. Karasch, *Slave Life and Culture in Rio de Janeiro, 1808–1850* (1986); and Stuart B. Schwartz, *Sugar Plantations in the Formation of Brazilian Society: Bahia, 1550–1835* (1985), are excellent introductions to the African experience in two very different Latin American societies.

Among the useful general studies of the British colonies are Charles M. Andrews, *The Colonial Period of American History: The Settlements*, 3 vols. (1934–1937); David Hackett Fischer, *Albion's Seed: Four British Folkways in America* (1989); and Gary B. Nash, *Red, White, and Black: The Peoples of Early America*, 2d ed. (1982). On the economy see John J. McCusker and Russell R. Menard, *The Economy of British America, 1607–1789* (1979). For slavery see David Brion Davis, *The Problem of Slavery in Western Culture* (1966); Allan Kulikoff, *Tobacco and Slaves: The Development of Southern Cultures in the Chesapeake, 1680–1800* (1986); and Peter H. Wood, *Black Majority: Negroes in Colonial South Carolina from 1670 Through the Stono Rebellion* (1974). Two very useful works on the relations between Europeans and Indians are James Merrill, *The Indians' New World: Catawbas and Their Neighbors from European Contact Through the Era of Removal* (1989); and Daniel H. Usner, Jr., *Indians, Settlers, and Slaves in a Frontier Exchange Economy: The Lower Mississippi Valley Before 1783* (1992).

For late colonial politics see Gary B. Nash, *Urban Crucible: Social Change, Political Consciousness, and the Origins of the American Revolution* (1979); Bernard Bailyn, *The Origins of American Politics* (1986); Jack P. Greene, *The Quest for Power: The Lower Houses of Assembly in the Southern Royal Colonies* (1963); and Richard Bushman, *King and People in Provincial Massachusetts* (1985). On immigration see Bernard Bailyn, *The Peopling of British North America* (1986).

On French North America, William J. Eccles, *France in America*, rev. ed. (1990), is an excellent overview; see also his *The Canadian Frontier, 1534–1760* (1969). G. F. G. Stanley, *New France, 1701–1760* (1968), is also an important resource. R. Cole Harris, *The Seigneurial System in Canada: A Geographical Study* (1966), provides an excellent analysis of the topic. Harold Innis, *The Fur Trade in Canada: An Introduction to Canadian Economic History* (1927), remains indispensable. Also of value are Cornelius Jaenen, *The Role of the Church in New France* (1976), Carole Blackburn, *Harvest of Souls: The Jesuit Missions and Colonialism in North America, 1632–1650* (2000); and Alison L. Prentice, *Canadian Women: A History* (1988).

Notes

1. Quoted in Alfred W. Crosby, Jr., *The Columbian Exchange: Biological and Cultural Consequences of 1492* (Westport, CT: Greenwood, 1972), 58.
2. Ibid.
3. Quoted in R. Douglas Francis, Richard Jones, and Donald B. Smith, *Origins: Canadian History to Confederation* (Toronto: Holt, Rinehart, and Winston of Canada, 1992), 52.
4. Quoted in Daniel H. Usner, Jr., *Indians, Settlers and Slaves in a Frontier Exchange Economy: The Lower Mississippi Valley Before 1783*, Institute of Early American History and Culture Series (Chapel Hill: University of North Carolina Press, 1992), 96.
5. Quoted in Cornelius J. Jaenen, "French and Native Peoples in New France," in J. M. Bumsted, *Interpreting Canada's Past*, vol. 1, 2d ed. (Toronto: Oxford University Press, 1993), 73.

19

The Atlantic System and Africa, 1550–1800

Caribbean Sugar Mill The wind mill crushes sugar cane whose juice is boiled down in the smoking building next door.

CHAPTER OUTLINE

In 1694 the English ship *Hannibal* called at the West African port of Whydah° to purchase slaves. The king of Whydah welcomed Captain Thomas Phillips and others of the ship's officers and invited them to his residence. Phillips gave the African ruler the rich presents required for Europeans to trade there and negotiated an agreement on the prices for slaves.

The ship's doctor carefully inspected the naked captives to be sure they were of sound body, young, and free of disease. After their purchase, the slaves were branded with an H (for *Hannibal*) to establish ownership. Once they were loaded on the ship, the crew put shackles on the men to prevent their escape. Phillips recorded that the shackles were removed once the ship was out of sight of land and the risk of a slave revolt had passed. In all, the *Hannibal* purchased 692 slaves, of whom about a third were women and girls.

This was not a private venture. The *Hannibal* had been hired by the **Royal African Company** (RAC), an association of English investors that in 1672 had received a charter from the English monarchy giving them exclusive rights to trade along the Atlantic coast of Africa. Besides slaves, the RAC purchased ivory and other products.

Under the terms of their agreement, the RAC would pay the owners of the *Hannibal* £10.50 for each slave brought to Barbados—but only for those delivered alive. To keep the slaves healthy, Captain Phillips had the crew feed them twice a day on boiled corn meal and beans brought from Europe flavored with hot peppers and palm oil purchased in Africa. Each slave received a pint (half a liter) of water with every meal. In addition, the slaves were made to "jump and dance for an hour or two to our bagpipe, harp, and fiddle" every evening to keep them fit. Despite the incentives and precautions for keeping the cargo alive, deaths were common among the hundreds of people crammed into every corner of a slave ship. The *Hannibal*'s experience was worse than most, losing 320 slaves and 14 crew members during the seven-week voyage to Barbados. One hundred slaves came down with smallpox, an infection one must have brought on board. Only a dozen died of that disease, but, the captain lamented, "what the small-pox spar'd, the flux [dysentery] swept off, to our great regret, after all our pains and care to give them their messes [meals] in due order and season, keeping their lodgings as clean as possible, and enduring so much misery and stench so long among a parcel of creatures nastier than swine." One wonders what one of the Africans might have written about the nasty creatures who put them in these conditions.

The *Hannibal*'s high losses, nearly double the average losses of an English slaver during the passage to Barbados in the last quarter of the seventeenth century, destroyed the profitability of the voyage. The 372 Africans who were landed alive netted the RAC about £7,000, but the purchase price of 692 slaves at Whydah and the costs of their transportation on the *Hannibal* amounted to about £10,800.

As the *Hannibal*'s experience suggests, the Atlantic slave trade took a devastating toll in African lives and was far from a sure-fire money maker for European investors. Nevertheless, the slave trade and plantation slavery were crucial pieces of a booming new **Atlantic system** that moved goods and wealth, as well as people and cultures, around the Atlantic.

As you read this chapter, ask yourself the following questions:

- How did the Atlantic system affect Europe, Africa, and the Americas?
- How and why did European businessmen, with the help of their governments, put this trading system together?
- How and why did the West Indies and other places in the Americas become centers of African population and culture?
- How did sub-Saharan Africa's expanding contacts in the Atlantic compare with its contacts with the Islamic world?

Whydah (WEE-duh)

CHRONOLOGY

	West Indies	Atlantic	Africa
1500	**ca. 1500** Spanish settlers introduce sugar-cane cultivation	**1530** Amsterdam Exchange opens	**1500–1700** Gold trade predominates **1591** Morocco conquers Songhai
1600	**1620s and 1630s** English and French colonies in Caribbean **1640s** Dutch bring sugar plantation system from Brazil **1655** English take Jamaica **1670s** French occupy western half of Hispaniola	**1621** Dutch West India Company chartered **1660s** English Navigation Acts **1672** Royal African Company chartered **1698** French *Exclusif*	**1638** Dutch take Elmina **1680s** Rise of Asante
1700	**1700** West Indies surpass Brazil in sugar production **1760** Tacky's rebellion in Jamaica **1795** Jamaican Maroon rebellion	**1700 to present** Atlantic system flourishing	**1700–1830** Slave trade predominates **1720s** Rise of Dahomey **1730** Oyo makes Dahomey pay tribute

Plantations in the West Indies

The West Indies was the first place in the Americas reached by Columbus and the first part of the Americas where native populations collapsed. It took a long time to repopulate these islands from abroad and forge new economic links between them and other parts of the Atlantic. But after 1650 sugar plantations, African slaves, and European capital made these islands a major center of the Atlantic economy.

Colonization Before 1650

Spanish settlers introduced sugar-cane cultivation into the West Indies shortly after 1500, but these colonies soon fell into neglect as attention shifted to colonizing the American mainland. After 1600 the West Indies revived as a focus of colonization, this time by northern Europeans interested in growing tobacco and other crops. In the 1620s and 1630s English colonization societies founded small European settlements on Montserrat°, Barbados°, and other Caribbean islands, while the French colonized Martinique°, Guadeloupe°, and some other islands. Because of greater support from their government, the English colonies prospered first, largely by growing tobacco for export.

This New World leaf, long used by Amerindians for recreation and medicine, was finding a new market among seventeenth-century Europeans. Despite the opposition of individuals like King James I of England, who condemned tobacco smoke as "dangerous to the eye, hateful to the nose, harmful to the brain, and dangerous to the lungs," the habit spread. By 1614 tobacco was reportedly being sold in seven thousand shops in and around London, and some English businessmen were dreaming of a tobacco trade as valuable as Spain's silver fleets.

Turning such pipe dreams into reality was not easy. Diseases, hurricanes, and attacks by the Carib and the Spanish scourged the early French and English West

Montserrat (mont-suh-RAHT) **Barbados** (bahr-BAY-dohs)
Martinique (mahr-tee-NEEK) **Guadeloupe** (gwah-duh-LOOP)

Indies colonists. They also suffered from shortages of supplies from Europe and shortages of labor sufficient to clear and plant virgin land with tobacco. Two changes improved the colonies' prospects. One was the formation of **chartered companies.** To promote national claims without government expense, France and England gave groups of private investors monopolies over trade to their West Indies colonies in exchange for the payment of annual fees. The other change was that the companies began to provide free passage to the colonies for poor Europeans. These indentured servants paid off their debt by working three or four years for the established colonists (see Chapter 18).

Under this system the French and English population on several tobacco islands grew rapidly in the 1630s and 1640s. By the middle of the century, however, the Caribbean colonies were in crisis because of stiff competition from milder Virginia-grown tobacco, also cultivated by indentured servants. The cultivation of sugar cane, introduced in the 1640s by Dutch investors expelled from Brazil, provided a way out of this crisis. In the process, the labor force changed from mostly European to mostly African.

The Portuguese had introduced sugar cultivation into Brazil from islands along the African coast after 1550 and had soon introduced enslaved African labor as well (see Chapter 18). By 1600 Brazil was the Atlantic world's greatest sugar producer. Some Dutch merchants invested in Brazilian sugar plantations so that they might profit from transporting the sugar across the Atlantic and distributing it in Europe. However, in the first half of the seventeenth century the Dutch were fighting for their independence from the Spanish crown, which then ruled Portugal and Brazil. As part of that struggle, the Dutch government chartered the **Dutch West India Company** in 1621 to carry the conflict to Spain's overseas possessions.

Not just a disguised form of the Dutch navy, the Dutch West India Company was a private trading company. Its investors expected the company's profits to cover its expenses and pay them dividends. After the capture of a Spanish treasure fleet in 1628, the company used some of the windfall to pay its stockholders a huge dividend and the rest to finance an assault on Brazil's valuable sugar-producing areas. By 1635 the Dutch company controlled 1,000 miles (1,600 kilometers) of northeastern Brazil's coast. Over the next fifteen years the new Dutch owners improved the efficiency of the Brazilian sugar industry, and the company prospered by supplying the plantations with enslaved Africans and European goods and carrying the sugar back to Europe.

Like its assault on Brazil, the Dutch West India Company's entry into the African slave trade combined economic and political motives. It seized the important West African trading station of Elmina from the Portuguese in 1638 and took their port of Luanda° on the Angolan coast in 1641. From these coasts the Dutch shipped slaves to Brazil and the West Indies. Although the Portuguese were able to drive the Dutch out of Angola after a few years, Elmina remained the Dutch West India Company's headquarters in West Africa.

Once free of Spanish rule in 1640, the Portuguese crown turned its attention to reconquering Brazil. By 1654 Portuguese armies had driven the last of the Dutch sugar planters from Brazil. Some of the expelled planters transplanted their capital and knowledge of sugar production to small Caribbean colonies, which the Dutch had founded earlier as trading bases with Spanish colonies; others introduced the Brazilian system into English and French Caribbean islands. This was a momentous turning point in the history of the Atlantic economy.

Sugar and Slaves

The Dutch infusion of expertise and money revived the French colonies of Guadeloupe and Martinique, but the English colony of Barbados best illustrates the dramatic transformation that sugar brought to the seventeenth-century Caribbean. In 1640 Barbados's economy depended largely on tobacco, mostly grown by European settlers, both free and indentured. By the 1680s sugar had become the colony's principal crop, and enslaved Africans were three times as numerous as Europeans. Exporting up to 15,000 tons of sugar a year, Barbados had become the wealthiest and most populous of England's American colonies. By 1700 the West Indies had surpassed Brazil as the world's principal source of sugar.

The expansion of sugar plantations in the West Indies required a sharp increase in the volume of the slave trade from Africa (see Figure 19.1). During the first half of the seventeenth century about ten thousand slaves a year had arrived from Africa. Most were destined for Brazil and the mainland Spanish colonies. In the second half of the century the trade averaged twenty thousand slaves a year. More than half were intended for the English, French, and Dutch West Indies and most of the rest for Brazil. A century later the volume of the Atlantic slave trade was three times larger.

The shift in favor of African slaves was a product of many factors. Recent scholarship has cast doubt on the once-common assertion that Africans were more suited than Europeans to field labor, since newly arrived Africans

Luanda (loo-AHN-duh)

Figure 19.1 Transatlantic Slave Trade from Africa, 1551–1850

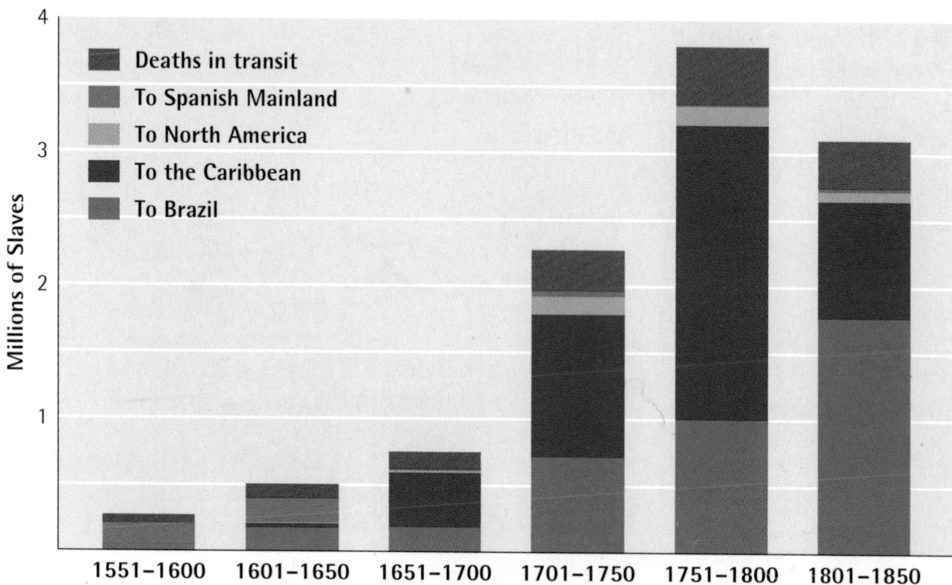

Source: Data from David Eltis, "The Volume and Structure of the Transatlantic Slave Trade: A Reassessment," *William and Mary Quarterly*, 3d Series, 58 (2001), tables II and III.

and Europeans both died in large numbers in the American tropics. Africans' slightly higher survival rate was not decisive because mortality was about the same among later generations of blacks and whites born in the West Indies and acclimated to its diseases.

The West Indian historian Eric Williams also refuted the idea that the rise of African slave labor was primarily motivated by prejudice. Citing the West Indian colonies' prior use of enslaved Amerindians and indentured Europeans, along with European convicts and prisoners of war, he argued that "Slavery was not born of racism: rather, racism was the consequence of slavery."[1] Williams suggested that the shift was due to the lower cost of African labor.

Yet slaves were far from cheap. Cash-short tobacco planters in the seventeenth century preferred indentured Europeans because they cost half as much as African slaves. Poor European men and women were willing to work for little in order to get to the Americas, where they could acquire their own land cheaply at the end of their terms of service. However, as the cultivation of sugar spread after 1750, rich speculators drove the price of land in the West Indies so high that end-of-term indentured servants could not afford to buy it. As a result, poor Europeans chose to indenture themselves in the mainland North American colonies, where cheap land was still available. Rather than raise wages to attract European laborers, Caribbean sugar planters switched to slaves.

Rising sugar prices helped the West Indian sugar planters afford the higher cost of African slaves. The fact that the average slave lived seven years, while the typical indentured labor contract was for only three or four years, also made slaves a better investment. The planters could rely on the Dutch and other traders to supply them with enough new slaves to meet the demands of the expanding plantations. Rising demand for slaves (see Figure 19.1) drove their sale price up steadily during the eighteenth century. These high labor costs were one more factor favoring large plantations over smaller operations.

Plantation Life in the Eighteenth Century

To find more land for sugar plantations, France and England founded new Caribbean colonies. In 1655 the English had wrested the island of Jamaica from the Spanish (see Map 18.1). The French seized the western half of the large Spanish island of Hispaniola in the 1670s. During the eighteenth century this new French colony of Saint Domingue° (present-day Haiti) became the greatest producer of sugar in the Atlantic world,

Saint Domingue (san doh-MANGH)

Plantation Scene, Antigua, British West Indies The sugar made at the mill in the background was sealed in barrels and loaded on carts that oxen and horses drew to the beach. By means of a succession of vessels the barrels were taken to the ship that hauled the cargo to Europe. The importance of African labor is evident from the fact that only one white person appears in the painting. (Courtesy of the John Carter Brown Library at Brown University)

while Jamaica surpassed Barbados as England's most important sugar colony. The technological, environmental, and social transformation of these island colonies illustrates the power of the new Atlantic system.

Technology and Environment

The cultivation of sugar cane was fairly straightforward. From fourteen to eighteen months after planting, the canes were ready to be cut. The roots continued to produce new shoots that could be harvested about every nine months. Only simple tools were needed: spades for planting, hoes to control the weeds, and sharp machetes to cut the canes. What made the sugar plantation a complex investment was that it had to be a factory as well as a farm. Freshly cut canes needed to be crushed within a few hours to extract the sugary sap. Thus, for maximum efficiency, each plantation needed its own expensive crushing and processing equipment.

At the heart of the sugar works was the mill where canes were crushed between sets of heavy rollers. Small mills could be turned by animal or human power, but larger, more efficient mills needed more sophisticated sources of power. Eighteenth-century Barbados went in heavily for windmills, and the French sugar islands and Jamaica used costly water-powered mills, often fed by elaborate aqueducts.

From the mill, lead-lined wooden troughs carried the cane juice to a series of large copper kettles in the boiling shed, where the excess water boiled off, leaving a thick syrup. Workers poured the syrup into conical molds in the drying shed. The sugar crystals that formed in the molds were packed in wooden barrels for shipment to Europe. The dark molasses that drained off was made into rum in yet another building, or it was barreled for export.

To make the operation more efficient and profitable, investors gradually increased the size of the typical West Indian plantation from around 100 acres (40 hectares) in the seventeenth century to at least twice that size in the eighteenth century. Some plantations were even larger. In 1774 Jamaica's 680 sugar plantations averaged 441 acres (178 hectares) each; some spread over 2,000 acres

(800 hectares). Jamaica specialized so heavily in sugar production that the island had to import most of its food. Saint Domingue had a comparable number of plantations of smaller average size but generally higher productivity. The French colony was also more diverse in its economy. Although sugar production was paramount, some planters raised provisions for local consumption and crops such as coffee and cacao for export.

In some ways the mature sugar plantation was environmentally responsible. The crushing mill was powered by water, wind, or animals, not fossil fuels. The boilers were largely fueled by burning the crushed canes, and the fields were fertilized by manure from the cattle. In two respects, however, the plantation was very damaging to the environment: soil exhaustion and deforestation.

Repeated cultivation of a single crop removes more nutrients from the soil than animal fertilizer and fallow periods can restore. Instead of rotating sugar with other crops in order to restore the nutrients naturally, planters found it more profitable to clear new lands when yields declined too much in the old fields. When land close to the sea was exhausted, planters moved on to new islands. Many of the English who first settled Jamaica were from Barbados, and the pioneer planters on Saint Domingue came from older French sugar colonies. In the second half of the eighteenth century, Jamaican sugar production began to fall behind that of Saint Domingue, which still had access to virgin land. Thus the plantations of this period were not a stable form of agriculture but rather gradually laid waste to the landscape.

Deforestation, the second form of environmental damage, continued a trend begun in the sixteenth century. The Spanish had cut down some forests in the Caribbean to make pastures for the cattle they introduced. Sugar cultivation rapidly accelerated land clearing. Forests near the coast were the first to disappear, and by the end of the eighteenth century only land in the interior of the islands retained dense forests.

Combined with soil exhaustion and deforestation, other changes profoundly altered the ecology balance of the West Indies. By the eighteenth century nearly all of the domesticated animals and cultivated plants in the Caribbean were ones that Europeans had introduced. The Spanish had brought cattle, pigs, and horses, all of which multiplied so rapidly that no new imports had been necessary after 1503. They had also introduced new plants. Of these, bananas and plantain from the Canary Islands were a valuable addition to the food supply, and sugar and rice formed the basis of plantation agriculture, along with native tobacco. Other food crops arrived with the slaves from Africa, including okra, black-eyed peas, yams, grains such as millet and sorghum, and mangoes. Many of these new animals and plants were useful additions to the islands, but they crowded out indigenous species. New World foods also found their way to Africa (see Environment and Technology: Amerindian Foods in Africa).

The most tragic and dramatic transformation in the West Indies occurred in the human population. Chapter 16 detailed how the indigenous Arawak peoples of the large islands were wiped out by disease and abuse within fifty years of Columbus's first voyage. As the plantation economy spread, the Carib surviving on the smaller islands were also pushed to the point of extinction. Far earlier and more completely than in any mainland colony, the West Indies were repeopled from across the Atlantic—first from Europe and then from Africa.

Slaves' Lives

During the eighteenth century West Indian plantation colonies were the world's most polarized societies. On most islands 90 percent or more of the inhabitants were slaves. Power resided in the hands of a **plantocracy,** a small number of very rich men who owned most of the slaves and most of the land. Between the slaves and the masters might be found only a few others—some estate managers and government officials and, in the French islands, small farmers, both white and black. Thus it is only a slight simplification to describe eighteenth-century Caribbean society as being made up of a large, abject class of slaves and a small, powerful class of masters.

The profitability of a Caribbean plantation depended on extracting as much work as possible from the slaves. Their long workday might stretch to eighteen hours or more when the cane harvest and milling were in full swing. Sugar plantations achieved exceptional productivity through the threat and use of force. As Table 19.1 shows (see page 507), on a typical Jamaican plantation about 80 percent of the slaves actively engaged in productive tasks; the only exceptions were infants, the seriously ill, and the very old. Everyone on the plantation, except those disabled by age or infirmity, had an assigned task.

Table 19.1 also illustrates how slave labor was organized by age, sex, and ability. As in other Caribbean colonies, only 2 or 3 percent of the slaves were house servants. About 70 percent of the able-bodied slaves worked in the fields, generally in one of three labor gangs. A "great gang," made up of the strongest slaves in the prime of life, did the heaviest work, such as breaking up the soil at the beginning of the planting season. A second gang of youths, elders, and less fit slaves did somewhat lighter work. A "grass gang," composed of children under the supervision of an elderly slave, was responsible for weeding and other simple work, such as collecting grass

ENVIRONMENT + TECHNOLOGY

Amerindian Foods in Africa

The migration of European plants and animals across the Atlantic to the New World was one side of the Columbian Exchange (see Chapter 18). The Andean potato, for example, became a staple crop of the poor in Europe, and cassava (a Brazilian plant cultivated for its edible roots) and maize (corn) moved across the Atlantic to Africa.

Maize was a high-yielding grain that could produce much more food per acre than many grains indigenous to Africa. The varieties of maize that spread to Africa were not modern high-bred "sweet corn" but starchier types found in white and yellow corn meal. Cassava—not well known to modern North Americans except perhaps in the form of tapioca—became the most important New World food in Africa. Truly a marvel, cassava had the highest yield of calories per acre of any staple food and thrived even in poor soils and during droughts. Both the leaves and the root could be eaten. Ground into meal, the root could be made into a bread that would keep for up to six months, or it could be fermented into a beverage.

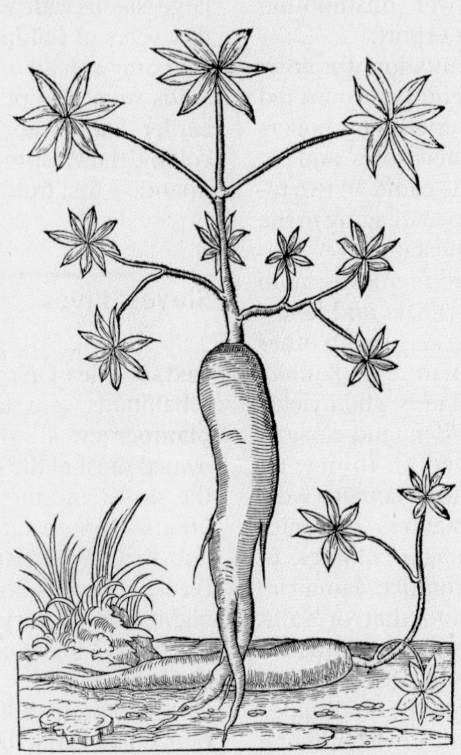

Cassava Plant Both the leaves and the starchy root of the cassava plant could be eaten. (Engraving from André Thevet, *Les Singularitez de la France Antarctique*. Paris: Maurice de la Porte, 1557. Courtesy of the James Bell Library, University of Minnesota)

Cassava and maize were probably accidentally introduced into Africa by Portuguese ships from Brazil that discarded leftover supplies after reaching Angola. It did not take long for local Africans to recognize the food value of these new crops, especially in drought-prone areas. As the principal farmers in Central Africa, women must have played an important role in learning how to cultivate, harvest, and prepare these foods. By the eighteenth century Lunda rulers hundreds of miles from the Angolan coast were actively promoting the cultivation of maize and cassava on their royal estates in order to provide a more secure food supply.

Some historians of Africa believe that in the inland areas these Amerindian food crops provided the nutritional base for a population increase that partially offset losses due to the Atlantic slave trade. By supplementing the range of food crops available and by enabling populations to increase in once lightly settled or famine-prone areas, cassava and maize, along with peanuts and other New World legumes, permanently altered Africans' environmental prospects.

for the animals. Women formed the majority of the field laborers, even in the great gang. Nursing mothers took their babies with them to the fields. Slaves too old for field labor tended the toddlers.

Because slave ships brought twice as many males as females from Africa, men outnumbered women on Caribbean plantations. As Table 19.1 shows, a little over half of the adult males were employed in nongang work. Some tended the livestock, including the mules and oxen that did the heavy carrying work; others were skilled tradesmen, such as blacksmiths and carpenters. The most important artisan slave was the head boiler, who oversaw the delicate process of reducing the cane sap to crystallized sugar and molasses.

Skilled slaves received rewards of food and clothing or time off for good work, but the most common reason for working hard was to escape punishment. A slave gang was headed by a privileged male slave, appropriately called the **"driver,"** whose job was to ensure that the gang completed its work. Since production quotas

Table 19.1 Slave Occupations on a Jamaican Sugar Plantation, 1788

Occupations and Conditions	Men	Women	Boys and Girls	Total
Field laborers	62	78		140
Tradesmen	29			29
Field drivers	4			4
Field cooks		4		4
Mule-, cattle-, and stablemen	12			12
Watchmen	18			18
Nurse		1		1
Midwife		1		1
Domestics and gardeners		5	3	8
Grass-gang			20	20
Total employed	**125**	**89**	**23**	**237**
Infants			23	23
Invalids (18 with yaws)				32
Absent on roads				5
Superannuated [elderly]				7
Overall total				**304**

Source: Adapted from "Edward Long to William Pitt," in Michael Craton, James Walvin, and David Wright, eds., *Slavery, Abolition, and Emancipation* (London: Longman, 1976), 103. © Michael Craton, James Walvin, and David Wright, reprinted by permission of Pearson Education Limited.

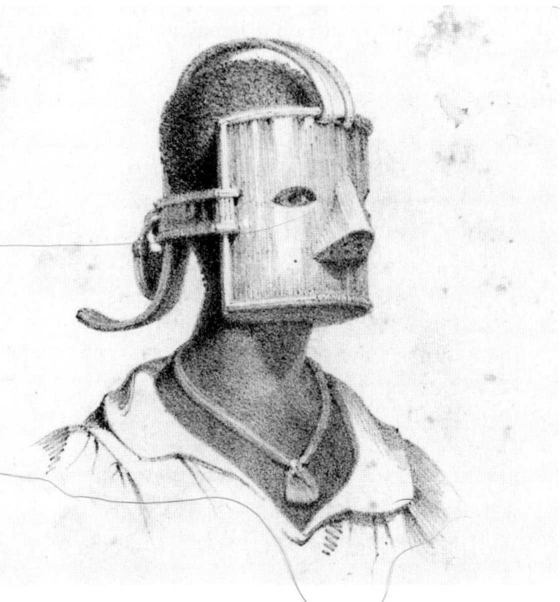

Punishment for Slaves In addition to whipping and other cruel punishments, slave owners devised other ways to shame and intimidate slaves into obedience. This metal face mask prevented the wearer from eating or drinking. (By permission of the Syndics of Cambridge University Library)

were high, slaves toiled in the fields from sunup to sunset, except for meal breaks. Those who fell behind due to fatigue or illness soon felt the sting of the whip. Openly rebellious slaves who refused to work, disobeyed orders, or tried to escape were punished with flogging, confinement in irons, or mutilation. Sometimes slaves were punished with an "iron muzzle," which covered their faces and kept them from eating and drinking.

Even though slaves did not work in the fields on Sunday, it was no day of rest, for they had to farm their own provisioning grounds, maintain their dwellings, and do other chores, such as washing and mending their rough clothes. Sunday markets, where slaves sold small amounts of produce or animals they had raised to get a little spending money, were common in the British West Indies.

Except for occasional holidays—including the Christmas-week revels in the British West Indies—there was little time for recreation and relaxation. Slaves might sing in the fields, but singing was simply a way to distract themselves from their fatigue and the monotony of the work. There was certainly no time for schooling, nor was there willingness to educate slaves beyond skills useful to the plantation.

Time for family life was also inadequate. Although the large proportion of young adults in plantation colonies ought to have had a high rate of natural increase, the opposite occurred. Poor nutrition and overwork lowered fertility. A woman who did become pregnant found it difficult to carry a child to term while continuing heavy fieldwork or to ensure her infant's survival. As a result of these conditions along with disease and accidents from dangerous mill equipment, deaths heavily outnumbered births on West Indian plantations (see Table 19.2). Life expectancy for slaves in nineteenth-century Brazil was only 23 years of age for males and 25.5 years for females. The figures were probably similar for the eighteenth-century Caribbean. A callous opinion, common among slave owners in the Caribbean and in parts of Brazil, held that it was cheaper to import a youthful new slave from Africa than to raise one to the same age on a plantation.

The harsh conditions of plantation life played a major role in shortening slaves' lives, but the greatest killer

Table 19.2 Birth and Death on a Jamaican Sugar Plantation, 1779–1785

	Born			Died		
Year	Males	Females	Purchased	Males	Females	Proportion of Deaths
1779	5	2	6	7	5	1 in 26
1780	4	3	–	3	2	1 in 62
1781	2	3	–	4	2	1 in 52
1782	1	3	9	4	5	1 in 35
1783	3	3	–	8	10	1 in 17
1784	2	1	12	9	10	1 in 17
1785	2	3	–	0	3	1 in 99
Total	19	18	27	35	37	
	Born 37			Died 72		

Source: From "Edward Long to William Pitt," in Michael Craton, James Walvin, and David Wright, eds., *Slavery, Abolition, and Emancipation* (London: Longman, 1976), 105.

was disease. The very young were carried off by dysentery caused by contaminated food and water. Slaves newly arrived from Africa went through the period of adjustment to a new environment known as **seasoning,** during which one-third, on average, died of unfamiliar diseases. Slaves also suffered from diseases brought with them, including malaria. On the plantation profiled in Table 19.1, for example, more than half of the slaves incapacitated by illness had yaws, a painful and debilitating skin disease common in Africa. As a consequence, only slave populations in the healthier temperate zones of North America experienced natural increase; those in tropical Brazil and the Caribbean had a negative rate of growth.

Such high mortality greatly added to the volume of the Atlantic slave trade, since plantations had to purchase new slaves every year or two just to replace those who died (see Table 19.2). The additional imports of slaves to permit the expansion of the sugar plantations meant that the majority of slaves on most West Indian plantations were African-born. As a result, African religious beliefs, patterns of speech, styles of dress and adornment, and music were prominent parts of West Indian life.

Given the harsh conditions of their lives, it is not surprising that slaves in the West Indies often sought to regain the freedom into which most had been born. Individual slaves often ran away, hoping to elude the men and dogs who would track them. Sometimes large groups of plantation slaves rose in rebellion against their bondage and abuse. For example, a large rebellion in Jamaica in 1760 was led by a slave named Tacky, who had been a chief on the Gold Coast of Africa. One night his followers broke into a fort and armed themselves. Joined by slaves from nearby plantations, they stormed several plantations, setting them on fire and killing the planter families. Tacky died in the fighting that followed, and three other rebel leaders stoically endured cruel deaths by torture that were meant to deter others from rebellion.

Because they believed rebellions were usually led by slaves with the strongest African heritage, European planters tried to curtail African cultural traditions. They required slaves to learn the colonial language and discouraged the use of African languages by deliberately mixing slaves from different parts of Africa. In French and Portuguese colonies, slaves were encouraged to adopt Catholic religious practices, though African deities and beliefs also survived. In the British West Indies, where only Quaker slave owners encouraged Christianity among their slaves before 1800, African herbal medicine remained strong, as did African beliefs concerning nature spirits and witchcraft.

Free Whites and Free Blacks

The lives of the small minority of free people were very different from the lives of slaves. In the French colony of Saint Domingue, which had nearly half of the slaves in the Caribbean in the eighteenth century, free people fell into three distinct groups. At the top of free society were the wealthy owners of large sugar plantations (the *grands*

The Unknown Maroon of Saint-Domingue This modern sculpture by Albert Mangonès celebrates the brave but perilous life of a runaway slave, who is shown drinking water from a seashell. (Albert Mangonès, "The Unknown Maroon of Saint-Domingue." From Richard Price, *Maroon Societies*, Johns Hopkins University Press. Reproduced with permission.)

blancs°, or "great whites"), who dominated the economy and society of the island. Second came less-well-off Europeans (*petits blancs*°, or "little whites"). Most of them raised provisions for local consumption and crops such as coffee, indigo, and cotton for export, relying on their own and slave labor. Third came the free blacks. Though nearly as numerous as the free whites and engaged in similar occupations, they ranked below whites socially. A few free blacks became wealthy enough to own their own slaves.

The dominance of the plantocracy was even greater in British colonies. Whereas sugar constituted about half of Saint Domingue's exports, in Jamaica the figure was over 80 percent. Such concentration on sugar cane left much less room for small cultivators, white or black, and confined most landholding to a few larger owners. At midcentury three-quarters of the farmland in Jamaica belonged to individuals who owned 1,000 acres (400 hectares) or more.

One source estimated that a planter had to invest nearly £20,000 ($100,000) to acquire even a medium-size Jamaican plantation of 600 acres (240 hectares) in 1774. A third of this money went for land on which to grow sugar and food crops, pasture animals, and cut timber and firewood. A quarter of the expense was for the sugar works and other equipment. The largest expense was to purchase 200 slaves at about £40 ($200) each. In comparison, the wage of an English rural laborer at this time was about £10 ($50) a year (one-fourth the price of a slave), and the annual incomes in 1760 of the ten wealthiest noble families in Britain averaged only £20,000 each.

Reputedly the richest Englishmen of this time, West Indian planters often translated their wealth into political power and social prestige. The richest planters put their plantations under the direction of managers and lived in Britain, often on rural estates that once had been the preserve of country gentlemen. Between 1730 and 1775 seventy of these absentee planters secured election to the British Parliament, where they formed an influential voting bloc. Those who resided in the West Indies had political power as well, for the British plantocracy controlled the colonial assemblies.

Most Europeans in plantation colonies were single males. Many of them took advantage of slave women for sexual favors or took slave mistresses. A slave owner who fathered a child by a female slave often gave both mother and child their freedom. In some colonies such **manumission** (a legal grant of freedom to an individual slave) produced a significant free black population. By the late eighteenth century free blacks were more numerous than slaves in most of the Spanish colonies. They made up almost 30 percent of the black population of Brazil, and they existed in significant numbers in the French colonies. Free blacks were far less common in the British colonies and the United States, where manumission was rare.

As in Brazil (see Chapter 18), escaped slaves constituted another part of the free black population. In the Caribbean runaways were known as **maroons.** Maroon communities were especially numerous in the mountainous interiors of Jamaica and Hispaniola as well as in the island parts of the Guianas°. Jamaican maroons, after withstanding several attacks by the colony's militia, signed a treaty in 1739 that recognized their independence in return for their cooperation in stopping new runaways and suppressing slave revolts. Similar treaties with the large maroon population in the Dutch colony of Surinam (Dutch Guiana) recognized their possession of large inland regions.

---

grands blancs (grawn blawnk) **petits blancs** (pay-TEE blawnk)

Guianas (guy-AHN-uhs)

CREATING THE ATLANTIC ECONOMY

At once archaic in their cruel system of slavery and oddly modern in their specialization in a single product, the West Indian plantation colonies were the bittersweet fruits of a new Atlantic trading system. Changes in the type and number of ships crossing the Atlantic illustrate the rise of this new system. The Atlantic trade of the sixteenth century calls to mind the treasure fleet, an annual convoy of from twenty to sixty ships laden with silver and gold bullion from Spanish America. Two different vessels typify the far more numerous Atlantic voyages of the late seventeenth and eighteenth centuries. One was the sugar ship, returning to Europe from the West Indies or Brazil crammed with barrels of brown sugar destined for further refinement. At the end of the seventeenth century an average of 266 sugar ships sailed every year just from the small island of Barbados. The second type of vessel was the slave ship. At the trade's peak between 1760 and 1800, some 300 ships, crammed with an average of 250 African captives each, crossed the Atlantic to the Americas each year.

Many separate pieces went into the creation of the new Atlantic economy. Besides the plantation system itself, three other elements merit further investigation: new economic institutions, new partnerships between private investors and governments in Europe, and new working relationships between European and African merchants. The new trading system is a prime example of how European capitalist relationships were reshaping the world.

Capitalism and Mercantilism

The Spanish and Portuguese voyages of exploration in the fifteenth and sixteenth centuries were government ventures, and both countries tried to keep their overseas trade and colonies royal monopolies (see Chapters 16 and 18). Monopoly control, however, proved both expensive and inefficient. The success of the Atlantic economy in the seventeenth and eighteenth centuries owed much to private enterprise, which made trading venues more efficient and profitable. European private investors were attracted by the profits they could make from an established and growing trading and colonial system, but their successful participation in the Atlantic economy depended on new institutions and a significant measure of government protection that reduced the likelihood of catastrophic loss.

Two European innovations enabled private investors to fund the rapid growth of the Atlantic economy. One was the ability to manage large financial resources through mechanisms that modern historians have labeled **capitalism.** The essence of early modern capitalism was a system of large financial institutions—banks, stock exchanges, and chartered trading companies—that enabled wealthy investors to reduce risks and increase profits. Originally developed for business dealings within Europe, the capitalist system expanded overseas in the seventeenth century, when slow economic growth in Europe led many investors to seek greater profits abroad.

Banks were a central capitalist institution. By the early seventeenth century Dutch banks had developed such a reputation for security that individuals and governments from all over western Europe entrusted them with large sums of money. To make a profit, the banks invested these funds in real estate, local industries, loans to governments, and overseas trade.

Individuals seeking returns higher than the low rate of interest paid by banks could purchase shares in a joint-stock company, a sixteenth-century forerunner of the modern corporation. Shares were bought and sold in specialized financial markets called stock exchanges. The Amsterdam Exchange, founded in 1530, became the greatest stock market in the seventeenth and eighteenth centuries. To reduce risks in overseas trading, merchants and trading companies bought insurance on their ships and cargoes from specialized companies that agreed to cover losses.

The capitalism of these centuries was buttressed by **mercantilism,** policies adopted by European states to promote their citizens' overseas trade and accumulate capital in the form of precious metals, especially gold and silver. Mercantilist policies strongly discouraged citizens from trading with foreign merchants and used armed force when necessary to secure exclusive relations.

Chartered companies were one of the first examples of mercantilist capitalism. A charter issued by the government of the Netherlands in 1602 gave the Dutch East India Company a legal monopoly over all Dutch trade in the Indian Ocean. This privilege encouraged private investors to buy shares in the company. They were amply rewarded when Dutch East India Company captured control of long-distance trade routes in the Indian Ocean from the Portuguese (see Chapter 20). As we have seen, a sister firm, the Dutch West India Company, was chartered in 1621 to engage in the Atlantic trade and to seize sugar-producing areas in Brazil and African slaving ports from the Portuguese.

Such successes inspired other governments to set up their own chartered companies. In 1672 a royal charter placed all English trade with West Africa in the hands of a new Royal African Company, which established its headquarters at Cape Coast Castle, just east of Elmina on the Gold Coast. The French government also played an active role in chartering companies and promoting overseas trade and colonization. Jean Baptiste Colbert°, King Louis XIV's minister of finance from 1661 to 1683, chartered French East India and French West India Companies to reduce French colonies' dependence on Dutch and English traders.

French and English governments also used military force in pursuit of commercial dominance, especially to break the trading advantage of the Dutch in the Americas. Restrictions on Dutch access to French and English colonies provoked a series of wars with the Netherlands between 1652 and 1678 (see Chapter 18), during which the larger English and French navies defeated the Dutch and drove the Dutch West India Company into bankruptcy.

With Dutch competition in the Atlantic reduced, the French and English governments moved to revoke the monopoly privileges of their chartered companies. England opened trade in Africa to any English subject in 1698 on the grounds that ending monopolies would be "highly beneficial and advantageous to this kingdom." It was hoped that such competition would also cut the cost of slaves to West Indian planters, though the demand for slaves soon drove the prices up again.

Such new mercantilist policies fostered competition among a nation's own citizens, while using high tariffs and restrictions to exclude foreigners. In the 1660s England had passed a series of Navigation Acts that confined trade with its colonies to English ships and cargoes. The French called their mercantilist legislation, first codified in 1698, the *Exclusif*°, highlighting its exclusionary intentions. Other mercantilist laws defended manufacturing and processing interests in Europe against competition from colonies, imposing prohibitively high taxes on any manufactured goods and refined sugar imported from the colonies.

As a result of such mercantilist measures, the Atlantic became Britain, France, and Portugal's most important overseas trading area in the eighteenth century. Britain's imports from its West Indian colonies in this period accounted for over one-fifth of the value of total British imports. The French West Indian colonies played an even larger role in France's overseas trade. Only the Dutch, closed out of much of the American trade, found Asian trade of greater importance (see Chapter 20). Profits from the Atlantic economy, in turn, promoted further economic expansion and increased the revenues of European governments.

Colbert (kohl-BEAR) ***Exclusif*** (ek-skloo-SEEF)

The Atlantic Circuit

At the heart of this trading system was a clockwise network of sea routes known as the **Atlantic Circuit** (see Map 19.1). It began in Europe, ran south to Africa, turned west across the Atlantic Ocean to the Americas, and then swept back to Europe. Like Asian sailors in the Indian Ocean, Atlantic mariners depended on the prevailing winds and currents to propel their ships. What drove the ships as much as the winds and currents was the desire for the profits that each leg of the circuit was expected to produce.

The first leg, from Europe to Africa, carried European manufactures—notably metal bars, hardware, and guns—as well as great quantities of cotton textiles brought from India. Some of these goods were traded for West African gold, timber, and other products, which were taken back to Europe. More goods went to purchase slaves, who were transported across the Atlantic to the plantation colonies in the part of the Atlantic Circuit known as the **Middle Passage.** On the third leg, plantation goods from the colonies returned to Europe. Each leg carried goods from where they were abundant and relatively cheap to where they were scarce and therefore more valuable. Thus, in theory, each leg of the Atlantic Circuit could earn much more than its costs, and a ship that completed all three legs could return a handsome profit to its owners. In practice, shipwrecks, deaths, piracy, and other risks could turn profit into loss.

The three-sided Atlantic Circuit is only the simplest model of Atlantic trade. Many other trading voyages supplemented the basic circuit. Cargo ships made long voyages from Europe to the Indian Ocean, passed southward through the Atlantic with quantities of African gold and American silver, and returned with the cotton textiles necessary to the African trade. Other sea routes brought the West Indies manufactured goods from Europe or foodstuffs and lumber from New England. In addition, some Rhode Island and Massachusetts merchants participated in a "Triangular Trade" that carried rum to West Africa, slaves to the West Indies, and molasses and rum back to New England. There was also a considerable two-way trade between Brazil and Angola that exchanged Brazilian liquor and other goods for slaves. On another route, Brazil and Portugal exchanged sugar and gold for European imports.

European interests dominated the Atlantic system. The manufacturers who supplied the trade goods and the investors who provided the capital were all based in Europe, but so too were the principal consumers of the plantation products. Before the seventeenth century, sugar had been rare and fairly expensive in western Europe. By 1700 annual consumption of sugar in England had risen to about 4 pounds (nearly 2 kilograms) per

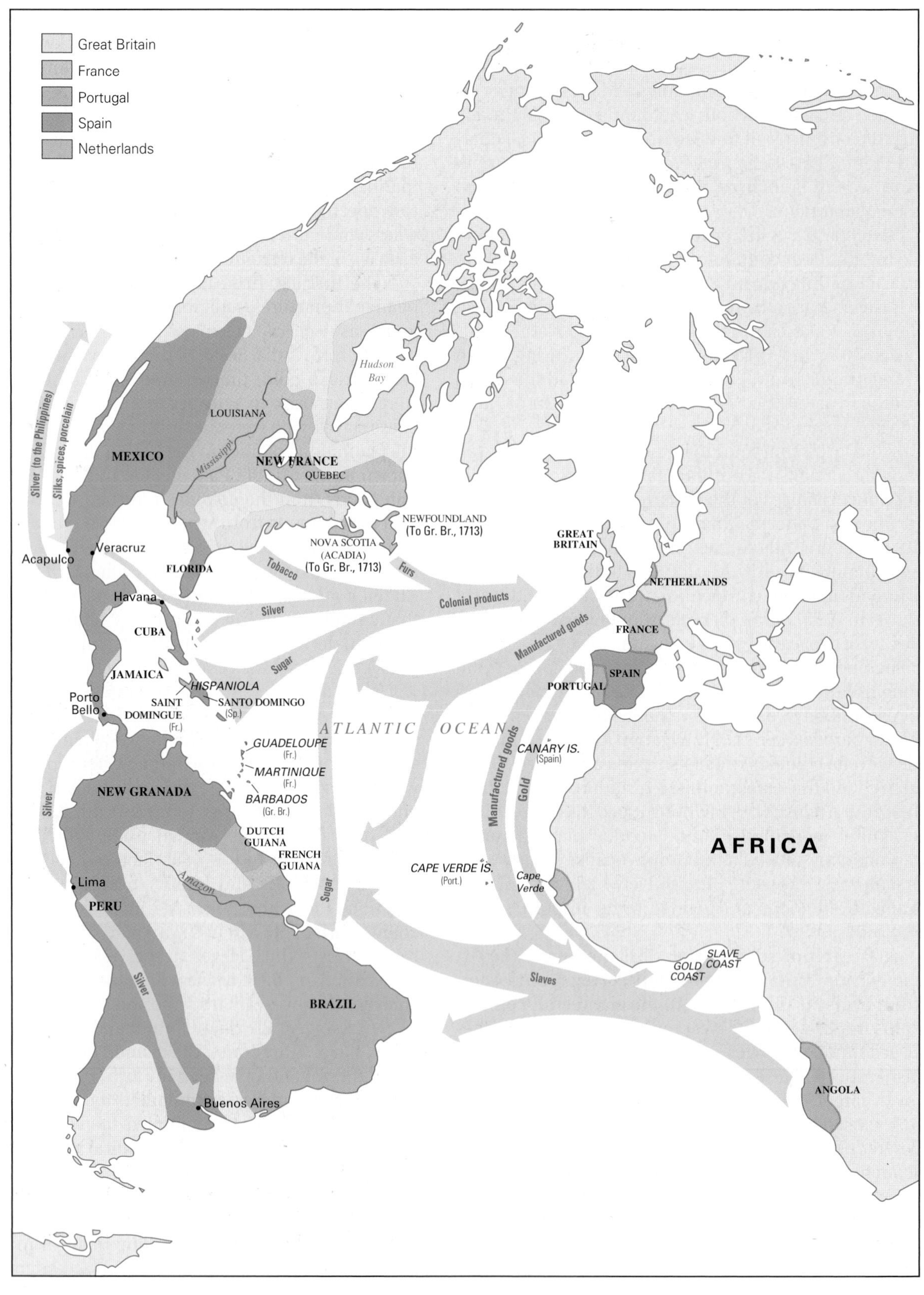
Great Britain
France
Portugal
Spain
Netherlands
Silver (to the Philippines)
Silks, spices, porcelain
MEXICO
LOUISIANA
Mississippi
NEW FRANCE
QUEBEC
Hudson Bay
NEWFOUNDLAND
(To Gr. Br., 1713)
NOVA SCOTIA
(ACADIA)
(To Gr. Br., 1713)
Acapulco
Veracruz
FLORIDA
Tobacco
Furs
Colonial products
GREAT BRITAIN
NETHERLANDS
Havana
Silver
CUBA
Sugar
Manufactured goods
FRANCE
JAMAICA
HISPANIOLA
SPAIN
PORTUGAL
Porto Bello
SAINT DOMINGUE (Fr.)
SANTO DOMINGO (Sp.)
ATLANTIC OCEAN
GUADELOUPE (Fr.)
MARTINIQUE (Fr.)
BARBADOS (Gr. Br.)
CANARY IS. (Spain)
Manufactured goods
Gold
Silver
NEW GRANADA
DUTCH GUIANA
FRENCH GUIANA
AFRICA
CAPE VERDE IS. (Port.)
Cape Verde
Lima
Amazon
Sugar
PERU
Slaves
GOLD COAST
SLAVE COAST
Silver
BRAZIL
ANGOLA
Buenos Aires

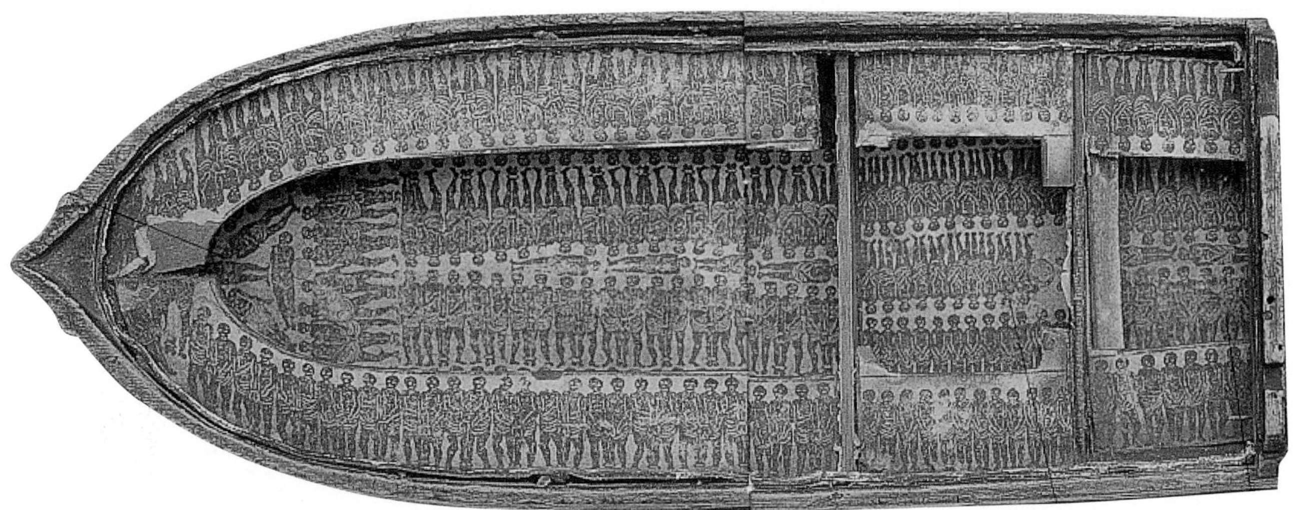

Slave Ship This model of the English vessel *Brookes* shows the specially built section of the hold where enslaved Africans were packed together during the Middle Passage. Girls, boys, and women were confined separately. (Wilberforce House Museum, Hull, Humberside, UK/The Bridgeman Art Library, London and New York)

person. Rising western European prosperity and declining sugar prices promoted additional consumption, starting with the upper classes and working its way down the social ladder. People spooned sugar into popular new beverages imported from overseas—tea, coffee, and chocolate—to overcome the beverages' natural bitterness. By 1750 annual sugar consumption in Britain had doubled, and it doubled again to about 18 pounds (8 kilograms) per person by the early nineteenth century (well below the American average of about 100 pounds [45 kilograms] a year in 1960).

The flow of sugar to Europe depended on another key component of the Atlantic trading system: the flow of slaves from Africa (see Map 19.2). The rising volume of the Middle Passage also measures the Atlantic system's expansion. During the first 150 years after the European discovery of the Americas, some 800,000 Africans had begun the journey across the Atlantic. During the boom in sugar production between 1650 and 1800, the slave trade amounted to nearly 7.5 million. Of the survivors, over half landed in the West Indies and nearly a third in Brazil. Plantations in North America imported another 5 percent, and the rest went to other parts of Spanish America (see Figure 19.1).

Map 19.1 The Atlantic Economy By 1700 the volume of maritime exchanges among the Atlantic continents had begun to rival the trade of the Indian Ocean basin. Notice the trade in consumer products, slave labor, precious metals, and other goods. Silver trade to East Asia laid the basis for a Pacific Ocean economy.

In these peak decades, the transportation of slaves from Africa was a highly specialized trade, although it regularly attracted some amateur traders hoping to make a quick profit. Most slaves were carried in ships that had been specially built or modified for the slave trade by the construction between the ships' decks of additional platforms on which the human cargo was packed as tightly as possible.

Seventeenth-century mercantilist policies placed much of the Atlantic slave trade in the hands of chartered companies. During their existence the Dutch West India Company and the English Royal African Company each carried about 100,000 slaves across the Atlantic. In the eighteenth century private English traders from Liverpool and Bristol controlled about 40 percent of the slave trade. The French, operating out of Nantes and Bordeaux, handled about half as much, but the Dutch hung on to only 6 percent. The Portuguese supplying Brazil and other places had nearly 30 percent of the Atlantic slave trade, in contrast to the 3 percent carried in North American ships.

To make a profit, European slave traders had to buy slaves in Africa for less than the cost of the goods they traded in return. Then they had to deliver as many

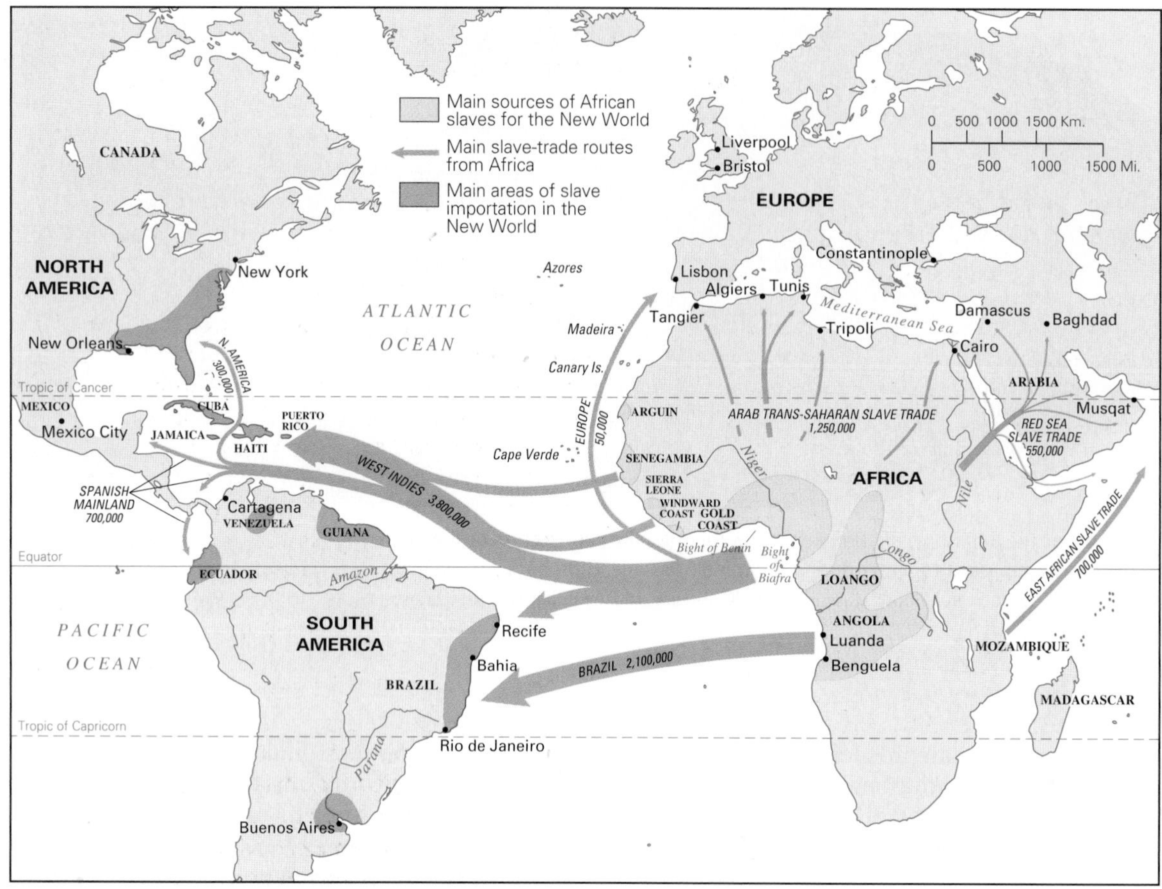

Map 19.2 The African Slave Trade, 1500–1800 After 1500 a vast new trade in slaves from sub-Saharan Africa to the Americas joined the ongoing slave trade to the Islamic states of North Africa, the Middle East, and India. The West Indies were the major destination of the Atlantic slave trade, followed by Brazil.

healthy slaves as possible across the Atlantic for resale in the plantation colonies. The treacherous voyage to the Americas lasted from six to ten weeks. Some ships completed it with all of their slaves alive, but large, even catastrophic, losses of life were common (see Figure 19.1). On average, however, slave transporters succeeded in lowering mortality during the Middle Passage from about 23 percent on voyages before 1700 to half that in the last half of the eighteenth century.

Some deaths resulted from the efforts of the captives to escape. As on the voyage of the *Hannibal* recounted at the beginning of the chapter, male slaves were shackled together to prevent them from trying to escape while they were still in sight of land. Because some still managed to jump overboard in pairs, slave ships were outfitted with special netting around the outside. Some slaves developed deep psychological depression, known to contemporaries as "fixed melancholy." Crews force-fed slaves who refused to eat, but some successfully willed themselves to death.

When opportunities presented themselves (nearness to land, illness among the crew), some enslaved Africans tried to overpower their captors. To inhibit such mutinies, African men were confined below deck during most of the voyage, except at mealtimes when they were brought up in small groups under close supervision. In any event, "mutinies" were rarely successful and were put down with brutality that occasioned further losses of life.

Other deaths during the Middle Passage were due to ill treatment. Although it was in the interests of the captain and crew to deliver their slave cargo in good condition, whippings, beatings, and even executions were used to maintain order or force captives to take nourishment. Moreover, the dangers and brutalities of the slave trade were so notorious that many ordinary seamen shunned such work. As a consequence, cruel and brutal officers and crews abounded on slave ships.

Although examples of unspeakable cruelties are common in the records, most deaths in the Middle Passage were the result of disease rather than abuse, as the voyage of the *Hannibal* illustrated. Dysentery spread by contaminated food and water caused many deaths. Other slaves died of contagious diseases such as smallpox carried by persons whose infections were not detected during medical examinations prior to boarding. Such maladies spread quickly in the crowded and unsanitary confines of the ships, claiming the lives of many slaves already physically weakened and mentally traumatized by their ordeals.

Crew members in close contact with the slaves were exposed to the same epidemics and also died in great numbers. Moreover, sailors often fell victim to tropical diseases, such as malaria, to which Africans had acquired resistance. It is a measure of the callousness of the age, as well as the cheapness of European labor, that over the course of a round-trip voyage from Europe the proportion of crew deaths could be as high as the slave deaths.

Africa, the Atlantic, and Islam

The Atlantic system took a terrible toll in African lives both during the Middle Passage and under the harsh conditions of plantation slavery. Many other Africans died while being marched to African coastal ports for sale overseas. The overall effects on Africa of these losses and of other aspects of the slave trade have been the subject of considerable historical debate. It is clear that the trade's impact depended on the intensity and terms of different African regions' involvement.

Any assessment of the Atlantic system's effects in Africa must also take into consideration the fact that some Africans profited from the trade by capturing and selling slaves. They chained the slaves together or bound them to forked sticks for the march to the coast, then bartered them to the European slavers for trade goods. The effects on the enslaver were different from the effects on the enslaved. Finally, a broader understanding of the Atlantic system's effects in sub-Saharan Africa comes from comparisons with the effects of Islamic contacts.

The Gold Coast and the Slave Coast

As Chapter 16 showed, early European visitors to Africa's Atlantic coast were interested more in trading than in colonizing or controlling the continent. As the Africa trade mushroomed after 1650, this pattern continued. African kings and merchants sold slaves and goods at many new coastal sites, but the growing slave trade did not lead to substantial European colonization.

The transition to slave trading was not sudden. Even as slaves were becoming Atlantic Africa's most valuable export, goods such as gold, ivory, and timber remained a significant part of the total trade. For example, during its eight decades of operation from 1672 to 1752, the Royal African Company made 40 percent of its profits from dealings in gold, ivory, and forest products. In some parts of West Africa, such nonslave exports remained predominant even at the peak of the trade.

African merchants were very discriminating about what merchandise they received in return for slaves or goods. A European ship that arrived with goods of low quality or not suited to local tastes found it hard to purchase a cargo at a profitable price. European guidebooks to the African trade carefully noted the color and shape of beads, the pattern of textiles, the type of guns, and the sort of metals that were in demand on each section of the coast. In the early eighteenth century the people of Sierra Leone had a strong preference for large iron kettles; brass pans were preferred on the Gold Coast; and iron and copper bars were in demand in the Niger Delta, where smiths turned them into useful objects (see Map 19.3).

Although preferences for merchandise varied, Africans' greatest demands were for textiles, hardware, and guns. Of the goods the Royal African Company traded in West Africa in the 1680s, over 60 percent were Indian and European textiles and 30 percent were hardware and weaponry. Beads and other jewelry made up 3 percent. The rest consisted of cowrie shells that were used as money. In the eighteenth century, tobacco and rum from the Americas became welcome imports.

Both Europeans and Africans attempted to drive the best bargain for themselves and sometimes engaged in deceitful practices. The strength of the African bargaining position, however, may be inferred from the fact that as the demand for slaves rose, so too did their price in Africa. In the course of the eighteenth century the goods needed to purchase a slave on the Gold Coast doubled and in some places tripled or quadrupled.

West Africans' trading strengths were reinforced by African governments on the Gold and Slave Coasts that made Europeans observe African trading customs and

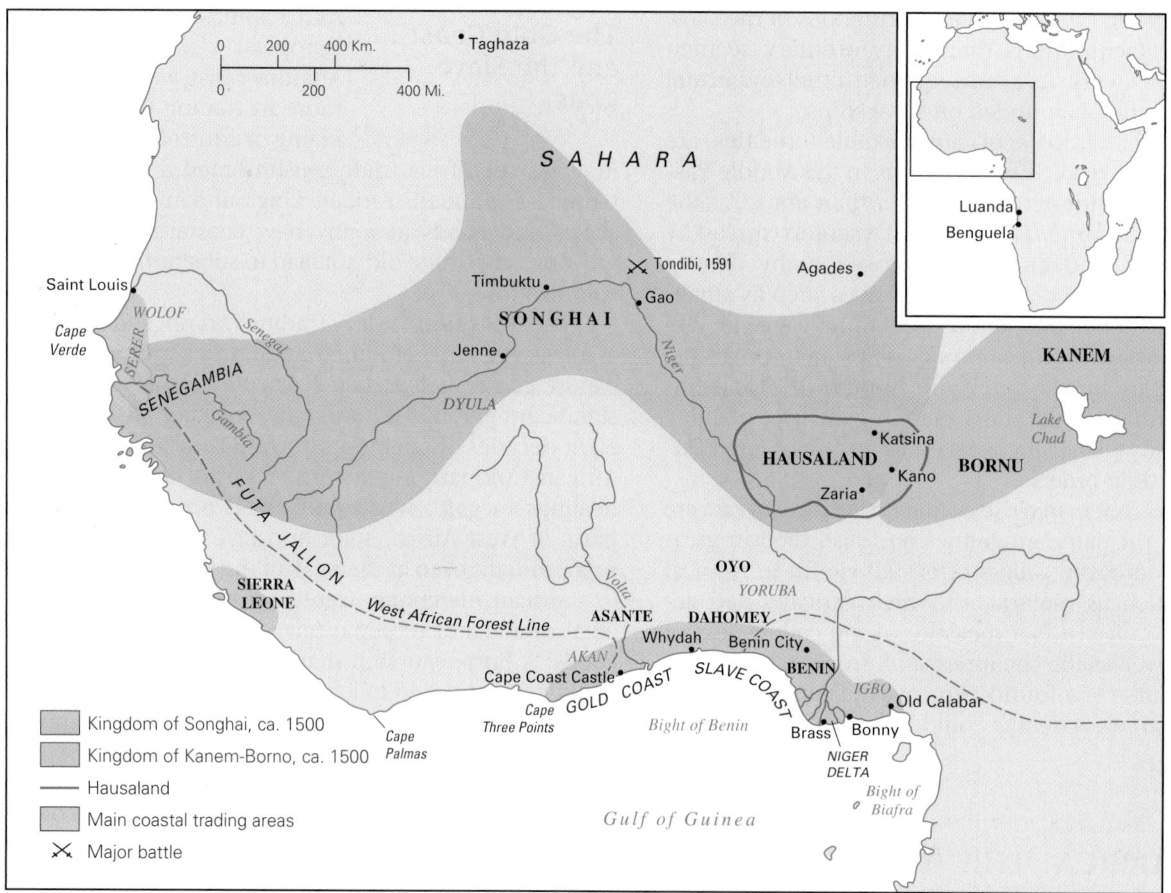

Map 19.3 West African States and Trade, 1500–1800 The Atlantic and the trans-Saharan trade brought West Africans new goods and promoted the rise of powerful states and trading communities. The Moroccan invasion of Songhai and Portuguese colonization of the Angolan ports of Luanda and Benguela showed the political dangers of such relations.

prevented them from taking control of African territory. Rivalry among European nations, each of which established its own trading "castles" along the Gold Coast, also reduced Europeans' bargaining strength. In 1700 the head of the Dutch East India Company in West Africa, Willem Bosman°, bemoaned the fact that, to stay competitive against the other European traders, his company had to include large quantities of muskets and gunpowder in the goods it exchanged, thereby adding to Africans' military power.

Bosman also related that before being allowed to buy slaves at Whydah on the Slave Coast, his agents first had to pay the king a substantial customs duty and then pay a premium price for whatever slaves the king had to sell. By African standards, Whydah was a rather small kingdom controlling only that port and its immediate hinterland. In 1727 it was annexed by the larger kingdom of Dahomey°, which maintained a strong trading position with Europeans at the coast. Dahomey's rise in the 1720s depended heavily on the firearms that the slave trade supplied for its well-trained armies of men and women.

In the cases of two of Dahomey's neighbors, the connections between state growth and the Atlantic trade were more complex. One was the inland Oyo° kingdom to the northeast. Oyo cavalry overran Dahomey in 1730 and forced it to pay an annual tribute to keep its independence. The other was the newer kingdom of Asante°,

Willem Bosman (VIL-uhm boos-MAHN)

Dahomey (dah-HOH-mee) **Oyo** (aw-YOH)
Asante (uh-SHAN-tee)

west of Dahomey along the Gold Coast, which expanded rapidly after 1680. Both Oyo and Asante participated in the Atlantic trade, but neither kingdom was as dependent on it as Dahomey. Overseas trade formed a relatively modest part of the economies of these large and populous states and was balanced by their extensive overland trade with their northern neighbors and with states across the Sahara. Like the great medieval empires of the western Sudan, Oyo and Asante were stimulated by external trade but not controlled by it.

How did African kings and merchants obtain slaves for sale? Bosman dismissed misconceptions prevailing in Europe in his day. "Not a few in our country," he wrote to a friend in 1700, "fondly imagine that parents here sell their children, men their wives, and one brother the other. But those who think so, do deceive themselves; for this never happens on any other account but that of necessity, or some great crime; but most of the slaves that are offered to us are prisoners of war, which are sold by the victors as their booty."[2] Other accounts agree that prisoners taken in war were the greatest source of slaves for the Atlantic trade, but it is difficult to say how often capturing slaves for export was the main cause of warfare. "Here and there," conclude two respected historians of Africa, "there are indications that captives taken in the later and more peripheral stages of these wars were exported overseas, but it would seem that the main impetus of conquest was only incidentally concerned with the slave-trade in any external direction."[3]

An early-nineteenth-century king of Asante had a similar view: "I cannot make war to catch slaves in the bush, like a thief. My ancestors never did so. But if I fight a king, and kill him when he is insolent, then certainly I must have his gold, and his slaves, and his people are mine too. Do not the white kings act like this?"[4] English rulers had indeed sentenced seventeenth-century Scottish and Irish prisoners to forced labor in the West Indies. One may imagine that the African and the European prisoners did not share their kings' view that such actions were legitimate.

The Bight of Biafra and Angola

In the eighteenth century the slave trade expanded eastward to the Bight° of Biafra. In contrast to the Gold and Slave Coasts, where strong kingdoms predominated, the densely populated interior of the Bight of Biafra contained no large states. Even so, the powerful merchant princes of the coastal ports made European traders give them rich presents. Because of the absence of sizable states, there were no large-scale wars and consequently few prisoners of war. Instead, kidnapping was the major source of slaves.

Through a network of markets and inland routes, some inland African merchants supplied European slave traders at the coast with debtors, victims of kidnapping, and convicted criminals. The largest inland traders of the Bight of Biafra were the Aro of Arochukwu, who used their control of a famous religious oracle to enhance their prestige. The Aro cemented their business links with powerful inland families and the coastal merchants through gifts and marriage alliances.

As the volume of the Atlantic trade along the Bight of Biafra expanded in the late eighteenth century, some inland markets evolved into giant fairs with different sections specializing in slaves and imported goods. In the 1780s an English ship's doctor reported that slaves were "bought by the black traders at fairs, which are held for that purpose, at a distance of upwards of two hundred miles from the sea coast." He reported seeing between twelve hundred and fifteen hundred enslaved men and women arriving at the coast from a single fair.[5]

The local context of the Atlantic trade was different south of the Congo estuary at Angola, the greatest source of slaves for the Atlantic trade (see Map 19.2). This was also the one place along the Atlantic coast where a single European nation, Portugal, controlled a significant amount of territory. Except when overrun by the Dutch for a time in the seventeenth century, Portuguese residents of the main coastal ports of Luanda and Benguela° served as middlemen between the caravans that arrived from the far interior and the ships that crossed from Brazil. From the coastal cities Afro-Portuguese traders guided large caravans of trade goods inland to exchange for slaves at special markets. Some markets met in the shadow of Portuguese frontier forts; powerful African kings controlled others.

Many of the slaves sold at these markets were prisoners of war captured by expanding African states. By the late eighteenth century slaves sold from Angolan ports were prisoners of wars fought as far as 600 to 800 miles (1,000 to 1,300 kilometers) inland. Many were victims of wars of expansion fought by the giant federation of Lunda kingdoms. As elsewhere in Africa, such prisoners usually seem to have been a byproduct of African wars rather than the purpose for which the wars were fought.

Research has linked other enslavement with environmental crises in the hinterland of Angola.[6] During

Bight (bite)

Benguela (ben-GWAY-luh)

Queen Nzinga of Angola, 1622 This formidable African woman went to great lengths to maintain her royal dignity when negotiating a treaty for her brother with the Portuguese governor of Luanda. To avoid having to stand in his presence, she had one of her women bend herself into a human seat. Nzinga later ruled in her own name and revolted against the Portuguese with the aid of Dutch and African allies. (Jean-Loup Charmet)

the eighteenth century these southern grasslands periodically suffered severe droughts, which drove famished refugees to better-watered areas. Powerful African leaders gained control of such refugees in return for supplying them with food and water. These leaders built up their followings by assimilating refugee children, along with adult women, who were valued as food producers and for reproduction. However, they often sold into the Atlantic trade the adult male refugees, who were more likely than the women and children to escape or challenge the ruler's authority. Rising Angolan leaders parceled out the Indian textiles, weapons, and alcohol they received in return for such slaves as gifts to attract new followers and to cement the loyalty of their established allies.

The most successful of these inland Angolan leaders became heads of powerful new states that stabilized areas devastated by war and drought and repopulated them with the refugees and prisoners they retained. The slave frontier then moved farther inland. This cruel system worked to the benefit of a few African rulers and merchants at the expense of the many thousands of Africans who were sent to death or perpetual bondage in the Americas.

Although the organization of the Atlantic trade in Africa varied, it was based on a partnership between European and African elites. To obtain foreign textiles, metals, and weapons, African rulers and merchants sold slaves and many products. Most of the exported slaves were prisoners taken in wars associated with African state growth. But strong African states also helped offset the Europeans' economic advantage and hindered them from taking control of African territory. Even in the absence of strong states, powerful African merchant communities everywhere dominated the movement of goods and people. The Africans who gained from these exchanges were the rich and powerful few. Many more Africans were losers in the exchanges.

Africa's European and Islamic Contacts

The ways in which sub-Saharan Africans were establishing new contacts with Europe paralleled their much older pattern of relations with the Islamic world. There were striking similarities and differences in Africans' political, commercial, and cultural interactions with these two external influences between 1500 and 1800.

Traders Approaching Timbuktu As they had done for centuries, traders brought their wares to this ancient desert-edge city. Timbuktu's mosques tower above the ordinary dwellings of the fabled city. (The Art Archive)

During the three and a half centuries of contact up to 1800, Africans ceded very little territory to Europeans. Local African rulers kept close tabs on the European trading posts they permitted along the Gold and Slave Coasts and collected lucrative rents and fees from the traders who came there. Aside from some uninhabited islands off the Atlantic coast, Europeans established colonial beachheads in only two places. One was the Portuguese colony of Angola; the other was the Dutch East India Company's Cape Colony at the southern tip of the continent, which was tied to the Indian Ocean trade, not to the Atlantic trade. Unlike Angola, the Cape Colony did not export slaves; rather, most of the 25,750 slaves in its population in 1793 were imported from Madagascar, South Asia, and the East Indies.

North Africa had become a permanent part of the Islamic world in the first century of Islamic expansion. Sub-Saharan Africans had learned of Muslim beliefs and practices more gradually from the traders who crossed the Sahara from North Africa or who sailed from the Middle East to the Swahili trading cities of East Africa. However, the geography, trading skills, and military prowess of sub-Saharan Africans had kept them from being conquered by expansive Middle Eastern empires. During the sixteenth century all of North Africa except Morocco was annexed to the new Ottoman Islamic empire, and Ethiopia lost extensive territory to other Muslim conquerors, but until 1590 the Sahara was an effective buttress against invasion.

The great **Songhai**° Empire of West Africa was pushing its dominion into the Sahara from the south. Like its predecessor Mali, Songhai drew its wealth from the trans-Saharan trade and was ruled by an indigenous Muslim dynasty (see Map 19.3). However, Songhai's rulers faced a challenge from the northwestern kingdom of Morocco, whose Muslim rulers sent a military expedition of four thousand men and ten thousand camels across the desert. Half the men perished on their way across the desert. Songhai's army of forty thousand cavalry and foot soldiers faced the survivors in 1591, but could not withstand the Moroccans' twenty-five hundred muskets. Although Morocco was never able to annex the western Sudan, for the next two centuries the occupying troops extracted a massive tribute of slaves

Songhai (song-GAH-ee)

DIVERSITY AND DOMINANCE

SLAVERY IN WEST AFRICA AND THE AMERICAS

Social diversity was common in Africa and the domination of masters over slaves was a feature of many societies. Ahmad Baba (1556–1627) was an outstanding Islamic scholar in the city of Timbuktu. He came from an old Muslim family of the city. In about 1615 he replied to some questions that had been sent to him. His answers reveal a great deal about the official and unofficial condition of slavery in the Sudan of West Africa, especially in the Hausa states of Kano and Katsina (see Map 19.3).

You asked: What have you to say concerning the slaves imported from the lands of the Sudan whose people are acknowledged to be Muslims, such as Bornu, . . . Kano, Goa, Songhay, Katsina and others among whom Islam is widespread? Is it permissible to possess them [as slaves] or not?

Know—may God grant us and you success—that these lands, as you have stated are Muslim. . . . But close to each of them are lands in which are unbelievers whom the Muslim inhabitants of these lands raid. Some of these unbelievers are under the Muslims' protection and pay them [taxes]. . . . Sometimes there is war between the Muslim sultans of some of these lands and one attacks the other, taking as many prisoners as he can and selling the captive though he is a free-born Muslim. . . . This is a common practice among them in Hausaland; Katsina raids Kano, as do others, though their language is one and their situations parallel; the only difference they recognize among themselves is that so-and-so is a born Muslim and so-and-so is a born unbeliever. . . .

Whoever is taken prisoner in a state of unbelief may become someone's property, whoever he is, as opposed to those who have become Muslims of their own free will . . . and may not be possessed at all.

A little over a century later another African provided information about enslavement practices in the Western Sudan. Ayuba Suleiman Diallo (ah-YOO-bah SOO-lay-mahn JAH-loh) (1701–?) of the state of Bondu some 200 miles from the Gambia River was enslaved and transported to Maryland, where he was a slave from 1731 to 1733. When an Englishman learned of Ayuba's literacy in Arabic, he recorded his life story, anglicizing his name to Job Solomon. According to the account, slaves in Bondu did much of the hard work, while men of Ayuba's class were free to devote themselves to the study of Islamic texts.

In February, 1730, Job's father hearing of an English ship at Gambia River, sent him, with two servants to attend him, to sell two Negroes, and to buy paper, and some other necessaries; but desired him not to venture over the river, because the country of the Mandingoes, who are enemies to the people of Futa, lies on the other side. Job not agreeing with Captain Pike (who commanded the ship, lying then at Gambia, in the service of Captain Henry Hunt, brother to Mr. William Hunt, merchant, in Little Tower-street, London) sent back the two servants to acquaint his father with it, and to let him know that he intended to go no farther. Accordingly . . . he crossed the River Gambia, and disposed of his Negroes for some cows. As he was returning home, he stopped for some refreshment at the house of an old acquaintance; and the weather being hot, he hung up his arms in the house, while he refreshed himself. . . . It happened that a company of the Mandingoes, . . . passing by at that time, and observing him unarmed, rushed in, to the number of seven or eight at once, at a back door, and pinioned Job, before he could get his arms, together with his interpreter, who is a slave in Maryland still. They then shaved their heads and beards, which Job and his man resented as the highest indignity; tho' the Mandingoes meant no more by it, than to make them appear like slaves taken in war. On the 27th of February, 1730, they carried them to Captain Pike at Gambia, who purchased them; and on the first of March they were put on board. Soon after Job found means to acquaint Captain Pike that he was the same person that came to trade with him a few days before, and after what manner he had been taken. Upon this Captain Pike gave him free leave to redeem himself and his man; and Job sent to an acquaintance of his father's, near Gambia, who promised to send to Job's father, to inform him of what had happened, that he might take some course to have him set at liberty. But it being a fortnight's [two weeks'] journey between that friend's house and his father's, and the ship sailing in about a week after, Job was brought with the rest of the slaves to Annapolis in Maryland, and delivered to Mr. Vachell Denton. . . .

Mr. Vachell Denton sold Job to one Mr. Tolsey in Kent Island in Maryland, who put him to work in making tobacco; but he was soon convinced that Job had never been used to such labour. He every day showed more and more uneasiness under this exercise, and at last grew sick, being no way able to bear it; so his master was obliged to find easier work for him, and therefore put him to tend the cattle. Job would often leave the cattle, and withdraw into the woods to pray; but a white boy frequently watched him, and whilst he was at his devotion would mock him and throw dirt in his face. This very much disturbed Job, and added considerably to his other misfortunes; all which were increased by his ignorance of the English language, which prevented his complaining, or telling his case to any person about him. Grown in some measure desperate, by reason of his present hardships, he resolved to travel at a venture; thinking he might possibly be taken up by some master, who would use him better, or otherwise meet with some lucky accident, to divert or abate his grief. Accordingly, he travelled thro' the woods, till he came to the County of Kent, upon Delaware Bay. . . . There is a law in force, throughout the [mid-Atlantic] colonies . . . as far as Boston in New England, viz. that any Negroe, or white servant who is not known in the county, or has no pass, may be secured by any person, and kept in the common [jail], till the master of such servant shall fetch him. Therefore Job being able to give no account of himself, was put in prison there.

This happened about the beginning of June 1731, when I, who was attending the courts there, and heard of Job, went with several gentlemen to the [jailer's] house, being a tavern, and desired to see him. He was brought into the tavern to us, but could not speak one word of English. Upon our talking and making signs to him, he wrote a line to two before us, and when he read it, pronounced the words Allah and Mahommed; by which, and his refusing a glass of wine we offered him, we perceived he was a Mahometan [Muslim], but could not imagine of what country he was, or how he got thither; for by his affable carriage, and the easy composure of his countenance, we could perceive he was no common slave.

When Job had been some time confined, an old Negroe man, who lived in that neighborhood, and could speak the Jalloff [Wolof] language, which Job also understood, went to him, and conversed with him. By this Negroe the keeper was informed to whom Job belonged, and what was the cause of his leaving his master. The keeper thereupon wrote to his master, who soon after fetched him home, and was much kinder to him than before; allowing him place to pray in, and in some other conveniences, in order to make his slavery as easy as possible. Yet slavery and confinement was by no means agreeable to Job, who had never been used to it; he therefore wrote a letter in Arabick to his father, acquainting him with his misfortunes, hoping he might yet find means to redeem him. . . . It happened that this letter was seen by James Oglethorpe, Esq. [founder of the colony of Georgia and director of the Royal African Company]; who, according to his usual goodness and generosity, took compassion on Job, and [bought him from his master]; his master being very willing to part with him, as finding him no ways fit for his business.

Ayuba Suleiman Diallo (1701–??) (British Library)

In spring 1733 Job's benefactors took him to England, teaching him passable English during the voyage, and introduced him to the English gentry. Job attracted such attention that local men took up a collection to buy his freedom and pay his debts, and introduced him at the royal court. In 1735 Job returned to Gambia in a Royal African Company ship, richly clothed and accompanied by many gifts.

QUESTIONS FOR ANALYSIS

1. **Since Ahmad Baba points out that Islamic law permitted a Muslim to raid and enslave non-Muslims, do you think that the non-Mulsim Mandinka (Mandingos) would have considered it justifiable to enslave Ayuba, since he was a Muslim?**
2. **What aspects of Ayuba Suleiman's experiences of enslavement were normal, and which unusual?**
3. **How different might Ayuba's experiences of slavery have been had he been sold to Jamaica rather than Maryland?**
4. **How strictly was the ban against enslaving Muslims observed in Hausaland?**

Source: Thomas Hodgkin, ed., *Nigerian Perspectives: An Historical Anthology*, 2d ed. (London: Oxford University Press, 1975), 154–156; Thomas Bluett, *Some Memoirs of the Life of Job, the Son of Solomon the High Priest of Boonda in Africa* (London: Richard Ford, 1734), 16–24.

and goods from the local population and collected tolls from passing merchants.

Morocco's destruction of Songhai weakened the trans-Saharan trade in the western Sudan. The **Hausa** trading cities in the central Sudan soon attracted most of the caravans bringing textiles, hardware, and weapons across the Sahara. The goods the Hausa imported and distributed through their trading networks were similar to those coastal African traders commanded from the Atlantic trade, except for the absence of alcohol (which was prohibited to Muslims). The goods they sent back in return also resembled the major African exports into the Atlantic: gold and slaves. One unique export to the north was the caffeine-rich kola nut, a stimulant that was much in demand among Muslims in North Africa. The Hausa also exported cotton textiles and leather goods.

Few statistics of the slave trade to the Islamic north exist, but the size of the trade seems to have been substantial, if smaller than the transatlantic trade at its peak. Between 1600 and 1800, by one estimate, about 850,000 slaves trudged across the desert's various routes (see Map 19.2). A nearly equal number of slaves from sub-Saharan Africa entered the Islamic Middle East and India by way of the Red Sea and the Indian Ocean.

In contrast to the plantation slavery of the Americas, most African slaves in the Islamic world were soldiers and servants. In the late seventeenth and eighteenth centuries Morocco's rulers employed an army of 150,000 African slaves obtained from the south, whose loyalty they trusted more than the loyalty of recruits from their own lands. Other slaves worked for Moroccans on sugar plantations, as servants, and as artisans. Unlike the case in the Americas, the majority of African slaves in the Islamic world were women who served wealthy households as concubines, servants, and entertainers. The trans-Saharan slave trade also included a much higher proportion of children than did the Atlantic trade, including eunuchs meant for eventual service as harem guards. It is estimated that only one in ten of these boys survived the surgical removal of their genitals.

The central Sudanese kingdom of **Bornu** illustrates several aspects of trans-Saharan contacts. Ruled by the same dynasty since the ninth century, this Muslim state had grown and expanded in the sixteenth century as the result of guns imported from the Ottoman Empire. Bornu retained many captives from its wars or sold them as slaves to the north in return for the firearms and horses that underpinned the kingdom's military power. One Bornu king, Mai Ali, conspicuously displayed his kingdom's new power and wealth while on four pilgrimages to Mecca between 1642 and 1667. On the last, an enormous entourage of slaves—said to number fifteen thousand—accompanied him.

Like Christians of this period, Muslims saw no moral impediment to owning or trading in slaves. Indeed, Islam considered enslaving "pagans" to be a meritorious act because it brought them into the faith. Although Islam forbade the enslavement of Muslims, Muslim rulers in Bornu, Hausaland, and elsewhere were not strict observers of that rule (see Diversity and Dominance: Slavery in West Africa and the Americas).

Sub-Saharan Africans had much longer exposure to Islamic cultural influences than to European cultural influences. Scholars and merchants learned to use the Arabic language to communicate with visiting North Africans and to read the Quran. Islamic beliefs and practices as well as Islamic legal and administrative systems were influential in African trading cities on the southern edge of the Sahara and on the Swahili coast. In some places Islam had extended its influence among rural people, but in 1750 it was still very much an urban religion.

European cultural influence in Africa was even more limited. Some coastal Africans had shown an interest in Western Christianity during the first century of contact with the Portuguese, but in the 1700s only Angola had a significant number of Christians. Coastal African traders found it useful to learn one or more European languages, but African languages dominated inland trade routes. A few African merchants sent their sons to Europe to learn European ways. One of these young men, Philip Quaque°, who was educated in England, was ordained as a priest in the Church of England and became the official chaplain of the Cape Coast Castle from 1766 until his death in 1816. A few other Africans learned to write in a European language, such as the Old Calabar trader Antera Duke who kept a diary in English in the late eighteenth century.

Overall, how different and similar were the material effects of Islam and Europe in sub-Saharan Africa by 1800? The evidence is incomplete, but some assessment is possible with regard to population and possessions.

Although both foreign Muslims and Europeans obtained slaves from sub-Saharan Africa, there was a significant difference in the numbers they obtained. Between 1550 and 1800 some 8 million Africans were exported into the Atlantic trade, compared to perhaps 2 million in the Islamic trade to North Africa and the Middle East. What effect did these losses have on Africa's population? Scholars who have looked deeply into the question generally agree on three points: (1) even at the

Quaque (KWAH-kay)

peak of the trade in the 1700s sub-Saharan Africa's overall population remained very large; (2) localities that contributed heavily to the slave trade, such as the lands behind the Slave Coast, suffered acute losses; (3) the ability of a population to recover from losses was related to the proportion of fertile women who were shipped away. The fact that Africans sold fewer women than men into the larger Atlantic trade somewhat reduced its long-term effects.

Many other factors played a role. Angola, for example, supplied more slaves over a longer period than any other part of Africa, but the trade drew upon different parts of a vast and densely populated hinterland. Moreover, the periodic population losses due to famine in this region may have been reduced by the increasing cultivation of high-yielding food plants from the Americas (see Environment and Technology: Amerindian Foods in Africa).

The impact of the goods received in sub-Saharan Africa from these trades is another topic of research. Africans were very particular about what they received, and their experience made them very adept at assessing the quality of different goods. Economic historians have questioned the older idea that the imports of textiles and metals undermined African weavers and metalworkers. First, they point out that on a per capita basis the volume of these imports was too small to have idled many African artisans. Second, the imports are more likely to have supplemented rather than replaced local production. The goods received in sub-Saharan Africa were intended for consumption and thus did not serve to develop the economy. Likewise, the sugar, tea, and chocolate Europeans consumed did little to promote economic development in Europe. However, both African and European merchants profited from trading these consumer goods. Because they directed the whole Atlantic system, Europeans gained far more wealth than Africans.

Historians disagree in their assessment of how deeply European capitalism dominated Africa before 1800, but Europeans clearly had much less political and economic impact in Africa than in the West Indies or on the mainland of the Americas. Still, it is significant that Western capitalism was expanding rapidly in the seventeenth century, while the Ottoman Empire, the dominant state of the Middle East, was entering a period of economic and political decline (see Chapter 20). The tide of influence in Africa was thus running in the Europeans' direction.

Conclusion

The new Atlantic trading system had great importance in and momentous implications for world history. In the first phase of their expansion Europeans had conquered and colonized the Americas and captured major Indian Ocean trade routes. The development of the Atlantic system showed their ability to move beyond the conquest and capture of existing systems to create a major new trading system that could transform a region almost beyond recognition.

The West Indies felt the transforming power of capitalism more profoundly than did any other place outside Europe in this period. The establishment of sugar plantation societies was not just a matter of replacing native vegetation with alien plants and native peoples with Europeans and Africans. More fundamentally, it made these once-isolated islands part of a dynamic trading system controlled from Europe. To be sure, the West Indies was not the only place affected. Parts of northern Brazil were touched as deeply by the sugar revolution, and other parts of the Americas were yielding to the power of European colonization and capitalism.

Africa played an essential role in the Atlantic system, importing trade goods and exporting slaves to the Americas. Africa, however, was less dominated by the Atlantic system than were Europe's American colonies. Africans remained in control of their continent and interacted culturally and politically with the Islamic world more than with the Atlantic.

Historians have seen the Atlantic system as a model of the kind of highly interactive economy that became global in later centuries. For that reason the Atlantic system was a milestone in a much larger historical process, but not a monument to be admired. Its transformations were destructive as well as creative, producing victims as well as victors. Yet one cannot ignore that the system's awesome power came from its ability to create wealth. As the next chapter describes, southern Asia and the Indian Ocean basin were also beginning to feel the effects of Europeans' rising power.

Key Terms

Royal African Company	**maroon**
Atlantic system	**capitalism**
chartered company	**mercantilism**
Dutch West India Company	**Atlantic Circuit**
plantocracy	**Middle Passage**
driver	**Songhai**
seasoning	**Hausa**
manumission	**Bornu**

Suggested Reading

The global context of early modern capitalism is examined by Immanuel Wallerstein, *The Modern World-System,* 3 vols. (1974–1989); by Fernand Braudel, *Civilization and Capitalism, 15th–18th Century,* 3 vols. (1982–1984); and in two volumes of scholarly papers edited by James D. Tracy, *The Rise of Merchant Empires* (1990) and *The Political Economy of Merchant Empires* (1991). Especially relevant are the chapters in *The Rise of Merchant Empires* by Herbert S. Klein, summarizing scholarship on the Middle Passage, and by Ralph A. Austen, on the trans-Saharan caravan trade between 1500 and 1800.

The best general introductions to the Atlantic system are Philip D. Curtin, *The Rise and Fall of the Plantation Complex* (1990); David Ellis, *The Rise of African Slavery in the Americas* (2000); and Robin Blackburn, *The Making of New World Slavery* (1997). Recent scholarly articles on subjects considered in this chapter are available in *The Atlantic Slave Trade: Effects on Economies, Societies, and Peoples in Africa, the Americas and Europe,* ed. Joseph E. Inikori and Stanley L. Engerman (1992); in *Slavery and the Rise of the Atlantic System,* ed. Barbara L. Solow (1991); and in *Africans in Bondage: Studies in Slavery and the Slave Trade,* ed. Paul Lovejoy (1986). Pieter Emmer has edited a valuable collection of articles on *The Dutch in the Atlantic Economy, 1580–1880: Trade, Slavery, and Emancipation* (1998).

Herbert S. Klein's *The Atlantic Slave Trade* (1999) provides a brief overview of research on that subject. A useful collection of debates is David Northrup, ed., *The Atlantic Slave Trade,* 2d ed. (2002). Hugh Thomas's *The Slave Trade: The Story of the Atlantic Slave Trade, 1440–1870* (1999) and Basil Davidson's *The Atlantic Slave Trade,* rev. ed. (1980) are other useful historical narratives. More global in its conception is Patrick Manning, *Slave Trades, 1500–1800: Globalization of Forced Labor* (1996).

The connections of African communities to the Atlantic are explored by David Northrup, *Africa's Discovery of Europe, 1450–1850* (2002); John Thornton, *Africa and Africans in the Making of the Atlantic World, 1400–1800,* 2d ed. (1998); and the authors of *Captive Passage: The Transatlantic Slave Trade and the Making of the Americas* (2002). Still valuable are Margaret E. Crahan and Franklin W. Knight, eds., *Africa and the Caribbean: The Legacies of a Link* (1979), and Richard Price, ed., *Maroon Societies: Rebel Slave Communities in the Americas,* 2d ed. (1979).

Herbert S. Klein's *African Slavery in Latin America and the Caribbean* (1986) is an exceptionally fine synthesis of recent research on New World slavery. The larger context of Caribbean history is skillfully surveyed by Eric Williams, *From Columbus to Castro: The History of the Caribbean* (1984), and more simply surveyed by William Claypole and John Robottom, *Caribbean Story,* vol. 1, *Foundations,* 2d ed. (1990). A useful collection of sources and readings is Stanley Engerman, Seymour Drescher, and Robert Paquette, eds., *Slavery* (2001).

Roland Oliver and Anthony Atmore, *The African Middle Ages, 1400–1800,* 2d ed. (2003), summarize African history in this period. Students can pursue specific topics in more detail in Richard Gray, ed., *The Cambridge History of Africa,* vol. 4 (1975), and B. A. Ogot, ed., *UNESCO General History of Africa,* vol. 5 (1992). For recent research on slavery and the African, Atlantic, and Muslim slave trades with Africa, see Paul Lovejoy, *Transformations in Slavery: A History of Slavery in Africa,* 2d ed. (2000); Claire C. Robertson and Martin A. Klein, eds., *Women and Slavery in Africa* (1983); and Patrick Manning, *Slavery and African Life: Occidental, Oriental, and African Slave Trades* (1990). See also Philip D. Curtin, ed., *Africa Remembered: Narratives by West Africans from the Era of the Slave Trade* (1968, 1997).

Those interested in Islam's cultural and commercial contacts with sub-Saharan Africa will find useful information in James L. A. Webb, Jr., *Desert Frontier: Ecological and Economic Change Along the Western Sahel, 1600–1850* (1995); Elizabeth Savage, ed., *The Human Commodity: Perspectives on the Trans-Saharan Slave Trade* (1992); and J. Spencer Trimingham, *The Influence of Islam upon Africa* (1968).

Notes

1. Eric Williams, *Capitalism and Slavery* (Charlotte: University of North Carolina Press, 1944), 7.
2. Willem Bosman, *A New and Accurate Description of Guinea, etc.* (London, 1705), quoted in David Northrup, ed., *The Atlantic Slave Trade* (Lexington, MA: D. C. Heath, 1994), 72.
3. Roland Oliver and Anthony Atmore, *The African Middle Ages, 1400–1800* (Cambridge, England: Cambridge University Press, 1981), 100.
4. King Osei Bonsu, quoted in Northrup, ed., *The Atlantic Slave Trade,* 93.
5. Alexander Falconbridge, *Account of the Slave Trade on the Coast of Africa* (London: J. Phillips, 1788), 12.
6. Joseph C. Miller, "The Significance of Drought, Disease, and Famine in the Agriculturally Marginal Zones of West-Central Africa," *Journal of African History* 23 (1982), 17–61.

20 Southwest Asia and the Indian Ocean, 1500–1750

Building a Palace This miniature painting from the reign of the Mughal emperor Akbar illustrates the building techniques of seventeenth-century India.

CHAPTER OUTLINE

Anthony Jenkinson, merchant-adventurer for the Muscovy Company, which was founded in 1555 to develop trade with Russia, became the first Englishman to set foot in Iran. In 1561 he sailed to Archangel in Russia's frigid north, and from there found his way down the Volga River and across the Caspian Sea. The local ruler he met in northwestern Iran was an object of wonder:

> richly appareled with long garments of silk, and cloth of gold, embroidered with pearls of stone; upon his head was a *tolipane* [headdress shaped like a tulip] with a sharp end pointing upwards half a yard long, of rich cloth of gold, wrapped about with a piece of India silk of twenty yards long, wrought in gold richly enameled, and set with precious stones; his earrings had pendants of gold a handful long, with two rubies of great value, set in the ends thereof.

Moving on to Qazvin°, Iran's capital, Jenkinson met the shah, whom the English referred to as the "Great Sophie" (apparently from Safavi°, the name of the ruling family). "In lighting from my horse at the Court gate, before my feet touched the ground, a pair of the Sophie's own shoes . . . were put upon my feet, for without the same shoes I might not be suffered to tread upon his holy ground."[1] Finding no one capable of reading a letter he carried from Queen Elizabeth, written in Latin, English, Hebrew, and Italian, he nevertheless managed to propose trade between England and Iran. The shah, who was in the midst of negotiations with the Ottoman sultan to end a half-century of hostilities, rejected the idea of diverting Iranian silk from Ottoman markets.

Though Jenkinson and later merchants discovered that Central Asia's bazaars were only meagerly supplied with goods, the idea of bypassing the Ottomans in the eastern Mediterranean and trading directly with Iran through Russia remained tempting. The Ottomans, too, dreamed of outflanking Safavid Iran. In 1569 an Ottoman army unsuccessfully tried to dig a 40-mile (64-kilometer) canal between the Don River, which opened into the Black Sea, and the Volga, which flowed into the Caspian. Putting Ottoman ships in the Caspian would have facilitated an attack on Iran from the north.

Russia, then ruled by Tsar Ivan IV (r. 1533–1584), known as Ivan the Terrible or Awesome, stood in the Ottoman path. Ivan transformed his principality from a second-rate power into the sultan's primary competitor in Central Asia. In the river-crossed steppe, where Turkic nomads had long enjoyed uncontested sway, Slavic Christian Cossacks from the region of the Don and Dnieper Rivers used armed wagon trains and river craft fitted with small cannon to push southward and establish a Russian presence.

A contest for trade with or control of Central Asia, and beyond that with the Muslim Mughal empire in India, grew out of the centrality conferred on the region by three centuries of Mongol and Turkic conquest. Nevertheless, changes in the organization of world trade were sapping the vitality of the Silk Road, and power was shifting to European seafaring empires linking the Atlantic with the Indian Ocean. For all their naval power in the Mediterranean, neither the Ottomans, the Safavid shahs in Iran, nor the Mughal emperors of India deployed more than a token navy in the southern seas.

As you read this chapter, ask yourself the following questions:

- What were the advantages and disadvantages of a land empire as opposed to a maritime empire?
- What role did religion play in political alliances and rivalries and in the formation of states?
- How did trading patterns change between 1500 and 1750?
- How did imperial rulers maintain dominance over their diverse populations?

The Ottoman Empire, to 1750

The most long-lived of the post-Mongol Muslim empires, the **Ottoman Empire** grew from a tiny nucleus in 1300 to encompass most of southeastern Europe by

Qazvin (kaz-VEEN) **Safavi** (SAH-fah-vee)

CHRONOLOGY

	Ottoman Empire	Safavid Empire	Mughal Empire	Europeans in the Indian Ocean States
1500		**1502–1524** Shah Ismail establishes Safavid rule in Iran		**1511** Portuguese seize Malacca from local Malay ruler
	1514 Selim I defeats Safavid shah at Chaldiran; conquers Egypt and Syria (1516–1517)	**1514** Defeat by Ottomans at Chaldiran limits Safavid growth		
	1520–1566 Reign of Suleiman the Magnificent; peak of Ottoman Empire			
	1529 First Ottoman siege of Vienna		**1526** Babur defeats last sultan of Delhi at Panipat	
			1539 Death of Nanak, founder of Sikh religion	
			1556–1605 Akbar rules in Agra; peak of Mughal Empire	**1565** Spanish establish their first fort in the Philippines
	1571 Ottoman naval defeat at Lepanto	**1587–1629** Reign of Shah Abbas the Great; peak of Safavid Empire		
1600				**1600** English East India company founded
				1602 Dutch East India Company founded
	1610 End of Anatolian revolts	**1622** Iranians oust Portuguese from Hormuz after 108 years		**1606** Dutch reach Australia
				1641 Dutch seize Malacca from Portuguese
			1658–1707 Aurangzeb imposes conservative Islamic regime	**1650** Omani Arabs capture Musqat from Portuguese
			1690 British found city of Calcutta	
1700	**1718–1730** Tulip Period; military decline apparent to Austria and Russia	**1722** Afghan invaders topple last Safavid shah		**1698** Omani Arabs seize Mombasa from Portuguese
		1736–1747 Nadir Shah temporarily reunites Iran; invades India (1739)	**1739** Iranians under Nadir Shah sack Delhi	**1742** Expansion of French Power in India

the late fifteenth century. Mamluk Syria and Egypt succumbed in the early sixteenth century, leaving the Ottomans with the largest Muslim empire since the original Islamic caliphate in the seventh century. However, the empire resembled the new centralized monarchies of France and Spain (see Chapter 17) more than any medieval model.

Enduring more than five centuries until 1922, the Ottoman Empire survived several periods of wrenching change, some caused by internal problems, others by the growing power of European adversaries. These periods of change reveal the problems faced by huge, land-based empires around the world.

Expansion and Frontiers

At first a tiny state in northwestern Anatolia built by Turkish nomad horsemen, zealous Muslim warriors, and a few Christian converts to Islam (see Map 20.1), the empire grew because of three factors: (1) the shrewdness of its founder Osman (from which the name "Ottoman" comes) and his descendants, (2) control of a strategic link between Europe and Asia at Gallipoli° on the Dardanelles strait, and (3) the creation of an army that took advantage of the traditional skills of the Turkish cavalryman and new military possibilities presented by gunpowder and Christian prisoners of war.

At first, Ottoman armies concentrated on Christian enemies in Greece and the Balkans, conquering a strong Serbian kingdom at the Battle of Kosovo° (in present-day Yugoslavia) in 1389. Much of southeastern Europe and Anatolia was under the control of the sultans by 1402, when Bayazid° I, "the Thunderbolt," confronted Timur's challenge from Central Asia. After Timur defeated and captured Bayazid at the Battle of Ankara (1402), a generation of civil war followed, until Mehmed° I reunified the sultanate.

During a century and a half of fighting for territory both east and west of Constantinople, the sultans repeatedly eyed the heavily fortified capital of the slowly dying Byzantine Empire. In 1453 Sultan Mehmed II, "the Conqueror," laid siege to Constantinople, using enormous cannon to bash in the city's walls, dragging warships over a high hill from the Bosporus strait to the city's inner harbor to avoid its sea defenses, and finally penetrating the city's land walls through a series of infantry assaults. The fall of Constantinople—henceforth commonly known as Istanbul—brought over eleven hundred years of Byzantine rule to an end and made the Ottomans seem invincible.

In 1514, at the Battle of Chaldiran (in Armenia), Selim° I, "the Inexorable," ended a potential threat on his eastern frontier from the new and expansive realm of the Safavid shah in Iran (see below). Although warfare between the two recurred, the general border between the Ottomans and their eastern neighbor dates to this battle. Iraq became a contested and repeatedly ravaged frontier zone.

When Selim conquered the Mamluk Sultanate of Egypt and Syria in 1516 and 1517, the Red Sea became the Ottomans' southern frontier. In the west, the rulers of the major port cities of Algeria and Tunisia, some of them Greek or Italian converts to Islam, voluntarily joined the empire in the early sixteenth century, thereby strengthening its Mediterranean fleets.

The son of Selim I, **Suleiman° the Magnificent** (r. 1520–1566), known to his subjects as Suleiman Kanuni, "the Lawgiver," commanded the greatest Ottoman assault on Christian Europe. Suleiman seemed unstoppable as he conquered Belgrade in 1521, expelled the Knights of the Hospital of St. John from the island of Rhodes the following year, and laid siege to Vienna in 1529. Only the lateness of the season and the need to retreat before the onset of winter saved Vienna's overmatched Christian garrison. In later centuries, Ottoman historians looked back on Suleiman's reign as a golden age when the imperial system worked to perfection.

While Ottoman armies pressed deeper and deeper into eastern Europe, the sultans also sought to control the Mediterranean. Between 1453 and 1502 the Ottomans fought the opening rounds of a two-century war with Venice, the most powerful of Italy's commercial city-states. From the Fourth Crusade of 1204 onward, Venice had assembled a profitable maritime empire that included major islands such as Crete and Cyprus along with strategic coastal strongpoints in Greece. Venice thereby became more than just a trading nation. Its island sugar plantations, exploiting cheap slave labor, competed favorably with Egypt in the international trade of the fifteenth century. With their rivals the Genoese, who traded through the strategic island of Chios, the Venetians stifled Ottoman maritime activities in the Aegean Sea.

The initial fighting left Venice with reduced military power and subject to an annual tribute payment, but it controlled its lucrative islands for another century. The Ottomans, like the Chinese, were willing to let other nations carry trade to and from their ports; they preferred trade of this sort as long as the other nations acknowledged Ottoman authority. It never occurred to them that a sea empire held together by flimsy ships could rival a great land empire fielding an army of a hundred thousand.

In the south Muslims of the Red Sea and Indian Ocean region customarily traded by way of Egypt and Syria. In the early sixteenth century merchants from southern India and Sumatra sent emissaries to Istanbul requesting naval support against the Portuguese. The Ottomans responded vigorously to Portuguese threats close to their territories, such as at Aden at the southern entrance to the Red Sea, but their efforts farther afield fell short of stopping the Portuguese.

So long as eastern luxury products still flowed to Ottoman markets, why commit major resources to subduing an enemy whose main threat was a demand that merchant vessels, mostly belonging to non-Ottoman

---

Gallipoli (gah-LIP-po-lee) **Kosovo** (KO-so-vo)
Bayazid (BAY-yah-zeed) **Mehmed** (MEH-met)
Selim (seh-LEEM)

Suleiman (SOO-lay-man)

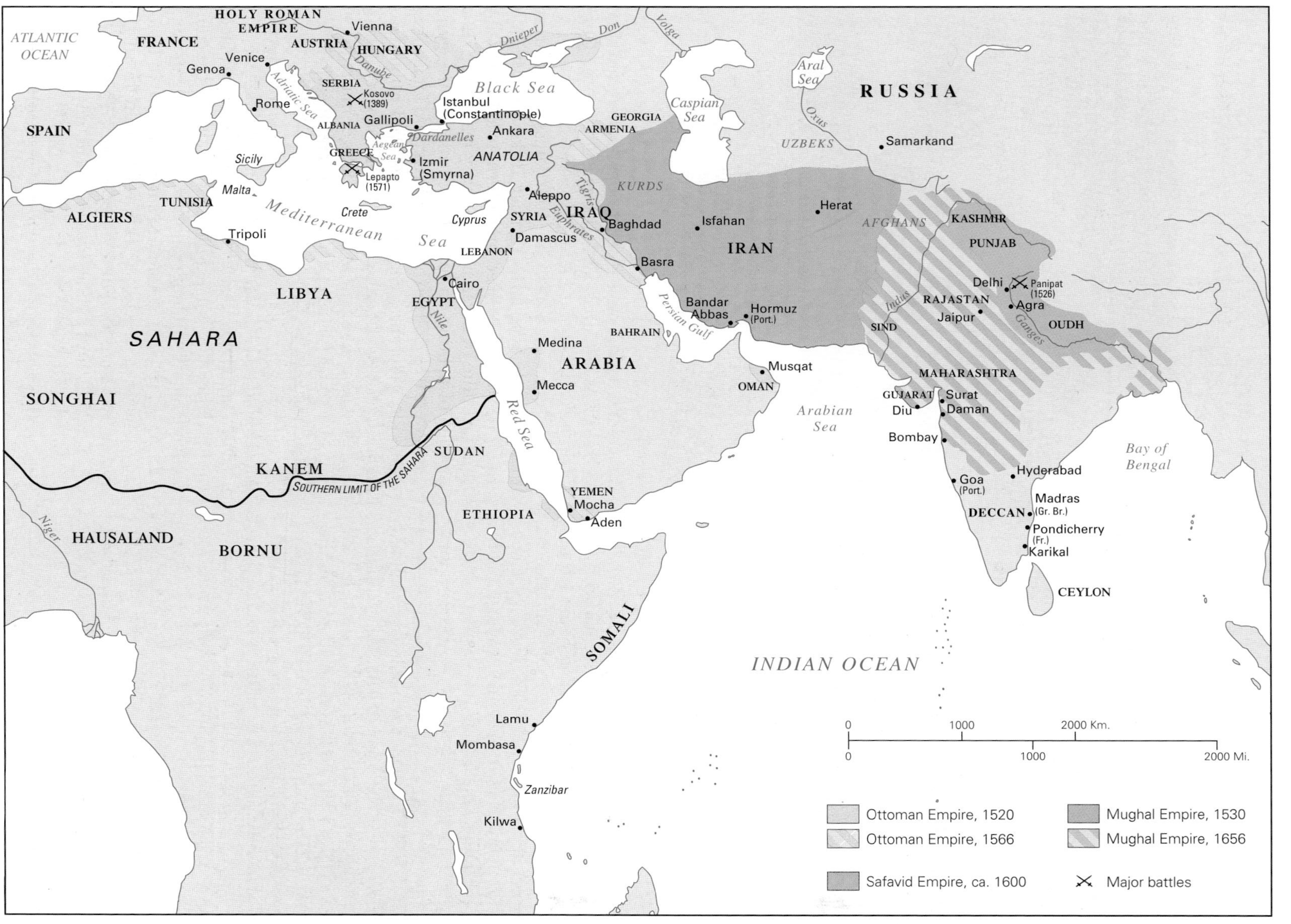

Map 20.1 Muslim Empires in the Sixteenth and Seventeenth Centuries Iran, a Shi'ite state flanked by Sunni Ottomans on the west and Sunni Mughals on the east, had the least exposure to European influences. Ottoman expansion across the southern Mediterranean Sea intensified European fears of Islam. The areas of strongest Mughal control dictated that Islam's spread into southeast Asia would be heavily influenced by merchants and religious figures from Gujarat instead of from eastern India.

Aya Sofya Mosque in Istanbul Orginally a Byzantine cathedral, Aya Sofya (in Greek, Hagia Sophia) was transformed into a mosque after 1453, and four minarets were added. It then became a model for subsequent Ottoman mosques. To the right behind it is the Bosporus strait dividing Europe and Asia, to the left the Golden Horn inlet separating the old city of Istanbul from the newer parts. The gate to the Ottoman sultan's palace is to the right of the mosque. The pointed tower to the left of the dome is part of the palace. (Robert Frerck/Woodfin Camp & Associates)

Muslims, buy protection from Portuguese attack? Portuguese power was territorially limited to fortified coastal points, such as Hormuz at the entrance to the Persian Gulf, Goa in western India, and Malacca in Malaya (see Chapter 16). The Ottomans did send a small naval force to Indonesia, but they never acted consistently or aggressively in the Indian Ocean.

Central Institutions

Heirs of the military traditions of Central Asia, the Ottoman army originally consisted of lightly armored mounted warriors skilled at shooting short bows made of compressed layers of bone, wood, and leather. The conquest of Christian territories in the Balkans in the late fourteenth century, however, gave the Ottomans access to a new military resource: Christian prisoners of war induced to serve as military slaves.

Slave soldiery had a long history in Islamic lands. The Mamluk Sultanate of Egypt and Syria was built on that practice. The Mamluks, however, acquired their new blood from slave markets in Central Asia and the Caucasus. Enslaving Christian prisoners, an action of questionable legality in Islamic law, was an Ottoman innovation. Converted to Islam, these "new troops," called yeni cheri in Turkish and **"Janissary"**° in English, gave the Ottomans great military flexibility.

Christians by upbringing, the Janissaries had no misgivings about fighting against Turks and Muslims when the sultans attacked in western Asia. Not coming from a culture of horse nomads, they readily accepted the idea of fighting on foot and learning to use guns, which were then still too heavy and awkward for a horseman to load and fire. The Janissaries lived in barracks and trained all year round. Until the mid-sixteenth century, they were barred from holding jobs or marrying.

Selection for Janissary training changed early in the fifteenth century. The new system, called the **devshirme**° (literally "selection"), imposed a regular levy of male children on Christian villages in the Balkans and occasionally elsewhere. Devshirme children were placed with Turkish families to learn their language before commencing military training. The most promising of them received their education at the sultan's palace in Istanbul, where they studied Islam and what we might call the liberal arts in addition to military matters. This regime, sophisticated for its time, produced not only the Janis-

Janissary (JAN-nih-say-ree) **devshirme** (dev-sheer-MEH) sary soldiers but also, from among the few who received special training in the inner service of the palace, senior military commanders and heads of government departments up to the rank of grand vizier.

The Ottoman Empire became cosmopolitan in character. The sophisticated court language, Osmanli° (the Turkish form of Ottoman), shared basic grammar and vocabulary with the Turkish spoken by Anatolia's nomads and villagers, but Arabic and Persian elements made it as distinct from that language as the Latin of educated Europeans was from the various Latin-derived Romance languages. People who served in the military or the bureaucracy and conversed in Osmanli belonged to the askeri°, or "military," class, which made them exempt from taxes and dependent on the sultan for their well-being. The mass of the population, whether Muslims, Christians, or Jews—Jews flooded into Ottoman territory after their expulsion from Spain in 1492 (see Chapter 17)—constituted the raya°, literally "flock of sheep."

By the beginning of the reign of Sultan Suleiman, the Ottoman Empire was the most powerful and best-organized state in Europe and the Islamic world. Its military balanced mounted archers, primarily Turks supported by grants of land in return for military service, with Janissaries—Turkified Albanians, Serbs, and Macedonians paid from the central treasury and trained in the most advanced weaponry. Greek, Turkish, Algerian, and Tunisian sailors manned the galley-equipped navy, usually under the command of an admiral from one of the North African ports.

The balance of the Ottoman land forces brought success to Ottoman arms in recurrent wars with the Safavids, who were much slower to adopt firearms, and in the inexorable conquest of the Balkans. In naval matters, a major expedition against Malta that would have given the Ottomans a foothold in the western Mediterranean failed in 1565. Combined Christian forces also achieved a massive naval victory at the Battle of Lepanto, off Greece, in 1571. In a year's time, however, the sultan had replaced all of the galleys sunk in that battle.

Under the land-grant system, resident cavalrymen administered most rural areas in Anatolia and the Balkans. They maintained order, collected taxes, and reported for each summer's campaign with their horses, retainers, and supplies, all paid for from the taxes they collected. When not campaigning, they stayed at home. Some historians maintain that these cavalrymen, who did not own their land, had little interest in encouraging production or introducing new technologies; but since a militarily able son usually succeeded his father, the grant holders did have some interest in productivity.

Ottoman Glassmakers on Parade Celebrations of the circumcisions of the sultan's sons featured parades organized by the craft guilds of Istanbul. This float features glassmaking, a common craft in Islamic realms. The most elaborate glasswork included oil lamps for mosques and colored glass for the small stained-glass windows below mosque domes. (Topkapi Saray Museum)

The Ottoman conception of the world saw the sultan providing justice for his raya and the military protecting them. In return, the raya paid the taxes that supported both the sultan and the military. In reality, the central government, like most large territorial governments in premodern times, seldom intersected the lives of most subjects. Arab, Turkish, and Balkan townsfolk sought justice in religious law courts and depended on local notables and religious leaders to represent them before Ottoman provincial officials. Balkan regions such as Albania and Bosnia had large numbers of converts, and Islam gradually became the majority religion. Thus the law of Islam (the Shari'a°), as interpreted by local ulama° (religious scholars), conditioned urban institutions and social life (see Diversity and Dominance: Islamic Law and Ottoman Rule). Local customs prevailed among non-Muslims and in many rural areas. Non-Muslims also looked to their own religious leaders for guidance in family and spiritual matters.

Osmanli (os-MAHN-lee) **askeri** (AS-keh-ree) **raya** (RAH-yah)

Shari'a (sha-REE-ah) **ulama** (oo-leh-MAH)

DIVERSITY AND DOMINANCE

ISLAMIC LAW AND OTTOMAN RULE

Ebu's-Su'ud was the Mufti of Istanbul from 1545 to 1574, serving under the sultans Suleiman the Magnificent (1520–1566) and his son Selim II (1566–1574). Originally one of many city-based religious scholars giving opinions on matters of law, the mufti of Istanbul by Ebu's-Su'ud's time had become the top religious official in the empire and the personal adviser to the sultan on religious and legal matters. The position would later acquire the title Shaikh al-Islam.

Historians debate the degree of independence these muftis had. Since the ruler, as a Muslim, was subject to the Shari'a, the mufti could theoretically veto his policies. On important matters, however, the mufti more often seemed to come up with the answer that best suited the sultan who appointed him. This bias is not apparent in more mundane areas of the law.

The collection of Ebu's-Su'ud's fatwas, or legal opinions, from which the examples below are drawn shows the range of matters that came to his attention. They are also an excellent source for understanding the problems of his time, the relationship between Islamic law and imperial governance, and the means by which the state asserted its dominance over the common people. Some opinions respond directly to questions posed by the sultan. Others are hypothetical, using the names Zeyd, 'Amr, and Hind the way police today use John Doe and Jane Doe. While qadis, or Islamic judges, made findings of fact in specific cases on trial, muftis issued only opinions on matters of law. A qadi as well as a plaintiff or defendant might ask a question of a mufti. Later jurists consulted collections of fatwas for precedents, but the fatwas had no permanent binding power.

On the plan of Selim II to attack the Venetians in Crete in 1570 A land was previously in the realm of Islam. After a while, the abject infidels overran it, destroyed the colleges and mosques, and left them vacant. They filled the pulpits and the galleries with the tokens of infidelity and error, intending to insult the religion of Islam with all kinds of vile deeds, and by spreading their ugly acts to all corners of the earth.

His Excellency the Sultan, the Refuge of Religion, has, as zeal for Islam requires, determined to take the aforementioned land from the possession of the shameful infidels and to annex it to the realm of Islam.

When peace was previously concluded with the other lands in the possession of the said infidels, the aforenamed land was included. An explanation is sought as to whether, in accordance with the Pure shari'a, this is an impediment to the Sultan's determining to break the treaty.

Answer: There is no possibility that it could ever be an impediment. For the Sultan of the People of Islam (may God glorify his victories) to make peace with the infidels is legal only when there is a benefit to all Muslims. When there is no benefit, peace is never legal. When a benefit has been seen, and it is then observed to be more beneficial to break it, then to break it becomes absolutely obligatory and binding.

His Excellency [Muhammad] the Apostle of God (may God bless him and give him peace) made a ten-year truce with the Meccan infidels in the sixth year of the Hegira. His Excellency 'Ali (may God ennoble his face) wrote a document that was corroborated and confirmed. Then, in the following year, it was considered more beneficial to break it and, in the eighth year of the Hegira, [the Prophet] attacked [the Meccans], and conquered Mecca the Mighty.

On war against the Shi'ite Muslim Safavids of Iran Is it licit according to the shari'a to fight the followers of the Safavids? Is the person who kills them a holy warrior, and the person who dies at their hands a martyr?

Answer: Yes, it is a great holy war and a glorious martyrdom.

Assuming that it is licit to fight them, is this simply because of their rebellion and enmity against the [Ottoman] Sultan of the People of Islam, because they drew the sword against the troops of Islam, or what?

Answer: They are both rebels and, from many points of view, infidels.

Can the children of Safavid subjects captured in the Nakhichevan campaign be enslaved?

Answer: No.

The followers of the Safavids are killed by order of the Sultan. If it turns out that some of the prisoners, young and old, are [Christian] Armenian[s], are they set free?

Answer: Yes. So long as the Armenians have not joined the Safavid troops in attacking and fighting against the troops of Islam, it is illegal to take them prisoner.

On the Holy Land Are all the Arab realms Holy Land, or does it have specific boundaries, and what is the difference between the Holy Land and other lands?

Answer: Syria is certainly called the Holy Land. Jerusalem, Aleppo and its surroundings, and Damascus belong to it.

On land-grants What lands are private property, and what lands are held by feudal tenure [i.e., assignment in exchange for military service]?

Answer: Plots of land within towns are private property. Their owners may sell them, donate them or convert them to trust. When [the owner] dies, [the land] passes to all the heirs. Lands held by feudal tenure are cultivated lands around villages, whose occupants bear the burden of their services and pay a portion of their [produce in tax]. They cannot sell the land, donate it or convert it to trust. When they die, if they have sons, these have the use [of the land]. Otherwise, the cavalryman gives [it to someone else] by *tapu* [title deed].

On the consumption of coffee Zeyd drinks coffee to aid concentration or digestion. Is this licit?

Answer: How can anyone consume this reprehensible [substance], which dissolute men drink when engaged in games and debauchery?

The Sultan, the Refuge of Religion, has on many occasions banned coffee-houses. However, a group of ruffians take no notice, but keep coffee-houses for a living. In order to draw the crowds, they take on unbearded apprentices, and have ready instruments of entertainment and play, such as chess and backgammon. The city's rakes, rogues and vagabond boys gather there to consume opium and hashish. On top of this, they drink coffee and, when they are high, engage in games and false sciences, and neglect the prescribed prayers. In law, what should happen to a judge who is able to prevent the said coffee-sellers and drinkers, but does not do so?

Answer: Those who perpetrate these ugly deeds should be prevented and deterred by severe chastisement and long imprisonment. Judges who neglect to deter them should be dismissed.

On matters of theft How are thieves to be "carefully examined"?

Answer: His Excellency 'Ali (may God ennoble his face) appointed Imam Shuraih as judge. It so happened that, at that time, several people took a Muslim's son to another district. The boy disappeared and, when the people came back, the missing boy's father brought them before Judge Shuraih. [When he brought] a claim [against them on account of the loss of his son], they denied it, saying: "No harm came to him from us." Judge Shuraih thought deeply and was perplexed.

When the man told his tale to His Excellency 'Ali, [the latter] summoned Judge Shuraih and questioned him. When Shuraih said; "Nothing came to light by the shari'a," ['Ali] summoned all the people who had taken the man's son, separated them from one another, and questioned them separately. For each of their stopping places, he asked: "What was the boy wearing in that place? What did you eat? And where did he disappear?" In short, he made each of them give a detailed account, and when their words contradicted each other, each of their statements was written down separately. Then he brought them all together, and when the contradictions became apparent, they were no longer able to deny [their guilt] and confessed to what had happened.

This kind of ingenuity is a requirement of the case.

[This fatwa appears to justify investigation of crimes by the state instead of by the qadi. Judging from court records, which contain very few criminal cases, it seems likely that in practice, many criminal cases were dealt with outside the jurisdiction of the qadi's court.]

Zeyd takes 'Amr's donkey without his knowledge and sells it. Is he a thief?

Answer: His hand is not cut off.

Zeyd mounts 'Amr's horse as a courier and loses it. Is compensation necessary?

Answer: Yes

In which case: What if Zeyd has a Sultanic decree [authorising him] to take horses for courier service?

Answer: Compensation is required in any case. He was not commanded to lose [the horse]. Even if he were commanded, it is the person who loses it who is liable.

On homicides Zeyd enters Hind's house and tries to have intercourse forcibly. Since Hind can repel him by no other means, she strikes and wounds him with an axe. If Zeyd dies of the wound, is Hind liable for anything?

Answer: She has performed an act of Holy War.

QUESTIONS FOR ANALYSIS

1. **What do these fatwas indicate with regard to the balance between practical legal reasoning and religious dictates?**
2. **How much was the Ottoman government constrained by the Shari'a?**
3. **What can be learned about day-to-day life from materials of this sort?**

Source: Excerpts from Colin Imber, *Ebu's-Su'ud: The Islamic Legal Tradition* (Stanford, CA: University Press, 1997), 84–88, 93–94, 223–226, 250, 257.

Crisis of the Military State, 1585–1650

As military technology evolved, cannon and lighter-weight firearms played an ever-larger role on the battlefield. Accordingly, the size of the Janissary corps—and its cost to the government—grew steadily, and the role of the Turkish cavalry, which continued to disdain firearms, diminished. In the mid-sixteenth century, to fill state coffers and pay the Janissaries, the sultan started reducing the number of landholding cavalrymen. Revenues previously spent on their living expenses and military equipment went directly into the imperial treasury. Some of the displaced cavalrymen, armed and unhappy, became a restive element in rural Anatolia.

In the late sixteenth century, inflation caused by a flood of cheap silver from the New World (see Environment and Technology: Metal Currency and Inflation), affected many of the remaining landholders, who collected taxes according to legally fixed rates. Some saw their purchasing power decline so much that they could not report for military service. This delinquency played into the hands of the government, which wanted to reduce the cavalry and increase the Janissary corps. As the central government recovered control of the land, more and more cavalrymen joined the ranks of dispossessed troopers. Students and professors in madrasas (religious colleges) similarly found it impossible to live on fixed stipends from madrasa endowments.

Constrained by religious law from fundamentally reforming the tax system, the government levied emergency surtaxes to obtain enough funds to pay the Janissaries and bureaucrats. For additional military strength, particularly in wars with Iran, the government reinforced the Janissaries with partially trained, salaried soldiers hired for the duration of a campaign. Once the summer campaign season ended, these soldiers found themselves out of work and short on cash.

This complicated situation resulted in revolts that devastated Anatolia between 1590 and 1610. Former landholding cavalrymen, short-term soldiers released at the end of a campaign, peasants overburdened by emergency taxes, and even impoverished students of religion formed bands of marauders. Anatolia experienced the worst of the rebellions and suffered greatly from emigration and loss of agricultural production. Banditry, made worse by the government's inability to stem the spread of muskets among the general public, beset other parts of the empire as well.

In the meantime, the Janissaries took advantage of their growing influence to gain relief from prohibitions on marrying and engaging in business. Janissaries who involved themselves in commerce lessened the burden on the state budget. Married Janissaries who enrolled sons or relatives in the corps made it possible in the seventeenth century for the government to save state funds by abolishing the devshirme system with its traveling selection officers. However, the increase in the total number of Janissaries and their steady deterioration as a military force more than offset these savings.

Economic Change and Growing Weakness, 1650–1750

A very different Ottoman Empire emerged from this period of crisis. The sultan once had led armies. Now he mostly resided in his palace and had little experience of the real world. This manner of living resulted from a gradually developed policy of keeping the sultan's male relatives confined to the palace to prevent them from plotting coups or meddling in politics. The sultan's mother and the chief eunuch overseeing the private quarters of the palace thus became important arbiters of royal favor, and even of succession to the sultanate, while the chief administrators—the grand viziers—oversaw the affairs of government. (Ottoman historians draw special attention to the negative influence of women in the palace after the time of Suleiman, but to some degree they reflect stereotypical male, and Muslim, fears about women in politics.)

The devshirme had been discontinued, and the Janissaries had taken advantage of their increased power and privileges to make membership in their corps hereditary. Together with several other newly prominent infantry regiments, they involved themselves in crafts and trading, both in Istanbul and in provincial capitals such as Cairo, Aleppo, and Baghdad. This activity took a toll on their military skills, but they continued to be a powerful faction in urban politics that the sultans could neither ignore nor reform.

Land grants in return for military service also disappeared. Tax farming arose in their place. Tax farmers paid specific taxes, such as customs duties, in advance in return for the privilege of collecting greater amounts from the actual taxpayers. In one instance, two tax farmers advanced the government 18 million akches° (small silver coins) for the customs duties of the Aegean port of Izmir° and collected a total of 19,169,203 akches, for a profit of 6.5 percent.

Rural administration, already disrupted by the rebellions, suffered from the transition to tax farms. The military landholders had kept order on their lands to maintain their incomes. Tax farmers seldom lived on the land, and their tax collection rights could vary from year to year. The imperial government, therefore, faced

akches (ahk-CHEH) **Izmir** (IZ-meer)

Metal Currency and Inflation

Inflation occurs when the quantity of goods and services available for purchase remains stable while the quantity of money in circulation increases. With more money in their pockets, people are willing to pay more to get what they want. Prices go up, and what people think of as the value of money goes down.

Today, with paper money and electronic banking, governments try to control inflation by regulating the printing of money or by other means. Prior to the nineteenth century, money consisted of silver and gold coins, and governments did not keep track of how much money was in circulation. As long as the annual production of gold and silver mines was quite small, inflation was not a worry. In the sixteenth and seventeenth centuries, however, precious metal poured into Spain from silver and gold mines in the New World, but there was no increase in the availability of goods and services. The resulting inflation triggered a "price revolution" in Europe—a general tripling of prices between 1500 and 1650. In Paris in 1650 the price of wheat and hay was fifteen times higher than the price had been in 1500.

This wave of inflation worked its way east, contributing to social disorder in the Ottoman Empire. European traders had more money available than Ottoman merchants and could outbid them for scarce commodities. Lacking silver and gold mines, the Ottoman government reduced the amount of precious metal in Ottoman coins. This made the problem worse. Hit hardest were people who had fixed incomes. Cavalrymen holding land grants worth a set amount each year were unable to equip themselves for military campaigns. Students living on fixed scholarships went begging.

Safavid Iran needed silver and gold to pay for imports from Mughal India, which imported few Iranian goods. Iranians sold silk to the Ottoman Empire for silver and gold, worsening the Ottoman situation, and then passed the precious metal on to India. Everyday life in Iran depended on barter or locally minted copper coinage, both more resistant to inflation. Copper for coins was sometimes imported from China.

Though no one then grasped the connection between silver production in Mexico and the trade balance between Iran and India, the world of the sixteenth and seventeenth centuries was becoming more closely linked economically than it had ever been before.

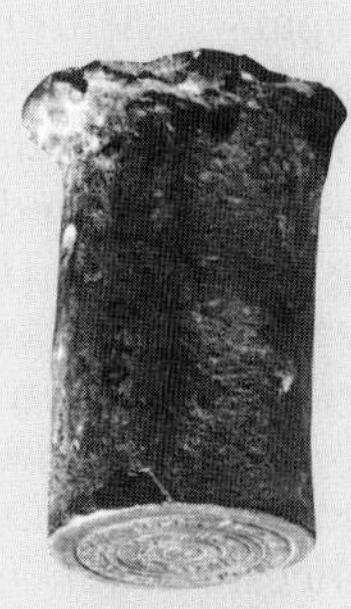

Set of Coin Dies The lower die, called the anvil die, was set in a piece of wood. A blank disk of gold, silver or copper was placed on top of it. The hammer die was placed on top of the blank and struck with a hammer to force the coin's image onto it. (Courtesy, Israel Museum, Jerusalem)

greater administrative burdens and came to rely heavily on powerful provincial governors or on wealthy men who purchased lifelong tax collection rights that prompted them to behave more or less as private landowners.

Rural disorder and decline in administrative control sometimes opened the way for new economic opportunities. The port of Izmir, known to Europeans by the ancient name "Smyrna," had a population of around two thousand in 1580. By 1650 the population had increased to between thirty thousand and forty thousand. Along with refugees from the Anatolian uprisings and from European pirate attacks along the coast came European merchants and large colonies of Armenians, Greeks, and Jews. A French traveler in 1621 wrote: "At present, Izmir has a great traffic in wool, beeswax, cotton, and silk, which the Armenians bring there instead of going to Aleppo . . . because they do not pay as many dues."[2]

Izmir transformed itself between 1580 and 1650 from a small Muslim Turkish town into a multiethnic, multireligious, multilinguistic entrepôt because of the Ottoman government's inability to control trade and the slowly growing dominance of European traders in the Indian Ocean. Spices from the East, though still traded in Aleppo and other long-established Ottoman centers, were not to be found in Izmir. Aside from Iranian silk brought in by caravan, European traders at Izmir purchased local agricultural products—dried fruits, sesame seeds, nuts, and olive oil. As a consequence, local farmers who previously had grown grain for subsistence shifted their plantings more and more to cotton and other cash crops, including, after its introduction in the 1590s, tobacco, which quickly became popular in the Ottoman Empire despite government prohibitions. In this way, the agricultural economy of western Anatolia, the Balkans, and the Mediterranean coast—the Ottoman lands most accessible to Europe (see Map 20.1)—became enmeshed in a growing European commercial network.

At the same time, military power slowly ebbed. The ill-trained Janissaries sometimes resorted to hiring substitutes to go on campaign, and the sultans relied on partially trained seasonal recruits and on armies raised by the governors of frontier provinces. By the middle of the eighteenth century it was obvious to the Austrians and Russians that the Ottoman Empire was weakening. On the eastern front, however, Ottoman exhaustion after many wars was matched by the demise in 1722 of their perennial adversary, the Safavid state of Iran.

The Ottoman Empire lacked both the wealth and the inclination to match European economic advances. Overland trade from the east dwindled as political disorder in Safavid Iran cut deeply into Iranian silk production (see below). Coffee from the highlands of Yemen, a product that rose from obscurity in the fifteenth century to become the rage first in the Ottoman Empire and then in Europe, traditionally reached the market by way of Egypt. By 1770, however, Muslim merchants trading in the Yemeni port of Mocha° (literally "the coffee place") paid 15 percent in duties and fees. But European traders, benefiting from long-standing trade agreements with the sultans, paid little more than 3 percent.

Such trade agreements, called capitulations, led to European domination of Ottoman seaborne trade. Nevertheless, the Europeans did not control strategic ports in the Mediterranean comparable to Malacca in the Indian Ocean and Hormuz on the Persian Gulf, so their economic power stopped short of colonial settlement or direct control in Ottoman territories.

A few astute Ottoman statesmen observed the growing disarray of the empire and advised the sultans to reestablish the land-grant and devshirme systems of Suleiman's reign. Most people, however, could not perceive the downward course of imperial power, much less the reasons behind it. Ottoman historians named the period between 1718 and 1730 the **"Tulip Period"** because of the craze for high-priced tulip bulbs that swept Ottoman ruling circles. The craze echoed a Dutch tulip mania that had begun in the mid-sixteenth century, when the flower was introduced into Holland from Istanbul, and had peaked in 1636 with particularly rare bulbs going for 2,500 florins apiece—the value of twenty-two oxen. Far from seeing Europe as the enemy that would eventually dismantle the empire, the Istanbul elite experimented with European clothing and furniture styles and purchased printed books from the empire's first (and short-lived) press.

In 1730, however, the gala soirees, at which guests watched turtles with candles on their backs wander in the dark through massive tulip beds, gave way to a conservative Janissary revolt with strong religious overtones. Sultan Ahmed III abdicated, and the leader of the revolt, Patrona Halil°, an Albanian former seaman and stoker of the public baths, swaggered around the capital for several months dictating government policies before he was seized and executed.

The Patrona Halil rebellion confirmed the perceptions of a few that the Ottoman Empire was facing severe difficulties. Yet decay at the center spelled benefit elsewhere. In the provinces, ambitious and competent governors, wealthy landholders, urban notables, and nomad chieftains took advantage of the central government's weakness. By the middle of the eighteenth century groups of Mamluks had regained a dominant position in Egypt, and Janissary commanders had become virtually independent rulers in Baghdad. In central Arabia a conservative Sunni movement inspired by Muhammad ibn Abd al-Wahhab began a remarkable rise beyond the reach of Ottoman power. Although no region declared full independence, the sultan's power was slipping away to the advantage of a broad array of lower officials and upstart chieftains in all parts of the empire while the Ottoman economy was reorienting itself toward Europe.

THE SAFAVID EMPIRE, 1502–1722

The **Safavid Empire** of Iran (see Map 20.1) resembled its longtime Ottoman foe in many ways: it initially used land grants to support its all-important cavalry; its population spoke several languages; it focused on land rather than sea power; and urban notables, nomadic chieftains, and religious scholars served as intermediaries between the people and the government. Certain other qualities, such as a royal tradition rooted in pre-Islamic legends and adoption of Shi'ism, continue to the present day to set Iran off from its neighbors.

Mocha (MOH-kuh)

Patrona Halil (pa-TROH-nuh ha-LEEL)

Safavid Shah with Attendants and Musicians This painting by Ali-Quli Jubbadar, a European convert to Islam working for the Safavid armory, reflects Western influences. Notice the use of light and shadow to model faces and the costume of the attendant to the shah's right. The shah's waterpipe indicates the spread of tobacco, a New World crop, to the Middle East. (Courtesy of Oriental Institute, Academy of Sciences, Leningrad. Reproduced from Album of Persian and Indian Miniatures [Moscow, 1962], ill. no. 98)

The Rise of the Safavids

Timur had been a great conqueror, but his children and grandchildren contented themselves with modest realms in Afghanistan and Central Asia, while a number of would-be rulers vied for control elsewhere. In Iran itself, the ultimate victor in a complicated struggle for power among Turkish chieftains was a boy of Kurdish, Iranian, and Greek ancestry named Ismail°, the hereditary leader of a militant Sufi brotherhood called the "Safaviya" for his ancestor Safi al-Din. In 1502, at age sixteen, Ismail proclaimed himself shah of Iran. At around the same time, he declared that henceforward his realm would practice **Shi'ite Islam** and revere the family of Muhammad's son-in-law Ali. He called on his subjects to abandon their Sunni beliefs.

Most of the members of the Safaviya spoke Turkish and belonged to nomadic groups known as qizilbash°, or "redheads," because of their distinctive turbans. Many considered Ismail god incarnate and fought ferociously on his behalf. If Ismail wished his state to be Shi'ite, his word was law to the qizilbash. The Iranian subject population, however, resisted. Neighboring lands gave asylum to Sunni refugees whose preaching and intriguing helped stoke the fires that kept Ismail (d. 1524) and his son Tahmasp° (d. 1576) engaged in war after war. It took a century and a series of brutal persecutions to make Iran an overwhelmingly Shi'ite land. The transformation also involved the importation of Arab Shi'ite scholars from Lebanon and Bahrain to institute Shi'ite religious education at a high level.

Ismail (IS-ma-eel) **qizilbash** (KIH-zil-bahsh)
Tahmasp (tah-MAHSP)

Society and Religion

Although Ismail's reasons for compelling Iran's conversion are unknown, the effect was to create a deep chasm between Iran and its neighbors, all of which were Sunni. Iran's distinctiveness had been long in the making, however. Persian, written in the Arabic script from the tenth century onward, had emerged as the second language of Islam. By 1500 an immense library of legal and theological writings; epic, lyric, and mystic poetry; histories; and drama and fiction had come into being. Iranian scholars and writers normally read Arabic as well as Persian and sprinkled their writings with Arabic phrases, but their Arab counterparts were much less inclined to learn Persian. Even handwriting styles differed, Iranians preferring highly cursive forms of the Arabic script.

This divergence between the two language areas had intensified after 1258 when the Mongols destroyed Baghdad, the capital of the Islamic caliphate, and thereby diminished the importance of Arabic-speaking Iraq. Syria and Egypt, under Mamluk rule, had become the heartland of the Arab world, while Iran developed largely on its own, building extensive contacts with India, whose Muslim rulers favored the Persian language.

Where cultural styles had radiated in all directions from Baghdad during the heyday of the Islamic caliphate in the seventh through ninth centuries, now Iraq separated an Arab zone from a Persian zone. The post-Mongol period saw an immense burst of artistic creativity and innovation in Iran, Afghanistan, and Central Asia. Painted and molded tiles and tile mosaics, often in vivid turquoise blue, became the standard exterior decoration of mosques in Iran. Architects in Syria and Egypt never used them. The Persian poets Hafez (1319–1389?) and Sa'di (1215–1291) raised morally instructive and mystical-allegorical verse to a peak of perfection. Arabic poetry languished.

The Turks, who steadily came to dominate the political scene from Bengal to Istanbul, generally preferred Persian as a vehicle for literary and religious expression. The Mamluks in Egypt and Syria, however, showed greatest respect for Arabic. The Turkish language, which had a vigorous tradition of folk poetry, developed only slowly, primarily in the Ottoman Empire, as a language of literature and administration. Ironically, Ismail Safavi was a noted religious poet in the Turkish language of his qizilbash followers, while his mortal adversary, the Ottoman Selim I (r. 1512–1520), composed elegant poetry in Persian.

To be sure, Islam itself provided a tradition that crossed ethnic and linguistic borders. Mosque architecture differed, but Iranians, Arabs, and Turks, as well as Muslims in India, all had mosques. They also had madrasas that trained the ulama to sustain and interpret the Shari'a as the all-encompassing law of Islam. Yet local understandings of the common tradition differed substantially.

Each Sufi brotherhood had distinctive rituals and concepts of mystical union with God, but Iran stood out as the land where Sufism most often fused with militant political objectives. The Safaviya was not the first brotherhood to deploy armies and use the point of a sword to promote love of God. The later Safavid shahs, however, banned (somewhat ineffectively) all Sufi orders from their domain.

Even prior to Shah Ismail's imposition of Shi'ism, therefore, Iran had become a distinctive society. Nevertheless, the impact of Shi'ism was significant. Shi'ite doctrine says that all temporal rulers, regardless of title, are temporary stand-ins for the **"Hidden Imam,"** the twelfth descendant of Ali, who was the prophet Muhammad's cousin and son-in-law. Shi'ites believe that leadership of the Muslim community rests solely with divinely appointed Imams from Ali's family, that the twelfth descendant (the Hidden Imam) disappeared as a child in the ninth century, and that the Shi'ite community will lack a proper religious authority until he returns. Some Shi'ite scholars concluded that the faithful should calmly accept the world as it was and wait quietly for the Hidden Imam's return. Others maintained that they themselves should play a stronger role in political affairs because they were best qualified to know the Hidden Imam's wishes. These two positions, which still play a role in Iranian Shi'ism, tended to enhance the self-image of the ulama as independent of imperial authority and slowed the trend of religious scholars' becoming subordinate government functionaries, as happened with many Ottoman ulama.

Shi'ism also affected the psychological life of the people. Commemoration of the martyrdom of Imam Husayn (d. 680), Ali's son and the third Imam, during the first two weeks of every lunar year regularized an emotional outpouring with no parallel in Sunni lands. Day after day for two weeks (as they do today) preachers recited the woeful tale to crowds of weeping believers, and chanting and self-flagellating men paraded past crowds of reverent onlookers in elaborate street processions, often organized by craft guilds. Passion plays in which Husayn and his family are mercilessly killed by the Sunni caliph's general became a unique form of Iranian public theater.

Of course, Shi'ites elsewhere observed some of the same rites of mourning for Imam Husayn, particularly in the Shi'ite pilgrimage cities of Karbala and Najaf° in Ottoman Iraq. But Iran, with over 90 percent of its population professing Shi'ism, felt the impact of these rites most strongly. Over time, the subjects of the Safavid shahs came to feel more than ever a people apart, even though many of them had been Shi'ite for only two or three generations.

A Tale of Two Cities: Isfahan and Istanbul

Isfahan° became Iran's capital in 1598 by decree of **Shah Abbas I** (r. 1587–1629). Outwardly, Istanbul and Isfahan looked quite different. Built on seven hills on the south side of the narrow Golden Horn inlet, Istanbul boasted a skyline punctuated by the gray stone domes and thin, pointed minarets of the great imperial mosques. Their design derived from Hagia Sophia, the Byzantine cathedral converted to a mosque and renamed Aya Sofya° after 1453. By contrast, the mosques surrounding the royal plaza in Isfahan featured brightly tiled domes rising to gentle peaks and unobtrusive minarets. High walls surrounded the sultan's palace in Istanbul. Shah Abbas focused Isfahan on the giant royal plaza, which was large enough for his army to play polo, and he used an airy palace overlooking the plaza to receive dignitaries and review his troops. This public image contributed to Shah Abbas' being called "the Great."

Najaf (NAH-jaf) **Isfahan** (is-fah-HAHN)
Aya Sofya (AH-yah SOAF-yah)

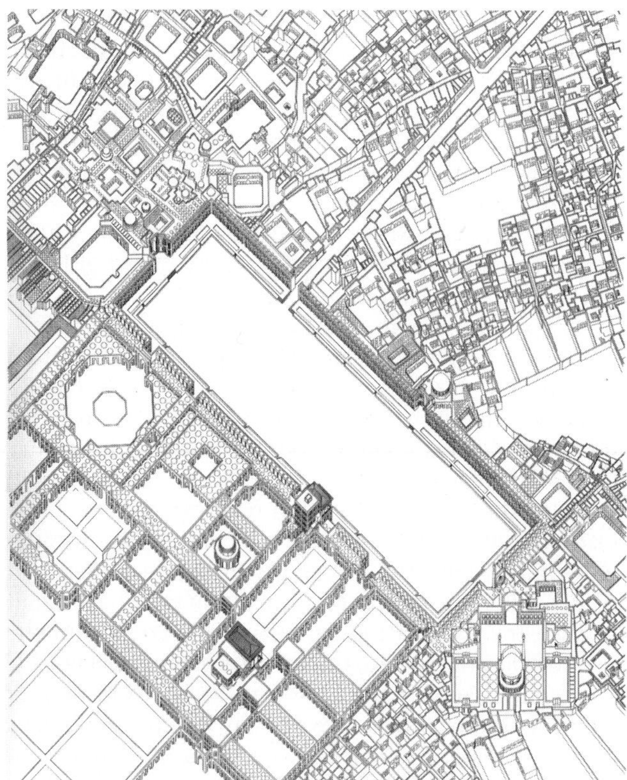

Royal Square in Isfahan Built by the order Shah Abbas over a period of twenty years starting in 1598, the open space is as long as five football fields (555 by 172 yards). At the upper left end of the square in this drawing is the entrance to the covered bazaar, at the bottom the immense Royal Mosque. The left hand side adjoins the Shah's palace and state administrative office. A multi-story pavilion for reviewing troops and receiving guests overlooks the square across from the smaller domed personal mosque of the Shah. [Reproduced with permission from Klaus Herdeg, *Formal Structure in Islamic Architecture of Iran and Turkestan* (New York: Rizzoli, 1990)]

The harbor of Istanbul, the primary Ottoman seaport, teemed with sailing ships and smaller craft, many of them belonging to a colony of European merchants perched on a hilltop on the north side of the Golden Horn. Isfahan, far from the sea, only occasionally received European visitors. Along with Jews and Hindus, a colony of Armenian Christians brought in by Shah Abbas who settled in a suburb of the city handled most of its trade.

Beneath these superficial differences, the two capitals had much in common. Wheeled vehicles were scarce in hilly Istanbul and nonexistent in Isfahan, which was within the broad zone where camels supplanted wheeled transport after the rise of the Arab caravan cities in the pre-Islamic centuries. In size and layout both cities favored walking and, aside from the royal plaza in Isfahan, lacked the open spaces common in contemporary European cities. Away from the major mosque complexes, streets were narrow and irregular. Houses crowded against each other in dead-end lanes. Residents enjoyed the privacy of interior courtyards. Artisans and merchants organized themselves into guilds that had strong social and religious as well as economic bonds. The shops of the guilds adjoined each other in the markets.

Women seldom appeared in public, even in Istanbul's mazelike covered market or in Isfahan's long, serpentine bazaar. At home, the women's quarters—called anderun°, or "interior," in Iran and harem, or "forbidden area," in Istanbul—were separate from the public rooms where the men of the family received visitors. Low cushions, charcoal braziers for warmth, carpets, and small tables constituted most of the furnishings. In Iran and the Arab provinces, shelves and niches for books could be cut into thick, mud-brick walls. Residences in Istanbul were usually built of wood. Glazed tile in geometric or floral patterns covered the walls of wealthy men's reception areas.

The private side of family life has left few traces, but it is apparent that women's society—consisting of wives, children, female servants, and sometimes one or more eunuchs (castrated male servants)—had some connections with the outside world. Ottoman court records reveal that women using male agents bought and sold urban real estate, often dealing with inherited shares of their fathers' estates. Some even established religious endowments for pious purposes. The fact that Islamic law, unlike most European codes, permitted a wife to retain her property after marriage gave some women a stake in the general economy and a degree of independence from their spouses. Women also appeared in other types of court cases, where they often testified for themselves, for Islamic courts did not recognize the role of attorney. Although comparable Safavid court records do not survive, historians assume that a parallel situation prevailed in Iran.

European travelers commented on the veiling of women outside the home, but miniature paintings indicate that ordinary female garb consisted of a long, ample dress with a scarf or long shawl pulled tight over the forehead to conceal the hair. Lightweight trousers, either close-fitting or baggy, were worn under the dress. This mode of dress differed little from that of men. Poor men wore light trousers, a long shirt, a jacket, and a brimless cap or turban. Wealthier men wore ankle-length caftans, often closely fitted around the chest, over their trousers. The norm for both sexes was complete coverage of arms, legs, and hair.

---

anderun (an-deh-ROON)

Istanbul Family on the Way to a Bath House Public baths, an important feature of Islamic cities, set different hours for men and women. Young boys, such as the lad in the turban shown here, went with their mothers and sisters. Notice that the children wear the same styles as the adults. (Osterreichische Nationalbibliothek)

Men monopolized public life. Poetry and art, both somewhat more elegantly developed in Isfahan than in Istanbul, centered as much on the charms of beardless boys as of pretty maidens. Despite religious disapproval of homosexuality, attachments to adolescent boys were neither unusual nor hidden. Women on city streets included non-Muslims, the aged, the very poor, and slaves. Miniature paintings frequently depict female dancers, musicians, and even acrobats in attitudes and costumes that range from decorous to decidedly erotic.

Despite social similarities, the overall flavors of Isfahan and Istanbul were not the same. Isfahan had a prosperous Armenian quarter across the river from the city's center, but it was not a truly cosmopolitan capital. Like other rulers of extensive land empires, Shah Abbas located his capital toward the center of his domain, within comparatively easy reach of any threatened frontier. Istanbul, in contrast, was a great seaport and crossroads located on the straits separating the sultan's European and Asian possessions. People of all sorts lived or spent time in Istanbul—Venetians, Genoese, Arabs, Turks, Greeks, Armenians, Albanians, Serbs, Jews, Bulgarians, and more. In this respect, Istanbul conveyed the cosmopolitan character of major seaports from London to Canton (Guangzhou) and belied the fact that its prosperity rested on the vast reach of the sultan's territories rather than on the voyages of its merchants.

Economic Crisis and Political Collapse

The silk fabrics of northern Iran, monopolized by the shahs, provided the mainstay of the Safavid Empire's foreign trade. However, the manufacture that eventually became most powerfully associated with Iran was the deep-pile carpet made by knotting colored yarns around stretched warp threads. Different cities produced distinctive carpet designs. Women and girls did much of the actual knotting work.

Carpets with geometrical or arabesque designs appear in Timurid miniature paintings, but no knotted "Persian rug" survives from the pre-Safavid era. One of the earliest dated carpets was produced in 1522 to adorn the tomb of Shaikh Safi al-Din, the fourteenth-century founder of the Safaviya. This use indicates the high value accorded these products within Iran. One German visitor to Isfahan remarked: "The most striking adornment of the banqueting hall was to my mind the carpets laid out over all three rostra [platforms to sit on for eating] in a most extravagant fashion, mostly woolen rugs from Kirman with animal patterns and woven of the finest wool."[3]

Overall, Iran's manufacturing sector was neither large nor notably productive. Most of the shah's subjects, whether Iranians, Turks, Kurds, or Arabs, lived by subsistence farming or herding. Neither area of activity recorded significant technological advances during the Safavid period. The shahs granted large sections of the country to the qizilbash nomads in return for mounted warriors for the army. Nomad groups held these lands in common, however, and did not subdivide them into individual landholdings as in the Ottoman Empire. Thus, many people in rural areas lived according to the will of a nomad chieftain who had little interest in building the agricultural economy.

The Safavids, like the Ottomans, had difficulty finding the money to pay troops armed with firearms. This crisis occurred somewhat later in Iran because of its greater distance from Europe. By the end of the sixteenth century, it was evident that a more systematic adoption of cannon and firearms in the Safavid Empire would be needed to hold off the Ottomans and the Uzbeks° (Turkish rulers who had succeeded the Timurids on Iran's Central Asian frontier; see Map 20.1). Like the Ottoman cavalry a century earlier, however, the nomad warriors refused to trade in their bows for firearms. Shah Abbas responded by establishing a slave corps of year-round soldiers and arming them with guns.

The Christian converts to Islam who initially provided the manpower for the new corps came mostly

Uzbeks (UHZ-bex)

from captives taken in raids on Georgia in the Caucasus°. Some became powerful members of the court. They formed a counterweight to the nomad chiefs just as the Janissaries had earlier challenged the landholding Turkish cavalry in the Ottoman Empire. The strong hand of Shah Abbas kept the inevitable rivalries and intrigues between the factions under control. His successors showed less skill.

In the late sixteenth century the inflation caused by cheap silver spread into Iran; then overland trade through Safavid territory declined because of mismanagement of the silk monopoly after Shah Abbas's death in 1629. As a result, the country faced the unsolvable problem of finding money to pay the army and bureaucracy. Trying to remove the nomads from their lands to regain control of taxes proved more difficult and more disruptive militarily than the piecemeal dismantling of the land-grant system in the Ottoman Empire. Demands from the central government caused the nomads, who were still a potent military force, to withdraw to their mountain pastures until the pressure subsided. By 1722 the government had become so weak and commanded so little support from the nomadic groups that an army of marauding Afghans was able to capture Isfahan and effectively end Safavid rule.

Despite Iran's long coastline, the Safavids never possessed a navy. The Portuguese seized the strategic Persian Gulf island of Hormuz in 1517 and were expelled only in 1622, when the English ferried Iranian soldiers to the attack. Entirely land-oriented, the shahs relied on the English and Dutch for naval support and never considered confronting them at sea. Nadir Shah, a general who emerged from the confusion of the Safavid fall to reunify Iran briefly between 1736 and 1747, purchased some naval vessels from the English and used them in the Persian Gulf. But his navy decayed after his death, and Iran did not have a navy again until the twentieth century.

THE MUGHAL EMPIRE, 1526–1761

As a land of Hindus ruled by a Muslim minority, the realm of the Mughal° sultans of India differed substantially from the empires of the Ottomans and Safavids. To be sure, the Ottoman provinces in the Balkans, except for Albania and Bosnia, remained mostly Christian; but the remainder of the Ottoman Empire was overwhelmingly Muslim with small Christian and Jewish minorities. The Ottoman sultans made much of their control of Mecca and Medina and resulting supervision of the annual pilgrimage caravans just as the Safavids fostered pilgrimages to a shrine in Mashhad in northeastern Iran for their overwhelmingly Shi'ite subjects.

India, in contrast, lay far from the Islamic homelands (see Map 20.1). Muslim dominion in northern India began with repeated military campaigns in the early eleventh century, and the Mughals had to contend with the Hindus' long-standing resentment of the destruction of their culture. Unlike the Balkan peoples who had struggled to maintain their separate identities in relation to the Byzantines, the crusaders, and one another before arrival of the Turks, the peoples of the Indian subcontinent had used centuries of freedom from foreign intrusion to forge a distinctive Hindu civilization that could not easily accommodate the worldview of Islam. Thus, the Mughals faced the challenge not just of conquering and organizing a large territorial state but also of finding a formula for Hindu-Muslim coexistence.

Political Foundations

Babur° (1483–1530), the founder of the **Mughal Empire,** descended from Timur. Though Mughal means "Mongol" in Persian, the Timurids were of Turkic rather than Mongol origin. Timur's marriage to a descendant of Genghis Khan had earned him the Mongol designation "son-in-law," but like the Ottomans, his family did not enjoy the political legitimacy that came with Genghisid decent experienced by lesser rulers in Central Asia and in the Crimea north of the Black Sea.

Invading from Central Asia, Babur defeated the last Muslim sultan of Delhi at the Battle of Panipat in 1526. Even though this victory marked the birth of a brilliant and powerful state in India, Babur's descendants continued to think of Central Asia as their true home, from time to time expressing intentions of recapturing Samarkand and referring to its Uzbek ruler—a genuine descendant of Genghis Khan—as a governor rather than an independent sovereign.

India proved to be the primary theater of Mughal accomplishment, however. Babur's grandson **Akbar** (r. 1556–1605), a brilliant but mercurial man whose illiteracy betrayed his upbringing in the wilds of Afghanistan, established the central administration of the expanding state. Under him and his three successors—the last of whom died in 1707—all but the southern tip of India

Caucasus (CAW-kuh-suhs) **Mughal** (MOH-guhl)

Babur (BAH-bur)

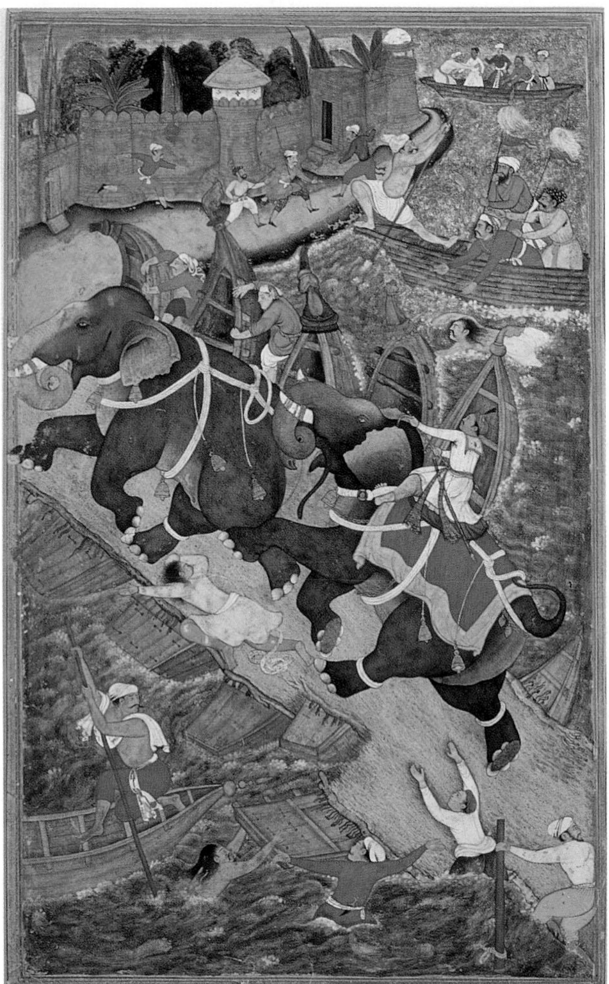

Elephants Breaking Bridge of Boats This illustration of an incident in the life of Akbar illustrates the ability of Mughal miniature painters to depict unconventional action scenes. Because the flow of rivers in India and the Middle East varied greatly from dry season to wet season, boat bridges were much more common than permanent constructions. (Victoria and Albert Museum, London/Bridgeman Art Library)

fell under Mughal rule, administered first from Agra and then from Delhi°.

Akbar granted land revenues to military officers and government officials in return for their service. Ranks called **mansabs°**, some high and some low, entitled their holders to revenue assignments. As in the other Islamic empires, the central government kept careful track of these nonhereditary grants.

With a population of 100 million, a thriving trading economy based on cotton cloth, and a generally efficient administration, India under Akbar enjoyed great prosperity in the sixteenth century. Akbar and his successors faced few external threats and experienced generally peaceful conditions in their northern Indian heartland. Nevertheless, they were capable of squandering immense amounts of blood and treasure fighting Hindu kings and rebels in the Deccan region or Afghans on their western frontier (see Map 20.1).

Foreign trade boomed at the port of Surat in the northwest, which also served as an embarkation point for pilgrims headed for Mecca. Like the Safavids, the Mughals had no navy or merchant ships. The government saw the Europeans—now primarily Dutch and English, the Portuguese having lost most of their Indian ports—less as enemies than as shipmasters whose naval support could be procured as needed in return for trading privileges. It never questioned the wisdom of selling Indian cottons for European coin—no one understood how cheap silver had become in Europe—and shipping them off to European customers in English and Dutch vessels.

Hindus and Muslims

India had not been dominated by a single ruler since the time of Harsha Vardhana (r. 606–647). Muslim destruction of Hindu cultural monuments, the expansion of Muslim territory, and the practice, until Akbar's time, of enslaving prisoners of war and compelling them to convert to Islam horrified the Hindus. But the politically divided Hindus did not put up a combined resistance. The Mughal state, in contrast, inherited traditions of unified imperial rule from both the Islamic caliphate and the more recent examples of Genghis Khan and Timur.

Those Mongol-based traditions did not necessarily mean religious intolerance. Seventy percent of the mansabdars° (officials holding land grants) appointed under Akbar were Muslim soldiers born outside India, but 15 percent were Hindus, mostly warriors from the north called **Rajputs°.** One of them rose to be a powerful revenue minister. Their status as mansabdars confirmed the policy of religious accommodation adopted by Akbar and his successors.

Akbar, the most illustrious Mughal ruler, differed from his Ottoman and Safavid counterparts—Suleiman the Magnificent and Shah Abbas the Great—in his striving for social harmony and not just for more territory and revenue. He succeeded to the throne at age thirteen, and his actions were dominated at first by a regent and then by his strong-minded childhood nurse. On reach-

Delhi (DEL-ee) **mansabs** (MAN-sabz)

mansabdars (man-sab-DAHRZ) **Rajputs** (RAHJ-putz)

ing twenty, Akbar took command of the government. He married a Hindu Rajput princess, whose name is not recorded, and welcomed her father and brother to the court in Agra.

Other rulers might have used such a marriage as a means of humiliating a subject group, but Akbar signaled his desire for Muslim-Hindu reconciliation. A year later he rescinded the head tax that Muslim rulers traditionally levied on tolerated non-Muslims. This measure was more symbolic than real because the tax had not been regularly collected, but the gesture helped cement the allegiance of the Rajputs.

Akbar longed for an heir. Much to his relief, his Rajput wife gave birth to a son in 1569, ensuring that future rulers would have both Muslim and Hindu ancestry.

Akbar ruled that in legal disputes between two Hindus, decisions would be made according to village custom or Hindu law as interpreted by local Hindu scholars. Muslims followed Shari'a law. Akbar made himself the legal court of last resort in a 1579 declaration that he was God's infallible earthly representative. Thus, appeals could be made to Akbar personally, a possibility not usually present in Islamic jurisprudence.

He also made himself the center of a new "Divine Faith" incorporating Muslim, Hindu, Zoroastrian, Sikh°, and Christian beliefs. Sufi ideas attracted him and permeated the religious rituals he instituted at his court. To promote serious consideration of his religious principles, he monitored, from a high catwalk, debates among scholars of all religions assembled in his private octagonal audience chamber. When courtiers uttered the Muslim exclamation "Allahu Akbar"—"God is great"—its second grammatical meaning, "God is Akbar," was not lost on them. Akbar's religious views did not survive him, but the court culture he fostered, reflecting a mixture of Muslim and Hindu traditions, flourished until his zealous great-grandson Aurangzeb° (r. 1658–1707) reinstituted many restrictions on Hindus.

Mughal and Rajput miniature portraits of political figures and depictions of scantily clad women brought frowns to the faces of pious Muslims, who deplored the representation of human beings in art. Most of the leading painters were Hindus. In literature, in addition to the florid style of Persian verse favored at court, a new taste developed for poetry and prose in the popular language of the Delhi region. The modern descendant of this language is called Urdu in Pakistan, from the Turkish word *ordu*, meaning "army" (in India it is called Hindi).

Akbar's policy of toleration does not explain the pattern of conversion in Mughal India, most of which was to Sunni Islam. Some scholars maintain that most converts came from the lowest Hindu social groups, or castes, who hoped to improve their lot in life, but little data confirm this theory. Others argue that Sufi brotherhoods, which developed strongly in India, led the way in converting people to Islam, but this proposition has not been proved. The most heavily Muslim regions developed in the valley of the Indus River and in Bengal. The Indus center dates from the isolated establishment of Muslim rule there as early as the eighth century.

A careful study of local records and traditions from east Bengal indicates that the eastward movement of the delta of the Ganges River, caused by silting, and the spread of rice cultivation into forest clearings played the primary role in conversions to Islam there. Mansabdars (mostly Muslims) with land grants in east Bengal contracted with local entrepreneurs to collect a labor force, cut down the forest, and establish rice paddies. Though some entrepreneurs were Hindu, most were non-Sufi Muslim religious figures. The latter centered their farming communities on mosques and shrines, using religion as a social cement. Most natives of the region were accustomed to worshiping local forest deities rather than the main Hindu gods. So the shift to Islam represented a move to a more sophisticated, literate culture appropriate to their new status as farmers producing for the commercial rice market. Gradual religious change of this kind often produced Muslim communities whose social customs differed little from those in neighboring non-Muslim communities. In east Bengal, common Muslim institutions, such as madrasas, the ulama, and law courts, were little in evidence.

The emergence of **Sikhism** in the Punjab region of northwest India constituted another change in Indian religious life in the Mughal period. Nanak (1469–1539), the religion's first guru (spiritual teacher), stressed meditation as a means of seeking enlightenment and drew upon both Muslim and Hindu imagery in his teachings. His followers formed a single community without differences of caste. However, after Aurangzeb ordered the ninth guru beheaded in 1675 for refusing to convert to Islam, the tenth guru dedicated himself to avenging his father's death and reorganized his followers into "the army of the pure," a religious order dedicated to defending Sikh beliefs. These devotees signaled their faith by leaving their hair uncut beneath a turban; carrying a comb, a steel bracelet, and a sword or dagger; and wearing military-style breeches. By the eighteenth century, the Mughals were encountering fierce opposition from the Sikhs as well as from Hindu guerrilla forces in the rugged and ravine-scarred province of Maharashtra on India's west coast.

Sikh (sick) **Aurangzeb** (ow-rang-ZEB)

Central Decay and Regional Challenges, 1707–1761

Mughal power did not long survive Aurangzeb's death in 1707. Some historians consider the land-grant system a central element in the rapid decline of imperial authority, but other factors played a role as well. Aurangzeb failed to effectively integrate new Mughal territories in southern India into the imperial structure, and a number of strong regional powers challenged Mughal military supremacy. The Marathas proved a formidable enemy as they carved out a swath of territory across India's middle, and Sikhs, Hindu Rajputs, and Muslim Afghans exerted intense pressure from the northwest. A climax came in 1739 when Nadir Shah, the general who had seized power in Iran after the fall of the Safavids, invaded the subcontinent and sacked Delhi, which Akbar's grandson had rebuilt and beautified as the Mughal capital some decades before. He carried off to Iran, as part of the booty, the priceless, jewel-encrusted "peacock throne," symbol of Mughal grandeur. The later Mughals found another throne to sit on; but their empire, which survived in name to 1857, was finished.

In 1723 Nizam al-Mulk°, the powerful vizier of the Mughal sultan, gave up on the central government and established his own nearly independent state at Hyderabad in the eastern Deccan. Other officials bearing the title nawab° (from Arabic *na'ib* meaning "deputy" and Anglicized as "nabob") became similarly independent in Bengal and Oudh° in the northeast, as did the Marathas farther west. In the northwest, simultaneous Iranian and Mughal weakness allowed the Afghans to establish an independent kingdom.

Some of these regional powers and smaller princely states flourished with the removal of the sultan's heavy hand. Linguistic and religious communities, freed from the religious intolerance instituted during the reign of Aurangzeb, similarly enjoyed greater opportunity for political expression. However, this disintegration of central power favored the intrusion of European adventurers.

Joseph François Dupleix° took over the presidency of the east coast French stronghold of Pondicherry° in 1741 and began a new phase of European involvement in India. He captured the English trading center of Madras and used his small contingent of European and European-trained Indian troops to become a power broker in southern India. Though offered the title nawab, Dupleix preferred to operate behind the scenes, using Indian princes as puppets. His career ended in 1754 when he was called home. Deeply involved in European wars, the French government declined to pursue further adventures in India. Dupleix's departure cleared the way for the British, whose ventures in India are described in Chapter 25.

Nizam al-Mulk (nee-ZAHM al-MULK) **nawab** (NAH-wab)
Oudh (OW-ad) **Dupleix** (doo-PLAY)
Pondicherry (pon-dir-CHEH-ree)

TRADE EMPIRES IN THE INDIAN OCEAN, 1600–1729

It is no coincidence that the Mughal, Safavid, and Ottoman Empires declined simultaneously in the seventeenth and eighteenth centuries. Complex changes in military technology and in the world economy, along with the increasing difficulty of basing an extensive land empire on military forces paid through land grants, affected them all adversely. The opposite held for seafaring countries intent on turning trade networks into maritime empires. Improvements in ship design, navigation accuracy, and the use of cannon gave an ever-increasing edge to European powers competing with local seafaring peoples. Moreover, the development of joint-stock companies, in which many merchants pooled their capital, provided a flexible and efficient financial instrument for exploiting new possibilities. The English East India Company was founded in 1600, the Dutch East India Company in 1602.

Although the Ottomans, Safavids, and Mughals did not effectively contest the growth of Portuguese and then Dutch, English, and French maritime power, the majority of non-European shipbuilders, captains, sailors, and traders were Muslim. Groups of Armenian, Jewish, and Hindu traders were also active, but they remained almost as aloof from the Europeans as the Muslims did. The presence in every port of Muslims following the same legal traditions and practicing their faith in similar ways cemented the Muslims' trading network. Islam, from its very outset in the life and preaching of Muhammad (570–632), had favored trade and traders. Unlike Hinduism, it was a proselytizing religion, a factor that encouraged the growth of coastal Muslim communities as local non-Muslims associated with Muslim commercial activities converted and intermarried with Muslims from abroad.

Although European missionaries, particularly the Jesuits, tried to extend Christianity into Asia and Africa (see Chapters 16 and 21), most Europeans, the Portuguese excepted, did not treat local converts or the offspring of mixed marriages as full members of their communities. Islam was generally more welcoming. As a consequence, Islam spread extensively into East Africa and Southeast Asia during precisely the time of rapid European commercial expansion. Even without the support of the Muslim land empires, Islam became a source of resistance to growing European domination.

Muslims in the East Indies

Historians disagree about the chronology and manner of Islam's spread in Southeast Asia. Arab traders appeared in southern China as early as the eighth century, so Muslims probably reached the East Indies at a similarly early date. Nevertheless, the dominance of Indian cultural influences in the area for several centuries thereafter indicates that early Muslim visitors had little impact on local beliefs. Clearer indications of conversion and the formation of Muslim communities date from roughly the fourteenth century, with the strongest overseas linkage being to the port of Cambay in India (see Map 20.2) rather than to the Arab world. Islam first took root in port cities and in some royal courts and spread inland only slowly, possibly transmitted by itinerant Sufis.

Although appeals to the Ottoman sultan for support against the Europeans ultimately proved futile, Islam strengthened resistance to Portuguese, Spanish, and Dutch intruders. When the Spaniards conquered the Philippines during the decades following the establishment of their first fort in 1565, they encountered Muslims on the southern island of Mindanao° and the nearby Sulu archipelago. They called them "Moros," the Spanish term for their old enemies, the Muslims of North Africa. In the ensuing Moro wars, the Spaniards portrayed the Moros as greedy pirates who raided non-Muslim territories for slaves. In fact, they were political, religious, and commercial competitors whose perseverance enabled them to establish the Sulu Empire based in the southern Philippines, one of the strongest states in Southeast Asia from 1768 to 1848.

Other local kingdoms that looked on Islam as a force to counter the aggressive Christianity of the Europeans included the actively proselytizing Brunei° Sultanate in northern Borneo and the **Acheh° Sultanate** in northern Sumatra. At its peak in the early seventeenth century, Acheh succeeded Malacca as the main center of Islamic expansion in Southeast Asia. It prospered by trading pepper for cotton cloth from Gujarat in India. Acheh declined after the Dutch seized Malacca from Portugal in 1641.

Mindanao (min-duh-NOW) **Brunei** (BROO-nie)
Acheh (AH-cheh)

How well Islam was understood in these Muslim kingdoms is open to question. In Acheh, for example, a series of women ruled between 1641 and 1699. This practice ended when local Muslim scholars obtained a ruling from scholars in Mecca and Medina that Islam did not approve of female rulers. After this ruling scholarly understandings of Islam gained greater prominence in the East Indies.

Historians have looked at merchants, Sufi preachers, or both as the first propagators of Islam in Southeast Asia. The scholarly vision of Islam, however, took root in the sixteenth century by way of pilgrims returning from years of study in Mecca and Medina. Islam promoted the dissemination of writing in the region. Some of the returning pilgrims wrote in Arabic, others in Malay or Javanese. As Islam continued to spread, adat ("custom"), a form of Islam rooted in pre-Muslim religious and social practices, retained its preeminence in rural areas over practices centered on the Shari'a, the religious law. But the royal courts in the port cities began to heed the views of the pilgrim teachers. Though different in many ways, both varieties of Islam provided believers with a firm basis of identification in the face of the growing European presence. Christian missionaries gained most of their converts in regions that had not yet converted to Islam, such as the northern Philippines.

Muslims in East Africa

Muslim rulers also governed the East African ports that the Portuguese began to visit in the fifteenth century, though they were not allied politically (see Map 20.2). People living in the millet and rice lands of the Swahili Coast—from the Arabic sawahil° meaning "coasts"—had little contact with those in the dry hinterlands. Throughout this period, the East African lakes region and the highlands of Kenya witnessed unprecedented migration and relocation of peoples because of drought conditions that persisted from the late sixteenth through most of the seventeenth century.

Cooperation among the trading ports of Kilwa, Mombasa, and Malindi was hindered by the thick bush country that separated the cultivated tracts of coastal land and by the fact that the ports competed with one another in the export of ivory; ambergris° (a whale byproduct used in perfumes); and forest products such as beeswax, copal tree resin, and wood. Kilwa also exported gold. In the eighteenth century slave trading, primarily to Arabian ports but also to India, increased in

sawahil (suh-WAH-hil) **ambergris** (AM-ber-grees)

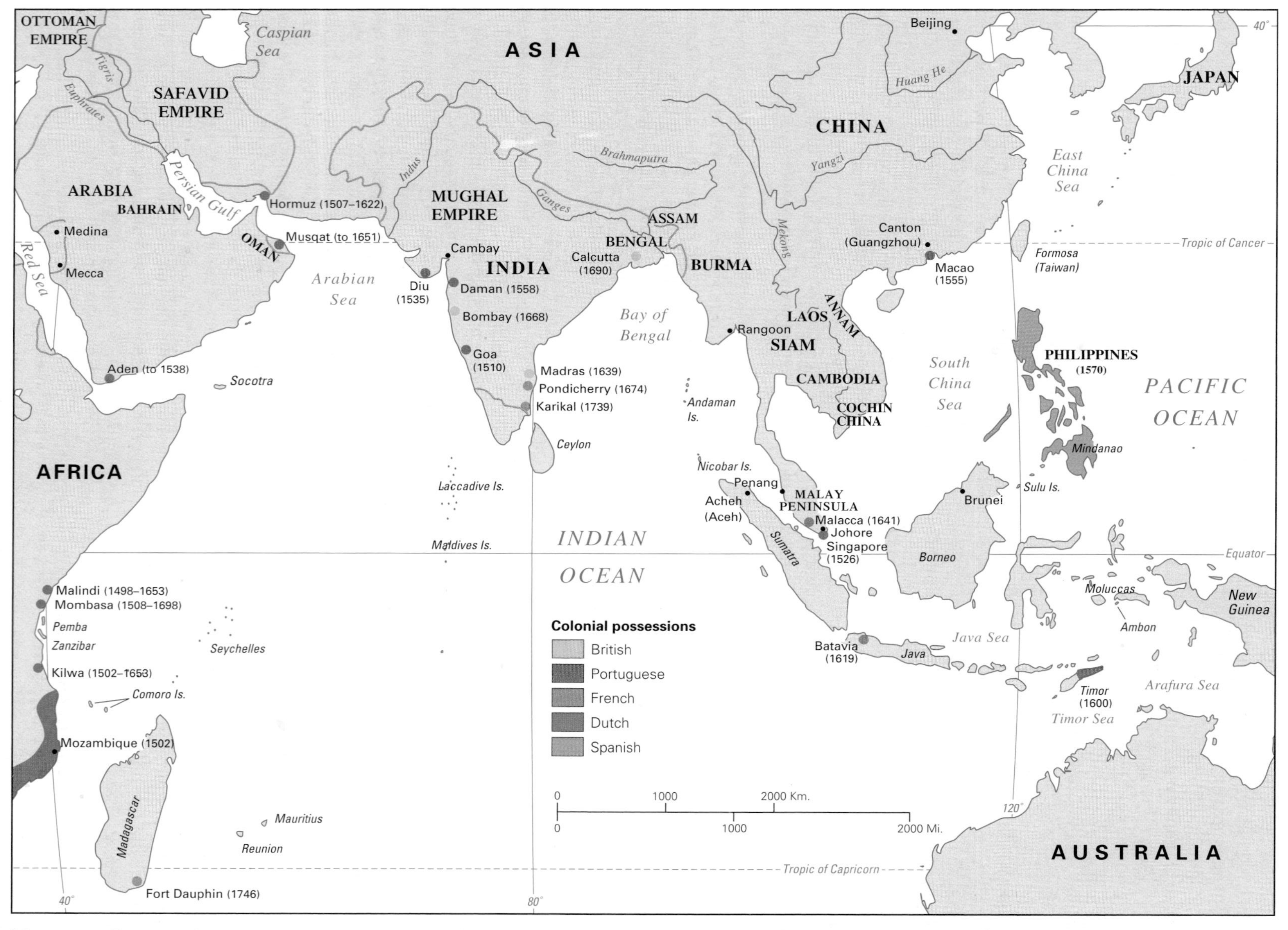

Map 20.2 European Colonization in the Indian Ocean to 1750 Since Portuguese explorers were the first Europeans to reach India by rounding Africa, Portugal gained a strong foothold in both areas. Rival Spain was barred from colonizing the region by the Treaty of Tordesillas in 1494, which limited Spanish efforts to lands west of a line drawn through the mid-Atlantic Ocean. The line carried around the globe provided justification of Spanish colonization in the Philippines. French, British, and Dutch colonies date from after 1600, when joint-stock companies provided a new stimulus for overseas commerce.

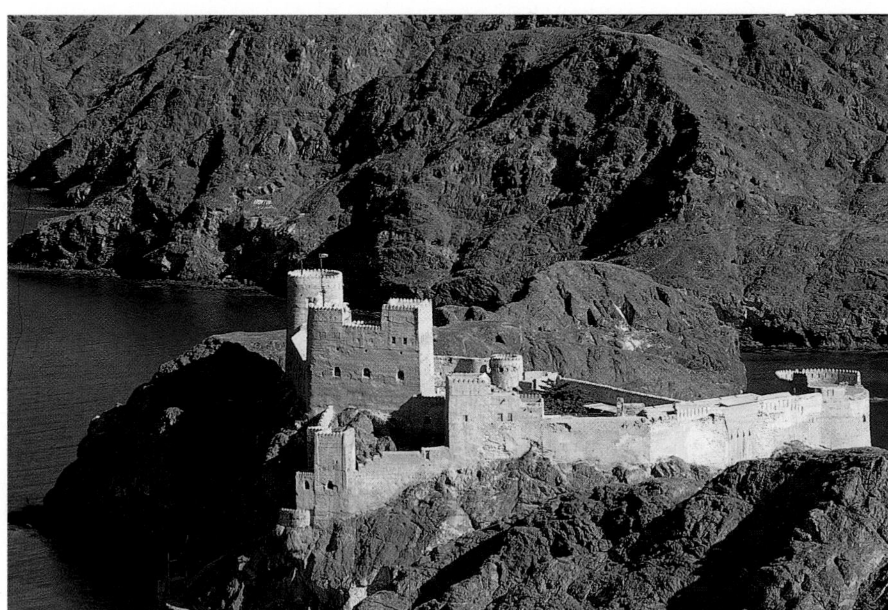

Portuguese Fort Guarding Musqat Harbor Musqat in Oman and Aden in Yemen, the best harbors in southern Arabia, were targets for imperial navies trying to establish dominance in the Indian Ocean. Musqat's harbor is small and circular, with one narrow entrance overlooked by this fortress. The palace of the sultan of Oman is still located at the opposite end of the harbor. (Robert Harding Picture Library)

importance. Because Europeans—the only peoples who kept consistent records of slave-trading activities—played a minor role in this slave trade, few records have survived to indicate its extent. Perhaps the best estimate is that 2.1 million slaves were exported between 1500 and 1890, a little over 12.5 percent of the total traffic in African slaves during that period (see Chapter 19).

The Portuguese conquered all the coastal ports from Mozambique northward except Malindi, with whose ruler Portugal cooperated. A Portuguese description of the ruler names some of the cloth and metal goods that Malindi imported, as well as some local manufactures:

> The King wore a robe of damask trimmed with green satin and a rich [cap]. He was seated on two cushioned chairs of bronze, beneath a rough sunshade of crimson satin attached to a pole. An old man, who attended him as a page, carried a short sword in a silver sheath. There were many players on [horns], and two trumpets of ivory richly carved and of the size of a man, which were blown through a hole in the side, and made sweet harmony with the [horns].[4]

Initially, the Portuguese favored the port of Malindi, which caused the decline of Kilwa and Mombasa. Repeatedly plagued by local rebellion, Portuguese power suffered severe blows when the Arabs of **Oman** in southeastern Arabia captured their south Arabian stronghold at Musqat (1650) and then went on to seize Mombasa (1698), which had become the Portuguese capital in East Africa. The Portuguese briefly retook Mombasa but lost control permanently in 1729. From then on, the Portuguese had to content themselves with Mozambique in East Africa and a few remaining ports in India (Goa) and farther east (Macao and Timor).

The Omanis created a maritime empire of their own, one that worked in greater cooperation with the African populations. The Bantu language of the coast, broadened by the absorption of Arabic, Persian, and Portuguese loanwords, developed into **Swahili°,** which was spoken throughout the region. Arabs and other Muslims who settled in the region intermarried with local families, giving rise to a mixed population that played an important role in developing a distinctive Swahili culture.

Islam also spread in the southern Sudan in this period, particularly in the dry areas away from the Nile River. This growth coincided with a waning of Ethiopian power as a result of Portugal's stifling of trade in the Red Sea. Yet no significant contact developed between the emerging Muslim Swahili culture and that of the Muslims in the Sudan to the north.

The Dutch played a major role in driving the Portuguese from their possessions in the East Indies. They were better organized than the Portuguese through the Dutch East India Company. Just as the Portuguese had tried to dominate the trade in spices, so the Dutch

Swahili (swah-HEE-lee)

concentrated at first on the spice-producing islands of Southeast Asia. The Portuguese had seized Malacca, a strategic town on the narrow strait at the end of the Malay Peninsula, from a local Malay ruler in 1511 (see Chapter 16). The Dutch took it away from them in 1641, leaving Portugal little foothold in the East Indies except the islands of Ambon° and Timor (see Map 20.2).

Although the United Netherlands was one of the least autocratic countries of Europe, the governors-general appointed by the Dutch East India Company deployed almost unlimited powers in their efforts to maintain their trade monopoly. They could even order the execution of their own employees for "smuggling"—that is, trading on their own. Under strong governors-general, the Dutch fought a series of wars against Acheh and other local kingdoms on Sumatra and Java. In 1628 and 1629 their new capital at **Batavia,** now the city of Jakarta on Java, was besieged by a fleet of fifty ships belonging to the sultan of Mataram°, a Javanese kingdom. The Dutch held out with difficulty and eventually prevailed when the sultan was unable to get effective help from the English.

Suppressing local rulers, however, was not enough to control the spice trade once other European countries adopted Dutch methods, learned more about where goods might be acquired, and started to send more ships to Southeast Asia. In the course of the eighteenth century, therefore, the Dutch gradually turned from being middlemen between Southeast Asian producers and European buyers to producing crops in areas they controlled, notably in Java. Javanese teak forests yielded high-quality lumber, and coffee, transplanted from Yemen, grew well in the western hilly regions. In this new phase of colonial export production, Batavia developed from being the headquarters town of a far-flung enterprise to being the administrative capital of a conquered land.

Beyond the East Indies, the Dutch utilized their discovery of a band of powerful eastward-blowing winds (called the "Roaring Forties" because they blow throughout the year between 40 and 50 degrees south latitude) to reach Australia in 1606. In 1642 and 1643 Abel Tasman became the first European to set foot on Tasmania and New Zealand and to sail around Australia, signaling European involvement in that region (see Chapter 25).

Ambon (am-BOHN) **Mataram** (MAH-tah-ram)

CONCLUSION

Asians and Africans ruled by the Ottoman and Mughal sultans and the Safavid shahs did not perceive that a major shift in world economic and political alignments was under way by the late seventeenth century. The rulers focused their efforts on conquering more and more land, sometimes at the expense of Christian Europe and Hindu India, but also at one another's expense, since the Sunni-Shi'ite division justified Iranian attacks on its neighbors and vice versa.

To be sure, more and more trade was being carried in European vessels, particularly after the advent of joint-stock companies in 1600; and Europeans had enclaves in a handful of port cities and islands. But the age-old tradition of Asia was that imperial wealth came from control of broad expanses of agricultural land. Except for state monopolies, such as Iranian silk, governments did not greatly concern themselves with what farmers did. They relied mostly on land taxes, usually indirectly collected via holders of land grants or tax farmers, rather than on customs duties or control of markets to fill the government coffers.

With ever-increasing military expenditures, these taxes fell short of the rulers' needs. Few people realized, however, that this problem was basic to the entire economic system rather than a temporary revenue shortfall. Imperial courtiers pursued their luxurious ways; poetry and the arts continued to flourish; and the quality of manufacturing and craft production remained generally high. Eighteenth-century European observers, luxuriating in the prosperity gained from their ever-increasing control of the Indian Ocean, marveled no less at the riches and industry of these eastern lands than at the fundamental weakness of their political and military systems.

Key Terms

Ottoman Empire
Suleiman the Magnificent
Janissary
devshirme
Tulip Period
Safavid Empire
Shi'ite Islam
Hidden Imam
Shah Abbas I
Mughal Empire
Akbar
mansabs
Rajputs
Sikhism
Acheh Sultanate
Oman
Swahili
Batavia

Suggested Reading

The best comprehensive and comparative account of the post-Mongol Islamic land empires, with an emphasis on social history, is Ira Lapidus, *A History of Islamic Societies* (1988). For a work of similar scope concentrating on intellectual history see Marshall G. S. Hodgson, *The Venture of Islam*, vol. 3, *The Gunpowder Empires and Modern Times* (1974).

On the Ottoman Empire in its prime see Colin Imber, *The Ottoman Empire, 1300–1650: The Structure of Power* (2002). Daniel Goffman, *The Ottoman Empire and Early Modern Europe* (2002), compares the Ottomans with contemporary European kingdoms. Jason Goodwin, *Lords of the Horizons: A History of the Ottoman Empire* (1999), offers a brief journalistic account. Ottoman origins are well covered in Cemal Kafadar, *Between Two Worlds* (1995). For a collection of articles on nonpolitical matters see Halil Inalcik and Donald Quataert, eds., *An Economic and Social History of the Ottoman Empire, 1300–1914* (1994). For a sociological analysis of change in the seventeenth century see Karen Barkey, *Bandits and Bureaucrats* (1994).

Some specialized studies of cities and regions give a sense of the major changes in Ottoman society and economy after the sixteenth century: Daniel Goffman, *Izmir and the Levantine World, 1550–1650* (1990); Abraham Marcus, *The Middle East on the Eve of Modernity: Aleppo in the Eighteenth Century* (1989); Bruce McGowan, *Economic Life in the Ottoman Empire: Taxation, Trade, and the Struggle for Land, 1600–1800* (1981); and Dina Rizk Khoury, *State and Provincial Society in the Ottoman Empire: Mosul, 1540–1834* (1997).

Articles in Benjamin Braude and Bernard Lewis, eds., *Christians and Jews in the Ottoman Empire: The Functioning of a Plural Society* (1982), deal with questions relating to religious minorities. Leslie Pierce skillfully treats the role of women in the governance of the empire in *The Imperial Harem: Women and Sovereignty in the Ottoman Empire* (1993). Ralph S. Hattox, *Coffee and Coffeehouses: The Origins of a Social Beverage in the Medieval Near East* (1988), is an excellent contribution to Ottoman social history.

The most comprehensive treatment of the history of Safavid Iran is in the articles in Peter Jackson and Laurence Lockhart, eds., *The Cambridge History of Iran*, vol. 6, *The Timurid and Safavid Periods* (1986). The articles by Hans Roemer in this volume provide solid political narratives of the pre-Safavid and Safavid periods. Roger Savory's important article on the structure of the Safavid state is available in a more extensive form in his *Iran Under the Safavids* (1980).

For the artistic side of Safavid history, abundantly illustrated, see Anthony Welch, *Shah Abbas and the Arts of Isfahan* (1973). Said Amir Arjomand, *The Shadow of God and the Hidden Imam: Religion, Political Order, and Societal Change in Shiite Iran from the Beginning to 1890* (1984), contains the best analysis of the complicated relationship between Shi'ism and monarchy. For Safavid economic history see Willem Floor, *A Fiscal History of Iran in the Safavid and Qajar Periods, 1500–1925* (1998); and Rudoph Matthee, *The Politics of Trade in Safavid Iran: Silk for Silver, 1600–1730* (1999).

A highly readable work that situates the Mughal Empire within the overall history of the subcontinent is Stanley Wolpert, *A New History of India*, 6th ed. (1999). For a broad treatment of the entire development of Islamic society in India with emphasis on the Mughal period, see S. M. Ikram, *History of Muslim Civilization in India and Pakistan* (1989). Wheeler Thackston has made a lively translation of Babur's autobiography in *The Baburnama: Memoirs of Babur, Prince and Emperor* (1996). For a comprehensive history of the Mughals see John F. Richards, *The Mughal Empire* (1993). See also Richard Foltz, *Mughal India and Central Asia* (1999). Irfan Habib has edited an extensive collection of articles on the Mughal Empire in its prime entitled *Akbar and His India* (1997). For the history of the Sikhs see W. H. McLeod, *The Sikhs: History, Religion, and Society* (1989). Two specialized works on the economic and trading history of India are Ashin Das Gupta and M. N. Pearson, eds., *India and the Indian Ocean, 1500–1800* (1987), and Stephen Frederic Dale, *Indian Merchants and Eurasian Trade, 1600–1750* (1994).

The history of East Africa in this period is not well documented, but B. A. Ogot, ed., *UNESCO General History of Africa*, vol. 5, *Africa from the Sixteenth to the Eighteenth Century* (1992), provides a useful collection of articles. See also Tom Spear, *The Swahili* (1984), and James de Vere Allen, *Swahili Origins* (1993).

For a brief, general introduction to the relations between the Muslim land empires and the development of Indian Ocean trade, see Patricia Risso, *Merchants and Faith: Muslim Commerce and Culture in the Indian Ocean* (1995). Esmond Bradley Martin and Chryssee Perry Martin have written a popular and well-illustrated work on the western Indian Ocean entitled *Cargoes of the East: The Ports, Trade and Culture of the Arabian Seas and Western Indian Ocean* (1978). C. R. Boxer, *The Dutch Seaborne Empire, 1600–1800* (1973), is a classic account of all aspects of Dutch maritime expansion.

Notes

1. Quoted in Sarah Searight, *The British in the Middle East* (New York: Atheneum 1970), 36.
2. Daniel Goffman, *Izmir and the Levantine World, 1550–1650* (Seattle: University of Washington Press, 1990), 52.
3. Quoted in Peter Jackson and Laurence Lockhart, eds., *The Cambridge History of Iran*, vol. 6, *The Timurid and Safavid Periods* (New York: Cambridge University Press, 1986), 703.
4. Esmond Bradley Martin and Chryssee Perry Martin, *Cargoes of the East: The Ports, Trade and Culture of the Arabian Seas and Western Indian Ocean* (1978), 17.

21 Northern Eurasia, 1500–1800

Russian Ambassadors to Holland Display Their Furs, 1576 Representatives from Muscovy impressed the court of King Maximilian II of Bohemia with their sable coats and caps.

CHAPTER OUTLINE

Li Zicheng° was an apprentice ironworker in a barren northern Chinese province. His dreams for the future were dashed when, in a desperate effort to save money, the Hanli emperor ordered the elimination of Li's job and those of many other government employees. The savings went to fund more troops to defend the capital city of Beijing° against attacks by **Manchu** armies from Manchuria in the northeast. By 1630 Li Zicheng had found work as a soldier, but he and his fellow soldiers mutinied when the government failed to provide them with needed supplies. A natural leader, Li soon headed a group of several thousand Chinese rebels. In 1635 he and other rebel leaders were strong enough to control much of north central China.

Wedged between the armies of the Manchu pressing from the north and the rebels to the southwest, the Ming government grew ever weaker. Taking advantage of the weakness, Li Zicheng's forces began to move toward Beijing. Along the way they captured towns and conscripted young men into their army. The rebels also won popular support with promises to end the abuses of the Ming and restore peace and prosperity. In April 1644 Li's armies were able to take over Beijing without a fight. The last Ming emperor hanged himself in the palace garden, bringing to an end the dynasty that had ruled China since 1368.

The rebels' success was short-lived. Believing there was more to fear from uneducated, violent men like Li, the Ming general Wu Sangui joined forces with the Manchu. Wu may have been influenced by the fact that Li had captured one of the general's favorite concubines and taken her for himself. Together Wu and the Manchu retook Beijing in June. Li's forces scattered, and a year later he was dead, either a suicide or beaten to death by peasants whose food he tried to steal.[1]

Meanwhile, the Manchu were making it clear that they intended to be the new masters of China. They installed their young sovereign as the new emperor and over the next two decades hunted down the last of the Ming loyalists and heirs to the throne.

China was not the only state in Northern Eurasia facing uprisings from within and foreign threats. In the period from 1500 to 1800 Japan and Russia experienced turbulence as they underwent massive political change and economic growth. Besides challenges from nearby neighbors, the three also faced new contacts and challenges from the commercially and militarily powerful European states.

As you read this chapter, ask yourself the following questions:

- How did Japan, China, and Russia respond to internal social, economic, and political pressures?
- How did China and Russia deal with military challenges from their immediate neighbors?
- How did Japan, China, and Russia differ in the ways they reacted to western European commercial and cultural contacts?

Japanese Reunification

Like China and Russia in the centuries between 1500 and 1800, Japan experienced three major changes: internal and external military conflicts, political growth and strengthening, and expanded commercial and cultural contacts. Along with its culturally homogenous population and natural boundaries, Japan's smaller size made the process of political unification shorter than in the great empires of China and Russia. Japan also differed in its responses to new contacts with western Europeans.

Civil War and the Invasion of Korea, 1500–1603

In the twelfth century Japan's imperial unity had disintegrated, and the country fell under the rule of numerous warlords known as ***daimyo*°.** Each of the daimyo had his own castle town, a small bureaucracy, and an army of warriors, the ***samurai*°.** Daimyo pledged a loose allegiance to the hereditary commander of the armies, the shogun, as well as to the Japanese emperor residing in the capital city of Kyoto°. The emperor and shogun were symbols of national unity but lacked political power.

Warfare among the different daimyo was common. In the late 1500s Japan experienced a prolonged civil war

Li Zicheng (lee ZUH-cheng) **Beijing** (bay-JING)

daimyo (DIE-mee-oh) **samurai** (SAH-moo-rye)
Kyoto (KYOH-toh)

that brought the separate Japanese islands under powerful warlords. The most successful of these warlords was Hideyoshi°. In 1592, buoyed with his success in Japan, the supremely confident Hideyoshi launched an invasion of the Asian mainland with 160,000 men. His apparent intention was not just to conquer the Korean peninsula but to make himself emperor of China as well.

The Korean and Japanese languages are closely related, but the dominant influence on Korean culture had long been China. Korea generally accepted a subordinate relationship with its giant neighbor and paid tribute to the Chinese dynasty in power. In many ways the Yi dynasty that ruled Korea from 1392 to 1910 was a model Confucian state. Although Korea had developed its own system of writing in 1443 and made extensive use of printing with movable type from the fifteenth century, most printing continued to use Chinese characters.

Against Hideyoshi's invaders the Koreans employed all the technological and military skill for which the Yi period was renowned. Ingenious covered warships, or "turtle boats," intercepted a portion of the Japanese fleet. The mentally unstable Hideyoshi countered with brutal punitive measures. The Koreans and their Chinese allies could not stop the Japanese conquest of the peninsula and into the Chinese province of Manchuria. However, after Hideyoshi's death in 1598, the other Japanese military leaders withdrew their forces, and the Japanese government made peace in 1606.

Korea was severely devastated by the invasion. In the confusion after the Japanese withdrawal, the Korean *yangban* (nobility) and lesser royals were able to lay claim to so much tax-paying land that royal revenues may have fallen by two-thirds. But the most dramatic consequences of the Japanese invasion were in China. The battles in Manchuria weakened Chinese garrisons there, permitting Manchu opposition to consolidate. Manchu forces invaded Korea in the 1620s and eventually compelled the Yi to become a tributary state. As already related, the Manchu would be in possession of Beijing, China's capital, by 1644.

The Tokugawa Shogunate, to 1800

After Hideyoshi's demise, Japanese leaders brought the civil wars to an end, and in 1603 they established a more centralized government. A new shogun, Tokugawa Ieyasu° (1543–1616), had gained the upper hand in the conflict and established a new military government known as the **Tokugawa Shogunate.** The shoguns created a new administrative capital at Edo° (now Tokyo). Trade along the well-maintained road between Edo and the imperial capital of Kyoto promoted the development of the Japanese economy and the formation of other trading centers (see Map 26.3).

Although the Tokugawa Shogunate gave Japan more political unity than the islands had seen in centuries, the regional lords, the daimyo, still had a great deal of power and autonomy. Ieyasu and his successor shoguns had to work hard to keep this decentralized political system from disintegrating.

In some ways, economic integration was more a feature of Tokugawa Japan than was political centralization. Because Tokugawa shoguns required the daimyo to visit Edo frequently, good roads and maritime transport linked the city to the castle towns on three of the four main islands of Japan. Commercial traffic also developed along these routes. The shogun paid the lords in rice, and the lords paid their followers in rice. To meet their personal expenses, recipients of rice had to convert much of it into cash. This transaction stimulated the development of rice exchanges at Edo and at Osaka°, where merchants speculated in rice prices. By the late seventeenth century Edo was one of the largest cities in the world, with nearly a million inhabitants.

The domestic peace of the Tokugawa era forced the warrior class to adapt itself to the growing bureaucratic needs of the state. As the samurai became better educated, more attuned to the tastes of the civil elite, and more interested in conspicuous consumption, they became important customers for merchants dealing in silks, *sake*° (rice wine), fans, porcelain, lacquer ware, books, and moneylending. The state attempted—unsuccessfully—to curb the independence of the merchants when the economic well-being of the samurai was threatened, particularly when rice prices went too low or interest rates on loans were too high.

The 1600s and 1700s were centuries of high achievement in artisanship, and Japanese skills in steel making, pottery, and lacquer ware were joined by excellence in the production and decoration of porcelain (see Environment and Technology: East Asian Porcelain), thanks in no small part to Korean experts brought back to Japan after the invasion of 1592. In the early 1600s manufacturers and merchants amassed enormous family fortunes. Several of the most important industrial and financial companies—for instance, the Mitsui° companies—had their origins in sake breweries of the early Tokugawa period, then branched out into manufacturing, finance, and transport.

Hideyoshi (HEE-duh-YOH-shee)
Tokugawa Ieyasu (TOH-koo-GAH-wah ee-ay-YAH-soo)

Edo (ED-oh) **Osaka** (OH-sah-kah) **sake** (SAH-kay)
Mitsui (MIT-soo-ee)

CHRONOLOGY

	Korea and Japan	China and Central Asia	Russia
1500	**1543** First Portuguese contacts **1592** Japanese invasion of Korea	**1517** Portuguese embassy to China	**1547** Ivan IV tsar **1582** Russians conquer Khanate of Sibir
1600	**1603** Tokugawa Shogunate formed **1633–1639** Edicts close down trade with Europe	**1601** Matteo Ricci allowed to reside in Beijing **1644** Qing conquest of Beijing **1662–1722** Rule of Emperor Kangxi **1689** Treaty of Nerchinsk with Russia **1691** Qing control of Inner Mongolia	**1613–1645** Rule of Mikhail, the first Romanov tsar **1649** Subordination of serfs complete **1689–1725** Rule of Peter the Great
1700	**1702** Trial of the Forty-Seven Ronin **1792** Russian ships first spotted off the coast of Japan	**1736–1795** Rule of Emperor Qianlong	**1712** St. Petersburg becomes Russia's capital **1762–1796** Rule of Catherine the Great **1799** Alaska becomes a Russian colony

Wealthy merchant families usually cultivated close alliances with their regional daimyo and, if possible, with the shogun himself. In this way they could weaken the strict control of merchant activity that was an official part of Tokugawa policy. By the end of the 1700s the merchant families of Tokugawa Japan held the key to future modernization and the development of heavy industry, particularly in the prosperous provinces.

Japan and the Europeans

Direct contacts with Europeans from the mid-sixteenth century presented Japan with new opportunities and problems. The first major impact was on Japanese military technology. Within thirty years of the arrival of the first Portuguese in 1543, the daimyo were fighting with Western-style firearms, copied and improved upon by Japanese armorers. Japan's civil conflicts of the late sixteenth century launched the first East Asian "gunpowder revolution."

The Japanese also welcomed new trade with merchants from distant Portugal, Spain, the Netherlands, and England, but the government closely regulated their activities. Aside from the brief boom in porcelain exports in the seventeenth century, few Japanese goods went to Europe, and not much from Europe found a market in Japan. The Japanese sold the Dutch copper and silver, which the Dutch exchanged in China for silks that they then resold in Japan. The Japanese, of course, had their own trade with China.

Portuguese and Spanish merchant ships also brought Catholic missionaries. One of the first, Francis Xavier, went to India in the mid-sixteenth century looking for converts and later traveled throughout Southeast and East Asia. He spent two years in Japan and died in 1552, hoping to gain entry to China.

Japanese responses were decidedly mixed to Xavier and other Jesuits (members of the Catholic religious order the Society of Jesus). Large numbers of ordinary Japanese found the new faith deeply meaningful, but

ENVIRONMENT + TECHNOLOGY

East Asian Porcelain

By the 1400s artisans in China, Korea, and Japan were all producing high-quality pottery with lustrous surface glazes. The best quality, intended for the homes of the wealthy and powerful, was made of pure white clay and covered with a hard translucent glaze. Artisans often added intricate decorations in cobalt blue and other colors. Cheaper pottery found a huge market in East Asia.

Such pottery was also exported to Southeast Asia, the Indian Ocean, and the Middle East. Little found its way to Europe before 1600, but imports soared once the Dutch established trading bases in East Asia. Europeans called the high-quality ware "porcelain." Blue and white designs were especially popular.

One of the great centers of Chinese production was at the large artisan factory at Jingdezhen (JING-deh-JUHN). No sooner had the Dutch tapped into this source than the civil wars and Manchu conquests disrupted production in the middle 1600s. Desperate for a substitute source, the Dutch turned to porcelain from Japanese producers at Arita and Imari, near Nagasaki. Despite Japan's restriction of European trade, the Dutch East India Company transported some 190,000 pieces of Japanese ceramic ware to the Netherlands between 1653 and 1682.

In addition to a wide range of Asian designs, Chinese and Japanese artisans made all sorts of porcelain for the European market. These included purely decorative pottery birds, vases, and pots as well as utilitarian vessels and dishes intended for table use. The serving dish illustrated here came from dinnerware sets the Japanese made especially for the Dutch East India Company. The VOC logo at the center represents the first letters of the company's name in Dutch. It is surrounded by Asian design motifs.

After the return of peace in China, the VOC imported tens of thousands of Chinese porcelain pieces a year. The Chinese artisans sometimes produced imitations of Japanese designs that had become popular in Europe. Meanwhile, the Dutch were experimenting with making their own imitations of East Asian porcelain, right down to the Asian motifs and colors that had become so fashionable in Europe.

Japanese Export Porcelain Part of a larger set made for the Dutch East India Company (Photograph courtesy Peabody Essex Museum, #83830).

members of the Japanese elite were inclined to oppose it as disruptive and foreign. By 1580 more than 100,000 Japanese had become Christians, and one daimyo gave Jesuit missionaries the port city of Nagasaki°. In 1613 Date Masamune°, the fierce and independent daimyo of northern Honshu°, sent his own embassy to the Vatican, by way of the Philippines (where there were significant communities of Japanese merchants and pirates) and Mexico City. Some daimyo converts ordered their subjects to become Christians as well. Other Japanese were won over by the Jesuit, Dominican, and Franciscan missionaries.

By the early seventeenth century there were some 300,000 Japanese Christians and a few newly ordained Japanese priests. But these extraordinary events could not stand apart from the fractious politics of the day and suspicions about the larger intentions of the Europeans and their well-armed ships. The new shogunate in Edo became the center of hostility to Christianity. In 1614 a decree charging the Christians with seeking to overthrow true doctrine, change the government, and seize

Nagasaki (NAH-guh-SAHK-kee) **Date Masamune** (DAH-tay mah-suh-MOO-nay) **Honshu** (HOHN-shoo)

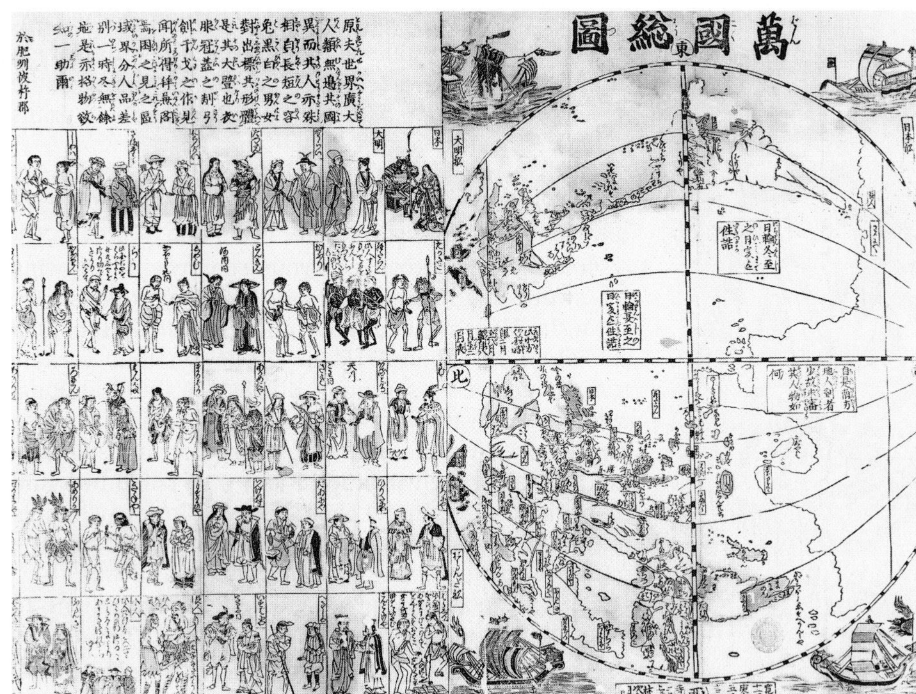

Comprehensive Map of the Myriad Nations Thanks to the "Dutch studies" scholars and to overseas contacts, many Japanese were well informed about the cultures, technologies, and political systems of various parts of the world. This combination map and ethnographic text of 1671 enthusiastically explores the differences among the many peoples living or traveling in Asia. The map of the Pacific hemisphere has the north pole on the left and the south pole on the extreme right of the drawing. (British Museum/Fotomas Index)

the land ordered the movement eliminated. Some missionaries left Japan, but others took their movement underground. The government began its persecutions in earnest in 1617, and the beheadings, crucifixions, and forced recantations over the next several decades destroyed almost the entire Christian community.

A series of decrees issued between 1633 and 1639 went much farther, ordering an end to European trade as the price to be paid for eliminating Christian influences. Europeans who entered illegally faced the death penalty. A new government office made sure Christianity did not reemerge; people were required to produce certificates from Buddhist temples attesting to their religious orthodoxy and thus their loyalty to the regime.

The closing of Japan to European influence was not total. A few Dutch were permitted to reside on a small artificial island in Nagasaki's harbor, and a few Japanese were licensed to supply their needs. The information these intermediaries acquired about European weapons technology, shipbuilding, mathematics and astronomy, anatomy and medicine, and geography was known as "Dutch studies."

The Tokugawa government also placed restrictions on the number of Chinese ships that could trade in Japan, but these were harder to enforce. Regional lords in northern and southern Japan not only pursued overseas trade and piracy but also claimed dominion over islands between Japan and Korea to the east and between Japan and Taiwan to the south, including present-day Okinawa. Despite such evasions, the larger lesson is the substantial success of the new shogunate in exercising its authority.

Elite Decline and Social Crisis

During the 1700s population growth put a great strain on the well-developed lands of central Japan. In more remote provinces, where the lords promoted new settlements and agricultural expansion, the rate of economic growth far outstripped the growth rate in central Japan.

Also destabilizing the Tokugawa government in the 1700s was the shogunate's inability to stabilize rice prices and halt the economic decline of the samurai. To finance their living, the samurai had to convert their rice to cash in the market. The Tokugawa government realized that the rice brokers might easily enrich themselves at the expense of the samurai if the price of rice and the rate of interest were not strictly controlled. Laws designed to regulate both had been passed early in the Tokugawa period, and laws requiring moneylenders to forgive samurai debts were added later. But these laws were not always enforced, sometimes because neither the lords nor the samurai wished them to be. By the early 1700s members of both groups were dependent on the willingness of merchants to provide credit.

The Tokugawa shoguns sought to protect the samurai from decline while curbing the growing power of the

Woodblock Print of the "Forty-Seven Ronin" Story The saga of the forty-seven ronin and the avenging of their fallen leader has fascinated the Japanese public since the event occurred in 1702. This watercolor from the Tokugawa period shows the leaders of the group pausing on the snowy banks of the Sumida River in Edo (Tokyo) before storming their enemy's residence. (Jean-Pierre Hauchecorne Collection)

merchant class. Their legitimacy rested on their ability to reward and protect the interests of the lords and samurai who had supported the Tokugawa conquest. But the Tokugawa government, like the governments of China, Korea, and Vietnam, accepted the Confucian idea that agriculture should be the basis of state wealth and that merchants should occupy lowly positions in society because of their reputed lack of moral character.

Governments throughout East Asia used Confucian philosophy to attempt to limit the influence and power of merchants. The Tokugawa government, however, was at a special disadvantage. Its decentralized system limited its ability to regulate merchant activities and actually stimulated the growth of commercial activities. From the founding of the Tokugawa Shogunate in 1603 until 1800, the economy grew faster than the population. Household amenities and cultural resources that in China were found only in the cities were common in the Japanese countryside. Despite official disapproval, merchants and others involved in the growing economy enjoyed relative freedom and influence in eighteenth-century Japan. They produced a vivid culture of their own, fostering the development of *kabuki* theater, colorful woodblock prints and silk-screened fabrics, and restaurants.

The ideological and social crisis of Tokugawa Japan's transformation from a military to a civil society is captured in the "Forty-Seven Ronin°" incident of 1701–1703. A senior minister provoked a young daimyo into drawing his sword at the shogun's court. For this offense the young lord was sentenced to commit *seppuku*°, the ritual suicide of the samurai. His own followers then became *ronin,* "masterless samurai," obliged by the traditional code of the warrior to avenge their deceased master. They broke into the house of the senior minister who had provoked their own lord, and they killed him and others in his household. Then they withdrew to a temple in Edo and notified the shogun of what they had done out of loyalty to their lord and to avenge his death.

A legal debate began in the shogun's government. To deny the righteousness of the ronin would be to deny samurai values. But to approve their actions would create social chaos, undermine laws against murder, and deny the shogunal government the right to try cases of samurai violence. The shogun ruled that the ronin had to die but would be permitted to die honorably by committing *seppuku.* Traditional samurai values had to surrender to the supremacy of law. The purity of purpose of the ronin is still celebrated in Japan, but since then Japanese writers, historians, and teachers have recognized that the self-sacrifice of the ronin for the sake of upholding civil law was necessary.

The Tokugawa Shogunate put into place a political and economic system that fostered innovation, but the government itself could not exploit it. Thus, during the Tokugawa period the government remained quite traditional while other segments of society developed new methods of productivity and management.

THE LATER MING AND EARLY QING EMPIRES

Like Japan, China after 1500 experienced civil and foreign wars, an important change in government, and new trading and cultural relations with Europe and its neighbors. The internal and external forces at work in China were different in detail and operated on a much larger scale, but they led in similar directions. By 1800

ronin (ROH-neen) **seppuku** (SEP-poo-koo)

China had a greatly enhanced empire, an expanding economy, and growing doubts about the importance of European trade and Christianity.

The Ming Empire, 1500–1644

The brilliant economic and cultural achievements of the early **Ming Empire** continued during the 1500s. Ming manufacturers had transformed the global economy with their techniques for the assembly-line production of porcelain. An international market eager for Ming porcelain, as well as for silk and lacquered furniture, stimulated the commercial development of East Asia, the Indian Ocean, and Europe. But this golden age was followed by many decades of political weakness, warfare, and rural woes until a new dynasty, the Qing° from Manchuria, guided China back to peace and prosperity.

The Europeans whose ships began to seek out new contacts with China in the early sixteenth century left many accounts of their impressions. Like others before them, they were astonished at Ming China's imperial power, exquisite manufactures, and vast population. European merchants bought such large quantities of the high-grade blue-on-white porcelain commonly used by China's upper classes that in English all fine dishes became known simply as "china."

The growing integration of China into the world economy stimulated rapid growth in the silk, cotton, and porcelain industries. Agricultural regions that supplied raw materials to these industries and food for the expanding urban populations also prospered. In exchange for Chinese porcelain and textiles, tens of thousands of tons of silver from Japan and Latin America flooded into China in the century before 1640. The influx of silver led many Chinese to substitute payments in silver for various land taxes, labor obligations, and other kinds of dues.

Ming cities had long been culturally and commercially vibrant. Many large landowners and absentee landlords lived in the cities, as did officials, artists, and rich merchants who had purchased ranks or prepared their sons for the examinations. The elite classes had created a brilliant culture in which novels, operas, poetry, porcelain, and painting were all closely interwoven. Owners of small businesses catering to the urban elites could make money through printing, tailoring, running restaurants, or selling paper, ink, ink-stones, and writing brushes. The imperial government operated factories for the production of ceramics and silks. Enormous government complexes at Jingdezhen and elsewhere invented assembly-line techniques and produced large quantities of high-quality ceramics for sale in China and abroad.

Despite these achievements, serious problems were developing that left the Ming Empire economically exhausted, politically deteriorating, and technologically lagging behind both its East Asian neighbors and some European countries. Some of these problems were the result of natural disasters associated with climate change and disease. There is evidence that the climate changes known as the Little Ice Age in seventeenth-century Europe affected the climate in China as well (see Issues in World History: The Little Ice Age). Annual temperatures dropped, reached a low point about 1645, and remained low until the early 1700s. The resulting agricultural distress and famine fueled large uprisings that speeded the end of the Ming Empire. The devastation caused by these uprisings and the spread of epidemic disease resulted in steep declines in local populations.

Along with many benefits, the rapid growth in the trading economy also led to such problems as rapid urban growth and business speculation. Some provinces suffered from price inflation that the flood of silver caused. In contrast to the growing involvement of European governments in promoting economic growth, the Ming government showed little interest in developing the economy and pursued some policies that were inimical to it. Despite the fact that paper currency had failed to find general acceptance as far back as the 1350s, Ming governments persisted in issuing new paper money and promoting copper coins, even after abundant supplies of silver had won the approval of the markets. Corruption was also a serious government problem. By the end of the Ming period the factories were plagued by disorder and inefficiency. The situation became so bad during the late sixteenth and seventeenth centuries that workers held strikes with increasing frequency. During a labor protest at Jingdezhen in 1601, workers threw themselves into the kilns to protest working conditions.

Yet the urban and industrial sectors of later Ming society fared much better than the rural, agricultural sector. After a period of economic growth and recovery from the population decline of the thirteenth century, the rural Ming economy did not maintain strong growth. After the beginning of the sixteenth century, China had knowledge, gained from European traders, of new crops from Africa and America. But they were introduced very slowly, and neither rice-growing regions in southern China nor wheat-growing regions in northern China experienced a meaningful increase in productivity under the later Ming. After 1500 economic depression in the countryside, combined with recurring epidemics in central and southern China, kept rural population growth in check.

Qing (ching)

Ming Collapse and the Rise of the Qing

Rising environmental, economic, and administrative problems weakened the Ming Empire but did not cause its fall. That was the result of growing rebellion within and the rising power of the Manchu outside the borders.

Insecure boundaries are an indication of the later Ming Empire's difficulties. The Ming had long been under pressure from the powerful Mongol federations of the north and west. In the late 1500s large numbers of Mongols were unified by their devotion to the Dalai Lama°, or universal teacher, of Tibetan Buddhism, whom they regarded as their spiritual leader. Building on this spiritual unity, a brilliant leader named Galdan restored Mongolia as a regional military power around 1600. The Manchu, an agriculturally based people who controlled the region north of Korea, grew stronger in the northeast.

In the southwest, there were repeated uprisings among native peoples crowded by the immigration of Chinese farmers. Pirates, many Japanese, based in Okinawa and Taiwan frequently looted the southeastern coastal towns. Ming military resources, concentrated against the Mongols and the Manchu in the north, could not be deployed to defend the coasts. As a result, many southern Chinese migrated to Southeast Asia to profit from the sea-trading networks of the Indian Ocean.

As the previous section related, the Japanese invasion of 1592 to 1598 set the Ming collapse in motion. To stop the Japanese the Ming brought Manchu troops into an international force and eventually paid a high price for that invitation. Weakened by the strain of repelling the Japanese, Chinese defenses in the northeast could not stop the advance of Manchu troops, who had already brought Korea under their sway.

Taking advantage of this situation, as the opening of this chapter related, the Chinese rebel leader Li Zicheng advanced and captured Beijing. With the emperor dead by his own hand and the imperial family in flight, a Ming general invited Manchu leaders to help his forces take Beijing from the rebels. The Manchu did so in the summer of 1644. Rather than restoring the Ming, they claimed China for their own and began a forty-year conquest of the rest of the Ming territories (see Diversity and Dominance: Gendered Violence: The Yangzhou Massacre). By the end of the century, the Manchu had gained control of south China and incorporated the island of Taiwan into imperial China for the first time (see Map 21.1). They also conquered parts of Mongolia and Central Asia.

A Manchu family headed the new **Qing Empire,** and Manchu generals commanded the military forces. But Manchu were a very small portion of the population, and one of several minority populations. The overwhelming majority of Qing officials, soldiers, merchants, and farmers were ethnic Chinese. Like other successful invaders of China, the Qing soon adopted Chinese institutions and policies.

Trading Companies and Missionaries

For the European mariners who braved the long voyages to Asia, the China trade was second in importance only to the spice trade of southern Asia. China's vast population and manufacturing skills drew a steady supply of ships from western Europe, but enthusiasm for the trade developed more slowly, especially at the imperial court.

A Portuguese ship reached China at the end of 1513, but was not permitted to trade. A formal Portuguese embassy in 1517 got bogged down in Chinese protocol and procrastination, and China expelled the Portuguese in 1522. Finally, in 1557 the Portuguese gained the right to trade from a base in Macao°. Spain's Asian trade was conducted from Manila in the Philippines, which served as the terminus of trans-Pacific trade routes from South America. For a time, the Spanish and the Dutch both maintained outposts for trade with China and Japan on the island of Taiwan, but in 1662 they were forced to concede control over the island to the Qing, who incorporated Taiwan for the first time as a part of China.

By then, the Dutch East India Company (VOC) had displaced the Portuguese as the major European trader in the Indian Ocean and, despite the setback on Taiwan, was establishing itself as the main European trader in East Asia. VOC representatives courted official favor in China by acknowledging the moral superiority of the emperor. They performed the ritual kowtow (in which the visitor knocked his head on the floor while crawling toward the throne) to the Ming emperor.

Catholic missionaries accompanied the Portuguese and Spanish merchants to China, just as they did to Japan. While the Franciscans and Dominicans sought to replicate the conversion efforts at the bottom of society that had worked so well in Japan, the Jesuits concentrated their efforts among China's intellectual and political elite. In this they were far more successful than they had been in Japan—at least until the eighteenth century.

The outstanding Jesuit of late Ming China, Matteo Ricci° (1552–1610), became expert in the Chinese language and an accomplished scholar of the Confucian

Dalai Lama (DAH-lie LAH-mah)

Macao (muh-KOW) **Matteo Ricci** (mah-TAY-oh REE-chee)

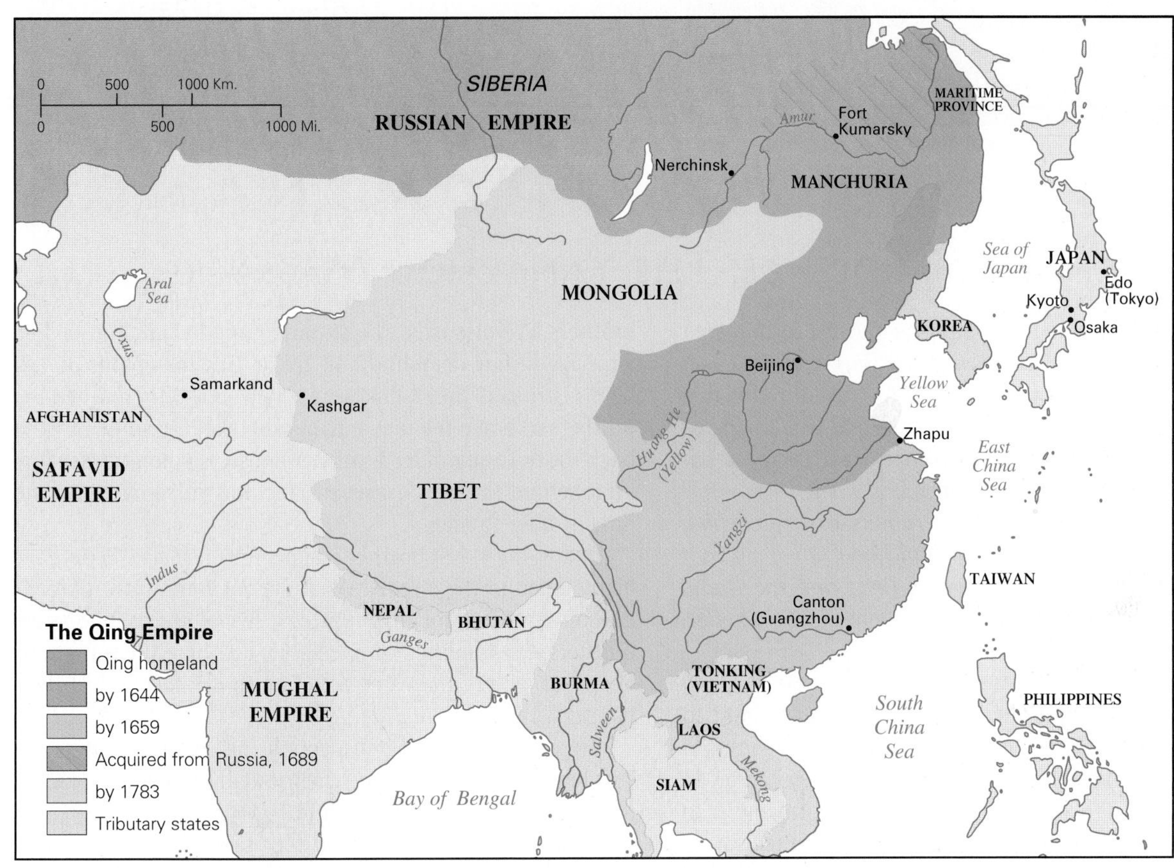

Map 21.1 The Qing Empire, 1644–1783 The Qing Empire began in Manchuria and captured north China in 1644. Between 1644 and 1783 the Qing conquered all the former Ming territories and added Taiwan, the lower Amur River basin, Inner Mongolia, eastern Turkestan, and Tibet. The resulting state was more than twice the size of the Ming Empire.

classics. Under Ricci's leadership, the Jesuits sought to adapt Catholic Christianity to Chinese cultural traditions while enhancing their status by introducing the Chinese to the latest science and technology from Europe. From 1601 Ricci was allowed to reside in Beijing on an imperial stipend as a Western scholar. Later Jesuits headed the office of astronomy that issued the official calendar.

Emperor Kangxi (r. 1662–1722)

The seventeenth and eighteenth centuries—particularly the reigns of the **Kangxi**° (r. 1662–1722) and Qianlong° (r. 1736–1796) emperors—were a period of great economic, military, and cultural achievement in China. The early Qing emperors wished to foster economic and demographic recovery in China. They repaired the roads and waterworks, lowered transit taxes, mandated comparatively low rents and interest rates, and established economic incentives for resettlement of the areas devastated during the peasant rebellions of the late Ming period. Foreign trade was encouraged. Vietnam, Burma, and Nepal sent regular embassies to the Qing tribute court and carried the latest Chinese fashions back home. Overland routes of communication from Korea to Central Asia were revived, and through its conquests the Qing Empire gained access to the superior horses of Afghanistan.

The early Qing conquest of Beijing and north China was carried out under the leadership of a group of Manchu aristocrats who dominated the first Qing emperor based in China and were regents for his young son, who was declared emperor in 1662. This child-emperor, Kangxi, spent several years doing political battle with his regents, and in 1669 he gained real as well as formal control of the government by executing his chief regent.

Kangxi (KAHNG-shee) **Qianlong** (chee-YEN-loong)

Diversity and Dominance

Gendered Violence: The Yangzhou Massacre

After the fall of Beijing to the Manchu, the rest of China felt the dominance of the conquerors. The Qing were not eager for reminders of their brutal takeover to circulate. This rare eyewitness account, which survived because it was smuggled out of China, reveals not just the violence of the conquest but also the diversity of its impact on men and women.

The account begins in 1645 as rumors of approaching Manchu soldiers spread through Yangzhou, an important city near the juncture of the Yangzi River and the Grand Canal, and the soldiers charged with its defense begin to flee.

Crowds of barefoot and disheveled refugees were flocking into the city. When questioned, they were too distraught to reply. At that point dozens of mounted soldiers in confused waves came surging south looking as though they had given up all hope. Along them appeared a man who turned out to be the commandant himself. It seems he had intended to leave by the east gate but could not because the enemy soldiers outside the wall were drawing too near; he was therefore forced to cut across this part of town to reach the south gate. This is how we first learned for sure that the enemy troops would enter the city. . . .

My house backed against the city wall, and peeping through the chinks in my window, I saw the soldiers on the wall marching south then west, solemn and in step. Although the rain was beating down, it did not seem to disturb them. This reassured me because I gathered that they were well disciplined units.

. . . For a long time no one came. I retreated again to the back window and found that the regiment on the wall had broken ranks; some soldiers were walking about, others standing still.

All of a sudden I saw some soldiers escorting a group of women dressed in Yangzhou fashion. This was my first real shock. Back in the house, I said to my wife, "Should things go badly when the soldiers enter the city, you may need to end your life."

"Yes," she replied, "Whatever silver we have you should keep. I think we women can stop thinking about life in this world." She gave me all the silver, unable to control her crying. . . .

Soon my younger brother arrived, then my two older brothers. We discussed the situation and I said, "The people who live in our neighborhood are all rich merchants. It will be disastrous if they think we are rich too." I then urged my brothers to brave the rain and quickly take the women by the back route to my older brother's house. His home was situated behind Mr. He's graveyard and was surrounded by the huts of poor families. . . .

Finally, my eldest brother reappeared and said, "People are being killed in the streets! What are we waiting for here? It doesn't matter so much whether we live or die, as long as we brothers stay together." Immediately I gathered together our ancestral tablets and went with him to our second brother's house. . . .

The cunning soldiers, suspecting that many people were still hidden, tried to entice them out by posting a placard promising clemency. About fifty to sixty people, half of them women, emerged. My elder brother said, "We four by ourselves will never survive if we run into these vicious soldiers, so we had better join the crowd. Since there are so many of them, escape will be easier. Even if things do not turn out well, as long as we are together, we will have no cause for regret." In our bewilderment we could think of no other way to save our lives. Thus agreed, we went to join the group.

The leaders were three Manchu soldiers. They searched my brothers and found all the silver they were carrying, but left me untouched. At that point some women appeared, two of whom called out to me. I recognized them as the concubines of my friend Mr. Zhu Shu and stopped them anxiously. They were disheveled and partly naked, their feet bare and covered with mud up to the ankles. One was holding a girl whom the soldiers hit with a whip and threw into the mud. Then we were immediately driven on. One soldier, sword in hand, took the lead; another drove us from behind with a long spear; and a third walked along on our right and left flanks alternately, making sure no one escaped. In groups of twenty or thirty we were herded along like sheep and cattle. If we faltered we were struck, and some people were even killed on the spot. The women were tied together with long chains around their necks, like a clumsy string of pearls. Stumbling at every step, they were soon covered with mud. Here and there on the ground lay babies, trampled by people or horses. Blood and gore soaked the fields, which were filled with the sound of sobbing. We passed gutters and ponds piled high with corpses; the blood had turned the water to a deep greenish-red color and filled the ponds to the brim.

. . . We then entered the house of [a] merchant, . . . which had been taken over by the three soldiers. Another soldier was already there. He had seized several attractive women and was rifling their trunks for fancy silks, which he piled in a heap. Seeing the three soldiers arrive, he laughed and pushed several dozen of us into the back hall. The women he led into a side chamber. . . .

The three soldiers stripped the women of their wet clothing all the way to their underwear, then ordered the seamstress to measure them and give them new garments. The women, thus coerced, had to expose themselves and stand naked. What shame they endured! Once they had changed, the soldiers grabbed them and forced them to join them in eating and drinking, then did whatever they pleased with them, without any regard for decency.

[The narrator escapes and hides atop a wooden canopy over a bed.] Later on a soldier brought a woman in and wanted her to sleep with him in the bed below me. Despite her refusal he forced her to yield. "This is too near the street. It is not a good place to stay," the woman said. I was almost discovered, but after a time the soldier departed with the woman. . . . [The narrator flees again and is reunited with his wife and relatives.]

At length, however, there came a soldier of the "Wolf Men" tribe, a vicious-looking man with a head like a mouse and eyes like a hawk. He attempted to abduct my wife. She was obliged to creep forward on all fours, pleading as she had with the others, but to no avail. When he insisted that she stand up, she rolled on the ground and refused. He then beat her so savagely with the flat of his sword that the blood flowed out in streams, totally soaking her clothes. Because my wife had once admonished me, "If I am unlucky I will die no matter what; do not plead for me as a husband or you will get caught too," I acted as if I did not know she was being beaten and hid far away in the grass, convinced she was about to die. Yet the depraved soldier did not stop there; he grabbed her by the hair, cursed her, struck her cruelly, and then dragged her away by the leg. . . . Just then they ran into a body of mounted soldiers. One of them said a few words to the soldier in Manchu. At this he dropped my wife and departed with them. Barely able to crawl back, she let out a loud sob, every part of her body injured. . . .

Unexpectedly there appeared a handsome looking man of less than thirty, a double-edged sword hung by his side, dressed in Manchu-style hat, red coat, and a pair of black boots. His follower, in a yellow jacket, was also very gallant in appearance. Immediately behind them were several residents of Yangzhou. The young man in red, inspecting me closely, said, "I would judge from your appearance that you are not one of these people. Tell me honestly, what class of person are you?"

I remembered that some people had obtained pardons and others had lost their lives the moment they said that they were poor scholars. So I did not dare come out at once with the truth and instead concocted a story. He pointed to my wife and son and asked who they were, and I told him the truth. "Tomorrow the prince will order that all swords be sheathed and all, of you will be spared," he said and then commanded his followers to give us some clothes and an ingot of silver. He also asked me, "How many days have you been without food?"

"Five days," I replied.

"Then come with me," he commanded. Although we only half trusted him, we were afraid to disobey. He led us to a well-stocked house, full of rice, fish, and other provisions. "Treat these four people well," he said to a woman in the house and then left. . . .

The next day was [April 30]. Killing and pillaging continued, although not on the previous scale. Still the mansions of the rich were thoroughly looted, and almost all the teenage girls were abducted. . . . every grain of rice, every inch of silk now entered these tigers' mouths. The resulting devastation is beyond description.

[May 2]. Civil administration was established in all the prefectures and counties; proclamations were issued aimed at calming the people, and monks from each temple were ordered to burn corpses. The temples themselves were clogged with women who had taken refuge, many of whom had died of fright or starvation. The "List of Corpses Burned" records more than eight hundred thousand, and this list does not include those who jumped into wells, threw themselves into the river, hanged themselves, were burned to death inside houses, or were carried away by the soldiers. . . .

When this calamity began there had been eight of us: my two elder brothers, my younger brother, my elder brother's wife, their son, my wife, my son, and myself. Now only three of us survived for sure, though the fate of my wife's brother and sister-in-law was not yet known. . . .

From the 25th of the fourth month to the 5th of the fifth month was a period of ten days. I have described here only what I actually experienced or saw with my own eyes; I have not recorded anything I picked up from rumor or hearsay.

QUESTIONS FOR ANALYSIS

1. **What accounts for the soldiers' brutal treatment of the women.**
2. **What did different women do to protect themselves?**
3. **Having conquered, what did the Manchu do to restore order?**

Emperor Kangxi In a portrait from about 1690, the young Manchu ruler is portrayed as a refined scholar in the Confucian tradition. He was a scholar and had great intellectual curiosity, but this portrait would not suggest that he was also capable of leading troops in battle. (The Palace Museum, Beijing)

Kangxi was then sixteen. He was an intellectual prodigy who mastered classical Chinese, Manchu, and Mongolian at an early age and memorized the Chinese classics. His reign, lasting until his death in 1722, was marked not only by great expansion of the empire but by great stability as well.

The Qing rulers were as anxious as the Ming to consolidate their northern frontiers, especially as they feared an alliance between Galdan's Mongol state and the expanding Russian presence along the **Amur° River.** In the 1680s the Kangxi sent forces to attack the wooden forts on the northern bank of the Amur that hardy Russian scouts had built. Neither empire sent large forces into the Amur territories, and the contest was partly a struggle for the goodwill of the local Evenk and Dagur peoples. The Qing emperor emphasized the importance of treading lightly in the struggle and well understood the principles of espionage:

> Upon reaching the lands of the Evenks and the Dagurs you will send to announce that you have come to hunt deer. Meanwhile, keep a careful record of the distance and go, while hunting, along the northern bank of the Amur until you come by the shortest route to the town of Russian settlement at Albazin. Thoroughly reconnoiter its location and situation. I don't think the Russians will take a chance on attacking you. If they offer you food, accept it and show your gratitude. If they do attack you, don't fight back. In that case, lead your people and withdraw into our own territories. For I have a plan of my own.[2]

That delicacy gives a false impression of the intensity of the struggle between these two great empires. Qing forces twice attacked Albazin. The Qing were worried about Russian alliances with other frontier peoples, while Russia wished to protect its access to the furs, timber, and metals concentrated in Siberia, Manchuria, and Yakutsk. The Qing and Russians were also rivals for control of northern Asia's Pacific coast. Continued conflict would benefit neither side. In 1689 the Qing and Russian Empires negotiated the Treaty of Nerchinsk, using Jesuit missionaries as interpreters. The treaty fixed the border along the Amur River and regulated trade across it. Although this was a thinly settled area, the treaty proved important since the frontier it demarcated has long endured.

The next step was to settle the Mongolian frontier. Kangxi personally led troops in the great campaigns that defeated Galdan and brought Inner Mongolia under Qing control by 1691.

Kangxi was distinguished by his openness to new ideas and technologies from different regions. Unlike the rulers of Japan, who drove Christian missionaries out, he welcomed Jesuit advisers and put them in important offices. Jesuits helped create maps in the European style as practical guides to newly conquered regions and as symbols of Qing dominance. Kangxi considered introducing the European calendar, but protests from the Confucian elite were so strong that the plan was dropped. The emperor frequently discussed scientific and philosophical issues with the Jesuits. When he fell ill with malaria in the 1690s, Jesuit medical expertise (in this case, the use of quinine) aided his recovery. Kangxi also ordered the creation of illustrated books in Manchu detailing European anatomical and pharmaceutical knowledge.

To gain converts among the Chinese elite, the Jesuits made important compromises in their religious teaching. The most important was their toleration of Confucian ancestor worship. The matter caused great controversy

---

Amur (AH-moor)

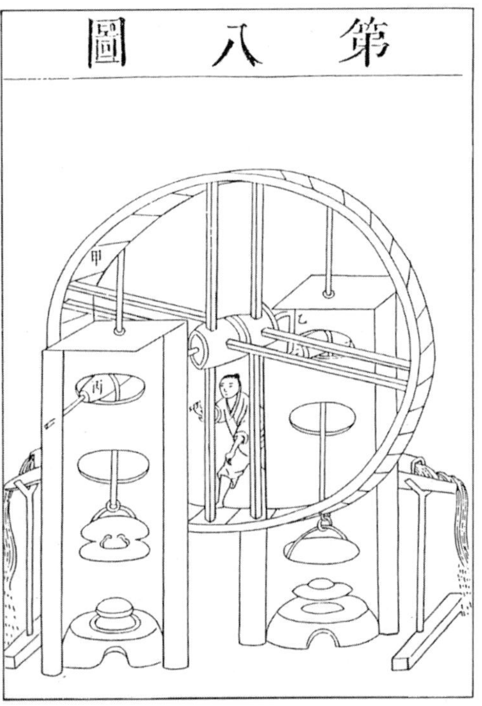

From the Jesuit Library at Beijing Jesuits such as Matteo Ricci were willing to share books on technology and science with Chinese scholars. But without firsthand experience it was impossible for Chinese translators to convey how the devices actually worked. Here, a man walking in a wheel drives a shaft that changes the pressure inside two pumps. In the Chinese translation of the drawing, the mechanisms were all lost. (Left: From Zonca, *Trombe da Rota per Cavar Aqua* [1607]. Right: "Diagram Number Eight" from *Qi tushuo* [*Illustrations on Energy*] [1627]. Both courtesy of Joseph Needham, *Science and Civilization in China*, vol. 4)

between the Jesuits and their Catholic rivals in China, the Franciscans and Dominicans, and also between the Jesuits and the pope. In 1690 the disagreement reached a high pitch. Kangxi wrote to Rome supporting the Jesuit position. Further disagreement with a papal legate to China led Kangxi to order the expulsion of all missionaries who refused to sign a certificate accepting his position. Most of the Jesuits signed, but relations with the imperial court were irreparably harmed. Jesuit presence in China declined in the eighteenth century, and later Qing emperors persecuted Christians rather than naming them to high offices.

Chinese Influences on Europe

The exchange of information between the Qing and the Europeans that Kangxi had fostered was never one-way. When the Jesuits informed the Qing court on matters of anatomy, for instance, the Qing were able to demonstrate an early form of inoculation, called "variolation," that had been used to stem the spread of smallpox after the Qing conquest of Beijing. The technique helped inspire the development of other vaccines later in Europe.

Similarly, Jesuit writings about the intellectual and cultural achievements of China excited admiration in Europe. The wealthy and the aspiring middle classes of Europe demanded Chinese things—or things that looked to Europeans as if they could be Chinese. Not only silk, porcelain, and tea were avidly sought, but also cloisonné jewelry, tableware and decorative items, lacquered and jeweled room dividers, painted fans, and carved jade and ivory (which originated in Africa and was finished in China). One of the most striking Chinese influences on European interior life in this period was wallpaper—an adaptation of the Chinese practice of covering walls with enormous loose-hanging watercolors or calligraphy scrolls. By the mid-1700s special workshops throughout China were producing wallpaper and other consumer items according to the specifications of European merchants. The items were shipped to Canton for export to Europe.

In political philosophy, too, the Europeans felt they had something to learn from the early Qing emperors. In the late 1770s poems supposedly written by Emperor Qianlong were translated into French and disseminated through the intellectual circles of western Europe. These works depicted the Qing emperors as benevolent despots who campaigned against superstition and ignorance, curbed the excesses of the aristocracy, and patronized science and the arts. European intellectuals who were questioning their own political systems found the image of a practical, secular, compassionate ruler intriguing. The French thinker Voltaire proclaimed the

Qing emperors model philosopher-kings and advocated such rulership as a protection against the growth of aristocratic privilege.

Tea and Diplomacy

The Qing were eager to expand China's economic influence but were determined to control the trade very strictly. To make trade easier to tax and to limit piracy and smuggling, the Qing permitted only one market point for each foreign sector. Thus Europeans were permitted to trade only at Canton.

This system worked well enough for European traders until the late 1700s, when Britain became worried about its massive trade deficit with China. From bases in India and Singapore, British traders moved eastward to China and eventually displaced the Dutch as China's leading European trading partner. The directors of the East India Company (EIC) believed that China's technological achievements and gigantic potential markets made it the key to limitless profit. China had tea, rhubarb, porcelain, and silk to offer. By the early 1700s the EIC dominated European trading in Canton.

Tea from China had spread overland on Eurasian routes in medieval and early modern times to become a prized import in Russia, Central Asia, and the Middle East, all of which know it by its northern Chinese name, *cha*—as do the Portuguese. Other western Europeans acquired tea from the sea routes and thus know it by its name in the Fujian province of coastal China and Taiwan: *te*. In much of Europe, tea competed with chocolate and coffee as a fashionable drink by the mid-1600s.

Great fortunes were being made in the tea trade, but the English had not found a product to sell to China. They believed that China was a vast unexploited market, with hundreds of millions of potential consumers of lamp oil made from whale blubber, cotton grown in India or the American South, or guns manufactured in London or Connecticut. Particularly after the loss of the thirteen American colonies, Britain feared that its markets would diminish, and the EIC and other British merchants believed that only the Qing trade system—the "Canton system," as the British called it—stood in the way of opening new paths for commerce.

The British government also worried about Britain's massive trade deficit with China. Because the Qing Empire rarely bought anything from Britain, British silver poured into China to pay for imported tea and other products. The Qing government, whose revenues were declining in the later 1700s while its expenses rose, needed the silver. But in Britain the imbalance of payments stirred anxiety and anger over the restrictions that the Qing placed on imported foreign goods. To make matters worse, the East India Company had managed its worldwide holdings badly, and as it teetered on bankruptcy, its attempts to manipulate Parliament became increasingly intrusive. In 1792 the British government dispatched Lord George Macartney, a well-connected peer with practical experience in Russia and India, to China. Including scientists, artists, and translators as well as guards and diplomats, the **Macartney mission** showed Britain's great interest in the Qing Empire as well as the EIC's desire to revise the trade system.

China was not familiar with the European system of ambassadors, and Macartney struggled to portray himself in Chinese terms as a "tribute emissary" come to salute the Qianlong emperor's eightieth birthday. He steadfastly refused to perform the kowtow to the emperor, but did agree to bow on one knee as he would to his own monarch, King George III. The Qianlong emperor received Macartney courteously in September 1793, but refused to alter the Canton trading system, open new ports of trade, or allow the British to establish a permanent mission in Beijing, The Qing had no interest in changing a system that provided revenue to the imperial family and lessened serious piracy problems. Qianlong sent a letter to King George explaining that China had no need to increase its foreign trade, had no use for Britain's ingenious devices and manufacturers, and set no value on closer diplomatic ties.

Dutch, French, and Russian embassies soon attempted to achieve what Macartney had failed to do. When they also failed, European frustration with the Qing mounted. The great European admiration for China faded, and China was considered despotic, self-satisfied, and unrealistic. Political solutions seemed impossible because the Qing court would not communicate with foreign envoys or observe the simplest rules of the diplomatic system familiar to Europeans. In Macartney's view, China was like a venerable old warship, well maintained and splendid to look at, but obsolete and no longer up to the task.

Population and Social Stress

The Chinese who escorted Macartney and his entourage in 1792–1793 took them through China's prosperous cities and productive farmland. The visitors did not see evidence of the economic and environmental decline that had begun to affect China in the last decades of the 1700s. The population explosion had intensified demand for rice and wheat, for land to be opened for the planting of crops imported from Africa and the Americas, and for more thorough exploitation of land already in use.

East Meets West In a large procession, sixteen men carry the seated Qianlong emperor to a meeting with the English ambassador Lord Macartney at the emperor's extensive summer palace on 14 September 1793. The British are on the right. (British Museum, Department of Prints and Drawings)

In the peaceful decades of Qing rule, China's population had grown to three times its size in 1500. If one accepts an estimate of some 350 million in the late 1700s, China had twice the population of all of Europe. Despite the efficiency of Chinese agriculture and the gradual adoption of New World crops such as corn and sweet potatoes, population growth led to social and environmental problems. More people meant less land per person for farming. Increased demand for building materials and firewood sharply reduced China's remaining woodlands. Deforestation, in turn, accelerated wind and water erosion and increased the danger of flooding. Dams and dikes were not maintained, and silted-up river channels were not dredged. By the end of the eighteenth century parts of the thousand-year-old Grand Canal linking the rivers of north and south China were nearly unusable, and the towns that bordered it were starved for commerce.

The result was misery in many parts of interior China. Some districts responded by increasing production of cash crops such as tea, cotton, and silk that were tied to the export market. Some peasants sought seasonal jobs in better-off agricultural areas or worked in low-status jobs such as barge puller, charcoal burner, or night soil carrier. Many drifted to the cities to make their way by begging, prostitution, or theft. In central and southwestern China, where serious floods had impoverished many farmers, rebellions became endemic. Often joining in revolt were various indigenous peoples, who were largely concentrated in the less fertile lands in the south and in the northern and western borderlands of the empire (see Map 21.2).

The Qing government was not up to controlling its vast empire. The Qing Empire was twice the size of the Ming geographically, but employed about the same number of officials. The government's dependence on working alliances with local elites had led to widespread corruption and shrinking government revenues. As was the case with other empires, the Qing's spectacular rise had ended, and decline had set in.

The Russian Empire

From modest beginnings in 1500, Russia expanded rapidly during the next three centuries to create an empire that stretched from eastern Europe across northern Asia and into North America. Russia also became one of the major powers of Europe by 1750, with armies capable of mounting challenges to its Asian and European neighbors.

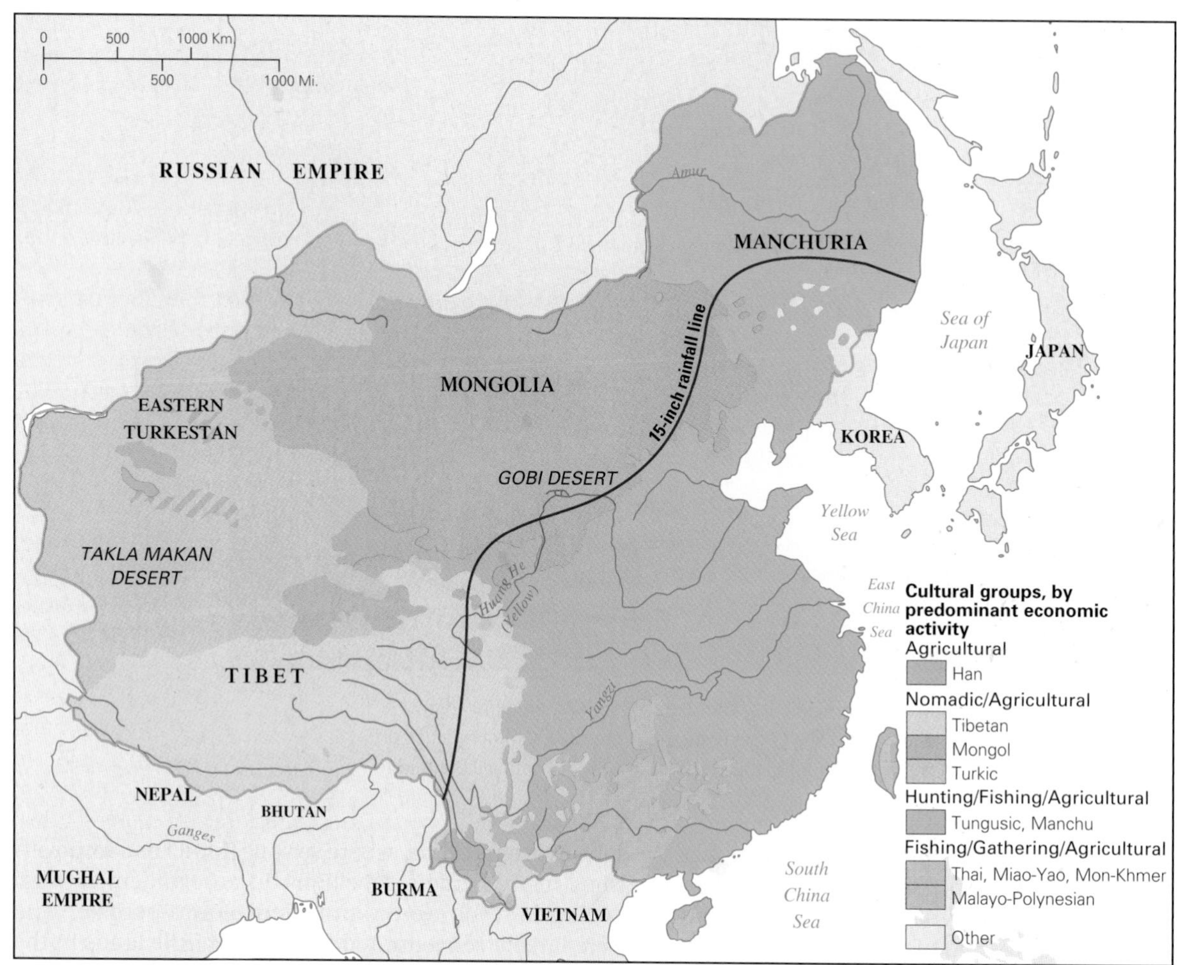

Map 21.2 Climate and Diversity in the Qing Empire The Qing Empire encompassed different environmental zones, and the climate differences corresponded to population density and cultural divisions. Wetter regions to the east of the 15-inch rainfall line also contained the most densely populated 20 percent of Qing land. The drier, less densely populated 80 percent of the empire was home to the greatest portion of peoples who spoke languages other than Chinese. Many were nomads, fishermen, hunters, and farmers who raised crops other than rice.

The Drive Across Northern Asia

The Russians were a branch of the Slavic peoples of eastern Europe, and most were Orthodox Christians like the Greeks. During the centuries just before 1500, their history had been dominated by Asian rule. The Mongol Khanate of the Golden Horde had ruled the Russians and their neighbors from the 1240s until 1480.

Under the Golden Horde Moscow became the most important Russian city and the center of political power. Moscow lay in the forest that stretched across northern Eurasia, in contrast to the treeless steppe (plains) favored by Mongol horsemen for pasture. The princes of **Muscovy°**, the territory surrounding the city of Moscow, led the movement against the Golden Horde and ruthlessly annexed the great territories of the neighboring Russian state of Novgorod in 1478.

Once free from Mongol domination, the princes of Moscovy set out on conquests that in time made them masters of the old dominions of the Golden Horde and then of a far greater empire. Prince Ivan IV (r. 1533–1584) pushed the conquests south and east, expanding Rus-

Muscovy (MUSS-koe-vee)

sia's borders far to the east through the conquest of the Khanates of Kazan and Astrakhan and the northern Caucasus region (see Map 21.3).

At the end of the sixteenth century, Russians ruled the largest state in Europe and large territories on the Asian side of the **Ural Mountains** as well. Since 1547 the Russian ruler used the title **tsar**° (from the Roman imperial title "caesar"), the term Russians had used for the rulers of the Mongol Empire. The Russian church promoted the idea of Moscow as the "third Rome," successor to the Roman Empire's second capital, Constantinople, which had fallen to the Ottoman Turks in 1453. But such foreign titles were a thin veneer over a very Russian pattern of expansion.

These claims to greatness were also exaggerated: in 1600 the Russian Empire was poor, backward, and landlocked. Only the northern city of Arkangelsk was connected by water to the rest of the world—when its harbor was not frozen. The independent Crimean peoples to the south were powerful enough to sack Moscow in 1571. Beyond them, the still vigorous Ottoman Empire controlled the shores of the Black Sea, while the Safavid rulers of Iran dominated the trade routes of southern Central Asia. The powerful kingdoms of Sweden and Poland-Lithuania to the west turned back Russian forces trying to gain access to the warmer waters of the Baltic Sea and pummeled them badly.

A path of less resistance lay to the east across **Siberia,** and it had much to recommend it. Many Russians felt more at home in the forested northern part of Siberia than on the open steppes, and the thinly inhabited region teemed with valuable resources. Most prominent of these resources was the soft, dense fur that forest animals grew to survive the long winter cold. Like their counterparts in Canada (see Chapter 18), hardy Russian pioneers in Siberia made a living from animal pelts. The merchants from western Europe and other lands who came to buy these furs in Moscow provided the tsars with revenues and access to European technology.

Early Russian exploration of Siberia was not the work of the state but of the Strogonovs, a wealthy Russian trading family. The small bands of hunting and fishing peoples who inhabited this cold and desolate region had no way of resisting the armed adventurers hired by the Strogonovs. Their troops attacked the only political power in the region, the Khanate of Sibir, and they used their rifles to destroy the khanate in 1582. Taking advantage of rivers to move through the almost impenetrable forests, Russian fur trappers reached the Pacific during the seventeenth century and soon crossed over into Alaska. Russian political control followed at a much slower pace. In the seventeenth century Siberia was a frontier zone with widely scattered forts, not a province under full control. Native Siberian peoples continued to resist Russian control fiercely, and the Russians had to placate local leaders with gifts and acknowledge their rights and authority. From the early seventeenth century the tsar also used Siberia as a penal colony for criminals and political prisoners.

The trade in furs and forest products helped ease Russian isolation and fund further conquests. The eastward expansion of the Russian state took second place during the seventeenth century to the tsars' efforts to build political and military power and establish control over the more numerous peoples of Siberia and the steppe.

In the 1640s Russian settlers had begun to move into the valley of the Amur River east of Mongolia in order to grow grain. The government's wooden forts aroused the concerns of the Ming about yet another threat on their northern frontier. As seen already, by the time the Qing were in a position to deal with the Russian presence, the worrisome threat of Galdan's Mongol military power had arisen. Equally concerned about the Mongols, the Russians were pleased to work out a frontier agreement with China. The 1689 Treaty of Nerchinsk recognized Russian claims west of Mongolia but required the Russians to withdraw their settlements east. Moreover, the negotiations showed China's recognition of Russia as an important and powerful neighbor.

Russian Society and Politics to 1725

Russian expansion produced far-reaching demographic changes and more gradual changes in the relations of the tsar with the elite classes. A third transformation was in the freedom and mobility of the Russian peasantry.

As the empire expanded, it incorporated people with different languages, religious beliefs, and ethnic identities. The emerging Russian Empire included peoples who spoke Asian languages and who were not Christians. Language differences were not hard to overcome, but religious and other cultural differences often caused tensions, especially when differences were manipulated for political purposes. Orthodox missionaries made great efforts to turn people in Siberia into Christians, in much the same way that Catholic missionaries did in Canada. But among the more populous steppe peoples, Islam eventually replaced Christianity as the dominant religion. More fundamental than language, ethnicity, or religion were the differences in how people made their living. Russians tended to live as

---

tsar (zahr)

Map 21.3 The Expansion of Russia, 1500–1800 Sweden and Poland initially blocked Russian expansion in Europe, while the Ottoman Empire blocked the southwest. In the sixteenth century, Russia began to expand east, toward Siberia and the Pacific Ocean. By the end of the rule of Catherine the Great in 1796, Russia encompassed all of northern and northeastern Eurasia.

farmers, hunters, builders, scribes, or merchants, while those newly incorporated into the empire were mostly herders, caravan workers, and soldiers.

As people mixed, individual and group identities could become quite complex. Even among Russian speakers who were members of the Russian Orthodox Church there was wide diversity of identity. The **Cossacks** are a revealing example. The name probably came from a Turkic word for a warrior or mercenary soldier and referred to bands of people living on the steppes between Moscovy and the Caspian and Black Seas. In practice, Cossacks became highly diverse in their origins and beliefs. What mattered was that they belonged to close-knit bands, were superb riders and fighters, and were feared by both the villagers and the legal authorities. Cossacks made temporary allegiances with many rulers but were most loyal to their bands and to whoever was currently paying for their military services.

Many Cossacks were important allies in the expansion of the Russian Empire. They formed the majority of the soldiers and early settlers employed by the Strogonovs in the penetration of Siberia. Most historians believe that Cossacks founded all the major towns of Russian Siberia. They also manned the Russian camps on the Amur River. The Cossacks west of the Urals performed distinctive service for Russia in defending against Swedish and Ottoman incursions, but they also resisted any efforts to undermine their own political autonomy. Those in the rich and populous lands of the Ukraine, for example, rebelled when the tsar agreed to a division of their lands with Poland-Lithuania in 1667.

In the early seventeenth century Swedish and Polish forces briefly occupied Moscow on separate occasions. In the midst of this "Time of Troubles" the old line of Muscovite rulers was finally deposed, and the Russian aristocracy—the boyars°—allowed one of their own, Mikhail Romanov°, to become tsar (r. 1613–1645). The early Romanov rulers saw a close connection between the consolidation of their own authority and successful competition with neighboring powers. They tended to represent conflicts between Slavic Russians and Turkic peoples of Central Asia as being between Christians and "infidels" or between the civilized and the "barbaric." Despite this rhetoric, it is important to understand that these cultural groups were defined less by blood ties than by the way in which they lived.

The political and economic transformations of the Russian Empire had serious repercussions for the peasants who tilled the land in European Russia. As centralized power rose, the freedom of the peasants fell. The process was longer and more complex than the rise of slavery in the Americas. The Moscovy rulers and early tsars rewarded their loyal nobles with grants of land that included obligations of the local peasants to work for these lords. Law and custom permitted peasants to change masters during a two-week period each year, which encouraged lords to treat their peasants well, but the rising commercialization of agriculture also raised the value of these labor obligations.

The long periods of civil and foreign warfare in the late sixteenth and early seventeenth centuries caused such disruption and economic decline that many peasants fled to the Cossacks or across the Urals to escape. Some who couldn't flee sold themselves into slavery to ensure a steady supply of food. When peace returned, landlords sought to recover these runaway peasants and bind them more firmly to their land. A law change in 1649 completed the transformation of peasants into **serfs** by eliminating the period when they could change masters and removing limitations on the length of the period during which runaways could be forced to return to their masters.

Like slavery, serfdom was a hereditary status, but in theory the serf was tied to a piece of land, not owned by a master. In practice, the difference between serfdom and slavery grew finer as the laws regulating selfdom became stricter. By 1723 all Russian slaves were transformed into serfs. In the Russian census of 1795, serfs made up over half the population of Russia. The serfs were under the control of landowners who made up only 2 percent of Russia's population, similar to the size of the slave-owning class in the Caribbean.

Peter the Great

The greatest of the Romanovs was Tsar **Peter the Great** (r. 1689–1725), who made major changes to reduce Russia's isolation and increase the empire's size and power. Tsar Peter is remembered for his efforts to turn Russia away from its Asian cultural connections and toward what he deemed the civilization of the West. In fact, he accelerated trends under way for some time. By the time he ascended the throne, there were hundreds of foreign merchants in Moscow; western European soldiers had trained a major part of the army in new weapons and techniques; and Italian architects had made an impression on the city's churches and palaces. It was on this substantial base that Peter erected a more rapid transformation of Russia.

Peter matured quickly both physically and mentally. In his youth the government was in the hands of his half-sister Sophia, who was regent on behalf of him and her sickly brother Ivan. Living on an estate near the foreigners' quarter outside Moscow, Peter learned what he could

---

boyar (BOY-ar)
Romanov (ROH-man-off or roh-MAN-off)

of life outside Russia and busied himself with gaining practical skills in blacksmithing, carpentry, shipbuilding, and the arts of war. He organized his own military drill unit among other young men. When Princess Sophia tried to take complete control of the government in 1689, Peter rallied enough support to send her to a monastery, secure the abdication of Ivan, and take charge of Russia. He was still in his teens.

Peter concerned himself with Russia's expansion and modernization. To secure a warm-water port on the Black Sea, he constructed a small but formidable navy that could blockade Ottoman ports. Describing his wars with the Ottoman Empire as a new crusade to liberate Constantinople from the Muslim sultans, Peter also saw himself as the legal protector of Orthodox Christians living under Ottoman rule. Peter's forces had seized the port of Azov in 1696, but the fortress was lost again in 1713, and Russian expansion southward was blocked for the rest of Peter's reign.

In the winter of 1697–1698, after his Black Sea campaign, Peter traveled in disguise across Europe to discover how western European societies were becoming so powerful and wealthy. The young tsar paid special attention to ships and weapons, even working for a time as a ship's carpenter in the Netherlands. With great insight, he perceived that western European success owed as much to trade and toleration as to technology. Trade generated the money to spend on weapons, while toleration attracted talented persons fleeing persecution. Upon his return to Russia, Peter resolved to expand and reform his vast and backward empire.

In the long and costly Great Northern War (1700–1721), his modernized armies broke Swedish control of the Baltic Sea, establishing more direct contacts between Russia and Europe. Peter's victory forced the European powers to recognize Russia as a major power for the first time.

On land captured from Sweden at the eastern end of the Baltic, Peter built St. Petersburg, a new city that was to be his window on the West. In 1712 the city became Russia's capital. To demonstrate Russia's new sophistication, Peter ordered architects to build St. Petersburg's houses and public buildings in the baroque style then fashionable in France.

Peter also pushed the Russian elite to imitate western European fashions. He personally shaved off his noblemen's long beards to conform to Western styles and ordered them to wear Western clothing. To end the traditional seclusion of upper-class Russian women, Peter required officials, officers, and merchants to bring their wives to the social gatherings he organized in the capital. He also directed the nobles to educate their children.

Another of Peter's strategies was to reorganize Russian government along the lines of the powerful German state of Prussia. To break the power of the boyars he sharply reduced their traditional roles in government and the army. The old boyar council of Moscow was replaced by a group of advisers in St. Petersburg whom the tsar appointed. Members of the traditional nobility continued to serve as generals and admirals, but officers in Peter's modern, professional army and navy were promoted according to merit, not birth.

Peter the Great This portrait from his time as a student in Holland in 1697 shows Peter as ruggedly masculine and practical, quite unlike most royal portraits of the day that posed rulers in foppish elegance and haughty majesty. Peter was a popular military leader as well as an autocratic ruler. (Collection, Countess Bobrinskoy/Michael Holford)

The goal of Peter's westernization strategy was to strengthen the Russian state and increase the power of the tsar. A decree of 1716 proclaimed that the tsar "is not obliged to answer to anyone in the world for his doings, but possesses power and authority over his kingdom and land, to rule them at his will and pleasure as a Christian ruler." Under this expansive definition of his role, Peter brought the Russian Orthodox Church more firmly under state control, built factories and iron and copper foundries to provide munitions and supplies for the military, and increased the burdens of taxes and forced labor on the serfs. Peter was an absolutist ruler of the sort then popular in western Europe, and he had no more intention of improving the conditions of the serfs, on whose labors the production of basic foodstuffs depended, than did the European slave owners of the Americas.

The Fontanka Canal in St. Petersburg in 1753 The Russian capital continued to grow as a commercial and administrative center. As in Amsterdam, canals were the city's major arteries. On the right is a new summer palace built by Peter's successor. (Engraving, after M. I. Makhaiev, from the official series of 1753, British Museum)

Consolidation of the Empire

Russia's eastward expansion also continued under Peter the Great and his successors. The frontier settlement with China and Qianlong's quashing of Inner Mongolia in 1689 freed Russians to concentrate on the northern Pacific. The Pacific northeast was colonized, and in 1741 an expedition led by Captain Vitus Bering crossed the strait (later named for him) into North America. In 1799 a Russian company of merchants received a monopoly over the Alaskan fur trade, and its agents were soon active along the entire northwestern coast of North America.

Far more important than these immense territories in the cold and thinly populated north were the populous agricultural lands to the west acquired during the reign of Catherine the Great (r. 1762–1796). A successful war with the Ottoman Empire gave Russia control of the rich north shore of the Black Sea by 1783. As a result of three successive partitions of the once powerful kingdom of Poland between 1772 and 1795, Russia's frontiers advanced 600 miles (nearly 1,000 km.) to the west (see Map 21.3). When Catherine died, the Russian Empire extended from Poland in the west to Alaska in the east, from the Barents Sea in the north to the Black Sea in the south.

Catherine also made important additions to Peter's policies of promoting industry and building a canal system to improve trade. Besides furs, the Russians had also become major exporters of gold, iron, and timber. Catherine implemented administrative reforms and showed a special talent for diplomacy. Through her promotion of the ideas of the Enlightenment, she expanded Peter's policies of westernizing the Russian elite.

Comparative Perspectives

Looked at separately, the histories of Japan, China, and Russia seem to have relatively little in common. Contacts with each other and with other parts of the world appear far less important than forces within each state. However, when examined comparatively these separate histories reveal similarities and differences that help explain the global dynamics of this period and the larger historical patterns of which it is a part.

Political Comparisons

China and Russia are examples of the phenomenal flourishing of empires in Eurasia between 1500 and 1800. Already a vast empire under the Ming, China doubled in size under the Qing, mostly through westward expansion into less densely populated areas. In expanding from a modestly sized principality into the world's largest land empire, Russia added rich and well-populated lands to the west and south and far larger but less populous lands to the east. Russia and China were land based, just like the Ottoman and Mughal Empires, with the strengths and problems of administrative control and tax collection that size entailed.

Although western Europe is often seen as particularly imperialist in the centuries after 1500, only Spain's empire merits comparison with Russia's in the speed of its growth, its land size, and its presence on three continents. The more typical western European empires of this era, the new seaborne trading empires of the Portuguese, Dutch, French, and English, had much less territory, far tighter administration, and a much more global sweep.

Japan was different. Though nominally headed by an emperor, Japan's size and ethnic homogeneity do not support calling it an empire in the same breath with China and Russia. Tokugawa Japan was similar in size and population to France, the most powerful state of western Europe, but its political system was much more decentralized. Japan's efforts to add colonies on the East Asian mainland had failed.

China had once led the world in military innovation (including the first uses of gunpowder), but the modern "gunpowder revolution" of the fifteenth and sixteenth centuries was centered in the Ottoman Empire and western European states. Although the centuries after 1500 were full of successful military operations, Chinese armies continued to depend on superior numbers and tactics for their success, rather than on new technology. As in the past, infantrymen armed with guns served alongside others armed with bows and arrows, swords, and spears.

The military forces of Japan and Russia underwent more innovative changes than those of China, in part through Western contacts. In the course of its sixteenth-century wars of unification, Japan produced its own gunpowder revolution but thereafter lacked the motivation and the means to stay abreast of the world's most advanced military technology. By the eighteenth century Russia had made greater progress in catching up with its European neighbors, but its armies still relied more on their size than on the sophistication of their weapons.

Naval power provides the greatest military contrast among the three. Eighteenth-century Russia constructed modern fleets of warships in the Baltic and the Black Seas, but neither China nor Japan developed navies commensurate with their size and coastlines. China's defenses against pirates and other sea invaders were left to its maritime provinces, whose small war junks were armed with only a half-dozen cannon. Japan's naval capacity was similarly decentralized. In 1792, when Russian ships exploring the North Pacific turned toward the Japanese coast, the local daimyo used his own forces to chase them away. All Japanese daimyo understood that they would be on their own if foreign incursions increased.

Cultural, Social, and Economic Comparisons

The expansion of China and Russia incorporated not just new lands but also diverse new peoples. Both empires pursued policies that tolerated diversity along with policies to promote cultural assimilation. In contrast, Japan remained more culturally homogeneous, and the government reacted with great intolerance to the growing influence of converts to western Christianity.

Chinese society had long been diverse, and its geographical, occupational, linguistic, and religious differences grew as the Qing expanded (see Map 21.2). China had also long used Confucian models, imperial customs, and a common system of writing to transcend such differences. These techniques were most effective in assimilating elites. It is striking how quickly and thoroughly the Manchu conquerors adopted Chinese imperial ways of thinking and acting as well as of dressing, speaking, and writing.

Kangxi's reign is a notable example of how tolerant the Chinese elite could be of new ideas from the Jesuits and other sources. Yet it is important to note that the Jesuits' success owed much to their portraying themselves as supporters of Confucian values and learning. Although Chinese converts to Catholicism were instrumental in introducing European techniques of crop production and engineering, influential members of China's government were highly suspicious of the loyalties of these converts, persecuted them, and eventually moved to prohibit or severely limit missionary activity.

Russia likewise approached its new peoples with a mixture of pragmatic tolerance and a propensity for seeing Russian ways and beliefs as superior. Religion was a particular sore point. With the support of the tsars, Russian Orthodox missionaries encouraged conversion of Siberian peoples. In the new lands of Eastern Europe, Or-

PART SIX

Revolutions Reshape the World, 1750–1870

Between 1750 and 1870, nearly every part of the world experienced dramatic political, economic, and social change. The beginnings of industrialization, the American and French Revolutions, and the revolutions for independence in Latin America transformed political and economic life in Europe and the Americas. The most powerful nations challenged existing borders and ethnic boundaries. European nations expanded into Africa, Asia, and the Middle East while Russia and the United States acquired vast new territories.

The American, French, and Latin American revolutions created new political institutions and unleashed the forces of nationalism and social reform. The Industrial Revolution introduced new technologies and patterns of work that made industrial societies wealthier, more fluid socially, and militarily more powerful. Western intellectual life became more secular as the practical benefits of science and technology became evident. Reformers led successful efforts to abolish the Atlantic slave trade and, later, slavery itself in the Western Hemisphere. Efforts to expand voting rights and improve the status of women also gained support in Europe and the Americas.

European empires in the Western Hemisphere were largely dismantled by 1825. But the Industrial Revolution led to a new wave of economic and imperial expansion. France conquered the North African state of Algeria, while Great Britain expanded its colonial rule in India and established new colonies in Australia and New Zealand. Of these, India alone had a larger population than that of all the colonies Europe had lost in the Americas.

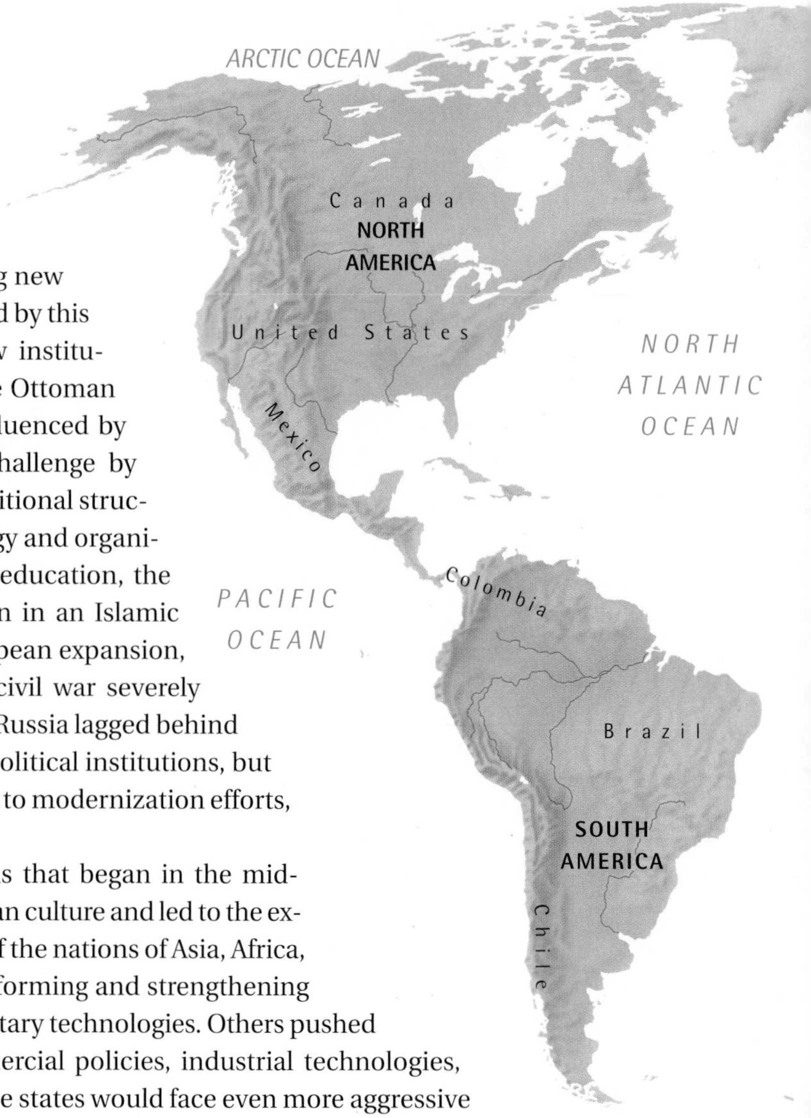

Throughout Africa, European economic influence greatly expanded, deepening the region's connection to the Atlantic economy and generating new political forces. Some African states were invigorated by this era of intensified cultural exchange, creating new institutions and developing new products for export. The Ottoman Empire and the Qing Empire were also deeply influenced by Western expansionism. Both empires met this challenge by implementing reform programs that preserved traditional structures while adopting elements of Western technology and organization. The Ottoman court introduced reforms in education, the military, and law and created the first constitution in an Islamic state. The Qing Empire survived the period of European expansion, but a series of military defeats and a prolonged civil war severely weakened the authority of the central government. Russia lagged behind Western Europe in transforming its economy and political institutions, but military weakness and internal reform pressures led to modernization efforts, including the abolition of serfdom.

The economic, political, and social revolutions that began in the mid-eighteenth century shook the foundations of European culture and led to the expansion of Western power around the globe. Some of the nations of Asia, Africa, and Latin America resisted foreign intrusions by reforming and strengthening their own institutions, forms of production, and military technologies. Others pushed for more radical change, adopting Western commercial policies, industrial technologies, and government institutions. But after 1870, all these states would face even more aggressive Western imperialism, which few of them were able to resist.

	1750	1775	1800
Americas	**1754–1763** French and Indian War	U.S. Declaration of Independence **1776**	Louisiana Purchase by United States **1803**; **1789** U.S. Constitution ratified; **1791** Slaves revolt in Haiti; **1809–1825** Wars for independence in Spanish America
Europe	**ca. 1750** Industrial Revolution begins in Britain; **1756–1763** Seven Years War		**1789–1799** French Revolution; **1814–1815** Congress of Vienna; **1799–1815** Rule of Napoleon in France
Africa	**1750–1800** Growing slave trade reduces population		Sokoto Caliphate founded **1809**; Britain takes Cape Colony **1795**; Shaka founds Zulu kingdom **1818**
Middle East	**1769–1772** High point of restored Mamluk influence in Egypt		**1789–1807** Reign of Ottoman sultan Selim III; **1798** Napoleon invades Egypt; Muhammad Ali founds dynasty in Egypt **1805**
Asia and Oceania	**1755** Qing conquest of Turkestan; East India Company rule of Bengal begins **1765**	**1769–1778** Captain Cook's exploration of Australia, New Zealand	White Lotus Rebellion in China **1796–1804**; Britain takes Ceylon **1798**; East India Company creates Bombay presidency **1818**

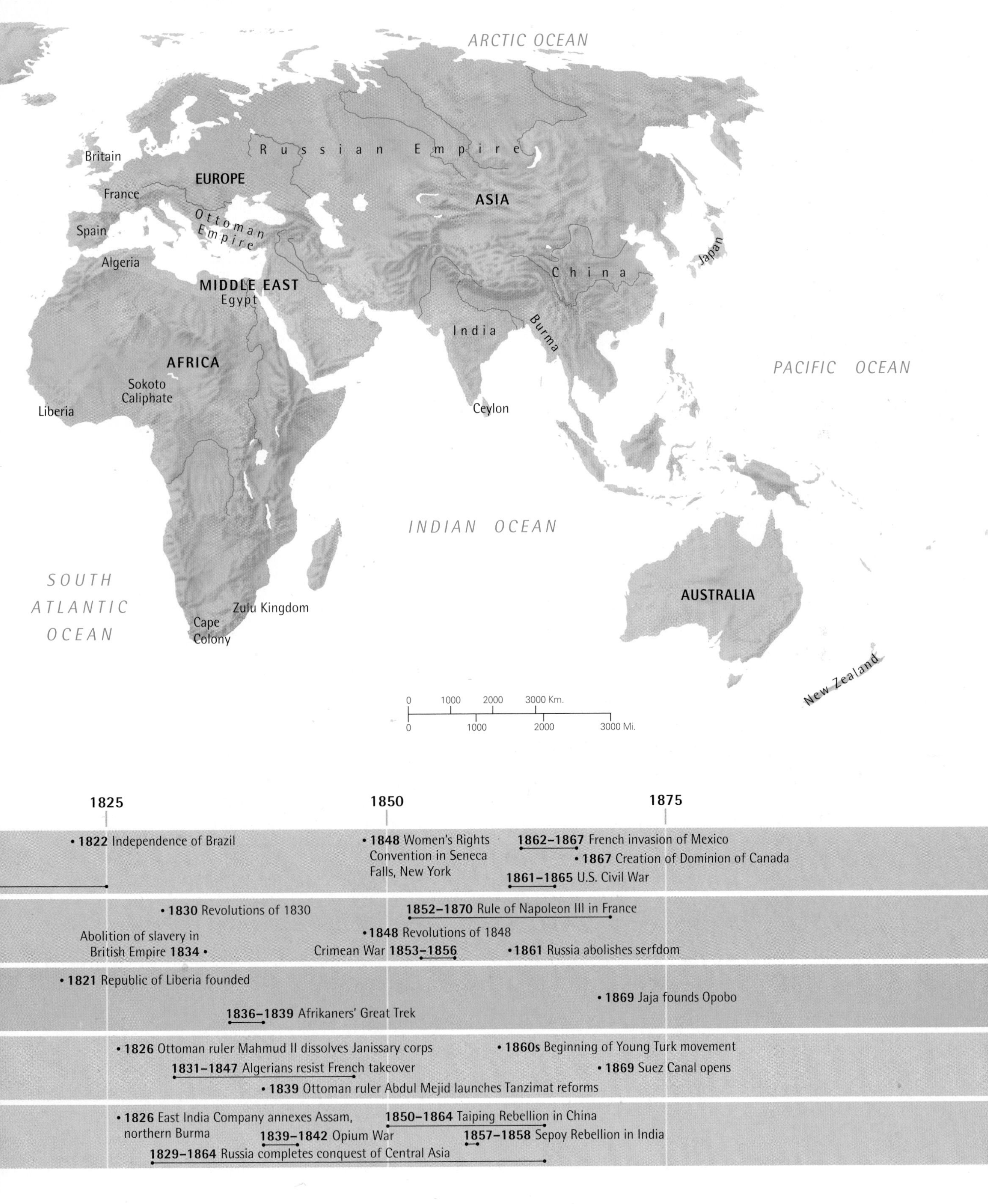

ARCTIC OCEAN
Britain
Russian Empire
EUROPE
France
ASIA
Ottoman Empire
Spain
Japan
Algeria
China
MIDDLE EAST
Egypt
Burma
India
PACIFIC OCEAN
AFRICA
Sokoto Caliphate
Liberia
Ceylon
INDIAN OCEAN
SOUTH ATLANTIC OCEAN
AUSTRALIA
Zulu Kingdom
Cape Colony
New Zealand
0 1000 2000 3000 Km.
0 1000 2000 3000 Mi.
1825
1850
1875
• 1822 Independence of Brazil
• 1848 Women's Rights Convention in Seneca Falls, New York
1862–1867 French invasion of Mexico
• 1867 Creation of Dominion of Canada
1861–1865 U.S. Civil War
• 1830 Revolutions of 1830
1852–1870 Rule of Napoleon III in France
Abolition of slavery in British Empire 1834 •
• 1848 Revolutions of 1848
Crimean War 1853–1856
• 1861 Russia abolishes serfdom
• 1821 Republic of Liberia founded
• 1869 Jaja founds Opobo
1836–1839 Afrikaners' Great Trek
• 1826 Ottoman ruler Mahmud II dissolves Janissary corps
• 1860s Beginning of Young Turk movement
1831–1847 Algerians resist French takeover
• 1869 Suez Canal opens
• 1839 Ottoman ruler Abdul Mejid launches Tanzimat reforms
• 1826 East India Company annexes Assam, northern Burma
1850–1864 Taiping Rebellion in China
1839–1842 Opium War
1857–1858 Sepoy Rebellion in India
1829–1864 Russia completes conquest of Central Asia

22 Revolutionary Changes in the Atlantic World, 1750–1850

Burning of Cap Français, St. Domingue in 1793 In 1791, the slaves of St. Domingue, France's richest colony, began a rebellion that, after years of struggle, ended slavery and created the Western Hemisphere's second independent nation, Haiti.

CHAPTER OUTLINE

On the evening of August 14, 1791, more than two hundred slaves and black freedmen met in secret in the plantation district of northern Saint Domingue° (present-day Haiti) to set the date for an armed uprising against local slave owners. Although the delegates agreed to delay the attack for a week, violence began almost immediately. During the following decade, slavery was abolished; military forces from Britain and France were defeated; and Haiti achieved independence.

The meeting was provoked by news and rumors about revolutionary events in France that had spread through the island's slave community. Events in France had also divided the island's white population into competing camps of royalists (supporters of France's King Louis XVI) and republicans (who sought an end to monarchy). The free mixed-race population initially gained some political rights from the French Assembly but was then forced to rebel when the local slave-owning elite reacted violently.

A black freedman named François Dominique Toussaint eventually became leader of the insurrection. He proved to be one of the most remarkable representatives of the revolutionary era, later taking the name Toussaint L'Ouverture°. He organized the rebels into a potent military force, negotiated with the island's royalist and republican factions and with representatives of Great Britain and France, and wrote his nation's first constitution. Commonly portrayed as a fiend by slave owners throughout the Western Hemisphere, to the slaves Toussaint became a towering symbol of resistance to oppression.

The Haitian slave rebellion was an important episode in the long and painful political and cultural transformation of the modern Western world. Economic expansion and the growth of trade were creating unprecedented wealth. The first stage of the Industrial Revolution (see Chapter 23) increased manufacturing productivity and led to greater global interdependence, new patterns of consumerism, and altered social structures. At the same time, intellectuals were questioning the traditional place of monarchy and religion in society. An increasingly powerful class of merchants, professionals, and manufacturers created by the emerging economy provided an audience for these new intellectual currents and began to press for a larger political role.

This revolutionary era turned the Western world "upside down." The *ancien régime*°, the French term for Europe's old order, rested on medieval principles: politics dominated by powerful monarchs, intellectual and cultural life dominated by religion, and economics dominated by a hereditary agricultural elite. In the West's new order, politics was opened to vastly greater participation; science and secular inquiry took the place of religion in intellectual life; and economies were increasingly opened to competition.

This radical transformation did not take place without false starts and temporary setbacks. Imperial powers resisted the loss of colonies; monarchs and nobles struggled to retain their ancient privileges; and the church fought against the claims of science. Revolutionary steps forward were often matched by reactionary steps backward. The liberal and nationalist ideals of the eighteenth-century revolutionary movements were only imperfectly realized in Europe and the Americas in the nineteenth century. Despite setbacks, belief in national self-determination and universal suffrage and a passion for social justice continued to animate reformers into the twentieth century.

As you read this chapter, ask yourself the following questions:

- How did imperial wars among European powers provoke revolution?
- In what ways were the revolutions, expanded literacy, and new political ideas linked?
- How did revolution in one country help incite revolution elsewhere?
- Why were the revolutions in France and Haiti more violent than the American Revolution?

Saint Domingue (san doe-MANG) **Toussaint L'Ouverture** (too-SAN loo-ver-CHORE)

ancien régime (ahn-see-EN ray-ZHEEM)

PRELUDE TO REVOLUTION: THE EIGHTEENTH-CENTURY CRISIS

In large measure, the cost of wars fought among Europe's major powers over colonies and trade precipitated the revolutionary era that began in 1775 with the American Revolution. Britain, France, and Spain were the central actors in these global struggles, but other imperial powers were affected as well. Unpopular and costly wars had been fought earlier and paid for with new taxes. But changes in the Western intellectual and political environments led to a much more critical response. Any effort to extend the power of a monarch or impose new taxes now raised questions about the rights of individuals and the authority of political institutions.

Colonial Wars and Fiscal Crises

The rivalry among European powers intensified in the early 1600s when the newly independent Netherlands began an assault on the American and Asian colonies of Spain and Portugal. The Dutch attacked Spanish treasure fleets in the Caribbean and Pacific and seized parts of Portugal's colonial empire in Brazil and Angola. Europe's other emerging sea power, Great Britain, also attacked Spanish fleets and seaports in the Americas. By the end of the seventeenth century expanding British sea power had checked Dutch commercial and colonial ambitions and ended the Dutch monopoly of the African slave trade.

As Dutch power ebbed, Britain and France began a long struggle for political preeminence in western Europe and for territory and trade outlets in the Americas and Asia. Both the geographic scale and the expense of this conflict expanded during the eighteenth century. Nearly all of Europe's great powers were engaged in the War of the Spanish Succession (1701–1714). In 1739 a war between Britain and Spain over smuggling in the Americas quickly broadened into a generalized European conflict, the War of the Austrian Succession (1740–1748). Conflict between French and English settlers in North America then helped ignite a long war that altered the colonial balance of power. War began along the American frontier between French and British forces and their Amerindian allies. Known as the French and Indian War, this conflict helped lead to a wider struggle, the Seven Years War (1756–1763). British victory led to undisputed control of North America east of the Mississippi River while also forcing France to surrender most of its holdings in India.

The enormous costs of these conflicts distinguished them from earlier wars. Traditional taxes collected in traditional ways no longer covered the obligations of governments. For example, at the end of the Seven Years War in 1763, Britain's war debt reached £137 million. Britain's total budget before the war had averaged only £8 million. With the legacy of war debt, Britain's interest payments alone came to exceed £5 million. Even as European economies expanded because of increased trade and the early stages of the Industrial Revolution, fiscal crises overtook one European government after another. In an intellectual environment transformed by the Enlightenment, the need for new revenues provoked debate and confrontation within a vastly expanded and more critical public.

The Enlightenment and the Old Order

The complex and diverse intellectual movement called the **Enlightenment** applied the methods and questions of the Scientific Revolution of the seventeenth century to the study of human society. Dazzled by Copernicus's ability to explain the structure of the solar system and Newton's representation of the law of gravity, European intellectuals began to apply the logical tools of scientific inquiry to other questions. Some labored to systematize knowledge or organize reference materials. For example, Carolus Linnaeus° (a Swedish botanist known by the Latin form of his name) sought to categorize all living organisms, and Samuel Johnson published a comprehensive English dictionary with over forty thousand definitions. In France Denis Diderot° worked with other Enlightenment thinkers to create a compendium of human knowledge, the thirty-five-volume *Encyclopédie*.

Other thinkers pursued lines of inquiry that challenged long-established religious and political institutions. Some argued that if scientists could understand the laws of nature, then surely similar forms of disciplined investigation might reveal laws of human nature. Others wondered whether society and government might be better regulated and more productive if guided by science rather than by hereditary rulers and the church. These new perspectives and the intellectual optimism that fed them were to help guide the revolutionary movements of the late eighteenth century.

The English political philosopher John Locke (1632–1704) argued in 1690 that governments were created to

Carolus Linnaeus (kar-ROLL-uhs lin-NEE-uhs) **Denis Diderot** (duh-nee DEE-duh-roe)

CHRONOLOGY

	The Americas	Europe
1750		
	1754–1763 French and Indian War	**1756–1763** Seven Years War
	1770 Boston Massacre	
1775	**1776** American Declaration of Independence	
	1778 United States alliance with France	**1778** Death of Voltaire and Rousseau
	1781 British surrender at Yorktown	
	1783 Treaty of Paris ends American Revolution	
	1791 Slaves revolt in Saint Domingue (Haiti)	**1789** Storming of Bastille begins French Revolution; Declaration of Rights of Man and Citizen in France
		1793–1794 Reign of Terror in France
	1798 Toussaint L'Ouverture defeats British in Haiti	**1795–1799** The Directory rules France
1800		**1799** Napoleon overthrows the Directory
	1804 Haitians defeat French invasion and declare independence	**1804** Napoleon crowns himself emperor
		1814 Napoleon abdicates; Congress of Vienna opens
		1815 Napoleon defeated at Waterloo
		1830 Greece gains independence; revolution in France overthrows Charles X
		1848 Revolutions in France, Austria, Germany, Hungary, and Italy

protect life, liberty, and property and that the people had a right to rebel when a monarch violated these natural rights. Locke's closely reasoned theory began with the assumption that individual rights were the foundation of civil government. In *The Social Contract*, published in 1762, the French-Swiss intellectual Jean-Jacques Rousseau° (1712–1778) asserted that the will of the people was sacred and that the legitimacy of the monarch depended on the consent of the people. Although both men believed that government rested on the will of the people rather than on divine will, Locke emphasized the importance of individual rights, and Rousseau envisioned the people acting collectively because of their shared historical experience.

All Enlightenment thinkers were not radicals like Rousseau. There was never a uniform program for political and social reform, and the era's intellectuals often disagreed about principles and objectives. The Enlightenment is commonly associated with hostility toward religion and monarchy, but few European intellectuals openly expressed republican or atheist sentiments. The church was most commonly attacked when it attempted to censor ideas or ban books. Critics of monarchial authority were as likely to point out violations of ancient custom as to suggest democratic alternatives. Even Voltaire, one of the Enlightenment's most critical intellects and great celebrities, believed that Europe's monarchs were likely agents of political and economic reform and even wrote favorably of China's Qing° emperors.

Indeed, sympathetic members of the nobility and reforming European monarchs such as Charles III of Spain (r. 1759–1788), Catherine the Great of Russia (r. 1762–1796), Joseph II of Austria (r. 1780–1790), and Frederick the Great of Prussia (r. 1740–1786) actively sponsored and promoted the dissemination of new ideas, providing patronage for many intellectuals. They recognized that elements of the Enlightenment critique of the ancien régime buttressed their own efforts to expand royal authority at the expense of religious institutions, the nobility, and regional autonomy. Goals such as the development of national bureaucracies staffed by civil servants selected on merit, the creation of national legal systems, and the modernization of tax systems united many of Europe's monarchs and intellectuals. Monarchs also understood that the era's passion for science and technology held the potential of fattening

Jean-Jacques Rousseau (zhah-zhock roo-SOE)

Qing (ching)

ENVIRONMENT + TECHNOLOGY

The Pencil

From early times Europeans had used sharp points, lead, and other implements to sketch, make marks, and write brief notes. At the end of the seventeenth century a source of high-quality graphite was discovered at Borrowdale in northwestern England. Borrowdale graphite gained acceptance among artists, artisans, and merchants. At first, pure graphite was simply wrapped in string. By the eighteenth century, pieces of graphite were being encased in wooden sheaths and resembled modern pencils. Widespread use of this useful tool was retarded by the limited supply of high-quality graphite from the English mines.

The English crown periodically closed the Borrowdale mines or restricted production to keep prices high and maintain adequate supplies for future needs. As a result, artisans in other European nations developed alternatives that used lower-quality graphite or, most commonly, graphite mixed with sulfur and glues.

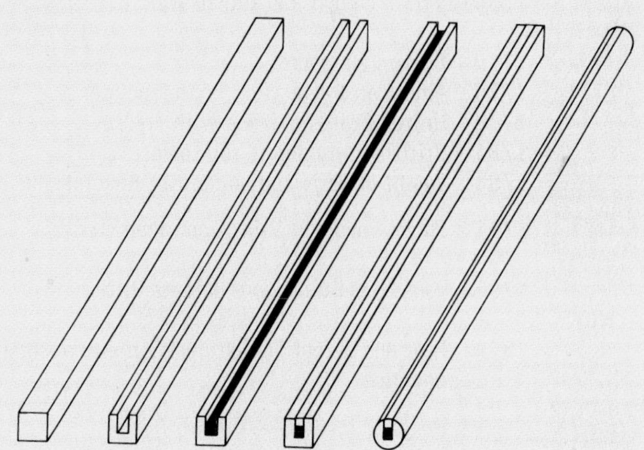

Pencils Wartime necessity led to invention of the modern pencil in France. (Drawing by Fred Avent for Henry Petroski. Reproduced by permission)

The major breakthrough occurred in 1793 in France when war with England ruptured trade links. The government of revolutionary France responded to the shortage of graphite by assigning a thirty-nine-year-old scientist, Nicolas-Jacques Conté, to find an alternative. Conté had earlier promoted the military use of balloons and conducted experiments with hydrogen. He had also used graphite alloys in the development of crucibles for melting metal.

Within a short period, Conté produced a graphite that is the basis for most lead pencils today. He mixed finely ground graphite with potter's clay and water. The resulting paste was dried in a long mold, sealed in a ceramic box, and fired in an oven. The graphite strips were then placed in wooden cases. Although some believed the Conté pencils were inferior to the pencils made from Borrowdale graphite, Conté produced a very serviceable pencil that could be produced in uniform quality and unlimited amounts.

Summarizing the achievement of Conté in *The Pencil*, Henry Petroski wrote: "The laboratory is really the modern workshop. And modern engineering results when the scientific method is united with experience with the tools and products of craftsmen. . . . Modern engineering, in spirit if not in name, would come to play a more and more active role in turning the craft tradition into modern technology, with its base of research and development."

Source: This discussion depends on Henry Petroski, *The Pencil: A History of Design and Circumstance* (New York: Knopf, 1990); the quotation is from pp. 50–78. Drawing by Fred Avent for Henry Petroski. Reproduced by permission.

national treasuries and improving economic performance (see Environment and Technology: The Pencil). Periodicals disseminating new technologies often gained the patronage of these reforming monarchs.

Though willing to embrace reform proposals when they served royal interests, Europe's monarchs moved quickly to suppress or ban radical ideas that promoted republicanism or directly attacked religion. However, too many channels of communication were open to permit a thoroughgoing suppression of ideas. In fact, censorship tended to enhance intellectual reputations, and persecuted intellectuals generally found patronage in the courts of foreign rivals.

Many of the major intellectuals of the Enlightenment maintained extensive correspondence with each other as well as with political leaders. This communication led to numerous firsthand contacts among the intellectuals of different nations and helped create a coherent assault on what was typically called ignorance—beliefs and values associated with the ancien régime. Rousseau, for example, briefly sought refuge in Britain, where the Scottish philosopher David Hume befriended him. Similarly, Voltaire sought patronage and protection in England and later in Prussia.

Women were instrumental in the dissemination of the new ideas. In England educated middle-class women purchased and discussed the books and pamphlets of the era. Some were important contributors to intellectual life as writers and commentators, raising by example and in argument the issue of the rights of women. In Paris wealthy women made their homes centers of debate, intellectual speculation, and free inquiry. Their salons brought together philosophers, social critics, artists, and members of the aristocracy and commercial elite. Unlike their contemporaries in England, the women of the Parisian salons used their social standing more to direct the conversations of men than to give vent to their own opinions.

The intellectual ferment of the era deeply influenced the expanding middle class in Europe and the Western Hemisphere. Members of this class were eager consumers of books and the inexpensive newspapers and journals that were widely available. This broadening of the intellectual audience overwhelmed traditional institutions of censorship. Scientific discoveries, new technologies, and controversial work on human nature and politics also were discussed in the thousands of coffeehouses and teashops opening in major cities and market towns.

Many European intellectuals were interested in the Americas. Some Europeans continued to dismiss the New World as barbaric and inferior, but others used idealized accounts of the New World to support their critiques of European society. These thinkers looked to Britain's North American colonies for confirmation of their belief that human nature unconstrained by the corrupted practices of Europe's old order would quickly produce material abundance and social justice. More than any other American, the writer and inventor **Benjamin Franklin** came to symbolize both the natural genius and the vast potential of America.

Born in 1706 in Boston, the young Franklin was apprenticed to his older brother, a printer. At seventeen he ran away to Philadelphia, where he succeeded as a printer and publisher and was best known for his *Poor Richard's Almanac*. By age forty-two he was a wealthy man. He retired from active business to pursue writing, science, and public affairs. In Philadelphia Franklin was instrumental in the creation of the organizations that later became the Philadelphia Free Library, the American Philosophical Society, and the University of Pennsylvania.

Franklin's contributions were both practical and theoretical. He was the inventor of bifocal glasses, the lightning rod, and an efficient wood-burning stove. In 1751 he published a scientific work, *Experiments and Observations on Electricity*, that established his intellectual reputation in Europe. Intellectuals heralded the book as proof that the simple and unsophisticated world of America was a particularly hospitable environment for genius.

Franklin was also an important political figure. He served Pennsylvania as a delegate to the Albany (New York) Congress in 1754, which sought to coordinate colonial defense against attacks by the French and their Amerindian allies. Later he was a Pennsylvania delegate to the Continental Congress that issued the Declaration of Independence in 1776. His service in England as colonial lobbyist and later as the Continental Congress's ambassador to Paris allowed him to cultivate his European reputation. Franklin's wide achievement, witty conversation, and careful self-promotion make him a symbol of the era. In him the Enlightenment's most radical project, the freeing of human potential from the inhibitions of inherited privilege, found its most agreeable confirmation.

As Franklin's career demonstrates, the Western Hemisphere shared in the debates of Europe. New ideas penetrated the curricula of many colonial universities and appeared in periodicals and books published in the New World. As scientific method was applied to economic and political questions, colonial writers, scholars, and artists on both sides of the Atlantic were drawn into a debate that eventually was to lead to the rejection of colonialism itself. This radicalization of the colonial intellectual community was provoked by the European monarchies' efforts to reform colonial policies. As European authorities swept away colonial institutions and long-established political practices without consultation, colonial residents had to acknowledge that their status as colonies meant perpetual subordination to European rulers. Among people compelled to recognize this structural dependence and inferiority, the idea that government authority ultimately rested on the consent of the governed was potentially explosive.

In Europe and the colonies, many intellectuals resisted the Enlightenment, seeing it as a dangerous assault on the authority of the church and monarchy. This Counter Enlightenment was most influential in France and other Catholic nations. Its adherents argued the importance of faith to human happiness and social well-being. They also emphasized duty and obligation to the community of believers in opposition to the concern for

Beer Street (1751) This engraving by William Hogarth shows an idealized London street scene where beer drinking is associated with manly strength, good humor, and prosperity. The self-satisfied corpulent figure in the left foreground has been reading a copy of the king's speech to Parliament. We can imagine him offering a running commentary to his drinking companions as he reads. (The Art Archive)

individual rights and individual fulfillment common in the works of the Enlightenment. Most importantly for the politics of the era, they rejected their enemies' enthusiasm for change and utopianism, reminding their readers of human fallibility and the importance of history. While the central ideas of the Enlightenment gained strength across the nineteenth century, the Counter Enlightenment provided the ideological roots of both conservatism and popular antidemocratic movements.

Folk Cultures and Popular Protest

While intellectuals and the reforming royal courts of Europe debated the rational and secular enthusiasms of the Enlightenment, most people in Western society remained loyal to competing cultural values grounded in the preindustrial past. These regionally distinct folk cultures were framed by the memory of shared local historical experience and nourished by religious practices encouraging emotional release. They emphasized the obligations that people had to each other and local, rather than national, loyalties. Though never formally articulated, these cultural traditions composed a coherent expression of the mutual rights and obligations connecting the people and their rulers. Rulers who violated the constraints of these understandings were likely to face violent opposition.

In the eighteenth century, European monarchs sought to increase their authority and to centralize power by reforming tax collection, judicial practice, and public administration. Although monarchs viewed these changes as reforms, the common people often saw them as violations of sacred customs and sometimes expressed their outrage in bread riots, tax protests, and attacks on royal officials. These violent actions were not efforts to overturn traditional authority but were instead efforts to preserve custom and precedent. In Spain and the Spanish colonies, for example, protesting mobs commonly asserted the apparently contradictory slogan "Long live the King. Death to bad government." They expressed loyalty to and love for their monarch while at the same time assaulting his officials and preventing the implementation of changes to long-established customs.

Folk cultures were threatened by other kinds of reform as well. Rationalist reformers of the Enlightenment sought to bring order and discipline to the citizenry by banning or by altering the numerous popular cultural traditions—such as harvest festivals, religious holidays, and country fairs—that enlivened the drudgery of everyday life. These events were popular celebrations of sexuality and individuality as well as opportunities for masked and costumed celebrants to mock the greed, pretension, and foolishness of government officials, the wealthy, and the clergy. Hard drinking, gambling, and blood sports like cockfighting and bearbaiting were popular in this preindustrial mass culture. Because these customs were viewed as corrupt and decadent by reformers influenced by the Enlightenment, governments undertook efforts to substitute civic rituals, patriotic anniversaries, and institutions of self-improvement. These challenges to custom—like the efforts at political reform—often provoked protests, rebellions, and riots.

The efforts of ordinary men and women to resist the growth of government power and the imposition of new cultural forms provide an important political undercurrent to much of the revolutionary agitation and conflict between 1750 and 1850. Spontaneous popular uprisings and protests punctuated nearly every effort at reform in the eighteenth century. But these popular actions gained revolutionary potential only when they coincided with ideological divisions and conflicts within the governing class itself. In America and France the old order was swept away when the protests and rebellions of the rural and urban poor coincided with the appearance of revolutionary leaders who followed Enlightenment ideals in efforts to create secular republican states. Likewise, the slave rebellion in Saint Domingue (Haiti) achieved revolutionary potential when it attracted the support of black freedmen and disaffected poor whites radicalized by news of the French Revolution.

The American Revolution, 1775–1800

In British North America, clumsy efforts to reform colonial tax policy to cover rising defense expenditures and to diminish the power of elected colonial legislatures outraged a populace accustomed to greater local autonomy. Once begun, the American Revolution ushered in a century-long process of political and cultural transformation in Europe and the Americas. By the end of this revolutionary century the authority of monarchs had been swept away or limited by constitutions, and religion had lost its dominating place in Western intellectual life. Moreover, the medieval idea of a social order determined by birth had been replaced by a capitalist vision that emphasized competition and social mobility.

Frontiers and Taxes

After defeating the French in 1763, the British government faced two related problems in its North American colonies. As settlers pushed west into Amerindian lands, the government saw the likelihood of renewed conflict and rising military expenses. Already burdened with heavy debts from the French and Indian War, Britain tried to limit settler pressure on Amerindian lands and get colonists to shoulder more of the costs of imperial defense and colonial administration.

In the Great Lakes region the British tried to contain costs by reducing the prices paid for furs and refusing to honor the French practice of giving gifts and paying rent for frontier forts to Amerindian communities that had become dependent on European trade goods, especially firearms, gunpowder, textiles, and alcohol. When the British forced down the trade value of furs, Amerindians had to hunt more aggressively to get the volume of commodities they required, putting new pressures on the environment and endangering some species. The situation got worse as settlers and white trappers pushed across the Appalachians to compete with indigenous hunters.

At the end of the Seven Years War (see Chapter 18), Pontiac, an Ottawa chief, led a broad alliance of native peoples that drove the British military from western outposts and raided settled areas of Virginia and Pennsylvania. Although this Amerindian alliance was defeated within a year, the potential for new violence existed all along the frontier.

The British government's panicked reaction was the Proclamation of 1763, which sought to establish an effective western limit for settlement, throwing into question the claims of thousands of established farmers without effectively protecting Amerindian land. No one was satisfied. In 1774 the British government annexed disputed western territory to the province of Quebec, thus denying eastern colonies the authority to distribute additional lands.

Frontier issues increased hostility and suspicion between the British government and many of the colonists but did not directly lead to a breach. However, when the British government sought relief from the cost of imperial wars with a campaign of fiscal reforms and new taxes, it sparked a political confrontation that would lead to rebellion. New commercial regulations increased the cost of foreign molasses and endangered New England's profitable trade with Spanish and French Caribbean sugar colonies. The colonial practice of issuing paper money, a custom made necessary by the colonies' chronic balance-of-payments deficits, was outlawed. Colonial legislatures formally protested these measures, and angry colonists organized boycotts of British goods.

The Stamp Act of 1765, which imposed a tax, to be paid in scarce coin, on all legal documents, newspapers, pamphlets, and nearly all other printed material, proved incendiary. Propertied colonists, including holders of high office and members of the colonial elite, now assumed leading roles in protests, using fiery political language that identified Britain's rulers as "parricides" and "tyrants." Women from many of the most prominent colonial families organized boycotts of British goods. The production of homespun textiles by colonial women now became a patriotic enterprise. A young girl in Boston proclaimed that she was a "daughter of liberty" because she had learned to spin.[1] Organizations such as the Sons of Liberty held public meetings, intimidated royal officials, and developed committees to enforce the boycotts. The combination of violent protest and trade boycott forced the repeal of the Stamp Act, but new taxes and duties were soon imposed, and Parliament sent British troops to quell urban riots. One indignant woman later sent her poignant perception of this injustice to a British officer:

The Tarring and Feathering of a British Official, 1774 This illustration from a British periodical shows the unfortunate John Malcomb, commissioner of customs at Boston. By the mid-1770s British periodicals were focusing public opinion on mob violence and the breakdown of public order in the colonies. British critics of colonial political protests viewed the demand for liberty as little more than an excuse for mob violence. (The Granger Collection, New York)

> [T]he most ignorant peasant knows, and [it] is clear to the weakest capacity, that no man has the right to take their money without their consent. The supposition is ridiculous and absurd, as none but highwaymen and robbers attempt it. Can you, my friend, reconcile it with your own good sense, that a body of men in Great Britain, who have little intercourse with America . . . shall invest themselves with a power to command our lives and properties [?][2]

New colonial boycotts cut the importation of British goods by two-thirds. Angry colonists also destroyed property and bullied or attacked royal officials. British authorities reacted by threatening traditional liberties, even dissolving the colonial legislature of Massachusetts, and by dispatching two regiments of soldiers to reestablish control of Boston's streets. Support for a complete break with Britain grew after March 5, 1770, when a British force fired on an angry Boston crowd, killing five civilians. This "Boston Massacre," which seemed to expose the naked force on which colonial rule rested, radicalized public opinion throughout the colonies.

Parliament attempted to calm public opinion by repealing some taxes and duties, but then stumbled into another crisis by granting a monopoly for importing tea to the colonies to the British East India Company, raising anew the constitutional issue of Parliament's right to tax the colonies. The crisis came to a head when protesters dumped tea worth £10,000 into Boston harbor. Britain responded by appointing a military man, Thomas Gage, as governor of Massachusetts and by closing the port of Boston. Public order in Boston now depended on British troops, and public administration was in the hands of a general. This militarization of colonial government in Boston undermined Britain's constitutional authority and made a military test of strength inevitable.

The Course of Revolution, 1775–1783

As the crisis mounted, patriot leaders created new governing bodies that made laws, appointed justices, and even took control of colonial militias, thus effectively deposing many British governors, judges, and customs officers. Simultaneously, radical leaders organized crowds to intimidate loyalists—people who were pro-British—and organized women to enforce boycotts of British goods.

When representatives elected to the Continental Congress met in Philadelphia in 1775, patriot militia had met British troops at Lexington and Concord, Massachusetts (see Map 22.1), and blood had already been shed. Events were propelling the colonies toward revolution. Congress assumed the powers of government, creating a currency and organizing an army led by **George Washington** (1732–1799), a Virginia planter who had served in the French and Indian War.

Popular support for independence was given a hard edge by the angry rhetoric of thousands of street-corner speakers and the inflammatory pamphlet *Common Sense,* written by Thomas Paine, a recent immigrant from England. Paine's pamphlet sold 120,000 copies. On July 4, 1776, Congress approved the Declaration of Independence, the document that proved to be the most enduring statement of the revolutionary era's ideology:

> We hold these truths to be self evident: That all men are created equal; that they are endowed by their creator with certain unalienable rights; that among these are life, liberty and the pursuit of happiness; that, to secure these rights, governments are instituted among men, deriving their just powers from the consent of the governed.

The Declaration's affirmation of popular sovereignty and individual rights would influence the language of revolution and popular protest around the world.

Hoping to shore up British authority, Great Britain sent additional military forces to pacify the colonies. By 1778 British land forces numbered 50,000 and were supported by 30,000 German mercenaries. This military commitment proved futile. Despite the existence of a large loyalist community, the British army found it difficult to control the countryside. Although British forces won most of the battles, Washington slowly built a competent Continental army as well as the civilian support networks that provided supplies and financial resources.

The real problem for the British government was its inability to discover a compromise solution that would satisfy colonial grievances. Half-hearted efforts to resolve the bitter conflict over taxes failed, and a later offer to roll back the clock and reestablish the administrative arrangements of 1763 made little headway. Overconfidence and poor leadership prevented the British from finding a political solution before revolutionary institutions were in place and the armies engaged. By allowing confrontation to occur, the British government lost the opportunity to mobilize and give direction to the large numbers of loyalists and pacifists in the colonies.

Along the Canadian border, both sides solicited Amerindians as potential allies and feared them as potential enemies. For over a hundred years, members of the powerful Iroquois Confederacy—Mohawk, Oneida, Onondaga, Cayuga, Seneca, and (after 1722) Tuscarora—had protected their traditional lands with a combination of diplomacy and warfare, playing a role in all the colonial wars of the eighteenth century. Just as the American Revolution forced neighbors and families to join the rebels or remain loyal, it divided the Iroquois, who fought on both sides.

The Mohawk proved to be the most valuable British allies among the Iroquois. Their loyalist leader **Joseph Brant** (Thayendanegea°) organized Britain's most potent fighting force along the Canadian border. His raids along the northern frontier earned him the title "Monster" Brant, but he was actually a man who moved easily between European and Amerindian cultures. Educated by missionaries, he was fluent in English and helped translate Protestant religious tracts into Mohawk. He was tied to many of the wealthiest loyalist families through his sister, formerly the mistress of Sir William Johnson, Britain's superintendent of Indian affairs for North America. Brant had traveled to London, had an audience with George III, (r. 1760–1820) and had been embraced by London's aristocratic society.

The defeat in late 1777 of Britain's general John Burgoyne by General Horatio Gates at Saratoga, New York, put the future of the Mohawk at risk. This victory, which gave heart to patriot forces that had recently suffered a string of defeats, led to destructive attacks on Iroquois villages. Brant's supporters fought on to the end of the war, but patriot victories along the frontier curtailed their political and military power. Brant eventually joined the loyalist exodus to Canada. For these Ameri-

---

Thayendanegea (ta YEHN dah NEY geh ah)

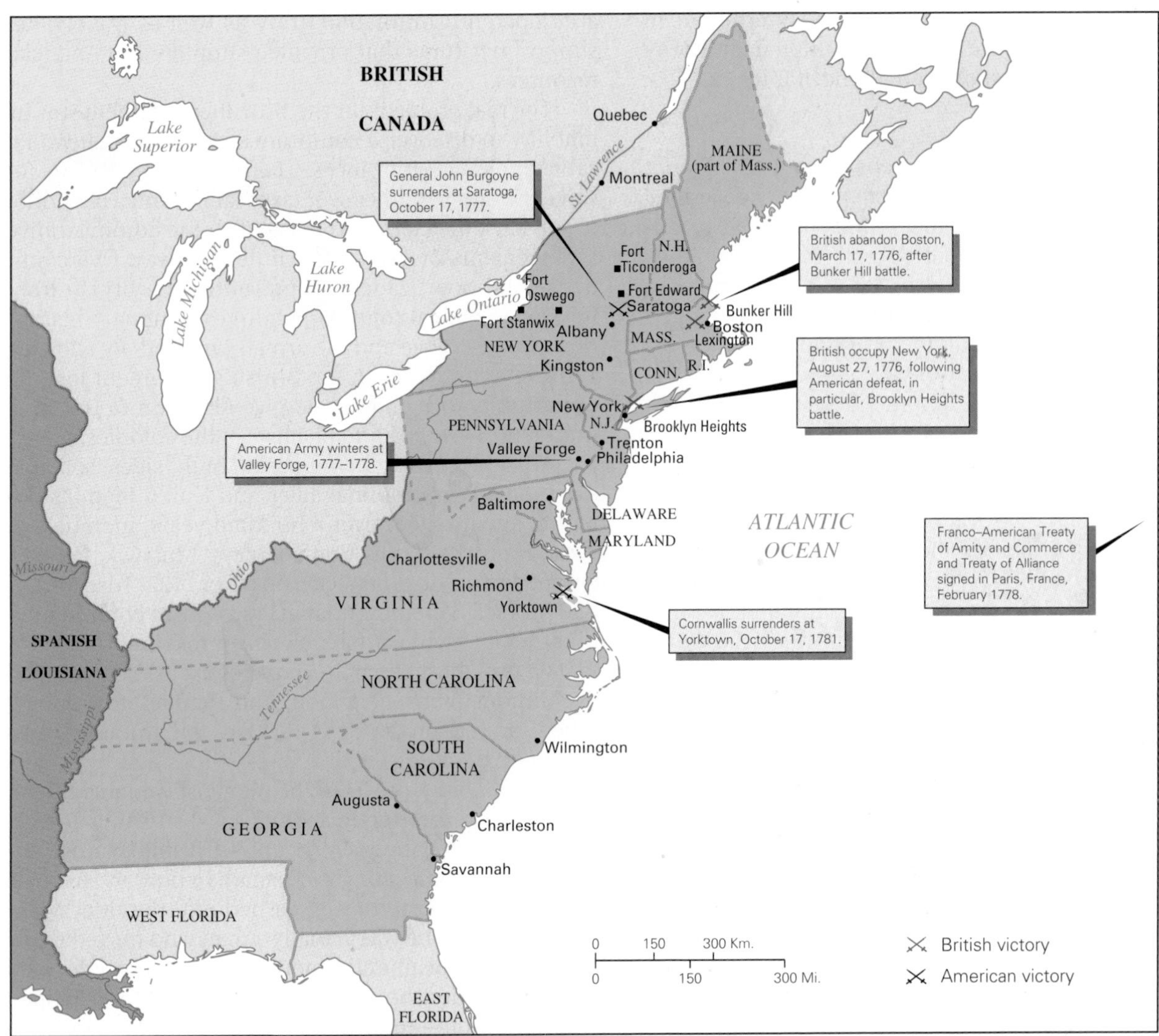

Map 22.1 The American Revolutionary War The British army won most of the major battles, and British troops held most of the major cities. Even so, the American revolutionaries eventually won a comprehensive military and political victory.

cans the revolution did not mean the protection of life and property.

The British defeat at Saratoga also convinced France to enter the war as an ally of the United States in 1778. French military help proved crucial, supplying American forces and forcing the British to defend their colonies in the Caribbean. The French contribution was most clear in the final decisive battle, fought at Yorktown, Virginia (see Map 22.1). With the American army supported by French soldiers and a French fleet, General Charles Cornwallis surrendered to Washington as the British military band played "The World Turned Upside-Down."

This victory effectively ended the war. The Continental Congress sent representatives to the peace conference that followed with instructions to work in tandem with the French. Believing that France was more concerned with containing British power than with guaranteeing a strong United States, America's peace delegation chose to negotiate directly with Britain and gained a generous settlement. The Treaty of Paris (1783) granted unconditional independence and established generous boundaries for the former colonies. In return the United States promised to repay prewar debts due to British merchants and to allow loyalists to recover property confiscated by patriot forces. In the end, loyalists were poorly treated, and thousands of them decided to leave for Canada.

The Construction of Republican Institutions, to 1800

Even before the Declaration of Independence, many colonies had created new governments independent of British colonial authorities. After independence leaders in each of the new states (as the former colonies were called) summoned constitutional conventions to draft formal charters and submitted the results to voters for ratification. Europeans were fascinated by the drafting of written constitutions and by the formal ratification of these constitutions by a vote of the people. Many of these documents were quickly translated and published in Europe. Remembering conflicts between royal governors and colonial legislatures, the authors of state constitutions placed severe limits on executive authority but granted legislatures greater powers than in colonial times. Many state constitutions also included bills of rights to provide further protection against government tyranny.

An effective constitution for the new national government was developed with difficulty. The Second Continental Congress sent the Articles of Confederation—the first constitution of the United States—to the states for approval in 1777, but it was not accepted by all the states until 1781. It created a one-house legislature in which each state was granted a single vote. A simple majority of the thirteen states was sufficient to pass minor legislation, but nine votes were necessary for declaring war, imposing taxes, and coining or borrowing money. Executive power was exercised by committees, not by a president. Given the intended weakness of this government, it is remarkable that it successfully organized the human and material resources to defeat Great Britain.

With the coming of peace, many of the most powerful political figures in the United States recognized that the Confederation was unable to enforce unpopular requirements of the peace treaty such as the recognition of loyalist property claims, the payment of prewar debts, and even the payment of military salaries and pensions to veterans. In September 1786 Virginia invited the other states to discuss the government's failure to deal with trade issues. This led to a call for a new convention to meet in Philadelphia nine months later. A rebellion led by Revolutionary War veterans in western Massachusetts gave the assembling delegates a sense of urgency.

The **Constitutional Convention,** which began meeting in May 1787, achieved a nonviolent second American Revolution. The delegates pushed aside the announced purpose of the convention—"to render the constitution of the federal government adequate to the exigencies of the union"—and secretly undertook the creation of a new constitution. George Washington was elected presiding officer. His reputation and popularity provided a solid foundation on which the delegates could contemplate an alternative political model.

Debate focused on representation, electoral procedures, executive powers, and the relationship between the federal government and the states. Compromise solutions included distribution of political power among the executive, legislative, and judicial branches and the division of authority between the federal government and the states. The final compromise provided for a two-house legislature: the lower house (the House of Representatives) to be elected directly by voters and the upper house (the Senate) to be elected by state legislatures. The chief executive—the president—was to be elected indirectly by "electors" selected by ballot in the states.

Although the U.S. Constitution created the most democratic government of the era, only a minority of the adult population was given full rights. In some northern states where large numbers of free blacks had fought with patriot forces, there was some hostility to the continuation of slavery, but southern leaders were able to protect the institution. Although slaves were denied participation in the political process, slave states were permitted to count three-fifths of the slave population in the calculations that determined the number of congressional representatives, thus multiplying the political power of the slave-owning class. Southern delegates also gained a twenty-year continuation of the slave trade to 1808 and a fugitive slave clause that required all states to return runaway slaves to their masters.

Women were powerfully affected by their participation in revolutionary politics and by the changes in the economy brought on by the break with Britain. They had led prewar boycotts and had organized relief and charitable organizations during the war. Some had served in the military as nurses, and a smaller number had joined the ranks disguised as men. Nevertheless, they were denied political rights in the new republic. Only New Jersey did not specifically bar women from voting, granting the right to vote to all free residents who met modest property-holding requirements. As a result, women and

African-Americans who met property requirements were able to vote in New Jersey until 1807, when lawmakers eliminated this right.

THE FRENCH REVOLUTION, 1789–1815

The French Revolution undermined traditional monarchy as well as the power of the Catholic Church and the hereditary aristocracy but, unlike the American Revolution, did not create an enduring form of representative democracy. The colonial revolution in North America, however, did not confront so directly the entrenched privileges of an established church, monarchy, and aristocracy, and the American Revolution produced no symbolic drama comparable to the public beheading of the French king Louis XVI in early 1793. Among its achievements, the French Revolution expanded mass participation in political life and radicalized the democratic tradition inherited from the English and American experiences. But in the end, the passions unleashed by revolutionary events in France could not be sustained, and popular demagogues and the dictatorship of Napoleon stalled democratic reform.

Parisian Stocking Mender The poor lived very difficult lives. This woman uses a discarded wine barrel as a shop where she mends socks. (Private collection)

French Society and Fiscal Crisis

French society was divided into three groups. The clergy, called the First Estate, numbered about 130,000 in a nation of 28 million. The Catholic Church owned about 10 percent of the nation's land and extracted substantial amounts of wealth from the economy in the form of tithes and ecclesiastical fees. Despite its substantial wealth, the church was exempted from nearly all taxes. The clergy was organized hierarchically, and members of the hereditary nobility held almost all the upper positions in the church.

The 300,000 members of the nobility, the Second Estate, controlled about 30 percent of the land and retained ancient rights on much of the rest. Nobles held the vast majority of high administrative, judicial, military, and church positions. Though traditionally barred from some types of commercial activity, nobles were important participants in wholesale trade, banking, manufacturing, and mining. Like the clergy, this estate was hierarchical: important differences in wealth, power, and outlook separated the higher from the lower nobility. The nobility was also a highly permeable class: the Second Estate in the eighteenth century saw an enormous infusion of wealthy commoners who purchased administrative and judicial offices that conferred noble status.

The Third Estate included everyone else, from wealthy financier to homeless beggar. The bourgeoisie°, or middle class, grew rapidly in the eighteenth century. There were three times as many members of this class in 1774, when Louis XVI took the throne, as there had been in 1715, at the end of Louis XIV's reign. Commerce, finance, and manufacturing accounted for much of the wealth of the Third Estate. Wealthy commoners also owned nearly a third of the nation's land. This literate and socially ambitious class supported an expanding publishing industry, subsidized the fine arts, and purchased many of the extravagant new homes being built in Paris and other cities.

bourgeoisie (boor-zwah-ZEE)

Peasants accounted for 80 percent of the French population. Artisans and other skilled workers, small shopkeepers and peddlers, and small landowners held a more privileged position in society. They owned some property and lived decently when crops were good and prices stable. By 1780 poor harvests had increased their cost of living and led to a decline in consumer demand for their products. They were rich enough to fear the loss of their property and status, well educated enough to be aware of the growing criticism of the king, but too poor and marginalized to influence policy.

The nation's poor were a large, growing, and troublesome sector. The poverty and vulnerability of peasant families forced younger children to seek seasonal work away from home and led many to crime and beggary. That raids by roving vagabonds threatened isolated farms was one measure of this social dislocation. In Paris and other French cities the vile living conditions and unhealthy diet of the working poor were startling to visitors from other European nations. Urban streets swarmed with beggars and prostitutes. Paris alone had 25,000 prostitutes in 1760. The wretchedness of the French poor is perhaps best indicated by the growing problem of child abandonment. On the eve of the French Revolution at least 40,000 children a year were given up by their parents. The convenient fiction was that these children would be adopted; in reality the majority died of neglect.

Unable to afford decent housing, obtain steady employment, or protect their children, the poor periodically erupted in violent protest and rage. In the countryside violence was often the reaction when the nobility or clergy increased dues and fees. In towns and cities an increase in the price of bread often provided the spark, for bread prices largely determined the quality of life of the poor. These explosive episodes, however, were not revolutionary in character. The remedies sought were conventional and immediate rather than structural and long-term. That was to change when the Crown tried to solve its fiscal crisis.

The expenses of the War of the Austrian Succession began the crisis. Louis XV (r. 1715–1774) first tried to impose new taxes on the nobility and on other groups that in the past had enjoyed exemptions. This effort failed in the face of widespread protest and the refusal of the Parlement of Paris, a court that heard appeals from local courts throughout France, to register the new tax. The crisis deepened when debts from the Seven Years War compelled the king to impose emergency fiscal measures. Again, the king met resistance from the Parlement of Paris. In 1768 frustrated authorities exiled the members of that Parlement and pushed through a series of unpopular fiscal measures. When the twenty-two-year-old Louis XVI assumed the throne in 1774, he attempted to gain popular support by recalling the exiled members of the Parlement of Paris, but he soon learned that provincial parlements had also come to see themselves as having a constitutional power to check any growth in monarchial authority.

In 1774 Louis's chief financial adviser warned that the government could barely afford to operate; as he put it, "the first gunshot [act of war] will drive the state to bankruptcy." Despite this warning, the French took on the heavy burden of supporting the American Revolution, delaying collapse by borrowing enormous sums and disguising the growing debt in misleading fiscal accounts. By the end of the war with Britain, more than half of France's national budget was required to service the resulting debt. It soon became clear that fiscal reforms and new taxes, not new loans, were necessary.

In 1787 the desperate king called an Assembly of Notables to approve a radical and comprehensive reform of the economy and fiscal policy. Despite the fact that the members of this assembly were selected by the king's advisers from the high nobility, the judiciary, and the clergy, it proved unwilling to act as a rubber stamp for the proposed reforms or new taxes. Instead, these representatives of France's most privileged classes sought to protect their interests by questioning the competence of the king and his ministers to supervise the nation's affairs.

Protest Turns to Revolution, 1789–1792

In frustration, the king dismissed the Notables and attempted to implement some reforms on his own, but his effort was met by an increasingly hostile judiciary and by popular demonstrations. Because the king was unable to extract needed tax concessions from the French elite, he was forced to call the **Estates General,** the French national legislature, which had not met since 1614. The narrow self-interest and greed of the rich—who would not tolerate an increase in their taxes—rather than the grinding poverty of the common people had created the conditions for political revolution.

In late 1788 and early 1789 members of the three estates came together throughout the nation to discuss grievances and elect representatives who would meet at Versailles°. The Third Estate's representatives were mostly men of property, but there was anger directed against the king's ministers and an inclination to move France toward constitutional monarchy with an elected

Versailles (vuhr-SIGH)

Parisians Storm the Bastille This depiction of the storming of the Bastille on July 14, 1789, was painted by an artist who witnessed the epochal event still celebrated by the French as a national holiday. (Photos12.com-ARJ)

legislature. Many nobles and members of the clergy sympathized with the reform agenda of the Third Estate, but deep internal divisions over procedural and policy issues limited the power of the First and the Second Estates.

Traditionally, the three estates met separately, and a positive vote by two of the three was required for action. Tradition, however, was quickly overturned when the Third Estate refused to conduct business until the king ordered the other two estates to sit with it in a single body. During a six-week period of stalemate, many parish priests from the First Estate began to meet with the commoners. When this expanded Third Estate declared itself the **National Assembly,** the king and his advisers recognized that the reformers intended to force them to accept a constitutional monarchy.

After being locked out of their meeting place, the Third Estate appropriated an indoor tennis court and pledged to write a constitution. The Oath of the Tennis Court ended Louis's vain hope that he could limit the agenda to fiscal reform. The king's effort to solve the nation's fiscal crisis was being connected in unpredictable ways to the central ideas of the era: the people were sovereign, and the legitimacy of political institutions and individual rulers ultimately depended on their carrying out the people's will. Louis prepared for a confrontation with the National Assembly by moving military forces to Versailles. Before he could act, the people of Paris intervened.

A succession of bad harvests beginning in 1785 had propelled bread prices upward throughout France and provoked an economic depression as demand for nonessential goods collapsed. By the time the Estates General met, nearly a third of the Parisian work force was unemployed. Hunger and anger marched hand in hand through working-class neighborhoods.

When the people of Paris heard that the king was massing troops in Versailles to arrest the representatives, crowds of common people began to seize arms and mobilize. On July 14, 1789, a crowd searching for military supplies attacked the Bastille, a medieval fortress used as a prison. The futile defense of the Bastille° cost ninety-eight lives before its garrison surrendered. Enraged, the attackers hacked the commander to death and then paraded through the city with his head and that of Paris's chief magistrate stuck on pikes.

These events coincided with uprisings by peasants in the country. Peasants sacked manor houses and destroyed documents that recorded their traditional obligations. They refused to pay taxes and dues to landowners and seized common lands. Forced to recognize the fury raging through rural areas, the National Assembly voted to end traditional obligations and to reform the tax system. Having forced acceptance of their narrow agenda, the peasants ceased their revolt.

These popular uprisings strengthened the hand of the National Assembly in its dealings with the king. One manifestation of this altered relationship was passage of the **Declaration of the Rights of Man.** There were clear similarities between the language of this declaration and the U.S. Declaration of Independence. Indeed, Thomas Jefferson, who had written the American document, was U.S. ambassador to Paris and offered his opinion to those drafting the French statement. The French declaration, however, was more sweeping in its language than the American. Among the enumerated natural rights were "liberty, property, security, and resistance to oppression." The Declaration of the Rights of Man also guaranteed free expression of ideas, equality before the law, and representative government.

While delegates debated political issues in Versailles, the economic crisis worsened in Paris. Women employed in the garment industry and in small-scale retail businesses were particularly hard hit. Because the working women of Paris faced high food prices everyday as they struggled to feed their families, their anger had a hard edge. Public markets became political arenas where the urban poor met daily in angry assembly. Here the revolutionary link between the material deprivation of the French poor and the political aspirations of the French bourgeoisie was forged.

On October 5, market women organized a crowd of thousands to march the 12 miles (19 kilometers) to Versailles. Once there, they forced their way into the National Assembly to demand action from the frightened representatives: "the point is that we want bread." The crowd then entered the royal apartments, killed some of the king's guards, and searched for Queen Marie Antoinette°, whom they loathed as a symbol of extravagance. Eventually, the crowd demanded that the royal family return to Paris. Preceded by the heads of two aristocrats carried on pikes and hauling away the palace's supply of flour, the triumphant crowd escorted the royal family to Paris.

With the king's ability to resist democratic change overcome by the Paris crowd, the National Assembly achieved a radically restructured French society in the next two years. It passed a new constitution that dramatically limited monarchial power and abolished the nobility as a hereditary class. Economic reforms swept away monopolies and trade barriers within France. The Legislative Assembly (the new constitution's name for the National Assembly) seized church lands to use as collateral for a new paper currency, and priests—who were to be elected—were put on the state payroll. When the government tried to force priests to take a loyalty oath, however, many Catholics joined a growing counterrevolutionary movement.

At first, many European monarchs had welcomed the weakening of the French king, but by 1791 Austria and Prussia threatened to intervene in support of the monarchy. The Legislative Assembly responded by declaring war. Although the war went badly at first for French forces, people across France responded patriotically to foreign invasions, forming huge new volunteer armies and mobilizing national resources to meet the challenge. By the end of 1792 French armies had gained a stalemate with the foreign forces.

The Terror, 1793–1794

In this period of national crisis and foreign threat, the French Revolution entered its most radical phase. A failed effort by the king and queen to escape from Paris and find foreign allies cost the king any remaining popular support. As foreign armies crossed into France, his behavior was increasingly viewed as treasonous. On August 10, 1792, a crowd similar to the one that had marched on Versailles invaded his palace in Paris and forced the king to seek protection in the Legislative Assembly. The Assembly suspended the king, ordered his imprisonment, and called for the formation of a new National Convention to be elected by the vote of all men.

Rumors of counterrevolutionary plots kept working-class neighborhoods in an uproar. In September mobs surged through the city's prisons, killing nearly half the prisoners. Swept along by popular passion, the newly elected National Convention convicted Louis XVI of treason, sentencing him to death and proclaiming France a republic. The guillotine ended the king's life in January

Bastille (bass-TEEL) **Antoinette** (ann twah-NET)

Playing Cards from the French Revolution Even playing cards could be used to attack the aristocracy and Catholic Church. In this pack of cards, "Equality" and "Liberty" replaced kings and queens. (Jean-Loup Charmet/The Bridgeman Art Library)

1793. Invented in the spirit of the era as a more humane way to execute the condemned, this machine was to become the bloody symbol of the revolution. These events helped by February 1793 to precipitate a wider war with France now confronting nearly all of Europe's major powers.

The National Convention—the new legislature of the new First Republic of France—convened in September. Almost all of its members were from the middle class, and nearly all were **Jacobins**°—the most uncompromising democrats. Deep political differences, however, separated moderate Jacobins—called "Girondists°," after a region in southern France—and radicals known as "the Mountain." Members of the Mountain—so named because their seats were on the highest level in the assembly hall—were more sympathetic than the Girondists to the demands of the Parisian working class and more impatient with parliamentary procedure and constitutional constraints on government action. The Mountain came to be dominated by **Maximilien Robespierre°**, a young, little-known lawyer from the provinces who had been influenced by Rousseau's ideas.

With the French economy still in crisis and Paris suffering from inflation, high unemployment, and scarcity, Robespierre used the popular press and political clubs to forge an alliance with the volatile Parisian working class. His growing strength in the streets allowed him to purge the National Convention of his enemies and to restructure the government. Executive power was placed in the hands of the newly formed Committee of Public Safety, which created special courts to seek out and punish domestic enemies.

Jacobin (JAK-uh-bin) **Girondist** (juh-RON-dist) **Robespierre** (ROBES-pee-air)

Among the groups that lost ground were the active feminists of the Parisian middle class and the working-class women who had sought the right to bear arms in defense of the Revolution. These women had provided decisive leadership at crucial times, helping propel the Revolution toward widened suffrage and a more democratic structure. Armed women had actively participated in every confrontation with conservative forces. It is ironic that the National Convention—the revolutionary era's most radical legislative body, elected by universal male suffrage—chose to repress the militant feminist forces that had prepared the ground for its creation.

Faced with rebellion in the provinces and foreign invasion, Robespierre and his allies unleashed a period of repression called the Reign of Terror (1793–1794) (see Diversity and Dominance: Robespierre and Wollstonecraft Defend and Explain the Terror). During the Terror, approximately 40,000 people were executed or died in prison, and another 300,000 were imprisoned. New actions against the clergy were also approved, including the provocative measure of forcing priests to marry. Even time was subject to revolutionary change. A new republican calendar created twelve thirty-day months divided into ten-day weeks. Sunday, with its Christian meanings, disappeared from the calendar.

By spring 1794 the Revolution was secure from foreign and domestic enemies, but repression, now institutionalized, continued. Among the victims were some who had been Robespierre's closest political collaborators during the early stage of the Terror. The execution of these former allies prepared the way for Robespierre's own fall by undermining the sense of invulnerability that had secured the loyalty of his remaining partisans in the National Convention. After French victories eliminated the immediate foreign threat, conservatives in the

Convention felt secure enough to vote for the arrest of Robespierre on July 27, 1794. Over the next two days, Robespierre and nearly a hundred of his remaining allies were executed by guillotine.

Reaction and Dictatorship, 1795–1815

Purged of Robespierre's collaborators, the Convention began to undo the radical reforms. It removed many of the emergency economic controls that had been holding down prices and protecting the working class. Gone also was toleration for violent popular demonstrations. When the Paris working class rose in protest in 1795, the Convention approved the use of overwhelming military force. Another retreat from radical objectives was signaled when the Catholic Church was permitted to regain much of its former influence. The church's confiscated wealth, however, was not returned. A more conservative constitution was also ratified. It protected property, established a voting process that reduced the power of the masses, and created a new executive authority, the Directory. Once installed in power, however, the Directory proved unable to end the foreign wars or solve domestic economic problems.

After losing the election of 1797 the Directory suspended the results. The republican phase of the Revolution was clearly dead. Legitimacy was now based on coercive power rather than on elections. Two years later, **Napoleon Bonaparte** (1769–1821), a brilliant young general in the French army, seized power. Just as the American and French Revolutions had been the start of the modern democratic tradition, the military intervention that brought Napoleon to power in 1799 marked the advent of another modern form of government: popular authoritarianism.

The American and French Revolutions had resulted in part from conflicts over representation. If the people were sovereign, what institutions best expressed popular will? In the United States the answer was to expand the electorate and institute representative government. The French Revolution had taken a different direction with the Reign of Terror. Interventions on the floor of the National Convention by market women and soldiers, the presence of common people at revolutionary tribunals and at public executions, and expanded military service were all forms of political communication that temporarily satisfied the French people's desire to influence their government. Napoleon tamed these forms of political expression to organize Europe's first popular dictatorship. He succeeded because his military reputation promised order to a society exhausted by a decade of crisis, turmoil, and bloodshed.

In contrast to the National Convention, Napoleon proved capable of realizing France's dream of dominating Europe and providing effective protection for persons and property at home. Negotiations with the Catholic Church led to the Concordat of 1801. This agreement gave French Catholics the right to freely practice their religion, and it recognized the French government's authority to nominate bishops and retain priests on the state payroll. In his comprehensive rewriting of French law, the Civil Code of 1804, Napoleon won the support of the peasantry and of the middle class by asserting two basic principles inherited from the moderate first stage of the French Revolution: equality in law and protection of property. Even some members of the nobility became supporters after Napoleon declared himself emperor and France an empire in 1804. However, the discrimination against women that had begun during the Terror was extended by the Napoleonic Civil Code. Women were denied basic political rights and were able to participate in the economy only with the guidance and supervision of their fathers and husbands.

While providing personal security, the Napoleonic system denied or restricted many individual rights. Free speech and free expression were limited. Criticism of the government, viewed as subversive, was proscribed, and most opposition newspapers disappeared. Spies and informers directed by the minister of police enforced these limits to political freedom. Thousands of the regime's enemies and critics were questioned or detained in the name of domestic tranquility.

Ultimately, the Napoleonic system depended on the success of French arms and French diplomacy (see Map 22.2). From Napoleon's assumption of power until his fall, no single European state could defeat the French military. Even powerful alliances like that of Austria and Prussia were brushed aside with humiliating defeats and forced to become allies of France. Only Britain, protected by its powerful navy, remained able to thwart Napoleon's plans to dominate Europe. His effort to mobilize forces for an invasion of Britain failed in late 1805 when the British navy defeated the French and allied Spanish fleets off the coast of Spain at the Battle of Trafalgar.

Desiring to again extend French power to the Americas, Napoleon invaded Portugal in 1807 and Spain in 1808. French armies soon became tied down in a costly conflict with Spanish and Portuguese patriots who had forged an alliance with the only available European power, Great Britain. Frustrated by events on the Iberian Peninsula and faced with a faltering economy, Napoleon made the fateful decision to invade Russia. In June 1812

Diversity and Dominance

Robespierre and Wollstonecraft Defend and Explain the Terror

Many Europeans who had initially been sympathetic to the French Revolution were repelled by the Terror. In 1793 and 1794 while France was at war with Austria, Prussia, Great Britain, Holland, and Spain about 2,600 people were executed in Paris, including the king and queen, members of the nobility, and Catholic clergy. The public nature of the judicial procedures and executions outraged many. Critics of the Revolution asked if these excesses were not worse than those committed by the French monarchy. Others defended the violence as necessary, arguing that the Terror had been provoked by enemies of the Revolution or was the consequence of earlier injustices.

The following two opinions date from 1794. Maximilien Robespierre was the head of the Committee of Public Safety, the effective head of the revolutionary government. Robespierre was a provincial lawyer who rose to power in Paris as the Revolution was radicalized. In the statement that follows he is unrepentant, arguing that violence was necessary in the defense of liberty. He made this statement on the eve of his political demise; in 1794 he was driven from power and executed by the revolutionary movement he had helped create.

Mary Wollstonecraft, an English intellectual and advocate for women's rights who was living in Paris at the time of the execution of Louis XVI, was troubled by the violence, and her discussion of these events is more an apology than a defense. She had published her famous A Vindication of the Rights of Woman *in 1792, after which she left for Paris. Wollstonecraft left Paris after war broke out between France and Britain. She remained an important force in European intellectual life until her death from complications of childbirth in 1797.*

MAXIMILIEN ROBESPIERRE, "ON THE MORAL AND POLITICAL PRINCIPLES OF DOMESTIC POLICY"

[L]et us deduce a great truth: the characteristic of popular government is confidence in the people and severity towards itself.

The whole development of our theory would end here if you had only to pilot the vessel of the Republic through calm waters; but the tempest roars, and the revolution imposes on you another task.

This great purity of the French revolution's basis, the very sublimity of its objective, is precisely what causes both our strength and our weakness. Our strength, because it gives to us truth's ascendancy over imposture, and the rights of the public interest over private interests; our weakness, because it rallies all vicious men against us, all those who in their hearts contemplated despoiling the people and all those who intend to let it be despoiled with impunity, both those who have rejected freedom as a personal calamity and those who have embraced the revolution as a career and the Republic as prey. Hence the defection of so many ambitious or greedy men who since the point of departure have abandoned us along the way because they did not begin the journey with the same destination in view. The two opposing spirits that have been represented in a struggle to rule nature might be said to be fighting in this great period of human history to fix irrevocably the world's destinies, and France is the scene of this fearful combat. Without, all the tyrants encircle you; within, all tyranny's friends conspire; they will conspire until hope is wrested from crime. We must smother the internal and external enemies of the Republic or perish with it; now in this situation, the first maxim of your policy ought to be to lead the people by reason and the people's enemies by terror.

If the spring of popular government in time of peace is virtue, the springs of popular government in revolution are at once virtue and terror: virtue, without which terror is fatal; terror, without which virtue is powerless. Terror is nothing other than justice, prompt, severe, inflexible; it is therefore an emanation of virtue; it is not so much a special principle as it is a consequence of the general principle of democracy applied to our country's most urgent needs.

It has been said that terror is the principle of despotic government. Does your government therefore resemble despotism? Yes, as the sword that gleams in the hands of the heroes of liberty resembles that with which the henchmen of tyranny are armed. Let the despot govern by terror his brutalized subjects; he is right, as a despot. Subdue by terror the enemies of liberty, and you will be right, as founders of the Republic. The government of the revolution is liberty's despotism against tyranny. Is force made only to protect crime? And is the thunderbolt not destined to strike the heads of the proud?

. . . Society owes protection only to peaceable citizens; the only citizens in the Republic are the republicans. For it, the royalists, the conspirators are only strangers or, rather, enemies. This terrible war waged by liberty against tyranny-is it not indivisible? Are the enemies within not the allies of the enemies without? The assassins who tear our country apart, the intriguers who buy the consciences that hold the people's mandate; the traitors who sell them; the mercenary pamphleteers hired to dishonor the people's cause, to kill public virtue, to stir up the fire of civil discord, and to prepare political counterrevolution by moral counterrevolution—are all those men less guilty or less dangerous than the tyrants whom they serve?

MARY WOLLSTONECRAFT, "AN HISTORICAL AND MORAL VIEW OF THE ORIGIN AND PROGRESS OF THE FRENCH REVOLUTION"

Weeping scarcely conscious that I weep, O France! Over the vestiges of thy former oppression, which, separating man from man with a fence of iron, sophisticated [complicated] all, and made many completely wretched; I tremble, lest I should meet some unfortunate being, fleeing from the despotism of licentious freedom, hearing the snap of the guillotine at his heels, merely because he was once noble, or has afforded an asylum to those whose only crime is their name—and, if my pen almost bound with eagerness to record the day that leveled the Bastille [an abbey used as a prison before the Revolution] with the dust, making the towers of despair tremble to their base, the recollection that still the abbey is appropriated to hold the victims of revenge and suspicion [she means that the Bastille remained a prison for those awaiting revolutionary justice]. . . .

Excuse for the Ferocity of the Parisians The deprivation of natural, equal, civil, and political rights reduced the most cunning the lower orders to practice fraud, and the rest to habits of stealing, audacious robberies, and murders. And why? Because the rich and poor were separated into bands of tyrants and slaves, and the retaliation of slaves is always terrible. In short, every sacred feeling, moral and divine, has been obliterated, and the dignity of man sullied, by a system of policy and jurisprudence as repugnant to reason as at variance with humanity.

The only excuse that can be made for the ferocity of the Parisians is then simply to observe that they had not any confidence in the laws, which they had always found to be merely cobwebs to catch small flies [the poor]. Accustomed to be punished themselves for every trifle, and often for only being in the way of the rich, or their parasites, when, in fact, had the Parisians seen the execution of a noble, or priest, though convicted of crimes beyond the daring of vulgar minds? When justice, or the law, is so partial, the day of retribution will come with the red sky of vengeance, to confound the innocent with the guilty. The mob were barbarous beyond the tiger's cruelty.

. . .

Let us cast our eyes over the history of man, and we shall scarcely find a page that is not tarnished by some foul deed or bloody transaction. Let us examine the catalogue of the vices of men in a savage state, and contrast them with those of men civilized; we shall find that a barbarian, considered as a moral being, is an angel, compared with the refined villain of artificial life. Let us investigate the causes which have produced this degeneracy, and we shall discover that they are those unjust plans of government which have been formed by peculiar circumstances in every part of the globe.

Then let us coolly and impartially contemplate the improvements which are gaining ground in the formation of principles of policy; and I flatter myself it will be allowed by every humane and considerate being that a political system more simple than has hitherto existed would effectually check those aspiring follies, which, by imitation, leading to vice, have banished from governments the very shadow of justice and magnanimity.

Thus had France grown up and sickened on the corruption of a state diseased. . . . it is only the philosophical eye, which looks into the nature and weighs the consequences of human actions, that will be able to discern the cause, which has produced so many dreadful effects.

QUESTIONS FOR ANALYSIS

1. **Why does Robespierre believe that revolution cannot tolerate diversity of opinion? Are his reasons convincing?**
2. **How does Robespierre distinguish the terror of despots from the terror of liberty?**
3. **How does Wollstonecraft explain the "ferocity" of the Parisians?**
4. **What does Wollstonecraft believe will come from this period of violence?**

Sources: Maximilien Robespierre, "On the Moral and Political Principles of Domestic Policy," February 5, 1794, *Modern History Sourcebook: Robespierre: Terror and Virtue, 1794, http://www.fordham.edu/halsall/mod/robespierre-terror.html*; Mary Wollstonecraft, "An Historical and Moral View of the Origin and Progress of the French Revolution," *A Mary Wollstonecraft Reader,* ed. Barbara H. Solomon and Paula S. Berggren (New York: New American Library, 1983), 374–375, 382–383.

Map 22.2 Napoleon's Europe, 1810 By 1810 Great Britain was the only remaining European power at war with Napoleon. Because of the loss of the French fleet at the Battle of Trafalgar in 1805, Napoleon was unable to threaten Britain with invasion, and Britain was able to actively assist the resistance movements in Spain and Portugal, thereby helping weaken French power.

he began his campaign with the largest army ever assembled in Europe, approximately 600,000 men. After fighting an inconclusive battle at Borodino, Napoleon pressed on to Moscow. Five weeks after occupying Moscow, he was forced to retreat by Russian patriots who set the city on fire and by approaching armies. During the retreat, the brutal Russian winter and attacks by Russian forces destroyed his army. A broken and battered fragment of 30,000 men returned home to France.

After the debacle in Russia, Austria and Prussia deserted Napoleon and entered an alliance with England and Russia. Unable to defend Paris, Napoleon was forced to abdicate the French throne in April 1814. The allies exiled Napoleon to the island of Elba off the coast of Italy and restored the French monarchy. The next year Napoleon escaped from Elba and returned to France. But his moment had passed. He was defeated by an allied army at Waterloo, in Belgium, after only one hundred days in power. His final exile was on the distant island of St. Helena in the South Atlantic, where he died in 1821.

Revolution Spreads, Conservatives Respond, 1789–1850

Even as the dictatorship of Napoleon eliminated the democratic legacy of the French Revolution, revolutionary ideology was spreading and taking hold in Europe and the Americas. In Europe the French Revolution promoted nationalism and republicanism. In the Americas the legacies of the American and French Revolutions led to a new round of struggles for independence. News of revolutionary events in France destabilized the colonial regime in Saint Domingue (present-day Haiti), a small French colony on the western half of the island of Hispaniola, and resulted in the first successful slave rebellion. In Europe, however, the spread of revolutionary fervor was checked by reaction as monarchs formed an alliance to protect themselves from further revolutionary outbreaks.

The Haitian Revolution, 1789–1804

In 1789 the French colony of Saint Domingue was among the richest European colonies in the Americas. Its plantations produced sugar, cotton, indigo, and coffee. The colony produced two-thirds of France's tropical imports and generated nearly one-third of all French foreign trade. This impressive wealth depended on a brutal slave regime. Saint Domingue's harsh punishments and poor living conditions were notorious throughout the Caribbean. The colony's high mortality and low fertility rates created an insatiable demand for African slaves. As a result, in 1790 the majority of the colony's 500,000 slaves were African-born.

In 1789, when news of the calling of France's Estates General arrived on the island, wealthy white planters sent a delegation to Paris charged with seeking more home rule and greater economic freedom for Saint Domingue. The free mixed-race population, the ***gens de couleur*°,** also sent representatives. These nonwhite delegates were mostly drawn from the large class of slave-owning small planters and urban merchants. They focused on ending race discrimination and achieving political equality with whites. They did not seek freedom for slaves; the most prosperous gens de couleur were slave owners themselves. As the French Revolution became more radical, the gens de couleur forged an alliance with sympathetic French radicals, who came to identify the colony's wealthy planters as royalists and aristocrats.

The political turmoil in France weakened the ability of colonial administrators to maintain order. The authority of colonial officials was no longer clear, and the very legitimacy of slavery was being challenged in France. In the vacuum that resulted, rich planters, poor whites, and the gens de couleur pursued their narrow interests, engendering an increasingly bitter and confrontational struggle. Given the slaves' hatred of the brutal regime that oppressed them and the accumulated grievances of the free people of color, there was no way to limit the violence once the control of the slave owners slipped. When Vincent Ogé°, leader of the gens de couleur mission to France, returned to Saint Domingue in 1790 to organize a military force, the planters captured, tortured, and executed him. This cruelty was soon repaid in kind.

By 1791 whites, led by the planter elite, and the gens de couleur were engaged in open warfare. This breach between the two groups of slave owners gave the slaves an opening. A slave rebellion began on the plantations of the north and spread throughout the colony (see Map 22.3). Plantations were destroyed, masters and overseers killed, and crops burned. An emerging rebel leadership that combined elements of African political culture with revolutionary ideology from France mobilized and directed the rebelling slaves.

The rebellious slaves eventually gained the upper hand under the leadership of **François Dominique Toussaint L'Ouverture,** a former domestic slave, who created a disciplined military force. Toussaint was politically

gens de couleur (zhahn deh koo-LUHR) **Ogé** (oh-ZHAY)

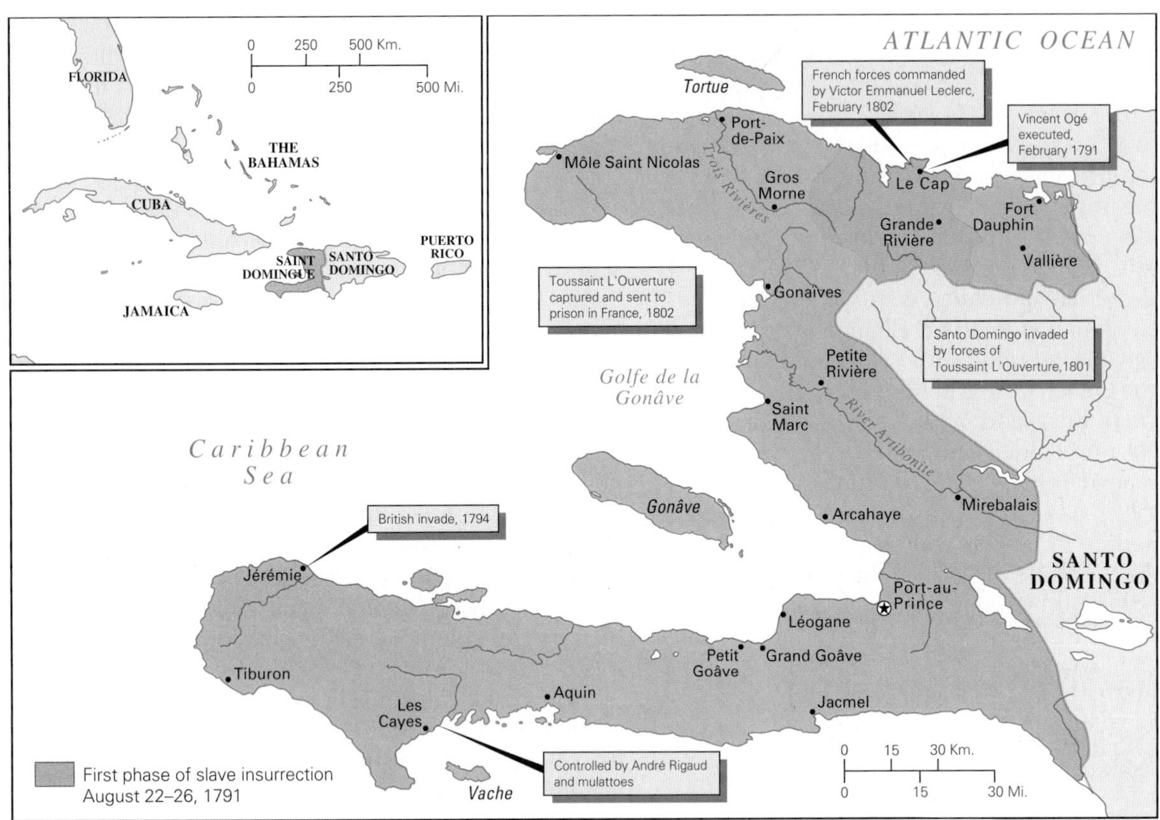

Map 22.3 The Haitian Revolution On their way to achieving an end to slavery and gaining national independence, the Haitian revolutionaries were forced to defeat British and French military interventions as well as the local authority of the slave masters.

strengthened in 1794 when the radical National Convention in Paris abolished slavery in all French possessions. He overcame his rivals in Saint Domingue, defeated a British expeditionary force in 1798, and then led an invasion of the neighboring Spanish colony of Santo Domingo, freeing the slaves there. Toussaint continued to assert his loyalty to France but gave the French government no effective role in local affairs.

As reaction overtook revolution in France, both the abolition of slavery and Toussaint's political position were threatened. When the Directory contemplated the reestablishment of slavery, Toussaint protested:

> Do they think that men who have been able to enjoy the blessing of liberty will calmly see it snatched away? They supported their chains only so long as they did not know any condition of life more happy than slavery. But today when they have left it, if they had a thousand lives they would sacrifice them all rather than be forced into slavery again.[3]

In 1802 Napoleon sent a large military force to Saint Domingue to reestablish both French colonial authority and slavery (see Map 22.3). At first the French forces were successful. Toussaint was captured and sent to France, where he died in prison. Eventually, however, the loss of thousands of lives to yellow fever and the resistance of the revolutionaries turned the tide. Visible in the resistance to the French were small numbers of armed women. During the early stages of the Haitian Revolution, very few slave women had taken up arms, although many had aided Toussaint's forces in support roles. But after a decade of struggle and violence, more Haitian women were politically aware and willing to join the armed resistance. In 1804 Toussaint's successors declared independence, and the free republic of Haiti joined the United States as the second independent nation in the Western Hemisphere. But independence and emancipation were achieved at a terrible price. Tens of thousands had died; the economy was destroyed; and public administration was corrupted by more than a decade of vio-

Haiti's Former Slaves Defend Their Freedom In this representation, a veteran army sent by Napoleon to reassert French control in Haiti battles with Haitian forces in a tropical forest. The combination of Haitian resistance and yellow fever defeated the French invasion. (Bettmann/Corbis)

lence. Political violence and economic stagnation were to trouble Haiti throughout the nineteenth century.

The Congress of Vienna and Conservative Retrenchment, 1815–1820

From 1814 to 1815 representatives of Britain, Russia, Austria, and Prussia met as the **Congress of Vienna** to reestablish political order in Europe. While they were meeting, Napoleon escaped from Elba, then was defeated at Waterloo. The French Revolution and Napoleon's imperial ambitions had threatened the very survival of Europe's old order. Ancient monarchies had been overturned and dynasties replaced with interlopers. Long-established political institutions had been tossed aside, and long-recognized international borders had been ignored. The very existence of the nobility and church had been put at risk. Under the leadership of the Austrian foreign minister, Prince Klemens von Metternich° (1773–1859), the allies worked together in Vienna to create a comprehensive peace settlement that they hoped would safeguard the conservative order.

The central objective of the Congress of Vienna was to roll back the clock in France. Because the participants believed that a strong and stable France was the best guarantee of future peace, the French monarchy was reestablished, and France's 1792 borders were recognized. Most of the continental European powers received some territorial gains, for Metternich sought to offset French strength with a balance of power. In addition, Austria, Russia, and Prussia formed a separate alliance to more actively confront the revolutionary and nationalist energies that the French Revolution had unleashed. In 1820 this "Holy Alliance" acted decisively to defeat liberal revolutions in Spain and Italy. By repressing republican and nationalist ideas in universities and the press, the Holy Alliance also attempted to meet the potential challenge posed by subversive ideas. Metternich's program of conservative retrenchment succeeded in the short term, but powerful ideas associated with liberalism and nationalism remained a vital part of European political life throughout the nineteenth century.

Metternich (MET-uhr-nik)

Nationalism, Reform, and Revolution, 1821–1850

Despite the power of the conservative monarchs, popular support for national self-determination and democratic reform grew throughout Europe. Greece had been under Ottoman control since the fifteenth century. In 1821 Greek patriots launched an independence movement. Metternich and other conservatives opposed Greek independence, but European artists and writers enamored with the cultural legacy of ancient Greece rallied political support for intervention. After years of struggle, Russia, France, and Great Britain forced the Ottoman Empire to recognize Greek independence in 1830.

Louis XVIII, brother of the executed Louis XVI, had been placed on the throne of France by the victorious allies in 1814. He ruled as a constitutional monarch until his death in 1824 and was followed to the throne by his brother Charles X. Charles attempted to rule in the prerevolutionary style of his ancestors, repudiating the constitution in 1830. Unwilling to accept this reactionary challenge, the people of Paris rose up and forced Charles to abdicate. His successor was his cousin Louis Philippe° (r. 1830–1848), who accepted the reestablished constitution and extended voting privileges.

At the same time democratic reform movements appeared in both the United States and Great Britain. In the United States after 1790 the original thirteen states were joined by new states with constitutions granting voting rights to most free males. After the War of 1812 the right to vote was expanded in the older states as well. This broadening of the franchise led to the election of the populist president Andrew Jackson in 1828 (see Chapter 24).

However, revolutionary violence in France made the British aristocracy and the conservative Tory Party fearful of expanded democracy and mass movements of any kind. In 1815 the British government passed the Corn Laws, which limited the importation of foreign grains. The laws favored the profits of wealthy landowners who produced grain at the expense of the poor who were forced to pay more for their bread. When poor consumers organized to overturn these laws, the government outlawed most public meetings, using troops to crush protest in Manchester. Reacting against these policies, reformers gained the passage of laws that increased the power of the House of Commons, redistributed votes from agricultural to industrial districts, and increased the number of voters by nearly 50 percent. Although the most radical demands of these reformers, called Chartists, were defeated, new labor and economic reforms addressing the grievances of workers were passed (see Chapter 23).

Despite the achievement of Greek independence and limited political reform in France and Great Britain, conservatives continued to hold the upper hand in Europe. Finally, in 1848 the desire for democratic reform and national self-determination and the frustrations of urban workers led to upheavals across Europe. The **Revolutions of 1848** began in Paris, where members of the middle class and workers united to overthrow the regime of Louis Philippe and create the Second French Republic. Adult men were given voting rights; slavery was abolished in French colonies; the death penalty was ended; and a ten-hour workday was legislated for Paris. But Parisian workers' demands for programs to reduce unemployment and prices provoked conflicts with the middle class, which wanted to protect property rights. When workers rose up against the government, French troops were called out to crush them. Desiring the reestablishment of order, the French elected Louis Napoleon, nephew of the former emperor, president in December 1848. Three years later, he overturned the constitution as a result of popular plebiscite and, after ruling briefly as dictator, became Emperor Napoleon III. He remained in power until 1871.

Reformers in Hungary, Italy, Bohemia, and elsewhere pressed for greater national self-determination in 1848. When the Austrian monarchy did not meet their demands, students and workers in Vienna took to the streets to force political reforms similar to those sought in Paris. With revolution spreading throughout the Austrian Empire, Metternich, the symbol of reaction, fled Vienna in disguise. Little lasting change occurred, however, because the new Austrian emperor, Franz Joseph (r. 1848–1916) was able to use Russian military assistance and loyal Austrian troops to reestablish central authority.

Middle-class reformers and workers in Berlin joined forces in an attempt to compel the Prussian king to accept a liberal constitution and seek unification of the German states. But the Constituent Assembly called to write a constitution and arrange for national integration became entangled in diplomatic conflicts with Austria and Denmark. As a result, Frederick William IV (r. 1840–1861) was able to reassert his authority, thwarting both constitutional reform and unification.

Despite their heroism on the barricades of Paris, Vienna, Rome, and Berlin, the revolutionaries of 1848 failed to gain either their nationalist or their republican objectives. Monarchs retained the support not only of aristocrats but also of professional militaries, largely re-

Louis Philippe (loo-EE-fee-LEEP)

The Revolution of 1830 in Belgium After the 1830 uprising that overturned the restored monarchy in France, Belgians rose up to declare their independence from Holland. In Poland and Italy, similar uprisings combining nationalism and a desire for self-governance failed. This painting by Baron Gustaf Wappers romantically illustrates the popular nature of the Belgian uprising by bringing to the barricades men, women, and children drawn from both the middle and the working classes. (Musées royaux des Beaux-Arts de Belgique, Brussels)

cruited from among peasants who had little sympathy for urban workers. Revolutionary coalitions, in contrast, were fragile and lacked clear objectives. Workers' demands for higher wages, lower prices, and labor reform often drove their middle-class allies into the arms of the reactionaries.

Conclusion

This era of revolution was, in large measure, the product of a long period of costly warfare among the imperial nations of Europe. Using taxes and institutions inherited from the past, England and France found it increasingly difficult to fund distant wars in the Americas or in Asia. Royal governments attempting to impose new taxes met with angry resistance. The spread of literacy and the greater availability of books helped create a European culture more open to reform or the revolutionary change of existing institutions. The ideas of Locke and Rousseau guided critics of monarchy toward a new political culture of elections and representative institutions. Each new development served as example and provocation for new revolutionary acts. French officers who took part in the American Revolution helped ignite the French Revolution. Black freemen from Haiti traveled to France to seek their rights and returned to spread revolutionary passions. Each revolution had its own character. The revolutions in France and Haiti proved to be more violent and destructive than the American Revolution. Revolutionaries in France and Haiti, facing a more strongly entrenched and more powerful opposition and greater social inequalities, responded with greater violence.

The conservative retrenchment that followed the defeat of Napoleon succeeded in the short term. Monarchy, multinational empires, and the established church retained their hold on the loyalty of millions of Europeans and could count on the support of many of Europe's wealthiest and most powerful individuals. But liberalism and nationalism continued to stir revolutionary sentiment. The contest between adherents of the old order and partisans of change was to continue well into the nineteenth century. In the end, the nation-state, the Enlightenment legacy of rational inquiry, broadened political participation, and secular intellectual culture prevailed. This outcome was determined in large measure by the old order's inability to satisfy the new social classes that appeared with the emerging industrial economy. The material transformation produced by industrial capitalism could not be contained in the narrow confines of a hereditary social system, nor could the rapid expansion of scientific learning be contained within the doctrines of traditional religion.

The revolutions of the late eighteenth century began the transformation of Western society, but they did not complete it. Only a minority gained full political rights. Women did not achieve full political rights until the twentieth century. Democratic institutions, as in revolutionary France, often failed. Moreover, as Chapter 24 discusses, slavery endured in the Americas past the mid-1800s, despite the revolutionary era's enthusiasm for individual liberty.

Key Terms

Enlightenment
Benjamin Franklin
George Washington
Joseph Brant
Constitutional Convention
Estates General
National Assembly
Declaration of the Rights of Man
Jacobins
Maximilien Robespierre
Napoleon Bonaparte
gens de couleur
François Dominique Toussaint L'Ouverture
Congress of Vienna
Revolutions of 1848

Suggested Reading

The American Revolution has received a great amount of attention from scholars. Colin Bonwick, *The American Revolution* (1991), and Edward Countryman, *The American Revolution* (1985), provide excellent introductions. Edmund S. Morgan, *The Challenge of the American Revolution* (1976), remains a major work of interpretation. Gordon S. Wood, *The Radicalism of the American Revolution* (1992), is a brilliant examination of the ideological and cultural meanings of the Revolution. A contrarian view is offered by Francis Jennings, *The Creation of America Through Revolution to Empire* (2003). See also William Howard Adams, *The Paris Years of Thomas Jefferson* (1997). Lance Banning, *The Sacred Fire of Liberty: James Madison and the Founding of the Federal Republic* (1995), is a convincing revision of the story of Madison and his era. For the role of women in the American Revolution see Linda K. Kerber, *Women of the Republic: Intellect and Ideology in Revolutionary America* (1980), and Mary Beth Norton, *Liberty's Daughters: The Revolutionary Experience of American Women, 1750–1800* (1980). Also recommended is Norton's *Founding Mothers and Fathers: Gendered Power and the Forming of American Society* (1996). Among the many works that deal with African-Americans and Amerindians during the era, see Sylvia Frey, *Water from Rock: Black Resistance in a Revolutionary Age* (1991); Barbara Graymont, *The Iroquois in the American Revolution* (1972); and William N. Fenton, *The Great Law and the Longhouse: A Political History of the Iroquois Confederacy* (1998).

For intellectual life in the era of the French Revolution see Anne Goldgar, *Impolite Learning: Conduct and Community in the Republic of Letters, 1680–1750* (1995); Dena Goodman, *The Republic of Letters: A Cultural History of the Enlightenment* (1994); and James Swenson, *On Jean-Jacques Rousseau Considered as One of the First Authors of the Revolution* (2002). For the Counter Enlightenment see Darrin M. McMahon, *Enemies of the Enlightenment, The French Counter-Enlightenment and the Making of Modernity* (2001). For the "underside" of this era see the discussion of "folk culture" in *Shaping History: Ordinary People in European Politics, 1500–1700* (1998), by Wayne Te Brake. François Furet, *Interpreting the French Revolution* (1981), breaks with interpretations that emphasize class and ideology. Georges Lefebve, *The Coming of the French Revolution*, trans. R. R. Palmer (1947), presents the classic class-based analysis. George Rudé, *The Crowd in History: Popular Disturbances in France and England* (1981), remains the best introduction to the role of mass protest in the period. Lynn Hunt, *The Family Romance of the French Revolution* (1992), examines the gender content of revolutionary politics. For the role of women see Joan Landes, *Women and the Public Sphere in the Age of the French Revolution* (1988), and the recently published *The Women of Paris and Their French Revolution* (1998) by Dominique Godineau. Felix Markham, *Napoleon* (1963), and Robert B. Holtman, *The Napoleonic Revolution* (1967), provide reliable summaries of the period.

The Haitian Revolution has received less extensive coverage than the revolutions in the United States and France. C. L. R.

James, *The Black Jacobins,* 2d ed. (1963), is the classic study. Anna J. Cooper, *Slavery and the French Revolutionists, 1788–1805* (1988), also provides an overview of this important topic. Carolyn E. Fick, *The Making of Haiti: The Saint Domingue Revolution from Below* (1990), is the best recent synthesis. David P. Geggus, *Slavery, War, and Revolution* (1982), examines the British role in the revolutionary period. See also David Barry Gaspar and David Patrick Geggus, eds., *A Turbulent Time: The French Revolution and the Greater Caribbean* (1997).

For the revolutions of 1830 and 1848 see Arthur J. May's brief survey in *The Age of Metternich, 1814–48,* rev. ed. (1963). Henry Kissinger's *A World Restored* (1957) remains among the most interesting discussions of the Congress of Vienna. Eric Hobsbawm's *The Age of Revolution* (1962) provides a clear analysis of the class issues that appeared during this era. Paul Robertson's *Revolutions of 1848: A Social History* (1960) remains a valuable introduction. See also Peter Stearns and Herrick Chapman, *European Society in Upheaval* (1991). For the development of European social reform movements see Albert Lindemann, *History of European Socialism* (1983).

For national events in Hungary see István Deák's examination of Hungary, *The Lawful Revolution: Louis Kossuth and the Hungarians, 1848–49* (1979). On Germany see Theodore S. Hamerow, *Restoration, Revolution, and Reaction, 1815–1871* (1966). For French events see Roger Price, *A Social History of Nineteenth-Century France* (1987). Barbara Taylor, *Eve and the New Jerusalem: Socialism and Feminism in the Nineteenth Century* (1983), analyzes connections between workers' and women's rights issues in England.

Notes

1. Quoted in Ray Raphael, *A People's History of the American Revolution* (New York: Perenial, 2001), 142.
2. Ibid., 141.
3. Quoted in C. L. R. James, *The Black Jacobins,* 2d ed., (New York: Vintage Books, 1963), 196.

23 The Early Industrial Revolution, 1760–1851

Mr. Watt's Engine This drawing shows the functioning parts of a Watt engine used to pump water from a mine: the boiler, cylinder Q, condenser N, rocking horse, and pump S.

CHAPTER OUTLINE

From 1765 until the 1790s a small group of men calling themselves the Lunar Society met once a month in Birmingham, England. They gathered on nights when the moon was full, so they could find their way home in the dark. Among them were the pottery manufacturer Josiah Wedgwood, the engine designer James Watt, the chemist Joseph Priestley, the iron manufacturer Matthew Boulton, and the naturalist Erasmus Darwin. They did not leave a record of what they discussed, but the fact that businessmen, craftsmen, and scientists had interests in common was something new in the history of the world. Though members of very different professions, they were willing to exchange ideas and discoveries in an atmosphere of experimentation and innovation. They invited experts in industry, science, and engineering to speak at their meetings in order to obtain the latest information in their fields.

Meanwhile, similar societies throughout Britain were creating a vogue for science and were giving the word *progress* a new meaning: "change for the better." By focusing on the practical application of knowledge, groups like the Lunar Society laid the groundwork for the economic and social transformations that historians call the **Industrial Revolution.** This revolution involved dramatic innovations in manufacturing, mining, transportation, and communications and equally rapid changes in society and commerce. New relationships between social groups created an environment that was conducive to technical innovation and economic growth. New technologies and new social and economic arrangements allowed the industrializing countries—first Britain, then western Europe and the United States—to unleash massive increases in production and productivity, exploit the world's natural resources as never before, and transform the environment and human life in unprecedented ways.

The distribution of power and wealth generated by the Industrial Revolution was very uneven, for industrialization widened the gap between rich and poor. The people who owned and controlled the innovations amassed wealth and power over nature and over other people. Some of them lived lives of spectacular luxury. Workers, including children, worked long hours in dangerous factories and lived crowded together in unsanitary tenements.

The effect of the Industrial Revolution around the world was also very uneven. The first countries to industrialize grew rich and powerful. In Egypt and India, the economic and military power of the European countries stifled the tentative beginnings of industrialization. Regions that had little or no industry were easily taken advantage of. The disparity between the industrial and the developing countries that exists today has its origins in the early nineteenth century.

As you read this chapter, ask yourself the following questions:

- What caused the Industrial Revolution?
- What were the key innovations that increased productivity and drove industrialization?
- What was the impact of these changes on the society and environment of the industrializing countries?
- How did the Industrial Revolution affect the relations between the industrialized and the nonindustrialized parts of the world?

Causes of the Industrial Revolution

What caused the Industrial Revolution, and why did it begin in England in the late eighteenth century? These are two of the great questions of history. The basic preconditions of this momentous event seem to have been economic development propelled by population growth, an agricultural revolution, the expansion of trade, and an openness to innovation.

Population Growth

The population of Europe rose in the eighteenth century—slowly at first, faster after 1780, then even faster in the early nineteenth century. The fastest growth took place in England and Wales. Population there rose from 5.5 million in 1688 to 9 million in 1801 and 18 million by 1851—increases never before experienced in European history.

The growth of population resulted from more widespread resistance to disease and more reliable food supplies, thanks to the new crops that originated in the Americas (see Chapter 17). More dependable food supplies and better job opportunities led people to marry at earlier ages and have more children. A high birthrate meant a large percentage of children in the general population. In the early nineteenth century some 40 percent of the population of Britain was under fifteen years of age. This high proportion of youths explains both the vitality of the British people in that period and the widespread use of child labor. People also migrated at an unprecedented rate—from the countryside to the cities, from Ireland to England, and, more generally, from Europe to the Americas. Thanks to immigration, the population of the United States rose from 4 million in 1791 to 9.6 million in 1820 and 31.5 million in 1860—faster growth than in any other part of the world at the time.

The Agricultural Revolution

Innovations in manufacturing could only have taken place alongside a simultaneous revolution in farming that provided food for city dwellers and forced poorer peasants off the land. This **agricultural revolution** had begun long before the eighteenth century. One important aspect was the acceptance of the potato, introduced from South America in the sixteenth century. In the cool and humid regions of Europe from Ireland to Russia, potatoes yielded two or three times more food per acre than did the wheat, rye, and oats they replaced. Maize (American corn) was grown across Europe from northern Iberia to the Balkans. Turnips, legumes, and clover did not deplete the soil and could be fed to cattle, which were sources of milk and meat. Manure from cattle in turn fertilized the soil for other crops.

The security of small-scale tenant farmers and sharecroppers depended on traditional methods and rural customs such as collecting plants left over in the fields after the harvest, pasturing their animals on common village lands, and gathering firewood in common woods. Only prosperous landowners with secure titles to their land could afford to bear the risk of trying new methods and new crops. Rich landowners therefore "enclosed" the land—that is, consolidated their holdings—and got Parliament to give them title to the commons that in the past had been open to all. Once in control of the land, they could drain and improve the soil, breed better livestock, and introduce crop rotation. This "enclosure movement" turned tenants and sharecroppers into landless farm laborers. Many moved to the cities to seek work; others became homeless migrants and vagrants; and still others emigrated to Canada, Australia, and the United States.

In eastern Europe, as in Britain, large estates predominated, and aristocratic landowners used such improvements to increase their wealth and political influence. In western Europe enclosure was hampered by the fact that the law gave secure property rights to numerous small farmers.

Trade and Inventiveness

In most of Europe the increasing demand that accompanied the growth of population was met by increasing production in traditional ways. Roads were improved so stagecoaches could travel faster. Royal manufacturers trained additional craftsmen to produce fine china, silks, and carpets by hand. In rural areas much production was carried out through cottage industries. Merchants delivered fibers, leather, and other raw materials to craftspeople (often farmers in the off-season) and picked up the finished products. The growth of the population and food supply was accompanied by the growth of trade. Most of it was local trade in traditional goods and services. But a growing share consisted of simple goods that even middle-class people could afford: sugar, tea, cotton textiles, iron hardware, pottery. Products from other parts of the world like tea and sugar required extensive networks of shipping and finance.

As the story of the Lunar Society demonstrates, scientific discoveries, commercial enterprise, and technical skills became closely connected. Technology and innovation fascinated educated people throughout Europe and eastern North America. The French *Encyclopédie* contained thousands of articles and illustrations of crafts and manufacturing (see Diversity and Dominance: Adam Smith and the Division of Labor). The French and British governments sent expeditions around the world to collect plants that could profitably be grown in their colonies. They also offered prizes to anyone who could find a method of determining the longitude of a ship at sea to avoid the shipwrecks that had cost the lives of thousands of sailors. The American Benjamin Franklin, like many others, experimented with electricity. In France, the Montgolfier brothers invented a hot-air balloon. Claude Chappe° created the first semaphore telegraph. French artillery officers proposed making guns with interchangeable parts. The American Eli Whitney and his associate John Hall invented machine tools, that

Chappe (SHAPP)

CHRONOLOGY

	Technology	Economy, Society, and Politics
1750	**1759** Josiah Wedgwood opens pottery factory **1764** Spinning jenny **1769** Richard Arkwright's water frame; James Watt patents steam engine **1779** First iron bridge **1785** Boulton and Watt sell steam engines; Samuel Crompton's mule **1793** Eli Whitney's cotton gin	**1776** Adam Smith's *Wealth of Nations* **1776–1783** American Revolution **1789–1799** French Revolution
1800	**1800** Alessandro Volta's battery **1807** Robert Fulton's *Clermont* **1820s** Construction of Erie Canal **1829** *Rocket,* first steam-powered locomotive **1837** Wheatstone and Cooke's telegraph **1838** First ships steam across the Atlantic **1840** *Nemesis* sails to China **1843** Samuel Morse's Baltimore-to-Washington telegraph	**1804–1815** Napoleonic Wars **1820s** U.S. cotton industry begins **1833** Factory Act in Britain **1834** German Zollverein; Robert Owen's Grand National Consolidated Trade Union **1846** Repeal of British Corn Laws **1847–1848** Irish famine **1848** Collapse of Chartist movement; Revolutions in Europe
1850	**1851** Crystal Palace opens in London	**1854** First cotton mill in India

is, machines capable of making other machines. These machines greatly increased the productivity of manufacturing.

Britain and Continental Europe

Economic growth was evident throughout the North Atlantic area, yet industrialization did not take place everywhere at once. To understand why, we must look at the peculiar role of Great Britain. Britain enjoyed a rising standard of living during the eighteenth century, thanks to good harvests, a growing population, and a booming overseas trade. Britain was the world's leading exporter of tools, guns, hardware, clocks, and other craft goods (see Map 23.1). Its mining and metal industries employed engineers willing to experiment with new ideas. It had the largest merchant marine and produced more ships, naval supplies, and navigation instruments than other countries.

Until the mid-eighteenth century the British were better known for their cheap imitations than for their innovations or quality products. But they put inventions into practice more quickly than other people, as the engineer John Farey told a parliamentary committee in 1829: "The prevailing talent of English and Scotch people is to apply new ideas to use and to bring such applications to perfection, but they do not imagine as much as foreigners" (see Environment and Technology: The Origin of Graphs).

Before 1790 Britain had a more fluid society than did the rest of Europe. The English royal court was less ostentatious than the courts of France, Spain, and Austria. Its aristocracy was less powerful, and the lines separating the social classes were not as sharply drawn. Political power was not as centralized as on the European continent, and the government employed fewer bureaucrats and officials. Members of the gentry, and even some aristocrats, married into merchant families. Intermarriage among the families of petty merchants, yeoman farmers, and town craftsmen was common. Guilds, which resisted innovation, were relatively weak. Ancestry remained important, but wealth also commanded respect. A businessman with enough money could buy a landed estate,

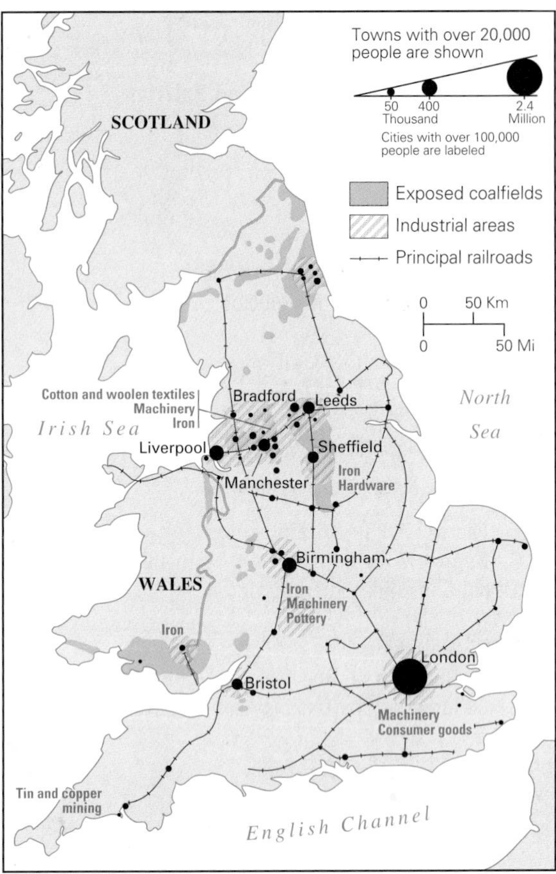

Map 23.1 The Industrial Revolution in Britain, ca. 1850 The first industries arose in northern and western England. These regions had abundant coal and iron-ore deposits for the iron industry and moist climate and fast-flowing rivers, factors imporant for the cotton textile industry.

a seat in Parliament, and the social status that accompanied them.

At a time when transportation by land was very costly, Great Britain had good water transportation thanks to its indented coastline, navigable rivers, and growing network of canals. It had a unified internal market with none of the duties and tolls that goods had to pay every few miles in France. This encouraged regional specialization, such as tin mining in Cornwall and cotton manufacturing in Lancashire, and a growing trade between regions.

Britain was highly commercial; more people were involved in production for export and in trade and finance than in any other major country. It was especially active in overseas trade with the Americas, West Africa, the Middle East, and India. It had financial and insurance institutions able to support growing business enterprises and a patent system that offered inventors the hope of rich rewards. The example of men who became wealthy and respected for their inventions—such as Richard Arkwright, the cotton magnate, and James Watt, the steam engine designer—stimulated others.

In the eighteenth century, the economies of continental Europe also underwent a dynamic expansion, thanks to the efforts of individual entrepreneurs and investors. Yet growth was still hampered by high transportation costs, misguided government regulations, and rigid social structures. The Low Countries were laced with canals, but the terrain elsewhere in Europe made canal building costly and difficult. The ruling monarchies made some attempts to import British techniques and organize factory production, but they all foundered for lack of markets or management skills. From 1789 to 1815 Europe was scarred by revolutions and wars. War created opportunities for suppliers of weapons, uniforms, and horses produced by traditional methods. But the interruption of trade between Britain and continental Europe slowed the diffusion of new techniques, and the insecurity of countries at war discouraged businessmen from investing in factories and machinery.

The political revolutions swept away the restrictions of the old regimes. After 1815 the economies of western Europe were ready to begin industrializing. Industrialization took hold in Belgium and northern France, as businessmen visited Britain to observe the changes and spy out industrial secrets. In spite of British laws forbidding the emigration of skilled workers and the export of textile machinery, many workers slipped through. By the 1820s several thousand Britons were at work on the continent of Europe setting up machines, training workers in the new methods, and even starting their own businesses.

Acutely aware of Britain's head start and the need to stimulate their own industries, European governments took action. They created technical schools. They eliminated internal tariff barriers, tolls, and other hindrances to trade. They encouraged the formation of joint-stock companies and banks to channel private savings into industrial investments. On the European continent, as in Britain, cotton cloth was the first industry. The mills of France, Belgium, and the German states served local markets but could not compete abroad with the more advanced British industry. By 1830 the political climate in western Europe was as favorable to business as Britain's had been a half-century earlier.

Abundant coal and iron-ore deposits determined the concentration of industries in a swath of territories running from northern France through Belgium and the

ENVIRONMENT + TECHNOLOGY

The Origin of Graphs

Not all technologies involve hardware. There are also information technologies, such as graphs, the visual representation of numerical tables. We see graphs so often in textbooks, magazines, and newspapers that we take them for granted. But they too have a history.

Scientists in France and England created the first graphs in the seventeenth century to illustrate natural phenomena. Some represented tables of data, such as the movements of stars and atmospheric pressure. Until the late eighteenth century few people outside of scientific circles knew or cared about such graphs. This changed with the growing public interest in economic data, population statistics, and other secular subjects that were so much a part of the Enlightenment.

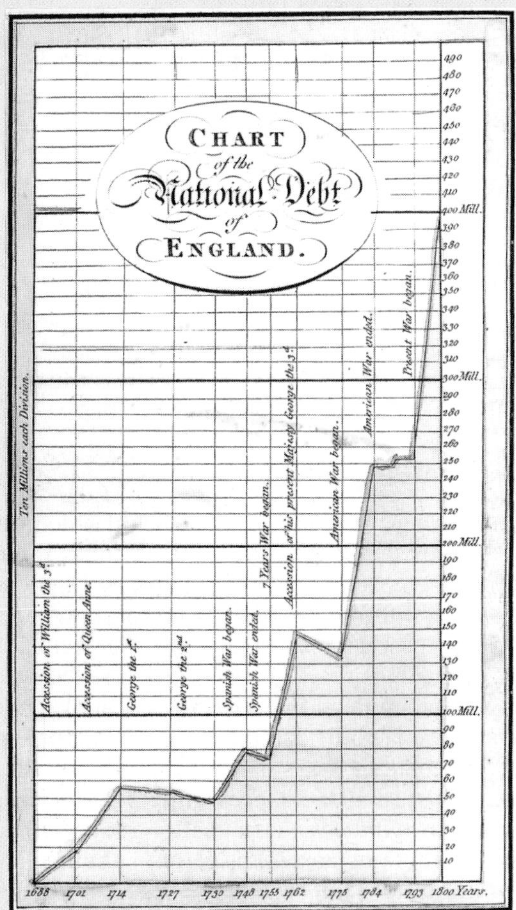

Line Graph of National Debt of England 1803
This graph by William Playfair is designed to shock the viewer by showing the national debt of Britain skyrocketing out of control, especially during the country's many wars. (British Library)

The first person to publish graphs of interest to the general public was William Playfair (1729–1823), an Englishman who started his career as a draftsman for the engine manufacturing firm of Boulton and Watt. In 1786 he published *The Commercial and Political Atlas*, a book that was widely read and went though several editions. All but one of the forty-four graphs in it were line graphs with the vertical axis showing economic data and the horizontal axis representing time. Playfair explained to skeptical readers how a line could represent money:

> *This method has struck several persons as being fallacious, because geometrical measurement has not any relation to money or to time; yet here it is made to represent both. The most familiar and simple answer to this objection is by giving an example. Suppose the money received by a man in trade were all in guineas, and that every evening he made a single pile of all the guineas received during the day, each pile would represent a day, and its height would be proportioned to the receipts of that day; so that by this plain operation,* time, proportion, *and* amount *would all be physically combined.*
>
> *Lineal arithmetic then, it may be averred, is nothing more than those piles of guineas represented on paper, and on a small scale, in which an inch (suppose) represents the thickness of five millions of guineas, as in geography it does the breadth of a river, or any other extent of country.*

As for why it was necessary to show economic data in the form of a graph, Playfair explained:

> *Men of high rank, or active business, can only pay attention to general outlines; nor is attention to particulars of use, any further than they give a general information; it is hoped that, with the Assistance of these Charts, such information will be got, without the fatigue and trouble of studying the particulars of which it is composed.*

Today, graphs are an indispensable means of conveying information in business and finance, in the sciences, and in government. We need graphs because they give us information quickly and efficiently, "without the fatigue and trouble of studying the particulars."

Source: William Playfair, *The Commercial and Political Atlas*, 3rd ed. (London: J. Wallis, 1801), ix, xiv–xv.

Ruhr district of western Germany to Silesia in Prussia (now part of Poland). By the 1850s France, Belgium, and the German states were in the midst of an industrial boom like that of Britain, based on iron, cotton, steam engines, and railroads.

THE TECHNOLOGICAL REVOLUTION

Five innovations spurred industrialization: (1) mass production through the division of labor, (2) new machines and mechanization, (3) a great increase in the manufacture of iron, (4) the steam engine and the changes it made possible in industry and transportation, and (5) the electric telegraph. China had achieved the first three of these during the Song dynasty (960–1279), but had not developed the steam engine or electricity. The continued success of Western industrialization depended heavily on these new forms of energy.

Wedgwood's Potteries In Staffordshire, England, Josiah Wedgwood established a factory to mass-produce beautiful and inexpensive china. The bottle-shaped buildings are kilns in which thousands of pieces of china could be fired at one time. Kilns, factories, and housing were all mixed together in pottery towns, and smoke from burning coal filled the air. (Mary Evans Picture Library)

Mass Production: Pottery

The pottery industry offers a good example of **mass production,** the making of many identical items by breaking the process into simple repetitive tasks. East Asian potters had long known how to make fine glazed porcelain, or "china," but the high cost of transporting it to Europe before the mid-eighteenth century meant that only the wealthy could afford fine Chinese porcelain. Middle-class people used pewter tableware, and the poor ate from wooden or earthenware bowls. Several royal manufactures—Meissen° in Saxony, Delft in Holland, and Sèvres° in France—produced exquisite handmade products for the courts and aristocracy, but their products were much too expensive for mass consumption. Meanwhile, more and more Europeans acquired a taste for Chinese tea as well as for cocoa and coffee, and they wanted porcelain that would not spoil the flavor of hot beverages. This demand created opportunities for inventive entrepreneurs.

Like other countries, Britain had many small pottery workshops where craftsmen made a few plates and cups at a time. Much of this activity took place in a part of the Midlands that possessed good clay, coal for firing, and lead for glazing. There **Josiah Wedgwood,** the son of a potter, started his own pottery business in 1759. He had a scientific bent and invented the pyrometer, a device to measure the extremely high temperatures that are found in kilns during the firing of pottery, for which he was elected a member of the Royal Society. Today the name Wedgwood is associated with expensive, highly decorated china. But Wedgwood's most important contribution lay in producing ordinary porcelain cheaply by means of the **division of labor** (see Diversity and Dominance: Adam Smith and the Division of Labor).

Wedgwood subdivided the work into highly specialized and repetitive tasks, such as unloading the clay, mixing it, pressing flat pieces, dipping the pieces in glaze, putting handles on cups, packing kilns, and carrying things from one part of his plant to another. To prevent interruptions in production, he instituted strict discipline among his workers. He substituted the use of molds for the potter's wheel wherever possible, a change that not only saved labor but also created identical plates and bowls that could be stacked. He invested in toll

Meissen (MY-sen) **Sèvres** (SEV-ruh)

roads and canals so that special pottery clay found in southwestern England could be economically shipped to his factories in the Midlands.

Wedgwood's interest in applying technology to manufacturing was sparked by his membership in the Lunar Society. In 1782 the naturalist Erasmus Darwin encouraged him to purchase a steam engine from Boulton and Watt, the firm founded by two other members of the society. The engine that Wedgwood bought to mix clay and grind flint was one of the first to be installed in a factory.

These were radical departures from the age-old methods of craftsmanship. But the division of labor and new machinery allowed Wedgwood to lower the cost of his products while improving their quality, and to offer his wares for sale at lower prices. His factory grew far larger than his competitors' factories and employed several hundred workers. His salesmen traveled throughout England touting his goods, and his products were sold on the European continent as well.

Mechanization: The Cotton Industry

The cotton industry, the largest industry in this period, illustrates the role of **mechanization,** the use of machines to do work previously done by hand. Cotton cloth had long been the most common fabric in China, India, and the Middle East, where it was spun and woven by hand. The cotton plant did not grow in Europe, but the cloth was so much cooler, softer, and cleaner than wool that wealthy Europeans developed a liking for the costly import. When the powerful English woolen industry persuaded Parliament to forbid the import of cotton cloth into England, that prohibition stimulated attempts to import cotton fiber and make the cloth locally. Here was an opportunity for enterprising inventors to reduce costs with labor-saving machinery.

To turn inventions into successful businesses, inventors had to link up with entrepreneurs or become businessmen themselves. Making a working prototype often took years, even decades, and many inventions led to dead ends. History remembers the successful, but even they struggled against great odds.

Beginning in the 1760s a series of inventions revolutionized the spinning of cotton thread. The first was the spinning jenny, invented in 1764, which mechanically drew out the cotton fibers and twisted them into thread. The jenny was simple, cheap to build, and easy for one person to operate. Early models spun six or seven threads at once, later ones up to eighty. The thread, however, was soft and irregular and could be used only in combination with linen, a strong yarn derived from the flax plant.

In 1769 **Richard Arkwright** invented another spinning machine, the water frame, which produced thread strong enough to be used without linen. Arkwright was both a gifted inventor and a successful businessman. His machine was larger and more complex than the jenny and required a source of power such as a water wheel, hence the name "water frame." To obtain the necessary energy he installed dozens of machines in a building next to a fast-flowing river. The resemblance to a flour mill gave such enterprises the name cotton mill.

In 1785 Samuel Crompton patented a machine that combined the best features of the jenny and the water frame. This device, called a mule, produced a strong thread that was thin enough to be used to make a better type of cotton cloth called muslin. The mule could make a finer, more even thread than could any human being, and at a lower cost. At last British industry could undersell high-quality handmade cotton cloth from India, and British cotton output increased tenfold between 1770 and 1790.

The boom in thread production and the soaring demand for cloth created bottlenecks in weaving, stimulating inventors to mechanize the rest of textile manufacturing. The first power loom was introduced in 1784 but was not perfected until after 1815. Other inventions of the period included carding machines, chlorine bleach, and cylindrical presses to print designs on fabric. By the 1830s large English textile mills powered by steam engines were performing all the steps necessary to turn raw cotton into printed cloth. This was a far cry from the cottage industries of the previous century.

Mechanization offered two advantages: (1) increased productivity for the manufacturer and (2) lower prices for the consumer. Whereas in India it took five hundred hours to spin a pound of cotton, the mule of 1790 could do so in three person-hours, and the self-acting mule—an improved version introduced in 1830—required only eighty minutes. Cotton mills needed very few skilled workers, and managers often hired children to tend the spinning machines. The same was true of power looms, which gradually replaced handloom weaving: the number of power looms rose from 2,400 in 1813 to 500,000 by 1850. Meanwhile, the price of cloth fell by 90 percent between 1782 and 1812 and kept on dropping.

The industrialization of Britain made cotton America's most valuable crop. In the 1790s most of Britain's cotton came from India, as the United States produced a mere 750 tons (729 metric tons), mostly from South Carolina. In 1793 the American Eli Whitney patented his cotton gin, a simple device that separated the bolls or seed pods from the fiber and made cotton growing economical. This invention permitted the spread of cotton

DIVERSITY AND DOMINANCE

ADAM SMITH AND THE DIVISION OF LABOR

Adam Smith (1723–1790), a Scottish social philosopher, is famous for one book, An Inquiry into the Nature and Causes of the Wealth of Nations, *which was first published in 1776 and has been reprinted many times and translated into many languages. It was the first work to explain the economy of a nation as a system. In it, Smith criticized the notion, common in the eighteenth century, that a nation's wealth was synonymous with the amount of gold and silver in the government's coffers. Instead, he defined wealth as the amount of goods and services produced by a nation's people. By this definition, labor and its products are an essential element in a nation's prosperity.*

In the passage that follows, Smith discusses the increase in productivity (to use a modern term) that results from dividing a craft into separate tasks, each of which is performed over and over by one worker. He contrasts two methods of making pins. In one a team of workers divided up the job of making pins and produced a great many every day; in the other pin-workers "wrought separately and independently" and produced very few pins per day. It is clear that the division of labor produces more pins per worker per day. But who benefits? Left unsaid is that a pin factory had to be owned and operated by a manufacturer who hired workers and assigned a task to each one. Thus did industrialization reduce the diversity of self-employed craftsmen by replacing them with a system of dominance.

The illustration shows a pin-makers' workshop in late eighteenth-century France. Each worker is performing a specific task on a few pins at once, and all the energy comes from human muscles. These are the characteristics of a proto-industrial workshop.

To take an example, therefore, from a very trifling manufacture—but one in which the division of labour has been very often taken notice of—the trade of the pin-maker: a workman not educated to this business (which the division of labour has rendered a distinct trade), nor acquainted with the use of machinery employed in it (to the invention of which the same division of labour has probably given occasion), could scarce, perhaps, with his utmost industry, make one pin in a day, and certainly could not make twenty. But in the way in which this business is now carried on, not only the whole work is a peculiar trade, but it is divided into a number of branches, of which the greater part are likewise peculiar trades. One man draws out the wire, another straights it, a third cuts it, a fourth points it, a fifth grinds it at the top for receiving the head; to make the head requires two or three distinct operations, to put it on, is a peculiar business, to whiten the pins is another; it is even a trade by itself to put them into the paper; and the important business of making a pin is, in this manner, divided into about eighteen distinct operations, which, in some manufactories, are all performed by distinct hands, though in others the same man will sometimes perform two or three of them. I have seen a small manufactory of this kind where ten men only were employed, and where some of them, conse-

farming into Georgia, then into Alabama, Mississippi, and Louisiana, and finally as far west as Texas. By the late 1850s the southern states were producing a million tons of cotton a year, five-sixths of the world's total.

With the help of British craftsmen who introduced jennies, mules, and power looms, Americans developed their own cotton industry in the 1820s. By 1840 the United States had twelve hundred cotton mills, two-thirds of them in New England, that served the booming domestic market.

The Iron Industry

Iron making also was transformed during the Industrial Revolution. Throughout Eurasia and Africa, iron had been in use for thousands of years for tools, swords and other weapons, and household items such as knives, pots, hinges, and locks. In the eleventh century, during the Song period, Chinese forges had produced cast iron in large quantities. Production declined after the Song, but iron continued to be common and inexpensive in China. Wherever iron was pro-

A Pin-Makers Workshop The man in the middle (Figure 2) is pulling wire off a spindle (G) and through a series of posts (HK in Figure 17). This ensures that the wire will be perfectly straight. The worker seated on the lower right (Figure 3) takes the long pieces of straightened wire and cuts them into shorter lengths. The man in the lower left-hand corner (Figure 5) sharpens twelve to fifteen wires at a time by holding them against a grindstone turned by the worker in Figure 6. Figure 16 shows a close-up of this operation. The men in Figures 7 and 8 put the finishing touches on the points. The one in Figure 4 cuts the sharpened pins using the tool shown in Figures 21. Other operations—such as forming the wire to the proper thickness, cleaning and coating it with tin, attaching the heads—are depicted in other engravings in the same encyclopedia. (Division of Rare and Manuscript Collections, Cornell University Library).

quently, performed two or three distinct operations. But though they were very poor, and therefore but indifferently accommodated with the necessary machinery, they could, when they exerted themselves, make among them about twelve pounds of pins in a day. There are in a pound upwards of four thousand pins of a middling size. Those ten persons, therefore, could make among them upwards of forty-eight thousand pins in a day. Each person, therefore, making a tenth part of forty-eight thousand pins, might be considered as making four thousand eight hundred pins a day. But if they had all wrought separately and independently, and without any of them having been educated to this peculiar business, they certainly could not each of them have made twenty, perhaps not one pin in a day; that is, certainly, not the two hundred and fortieth, perhaps not the four thousand eight hundredth part of what they are at present capable of performing, in consequence of a proper division and combination of their different operations.

QUESTIONS FOR ANALYSIS

1. **Why does dividing the job of pin-making into ten or more operations result in the production of more pins per worker? How much more productive are these workers than if each one made complete pins from start to finish?**
2. **How closely does the picture of a pin-maker's workshop illustrate Smith's verbal description?**
3. **What disadvantage would there be to working in a pin manufacture where the job was divided as in Smith's example, compared to making entire pins from start to finish?**
4. **What other examples can you think of, from Adam Smith's day or from more recent times, of the advantages of the division of labor?**

Source: Adam Smith, *An Inquiry into the Nature and Causes of the Wealth of Nations*, ed. Edward Gibbon Wakefield (London: Charles Knight & Co., 1843), 7–9.

duced, however, deforestation eventually drove up the cost of charcoal (used for smelting) and restricted output. Furthermore, iron had to be repeatedly heated and hammered to drive out impurities, a difficult and costly process. Because of limited wood supplies and the high cost of skilled labor, iron was a rare and valuable metal outside China before the eighteenth century.

A first breakthrough occurred in 1709 when Abraham Darby discovered that coke (coal from which the impurities have been cooked out) could be used in place of charcoal. The resulting metal was of lower quality than charcoal-smelted iron but much cheaper to produce, for coal was plentiful. Just as importantly, in 1784 Henry Cort found a way to remove some of the impurities in coke-iron by puddling—stirring the molten iron with long rods. Cort's process made it possible to turn high-sulfur English coal into coke to produce wrought iron (a soft and malleable form of iron) very cheaply. By 1790 four-fifths of Britain's iron was made with coke, while other countries still used charcoal. Coke-iron was cheaper and

Pit Head of a Coal Mine This is a small coal mine. In the center of this picture stands a Newcomen engine used to pump water. The work of hauling coal out of the mine was still done by horses and mules. The smoke coming out of the smokestack is a trademark of the early industrial era. (National Museums and Galleries on Merseyside, Walker Art Gallery [WAG 659])

less destructive of forests, and it allowed a great expansion in the size of individual blast furnaces, substantially reducing the cost of iron. There seemed almost no limit to the quantity of iron that could be produced with coke. Britain's iron production began rising fast, from 17,000 tons in 1740 to 3 million tons in 1844, as much as in the rest of the world put together.

In turn, there seemed no limit to the amount of iron that an industrializing society would purchase or to the novel applications for this cheap and useful material. In 1779 the iron manufacturer Abraham Darby III (grandson of the first Abraham Darby) built a bridge of iron across the Severn River. In 1851 Londoners marveled at the **Crystal Palace,** a huge greenhouse made entirely of iron and glass and large enough to enclose the tallest trees.

The availability of cheap iron made the mass production of objects such as guns, hardware, and tools appealing. However, fitting together the parts of these products required a great deal of labor. To reduce labor costs, manufacturers turned to the idea of interchangeable parts. This idea originated in the eighteenth century when French army officers attempted, without success, to persuade gun makers to produce precisely identical parts. Craftsmen continued to use traditional methods to make gun parts that had to be fitted together by hand. By the mid-nineteenth century, however, interchangeable-parts manufacturing had been adopted in the manufacture of firearms, farm equipment, and sewing machines. At the Crystal Palace exhibition of 1851, Europeans called it the "American system of manufactures." In the next hundred years the use of machinery to mass-produce consumer items was to become the hallmark of American industry.

The Steam Engine

In the history of the world, there had been a number of periods of great technological inventiveness and economic growth. But in all previous cases, the dynamism eventually faltered for various reasons, such as the Mongol invasions that overthrew the Song dynasty in China and the Abassid Caliphate (750–1258) in the Middle East.

The Industrial Revolution that began in the eighteenth century, in contrast, has never slowed down but has instead only accelerated. One reason has been increased interactions between scientists, technicians, and businesspeople. Another has been access to an inexhaustible source of cheap energy, namely fossil fuels.

The first machine to transform fossil fuel into mechanical energy was the **steam engine,** a substitute for human and animal power as well as for wind and water power. Although the mechanization of manufacturing was very important, the steam engine was what set the Industrial Revolution apart from all previous periods of growth and innovation.

Before the eighteenth century, many activities had been limited by the lack of energy. For example, deep

Transatlantic Steamship Race In 1838, two ships equipped with steam engines, the *Sirius* and the *Great Western*, steamed from England to New York. Although the *Sirius* left a few days earlier, the *Great Western*—shown here arriving in New York harbor—almost caught up with it, arriving just four hours after the *Sirius*. This race inaugurated regular transatlantic steamship service. (Courtesy of the Mariners' Museum, Newport News, VA)

mines filled with water faster than horses could pump it out. Scientists understood the concept of atmospheric pressure and had created experimental devices to turn heat into motion, but they had not found a way to put those devices to practical use. Then, between 1702 and 1712 Thomas Newcomen developed the first practical steam engine, a crude but effective device. One engine could pump water out of mines as fast as four horses, and it could run day and night without getting tired.

The Newcomen engine's voracious appetite for fuel mattered little in coal mines, where fuel was cheap, but made the engine too costly for other uses. In 1764 **James Watt,** a maker of scientific instruments at Glasgow University in Scotland, was asked to repair the university's model Newcomen engine. Watt realized that the engine wasted fuel because the cylinder had to be alternately heated and cooled. He developed a separate condenser—a vessel into which the steam was allowed to escape after it had done its work, leaving the cylinder always hot and the condenser always cold. Watt patented his idea in 1769. He enlisted the help of the iron manufacturer Matthew Boulton to turn his invention into a commercial product. Their first engines were sold to pump water out of copper and tin mines, where fuel was too costly for Newcomen engines. In 1781 Watt invented the sun-and-planet gear, which turned the back-and-forth action of the piston into rotary motion. This allowed steam engines to power machinery in flour and cotton mills, pottery manufactures, and other industries. Watt's steam engine was the most celebrated invention of the eighteenth century. Because there seemed almost no limit to the amount of coal in the ground, steam-generated energy appeared to be an inexhaustible source of power, and steam engines could be used where animal, wind, and water power were lacking.

Inspired by the success of Watt's engine, inventors in France in 1783, in the United States in 1787, and in England in 1788 put steam engines on boats. The need to travel great distances in the United States explains why the first commercially successful steamboat was Robert Fulton's *North River*, which steamed up and down the Hudson River between New York City and Albany, New York, in 1807.

Soon steamboats were launched on other American rivers, especially the Ohio and the Mississippi, gateways to the Midwest. In the 1820s the Erie Canal linked the Atlantic seaboard with the Great Lakes and opened Ohio, Indiana, and Illinois to European settlement. Steamboats proliferated west of the Appalachian Mountains; by 1830 some three hundred plied the Mississippi and its tributaries. To counter the competition from New York State, Pennsylvania built a thousand miles of canals by 1840. The United States was fast becoming a nation that moved by water.

Oceangoing steam-powered ships were much more difficult to build than river boats, for the first steam engines used so much coal that no ship could carry more than a few days' supply. The *Savannah*, which crossed the Atlantic in 1819, was a sailing ship with an auxiliary steam engine that was used for only ninety hours of its twenty-nine-day trip. Engineers soon developed more efficient engines, and in 1838 two steamers, the *Great Western* and the *Sirius*, crossed the Atlantic on steam power alone. Elsewhere, sailing ships held their own until late in the century. World trade was growing so fast that there was enough business for ships of every kind.

Railroads

On land as on water, the problem was not imagining uses for steam-powered vehicles but building ones that worked, for steam engines were too heavy and weak to pull any weight. After Watt's patent expired in 1800, inventors experimented with lighter, more powerful high-pressure engines—an idea Watt had rejected as too dangerous. In 1804 the engineer Richard Trevithick built an engine that consumed twelve times less coal than Newcomen's and three times less than Watt's. With it, he built several steam-powered vehicles able to travel on roads or rails.

By the 1820s England had many railways on which horses pulled heavy wagons. On one of them, the Stockton and Darlington Railway, chief engineer George Stephenson began using steam locomotives in 1825. Four years later the owners of the Liverpool and Manchester Railway organized a contest between steam-powered locomotives and horse-drawn wagons. Stephenson and his son Robert easily won the contest with their locomotive *Rocket*, which pulled a 20-ton train at up to 30 miles (48 kilometers) per hour. After that triumph, a railroad-building mania that lasted for twenty years swept Britain. The first lines linked towns and mines with the nearest harbor or waterway. In the late 1830s passenger traffic soared, and entrepreneurs built lines between the major cities and then to small towns as well. Railroads were far cheaper, faster, and more comfortable than stagecoaches, and millions of people got in the habit of traveling.

In the United States entrepreneurs built railroads as quickly and cheaply as possible with an eye to fast profits, not long-term durability. By the 1840s, 6,000 miles (10,000 kilometers) of track connected and radiated westward from Boston, New York, Philadelphia, and Baltimore. The boom of the 1840s was dwarfed by the mania of the 1850s, when 21,000 miles (34,000 kilometers) of new track were laid, much of it westward across the Appalachians to Memphis, St. Louis, and Chicago. After 1856 the trip from New York to Chicago, which had once taken three weeks by boat and on horseback, could be made in forty-eight hours. More than anything else, it was the railroads that opened up the Midwest, turning the vast prairie into wheat fields and pasture for cattle to feed the industrial cities of the eastern United States.

The De Witt Clinton Locomotive, 1835–1840 The De Witt Clinton was the first steam locomotive built in the United States. The high smokestack let the hot cinders cool so they would not set fire to nearby trees, an important consideration at a time when eastern North America was still covered with forest. The three passenger cars are clearly horse carriages fitted with railroad wheel. (Corbis)

Railways triggered the industrialization of Europe (see Map 23.2). Belgium, independent since 1830, quickly copied the British railways. In France and Prussia, the state planned and supervised railroad construction from the start. This delayed construction until the mid-1840s. When it began, however, it had an even greater impact than in Britain, for it not only satisfied the long-standing need for transportation, but also stimulated the iron, machinery, and construction industries.

Communication over Wires

After the Italian scientist Alessandro Volta invented the battery in 1800, making it possible to produce an electric current, many inventors tried to apply electricity to communication. The first practical **electric telegraph** systems were developed almost simultaneously in England and Amer-

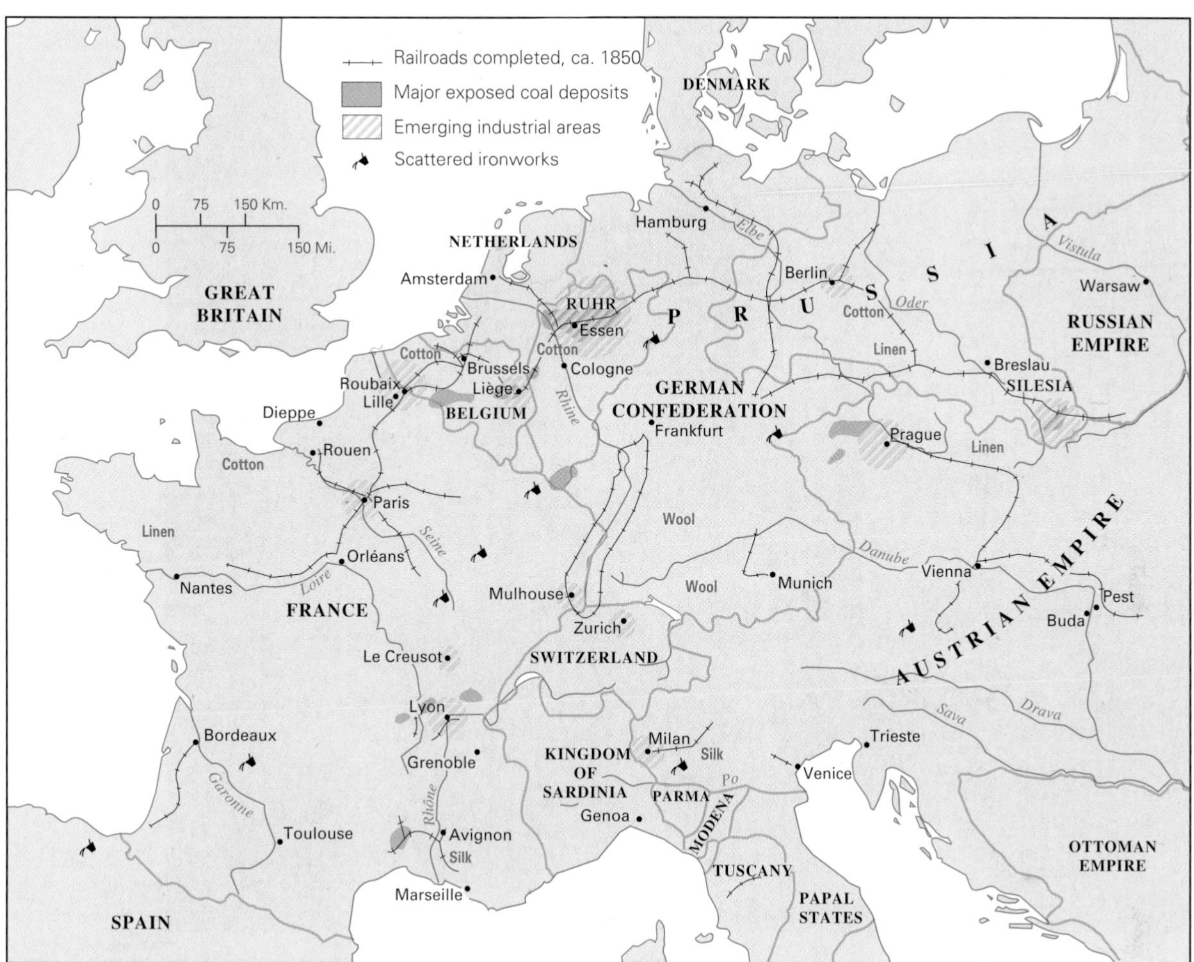

Map 23.2 Industrialization in Europe, ca. 1850 In 1850 industrialization was in its early stages on the European continent. The first industrial regions were comparatively close to England and possessed rich coal deposits: Belgium and the Ruhr district of Germany. Politics determined the location of railroads. Notice the star-shaped French network of rail lines emanating from Paris and the lines linking the different parts of the German Confederation.

ica. In 1837 in England Charles Wheatstone and William Cooke introduced a five-wire telegraph that remained in use until the early twentieth century. That same year, the American Samuel Morse introduced a code of dots and dashes that could be transmitted with a single wire; in 1843 he erected a telegraph line between Washington and Baltimore.

The railroad companies were among the first users of the new electric telegraph. They allowed telegraph companies to string wires along the tracks in exchange for the right to send telegrams from station to station announcing the departure and arrival of trains. Such messages made railroads much safer as well as more efficient.

By the late 1840s telegraph wires were being strung throughout the eastern United States and western Europe. In 1851 the first submarine telegraph cable was laid across the English Channel from England to France; it was the beginning of a network that eventually connected the entire globe. The world was rapidly shrinking, to the applause of Europeans and Americans for whom speed was a clear measure of progress. No longer were communications limited to the speed of a sailing ship, a galloping horse, or a fast-moving train.

Overcrowded London The French artist Gustave Doré depicted the tenements of industrial London where workers and their families lived. This drawing shows crowded and unsanitary row houses, each one room wide, with tiny back yards, and a train steaming across a viaduct overhead. (Prints Division, New York Public Library, Astor, Lenox, and Tilden Foundations)

THE IMPACT OF THE EARLY INDUSTRIAL REVOLUTION

The Industrial Revolution led to profound changes in society, politics, and the economy. At first, the changes were local. While some people became wealthy and built beautiful mansions, others lived in slum neighborhoods with polluted water and smoke-filled air. By the mid-nineteenth century, the worst local effects were being alleviated and cities became cleaner and healthier. Replacing them on a national scale were more complex problems: business cycles, labor conflicts, and the transformation of entire regions into industrial landscapes. At the international and global level, industrialization empowered the nations of western Europe and North America at the expense of the rest of the world.

The New Industrial Cities

The most dramatic environmental changes brought about by industrialization occurred in the towns. Never before had towns grown so fast. London, one of the largest cities in Europe in 1700 with 500,000 inhabitants, grew to 959,000 by 1800 and to 2,363,000 by 1850; it was then the largest city the world had ever known. Smaller towns grew even faster. Manchester, a small town of 20,000 in 1758, reached 400,000 a century later, a twentyfold increase. Liverpool grew sixfold in sixty years, from 82,000 in 1801 to 472,000 in 1861. New York City, already 100,000 strong in 1815, reached 600,000 (including Brooklyn) in 1850. European cities also grew, but more slowly; their fastest growth occurred after 1850 with increasing industrialization. In some areas, towns merged and formed megalopolises, such as Greater London, the English Midlands, central Belgium, and the Ruhr district of western Germany.

Industrialization made some people very prosperous. A great deal of this new wealth went into the building of fine homes, churches, museums, and theaters in wealthy neighborhoods in London, Berlin, and New York. Much of the beauty of London dates from the time of the Industrial Revolution. Yet, by all accounts, the industrial cities grew much too fast, and much of the growth occurred in the poorest neighborhoods. As poor migrants streamed in from the countryside, developers built cheap, shoddy row houses for them to rent. These tenements were dangerously overcrowded. Often, several families had to live in one small room.

Sudden population growth, overcrowding, and inadequate municipal services conspired to make urban problems more serious than in earlier times. Town dwellers recently arrived from the country brought country ways with them. People threw their sewage and trash out the windows to be washed down the gutters in the streets. The poor kept pigs and chickens; the rich kept horses; and pedestrians stepped into the street at their own risk. Factories and workers' housing were mixed together. Air pollution from burning coal, a problem since the sixteenth century, got steadily worse. Londoners in particular breathed dense and noxious coal smoke. People drank water drawn from wells and rivers contaminated by sewage and industrial runoff. The River Irwell, which ran through Manchester, was, in the words of one visitor, "considerably less a river than a flood of liquid manure."[1]

"Every day that I live," wrote an American visitor to Manchester, "I thank Heaven that I am not a poor man with a family in England."[2] In his poem "Milton," William Blake (1757–1827) expressed the revulsion of sensitive people at the spoliation of England's "mountains green" and "pleasant pastures":

> And did the Countenance Divine
> Shine forth upon our clouded hills?
> And was Jerusalem builded here
> Among these dark Satanic Mills?

Railroads invaded the towns, bringing noise and smoke into densely populated neighborhoods. Railroad companies built their stations as close to the heart of cities as they could. On the outskirts of cities, railroad yards, sidings, and repair shops covered acres of land, surrounded by miles of warehouses and workers' housing. Farther out, far from the dangerous and polluted cities where their factories were located, newly rich industrialists created an environment halfway between country homes and townhouses: the first suburbs.

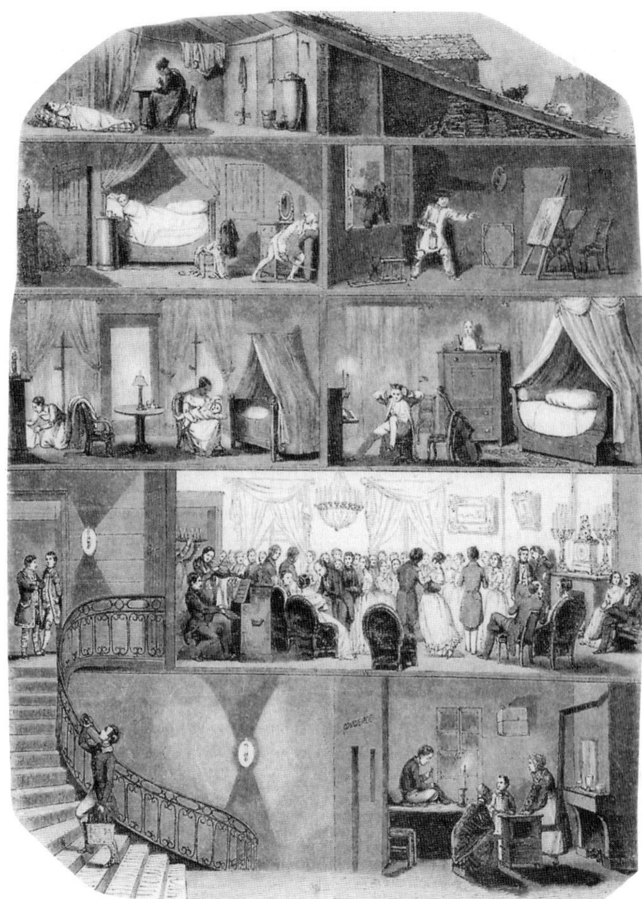

Paris Apartment at Night This cutaway drawing in a French magazine shows the vertical segregation by social class that prevailed in the 1840s. The lower level is occupied by the concierge and her family. The first floor belongs to a wealthy family throwing a party for high-society friends. Middle-class people living on the next floor seem annoyed by the noise coming from below. Above them, a thief has entered an artist's studio. A poor seamstress and her child live in the garret under the roof. When elevators were introduced in the late nineteenth century, people of different income levels became segregated by neighborhoods instead of by floors. (Bibliothèque nationale de France)

Under these conditions, diseases proliferated. To the long list of preindustrial urban diseases such as smallpox, dysentery, and tuberculosis, industrialization added new ailments. Rickets, a bone disease caused by lack of sunshine, became endemic in dark and smoky industrial cities. Steamships brought cholera from India, causing great epidemics that struck poor neighborhoods especially hard. In the 1850s, when the average life expectancy in England was forty years, it was only twenty-four years in Manchester, and around seventeen years in Manchester's poorest neighborhoods, because of high rates of infant mortality. Observers of nineteenth-century industrial cities documented the horrors of slum life in vivid detail. Their shocking reports led to municipal reforms, such as garbage removal, water and sewage systems, and parks and schools. These measures began to alleviate the ills of urban life after the mid-nineteenth century.

Rural Environments

Long before the Industrial Revolution began, practically no wilderness areas were left in Britain and very few in western Europe. Almost every piece of land was covered with fields, forests, or pastures shaped by human activity, or by towns; yet humans continued to alter the environment. The most serious problem was deforestation. As they had been doing for centuries, people cut timber to build ships and houses, to heat homes, and to manufacture bricks, iron, glass, beer, bread, and many other items (see Chapter 17).

Americans transformed their environment even faster than Europeans. In North America, the Canadian and American governments seized land from the Indians and made it available at low cost to white farmers and logging companies. After shipbuilding and construction had depleted the British forests in the early nineteenth century, Britain relied heavily on imports of Canadian lumber. East of the Appalachian Mountains, settlers viewed forests not as a valuable resource but as a hindrance to development. In their haste to "open up the West," pioneers felled trees and burned them, built houses and abandoned them, and moved on. The cultivation of cotton in the southern United States was especially harmful. Planters cut down forests, grew cotton for a few years until it depleted the soil, then moved west, abandoning the land to scrub pines. This was slash-and-burn agriculture on an industrial scale.

At that time, America seemed immune to human depredations. Americans thought of nature as an obstacle to be overcome and dominated. This mindset persisted long after the entire continent was occupied and the environment truly endangered.

Paradoxically, in some ways industrialization relieved pressures on the environment in Europe. Raw materials once grown on the land—such as wood, hay, and wool—were replaced by materials found underground, like iron ore and coal, or obtained overseas, like cotton. While Russia, Sweden, the United States, and other forested countries continued to smelt iron with charcoal, the British and western Europeans substituted coke made from coal. As the population increased and land grew scarcer, the cost of growing feed for horses rose, creating incentives to find new, less land-hungry means of transportation. Likewise, as iron became cheaper and wood more expensive, ships and many other objects formerly made of wood began to be made of iron.

To contemporaries, the most obvious changes in rural life were brought about by the new transportation systems. In the eighteenth century France had a national network of quality roads, which Napoleon extended into Italy and Germany. In Britain local governments' neglect of the roads that served long-distance traffic led to the formation of private enterprises—"Turnpike Trusts"—that built numerous toll roads. For heavy goods, horse-drawn wagons were costly even on good roads because of the need to feed the horses. The growing volume of heavy freight triggered canal-building booms in Britain, France, and the Low Countries in the late eighteenth century. Some canals, like the duke of Bridgewater's canal in England, connected coal mines to towns or navigable rivers. Others linked navigable rivers and created national transportation networks.

Canals were marvels of construction, with deep cuts, tunnels, and even aqueducts that carried barges over rivers. They also were a sort of school where engineers learned skills they were able to apply to the next great transportation system: the railroads. They laid track across rolling country by cutting deeply into hillsides and erecting daringly long bridges of stone and iron across valleys. Lesser lines snaked their way to small towns hidden in remote valleys. Soon, clanking trains pulled by puffing, smoke-belching locomotives were invading long-isolated districts.

Thus, in the century after industrialization began, the landscape of industrializing countries was transformed more rapidly than ever before. But the ecological changes, like the technological and economic changes that caused them, were only beginning.

Working Conditions

Industrialization offered new opportunities to the enterprising. Carpenters, metalworkers, and machinists were in great demand. Since industrial machines were fairly simple, some workers became engineers or went into business for themselves. The boldest in England moved to the European continent, the Americas, or India, using their skills to establish new industries.

The successful, however, were a minority. Most industrial jobs were unskilled, repetitive, and boring. Factory work did not vary with the seasons or the time of day but began and ended by the clock. Workdays were long; there were few breaks; and foremen watched constantly. Workers who performed one simple task over and over had little sense of achievement or connection to the final product. Industrial accidents were common and could ruin a family. Unlike even the poorest preindustrial farmer or artisan, factory workers had no control over their tools, jobs, or working hours.

Industrial work, by definition, was physically removed from the home. This had a major impact on women and family life. Women workers were concentrated in textile mills, partly because of ancient traditions, partly because textile work required less strength than metalworking, construction, or hauling. On average, women earned one-third to one-half as much as men. Young unmarried women worked to support themselves or to save for marriage. Married women took factory jobs when their husbands were unable to support the family. Mothers of infants faced a hard choice: whether to leave their babies with wet-nurses at great expense and danger or bring them to the factory and keep them drugged. Rather than working together as family units, husbands and wives increasingly worked in different places.

In the early years of industrialization, even where factory work was available, it was never the main occupation of working women. Most young women who sought paid employment became domestic servants in spite of the low pay, drudgery, and risk of sexual abuse by male employers. Women with small children tried hard to find work they could do at home, such as laundry, sewing, embroidery, millinery, or taking in lodgers.

Even with both parents working, poor families found it hard to make ends meet. As in preindustrial societies, parents thought children should contribute to their upkeep as soon as they were able to. The first generation of workers brought children as young as five or six with them to the factories and mines; they had little choice, since there were no public schools or daycare centers. Employers encouraged the practice and even hired orphans. They preferred children because they were cheaper and more docile than adults and were better able to tie broken threads or crawl under machines to sweep the dust.

In Arkwright's cotton mills two-thirds of the workers were children. In another mill 17 percent were under ten years of age, and 53 percent were between ten and seventeen; they worked fourteen to sixteen hours a day and were beaten if they made mistakes or fell asleep. Mine operators used children to pull coal carts along the low passageways from the coal face to the mine shaft. In the mid-nineteenth century, when the British government began restricting child labor, mill owners increasingly recruited adult immigrants from Ireland.

"Love Conquers Fear" This is a sentimental Victorian drawing of children in a textile mill. Child labor was common in the first half of the nineteenth century, and workers were exposed to dangerous machines and moving belts, as well as to dust and dirt. (British Library)

American industry began on a somewhat different note than the British. In the early nineteenth century Americans still remembered their revolutionary ideals. When Francis Cabot Lowell built a cotton mill in Massachusetts, he hired the unmarried daughters of New England farmers, promising them decent wages and housing in dormitories under careful moral supervision. Other manufacturers eager to combine profits with morality followed his example. Soon the profit motive won out, and manufacturers imposed longer hours, harsher working conditions, and lower wages. The young women protested: "As our fathers resisted with blood the lordly avarice of the British ministry, so we, their daughters, never will wear the yoke which has been prepared for us."[3] When they went on strike, the mill owners replaced them with Irish immigrant women willing to accept lower pay and worse conditions.

While the cotton boom enriched planters, merchants, and manufacturers, African-Americans paid for it with their freedom. In the 1790s, 700,000 slaves of African descent lived in the United States. The rising demand for cotton and the British and American prohibition of the African slave trade in 1808 caused an increase in the price of slaves. As the "Cotton Kingdom" expanded, the number of slaves rose through natural increase and the reluctance of slave owners to free their slaves. By 1850 there were 3.2 million slaves in the United States, 60 percent of whom grew cotton. Similarly, Europe's and North America's surging demand for tea and coffee prolonged slavery in the sugar plantations of the West Indies and caused it to spread to the coffee-growing regions of southern Brazil. In the British West Indies slavery was abolished in 1833, but elsewhere in the Americas it persisted for another thirty to fifty years.

Slavery was not, as white American southerners maintained, a "peculiar institution"—a consequence of biological differences, biblical injunctions, or African traditions. Slavery was just as much part and parcel of the Industrial Revolution as child labor in Britain, the clothes that people wore, and the beverages they drank.

Changes in Society

Industrialization accentuated the polarization of society and income disparities. In his novel *Sybil; or, The Two Nations*, the British politician Benjamin Disraeli° (1804–1881) spoke of "Two nations between whom there is no intercourse and no sympathy, who are as ignorant of each other's habits, thoughts, and feelings as if they were dwellers in different zones, or inhabitants of different planets . . . the rich and the poor."

In Britain the worst-off were those who clung to an obsolete skill or craft. The cotton-spinning boom of the 1790s briefly brought prosperity to weavers. Their high wages and low productivity, however, induced inventors to develop power looms. As a result, by 1811 the wages of handloom weavers had fallen by a third; by 1832, by two-thirds. Even by working longer hours, they could not escape destitution.

Disraeli (diz-RAY-lee)

In the industrial regions of Britain and continental Europe, the wages and standard of living of factory workers did not decline steadily like those of handloom weavers; they fluctuated wildly. During the war years of 1792 to 1815, the price of food, on which the poor spent most of their income, rose faster than wages. The result was widespread hardship. Then, in the 1820s real wages and public health began to improve. Industrial production grew at over 3 percent a year, pulling the rest of the economy along. Prices fell and wages rose. Even the poor could afford comfortable, washable cotton clothes and underwear.

Improvement, however, was not steady. One reason was the effect of **business cycles**—recurrent swings from economic hard times to recovery and growth, then back to hard times. When demand fell, businesses contracted or closed, and workers found themselves unemployed. Most had few or no savings, and no government at the time provided unemployment insurance. Hard times returned in the "hungry forties." In 1847–1848 the potato crop failed in Ireland. One-quarter of the Irish population died in the resulting famine, and another quarter emigrated to England and North America. On the European continent the negative effects of economic downturns were tempered by the existence of small family farms to which urban workers could return when they were laid off.

Only in the 1850s did the benefits of industrialization—cheaper food, clothing, and utensils—begin to improve workers' standard of living. The real beneficiary of the early Industrial Revolution was the middle class. In Britain landowning gentry and merchants had long shared wealth and influence. In the late eighteenth century a new group arose: entrepreneurs whose money came from manufacturing. Most, like Arkwright and Wedgwood, were the sons of middling shopkeepers, craftsmen, or farmers. Their enterprises were usually self-financed, for little capital was needed to start a cotton-spinning or machine-building business. Many tried and some succeeded, largely by plowing their profits back into the business. A generation later, in the nineteenth century, some newly rich industrialists bought their way into high society. The same happened in western Europe after 1815.

Before the Industrial Revolution, wives of merchants had often participated in the family business; widows occasionally managed sizable businesses on their own. With industrialization came a "cult of domesticity" to justify removing middle-class women from contact with the business world. Instead, they became responsible for the home, the servants, the education of children, and the family's social life (see Chapter 27).

Middle-class people who attributed their success, often correctly, to their own efforts and virtues believed in individual responsibility: if some people could succeed through hard work, thrift, and temperance, then those who did not succeed had no one but themselves to blame. Many workers, however, were newly arrived from rural districts and earned too little to save for the long stretches of unemployment they experienced. The squalor and misery of life in factory towns led to a noticeable increase in drunkenness on paydays. While the life of the poor remained hard, the well-to-do attributed their own success to sobriety, industriousness, thrift, and responsibility. The moral position of the middle-class mingled condemnation with concern, coupled with feelings of helplessness in the face of terrible social problems, such as drunkenness, prostitution, and child abandonment.

New Economic and Political Ideas

Changes as profound as the Industrial Revolution triggered political ferment and ideological conflict. So many other momentous events took place during those years—the American Revolution (1776–1783), the French Revolution (1789–1799), the Napoleonic Wars (1804–1815), the reactions and revolts that periodically swept over Europe after 1815—that we cannot neatly separate out the consequences of industrialization from the rest. But it is clear that by undermining social traditions and causing a growing gap between rich and poor, the Industrial Revolution strengthened the ideas of laissez faire° and socialism and sparked workers' protests.

Laissez Faire and Its Critics

The most celebrated exponent of **laissez faire** ("let them do") was Adam Smith (1723–1790), a Scottish economist. In *The Wealth of Nations* (1776) Smith argued that if individuals were allowed to seek personal gain, the effect, as though guided by an "invisible hand," would be to increase the general welfare. The government should refrain from interfering in business, except to protect private property; it should even allow duty-free trade with foreign countries. By advocating free-market capitalism, Smith was challenging the prevailing economic doctrine of earlier centuries, **mercantilism,** which argued that governments should regulate trade in order to maximize their hoard of precious metals (see Chapter 19).

Persuaded by Adam Smith's arguments, governments dismantled many of their regulations in the decades after 1815. Britain even lowered its import duties, though other countries kept theirs. Nonetheless, it was obvious that industrialization was not improving the general welfare but was instead causing widespread misery. Two other thinkers, Thomas Malthus (1766–1834) and David Ricardo (1772–1832), attempted to explain the poverty they saw without challenging the basic premises of laissez faire. The cause of the workers' plight, Malthus and Ricardo said, was the population boom, which outstripped the food supply and led to falling wages. The workers' poverty, they claimed, was as much a result of "natural law" as the wealth of successful businessmen, and the only way the working class could avoid mass famine was to delay marriage and practice self-restraint and sexual abstinence.

Laissez faire provided an ideological justification for a special kind of capitalism: banks, stock markets, and chartered companies allowed investors to obtain profits with reasonable risks but with much less government control and interference than in the past. In particular, removing guild and other restrictions allowed businesses to employ women and children and keep wages low.

Businesspeople in Britain eagerly adopted laissez-faire ideas that justified their activities and kept the government at bay. But not everyone accepted the grim conclusions of the "dismal science," as economics was then known. The British philosopher Jeremy Bentham (1748–1832) believed that it was possible to maximize "the greatest happiness of the greatest number," if only a Parliament of enlightened reformers would study the social problems of the day and pass appropriate legislation.

The German economist Friedrich List (1789–1846) rejected laissez faire and free trade as a British trick "to make the rest of the world, like the Hindus, its serfs in all industrial and commercial relations." To protect their "infant industries" from British competition, he argued, the German states had to eliminate tariff barriers between them but erect high barriers against imports from Britain. On the European continent, List's ideas were as influential as those of Smith and Ricardo and led in 1834 to the formation of the Zollverein,° a customs union of most of the German states.

laissez faire (LAY-say fair)

Zollverein (TSOLL-feh-rine)

Positivists and Utopian Socialists

Bentham optimistically advocated gradual improvements. In contrast, three French social thinkers, moved by sincere concern for the poor, offered a radically new vision of a just civilization. Espousing a philosophy called **positivism,** the count of Saint-Simon (1760–1825) and his disciple Auguste Comte° (1798–1857) argued that the scientific method could solve social as well as technical problems. They recommended that the poor, guided by scientists and artists, form workers' communities under the protection of benevolent business leaders. These ideas found no following among workers, but they attracted the enthusiastic support of bankers and entrepreneurs, for whom positivism provided a rationale for investing in railroads, canals, and other symbols of modernity. The third French thinker, Charles Fourier° (1768–1837), loathed capitalists and imagined an ideal society in which groups of sixteen hundred workers would live in dormitories and work together on the land and in workshops where music, wine, and pastries would soften the hardships of labor. Critics called his ideas **utopian° socialism,** from the Greek word *utopia* meaning "nowhere." Fourier's ideas are now considered a curiosity, but positivism resonates to this day among liberal thinkers, especially in Latin America.

The person who came closest to creating a utopian community was the Englishman Robert Owen (1771–1858), a successful cotton manufacturer who believed that industry could provide prosperity for all. Conscience-stricken by the plight of British workers, Owen took over the management of New Lanark, a mill town south of Glasgow. He improved the housing and added schools, a church, and other amenities. He also testified in Parliament against child labor and for government inspection of working conditions, angering his fellow industrialists, but helping bring about long-overdue reforms.

Protests and Reforms

Workers benefited little from the ideas of these middle-class philosophers. Instead, they resisted the harsh working conditions in their own ways. They changed jobs frequently. They were often absent, especially on Mondays. When they were not closely watched, the quality of their work was likely to be poor.

Periodically, workers rioted or went on strike, especially when food prices were high and when downturns in the business cycle left many unemployed. In some places, craftsmen broke into factories and destroyed the machines that threatened their livelihoods. Such acts of resistance did nothing to change the nature of industrial work. Not until workers learned to act together could they hope to have much influence.

Gradually, workers formed benevolent societies and organizations to demand universal male suffrage and shorter workdays. In 1834 Robert Owen organized the Grand National Consolidated Trade Union to lobby for an eight-hour workday; it quickly gained half a million members but collapsed a few months later in the face of government prosecution of trade-union activities. A new movement called Chartism arose soon thereafter. It was led by the London cabinetmaker William Lovett and the Irish landlord Fergus O'Connor and appealed to miners and industrial workers. It demanded universal male suffrage, equal electoral districts, the secret ballot, salaries for members of Parliament, and annual elections. It gathered 1.3 million signatures on a petition, but Parliament rejected it. Chartism collapsed in 1848, but left a legacy of labor organizing.

Eventually, mass movements persuaded political leaders to look into the abuses of industrial life, despite the prevailing laissez-faire philosophy. In the 1820s and 1830s the British Parliament began investigating conditions in factories and mines. The Factory Act of 1833 prohibited the employment of children younger than nine in textile mills. It also limited the working hours of children between the ages of nine and thirteen to eight hours a day and of fourteen- to eighteen-year-olds to twelve hours. The Mines Act of 1842 prohibited the employment of women and boys under age ten underground. Several decades passed before the government appointed enough inspectors to enforce the new laws.

Most important was the struggle over the Corn Laws—tariffs on imported grain. Their repeal in 1846, in the name of "free trade," was designed to lower the cost of food for workers and thereby allow employers to pay lower wages. A victory for laissez faire, the repeal also represented a victory for the rising class of manufacturers and other employers over the conservative landowners who had long dominated politics and whose harvests faced competition from cheaper imported food.

The British learned to seek reform through accommodation. On the European continent, in contrast, the revolutions of 1848 revealed widespread discontent with repressive governments but failed to soften the hardships of industrialization (see Chapter 27).

Comte (COME-tuh) **Fourier** (FOOR-yeh) **utopian** (you-TOE-pee-uhn)

Industrialization and the Nonindustrial World

The spread of the Industrial Revolution in the early nineteenth century transformed the relations of western Europe and North America with the rest of the world. For most of the world, trade with the industrial countries meant exporting raw materials, not locally made handicraft products. China was defeated and humiliated by the products of industrial manufacture. In Egypt and India cheap industrial imports, backed by the power of Great Britain, delayed industrialization for a century or more. In these three cases, we can discern the outlines of the Western domination that has characterized the history of the world since the late nineteenth century.

In January 1840 a shipyard in Britain launched a radically new ship. The *Nemesis* had an iron hull, a flat bottom that allowed it to navigate in shallow waters, and a steam engine to power it upriver and against the wind. The ship was heavily armed. In November it arrived off the coast of China. Though ships from Europe had been sailing to China for three hundred years, the *Nemesis* was the first steam-powered iron gunboat seen in Asian waters. A Chinese observer noted: "Iron is employed to make it strong. The hull is painted black, weaver's shuttle fashion. On each side is a wheel, which by the use of coal fire is made to revolve as fast as a running horse. . . . At the vessel's head is a Marine God, and at the head, stern, and sides are cannon, which give it a terrific appearance. Steam vessels are a wonderful invention of foreigners, and are calculated to offer delight to many."[4]

Instead of offering delight, the *Nemesis* and other steam-powered warships that soon joined it steamed up the Chinese rivers, bombarded forts and cities, and transported troops and supplies from place to place along the coast and up rivers far more quickly than Chinese soldiers could move on foot. With this new weapon, Britain, a small island nation half a world away, was able to defeat the largest and most populated country in the world (see Chapter 26).

Egypt, strongly influenced by European ideas since the French invasion of 1798, began to industrialize in the early nineteenth century. The driving force was its ruler, Muhammad Ali (1769–1849), a man who was to play a major role not only in the history of Egypt but in the Middle East and East Africa as well (see Chapter 25). He wanted to build up the Egyptian economy and military in order to become less dependent on the Ottoman sultan, his nominal overlord. To do so, he imported advisers and technicians from Europe and built cotton mills, foundries, shipyards, weapons factories, and other industrial enterprises. To pay for all this, he made the peasants grow wheat and cotton, which the government bought at a low price and exported at a profit. He also imposed high tariffs on imported goods in order to force the pace of industrialization.

Steam Tractor in India Power machinery was introduced into India because of the abundance of skilled low-cost labor. In this scene, a steam tractor fords a shallow stream to the delight of onlookers. The towerlike construction on the right is probably a pier for a railroad bridge. (Billie Love Historical Society)

Muhammad Ali's efforts fell afoul of the British, who did not want a powerful country threatening to interrupt the flow of travelers and mail across Egypt, the shortest route between Europe and India. When Egypt went to war against the Ottoman Empire in 1839, Britain intervened and forced Muhammad Ali to eliminate all import duties in the name of free trade. Unprotected, Egypt's fledgling industries could not compete with the flood of cheap British products. Thereafter, Egypt exported raw cotton, imported manufactured goods, and became, in effect, an economic dependency of Britain.

Until the late eighteenth century, India had been the world's largest producer and exporter of cotton textiles, handmade by skilled spinners and weavers. The British

East India Company took over large parts of India just as the Industrial Revolution was beginning in Britain (see Chapter 25 and Map 25.2). It allowed cheap British factory-made yarn and cloth to flood the Indian market duty-free, putting spinners and later handloom weavers out of work. Unlike Britain, India had no factories to which displaced handicraft workers could turn for work. Most of them became landless peasants, eking out a precarious living.

Like other tropical regions, India became an exporter of raw materials and an importer of British industrial goods. To hasten the process, British entrepreneurs and colonial officials introduced railroads into the subcontinent. The construction of India's railroad network began in the mid-1850s, along with coal mining to fuel the locomotives and the installation of telegraph lines to connect the major cities.

Some Indian entrepreneurs saw opportunities in the atmosphere of change that the British created. In 1854 the Bombay merchant Cowasjee Nanabhoy Davar imported an engineer, four skilled workers, and several textile machines from Britain and started India's first textile mill. This was the beginning of India's mechanized cotton industry. Despite many gifted entrepreneurs, India's industrialization proceeded at a snail's pace, for the government was in British hands and the British did nothing to encourage Indian industry.

The cases of Egypt, India, and China show how the demands of Western nations and the military advantage that industrialization gave them led them to interfere in the internal affairs of nonindustrial societies. As we shall see in Chapter 28, this was the start of a new age of Western dominance.

Conclusion

The great change we call the Industrial Revolution began in Great Britain, a society that was open to innovation, commercial enterprise, and the cross-fertilization of science, technology, and business. New machines and processes in the cotton and iron industries were instrumental in launching the Industrial Revolution, but what made industrialization an ongoing phenomenon was a new source of energy, the steam engine.

In the period from 1760 to 1851 the new technologies of the Industrial Revolution greatly increased humans' power over nature. Goods could be manufactured in vast quantities at low cost. People and messages could travel at unprecedented speeds. Most important, humans gained access to the energy stored in coal and used it to power machinery and propel ships and trains faster than vehicles had ever traveled before. With their newfound power, humans turned woodland into farmland, dug canals and laid tracks, bridged rivers and cut through mountains, and covered the countryside with towns and cities.

The ability to command nature, far from benefiting everyone, increased the disparities between individuals and societies. Industrialization brought forth entrepreneurs—whether in the mills of England or on plantations in the American South—with enormous power over their employees or slaves, a power that they found easy and profitable to abuse. Some people acquired great wealth, while others lived in poverty and squalor. While middle-class women were restricted to caring for their homes and children, many working-class women had to leave home to earn wages in factories or as domestic servants. These changes in work and family life provoked intense debates among intellectuals. Some defended the disparities in the name of laissez faire; others criticized the injustices that industrialization brought. Society was slow to bring these abuses under control.

By the 1850s the Industrial Revolution had spread from Britain to western Europe and the United States, and its impact was being felt around the world. To make a product that was sold on every continent, the British cotton industry used African slaves, American land, British machines, and Irish workers. As we shall see in Chapter 24, industrialization brought even greater changes to the Americas than it did to the Eastern Hemisphere.

Key Terms

Industrial Revolution
agricultural revolution
mass production
Josiah Wedgwood
division of labor
mechanization
Richard Arkwright
Crystal Palace
steam engine
James Watt
electric telegraph
business cycles
laissez faire
mercantilism
positivism
utopian socialism

Suggested Reading

General works on the history of technology give pride of place to industrialization. For an optimistic overview see Joel Mokyr, *The Lever of Riches: Technological Creativity and Economic Progress* (1990). Other important recent works include James McClellan III and Harold Dorn, *Science and Technology in World History* (1999); David Landes, *The Wealth and Poverty of Nations* (1998); and Ian Inkster, *Technology and Industrialization: Historical Case Studies and International Perspectives* (1998).

There is a rich literature on the British industrial revolution, beginning with T. S. Ashton's classic *The Industrial Revolution, 1760–1830,* published in 1948 and often reprinted. The interactions between scientists, technologists, and businessmen are described in Jenny Uglow, *The Lunar Men: Five Friends Whose Curiosity Changed the World* (2002), but see also Joel Mokyr, *The Gifts of Athena: Historical Origins of the Knowledge Economy* (2002). The importance of the steam engine is the theme of Jack Goldstone, "Efflorescences and Economic Growth in World History: Rethinking the 'Rise of the West' and the Industrial Revolution," in *Journal of World History* (Fall 2002).

The impact of industrialization on workers is the theme of E. P. Thompson's classic work *The Making of the English Working Class* (1963), but see also E. R. Pike, *"Hard Times": Human Documents of the Industrial Revolution* (1966). The role of women is most ably revealed in Lynn Y. Weiner, *From Working Girl to Working Mother: The Female Labor Force in the United States, 1820–1980* (1985), and in Louise Tilly and Joan Scott, *Women, Work, and Family* (1978).

European industrialization is the subject of J. Goodman and K. Honeyman, *Gainful Pursuits: The Making of Industrial Europe: 1600–1914* (1988); John Harris, *Industrial Espionage and Technology Transfer: Britain and France in the Eighteenth Century* (1998); and David Landes, *The Unbound Prometheus: Technological Change and Industrial Development in Western Europe from 1750 to the Present* (1972). On the beginnings of American industrialization see David Jeremy, *Artisans, Entrepreneurs and Machines: Essays on the Early Anglo-American Textile Industry, 1770–1840* (1998).

On the environmental impact of industrialization see Richard Wilkinson, *Poverty and Progress: An Ecological Perspective on Economic Development* (1973), and Richard Tucker and John Richards, *Global Deforestation in the Nineteenth-Century World Economy* (1983).

The first book to treat industrialization as a global phenomenon is Peter Stearns, *The Industrial Revolution in World History* (1993); see also Louise Tilly's important article "Connections" in *American Historical Review* (February 1994).

Notes

1. Quoted in Lewis Mumford, *The City in History* (New York: Harcourt Brace, 1961), 460.
2. Quoted in F. Roy Willis, *Western Civilization: An Urban Perspective,* vol. II (Lexington, MA: D.C. Heath, 1973), 675.
3. Alice Kessler-Harris, *Women Have Always Worked: A Historical Overview* (Old Westbury, New York: The Feminist Press, 1981), 59.
4. *Nautical Magazine* 12 (1843): 346.

24 Nation Building and Economic Transformation in the Americas, 1800–1890

The Train Station in Orizaba, Mexico, 1877 In the last decades of the nineteenth century Mexico's political leaders actively promoted economic development. The railroad became the symbol of this ideal.

CHAPTER OUTLINE

Between 1836 and 1848 Mexico lost 50 percent of its territory to the United States. In the political crisis that followed, reformers, called liberals, fought conservatives for control of the nation. The liberal Benito Juárez° dominated this era as a war leader and a symbol of Mexican nationalism. Many have compared him to his contemporary, Abraham Lincoln. Juárez began his life in poverty. An Amerindian orphan, he became a lawyer and political reformer. He helped drive the dictator Antonio López de Santa Anna from power in 1854 and helped lead efforts to reduce the power of the Catholic Church and the military. He later served as chief justice of the Supreme Court and as president.

When conservatives rebelled against the Constitution of 1857, Juárez assumed the presidency and led liberal forces to victory. Mexico's conservatives turned to Napoleon III of France, who sent an army that suspended the constitution and imposed Archduke Maximilian of Habsburg, brother of Emperor Franz Joseph of Austria, as emperor. But the French army could not defeat Juárez, and Mexican resistance was eventually supported by U.S. diplomatic pressure. When the French left, Maximilian was captured and executed. This victory over a powerful foreign enemy redeemed a nation that had earlier been humiliated by the United States. But the creation of democracy proved more elusive than the protection of Mexican sovereignty. Despite the Mexican constitution's prohibition of presidential reelection, Juárez would serve as president until his death in 1872.

Despite cycles of political violence like that experienced by Mexico, the nineteenth century witnessed a radical transformation of the Western Hemisphere. Spurred by the American and French revolutions see Chapter 22) and encouraged by nationalism and the ideal of political freedom, most of the region's nations achieved independence, although Mexico and others faced foreign interventions.

Throughout the nineteenth century the new nations in the Western Hemisphere wrestled with the difficult questions that independence raised. If colonies could reject submission to imperial powers, could not regions with distinct cultures, social structures, and economies refuse to accept the political authority of the newly formed nation-states? How could nations born in revolution accept the political strictures of written constitutions—even those they wrote themselves? How could the ideals of liberty and freedom expressed in those constitutions be reconciled with the denial of rights to Amerindians, slaves, recent immigrants, and women?

While trying to resolve these political questions, the new nations also attempted to promote economic growth. But colonial economic development, with its emphasis on agricultural and mining exports, inhibited efforts to promote diversification and industrialization, just as the legacy of class and racial division thwarted the realization of political ideals.

As you read this chapter, ask yourself the following questions:

- What were the causes of the revolutions for independence in Latin America?
- What major political challenges did Western Hemisphere nations face in the nineteenth century?
- How did abolitionism, the movement for women's rights, and immigration change the nations of the Western Hemisphere?
- How did industrialization and new agricultural technologies affect the environment?

Independence in Latin America, 1800–1830

As the eighteenth century drew to a close, Spain and Portugal held vast colonial possessions in the Western Hemisphere, although their power had declined relative to that of their British and French rivals. Both Iberian empires had reformed their colonial administration and strengthened their military forces in the eighteenth century. Despite these efforts, the same economic and political forces that had undermined British

Benito Juárez (beh-NEE-toh WAH-rez)

rule in the colonies that became the United States were present in Spanish America and Brazil.

Roots of Revolution, to 1810

The great works of the Enlightenment as well as revolutionary documents like the Declaration of Independence and the Declaration of the Rights of Man circulated widely in Latin America by 1800, but very few colonial residents desired to follow the examples of the American and French Revolutions (see Chapter 22). Local-born members of Latin America's elites and middle classes were frustrated by the political and economic power of colonial officials and angered by high taxes and imperial monopolies. But it was events in Europe that first pushed the colonies towards independence. Napoleon's decision to invade Portugal (1807) and Spain (1808), not revolutionary ideas, created the crisis of legitimacy that undermined the authority of colonial officials, and ignited Latin America's struggle for independence.

In 1808 as a French army neared Lisbon, the royal family of Portugal fled to Brazil. King John VI maintained his court there for over a decade. In Spain, in contrast, Napoleon forced King Ferdinand VII to abdicate and placed his own brother, Joseph Bonaparte, on the throne. Spanish patriots fighting against the French created a new political body, the Junta° Central, to administer the areas they controlled. Most Spaniards viewed the Junta as a temporary patriotic institution created to govern Spain while the king remained a French prisoner. The Junta, however, claimed the right to exercise the king's powers over Spain's colonies, and this claim provoked a crisis.

Large numbers of colonial residents in Spanish America, perhaps a majority, favored obedience to the Junta Central. A vocal minority, which included many wealthy and powerful individuals, objected. The dissenters argued that they were subjects of the king, not dependents of the Spanish nation. They wanted to create local juntas and govern their own affairs until Ferdinand regained the throne. Spanish loyalists in the colonies resisted this tentative assertion of local autonomy and thus provoked armed uprisings. In late 1808 and 1809 popular movements overthrew Spanish colonial officials in Venezuela, Mexico, and Alto Peru (modern Bolivia) and created local juntas. In each case, Spanish officials quickly reasserted control and punished the leaders. Their harsh repression, however, further polarized public opinion in the colonies and gave rise to a greater sense of a separate American nationality. By 1810 Spanish colonial authorities were facing a new round of revolutions more clearly focused on the achievement of independence.

Spanish South America, 1810–1825

In Caracas (the capital city of modern Venezuela) a revolutionary Junta led by creoles (colonial-born whites) declared independence in 1811. Although this group espoused popular sovereignty and representative democracy, its leaders were large landowners who defended slavery and opposed full citizenship for the black and mixed-race majority. Their aim was to expand their own privileges by eliminating Spaniards from the upper levels of Venezuela's government and from the church. The junta's narrow agenda spurred loyalists in the colonial administration and church hierarchy to rally thousands of free blacks and slaves to defend the Spanish Empire. Faced with this determined resistance, the revolutionary movement placed overwhelming political authority in the hands of its military leader **Simón Bolívar**° (1783–1830), who later became the preeminent leader of the independence movement in Spanish South America.

The son of wealthy Venezuelan planters, Bolívar had studied both the classics and the works of the Enlightenment. He used the force of his personality to mobilize political support and to hold the loyalty of his troops. Defeated on many occasions, Bolívar successfully adapted his objectives and policies to attract new allies and build coalitions. Although initially opposed to the abolition of slavery, for example, he agreed to support emancipation in order to draw slaves and freemen to his cause and to gain supplies from Haiti. Bolívar was also capable of using harsh methods to ensure victory. Attempting to force resident Spaniards to join the rebellion in 1813 he proclaimed: "Any Spaniard who does not . . . work against tyranny in behalf of this just cause will be considered an enemy and punished; as a traitor to the nation, he will inevitably be shot by a firing squad."[1]

Between 1813 and 1817 military advantage shifted back and forth between the patriots and loyalists. Bolívar's ultimate success was aided by his decision to enlist demobilized English veterans of the Napoleonic Wars and by a military revolt in Spain in 1820. The English veterans, hardened by combat, helped improve the battlefield performance of Bolívar's army. The revolt in Spain forced Ferdinand VII—restored to the throne in 1814 after the defeat of Napoleon—to accept a constitution that

Junta (HUN-tah)

Simón Bolívar (see-MOAN bow-LEE-varh)

CHRONOLOGY

	United States and Canada	Mexico and Central America	South America
	1789 U.S. Constitution ratified		
1800	**1803** Louisiana Purchase **1812–1815** War of 1812	**1810–1821** Mexican movement for independence	**1808** Portuguese royal family arrives in Brazil **1808–1809** Revolutions for independence begin in Spanish South America **1822** Brazil gains independence
1825	**1836** Texas gains independence from Mexico **1845** Texas admitted as a state	**1846–1848** War between Mexico and the United States **1847–1870** Caste War	
1850	**1848** Women's Rights Convention in Seneca Falls, New York **1861–1865** Civil War **1867** Creation of Dominion of Canada	**1857** Mexico's new constitution limits power of Catholic church and military **1862–1867** French invade Mexico **1867** Emperor Maximilian executed	**1850** Brazilian slave trade ends **1865–1870** Argentina, Uruguay, and Brazil wage war against Paraguay **1870s** Governments of Argentina and Chile begin final campaigns against indigenous peoples
1875	**1876** Sioux and allies defeat U.S. Army in Battle of Little Bighorn **1879** Thomas Edison develops incandescent lamp **1890** "Jim Crow" laws enforce segregation in South **1890s** United States becomes world's leading steel producer		**1879–1881** Chile wages war against Peru and Bolivia; telegraph, barbed wire, and refrigeration introduced in Argentina **1888** Abolition of slavery in Brazil

limited the powers of both the monarch and the church. Colonial loyalists who for a decade had fought to maintain the authority of monarch and church viewed those reforms as unacceptably liberal.

With the king's supporters divided, momentum swung to the patriots. After liberating present-day Venezuela, Colombia, and Ecuador, Bolívar's army occupied the area that is now Peru and Bolivia (named for Bolívar). Finally defeating the last Spanish armies in 1824, Bolívar and his closest supporters attempted to draw the former Spanish colonies into a formal confederation. The first step was to forge Venezuela, Colombia, and Ecuador into the single nation of Gran Colombia (see Map 24.1). With Bolívar's encouragement, Peru and Bolivia also experimented with unification. Despite his prestige, however, all of these initiatives had failed by 1830.

Buenos Aires (the capital city of modern Argentina) was the second important center of revolutionary activity in Spanish South America. In Buenos Aires news of Ferdinand VII's abdication led to the creation of a junta organized by militia commanders, merchants, and ranchers, which overthrew the viceroy in 1810. To deflect the opposition of loyalists and Spanish colonial officials, the junta claimed loyalty to the imprisoned king. After Ferdinand regained the Spanish throne, however, junta

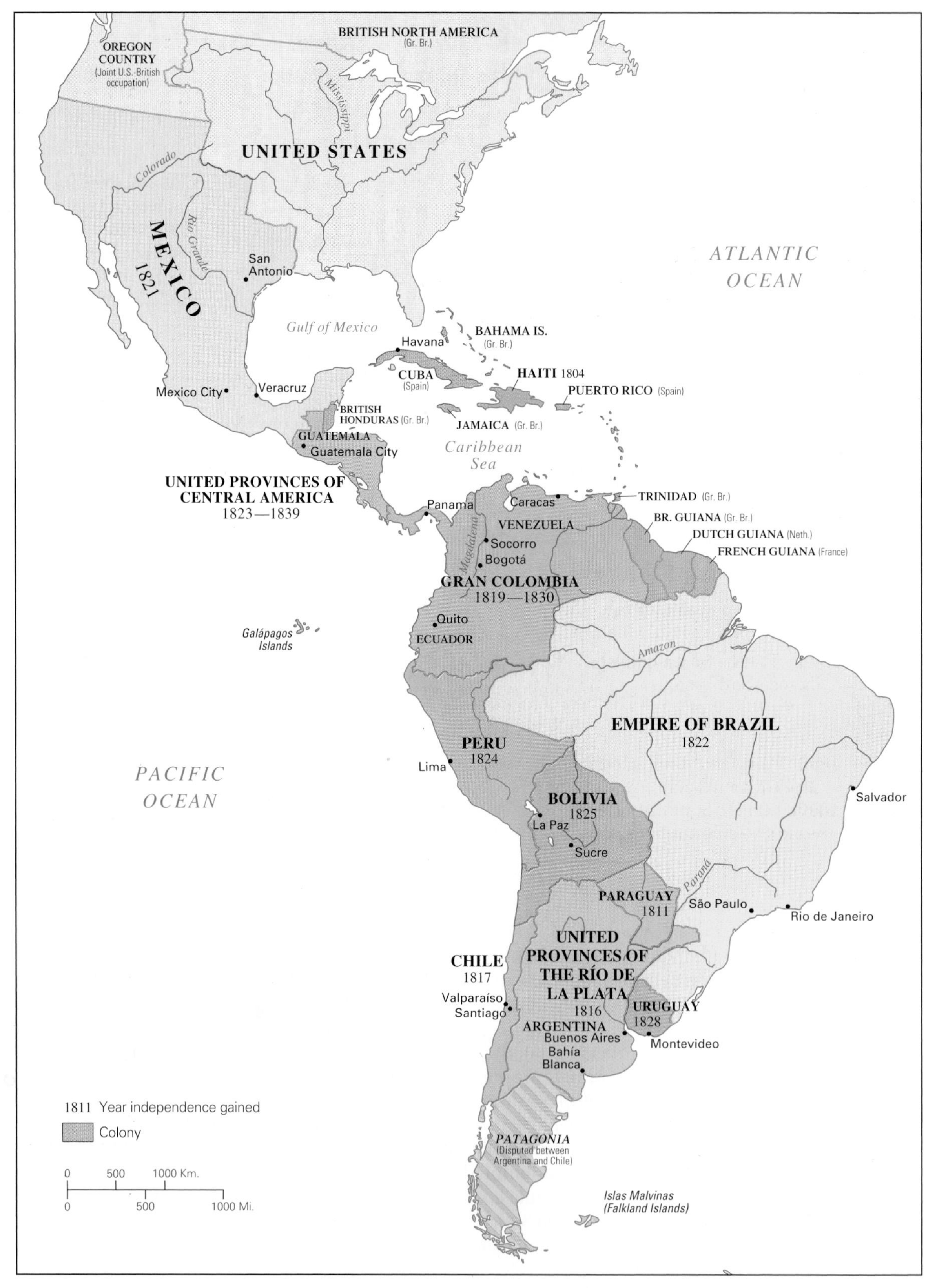
BRITISH NORTH AMERICA
(Gr. Br.)
OREGON COUNTRY
(Joint U.S.-British occupation)
Mississippi
UNITED STATES
Colorado
Rio Grande
MEXICO
1821
San Antonio
ATLANTIC OCEAN
Gulf of Mexico
Havana
BAHAMA IS.
(Gr. Br.)
CUBA
(Spain)
HAITI 1804
PUERTO RICO (Spain)
Mexico City
Veracruz
BRITISH HONDURAS (Gr. Br.)
JAMAICA (Gr. Br.)
GUATEMALA
Guatemala City
Caribbean Sea
UNITED PROVINCES OF CENTRAL AMERICA
1823—1839
Panama
Caracas
TRINIDAD (Gr. Br.)
BR. GUIANA (Gr. Br.)
DUTCH GUIANA (Neth.)
FRENCH GUIANA (France)
VENEZUELA
Magdalena
Socorro
Bogotá
GRAN COLOMBIA
1819—1830
Quito
ECUADOR
Galápagos Islands
Amazon
EMPIRE OF BRAZIL
1822
PERU
1824
Lima
PACIFIC OCEAN
BOLIVIA
1825
La Paz
Sucre
Salvador
Paraná
PARAGUAY
1811
São Paulo
Rio de Janeiro
CHILE
1817
UNITED PROVINCES OF THE RÍO DE LA PLATA
1816
ARGENTINA
Valparaíso
Santiago
URUGUAY
1828
Buenos Aires
Montevideo
Bahía Blanca
1811 Year independence gained
Colony
0 500 1000 Km.
0 500 1000 Mi.
PATAGONIA
(Disputed between Argentina and Chile)
Islas Malvinas
(Falkland Islands)

Map 24.1 Latin America by 1830 By 1830 patriot forces had overturned the Spanish and Portuguese Empires of the Western Hemisphere. Regional conflicts, local wars, and foreign interventions challenged the survival of many of these new nations following independence.

leaders dropped this pretense. In 1816 they declared independence as the United Provinces of the Río de la Plata.

Patriot leaders in Buenos Aires at first sought to retain control over the territory of the Viceroyalty of Río de la Plata, which had been created in 1776 and included modern Argentina, Uruguay, Paraguay, and Bolivia. But Spanish loyalists in Uruguay and Bolivia and a separatist movement in Paraguay defeated these ambitions. Even within the territory of Argentina, the government in Buenos Aires was unable to control regional rivalries and political differences. As a result, the region rapidly descended into political chaos.

A weak succession of juntas, collective presidencies, and dictators soon lost control over much of the interior of Argentina. However, in 1817 the government in Buenos Aires did manage to support a mixed force of Chileans and Argentines led by José de San Martín° (1778–1850), who crossed the Andes Mountains to attack Spanish military forces in Chile and Peru. During this campaign San Martín's most effective troops were former slaves, who had gained their freedom by enlisting in the army, and gauchos, the cowboys of the Argentine pampas (prairies). After gaining victory in Chile San Martín pushed on to Peru in 1820, but failed to gain a clear victory there. The violent and destructive uprising of Tupac Amaru II in 1780 had traumatized the Andean region and made colonists fearful that support for independence might unleash another Amerindian uprising (see Chapter 18). Unable to make progress, San Martín surrendered command of patriot forces in Peru to Simón Bolívar, who overcame final Spanish resistance in 1824.

Mexico, 1810–1823

In 1810 Mexico was Spain's wealthiest and most populous colony. Its silver mines were the richest in the world, and the colony's capital, Mexico City, was larger than any city in Spain. Mexico also had the largest population of Spanish immigrants among the colonies. Spaniards dominated the government, church, and economy. When news of Napoleon's invasion of Spain reached Mexico, conservative Spaniards in Mexico City overthrew the local viceroy because he was too sympathetic to the creoles. This action by Spanish loyalists underlined the new reality: with the king of Spain removed from his throne by the French, colonial authority now rested on brute force.

Padre Hidalgo The first stage of Mexico's revolution for independence was led by Padre Miguel Hidalgo y Costilla, who rallied the rural masses of central Mexico to his cause. His defeat, trial, and execution made him one of Mexico's most important political martyrs. (Schaalkwijk/Art Resource, NY)

The first stage of the revolution against Spain occurred in central Mexico. In this region wealthy ranchers and farmers had aggressively forced many Amerindian communities from their traditional agricultural lands. Crop failures and epidemics further afflicted the region's rural poor. Miners and the urban poor faced higher food prices and rising unemployment. With the power of colonial authorities weakened by events in Spain, anger and fear spread through towns and villages in central Mexico.

On September 16, 1810, **Miguel Hidalgo y Costilla**°, parish priest of the small town of Dolores, rang the

José de San Martín (hoe-SAY deh san mar-TEEN)

Miguel Hidalgo y Costilla (mee-GEHL ee-DAHL-go ee cos-TEA-ah)

church bells, attracting thousands. In a fiery speech he urged the crowd to rise up against the oppression of Spanish officials. Tens of thousands of the rural and urban poor joined his movement. They lacked military discipline and adequate weapons but knew who their oppressors were, spontaneously attacking the ranches and mines that had been exploiting them. Many Spaniards and colonial-born whites were murdered or assaulted. At first wealthy Mexicans were sympathetic to Hidalgo's objectives, but they eventually supported Spanish authorities when they recognized the threat that the angry masses following Hidalgo posed to them. The military tide quickly turned against Hidalgo and he was captured, tried, and executed in 1811.

The revolution continued under the leadership of another priest, **José María Morelos**°, a former student of Hidalgo's. A more adept military and political leader than his mentor, Morelos created a formidable fighting force and, in 1813, convened a congress that declared independence and drafted a constitution. Despite these achievements, loyalist forces also proved too strong for Morelos. He was defeated and executed in 1815.

Although small numbers of insurgents continued to wage war against Spanish forces, colonial rule seemed secure in 1820. However, news of the military revolt in Spain unsettled the conservative groups and church officials who had defended Spanish rule against Hidalgo and Morelos. In 1821 Colonel Agustín de Iturbide° and other loyalist commanders forged an alliance with remaining insurgents and declared Mexico's independence. The conservative origins of Mexico's transition to independence were highlighted by the decision to create a monarchial form of government and crown Iturbide as emperor. In early 1823, however, the army overthrew Iturbide and Mexico became a republic.

Brazil, to 1831

The arrival of the Portuguese royal family in Brazil in 1808 helped maintain the loyalty of the colonial elite and stimulate the local economy. After the defeat of Napoleon in Europe, the Portuguese government called for King John VI to return to Portugal. He at first resisted this pressure. Then in 1820 the military uprising in Spain provoked a sympathetic liberal revolt in Portugal, and the Portuguese military garrison in Rio de Janeiro forced the king to permit the creation of juntas. John recognized that he needed to take dramatic action to protect his throne. In 1821 he returned to Portugal. Hoping to protect his claims to Brazil, he left his son Pedro in Brazil as regent.

By 1820 the Spanish colonies along Brazil's borders had experienced ten years of revolution and civil war, and some, like Argentina and Paraguay, had gained independence. Unable to ignore these struggles, some Brazilians began to reevaluate Brazil's relationship with Portugal. Many Brazilians resented their homeland's economic subordination to Portugal. The arrogance of Portuguese soldiers and bureaucrats led others to talk openly of independence. Rumors circulated that Portuguese troops were being sent to discipline Brazil and force the regent Pedro to join his father in Lisbon.

Unwilling to return to Portugal and committed to maintaining his family's hold on Brazil, Pedro aligned himself with the rising tide of independence sentiment. In 1822 he declared Brazilian independence. Pedro's decision launched Brazil into a unique political trajectory. Unlike its neighbors, which became constitutional republics, Brazil gained independence as a constitutional monarchy with Pedro I, heir to the throne of Portugal, as emperor.

Pedro I was committed to both monarchy and many liberal principles. He directed the writing of the constitution of 1824, which provided for an elected assembly and granted numerous protections for political opposition. But he made powerful enemies by attempting to protect the Portuguese who remained in Brazil from arbitrary arrest and seizure of their property. More dangerously still, he opposed slavery in a nation dominated by a slave-owning class. In 1823 Pedro I anonymously published an article that characterized slavery as a "cancer eating away at Brazil" (see Diversity and Dominance: The Afro-Brazilian Experience, 1828). Despite opposition, in 1830 he concluded a treaty with Great Britain to end Brazilian participation in the slave trade. The political elite of Brazil's slave-owning regions opposed the treaty and for nearly two decades worked tirelessly to prevent enforcement. Pedro also continued his father's costly commitment of military forces to control neighboring Uruguay. As military losses and costs rose, the Brazilian public grew impatient. A small but vocal minority that opposed the monarchy and sought the creation of a democracy used these issues to rally public opinion against the emperor.

Confronted by street demonstrations and violence between Brazilians and Portuguese, Pedro I abdicated the throne in 1831 in favor of his five-year-old son Pedro II. After a nine-year regency, Pedro II assumed full powers as emperor of Brazil. He reigned until he was overthrown by republicans in 1889.

José María Morelos (hoe-SAY mah-REE-ah moh-RAY-los)
Agustín de Iturbide (ah-goos-TEEN deh ee-tur-BEE-deh)

The Problem of Order, 1825–1890

All the newly independent nations of the Western Hemisphere had difficulties establishing stable political institutions. The idea of popular sovereignty found broad support across the hemisphere. As a result, written constitutions and elected assemblies were put in place, often before the actual achievement of independence. Even in the hemisphere's two monarchies, Mexico and Brazil, the emperors sought to legitimize their rule by accepting constitutional limits on their authority and by the creation of representative assemblies. Nevertheless, widespread support for constitutional order and for representative government failed to prevent bitter factional conflict, regionalism, and the appearance of charismatic political leaders and military uprisings.

Constitutional Experiments

In reaction to the arbitrary and tyrannical authority of colonial rulers, revolutionary leaders in both the United States and Latin America espoused constitutionalism. They believed that the careful description of political powers in written constitutions offered the best protection for individual rights and liberties. In practice, however, many new constitutions proved unworkable. In the United States George Washington, James Madison, and other leaders became dissatisfied with the nation's first constitution, the Articles of Confederation. They led the effort to write a new constitution, which was put into effect in 1789. In Latin America few constitutions survived the rough-and-tumble of national politics. Between 1811 and 1833 Venezuela and Chile ratified and then rejected a combined total of nine constitutions.

Important differences in colonial political experience influenced later political developments in the Americas. The ratification of a new constitution in the United States was the culmination of a long historical process that had begun with the development of English constitutional law and continued under colonial charters. Many more residents of the British North American colonies had had the experience of voting and holding political office than did people in Portuguese and Spanish colonies. The British colonies provided opportunities for holding elective offices in town governments and colonial legislatures, and, by the time of independence, citizens had grown accustomed to elections, political parties, and factions. In contrast, constitutional government and elections were only briefly experienced in Spanish America between 1812 and 1814—while Ferdinand VII was a prisoner of Napoleon—and this short period was disrupted by the early stages of the revolutions for independence. Brazil had almost no experience with popular politics before independence. Despite these differences in experience and constitutional forms, every new republic in the Americas initially limited the right to vote to free men of property.

Democratic passions and the desire for effective self-rule led to significant political reform in the Americas, even in some of the region's remaining colonies. British Canada was divided into separate colonies and territories, each with a separate and distinct government. Political life in each colony was dominated by a provincial governor and appointed advisory councils drawn from the local elite. Elected assemblies existed within each province, but they exercised limited power. Agitation to end oligarchic rule and make government responsive to the will of the assemblies led to armed rebellion in 1837. In the 1840s Britain responded by establishing responsible government in each of the Canadian provinces, allowing limited self-rule. By the 1860s regional political leaders interested in promoting economic development realized that railroads and other internal improvements required a government with a "national" character. Both the U.S. Civil War and raids from U.S. territory into Canada by Irish nationalists attempting to force an end to British control of Ireland gave the reform movement a sense of urgency and focused attention on the need to protect the border. Negotiations led to the **Confederation of 1867,** which included the provinces of Ontario, Quebec, New Brunswick, and Nova Scotia. The Confederation that created the new Dominion of Canada with a central government in Ottawa (see Map 24.2) was hailed by one observer as the "birthday of a new nationality."[2] The path to effective constitutional government was rockier to the south. Because neither Spain nor Portugal had permitted anything like the elected legislatures and municipal governments of colonial North America, the drafters of Latin American constitutions were less constrained by practical political experience. As a result, many of the new Latin American nations experimented with untested political institutions. For example, Simón Bolívar, who wrote the first constitutions of five South American republics, included in Bolivia's constitution a fourth branch of government that had "jurisdiction over the youth, the hearts of men, public spirit, good customs, and republican ethics."

Most Latin American nations found it difficult to define the political role of the Catholic Church after independence. In the colonial period the Catholic Church

DIVERSITY AND DOMINANCE

THE AFRO-BRAZILIAN EXPERIENCE, 1828

Brazil was the most important destination for the Atlantic slave trade. From the sixteenth century to the 1850s more than 2 million African slaves were imported by Brazil, roughly twice the number of free European immigrants who arrived in the same period. Beginning in the 1820s Great Britain, Brazil's main trading partner, began to press for an end to the slave trade. British visitors to Brazil became an important source of critical information for those who sought to end the trade.

The following opinions were provided by a British clergyman, Robert Walsh, who traveled widely in Brazil in 1828 and 1829. Walsh's account reflects the racial attitudes of his time, but his testimony is valuable because of his ability to recognize the complex and sometime unexpected ways that slaves and black freedmen were integrated into Brazilian society.

[At the Alfandega, or custom house,] . . . for the first time I saw the Negro population under circumstances so striking to a stranger. The whole labour of bearing and moving burdens is performed by these people, and the state in which they appear is revolting to humanity. Here were a number of beings entirely naked, with the exception of a covering of dirty rags tied about their waists. Their skins, from constant exposure to the weather, had become hard, crusty, and seamed, resembling the coarse black covering of some beast, or like that of an elephant, a wrinkled hide scattered with scanty hairs. On contemplating their persons, you saw them with a physical organization resembling beings of a grade below the rank of man . . . . Some of these beings were yoked to drays, on which they dragged heavy burdens. Some were chained by the necks and legs, and moved with loads thus encumbered. Some followed each other in ranks, with heavy weights on their heads, chattering the most inarticulate and dismal cadence as they moved along. Some were munching young sugar-canes, like beasts of burden eating green provender [animal feed], and some were seen near water, lying on the bare ground among filth and offal, coiled up like dogs, and seeming to expect or require no more comfort or accommodation, exhibiting a state and conformation so unhuman, that they not only seemed, but actually were, far below the inferior animals around them. Horses and mules were not employed in this way; they were used only for pleasure, and not for labour. They were seen in the same streets, pampered, spirited, and richly caparisoned, enjoying a state far superior to the negroes, and appearing to look down on the fettered and burdened wretches they were passing, as on beings of an inferior rank in the creation to themselves. . . .

The first impression of all this on my mind, was to shake the conviction I had always felt, of the wrong and hardship inflicted on our black fellow creatures, and that they were only in that state which God and nature had assigned them; that they were the lowest grade of human existence, and the link that connected it with the brute, and that the gradation was so insensible, and their natures so intermingled, that it was impossible to tell where one had terminated and the other commenced; and that it was not surprising that people who contemplated them every day, so formed, so employed, and so degraded, should forget their claims to that rank in the scale of beings in which modern philanthropists are so anxious to place them. I did not at the moment myself recollect, that the white man, made a slave on the coast of Africa, suffers not only a similar mental but physical deterioration from hardships and emaciation, and becomes in time the dull and deformed beast I now saw yoked to a burden.

A few hours only were necessary to correct my first impressions of the negro population, by seeing them under a different aspect. We were attracted by the sound of military music, and found it proceeded from a regiment drawn up in one of the streets. Their colonel had just died, and they attended to form a procession to celebrate his obsequies. They were all of different shades of black, but the majority were negroes. Their equipment was excellent; they wore dark jackets, white pantaloons, and black leather caps and belts, all which, with their arms, were in high order. Their band produced sweet and agreeable music, of the leader's own composition, and the men went through some evolutions with regularity and dexterity. They were only a militia regiment, yet were as well appointed and disciplined as one of our regiments of the line. Here then was the first step in that gradation by which the black population of this country ascend in the scale of humanity; he advances from the state below that of a beast of burden into a military rank, and he shows himself as capable of discipline and improvement as a human being of any other colour.

Our attention was next attracted by negro men and women bearing about a variety of articles for sale; some in baskets, some on boards and cases carried on their heads. They belonged to a class of small shopkeepers, many of whom vend their wares at home, but the greater number send them about in this way, as in itinerant shops. A few of these people were still in a state of bondage, and brought a certain sum every evening to their owners, as the produce of their daily labour. But a large proportion, I was informed, were free, and exercised this little calling on their own account. They were all very neat and clean in their persons, and had a decorum and sense of respectability about them, superior to whites of the same class and calling. All their articles were good in their kind, and neatly kept, and they sold them with simplicity and confidence, neither wishing to take advantage of others, nor suspecting that it would be taken of themselves. I bought some confectionary from one of the females, and I was struck with the modesty and propriety of her manner; she was a young mother, and had with her a neatly dressed child, of which she seemed very fond. I gave it a little comfit [candy covered nut], and it turned up its dusky countenance to her and then to me, taking my sweetmeat, and at the same time kissing my hand. As yet unacquainted with the coin of the country, I had none that was current about me, and was leaving the articles; but the poor young woman pressed them on me with a ready confidence, repeating in broken Portuguese, outo tempo, I am sorry to say, the "other time" never came, for I could not recognize her person afterwards to discharge her little debt, though I went to the same place for the purpose.

It soon began to grow dark, and I was attracted by a number of persons bearing large lighted wax tapers, like torches, gathering before a house. As I passed by, one was put into my hand by a man who seemed in some authority, and I was requested to fall into a procession that was forming. It was the preparation for a funeral, and on such occasions, I learned that they always request the attendance of a passing stranger, and feel hurt if they are refused. I joined the party, and proceeded with them to a neighbouring church. When we entered we ranged ourselves on each side of a platform which stood near the choir, on which was laid an open coffin, covered with pink silk and gold borders. The funeral service was chanted by a choir of priests, one of whom was a negro, a large comely man, whose jet black visage formed a strong and striking contrast to his white vestments. He seemed to perform his part with a decorum and sense of solemnity, which I did not observe in his brethren. After scattering flowers on the coffin, and fumigating it with incense, they retired, the procession dispersed, and we returned on board. I had been but a few hours on shore, for the first time, and I saw an African negro under four aspects of society; and it appeared to me, that in every one his character depended on the state in which he was placed, and the estimation in which he was held. As a despised slave, he was far lower than other animals of burthen that surrounded him; more miserable in his look, more revolting in his nakedness, more distorted in his person, and apparently more deficient in intellect than the horses and mules that passed him by. Advanced to the grade of a soldier, he was clean and neat in his person, amenable to discipline, expert at his exercises, and showed the port [sic.] and being of a white man similarly placed. As a citizen, he was remarkable for the respectability of his appearance, and the decorum of his manners in the rank assigned him; and as a priest, standing in the house of God, appointed to instruct society on their most important interests, and in a grade in which moral and intellectual fitness is required, and a certain degree of superiority is expected, he seemed even more devout in his impressions, and more correct in his manners, than his white associates. I came, therefore, to the irresistible conclusion in my mind, that colour was an accident affecting the surface of a man, and having no more to do with his qualities than his clothes—that God had equally created an African in the image of his person, and equally given him an immortal soul; and that an European had no pretext but his own cupidity, for impiously thrusting his fellow man from that rank in the creation which the Almighty had assigned him, and degrading him below the lot of the brute beasts that perish.

QUESTIONS FOR ANALYSIS

1. **What was the author's first impression of the Brazilian slave population?**
2. **How does slavery dehumanize slaves?**
3. **What does the author later observe that changes this opinion?**
4. **What circumstances or opportunities permitted Brazil's free blacks to improve their lives?**

Source: Robert Edgar Conrad, *Children of God's Fire, A Documentary History of Black Slavery in Brazil* (Princeton, NJ: Princeton University Press, 1983), 216–220. Reprinted by permission of the author.

Map 24.2 Dominion of Canada, 1873 Although independence was not yet achieved and settlement remained concentrated along the U.S. border, Canada had established effective political and economic control over its western territories by 1873.

was a religious monopoly that controlled all levels of education, and dominated intellectual life. Many early constitutions aimed to reduce this power by making education secular and by permitting the practice of other religions. The church reacted by organizing its allies and financing conservative political movements. In Mexico, Colombia, Chile, and Argentina conflicts between liberals who sought the separation of church and state and supporters of the church's traditional powers dominated political life until late in the nineteenth century.

Limiting the power of the military proved to be another significant stumbling block to the creation of constitutional governments in Latin America. The wars for independence elevated the prestige of military leaders. When the wars were over, Bolívar and other military commanders seldom proved willing to subordinate themselves to civilian authorities. At the same time, frustrated by the often-chaotic workings of constitutional democracy, few citizens were willing to support civilian politicians in any contest with the military. As a result, many Latin American militaries successfully resisted civilian control. Brazil, ruled by Emperor Pedro I, was the principal exception to this pattern.

Personalist Leaders

Successful patriot leaders in both the United States and Latin America gained mass followings during the wars for independence. They recruited and mobilized popular support by using patriotic symbols and by carefully associating their actions with national objectives. After independence, many patriot military leaders were able to use their personal followings to gain national political leadership. George Washington's ability to dominate the political scene in the early republican United States anticipated the later political ascendancy of revolutionary heroes such as Iturbide in Mexico and Bolívar in Gran Colombia. In each case, military reputation provided the foundation for personal political power. Washington was distinguished from most other early leaders by his willingness to surrender power. More commonly, **personalist leaders** relied on their ability to mobilize and direct the masses of these new nations rather than on the authority of constitutions and laws. Their model was Napoleon, who rose from the French army to become emperor, not James Madison, the primary author of the U.S. Constitution. In Latin America, a personalist leader who gained and held political power without constitutional sanction was called a *caudillo*°.

Latin America's slow development of stable political institutions made personalist politics more influential than they were in the United States. Nevertheless, charismatic politicians in the United States such as Andrew Jackson did sometimes challenge constitutional limits to their authority, as did the *caudillos* of Latin America.

Throughout the Western Hemisphere charismatic military men played key roles in attracting mass support for independence movements that were commonly dominated by colonial elites. Although this popular support was often decisive in the struggle for independence, the first constitutions of nearly all the American republics excluded large numbers of poor citizens from full political participation. But nearly everywhere in the Americas marginalized groups found populist leaders to articulate their concerns and challenge limits on their participation. Using informal means, these leaders sought to influence the selection of officeholders and to place their concerns in the public arena. Despite their success in overturning the deference-based politics of the colonial past, this populist political style at times threatened constitutional order and led to dictatorship.

Powerful personal followings allowed **Andrew Jackson** of the United States and **José Antonio Páez**° of Venezuela to challenge constitutional limits to their authority. During the independence wars in Venezuela and Colombia, Páez (1790–1873) organized and led Bolívar's most successful cavalry force. Like most of his followers, Páez was uneducated and poor, but his physical strength, courage, and guile made him a natural guerrilla leader and helped him build a powerful political base in Venezuela. Páez described his authority in the following manner: "[The soldiers] resolved to confer on me the supreme command and blindly to obey my will, confident . . . that I was the only one who could save them."[3] Able to count on the personal loyalty of his followers, Páez was seldom willing to accept the constitutional authority of a distant president.

After defeating the Spanish armies, Bolívar pursued his dream of forging a permanent union of former Spanish colonies modeled on the federal system of the United States. But he underestimated the strength of nationalist sentiment unleashed during the independence wars. Páez and other Venezuelan leaders resisted the surrender of their hard-won power to Bolívar's Gran Colombian government in distant Bogotá (the capital city of modern Colombia). When Bolívar's authority was challenged by political opponents in 1829 Páez declared Venezuela's independence. Merciless to his enemies and indulgent with his followers, Páez ruled the country as president or dictator for the next eighteen years. Despite implementing an economic program favorable to the elite, Páez remained popular with the masses by skillfully manipulating popular political symbols. Even as his personal wealth grew through land acquisitions and commerce, Páez took care to present himself as a common man.

Andrew Jackson (1767–1845) was the first U.S. president born in humble circumstances. A self-made man who eventually acquired substantial property and owned over a hundred slaves, Jackson was extremely popular among frontier residents, urban workers, and small farmers. Although he was notorious for his untidy personal life as well as for dueling, his courage, individualism, and willingness to challenge authority helped attain political success as judge, general, congressman, senator, and president.

During his military career, Jackson proved to be impatient with civilian authorities. Widely known because of his victories over the Creek and Seminole peoples, he was elevated to the pinnacle of American politics by his celebrated defeat of the British at the Battle of New Orleans in 1815 and by his seizure of Florida from the Spanish in 1818. In 1824 he received a plurality of the popular votes cast for the presidency, but he failed to win a majority of the electoral votes and was denied the presidency when the House of Representatives chose John Quincy Adams.

Jackson's followers viewed his landslide election victory in 1828 and reelection in 1832 as the triumph of democracy over the entrenched aristocracy. In office Jackson challenged constitutional limits on his authority, substantially increasing presidential power at the expense of Congress and the Supreme Court. Like Páez, Jackson was able to dominate national politics by blending a populist political style that celebrated the virtues and cultural enthusiasms of common people with support for policies that promoted the economic interests of some of the nation's most powerful propertied groups.

Personalist leaders were common in both Latin America and the United States, but Latin America's

---

caudillo (kouh-DEE-yoh) **José Antonio Páez** (hoe-SAY an-TOE-nee-oh PAH-ays) weaker constitutional tradition, more limited protection of property rights, lower literacy levels, and less-developed communications systems provided fewer checks on the ambitions of popular politicians. The Constitution of the United States was never suspended, and no national election result in the United States was ever successfully overturned by violence. Latin America's personalist leaders, however, often ignored constitutional restraints on their authority, and election results seldom determined access to presidential power. As a result, by 1900 every Latin American nation had experienced periods of dictatorship.

The Threat of Regionalism

After independence, new national governments were generally weaker than the colonial governments they replaced. In debates over tariffs, tax and monetary policies, and, in many nations, slavery and the slave trade, regional elites often were willing to lead secessionist movements or to provoke civil war rather than accept laws that threatened their interests. Some of the hemisphere's newly independent nations did not survive these struggles; others lost territories to aggressive neighbors.

In Spanish America all of the postindependence efforts to forge large multistate federations failed. Central America and Mexico had been united in the Viceroyalty of New Spain and briefly maintained their colonial-era administrative ties following independence in 1821. After the overthrow of Iturbide's imperial rule in Mexico in 1823, however, regional politicians split with Mexico and created the independent Republic of Central America. Regional rivalries and civil wars during the 1820s and 1830s forced the breakup of that entity as well and led to the creation of five separate nations. Bolívar attempted to maintain the colonial unity of Venezuela, Colombia, and Ecuador by creating the nation of Gran Colombia with a capital in Bogotá. But even before his death in 1830 Venezuela and Ecuador had become independent states.

During colonial times Argentina, Uruguay, Paraguay, and Bolivia had been united in a single viceroyalty with its capital in Buenos Aires. With the defeat of Spain, political leaders in Paraguay, Uruguay, and Bolivia declared their independence from Buenos Aires. Argentina, the area that remained after this breakup, was itself nearly overwhelmed by these powerful centrifugal forces. After independence, Argentina's liberals took power in Buenos Aires. They sought a strong central government to promote secular education, free trade, and immigration from Europe. Conservatives dominated the interior provinces. They supported the Catholic Church's traditional control of education as well as the protection of local textile and winemaking industries from European imports.In 1819, when political leaders in Buenos Aires imposed a national constitution that ignored these concerns, the conservatives of the interior rose in rebellion.

After a decade of civil war and rebellions a powerful local *caudillo*, Juan Manuel de Rosas°, came to power. For more than two decades he dominated Argentina, running the nation as if it were his private domain. The economy expanded under Rosas, but his use of intimidation, mob violence, and assassination created many enemies. In 1852 an alliance of foreign and domestic enemies overthrew him, but a new cycle of provincial rivalry and civil war prevented the creation of a strong central government until 1861.

Regionalism threatened the United States as well. The defense of state and regional interests played an important role in the framing of the U.S. Constitution. Many important constitutional provisions represented compromises forged among competing state and regional leaders. The creation of a Senate with equal representation from each state, for example, was an attempt to calm small states, which feared they might be dominated by larger states. The formula for representation in the House of Representatives was also an effort to compromise the divisions between slave and free states. Yet, despite these constitutional compromises, the nation was still threatened by regional rivalries.

Slavery increasingly divided the nation into two separate and competitive societies. A rising tide of immigration to the northern states in the 1830s and 1840s began to move the center of political power in the House of Representatives away from the south. Many southern leaders sought to protect slavery by expanding it to new territories. They supported the Louisiana Purchase in 1803 (see Map 24.3), an agreement with France that transferred to the United States a vast territory extending from the Gulf of Mexico to Canada. Southern leaders also supported statehood for Texas and war with Mexico (discussed later in the chapter).

The territorial acquisitions proved a mixed blessing to the defenders of slavery because they forced a national debate about slavery itself. Should slavery be allowed to expand into new territories? Could slavery be protected if new territories eligible for statehood were overwhelmingly free?

In 1860 Abraham Lincoln (1809–1865), who was committed to checking the spread of slavery, was elected president of the United States. In response, the planter elite in the southern states chose the dangerous course

Juan Manuel de Rosas (huan man-WELL deh ROH-sas)

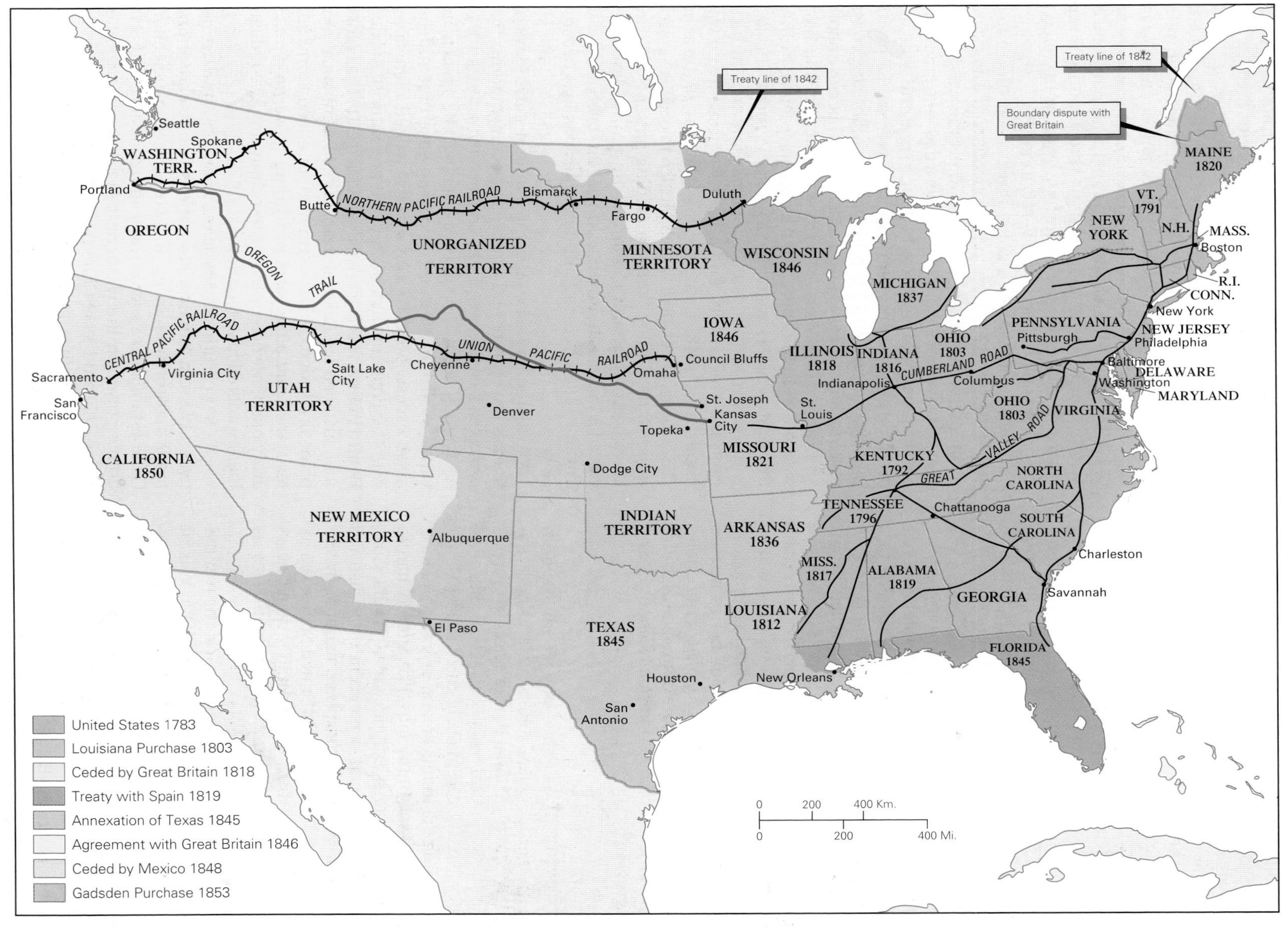

Map 24.3 Territorial Growth of the United States, 1783–1853 The rapid western expansion of the United States resulted from aggressive diplomacy and warfare against Mexico and Amerindian peoples. Railroad development helped integrate the trans-Mississippi west and promote economic expansion.

of secession from the federal Union. The seceding states formed a new government, the Confederate States of America, known as the Confederacy. Lincoln was able to preserve the Union, but his victory was purchased at an enormous cost. The U.S. Civil War (1861–1865), waged by southern Confederate forces and northern Union (U.S.) forces, was the most destructive conflict in the history of the Western Hemisphere. More than 600,000 lives were lost before the Confederacy surrendered in 1865. The Union victory led to the abolition of slavery. It also transferred national political power to a northern elite committed to industrial expansion and federal support for the construction of railroads and other internal improvements.

The Confederate States of America was better prepared politically and economically for independence than were the successful secessionist movements that broke up Gran Colombia and other Spanish American federations. Nevertheless, the Confederacy failed, in part because of poor timing. The new nations of the Western Hemisphere were most vulnerable during the early years of their existence; indeed, all the successful secessions occurred within the first decades following independence. In the case of the United States, southern secession was defeated by an experienced national government legitimated and strengthened by more than seven decades of relative stability reinforced by dramatic economic and population growth.

Foreign Interventions and Regional Wars

In the nineteenth century wars often determined national borders, access to natural resources, and control of markets in the Western Hemisphere. Even after the achievement of independence, some Western Hemisphere nations, like Mexico, had to defend themselves against Europe's great powers. Contested national borders and regional rivalries also led to wars between Western Hemisphere nations. By the end of the nineteenth century the United States, Brazil, Argentina, and Chile had successfully waged wars against their neighbors and established themselves as regional powers.

Within thirty years of independence the United States fought a second war with England—the War of 1812 (1812–1815). The weakness of the new republic was symbolized by the burning of the White House and Capitol by British troops in 1814. This humiliation was soon overcome, however, and by the end of the nineteenth century the United States was the hemisphere's greatest military power. Its war against Spain in 1898–1899 created an American empire that reached from the Philippines in the Pacific Ocean to Puerto Rico in the Caribbean Sea (see Chapter 28).

Europe also challenged the sovereignty of Latin American nations. During the first decades after independence Argentina faced British and French naval blockades, and British naval forces systematically violated Brazil's territorial waters to stop the importation of slaves. Mexico faced more serious threats to its sovereignty, defeating a weak Spanish invasion in 1829 and a French assault on the city of Veracruz in 1838.

Mexico also faced a grave threat from the United States. In the 1820s Mexico had encouraged Americans to immigrate to Texas, which at that time was part of Mexico. By the early 1830s Americans outnumbered Mexican nationals in Texas by four to one and were aggressively challenging Mexican laws such as the prohibition of slavery. In 1835 political turmoil in Mexico led to a rebellion in Texas by an alliance of Mexican liberals and American settlers. Mexico was defeated in a brief war, and in 1836 Texas gained its independence. In 1845 the United States made Texas a state, provoking war with Mexico a year later. American forces eventually captured Mexico City, and a punitive peace treaty was imposed in 1848. Compounding the loss of Texas in 1837, the treaty of 1848 forced Mexico to cede vast territories to the United States, including present-day New Mexico, Arizona, and California. In return Mexico received $15 million. When gold was discovered in California in 1848, the magnitude of Mexico's loss became clear.

With the very survival of the nation at stake, Mexico's liberals took power and imposed sweeping reforms that provoked a civil war with the conservatives (1858–1861). As mentioned in the chapter opening, the French invaded Mexico in 1862, using unpaid government debts as an excuse. Mexico's conservatives allied themselves with the French invaders, and the president of Mexico, **Benito Juárez,** was forced to flee Mexico City. The French then installed the Austrian Habsburg Maximilian as emperor of Mexico. Juárez organized an effective military resistance and after years of warfare drove the French army out of Mexico in 1867. After capturing Maximilian, Juárez ordered his execution.

As was clear in the Mexican-American War, wars between Western Hemisphere nations could lead to dramatic territorial changes. In two wars with neighbors Chile established itself as the leading military and economic power on the west coast of South America. Between 1836 and 1839 Chile defeated the Confederation of Peru and Bolivia. In 1879 Chilean and British investors in nitrate mines located in the Atacama Desert, a dis-

Benito Juárez's Triumph over the French Benito Juárez overcame humble origins to lead the overthrow of Emperor Maximilian and the defeat of French imperialism. He remains a powerful symbol of secularism and republican virtue in Mexico. In this 1948 mural by José Clemente Orozco, Juárez's face dominates a scene of struggle that pits Mexican patriots against the allied forces of the Catholic Church, Mexican conservatives, and foreign invaders. The artist also celebrates the struggle of Mexico's Amerindians and mestizos against the white elite. (Museo Nacional de Historia/CENIDIAP-INBA)

puted border region, provoked a new war with Peru and Bolivia (War of the Pacific). The Chilean army and navy won a crushing victory in 1881, forcing Bolivia to cede its only outlet to the sea and Peru to yield the rich mining districts.

Argentina and Brazil fought over control of Uruguay in the 1820s, but a military stalemate eventually forced them to recognize Uruguayan independence. In 1865 Argentina and Uruguay joined Brazil to wage war against Paraguay (War of the Triple Alliance, or Paraguayan War). After five years of warfare the Paraguayan dictator Francisco Solano López° and more than 20 percent of the population of Paraguay had died. Paraguay suffered military occupation, lost territory to the victors, and was forced to open its markets to foreign trade.

Francisco Solano López (fran-CEES-co so-LAN-oh LOH-pehz)

Native Peoples and the Nation-State

Both diplomacy and military action shaped relations between the Western Hemisphere's new nation-states and the indigenous peoples living within them. During late colonial times, to avoid armed conflict and to limit the costs of frontier defense, Spanish, Portuguese, and British imperial governments attempted to restrict the expansion of settlements into territories already occupied by Amerindians. With independence, the colonial powers' role as mediator for and protector of native peoples ended.

Still-independent Amerindian peoples posed a significant military challenge to many Western Hemisphere republics. Weakened by civil wars and constitutional crises, many of the new nations were less able to maintain frontier peace than the colonial governments had been. After independence Amerindian peoples in Argentina, the United States, Chile, and Mexico succeeded

Navajo Leaders Gathered in Washington to Negotiate As settlers, ranchers, and miners pushed west in the nineteenth century, leaders of Amerindian peoples were forced to negotiate territorial concessions with representatives of the U.S. government. In order to impress Amerindian peoples with the wealth and power of the United States, many of their leaders were invited to Washington, D.C. This photo shows Navajo leaders and their Anglo translators in Washington, D.C., in 1874. (#5851 Frank McNill Collection, State Records Center & Archives, Sante Fe, NM)

in pushing back some frontier settlements. But despite these early victories, by the end of the 1880s native military resistance was finally overcome in both North and South America.

After the American Revolution, the rapid expansion of agricultural settlements threatened native peoples in North America. Between 1790 and 1810 tens of thousands of settlers entered territories guaranteed to Amerindians in treaties with the United States. More than 200,000 white settlers were present in Ohio alone by 1810. Indigenous leaders responded by seeking the support of British officials in Canada and by forging broad indigenous alliances. American forces decisively defeated one such Amerindian alliance in 1794 at the Battle of Fallen Timbers in Ohio. After 1800 two Shawnee leaders, the brothers **Tecumseh**° and Prophet (Tenskwatawa), created a larger and better-organized alliance among Amerindian peoples in the Ohio River Valley and gained some support from Great Britain. In 1811 American military forces attacked and destroyed the ritual center of the alliance, Prophet Town. The final blow came during the War of 1812 when Tecumseh, fighting alongside his British allies, was killed in battle.

In the 1820s white settlers forced native peoples living in Ohio, southern Indiana and Illinois, southwestern Michigan, most of Missouri, central Alabama, and southern Mississippi to cede their land. The 1828 presidential election of Andrew Jackson, a veteran of wars against native peoples, brought matters to a head. In 1830 Congress passed the Indian Removal Act, forcing the resettlement of the Cherokee, Creek, Choctaw, and other eastern peoples to land west of the Mississippi River. The removal was carried out in the 1830s, and nearly half of the forced migrants died on this journey, known as the Trail of Tears.

Tecumseh (teh-CUM-sah)

Amerindians living on the Great Plains offered formidable resistance to the expansion of white settlement. By the time substantial numbers of white buffalo hunters, cattlemen, and settlers reached the American west, indigenous peoples were skilled users of horses and firearms. These technologies had transformed the cultures of the Sioux, Comanche, Pawnee, Kiowa, and other Plains peoples. The improved efficiency of the buffalo hunt reduced their dependence on agriculture. As a result, women, whose primary responsibility had been raising crops, lost prestige and social power to male hunters. Living arrangements also changed as the single-family tepees of migratory buffalo hunters replaced the multigenerational lodges of the traditional farming economy.

During the U.S. Civil War, native peoples experienced a disruption of their trade with Eastern merchants and the suspension of payments pledged by previous treaties. After the war ever more settlers pushed onto the plains. Buffalo herds were hunted to near extinction for their hides, and land was lost to farmers and ranchers. During nearly four decades of armed conflict with the United States Army, Amerindian peoples were forced to give up their land and their traditional ways. The Comanche, who had dominated the southern plains during the period of Spanish and Mexican rule, were forced by the U.S. government to cede most of their land in Texas in 1865. The Sioux and their allies resisted. In 1876 they overwhelmed General George Armstrong Custer and the Seventh Cavalry in the Battle of Little Bighorn (in the southern part of the present-day state of Montana). But finally the Sioux were also forced to accept reservation life. Military campaigns in the 1870s and 1880s then broke the resistance of the Apache.

The indigenous peoples of Argentina and Chile experienced a similar trajectory of adaptation, resistance, and defeat. Herds of wild cattle provided indigenous peoples with a limitless food supply, and horses and metal weapons increased their military capacities. Thus, for a while, the native peoples of Argentina and Chile effectively checked the southern expansion of agriculture and ranching. Amerindian raiders operated within 100 miles (160 kilometers) of Buenos Aires into the 1860s. Unable to defeat these resourceful enemies, the governments of Argentina and Chile relied on an elaborate system of gift giving and prisoner exchanges to maintain peace on the frontier. By the 1860s, however, population increase, political stability, and military modernization allowed Argentina and Chile to take the offensive.

In the 1870s the government of Argentina used overwhelming military force to crush native resistance. Thousands of Amerindians were killed, and survivors were driven onto marginal land. In Chile the story was the same. When civil war and an economic depression weakened the Chilean government at the end of the 1850s, the Mapuches° (called "Araucanians" by the Spanish) attempted to push back frontier settlements. Despite early successes the Mapuches were defeated in the 1870s by modern weaponry. In Chile, as in Argentina and the United States, government authorities justified military campaigns against native peoples by demonizing them. Newspaper editorials and the speeches of politicians portrayed Amerindians as brutal and cruel, and as obstacles to progress. In April 1859 a Chilean newspaper commented:

> The necessity, not only to punish the Araucanian race, but also to make it impotent to harm us, is well recognized . . . as the only way to rid the country of a million evils. It is well understood that they are odious and prejudicial guests in Chile . . . conciliatory measures have accomplished nothing with this stupid race—the infamy and disgrace of the Chilean nation.[4]

Political divisions and civil wars within the new nations sometimes provided an opportunity for long-pacified native peoples to rebel. In the Yucatán region of Mexico, the owners of henequen (the agave plant that produces fiber used for twine) and sugar plantations had forced many Maya° communities off their traditional agricultural lands, reducing thousands to peonage. This same regional elite declared itself independent of the government in Mexico City that was convulsed by civil war in the late 1830s. The Mexican government was unable to reestablish control because it faced the greater threat of invasion by the United States. Seeing their oppressors divided, the Maya rebelled in 1847. This well-organized and popular uprising, known as the **Caste War,** nearly returned the Yucatán to Maya rule. Grievances accumulated over more than three hundred years led to great violence and property destruction. The Maya were not defeated until the war with the United States ended. Even then Maya rebels retreated to unoccupied territories and created an independent state, which they called the "Empire of the Cross." Organized around a mix of traditional beliefs and Christian symbols, this indigenous state resisted Mexican forces to 1870. A few defiant Maya strongholds survived until 1901.

Mapuches (mah-POO-chez)
Maya (MY-ah)

The Challenge of Social and Economic Change

During the nineteenth century the newly independent nations of the Western Hemisphere struggled to realize the Enlightenment ideals of freedom and individual liberty that had helped ignite the revolutions for independence. The achievement of these objectives was slowed by the persistence of slavery and other oppressive colonial-era institutions. Cultural and racial diversity also presented obstacles to reform. Nevertheless, by century's end reform movements in many of the hemisphere's nations had succeeded in ending the slave trade, abolishing slavery, expanding voting rights, and assimilating immigrants from Asia and Europe.

Increased industrialization and greater involvement in the evolving world economy challenged the region's political stability and social arrangements. A small number of nations embraced industrialization, but most Western Hemisphere economies became increasingly dependent on the export of agricultural goods and minerals during the nineteenth century. While the industrializing nations of the hemisphere became richer than the nations that remained exporters of raw materials, all the region's economies became more vulnerable and volatile as a result of greater participation in international markets. Like contemporary movements for social reform, efforts to assert national economic control produced powerful new political forces.

The Abolition of Slavery

In both the United States and Latin America strong antislavery sentiments were expressed during the struggles for independence. Revolutionary leaders of nearly all the new nations of the Western Hemisphere asserted ideals of universal freedom and citizenship that contrasted sharply with the reality of slavery. Men and women who wanted to outlaw slavery were called **abolitionists.** Despite their efforts, slavery survived in much of the hemisphere until the 1850s. In regions where the export of plantation products was most important—such as the United States, Brazil, and Cuba—the abolition of slavery was achieved with great difficulty.

In the United States slavery was weakened by abolition in some northern states and by the termination of the African slave trade in 1808. But this progress was stalled by the profitable expansion of cotton agriculture after the War of 1812. In Spanish America tens of thousands of slaves gained freedom by joining revolutionary armies during the wars for independence. After independence, most Spanish American republics prohibited the slave trade. Counteracting that trend was the growing international demand for sugar and coffee, products traditionally produced on plantations by slaves. As prices rose for plantation products in the first half of the nineteenth century, Brazil and Cuba (the island remained a Spanish colony until 1899) increased their imports of slaves.

During the long struggle to end slavery in the United States, American abolitionists argued that slavery offended both morality and the universal rights asserted in the Declaration of Independence. Abolitionist Theodore Weld articulated the religious objection to slavery in 1834:

> No condition of birth, no shade of color, no mere misfortune of circumstance, can annul the birth-right charter, which God has bequeathed to every being upon whom he has stamped his own image, by making him a free *moral agent* [emphasis in original], and that he who robs his fellow man of this tramples upon right, subverts justice, outrages humanity . . . and sacrilegiously assumes the prerogative of God.[5]

Two groups denied full rights of citizenship under the Constitution, women and free African-Americans, played important roles in the abolition of slavery. Women served on the executive committee of the American Anti-Slavery Society and produced some of the most effective propaganda against slavery. Eventually, thousands of women joined the abolitionist cause, where they provided leadership and were effective speakers and propagandists. When social conservatives attacked this highly visible public role, many women abolitionists responded by becoming public advocates of female suffrage as well.

Frederick Douglass, a former slave, became one of the most effective abolitionist speakers and writers. Other, more radical black leaders pushed the abolitionist movement to accept the inevitability of violence. They saw civil war or slave insurrection as necessary for ending slavery. In 1843 Henry Highland Garnet stirred the National Colored Convention when he demamded, "Brethren, arise, arise, arise! . . . Let every slave in the land do this and the days of slavery are numbered."[6] In the 1850s the growing electoral strength of the newly formed Republican Party forced a confrontation between slave and free states. After the election of Abraham Lincoln in 1860, the first of the eleven southern states that formed the Confederacy seceded from the Union. During the Civil War pressure for emancipation rose as tens of thousands of black freemen and escaped slaves joined the Union army. Hundreds of thousands of other slaves fled their masters' plantations and farms for the protection of advancing northern armies. In 1863, in the midst of the Civil War and two years after the abolition of serfdom in Russia (see Chapter 26), President Lincoln began the abolition of slavery by issuing the Emancipation Proclamation, which ended slavery in rebel states not occupied by the Union army. Final abolition was accomplished after the war, in 1865, by the Thirteenth Amendment to the Constitution. By the 1880s, however, most African-Americans lived in harsh conditions as sharecroppers, and by the end of the century nearly all southern states had instituted "Jim Crow" laws that segregated blacks in public transportation, jobs, and schools. This coincided with increased racial violence that saw an average of fifty blacks lynched each year.

In Brazil slavery survived for more than two decades after it was abolished in the United States. Progress toward abolition was not only slower but also depended on foreign pressure. In 1830 Brazil signed a treaty with the British ending the slave trade. Despite this agreement, Brazil illegally imported over a half-million more African slaves before the British navy finally forced compliance in the 1850s. In the 1850s and 1860s the Brazilian emperor, Pedro II, and many liberals worked to abolish slavery, but their desire to find a form of gradual emancipation acceptable to slave owners slowed progress.

During the war with Paraguay (1865–1870) large numbers of slaves joined the Brazilian army in exchange for freedom. Their loyalty and heroism undermined the military's support for slavery. Educated Brazilians increasingly viewed slavery as an obstacle to economic development and an impediment to democratic reform. In the 1870s, as abolitionist sentiment grew, reformers forced the passage of laws providing for the gradual emancipation of slaves. When political support for slavery weakened in the 1880s, growing numbers of slaves forced the issue by fleeing from bondage. By then army leaders were resisting demands to capture and return runaway slaves. Legislation abolishing slavery finally was passed by the Brazilian parliament and accepted by the emperor in 1888.

The plantations of the Caribbean region received almost 40 percent of all African slaves shipped to the New World. Throughout the region tiny white minorities lived surrounded by slave and free colored majorities. At the end of the eighteenth century the slave rebellion in Saint Domingue (see Chapter 22) spread terror among slave owners across the Caribbean. Because of fear that any effort to overthrow colonial rule might unleash new slave rebellions, there was little enthusiasm among free settlers in Caribbean colonies for independence. Nor did local support for abolition appear among white settlers or free colored populations. Thus abolition in most Caribbean colonies commonly resulted from political decisions made in Europe by colonial powers.

A Former Brazilian Slave Returns from Military Service The heroic participation of black freemen and slaves in the Paraguayan War (1865–1870) led many Brazilians to advocate the abolition of slavery. The original caption for this drawing reads: "On his return from the war in Paraguay: Full of glory, covered with laurels, after having spilled his blood in defense of the fatherland and to free a people from slavery, the volunteer sees his own mother bound and whipped! Awful reality!" (Courtesy, Fundacao Biblioteca Nacional, Brazil)

Nevertheless, like slaves in Brazil, the United States, and Spanish America, slaves in the Caribbean helped propel the movement toward abolition by rebelling, running away, and resisting in more subtle ways. Although initially unsuccessful, the rebellions that threatened other French Caribbean colonies after the Haitian Revolution (1789–1804)) weakened France's support for slavery. Jamaica and other British colonies also experienced rebellions and saw the spread of communities of runaways. In Spanish Cuba as well, slave resistance forced increases in expenditures for police forces in the nineteenth century.

After 1800 the profitability of sugar plantations in the British West Indian colonies declined with increased competition from Cuba, and a coalition of labor groups, Protestant dissenters, and free traders in Britain pushed for the abolition of slavery. Britain, the major participant in the eighteenth-century expansion of slavery in the Americas, ended its participation in the slave trade in 1807. It then negotiated a series of treaties with Spain, Brazil, and other importers of slaves to eliminate the slave trade to the Americas. Once these treaties were in place, British naval forces acted to force compliance.

Slavery in British colonies was abolished in 1833. However, the law compelled "freed" slaves to remain with former masters as "apprentices." Abuses by planters and resistance to apprenticeship by former slaves led to complete abolition in 1838. A decade later slavery in the French Caribbean was abolished after upheavals in France led to the overthrow of the government of Louis Philippe (see Chapter 22). The abolition of slavery in the Dutch Empire in 1863 freed 33,000 slaves in Surinam and 12,000 in the Antilles. Slave owners were compensated for their loss, and the freedmen of Surinam were required to provide ten years of compensated labor to their former owners.

In the Caribbean, slavery lasted longest in Cuba and Puerto Rico, Spain's remaining colonies. Britain's use of diplomatic pressure and naval force to limit the arrival of African slaves weakened slavery after 1820. More important, however, was the growth of support for abolition in these colonies. Both Cuba and Puerto Rico had larger white and free colored populations than did the Caribbean colonies of Britain and France. As a result, there was less fear in Cuba and Puerto Rico that abolition would lead to the political ascendancy of former slaves (as had occurred in Haiti). In Puerto Rico, where slaves numbered approximately thirty thousand, local reformers secured the abolition of slavery in 1873. In the midst of a decade-long war to defeat forces seeking the independence of Cuba, the Spanish government gradually moved toward abolition. Initially, slave children born after September 18, 1868, were freed but obligated to work for their former masters for eighteen years. In 1880 all other slaves were freed on the condition that they serve their masters for eight additional years. Finally, in 1886 these conditions were eliminated; slavery was abolished; and Cuban patriots forged the multiracial alliance that was to initiate a war for Cuban independence in 1895 (see Chapter 28).

Immigration

During the colonial period free Europeans were a minority among immigrants to the Western Hemisphere. Between 1500 and 1760 African slaves entering the Western Hemisphere outnumbered European immigrants by nearly two to one. Another 4 million or so African slaves were imported before the effective end of the slave trade at the end of the 1850s. As the African slave trade came to an end, the arrival of millions of immigrants from Europe and Asia contributed to the further transformation of the Western Hemisphere. This nineteenth-century wave of immigration fostered rapid economic growth and the occupation of frontier regions in the United States, Canada, Argentina, Chile, and Brazil. It also promoted urbanization. By century's end nearly all of the hemisphere's fastest-growing cities (Buenos Aires, Chicago, New York, and São Paulo, for example) had large immigrant populations.

Europe provided the majority of immigrants to the Western Hemisphere during the nineteenth century. For much of the century they came primarily from western Europe, but after 1870 most came from southern and eastern Europe. The scale of immigration increased dramatically in the second half of the century. The United States received approximately 600,000 European immigrants in the 1830s, 1.5 million in the 1840s, and then 2.5 million per decade until 1880. In the 1890s an astonishing total of 5.2 million immigrants arrived. This helped push the national population from 39 million in 1871 to 63 million in 1891, an increase of 62 percent. Most of the immigrants ended up in cities. Chicago, for example, grew from 444,000 in 1870 to 1.7 million in 1900.

European immigration to Latin America also increased dramatically after 1880. Combined immigration to Argentina and Brazil rose from just under 130,000 in the 1860s to 1.7 million in the 1890s. By 1910, 30 percent of the Argentine population was foreign-born, more than twice the proportion in the U.S. population. Argentina was an extremely attractive destination for European immigrants, receiving more than twice as many immigrants as Canada between 1870 and 1930. Even so, immigration to Canada increased tenfold during this period.

Asian immigration to the Western Hemisphere increased after 1850. Between 1849 and 1875 approximately 100,000 Chinese immigrants arrived in Peru and another 120,000 entered Cuba. Canada attracted about 50,000 Chinese in the second half of the century. The United States, however, was the primary North American destination for Chinese immigrants, receiving 300,000 between 1854 and 1882. India also contributed to the social transformation of the Western Hemisphere, sending more than a half-million immigrants to the Caribbean region. British Guiana alone received 238,000 immigrants, mostly indentured laborers, from the Asian subcontinent.

Despite the obvious economic benefits that accompanied this inflow of people, hostility to immigration mounted in many nations. Nativist political movements

Chinese Funeral in Vancouver, Canada In the 1890s Vancouver was an important Western Hemisphere destination for Chinese immigrants. This photo shows how an important element of traditional Chinese culture thrived among the storefronts and streetcar lines of the late-Victorian Canadian city. (Vancouver Public Library, Special Collections, VPL1234)

argued that large numbers of foreigners could not be successfully integrated into national political cultures. By the end of the century fear and prejudice led many governments in the Western Hemisphere to limit immigration or to distinguish between "desirable" and "undesirable" immigrants, commonly favoring Europeans over Asians.

Asians faced more obstacles to immigration than did Europeans and were more often victims of violence and extreme forms of discrimination in the New World. In the 1870s and 1880s anti-Chinese riots erupted in many western cities in the United States. Congress responded to this wave of racism by passing the Chinese Exclusion Act in 1882, which eliminated most Chinese immigration. In 1886 fears that Canada was being threatened by "inferior races" led to the imposition of a head tax that made immigration to Canada more difficult for Chinese families. During this same period strong anti-Chinese prejudice surfaced in Peru, Mexico, and Cuba. Japanese immigrants in Brazil and East Indians in the English-speaking Caribbean faced similar prejudice.

Immigrants from Europe also faced prejudice and discrimination. In the United States, Italians were commonly portrayed as criminals or anarchists. In Argentina, social scientists attempted to prove that Italian immigrants were more violent and less honest than the native-born population. Immigrants from Spain were widely stereotyped in Argentina as miserly and dishonest. Eastern European Jews seeking to escape pogroms and discrimination at home found themselves barred from many educational institutions and professional careers in both the United States and Latin America. Negative stereotypes were invented for Irish, German, Swedish, Polish, and Middle Eastern immigrants as well. The perceived grievances used to justify these common prejudices were remarkably similar from Canada to Argentina. Immigrants, it was argued, threatened the well-being of native-born workers by accepting low wages, and they threatened national culture by resisting assimilation.

Many intellectuals and political leaders wondered if the evolving mix of culturally diverse populations could sustain a common citizenship. As a result, efforts were directed toward compelling immigrants to assimilate. Schools became cultural battlegrounds where language, cultural values, and patriotic feelings were transmitted to the children of immigrants. Across the hemisphere, school curricula were revised to promote national culture. Ignoring Canada's large French-speaking population, an English-speaking Canadian reformer commented on recent immigration: "If Canada is to become in a real sense a nation, if our people are to become one people, we must have one language."[7] Fear and prejudice were among the emotions promoting the singing of patriotic songs, the veneration of national flags and other symbols, and the writing of national histories that emphasized patriotism and civic virtue. Nearly everywhere in the Americas schools worked to create homogeneous national cultures.

American Cultures

Despite discrimination, immigrants continued to stream into the Western Hemisphere, introducing new languages, living arrangements, technologies, and work customs. Immigrants altered the politics of many of the hemisphere's nations as they sought to influence government policies. Where immigrants arrived in the greatest numbers, they put enormous pressure on housing, schools, and social welfare services. To compensate for their isolation from home, language, and culture, immigrants often created ethnically based mutual aid societies, sports and leisure clubs, and neighborhoods. Ethnic organizations and districts provided valuable social and economic support for recent arrivals while sometimes worsening the fears of the native-born that immigration posed a threat to national culture.

Immigrants were changed by their experiences in their adopted nations and by programs that forced them to accept new cultural values through education or, in some cases, service in the military. Similar efforts to forge national cultures were put in place in Europe by modernizing governments at the same time. The modification of the language, customs, values, and behaviors of a group as a result of contact with people from another culture is called **acculturation.**

Immigrants and their children, in turn, made their mark on the cultures of their adopted nations in the Americas. They learned the language spoken in their adopted countries as fast as possible in order to improve their earning capacity. At the same time, words and phrases from their languages entered the vocabularies of the host nations. Languages as diverse as Yiddish and Italian strongly influenced American English, Argentine Spanish, and Brazilian Portuguese. Dietary practices introduced from Europe and Asia altered the cuisine of nearly every American nation. In turn, immigrants commonly added native foods to their diets, especially the hemisphere's abundant and relatively cheap meats.

Throughout the hemisphere culture and popular music changed as well. For example, the Argentine tango, based on African-Argentine rhythms, was transformed by new instrumentation and orchestral arrangements brought by Italian immigrants. Mexican ballads blended

Arrest of Labor Activist in Buenos Aires The labor movement in Buenos Aires grew in numbers and became more radical with the arrival of tens of thousands of Italian and Spanish immigrants. Fearful of socialist and anarchist unions, the government of Argentina used an expanded police force to break strikes by arresting labor leaders. (Archivo General de la Nación, Buenos Aires)

with English folk music in the U.S. southwest, and Italian operas played to packed houses in Buenos Aires. Sports, games of chance, and fashion also experienced this process of borrowing and exchange.

Union movements and electoral politics in the hemisphere also felt the influence of new arrivals who aggressively sought to influence government and improve working conditions. The labor movements of Mexico, Argentina, and the United States, in particular, were influenced by the anarchist and socialist beliefs of European immigrants. Mutual benevolent societies and less-formal ethnic associations pooled resources to help immigrants open businesses, aid the immigration of relatives, or bury family members. They also established links with political movements, sometimes exchanging votes for favors.

Women's Rights and the Struggle for Social Justice

The abolition of slavery in the Western Hemisphere did not end racial discrimination or provide full political rights for every citizen. Not only blacks but also women, new immigrants, and native peoples in nearly every Western Hemisphere nation suffered the effects of political and economic discrimination. During the second half of the nineteenth century reformers struggled to remove these limits on citizenship while also addressing the welfare needs of workers and the poor.

In 1848 a group of women angered by their exclusion from an international antislavery meeting issued a call for a meeting to discuss women's rights. The **Women's Rights Convention** at Seneca Falls, New York, issued a statement that said, in part, "We hold these truths to be self-evident: that all men and women are equal." While moderates focused on the issues of greater economic independence and full legal rights, increasing numbers of women demanded the right to vote. Others lobbied to provide better conditions for women working outside the home, especially in textile factories. Sarah Grimké responded to criticism of women's activism:

> This has been the language of man since he laid aside the whip as a means to keep woman in subjection. He spares her body, but the war he has waged against her mind, her heart, and her soul, has been no less destructive to her as a moral being. How monstrous is the doctrine that woman is to be dependent on man![8]

Progress toward equality between men and women was equally slow in Canada and Latin America. Canada's first women doctors received their training in the United States because no woman was able to receive a medical degree in Canada until 1895. Full enfranchisement occurred in Canada in the twentieth century, but Canadian women did gain the right to vote in some provincial and municipal elections before 1900. Like women in the United States, Canadian women provided leadership in temperance, child welfare, and labor reform movements.

Argentina and Uruguay were among the first Latin American nations to provide public education for women. Both nations introduced coeducation in the 1870s. Chilean women gained access to some careers in medicine and law in the 1870s. In Argentina the first woman doctor graduated from medical school in 1899. In Brazil, where many women were active in the abolitionist movement, four women graduated in medicine by 1882. Throughout the hemisphere more rapid progress was achieved in lower-status careers that threatened male economic power less directly, and by the end of the century women dominated elementary school teaching throughout the Western Hemisphere.

From Canada to Argentina and Chile, the majority of working-class women had no direct involvement in these reform movements, but they succeeded in transforming gender relations in their daily lives. By the end of the nineteenth century, large numbers of poor women worked outside the home on farms, in markets, and, increasingly, in factories. Many bore full responsibility for providing for their children. Whether men thought women should remain in the home or not, by the end of the century women were unambiguously present in the economy (see also Chapter 27).

Throughout the hemisphere there was little progress toward eliminating racial discrimination. Blacks were denied the vote throughout the southern United States. They also were subjected to the indignity of segregation—consigned to separate schools, hotels, restaurants, seats in public transportation, and even water fountains. Racial discrimination against men and women of African descent was also common in Latin America, though seldom spelled out in legal codes. Unlike the southern states of the United States, Latin American nations did not insist on formal racial segregation or permit lynching. Nor did they enforce a strict color line. Many men and women of mixed background were able to enter the skilled working class or middle class. Latin Americans tended to view racial identity across a continuum of physical characteristics rather than in the narrow terms of black and white that defined race relations in the United States.

The abolition of slavery in Latin America did not lead to an end to racial discrimination. Some of the participants in the abolition struggles later organized to promote racial integration. They demanded access to education, the right to vote, and greater economic opportunity, pointing out the economic and political costs of denying full rights to all citizens. Their success depended on effective political organization and on forging alliances with sympathetic white politicians. Black intellectuals also struggled to overturn racist stereotypes. In Brazil, Argentina, and Cuba, as in the United States, political and literary magazines celebrating black cultural achievement became powerful weapons in the struggle against racial discrimination. Although men and women of African descent continued to experience prejudice and discrimination everywhere in the Americas, successful men and women of mixed descent in Latin America confronted fewer obstacles to their advancement than did similar groups in the United States.

Development and Underdevelopment

The Atlantic economy experienced three periods of economic contraction during the nineteenth century, but nearly all the nations of the Western Hemisphere were richer in 1900 than in 1800. The Industrial Revolution, worldwide population growth, and an increasingly integrated world market stimulated economic expansion (see Environment and Technology: Constructing the Port of Buenos Aires, Argentina). Wheat, corn, wool, meats, and nonprecious minerals joined the region's earlier exports of silver, sugar, dyes, coffee, and cotton. During the nineteenth century the United States was the only Western Hemisphere nation to industrialize, but nearly every government promoted new economic activities. Governments and private enterprises invested in roads, railroads, canals, and telegraphs to better serve distant markets. Most governments adopted tariff and monetary policies to foster economic diversification and growth. Despite these efforts, by 1900 only three Western Hemisphere nations—the United States, Canada, and Argentina—achieved individual income levels similar to those of western Europe. All three nations had open land, temperate climates, diverse resources, and large inflows of immigrants.

New demands for copper, zinc, lead, coal, and tin unleashed by the Industrial Revolution led to mining booms in the western United States, Mexico, and Chile. Unlike the small-scale and often short-term gold- and silver-mining operations of the colonial era, the mining companies of the late nineteenth century were heavily capitalized international corporations that could bully governments and buy political favors. During this period, European and North American corporations owned most new mining enterprises in Latin America. Petroleum development, which occurred at the end of the century in Mexico and elsewhere, would follow this pattern as well (see the discussion of the Mexican economy during the Díaz dictatorship in Chapter 31).

New technology accelerated economic integration, but the high cost of this technology often increased dependence on foreign capital. Many governments promoted railroads by granting tax benefits, free land, and monopoly rights to both domestic and foreign investors. By 1890 vast areas of the Great Plains in the United States, the Canadian prairie, the Argentine pampas, and parts of northern Mexico were producing grain and livestock for foreign markets opened by the development of railroads. Steamships also lowered the cost of transportation to distant markets, and the telegraph stimulated expansion by speeding information about the demand for and availability of products.

The simultaneous acquisition of several new technologies multiplied the effects of individual technologies. In Argentina the railroad, the telegraph, barbed wire, and refrigeration all appeared in the 1870s and 1880s. Although Argentina had had abundant livestock herds since the colonial period, the distance from Europe's markets prevented Argentine cattle raisers from exporting fresh meat or live animals. Technology overcame these obstacles. The combination of railroads and the telegraph lowered freight costs and improved information about markets. Steamships shortened trans-Atlantic crossings. Refrigerated ships made it possible to sell meat in the markets of Europe. As land values rose and livestock breeding improved, new investments were protected by barbed wire, the first inexpensive fencing available on the nearly treeless plains.

Growing interdependence and increased competition produced deep structural differences among Western Hemisphere economies by 1900. Two distinct economic tracks became clearly visible. One led to industrialization and prosperity, what is now called **development.** The other continued colonial dependence on exporting raw materials and on low-wage industries, now commonly called **underdevelopment.** By 1900 material prosperity was greater and economic development more diversified in English-speaking North America than in the nations of Latin America. With a temperate climate, vast fertile prairies, and an influx of European immigrants, Argentina was the only Latin American nation to approach the prosperity of the United States and Canada.

The Introduction of New Technologies Changes the Mining Industry Powerful hydraulic technologies were introduced in western mining sites in the United States. This early photo shows how high-power water jets could transform the natural environment. (Colorado Historical Society)

Changes in the performance of international markets helped determine the trajectory of Western Hemisphere economies as new nations promoted economic development. When the United States gained independence the world capitalist economy was in a period of rapid growth. With a large merchant fleet, a diversified economy that included some manufacturing, and adequate banking and insurance services, the United States benefited from the expansion of the world economy. Rapid population growth due in large measure to immigration, high levels of individual wealth, widespread landownership, and relatively high literacy rates also fostered rapid economic development in the United States. The rapid expansion of railroad mileage suggests this success. In 1865 the United States had the longest network in the world. By 1915 it had multiplied eleven-fold (see Map 24.4). Steel production grew rapidly as well, with the United States overtaking Britain and Germany in the 1890s. One cost of the nation's industrialization was the vastly expanded power of monopolies, like Standard Oil, over political life.

Canada's struggle for greater political autonomy led to the Confederation of 1867, which coincided with a second period of global economic expansion. Canada also benefited from a special trading relationship with Britain, the world's preeminent industrial nation, and from a rising tide of immigrants after 1850. Nevertheless, some regions within each of these prosperous North American nations—Canada's Maritime Provinces and the southern part of the United States, for example—demonstrated the same patterns of underdevelopment found in Latin America.

Latin American nations gained independence in the 1820s, when the global economy was contracting due to the end of the Napoleonic Wars and market saturation provoked by the early stages of European industrialization. In the colonial period Spain and Portugal had promoted the production of agricultural and mining

Constructing the Port of Buenos Aires, Argentina

Located on the banks of the Río de la Plata, Buenos Aires had been a major commercial center and port since the late eighteenth century. But Buenos Aires was not a natural harbor. Because of the shallowness of the river, the largest oceangoing ships were forced to anchor hundreds of yards offshore while goods and passengers were unloaded by small boats or by specially built ox carts with huge wheels. Smaller vessels docked at a river port to the city's south.

By the 1880s the Argentine economy was being transformed by the growing demands of European consumers for meat and grain. As exports surged and land values exploded, the wages of Argentines rose, and the nation became a favored destination for European immigrants. Argentina was becoming the wealthiest nation in Latin America.

The nation's political and economic elites decided that future growth required the modernization and expansion of port facilities. Two competing plans were debated. The first emphasized the incremental expansion and dredging of the river port. This was supported by local engineers and political groups suspicious of foreign economic interests. The second, and ultimately successful, plan involved dredging a port and deep-water channel from the low mud flats near the city center. This plan was more expensive, relying on British engineering firms, British banks, and British technology. It was supported by Argentine economic interests most closely tied to the European export trade and by national political leaders who believed progress and prosperity required the imitation of European models. Already the British were the nation's primary creditors as well as leaders in the development of the nation's railroads, streetcar lines, and gas works in Buenos Aires.

The photograph below shows the construction of Puerto Madero, the new port of Buenos Aires, in the 1890s. The work force was almost entirely recruited from recent immigrants. The engineering staff was dominated by British experts. Most of the profits were culled by the local elite through real estate deals and commissions associated with construction. Puerto Madero, named after its local promoter, was opened in stages beginning in 1890. Cost overruns and corruption stretched out completion to 1898. By 1910 arrivals and departures reached thirty thousand ships and 18 million tons. But the project was poorly designed, and "improvements" were still being made in the 1920s.

Excavation of Port of Buenos Aires, Argentina Relying on foreign capital and engineering, the government of Argentina improved the port to facilitate the nation's rapidly expanding export economy. (Courtesy, Hack Hoffenburg, South American Resources)

Why had the government of Argentina chosen the costliest and most difficult design? Argentine politicians were seduced by the idea of modernity; they chose the most complex and technologically sophisticated solution to the port problem. And they believed that British engineering and British capital were guarantees of modernity. The new port facilities did facilitate a boom in exports and imports, and the huge public works budget did provide incomes for thousands of laborers. However, debts, design flaws, and the increased influence of foreign capital in Argentina left a legacy of problems that Argentina would be forced to deal with in the future. (See the discussion of Juan Perón in Chapter 31.)

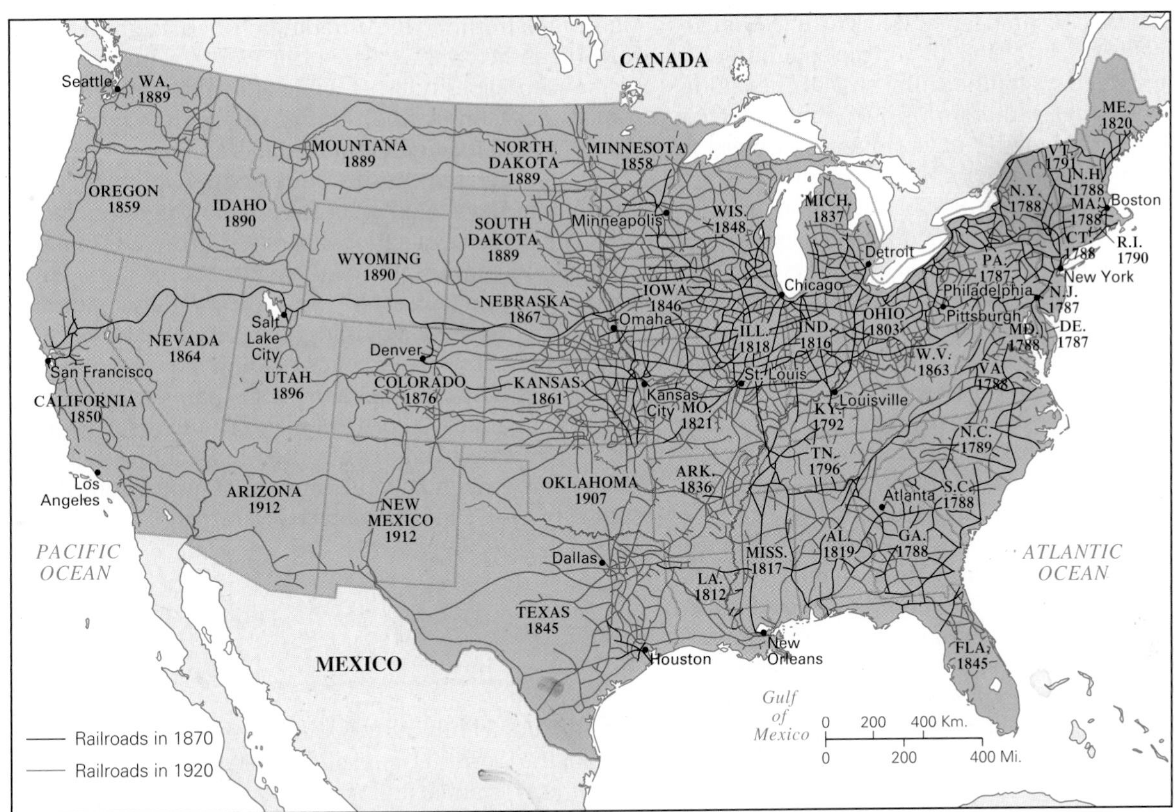

Map 24.4 The Expansion of the United States, 1850–1920. The settlement of western territories and their admission as states depended on migration, the exploitation of natural resources and important new technologies like railroads and telegraphs that facilitated economic and political integration.

exports. After independence those raw-material exports faced increased competition. Although these sectors experienced periods of great prosperity in the nineteenth century, they also faced stiff competition and falling prices as new regions began production or new products captured markets. Sugar, coffee, nitrates, and copper all followed this pattern.

The history of the specialized Latin American economies, subject to periodic problems of oversupply and low prices, was one of boom and bust. Many Latin American governments sought to promote exports in the face of increased competition and falling prices by resisting union activity and demands for higher wages and by opening domestic markets to foreign manufactures. Resulting low wages and an abundance of foreign manufactured goods, in turn, undermined efforts to promote industrialization in Latin America.

Weak governments, political instability, and, in some cases, civil war also slowed Latin American economic development. A comparative examination of Western Hemisphere economic history makes clear that stable and reliable public administration is a necessary part of the development process. Because Latin America was dependent on capital and technology from abroad, Great Britain and, by the end of the century, the United States were often able to impose unfavorable trade conditions or even intervene militarily to protect investments. The combined impact of these domestic and international impediments to development became clear when Mexico, Chile, and Argentina failed to achieve high levels of domestic investment in manufacturing late in the nineteenth century, despite a rapid accumulation of wealth derived from traditional exports.

Altered Environments

Population growth, economic expansion, new technologies, and the introduction of plants and animals to new regions dramatically altered the environment of the Western Hemisphere. Cuba's planters cut down many of the island's forests in the early nineteenth century to expand sugar production. Growing demand for meat led ranchers to expand livestock-raising into fragile environments in Argentina, Uruguay, southern Brazil, and the southwestern United States. Other forms of commercial agriculture also threatened the environment. Farmers in South Carolina and Georgia gained a short-term increase in cotton production by abandoning crop rotation after 1870, but this practice quickly led to soil exhaustion and erosion. The use of steel plows on North American prairies and Argentine pampas eliminated many native grasses and increased the threat of soil erosion. Coffee planters in Brazil exhausted soil fertility with a destructive cycle of overplanting followed by expansion onto forest reserves cleared by cutting and burning. Similarly massive transfers of land from public to private ownership occurred in Argentina and Brazil in order to promote livestock-raising and agriculture.

Rapid urbanization also put heavy pressure on the environment. New York, Chicago, Rio de Janeiro, Buenos Aires, and Mexico City were among the world's fastest-growing cities in the nineteenth century. Governments strained to provide adequate sewers, clean water, and garbage disposal. Timber companies clear-cut large areas of Michigan, Wisconsin, and the Appalachian Mountains to provide lumber for railroad ties and frame houses, pulp for paper, and fuel for locomotives and foundries. Under the Timber and Stone Act of 1878, the U.S. government sold more than 3.5 million additional acres (1.4 million hectares) of public land to individual and corporations at low cost by 1900. At the same time, the forest industries of British Honduras (now Belize), Nicaragua, and Guatemala grew rapidly in response to demand in Europe and North America for tropical hardwoods like mahogany. As forest throughout the hemisphere was cleared, animal habitats and native plant species disappeared.

The scale of mining operation grew in Nevada, Montana, and California, accelerating erosion and pollution. Similar results occurred in other mining areas. The expansion of nitrate mining and, later, open-pit copper mining in Chile scarred and polluted the environment. The state of Minas Gerais° in Brazil experienced a series of mining booms that began with gold in the late seventeenth century and continued with iron ore in the nineteenth. By the end of the nineteenth century its red soil was ripped open, its forests were depleted, and erosion was uncontrolled. Similar devastation afflicted parts of ·olivia and Mexico.

Efforts to meet increasing domestic demand for food ·using and to satisfy foreign demands for exports led to environmental degradation but also contributed significantly to the growth of the world economy and to regional prosperity. By the end of the nineteenth century small-scale conservation efforts were under way in many nations, and the first national parks and nature reserves had been created. In the United States large areas remained undeveloped. A few particularly beautiful areas were preserved in a national park system. In 1872 Yellowstone in Wyoming became the first national park. President Theodore Roosevelt (1901–1909) and the naturalist John Muir played major roles in preserving large areas of the western states. In Canada the first national park was created at Banff in 1885 and was expanded from 10 to 260 square miles (26 to 673 square kilometers) two years later. However, when confronted by a choice between economic growth and environmental protection, all the hemisphere's nations embraced growth.

° (ME-nas JER-aize)

CONCLUSION

The nineteenth century witnessed enormous changes in the Western Hemisphere. Except in Canada, many Caribbean islands, and a handful of mainland colonies like Surinam, the Guyanas, and Belize, colonial controls were removed by century's end. The powerful new political ideas of the Enlightenment and an increased sense of national identity contributed to the desire for independence and self-rule. The success of the American and Haitian Revolutions began the assault on the colonial order, transforming the hemisphere's politics. Napoleon's invasion of Portugal and Spain then helped initiate the movement toward independence in Latin America.

Once colonial rule was overturned, the creation of stable and effective governments proved difficult. Powerful personalist leaders resisted the constraints imposed by constitutions. National governments often confronted divisive regional political movements. From Argentina in the south to the United States in the north, regional political rivalries provoked civil wars that challenged the very survival of the new nations. Foreign military interventions and wars with native peoples also consumed resources and determined national boundaries. The effort to fulfill the promise of universal citizenship led to struggles to end slavery, extend civil and political rights to women and minorities, and absorb new immigrants. These objectives were only partially achieved.

Industrialization had a transforming effect on the hemisphere as well. Wealth, political power, and population were increasingly concentrated in urban areas. In most countries, bankers and manufacturers, rather than farmers and plantation owners, directed national destinies. The United States, the most industrialized nation in the Americas, played an aggressive economic role in the region's affairs and used its growing military power as well. Industrialization altered the natural environment in dramatic ways. Modern factories consumed huge amounts of raw materials and energy. Copper mines in Chile and Mexico, Cuban sugar plantations, Brazilian coffee plantations, and Canadian lumber companies all left their mark on the natural environment, and all had ties to markets in the United States. The concentration of people in cities in the United States and Latin America put pressure on water supplies, sewage treatment, and food supplies.

By 1900, however, the hemisphere's national governments were much stronger than they had been at independence. Latin America lagged behind the United States and Canada in institutionalizing democratic political reforms, but Latin American nations in 1900 were stronger and more open than they had been in 1850. By 1900 all the hemisphere's nations also were better able to meet the threats of foreign intervention and regionalism. Among the benefits resulting from the increased strength of national governments were the abolition of slavery and the extension of political rights to formerly excluded citizens.

Serious challenges remained. Amerindian peoples were forced to resettle on reservations, were excluded from national political life, and, in some countries, remained burdened with special tribute and tax obligations. Women began to enter occupations previously reserved to men but still lacked full citizenship rights. The baneful legacy of slavery and colonial racial stratification remained a barrier to many men and women. The benefits of economic growth were not equitably distributed among the nations of the Western Hemisphere or within individual nations. In 1900 nearly every American nation was wealthier, better educated, more democratic, and more populous than at independence. But these nations were also more vulnerable to distant economic forces, more profoundly split between haves and have-nots, and more clearly divided into a rich north and a poorer south.

Key Terms

Simón Bolívar
Miguel Hidalgo y Costilla
José María Morelos
Confederation of 1867
personalist leaders
Andrew Jackson
José Antonio Páez
Benito Juárez
Tecumseh
Caste War
abolitionists
acculturation
Women's Rights Convention
development
underdevelopment

Suggested Reading

For the independence era in Latin America see John Lynch, *The Spanish American Revolutions, 1808–1826,* 2d ed. (1986); Jay Kinsbruner, *Independence in Spanish America* (1994); and A. J. R. Russell-Wood, ed., *From Colony to Nation: Essays on the Independence of Brazil* (1976).

The postindependence political and economic struggles in Latin America can be traced in David Bushnell and Neil Macaulay, *The Emergence of Latin America in the Nineteenth Century* (1988). Tulio Halperin-Donghi, *The Contemporary History of Latin America* (1993), and E. Bradford Burns, *The Poverty of Progress: Latin America in the Nineteenth Century* (1980), argue in different ways that Latin America's economic and social problems originated in unfavorable trade relationships with more-developed nations. See also an excellent collection of essays, Leslie Bethell, ed., *The Cambridge History of Latin America,* vol. 3, *From Independence to c. 1870* (1985).

There is an enormous literature on politics and nation building in the United States and Canada. Among the many worthy studies of the United States are John Lauritz Larson, *Internal Improvement: National Public Works and the Promise of Popular Government in the Early United States* (2001); William J. Cooper, *The South and the Politics of Slavery, 1828–1856* (1978); Kenneth M. Stampp, *America in 1857* (1991); and Lawrence Frederick Kohl, *The Politics of Individualism: Parties and the American Character in the Jacksonian Era* (1989). For Canada see J. M. S. Careless, *The Union of the Canadas: The Growth of Canadian Institutions, 1841–1857* (1967); Ged Martin, ed., *The Causes of Canadian Confederation* (1990); and Arthur I. Silver, *The French-Canadian Idea of Confederation, 1864–1900* (1982).

The social and cultural issues raised in this chapter are also th subject of a vast literature. For an excellent history of the imm gration era see Walter Nugent, *Crossing: The Great Transatlan*

Migrations, 1870–1914 (1992). See also Gunther Barth, *Bitter Strength: A History of Chinese in the United States, 1850–1870* (1964), and Nicolás Sánchez-Albornoz, *The Population of Latin America: A History* (1974).

On the issue of slavery see David Brion Davis, *Slavery and Human Progress* (1984), and George M. Frederickson, *The Black Image in the White Mind: The Debate on Afro-American Character and Destiny, 1817–1914* (1971). Among the many fine studies of abolition see Benjamin Quarles, *Black Abolitionists* (1969), and John Stauffer, *The Black Hearts of Men* (2001). For the women's rights movement see Ellen C. Du Bois, *Feminism and Suffrage: The Emergence of an Independent Woman's Movement in the Nineteenth Century* (1984), and Lori D. Ginzberg, *Women and the Work of Benevolence: Morality, Politics, and Class in the Nineteenth-Century United States* (1990). Among numerous excellent studies of Indian policies see Robert M. Utley, *The Indian Frontier of the American West, 1846–1890* (1984), and the recent *Andrew Jackson and His Indian Wars* (2001) by Robert V. Remini. On those topics for Canada see J. R. Miller, *Skyscrapers Hide the Heavens: A History of Indian White Relations in Canada* (1989); Olive Patricia Dickason, *Canada's First Nations* (1993); and Alison Prentice, *Canadian Women: A History* (1988).

For abolition in Latin America and the Caribbean see Rebecca Scott, *Slave Emancipation in Cuba: The Transition to Free Labor, 1860–1899* (1985); Robert Conrad, *The Destruction of Brazilian Slavery, 1850–1888* (1973); and William A. Green, *British Slave Emancipation: The Sugar Colonies and the Great Experiment, 1830–1865* (1973). An introduction to the place of women in Latin American society is found in Francesca Miller, *Latin American Women and the Search for Social Justice* (1991), and Jane Jaquette, ed., *The Women's Movement in Latin America* (1989). See also David Barry Gaspar and Darlene Clark Hine, eds., *More Than Chattel: Black Women and Slavery in the Americas* (1996).

An introduction to environmental consequence of North American development is provided by William Cronon, *Nature's Metropolis: Chicago and the Great West* (1991); Joseph M. Petulla, *American Environmental History* (1973); and Donald Worster, *Rivers of Empire: Water, Aridity, and the Growth of the American West* (1985). For Brazil see Warren Dean, *With Broadax and Firebrand: The Destruction of the Brazilian Atlantic Forest* (1995); and for Argentina, Uruguay, and Chile, Alfred Crosby, *Ecological Imperialism: The Biological Expansion of Europe, 900–1900* (1986).

Notes

1. Quoted in Lyman L. Johnson, "Spanish American Independence and Its Consequences," in *Problems in Modern Latin American History: A Reader,* ed. John Charles Chasteen and Joseph S. Tulchin (Wilmington, DE: Scholarly Resources, 1994), 21.
2. Quoted in Margaret Conrad, Alvin Finkel, and Cornelius Jaenen, *History of the Canadian Peoples,* vol. 1 (Toronto: Copp Clark Pittman Ltd., 1993), 606–607.
3. José Antonio Páez, *Autobiografía del General José Antonio Páez,* vol. 1 (New York: Hallety Breen, 1869), 83.
4. Quoted in Brian Loveman, *Chile: The Legacy of Hispanic Capitalism* (New York: Oxford University Press, 1979), 170.
5. Quoted in Bernard Bailyn, David Brion Davis, David Herbert Donald, John L. Thomas, Robert H. Wiebe, and Gordon S. Wood, *The Great Republic: A History of the American People* (Lexington, MA: D. C. Heath, 1981), 398.
6. Quoted in Mary Beth Norton, et al, A People and a Nation. A History of the United States, 6th edition (Boston, MA: Houghton Mifflin Company, 2001), 284.
7. J. S. Woodsworth in 1909, quoted in R. Douglas Francis, Richard Jones, and Donald B. Smith, *Destinies: Canadian History Since Confederation,* 2d ed. (Toronto: Holt, Rinehart and Winston, 1992), 141.
8. Sarah Grimké, "Reply to the Massachusetts Clergy," in Nancy Woloch, ed., *Early American Women: A Documentary History, 1600–1900* (Belmont, CA: Wadsworth, 1992), 343.

25

Africa, India, and the New British Empire, 1750–1870

Indian Railroad Station, 1866 British India built the largest network of railroads in Asia. People of every social class traveled by train.

CHAPTER OUTLINE

Changes and Exchanges in Africa

India Under British Rule

Britain's Eastern Empire

DIVERSITY AND DOMINANCE: Ceremonials of Imperial Domination

ENVIRONMENT AND TECHNOLOGY: Whaling

In 1782 Tipu Sultan inherited the throne of the state of Mysore°, which his father had made the most powerful state in South India. The ambitious and talented new ruler also inherited a healthy distrust of the territorial ambitions of Great Britain's East India Company. In 1785, before the company could invade Mysore, Tipu Sultan launched his own attack. He then sent an embassy to France in 1788, seeking an alliance against Britain. Neither of these ventures was immediately successful.

Not until a decade later did the French agree to a loose alliance with Tipu Sultan as part of their plan to challenge Britain's colonial and commercial supremacy in the Indian Ocean. General Napoleon Bonaparte invaded Egypt in 1798 to threaten British trade routes to India and hoped to use the alliance with Tipu Sultan to drive the British out of India. The French invasion of Egypt went well enough at first, but a British naval blockade and the ravages of disease crippled the French force. When the French withdrew, another military adventurer, Muhammad Ali, commander of the Ottoman army in Egypt, took advantage of the situation to revitalize Egypt and expand its rule.

Meanwhile, Tipu's struggle with the East India Company was going badly. A military defeat in 1792 forced him to surrender most of his coastal lands. Despite the loose alliance with France, he was unable to stop further British advances. Tipu lost his life in 1799 while defending his capital against a British assault. Mysore was divided between the British and their Indian allies.

As these events illustrate, talented local leaders and European powers were all vying to expand their influence in South Asia and Africa between 1750 and 1870. Midway through that period, it was by no means
ar who would gain the upper hand. Britain and
e were as likely to fight each other as they were
an Asian or African state. In 1800 the two na-
engaged in their third major war for over-
cy since 1750. By 1870, however, Britain
cisive advantage over France.

The new British Empire in the East included the subcontinent of India, settler colonies in Australia and New Zealand, and a growing network of trading outposts. By 1870 Britain had completed the campaign to replace the overseas slave trade from Africa with "legitimate" trade and had spearheaded new Asian and South Pacific labor migrations into a rejuvenated string of tropical colonies.

As you read this chapter, ask yourself the following questions:

- Why were the British able to gain decisive advantages in distant lands?
- Why were Asians and Africans so divided, some choosing to cooperate with the Europeans and others resisting their advances?
- How important an advantage were Britain's weapons, ships, and economic motives?
- How much of the outcome was the result of advance planning, and how much was due to particular individuals or to chance?
- By 1870, how much had the British and the different peoples of Africa and Asia gained or lost?

Changes and Exchanges in Africa

In the century before 1870 Africa underwent dynamic political changes and a great expansion of foreign trade. Indigenous African leaders as well as Middle Eastern and European imperialists built powerful new states and expanded old ones. As the continent's external slave trades to the Americas and to Islamic lands died slowly under British pressure, trade in goods such as palm oil, ivory, timber, and gold grew sharply. In return Africans imported large quantities of machine-made textiles and firearms. These complex changes are best understood by looking at African regions separately.

CHRONOLOGY

	Empire	Africa	India
1750	**1763** End of Seven Years War **1769–1778** Captain James Cook explores New Zealand and eastern Australia **1795** End of Dutch East India Company	**1795** Britain takes Cape Colony **1798** Napoleon invades Egypt	**1756** Black Hole of Calcutta **1765** East India Company (EIC) rule of Bengal begins **1798** Britain annexes Ceylon **1799** EIC defeats Mysore
1800	**1808** Britain outlaws slave trade **1834** Britain abolishes slavery	**1805** Muhammad Ali seizes Egypt **1808** Britain takes over Sierra Leone **1809** Sokoto Caliphate founded **1818** Shaka founds Zulu kingdom **1821** Foundation of Republic of Liberia; Egypt takes control of Sudan **1831–1847** Algerians resist French takeover **1836–1839** Afrikaners' Great Trek **1840** Omani sultan moves capital to Zanzibar	**1818** EIC creates Bombay Presidency **1826** EIC annexes Assam and northern Burma **1828** Brahmo Samaj founded **1834** Indentured labor migrations begin
1850	**1867** End of Atlantic slave trade **1877** Queen Victoria becomes Empress of India	**1869** Jaja founds Opobo **1889** Menelik unites modern Ethiopia	**1857–1858** Sepoy Rebellion leads to end of EIC rule and Mughal rule **1885** First Indian National Congress

New Africa States

Internal forces produced clusters of new states in two parts of sub-Saharan Africa between 1750 and 1870. In southern Africa changes in warfare gave rise to a powerful Zulu kingdom and other new states. In inland West Africa Islamic reformers created the gigantic Sokoto° Caliphate and companion states (see Map 25.1).

For many centuries the Nguni° peoples had pursued a life based on cattle and agriculture in the fertile coastlands of southeastern Africa (in modern South Africa). Small independent chiefdoms suited their political needs until a serious drought hit the region at the beginning of the nineteenth century. Out of the conflict for grazing and farming lands, an upstart military genius named Shaka (r. 1818–1828) created the **Zulu** kingdom in 1818. Strict military drill and close-combat warfare featuring ox-hide shields and lethal stabbing spears made the Zulu the most powerful and most feared fighters in southern Africa.

Shaka expanded his kingdom by raiding his African neighbors, seizing their cattle, and capturing their women and children. Breakaway military bands spread this system of warfare and state building inland to the high plateau country, across the Limpopo River (in modern Zimbabwe°), and as far north as Lake Victoria. As the power and population of these new kingdoms increased, so too did the number of displaced and demoralized refugees around them.

To protect themselves from the Zulu, some neighboring Africans created their own states. The Swazi kingdom consolidated north of the Zulu, and the kingdom of

Sokoto (SOH-kuh-toh) **Nguni** (ng-GOO-nee)

Zimbabwe (zim-BAH-bway)

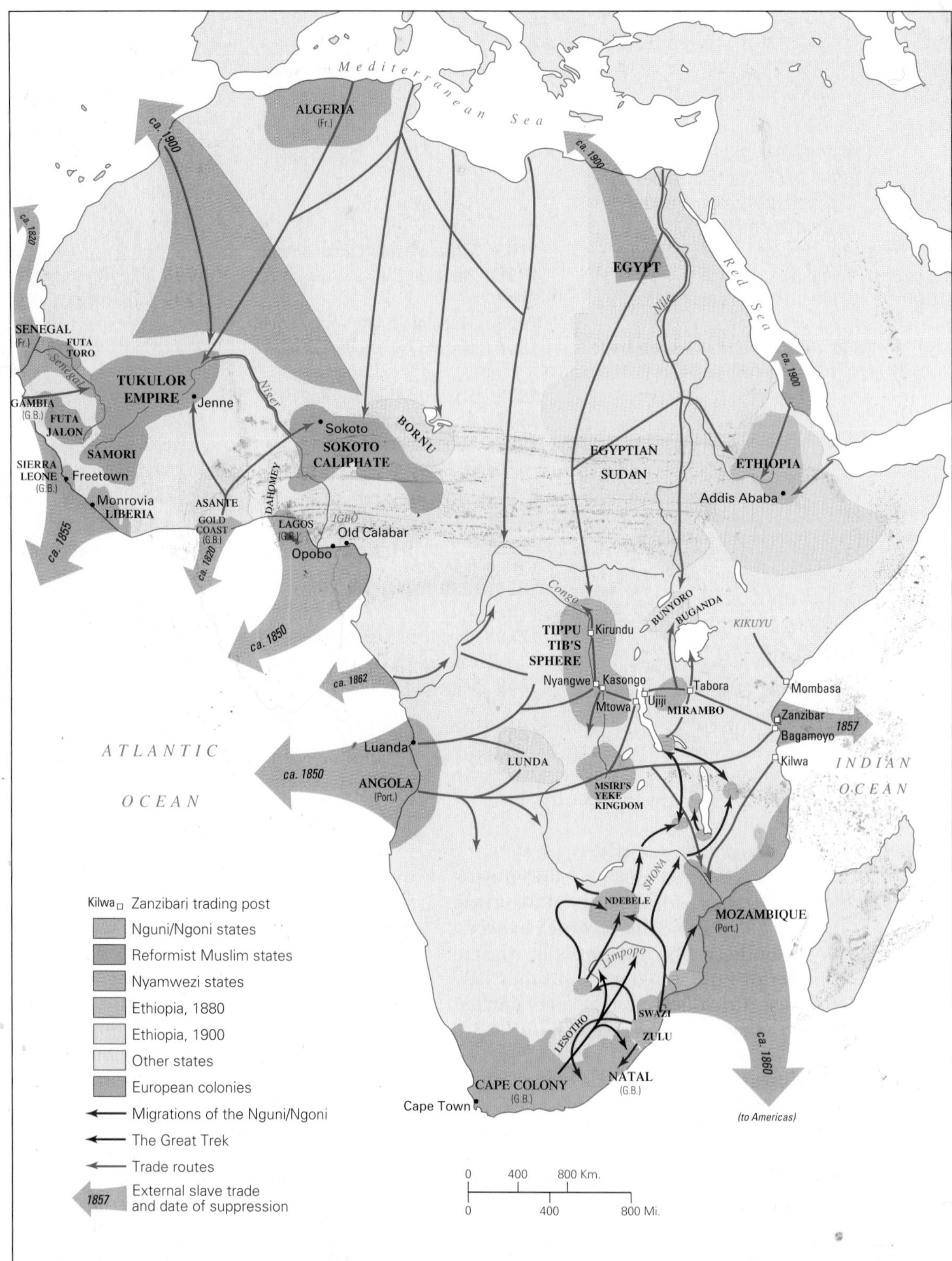

Map 25.1 Africa in the Nineteenth Century Expanding internal and overseas trade drew much of Africa into global networks, but foreign colonies in 1870 were largely confined to Algeria and southern Africa. Growing trade, Islamic reform movements, and other internal forces created important new states throughout the continent.

Lesotho° grew by attracting refugees to strongholds in southern Africa's highest mountains. Both Lesotho and Swaziland survive as independent states to this day.

Although Shaka ruled for little more than a decade, he succeeded in creating a new national identity as well as a new kingdom. He grouped all the young people in his domains by age into regiments. Regiment members lived together and immersed themselves in learning Zulu lore and customs, including fighting methods for the males. A British trader named Henry Francis Fynn expressed his "astonishment at the order and discipline" he found everywhere in the Zulu kingdom. He witnessed public festivals of loyalty to Shaka at which regiments of young men and women numbering in the tens of thousands danced around the king for hours. Parades showed off the king's enormous herds of cattle, a Zulu measure of wealth.

Meanwhile, Islamic reform movements were creating another cluster of powerful states in the savannas of West Africa. Islam had been a force in the politics and cities of this region for centuries, but it had made only slow progress among most rural people. As a consequence, most Muslim rulers had found it prudent to tolerate the older religious practices of their rural subjects. In the 1770s local Muslim scholars began preaching the need for a vigorous reform of Islamic practices. They condemned the accommodations Muslim rulers had made with older traditions and called for a forcible conquest of rural "pagans." The reformers followed a classic Muslim pattern: a *jihad* (holy war) added new lands, where governments enforced Islamic laws and promoted the religion's spread among conquered people.

The largest of the new Muslim reform movements occurred in the Hausa° states (in what is now northern Nigeria) under the leadership of Usuman dan Fodio° (1745–1817), a Muslim cleric of the Fulani° people. He charged that the Hausa kings, despite their official profession of Islam, were "undoubtedly unbelievers . . . because they practice polytheistic rituals and turn people away from the path of God." Distressed by the lapses of a former pupil, the king of Gobir, Usuman issued a call in 1804 for a jihad to overthrow him. Muslims unhappy with their social or religious position spread the movement to other Hausa states. The successful armies united the conquered Hausa states and neighboring areas under a caliph (sultan) who ruled from the city of Sokoto. The **Sokoto Caliphate** (1809–1906) was the largest state in West Africa since the fall of Songhai in the sixteenth century.

Zulu in Battle Dress, 1838 Elaborate costumes helped impress opponents with the Zulu's strength. Shown here are long-handled spears and thick leather shields. The stabbing spear is not shown. (Killie Campbell Africana Library. Photo: Jane Taylor/Sonia Halliday)

As in earlier centuries, these new Muslim states became centers of Islamic learning and reform. Schools for training boys in Quranic subjects spread rapidly, and the great library at Sokoto attracted many scholars. Although officials permitted non-Muslims within the empire to follow their religions in exchange for paying a special tax, they suppressed public performances of dances and ceremonies associated with traditional religions. During the jihads, many who resisted the expansion of Muslim rule were killed, enslaved, or forced to convert.

Sokoto's leaders sold some captives into the Atlantic slave trade and many more into the trans-Saharan slave trade, which carried ten thousand slaves a year, mostly women and children, across the desert to North Africa

Lesotho (luh-SOO-too) **Hausa** (HOW-suh)
Usuman dan Fodio (OO-soo-mahn dahn FOH-dee-oh)
Fulani (foo-LAH-nee)

and the Middle East. Slavery also increased greatly within the Sokoto Caliphate and other new Muslim states. It is estimated that by 1865 there were more slaves in the Sokoto Caliphate than in any remaining slave-holding state in the Americas.[1] Most of the enslaved persons raised food, making possible the seclusion of free women in their homes in accordance with reformed Muslim practice.

Modernization in Egypt and Ethiopia

While new states were arising elsewhere, in northeastern Africa the ancient states of Egypt and Ethiopia were undergoing growth and **modernization.** Napoleon's invading army had withdrawn from Egypt by 1801, but the shock of this display of European strength and Egyptian weakness was long-lasting. The successor to Napoleon's rule was **Muhammad Ali** (1769– 1849), who eliminated his rivals and ruled Egypt from 1805 to 1848. He began the political, social, and economic reforms that created modern Egypt.

Muhammad Ali's central aim was to give Egypt sufficient military strength to prevent another European conquest, but he was pragmatic enough to make use of European experts and techniques to achieve that goal. His reforms transformed Egyptian landholding, increased agricultural production, and created a modern administration and army. To train candidates for the army and administration, Muhammad Ali set up a European-style state school system and opened a military college at Aswan°. To pay for these ventures and for the European experts and equipment he imported, he required Egyptian peasants to cultivate cotton and other crops for export.

In the 1830s Muhammad Ali headed the strongest state in the Islamic world and the first to employ Western methods and technology for modernization. The process was far from blind imitation of the West. Rather, the technical expertise of the West was combined with Islamic religious and cultural traditions. For example, the Egyptian printing industry, begun to provide Arabic translations of technical manuals, turned out critical editions of Islamic classics and promoted a revival of Arabic writing and literature later in the century.

By the end of Muhammad Ali's reign in 1848, the modernization of Egypt was well underway. The population had nearly doubled; trade with Europe had expanded by almost 600 percent; and a new class of educated Egyptians had begun to replace the old ruling aristocracy. Egyptians were replacing many of the foreign experts, and the fledgling program of industrialization was providing the country with its own textiles, paper, weapons, and military uniforms. The demands on peasant families for labor and military service, however, were acutely disruptive.

Ali's grandson Ismail° (r. 1863–1879) placed even more emphasis on westernizing Egypt. "My country is no longer in Africa," Ismail declared, "it is in Europe."[2] His efforts increased the number of European advisers in Egypt—and Egypt's debts to French and British banks. In the first decade of his reign, revenues increased thirty-fold and exports doubled (largely because of a huge increase in cotton exports during the American Civil War). By 1870 Egypt had a network of new irrigation canals, 800 miles (1,300 kilometers) of railroads, a modern postal service, and the dazzling new capital city of Cairo. When the market for Egyptian cotton collapsed after the American Civil War, however, Egypt's debts to British and French investors led to the country's partial occupation.

From the middle of the century, state building and reform also were underway in the ancient kingdom of Ethiopia, whose rulers had been Christian for fifteen hundred years. Weakened by internal divisions and the pressures of its Muslim neighbors, Ethiopia was a shadow of what it had been in the sixteenth century, but under Emperor Téwodros° II (r. 1833–1868) and his successor Yohannes° IV (r. 1872–1889) most highland regions were brought back under imperial rule. The only large part of ancient Ethiopia that remained outside Emperor Yohannes's rule was the Shoa kingdom, ruled by King Menelik° from 1865. When Menelik succeeded Yohannes as emperor in 1889, the merger of their separate realms created the modern boundaries of Ethiopia.

Beginning in the 1840s Ethiopian rulers purchased modern weapons from European sources and created strong armies loyal to the ruler. Emperor Téwodros also encouraged the manufacture of weapons locally. With the aid of Protestant missionaries his craftsmen even constructed a giant cannon capable of firing a half-ton shell. However, his efforts to coerce more technical aid by holding some British officials captive backfired when the British invaded instead. As the British forces advanced, Téwodros committed suicide to avoid being taken prisoner. Satisfied that their honor was avenged, the British withdrew. Later Ethiopian emperors kept up the program of reform and modernization.

Aswan (AS-wahn)

Ismail (is-MAH-eel) **Téwodros** (tay-WOH-druhs)
Yohannes (yoh-HAHN-nehs) **Menelik** (MEN-uh-lik)

Téwodros's Mighty Cannon Like other modernizers in the nineteenth century, Emperor Téwodros of Ethiopia sought to reform his military forces. In 1861 he forced resident European missionaries and craftsmen to build guns and cannon, including this 7-ton behemoth nicknamed "Sebastapol" after the Black Sea port that had been the center of the Crimean War. It took five hundred men to haul the cannon across Ethiopia's hilly terrain. (From Hormuzd Rassam, *Narrative of the British Mission to Theodore, King of Abyssinia, II*, London 1869, John Murray)

European Penetration

More lasting than Britain's punitive invasion of Ethiopia was France's conquest of Algeria, a move that anticipated the general European "scramble" for Africa after 1870. Equally pregnant with future meaning was the Europeans' exploration of the inland parts of Africa in the middle decades of the century.

Long an exporter of grain and olive oil to France, the North African state of Algeria had even supplied Napoleon with grain for his 1798 invasion of Egypt. The failure of French governments to repay this debt led to many disputes between Algeria and France and eventually to a severing of diplomatic relations in 1827 after the ruler of Algeria, annoyed with the French ambassador, allegedly struck him with a fly whisk. Three years later an unpopular French government, hoping to stir French nationalism with an easy overseas victory, attacked Algeria on the pretext of avenging this insult.

The invasion of 1830 proved a costly mistake. The French government was soon overthrown, but the war in Algeria dragged on for eighteen years. The attack by an alien Christian power united the Algerians behind 'Abd al-Qadir°, a gifted and resourceful Muslim holy man. To achieve victory, the French built up an army of over 100,000 that broke Algerian resistance by destroying farm animals and crops and massacring villagers by the tens of thousands. After 'Abd al-Qadir was captured and exiled in 1847, the resistance movement fragmented, but the French occupiers faced resistance in the mountains for another thirty years. Poor European settlers,

'Abd al-Qadir (AHB-dahl-KAH-deer)

who rushed in to take possession of Algeria's rich coastlands, numbered 130,000 by 1871.

Meanwhile, a more peaceful European intrusion was penetrating Africa's geographical secrets. Small expeditions of adventurous explorers, using their own funds or financed by private geographical societies, were seeking to uncover the mysteries of inner Africa that had eluded Europeans for four centuries. Besides discovering more about the course of Africa's mighty rivers, these explorers wished to assess the continent's mineral wealth or convert the African millions to Christianity.

Many of the explorers were concerned with tracing the course of Africa's great rivers. Explorers learned in 1795 that the Niger River in West Africa flowed from west to east (not the other way, as had often been supposed) and in 1830 that the great morass of small streams entering the Gulf of Guinea was in fact the Niger Delta.

The north-flowing Nile, whose annual floods made Egypt bloom, similarly attracted explorers bent on finding the headwaters of the world's longest river. In 1770 Lake Tana in Ethiopia was established as a major source, and in 1861–1862 Lake Victoria (named for the British sovereign) was found to be the other main source.

In contrast to the heavily financed expeditions with hundreds of African porters that searched the Nile, the Scottish missionary David Livingstone (1813–1873) organized modest treks through southern and Central Africa. The missionary doctor's primary goal was to scout out locations for Christian missions, but he was also highly influential in tracing the course of the Zambezi River between 1853 and 1856. He named its greatest waterfall for the British monarch Queen Victoria. Livingstone also traced the course of the upper Congo River, where in 1871 he was met by the Welsh-American journalist Henry Morton Stanley (1841–1904) on a publicity-motivated search for the "lost" missionary doctor. On an expedition from 1874 to 1877, Stanley descended the Congo River to its mouth.

One of the most remarkable features of the explorers' experiences in Africa was their ability to move unmolested from place to place. The strangers were seldom harmed without provocation. Stanley preferred large expeditions that fought their way across the continent, but Livingstone's modest expeditions, which posed no threat to anyone, regularly received warm hospitality.

Abolition and Legitimate Trade

No sooner was the mouth of the Niger River discovered than eager entrepreneurs began to send expeditions up the river to scout out its potential for trade. Along much of coastal West Africa, commercial relations with Europeans remained dominant between 1750 and 1870. The value of trade between Africa and the other Atlantic continents more than doubled between the 1730s and the 1780s, then doubled again by 1870.[3] Before about 1825 the slave trade accounted for most of that increase, but thereafter African exports of vegetable oils, gold, ivory, and other goods drove overseas trade to new heights.

Europeans played a critical role in these changes in Africa's overseas trade. The Atlantic trade had arisen to serve the needs of the first European empires, and its transformation was linked to the ideas and industrial needs of Britain's new economy and empire.

One step in the Atlantic slave trade's extinction was the successful slave revolt in Saint Domingue in the 1790s (see Chapter 22). It ended slavery in the largest plantation colony in the West Indies, and elsewhere in the Americas it inspired slave revolts that were brutally repressed. As news of the slave revolts and their repression spread, humanitarians and religious reformers called for an end to the trade. Since it was widely believed that African-born slaves were more likely to rebel than were persons born into slavery, support for abolition of the slave trade was found even among Americans wanting to preserve slavery. In 1808 both Great Britain and the United States made carrying and importing slaves from Africa illegal for their citizens. Most other Western countries followed suit by 1850, but few enforced abolition with the vigor of the British.

Once the world's greatest slave traders, the British became the most aggressive abolitionists. Britain sent a naval patrol to enforce the ban along the African coast and negotiated treaties allowing the patrol to search other nations' vessels suspected of carrying slaves. During the half-century after 1815, Britain spent some $60 million (£12 million) to end the slave trade, a sum equal to the profits British slave traders had made in the fifty years before 1808.

Although British patrols captured 1,635 slave ships and liberated over 160,000 enslaved Africans, the trade proved difficult to stop. Cuba and Brazil continued to import huge numbers of slaves, which drove prices up and persuaded some African rulers and merchants to continue to sell slaves and to help foreign slavers evade the British patrols. After British patrols quashed the slave trade along the Gold Coast, the powerful king of Asante° even tried to persuade a British official in 1820 that reopening the trade would be to their mutual profit. Because the slave trade moved to other parts of Africa, the trans-Atlantic slave trade did not end until 1867.

Asante (uh-SHAHN-tee)

The demand for slaves in the Americas claimed the lives and endangered the safety of untold numbers of Africans, but the trade also satisfied other Africans' desires for the cloth, metals, and other goods that European traders brought in return. To continue their access to those imports, Africans expanded their **"legitimate" trade** (exports other than slaves). They revived old exports or developed new ones as the Atlantic slave trade was shut down. On the Gold Coast, for example, annual exports of gold climbed to nearly 25,000 ounces (750 kilograms) in the 1840s and 1850s, compared to 10,000 ounces (300 kilograms) in the 1790s.

The most successful of the new exports from West Africa was palm oil, a vegetable oil used by British manufacturers for soap, candles, and lubricants. Though still a major source of slaves until the mid-1830s, the trading states of the Niger Delta simultaneously emerged as the premier exporters of palm oil. In inland forests men climbed tall oil palms and cut down large palm-nut clusters, which women pounded to extract the thick oil. Coastal African traders bought the palm oil at inland markets and delivered it to European ships at the coast.

The dramatic increase in palm-oil exports—from a few hundred tons at the beginning of the century to tens of thousands of tons by midcentury—did not require any new technology, but it did alter the social structure of the coastal trading communities. Coastal traders grew rich and used their wealth to buy large numbers of male slaves to paddle the giant dugout canoes that transported palm oil from inland markets along the narrow delta creeks to the trading ports. Niger Delta slavery could be as harsh and brutal as slavery on New World plantations, but it offered some male and female slaves a chance to gain wealth and power. Some female slaves who married big traders exercised great authority over junior members of trading households. Male slaves who supervised canoe fleets were well compensated, and a few even became wealthy enough to take over the leadership of the coastal "canoe houses" (companies). The most famous, known as "Jaja" (ca. 1821–1891), rose from canoe slave to become the head of a major canoe house. In 1869, to escape discrimination by free-born Africans, he founded the new port of Opobo, which he ruled as king. In the 1870s Jaja of Opobo was the greatest palm-oil trader in the Niger Delta.

Another effect of the suppression of the slave trade was the spread of Western cultural influences in West Africa. To serve as a base for their anti-slave-trade naval squadron, the British had taken over the small colony of Sierra Leone° in 1808. Over the next several years, 130,000 men, women, and children taken from "captured" vessels were liberated in Sierra Leone. Christian missionaries helped settle these impoverished and dispirited **recaptives** in and around Freetown, the capital. In time the mission churches and schools made many willing converts among such men and women.

Sierra Leone's schools also produced a number of distinguished graduates. For example, Samuel Adjai

King Jaja of Opobo This talented man rose from slavery in the Niger Delta port of Bonny to head one of the town's major palm-oil trading firms, the Anna Pepple House, in 1863. Six years later, Jaja founded and ruled his own trading port of Opobo. (Reproduced from *West Africa: An Introduction to Its History*, by Michael Crowder, by courtesy of the publishers, Addison Wesley Longman)

Sierra Leone (see-ER-uh lee-OWN)

Crowther (1808–1891), freed as a youth from a slave ship by the British squadron in 1821, became the first Anglican bishop in West Africa in 1864, administering a pioneering diocese along the lower Niger River. James Africanus Horton (1835–1882), the son of slaves liberated in Sierra Leone, became a doctor and the author of many studies of West Africa.

Other Western cultural influences came from people of African birth or descent returning to their ancestral homeland. In 1821, to the south of Sierra Leone, free black Americans began a settlement that grew into the Republic of Liberia, a place of liberty at a time when slavery was legal and flourishing in the United States. After their emancipation in 1865 other African-Americans moved to Liberia. Emma White, a literate black woman from Kentucky, moved from Liberia to Opobo in 1875, where King Jaja employed her to write his commercial correspondence and run a school for his children. Edward Wilmot Blyden (1832–1912), born in the Danish West Indies and proud of his West African parentage, emigrated to Liberia in 1851 and became a professor of Greek and Latin (and later Arabic) at the fledgling Liberia College. Free blacks from Brazil and Cuba chartered ships to return to their West African homelands, bringing Roman Catholicism, architectural motifs, and clothing fashions from the New World. Although the number of Africans exposed to Western culture in 1870 was still small, this influence grew rapidly.

Secondary Empires in Eastern Africa

When British patrols hampered the slave trade in West Africa, slavers moved southward and then around the tip of southern Africa to eastern Africa. There the Atlantic slave trade joined an existing trade in slaves to the Islamic world that also was expanding. Two-thirds of the 1.2 million slaves exported from eastern Africa in the nineteenth century went to markets in North Africa and the Middle East; the other third went to plantations in the Americas and to European-controlled Indian Ocean islands.

Slavery also became more prominent within eastern Africa itself. Between 1800 and 1873 Arab and Swahili° owners of clove plantations along the coast purchased some 700,000 slaves from inland eastern Africa to do the labor-intensive work of harvesting this spice. The plantations were on Zanzibar Island and in neighboring territories belonging to the Sultanate of Oman, an Arabian kingdom on the Persian Gulf that had been expanding its control over the East African coast since 1698. The sultan had even moved his court to Zanzibar in 1840 to take better advantage of the burgeoning trade in cloves. Zanzibar also was an important center of slaves and ivory. Most of the ivory was shipped to India, where much of it was carved into decorative objects for European markets.

Ivory caravans came to the coast from hundreds of miles inland under the direction of African and Arab merchants. Some of these merchants brought large personal empires under their control by using capital they had borrowed from Indian bankers and modern firearms they had bought from Europeans and Americans. Some trading empires were created by inland Nyamwezi° traders, who worked closely with the indigenous Swahili and Arabs in Zanzibar to develop the long-distance caravan routes.

The largest of these personal empires, along the upper Congo River, was created by Tippu Tip (ca. 1830–1905), a trader from Zanzibar, who was Swahili and Nyamwezi on his father's side and Omani Arab on his mother's. Livingstone, Stanley, and other explorers who received Tippu Tip's gracious hospitality in the remote center of the continent praised their host's intelligence and refinement. On an 1876 visit, for example, Stanley recorded in his journal that Tippu Tip was "a remarkable man," a "picture of energy and strength" with "a fine intelligent face: almost courtier-like in his manner."

Tippu Tip also composed a detailed memoir of his adventures in the heart of Africa, written in the Swahili language of the coast. In it he mocked innocent African villagers for believing that his gunshots were thunder. As the memoir and other sources make clear, modern rifles not only felled countless elephants for their ivory tusks but also inflicted widespread devastation and misery on the people of this isolated area.

One can blame Tippu Tip and other Zanzibari traders, along with their master, the sultan of Oman, for the pillage and havoc in the once-peaceful center of Africa. However, the circle of responsibility was broader. Europeans supplied the weapons and were major consumers of ivory and cloves. For this reason histories have referred to the states carved out of eastern Africa by the sultans of Oman, Tippu Tip, and others as "secondary empires," in contrast to the empire that Britain was establishing directly. At the same time, British officials pressured the sultan of Oman into halting the Indian Ocean slave trade from Zanzibar in 1857 and ending the import of slaves into Zanzibar in 1873.

Swahili (swah-HEE-lee)

Nyamwezi (nn-nyahm-WAY-zee)

Egypt's expansion southward during the nineteenth century can also be considered a secondary empire. Muhammad Ali had pioneered the conquest of the upper Nile, in 1821 establishing a major base at Khartoum° that became the capital of Egyptian Sudan. A major reason for his invasion of Sudan was to secure slaves for his army so that more Egyptian peasants could be left free to grow cotton for export. From the 1840s unscrupulous traders of many origins, leading forces armed with European weapons, pushed south to the modern frontiers of Uganda and Zaire in search of cattle, ivory, and slaves. They set one African community against another and reaped profit from the devastation they sowed.

India Under British Rule

The people of South Asia felt the impact of European commercial, cultural, and colonial expansion more immediately and profoundly than did the people of Africa. While Europeans were laying claim to only small parts of Africa between 1750 and 1870, nearly all of India (with three times the population of all of Africa) came under Britain's direct or indirect rule. During the 250 years after the founding of East India Company in 1600, British interests commandeered the colonies and trade of the Dutch, fought off French and Indian challenges, and picked up the pieces of the decaying Mughal° Empire. By 1763 the French were stymied; in 1795 the Dutch East India Company was dissolved; and in 1858 the last Mughal emperor was dethroned, leaving the vast subcontinent in British hands.

Company Men

As Mughal power weakened in the eighteenth century, Europeans were not the first outsiders to make a move. In 1739 Iranian armies defeated the Mughal forces, sacked Delhi, and returned home with vast amounts of booty. Indian states also took advantage of Mughal weakness to assert their independence. By midcentury, the Maratha° Confederation, a coalition of states in central India, controlled more land than the Mughals did (see Map 25.2). Also ruling their own powerful states were the **nawabs**° (a term used for Muslim princes who were deputies of the Mughal emperor, though in name only): the nawab of Bengal in the northeast; the nawab of Arcot in the southeast, Haidar Ali (1722–1782)—the father of Tipu Sultan and ruler of the southwestern state of Mysore; and many others.

British, Dutch, and French companies were also eager to expand their profitable trade into India in the eighteenth century. Such far-flung European trading companies were speculative and risky ventures in 1750. Their success depended on hard-drinking and ambitious young "company men," who used hard bargaining, and hard fighting when necessary, to persuade Indian rulers to allow them to establish trading posts at strategic points along the coast. To protect their fortified warehouses from attack by other Europeans or by native states, the companies hired and trained Indian troops known as **sepoys**°. In divided India these private armies came to hold the balance of power.

In 1691 Great Britain's East India Company (EIC) had convinced the nawab of the large state of Bengal in northeast India to let the company establish a fortified outpost at the fishing port of Calcutta. A new nawab, pressing claims for additional tribute from the prospering port, overran the fort in 1756 and imprisoned a group of EIC men in a cell so small that many died of suffocation. To avenge their deaths in this "Black Hole of Calcutta," a large EIC force from Madras, led by the young Robert Clive, overthrew the nawab. The weak Mughal emperor was persuaded to acknowledge the East India Company's right to rule Bengal in 1765. Fed by the tax revenues of Bengal as well as by profits from trade, the EIC was on its way. Calcutta grew into a city of 250,000 by 1788.

In southern India, Clive had used EIC forces from Madras to secure victory for the British Indian candidate for nawab of Arcot during the Seven Years War (1756–1763), thereby gaining an advantage over French traders who had supported the loser. The defeat of Tipu Sultan of Mysore at the end of the century (described at the start of the chapter) secured south India for the company and prevented a French resurgence.

Along with Calcutta and Madras, the third major center of British power in India was Bombay, on the western coast. There, after a long series of contests with Maratha Confederation rulers, the East India Company gained a decisive advantage in 1818, annexing large territories to form the core of what was called the "Bombay Presidency." Some states were taken over completely, as Bengal had been, but very many others remained in the hands of local princes who accepted the political control of the company.

Khartoum (khar-TOOM) **Mughal** (MOO-guhl)
Maratha (muh-RAH-tuh) **nawab** (NAH-wab)

sepoy (SEE-poy)

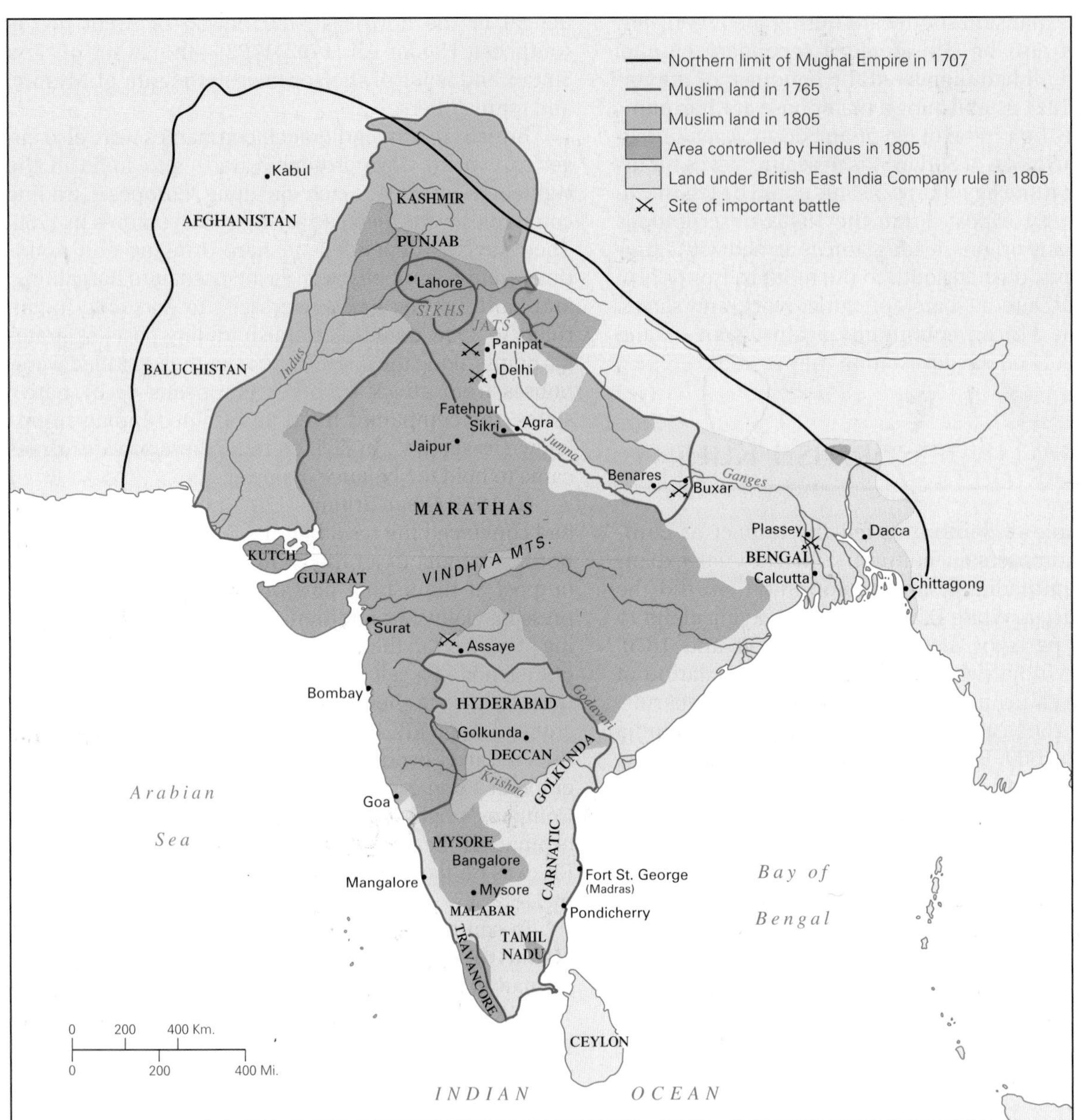

Map 25.2 India, 1707–1805 As Mughal power weakened during the eighteenth century, other Indian states and the East India Company expanded their territories.

Raj and Rebellion, 1818–1857

In 1818 the East India Company controlled an Empire with more people than in all of western Europe and fifty times the population of the colonies the British had lost in North America. One thrust of **British raj** (reign) was to remake India on a British model through administrative and social reform, economic development, and the introduction of new technology. But at the same time the company men—like the Mughals before them—had to temper their interference with Indian social and religious customs lest they provoke rebellion or lose the support of their Indian princely allies. For this reason and because of the complexity of the task of ruling such a vast empire, there were many inconsistencies in Britain's policies toward India.

The main policy was to create a powerful and efficient system of government. British rule before 1850 relied heavily on military power—170 sepoy regiments and 16 European regiments. Another policy very much in the interests of India's new rulers was to disarm approximately 2 million warriors who had served India's many states and turn them to civilian tasks, mostly cultivation. A third policy was to give freer rein to Christian missionaries eager to convert and uplift India's masses. Few converts were made, but the missionaries kept up steady pressure for social reforms.

Another key British policy was to substitute ownership of private property for India's complex and overlapping patterns of landholding. In Bengal this reform worked to the advantage of large landowners, but in Mysore the peasantry gained. Private ownership made it easier for the state to collect the taxes that were needed to pay for administration, the army, and economic reform.

Such policies of "westernization, Anglicization, and modernization," as they have been called, were only one side of British rule. The other side was the bolstering of "traditions"—both real and newly invented. In the name of tradition the Indian princes who ruled nearly half of British India were frequently endowed by their British overlords with greater power and splendor and longer tenure than their predecessors had ever had. Hindu and Muslim holy men were able to expand their "traditional" power over property and people far beyond what had been the case in earlier times. Princes, holy men, and other Indians frequently used claims of tradition to resist British rule as well as to turn it to their advantage. The British rulers themselves invented many "traditions"—including elaborate parades and displays—half borrowed from European royal pomp, half freely improvised from Mughal ceremonies.

The British and Indian elites danced sometimes in close partnership, sometimes in apparent opposition. But the ordinary people of India suffered. Women of every status, members of subordinate Hindu castes, the "untouchables" and "tribals" outside the caste system, and the poor generally experienced less benefit from the British reforms and much new oppression from the taxes and "traditions" that exalted their superiors' status.

The transformation of British India's economy was also doubled-edged. On the one hand, British raj created many new jobs as a result of the growth of internal and external trade and the expansion of agricultural production, such as in opium in Bengal—largely for export to China (see Chapter 26)—coffee in Ceylon (an island off the tip of India), and tea in Assam (a state in northeastern India). On the other hand, competition from cheap cotton goods produced in Britain's industrial mills drove many Indians out of the handicraft textile industry. In the eighteenth century India had been the world's greatest exporter of cotton textiles; in the nineteenth century India increasingly shipped raw cotton fiber to Britain.

Even the beneficial economic changes introduced under Britain rule were disruptive, and there were no safety nets for the needy. Displaced ruling elites, disgruntled religious traditionalists, and the economically dispossessed fomented almost constant local rebellions during the first half of the nineteenth century. British rulers readily handled these isolated uprisings, but they were more concerned about the continuing loyalty of Indian sepoys in the East India Company's army. The EIC employed 200,000 sepoys in 1857, along with 38,000 British officers. Armed with the latest rifles and disciplined in fighting methods, the sepoys had a potential for successful rebellion that other groups lacked.

In fact, discontent was growing among Indian soldiers. In the early decades of EIC rule, most sepoys came from Bengal, one of the first states the company had annexed. The Bengali sepoys resented the active recruitment of other ethnic groups into the army after 1848, such as Sikhs° from Punjab and Gurkhas from Nepal. Many high-caste Hindus objected to a new law in 1856 requiring new recruits to be available for service overseas in the growing Indian Ocean empire, for their religion prohibited ocean travel. The replacement of the standard military musket by the far more accurate Enfield rifle in 1857 also caused problems. Soldiers were ordered to use their teeth to tear open the ammunition cartridges, which were greased with animal fat. Hindus were offended by this order if the fat came from cattle, which they considered sacred. Muslims were offended if the fat came from pigs, which they considered unclean.

Although the cartridge-opening procedure was quickly changed, the initial discontent grew into rebellion by Hindu sepoys in May 1857. British troubles mushroomed when Muslim sepoys, peasants, and discontented elites joined in. The rebels asserted old traditions to challenge British authority: sepoy officers in Delhi proclaimed their loyalty to the Mughal emperor; others rallied behind the Maratha leader Nana Sahib. The rebellion was put down by March 1858, but it shook this piecemeal empire to its core.

Historians have attached different names and meanings to the events of 1857 and 1858. Concentrating on

---

Sikh (seek)

the technical fact that the uprising was an unlawful action by soldiers, nineteenth-century British historians labeled it the **"Sepoy Rebellion"** or the "Mutiny," and these names are still commonly used. Seeing in these events the beginnings of the later movement for independence, some modern Indian historians have termed it the "Revolution of 1857." In reality, it was much more than a simple mutiny, because it involved more than soldiers, but it was not yet a nationalist revolution, for the rebels' sense of a common Indian national identity was weak.

Political Reform and Industrial Impact

Whatever it is called, the rebellion of 1857–1858 was a turning point in the history of modern India. Some say it marks the beginning of modern India. In its wake Indians gained a new centralized government, entered a period of rapid economic growth, and began to develop a new national consciousness.

The changes in government were immediate. In 1858 Britain eliminated the last traces of Mughal and Company rule. In their place, a new secretary of state for India in London oversaw Indian policy, and a new government-general in Delhi acted as the British monarch's viceroy on the spot. A proclamation by Queen Victoria in November 1858 guaranteed all Indians equal protection of the law and the freedom to practice their religions and social customs; it also assured Indian princes that so long as they were loyal to the queen British India would respect their control of territories and "their rights, dignity and honour."[4]

British rule continued to emphasize both tradition and reform after 1857. At the top, the British viceroys lived in enormous palaces amid hundreds of servants and gaudy displays of luxury meant to convince Indians that the British viceroys were legitimate successors to the Mughal emperors. They treated the quasi-independent Indian princes with elaborate ceremonial courtesy and maintained them in splendor. When Queen Victoria was proclaimed "Empress of India" in 1877 and periodically thereafter, the viceroys put on great pageants known as **durbars.** The most elaborate was the durbar at Delhi in 1902–1903 to celebrate the coronation of King Edward VII, at which Viceroy Lord Curzon honored himself with a 101-gun salute and a parade of 34,000 troops in front of 50 princes and 173,000 visitors (see Diversity and Dominance: Ceremonials of Imperial Domination).

Behind the pomp and glitter, a powerful and efficient bureaucracy controlled the Indian masses. Members of the elite **Indian Civil Service** (ICS), mostly graduates of Oxford and Cambridge Universities, held the senior administrative and judicial posts. Numbering only a thousand at the end of the nineteenth century, these men visited the villages in their districts, heard lawsuits and complaints, and passed judgments. Beneath them were a far greater number of Indian officials and employees. Recruitment into the ICS was by open examinations. In theory any British subject could take these exams. But they were given in England, so in practice the system worked to exclude Indians. In 1870 only one Indian was a member of the ICS. Subsequent reforms by Viceroy Lord Lytton led to fifty-seven Indian appointments by 1887, but there the process stalled.

The key reason qualified Indians were denied entry into the upper administration of their country was the racist contempt most British officials felt for the people they ruled. When he became commander-in-chief of the Indian army in 1892, Lord Kitchener declared:

> It is this consciousness of the inherent superiority of the European which had won for us India. However well educated and clever a native may be, and however brave he may have proved himself, I believe that no rank we can bestow on him would cause him to be considered an equal of the British officer.

A second transformation of India after 1857 resulted from involvement with industrial Britain. The government invested millions of pounds sterling in harbors, cities, irrigation canals, and other public works. British interests felled forests to make way for tea plantations, persuaded Indian farmers to grow cotton and jute for export, and created great irrigation systems to alleviate the famines that periodically decimated whole provinces. As a result, India's trade expanded rapidly.

Most of the exports were agricultural commodities for processing elsewhere: cotton fiber, opium, tea, silk, and sugar. In return India imported manufactured goods from Britain, including the flood of machine-made cotton textiles that severely undercut Indian hand-loom weavers. The effects on individual Indians varied enormously. Some women found new jobs, though at very low pay, on plantations or in the growing cities, where prostitution flourished. Others struggled to hold families together or ran away from abusive husbands. Everywhere in India poverty remained the norm.

The Indian government also promoted the introduction of new technologies into India not long after their appearance in Britain. Earlier in the century there were steamboats on the rivers and a massive program of canal building for irrigation. Beginning in the 1840s a

Delhi Durbar, January 1, 1903 The parade of Indian princes on ornately decorated elephants and accompanied by retainers fostered their sense of belonging to the vast empire of India that British rule had created. The durbar was meant to evoke the glories of India's earlier empires, but many of the details and ceremonies were nineteenth-century creations. (British Empire and Commonwealth Museum, Bristol, UK/The Bridgeman Art Library)

railroad boom (paid for out of government revenues) gave India its first national transportation network, followed shortly by telegraph lines. Indeed, in 1870 India had the greatest rail network in Asia and the fifth largest in the world. Originally designed to serve British commerce, the railroads were owned by British companies, constructed with British rails and equipment, and paid dividends to British investors. Ninety-nine percent of the railroad employees were Indians, but Europeans occupied all the top positions—"like a thin film of oil on top of a glass of water, resting upon but hardly mixing with [those] below," as one official report put it.

Although some Indians opposed the railroads at first because the trains mixed people of different castes, faiths, and sexes, the Indian people took to rail travel with great enthusiasm. Indians rode trains on business, on pilgrimage, and in search of work. In 1870 over 18 million passengers traveled along the network's 4,775 miles (7,685 kilometers) of track, and more than a half-million messages were sent up and down the 14,000 miles (22,500 kilometers) of telegraph wire. By 1900 India's trains were carrying 188 million passengers a year.

But the freer movement of Indian pilgrims and the flood of poor Indians into the cities also promoted the spread of cholera°, a disease transmitted through water contaminated by human feces. Cholera deaths rose rapidly during the nineteenth century, and eventually the disease spread to Europe. In many Indian minds *kala mari* ("the black death") was a divine punishment for failing to prevent the British takeover. This chastisement also fell heavily on British residents, who died in large numbers. In 1867 officials demonstrated the close connection between cholera and pilgrims who bathed in and drank from sacred pools and rivers. The installation of a new sewerage system (1865) and a filtered water

cholera (KAHL-uhr-uh)

Diversity and Dominance

Ceremonials of Imperial Domination

This letter to Queen Victoria from Edward Robert Bulwer-Lytton, the Earl of Lytton and the viceroy of India, describes the elaborate durbar that the government of India staged in 1876 in anticipation of her being named "Empress of India." It highlights the effects these ceremonies had on the Indian princes who governed many parts of India as agents ("feudatories") of the British or as independent rulers.

British India's power rested on the threat of military force, but the letter points up how much it also depended on cultivating the allegiance of powerful Indian rulers. For their part, as the letter suggests, such rulers were impressed with such displays of majesty and organization and found much to be gained from granting the British their support.

The day before yesterday (December 23), I arrived, with Lady Lytton and all my staff at Delhi. . . . I was received at the [railroad] station by all the native chiefs and princes, and, . . . after shaking hands . . . , I immediately mounted my elephant, accompanied by Lady Lytton, our two little girls following us on another elephant. The procession through Delhi to the camp . . . lasted upwards of three hours. . . . The streets were lined for many miles with troops; those of the native princes being brigaded with those of your Majesty. The crowd along the way, behind the troops, was dense, and apparently enthusiastic; the windows, walls, and housetops being thronged with natives, who salaamed, and Europeans, who cheered as we passed along. . . .

My reception by the native princes at the station was most cordial. The Maharaja of Jeypore informed Sir John Strachey that India had never seen such a gathering as this, in which not only all the great native princes (many of whom have never met before), but also chiefs and envoys from Khelat, Burmah, Siam, and the remotest parts of the East, are assembled to do homage to your Majesty. . . .

On Tuesday (December 26) from 10 A.M. till past 7 P.M., I was, without a moment's intermission, occupied in receiving visits from native chiefs, and bestowing on those entitled to them the banners, medals, and other honours given by your Majesty. The durbar, which lasted all day and long after dark, was most successful. . . . Your Majesty's portrait, which was placed over the Viceregal throne in the great durbar tent, was thought by all to be an excellent likeness of your Majesty. The native chiefs examined it with special interest.

On Wednesday, the 27th, I received visits from native chiefs, as before, from 10 A.M. til 1 P.M., and from 1:30 P.M. to 7:30 P.M., was passed in returning visits. I forgot to mention that on Tuesday and Wednesday evenings I gave great State dinners to the Governors of Bombay and Madras. Every subsequent evening of my stay at Delhi was similarly occupied by state banquets and receptions [for officials, foreign dignitaries, and] many distinguished natives. After dinner on Thursday, I held a levee [reception], which lasted till one o'clock at night, and is said to have been attended by 2,500 persons—the largest, I believe, ever held by any Viceroy or Governor-General in India. . . .

The satisfactory and cordial assurances received from [the ruler of] Kashmir are, perhaps, less important, because his loyalty was previously assumed. But your Majesty will, perhaps, allow me to mention, in connection with the name of this prince, one little circumstance which appears to me very illustrative of the effect which the assemblage has had on him and others. In the first interviews which took place months ago between myself and Kashmir, which resulted in my securing his assent to the appointment of a British officer at Gilgit, I noticed that, though perfectly courteous, he was extremely mistrustful of the British Government and myself. He seemed to think that every word I had said to him must have a hidden meaning against which he was bound to be on his guard. During our negotiations he carefully kept all his councillors round him, and he referred to them before answering any question I put to him, and, although he finally agreed to my proposals, he did so with obvious reluctance and suspicion, after taking a night to think them over. On the day following the Imperial assemblage, I had another private interview with Kashmir for the settlement of some further details. His whole manner and language on this last occasion were strikingly different. [He said:] "I am now convinced that you mean nothing that is not for the good of me and mine. Our interests are identical with those of the empire. Give me your orders and they shall be obeyed."

I have already mentioned to your Majesty that one of the sons of Kashmir acted as my page at the assemblage. I can truly affirm that all the native princes, great and small, with whom I was previously acquainted vied with each other in doing honor to the occasion, and I sincerely believe that this great gathering has also enabled me to establish the most cordial and confidential personal relations with a great many others whom I then met for the first time.

. . . If the vast number of persons collected together at Delhi, and all almost entirely under canvas, be fairly taken into consideration—a number alluding the highest executive officers of your Majesty's administration from every part of India, each with his own personal staff; all the members of my own Council, with their wives and families, who were entertained as the Viceroy's personal guests; all the representatives of the Press, native and European; upwards of 15,000 British troops, besides about 450 native princes and nobles, each with a following of from 2 to 500 attendants; the foreign ambassadors with their suites; the foreign consuls; a large number of the rudest and most unmanageable trans-frontier chieftains with their horses and camels, &c.; and then an incalculably large concourse of private persons attracted by curiosity from every corner of the country—I say if all this be fairly remembered, no candid person will, I think, deny that to bring together, lodge, and feed so vast a crowd without a single case of sickness, or a single accident due to defective arrangements, without a moment's confusion or an hour's failure in the provision of supplies, and then to have sent them all away satisfied and loud in their expressions of gratitude for the munificent hospitality with which they had been entertained (at an expenditure of public money scrupulously moderate), was an achievement highly creditable to all concerned in carrying it out. Sir Dinkur Rao (Sindiah's great Minister) said to one of my colleagues: "If any man would understand why it is that the English are, and must necessarily remain, the masters of India, he need only go up to the Flagstaff Tower, and look down upon this marvellous camp. Let him notice the method, the order, the cleanliness, the discipline, the perfection of its whole organisation, and he will recognise in it at once the epitome of every title to command and govern which one race can possess over others." This anecdote reminds me of another which may perhaps please your Majesty. [The ruler of] Holkar said to me when I took leave of him: "India has been till now a vast heap of stones, some of them big, some of them small. Now the house is built, and from roof to basement each stone of it is in the right place."

The Khan of Khelat and his wild Sirdars were, I think, the chief objects of curiosity and interest to our Europeans. . . . On the Khan himself and all his Sirdars, the assemblage seems to have made an impression more profound even than I had anticipated. Less than a year ago they were all at war with each other, but they have left Delhi with mutual embraces, and a very salutary conviction that the Power they witnessed there is resolved that they shall henceforth keep the peace and not disturb its frontiers with their squabbles. The Khan asked to have a banner given to him. It was explained to His Highness that banners were only given to your Majesty's feudatories, and that he, being an independent prince, could not receive one without compromising his independence. He replied: "But I am a feudatory of the Empress, a feudatory quite as loyal and obedient as any other. I don't want to be an independent prince, and I do want to have my banner like all the rest. Pray let me have it."

I anticipate an excellent effect by and by from the impressions which the yet wilder envoys and Sirdars of Chitral and Yassin will carry with them from Delhi, and propagate throughout that important part of our frontier where the very existence of the British Government has hitherto been almost unrealised, except as that of a very weak power, popularly supposed in Kafristan to be exceedingly afraid of Russia. Two Burmese noblemen, from the remotest part of Burmah, said to me: "The King of Burmah fancies he is the greatest prince upon earth. When we go back, we shall tell all his people that he is nobody. Never since the world began has there been in it such a power as we have witnessed here." These Burmese are writing a journal or memoir of their impressions and experiences at Delhi, of which they have promised me a copy. I have no doubt it will be very curious and amusing. Kashmir and some other native princes have expressed a wish to present your Majesty with an imperial crown of great value; but as each insists upon it that the crown shall be exclusively his own gift, I have discouraged an idea which, if carried out, would embarrass your Majesty with the gift of half a dozen different crowns, and probably provoke bitter heart-burnings amongst the donors. The Rajpootana Chiefs talk of erecting a marble statue of the Empress on the spot where the assemblage was held; native noblemen have already intimated and several to me their intention of building bridges, or other public works, and founding charities, to be called after your Majesty in commemoration of the event.

QUESTIONS FOR ANALYSIS

1. **What is significant about the fact that Lord Lytton and his family arrived in Delhi by train and then chose to move through the city on elephants?**
2. **What impression did the viceroy intend to create in the minds of the Indian dignitaries by assembling so many of them together and bestowing banners, medals, and honors on them?**
3. **What might account for some Indians' remarkable changes of attitude toward the viceroy and the empire? How differently might a member of the Indian middle class or an unemployed weaver have reacted?**

Source: Lady Betty Balfour, *The History of Lord Lytton's Indian Administration, 1876 to 1880* (London: Longmans, Green, and Co., 1899), 116–125.

supply (1869) in Calcutta dramatically reduced cholera deaths there. Similar measures in Bombay and Madras also led to great reductions, but most Indians lived in small villages where famine and lack of sanitation kept cholera deaths high. In 1900 an extraordinary four out of every thousand residents of British India died of cholera. Sanitary improvements lowered the rate later in the twentieth century.

Rising Indian Nationalism

Ironically, both the successes and the failures of British India stimulated the development of Indian nationalism. Stung by the inability of the rebellion of 1857 to overthrow British rule, some thoughtful Indians began to argue that the only way for Indians to regain control of their destiny was to reduce their country's social and ethnic divisions and promote Pan-Indian nationalism.

Individuals such as Rammohun Roy (1772–1833) had promoted development along these lines a generation earlier. A Western-educated Bengali from a Brahmin family, Roy was a successful administrator for the East India Company and a thoughtful student of comparative religion. His Brahmo Samaj° (Divine Society), founded in 1828, attracted Indians who sought to reconcile the values they found in the West with the ancient religious traditions of India. They supported efforts to reform some Hindu customs, including the restrictions on widows and the practice of child marriage. They advocated reforming the caste system, encouraged a monotheistic form of Hinduism, and urged a return to the founding principles of the Upanishads, ancient sacred writings of Hinduism.

Roy and his supporters had backed earlier British efforts to reform or ban some practices they found repugnant. Widow burning (*sati*°) was outlawed in 1829 and slavery in 1843. Reformers sought to correct other abuses of women: prohibitions against widows remarrying were revoked in 1856, and female infanticide was made a crime in 1870.

Although Brahmo Samaj remained an influential movement after the rebellion of 1857, many Indian intellectuals turned to Western secular values and nationalism as the way to reclaim India for its people. In this process the spread of Western education played an important role. Roy had studied both Indian and Western subjects, mastering ten languages in the process, and helped found the Hindu College in Calcutta in 1816. Other Western-curriculum schools quickly followed, including Bethune College in Calcutta, the first secular school for Indian women, in 1849. European and American missionaries played a prominent role in the spread of Western education. In 1870 there were 790,000 Indians in over 24,000 elementary and secondary schools, and India's three universities (established in 1857) awarded 345 degrees. Graduates of these schools articulated a new Pan-Indian nationalism that transcended regional and religious differences.

Rammohun Roy This romantic portrait of the Indian reformer emphasizes his scholarly accomplishments and India's traditional architecture and natural beauty. (Bristol City Museum and Art Gallery, UK/The Bridgemen Art Library)

Bramo Samaj (BRAH-moh suh-MAHJ) **sati** (suh-TEE)

Many of the new nationalists came from the Indian middle class, which had prospered from the increase of trade and manufacturing. Such educated and ambitious people were angered by the obstacles that British rules and prejudices put in the way of their advancement. Hoping to increase their influence and improve their employment opportunities in the Indian government, they convened the first **Indian National Congress** in 1885. The members sought a larger role for Indians in the Civil Service. They also called for reductions in military expenditures, which consumed 40 percent of the government's budget, so that more could be spent on alleviating the poverty of the Indian masses. The Indian National Congress promoted unity among the country's many religions and social groups, but most early members were upper-caste Western-educated Hindus and Parsis (members of a Zoroastrian religious sect descended from Persians). The Congress effectively voiced the opinions of elite Indians, but until it attracted the support of the masses, it could not hope to challenge British rule.

Britain's Eastern Empire

In 1750 Britain's empire was centered on slave-based plantation and settler colonies in the Americas. A century later its main focus was on commercial networks and colonies in the East. In 1750 the French and Dutch were also serious contenders for global dominion. A century later they had been eclipsed by the British colossus that was straddling the world.

Several distinct changes facilitated the expansion and transformation of Britain's overseas empire. A string of military victories pushed aside other rivals for overseas trade and colonies; new policies favored free trade over mercantilism; and changes in shipbuilding techniques increased the speed and volume of maritime commerce. Linked to these changes were new European settlements in southern Africa, Australia, and New Zealand and the growth of a new long-distance trade in indentured labor.

Colonies and Commerce

As the story of Tipu Sultan told at the beginning of this chapter illustrates, France was still a serious rival for dominion in the Indian Ocean at the end of the eighteenth century. However, defeats in the wars of the French Revolution (see Chapter 22) ended Napoleon's dream of restoring French dominance overseas. The wars also dismantled much of the Netherlands' Indian Ocean empire. When French armies occupied the Netherlands, the Dutch ruler, who had fled to Britain in January 1795, authorized the British to take over Dutch possessions overseas in order to keep them out of French hands. During 1795 and 1796 British forces quickly occupied the Cape Colony at the tip of southern Africa, the strategic Dutch port of Malacca on the strait between the Indian Ocean and the South China Sea, and the island of Ceylon (see Map 25.3).

Then the British occupied Dutch Guiana° and Trinidad in the southern Caribbean. In 1811 they even seized the island of Java, the center of the Netherlands' East Indian empire. British forces had also attacked French possessions, gaining control of the islands of Mauritius° and Réunion in the southwestern Indian Ocean. At the end of the Napoleonic Wars in 1814, Britain returned Java to the Dutch and Réunion to the French but kept the Cape Colony, British Guiana (once part of Dutch Guiana), Trinidad, Ceylon, Malacca, and Mauritius.

The Cape Colony was valuable because of Cape Town's strategic importance as a supply station for ships making the long voyages between Britain and India. With the port city came some twenty thousand descendants of earlier Dutch and French settlers who occupied far-flung farms and ranches in its hinterland. Despite their European origins, these people thought of themselves as permanent residents of Africa and were beginning to refer to themselves as "Afrikaners°" ("Africans" in their dialect of Dutch). British governors prohibited any expansion of the white settler frontier because such expansion invariably led to wars with indigenous Africans. This decision, along with the imposition of laws protecting African rights within Cape Colony (including the emancipation of slaves in 1834), alienated many Afrikaners.

Between 1836 and 1839 parties of Afrikaners embarked on a "Great Trek," leaving British-ruled Cape Colony for the fertile high *veld* (plateau) to the north that two decades of Zulu wars had depopulated. The Great Trek led to the foundation of three new settler colonies in southern Africa by 1850: the Afrikaners' Orange Free State and Transvaal on the high veld and the British colony of Natal on the Indian Ocean coast. Although firearms enabled the settlers to win some important battles against the Zulu and other Africans, they were still a tiny minority surrounded by the populous and powerful independent African kingdoms that had grown up at the beginning of the century. A few thousand British settlers came to Natal and the Cape Colony by midcentury, but

Guiana (ghee-AH-nuh) **Mauritius** (moh-RIHS-uhs) **Afrikaner** (af-rih-KAHN-uhr)

Map 25.3 European Possessions in the Indian Ocean and South Pacific, 1870 After 1750 French and British competition for new territories generally expanded the European presence established earlier by the Portuguese, Spanish, and Dutch. By 1870 the British controlled much of India, were settling Australia and New Zealand, and possessed important trading enclaves throughout the region.

these colonies were important to Britain only as stopovers for shipping between Britain and British India.

Meanwhile, another strategic British outpost was being established in Southeast Asia. One prong of the advance was led by Thomas Stamford Raffles, who had governed Java during the period of British occupation from 1811 to 1814. After Java's return to the Dutch, Raffles helped the British East India Company establish a new free port at Singapore in 1824, on the site of a small Malay fishing village with a superb harbor. By attracting British merchants and Chinese businessmen and laborers, Singapore soon became the center of trade and shipping between the Indian Ocean and China. Along with Malacca and other possessions on the strait, Singapore formed the "Straits Settlements," which British India administered until 1867.

Further British expansion in Malaya (now Malaysia) did not occur until after 1874, but it came more quickly in neighboring Burma. Burma had emerged as a powerful kingdom by 1750, with plans for expansion. In 1785 Burma tried to annex neighboring territories of Siam (now Thailand) to the east, but a coalition of Thai leaders thwarted Burmese advances by 1802. Burma next attacked Assam to the west, but this action led to war with British India, which was concerned for the security of its own frontier with Assam. After a two-year war, India annexed Assam in 1826 and occupied two coastal provinces of northern Burma. As rice and timber trade from these provinces grew important, the occupation became permanent, and in 1852 British India annexed the port of Rangoon and the rest of coastal Burma.

Great Trek Aided by African Servants The ox-drawn wagons of the Afrikaners struggled over the Drakensberg Mountains to the high plains in an effort to escape British control. (Hulton Getty/Liaison)

Imperial Policies and Shipping

Through such piecemeal acquisitions, by 1870 Britain had added several dozen colonies to the twenty-six colonies it had in 1792, after the loss of the thirteen in North America (see Chapter 22). Nevertheless, historians usually portray Britain in this period as a reluctant empire builder, its leaders unwilling to acquire new outposts that could prove difficult and expensive to administer. This apparent contradiction is resolved by the recognition that the underlying goal of most British imperial expansion during these decades was trade rather than territory. Most of the new colonies were meant to serve as ports in the growing network of shipping that encircled the globe or as centers of production and distribution for those networks.

This new commercial expansion was closely tied to the needs of Britain's growing industrial economy and reflected a new philosophy of overseas trade. Rather than rebuilding the closed, mercantilist network of trade with its colonies, Britain sought to trade freely with all parts of the world. Free trade was also a wise policy in light of the independence of so many former colonies in the Americas (see Chapter 24).

Whether colonized or not, more and more African, Asian, and Pacific lands were being drawn into the commercial networks created by British expansion and industrialization. As was pointed out earlier, uncolonized parts of West Asia became major exporters to Britain of vegetable oils for industrial and domestic use and forest products for dyes and construction, while areas of eastern Africa free of European control exported ivory that ended up as piano keys and decorations in the elegant homes of the industrial middle class. From the far corners of the world came coffee, cocoa, and tea (along with sugar to sweeten them) for the tables of the new industrial classes in Britain and other parts of Europe, and indigo dyes and cotton fibers for their expanding textile factories.

In return, the factories of the industrialized nations supplied manufactured goods at very attractive prices. By the mid-nineteenth century a major part of their textile production was destined for overseas markets. Sales of cotton cloth to Africa increased 950 percent from the 1820s to the 1860s. British trade to India grew 350 percent between 1841 and 1870, while India's exports increased 400 percent. Trade with other regions also expanded rapidly. In most cases such trade benefited both sides, but there is no question that the industrial nations were the dominant partners.

A second impetus to global commercial expansion was the technological revolution in the construction of oceangoing ships under way in the nineteenth century. The middle decades of the century were the golden age of the sailing ship. Using iron to fasten timbers together permitted shipbuilders to construct much larger vessels. Merchant ships in the eighteenth century rarely exceeded 300 tons, but after 1850 swift American-built **clipper ships** of 2,000 tons were commonplace in the British merchant fleet. Huge canvas sails hung from tall masts made the streamlined clippers faster than earlier vessels. Ships from the East Indies or India had taken six months to reach Europe in the seventeenth century; after 1850 the new ships could complete the voyage in half that time.

This increase in size and speed lowered shipping costs and further stimulated maritime trade. The growth in size and numbers of ships increased the tonnage of British merchant shipping by 400 percent between 1778 and 1860. To extend the life of such ships in tropical lands, clippers intended for Eastern service generally were built of teak and other tropical hardwoods from new British colonies in South and Southeast Asia. Although tropical forests began to be cleared for rice and sugar plantations as well as for timbers, the effects on the environment and people of Southeast Asia came primarily after 1870.

Colonization of Australia and New Zealand

The development of new ships and shipping contributed to a third form of British rule in the once-remote South Pacific. British settlers displaced indigenous populations in the new colonies of Australia and New Zealand, just as they had done in North America. This differs from India, where Britain ruled numerous indigenous populations, and Singapore and Cape Town, which were outposts of a commercial empire.

Portuguese mariners had sighted the continent of Australia in the early seventeenth century, but it was too remote to be of much interest to Europeans. However, after the English adventurer Captain James Cook systematically explored New Zealand and the fertile eastern coast of Australia between 1769 and 1778, expanding shipping networks brought in growing numbers of visitors and settlers.

At the time of Cook's visits Australia was the home of about 650,000 hunting-and-gathering people, whose Melanesian° ancestors had settled there some forty thousand years earlier. The two islands of New Zealand, lying 1,000 miles (1,600 kilometers) southeast of Australia, were inhabited by about 250,000 Maori°, who practiced hunting, fishing, and simple forms of agriculture, which their Polynesian ancestors had introduced around 1200 C.E. Because of their long isolation from the rest of humanity, the populations of Australia and New Zealand were as vulnerable as the Amerindians had been to unfamiliar diseases introduced by new overseas contacts. In the 1890s only 93,000 aboriginal Australians and 42,000 Maori survived. By then, British settler populations outnumbered and dominated the indigenous peoples.

The first permanent British settlers in Australia were 736 convicts, of whom 188 were women, sent into exile from British prisons in 1788. Over the next few decades, Australian penal colonies grew slowly and had only slight contact with the indigenous population, whom the British called "Aborigines." However, the discovery of gold in 1851 brought a flood of free European settlers (and some Chinese) and hastened the end of the penal colonies. When the gold rush subsided, government subsidies enabled tens of thousands of British settlers to settle "down under." Improved sailing ships made possible a voyage halfway around the world, although it still took more than three months to reach Australia from Britain. By 1860 Australia had a million immigrants, and the settler population doubled during the next fifteen years.

British settlers were drawn more slowly to New Zealand. Some of the first were temporary residents along the coast who slaughtered seals and exported seal pelts to Western countries to be made into men's felt hats. A single ship in 1806 took away sixty thousand sealskins. By the early 1820s overhunting had nearly exterminated the seal population. Special ships also hunted sperm whales extensively near New Zealand for their oil, used for lubrication, soap, and lamps; ambergris°, an ingredient in perfume; and bone, used in women's corsets (see Environment and Technology: Whaling). Military action that overcame Maori resistance, a brief gold rush, and the availability of faster ships and subsidized passages attracted more British immigrants after 1860. The colony especially courted women immigrants to offset

Melanesian (mel-uh-NEE-zhuhn) **Maori** (MOW-ree [*ow* as in *cow*]) **ambergris** (AM-ber-grees)

ENVIRONMENT + TECHNOLOGY

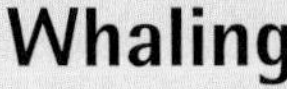

Whaling

The rapid expansion of whaling aptly illustrates the growing power of technology over nature in this period. Many contemporaries, like many people today, were sickened by the killing of the planet's largest living mammals. American novelist Herman Melville captured the conflicting sentiments in his epic whaling story, *Moby Dick* (1851). One of his characters enthusiastically explains why the grisly and dangerous business existed:

> *But, though the world scorns us as whale hunters, yet does it unwittingly pay us the profoundest homage; yea, an all abounding adoration! for almost all the tapers, lamps, and candles that burn around the globe, burn, as before so many shrines, to our glory!*

Melville's character overstates the degree to which whale oil dominated illumination and does not mention its many other industrial uses. Neither does he describe the commercial importance of whalebone (baleen). For a time its use in corsets allowed fashionable women to achieve the hourglass shape that fashion dictated. Whalebone's use for umbrella stays, carriage springs, fishing rods, suitcase frames, combs, brushes, and many other items made it the plastic of its day.

New manufacturing technologies went hand in hand with new hunting technologies. The revolution in ship design enabled whalers from Europe and North America to extend the hunt into the southern oceans off New Zealand. By the nineteenth century whaling ships were armed with guns that shot a steel harpoon armed with vicious barbs deep into the whale. In the 1840s explosive charges on harpoon heads ensured the whale's immediate death. Yet, as this engraving of an expedition off New Zealand shows, flinging small harpoons from rowboats in the open sea continued to be part of the dangerous work.

Another century of extensive hunting devastated many whale species before international agreements finally limited the killing of these giant sea creatures.

South Pacific Whaling One boat was swamped, but the hunters killed the huge whale. (The Granger Collection, New York)

Asian Laborers in British Guiana The manager of the sugar estate reposes on the near end of the gallery of his house with the proprietor's attorney. At the other end of the gallery European overseers review the plantation's record books. In the yard cups of lifeblood are being drained from bound Chinese and Indian laborers. This allegorical drawing by a Chinese laborer represents the exploitation of Asian laborers by Europeans. (Boston Athenaeum)

the preponderance of single men. By the early 1880s fertile agricultural lands of this most distant frontier of the British Empire had a settler population of 500,000.

Britain encouraged the settlers in Australia and New Zealand to become self-governing, following the 1867 model that had formed the giant Dominion of Canada out of the very diverse and thinly settled colonies of British North America. In 1901 a unified Australia emerged from the federation of six separate colonies. New Zealand became a self-governing dominion in 1907.

Britain's policies toward its settler colonies in Canada and the South Pacific reflected a desire to avoid the conflicts that had led to the American Revolution in the eighteenth century. By gradually turning over governing power to the colonies' inhabitants, Britain accomplished three things. It satisfied the settlers' desire for greater control over their own territories; it muted demands for independence; and it made the colonial governments responsible for most of their own expenses. Indigenous peoples were outvoted by the settlers or even excluded from voting.

North American patterns also shaped the indigenous peoples' fate. An 1897 Australian law segregated the remaining Aborigines onto reservations, where they lacked the rights of Australian citizenship. The requirement that voters had to be able to read and write English kept Maori from voting in early New Zealand elections, but four seats in the lower house of the legislature were reserved for Maori from 1867.

In other ways the new settler colonies were more progressive. Australia developed very powerful trade unions, which improved the welfare of skilled and semiskilled urban white male workers, promoted democratic values, and exercised considerable political clout. In New Zealand, where sheep raising was the main occupation, populist and progressive sentiments promoted the availability of land for the common person. Australia and New Zealand were also among the first states in the world to grant women the right to vote, beginning in 1894.

New Labor Migrations

Europeans were not the only people to transplant themselves overseas in the mid-nineteenth century. Between 1834 and 1870 many thousands of Indians, Chinese, and Africans responded to labor recruiters, especially to work overseas on sugar plantations. In the half-century after 1870 tens of thousands of Asians and Pacific Islanders made similar voyages.

In part these migrations were linked to the end of slavery. After their emancipation in British colonies in 1834, the freed men and women were no longer willing to put in the long hours they had been forced to work as slaves. When given full freedom of movement in 1839, many left the plantations. To compete successfully with sugar plantations in Cuba, Brazil, and the French Caribbean that were still using slave labor, British colonies had to recruit new laborers.

India's impoverished people seemed one obvious alternative. After planters on Mauritius successfully introduced Indian laborers, the Indian labor trade moved to the British Caribbean in 1838. In 1841 the British government also allowed Caribbean planters to recruit Africans whom British patrols had rescued from slave ships and liberated in Sierra Leone and elsewhere. By 1870 nearly 40,000 Africans had settled in British colonies, along with over a half-million Indians and over 18,000 Chinese. After the French and Dutch abolished slavery in 1848, their colonies also recruited over 150,000 new laborers from Asia and Africa.

Slavery was not abolished in Cuba until 1886, but the rising cost of slaves led the burgeoning sugar plantations to recruit 138,000 new laborers from China between 1847 and 1873. Indentured labor recruits also became the mainstay of new sugar plantations in places that had never known slave labor. After 1850 American planters in Hawaii recruited labor from China and Japan; British planters in Natal recruited from India; and those in Queensland (in northeastern Australia) relied on laborers from neighboring South Pacific islands.

Larger, faster ships made transporting laborers halfway around the world affordable, though voyages from Asia to the Caribbean still took an average of three months. Despite close regulation and supervision of shipboard conditions, the crowded accommodations encouraged the spread of cholera and other contagious diseases that took many migrants' lives.

All of these laborers served under **contracts of indenture,** which bound them to work for a specified period (usually from five to seven years) in return for free passage to their overseas destination. They were paid a small salary and were provided with housing, clothing, and medical care. Indian indentured laborers also received the right to a free passage home if they worked a second five-year contract. British Caribbean colonies required forty women to be recruited for every hundred men as a way to promote family life. So many Indians chose to stay in Mauritius, Trinidad, British Guiana, and Fiji that they constituted a third or more of the total population of these colonies by the early twentieth century.

Although many early recruits from China and the Pacific Islands were kidnapped or otherwise coerced into leaving their homes, in most cases the new indentured migrants had much in common with contemporary emigrants from Europe (described in Chapter 23). Both groups chose to leave their homelands in hopes of improving their economic and social conditions. Both earned modest salaries. Many saved to bring money back when they returned home, or they used their earnings to buy land or to start a business in their new countries, where large numbers chose to remain. One major difference was that people recruited as indentured laborers were generally so much poorer than emigrants from Europe that they had to accept lower-paying jobs in less desirable areas because they could not pay their own way. However, it is also true that many European immigrants into distant places like Australia and New Zealand had their passages subsidized but did not have to sign a contract of indenture. This shows that racial and cultural preferences, not just economics, shaped the flow of labor into European colonies.

A person's decision to accept an indentured labor contract could also be shaped by political circumstances. In India disruption brought by British colonial policies and the suppression of the 1857 rebellion contributed significantly to people's desire to emigrate. Poverty, famine, and warfare had not been strangers in precolonial India. Nor were these causes of emigration absent in China and Japan (see Chapter 26).

The indentured labor trade reflected the unequal commercial and industrial power of the West, but it was not an entirely one-sided creation. The men and women who signed indentured contracts were trying to improve their lives by emigrating, and many succeeded. Whether for good or ill, more and more of the world's peoples saw their lives being influenced by the existence of Western colonies, Western ships, and Western markets.

Conclusion

What is the global significance of these complex political and economic changes in southern Asia, Africa, and the South Pacific? One perspective stresses the continuing exploitation of the weak by the strong, of African, Asian, and Pacific peoples by aggressive Europeans. In this view, the emergence of Britain as a dominant power in the Indian Ocean basin and South Pacific continues the European expansion that the

Portuguese and the Spanish pioneered and the Dutch took over. Likewise, Britain's control over the densely populated lands of South and Southeast Asia and over the less populated lands of Australia and New Zealand can be seen as a continuation of the conquest and colonization of the Americas.

From another perspective what was most important about this period was not the political and military strength of the Europeans but their growing domination of the world's commerce, especially through long-distance ocean shipping. In this view, like other Europeans, the British were drawn to Africa and southern Asia by a desire to obtain new materials.

However, Britain's commercial expansion in the nineteenth century was also the product of Easterners' demand for industrial manufactures. The growing exchanges could be mutually beneficial. African and Asian consumers found industrially produced goods far cheaper and sometimes better than the handicrafts they replaced or supplemented. Industrialization created new markets for African and Asian goods, as in the case of the vegetable-oil trade in West Africa or cotton in Egypt and India. There were also negative impacts, as in the case of the weavers of India and the damage to species of seals and whales.

Europeans' military and commercial strength did not reduce Africa, Asia, and the Pacific to mere appendages of Europe. While the balance of power shifted in the Europeans' favor between 1750 and 1870, other cultures were still vibrant and local initiatives often dominant. Islamic reform movements and the rise of the Zulu nation had greater significance for their respective regions of Africa than did Western forces. Despite some ominous concessions to European power, Southeast Asians were still largely in control of their own destinies. Even in India, most people's lives and beliefs showed more continuity with the past than the change due to British rule.

Finally, it must not be imagined that Asians and Africans were powerless in dealing with European expansion. The Indian princes who extracted concessions from the British in return for their cooperation and the Indians who rebelled against the raj both forced the system to accommodate their needs. Moreover, some Asians and Africans were beginning to use European education, technology, and methods to transform their own societies. Leaders in Egypt, India, and other lands, like those in Russia, the Ottoman Empire, China, and Japan—the subject of Chapter 26—were learning to challenge the power of the West on its own terms. In 1870 no one could say how long and how difficult that learning process would be, but Africans and Asians would continue to shape their own futures.

Key Terms

Zulu
Sokoto Caliphate
modernization
Muhammad Ali
"legitimate" trade
recaptives
nawab
sepoy
British raj
Sepoy Rebellion
durbar
Indian Civil Service
Indian National Congress
clipper ship
contract of indenture

Suggested Reading

Volumes 2 and 3 of *The Oxford History of the British Empire*, ed. William Roger Louis, (1998, 1999), are the most up-to-date global surveys of this period. Less Anglocentric in their interpretations are Immanuel Wallerstein's *The Modern World-System III: The Second Era of Great Expansion of the Capitalist World-Economy, 1730–1840s* (1989) and William Wodruff's *Impact of Western Man: A Study of Europe's Role in the World Economy, 1750–1960* (1982). Atlantic relations are well handled by David Eltis, *Economic Growth and the Ending of the Transatlantic Slave Trade* (1987). For the Indian Ocean basin see Sugata Bose, *The Indian Ocean Rim: An Inter-Regional Arena in the Age of Global Empire* (2003).

Roland Oliver and Anthony Atmore provide a brief introduction to Africa in *Africa Since 1800*, 4th ed. (1994). More advanced works are J. F. Ade Ajayi, ed., *UNESCO General History of Africa*, vol. 6, *Africa in the Nineteenth Century until the 1880s* (1989), and John E. Flint, ed., *The Cambridge History of Africa*, vol. 5, *From c. 1790 to c. 1870* (1976). Although specialized literature has refined some of their interpretations, the following are excellent introductions to their subjects: J. D. Omer-Cooper, *The Zulu Aftermath* (1966); Murray Last, *The Sokoto Caliphate* (1967); A. G. Hopkins, *An Economic History of West Africa* (1973); Robert W. July, *The Origins of Modern African Thought* (1967); and Robert I. Rotberg, ed., *Africa and Its Explorers: Motives, Methods, and Impact* (1970). For eastern and northeastern Africa see Norman R. Bennett, *Arab Versus European: War and Diplomacy in Nineteenth Century East Central Africa* (1985); P. J. Vatikiotis, *The History of Modern Egypt: From Muhammad Ali to Mubarak*, 4th ed. (1991); and, for the negative social impact of Egyptian modernization, Judith Tucker, "Decline of the Family Economy in Mid-Nineteenth-Century Egypt," *Arab Studies Quarterly 1* (1979): 245–271.

Very readable introductions to India in this period are Sugata Bose and Ayeshia Jalal, *Modern South India* (1998); Burton Stein, *A History of India* (1998); and Stanley Wolpert, *A New History of India,* 6th ed. (1999). More advanced treatments in the "New Cambridge History of India" series are P. J. Marshall, *Bengal: The British Bridgehead: Eastern India, 1740–1828* (1988); C. A. Bayly, *Indian Society and the Making of the British Empire* (1988); Sugata Bose, *Peasant Labour and Colonial Capital: Rural Bengal Since 1700* (1993); and Kenneth W. Jones, *Socio-Religious Reform Movements in British India* (1989). Environmental and technological perspectives on India are offered in the appropriate parts of Daniel Headrick, *The Tentacles of Progress: Technology Transfer in the Age of Imperialism, 1850–1940* (1988); Mashav Gadgil and Ramachandra Guha, *This Fissured Land: An Ecological History of India* (1992). For Tipu Sultan see Kate Brittlebank, *Tipu Sultan's Search for Legitimacy: Islam and Kingship in a Hindu Domain* (1997).

A good introduction to the complexities of Southeast Asian history is D. R. SarDesai, *Southeast Asia: Past and Present,* 2nd ed. (1989). More detail can be found in the appropriate chapters of Nicholas Tarling, ed., *The Cambridge History of South East Asia,* 2 vols. (1992). The second and third volumes of *The Oxford History of Australia,* ed. Geoffrey Bolton (1992, 1988), deal with the period covered by this chapter. A very readable multicultural and gendered perspective is provided by *Images of Australia,* ed. Gillian Whitlock and David Carter (1992). *The Oxford Illustrated History of New Zealand,* ed. Keith Sinclair (1990), provides a wide-ranging introduction to that nation.

For summaries of recent scholarship on the indentured labor trade see David Northrup, *Indentured Labor in the Age of Imperialism, 1834–1922* (1995), and Robin Cohen, ed., *The Cambridge Survey of World Migration,* part 3, "Asian Indentured and Colonial Migration" (1995).

An outstanding analysis of British whaling is Gordon Jackson's *The British Whaling Trade* (1978). Edouard A. Stackpole's *Whales & Destiny: The Rivalry Between America, France, and Britain for Control of the Southern Whale Fishery, 1785–1825* (1972) is more anecdotal.

Notes

1. Paul E. Lovejoy and Jan S. Hogendorn, *Slow Death for Slavery: The Course of Abolition in Northern Nigeria, 1897–1936* (New York: Cambridge University Press, 1993).
2. Quoted in P. J. Vatikiotis, *The History of Modern Egypt: From Muhammad Ali to Mubarak,* 4th ed. (Baltimore: Johns Hopkins University Press, 1991), 74.
3. David Eltis, "Precolonial Western Africa and the Atlantic Economy," in *Slavery and the Rise of the Atlantic Economy,* ed. Barbara Solow (New York: Cambridge University Press, 1991), table 1.
4. Quoted by Bernard S. Cohn, "Representing Authority in Victorian India," in *The Invention of Tradition,* ed. Eric Hobsbawm and Terence Ranger (Cambridge, England: Cambridge University Press, 1983), 165.

26 Land Empires in the Age of Imperialism, 1800–1870

Muhammad Ali Meets with European Representatives in 1839 This meeting came after the European powers brought the expansive portion of the Egyptian governor's meteoric career to an end.

CHAPTER OUTLINE

When the emperor of the Qing° (the last empire to rule China) died in 1799, the imperial court received a shock. For decades officials had known that the emperor was indulging his handsome young favorite, Heshen°, allowing him extraordinary privileges and power. Senior bureaucrats hated Heshen, suspecting him of overseeing a widespread network of corruption. They believed he had been scheming to prolong the inconclusive wars against the native Miao° peoples of southwest China in the late 1700s. Glowing reports of successes against the rebels had poured into the capital, and enormous sums of government money had flowed to the battlefields. But there was no adequate accounting for the funds, and the war persisted.

After the emperor's death, Heshen's enemies ordered his arrest. When they searched his mansion, they discovered a magnificent hoard of silk, furs, porcelain, furniture, and gold and silver. His personal cash alone exceeded what remained in the imperial treasury. The new emperor ordered Heshen to commit suicide with a rope of gold silk. The government seized Heshen's fortune, but the financial damage could not be undone. The declining agricultural base could not replenish the state coffers, and much of the income that did flow in was squandered by an increasingly corrupt bureaucracy. In the 1800s the Qing Empire faced increasing challenges from Europe and the United States with an empty treasury, a stagnant economy, and a troubled society.

The Qing Empire's problems were not unique. They were common to all the land-based empires of Eurasia, where old and inefficient ways of governing put states at risk. The international climate was increasingly dominated by industrializing European economies drawing on the wealth of their overseas colonies. During the early 1800s rapid population growth and slow agricultural growth affected much of Eurasia. Earlier military expansion had stretched the resources of imperial treasuries (see Chapter 21), leaving the land-based empires vulnerable to European military pressure. Responses to this pressure varied, with reform and adaptation gaining headway in some lands and tradition being reasserted in others. In the long run, attempts to meet western Europe's economic and political demands produced financial indebtedness to France, Britain, and other Western powers.

This chapter contrasts the experiences of the Qing Empire with the Russian and Ottoman Empires, with a particular look at the Ottomans' semi-independent province of Egypt. While the Qing opted for resistance, the others made varying attempts to adapt and reform. Russia eventually became part of Europe and shared in many aspects of European culture, while the Ottomans and the Qing became subject to ever greater imperialist pressure. These different responses raise the question of the role of culture in shaping western Europe's relations with the rest of the world in the nineteenth century.

As you read this chapter, ask yourself the following questions:

- Why did the Ottoman and Qing Empires find themselves on the defensive in their encounters with Europeans in the 1800s?
- By what strategies did the land-based empires try to adapt to nineteenth-century economic and political conditions?
- How did the Russian Empire maintain its status as both a European power and a great Asian land empire?

The Ottoman Empire

During the eighteenth century the central government of the Ottoman Empire lost much of its power to provincial governors, military commanders, ethnic leaders, and bandit chiefs. In several parts of the empire local officials and large landholders tried to increase their independence and divert imperial funds into their own coffers.

Qing (ching) **Heshen** (huh-shun) **Miao** (mee-ow)

A kingdom in Arabia led by the Saud family, and following the puritanical and fundamentalist religious views of an eighteenth-century leader named Muhammad ibn Abd al-Wahhab°, took control of the holy cities of Mecca and Medina and deprived the sultan of the honor of organizing the annual pilgrimage. In Egypt the Mamluk slave-soldiers purchased as boys in Georgia and nearby parts of the Caucasus and educated for war reasserted their influence. Between 1260 and 1517, when they were defeated by the Ottomans, Egypt's sultans had come from the ranks of the Mamluks. Now Ottoman weakness allowed the Mamluk factions to reemerge as local military forces.

For the sultans, hopes of escaping still further decline were few. The inefficient Janissary corps wielded great political power in Istanbul. It used this power to force Sultan Selim III to abandon efforts to train a modern, European-style army at the end of the eighteenth century. This situation unexpectedly changed when France invaded Egypt.

Egypt and the Napoleonic Example, 1798–1840

Napoleon Bonaparte and an invasion force of 36,000 men and four hundred ships invaded Egypt in May 1798 (see Diversity and Dominance: The French Occupation of Egypt). The French quickly defeated the Mamluk forces that for several decades had dominated the country under the loose jurisdiction of the Ottoman sultan in Istanbul. Fifteen months later, after being stopped by Ottoman land and British naval forces in an attempted invasion of Syria, Napoleon secretly left Cairo and returned to France. Three months later he seized power and made himself emperor.

Back in Egypt, his generals tried to administer a country that they only poorly understood. Cut off from France by British ships in the Mediterranean, they had little hope of remaining in power and agreed to withdraw in 1801. For the second time in three years, a collapse of military power produced a power vacuum in Egypt. The winner of the ensuing contest was **Muhammad Ali°**, the commander of a contingent of Albanian soldiers sent by the sultan to restore imperial control. By 1805 he had taken the place of the official Ottoman governor, and by 1811 he had dispossessed the Mamluks of their lands and privileges.

Muhammad ibn Abd al-Wahhab (Moo-HAH-muhd ib-uhn ab-dahl-wa HAHB)
Muhammad Ali (moo-HAM-mad AH-lee)

Muhammad Ali's rise to power coincided with the meteoric career of Emperor Napoleon I. It is not surprising, therefore, that he adopted many French practices in rebuilding the Egyptian state. Militarily, he dutifully sent an army against the Saudi kingdom in Arabia to reclaim Mecca and Medina for the sultan. Losses during the successful war greatly reduced his contingent of Albanians, leaving him free to construct a new army. Instead of relying on picked groups of warriors like the Mamluks, Muhammad Ali instituted the French practice of conscription. For the first time since the days of the pharaohs, Egyptian peasants were compelled to become soldiers.

He also established special schools for training artillery and cavalry officers, army surgeons, military bandmasters, and others. The curricula of these schools featured European skills and sciences, and Muhammad Ali began to send promising young Turks and Circassians (an ethnic group from the Caucasus), the only people permitted to serve as military officers, to France for education. In 1824 he started a gazette devoted to official affairs, the first newspaper in the Islamic world.

To outfit his new army Muhammad Ali built all sorts of factories. These did not prove efficient enough to survive, but they showed a determination to achieve independence and parity with the European powers.

Money for these enterprises came from confiscation of lands belonging to Muslim religious institutions, under the pretext that the French occupation had canceled religious trusts established in earlier centuries, and from forcing farmers to sell their crops to the government at fixed prices. Muhammad Ali resold some of the produce abroad, making great profits as long as the Napoleonic wars kept European prices for wheat at a high level.

In the 1830s Muhammad Ali's son Ibrahim invaded Syria and instituted some of the changes already underway in Egypt. The improved quality of the new Egyptian army had been proven during the Greek war of independence (see below), when Ibrahim had commanded an expeditionary force to help the sultan. In response, the sultan embarked on building his own new army in 1826. The two armies met in 1839 when Ibrahim attacked northward into Anatolia. The Egyptian army was victorious, and Istanbul would surely have fallen if not for European intervention.

In 1841 European pressure, highlighted by British naval bombardment of coastal cities in Egyptian-controlled Syria, forced Muhammad Ali to withdraw to the present-day border between Egypt and Israel. The great powers imposed severe limitations on his army and navy and forced him to dissolve his economic mo-

CHRONOLOGY

	Ottoman Empire	Russian Empire	Qing Empire
1800	**1805–1849** Muhammad Ali governs Egypt **1808–1839** Rule of Mahmud II **1826** Janissary corps dissolved **1829** Greek independence **1839** Abdul Mejid begins Tanzimat reforms	**1801–1825** Reign of Alexander I **1812** Napoleon's retreat from Moscow **1825** Decembrist revolt **1825–1855** Reign of Nicholas I	**1794–1804** White Lotus Rebellion **1839–1842** Opium War
1850	**1853–1856** Crimean War **1876** First constitution by an Islamic government	**1853–1856** Crimean War **1855–1881** Reign of Alexander II **1861** Emancipation of the serfs	**1850–1864** Taiping Rebellion **1856–1860** Arrow War **1860** Sack of Beijing **1862–1875** Reign of Tongzhi

nopolies and allow Europeans to undertake business ventures in Egypt.

Muhammad Ali remained Egypt's ruler, under the suzerainty of the sultan, until his death in 1849; and his family continued to rule the country until 1952. But his dream of making Egypt a mighty country capable of standing up to Europe faded. What survived was the example he had set for the sultans in Istanbul.

Ottoman Reform and the European Model, 1807–1853

At the end of the eighteenth century Sultan Selim° III (r. 1789–1807), an intelligent and forward-looking ruler who stayed well informed about events in Europe, introduced reforms to create European-style military units, bring provincial governors under the control of the central government, and standardize taxation and land tenure. The rise in government expenditures to implement the reforms was supposed to be offset by taxes on selected items, primarily tobacco and coffee.

These reforms failed for political, more than economic, reasons. The most violent and persistent opposition came from the **Janissaries°**. Originally Christian boys taken from their homes in the Balkans, converted to Islam, and required to serve for life in the Ottoman army, in the eighteenth century the Janissaries became a significant political force in Istanbul and in provincial capitals like Baghdad. Their interest in preserving special economic privileges made them resist the creation of new military units.

At times, the disapproval of the Janissaries produced military uprisings. An early example occurred in the Balkans, in the Ottoman territory of **Serbia,** where Janissaries acted as provincial governors. Their control in Serbia was intensely resented by the local residents, particularly Orthodox Christians who claimed that the Janissaries abused them. In response to the charges, Selim threatened to reassign the Janissaries to the Ottoman capital at Istanbul. Suspecting that the sultan's threat signaled the beginning of the end of their political power, in 1805 the Janissaries revolted against Selim and massacred Christians in Serbia. Selim was unable to reestablish central Ottoman rule over Serbia. Instead, the Ottoman court had to rely on the ruler of Bosnia, another Balkan province, who joined his troops with the peasants of Serbia to suppress the Janissary uprising. The threat of Russian intervention prevented the Ottomans from disarming the victorious Serbians, so Serbia became effectively independent.

Other opponents of reform included ulama, or Muslim religious scholars, who distrusted the secularization of law and taxation that Selim proposed. In the face of widespread rejection of his reforms, Selim suspended his program in 1806. Nevertheless, a massive military uprising occurred at Istanbul, and the sultan was deposed and imprisoned. Reform forces rallied and recaptured

Selim (seh-LEEM) **Janissaries** (JAN-nih-say-rees)

DIVERSITY AND DOMINANCE

THE FRENCH OCCUPATION OF EGYPT

Napoleon's invasion of Egypt in 1798 strikingly illustrates the techniques of dominance employed by the French imperial power and the means of resistance available to noncombatant Egyptian intellectuals in reasserting their cultural diversity and independence. Abd al-Rahman al-Jabarti (1753–1826), from whose writings the first four passages are drawn, came from a family of ulama, or Muslim religious scholars. His three works concerning the French occupation, which lasted until 1801, provide the best Egyptian account of that period. The selections below start with the first half of Napoleon's first proclamation to the Egyptian people, which was published in Arabic at the time of the invasion and is quoted here from al-Jabarti's text.

In the Name of God the Compassionate the Merciful: There is no god but God. He has not begotten a son, and does not share in His Kingship.

On behalf of the French Republic, which is founded upon the principles of liberty and equality, the Commander-in-Chief of the French armies, the great head-general Bonaparte, hereby declares to all inhabitants of Egyptian lands that the Sanjaqid rulers of Egypt [i.e., the Mamluk commanders] have persisted far too long in their maltreatment and humiliation of the French nation and have unjustly subjected French merchants to all manner of abuse and extortion. The hour of their punishment has now come.

It is a great pity that this group of slave fighters [Mamluks], caught in the mountains of Abkhazia and Georgia, have for such a long time perpetrated so much corruption in the fairest of all lands on the face of the globe. Now, the omnipotent Lord of the Universe has ordained their demise.

O people of Egypt, should they say to you that I have only come hither to defile your religion, this is but an utter lie that you must not believe. Say to my accusers that I have only come to rescue your rights from the hands of tyrants, and that I am a better servant of God—may He be praised and exalted—and that I revere His Prophet Muhammad and the grand Koran more than the group of slave fighters do.

Tell them also that all people stand equally before God and that reason, virtue, and knowledge comprise the only distinguishing qualities among them. Now, what do the group of slave fighters possess of reason, virtue, and knowledge that would distinguish them from the rest of the people and qualify them exclusively to benefit from everything that is desirable in this worldly life?

The most fertile of all agricultural lands, the prettiest concubines, the best horses, and most attractive residences, all are appropriated exclusively by them. If the land of Egypt was ever conferred upon this group of slave fighters exclusively, let them show us the document that God has written for them: of course, the Lord of the Universe acts with compassion and equity toward mankind. With His help—may He be Exalted—from this day on no Egyptian shall be excluded from high positions nor barred from acquiring high ranks, and men of reason, virtue and learning from among them will administer the affairs, and as a result the welfare of the entire Muslim community (*umma*) shall improve.

The following passages provide examples of al-Jabarti's line-by-line commentary on the proclamation and two examples of his more general comments on the French and on French rule.

Explanation of the wretched proclamation composed of incoherent words and vulgar phrases:

By saying, "in the Name of God the Compassionate the Merciful: There is no god but God. He has not begotten a son, and does not share in His Kingship" [the French] implicitly claim in three propositions that they concur with the three religions [Islam, Christianity, and Judaism] whereas in truth they falsify all three and indeed any other [viable] doctrine. They concur with the Muslims in opening [the statement] with the name of God and in rejecting His begetting a son or sharing in His Kingship. They differ from them in not professing the two essential Articles of Faith: refusing to recognize Prophet Muhammad, and rebuffing the essential teachings of Islam in word and deed. They concur with the Christians in most of what they say and do, but diverge over the question of Trinity, in their rejection of the vocation [of Christ], and furthermore in rebuffing their beliefs and rituals, killing the priests, and desecrating places of worship. They concur with the Jews in believing in one God, as the Jews also do not believe in the Trinity but hold on to anthropomorphism. [The French Republicans] do not share in the religious beliefs and practices of the Jews either. Apparently they do not follow any particular religion and do not adhere to a set of specific rituals: each of them fathoms a religion as it suits his own reason. The rest of the [people of France] are Christians but keep it hidden, and there are some real Jews among them as well. However, even those who may follow a religion, when they come to Egypt, they concur with the agents of the Republic in their insistence upon leading the Egyptians astray.

Their saying "On behalf of the French Republic, etc." implies that the proclamation comes from the Republic or their people directly, because unlike other nations they have no overlord or sovereign whom they unanimously appoint, and who has exclusive authority to speak on their behalf. It is now six years since they revolted against their sovereign and murdered him. Subsequently, the people agreed not to have a single ruler but rather to put the affairs of the government, provincial issues, legislation and administration, into the hands of men of discretion and reason among themselves. They chose and appointed men in a hierarchy: a head of the entire army followed in rank by generals and military commanders each in charge of groups of a thousand, two hundred, or ten men. They similarly appointed administrators and advisers by observing their essential equality and non-supremacy of one over the others, in the same way that people are created equally in essence. This constitutes the foundation and touchstone of their system, and this is what "founded upon the principles of liberty and equality" means. The reference to "liberty" implies that unlike the slaves and [the slave fighters ruling over Egypt] they are not anybody's slaves; the meaning of "equality" has already been explained.

[On that day the French] started to operate a new court bureau, which they named the Ad hoc Court (*mahkamat al-qadaya*). On this occasion they drafted a decree that included clauses framed in most unacceptable terms that sounded rather repellant to the ear. Six Copts and six Muslim merchants were appointed to the bureau, and the presiding judge and chief of the bureau was the Copt from Malta who used to work as secretary to Ayyub Bey, the notary (*daftardar*). Ad hoc cases involving commercial, civil, inheritance disputes, and other suits were referred to this bureau. [The French] formulated corrupt principles for this institution that were based on heresy, founded in tyranny, and rooted in all sorts of abominable unprecedented rulings (*bid'a al-sayyi'a*).

[The French] devastated the palace of Yusuf Salah al-Din including the cites where sovereigns and sultans held audiences, and they tore down strong foundations and demolished towering columns. They also destroyed mosques, meditation spots (*zawaya*), and shrines of martyrs (*mashahid*). They defaced the Grand Congregational Mosque, built by the venerable Muhammad b. Qalawan al-Malik al-Nasir: wrecked the pulpit, spoiled the mosque's courtyard, looted its lumber, undermined its columns, and razed the well-wrought iron enclosure inside of which the sultan used to pray.

The final passage, which is not in any of al-Jabarti's chronicles, is the full text of an announcement distributed to Napoleon's thirty-six thousand troops on board ship as they headed for Egypt.

Soldiers,—You are about to undertake a conquest the effects of which on civilization and commerce are incalculable. The blow you are about to give to England will be the best aimed, and the most sensibly felt, she can receive until the time arrive when you can give her her death-blow.

We must make some fatiguing marches; we must fight several battles; we shall succeed in all we undertake. The destinies are with us. The Mameluke Beys, who favour exclusively English commerce, whose extortions oppress our merchants , and who tyrannise over the unfortunate inhabitants of the Nile, a few days after our arrival will no longer exist.

The people amongst whom we are going to live are Mahometans. The first article of their faith is this: "there is no God but God, and Mahomet is His prophet." Do not contradict them. Behave to them as you have behaved to the Jews—to the Italians. Pay respect to their muftis [jurists], and their Imaums [sic], as you did to the rabbis and the bishops. Extend to the ceremonies prescribed by the Koran and to the mosques the same toleration which you showed to the synagogues, to the religion of Moses and of Jesus Christ.

The Roman legions protected all religions. You will find here customs different from those of Europe. You must accommodate yourselves to them. The people amongst whom we are to mix differ from us in the treatment of women; but in all countries he who violates is a monster. Pillage enriches only a small number of men; it dishonours us; it destroys our resources; it converts into enemies the people whom it is our interest to have for friends.

The first town we shall come to was built by Alexander. At every step we shall meet with grand recollections, worthy of exciting the emulations of Frenchmen.

Bonaparte

QUESTIONS FOR ANALYSIS

1. **Why are the reasons for invading Egypt given to the French soldiers different from those announced to the Egyptians?**
2. **How do Napoleon and al-Jabarti use religious feeling as a political tool?**
3. **What do texts like these suggest about the role culture plays in confrontations between imperial powers and imperialized peoples?**

Source: First selection from *Abd al-Rahman al-Jabarti's History of Egypt*, ed. Thomas Phillipp and Moshe Perlmann (Stuttgart, 1994), translated by Hossein Kamaly. Second selection from Louis Antoine Fauvelet de Bourrienne, *Memoirs of Napoleon Bonaparte* (1843).

the capital, but not before Selim had been executed. Selim's cousin Sultan Mahmud° II (r.1808–1839) cautiously revived the reform movement. The fate of Selim III had taught the Ottoman court that reform needed to be more systematic and imposed more forcefully, but it took the concrete evidence of the effectiveness of radical reform in Muhammad Ali's Egypt to drive this lesson home. Mahmud II was able to use an insurrection in Greece, and the superior performance of Egyptian forces in the unsuccessful effort to suppress it, as a sign of the weakness of the empire and the pressing need for reform.

Greek independence in 1829 was a complex event that had dramatic international significance. A combination of Greek nationalist organizations and interlopers from Albania formed the independence movement. By the early nineteenth century interest in the classical age of Greece and Rome had intensified European desires to encourage and if possible aid the struggle for independence. Europeans considered the war for Greek independence a campaign to recapture the classical roots of their civilization from Muslim despots, and many—including the "mad, bad and dangerous to know" English poet Lord Byron, who lost his life in the war—went to Greece to fight as volunteers. The Ottomans called on Ibrahim Pasha° of Egypt, the son of Muhammad Ali, to help preserve their rule in Greece; but when the combined squadrons of the British, French, and Russian fleets, under orders to observe but not intervene in the war, made an unauthorized attack that sank the Ottoman fleet at the Battle of Navarino, not even Ibrahim's help could prevent defeat (see Map 26.1).

Europeans trumpeted the victory of the Greeks as a triumph of European civilization over the Ottoman Empire, and Mahmud II agreed that the loss of Greece indicated a profound weakness—he considered it backwardness—in Ottoman military and financial organization. With popular outrage over the military setbacks in Greece strong, the sultan made his move in 1826. First he announced the creation of a new artillery unit, which he had secretly been training. When the Janissaries rose in revolt, he ordered the new unit to bombard the Janissary barracks. The Janissary corps was officially dissolved.

Like Muhammad Ali, Mahmud felt he could not implement major changes without reducing the political power of the religious elite. He visualized restructuring the bureaucracy and the educational and legal systems, where ulama power was strongest. Before such strong measures could be undertaken, however, Ibrahim attacked from Syria in 1839. Battlefield defeat, the decision of the rebuilt Ottoman navy to switch sides and support Egypt, and the death of Mahmud, all in the same year, left the empire completely dependent on the European powers for survival.

Mahmud's reforming ideas received their widest expression in the **Tanzimat**° ("reorganization"), a series of reforms announced by his sixteen-year-old son and successor, Abdul Mejid°, in 1839 and strongly endorsed by the European ambassadors. One proclamation called for public trials and equal protection under the law for all, whether Muslim, Christian, or Jew. It also guaranteed some rights of privacy, equalized the eligibility of men for conscription into the army (a practice copied from Egypt), and provided for a new, formalized method of tax collection that legally ended tax farming in the Ottoman Empire. It took many years and strenuous efforts by reforming bureaucrats, known as the "men of the Tanzimat," to give substance to these reforms. At a theoretical level, however, they opened a new chapter in the history of the Islamic world. European observers praised them for their noble principles and rejection of religious influences in government. Ottoman citizens were more divided; the Christians and Jews, about whom the Europeans showed the greatest concern, were generally more enthusiastic than the Muslims. Many historians see the Tanzimat as the dawn of modern thought and enlightened government in the Middle East. Others point out that removing the religious elite from influence in government also removed the one remaining check on authoritarian rule.

With the passage of time, one legal code after another—commercial, criminal, civil procedure—was introduced to take the place of the corresponding areas of religious legal jurisdiction. All the codes were modeled closely on those of Europe. The sharia, or Islamic law, gradually became restricted to matters of family law such as marriage and inheritance. As the sharia was displaced, job opportunities for the ulama shrank, as did the value of a purely religious education.

Like Muhammad Ali, Sultan Mahmud sent military cadets to France and the German states for training. Military uniforms were modeled on those of France. In the 1830s an Ottoman imperial school of military sciences, later to become Istanbul University, was established at Istanbul. Instructors imported from western Europe taught chemistry, engineering, mathematics, and physics in addition to military history. Reforms in military education became the model for more general educational reforms. In 1838 the first medical school was established

---

Mahmud (MAH-mood)
Ibrahim Pasha (ib-rah-HEEM PAH-shah)

Tanzimat (TAHNZ-ee-MAT) **Abdul Mejid** (ab-dul meh-JEED)

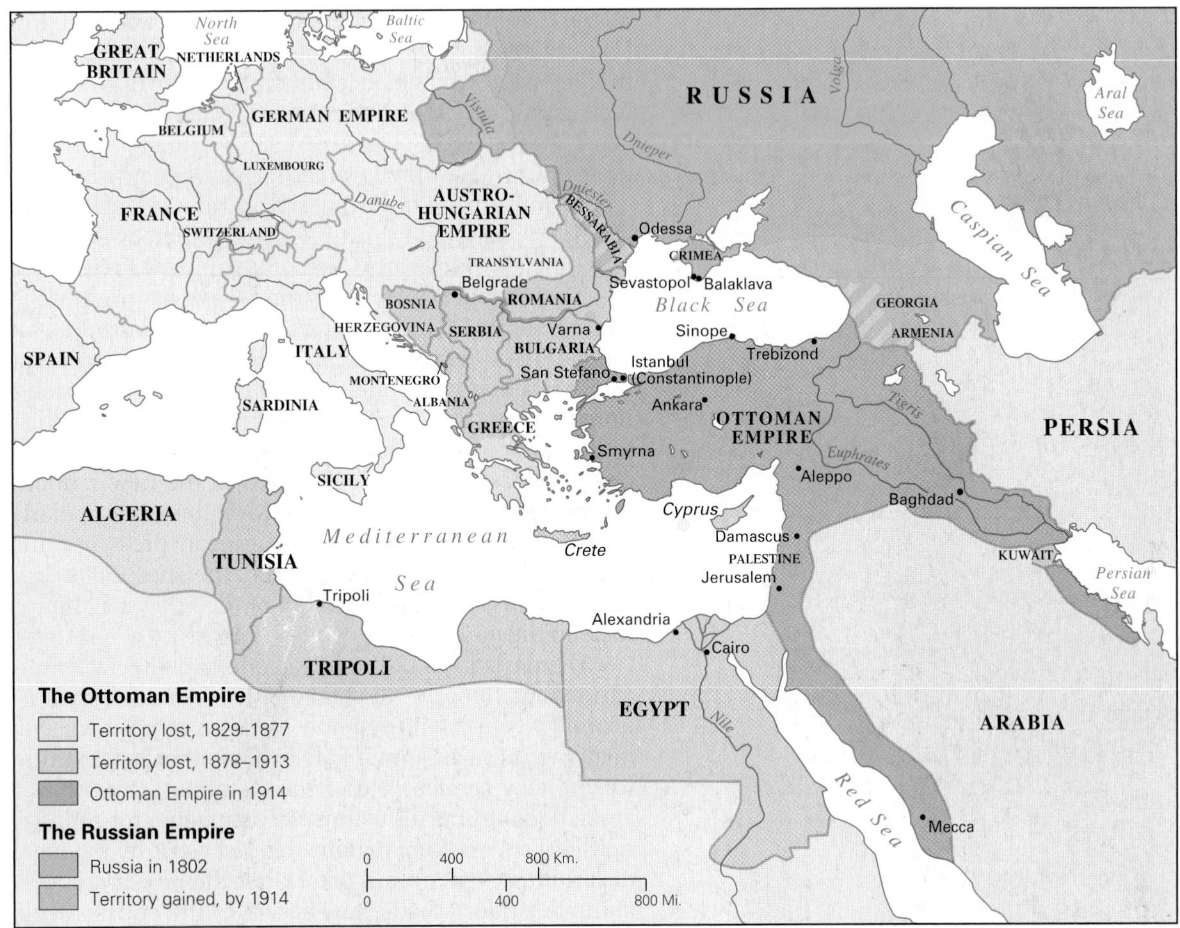

Map 26.1 The Ottoman and Russian Empires, 1829–1914 At its height the Ottoman Empire controlled most of the perimeter of the Mediterranean Sea. But in the 1800s Ottoman territory shrank as many countries gained their independence. The Black Sea, where the Turkish coast was vulnerable to assault, became a weak spot as Russian naval power grew. Russian challenges to the Ottomans at the eastern end of the Black Sea, and to the Persians east and west of the Caspian aroused fears in Europe that Russia was trying to reach the Indian Ocean.

to train army doctors and surgeons. Later, a national system of preparatory schools was created to feed graduates into the military schools. The subjects that were taught and many of the teachers were foreign, so the issue of whether Turkish would be a language of instruction in the new schools was a serious one. Because it was easier to import and use foreign textbooks than to write new ones in Turkish, French became the preferred language in all advanced professional and scientific training. In numerical terms, however, the great majority of students still learned to read and write in Quran schools down to the twentieth century.

In the capital city of Istanbul, the reforms stimulated the growth of a small but cosmopolitan milieu embracing European language and culture. The first Turkish newspaper, a government gazette modeled on that of Muhammad Ali, appeared in 1831. Other newspapers followed, many written in French. Travel to Europe—particularly to England and France—became more common among wealthy Turks. Interest in importing European military, industrial, and communications technology remained strong through the 1800s.

The Ottoman rulers quickly learned that limited improvements in military technology had unforeseen cultural and social effects. Accepting the European notion that modern weapons and drill required a change in traditional military dress, beards were deemed unhygienic and, in artillery units, a fire hazard. They were restricted,

Change with Tradition Change in the Ottoman armies was gradual, beginning with the introduction of European guns and artillery. To use the new weapons efficiently and safely, the Janissaries were required to modify their dress and beards. Beards were trimmed, and elaborate headgear was reserved for ritual occasions. Traditional military units attempted to retain distinctive dress whenever possible, and one compromise was the brimless cap adapted from the high hats that some Janissaries had traditionally worn. (Courtesy, Turkish Ministry of Culture and Tourism. Photo: Necmettin Kulahci)

along with the wearing of loose trousers and turbans. Military headgear also became controversial. European military caps, which had leather bills on the front to protect against the glare of the sun, were not acceptable because they interfered with Muslim soldiers' touching their foreheads to the ground during daily prayers. The compromise was the brimless cap now called the *fez*, which was adopted by the military and then by Ottoman civil officials in the early years of Mahmud II's reign.

The changes in military dress—so soon after the suppression of the Janissaries—were recognized as an indication of the empire's new orientation. Government ministries that traditionally drew young men from traditional bureaucratic families and trained them for ministerial service were gradually transformed into formal civil services hiring men educated in the new schools. Among self-consciously progressive men, particularly those in government service, European dress became the fashion in the Ottoman cities of the later 1800s. Traditional dress became a symbol of the religious, the rural, and the parochial.

Secularization of the legal code had special implications for the non-Muslim subjects of the Ottomans. Islamic law had required non-Muslims to pay a special head tax that was sometimes explained as a substitute for military service. Under the Tanzimat, the tax was abolished and non-Muslims became liable for military service—unless they bought their way out by paying a new military exemption tax. Under the new law codes, all male subjects had equal access to the courts, while the sphere of operation of the Islamic law courts shrank. Perhaps the biggest enhancement of the status of non-Muslims, however, was the strong and direct concern for their welfare consistently expressed by the European powers. The Ottoman Empire became a rich field of operation for Christian missionaries and European supporters of Jewish community life in the Muslim world.

The public rights and political participation granted during the Tanzimat applied specifically to men. Private life, including everything connected to marriage and divorce, remained within the sphere of religious law, and at no time was there a question of political participation or reformed education for women. Indeed, the reforms may have decreased the influence of women. The political changes ran parallel to economic changes that also narrowed women's opportunities.

The influx of silver from the Americas that had begun in the 1600s increased the monetarization of some sectors of the Ottoman economy, particularly in the cities. Workers were increasingly paid in cash rather than in goods, and businesses associated with banking, finance, and law developed. Competition drove women from the work force. Early industrial labor and the professions were not open to women, and traditional "woman's work" such as weaving was increasingly mechanized and done by men.

Nevertheless, women retained considerable power in the management and disposal of their own property, gained mostly through fixed shares of inheritance, well into the 1800s. After marriage a woman was often pressured to convert her landholdings to cash in order to transfer her personal wealth to her husband's family, with whom she and her husband would reside; but this was not a requirement, since men were legally obligated to support their families single-handedly. Until the 1820s many women retained their say in the distribution of property through the creation of charitable trusts for their sons. Because these trusts were set up in the religious courts, they could be designed to conform to the wishes of family members, and they gave women of wealthy families an opportunity to exercise significant indirect control over property. Then, in the 1820s and 1830s the secularizing reforms of Mahmud II, which did not always produce happy results, transferred jurisdiction over the charitable trusts from religious courts to the state and ended women's control over this form of property. In addition, reforms in the military, higher education, the professions, and commerce all bypassed women.

The Crimean War and Its Aftermath, 1853–1877

Since the reign of Peter the Great (r. 1689–1725) the Russian Empire had been attempting to expand southward at the Ottomans' expense (see "Russia and Asia," below). By 1815 Russia had pried the Georgian region of the Caucasus away from the Ottomans, and the threat of Russian intervention had prevented the Ottomans from crushing Serbian independence. Russia seemed poised to exploit Ottoman weakness and acquire the long-sought goal of free access to the Mediterranean Sea. In the eighteenth century Russia had claimed to be the protector of Ottoman subjects of Orthodox Christian faith in Greece and the Balkans. When Muhammad Ali's Egyptian army invaded Syria in 1833, Russia signed a treaty in support of the Ottomans. In return, the sultan recognized an extension of this claim to cover all of the empire's Orthodox subjects. This set the stage for an obscure dispute that resulted in war.

In 1852 the sultan bowed to British and French pressure and named France Protector of the Holy Sepulchre in Jerusalem, a position with certain ecclesiastical privileges. Russia protested, but the sultan held firm. So Russia invaded Ottoman territories in what is today Romania, and Britain and France went to war as allies of the sultan. The real causes of the war went beyond church quarrels in Jerusalem. Diplomatic maneuvering among European powers over whether the Ottoman Empire should continue to exist and, if not, who should take over its territory lasted until the empire finally disappeared after World War I. The Eastern Question was the simple name given to this complex issue. Though the

Street Scene in Cairo This engraving from Edward William Lane's influential travel book, *Account of the Manners and Customs of the Modern Egyptians Written in Egypt During the Years 1833–1835* conveys the image of narrow lanes and small stores that became stock features of European thinking about Middle Eastern cities. (From Edward William Lane, *The Manners and Customs of the Modern Egyptians,* (London: J. M. D & Co. 1860)

Interior of the Ottoman Financial Bureau This engraving from the eighteenth century depicts the governing style of the Ottoman Empire before the era of westernizing reforms. By the end of the Tanzimat period in 1876, government offices and the costumes of officials looked much more like those in contemporary European capitals. (From Ignatius Mouradgea d'Ohsson, *Tableau General de l'Empire Ottoman,* large folio edition, Paris, 1787–1820, pl. 178, following p. 340)

powers had agreed to save the empire from Ibrahim's invasion in 1839, Britain subsequently became very suspicious of Russian ambitions. A number of prominent British politicians were strongly anti-Russian. They feared that Russia would threaten the British hold on India either overland through Central Asia or by placing its navy in the Mediterranean Sea.

Between 1853 and 1856 the **Crimean° War** raged in Romania, on the Black Sea, and on the Crimean peninsula. Britain, France, and the Italian kingdom of Sardinia-Piedmont sided with the Ottomans, allowing Austria to mediate the final outcome. Britain and France trapped the Russian fleet in the Black Sea, where its commanders decided to sink the ships to protect the approaches to Sevastopol, their main base in Crimea. An army largely made up of British and French troops landed and laid siege to the city. A lack of railways and official corruption hampered Russian attempts to supply both its land and its sea forces. On the Romanian front, the Ottomans resisted effectively. At Sevastopol, the Russians were outmatched militarily and suffered badly from disease. Tsar Nicholas died as defeat became apparent, leaving his successor, Alexander II (r. 1855–1881), to sue for peace when Sevastopol finally fell three months later.

A formal alliance among Britain, France, and the Ottoman Empire blocked further Russian expansion into eastern Europe and the Middle East. The terms of peace also gave Britain and France a means of checking each other's colonial ambitions in the Middle East; neither, according to the agreement that ended the war, was entitled to take Ottoman territory for its exclusive use.

Crimean (cry-ME-uhn)

The Crimean War brought significant changes to all the combatants. The tsar and his government, already beset by demands for the reform of serfdom, education, and the military (discussed later), were further discredited. In Britain and France, the conflict was accompanied by massive propaganda campaigns. For the first time newspapers were an important force in mobilizing public support for a war. Press accounts of British participation in the war were often so glamorized that the false impression has lingered ever since that Ottoman troops played a negligible role in the conflict. At the time, however, British and French military commanders noted the massive losses among Turkish troops in particular. The French press, dominant in Istanbul, promoted a sense of unity between Turkish and French society that continued to influence many aspects of Turkish urban culture.

The larger significance of the Crimean War was that it marked the transition from traditional to modern warfare (see Environment and Technology: The Web of War). A high casualty count resulted in part from the clash of mechanized and unmechanized means of killing. All the combatant nations had previously prided themselves on the effective use of highly trained cavalry to smash through the front lines of infantry. Cavalry coexisted with firearms until the early 1800s, primarily because early rifles were awkward to load, vulnerable to explosion, and not very accurate. Swift and expert cavalry could storm infantry lines during the intervals between volleys and even penetrate artillery barrages. In the 1830s and 1840s percussion caps that did away with pouring gunpowder into the barrel of a musket were widely adopted in Europe. In Crimean War battles many cavalry units were destroyed by the rapid and relatively accurate fire of rifles that loaded at the breech rather than down the barrel. That was the fate of the British Light Brigade, which was sent to relieve an Ottoman unit surrounded by Russian troops. Ironically, in the charge of the Light Brigade, the heroic but obsolete horsemen were on the side with the most advanced weaponry. In the long run, despite the pathos of Alfred Lord Tennyson's famous poem, the new military technologies pioneered in the Crimean War, not its heroic events, made the conflict a turning point in the history of war.

After the Crimean War, declining state revenues and increasing integration with European commercial networks created hazardous economic conditions in the Ottoman Empire. The men of the Tanzimat dominated government affairs under Abdul Mejid's successors and continued to secularize Ottoman financial and commercial institutions, modeling them closely on European counterparts. The Ottoman imperial bank was founded in 1840, and a few years later currency reform pegged the value of Ottoman gold coins to the British pound. Sweeping changes in the 1850s expedited the creation of banks, insurance companies, and legal firms throughout the empire. These and other reforms facilitating trade contributed to a strong demographic shift in the Ottoman Empire between about 1850 and 1880, as many rural people headed to the cities. Within this period many of the major cities of the empire—Istanbul, Damascus, Beirut, Alexandria, Cairo—expanded. A small but influential urban professional class emerged, as did a considerable class of wage laborers. This shift was magnified by an influx into the northern Ottoman territories of refugees from Poland and Hungary, where rivalry between the European powers and the Russian Empire caused political tension and sporadic warfare, and from Georgia and other parts of the Caucasus, where Russian expansion forced many Muslims to emigrate (discussed later).

The Ottoman reforms stimulated commerce and urbanization, but no reform could repair the chronic insolvency of the imperial government. Declining revenues from agricultural yields and widespread corruption damaged Ottoman finances. Some of the corruption was exposed in the early 1840s. From the conclusion of the Crimean War in 1856 on, the Ottoman government became heavily dependent on foreign loans. In return the Ottoman government lowered tariffs to favor European imports, and European banks opened in Ottoman cities. Currency changes allowed more systematic conversion to European currencies. Europeans were allowed to live in their own enclaves in Istanbul and other commercial centers, subject to their own laws and exempt from Ottoman jurisdiction. This status was known as **extraterritoriality.**

As the cities prospered, they became attractive to laborers, and still more people moved from the countryside. But opportunities for wage workers reached a plateau in the bloated cities. Foreign trade brought in large numbers of imports, but—apart from tobacco and the Turkish opium that American traders took to China to compete against the Indian opium of the British—few exports were sent abroad from Anatolia. Together with the growing national debt, these factors aggravated inflationary trends that left urban populations in a precarious position in the mid-1800s. By contrast, Egyptian cotton exports soared during the American Civil War, when American cotton exports plummeted, but the profits benefited Muhammad Ali's descendants, who had become the hereditary governors of Egypt, rather than the Ottoman government. The Suez Canal, which

The Web of War

The lethal military technologies of the mid-nineteenth century that were used on battlefields in the United States, Russia, India, and China were rapidly transmitted from one conflict to the next. This dissemination was due not only to the rapid development of communications but also to the existence of a new international network of soldiers who moved from one trouble spot to another, bringing expertise in the use of new techniques.

General Charles Gordon (1833–1885), for instance, was commissioned in the British army in 1852, then served in the Crimean War after Britain entered on the side of the Ottomans. In 1860 he was dispatched to China. He served with British forces during the Arrow War and took part in the sack of Beijing. Afterward, he stayed in China and was seconded to the Qing imperial government until the suppression of the Taipings in 1864, earning himself the nickname "Chinese" Gordon. Gordon later served the Ottoman rulers of Egypt as governor of territory along the Nile. He was killed in Egypt in 1885 while leading his Egyptian troops in defense of the city of Khartoum against an uprising by the Sudanese religious leader, the Mahdi.

Journalism played an important part in the developing web of telegraph communications that sped orders to and from the battlefields. Readers in London could learn details of the drama occurring in the Crimea or in China within a week—or in some cases days—after they occurred. Print and, later, photographic journalism created new "stars" from these war experiences. Charles Gordon was one. Florence Nightingale was another.

In the great wars of the 1800s, the vast majority of deaths resulted from infection or excessive bleeding, not from the wounds themselves. Florence Nightingale (1820–1910), while still a young woman, became interested in hospital management and nursing. She went to Prussia and France to study advanced techniques. Before the outbreak of the Crimean War she was credited with bringing about marked improvement in British health care. When the public reacted to news reports of the suffering in the Crimea, the British government sent Nightingale to the region. Within a year of her arrival the death rate in the military hospitals there dropped from 45 percent to under 5 percent. Her techniques for preventing septicemia and dysentery and for promoting healing therapies were quickly adopted by those working for and with her. On her return to London, Nightingale established institutes for nursing that soon were recognized around the world as leaders. She herself was lionized by the British public and received the Order of Merit in 1907, three years before her death.

With Florence Nightingale in Crimea Readers could read about war dramas in telegraphed copy and see them in vivid illustrations. (The Granger Collection, New York)

The importance of Nightingale's innovations in public hygiene is underscored by the life of her contemporary, Mary Seacole (1805–1881). A Jamaican woman who volunteered to nurse British troops in the Crimean War, Seacole was repeatedly excluded from nursing service by British authorities. She eventually went to Crimea and used her own funds to run a hospital there, bankrupting herself in the process. The drama of the Crimean War moved the British public to support Seacole after her sacrifices were publicized. She was awarded medals by the British, French, and Turkish governments and today is recognized with her contemporary Florence Nightingale as an innovative field nurse and a champion of public hygiene in peacetime.

was partly financed by cotton profits, opened in 1869, and Cairo was redesigned and beautified. Eventually overexpenditure on such projects plunged Egypt into the same debt crisis that plagued the empire as a whole.

In the 1860s and 1870s reform groups demanded a constitution and entertained the possibility of a law permitting all men to vote. Spokesmen for the Muslim majority expressed dismay at the possibility that the Ottoman Empire would no longer be a Muslim society. Muslims were also suspicious of the motives of Christians, many of whom enjoyed close relations with European powers. Memories of attempts by Russia and France to interfere in Ottoman affairs for the benefit of Christians seemed to some to warrant hostility toward Christians in Ottoman territories.

The decline of Ottoman power and prosperity had a strong impact on a group of well-educated young urban men who aspired to wealth and influence. They believed that the empire's rulers and the Tanzimat officials who worked for them would be forced to—or would be willing to—allow the continued domination of the empire's political, economic, and cultural life by Europeans. Though lacking a sophisticated organization, these **Young Ottomans** (who are sometimes called Young Turks, though that term properly applies to a later movement) promoted a mixture of liberal ideas derived from Europe, national pride in Ottoman independence, and modernist views of Islam. Prominent Young Ottomans helped draft a constitution that was promulgated in 1876 by a new and as yet untried sultan, Abdul Hamid II. This apparent triumph of liberal reform was short-lived. With war against Russia again threatening in the Balkans in 1877, Abdul Hamid suspended the constitution and the parliament that had been elected that year. He ruthlessly opposed further political reforms, but the Tanzimat programs of extending modern schooling, utilizing European military practices and advisers, and making the government bureaucracy more orderly continued during his reign.

The Russian Empire

Awareness of western Europe among Russia's elite began with the reign of Peter the Great (r. 1689–1725), but knowledge of the French language, considered by Russians to be the language of European culture, spread only slowly among the aristocracy in the second half of the eighteenth century. In 1812, when Napoleon's march on Moscow ended in a disastrous retreat brought on more by what a later tsar called "Generals January and February" than by Russian military action, the European image of Russia changed. Just as Napoleon's withdrawal from Egypt paved the way for the brief emergence of Muhammad Ali's Egypt as a major power, so his withdrawal from Russia conferred status on another autocrat. Conservative Europeans still saw Russia as an alien, backward, and oppressive land, but they acknowledged its immensity and potential power and included Tsar Alexander I (r. 1801–1825) as a major partner in efforts to restore order and suppress revolutionary tendencies throughout Europe. Like Muhammad Ali, Alexander attempted reforms in the hope of strengthening his regime. Unlike Muhammad Ali, acceptance by the other European monarchs saved a rising Russia from being strangled in its cradle.

In several important respects Russia resembled the Ottoman Empire more than the conservative kingdoms of Europe whose autocratic practices it so staunchly supported. Socially dominated by nobles whose country estates were worked by unfree serfs, Russia had almost no middle class. Industry was still at the threshold of development by the standards of the rapidly industrializing European powers, though it was somewhat more dynamic than Ottoman industry. And the absolute power of the tsar was unchallenged. Like Egypt and the Ottoman Empire, Russia engaged in reforms from the top down under Alexander I, but when his conservative brother Nicholas I (r. 1825–1855) succeeded to the throne, iron discipline and suspicion of modern ideas took priority over reform.

Russia and Europe

In 1700 only 3 percent of the Russian people lived in cities, two-thirds of them in Moscow alone. By the middle of the nineteenth century the town population had grown tenfold, though it still accounted for only 6 percent of the population because the territories of the tsars had grown greatly through wars and colonization (see Chapter 21). Since mining and small-scale industry can be carried out in small communities, urbanization is only a general indicator of modern economic developments. These figures do demonstrate, however, that, like the Ottoman Empire, Russia was an overwhelmingly agricultural land. Moreover, Russian transportation was even worse than that of the Ottomans, since many of the latter's major cities were seaports. Both empires encompassed peoples speaking many different languages.

Well-engineered roads did not begin to appear until 1817, and steam navigation commenced on the Volga in 1843. Tsar Nicholas I built the first railroad in Russia

Raising of the Alexander Monument in St. Petersburg The death of Alexander I in 1825 brought to power his conservative brother Nicholas I. Yet Alexander remained a heroic figure for his resistance to Napoleon. This monument in Winter Palace Square was erected in 1829. (Novosti Photo Library)

from St. Petersburg, the capital, to his summer palace in 1837. A few years later his commitment to strict discipline led him to insist that the trunk line from St. Petersburg to Moscow run in a perfectly straight line. American engineers, among them the father of the painter James McNeill Whistler, who learned to paint in St. Petersburg, oversaw the laying of track and built locomotive workshops. This slow start in modern transportation compares better with that of Egypt, where work on the first railroad began in 1851, than with France, which saw railroad building soar during the 1840s. Industrialization projects depended heavily on foreign expertise. British engineers set up the textile mills that gave wool and cotton a prominent place among Russia's industries.

Until the late nineteenth century the Russian government's interest in industry was limited and hesitant. To be successful, an industrial revolution required large numbers of educated and independent-minded artisans and entrepreneurs. Suspicious of Western ideas, especially anything smacking of liberalism, socialism, or revolution, Nicholas feared the spread of literacy and modern education beyond the minimum needed to train the officer corps and the bureaucracy. Rather than run the risk of allowing the development of a middle class and a working class that might challenge his control, Nicholas I kept the peasants in serfdom and preferred to import most industrial goods and pay for them with exports of grain and timber.

Like Egypt and the Ottoman Empire, Russia aspired to Western-style economic development. But fear of political change caused the country to fall farther behind western Europe, economically and technologically, than it had been a half-century before. When France and Britain entered the Crimean War, they faced a Russian army equipped with obsolete weapons and bogged down by lack of transportation. At a time when European engineers were making major breakthroughs in fast loading of cannon through an opening at the breech end, muzzle-loading artillery remained the Russian standard.

Despite these deficiencies in technology and its institutional supports, in some ways Russia bore a closer resemblance to other European countries than the Ottoman Empire did. From the point of view of the French and the British, the Cyrillic alphabet and the Russian Orthodox form of Christianity seemed foreign, but they were not nearly as foreign as the Arabic alphabet and the Muslim faith of the Turks, Arabs, Persians, and Muslim Indians. Britain and France feared Russia as a rival for power in eastern Europe and the eastern Mediterranean lands, but they increasingly accepted Tsar Nicholas's view of the Ottoman Empire as "the sick man of Europe," capable of surviving only so long as the European powers found it a useful buffer state.

From the Russian point of view, kinship with western Europe was of questionable value. Westernizers, like the men of the Tanzimat in the Ottoman Empire, put their trust in technical advances and governmental reform. Opposing them were intellectuals known as **Slavophiles,** who in some respects resembled the Young Ottomans and considered the Orthodox faith, the solidity of peasant life, and the tsar's absolute rule to be the proper bases of Russian civilization. After Russia's humiliating defeat in the Crimea, the Slavophile tendency gave rise to **Pan-Slavism,** a militant political doctrine advocating unity of all the Slavic peoples, including those living under Austrian and Ottoman rule.

On the diplomatic front, the tsar's inclusion among the great powers of Europe contrasted sharply with the sultan's exclusion. However, this did not prevent the development of a powerful sense of Russophobia in the west. Britain in particular saw Russia as a geostrategic threat and despised the continuing subjection of the serfs, who were granted their freedom by Tsar Alexander II only in 1861, twenty-eight years after the British had abolished slavery. The passions generated by the Crimean War and its outcome affected the relations of Russia, Europe, and the Ottoman Empire for the remainder of the nineteenth century.

Russia and Asia

The Russian drive to the east in the eighteenth century brought the tsar's empire to the Pacific Ocean and the frontiers of China (see Map 21.1) by century's end. In the nineteenth century Russian expansionism continued with a drive to the south. The growing inferiority of the Russian military in comparison with the European powers did not affect these Asian battlefronts, since the peoples they faced were even less industrialized and technologically advanced than Russians. In 1860 Russia established a military outpost on the Pacific coast that would eventually grow into the great naval port of Vladivostok, today Russia's most southerly city. In Central Asia the steppe lands of the Kazakh nomads came under Russian control early in the century, setting the stage for a confrontation with three Uzbek states farther south. They succumbed to Russian pressure and military action one by one, beginning in 1865, giving rise to the new province of Turkestan, with its capital at Tashkent in present-day Uzbekistan. In the region of the Caucasus Mountains, the third area of southward expansion, Russia first took over Christian Georgia (1786), Muslim Azerbaijan° (1801), and Christian Armenia (1813) before embarking on the conquest of the many small principalities, each with its own language or languages, in the heart of the mountains. Between 1829 and 1864 Dagestan, Chechnya°, Abkhazia°, and other regions that were to gain political prominence only after the breakup of the Soviet Union at the end of the twentieth century became parts of the Russian Empire.

The drive to the south intensified political friction with Russia's new neighbors: Qing China and Japan in the east, Iran on the Central Asian and Caucasus frontiers, and the Ottoman Empire at the eastern end of the Black Sea. In the latter two instances, a flow of Muslim refugees from the territories newly absorbed by Russia increased anti-Russian feelings, but in some cases also brought talented people into Iran and the Ottoman lands. Armenian, Azerbaijani, and Bukharan exiles who had been exposed to Russian administration and education brought new ideas to Iran in the later decades of the century, and a massive migration of Crimean Turks and Circassians from Russia's Caucasian territories affected the demography of the Ottoman Empire, which resettled some of the immigrants as far away as Syria and Jordan and others as buffer populations on the Russian frontiers.

In a broader political perspective, the Russian drive to the south added a new element to the Eastern Question. Many British statesmen and strategists reckoned that a warlike Russia would press on until it had conquered all the lands separating it from British India, a prospect that made them shudder, given India's enormous contribution to Britain's prosperity. The competition that ensued over which power would control southern Central Asia resulted in a standoff in Afghanistan, which became a buffer zone under the control of neither, and direct competition in Iran, where both powers sought to gain an economic and political advantage while preserving the independence of the Qajar dynasty of shahs.

Azerbaijan (ah-zer-by-JAHN) **Chechnya** (CHECH-nee-yah)
Abkhazia (ab-KAH-zee-yah)

Cultural Trends

Unlike Egypt and the Ottoman Empire, which began to send students to Europe for training only in the nineteenth century, Russia had been in cultural contact with western Europe since the time of Peter the Great (r. 1689–1725). Members of the Russian court knew western languages, and the tsars employed officials and advisers from western countries. Peter had also enlisted the well-educated Ukrainian clerics who headed the Russian Orthodox Church to help spread a western spirit of education. As a result, Alexander I's reforms met a more positive reception than those of Muhammad Ali and Mahmud II.

While Muhammad Ali put his efforts into building a modern army and an economic system to support it, the reforms of Sultan Mahmud II and Alexander promised more on paper than they brought about in practice. Both monarchs hoped to create better organized and more efficient government bureaus, but it took many years to develop a sufficient pool of trained bureaucrats to make the reforms effective. Alexander's Council of State worked better than the new ministerial system he devised. The council coordinated ministry affairs and deliberated over new legislation. As for the ministries, Alexander learned a lesson from Napoleon's military organization. He made each minister theoretically responsible for a strict hierarchy of officers below him, and ordered them to report directly to him as commander-in-chief. But this system remained largely ineffective, as did the provincial advisory councils that were designed to extend the new governing ideas into outlying areas.

Ironically, much of the opposition to these reforms came from well-established families that were not at all unfriendly to western ideas. Their fear was that the new government bureaucrats, who often came from humbler social origins, would act as agents of imperial despotism. This fear was realized during the conservative reign of Nicholas I in the same way that the Tanzimat-inspired bureaucracy of the Ottoman Empire served the despotic purposes of Sultan Abdul al-Hamid II after 1877. In both cases, historians have noted that administrative reforms made by earlier rulers began to take hold under conservative despots, though more because of accumulating momentum and training than because of those rulers' policies.

Individuals favoring more liberal reforms, including military officers who had served in western Europe, intellectuals who read western political tracts, and members of Masonic lodges who exchanged views with Freemasons in the west, formed secret societies of opposition. Some placed their highest priority on freeing the serfs; others advocated a constitution and a republican form of government. When Alexander I died in December 1825, confusion over who was to succeed him encouraged a group of reform-minded army officers to try to take over the government and provoke an uprising. The so-called **Decembrist revolt** failed, and many of the participants were severely punished. These events ensured that the new tsar, Nicholas I, would pay little heed to calls for reform over the next thirty years.

Though the great powers meeting in Paris to settle the Crimean War in 1856 compelled the Ottoman sultan to issue new reform decrees improving the status of non-Muslim subjects, Russia faced a heavier penalty, being forced to return land to the Ottomans in both Europe and Asia. This humiliation contributed to the determination of Nicholas's son and successor, Alexander II, to institute major new reforms to reinvigorate the country. The greatest of his reforms was the emancipation of the serfs in 1861 and the conferral on them of property rights to prevent them from simply becoming hired laborers of big landowners (see Chapter 27). He also authorized new joint stock companies, projected a railroad network to tie the country together, and modernized the legal and administrative arms of government.

Intellectual and cultural trends that began to germinate under Alexander I, and continued to grow under Nicholas, flourished under Alexander II. More and more people became involved in intellectual, artistic, and professional life. Under Alexander I education expanded both at the preparatory and university levels, though Alexander imposed curbs on liberal thought in his later years. Most prominent intellectuals received some amount of instruction at Moscow University, and some attended German universities. Universities also appeared in provincial cities like Kharkov and Kazan. Student clubs, along with Masonic lodges, became places for discussing new ideas.

Nicholas continued his brother's crackdown on liberal education in the universities, but he encouraged professional and scientific training. By the end of his reign Russian scholars and scientists were achieving recognition for their contributions to European thought. Scholarly careers attracted many young men from clerical families, and this helped stimulate reforms in religious education. Perhaps because political activism was prohibited, clubs, salons, and organizations promoting scientific and scholarly activities became more and more numerous. The ideas of Alexander Herzen (1812–1870), a Russian intellectual working abroad who praised traditional peasant assemblies as the heart of Russia, encouraged socialist and Slavophile thinking and gave rise, under Alexander II, to the *narodniki*, a political movement dedicated to making Russia a land of peasant communes. Feodor Dostoyevsky° (1821–1881) and Count Leo Tolstoy (1828–1910), both of whom began to publish their major novels during the reign of Alexander II, aired these and other reforming ideas in the debates of the characters they created.

Just as the Tanzimat reforms of the Ottoman Empire preceded the emergence of the Young Ottomans as a new and assertive political and intellectual force in the second half of the nineteenth century, so the initially ineffective bureaucratic reforms of Alexander I set in motion cultural currents that would make Russia a dynamic center of intellectual, artistic, and political life under his nephew Alexander II. Thus Russia belonged to two different spheres of development. It entered the nineteenth century as a recognized political force in European politics, but in other ways it had a greater resemblance to the Ottoman Empire. Rulers in both empires instituted reforms, overcame opposition, and increased the power of their governments. These activities also stimulated intellectual and political trends that would ultimately work against the absolute rule of tsar and sultan. Yet Russia would eventually develop much closer relations with western Europe and become an arena for every sort of European intellectual, artistic, and political tendency, while the Ottoman Empire would ultimately succumb to European imperialism.

THE QING EMPIRE

In 1800 the Qing Empire faced many of the crises the Ottomans had encountered, but no early reform movement of the kind initiated by Sultan Selim III emerged in China. The reasons are not difficult to understand. The Qing Empire, created by the Manchus, had skillfully countered Russian strategic and diplomatic moves in the 1600s. Instead of a Napoleon threatening them with invasion, the Qing rulers enjoyed the admiration of Jesuit priests who likened them to enlightened philosopher-kings. In 1793, however, a British attempt to establish diplomatic and trade relations—the Macartney mission—turned European opinion against China (see Chapter 21).

For their part, the Qing rulers and bureaucrats faced serious crises of a depressingly familiar sort: rebellions by displaced indigenous peoples and the poor, and protests against the injustice of the local magistrates. They dealt with these problems in the usual way, by suppressing rebels and dismissing incompetent or untrustworthy officials, and paid little attention to contacts with far-off Europeans. Complaints from European merchants at Canton, who chafed against the restrictions of the "Canton system" by which the Qing limited and controlled foreign trade, were brushed off.

Economic and Social Disorder, 1800–1839

Early Qing successes and territorial expansion sowed the seeds of the domestic and political chaos of the later period. The Qing conquest in the 1600s brought stability to central China after decades of rebellion and agricultural shortages. The new emperors encouraged the recovery of farmland, the opening of previously uncultivated areas, and the restoration and expansion of the road and canal systems. The result was a great expansion of the agricultural base together with a doubling of the population between about 1650 and 1800. Enormous numbers of farmers, merchants, and day laborers migrated in search of less crowded conditions, and a permanent floating population of the unemployed and homeless emerged. By 1800 population strain on the land had caused serious environmental damage in some parts of central and western China.

While farmers tried to cope with agricultural deterioration, other groups vented grievances against the government: Minority peoples in central and southwestern China complained about being driven off their lands during the boom of the 1700s; Mongols resented appropriation of their grazing lands and the displacement of their traditional elites. In some regions, village vigilante organizations took over policing and governing functions from Qing officials who had lost control. Growing numbers of people mistrusted the government, suspecting that all officials were corrupt. The growing presence of foreign merchants and missionaries in Canton and in the Portuguese colony of Macao aggravated discontent in neighboring districts.

In some parts of China the Qing were hated as foreign conquerors and were suspected of sympathy with the Europeans. Indeed, the White Lotus Rebellion (1794–1804)—partly inspired by a messianic ideology that predicted the restoration of the Chinese Ming dynasty and the coming of the Buddha—raged across central China and was not suppressed until 1804. It initiated a series of internal conflicts that continued through the

Feodor Dostoyevsky (FE-oh-dor doh-stoh-YEHV-skee)

1800s. Ignited by deepening social instabilities, these movements were sometimes intensified by local ethnic conflicts and by unapproved religions. The ability of some village militias to defend themselves and attack others intensified the conflicts, though the same techniques proved useful to southern coastal populations attempting to fend off British invasion.

The Opium War and Its Aftermath, 1839–1850

Unlike the Ottomans, the Qing believed that the Europeans were remote and only casually interested in trade. They knew little of the enormous fortunes being made in the early 1800s by European and American merchants smuggling opium into China. They did not know that silver gained in this illegal trade was helping finance the industrial transformation of England and the United States. But Qing officials slowly became aware of British colonies in India that grew and exported opium, and of the major naval base at Singapore through which British opium reached East Asia.

For more than a century, British officials had been frustrated by the trade deficit caused by the British demand for tea and the Qing refusal to facilitate the importation of any British product. In the early 1700s a few European merchants and their Chinese partners were importing small quantities of opium. In 1729 the first Qing law banning opium imports was promulgated. By 1800, however, opium smuggling had swelled the annual import level to as many as four thousand chests. British merchants had pioneered this extremely profitable trade; Chinese merchants likewise profited from distributing the drugs. A price war in the early 1820s stemming from competition between British and American importers raised demand so sharply that as many as thirty thousand chests were being imported by the 1830s. Addiction spread to people at all levels of Qing society, including very high-ranking officials. The Qing emperor and his officials debated whether to legalize and tax opium or to enforce the existing ban more strictly. Having decided to root out the use and importation of opium, in 1839 they sent a high official to Canton to deal with the matter.

Britain considered the ban on opium importation an intolerable limitation on trade, a direct threat to Britain's economic health, and a cause for war. British naval and marine forces arrived at the south China coast in late 1839. The power of modern naval forces dawned on the Qing slowly. Indeed, Qing strategists did not learn to distinguish a naval invasion from piracy until the Opium War was nearly ended.

The **Opium War** (1839–1842) broke out when negotiations between the Qing official and British representatives reached a stalemate. The war exposed the fact that the traditional, hereditary soldiers of the Qing Empire—the **Bannermen**—were, like the Janissaries of the Ottoman Empire, hopelessly obsolete. As in the Crimean War, the British excelled at sea, where they deployed superior technology. British ships landed marines who pillaged coastal cities and then sailed to new destinations (see Map 26.2). The Qing had no imperial navy, and until they were able to engage the British in prolonged fighting on land, they were unable to defend themselves against British attacks. Even in the land engagements, Qing resources proved woefully inadequate. The British could quickly transport their forces by sea along the coast; Qing troops moved primarily on foot. Moving Qing reinforcements from central to eastern China took more than three months, and when the defense forces arrived, they were exhausted and basically without weapons.

The Bannermen used the few muskets the Qing had imported during the 1700s. The weapons were matchlocks, which required the soldiers to ignite the load of gunpowder in them by hand. Firing the weapons was dangerous, and the canisters of gunpowder that each musketeer carried on his belt were likely to explode if a fire broke out nearby—a frequent occurrence in encounters with British artillery. Most of the Bannermen, however, had no guns and fought with swords, knives, spears, and clubs. Soldiers under British command—many of them were Indians—carried percussion-cap rifles, which were far quicker, safer, and more accurate than the matchlocks. In addition, the long-range British artillery could be moved from place to place and proved deadly in the cities and villages of eastern China.

Qing commanders thought that British gunboats rode so low in the water that they could not sail up the Chinese rivers. Hence, evacuating the coasts, they believed, would protect the country from the British threat. But the British deployed new gunboats for shallow waters and moved without difficulty up the Yangzi River.

When the invaders approached Nanjing, the former Ming capital, the Qing decided to negotiate. In 1842 the terms of the **Treaty of Nanking** (the British name for Nanjing) dismantled the old Canton system. The number of **treaty ports**—cities opened to foreign residents—increased from one (Canton) to five (Canton, Xiamen, Fuzhou, Ningbo, and Shanghai°), and the island of Hong

Shanghai (shahng-hie)

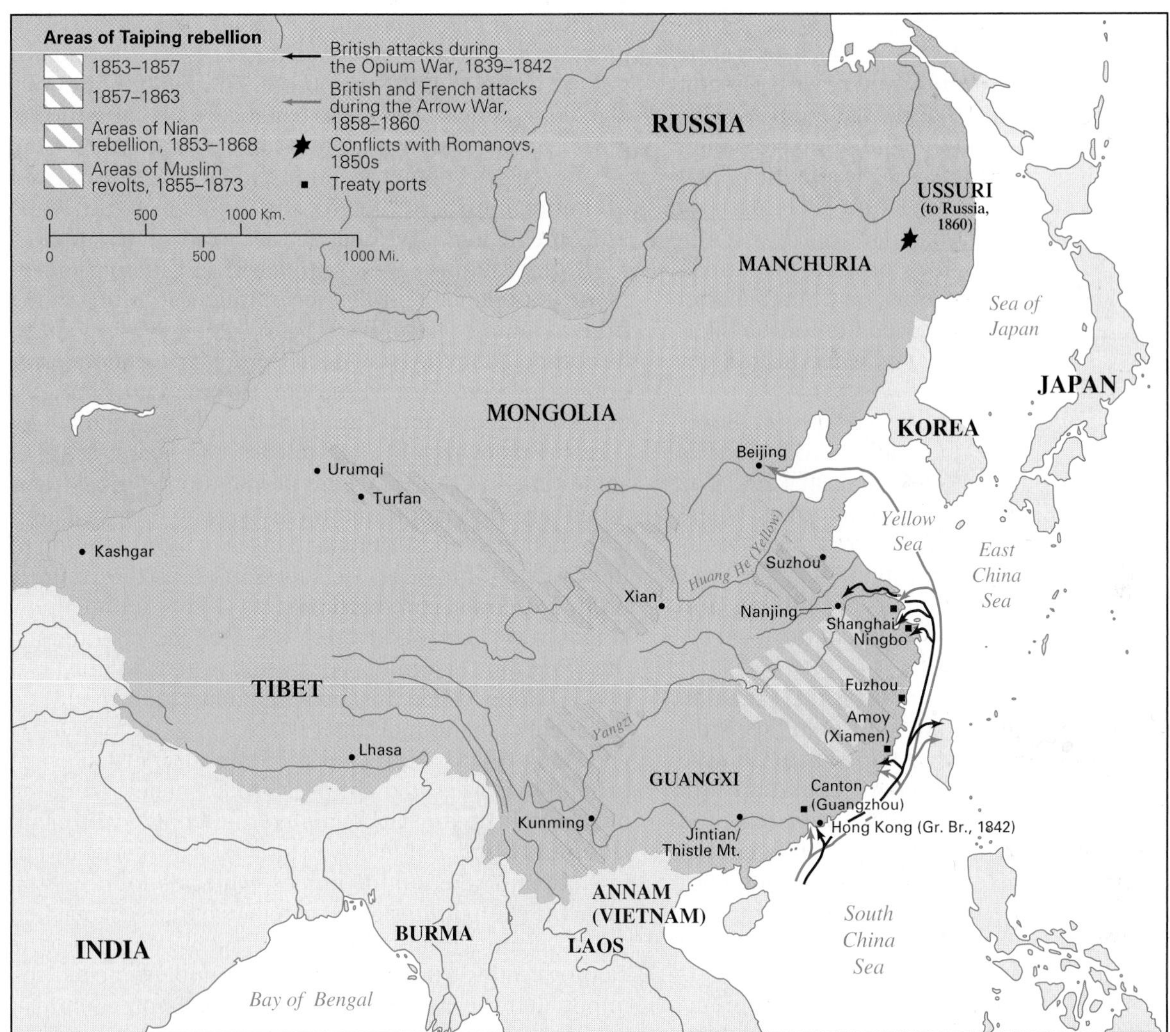

Map 26.2 Conflicts in the Qing Empire, 1839–1870 In both the Opium War of 1839–1842 and the Arrow War of 1856–1860, the seacoasts saw most of the action. Since the Qing had no imperial navy, the well-armed British ships encountered little resistance as they shelled the southern coasts. In inland conflicts, such as the Taiping Rebellion, the opposing armies were massive and slow moving. Battles on land were often prolonged attempts by one side to starve out the other side before making a major assault.

Kong became a permanent British colony. British residents in China gained extraterritorial rights. The Qing government agreed to set a low tariff of 5 percent on imports and to pay Britain an indemnity of 21 million ounces of silver as a penalty for having started the war. A supplementary treaty the following year guaranteed **most-favored-nation status** to Britain; any privileges that China granted to another country would be automatically extended to Britain as well. This provision effectively prevented the colonization of China, because giving land to one country would have necessitated giving it to all.

With each round of treaties came a new round of privileges for foreigners. In 1860 a new treaty legalized their right to import opium. Later, French treaties established the rights of foreign missionaries to travel extensively in the Chinese countryside and preach their religion. The number of treaty ports grew, too; by 1900 they numbered more than ninety.

The treaty system and the principle of extraterritoriality resulted in the colonization of small pockets of Qing territory, where foreign merchants lived at ease. Greater territorial losses resulted when outlying regions gained independence or were ceded to neighboring countries. Districts north and south of the Amur River in the northeast fell to Russia by treaty in 1858 and 1860; parts of modern Kazakhstan and Kirgizstan in the northwest met the same fate in 1864. From 1865 onward the British gradually gained control of territories on China's Indian frontier. In the late 1800s France forced the court of Vietnam to end its vassalage to the Qing, while Britain encouraged Tibetan independence.

In Canton, Shanghai, and other coastal cities, Europeans and Americans maintained offices and factories that employed local Chinese as menial laborers. The foreigners built comfortable housing in zones where Chinese were not permitted to live, and they entertained themselves in exclusive restaurants and bars. Around the foreign establishments, gambling and prostitution offered employment to part of the local urban population.

Whether in town or in the countryside, Christian missionaries whose congregations sponsored hospitals, shelters, and soup kitchens or gave stipends to Chinese who attended church enjoyed a good reputation. But just as often the missionaries themselves were regarded as another evil. They seemed to subvert Confucian beliefs by condemning ancestor worship, pressuring poor families to put their children into orphanages, or fulminating against foot-binding. The growing numbers of foreigners, and their growing privileges, became targets of resentment for a deeply dissatisfied, daily more impoverished, and increasingly militarized society.

The Taiping Rebellion, 1850–1864

The inflammatory mixture of social unhappiness and foreign intrusion exploded in the great civil war usually called the **Taiping° Rebellion.** In Guangxi, where the Taiping movement originated, entrenched social problems had been generating disorders for half a century. Agriculture in the region was unstable, and many people made their living from arduous and despised trades such as disposing of human waste, making charcoal, and mining. Ethnic divisions complicated economic distress. The lowliest trades frequently involved a minority group, the Hakkas, and tensions between them and the majority were rising. Problems may have been intensified by the sharp rises and falls in the trade of opium, which flooded the coastal and riverine portions of China after 1842, then collapsed as domestically grown opium began to dominate the market. Also, the area was close enough to Canton to feel the cultural and economic impact of the growing number of Europeans and Americans.

Hong Xiuquan°, the founder of the Taiping movement, experienced all of these influences. Hong came from a humble Hakka background. After years of study, he competed in the provincial Confucian examinations, hoping for a post in government. He failed the examinations repeatedly, and it appears that he suffered a nervous breakdown in his late thirties. Afterward he spent some time in Canton, where he met both Chinese and American Protestant missionaries, who inspired him with their teachings. Hong had his own interpretation of the Christian message. He saw himself as the younger brother of Jesus, commissioned by God to found a new kingdom on Earth and drive the Manchu conquerors, the Qing, out of China. The result would be universal peace. Hong called his new religious movement the "Heavenly Kingdom of Great Peace."

Hong quickly attracted a community of believers, primarily Hakkas like himself. They believed in the prophecy of dreams and claimed they could walk on air. Hong and his rivals for leadership in the movement went in and out of ecstatic trances. They denounced the Manchus as creatures of Satan. News of the sect reached the government, and Qing troops arrived to arrest the Taiping leaders. But the Taipings soundly repelled the imperial troops. Local loyalty to the Taipings spread quickly; their numbers multiplied; and they began to enlarge their domain.

The Taipings relied at first on Hakka sympathy and the charismatic appeal of their religious doctrine to attract followers. But as their numbers and power grew, they altered their methods of preaching and governing. They replaced the anti-Chinese appeals used to enlist Hakkas with anti-Manchu rhetoric designed to enlist Chinese. They forced captured villages to join their movement. Once people were absorbed, the Taipings strictly monitored their activities. They segregated men and women and organized them into work and military teams. Women were forbidden to bind their feet (the Hakkas had never practiced foot-binding) and participated fully in farming and labor. Brigades of women soldiers took to the field against Qing forces.

Taiping (tie-PING)

Hong Xiuquan (hoong shee-OH-chew-an)

As the movement grew, it began to move toward eastern and northern China (see Map 26.2). Panic preceded the Taipings. Villagers feared being forced into Taiping units, and Confucian elites recoiled in horror from the bizarre ideology of foreign gods, totalitarian rule, and walking, working, warring women. But the huge numbers the Taipings were able to muster overwhelmed attempts at local defense. The tremendous growth in the number of Taiping followers required the movement to establish a permanent base. When the rebel army conquered Nanjing in 1853, the Taiping leaders decided to settle there and make it the capital of the new "Heavenly Kingdom of Great Peace."

Qing forces attempting to defend north China became more successful as problems of organization and growing numbers slowed Taiping momentum. Increasing Qing military success resulted mainly from the flexibility of the imperial military commanders in the face of an unprecedented challenge. In addition, the military commanders received strong backing from a group of civilian provincial governors who had studied the techniques developed by local militia forces for self-defense. Certain provincial governors combined their knowledge of civilian self-defense and local terrain with more efficient organization and the use of modern weaponry. The result was the formation of new military units, in which many of the Bannermen voluntarily served under civilian governors. The Qing court agreed to special taxes to fund the new armies and acknowledged the new combined leadership of the civilian and professional force.

When the Taipings settled into Nanjing, the new Qing armies surrounded the city, hoping to starve out the rebels. The Taipings, however, had provisioned and fortified themselves well. They also had the services of several brilliant young military commanders, who mobilized enormous campaigns in nearby parts of eastern China, scavenging supplies and attempting to break the encirclement of Nanjing. For more than a decade the Taiping leadership remained ensconced at Nanjing, and the "Heavenly Kingdom" endured.

In 1856 Britain and France, freed from their preoccupation with the Crimean War, turned their attention to China. European and American missionaries had visited Nanjing, curious to see what their fellow Christians were up to. Their reports were discouraging. Hong Xiuquan and the other leaders appeared to lead lives of indulgence and abandon, and more than one missionary accused them of homosexual practices. Relieved of the possible accusation of quashing a pious Christian movement, the British and French surveyed the situation. Though the Taipings were not going to topple the Qing, rebellious Nian ("Bands") in northern China added a new threat in the 1850s. A series of simultaneous large insurrections might indeed destroy the empire. Moreover, since the Qing had not observed all the provisions of the treaties signed after the Opium War, Britain and France were now considering renewing war on the Qing themselves.

In 1856 the British and French launched a series of swift, brutal coastal attacks—a second opium war, called the Arrow War (1856–1860)—which culminated in a British and French invasion of Beijing and the sacking of the Summer Palace in 1860. A new round of treaties punished the Qing for not enacting all the provisions of the Treaty of Nanking. Having secured their principal objective, the British and French forces joined the Qing campaign against the Taipings. Attempts to coordinate the international forces were sometimes riotous and sometimes tragic, but the injection of European weaponry and money helped quell both the Taiping and the Nian rebellions during the 1860s.

The Taiping Rebellion ranks as the world's bloodiest civil war and the greatest armed conflict before the twentieth century. Estimates of deaths range from 20 million to 30 million. The loss of life came primarily from starvation and disease, for most engagements consisted of surrounding fortified cities and waiting until the enemy forces died, surrendered, or were so weakened that they could be easily defeated. Many sieges continued for months, and after starving for a year under the occupation of the rebels, people within some cities had to starve for another year under the occupation of the imperial forces. Reports of people eating grass, leather, hemp, and human flesh were widespread. The dead were rarely buried properly, and epidemic disease was common.

The area of early Taiping fighting was close to the regions of southwest China in which bubonic plague had been lingering for centuries. When the rebellion was suppressed, many Taiping followers sought safety in the highlands of Laos and Vietnam, which soon showed infestation by plague. Within a few years the disease reached Hong Kong. From there it spread to Singapore, San Francisco, Calcutta, and London. In the late 1800s there was intense apprehension over the possibility of a worldwide outbreak, and Chinese immigrants were regarded as likely carriers. This fear became a contributing factor in the passage of discriminatory immigration bans on Chinese in the United States in 1882.

The Taiping Rebellion devastated the agricultural centers of China. Many of the most intensely cultivated regions of central and eastern China were depopulated and laid barren. Some were still uninhabited decades

Nanjing Encircled For a decade the Taipings held the city of Nanjing as their capital. For years Qing and international troops attempted to break the Taiping hold. By the summer of 1864, Qing forces had built tunnels leading to the foundations of Nanjing's city walls and had planted explosives. The detonation of the explosives signaled the final Qing assault on the rebel capital. As shown here, the common people of the city, along with their starving livestock, were caught in the cross-fire. Many of the Taiping leaders escaped the debacle at Nanjing, but nearly all were hunted down and executed. (Roger-Viollet/Getty Images)

later, and major portions of the country did not recover until the twentieth century.

Cities, too, were hard hit. Shanghai, a treaty port of modest size before the rebellion, saw its population multiplied many times by the arrival of refugees from war-blasted neighboring provinces. The city then endured months of siege by the Taipings. Major cultural centers in eastern China lost masterpieces of art and architecture; imperial libraries were burned or their collections exposed to the weather; and the printing blocks used to make books were destroyed. While the empire faced the mountainous challenge of dealing with the material and cultural destruction of the war, it also was burdened by a major ecological disaster in the north. The Yellow River changed course in 1855, destroying the southern part of impoverished Shandong province with flood and initiating decades of drought along the former riverbed in northern Shandong.

Decentralization at the End of the Qing Empire, 1864–1875

The Qing government emerged from the 1850s with no hope of achieving solvency. The corruption of the 1700s, attempts in the very early 1800s to restore waterworks and roads, and de-

We Have Got the Maxim Gun These two representatives of the Qing Empire visited northern England after the Taiping Rebellion to examine and, if possible, purchase new weapons. They posed for a photograph after watching the famous Maxim gun, one of the first machine guns, shoot a tree in half. (Peter Newark's Military Pictures)

clining yields from land taxes had bankrupted the treasury. By 1850, before the Taiping Rebellion, Qing government expenditures were ten times revenues. The indemnities demanded by Europeans after the Opium and Arrow Wars foreclosed any hope that the Qing would get out of debt. Vast stretches of formerly productive rice land were devastated, and the population was dispersed. Refugees pleaded for relief, and the imperial, volunteer, foreign, and mercenary troops that had suppressed the Taipings demanded unpaid wages.

Britain and France became active participants in the period of recovery that followed the rebellion. To insure repayment of the debt to Britain, Robert Hart was installed as inspector-general of a newly created Imperial Maritime Customs Service. Britain and the Qing split the revenues he collected. Britons and Americans worked for the Qing government as advisers and ambassadors, attempting to smooth communications between the Qing, Europe, and the United States.

The real work of the recovery, however, was managed by provincial governors who had come to the forefront in the struggle against the Taipings. To prosecute the war, they had won the right to levy their own taxes, raise their own troops, and run their own bureaucracies. These special powers were not entirely canceled when the war ended. Chief among these governors was Zeng Guofan°, who oversaw programs to restore agriculture, communications, education, and publishing, as well as

Zeng Guofan (zung gwoh-FAN)

Cixi's Allies In the 1860s and 1870s, Cixi was a supporter of reform. In later years she was widely regarded as corrupt and self-centered and as an obstacle to reform. Her greatest allies were the court eunuchs. Introduced to palace life in early China as managers of the imperial harems, eunuchs became powerful political parties at court. The first Qing emperors refused to allow the eunuchs any political influence, but by Cixi's time the eunuchs once again were a political factor. (Freer Gallery, Smithsonian Institution)

efforts to reform the military and industrialize armaments manufacture.

Like many provincial governors, Zeng preferred to look to the United States rather than to Britain for models and aid. He hired American advisers to run his weapons factories, shipyards, and military academies. He sponsored a daring program in which promising Chinese boys were sent to Hartford, Connecticut, a center of missionary activity, to learn English, science, mathematics, engineering, and history. They returned to China to assume some of the positions previously held by foreign advisers. Though Zeng was never an advocate of participation in public life by women, his Confucian convictions taught him that educated mothers were more than ever a necessity. He not only encouraged but partly oversaw the advanced classical education of his own daughters. Zeng's death in 1872 deprived the empire of a major force for reform.

The period of recovery marked a fundamental structural change in the Qing Empire. Although the emperors after 1850 were ineffective rulers, a coalition of aristocrats supported the reform and recovery programs. Without their legitimization of the new powers of provincial governors like Zeng Guofan, the empire might have evaporated within a generation. A crucial member of this alliance was Cixi°, who was known as the "Empress Dowager" after the 1880s. Later observers, both Chinese and foreign, reviled her as a monster of corrup-

Cixi (tsuh-shee)

tion and arrogance. But in the 1860s and 1870s Cixi supported the provincial governors, some of whom became so powerful that they were managing Qing foreign policy as well as domestic affairs.

No longer a conquest regime dominated by a Manchu military caste and its Chinese civilian appointees, the empire came under the control of a group of reformist aristocrats and military men, independently powerful civilian governors, and a small number of foreign advisers. The Qing lacked strong, central, unified leadership and could not recover their powers of taxation, legislation, and military command once they had been granted to the provincial governors. From the 1860s forward, the Qing Empire disintegrated into a number of large power zones in which provincial governors handed over leadership to their protégés in a pattern that the Qing court eventually could only ritually legitimate.

Conclusion

Most of the subjects of the Ottoman, Russian, and Qing rulers did not think of European pressure or competition as determining factors in their lives during the first half of the nineteenth century. They continued to live according to the social and economic institutions they inherited from previous generations. By the 1870s, however, the challenge of Europe had become widely realized. The Crimean War, where European allies achieved a hollow victory for the Ottomans and then pressured the sultan for more reforms, confirmed both Ottoman and Russian military weakness. The Opium War did the same for China. Though all three empires faced similar problems of reform and military rebuilding, Russia enjoyed a comparative advantage in being less appealing to rapacious European merchants and strategists concerned with protecting overseas empires.

The policies adopted by the three imperial governments responded both to traditional concerns and to European demands. The sultans gave first priority to strengthening the central government to prevent territorial losses that began when Serbia, Egypt, and Greece became fully or partially independent. The Qing emperors confronted population growth and agricultural decline that resulted in massive rebellions. The tsars focused on continued territorial expansion. However, each faced different European pressures. In China, the Europeans and Americans wanted trade rights. In the Ottoman Empire, Britain, France, and Russia wanted equality for Christians and freedom from naval and commercial competition in the eastern Mediterranean. In Russia, moral demands for the abolition of serfdom accompanied British determination to stop territorial advances in Asia that might threaten India.

Repeated crises in all three empires would eventually result in the fall of the Qing, Romanov, and Ottoman dynasties in the first two decades of the twentieth century, but in 1870 it was still unclear whether the traditional land empires of Asia would be capable of weathering the storm. One thing that had become clear, however, at least to European eyes, was that Russia was part of Europe, while the other two empires were fundamentally alien. This judgment was based partly on religion, partly on the enthusiasm of westernizing Russian artists and intellectuals for European cultural trends, and partly on the role Russia had played in defeating Napoleon at the beginning of the century, a role that brought the tsars into the highest councils of royal decision making in Europe.

Key Terms

Muhammad Ali
Janissaries
Serbia
Tanzimat
Crimean War
extraterritoriality
Young Ottomans
Slavophile
Pan-Slavism
Decembrist revolt
Opium War
Bannermen
Treaty of Nanking
treaty ports
most-favored-nation status
Taiping Rebellion

Suggested Reading

For widely available general histories of the Ottoman Empire see Stanford Shaw, *History of the Ottoman Empire and Modern Turkey* (1976–1977), and J. P. D. B. Kinross, *The Ottoman Centuries: The Rise and Fall of the Turkish Empire* (1977).

On the economy and society of the nineteenth-century Ottoman Empire see Huri Islamoglu-Inan, ed., *The Ottoman Empire and the World-Economy* (1987); Resat Kasaba, *The Ottoman Empire and the World Economy: The Nineteenth Century* (1988); Sevket Pamuk, *The Ottoman Empire and European Capitalism, 1820–1913: Trade, Investment, and Production* (1987); Kemal H. Karpat, *Ottoman Population, 1830–1914: Demographic and Social Characteristics* (1985); and Carter V. Findley, *Bureaucratic Reform in the Ottoman Empire: The Sublime Porte, 1789–1922*

(1980). On the reform program and the emergence of national concepts see also Selim Deringil, *The Well-Protected Domains: Ideology and the Legitimation of Power in the Ottoman Empire, 1876–1909* (1998).

Marc Raeff, *Understanding Imperial Russia* (1984), sets nineteenth-century Russian developments in a broad context and challenges many standard ideas. Andreas Kappeler, *The Russian Multi-Ethnic Empire* (2001), and Mark Bassin, *Imperial Visions: Nationalist Imagination and Geographical Expansion in the Russian Far East, 1840–1865* (1999), address Russian expansion and the problems inherent in diversity of population. On economic matters see W. L. Blackwell, *The Beginnings of Russian Industrialization, 1800–1860* (1968). Daniel Field, *The End of Serfdom: Nobility and Bureaucracy in Russia, 1855–1861* (1976), addresses the primary problem besetting Russian society during this period. On the intellectual debates see M. Malia, *Alexander Herzen and the Birth of Russian Socialism* (1961), and Andrzej Walicki, *The Slavophile Controversy* (1975).

On the Qing Empire of the nineteenth century see Pamela Kyle Crossley, *Orphan Warriors: Three Manchu Generations and the End of the Qing World* (1990), and for a more detailed political history see Mary C. Wright, *The Last Stand of Chinese Conservatism: The T'ung-chih Restoration, 1862–1874* (1971). There is a very large literature on both the Opium War and the Taiping Rebellion, including reprinted editions of contemporary observers. For general histories of the Opium War see Peter Ward Fay, *The Opium War, 1840–1842: Barbarians in the Celestial Empire in the Early Part of the Nineteenth Century and the War by Which They Forced Her Gates Ajar* (1975); Christopher Hibbert, *The Dragon Wakes: China and the West, 1793–1911* (1970); and the classic study by Chang Hsin-pao, *Commissioner Lin and the Opium War* (1964). For a recent, more monographic study on Qing political thought in the period of the Opium War see James M. Polachek, *The Inner Opium War* (1992). On the Taiping Rebellion, enduring sources are S. Y. Têng, *The Taiping Rebellion and the Western Powers: A Comprehensive Survey* (1971), and C. A. Curwen, *Taiping Rebel: The Deposition of Li Hsiu-ch'eng* (1976); see also Caleb Carr, *The Devil Soldier: The Story of Frederick Townsend Ward* (1992). The most recent study is Jonathan D. Spence, *God's Chinese Son: The Taiping Heavenly Kingdom of Hong Xiuquan* (1996).

State Power, the Census, and the Question of Identity

Between the American Revolution and the last decades of the nineteenth century, Europe and the Americas were transformed. The ancient power of kings and the authority of religion were eclipsed by muscular new ways of organizing political, economic, and intellectual life. The Western world was vastly different in 1870 than it had been a century earlier. One of the less heralded but enduringly significant changes was the huge expansion of government statistical services.

The rise of the nation-state was associated with the development of modern bureaucratic departments that depended on reliable statistics to measure the nation's achievements and discover its failures. The nation-state, whether democratic or not, mobilized resources on a previously unimaginable scale. Modern states were more powerful and wealthier, and they were also more ambitious and more intrusive. The growth of their power can be seen in the modernization of militaries, the commitment to internal improvements such as railroads, and the growth in state revenues. In recent years historians have begun to examine a less visible but equally important manifestation of growing state power: census taking.

Governments and religious authorities have counted people since early times. Our best estimates of the Amerindian population of the Western Hemisphere in 1500 rest almost entirely on what were little more than missionaries' guesses about the numbers of people they baptized. Spanish and Portuguese kings were eager to count native populations, since "indios" (adult male Amerindians) were subject to special labor obligations and tribute payments. So, from the mid-sixteenth century onward, imperial officials conducted regular censuses of Amerindians, adapting practices already in place in Europe.

The effort to measure and categorize populations was transformed in the last decades of the eighteenth century when the nature of European governments began to change. The Enlightenment belief that the scientific method could be applied to human society proved to be attractive both to political radicals, like the French Revolutionaries, and to reforming monarchs like Maria Theresa of Austria. Enlightenment philosophers had argued that a science of government could remove the inefficiencies and irrationalities that had long subverted the human potential for prosperity and happiness. The French intellectual Condorcet wrote in 1782:

> Those sciences, created almost in our own days, the object of which is man himself, the direct goal of which is the happiness of man, will enjoy a progress no less sure than that of the physical sciences. . . . In meditating on the nature of the moral sciences [what we now call the social sciences], one cannot help seeing that, as they are based like the physical sciences on the observation of fact, they must follow the method, acquire a language equally exact and precise, attaining the same degree of certainty.[1]

As confidence in this new "science" grew, the term previously used to describe the collection of numbers about society, *political arithmetic*, was abandoned by governments and practitioners in favor of *statistics*, a term that clearly suggests its close ties to the "state." In the nineteenth century the new objectives set out by Condorcet and others led to both the formal university training of statisticians and the creation of government statistical services.

The ambitions of governments in this new era were great. Nation-states self-consciously sought to transform society, sponsoring economic development, education, and improvements in health and welfare. They depended on statistics to measure the effectiveness of their policies and, as a result, were interested in nearly everything. They counted taverns, urban buildings, births and deaths, and arrests and convictions. They also counted their populations with a thoroughness never before seen. As statistical reporting became more uniform across Europe and the Americas, governments could measure not only their own progress but also that of their neighbors and rivals.

The revolutionary governments of France modernized the census practices of the overthrown monarchy. They spent much more money, hired many more census takers, and devoted much more energy to training the staff that designed censuses and analyzed results. Great Britain set up an official census in 1801, but established a special administrative structure only in the 1830s. In the Western Hemisphere nearly every independent nation provided for "scientific" censuses. In the United States the federal constitution required that a census be taken every ten years. Latin American nations, often torn by civil war in the nineteenth century, took censuses less regularly, but even the poorest nations took censuses when they could. It was as if the census itself confirmed the existence of the government, demonstrating its modernity and seriousness.

Until recently, historians who relied on these documents in their research on economic performance, issues of race and ethnicity, family life, and fertility and mortality asked few questions about the politics of census design. What could be more objective than rows of numbers? But the advocates of statistics who managed census taking were uninhibited in advertising the usefulness of reliable numbers to the governments that employed them. At the 1860 International Statistical Congress held in London one speaker said, "I think the true meaning to be attached to 'statistics' is not every collection of figures, but figures collected with the sole purpose of applying the principles deduced from them to questions of importance to the state."[2] The desire to be useful meant that statistics could not be fully objective.

Subjectivity was an unavoidable problem with censuses. Censuses identified citizens and foreign residents by place of residence, sex, age, and family relationships within households as well as profession and literacy. These determinations were sometimes subjective. Modern scholars have demonstrated that census takers also often undercounted the poor and those living in rural areas.

Because census takers, as agents of nation-states, were determined to be useful, they were necessarily concerned with issues of nationality and, in the Americas, with race because these characteristics commonly determined political rights and citizenship. The assessment and recording of nationality and race would prove to be among the most politically problematic objectives of the new social sciences.

Nationality had not been a central question for traditional monarchies. For the emerging nation-state, nationality was central. A nation's strength was assumed to depend in large measure on the growth of its population, a standard that, once articulated, suggested that the growth of minority populations was dangerous. Who was French? Who was Austrian or Hungarian? European statisticians relied on both *language of use* and *mother tongue* as proxies for *nationality*, the first term being flexible enough to recognize the assimilation of minorities, the second suggesting a more permanent identity based on a person's original language. Both terms forced bilingual populations to simplify their more complex identities. Ethnic minorities, once identified, were sometimes subject to discrimination such as exclusion from military careers or from universities. In parts of Spanish America language was used as a proxy for *race*. Those who spoke Spanish were citizens in the full sense, even if they were indistinguishable from Amerindians in appearance. Those who spoke indigenous languages were "indios" and therefore subject to special taxes and labor obligations and effectively denied the right to vote.

Beyond providing a justification for continuing discrimination, census categories compressed and distorted the complexity and variety of human society to fit the preconceptions of bureaucrats and politicians. Large percentages of the residents of Mexico, Peru, and Bolivia, among other parts of the Americas, were descended from both Europeans and Amerindians and, in the Caribbean region, from Europeans and Africans. Census categories never adequately captured the complexities of these biological and cultural mixtures. We now know that the poor were often identified as "indios" or "blacks" and the better-off were often called something else, "Americanos," "criollos" (creoles), or even whites. Since this process flattened and streamlined the complexities of identity, censuses on their own are not reliable guides to the distribution of ethnicity and race in a population.

In Europe the issue of nationality proved similarly perplexing for census takers and similarly dangerous to those identified as minorities. Linguistic and ethnic minorities had always lived among the politically dominant majorities: Jewish and Polish minorities in areas controlled by German speakers, German speakers among the French, and Serbo-Croatian speakers among Hungarians, for example. The frontiers between these minority populations and their neighbors were always porous. Sexual unions and marriages were common, and two or more generations of a family often lived together in the same household, with the elder members speaking one language and the younger members another. Who was what? In a very real sense, nationality, like race in the Americas, was ultimately fixed by the census process, where the nation-state forced a limited array of politically utilitarian categories onto the rich diversity of ethnicity and culture.

Notes

1. Quoted in James C. Scott, *Seeing Like a State. How Certain Schemes to Improve the Human Condition Have Failed* (New Haven: Yale University Press, 1998), 91.
2. This discussion relies heavily on Eliza Johnson (now Ablovatski), "Counting and Categorizing: The Hungarian Gypsy Census of 1893" (M.A. Thesis, Columbia University, 1996), especially Chapter III. She quotes from the *Proceedings of the Sixth International Statistical Congress Held in London*, 1860, 379.

PART SEVEN

Global Diversity and Dominance, 1850–1945

In 1850, despite centuries of global contacts, the world still embraced a huge diversity of societies and cultures and of independent states. During the century that followed, much of the world came to be dominated by a few European nations, along with the United States and Japan.

After 1870, the industrializing nations used their newfound power to dominate Africa, South and Southeast Asia, and the Pacific in a wave of conquest we call the New Imperialism. Their domination was more than military or economic, for their agents—soldiers, administrators, missionaries, teachers, and merchants—tried to convert their new subjects to their own cultures, business practices, and ways of life. They were partly successful, as the spread of Western religions, languages, clothing, and political ideas testifies.

By 1900, Europe had been largely at peace for almost a century. As memories of war faded, the rise of nationalism and the awesome power of modern armies and navies made national rivalries dangerously inflammable. Germany, a latecomer to national unity, found its imperial ambitions frustrated by the earlier conquests of France, Britain, and Russia. Mounting tensions between the great powers led to the devastating Great War of 1914–1918. Far from settling issues, this war destabilized the victors as much as the vanquished. Russia and China erupted in revolution. The collapse of the Ottoman Empire led to the emergence of modern Turkey, while its Arab provinces were taken over by France and Britain. In the 1920s, the European powers struggled to maintain a precarious peace.

By the 1930s, the political and economic system they had crafted after the Great War fell apart. While the capitalist nations fell into a deep economic depression that their governments seemed helpless to stop, the Soviet Union industrialized at breakneck speed. Social disruption in Germany and Japan brought to power extremist politicians who sought to solve their countries' economic woes and political grievances by military conquest. Nationalism and industrial warfare assumed their most hideous forms in World War II, leading to the massacre of millions of innocent people and the destruction of countless cities.

World War II weakened European control of their overseas empires. Leaders of liberation movements in Asia, Latin America, and Africa were inspired by Western ideas of nationalism and communism and by the desire to acquire the benefits of industrialization. After decades of struggle India gained its independence in 1947. Two years later, Chinese communists led by Mao Zedong overthrew a government they viewed as subservient to the West. In Latin America, leaders turned to nationalist economic and social policies. Of all the once great powers, only the United States and the Soviet Union remained to compete for global dominance. In the face of their military and economic might, other nations continued to assert the diversity of their cultures and political aspirations.

	1850	1870	1890
Americas	U.S. Civil War **1861–1865**; Creation of Dominion of Canada **1867**	British build railroads in Brazil and Argentina **1880s**; **1880–1914** Immigration from southern and eastern Europe surges	**1890** U.S. is leading steel producer; Spanish-American War **1898**
Europe	**1851** Majority of British population living in cities; **1856** Transformation of steel and chemical industries begins	**1870–1914** Era of the New Imperialism; **1871** Unification of Germany, Italy	**1894–1906** Dreyfus affair in France
Africa	**1853–1877** Livingstone, Stanley expeditions in central Africa; End of transatlantic slave trade **1867**	**1880s** West Africa conquered by France and Britain; Berlin Africa Conference **1884–1885**	**1896** Ethiopians defeat Italian army at Adowa; Nigeria becomes British protectorate **1899**
Middle East	**1863–1879** Ismail westernizes Egypt; Suez Canal opens **1869**	**1878** Ottoman Empire loses most of its European territories; **1882** British occupy Egypt	**1904** Young Turk reforms in Ottoman Empire
Asia and Oceania	Direct British rule in India **1858**; **1862** French conquer Indochina; Meiji Restoration in Japan **1868**	First Indian National Congress **1885**; Russia conquers Central Asia **1884–1887**	Sino-Japanese War **1894**; Boxer Rebellion in China **1900**; **1904–1905** Russo-Japanese War

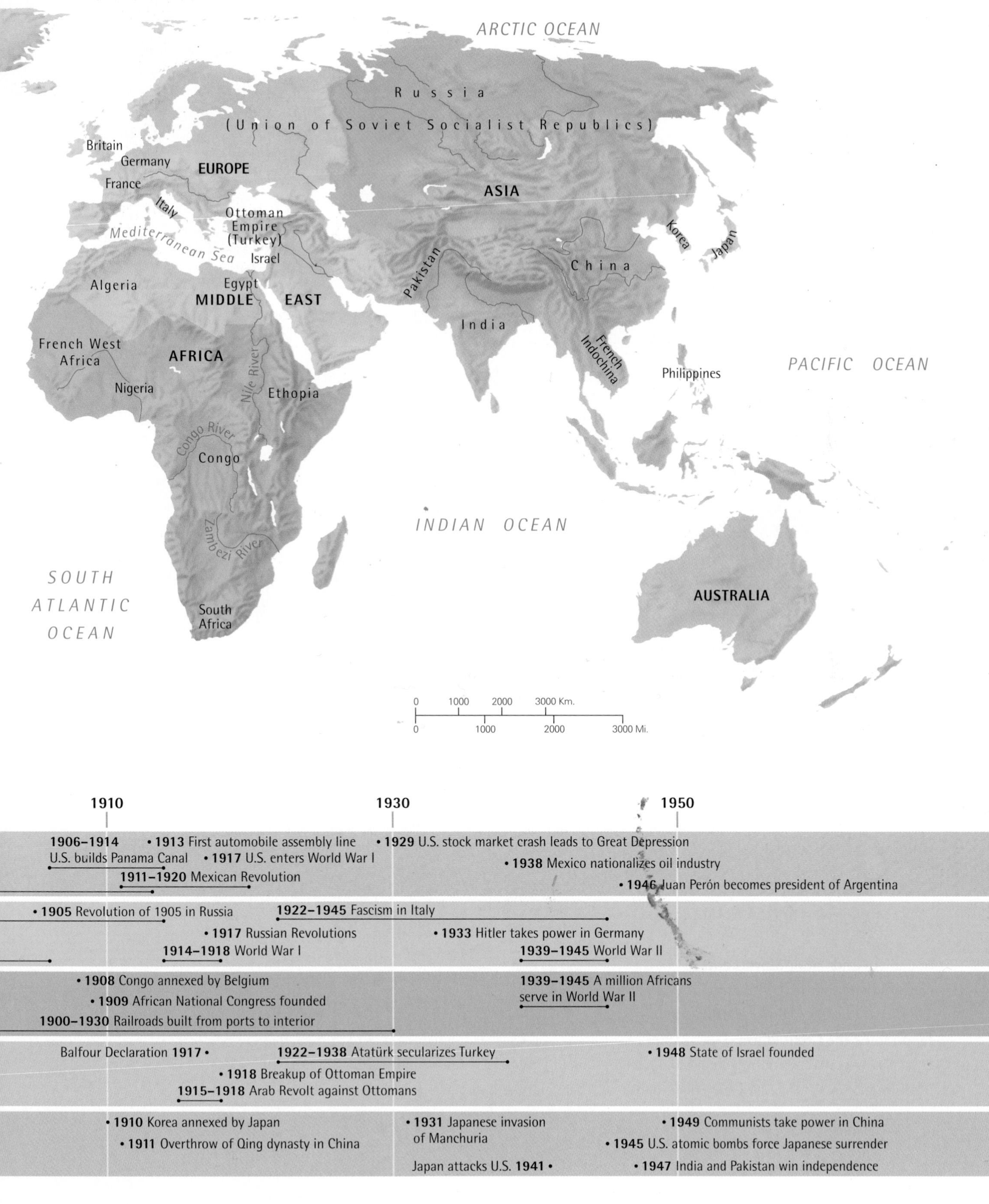

ARCTIC OCEAN
Russia
(Union of Soviet Socialist Republics)
Britain
Germany
EUROPE
France
Italy
Ottoman Empire (Turkey)
Mediterranean Sea
Israel
ASIA
Korea
Japan
Pakistan
China
Algeria
Egypt
MIDDLE EAST
India
French Indochina
French West Africa
AFRICA
Nile River
Nigeria
Ethopia
Philippines
PACIFIC OCEAN
Congo River
Congo
INDIAN OCEAN
Zambezi River
SOUTH ATLANTIC OCEAN
South Africa
AUSTRALIA
0 1000 2000 3000 Km.
0 1000 2000 3000 Mi.
1910
1930
1950
1906–1914 U.S. builds Panama Canal
• 1913 First automobile assembly line
• 1917 U.S. enters World War I
1911–1920 Mexican Revolution
• 1929 U.S. stock market crash leads to Great Depression
• 1938 Mexico nationalizes oil industry
• 1946 Juan Perón becomes president of Argentina
• 1905 Revolution of 1905 in Russia
1922–1945 Fascism in Italy
• 1917 Russian Revolutions
• 1933 Hitler takes power in Germany
1914–1918 World War I
1939–1945 World War II
• 1908 Congo annexed by Belgium
• 1909 African National Congress founded
1900–1930 Railroads built from ports to interior
1939–1945 A million Africans serve in World War II
Balfour Declaration 1917 •
1922–1938 Atatürk secularizes Turkey
• 1948 State of Israel founded
• 1918 Breakup of Ottoman Empire
1915–1918 Arab Revolt against Ottomans
• 1910 Korea annexed by Japan
• 1911 Overthrow of Qing dynasty in China
• 1931 Japanese invasion of Manchuria
Japan attacks U.S. 1941 •
• 1949 Communists take power in China
• 1945 U.S. atomic bombs force Japanese surrender
• 1947 India and Pakistan win independence

27 The New Power Balance, 1850–1900

Silk Factory in Japan Silk manufacture, Japan's best known industry, began to be mechanized in the 1870s. In this factory, as in most textile mills, the workers were women.

CHAPTER OUTLINE

On January 18, 1871, in the Hall of Mirrors of the palace of Versailles, King Wilhelm I of Prussia was proclaimed emperor of Germany before a crowd of officers and other German rulers. This ceremony marked the unification of many small German states into one nation. In the center stood Prussian chancellor Otto von Bismarck°, the man most responsible for the creation of a united Germany. A few years earlier, he had declared: "The great issues of the day will be decided not by speeches and votes of the majority—that was the great mistake of 1848 and 1849—but by iron and blood." Indeed it was "blood"—that is, victories on the battlefield—rather than popular participation that had led to the unification of Germany. The "iron" was not only weapons but, more importantly, the industries that produced weapons. Thus, after 1871, nationalism, once a dream of revolutionaries and romantics, became ever more closely associated with military force and with industry.

In the late nineteenth century a very small number of states, known as "great powers," dominated the world. Great Britain, France, and Russia had been recognized as great powers long before the industrial age. Russia began industrializing in the late nineteenth century, as did Germany, the United States, and Japan. The rise of the United States was covered in Chapter 24; in this chapter we will turn to the other great powers of the age. In the next chapter, which deals with the era of the "New Imperialism" (1870–1914), we will see how these nations used their power to establish colonial empires in Asia and Africa and to control Latin America. Together, Chapters 27 and 28 describe an era in which a handful of wealthy industrialized nations imposed on the other peoples of the world a domination more powerful than any experienced before or since.

As you read this chapter, ask yourself the following questions:

- What new technologies and industries appeared between 1850 and 1900, and how did they affect the world economy?
- How did the societies of the industrial countries change during this period?
- How was nationalism transformed from a revolutionary to a conservative ideology?
- How did China and Japan respond to the challenge of the Western powers?

Otto von Bismarck (UTT-oh fun BIS-mark)

New Technologies and the World Economy

The Industrial Revolution marked the beginning of a massive transformation of the world. In the nineteenth century the technologies discussed in Chapter 23—textile mills, railroads, steamships, the telegraph, and others—spread from Britain to other parts of the world. By 1890 Germany and the United States had surpassed Great Britain as the world's leading industrial powers. Small companies, like those that flourished in Britain, were overshadowed by large corporations, some owned by wealthy capitalists, others (especially in Russia and Japan) by governments.

Industrialization did not consist only of familiar technologies spreading to new areas, but also of entirely new technologies that revolutionized everyday life and transformed the world economy. The motive force behind this second phase of industrialization consisted of deliberate combinations of business entrepreneurship, engineering, and science, especially physics and chemistry. The first Industrial Revolution that you read about in Chapter 23 also involved the interactions of science, crafts, and business through the friendships of people with different interests, as in the Lunar Society. By the mid-nineteenth century this potent combination was institutionalized in the creation of engineering schools and research laboratories, first in Germany and then in the United States. Electricity and the steel and chemical industries were the first results of this new force. Let us turn first to the diffusion of earlier technologies, and then to the newer industries of the late nineteenth century.

Railroads

By the mid-nineteenth century, steam engines had become the prime mover of industry and commerce. Nowhere was this more evident than in the spread of **railroads.** By 1850 the first railroads had proved so successful that every industrializing country, and many that aspired to become industrial, began to build lines. The next fifty years saw a tremendous expansion of the world's rail networks. After a rapid spurt of building new lines, British railroad mileage leveled off at around 20,000 miles (over 32,000 kilometers) in the 1870s. France and Germany built networks longer than Britain's, as did Canada and Russia. When Japan began building its railway network in the 1870s, it imported several hundred engineers from the United States and Britain, then replaced them with newly trained Japanese engineers in the 1880s. By the early twentieth century, rail lines reached every city and province in Japan (see Map 27.3).

The largest rail network by far was in the United States. At the end of its Civil War in 1865 the United States already had 35,000 miles (over 56,000 kilometers) of track, three times as much as Britain. By 1915 the American network reached 390,000 miles (around 628,000 kilometers), more than the next seven longest networks combined.

Railroads were not confined to the industrialized nations; they could be constructed almost anywhere they would be of value to business or government. That included regions with abundant raw materials or agricultural products, like South Africa, Mexico, and Argentina, and densely populated countries like Egypt. The British built the fourth largest rail network in the world in India in order to reinforce their presence and develop trade with their largest colony. Before the opening of the Panama Canal in 1915, a railroad across the isthmus carried freight between the Atlantic and Pacific Oceans.

Railroads consumed huge amounts of land. Many old cities doubled in size to accommodate railroad stations, sidings, tracks, warehouses, and repair shops. In the countryside, railroads required bridges, tunnels, and embankments. Railroads also consumed vast quantities of timber for ties to hold the rails and for bridges, often using up whole forests for miles on either side of the tracks. Throughout the world, they opened new land to agriculture, mining, and other human exploitation of natural resources, whether for the benefit of the local inhabitants, as in Europe and North America, or for a distant power, as in the colonial empires.

Steamships and Telegraph Cables

Steam-powered ships dated back to the 1830s but were initially too costly for anything but first-class passenger traffic. Then, by midcentury, a series of developments radically transformed ocean shipping. First iron, then steel, replaced the wood that had been used for hulls since shipbuilding began. Propellers replaced paddle wheels. Engineers built more powerful and fuel-efficient engines. By the turn of the century a marine engine could convert the heat produced by burning a single sheet of paper into the power to move one ton over half a mile. The average size of freighters increased from 200 tons in 1850 to 7,500 tons in 1900. Coaling stations and ports able to handle large ships were built around the world. Most of all, the Suez Canal, constructed in 1869, shortened the distance between Europe and Asia and triggered a massive switch from sail power to steam (see Chapter 28).

The steamers of the turn of the century were so costly they had to be used as efficiently as possible. As the world's fleet of merchant ships grew from 9 million tons in 1850 to 35 million tons in 1910, new organizations developed to make the best use of them. One such organization was the shipping line, a company that offered fast, punctual, and reliable service on a fixed schedule. Passengers, mail, and perishable freight traveled on scheduled liners. Most ships, however, were tramp freighters that voyaged from one port to another under orders from their company headquarters in Europe or North America.

To control their ships around the globe, shipping companies used a new medium of communications: **submarine telegraph cables** laid on the ocean floor. Cables were laid across the Atlantic in 1866, to India in 1870, to China, Japan, and Australia in 1871 and 1872, to Latin America in 1872 and 1873, to East and South Africa in 1879, and to West Africa in 1886. By the turn of the century cables connected every country and almost every inhabited island. As cables became the indispensable tools of modern shipping and business, the public and the press extolled the "annihilation of time and space."

The Steel and Chemical Industries

Steel is a special form of iron, both hard and elastic. Until the nineteenth century it could be made only by skilled blacksmiths in very small quantities at a very high cost and was reserved for swords, knives, axes, and watch springs. Then came a series of inventions that made steel the cheapest and most versatile metal ever known. In the 1850s William Kelly, a Kentucky iron master, discovered that air forced through molten pig iron by powerful pumps turned the iron into steel without additional fuel. In 1856 the Englishman Henry Bessemer improved Kelly's method, producing steel at one-tenth the cost of earlier methods. Other new processes permitted steel to be made from scrap iron, an increasingly important raw material, and from the phosphoric iron ores common in western Europe. As a result,

CHRONOLOGY

	Europe and United States	East Asia
1850	**1851** Majority of British population living in cities	**1853–1854** Commodore Matthew Perry visits Japan
	1856 Bessemer converter; first synthetic dye	
	1859 Charles Darwin, *On the Origin of Species*	
	1861 Emancipation of serfs (Russia)	**1862–1908** Rule of Dowager Empress Cixi (China)
	1866 Alfred Nobel develops dynamite	
	1867 Karl Marx, *Das Kapital*	**1868** Meiji Restoration begins modernization drive in Japan
1870	**1860–1870** Unification of Italy	
	1871 Unification of Germany	
	1875 Social Democratic Party founded in Germany	
	1879 Thomas Edison develops incandescent lamp	
	1882 Married Women's Property Act (Britain)	
1890	**1894–1906** Dreyfus affair (France)	**1894** Sino-Japanese War
	1905 Revolution of 1905 (Russia)	**1900** Boxer Uprising (China)
		1904–1905 Russo-Japanese War
		1910 Japan annexes Korea

world steel production rose from a half-million tons in 1870 to 28 million in 1900, of which the United States produced 10 million, Germany 8 million, and Britain 4.9 million. Steel became cheap and abundant enough to make rails, bridges, ships, and even "tin" cans meant to be used once and thrown away.

The chemical industry followed a similar pattern. Until the late eighteenth century chemicals were produced by trial and error in small workshops. By the early nineteenth century soda, sulfuric acid, and chlorine bleach (used in the cotton industry) were manufactured on a large scale, especially in Britain. In 1856 the Englishman William Perkin created the first synthetic dye, aniline purple, from coal tar; the next few years were known in Europe as the "mauve decade" from the pale purple color of fashionable women's clothes. Industry began mass-producing other organic chemicals—compounds containing carbon atoms. Toward the end of the century German chemists synthesized red, violet, blue, brown, and black dyes as well. These bright, long-lasting colors were cheaper to manufacture and could be produced in much greater quantities than natural dyes. They delighted consumers but ruined the natural-dye producers in tropical countries, such as the indigo plantations of India.

Chemistry also made important advances in the manufacture of explosives. The first of these, nitroglycerin, was so dangerous that it exploded when shaken. In 1866 the Swedish scientist Alfred Nobel found a way to turn nitroglycerin into a stable solid—dynamite. This and other new explosives were useful in mining and were critical in the construction of railroads and canals, including the all-important Suez Canal. They also enabled the armies and navies of the great powers to arm themselves with increasingly accurate and powerful rifles and cannon.

The growing complexity of industrial chemistry made it one of the first fields where science and technology interacted on a daily basis. This development gave a great advantage to Germany, which had the most advanced engineering schools and scientific institutes of the time. While the British government paid little attention to science and engineering, the German government funded research and encouraged cooperation between universities and industries. By the end of the nineteenth century, Germany was the world's leading producer of dyes, drugs, synthetic fertilizers, ammonia, and nitrates used in making explosives.

Industrialization affected entire regions such as the English Midlands, the German Ruhr, and parts of Pennsylvania in the United States. The new steel mills were hungry consumers of coal, iron ore, limestone, and other raw materials that were extracted from the ground. They took up as much space as whole towns, belched smoke and particulates, and left behind huge hills of slag and other waste products. Railroad locomotives and other steam engines polluted the air with coal smoke. The dyestuff and other chemical industries left behind toxic wastes that were usually dumped into nearby rivers. This phase of industrialization, unrestrained by

Paris Lit Up by Electricity, 1900 The electric light bulb was invented in the United States and Britain, but Paris made such extensive use of the new technology that it was nicknamed "City of Lights." To mark the Paris Exposition of 1900, the Eiffel Tower and all the surrounding buildings were illuminated with strings of light bulbs while powerful spotlights swept the sky. (Courtesy, Civiche Raccolte d'Art Applicata ed Incisioni (Raccolte Bertarelli) Photo: Foto Saporetti)

environmental regulations, caused considerable damage to nature and to the health of nearby inhabitants.

Electricity

No innovation of the late nineteenth century changed people's lives as radically as **electricity.** At first, producing electric current was so costly that it was used only for electroplating and telegraphy. In 1831 the Englishman Michael Faraday° showed that the motion of a copper wire through a magnetic field induced an electric current in the wire. Based on his discovery, inventors in the 1870s devised efficient generators that turned mechanical energy into electric current. As an energy source, electricity was more flexible and much easier to use than water power or the stationary steam engine, which had powered industrialization until then. This opened the way to a host of new applications.

Arc lamps lit up public squares, theaters, and stores. For a while, homes continued to rely on gas lamps, which produced a softer light. Then in 1879 in the United States **Thomas Edison** developed an incandescent lamp well suited to lighting small rooms. In 1882 Edison created the world's first electrical distribution network in New York City. By the turn of the century electric lighting was rapidly replacing dim and smelly gas lamps in the cities of Europe and North America.

Other uses of electricity quickly appeared. Electric streetcars and, later, subways helped reduce the traffic jams that clogged the large cities of Europe and North America. Electric motors replaced steam engines and power belts, increasing productivity and improving workers' safety. As demand for electricity grew, engineers learned to use waterpower to produce electricity, and hydroelectric plants were built. The plant at Niagara Falls, on the border between Ontario, Canada, and New York State, produced an incredible 11,000 horsepower when it opened in 1895.

World Trade and Finance

World trade expanded tenfold between 1850 and 1913. Europe imported wheat from the United States and India, wool from Australia, and beef from Argentina, and exported coal, railroad equipment, textiles, and machinery to Asia and the Americas. Because steamships were much more efficient than sailing ships, the cost of freight dropped between 50 and 95 percent, making it worthwhile to ship even cheap and heavy products over very long distances. The advantage that steamers had over sailing ships was

Faraday (FAIR-ah-day)

especially pronounced close to industrial countries that produced coal, such as Britain and the United States. On seas and oceans to which coal had to be shipped halfway around the world, such as the Pacific Ocean, sailing ships retained a competitive advantage until the early twentieth century.

The growth of world trade transformed the economies of different parts of the world in different ways. The economics of western Europe and North America, the first to industrialize, grew more diversified and prosperous. Industries mass produced consumer goods for a growing number of middle-class and even working-class customers: soap, canned and packaged foods, ready-made clothes, household items, and small luxuries like cosmetics and engravings.

Capitalist economies, however, were prey to sudden swings in the business cycle—booms followed by deep depressions in which workers lost their jobs and investors their fortunes. For example, because of the close connections among the industrial economies, the collapse of a bank in Austria in 1873 triggered a depression that spread to the United States, causing mass unemployment. Worldwide recessions occurred in the mid-1880s and mid-1890s as well.

In the late 1870s and early 1880s Germany, the United States, and other late-industrializing Western nations raised tariffs to protect their industries from British competition. Yet trade barriers could not insulate them from the business cycle, for money continued to flow almost unhindered around the world. One of the main causes of the growing interdependence of the global economy was the financial power of Great Britain. Long after German and American industries surpassed the British, Britain continued to dominate the flow of trade, finance, and information. In 1900 two-thirds of the world's submarine cables were British or passed through Britain. Over half of the world's shipping was British owned. Britain invested one-fourth of its national wealth overseas, much of it in the United States and Argentina. British money financed many of the railroads, harbors, mines, and other big projects outside Europe. While other currencies fluctuated, the pound sterling was as good as gold, and nine-tenths of international transactions used sterling.

Nonindustrial areas also were tied to the world economy as never before. They were more vulnerable to changes in price and demand than were the industrialized nations, for many of them produced raw materials that could be replaced by synthetic substitutes (like dyestuffs) or alternative sources of supply (like coffee from Brazil). Electricity created a huge demand for copper, tying Chile, Montana, and southern Africa to the world economy as never before. Even products in constant demand, like Cuban sugar or Bolivian tin, were subject to wild swings in price on the world market. Nevertheless, until World War I, the value of exports from the tropical countries generally kept up with the growth of their populations.

Social Changes

The technological and economic changes of the late nineteenth century sparked profound social changes in the industrial nations. A fast-growing population swelled cities to unprecedented size, and millions of Europeans emigrated to the Americas. Strained relations between industrial employers and workers spawned labor movements and new forms of radical politics. Women found their lives dramatically altered, both in the home and in the public sphere.

Population and Migrations

The population of Europe grew faster from 1850 to 1914 than ever before or since, almost doubling from 265 million to 468 million. In non-European countries with predominantly white populations—the United States, Canada, Australia, New Zealand, and Argentina—the increase was even greater because of the inflow of Europeans. There were many reasons for the mass migrations of this period: the Irish famine of 1847–1848; the persecution of Jews in Russia; poverty and population growth in Italy, Spain, Poland, and Scandinavia; and the cultural ties between Great Britain and English-speaking countries overseas. Equally important was the availability of cheap and rapid steamships and railroads serving travelers at both ends (see Environment and Technology: Railroads and Immigration). Between 1850 and 1900, on average, 400,000 Europeans migrated overseas every year; between 1900 and 1914 the flood rose to over 1 million a year. From 1850 to 1910 the population of the United States and Canada rose from 25 million to 98 million, nearly a fourfold increase. The proportion of people of European ancestry in the world's population rose from one-fifth to one-third.

Why did the number of Europeans and their descendants overseas jump so dramatically? Much of the increase came from a drop in the death rate, as epidemics and starvation became less common. The Irish famine was the last peacetime famine in European history. As farmers plowed up the plains of North America and

ENVIRONMENT + TECHNOLOGY

Railroads and Immigration

Why did so many Europeans emigrate to North America in the late nineteenth and early twentieth centuries? The quick answer is that they wanted to. Millions of people longed to escape the poverty or tyranny of their home countries and start new lives in a land of freedom and opportunity. Personal desire alone, however, does not account for the migrations. After all, poverty and tyranny existed long before the late nineteenth century. Two other factors helped determine when and where people migrated: whether they were allowed to migrate, and whether they were able to.

In the nineteenth century Asians were recruited to build railroads and work on farms. But from the 1890s on, the United States and Canada closed their doors to non-Europeans, so regardless of what they wanted, they could not move to North America. In contrast, emigrants from Europe were admitted until after the First World War.

The ability to travel was a result of improvements in transportation. Until the 1890s most immigrants came from Ireland, England, or Germany—countries with good rail transportation to their own harbors and low steamship fares to North America. As rail lines were extended into eastern and southern Europe, more and more immigrants came from Italy, Austria-Hungary, and Russia.

Similarly, until the 1870s most European immigrants to North America settled on the east coast. Then, as the railroads pushed west, more of them settled on farms in the central and western parts of the continent. The power of railroads moved people as much as their desires did.

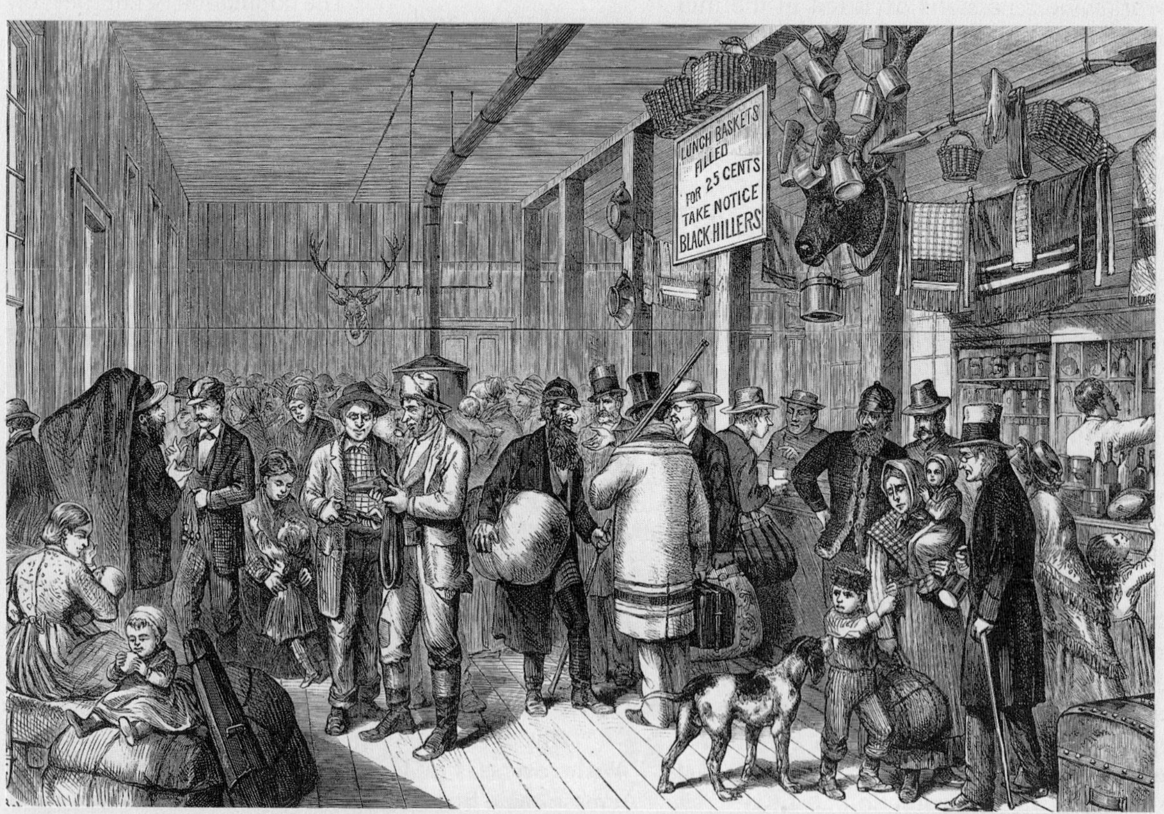

Emigrant Waiting Room The opening of the western region of the United States attracted settlers from the east coast and from Europe. These migrants are waiting for a train to take them to the Black Hills of Dakota during one of the gold rushes of the late nineteenth century. (Library of Congress)

planted wheat, much of which was shipped to Europe, food supplies increased faster than the population. Fertilizers boosted crop yields, and canning and refrigeration made food abundant year-round. The diet of Europeans and North Americans improved as meat, fruit, vegetables, and oils became part of the daily fare of city dwellers in winter as well as in summer.

Asians also migrated in large numbers during this period, often as indentured laborers recruited to work on plantations, in mines, and on railroads. Indians went mainly to Africa, Southeast Asia, and other tropical colonies of Great Britain. Chinese emigrated to Southeast Asia and the East Indies. Indian and Chinese workers were brought to the Caribbean to work in the sugar plantations after the emancipation of African slaves. Japanese migrated to Brazil and other parts of Latin America. Many Chinese, as well as Japanese and Filipinos, went to Hawaii and California, where they encountered growing hostility from European-Americans.

Urbanization and Urban Environments

In 1851 Britain became the first nation with a majority of its population living in towns and cities. By 1914, 80 percent of its population was urban, as were 60 percent of the German and 45 percent of the French populations. Cities grew to unprecedented size. London grew from 2.7 million in 1850 to 6.6 million in 1900. New York, a small town of 64,000 people in 1800, reached 3.4 million by 1900, a fiftyfold increase. Population growth and the building of railroads and industries allowed cities to invade the countryside, swallowing nearby towns and villages. In 1800 New York had covered only the southernmost quarter of Manhattan Island, some 3 square miles (nearly 8 square kilometers); by 1900 it covered 150 square miles (390 square kilometers). London in 1800 measured about 4 square miles (about 10 square kilometers); by 1900 it covered twenty times more area. In the English Midlands, in the German Ruhr, and around Tokyo Bay, towns fused into one another, filling in the fields and woods that once had separated them.

As cities grew, they changed in character. Newly built railroads not only brought goods into the cities on a predictable schedule but also allowed people to live farther apart. At first, only the well-to-do could afford to commute by train; by the end of the century, electric streetcars and subways allowed working-class people to live miles from their workplaces.

In preindustrial and early industrial cities, the poor crowded together in tenements; sanitation was bad; water often was contaminated with sewage; and darkness made life dangerous. New urban technologies and the growing powers and responsibilities of governments transformed city life for all but the poorest residents. The most important change was the installation of pipes to bring in clean water and to carry away sewage. First gas lighting and then electric lighting made cities safer and more pleasant at night. By the turn of the twentieth century municipal governments provided police and fire protection, sanitation and garbage removal, building and health inspection, schools, parks, and other amenities unheard of a century earlier.

As sanitation improved, epidemics became rare. For the first time, urban death rates fell below birthrates. The decline in infant mortality was especially significant. Confident that their children would survive infancy, couples began to limit the number of children they had, and ancient scourges like infanticide and child abandonment became less frequent. By the beginning of the twentieth century middle-class and even working-class couples began using contraceptives.

To accommodate the growing population, builders created new neighborhoods, from crowded tenements for the poor to opulent mansions for the newly rich. In the United States planners laid out new cities, such as Chicago, on rectangular grids, and middle-class families moved to new developments on the edges of cities. In Paris older neighborhoods with narrow crooked streets and rickety tenements were torn down to make room for broad boulevards and modern apartment buildings. Brilliantly lit by gas and electricity, Paris became the "city of lights," a model for city planners from New Delhi to Buenos Aires. The rich continued to live in inner cities that contained the monuments, churches, and palaces of preindustrial times, while workers moved to the outskirts.

Lower population densities and better transportation divided cities into industrial, commercial, and residential zones occupied by different social classes. Improvements such as water and sewerage, electricity, and streetcars always benefited the wealthy first, then the middle class, and finally the working class. In the complex of urban life, businesses of all kinds arose, and the professions—engineering, accounting, research, journalism, and the law, among others—took on increased importance. The new middle class exhibited its wealth in fine houses with servants and in elegant entertainment.

In fast-growing cities such as London, New York, or Chicago, newcomers arrived so quickly that housing construction and municipal services could not keep up. Immigrants who saved their money to reunite their families could not afford costly municipal services. As a result, the poorest neighborhoods remained as overcrowded,

Separate Spheres in Great Britain In the Victorian Age, men and women of the middle and upper classes led largely separate lives. In *Aunt Emily's Visit* (1845), we see women and children at home, tended by a servant. *The Royal Exchange*, meanwhile, was a place for men to transact business. (Mary Evans Picture Library)

unhealthy, and dangerous as they had been since the early decades of industrialization.

While urban environments improved in many ways, air quality worsened. Coal, burned to power steam engines and heat buildings, polluted the air, creating unpleasant and sometimes dangerous "pea-soup" fog and coating everything with a film of grimy dust. The thousands of horses that pulled the carts and carriages covered the streets with their wastes, causing a terrible stench. The introduction of electricity helped alleviate some of these environmental problems. Electric motors and lamps did not pollute the air. Power plants were built at a distance from cities. As electric trains and streetcars began replacing horse-drawn trolleys and coal-burning locomotives, cities became cleaner and healthier. However, most of the environmental benefits of electricity were to come in the twentieth century.

Middle-Class Women's "Separate Sphere"

In English-speaking countries the period from about 1850 to 1901 is known as the **"Victorian Age."** The expression refers not only to the reign of Queen Victoria of England (r. 1837–1901) but also to rules of behavior and to an ideology surrounding the family and the relations between men and women. The Victorians contrasted the masculine ideals of strength and courage with the feminine virtues of beauty and kindness, and they idealized the home as a peaceful and loving refuge from the dog-eat-dog world of competitive capitalism.

Victorian morality claimed to be universal, yet it best fit upper- and middle-class European families. Men and women were thought to belong in **"separate spheres."** Successful businessmen spent their time at work or relaxing in men's clubs. They put their wives in charge of rearing the children, running the household, and spending the family money to enhance the family's social status.

Before electric appliances, maintaining a middle-class home involved enormous amounts of work. Not only were families larger, but middle-class couples entertained often and lavishly. Carrying out these tasks required servants. A family's status and the activities and lifestyle of the "mistress of the house" depended on the availability of servants to help with household tasks. Only families that employed at least one full-time servant were considered middle class.

Toward the turn of the century modern technology began to transform middle-class homes. Plumbing eliminated the pump and the outhouse. Central heating replaced fireplaces, stoves, trips to the basement for coal, and endless dusting. Gas and electricity lit houses and cooked food without soot, smoke, and ashes. In the early twentieth century wealthy families acquired the first vacuum cleaners and washing machines. These technological advances did not mean less housework for women. As families acquired new household technologies, they raised their standards of cleanliness, thus demanding just as much labor as before.

The most important duty of middle-class women was raising children. Unlike the rich of previous eras who handed their children over to wet nurses and tutors, Victorian mothers nursed their own babies and show-

Emmeline Pankhurst Under Arrest The leader of the British women's suffrage movement frequently called attention to her cause by breaking the law to protest discrimination against women. Here she is being arrested and carried off to jail by the police. (Mary Evans Picture Library)

ered their children with love and attention. Even those who could afford nannies and governesses remained personally involved in their children's education. Girls received an education very different from that of boys. While boys were being prepared for the business world or the professions, girls were taught such skills as embroidery, drawing, and music, which offered no monetary reward or professional preparation but enhanced their social graces and marriage prospects.

Victorian morality frowned on careers for middle-class women. Young women could work until they got married, but only in genteel places like stores and offices, never in factories. When the typewriter and telephone were introduced into the business world in the 1880s, businessmen found that they could get better work at lower wages from educated young women than from men, and operating these machines was typecast as women's work.

Most professional careers were closed to women. Until late in the century few universities granted degrees to women. In the United States higher education was available to women only at elite colleges in the East and teachers' colleges in the Midwest. European women had fewer opportunities. Before 1914 very few women became doctors, lawyers, or professional musicians.

The first profession open to women was teaching, due to laws calling for universal compulsory education. By 1911, for instance, 73 percent of all teachers in England were women. They were considered well suited to teaching young children and girls—an extension of the duties of Victorian mothers. Teaching, however, was judged suitable only for single women. A married woman was expected to get pregnant right away and to stay home taking care of her own children rather than the children of other people.

A home life, no matter how busy, did not satisfy all middle-class women. Some became volunteer nurses or social workers, receiving little or no pay. Others organized to fight prostitution, alcohol, and child labor. By the turn of the century a few were challenging male domination of politics and the law. Women suffragists, led in Britain by Emmeline Pankhurst and in the United States by Elizabeth Cady Stanton and Susan B. Anthony, demanded the right to vote. By 1914 U.S. women had won the right to vote in twelve states. British women did not vote until 1918.

Working-Class Women

In the new industrial cities, men and women no longer worked together at home or in the fields. The separation of work and home affected women's lives even more than men's lives. Women formed a majority of the workers in the textile industries and in domestic service. Yet working-class women needed to keep homes and raise children as well as earn their living. As a result, they led lives of toil and pain, considerably harder than the lives of their menfolk. Parents expected girls as young as ten to contribute to the household. Many became domestic servants, commonly working sixteen or more hours a day, six-and-a-half days a week, for little more than room and board. Their living quarters, usually in attics or basements, contrasted with the luxurious quarters of their masters. Without appliances, much of their work was physically hard: hauling coal and water up stairs, washing laundry by hand.

Female servants were vulnerable to sexual abuse by their masters or their masters' sons. A well-known case is that of Helene Demuth, who worked for Karl and Jenny Marx all her life. At age thirty-one she bore a son by Karl

Marx and put him with foster parents rather than leave the family. She was more fortunate than most; the majority of families fired servants who got pregnant, rather than embarrass the master of the house.

Young women often preferred factory work to domestic service. Here, too, Victorian society practiced a strict division of labor by gender. Men worked in construction, iron and steel, heavy machinery, or on railroads; women worked in textiles and the clothing trades, extensions of traditional women's household work. Appalled by the abuses of women and children in the early years of industrialization, most industrial countries passed protective legislation limiting the hours or forbidding the employment of women in the hardest and most dangerous occupations, such as mining and foundry work. Such legislation limited abuses but also reinforced gender divisions in industry, keeping women in low-paid, subordinate positions. Denied access to the better-paid jobs of foremen or machine repairmen, female factory workers earned between one-third and two-thirds of men's wages.

Married women with children were expected to stay home, even if their husbands did not make enough to support the family. Most working-class married women had double responsibilities within the home: not only the work of child-rearing and housework but also that of contributing to the family's income. Families who had room to spare, even a bed or a corner in the kitchen, took in boarders. Many women did piecework such as sewing dresses, making hats or gloves, or weaving baskets. The hardest and worst-paid work was washing other people's clothes. Many women worked at home ten to twelve hours a day and enlisted the help of their small children, perpetuating practices long outlawed in factories. Since electric lighting and indoor plumbing cost more than most working-class families could afford, even ordinary household duties like cooking and washing remained heavy burdens.

SOCIALISM AND LABOR MOVEMENTS

Industrialization combined with the revolutionary ideas of the late eighteenth century to produce two kinds of movements calling for further changes: socialism and labor unions. **Socialism** was an ideology developed by radical thinkers who questioned the sanctity of private property and argued in support of industrial workers against their employers. **Labor unions** were organizations formed by industrial workers to defend their interests in negotiations with employers. The socialist and labor movements were never identical. Most of the time they were allies; occasionally they were rivals.

Marx and Socialism

Socialism began as an intellectual movement. By far the best-known socialist was **Karl Marx** (1818–1883), a German journalist and writer who spent most of his life in England and collaborated with another socialist, Friedrich Engels (1820–1895), author of *The Condition of the Working Class in England in 1844* (1845). Together, they combined German philosophy, French revolutionary ideas, and knowledge of British industrial conditions.

Marx expressed his ideas succinctly in the *Communist Manifesto* (1848) (see Diversity and Dominance: Marx and Engels on Global Trade and the Bourgeoisie) and in great detail in *Das Kapital*° (1867). He saw history as a long series of conflicts between social classes, the latest being between property owners (the bourgeoisie) and workers (the proletariat). He argued that the capitalist system allowed the bourgeoisie to extract the "surplus value" of workers' labor—that is, the difference between their wages and the value of the goods they manufactured. He saw business enterprises becoming larger and more monopolistic and workers growing more numerous and impoverished with every downturn in the business cycle. He concluded that this conflict would inevitably lead to a revolution and the overthrow of the bourgeoisie, after which the workers would establish a communist society without classes.

What Marx called "scientific socialism" provided an intellectual framework for the growing dissatisfaction with raw industrial capitalism. In the late nineteenth century business tycoons spent money lavishly on mansions, yachts, private railroad cars, and other displays of wealth that contrasted sharply with the poverty of the workers. Even though industrial workers were not becoming poorer as Marx believed, the class struggle between workers and employers was brutally real. What Marx did was to offer a persuasive explanation of the causes of this contrast and the antagonisms it bred.

Marx was not just a philosopher; he also had a direct impact on politics. In 1864 he helped found the International Working Man's Association (later known as the First International), a movement he hoped would bring about the overthrow of the bourgeoisie. However, it attracted more intellectuals than workers. Workers found

Das Kapital (DUSS cop-ee-TALL)

other means of redressing their grievances, such as the vote and labor unions.

Labor Movements

Since the beginning of the nineteenth century, workers had united to create "friendly societies" for mutual assistance in times of illness, unemployment, or disability. Anticombination laws, however, forbade workers to strike. These laws were abolished in Britain in the 1850s and in the rest of Europe in subsequent decades. Labor unions sought not only better wages but also improved working conditions and insurance against illness, accidents, disability, and old age. They grew slowly because they required a permanent staff and a great deal of money to sustain their members during strikes. By the end of the century British labor unions counted 2 million members, and German and American unions had 1 million members each.

Just as labor unions strove to enable workers to share in the benefits of a capitalist economy, so did electoral politics persuade workers to become part of the existing political system instead of seeking to overthrow it. The nineteenth century saw a gradual extension of the right to vote throughout Europe and North America. Universal male suffrage became law in the United States in 1870, in France and Germany in 1871, in Britain in 1885, and in the rest of Europe soon thereafter. Because there were so many newly enfranchised workers, universal male suffrage meant that socialist politicians could expect to capture many seats in their nations' parliaments. Unlike Marx, who predicted that workers would seize power through revolution, the socialists expected workers to use their voting power to obtain concessions from government and eventually even to form a government.

The classic case of socialist electoral politics is the Social Democratic Party of Germany. Founded in 1875 with a revolutionary socialist program, within two years it won a half-million votes and several seats in the Reichstag° (the lower house of the German parliament). Through superb organizing efforts and important concessions wrung from the government, the party grew fast, garnering 4.2 million votes in 1912 and winning more seats in the Reichstag than any other party. In pursuit of electoral success, the Social Democrats became more reformist and less radical. By joining the electoral process, they abandoned the idea of violent revolution.

Working-class women, burdened with both job and family responsibilities, found little time for politics and were not welcome in the male-dominated trade unions or radical political parties. A few radical women, such as the German socialist Rosa Luxemburg and Emma Goldman in the United States, an **anarchist** who believed in the abolition of all governments, became famous but did not have a large following. It was never easy to reconcile the demands of workers and those of women. In 1889 the German socialist Clara Zetkin wrote: "Just as the male worker is subjected by the capitalist, so is the woman by the man, and she will always remain in subjugation until she is economically independent. Work is the indispensable condition for economic independence." Six years later, she recognized that the liberation of women would have to await a change in the position of the working class as a whole: "The proletarian woman cannot attain her highest ideal through a movement for the equality of the female sex, she attains salvation only through the fight for the emancipation of labor."[1]

Reichstag (RIKES-tog)

Nationalism and the Unification of Germany and Italy

The most influential idea of the nineteenth century was **nationalism.** The French revolutionaries had defined people, who had previously been considered the subjects of a sovereign, as the citizens of a *nation*—a concept identified with a territory, the state that ruled it, and the culture of its people.

Language and National Identity Before 1871

Language was usually the crucial element in creating a feeling of national unity. It was important both as a way to unite the people of a nation and as the means of persuasion by which political leaders could inspire their followers. Language was the tool of the new generation of political activists, most of them lawyers, teachers, students, and journalists. Yet language and citizenship seldom coincided.

The fit between France and the French language was closer than in most large countries, though some French-speakers lived outside of France and some French people spoke other languages. Italian- and German-speaking people, however, were divided among many small states. Living in the Austrian Empire were peoples who spoke German, Czech, Slovak, Hungarian, Polish, and other languages. Even where people spoke a common language, they could be divided by religion or

DIVERSITY AND DOMINANCE

MARX AND ENGELS ON GLOBAL TRADE AND THE BOURGEOISIE

In 1848 the German philosophers Karl Marx (1818–1883) and Friedrich Engels (1820–1895), who were living in England at the time, published a small book called Manifesto of the Communist Party. *In it, they tried to explain why owners of manufactures and business—the "bourgeoisie"—had become the wealthiest and most powerful class of people in industrializing countries like Britain, and why urban and industrial workers—the "proletariat"—lived in poverty. In their view, the dominance of the European commercial and industrial bourgeoisie was in the process of destroying the diversity of human cultures, reducing all classes in Europe and all cultures to the status of proletarians selling their labor.*

In the Manifesto, *Marx and Engels did not limit themselves to publicizing social inequities. They also called for a social revolution in which the workers would overthrow the bourgeoisie and establish a new society without private property or government. Their* Manifesto *was soon translated into many languages and became the best-known expression of radical communist ideology.*

Whatever one may think of their call to revolution, Marx and Engels's analysis of class relations has had a lasting impact on social historians. Their ideas are especially interesting from the perspective of global history because of the way in which they connect the rise of the bourgeois with world trade and industrial technology. The following paragraphs explain these connections.

The history of all hitherto existing society is the history of class struggles.

Freeman and slave, patrician and plebeian, lord and serf, guild-master and journeyman, in a word, oppressor and oppressed, stood in constant opposition to one another, carried on an uninterrupted, now hidden, now open fight, a fight that each time ended, either in a revolutionary re-constitution of society at large, or in the common ruin of the contending classes.

In the earlier epochs of history, we find almost everywhere a complicated arrangement of society into various orders, a manifold gradation of social rank. In ancient Rome we have patricians, knights, plebeians, slaves; in the middle ages, feudal lords, vassals, guild-masters, journeymen, apprentices, serfs; in almost all of these classes, again, subordinate gradations.

The modern bourgeois society that has sprouted from the ruins of feudal society, has not done away with class antagonisms. It has but established new classes, new conditions of oppression, new forms of struggle in place of the old ones.

Our epoch, the epoch of the bourgeoisie, possesses, however, this distinctive feature; it has simplified the class antagonisms. Society as a whole is more and more splitting up into two great hostile camps, into two great classes directly facing each other: Bourgeoisie and Proletariat.

From the serfs of the middle ages sprang the chartered burghers of the earliest towns. From these burgesses the first elements of the bourgeoisie were developed.

The discovery of America, the rounding of the Cape, opened up fresh ground for the rising bourgeoisie. The East-Indian and Chinese markets, the colonization of America, trade with the colonies, the increase in the means of exchange and in commodities generally, gave to commerce, to navigation, to industry, an impulse never before known, and thereby, to the revolutionary element in the tottering feudal society, a rapid development.

The feudal system of industry, under which industrial production was monopolised by close guilds, now no longer sufficed for the growing wants of the new markets. The manufacturing system took its place. The guild-masters were pushed on one side by the manufacturing middle-class; division of labour between the different corporate guilds vanished in the face of division of labour in each single workshop.

Meantime the markets kept ever growing, the demand, ever rising. Even manufacture no longer sufficed. Thereupon, steam and machinery revolutionised industrial production. The place of manufacture was taken by the giant, Modern Industry, the place of the industrial middle-class, by industrial millionaires, the leaders of whole industrial armies, the modern bourgeois.

Modern industry has established the world-market, for which the discovery of America paved the way. This market has given an immense importance to commerce, to navigation, to communication by land. This development has, in its turn, reacted on the extension of industry; and in proportion as industry, commerce, navigation, railways extended, in the same proportion the bourgeoisie developed, increased its capital, and pushed into the background every class handed down from the Middle Ages.

We see, therefore, how the modern bourgeoisie is itself the product of a long course of development, of a series of revolutions in the modes of production and of exchange. . . .

[T]he bourgeoisie has at last, since the establishment of Modern Industry and of the world-market, conquered for itself, in the modern representative State, exclusive political sway. The executive of the modern State is but a committee for managing the common affairs of the whole bourgeoisie.

The bourgeoisie, historically, has played a most revolutionary part. . . .

It has been the first to shew what man's activity can bring about. It has accomplished wonders far surpassing Egyptian pyramids, Roman aqueducts, and Gothic cathedrals; it has conducted expeditions that put in the shade all former Exoduses of nations and crusades.

The bourgeoisie cannot exist without constantly revolutionising the instruments of production, and thereby the relations of production, and with them the whole relations of society. Conservation of the old modes of production in unaltered form, was, on the contrary, the first condition of existence for all earlier industrial classes. Constant revolutionising of production, uninterrupted disturbance of all social conditions, everlasting uncertainty and agitation distinguish the bourgeois epoch from all earlier ones. All fixed, fast-frozen relations, with their train of ancient and venerable prejudices and opinions, are swept away, all new-formed ones become antiquated before they can ossify. All that is solid melts into air, all that is holy is profaned, and man is at last compelled to face with sober senses, his real conditions of life, and his relations with his kind.

The need of a constantly expanding market for its products chases the bourgeoisie over the whole surface of the globe. It must nestle everywhere, settle everywhere, establish connexions everywhere.

The bourgeoisie has through its exploitation of the world-market given a cosmopolitan character to production and consumption in every country. To the great chagrin of Reactionists, it has drawn from under the feet of industry the national ground on which it stood. All old-fashioned national industries have been destroyed or are daily being destroyed. They are dislodged by new industries, whose introduction becomes a life or death question for all civilised nations, by industries that no longer work up indigenous raw material, but raw material drawn from the remotest zones; industries whose products are consumed, not only at home, but in every quarter of the globe. In place of the old wants, satisfied by the productions of the country, we find new wants, requiring for their satisfaction the products of distant lands and climes. In place of the old local and national seclusion and self-sufficiency, we have intercourse in every direction, universal inter-dependence of nations. And as in material, so also in intellectual production. The intellectual creations of individual nations become common property. National one-sidedness and narrow-mindedness become more and more impossible, and from the numerous national and local literatures there arises a world-literature.

The bourgeoisie, by the rapid improvement of all instruments of production, by the immensely facilitated means of communication, draws all, even the most barbarian, nations into civilisation. The cheap prices of its commodities are the heavy artillery with which it batters down all Chinese walls, with which it forces the barbarians' intensely obstinate hatred of foreigners to capitulate. It compels all nations, on pain of extinction, to adopt the bourgeois mode of production; it compels them to introduce what it calls civilisation into their midst, i.e., to become bourgeois themselves. In a word, it creates a world after its own image.

The bourgeoisie has subjected the country to the rule of the towns. It has created enormous cities, has greatly increased the urban population as compared with the rural, and has thus rescued a considerable part of the population from the idiocy of rural life. Just as it has made the country dependent on the towns, so it has made barbarian and semi-barbarian countries dependent on the civilised ones, nations of peasants on nations of bourgeois, the East on the West. . . .

The bourgeoisie, during its rule of scarce one hundred years, has created more massive and more colossal productive forces than have all preceding generations together. Subjection of Nature's forces to man, machinery, application of chemistry to industry and agriculture, steam-navigation, railways, electric telegraphs, clearing of whole continents for cultivation, canalization of rivers, whole populations conjured out of the ground—what earlier century had even a presentiment that such productive forces slumbered in the lap of social labour?

QUESTIONS FOR ANALYSIS

1. **How did the growth of world trade since the European discovery of America affect relations between social classes in Europe?**
2. **What effect did the growth of trade and industry have on products, intellectual creations, and consumer tastes around the world?**
3. **Why does Marx think the bourgeoisie requires constant changes in technology and social relations? How well does that description fit the world you live in?**
4. **Can you think of recent examples of the Western bourgeoisie's creating "a world after its own image"?**

Source: Karl Marx and Frederick Engels, *Manifesto of the Communist Party,* Authorized English Translation: Edited and Annotated by Frederick Engels (Chicago: Charles H. Kerr & Company, 1906), 12–20.

institutions. The Irish, though English-speaking, were mostly Catholic, whereas the English were primarily Protestant; and in the United States, different economic systems and the issue of slavery divided the south from the north.

The idea of redrawing the boundaries of states to accommodate linguistic, religious, or cultural differences was revolutionary. In Italy and Germany it led to the forging of large new states out of many small ones in 1871. In central and eastern Europe, nationalism threatened to break up large states into smaller ones.

Until the 1860s nationalism was associated with **liberalism,** the revolutionary middle-class ideology that emerged from the French Revolution, asserted the sovereignty of the people, and demanded constitutional government, a national parliament, and freedom of expression. The most famous nationalist of the early nineteenth century was the Italian liberal Giuseppe Mazzini° (1805–1872), the leader of the failed revolution of 1848 in Italy. Mazzini not only sought to unify the Italian peninsula into one nation but also associated with like-minded revolutionaries elsewhere to bring nationhood and liberty to all peoples oppressed by tyrants and foreigners. Although the governments of Russia, Prussia, and Austria censored the new ideas, they could not be quashed. To staff bureaucracies and police forces to maintain law and order, even conservative regimes required educated personnel, and education meant universities, the seedbeds of new ideas transmitted by a national language.

Although the revolutions of 1848 failed except in France, the strength of the revolutionary movements convinced conservatives that governments could not forever keep their citizens out of politics, and that mass politics, if properly managed, could strengthen rather than weaken the state. A new generation of conservative political leaders learned how to preserve the social status quo through public education, universal military service, and colonial conquests, all of which built a sense of national unity.

The Unification of Italy, 1860–1870

The Austrian statesman Prince Metternich had famously described Italy as "a geographical expression." By midcentury, however, popular sentiment was building throughout Italy for unification. Opposing it were Pope Pius IX, who abhorred everything modern, and Austria, which controlled two Italian provinces, Lombardy and Venetia (see Map 27.1). The prime minister of the Kingdom of Piedmont-Sardinia, Count Camillo Benso di Cavour, saw the rivalry between France and Austria as an opportunity to unify Italy. He secretly formed an alliance with France, then instigated a war with Austria in 1858. The war was followed by uprisings throughout northern and central Italy in favor of joining Piedmont-Sardinia, a moderate constitutional monarchy under King Victor Emmanuel.

If the conservative, top-down approach to unification prevailed in the north, a more radical approach was still possible in the south. In 1860 the fiery revolutionary **Giuseppe Garibaldi**° and a small band of followers landed in Sicily and then in southern Italy, overthrew the Kingdom of the Two Sicilies, and prepared to found a democratic republic. The royalist Cavour, however, took advantage of the unsettled situation to sideline Garibaldi and expand Piedmont-Sardinia into a new Kingdom of Italy. Unification was completed with the addition of Venetia in 1866 and the Papal States in 1870. The process of unification illustrates the shift of nationalism from a radical democratic idea to a conservative method of building popular support for a strong centralized government, even an aristocratic and monarchical one.

The Unification of Germany, 1866–1871

Because the most widely spoken language in nineteenth-century Europe was German, the unification of most German-speaking people into a single state in 1871 had momentous consequences for the world. Until the 1860s the region of Central Europe where people spoke German (the former Holy Roman Empire) consisted of Prussia, the western half of the Austrian Empire, and numerous smaller states (see Map 27.2). Some German nationalists wanted to unite all Germans under the Austrian throne. Others wanted to exclude Austria with its many non-Germanic peoples and unite all other German-speaking areas under Prussia. The divisions were also religious: Austria and southwestern Germany were Catholic; Prussia and the northeast were Lutheran. The Prussian state had two advantages: (1) the newly developed industries of the Rhineland, and (2) the first European army to make use of railroads, telegraphs, breechloading rifles, steel artillery, and other products of modern industry.

During the reign of King Wilhelm I (r. 1861–1888) Prussia was ruled by the brilliant and authoritarian aris-

Giuseppe Mazzini (jew-SEP-pay mots-EE-nee)

Giuseppe Garibaldi (jew-SEP-pay gary-BAHL-dee)

Map 27.1 Unification of Italy, 1859–1870 The unification of Italy was achieved by the expansion of the kingdom of Piedmont-Sardinia, with the help of France.

tocrat, Chancellor **Otto von Bismarck** (1815–1898). Bismarck was determined to use Prussian industry and German nationalism to make his state the dominant power in Germany. In 1866 Prussia attacked and defeated Austria. To everyone's surprise, Prussia took no Austrian territory. Instead, Prussia and some smaller states formed the North German Confederation, the nucleus of a future Germany. Then in 1870, confident that Austria would not hinder him, Bismarck took advantage of French Emperor Napoleon III's hostility to the North

Wilhelm I Proclaimed Emperor of Germany On January 18, 1871, Prussia and the smaller states of Germany united to form the German Reich (empire). King Wilhelm I of Prussia was proclaimed kaiser (emperor) as his chancellor, Otto von Bismarck (in a white jacket), and dozens of generals and lesser princes cheered. The ceremony took place in the Great Hall of Mirrors in the palace of Versailles, near Paris, to mark Prussia's stunning victory over France. (Bismarck Museum, Friedrichsruh)

German Confederation to start a war with France. Prussian armies, joined by troops from southern as well as northern Germany, used their superior firepower and tactics to achieve a quick victory. "Blood and iron" were the foundation of the new German Empire.

The spoils of victory included a large indemnity and two provinces of France bordering on Germany: Alsace and Lorraine. The French paid the indemnity easily enough but resented the loss of their provinces. To the Germans, this region was German because a majority of its inhabitants spoke German. To the French, it was French because it had been so when the nation of France was forged in the Revolution and because most of its inhabitants considered themselves French. These two conflicting definitions of nationalism kept enmity between France and Germany smoldering for decades. In this case, nationalism turned out to be a divisive rather than a unifying force.

Nationalism After 1871

The Franco-Prussian War of 1870–1871 changed the political climate of Europe. France became more liberal. The kingdom of Italy completed the unification of the peninsula. Germany, Austria-Hungary (as the Austrian Empire had renamed itself in 1867), and Russia remained conservative and used nationalism to maintain the status quo.

Nationalism and parliamentary elections made politicians of all parties appeal to public opinion. They were greatly aided by the press, especially cheap daily newspapers that sought to increase circulation by publishing sensational articles about overseas conquests and foreign threats. As governments increasingly came to recognize the advantages of an educated population in the competition between states, they opened public schools in every town and admitted women into public-

Map 27.2 The Unification of Germany, 1866–1871 Germany was united after a series of short, successful wars by the kingdom of Prussia against Austria in 1866 and against France in 1871.

service jobs for the first time. The spread of literacy allowed politicians and journalists to appeal to the emotions of the poor, diverting their anger from their employers to foreigners and their votes from socialist to nationalist parties.

In many countries the dominant group used nationalism to justify imposing its language, religion, or customs on minority populations. The Russian Empire attempted to "Russify" its diverse ethnic populations. The Spanish government made the Spanish language compulsory in the schools, newspapers, and courts of its Basque- and Catalan-speaking provinces. Immigrants to the United States were expected to learn English to safeguard national unity.

Nationalism soon spread. By the 1880s signs of national consciousness appeared in Egypt, Japan, India, and other non-Western countries, inspiring anti-Western and anticolonial movements.

THE GREAT POWERS OF EUROPE, 1871–1900

After the middle of the century, politicians and journalists discovered that minor incidents involving foreigners could be used to stir up popular indignation against neighboring countries. Military officers, impressed by the awesome power of the weapons that industry provided, began to think that the weapons were invincible. Rivalries over colonial territories, ideological differences between liberal and conservative governments, and even minor border incidents or trade disagreements contributed to a growing atmosphere of international tension.

Germany at the Center of Europe

International relations revolved around a united Germany because Germany was located in the center of Europe and had the most powerful army on the European continent. After creating a unified Germany in 1871, Bismarck declared that his country had no further territorial ambitions, and he put his effort into maintaining the peace in Europe. To isolate France, the only country with a grudge against Germany, he forged a loose coalition with Austria-Hungary and Russia, the other two conservative powers. Despite the competing ambitions of Austria and Russia in the Balkans, he was able to keep his coalition together for twenty years.

Bismarck proved equally adept at strengthening German national unity at home. To weaken the influence of middle-class liberals, he extended the vote to all adult men, thereby allowing Socialists to win seats in the *Reichstag* or parliament. By imposing high tariffs on manufactured goods and wheat, he gained the support of both the wealthy industrialists of the Rhineland and the great landowners of eastern Germany, traditional rivals for power. Though he repressed labor unions, he gained the acquiescence of industrial workers by introducing social legislation—medical, unemployment, and disability insurance and old-age pensions—long before other industrial countries. His government supported public and technical education. Under his leadership, the German people developed a strong sense of national unity and pride in their industrial and military power.

In 1888 Wilhelm I was succeeded by his grandson Wilhelm II (r. 1888–1918), an insecure and arrogant man who tried to gain respect by using bullying tactics. Within two years he had dismissed Chancellor Bismarck and surrounded himself with yes men. Whereas Bismarck had shown little interest in acquiring colonies overseas, Wilhelm II talked about his "global policy" and demanded a colonial empire. Ruler of the nation with the mightiest army and the largest industrial economy in Europe, he felt that Germany deserved "a place in the sun." His intemperate speeches made him seem far more belligerent than he really was.

The Liberal Powers: France and Great Britain

France, once the dominant nation in Europe, had difficulty reconciling itself to being in second place. Though a prosperous country with flourishing agriculture and a large colonial empire, the French republic had some serious weaknesses. Its population was scarcely growing; in 1911 France had only 39 million people compared to Germany's 64 million. In an age when the power of nations was roughly proportional to the size of their armies, France could field an army only two-thirds the size of Germany's. Another weakness was the slow growth of French industry compared to Germany's, due in part to the loss of the iron and coal mines of Lorraine.

The French people were deeply divided over the very nature of the state: some were monarchists and Catholic; a growing number held republican and anticlerical views. These divisions came to a head at the turn of the century over the case of Captain Alfred Dreyfus, a Jewish officer falsely convicted of spying for the Germans in 1894. French society, even families, split between those who felt that reopening the case would only dishonor the army and those who believed that letting injustice go unchallenged dishonored the nation. The case reawakened the dormant anti-Semitism in French society. Not until 1906, after twelve painful years, was Dreyfus exonerated. Yet if French political life seemed fragile and frequently in crisis, a long tradition of popular participation in politics and a strong sense of nationhood, reinforced by a fine system of public education, gave the French people a deeper cohesion than appeared on the surface.

Great Britain had a long experience with parliamentary elections and competing parties. The British government alternated smoothly between the Liberal and Conservative Parties, and the income gap between rich

The Doss House Late-nineteenth-century cities showed more physical than social improvements. This painting by Makovsky of a street in St. Petersburg contrasts the broad avenue and impressive new buildings with the poverty of the crowd. (The State Russian Museum/Smithsonian Institution Traveling Exhibit)

and poor gradually narrowed. Nevertheless, Britain had problems that grew more apparent as time went on. One problem was Irish resentment of English rule. Nationalism had strengthened the allegiance of the English, Scots, and Welsh to the British crown and state. But the Irish, excluded because they were Catholic and predominantly poor, saw the British as a foreign occupying force.

Another problem was the British economy. Once the workshop of the world, Great Britain had fallen behind the United States and Germany in such important industries as iron and steel, chemicals, electricity, and textiles. Even in shipbuilding and shipping, Britain's traditional specialties, Germany was catching up.

Also, Britain was preoccupied with its enormous and fast-growing empire. A source of wealth for investors and the envy of other imperialist nations, the empire was also a constant drain on Britain's finances. The revolt of 1857 against British rule in India (see Chapter 25) was crushed with difficulty and kept British politicians worried thereafter. The empire required Britain to station several costly fleets of warships throughout the world.

For most of the nineteenth century Britain turned its back on Europe and pursued a policy of "splendid isolation." Only in 1854 did it intervene militarily in Europe, joining France in the Crimean War of 1854–1856 against Russia (see Chapter 26). Britain's preoccupation with India and the shipping routes through the Mediterranean led British statesmen to exaggerate the Russian threat to the Ottoman Empire and to the Central Asian approaches to India. Periodic "Russian scares" and Britain's age-old rivalry with France for overseas colonies diverted the attention of British politicians away from the rise of a large, powerful, united Germany.

The Conservative Powers: Russia and Austria-Hungary

The forces of nationalism weakened rather than strengthened Russia and Austria-Hungary. Their populations were far more divided, socially and ethnically, than were the German, French, or British peoples.

Nationalism was most divisive in south-central Europe, where many different language groups lived in close proximity. In 1867 the Austrian Empire renamed itself the Austro-Hungarian Empire to appease its Hungarian critics. Its attempts to promote the cultures of its Slavic-speaking minorities did little to gain their political allegiance. The Austro-Hungarian Empire still thought of itself as a great power, but instead of seeking conquests in Asia or Africa, it attempted to dominate the Balkans. This strategy irritated Russia, which thought of itself as the protector of Slavic peoples everywhere. The Austrian annexation of the former Turkish province of Bosnia-Herzegovina in 1908 worsened relations between the Austro-Hungarian and Russian Empires. As we will see in Chapter 29, festering quarrels over the Balkans—the "tinderbox of Europe"—eventually pushed Europe into war.

Ethnic diversity also contributed to the instability of imperial Russia. The Polish people, never reconciled to being annexed by Russia in the eighteenth century, rebelled in 1830 and 1863–1864. The tsarist empire also included Finland, Estonia, Latvia, Lithuania, and Ukraine, the very mixed peoples of the Caucasus, and the Muslim population of Central Asia conquered between 1865 and 1881. Furthermore, Russia had the largest Jewish population in Europe, despite the harshness of its anti-Semitic laws and periodic *pogroms* (massacres), which prompted many Jews to flee to America. All in all, only 45 percent of the peoples of the tsarist empire spoke Russian. This meant that Russian nationalism and the state's attempts to impose the Russian language on its subjects were divisive instead of unifying forces.

In 1861 the moderate conservative Tsar Alexander II (r. 1855–1881) emancipated the peasants from serfdom. He did so partly out of a genuine desire to strengthen the bonds between the monarchy and the Russian people, and partly to promote industrialization by enlarging the labor pool. That half-hearted measure, however, did not create a modern society on the western European model. It only turned serfs into communal farmers with few skills and little capital. Though technically "emancipated," the great majority of Russians had little education, few legal rights, and no say in the government. After Alexander's assassination in 1881, his successors Alexander III (r. 1881–1894) and Nicholas II (r. 1894–1917) reluctantly permitted half-hearted attempts at social change. Although the Russian government employed many bureaucrats and policemen, its commercial middle class was small and had little influence. Industrialization consisted largely of state-sponsored projects, such as railroads, iron foundries, and armament factories, and led to social unrest among urban workers. Wealthy landowning aristocrats continued to dominate the Russian court and administration and succeeded in blocking most reforms.

The weaknesses in Russia's society and government became glaringly obvious during a war with Japan in 1904 and 1905. The fighting in the Russo-Japanese War took place in Manchuria, a province in northern China far from European Russia. The Russian army, which received all its supplies by means of the inefficient Trans-Siberian Railway, was soon defeated by the better trained and equipped Japanese. The Russian navy, after a long journey around Europe, Africa, and Asia, was met and sunk by the Japanese fleet at the Battle of Tsushima Strait in 1905.

The shock of defeat caused a popular uprising, the Revolution of 1905, that forced Tsar Nicholas II to grant a constitution and an elected Duma (parliament). But as soon as he was able to rebuild the army and the police, he reverted to the traditional despotism of his forefathers. Small groups of radical intellectuals, angered by the contrast between the wealth of the elite and the poverty of the common people, began plotting the violent overthrow of the tsarist autocracy.

Japan Joins the Great Powers, 1865–1905

Since the seventeenth century Europeans had come to regard their continent as the center of the universe and their states as the only great powers in the world. The rest of the world was either ignored or used as bargaining chips in the game of power politics. The late nineteenth century marked the high point of European power and arrogance, as the nations of Europe, in a frenzy known as the "New Imperialism," rushed to gobble up the last remaining unclaimed pieces of the world, as we will see in Chapter 28.

Yet at that very moment two nations outside Europe were becoming great powers. One of them, the United States, was inhabited mainly by people of European origin. As we saw in Chapter 24, its rise to great-power status had been predicted early in the nineteenth century by astute observers like the French statesman Alexis de Tocqueville. The other one, Japan, seemed so distant and exotic in 1850 that no European had guessed that it would join the ranks of the great powers.

China, Japan, and the Western Powers, to 1867

After 1850 China and Japan—the two largest countries in East Asia—felt the influence of the Western powers as never before, but their responses were completely opposite. China resisted Western influence and became weaker, while Japan transformed itself into a major industrial and military power. One reason for this difference was the Western powers' heavy involvement in China and the distance to Japan, the nation most remote from Europe by ship. More important was the difference between the Chinese and Japanese elites' attitudes toward foreign cultures.

China had been devastated by the Taiping° Rebellion that raged from 1850 to 1864 (see Chapter 26). The French and British took advantage of China's weakness to demand treaty ports where they could trade at will. The British took over China's customs and allowed the free import of opium until 1917. A Chinese "self-strengthening movement" tried in vain to bring about significant reforms by reducing government expenditures and eliminating corruption. The **Empress Dowager Cixi**° (r. 1862–1908), who had once encouraged the construction of shipyards, arsenals, and telegraph lines, opposed railways and other foreign technologies that could carry foreign influences to the interior. Government officials, who did not dare resist the Westerners outright, secretly encouraged crowds to attack and destroy the intrusive devices. They were able to slow the foreign intrusion, but in doing so, they denied themselves the best means of defense against foreign pressure.

In Japan a completely different political organization was in place. The emperor was revered but had no power. Instead, Japan was governed by the Tokugawa shogunate—a secular government under a military leader, or *shogun*, that had come to power in 1600 (see Chapter 21). Local lords, called *daimyos*, were permitted to control their lands and populations with very little interference from the shogunate.

When threatened from outside, this system showed many weaknesses. It did not permit the coordination of resources necessary to resist a major invasion. Shoguns attempted to minimize exposure to foreign powers. In the early 1600s they prohibited foreigners from entering Japan and Japanese from going abroad. The penalties for breaking these laws was death, but many Japanese ignored them anyway. The most flagrant violators were powerful lords in southern Japan who ran large and very successful pirate or black-market operations. In their entrepreneurial activities these lords benefited from the decentralization of the shogunal political system. But when a genuine foreign threat was suggested—as when, in 1792, Russian and British ships were spotted off the Japanese coast—the local lords realized that Japan was too weak and decentralized to resist a foreign invasion. As a result, a few of the regional lords began to develop their own reformed armies, arsenals, and shipyards.

By the 1800s Satsuma° and Choshu,° two large domains in southern Japan, had become wealthy and ambitious. They enjoyed high rates of revenue and population growth. Their remoteness from the capital Edo (now Tokyo) and their economic vigor also fostered a strong sense of local self-reliance.

In 1853 the American Commodore Matthew C. Perry arrived off the coast of Japan with a fleet of steam-powered warships that the Japanese called "black ships." He demanded that Japan open its ports to trade and allow American ships to refuel and take on supplies during their voyages between China and California. He promised to return a year later to receive the Japanese answer.

Perry's demands sparked a crisis in the shogunate. After consultation with the provincial daimyos, the shogun's advisers advocated capitulation to Perry. They pointed to China's humiliating defeats in the Opium and Arrow Wars. In 1854, when Perry returned, representatives of the shogun indicated their willingness to sign the Treaty of Kanagawa,° modeled on the unequal treaties between China and the Western powers. Angry and disappointed, some provincial governors began to encourage an underground movement calling for the destruction of the Tokugawa regime and the banning of foreigners from Japan.

Tensions between the shogunate and some provincial leaders, particularly in Choshu and Satsuma, increased in the early 1860s. When British and French ships shelled the southwestern coasts in 1864 to protest the treatment of foreigners, the action enraged the provincial samurai who rejected the Treaty of Kanagawa and resented the shogunate's inability to protect the country. Young, ambitious, educated men who faced mediocre prospects under the rigid Tokugawa class system emerged as provincial leaders. In 1867 the Choshu leaders Yamagata Aritomo and Ito Hirobumi finally realized that they should stop warring with their rival province, Satsuma, and join forces to lead a rebellion against the shogunate.

The Meiji Restoration and the Modernization of Japan, 1868–1894

The civil war was intense but brief. In 1868 provincial rebels overthrew the Tokugawa Shogunate and declared the young emperor Mutsuhito° (r. 1868–1912) "restored." The new leaders called their regime the

Taiping (tie-PING) **Cixi** (TSUH-shee)

Satsuma (SAT-soo-mah) **Choshu** (CHOE-shoo)
Kanagawa (KAH-nah-GAH-wah) **Mutsuhito** (moo-tsoo-HE-toe)

Arrivals from the East In 1853 Commodore Matthew Perry's ships surprised the Tokugawa Shogunate by appearing not in Kyushu or southern Honshu, where European ships previously had been spotted, but at Uraga on the coast of eastern Honshu. The Japanese soon learned that Perry had come not from the south but across the Pacific from the east. The novelty of the threat unsettled the provincial leaders, who were largely responsible for their own defense. In this print done after the Meiji Restoration, the traditionally dressed local samurai go out to confront the mysterious "black ships." (Courtesy of the Trustees of the British Museum)

"Meiji° Restoration," after Mutsuhito's reign name (*Meiji* means "enlightened rule"). The "Meiji oligarchs," as the new rulers were known, were extraordinarily talented and far-sighted. Determined to protect their country from Western imperialism, they encouraged its transformation into "a rich country with a strong army" with world-class industries. Though imposed from above, the Meiji Restoration marked as profound a change as the French Revolution.

The oligarchs were under no illusion that they could fend off the Westerners without changing their institutions and their society. In the Charter Oath issued in 1868, the young emperor included a prophetic phrase: "Knowledge shall be sought throughout the world and thus shall be strengthened the foundation of the imperial polity." It was to be the motto of a new Japan, which embraced all foreign ideas, institutions, and techniques that could strengthen the nation. The literacy rate in Japan was the highest in Asia at the time, and the oligarchs shrewdly exploited it in their introduction of new educational systems, a conscript army, and new communications. The government was able to establish heavy industry through the use of judicious deficit financing without extensive foreign debt, thanks to decades of experimentation with industrial development and financing in the provinces in the earlier 1800s. With a conscript army and a revamped educational system, the oligarchs attempted to create a new citizenry that was literate and competent but also loyal and obedient.

The Meiji leaders copied the government structure of imperial Germany. They modeled the new Japanese navy on the British and the army on the Prussian. They

Meiji (MAY-gee)

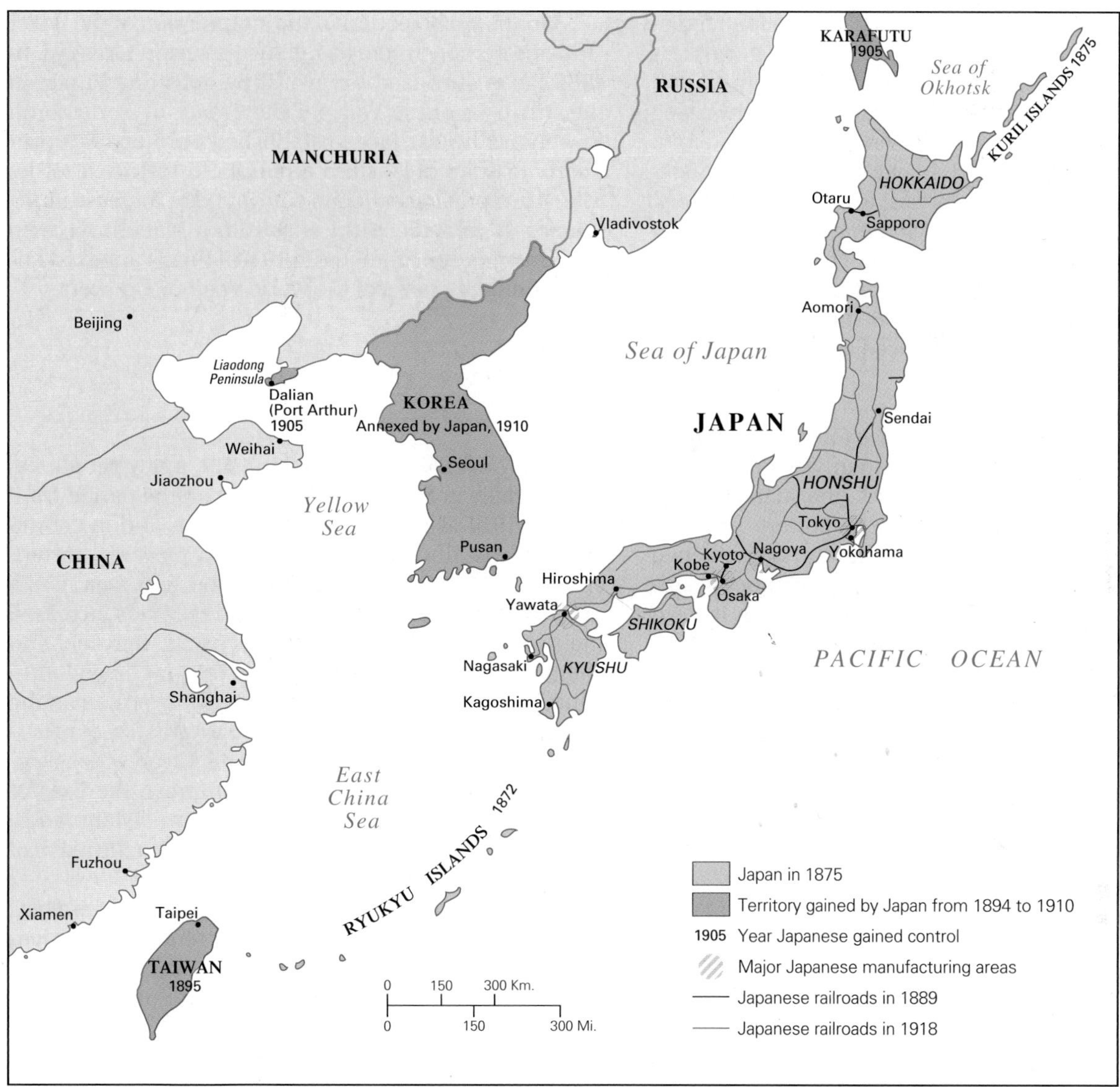

Map 27.3 Expansion and Modernization of Japan, 1868–1918 As Japan acquired modern industry, it followed the example of the European powers in seeking overseas colonies. Its colonial empire grew at the expense of its neighbors: Taiwan was taken from China in 1895; Karafutu (Sakhalin) from Russia in 1905; and all of Korea became a colony in 1910.

introduced Western-style postal and telegraph services, railroads and harbors, banking, clocks, and calendars. To learn the secrets of Western strength, they sent hundreds of students to Britain, Germany, and the United States. They even encouraged foreign clothing styles and pastimes.

The government was especially interested in Western technology. It opened vocational, technical, and agricultural schools and founded four imperial universities. It brought in foreign experts to advise on medicine, science, and engineering. At the newly created Imperial College of Engineering, an Englishman, William Ayrton, became the first professor of electrical engineering anywhere in the world. His students later went on to found major corporations and government research institutes.

To encourage industrialization, the government set up state-owned enterprises to manufacture cloth and inexpensive consumer goods for sale abroad. The first

Japanese industries, some of which had been founded in the early nineteenth century, exploited their workers ruthlessly, just as the first industries in Europe and America had done. Peasant families, squeezed by rising taxes and rents, were forced to send their daughters to work in textile mills. In 1881, to pay off its debts, the government sold these enterprises to private investors, mainly large *zaibatsu*°, or conglomerates. It encouraged individual technological innovation. Thus the carpenter Toyoda Sakichi founded the Toyoda Loom Works (now Toyota Motor Company) in 1906; ten years later he patented the world's most advanced automatic loom.

The Birth of Japanese Imperialism, 1894–1905

The motive for the transformation of Japan was defensive—to protect the nation from the Western powers—but the methods that strengthened Japan against the imperial ambitions of others could also be used to carry out its own conquests. Japan's path to imperialism was laid out by **Yamagata Aritomo,** a leader of the Meiji oligarchs. He believed that to be independent Japan had to define a "sphere of influence" that included Korea, Manchuria, and part of China (see Map 27.3). If other countries controlled this sphere, Japan would be at risk. To protect this sphere of influence, Yamagata insisted, Japan must sustain a vigorous program of military industrialization, culminating in the building of battleships.

Meanwhile, as Japan grew stronger, China was growing weaker. In 1894 the two nations went to war over Japanese encroachments in Korea. The Sino-Japanese War lasted less than six months, and forced China to evacuate Korea, cede Taiwan and the Liaodong° Peninsula, and pay a heavy indemnity. France, Germany, Britain, Russia, and the United States, upset at seeing a newcomer join the ranks of the imperialists, made Japan give up Liaodong in the name of the "territorial integrity" of China. In exchange for their "protection," the Western powers then made China grant them territorial and trade concessions, including ninety treaty ports.

In 1900 Chinese officials around the Empress Dowager Cixi encouraged a series of antiforeign riots known as the Boxer Uprising. Military forces from the European powers, Japan, and the United States put down the riots and occupied Beijing. Emboldened by China's obvious weakness, Japan and Russia competed for possession of the mineral-rich Chinese province of Manchuria.

zaibatsu (zye-BOT-soo) **Liaodong** (li-AH-oh-dong)

Japan's participation in the suppression of the Boxer Uprising demonstrated its military power in East Asia. In 1905 Japan surprised the world by defeating Russia in the Russo-Japanese War. By the Treaty of Portsmouth that ended the war, Japan established a protectorate over Korea. In spite of Western attempts to restrict it to the role of junior partner, Japan continued to increase its influence. It gained control of southern Manchuria, with its industries and railroads. In 1910 it finally annexed Korea, joining the ranks of the world's colonial powers.

Conclusion

After World War I broke out in 1914, many people, especially in Europe, looked back on the period from 1850 to 1914 as a golden age. For some, and in certain ways, it was. Industrialization was a powerful torrent changing Europe, North America, and East Asia. While other technologies like shipping and railroads increased their global reach, new ones—electricity, the steel and chemical industries, and the global telegraph network—contributed to the enrichment and empowerment of the industrial nations. Memories of the great scourges—famines, wars, and epidemics—faded. Clean water, electric lights, and railways began to improve the lives of city dwellers, even the poor. Goods from distant lands, even travel to other continents, came within the reach of millions.

European society seemed to be heading toward better organization and greater security. Municipal services made city life less dangerous and chaotic. Through labor unions, workers achieved some measure of recognition and security. By the turn of the century, liberal political reforms had taken hold in western Europe and seemed about to triumph in Russia as well. Morality and legislation aimed at providing security for women and families, though equality between the sexes was still beyond reach.

The framework for all these changes was the nation-state. The world economy, international politics, even cultural and social issues revolved around a handful of countries—the great powers—that believed they controlled the destiny of the world. These included the most powerful European nations of the previous century, as well as three newcomers—Germany, the United States, and Japan—that were to play important roles in the future.

The strength of the dominant countries rested not only on their industries and trade, but also on the enthusiasm of their peoples for the national cause. The feeling of unity and identity that we call nationalism was a two-edged sword, for it could also be divisive for multiethnic states like Russia and Austria-Hungary, and even Great Britain. It was also a Western concept that did not spread easily to other cultures. Thus Japan and China reacted very differently to the Western intrusion. China, long in contact with the West, was ruled by a conservative elite that associated modern technology with Western interference and resisted both. Japan, after a period of turmoil, accepted not only Western technology but also the nationalist and expansionist ideology of the West.

The success of the great powers rested on their ability to extract resources from nature and from other societies, especially in Asia, Africa, and Latin America. In a global context, the counterpart of the rise of the great powers is the story of imperialism and colonialism. To complete our understanding of the period before 1914, let us turn now to the relations between the great powers and the rest of the world.

Key Terms

railroads
submarine telegraph cables
steel
electricity
Thomas Edison
Victorian Age
"separate spheres"
socialism
labor unions
Karl Marx
anarchist
nationalism
liberalism
Giuseppe Garibaldi
Otto von Bismarck
Empress Dowager Cixi
Meiji Restoration
Yamagata Aritomo

Suggested Reading

More has been written on the great powers in the late nineteenth century than on any previous period in their histories. The following are some interesting recent works and a few classics.

Industrialization is the subject of Peter Stearns, *The Industrial Revolution in World History* (1993), and David Landes, *The Unbound Prometheus: Technological Change and Industrial Development in Western Europe from 1750 to the Present* (1969). Two interesting works on nationalism are E. J. Hobsbawm, *Nation and Nationalism Since 1780* (1990), and Benedict Anderson, *Imagined Communities: Reflections on the Origin and Spread of Nationalism* (1991).

Barrington Moore, *The Social Origins of Dictatorship and Democracy* (1966), is a classic essay on European society. On European women see Renate Bridenthal, Susan Mosher Stuard, and Merry E. Wiesner, eds., *Becoming Visible: Women in European History,* 3d ed. (1998); Patricia Branca, *Silent Sisterhood: Middle-Class Women in the Victorian Home* (1975); Louise Tilly and Joan Scott, *Women, Work, and Family* (1987); and Theresa McBride, *The Domestic Revolution: The Modernization of Household Service in England and France, 1820–1920* (1976). The history of family life is told in Beatrice Gottlieb, *The Family in the Western World from the Black Death to the Industrial Age* (1993). Albert Lindemann, *A History of European Socialism* (1983), covers the labor movements as well.

There are many excellent histories of individual countries. On Germany in the nineteenth century see David Blackbourne, *The Long Nineteenth Century: A History of Germany, 1780–1918* (1998), and Gordon A. Craig, *Germany, 1866–1945* (1980). The standard works on Bismarck and the unification of Germany are Otto Pflanze, *Bismarck and the Development of Germany* (1990), and Lothar Gall, *Bismarck, the White Revolutionary* (1986). On Britain see Donald Read, *The Age of Urban Democracy: England, 1868–1914* (1994), and David Thomson, *England in the Nineteenth Century, 1815–1914* (1978). On France Eugen Weber, *Peasants into Frenchmen* (1976), and Roger Price, *A Social History of Nineteenth-Century France* (1987), are especially recommended. For Austria see Alan Sked, *The Decline and Fall of the Habsburg Empire, 1815–1918* (1989). Two good introductions to Russian history are Hans Rogger, *Russia in the Age of Modernization and Revolution, 1881–1917* (1983), and Gregory L. Freeze, ed., *Russia: A History* (1997).

There are several interesting books on Japan, in particular Peter Duus, *The Rise of Modern Japan,* 2d ed. (1998), and Tessa Morris-Suzuki, *The Technological Transformation of Japan* (1994). Two fine books that cover the history of modern China: John King Fairbank, *The Great Chinese Revolution, 1800–1985* (1987), and Jonathan D. Spence, *The Search for Modern China* (1990).

Notes

1. Quoted in Bonnie S. Anderson and Judith P. Zinsser, *A History of Their Own: Women in Europe from Prehistory to the Present,* vol. 2 (New York: Harper & Row, 1988), 372, 387.

28 The New Imperialism, 1869–1914

Opening the Suez Canal When the canal opened in 1869, thousands of dignitaries and ordinary people gathered to watch the ships go by.

CHAPTER OUTLINE

In 1869 Ismail°, the khedive° (ruler) of Egypt, invited all the Christian princes of Europe and all the Muslim princes of Asia and Africa—except the Ottoman sultan, his nominal overlord—to celebrate the inauguration of the greatest construction project of the century: the **Suez Canal.** Among the sixteen hundred dignitaries from the Middle East and Europe who assembled at Port Said° were Emperor Francis Joseph of Austria-Hungary and Empress Eugénie of France. A French journalist wrote:

> This multitude, coming from all parts of the world, presented the most varied and singular spectacle. All races were represented. . . . We saw, coming to attend this festival of civilization, men of the Orient wearing clothes of dazzling colors, chiefs of African tribes wrapped in their great coats, Circassians in war costumes, officers of the British army of India with their shakos [hats] wrapped in muslin, Hungarian magnates wearing their national costumes.[1]

Ismail used the occasion to emphasize the harmony and cooperation between the peoples of Africa, Asia, and Europe and to show that Egypt was not only independent but was also an equal of the great powers. To bless the inauguration, Ismail had invited clergy of the Muslim, Orthodox, and Catholic faiths. A reporter noted: "The Khedive . . . wished to symbolize thereby the unity of men and their brotherhood before God, without distinction of religion; it was the first time that the Orient had seen such a meeting of faiths to celebrate and bless together a great event and a great work."[2]

The canal was a great success, but not in the way Ismail intended. Ships using it could travel between Europe and India in less than two weeks—much less time than the month or longer consumed by sailing around Africa and across the Indian Ocean. By lowering freight costs, the canal stimulated shipping and the construction of steamships, giving an advantage to nations that had heavy industry and a large maritime trade over land-based empires and countries with few merchant ships. Great Britain, which long opposed construction of the canal for fear that it might fall into enemy hands, benefited more than any other nation. France, which provided half the capital and most of the engineers, came in a distant second, for it had less trade with Asia than Britain did. Egypt, which contributed the other half of the money and most of the labor, was the loser. Instead of making Egypt powerful and independent, the Suez Canal provided the excuse for a British invasion and occupation of Egypt.

Far from inaugurating an era of harmony among the peoples of three continents and three faiths, the canal triggered a wave of European domination over Africa and Asia. Between 1869 and 1914 Germany, France, Britain, Russia, Japan, and the United States used industrial technology to impose their will on the nonindustrial parts of the world. Historians use the expression **New Imperialism** to describe this exercise of power.

As you read this chapter, ask yourself the following questions:

- What motivated the industrial nations to conquer new territories, and what means did they use?
- Why were some parts of the world annexed to the new empires, while others became economic dependencies of the great powers?
- How did the environment change in the lands subjected to the New Imperialism?

The New Imperialism: Motives and Methods

Europe had a long tradition of imperialism reaching back to the twelfth-century Crusades against the Arabs, and the United States greatly expanded its territory after achieving independence in 1783 (see Map 24.3). During the first two-thirds of the nineteenth century the European powers continued to increase their

Ismail (is-mah-EEL) **khedive** (kuh-DEEV) **Port Said** (port sah-EED)

influence overseas (see Chapter 25). The New Imperialism was characterized by an explosion of territorial conquests even more rapid than the Spanish conquests of the sixteenth century. Between 1869 and 1914, in a land grab of unprecedented speed, Europeans seized territories in Africa and Central Asia, and both Europeans and Americans took territories in Southeast Asia and the Pacific. Approximately 10 million square miles (26 million square kilometers) and 150 million people fell under the rule of Europe and the United States in this period.

The New Imperialism was more than a land grab. The imperial powers used economic and technological means to reorganize dependent regions and bring them into the world economy as suppliers of foodstuffs and raw materials and as consumers of industrial products. In Africa and other parts of the world, this was done by conquest and colonial administration. In the Latin American republics the same result was achieved indirectly. Even though they remained politically independent, they became economic dependencies of the United States and Europe.

What inspired Europeans and Americans to venture overseas and impose their will on other societies? There is no simple answer to this question. Economic, cultural, and political motives were involved in all cases.

Political Motives

The great powers of the late nineteenth century, as well as less powerful countries like Italy, Portugal, and Belgium, were competitive and hypersensitive about their status. French leaders, humiliated by their defeat by Prussia in 1871 (see Chapter 27), sought to reestablish their nation's prestige through territorial acquisitions overseas. Great Britain, already in possession of the world's largest and richest empire, felt the need to protect India, its "jewel in the crown," by acquiring colonies in East Africa and Southeast Asia. German Chancellor Otto von Bismarck had little interest in acquiring colonies, but many Germans believed that a country as important as theirs required an impressive empire overseas.

Political motives were not limited to statesmen in the capital cities. Colonial governors, even officers posted to the farthest colonial outposts, practiced their own diplomacy. They often decided on their own to claim a piece of land before some rival got it. Armies fighting frontier wars found it easier to defeat their neighbors than to make peace with them. In response to border skirmishes with neighboring states, colonial agents were likely to send in troops, take over their neighbors' territories, and then inform their home governments. Governments felt obligated to back up their men-on-the-spot in order not to lose face. The great powers of Europe acquired much of West Africa, Southeast Asia, and the Pacific islands in this manner.

Cultural Motives

The late nineteenth century saw a Christian revival in Europe and North America, as both Catholics and Protestants founded new missionary societies. Their purpose was not only religious—to convert nonbelievers, whom they regarded as "heathen"—but also cultural in a broader sense. They sought to export their own norms of "civilized" behavior: they were determined to abolish slavery in Africa and bring Western education, medicine, hygiene, and monogamous marriage to all the world's peoples.

Among those attracted by religious work overseas were many women who joined missionary societies to become teachers and nurses, positions of greater authority than they could hope to find at home. Although they did not challenge colonialism directly, their influence often helped soften the harshness of colonial rule—for example, by calling attention to issues of maternity and women's health. Mary Slessor, a British missionary who lived for forty years among the people of southeastern Nigeria, campaigned against slavery, human sacrifice, and the killing of twins and, generally, for women's rights. In India missionaries denounced the customs of child marriages and *sati* (the burning of widows on their husbands' funeral pyres). Such views often clashed with the customs of the people among whom they settled.

The sense of moral duty and cultural superiority was not limited to missionaries. Many Europeans and Americans equated technological innovations with "progress" and "change for the better." They believed that Western technology proved the superiority of Western ideas, customs, and culture. This attitude included the idea that non-Western peoples could achieve, through education, the same cultural level as Europeans and Americans. More harmful were racist ideas that relegated non-Europeans to a status of permanent inferiority. Racists assigned different stages of biological development to peoples of different races and cultures. They divided humankind into several races based on physical appearance and ranked these races in a hierarchy that ranged from "civilized" at the highest level down through "semi-barbarous," "barbarian," and finally, at the bottom, "savage." Caucasians—whites—were always at the top of this ranking. Such ideas were often presented as an excuse for permanent rule over Africans and Asians.

Imperialism first interested small groups of explorers, clergy, and businessmen but soon attracted people

CHRONOLOGY

	The Scramble for Africa	Asia and Western Dominance	Imperialism in Latin America
		1862–1895 French conquer Indochina **1865–1876** Russian forces advance into Central Asia	
1870	**1869** Opening of the Suez Canal **1874** Warfare between the British and the Asante (Gold Coast) **1877–1879** Warfare between the British and the Xhosa and between the British and the Zulu (South Africa) **1882** British forces occupy Egypt **1884–1885** Berlin Conference; Leopold II obtains Congo Free State	**1878** United States obtains Pago Pago Harbor (Samoa) **1885** Britain completes conquest of Burma **1887** United States obtains Pearl Harbor (Hawaii)	**1870–1910** Railroad building boom; British companies in Argentina and Brazil; U.S. companies in Mexico.
1890	**1896** Ethiopians defeat Italian army at Adowa; warfare between the British and the Asante **1898** Battle of Omdurman **1899–1902** South African War between Afrikaners and the British **1902** First Aswan Dam completed (Egypt) **1908** Belgium annexes Congo	**1894–1895** China defeated in Sino-Japanese War **1895** France completes conquest of Indochina **1898** United States annexes Hawaii and purchases Philippines from Spain **1899–1902** U.S. forces conquer and occupy Philippines **1903** Russia completes Trans-Siberian Railway **1904–1905** Russia defeated in Russo-Japanese War	**1895–1898** Cubans revolt against Spanish rule **1898** Spanish-American War; United States annexes Puerto Rico and Guam **1901** United States imposes Platt Amendment on Cuba **1903** United States backs secession of Panama from Colombia **1904–1907, 1916** U.S. troops occupy Dominican Republic **1904–1914** United States builds Panama Canal **1912** U.S. troops occupy Nicaragua and Honduras
1910			

from other walks of life. Young men, finding few opportunities for adventure and glory at home in an era of peace, sought them overseas as the Spanish conquistadors had done over three centuries earlier. At first, European people and parliaments were indifferent or hostile to overseas adventures, but a few easy victories in the 1880s helped to overcome their reluctance. The United States was fully preoccupied with its westward expansion until the 1880s, but in the 1890s popular attention shifted to lands outside U.S. borders. Newspapers, which achieved wide readership in the second half of the nineteenth century, discovered that they could boost circulation with reports of wars and conquests. By the 1890s imperialism was a popular cause; it was the overseas extension of the nationalism propelling the power politics of the time.

Economic Motives

The industrialization of Europe and North America stimulated the demand for minerals—copper for electrical wiring, tin for canning, chrome and manganese for the steel industry, coal for steam engines, and, most of all, gold and

Pears Soap Is Best This advertisement appeared in the *Illustrated London News* in 1887. In identifying a brand of soap as "the formula for British conquest," it credited British manufactured products with the power to overawe spear-wielding indigenous warriors. (*Illustrated London News* Picture Library)

diamonds. The demand for such industrial crops as cotton and rubber and for stimulants such as sugar, coffee, tea, and tobacco also grew. These products were found in the tropics, but never in sufficient quantities.

An economic depression lasting from the mid-1870s to the mid-1890s caused European merchants, manufacturers, and shippers to seek protection against foreign competition (see below). They argued that their respective countries needed secure sources of tropical raw materials and protected markets for their industries. Declining business opportunities at home prompted entrepreneurs and investors to look for profits from mines, plantations, and railroads in Asia, Africa, and Latin America. Since investment in countries so different from their own was extremely risky, businessmen sought the backing of their governments, preferably with soldiers.

These reasons explain why Europeans and Americans wished to expand their influence over other societies in the late nineteenth and early twentieth centuries. Yet motives do not adequately explain the events of that time. It was possible to conquer a piece of Africa, convert the "heathen," and start a plantation because of the sudden increase in the power that industrial peoples could wield over nonindustrial peoples and over the forces of nature. Technological advances explain both the motives and the outcome of the New Imperialism.

The Tools of the Imperialists

To succeed, empire builders needed the means to achieve their objectives at a reasonable cost. These means were provided by the Industrial Revolution (see Chapter 23). In the early part of the nineteenth century technological innovations began to tip the balance of power in favor of Europe.

Europeans had dominated the oceans since about 1500, and their naval power increased still more with the introduction of steamships. The first steamer reached India in 1825 and was soon followed by regular mail service in the 1830s. The long voyage around Africa was at first too costly for cargo steamers, for coal had to be shipped from England. The building of the Suez Canal and the development of increasingly efficient engines solved this problem and led to a boom in shipping to the Indian Ocean and East Asia. Whenever fighting broke out, passenger liners were requisitioned as troopships, giving European forces greater mobility than Asians and Africans. Their advantage was enhanced even more by the development of a global network of submarine telegraph cables connecting Europe with North America in the 1860s, with Latin America and Asia in the 1870s, with Africa in the 1880s, and finally across the Pacific in 1904.

Until the middle of the nineteenth century, western Europeans were much weaker on land than at sea. Thereafter, Europeans used gunboats with considerable success in China, Burma, Indochina, and the Congo Basin. Although gunboats opened the major river basins to European penetration, the invaders often found themselves hampered by other natural obstacles. *Falciparum* malaria, found only in Africa, was so deadly to Europeans that few explorers survived before the 1850s. In 1854 a British doctor discovered that the drug quinine, taken regularly during one's stay in Africa, could prevent the disease. This and a few sanitary precautions reduced the annual death rate among whites in West Africa from between 250 and 750 per thousand in the early nineteenth century to between 50 and 100 per thousand after

The Battle of Omdurman In the late nineteenth century, most battles between European (or European-led) troops and African forces were one-sided encounters because of the disparity in the opponents' firearms and tactics. The Battle of Omdurman in Sudan in 1898 is a dramatic example. The forces of the Mahdi, some on horseback, were armed with spears and single-shot muskets. The British troops and their Egyptian allies, lined up in the foreground, used repeating rifles and machine guns able to shoot much farther than the Sudanese weapons. As a result, there were many Sudanese casualties but very few British or Egyptian. (The Art Archive)

1850. This reduction was sufficient to open the continent to merchants, officials, and missionaries.

Muzzle-loading smoothbore muskets had been used in Europe, Asia, and the Americas since the late seventeenth century, and by the early nineteenth century they were also common in much of Africa. The development of new and much deadlier firearms in the 1860s and 1870s shifted the balance of power on land between Westerners and other peoples. One of these was the breechloader, which could be fired accurately ten times as fast as, and five or six times farther than, a musket. By the 1870s all armies in Europe and the United States had switched to these new rifles. Two more innovations appeared in the 1880s: smokeless powder, which did not foul the gun or reveal the soldier's position, and repeating rifles, which could shoot fifteen rounds in fifteen seconds. In the 1890s European and American armies began using machine guns, which could fire eleven bullets per second.

In the course of the century Asians and Africans also acquired better firearms, mostly old weapons that European armies had discarded. As European firearms improved, the firepower gap widened, making colonial conquests easier than ever before. By the 1880s and 1890s European-led forces of a few hundred could defeat non-European armies of thousands. Against the latest weapons, African and Asian soldiers armed with muskets or, in some cases, with spears did not stand a chance, no matter how numerous and courageous they were.

A classic example is the **Battle of Omdurman** in Sudan. On September 2, 1898, forty thousand Sudanese attacked an Anglo-Egyptian expedition that had come up the Nile on six steamers and four other boats. General Horatio Kitchener's troops had twenty machine guns and four artillery pieces; the Sudanese were equipped with muskets and spears. Within a few hours eleven thousand Sudanese and forty-eight British lay dead. Winston Churchill, the future British prime minister, witnessed the battle and called it

> The most signal triumph ever gained by the arms of science over barbarians. Within the space of five hours the strongest and best-armed savage army yet arrayed against a modern European Power had been destroyed and dispersed, with hardly any difficulty, comparatively small risk, and insignificant loss to the victors.[3]

Colonial Agents and Administration

Once colonial agents took over a territory, their home government expected them to cover their own costs and, if possible, return some profit to the home country. The system of administering and exploiting colonies for the benefit of the home country is known as **colonialism.** In some cases, such as along the West African coast or in Indochina, there was already a considerable trade that could be taxed. In other places profits could come only from investments and a thorough reorganization of the indigenous societies. In applying modern scientific and industrial methods to their colonies, colonialists started the transformation of Asian and African societies and landscapes that has continued to our day.

Legal experts and academics emphasized the differences between various systems of colonial government and debated whether colonies eventually should be assimilated into the ruling nation, associated in a federation, or allowed to rule themselves. Colonies that were protectorates retained their traditional governments, even their monarchs, but had a European "resident" or "consul-general" to "advise" them. Other colonies were directly administered by a European governor. In fact, the impact of colonial rule depended much more on economic and social conditions than on narrow legal distinctions.

One important factor was the presence or absence of European settlers. In Canada, Australia, and New Zealand, whites were already in the majority by 1869, and their colonial "mother-country," Britain, encouraged them to elect parliaments and rule themselves. Where European settlers were numerous but still a minority of the population, as in Algeria and South Africa, settlers and the home country struggled for control over the indigenous population. In colonies with few white settlers, the European governors ruled autocratically.

In the early years of the New Imperialism, colonial administrations consisted of a governor and his staff, a few troops to keep order, and a small number of tax collectors and magistrates. Nowhere could colonialism operate without the cooperation of indigenous elites, because no colony was wealthy enough to pay the salaries of more than a handful of European officials. In most cases the colonial governors exercised power through traditional rulers willing to cooperate, as in the Princely States of India (see Chapter 25). In addition, colonial governments educated a few local youths for "modern" jobs as clerks, nurses, policemen, customs inspectors, and the like. Thus colonialism relied on two rival indigenous elites.

European and American women seldom took part in the early stages of colonial expansion. As conquest gave way to peaceful colonialism and as steamships and railroads made travel less difficult, colonial officials and settlers began bringing their wives to the colonies. By the 1880s the British Women's Emigration Association was recruiting single women to go out to the colonies to marry British settlers. As one of its founders, Ellen Joyce, explained, "The possibility of the settler marrying his own countrywoman is of imperial as well as family importance."

The arrival of white women in Asia and Africa led to increasing racial segregation. Sylvia Leith-Ross, wife of a colonial officer in Nigeria, explained: "When you are alone, among thousands of unknown, unpredictable people, dazed by unaccustomed sights and sounds, bemused by strange ways of life and thought, you need to remember who you are, where you come from, what your standards are." Many colonial wives found themselves in command of numerous servants and expected to follow the complex etiquette of colonial entertainment in support of their husbands' official positions. Occasionally they found opportunities to exercise personal initiatives, usually charitable work involving indigenous women and children. However well meaning, their efforts were always subordinate to the work of men.

THE SCRAMBLE FOR AFRICA

Until the 1870s African history was largely shaped by internal forces and local initiatives (see Chapter 25). Outside Algeria and southern Africa, only a handful of Europeans had ever visited the interior of Africa, and European countries possessed only small enclaves on the coasts. As late as 1879 Africans ruled more than 90 percent of the continent. Then, within a decade, Africa was invaded and divided among the European powers in a movement often referred to as the **"scramble" for Africa** (see Map 28.1). This invasion affected all regions of the continent. Let us look at the most significant cases, beginning with Egypt, the wealthiest and most populated part of the continent.

Egypt

Ironically, European involvement in Egypt resulted from Egypt's attempt to free itself from Ottoman Turkish rule. Throughout the mid-nineteenth century the khedives of Egypt had tried to modernize their armed forces; build canals, harbors, railroads, and other public works; and reorient agriculture toward export crops, especially cotton (see Chapters 23 and 25). Their interest in the Suez Canal was also part of this policy. Khedive Ismail even tried to make Egypt the center of an empire reaching south into Sudan and Ethiopia.

These ambitions cost vast sums of money, which the khedives borrowed from European creditors at high interest rates. By 1876 Egypt's foreign debt had risen to £100 million sterling, and the interest payments alone consumed one-third of its foreign export earnings. To avoid bankruptcy the Egyptian government sold its shares in the Suez Canal to Great Britain and accepted four foreign "commissioners of the debt" to oversee its finances. French and British bankers, still not satisfied, lobbied their governments to secure the loans by stronger measures. In 1878 the two governments obliged Ismail to appoint a Frenchman as minister of public works and a Briton as minister of finance. When high taxes caused hardship and popular discontent, the French and British persuaded the Ottoman sultan to depose Ismail. This foreign intervention provoked a military uprising under Egyptian army colonel Arabi Pasha, which threatened the Suez Canal.

Fearing for their investments, the British sent an army into Egypt in 1882. They intended to occupy Egypt for only a year or two. But theirs was a seaborne empire that depended on secure communications between Britain and India. So important was the Suez Canal to their maritime supremacy that they stayed for seventy years. During those years the British ruled Egypt "indirectly"—that is, they maintained the Egyptian government and the fiction of Egyptian sovereignty but retained real power in their own hands.

Eager to develop Egyptian agriculture, especially cotton production, the British brought in engineers and contractors to build the first dam across the Nile, at Aswan in upper Egypt. When completed in 1902, it was one of the largest dams in the world. It captured the annual Nile flood and released its waters throughout the year, allowing farmers to grow two, sometimes three, crops a year. This doubled the effective acreage compared with the basin system of irrigation practiced since the time of the pharaohs, in which the annual floodwaters of the Nile were retained by low dikes around the fields.

The economic development of Egypt by the British enriched a small elite of landowners and merchants, many of them foreigners. Egyptian peasants got little relief from the heavy taxes collected to pay for their country's crushing foreign debt and the expenses of the British army of occupation. Western ways that conflicted with the teachings of Islam—such as the drinking of alcohol and the relative freedom of women—offended Muslim religious leaders. Most Egyptians found British rule more onerous than that of the Ottomans. By the 1890s Egyptian politicians and intellectuals were demanding that the British leave, to no avail.

Western and Equatorial Africa

While the British were taking over Egypt, the French were planning to extend their empire into the interior of West Africa. Starting from the coast of Senegal, which had been in French hands for centuries, they hoped to build a railroad from the upper Senegal River to the upper Niger in order to open the interior to French merchants. This in turn led the French military to undertake the conquest of western Sudan.

Meanwhile, the actions of three individuals, rather than a government, brought about the occupation of the Congo Basin, an enormous forested region in the heart of equatorial Africa (see Map 28.1). In 1879 the American journalist **Henry Morton Stanley,** who had explored the area, persuaded **King Leopold II** of Belgium to invest his personal fortune in "opening up" equatorial Africa. With Leopold's money, Stanley returned to Africa from 1879 to 1884 to establish trading posts along the southern bank of the Congo River. At the same time, **Savorgnan de Brazza**, an Italian officer serving in the French army, obtained from an African ruler living on the opposite bank a treaty that placed the area under the "protection" of France.

These events sparked a flurry of diplomatic activity. German chancellor Bismarck called the **Berlin Conference** on Africa of 1884 and 1885. There the major powers agreed that henceforth "effective occupation" would replace the former trading relations between Africans and Europeans. This meant that every country with colonial ambitions had to send troops into Africa and participate in the division of the spoils. As a reward for

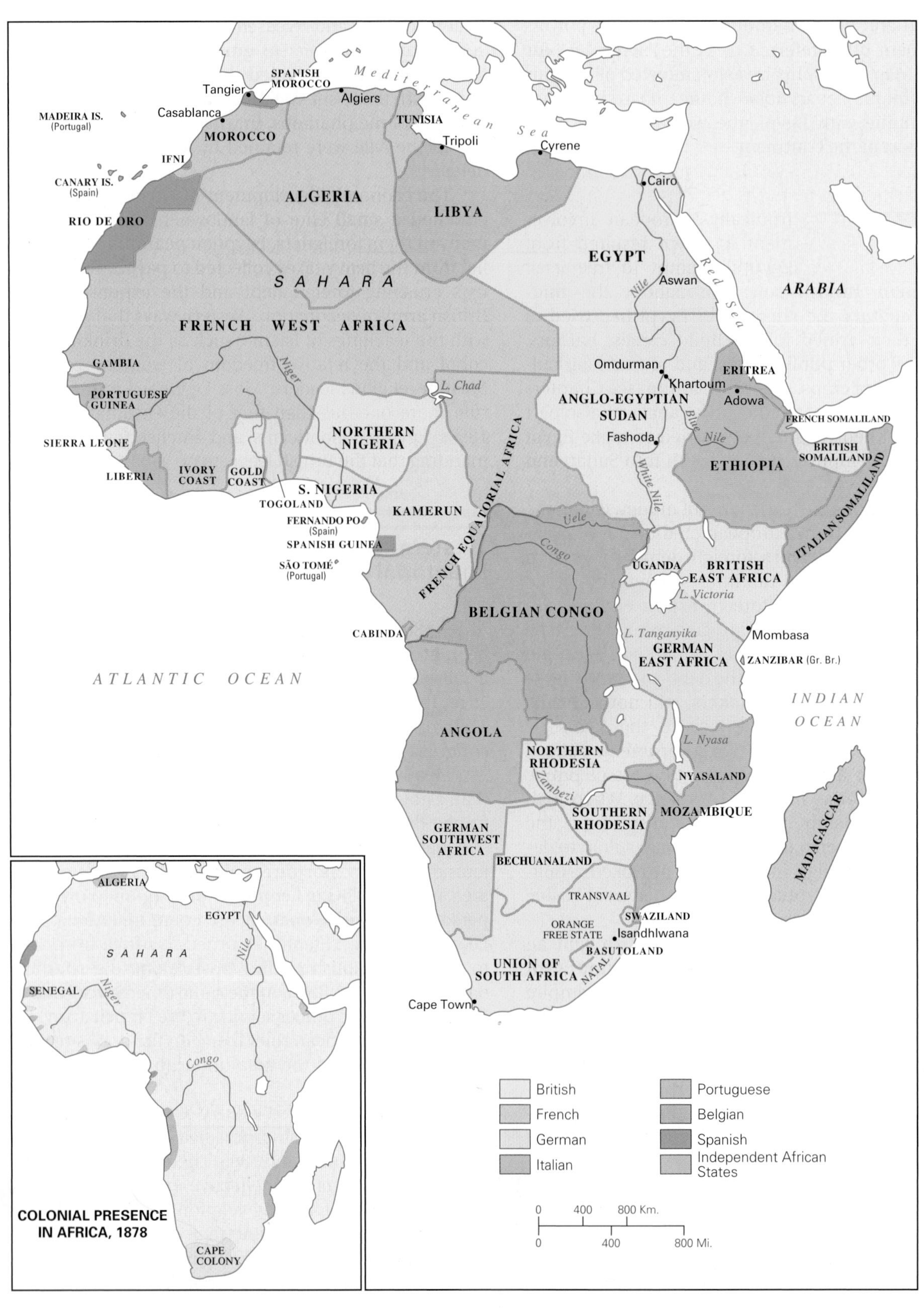

Mediterranean Sea
Tangier
SPANISH MOROCCO
Algiers
MADEIRA IS. (Portugal)
Casablanca
MOROCCO
TUNISIA
Tripoli
Cyrene
IFNI
CANARY IS. (Spain)
ALGERIA
LIBYA
Cairo
RIO DE ORO
EGYPT
Aswan
Red Sea
ARABIA
SAHARA
Nile
FRENCH WEST AFRICA
GAMBIA
Niger
Omdurman
Khartoum
ERITREA
PORTUGUESE GUINEA
L. Chad
ANGLO-EGYPTIAN SUDAN
Adowa
FRENCH SOMALILAND
NORTHERN NIGERIA
SIERRA LEONE
Blue Nile
Fashoda
BRITISH SOMALILAND
LIBERIA
IVORY COAST
GOLD COAST
ETHIOPIA
S. NIGERIA
TOGOLAND
White Nile
FRENCH EQUATORIAL AFRICA
KAMERUN
FERNANDO PO (Spain)
Uele
SPANISH GUINEA
Congo
ITALIAN SOMALILAND
SÃO TOMÉ (Portugal)
UGANDA
BRITISH EAST AFRICA
L. Victoria
BELGIAN CONGO
CABINDA
L. Tanganyika
Mombasa
GERMAN EAST AFRICA
ZANZIBAR (Gr. Br.)
ATLANTIC OCEAN
INDIAN OCEAN
ANGOLA
L. Nyasa
NORTHERN RHODESIA
NYASALAND
Zambezi
SOUTHERN RHODESIA
MOZAMBIQUE
GERMAN SOUTHWEST AFRICA
MADAGASCAR
BECHUANALAND
TRANSVAAL
SWAZILAND
ORANGE FREE STATE
Isandhlwana
BASUTOLAND
UNION OF SOUTH AFRICA
NATAL
Cape Town
British
French
German
Italian
Portuguese
Belgian
Spanish
Independent African States
0 400 800 Km.
0 400 800 Mi.
ALGERIA
EGYPT
SAHARA
Nile
SENEGAL
Niger
Congo
COLONIAL PRESENCE IN AFRICA, 1878
CAPE COLONY

Map 28.1 Africa in 1878 and 1914 In 1878 the European colonial presence was limited to a few coastal enclaves, plus portions of Algeria and South Africa. By 1914, Europeans had taken over all of Africa except Ethiopia and Liberia.

triggering the "scramble" for Africa, Leopold II acquired a personal domain under the name "Congo Free State," while France and Portugal took most of the rest of equatorial Africa. In this manner, the European powers and King Leopold managed to divide Africa among themselves, at least on paper.

"Effective occupation" required many years of effort. In the interior of West Africa, Muslim rulers resisted the French invasion for up to thirty years. The French advance encouraged the Germans to stake claims to parts of the region and the British to move north from their coastal enclaves, until the entire region was occupied by Britain, France, and Germany.

Because West Africa had long had a flourishing trade, the new rulers took advantage of existing trade networks, taxing merchants and farmers, investing the profits in railroads and harbors, and paying dividends to European stockholders. In the Gold Coast (now Ghana) British trading companies bought the cocoa grown by African farmers at low prices and resold it for large profits. The interior of French West Africa lagged behind. Although the region could produce cotton, peanuts, and other crops, the difficulties of transportation limited its development before 1914.

Compared to West Africa, equatorial Africa had few inhabitants and little trade. Rather than try to govern these vast territories directly, authorities in the Congo Free State, the French Congo, and the Portuguese colonies of Angola and Mozambique farmed out huge pieces of land to private concession companies, offering them monopolies on the natural resources and trade of their territories and the right to employ soldiers and tax the inhabitants. The inhabitants, however, had no cash crops that they could sell to raise the money they needed to pay their taxes.

Freed from outside supervision, the companies forced the African inhabitants at gunpoint to produce cash crops and carry them, on their heads or backs, to the nearest railroad or navigable river. The worst abuses took place in the Congo Free State, where a rubber boom

A Steamboat for the Congo River Soon after the Congo Basin was occupied by Europeans, the new colonial rulers realized they needed to improve transportation. Since access from the sea was blocked by rapids on the lower Congo River, steamboats had to be brought in sections, hauled from the coast by thousands of Congolese over very difficult terrain. This picture shows the pieces arriving at Stanley Pool, ready to be reassembled. (From H. M. Stanley, *The Congo*, vol. 2, London, 1885)

lasting from 1895 to 1905 made it profitable for private companies to coerce Africans to collect latex from vines that grew in the forests. One Congolese refugee told the British consul Roger Casement who investigated the atrocities:

> We begged the white men to leave us alone, saying we could get no more rubber, but the white men and their soldiers said: "Go. You are only beasts yourselves, you are only *nyama* (meat)." We tried, always going further into the forest, and when we failed and our rubber was short, the soldiers came to our towns and killed us. Many were shot, some had their ears cut off; others were tied up with ropes around their necks and bodies and taken away.[4]

After 1906 the British press began publicizing the horrors. The public outcry that followed, coinciding with the end of the rubber boom, convinced the Belgian government to take over Leopold's private empire in 1908.

Southern Africa

The history of southern Africa between 1869 and 1914 differs from that of the rest of the continent in several important respects. One was that the land had long attracted settlers. African pastoralists and farmers had inhabited the region for centuries. **Afrikaners,** descendants of Dutch settlers on the Cape of Good Hope, moved inland throughout the nineteenth century; British prospectors and settlers arrived later in the century; and, finally, Indians were brought over by the British and stayed.

Southern Africa attracted European settlers because of its good pastures and farmland and its phenomenal deposits of diamonds, gold, and copper, as well as coal and iron ore. This was the new El Dorado that imperialists had dreamed of since the heyday of the Spanish Empire in Peru and Mexico in the sixteenth century.

The discovery of diamonds at Kimberley in 1868 lured thousands of European prospectors as well as Africans looking for work. It also attracted the interest of Great Britain, colonial ruler of the Cape Colony, which annexed the diamond area in 1871, thereby angering the Afrikaners. Once in the interior, the British defeated the Xhosa° people in 1877 and 1878. Then in 1879 they confronted the Zulu, militarily the most powerful of the African peoples in the region.

The Zulu, led by their king Cetshwayo°, resented their encirclement by Afrikaners and British. A growing sense of nationalism and their proud military tradition led them into a war with the British in 1879. At first they held their own, defeating the British at Isandhlwana°, but a few months later they were defeated. Cetshwayo was captured and sent into exile, and the Zulu lands were given to white ranchers. Yet throughout those bitter times, the Zulu's sense of nationhood remained strong.

Relations between the British and the Afrikaners, already tense as a result of British encroachment, took a turn for the worse when gold was discovered in the Afrikaner republic of Transvaal° in 1886. In the gold rush that ensued, the British soon outnumbered the Afrikaners.

Britain's invasion of southern Africa was driven in part by the ambition of **Cecil Rhodes** (1853–1902), who once declared that he would "annex the stars" if he could. Rhodes made his fortune in the Kimberley diamond fields, founding De Beers Consolidated, a company that has dominated the world's diamond trade ever since. He then turned to politics. He encouraged a concession company, the British South Africa Company, to push north into Central Africa, where he named two new colonies after himself: Southern Rhodesia (now Zimbabwe) and Northern Rhodesia (now Zambia). The Ndebele° and Shona peoples, who inhabited the region, resisted this invasion, but the machine guns of the British finally defeated them.

British attempts to annex the two Afrikaner republics, Transvaal and Orange Free State, and the inflow of English-speaking whites into the gold- and diamond-mining areas led to the South African War, which lasted from 1899 to 1902. At first the Afrikaners had the upper hand, for they were highly motivated, possessed modern rifles, and knew the land. In 1901, however, Great Britain brought in 450,000 troops and crushed the Afrikaner armies. Ironically, the Afrikaners' defeat in 1902 led to their ultimate victory. Wary of costly commitments overseas, the British government expected European settlers in Africa to manage their own affairs, as they were doing in Canada, Australia, and New Zealand. Thus, in 1910 the European settlers created the Union of South Africa, in which the Afrikaners eventually emerged as the ruling element.

Unlike Canada, Australia, and New Zealand, South Africa had a majority of indigenous inhabitants and substantial numbers of Indians and "Cape Coloureds" (people of mixed ancestry). Yet the Europeans were both numerous enough to demand self-rule and powerful enough to deny the vote and other civil rights to the majority. In 1913 the South African parliament passed the Natives Land Act, assigning Africans to reservations and

Xhosa (KOH-sah) **Cetshwayo** (set-SHWAH-yo)

Isandhlwana (ee-sawn-dull-WAH-nuh) **Transvaal** (trans-VAHL)
Ndebele (en-duh-BELL-ay)

forbidding them to own land elsewhere. This and other racial policies turned South Africa into a land of segregation, oppression, and bitter divisions.

Political and Social Consequences

At the time of the European invasion, Africa contained a wide variety of societies. Some parts of the continent had long-established kingdoms with aristocracies or commercial towns dominated by a merchant class. In other places agricultural peoples lived in villages without any outside government. Still elsewhere pastoral nomads were organized along military lines. In some remote areas people lived from hunting and gathering. Not surprisingly, these societies responded in very different ways to the European invasion.

Some peoples welcomed the invaders as allies against local enemies. Once colonial rule was established, they sought work in government service or in European firms and sent their children to mission schools. In exchange, they were often the first to receive benefits such as clinics and roads.

Others, especially peoples with a pastoral or a warrior tradition, fought tenaciously. Examples abound, from the Zulu and Ndebele of southern Africa to the pastoral Herero° people of Southwest Africa (now Namibia), who rose up against German invaders in 1904; in repressing their uprising, the Germans exterminated two-thirds of them. In the Sahel, a belt of grasslands south of the Sahara, charismatic leaders rose up in the name of a purified Islam, gathered a following of warriors, and led them on part-religious, part empire-building campaigns called *jihads*. These leaders included Samori Toure in western Sudan (now Mali), Rabih in the Chad basin, and the Mahdi° in eastern Sudan. All of them eventually came into conflict with European-led military expeditions and were defeated.

Some commercial states with long histories of contact with Europeans also fought back. The kingdom of **Asante**° in Gold Coast rose up in 1874, 1896, and 1900 before it was finally overwhelmed. In the Niger Delta, the ancient city of Benin, rich with artistic treasures, resisted colonial control until 1897, when a British "punitive expedition" set it on fire and carted its works of art off to Europe.

One resistance movement succeeded, to the astonishment of Europeans and Africans alike. When **Menelik** became emperor of Ethiopia in 1889 (see Chapter 25), his country was threatened by Sudanese Muslims to the west and by France and Italy, which controlled the coast of the Red Sea to the east. For many years, Ethiopia had been purchasing weapons. By the Treaty of Wichelle (1889), Italy agreed to sell more weapons to Ethiopia. Six years later, when Italians attempted to establish a protectorate over Ethiopia, they found the Ethiopians armed with thousands of rifles and even a few machine guns and artillery pieces. Although Italy sent twenty thousand troops to attack Ethiopia, in 1896 they were defeated at Adowa° by a larger and better-trained Ethiopian army.

Most Africans neither joined nor fought the European invaders but tried to continue living as before. They found this increasingly difficult because colonial rule disrupted every traditional society. The presence of colonial officials meant that rights to land, commercial transactions, and legal disputes were handled very differently, and that traditional rulers lost all authority, except where Europeans used them as local administrators.

Changes in landholding were especially disruptive, for most Africans were farmers or herders for whom access to land was a necessity. In areas with a high population density, such as Egypt and West Africa, colonial rulers left peasants in place, encouraged them to grow cash crops, and collected taxes on the harvest. Elsewhere, the new rulers declared any land that was not farmed to be "waste" or "vacant" and gave it to private concession companies or to European planters and ranchers. In Kenya, Northern Rhodesia, and South Africa, Europeans found the land and climate to their liking, in contrast to other parts of Africa, where soldiers, officials, missionaries, or traders stayed only a few years. White settlers forced Africans to become squatters, sharecroppers, or ranch hands on land they had farmed for generations. In South Africa they forced many Africans off their lands and onto "reserves," much like the nomadic peoples of North America, Russia, and Australia (see Chapter 24).

Although the colonial rulers harbored designs on the land, they were even more interested in African labor. They did not want to pay wages high enough to attract workers voluntarily. Instead, they imposed various taxes, such as the hut tax and the head tax, which Africans had to pay regardless of their income. To find the money, Africans had little choice but to accept whatever work the Europeans offered. In this way Africans were recruited to work on plantations, railroads, and other modern enterprises. In the South African mines Africans were paid, on average, one-tenth as much as Europeans.

Some Africans came to the cities and mining camps seeking a better life than they had on the land. Many migrated great distances and stayed away for years at a

Herero (hair-AIR-oh) **Mahdi** (MAH-dee) **Asante** (uh-SAWN-tay)

Adowa (AH-do-ah)

Victorious Ethiopians Among the states of Africa, Ethiopia alone was able to defend itself against European imperialism. In the 1880s, hemmed in by Italian advances to its east and north and by British advances to its south and west, Ethiopia purchased modern weapons and trained its army to use them. Thus prepared, the Ethiopians defeated an Italian invasion at Adowa in 1896. These Ethiopian army officers wore their most elaborate finery to pose for a photograph after their victory. (National Archives)

time. Most migrant workers were men who left their wives and children behind in villages and on reserves. In some cases the authorities did not allow them to bring their families and settle permanently in the towns. This caused great hardship for African women, who had to grow food for their families during the men's absences and care for sick and aged workers. Long separations between spouses also led to an increase in prostitution and to the spread of sexually transmitted diseases.

Some African women welcomed colonial rule, for it brought an end to fighting and slave raiding, but others were led into captivity (see Diversity and Dominance: Two Africans Recall the Arrival of the Europeans). A few succeeded in becoming wealthy traders or owners of livestock. On the whole, however, African women benefited less than men from the economic changes that colonialism introduced. In areas where the colonial rulers replaced communal property (traditional in most of Africa) with private property, property rights were assigned to the head of the household—that is, to the man. Almost all the jobs open to Africans, even those considered "women's work" in Europe, such as nursing and domestic service, were reserved for men.

Cultural Responses

More Africans came into contact with missionaries than with any other Europeans. Missionaries, both men and women, opened schools to teach reading, writing, and arithmetic to village children. Boys were taught crafts such as carpentry and blacksmithing, while girls learned domestic skills such as cooking, laundry, and child care.

Along with basic skills, the first generation of Africans educated in mission schools acquired Western ideas of justice and progress. Samuel Ajayi Crowther, a Yoruba rescued from slavery as a boy and educated in mission schools in Sierra Leone, went on to become an Anglican minister and, in 1864, the first African bishop. Crowther thought that Africa needed European assistance in achieving both spiritual and economic development:

> Africa has neither knowledge nor skill . . . to bring out her vast resources for her own improvement. . . . Therefore to claim Africa for the Africans alone, is to claim for her the right of a continued ignorance. . . . For it is certain, unless help [comes] from without, a nation can never rise above its present state.[5]

After the first generation, many of the teachers in mission schools were African, themselves the products of a mission education. They discovered that Christian ideals clashed with the reality of colonial exploitation. One convert wrote in 1911:

> There is too much failure among all Europeans in Nyasaland. The three combined bodies—Missionaries, Government and Companies or gainers of money—do form the same rule to look upon the native with mock-

> ery eyes. . . . If we had enough power to communicate ourselves to Europe, we would advise them not to call themselves Christendom, but Europeandom. Therefore the life of the three combined bodies is altogether too cheaty, too thefty, too mockery. Instead of "Give," they say "Take away from." There is too much breakage of God's pure law.[6]

Christian missionaries from Europe and America were not the only ones to bring religious change to Africa. In southern and Central Africa indigenous preachers adapted Christianity to African values and customs and founded new denominations known as "Ethiopian" churches.

Christianity proved successful in converting followers of traditional religions but made no inroads among Muslims. Instead, Islam, long predominant in northern and eastern Africa, spread southward as Muslim teachers established Quranic schools in the villages and founded Muslim brotherhoods. European colonialism unwittingly helped the diffusion of Islam. By building cities and increasing trade, colonial rule permitted Muslims to settle in new areas. As Islam—a universal religion without the taint of colonialism—became increasingly relevant to Africans, the number of Muslims in sub-Saharan Africa probably doubled between 1869 and 1914.

ASIA AND WESTERN DOMINANCE

From 1869 to 1914 the pressure of the industrial powers was felt throughout Asia, the East Indies, and the Pacific islands. As trade with these regions grew in the late nineteenth century, so did their attractiveness to imperialists eager for economic benefits and national prestige.

Europeans had traded along the coasts of Asia and the East Indies since the early sixteenth century. By 1869 Britain already controlled most of India and Burma; Spain occupied the Philippines; and the Netherlands held large parts of the East Indies (now Indonesia). Between 1862 and 1895 France conquered Indochina (now Vietnam, Kampuchea, and Laos). The existence of these Asian colonial possessions had inspired the building of the Suez Canal.

We have already seen the special cases of British imperialism in India (Chapter 25) and of Japanese imperialism in China and Korea (Chapter 27). Here let us look at the impact of the New Imperialism on Central and Southeast Asia, Indonesia, the Philippines, and Hawaii (see Map 28.2)

Central Asia

For over seven centuries Russians had been at the mercy of the nomads of the Eurasian steppe extending from the Black Sea to Manchuria. When the nomadic tribesmen were united, as they were under the Mongol ruler Genghis Khan (r. 1206–1227), they could defeat the Russians; when they were not, the Russians moved into the steppe. This age-old ebb and flow ended when Russia acquired modern rifles and artillery.

Between 1865 and 1876 Russian forces advanced into Central Asia. Nomads like the Kazakhs, who lived east of the Caspian Sea, fought bravely but in vain. The fertile agricultural land of Kazakhstan attracted 200,000 Russian settlers. Although the governments of Tsar Alexander II (r. 1855–1881) and Tsar Alexander III (r. 1881–1894) claimed not to interfere in indigenous customs, they declared communally owned grazing lands "waste" or "vacant" and turned them over to farmers from Russia. By the end of the nineteenth century the nomads were fenced out and reduced to starvation. Echoing the beliefs of other European imperialists, an eminent Russian jurist declared: "International rights cannot be taken into account when dealing with semibarbarous peoples."

South of the Kazakh steppe land were deserts dotted with oases where the fabled cities of Tashkent, Bukhara, and Samarkand served the caravan trade between China and the Middle East. For centuries the peoples of the region had lived under the protection of the Mongols and later the Qing Empire. But by the 1860s and 1870s the Qing Empire was losing control over Central Asia, so it was fairly easy for Russian expeditions to conquer the indigenous peoples. Russia thereby acquired land suitable for cotton, along with a large and growing Muslim population.

Russian rule brought few benefits to the peoples of the Central Asian oases and few real changes. The Russians abolished slavery, built railroads to link the region with Europe, and planted hundreds of thousands of acres of cotton. Unlike the British in India, however, they did not attempt to change the customs, languages, or religious beliefs of their subjects.

Southeast Asia and Indonesia

The peoples of the Southeast Asian peninsula and the Indonesian archipelago had been in contact with outsiders—Chinese, Indians, Arabs, Europeans—for centuries. Java and the smaller islands—the fabled Spice Islands (the Moluccas)—had long been subject to Portuguese and later to Dutch domination. Until the mid-nineteenth

DIVERSITY AND DOMINANCE

TWO AFRICANS RECALL THE ARRIVAL OF THE EUROPEANS

We know a great deal about the arrival of the Europeans into the interior of Africa from the perspective of the conquerors, but very little about how the events were experienced by Africans. Here are two accounts by African women, one from northern Nigeria whose land was occupied by the British, the other from the Congo Free State, a colony of King Leopold II of Belgium. They show not only how Africans experienced European colonial dominance, but also the great diversity of experiences of Africans.

BABA OF KARO, A NIGERIAN WOMAN, REMEMBERS HER CHILDHOOD

When I was a maiden the Europeans first arrived. Ever since we were quite small the *malams* had been saying that the Europeans would come with a thing called a train, they would come with a thing called a motor-car, in them you would go and come back in a trice. They would stop wars, they would repair the world, they would stop oppression and lawlessness, we should live at peace with them. We used to go and sit quietly and listen to the prophecies. They would come, fine handsome people, they would not kill anyone, they would not oppress anyone, they would bring all their strange things. . . .

I remember when a European came to Karo on a horse, and some of his foot soldiers went into the town. Everyone came out to look at them, but in Zerewa they didn't see the European. Everyone at Karo ran away—"There's a European, there's a European!" He came from Zaria with a few black men, two on horses and four on foot. We were inside the town. Later on we heard that they were there in Zaria in crowds, clearing spaces and building houses. One of my younger "sisters" was at Karo, she was pregnant, and when she saw the European she ran away and shut the door.

At that time Yusufu was the king of Kano. He did not like the Europeans, he did not wish them, he would not sign their treaty. Then he say that perforce he would have to agree, so he did. We Habe wanted them to come, it was the Fulani who did not like it. When the Europeans came the Habe saw that if you worked for them they paid you for it, they didn't say, like the Fulani, "Commoner, give me this! Commoner, bring me that!" Yes, the Habe wanted them; they saw no harm in them. From Zaria they came to Rogo, they were building their big road to Kano City. They called out the people and said they were to come and make the road, if there were trees in the way they cut them down. The Europeans paid them with goods, they collected the villagers together and each man brought his large hoe. Money was not much use to them, so the Europeans paid them with food and other things.

The Europeans said that there were to be no more slaves; if someone said "Slave!" you could complain to the *alkali* who would punish the master who said it, the judge said, "That is what the Europeans have decreed." The first order said that any slave, if he was younger than you, was your younger brother, if he was older than you was your elder brother—they were all brothers of their master's family. No one used the word "slave" any more. When slavery was stopped, nothing much happened at our *rinji* except that some slaves whom we had bought in the market ran away. Our own father went to his farm and worked, he and his son took up their large hoes; they loaned out their spare farms. Tsoho our father and Kadiri my brother with whom I live now and Babambo worked, they farmed guineacorn and millet and groundnuts and everything; before this they had supervised the slaves' work—now they did their own. When the midday food was ready, the women of the compound would give us children the food, one of us drew water, and off we went to the farm to take the men their food at the foot of a tree; I was about eight or nine at that time, I think. . . .

In the old days if the chief liked the look of your daughter he would take her and put her in his house; you could do nothing about it. Now they don't do that.

ILANGA, A CONGOLESE WOMAN, RECOUNTS HER CAPTURE BY AGENTS OF THE CONGO FREE STATE

Our village is called Waniendo, after our chief Niendo. . . . It is a large village near a small stream, and surrounded by large fields of *mohago* (cassava) and *muhindu* (maize) and other foods, for we all worked hard at our plantations, and always had plenty to eat. The men always worked in the fields clearing the ground, or went hunting, . . . We never had war in our country, and the men had not many arms except knives; but our chief Niendo had a gun, which he had bought long ago from another chief for forty-three beads, but he had no powder or caps, and only carried it when he went on a journey.

. . . we were all busy in the fields hoeing our plantations, for it was the rainy season, and the weeds sprang quickly up, when a runner came to the village saying that a large band of men was coming, that they all wore red caps and blue cloth, and carried guns and long knives, and that many white men were with them, the chief of whom was *Kibalanga* (Michaux). Niendo at once called all the chief men to his house, while the drums were beaten to summon the people to the village. A long consultation was held, and finally we were all told to go quietly to the fields and bring in ground-nuts, plantains, and cassava for the warriors who were coming, and goats and fowl for the white men. The women all went with baskets and filled them, and put them in the road, which was blocked up, so many were there. Niendo then commanded everyone to go and sit quietly in the houses until he gave other orders. This we did, everyone remaining quietly seated while Niendo went up the road with the head men to meet the white chief. We did not know what to think, for most of us feared that so many armed men coming boded evil; but Niendo thought that, by giving presents of much food, he would induce the strangers to pass on without harming us. And so it proved, for the soldiers took the baskets, and were then ordered by the white men to move off through the village. Many of the soldiers looked into the houses and shouted at us words we did not understand. We were glad when they were all gone, for we were much in fear of the white men and the strange warriors, who are known to all the people as being great fighters, bringing war wherever they go. . . .

When the white men and their warriors had gone, we went again to our work, and were hoping that they would not return; but this they did in a very short time. As before, we brought in great heaps of food; but this time *Kibalanga* did not move away directly, but camped near our village, and his soldiers came and stole all our fowl and goats and tore up our cassava; but we did not mind as long as they did not harm us. The next morning it was reported that the white men were going away; but soon after the sun rose over the hill, a large band of soldiers came into the village, and we all went into the houses and sat down. We were not long seated when the soldiers came rushing in shouting, and threatening Niendo with their guns. They rushed into the houses and dragged the people out. Three or four came to our house and caught hold of me, also my husband Oleka and my sister Katinga. We were dragged into the road, and were tied together with cords about our necks, so that we could not escape. We were all crying, for now we knew that we were to be taken away to be slaves. The soldiers beat us with the iron sticks from their guns, and compelled us to march to the camp of *Kibalanga*, who ordered the women to be tied up separately, ten to each cord, and the men in the same way. When we were all collected—and there were many from other villages whom we now saw, and many from Waniendo—the soldiers brought baskets of food for us to carry, in some of which was smoked human flesh (*niama na nitu*).

We then set off marching very quickly. My sister Katinga had her baby in her arms, and was not compelled to carry a basket; but my husband Oleka was made to carry a goat. We marched until the afternoon, when we camped near a stream, where we were glad to drink, for we were much athirst. We had nothing to eat, for the soldiers would give us nothing, so we lay upon the ground, and at night went to sleep. The next day we continued the march, and when we camped at noon were given some maize and plantains, which were gathered near a village from which the people had run away. So it continued each day until the fifth day, when the soldiers took my sister's baby and threw it in the grass, leaving it to die, and made her carry some cooking pots which they found in the deserted village. On the sixth day we became very weak from lack of food and from constant marching and sleeping in the damp grass, and my husband, who marched behind us with the goat, could not stand up longer, and so he sat down beside the path and refused to walk more. The soldiers beat him, but still he refused to move. Then one of them struck him on the head with the end of his gun, and he fell upon the ground. One of the soldiers caught the goat, while two or three others stuck the long knives they put on the ends of their guns into my husband. I saw the blood spurt out, and then saw him no more, for we passed over the brow of a hill and he was out of sight. Many of the young men were killed the same way, and many babies thrown into the grass to die. A few escaped; but we were so well guarded that it was almost impossible.

After marching ten days we came to the great water (Lualaba) and were taken in canoes across to the white men's town at Nyangwe. Here we stayed for six or seven days, and were then put in canoes and sent down the river; . . . but on the way we could get nothing to eat, and were glad to rest here, where there are good houses and plenty of food; and we hope we will not be sent away.

QUESTIONS FOR ANALYSIS

1. **How do Baba and Ilanga recall their existence before the Europeans came?**
2. **What did they expect when they first heard of the arrival of Europeans? Instead, what happened to them, their relatives, and their towns?**
3. **How do you explain the difference between these two accounts?**

Source: From M. F. Smith, ed., *Baba of Karo: A Woman of the Muslim Hausa* (New York: Philosophical Library, 1955), 66–68. Edgar Canisius, *A Campaign Amongst Cannibals* (London: R. A. Everett & Co., 1903), 250–256. Used by permission of the Philosophical Library.

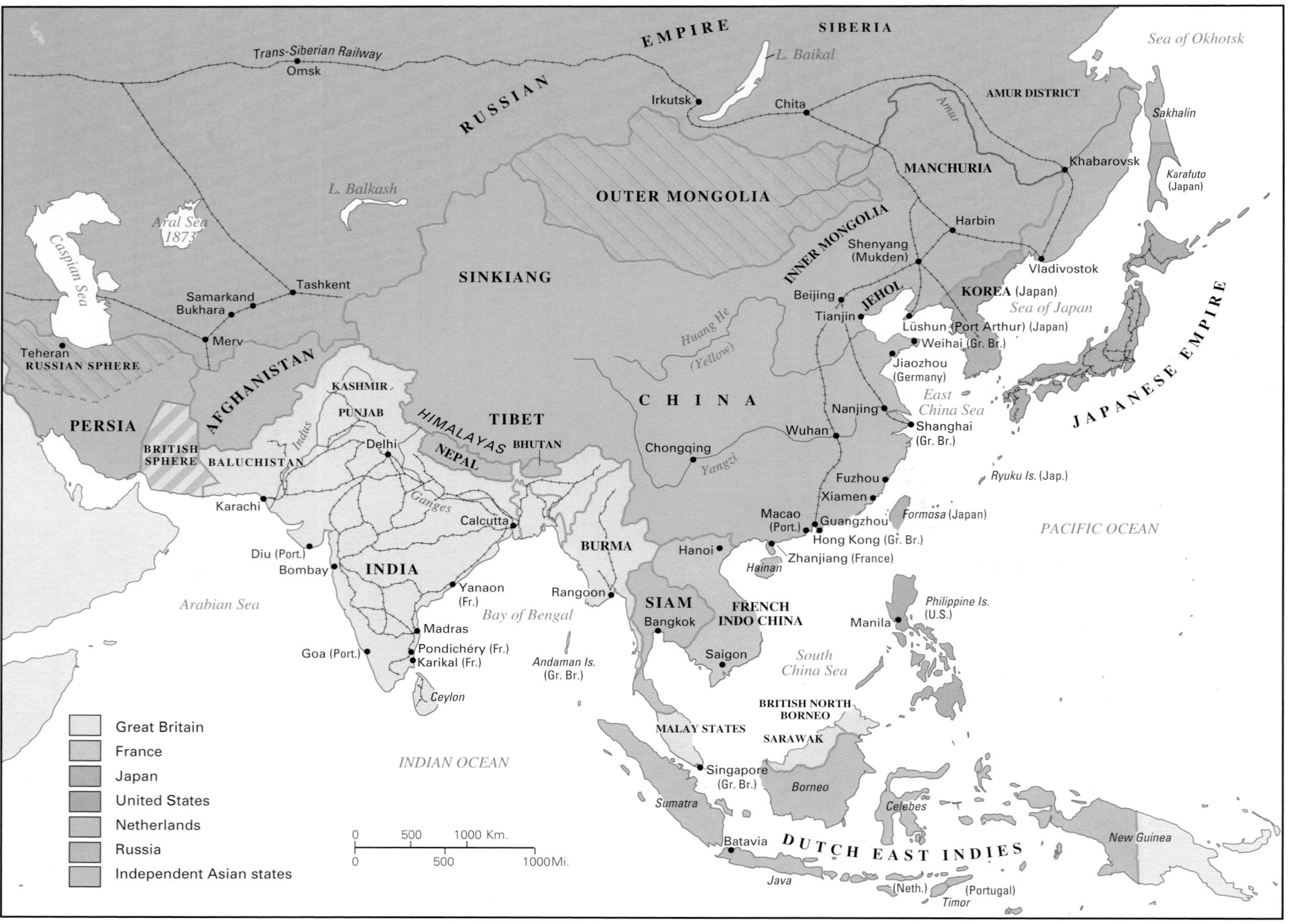

Map 28.2 Asia in 1914 By 1914, much of Asia was claimed by colonial powers. The southern rim, from the Pacific Gulf to the Pacific, was occupied by Great Britain, France, the Netherlands, and the United States. Central Asia had been incorporated into the Russian Empire. Japan, now industrialized, had joined the Western imperialist powers in expanding its territory and influence at the expense of China.

Lim Nee Soon's Plantation In British Malaya, pineapples and rubber trees were often cultivated together, because pineapples could be grown between the trees during the five or six years it took for the saplings to grow large enough to be tapped. Not all plantation owners were British. In this picture, Lim Nee Soon, known as the "Pineapple King," stands next to a truck that is taking pineapples to his canning factory. (National Archives of Singapore)

century, however, most of the region was made up of independent kingdoms.

As in Africa, there is considerable variation in the history of different parts of the region, yet all came under intense imperialist pressure during the nineteenth century. Burma (now Myanmar), nearest India, was gradually taken over by the British in the course of the century, until the last piece was annexed in 1885. Indochina fell under French control piece by piece until it was finally subdued in 1895. Similarly, Malaya (now Malaysia) came under British rule in stages during the 1870s and 1880s. By the early 1900s the Dutch had subdued northern Sumatra, the last part of the Dutch East Indies to be conquered. Only Siam (now Thailand) remained independent, although it lost several border provinces.

Despite their varied political histories, all these regions had features in common. They all had fertile soil, constant warmth, and heavy rains. Furthermore, the peoples of the region had a long tradition of intensive gardening, irrigation, and terracing. In parts of the region where the population was not very dense, Europeans found it easy to import landless laborers from China and India seeking better opportunities overseas. Another reason for the region's wealth was the transfer of commercially valuable plants from other parts of the world. Tobacco, cinchona° (an antimalarial drug), manioc (an edible root crop), maize (corn), and natural rubber were brought from the Americas; sugar from India; tea from China; and coffee and oil palms from Africa. By 1914 much of the world's supply of these valuable products—in the case of rubber, almost all—came from Southeast Asia and Indonesia (see Environment and Technology: Imperialism and Tropical Ecology).

Most of the wealth of Southeast Asia and Indonesia was exported to Europe and North America. In exchange, the inhabitants of the region received two benefits from colonial rule: peace and a reliable food supply. As a result, their numbers increased at an unprecedented rate. For instance, the population of Java (an island the size of Pennsylvania) doubled from 16 million in 1870 to over 30 million in 1914.

Colonialism and the growth of population brought many social changes. The more numerous agricultural and commercial peoples gradually moved into mountainous and forested areas, displacing the earlier inhabitants who practiced hunting and gathering or shifting

---

cinchona (sin-CHO-nah)

agriculture. The migrations of the Javanese to Borneo and Sumatra are but one example. Immigrants from China and India (see Chapter 25) changed the ethnic composition and culture of every country in the region. Thus the population of the Malay Peninsula became one-third Malay, one-third Chinese, and one-third Indian.

As in Africa, European missionaries attempted to spread Christianity under the colonial umbrella. Islam, however, was much more successful in gaining new converts, for it had been established in the region for centuries and people did not consider it a religion imposed on them by foreigners.

Education and European ideas had an impact on the political perceptions of the peoples of Southeast Asia and Indonesia. Just as important was their awareness of events in neighboring Asian countries: India, where a nationalist movement arose in the 1880s; China, where modernizers were undermining the authority of the Qing; and especially Japan, whose rapid industrialization culminated in its brilliant victory over Russia in the Russo-Japanese War (1904–1905; see Chapter 27). The spirit of a rising generation was expressed by a young Vietnamese writing soon after the Russo-Japanese War:

> I, . . . an obscure student, having had occasion to study new books and new doctrines, have discovered in a recent history of Japan how they have been able to conquer the impotent Europeans. This is the reason why we have formed an organization. . . . We have selected from young Annamites [Vietnamese] the most energetic, with great capacities for courage, and are sending them to Japan for study. . . . Several years have passed without the French being aware of the movement. . . . Our only aim is to prepare the population for the future.[7]

Hawaii and the Philippines, 1878–1902

By the 1890s the United States had a fast-growing population and industries that produced more manufactured goods than they could sell at home. Merchants and bankers began to look for export markets. The political mood was also expansionist, and many echoed the feelings of the naval strategist Alfred T. Mahan°: "Whether they will or no, Americans must now begin to look outward. The growing production of the country requires it."

Some Americans had been looking outward for quite some time, especially across the Pacific to China and Japan. In 1878 the United States obtained the harbor of Pago Pago in Samoa as a coaling and naval station, and in 1887 it secured the use of Pearl Harbor in Hawaii for the same purpose. Six years later American settlers in Hawaii deposed Queen Liliuokalani (1838–1917) and offered the Hawaiian Islands to the United States. At the time President Grover Cleveland (1893–1897) was opposed to annexation, and the settlers had to content themselves with an informal protectorate. By 1898, however, the United States under President William McKinley (1897–1901) had become openly imperialistic, and it annexed Hawaii as a steppingstone to Asia. As the United States became ever more involved in Asian affairs, Hawaii's strategic location brought an inflow of U.S. military personnel, and its fertile land caused planters to import farm laborers from Japan, China, and the Philippines. These immigrants soon outnumbered the native Hawaiians.

While large parts of Asia were falling under colonial domination, the people of the Philippines were chafing under their Spanish rulers. The movement for independence began among young Filipinos studying in Europe. José Rizal, a young doctor working in Spain, was arrested and executed in 1896 for writing patriotic and anticlerical novels. Thereafter, the center of resistance shifted to the Philippines, where **Emilio Aguinaldo,** leader of a secret society, rose in revolt and proclaimed a republic in 1898. The revolutionaries had a good chance of winning independence, for Spain had its hands full with a revolution in Cuba (see below).

Unfortunately for Aguinaldo and his followers, the United States went to war against Spain in April 1898 and quickly overcame Spanish forces in the Philippines and Cuba. President McKinley had not originally intended to acquire the Philippines, but after the Spanish defeat, he realized that a weakened Spain might lose the islands to another imperialist power. Japan, having recently defeated China in the Sino-Japanese War (1894–1895) and annexed Taiwan (see Chapter 27), was eager to expand its empire. So was Germany, which had taken over parts of New Guinea and Samoa and several Pacific archipelagoes during the 1880s. To forestall them, McKinley purchased the Philippines from Spain for $20 million.

The Filipinos were not eager to trade one master for another. For a while, Aguinaldo cooperated with the Americans in the hope of achieving full independence. When his plan was rejected, he rose up again in 1899 and proclaimed the independence of his country. In spite of protests by anti-imperialists in the United States, the U.S. government decided that its global interests outweighed the interests of the Filipino people. In rebel areas, a U.S. army of occupation tortured prisoners, burned villages and crops, and forced the inhabitants into "reconcentration camps." Many American soldiers tended to look on Filipinos with the same racial contempt with

Mahan (mah-HAHN)

Imperialism and Tropical Ecology

Like all conquerors before them, the European imperialists of the nineteenth century exacted taxes and rents from the peoples they conquered. But they also sent botanists and agricultural experts to their tropical colonies to increase the production of commercial crops, radically changing the landscapes.

The most dramatic effects were brought about by the deliberate introduction of new crops—an acceleration of the Columbian Exchange that had begun in the fifteenth century. In the early nineteenth century tea was transferred from China to India and Ceylon. In the 1850s British and Dutch botanists smuggled seeds of the cinchona tree from the Andes in South America to India and Java. They had to operate in secret because the South American republics, knowing the value of this crop, prohibited the export of seeds. With the seeds, the British and Dutch established cinchona plantations in Ceylon and Java, respectively, to produce quinine, which was essential as an antimalarial drug and a flavoring for tonic water. Similarly, in the 1870s British agents stole seeds of rubber trees from the Amazon rain forest and transferred them to Malaya and Sumatra.

Before these transfers, vast forests covered the highlands of India, Southeast Asia, and Indonesia, precisely the lands where the new plants grew best. So European planters had the forests cut down and replaced with thousands of acres of commercially profitable trees and bushes, all lined up in perfect rows and tended by thousands of indigenous laborers to satisfy the demands of customers in faraway lands. The crops that poured forth from the transformed environments brought great wealth to the European planters and the imperial powers. In 1909 the British botanist John Willis justified the transformation in these terms:

> *Whether planting in the tropics will always continue to be under European management is another question, but the northern powers will not permit that the rich and as yet comparatively undeveloped countries of the tropics should be entirely wasted by being devoted merely to the supply of the food and clothing wants of their own people, when they can also supply the wants of the colder zones in so many indispensable products.*

This quotation raises important questions about trade versus self-sufficiency. If a region's economy supplies the food and clothing wants of its own people, is its output "entirely wasted"? What is the advantage of trading the products of one region (such as the tropics) for those of another (such as the colder zones)? Is this trade an obligation? Should one part of the world (such as the "northern powers") let another refuse to develop and sell its "indispensable products"? Can you think of a case where a powerful country forced a weaker one to trade?

Branch of a Cinchona Tree The bark of the cinchona tree was the source of quinine, the only antimalarial drug known before the 1940s. Quinine made it much safer for Europeans to live in the tropics. (From Bentley & Trimen's Medicinal Plants. Hunt Institute for Botanical Documentation, Carnegie Mellon University)

Source: The quotation is from John Christopher Willis, *Agriculture in the Tropics: An Elementary Treatise* (Cambridge: Cambridge University Press, 1909), 38–39.

Emilio Aguinaldo In 1896, a revolt led by Emilio Aguinaldo attempted to expel Spaniards from the Philippines. When the United States purchased the Philippines from Spain two years later, the Filipino people were not consulted. Aguinaldo continued his campaign, this time against the American occupation forces, until his capture in 1901. In this picture, he appears on horseback, surrounded by some of his troops. (Corbis)

which Europeans viewed their colonial subjects. By the end of the insurrection in 1902, the war had cost the lives of 5,000 Americans and 200,000 Filipinos.

After the insurrection ended, the United States attempted to soften its rule with public works and economic development projects. New buildings went up in the city of Manila; roads, harbors, and railroads were built; and the Philippine economy was tied ever more closely to that of the United States. In 1907 Filipinos were allowed to elect representatives to a legislative assembly, but ultimate authority remained in the hands of a governor appointed by the president of the United States. In 1916 the Philippines were the first U.S. colony to be promised independence, a promise fulfilled thirty years later.

IMPERIALISM IN LATIN AMERICA

Nations in the Americas followed two divergent paths (see Chapter 24). In Canada and the United States manufacturing industries, powerful corporations, and wealthy financial institutions arose. Latin America and the Caribbean exported raw materials and foodstuffs and imported manufactured goods. The poverty of their people, the preferences of their elites, and the pressures of the world economy made them increasingly dependent on the industrialized countries. Their political systems saved them from outright annexation by the colonial empires. But their natural resources made them attractive targets for manipulation by the industrial powers, including the United States, in a form of economic dependence called **free-trade imperialism.**

In the Western Hemisphere, therefore, the New Imperialism manifested itself not by a "scramble" for territories but in two other ways. In the larger republics of South America, the pressure was mostly financial and economic. In Central America and the Caribbean, it also included military intervention by the United States.

Railroads and the Imperialism of Free Trade

Latin America's economic potential was huge, for the region could produce many agricultural and mineral products in demand in the industrial countries. What was needed was a means of opening the interior to development. Railroads seemed the perfect answer.

Foreign merchants and bankers as well as Latin American landowners and politicians embraced the new technology. Starting in the 1870s almost every country in Latin America acquired railroads, usually connecting mines or agricultural regions with the nearest port rather than linking up the different parts of the interior. Since Latin America did not have any steel or mechanical industries, all the equipment and building material came from Britain or the United States. So did the money to build the networks, the engineers who designed and maintained them, and the managers who ran them.

Argentina, a land of rich soil that produced wheat, beef, and hides, gained the longest and best-developed rail network south of the United States. By 1914, 86 percent of the railroads in Argentina were owned by British firms; 40 percent of the employees were British; and the official language of the railroads was English, not Spanish. The same was true of mining and industrial enterprises and public utilities throughout Latin America.

In many ways, the situation resembled those of India and Ireland, which also obtained rail networks in exchange for raw materials and agricultural products. The Argentine nationalist Juan Justo saw the parallel:

> English capital has done what English armies could not do. Today our country is tributary to England . . . the gold that the English capitalists take out of Argentina or carry off in the form of products does us no more good than the Irish get from the revenues that the English lords take out of Ireland.[8]

The difference was that the Indians and Irish had little say in the matter because they were under British rule. But in Latin America the political elites encouraged foreign companies with generous concessions as the most rapid way to modernize their countries and enrich

Railroads Penetrate South America The late nineteenth century saw the construction of several railroad networks in South America, often through rugged and dangerous terrain. This photograph shows the opening of a bridge on the Transandine Railroad in Peru. Flags were raised in honor of American construction and British ownership of the railroad. (Tony Morrison/South American Pictures)

the property owners. In countries where the majority of the poor were Indians (as in Mexico and Peru) or of African origin (as in Brazil), they were neither consulted nor allowed to benefit from the railroad boom.

American Expansionism and the Spanish-American War, 1898

After 1865 Europeans used their financial power to penetrate Latin America. But they avoided territorial acquisitions for four reasons: (1) they were overextended in Africa and Asia; (2) there was no need, because the Latin American governments provided the political backing for the economic arrangements; (3) the Latin Americans had shown themselves capable of resisting invasions, most recently when Mexico fought off the French in the 1860s (see Chapter 24); and (4) the United States, itself a former colony, claimed to defend the entire Western Hemisphere against all outside intervention. This claim, made in the Monroe Doctrine (1823), did not prevent the United States itself from intervening in Latin American affairs.

The United States had long had interests in Cuba, the closest and richest of the Caribbean islands and a Spanish colony. American businesses had invested great sums of money in Cuba's sugar and tobacco industries, and tens of thousands of Cubans had migrated to the United States. In 1895 the Cuban nationalist José Martí started a revolution against Spanish rule. American newspapers thrilled readers with lurid stories of Spanish atrocities; businessmen worried about their investments; and politicians demanded that the U.S. government help liberate Cuba.

On February 15, 1898, the U.S. battleship *Maine* accidentally blew up in Havana harbor, killing 266 American sailors. The U.S. government immediately blamed Spain and issued an ultimatum that the Spanish evacuate Cuba. Spain agreed to the ultimatum, but the American press and Congress were eager for war, and President McKinley did not restrain them.

The Spanish-American War was over quickly. On May 1, 1898, U.S. warships destroyed the Spanish fleet at Manila in the Philippines. Two months later the United States Navy sank the Spanish Atlantic fleet off Santiago, Cuba. By mid-August Spain was suing for peace. U.S. Secretary of State John Hay called it "a splendid little war." The United States purchased the Philippines from Spain but took over Puerto Rico and Guam as war booty. The two islands remain American possessions to this day. Cuba became an independent republic, subject, however, to intense interference by the United States.

American Intervention in the Caribbean and Central America, 1901–1914

The nations of the Caribbean and Central America were small and poor, and their governments were corrupt, unstable, and often bankrupt. They seemed to offer an open invitation to foreign interference. A government would borrow money to pay for railroads, harbors, electric power, and other symbols of modernity. When it could not repay the loan, the lending banks in Europe or the United States would ask for assistance from their home governments, which sometimes threatened to intervene. To ward off European intervention, the United States sent in the marines on more than one occasion.

Presidents Theodore Roosevelt (1901–1909), William Taft (1909–1913), and Woodrow Wilson (1913–1921) felt impelled to intervene in the region, though they differed sharply on the proper policy the United States should follow toward the small nations to the south. Roosevelt encouraged regimes friendly to the United States, like Porfirian Mexico; Taft sought to influence them through loans from American banks; and the moralist Wilson tried to impose clean governments through military means.

Having "liberated" Cuba from Spain, the United States forced the Cuban government to accept the Platt Amendment in 1901. The amendment gave the United States the "right to intervene" to maintain order on the island. The United States used this excuse to occupy Cuba militarily from 1906 to 1909, in 1912, and again from 1917 to 1922. In all but name Cuba became an American protectorate. U.S. troops also occupied the Dominican Republic from 1904 to 1907 and again in 1916, Nicaragua and Honduras in 1912, and Haiti in 1915. They brought sanitation and material progress but no political improvements.

The United States was especially forceful in Panama, which was a province of Colombia. Here the issue was not corruption or debts but a more vital interest: the construction of a canal across the isthmus of Panama to speed shipping between the east and west coasts of the United States. In 1878 the Frenchman Ferdinand de Lesseps, builder of the Suez Canal, had obtained a concession from Colombia to construct a canal across the isthmus, which lay in Colombian territory. Financial scandals and yellow fever, however, doomed his project.

When the United States acquired Hawaii and the Philippines, it recognized the strategic value of a canal that would allow warships to move quickly between the Atlantic and Pacific Oceans. The main obstacle was Colombia, whose senate refused to give the United

States a piece of its territory. In 1903 the U.S. government supported a Panamanian rebellion against Colombia and quickly recognized the independence of Panama. In exchange, it obtained the right to build a canal and to occupy a zone 5 miles (8 kilometers) wide on either side of it. Work began in 1904, and the **Panama Canal** opened on August 15, 1914.

The World Economy and the Global Environment

The New Imperialists were not traditional conquerors or empire builders like the Spanish conquistadors. Although their conquests were much larger (see Map 28.3), their aim was not only to extend their power over new territories and peoples but also to control both the natural world and indigenous societies and put them to work more efficiently than had ever been done before. Both their goals and their methods were industrial. A railroad, for example, was an act of faith as well as a means of transportation. They expressed their belief in progress and their good intentions in the clichés of the time: "the conquest of nature," "the annihilation of time and space," "the taming of the wilderness," and "our civilizing mission."

Expansion of the World Economy

For centuries Europe had been a ready market for spices, sugar, silk, and other exotic or tropical products. The Industrial Revolution vastly expanded this demand. Imports of foods and stimulants such as tea, coffee, and cocoa increased substantially during the nineteenth century. The trade in industrial raw materials grew even faster. Some were the products of agriculture, such as cotton, jute for bags, and palm oil for soap and lubricants. Others were minerals such as diamonds, gold, and copper. There also were wild forest products that only later came to be cultivated: timber for buildings and railroad ties, cinchona bark, rubber for rainwear and tires, and gutta-percha° to insulate electric cables.

The growing needs of the industrial world could not be met by the traditional methods of production and transportation of the nonindustrial world. When the U.S. Civil War interrupted the export of cotton to England in the 1860s, the British turned to India. But they found that Indian cotton was ruined by exposure to rain and dust during the long trip on open carts from the interior of the country to the harbors. To prevent the expansion of their industry from being stifled by the technological backwardness of their newly conquered territories, the imperialists made every effort to bring those territories into the mainstream of the world market.

One great change was in transportation. The Suez and Panama Canals cut travel time and lowered freight costs dramatically. Steamships became more numerous, and as their size increased, new, deeper harbors were needed. The Europeans also built railroads throughout the world; India alone had 37,000 miles (nearly 60,000 kilometers) of track by 1915, almost as much as Germany or Russia. Railroads reached into the interior of Latin America, Canada, China, and Australia. In 1903 the Russians completed the Trans-Siberian Railway from Moscow to Vladivostok on the Pacific. Visionaries even made plans for railroads from Europe to India and from Egypt to South Africa.

Transformation of the Global Environment

The economic changes brought by Europeans and Americans also altered environments around the world. The British, whose craving for tea could not be satisfied with the limited exports available from China, introduced tea into the warm, rainy hill country of Ceylon and northeastern India. In those areas and in Java thousands of square miles of tropical rain forests were felled to make way for tea plantations.

Economic botany and agricultural science were applied to every promising plant species. European botanists had long collected and classified exotic plants from around the world. In the nineteenth century they founded botanical gardens in Java, India, Mauritius°, Ceylon, Jamaica, and other tropical colonies. These gardens not only collected local plants but also exchanged plants with other gardens. They were especially active in systematically transferring commercially valuable plant species from one tropical region to another. Cinchona, tobacco, sugar, and other crops were introduced, improved, and vastly expanded in the colonies of Southeast Asia and Indonesia (see Environment and Technology: Imperialism and Tropical Ecology). Cocoa and coffee growing spread over large areas of Brazil and Africa; oil-palm plantations were established in Nigeria and the Congo Basin. Rubber, used to make waterproof garments and bicycle tires, originally came from the latex of *Hevea*

gutta-percha (gut-tah-PER-cha)

Mauritius (maw-REE-shuss)

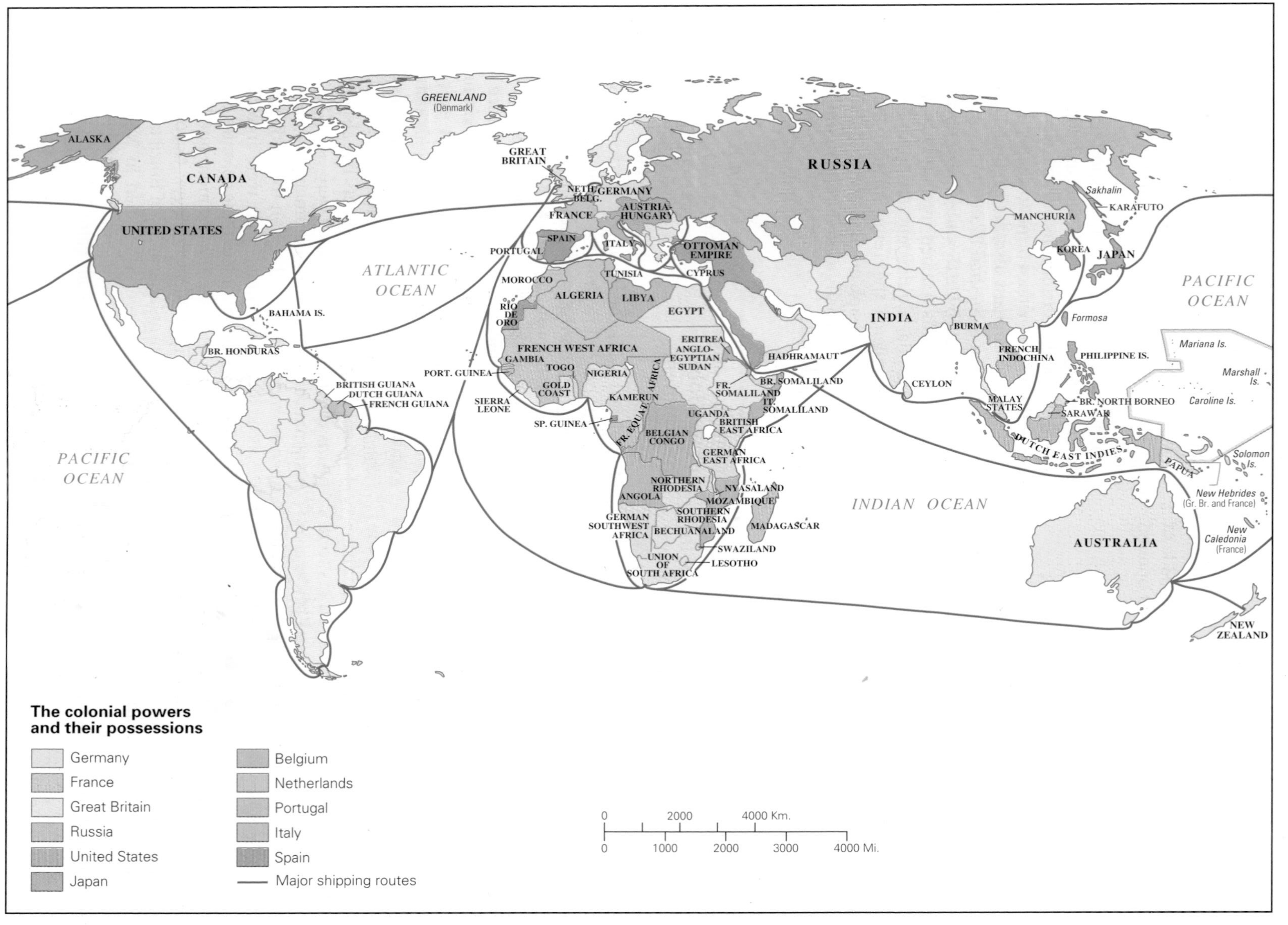

Map 28.3 The Great Powers and Their Colonial Possessions in 1913 By 1913, a small handful of countries claimed sovereignty over more than half the land area of the earth. Global power was closely connected with industries and a merchant marine, rather than with a large territory. This explains why Great Britain, the smallest of the great powers, possessed the largest empire.

trees growing wild in the Brazilian rain forest. Then, in the 1870s, British agents smuggled seedlings from Brazil to the Royal Botanic Gardens at Kew near London, and from there to the Botanic Garden of Singapore. These plants formed the nucleus of the enormous rubber economy of Southeast Asia.

Throughout the tropics land once covered with forests or devoted to shifting slash-and-burn agriculture was transformed into permanent farms and plantations. Even in areas not developed to export crops, growing populations put pressure on the land. In Java and India farmers felled trees to obtain arable land and firewood. They terraced hillsides, drained swamps, and dug wells.

Irrigation and water control transformed the dry parts of the tropics as well. In the 1830s British engineers in India had restored ancient canals that had fallen into disrepair. Their success led them to build new irrigation canals, turning thousands of previously barren acres into well-watered, densely populated farmland. The migration of European experts spread the newest techniques of irrigation engineering around the world. By the turn of the century irrigation projects were under way wherever rivers flowed through dry lands. In Egypt and Central Asia irrigation brought more acres under cultivation in one forty-year span than in all previous history.

Railroads had voracious appetites for land and resources. They cut into mountains, spanned rivers and canyons with trestles, and covered as much land with their freight yards as whole cities had needed in previous centuries. They also consumed vast quantities of iron, timber for ties, and coal or wood for fuel. Most important of all, railroads brought people and their cities, farms, and industries to areas previously occupied by small, scattered populations.

Prospectors looking for valuable minerals opened the earth to reveal its riches: gold in South Africa, Australia, and Canada; tin in Nigeria, Malaya, and Bolivia; copper in Chile and Central Africa; iron ore in northern India; and much else. Where mines were dug deep inside the earth, the dirt and rocks brought up with the ores formed huge mounds near mine entrances. Open mines dug to obtain ores lying close to the surface created a landscape of lunar craters, and runoff from the minerals poisoned the water for miles around. Refineries that processed the ores fouled the environment with slag heaps and more toxic runoff.

The transformation of the land by human beings, a constant throughout history, accelerated sharply. Only the changes occurring since 1914 can compare with the transformation of the global environment that took place between 1869 and 1914.

Conclusion

The industrialization of the late nineteenth century increased the power of Europeans and North Americans over nature and over the peoples of other continents. They used their newfound power to conquer empires.

The opening of the Suez Canal in 1869 was the symbolic beginning of the New Imperialism. It demonstrated the power of modern industry to subdue nature by carving the land. It stimulated shipping and trade between the industrial countries and the tropics. It deepened the involvement of Europeans in the affairs of the Middle East, Africa, and Asia. From that year until 1914, not only the great powers but smaller countries too—even, in some cases, individual Europeans or Americans—had the power to decide the fate of whole countries. The motivation to conquer or control other lands surely helps explain the New Imperialism. But the means at the disposal of the imperialists—that is, the gap that opened between their technologies and forms of organization and those available to Asians, Africans, and Latin Americans—is equally important.

The new technological means and the enhanced motivations of the imperialists resulted in the most rapid conquest of territories in the history of the world. In less than half a century almost all of Africa and large parts of Asia and Oceania were added to the colonial empires, while Latin America, nominally independent, was turned into an economic colony of the industrial powers. In the process of developing the economic potential of their empires, the colonial powers transformed natural environments around the world.

The opening of the Panama Canal in August 1914 confirmed the new powers of the industrializing nations—but with a twist, for it was the United States, a latecomer to the game of imperialism, that created the canal. In that same month, the other imperialist nations turned their weapons against one another and began a life-or-death struggle for supremacy in Europe. That conflict is the subject of the next chapter.

Key Terms

Suez Canal
New Imperialism
Battle of Omdurman
colonialism
"scramble" for Africa
Henry Morton Stanley
King Leopold II
Savorgnan de Brazza
Berlin Conference
Afrikaners
Cecil Rhodes
Asante
Menelik
Emilio Aguinaldo
free-trade imperialism
Panama Canal

Suggested Reading

Two good introductions to imperialism are D. K. Fieldhouse, *Colonialism, 1870–1945* (1981), and Scott B. Cook, *Colonial Encounters in the Age of High Imperialism* (1996). The debate on the theories of imperialism is presented in Roger Owen and Robert Sutcliffe, *Studies in the Theory of Imperialism* (1972), and in Winfried Baumgart, *Imperialism* (1982). The British Empire is the subject of Bernard Porter, *The Lion's Share: A Short History of British Imperialism, 1850–1970* (1976).

On Africa in this period see Roland Oliver and Anthony Atmore, *Africa Since 1800*, new ed. (1994); Roland Oliver and G. N. Sanderson, eds., *From 1870 to 1905* (1985), and A. D. Roberts, ed., *From 1905 to 1940* (1986), in *The Cambridge History of Africa*; and A. Adu Boahen, ed., *Africa Under Colonial Domination, 1880–1935* (1985), in *UNESCO General History of Africa.* The European conquest of Africa is recounted in Thomas Pakenham, *The Scramble for Africa* (1991); Bruce Vandervort, *Wars of Imperial Conquest in Africa, 1830–1914* (1998); and Ronald Robinson and John Gallagher, *Africa and the Victorians: The Climax of Imperialism* (1961). Adam Hochschild's *King Leopold's Ghost: A Story of Greed, Terror, and Heroism in Colonial Africa* (1998) is a very readable account of imperialism in the Belgian Congo. The classic novel about the impact of colonial rule on African society is Chinua Achebe's *Things Fall Apart* (1958).

Imperial rivalries in Asia are the subject of Akira Iriye, *Across the Pacific: An Inner History of American-East Asian Relations*, rev. ed. (1992); David Gillard, *The Struggle for Asia, 1828–1914: A Study in British and Russian Imperialism* (1977); and Peter Hopkirk, *The Great Game: The Struggle for Empire in Central Asia* (1994). On other aspects of imperialism in Asia see Clifford Geertz, *Agricultural Involution: The Process of Ecological Change in Indonesia* (1963), especially chapters 4 and 5, and Stanley Karnow, *In Our Image: America's Empire in the Philippines* (1989).

On Latin America in this period see David Bushnell and Neill Macauley, *The Emergence of Latin America in the Nineteenth Century* (1994). Free-trade imperialism is the subject of D. C. M. Platt, *Latin America and British Trade, 1806–1914* (1973). On American expansionism see David Healy, *Drive to Hegemony: The United States in the Caribbean, 1898–1917* (1989), and Walter LaFeber, *The Panama Canal*, rev. ed. (1990).

On race relations in the colonial world see Noel Mostert, *Frontiers: The Epic of South Africa's Creation and the Tragedy of the Xhosa People* (1992), and Robert Huttenback, *Racism and Empire: White Settlers and Colored Immigrants in the British Self-Governing Colonies, 1830–1910* (1976). Gender relations are the subject of Caroline Oliver, *Western Women in Colonial Africa* (1982), and Cheryl Walker, ed., *Women and Gender in Southern Africa to 1945* (1990). David Northrup's *Indentured Labor in the Age of Imperialism, 1834–1922* (1995) discusses migrations and labor. Franz Fanon, *The Wretched of the Earth* (1966), and Albert Memmi, *The Colonizer and the Colonized* (1967), examine colonialism from the point of view of the colonized.

The impact of technology on the New Imperialism is the subject of Daniel R. Headrick, *The Tools of Empire: Technology and European Imperialism in the Nineteenth Century* (1981) and *The Tentacles of Progress: Technology Transfer in the Age of Imperialism, 1850–1940* (1988), and Clarence B. Davis and Kenneth E. Wilburn, Jr., eds., *Railway Imperialism* (1991).

On the economic and demographic transformation of Africa and Asia see Eric Wolf, *Europe and the People Without History* (1982), especially chapters 11 and 12. The impact on the environment is the subject of R. P. Tucker and J. F. Richards, *Deforestation and the Nineteenth-Century World Economy* (1983); Donal McCracken, *Gardens of Empire: Botanical Institutions of the Victorian British Empire* (1997); Lucile H. Brockway, *Science and Colonial Expansion: The Role of the British Royal Botanic Gardens* (1979); and David Arnold and Ramchandra Guha, eds., *Nature, Culture, Imperialism: Essays on the Environmental History of South Asia* (1995). In *Late Victorian Holocausts: El Niño Famines and the Making of the Third World* (2001), Mike Davis argues that imperialism exacerbated the social and demographic effects of famines.

Notes

1. *Journal Officiel* (November 29, 1869), quoted in Georges Douin, *Histoire du Règne du Khédive Ismaïl* (Rome: Reale Societá di Geografia d'Egitto, 1933), 453.
2. E. Desplaces in *Journal de l'Union des Deux Mers* (December 15, 1869), quoted ibid., 453.
3. Winston Churchill, *The River War: An Account of the Reconquest of the Soudan* (New York: Charles Scribner's Sons, 1933), 300.
4. "Correspondence and Report from His Majesty's Consul at Boma respecting the Administration of the Independent State of the Congo," *British Parliamentary Papers, Accounts and Papers*, 1904 (Cd. 1933), lxii, 357.
5. Robert W. July, *A History of the Africa People*, 3d ed. (New York: Charles Scribner's Sons, 1980), 323.
6. George Shepperson and Thomas Price, *Independent African* (Edinburgh: University Press, 1958), 163–164, quoted in Roland Oliver and Anthony Atmore, *Africa Since 1800*, 4th ed. (Cambridge: Cambridge University Press, 1994), 150.
7. Thomas Edson Ennis, *French Policy and Development in Indochina* (Chicago: University of Chicago Press, 1936), 178, quoted in K. M. Panikkar, *Asia and Western Dominance* (New York: Collier, 1969), 167.
8. Quoted in Stanley J. Stein and Barbara H. Stein, *The Colonial Heritage of Latin America* (New York: Oxford University Press, 1970), 151.

29

The Crisis of the Imperial Order, 1900–1929

The Western Front in World War I In a landscape ravaged by artillery fire, two soldiers dash for cover amid shell holes and the charred remains of a forest.

CHAPTER OUTLINE

On June 28, 1914, Archduke Franz Ferdinand, heir to the throne of Austria-Hungary, was riding in an open carriage through Sarajevo, capital of Bosnia-Herzegovina, a province Austria had annexed six years earlier. When the carriage stopped momentarily, Gavrilo Princip, member of a pro-Serbian conspiracy, fired his pistol twice, killing the archduke and his wife.

Those shots ignited a war that spread throughout Europe, then became global as the Ottoman Empire fought against Britain in the Middle East and Japan attacked German positions in China. France and Britain involved their empires in the war and brought Africans, Indians, Australians, and Canadians to Europe to fight and labor on the front lines. Finally, in 1917, the United States entered the fray.

The next three chapters tell a story of violence and hope. In this chapter, we will look at the causes of war between the great powers, the consequences of that conflict in Europe, the Middle East, and Russia, and the upheavals in China and Japan. At the same time, we will review the accelerating rate of technological change, which made the first half of the twentieth century so violent and so hopeful. Industrialization continued apace. Entirely new technologies, and the organizations that produced and applied them, made war more dangerous, yet also allowed far more people to live healthier, more comfortable, and more interesting lives than ever before.

As you read this chapter, ask yourself the following questions:

- How did the First World War lead to revolution in Russia and the disintegration of several once-powerful empires?
- What role did the war play in eroding European dominance in the world?
- Why did China and Japan follow such divergent paths in this period?
- How did European and North American society and technology change in the aftermath of the war?

Origins of the Crisis in Europe and the Middle East

When the twentieth century opened, the world seemed firmly under the control of the great powers that you read about in Chapter 27. The first decade of the twentieth century was a period of relative peace and economic growth in most of the world. Trade boomed. Several new technologies—airplanes, automobiles, radio, and cinema—aroused much excitement. The great powers consolidated their colonial conquests of the previous decades. Their alliances were so evenly matched that they seemed, to observers at the time, likely to maintain peace. The only international war of the period, the Russo-Japanese War (1904–1905), ended quickly with a decisive Japanese victory.

However, two major changes were undermining the apparent stability of the world. In Europe, tensions mounted as Germany, with its growing industrial and military might, challenged Britain at sea and France in Morocco. The Ottoman Empire grew weaker, leaving a dangerous power vacuum. The resulting chaos in the Balkans, the unstable borderlands between a predominantly Christian Europe and a predominantly Muslim Middle East, gradually drew the European powers into a web of hostilities.

The Ottoman Empire and the Balkans

From the fifteenth to the nineteenth centuries the Ottoman Empire was one of the world's richest and most powerful states. By the late nineteenth century, however, it had fallen behind economically, technologically, and militarily, and Europeans referred to it as the "sick man of Europe."

As the Ottoman Empire weakened, it began losing outlying provinces situated closest to Europe. Macedonia rebelled in 1902–1903. In 1908 Austria-Hungary annexed Bosnia. Crete, occupied by European "peacekeepers" since 1898, merged with Greece in 1909. A year later Albania became independent. In 1912 Italy conquered Libya, the Ottomans' last foothold in Africa. In 1912–1913 in rapid succession came two Balkan Wars in which Serbia, Bulgaria, Romania, and Greece chased the Turks out of Europe, except for a small enclave around Constantinople.

The European powers meddled in the internal affairs of the Ottoman Empire, sometimes cooperatively but often as rivals. Russia saw itself as the protector of

CHRONOLOGY			
	Europe and North America	**Middle East**	**East Asia**
1900	**1904** British-French Entente **1907** British-Russian Entente	**1909** Young Turks overthrow Sultan Abdul Hamid	**1900** Boxer Rebellion in China **1904–1905** Russo-Japanese War
1910	**1912–1913** Balkan Wars **1914** Assassination of Archduke Franz Ferdinand sparks World War I **1916** Battles of Verdun and the Somme **1917** Russian Revolutions; United States enters the war **1918** Armistice ends World War I **1918–1921** Civil war in Russia **1919** Treaty of Versailles	**1912** Italy conquers Libya, last Ottoman territory in Africa **1915** British defeat at Gallipoli **1916** Arab Revolt in Arabia **1917** Balfour Declaration **1919–1922** War between Turkey and Greece	**1911** Chinese revolutionaries led by Sun Yat-sen overthrow Qing dynasty **1915** Japan presents Twenty-One Demands to China **1919** May Fourth Movement in China
1920	**1920** First commercial radio broadcast (United States) **1921** New Economic Policy in Russia **1927** Charles Lindbergh flies alone across the Atlantic	**1922** Egypt nominally independent **1923** Mustafa Kemal proclaims Turkey a republic	**1927** Guomindang forces occupy Shanghai and expel Communists

the Slavic peoples of the Balkans. France and Britain, posing as protectors of Christian minorities, controlled Ottoman finances, taxes, railroads, mines, and public utilities. Austria-Hungary coveted Ottoman lands inhabited by Slavs, thereby angering the Russians.

In reaction, the Turks began to assert themselves against rebellious minorities and meddling foreigners. Many officers in the army, the most Europeanized segment of Turkish society, blamed Sultan Abdul Hamid II (r. 1876–1909) for the decline of the empire. The group known as "Young Turks" began conspiring to force a constitution on the Sultan. They alienated other anti-Ottoman groups by advocating centralized rule and the Turkification of ethnic minorities.

In 1909 the parliament, dominated by Young Turks, overthrew Abdul Hamid and replaced him with his brother. The new regime began to reform the police, the bureaucracy, and the educational system. At the same time, it cracked down on Greek and Armenian minorities. Galvanized by their defeat in the Balkan Wars, the Turks turned to Germany, the European country that had meddled least in Ottoman affairs, and hired a German general to modernize their armed forces.

Nationalism, Alliances, and Military Strategy

The assassination of Franz Ferdinand triggered a chain of events over which military and political leaders lost control. The escalation from assassination to global war had causes that went back many years. One was nationalism, which bound citizens to their ethnic group and led them, when called upon, to kill people they viewed as enemies. Another was the system of alliances and military plans that the great powers had devised to protect themselves from their rivals. A third was Germany's yearning to dominate Europe.

Nationalism was deeply rooted in European culture. As we saw in Chapter 27, it united the citizens of France, Britain, and Germany behind their respective governments and gave them tremendous cohesion and strength of purpose. Only the most powerful feelings could inspire millions of men to march obediently into battle and could sustain civilian populations through years of hardship.

Nationalism could also be a dividing force. The large but fragile multinational Russian, Austro-Hungarian, and Ottoman Empires contained numerous ethnic and religious minorities. Having repressed them for centuries, the governments could never count on their full support. The very existence of an independent Serbia threatened Austria-Hungary by stirring up the hopes and resentments of its Slavic populations.

Because of the spread of nationalism, most people viewed war as a crusade for liberty or as long-overdue revenge for past injustices. In the course of the nineteenth century, as memories of the misery and carnage caused by the Napoleonic Wars faded, revulsion against war gradually weakened. The few wars fought in Europe after 1815, such as the Crimean War of 1853–1856 and the Franco-Prussian War of 1871, had been short and caused few casualties or long-term consequences. And in the wars of the New Imperialism (see Chapter 28), Europeans almost always had been victorious at a small cost in money and manpower. The well-to-do began to believe that only war could heal the class divisions in their societies and make workers unite behind their "natural" leaders.

What turned an incident in a small town in the Balkans into a conflict involving all the great powers was the system of alliances that had grown up over the previous decades. At the center of Europe stood Germany, the most heavily industrialized country in Europe. Its army was the best trained and equipped. It challenged Great Britain's naval supremacy by building "dreadnoughts"—heavily armed battleships. It joined Austria-Hungary and Italy in the Triple Alliance in 1882, while France allied itself with Russia. In 1904 Britain joined France in an Entente° ("understanding"), and in 1907 Britain and Russia buried their differences and formed an Entente. Europe was thus divided into two blocs of roughly equal power (see Map 29.1).

The alliance system was cursed by inflexible military planning. In 1914 western and central Europe had highly developed railroad networks but very few motor vehicles. European armies had grown to include millions of soldiers and more millions of reservists. To mobilize these forces and transport them to battle would be an enormous project requiring thousands of trains running on precise schedules. As a result, once under way, a country's mobilization could not be canceled or postponed without causing chaos.

In the years before World War I, military planners in France and Germany had worked out elaborate railroad timetables to mobilize their respective armies in a few days. Other countries were less prepared. Russia, a large country with an underdeveloped rail system, needed several weeks to mobilize its forces. Britain, with a tiny volunteer army, had no mobilization plans, and German planners believed that the British would stay out of a war on the European continent. So that Germany could avoid having to fight France and Russia at the same time, German war plans called for German generals to defeat France in a matter of days, then transport the entire army across Germany to the Russian border by train before Russia could fully mobilize.

On July 28, emboldened by the backing of Germany, Austria-Hungary declared war on Serbia. Diplomats, statesmen, and monarchs sent one another frantic telegrams, but they had lost control of events, for the declaration of war triggered the general mobilization plans of Russia, France, and Germany. On July 29 the Russian government ordered general mobilization to force Austria to back down. On August 1 France honored its treaty obligation to Russia and ordered general mobilization. Minutes later Germany did likewise. Because of the rigid railroad timetables, war was now automatic.

The German plan was to wheel around through neutral Belgium and into northwestern France. The German General Staff expected France to capitulate before the British could get involved. But on August 3, when German troops entered Belgium, Britain demanded their withdrawal. When Germany refused, Britain declared war on Germany.

THE "GREAT WAR" AND THE RUSSIAN REVOLUTIONS, 1914–1918

Throughout Europe, people greeted the outbreak of war with parades and flags, expecting a quick victory. German troops marched off to the front shouting "To Paris!" Spectators in France encouraged marching French troops with shouts of "Send me the Kaiser's moustache!" The British poet Rupert Brooke began a poem with the line "Now God be thanked Who has matched us with His hour." The German sociologist Max Weber wrote: "This war, with all its ghastliness, is nevertheless grand and wonderful. It is worth experiencing." When the war began, very few imagined that their side might not win, and no one foresaw that everyone would lose.

In Russia the effect of the war was especially devastating, for it destroyed the old society, opened the door to revolution and civil war, and introduced a radical new

---

Entente (on-TONT)

Map 29.1 **Europe in 1913** On the eve of World War I, Europe was divided between two great alliance systems—the Central Powers (Germany, Austria-Hungary, and Italy) and the Entente (France, Great Britain, and Russia)—and their respective colonial empires. These alliances were not stable. When war broke out, the Central Powers lost Italy but gained the Ottoman Empire.

political system. By clearing away the old, the upheaval of war prepared Russia to industrialize under the leadership of professional revolutionaries.

Stalemate, 1914–1917

The war that erupted in 1914 was known as the "Great War" until the 1940s, when a far greater one overshadowed it. Its form came as a surprise to all belligerents, from the generals on down. In the classic battles—from Alexander's to Napoleon's—that every officer studied, the advantage always went to the fastest-moving army led by the boldest general. In 1914 the generals' carefully drawn plans went awry from the start. Believing that a spirited attack would always prevail, French generals hurled their troops, dressed in bright blue-and-red uniforms, against the well-defended German border and suffered a crushing defeat. In battle after battle the much larger German armies defeated the French and the British. By early September the Germans held Belgium and northern France and were fast approaching Paris.

German victory seemed assured. But German troops, who had marched and fought for a month, were exhausted, and their generals wavered. When Russia attacked eastern Germany, troops needed for the final push into France were shifted to the Russian front. A gap opened between two German armies along the Marne River, into which General Joseph Joffre moved France's last reserves. At the Battle of the Marne (September 5–12, 1914), the Germans were thrown back several miles.

During the next month, both sides spread out until they formed an unbroken line extending over 300 miles (some 500 kilometers) from the North Sea to the border of Switzerland. All along this **Western Front,** the opposing troops prepared their defenses. Their most potent weapons were machine guns, which provided an almost impenetrable defense against advancing infantry but were useless for the offensive because they were too heavy for one man to carry and took too much time to set up.

Trench Warfare in World War I German and Allied soldiers on the Western Front faced each other from elaborate networks of trenches. Attacking meant jumping out of the trenches and racing across a no-man's land of mud and barbed wire. Here we see Princess Patricia's Canadian Light Infantry repelling a German attack near Ypres, in northern France, in March 1915, using machine guns, rifles, and hand grenades. (Courtesy, The Princess Patricia's Canadian Light Infantry, Regimental Museum and Archives)

To escape the deadly streams of bullets, soldiers dug holes in the ground, connected the holes to form shallow trenches, then dug communications trenches to the rear. Within weeks, the battlefields were scarred by lines of trenches several feet deep, their tops protected by sandbags and their floors covered with planks. Despite all the work they put into the trenches, the soldiers spent much of the year soaked and covered with mud. Trenches were nothing new. What was extraordinary was that the trenches along the entire Western Front were connected, leaving no gaps through which armies could advance (see Map 29.2). How, then, could either side ever hope to win?

For four years, generals on each side again and again ordered their troops to attack. They knew the casualties would be enormous, but they expected the enemy to run out of young men before their own side did. In battle after battle, thousands of young men on one side climbed out of their trenches, raced across the open fields, and were mowed down by enemy machine-gun fire. Hoping to destroy the machine guns, the attacking force would saturate the entrenched enemy lines with artillery barrages. But this tactic alerted the defenders to an impending attack and allowed them to rush in reinforcements and set up new machine guns.

The year 1916 saw the bloodiest and most futile battles of the war. The Germans attacked French forts at Verdun, losing 281,000 men and causing 315,000 French casualties. In retaliation, the British attacked the Germans at the Somme River and suffered 420,000 casualties—60,000 on the first day alone—while the Germans lost 450,000 and the French 200,000.

Warfare had never been waged this way before. It was mass slaughter in a moonscape of mud, steel, and flesh. Both sides attacked and defended, but neither side could win, for the armies were stalemated by trenches and machine guns. During four years of the bloodiest fighting the world had ever seen, the Western Front moved no more than a few miles one way or another.

At sea, the war was just as inconclusive. As soon as war broke out, the British cut the German overseas telegraph cables, blockaded the coasts of Germany and Austria-Hungary, and set out to capture or sink all enemy ships still at sea. The German High Seas Fleet, built at enormous cost, seldom left port. Only once, in May 1916, did it confront the British Grand Fleet. At the Battle of Jutland, off the coast of Denmark, the two fleets lost roughly equal numbers of ships, and the Germans escaped back to their harbors.

Britain ruled the waves but not the ocean below the surface. In early 1915, in retaliation for the British naval blockade, Germany announced a blockade of Britain by submarines. Unlike surface ships, submarines could not rescue the passengers of a sinking ship or distinguish between neutral and enemy ships. German submarines attacked every vessel they could. One of their victims was the British ocean liner *Lusitania*. The death toll from that attack was 1,198 people, 139 of them Americans. When the United States protested, Germany ceased its submarine campaign, hoping to keep America neutral.

Other than machine guns and submarines, military innovations had only minor effects. Airplanes were used for reconnaissance and engaged in spectacular but inconsequential dogfights above the trenches. Poison gas, introduced on the Western Front in 1915, killed and wounded attacking soldiers as well as their intended victims, adding to the horror of battle. Primitive tanks aided, but did not cause, the collapse of the German army in the last weeks of the war. Although these weapons were of limited effectiveness in World War I, they offered an insight into the future of warfare.

The Home Front and the War Economy

Trench-bound armies demanded ever more weapons, ammunition, and food, so civilians had to work harder, eat less, and pay higher taxes. Textiles, coal, meat, fats, and imported products such as tea and sugar were strictly rationed. Governments gradually imposed stringent controls over all aspects of their economies. Socialists and labor unions participated actively in the war effort, for they found government regulation more to their liking than unfettered free enterprise.

The war economy transformed civilian life. In France and Britain food rations were allocated according to need, improving nutrition among the poor. Unemployment vanished. Thousands of Africans, Indians, and Chinese were recruited for heavy labor in Europe. Employers hired women to fill jobs in steel mills, mines, and munitions plants vacated by men off to war. Some women became streetcar drivers, mail carriers, and police officers. Others found work in the burgeoning government bureaucracies. Many joined auxiliary military services as doctors, nurses, mechanics, and ambulance drivers; after 1917, as the war took its toll of young men, the British government established women's auxiliary units for the army, navy, and air force. Though clearly intended "for the duration only," these positions gave thousands of women a sense of participation in the war effort and a taste of personal and financial independence.

German civilians paid an especially high price for the war, for the British naval blockade severed their

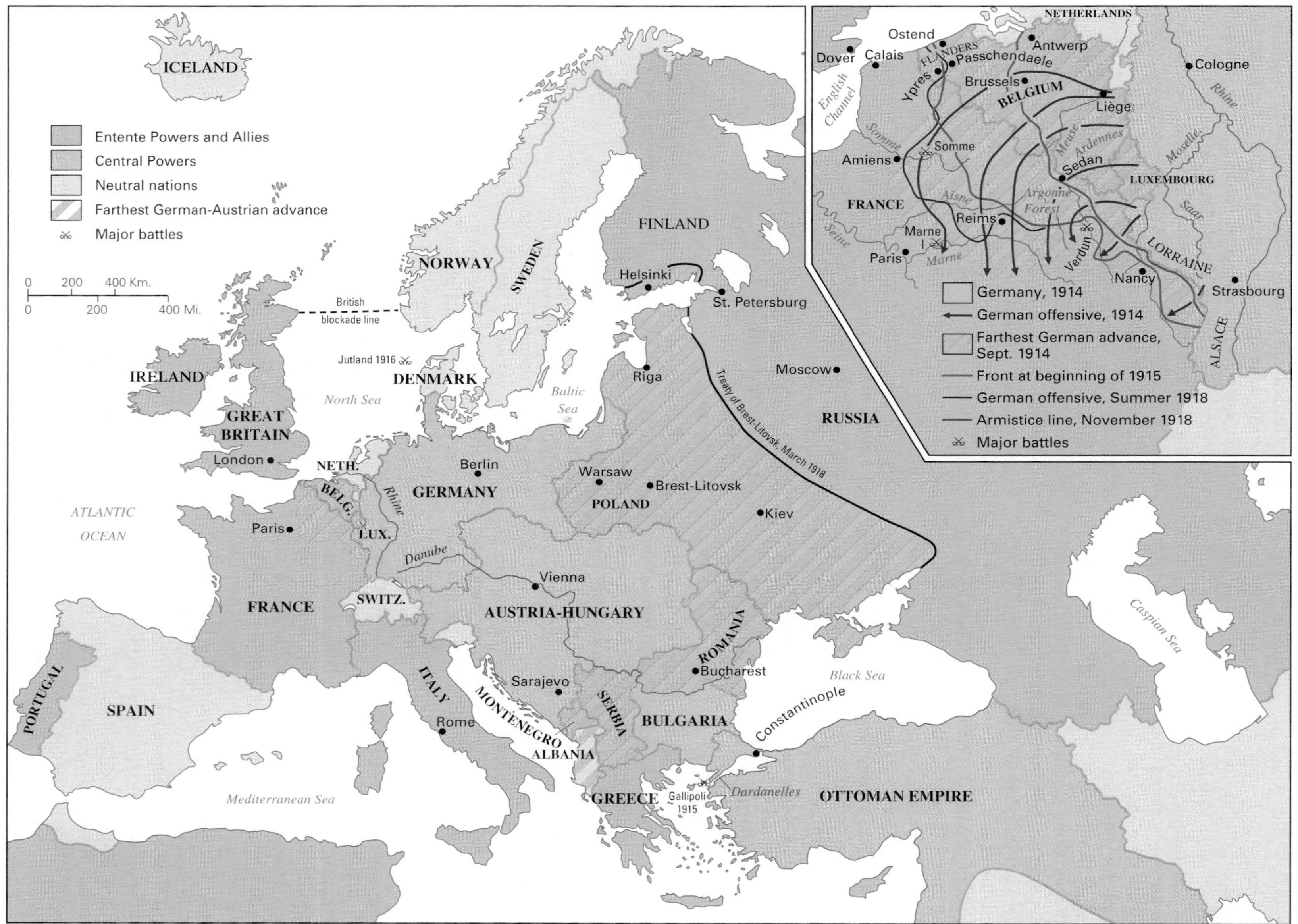

Map 29.2 The First World War in Europe Most of the fighting in World War I took place on two fronts. After an initial surge through Belgium into northern France, the German offensive bogged down for four years along the Western Front. To the East, the German armies conquered a large part of Russia during 1917 and early 1918. Despite spectacular victories in the east, Germany lost the war because its armies collapsed along the strategically important Western Front.

ON HER
THEIR LIVES DEPEND
WOMEN
MUNITION
WORKERS
Enrol at once

Women in World War I Women played a more important role in World War I than in previous wars. As the armies drafted millions of men, employers hired women for essential war work. This poster extolling the importance of women workers in supplying munitions was probably designed to recruit women for factory jobs. (Imperial War Museum)

overseas trade. The German chemical industry developed synthetic explosives and fuel, but synthetic food was not an option. Wheat flour disappeared, replaced first by rye, then by potatoes and turnips, then by acorns and chestnuts, and finally by sawdust. After the failure of the potato crop in 1916 came the "turnip winter," when people had to survive on 1,000 calories per day, half the normal amount that an active adult needed. Women, children, and the elderly were especially hard hit. Soldiers at the front went hungry and raided enemy lines to scavenge food.

When the war began, the British and French overran German Togo on the West African coast. The much larger German colonies of Southwest Africa and German Cameroon were conquered in 1915. In Tanganyika the Germans remained undefeated until the end of the war.

The war also brought hardships to Europe's African colonies. The Europeans requisitioned foodstuffs, imposed heavy taxes, and forced Africans to grow export crops and sell them at low prices. Many Europeans stationed in Africa joined the war, leaving large areas with little or no European presence. In Nigeria, Libya, Nyasaland (now Malawi), and other colonies, the combination of increased demands on Africans and fewer European officials led to uprisings that lasted for several years.

Over a million Africans served in the various armies, and perhaps three times that number were drafted as porters to carry army equipment. Faced with a shortage of young Frenchmen, France drafted Africans into its army, where many fought side by side with Europeans. The Senegalese Blaise Diagne°, the first African elected to France's Chamber of Deputies in 1914, campaigned for African support of the war effort. Put in charge of recruiting African soldiers, he insisted on equal rights for African and European soldiers and an extension of the franchise to educated Africans. These demands were only partially met.

One country grew rich during the war: the United States. For two and a half years the United States stayed technically neutral—that is, it did not fight but did a roaring business supplying France and Britain. When the United States entered the war in 1917 businesses engaging in war production made spectacular profits. Civilians were exhorted to help the war effort by investing their savings in war bonds and growing food in backyard "victory gardens." Facing labor shortages, employers hired women and African-Americans. Employment opportunities created by the war played a major role in the migration of black Americans from the rural south to the cities of the north.

The Ottoman Empire at War

On August 2, 1914, the Turks signed a secret alliance with Germany. In November they joined the fighting, hoping to gain land at Russia's expense. But the campaign in the Caucasus proved disastrous for both armies and for the civilian populations as well. The Turks deported the Armenians, whom they suspected of being pro-Russian, from their homelands in eastern Anatolia to Syria and other parts of the Ottoman Empire. During the forced march across the mountains in the winter, hundreds of thousands of Armenians died of hunger and exposure.

Blaise Diagne (blez dee-AHN-yuh)

This massacre was a precedent for even ghastlier tragedies still to come.

The Turks also closed the Dardanelles, the strait between the Mediterranean and Black Seas (see Map 29.2). Seeing little hope of victory on the Western Front, British officials tried to open the Dardanelles by landing troops on the nearby Gallipoli Peninsula in 1915. Turkish troops pushed the invaders back into the sea.

Having failed at the Dardanelles, the British tried to subvert the Ottoman Empire from within by promising the emir (prince) of Mecca, Hussein ibn Ali, a kingdom of his own if he would lead an Arab revolt against the Turks. In 1916 Hussein rose up and was proclaimed king of Hejaz° (western Arabia). His son **Faisal**° led an Arab army in support of the British advance from Egypt into Palestine and Syria. The Arab Revolt of 1916 did not affect the struggle in Europe, but it did contribute to the defeat of the Ottoman Empire.

The British made promises to Jews as well as Arabs. For centuries, Jewish minorities had lived in eastern and central Europe, where they developed a thriving culture despite frequent persecutions. By the early twentieth century a nationalist movement called Zionism, led by **Theodore Herzl,** arose among those who wanted to return to their ancestral homeland in Palestine. The concept of a Jewish homeland appealed to many Europeans, Jews and gentiles alike, as a humanitarian solution to the problem of anti-Semitism.

By 1917 Chaim Weizmann°, leader of the British Zionists, had persuaded several British politicians that a Jewish homeland in Palestine should be carved out of the Ottoman Empire and placed under British protection, thereby strengthening the Allied cause (as the Entente was now called). In November, as British armies were advancing on Jerusalem, Foreign Secretary Sir Arthur Balfour wrote:

> His Majesty's Government view with favor the establishment in Palestine of a national home for the Jewish people and will use their best endeavours to facilitate the achievement of that object, it being clearly understood that nothing shall be done which may prejudice the civil and religious rights of existing non-Jewish communities in Palestine.

The British did not foresee that this statement, known as the **Balfour Declaration,** would lead to conflicts between Palestinians and Jewish settlers.

Britain also sent troops to southern Mesopotamia to secure the oil pipeline from Iran. Then they moved north, taking Baghdad in early 1917. The officers for the Mesopotamian campaign were British, but most of the troops and equipment came from India. Most Indians, like other colonial subjects of Britain, supported the war effort despite the hardships it caused. Their involvement in the war bolstered the movement for Indian independence (see Chapter 31).

Double Revolution in Russia, 1917

At the beginning of the war Russia had the largest army in the world, but its generals were incompetent, supplies were lacking, and soldiers were poorly trained and equipped. In August 1914 two Russian armies invaded eastern Germany but were thrown back. The Russians defeated the Austro-Hungarian army several times, only to be defeated in turn by the Germans.

In 1916, after a string of defeats, the Russian army ran out of ammunition and other essential supplies. Soldiers were ordered into battle unarmed and told to pick up the rifles of fallen comrades. With so many men in the army, railroads broke down for lack of fuel and parts, and crops rotted in the fields. Civilians faced shortages and widespread hunger. In the cities food and fuel became scarce. During the bitterly cold winter of 1916–1917 factory workers and housewives had to line up in front of grocery stores before dawn to get food. The court of Tsar° Nicholas II, however, remained as extravagant and corrupt as ever.

In early March 1917 (February by the old Russian calendar) food ran out in Petrograd (St. Petersburg), the capital. Housewives and women factory workers staged mass demonstrations. Soldiers mutinied and joined striking workers to form soviets (councils) to take over factories and barracks. A few days later the tsar abdicated, and leaders of the parliamentary parties, led by Alexander Kerensky, formed a Provisional Government. Thus began what Russians called the "February Revolution."

Revolutionary groups formerly hunted by the tsar's police came out of hiding. Most numerous were the Social Revolutionaries, who advocated the redistribution of land to the peasants. The Social Democrats, a Marxist party, were divided into two factions: Mensheviks and Bolsheviks. The Mensheviks advocated electoral politics and reform in the tradition of European socialists and had a large following among intellectuals and factory workers. The **Bolsheviks,** their rivals, were a small but tightly disciplined group of radicals obedient to the will of their leader, **Vladimir Lenin** (1870–1924).

Lenin, the son of a government official, became a revolutionary in his teens when his older brother was ex-

Hejaz (HEE-jaz) **Faisal** (fie-SAHL) **Chaim Weizmann** (hi-um VITES-mun)

tsar (zahr)

ecuted for plotting to kill the tsar. He spent years in exile, first in Siberia and later in Switzerland, where he devoted his full attention to organizing his followers. He professed Marx's ideas about class conflict (see Chapter 27), but he never visited a factory or a farm. His goal was to create a party that would lead the revolution rather than wait for it. He explained: "Classes are led by parties and parties are led by individuals. . . . The will of a class is sometimes fulfilled by a dictator."

In early April 1917 the German government, hoping to destabilize Russia, allowed Lenin to travel from Switzerland to Russia in a sealed railway car. As soon as he arrived in Petrograd, he announced his program: immediate peace, all power to the soviets, and transfers of land to the peasants and factories to the workers. This plan proved immensely popular among soldiers and workers exhausted by the war.

The next few months witnessed a tug-of-war between the Provisional Government and the various revolutionary factions in Petrograd. When Kerensky ordered another offensive against the Germans, Russian soldiers began to desert by the hundreds of thousands, throwing away their rifles and walking back to their villages. As the Germans advanced, Russian resistance melted, and the government lost the little support it had.

Meanwhile, the Bolsheviks were gaining support among the workers of Petrograd and the soldiers and sailors stationed there. On November 6, 1917 (October 24 in the Russian calendar), they rose up and took over the city, calling their action the "October Revolution." Their sudden move surprised rival revolutionary groups that believed that a "socialist" revolution could happen only after many years of "bourgeois" rule. Lenin, however, was more interested in power than in the fine points of Marxist doctrine. He overthrew the Provisional Government and arrested Mensheviks, Social Revolutionaries, and other rivals.

Seizing Petrograd was only the first step, for the rest of Russia was in chaos. The Bolsheviks nationalized all private land and ordered the peasants to hand over their crops without compensation. The peasants, having seized their landlords' estates, resisted. In the cities the Bolsheviks took over the factories and drafted the workers into compulsory labor brigades. To enforce his rule Lenin created the Cheka, a secret police force with powers to arrest and execute opponents.

The Bolsheviks also sued for peace with Germany and Austria-Hungary. By the Treaty of Brest-Litovsk, signed on March 3, 1918, Russia lost territories containing a third of its population and wealth. Poland, Finland, and the Baltic states (Estonia, Latvia, and Lithuania) became independent republics. Russian colonies in Central Asia and the Caucasus broke away temporarily.

The End of the War in Western Europe, 1917–1918

Like many other Americans, President **Woodrow Wilson** wanted to stay out of the European conflict. For nearly three years he kept the United States neutral and tried to persuade the belligerents to compromise. But in late 1916 German leaders decided to starve the British into submission by using submarines to sink merchant ships carrying food supplies to Great Britain. The Germans knew that unrestricted submarine warfare was likely to bring the United States into the war, but they were willing to gamble that Britain and France would collapse before the United States could send enough troops to help them.

The submarine campaign resumed on February 1, 1917, and the German gamble failed. The British organized their merchant ships into convoys protected by destroyers, and on April 6 President Wilson asked the United States Congress to declare war on Germany.

On the Western Front, the two sides were so evenly matched in 1917 that the war seemed unlikely to end until one side or the other ran out of young men. Losing hope of winning, soldiers began to mutiny. In May 1917, before the arrival of U.S. forces, fifty-four of one hundred French divisions along the Western Front refused to attack. During the summer Italian troops also mutinied, panicked, or deserted.

Between March and August 1918 General Erich von Ludendorff launched a series of surprise attacks that broke through the front at several places and pushed to within 40 miles (64 kilometers) of Paris. But victory eluded him. Meanwhile, every month was bringing another 250,000 American troops to the front. In August the Allies counterattacked, and the Germans began a retreat that could not be halted, for German soldiers, many of them sick with the flu, had lost the will to fight.

In late October Ludendorff resigned, and sailors in the German fleet mutinied. Two weeks later Kaiser Wilhelm fled to Holland as a new German government signed an armistice. On November 11 at 11 A.M. the guns on the Western Front went silent.

Peace and Dislocation in Europe, 1919–1929

The Great War lasted four years. It took almost twice as long for Europe to recover. Millions of people had died or been disabled; political tensions and resentments lingered; and national economies remained depressed until the mid-1920s. In the late 1920s peace and prosperity finally seemed assured, but this hope proved to be illusory.

The Impact of the War

The war left more dead and wounded and more physical destruction than any previous conflict. It is estimated that between 8 million and 10 million people died, almost all of them young men. Perhaps twice that many returned home wounded, gassed, or shell-shocked, many of them injured for life. Among the dead were about 2 million Germans, 1.7 million Russians, and 1.7 million Frenchmen. Austria-Hungary lost 1.5 million, the British Empire a million, Italy 460,000, and the United States 115,000.

Besides ending over 8 million lives, the war dislocated whole populations, creating millions of refugees. War and revolution forced almost 2 million Russians, 750,000 Germans, and 400,000 Hungarians to flee their homes. War led to the expulsion of hundreds of thousands of Greeks from Anatolia and Turks from Greece.

Many refugees found shelter in France, which welcomed 1.5 million people to bolster its declining population. The preferred destination, however, was the United States, the most prosperous country in the world. About 800,000 immigrants succeeded in reaching the United States before immigration laws passed in 1921 and 1924 closed the door to eastern and southern Europeans. Canada, Australia, and New Zealand adopted similar restrictions on immigration. The Latin American republics welcomed European refugees, but their economies were hard hit by the drop in the prices of their main exports, and their poverty discouraged potential immigrants.

One unexpected byproduct of the war was the great influenza epidemic of 1918–1919, which started among soldiers heading for the Western Front. This was no ordinary flu but a virulent strain that infected almost everyone on earth and killed one person in every forty. It caused the largest number of deaths in so short a time in the history of the world. Half a million Americans perished in the epidemic—five times as many as died in the war. Worldwide, some 20 million people died.

The war also caused serious damage to the environment. No place was ever so completely devastated as the scar across France and Belgium known as the Western Front. The fighting ravaged forests and demolished towns. The earth was gouged by trenches, pitted with craters, and littered with ammunition, broken weapons, chunks of concrete, and the bones of countless soldiers. After the war, it took a decade to clear away the debris, rebuild the towns, and create dozens of military cemeteries with neat rows of crosses stretching for miles. To this day, farmers plow up fragments of old weapons and ammunition, and every so often a long-buried shell explodes. The war also hastened the buildup of industry, with mines, factories, and railroad tracks.

The Peace Treaties

In early 1919 delegates of the victorious powers met in Paris. The defeated powers were kept out until the treaties were ready for signing. Russia, in the throes of civil war, was not invited.

From the start, three men dominated the Paris Peace Conference: U.S. president Wilson, British prime minister David Lloyd George, and French premier Georges Clemenceau°. They ignored the Italians, who had joined the Allies in 1915. They paid even less attention to the delegates of smaller European nations and none at all to non-European nationalities. They rejected the Japanese proposal that all races be treated equally. They ignored the Pan-African Congress organized by the African-American W. E. B. Du Bois to call attention to the concerns of African peoples around the world. They also ignored the ten thousand other delegates of various nationalities that did not represent sovereign states—the Arab leader Faisal, the Zionist Chaim Weizmann, and several Armenian delegations—who came to Paris to lobby for their causes. They were, in the words of Britain's Foreign Secretary Balfour, "three all-powerful, all-ignorant men, sitting there and carving up continents" (see Map 29.3).

Each had his own agenda. Wilson, a high-minded idealist, wanted to apply the principle of self-determination to European affairs, by which he meant creating nations that reflected ethnic or linguistic divisions. He proposed a **League of Nations,** a world organization to safeguard the peace and foster international cooperation. His idealism clashed with the more hard-headed and self-serving nationalism of the Europeans. To satisfy his constituents, Lloyd George insisted that Germany pay a heavy indemnity. Clemenceau wanted Germany to give Alsace and Lorraine (a part of France before 1871) and the industrial Saar region to France and demanded that the Rhineland be detached from Germany to form a buffer state.

The result was a series of compromises that satisfied no one. The European powers formed a League of Nations, but the United States Congress, reflecting the isolationist feelings of the American people, refused to let the United States join. France recovered Alsace and Lorraine but was unable to detach the Rhineland and had to

Georges Clemenceau (zhorzh cluh-mon-SO)

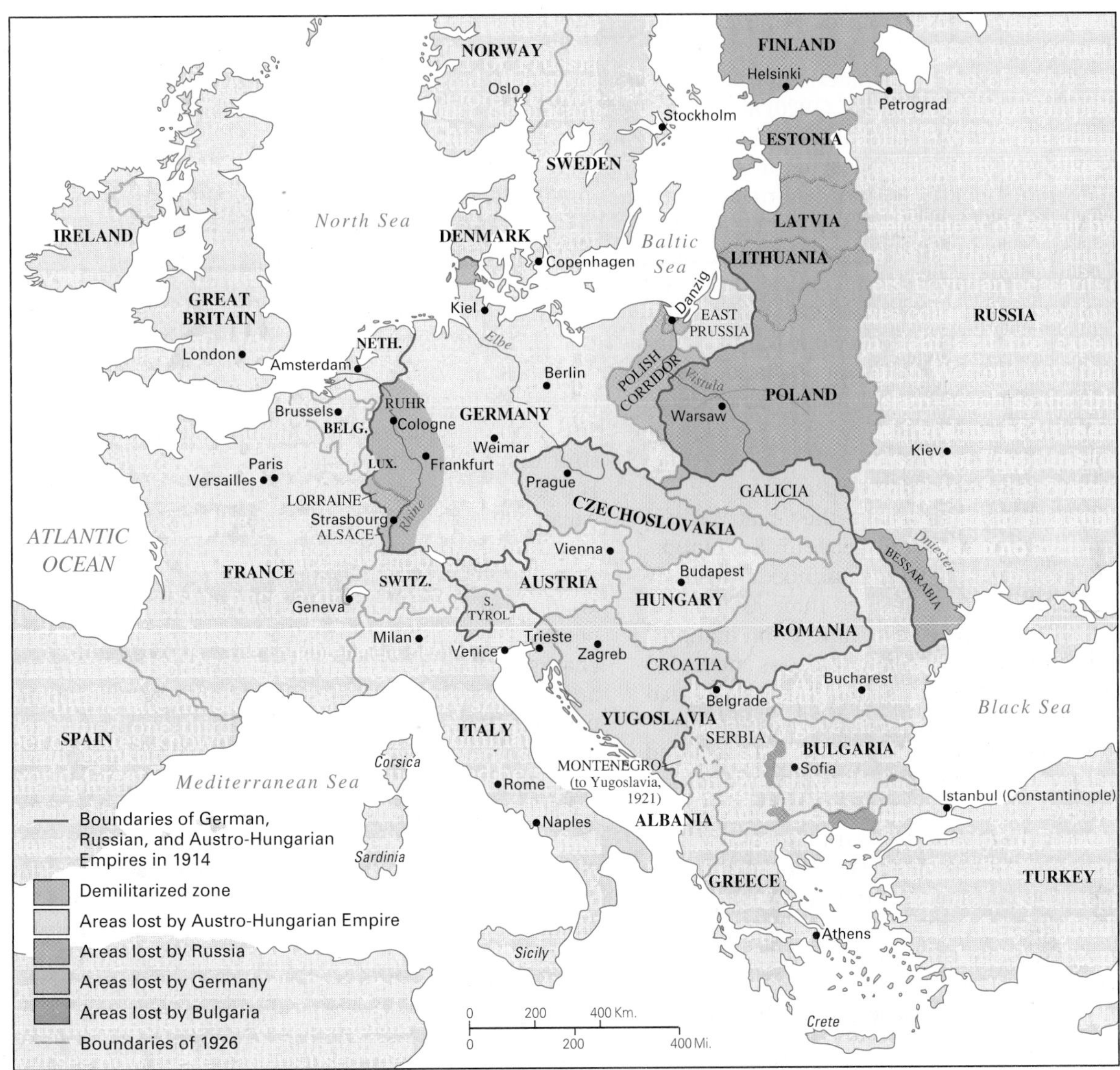

Map 29.3 Territorial Changes in Europe After World War I Although the heaviest fighting took place in western Europe, the territorial changes there were relatively minor; the two provinces taken by Germany in 1871, Alsace and Lorraine, were returned to France. In eastern Europe, in contrast, the changes were enormous. The disintegration of the Austro-Hungary Empire and the defeat of Russia allowed a belt of new countries to arise, stretching from Finland in the north to Yugoslavia in the south.

content itself with vague promises of British and American protection if Germany ever rebuilt its army. Britain acquired new territories in Africa and the Middle East but was greatly weakened by human losses and the disruption of its trade.

On June 28, 1919, the German delegates reluctantly signed the **Treaty of Versailles°**. Germany was forbidden to have an air force and was permitted only a token army and navy. It gave up large parts of its eastern territory to a newly reconstituted Poland. The Allies made Germany promise to pay reparations to compensate the victors for their losses, but they did not set a figure or a period of time for payment. A "guilt clause," which was to rankle for years to come, obliged the Germans to accept "responsibility for causing all the loss and damage" of the war. The Treaty of Versailles left Germany humiliated but largely intact and potentially the most powerful nation in Europe. Establishing a peace neither of punishment

Versailles (vuhr-SIGH)

nor of reconciliation, the treaty was one of the great failures in history.

Meanwhile, the Austro-Hungarian Empire had fallen apart. In the Treaty of Saint-Germain° (1920) Austria and Hungary each lost three-quarters of its territory. New countries appeared in the lands lost by Russia, Germany, and Austria-Hungary: Poland, resurrected after over a century; Czechoslovakia, created from the northern third of Austria-Hungary; and Yugoslavia, combining Serbia and the former south Slav provinces of Austria-Hungary. The new boundaries coincided with the major linguistic groups of eastern Europe, but they all contained disaffected minorities. These small nations were safe only as long as Germany and Russia lay defeated and prostrate.

Russian Civil War and the New Economic Policy

The end of the Great War did not bring peace to all of Europe. Fighting continued in Russia for another three years. The Bolshevik Revolution had provoked Allied intervention. French troops occupied Odessa in the south; the British and Americans landed in Archangel and Murmansk in the north; and the Japanese occupied Vladivostok in the far east. Liberated Czech prisoners of war briefly seized the Trans-Siberian Railway.

Also, in December 1918, civil war broke out in Russia. The Communists—as the Bolsheviks called themselves after March 1918—held central Russia, but all the surrounding provinces rose up against them. Counterrevolutionary armies led by former tsarist officers obtained weapons and supplies from the Allies. For three years the two sides fought each other. They burned farms and confiscated crops, causing a famine that claimed 3 million victims, more than had died in Russia in seven years of fighting. By 1921 the Communists had defeated most of their enemies, for the anti-Bolshevik forces were never united, and the peasants feared that a tsarist victory would mean the return of their landlords. The Communists' victory was also due to the superior discipline of their Red Army and the military genius of their army commander, Leon Trotsky.

Finland, the Baltic states, and Poland remained independent, but the Red Army reconquered other parts of the tsar's empire one by one. In December 1920 Ukrainian Communists declared the independence of a Soviet Republic of Ukraine, which merged with Russia in 1922 to create the Union of Soviet Socialist Republics (USSR), or Soviet Union. The provinces of the Russian Empire in the Caucasus and Central Asia had also declared their independence in 1918. Although the Bolsheviks staunchly supported anticolonialist movements in Africa and Asia, they opposed what they called "feudalism" in the former Russian colonies. They were also eager to control the oil fields in both regions. In 1920–1921 the Red Army reconquered the Caucasus and replaced the indigenous leaders with Russians. In 1922 the new Soviet republics of Georgia, Armenia, and Azerbaijan joined the USSR. In this way the Bolsheviks rid Russia of the taint of tsarist colonialism but retained control over lands and peoples that had been part of the tsar's empire.

Years of warfare, revolution, and mismanagement ruined the Russian economy. By 1921 it had declined to one-sixth of its prewar level. Factories and railroads had shut down for lack of fuel, raw materials, and parts. Farmland had been devastated and livestock killed, causing hunger in the cities. Finding himself master of a country in ruin, Lenin decided to release the economy from party and government control. In March 1921 he announced The **New Economic Policy** (N.E.P.). It allowed peasants to own land and sell their crops, private merchants to trade, and private workshops to produce goods and sell them on the free market. Only the biggest businesses, such as banks, railroads, and factories, remained under government ownership.

The relaxation of controls had an immediate effect. Production began to climb, and food and other goods became available. In the cities food remained scarce because farmers used their crops to feed their livestock rather than sell them. But the N.E.P. reflected no change in the ultimate goals of the Communist Party. It merely provided breathing space, what Lenin called "two steps back to advance one step forward." The Communists had every intention of creating a modern industrial economy without private property, under party guidance. This meant investing in heavy industry and electrification and moving farmers to the cities to work in the new industries. It also meant providing food for the urban workers without spending scarce resources to purchase it from the peasants. In other words, it meant making the peasants, the great majority of the Soviet people, pay for the industrialization of Russia. This turned them into bitter enemies of the Communists.

When Lenin died in January 1924 his associates jockeyed for power. The leading contenders were Leon Trotsky, commander of the Red Army, and Joseph Stalin, general secretary of the Communist Party. Trotsky had the support of many "Old Bolsheviks" who had joined the party before the Revolution. Having spent years in exile, he saw the revolution as a spark that would ignite a world revolution of the working class.

Saint-Germain (san-zhair-MEN)

Lenin the Orator The leader of the Bolshevik revolutionaries was a spellbinding orator. Here Lenin is addressing Red Army soldiers in Sverdlov Square, Moscow, in 1920. At the time, the Bolsheviks were mopping up the last of the anti-Bolshevik forces and were fully engaged in a war with Poland. The fate of the Revolution depended on the fighting spirit of the Red Army soldiers and on their loyalty to Lenin. (David King Collection)

Stalin, the only leading Communist who had never lived abroad, insisted that socialism could survive "in one country."

Stalin filled the party bureaucracy with individuals loyal to himself. In 1926–1927 he had Trotsky expelled for "deviation from the party line." In January 1929 he forced Trotsky to flee the country. Then, as absolute master of the party, he prepared to industrialize the Soviet Union at breakneck speed.

An Ephemeral Peace

The 1920s were a decade of apparent progress hiding irreconcilable tensions. Conservatives in Britain and France longed for a return to the stability of the prewar era—the hierarchy of social classes, prosperous world trade, and European dominance over the rest of the world. All over the rest of the world, people's hopes had been raised by the rhetoric of the war, then dashed by its outcome. In Europe, Germans felt cheated out of a victory that had seemed within their grasp, and Italians were disappointed that their sacrifices had not been rewarded at Versailles with large territorial gains. In the Middle East and Asia, Arabs and Indians longed for independence; the Chinese looked for social justice and a lessening of foreign intrusion; and the Japanese hoped to expand their influence in China. In Russia, the Communists were eager to consolidate their power and export their revolution to the rest of the world.

The decade after the end of the war can be divided into two distinct periods: five years of painful recovery and readjustment (1919–1923), followed by six years of growing peace and prosperity (1924–1929). In 1923 Germany suspended reparations payments. In retaliation for the French occupation of the Ruhr, the German government began printing money recklessly, causing the most severe inflation the world had ever seen. Soon German money was worth so little that it took a wheelbarrow full of it to buy a loaf of bread. As Germany teetered on the brink of civil war, radical nationalists called for revenge and tried to overthrow the government. Finally, the German government issued a new currency and promised to resume reparations payments, and the French agreed to withdraw their troops from the Ruhr.

Beginning in 1924 the world enjoyed a few years of calm and prosperity. After the end of the German crisis of 1923, the western European nations became less confrontational, and Germany joined the League of Nations. The vexed issue of reparations also seemed to vanish, as Germany borrowed money from New York banks to make its payments to France and Britain, which used the money to repay their wartime loans from the United States. This triangular flow of money, based on credit, stimulated the rapid recovery of the European economies. France began rebuilding its war-torn northern zone; Germany recovered from its hyperinflation; and a boom began in the United States that was to last for five years.

While their economies flourished, governments grew more cautious and businesslike. Even the Communists, after Lenin's death, seemed to give up their attempts to spread revolution abroad. Yet neither Germany nor the Soviet Union accepted its borders with the small nations that had arisen between them. In 1922 they signed a secret pact allowing the German army to conduct maneuvers in Russia (in violation of the Versailles treaty) in exchange for German help in building up Russian industry and military potential.

The League of Nations proved adept at resolving numerous technical issues pertaining to health, labor relations, and postal and telegraph communications. But the League could carry out its main function, preserving the peace, only when the great powers (Britain, France, and Italy) were in agreement. Without U.S. participation, sanctions against states that violated League rules carried little weight.

China and Japan: Contrasting Destinies

China and Japan share a common civilization, and both were subject to Western pressures, but their modern histories have been completely opposite. China clung much longer than Japan to a traditional social structure and economy, then collapsed into chaos and revolution. Japan experienced reform from above (see Chapter 27), acquiring industry and a powerful military, which it used to take advantage of China's weakness. Their different reactions to the pressures of the West put these two great nations on a collision course.

Social and Economic Change

China's population—about 400 million in 1900—was the largest of any country in the world and growing fast. But China had little new land to put into cultivation. In 1900 peasant plots averaged between 1 and 4 acres (less than 2 hectares) apiece, half as large as they had been two generations earlier. Farming methods had not changed in centuries. Landlords and tax collectors took more than half of the harvest. Most Chinese worked incessantly, survived on a diet of grain and vegetables, and spent their lives in fear of floods, bandits, and tax collectors.

Constant labor was needed to prevent the Yellow River from bursting its dikes and flooding the low-lying fields and villages on either side. In times of war and civil disorder, when flood-control precautions were neglected, disasters ensued. Between 1913 and 1938 the river burst its dikes seventeen times, each time killing thousands of people and making millions homeless.

Japan had few natural resources and very little arable land on which to grow food for its rising population. It did not suffer from devastating floods like China, but it was subject to other natural calamities. Typhoons regularly hit its southern regions. Earthquakes periodically shook the country, which lies on the great ring of tectonic fault lines that surround the Pacific Ocean. The Kanto earthquake of 1923 destroyed all of Yokohama and half of Tokyo and killed as many as 200,000 people.

Above the peasantry, Chinese society was divided into many groups and strata. Landowners lived off the rents of their tenants. Officials, chosen through an elaborate examination system, enriched themselves from taxes and the government's monopolies on salt, iron, and other products. Wealthy merchants handled China's growing import-export trade in collaboration with foreign companies. Shanghai, China's financial and commercial center, was famous for its wealthy foreigners and its opium addicts, prostitutes, and gangsters.

Although foreign trade represented only a small part of China's economy, contact with the outside world had a tremendous impact on Chinese politics. Young men living in the treaty ports saw no chance for advancement in the old system of examinations and official positions. Some learned foreign ideas in Christian mission schools or abroad. The contrast between the squalor in which most urban residents lived and the luxury of the foreigners' enclaves in the treaty ports sharpened the resentment of educated Chinese.

Japan's population reached 60 million in 1925 and was increasing by a million a year. The crash program of industrialization begun in 1868 by the Meiji oligarchs (see Chapter 27) accelerated during the First World War, when Japan exported textiles, consumer goods, and munitions. In the war years, its economy grew four times as fast as western Europe's, eight times faster than China's.

In the 1880s electrification was still in its infancy, so Japan became competitive very early on. Blessed with a rainy climate and many fast-flowing rivers, Japan quickly expanded its hydroelectric capacity. By the mid-1930s, 89 percent of Japanese households had electric lights, compared with 68 percent of U.S. and 44 percent of British households.

Economic growth aggravated social tensions. The *narikin* ("new rich") affected Western ways and lifestyles that clashed with the austerity of earlier times. In the big

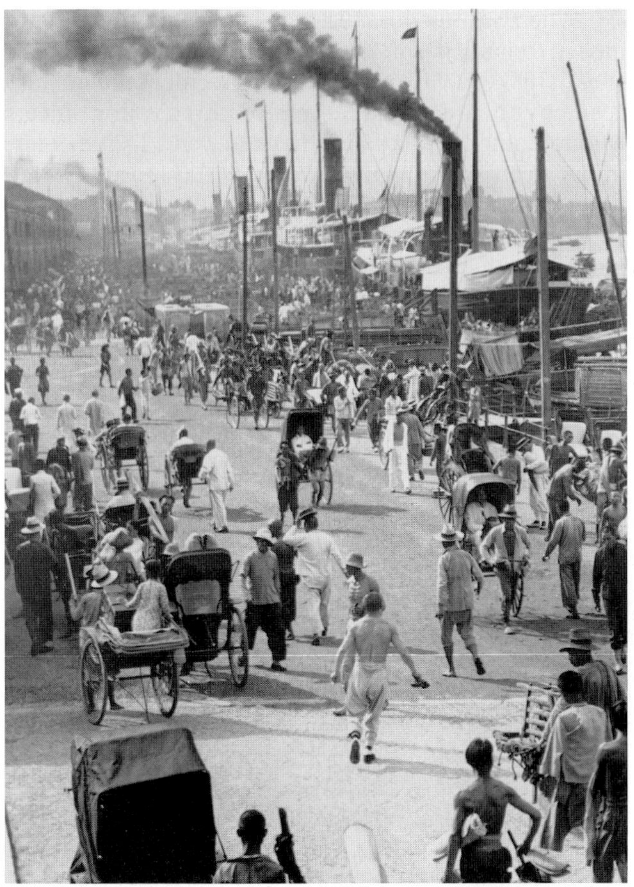

The Bund, Shanghai Shanghai was the most important port and industrial city in China. This picture shows the Bund, or waterfront, where ocean-going ships docked and where Chinese and foreign merchants did business. Many of the people you see in the picture were stevedores, who loaded and unloaded ships, and drivers of rickshaws or man-powered taxis. (Corbis)

cities *mobos* (modern boys) and *mogas* (modern girls) shocked traditionalists with their foreign ways: dancing together, wearing short skirts and tight pants, and behaving like Americans. Students who flirted with dangerous thoughts were called "Marx boys."

The main beneficiaries of prosperity were the *zaibatsu*°, or conglomerates, four of which—Mitsubishi, Sumitomo, Yasuda, and Mitsui—controlled most of Japan's industry and commerce. Farmers, who constituted half of the population, remained poor; in desperation some sold their daughters to textile mills or into domestic service, where young women formed the bulk of the labor force. Labor unions were weak and repressed by the police.

zaibatsu (zie-BOT-soo)

Japanese prosperity depended on foreign trade and imperialism in Asia. The country exported silk and light manufactures and imported almost all its fuel, raw materials, and machine tools, and even some of its food. Though less at the mercy of the weather than China, Japan was much more vulnerable to swings in the world economy.

Revolution and War, 1900–1918

In 1900 China's Empress Dowager Cixi°, who had seized power in a palace coup two years earlier, encouraged a secret society, the Righteous Fists, or Boxers, to rise up and expel all the foreigners from China. When the Boxers threatened the foreign legation in Beijing, an international force from the Western powers and Japan captured the city and forced China to pay a huge indemnity. Shocked by these events, many Chinese students became convinced that China needed a revolution to get rid of the Qing dynasty and modernize their country. In Shanghai dissidents published works that would have been forbidden elsewhere in China.

When Cixi died in 1908, the Revolutionary Alliance led by **Sun Yat-sen**° (Sun Zhongshan, 1867–1925) prepared to take over. Sun had spent much of his life in Japan, England, and the United States, plotting the overthrow of the Qing dynasty. His ideas were a mixture of nationalism, socialism, and Confucian philosophy. His patriotism, his powerful ambition, and his tenacious spirit attracted a large following.

The military thwarted Sun's plans. After China's defeat in the war with Japan in 1895, the government had agreed to equip the army with modern rifles and machine guns. The combination of traditional regional autonomy with modern tactics and equipment led to the creation of local armies beholden to local generals known as warlords, rather than to the central government. When a regional army mutinied in October 1911, **Yuan Shikai**°, the most powerful of the regional generals, refused to defend the Qing. A revolutionary assembly at Nanjing elected Sun president of China in December 1911, and the last Qing ruler, the boy-emperor Puyi, abdicated the throne. But Sun had no military forces at his command. To avoid a clash with the army, he resigned after a few weeks, and a new national assembly elected Yuan president of the new Chinese republic.

Yuan was an able military leader, but he had no political program. When Sun reorganized his followers into a political party called **Guomindang**° (National

Cixi (TSUH-shee) **Sun Yat-sen** (soon yot-SEN)
Yuan Shikai (you-AHN she-KIE) **Guomindang** (gwo-min-dong)

People's Party), Yuan quashed every attempt at creating a Western-style government and harassed Sun's followers. Victory in the first round of the struggle to create a new China went to the military.

The Japanese were quick to join the Allied side in World War I. They saw the war as an opportunity to advance their interests while the Europeans were occupied elsewhere. The war created an economic boom, as the Japanese suddenly found their products in greater demand. But it also created hardships for workers, who rioted when the cost of rice rose faster than their wages.

The Japanese soon conquered the German colonies in the northern Pacific and on the coast of China, then turned their attention to the rest of China. In 1915 Japan presented China with Twenty-One Demands, which would have turned it into a virtual protectorate. Britain and the United States persuaded Japan to soften the demands but could not prevent it from keeping the German coastal enclaves and extracting railroad and mining concessions at China's expense. In protest, anti-Japanese riots and boycotts broke out throughout China. Thus began a bitter struggle between the two countries that was to last for thirty years.

Chinese Warlords and the Guomindang, 1919–1929

At the Paris Peace Conference, the great powers accepted Japan's seizure of the German enclaves in China. To many educated Chinese, this decision was a cruel insult. On May 4, 1919, students demonstrated in front of the Forbidden City of Beijing. Despite a government ban, the May Fourth Movement spread to other parts of China. A new generation was growing up to challenge the old officials, the regional generals, and the foreigners.

China's regional generals—the warlords—still supported their armies through plunder and arbitrary taxation. They frightened off trade and investment in railroads, industry, and agricultural improvement. While neglecting the dikes and canals on which the livelihood of Chinese farmers depended, they fought one another and protected the gangsters who ran the opium trade. During the warlord era only the treaty ports prospered, while the rest of China grew poorer and weaker.

Sun Yat-sen tried to make a comeback in Canton (Guangzhou) in the early 1920s. Though not a Communist, he was impressed with the efficiency of Lenin's revolutionary tactics and let a Soviet adviser reorganize the Guomindang along Leninist lines. He also welcomed members of the newly created Chinese Communist Party into the Guomindang.

When Sun died in 1925 the leadership of his party passed to Jiang Jieshi, known in the West as **Chiang Kai-shek**° (1887–1975). An officer and director of the military academy, Chiang trained several hundred young officers who remained loyal to him thereafter. In 1927 he determined to crush the regional warlords. As his army moved north from its base in Canton, he briefly formed an alliance with the Communists. Once his troops had occupied Shanghai, however, he allied himself with local gangsters to crush the labor unions and decimate the Communists, whom he considered a threat. He then defeated or co-opted most of the other warlords and established a dictatorship.

Chiang's government issued ambitious plans to build railroads, develop agriculture and industry, and modernize China from the top down. However, his followers were neither competent administrators like the Japanese officials of the Meiji Restoration nor ruthless modernizers like the Russian Bolsheviks. Instead, the government attracted thousands of opportunists whose goals were to "become officials and get rich" by taxing and plundering businesses. In the countryside tax collectors and landowners squeezed the peasants ever harder, even in times of natural disasters. What little money reached the government's coffers went to the military. For twenty years after the fall of the Qing, China remained mired in poverty, subject to corrupt officials and the whims of nature.

The New Middle East

Having contributed to the Allied victory, the Arab peoples expected to have a say in the outcome of the Great War. But the victorious French and British planned to treat the Middle East like a territory open to colonial rule. The result was a legacy of instability that has persisted to this day.

The Mandate System

At the Paris Peace Conference France, Britain, Italy, and Japan proposed to divide the former German colonies and the territories of the Ottoman Empire among themselves, but their ambitions clashed with President Wilson's ideal of national self-determination. Eventually, the victors arrived at a compromise solution called the **mandate system:** colonial rulers would administer the territories but would be accountable to the League of Nations for "the

---

Chiang Kai-shek (chang kie-shek)

material and moral well-being and the social progress of the inhabitants."

Class C Mandates—those with the smallest populations—were treated as colonies by their conquerors. South Africa replaced Germany in Southwest Africa (now Namibia). Britain, Australia, New Zealand, and Japan took over the German islands in the Pacific. Class B Mandates, larger than Class C but still underdeveloped, were to be ruled for the benefit of their inhabitants under League of Nations supervision. They were to receive autonomy at some unspecified time in the future. Most of Germany's African colonies fell into this category.

The Arab-speaking territories of the old Ottoman Empire were Class A Mandates. The League of Nations declared that they had "reached a state of development where their existence as independent nations can be provisionally recognized subject to the rendering of administrative advice and assistance by a Mandatory, until such time as they are able to stand alone." Arabs interpreted this ambiguous wording as a promise of independence. Britain and France sent troops into the region "for the benefit of its inhabitants." Palestine (now Israel), Transjordan (now Jordan), and Iraq (formerly Mesopotamia) became British mandates; France claimed Syria and Lebanon (see Map 29.4). (See Diversity and Dominance: The Middle East After World War I.)

Mustafa Kemal Atatürk After World War I, Mustafa Kemal was determined to modernize Turkey on the western model. Here he is shown wearing a European-style suit and teaching the Latin alphabet. (Stock Montage)

The Rise of Modern Turkey

At the end of the war, as the Ottoman Empire teetered on the brink of collapse, France, Britain, and Italy saw an opportunity to expand their empires, and Greece eyed those parts of Anatolia inhabited by Greeks. In 1919 French, British, Italian, and Greek forces occupied Constantinople and parts of Anatolia. By the Treaty of Sèvres (1920) the Allies made the sultan give up most of his lands.

In 1919 Mustafa Kemal, a hero of the Gallipoli campaign, had formed a nationalist government in central Anatolia with the backing of fellow army officers. In 1922, after a short but fierce war against invading Greeks, his armies reconquered Anatolia and the area around Constantinople. The victorious Turks forced hundreds of thousands of Greeks from their ancestral homes in Anatolia. In response the Greek government expelled all Muslims from Greece. The ethnic diversity that had prevailed in the region for centuries ended.

As a war hero and proclaimed savior of his country, Kemal was able to impose wrenching changes on his people faster than any other reformer would have dared. An outspoken modernizer, he was eager to bring Turkey closer to Europe as quickly as possible. He abolished the sultanate, declared Turkey a secular republic, and introduced European laws. In a radical break with Islamic tradition, he suppressed Muslim courts, schools, and religious orders and replaced the Arabic alphabet with the Latin alphabet.

Kemal attempted to westernize the traditional Turkish family. Women received civil equality, including the right to vote and to be elected to the national assembly. Kemal forbade polygamy and instituted civil marriage and divorce. He even changed people's clothing, strongly discouraging women from veiling their faces, and replaced the fez, until then the traditional Turkish men's hat, with the European brimmed hat. He ordered everyone to take a family name, choosing the name Atatürk ("father of the Turks") for himself. His reforms spread quickly in the cities; but in rural areas, where Islamic traditions remained strong, people resisted them for a long time.

Diversity and Dominance

The Middle East After World War I

During the First World War, Entente forces invaded the Arab provinces of the Ottoman Empire and occupied Palestine, Mesopotamia, and Syria. This raised the question of what to do with these territories after the war. Would they be returned to the Ottoman Empire? Would they simply be added to the colonial empires of Britain and France? Or would they become independent Arab states?

The following documents illustrate the diversity of opinions among various groups planning the postwar settlement: Great Britain concerned with defeating Germany and maintaining its empire; the United States, basing its policies on lofty principles; and Arab delegates from the Middle East, seeking self-determination.

In the early twentieth century, in response to the rise of anti-Semitism in Europe, a movement called Zionism had arisen among European Jews. Zionists, led by Theodore Herzl, hoped for a return to Israel, the ancestral homeland of the Jewish people. For two thousand years this land had been a province of various empires—the Roman, Byzantine, Arab, and Ottoman—and was inhabited by Arabic-speaking people who practiced the Islamic religion.

During the war the British government eagerly sought the support of the American Jewish community to balance the hostility of Irish-Americans and German-Americans toward the British war effort. It was therefore receptive to the idea of establishing a Jewish homeland in Palestine. The British government therefore found itself torn between two contradictory impulses, both motivated by the short-term need to win the war, but not without thought of the more distant future. The result was a policy statement, sent by Foreign Secretary Arthur James Balfour to Baron Rothschild, a prominent supporter of the Zionist movement in England. This statement, called the "Balfour Declaration," has haunted the Middle East ever since.

THE BALFOUR DECLARATION OF 1917

Foreign Office
November 2nd, 1917

Dear Lord Rothschild:

I have much pleasure in conveying to you, on behalf of His Majesty's Government, the following declaration of sympathy with Jewish Zionist aspirations which have been submitted to, and approved by, the Cabinet:

> His Majesty's Government view with favor the establishment in Palestine of a national home for the Jewish people, and will use their best endeavors to facilitate the achievement of this object, it being clearly understood that nothing shall be done which may prejudice the civil and religious rights of existing non-Jewish communities in Palestine, or the rights and political status enjoyed by Jews in any other country.

I should be grateful if you would bring this declaration to the knowledge of the Zionist Federation.

Yours,
Arthur James Balfour

On January 8, 1918, the American president Woodrow Wilson issued his famous Fourteen Points proposal to end the war. Much of his speech was devoted to European affairs or to international relations in general, but two of his fourteen points were understood as referring to the Arab world.

WOODROW WILSON'S FOURTEEN POINTS

We entered this war because violations of right had occurred which touches us to the quick and made the life of our own people impossible unless they were corrected and the world secured once for all against their recurrence. What we demand in this war, therefore, is nothing peculiar to ourselves. It is that the world be made fit and safe to live in; and particularly that it be made safe for every peace-loving nation which, like our own, wishes to live its own life, determine its own institutions, be assured of justice and fair dealing by the other peoples of the world as against force and selfish aggression. All the peoples of the world are in effect partners in this interest, and for our own part we see very clearly that unless justice be done to others it will not be done to us. The programme of the world's peace, therefore, is our programme; and that programme, the only possible programme, as we see it, is this:

V. A free, open-minded, and absolutely impartial adjustment of all colonial claims, based upon a strict observance of the principle that in determining all such questions of sovereignty the interests of the populations concerned must have equal weight with the equitable claims of the government whose title is to be determined.

XII. The Turkish portions of the present Ottoman Empire should be assured a secure sovereignty, but the other nationalities which are now under Turkish rule should be assured an undoubted security of life and an absolutely unmolested opportunity of autonomous development. . . .

When the war ended, the victorious Allies assembled in Paris to determine, among other things, the fate of the former Arab provinces of the Ottoman Empire. This was a matter of grave concern to both Zionists and leaders of the Arab populations. Arab leaders, in particular, had reason to doubt the intentions of the great powers, especially Britain and France. When the Allies decided to create mandates in the Arab territories on the grounds that the Arab peoples were not ready for independence, Arab leaders expressed their misgivings, as the following statement shows:

MEMORANDUM OF THE GENERAL SYRIAN CONGRESS, JULY 2, 1919

We the undersigned members of the General Syrian Congress, meeting in Damascus on Wednesday, July 2nd, 1919, made up of representatives from the three Zones, viz., The Southern, Eastern, and Western, provided with credentials and authorizations by the inhabitants of our various districts, Moslems, Christians, and Jews, have agreed upon the following statement of the desires of the people of the country who have elected us. . . .

1. We ask absolutely complete political independence for Syria. . . .
2. We ask that the government of this Syrian country should be a democratic civil constitutional Monarchy on broad decentralization principles, safeguarding the rights of minorities, and that the King be the Emir Feisal, who carried on a glorious struggle in the cause of our liberation and merited our full confidence and entire reliance.
3. Considering the fact that the Arabs inhabiting the Syrian area are not naturally less gifted than other more advanced races and that they are by no means less developed than the Bulgarians, Serbians, Greeks, and Roumanians at the beginning of their independence, we protest against Article 22 of the Covenant of the League of Nations, placing us among the nations in their middle stage of development which stand in need of a mandatory power.
4. In the event of the rejection of the Peace Conference of this just protest for certain considerations that we may not understand, we, relying on the declarations of President Wilson that his object in waging war was to put an end to the ambition of conquest and colonization, we can only regard the mandate mentioned in the Covenant of the League of Nations as equivalent to the rendering of economical and technical assistance that does not prejudice our complete independence. And desiring that our country should not fall a prey to colonization and believing that the American Nation is furthest from any thought of colonization and has no political ambition in our country, we will seek the technical and economic assistance from the United States of America, provided that such assistance does not exceed 20 years.
5. In the event of America not finding herself in a position to accept our desire for assistance, we will seek this assistance from Great Britain, also provided that such does not prejudice our complete independence and unity of our country and that the duration of such assistance does not exceed that mentioned in the previous article.
6. We do not acknowledge any right claimed by the French Government in any part whatever of our Syrian country and refuse that she should assist us or have a hand in our country under any circumstances and in any place.
7. We opposed the pretensions of the Zionists to create a Jewish commonwealth in the southern part of Syria, known as Palestine, and oppose Zionist migration to any part of our country; for we do not acknowledge their title but consider them a grave peril to our people from the national, economical, and political points of view. Our Jewish compatriots shall enjoy our common rights and assume our common responsibilities.

QUESTIONS FOR ANALYSIS

1. **Was there a contradiction between Balfour's proposal to establish "a national home for the Jewish people" and the promise "that nothing shall be done which may prejudice the civil and religious rights of existing non-Jewish communities in Palestine"? If so, why did he make two contradictory promises?**
2. **How would Woodrow Wilson's statements about "the interests of the populations concerned" and "an absolutely unmolested opportunity of autonomous development" apply to Palestine?**
3. **Why did the delegates to the Syrian General Congress object to the plan to create mandates in the former Ottoman provinces? What alternatives did they offer?**
4. **Why did the delegates object to the creation of a Jewish commonwealth?**

Source: The Balfour Declaration, *The Times* (London), November 9, 1917. Memorandum of the General Syrian Congress, *Foreign Relations of the United States: Paris Peace Conference*, vol. 12 (Washington, DC: Government Printing Office, 1919), 780–781.

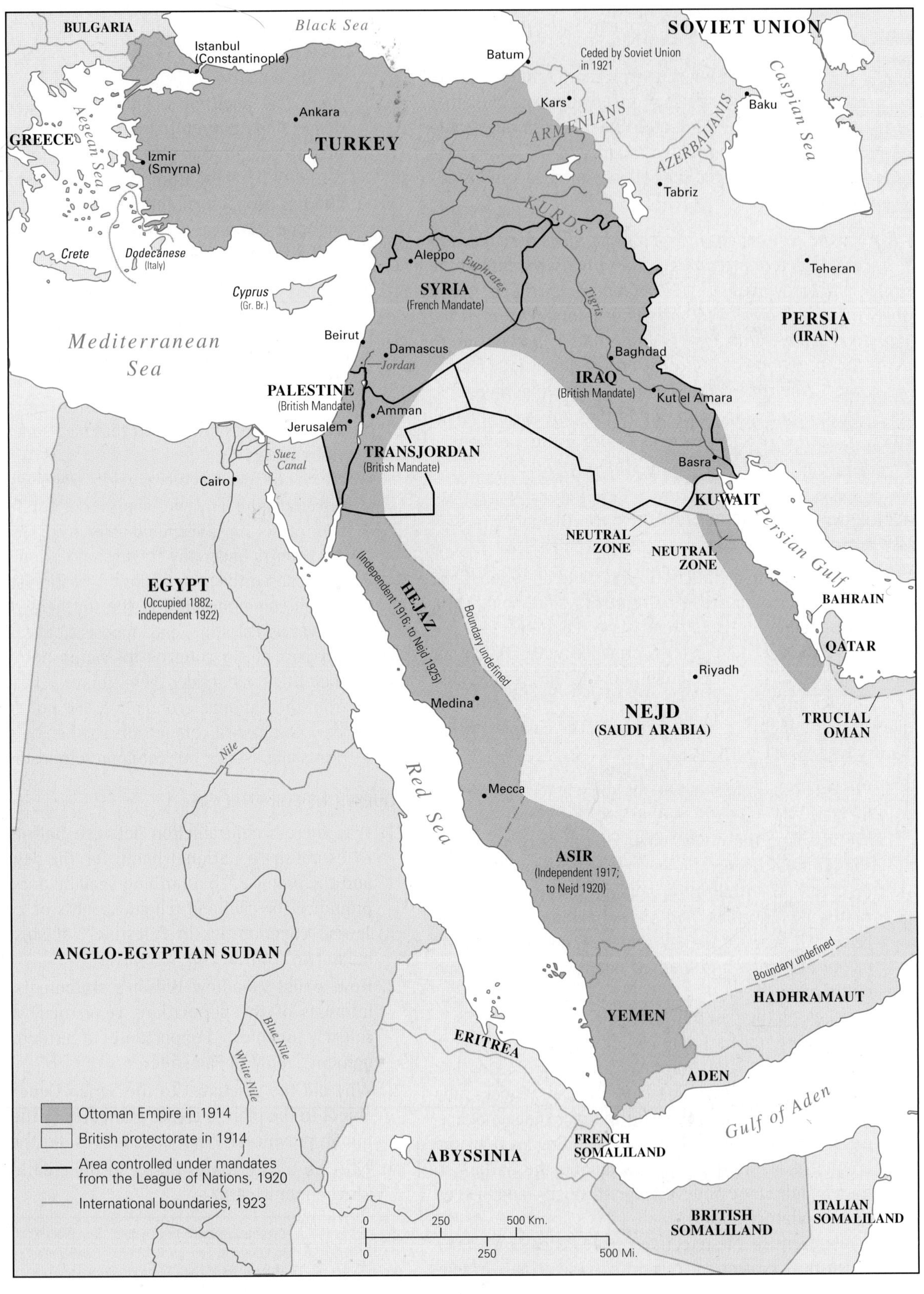
BULGARIA
Black Sea
SOVIET UNION
Istanbul (Constantinople)
Batum
Ceded by Soviet Union in 1921
Kars
ARMENIANS
AZERBAIJANIS
Baku
Caspian Sea
Ankara
GREECE
Aegean Sea
Izmir (Smyrna)
TURKEY
Tabriz
KURDS
Crete
Dodecanese (Italy)
Aleppo
Euphrates
Tigris
Teheran
Cyprus (Gr. Br.)
SYRIA (French Mandate)
PERSIA (IRAN)
Mediterranean Sea
Beirut
Damascus
Jordan
Baghdad
PALESTINE (British Mandate)
IRAQ (British Mandate)
Kut el Amara
Amman
Jerusalem
Suez Canal
TRANSJORDAN (British Mandate)
Basra
Cairo
KUWAIT
NEUTRAL ZONE
NEUTRAL ZONE
Persian Gulf
EGYPT (Occupied 1882; independent 1922)
HEJAZ (Independent 1916; to Nejd 1925)
Boundary undefined
BAHRAIN
QATAR
Riyadh
Medina
NEJD (SAUDI ARABIA)
TRUCIAL OMAN
Nile
Red Sea
Mecca
ASIR (Independent 1917; to Nejd 1920)
ANGLO-EGYPTIAN SUDAN
Boundary undefined
HADHRAMAUT
YEMEN
Blue Nile
White Nile
ERITREA
ADEN
Gulf of Aden
Ottoman Empire in 1914
British protectorate in 1914
Area controlled under mandates from the League of Nations, 1920
International boundaries, 1923
FRENCH SOMALILAND
ABYSSINIA
BRITISH SOMALILAND
ITALIAN SOMALILAND
0
250
500 Km.
0
250
500 Mi.

Map 29.4 Territorial Changes in the Middle East After World War I The defeat and dismemberment of the Ottoman Empire at the end of World War I resulted in an entirely new political map of the region. The Turkish Republic inherited Anatolia and a small piece of the Balkans, while the Ottoman Empire's Arab provinces were divided between France and Great Britain as "Class A Mandates." The French acquired Syria and Lebanon, and the British got Palestine (now Israel), Transjordan (now Jordan), and Iraq. Only Iran and Egypt remained as they had been.

Arab Lands and the Question of Palestine

Among the Arab people, the thinly disguised colonialism of the mandate system set off protests and rebellions not only in the mandated territories, but even as far away as Morocco. Arabs viewed the European presence not as "liberation" from Ottoman "oppression," but as foreign occupation.

After World War I Middle Eastern society underwent dramatic changes. Nomads disappeared from the deserts as trucks replaced camel caravans. The rural population grew fast, and many landless peasants migrated to the swelling cities. The population of the region is estimated to have increased by 50 percent between 1914 and 1939, while that of large cities such as Constantinople, Baghdad, and Cairo doubled.

The urban and mercantile middle class, encouraged by the transformation of Turkey, adopted Western ideas, customs, and styles of housing and clothing. Some families sent their sons to European secular or mission schools, then to Western colleges in Cairo and Beirut or universities abroad, to prepare for jobs in government and business. Among the educated elite were a few women who became schoolteachers or nurses. There were great variations, ranging from Lebanon, with its strong French influence, to Arabia and Iran, which retained their cultural traditions.

The region in closest contact with Europe was the Maghrib—Algeria, Tunisia, and Morocco—which the French army considered its private domain. Alongside the old native quarters, the French built modern neighborhoods inhabited mainly by Europeans (see Environment and Technology: Cities Old and New). France had occupied Algeria since 1830 and had encouraged European immigration. The settlers owned the best lands and monopolized government jobs and businesses, while Arabs and Berbers remained poor and suffered intense discrimination. Nationalism was only beginning to appear before World War II, and the settlers quickly blocked attempts at reform.

The British attempted to control the Middle East with a mixture of bribery and intimidation. They helped Faisal, leader of the Arab Revolt, become king of Syria. When the French ousted him, the British made him king of Iraq. They used bombers to quell rural insurrections in Iraq. In 1931 they reached an agreement with King Faisal's government: official independence for Iraq in exchange for the right to keep two air bases, a military alliance, and an assured flow of petroleum. France, meanwhile, sent thousands of troops to Syria and Lebanon to crush nationalist uprisings.

In Egypt, as in Iraq, the British substituted a phony independence for official colonialism. They declared Egypt independent in 1922 but reserved the right to station troops along the Suez Canal to secure their link with India in the event of war. Most galling to the Wafd (Nationalist) Party was the British attempt to remove Egyptian troops from Sudan, a land many Egyptians considered a colony of Egypt. Britain was successful in keeping Egypt in limbo—neither independent nor a colony—thanks to an alliance with King Farouk and conservative Egyptian politicians who feared both secular and religious radicalism.

Before the war, a Jewish minority lived in Palestine, as in other Arab countries. As soon as Palestine became a British mandate in 1920, Jewish immigrants began arriving from Europe, encouraged by the Balfour Declaration of 1917. Most settled in the cities, but some purchased land to establish *kibbutzim,* communal farms. Their goals were to become self-sufficient and to reestablish their ties to the land of their ancestors. The purchases of land by Jewish agencies angered the indigenous Palestinians, especially tenant farmers who had been evicted to make room for settlers. In 1920–1921 riots erupted between Jews and Arabs. When far more Jewish immigrants arrived than they had anticipated, the British tried to limit immigration, thereby alienating the Jews without mollifying the Arabs. Increasingly, Jews arrived without papers, smuggled in by militant Zionist organizations. In the 1930s the country was torn by strikes and guerrilla warfare that the British could not control. In the process, Britain earned the hatred of both sides and of much of the Arab world as well.

Society, Culture, and Technology in the Industrialized World

With the signing of the peace treaties, the countries that had fought for four years turned their efforts toward building a new future. The war had left a deep imprint on European society and culture. Advances

ENVIRONMENT + TECHNOLOGY

Cities Old and New

Cities do not just grow larger; they change, sometimes radically, in response to culture and technology. The impact of cultural dominance and technological innovations on urban design is evident in these photographs of Cairo.

The European colonial presence was felt more strongly in cities than in the countryside. Cairo, the largest city in the Arab world before the British conquest, grew much larger after 1882. However, the construction of modern quarters for Europeans and wealthy Egyptians had little impact on the older quarters where most Cairenes lived. In the picture of the old quarter of Cairo in 1900 with its narrow streets and open stalls, men wear the burnoose and women cover their faces with a veil. The later picture, taken in 1904, shows Shepheard's hotel, one of the most luxurious hotels in the world, built on a broad avenue in the city's modern quarter.

The picture at left reflects the traditional architecture of hot desert countries: narrow streets, thick whitewashed walls, small windows, and heavy doors, all designed to keep out the heat of the day and protect privacy. The picture below shows the ideas Europeans brought with them about how a city should look. The wide streets and high airy buildings with windows and balconies mimic the urban design of late-nineteenth-century Paris, London, and Rome.

Cairo—Modern and Traditional The luxurious Shepheard's Hotel (below) was built in the European style on a broad avenue in the new quarter of Cairo. In stark contrast is the street (above) in the old quarter of the city: the street is narrow, the walls of the buildings are thick, and the windows small in order to protect the interiors from the heat of the sun. (Billie Love Historical Collection)

in science offered astonishing new insights into the mysteries of nature and the universe. New technologies, many of them pioneered in the United States, promised to change the daily lives of millions of people.

Class and Gender

After the war, class distinctions began to fade. Many European aristocrats had died on the battlefields, and with them went their class's long domination of the army, the diplomatic corps, and other elite sectors of society. The United States and Canada had never had as rigidly defined a class structure as European societies or as elaborate a set of traditions and manners. During the war, displays of wealth and privilege seemed unpatriotic. On both sides of the Atlantic, engineers, businessmen, lawyers, and other professionals rose to prominence, increasing the relative importance of the middle class.

The activities of governments had expanded during the war and continued to grow. Governments provided housing, highways, schools, public health facilities, broadcasting, and other services. This growth of government influence created a need for thousands more bureaucrats. Department stores, banks, insurance companies, and other businesses also increased the white-collar work force.

In contrast with the middle class, the working class did not expand. The introduction of new machines and new ways of organizing work, such as the automobile assembly line that Henry Ford devised, increased workers' productivity so that greater outputs could be achieved without a larger labor force.

Women's lives changed more rapidly in the 1920s than in any previous decade. Although the end of the war marked a retreat from wartime job opportunities, some women remained in the work force as wage earners and as salaried professionals. The young and wealthy enjoyed more personal freedoms than their mothers had before the war; they drove cars, played sports, traveled alone, and smoked in public. For others the upheavals of war brought more suffering than liberation. Millions of women had lost their fathers, brothers, sons, husbands, and fiancés in the war or in the great influenza epidemic. After the war the shortage of young men caused many single women to lead lives of loneliness and destitution.

In Europe and North America advocates of women's rights had been demanding the vote for women since the 1890s. New Zealand was the only nation to grant women the vote before the twentieth century. Women in Norway were the first to obtain it in Europe, in 1915. Russian women followed in 1917, and Canadians and Germans in 1918. Britain gave women over age thirty the vote in 1918 and later extended it to younger women. The Nineteenth Amendment to the U.S. Constitution granted suffrage to American women in 1920. Women in Turkey began voting in 1934. Most other countries did not allow women to vote until after 1945.

In dictatorships voting rights for women made no difference, and in democratic countries women tended to vote like their male relatives. In the British elections of 1918—the first to include women—they overwhelmingly voted for the Conservative Party. Everywhere, their influence on politics was less radical than feminists had hoped and conservatives had feared. Even when it did not alter politics and government, however, the right to vote was a potent symbol.

Women were active in many other areas besides the suffrage movement. On both sides of the Atlantic women participated in social reform movements to prevent mistreatment of women and children and of industrial workers. In the United States such reforms were championed by Progressives such as Jane Addams (1860–1935), who founded a settlement house in a poor neighborhood and received the Nobel Peace Prize in 1931. In Europe reformers were generally aligned with Socialist or Labour Parties.

Since 1874 the Women's Christian Temperance Union had campaigned against alcohol and taverns. In the early twentieth century the American Carrie Nation (1846–1911) became famous for destroying saloons and for lectures in the United States and Europe against the evils of liquor. As a result of this campaign the Eighteenth Amendment imposed prohibition in the United States from 1919 until it was revoked by the Twenty-First Amendment fourteen years later.

Among the most controversial, and eventually most effective of the reformers, were those who advocated contraception, such as the American **Margaret Sanger** (1883–1966). Her campaign brought her into conflict with the authorities, who equated birth control with pornography. Finally, in 1923 she was able to found a birth control clinic in New York. In France, however, the government prohibited contraception and abortion in 1920 in an effort to increase the birthrate and make up for the loss of so many young men in the war. Only the Russian communists allowed abortion, for ideological reasons (see Diversity and Dominance: Women, Family Values, and the Russian Revolution in Chapter 30).

Revolution in the Sciences

For two hundred years scientists following in Isaac Newton's footsteps had applied the same laws and equations to astronomical observations and to laboratory experiments. At the end of the nineteenth century, however, a revolution in physics undermined all the old certainties about nature. Physicists discovered that atoms, the building blocks of matter, are not indivisible, but consist of far smaller subatomic particles. In 1900 the German physicist **Max Planck** (1858–1947) found that atoms emit or absorb energy only in discrete amounts, called *quanta,* instead of continuously, as assumed in Newtonian physics. These findings seemed strange enough, but what really undermined Newtonian physics was the general theory of relativity developed by **Albert Einstein** (1879–1955), another German physicist. In 1916 Einstein announced that not only is matter made of insubstantial particles, but that time, space, and mass are not fixed but are relative to one another. Other physicists said that light is made up of either waves or particles, depending on the observer, and that an experiment could determine either the speed or the position of a particle of light, but never both.

To nonscientists it seemed as though theories expressed in arcane mathematical formulas were replacing truth and common sense. Far from being mere speculation, however, the new physics promised to unlock the secrets of matter and provide humans with plentiful—and potentially dangerous—sources of energy.

The new social sciences were even more unsettling than the new physics, for they challenged Victorian morality, middle-class values, and notions of Western superiority. Sigmund Freud (1856–1939), a Viennese physician, developed the technique of psychoanalysis to probe the minds of his patients. He found not only rationality but also hidden layers of emotion and desire repressed by social restraints. "The primitive, savage and evil impulses have not vanished from any individual, but continue their existence, although in a repressed state," he warned. Meanwhile, sociologists and anthropologists had begun the empirical study of societies, both Western and non-Western. Before the war the French sociologist Emile Durkheim (1858–1917) had come to the then-shocking conclusion that "there are no religions that are false. All are true in their own fashion."

If the words *primitive* and *savage* applied to Europeans as well as to other peoples, and if religions were all equally "true," then what remained of the superiority of Western civilization? Cultural relativism, as the new approach to human societies was called, was as unnerving as relativity in physics.

Although these ideas had been expressed before 1914, wartime experiences called into question the West's faith in reason and progress. Some people accepted the new ideas with enthusiasm. Others condemned and rejected them, clinging to the sense of order and faith in progress that had energized European and American culture before the war.

The New Technologies of Modernity

Some Europeans and Americans viewed the sciences with mixed feelings, but the new technologies aroused almost universal excitement. In North America even working-class people could afford some of the new products of scientific research, inventors' ingenuity, and industrial production. Mass consumption lagged in Europe, but science and technology were just as advanced, and public fascination with the latest inventions—the cult of the modern—was just as strong.

Of all the innovations of the time, none attracted public interest as much as airplanes. In 1903 two young American mechanics, **Wilbur and Orville Wright,** built the first aircraft that was heavier than air and could be maneuvered in flight. From that moment on, wherever they appeared, airplanes fascinated people. During the war the exploits of air aces relieved the tedium of news from the front. In the 1920s aviation became a sport and a form of entertainment, and flying daredevils achieved extraordinary fame by pushing their planes to the very limit—and often beyond. Among the most celebrated pilots were three Americans. Amelia Earhart was the first woman to fly across the Atlantic Ocean, and her example encouraged other women to fly. Richard Byrd flew over the North Pole in 1926. The most admired of all was Charles Lindbergh, the first person to fly alone across the Atlantic in 1927. The heroic age of flight lasted until the late 1930s, when aviation became a means of transportation, a business, and a male preserve.

Electricity, produced in industrial quantities since the 1890s (see Chapter 27), began to transform home life. The first home use of electricity was for lighting, thanks to the economical and long-lasting tungsten bulb. Then, having persuaded people to wire their homes, electrical utilities joined manufacturers in advertising electric irons, fans, washing machines, hot plates, and other appliances.

Radio—or wireless telegraphy, as it was called—had served ships and the military during the war as a means of point-to-point telecommunication. After the war, amateurs used surplus radio equipment to talk to one another. The first commercial station began broadcasting in Pittsburgh in 1920. By the end of 1923 six hundred stations were broadcasting news, sports, soap operas, and advertising to homes throughout North America. By 1930, 12 million families owned radio receivers. In Europe radio spread more slowly because governments reserved the airwaves for cultural and official programs and taxed radio owners to pay for the service.

Another medium that spread explosively in the 1920s was film. Motion pictures had begun in France in 1895 and flourished there and elsewhere in Europe, where the dominant concern was to reproduce stage plays. In the United States filmmaking started at almost the same time, but American filmmakers considered it their business to entertain audiences rather than preserve outstanding theatrical performances. In competing for audiences they looked to cinematic innovation, broad humor, and exciting spectacles, in the process developing styles of filmmaking that became immensely popular.

Diversity was a hallmark of the early film industry. After World War I filmmaking took root and flourished in Japan, India, Turkey, Egypt, and a suburb of Los Angeles, California, called Hollywood. American and European movie studios were successful in exporting films, since silent movies presented no language problems. In 1929, out of an estimated 2,100 films produced worldwide, 510 were made in the United States and 750 in Japan. But by then the United States had introduced the first "talking" motion picture, *The Jazz Singer* (1927), which changed all the rules.

The number of Americans who went to see their favorite stars in thrilling adventures and heart-breaking romances rose from 40 million in 1922 to 100 million in 1930, at a time when the population of the country was about 120 million. Europeans had the technology and the art but neither the wealth nor the huge market of the United States. Hollywood studios began the diffusion of American culture that has continued to this day.

Health and hygiene were also part of the cult of modernity. Advances in medicine—some learned in the war—saved many lives. Wounds were regularly disinfected, and x-ray machines helped diagnose fractures. Since the late nineteenth century scientists had known that disease-causing bacteria could be transmitted through contaminated water, spoiled food, or fecal matter. After the war cities built costly water supply and sewage treatment systems. By the 1920s indoor plumbing and flush toilets were becoming common even in working-class neighborhoods.

Interest in cleanliness altered private life. Doctors and home economists bombarded women with warnings and advice on how to banish germs. Soap and appliance manufacturers filled women's magazines with advertisements for products to help housewives keep their family's homes and clothing spotless and their meals fresh and wholesome. The decline in infant mortality and improvements in general health and life expectancy in this period owe as much to the cult of cleanliness as to advances in medicine.

Technology and the Environment

Two new technologies—the skyscraper and the automobile—transformed the urban environment even more radically than the railroad had done in the nineteenth century. At the end of the nineteenth century architects had begun to design ever-higher buildings using load-bearing steel frames and passenger elevators. Major corporations in Chicago and New York competed to build the most daring buildings in the world, such as New York's fifty-five-story Woolworth Building (1912) and Chicago's thirty-four-story Tribune Tower (1923). A building boom in the late 1920s produced dozens of skyscrapers, culminating with the eighty-six-story, 1,239-foot (377-meter) Empire State Building in New York, completed in 1932.

European cities restricted the height of buildings to protect their architectural heritage; Paris forbade buildings over 56 feet (17 meters) high. In innovative designs, however, European architects led the way. In the 1920s the Swiss architect Charles Edouard Jeanneret (1887–1965), known as Le Corbusier°, outlined a new approach to architecture that featured simplicity of form, absence of surface ornamentation, easy manufacture, and inexpensive materials. Other architects—including the Finn Eero Saarinen, the Germans Ludwig Mies van der Rohe° and Walter Gropius, and the American Frank Lloyd Wright—also contributed their own designs to create what became known as the International Style.

While central business districts were reaching for the sky, outlying areas were spreading far into the countryside, thanks to the automobile. The assembly line pioneered by Henry Ford mass-produced vehicles in ever-greater volume and at falling prices. By 1929 the United States had one car for every five people, five-sixths of the world's automobiles. Far from being blamed for their exhaust emissions, automobiles were praised as the solution to urban pollution. As cars replaced carts and carriages, horses disappeared from city streets, as did tons of manure.

The most important environmental effect of automobiles was suburban sprawl. Middle-class families could now live in single-family homes too spread apart to be served by public transportation. By the late 1920s paved roads rivaled rail networks both in length and in the surface they occupied. As middle- and working-class

Le Corbusier (luh cor-booz-YEH)
Ludwig Mies van der Rohe (LOOD-vig MEES fon der ROW-uh)

The Archetypal Automobile City As Los Angeles grew from a modest town into a sprawling metropolis, broad avenues, parking lots, and garages were built to accommodate automobiles. By 1929, most families owned a car and streetcar lines had closed for lack of passengers. This photograph shows a street in the downtown business district. (Ralph Morris Archives/Los Angeles Public Library)

families bought cars, cities acquired rings of automobile suburbs. Los Angeles, the first true automobile city, consisted of suburbs spread over hundreds of square miles and linked together by broad avenues. In sections of the city where streetcar lines went out of business, the automobile, at first a plaything for the wealthy, became a necessity for commuters. Many Americans saw Los Angeles as the portent of a glorious future in which everyone would have a car; only a few foresaw the congestion and pollution that would ensue.

Technological advances also transformed rural environments. Automobile owners quickly developed an interest in "motoring"—driving their vehicles out into the country on weekends or on holiday trips. Farmers began buying cars and light trucks, using them to transport produce as well as passengers. Governments obliged by building new roads and paving old ones to make automobile travel smoother and safer.

Until the 1920s horses remained the predominant source of energy for pulling plows and reapers and powering threshing machines on American farms. Only the wealthiest farmers could afford the slow and costly steam tractors. In 1915 Ford introduced a gasoline-powered tractor, and by the mid-1920s these versatile machines began replacing horses. Larger farms profited most from this innovation, while small farmers sold their land and moved to the cities. Tractors and other expensive equipment hastened the transformation of agriculture from family enterprises to the large agribusinesses of today.

In India, Australia, and the western United States, where there was little virgin rain-watered land left to cultivate, engineers built dams and canals to irrigate dry lands. Dams offered the added advantage of producing electricity, for which there was a booming demand. The immediate benefits of irrigation—land, food, and electricity—far outweighed such distant consequences as salt deposits on irrigated lands and harm to wildlife.

CONCLUSION

In the late 1920s it seemed as though the victors in the Great War might reestablish the prewar prosperity and European dominance of the globe. But the spirit of the 1920s was not real peace; instead it was the eye of a hurricane.

The Great War caused a major realignment among the nations of the world. France and Britain, the two leading colonial powers, emerged economically weakened despite their victory. The war brought defeat and humiliation to Germany but did not reduce its military or industrial potential. It destroyed the old regime and the aristocracy of Russia, leading to civil war and revolution from which the victorious powers sought to isolate themselves. Two other old empires—the Austro-Hungarian and the Ottoman—were divided into many smaller and weaker nations. For a while, the Middle East seemed ripe for a new wave of imperialism. But there and throughout Asia the war unleashed revolutionary nationalist movements that challenged European influence.

Only two countries benefited from the war. Japan took advantage of the European conflict to develop its industries and press its demands on a China weakened by domestic turmoil and social unrest. The United States emerged as the most prosperous and potentially most powerful nation, restrained only by the isolationist sentiments of many Americans.

Modern technology and industrial organization had long been praised in the name of "progress" for their ability to reduce toil and disease and improve living standards. The war showed that they possessed an equally awesome destructive potential. As we shall see in the next chapter, most survivors wanted no repeat of such a nightmare. But a small minority worshiped violence and saw the new weaponry as a means to dominate those who feared conflict and death.

Key Terms

Western Front	**Sun Yat-sen**
Faisal	**Yuan Shikai**
Theodore Herzl	**Guomindang**
Balfour Declaration	**Chiang Kai-shek**
Bolsheviks	**mandate system**
Vladimir Lenin	**Margaret Sanger**
Woodrow Wilson	**Max Planck**
League of Nations	**Albert Einstein**
Treaty of Versailles	**Wilbur and Orville Wright**
New Economic Policy	

Suggested Reading

Bernadotte Schmitt and Harold C. Bedeler, *The World in the Crucible, 1914–1918* (1984), and John Keegan, *The First World War* (1999), are two engaging overviews of World War I. Imanuel Geiss, *July 1914: The Outbreak of the First World War* (1967), argues that Germany caused the conflict. Barbara Tuchman's *The Guns of August* (1962) and Alexander Solzhenitsyn's *August 1914* (1972) recount the first month of the war in detail. Keegan's *The Face of Battle* (1976) vividly describes the Battle of the Somme from the soldiers' perspective. On the technology of warfare see William H. McNeill, *The Pursuit of Power: Technology, Armed Force, and Society* (1982), and John Ellis, *The Social History of the Machine Gun* (1975). The role of women and the home front is the subject of essays in Margaret Higonnet et al., eds., *Behind the Lines: Gender and the Two World Wars* (1987), and sections of Lynn Weiner, *From Working Girl to Working Mother* (1985). The definitive work on the flu epidemic is Alfred W. Crosby, *America's Forgotten Pandemic: The Influenza of 1918* (1989). Two famous novels about the war are Erich Maria Remarque's *All Quiet on the Western Front* (1928) and Robert Graves's *Goodbye to All That* (1929). The war in English literature is the subject of Paul Fussell, *The Great War and Modern Memory* (1975).

For the background to the Russian Revolution read Theodore von Laue's *Why Lenin? Why Stalin?* 2d ed. (1971); but see also Richard Pipes, *The Russian Revolution* (1990), and Orlando Figes, *A People's Tragedy: The Russian Revolution, 1891–1924* (1996). The classic eyewitness account of the Revolution is John Reed's *Ten Days That Shook the World* (1919). On gender issues see Wendy Goldman, *Women, the State, and Revolution: Soviet Family Policy and Social Life, 1917–1936* (1993). The best-known novel about the Revolution and civil war is Boris Pasternak's *Doctor Zhivago* (1958).

John Maynard Keynes's *The Economic Consequences of the Peace* (1920) is a classic critique of the Paris Peace Conference. Arno Mayer's *Political Origins of the New Diplomacy, 1917–1918* (1959) analyzes the tensions and failures of great-power politics. The 1920s are discussed in Raymond Sontag's *A Broken World, 1919–1939* (1971).

The best recent book on Japan in the twentieth century is Daikichi Irokawa's *The Age of Hirohito: In Search of Modern Japan* (1995). See also Richard Storry, *A History of Modern Japan* (1982), and Tessa Morris-Suzuki, *The Technological Transformation of Japan* (1994). In the large and fast-growing literature on twentieth-century China, two general introductions are especially useful: John K. Fairbank, *The Great Chinese Revolution, 1800–1985* (1986), and Jonathan Spence, *The Search for Modern China* (1990). On the warlord and Guomindang periods see Lucien Bianco, *Origins of the Chinese Revolution, 1915–1949* (1971).

On the war and its aftermath in the Middle East see David Fromkin, *A Peace to End All Peace* (1989), and M. E. Yapp, *The Near East Since the First World War* (1991). Bernard Lewis, *The Emergence of Modern Turkey* (1968), is a good introduction. On Africa in this period see A. Adu Boahen, ed., *Africa Under Colonial Domination, 1880–1935*, vol. 7 of the *UNESCO General History of Africa* (1985), and A. D. Roberts, ed., *Cambridge History of Africa*, vol. 7, *1905–1940* (1986).

The cultural transformation of Europe is captured in H. Stuart Hughes, *Consciousness and Society: The Reorientation of European Social Thought, 1890–1930* (1958). The towering intellectuals of that era are the subject of Peter Gay, *Freud: A Life for Our Time* (1988), and Abraham Pais, *Subtle Is the Lord: The Science and Life of Albert Einstein* (1982). Three books capture the enthusiastic popular response to technological innovations: David E. Nye, *Electrifying America: Social Meanings of a New Technology* (1990); Peter Fritzsche, *A Nation of Fliers: German Aviation and the Popular Imagination* (1992); and the sweeping overview by Thomas Hughes, *American Genesis: A Century of Invention and Technological Enthusiasm, 1870–1970* (1989). On the role of women is this period, see Ellen DuBois, *Woman Suffrage and Women's Rights* (1998); Sheila Rowbotham, *A Century of Women: The History of Women in Britain and the United States* (1997); and Renate Bridenthal, Claudia Koonz, and Susan Stuard, eds., *Becoming Visible: Women in European History* (1987).

30 The Collapse of the Old Order, 1929–1949

German Dive-Bomber over Eastern Europe A German ME-100 fighter plane attacks a Soviet troop convoy on the Eastern Front.

CHAPTER OUTLINE

The Stalin Revolution

The Depression

The Rise of Fascism

East Asia, 1931–1945

The Second World War

The Character of Warfare

Diversity and Dominance: Women, Family Values, and the Russian Revolution

Environment and Technology: Biomedical Technologies

Before the First World War the Italian futurist poet Filippo Marinetti exalted violence as noble and manly: "We want to glorify war, the world's only hygiene—militarism, deed, destroyer of anarchisms, the beautiful ideas that are death-bringing, and the subordination of women." His friend Gabriele d'Annunzio added: "If it is a crime to incite citizens to violence, I shall boast of this crime." Poets are sometimes more prescient than they imagine.

In the nineteenth century the great powers had created a world order with three dimensions. Their constitutional governments were manipulated by politicians—some liberal, some conservative—through appeals to popular nationalism. Internationally, the world order relied on the maintenance of empires, formal or informal, by military or economic means. And the global economy was based on free-market capitalism in which the industrial countries exchanged manufactured goods for the agricultural and mineral products of the nonindustrial world.

After the trauma of World War I the world seemed to return to what U.S. president Warren Harding called "normalcy": prosperity in Europe and America, European colonialism in Asia and Africa, American domination of Latin America, and peace almost everywhere. But the old order, like Humpty Dumpty, could not be put back together again, for its economic underpinnings were fragile and its political support was superficial.

In 1929 the normalcy of the twenties fell apart. Stocks plummeted; businesses went bankrupt; prices fell; factories closed; and workers were laid off. As the Great Depression spread around the world, governments turned against one another in a desperate attempt to protect their people's livelihood. Even wholly agricultural nations and colonies suffered as markets for their exports shriveled.

Most survivors of the war had learned to abhor violence. For a few, however, war and domination became a creed, a goal, and a solution to their problems. The Japanese military tried to save their country from the Depression by conquering China, which erupted in revolution. In Germany the Depression reawakened resentments against the victors of the Great War; people who blamed their troubles on Communists and Jews turned to the Nazis, who promised to save German society by crushing others. In the Soviet Union Stalin used energetic and murderous means to force his country into a Communist version of the Industrial Revolution.

As the old order collapsed, the world was engulfed by a second Great War, far more global and destructive than the first. At the end of World War II much of Europe and East Asia lay in ruins, and millions of destitute refugees sought safety in other lands. The colonial powers were either defeated or so weakened that they could no longer hold onto their empires when Asian and African peoples asserted their desire for independence.

This, then, is the theme of this chapter. As you read it, ask yourself the following questions:

- How did the Soviet Union change under Stalin, and at what cost?
- What caused the Depression, and what effects did it have on the world?
- How did the Depression lead to the Second World War?
- How was the war fought, and why did Japan and Germany lose?

The Stalin Revolution

During the 1920s other countries ostracized the Soviet Union as it recovered from the Revolutions of 1917 and the civil war that followed (see Chapter 29). After Stalin achieved total mastery over this huge nation in early 1929, he led it through another revolution—an economic and social transformation that turned it into a great industrial and military power and intensified both admiration for and fear of communism throughout the world.

Five-Year Plans

Joseph Stalin (1879–1953) was born Joseph Vissarionovich Dzhugashvili into the family of a poor shoemaker. Before becoming a revolutionary, he studied for the priesthood. Under the name "Stalin"

(Russian for "man of steel") he played a small part in the Revolutions of 1917. He was a hard-working and skillful administrator who rose within the party bureaucracy and filled its upper ranks with men loyal to himself. By 1927 he had ousted Leon Trotsky, the best-known revolutionary after Lenin, from the party. He then proceeded to squeeze all other rivals out of positions of power, make himself absolute dictator, and transform Soviet society.

Stalin's ambition was to turn the Union of Soviet Socialist Republics (USSR) into an industrial nation. Industrialization was to serve a different purpose in the USSR than in other countries, however. It was not expected to produce consumer goods for a mass market, as in Britain and the United States, or to enrich individuals. Instead, its aim was to increase the power of the Communist Party domestically and the power of the Soviet Union in relation to other countries.

By building up Russia's industry, Stalin was determined to prevent a repetition of the humiliating defeat Russia had suffered at the hands of Germany in 1917. His goal was to quintuple the output of electricity and double that of heavy industry—iron, steel, coal, and machinery—in five years. To do so, he devised the first of a series of **Five-Year Plans,** a system of centralized control copied from the German experience of World War I.

Beginning in October 1928 the Communist Party and government created whole industries and cities from scratch, then trained millions of peasants to work in the new factories, mines, and offices. In every way except actual fighting, Stalin's Russia resembled a nation at war.

Rapid industrialization hastened environmental changes. Hydroelectric dams turned rivers into strings of reservoirs. Roads, canals, and railroad tracks cut the landscape. Forests and grassland were turned into farmland. From an environmental perspective, the outcome of the Five-Year Plans resembled the transformation that had occurred in the United States and Canada a few decades earlier.

The Collectivization of Soviet Agriculture One of the goals of collectivization was to introduce modern farm machinery. This poster shows delighted farmers operating new tractors and threshers. (David King Collection)

Collectivization of Agriculture

Since the Soviet Union was still a predominantly agrarian country, the only way to pay for these massive investments, provide the labor, and feed the millions of new industrial workers was to squeeze the peasantry. Stalin therefore proceeded with the most radical social experiment conceived up to that time: the collectivization of agriculture.

Collectivization meant consolidating small private farms into vast collectives and making the farmers work together in commonly owned fields. Each collective was expected to supply the government with a fixed amount of food and distribute what was left among its members. Machine Tractor Stations leased agricultural machinery to several farms in exchange for the government's share of the crop. Collectives were to become outdoor factories where food was manufactured through the techniques of mass production and the application of machinery. Collectivization was an attempt to replace what Lenin called the peasants' "petty bourgeois" attitudes with an industrial way of life, the only one Communists respected. Collectivization was expected to bring the peasants under government control so they never again could withhold food supplies, as they had done during the Russian civil war of 1918–1921.

CHRONOLOGY

	Europe and North Africa	Asia and the Pacific
1930	**1931** Great Depression reaches Europe	**1931** Japanese forces occupy Manchuria
	1933 Hitler comes to power in Germany	**1934–1935** Mao leads Communists on Long March
1935	**1936** Hitler invades the Rhineland	
		1937 Japanese troops invade China, conquer coastal provinces; Chiang Kai-shek flees to Sichuan
	1939 (Sept. 1) German forces invade Poland	**1937–1938** Japanese troops take Nanjing
1940	**1940 (March–April)** German forces conquer Denmark, Norway, the Netherlands, and Belgium	
	1940 (May–June) German forces conquer France	
	1940 (June–Sept.) Battle of Britain	
	1941 (June 21) German forces invade USSR	**1941 (Dec. 7)** Japanese aircraft bomb Pearl Harbor
	1942–1943 Allies and Germany battle for control of North Africa	**1942 (Jan–March)** Japanese conquer Thailand, Philippines, Malaya
	1943 Soviet victory in Battle of Stalingrad	**1942 (June)** United States Navy defeats Japan at Battle of Midway
	1943–1944 Red Army slowly pushes Wehrmacht back to Germany	
	1944 (June 6) D-day: U.S., British, and Canadian troops land in Normandy	
1945	**1945 (May 7)** Germany surrenders	**1945 (Aug. 6)** United States drops atomic bomb on Hiroshima
		1945 (Aug. 14) Japan surrenders
		1945–1949 Civil war in China
		1949 Communist defeat Guomindang; Mao proclaims People's Republic (Oct. 1)

When collectivization was announced, the government mounted a massive propaganda campaign and sent party members into the countryside to enlist the farmers' support. At first all seemed to go well, but soon *kulaks*° ("fists"), the better-off peasants, began to resist giving up all their property. When soldiers came to force them into collectives at gunpoint, the kulaks burned their own crops, smashed their own equipment, and slaughtered their own livestock. Within a few months they slaughtered half of the Soviet Union's horses and cattle and two-thirds of the sheep and goats. In retaliation, Stalin ruthlessly ordered the "liquidation of kulaks as a class" and incited the poor peasants to attack their wealthier neighbors. Over 8 million kulaks were arrested. Many were executed. The rest were sent to slave labor camps, where most starved to death.

The peasants who were left had been the least successful before collectivization and proved to be the least competent after. Many were sent to work in factories. The rest were forbidden to leave their farms. With half of their draft animals gone, they could not plant or harvest enough to meet the swelling demands of the cities. Yet government agents took whatever they could find, leaving little or nothing for the farmers themselves. After bad harvests in 1933 and 1934, a famine swept through the countryside, killing some 5 million people, about one in every twenty farmers.

Stalin's second Five-Year Plan, designed to run from 1933 to 1937, was originally intended to increase the output of consumer goods. But when the Nazis took over Germany in 1933 (see below), Stalin changed the plan to emphasize heavy industries that could produce armaments. Between 1927 and 1937 the Soviet output of metals and machines increased fourteen-fold while consumer goods became scarce and food was rationed. After a decade of Stalinism, the Soviet people were more poorly clothed, fed, and housed than they had been during the years of the New Economic Policy.

---

kulaks (COO-lox)

Terror and Opportunities

The 1930s brought both terror and new opportunities to the Soviet people. The forced pace of industrialization, the collectivization of agriculture, and the uprooting of millions of people could be accomplished only under duress. To prevent any possible resistance or rebellion, the NKVD, Stalin's secret police force, created a climate of suspicion and fear. The terror that pervaded the country was a reflection of Stalin's own paranoia, for he distrusted everyone and feared for his life.

As early as 1930 Stalin had hundreds of engineers and technicians arrested on trumped-up charges of counterrevolutionary ideas and sabotage. Three years later, he expelled a million members of the Communist Party—one-third of the membership—on similar charges. He then turned on his most trusted associates.

In December 1934 Sergei Kirov, the party boss of Leningrad (formerly called Petrograd), was assassinated, perhaps on Stalin's orders. Stalin made a public display of mourning Kirov while blaming others for the crime. He then ordered a series of spectacular purge trials in which he accused most of Lenin's associates of "antiparty activities," the worst form of treason. In 1937 he had his eight top generals and many lesser officers charged with treason and executed, leaving the Red Army dangerously weakened. He even executed the head of the dreaded NKVD, which was enforcing the terror. Under torture or psychological pressure, almost all the accused confessed to the "crimes" they were charged with.

While "Old Bolsheviks" and high officials were being put on trial, terror spread steadily downward. The government regularly made demands that people could not meet, so everyone was guilty of breaking some regulation or other. People from all walks of life were arrested, sometimes on mere suspicion or because of a false accusation by a jealous coworker or neighbor, sometimes for expressing a doubt or working too hard or not hard enough, sometimes for being related to someone previously arrested, sometimes for no reason at all. Millions of people were sentenced without trials. At the height of the terror, some 8 million were sent to *gulags*° (labor camps), where perhaps a million died each year of exposure or malnutrition. To its victims the terror seemed capricious and random. Yet it turned a sullen and resentful people into docile hard-working subjects of the party.

In spite of the fear and hardships, many Soviet citizens supported Stalin's regime. Suddenly, with so many people gone and new industries and cities being built everywhere, there were opportunities for those who remained, especially the poor and the young. Women entered careers and jobs previously closed to them, becoming steelworkers, physicians, and office managers; but they retained their household and child-rearing duties, receiving little help from men (see Diversity and Dominance: Women, Family Values, and the Russian Revolution). People who moved to the cities, worked enthusiastically, and asked no questions could hope to rise into the upper ranks of the Communist Party, the military, the government, or the professions—where the privileges and rewards were many.

Stalin's brutal methods helped the Soviet Union industrialize faster than any country had ever done. By the late 1930s the USSR was the world's third largest industrial power, after the United States and Germany. To foreign observers it seemed to be booming with construction projects, production increases, and labor shortages. Even anti-Communist observers admitted that only a planned economy subject to strict government control could avoid the Depression. To millions of Soviet citizens who took pride in the new strength of their country, and to many foreigners who contrasted conditions in the Soviet Union with the unemployment and despair in the West, Stalin's achievement seemed worth any price.

gulag (GOO-log)

THE DEPRESSION

On October 24, 1929—"Black Thursday"—the New York stock market went into a dive. Within days stocks had lost half their value. The fall continued for three years. Millions of investors lost money, as did the banks and brokers from whom they had borrowed the money. People with savings accounts rushed to make withdrawals, causing thousands of banks to collapse.

Economic Crisis

What began as a stock-market crash soon turned into the deepest and most widespread depression in history. As consumers reduced their purchases, businesses cut production. Companies laid off thousands of workers, throwing them onto public charity. Business and government agencies laid off their female employees, arguing that men had to support families while women worked only for "pin money." Jobless men deserted their families. As farm prices fell, small farmers went bankrupt and lost their land. By mid-1932 the American economy had shrunk by half, and unemployment had risen to an unprecedented 25 percent of the work force. Many observers thought that free-enterprise capitalism was doomed.

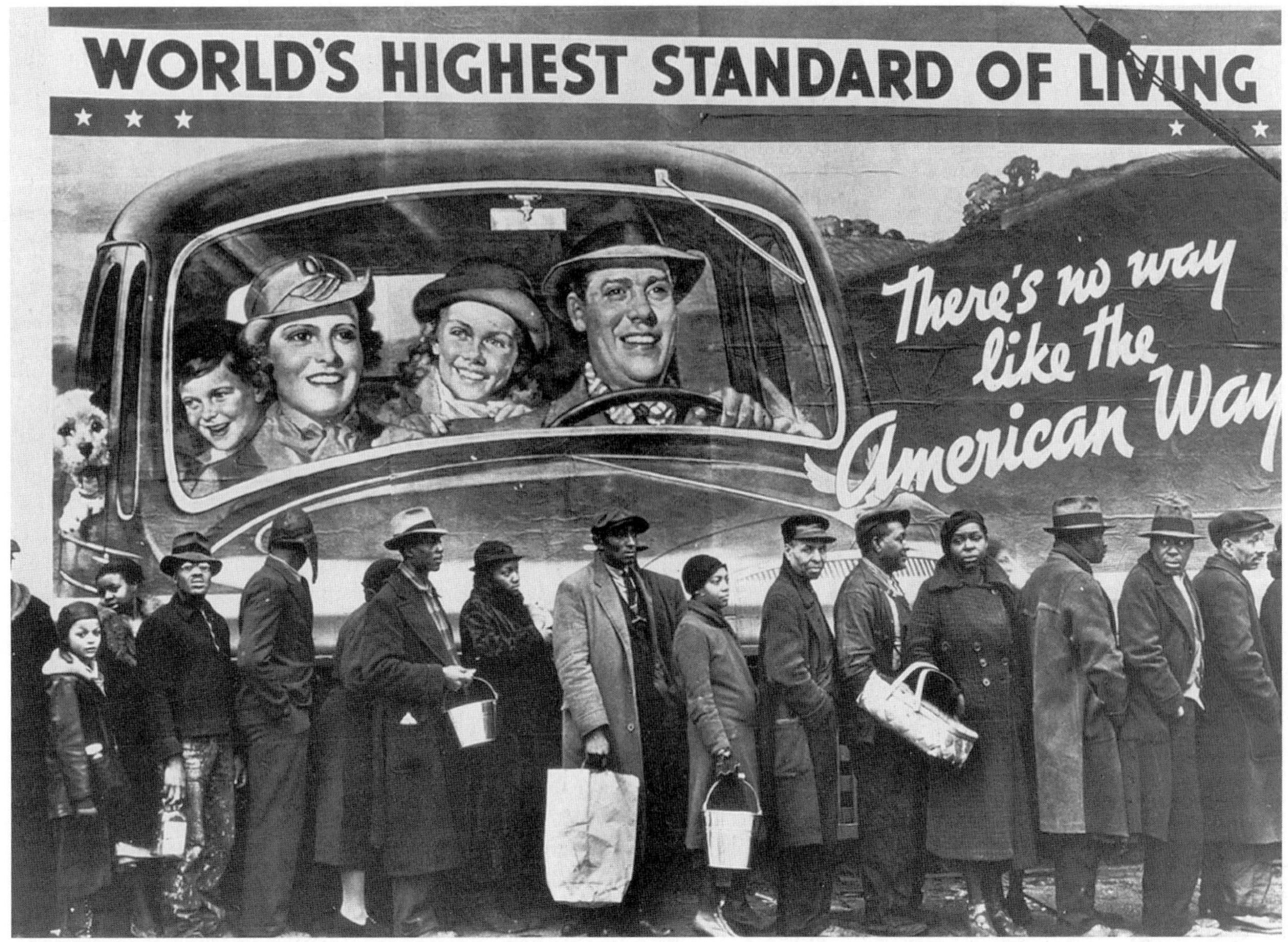

Two Views of the American Way In this classic photograph, *Life* magazine photographer Margaret Bourke-White captured the contrast between advertisers' view of the ideal American family and the reality of mass poverty in a land of plenty. (TimeLife Pictures/Getty Images)

In 1930 the U.S. government, hoping to protect American industries from foreign competition, imposed the Smoot-Hawley tariff, the highest import duty in American history. In retaliation, other countries raised their tariffs in a wave of "beggar thy neighbor" protectionism. The result was crippled export industries and shrinking world trade. While global industrial production declined by 36 percent between 1929 and 1932, world trade dropped by a breathtaking 62 percent.

Depression in Industrial Nations

Frightened by the stock-market collapse, the New York banks called in their loans to Germany and Austria. Without American money, Germany and Austria stopped paying reparations to France and Britain, which then could not repay their war loans to America. By 1931 the Depression had spread to Europe. Governments canceled reparations payments and war loans, but it was too late to save the world economy.

Though their economies stagnated, France and Britain weathered the Depression by making their colonial empires purchase their products rather than the products of other countries. Nations that relied on exports to pay for imported food and fuel, in particular Japan and Germany, suffered much more. In Germany unemployment reached 6 million by 1932, twice as high as in Britain. Half the German population lived in poverty. Thousands of teachers and engineers were laid off, and those who kept their jobs saw their salaries cut and their living standards fall. In Japan the burden of the Depression fell hardest on the farmers and fishermen, who saw their incomes drop sharply.

Diversity and Dominance

Women, Family Values, and the Russian Revolution

The Bolsheviks were of two minds on the subject of women. Following in the footsteps of Marx, Engels, and other revolutionaries, they were opposed to bourgeois morality and to the oppression of women, especially working-class women, under capitalism, with its attendant evils of prostitution, sexual abuse, and the division of labor. But what to put in its place?

Alexandra Kollontai was the most outspoken of the Bolsheviks on the subject of women's rights and the equality of the sexes. Before and during the Russian Revolution, she advocated the liberation of women, the replacement of housework by communal kitchens and laundries, and divorce on demand. Under socialism, love, sex, and marriage would be entirely equal, reciprocal, and free of economic obligations. Childbearing would be encouraged, but children would be raised communally, rather than individually by their fathers and mothers: "The worker mother . . . must remember that there are henceforth only our *children, those of the communist state, the common possession of all workers."*

In a lecture she gave at Sverdlov University in 1921, Kollontai declared:

. . . it is important to preserve not only the interests of the woman but also the life of the child, and this is to be done by giving the woman the opportunity to combine labour and maternity. Soviet power tries to create a situation where a woman does not have to cling to a man she has learned to loathe only because she has nowhere else to go with her children, and where a woman alone does not have to fear her life and the life of her child. In the labour republic it is not the philanthropists with their humiliating charity but the workers and peasants, fellow-creators of the new society, who hasten to help the working woman and strive to lighten the burden of motherhood. The woman who bears the trials and tribulations of reconstructing the economy on an equal footing with the man, and who participated in the civil war, has a right to demand that in this most important hour of her life, at the moment when she presents society with a new member, the labour republic, the collective, should take upon itself the job of caring for the future of the new citizen. . . .

I would like to say a few words about a question which is closely connected with the problem of maternity—the question of abortion, and Soviet Russia's attitude toward it. On 20 November 1920 the labour republic issued a law abolishing the penalties that had been attached to abortion. What is the reason behind this new attitude? Russia after all suffers not from an overproduction of living labour but rather from a lack of it. Russia is thinly, not densely populated. Every unit of labour power is precious. Why then have we declared abortion to be no longer a criminal offence? Hypocrisy and bigotry are alien to proletarian politics. Abortion is a problem connected with the problem of maternity, and likewise derives from the insecure position of women (we are not speaking here of the bourgeois class, where abortion has other reasons—the reluctance to "divide" an inheritance, to suffer the slightest discomfort, to spoil one's figure or miss a few months of the season, etc.)

Abortion exists and flourishes everywhere, and no laws or punitive measures have succeeded in rooting it out. A way round the law is always found. But "secret help" only cripples women; they become a burden on the labour government, and the size of the labour force is reduced. Abortion, when carried out under proper medical conditions, is less harmful and dangerous, and the woman can get back to work quicker. Soviet power realizes that the need for abortion will only disappear on the one hand when Russia has a broad and developed network of institutions protecting motherhood and providing social education, and on the other hand when women understand that *childbirth is a social obligation*; Soviet power has therefore allowed abortion to be performed openly and in clinical conditions.

Besides the large-scale development of motherhood protection, the task of labour Russia is to strengthen in women the healthy instinct of motherhood, to make motherhood and labour for the collective compatible and thus do away with the need for abortion. This is the approach of the labour republic to the question of abortion, which still faces women in the bourgeois countries in all its magnitude. In these countries women are exhausted by the dual burden of hired labour for capital and motherhood. In Soviet Russia the working woman and peasant woman are helping the Communist Party to build a new society and to undermine the old way of life that has enslaved women. As soon as woman is viewed as being essentially a labour unit, the key to the solution of the complex question of maternity can be found. In bourgeois society, where housework complements the system of capitalist economy and private property creates a stable basis for the isolated form of the family, there is no way out for the working woman. The emancipation of women can only be completed when a fundamental transformation of living is effected; and life-styles will change only with the fundamental transformation of all production and the establishment of a communist economy. The revolution in everyday life is unfolding before our very eyes, and in this process the liberation of women is being introduced in practice.

Fifteen years later Joseph Stalin reversed the Soviet policy on abortion.

The published draft of the law prohibiting abortion and providing material assistance to mothers has provoked a lively reaction throughout the country. It is being heatedly discussed by tens of millions of people and there is no doubt that it will serve as a further strengthening of the Soviet family. Parents' responsibility for the education of their children will be increased and a blow will be dealt at the lighthearted, negligent attitude toward marriage.

When we speak of strengthening the Soviet family, we are speaking precisely of the struggle against the survivals of a bourgeois attitude towards marriage, women, and children. So-called "free love" and all disorderly sex life are bourgeois through and through, and have nothing to do with either socialist principles or the ethics and standards of conduct of the Soviet citizens. Socialist doctrine shows this, and it is proved by life itself.

The elite of our country, the best of the Soviet youth, are as a rule also excellent family men who dearly love their children. And vice versa: the man who does not take marriage seriously, and abandons his children to the whims of fate, is usually also a bad worker and a poor member of society.

Fatherhood and motherhood have long been virtues in this country. This can be seen at first glance, without searching enquiry. Go through the parks and streets of Moscow or of any other town in the Soviet Union on a holiday, and you will see not a few young men walking with pink-cheeked, well-fed babies in their arms. . . .

It is impossible even to compare the present state of the family with that which obtained before the Soviet regime—so great has been the improvement towards greater stability and, above all, greater humanity and goodness. The single fact that millions of women have become economically independent and are no longer at the mercy of men's whims, speaks volumes. Compare, for instance, the modern woman collective farmer who sometimes earns more than her husband, with the pre-revolutionary peasant women who completely depended on her husband and was a slave in the household. Has not this fundamentally changed family relations, has it not rationalized and strengthened the family? The very motives for setting up a family, for getting married, have changed for the better, have been cleansed of atavistic and barbaric elements. Marriage has ceased to be matter of sell-and-buy. Nowadays a girl from a collective farm is not given away (or should we say "sold away"?) by her father, for now she is her own mistress, and no one can give her away. She will marry the man she loves. . . .

We alone have all the conditions under which a working woman can fulfill her duties as a citizen and as a mother responsible for the birth and early upbringing of her children.

A woman without children merits our pity, for she does not know the full joy of life. Our Soviet women, full-blooded citizens of the freest country in the world, have been given the bliss of motherhood. We must safeguard the family and raise and rear healthy Soviet heroes!

QUESTIONS FOR ANALYSIS

1. **How does Kollontai expect women to be both workers and mothers without depending on a man? How would Soviet society make this possible?**
2. **Why does Alexandra Kollontai advocate the legalization of abortion in Soviet Russia? Does she view abortion as a permanent right or as a temporary necessity?**
3. **Why does Stalin characterize a "lighthearted, negligent attitude toward marriage" and "all disorderly sex life" as "bourgeois through and through"?**
4. **How does Stalin's image of the Soviet family differ from Kollontai's? Are his views a variation of her views, or the opposite?**
5. **Do the views of Kollontai and Stalin on the role of women represent a diversity of opinions within the Communist Party, or the dominance of one view over others?**

Source: First selection from *Selected Writings of Alexandra Kollontai,* translated by Alix Holt (Lawrence Hill Books, 1978). Reprinted with permission. Second selection from Joseph Stalin, *Law on the Abolition of Legal Abortion* (1936).

This massive economic upheaval had profound political repercussions. Nationalists everywhere called for autarchy, or independence from the world economy. Many people in capitalist countries began calling for government intervention in the economy. In the United States Franklin D. Roosevelt was elected president in 1932 on a "New Deal" platform of government programs to stimulate and revitalize the economy. Although the American, British, and French governments intervened in their economies, they remained democratic. In Germany and Japan, as economic grievances worsened long-festering political resentments, radical leaders came to power and turned their nations into military machines, hoping to acquire, by war if necessary, empires large enough to support self-sufficient economies.

Depression in Nonindustrial Regions

The Depression also spread to Asia, Africa, and Latin America, but very unevenly. In 1930 India erected a wall of import duties to protect its infant industries from foreign competition; its living standards stagnated but did not drop. Except for its coastal regions, China was little affected by trade with other countries; as we shall see, its problems were more political than economic.

Countries that depended on exports—sugar from the Caribbean, coffee from Brazil and Colombia, wheat and beef from Argentina, tea from Ceylon and Java, tin from Bolivia, and many other products—were hard hit by the Depression. Malaya, Indochina, and the Dutch East Indies produced most of the world's natural rubber; when automobile production dropped by half in the United States and Europe, so did imports of rubber, devastating their economies. Egypt's economy, dependent on cotton exports, was also affected, and in the resulting political strife, the government became autocratic and unpopular.

Throughout Latin America unemployment and homelessness increased markedly. The industrialization of Argentina and Brazil was set back a decade or more. During the 1920s Cuba had been a playground for Americans who basked in the sun and quaffed liquor forbidden at home by Prohibition; when the Depression hit, the tourists vanished, and with them went Cuba's prosperity. Disenchanted with liberal politics, military officers seized power in several Latin American countries. Consciously imitating dictatorships emerging in Europe, they imposed authoritarian control over their economies, hoping to stimulate local industries and curb imports.

Other than the USSR, only southern Africa boomed during the 1930s. As other prices dropped, gold became relatively more valuable. Copper deposits, found in Northern Rhodesia (now Zambia) and the Belgian Congo, proved to be cheaper to mine than Chilean copper. But this mining boom benefited only a small number of European and white South African mine owners. For Africans it was a mixed blessing; mining provided jobs and cash wages to men while women stayed behind in the villages, farming, herding, and raising children without their husbands' help.

THE RISE OF FASCISM

The Russian Revolution and its Stalinist aftermath frightened property owners in Europe and North America. In the democracies of western Europe and North America, where there was little fear of Communist uprisings or electoral victories, middle- and upper-income voters took refuge in conservative politics. Political institutions in southern and central Europe, in contrast, were frail and lacked popular legitimacy. The war had turned people's hopes of victory to bitter disappointment. Many were bewildered by modernity—with its cities, factories, and department stores—which they blamed on ethnic minorities, especially Jews. In their yearning for a mythical past of family farms and small shops, increasing numbers rejected representative government and sought more dramatic solutions.

Radical politicians quickly learned to apply wartime propaganda techniques to appeal to a confused citizenry, especially young and unemployed men. They promised to use any means necessary to bring back full employment, stop the spread of communism, and achieve the territorial conquests that World War I had denied them. While defending private property from communism, they borrowed the communist model of politics: a single party and a totalitarian state with a powerful secret police that ruled by terror and intimidation.

Mussolini's Italy

The first country to seek radical answers was Italy. World War I, which had never been popular, left thousands of veterans who found neither pride in their victory nor jobs in the postwar economy. Unemployed veterans and violent youths banded together into *fasci di combattimento* (fighting units) to demand action and intimidate politicians. When workers threatened to strike, factory and property owners hired gangs of these *fascisti* to defend them.

Benito Mussolini (1883–1945) had been expelled by the Socialist Party for supporting Italy's entry into the war. A spellbinding orator, he quickly became the leader of the **Fascist Party,** which glorified warfare and the Italian nation. By 1921 the party had 300,000 members, many of whom used violent methods to repress strikes, intimidate voters, and seize municipal governments. A year later Mussolini threatened to march on Rome if he was not appointed prime minister. The government, composed of timid parliamentarians, gave in.

Mussolini proceeded to install Fascist Party members in all government jobs, crush all opposition parties, and jail anyone who criticized him. The party took over the press, public education, and youth activities and gave employers control over their workers. The Fascists lowered living standards but reduced unemployment and provided social security and public services. On the whole, they proved to be neither ruthless radicals nor competent administrators.

What Mussolini and the Fascist movement really excelled at was publicity: bombastic speeches, spectacular parades, and signs everywhere proclaiming "Il Duce° [the Leader] is always right!" Mussolini's genius was to apply the techniques of modern mass communications and advertisement to political life. Movie footage and radio news bulletins galvanized the masses in ways never before done in peacetime. His techniques of whipping up public enthusiasm were not lost on other radicals. By the 1930s fascist movements had appeared in most European countries, as well as in Latin America, China, and Japan. Of all of Mussolini's imitators, none was as sinister as Adolf Hitler.

Hitler the Orator A masterful public speaker, Adolf Hitler often captivated mass audiences at Nazi Party rallies. (Getty Images)

Hitler's Germany

Germany had lost the First World War after coming very close to winning. The hyperinflation of 1923 wiped out the savings of middle-class families. Less than ten years later the Depression caused more unemployment and misery than in any other country. Millions of Germans blamed Socialists, Jews, and foreigners for their troubles. Few foresaw that they were about to get a dictatorship dedicated to war and mass murder.

Adolf Hitler (1889–1945) joined the German army in 1914 and was wounded at the front. He later looked back fondly on the clear lines of authority and the camaraderie he had experienced in battle. After the war he used his gifts as an orator to lead a political splinter group called the National Socialist German Workers' Party—**Nazis** for short. While serving a brief jail sentence he wrote *Mein Kampf*° (*My Struggle*), in which he outlined his goals and beliefs.

Il Duce (eel DOO-chay) ***Mein Kampf*** (mine compf)

When it was published in 1925 *Mein Kampf* attracted little notice. Its ideas seemed so insane that almost no one took it, or its author, seriously. Hitler's ideas went far beyond ordinary nationalism. He believed that Germany should incorporate all German-speaking areas, even those in neighboring countries. He distinguished among a "master race" of Aryans (he meant Germans, Scandinavians, and Britons), a degenerate "Alpine" race of French and Italians, and an inferior race of Russian and eastern European Slavs, fit only to be slaves of the master race. He reserved his most intense hatred for Jews, on whom he blamed every disaster that had befallen Germany, especially the defeat of 1918. He glorified violence and looked forward to a future war in which the "master race" would defeat and subjugate all others.

Hitler's first goal was to repeal the humiliation and military restrictions of the Treaty of Versailles. Then he planned to annex all German-speaking territories to a greater Germany, then conquer *Lebensraum*° (room to live) at the expense of Poland and the USSR. Finally, he planned to eliminate all Jews from Europe.

From 1924 to 1930 Hitler's followers remained a tiny minority, for most Germans found his ideas too extreme. But when the Depression hit, the Nazis gained supporters among the unemployed, who believed their promises of jobs for all, and among property owners frightened by the growing popularity of Communists. In March 1933 President Hindenburg called on Hitler to become chancellor of Germany.

Once in office Hitler quickly assumed dictatorial power. He put Nazis in charge of all government agencies, educational institutions, and professional organizations. He banned all other political parties and threw their leaders into concentration camps. The Nazis deprived Jews of their citizenship and civil rights, prohibited them from marrying "Aryans," ousted them from the professions, and confiscated their property. In August 1934 Hitler proclaimed himself *Führer*° ("leader") and called Germany the "Third Reich" (empire)—the third after the Holy Roman Empire of medieval times and the German Empire of 1871 to 1918.

The Nazis' economic and social policies were spectacularly effective. The government undertook massive public works projects. Businesses got contracts to manufacture weapons for the armed forces. Women, who had entered the work force during and after World War I, were urged to return to "Kinder, Kirche, Küche" (children, church, kitchen), releasing jobs for men. By 1936 business was booming; unemployment was at its lowest level since the 1920s; and living standards were rising. Hitler's popularity soared because most Germans believed that their economic well-being outweighed the loss of liberty.

The Road to War, 1933–1939

Hitler's goal was not prosperity or popularity, but conquest. As soon as he came to office, he began to build up the armed forces. Meanwhile, he tested the reactions of the other powers through a series of surprise moves followed by protestations of peace.

In 1933 Hitler withdrew Germany from the League of Nations. Two years later he announced that Germany was going to introduce conscription, build up its army, and create an air force—in violation of the Versailles treaty. Instead of protesting, Britain signed a naval agreement with Germany. The message was clear: neither Britain nor France was willing to risk war by standing up to Germany. The United States, absorbed in its domestic economic problems, reverted to isolationism.

In 1935, emboldened by the weakness of the democracies, Italy invaded Ethiopia, the last independent state in Africa and a member of the League of Nations. The League and the democracies protested but refused to close the Suez Canal to Italian ships or impose an oil embargo. The following year, when Hitler sent troops into the Rhineland on the borders of France and Belgium, the other powers merely protested.

By 1938 Hitler decided that his rearmament plans were far enough advanced that he could afford to escalate his demands. In March Germany invaded Austria. Most Austrians were German-speakers and accepted the annexation of their country without protest. Then came Czechoslovakia, where a German-speaking minority lived along the German border. Hitler first demanded their autonomy from Czech rule, then their annexation to Germany. Throughout the summer he threatened to go to war. At the Munich Conference of September 1938 he met with the leaders of France, Britain, and Italy, who gave him everything he wanted without consulting Czechoslovakia. Once again, Hitler learned that aggression paid off and that the democracies would always give in.

The weakness of the democracies—now called "appeasement"—ran counter to the traditional European balance of power. It had three causes. The first was the deep-seated fear of war among people who had lived through World War I. Unlike the dictators, politicians in the democracies could not ignore their constituents' yearnings for peace. Politicians and most other people believed that the threat of war might go away if they wished for peace fervently enough.

The second cause of appeasement was fear of communism among conservative politicians who were more afraid of Stalin than of Hitler, because Hitler claimed to respect Christianity and private property. Distrust of the Soviet Union prevented them from re-creating the only viable counterweight to Germany: the prewar alliance of Britain, France, and Russia.

The third cause was the very novelty of fascist tactics. Britain's Prime Minister Neville Chamberlain assumed that political leaders (other than the Bolsheviks) were honorable men and that an agreement was as valid

Lebensraum (LAY-bens-rowm) **Führer** (FEW-rer)

as a business contract. Thus, when Hitler promised to incorporate only German-speaking people into Germany and said he had "no further territorial demands," Chamberlain believed him.

After Munich it was too late to stop Hitler, short of war. Germany and Italy signed an alliance called the Axis. In March 1939 Germany invaded what was left of Czechoslovakia. Belatedly realizing that Hitler could not be trusted, France and Britain sought Soviet help. Stalin, however, distrusted the "capitalists" as much as they distrusted him. When Hitler offered to divide Poland between Germany and the Soviet Union, Stalin accepted. The Nazi-Soviet Pact of August 23, 1939, freed Hitler from the fear of a two-front war and gave Stalin time to build up his armies. One week later, on September 1, German forces swept into Poland, and the war was on.

East Asia, 1931–1945

When the Depression hit, China and the United States erected barriers against Japanese imports. The collapse of demand for silk and rice ruined thousands of Japanese farmers; to survive, many sold their daughters into prostitution while their sons flocked to the military. Ultra-nationalists, including young army officers, resented their country's dependence on foreign trade. If only Japan had a colonial empire, they thought, it would not be beholden to the rest of the world. But Europeans and Americans had already taken most potential colonies in Asia. Japan had only Korea, Taiwan, and a railroad in Manchuria. China, however, had not yet been conquered. Japanese nationalists saw the conquest of China, with its vast population and resources, as the solution to their country's problems.

The Manchurian Incident of 1931

Meanwhile, in China the Guomindang° was becoming stronger and preparing to challenge the Japanese presence in Manchuria, a province rich in coal and iron ore. Junior officers in the Japanese army guarding the South Manchurian Railway, frustrated by the caution of their superiors, wanted to take action. In September 1931 an explosion on a railroad track, probably staged, gave them an excuse to conquer the entire province. In Tokyo weak civilian ministers were intimidated by the military. Informed after the fact, they acquiesced to the attack to avoid losing face, but privately one said: "From beginning to end the government has been utterly fooled by the army."

When Chinese students, workers, and housewives boycotted Japanese goods, Japanese troops briefly took over Shanghai, China's major industrial city, and the area around Beijing. Japan thereupon recognized the "independence" of Manchuria under the name "Manchukuo."°

The U.S. government condemned the Japanese conquest. The League of Nations refused to recognize Manchukuo and urged the Japanese to remove their troops from China. Persuaded that the Western powers would not fight, Japan simply resigned from the League.

During the next few years the Japanese built railways and heavy industries in Manchuria and northeastern China and sped up their rearmament. At home, production was diverted to the military, especially to building warships. The government grew more authoritarian, jailing thousands of dissidents. On several occasions, superpatriotic junior officers mutinied or assassinated leading political figures. The mutineers received mild punishments, and generals and admirals sympathetic to their views replaced more moderate civilian politicians.

The Chinese Communists and the Long March

Until the Japanese seized Manchuria, the Chinese government seemed to be consolidating its power and creating conditions for a national recovery. The main challenge to the government of **Chiang Kai-shek**° came from the Communists. The Chinese Communist Party was founded in 1921 by a handful of intellectuals. For several years it lived in the shadow of the Guomindang, kept there by orders of Joseph Stalin, who expected it to subvert the government from within. All its efforts to manipulate the Guomindang and to recruit members among industrial workers came to naught in 1927, when Chiang Kai-shek arrested and executed Communists and labor leaders alike. The few Communists who escaped the mass arrests fled to the remote mountains of Jiangxi°, in southeastern China.

Among them was **Mao Zedong**° (1893–1976), a farmer's son who had left home to study philosophy. He was not a contemplative thinker, but rather a man of action whose first impulse was to call for violent effort: "To be able to leap on horseback and to shoot at the same time; to go from battle to battle; to shake the mountains by one's cries, and the colors of the sky by one's roars of

Guomindang (gwo-min-dong)

Manchukuo (man-CHEW-coo-oh) **Chiang Kai-shek** (chang kie-shek) **Jiangxi** (jang-she) **Mao Zedong** (ma-oh zay-dong)

anger." In the early 1920s Mao discovered the works of Karl Marx, joined the Communist Party, and soon became one of its leaders.

In Jiangxi Mao began studying conditions among the peasants, in whom Communists had previously shown no interest. He planned to redistribute land from the wealthier to the poorer peasants, thereby gaining adherents for the coming struggle with the Guomindang army. In this, he was following the example of innumerable leaders of peasant rebellions over the centuries. His goal, however, was not just a nationalist revolution against the traditional government and foreign intervention, but a complete social revolution from the bottom up. Mao's reliance on the peasantry was a radical departure from Marxist-Leninist ideology, which stressed the backwardness of the peasants and pinned its hopes on industrial workers. Mao therefore had to be careful to cloak his pragmatic tactics in Communist rhetoric in order to allay the suspicions of Stalin and his agents.

Mao was also an advocate of women's equality. Radical ideas such as those of Margaret Sanger, the American leader of the birth-control movement, and the feminist play *A Doll's House* by the Norwegian playwright Henrik Ibsen inspired veterans of the May Fourth Movement (see Chapter 29) and young women attending universities and medical or nursing schools. Before 1927 the Communists had organized the women who worked in Shanghai's textile mills, the most exploited of all Chinese workers. Later, in their mountain stronghold in Jiangxi, they organized women farmers, allowed divorce, and banned arranged marriages and footbinding. But they did not admit women to leadership positions, for the party was still run by men whose primary task was warfare.

The Guomindang army pursued the Communists into the mountains, building small forts throughout the countryside. Rather than risk direct confrontations, Mao responded with guerrilla warfare. He harassed the army at its weak points with hit-and-run tactics, relying on the terrain and the support of the peasantry. Government troops often mistreated civilians, but Mao insisted that his soldiers help the peasants, pay a fair price for food and supplies, and treat women with respect.

In spite of their good relations with the peasants of Jiangxi, the Communists gradually found themselves encircled by government forces. In 1934 Mao and his followers decided to break out of the southern mountains and trek to Shaanxi°, an even more remote province in northwestern China. The so-called **Long March** took them 6,000 miles (nearly 9,700 kilometers) in one year, 17 miles (27 kilometers) a day over desolate mountains and through swamps and deserts, pursued by the army and bombed by Chiang's aircraft. Of the 100,000 Communists who left Jiangxi in October 1934, only 4,000 reached Shaanxi a year later (see Map 30.1). Chiang's government thought it was finally rid of the Communists.

Shaanxi (SHAWN-she)

The Sino-Japanese War, 1937–1945

In Japan politicians, senior officers, and business leaders disagreed on how to solve their country's economic problems. Some proposed a quick conquest of China; others advocated war with the Soviet Union. While their superiors hesitated, junior officers decided to take matters into their own hands.

On July 7, 1937, Japanese troops attacked Chinese forces near Beijing. As in 1931, the junior officers who ordered the attack quickly obtained the support of their commanders and then, reluctantly, of the government. Within weeks Japanese troops seized Beijing, Tianjin, Shanghai, and other coastal cities, and the Japanese navy blockaded the entire coast of China.

Once again, the United States and the League of Nations denounced the Japanese atrocities. Yet the Western powers were too preoccupied with events in Europe and with their own economic problems to risk a military confrontation in Asia. When the Japanese sank a U.S. gunboat and shelled a British ship on the Yangzi River, the U.S. and British governments responded only with righteous indignation and pious resolutions.

The Chinese armies were large and fought bravely, but they were poorly led and armed and lost every battle. Japanese planes bombed Hangzhou, Nanjing, and Guangzhou, while soldiers on the ground broke dikes and burned villages, killing thousands of civilians. Within a year Japan controlled the coastal provinces of China and the lower Yangzi and Yellow River Valleys, China's richest and most populated regions (see Map 30.1).

In spite of Japanese organizational and fighting skills, the attack on China did not bring the victory Japan had hoped for. The Chinese people continued to resist,

Map 30.1 Chinese Communist Movement and the Sino-Japanese War, to 1938 During the 1930s, China was the scene of a three-way war. The Nationalist government attacked and pursued the Communists, who escaped into the mountains of Shaanxi. Meanwhile, Japanese forces, having seized Manchuria in 1931, attacked China in 1937 and quickly conquered its eastern provinces.

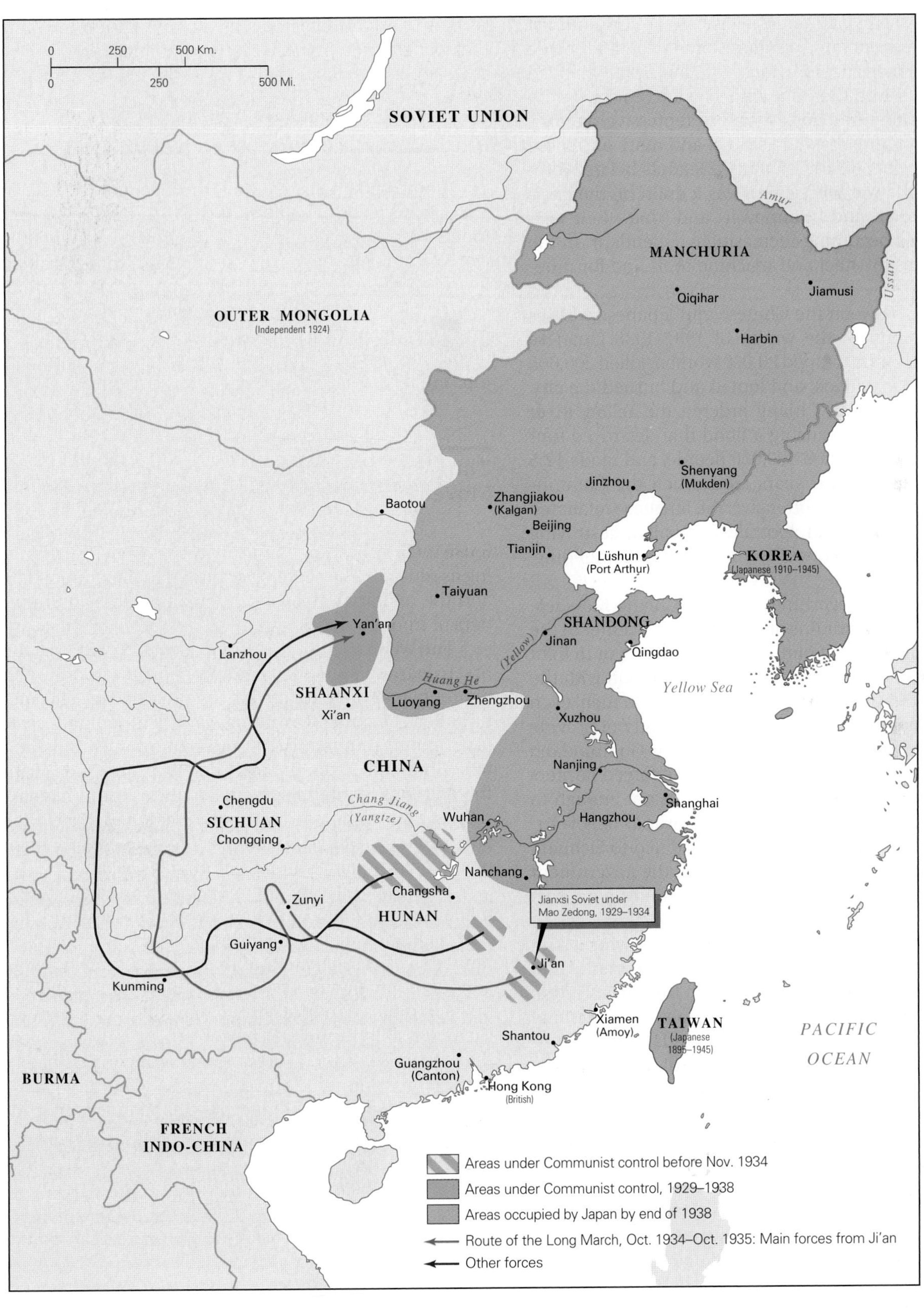

0 250 500 Km.
0 250 500 Mi.
SOVIET UNION
Amur
MANCHURIA
Ussuri
Qiqihar
Jiamusi
Harbin
OUTER MONGOLIA
(Independent 1924)
Shenyang
(Mukden)
Jinzhou
Zhangjiakou
(Kalgan)
Baotou
Beijing
Tianjin
Lüshun
(Port Arthur)
KOREA
(Japanese 1910–1945)
Taiyuan
SHANDONG
Yan'an
Jinan
(Yellow)
Lanzhou
Qingdao
Yellow Sea
Huang He
SHAANXI
Xi'an
Luoyang
Zhengzhou
Xuzhou
CHINA
Nanjing
Chengdu
Chang Jiang
(Yangtze)
Shanghai
SICHUAN
Chongqing
Wuhan
Hangzhou
Nanchang
Zunyi
Changsha
Jianxsi Soviet under
Mao Zedong, 1929–1934
HUNAN
Guiyang
Ji'an
Kunming
Xiamen
(Amoy)
TAIWAN
(Japanese
1895–1945)
PACIFIC
OCEAN
Shantou
Guangzhou
(Canton)
Hong Kong
(British)
BURMA
FRENCH
INDO-CHINA
Areas under Communist control before Nov. 1934
Areas under Communist control, 1929–1938
Areas occupied by Japan by end of 1938
Route of the Long March, Oct. 1934–Oct. 1935: Main forces from Ji'an
Other forces

either in the army or, increasingly, with the Communist guerrilla forces. Japan's periodic attempts to turn the tide by conquering one more piece of China only pushed Japan deeper into the quagmire. For the Japanese people, life became harsher and more repressive as taxes rose, food and fuel became scarce, and more and more young men were drafted. Japanese leaders belatedly realized that the war with China was a drain on the Japanese economy and manpower and that their war machine was becoming increasingly dependent on the United States for steel and machine tools and for nine-tenths of its oil.

Warfare between the Chinese and Japanese was incredibly violent. In the winter of 1937–1938 Japanese troops took Nanjing, raped 20,000 women, killed 200,000 prisoners and civilians, and looted and burned the city. To slow them down, Chiang ordered the Yellow River dikes blasted open, causing a flood that destroyed four thousand villages, killed 890,000 people, and made 12.5 million homeless. Two years later, when the Communists ordered a massive offensive, the Japanese retaliated with a "kill all, burn all, loot all" campaign, destroying hundreds of villages down to the last person, building, and farm animal.

The Chinese government, led by Chiang Kai-shek, escaped to the mountains of Sichuan in the center of the country. There Chiang built up a huge army, not to fight Japan but to prepare for a future confrontation with the Communists. The army drafted over 3 million men, even though it had only a million rifles and could not provide food or clothing for all its soldiers. The Guomindang raised farmers' taxes, even when famine forced farmers to eat the bark of trees. Such taxes were not enough to support both a large army and the thousands of government officials and hangers-on who had fled to Sichuan. To avoid taxing its wealthy supporters the government printed money, causing inflation, hoarding, and corruption.

From his capital of Yan'an in Shaanxi province, Mao also built up his army and formed a government. Until early 1941 he received a little aid from the Soviet Union; then, after Stalin signed a Soviet-Japanese Neutrality Pact, none at all. Unlike the Guomindang, the Communists listened to the grievances of the peasants, especially the poor, to whom they distributed land confiscated from wealthy landowners. They imposed rigid discipline on their officials and soldiers and tolerated no dissent or criticism from intellectuals. Though they had few weapons, the Communists obtained support and intelligence from farmers in Japanese-occupied territory. They turned military reversals into propaganda victories, presenting themselves as the only group in China that was serious about fighting the Japanese.

THE SECOND WORLD WAR

Many people feared that the Second World War would be a repetition of the First. Instead, it was much bigger in every way. It was fought around the world, from Norway to New Guinea and from Hawaii to Egypt, and on every ocean. It killed far more people than World War I. It was a total war, involving all productive forces and all civilians, and it showed how effectively industry, science, and nationalism could be channeled into mass destruction.

The War of Movement

Defensive maneuvers had dominated in World War I. In World War II motorized weapons gave back the advantage to the offensive. Opposing forces moved fast, their victories hinging as much on the aggressive spirit of their commanders and the military intelligence they obtained as on numbers of troops and firepower.

The Wehrmacht°, or German armed forces, was the first to learn this lesson. It not only had tanks, trucks, and fighter planes but perfected their combined use in a tactic called *Blitzkrieg*° (lightning war): fighter planes scattered enemy troops and disrupted communications, and tanks punctured the enemy's defenses and then, with the help of the infantry, encircled and captured enemy troops. At sea, the navies of both Japan and the United States had developed aircraft carriers that could launch planes against targets hundreds of miles away.

Yet the very size and mobility of the opposing forces made the fighting far different from any the world had ever seen. Instead of engaging in localized battles, armies ranged over vast theaters of operation. Countries were conquered in days or weeks. The belligerents mobilized the economies of entire continents, squeezing them for every possible resource. They tried not only to defeat their enemies' armed forces but—by means of blockades, submarine attacks on shipping, and bombing raids on industrial areas—to damage the economies that supported those armed forces. They thought of civilians not as innocent bystanders but as legitimate targets and, later, as vermin to be exterminated.

Wehrmacht (VAIR-mokt) **Blitzkrieg** (BLITS-creeg)

War in Europe and North Africa

It took less than a month for the Wehrmacht to conquer Poland. Britain and France declared war on Germany but took no military action. Meanwhile, the Soviet Union invaded eastern Poland and the Baltic republics of Lithuania, Latvia, and Estonia. Although the Poles fought bravely, the Polish infantry and cavalry were no match for German and Russian tanks. During the winter of 1939–1940 Germany and the Western democracies faced each other in what soldiers called a "phony war" and watched as the Soviet Union attacked Finland, which resisted for many months.

In March 1940 Hitler went on the offensive again, conquering Denmark, Norway, the Netherlands, and Belgium in less than two months. In May he attacked France. Although the French army had as many soldiers, tanks, and aircraft as the Wehrmacht, its morale was low and it quickly collapsed. By the end of June Hitler was master of all of Europe between Russia and Spain.

Germany still had to face one enemy: Britain. The British had no army to speak of, but they had other assets: the English Channel, the Royal Navy and Air Force, and a tough new prime minister, Winston Churchill. The Germans knew they could invade Britain only by gaining control of the airspace over the Channel, so they launched a massive air attack—the Battle of Britain—lasting from June through September. The attack failed, however, because the Royal Air Force had better fighters and used radar and code-breaking to detect approaching German planes.

Frustrated in the west, Hitler turned his attention eastward, even though it meant fighting a two-front war. So far he had gotten the utmost cooperation from Stalin, who supplied Germany with grain, oil, and strategic raw materials. Yet he had always wanted to conquer Lebensraum in the east and enslave the Slavic peoples who lived there, and he feared that if he waited, Stalin would build a dangerously strong army. In June 1941 Hitler launched the largest attack in history, with 3 million soldiers and thousands of planes and tanks. Within five months the Wehrmacht conquered the Baltic states, Ukraine, and half of European Russia; captured a million prisoners of war; and stood at the very gates of Moscow and Leningrad. The USSR seemed on the verge of collapse when the weather turned cold, machines froze, and the fighting came to a halt. Like Napoleon, Hitler had ignored the environment of Russia to his peril.

The next spring the Wehrmacht renewed its offensive. It surrounded Leningrad in a siege that was to cost a million lives. Leaving Moscow aside, it turned toward the Caucasus and its oil wells. In August the Germans attacked **Stalingrad** (now Volgagrad), the key to the Volga River and the supply of oil. For months German and Soviet soldiers fought over every street and every house. When winter came the Red Army counterattacked and encircled the city. In February 1943 the remnants of the German army in Stalingrad surrendered. Hitler had lost an army of 200,000 men and his last chance of defeating the Soviet Union and of winning the war (see Map 30.2).

The Enigma Machine During World War II, German armed forces used Enigma machines like the one seen here in the vehicle of a German tank commander. With Enigmas, they could encrypt and decode radio messages, keeping them secret (they believed) from enemy code-breakers. (Brian Johnson)

From Europe the war spread to Africa. When France fell in 1940 Mussolini began imagining himself a latter-day Roman emperor and decided that the time had come to realize his imperial ambitions. Italian forces quickly overran British Somaliland, then invaded Egypt. Their victories were ephemeral, however, for when the

Map 30.2 World War II in Europe and North Africa In a series of quick and decisive campaigns from September 1939 to December 1941, German forces overran much of Europe and North Africa. There followed three years of bitter fighting as the Allies slowly pushed the Germans back. This map shows the maximum extent of Germany's conquests and alliances, as well as the key battles and the front lines at various times.

British counterattacked, Italian resistance crumbled. During 1941 British forces conquered Italian East Africa and invaded Libya as well. The Italian rout in North Africa brought the Germans to their rescue. During 1942 the German army and the forces of the British Empire (now known as the Commonwealth) seesawed back and forth across the deserts of Libya and Egypt. At **El Alamein** in northern Egypt the British prevailed because they had more weapons and supplies. Thanks to their success at breaking German codes, they also were better informed about their enemies' plans. The Germans were finally expelled from Africa in May 1943.

War in Asia and the Pacific

The fall of France and the involvement of Britain and the USSR against Germany presented Japan with the opportunity it had been looking for. Suddenly the European colonies in Southeast Asia, with their abundant oil, rubber, and other strategic materials, seemed ripe for the taking. In July 1941 the French government allowed Japanese forces to occupy Indochina. In retaliation, the United States and Britain stopped shipments of steel, scrap iron, oil, and other products that Japan desperately needed. This left Japan with three alternatives: accept the shame and humiliation of giving up its conquests, as the Americans insisted; face economic ruin; or widen the war. Japan chose war.

Admiral Isoroku Yamamoto, commander of the Japanese fleet, told Prime Minister Fumimaro Konoye: "If I am told to fight regardless of the consequences, I shall run wild for the first six months or a year, but I have utterly no confidence for the second or third year. . . . I hope that you will endeavor to avoid a Japanese-American war." Ignoring his advice, the war cabinet made plans for a surprise attack on the United States Navy, followed by an invasion of Southeast Asia. They knew they could not hope to defeat the United States, but they calculated that the shock of the attack would be so great that isolationist Americans would accept the Japanese conquest of Southeast Asia as readily as they had acquiesced to Hitler's conquests in Europe.

On December 7, 1941, Japanese planes bombed the U.S. naval base at **Pearl Harbor,** Hawaii, sinking or damaging scores of warships, but missing the aircraft carriers, which were at sea. Then, between January and March 1942, the Japanese bombed Hong Kong and Singapore and invaded Thailand, the Philippines, and Malaya. Within a few months they occupied all of Southeast Asia and the Dutch East Indies. The Japanese claimed to be liberating the inhabitants of these lands from European colonialism. But they soon began to confiscate food and raw materials and demand heavy labor from the inhabitants, whom they treated with contempt. Those who protested were brutally punished.

Japan's dream of an East Asian empire seemed within reach, for its victories surpassed even Hitler's in Europe. Yamamoto's fears were justified, however, because the United States, far from being cowed into submission, joined Britain and the Soviet Union in an alliance called the United Nations (or the Allies) and began preparing for war. In April 1942 American planes bombed Tokyo. In May the United States Navy defeated a Japanese fleet in the Coral Sea, ending Japanese plans to conquer Australia. A month later, at the **Battle of Midway,** Japan lost four of its six largest aircraft carriers. Japan did not have enough industry to replace them, for its war production was only one-tenth that of the United States. In the vastness of the Pacific Ocean aircraft carriers held the key to victory, and without them, Japan faced a long and hopeless war (see Map 30.3).

The End of the War

After the Battle of Stalingrad the advantage on the Eastern Front shifted to the Soviet Union. By 1943 the Red Army was receiving a growing stream of supplies from factories in Russia and the United States. Slowly at first and then with increasing vigor, it pushed the Wehrmacht back toward Germany.

The Western powers, meanwhile, staged two invasions of Europe. Beginning in July 1943 they captured Sicily and invaded Italy. Italy signed an armistice, but German troops held off the Allied advance for two years. In November, at a meeting with Stalin in Teheran, Roosevelt and Churchill promised to open another front in France as soon as possible. On June 6, 1944—forever after known as D-day—156,000 British, American, and Canadian troops landed on the coast of Normandy in western France—the largest shipborne assault ever staged. Within a week the Allies had more troops in France than Germany did, and by September Germany faced an Allied army of over 2 million men with half a million vehicles of all sorts.

Although the Red Army was on the eastern border of Germany, ready for the final push, Hitler transferred part of the Wehrmacht westward. Despite overwhelming odds, Germany held out for almost a year, a result of the fighting qualities of its soldiers and the terror inspired by the Nazi regime, which commanded obedience to the end. In February 1945 the three Allied leaders met again in Yalta on the Black Sea to plan the future of Europe

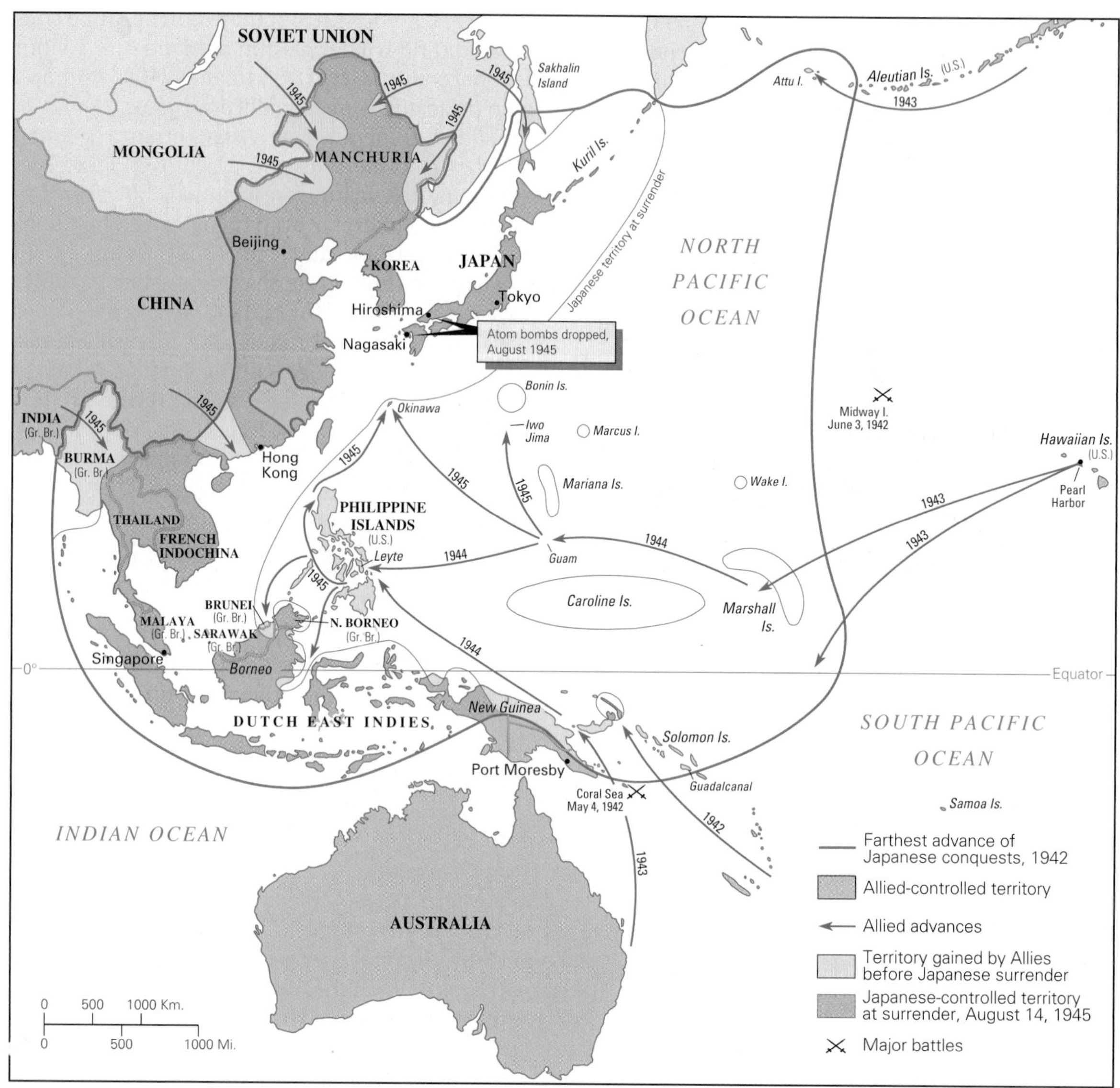

Map 30.3 World War II in Asia and the Pacific After having conquered much of China between 1937 and 1941, Japanese forces launched a sudden attack on Southeast Asia, Indonesia, and the Pacific in late 1941 and early 1942. American forces slowly reconquered the Pacific islands and the Philippines until August 1945, when the atomic bombing of Hiroshima and Nagasaki forced Japan's surrender.

after the war. On May 7, 1945, a week after Hitler committed suicide, German military leaders surrendered.

Japan fought on a while longer, in large part because the United States had aimed most of its war effort at Germany. In the Pacific U.S. forces "leap-frogged" some heavily fortified Japanese island bases in order to capture others closer to Japan itself. By June 1944 U.S. bombers were able to attack Japan. Meanwhile, U.S. submarines sank ever larger numbers of Japanese merchant ships, gradually cutting Japan off from its sources of oil and other raw materials. In 1944 a terrible earthquake devastated the city of Nagoya, compounding the misery of war and bombing raids. After May 1945, with the Japanese air force grounded for lack of fuel, U.S. planes began destroying Japanese shipping, industries, and cities at will.

Even as their homeland was being pounded, the Japanese still held strong positions in Asia. At first, Asian

Hiroshima After the Atomic Bomb On August 6, 1945, an atomic bomb destroyed the city, killing over fifty thousand people. This photo shows the devastation of the city center, where only a few concrete buildings remained standing. (Wide World Photos)

nationalists such as the Indonesian Achmed Sukarno were glad to get rid of the white colonialists and welcomed the Japanese. Yet despite its name, "Greater East Asian Co-Prosperity Sphere," the Japanese occupation was harsh and brutal. By 1945 Asians were eager to see the Japanese leave, but not to welcome back the Europeans. Instead, they looked forward to independence (see Chapters 31 and 32).

On August 6, 1945, the United States dropped an atomic bomb on **Hiroshima,** killing some 80,000 people in a flash and leaving about 120,000 more to die in agony from burns and radiation. Three days later another atomic bomb destroyed Nagasaki. Were these atomic weapons necessary? At the time, Americans believed that the conquest of the Japanese homeland would take more than a year and cost the lives of hundreds of thousands of American soldiers. Although some Japanese were determined to fight to the bitter end, others were willing to surrender if they could retain their emperor. Had the Allies agreed sooner to keep the monarchy, Japan might have surrendered without the nuclear devastation. On August 14 Japan offered to surrender, and Emperor Hirohito himself gave the order to lay down arms. Two weeks later Japanese leaders signed the terms of surrender. The war was officially over.

Chinese Civil War and Communist Victory

The formal Japanese surrender in September 1945 came as a surprise to the Guomindang. American transport planes flew Guomindang officials and troops to all the cities of China. The United States gave millions of dollars of aid and weapons to the Guomindang, all the while urging "national unity" and a "coalition government" with the Communists. But Chiang used American aid and all other means available to prepare for a civil war. By late 1945 he had an army of 2.7 million, more than twice the size of the Communist forces.

From 1945 to 1949 the contest between the Guomindang and the Communists intensified. Guomindang forces started with more troops and weapons, U.S. support, and control of China's cities. But their behavior

Sale of Gold in the Last Days of the Guomindang This picture was taken by famed French photojournalist Henri Cartier-Bresson in Shanghai just before the arrival of the Communist-led People's Liberation Army in 1949. It shows people desperate to buy gold before their Guomindang currency becomes worthless. (Henri Cartier-Bresson/Magnum Photos)

eroded whatever popular support they had. As they moved into formerly Japanese-held territory, they acted like an occupation force. They taxed the people they "liberated" more heavily than the Japanese had, looted businesses, confiscated supplies, and enriched themselves at the expense of the population. To pay its bills Chiang's government printed money so fast that it soon lost all its value, ruining merchants and causing hoarding and shortages. In the countryside the Guomindang's brutality alienated the peasants.

Meanwhile, the Communists obtained Japanese equipment seized by the Soviets in the last weeks of the war and American weapons brought over by deserting Guomindang soldiers. In Manchuria, where they were strongest, they pushed through a radical land reform program, distributing the properties of wealthy landowners among the poorest peasants. In battles against government forces, the higher morale and popular support they enjoyed outweighed the heavy equipment of the Guomindang, whose soldiers began deserting by the thousands.

In April 1947, as Chinese Communist forces surrounded Nanjing, the British frigate *Amethyst* sailed up the Yangzi River to evacuate British civilians. Dozens of times since the Opium War of 1839–1842, foreign powers had dispatched warships up the rivers of China to rescue their citizens, enforce their treaty rights, or intimidate the Chinese. Foreign warships deep in the heart of China were the very symbols of its weakness. This time, however, Chinese Communist artillery damaged the *Amethyst* and beat back other British warships sent to its rescue.

By 1949 the Guomindang armies were collapsing everywhere, defeated more by their own greed and ineptness than by the Communists. As the Communists advanced, high-ranking members of the Guomindang fled to Taiwan, protected from the mainland by the United States Navy. On October 1, 1949, Mao Zedong announced the founding of the People's Republic of China.

The Character of Warfare

The war left an enormous death toll. Recent estimates place the figure at close to 60 million deaths, six to eight times more than in World War I. Over half of the dead were civilian victims of massacres, famines, and bombs. The Soviet Union lost between 20 million and 25 million people, more than any other country. China suffered 15 million deaths; Poland lost some 6 million, of whom half were Jewish; the Jewish people lost another 3 million outside Poland. Over 4 million Germans and over 2 million Japanese died. Great Britain lost 400,000 people, and the United States 300,000. In much of the world, almost every family mourned one or more of its members.

Many parts of the world were flooded with refugees. Some 90 million Chinese fled the Japanese advance. In Europe millions fled from the Nazis or the Red Army or were herded back and forth on government orders. Many refugees never returned to their homes, creating new ethnic mixtures more reminiscent of the New World than of the Old.

One reason for the terrible toll in human lives and suffering was a change in moral values, as belligerents identified not just soldiers but entire peoples as enemies. Some belligerents even labeled their own ethnic minorities as "enemies." Another reason for the devastation was the appearance of new technologies that carried destruction deep into enemy territory, far beyond the traditional battlefields. Let us consider the new technologies of warfare, the changes in morality, and their lethal combination.

The War of Science

As fighting spread around the world, the features that had characterized the early years of the war—the mobilization of manpower and economies and the mobility of the armed forces—grew increasingly powerful. Meanwhile, new aspects of war took on a growing importance. One of these was the impact of science on the technology of warfare. Chemists found ways to make synthetic rubber from coal or oil. Physicists perfected radar, which warned of approaching enemy aircraft and submarines. Cryptanalysts broke enemy codes and were able to penetrate secret military communications. Pharmacologists developed antibiotics that saved the lives of countless wounded soldiers, who in any earlier war would have died of infections (see Environment and Technology: Biomedical Technologies).

Aircraft development was especially striking. As war approached, German, British, and Japanese aircraft manufacturers developed fast, maneuverable fighter planes. U.S. industry produced aircraft of every sort but was especially noted for heavy bombers designed to fly in huge formations and drop tons of bombs on enemy cities. The Japanese developed the Mitsubishi "Zero" fighter plane—light, fast, and agile, but dangerous to fly. Unable to produce heavy planes in large numbers, Germany responded with radically new designs, including the first jet fighters, low-flying buzz bombs, and, finally, V-2 missiles, against which there was no warning or defense.

Military planners no longer dismissed the creations of civilian inventors, as they had done before World War I. Now they expected scientists to furnish secret weapons that could doom the enemy. In October 1939 President Roosevelt received a letter from physicist Albert Einstein, a Jewish refugee from Nazism, warning of the dangers of nuclear power: "There is no doubt that sub-atomic energy is available all around us, and that one day man will release and control its almost infinite power. We cannot prevent him from doing so and can only hope that he will not use it exclusively in blowing up his next door neighbor." Fearing that Germany might develop a nuclear bomb first, Roosevelt placed the vast resources of the U.S. government at the disposal of physicists and engineers, both Americans and refugees from Europe. By 1945 they had built two atomic bombs, each one powerful enough to annihilate an entire city.

Bombing Raids

German bombers damaged Warsaw in 1939 and Rotterdam and London in 1940. Yet Germany lacked a strategic bomber force capable of destroying whole cities. In this area, the British and Americans excelled. Since it was very hard to pinpoint individual buildings, especially at night, the British Air Staff under British Air Chief Marshal Arthur "Bomber" Harris decided that "operations should now be focused on the morale of the enemy civilian population and in particular the industrial workers."

In May 1942, 1,000 British planes dropped incendiary bombs on Cologne, setting fire to most of the old city. Between July 24 and August 2, 1943, 3,330 British and American bombers set fire to Hamburg, killing 50,000

ENVIRONMENT + TECHNOLOGY

Biomedical Technologies

Life expectancy at birth has nearly doubled in the past 150 years. Even in the poorest countries, life expectancy has risen from forty to sixty or seventy years. The cause of this remarkable change is threefold: clean water, immunizations, and antibiotics.

The realization that drinking water can spread disease came first to Dr. Charles Snow, who noticed the correlation between deaths from cholera and the water from a particular pump in London during an epidemic in 1854. Since then, public health officials have been very conscious of the quality of drinking water, although only wealthy cities can afford to purify and chlorinate water for all their inhabitants.

The practice of immunization goes back to the eighteenth century, when physicians in Turkey and in Europe applied infected pus from a person with smallpox (variolation) or an animal with cowpox (vaccination) to healthy persons to build up their resistance to smallpox. By the end of the nineteenth century it became clear that immunity to many diseases could be conferred by injections of weakened bacteria. Immunizations offer the single most effective way to prevent childhood diseases and thereby increase life expectancy.

Antibiotics are more recent. In 1928 Dr. Alexander Fleming discovered that a certain mold, *Penicillin notatum*, could kill bacteria. Antibiotics were first used in large quantities in the Second World War. Along with two other innovations—synthetic antimalarial drugs and blood transfusions—antibiotics helped cut the fatality of battlefield wounds from 11 percent in World War I to 3 percent in World War II.

The remarkable success of these technologies has led people to consider good health their natural birthright. Unfortunately, the victory over disease is temporary at best. The abuse of antibiotics and of antibacterial products encourages the growth of new strains of old diseases, such as tuberculosis, which can resist all known antibiotics. And although bacterial diseases are no longer as prevalent as they once were, humans are still susceptible to viral afflictions such as influenza and AIDS.

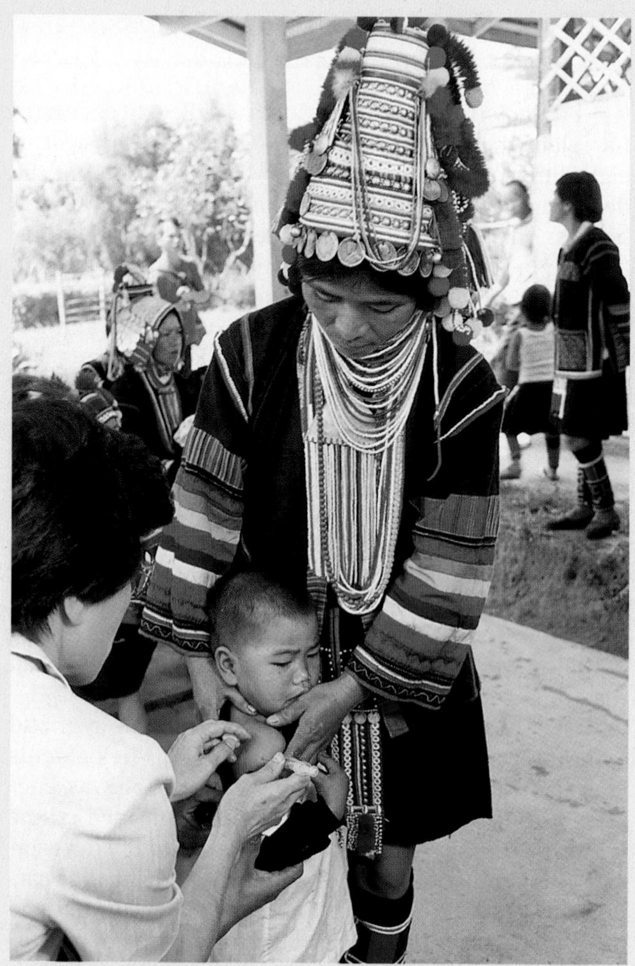

Biotechnology in Action Campaigns to immunize children against diseases reached even remote villages, as here in Thailand. (Peter Charlesworth/Corbis Saba)

people, mostly women and children. Later raids destroyed Berlin, Dresden, and other German cities. All in all, the bombing raids against Germany killed 600,000 people—more than half of them women and children—and injured 800,000. If the air strategists had hoped thereby to break the morale of the German people, they failed. German armament production continued to increase until late 1944, and the population remained obedient and hard working. The only effective bombing raids were those directed against oil depots and synthetic fuel plants; by early 1945 they had almost brought the German war effort to a standstill.

Japanese cities were also the targets of American bombing raids. As early as April 1942 sixteen planes launched from an aircraft carrier bombed Tokyo. Later, as American forces captured islands close to Japan, the raids intensified. Their effect was even more devastating than the fire-bombing of German cities, for Japanese cities were made of wood. In March 1945 bombs set Tokyo ablaze, killing 80,000 people and leaving a million homeless. It was a portent of worse destruction to come.

The Holocaust

In World War II, for the first time, more civilians than soldiers were deliberately put to death. The champions in the art of killing defenseless civilians were the Nazis. Their murders were not the accidental byproducts of some military goal but a calculated policy of exterminating whole races of people.

Their first targets were Jews. Soon after Hitler came to power, he deprived German Jews of their citizenship and legal rights. When eastern Europe fell under Nazi rule, the Nazis herded its large Jewish population into ghettos in the major cities, where many died of starvation and disease. Then, in early 1942, the Nazis decided to carry out Hitler's "final solution to the Jewish problem" by applying modern industrial methods to the slaughter of human beings. German companies built huge extermination camps in eastern Europe, while thousands of ordinary German citizens supported and aided the genocide. Every day trainloads of cattle cars arrived at the camps and disgorged thousands of captives and the corpses of those who had died of starvation or asphyxiation along the way. The strongest survivors were put to work and fed almost nothing until they died. Women, children, the elderly, and the sick were shoved into gas chambers and asphyxiated with poison gas. **Auschwitz,** the biggest camp, was a giant industrial complex designed to kill up to twelve thousand people a day. Most horrifying of all were the tortures inflicted on prisoners selected by Nazi doctors for "medical experiments." This mass extermination, now called the **Holocaust** ("burning"), claimed some 6 million Jewish lives.

Besides the Jews, the Nazis also killed 3 million Polish Catholics—especially professionals, army officers, and the educated—in an effort to reduce the Polish people to slavery. They also exterminated homosexuals, Jehovah's Witnesses, Gypsies, the disabled, and the mentally ill—all in the interests of "racial purity." Whenever a German was killed in an occupied country, the Nazis retaliated by burning a village and all its inhabitants. After the invasion of Russia the Wehrmacht was given orders to execute all captured communists, government employees, and officers. They also worked millions of prisoners of war to death or let them die of starvation.

U.S. Army Medics and Holocaust Victims At the end of World War II, Allied troops entered the Nazi concentration camps, where they found the bodies of thousands of victims of the Holocaust. In this picture, taken at Dachau in southern Germany, two U.S. Army medics are overseeing a truckload of corpses to be taken to a burial site. (Hulton Deutsch Collection/Corbis)

The Home Front in Europe and Asia

In the First World War there had been a clear distinction between the "front" and the "home front." Not so in World War II, where rapid military movements and air power carried the war into people's homes. For the civilian populations of China, Japan, Southeast Asia, and Europe, the war was far more terrifying than their worst nightmares. Armies swept through the land, confiscating food, fuel, and anything else of value. Bombers and heavy artillery pounded cities into rubble, leaving only the skeletons of buildings, while survivors cowered in cellars and scurried like rats. Even when a city was not targeted, air-raid sirens awakened people throughout the night. In countries occupied by the Germans the police arrested civilians, deporting many to die in concentration camps or to work as slave laborers in armaments factories. Millions fled their homes in terror, losing their families and friends. Even in Britain, which was never invaded, children and the elderly were taken from their families for their own safety and sent to live in the countryside.

The war demanded an enormous and sustained effort from all civilians, but more so in some countries than in others. In 1941, even as the Wehrmacht was routing the Red Army, the Soviets dismantled over fifteen hundred factories and rebuilt them in the Ural Mountains and Siberia, where they soon turned out more tanks and artillery than the Axis.

Half of the ships afloat in 1939 were sunk during the war, but the Allied losses were more than made up for by American shipyards, while Axis shipping was reduced to nothing by 1945. The production of aircraft, trucks, tanks, and other materiel showed a similar imbalance. Although the Axis powers made strenuous efforts to increase their production, they could not compete with the vast outpouring of Soviet tanks and American materiel.

The Red Army eventually mobilized 22 million men; Soviet women took over half of all industrial and three-quarters of all agricultural jobs. In the other belligerent countries women also played major roles in the war effort, replacing men in fields, factories, and offices. The Nazis, in contrast, believed that German women should stay home and bear children, and they imported 7 million "guest workers"—a euphemism for war prisoners and captured foreigners.

The Home Front in the United States

The United States flourished during the war. Safe behind their oceans, Americans felt no bombs, saw no enemy soldiers, had almost no civilian casualties, and suffered fewer military casualties than other belligerents. The economy, still depressed in 1939, went into a prolonged boom after 1940. By 1944 the United States was producing twice as much as all the Axis powers combined. Thanks to huge military orders, jobs were plentiful and opportunities beckoned. Bread lines disappeared, and nutrition and health improved. Consumer goods ranging from automobiles to nylon stockings were in short supply, and most Americans saved part of their paychecks, laying the basis for a phenomenal postwar consumer boom. Many Americans later looked back on the conflict as the "good war."

War always exalts such supposedly masculine qualities as physical courage, violence, and domination. These were the official virtues of the Axis powers, but they were highly valued in the United States as well. Yet World War II also did much to weaken the hold of traditional ideas, as employers recruited women and members of racial minorities to work in jobs once reserved for white men. For example, 6 million women entered the labor force during the war, 2.5 million of them in manufacturing jobs previously considered "men's work." In a book entitled *Shipyard Diary of a Woman Welder* (1944), Augusta Clawson recalled her experiences in a shipyard in Oregon:

> The job confirmed my strong conviction—I have stated it before—what exhausts the woman welder is not the work, not the heat, nor the demands upon physical strength. It is the apprehension that arises from inadequate skill and consequent lack of confidence; and this *can* be overcome by the right kind of training. . . . I know I can do it if my machine is correctly set, and I have learned enough of the vagaries of machines to be able to set them. And so, in spite of the discomforts of climbing, heavy equipment, and heat, I enjoyed the work today because *I could do it.*

At the beginning, many men resisted the idea that women, especially mothers of young children, should take jobs that would take them away from their families. As the labor shortage got worse, however, employers and politicians grudgingly admitted that the government ought to help provide day care for the children of working mothers. The entry of women into the labor force proved to be one of the most significant consequences of the war. As one woman put it: "War jobs have uncovered unsuspected abilities in American women. Why lose all these abilities because of a belief that 'a woman's place is in the home?' For some it is, for others not."

The war loosened racial bonds as well, bringing hardships for some and benefits for others. Seeking work in war industries, 1.2 million African-Americans migrated to the north and west. In the southwest Mexican immigrants took jobs in agriculture and war industries. But no new housing was built to accommodate the influx of migrants to the industrial cities, and as a result many suffered from overcrowding and discrimination. Much worse was the fate of 112,000 Japanese-Americans living on the west coast of the United States; they were rounded up and herded into internment camps in the desert until the war was over, ostensibly for fear of spying and sabotage, but actually because of their race.

War and the Environment

During the Depression, construction and industry had slowed to a crawl, reducing environmental stress. The war reversed this trend, sharply accelerating pressures on the environment.

One reason for the change was the fighting itself. Battles scarred the landscape, leaving behind spent ammunition and damaged equipment. Retreating armies flooded large areas of China and the Netherlands. The bombing of cities left ruins that remained visible for a generation or more. Much of the damage eventually was repaired, although the rusted hulls of ships still darken the lagoons of once-pristine coral islands in the Pacific.

The main cause of environmental stress, however, was not the fighting but the economic development that sustained it. The war's half-million aircraft required thousands of air bases, many of them in the Pacific, China, Africa, and other parts of the world that had seldom seen an airplane before. Barracks, shipyards, docks, warehouses, and other military construction sprouted on every continent.

As war industries boomed—the United States increased its industrial production fourfold during the war—so did the demand for raw materials. Mining companies opened new mines and towns in Central Africa to supply strategic minerals. Brazil, Argentina, and other Latin American countries deprived of manufactured imports began building their own steel mills, factories, and shipyards. In India, China, and Europe, timber felling accelerated far beyond the reproduction rate of trees, replacing forests with denuded land. In a few instances the war was good for the environment. For example, submarine warfare made fishing and whaling so dangerous that fish and whale populations had a few years in which to increase.

We must keep the environmental effects of the war in perspective. Except for the destruction of cities, much of the war's impact was simply the result of industrial development only temporarily slowed by the Depression. During the war the damage that military demand caused was tempered by restraints on civilian consumption. From the vantage point of the present, the environmental impact of the war seems quite modest in comparison with the damage inflicted on the earth by the long consumer boom that began in the post–World War II years.

Conclusion

Between 1929 and 1949 the old global order—conservative, colonialist, and dominated by Great Britain and France—was shattered by the Depression, the politics of violence, and the most devastating war in history. Stalin transformed the Soviet Union into an industrial giant at enormous human cost. Reacting to the Depression, which weakened the Western democracies, Hitler in Germany and military leaders in Japan prepared for a war of conquest. Though Germany and Japan achieved stunning victories at first, their forces soon faltered in the face of the greater industrial production of the United States and the Soviet Union.

The war was so destructive and spread to so much of the globe because rapidly advancing technology was readily converted from civilian to military production. Machines that had made cars could also manufacture bombers or tanks. Engineers could design factories to kill people with maximum efficiency. The accelerating technology of missiles and nuclear bombs made the entire planet vulnerable to human destruction for the first time in history.

Into the power vacuum left by the collapse of Germany and Japan stepped the two superpowers: the United States and the USSR. When the war ended, U.S. soldiers were stationed in Australia, Japan, and western Europe, and the Red Army occupied all of eastern Europe and parts of northern China. Within months of their victory, these one-time allies became ideological enemies, hovering on the brink of war.

World War I had rearranged the colonial empires. In contrast, the global impact of World War II was drastic and almost immediate, because the war weakened the European colonial powers and because so much of the fighting took place in North Africa, Southeast Asia, and other colonial areas. Within fifteen years of the end of the war almost every European colonial empire had disappeared. As the long era of European domination receded, Asians and Africans began reclaiming their independence.

Key Terms

Joseph Stalin	**Long March**
Five-Year Plans	**Stalingrad**
Benito Mussolini	**El Alamein**
Fascist Party	**Pearl Harbor**
Adolf Hitler	**Battle of Midway**
Nazi Party	**Hiroshima**
Chiang Kai-shek	**Auschwitz**
Mao Zedong	**Holocaust**

Suggested Reading

The literature on the period from 1929–1945 is enormous and growing fast. The following list is but a very brief introduction.

Charles Kindelberger's *The World in Depression, 1929–39* (1973) and Robert McElvaine's *The Great Depression: America, 1929–1941* (1984) provide sophisticated economic analyses of the Depression. A. J. H. Latham's *The Depression and the Developing World, 1914–1939* (1981) gives a global perspective.

The best recent book on Japan in the twentieth century is Daikichi Irokawa's *The Age of Hirohito: In Search of Modern Japan* (1995). On Japanese expansion see W. G. Beasley, *Japanese Imperialism, 1894–1945* (1987). The race to war is covered in Akira Iriye, *The Origins of the Second World War in Asia and the Pacific* (1987); Michael Barnhart, *Japan Prepares for Total War* (1987), is short and well written.

In the large and fast-growing literature on twentieth-century China, two general introductions are especially useful: John K. Fairbank, *The Great Chinese Revolution, 1800–1985* (1986), and Jonathan Spence, *The Search for Modern China* (1990). On the warlord and Guomindang periods see Lucien Bianco, *Origins of the Chinese Revolution, 1915–1949* (1971). The Japanese invasion of China is the subject of Iris Chang, *The Rape of Nanking: The Forgotten Holocaust of World War II* (1997). Jung Chang, *Wild Swans: Three Daughters of China* (1991), is a fascinating account of women's experiences during the Revolution and the Mao era by the daughter of two Communist officials.

Among recent biographies of Stalin, see Dmitrii Volkogonov's *Stalin: Triumph and Tragedy* (1991) and Robert Tucker's *Stalin as Revolutionary, 1879–1929* (1973) and *Stalin in Power: The Revolution from Above, 1928–1941* (1990). On the transformation of the USSR, see Roy Medvedev's *Let History Judge: The Origins and Consequences of Stalinism* (1989) and Stephen Kotkin's *Magnetic Mountain: Stalinism as Civilization* (1995). Stalin's collectivization of agriculture is vividly portrayed in Robert Conquest's *Harvest of Sorrow* (1986); see also Sheila Fitzpatrick's *Stalin's Peasants: Resistance and Survival in the Russian Village After Collectivization* (1994). Conquest's *The Great Terror: A Reassessment* (1990) describes the purges of the 1930s. Alexander Solzhenitsyn, a veteran of Stalin's prisons, explores them in a detailed history, *The Gulag Archipelago, 1918–1956* (3 vols. 1974–1978), and in a short but brilliant novel *One Day in the Life of Ivan Denisovich* (1978).

Alexander De Grand provides an excellent interpretation of fascism in *Italian Fascism: Its Origins and Development*, 2d ed. (1989). William Shirer's *The Rise and Fall of the Third Reich* (1960) is a long but very dramatic eyewitness description of Nazi Germany by a journalist. The dictators are the subject of two fine biographies: Denis Mack Smith's *Mussolini* (1982) and Ian Kershaw's *Hitler* (2001). See also A. J. P. Taylor's controversial classic *The Origins of the Second World War* (1966) and Michael Burleigh's *Third Reich: A New History* (2000).

Two very detailed books on World War II are John Keegan, *The Second World War* (1990), and Gerhard Weinberg, *A World at Arms: A Global History of World War II* (1994). Particular aspects of the war in Europe are covered in Alexander Werth, *Russia at War, 1941–1945* (1965), and Conrad Crane, *Bombs, Cities, and Civilians* (1993). One of the most readable accounts of the war in Asia and the Pacific is Ronald Spector's *Eagle Against the Sun* (1988). Also see Akira Iriye, *Power and Culture: The Japanese-American War, 1941–1945* (1981), and James Hsiung and Steven Levine, eds., *China's Bitter Victory: The War with Japan, 1937–1945* (1992).

The terror of life under Nazi rule is the subject of two powerful memoirs: Anne Frank's *The Diary of a Young Girl* and Eli Wiesel's *Night* (1960). On the Holocaust see Lucy Dawidowicz, *The War Against the Jews, 1933–1945,* 2d ed. (1986); Leni Yahil, *The Holocaust: The Fate of European Jewry* (1990); and Christopher Browning's *Ordinary Men: Reserve Police Battalion 101 and the Final Solution in Poland* (1992).

Among the many books that capture the scientific side of warfare, two are especially recommended: Richard Rhodes's long but fascinating *The Making of the Atomic Bomb* (1986), and F. H. Hinsley and Alan Stripp, eds., *Code Breakers* (1993).

Among the many books on the home front in the United States, the most vivid is Studs Terkel, *"The Good War": An Oral History of World War Two* (1984). Margaret Higonnet et al., eds., *Behind the Lines: Gender and the Two World Wars* (1987), discusses the role of women in the war.

Striving for Independence: Africa, India, and Latin America, 1900–1949

31

Rush Hour in Brazil In Latin American countries, modern conveniences, when first introduced, were often insufficient to meet the demand from eager customers. Here the Sao Januario streetcar in Rio de Janeiro carries twice as may passengers as it was designed for.

CHAPTER OUTLINE

Emiliano Zapata°, leader of a peasant rebellion in the Mexican Revolution, liked to be photographed on horseback, carrying a sword and a rifle and draped with bandoliers of bullets. Mahatma Gandhi°, who led the independence movement in India, preferred to be seen sitting at a spinning wheel, dressed in a *dhoti*°, the simple loincloth worn by Indian farmers. The images they liked to project and the methods they used could not have been more opposed. Yet their goals were similar: each wanted social justice and a better life for the poor in a country free of foreign domination.

The previous two chapters focused on a world convulsed by war and revolution. The world wars involved Europe, East Asia, the Middle East, and the United States, and they sparked violent revolutions in Russia and China. They accelerated the development of aviation, electronics, nuclear power, and other technologies. Although these momentous events dominate the history of the first half of the twentieth century, parts of the world that were little touched by war also underwent profound changes in this period, partly for internal reasons and partly because of the warfare and revolution in other parts of the world.

In this chapter we examine the changes that took place in sub-Saharan Africa, in India, and in three major countries of Latin America—Mexico, Brazil, and Argentina. These three regions represent three very distinct cultures, yet they had much in common. Africa and India were colonies of Europe, both politically and economically. Though politically independent the Latin American republics were dependent on Europe and the United States for the sale of raw materials and commodities and for imports of manufactured goods, technology, and capital. In all three regions independence movements tried to wrest control from distant foreigners and improve the livelihood of their peoples. Their success was partial at best.

As you read this chapter, ask yourself the following questions:

Zapata (sah-PAH-tah) **Gandhi** (GAHN-dee) ***dhoti*** (DOE-tee)

- How did wars and revolutions in Europe and East Asia affect the countries of the Southern Hemisphere?
- Why did educated Indians and Africans want independence?
- What could Latin Americans do to achieve social justice and economic development? Were these two goals compatible?

Sub-Saharan Africa, 1900–1945

Of all the continents, Africa was the last to come under European rule (see Chapter 28). The first half of the twentieth century, the time when nationalist movements threatened European rule in Asia (see Diversity and Dominance: A Vietnamese Nationalist Denounces French Colonialism), was Africa's period of classic colonialism. After World War I Britain, France, Belgium, and South Africa divided Germany's African colonies among themselves. In the 1930s Italy invaded Ethiopia. The colonial empires reached their peak shortly before World War II.

Colonial Africa: Economic and Social Changes

Outside of Algeria, Kenya, and South Africa, few Europeans lived in Africa. In 1930 Nigeria, with a population of 20 million, was ruled by 386 British officials and by 8,000 policemen and military, of whom 150 were European. Yet even such a small presence stimulated deep social and economic changes.

Since the turn of the century the colonial powers had built railroads from coastal cities to mines and plantations in the interior, in order to provide raw materials to the industrial world. The economic boom of the interwar years benefited few Africans. Colonial governments took lands that Africans owned communally and sold or leased them to European companies or, in eastern and southern Africa, to white settlers. Large European companies dominated wholesale commerce, while immigrants from various countries—Indians in East Africa, Greeks and Syrians in West Africa—handled much of the retail trade. Airplanes and automobiles were even more alien to the experience of Africans than railroads had been to an earlier generation.

CHRONOLOGY

	Africa	India	Latin America
			1876–1910 Porfirio Díaz, dictator of Mexico
1900	**1900s** Railroads connect ports to the interior	**1905** Viceroy Curzon splits Bengal; mass demonstrations	
	1909 African National Congress founded	**1906** Muslims found All-India Muslim League	
		1911 British transfer capital from Calcutta to Delhi	**1911–1919** Mexican Revolution; Emiliano Zapata and Pancho Villa against the Constitutionalists
			1917 New constitution proclaimed in Mexico
1920	**1920s** J. E. Casely Hayford organizes political movement in British West Africa	**1919** Amritsar Massacre	
		1929 Gandhi leads March to the Sea	**1928** Plutarco Elías Calles founds Mexico's National Revolutionary Party
		1930s Gandhi calls for independence; he is repeatedly arrested	**1930–1945** Getulio Vargas, dictator of Brazil
			1934–1940 Lázaro Cárdenas, president of Mexico
			1938 Cárdenas nationalizes Mexican oil industry; Vargas proclaims Estado Novo in Brazil
	1939–1945 A million Africans serve in World War II	**1939** British bring India into World War II	
1940		**1940** Muhammad Ali Jinnah demands a separate nation for Muslims	**1943** Juan Perón leads military coup in Argentina
		1947 Partition and independence of India and Pakistan	**1946** Perón elected president of Argentina

Where land was divided into small farms, some Africans benefited from the boom. Farmers in the Gold Coast (now Ghana°) profited from the high price of cocoa, as did palm-oil producers in Nigeria and coffee growers in East Africa. In most of Africa women played a major role in the retail trades, selling pots and pans, cloth, food, and other items in the markets. Many maintained their economic independence and kept their household finances separate from those of their husbands, following a custom that predated the colonial period.

For many Africans economic development meant working in European-owned mines and plantations, often under compulsion. Colonial governments were eager to develop the resources of the territories under their control but could not afford to pay high enough wages to attract workers. Instead, they used their police powers to force Africans to work under harsh conditions for little or no pay. In the 1920s, when the government of French Equatorial Africa decided to build a railroad from Brazzaville to the Atlantic coast, a distance of 312 miles (502 kilometers), it drafted 127,000 men to carve a roadbed across mountains and through rain forests. For lack of food, clothing, and medical care, 20,000 of them died, an average of 64 deaths per mile of track.

Europeans prided themselves on bringing modern health care to Africa; yet before the 1930s there was too little of it to help the majority of Africans, and other aspects of colonialism actually worsened public health. Migrants to cities, mines, and plantations and soldiers moving from post to post spread syphilis, gonorrhea, tuberculosis, and malaria. Sleeping sickness and smallpox epidemics raged throughout Central Africa. In recruiting men to work, colonial governments depleted rural areas of farmers needed to plant and harvest crops. Forced requisitions of food to feed the workers left the remaining populations

Ghana (GAH-nuh)

DIVERSITY AND DOMINANCE

A VIETNAMESE NATIONALIST DENOUNCES FRENCH COLONIALISM

The regions described in this chapter were not the only ones whose inhabitants chafed at the dominance of the great powers and sought more control over their own national destinies. Movements for independence were a worldwide phenomenon. The tactics that different peoples used to achieve their goals differed widely. Among countries that were formal colonies, the case of India is unique in that its nationalist movement was led by Mahatma Gandhi, a man who subordinated the goal of national independence to his commitment to nonviolent passive resistance. In Mexico, as in China, Russia, and other parts of the world, revolutionary movements were often associated with violent uprisings. French Indochina is a case in point.

Indochina, comprising the countries we now call Vietnam, Kampuchea, and Laos, was conquered piecemeal by the French from 1862 to 1895, but only after overcoming fierce resistance. Thereafter, France modernized the cities and irrigation systems and transformed the country into a leading producer of tea, rice, and natural rubber. This meant transferring large numbers of landless peasants to new plantations and destroying the traditional social structure. To govern Indochina, the French brought in more soldiers and civil administrators than the British had in all of India, a far larger colony. Even though they succeeded in crushing the resistance of the peasants and the old Confucian elites, the French were educating a new elite in the French language. These newly educated youths, inspired by French ideas of liberty and nationhood and by the examples of the Guomindang and the Communist Party in neighboring China, formed the core of two new revolutionary movements.

One movement was the Vietnamese Revolutionary Youth League founded by Ho Chi Minh (1890–1969) in 1925, which later became the Indochinese Communist Party. The other was the Viet Nam Quoc Dan Dang, or Vietnamese Nationalist Party, modeled after Sun Yat-sen's Guomindang, founded in 1927 by a schoolteacher named Nguyen Thai Hoc (1904–1930). This party attracted low-level government employees, soldiers, and small businessmen. At first Nguyen Thai Hoc lobbied the colonial government for reforms, but in vain. Two years later he turned to revolutionary action. In February 1930 he led an uprising at Yen Bay that the French quickly crushed. He and many of his followers were executed four months later, leaving Ho Chi Minh's Communists as the standard-bearers of nationalist revolution in Vietnam.

While awaiting his execution, Nguyen Thai Hoc wrote the following letter to the French Chamber of Deputies to justify his actions.

Gentlemen:

I, the undersigned, Nguyen Thai Hoc, a Vietnamese citizen, twenty-six years old, chairman and founder of the Vietnamese Nationalist Party, at present arrested and imprisoned at the jail of Yen Bay, Tongking, Indochina, have the great honor to inform you of the following facts:

According to the tenets of justice, everyone has the right to defend his own country when it is invaded by foreigners, and according to the principles of humanity, everyone has the duty to save his compatriots when they are in difficulty or in danger. As for myself, I have assessed the fact that my country has been annexed by you French for more than sixty years. I realize that under your dictatorial yoke, my compatriots have experienced a very hard life, and my people will without doubt be completely annihilated, by the naked principle of natural selection. Therefore, my right and my duty have compelled me to seek every way to defend my country which has been invaded and occupied, and to save my people who are in great danger.

At the beginning, I had thought to cooperate with the French in Indochina in order to serve my compatriots, my country and my people, particularly in the areas of cultural and economic development. As regards economic development, in 1925 I sent a memorandum to Governor General Varenne, describing to him all our aspirations concerning the protection of local industry and commerce in Indochina. I urged strongly in the same letter the creation of a Superior School of Industrial Development in Tongking. In 1926 I again addressed another letter to the then Governor General of Indochina in which I included some explicit suggestions to relieve the hardships of our poor people. In 1927, for a third time, I sent a letter to the Résident Supérieur [provincial administrator] in Tongking, requesting permission to publish a weekly magazine with the aim of safeguarding and encouraging local industry and commerce. With regard to the cultural domain, I sent a letter to the Governor General in 1927, requesting (1) the privilege of opening tuition-free schools for the children of the lower classes, particularly children of workers and peasants; (2) freedom to open popular publishing houses and libraries in industrial cènters.

It is absolutely ridiculous that every suggestion has been rejected. My letters were without answer; my plans have not been considered; my requests have been ignored; even the articles that I sent to newspapers have been censored and rejected. From the experience of these rejections, I have come to the conclusion that the French have no sincere intention of helping my country or my people. I also concluded that we have to expel France. For this reason, in 1927, I began to organize a revolutionary party, which I named the Vietnamese Nationalist Party, with the aim of overthrowing the dictatorial and oppressive administration of our country. We aspire to create a Republic of Vietnam, composed of persons sincerely concerned with the happiness of the people. My party is a clandestine organization, and in February 1929, it was uncovered by the security police. Among the members of my party, a great number have been arrested. Fifty-two persons have been condemned to forced labor ranging from two to twenty years. Although many have been detained and many others unjustly condemned, my party has not ceased its activity. Under my guidance, the Party continues to operate and progress towards its aim.

During the Yen Bay uprising someone succeeded in killing some French officers. The authorities accused my party of having organized and perpetrated this revolt. They have accused me of having given the orders for the massacre. In truth, I have never given such orders, and I have presented before the Penal Court of Yen Bay all the evidence showing the inanity of this accusation. Even so, some of the members of my party completely ignorant of that event have been accused of participating in it. The French Indochinese government burned and destroyed their houses. They sent French troops to occupy their villages and stole their rice to divide it among the soldiers. Not just members of my party have been suffering from this injustice—we should rather call this cruelty rather than injustice—but also many simple peasants, interested only in their daily work in the rice fields, living miserable lives like buffaloes and horses, have been compromised in this reprisal. At the present time, in various areas there are tens of thousands of men, women, and children, persons of all ages, who have been massacred. They died either of hunger or exposure because the French Indochinese government burned their homes. I therefore beseech you in tears to redress this injustice which otherwise will annihilate my people, which will stain French honor, and which will belittle all human values.

I have the honor to inform you that I am responsible for all events happening in my country under the leadership of my party from 1927 until the present. You only need to execute me. I beg your indulgence for all the others who at the present time are imprisoned in various jails. I am the only culprit, all the others are innocent. They are innocent because most of them are indeed members of my party, and have joined it only because I have succeeded in convincing them of their duties as citizens of this country, and of the humiliations of a slave with a lost country. Some of them are not even party members. They have been wrongly accused by their enemy or by the security police; or they simply are wrongly accused by their friends who have not been able to bear the tortures inflicted by the security police. I have the honor to repeat once again that you need execute only me. If you are not satisfied with killing one man, I advise you to kill also the members of my family, but I strongly beg your indulgence towards those who are innocent.

Finally, I would like to declare in conclusion: if France wants to stay in peace in Indochina, if France does not want to have increasing troubles with revolutionary movements, she should immediately modify the cruel and inhuman policy now practiced in Indochina. The French should behave like friends to the Vietnamese, instead of being cruel and oppressive masters. They should be attentive to the intellectual and material sufferings of the Vietnamese people, instead of being harsh and tough.

Please, Gentlemen, receive my gratitude.

QUESTIONS FOR ANALYSIS

1. **When he first became involved in politics, what were Nguyen Thai Hoc's views of French colonialism?**
2. **What were his first initiatives, and what response did he get from the French colonial administration?**
3. **What motivated Nguyen Thai Hoc to organize an uprising, and what was the response of the French?**
4. **Compare Nguyen Thai Hoc's views and methods and the French response with the situation in India.**

Source: Harry Benda and John Larkin, *The World of Southeast Asia* (New York: Harper & Row, 1967), 182–185. Reprinted by permission of the author.

African Farmers in the Gold Coast African farmers in the Gold Coast (now Ghana) sold their cocoa beans to government agents. The government kept the prices artificially low in order to profit on the transactions. (Popperfoto/Archive Photos)

undernourished and vulnerable to diseases. Not until the 1930s did colonial governments realize the negative consequences of their labor policies and begin to invest in agricultural development and health care for Africans.

In 1900 Ibadan° in Nigeria was the only city in sub-Saharan Africa with more than 100,000 inhabitants; fifty years later, dozens of cities had reached that size, including Nairobi° in Kenya, Johannesburg in South Africa, Lagos in Nigeria, Accra in Gold Coast, and Dakar in Senegal. Africans migrated to cities because they offered hope of jobs and excitement and, for a few, the chance to become wealthy.

However, migrations damaged the family life of those involved, for almost all the migrants were men leaving women in the countryside to farm and raise children. Cities built during the colonial period reflected the colonialists' attitudes with racially segregated housing, clubs, restaurants, hospitals, and other institutions. Patterns of racial discrimination were most rigid in the white-settler colonies of eastern and southern Africa.

Religious and Political Changes

Traditional religious belief could not explain the dislocations that foreign rule, migrations, and sudden economic changes brought to the lives of Africans. Many therefore turned to one of the two universal religions, Christianity and Islam, for guidance.

Christianity was introduced into Africa by Western missionaries, except in Ethiopia, where it was indigenous. It was most successful in the coastal regions of West and South Africa, where the European influence was strongest. A major attraction of the Christian denominations was their mission schools, which taught both craft skills and basic literacy, providing access to employment as minor functionaries, teachers, and shopkeepers. These schools educated a new elite, many of whom learned not only skills and literacy but Western political ideas as well. Many Africans accepted Christianity enthusiastically, reading the suffering of their own peoples into the biblical stories of Moses and the parables of Jesus. The churches trained some of the brighter pupils to become catechists, teachers, and clergymen. A few rose to high positions, such as James Johnson, a Yoruba who became the Anglican bishop of the Niger Delta Pastorate. Independent Christian churches—known as "Ethiopian" churches—associated Christian beliefs with radical ideas of racial equality and participation in politics.

Islam spread inland from the East African coast and southward from the Sahel° toward the West African coast, through the influence and example of Arab and African merchants. Islam also emphasized literacy—in

Ibadan (ee-BAH-dahn) **Nairobi** (nie-ROE-bee)

Sahel (SAH-hel)

Diamond Mining in Southern Africa The discovery of diamonds in the Transvaal in 1867 attracted prospectors to the area around Kimberley. The first wave of prospectors consisted of individual "diggers," including a few Africans. By the late 1870s, surface deposits had been exhausted and further mining required complex and costly machinery. After 1889, one company, De Beers Consolidated, owned all the diamond mines. This photograph shows the entrance to a mine shaft and mine workers surrounded by heavy equipment. (Royal Commonwealth Society. By permission of the Syndics of Cambridge University Library.)

Arabic through Quaranic schools rather than in a European language—and was less disruptive of traditional African customs such as polygamy.

In a few places, such as Dakar in Senegal and Cape Town in South Africa, small numbers of Africans could obtain secondary education. Even smaller numbers went on to college in Europe or America. Though few in number, they became the leaders of political movements. The contrast between the liberal ideas imparted by Western education and the realities of racial discrimination under colonial rule contributed to the rise of nationalism among educated Africans. In Senegal **Blaise Diagne**° agitated for African participation in politics and fair treatment in the French army. In the 1920s J. E. Casely Hayford began organizing a movement for greater autonomy in British West Africa. In South Africa Western-educated lawyers and journalists founded the **African National Congress** in 1909 to defend the interests of Africans. These nationalist movements were inspired by the ideas of Pan-Africanists from America such as W. E. B. Du Bois and Marcus Garvey, who advocated the unity of African peoples around the world, as well as by European ideas of liberty and nationhood. Before World War II, however, they were small and had little influence.

The Second World War (1939–1945) had a profound effect on the peoples of Africa, even those far removed from the theaters of war. The war brought hardships, such as increased forced labor, inflation, and requisitions of raw materials. Yet it also brought hope. During

Diagne (dee-AHN-yuh)

the campaign to oust the Italians from Ethiopia, Emperor **Haile Selassie**° (r. 1930–1974) led his own troops into Addis Ababa, his capital, and reclaimed his title. A million Africans served as soldiers and carriers in Burma, North Africa, and Europe, where many became aware of Africa's role in helping the Allied war effort. They listened to Allied propaganda in favor of European liberation movements and against Nazi racism, and they returned to their countries with new and radical ideas.

The early twentieth century was a relatively peaceful period for sub-Saharan Africa. But this peace—enforced by the European occupiers—masked profound changes that were to transform African life after the Second World War. The building of cities, railroads, and other enterprises brought Africa into the global economy, often at great human cost. Colonialism also brought changes to African culture and religion, hastening the spread of Christianity and Islam. And the foreign occupation awakened political ideas that inspired the next generation of Africans to demand independence (see Chapter 32).

THE INDIAN INDEPENDENCE MOVEMENT, 1905–1947

India was a colony of Great Britain from the late eighteenth to the mid-twentieth centuries. Under British rule the subcontinent acquired many of the trappings of Western-style economic development, such as railroads, harbors, modern cities, and cotton and steel mills, as well as an active and worldly middle class. The economic transformation of the region awakened in this educated middle class a sense of national dignity that demanded political fulfillment. In response, the British gradually granted India a limited amount of political autonomy while maintaining overall control. Religious and communal tensions among the Indian peoples were carefully papered over under British rule. Violent conflicts tore India apart after the withdrawal of the British in 1947 (see Map 31.1).

The Land and the People

Much of India is fertile land, but it is vulnerable to the vagaries of nature, especially droughts caused by the periodic failure of the monsoons. When the rains failed from 1896 to 1900, 2 million people died of starvation.

Despite periodic famines the Indian population grew from 250 million in 1900 to 319 million in 1921 and 389 million in 1941. This growth created pressures in many areas. Landless young men converged on the cities, exceeding the number of jobs available in the slowly expanding industries. To produce timber for construction and railroad ties, and to clear land for tea and rubber plantations, government foresters cut down most of the tropical hardwood forests that had covered the subcontinent in the nineteenth century. In spite of deforestation and extensive irrigation, the amount of land available to peasant families shrank with each successive generation. Economic development—what the British called the "moral and material progress of India"—hardly benefited the average Indian.

Indians were divided into many classes. Peasants, always the great majority, paid rents to the landowner, interest to the village moneylender, and taxes to the government and had little left to improve their land or raise their standard of living. The government protected property owners, from village moneylenders all the way up to the maharajahs,° or ruling princes, who owned huge tracts of land. The cities were crowded with craftsmen, traders, and workers of all sorts, most very poor. Although the British had banned the burning of widows on their husbands' funeral pyres, in other respects women's lives changed little under British rule.

The peoples of India spoke many different languages: Hindi in the north, Tamil in the south, Bengali in the east, Gujerati around Bombay, Urdu in the northwest, and dozens of others. As a result of British rule and increasing trade and travel, English became, like Latin in medieval Europe, the common medium of communication of the Western-educated middle class. This new class of English-speaking government bureaucrats, professionals, and merchants was to play a leading role in the independence movement.

The majority of Indians practiced Hinduism and were subdivided into hundreds of castes, each affiliated with a particular occupation. Hinduism discouraged intermarriage and other social interactions among the castes and with people who were not Hindus. Muslims constituted one-quarter of the people of India but formed a majority in the northwest and in eastern Bengal. Muslim rulers had dominated northern and central India until they were displaced by the British in the eighteenth century. More reluctant than Hindus to learn English, Muslims felt discriminated against by both British and Hindus.

Haile Selassie (HI-lee seh-LASS-ee)

maharajah (mah-huh-RAH-juh)

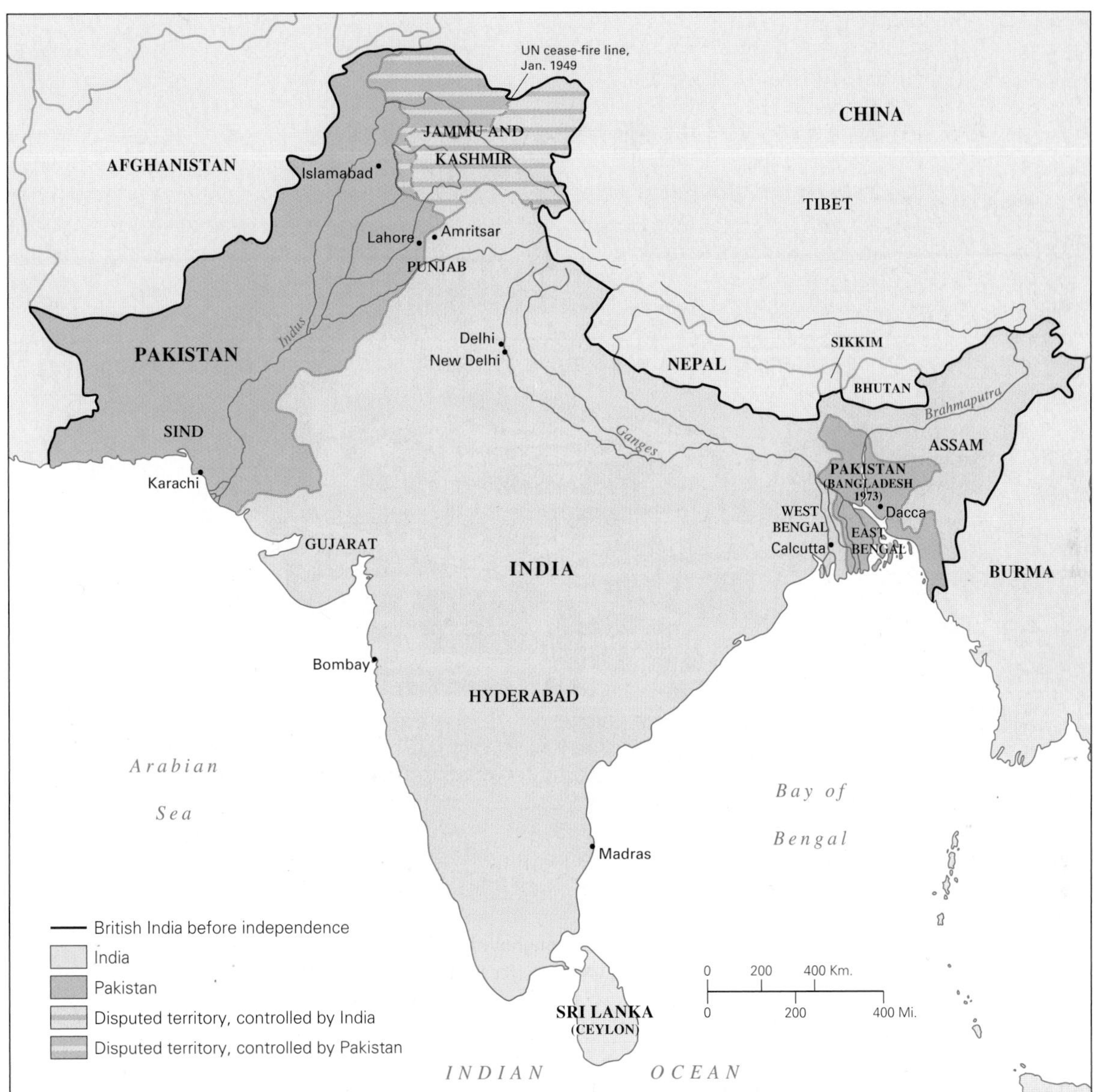

Map 31.1 The Partition of India, 1947 Before the British, India was divided among many states, ethnic groups, and religions. When the British left in 1947, the subcontinent split along religious lines. The predominantly Muslim regions of Sind and Punjab in the northwest and East Bengal in the east formed the new nation of Pakistan. The predominantly Hindu center became the Republic of India. Jammu and Kashmir remained disputed territories and poisoned relations between the two new countries.

British Rule and Indian Nationalism

Colonial India was ruled by a viceroy appointed by the British government and administered by a few thousand members of the Indian Civil Service. These men, imbued with a sense of duty toward their subjects, formed one of the more honest (if not efficient) bureaucracies of all time. Drawn mostly from the English gentry, they liked to think of India as a land of lords and peasants. They believed it was their duty to protect the Indian people from the dangers of industrialization, while defending their own positions from Indian nationalists.

As Europeans they admired modern technology but tried to control its introduction into India so as

Construction Site in Colonial India British civil engineers were active throughout India building roads, railroads, and canals. Here, a British official supervises Indian workers building a bridge. (The Billie Love Collection)

to maximize the benefits to Britain and to themselves. For example, they encouraged railroads, harbors, telegraphs, and other communications technologies, as well as irrigation and plantations, because they increased India's foreign trade and strengthened British control. At the same time, they discouraged the cotton and steel industries and limited the training of Indian engineers, ostensibly to spare India the social upheavals that had accompanied the Industrial Revolution in Europe, while protecting British industry from Indian competition.

At the turn of the century the majority of Indians—especially the peasants, landowners, and princes—accepted British rule. But the Europeans' racist attitude toward dark-skinned people increasingly offended Indians who had learned English and absorbed English ideas of freedom and representative government, only to discover that thinly disguised racial quotas excluded them from the Indian Civil Service, the officer corps, and prestigious country clubs.

In 1885 a small group of English-speaking Hindu professionals founded a political organization called the **Indian National Congress.** For twenty years its members respectfully petitioned the government for access to the higher administrative positions and for a voice in official decisions, but they had little influence outside intellectual circles. Then, in 1905, Viceroy Lord Curzon divided the province of **Bengal** in two to improve the efficiency of its administration. This decision, made without consulting anyone, angered not only educated Indians, who saw it as a way to lessen their influence, but also millions of uneducated Hindu Bengalis, who suddenly found themselves outnumbered by Muslims in East Bengal. Soon Bengal was the scene of demonstrations, boycotts of British goods, and even incidents of violence against the British.

In 1906, while the Hindus of Bengal were protesting the partition of their province, Muslims, fearful of Hindu dominance elsewhere in India, founded the **All-India Muslim League.** Caught in an awkward situation, the government responded by granting Indians a limited franchise based on wealth. Muslims, however, were on average poorer than Hindus, for many poor and low-caste Hindus had converted to Islam to escape caste discrimination. Taking advantage of these religious divisions, the British instituted separate representation and different voting qualifications for Hindus and Muslims. Then, in 1911, the British transferred the capital of India from Calcutta to Delhi°, the former capital of the Mughal° emperors. These changes disturbed Indians of all classes and religions and raised their political consciousness. Politics, once primarily the concern of westernized intellectuals, turned into two mass movements: one by Hindus and one by Muslims.

To maintain their commercial position and prevent social upheavals, the British resisted the idea that India could, or should, industrialize. Their geologists looked for minerals, such as coal or manganese, that British industry required. However, when the only Indian member of the Indian Geological Service, Pramatha Nath Bose, wanted to prospect for iron ore, he had to resign because the government wanted no part of an Indian steel industry that could compete with that of Britain. Bose joined forces with Jamsetji Tata, a Bombay textile magnate who decided to produce steel in spite of British opposition. With the help of German and American engineers and equipment, Tata's son Dorabji opened the first steel mill in India in 1911, in a town called Jamshedpur in honor of his father. Although it produced only a fraction of the steel that India required, Jamshedpur became a powerful symbol of Indian national pride. It prompted Indian nationalists to ask why a country that could produce its own steel needed foreigners to run its government.

During World War I Indians supported Britain enthusiastically; 1.2 million men volunteered for the army, and millions more voluntarily contributed money to the government. Many expected the British to reward their loyalty with political concessions. Others organized to demand concessions and a voice in the government. In 1917, in response to the agitation, the British government announced "the gradual development of self-governing institutions with a view to the progressive realization of responsible government in India as an integral part of the British Empire." This sounded like a promise of self-government, but the timetable was so vague that nationalists denounced it as a devious maneuver to postpone India's independence.

In late 1918 and early 1919 a violent influenza epidemic broke out among soldiers in the war zone of northern France. Within a few months it spread to every country on earth and killed over 20 million people. India was especially hard hit; of the millions who died, two out of three was Indian. This dreadful toll increased the mounting political tensions. Leaders of the Indian National Congress declared that the British reform proposals were too little, too late.

On April 13, 1919, in the city of Amritsar in Punjab, General Reginald Dyer ordered his troops to fire into a peaceful crowd of some 10,000 demonstrators, killing at least 379 and wounding 1,200. Waves of angry demonstrations swept over India, but the government waited six months to appoint a committee to investigate the massacre. After General Dyer retired, the British House of Lords voted to approve his actions, and a fund was raised in appreciation of his services. Indians interpreted these gestures as showing British contempt for their colonial subjects. In the charged atmosphere of the time, the period of gradual accommodation between the British and the Indians came to a close.

Mahatma Gandhi and Militant Nonviolence

For the next twenty years India teetered on the edge of violent uprisings and harsh repression, possibly even war. That it did not succumb was due to **Mohandas K. Gandhi** (1869–1948), a man known to his followers as "Mahatma," the "great soul."

Gandhi began life with every advantage. His family was wealthy enough to send him to England for his education. After his studies he lived in South Africa and practiced law for the small Indian community there. During World War I he returned to India and was one of many Western-educated Hindu intellectuals who joined the Indian National Congress.

Gandhi had some unusual political ideas. Unlike many radical political thinkers of his time, he denounced the popular ideals of power, struggle, and combat. Instead, inspired by both Hindu and Christian concepts, he preached the saintly virtues of *ahimsa*° (nonviolence) and *satyagraha*° (the search for truth). He refused to countenance violence among his followers,

Delhi (DEL-ee) **Mughal** (MOO-guhl)

ahimsa (uh-HIM-sah) ***satyagraha*** (suh-TYAH-gruh-huh)

and he called off several demonstrations when they turned violent.

Gandhi had an affinity for the poor that was unusual even among socialist politicians. In 1921 he gave up the Western-style suits worn by lawyers and the fine raiment of wealthy Indians and henceforth wore simple peasant garb: a length of homespun cloth below his waist and a shawl to cover his torso (see Environment and Technology: Gandhi and Technology). He spoke for the farmers and the outcasts, whom he called *harijan*°, "children of God." He attracted ever-larger numbers of followers among the poor and the illiterate, who soon began to revere him; and he transformed the cause of Indian independence from an elite movement of the educated into a mass movement with a quasi-religious aura.

Gandhi was a brilliant political tactician and a master of public relations gestures. In 1929, for instance, he led a few followers on an 80-mile (129-kilometer) walk, camped on a beach, and gathered salt from the sea in a blatant and well-publicized act of civil disregard for the government's monopoly on salt. But he discovered that unleashing the power of popular participation was one thing and controlling its direction was quite another. Within days of his "Walk to the Sea," demonstrations of support broke out all over India, in which the police killed a hundred demonstrators and arrested over sixty thousand.

Many times during the 1930s Gandhi threatened to fast "unto death," and several times he did come close to death, to protest the violence of both the police and his followers and to demand independence. He was repeatedly arrested and spent a total of six years in jail. But every arrest made him more popular. He became a cult figure not only in his own country but also in the Western media. He never won a battle or an election; instead, in the words of historian Percival Spear, he made the British "uncomfortable in their cherished field of moral rectitude," and he gave Indians the feeling that theirs was the ethically superior cause.

India Moves Toward Independence

In the 1920s, slowly and reluctantly, the British began to give in to the pressure of the Indian National Congress and the Muslim League. They handed over control of "national" areas such as education, the economy, and public works. They also gradually admitted more Indians into the Civil Service and the officer corps.

India took its first tentative steps toward industrialization in the years before the First and then the Second World Wars. Indian politicians obtained the right to erect high tariff barriers against imports in order to protect India's infant industries from foreign, even British, competition. Behind these barriers, Indian entrepreneurs built plants to manufacture iron and steel, cement, paper, cotton and jute textiles, sugar, and other products. This early industrialization provided jobs, though not enough to improve the lives of the Indian peasants or urban poor. These manufactures, however, helped create a class of wealthy Indian businessmen. Far from being satisfied by the government's policies, they supported the Indian National Congress and its demands for independence. Though paying homage to Gandhi, they preferred his designated successor as leader of the Indian National Congress, **Jawaharlal Nehru**° (1889–1964). A highly educated nationalist and subtle thinker, Nehru, unlike Gandhi, looked forward to creating a modern industrial India.

Congress politicians won regional elections but continued to be excluded from the viceroy's cabinet, the true center of power. When World War II began in September 1939 Viceroy Lord Linlithgow declared war without consulting a single Indian. The Congress-dominated provincial governments resigned in protest and found that boycotting government office increased their popular support. When the British offered to give India its independence once the war ended, Gandhi called the offer a "postdated cheque on a failing bank" and demanded full independence immediately. His "Quit India" campaign aroused popular demonstrations against the British and provoked a wave of arrests, including his own. Nehru explained: "I would fight Japan sword in hand, but I can only do so as a free man."

The Second World War divided the Indian people. Most Indian soldiers felt they were fighting to defend their country rather than to support the British Empire. As in World War I, Indians contributed heavily to the Allied war effort, supplying 2 million soldiers and enormous amounts of resources, especially the timber needed for emergency construction. A small number of Indians, however, were so anti-British that they joined the Japanese side.

India's subordination to British interests was vividly demonstrated in the famine of 1943 in Bengal. Unlike previous famines, this one was caused not by drought but by the Japanese conquest of Burma, which cut off supplies of Burmese rice that normally went to Bengal. Although food was available elsewhere in India, the

harijan (HAH-ree-jahn)

Nehru (NAY-roo)

ENVIRONMENT + TECHNOLOGY

Gandhi and Technology

In the twentieth century all political leaders but one embraced modern industrial technology. That one exception is Gandhi.

After deciding to wear only handmade cloth, Gandhi made a bonfire of imported factory-made cloth and began spending half an hour every day spinning yarn on a simple spinning wheel, a task he called a "sacrament." The spinning wheel became the symbol of his movement. Any Indian who wished to come before him had to dress in handwoven cloth.

Gandhi had several reasons for reviving this ancient craft. One was his revulsion against "the incessant search for material comforts," an evil to which he thought Europeans were "becoming slaves." Not only had materialism corrupted the people of the West, it had also caused massive unemployment in India. In particular, he blamed the impoverishment of the Indian people on the cotton industries of England and Japan, which had ruined the traditional cotton manufacturing by which India had once supplied all her own needs.

Gandhi looked back to a time before India became a colony of Britian, when "our women spun fine yarns in their own cottages, and supplemented the earnings of their husbands." The spinning wheel, he believed, was "presented to the nation for giving occupation to the millions who had, at least four months of the year, nothing to do." Not only would a return to the spinning wheel provide employment to millions of Indians, it would also become a symbol of "national consciousness and a contribution by every individual to a definite constructive national work."

Nevertheless, Gandhi was a shrewd politician who understood the usefulness of modern devices for mobilizing the masses and organizing his followers. He wore a watch and used the telephone and the printing press to keep in touch with his followers. When he traveled by train, he rode third class—but in a third-class railroad car of his own. His goal was the independence of his country, and he pursued it with every nonviolent means he could find.

Gandhi's ideas challenge us to rethink the purpose of technology. Was he opposed on principle to all modern devices? Was he an opportunist who used those devices that served his political ends and rejected those that did not? Or did he have a higher principle that accounts for his willingness to use the telephone and the railroad but not factory-made cloth?

Source: Quotations from Louis Fischer, *Gandhi: His Life and Message for the World* (New York: New American Library, 1954), 82–83.

Gandhi at the Spinning Wheel Mahatma Gandhi chose the spinning wheel as his symbol because it represented the traditional activity of millions of rural Indians whose livelihoods were threatened by industrialization. (Margaret Bourke-White, *LIFE Magazine* © Time Warner Inc.)

The Partition of India When India became independent, Muslims fled from Hindu regions, and Hindus fled from Muslims. Margaret Bourke-White photographed a long line of refugees, with their cows, carts, and belongings, trudging down a country road toward safety. (Margaret Bourke-White, *LIFE Magazine* © Time Inc.)

British army had requisitioned the railroads to transport troops and equipment in preparation for a Japanese invasion. As a result, supplies ran short in Bengal and surrounding areas, while speculators hoarded whatever they could find. Some 2 million people starved to death before the army was ordered to supply food.

Partition and Independence

When the war ended, Britain's new Labour Party government prepared for Indian independence, but deep suspicions between Hindus and Muslims complicated the process. The break between the two communities had started in 1937, when the Indian National Congress won provincial elections and refused to share power with the Muslim League. In 1940 the leader of the League, **Muhammad Ali Jinnah**° (1876–1948) demanded what many Muslims had been dreaming of for years: a country of their own, to be called Pakistan (from "Punjab-Afghans-Kashmir-Sind" plus the Persian suffix *-stan* meaning "kingdom").

As independence approached, talks between Jinnah and Nehru broke down and battle lines were drawn. Violent rioting between Hindus and Muslims broke out in Bengal and Bihar. Gandhi's appeals for tolerance and cooperation fell on deaf ears. In despair, he retreated to his home near Ahmedabad. The British made frantic proposals to keep India united, but their authority was waning fast.

By early 1947 the Indian National Congress had accepted the idea of a partition of India into two states, one secular but dominated by Hindus, the other Muslim. In June Lord Mountbatten, the last viceroy, decided that independence must come immediately. On August 15 British India gave way to a new India and Pakistan. The Indian National Congress, led by Nehru, formed the first government of India; Jinnah and the Muslim League established a government for the provinces that made up Pakistan.

The rejoicing over independence was marred by violent outbreaks between Muslims and Hindus. In protest against the mounting chaos, Gandhi refused to attend the independence day celebration. Throughout the land, Muslim and Hindu neighbors turned on one another,

Jinnah (jee-NAH)

and armed members of one faith hunted down people of the other faith. For centuries Hindus and Muslims had intermingled throughout most of India. Now, leaving most of their possessions behind, Hindus fled from predominantly Muslim areas, and Muslims fled from Hindu areas. Trainloads of desperate refugees of one faith were attacked and massacred by members of the other or were left stranded in the middle of deserts. Within a few months some 12 million people had abandoned their ancestral homes and a half-million lay dead. In January 1948 Gandhi died too, gunned down by an angry Hindu refugee.

After the sectarian massacres and flights of refugees, few Hindus remained in Pakistan, and Muslims were a minority in all but one state of India. That state was Kashmir, a strategically important region in the foothills of the Himalayas. India annexed Kashmir because the local maharajah was Hindu and because the state held the headwaters of the rivers that irrigated millions of acres of farmland in the northwestern part of the subcontinent. The majority of the inhabitants of Kashmir were Muslims, however, and would probably have joined Pakistan if they had been allowed to vote on the matter. The consequence of the partition and of Kashmir in particular was to turn India and Pakistan into bitter enemies that have fought several wars in the past half-century.

The Mexican Revolution, 1910–1940

In the nineteenth century Latin America achieved independence from Spain and Portugal but did not industrialize. Throughout much of the century most Latin American republics suffered from ideological divisions, unstable governments, and violent upheavals. By trading their raw materials and agricultural products for foreign manufactured goods and capital investments, they became economically dependent on the wealthier countries to the north, especially on the United States and Great Britain. Their societies, far from fulfilling the promises of their independence, remained deeply split between wealthy landowners and desperately poor peasants.

Mexico, Brazil, and Argentina contained well over half of Latin America's land, population, and wealth, and their relations with other countries and their economies were quite similar. Mexico, however, underwent a traumatic social revolution, while Argentina and Brazil evolved more peaceably.

Mexico in 1910

Few countries in Latin America suffered as many foreign invasions and interventions as Mexico. A Mexican saying observed wryly: "Poor Mexico: so far from God, so close to the United States." In Mexico the chasm between rich and poor was so deep that only a revolution could move the country toward prosperity and democracy.

Mexico was the Latin American country most influenced by the Spanish during three centuries of colonial rule. After independence in 1821 it suffered from a half-century of political turmoil. At the beginning of the twentieth century Mexican society was divided into rich and poor and into persons of Spanish, Indian, and mixed ancestry. A few very wealthy families of Spanish origin, less than 1 percent of the population, owned 85 percent of Mexico's land, mostly in huge *haciendas* (estates). Closely tied to this elite were the handful of American and British companies that controlled most of Mexico's railroads, silver mines, plantations, and other productive enterprises. At the other end of the social scale were Indians, many of whom did not speak Spanish. *Mestizos*°, people of mixed Indian and European ancestry, were only slightly better off; most of them were peasants who worked on the haciendas or farmed small communal plots near their ancestral villages.

The urban middle class was small and had little political influence. Few professional and government positions were open to them, and foreigners owned most businesses. Industrial workers also were few in number; the only significant groups were textile workers in the port of Veracruz on the Gulf of Mexico and railroad workers spread throughout the country.

During the colonial period, the Spanish government had made halfhearted efforts to defend Indians and mestizos from the land-grabbing tactics of the haciendas. After independence in 1821 wealthy Mexican families and American companies used bribery and force to acquire millions of acres of good agricultural land from villages in southern Mexico. Peasants lost not only their fields but also their access to firewood and pasture for their animals. Sugar, cotton, and other commercial crops replaced corn and beans, and peasants had little choice but to work on haciendas. To survive, they had to buy food and other necessities on credit from the landowner's store; eventually, they fell permanently into debt. Sometimes whole communities were forced to relocate.

In the 1880s American investors purchased from the Mexican government dubious claims to more than

mestizo (mess-TEE-zoh)

2.5 million acres (1 million hectares) traditionally held by the Yaqui people of Sonora, in northern Mexico. When the Yaqui resisted the expropriation of their lands, they were brutally repressed by the Mexican army.

Northern Mexicans had no peasant tradition of communal ownership, for the northern half of the country was too dry for farming, unlike the tropical and densely populated south. The north was a region of silver mines and cattle ranches, some of them enormous. It was thinly populated by cowboys and miners. The harshness of their lives and vast inequities in the distribution of income made northern Mexicans as resentful as people in the south.

Despite many upheavals in Mexico in the nineteenth century, in 1910 the government seemed in control. For thirty-four years General Porfirio Díaz° (1830–1915) had ruled Mexico under the motto "Liberty, Order, Progress." To Díaz "liberty" meant freedom for rich hacienda owners and foreign investors to acquire more land. The government imposed "order" through rigged elections and a policy of *pan o palo* (bread or the stick)—that is, bribes for Díaz's supporters and summary justice for those who opposed him. "Progress" meant mainly the importing of foreign capital, machinery, and technicians to take advantage of Mexico's labor, soil, and natural resources.

During the Díaz years (1876–1910) Mexico City—with paved streets, streetcar lines, electric street lighting, and public parks—became a showplace, and new telegraph and railroad lines connected cities and towns throughout Mexico. But this material progress benefited only a handful of well-connected businessmen. The boom in railroads, agriculture, and mining at the turn of the century actually caused a decline in the average Mexican's standard of living.

Though a mestizo himself, Díaz discriminated against the nonwhite majority of Mexicans. He and his supporters tried to eradicate what they saw as Mexico's embarrassingly rustic traditions. On many middle- and upper-class tables French cuisine replaced traditional Mexican dishes. The wealthy replaced sombreros and ponchos with European garments. Though bullfighting and cockfighting remained popular, the well-to-do preferred horse racing and soccer. To the educated middle class—the only group with a strong sense of Mexican nationhood—this devaluation of Mexican culture became a symbol of the Díaz regime's failure to defend national interests against foreign influences.

Revolution and Civil War, 1911–1920

Many Mexicans feared or anticipated a popular uprising after Díaz. Unlike the independence movement in India, the Mexican Revolution was not the work of one party with a well-defined ideology. Instead, it developed haphazardly, led by a series of ambitious but limited leaders, each representing a different segment of Mexican society.

The first was Francisco I. Madero (1873–1913), the son of a wealthy landowning and mining family, educated in the United States. When minor uprisings broke out in 1911, the government collapsed and Díaz fled into exile. The Madero presidency was welcomed by some, but aroused opposition from peasant leaders like **Emiliano Zapata** (1879–1919). In 1913, after two years as president, Madero was overthrown and murdered by one of his former supporters, General Victoriano Huerta. Woodrow Wilson (1856–1924), president of the United States, showed his displeasure by sending the United States Marines to occupy Veracruz.

The inequities of Mexican society and foreign intervention in Mexico's affairs angered Mexico's middle class and industrial workers. They found leaders in Venustiano Carranza, a landowner, and in Alvaro Obregón°, a schoolteacher. Calling themselves Constitutionalists, Carranza and Obregón organized private armies and succeeded in overthrowing Huerta in 1914. By then, the revolution had spread to the countryside.

As early as 1911 Zapata, an Indian farmer, had led a revolt against the haciendas in the mountains of Morelos, south of Mexico City (see Map 31.2). His soldiers were peasants, some of them women, mounted on horseback and armed with pistols and rifles. For several years they periodically came down from the mountains, burned hacienda buildings, and returned land to the Indian villages to which it had once belonged.

Another leader appeared in Chihuahua, a northern state where seventeen individuals owned two-fifths of the land and 95 percent of the people had no land at all. Starting in 1913 **Francisco "Pancho" Villa** (1877–1923), a former ranch hand, mule driver, and bandit, organized an army of three thousand men, most of them cowboys. They too seized land from the large haciendas, not to rebuild traditional communities as in southern Mexico but to create family ranches.

Zapata and Villa were part agrarian rebels, part social revolutionaries. They enjoyed tremendous popular support but could never rise above their regional and peasant origins and lead a national revolution. The Con-

Díaz (DEE-as)

Obregón (oh-bray-GAWN)

Emiliano Zapata Zapata, the leader of a peasant rebellion in southern Mexico during the Mexican Revolution, stands in full revolutionary regalia: sword, rifles, bandoleers, boots, and sombrero. (Brown Brothers)

stitutionalists had fewer soldiers than Zapata and Villa; but they held the major cities, controlled the country's exports of oil, and used the proceeds of oil sales to buy modern weapons. Fighting continued for years, and gradually the Constitutionalists took over most of Mexico. In 1919 they defeated and killed Zapata; Villa was assassinated four years later. An estimated 2 million people lost their lives in the civil war, and much of Mexico lay in ruins.

During their struggle to win support against Zapata and Villa, the Constitutionalists adopted many of their rivals' agrarian reforms, such as restoring communal lands to the Indians of Morelos. The Constitutionalists also proposed social programs designed to appeal to workers and the middle class. The Constitution of 1917 promised universal suffrage and a one-term presidency; state-run education to free the poor from the hold of the Catholic Church; the end of debt peonage; restrictions on foreign ownership of property; and laws specifying minimum wages and maximum hours to protect laborers. Although these reforms were too costly to implement right away, they had important symbolic significance, for they enshrined the dignity of Mexicans and the equality of Indians, mestizos, and whites, as well as of peasants and city people.

The Revolution Institutionalized, 1920–1940

In the early 1920s, after a decade of violence that exhausted all classes, the Mexican Revolution lost momentum. Only in Morelos did peasants receive land, and President Obregón and his closest associates made all the important decisions. Nevertheless, the Revolution changed the social makeup of the governing class. For the first time in Mexico's history, representatives of rural communities, unionized workers, and public employees were admitted to the inner circle.

In the arts the Mexican Revolution sparked a surge of creativity. The political murals of José Clemente Orozco and Diego Rivera and the paintings of Frida Kahlo focused on social themes, showing peasants, workers, and soldiers in scenes from the Revolution.

In 1928 Obregón was assassinated. His successor, Plutarco Elías Calles°, founded the National Revolutionary Party, or PNR (the abbreviation of its name in Spanish). The PNR was a forum where all the pressure groups and vested interests—labor, peasants, businessmen, landowners, the military, and others—worked out compromises. The establishment of the PNR gave the Mexican Revolution a second wind.

Lázaro Cárdenas°, chosen by Calles to be president in 1934, brought peasants' and workers' organizations into the party, renamed it the Mexican Revolutionary Party (PRM), and removed the generals from government positions. Then he set to work implementing the reforms promised in the Constitution of 1917. Cárdenas redistributed 44 million acres (17.6 million hectares) to peasant communes. He closed church-run schools, replacing them with government schools. He nationalized the railroads and numerous other businesses.

Calles (KAH-yace)
Lázaro Cárdenas (LAH-sah-roe KAHR-dih-nahs)

Map 31.2 The Mexican Revolution The Mexican Revolution began in two distinct regions of the country. One was the mountainous and densely populated area south of Mexico City, particularly Morelos, homeland of Emiliano Zapata. The other was the dry and thinly populated ranch country of the north, such as Chihuahua, home of Pancho Villa. The fighting that ensued crisscrossed the country along the main railroad lines, shown on the map.

Cárdenas's most dramatic move was the expropriation of foreign-owned oil companies. In the early 1920s Mexico was the world's leading producer of oil, but a handful of American and British companies exported almost all of it. In 1938 Cárdenas seized the foreign-owned oil industry, more as a matter of national pride than of economics. The oil companies expected the governments of the United States and Great Britain to come to their rescue, perhaps with military force. But Mexico and the United States chose to resolve the issue through negotiation, and Mexico retained control of its oil industry.

When Cárdenas's term ended in 1940, Mexico, like India, was still a land of poor farmers with a small industrial base. The Revolution had brought great changes, however. The political system was free of both chaos and dictatorships. A small group of wealthy people no longer monopolized land and other resources. The military was tamed; the Catholic Church no longer controlled education; and the nationalization of oil had demonstrated Mexico's independence from foreign corporations and military intervention.

What did the Mexican Revolution accomplish? It did not fulfill the democratic promise of Madero's campaign, for it brought to power a party that monopolized the government for eighty years. However it allowed far more sectors of the population to participate in politics and made sure no president stayed in office more than six years. The Revolution also promised far-reaching social reforms, such as free education, higher wages and more security for workers, and the redistribution of land to the peasants. These long-delayed reforms began to be implemented during the Cárdenas administration. They fell short of the ideals expressed by the revolutionaries, but they laid the foundation for the later industrialization of Mexico.

***The Agitator*, a Mural by Diego Rivera** Diego Rivera (1886–1957) was politically committed to the Mexican Revolution and widely admired as an artist. This mural, painted at the National Agricultural School at Chapingo near Mexico City, shows a political agitator addressing peasants and workers. With one hand, the speaker points to miners laboring in a silver mine; with the other, to a hammer and sickle. (Universidad Autonoma de Chapingo/ CENIDIAP-INBA)

ARGENTINA AND BRAZIL, 1900–1949

On the surface, Argentina and Brazil seem very different. Argentina is Spanish-speaking, temperate in climate, and populated almost exclusively by people of European origin. Brazil is tropical and Portuguese-speaking, and its inhabitants are of mixed European and African origin, with a substantial Indian minority. Yet in the twentieth century their economic, political, and technological experiences were remarkably similar.

The Transformation of Argentina

Most of Argentina consists of *pampas*°, flat, fertile land that is easy to till, much like the prairies of the midwestern United States and Canada. Throughout the nineteenth century Argentina's economy was based on two exports: the hides of longhorn creole cattle and the wool of merino sheep, which roamed the pampas in huge herds. Centuries earlier, Europeans had haphazardly introduced the animals and the grasses they ate. Natural selection had made the animals tough and hardy.

At the end of the nineteenth century railroads and refrigerator ships, which allowed the safe transportation of meat, changed not only the composition of Argentina's exports but also the way they were produced—in other words, the land itself. European consumers preferred the soft flesh of Lincoln sheep and Hereford cattle to the tough sinewy meat of creole cattle and merino sheep. The valuable Lincolns and Herefords could not be allowed to roam and graze on the pampas. They were carefully bred and received a diet of alfalfa and oats. To safeguard them, the pampas had to be divided, plowed, cultivated, and fenced with barbed wire to keep out predators and other unwelcome animals. Once fenced, the land could be used to produce wheat as well as beef and mutton. Within a few years grasslands that had stretched to the horizon were transformed into farmland. Like the North American midwest, the pampas became one of the world's great producers of wheat and meat.

Argentina's government represented the interests of the *oligarquía*°, a very small group of wealthy landowners. Members of this elite controlled enormous haciendas

pampas (POM-pus)

oligarquía (oh-lee-gar-KEE-ah)

where they raised cattle and sheep and grew wheat for export. They also owned fine homes in Buenos Aires°, a city that was built to look like Paris. They traveled frequently to Europe and spent so lavishly that the French coined the superlative "rich as an Argentine." They showed little interest in any business other than farming, however, and were content to let foreign companies, mainly British, build Argentina's railroads, processing plants, and public utilities. In exchange for its agricultural exports Argentina imported almost all its manufactured goods from Europe and the United States. So important were British interests in the Argentinean economy that English, not Spanish, was used on the railroads, and the biggest department store in Buenos Aires was a branch of Harrods of London.

Brazil and Argentina, to 1929

Before the First World War Brazil produced most of the world's coffee and cacao, grown on vast estates, and natural rubber, gathered by Indians from rubber trees growing wild in the Amazon rain forest. Brazil's elite was made up of coffee and cacao planters and rubber exporters. Like their Argentinean counterparts, they spent their money lavishly, building palaces in Rio de Janeiro° and one of the world's most beautiful opera house in Manaus°, deep in the Amazon. They had little interest in other forms of development; let British companies build railroads, harbors, and other infrastructure; and imported most manufactured goods. At the time this seemed to allow each country to do what it did best. If the British did not grow coffee, why should Brazil build locomotives?

Both Argentina and Brazil had small but outspoken middle classes that demanded a share in government and looked to Europe as a model. Beneath each middle class were the poor. In Argentina these were mainly Spanish and Italian immigrants who had ended up as landless farm laborers or workers in urban packing plants. In Brazil there was a large class of sharecroppers and plantation workers, many of them descendants of slaves.

Rubber exports collapsed after 1912, replaced by cheaper plantation rubber from Southeast Asia. The outbreak of war in 1914 put an end to imports from Europe as Britain and France focused all their industries on war production and Germany was cut off entirely. The disruption of the old trade patterns weakened the landowning class. In Argentina the urban middle class obtained the secret ballot and universal male suffrage in 1916 and elected a liberal politician, **Hipólito Irigoyen°**, as president. To a certain extent, the United States replaced the European countries as suppliers of machinery and consumers of coffee. European immigrants built factories to manufacture textiles and household goods. Desperate for money to pay for the war, Great Britain sold many of its railroad, streetcar, and other companies to the governments of Argentina and Brazil.

In contrast to Mexico, the postwar years were a period of prosperity in South America. Trade with Europe resumed; prices for agricultural exports remained high; and both Argentina and Brazil used profits accumulated during the war to industrialize and improve their transportation systems and public utilities. Yet it was also a time of social turmoil, as workers and middle-class professionals demanded social reforms and a larger voice in politics. In Argentina students' and workers' demonstrations were brutally crushed. In Brazil junior officers rose up several times against the government, calling for universal suffrage, social reforms, and freedom for labor unions. Though they accomplished little, they laid the groundwork for later reformist movements. In neither country did the urban middle class take power away from the wealthy landowners. Instead, the two classes shared power at the expense of both the landless peasants and the urban workers.

Yet as Argentina and Brazil were moving forward, new technologies again left them dependent on the advanced industrial countries. Brazilians are justly proud that the first person to fly an airplane outside the United States was Alberto Santos-Dumont, a Brazilian. He did so in 1906 in France, where he lived most of his life and had access to engine manufacturers and technical assistance. Aviation reached Latin America after World War I, when European and American companies such as Aéropostale and Pan American Airways introduced airmail service between cities and linked Latin America with the United States and Europe.

Before and during World War I radio, then called "wireless telegraphy," was used not for broadcasting but for point-to-point communications. Transmitters powerful enough to send messages across oceans or continents were extraordinarily complex and expensive: their antennas covered many acres; they used as much electricity as a small town; and they cost tens of thousands of pounds sterling (millions of dollars in today's money).

Right after the war, the major powers scrambled to build powerful transmitters on every continent to com-

Buenos Aires (BWAY-nihs AIR-eze) **Rio de Janeiro** (REE-oh day zhuh-NAIR-oh) **Manaus** (meh-NOWSE)

Hipólito Irigoyen (ee-POH-lee-toe ee-ree-GO-yen)

pete with the telegraph cable companies and to take advantage of the boom in international business and news reporting. At the time, no Latin American country possessed the knowledge or funds to build its own transmitters. In 1919, therefore, President Irigoyen of Argentina granted a radio concession to a German firm. France and Britain protested this decision, and eventually four powerful radio companies—one British, one French, one German, and one American—formed a cartel to control all radio communications in Latin America. This cartel set up a national radio company in each Latin American republic, installing a prominent local politician as its president, but the cartel held all the stock and therefore received all the profits. Thus, even as Brazil and Argentina were taking over their railroads and older industries, the major industrial countries controlled the diffusion of the newer aviation and radio technologies.

The Depression and the Vargas Regime in Brazil

The Depression hit Latin America as hard as it hit Europe and the United States; in many ways, it marks a more important turning point for the region than either of the world wars. As long-term customers cut back their orders, the value of agricultural and mineral exports fell by two-thirds between 1929 and 1932. Argentina and Brazil could no longer afford to import manufactured goods. An imploding economy also undermined their shaky political systems. Like European countries, Argentina and Brazil veered toward authoritarian regimes that promised to solve their economic problems.

In 1930 **Getulio Vargas°,** (1883–1953), a state governor, staged a coup and proclaimed himself president of Brazil. He proved to be a masterful politician. He wrote a new constitution that broadened the franchise and limited the president to one term. He raised import duties and promoted national firms and state-owned enterprises, culminating in the construction of the Volta Redonda steel mill in the 1930s. By 1936 industrial production had doubled, especially in textiles and small manufactures. Under his guidance, Brazil was on its way to becoming an industrial country. Vargas's policy, called **import-substitution industrialization,** became a model for other Latin American countries as they attempted to break away from neocolonial dependency.

The industrialization of Brazil brought all the familiar environmental consequences. Powerful new machines allowed the reopening of old mines and the digging of new ones. Cities grew as poor peasants looking for work arrived from the countryside. Around the older neighborhoods of Rio de Janeiro and São Paulo°, the poor turned steep hillsides and vacant lands into immense *favelas*° (slums) of makeshift shacks.

The countryside also was transformed. Scrubland was turned into pasture, and new acreage was planted in wheat, corn, and sugar cane. Even the Amazon rain forest—half of the land area of Brazil—was affected. In 1930 American industrialist Henry Ford invested $8 million to clear land along the Tapajós River and prepare it to become the site of the world's largest rubber plantation. Ford encountered opposition from Brazilian workers and politicians; the rubber trees proved vulnerable to diseases; and he had to abandon the project—but not before leaving 3 million acres (1.2 million hectares) denuded of trees. The ecological changes of the Vargas era, however, were but a tiny forerunner of the degradation of the Brazilian environment that was to take place later in the century.

Vargas instituted many reforms favorable to urban workers, such as labor unions, pension plans, and disability insurance, but he refused to take any measures that might help the millions of landless peasants or harm the interests of the great landowners. Although the Brazilian economy recovered from the Depression, the benefits of recovery were so unequally distributed that communist and fascist movements demanded even more radical changes.

In 1938, prohibited by his own constitution from being reelected, Vargas staged another coup, abolished the constitution, and instituted the Estado Novo°, or "New State," with himself as supreme leader. He abolished political parties, jailed opposition leaders, and turned Brazil into a fascist state. When the Second World War broke out, however, Vargas aligned Brazil with the United States and contributed troops and ships to the Allied war effort.

Despite his economic achievements, Vargas harmed Brazil. By running roughshod over laws, constitutions, and rights, he infected not only Brazil but all of South America with the temptations of political violence. It is ironic, but not surprising, that Vargas was overthrown in 1945 by a military coup.

Argentina After 1930

Economically, the Depression hurt Argentina almost as badly as it hurt Brazil. Politically, however, the consequences were

Getulio Vargas (jay-TOO-lee-oh VAR-gus)

São Paulo (sow PAL-oh) ***favela*** (feh-VEL-luh) **Estado Novo** (esh-TAH-doe NO-vo)

The Peróns in Front of the TZ Hotel In 1945, Juan Perón, the dictator of Argentina, married the actress Eva Duarte. Her charms and gifts as an orator attracted the support of the labor unions to the Perón regime. The Peróns are shown riding through Buenos Aires following Perón's second inauguration on June 4, 1952. Eva died a month later, reportedly of cancer. (Bettemann/Corbis)

delayed for many years. In 1930 General José Uriburu° overthrew the popularly elected President Irigoyen. The Uriburu government represented the large landowners and big business interests. For thirteen years the generals and the oligarquía ruled, doing nothing to lessen the poverty of the workers or the frustrations of the middle class. When World War II broke out, Argentina sympathized with the Axis but remained officially neutral.

In 1943 another military revolt flared, this one among junior officers angry at conservative politicians. It was led by Colonel **Juan Perón**° (1895–1974). The intentions of the rebels were clear:

> Civilians will never understand the greatness of our ideal; we shall therefore have to eliminate them from the government and give them the only mission which corresponds to them: work and obedience.[1]

Once in power the officers took over the highest positions in government and business and began to lavish money on military equipment and their own salaries. Their goal, inspired by Nazi victories, was nothing less than the conquest of South America.

As the war turned against the Nazis, the officers saw their popularity collapse. Perón, however, had other plans. Inspired by his charismatic wife **Eva Duarte Perón**° (1919–1952), he appealed to the urban workers. Eva Perón became the champion of the *descamisados*°, or "shirtless ones," and campaigned tirelessly for social benefits and for the cause of women and children. With his wife's help, Perón won the presidency in 1946 and created a populist dictatorship in imitation of the Vargas regime in Brazil.

Like Brazil, Argentina industrialized rapidly under state sponsorship. Perón spent lavishly on social welfare projects as well as on the military, depleting the capital that Argentina had earned during the war. Though a skillful demagogue who played off the army against the navy and both against the labor unions, Perón could not create a stable government out of the chaos of coups and conspiracies. He had to back down from a plan to make Eva his vice president. When she died in 1952, he lost his political skills (or perhaps they were hers), and soon thereafter he was overthrown in yet another military coup.

José Uriburu (hoe-SAY oo-ree-BOO-roo) **Juan Perón** (hoo-AHN pair-OWN)

Eva Duarte Perón (AY-vuy doo-AR-tay pair-OWN) ***descamisados*** (des-cah-mee-SAH-dohs)

Mexico, Argentina, and Brazil: A Comparison

Until 1910 Mexico, Argentina, and Brazil shared a common history and similar cultures. In the first half of the twentieth century their economies followed parallel trajectories, based on unequal relations with the industrialized countries of Europe and North America. All three countries—indeed, all of Latin America—struggled with the failure of neocolonial economics to improve the lives of the middle class, let alone the peasants. And when the Depression hit, all three turned to state intervention and import-substitution industrialization. Like all industrializing countries, they did so by mining, farming, ranching, cutting down forests, and irrigating land, all at the expense of the natural environment.

Yet their political histories diverged radically. Mexico underwent a traumatic and profound social revolution. Argentina and Brazil, meanwhile, languished under conservative regimes devoted to the interests of wealthy landowners, sporadically interrupted by military coups and populist demagogues. Mexicans, thanks to their experience of revolution, developed an acute sense of their national identity and civic pride in their history—pride largely missing in South America. Despite shortcomings, Mexico seriously committed itself to education, land reform, social justice, and political stability as national goals, not merely as the campaign platform of a populist dictator.

Conclusion

Sub-Saharan Africa, India, and Latin America lay outside the theaters of war that engulfed most of the Northern Hemisphere, but they were deeply affected by global events and by the demands of the industrial powers. Sub-Saharan Africa and India were still under colonial rule, and their political life revolved around the yearnings of their elites for political independence and their masses for social justice. Mexico, Argentina, and Brazil were politically independent, but their economies, like those of Africa and India, were closely tied to the economies of the industrial nations with which they traded. Their deeply polarized societies and the stresses caused by their dependence on the industrial countries clashed with the expectations of ever larger numbers of their peoples.

In Mexico these stresses brought about a long and violent revolution, out of which Mexicans forged a lasting sense of national identity. Argentina and Brazil moved toward greater economic independence, but the price was social unrest, militarism, and dictatorship. In India the conflict between growing expectations and the reality of colonial rule produced both a movement for independence and an ethnic split that tore the nation apart. In sub-Saharan Africa demands for national self-determination and economic development were only beginning to be voiced by 1949 and did not come to fruition until the second half of the century.

Nationalism and the yearning for social justice were the two most powerful forces for change in the early twentieth century. These ideas originated in the industrialized countries but resonated in the independent countries of Latin America as well as in colonial regions such as the Indian subcontinent and sub-Saharan Africa. However, they did not always unite people against their colonial rulers or foreign oppressors; instead, they often divided them along social, ethnic, or religious lines. Western-educated elites looked to industrialization as a means of modernizing their country and ensuring their position in it, while peasants and urban workers supported nationalist and revolutionary movements in the hope of improving their lives. Often these goals were not compatible.

Key Terms

Blaise Diagne
African National Congress
Haile Selassie
Indian National Congress
Bengal
All-India Muslim League
Mohandas K. (Mahatma) Gandhi
Jawaharlal Nehru
Muhammad Ali Jinnah
Emiliano Zapata
Francisco "Pancho" Villa
Lázaro Cárdenas
Hipólito Irigoyen
Getulio Vargas
import-substitution industrialization
Juan Perón
Eva Duarte Perón

Suggested Reading

On Africa under colonial rule the classic overview is Melville Herskovits, *The Human Factor in Changing Africa* (1958). Two excellent general introductions are Roland Oliver and Anthony Atmore, *Africa Since 1800*, 4th ed. (1994), and A. E. Afigbo et al.,

The Making of Modern Africa, vol. 2, *The Twentieth Century* (1986). More detailed and challenging are *UNESCO General History of Africa*, vols. 7 and 8; *The Cambridge History of Africa*, vols. 7 and 8; and Adu Boahen, *African Perspectives on Colonialism* (1987). Outstanding novels about Africa in the colonial era include Chinua Achebe, *Arrow of God* (1964); Buchi Emecheta, *The Joys of Motherhood* (1980); and Peter Abraham, *Mine Boy* (1946).

For a general introduction to Indian history see Sumit Sarkar, *Modern India, 1885–1947* (1983), and Percival Spear, *India: A Modern History*, rev. ed. (1972). On the influenza epidemic of 1918–1919 see Alfred W. Crosby, *America's Forgotten Pandemic: The Influenza of 1918* (1989). The Indian independence movement has received a great deal of attention. Judith M. Brown's most recent book on Gandhi is *Gandhi: Prisoner of Hope* (1989). *Gandhi's Truth: On the Origin of Militant Nonviolence* (1969) by noted psychoanalyst Erik Erikson is also recommended. Two collections of memoirs of the last decades of British rule are worth looking at: Charles Allen, ed., *Plain Tales of the Raj: Image of British India in the Twentieth Century* (1975), and Zareer Masani, ed., *Indian Tales of the Raj* (1988). The transition from colonialism to partition and independence is the subject of the very readable *Freedom at Midnight* (1975) by Larry Collins and Dominique Lapierre. The environment is discussed in M. Gadgil and R. Guha, *This Fissured Land: An Ecological History of India* (1993).

Thomas Skidmore and Peter Smith, *Modern Latin America*, 3d ed. (1992), offers the best brief introduction. Two fine general overviews of modern Mexican history are Enrique Krauze, *Mexico: Biography of Power: A History of Modern Mexico, 1810–1996* (1997), and Colin MacLachlan and William Beezley, *El Gran Pueblo: A History of Greater Mexico* (1994). On the Mexican Revolution, two recent books are essential: Alan Knight, *The Mexican Revolution*, 2 vols. (1986), and John M. Hart, *Revolutionary Mexico: The Coming and Process of the Mexican Revolution* (1987). But see also two classics by sympathetic Americans: Frank Tannenbaum, *Peace by Revolution: Mexico After 1910* (1933), and Robert E. Quirk, *The Mexican Revolution, 1914–1915* (1960). Mexico's most celebrated revolutionary is the subject of Manuel Machado, *Centaur of the North: Francisco Villa, the Mexican Revolution, and Northern Mexico* (1988). Mariano Azuela, *The Underdogs* (1988), is an interesting fictional account of this period. The standard work on Brazil is E. Bradford Burns, *A History of Brazil*, 3d ed. (1993). On the environmental history of Brazil, see Warren Dean, *Brazil and the Struggle for Rubber: A Study in Environmental History* (1987). The history of modern Argentina is ably treated in David Rock, *Argentina, 1517–1987: From Spanish Colonization to Alfonsín* (1987). Mark Jefferson, *Peopling the Argentine Pampas* (1971), and Jeremy Adelman, *Frontier Development: Land, Labour and Capital on the Wheatlands of Argentina and Canada, 1890–1914* (1994), describe the transformation of the Argentinean environment.

Notes

1. George Blanksten, *Perón's Argentina* (Chicago: University of Chicago Press, 1953), 37.

Famines and Politics

Nature is never reliable, and all living things periodically suffer from a catastrophic drop in food supplies. Human history is filled with tales of famines—times when crops failed, food supplies ran out, and people starved.

Natural famines India, dependent on the monsoon rains, has been particularly prone to such calamities, with famines striking two to four times a century, whenever the rains failed for several years in succession. Three times in the eighteenth century (1702–1704, 1769–1770, and 1790–1792) famines killed several million people in different parts of the subcontinent. The nineteenth century was worse, with famines in 1803–1804, 1837–1838, 1868–1870, and 1876–1878. The latter also afflicted northern China, causing between 9 and 13 million deaths from hunger and from the diseases of malnutrition. There were even incidents of cannibalism, as starving adults killed and ate starving children.

When a drought hit a region, it decimated not only the human population but also the animals they relied on to transport goods and plow the land. Likewise, droughts lowered the water levels in rivers and canals, so food could not be moved from one place to another.

Commerical famines That all changed in the nineteenth century. Railroads and steamships could transport foodstuffs across great distances in a matter of days or weeks, regardless of drought or heavy rains. Great Britain became dependent on imports of wheat from Russia and the American Midwest, and later of beef from Argentina. Yet famines were worse than ever, and the global death toll from starvation has been far higher since the mid-nineteenth century than it ever was in earlier times. Why?

Consider the Irish famine of 1845–1848. By the early nineteenth century the potato had become the main source of nutrition for the Irish people. Potatoes grew abundantly in the cool, moist climate of Ireland and produced more calories per acre than any other crop. Most of the Irish were poor tenant farmers, and potatoes had allowed their population to increase far more than wheat or rye could have.

In fall 1845 the blight turned the potatoes in the fields black, mushy, and inedible. The harvest was ruined the following year as well. It recovered slightly in 1847, but was bad again in 1848. Tens of thousands died of starvation, while hundreds of thousands died from the diseases that strike malnourished people, especially dysentery, typhus, and cholera. Travelers saw corpses rotting in their hovels or on the sides of roads. Altogether, a million or more people died, while another million managed to emigrate, reducing the population of Ireland by half.

Throughout those years, wheat grew in Ireland, but much of it was exported to England, where customers had money to pay for it. Like any other commodity, food cost money. The Irish farmers, poor even before the famines, were destitute and could not afford to buy the wheat. The British government, wedded to the ideology of laissez-faire, was convinced that interfering with the free market would only make things worse. Relief efforts were half-hearted at best; the official responsible for Irish affairs preferred to leave the situation to "the operation of natural causes."

The same held true in India, like Ireland a colony of Great Britain. The drought of 1876–1878 killed over 5 million Indians in the Deccan region, while British officials were helpless or indifferent. Part of the problem was transportation. In the 1870s only a few railway lines connected major cities. Most goods were still transported in bullock carts, but the bullocks also starved during the drought. Another obstacle was political. The idea that a government should be responsible for feeding the population was unthinkable at the time. And so, while millions were starving in the Deccan, the Punjab region was exporting wheat to Britain.

Over the next twenty years so-called famine railways were built in the regions historically most affected by the failures of the monsoon. When drought struck again at the end of the century, the railways were ready to transport food to areas that had previously been accessible only by bullock carts. However, the inhabitants of the affected regions had no money with which to buy what little food there was, and the government was still reluctant to interfere with free enterprise. Grain merchants bought all the stocks, hoarded them until the price rose, then used the railways to transport them out of the famine regions to regions where the harvests were better and people had more money.

In the twentieth century commercial famines have become rare, as governments have come to realize that they have a responsibility for food supplies not only for their own people, but for people in other countries as well. Yet commercial famines have not entirely disappeared. In

1974, when a catastrophic flood covered half of Bangladesh, the government was too disorganized to distribute its stocks of rice, while merchants bought what they could and exported it to India. Thousands died, and thousands more survived only because of belated shipments of food from donor countries.

Political families To say that governments are responsible for food supplies does not mean that they exercise that responsibility for the good of the people. Some do, but in many instances food is used as a weapon. In the twentieth century global food supplies were always adequate for the population of the world, and transportation was seldom a problem. Yet the century witnessed the most murderous famines ever recorded.

War-induced famines were not new. In 1812, as the Russian army retreated, it practiced a "scorched-earth" policy of burning food stocks to prevent them from falling into the hands of Napoleon's army. In doing so, it also caused a famine among Russian peasants. Similar famines resulted from the destruction or requisitioning of crops in the Russian civil war of 1921–1922, the Japanese occupation of Indochina in 1942–1945, and the Biafran war in Nigeria in 1967–1969.

The Bengal famine of 1943 was also war-related. In 1942 the Japanese army had conquered Burma, a rich rice-producing colony. Food supplies in Bengal, which imported rice from Burma, dropped by 5 percent. As prices began to rise, merchants bought stocks of rice and held them in the hope that prices would continue to increase. Sharecroppers sold their stocks to pay off their debts to landlords and village moneylenders. Meanwhile, the railroads that in peacetime would have carried food from other parts of India were fully occupied with military traffic. In October 1943, when a new viceroy, Lord Wavell, arrived in India and ordered the army to transport food to Bengal, food prices dropped to a level that the poor could afford. By then, however, between 1.5 and 2 million Bengalis had starved to death.

Worst of all were the famines that happened in peacetime as a result of the deliberate decisions of governments. The most famous of these political famines was caused by Stalin's collectivization of agriculture in 1932–1934. The Communist Party tried to force the peasants to give up their land and livestock and join collectives, where they could be made to work harder and provide food for the growing cities and industries. When they resisted, their crops were seized. Millions were sent to prison camps and millions of others died of starvation. Stalin chided the overly enthusiastic party members who had caused the famine for being "dizzy with success."

An even worse famine took place in China from 1958 to 1961 during the "Great Leap Forward" (see Chapter 32). Communist Party Chairman Mao Zedong decided to hasten the transformation of China into a communist state and industrial power by relying not on the expertise of economists and technocrats but on the enthusiasm of the masses. All farms were consolidated into huge communes. Peasants were mobilized to work on giant construction projects or to make steel out of household utensils and tools in backyard furnaces. The harvest of 1959 was poor, and later ones were even worse. The amount of grain per person declined from 452 pounds (205 kilograms) in 1957 to 340 pounds (154 kilograms) in 1961. Since the Central Statistical Bureau had been shut down, the central government was unaware of the shortages and demanded ever higher requisitions of food to feed the army and urban and industrial workers and to export to the Soviet Union to pay off China's debts. The amount of food left to the farmers was between one-fifth and one-half of their usual subsistence diet. From 1958 to 1961 20 to 30 million Chinese are estimated to have starved or died of the diseases of malnutrition in the most catastrophic famine in the history of the world. The leaders of the Communist Party either were unaware of its extent or, if they knew, did not dare mention it for fear of displeasing Mao, who denied its existence.

Nothing quite as horrible has happened since the Great Leap Forward. During the droughts in Africa in the 1970s and 1980s, most people in the affected regions received international food aid, but the governments of Ethiopia and Sudan either denied that their people were hungry or prevented food shipments from reaching drought victims in order to crush rebellions.

In the world today, natural disasters are as frequent as ever, and many countries are vulnerable to food shortages. No one now claims, as many did in the nineteenth century, that governments have no business providing free food to the starving. Though food is not equitably distributed, there is enough for all human beings now, and there will be enough for the foreseeable future. However, humanitarian feelings compete with other political agendas, and the specter of politically motivated famines still stalks the world.

PART EIGHT

Perils and Promises of a Global Community, 1945 to the Present

The years after World War II brought many promising changes to an increasingly interconnected world. Major efforts were made to promote peace and international cooperation, and most countries agreed to human rights standards to be enforced through the United Nations. Colonized peoples in Asia and Africa gained their independence, and expanding global trade offered the hope of economic growth. However, these decades also saw major threats to peace, prosperity, and the environment.

A Cold War of rhetoric and frayed nerves between communist and anticommunist states disrupted dreams of a new era of international peace and cooperation. The Iron Curtain divided Soviet-dominated eastern Europe from American-supported western Europe. Regional wars in Korea and Vietnam pitted the United States and its allies against communist regimes. Cold War rivalries sometimes provided a windfall of aid for new states but also intensified civil conflicts in Latin America, Africa, and elsewhere.

Tensions eased in the 1970s, and the United States and the Soviet Union signed agreements to curtail nuclear arms and testing. With the collapse of communism in the Soviet Union in 1991, the Cold War finally ended. The United Nations and other multinational organizations moved to stop the spread of weapons of mass destruction and promote global justice and equality. As the sole remaining superpower, the United States had a unique capacity to act globally and a unique burden of suspicion of its motives.

Economic promises and perils also abounded in the post-war world. The wartime victors experienced rapid economic recovery, as did Germany and Japan, but in less developed lands prosperity came slowly or not at all. Global markets seemed to favor the industrialized nations. After 1975 a number of countries, including China, South Korea, Brazil, and Argentina, made dramatic strides in industrialization. But less developed nations had to struggle, and rapid population growth often offset their economic gains. The divide between rich and poor nations remained—or even widened.

Economic development meant new possibilities and perils for the environment. In the 1960s, the Green Revolution in agriculture greatly increased food supplies in Asia, and in the 1990s genetic engineering advances produced plants that yielded more food and were resistant to disease, drought, and insect damage. But industrial growth added immeasurably to the pollution of water and land. Atmospheric pollution increased exposure to harmful ultraviolet rays and led to increased global temperatures. Over-fishing and over-hunting imperiled many animal species, while thousands of acres of tropical forests were cut or burned for timber and farmland.

Finally, growing global interconnectedness held its own promises and perils. Many welcomed the emergence of English as the global language and the rapid spread of news, money, and ideas via the Internet. Others feared that Western material values and political and economic dominance posed a severe threat to cultural diversity around the world. A dangerous few reacted with violence.

1950
1960
1970
Americas
• 1945 United Nations charter signed in San Francisco
• 1946 International Monetary Fund and World Bank founded
• 1952 U.S. tests first hydrogen bomb
• 1959 Cuban Revolution
• 1962 Cuban missile crisis
• 1964 Military takes power in Brazil
Neil Armstrong walks on moon 1969 •
Europe
1948–1952 Marshall Plan helps rebuild western Europe
• 1949 NATO founded
• 1955 Warsaw Pact formed
Soviet troops crush revolt in Hungary 1956 •
• 1957 Common Market founded
• 1961 Berlin Wall built
Student uprising in France 1968 •
Africa
• 1948 Apartheid becomes official in South Africa
Ghana first British colony in West Africa to win independence 1957 •
• 1958 Guinea wins independence from France
• 1960 Nigeria, Congo, Somalia, Togo win independence
• 1963 Kenya independent
Middle East
• 1948 State of Israel founded; first Arab-Israeli War
• 1956 Suez crisis
1954–1962 Algerian war for Independence
Organization of Petroleum Exporting Countries founded 1960 •
• 1967 Six Day Arab-Israeli War
Asia and Oceania
Communist Revolution in China 1949 •
1951–1953 Korean War
1954–1975 Vietnam War
• 1949 Indonesia wins independence from Netherlands
Cultural Revolution in China 1966–1969
Japan becomes world economic power 1970s •

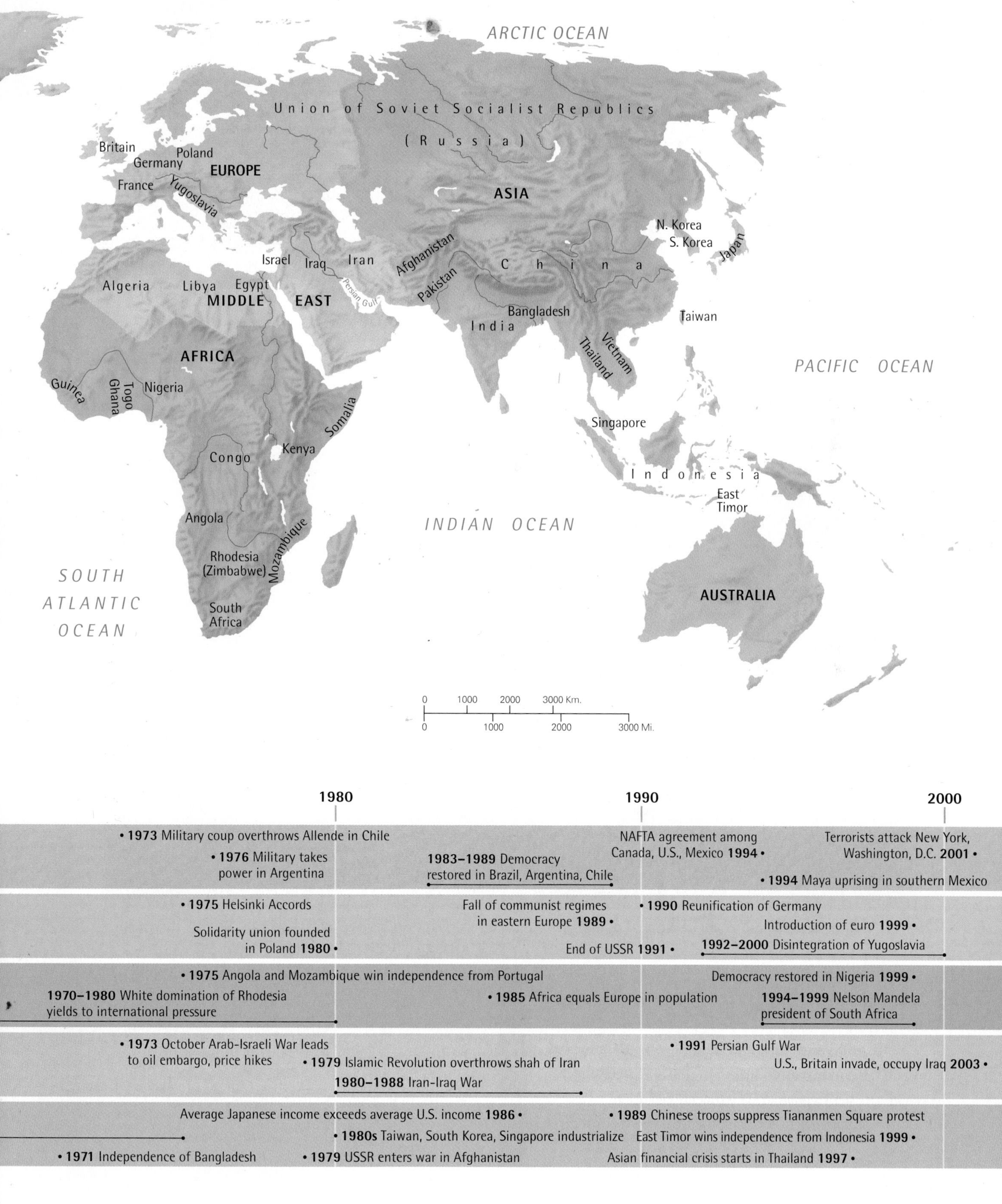
ARCTIC OCEAN
Union of Soviet Socialist Republics
(Russia)
Britain
Poland
Germany
EUROPE
France
Yugoslavia
ASIA
N. Korea
S. Korea
Japan
Israel
Iraq
Iran
Afghanistan
China
Algeria
Libya
Egypt
Persian Gulf
Pakistan
MIDDLE EAST
Bangladesh
India
Taiwan
AFRICA
Vietnam
Thailand
PACIFIC OCEAN
Guinea
Togo
Ghana
Nigeria
Somalia
Singapore
Kenya
Congo
Indonesia
East Timor
Angola
INDIAN OCEAN
Mozambique
Rhodesia (Zimbabwe)
SOUTH ATLANTIC OCEAN
South Africa
AUSTRALIA
0 1000 2000 3000 Km.
0 1000 2000 3000 Mi.
1980
1990
2000
• 1973 Military coup overthrows Allende in Chile
• 1976 Military takes power in Argentina
1983–1989 Democracy restored in Brazil, Argentina, Chile
NAFTA agreement among Canada, U.S., Mexico 1994 •
Terrorists attack New York, Washington, D.C. 2001 •
• 1994 Maya uprising in southern Mexico
• 1975 Helsinki Accords
Solidarity union founded in Poland 1980 •
Fall of communist regimes in eastern Europe 1989 •
• 1990 Reunification of Germany
Introduction of euro 1999 •
End of USSR 1991 •
1992–2000 Disintegration of Yugoslavia
• 1975 Angola and Mozambique win independence from Portugal
Democracy restored in Nigeria 1999 •
1970–1980 White domination of Rhodesia yields to international pressure
• 1985 Africa equals Europe in population
1994–1999 Nelson Mandela president of South Africa
• 1973 October Arab-Israeli War leads to oil embargo, price hikes
• 1979 Islamic Revolution overthrows shah of Iran
1980–1988 Iran-Iraq War
• 1991 Persian Gulf War
U.S., Britain invade, occupy Iraq 2003 •
Average Japanese income exceeds average U.S. income 1986 •
• 1989 Chinese troops suppress Tiananmen Square protest
• 1980s Taiwan, South Korea, Singapore industrialize
East Timor wins independence from Indonesia 1999 •
• 1971 Independence of Bangladesh
• 1979 USSR enters war in Afghanistan
Asian financial crisis starts in Thailand 1997 •

32 The Cold War and Decolonization, 1945–1975

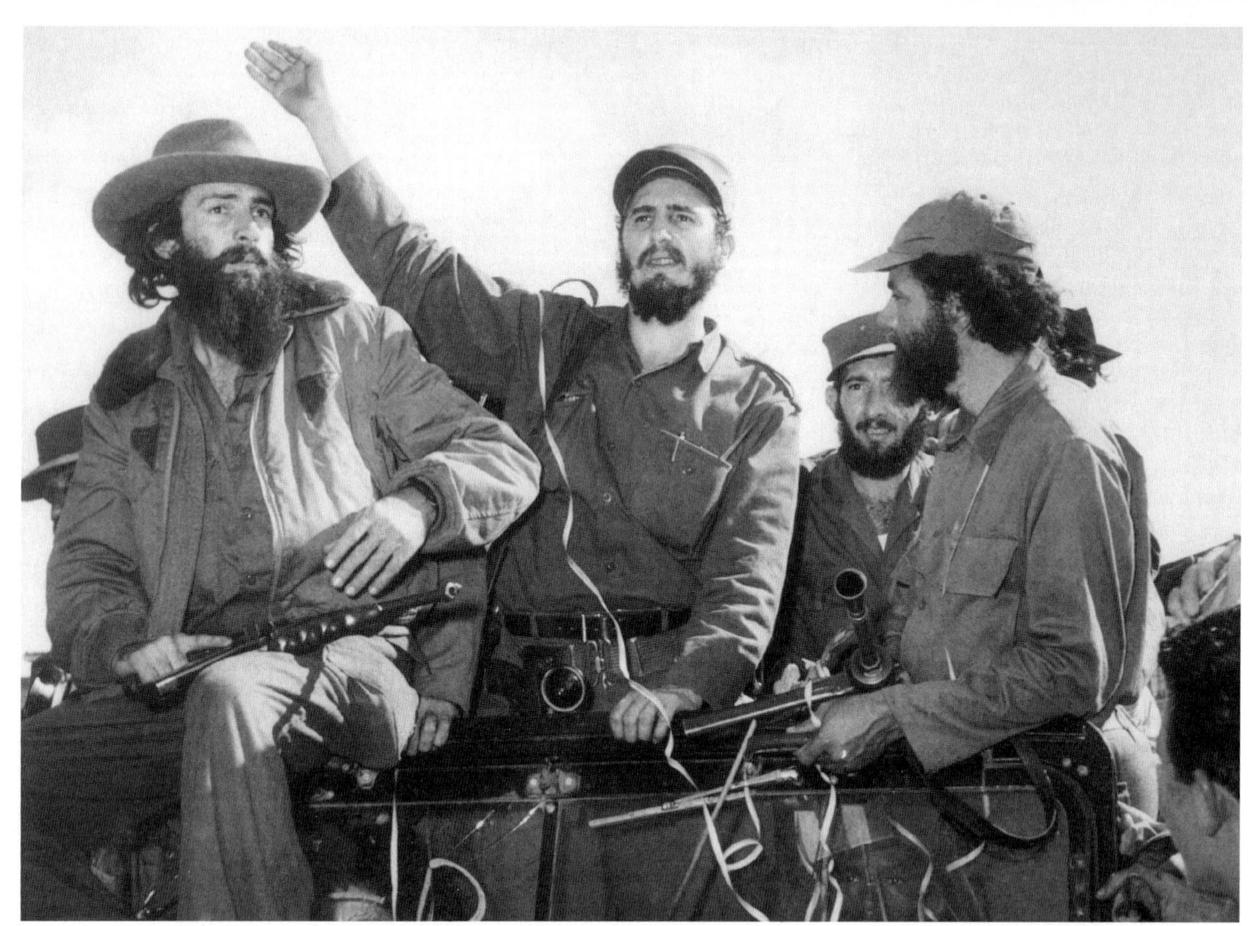

Fidel Castro Arrives in Havana Castro and his supporters overthrew a brutal dictatorship and began the revolutionary transformation of Cuba. This led to a confrontation with the United States.

CHAPTER OUTLINE

In 1946, in a speech at Fulton, Missouri, Great Britain's wartime leader Winston Churchill said: "From Stettin in the Baltic to Trieste in the Adriatic, an iron curtain has descended across the Continent. . . . I am convinced there is nothing they [the communists] so much admire as strength, and there is nothing for which they have less respect than weakness, especially military weakness." The phrase **"iron curtain"** became a watchword of the **Cold War,** the state of political tension and military rivalry that was then beginning between the United States and its allies ("running dogs of imperialism," in Chinese communist parlance) and the Soviet Union and its allies ("satellites," in American parlance).

The Atlantic Charter issued by Churchill and President Franklin Roosevelt four months before the United States entered World War II in 1941 and the 1942 declaration signed by twenty-six "United Nations" (Roosevelt's term for the alliance against the Axis) had looked forward to economic cooperation, restoration of sovereignty to nations occupied by the Axis, and above all to a world in which war and territorial conquest were not tolerated. By the time Churchill delivered his "iron curtain" speech, however, Britain's electorate had voted him out of power, Harry S Truman had succeeded to the presidency after Roosevelt's death, Communist Yugoslavia was supporting the communists in Greece, and the Soviet Union was dominating eastern Europe and supporting communist movements in China, Iran, Turkey, and Korea. Although Soviet diplomats joined their former allies in the newly founded United Nations organization, confrontation, not cooperation, was the hallmark of relations between East and West.

The intensity of the Cold War, with its accompanying threat of nuclear destruction, sometimes obscured a postwar phenomenon of more enduring importance. Western domination was greatly reduced in most of Asia, Africa, and Latin America and the colonial empires of the New Imperialism were gradually dismantled. The new generation of national leaders heading the states in these regions sometimes skillfully used Cold War antagonism to their own advantage. Their real business, however, was nation building, an enterprise charged with almost insurmountable problems and conflicts.

Each region subjected to imperialism had its own history and conditions and followed its own route to independence. Thus the new nations had difficulty finding a collective voice in a world increasingly oriented toward two superpowers, the United States and the Soviet Union. Some sided openly with one or the other. Others banded together in a posture of neutrality and spoke with one voice about their need for economic and technical assistance and the obligation of the wealthy nations to satisfy those needs.

The Cold War military rivalry stimulated extraordinary advances in weaponry and associated technologies, but many new nations faced basic problems of educating their citizens, nurturing industry, and escaping the economic constraints imposed by their former imperialist masters. The environment suffered severe pressures from oil exploration and transport to support the growing economies of the wealthy nations and from deforestation in poor regions challenged by the need for cropland. Neither rich nor poor nations understood the costs associated with these environmental changes.

As you read this chapter, ask yourself the following questions:

- What impact did economic philosophy have on both the Cold War and the decolonization movement?
- How was a third world war averted?
- Was world domination by the superpowers good or bad for the rest of the world?
- How were the experiences of Asia, Africa, and Latin America similar in this period?

THE COLD WAR

The wartime alliance between the United States, Great Britain, and the Soviet Union had been uneasy. Fear of working-class revolution, which the Nazis had played on in their rise to power, was not confined to Germany. For more than a century political and economic leaders committed to free markets and untrammeled capital investment had loathed socialism in its several forms. After World War II the iron curtain in Europe and communist insurgencies in China and elsewhere seemed to confirm the threat of worldwide revolution.

Western leaders quickly came to perceive the Soviet Union as the nerve center of world revolution and as a military power capable of launching a war as destructive and terrible as the one that had recently ended. But particularly after the United States and the countries of western Europe established the **North Atlantic Treaty Organization (NATO)** military alliance in 1949, Soviet leaders felt surrounded by hostile forces just when they were trying to recover from the terrible losses sustained in the war against the Axis. The distrust and suspicion between the two sides played out on a worldwide stage. The United Nations provided the venue for face-to-face debate.

The United Nations

In 1944 representatives from the United States, Great Britain, the Soviet Union, and China drafted proposals that finally bore fruit in the treaty called the United Nations Charter, ratified on October 24, 1945. Like the earlier League of Nations, the **United Nations** had two main bodies: the General Assembly, with representatives from all member states; and the Security Council, with five permanent members—China, France, Great Britain, the United States, and the Soviet Union—and seven rotating members. A full-time bureaucracy headed by a Secretary General carried out the day-to-day business of both bodies. Various agencies focused on specialized international problems—for example, UNICEF (United Nations Children's Emergency Fund), FAO (Food and Agriculture Organization), and UNESCO (United Nations Educational, Scientific and Cultural Organization) (see Environment and Technology: The Green Revolution). Unlike the League of Nations, which required unanimous agreement in both deliberative bodies, the United Nations operated by majority vote, except that the five permanent members of the Security Council had veto power in that chamber.

All signatories to the United Nations Charter renounced war and territorial conquest. Nevertheless, peacekeeping, the sole preserve of the Security Council, became a vexing problem. The permanent members exercised their vetoes to protect their friends and interests. Throughout the Cold War the United Nations was seldom able to forestall or quell international conflicts, though from time to time it sent observers or peacekeeping forces to monitor truces or agreements otherwise arrived at.

The decolonization of Africa and Asia greatly swelled the size of the General Assembly but not of the Security Council. Many of the new nations looked to the United Nations for material assistance and access to a wider political world. While the vetoes of the Security Council's permanent members often stymied actions that even indirectly touched on Cold War concerns, the General Assembly became an arena for opinions on many issues involving decolonization, a movement that the Soviet Union strongly encouraged but the Western colonial powers resisted.

In the early years of the United Nations, General Assembly resolutions carried great weight. An example is a 1947 resolution that sought to divide Palestine into sovereign Jewish and Arab states. Gradually, though, the flood of new members produced a voting majority concerned more with poverty, racial discrimination, and the struggle against imperialism than with the Cold War. As a result, the Western powers increasingly disregarded the General Assembly, in effect allowing the new nations of the world to have their say, but not the means to act collectively.

Capitalism and Communism

In July 1944, with Allied victory a foregone conclusion, economic specialists representing over forty countries met at Bretton Woods, a New Hampshire resort, to devise a new international monetary system. The signatories eventually agreed to fix exchange rates and to create the International Monetary Fund (IMF) and World Bank (formally the International Bank for Reconstruction and Development). The IMF was to use currency reserves from member nations to finance temporary trade deficits, and the **World Bank** was to provide funds for reconstructing Europe and helping needy countries after the war.

The Soviet Union attended the Bretton Woods Conference and signed the agreements, which went into effect in 1946. But deepening suspicion and hostility between the Soviet Union and the United States and Britain undermined cooperation. While the United States held reserves of gold and the rest of the world held reserves of dollars in order to maintain the stability of the monetary system, the Soviet Union established a closed monetary system for itself and the new communist regimes in eastern Europe. Similar differences were found across the economies of the two alliances. In the Western countries, supply and demand determined prices; in the Soviet command economy, government agencies allocated goods and set prices ac-

CHRONOLOGY

	Cold War	Decolonization
1945		
	1948–1949 Berlin airlift **1949** NATO formed	**1947** Partition of India **1949** Dutch withdraw from Indonesia
1950	**1950–1953** Korean War **1952** United States detonates first hydrogen bomb **1954** Jacobo Arbenz overthrown in Guatemala, supported by CIA **1955** Warsaw Pact concluded **1956** Soviet Union suppresses Hungarian revolt **1957** Soviet Union launches first artificial satellite into Earth orbit	**1952** Bolivian Revolution **1954** CIA intervention in Guatemala; defeat at Dienbienphu ends French hold on Vietnam **1955** Bandung Conference **1957** Ghana becomes first British colony in Africa to gain independence **1959** Fidel Castro leads revolution in Cuba
1960	**1961** East Germany builds Berlin Wall **1961** Bay of Pigs (Cuba) **1962** Cuban missile crisis **1968** Nuclear Non-Proliferation Treaty	**1960** Shootings in Sharpeville intensify South African struggle against apartheid; Nigeria becomes independent **1962** Algeria wins independence
1970	**1975** Helsinki Accords; end of Vietnam War	**1971** Bangladesh secedes from Pakistan

cording to governmental priorities, irrespective of market forces.

Many leaders of newly independent states, having won the struggle against imperialism, preferred the Soviet Union's socialist example to the capitalism of their former colonizers. Thus, the relative success of economies patterned on Eastern or Western models became part of Cold War rivalry. Each side trumpeted economic successes measured by industrial output, changes in per capita income, and productivity gains.

During World War II the U.S. economy finally escaped the lingering effects of the Great Depression (see Chapter 30). Increased military spending and the draft brought full employment and high wages. The wartime conversion of factories from the production of consumer goods had created demand for those goods. With peace, the United States enjoyed prosperity and an international competitive advantage because of massive destruction in Europe.

The economy of western Europe was heavily damaged during World War II, and the early postwar years were bleak in many European countries. With prosperity, the United States was able to support the reconstruction of western Europe. The **Marshall Plan** provided $12.5 billion in aid to friendly European countries between 1948 and 1952. Most of the aid was in the form of food, raw materials, and other goods. By 1961 more than $20 billion in economic aid had been disbursed. European determination backed by American aid spurred recovery, and by 1963 the resurgent European economy had doubled its 1940 output.

Western European governments generally increased their role in economic management during this period. In Great Britain, for example, the Labour Party government of the early 1950s nationalized coal, steel, railroads, and health care. Similarly, the French government nationalized public utilities; the auto, banking, and insurance industries; and parts of the mining industry. These steps provided large infusions of capital for rebuilding and acquiring new technologies.

In 1948 European governments also launched a process of economic cooperation and integration with the creation of the Organization of European Economic Cooperation (OEEC). Cooperative policies were first focused on coal and steel. Often located in disputed border areas, these industries had previously been flash points that led to war. Successes in these crucial areas encouraged some OEEC countries to begin lowering tariffs to

ENVIRONMENT + TECHNOLOGY

The Green Revolution

Concern about world food supplies grew directly out of serious shortages caused by the devastation and trade disruptions of World War II. The Food and Agriculture Organization of the United Nations, the Rockefeller Foundation, and the Ford Foundation took leading roles in fostering crop research and educating farmers about agricultural techniques. In 1966 the International Rice Research Institute (established in 1960–1962) began distributing seeds for an improved rice variety known as IR-8. Crop yields from this and other new varieties, along with improved farming techniques, were initially so impressive that the term *Green Revolution* was coined to describe a new era in agriculture.

On the heels of the successful new rice strains, new varieties of corn and wheat were introduced. Building on twenty years of Rockefeller-funded research in Mexico, the Centro Internacional de Mejoramiento de Maiz y Trigo (International Center for the Improvement of Maize and Wheat) was established in 1966 under Norman Borlaug, who was awarded the Nobel Peace Prize four years later. This organization distributed short, stiff-strawed varieties of wheat that were resistant to disease and responsive to fertilizer.

By 1970 other centers for research on tropical agriculture had been established in Ibadan, Nigeria, and Cali, Colombia. But the success of the Green Revolution and the growing need for its products called for a more comprehensive effort. The Consultative Group on International Agricultural Research brought together World Bank expertise, private foundations, international organizations, and national foreign aid agencies to undertake worldwide support of efforts to increase food productivity and improve natural resource management. More recently, the optimism that followed these innovations has been muted by the realization that population growth, soil depletion, the costs of irrigation and fertilizer, and the growing concentration of land in the export sector combined to reduce the effects of improved crop technology in poor countries.

Miracle Rice New strains of so-called "miracle rice" made many nations in South and Southeast Asia self-sufficient in food production after decades of worry that population growth would outstrip agricultural productivity. (Victor Englebert)

encourage the movement of goods and capital. In 1957 France, West Germany, Italy, the Netherlands, Belgium, and Luxembourg signed a treaty creating the European Economic Community, also known as the Common Market. By the 1970s the Common Market nations had nearly overtaken the United States in industrial production. The economic alliance expanded after 1970, when Great Britain, Denmark, Greece, Ireland, Spain, Portugal, Finland, Sweden, and Austria joined. The enlarged alliance called itself the **European Community (EC).**

Prosperity brought dramatic changes to the societies of western Europe. Average wages increased, unemployment fell, and social welfare benefits were expanded. Governments increased spending on health care, unemployment benefits, old-age pensions, public housing, and grants to poor families with children. The combination of economic growth and income redistribution raised living standards and fueled demand for consumer goods, leading to the development of a mass consumer society. Automobile ownership, for example, grew approximately ninefold between 1950 and 1970.

The Soviet experience was dramatically different. The rapid growth of a powerful Soviet state after 1917 had challenged traditional Western assumptions about economic development and social policy. From the 1920s the Soviet state relied on bureaucratic agencies and political processes to determine the production, distribution, and price of goods. Housing, medical services, retail shops, factories, the land—even musical compositions and literary works—were viewed as collective property and were therefore regulated and administered by the state.

The economies of the Soviet Union and its eastern European allies were just as devastated at the end of the Second World War as those of western Europe. However, the Soviet command economy had enormous natural resources, a large population, and abundant energy at its disposal. Moreover, Soviet planners had made large investments in technical and scientific education, and the Soviet state had developed heavy industry in the 1930s and during the war years. Finally, Soviet leadership was willing to use forced labor on an enormous scale. For example, Bulgaria's postwar free work force of 361,000 was supplemented by 100,000 slave laborers.[1]

As a result, recovery was rapid at first, creating the structural basis for modernization and growth. Then, as the postwar period progressed, bureaucratic control of the economy grew less responsive and efficient at the same time that industrial might came to be more commonly measured by the production of consumer goods

Cold War Confrontation in 1959 U.S. Vice President Richard M. Nixon and Soviet premier Nikita Khrushchev had a heated exchange of views during Nixon's visit to a Moscow trade fair. Two years earlier, the Soviet Union had launched the world's first space satellite. (Seymour Raskin/Magnum Photos, Inc.)

such as television sets and automobiles, rather than by tons of coal and steel. In the 1970s the gap with the West widened. Soviet industry failed to meet domestic demand for clothing, housing, food, automobiles, and consumer electronics, while Soviet agricultural inefficiency compelled increased reliance on food imports.

The socialist nations of eastern Europe were compelled to follow the Soviet economic model, with some national differences. Poland and Hungary, for example, implemented agricultural collectivization more slowly than did Czechoslovakia. Nevertheless, economic planners throughout the region coordinated industrialization and production plans with the Soviet Union. Significant growth occurred in all the socialist economies, but the inefficiencies and failures that plagued the Soviet economy troubled them as well.

Outside Europe, the United States and the Soviet Union competed in providing loans and grants and supplying arms (at bargain prices) to countries willing to align with them. Thus the relative success or failure of capitalism and communism in Europe and the United States was not necessarily the strongest consideration in other parts of the world when the time came to construct new national economies.

West Versus East in Europe and Korea

For Germany, Austria, and Japan, peace brought foreign military occupation and new governments that were initially controlled by the occupiers. When relations with the Western powers cooled at the end of the war, the Soviet Union sought to prevent the reappearance of hostile regimes on its borders. Initially, the Soviet Union seemed willing to accept governments in neighboring states that included a mix of parties as long as they were not hostile to local communist groups or to the Soviets. The nations of central and eastern Europe were deeply split by the legacies of the war, and many were willing to embrace the communists as a hedge against those who had supported fascism or cooperated with the Germans. As relations between the Soviets and the West worsened in the late 1940s, local communists, their strength augmented by Soviet military occupation, gained victories across eastern Europe. Western leaders saw the rapid emergence of communist regimes in Poland, Czechoslovakia, Hungary, Bulgaria, Romania, Yugoslavia, and Albania as a threat.

It took two years for the United States to shift from viewing the Soviet Union as an ally against Germany to seeing it as a worldwide enemy. In the waning days of World War II the United States had seemed amenable to the Soviet desire for free access to the Bosporus and Dardanelles straits that, under Turkish control, restricted naval deployments from the Black Sea to the Mediterranean. But in July 1947 the **Truman Doctrine** offered military aid to help both Turkey and Greece resist Soviet military pressure and subversion, and in 1951 both were admitted to NATO. NATO's Soviet counterpart, the **Warsaw Pact,** emerged in 1955 in response to the Western powers' decision to allow West Germany to rearm within limits set by NATO (see Map 32.1).

The much-feared and long-prepared-for third great war in Europe did not occur. The Soviet Union tested Western resolve in 1948–1949 by blockading the British, French, and American zones in Berlin (located in Soviet-controlled East Germany). Airlifts of food and fuel defeated the blockade. In 1961 the East German government accentuated Germany's political division by building the Berlin Wall, a structure designed primarily to prevent its citizens from fleeing to the noncommunist western part of the city. In turn, the West tested the East by encouraging a rift between the Soviet Union and Yugoslavia. Western aid and encouragement resulted in Yugoslavia's signing a defensive treaty with Greece and Turkey (but not with NATO) and deciding against joining the Warsaw Pact.

Soviet power set clear limits on how far any eastern European country might stray from Soviet domination. In 1956 Soviet troops crushed an armed anti-Soviet revolt in Hungary. Then in 1968 Soviet troops repressed a peaceful reform effort in Czechoslovakia. The West, a passive onlooker, could only acknowledge that the Soviet Union had the right to intervene in the domestic affairs of any Soviet-bloc nation whenever it wished.

A more explosive crisis erupted in Korea, where the Second World War had left Soviet troops in control north of the thirty-eighth parallel and American troops in control to the south. When no agreement could be reached on holding countrywide elections, communist North Korea and noncommunist South Korea became independent states in 1948. Two years later North Korea invaded South Korea. The United Nations Security Council, in the absence of the Soviet delegation, voted to condemn the invasion and called on members of the United Nations to come to the defense of South Korea. The ensuing **Korean War** lasted until 1953. The United States was the primary ally of South Korea. The People's Republic of China supported North Korea.

The conflict in Korea remained limited to the Korean peninsula because the United States feared that launching attacks into China might prompt China's ally, the Soviet Union, to retaliate, beginning the dreaded third world war. Americans and South Koreans advanced from a toehold in the south to the North Korean–Chinese bor-

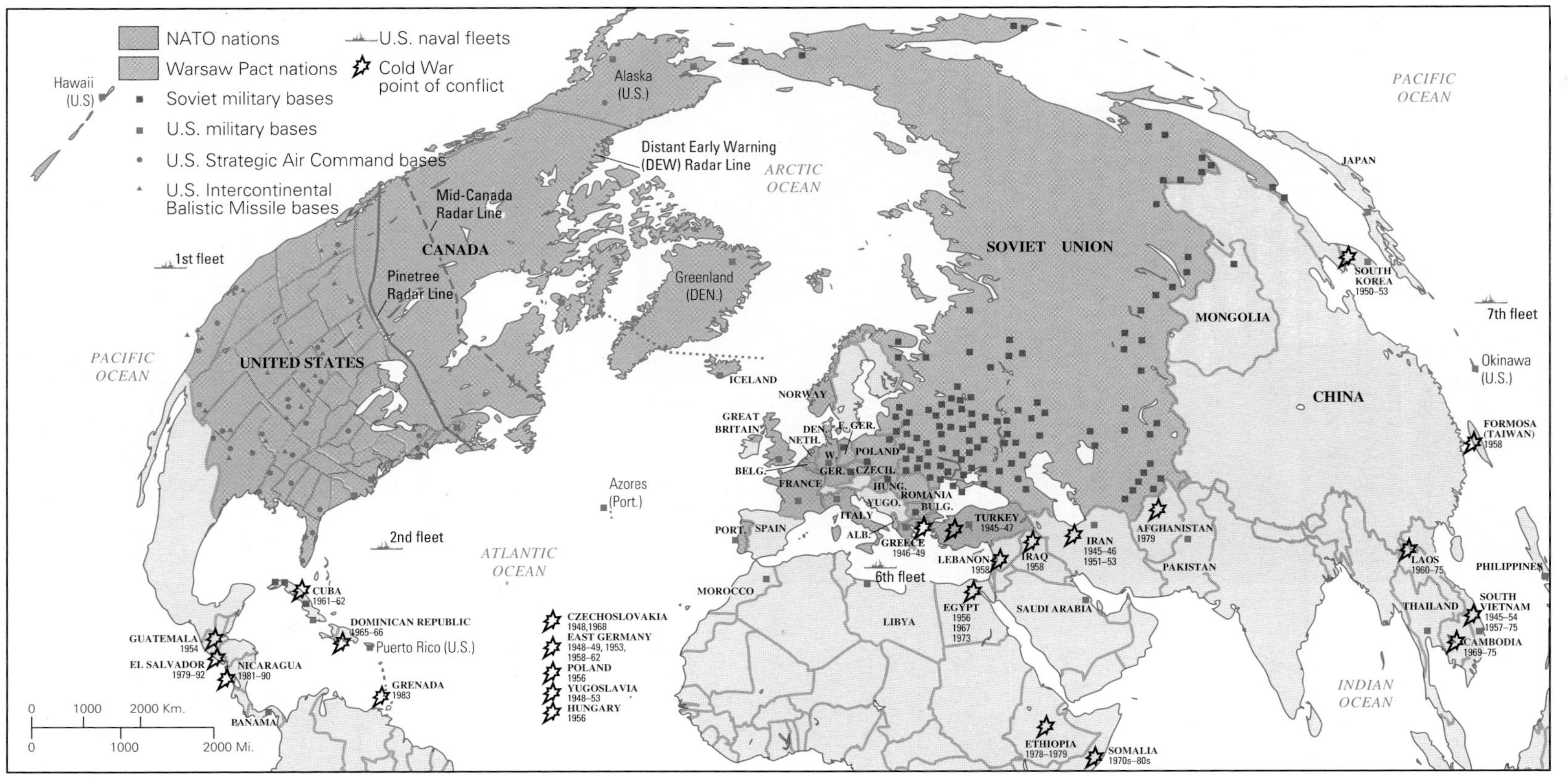

Map 32.1 Cold War Confrontation A polar projection is shown on this map because Soviet and U.S. strategists planned to attack one another by missile in the polar region; hence the Canadian-American radar lines. Military installations along the southern border of the Soviet Union were directed primarily at China.

der. China sent troops across the border, and the North Koreans and Chinese pushed the Americans and South Koreans back. The fighting then settled into a static war in the mountains along the thirty-eighth parallel. The two sides eventually agreed to a truce along that line; but the cease-fire lines remained fortified, and no peace treaty was concluded. The possibility of renewed warfare between the two Koreas continued well past the end of the Cold War and remains a disturbing possibility today.

Japan benefited from the Korean War in an unexpected way. Massive purchases of supplies by the United States and spending by American servicemen on leave stimulated the Japanese economy similar to the way the Marshall Plan had stimulated Europe's economy.

United States Defeat in Vietnam

The most important postwar communist movement arose in the part of Southeast Asia known as French Indochina. Ho Chi Minh° (1890–1969), who had spent several years in France during World War I, played the pivotal role. Ho had helped form the Communist Party in France. In 1930, after training in Moscow, he returned to Vietnam to found the Indochina Communist Party. He and his supporters took refuge in China during World War II.

At war's end the new French government was determined to keep its prewar colonial possessions. Ho Chi Minh's nationalist coalition, then called the Viet Minh, fought the French with help from the People's Republic of China. After a brutal struggle, the French stronghold of Dienbienphu° fell in 1954, marking the end of France's colonial enterprise. Ho's Viet Minh government took over in the north, and a noncommunist nationalist government ruled in the south.

The United States had given some support to the French. President Dwight D. Eisenhower (1953–1961) and his foreign policy advisers debated long and hard about whether to aid France militarily during the battle for Dienbienphu. They decided not to prop up French colonial rule in Vietnam, perceiving that the European colonial empires were doomed. After winning independence, communist North Vietnam eventually supported a communist guerrilla movement—the Viet Cong—against the noncommunist government of South Vietnam. At issue was the ideological and economic orientation of an independent Vietnam.

President John F. Kennedy (served 1961–1963) and his advisers decided to support the South Vietnamese government of President Ngo Dinh Diem°. While they knew that the Diem government was corrupt and unpopular, they feared that a communist victory would encourage communist movements throughout Southeast Asia and alter the Cold War balance of power. Kennedy steadily increased the number of American military advisers from 685 to almost 16,000, while secretly encouraging the overthrow of Diem. The execution of Diem following his overthrow instigated a public debate as well as a critical reevaluation within the administration.

The Vietnamese People at War American and South Vietnamese troops burned many villages to deprive the enemy of civilian refuges. This policy undermined support for the South Vietnamese government in the countryside. (Dana Stone/stockphoto.com)

Ho Chi Minh (hoe chee min)
Dienbienphu (dee-yen-bee-yen-FOO)

Diem (dee-YEM)

Lyndon Johnson, who became president (served 1963–1969) after Kennedy was assassinated, obtained support from Congress for unlimited expansion of U.S. military deployment after an apparent North Vietnamese attack on two U.S. destroyers in the Gulf of Tonkin. But in South Vietnam there was little support for the nation's new rulers who soon revealed themselves to be just as corrupt and unpopular as the earlier Diem government. Instead, many South Vietnamese were drawn to the heroic nationalist image of North Vietnam's leader Ho Chi Minh who had led the struggles against the Japanese and French. By the end of 1966, 365,000 U.S. troops were engaged in the **Vietnam War,** but they were unable to achieve a comprehensive victory. The Viet Cong guerrillas and their North Vietnamese allies gained significant military credibility in the massive 1968 Tet Offensive. With a battlefield victory unlikely, the antiwar movement in the United States grew and Lyndon Johnson decided to not seek reelection.

In 1973 a treaty between North Vietnam and the United States ended U.S. involvement in the war and promised future elections. Two years later, in violation of the treaty, Viet Cong and North Vietnamese troops overran the South Vietnamese army and captured the southern capital of Saigon, renaming it Ho Chi Minh City. The two parts of Vietnam were reunited in a single state ruled from the north. Over a million Vietnamese and 58,000 Americans had been killed in the war.

President Johnson had begun his administration committed to a broad program of social reforms and civil rights initiatives, called the Great Society. The civil rights campaign in the South led by Martin Luther King, Jr., and others led to a broad examination of issues of social justice and spawned numerous organizations that challenged the status quo. As the commitment of U.S. troops grew, a massive antiwar movement applied the tactics of the civil rights movement to government military policies. Many members of the military and their civilian supporters, on the other hand, were angered by limitations placed on the conduct of operations, despite fears that a wider war would lead to Chinese involvement and possible nuclear confrontation. The rising tide of antiwar rallies, now international in character, and growing economic problems undermined support for Johnson, who declined to seek reelection. By the mid 1970s both antiwar and pro-war groups had drawn lessons from Vietnam, the former seeing any use of military force overseas as dangerous and unnecessarily destructive, and the latter believing that overwhelming force was required in warfare.

The Race for Nuclear Supremacy

Fear of nuclear warfare affected strategic decisions in the Korean and Vietnam Wars. It also affected all other aspects of Cold War confrontation. The devastation of Hiroshima and Nagasaki by atomic weapons (see Chapter 30) had ushered in a new era. Nuclear weapons fed into a logic of total war that was already reaching a peak in Nazi genocide and terror bombing and in massive Allied air raids on large cities. After the Soviet Union exploded its first nuclear device in 1949, fears of a worldwide holocaust grew. Fears increased when the United States exploded a far more powerful weapon, the hydrogen bomb, in 1952 and the Soviet Union followed suit less than a year later. The possibility of the theft of nuclear secrets by Soviet spies fostered paranoia in the United States, and the conviction that the nuclear superpowers were willing to use their terrible weapons if their vital interests were threatened spread despair around the world.

In 1954 President Eisenhower warned Soviet leaders against attacking western Europe. In response to such an attack, he said, the United States would reduce the Soviet Union to "a smoking, radiating ruin at the end of two hours." A few years later the Soviet leader Nikita Khrushchev° made an equally stark promise: "We will bury you." He was referring to economic competition, but Americans interpreted the statement to mean literal burial. Rhetoric aside, both men—and their successors—had the capacity to deliver on their threats, and everyone in the world knew that all-out war with nuclear weapons would produce the greatest global devastation in human history.

Everyone's worst fears seemed about to be realized in 1962 when the Soviet Union deployed nuclear missiles in Cuba. Khrushchev and Cuban president Fidel Castro were reacting to U.S. efforts to overthrow the government of Cuba. When the missiles were discovered, the United States prepared for an invasion of Cuba. Confronted by unyielding diplomatic pressure and military threats, Khrushchev pulled the missiles from Cuba. Subsequently, the United States removed its missiles from Turkey. As frightening as the **Cuban missile crisis** was, the fact that the superpower leaders accepted tactical defeat rather than launch an attack gave reason for hope that nuclear weapons might be contained.

The number, means of delivery, and destructive force of nuclear weapons increased enormously. The bomb dropped on Hiroshima, equal in strength to 12,500 tons of TNT, had destroyed an entire city. By the 1960s explosive yields were measured in megatons (millions of

Khrushchev (KROOSH-chef)

tons) of TNT, and a single missile could contain several weapons of this scale, each of which could be targeted to a different site. When the missiles were placed on submarines, a major component of U.S. nuclear forces, defending against them seemed impossible.

Arms limitation also progressed. In 1963 Great Britain, the United States, and the Soviet Union agreed to ban the testing of nuclear weapons in the atmosphere, in space, and underwater, thus reducing the environmental danger of radioactive fallout. In 1968 the United States and the Soviet Union together proposed a world treaty against further proliferation of nuclear weapons. The Nuclear Non-Proliferation Treaty (NPT) was signed by 137 countries later that year. Not until 1972, however, did the two superpowers truly recognize the futility of squandering their wealth on ever-larger missile forces. They began the arduous and extremely slow process of negotiating weapons limits, a process made even slower by the vested interests of military officers and arms industries in each country—what President Eisenhower had called the "military-industrial complex."

In Europe, the Soviet-American arms race outran the economic ability of atomic powers France and Britain to keep pace. Instead, the European states sought to relax tensions. Between 1972 and 1975 the Conference on Security and Cooperation in Europe (CSCE) brought delegates from thirty-seven European states, the United States, and Canada to Helsinki. The goal of the Soviet Union was European acceptance of the political boundaries of the Warsaw Pact nations. The Helsinki Final Act—commonly known as the **Helsinki Accords**—affirmed that no boundaries should be changed by military force. It also contained formal (but nonbinding) declarations calling for economic, social, and governmental contacts across the iron curtain, and for cooperation in humanitarian fields, a provision that paved the way for dialogue about human rights.

Space exploration was another offshoot of the nuclear arms race. The contest to build larger and more accurate missiles prompted the superpowers to prove their skills in rocketry by launching space satellites. The Soviet Union placed a small Sputnik satellite into orbit around the earth in October 1957. The United States responded with its own satellite three months later. The space race was on, a contest in which accomplishments in space were understood to signify equivalent achievements in the military sphere. Sputnik administered a deep shock to American pride and confidence, but in 1969 two Americans, Neil A. Armstrong and Edwin E. ("Buzz") Aldrin, became the first humans to walk on the moon.

Despite rhetorical Cold War saber-rattling by Soviet and American leaders, the threat of nuclear war forced a measure of restraint on the superpower adversaries. Because fighting each other directly would have risked escalation to the level of nuclear exchange, they carefully avoided crises that might provoke such confrontations. Even when arming third parties to do their fighting by proxy, they set limits on how far such fighting could go. Some of these proxy combatants, however, understood the limitations of the superpowers well enough to manipulate them for their own purposes.

DECOLONIZATION AND NATION BUILDING

After World War I Germany, Austria-Hungary, and the Ottoman Empire lost their empires, and many foreign colonies and dependencies were transferred to the victors, especially to Great Britain and France. Following World War II the victors lost nearly all their imperial possessions. As a result of independence movements in Africa, Asia, and the Americas and growing anti-imperialist movements at home, most of the colonies of Great Britain, France, the Netherlands, Belgium, and the United States were transformed into independent states (see Map 32.2).

Circumstances differed profoundly from place to place. In some Asian countries, where colonial rule was of long standing, newly independent states found themselves in possession of viable industries, communications networks, and education systems. In other countries, notably in Africa, decolonized nations faced dire economic problems and internal disunity that resulted from language and ethnic differences. Political independence had been achieved by most of Latin America in the nineteenth century (see Chapter 22). Following World War II mass political movements in this region focused on the related issue of economic sovereignty—freedom from growing American economic domination.

Despite their differences, a sense of kinship arose among the new and old nations of Latin America, Africa, and Asia. All shared feelings of excitement and rebirth. As the North Americans, Europeans, and Chinese settled into the exhausting deadlock of the Cold War, visions of independence and national growth captivated the rest of the world.

New Nations in South and Southeast Asia

After partition in 1947 the independent states of India and Pakistan were strikingly dissimilar. Muslim Pakistan defined itself according to religion and quickly fell under the control of military leaders. India, a secular republic led by Prime Minister

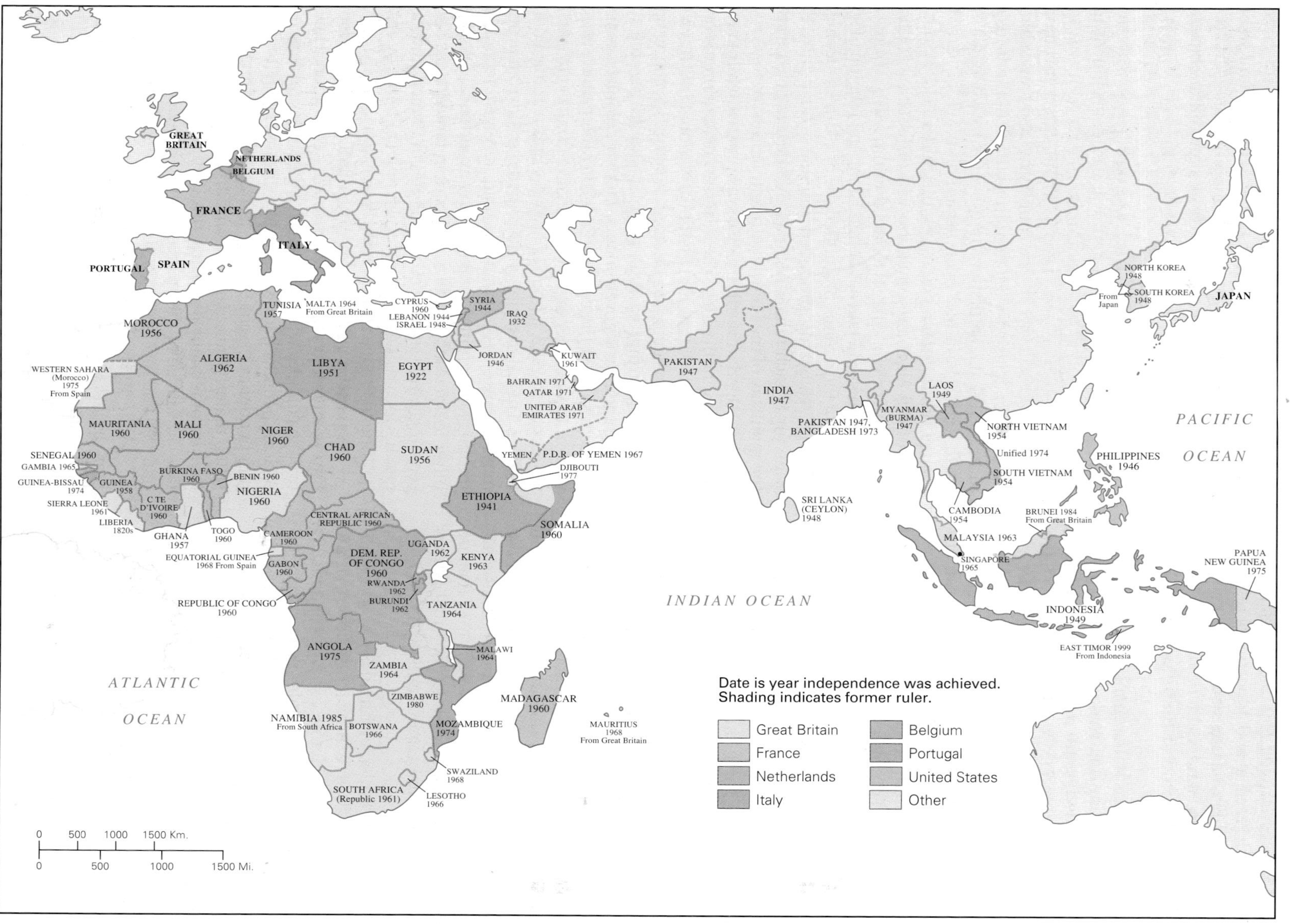

Map 32.2 Decolonization, 1947–1990 Notice that independence came a decade or so earlier in South and Southeast Asia than in Africa. Numerous countries that gained independence after World War II in the Caribbean, in South and Central America, and in the Pacific are not shown.

Jawaharlal Nehru, was much larger and inherited most of the considerable industrial and educational resources the British had developed, along with the larger share of trained civil servants and military officers. Ninety percent of its population was Hindu, most of the rest Muslim.

Adding to the tensions of independence (see Chapter 31) was the decision by the Hindu ruler of the northwestern state known as Jammu and Kashmir, without consulting his overwhelmingly Muslim subjects, to join India. War between India and Pakistan over Kashmir broke out in 1947 and ended with an uneasy truce, only to resume briefly in 1965. Though Kashmir remained a flash point of patriotic feeling, the two countries managed to avoid further warfare.

Despite recurrent predictions that multilingual India might break up into a number of linguistically homogeneous states, most Indians recognized that unity benefited everyone; and the country pursued a generally democratic and socialist line of development. Pakistan, in contrast, did break up. In 1971 its Bengali-speaking eastern section seceded to become the independent country of Bangladesh. Their shared political heritage notwithstanding, India, Pakistan, and Bangladesh grew steadily apart, following markedly different economic, political, religious, and social paths.

As the Japanese had supported anti-British Indian nationalists, so they encouraged the dreams of some anticolonialists in the countries they had occupied in Southeast Asia. Other nationalists, particularly those belonging to communist groups, saw the Japanese as an imperialist enemy; and the harsh character of Japanese occupation eventually alienated most people in the occupied countries. Nevertheless, the defeats the Japanese inflicted on British, French, and Dutch colonial armies set an example of an Asian people standing up to European colonizers.

In the Dutch East Indies, Achmad Sukarno (1901–1970) cooperated with the Japanese in the hope that the Dutch, who had dominated the region economically since the seventeenth century, would never return. After military confrontation, Dutch withdrawal was finally negotiated in 1949, and Sukarno became the dictator of the resource-rich but underdeveloped island nation. He ruled until 1965, when a military coup ousted him andbrutally eliminated Indonesia's powerful communist party.

Elsewhere in the region, nationalist movements won independence as well. Britain granted independence to Burma (now Myanmar°) in 1948 and established the Malay Federation the same year. Singapore, once a member of the federation, became an independent city-state in 1965. In 1946 the United States kept its promise of postwar independence for the Philippine Islands but retained close economic ties and leases on military bases.

The Struggle for Independence in Africa

The postwar French government was as determined to hold onto Algeria as it was to keep Vietnam. Since invading the country in 1830 France had followed policies very different from those of the British in India. French settlement had been strongly encouraged, and Algeria had been declared an actual part of France rather than a colony. By the mid-1950s, 10 percent of the Algerian population was of French or other European origin. The Algerian economy was strongly oriented toward France. Though Islam, the religion of 90 percent of the people, prohibited the drinking of alcohol, Algerian vineyards produced immense quantities of wine for French tables. Algerian oil and gas fields were the mainstay of the French petroleum industry.

The Algerian revolt in 1954 was pursued with great brutality by both sides. The Algerian revolutionary organization, the Front de Libération National (FLN), was supported by Egypt and other Arab countries acting on the principle that all Arab peoples should be able to choose their own governments. French colonists, however, considered the country rightfully theirs and swore to fight to the bitter end. When Algeria finally won independence in 1962, a flood of angry colonists returned to France. Their departure undermined the Algerian economy because very few Arabs had received technical training or acquired management experience. Despite bitter feelings left by the war, Algeria retained close and seemingly indissoluble economic ties to France, and Algerians increasingly fled unemployment at home by emigrating to France and taking low-level jobs.

In most of sub-Saharan Africa independence from European rule was achieved through negotiation. However, in colonies with significant white settler minorities, African peoples had to resort to armed struggle to gain independence, since settler populations strongly resisted majority rule. Throughout Africa, nationalists had to overcome many obstacles, but they were also able to take advantage of the consequential changes that colonial rule had brought.

In the 1950s and 1960s economic growth and growing support for liberation overcame worries about economic and environmental problems that would develop after independence. In the cities that hosted colonial authorities, educated African nationalists used the languages introduced by colonial governments to help

Myanmar (myahn-MAH)

build multiethnic coalitions within the artificial colonial boundaries. Missionary and colonial schools had produced few high school and college graduates, but graduates of these colonial school systems were often frustrated by obstacles to their advancement and joined the independence movements. Africans who had obtained advanced education in Europe and the United States also played an important role in the struggle for independence as did African veterans of allied armies during World War II.

The networks of roads and railroads built to facilitate colonial exports were used by African truckers and railroad workers to promote Africa's new political consciousness and spread anticolonial ideas. Improvements in medical care and public health had led to rapid population growth. The region's young population enthusiastically embraced the goal of self-rule.

The young politicians who led the nationalist movements devoted their lives to ridding their homelands of foreign occupation. An example is Kwame Nkrumah° (1909–1972), who in 1957 became prime minister of Ghana (formerly the Gold Coast), the first British colony in West Africa to achieve independence. After graduating from a Catholic mission school and a government teacher-training college, Nkrumah spent a decade studying philosophy and theology in the United States, where he absorbed ideas about black pride and independence then being propounded by W. E. B. Du Bois and Marcus Garvey.

During a brief stay in Britain, Nkrumah joined Kenyan nationalist Jomo Kenyatta, a Ph.D. in anthropology, to found an organization devoted to African freedom. In 1947 Nkrumah returned to the Gold Coast to work for independence. The time was right. There was no longer strong public support in Britain for colonialism and, as a result, Britain's political leadership was not enthusiastic about investing resources to hold restive colonies. After Nkrumah's party won a decisive election victory in 1951, the Gold Coast governor released him from prison (where he had been held on "sedition" charges) and appointed him prime minister. Full independence came in 1957. Nkrumah turned out to be more effective as an international spokesman for colonized peoples than as an administrator, and in 1966 a group of army officers ousted him.

After Ghana won independence, Britain quickly granted independence to its other West African colonies, including large and populous Nigeria in 1960. However, white settler opposition in some British colonies in eastern and southern Africa delayed this process. In Kenya a small but influential group of wealthy coffee planters seized upon a protest movement among the Kikuyu people as proof that Africans were unready for self-government. The settlers called the movement "Mau Mau," a made-up name meant to evoke primitive savagery. When violence between settlers and Mau Mau fighters escalated after 1952, British troops hunted down the Mau Mau leaders and resettled the Kikuyu° in fortified villages to prevent contact with rebel bands. The British also declared a state of emergency, banned all African political protest, and imprisoned Kenyatta and many other nationalists for eight years on charges of being Mau Mau leaders. Released in 1961, Kenyatta negotiated with the British to write a constitution for an independent Kenya. In 1964 he was elected the first president of the Republic of Kenya. He proved to be an effective, though autocratic, ruler. Kenya benefited from greater stability and prosperity than Ghana.

African Leaders Meet for Conference Prime Minister Jomo Kenyatta of Kenya (right) waves to the crowd before entering the East African Heads of Government Conference held in Nairobi in 1964. With him are President Julius Nyerere (far left) of Tanzania and Dr. Milton Obote (center), president of Uganda. (Bettmann/Corbis)

Kwame Nkrumah (KWAH-mee nn-KROO-muh)

Kikuyu (kih-KOO-you)

African leaders in the sub-Saharan French colonies were more reluctant than their counterparts in British colonies to call for full independence. They visualized political change in terms of promises made in 1944 by the Free French movement of General Charles de Gaulle at a conference in Brazzaville, in French Equatorial Africa. Acknowledging the value of his African territorial base, his many African troops, and the food supplied by African farmers, de Gaulle had promised more democratic government and broader suffrage, though not representation in the French National Assembly. He also had promised to abolish forced labor and imprisonment of Africans without charge; to expand French education down to the village level; to improve health services; and to open more administrative positions, though not the top ones, to Africans. The word *independence* was never mentioned at Brazzaville, but the politics of postwar colonial self-government led in that direction.

Most new African politicians who sought election in the colonies of French West Africa were civil servants. Because of the French policy of job rotation, they had typically served in a number of different colonies and thus had a broad outlook. They realized that some colonies—such as Ivory Coast, with coffee and cacao exports, fishing, and hardwood forests—had good economic prospects and others, such as landlocked, desert Niger, did not. Furthermore, they recognized the importance of French public investment in the region—a billion dollars between 1947 and 1956—and their own dependence on civil service salaries, which in places totaled 60 percent of government expenditures. The Malagasy politician Philibert Tsirinana° said at a press conference in 1958: "When I let my heart talk, I am a partisan of total and immediate independence [for Madagascar]; when I make my reason speak, I realize that it is impossible."

When Charles de Gaulle returned to power in France in 1958, at the height of the Algerian war, he warned that a rush to independence would have costs, saying: "One cannot conceive of both an independent territory and a France which continues to aid it." Ultimately, African patriotism prevailed in all of France's West African and Equatorial African colonies. Guinea, under the dynamic leadership of Sékou Touré°, gained full independence in 1958 and the rest in 1960.

Independence in the Belgian Congo was chaotic and violent. Contending political and ethnic groups found external allies; some were aided by Cuba and the Soviet Union, others by the West or by business groups tied to the rich mines. Civil war, the introduction of foreign mercenaries, and the rhetoric of Cold War confrontation roiled the waters and led to heavy loss of life as well as property destruction. In 1965 Mobuto Sese Seko seized the reins in a military coup that included the assassination of Patrice Lumumba, the first prime minister, and held on in one of the region's most corrupt governments until driven from power in 1997.

Decolonization in southern Africa was delayed by the opposition of European settlers, some with deep roots in Africa but many others who were new arrivals after 1945. While the settler minority tried to defend white supremacy, African-led liberation movements were committed to the creation of nonracial societies and majority rule. In the 1960s Africans began guerrilla movements against Portuguese rule in Angola and Mozambique, eventually prompting the Portuguese army to overthrow the undemocratic government of Portugal in 1974. The new Portuguese government granted independence to Angola and Mozambique the following year. In 1980, after a ten-year fight, European settlers in the British colony of Southern Rhodesia accepted African majority rule. The new government changed the country's name, which had honored the memory of the British imperialist Cecil Rhodes, to Zimbabwe, the name of a great stone city built by Africans long before the arrival of European settlers. This left only South Africa and neighboring Namibia in the hands of ruling European minorities.

A succession of South African governments had constructed a state and society based on a policy of racial separation, or *apartheid*°, after World War II. Fourteen percent of the population was descended from Dutch and English settlers. By law, whites controlled the most productive tracts of land, the industrial, mining, and commercial enterprises, and the government. Other laws imposed segregated housing, schools, and jobs on South Asians and people of mixed parentage classified as "nonwhite." The 74 percent of the population made up of indigenous Africans were subjected to far stricter limitations on place of residence, right to travel, and access to jobs and public facilities. African "homelands," somewhat similar to Amerindian reservations in the United States, were created in parts of the country, often far from the more dynamic and prosperous urban and industrial areas. Overcrowded and lacking investment, these restricted "homelands" were very poor and squalid, with few services and fewer opportunities.

The African National Congress (ANC), formed in 1912, and other organizations led the opposition to apartheid (see Diversity and Dominance: Race and the Struggle for Justice in South Africa). After police fired on demonstrators in the African town of Sharpeville in 1960 and banned all peaceful political protest by Africans, an

---

Tsirinana (tsee-REE-nah-nah) **Sékou Touré** (SAY-koo too-RAY)

apartheid (uh-PAHRT-ate)

African lawyer named Nelson Mandela (b. 1918) organized guerrilla resistance by the ANC. Mandela was sentenced to life in prison in 1964. The ANC operated from outside the country. The armed struggle against apartheid continued until 1990 (see Chapter 34).

The Quest for Economic Freedom in Latin America

Latin American independence from European rule was achieved more than a hundred years earlier, but European and, by the end of the nineteenth century, American economic domination continued (see Chapters 28 and 31). Chile's copper, Cuba's sugar, Colombia's coffee, and Guatemala's bananas were largely controlled from abroad. The communications networks of several countries were in the hands of ITT (International Telephone and Telegraph Company), a U.S. corporation. From the 1930s, however, support for economic nationalism grew. During the 1930s and 1940s populist political leaders had experimented with programs that would constrain foreign investors or, alternatively, promote local efforts to industrialize (see discussion of Getulio Vargas and Juan Perón in Chapter 31).

In Mexico the revolutionary constitution of 1917 had begun an era of economic nationalism that culminated in the expropriation of foreign oil interests in 1938. Political stability had been achieved under the Institutional Revolutionary Party, or PRI (the abbreviation of its name in Spanish), which controlled the government until the 1990s. Stability allowed Mexico to experience significant economic expansion during the war years, but a yawning gulf between rich and poor, urban and rural, persisted. Although the government dominated important industries like petroleum and restricted foreign investment, rapid population growth, uncontrolled migration to Mexico City and other urban areas, and political corruption challenged efforts to lift the nation's poor. Economic power was concentrated at the top of society, with two thousand elite families benefiting disproportionally from the three hundred foreign and eight hundred Mexican companies that dominated the country. At the other end of the economic scale were the peasants, the 14 percent of the population classified as Indian, and the urban poor.

While Mexico's problems derived only partly from the effects of foreign influence, Guatemala's situation was more representative. Jacobo Arbenz Guzmán, elected in 1951, was typical of Latin American leaders, including Perón of Argentina and Vargas of Brazil (see Chapter 31), who tried to confront powerful foreign interests. An American corporation, the United Fruit Company, was Guatemala's largest landowner; it also controlled much of the nation's infrastructure, including port facilities and railroads. To suppress banana production and keep prices high, United Fruit kept much of its Guatemalan lands fallow. Arbenz attempted land reform, which would have transferred these fallow lands to the nation's rural poor. The threatened expropriation angered the United Fruit Company. Simultaneously, Arbenz tried to reduce U.S. political influence, raising fears in Washington that he sought closer ties to the Soviet Union. Reacting to the land reform efforts and to reports that Arbenz was becoming friendly to communism, the U.S. Central Intelligence Agency (CIA), in one of its first major overseas operations, sponsored a takeover by the Guatemalan military in 1954. CIA intervention removed Arbenz, but it also condemned Guatemala to decades of governmental instability and growing violence between leftist and rightist elements in society.

In Cuba economic domination by the United States prior to 1960 was overwhelming. U.S. companies effectively controlled sugar production, the nation's most important industry, as well as banking, transportation, tourism, and public utilities. The United States was the most important market for Cuba's exports and the most important source of Cuba's imports. The needs of the U.S. economy largely determined the ebb and flow of Cuban foreign trade. A 1934 treaty had granted preferential treatment (prices higher than world market prices) to Cuban sugar in the American market in return for access to the Cuban market by American manufacturers. Since U.S. companies dominated the sugar business, this was actually a kind of tax imposed on American consumers for the benefit of American corporations. By 1956 sugar accounted for 80 percent of Cuba's exports and 25 percent of Cuba's national income. But demand in the United States dictated keeping only 39 percent of the land owned by the sugar companies in production, while Cuba experienced chronic underemployment. Similarly, immense deposits of nickel in Cuba went untapped because the U.S. government, which owned them, considered them to be a reserve.

Profits went north to the United States or to a small class of wealthy Cubans, many of them, like the owners of the Bacardi rum company, of foreign origin. Between 1951 and 1958 Cuba's economy grew at 1.4 percent per year, less than the rate of population increase. Cuba's government was notoriously corrupt and subservient to the wishes of American interests. In 1953 Fulgencio Batista°, a former military leader and president, illegally returned to power in a coup. Cuban aversion to

---

Fulgencio Batista (ful-HEHN-see-oh bah-TEES-tah)

DIVERSITY AND DOMINANCE

RACE AND THE STRUGGLE FOR JUSTICE IN SOUTH AFRICA

One of South Africa's martyrs in the struggle against apartheid was Steve Biko (1946–1977), a thinker and activist especially concerned with building pride among Africans and asserting the importance of African cultures. Biko was one of the founders of the Black Consciousness Movement, focusing on the ways in which white settlers had stripped Africans of their freedom. As a result of his activism, he was restricted to his home town in 1973. Between 1975 and 1977 he was arrested and interrogated four times by the police. After his arrest in August 1977 he was severely beaten while in custody. He died days later without having received medical care. His death caused worldwide outrage.

But these are not the people we are concerned with [those who support apartheid]. We are concerned with that curious bunch of nonconformists who explain their participation in negative terms: that bunch of do-gooders that goes under all sorts of names—liberals, leftists etc. These are the people who argue that they are not responsible for white racism and the country's "inhumanity to the black man." These are the people who claim that they too feel the oppression just as acutely as the blacks and therefore should be jointly involved in the black man's struggle for a place under the sun. In short, these are the people who say that they have black souls wrapped up in white skins.

The role of the white liberal in the black man's history in South Africa is a curious one. Very few black organisations were not under white direction. True to their image, the white liberals always knew what was good for the blacks and told them so. The wonder of it all is that the black people have believed in them for so long. It was only at the end of the 50s that the blacks started demanding to be their own guardians.

Nowhere is the arrogance of the liberal ideology demonstrated so well as in their insistence that the problems of the country can only be solved by a bilateral approach involving both black and white. This has, by and large, come to be taken in all seriousness as the modus operandi in South Africa by all those who claim they would like a change in the status quo. Hence the multiracial political organisations and parties and the "nonracial" student organisations, all of which insist on integration not only as an end goal but also as a means.

The integration they talk about is first of all artificial in that it is a response to conscious manoeuvre rather than to the dictates of the inner soul. In other words the people forming the integrated complex have been extracted from various segregated societies with their in built complexes of superiority and inferiority and these continue to manifest themselves even in the "nonracial" setup of the integrated complex. As a result the integration so achieved is a one-way course, with the whites doing all the talking and the blacks the listening. Let me hasten to say that I am not claiming that segregation is necessarily the natural order; however, given the facts of the situation where a group experiences privilege at the expense of others, then it becomes obvious that a hastily arranged integration cannot be the solution to the problem. It is rather like expecting the slave to work together with the slave-master's son to remove all the conditions leading to the former's enslavement.

Secondly, this type of integration as a means is almost always unproductive. The participants waste lots of time in an internal sort of mudslinging designed to prove that A is more of a liberal than B. In other words the lack of common ground for solid identification is all the time manifested in internal strifes [sic] inside the group.

It will not sound anachronistic to anybody genuinely interested in real integration to learn that blacks are asserting themselves in a society where they are being treated as perpetual under-16s. One does not need to plan for or actively encourage real integration. Once the various groups within a given community have asserted themselves to the point that mutual respect has to be shown then you have the ingredients for a true and meaningful integration. At the heart of true integration is the provision for each man, each group to rise and attain the envisioned self. Each group must be able to attain its style of existence without encroaching on or being thwarted by another. Out of this mutual respect for each other and complete freedom of self-determination there will obviously arise a genuine fusion of the life-styles of the various groups. This is true integration.

From this it becomes clear that as long as blacks are suffering from [an] inferiority complex—a result of 300 years of deliberate oppression, denigration and derision—they will be useless as co-architects of a normal society where man is nothing else but man for his own sake. Hence what is necessary as a prelude to anything else that may come is a very strong grass-roots build-up of black consciousness such that blacks can learn to assert themselves and stake their rightful claim.

Thus in adopting the line of a nonracial approach, the liberals are playing their old game. They are claiming a "monopoly on intelligence and moral judgement" and setting the pattern and pace for the realisation of the black man's aspirations. They want to remain in good books with both the black and white worlds. They want to shy away from all forms of "extremisms," condemning "white supremacy" as being just as bad as "Black Power!" They vacillate between the two worlds, verbalising all the complaints of the blacks beautifully while skilfully extracting what suits them from the exclusive pool of white privileges. But ask them for a moment to give a concrete meaningful programme that they intend adopting, then you will see on whose side they really are. Their protests are directed at and appeal to white conscience, everything they do is directed at finally convincing the white electorate that the black man is also a man and that at some future date he should be given a place at the white man's table.

In the following selection Anglican bishop Desmond Tutu (b. 1931) expressed his personal anguish at the death of Steve Biko. He summarized Biko's contributions to the struggle for justice in South Africa. Tutu won the Noble Peace Prize in 1984 and was named archbishop in 1988. From 1995 to 1998 he chaired the Truth and Reconciliation Commission, which investigated atrocities in South Africa during the years of apartheid. He stated that his objective was to create "a democratic and just society without racial divisions."

When we heard the news "Steve Biko is dead" we were struck numb with disbelief. No, it can't be true! No, it must be a horrible nightmare, and we will awake and find that really it is different—that Steve is alive even if it be in detention. But no, dear friends, he is dead and we are still numb with grief, and groan with anguish "Oh God, where are you? Oh God, do you really care—how can you let this happen to us?"

It all seems such a senseless waste of a wonderfully gifted person, struck down in the bloom of youth, a youthful bloom that some wanted to see blighted. What can be the purpose of such wanton destruction? God, do you really love us? What must we do which we have not done, what must we say which we have not said a thousand times over, oh, for so many years—that all we want is what belongs to all God's children, what belongs as an inalienable right—a place in the sun in our own beloved mother country. Oh God, how long can we go on? How long can we go on appealing for a more just ordering of society where we all, black and white together, count not because of some accident of birth or a biological irrelevance—where all of us black and white count because we are human persons, human persons created in your own image.

God called Steve Biko to be his servant in South Africa—to speak up on behalf of God, declaring what the will of this God must be in a situation such as ours, a situation of evil, injustice, oppression and exploitation. God called him to be the founder father of the Black Consciousness Movement against which we have had tirades and fulminations. It is a movement by which God, through Steve, sought to awaken in the Black person a sense of his intrinsic value and worth as a child of God, not needing to apologise for his existential condition as a black person, calling on blacks to glorify and praise God that he had created them black. Steve, with his brilliant mind that always saw to the heart of things, realised that until blacks asserted their humanity and their personhood, there was not the remotest chance for reconciliation in South Africa. For true reconciliation is a deeply personal matter. It can happen only between persons who assert their own personhood, and who acknowledge and respect that of others. You don't get reconciled to your dog, do you? Steve knew and believed fervently that being pro-black was not the same thing as being anti-white. The Black Consciousness Movement is not a "hate white movement," despite all you may have heard to the contrary. He had a far too profound respect for persons as persons, to want to deal with them under readymade, shopsoiled [sic] categories.

All who met him had this tremendous sense of a warm-hearted man, and as a notable acquaintance of his told me, a man who was utterly indestructible, of massive intellect and yet reticent; quite unshakeable in his commitment to principle and to radical change in South Africa by peaceful means; a man of real reconciliation, truly an instrument of God's peace, unshakeable in his commitment to the liberation of all South Africans, black and white, striving for a more just and more open South Africa.

QUESTIONS FOR ANALYSIS

1. **What are Steve Biko's charges against white liberals in South Africa?**
2. **What was the proper role for whites in the antiapartheid movement according to Biko?**
3. **How does Bishop Tutu's eulogy differ from the political spirit and point of view expressed in Biko's 1970 essay?**
4. **According to Bishop Tutu, what were Biko's strongest characteristics? Were these characteristics demonstrated in Biko's essay?**

corruption, repression, and foreign economic domination spread quickly.

A popular rebellion forced Batista to flee the country in 1959. The dictator had been opposed by student groups, labor unions, and supporters of Cuba's traditional parties. The revolution was led by Fidel Castro, a young lawyer who had been jailed and then exiled when a 1953 uprising failed. Castro established his revolutionary base in the countryside and utilized guerrilla tactics. When he and his youthful followers took power, they vowed not to suffer the fate of Arbenz and the Guatemalan reformers. Ernesto ("Che") Guevara°, Castro's chief lieutenant who became the main theorist of communist revolution in Latin America, had been in Guatemala at the time of the CIA coup. He and Castro took for granted that confrontation with the United States was inevitable. As a result, they quickly removed the existing military leadership, executing many Batista supporters and creating a new military.

They also moved rapidly to transform Cuban society. Fidel Castro (b. 1927) gave a number of speeches in the United States in the wake of his victory and was cheered as a heroic enemy of dictatorship and American economic imperialism. Within a year his government redistributed land, lowered urban rents, and raised wages, effectively transferring 15 percent of the national income from the rich to the poor. Within twenty-two months the Castro government seized the property of almost all U.S. corporations in Cuba as well as the wealth of Cuba's elite.

To achieve his revolutionary transformation Castro sought economic support from the Soviet Union. The United States responded by suspending the sugar agreement and seeking to destabilize the Cuban economy. These punitive measures, the nationalization of so much of the economy, and the punishment of Batista supporters caused tens of thousands of Cubans to leave. Initially, most immigrants were from wealthy families and the middle-class, but when the economic failures of the regime eventually became clear, many poor Cubans fled to the United States or to other Latin American nations.

Little evidence supports the view that Castro undertook his revolution to install a communist government, but he certainly sought to break the economic and political power of the United States in Cuba and install dramatic social reforms based on an enhanced role for the state in the economy. With relations between Castro and Washington reaching crisis and Castro openly seeking the support of the Soviet Union, in April 1961 the United States attempted to apply the strategy that had removed Arbenz from power in Guatemala. Some fifteen hundred Cuban exiles trained and armed by the CIA were landed at the Bay of Pigs in an effort to overthrow Castro. The Cuban army defeated the attempted invasion in a matter of days, partly because the new U.S. president, John F. Kennedy, decided to provide less air support than had been planned by the Eisenhower administration.

Cuban Poster of Charismatic Leader Ernesto ("Che") Guevara A leading theorist of communist revolution in Latin America, Argentine-born Guevara was in Guatemala at the time of the CIA-sponsored coup against Jacobo Arbenz in 1954. He later met and had a strong influence on Fidel Castro. He was killed in 1967 while leading an insurgency in Bolivia. (Christopher Morris/stockphoto.com)

The failure of the Bay of Pigs tarnished the reputation of the United States and the CIA and gave heart to revolutionaries all over Latin America. The failed overthrow of Castro also helped precipitate the Cuban missile crisis. Fearful of a U.S. invasion, Castro and Khrushchev placed nuclear weapons as well as missiles and bombers in Cuba to forestall the anticipated attack. But the armed revolutionary movements that imitated the tactics, objectives, and even appearance of Cuba's bearded revolutionaries experienced little success. Among the thousands to lose their lives was Che Guevara who was executed after capture in Bolivia in 1967. Nevertheless, Castro had demonstrated that American power could be successfully challenged and that a radical program of economic and social reform could be put in place in the Western Hemisphere.

Che Guevara (chay guh-VAHR-uh)

Challenges of Nation Building

Decolonization occurred on a vast scale. Fifty-one nations signed the United Nations Charter in the closing months of 1945. During the United Nations' first decade twenty-five new members joined, a third of them upon gaining independence. During the next decade forty-six more new members were admitted, nearly all of them former colonial territories.

Each of these nations had to organize and institute some form of government. Comparatively few were able to do so without experiencing coups, rewritten constitutions, or regional rebellions. Leaders did not always agree on the form independence should take. In the absence of established constitutional traditions, leaders frequently tried to impose their own visions by force. Most of the new nations, while trying to establish political stability, also faced severe economic challenges, including foreign ownership and operation of key resources and the need to build infrastructure. Overdependence on world demand for raw materials and on imported manufactured goods persisted in many places long after independence.

Because the achievement of political and economic goals called for educated and skilled personnel, education was another common concern in newly emerging nations. Addressing that concern required more than building and staffing schools. In some countries, leaders had to decide which language to teach and how to inculcate a sense of national unity in students from different—and sometimes historically antagonistic—ethnic, religious, and linguistic groups. Another problem was how to provide satisfying jobs for new graduates, many of whom had high expectations because of their education.

Only rarely were the new nations able to surmount these hurdles. Even the most economically and educationally successful, such as South Korea, suffered from tendencies toward authoritarian rule. Similarly, Costa Rica, a country with a remarkably stable parliamentary regime from 1949 onward and a literacy rate of 90 percent, remained heavily dependent on world prices for agricultural commodities and on importation of manufactured goods.

Beyond a Bipolar World

Although no one doubted the dominating role of the East–West superpower rivalry in world affairs, the newly independent states had concerns that were primarily domestic and regional. Their challenge was to pursue their ends within the bipolar structure of the Cold War—and possibly to take advantage of the East–West rivalry. Where nationalist forces sought to assert political or economic independence, Cold War antagonists provided arms and political support even when the nationalist goals were quite different from those of the superpowers. For other nations, the ruinously expensive superpower arms race opened opportunities to expand industries and exports. In short, the superpowers dominated the world but did not control it. And as time progressed, they dominated it less and less.

The Third World

As one of the most successful leaders of the decolonization movement, Indonesia's President Sukarno was an appropriate figure to host a meeting in 1955 of twenty-nine African and Asian countries at Bandung, Indonesia. The conferees proclaimed solidarity among all peoples fighting against colonial rule. The Bandung Conference marked the beginning of an effort by the many new, poor, mostly non-European nations emerging from colonialism to gain more influence in world affairs by banding together. The terms **nonaligned nations** and **Third World,** which became commonplace in the following years, signaled these countries' collective stance toward the rival sides in the Cold War. If the West, led by the United States, and the East, led by the Soviet Union, represented two worlds locked in mortal struggle, the Third World consisted of everyone else.

Leaders of so-called Third World countries preferred the label *nonaligned,* which signified freedom from membership on either side. However, many leaders in the West noted that the Soviet Union supported national liberation movements and that the nonaligned movement included communist countries such as China and Yugoslavia. As a result, they decided not to take the term *nonaligned* seriously. In a polarized world, they saw Sukarno, Nehru, Nkrumah, and Egypt's Gamal Abd al-Nasir° as stalking horses for a communist takeover of the world. This may also have been the view of some Soviet leaders, since the Soviet Union was quick to offer some of these countries military and financial aid.

For the movement's leaders, however, nonalignment was primarily a way to extract money and support from one or both superpowers. By flirting with the Soviet Union or its ally, the People's Republic of China, a country could get cheap or free weapons, training, and barter agreements that offered an alternative to selling agricultural or mineral products on Western-dominated world markets. The same flirtation might also prompt the

Gamal Abd al-Nasir (gah-MAHL AHB-d al–NAH-suhr)

Bandung Conference, 1955 India's Jawaharlal Nehru (in white hat) was a central figure at the conference held in Indonesia to promote solidarity among nonaligned developing nations. The non-alignment movement failed to achieve the influence that Nehru, Egypt's Nasir, and Indonesia's Sukarno sought. (Wide World Photos)

United States and its allies to proffer grants and loans, cheap or free surplus grain, and investment in industry and infrastructure.

When skillful, nonaligned countries could play the two sides against each other and profit from both. Egypt under Nasir, who had led a military coup against the Egyptian monarchy in 1952, and under Nasir's successor Anwar al-Sadat° after 1970 played the game well. The United States offered to build a dam at Aswan°, on the Nile River, to increase Egypt's electrical generating and irrigation capacity. When Egypt turned to the Soviet Union for arms, the United States reneged on the dam project in 1956. The Soviet Union then picked it up and completed the dam in the 1960s. In 1956 Israel, Great Britain, and France conspired to invade Egypt. Their objective was to overthrow Nasir, regain the Suez Canal (he had recently nationalized it), and secure Israel from any Egyptian threat. The invasion succeeded militarily, but the United States and the Soviet Union both pressured the invaders to withdraw, thus saving Nasir's government. In 1972 Sadat evicted his Soviet military advisers, but a year later he used his Soviet weapons to attack Israel. After he lost that war, he announced his faith in the power of the United States to solve Egypt's political and economic problems.

al-Sadat (al-seh-DAT) **Aswan** (AS-wahn)

Numerous other countries adopted similar balancing strategies. In each case, local leaders were trying to develop their nation's economy and assert or preserve their nation's interests. Manipulating the superpowers was a means toward those ends and implied very little about true ideological orientation.

Japan and China

No countries took better advantage of the opportunities presented by the superpowers' preoccupation than did Japan and China. Japan signed a peace treaty with most of its former enemies in 1951 and regained independence from American occupation the following year. Renouncing militarism and its imperialist past (see Chapter 27), Japan remained on the sidelines throughout the Korean War. Its new constitution, written under American supervision in 1946, allowed only a limited self-defense force, banned the deployment of Japanese troops abroad, and gave the vote to women.

The Japanese turned their talents and energies to rebuilding their industries and engaging in world commerce. Peace treaties with countries in Southeast Asia specified reparations payable in the form of goods and services, thus reintroducing Japan to that region as a force for economic development rather than as a military occupier. Nevertheless, bitterness over wartime oppression remained strong, and Japan had to move slowly in developing new regional markets for its manufactured goods. The Cold War isolated Japan and excluded it from most world political issues. It thus provided an exceptionally favorable environment for Japan to develop its economic strength.

Three industries that took advantage of government aid and the newest technologies paved the way for Japan's emergence as an economic superpower after 1975. Electricity was in short supply in 1950; Tokyo itself suffered evening power outages. Projects producing 60 million kilowatts of electricity were completed between 1951 and 1970, almost a third through dams on Japan's many rivers. Between 1960 and 1970 steel production more than quadrupled, reaching 15.7 percent of the total capacity of countries outside the Soviet bloc. The shipbuilding industry produced six times as much tonnage in 1970 as in 1960, almost half the new tonnage produced worldwide outside the Soviet bloc.

While Japan benefited from being outside the Cold War, China was deeply involved in Cold War politics. When Mao Zedong° and the communists defeated the nationalists in 1949 and established the People's Republic of China (PRC), their main ally and source of arms was the Soviet Union. By 1956, however, the PRC and the Soviet Union were beginning to diverge politically, partly in reaction to the Soviet rejection of Stalinism and partly because of China's reluctance to be cast forever in the role of student. Mao had his own notions of communism, focusing strongly on the peasantry, whom the Soviets ignored in favor of the industrial working class.

Mao's Great Leap Forward in 1958 was supposed to vault China into the ranks of world industrial powers by maximizing the use of labor in small-scale, village-level industries and by mass collectivization in agriculture. These policies demonstrated Mao's willingness to carry out massive economic and social projects of his own devising in the face of criticism by the Soviets and by traditional economists. However, these revolutionary reforms failed comprehensively by 1962, leading to an estimated 30 million deaths.

In 1966 Mao instituted another radical nationwide program, the **Cultural Revolution.** Ordering the mass mobilization of Chinese youth into Red Guard units, his goal was to kindle revolutionary fervor in a new generation to ward off the stagnation and bureaucratization he saw in the Soviet Union. But this was also a strategy for increasing Mao's power within the Communist Party. Red Guard units criticized and purged teachers, party officials, and intellectuals for "bourgeois values." The young militants themselves suffered from factionalism, which caused more violence. Executions, beatings, and incarcerations were widespread, leading to a half-million deaths and three million purged by 1971. Finally, Mao admitted that attacks on individuals had gotten out of hand and intervened to reestablish order. The last years of the Cultural Revolution were dominated by radicals led by Mao's wife Jiang Qing°, who focused on restrictions on artistic and intellectual activity.

Chinese Red Guards During the Cultural Revolution young Chinese militants joined the Red Guards, identifying enemies of the Communist Party and Chairman Mao. They also turned on their teachers and sometimes their parents and neighbors, labeling them enemies of the people or members of the bourgeoisie. Here a victim wearing a dunce's cap on which his crimes are written is paraded. (Wide World Photos)

In the meantime, the rift between the PRC and the Soviet Union had opened so wide that U.S. President Richard Nixon (served 1969–1974), by reputation a

Mao Zedong (maow dzuh-dong)

Jiang Qing (jyahn ching)

staunch anticommunist, put out secret diplomatic feelers to revive relations with China. In 1971 the United States agreed to allow the PRC to join the United Nations and occupy China's permanent seat on the Security Council. This decision necessitated the expulsion of the Chinese nationalist government based on the island of Taiwan, which had persistently claimed to be the only legal Chinese authority. The following year, Nixon visited Beijing, initiating a new era of enhanced cooperation between the People's Republic of China and the United States.

Map 32.3 Middle East Oil and the Arab-Israeli Conflict, 1947–1973 Oil resources were long controlled by private European and American companies. In the 1960s most countries, guided by OPEC, negotiated agreements for sharing control, eventually leading to national ownership. This set the stage for the use of oil as a weapon in the 1973 Arab-Israeli war and for subsequent price increases.

The Middle East

The superpowers could not control all dangerous international disputes. Independence had come gradually to the Arab countries of the Middle East. Britain granted Syria and Lebanon independence after World War II. Iraq, Egypt, and Jordan enjoyed nominal independence between the two world wars but remained under indirect British control until the 1950s. Military coups overthrew King Faruq° of Egypt in 1952 and King Faysal° II of Iraq in 1958. King Husayn° of Jordan dismissed his British military commander in 1956 in response to the Suez crisis, but his poor desert country remained dependent on British and later American financial aid.

Overshadowing all Arab politics, however, was the struggle with Israel. British policy on Palestine between the wars oscillated between sentiment favoring Zionist Jews—who emigrated to Palestine, encouraged by the Balfour Declaration—and sentiment for the indigenous Palestinian Arabs, who felt themselves being pushed aside and suspected that the Zionists were aiming at an independent state. As more and more Jews sought a safe haven from persecution by the Nazis, Arabs felt more and more threatened. The Arabs unleashed a guerrilla uprising against the British in 1936, and Jewish groups turned to militant tactics a few years later. Occasionally, Arabs and Jews confronted each other in riots or killings, making it clear that peaceful coexistence in Palestine would be difficult or impossible to achieve.

After the war, under intense pressure to resettle European Jewish refugees, Britain conceded that it saw no way of resolving the dilemma and turned the Palestine problem over to the United Nations. In November 1947 the General Assembly voted in favor of partitioning Palestine into two states, one Jewish and the other Arab. The Jewish community made plans to declare independence, while the Palestinians, who felt that the proposed land division was unfair, reacted with horror and took up arms. When Israel declared its independence in May 1948, neighboring Arab countries sent armies to help the Palestinians crush the newborn state.

Israel prevailed on all fronts. Some 700,000 Palestinians became refugees, finding shelter in United Nations refugee camps in Jordan, Syria, Lebanon, and the Gaza Strip (a bit of coastal land on the Egyptian-Israeli border). The right of these refugees to return home remains a focal point of Arab politics. In 1967 Israel responded to threatening military moves by Egypt's Nasir by preemptively attacking Egyptian and Syrian air bases. In six days Israel won a smashing victory. When Jordan entered the war, Israel won control of Jerusalem, which it had previously split with Jordan, and the West Bank. Acquiring all of Jerusalem satisfied Jews' deep longing to return to their holiest city, but Palestinians continued to regard Jerusalem as their destined capital, and Muslims in many countries protested Israeli control of the Dome of the Rock, a revered Islamic shrine located in the city. Israel also occupied the Gaza Strip, the strategic Golan Heights in southern Syria, and the entire Sinai Peninsula (see Map 32.3). These acquisitions resulted in a new wave of Palestinian refugees.

The rival claims to Palestine continued to plague Middle Eastern politics. The Palestine Liberation Organization (PLO), headed by Yasir Arafat°, waged guerrilla war against Israel, frequently engaging in acts of terrorism. The militarized Israelis were able to blunt or absorb these attacks and launch counterstrikes that likewise involved assassinations and bombings. Though the United States was a firm friend to Israel and the Soviet Union armed the Arab states, neither superpower saw the struggle between Zionism and Palestinian nationalism as a vital concern—until oil became a political issue.

The phenomenal concentration of oil wealth in the Middle East—Saudi Arabia, Iran, Iraq, Kuwait, Libya, Qatar, Bahrain, and the United Arab Emirates—was not fully realized until after World War II, when demand for oil rose sharply as civilian economies recovered. In 1960, as a world oversupply diminished in the face of rising

Faruq (fuh-ROOK) **Faysal** (FIE-suhl) **Husayn** (hoo-SANE)

Arafat (AR-uh-fat)

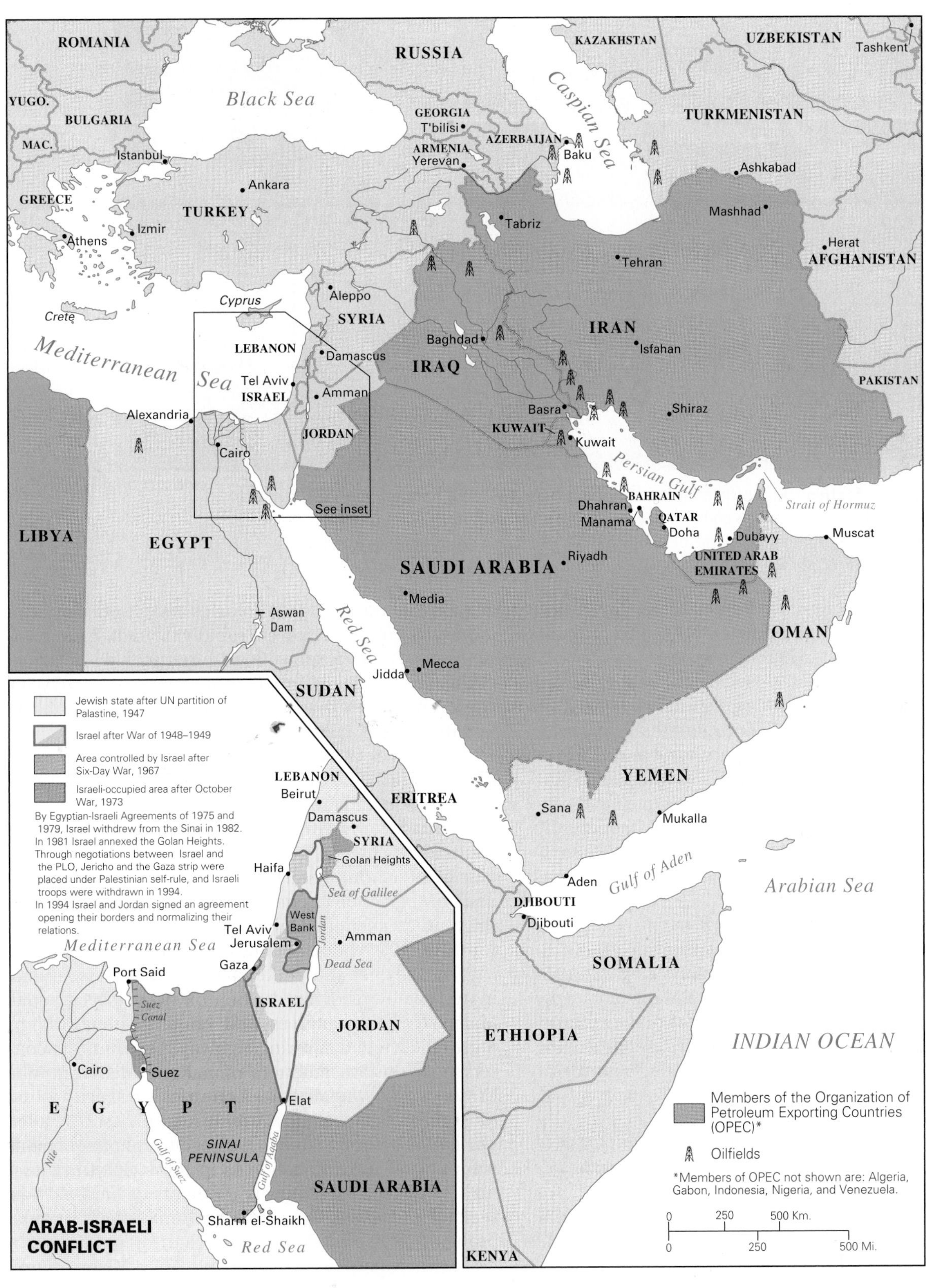

ROMANIA
RUSSIA
KAZAKHSTAN
UZBEKISTAN
Tashkent
YUGO.
Black Sea
Caspian Sea
BULGARIA
GEORGIA
T'bilisi
TURKMENISTAN
MAC.
ARMENIA
Yerevan
AZERBAIJAN
Baku
Istanbul
Ashkabad
Ankara
GREECE
TURKEY
Mashhad
Tabriz
Izmir
Athens
Herat
Tehran
AFGHANISTAN
Aleppo
Cyprus
SYRIA
Crete
IRAN
LEBANON
Damascus
Baghdad
Isfahan
Mediterranean Sea
IRAQ
Tel Aviv
ISRAEL
Amman
PAKISTAN
Basra
Shiraz
Alexandria
JORDAN
KUWAIT
Kuwait
Cairo
Persian Gulf
Strait of Hormuz
BAHRAIN
See inset
Dhahran
Manama
QATAR
Doha
Dubayy
Muscat
LIBYA
EGYPT
Riyadh
SAUDI ARABIA
UNITED ARAB EMIRATES
Media
Aswan Dam
Red Sea
OMAN
Mecca
Jidda
SUDAN
YEMEN
ERITREA
Sana
Mukalla
Aden
Gulf of Aden
Arabian Sea
DJIBOUTI
Djibouti
SOMALIA
ETHIOPIA
INDIAN OCEAN
KENYA
Members of the Organization of Petroleum Exporting Countries (OPEC)*
Oilfields
*Members of OPEC not shown are: Algeria, Gabon, Indonesia, Nigeria, and Venezuela.
0 250 500 Km.
0 250 500 Mi.
Jewish state after UN partition of Palestine, 1947
Israel after War of 1948–1949
Area controlled by Israel after Six-Day War, 1967
Israeli-occupied area after October War, 1973
By Egyptian-Israeli Agreements of 1975 and 1979, Israel withdrew from the Sinai in 1982. In 1981 Israel annexed the Golan Heights. Through negotiations between Israel and the PLO, Jericho and the Gaza strip were placed under Palestinian self-rule, and Israeli troops were withdrawn in 1994. In 1994 Israel and Jordan signed an agreement opening their borders and normalizing their relations.
LEBANON
Beirut
Damascus
SYRIA
Golan Heights
Haifa
Sea of Galilee
West Bank
Jordan
Tel Aviv
Jerusalem
Amman
Mediterranean Sea
Dead Sea
Port Said
Gaza
ISRAEL
Suez Canal
JORDAN
Cairo
Suez
Elat
E G Y P T
SINAI PENINSULA
Nile
Gulf of Suez
Gulf of Aqaba
SAUDI ARABIA
Sharm el-Shaikh
ARAB-ISRAELI CONFLICT
Red Sea

Oil Crisis at the Gas Station Dislocations in the oil industry caused by OPEC price increases that began in 1974 produced long lines at gas pumps and local shortages. The crisis brought Middle East politics home to consumers and created a negative stereotype of "oil sheikhs." (Keza/Liaison/Getty Images)

demand, oil-producing states formed the **Organization of Petroleum Exporting Countries (OPEC)** to promote their collective interest in higher revenues.

Oil politics and the Arab-Israeli conflict intersected in October 1973. A surprise Egyptian attack across the Suez Canal threw the Israelis into temporary disarray. Within days the war turned in Israel's favor, and an Egyptian army was trapped at the canal's southern end. The United States then arranged a cease fire and the disengagement of forces. But before that could happen, the Arab oil-producing countries voted to embargo oil shipments to the United States and the Netherlands as punishment for their support of Israel.

The implications of using oil as an economic weapon profoundly disturbed the worldwide oil industry. Prices rose—along with feelings of insecurity. In 1974 OPEC responded to the turmoil in the oil market by quadrupling prices, setting the stage for massive transfers of wealth to the producing countries and provoking a feeling of crisis throughout the consuming countries.

The Emergence of Environmental Concerns

The Cold War and the massive investments made in postwar economic recovery had focused public and governmental attention on technological innovations and enormous projects such as hydroelectric dams and nuclear power stations. Only a few people warned that untested technologies and all-out drives for industrial productivity were rapidly degrading the environment. The superpowers were particularly negligent of the environmental impact of pesticide and herbicide use, automobile exhaust, industrial waste disposal, and radiation.

The wave of student unrest that swept many parts of the world in 1968 and the early 1970s created a new awareness of environmental issues and a new constituency for environmental action. As the current of youth activism grew, governments in the West began to pass new environmental regulations. Earth Day, a benchmark of the new awareness, was first celebrated in 1970, the year in which the United States established its Environmental Protection Agency.

The problem of finite natural resources became more broadly recognized when oil prices skyrocketed. Making gasoline engines and home heating systems more efficient and lowering highway speed limits to conserve fuel became matters of national debate in the United States, while poorer countries struggled to find the money to import oil. A widely read 1972 study called *The Limits of Growth* forecast a need to cut back on consumption of natural resources in the twenty-first century. As the most dangerous moments of the Cold War seemed to be passing, ecological and environmental problems of worldwide impact vied for public attention with superpower rivalry and Third World nation building.

Conclusion

The impact of the Second World War was so immense that for several decades people commonly referred to the time they were living in as the "postwar era," not needing to specify which war they were referring to. The Cold War and the decolonization movement seemed to be logical extensions of World War II. The question of who would control the parts of Europe and Asia liberated from Axis occupation led to Churchill's notion of an iron curtain dividing East and West. The war exhaustion of the European imperialist powers encouraged Asian and African peoples to seek independence and embark on building their own nations.

Intellectuals often framed their understanding of the period in terms of a philosophical struggle between capitalism and socialism dating back to the nineteenth century. But for leaders facing the challenge of governing new nations and creating viable economies, economic philosophy was inextricably intertwined with questions of how to take advantage of the Cold War rivalry between the United States and the Soviet Union.

There is some disagreement among historians about whether the postwar era ended in 1975. The end of the Vietnam War, the beginning of the world oil crisis, and the signing of the Helsinki Accords that brought a measure of agreement among Europeans on both sides of the iron curtain were pivotal events for some countries. But the number of independent countries in the world had grown enormously, and each was in the process of working out its own problems. What marks the mid-1970s as the end of an era, therefore, is not a single event so much as the emergence of new concerns. Young people in particular—the new generation that had no memories of World War II—seemed less concerned with the Cold War and the specter of nuclear annihilation and more interested in newly recognized threats to the world environment and in seeking opportunities for making their way in the world. For those in wealthier nations, this meant taking advantage of economic growth and increasing technological sophistication. For those in the developing world, it meant seeking the education and employment needed for playing active roles in the drama of nation building.

Key Terms

iron curtain
Cold War
North Atlantic Treaty Organization (NATO)
United Nations
World Bank
Marshall Plan
European Community
Truman Doctrine
Warsaw Pact
Korean War
Vietnam War
Cuban missile crisis
Helsinki Accords
nonaligned nations
Third World
Cultural Revolution (China)
Organization of Petroleum Exporting Countries (OPEC)

Suggested Reading

The period since 1945 has been particularly rich in memoirs by government leaders. Some that are particularly relevant to the Cold War and decolonization are Dean Acheson (U.S. secretary of state under Truman), *Present at the Creation* (1969); Nikita Khrushchev, *Khrushchev Remembers* (1970); and Anthony Eden (British prime minister), *Full Circle* (1960).

Geoffrey Barraclough, *An Introduction to Contemporary History* (1964), is a remarkable early effort at understanding the broad sweep of history during this period. See also David Reynolds, *One World Divisible: A Global History Since 1945* (2000).

Scholarship on the origins of the Cold War is extensive and includes Akira Iriye, *The Cold War in Asia: A Historical Introduction* (1974); Bruce Kuniholm, *The Origins of the Cold War in the Middle East* (1980); Madelaine Kalb, *The Congo Cables: The Cold War in Africa—From Eisenhower to Kennedy* (1982); and Michael J. Hogan, *A Cross of Iron: Harry S Truman and the Origins of the National Security State* (1998). For a recent reconsideration of earlier historical viewpoints see Melvyn P. Leffler and David S. Painter, eds., *Origins of the Cold War: An International History* (1994).

Good general histories of the Cold War include Martin Walker, *The Cold War: A History* (1993), and Walter Lafeber, *America, Russia, and the Cold War, 1945–1992* (1993). The latter emphasizes how the Cold War eroded American democratic values. For a look at the Cold War from the Soviet perspective see William Taubman, *Stalin's America Policy* (1981); for the American perspective see John Lewis Gaddis, *Strategies of Containment: A Critical Appraisal of Postwar American National Security Policy* (1982). The Cuban missile crisis is well covered in Graham Allison, *Essence of Decision: Explaining the Cuban Missile Crisis* (1971), and Michael Beschloss, *The Crisis Years: Kennedy and Khrushchev, 1960–1963* (1991). Also see Aleksandr Fursenko and Timothy Naftali, *"One Hell of a Gamble": Khrushchev, Castro, and Kennedy, 1958–1964: The Secret History of the Cuban Missile Crisis* (1997); and the more recent John L. Gaddis, *We Now Know: Rethinking Cold War History* (1997); Mark Mazower, *Dark Continent* (1999); and William Hitchcock,

The Struggle for Europe: The Turbulent History of a Divided Continent 1945–2002 (2003).

The nuclear arms race and the associated Soviet–U.S. competition in space are well covered by McGeorge Bundy, *Danger and Survival: Choices About the Bomb in the First Fifty Years* (1988), and Walter MacDougall, *The Heavens and the Earth: A Political History of the Space Age* (1985). Among the many novels illustrating the alarming impact of the arms race on the general public are Philip Wylie, *Tomorrow!* (1954), and Nevil Shute, *On the Beach* (1970). At a technical and philosophical level, Herman Kahn's *On Thermonuclear War* (1961) had a similar effect.

The end of the European empires is broadly treated by D. K. Fieldhouse, *The Colonial Empires* (1982); a broad view is provided by D. A. Low, *The Egalitarian Moment: Asia and Africa, 1950–1980* (1996); for the British Empire in particular, Brian Lapping, *End of Empire* (1985). For a critical view of American policies toward the decolonized world see Gabriel Kolko, *Confronting the Third World: United States Foreign Policy, 1945–1980* (1988).

For books on some of the specific episodes of decolonization treated in this chapter see, on Algeria, Alistaire Horne, *A Savage War of Peace: Algeria, 1954–1962* (1987); on Africa, H. S. Wilson, *African Decolonization* (1994); and Frederick Cooper, *Decolonization and African Society: The Labor Question in French and British Africa* (1996); on Cuba, Hugh Thomas, *Cuba: The Pursuit of Freedom* (1971); on the Suez crisis of 1956, Keith Kyle, *Suez 1956* (1991); on Britain's role in the Middle East over the period of the birth of Israel, William Roger Louis, *The British Empire in the Middle East, 1945–1951* (1984); on Vietnam, George Herring, *America's Longest War: The United States and Vietnam, 1950–1975* (1986), and Stanley Karnow, *Vietnam: A History* (1991); and on Latin America, Thomas E. Skidmore and Peter H. Smith, *Modern Latin America*, 5th ed. (2001).

The special cases of Japan and China in this period are covered by Takafusa Nakamura, *A History of Showa Japan, 1926–1989* (1998); John Dower, *Embracing Defeat: Japan in the Wake of World War II* (1999); Marius B. Jansen, *Japan and China: From War to Peace, 1894–1972* (1975); and Maurice Meisner, *Mao's China and After: A History of the People's Republic* (1986). On the consequences of the Great Leap Forward see Jasper Becker, *Hungry Ghosts* (1998); and on the Cultural Revolution see Lynn T. White, *Policies of Chaos: The Organizational Causes of Violence in China's Cultural Revolution* (1989). John Merrill, *Korea: The Peninsular Origins of the War* (1989), presents the Korean War as a civil and revolutionary conflict as well as an episode of the Cold War. Among the hundreds of books on the Arab-Israeli conflict, Charles D. Smith, *Palestine and the Arab-Israel Conflict* (1992), and Trevor N. Dupuy, *Elusive Victory: The Arab-Israeli Wars, 1947–1974* (1978), stand out.

Notes

1. From Mark Mazower, *Dark Continent: Europe's Twentieth Century* (New York: Alfred A. Knopf, 1999), 271.

Crisis, Realignment, and the Dawn of the Post–Cold War World, 1975–1991

33

Dry Docks Owned by Korea's Hyundai Corporation Korea's rapid industrialization symbolizes Pacific Rim economic growth.

CHAPTER OUTLINE

On Thursday, July 22, 1993, police officers in Rio de Janeiro's banking district attempted to arrest a young boy caught sniffing glue. In the resulting scuffle, one police officer was injured by stones thrown by homeless children who lived in nearby streets and parks. Late the following night, hooded vigilantes in two cars fired hundreds of shots at a group of these children who were sleeping on the steps of a church, killing five of them at the church and two more in a park. The murderers were later identified as off-duty police officers.

At the time more than 350,000 abandoned children lived in Rio's streets and parks, begging, selling drugs, stealing, and engaging in prostitution to survive. In 1993 alone death squads and drug dealers killed more than 400 of them. Few people sympathized with the victims. One person living near the scene of the July shootings said, "Those street kids are bandits, and bandits have to die. They are a rotten branch that has to be pruned."

At the end of the twentieth century the brutality of those children's lives were common in the developing world, where rapid population growth was outstripping economic resources.[1] Problems of violence, poverty, and social breakdown could be found in most developing nations.

In wealthy industrialized nations as well, politicians and social reformers worried about the effects of unemployment, family breakdown, substance abuse, and homelessness. As had been true during the Industrial Revolution in the eighteenth century (see Chapter 23), dramatic economic growth, increased global economic integration, and rapid technological progress in the post–World War II period coincided with growing social dislocation and inequality. Among the most important events of the period were the emergence of new industrial powers in Asia and the precipitous demise of the Soviet Union and its socialist allies.

World population growth and large-scale migrations also created new challenges. Population grew most rapidly in the world's poorest nations, worsening social and economic problems and undermining fragile political institutions. In the industrialized nations the arrival of large numbers of culturally and linguistically distinct immigrants fueled economic growth but also gave rise to anti-immigrant political movements and, in some cases, violent ethnic conflict.

As you read this chapter, ask yourself the following questions:

- How did the Cold War affect politics in Latin America and the Middle East in the 1970s and 1980s?
- What forces led to the collapse of the Soviet Union?
- Why did the gap between rich and poor nations increase in this period?
- What is the relationship between the rate of population growth and the wealth of nations?
- How did technological change affect the global environment in the recent past?

Postcolonial Crises and Asian Economic Expansion, 1975–1991

Between 1975 and 1991 wars and revolutions provoked by a potent mix of ideology, nationalism, ethnic hatred, and religious fervor spread death and destruction through many of the world's least-developed regions. These conflicts often had ties to earlier colonialism and foreign intervention, but the character and objectives of each conflict reflected specific historical experiences. Throughout these decades of conflict the two superpowers sought to avoid direct military confrontation while working to gain strategic advantages. The United States and the Soviet Union each supplied arms and financial assistance to nations or insurgent forces hostile to its superpower rival. Once they became linked to the geopolitical rivalry of the superpowers, conflicts provoked by local and regional causes tended to become more deadly and long-lasting. Conflicts in which the rival super powers financed and armed competing factions or parties were called **proxy wars.**

In Latin America the rivalry of the superpowers helped transform conflicts over political rights, social justice, and economic policies into a violent cycle of revolution, military dictatorship, and foreign meddling. In

CHRONOLOGY

	The Americas	Middle East	Asia	Eastern Europe
	1964 Military takeover in Brazil			
1970	**1970** Salvador Allende elected president of Chile **1973** Allende overthrown **1976** Military takeover in Argentina **1979** Sandinistas overthrow Anastasio Somoza in Nicaragua	**1979** Islamic Revolution overthrows shah of Iran	**1975** Vietnam war ends **1978** China opens its economy	**1978** USSR sends troops to Afghanistan
1980	**1983–1990** Democracy returns in Argentina, Brazil, and Chile **1989** United States invades Panama	**1980–1988** Iran-Iraq War **1989** USSR withdraws from Afghanistan	**1986** Average Japanese income overtakes income in United States **1989** Tiananmen Square confrontation	**1985** Mikhail Gorbachev becomes Soviet head of state **1989** Berlin Wall falls **1989–1991** End of communism in eastern Europe
1990	**1990** Sandinistas defeated in elections in Nicaragua	**1990** Iraq invades Kuwait **1991** Persian Gulf War	**1990s** Japanese recession	**1990** Reunification of Germany

Iran and Afghanistan resentment against foreign intrusion and a growing religious hostility to modernization led to revolutionary transformations. Here again superpower ambitions and regional political instability helped provoke war and economic decline. These experiences were not universal. During this period some Asian nations experienced rapid transformation. Japan became one of the world's leading industrial powers, while a small number of other Asian economies quickly entered the ranks of industrial and commercial powers.

The collapse of the Soviet system in eastern Europe at the end of the 1980s ended the Cold War and undermined socialist economies elsewhere. As developing and former socialist nations opened their markets to foreign investment and competition, economic transformation was often accompanied by wrenching social change. The world's growing economic interconnectedness coincided with increased inequality. By the early 1990s it was clear that the world's wealthiest industrial nations were reaping most of the benefits of economic integration.

This period also witnessed a great increase in world population and international immigration. Population growth and increased levels of industrialization had a dramatic impact on the global environment. Every continent felt the destructive effects of forest depletion, soil erosion, and pollution. Wealthy nations with slow population growth found it easier to respond to these environmental challenges than did poor nations experiencing rapid population growth.

Revolutions, Repression, and Democratic Reform in Latin America

In the 1970s Latin America entered a dark era of political violence. As revolutionary movements challenged the established order in many nations, democratic governments were overturned by the military. A region of weak democracy in 1960 became a region of military dictatorships fifteen years later. The new authoritarian leaders had little patience with civil liberties and human rights.

The confrontation between Fidel Castro and the government of the United States that had led to the Bay of Pigs invasion and the missile crisis (see Chapter 32) helped propel the region toward crisis. The fact that the Cuban communist government survived efforts by the United States to overthrow it energized the revolutionary left throughout Latin America. Fearful that revolution would spread across Latin America and determined to defeat communism at all costs, the United States increased support for its political and military allies in Latin America. Many of the military leaders who would come to power in this period were trained by the United States.

Brazil was the first nation to experience the full effects of the conservative reaction to the Cuban Revolution. Claiming that Brazil's civilian political leaders could not protect the nation from communist subversion, the army overthrew the democratically elected government of President João Goulart° in 1964. The military suspended the constitution, outlawed all existing political parties, and exiled former presidents and opposition leaders. Death squads—illegal paramilitary organizations sanctioned by the government—detained, tortured, and executed thousands of citizens. The dictatorship also undertook an ambitious economic program that promoted industrialization through import substitution, using tax and tariff policies to compel foreign-owned companies to increase investment in manufacturing.

This combination of dictatorship, violent repression, and government promotion of industrialization came to be called the "Brazilian Solution" in Latin America. Elements of this "solution" were imposed across much of the region in the 1970s and early 1980s, beginning in Chile. In 1970 Chile's new president, **Salvador Allende°**, undertook an ambitious program of socialist reforms to redistribute wealth from the elite and middle classes to the poor. He also nationalized most of Chile's heavy industry and mines, including the American-owned copper companies that dominated the Chilean economy. From the beginning of Allende's presidency the administration of President Richard Nixon (served 1969–1973) worked to organize opposition to Allende's reforms and to overturn his election. Afflicted by inflation, mass consumer protests, and declining foreign trade, Allende was overthrown in 1973 by a military uprising led by General Augusto Pinochet° and supported by the United States. President Allende and thousands of Chileans died in the uprising, and thousands more were illegally seized, tortured, and imprisoned without trial. Once in power Pinochet rolled back Allende's social reforms, dramatically reduced state participation in the economy, and encouraged foreign investment.

In 1976 Argentina followed Brazil and Chile into dictatorship. Isabel Martínez de Perón° became president after the death of her husband Juan Perón in 1974 (see Chapter 31). Argentina was wracked by high inflation, terrorism, and labor protests. Impatient with the policies of the president, the military seized power and suspended the constitution. During the next seven years the military fought what it called the **Dirty War** against terrorism. More than nine thousand Argentines lost their lives, and thousands of others endured arrest, torture, and the loss of property.

Despite reverses in Brazil, Chile, and Argentina, however, revolutionary movements persisted elsewhere. The high-water mark of the revolutionary movement came in 1979 in Nicaragua with the overthrow of the corrupt dictatorship of Anastasio Somoza. The broad alliance of revolutionaries and reformers that took power called themselves **Sandinistas°**. They took their name from Augusto César Sandino, who had led Nicaraguan opposition to U.S. military intervention between 1927 and 1932. The Sandinistas received significant political and financial support from Cuba and, once in power, sought to imitate the command economies of Cuba and the Soviet Union, nationalizing properties owned by members of the Nicaraguan elite and U.S. citizens.

During his four-year term U.S. president Jimmy Carter (served 1977–1980) championed human rights in the hemisphere and stopped the flow of U.S. arms to regimes with the worst records. Carter sought to placate Latin American resentment for past U.S. interventions by agreeing to the reestablishment of Panamanian sovereignty in the Canal Zone at the end of 1999. He also tried and failed to find common ground with the Sandinistas. In 1981 Ronald Reagan became president and abandoned this policy of conciliation.

Reagan was committed to reversing the results of the Nicaraguan Revolution and defeating a revolutionary movement in neighboring El Salvador. His options, however, were limited by the U.S. Congress, which feared that Central America might become another Vietnam. Congress resisted using U.S. combat forces in Nicaragua and El Salvador and put strict limits on military aid. The Reagan administration sought to roll back the Nicaraguan Revolution by the use of punitive economic measures and by the recruitment and arming of anti-Sandinista Nicaraguans. Called Contras (counterrevolutionaries), this military force was financed by both legal and illegal funds provided by the Reagan administration.

The Contras were unable to defeat the Sandinistas, but they did gain a bloody stalemate by the end of the 1980s. Confident that they were supported by the majority of Nicaraguans and assured that the U.S. Congress

João Goulart (juwow go-LARHT)
Salvador Allende (sal-vah-DOR ah-YEHN-day) **Augusto Pinochet** (ah-GOOS-toh pin-oh-CHET) **Isabel Martínez de Perón** (EES-ah-bell mar-TEEN-ehz deh pair-OWN)

Sandinistas (sahn-din-EES-tahs)

The Nicaraguan Revolution Overturns Somoza A revolutionary coalition that included Marxists drove the dictator Anastasio Somoza from power in 1979. The Somoza family had ruled Nicaragua since the 1930s and maintained a close relationship with the United States. (Susan Meiselas/ Magnum Photos, Inc.)

was close to cutting off aid to the Contras, the Sandinistas called for free elections in 1990. But they had miscalculated politically. Exhausted by more than a decade of violence, a majority of Nicaraguan voters rejected the Sandinistas and elected a middle-of-the-road coalition led by Violeta Chamorro°.

The revolutionaries of El Salvador hoped to imitate the initial success of the Sandinistas of Nicaragua. Taking their name from a martyred leftist leader of the 1930s, the FMLN (Farabundo Martí° National Liberation Front) organized an effective guerrilla force. The United States responded by providing hundreds of millions of dollars in military assistance annually and by training units of the El Salvadoran army. These investments in military equipment and training failed to curb the Salvadoran military's human rights abuses.

The assassination of Archbishop Oscar Romero and other members of the Catholic clergy by death squads tied to the Salvadoran government as well as the murder of thousands of noncombatants by military units made it difficult for the Reagan administration to sustain its policy of military aid. Knowledge of human rights abuses led the U.S. Congress to place strict limits on the number of U.S. military advisers that could be sent to El Salvador and to try to force political reforms. External events finally brought peace to El Salvador. With the electoral defeat of the Sandinistas in Nicaragua and the collapse of the Soviet Union (see below), popular support for the rebels' vision of a socialist El Salvador waned, and the FMLN rebels negotiated an end to the war, transforming themselves into a civilian political party.

The military dictatorships established in Brazil, Chile, and Argentina all came to an end between 1983 and 1990. In each case reports of kidnappings, tortures, and corruption by military governments undermined public support. In Argentina the military junta's foolish decision in 1982 to seize the Falkland Islands—the Argentines called them the "Malvinas"—from Great Britain ended in an embarrassing military defeat and precipitated the return to civilian rule. The Argentine junta had helped President Reagan support the Contras in Nicaragua and believed he would keep Britain's Prime Minister Margaret Thatcher from taking military action. Instead the United States supported the British. With the surrender of the Argentine garrison in the Falklands, military rule in Argentina itself collapsed.

In Chile and Brazil the military dictatorships ended without the drama of foreign war. Despite significant economic growth under Pinochet, Chileans resented the violence and corruption of the military. In 1988 Pinochet called a plebiscite to extend his authority, but the majority vote went against him. A year later Chile elected its first civilian president in eighteen years. Brazil's military

Violeta Chamorro (vee-oh-LET-ah cha-MOR-roe) **Farabundo Martí** (fah-rah-BOON-doh mar-TEE)

initiated a gradual transition to civilian rule in 1985 and four years later had its first popular presidential election. By 1991 nearly 95 percent of Latin America's population lived under civilian rule.

By the end of the 1980s oil-importing and oil-exporting nations in Latin America were in economic trouble. Brazil and other oil importers had borrowed heavily to cover budget deficits caused by high oil prices engineered by OPEC. Oil exporters such as Mexico and Venezuela at first enjoyed a windfall as prices rose. Expecting prices to remain high, they borrowed to increase production and develop refining capacity. When oil prices fell in the 1980s, they were hard-pressed to repay debts. In 1982 Mexico was forced to declare that it could not make debt payments, triggering a world financial crisis. By 1988 Latin American nations owed more than $400 billion to external lenders, and Brazil alone owed $113 billion. Debt remained an impediment to economic development in Latin America into the 1990s.

In 1991 Latin America was more dominated by the United States than it had been in 1975. On a number of occasions in the 1980s the United States used military force to achieve its objectives. In 1983, for example, President Reagan authorized a military invasion of the tiny Caribbean nation of Grenada, using the need to protect a small number of American students from the actions of a pro-Cuban government as justification. Six years later President George H. W. Bush sent a large military force into Panama to overthrow and arrest dictator General Manuel Noriega°, who was associated with both drug smuggling and attacks on U.S. military personnel. These actions were powerful reminders to Latin Americans of prior foreign intervention and occupation (see Chapter 24).

With socialism discredited by the collapse of the Soviet bloc, most Latin American nations introduced economic reforms advocated by the United States that reduced the economic role of the state. Called neoliberalism in Latin America and other developing regions, these free-market policies reduced protections afforded local industries, government social welfare policies, and public-sector employment. Governments sold public-sector industries, like national airlines, manufacturing facilities, and public utilities, to foreign corporations. Popular support has been eroded by a succession of shocks since 1994, and new political movements are demanding an active role for government in the economy (see Diversity and Dominance: The Struggle for Women's Rights in an Era of Global Political and Economic Change).

Manuel Noriega (MAN-wel no-ree-EGG-ah)

Islamic Revolutions in Iran and Afghanistan

Although the Arab-Israel conflict and the oil crisis (see Chapter 32) concerned both superpowers, the prospect of direct military involvement remained remote. When unexpected crises developed in Iran and Afghanistan, however, significant strategic issues came to the foreground. Both countries adjoined Soviet territory, making Soviet military intervention more likely. Exercising post–Vietnam War caution, the United States reacted with restraint. The Soviet Union chose a bolder and ultimately disastrous course.

Muhammad Reza Pahlavi° succeeded his father as shah of Iran in 1941. In 1953 covert intervention by the U.S. Central Intelligence Agency (CIA) helped the shah retain his throne in the face of a movement to overturn royal power. Even when he finally nationalized the foreign-owned oil industry, the shah continued to enjoy special American support. As oil revenues increased following the price increases of the 1970s, the United States encouraged the shah to spend his nation's growing wealth on equipping the Iranian army with advanced American weaponry.

Resentment in Iran against the Pahlavi family's autocracy dated from the 1925 seizure of power by the shah's father. The shah's dependence on the United States stimulated further opposition. By the 1970s popular resentment against the ballooning wealth of the elite families that supported the shah and the brutality, inefficiency, malfeasance, and corruption of his government led to mass opposition.

Ayatollah Ruhollah Khomeini°, a Shi'ite° philosopher-cleric who had spent most of his eighty-plus years in religious and academic pursuits, became the voice and symbolic leader of the opposition. Massive street demonstrations and crippling strikes forced the shah to flee Iran and ended the monarchy in 1979. In the Islamic Republic of Iran, which replaced the monarchy, Ayatollah Khomeini was supreme arbiter of disputes and guarantor of religious legitimacy. He oversaw a parliamentary regime based on European models, but he imposed religious control of legislation and public behavior. Elections were held, but the electoral process was not open to all: monarchists, communists, and other groups opposed to the Islamic Republic were barred from running for office. Shi'ite clerics with little training for government service held many of the high-

Reza Pahlavi (REH-zah PAH-lah-vee) **Ayatollah Ruhollah Khomeini** (A-yat-ol-LAH ROOH-ol-LAH ko-MAY-nee)
Shi'ite (SHE-ite)

Muslim Women Mourning the Death of Ayatollah Khomeini in 1989 An Islamic revolution overthrew the shah of Iran in 1979. Ayatollah Khomeini sought to lead Iran away from the influences of Western culture and challenged the power of the United States in the Persian Gulf. (Alexandra Avakian/Woodfin Camp & Associates)

est posts, and stringent measures were taken to combat Western styles and culture. Universities were temporarily closed, and their faculties were purged of secularists and monarchists. Women were compelled to wear modest Islamic garments outside the house, and semi-official vigilante committees policed public morals and cast a pall over entertainment and social life.

The United States under President Carter had criticized the shah's repressive regime, but the overthrow of a long-standing ally and the creation of the Islamic Republic were blows to American prestige. The new Iranian regime was religiously doctrinaire. It also was anti-Israeli and anti-American. Khomeini saw the United States as a "Great Satan" opposed to Islam, and he helped foster Islamic revolutionary movements elsewhere, which threatened the interests of both the United States and Israel. In November 1979 Iranian radicals seized the U.S. embassy in Tehran and held fifty-two diplomats hostage for 444 days. Americans felt humiliated by their inability to do anything, particularly after the failure of a military rescue attempt.

In the fall of 1980, shortly after negotiations for the release of the hostages began, **Saddam Husain°,** the ruler of neighboring Iraq, invaded Iran to topple the Islamic Republic. His own dictatorial rule rested on a secular, Arab-nationalist philosophy and long-standing friendship with the Soviet Union, which had provided him with advanced weaponry. He feared that the fervor of Iran's revolutionary Shi'ite leaders would infect his own country's Shi'ite majority and threaten his power. The war pitted American weapons in the hands of the Iranians against Soviet weapons in the hands of the Iraqis, but the superpowers avoided overt involvement during eight years of bloodshed. Covertly, however, the United States sent arms to Iran, hoping to gain the release of other American hostages held by radical Islamic groups in Lebanon and to help finance the Contra war against the Sandinista government of Nicaragua. When this deal came to light in 1986, the resulting political scandal intensified American hostility to Iran. Openly tilting toward Iraq, President Reagan sent the United States Navy to the Persian Gulf, ostensibly to protect nonbelligerent shipping. The move helped force Iran to accept a cease-fire in 1988.

While the United States experienced anguish and frustration in Iran, the Soviet Union found itself facing even more serious problems in neighboring Afghanistan. Since World War II the Soviet Union had stayed out of shooting wars by using proxies to challenge the United States. But in 1978 the Soviet Union sent its army to Afghanistan to support a fledgling communist regime against a hodgepodge of local, religiously inspired guerrilla bands that had taken control of much of the countryside.

With the United States, Saudi Arabia, and Pakistan paying, equipping, and training the Afghan rebels, the Soviet Union found itself in an unwinnable war like the one the United States had stumbled into in Vietnam. Unable to justify the continuing drain on manpower, morale, and economic resources, and facing widespread domestic discontent over the war, Soviet leaders finally withdrew their troops in 1989. The Afghan communists held on for another three years. But once rebel groups took control of the entire country, they began to fight among themselves over who should rule.

Saddam Husain (sah-DAHM who-SANE)

Diversity and Dominance

The Struggle for Women's Rights in an Era of Global Political and Economic Change

The struggle for women's rights is one of the most important social movements of the twentieth century. Although fundamental similarities in objectives can be identified across cultural and political boundaries, women in less-developed nations are forced to recognize that their objectives and strategies must take into account international inequalities in power and wealth. In this section Gladys Acosta, a militant Peruvian feminist, discusses the appropriate agenda for this struggle in the era after the fall of the Soviet Union and the rise of **neo-liberalism.**

Neo-liberalism *is the term used in Latin America to identify the free-market economic policies advocated by the United States. Among its chief characteristics are an end to the protection of local industries, a reduction in government social welfare policies, a reduction in public-sector employment, a commitment to paying debts to international creditors, and the removal of impediments to foreign investment. Many Latin Americans believe neo-liberalism is a new form of imperialism.*

No one can abstain from the debate about the great historical systems of our time. Not even those of us who are trying to change the complex web of human relationships from a feminist perspective. Everywhere people are talking about the end of ideologies. But before we can grasp the significance of current events and their consequences, we need to pinpoint our various doubts and blank spots. Capitalism is the main pivot of our lives because we were born under its influence. It [has] hegemony. . . .

Gender, the main distinction between all people, is ignored in most philosophical, political or economic discussions. The reason for this lies partly in the low level of women's participation, but not entirely, because women are not always aware of the system of submission and repression to which we are subjected against our will. We need to find something which unites women in a gender-specific manner. That doesn't mean sweeping under the carpet all the differences between us, like social position, culture or age. . . .

NEO-LIBERALISM IN ACTION

For those of us who live under the influence of the capitalist system, the situation is different. When I talk of neo-liberalism, I mean austerity measures, foreign debts, and increased liberties for all those who have the power of money at their disposal and the power of repression over those who make demands. We have now reached a new form of capitalist accumulation. The world's economic system is in a state of change and capital has become more concentrated and centralised. I would not go as far as to say countries don't exist anymore but national identities do certainly play a different role now. It is important to understand the dynamics because otherwise historical responsibilities are obscured and we no longer know whom we're fighting against. If we look at the bare face of neo-liberalism from a woman's point of view, we cannot fail to notice its murderous consequences. To create a more humane society we must continue to reject neo-liberalism here and now in the hope of being able to change the dead present into a living future. Under neo-liberalism there is a breathtaking circulation of commodities, but also an exchange of ideas, illusions and dreams. At the moment we're experiencing capitalism's greatest ideological offensive. It's all business: everything is bought and sold and everything has its price.

THE CONSEQUENCES OF NEO-LIBERAL POLITICS

We women play an important role in this ever-more internationalized economy because we represent, as ever, a particularly exploitable workforce. A number of studies have revealed the existence of subcontractor chains who work for transnational companies "informally" and mainly employ women. Basically we are dealing with a kind of integration into the world market which often uses our own homes as its outlet. Obviously, this work is badly paid and completely unprotected and has to be done without any of those social rights which were formerly achieved by trade union struggles. The most important thing for us is to keep hold of just one thread of the enterprise so we can show how the commodities make their way to their final destination. As it advances worldwide, this capitalism also encourages the expansion of certain kinds of tourism. A visible increase in prostitution is part of this, whereby women from poor countries are smuggled into large, internationally-operated rings which exploit them. The reports of Filipina women traded on the West German market send shivers down our spines . . . What kind of freedom are you talking about there?

HOW THE ADOPTION OF AUSTERITY MEASURES AFFECTS WOMEN'S LIVES

It is obvious that foreign debt is one of the most inhuman forms of exploitation in our countries when one considers the ratio between work necessary for workers' needs and work producing profit for employers. The experts have already explained how the prevailing exchange and investment structures have created international finance systems which keep whole populations in inhuman conditions. Although many people might think it crazy, the development model of the global economy has a marked relation to gender. As long as prices were slapped on some luxury consumer items there weren't any serious problems; but now the snares have been set around basic commodities. Women in every household are suffering every day as a result of impoverished economies and those who are most exposed to the effects of foreign debt are women.

When it comes to shopping, caring for sick children or the impossibility of meeting their schooling costs, the illusion of "leaving poverty behind" evaporates. Yet the problem is not only of an economic nature because under such circumstances the constant tension leads to grave, often lasting exhaustion. The psychosocial damage is alarming. The situation is ready to explode, so to speak. . . . The adoption of austerity measures means a curtailment of the state's commitment to social services with a direct effect on women. Daily life becomes hell for them. The lack of even minimal state welfare presents women (and obviously children too) with crushing working days. There is a constant expenditure of human energy without any hope of rest! No relaxation, no breaks. . . . And if we consider what happens within the family, we notice that women keep the smallest portion of the meagre family income. They give everything to their children or those adults who bring home a pay packet. As a result malnutrition among women is increasing at an alarming rate and their frequent pregnancies represent a superhuman physical achievement.

Women's valiant achievements in defending life and survival are not acknowledged by society. The efforts of women's organisations, whether it be communal kitchens, the glass-of-milk committees [milk distribution among the poor] or health services don't get the appropriate social esteem. The social value of women cannot be calculated. Perhaps in years to come the fate of millions of women who sacrifice everything to support the children and youth of Peru and other countries in Latin America will be acknowledged. We should not ignore the fact that violence of every form . . . goes hand-in-hand with the difficult situation I have described.[1] It's nothing new for women because the open wounds of sexual violence, abuse at home and the contempt of this *machista* culture, have always featured in our lives and our mothers' lives. The challenge is to prevent these from also affecting our future generations.

AND THE FUTURE?

The neo-liberal offensive is international and demands international opposition strategies combined with political proposals by new social forces which address women's problems. We want to change estimations of our worth and achieve society's acknowledgement of what has been belittled until now as "women's affairs." Such important decisions as the right to the termination of unwanted pregnancies can no longer be ignored on the political stage. We want our place in the political decision-making process; we want to have a say in all problems which concern the Peruvian people and the whole world. We want to be informed so as not to be deceived by those who are used to practising politics for a flock of sheep. This road will be difficult but at least we shall regain the strengths of socialism and create social alternatives which are aimed at changing the destructive technological order as well as eliminating the international division of labour and the sexual hierarchy inherent within it. In so doing we shall try to create democratic structures which include the people in the decision-making process. The barriers thrown up by formal representative structures must be overcome urgently. A new democracy should be founded as the basic prerequisite for the society of the future.

QUESTIONS FOR ANALYSIS

1. **What is neo-liberalism?**
2. **According to Acosta, how does global economic integration fostered by neo-liberalism affect the lives of women as workers?**
3. **Acosta claims that indebtedness to foreign lenders leads to austerity measures. How does this impact families in poor countries?**
4. **What does Acosta advocate?**

[1] In the last report of the Comisaria de mujeres in Lima (the only one in the country at present) 4,800 rapes were filed for 1990, of which 4,200 went to trial. The police commissioner, in reading the document, personally acknowledged the alarming social problem which is posed by the violence of men who are connected to their victims in some way and. which, indeed, persists throughout all levels of society.

Source: Gaby Küppers, ed., *Compañeras. Voices from the Latin American Women's Movement* (London: Latin American Bureau, 1994), 167–172.

Asian Transformation

Japan has few mineral resources and is dependent on oil imports, but the Japanese economy weathered the oil price shocks of the 1970s better than did the economies of Europe and the United States. In fact, Japan experienced a faster rate of economic growth in the 1970s and 1980s than did any other major developed economy, growing at about 10 percent a year. Average income also increased rapidly, overtaking that of the United States in 1986 and surpassing it in the 1990s.

There are some major differences between the Japanese and U.S. industrial models. During the American occupation, Japanese industrial conglomerates known as *zaibatsu* (see Chapter 29) were broken up. Although ownership of major industries became less concentrated as a result, new industrial alliances appeared. There are now six major ***keiretsu***° each of which include a major bank and firms in industry, commerce, and construction tied together in an interlocking ownership structure. There are also minor keiretsu dominated by a major corporation, like Toyota, and including its major suppliers. These combinations of companies have close relationships with government. Government assistance in the form of tariffs and import regulations inhibiting foreign competition was crucial in the early stages of development of Japan's automobile and semiconductor industries, among others.

Through the 1970s and 1980s Japanese success at exporting manufactured goods produced huge trade surpluses with other nations, prompting the United States and the European Community to engage in tough negotiations to try to force open the Japanese market. These efforts had only limited success. In 1990 Japan's trade surplus with the rest of the world was double its size in 1985. Many experts assumed that Japan's competitive advantages would propel it past the United States as the world's preeminent industrial economy. But problems appeared at the end of the 1980s and have proved difficult to solve. Japanese housing and stock markets had become highly overvalued, in part because the large trade imbalances increased the monetary supply. Also, the close relationship of government, banks, and industries had led to speculation and corruption that undermined the nation's confidence. As the crisis deepened, the close relationships between industrial enterprises, government, and banks that had helped propel the postwar expansion proved to be a liability. These close ties propped up inefficient companies and made it next to impossible to write off a mountain of nonperforming loans.

The Japanese model of close cooperation between government and industry was imitated by a small number of Asian states in the 1970s. The most important was South Korea, which had a number of assets that helped promote economic development. The combination of inexpensive labor, strong technical education, and substantial domestic capital reserves allowed South Korea to overcome the devastation of the Korean War in little more than a decade. Despite large defense expenditures, South Korea developed heavy industries such as steel and shipbuilding as well as consumer industries such as automobiles and consumer electronics. Japanese investment and technology transfers accelerated this process. Led by four giant corporations, which accounted for nearly half of South Korea's gross domestic product (GDP) and produced a broad mix of goods, the Korean economy began to match Japanese economic growth rates by the 1980s. Hyundai, one of the four giant corporations, manufactured products ranging from supertankers and cars to electronics and housing.

Taiwan, Hong Kong, and Singapore also developed modern industrial and commercial economies. As a result of their rapid economic growth, these three nations and South Korea were often referred to as the **Asian Tigers.** Taiwan suffered a number of political reverses, including the loss of its United Nations seat to the People's Republic of China in 1971 and the withdrawal of diplomatic recognition by the United States. Nevertheless, it achieved remarkable economic progress. In contrast with South Korea, smaller, more specialized companies led development in Taiwan. Also, Taiwan was able to gain a foothold in the economy of the People's Republic of China while maintaining its traditional markets in the United States and South Asia. Between 1955 and 1990 Taiwan's per capita GDP increased from 10 percent of U.S. levels to 50 percent.

Hong Kong and Singapore—both small societies with extremely limited resources—also enjoyed rapid economic development. Singapore's initial economic takeoff was based on its busy port and on banking and commercial services. As capital accumulated in these profitable sectors, this society of around 3 million people diversified by building textile and electronics industries. Singapore's rate of growth in GDP was double that of Japan from 1970 to 1980. Hong Kong's economic prosperity was also tied to its port and to the development of banking and commercial services, which were increasingly involved with China's growing economy. Hong Kong developed a highly competitive industrial sector

keiretsu (kay-REHT-soo)

dominated by textile and consumer electronics production. Worried about Hong Kong's reintegration into the People's Republic of China in 1997, local capitalists moved significant amounts of capital to the United States, Canada, and elsewhere, slowing economic growth in Hong Kong.

These **newly industrialized economies (NIEs)** shared many characteristics that helped explain their rapid industrialization. All had disciplined and hard-working labor forces, and all invested heavily in education. For example, as early as 1980 Korea had as many engineering graduates as Germany, Britain, and Sweden combined. All had high rates of personal saving that allowed them to generously fund investment in new technology. In 1987 the saving rates in Taiwan and South Korea were three times higher than in the United States. All emphasized outward-looking export strategies. And, like Japan, these dynamic Pacific Rim economies benefited from government sponsorship and protection. They were also beneficiaries of the extraordinary expansion in world trade and international communication that permitted technology to be disseminated more rapidly than at any time in the past. As a result, newly industrializing nations began with current technologies.

China Rejoins the World Economy

In China after Mao Zedong's death in 1976 the communist leadership introduced comprehensive economic reforms that relaxed state control of the economy, allowing more initiative and permitting individuals to accumulate wealth. Beginning in 1978 the Communist Party in Sichuan province freed more than six thousand firms to compete for business outside the state planning process. The results were remarkable. Under China's leader **Deng Xiaoping°** these reforms were expanded across the nation. China also began to permit foreign investment for the first time since the communists came to power in 1949. Between 1978 and the end of the 1990s foreign investors committed more than $180 billion to the Chinese economy, and McDonald's, Coca-Cola, Airbus, and other foreign companies began doing business there. But more than 100 million workers were still employed in state-owned enterprises, and most foreign-owned companies were segregated in special economic zones. The result was a dual industrial sector—one modern, efficient, and connected to international markets, the other dominated by government and directed by political decisions.

When Mao came to power in 1949, the meaning of the Chinese Revolution was made clear in the countryside, where collective ownership and organization were imposed. Deng Xiaoping did not privatize land, but he did permit the contracting of land to individuals and families, who were free to consume or sell whatever they produced. By 1984, 93 percent of China's agricultural land was in effect in private hands and producing for the market, tripling agricultural output.

Perhaps the best measure of the success of Deng's reforms is that between 1980 and 1993 China's per capita output more than doubled, averaging more than 8 percent growth per year, in comparison with the world average of slightly more than 1 percent and Japan's average of 3.3 percent. This growth was overwhelmingly the result of exports to the developed nations of the West, especially to the United States. Nevertheless, per capita measures of wealth indicated that China remained a poor nation. In the early 1990s China's per capita GDP was roughly the same as Mexico's, about $3,600 per year. By comparison, Taiwan had a per capita GDP of $14,700. What is clear is that economic reforms combined with massive investments and technology transfers from the United States and Japan to propel China into the twenty-first century as one of the world's major industrial powers.

Much of China's command economy remained in place, and the leadership of the Chinese Communist Party resisted serious political reform. Deng Xiaoping's strategy of balancing change and continuity, however, helped China avoid some of the social costs and political consequences experienced by Russia and other European socialist countries that abruptly embraced capitalism and democracy. As Chinese officials put it, China was "changing a big earthquake into a thousand tremors." The nation's leadership faced a major challenge in 1989. Responding to inflation and to worldwide mass movements in favor of democracy, Chinese students and intellectuals, many of whom had studied outside China, led a series of protests demanding more democracy and an end to inflation and corruption. This movement culminated in **Tiananmen° Square,** in the heart of Beijing. Hundreds of thousands of protesters gathered and refused to leave. After weeks of standoff, tanks pushed into the square, killing hundreds, perhaps thousands. Many more protestors were arrested. Although the Communist Party survived this challenge, it was not clear whether rapid economic growth, increasing inequality, high levels of unemployment, and

Deng Xiaoping (dung shee-yao-ping)

Tiananmen (tee-yehn-ahn-men)

massive migration from the countryside to the cities would ultimately trigger a political transformation.

THE END OF THE BIPOLAR WORLD, 1989–1991

After the end of World War II competition between the United States and the Soviet Union and their respective allies created a bipolar world. Every conflict, no matter how local its origins, had the potential of engaging the attention of one or both of the superpowers. The Korean War, decolonization in Africa, the Vietnam War, the Cuban Revolution, hostilities between Israel and its neighbors, and numerous other events increased tension between the superpowers, each armed with nuclear weapons. Given this succession of provocations, budgets within both blocs were dominated by defense expenditures, and political culture everywhere was dominated by arguments over the relative merits of the two competing economic and political systems.

Few in 1980 predicted the startling collapse of the Soviet Union and the socialist nations of the Warsaw Pact. Western observers tended to see communist nations as both more uniform in character and more subservient to the Soviet Union than was true. Long before the 1980s deep divisions had appeared among communist states. Yugoslavia broke with the Soviet Union in the 1940s; China actually fought a brief border war with the Soviet Union in the 1960s; and the government of newly unified communist Vietnam invaded communist Cambodia in the 1970s. But in general, the once-independent nations and ethnic groups that had been brought within the Soviet Union seemed securely transformed by the experiences and institutions of communism. By 1990, however, nationalism was resurgent, and communism was nearly finished (see the discussion of the Balkans in Chapter 34).

Crisis in the Soviet Union

Under U.S. President Ronald Reagan and the Soviet Union's General Secretary Leonid Brezhnev°, the rhetoric of the Cold War remained intense. Massive new U.S. investments in armaments, including a space-based missile protection system that never became operational, placed heavy burdens on the Soviet economy, which was unable to absorb the cost of developing similar weapons. Soviet economic problems were systemic; shortages of food, consumer goods, and housing were an ongoing part of Soviet life. Obsolete industrial plants and centralized planning that stifled initiative and responsiveness to market demand led to a declining standard of living relative to the West. Government bureaucrats and Communist Party favorites received special privileges, including permission to shop in stores that stocked Western goods, but the average citizen faced long lines and waiting lists for goods. Soviet citizens contrasted their lot with the free and prosperous life of the West depicted in the increasingly accessible Western media. The arbitrariness of the bureaucracy, the cynical manipulation of information, and deprivations created a generalized crisis in morale.

Despite the unpopularity of the war in Afghanistan and growing discontent, Brezhnev refused to modify his rigid and unsuccessful policies. But he was unable to contain an underground current of protest. In a series of powerful books, the writer Alexander Solzhenitzyn° castigated the Soviet system and particularly the Stalinist prison camps. He won a Nobel Prize in literature but was charged with treason and expelled from the country in 1974. Self-published underground writings (*samizdat*°) by critics of the regime circulated widely despite government efforts to suppress them. The physicist Andrei Sakharov and his wife Yelena Bonner protested the nuclear arms race and human rights violations and were condemned to banishment within the country. Some Jewish dissidents spoke out against anti-Semitism, and many more left for Israel and the United States.

By the time **Mikhail Gorbachev**° took up the reins of the Soviet government in 1985, weariness with war in Afghanistan, economic decay, and vocal protest had reached critical levels. Casting aside Brezhnev's hard line, Gorbachev authorized major reforms in an attempt to stave off total collapse. His policy of political openness (*glasnost*) permitted criticism of the government and the Communist Party. His policy of ***perestroika***° ("restructuring") was an attempt to address long-suppressed economic problems by moving away from central state planning and toward a more open economic system. In 1989 he ended the war in Afghanistan, which had cost many lives and much money.

Leonid Brezhnev (leh-oh-NEED BREZ-nef)

Solzhenitzen (sol-zhuh-NEET-sin)
samizdat (sah-meez-DAHT) **Gorbachev** (GORE-beh-CHOF)
perestroika (per-ih-STROY-kuh)

The Collapse of the Socialist Bloc

Events in eastern Europe were important in forcing change on the Soviet Union. In 1980 protests by Polish shipyard workers in the city of Gdansk led to the formation of **Solidarity,** a labor union that soon enrolled 9 million members. The Roman Catholic Church in Poland, strengthened by the elevation of a Pole, Karol Wojtyla°, to the papacy as John Paul II in 1978, gave strong moral support to the protest movement.

The Polish government imposed martial law in 1981 in response to the growing power of Solidarity and its allies, giving the army effective political control. Seeing Solidarity under tight controls and many of its leaders in prison, the Soviet Union decided not to intervene. But Solidarity remained a potent force with a strong institutional structure and nationally recognized leaders. As Gorbachev loosened political controls in the Soviet Union after 1985, communist leaders elsewhere lost confidence in Soviet resolve, and critics and reformers in Poland and throughout eastern Europe were emboldened (see Map 33.1).

Beleaguered Warsaw Pact governments vacillated between relaxation of control and suppression of dissent. Just as the Catholic clergy in Poland had supported Solidarity, Protestant and Orthodox religious leaders aided the rise of opposition groups elsewhere. This combination of nationalism and religion provided a powerful base for opponents of the communist regimes. Threatened by these forces, communist governments sought to quiet opposition by seeking solutions to their severe economic problems. They turned to the West for trade and financial assistance. They also opened their nations to travelers, ideas, styles, and money from Western countries, all of which accelerated the demand for change.

By the end of 1989 communist governments across eastern Europe had fallen. The dismantling of the Berlin Wall, the symbol of a divided Europe and the bipolar world, vividly represented this transformation. Communist leaders in Poland, Hungary, Czechoslovakia, and Bulgaria decided that change was inevitable and initiated political reforms. In Romania the dictator Nicolae Ceausescu° refused to surrender power, thus provoking a rebellion that ended with his arrest and execution. The comprehensiveness of these changes became clear in 1990, when Solidarity leader Lech Walesa° was elected president of Poland and dissident playwright Vaclav Havel° was elected president of Czechoslovakia.

The Fall of the Berlin Wall The Berlin Wall was the most important symbol of the Cold War. Constructed to keep residents of East Germany from fleeing to the West and defended by armed guards and barbed wire, for many in the West it was the public face of communism. As the Soviet system fell apart, the residents of East and West Berlin broke down sections of the wall. Here young people straddle the wall, signaling the end of an era. (Bossu Regis/ Corbis Sygma)

Following the fall of the Berlin Wall, a tidal wave of patriotic enthusiasm swept aside the once-formidable communist government of East Germany. In the chaotic months that followed, East Germans crossed to West Germany in large numbers, and government services in the eastern sector nearly disappeared. Some Europeans recalled German militarism earlier in the century and worried about reunification. But there was little concrete opposition, and in 1990 Germany was reunified. Numerous problems followed reunification, including high levels of unemployment and budget deficits, but nearly fifty years of confrontation and tension across the heart of Europe seemed to end overnight.

Soviet leaders looked on with dismay at the collapse of communism in the Warsaw Pact countries. They knew

---

Karol Wojtyla (KAH-rol voy-TIL-ah) **Nicolae Ceausescu** (neh-koh-LIE chow-SHES-koo) **Lech Walesa** (leck wah-LESS-ah) **Vaclav Havel** (vah-SLAV hah-VEL)

Map 33.1 The End of Soviet Domination in Eastern Europe The creation of new countries out of Yugoslavia and Czechoslovakia and the reunification of Germany marked the most complicated changes of national borders since World War I. The Czech Republic and Slovakia separated peacefully, but Slovenia, Croatia, Macedonia, and Bosnia and Herzegovina achieved independence only after bitter fighting.

that similarly powerful nationalist sentiments existed within the Soviet Union as well. The year 1990 brought declarations of independence by Lithuania, Estonia, and Latvia, three small states on the Baltic Sea that the Soviet Union had annexed in 1939. Violent ethnic strife soon erupted in the Caucasus region. Gorbachev tried to accommodate the rising pressures for change, but the tide was running too fast.

The end of the Soviet Union came suddenly in 1991 (see Map 33.2). After communist hardliners botched a poorly conceived coup against Gorbachev, disgust with communism boiled over. Boris Yeltsin, the president of the Russian Republic and longtime member of the Communist Party, led popular resistance to the coup in Moscow and emerged as the most powerful leader in the country. Russia, the largest republic in the Soviet Union, was effectively taking the place of the disintegrating USSR. With the central government scarcely functioning, nationalism, long repressed by Soviet authorities, reappeared throughout the Soviet Union. In September 1991 the Congress of People's Deputies—the central legislature of the USSR, long subservient to the Communist Party—voted to dissolve the union. In December a loose successor organization with little central control, the Commonwealth of Independent States (CIS), was created. The same month Mikhail Gorbachev resigned.

The ethnic and religious passions that fueled the breakup of the Soviet Union soon challenged the survival of Yugoslavia and Czechoslovakia. The dismemberment of Yugoslavia began with declarations of independence in Slovenia and Croatia in 1991. Two years later Czechoslovakia peacefully divided into the Czech

Map 33.2 The End of the Soviet Union When Communist hardliners failed to overthrow Gorbachev in 1991, popular anticommunist sentiment swept the Soviet Union. Following Boris Yeltsin's lead in Russia, the republics that constituted the Soviet Union declared their independence.

Republic and Slovakia. East Germany was reunited with West Germany with little violence, but destructive ethnic and religious conflict characterized the transitional period in Armenia, Georgia, and Chechnya as well as the breakup of Yugoslavia (see Chapter 34).

The Persian Gulf War, 1990–1991

The first significant conflict to occur after the breakup of the Soviet Union and the end of the Cold War was the Persian Gulf War. The immediate causes were local and bilateral. Iraq's ruler, Saddam Husain, had borrowed a great deal of money from neighboring Kuwait and sought unsuccessfully to get Kuwait's royal family to reduce the size of this debt. He was also eager to gain control of Kuwait's oil fields. Husain believed that the smaller and militarily weaker nation could be quickly defeated, and he suspected, as a result of a conversation with an American diplomat, that the United States would not react. The invasion came in August 1990.

The United States convinced the government of Saudi Arabia that it was a possible target of Iraq's aggression. Saudi Arabia, an important regional ally of the United States and a major oil producer, was the key to any military action by the United States. The United States and its allies concentrated an imposing military force of 500,000 in the region. With his intention to use force endorsed by the United Nations and with many Islamic nations supporting military action, President George H. W. Bush ordered an attack in early 1991. Iraq proved incapable of countering the sophisticated weaponry of the coalition. The missiles and bombs of the United States destroyed not only military targets but also "relegated [Iraq] to a pre-industrial age," the United Nations reported after the war. Although Iraq's military defeat was comprehensive, Husain remained in power, and the country was not occupied. In fact Husain crushed an uprising in the months following this defeat. The United States and its key allies then imposed "no-fly" zones that denied Iraq's military aircraft access to the northern and southern regions of the country. As a result, military tensions and periodic armed confrontations continued.

In the United States the results were interpreted to mean that the U.S. military defeat in the Vietnam War could be forgotten and that U.S. military capability was unrivaled. Unable to deter military action by the U.S.-led coalition or to meaningfully influence the diplomacy that surrounded the war, Russia had been of little use to its former ally Iraq, and its impotence was clear.

THE CHALLENGE OF POPULATION GROWTH

For most of human history population growth was viewed as beneficial, and human beings were seen as a source of wealth. Since the late eighteenth century, however, population increases have been viewed with increasing alarm. At first it was feared that food supplies could not keep up with population growth. Then social critics expressed concern that growing population would lead to class and ethnic struggle as numbers overwhelmed resources. By the second half of the twentieth century population growth was increasingly seen as a threat to the environment. Are urban sprawl, pollution, and soil erosion inevitable results of population growth? The questions and debates continue today, but clearly population is both a cause and a result of increased global interdependency.

Demographic Transition

The population of Europe almost doubled between 1850 and 1914, putting enormous pressure on rural land and urban housing and overwhelming fragile public institutions that provided some crisis assistance (see Chapter 27). This dramatic growth forced a large wave of immigration across the Atlantic, helping to develop North and South America and invigorating the Atlantic economy (see Chapter 24). Population growth also contributed to Europe's Industrial Revolution by lowering labor costs and increasing consumer demand.

Educated Europeans of the nineteenth century were ambivalent about the rapid increase in human population. Some saw it as a blessing that would promote economic well-being. Others warned that the seemingly relentless increase would bring disaster. The best-known pessimist was the English cleric **Thomas Malthus,** who in 1798 argued convincingly that unchecked population growth would outstrip food production. When Malthus looked at Europe's future, he used a prejudiced image of China to terrify his European readers. A visitor to China, he claimed, "will not be surprised that mothers destroy or expose many of their children; that parents sell their daughters for a trifle; . . . and that there should be such a number of robbers. The surprise is that nothing still more dreadful should happen."[2]

The generation that came of age in the years immediately following World War II inherited a world in which the views of Malthus were casually dismissed. Industrial and agricultural productivity had multiplied supplies of food and other necessities. Cultural changes associated with expanded female employment, older age at marriage, and more effective family planning had combined to slow the rate of population increase. And by the late 1960s Europe and other industrial societies had made what was called the **demographic transition** to lower fertility rates (average number of births per woman) and reduced mortality. The number of births in the developed nations was just adequate for the maintenance of current population levels. Thus many experts argued that the population growth then occurring in developing nations was a short-term phenomenon that would be ended by the combination of economic and social changes that had altered European patterns.

By the late 1970s, however, the demographic transition had not occurred in the Third World, and the issue of population growth had become politicized. The leaders of some developing nations actively promoted large families, arguing that larger populations would increase national power. These arguments remained a persistent part of the debate between developed and developing nations. Industrialized, mostly white, nations raised concerns about rapid population growth in Asia, Africa, and Latin America. Populist political leaders in those regions asked whether these concerns were not fundamentally racist.

The question exposed the influence of racism in the population debate and temporarily disarmed Western advocates of birth control. However, once the economic shocks of the 1970s and 1980s revealed the vulnerability of developing economies, governments in the developing world jettisoned policies that promoted population growth. Mexico is a good example. In the 1970s the government had encouraged high fertility, and population growth rose to 3 percent per year. By the 1980s Mexico rejected these policies and promoted birth control, with the result that annual population growth fell to 2.3 percent.

Chinese Family-Planning Campaign Hoping to slow population growth, the Chinese government has sought to limit parents to a single child. Billboards and other forms of mass advertising have been an essential part of the campaign to gain compliance with national family-planning directives. (Picard/Sipa Press)

World population exploded in the twentieth century (see Table 33.1). Although there are indications that rates of growth are currently slowing, world population still increases by a number equal to the total population of the United States every three years. If fertility rates across the globe remain unchanged, world population will reach 256 billion in 2150, twenty-eight times the 2050 projection found in Table 33.1.

This is not likely. Fertility is already declining in some developing areas. Mortality rates have also increased in some areas as immigration, commercial expansion, and improved transportation facilitate the transmission of disease. The rapid spread of HIV/AIDS is an example of this phenomenon. Less-developed regions with poorly funded public health institutions and with few resources to invest in prevention and treatment experience the highest rates of infection and the greatest mortality. In Russia, for example, new HIV infections rose from under five thousand in 1997 to over ninety thousand in 2001. AIDS has spread at a similar pace in China. But the disease has developed most quickly and with the most devastating results in Africa, the home of 28 million of the world's 40 million infected people.

Unlike population growth in the eighteenth and nineteenth centuries, when much of the increase occurred in the wealthiest nations, population growth at the end of the twentieth century was overwhelmingly in the poorest nations. Although fertility rates dropped in most developing nations, they remained much higher than rates in the industrialized nations. At the same time, improvements in hygiene and medical treatment caused mortality rates to fall, despite recent catastrophies, such as HIV/AIDS. The result has been rapid population growth.

The Industrialized Nations

In the developed industrial nations of western Europe and in Japan at the beginning of the twenty-first century, fertility levels are so low that population will fall unless immigration increases. Japanese women have an average of 1.39 children; in Italy the number is 1.2. Although Sweden tries to promote fertility with cash payments, tax incentives, and job leaves to families with children, the average number of births per

Table 33.1 Population for World and Major Areas, 1750–2050

Population Size (Millions)

Major Area	1750	1800	1850	1900	1950	1995	(estimated) 2050
World	791	978	1,262	1,650	2,521	5,666	8,909
Africa	106	107	111	133	221	697	1,766
Asia	502	635	809	947	1,402	3,437	5,268
Europe	163	203	276	408	547	728	628
Latin America and the Caribbean	16	24	38	74	167	480	809
North America	2	7	26	82	172	297	392
Oceania	2	2	2	6	13	28	46

Percentage Distribution

Major Area	1750	1800	1850	1900	1950	1995	(estimated) 2050
World	100	100	100	100	100	100	100
Africa	13.4	10.9	8.8	8.1	8.8	12	19.8
Asia	63.5	64.9	64.1	57.4	55.6	61	59.1
Europe	20.6	20.8	21.9	24.7	21.7	13	7.0
Latin America and the Caribbean	2.0	2.5	3.0	4.5	6.6	8	9.1
North America	0.3	0.7	2.1	5.0	6.8	5	4.4
Oceania	0.3	0.2	0.2	0.4	0.5	1	0.5

Source: J. D. Durand, "Historical Estimates of World Population: An Evaluation" (Philadelphia: University of Pennsylvania, Population Studies Center, 1974, mimeographed); United Nations, *The Determinants and Consequences of Population Trends,* vol. 1 (New York: United Nations, 1973); United Nations, *World Population Prospects as Assessed in 1963* (New York: United Nations, 1966); United Nations, *World Population Prospects: The 1998 Revision* (New York: United Nations, forthcoming); United Nations Population Division, Department of Economic and Social Affairs, http://www.popin.org/pop1998/4.htm.

woman has fallen to 1.4 in recent years. The low fertility found in mature industrial nations is tied to higher levels of female education and employment, the material values of consumer culture, and access to contraception and abortion. Educated women now defer marriage and child rearing until they are established in careers. An Italian woman in Bologna, the city with the lowest fertility in the world, put it this way: "I'm an only child and if I could, I'd have more than one child. But most couples I know wait until their 30's to have children. People want to have their own life, they want to have a successful career. When you see life in these terms, children are an impediment."[3]

In industrialized nations life expectancy has improved as fertility has declined. The combination of abundant food, improved hygiene, and more effective medicines and medical care has lengthened human lives. In 2000 about 20 percent of the population in the more-developed nations was sixty-five or over. By 2050 this proportion should rise to one-third. Italy soon will have more than twenty adults fifty years old or over for each five-year-old child. Because of higher fertility and greater levels of immigration, the United States is moving in this direction more slowly than western Europe; by 2050 the median age in Europe will be fifty-two, while it will be thirty-five in the United States.

The combination of falling fertility and rising life expectancy in the industrialized nations presents a challenge very different from the one foreseen by Malthus. These nations generally offer a broad array of social services, including retirement income, medical services, and housing supplements for the elderly. As the number of retirees increases relative to the number of people who are employed, the costs of these services may become unsustainable. Economists track this problem using the PSR (potential support ratio). This is the ratio of persons fifteen to sixty-four years old (likely workers) to persons sixty-five or older (likely retirees). Between 1950 and 2000 the world's PSR fell from twelve to nine. By 2050 it will fall to four. Clearly, nations with the oldest populations, especially Japan and the nations of western Europe, will have to reexamine programs that encourage early retirement as the ratio of workers to retirees drops.

In Russia and other former socialist nations, current birthrates are now actually lower than death rates—

levels inadequate to sustain the current population size. Birthrates were already low before the collapse of the socialist system and have contracted further with recent economic problems. Since 1975 fertility rates have fallen between 20 and 40 percent across the former Soviet bloc. By the early 1980s abortions were as common as births in much of eastern Europe.

Life expectancy has also fallen. Life expectancy for Russian men is now only fifty-seven years, down almost ten years since 1980. In the Czech Republic, Hungary, and Poland, life expectancy is improving in response to improved economic conditions, but most of the rest of eastern Europe has experienced the Russian pattern of declining life expectancy. High unemployment, low incomes, food shortages, and the dismantling of the social welfare system of the communist era have all contributed to this decline.

The Developing Nations

Even if the industrialized nations decided to promote an increase in family size in the twenty-first century, they would continue to fall behind the developing nations as a percentage of world population. At current rates 95 percent of all future population growth will be in developing nations (see Map 33.3 and Table 33.1). A comparison between Europe and Africa illustrates these changes. In 1950 Europe had twice the population of Africa. By 1985 Africa's population had drawn even with Europe's. According to projections, Africa's population will be three times larger than Europe's by 2025. Given the performance of African economies, future generations of Africans will likely experience increased famine, epidemics, and social breakdown.

As the 1990s ended other developing regions had rapid population growth as well. While all developing nations had an average birthrate of 33.6 per thousand inhabitants, Muslim countries had a rate of 42.1. This rate is more than 300 percent higher than the 13.1 births per thousand in the developed nations of the West. The populations of Latin America and Asia were also expanding dramatically, but at rates slower than sub-Saharan Africa and the Muslim nations. Latin America's population increased from 165 million in 1950 to 405 million in 1985 and is projected to reach 778 million in 2025, despite declining birthrates.

In Asia, the populations of India and China continued to grow despite government efforts to reduce family size. Today these two nations account for roughly one-third of the world's population. In China efforts to enforce a limit of one child per family led to large-scale female infanticide as rural families sought to produce male heirs. India's policies of forced sterilization created widespread outrage and led to the electoral defeat of the ruling Congress Party. Yet both countries achieved some successes. Between 1960 and 1982 India's birthrate fell from 48 to 34 per thousand, while China's rate declined even more sharply—from 39 to 19 per thousand. Still, by 2025 both China, which today has 1.13 billion people, and India, with 853 million, will each reach 1.5 billion.

It is unclear whether the nations of Asia, Africa, and Latin America will undergo the lowered fertility and mortality rates experienced in the West during the Industrial Revolution. Yet real progress has occurred, and fertility rates have fallen where women have had access to education and employment outside the home.

Old and Young Populations

Population pyramids generated by demographers clearly illustrate the profound transformation in human reproductive patterns and life expectancy in the years since World War II. Figure 33.1 shows the 2001 age distributions in Pakistan, South Korea, and Sweden—nations at three different stages of economic development. Sweden is a mature industrial nation. South Korea is rapidly industrializing and has surpassed many European nations in both industrial output and per capita wealth. Pakistan is a poor, traditional Muslim nation with rudimentary industrialization, low educational levels, and little effective family planning.

In 2001 nearly 50 percent of Pakistan's population was under age sixteen. The resulting pressures on the economy have been extraordinary. Every year approximately 150,000 men reach age sixty-five—and another 1.2 million turn sixteen. Pakistan, therefore, has to create more than a million new jobs a year or face steadily growing unemployment and steadily declining wages. Sweden confronts a different problem. Sweden's aging population, growing demand for social welfare benefits, and declining labor pool means that its industries may become less competitive and living standards may decline. In South Korea, a decline in fertility dramatically altered the ratio of children to adults, creating an age distribution similar to that of western Europe earlier in the twentieth century. South Korea does not face Pakistan's impossible task of creating new jobs or Sweden's growing demands for welfare benefits for the aged.

The demographic challenges faced by Sweden and other developed nations are less daunting than those confronting the developing nations. Poor nations must overcome shortages of investment capital, poor transportation and communication networks, and low educational levels while they struggle to create jobs. Wealthy,

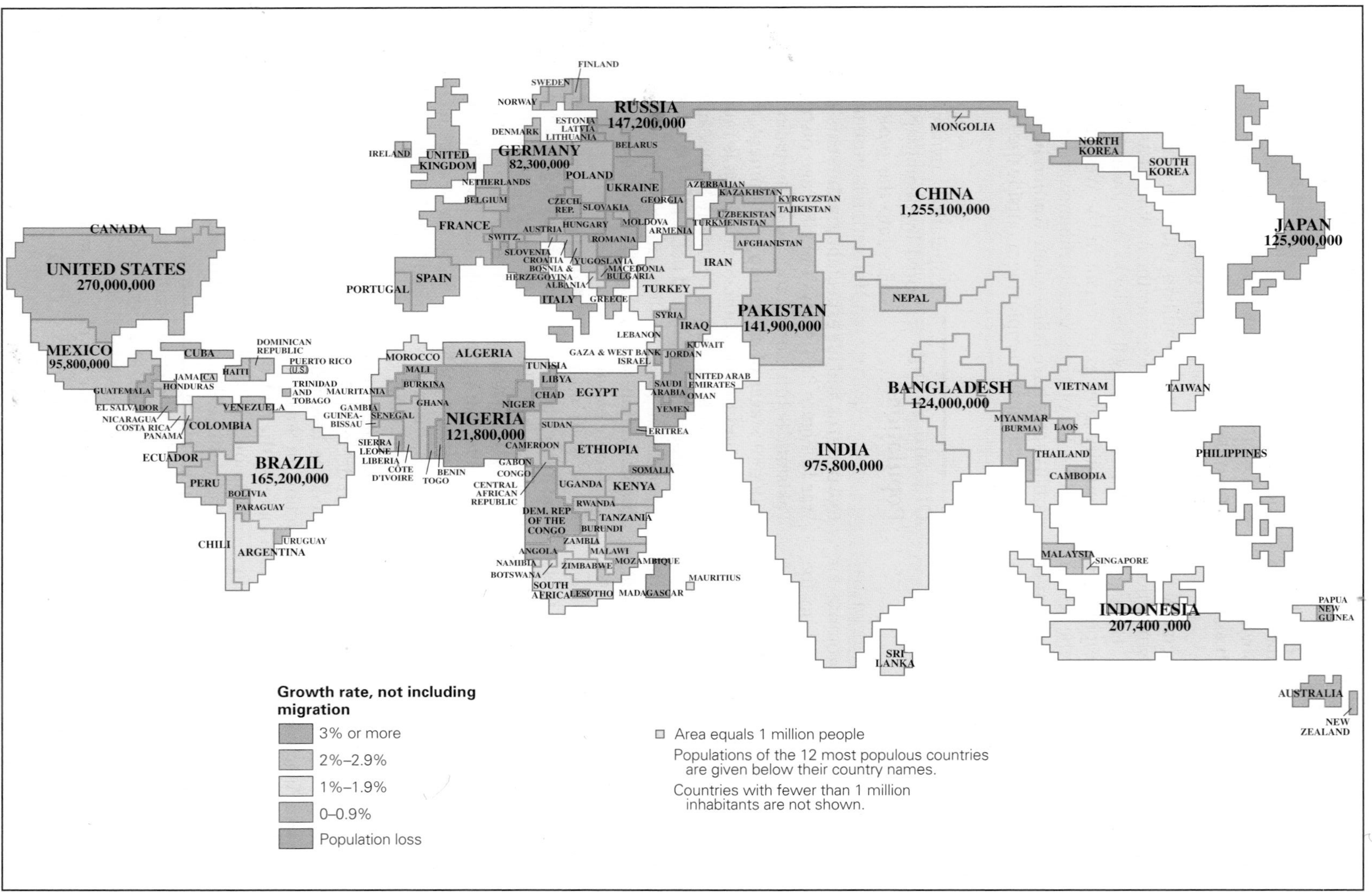

Map 33.3 World Population Growth At current rates of growth, every three years the world's population will increase by the equivalent of a nation the size of the United States. Most of this population increase will be in some of the world's poorest nations. By 2050, for example, Pakistan, a nation of only 40 million in 1950, will surpass the United States and become the country with the world's third largest population. *Source*: National Geographic Maps 1998/10 Map Supplement Population Growth. Used by permission of National Geographic Society.

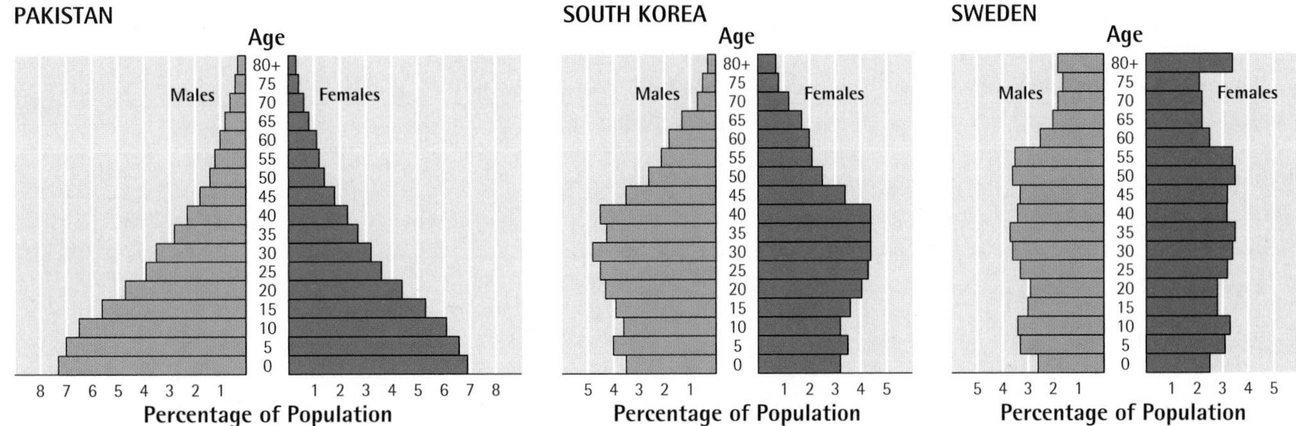

Figure 33.1 Age Structure Comparison: Islamic Nation (Pakistan), Non-Islamic Developing Nation (South Korea), and Developed Nation (Sweden), 2001 *Source:* U.S. Bureau of the Census, *International Database*, 2001.

well-educated, and politically stable nations can invest in robots and other new technologies to reduce labor needs and increase industrial and agricultural efficiency as their populations age.

The demographic problem and potential technological adjustments are most clearly visible in Japan. Japan has the oldest population in the world, with a current median age of forty-one. Large numbers of young immigrants from poorer nations are entering the work forces of Canada, Germany, the United States, and most other industrialized nations, slowing the aging of these populations. Japan has resisted immigration, instead investing heavily in technological solutions to the problems created by its aging labor force. As of 1994 Japan had 75 percent of the world's industrial robots. Although Japanese industries are able to produce more goods with fewer workers, Japan will still face long-term increases in social welfare payments.

The combination of intractable poverty and growing population generated a surge in international immigration. Few issues stirred more controversy. Even moderate voices sometimes framed the discussion of immigration as a competition among peoples. One commentator analyzed the situation this way: "As the better-off families of the northern hemisphere individually decide that having only one or at the most two children is sufficient, they may not recognize that they are in a small way vacating future space (that is, jobs, parts of inner cities, shares of population, shares of market preferences) to faster-growing ethnic groups both inside and outside their boundaries. But that, in fact, is what they are doing."[4]

Large numbers of legal and illegal immigrants from poor nations with growing populations are entering the developed industrial nations, with the exception of Japan. Large-scale migrations within developing countries are a related phenomenon. The movement of impoverished rural residents to the cities of Asia, Africa, and Latin America (see Map 33.3 and Table 33.2) has increased steadily since the 1970s. This internal migration often serves as the first step toward migration abroad.

Unequal Development and the Movement of Peoples

Two characteristics of the postwar world should now be clear. First, despite decades of experimentation with state-directed economic development, most nations that were poor in 1960 were as poor or poorer in 2003. The only exceptions were a few rapidly developing Asian industrial nations and an equally small number of oil-exporting nations. Second, world population increased to startlingly high levels, and most of the increase was in the poorest nations.

The Problem of Growing Inequality

Since 1945 global economic productivity has expanded more rapidly than at any other time in the past. Faster, cheaper communications and transportation have combined with improvements in industrial and agricultural technologies to create material abundance that would have amazed those who experienced the first Industrial Revolution (see Chapter 23). Despite this remarkable economic expansion and

Table 33.2 The World's Largest Cities (Population of 10 Million or More)

City	1950	City	1975	City	2000	City	2015
1 New York	12.3	1 Tokyo	19.8	1 Tokyo	26.4	1 Tokyo	26.4
		2 New York	15.9	2 Mexico City	18.1	2 Bombay	26.1
		3 Shanghai	11.4	3 Bombay	18.1	3 Lagos	23.2
		4 Mexico City	11.2	4 Sao Paulo	17.8	4 Dhaka	21.1
		5 Sao Paulo	10.0	5 New York	16.6	5 Sao Paulo	20.4
				6 Lagos	13.4	6 Karachi	19.2
				7 Los Angeles	13.1	7 Mexico City	19.2
				8 Calcutta	12.9	8 New York	17.4
				9 Shanghai	12.9	9 Jakarta	17.3
				10 Buenos Aires	12.6	10 Calcutta	17.3
				11 Dhaka	12.3	11 Delhi	16.8
				12 Karachi	11.8	12 Metro Manila	14.8
				13 Delhi	11.7	13 Shanghai	14.6
				14 Jakarta	11.0	14 Los Angeles	14.1
				15 Osaka	11.0	15 Buenos Aires	14.1
				16 Metro Manila	10.9	16 Cairo	13.8
				17 Beijing	10.8	17 Istanbul	12.5
				18 Rio de Janeiro	10.6	18 Beijing	12.3
				19 Cairo	10.6	19 Rio de Janeiro	11.9
						20 Osaka	11.0
						21 Tianjin	10.7
						22 Hyderabad	10.5
						23 Bangkok	10.1

Source: International Migration Report 2002, United Nations, Department of Economic and Social Affairs, Population Division, "World Urbanization Prospects: The 1999 Revision," p. 6. Reprinted by permission of United States Publications.

growing market integration, the majority of the world's population remains in poverty. The industrialized nations of the Northern Hemisphere now enjoy a larger share of the world's wealth than they did a century ago. The United States, Japan, and the nations of the European Union alone accounted for a startling 74 percent of the world's economy in 1998. The thousands of homeless street children who live among the gleaming glass and steel towers of Rio's banking district, on the other hand, can be seen as a metaphor for the social consequences of postwar economic development.

The gap between rich and poor nations has grown much wider since 1945. But among both groups dramatic changes have resulted from changes in competitiveness, technology transfers, and market conditions. In 2001 Luxemburg and Switzerland had the highest per capita GNI (gross national income)—$39,840 and $35,630, respectively; the U.S. figure was $34,280; and Greece, the poorest nation in the European Union, had a per capita GNI of $11,430. The nations of the former Soviet Union and eastern Europe have per capita GNIs lower than some developing nations in the Third World. Russia's per capita GNI was $1,750 in 2001, less than Mexico's $5,530, Brazil's $3,070, and South Africa's 2,820, but higher than Bolivia's $950 and the Philippines' $1,030. Among other developing economies, Algeria and Thailand had per capita GNIs of $1,650 and $1,940 respectively. Nigeria, India, and China had GNIs below $1,000. One billion of the world's people, approximately 20 percent, lived on less than $500 a year in 2001. This poverty was concentrated in Africa, Latin America, and Asia.

Wealth inequality within nations also grew. Regions tied to new technologies that provided competitive advantages became wealthier, while other regions lost ground. In the United States, for example, the South and Southwest grew richer in the last three decades relative to the older industrial regions of the Midwest. Regional inequalities also appeared in developing nations. Generally, capital cities such Buenos Aires, Argentina, and Lagos, Nigeria, attracted large numbers of migrants from rural areas because they offered more opportunities,

Garbage Dump in Manila, Philippines Garbage pickers are a common feature of Third World urban development. Thousands of poor families in nearly every Third World city sort and sell bottles, aluminum cans, plastic, and newspapers to provide household income. (Geoff Tompkinson/Aspect Picture Library Ltd.)

even if those opportunities could not compare to the ones available in developed nations.

Even in the industrialized world, people were divided into haves and have-nots. The tax reform program put in place during the presidency of Ronald Reagan (served 1981–1989) led to greater wealth inequality in the United States. This trend continued to the present, driven by the stock market boom of the 1990s and another round of tax reforms under President George W. Bush (elected 2001). Wealth inequality is now as great as on the eve of the 1929 stock market crash. Although this trend slowed in the 1990s, the households that make up the wealthiest 5 percent of American society are now relatively richer than at any time in the past. Scholars estimate that the wealthiest 1 percent of households in the United States control more than 30 percent of the nation's total wealth, while the poorest households have average incomes of under $5,000. Even in Europe, where tax and inheritance laws redistributed wealth, unemployment, homelessness, and substandard housing have become increasingly common.

Internal Migration: The Growth of Cities

In developing nations migration from rural areas to urban centers increased threefold between 1925 and 1950, and the pace accelerated after that (see Table 33.2). Shantytowns around major cities in developing nations are commonly seen as signs of social breakdown and economic failure. Nevertheless, city life was generally better than life in the countryside. A World Bank study estimated that three out of four migrants to cities made economic gains. Residents of cities in sub-Saharan Africa, for example, were six times more likely than rural residents to have safe water. An unskilled migrant from the depressed northeast of Brazil could triple his or her income by moving to Rio de Janeiro.

However, as the scale of rural-to-urban migration grew, these benefits proved more elusive. In many West African cities, basic services were crumbling under the pressure of rapid population growth. In 1990 in Mexico City, one of the world's largest cities, more than thirty thousand people lived in garbage dumps, where they scavenged for food and clothing. Worsening conditions and the threat of crime and political instability led many governments to try to slow migration to cities and, in some cases, to return people to the countryside. Indonesia, for example, has relocated more than a half-million urban residents since 1969. Despite some successes with slowing the rate of internal migration, nearly every poor nation still faces the challenge of rapidly growing cities.

Global Migration

Each year hundreds of thousands of men and women leave the developing world to emigrate to industrialized nations. After 1960 this movement increased in scale, and ethnic and racial tensions in the host nations worsened. Political refugees and immigrants faced murderous violence in Germany; growing anti-immigrant sentiment led to a new right-wing political movement in France; and an expanded border patrol attempted to more effectively seal the U.S. border with Mexico. By the 1990s levels of immigration posed daunting social and cultural challenges for both host nations and immigrants.

Immigrants from the developing nations brought host nations many of the same benefits that the great migration of Europeans to the Americas provided a century earlier (see Chapter 24). Many European nations actively promoted guest worker programs and other inducements to immigration in the 1960s, when an expanding European economy first confronted labor shortages. However, attitudes toward immigrants changed as the size of the immigrant population grew and as European economies slowed in the 1980s. Facing higher levels of unemployment, native-born workers saw immigrants as competitors willing to work for lower wages and less likely to support labor unions. However, because cultural and ethnic characteristics have traditionally formed the basis of national identity in many European countries (see Chapter 27), worsening relations between immigrants and the native-born may have been inevitable. Put simply, many Germans are unable to think of the German-born son or daughter of Turkish immigrants as a German.

Because immigrants are generally young adults and commonly retain positive attitudes toward early marriage and large families dominant in their native cultures, immigrants in Europe and the United States have tended to have higher fertility rates than do host populations. In Germany in 1975, for example, immigrants made up only 7 percent of the population but accounted for nearly 15 percent of all births. Although immigrant fertility rates decline with prolonged residence in industrialized societies, the family size of second-generation immigrants is still larger than that of the host population. Therefore, even without additional immigration, immigrant groups grow faster than longer-established populations. The fertility of the Hispanic population in the United States, for example, is lower than the rates in Mexico and other Latin American nations. Nevertheless, Hispanic groups will contribute well over 20 percent of all population growth in the United States during the next twenty-five years.

As the Muslim population in Europe and the Asian and Latin American populations in the United States expand in the twenty-first century, cultural conflicts will test definitions of citizenship and nationality. The United States will have some advantages in meeting these challenges because of long experience with immigration and relatively open access to citizenship. Yet in the 1990s the United States was moving slowly in the direction of restricting immigration and defending a culturally conservative definition of nationality.

TECHNOLOGICAL AND ENVIRONMENTAL CHANGE

Technological innovation powered the economic expansion that began after World War II. New technologies increased productivity and disseminated human creativity. They also altered the way people lived, worked, and played. Because most of the economic benefits were concentrated in the advanced industrialized nations, technology increased the power of those nations relative to the developing world. Even within developed nations, postwar technological innovations did not benefit all classes, industries, and regions equally. There were losers as well as winners.

Population growth and increased levels of migration and urbanization led to the global expansion of agricultural and industrial production. This multiplication of farms and factories intensified environmental threats. At the end of the twentieth century loss of rain forest, soil erosion, global warming, air and water pollution, and extinction of species threatened the quality of life and the survival of human societies. Here again, differences between nations were apparent. Environmental protection, like the acquisition of new technology, had progressed most in societies with the greatest economic resources.

New Technologies and the World Economy

Nuclear energy, jet engines, radar, and tape recording were among the many World War II developments that later had an impact on consumers' lives. When applied to industry, new technology increased productivity, reduced labor requirements, and improved the flow of information that made markets more efficient. Pent-up demand for consumer goods also spurred new research and the development of new technologies. As the Western economies recovered from the war and incomes rose, consumers wanted new products that reduced their workloads or provided entertainment. The consumer electronics industry rapidly developed new products, changes that can be summarized by the music industry's movement from vinyl records to 8-tracks, tapes, CDs, and MP3 technologies.

Improvements in existing technologies accounted for much of the developed world's productivity increases during the 1950s and 1960s. Larger and faster trucks, trains, and airplanes cut transportation costs. Both capitalist and socialist governments built highway systems, improved railroad tracks, and constructed airports. Governments also bore much of the cost of developing and constructing nuclear power plants.

No technology had greater significance than the computer. The first computers were expensive, large, and slow. Only large corporations, governments, and universities could afford them. But by the mid-1980s desktop computers had replaced typewriters in most of the developed world's offices, and the technology continued to advance. Each new generation of computers was smaller, faster, and more powerful than the one before (see Environment and Technology: The Personal Computer).

Computers also altered manufacturing. Small dedicated computers were used to control and monitor machinery in most industries. In the developed world companies forced by competition to improve efficiency and product quality brought robots into factories. Europe quickly followed Japan's lead in robotics, especially in automobile production and mining. The United States introduced robots more slowly because it enjoyed lower labor costs, but has now fully embraced this technology.

The transnational corporation became the primary agent of these technological changes. Since the eighteenth century powerful commercial companies have conducted business across national borders. By the twentieth century the growing economic power of corporations in industrialized nations allowed them to invest directly in the mines, plantations, and public utilities of less-developed regions. In the post–World War II years many of these companies became truly transnational, having multinational ownership and management. International trade agreements and open markets furthered the process. Ford Motor Company not only produced and sold cars internationally, but its shareholders, workers, and managers also came from numerous nations. Symbolic of these changes, the Japanese automaker Honda manufactured cars in Ohio and imported them into Japan, while Germany's Volkswagen made cars in Mexico for sale in the United States.

As transnational manufacturers, agricultural conglomerates, and financial giants became wealthier and more powerful, they increasingly escaped the controls imposed by national governments. If labor costs were too high in Japan, antipollution measures too intrusive in the United States, or taxes too high in Great Britain, transnational companies relocated—or threatened to do so. In 1945, for example, the U.S. textile industry was located in low-wage southern states, dominating the American market and exporting to the world. As wages in the South rose and global competition increased, producers began relocating plants to Puerto Rico in the 1980s, to Mexico after NAFTA went into effect in 1994 (see Chapter 34), and now to China. The relatively low Mexican wages that attracted investments in the early 1990s now appear high in comparison with China's wages. As industries moved around, searching for profits, the governments in the developing world were often hard-pressed to control their actions. As a result, the worst abuses of labor and of the environment usually occurred in poor nations.

Conserving and Sharing Resources

In the 1960s environmental activists and political leaders began warning about the devastating environmental consequences of population growth, industrialization, and the expansion of agriculture onto marginal lands. Assaults on rain forests and redwoods, the disappearance of species, and the poisoning of streams and rivers raised public consciousness. Environmental damage occurred both in the advanced industrial economies and in the poorest of the developing nations. Perhaps the worst environmental record was achieved in the former Soviet Union, where industrial and nuclear wastes were often dumped with little concern for environmental consequences. The accumulated effect of scientific studies and public debate led to national and international efforts to slow, if not undo, damage to the environment.

ENVIRONMENT + TECHNOLOGY

The Personal Computer

The period since World War II has witnessed wave after wave of technological innovations. Few of them have had a greater impact on the way people work, learn, and live than the personal computer. Until the 1970s most computing was done on large and expensive mainframe computers, and IBM (International Business Machines) dominated the industry. Access to computers was controlled by the government agencies, universities, and large corporations that owned them.

Few anticipated the technological innovations that revolutionized the computer industry in the next two decades. In rapid succession transistors replaced vacuum tubes in mainframes and then silicon chips replaced hard-wired transistors. The race to miniaturize was on. The key development was the microprocessor, a computer processor (in effect the computer's brains) on a silicon chip. Computers became smaller and cheaper as memory chips and microprocessors were made smaller and more powerful. As new companies entered the market, prices fell, and computers became a part of modern consumer culture.

Young physicists, engineers, and mathematicians working for small companies in Massachusetts and California were responsible for nearly all the most important innovations that led to desktops, then laptops, and more recently a variety of hand-held computers. Among the most important of these innovators were Steven Jobs and Stephen G. Wozniak. Part of an enterprising group of hobbyists, they joined forces to introduce the first mass-market home computer with color screen, keyboard, and built-in computing language, the Apple II, in 1977. IBM responded to these developments slowly, but in 1981 introduced its own personal computer, the IBM PC. Although IBM did not continue as the industry leader, the PC would begin a slow process of operating system standardization tied to the meteoric growth of Microsoft.

Each new generation of computers has been more powerful, smaller, and less expensive. A modern 1.8 gigahertz Intel Pentium 4 chip is 3,600 times as fast as the first desktop processor just forty years ago. By the mid-1990s desktop and laptop computers had replaced the mainframe for most uses. The Internet was developed to facilitate defense research in the 1960s. The establishment of the World Wide Web as a graphic interface in the 1990s allowed the smaller, faster computers to become research portals that accessed a vast international database of research, opinion, entertainment, and commerce. The computer revolution and the Web have had a revolutionary impact, allowing individuals and groups—without the support of governments, corporations, or other powerful institutions—to collect and disseminate information more freely than any time in the past (see Chapter 34).

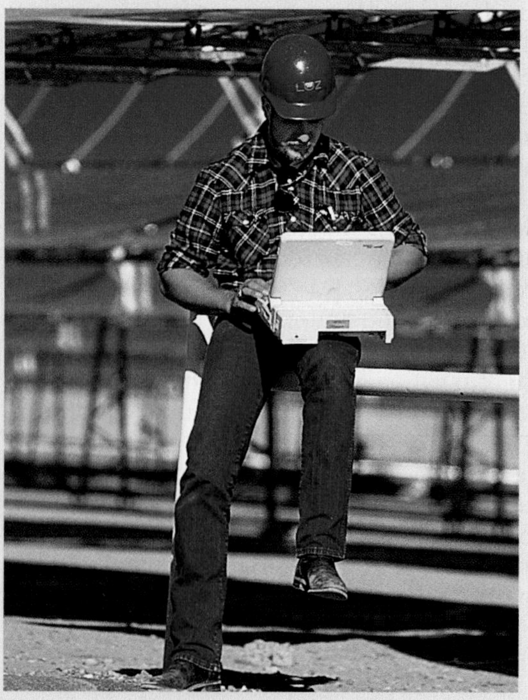

From Mainframe to Laptop During the last forty years the computer revolution has changed the way we work. (left: Courtesy, IBM Corporation; bottom: Dagmar Fabricius/Liaison/Getty Images)

Loss of Brazilian Rain Forest The destruction of large portions of Brazil's virgin rain forest has come to symbolize the growing threat to the environment caused by population growth and economic development. In this photograph we see a tragic moonscape of tree stumps and fragile topsoil ripped open by settlers. The name given to this place is "Bom Futuro" (Good Future in English). (Jacques Jangoux/Peter Arnold, Inc.)

The expanding global population required increasing quantities of food, fresh water, housing, energy, and other resources as the twentieth century ended (see Map 33.4). In the developed world industrial activity increased much more rapidly than population grew, and the consumption of energy (coal, electricity, and petroleum) rose proportionally. Indeed, the consumer-driven economic expansion of the post–World War II years became an obstacle to addressing environmental problems. Modern economies depend on the profligate consumption of goods and resources. Stock markets closely follow measures of consumer confidence—the willingness of people to make new purchases. When consumption slows, industrial nations enter a recession. How could the United States, Germany, or Japan change consumption patterns to protect the environment without endangering corporate profits, wages, and employment levels?

Since 1945 population growth has been most dramatic in the developing countries, where environmental pressures have also been extreme. In Brazil, India, and China, for example, the need to expand food production led to rapid deforestation and the extension of farming and grazing onto marginal lands. The results were predictable: erosion and water pollution. Population growth in Indonesia forced the government to permit the cutting of nearly 20 percent of the total forest area. These and many other poor nations also attempted to force industrialization because they believed that providing for their rapidly growing populations depended on the completion of the transition from agriculture to manufacturing. The argument was compelling: Why

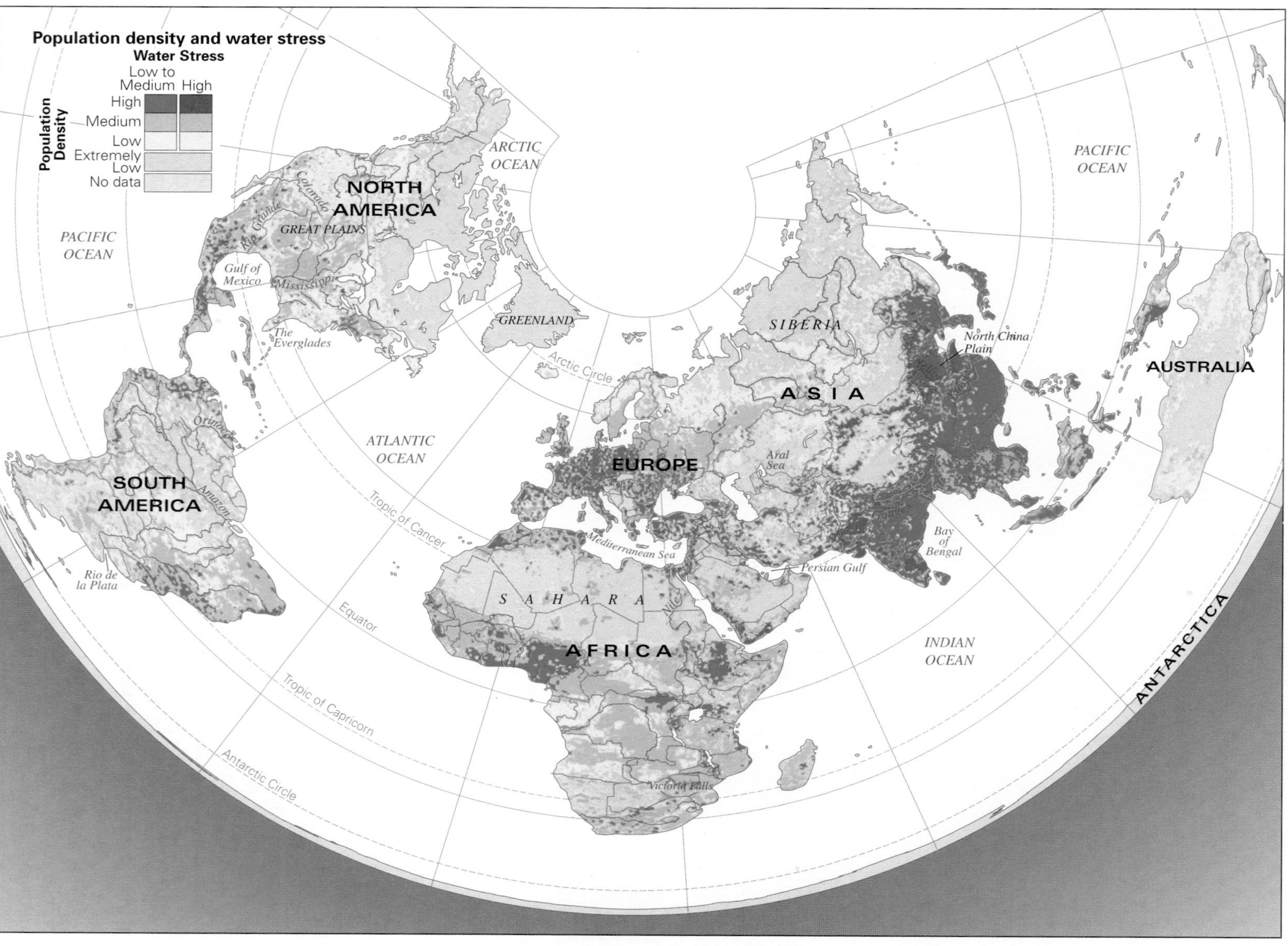

Map 33.4 Fresh Water Resources This map links population density and the availability of water. Red areas are highly stressed environments where populations use at least 40 percent or more of available water. Less stressed environments are blue. The deeper the shade of red or blue the greater the environmental stress. *Source: National Geographic*, September, 2002. Reprinted by permission of The National Geographic Society.

should Indians or Brazilians remain poor while Americans, Europeans, and Japanese remained rich?

Responding to Environmental Threats

Despite the gravity of environmental threats, there were many successful efforts to preserve and protect the environment. The Clean Air Act, the Clean Water Act, and the Endangered Species Act were passed in the United States in the 1970s as part of an environmental effort that included the nations of the European Community and Japan. Grassroots political movements and the media encouraged environmental awareness, and most nations in the developed world enforced strict antipollution laws and sponsored massive recycling efforts. Many also encouraged resource conservation by rewarding energy-efficient factories and manufacturers of fuel-efficient cars and by promoting the use of alternative energy sources such as solar and wind power. These efforts were implemented most comprehensively in Europe, where both energy conservation and new technologies like wind turbines were embraced.

Environmental efforts produced significant results. In western Europe and the United States air quality improved dramatically. Smog levels in the United States fell nearly a third from 1970 to 2000, even though the number of automobiles increased more than 80 percent. Emissions of lead and sulfur dioxide were down as well. The Great Lakes, Long Island Sound, and Chesapeake Bay were all much cleaner at the end of the century than they had been in 1970. The rivers of North America and Europe also improved. Still, in the United States more than thirty thousand deaths each year are attributed to exposure to pesticides and other chemicals.

New technologies made much of the improvement possible. Pollution controls on automobiles, planes, and factory smokestacks reduced harmful emissions. Scientists identified the chemicals that threaten the ozone layer, and their use in new appliances and cars began to be phased out.

Clearly, the desire to preserve the natural environment was growing around the world. In the developed nations continued political organization and enhanced awareness of environmental issues seemed likely to lead to step-by-step improvements in environmental policy. In the developing world and most of the former Soviet bloc, however, population pressures and weak governments were major obstacles to effective environmental policies. In China, for example, respiratory disease caused by industrial pollution was the leading cause of death.

Thus it was likely that the industrialized nations would have to fund global improvements, and the cost was likely to be high. Nevertheless, growing evidence of environmental degradation continued to propel reform efforts. The media drew attention to the precipitous shrinkage of Peru's Andean glaciers, which have lost a quarter of their volume in the last three decades; to oil spills, loss of rain forest in Brazil, and deforestation in Indonesia; and to erosion in parts of Africa. A growing, vocal movement pushed reluctant politicians to act.

In Kyoto, Japan, in 1997 representatives from around the world negotiated a far-reaching treaty to reduce greenhouse gases that contribute to global warning. Signed by President Clinton, the treaty was not ratified by the Senate, although it was affirmed by nearly all other industrial nations. Objections in the United States and elsewhere focused on costs. Without broad agreement among the rich nations, the economic and political power necessary for environmental protections on a global scale will be very difficult to institute.

Conclusion

The world was profoundly altered between 1975 and 1991. The Cold War dominated international relations to the end of the 1980s. Both the United States and the Soviet Union feared that every conflict and every regime change represented a potential threat to their strategic interests, and every conflict threatened to provoke confrontation between them. As a result, the superpowers were drawn into a succession of civil wars and revolutions. The costs in lives and property were terrible, the gains small. As defense costs escalated, the Soviet system crumbled. By 1991 the Soviet Union and the socialist Warsaw Pact had disappeared, transforming the international stage.

Latin America was pulled into the violence of the late Cold War period and paid a terrible price. The 1970s and 1980s witnessed a frontal assault on democratic institutions, a denial of human rights, and economic decline. This was the period of death squads and Dirty War. With the end of the Cold War, peace returned and democracy began to replace dictatorship.

In the Persian Gulf the end of the Cold War did not lead to peace. Iran and Iraq have experienced deep cycles of political turmoil, war, and foreign threats since the late 1970s.

The world was also altered by economic growth and integration, by population growth and movement, and by technological and environmental change. Led by the postwar recovery of the industrial powers and the remarkable economic expansion of Japan, the Asian Tigers, and more recently China, the world economy grew dramatically. The development and application of new technology contributed significantly to this process. International markets were more open and integrated than at any other time. The new wealth and exciting technologies of the postwar era were not shared equally, however. The capitalist West and a few Pacific Rim nations grew richer and more powerful, while most of the world's nations remained poor.

Population growth in the developing world was one reason for this divided experience. Unable to find adequate employment or, in many cases, bare subsistence, people in developing nations migrated across borders, hoping to improve their lives. These movements often provided valuable labor in the factories and farms of the developed world, but they also provoked cultural, racial, and ethnic tension. Problems of inequality, population growth, and international migration would continue to challenge the global community in the coming decades.

Technology seemed to offer some hope for meeting these challenges. Engineering, financial services, education, and other professions developed an international character, thanks to the communications revolution. Ambitious and talented people in the developing world could now fully participate in global intellectual and economic life. However, most people working in the developing world remained disconnected from this liberating technology by poverty. Technology also bolstered efforts to protect the environment, providing the means to clean auto and factory emissions—even while it helped produce much of the world's pollution. Technology has been intertwined with human culture since the beginning of human history. Our ability to control and direct its use will determine the future.

Key Terms

proxy wars
Salvador Allende
Dirty War
Sandinistas
Ayatollah Ruhollah Khomeini
Saddam Husain
neo-liberalism
keiretsu
Asian Tigers
newly industrialized economies (NIEs)
Deng Xiaoping
Tiananmen Square
Mikhail Gorbachev
perestroika
Solidarity
Thomas Malthus
demographic transition

Suggested Reading

Among the works devoted to postwar economic performance are W. L. M. Adriaasen and J. G. Waardensburg, eds., *A Dual World Economy: Forty Years of Development Experience* (1989); P. Krugman, *The Age of Diminished Expectations: U.S. Economic Policy in the 1990s* (1990); B. J. McCormick, *The World Economy: Patterns of Growth and Change* (1988); and H. van der Wee, *Prosperity and Upheaval: The World Economy, 1945–1980* (1986).

For Latin America, Thomas E. Skidmore and Peter H. Smith, *Modern Latin America,* 4th ed. (1996), provides an excellent general introduction to the period 1975 to 1991. The literature on the era of repression is large. *Nunca Mas* (1986), the official report of the Argentine government, provides a moving introduction. Also see news stories in 1999 and 2000 about the arrest of Augusto Pinochet in London and the resulting legal proceedings. The movie *Official Story* (available with subtitles or dubbed) offers an effective look at the legacy of the Dirty War in Argentina. For Central America see Walter La Feber, *Inevitable Revolutions: The United States in Central America* (1983).

For the Pacific Rim see Jonathan Spence, *The Search for Modern China* (1990); Edwin O. Reischauer, *The Japanese* (1988); H. Patrick and H. Rosovsky, *Asia's New Giant: How the Japanese Economy Works* (1976); and Staffan B. Linder, *Pacific Century: Economic and Political Consequences of Asian-Pacific Dynamism* (1986).

There are many fine studies of Europe and the Soviet system. See, for example, Richard Sakwa, *The Rise and Fall of the Soviet Union, 1917–1991* (1999). More focused examinations of the Soviet bloc are provided in Gale Stokes, *The Walls Came Tumbling Down: The Collapse of Communism in Eastern Europe* (1993); Barbara Engel and Christine Worobec, eds., *Russia's Women: Accommodation, Resistance, Transformation* (1990); David Remnick, *Lenin's Tomb: The Last Days of the Soviet Empire* (1993); and Charles Maier, *Dissolution: The Crisis of Communism and the End of East Germany* (1997). See also Katherine Verdery, *What Was Socialism, and What Comes Next?* (1996).

The story of the Iranian Revolution and the early days of the Islamic Republic of Iran is told well by Shaul Bakhash, *The Reign of the Ayatollahs: Iran and the Iranian Revolution* (1990). Barnet Rubin, *The Fragmentation of Afghanistan* (1995), provides excellent coverage of the struggle between Soviet forces and the Muslim resistance in that country.

A number of studies examine the special problems faced by women in the postwar period. See, for example, Elisabeth Croll,

Feminism and Socialism in China (1978); J. Ginat, *Women in Muslim Rural Society: Status and Role in Family and Community* (1982); June Hahner, *Women in Latin America* (1976); P. Hudson, *Third World Women Speak Out* (1979); A. de Souza, *Women in Contemporary India and South Asia* (1980); and M. Wolf, *Revolution Postponed: Women in Contemporary China* (1985).

For general discussions of economic, demographic, and environmental problems facing the world see R. N. Gwynne, *New Horizons? Third World Industrialization in an International Framework* (1990); W. Alonso, ed., *Population in an Interacting World* (1987); P. R. Ehrlich and A. E. Ehrlich, *The Population Explosion* (1990); James Fallows, *More Like Us: Making America Great Again* (1989); Paul M. Kennedy, *Preparing for the Twenty-first Century* (1993); W.W. Rostow, *The Great Population Spike and After: Reflections on the 21st Century* (1998); and J. L. Simon, *Population Matters: People, Resources, Environment and Immigration* (1990).

For issues associated with technological and environmental change see M. Feshbach and A. Friendly, *Ecocide in the U.S.S.R.* (1992); John Bellamy Foster, *Economic History of the Environment* (1994); S. Hecht and A. Cockburn, *The Fate of the Forest: Developers, Destroyers, and Defenders of the Amazon* (1989); K. Marton, *Multinationals, Technology, and Industrialization: Implications and Impact in Third World Countries* (1986); S. P. Huntington, *The Third Wave: Demoralization in the Late Twentieth Century* (1993); John R. McNeill, *Something New Under the Sun: An Environmental History of the Twentieth Century World* (2000); and B. L. Turner II et al., eds., *The Earth as Transformed by Human Action: Global and Regional Changes in the Biosphere over the Past 300 Years* (1990).

Notes

1. *New York Times,* July 24, 1993, 1.
2. Quoted in Antony Flew, "Introduction," in Thomas Robert Malthus, *An Essay on the Principle of Population and a Summary View of the Principle of Population* (New York: Penguin Books, 1970), 30.
3. "Population Implosion Worries a Graying Europe," *New York Times,* July 10, 1998.
4. Paul Kennedy, *Preparing for the Twenty-first Century* (New York: Random House, 1993), 45.

34 Globalization at the Turn of the Millennium

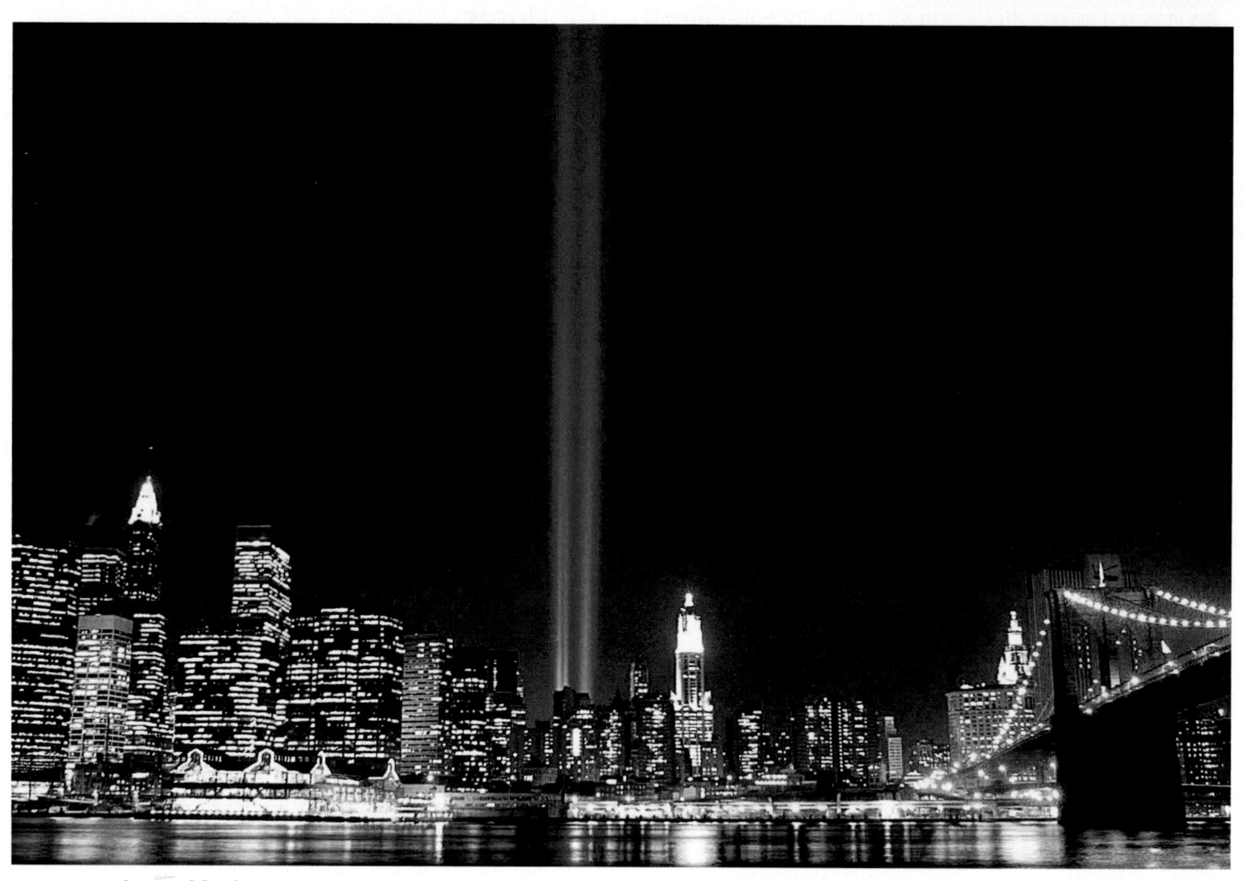

Lower Manhattan, 11 March 2002 Six months after the terrorist attacks, beams of light commemorated the destroyed twin towers of the World Trade Center and those who perished in them.

CHAPTER OUTLINE

The workday began normally at the World Trade Center in lower Manhattan on the morning of September 11, 2001. The 50,000 people who work there were making their way to the two 110-story towers, as were some 140,000 others who visit on a typical day. Suddenly, at 8:46 A.M., an American Airlines Boeing 767 with 92 people on board, traveling at a speed of 470 miles per hour (756 kilometers per hour), crashed into floors 94 to 98 of the north tower, igniting the 10,000 gallons (38,000 liters) of fuel in its tanks. Just before 9:03 A.M. a United Airlines flight with 65 people on board and a similar fuel load hit floors 78 to 84 of the south tower.

As the burning jet fuel engulfed the collision areas, the buildings' surviving occupants struggled through smoke-filled corridors and down dozens of flights of stairs. Many of those trapped above the crash sites used cell phones to say good-bye to loved ones. Rather than endure the flames and fumes, a few jumped to their deaths.

Just before 10 o'clock, temperatures that had risen to 2,300° Fahrenheit (1,260° Celsius) caused the steel girders in the impacted area of the south tower to give way. The collapsing upper floors crushed the floors underneath one by one, engulfing lower Manhattan in a dense cloud of dust. Twenty-eight minutes later the north tower pancaked in a similar manner. Miraculously, most of the buildings' occupants had escaped before the towers collapsed. Besides the people on the planes, nearly 2,600 lost their lives, including some 200 police officers and firefighters helping in the evacuation.

That same morning another American Airlines jet crashed into the Pentagon, killing all 64 people on board and 125 others inside the military complex near Washington, D.C. Passengers on a fourth plane managed to overpower their hijackers, and the plane crashed in rural Pennsylvania, killing all 45 on board.

The four planes had been hijacked by teams of Middle Eastern men who slit the throats of service and flight personnel and seized control. Of the nineteen hijackers, fifteen were from Saudi Arabia. All had links to an extremist Islamic organization, al Qaeda° (the base or foundation), supported by a rich Saudi named Usama bin Laden°, who was incensed with American political, military, and cultural influence in the Middle East. The men were educated and well-traveled, had lived in the United States, and spoke English. Some had trained as pilots so that they could fly the hijacked aircraft.

The hijackers left few records of their personal motives, but the acts spoke for themselves. The Pentagon was the headquarters of the American military, the most technologically sophisticated and powerful fighting force the world had even seen. The fourth plane was probably meant to hit the Capitol or the White House, the legislative and executive centers of the world's only superpower. The Twin Towers may have been targeted because they were the tallest buildings in New York, but they were not just American targets. The World Trade Center housed 430 companies involved in international commerce and finance. Among the dead were people from more than half the countries in the world. New York was the site of the attack, but the World Trade Center was a powerful symbol of the international economy.

The events of September 11 (9/11) can be understood on many levels. The hijackers and their supporters saw themselves as engaged in a holy struggle against economic, political, and military institutions they believed to be evil. They believed so deeply in their mission that they were willing to give their lives for it and to take as many other lives as they could. People directly affected and political leaders around the world tended to describe the attacks as evil acts against innocent victims.

To understand why the nineteen attackers were heroes to some and terrorists to others, one needs to explore the historical context of global changes at the turn of the millennium and the ideological tensions they have generated. While the advancing economic,

---

al Qaeda (ahl KIGH-duh or ahl kuh-EE-duh) **Usama bin Laden** (oo-SAH-mah bin LAH-din)

political, and cultural integration of the world is welcomed by some, it is hated or feared by others. The unique prominence of the United States in every major aspect of global integration also elicits sharply divergent views.

As you read this chapter, ask yourself the following questions:

- What are the main benefits and dangers of growing political, economic, and cultural integration?
- What roles do religious beliefs and secular ideologies play in the contemporary world?
- How has technology contributed to the process of global interaction?

GLOBAL POLITICAL ECONOMIES

The turn of the millennium saw the intensification of a **globalization** trend that had been building for some time. Growing trade and travel and new technologies were bringing all parts of the world into closer economic, political, and cultural integration and interaction. The collapse of the Soviet Union had completed the dissolution of empires that had been under way throughout the twentieth century. Autonomous national states (numbering about two hundred) became an almost universal norm, and a growing number of them have embraced democratic institutions. The rapid integration of world trade and markets have convinced world leaders of the need to balance national autonomy with international agreements and associations.

The Spread of Democracy

The last decades of the twentieth century saw rapid increases in democratic institutions and personal freedom. In 2003, 140 countries regularly held elections; people in 125 had access to free (or partly free) presses; and most people lived in fully democratic states.[1]

The great appeal of democracy has been that elections are a peaceful way to settle the inevitable differences among a country's social classes, cultural groups, and regions. Although majority votes might swing from one part of the political spectrum to another, democracies tend to encourage political moderation. For example, two of the world's oldest democracies saw two candidates win national elections in the 1990s by moving their political parties closer to the political center (and by exuding great personal charm). In 1992 Bill Clinton was the first Democrat to win the American presidency in twelve years. In 1997 Tony Blair became Great Britain's first Labour Party prime minister in eighteen years.

Very significant democratic gains have been made in the new nations of eastern Europe, where elections have also been more open to electoral mood swings. The Czech Republic, Poland, Romania, Ukraine, and most other formerly communist-ruled states have adopted democratic institutions. Likewise, after a shaky start, political institutions in the Russian Federation have begun to function more smoothly under President Vladimir Putin, elected in 2000.

Latin America has a long history of democracy, but an almost equally long history of authoritarian rule by military and personalist leaders (see Chapter 24). Since 1991, however, democracy has become almost universal in South and Central America. The region has also seen significant shifts in the balance of power within countries. In 2000 Mexican voters elected a reformist president with a centrist agenda, Vincente Fox, ending the half-century rule of the corrupt Institutional Revolutionary Party (PRI). In 2002 leftist Workers' Party candidate Luiz Inácio Lula da Silva° won the presidency of Brazil by appealing to nationalism and popular discontent with the economy. Other populist leaders won elections in Venezuela (1999), Chile (2000), and Argentina (2003).

Democratic governments continued to flourish in Asia. Beginning in 1999 the populous state of Indonesia moved from years of authoritarian and corrupt rule toward much more open political institutions. Since the death of long-time Communist leader Deng Xiaoping in 1997, China, the world's most populous country, has allowed a greater measure of free expression, but democracy is a long way off. India saw a major political shift in 1998 when a Bharatiya Janata Party (BJP) electoral victory ended four decades of Congress Party rule. The BJP success came through blatant appeals to Hindu nationalism, the condoning of violence against India's Muslims, and opposition to the social and economic progress of the Untouchables (those traditionally confined to the dirtiest jobs). The BJP also adopted a belligerent policy against neighboring Pakistan, centering on the two countries' long-standing claims to the state of Kashmir.

In sub-Saharan Africa, democracy has had mixed results. Many elected leaders have used their offices to

Luiz Inácio Lula da Silva (loo-EES ee-NAH-see-oh LOO-lah dah SEAL-vah)

CHRONOLOGY

	Politics	Economics and Society
1991		**1991** Mercosur free trade association formed
	1992 Yugoslavia disintegrates—Croatia and Slovenia become independent states **1992–1995** Bosnia crisis **1994** Nelson Mandela elected president of South Africa; Tutsi massacred in Rwanda	**1993** Nobel Peace Prize to Nelson Mandela **1994** North Atlantic Free Trade Agreement adopted
1995	**1995** Nerve gas released in Tokyo subway	**1995** World Trade Organization founded; United Nations women's conference in China
	1997 Hong Kong reunited with China **1998** Terrorists bomb U.S. embassies in Kenya and Tanzania; India and Pakistan test atomic bombs	**1997** Asian financial crisis begins
2000	**1999** East Timor secedes from Indonesia (officially independent 2002) **2001** Terrorists destroy the World Trade Center and damage the Pentagon on September 11 **2002** United Nations weapons inspectors return to Iraq **2003** United States and Britain invade and occupy Iraq	**1999** Nobel Peace Prize to Doctors Without Borders **2001** Start of global recession **2002** Euro the only currency in twelve European countries

enrich themselves and limit their opponents. Military coups and conflicts over resources such as diamonds have also been distressingly common. Southern Africa, however, has seen democratic progress and a decline in armed conflicts since 1991. A key change came in South Africa in 1994, when long-time political prisoner Nelson Mandela and his African National Congress (ANC) won the first national elections in which the African majority could participate equally. Since then, the lively politics of this ethnically diverse country have been a model of how democracy can resolve conflicts. Also hopeful has been the return to democracy of Nigeria, Africa's most populous state, after decades of military rulers. In 1999, after a succession of military governments, Nigerians elected President Olusegun Obasanjo° (a former coup leader) and a 2003 vote renewed his term, despite serious voting irregularities. In 2002 Kenyans voted out the party that had held power for thirty-nine years.

Democracy is as exceptional in the Middle East as it is in much of Africa. Some once-democratic states such as Algeria have manipulated elections because those in power fear the rising power of Islamic militants. On the other hand, in Turkey, the most democratic Muslim-majority state in the region, a once-strident Islamist party won a parliamentary majority in 2002 by moderating its tone and politics. Women have made gains in recent elections in Morocco, Turkey, and Bahrain. Recent regime changes in Afghanistan and Iraq may mark a move toward more democratic rule in these countries.

As examples later in the chapter will indicate, the growth (or decline) of democracy has only partly been due to internal changes in individual countries. Two international factors have also played important roles: the changed politics of the post–Cold War era and the demands of global economic forces.

Global Politics

Modern nation-states have considerable autonomy under international law. Other nations may intervene in a state's affairs only when seriously threatened or when the state is engaging in extreme human rights abuses. Although necessary to protect smaller, weaker countries from the imperial bullying that was once common, this autonomy greatly complicates international policing and peacekeeping efforts.

After the end of the Cold War, the United Nations struggled to reclaim its roles as defender of human rights and peacekeeper. This was especially noticeable under the leadership of Kofi Annan, who became United

Olusegun Obasanjo (oh-LOO-say-goon oh-bah-SAHN-joh)

Sectarian Strife in India Hours after these Hindu youths clambered atop the sixteenth-century Babri Mosque in December 1992 hundreds of angry Hindu nationalists completely demolished the structure. The Hindus claimed the Muslim place of worship in the northern Indian province of Uttar Pradesh had been erected upon the site of a temple commemorating the birthplace of Lord Ram, the incarnation of the Hindu god Vishnu. Thousands died in the riots that followed the razing of the temple. An Indian government archaeological team uncovered the foundation of an earlier temple-like structure. (Douglas E. Curran/Getty Images)

Nations secretary general in 1997. The members of the United Nations Security Council often had difficulty agreeing on a course of action. Individual countries often acted alone or with their neighbors to resolve conflicts in nearby countries, whether through peaceful negotiation or military intervention. Some interventions restored order and punished wrongdoers, but in other cases people suffered and died by the hundreds of thousands as world leaders hesitated or debated the wisdom and legitimacy of intervening. As the lone superpower, the United States was in a unique position to use its moral leadership, economic power, and military might to defend its national interests and promote the general good. However, interventions also brought charges of American imperialism.

There were some notable peacemaking successes. The United Nations, South Africa, and other countries helped end the long civil war in Mozambique in 1992 and struggled to do the same in Angola, where peace finally returned in 2002. In the 1990s Nigeria, the major military power in West Africa, helped end fighting in Sierra Leone in 1998, and again in 2003 in Liberia, which warlords and embezzlement has made the world's poorest country. The Clinton and George W. Bush administrations had some success in getting aggrieved parties in Israel, Ireland, and South Asia to negotiate their differences, even though lasting solutions were elusive.

However, in a number of cases the international community had great difficulty in agreeing on when and how to stop civil conflicts and abuses in individual countries. For example, in 1991 the Balkan state of Yugoslavia, which had existed since 1920 and was united by a common language (Serbo-Croatian), dissolved into a morass of separatism and warring ethnic and religious groups. Slovenia and Croatia, the most westerly provinces of Yugoslavia, both heavily Roman Catholic, became independent states in 1992 after brief struggles with federal Yugoslav forces. Reflecting centuries of Muslim, Catholic, and Orthodox competition in the Balkans, the people of the province of Bosnia and Herzegovina were more mixed—40 percent were Muslims, 30 percent Serbian Orthodox, and 18 percent Catholics. The murderous three-sided fighting that broke out with the declaration of Bosnian national independence in 1992 gave rise to **ethnic cleansing,** an effort by one racial, ethnic, or religious group to eliminate the people and culture of a different group. In this case, the Orthodox Serbs attempted to rid the state of Muslims.

At first, no European power acted to stop the growing tragedy in the Balkans. Finally, after much indecision—and extensive television coverage of atrocities and wanton destruction—the United States made a cautious intervention and eventually brokered a tentative settlement in 1995. In 1999 vicious new fighting and ethnic cleansing broke out in the southernmost Yugoslavian province of Kosovo, the ancient homeland of the Serbs, which had become predominantly Muslim and Albanian. When NATO's warnings went unheeded in Kosovo, the United States, with aid from Britain and France, launched an aerial war against Serbia. Suffering few casualties themselves, the NATO allies damaged military and infrastructure targets in Serbia and forced the withdrawal of Serbian forces from Kosovo. A trial of former Serbian president Slobodan Milosevic° at a special tribunal in the Hague on charges of crimes against humanity began in 2002 but was often delayed by his ill health.

Another tragedy unfolded in 1994, when political leaders in the Central African nation of Rwanda incited Hutu people to massacre their Tutsi neighbors. The major powers avoided characterizing the slaughter as genocide because an international agreement mandated intervention to stop genocide. Only after some 750,000 people were dead and millions of refugees had fled into neighboring states did the United States and other powers intervene. Belatedly, the United Nations set up a tribunal to try those responsible for the genocide. In 1998 violence spread from Rwanda to neighboring Congo, where growing opposition and ill-health had forced President Joseph Mobutu from office after over three decades of dictatorial misrule. Various peacemaking attempts failed to restore order. By mid-2003 more than 3 million Congolese had died from disease, malnutrition, and injuries related to the fighting.

Fear that intervention could result in long and costly commitments was one reason the major powers were reluctant to intervene. Nor was it easy to distinguish conflicts that would benefit from forceful intervention from those that might better be resolved by diplomatic pressure. Many conflicts reflected deep-seated differences that were difficult to resolve. Tamil-speaking Hindus in Sri Lanka have waged a merciless guerrilla struggle against the dominant Sinhalese-speaking Buddhists for decades. Militant Hindus and Muslims in South Asia continue a violent struggle over the territories of the state of Kashmir, which was divided between India and Pakistan at their independence in 1947. Sometimes it took decades of international pressure to bring a conflict to an end, as was the case in East Timor (a mostly Catholic former Portuguese colony that Indonesia had annexed in 1975), whose people voted to separate from Muslim Indonesia in 1999 and gained full independence in 2002.

Slobodan Milosevic (SLOH-boh-duhn mee-LOH-seh-vitch)

Arms Control and Terrorism

In addition to agreements on collective action against genocide and other crimes against humanity (see below), international treaties govern **weapons of mass destruction.** Nuclear, biological, and chemical devices pose especially serious dangers to global security because they can kill large numbers of people quickly.

For a time after international agreements were signed in the 1960s and 1970s (see Chapter 32), considerable progress was made in restricting the testing and spread of nuclear weapons and reducing their numbers. Fear increased when the breakup of the Soviet Union threatened to expand the number of states with nuclear weapons, but in the end only Russia retained nuclear arsenals. Meanwhile, China resumed nuclear weapons tests in 1992.

Anxiety over nuclear proliferation increased in 1998 when India and Pakistan openly tested nuclear bombs and missile delivery systems, acts that raised the stakes in any future conflict between them. Although North Korea was a signatory of the nuclear nonproliferation treaty, it secretly continued nuclear weapons programs and, beginning in 2002, belligerently challenged the rest of the world to try to stop them. Iran and Israel are also believed to have secret nuclear weapons programs. In violation of another agreement, the Bush administration is pushing for new nuclear weapons development in the United States.

Chemical and biological weapons are difficult to detect and can easily be produced in seemingly ordinary chemical and pharmaceutical plants. As part of the settlement of the 1991 Persian Gulf War, United Nations inspectors in Iraq uncovered and destroyed extensive stocks of chemical munitions and plants for producing nerve gas and lethal germs. However, in 1997 the government of Saddam Husain reneged on its agreement to allow United Nations weapons inspectors free access to all sites in Iraq.

What made the proliferation of weapons of mass destruction more worrisome was the fear that such weapons could be used for **terrorism.** Terrorists believe that horrendous acts of violence can provoke harsh reprisals that would win them sympathy or cause the regimes they oppose to lose legitimacy. Terrorism has a long history, but much recent concern focused on the network of terrorist organizations created by **Usama**

"All the News That's Fit to Print"

The New York Times

New England Edition
Boston: Windy, some clearing late. High 37. Mainly clear, brisk. Low 28. Tomorrow, partly sunny and not as cold, much lighter winds. High 42. Weather map appears on Page D12.

VOL. CLIII . . . . No. 52,698 Copyright © 2003 The New York Times MONDAY, DECEMBER 15, 2003 ONE DOLLAR

HUSSEIN CAUGHT IN MAKESHIFT HIDE-OUT; BUSH SAYS 'DARK ERA' FOR IRAQIS IS OVER

BETRAYED BY CLAN

Breakthrough Capped a Renewed Effort to Ferret Out Leads

By ERIC SCHMITT

BAGHDAD, Iraq, Dec. 14 — The hunt for Saddam Hussein ended late Saturday with information from a member of his tribal clan.

Seizing Mr. Hussein, a man who one senior general said had 20 to 30 hide-outs and moved as often as every three to four hours, had become a maddening challenge. Eleven previous times in the last several months, a brigade combat team from the Army's Fourth Infantry Division thought it had a bead on Mr. Hussein and began raids to kill or capture him, only to come up empty, sometimes missing its man by only a matter of hours, military officials here said.

But at 8:26 p.m. Saturday, less than 11 hours after receiving the decisive tip, 600 American soldiers and Special Operations forces backed by tanks, artillery and Apache helicopter gunships surrounded two farmhouses, and near one of them found Mr. Hussein hiding alone at the bottom of an eight-foot hole.

He surrendered without a shot.

"He was just caught like a rat," Maj. Gen. Raymond T. Odierno, the commander of the Fourth Infantry Division, told reporters at his headquarters in Tikrit on Sunday. "He could have been hiding in a hundred different places, a thousand different places like this all around Iraq. It just takes finding the right person who will give you a good idea where he might be."

In recent weeks, American officials had started a new effort to draw up a list of people likely to be hiding Mr. Hussein, including bodyguards, former palace functionaries, tribal

Arrest by U.S. Soldiers — President Still Cautious

By SUSAN SACHS

BAGHDAD, Iraq, Dec. 14 — Saddam Hussein, once the all-powerful leader of Iraq, was arrested without a fight on Saturday night by American soldiers who found him crouching in an eight-foot hole at an isolated farm near Tikrit, haggard, dirty and disoriented after eluding capture for nearly nine months.

News of Mr. Hussein's arrest, announced Sunday after being kept secret for 18 hours, electrified Iraq and much of the world, sending joyous Iraqis into the streets with the first real catharsis of liberation since the invasion toppled him in April.

For the Bush administration, which has been struggling to stabilize Iraq, the capture of Mr. Hussein was the most triumphal moment since American forces ousted him.

"In the history of Iraq, a dark and painful era is over," President Bush said in a televised noontime address from Washington. "A hopeful day has arrived. All Iraqis can now come together and reject violence and build a new Iraq." But Mr. Bush was careful to couch his message with caution that Iraq remains violent and dangerous.

American officials said Mr. Hussein was being held in Iraq, but they would not disclose the exact location. They said he had been unresistant in medical tests and other procedures but was not cooperating with interrogators on substantive matters.

American-appointed Iraqi leaders said he would eventually face a war crimes trial, but it was unclear when.

Reuters Television

President Bush, in a brief televised speech yesterday. Page A16.

Maj. Gen. Raymond T. Odierno, commander of the Fourth Infantry Division, which captured Mr. Hussein with a force of 600 soldiers, said he was armed with only a pistol and had surrendered without firing a shot. Two AK-47 rifles and $750,000 in American cash were found nearby.

It was an ignominious ending for Mr. Hussein, 66, who survived American attempts to kill him during the invasion and had eluded capture apparently by moving from one dingy hide-out to another.

Whether his arrest will undermine the insurgency against the American-led forces in Iraq is unclear. Hours after his capture but before it was announced publicly, a car bomb killed at least 17 people in a town west of Baghdad. [Page A12.]

Even in hiding, Mr. Hussein had

Continued on Page A12

In the Streets, a Shadow Lifts

By JOHN F. BURNS

Capture of Saddam in Iraq Acting on a tip from Iraqi sources, American troops captured Saddam Husain in December 2003. The bearded former dictator of Iraq was discovered in a small underground "spider hole" about ten miles southeast of the city of Tikrit. (©New York Times. Reprinted with permission.)

bin Laden, a wealthy Saudi. Because his methods were so repugnant, his own family disowned him and Saudi Arabia stripped him of his citizenship, but his anti-American stance and patronage attracted followers throughout the Islamic world. In 1992 bin Laden established himself in Sudan, where he invested in many projects. Suspecting that a pharmaceutical plant near the Sudanese capital Khartoum was being used for making chemical weapons, President Clinton had it destroyed by rockets in 1998, but no evidence of weapons production was found.

After being expelled from Sudan in 1996, bin Laden went to Afghanistan, where he had close ties with the Taliban, a fundamentalist Islamic organization that had taken control of most of that country in 1995. Bin Laden's agents bombed the American embassies in Kenya and Tanzania in 1998 as well as the destroyer USS *Cole,* which was making a port call in Yemen in 2000, before turning to targets in the United States itself. In response to the terrorist attacks of September 2001 and the subsequent panic caused by an unknown terrorist mailing spores of anthrax, a lethal disease, the U.S. government adopted a more aggressive policy against terrorism and weapons of mass destruction. In December 2001, American and other NATO forces joined with Afghan opposition groups to overthrow the Taliban-supported regime in Afghanistan, an act that President Bush declared to be the first step in a much larger "war on terrorism."

Such preemptive strikes are clearly speedier than collective action, but the issue of when military intervention is justified became the focus of a huge international debate after President Bush pushed for extension of the war on terrorism against the brutal regime of Saddam Husain in Iraq. Strong opposition to unilateral action came from America's NATO allies France and Germany, as well as from Russia and China. German Chancellor Gerhard Schröder won a close election in September 2002 by campaigning against American imperialism. Faced with this opposition, the Bush administration changed tactics. In November 2002 it persuaded the United Nations Security Council to unanimously pass a resolution ordering the return of United Nations weapons inspectors to Iraq and requiring the Iraqi government to specify what weapons of mass destruction it still possessed. It was a rare moment in which superpower America bowed to the authority of the international body and in which the Security Council acknowledged the need to take firm and forceful action to enforce its resolutions.

When the new United Nations inspectors in Iraq failed to find any evidence of banned weapons, the split widened between those nations wanting to continue inspections and those, led by the United States and Britain, wanting to intervene militarily. Abandoning efforts to gain Security Council authorization, an American-led "coalition of the willing" invaded Iraq in March 2003. On the eve of the invasion, General Brent Scowcroft, a former national security adviser to the elder President George Bush, predicted that the United States would pay a high price for the image of American arrogance and unilateralism that such actions fostered.

By the time the new Persian Gulf war began, the overwhelming international sympathy the United States had received after September 11 had evaporated. Public disapproval ran well over 80 percent in Russia and in NATO allies France, Germany, and Turkey (whose parliament voted not to allow American troops to attack Iraq from Turkish soil). Public opinion in most of the Muslim world was almost unanimously against the intervention. Even in Britain and Poland, which sent troops to Iraq, most people disapproved of the war. Not surprisingly, the war set off large antiwar demonstrations around the world and drew strong criticism from prominent religious leaders.

The war took only six weeks to drive Saddam's regime from power and showcased the technological precision of America's latest bombs and missiles. Iraqi looters did more damage to utility plants, oil well equipment, and government offices than had the bombing. However, the hidden weapons of mass destruction, on whose removal the Bush administration had justified the war, were not found.

In May the Security Council authorized the American and British occupation of Iraq and lifted the sanctions on petroleum exports that had been imposed on the old regime. But American efforts to secure a larger United Nations role in rebuilding Iraq faced resistance from other world powers, who insisted on curbing American control. Meanwhile, sniper attacks and car bombings took a steady toll.

Most Iraqis welcomed the end of Saddam's rule and applauded his capture, but were eager for American occupiers to leave. They criticized the slow pace of restoring electricity and water to the cities and the lack of law and order. They had little faith in the American-nominated Iraqi Governing Council. As in Afghanistan, reestablishing political and civil order in Iraq would be a long and costly process. In September 2003 President Bush anounced the price tag for the next year: $87 billion.

The Global Economy

The 1990s opened a new chapter in the history of global capitalism. After the collapse of the long experiment with state-managed socialist economies in eastern Europe and the Soviet Union, free-market capitalism seemed to be the only road to economic growth. Free trade could generate new wealth, but it also brought many problems.

From 1991 to 2000 the world experienced rapid expansion in manufacturing and trade. The burgeoning international trade of the 1990s tied the world more tightly together. Manufactured products were increasingly likely to be the product of materials and labor from many countries. Overall, the already developed economies increased their wealth the most, but the fastest rates of growth were in developing countries and in economies making a transition from communism. Net private capital flows to developing nations rose almost sevenfold between 1990 and 2000. This was not foreign aid. Investors put their funds in countries whose political stability, legal systems, level of education, and labor costs promised the most profitable returns.

The greatest single beneficiary was China. While officially espousing communism, the Chinese government took major steps to open its economy to freer trade and investment. Newly opened markets in eastern Europe and the former Soviet Union also received significant private investment. Stimulated by foreign investment, the Latin American nations of Brazil, Argentina, and Mexico experienced great economic growth. Investors put much less money into the shaky economies and political systems of sub-Saharan Africa, except for countries with significant petroleum resources.

Electronic transfers via the Internet made it possible to invest capital quickly; but when conditions became unfavorable, funds could be withdrawn just as fast. When investors lost faith in Thailand in 1997 and shifted their funds out, the country's currency and stock values plummeted. Political corruption and unrest in Indonesia brought on a similar capital flight the next year, and the widening Asian collapse eventually triggered a serious recession in Japan, business failures in South Korea, and a slowing of economic growth in China.

Government intervention sometimes helped. When Mexico's economy stumbled badly in 1995, U.S. loan guarantees helped it recover rapidly, and by 2001 Mexico had the largest economy in Latin America. However, when Argentina had to abandon its attempt to link its currency to the U.S. dollar in 2001, the value of the Argentine peso plummeted.

Although the largest economies were better able to weather tough times, they were not immune to economic downturns. The extraordinary economic and stock market economic boom of the 1990s cooled in 2000 and plunged deeper into recession in the wake of the September 11 attacks. The rate of growth in world trade fell from 13 percent in 2000 to only 1 percent in 2001.

As Map 34.1 shows, the economic boom of the 1990s

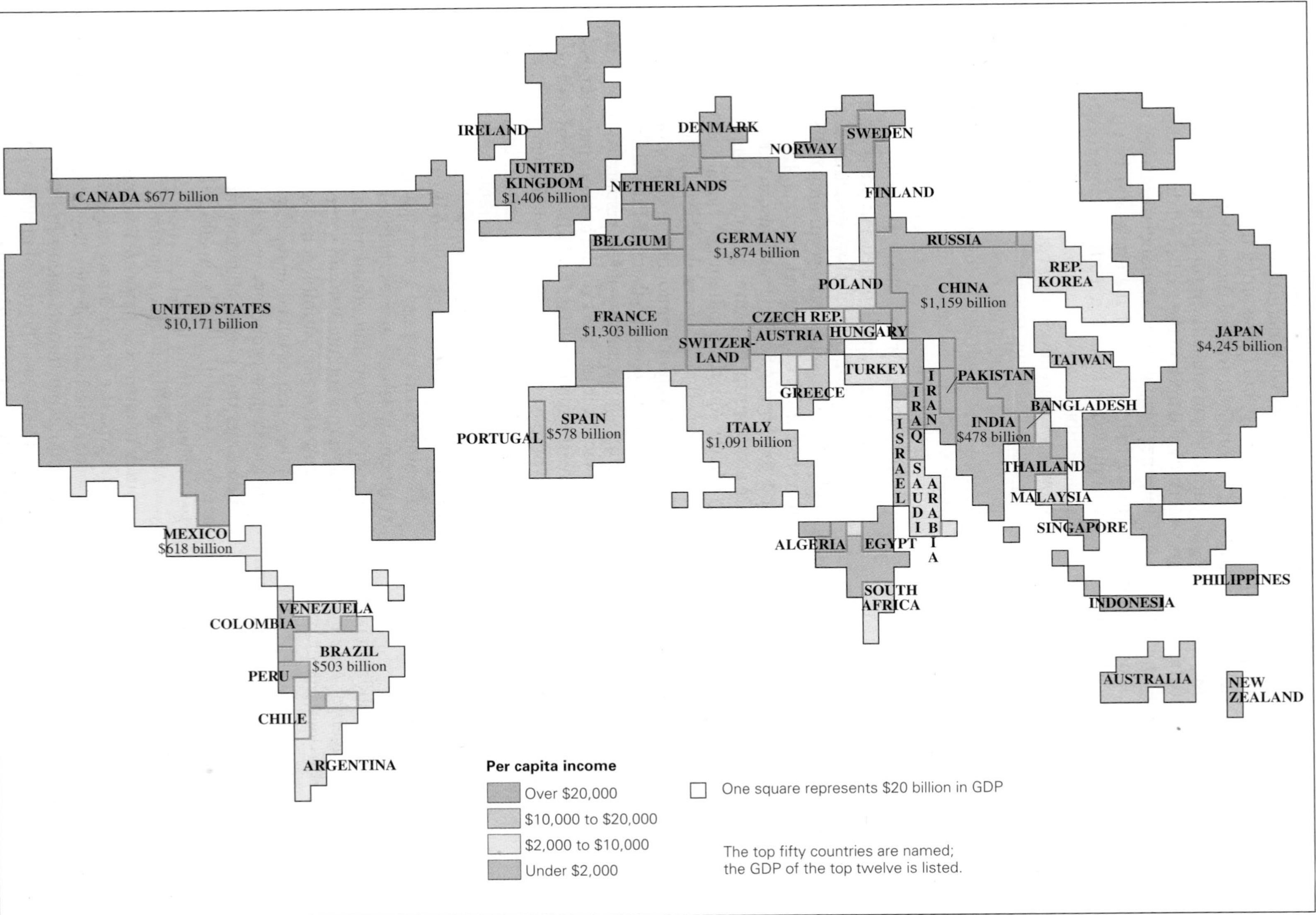

Map 34.1 Global Distribution of Wealth Industrialization and good government have given the citizens of Japan and Western countries access to tremendous wealth. Elsewhere, warfare and political mismanagement have slowed or reversed economic growth, while high population growth (see Map 33.3) has slowed increases in per capita wealth. In nearly all countries the distribution of wealth among individuals varies tremendously. Wealth is clearly concentrated in some parts of the world, but its geographical distribution is more complex than the often-cited divide between a rich north and a poor south.

did little to change historic disparities in regional economic size and in per capita income in 2002. The gigantic U.S. economy continued to be larger than the economies of the next five countries combined—Japan, Germany, Great Britain, China (including Hong Kong), and France. One person in six lived in a country whose per capita income was over $20,000, while four of every six lived in countries with per capita incomes of under $2,000. Some sixty countries grew poorer in the 1990s, but there were some remarkable overall improvements in the length and quality of life. The average lifespan grew by ten years in three decades. Infant mortality fell by 40 percent and adult illiteracy by 50 percent. However, every day many thousands still died of preventable diseases such as malaria, cholera, and tuberculosis.

Managing the Global Economy

To promote economic growth and reduce their vulnerabilities, many countries joined with their neighbors in free-trade zones and regional trade associations (see Map 34.2). The granddaddy of these is the European Union (EU), most of whose members replaced their coins and bills with a new common currency (the Euro) in 2002. Ten new members from eastern Europe and the Mediterranean were admitted in May 2004. Turkey, Bulgaria, and Romania were hoping to join. Despite the EU's expansion, the North American Free Trade Agreement (NAFTA), which eliminated tariffs among the United States, Canada, and Mexico in 1994, governed the world's largest free-trade zone. A South American free trade zone, Mercosur, created by Argentina, Brazil, Paraguay, and Uruguay in 1991 is the world's third largest trading group. In 2002 Mercosur decided to allow the free movement of people within its area and gave equal employment rights to the citizens of all member states. President Bush promoted a Free Trade Area of the Americas, which would include all the democracies of the Western Hemisphere. Chile was the first to sign on. Other free trade associations operate in West Africa, southern Africa, Southeast Asia, Central America, the Pacific basin, and the Caribbean.

Because of the inequalities and downturns that are intrinsic to capitalism, the global economic bodies that try to manage world trade and finance find it hard to convince poorer nations that they are not only concerned with the welfare of richer countries. In 1995 the world's major trading powers established the **World Trade Organization (WTO)** to replace GATT (see Chapter 32). The WTO encourages reduced trading barriers and enforces international trade agreements. Despite the membership of some 150 nations, the WTO has many critics, as became evident in Seattle in 1999, when street demonstrations, partly organized by American labor unions fearful of foreign competition, forced the organization to suspend a meeting. Moreover, the seven richest nations plus Russia form the Group of Eight (G-8), whose annual meetings have an enormous impact on international trade and politics and also attract a variety of protestors.

Countries in economic trouble have little choice but to turn to the international financial agencies for funds to keep things from getting worse. The International Monetary Fund (IMF) and World Bank make their assistance conditional on internal economic reforms that are often politically unpopular, such as terminating government subsidies for basic foodstuffs, cutting social programs, and liberalizing investment. While the bitter pill of economic reform may be good in the long run, it also fuels criticism of the international economic system.

The emphasis on free trade led to changes in the term of government-to-government aid programs. During the Cold War countries had often gained funds for economic development by allying themselves with one of the superpowers. In the decade after the Cold War ended, however, foreign economic aid to poor nations fell by a third. On an African tour in 2000 President Clinton told African countries that the days of large handouts were over and that they would have to rely on their own efforts to expand their economies.

In the face of rising criticism at home and protests at international meetings, world leaders in the 2000s have pledged to increase attention to the problem of economic backwardness, especially in Africa. At a Millennium Summit in September 2000 the states of the United Nations agreed to make sustainable development and the elimination of world poverty their highest priorities. A 2002 United Nations meeting in Monterrey, Mexico, called for special commitments to Africa. Recent G-8 summits endorsed new joint efforts to promote African development. Late in 2002 President Bush proposed a substantial increase in American foreign aid. If funded, his Millennium Challenge Account would increase the amount of nonmilitary foreign aid by 50 percent. First priority would be given to poor countries that cracked down on corruption, promoted civil liberties, increased spending on education and health, and followed free-market economic principles.

Freer trade has also put pressure on developed countries to change domestic aid programs. Though agriculture occupies a small part of the work force in Europe and the United States, agricultural interests are politically powerful. Government subsidies have led to vast overproduction of some products. Some of this surplus

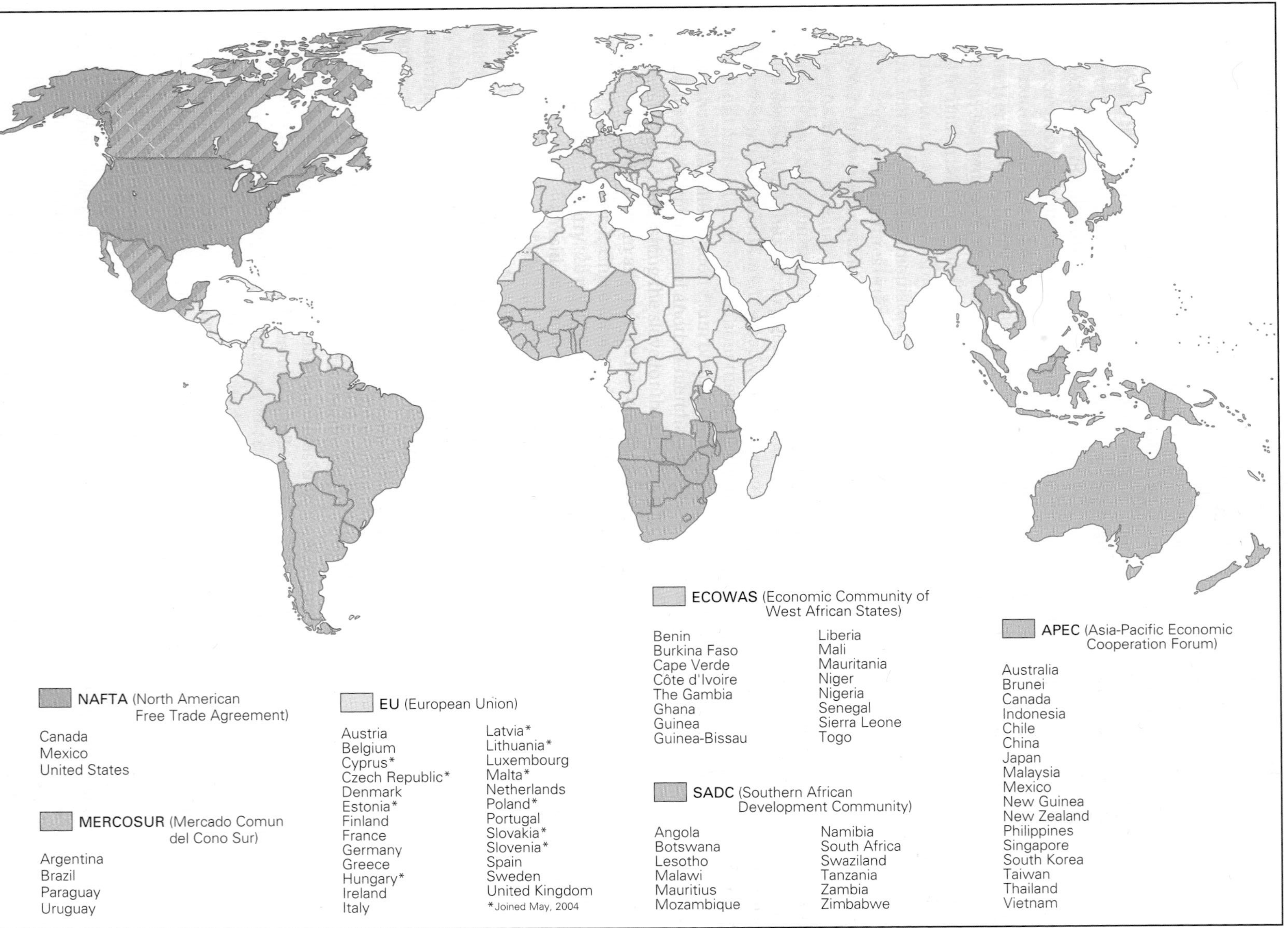

Map 34.2 Regional Trade Associations, 2004 International trade and development are major concerns of governments in developed and developing countries. NAFTA, Mercosur, and the EU are free-trade areas. The other associations promote trade and development.

Cheers for President Clinton in Nigeria In 2000 the first visit to sub-Saharan Africa by a sitting U.S. president brought out large, enthusiastic crowds everywhere, including this one outside the Nigerian capital city Abuja. The enthusiasm for President Clinton reflected his celebrity and his enthusiasm for Africa, but he was unable to promise much in the way of new American aid to this impoverished region. President Bush received a warm welcome when he visited Nigeria in 2003. (Brennan Linsley/AP/Wide World)

food is distributed as famine relief, but critics point out that subsidies to farmers in developed countries actually hurt farmers in poor countries who cannot compete with the artificially low prices that subsidies produce. A WTO meeting collapsed in 2003 when richer countries refused to meet the demands of delegates from poorer states to reduce agricultural subsidies.

Trends and Visions

As people around the world faced the opportunities and problems of globalization, they tried to make sense of these changes in terms of their own cultures and beliefs. With 6 billion people, the world is big enough to include a variety of different approaches, from intensely religious or local visions to broad secular views that champion a new universal value system. In some cases, however, conflicting visions fed violence.

A New Age?

In 1999 Thomas L. Friedman, a veteran Middle East and international reporter and columnist for the *New York Times*, published a penetrating analysis of the state of the planet. "The world is ten years old," proclaimed the opening essay of *The Lexus and the Olive Tree*. Friedman argued that the political and economic changes associated with the collapse of the Soviet Empire and the technological advances (computers, satellite and fiber optic communications, and the Internet) that had made possible a huge drop in telecommunications costs had ushered in a new age of political and economic globalization. In his view, global capitalism and American power and values characterized this new era of history, which held the promise (but not the certainty) of increased prosperity, peace, democracy, environmental protection, and human rights.

In Friedman's analysis, the Lexus, a splendidly engineered Japanese luxury car, produced for a global market on a computer-run assembly line of mechanical robots, symbolizes global progress and prosperity, and the international cooperation needed to achieve them. A Middle Eastern symbol, the olive tree, stands for the communal values of family, ethnicity, and religion that give people's lives stability, depth, and meaning.

To Friedman both the Lexus and the olive tree represent important human values, and his book suggests that they are mutually compatible. But his optimism about the new age is guarded. He believes that the benefits of global integration will offset its threats to established order. Still, his years of observation of Middle Eastern conflicts make him wary of the dangers that excessive devotion to parochial ethnic and religious values may pose to global progress. His book is less inclined to criticize the excesses of global capitalism.

The September 11 terrorist attacks that were being planned as Friedman wrote were a clear illustration of the extreme olive-tree mentalities he warned about, as are many other simmering conflicts around the world. The steeper declines in the value of the stock markets generally and especially of telecommunication companies that came in the wake of 9/11 and growing revelations of excessive greed and dishonesty by top executives in key companies shook many people's faith in free-market capitalism. Friedman and others would argue that such events were normal (and self-correcting) aspects of free markets, but they also suggest that the rapid pace of economic growth in the 1990s cannot be counted on. Moreover, the war on terrorism declared by President Bush in the wake of the 9/11 attacks promised to be a long and costly global struggle with an uncertain outcome.

Was Friedman too optimistic in seeing the dawning of an age of great promise? Many who thought so cited *The Clash of Civilizations and the Remaking of the World Order,* in which Harvard political scientist Samuel P. Huntington argues that the end of the Cold War left the world divided into distinct regional civilizations. For Huntington, religious and cultural differences are more likely to shape the future than are globalizing economic, political, and communication forces. It is impossible to predict whether global clashes or global convergence are more likely to dominate the future. Recent trends seem to point in both directions.

Christian Millenarianism

The turn of the millennium was an occasion for some very big parties. It also raised more serious issues. Fearing all sorts of mix-ups, businesses and governments spent vast sums to ensure that computers would recognize dates beginning with 2000. Some religious groups believed that a new era had arrived in which cosmic battles would be waged for the heart and soul of humanity.

Since the calendar now used around the world was devised to count the years since the birth of Jesus Christ, Christians had special reason to celebrate the millennium. The Catholic Church proclaimed the year 2000 a holy year and marked it with all sorts of special celebrations, including a vast gathering at its headquarters in Rome. With some 2 billion adherents, Christianity is the world's largest religious tradition and the most widespread globally (see Map 34.3). Well established in the Americas, Europe, and Africa, Christianity has been spreading rapidly in East Asia; for example, Christians are now more numerous than Buddhists in South Korea. After the fall of the official atheistic communist regime, many Russians returned to the Russian Orthodox Church or joined new evangelical Christian congregations.

As had sometimes happened in the past, some Christians looked for deeper meaning in the calendar change. Many turned to the prophetic account of the end of the world in the final book of the New Testament, the Apocalypse or Book of Revelation. This book foretold that three sets of seven violent struggles would lead to the final triumph of good over evil. With victory achieved, Christ would return to Earth, the good would be taken to Heaven, and the material world would come to an end. Guided by a tradition that held that since God had created the world in six days, the end of the world would come after the passage of six millennia, some Christians held that the year 2000 marked the beginning of the end, and they saw the events around them in terms of these prophecies.

The extent of this Christian **millenarianism** was suggested by the huge sales of the Left Behind series of novels, which described the events foretold in Revelation in vivid present-day settings. By the end of 2001 the ten novels by Tim LaHaye, a Baptist minister, and Jerry B. Jenkins, a syndicated cartoonist, had sold an unprecedented 50 million copies. Whatever the precise strength of Christian millenarianism, its supporters are well organized and skillfully use the Internet and other forms of mass communication to circulate their ideas.

While social scientists are inclined to interpret millenarian and other prophetic beliefs as efforts to find certainty in an uncertain world, believers accept the prophesies in Revelation as the guiding reality of their religious lives. To believers, the proliferation of secular values and permissive attitudes toward moral issues, disturbances in the weather, and the events of 9/11 are all signs of the impending confrontation between good and evil.

Because of their belief that only Christians can be saved, millenarian Christians have stepped up efforts to convert Muslims and Jews. These efforts have caused much resentment in Middle Eastern lands, where some Muslims have assaulted Christian missions. An American missionary in Lebanon was assassinated in 2002 for trying to convert Muslims.

A small part of millenarianism was associated with cult movements that came to violent ends. An armed confrontation with the FBI in Waco, Texas, in 1993 destroyed a small group called the Branch Davidians led by David Koresh. This was followed by ritual murders and collective suicides of members of the Heaven's Gate movement in California in 1997 and of members of the

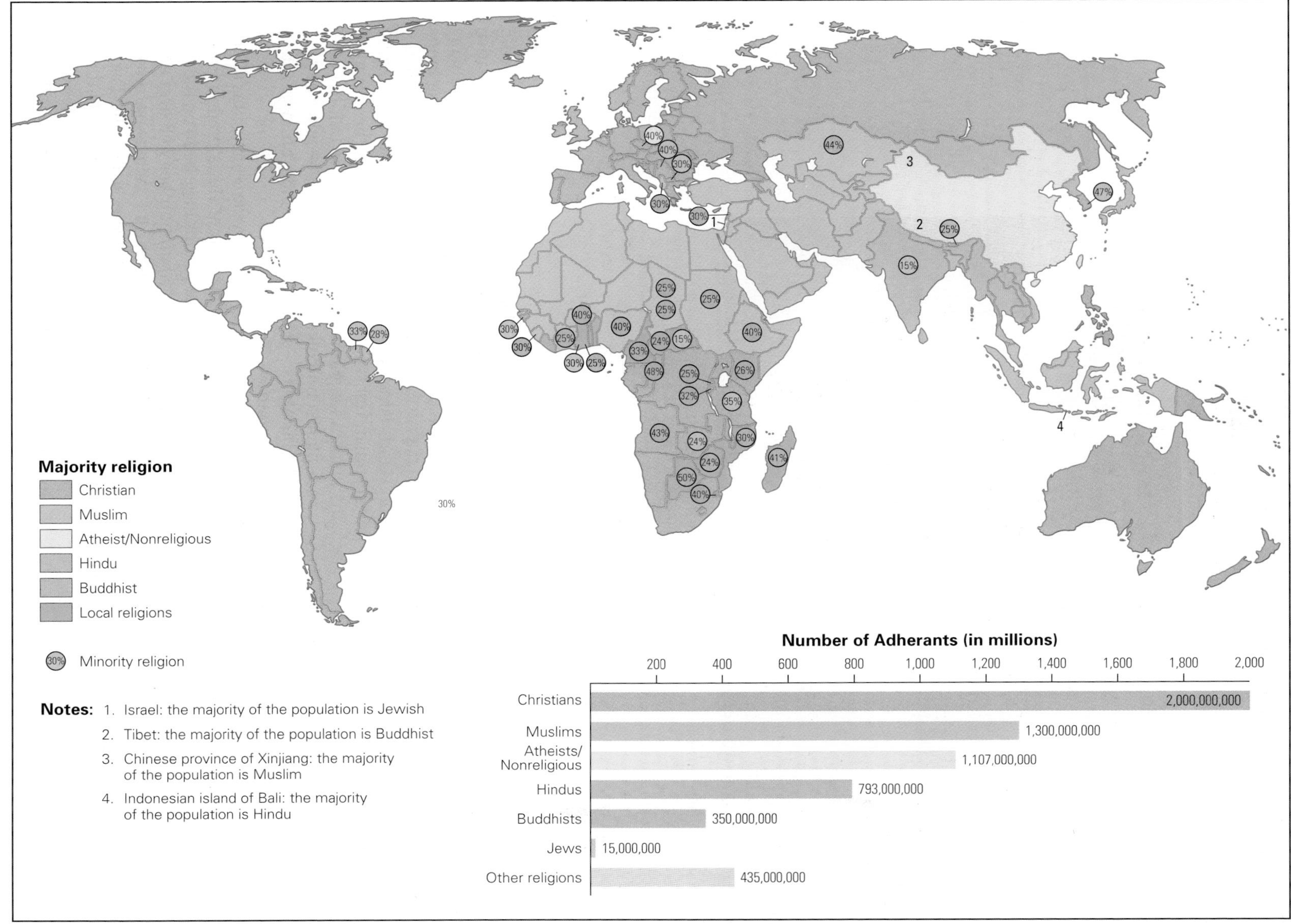

Map 34.3 World Religions The distribution of Buddhism, Christianity, and Islam reflects centuries of missionary efforts. Hinduism and Judaism have expanded primarily through trade and migration. Chinese governments have actively curtailed religious practice. As religion revives as a source of social identity or a rationale for political assertion or mass mobilization, the possibility of religious activism across broad geographic regions becomes greater, as does the likelihood of domestic discord in multireligious states. [Data from *The New York Times 2003 Almanac*, ed. John W. Wright (New York: Penguin Books, 2002), 484–488. Copyright © The New York Times Company, 2002.]

Millennium Celebration in Sydney Australia Uncertainties about what lay ahead for the world in the twenty-first century took a back seat to exuberant festivities as the millennium ended. The sleek modern silhouette of Sydney's opera house and the neon signs of major corporations epitomized the hopes of many. (Sydney Morning Herald/Sipa Press)

Order of the Solar Temple in France and Quebec in 1999. Such movements are easily dismissed as lunatic fringe groups, but they were not alone or uniquely Christian. In 1995 members of Aum Shinrikyo, a Buddhist sect whose founder had predicted that the world would end in 1999, released nerve gas in the Tokyo subway system.

Militant Islam

People in other faiths were also interpreting contemporary events from deeply religious perspectives. In the Jewish calendar a millennial change (the year 6000) will not arrive until 2240 C.E., but many on the religious right in Israel interpret the struggle of modern Israel to survive and prosper in term of the Biblical accounts of the Israelites' conquests more than four thousand years ago. Some Christian believers have gone to Israel to support Jewish settlers' efforts to reclaim the lands of the ancient Jewish kingdoms. In mid-2003, as President Bush was securing agreement to a new peace plan between Israel and the Palestinian Muslims who have occupied these lands for centuries, a conservative Jewish Israeli cabinet minister insisted that Palestinians must understand that God had given all of these lands to the Jews. The day the new peace plan was signed, ten thousand Israelis demonstrated against recognizing Palestinian rights to any territory that had been part of the ancient kingdom of Israel. Like others before it, the peace plan soon collapsed. For greater security against suicide bombers, Israel began walling off West Bank Palestinian lands.

Muslims have also drawn varying conclusions about the age of globalization. Moderate views predominate, but extreme and intolerant groups have been on the rise. Even though adherents to Islam number well over a billion globally and the numbers are increasing rapidly, many Muslims feel frustrated. The last of the Islamic empires disappeared after the defeat of the Ottoman Empire in the First World War, and three decades of European occupation of former Ottoman lands followed.

Since becoming independent in the 1950s, some Middle Eastern states have earned great wealth from petroleum exports, but per capita income in Muslim-majority countries in 2002 averaged half as much as in the world as a whole. No Muslim state is a major industrial or geopolitical power. The spread of mass media has also fed discontent by making ordinary Muslims more aware of life in the outside world and of the wide gaps in income and privilege within Muslim societies.

This failure of economic, social, and political modernization to advance along the lines envisioned by nationalist leaders of the twentieth century has led many Muslims to turn seek consolation in their sacred past. For some, it has also encouraged hostility to the seductions of the modern world and a rekindling of the Islamic struggle against non-Muslim infidels. In Indonesia, Nigeria, and other places, Muslim militants have assaulted non-Muslim minorities, often provoking retaliations.

Others have focused their hostility on external enemies. Much resentment centers on Israel, a Jewish state established in a part of the world that had been Muslim for many centuries. Israel's military victories over its Islamic neighbors have been particularly painful, as has been the failure to create the Palestinian state envisaged by the United Nations resolution in 1947. Israel's greater economic prosperity and technological sophistication are also frustrating to its Muslim neighbors.

Because American aid and support have helped Israel acquire the most powerful military force in the Middle East, much Islamic hatred and opposition has been directed against the United States. Many militants also denounce American support for unpopular and undemocratic governments in Muslim-majority countries, especially Saudi Arabia. Although most Muslims admire American technological and cultural achievements, a 2002 poll by the Pew Research Center for the People and the Press found that the majority of Egyptians, Jordanians, and Pakistanis held a "very unfavorable" opinion of the United States. America's extensive aid to Egypt and Pakistan seems to have won it few friends in those countries. The American-led liberation of the Muslim state of Kuwait in the Persian Gulf War of 1990–1991 after a violent takeover by Iraq actually became a rallying issue for many Islamic extremists, in part because of the American use of bases in Saudi Arabia, which they consider sacred territory.

This view of the world order has many roots, but it reflects an ideological vision of Muslims under attack that is widely published in the media in Muslim states and promoted by some Islamic leaders who use religious ideas to justify violent actions. From this perspective the Palestinian suicide bombers in Israel that others call terrorists are martyrs and heroes. Such a vision explains why some Muslims celebrated when the Twin Towers collapsed in New York.

While the actions of militant Muslims are based on their perception of complex realities, it is important to keep in mind that they are also the product of ideologies. A rational explanation of the 9/11 events makes no sense, according to Professor Richard Landes, director of the Center for Millennial Studies, because Usama bin Laden believes he is fighting "in a cosmic battle that pits the warriors for truth against the agents of Satan and evil in this world." Similarly, Bernard Lewis, a respected senior scholar of Islam, argues that for bin Laden "2001 marks the resumption of the war for the religious dominance of the world that began in the seventh century" when Islam was founded.[2] Such beliefs help explain why many Muslims also saw nothing positive in America's overthrow of the oppressive and unpopular Taliban regime in Afghanistan in 2001 and why a high proportion of Muslims regarded the American campaign to oust Saddam Husain from Iraq in 2003 as further American aggression against the Muslim world, rather than as the liberation of Muslims from an oppressive dictator.

Universal Rights and Values

At the same time as these religious visions have gained strength, efforts to promote adherence to universal standards of human rights have also gained wider acceptance. Religious leaders had first voiced the notion that all people are equal, but the modern human rights movement grew out of the secular statements of the French Declaration of the Rights of Man (1789) and the U.S. Constitution (1788) and Bill of Rights (1791). Over the next century, the logic of universal rights moved Westerners to undertake international campaigns to end slave trading and slavery throughout the world and to secure equal legal rights (and eventually voting rights) for women.

International organizations in the twentieth century secured agreement on labor standards, the rules of war, and the rights of refugees. The pinnacle of these efforts was the **Universal Declaration of Human Rights,** passed by the United Nations General Assembly in 1948, which proclaimed itself "a common standard of achievement for all peoples and nations." Its thirty articles condemned slavery, torture, cruel and inhuman punishment, and arbitrary arrest, detention, and exile. The Declaration called for freedom of movement, assembly, and thought. It asserted rights to life, liberty, and security of person; to impartial public trials; and to education, employment, and leisure. The principle of equality was most fully articulated in Article 2:

> Everyone is entitled to all the rights and freedoms set forth in this Declaration, without distinction of any kind, such as race, color, sex, language, religion, or political or other opinion, national or social origin, property, birth or other status.[3]

This passage reflected an international consensus against racism and imperialism and a growing acceptance of the importance of social and economic equality. Most newly independent countries joining the United Nations willingly signed the Declaration because it implicitly condemned European colonial regimes.

The idea of universal human rights has not gone unchallenged. Some have asked whether a set of principles whose origins were so clearly Western could be called universal. Others have been uneasy with the idea of subordinating the traditional values of their culture or religion to a broader philosophical standard. Despite these objections, important gains have been made in implementing these standards.

Besides the official actions of the United Nations and individual states, individual human rights activists, often working through international philanthropic bodies known as **nongovernmental organizations (NGOs),** have been important forces for promoting human rights. Amnesty International, founded in 1961 and numbering a million members in 162 countries by the 1990s, concentrates on gaining the freedom of people who have been tortured or imprisoned without trial and campaigns against summary execution by government death squads or other gross violations of rights. Arguing that no right is more fundamental than the right to life, other NGOs have devoted themselves to famine relief, refugee assistance, and health care around the world. Médecins Sans Frontières (Doctors Without Borders), founded in 1971, was awarded the Nobel Peace Prize for1999 for the medical assistance it offered in scores of crisis situations.

The rising tendency to see health care as a human right has made a new disease, acquired immune deficiency syndrome (AIDS), the focus of particular attention because its incidence and high mortality rate are closely associated with poverty, and treatments are very expensive. Over 40 million people worldwide are infected with the HIV retrovirus that causes AIDS. Of them, 70 percent live in sub-Saharan Africa (see Figure 34.1). The number of sick and dying is already large enough in some parts of Africa to pose a significant risk to the production of food, the care of the young and elderly, and the staffing of schools. Because sexual promiscuity among young men serving in the armed forces has made them especially likely to be infected, death and incapacitation from AIDS has significantly imperiled military preparedness in parts of Africa. Great international efforts are being made to provide drugs at a lower cost, so that more Africans can be treated. Because the disease is not contagious except by very intimate contact, education is a more cost-effective way of stemming the spread of AIDS. In Uganda, South Africa, and Ethiopia, for example, education campaigns have reduced the incidence of new HIV infections in targeted groups. An inexpensive drug has also been successful in cutting the transmission of the infection from mother to infant during childbirth.

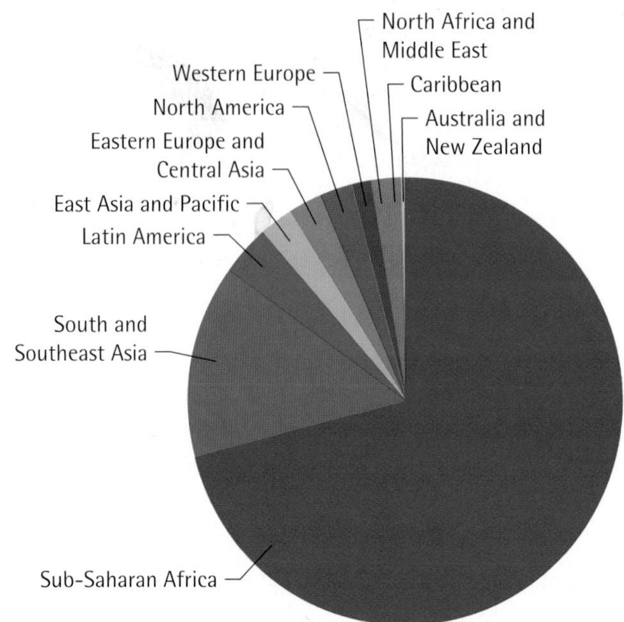

Figure 34.1 World Distribution of HIV/AIDS Cases (2001 estimates) *Source:* United Nations AIDS and World Health Organization, *Report on the Global HIV/AIDS Epidemic* (June 2000).

Other international agreements have made genocide a crime and have promoted environmental protection of the seas, of Antarctica, and of the atmosphere. The United States and a few other nations were greatly concerned that such treaties would unduly limit their sovereignty or threaten their national interests. For this reason the U.S. Congress delayed ratifying the 1949 convention on genocide until 1986. More recently the United States drew widespread international criticism for demanding exemption for Americans from the jurisdiction of the International Criminal Court, created in 2002 to try international criminals, and for withdrawing in 2001 from the 1997 Kyoto Protocol requiring industrial nations to sharply reduce emissions of pollutants that damage the atmosphere (see Environment and Technology: Global Warming). To many nations it seemed as if

Global Warming

Until the 1980s environmental alarms focused mainly on localized episodes of air and water pollution, exposure to toxic substances, waste management, and the disappearance of wilderness. The development of increasingly powerful computers and complex models of ecological interactions in the 1990s, however, made people aware of the global scope of certain environmental problems.

Many scientists and policymakers came to perceive global warming, the slow increase of the temperature of the Earth's lower atmosphere, as an environmental threat requiring preventive action on an international scale. The warming is caused by a layer of atmospheric gases (carbon dioxide, methane, nitrous oxide, and ozone) that allow solar radiation to reach Earth and warm it, but keep infrared energy (heat) from radiating from Earth's surface into space. Called the *greenhouse effect*, this process normally keeps the Earth's temperature at a level suitable for life. However, increases in greenhouse-gas emissions—particularly from the burning of fossil fuels in industry and transportation—have added to this insulating atmospheric layer.

Recent events have confirmed predictions of global temperature increases and melting glaciers and icecaps. Globally, the five warmest years on record were 1995, 1997, 1998, 2001, and 2002. Record heat hit northern Europe in the summer of 2003. Greenland glaciers and Arctic Ocean sea ice melted at record rates during 2002, and a huge section of the Antarctic ice shelf broke up and floated away. Andean glaciers are shrinking so fast they could disappear in a decade, imperiling water supplies for drinking, irrigation, and hydroelectric production. Drought has affected much of the United States in recent years, and in 2002 Australia experienced the "Big Dry," its worst drought in a century.

Despite this evidence, governments of the industrialized countries that produce the most greenhouse gasses have been slow to adopt measures stringent enough to reduce emissions because of the negative effects they believe this could have on their economies. There is also fear that it may be already too late to reverse global warming. The pledges that representatives from 178 countries made at the first Earth Summit in Rio de Janeiro in 1992 to limit their *increase* in greenhouse-gas production have so far been ineffective. Fearing limits on gas emissions could cripple their plans for industrial and economic expansion, many nations hesitated to sign the 1997 Kyoto Protocol, the first international agreement to impose penalties on countries that failed to cut greenhouse-gas emissions. It was a major environmental victory when Japan added its signature in March 2001, but to the consternation of many world leaders President George W. Bush has rejected the agreement. The war on terrorism also appears to have made the environment a lower American priority. Until the destructive effects of global warming, such as the inundation of coastal regions and large cities by rising sea levels, match the destruction of terrorists, the political focus is unlikely to shift.

Flooding in Bangladesh Typhoon-driven floods submerge the low-lying farmlands of Bangladesh with tragic regularity. Any significant rise in the sea level will make parts of the country nearly uninhabitable. (D. Aubert/Sygma)

Americans, with the world's greatest industrial economy, were trying to exempt themselves from standards that they wanted to impose on other nations.

Women's Rights

The women's rights movement, which began on both sides of the North Atlantic in the nineteenth century, became an important human rights issue in the twentieth century. Rights for women became accepted in Western countries and were enshrined in the constitutions of many nations newly freed from colonial rule. . A series of international conferences on the status of women sponsored by the Division for the Advancement of Women of the United Nations have shown the international importance of women's rights at the end of the twentieth century. The first meeting, held in Nairobi, Kenya, in 1985, attracted seventeen thousand women from all over the world. The delegates focused on equal access to education and jobs and on quality-of-life matters such as ending sexual exploitation and gaining control of reproduction. A second conference in Beijing in 1995 also examined a variety of women's issues and perspectives, in some cases to the discomfort of the Chinese government. The Beijing conference recognized the advances that had been made in the status of women and called for efforts to remove remaining obstacles to equality, including those caused by poverty.

Beijing Women's Conference in 1995 This gathering of women from every part of the world, under United Nations auspices, illustrated the challenges posed by women's search for equality. The Chinese government, consistent with its policies of suppressing dissent and closely regulating social life, tried to limit press access to the conference. As in many other instances, these efforts to silence or control women's voices on issues like abortion and family planning proved ineffective. (Boulat/Sipa Press)

Besides highlighting the similarity of the problems women faced around the world, the conferences also revealed great variety in the views and concerns of women. Feminists from the West, who had been accustomed to dictating the agenda and who had pushed for the liberation of women in other parts of the world, sometimes found themselves accused of having narrow concerns and condescending attitudes. Some non-Western women complained about Western feminists' endorsement of sexual liberation and about the deterioration of family life in the West. They found Western feminists' concern with matters such as comfortable clothing misplaced and trivial compared to the issues of poverty and disease.

Other cultures came in for their share of criticism. Western women and many secular leaders in Muslim countries protested Islam's requirement that a woman cover her head and wear loose-fitting garments to conceal the shape of her body, practices enforced by law in countries such as Iran and Saudi Arabia. Nevertheless, many outspoken Muslim women voluntarily donned concealing garments as expressions of personal belief, statements of resistance to secular dictatorship, or defense against coarse male behavior. Much Western criticism focused on the African custom of circumcising girls, a form of genital mutilation that can cause chronic infections or permanently impair sexual enjoyment. While not denying the problems this practice can lead to, many African women saw deteriorating economic conditions, rape, and AIDS as more important issues.

The conferences were more important for the attention they focused on women's issues than for the solutions they generated. The search for a universally accepted women's rights agenda proved elusive because of local concerns and strong disagreement on abortion and other issues. Nevertheless, increases in women's education, access to employment, political participation, and control of fertility augured well for the eventual achievement of gender equality.

Such efforts raised the prominence of human rights as a global concern and put pressure on governments to consider human rights when making foreign policy decisions. Skeptics observed, however, that a Western country could successfully prod a non-Western country to improve its human rights performance—for example, by granting women more equal access to education and careers—but that reverse criticism of a Western country often fell on deaf ears—for example, condemnation of the death penalty in the United States. For such critics the human rights movement was not as an effort to make the world more humane but another form of Western cultural imperialism, a club with which to beat former colonial societies into submission. Still, support for universal rights has grown, especially because increasing globalization has made common standards of behavior more important.

Global Culture

Along with the human rights movement, other kinds of cultural globalization were also proceeding rapidly at the turn of the millennium. A global language, a global educational system, and global forms of artistic expression have all come into being. Trade, travel, and migration have made a common culture necessary. Electronic communications that were once confined to members of a jet-setting elite have enabled global cultural influences to move deeper into many societies, and a sort of global popular culture has also emerged. These changes have angered some and delighted others.

The Media and the Message

Although cultural influences from every continent travel around the world, the fact that the most pervasive elements of global culture have their origins in the West raises concerns in many quarters about **cultural imperialism.** Critics complain that entertainment conglomerates are flooding the world's movie theaters and television screens with Western tastes and styles and that manufacturers are flooding world markets with Western goods—both relying on sophisticated advertising techniques that promote consumption and cultural conformity. In this view, global marketing is an especially insidious effort not only to overwhelm the world with a single Western outlook shaped by capitalist ideology, but also to suppress or devalue traditional cultures and alternative ideologies. As the leader of the capitalist world, the United States is seen as the primary culprit.

But in truth, technology plays a more central role than ideology in spreading Western culture. Even though imperialist forces old and new shape choices, strongly democratic forces are also at work as people around the world make their selections in the cultural marketplace. Thus, a diversity of voices is more characteristic of cultural globalization than the cultural imperialism thesis maintains.

The pace of cultural globalization began to quicken during the economic recovery after World War II. The Hollywood films and American jazz recordings that had become popular in Europe and parts of Asia continued to spread. But the birth of electronic technology opened contacts with large numbers of people who could never have afforded to go to a movie or buy a record.

The first step was the development of cheap transistor radios that could run for months on a couple of small batteries. Perfected by American scientists at Bell Telephone Laboratories in 1948, solid-state electronic transistors replaced power-hungry and less reliable electron tubes in radios and a wide array of other devices. Just as tube radios had spread in Europe and America in the decades before the war, small portable transistor radios, most made in Japan and elsewhere in Asia, spread rapidly in parts of the world where homes lacked electricity.

Because the transistor radios sold in Asia and Africa were designed to receive shortwave broadcasts, they brought people in remote villages the news, views, and music that American, European, Soviet, and Chinese transmitters beamed to the world. For the first time in history, the whole world could learn of major political and cultural events simultaneously. Although such broadcasts came in local and regional languages, many were in English. Electronic audiotape and CD players added to the diversity of music available to individuals everywhere.

Television, made possible by the invention of an electron scanning gun in 1928, became widely available to consumers in Western countries in the 1950s. In poorer parts of the world TVs were not common until the 1980s and 1990s, after mass production and cheap transistors made sets more affordable and reliable. Outside the United States, television broadcasting was usually a government monopoly at first, following the pattern of telegraph and postal service and radio broadcasting. Governments expected news reports and other programming to disseminate a unified national viewpoint.

Government monopolies eroded as the high cost of television production opened up global markets for rebroadcasts of American soap operas, adventure series, and situation comedies. By the 1990s a global network of satellites brought privately owned television broadcasting to even remote areas of the world, and the VCR (videocassette recorder) brought an even greater variety of programs to people everywhere. British programs found a secondary market in the United States, Canada, Australia, and other countries. As a result of wider circulation of programming, people often became familiar with different dialects of English and other languages. People in Portugal, for example, who in the 1960s had found it difficult to understand Brazilian Portuguese, have become avid fans of Brazilian soap operas. Immigrants from Albania and North Africa often arrive in Italy with a command of Italian learned from Italian stations whose signals they could pick up at home.

Further internationalization of culture resulted from satellite transmission of TV signals. Specializing in rock music videos aimed at a youth audience, MTV (Music Television) became an international enterprise offering special editions in different parts of the world. Music videos shown in Uzbekistan°, for example, often featured Russian bands, and Chinese groups appeared in MTV programs shown in Singapore. CNN (Cable News Network) expanded its international market after becoming the most-viewed and informative news source during the 1991 Persian Gulf War, when it broadcast live from Baghdad. Despite CNN's fundamentally American view of the news, its round-the-clock coverage and global resources began to supplant other commercial and government news programming as the best source of information about rapidly developing events. By the new millennium global satellite networks (Fox, Sky) assembled by Rupert Murdock and new regional networks competed for viewers.

The Internet, a linkage of academic, government, and business computer networks developed in the 1960s, became a major cultural phenomenon. Personal computers proliferated in the 1980s, and with the establishment of the easy-to-use graphic interface of the World Wide Web in 1994, the number of Internet users skyrocketed. Myriad new companies formed to exploit "e-commerce," the commercial dimension of the Internet. In the new century many college students spent less time studying conventional books and scholarly resources than they spent exploring the Web for information and entertainment.

As had happened so often throughout history, technological developments had unanticipated consequences. Although the new telecommunications and entertainment technologies derived disproportionately from American invention, industry, and cultural creativity, Japan and other East Asian nations came to dominate the manufacture and refinement of computer devices. In the 1990s Japan introduced digital television broadcasting at about the time that disks containing digitized movies and computer programs with movie-like action became increasingly available. In the early 2000s digital cameras, DVD players, and new generations of cell phones became popular, providing opportunities for companies in a variety of developing countries to capture a corner of the market. In contrast to these rapid changes in technology, Western, especially American, cultural domination of the content of the Web has changed more slowly, but people around the world can adapt the medium to their own purposes.

The Spread of Pop Culture

New technologies changed perceptions of culture as well as its distribution around the world and among different social classes. For most of history, popular culture was folk culture, highly localized ways of dress, food, music, and expression. Only the educated and urban few had access to the riches of a broader "great tradition," such as Confucianism in East Asia or Western culture in Europe and the Americas. The schools of modern nation-states promoted national values and beliefs, and tastes in painting, literature, and art. Governments also promoted a common language or dialect and frequently suppressed local traditions and languages. In a more democratic way, the transistor helped break down barriers and create a global popular culture that transcended regional great traditions and national cultures.

Initially, the content of global **pop culture** was heavily American. Singer Michael Jackson was almost as well known to the youth of Dar-es-Salaam (Tanzania) and Bangkok (Thailand) as to American fans. Basketball star Michael Jordan became a worldwide celebrity, heavily promoted by Nike, McDonald's, and television. American television programs such as Wheel of Fortune and Friends acquired immense followings and inspired local imitations. In the late twentieth century American movies, which had long had great popular appeal, substantially increased their share of world

Uzbekistan (ooz-BEK-ih-STAN)

markets. In the 1990s the vast majority of the most popular films in Europe were American made. Many Europeans complained loudly about this American cultural imperialism—and then bought tickets to see the latest Hollywood spectacular.

As with music and fast food, companies spent heavily to promote profitable overseas markets, but the United States did not have a lock on global pop culture. Latin American soap operas, *telenovelas*, have a vast following in the Americas, eastern Europe, and elsewhere. Bombay, India, long the largest producer of films in the world, is now making more films for an international audience, rather than just for the home market. Bruce Lee popularized kung fu (Chinese martial arts) movies. A sophisticated kung fu film, *Crouching Tiger, Hidden Dragon* by Hong Kong-born director Ang Lee, was very popular in the United States and won four Academy Awards for 2000, including one for the best foreign-language film.

In the post–World War II decades American, European, and Japanese companies sought international markets for their products. In the 1970s and 1980s American brand names like Levi's, Coca-Cola, Marlboro, Gillette, McDonald's, and Kentucky Fried Chicken were global phenomena. But in time Asian names—Hitachi, Sony, Sanyo, and Mitsubishi— were blazoned in neon and on giant video screens on the sides of skyscrapers, along with European brands such as Nestlé, Mercedes, Pirelli, and Benetton. The location of manufacturing plants overseas and the acquisition of corporate operations by foreign buyers rendered such global firms as transnational as the products they sell.

The content of international pop culture does not have to remain any more monolithic than the typical McDonald's lunch, which consists of a meat patty named for a German city, potatoes prepared in a French manner, and a soft drink named after the South American coca leaves and West African kola that were its original ingredients. Popular music also became increasingly international. Latin American styles extended their appeal beyond the Americas. The hybrid rhythms known as Afropop spread around Africa and found fans in Europe and the Americas.

Japanese Adult Male Comic Book After World War II comic magazines emerged as a major form of publication and a distinctive product of culture in Japan. Different series are directed to different age and gender groups. Issued weekly and running to some three hundred pages in black and white, the most popular magazines sell as many copies as do major newsmagazines in the United States. (Private Collection)

Emerging Global Culture

While the globalization of popular culture has been criticized, cultural links across national and ethnic boundaries at a more elite level have generated little controversy. The end of the Cold War reopened intellectual and cultural contacts between former adversaries, making possible such things as Russian-American collaboration on space missions and extensive business contacts among former rivals. The English language, modern science, and higher education became the key elements of this **global culture.**

The emergence of English as the first global language depended on developments that had been building for centuries. The British Empire introduced the language to far-flung colonies. When the last parts of the empire gained independence after World War II, most former colonies chose to continue using English as an official language because it provided national unity and a link to the outside world that the dozens or hundreds of local languages could not. After independence, representatives of former British colonies formed the Commonwealth on the basis of their shared language and commercial ties. Newly independent countries that made a local language official for nationalist reasons often found the decision counterproductive. Indian nationalists had pushed for Hindi to be India's official language, but they found that students taught in Hindi were unable to compete internationally because of poor knowledge of English. Sri Lanka, which had made Sinhala its official language in 1956, reversed itself after local reporters revealed in 1989 that prominent officials were sending their children to English-medium private schools.

The use of English as a second language was greatly stimulated by the importance of the United States in postwar world affairs. Individuals recognized the importance of mastering English for successful business, diplomatic, and military careers. After the collapse of Soviet domination, students in eastern Europe flocked to study English instead of Russian. Ninety percent of students in Cambodia (a former French colony) choose to study English, even though a Canadian agency offers a sizable cash bonus if they will study French. In the 1990s China made the study of English as a second language nearly universal from junior high school onwards, but also forced an English-medium school in Hong Kong to teach most subjects in Chinese.

English has become the language of choice for most international academic conferences, business meetings, and diplomatic gatherings. International organizations that provide equal status to many languages, such as the United Nations and the European Union, tend to conduct all informal committee meetings in English. English has even replaced Latin as the working language for international consultations in the Catholic Church. In cities throughout the world, signs and notices are now posted in the local language and English.

The utility of English as a global language is also evident in the emergence of an international literature in English (see Diversity and Dominance: World Literature in English). The trend has been evident for decades in former British colonies in Africa, where most writers use English to reach both a national audience and an international one. Wole Soyinka, the first sub-Saharan African to win the Nobel Prize in literature for 1986, wrote in English, the national language of Nigeria, rather than his native Yoruba. When Arundhati Roy won the prestigious Booker Prize in 1997 for *The God of Small Things,* a novel set in her native state of Kerala in southwest India, she was part of an English-language literary tradition that has been growing in India for a century. V. S. Naipaul of Trinidad, winner of the Nobel Prize in literature for 2001, is a good example of the way global migration has fostered the use of English. Naipaul's ancestors had emigrated from India in the nineteenth century.

V. S. Naipaul Receives the 2001 Nobel Prize for Literature
Of Indian descent and Trinidadian birth, Naipaul wrote critically of life in the West Indies, Africa, and the Islamic world. His selection for the world's most prestigious literary prize was a tribute to his talents and diligence and also highlighted the increasing globalization of writing in English. (Jonas Ekstromer/Pool/AP Wide)

World literature remains highly diverse in form and language, but science and technology have become standardized components of global culture. Though imperialism helped spread the Western disciplines of biology, chemistry, and physics around the world, their popularity continued to expand even after imperial systems ended because they worked so much better than other approaches to the natural world. Their truth was universal even if plants and animals continue to be classified in Latin and the less common elements are called by names originally derived from Latin and Greek. Global manufacturing could not function without a common system of applied science. Because of their scientific basis Western medicine and drugs are increasingly accepted as the best treatments, even though many cultures also use traditional remedies.

The third pillar of global elite culture is the university. The structure and curricula of modern universities are nearly indistinguishable around the world, permitting students today to cross national boundaries as freely as students in the medieval Latin West or the Muslim world. Instruction in the pure sciences varies little from place to place, and standardization is nearly as common in social science and applied sciences such as engineering and medicine. There may be more diversity in the humanities, but professors and students around the world pay attention to the latest literary theories and topics of historical interest.

While university subjects are taught in many languages, instruction in English is spreading rapidly. Because discoveries are often first published in English, advanced students in science, business, and international relations need to know that language to keep up with the latest developments. The global mobility of professors and students also promotes classroom instruction in the most global language. Many courses in the Netherlands and in Scandinavian countries have long been offered in English, and elsewhere in Europe offering more courses in English was the obvious way to facilitate the EU's efforts to encourage students to study outside their countries of origin. When South Africa ended the apartheid educational systems that had required people to study in their own languages, most students chose to study in English.

Because global elite culture is so deeply rooted in years of training, complex institutions, and practical utility, it is less subject to fads and commercial promotion than is global pop culture. Because such elite culture is confined to a distinct minority in most places, it poses little threat to national and folk cultures and, therefore, is much less controversial.

Enduring Cultural Diversity

Although protestors regularly denounce the "Americanization" of the world, a closer look suggests that cultural globalization is more complex and multifaceted. Just as English has largely spread as a second language, so global culture is primarily a second culture that dominates some contexts but does not displace other traditions. From this perspective, American music, fast food, and fashions are more likely to add to a society's options than to displace local culture. In any event, the amount of global change largely rests with the world's 6 billion people.

Japan first demonstrated that a country with a non-Western culture could perform at a high industrial level. Individuality was less valued in Japan than the ability of each person to fit into a group, whether as an employee, a member of an athletic team, or a student in a class. Moreover, the Japanese considered it unmannerly to directly contradict, correct, or refuse the request of another person. From a Western point of view, these Japanese customs seemed to discourage individual initiative and personality development and to preserve traditional hierarchies. Japanese women, for example, even though they often worked outside the home, responded only slowly to the American and European feminist advocacy of equality in economic and social relations. However, the Japanese approach to social relations was well suited to an industrial economy. The efficiency, pride in workmanship, and group solidarity of Japanese workers, supported by closely coordinated government and corporate policies, played a major role in transforming Japan from a defeated nation with a demolished industrial base in 1945 to an economic power by the 1980s.

Japan's success in the modern industrial world called into question the older assumption that successful industrialization required the adoption of Western culture. As awareness of the economic impact of Japanese culture and society began to spread, it became apparent that Taiwan and South Korea, along with Singapore and Hong Kong (a British colony before being reunited with China in 1997), were developing dynamic industrial economies of their own. Other countries seem likely to follow this model.

This does not mean that the world's culture diversity is secure. Every decade a number of languages cease to be spoken, usually as the result of the spread of national languages. Many religious practices are also disappearing in the face of the successful expansion of Islam, Christianity, and other religions, although secular values also play a role. Televised national ceremonies

DIVERSITY AND DOMINANCE

WORLD LITERATURE IN ENGLISH

The linguistic diversity of the world is part of its richness, but it is also an impediment to global communication. In this essay novelist and Indian diplomat Shashi Tharoor explains why he chooses to write in English. His decision to use English is not unusual among writers in India and many other lands where English is not the first language. Mr. Tharoor has worked for the United Nations since 1978. In 2002 he became Under-Secretary-General for Communications and Public Information.

For the record, the national languages of India are Hindi (spoken by 30 percent of the population) and English, which dominates communication among India's elite. Fourteen other languages are official at the provincial level, with English having official status in the provinces of East Bengal, Kerala, and Orissa.

As an Indian writer living in New York, I find myself constantly asked a question with which my American confreres never have to contend: "But whom do you write for?"

In my case, the question is complicated by both geography and language. I live in the United States (because of my work at the United Nations) and I write about India; and I do so in English, a language mastered, if the last census is to be believed, by only 2 percent of the Indian population. There is an unspoken accusation implicit in the question: Am I not guilty of the terrible sin of inauthenticity, of writing about my country for foreigners? . . .

This is ironic, because few developments in world literature have been more remarkable than the emergence, over the last two decades, of a new generation of Indian writers in English.

Beginning with Salman Rushdie's *Midnight's Children* in 1981, they have expanded the boundaries of their craft and their nation's literary heritage, enriching English with the rhythms of ancient legends and the larger-then-life complexities of another civilization, while reinventing India in the confident cadences of English prose. Of the unintended consequences of empire, it is hard to imagine one of greater value to both colonizers and colonized.

The new Indian writers dip into a deep well off memory, and experience far removed from those of their fellow novelists in the English language. But whereas Americans or Englishmen or Australians have also set their fictions in distant lands Indians write of India without exoticism, their insights undimmed by the dislocations of foreignness. And they do so in an English they have both learned and lived, an English of freshness and vigor, a language that is as natural to them as their quarrels at the school playground or the surreptitious notes they slipped each other in their classrooms.

Yet Indian critics still suggest that there is something artificial and un-Indian about an Indian writing in English. One critic disparagingly declared that the acid test ought to be, "Could this have been written only by an Indian?" I have never been much of a literary theoretician—I always felt that for a writer to study literature at university would be like learning about girls at medical school—but for most, though not all, of my own writing, I would answer that my works could not only have been written only by an Indian, but only by an Indian *in English*.

I write for anyone who will read me, but first of all for Indians like myself, Indians who have grown up speaking, writing, playing, wooing and quarreling in English, all over India. (No writer really chooses a language: the circumstances of his upbringing ensure that the language chooses him.)

Members of this class have entered the groves of academe and condemned themselves in terms of bitter self-reproach: one Indian scholar, Harish Trivedi, has asserted (in English) that Indian writers in that language are "cut off from the experiential mainstream and from that common cultural matrix . . . shared with writers of all other Indian languages." Dr. Trivedi metaphorically cites the fictional English-medium school in an R. K. Narayan story where the students must first rub off the sandalwood-paste caste marks from their foreheads before they enter its portals: "For this golden gate is only for the déraciné to pass through, for those who have erased their antecedents." [R. K. Narayan (1906–2001) pioneered writing in English in Madras in the 1930s, publishing three dozen novels and many short stories and essays.]

It's an evocative image, even though I thought the secular Indian state was supposed to encourage the erasure of casteism from the classroom. But the more important point is that writers like myself do share a "common cultural matrix," albeit one devoid of helpfully identifying caste marks.

It is one that consists of an urban upbringing and a pan-national outlook on the Indian reality. I do not think this is any less authentically "Indian" than the worldviews of writers in other Indian languages. Why should the rural peasant or the small-town schoolteacher with his sandalwood-smeared forehead be considered more quintessentially Indian than the punning collegian or the Bombay socialite, who are as much a part of the Indian reality?

India is a vast and complex country; in Whitman's phrase, it contains multitudes. I write of an India of multiple truths and multiple realities, an India that is greater than the sum of its parts. English expresses that diversity better than any Indian language precisely because it is not "rooted" in any one region of my vast country. At the same time, as an Indian, I remain conscious of, and connected to, my pre-urban and non-Anglophone antecedents: my novels reflect an intellectual heritage that embraces the ancient epic the Mahabharata, the Kerala folk dance called the ottamthullal (of which my father was a gifted practitioner) and the Hindi B-movies of Bollywood [the large movie-making industry of Bombay], as well as Shakespeare, Wodehouse and the Beatles.

As a first-generation urbanite myself, I keep returning to the Kerala villages of my parents, in my life as in my writing. Yet I have grown up in Bombay, Calicutta and Delhi, Indian cities a thousand miles apart from one another; the mother of my children is half-Kashmiri, half-Bengali; and my own mother now lives in the southern town of Coimbatore. This may be a wider cultural matrix than the good Dr. Trivedi imagined, but it draws from a rather broad range of Indian experience. And English is the language that brings those various threads of my India together, the language in which my wife could speak to her mother-in-law, the language that enables a Calcuttan to function in Coimbatore, the language that serves to express the complexity of that polyphonous Indian experience better than any other language I know.

As a novelist, I believe in distracting in order to instruct—my novels are, to some degree, didactic works masquerading as entertainments. Like Molière I believe that you have to entertain in order to edify. But the entertainment, and the edification, might strike different readers differently.

My first novel, *The Great Indian Novel*, as a satirical reinvention of the Mahabharata inevitably touches Indians in a way that most foreigners will not fully appreciate. But my publishers in the West enjoyed its stories and the risks it took with narrative form. My second, *Show Business*, did extremely well with American reviewers and readers, who enjoyed the way I tried to portray the lives and stories of Bollywood as a metaphor for Indian society. With *India: From Midnight to the Millennium*, an attempt to look back at the last 50 years of India's history; I found an additional audience of Indian-Americans seeking to rediscover their roots; their interest has helped the American edition outsell the Indian one.

In my new novel, *Riot*, for the first time I have major non-Indian characters, Americans as it happens, and that is bound to influence the way the book is perceived in the United States, and in India. Inevitably the English fundamentally affects the content of each book, but it does not determine the audience of the writer; as long as translations exist, language is a vehicle, not a destination.

Of course, there is no shame in acknowledging that English is the legacy of the colonial connection, but one no less useful and valid than the railway, the telegraphs or the law courts that were also left behind by the British. Historically, English helped us to find our Indian voice: that great Indian nationalist Jawaharlal Nehru wrote *The Discovery of India* in English. But the eclipse of that dreadful phrase "the Indo-Anglian novel" has occurred precisely because Indian writers have evolved well beyond the British connection to their native land.

The days when Indians wrote novels in English either to flatter or rail against their colonial masters are well behind us. Now we have Indians in India writing as naturally about themselves in English as Australians or South Africans do, and their tribe has been supplemented by India's rich diaspora in the United States, which has already produced a distinctive crop of impressive novelists, with Pulitzer Prizes and National Book Awards to their names.

Their addresses don't matter because writers really live inside their heads and on the page, and geography is merely a circumstance. They write secure of themselves in heritage of diversity, and they write free of the anxiety of audience, for theirs are narratives that appeal as easily to Americans as to Indians—and indeed to readers irrespective of ethnicity.

Surely that's the whole point about literature—that for a body of fiction to constitute a literature it must rise above its origins, its setting, even its language, to render accessible to a reader anywhere some insight into the human condition. Read my books and those of other Indian writers not because we're Indian, not necessarily because you are interested in India; but because they are worth reading in and of themselves. And dear reader, whoever you are, if you pick up one of my books, ask not for whom I write: I write for you.

QUESTIONS FOR ANALYSIS

1. **What does Shashi Tharoor mean when he states that his novels could only have been written in English?**
2. **What is the relationship between national literature and global literature?**
3. **What does the author mean when he says that for writers "geography is merely a circumstance"?**

Source: Shashi Tharoor, "A Bedeviling Question in the Cadence of English," *New York Times*, July 30, 2001.

or performances for tourists may prevent folk customs and costumes from dying out, but they also tend to standardize rituals that once had many local variations. While it was possible to recognize the nationality of people from their clothing and grooming a century ago, today most urban men dress the same the world over, although women's clothing shows much greater variety. As much as one may regret the disappearance or commercialization of some folkways, most anthropologists would agree that change is characteristic of all healthy cultures. What doesn't change risks extinction.

CONCLUSION

Have we entered a golden age, or is the world descending into a fiery abyss? The future is unknowable, but the study of history suggests that neither extreme is likely. Golden ages and dark ages are rare, and our understanding of our own time is easily swayed by hopes, fears, and other emotions. If the exuberant optimism of the 1990s now seems excessive, the pessimism of the early 2000s may in time seem equally far off the mark.

What is undeniable is that the turn of the millennium has been a time of important global changes. The Iron Curtain that had divided Europe since the end of the Second World War fell, taking with it the tensions and risks of the Cold War. The great Soviet Empire broke up, while dozens of countries joined new economic coalitions. The bastions of communism embraced capitalism with varying degrees of enthusiasm. As trading barriers tumbled, world trade surged, creating new wealth and new inequalities in its distribution.

Aided by new electronic marvels, individuals communicated around the planet and interacted across cultural barriers in ways never before imagined. News of disasters and human rights violations brought more rapid responses than ever before. Culturally, the English language, higher education, and science formed a viable global culture for the elite.

History teaches that change is always uneven. The rate of change in global telecommunications and international economic institutions was notably faster than in international political institutions. The nation-state remained supreme. The structure of the United Nations was little different than at its founding six decades earlier. States resisted limits on their autonomy, and the more powerful ones took unilateral actions, whether supported or opposed by international public opinion. Never before had one state, the United States, stood so far above the rest.

Rather than giving ground to globalization, many older ideas and values continued to be strong. The less powerful adapted slowly, dug in their heals to resist change, or raised voices and fists against it. Protests forced new attention on global poverty, disease, exploitation, and environmental damage that globalization caused or failed to relieve. Adjustments were made, but on the whole change on these fronts also came slowly.

In many places religious fundamentalism, ethnic nationalism, and social conservatism seemed to reach new levels of intensity. In some quarters globalization fomented and fostered violent responses and provoked a new war on terrorism led by the United States. The resulting clashes raised concerns and inspired apocalyptic visions. Adjusting to the new age of globalization would be neither quick nor easy.

Key Terms

globalization
ethnic cleansing
weapons of mass destruction
terrorism
Usama bin Laden
World Trade Organization (WTO)
millenarianism
Universal Declaration of Human Rights
nongovernmental organizations (NGOs)
cultural imperialism
pop culture
global culture

Suggested Reading

Among those attempting to describe the world at the turn of the millennium are Benjamin R. Barber, *Jihad vs. McWorld: How Globalism and Tribalism are Reshaping the World* (1995); Thomas L. Friedman, *The Lexus and the Olive Tree* (1999); Samuel P. Huntington, *The Clash of Civilizations and the Remaking of the World Order* (1996); and Paul Kennedy, *Preparing for the Twenty-First Century* (1993).

Recent studies of American military policies and the widening split with Europe include Dana Priest, *The Mission: Waging War and Keeping Peace with America's Military* (2003); Robert Kaplan, *Of Paradise and Power: America and Europe in the New World Order* (2002); Charles A. Kulpchan, *The End of the American Era: U.S. Foreign Policy and the Geopolitics of the Twenty-First Century* (2002); and Joseph S. Nye, Jr., *The Paradox of American Power: Why the World's Only Superpower Can't Go It Alone* (2002).

Mike Moore, a former director-general of the WTO, provides an insider's view of the global economy in *A World Without Walls: Freedom, Development, Free Trade and Global Governance* (2003). Amy Chua, *World on Fire: How Exporting Free Market Democracy Breeds Ethnic Hatred and Global Instability* (2003), offers a quite different perspective.

Gilles Kepel, *The Revenge of God: The Resurgence of Islam, Christianity and Judaism in the Modern World* (1994), Philip Jenkins, *The Next Christendom: The Coming of Global Christianity* (2002), and Bernard Lewis, *What Went Wrong? The Clash Between Islam and Modernity in the Middle East* (2003), deal with recent religious-political movements. Eugen Weber, *Apocalypses: Prophesies, Cults, and Millennial Beliefs Through the Ages* (1999), provides a deeper historical perspective. The Bosnian crisis is well covered in Susan L. Woodward, *Balkan Tragedy: Chaos and Dissolution After the Cold War* (1995). Other world crises involving international intervention are treated in William J. Durch, ed., *UN Peacekeeping, American Policy, and the Uncivil Wars of the 1990s* (1996). Terrorism is well covered by Bruce Hoffman, *Inside Terrorism* (1998).

Standard reviews of human rights include Thomas Buergenthal, et al., *International Human Rights in a Nutshell,* 3d ed. (2002); Carol Devine and Carol Rae Hansen, *Human Rights: The Essential Reference* (1999); and Jack Donnelly, *International Human Rights,* 2d ed. (1998). Ronald Inglehart and Pippa Norris, *Rising Tide: Gender Equality and Cultural Change Around the World* (2003), surveys the condition of women.

The interrelationships between high culture and popular culture during the twentieth century are treated from different perspectives in Arjun Appadurai, *Modernity at Large: Cultural Dimensions of Globalization* (1996); Peter L. Berger and Samuel Huntington, eds., *Many Globalizations: Cultural Diversity in the Contemporary World* (2002); Tyler Cowen, *Creative Destruction: How Globalization Is Changing the World's Cultures* (2002); and Diana Crane, Nobuko Kawashima, and Kenichi Kawasaka, eds., *Global Culture: Media Arts, Policy* (2002). Two very readable books by James B. Twitchell detail the rise of popular culture in the United States and present various reactions to this phenomenon: *Carnival Culture: The Trashing of Taste in America* (1992) and *Adcult USA: The Triumph of Advertising in American Culture* (1996). Walter LaFeber, *Michael Jordan and the New Global Capitalism* (1999), explores the relationship between a sports star and global marketing.

Some personal accounts of cultural change are Philippe Wamba, *Kinship: A Family's Journey in Africa and America* (1999); William Dalrymple, *The Age of Kali: Indian Travels and Encounters* (1998); V. S. Naipaul, *Beyond Belief: Islamic Excursions among the Converted Peoples* (1997); Fergal Keane, *A Season of Blood: A Rwandan Journey* (1995); Nelson Mandela, *Long Walk to Freedom* (1994); and Mark Mathabane, *African Women: Three Generations* (1994).

On global English see David Crystal, *English as a Global Language* (1997); Alistaire Pennycock, *The Cultural Politics of English as an International Language* (1994); and Robert Phillipson, *Linguistic Imperialism* (1992).

Notes

1. "Liberty's Great Advance," *The Economist,* June 28–July 4, 2003, pp. 5-6.
2. Richard Landes, "Apocalyptic Islam and bin Laden," available at http://www.mille.org; and Bernard Lewis, "The Revolt of Islam: When Did the Conflict with the West Begin?" *The New Yorker,* November 11, 2001.
3. "Universal Declaration of Human Rights," in *Twenty-five Human Rights Documents* (New York: Center for the Study of Human Rights, Columbia University, 1994), 6.

Thanks

Love,

Dar

Glossary

The glossary for *The Earth and Its Peoples,* 3/e is for the complete text, Chapters 1 through 34.

Abbasid Caliphate Descendants of the Prophet Muhammad's uncle, al-Abbas, the Abbasids overthrew the **Umayyad Caliphate** and ruled an Islamic empire from their capital in Baghdad (founded 762) from 750 to 1258. *(p. 238)*

abolitionists Men and women who agitated for a complete end to slavery. Abolitionist pressure ended the British transatlantic slave trade in 1808 and slavery in British colonies in 1834. In the United States the activities of abolitionists were one factor leading to the Civil War (1861–1865). *(p. 650)*

acculturation The adoption of the language, customs, values, and behaviors of host nations by immigrants. *(p. 654)*

Acheh Sultanate Muslim kingdom in northern Sumatra. Main center of Islamic expansion in Southeast Asia in the early seventeenth century, it declined after the Dutch seized **Malacca** from Portugal in 1641. *(p. 545)*

Aden Port city in the modern south Arabian country of Yemen. It has been a major trading center in the Indian Ocean since ancient times. *(p. 384)*

African National Congress An organization dedicated to obtaining equal voting and civil rights for black inhabitants of South Africa. Founded in 1912 as the South African Native National Congress, it changed its name in 1923. Though it was banned and its leaders were jailed for many years, it eventually helped bring majority rule to South Africa. *(p. 837)*

Afrikaners South Africans descended from Dutch and French settlers of the seventeenth century. Their Great Trek founded new settler colonies in the nineteenth century. Though a minority among South Africans, they held political power after 1910, imposing a system of racial segregation called apartheid after 1949. *(p. 758)*

Agricultural Revolution(s) (ancient) The change from food gathering to food production that occurred between ca. 8000 and 2000 B.C.E. Also known as the Neolithic Revolution. *(pp. 18, 610)*

agricultural revolution (eighteenth century) The transformation of farming that resulted in the eighteenth century from the spread of new crops, improvements in cultivation techniques and livestock breeding, and the consolidation of small holdings into large farms from which tenants and sharecroppers were forcibly expelled. *(p. 610)*

Aguinaldo, Emilio (1869–1964) Leader of the Filipino independence movement against Spain (1895–1898). He proclaimed the independence of the Philippines in 1899, but his movement was crushed and he was captured by the United States Army in 1901. *(p. 766)*

Akbar I (1542–1605) Most illustrious sultan of the Mughal Empire in India (r. 1556–1605). He expanded the empire and pursued a policy of conciliation with Hindus. *(p. 541)*

Akhenaten Egyptian pharaoh (r. 1353–1335 B.C.E.). He built a new capital at Amarna, fostered a new style of naturalistic art, and created a religious revolution by imposing worship of the sun-disk. The Amarna letters, largely from his reign, preserve official correspondence with subjects and neighbors. *(p. 86)*

Alexander (356–323 B.C.E.) King of Macedonia in northern Greece. Between 334 and 323 B.C.E. he conquered the Persian Empire, reached the Indus Valley, founded many Greek-style cities, and spread Greek culture across the Middle East. Later known as Alexander the Great. *(p. 143)*

Alexandria City on the Mediterranean coast of Egypt founded by Alexander. It became the capital of the Hellenistic kingdom of the **Ptolemies.** It contained the famous Library and the Museum—a center for leading scientific and literary figures. Its merchants engaged in trade with areas bordering the Mediterranean and the Indian Ocean. *(p. 145)*

Allende, Salvador (1908–1973) Socialist politician elected president of Chile in 1970 and overthrown by the military in 1973. He died during the military attack. *(p. 890)*

All-India Muslim League Political organization founded in India in 1906 to defend the interests of India's Muslim minority. Led by Muhammad Ali Jinnah, it attempted to negotiate with the **Indian National Congress.** In 1940, the League began demanding a separate state for Muslims, to be called Pakistan. (See also **Jinnah, Muhammad Ali.**) *(p. 841)*

amulet Small charm meant to protect the bearer from evil. Found frequently in archaeological excavations in Mesopotamia and Egypt, amulets reflect the religious practices of the common people. *(p. 36)*

Amur River This river valley was a contested frontier between northern China and eastern Russia until the settlement arranged in Treaty of Nerchinsk (1689). *(p. 562)*

anarchists Revolutionaries who wanted to abolish all private property and governments, usually by violence, and replace them with free associations of groups. *(p. 733)*

Anasazi Important culture of what is now the Southwest United States (1000–1300 C.E.). Centered on Chaco Canyon in New Mexico and Mesa Verde in Colorado, the Anasazi culture built multistory residences and worshipped in subterranean buildings called kivas. *(p. 317)*

aqueduct A conduit, either elevated or underground, using gravity to carry water from a source to a location—usually a city—that needed it. The Romans built many aqueducts in a period of substantial urbanization. *(p. 163)*

Arawak Amerindian peoples who inhabited the Greater Antilles of the Caribbean at the time of Columbus. *(p. 423)*

Arkwright, Richard (1732–1792) English inventor and entrepreneur who became the wealthiest and most successful textile manufacturer of the early **Industrial Revolution.** He invented the water frame, a machine that, with minimal human supervision, could spin many strong cotton threads at once. *(p. 615)*

Armenia One of the earliest Christian kingdoms, situated in eastern Anatolia and the western Caucasus and occupied by speakers of the Armenian language. *(p. 226)*

Asante African kingdom on the **Gold Coast** that expanded rapidly after 1680. Asante participated in the Atlantic economy, trading gold, slaves, and ivory. It resisted British imperial ambitions for a quarter century before being absorbed into Britain's Gold Coast colony in 1902. *(p. 759)*

Ashikaga Shogunate (1336–1573) The second of Japan's military governments headed by a shogun (a military ruler). Sometimes called the Muromachi Shogunate. *(p. 362)*

Ashoka Third ruler of the **Mauryan Empire** in India (r. 270–232 B.C.E.). He converted to Buddhism and broadcast his precepts on inscribed stones and pillars, the earliest surviving Indian writing. *(p. 189)*

Asian Tigers Collective name for South Korea, Taiwan, Hong Kong, and Singapore—nations that became economic powers in the 1970s and 1980s. *(p. 896)*

Atahualpa (1502?–1533) Last ruling Inca emperor of Peru. He was executed by the Spanish. *(p. 440)*

Atlantic Circuit The network of trade routes connecting Europe, Africa, and the Americas that underlay the Atlantic system. *(p. 511)*

Atlantic system The network of trading links after 1500 that moved goods, wealth, people, and cultures around the Atlantic Ocean basin. *(p. 500)*

Augustus (63 B.C.E.–14 C.E.) Honorific name of Octavian, founder of the **Roman Principate,** the military dictatorship that replaced the failing rule of the **Roman Senate.** After defeating all rivals, between 31 B.C.E. and 14 C.E. he laid the groundwork for several centuries of stability and prosperity in the Roman Empire. *(p. 157)*

Auschwitz Nazi extermination camp in Poland, the largest center of mass murder during the **Holocaust.** Close to a million Jews, Gypsies, Communists, and others were killed there. *(p. 827)*

australopithecines The several extinct species of humanlike primates that existed during the Pleistocene era (genus *Australopithecus*). *(p. 6)*

ayllu Andean lineage group or kin-based community. *(p. 321)*

Aztecs Also known as Mexica, the Aztecs created a powerful empire in central Mexico (1325–1521 C.E.). They forced defeated peoples to provide goods and labor as a tax. *(p. 314)*

Babylon The largest and most important city in Mesopotamia. It achieved particular eminence as the capital of the Amorite king **Hammurabi** in the eighteenth century B.C.E. and the Neo-Babylonian king Nebuchadnezzar in the sixth century B.C.E. *(p. 29)*

balance of power The policy in international relations by which, beginning in the eighteenth century, the major European states acted together to prevent any one of them from becoming too powerful. *(p. 468)*

Balfour Declaration Statement issued by Britain's Foreign Secretary Arthur Balfour in 1917 favoring the establishment of a Jewish national homeland in Palestine. *(p. 784)*

Bannermen Hereditary military servants of the **Qing Empire,** in large part descendants of peoples of various origins who had fought for the founders of the empire. *(p. 708)*

Bantu Collective name of a large group of sub-Saharan African languages and of the peoples speaking these languages. *(p. 224)*

Batavia Fort established ca. 1619 as headquarters of Dutch East India Company operations in Indonesia; today the city of Jakarta. *(p. 548)*

Battle of Midway U.S. naval victory over the Japanese fleet in June 1942, in which the Japanese lost four of their best aircraft carriers. It marked a turning point in World War II. *(p. 821)*

Battle of Omdurman British victory over the Mahdi in the Sudan in 1898. General Kitchener led a mixed force of British and Egyptian troops armed with rapid-firing rifles and machine guns. *(p. 753)*

Beijing China's northern capital, first used as an imperial capital in 906 and now the capital of the People's Republic of China. *(p. 352)*

Bengal Region of northeastern India. It was the first part of India to be conquered by the British in the eighteenth century and remained the political and economic center of British India throughout the nineteenth century. The 1905 split of the province into predominantly Hindu West Bengal and predominantly Muslim East Bengal (now Bangladesh) sparked anti-British riots. *(p. 840)*

Berlin Conference (1884–1885) Conference that German chancellor Otto von Bismarck called to set rules for the partition of Africa. It led to the creation of the Congo Free State under King **Leopold II** of Belgium. (See also **Bismarck, Otto von.**) *(p. 755)*

Bhagavad-Gita The most important work of Indian sacred literature, a dialogue between the great warrior Arjuna and the god Krishna on duty and the fate of the spirit. *(p. 190)*

bin Laden, Usama Saudi-born Muslim extremist who funded the al Qaeda organization that was responsible for several terrorist attacks, including those on the World Trade Center and the Pentagon in 2001. *(p. 923)*

bipedalism The ability to walk upright on two legs, characteristic of hominids. *(p. 7)*

Bismarck, Otto von (1815–1898) Chancellor (prime minister) of Prussia from 1862 until 1871, when he became chancellor of Germany. A conservative nationalist, he led Prussia to victory against Austria (1866) and France (1870) and was responsible for the creation of the German Empire in 1871. *(p. 737)*

Black Death An outbreak of **bubonic plague** that spread across Asia, North Africa, and Europe in the mid-fourteenth century, carrying off vast numbers of persons. *(p. 395)*

Bolívar, Simón (1783–1830) The most important military leader in the struggle for independence in South America. Born in Venezuela, he led military forces there and in Colombia, Ecuador, Peru, and Bolivia. *(p. 634)*

Bolsheviks Radical Marxist political party founded by Vladimir Lenin in 1903. Under Lenin's leadership, the Bolsheviks seized power in November 1917 during the Russian Revolution. (See also **Lenin, Vladimir.**) *(p. 784)*

Bonaparte, Napoleon. See **Napoleon I.**

Bornu A powerful West African kingdom at the southern edge of the Sahara in the Central Sudan, which was important in trans-Saharan trade and in the spread of Islam. Also known as Kanem-Bornu, it endured from the ninth century to the end of the nineteenth. (*p. 520*)

Borobodur A massive stone monument on the Indonesian island of Java, erected by the Sailendra kings around 800 C.E. The winding ascent through ten levels, decorated with rich relief carving, is a Buddhist allegory for the progressive stages of enlightenment. (*p. 199*)

bourgeoisie In early modern Europe, the class of well-off town dwellers whose wealth came from manufacturing, finance, commerce, and allied professions. (*p. 457*)

Brant, Joseph (1742–1807) Mohawk leader who supported the British during the American Revolution. (*p. 589*)

Brazza, Savorgnan de (1852–1905) Franco-Italian explorer sent by the French government to claim part of equatorial Africa for France. Founded Brazzaville, capital of the French Congo, in 1880. (*p. 755*)

British raj The rule over much of South Asia between 1765 and 1947 by the East India Company and then by a British government. (*p. 674*)

bronze An alloy of copper with a small amount of tin (or sometimes arsenic), it is harder and more durable than copper alone. The term *Bronze Age* is applied to the era—the dates of which vary in different parts of the world—when bronze was the primary metal for tools and weapons. The demand for bronze helped create long-distance networks of trade. (*p. 40*)

bubonic plague A bacterial disease of fleas that can be transmitted by flea bites to rodents and humans; humans in late stages of the illness can spread the bacteria by coughing. Because of its very high mortality rate and the difficulty of preventing its spread, major outbreaks have created crises in many parts of the world. (See also **Black Death.**) (*pp. 285, 344*)

Buddha (563–483 B.C.E.) An Indian prince named Siddhartha Gautama, who renounced his wealth and social position. After becoming "enlightened" (the meaning of *Buddha*) he enunciated the principles of Buddhism. This doctrine evolved and spread throughout India and to Southeast, East, and Central Asia. (See also **Mahayana Buddhism, Theravada Buddhism.**) (*p. 184*)

business cycles Recurrent swings from economic hard times to recovery and growth, then back to hard times and a repetition of the sequence. (*p. 626*)

Byzantine Empire Historians' name for the eastern portion of the Roman Empire from the fourth century onward, taken from "Byzantion," an early name for Constantinople, the Byzantine capital city. The empire fell to the Ottomans in 1453. (See also **Ottoman Empire.**) (*p. 254*)

caliphate Office established in succession to the Prophet Muhammad, to rule the Islamic empire; also the name of that empire. (See also **Abbasid Caliphate; Sokoto Caliphate; Umayyad Caliphate.**) (*p. 236*)

capitalism The economic system of large financial institutions—banks, stock exchanges, investment companies—that first developed in early modern Europe. *Commercial capitalism,* the trading system of the early modern economy, is often distinguished from *industrial capitalism,* the system based on machine production. (*p. 510*)

caravel A small, highly maneuverable three-masted ship used by the Portuguese and Spanish in the exploration of the Atlantic. (*p. 426*)

Cárdenas, Lázaro (1895–1970) President of Mexico (1934–1940). He brought major changes to Mexican life by distributing millions of acres of land to the peasants, bringing representatives of workers and farmers into the inner circles of politics, and nationalizing the oil industry. (*p. 847*)

Carthage City located in present-day Tunisia, founded by **Phoenicians** ca. 800 B.C.E. It became a major commercial center and naval power in the western Mediterranean until defeated by Rome in the third century B.C.E. (*p. 107*)

Caste War A rebellion of the Maya people against the government of Mexico in 1847. It nearly returned the Yucatán to Maya rule. Some Maya rebels retreated to unoccupied territories where they held out until 1901. (*p. 649*)

Catholic Reformation Religious reform movement within the Latin Christian Church, begun in response to the **Protestant Reformation.** It clarified Catholic theology and reformed clerical training and discipline. (*p. 453*)

Celts Peoples sharing a common language and culture that originated in Central Europe in the first half of the first millennium B.C.E.. After 500 B.C.E. they spread as far as Anatolia in the east, Spain and the British Isles in the west, and later were overtaken by Roman conquest and Germanic invasions. Their descendants survive on the western fringe of Europe (Brittany, Wales, Scotland, Ireland). (*p. 71*)

Champa rice Quick-maturing rice that can allow two harvests in one growing season. Originally introduced into Champa from India, it was later sent to China as a tribute gift by the Champa state. (See also **tributary system.**) (*p. 302*)

Chang'an City in the Wei Valley in eastern China. It became the capital of the Qin and early Han Empires. Its main features were imitated in the cities and towns that sprang up throughout the Han Empire. (*p. 171*)

Charlemagne (742–814) King of the Franks (r. 768–814); emperor (r. 800–814). Through a series of military conquests he established the Carolingian Empire, which encompassed all of Gaul and parts of Germany and Italy. Though illiterate himself, he sponsored a brief intellectual revival. (*p. 254*)

chartered companies Groups of private investors who paid an annual fee to France and England in exchange for a monopoly over trade to the West Indies colonies. (*p. 502*)

Chavín The first major urban civilization in South America (900–250 B.C.E.). Its capital, Chavín de Huántar, was located high in the Andes Mountains of Peru. Chavín became politically and economically dominant in a densely populated region that included two distinct ecological zones, the Peruvian coastal plain and the Andean foothills. (*p. 77*)

Chiang Kai-shek (1886–1975) Chinese military and political leader. Succeeded Sun Yat-sen as head of the **Guomindang** in 1923; headed the Chinese government from 1928 to 1948; fought against the Chinese Communists and Japanese invaders. After 1949 he headed the Chinese Nationalist government in Taiwan. (*pp. 792, 815*)

chiefdom Form of political organization with rule by a hereditary leader who held power over a collection of villages and towns. Less powerful than kingdoms and empires, chiefdoms were based on gift giving and commercial links. *(p. 318)*

Chimu Powerful Peruvian civilization based on conquest. Located in the region earlier dominated by **Moche.** Conquered by **Inca** in 1465. *(p. 323)*

chinampas Raised fields constructed along lake shores in Mesoamerica to increase agricultural yields. *(p. 309)*

city-state A small independent state consisting of an urban center and the surrounding agricultural territory. A characteristic political form in early Mesopotamia, Archaic and Classical Greece, Phoenicia, and early Italy. (See also **polis.**) *(p. 32)*

civilization An ambiguous term often used to denote more complex societies but sometimes used by anthropologists to describe any group of people sharing a set of cultural traits. *(p. 28)*

Cixi, Empress Dowager (1835–1908) Empress of China and mother of Emperor Guangxi. She put her son under house arrest, supported antiforeign movements, and resisted reforms of the Chinese government and armed forces. *(p. 743)*

clipper ship Large, fast, streamlined sailing vessel, often American built, of the mid-to-late nineteenth century rigged with vast canvas sails hung from tall masts. *(p. 684)*

Cold War (1945–1991) The ideological struggle between communism (Soviet Union) and capitalism (United States) for world influence. The Soviet Union and the United States came to the brink of actual war during the **Cuban missile crisis** but never attacked one another. The Cold War came to an end when the Soviet Union dissolved in 1991. (See also **North Atlantic Treaty Organization; Warsaw Pact.**) *(p. 831)*

colonialism Policy by which a nation administers a foreign territory and develops its resources for the benefit of the colonial power. *(p. 754)*

Columbian Exchange The exchange of plants, animals, diseases, and technologies between the Americas and the rest of the world following Columbus's voyages. *(p. 474)*

Columbus, Christopher (1451–1506) Genoese mariner who in the service of Spain led expeditions across the Atlantic, reestablishing contact between the peoples of the Americas and the Old World and opening the way to Spanish conquest and colonization. *(p. 430)*

Confederation of 1867 Negotiated union of the formerly separate colonial governments of Ontario, Quebec, New Brunswick, and Nova Scotia. This new Dominion of Canada with a central government in Ottawa is seen as the beginning of the Canadian nation. *(p. 639)*

Confucius Western name for the Chinese philosopher Kongzi (551–479 B.C.E.). His doctrine of duty and public service had a great influence on subsequent Chinese thought and served as a code of conduct for government officials. *(p. 64)*

Congress of Vienna (1814–1815) Meeting of representatives of European monarchs called to reestablish the old order after the defeat of **Napoleon I.** *(p. 603)*

conquistadors Early-sixteenth-century Spanish adventurers who conquered Mexico, Central America, and Peru. (See **Cortés, Hernán; Pizarro, Francisco.**) *(p.436)*

Constantine (285–337 C.E.) Roman emperor (r. 312–337). After reuniting the Roman Empire, he moved the capital to Constantinople and made Christianity a favored religion. *(p. 166)*

Constitutional Convention Meeting in 1787 of the elected representatives of the thirteen original states to write the Constitution of the United States. *(p. 591)*

contract of indenture A voluntary agreement binding a person to work for a specified period of years in return for free passage to an overseas destination. Before 1800 most **indentured servants** were Europeans; after 1800 most indentured laborers were Asians. *(p. 687)*

Cortés, Hernán (1485–1547) Spanish explorer and conquistador who led the conquest of Aztec Mexico in 1519–1521 for Spain. *(p. 436)*

Cossacks Peoples of the Russian Empire who lived outside the farming villages, often as herders, mercenaries, or outlaws. Cossacks led the conquest of Siberia in the sixteenth and seventeenth centuries. *(p. 569)*

Council of the Indies The institution responsible for supervising Spain's colonies in the Americas from 1524 to the early eighteenth century, when it lost all but judicial responsibilities. *(p. 477)*

***coureurs des bois* (runners of the woods)** French fur traders, many of mixed Amerindian heritage, who lived among and often married with Amerindian peoples of North America. *(p. 493)*

creoles In colonial Spanish America, term used to describe someone of European descent born in the New World. Elsewhere in the Americas, the term is used to describe all nonnative peoples. *(p. 483)*

Crimean War (1853–1856) Conflict between the Russian and Ottoman Empires fought primarily in the Crimean Peninsula. To prevent Russian expansion, Britain and France sent troops to support the Ottomans. *(p. 700)*

Crusades (1096–1291) Armed pilgrimages to the Holy Land by Christians determined to recover Jerusalem from Muslim rule. The Crusades brought an end to western Europe's centuries of intellectual and cultural isolation. *(p. 275)*

Crystal Palace Building erected in Hyde Park, London, for the Great Exhibition of 1851. Made of iron and glass, like a gigantic greenhouse, it was a symbol of the industrial age. *(p. 618)*

Cuban missile crisis (1962) Brink-of-war confrontation between the United States and the Soviet Union over the latter's placement of nuclear-armed missiles in Cuba. *(p. 869)*

cultural imperialism Domination of one culture over another by a deliberate policy or by economic or technological superiority. *(p. 937)*

Cultural Revolution (China) (1966–1969) Campaign in China ordered by **Mao Zedong** to purge the Communist Party of his opponents and instill revolutionary values in the younger generation. *(p. 881)*

culture Socially transmitted patterns of action and expression. *Material culture* refers to physical objects, such as dwellings, clothing, tools, and crafts. Culture also includes arts, beliefs, knowledge, and technology. *(p. 11)*

cuneiform A system of writing in which wedge-shaped symbols represented words or syllables. It originated in Mesopotamia and was used initially for Sumerian and Akkadian but later was adapted to represent other languages of western Asia. Because so many symbols had to be learned, literacy was confined to a relatively small group of administrators and **scribes.** *(p. 37)*

Cyrus (600–530 B.C.E.) Founder of the Achaemenid Persian Empire. Between 550 and 530 B.C.E. he conquered Media, Lydia, and Babylon. Revered in the traditions of both Iran and the subject peoples, he employed Persians and Medes in his administration and respected the institutions and beliefs of subject peoples. *(p. 122)*

czar See **tsar.**

daimyo Literally, great name(s). Japanese warlords and great landowners, whose armed **samurai** gave them control of the Japanese islands from the eighth to the later nineteenth century. Under the **Tokugawa Shogunate** they were subordinated to the imperial government. *(p. 551)*

Daoism Chinese school of thought, originating in the Warring States Period with Laozi (604–531 B.C.E.). Daoism offered an alternative to the Confucian emphasis on hierarchy and duty. Daoists believe that the world is always changing and is devoid of absolute morality or meaning. They accept the world as they find it, avoid futile struggles, and deviate as little as possible from the *Dao,* or "path" of nature. (See also **Confucius.**) *(p. 64)*

Darius I (ca. 558–486 B.C.E.) Third ruler of the Persian Empire (r. 521–486 B.C.E.). He crushed the widespread initial resistance to his rule and gave all major government posts to Persians rather than to Medes. He established a system of provinces and tribute, began construction of Persepolis, and expanded Persian control in the east (Pakistan) and west (northern Greece). *(p. 123)*

Decembrist revolt Abortive attempt by army officers to take control of the Russian government upon the death of Tsar Alexander I in 1825. *(p. 706)*

Declaration of the Rights of Man (1789) Statement of fundamental political rights adopted by the French **National Assembly** at the beginning of the French Revolution. *(p. 595)*

deforestation The removal of trees faster than forests can replace themselves. *(p. 460)*

Delhi Sultanate (1206–1526) Centralized Indian empire of varying extent, created by Muslim invaders. *(p. 370)*

democracy A system of government in which all "citizens" (however defined) have equal political and legal rights, privileges, and protections, as in the Greek city-state of Athens in the fifth and fourth centuries B.C.E. *(p. 135)*

demographic transition A change in the rates of population growth. Before the transition, both birthrates and death rates are high, resulting in a slowly growing population; then the death rate drops but the birthrate remains high, causing a population explosion; finally the birthrate drops and the population growth slows down. This transition took place in Europe in the late nineteenth and early twentieth centuries, in North America and East Asia in the mid-twentieth, and, most recently, in Latin America and South Asia. *(p. 902)*

Deng Xiaoping (1904–1997) Communist Party leader who forced Chinese economic reforms after the death of **Mao Zedong.** *(p. 897)*

development In the nineteenth and twentieth centuries, the economic process that led to industrialization, urbanization, the rise of a large and prosperous middle class, and heavy investment in education. *(p. 656)*

devshirme "Selection" in Turkish. The system by which boys from Christian communities were taken by the Ottoman state to serve as **Janissaries.** *(p. 530)*

dhow Ship of small to moderate size used in the western Indian Ocean, traditionally with a triangular sail and a sewn timber hull. *(p. 380)*

Diagne, Blaise (1872–1934) Senegalese political leader. He was the first African elected to the French National Assembly. During World War I, in exchange for promises to give French citizenship to Senegalese, he helped recruit Africans to serve in the French army. After the war, he led a movement to abolish forced labor in Africa. *(p. 837)*

Dias, Bartolomeu (1450?–1500) Portuguese explorer who in 1488 led the first expedition to sail around the southern tip of Africa from the Atlantic and sight the Indian Ocean. *(p. 428)*

Diaspora A Greek word meaning "dispersal," used to describe the communities of a given ethnic group living outside their homeland. Jews, for example, spread from Israel to western Asia and Mediterranean lands in antiquity and today can be found throughout the world. *(p. 101)*

Dirty War War waged by the Argentine military (1976–1982) against leftist groups. Characterized by the use of illegal imprisonment, torture, and executions by the military. *(p. 890)*

divination Techniques for ascertaining the future or the will of the gods by interpreting natural phenomena such as, in early China, the cracks on oracle bones or, in ancient Greece, the flight of birds through sectors of the sky. *(p. 60)*

division of labor A manufacturing technique that breaks down a craft into many simple and repetitive tasks that can be performed by unskilled workers. Pioneered in the pottery works of Josiah Wedgwood and in other eighteenth-century factories, it greatly increased the productivity of labor and lowered the cost of manufactured goods. (See also **Wedgwood, Josiah.**) *(p. 614)*

driver A privileged male slave whose job was to ensure that a slave gang did its work on a plantation. *(p. 506)*

Druids The class of religious experts who conducted rituals and preserved sacred lore among some ancient Celtic peoples. They provided education, mediated disputes between kinship groups, and were suppressed by the Romans as a potential focus of opposition to Roman rule. (See also **Celts.**) *(p. 73)*

durbar An elaborate display of political power and wealth in British India in the nineteenth century, ostensibly in imitation of the pageantry of the **Mughal Empire.** *(p. 676)*

Dutch West India Company (1621–1794) Trading company chartered by the Dutch government to conduct its merchants' trade in the Americas and Africa. *(p. 502)*

Edison, Thomas (1847–1931) American inventor best known for inventing the electric light bulb, acoustic recording on wax cylinders, and motion pictures. *(p. 726)*

Einstein, Albert (1879–1955) German physicist who developed the theory of relativity, which states that time, space, and mass are relative to each other and not fixed. *(p. 800)*

El Alamein Town in Egypt, site of the victory by Britain's Field Marshal Bernard Montgomery over German forces led by General Erwin Rommel (the "Desert Fox") in 1942–1943. *(p. 821)*

electricity A form of energy used in telegraphy from the 1840s on and for lighting, industrial motors, and railroads beginning in the 1880s. *(p. 726)*

electric telegraph A device for rapid, long-distance transmission of information over an electric wire. It was introduced in England and North America in the 1830s and 1840s and replaced telegraph systems that utilized visual signals such as semaphores. (See also **submarine telegraph cables.**) *(p. 620)*

encomienda A grant of authority over a population of Amerindians in the Spanish colonies. It provided the grant holder with a supply of cheap labor and periodic payments of goods by the Amerindians. It obliged the grant holder to Christianize the Amerindians. *(p. 482)*

English Civil War (1642-1649) A conflict over royal versus. Parliamentary rights, caused by King Charles I's arrest of his parliamentary critics and ending with his execution. Its outcome checked the growth of royal absolutism and, with the Glorious Revolution of 1688 and the English Bill of Rights of 1689, ensured that England would be a constitutional monarchy. *(p. 466)*

Enlightenment A philosophical movement in eighteenth-century Europe that fostered the belief that one could reform society by discovering rational laws that governed social behavior and were just as scientific as the laws of physics. *(pp. 456, 582)*

equites In ancient Italy, prosperous landowners second in wealth and status to the senatorial aristocracy. The Roman emperors allied with this group to counterbalance the influence of the old aristocracy and used the *equites* to staff the imperial civil service. *(p. 157)*

Estates General France's traditional national assembly with representatives of the three estates, or classes, in French society: the clergy, nobility, and commoners. The calling of the Estates General in 1789 led to the French Revolution. *(p. 593)*

Ethiopia East African highland nation lying east of the Nile River. (See also **Menelik II; Selassie, Haile.**) *(p. 226)*

ethnic cleansing Effort to eradicate a people and its culture by means of mass killing and the destruction of historical buildings and cultural materials. Ethnic cleansing was used by both sides in the conflicts that accompanied the disintegration of Yugoslavia in the 1990s. *(p. 922)*

European Community (EC) An organization promoting economic unity in Europe formed in 1967 by consolidation of earlier, more limited, agreements. Replaced by the European Union (EU) in 1993. *(p. 865)*

evolution The biological theory that, over time, changes occurring in plants and animals, mainly as a result of **natural selection** and genetic mutation, result in new species. *(p. 5)*

extraterritoriality The right of foreign residents in a country to live under the laws of their native country and disregard the laws of the host country. In the nineteenth and early twentieth centuries, European and American nationals living in certain areas of Chinese and Ottoman cities were granted this right. *(p. 701)*

Faisal I (1885–1933) Arab prince, leader of the Arab Revolt in World War I. The British made him king of Iraq in 1921, and he reigned under British protection until 1933. *(p.784)*

Fascist Party Italian political party created by Benito Mussolini during World War I. It emphasized aggressive nationalism and was Mussolini's instrument for the creation of a dictatorship in Italy from 1922 to 1943. (See also **Mussolini, Benito.**) *(p. 813)*

fief In medieval Europe, land granted in return for a sworn oath to provide specified military service. *(p. 263)*

First Temple A monumental sanctuary built in Jerusalem by King Solomon in the tenth century B.C.E. to be the religious center for the Israelite god Yahweh. The Temple priesthood conducted sacrifices, received a tithe or percentage of agricultural revenues, and became economically and politically powerful. The First Temple was destroyed by the Babylonians in 587 B.C.E., rebuilt on a modest scale in the late sixth century B.C.E., and replaced by King Herod's Second Temple in the late first century B.C.E. (destroyed by the Romans in 70 C.E.) *(p. 100)*

Five-Year Plans Plans that Joseph Stalin introduced to industrialize the Soviet Union rapidly, beginning in 1928. They set goals for the output of steel, electricity, machinery, and most other products and were enforced by the police powers of the state. They succeeded in making the Soviet Union a major industrial power before World War II. (See also **Stalin, Joseph.**) *(p. 806)*

foragers People who support themselves by hunting wild animals and gathering wild edible plants and insects. *(p. 12)*

Franklin, Benjamin (1706–1790) American intellectual, inventor, and politician He helped negotiate French support for the American Revolution. *(p. 585)*

free-trade imperialism Economic dominance of a weaker country by a more powerful one, while maintaining the legal independence of the weaker state. In the late nineteenth century, free-trade imperialism characterized the relations between the Latin American republics, on the one hand, and Great Britain and the United States, on the other. *(p. 768)*

Fujiwara Aristocratic family that dominated the Japanese imperial court between the ninth and twelfth centuries. *(p. 301)*

Funan An early complex society in Southeast Asia between the first and sixth centuries C.E. It was centered in the rich rice-growing region of southern Vietnam, and it controlled the passage of trade across the Malaysian isthmus. *(p. 198)*

Gama, Vasco da (1460?–1524) Portuguese explorer. In 1497–1498 he led the first naval expedition from Europe to sail to India, opening an important commercial sea route. *(p. 428)*

Gandhi, Mohandas K. (Mahatma) (1869–1948) Leader of the Indian independence movement and advocate of nonviolent resistance. After being educated as a lawyer in England, he returned to India and became leader of the **Indian National Congress** in 1920. He appealed to the poor, led nonviolent demonstrations against British colonial rule, and was jailed many times. Soon after independence he was assassinated for attempting to stop Hindu-Muslim rioting. *(p. 841)*

Garibaldi, Giuseppe (1807–1882) Italian nationalist and revolutionary who conquered Sicily and Naples and added them to a unified Italy in 1860. *(p. 736)*

Genghis Khan (ca. 1167–1227) The title of Temüjin when he ruled the Mongols (1206–1227). It means the "oceanic" or "universal" leader. Genghis Khan was the founder of the Mongol Empire. *(p. 337)*

gens de couleur Free men and women of color in Haiti. They sought greater political rights and later supported the Haitian Revolution. (See also **L'Ouverture, François Dominique Toussaint.**) *(p. 601)*

gentry In China, the class of prosperous families, next in wealth below the rural aristocrats, from which the emperors drew their administrative personnel. Respected for their education and expertise, these officials became a privileged group and made the government more efficient and responsive than in the past. The term *gentry* also denotes the class of landholding families in England below the aristocracy. *(pp. 171, 172, 459)*

Ghana First known kingdom in sub-Saharan West Africa between the sixth and thirteenth centuries C.E. Also the modern West African country once known as the Gold Coast. *(p. 221)*

global culture Cultural practices and institutions that have been adopted internationally, whether elite (the English language, modern science, and higher education) or popular (music, television, the Internet, food, and fashion). *(p. 939)*

globalization The economic, political, and cultural integration and interaction of all parts of the world brought about by increasing trade, travel, and technology. *(p. 920)*

Gold Coast (Africa) Region of the Atlantic coast of West Africa occupied by modern Ghana; named for its gold exports to Europe from the 1470s onward. *(p. 428)*

Golden Horde Mongol khanate founded by Genghis Khan's grandson Batu. It was based in southern Russia and quickly adopted both the Turkic language and Islam. Also known as the Kipchak Horde. *(p. 345)*

Gorbachev, Mikhail (b. 1931) Head of the Soviet Union from 1985 to 1991. His liberalization effort improved relations with the West, but he lost power after his reforms led to the collapse of communist governments in eastern Europe. *(p. 898)*

Gothic cathedrals Large churches originating in twelfth-century France; built in an architectural style featuring pointed arches, tall vaults and spires, flying buttresses, and large stained-glass windows. *(p. 404)*

Grand Canal The 1,100-mile (1,700-kilometer) waterway linking the Yellow and the Yangzi Rivers. It was begun in the **Han** period and completed during the Sui Empire. *(p. 282)*

Great Ice Age Geological era that occurred between ca. 2 million and 11,000 years ago. As a result of climate shifts, large numbers of new species evolved during this period, also called the Pleistocene epoch. (See also **Holocene.**) *(p. 8)*

"great traditions" Historians' term for a literate, well-institutionalized complex of religious and social beliefs and practices adhered to by diverse societies over a broad geographical area. (See also **"small traditions."**) *(p. 222)*

Great Western Schism A division in the Latin (Western) Christian Church between 1378 and 1417, when rival claimants to the papacy existed in Rome and Avignon. *(p. 412)*

Great Zimbabwe City, now in ruins (in the modern African country of Zimbabwe), whose many stone structures were built between about 1250 and 1450, when it was a trading center and the capital of a large state. *(p. 383)*

guild In medieval Europe, an association of men (rarely women), such as merchants, artisans, or professors, who worked in a particular trade and banded together to promote their economic and political interests. Guilds were also important in other societies, such as the Ottoman and Safavid empires. *(p. 401)*

Gujarat Region of western India famous for trade and manufacturing; the inhabitants are called Gujarati. *(p. 379)*

gunpowder A mixture of saltpeter, sulfur, and charcoal, in various proportions. The formula, brought to China in the 400s or 500s, was first used to make fumigators to keep away insect pests and evil spirits. In later centuries it was used to make explosives and grenades and to propel cannonballs, shot, and bullets. *(p. 296)*

Guomindang Nationalist political party founded on democratic principles by **Sun Yat-sen** in 1912. After 1925, the party was headed by **Chiang Kai-shek,** who turned it into an increasingly authoritarian movement. *(p. 791)*

Gupta Empire (320–550 C.E.) A powerful Indian state based, like its Mauryan predecessor, on a capital at Pataliputra in the Ganges Valley. It controlled most of the Indian subcontinent through a combination of military force and its prestige as a center of sophisticated culture. (See also **theater-state.**) *(p. 190)*

Habsburg A powerful European family that provided many Holy Roman Emperors, founded the Austrian (later Austro-Hungarian) Empire, and ruled sixteenth- and seventeenth-century Spain. *(p. 462)*

hadith A tradition relating the words or deeds of the Prophet Muhammad; next to the **Quran,** the most important basis for Islamic law. *(p. 243)*

Hammurabi Amorite ruler of **Babylon** (r. 1792–1750 B.C.E.). He conquered many city-states in southern and northern Mesopotamia and is best known for a code of laws, inscribed on a black stone pillar, illustrating the principles to be used in legal cases. *(p. 34)*

Han A term used to designate (1) the ethnic Chinese people who originated in the Yellow River Valley and spread throughout regions of China suitable for agriculture and (2) the dynasty of emperors who ruled from 206 B.C.E. to 220 C.E. *(p. 166)*

Hanseatic League An economic and defensive alliance of the free towns in northern Germany, founded about 1241 and most powerful in the fourteenth century. *(p. 398)*

Harappa Site of one of the great cities of the Indus Valley civilization of the third millennium B.C.E. It was located on the northwest frontier of the zone of cultivation (in modern

Pakistan), and may have been a center for the acquisition of raw materials, such as metals and precious stones, from Afghanistan and Iran. *(p. 49)*

Hatshepsut Queen of Egypt (r. 1473–1458 B.C.E.). She dispatched a naval expedition down the Red Sea to Punt (possibly northeast Sudan or Eretria), the faraway source of myrrh. There is evidence of opposition to a woman as ruler, and after her death her name and image were frequently defaced. *(p. 86)*

Hausa An agricultural and trading people of central Sudan in West Africa. Aside from their brief incorporation into the Songhai Empire, the Hausa city-states remained autonomous until the **Sokoto Caliphate** conquered them in the early nineteenth century. *(p. 520)*

Hebrew Bible A collection of sacred books containing diverse materials concerning the origins, experiences, beliefs, and practices of the Israelites. Most of the extant text was compiled by members of the priestly class in the fifth century B.C.E. and reflects the concerns and views of this group. *(p. 97)*

Hellenistic Age Historians' term for the era, usually dated 323–30 B.C.E., in which Greek culture spread across western Asia and northeastern Africa after the conquests of **Alexander** the Great. The period ended with the fall of the last major Hellenistic kingdom to Rome, but Greek cultural influence persisted until the spread of Islam in the seventh century C.E. *(p. 144)*

Helsinki Accords (1975) Political and human rights agreement signed in Helsinki, Finland, by the Soviet Union and western European countries. *(p. 870)*

Henry the Navigator (1394–1460) Portuguese prince who promoted the study of navigation and directed voyages of exploration down the western coast of Africa. *(p. 425)*

Herodotus (ca. 485–425 B.C.E.) Heir to the technique of *historia*—"investigation"—developed by Greeks in the late Archaic period. He came from a Greek community in Anatolia and traveled extensively, collecting information in western Asia and the Mediterranean lands. He traced the antecedents of and chronicled the **Persian Wars** between the Greek city-states and the Persian Empire, thus originating the Western tradition of historical writing. *(p. 136)*

Herzl, Theodore (1860–1904) Austrian journalist and founder of the Zionist movement urging the creation of a Jewish national homeland in Palestine. *(p. 784)*

Hidalgo y Costilla, Miguel (1753–1811) Mexican priest who led the first stage of the Mexican independence war in 1810. He was captured and executed in 1811. *(p. 637)*

Hidden Imam Last in a series of twelve descendants of Muhammad's son-in-law Ali, whom **Shi'ites** consider divinely appointed leaders of the Muslim community. In occlusion since ca. 873, he is expected to return as a messiah at the end of time. *(p. 538)*

hieroglyphics A system of writing in which pictorial symbols represented sounds, syllables, or concepts. It was used for official and monumental inscriptions in ancient Egypt. Because of the long period of study required to master this system, literacy in hieroglyphics was confined to a relatively small group of **scribes** and administrators. Cursive symbol-forms were developed for rapid composition on other media, such as **papyrus.** *(p. 44)*

Hinduism A general term for a wide variety of beliefs and ritual practices that have developed in the Indian subcontinent since antiquity. Hinduism has roots in ancient Vedic, Buddhist, and south Indian religious concepts and practices. It spread along the trade routes to Southeast Asia. *(p. 185)*

Hiroshima City in Japan, the first to be destroyed by an atomic bomb, on August 6, 1945. The bombing hastened the end of World War II. *(p. 823)*

history The study of past events and changes in the development, transmission, and transformation of cultural practices. *(p. 11)*

Hitler, Adolf (1889–1945) Born in Austria, Hitler became a radical German nationalist during World War I. He led the National Socialist German Workers' Party—the **Nazis**—in the 1920s and became dictator of Germany in 1933. He led Europe into World War II. *(p. 813)*

Hittites A people from central Anatolia who established an empire in Anatolia and Syria in the Late Bronze Age. With wealth from the trade in metals and military power based on chariot forces, the Hittites vied with New Kingdom Egypt for control of Syria-Palestine before falling to unidentified attackers ca. 1200 B.C.E. (See also **Ramesses II.**) *(p. 84)*

Holocaust Nazis' program during World War II to kill people they considered undesirable. Some 6 million Jews perished during the Holocaust, along with millions of Poles, Gypsies, Communists, Socialists, and others. *(p. 827)*

Holocene The geological era since the end of the **Great Ice Age** about 11,000 years ago. *(p. 21)*

Holy Roman Empire Loose federation of mostly German states and principalities, headed by an emperor elected by the princes. It lasted from 962 to 1806. *(pp. 267, 462)*

hominid The biological family that includes humans and humanlike primates. *(p. 7)*

Homo erectus An extinct human species. It evolved in Africa about 2 million years ago. *(p. 10)*

Homo habilis The first human species (now extinct). It evolved in Africa about 2.5 million years ago. *(p. 8)*

Homo sapiens The current human species. It evolved in Africa about 200,000 years ago. It includes archaic forms such as Neanderthals (now extinct) and all modern humans. *(p. 10)*

hoplite A heavily armored Greek infantryman of the Archaic and Classical periods who fought in the close-packed phalanx formation. Hoplite armies—militias composed of middle- and upper-class citizens supplying their own equipment—were for centuries superior to all other military forces. *(p. 133)*

horse collar Harnessing method that increased the efficiency of horses by shifting the point of traction from the animal's neck to the shoulders; its adoption favors the spread of horse-drawn plows and vehicles. *(p. 274)*

House of Burgesses Elected assembly in colonial Virginia, created in 1618. *(p. 489)*

humanists (Renaissance) European scholars, writers, and teachers associated with the study of the humanities (grammar, rhetoric, poetry, history, languages, and moral philosophy), influential in the fifteenth century and later. *(p. 407)*

Hundred Years War (1337–1453) Series of campaigns over

control of the throne of France, involving English and French royal families and French noble families. *(p. 413)*

Husain, Saddam (b. 1937) President of Iraq from 1979 until overthrown by an American-led invasion in 2003. Waged war on Iran from 1980 to 1988. His invasion of Kuwait in 1990 was repulsed in the Persian Gulf War in 1991. *(p. 893)*

Ibn Battuta (1304–1369) Moroccan Muslim scholar, the most widely traveled individual of his time. He wrote a detailed account of his visits to Islamic lands from China to Spain and the western Sudan. *(p. 370)*

Il-khan A "secondary" or "peripheral" khan based in Persia. The Il-khans' khanate was founded by Hülegü, a grandson of **Genghis Khan,** and was based at Tabriz in modern Azerbaijan. It controlled much of Iran and Iraq. *(p. 345)*

import-substitution industrialization An economic system aimed at building a country's industry by restricting foreign trade. It was especially popular in Latin American countries such as Mexico, Argentina, and Brazil in the mid-twentieth century. It proved successful for a time but could not keep up with technological advances in Europe and North America. *(p. 851)*

Inca Largest and most powerful Andean empire. Controlled the Pacific coast of South America from Ecuador to Chile from its capital of Cuzco. *(p. 327)*

indentured servant A migrant to British colonies in the Americas who paid for passage by agreeing to work for a set term ranging from four to seven years. *(p. 489)*

Indian Civil Service The elite professional class of officials who administered the government of British India. Originally composed exclusively of well-educated British men, it gradually added qualified Indians. *(p. 676)*

Indian National Congress A movement and political party founded in 1885 to demand greater Indian participation in government. Its membership was middle class, and its demands were modest until World War I. Led after 1920 by Mohandas K. Gandhi, it appealed increasingly to the poor, and it organized mass protests demanding self-government and independence. (See also **Gandhi, Mohandas K.**) *(pp. 681, 840)*

Indian Ocean Maritime System In premodern times, a network of seaports, trade routes, and maritime culture linking countries on the rim of the Indian Ocean from Africa to Indonesia. *(p. 213)*

indulgence The forgiveness of the punishment due for past sins, granted by the Catholic Church authorities as a reward for a pious act. Martin Luther's protest against the sale of indulgences is often seen as touching off the **Protestant Reformation.** *(p. 450)*

Industrial Revolution The transformation of the economy, the environment, and living conditions, occurring first in England in the eighteenth century, that resulted from the use of steam engines, the mechanization of manufacturing in factories, and innovations in transportation and communication. *(p. 609)*

investiture controversy Dispute between the popes and the Holy Roman Emperors over who held ultimate authority over bishops in imperial lands. *(p. 267)*

Irigoyen, Hipólito (1850–1933) Argentine politician, president of Argentina from 1916 to 1922 and 1928 to 1930. The first president elected by universal male suffrage, he began his presidency as a reformer, but later became conservative. *(p. 850)*

Iron Age Historians' term for the period during which iron was the primary metal for tools and weapons. The advent of iron technology began at different times in different parts of the world. *(p. 82)*

iron curtain Winston Churchill's term for the Cold War division between the Soviet-dominated East and the U.S.-dominated West. *(p. 861)*

Iroquois Confederacy An alliance of five northeastern Amerindian peoples (six after 1722) that made decisions on military and diplomatic issues through a council of representatives. Allied first with the Dutch and later with the English, the Confederacy dominated the area from western New England to the Great Lakes. *(p. 492)*

Islam Religion expounded by the Prophet Muhammad (570–632 C.E.) on the basis of his reception of divine revelations, which were collected after his death into the **Quran.** In the tradition of Judaism and Christianity, and sharing much of their lore, Islam calls on all people to recognize one creator god—Allah—who rewards or punishes believers after death according to how they led their lives. (See also **hadith.**) *(p. 235)*

Israel In antiquity, the land between the eastern shore of the Mediterranean and the Jordan River, occupied by the Israelites from the early second millennium B.C.E. The modern state of Israel was founded in 1948. *(p. 97)*

Jackson, Andrew (1767–1845) First president of the United States to be born in humble circumstances. He was popular among frontier residents, urban workers, and small farmers. He had a successful political career as judge, general, congressman, senator, and president. After being denied the presidency in 1824 in a controversial election, he won in 1828 and was reelected in 1832. *(p. 643)*

Jacobins Radical republicans during the French Revolution. They were led by Maximilien Robespierre from 1793 to 1794. (See also **Robespierre, Maximilien.**) *(p. 596)*

Janissaries Infantry, originally of slave origin, armed with firearms and constituting the elite of the Ottoman army from the fifteenth century until the corps was abolished in 1826. (See also ***devshirme.***) *(pp. 530, 693)*

jati. See ***varna.***

Jesus (ca. 5 B.C.E.–34 C.E.) A Jew from Galilee in northern Israel who sought to reform Jewish beliefs and practices. He was executed as a revolutionary by the Romans. Hailed as the Messiah and son of God by his followers, he became the central figure in Christianity, a belief system that developed in the centuries after his death. *(p. 162)*

Jinnah, Muhammad Ali (1876–1948) Indian Muslim politician who founded the state of Pakistan. A lawyer by training, he joined the **All-India Muslim League** in 1913. As leader of the League from the 1920s on, he negotiated with the British and the **Indian National Congress** for Muslim participation in Indian politics. From 1940 on, he led the movement for the independence of India's Muslims in a separate state of Pakistan, founded in 1947. *(p. 844)*

joint-stock company A business, often backed by a government charter, that sold shares to individuals to raise money for its trading enterprises and to spread the risks (and profits) among many investors. (*p. 459*)

Juárez, Benito (1806–1872) President of Mexico (1858–1872). Born in poverty in Mexico, he was educated as a lawyer and rose to become chief justice of the Mexican supreme court and then president. He led Mexico's resistance to a French invasion in 1863 and the installation of Maximilian as emperor. (*p. 646*)

junk A very large flatbottom sailing ship produced in the **Tang, Ming,** and **Song Empires,** specially designed for long-distance commercial travel. (*p. 295*)

Kamakura shogunate The first of Japan's decentralized military governments. (1185–1333). (*p. 302*)

kamikaze The "divine wind," which the Japanese credited with blowing Mongol invaders away from their shores in 1281. (*p. 361*)

Kangxi (1654–1722) Qing emperor (r. 1662–1722). He oversaw the greatest expansion of the **Qing Empire.** (*p. 559*)

karma In Indian tradition, the residue of deeds performed in past and present lives that adheres to a "spirit" and determines what form it will assume in its next life cycle. The doctrines of karma and reincarnation were used by the elite in ancient India to encourage people to accept their social position and do their duty. (*p. 183*)

keiretsu Alliances of corporations and banks that dominate the Japanese economy. (*p. 896*)

khipu System of knotted colored cords used by preliterate Andean peoples to transmit information. (*p. 321*)

Khomeini, Ayatollah Ruhollah (1900?–1989) Shi'ite philosopher and cleric who led the overthrow of the shah of Iran in 1979 and created an Islamic republic. (*p. 892*)

Khubilai Khan (1215–1294) Last of the Mongol Great Khans (r. 1260–1294) and founder of the **Yuan Empire.** (*p. 352*)

Kievan Russia State established at Kiev in Ukraine ca. 879 by Scandinavian adventurers asserting authority over a mostly Slavic farming population. (*p. 254*)

Korean War (1950–1953) Conflict that began with North Korea's invasion of South Korea and came to involve the United Nations (primarily the United States) allying with South Korea and the People's Republic of China allying with North Korea. (*p. 866*)

Koryo Korean kingdom founded in 918 and destroyed by a Mongol invasion in 1259. (*p. 301*)

Kush An Egyptian name for Nubia, the region alongside the Nile River south of Egypt, where an indigenous kingdom with its own distinctive institutions and cultural traditions arose beginning in the early second millennium B.C.E. It was deeply influenced by Egyptian culture and at times under the control of Egypt, which coveted its rich deposits of gold and luxury products from sub-Saharan Africa carried up the Nile corridor. (*p. 68*)

labor union An organization of workers in a particular industry or trade, created to defend the interests of members through strikes or negotiations with employers. (*p. 732*)

laissez faire The idea that government should refrain from interfering in economic affairs. The classic exposition of laissez-faire principles is Adam Smith's *Wealth of Nations* (1776). (*p. 627*)

lama In Tibetan Buddhism, a teacher. (*p. 352*)

Las Casas, Bartolomé de (1474–1566) First bishop of Chiapas, in southern Mexico. He devoted most of his life to protecting Amerindian peoples from exploitation. His major achievement was the New Laws of 1542, which limited the ability of Spanish settlers to compel Amerindians to labor for them. (See also **encomienda.**) (*p. 480*)

Latin West Historians' name for the territories of Europe that adhered to the Latin rite of Christianity and used the Latin language for intellectual exchange in the period ca. 1000–1500. (*p. 392*)

League of Nations International organization founded in 1919 to promote world peace and cooperation but greatly weakened by the refusal of the United States to join. It proved ineffectual in stopping aggression by Italy, Japan, and Germany in the 1930s, and it was superseded by the **United Nations** in 1945. (*p. 786*)

Legalism In China, a political philosophy that emphasized the unruliness of human nature and justified state coercion and control. The **Qin** ruling class invoked it to validate the authoritarian nature of their regime and its profligate expenditure of subjects' lives and labor. It was superseded in the **Han** era by a more benevolent Confucian doctrine of governmental moderation. (*p. 64*)

"legitimate" trade Exports from Africa in the nineteenth century that did not include the newly outlawed slave trade. (*p. 671*)

Lenin, Vladimir (1870–1924) Leader of the Bolshevik (later Communist) Party. He lived in exile in Switzerland until 1917, then returned to Russia to lead the Bolsheviks to victory during the Russian Revolution and the civil war that followed. (*p. 784*)

Leopold II (1835–1909) King of Belgium (r. 1865–1909). He was active in encouraging the exploration of Central Africa and became the ruler of the Congo Free State (to 1908). (*p. 755*)

liberalism A political ideology that emphasizes the civil rights of citizens, representative government, and the protection of private property. This ideology, derived from the **Enlightenment,** was especially popular among the property-owning middle classes of Europe and North America. (*p. 736*)

Library of Ashurbanipal A large collection of writings drawn from the ancient literary, religious, and scientific traditions of Mesopotamia. It was assembled by the sixth century B.C.E. Assyrian ruler Ashurbanipal. The many tablets unearthed by archaeologists constitute one of the most important sources of present-day knowledge of the long literary tradition of Mesopotamia. (*p. 97*)

Linear B A set of syllabic symbols, derived from the writing system of **Minoan** Crete, used in the Mycenaean palaces of the Late Bronze Age to write an early form of Greek. It was used primarily for palace records, and the surviving Linear B tablets provide substantial information about the economic organization of Mycenaean society and tantalizing clues about political, social, and religious institutions. (*p. 91*)

Li Shimin (599–649) One of the founders of the **Tang Empire** and its second emperor (r. 626–649). He led the expansion of the empire into Central Asia. (*p. 282*)

Little Ice Age A century-long period of cool climate that began in the 1590s. Its ill effects on agriculture in northern Europe were notable. (*p. 460*)

llama A hoofed animal indigenous to the Andes Mountains in South America. It was the only domesticated beast of burden in the Americas before the arrival of Europeans. It provided meat and wool. The use of llamas to transport goods made possible specialized production and trade among people living in different ecological zones and fostered the integration of these zones by **Chavín** and later Andean states. (*p. 77*)

loess A fine, light silt deposited by wind and water. It constitutes the fertile soil of the Yellow River Valley in northern China. Because loess soil is not compacted, it can be worked with a simple digging stick, but it leaves the region vulnerable to devastating earthquakes. (*p. 58*)

Long March (1934–1935) The 6,000-mile (9,600-kilometer) flight of Chinese Communists from southeastern to northwestern China. The Communists, led by **Mao Zedong,** were pursued by the Chinese army under orders from **Chiang Kai-shek.** The four thousand survivors of the march formed the nucleus of a revived Communist movement that defeated the **Guomindang** after World War II. (*p. 816*)

L'Ouverture, François Dominique Toussaint (1743–1803) Leader of the Haitian Revolution. He freed the slaves and gained effective independence for Haiti despite military interventions by the British and French. (*p. 601*)

ma'at Egyptian term for the concept of divinely created and maintained order in the universe. Reflecting the ancient Egyptians' belief in an essentially beneficent world, the divine ruler was the earthly guarantor of this order. (See also **pyramid.**) (*p. 43*)

Macartney mission (1792–1793) The unsuccessful attempt by the British Empire to establish diplomatic relations with the **Qing Empire.** (*p. 564*)

Magellan, Ferdinand (1480?–1521) Portuguese navigator who led the Spanish expedition of 1519–1522 that was the first to sail around the world. (*p. 431*)

Mahabharata A vast epic chronicling the events leading up to a cataclysmic battle between related kinship groups in early India. It includes the Bhagavad-Gita, the most important work of Indian sacred literature. (*p. 190*)

Mahayana Buddhism "Great Vehicle" branch of Buddhism followed in China, Japan, and Central Asia. The focus is on reverence for **Buddha** and for bodhisattvas, enlightened persons who have postponed nirvana to help others attain enlightenment. (*p. 185*)

Malacca Port city in the modern Southeast Asian country of Malaysia, founded about 1400 as a trading center on the Strait of Malacca. Also spelled Melaka. (*p. 385*)

Malay peoples A designation for peoples originating in south China and Southeast Asia who settled the Malay Peninsula, Indonesia, and the Philippines, then spread eastward across the islands of the Pacific Ocean and west to Madagascar. (*p. 196*)

Mali Empire created by indigenous Muslims in western Sudan of West Africa from the thirteenth to fifteenth century. It was famous for its role in the trans-Saharan gold trade. (See also **Mansa Kankan Musa** and **Timbuktu.**) (*p. 372*)

Malthus, Thomas (1766–1834) Eighteenth-century English intellectual who warned that population growth threatened future generations because, in his view, population growth would always outstrip increases in agricultural production. (*p. 902*)

Mamluks Under the Islamic system of military slavery, Turkic military slaves who formed an important part of the armed forces of the **Abbasid Caliphate** of the ninth and tenth centuries. Mamluks eventually founded their own state, ruling Egypt and Syria (1250–1517). (*p. 239*)

Manchu Federation of Northeast Asian peoples who founded the **Qing Empire.** (*p. 551*)

Mandate of Heaven Chinese religious and political ideology developed by the **Zhou,** according to which it was the prerogative of Heaven, the chief deity, to grant power to the ruler of China and to take away that power if the ruler failed to conduct himself justly and in the best interests of his subjects. (*p. 61*)

mandate system Allocation of former German colonies and Ottoman possessions to the victorious powers after World War I, to be administered under League of Nations supervision. (*p. 792*)

manor In medieval Europe, a large, self-sufficient landholding consisting of the lord's residence (manor house), outbuildings, peasant village, and surrounding land. (*p. 262*)

mansabs In India, grants of land given in return for service by rulers of the **Mughal Empire.** (*p. 542*)

Mansa Kankan Musa Ruler of Mali (r. 1312–1337). His pilgrimage through Egypt to **Mecca** in 1324–1325 established the empire's reputation for wealth in the Mediterranean world. (*p. 372*)

manumission A grant of legal freedom to an individual slave. (*p. 509*)

Mao Zedong (1893–1976) Leader of the Chinese Communist Party (1927–1976). He led the Communists on the **Long March** (1934–1935) and rebuilt the Communist Party and Red Army during the Japanese occupation of China (1937–1945). After World War II, he led the Communists to victory over the **Guomindang.** He ordered the **Cultural Revolution** in 1966. (*p. 815*)

maroon A slave who ran away from his or her master. Often a member of a community of runaway slaves in the West Indies and South America. (*p. 509*)

Marshall Plan U. S. program to support the reconstruction of western Europe after World War II. By 1961 more than $20 billion in economic aid had been dispersed. (*p. 863*)

Marx, Karl (1818–1883) German journalist and philosopher, founder of the Marxist branch of **socialism.** He is known for two books: *The Communist Manifesto* (1848) and *Das Kapital* (Vols. I–III, 1867–1894). (*p. 732*)

mass deportation The forcible removal and relocation of large numbers of people or entire populations. The mass deportations practiced by the Assyrian and Persian Empires were meant as a terrifying warning of the consequences of rebellion. They also brought skilled and unskilled labor to the imperial center. (*p. 95*)

mass production The manufacture of many identical products by the division of labor into many small repetitive tasks. This method was introduced into the manufacture of pottery by Josiah Wedgwood and into the spinning of cotton thread by Richard Arkwright. (See also **Arkwright, Richard; Industrial Revolution; Wedgwood, Josiah.**) (*p. 614*)

Mauryan Empire The first state to unify most of the Indian subcontinent. It was founded by Chandragupta Maurya in 324 B.C.E. and survived until 184 B.C.E. From its capital at Pataliputra in the Ganges Valley it grew wealthy from taxes on agriculture, iron mining, and control of trade routes. (See also **Ashoka.**) (*p. 188*)

Maya Mesoamerican civilization concentrated in Mexico's Yucatán Peninsula and in Guatemala and Honduras but never unified into a single empire. Major contributions were in mathematics, astronomy, and development of the calendar. (*p. 310*)

Mecca City in western Arabia; birthplace of the Prophet **Muhammad,** and ritual center of the Islamic religion. (*p. 234*)

mechanization The application of machinery to manufacturing and other activities. Among the first processes to be mechanized were the spinning of cotton thread and the weaving of cloth in late-eighteenth- and early-nineteenth-century England. (*p. 615*)

medieval Literally "middle age," a term that historians of Europe use for the period ca. 500 to ca. 1500, signifying its intermediate point between Greco-Roman antiquity and the Renaissance. (*p. 254*)

Medina City in western Arabia to which the Prophet Muhammad and his followers emigrated in 622 to escape persecution in Mecca. (*p. 235*)

megaliths Structures and complexes of very large stones constructed for ceremonial and religious purposes in **Neolithic** times. (*p. 23*)

Meiji Restoration The political program that followed the destruction of the **Tokugawa Shogunate** in 1868, in which a collection of young leaders set Japan on the path of centralization, industrialization, and imperialism. (See also **Yamagata Aritomo.**) (*p. 744*)

Memphis The capital of Old Kingdom Egypt, near the head of the Nile Delta. Early rulers were interred in the nearby **pyramids.** (*p. 43*)

Menelik II (1844–1911) Emperor of Ethiopia (r. 1889–1911). He enlarged Ethiopia to its present dimensions and defeated an Italian invasion at Adowa (1896). (*p. 759*)

mercantilism European government policies of the sixteenth, seventeenth, and eighteenth centuries designed to promote overseas trade between a country and its colonies and accumulate precious metals by requiring colonies to trade only with their motherland country. The British system was defined by the Navigation Acts, the French system by laws known as the *Exclusif.* (*p. 627*)

Meroë Capital of a flourishing kingdom in southern Nubia from the fourth century B.C.E. to the fourth century C.E. In this period Nubian culture shows more independence from Egypt and the influence of sub-Saharan Africa. (*p. 69*)

mestizo The term used by Spanish authorities to describe someone of mixed Amerindian and European descent. (*p. 487*)

Middle Passage The part of the **Atlantic Circuit** involving the transportation of enslaved Africans across the Atlantic to the Americas. (*p. 511*)

millenarianism Beliefs, based on prophetic revelations, in apocalyptic global transformations associated with the completion of cycles of a thousand years. (*p. 930*)

Ming Empire (1368–1644) Empire based in China that Zhu Yuanzhang established after the overthrow of the **Yuan Empire.** The Ming emperor **Yongle** sponsored the building of the Forbidden City and the voyages of **Zheng He.** The later years of the Ming saw a slowdown in technological development and economic decline. (*pp. 354, 557*)

Minoan Prosperous civilization on the Aegean island of Crete in the second millennium B.C.E. The Minoans engaged in far-flung commerce around the Mediterranean and exerted powerful cultural influences on the early Greeks. (*p. 88*)

mit'a Andean labor system based on shared obligations to help kinsmen and work on behalf of the ruler and religious organizations. (*p. 321*)

Moche Civilization of north coast of Peru (200–700 C.E.). An important Andean civilization that built extensive irrigation networks as well as impressive urban centers dominated by brick temples. (*p. 322*)

Moctezuma II (1466?–1520) Last Aztec emperor, overthrown by the Spanish conquistador Hernán Cortés. (*p. 436*)

modernization The process of reforming political, military, economic, social, and cultural traditions in imitation of the early success of Western societies, often with regard for accommodating local traditions in non-Western societies. (*p. 668*)

Mohenjo-Daro Largest of the cities of the Indus Valley civilization. It was centrally located in the extensive flood-plain of the Indus River in contemporary Pakistan. Little is known about the political institutions of Indus Valley communities, but the large-scale of construction at Mohenjo-Daro, the orderly grid of streets, and the standardization of building materials are evidence of central planning. (*p. 49*)

moksha The Hindu concept of the spirit's "liberation" from the endless cycle of rebirths. There are various avenues—such as physical discipline, meditation, and acts of devotion to the gods—by which the spirit can distance itself from desire for the things of this world and be merged with the divine force that animates the universe. (*p. 184*)

monasticism Living in a religious community apart from secular society and adhering to a rule stipulating chastity, obedience, and poverty. It was a prominent element of medieval Christianity and Buddhism. Monasteries were the primary centers of learning and literacy in medieval Europe. (*p. 268*)

Mongols A people of this name is mentioned as early as the records of the **Tang Empire,** living as nomads in northern Eurasia. After 1206 they established an enormous empire under **Genghis Khan,** linking western and eastern Eurasia. (*p. 337*)

monotheism Belief in the existence of a single divine entity. Some scholars cite the devotion of the Egyptian pharaoh **Akhenaten** to Aten (sun-disk) and his suppression of traditional gods as the earliest instance. The Israelite worship of Yahweh developed into an exclusive belief in one god, and this concept passed into Christianity and Islam. (*p. 101*)

monsoon Seasonal winds in the Indian Ocean caused by the differences in temperature between the rapidly heating and cooling landmasses of Africa and Asia and the slowly changing ocean waters. These strong and predictable winds have long been ridden across the open sea by sailors, and the large amounts of rainfall that they deposit on parts of India, Southeast Asia, and China allow for the cultivation of several crops a year. *(pp. 180, 368)*

Morelos, José María (1765–1814) Mexican priest and former student of Miguel Hidalgo y Costilla, he led the forces fighting for Mexican independence until he was captured and executed in 1814. (See also **Hidalgo y Costilla, Miguel.**) *(p. 638)*

most-favored-nation status A clause in a commercial treaty that awards to any later signatories all the privileges previously granted to the original signatories. *(p. 709)*

movable type Type in which each individual character is cast on a separate piece of metal. It replaced woodblock printing, allowing for the arrangement of individual letters and other characters on a page, rather than requiring the carving of entire pages at a time. It may have been invented in Korea in the thirteenth century. (See also **printing press.**) *(p. 297)*

Mughal Empire Muslim state (1526–1857) exercising dominion over most of India in the sixteenth and seventeenth centuries. *(p. 541)*

Muhammad (570–632 C.E.) Arab prophet; founder of religion of Islam. *(p. 234)*

Muhammad Ali (1769–1849) Leader of Egyptian modernization in the early nineteenth century. He ruled Egypt as an Ottoman governor, but had imperial ambitions. His descendants ruled Egypt until overthrown in 1952. *(p. 668)*

mulatto The term used in Spanish and Portuguese colonies to describe someone of mixed African and European descent. *(p. 488)*

mummy A body preserved by chemical processes or special natural circumstances, often in the belief that the deceased will need it again in the afterlife. In ancient Egypt the bodies of people who could afford mummification underwent a complex process of removing organs, filling body cavities, dehydrating the corpse with natron, and then wrapping the body with linen bandages and enclosing it in a wooden sarcophagus. *(p. 48)*

Muscovy Russian principality that emerged gradually during the era of Mongol domination. The Muscovite dynasty ruled without interruption from 1276 to 1598. *(p. 566)*

Muslim An adherent of the Islamic religion; a person who "submits" (in Arabic, *Islam* means "submission") to the will of God. *(p. 566)*

Mussolini, Benito (1883–1945) Fascist dictator of Italy (1922–1943). He led Italy to conquer Ethiopia (1935), joined Germany in the Axis pact (1936), and allied Italy with Germany in World War II. He was overthrown in 1943 when the Allies invaded Italy. *(p. 821)*

Mycenae Site of a fortified palace complex in southern Greece that controlled a Late Bronze Age kingdom. In Homer's epic poems Mycenae was the base of King Agamemnon, who commanded the Greeks besieging Troy. Contemporary archaeologists call the complex Greek society of the second millennium B.C.E. "Mycenaean." *(p. 90)*

Napoleon I (1769–1832) Overthrew French Directory in 1799 and became emperor of the French in 1804. Failed to defeat Great Britain and abdicated in 1814. Returned to power briefly in 1815 but was defeated and died in exile. *(p. 597)*

Nasir al-Din Tusi (1201–1274) Persian mathematician and cosmologist whose academy near Tabriz provided the model for the movement of the planets that helped to inspire the Copernican model of the solar system. *(p. 347)*

National Assembly French Revolutionary assembly (1789–1791). Called first as the Estates General, the three estates came together and demanded radical change. It passed the **Declaration of the Rights of Man** in 1789. *(p. 594)*

nationalism A political ideology that stresses people's membership in a nation—a community defined by a common culture and history as well as by territory. In the late eighteenth and early nineteenth centuries, nationalism was a force for unity in western Europe. In the late nineteenth century it hastened the disintegration of the Austro-Hungarian and Ottoman Empires. In the twentieth century it provided the ideological foundation for scores of independent countries emerging from **colonialism.** *(p. 733)*

nawab A Muslim prince allied to British India; technically, a semi-autonomous deputy of the Mughal emperor. *(p. 671)*

Nazis German political party joined by Adolf Hitler, emphasizing nationalism, racism, and war. When Hitler became chancellor of Germany in 1933, the Nazis became the only legal party and an instrument of Hitler's absolute rule. The party's formal name was National Socialist German Workers' Party. (See also **Hitler, Adolf.**) *(p. 813)*

Nehru, Jawaharlal (1889–1964) Indian statesman. He succeeded Mohandas K. Gandhi as leader of the **Indian National Congress.** He negotiated the end of British colonial rule in India and became India's first prime minister (1947–1964). *(p. 842)*

Neo-Assyrian Empire An empire extending from western Iran to Syria-Palestine, conquered by the Assyrians of northern Mesopotamia between the tenth and seventh centuries B.C.E. They used force and terror and exploited the wealth and labor of their subjects. They also preserved and continued the cultural and scientific developments of Mesopotamian civilization. *(p. 93)*

Neo-Babylonian kingdom Under the Chaldaeans (nomadic kinship groups that settled in southern Mesopotamia in the early first millennium B.C.E.), **Babylon** again became a major political and cultural center in the seventh and sixth centuries B.C.E. After participating in the destruction of Assyrian power, the monarchs Nabopolassar and Nebuchadnezzar took over the southern portion of the Assyrian domains. By destroying the **First Temple** in Jerusalem and deporting part of the population, they initiated the **Diaspora** of the Jews. *(p. 110)*

neo-Confucianism Term used to describe new approaches to understanding classic Confucian texts that became the basic ruling philosophy of China from the **Song** period to the twentieth century. *(p. 296)*

neo-liberalism The term used in Latin America and other developing regions to describe free-market policies that include reducing tariff protection for local industries; the sale of public-sector industries, like national airlines and public utilities, to private investors or foreign corporations;

and the reduction of social welfare policies and public-sector employment. *(p. 894)*

Neolithic The period of the Stone Age associated with the ancient **Agricultural Revolution(s).** It follows the **Paleolithic** period. *(p. 12)*

Nevskii, Alexander (1220–1263) Prince of Novgorod (r. 1236–1263). He submitted to the invading Mongols in 1240 and received recognition as the leader of the Russian princes under the **Golden Horde.** *(p. 349)*

New Economic Policy Policy proclaimed by Vladimir Lenin in 1924 to encourage the revival of the Soviet economy by allowing small private enterprises. Joseph Stalin ended the N.E.P. in 1928 and replaced it with a series of **Five-Year Plans.** (See also **Lenin, Vladimir.**) *(p. 788)*

New France French colony in North America, with a capital in Quebec, founded 1608. New France fell to the British in 1763. *(p. 493)*

New Imperialism Historians' term for the late-nineteenth- and early-twentieth-century wave of conquests by European powers, the United States, and Japan, which were followed by the development and exploitation of the newly conquered territories for the benefit of the colonial powers. *(p. 749)*

newly industrialized economies (NIEs) Rapidly growing, new industrial nations of the late twentieth century, including the **Asian Tigers.** *(p. 897)*

new monarchies Historians' term for the monarchies in France, England, and Spain from 1450 to 1600. The centralization of royal power was increasing within more or less fixed territorial limits. *(p. 413)*

nomadism A way of life, forced by a scarcity of resources, in which groups of people continually migrate to find pastures and water. *(p. 337)*

nonaligned nations Developing countries that announced their neutrality in the **Cold War.** *(p. 861)*

nongovernmental organizations (NGOs) Nonprofit international organizations devoted to investigating human rights abuses and providing humanitarian relief. Two NGOs won the Nobel Peace Prize in the 1990s: International Campaign to Ban Landmines (1997) and Doctors Without Borders (1999). *(p. 934)*

North Atlantic Treaty Organization (NATO) Organization formed in 1949 as a military alliance of western European and North American states against the Soviet Union and its east European allies. (See also **Warsaw Pact.**) *(p. 862)*

Olmec The first Mesoamerican civilization. Between ca. 1200 and 400 B.C.E., the Olmec people of central Mexico created a vibrant civilization that included intensive agriculture, wide-ranging trade, ceremonial centers, and monumental construction. The Olmec had great cultural influence on later Mesoamerican societies, passing on artistic styles, religious imagery, sophisticated astronomical observation for the construction of calendars, and a ritual ball game. *(p. 75)*

Oman Arab state based in Musqat, the main port in the southwest region of the Arabian peninsula. Oman succeeded Portugal as a power in the western Indian Ocean in the eighteenth century. *(p. 547)*

Opium War (1839–1842) War between Britain and the **Qing Empire** that was, in the British view, occasioned by the Qing government's refusal to permit the importation of opium into its territories. The victorious British imposed the one-sided **Treaty of Nanking** on China. *(p. 708)*

Organization of Petroleum Exporting Countries (OPEC) Organization formed in 1960 by oil-producing states to promote their collective interest in generating revenue from oil. *(p. 884)*

Ottoman Empire Islamic state founded by Osman in northwestern Anatolia ca. 1300. After the fall of the **Byzantine Empire,** the Ottoman Empire was based at Istanbul (formerly Constantinople) from 1453 to 1922. It encompassed lands in the Middle East, North Africa, the Caucasus, and eastern Europe. *(pp. 351, 526)*

Páez, José Antonio (1790–1873) Venezulean soldier who led Simón Bolívar's cavalry force. He became a successful general in the war and built a powerful political base. He was unwilling to accept the constitutional authority of Bolívar's government in distant Bogotá and declared Venezuela's independence from Gran Colombia in 1829. *(p. 643)*

Paleolithic The period of the Stone Age associated with the **evolution** of humans. It predates the **Neolithic** period. *(p. 12)*

Pan-Slavism Movement among Russian intellectuals in the second half of the nineteenth century to identify culturally and politically with the Slavic peoples of eastern Europe. *(p. 705)*

Panama Canal Ship canal cut across the isthmus of Panama by United States Army engineers; it opened in 1915. It greatly shortened the sea voyage between the east and west coasts of North America. The United States turned the canal over to Panama on January 1, 2000. *(p. 771)*

papacy The central administration of the Roman Catholic Church, of which the pope is the head. *(pp. 267, 450)*

papyrus A reed that grows along the banks of the Nile River in Egypt. From it was produced a coarse, paperlike writing medium used by the Egyptians and many other peoples in the ancient Mediterranean and Middle East. *(p. 44)*

Parthians Iranian ruling dynasty between ca. 250 B.C.E. and 226 C.E. *(p. 211)*

patron/client relationship In ancient Rome, a fundamental social relationship in which the patron—a wealthy and powerful individual—provided legal and economic protection and assistance to clients, men of lesser status and means, and in return the clients supported the political careers and economic interests of their patron. *(p. 155)*

Paul (ca. 5–65 C.E.) A Jew from the Greek city of Tarsus in Anatolia, he initially persecuted the followers of Jesus but, after receiving a revelation on the road to Syrian Damascus, became a Christian. Taking advantage of his Hellenized background and Roman citizenship, he traveled throughout Syria-Palestine, Anatolia, and Greece, preaching the new religion and establishing churches. Finding his greatest success among pagans ("gentiles"), he began the process by which Christianity separated from Judaism. *(p. 162)*

pax romana Literally, "Roman peace," it connoted the stability and prosperity that Roman rule brought to the lands of the Roman Empire in the first two centuries C.E. The movement of people and trade goods along Roman roads and safe seas allowed for the spread of cultural practices, technologies, and religious ideas. *(p. 161)*

Pearl Harbor Naval base in Hawaii attacked by Japanese aircraft on December 7, 1941. The sinking of much of the U.S. Pacific Fleet brought the United States into World War II. *(p. 821)*

Peloponnesian War A protracted (431–404 B.C.E.) and costly conflict between the Athenian and Spartan alliance systems that convulsed most of the Greek world. The war was largely a consequence of Athenian imperialism. Possession of a naval empire allowed Athens to fight a war of attrition. Ultimately, Sparta prevailed because of Athenian errors and Persian financial support. *(p. 142)*

perestroika Policy of "openness" that was the centerpiece of Mikhail Gorbachev's efforts to liberalize communism in the Soviet Union. (See also **Gorbachev, Mikhail.**) *(p. 898)*

Pericles (ca. 495–429 B.C.E.) Aristocratic leader who guided the Athenian state through the transformation to full participatory democracy for all male citizens, supervised construction of the Acropolis, and pursued a policy of imperial expansion that led to the **Peloponnesian War.** He formulated a strategy of attrition but died from the plague early in the war. *(p. 138)*

Perón, Eva Duarte (1919–1952) Wife of **Juan Perón** and champion of the poor in Argentina. She was a gifted speaker and popular political leader who campaigned to improve the life of the urban poor by founding schools and hospitals and providing other social benefits. *(p. 852)*

Perón, Juan (1895–1974) President of Argentina (1946–1955, 1973–1974). As a military officer, he championed the rights of labor. Aided by his wife **Eva Duarte Perón,** he was elected president in 1946. He built up Argentinean industry, became very popular among the urban poor, but harmed the economy. *(p. 852)*

Persepolis A complex of palaces, reception halls, and treasury buildings erected by the Persian kings **Darius I** and Xerxes in the Persian homeland. It is believed that the New Year's festival was celebrated here, as well as the coronations, weddings, and funerals of the Persian kings, who were buried in cliff-tombs nearby. *(p. 124)*

Persian Wars Conflicts between Greek city-states and the Persian Empire, ranging from the Ionian Revolt (499–494 B.C.E.) through Darius's punitive expedition that failed at Marathon (490 B.C.E.) and the defeat of Xerxes' massive invasion of Greece by the Spartan-led Hellenic League (480–479 B.C.E.). This first major setback for Persian arms launched the Greeks into their period of greatest cultural productivity. **Herodotus** chronicled these events in the first "history" in the Western tradition. *(p. 138)*

personalist leaders Political leaders who rely on charisma and their ability to mobilize and direct the masses of citizens outside the authority of constitutions and laws. Nineteenth-century examples include José Antonio Páez of Venezuela and Andrew Jackson of the United States. Twentieth-century examples include Getulio Vargas of Brazil and Juan Perón of Argentina. (See also **Jackson, Andrew; Páez, José Antonio; Perón, Juan; Vargas, Getulio.**) *(p. 643)*

Peter the Great (1672–1725) Russian tsar (r. 1689–1725). He enthusiastically introduced Western languages and technologies to the Russian elite, moving the capital from Moscow to the new city of St. Petersburg. *(p. 569)*

pharaoh The central figure in the ancient Egyptian state. Believed to be an earthly manifestation of the gods, he used his absolute power to maintain the safety and prosperity of Egypt. *(p. 43)*

Phoenicians Semitic-speaking Canaanites living on the coast of modern Lebanon and Syria in the first millennium B.C.E. From major cities such as Tyre and Sidon, Phoenician merchants and sailors explored the Mediterranean, engaged in widespread commerce, and founded **Carthage** and other colonies in the western Mediterranean. *(p. 104)*

pilgrimage Journey to a sacred shrine by Christians seeking to show their piety, fulfill vows, or gain absolution for sins. Other religions also have pilgrimage traditions, such as the Muslim pilgrimage to **Mecca** and the pilgrimages made by early Chinese Buddhists to India in search of sacred Buddhist writings. *(p. 276)*

Pilgrims Group of English Protestant dissenters who established Plymouth Colony in Massachusetts in 1620 to seek religious freedom after having lived briefly in the Netherlands. *(p. 490)*

Pizarro, Francisco (1475?–1541) Spanish explorer who led the conquest of the **Inca** Empire of Peru in 1531–1533. *(p. 440)*

Planck, Max (1858–1947) German physicist who developed quantum theory and was awarded the Nobel Prize for physics in 1918. *(p. 800)*

plantocracy In the West Indian colonies, the rich men who owned most of the slaves and most of the land, especially in the eighteenth century. *(p. 505)*

polis The Greek term for a **city-state,** an urban center and the agricultural territory under its control. It was the characteristic form of political organization in southern and central Greece in the Archaic and Classical periods. Of the hundreds of city-states in the Mediterranean and Black Sea regions settled by Greeks, some were oligarchic, others democratic, depending on the powers delegated to the Council and the Assembly. *(p. 132)*

pop culture Entertainment spread by mass communications and enjoying wide appeal. *(p. 938)*

positivism A philosophy developed by the French count of Saint-Simon. Positivists believed that social and economic problems could be solved by the application of the scientific method, leading to continuous progress. Their ideas became popular in France and Latin America in the nineteenth century. *(p. 628)*

Potosí Located in Bolivia, one of the richest silver mining centers and most populous cities in colonial Spanish America. *(p. 480)*

printing press A mechanical device for transferring text or graphics from a woodblock or type to paper using ink. Presses using movable type first appeared in Europe in about 1450. See also **movable type.** *(p. 409)*

Protestant Reformation Religious reform movement within the Latin Christian Church beginning in 1519. It resulted in the "protesters" forming several new Christian denominations, including the Lutheran and Reformed Churches and the Church of England. *(p. 450)*

proxy wars During the **Cold War,** local or regional wars in which the superpowers armed, trained, and financed the combatants. *(p. 888)*

Ptolemies The Macedonian dynasty, descended from one of Alexander the Great's officers, that ruled Egypt for three centuries (323–30 B.C.E.). From their magnificent capital at Alexandria on the Mediterranean coast, the Ptolemies largely took over the system created by Egyptian pharaohs to extract the wealth of the land, rewarding Greeks and Hellenized non-Greeks serving in the military and administration. *(p. 145)*

Puritans English Protestant dissenters who believed that God predestined souls to heaven or hell before birth. They founded Massachusetts Bay Colony in 1629. *(p. 490)*

pyramid A large, triangular stone monument, used in Egypt and Nubia as a burial place for the king. The largest pyramids, erected during the Old Kingdom near Memphis with stone tools and compulsory labor, reflect the Egyptian belief that the proper and spectacular burial of the divine ruler would guarantee the continued prosperity of the land. (See also **ma'at.**) *(p. 43)*

Qin A people and state in the Wei Valley of eastern China that conquered rival states and created the first Chinese empire (221–206 B.C.E.). The Qin ruler, **Shi Huangdi,** standardized many features of Chinese society and ruthlessly marshaled subjects for military and construction projects, engendering hostility that led to the fall of his dynasty shortly after his death. The Qin framework was largely taken over by the succeeding **Han** Empire. *(p. 166)*

Qing Empire Empire established in China by Manchus who overthrew the **Ming Empire** in 1644. At various times the Qing also controlled Manchuria, Mongolia, Turkestan, and Tibet. The last Qing emperor was overthrown in 1911. *(p. 558)*

Quran Book composed of divine revelations made to the Prophet Muhammad between ca. 610 and his death in 632; the sacred text of the religion of **Islam.** *(p. 236)*

railroads Networks of iron (later steel) rails on which steam (later electric or diesel) locomotives pulled long trains at high speeds. The first railroads were built in England in the 1830s. Their success caused a railroad-building boom throughout the world that lasted well into the twentieth century. *(p. 723)*

Rajputs Members of a mainly Hindu warrior caste from northwest India. The Mughal emperors drew most of their Hindu officials from this caste, and **Akbar I** married a Rajput princess. *(p. 542)*

Ramesses II A long-lived ruler of New Kingdom Egypt (r. 1290–1224 B.C.E.). He reached an accommodation with the **Hittites** of Anatolia after a standoff in battle at Kadesh in Syria. He built on a grand scale throughout Egypt. *(p. 87)*

Rashid al-Din (d.1318) Adviser to the **Il-khan** ruler Ghazan, who converted to Islam on Rashid's advice. *(p. 347)*

recaptives Africans rescued by Britain's Royal Navy from the illegal slave trade of the nineteenth century and restored to free status. *(p. 671)*

reconquest of Iberia Beginning in the eleventh century, military campaigns by various Iberian Christian states to recapture territory taken by Muslims. In 1492 the last Muslim ruler was defeated, and Spain and Portugal emerged as united kingdoms. *(p. 414)*

Renaissance (European) A period of intense artistic and intellectual activity, said to be a "rebirth" of Greco-Roman culture. Usually divided into an Italian Renaissance, from roughly the mid-fourteenth to mid-fifteenth century, and a Northern (trans-Alpine) Renaissance, from roughly the early fifteenth to early seventeenth century. *(pp. 406, 449)*

Revolutions of 1848 Democratic and nationalist revolutions that swept across Europe. The monarchy in France was overthrown. In Germany, Austria, Italy, and Hungary the revolutions failed. *(p. 604)*

Rhodes, Cecil (1853–1902) British entrepreneur and politician involved in the expansion of the British Empire from South Africa into Central Africa. The colonies of Southern Rhodesia (now Zimbabwe) and Northern Rhodesia (now Zambia) were named after him. *(p. 758)*

Robespierre, Maximilien (1758–1794) Young provincial lawyer who led the most radical phases of the French Revolution. His execution ended the Reign of Terror. See **Jacobins.** *(p. 596)*

Romanization The process by which the Latin language and Roman culture became dominant in the western provinces of the Roman Empire. The Roman government did not actively seek to Romanize the subject peoples, but indigenous peoples in the provinces often chose to Romanize because of the political and economic advantages that it brought, as well as the allure of Roman success. *(p. 161)*

Roman Principate A term used to characterize Roman government in the first three centuries C.E., based on the ambiguous title *princeps* ("first citizen") adopted by Augustus to conceal his military dictatorship. *(p. 157)*

Roman Republic The period from 507 to 31 B.C.E., during which Rome was largely governed by the aristocratic **Roman Senate.** *(p. 154)*

Roman Senate A council whose members were the heads of wealthy, landowning families. Originally an advisory body to the early kings, in the era of the **Roman Republic** the Senate effectively governed the Roman state and the growing empire. Under Senate leadership, Rome conquered an empire of unprecedented extent in the lands surrounding the Mediterranean Sea. In the first century B.C.E. quarrels among powerful and ambitious senators and failure to address social and economic problems led to civil wars and the emergence of the rule of the emperors. *(p. 154)*

Royal African Company A trading company chartered by the English government in 1672 to conduct its merchants' trade on the Atlantic coast of Africa. *(p. 400)*

sacrifice A gift given to a deity, often with the aim of creating a relationship, gaining favor, and obligating the god to provide some benefit to the sacrificer, sometimes in order to sustain the deity and thereby guarantee the continuing vitality of the natural world. The object devoted to the deity could be as simple as a cup of wine poured on the ground, a live animal slain on the altar, or, in the most extreme case, the ritual killing of a human being. *(p. 135)*

Safavid Empire Iranian kingdom (1502–1722) established by Ismail Safavi, who declared Iran a Shi'ite state. *(p. 536)*

Sahel Belt south of the Sahara; literally "coastland" in Arabic. *(p. 220)*

samurai Literally "those who serve," the hereditary military elite of the **Tokugawa Shogunate.** *(p. 551)*

Sandinistas Members of a leftist coalition that overthrew the Nicaraguan dictatorship of Anastasia Somoza in 1979 and attempted to install a socialist economy. The United States financed armed opposition by the Contras. The Sandinistas lost national elections in 1990. *(p. 890)*

Sanger, Margaret (1883–1966) American nurse and author; pioneer in the movement for family planning; organized conferences and established birth control clinics. *(p. 799)*

Sasanid Empire Iranian empire, established ca. 226, with a capital in Ctesiphon, Mesopotamia. The Sasanid emperors established **Zoroastrianism** as the state religion. Islamic Arab armies overthrew the empire ca. 640. *(p. 230)*

satrap The governor of a province in the Achaemenid Persian Empire, often a relative of the king. He was responsible for protection of the province and for forwarding tribute to the central administration. Satraps in outlying provinces enjoyed considerable autonomy. *(p. 123)*

savanna Tropical or subtropical grassland, either treeless or with occasional clumps of trees. Most extensive in **sub-Saharan Africa** but also present in South America. *(p. 222)*

schism A formal split within a religious community. See **Great Western Schism.** *(p. 256)*

scholasticism A philosophical and theological system, associated with Thomas Aquinas, devised to reconcile Aristotelian philosophy and Roman Catholic theology in the thirteenth century. *(p. 407)*

Scientific Revolution The intellectual movement in Europe, initially associated with planetary motion and other aspects of physics, that by the seventeenth century had laid the groundwork for modern science. *(p. 454)*

"scramble" for Africa Sudden wave of conquests in Africa by European powers in the 1880s and 1890s. Britain obtained most of eastern Africa, France most of northwestern Africa. Other countries (Germany, Belgium, Portugal, Italy, and Spain) acquired lesser amounts. *(p. 755)*

scribe In the governments of many ancient societies, a professional position reserved for men who had undergone the lengthy training required to be able to read and write using **cuneiforms, hieroglyphics,** or other early, cumbersome writing systems. *(p. 35)*

seasoning An often difficult period of adjustment to new climates, disease environments, and work routines, such as that experienced by slaves newly arrived in the Americas. *(p. 508)*

Selassie, Haile (1892–1975) Emperor of Ethiopia (r. 1930–1974) and symbol of African independence. He fought the Italian invasion of his country in 1935 and regained his throne during World War II, when British forces expelled the Italians. He ruled **Ethiopia** as a traditional autocracy until he was overthrown in 1974. *(p. 838)*

Semitic Family of related languages long spoken across parts of western Asia and northern Africa. In antiquity these languages included Hebrew, Aramaic, and Phoenician. The most widespread modern member of the Semitic family is Arabic. *(p. 32)*

"separate spheres" Nineteenth-century idea in Western societies that men and women, especially of the middle class, should have clearly differentiated roles in society: women as wives, mothers, and homemakers; men as breadwinners and participants in business and politics. *(p. 730)*

sepoy A soldier in South Asia, especially in the service of the British. *(p. 673)*

Sepoy Rebellion The revolt of Indian soldiers in 1857 against certain practices that violated religious customs; also known as the Sepoy Mutiny. *(p. 676)*

Serbia The Ottoman province in the Balkans that rose up against **Janissary** control in the early 1800s. After World War II the central province of Yugoslavia. Serb leaders struggled to maintain dominance as the Yugoslav federation dissolved in the 1990s. *(p. 693)*

serf In medieval Europe, an agricultural laborer legally bound to a lord's property and obligated to perform set services for the lord. In Russia some serfs worked as artisans and in factories; serfdom was not abolished there until 1861. *(pp. 262, 569)*

shaft graves A term used for the burial sites of elite members of Mycenaean Greek society in the mid-second millennium B.C.E. At the bottom of deep shafts lined with stone slabs, the bodies were laid out along with gold and bronze jewelry, implements, weapons, and masks. *(p. 90)*

Shah Abbas I (r. 1587–1629) The fifth and most renowned ruler of the **Safavid** dynasty in Iran. Abbas moved the royal capital to Isfahan in 1598. *(p. 538)*

shamanism The practice of identifying special individuals (shamans) who will interact with spirits for the benefit of the community. Characteristic of the Korean kingdoms of the early medieval period and of early societies of Central Asia. *(p. 300)*

Shang The dominant people in the earliest Chinese dynasty for which we have written records (ca. 1750–1027 B.C.E.). Ancestor worship, divination by means of oracle bones, and the use of bronze vessels for ritual purposes were major elements of Shang culture. *(p. 60)*

Shi Huangdi Founder of the short-lived **Qin** dynasty and creator of the Chinese Empire (r. 221–210 B.C.E.). He is remembered for his ruthless conquests of rival states, standardization of practices, and forcible organization of labor for military and engineering tasks. His tomb, with its army of life-size terracotta soldiers, has been partially excavated. *(p. 166)*

Shi'ites Muslims belonging to the branch of Islam believing that God vests leadership of the community in a descendant of Muhammad's son-in-law Ali. Shi'ism is the state religion of Iran. (See also **Sunnis.**) *(pp. 230, 537)*

Siberia The extreme northeastern sector of Asia, including the Kamchatka Peninsula and the present Russian coast of the Arctic Ocean, the Bering Strait, and the Sea of Okhotsk. *(p. 567)*

Sikhism Indian religion founded by the guru Nanak (1469–1539) in the Punjab region of northwest India. After the Mughal emperor ordered the beheading of the ninth guru in 1675, Sikh warriors mounted armed resistance to Mughal rule. *(p. 543)*

Silk Road Caravan routes connecting China and the Middle East across Central Asia and Iran. *(p. 209)*

Slavophiles Russian intellectuals in the early nineteenth century who favored resisting western European influences and taking pride in the traditional peasant values and institutions of the Slavic people. *(p. 705)*

"small traditions" Historians' term for a localized, usually nonliterate, set of customs and beliefs adhered to by a single society, often in conjunction with a **"great tradition."** *(p. 222)*

socialism A political ideology that originated in Europe in the 1830s. Socialists advocated government protection of workers from exploitation by property owners and government ownership of industries. This ideology led to the founding of socialist or labor parties throughout Europe in the second half of the nineteenth century. (See also **Marx, Karl.**) *(p. 732)*

Socrates Athenian philosopher (ca. 470–399 B.C.E.) who shifted the emphasis of philosophical investigation from questions of natural science to ethics and human behavior. He attracted young disciples from elite families but made enemies by revealing the ignorance and pretensions of others, culminating in his trial and execution by the Athenian state. *(p. 140)*

Sokoto Caliphate A large Muslim state founded in 1809 in what is now northern Nigeria. *(p. 667)*

Solidarity Polish trade union created in 1980 to protest working conditions and political repression. It began the nationalist opposition to communist rule that led in 1989 to the fall of communism in eastern Europe. *(p. 899)*

Song Empire Empire in central and southern China (960–1126) while the Liao people controlled the north. Empire in southern China (1127–1279; the "Southern Song") while the Jin people controlled the north. Distinguished for its advances in technology, medicine, astronomy, and mathematics. *(p. 292)*

Songhai A people, language, kingdom, and empire in western Sudan in West Africa. At its height in the sixteenth century, the Muslim Songhai Empire stretched from the Atlantic to the land of the **Hausa** and was a major player in the trans-Saharan trade. *(p. 519)*

Srivijaya A state based on the Indonesian island of Sumatra, between the seventh and eleventh centuries C.E. It amassed wealth and power by a combination of selective adaptation of Indian technologies and concepts, control of the lucrative trade routes between India and China, and skillful showmanship and diplomacy in holding together a disparate realm of inland and coastal territories. (See also **theater-state.**) *(p. 198)*

Stalin, Joseph (1879–1953) Bolshevik revolutionary, head of the Soviet Communist Party after 1924, and dictator of the Soviet Union from 1928 to 1953. He led the Soviet Union with an iron fist, using **Five-Year Plans** to increase industrial production and terror to crush all opposition. *(p. 805)*

Stalingrad City in Russia, site of a Red Army victory over the German army in 1942–1943. The Battle of Stalingrad was the turning point in the war between Germany and the Soviet Union. Today Volgograd. *(p. 819)*

Stanley, Henry Morton (1841–1904) British-American explorer of Africa, famous for his expeditions in search of Dr. David Livingstone. Stanley helped King **Leopold II** establish the Congo Free State. *(p. 755)*

steam engine A machine that turns the energy released by burning fuel into motion. Thomas Newcomen built the first crude but workable steam engine in 1712. **James Watt** vastly improved his device in the 1760s and 1770s. Steam power was later applied to moving machinery in factories and to powering ships and locomotives. *(p. 618)*

steel A form of iron that is both durable and flexible. It was first mass-produced in the 1860s and quickly became the most widely used metal in construction, machinery, and railroad equipment. *(p. 724)*

steppes Treeless plains, especially the high, flat expanses of northern Eurasia, which usually have little rain and are covered with coarse grass. They are good lands for nomads and their herds. Living on the steppes promoted the breeding of horses and the development of military skills that were essential to the rise of the Mongol Empire. *(p. 222)*

stirrup Device for securing a horseman's feet, enabling him to wield weapons more effectively. First evidence of the use of stirrups was among the Kushan people of northern Afghanistan in approximately the first century C.E. *(p. 213)*

stock exchange A place where shares in a company or business enterprise are bought and sold. *(p. 459)*

Stone Age The historical period characterized by the production of tools from stone and other nonmetallic substances. It was followed in some places by the Bronze Age and more generally by the Iron Age. *(p. 11)*

submarine telegraph cables Insulated copper cables laid along the bottom of a sea or ocean for telegraphic communication. The first short cable was laid across the English Channel in 1851; the first successful transatlantic cable was laid in 1866. (See also **electric telegraph.**) *(p. 724)*

sub-Saharan Africa Portion of the African continent lying south of the Sahara. *(p. 222)*

Suez Canal Ship canal dug across the isthmus of Suez in Egypt, designed by Ferdinand de Lesseps. It opened to shipping in 1869 and shortened the sea voyage between Europe and Asia. Its strategic importance led to the British conquest of Egypt in 1882. *(p. 749)*

Suleiman the Magnificent (1494–1566) The most illustrious sultan of the **Ottoman Empire** (r. 1520–1566); also known as Suleiman Kanuni, "The Lawgiver." He significantly expanded the empire in the Balkans and eastern Mediterranean. *(p. 528)*

Sumerians The people who dominated southern Mesopotamia through the end of the third millennium B.C.E. They were responsible for the creation of many fundamental elements of Mesopotamian culture—such as irrigation technology, **cuneiform,** and religious conceptions—taken over by their **Semitic** successors. *(p. 31)*

Sunnis Muslims belonging to branch of Islam believing that the community should select its own leadership. The majority religion in most Islamic countries. (See also **Shi'ites.**) *(p. 230)*

Sun Yat-sen (1867–1925) Chinese nationalist revolutionary, founder and leader of the **Guomindang** until his death. He attempted to create a liberal democratic political movement in China but was thwarted by military leaders. *(p. 791)*

Swahili Bantu language with Arabic loanwords spoken in coastal regions of East Africa. (*p. 547*)

Swahili Coast East African shores of the Indian Ocean between the Horn of Africa and the Zambezi River; from the Arabic *sawahil,* meaning "shores." (*p. 383*)

Taiping Rebellion (1853–1864) The most destructive civil war before the twentieth century. A Christian-inspired rural rebellion threatened to topple the **Qing Empire.** (*p. 710*)

Tamil kingdoms The kingdoms of southern India, inhabited primarily by speakers of Dravidian languages, which developed in partial isolation, and somewhat differently, from the Aryan north. They produced epics, poetry, and performance arts. Elements of Tamil religious beliefs were merged into the Hindu synthesis. (*p. 190*)

Tang Empire Empire unifying China and part of Central Asia, founded 618 and ended 907. The Tang emperors presided over a magnificent court at their capital, Chang'an. (*p. 282*)

Tanzimat "Restructuring" reforms by the nineteenth-century Ottoman rulers, intended to move civil law away from the control of religious elites and make the military and the bureaucracy more efficient. (*p. 696*)

Tecumseh (1768–1813) Shawnee leader who attempted to organize an Amerindian confederacy to prevent the loss of additional territory to American settlers. He became an ally of the British in War of 1812 and died in battle. (*p. 648*)

Tenochtitlan Capital of the Aztec Empire, located on an island in Lake Texcoco. Its population was about 150,000 on the eve of Spanish conquest. Mexico City was constructed on its ruins. (*p. 314*)

Teotihuacan A powerful **city-state** in central Mexico (100 B.C.E.–750 C.E.). Its population was about 150,000 at its peak in 600. (*p. 30*)

terrorism Political belief that extreme and seemingly random violence will destabilize a government and permit the terrorists to gain political advantage. Though an old technique, terrorism gained prominence in the late twentieth century with the growth of worldwide mass media that, through their news coverage, amplified public fears of terrorist acts. (*p. 923*)

theater-state Historians' term for a state that acquires prestige and power by developing attractive cultural forms and staging elaborate public ceremonies (as well as redistributing valuable resources) to attract and bind subjects to the center. Examples include the **Gupta Empire** in India and **Srivijaya** in Southeast Asia. (*p. 191*)

Thebes Capital city of Egypt and home of the ruling dynasties during the Middle and New Kingdoms. Amon, patron deity of Thebes, became one of the chief gods of Egypt. Monarchs were buried across the river in the Valley of the Kings. (*p. 43*)

Theravada Buddhism "Way of the Elders" branch of Buddhism followed in Sri Lanka and much of Southeast Asia. Therevada remains close to the original principles set forth by the **Buddha;** it downplays the importance of gods and emphasizes austerity and the individual's search for enlightenment. (*p. 185*)

third-century crisis Historians' term for the political, military, and economic turmoil that beset the Roman Empire during much of the third century C.E.: frequent changes of ruler, civil wars, barbarian invasions, decline of urban centers, and near-destruction of long-distance commerce and the monetary economy. After 284 C.E. Diocletian restored order by making fundamental changes. (*p. 163*)

Third World Term applied to a group of developing countries who professed nonalignment during the **Cold War.** (*p. 879*)

three-field system A rotational system for agriculture in which one field grows grain, one grows legumes, and one lies fallow. It gradually replaced two-field system in medieval Europe. (*p. 395*)

Tiananmen Square Site in Beijing where Chinese students and workers gathered to demand greater political openness in 1989. The demonstration was crushed by Chinese military with great loss of life. (*p. 897*)

Tibet Country centered on the high, mountain-bounded plateau north of India. Tibetan political power occasionally extended farther to the north and west between the seventh and thirteen centuries. (*p. 289*)

Timbuktu City on the Niger River in the modern country of Mali. It was founded by the Tuareg as a seasonal camp sometime after 1000. As part of the **Mali** empire, Timbuktu became a major terminus of the trans-Saharan trade and a center of Islamic learning. (*p. 386*)

Timur (1336–1405) Member of a prominent family of the Mongols' Jagadai Khanate, Timur through conquest gained control over much of Central Asia and Iran. He consolidated the status of Sunni Islam as orthodox, and his descendants, the Timurids, maintained his empire for nearly a century and founded the **Mughal Empire** in India. (*p. 346*)

Tiwanaku Name of capital city and empire centered on the region near Lake Titicaca in modern Bolivia (375–1000 C.E.). (*p. 323*)

Tokugawa Shogunate (1600–1868) The last of the three shogunates of Japan. (*p. 552*)

Toltecs Powerful postclassic empire in central Mexico (900–1168 C.E.). It influenced much of Mesoamerica. Aztecs claimed ties to this earlier civilization. (*p. 313*)

trans-Saharan caravan routes Trading network linking North Africa with **sub-Saharan Africa** across the Sahara. (*p. 219*)

Treaty of Nanking (1842) The treaty that concluded the **Opium War.** It awarded Britain a large indemnity from the **Qing Empire,** denied the Qing government tariff control over some of its own borders, opened additional ports of residence to Britons, and ceded the island of Hong Kong to Britain. (*p. 708*)

Treaty of Versailles (1919) The treaty imposed on Germany by France, Great Britain, the United States, and other Allied Powers after World War I. It demanded that Germany dismantle its military and give up some lands to Poland. It was resented by many Germans. (*p. 787*)

treaty ports Cities opened to foreign residents as a result of the forced treaties between the **Qing Empire** and foreign signatories. In the treaty ports, foreigners enjoyed **extraterritoriality.** (*p. 708*)

tributary system A system in which, from the time of the **Han** Empire, countries in East and Southeast Asia not under the direct control of empires based in China nevertheless enrolled as tributary states, acknowledging the superiority of the emperors in China in exchange for trading rights or strategic alliances. *(p. 285)*

tribute system A system in which defeated peoples were forced to pay a tax in the form of goods and labor. This forced transfer of food, cloth, and other goods subsidized the development of large cities. An important component of the Aztec and Inca economies. *(p. 315)*

trireme Greek and Phoenician warship of the fifth and fourth centuries B.C.E. It was sleek and light, powered by 170 oars arranged in three vertical tiers. Manned by skilled sailors, it was capable of short bursts of speed and complex maneuvers. *(p. 139)*

tropical rain forest High-precipitation forest zones of the Americas, Africa, and Asia lying between the Tropic of Cancer and the Tropic of Capricorn. *(p. 222)*

tropics Equatorial region between the Tropic of Cancer and the Tropic of Capricorn. It is characterized by generally warm or hot temperatures year-round, though much variation exists due to altitude and other factors. Temperate zones north and south of the tropics generally have a winter season. *(p. 367)*

Truman Doctrine Foreign policy initiated by U.S. president Harry Truman in 1947. It offered military aid to help Turkey and Greece resist Soviet military pressure and subversion. *(p. 866)*

tsar (czar) From Latin *caesar,* this Russian title for a monarch was first used in reference to a Russian ruler by Ivan III (r. 1462–1505). *(pp. 350, 567)*

Tulip Period (1718–1730) Last years of the reign of Ottoman sultan Ahmed III, during which European styles and attitudes became briefly popular in Istanbul. *(p. 536)*

Tupac Amaru II Member of Inca aristocracy who led a rebellion against Spanish authorities in Peru in 1780–1781. He was captured and executed with his wife and other members of his family. *(p. 496)*

tyrant The term the Greeks used to describe someone who seized and held power in violation of the normal procedures and traditions of the community. Tyrants appeared in many Greek **city-states** in the seventh and sixth centuries B.C.E., often taking advantage of the disaffection of the emerging middle class and, by weakening the old elite, unwittingly contributing to the evolution of **democracy.** *(p. 134)*

Uighurs A group of Turkic-speakers who controlled their own centralized empire from 744 to 840 in Mongolia and Central Asia. *(p. 289)*

ulama Muslim religious scholars. From the ninth century onward, the primary interpreters of Islamic law and the social core of Muslim urban societies. *(p. 241)*

Umayyad Caliphate First hereditary dynasty of Muslim caliphs (661 to 750). From their capital at Damascus, the Umayyads ruled an empire that extended from Spain to India. Overthrown by the **Abbasid Caliphate.** *(p. 236)*

umma The community of all Muslims. A major innovation against the background of seventh-century Arabia, where traditionally kinship rather than faith had determined membership in a community. *(p. 235)*

underdevelopment The condition experienced by economies that depend on colonial forms of production such as the export of raw materials and plantation crops with low wages and low investment in education. *(p. 656)*

United Nations International organization founded in 1945 to promote world peace and cooperation. It replaced the **League of Nations.** *(p. 862)*

Universal Declaration of Human Rights A 1946 United Nations covenant binding signatory nations to the observance of specified rights. *(p. 933)*

universities Degree-granting institutions of higher learning. Those that appeared in Latin West from about 1200 onward became the model of all modern universities. *(p. 406)*

Ural Mountains This north-south range separates Siberia from the rest of Russia. It is commonly considered the boundary between the continents of Europe and Asia. *(p. 567)*

Urdu A Persian-influenced literary form of Hindi written in Arabic characters and used as a literary language since the 1300s. *(p. 386)*

utopian socialism A philosophy introduced by the Frenchman Charles Fourier in the early nineteenth century. Utopian socialists hoped to create humane alternatives to industrial capitalism by building self-sustaining communities whose inhabitants would work cooperatively. (See also **socialism.**) *(p. 628)*

Vargas, Getulio (1883–1954) Dictator of Brazil from 1930 to 1945 and from 1951 to 1954. Defeated in the presidential election of 1930, he overthrew the government and created Estado Novo ("New State"), a dictatorship that emphasized industrialization and helped the urban poor but did little to alleviate the problems of the peasants. *(p. 851)*

varna/jati Two categories of social identity of great importance in Indian history. *Varna* are the four major social divisions: the *Brahmin* priest class, the *Kshatriya* warrior/administrator class, the *Vaishya* merchant/farmer class, and the *Shudra* laborer class. Within the system of *varna* are many *jati,* regional groups of people who have a common occupational sphere, and who marry, eat, and generally interact with other members of their group. *(pp. 182, 183)*

vassal In medieval Europe, a sworn supporter of a king or lord committed to rendering specified military service to that king or lord. *(p. 263)*

Vedas Early Indian sacred "knowledge"—the literal meaning of the term—long preserved and communicated orally by Brahmin priests and eventually written down. These religious texts, including the thousand poetic hymns to various deities contained in the Rig Veda, are our main source of information about the Vedic period (ca. 1500–500 B.C.E.). *(p. 180)*

Versailles The huge palace built for French King Louis XIV south of Paris in the town of the same name. The palace symbolized the preeminence of French power and architecture in Europe and the triumph of royal authority over the French nobility. *(p. 466)*

Victorian Age The reign of Queen Victoria of Great Britain (r. 1837–1901). The term is also used to describe late-nineteenth-century society, with its rigid moral standards and sharply differentiated roles for men and women and for middle-class and working-class people. (See also **"separate spheres."**) *(p. 730)*

Vietnam War (1954–1975) Conflict pitting North Vietnam and South Vietnamese communist guerrillas against the South Vietnamese government, aided after 1961 by the United States. *(p. 869)*

Villa, Francisco "Pancho" (1878–1923) A popular leader during the Mexican Revolution. An outlaw in his youth, when the revolution started, he formed a cavalry army in the north of Mexico and fought for the rights of the landless in collaboration with **Emiliano Zapata.** He was assassinated in 1923. *(p. 846)*

Wari Andean civilization culturally linked to **Tiwanaku,** perhaps beginning as a colony of Tiwanaku. *(p. 323)*

Warsaw Pact The 1955 treaty binding the Soviet Union and countries of eastern Europe in an alliance against the **North Atlantic Treaty Organization.** *(p. 866)*

Washington, George (1732–1799) Military commander of the American Revolution. He was the first elected president of the United States (1789–1799). *(p. 589)*

water wheel A mechanism that harnesses the energy in flowing water to grind grain or to power machinery. It was used in many parts of the world but was especially common in Europe from 1200 to 1900. *(p. 397)*

Watt, James (1736–1819) Scot who invented the condenser and other improvements that made the **steam engine** a practical source of power for industry and transportation. The watt, an electrical measurement, is named after him. *(p. 619)*

weapons of mass destruction Nuclear, chemical, and biological devices that are capable of injuring and killing large numbers of people. *(p. 923)*

Wedgwood, Josiah (1730–1795) English industrialist whose pottery works were the first to produce fine-quality pottery by industrial methods. *(p. 614)*

Western Front A line of trenches and fortifications in World War I that stretched without a break from Switzerland to the North Sea. Scene of most of the fighting between Germany, on the one hand, and France and Britain, on the other. *(p. 780)*

Wilson, Woodrow (1856–1924) President of the United States (1913–1921) and the leading figure at the Paris Peace Conference of 1919. He was unable to persuade the U.S. Congress to ratify the **Treaty of Versailles** or join the **League of Nations.** *(p. 785)*

witch-hunt The pursuit of people suspected of witchcraft, especially in northern Europe in the late sixteenth and seventeenth centuries. *(p. 453)*

Women's Rights Convention An 1848 gathering of women angered by their exclusion from an international antislavery meeting. They met at Seneca Falls, New York to discuss women's rights. *(p. 655)*

World Bank A specialized agency of the United Nations that makes loans to countries for economic development, trade promotion, and debt consolidation. Its formal name is the International Bank for Reconstruction and Development. *(p. 862)*

World Trade Organization (WTO) An international body established in 1995 to foster and bring order to international trade. *(p. 927)*

Wright, Wilbur (1867-1912), and Orville (1871-1948) American bicycle mechanics; the first to build and fly an airplane, at Kitty Hawk, North Carolina, December 7, 1903. *(p. 800)*

Xiongnu A confederation of nomadic peoples living beyond the northwest frontier of ancient China. Chinese rulers tried a variety of defenses and stratagems to ward off these "barbarians," as they called them, and finally succeeded in dispersing the Xiongnu in the first century C.E. *(p. 173)*

Yamagata Aritomo (1838–1922) One of the leaders of the **Meiji Restoration.** *(p. 746)*

Yi (1392–1910) The Yi dynasty ruled Korea from the fall of the **Koryo** kingdom to the colonization of Korea by Japan. *(p. 359)*

yin/yang In Chinese belief, complementary factors that help to maintain the equilibrium of the world. Yin is associated with masculine, light, and active qualities; yang with feminine, dark, and passive qualities. *(p. 65)*

Yongle Reign period of Zhu Di (1360–1424), the third emperor of the **Ming Empire** (r. 1403–1424). He sponsored the building of the **Forbidden City,** a huge encyclopedia project, the expeditions of **Zheng He,** and the reopening of China's borders to trade and travel. *(p. 355)*

Young Ottomans Movement of young intellectuals to institute liberal reforms and build a feeling of national identity in the Ottoman Empire in the second half of the nineteenth century. *(p. 703)*

Yuan Empire (1271–1368) Empire created in China and Siberia by **Khubilai Khan.** *(p. 342)*

Yuan Shikai (1859–1916) Chinese general and first president of the Chinese Republic (1912–1916). He stood in the way of the democratic movement led by **Sun Yat-sen.** *(p. 791)*

Zapata, Emiliano (1879–1919) Revolutionary and leader of peasants in the Mexican Revolution. He mobilized landless peasants in south-central Mexico in an attempt to seize and divide the lands of the wealthy landowners. Though successful for a time, he was ultimately defeated and assassinated. *(p. 846)*

Zen The Japanese word for a branch of **Mahayana Buddhism** based on highly disciplined meditation. It is known in Sanskrit as *dhyana,* in Chinese as *chan,* and in Korean as *son.* *(p. 296)*

Zheng He (1371–1433) An imperial eunuch and Muslim, entrusted by the Ming emperor **Yongle** with a series of state voyages that took his gigantic ships through the Indian Ocean, from Southeast Asia to Africa. *(pp. 356, 422)*

Zhou The people and dynasty that took over the dominant position in north China from the **Shang** and created the concept of the **Mandate of Heaven** to justify their rule. The Zhou era, particularly the vigorous early period (1027–771 B.C.E.), was remembered in Chinese tradition as a time of prosperity and benevolent rule. In the later Zhou period (771–221 B.C.E.), centralized control broke down, and warfare among many small states became frequent. *(p. 63)*

ziggurat A massive pyramidal stepped tower made of

mudbricks. It is associated with religious complexes in ancient Mesopotamian cities, but its function is unknown. (*p. 36*)

Zoroastrianism A religion originating in ancient Iran with the prophet Zoroaster. It centered on a single benevolent deity—Ahuramazda—who engaged in a twelve-thousand-year struggle with demonic forces before prevailing and restoring a pristine world. Emphasizing truth-telling, purity, and reverence for nature, the religion demanded that humans choose sides in the struggle between good and evil. Those whose good conduct indicated their support for Ahuramazda would be rewarded in the afterlife. Others would be punished. The religion of the Achaemenid and Sasanid Persians, Zoroastrianism may have spread within their realms and influenced Judaism, Christianity, and other faiths. (*p. 128*)

Zulu A people of modern South Africa whom King Shaka united in 1818. (*p. 665*)

Index

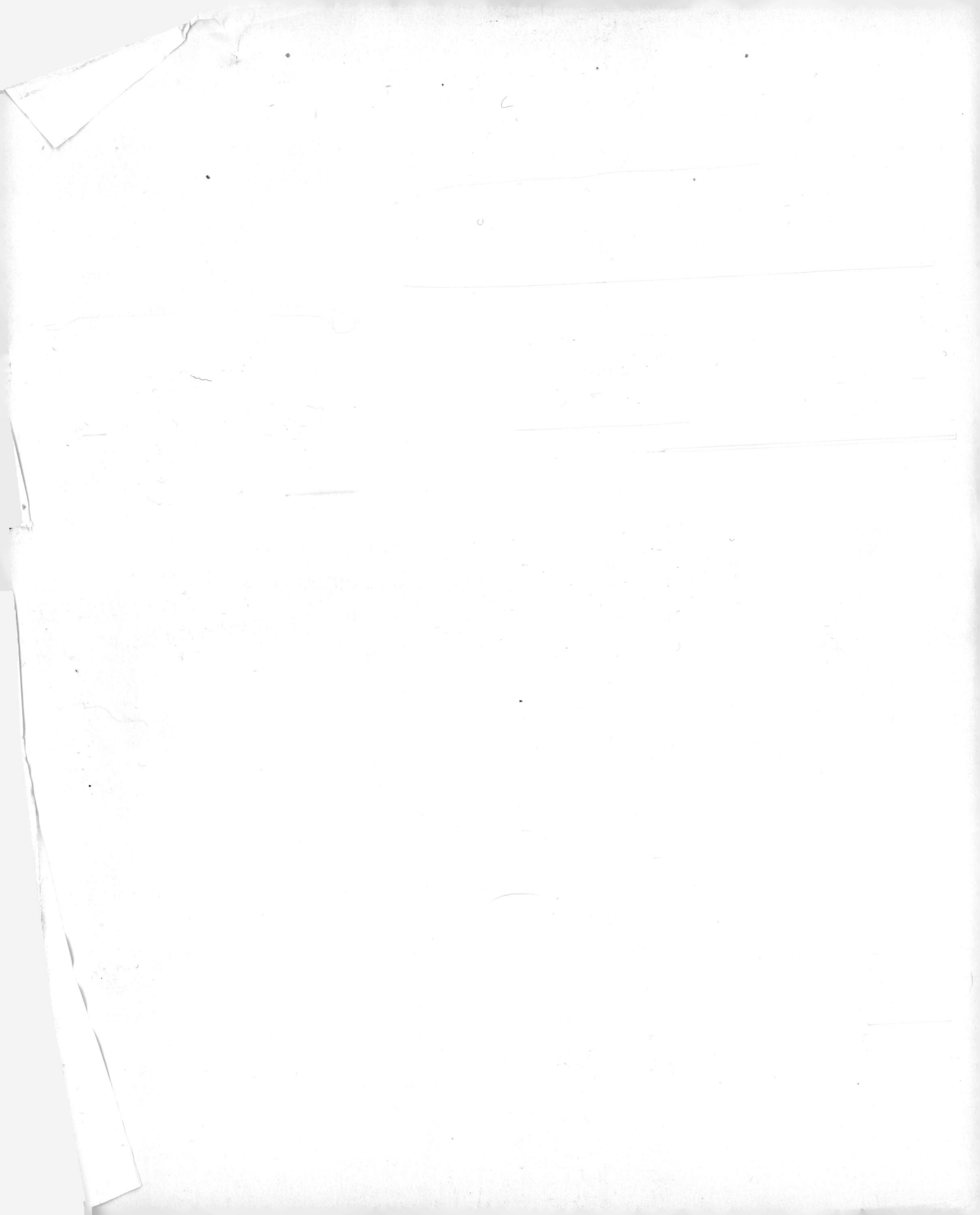